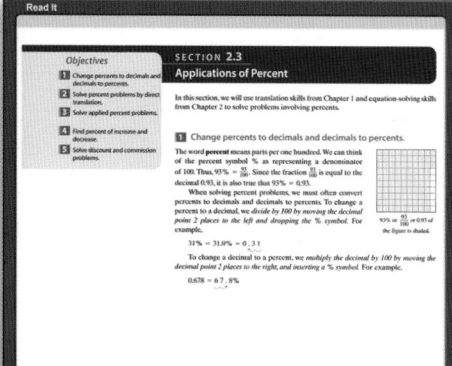

◀ *Read It*—links to excerpts from the text

If students don't have their textbook handy when they complete their online homework, all they have to do is click the *Read It* link under a problem. The link opens a relevant excerpt from the text that relates to the exercise, allowing them to review the context of the problem.

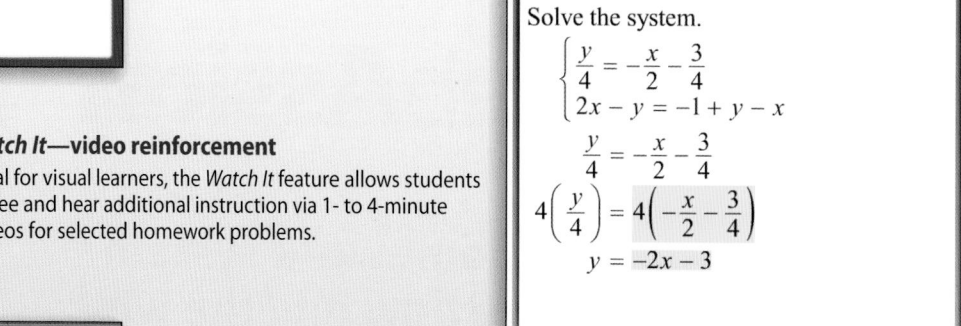

▶ *Watch It*—video reinforcement

Ideal for visual learners, the *Watch It* feature allows students to see and hear additional instruction via 1- to 4-minute videos for selected homework problems.

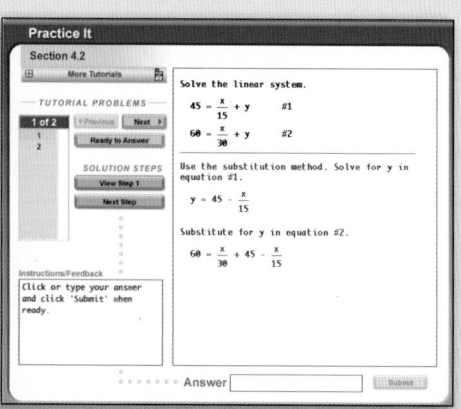

◀ *Practice It*—interactive text examples

If students are still hesitant to answer an exercise, they may have a *Practice It* link that launches a set of questions similar to the assigned exercise. Students can click through the solution in steps, attempt to answer at any point, and receive immediate feedback.

▶ *Master It*—step-by-step tutorials

For more comprehensive assistance, many problems include a *Master It* link to a tutorial that walks students through the solution to a similar problem in multiple steps, providing feedback along the way.

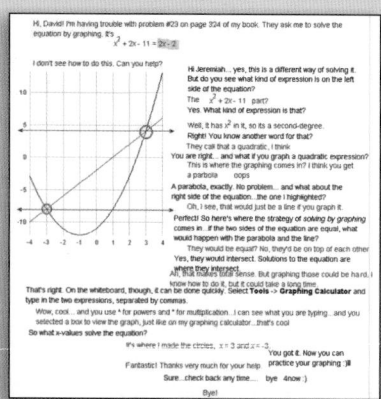

◀ *Chat About It*—live online tutoring

Students can also click the *Chat About It* link for live, one-on-one tutoring (via whiteboarding, email, and instant messaging) from an experienced mathematics instructor.

www.webassign.net/brookscole

Contact your Cengage Learning representative for information on packaging access to **Enhanced WebAssign** with each new text, or visit the URL noted above.

Enhanced WebAssign content is continually evolving; screenshots shown here are for illustrative purposes only.

What's *enhanced* about Enhanced WebAssign®?

▼ Enhanced homework management for you,
enhanced interactive learning for students ▶

ENHANCED

WebAssign

The most widely used online homework management system, **Enhanced WebAssign®** allows you to easily assign, collect, grade, and record homework assignments via the web.

▶ **Algorithmic problems for unlimited practice**

Choose from as many as 2,000 text items representing a variety of problem types. A blue triangle next to problem numbers in your *Instructor's Edition* identifies problems available online. **Enhanced WebAssign** generates algorithmic versions of the problems, allowing each student to see a unique version. You also have the option to let students "practice another version" of a problem with new values until they feel confident enough to work the original one.

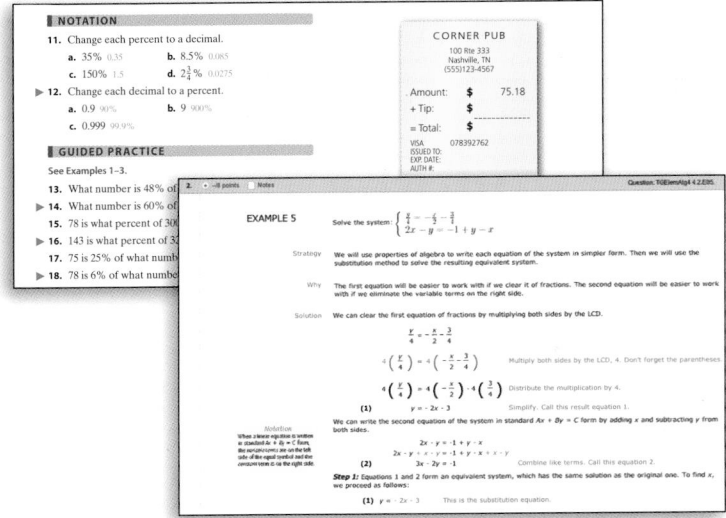

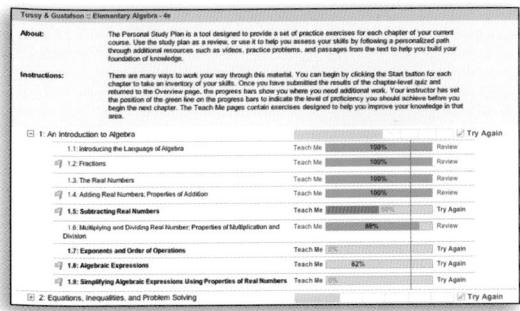

▲ **New! Personal Study Plans and a Premium eBook**

Diagnostic quizzing identifies concepts that students still need to master; the resulting *Personal Study Plans* direct them to appropriate review material. Also available to students when you choose **Enhanced WebAssign** is an interactive *Premium eBook*, which offers search, highlighting, and note-taking functionality, as well as links to multimedia resources.

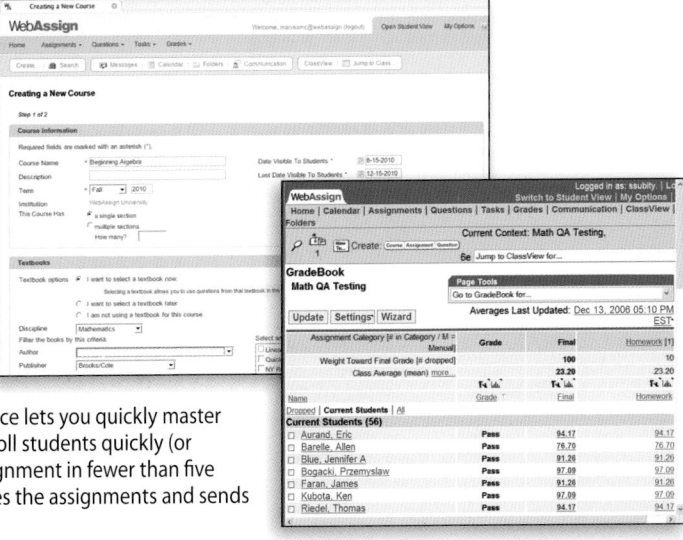

▶ **Simple course and assignment creation—automatic grading**

Enhanced WebAssign's simple, user-friendly interface lets you quickly master essential functions. Create a course in *two* steps, enroll students quickly (or let them self-enroll), and select problems for an assignment in fewer than five minutes. **Enhanced WebAssign** automatically grades the assignments and sends results to your gradebook.

Easy to assign, easy to use, easy to manage
Enhanced WebAssign® at a glance

Content Features

Online content for each of the Tussy/Gustafson/Koenig texts includes these features:

- *Algorithmic problems* based on as many as 2,000 text exercises
- *Step-by-step tutorials* for key problems from the text with complete algorithmic solutions
- *Videos* that provide additional instruction on selected problems
- *Careful feedback* to help guide students to deeper understanding
- *Access to relevant excerpts from the text* to provide the background students may need to answer problems, plus optional access to an interactive Premium eBook
- *Personal Study Plans* that identify concepts students still need to master, and direct them to the appropriate review resources
- *Live online tutoring* via whiteboarding, email, and instant messaging

Selected Program and Technical Features

- Simple, friendly user interface
- Course creation in two easy steps; assignment creation in five minutes
- Instructor gradebook with weighted categories and scores
- Automatic grading of online homework assignments
- Proper display of mathematical expressions
- Student forums, bulletin boards, messaging, and built-in calendar and communication tools
- Compatible with Windows®, Apple® Macintosh, and Linux®
- Works with most web browsers: Mozilla Firefox®, Internet Explorer®, and Safari™
- No proprietary plug-ins required
- Superior, reliable customer support

Note: Selected paperbound books are identified as such to differentiate them from their hardbound versions.

Texts Available with Enhanced WebAssign Content

Aufmann/Lockwood
New! Basic College Mathematics: An Applied Approach, 9th Edition
New! Essential Mathematics with Applications, 8th Edition
New! Introductory Algebra: An Applied Approach, 8th Edition
New! Intermediate Algebra: An Applied Approach, 8th Edition
New! Algebra: Introductory and Intermediate, 5th Edition
New! PREALG (4LTR Press)
Prealgebra, Enhanced Edition, 5th Edition
Beginning Algebra with Applications, Multimedia Edition, 7th Edition
Intermediate Algebra with Applications, Multimedia Edition, 7th Edition
Algebra: Beginning and Intermediate, Multimedia Edition, 2nd Edition

Gustafson/Karr/Massey
New! Beginning Algebra, 9th Edition
New! Intermediate Algebra, 9th Edition
New! Beginning and Intermediate Algebra: An Integrated Approach, 6th Edition

Kaufmann/Schwitters
Beginning Algebra (paperbound)
Intermediate Algebra (paperbound)
New! Elementary Algebra, 9th Edition
New! Intermediate Algebra, 9th Edition
Elementary and Intermediate Algebra, 5th Edition
New! Algebra for College Students, 9th Edition

Larson
Elementary Algebra, 5th Edition
Intermediate Algebra, 5th Edition
Elementary and Intermediate Algebra, 5th Edition

McKeague
Basic Mathematics: A Text/Workbook, 7th Edition
Basic College Mathematics: A Text/Workbook, 2nd Edition
Prealgebra: A Text/Workbook, 6th Edition
Beginning Algebra: A Text/Workbook, 8th Edition
Intermediate Algebra: A Text/Workbook, 8th Edition
Elementary Algebra, 8th Edition
Intermediate Algebra, 8th Edition
Elementary and Intermediate Algebra, 3rd Edition

Tussy/Gustafson
Developmental Mathematics for College Students, 2nd Edition
Elementary Algebra, 4th Edition
Intermediate Algebra, 4th Edition
Elementary and Intermediate Algebra, 4th Edition

Tussy/Gustafson/Koenig
New! Prealgebra, 4th Edition
New! Basic Mathematics for College Students, 4th Edition
New! Introductory Algebra, 4th Edition (paperbound)
New! Intermediate Algebra, 4th Edition (paperbound)

Van Dyke/Rogers/Adams
Fundamentals of Mathematics, Enhanced Edition, 9th Edition

For more information and sample assignments—

www.webassign.net/brookscole

EDITION
4

INTRODUCTORY ALGEBRA

ALAN S. TUSSY
CITRUS COLLEGE

R. DAVID GUSTAFSON
ROCK VALLEY COLLEGE

DIANE R. KOENIG
ROCK VALLEY COLLEGE

BROOKS/COLE
CENGAGE Learning™

Australia • Brazil • Japan • Korea • Mexico • Singapore • Spain • United Kingdom • United States

BROOKS/COLE
CENGAGE Learning™

Introductory Algebra, **Fourth Edition**
Alan S. Tussy, R. David Gustafson, Diane R. Koenig

Publisher: Charlie Van Wagner

Senior Developmental Editor: Danielle Derbenti

Senior Development Editor for Market Strategies:
Rita Lombard

Assistant Editor: Stefanie Beeck

Editorial Assistant: Jennifer Cordoba

Media Editors: Heleny Wong, Maureen Ross

Marketing Manager: Gordon Lee

Marketing Assistant: Angela Kim

Marketing Communications Manager: Katy
Malatesta

Content Project Manager: Jennifer Risden

Creative Director: Rob Hugel

Art Director: Vernon Boes

Print Buyer: Linda Hsu

Rights Acquisitions Account Manager, Text: Mardell
Glinksi-Schultz

Rights Acquisitions Account Manager, Image: Don
Schlotman

Production Service: Graphic World Inc.

Text Designer: Diane Beasley

Photo Researcher: Bill Smith Group

Illustrators: Lori Heckelman; Graphic World Inc.

Cover Designer: Terri Wright

Cover Image: Background: © J&L Images/Getty
Images RF, Y Button: © Art Parts/Fotosearch RF

Compositor: Graphic World Inc.

For product information and technology assistance, contact us at
Cengage Learning Customer & Sales Support, 1-800-354-9706

For permission to use material from this text or product,
submit all requests online at **www.cengage.com/permissions**

Further permissions questions can be e-mailed to
permissionrequest@cengage.com

Library of Congress Control Number: 2009933929

ISBN-13: 978-1-4390-4787-3

ISBN-10: 1-4390-4787-1

Brooks/Cole
20 Davis Drive
Belmont, CA 94002-3098
USA

Cengage Learning is a leading provider of customized learning solutions
with office locations around the globe, including Singapore, the United
Kingdom, Australia, Mexico, Brazil, and Japan. Locate your local office at
www.cengage.com/global

Cengage Learning products are represented in Canada by
Nelson Education, Ltd.

To learn more about Brooks/Cole, visit **www.cengage.com/brookscole**

Purchase any of our products at your local college store or at our preferred
online store **www.ichapters.com**

Printed in the United States of America
1 2 3 4 5 6 7 13 12 11 10 09

To the memory of my parents, Jeanene and Bill Tussy
ALAN S. TUSSY

■

To my parents, Roy and Lois Gustafson, with love and affection
R. DAVID GUSTAFSON

■

*In the memory of my parents, Darryl and Joan Vaupel, who taught me
to set my goals high and work hard to achieve them*
DIANE R. KOENIG

■

CONTENTS

CHAPTER 3

Graphs, Linear Equations, and Inequalities in Two Variables; Functions   211

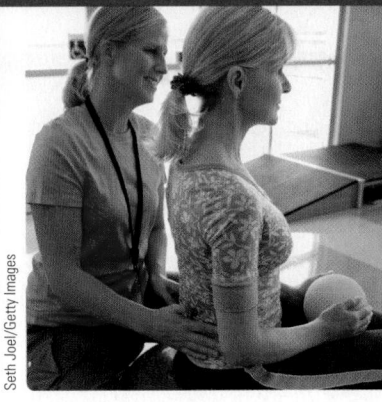

Seth Joel/Getty Images

CHAPTER 4

Solving Systems of Equations and Inequalities   319

Mark & Audrey Gibson/Jupiterimages

© BananaStock/SuperStock

CHAPTER 7

Rational Expressions and Equations   539

Ira Block/Getty Images

CHAPTER 8

Roots and Radicals   637

CHAPTER **9**

Quadratic Equations   719

© iStockphoto.com/Chris Schmidt

APPENDIXES

Introductory Algebra, Fourth Edition, is more than a simple upgrade of the third edition. Substantial changes have been made to the worked example structure, the *Study Sets,* and the pedagogy. Throughout the revision process, our objective has been to ease teaching challenges and meet students' educational needs.

Algebra, for many of today's developmental math students, is like a foreign language. They have difficulty translating the words, their meanings, and how they apply to problem solving. With these needs in mind (and as educational research suggests), our fundamental goal is to have students read, write, think, and speak using the *language of algebra.* Instructional approaches that include vocabulary, practice, and well-defined pedagogy, along with an emphasis on reasoning, modeling, communication, and technology skills have been blended to address this need.

The most common question that students ask as they watch their instructors solve problems and as they read the textbook is … *Why?* The new fourth edition addresses this question in a unique way. Experience teaches us that it's not enough to know *how* a problem is solved. Students gain a deeper understanding of algebraic concepts if they know *why* a particular approach is taken. This instructional truth was the motivation for adding a **Strategy** and **Why** explanation to the solution of each worked example. The fourth edition now provides, on a consistent basis, a concise answer to that all-important question: *Why?*

These are just two of several reasons we trust that this revision will make this course a better experience for both instructors and students.

NEW TO THIS EDITION

- **New Chapter Openers**
- **New Worked Example Structure**
- **New Study Skills Workshop Module**
- **New Language of Algebra, Success Tip, and Caution Boxes**
- **New Chapter Objectives**
- **New Guided Practice and Try It Yourself Sections in the Study Sets**
- **New Chapter Summary and Review**
- **New Study Skills Checklists**

Chapter Openers That Answer the Question: When Will I Use This?

Instructors are asked this question time and again by students. In response, we have written chapter openers called *From Campus to Careers.* This feature highlights vocations that require various algebraic skills. Designed to inspire career exploration, each includes job outlook, educational requirements, and annual earnings information. Careers presented in the openers are tied to an exercise found later in the *Study Sets.*

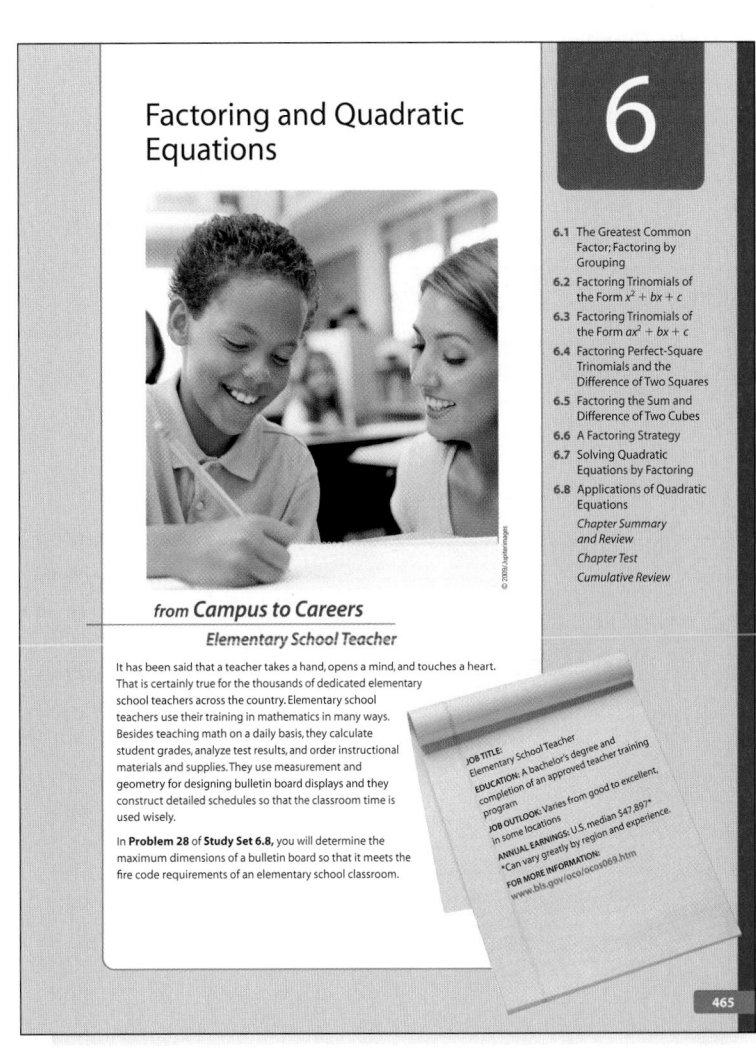

Factoring and Quadratic Equations

6

6.1 The Greatest Common Factor; Factoring by Grouping
6.2 Factoring Trinomials of the Form $x^2 + bx + c$
6.3 Factoring Trinomials of the Form $ax^2 + bx + c$
6.4 Factoring Perfect-Square Trinomials and the Difference of Two Squares
6.5 Factoring the Sum and Difference of Two Cubes
6.6 A Factoring Strategy
6.7 Solving Quadratic Equations by Factoring
6.8 Applications of Quadratic Equations
Chapter Summary and Review
Chapter Test
Cumulative Review

from Campus to Careers

Elementary School Teacher

It has been said that a teacher takes a hand, opens a mind, and touches a heart. That is certainly true for the thousands of dedicated elementary school teachers across the country. Elementary school teachers use their training in mathematics in many ways. Besides teaching math on a daily basis, they calculate student grades, analyze test results, and order instructional materials and supplies. They use measurement and geometry for designing bulletin board displays and they construct detailed schedules so that the classroom time is used wisely.

In **Problem 28** of **Study Set 6.8,** you will determine the maximum dimensions of a bulletin board so that it meets the fire code requirements of an elementary school classroom.

JOB TITLE: Elementary School Teacher
EDUCATION: A bachelor's degree and completion of an approved teacher training program
JOB OUTLOOK: Varies from good to excellent, in some locations
ANNUAL EARNINGS: U.S. median $47,897*
*Can vary greatly by region and experience.
FOR MORE INFORMATION:
www.bls.gov/oco/ocos069.htm

465

Examples That Tell Students Not Just How, But WHY

Why? That question is often asked by students as they watch their instructor solve problems in class and as they are working on problems at home. It's not enough to know *how* a problem is solved. Students gain a deeper understanding of the algebraic concepts if they know *why* a particular approach was taken. This instructional truth was the motivation for adding a *Strategy* and *Why* explanation to each worked example.

Examples That Offer Immediate Feedback

Each worked example includes a *Self Check*. These can be completed by students on their own or as classroom lecture examples, which is how Alan Tussy uses them. Alan asks selected students to read aloud the *Self Check* problems as he writes what the student says on the board. The other students, with their books open to that page, can quickly copy the *Self Check* problem to their notes. This speeds up the note-taking process and encourages student participation in his lectures. It also teaches students how to read mathematical symbols. Each *Self Check* answer is printed adjacent to the corresponding problem in the *Annotated Instructor's Edition* for easy reference. *Self Check* solutions can be found at the end of each section in the student edition before each *Study Set*.

Examples That Ask Students to Work Independently

Each worked example ends with a *Now Try* problem. These are the final step in the learning process. Each one is linked to a similar problem found within the *Guided Practice* section of the *Study Sets*.

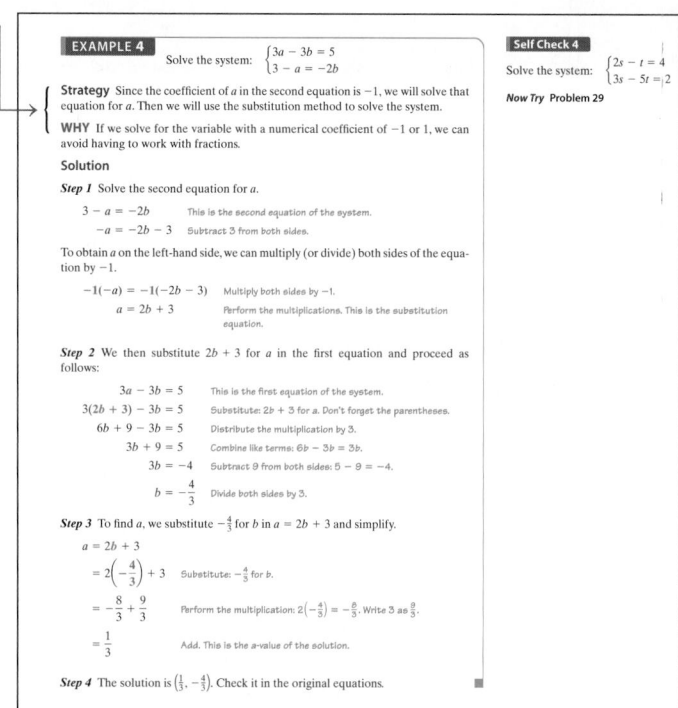

EXAMPLE 4   Solve the system: $\begin{cases} 3a - 3b = 5 \\ 3 - a = -2b \end{cases}$

Self Check 4

Solve the system: $\begin{cases} 2s - t = 4 \\ 3s - 5t = 2 \end{cases}$

Now Try Problem 29

Strategy Since the coefficient of a in the second equation is -1, we will solve that equation for a. Then we will use the substitution method to solve the system.

WHY If we solve for the variable with a numerical coefficient of -1 or 1, we can avoid having to work with fractions.

Solution

Step 1 Solve the second equation for a.

$$3 - a = -2b \qquad \text{This is the second equation of the system.}$$
$$-a = -2b - 3 \qquad \text{Subtract 3 from both sides.}$$

To obtain a on the left-hand side, we can multiply (or divide) both sides of the equation by -1.

$$-1(-a) = -1(-2b - 3) \qquad \text{Multiply both sides by } -1.$$
$$a = 2b + 3 \qquad \text{Perform the multiplications. This is the substitution equation.}$$

Step 2 We then substitute $2b + 3$ for a in the first equation and proceed as follows:

$$3a - 3b = 5 \qquad \text{This is the first equation of the system.}$$
$$3(2b + 3) - 3b = 5 \qquad \text{Substitute: } 2b + 3 \text{ for } a. \text{ Don't forget the parentheses.}$$
$$6b + 9 - 3b = 5 \qquad \text{Distribute the multiplication by 3.}$$
$$3b + 9 = 5 \qquad \text{Combine like terms: } 6b - 3b = 3b.$$
$$3b = -4 \qquad \text{Subtract 9 from both sides: } 5 - 9 = -4.$$
$$b = -\frac{4}{3} \qquad \text{Divide both sides by 3.}$$

Step 3 To find a, we substitute $-\frac{4}{3}$ for b in $a = 2b + 3$ and simplify.

$$a = 2b + 3$$
$$= 2\left(-\frac{4}{3}\right) + 3 \qquad \text{Substitute: } -\frac{4}{3} \text{ for } b.$$
$$= -\frac{8}{3} + \frac{9}{3} \qquad \text{Perform the multiplication: } 2\left(-\frac{4}{3}\right) = -\frac{8}{3}. \text{ Write 3 as } \frac{9}{3}.$$
$$= \frac{1}{3} \qquad \text{Add. This is the } a\text{-value of the solution.}$$

Step 4 The solution is $\left(\frac{1}{3}, -\frac{4}{3}\right)$. Check it in the original equations. ∎

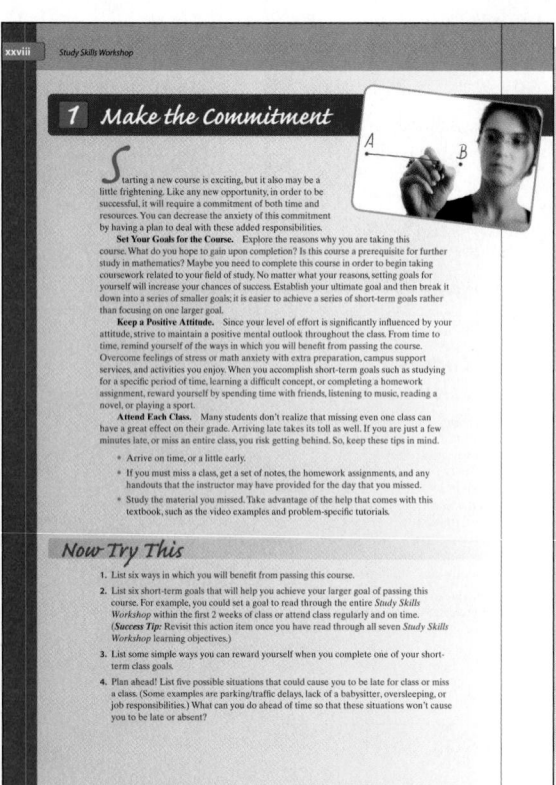

xxviii   *Study Skills Workshop*

1 Make the Commitment

Starting a new course is exciting, but it also may be a little frightening. Like any new opportunity, in order to be successful, it will require a commitment of both time and resources. You can decrease the anxiety of this commitment by having a plan to deal with these added responsibilities.

Set Your Goals for the Course. Explore the reasons why you are taking this course. What do you hope to gain upon completion? Is this course a prerequisite for further study in mathematics? Maybe you need to complete this course in order to begin taking coursework related to your field of study. No matter what your reasons, setting goals for yourself will increase your chances of success. Establish your ultimate goal and then break it down into a series of smaller goals; it is easier to achieve a series of short-term goals rather than focusing on one larger goal.

Keep a Positive Attitude. Since your level of effort is significantly influenced by your attitude, strive to maintain a positive mental outlook throughout the class. From time to time, remind yourself of the ways in which you will benefit from passing the course. Overcome feelings of stress or math anxiety with extra preparation, campus support services, and activities you enjoy. When you accomplish short-term goals such as studying for a specific period of time, learning a difficult concept, or completing a homework assignment, reward yourself by spending time with friends, listening to music, reading a novel, or playing a sport.

Attend Each Class. Many students don't realize that missing even one class can have a great effect on their grade. Arriving late takes its toll as well. If you are just a few minutes late, or miss an entire class, you risk getting behind. So, keep these tips in mind.

- Arrive on time, or a little early.
- If you must miss a class, get a set of notes, the homework assignments, and any handouts that the instructor may have provided for the day that you missed.
- Study the material you missed. Take advantage of the help that comes with this textbook, such as the video examples and problem-specific tutorials.

Now Try This

1. List six ways in which you will benefit from passing this course.
2. List six short-term goals that will help you achieve your larger goal of passing this course. For example, you could set a goal to read through the entire *Study Skills Workshop* within the first 2 weeks of class or attend class regularly and on time. (*Success Tip:* Revisit this action item once you have read through all seven *Study Skills Workshop* learning objectives.)
3. List some simple ways you can reward yourself when you complete one of your short-term class goals.
4. Plan ahead! List five possible situations that could cause you to be late for class or miss a class. (Some examples are parking/traffic delays, lack of a babysitter, oversleeping, or job responsibilities.) What can you do ahead of time so that these situations won't cause you to be late or absent?

Emphasis on Study Skills

Introductory Algebra begins with a *Study Skills Workshop* module. Instead of simple, unrelated suggestions printed in the margins, this module contains one-page discussions of study skills topics followed by a *Now Try This* section offering students actionable skills, assignments, and projects that will impact their study habits throughout the course.

> **The Language of Algebra**   The preposition *per* means for each, or for every. When we say the rate of change is 3 permits *per* month, we mean 3 permits for each month.

Integrated Focus on the Language of Algebra

Language of Algebra boxes draw connections between mathematical terms and everyday references to reinforce the language of algebra approach that runs throughout the text.

Guidance When Students Need It Most

Appearing at key teaching moments, *Success Tips* and *Caution* boxes improve students' problem-solving abilities, warn students of potential pitfalls, and increase clarity.

> **Success Tip**   The answers from Example 2 and the Self Check illustrate an important fact about slope: *The same value for the slope of a line will result no matter which two points on the line are used to determine the rise and the run.*

> **Caution!**   After checking a result, be careful when stating your conclusion. Here, it would be incorrect to say:
>
> The solution is -3.
>
> The number we were checking was 24, not -3.

Useful Objectives Help Keep Students Focused

Each section begins with a set of numbered *Objectives* that focus students' attention on the skills that they will learn. As each objective is discussed in the section, the number and heading reappear to the reader to remind them of the objective at hand.

Objectives
1. Determine whether a number is a solution.
2. Use the addition property of equality.
3. Use the subtraction property of equality.
4. Use the multiplication property of equality.
5. Use the division property of equality.

SECTION 2.1

Solving Equations Using Properties of Equality

In this section, we introduce four fundamental properties of equality that are used to solve equations.

1 Determine whether a number is a solution.

An **equation** is a statement indicating that two expressions are equal. An example is $x + 5 = 15$. The equal symbol $=$ separates the equation into two parts: The expression $x + 5$ is the **left side** and 15 is the **right side**. The letter x is the **variable** (or the **unknown**). The sides of an equation can be reversed, so we can write $x + 5 = 15$ or $15 = x + 5$.

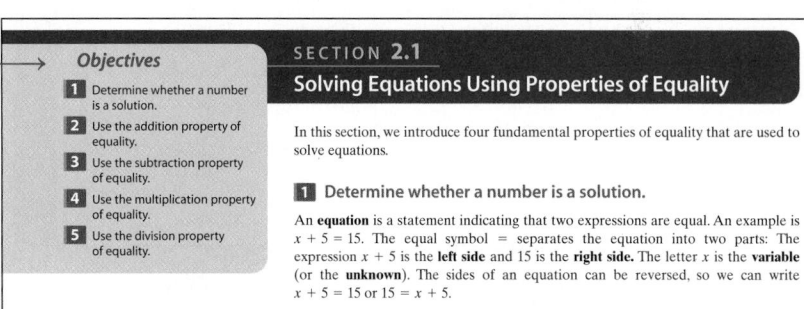

Thoroughly Revised Study Sets

The *Study Sets* have been thoroughly revised to ensure that every example type covered in the section is represented in the *Guided Practice* problems. Particular attention was paid to developing a gradual level of progression within problem types.

Guided Practice Problems

All of the problems in the *Guided Practice* portion of the *Study Sets* are linked to an associated worked example or objective from that section. This feature promotes student success by referring them to the proper worked example(s) or objective(s) if they encounter difficulties solving homework problems.

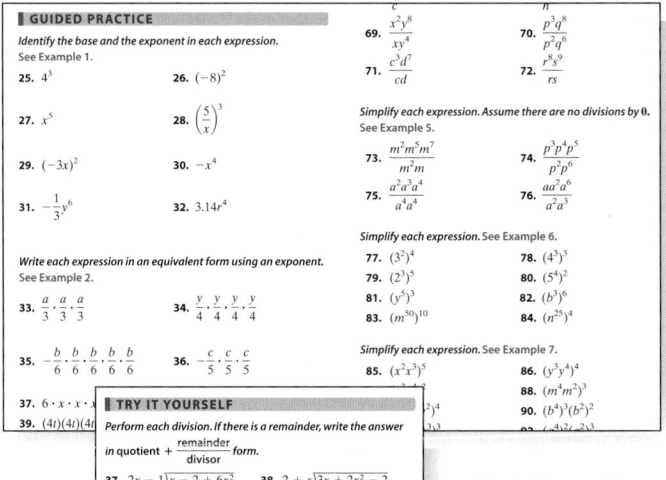

Try It Yourself

To promote problem recognition, many *Study Sets* now include a collection of *Try It Yourself* problems that *do not* link to worked examples. These problem types are thoroughly mixed, giving students an opportunity to practice decision making and strategy selection as they would when taking a test or quiz.

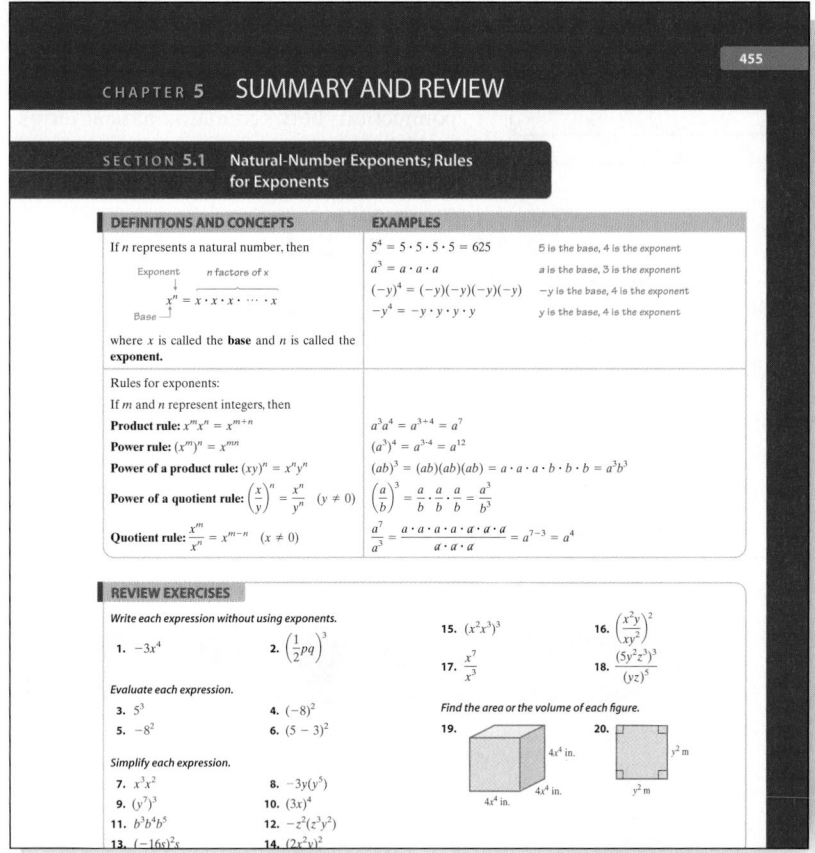

Comprehensive End-of-Chapter Summary with Integrated Chapter Review

The end-of-chapter material has been redesigned to function as a complete study guide for students. New chapter summaries that include definitions, concepts, and examples, by section, have been written. Review problems for each section immediately follow the summary for that section.

Study Skills That Point Out Common Student Mistakes

In Chapter 1, we have included four *Study Skills Checklists* designed to actively show students how to effectively use the key features in this text. Subsequent chapters include one checklist just before the *Chapter Summary and Review* that provides another layer of preparation to promote student success. These *Study Skills Checklists* warn students of common errors, giving them time to consider these pitfalls before taking their exam.

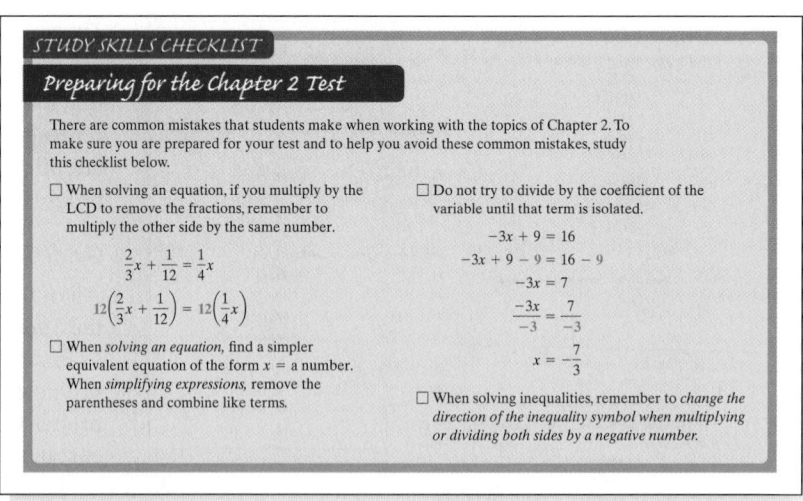

TRUSTED FEATURES

- **Study Sets** found in each section offer a multifaceted approach to practicing and reinforcing the concepts taught in each section. They are designed for students to methodically build their knowledge of the section concepts, from basic recall to increasingly complex problem solving, through reading, writing, and thinking mathematically.

  Vocabulary—Each *Study Set* begins with the important *Vocabulary* discussed in that section. The fill-in-the-blank vocabulary problems emphasize the main concepts taught in the chapter and provide the foundation for learning and communicating the language of algebra.

  Concepts—In *Concepts,* students are asked about the specific subskills and procedures necessary to successfully complete the *Guided Practice* and *Try It Yourself* problems that follow.

  Notation—In *Notation,* the students review the new symbols introduced in a section. Often, they are asked to fill in steps of a sample solution. This strengthens their ability to read and write mathematics and prepares them for the *Guided Practice* problems by modeling solution formats.

  Guided Practice—The problems in *Guided Practice* are linked to an associated worked example or objective from that section. This feature promotes student success by referring them to the proper examples if they encounter difficulties solving homework problems.

  Try It Yourself—To promote problem recognition, the *Try It Yourself* problems are thoroughly mixed and are *not* linked to worked examples, giving students an opportunity to practice decision-making and strategy selection as they would when taking a test or quiz.

  Applications—The *Applications* provide students the opportunity to apply their newly acquired algebraic skills to relevant and interesting real-life situations.

  Writing—The *Writing* problems help students build mathematical communication skills.

  Review—The *Review* problems consist of randomly selected problems from previous chapters. These problems are designed to keep students' successfully mastered skills up-to-date before they move on to the next section.

- **Detailed Author Notes** that guide students along in a step-by-step process appear in the solutions to every worked example.

- **The Five-Step Problem-Solving Strategy** guides students through applied worked examples using the *analyze, form, solve, state,* and *check* process. This approach clarifies the thought process and algebra skills necessary to solve a wide variety of problems. As a result, students' confidence is increased and their problem-solving abilities are strengthened.

- **Think It Through** features make the connection between mathematics and student life. These relevant topics often require algebra skills from the chapter to be applied to a real-life situation. Topics include tuition costs, student enrollment, job opportunities, credit cards, and many more.

- **Chapter Tests,** at the end of every chapter, can be used as preparation for the class exam.

- **Cumulative Reviews** follow the end-of-chapter material and keep students' skills current before moving on to the next chapter. For the Fourth Edition, each problem is now linked to the associated section from which the problem came for ease of reference. The final *Cumulative Review* is often used by instructors as a Final Exam Review.
- **Using Your Calculator** features (formerly called *Calculator Snapshots*) are designed for instructors who wish to use calculators as part of the instruction in this course. These features introduce keystrokes and show how scientific and graphing calculators can be used to solve problems. In the *Study Sets*, icons are used to denote problems that may be solved using a calculator.

CHANGES TO THE TABLE OF CONTENTS

Based on feedback from colleagues and users of the third edition, the following changes have been made to the table of contents in an effort to further streamline the text and make it even easier to use.

- In Chapter 1, *Adding Real Numbers* and *Subtracting Real Numbers* are now covered in two separate sections.
- The section *Simplifying Algebraic Expressions Using Properties of Real Numbers* has been moved from Chapter 2 to Section 1.9.
- Chapter 2 topics have been reorganized:

  2.1 *Solving Equations Using Properties of Equality*

  2.2 *More about Solving Equations*

  2.3 *Applications of Percent* (Commission and discount problems were added.)

  2.4 *Formulas*

  2.5 *Problem Solving* (Consecutive integer, commission, and set-up fee/cost per item problems were added.)

  2.6 *More about Problem Solving*

  2.7 *Solving Inequalities*

- The section *Graphing Linear Inequalities* has been moved from Chapter 7 to Section 3.7, and parallel and perpendicular lines are now introduced in Section 3.4 *Rate of Change and the Slope of a Line*.
- Former Chapter 7 *Solving Systems of Equations and Inequalities* has been moved up to Chapter 4, promoting the logical progression from linear equations and inequalities in two variables in Chapter 3 to systems of equations in two variables in Chapter 4. The built-in flexibility of the content allows instructors who prefer to cover this toward the end of the course to continue to do so.
- Chapter 6 topics have been reorganized:

  6.1 *The Greatest Common Factor; Factoring by Grouping*

  6.2 *Factoring Trinomials of the Form $x^2 + bx + c$*

  6.3 *Factoring Trinomials of the Form $ax^2 + bx + c$*

  6.4 *Factoring Perfect-Square Trinomials and the Difference of Two Squares*

  6.5 *Factoring the Sum and Difference of Two Cubes*

6.6 *A Factoring Strategy* (Factoring strategy is now covered in its own section.)

6.7 *Solving Quadratic Equations by Factoring*

6.8 *Applications of Quadratic Equations*

- Adding and subtracting rational expressions is now covered in two sections: 7.3 *Adding and Subtracting with Like Denominators; Least Common Denominators* and 7.4 *Adding and Subtracting with Unlike Denominators.*
- Applications of rational equations are now covered in their own section: 7.7 *Problem Solving Using Rational Equations.*
- Chapter 9 has been reorganized and two new sections have been added:

  9.1 *Solving Quadratic Equations: The Square Root Property* (Now covered in its own section.)

  9.2 *Solving Quadratic Equations: Completing the Square*

  9.3 *Solving Quadratic Equations: The Quadratic Formula*

  9.4 *Graphing Quadratic Equations*

  9.5 *Complex Numbers* (New to this edition.)

GENERAL REVISIONS AND OVERALL DESIGN

- We have edited the prose so that it is even more clear and concise.
- Strategic use of color has been implemented within the new design to help the visual learner.
- Added color in the solutions highlights key steps and improves readability.
- We have updated much of the data and graphs and have added scaling to all axes in all graphs.
- We have added more real-world applications.
- We have included more problem-specific photographs and improved the clarity of the illustrations.

INSTRUCTOR RESOURCES

Print Ancillaries

Instructor's Resource Binder (0-538-73675-5)
Maria H. Andersen, *Muskegon Community College*
NEW! Each section of the main text is discussed in uniquely designed *Teaching Guides* containing instruction tips, examples, activities, worksheets, overheads, assessments, and solutions to all worksheets and activities.

Complete Solutions Manual (0-538-73391-8)
Laurie McManus, *St. Louis Community College at Meramec*
The *Complete Solutions Manual* provides worked-out solutions to all of the problems in the text.

Annotated Instructor's Edition (1-4390-4865-7)
The *Annotated Instructor's Edition* provides the complete student text with answers next to each respective exercise. New to this edition: Teaching Examples have been added for each worked example.

Electronic Ancillaries

Enhanced WebAssign

Instant feedback and ease of use are just two reasons why WebAssign is the most widely used homework system in higher education. WebAssign's homework delivery system allows you to assign, collect, grade, and record homework assignments via the web. Personal Study Plans provide diagnostic quizzing for each chapter that identifies concepts that students still need to master, and directs them to the appropriate review material. And now, this proven system has been enhanced to include links to textbook sections, video examples, and problem-specific tutorials. For further utility, students will also have the option to purchase an online multimedia eBook of the text. Enhanced WebAssign is more than a homework system—it is a complete learning system for math students. Contact your local representative for ordering details.

Solution Builder (0-538-73392-6)

Easily build solution sets for homework or exams using *Solution Builder's* online solutions manual.

PowerLecture with ExamView® (0-538-73388-8)

This CD-ROM provides the instructor with dynamic media tools for teaching. Create, deliver, and customize tests (both print and online) in minutes with *ExamView® Computerized Testing Featuring Algorithmic Equations.* Easily build solution sets for homework or exams using *Solution Builder's* online solutions manual. Microsoft® PowerPoint® lecture slides, figures from the book, and Test Bank, in electronic format, are also included on this CD-ROM.

Text Specific Videos (0-538-73389-6)

Rena Petrello, *Moorpark College*

These 10- to 20-minute problem-solving lessons cover nearly every learning objective from each chapter in the Tussy/Gustafson/Koenig text. Recipient of the "Mark Dever Award for Excellence in Teaching," Rena Petrello presents each lesson using her experience teaching online mathematics courses. It was through this online teaching experience that Rena discovered the lack of suitable content for online instructors, which caused her to develop her own video lessons—and ultimately create this video project. These videos have won four awards: two Telly Awards, one Communicator Award, and one Aurora Award (an international honor). Students will love the additional guidance and support when they have missed a class or when they are preparing for an upcoming quiz or exam. The videos are available for purchase as a set of DVDs or online via ichapters.com.

STUDENT RESOURCES

Print Ancillaries

Student Workbook (0-538-49545-6)

Maria H. Andersen, *Muskegon Community College*

NEW! Get a head-start. The *Student Workbook* contains all of the assessments, activities, and worksheets from the *Instructor's Resource Binder* for classroom discussions, in-class activities, and group work.

Student Solutions Manual (0-538-73390-X)

Laurie McManus, *St. Louis Community College at Meramec*

The *Student Solutions Manual* provides worked-out solutions to the odd-numbered problems in the text.

Electronic Ancillaries

Enhanced WebAssign

Get instant feedback on your homework assignments with Enhanced WebAssign (assigned by your instructor). Personal Study Plans provide diagnostic quizzing for each chapter that identifies concepts that you still need to master, and directs you to the appropriate review material. This online homework system is easy to use and includes helpful links to textbook sections, video examples, and problem-specific tutorials. For further ease of use, purchase an online multimedia eBook via WebAssign.

Website *www.cengage.com/math/tussy*

Visit us on the web for access to a wealth of learning resources, including tutorials, final exams, chapter outlines, chapter reviews, web links, videos, flashcards, study skills handouts, and more!

ACKNOWLEDGMENTS

We want to express our gratitude to our accuracy checker, Paul McCombs, as well as many others for their help with this project: Steve Odrich, Mary Lou Wogan, Maria H. Andersen, Sheila Pisa, Laurie McManus, Alexander Lee, Ed Kavanaugh, Karl Hunsicker, Cathy Gong, Dave Ryba, Terry Damron, Marion Hammond, Lin Humphrey, Doug Keebaugh, Robin Carter, Tanja Rinkel, Bob Billups, Jeff Cleveland, Jo Morrison, Sheila White, Jim McClain, Paul Swatzel, and the Citrus College library staff (including Barbara Rugeley) for their help with this project. Your encouragement, suggestions, and insight have been invaluable to us.

We would also like to express our thanks to the Cengage Learning editorial, marketing, production, and design staff for helping us craft this new edition: Charlie Van Wagner, Danielle Derbenti, Gordon Lee, Rita Lombard, Greta Kleinert, Stefanie Beeck, Jennifer Cordoba, Angela Kim, Maureen Ross, Heleny Wong, Jennifer Risden, Vernon Boes, Diane Beasley, Carol O'Connell, and Graphic World.

Additionally, we would like to say that authoring a textbook is a tremendous undertaking. A revision of this scale would not have been possible without the thoughtful feedback and support from the following colleagues listed below. Their contributions to this edition have shaped this revision in countless ways.

Alan S. Tussy
R. David Gustafson
Diane R. Koenig

Advisory Board

J. Donato Fortin, *Johnson and Wales University*
Geoff Hagopian, *College of the Desert*
Jane Wampler, *Housatonic Community College*
Mary Lou Wogan, *Klamath Community College*
Kevin Yokoyama, *College of the Redwoods*

Reviewers

Darla Aguilar, *Pima Community College*
Sheila Anderson, *Housatonic Community College*
David Behrman, *Somerset Community College*
Michael Branstetter, *Hartnell College*
Joseph A. Bruno, Jr., *Community College of Allegheny County*

Joy Conner, *Tidewater Community College*
Ruth Dalrymple, *Saint Philip's College*
John D. Driscoll, *Middlesex Community College*
LaTonya Ellis, *Bishop State Community College*
Steven Felzer, *Lenoir Community College*
Rhoderick Fleming, *Wake Technical Community College*
Heather Gallacher, *Cleveland State University*
Kathirave Giritharan, *John A. Logan College*
Marilyn Green, *Merritt College and Diablo Valley College*
Joseph Guiciardi, *Community College of Allegheny County*
Deborah Hanus, *Brookhaven College*
A.T. Hayashi, *Oxnard College*
Susan Kautz, *Cy-Fair College*
Sandy Lofstock, *Saint Petersburg College–Tarpon Springs*
Mikal McDowell, *Cedar Valley College*
Gregory Perkins, *Hartnell College*
Euguenia Peterson, *City Colleges of Chicago–Richard Daley*
Carol Ann Poore, *Hinds Community College*
Christopher Quarles, *Shoreline Community College*
George Reed, *Angelina College*
John Squires, *Cleveland State Community College*
Sharon Testone, *Onondaga Community College*
Bill Thompson, *Red Rocks Community College*
Donna Tupper, *Community College of Baltimore County–Essex*
Andreana Walker, *Calhoun Community College*
Jane Wampler, *Housatonic Community College*
Mary Young, *Brookdale Community College*

Focus Groups

David M. Behrman, *Somerset Community College*
Eric Compton, *Brookdale Community College*
Nathalie Darden, *Brookdale Community College*
Joseph W. Giuciardi, *Community College of Allegheny County*
Cheryl Hobneck, *Illinois Valley Community College*
Todd J. Hoff, *Wisconsin Indianhead Technical College*
Jack Keating, *Massasoit Community College*
Russ Alan Killingsworth, *Seattle Pacific University*
Lynn Marecek, *Santa Ana College*
Lois Martin, *Massasoit Community College*
Chris Mirbaha, *The Community College of Baltimore County*
K. Maggie Pasqua, *Brookdale Community College*
Patricia C. Rome, *Delgado Community College*
Patricia B. Roux, *Delgado Community College*
Rebecca Rozario, *Brookdale Community College*
Barbara Tozzi, *Brookdale Community College*
Arminda Wey, *Brookdale Community College*
Valerie Wright, *Central Piedmont Community College*

Reviewers of Previous Editions

Cedric E. Atkins, *Mott Community College*
William D. Barcus, *SUNY, Stony Brook*
Kathy Bernunzio, *Portland Community College*
Linda Bettie, *Western New Mexico University*
Girish Budhwar, *United Tribes Technical College*
Sharon Camner, *Pierce College–Fort Steilacoom*
Robin Carter, *Citrus College*
John Coburn, *Saint Louis Community College–Florissant Valley*
Sally Copeland, *Johnson County Community College*
Ann Corbeil, *Massasoit Community College*
Ben Cornelius, *Oregon Institute of Technology*
Carolyn Detmer, *Seminole Community College*
James Edmondson, *Santa Barbara Community College*
David L. Fama, *Germanna Community College*
Maggie Flint, *Northeast State Technical Community College*
Charles Ford, *Shasta College*
Barbara Gentry, *Parkland College*
Kathirave Giritharan, *John A. Logan College*
Michael Heeren, *Hamilton College*
Laurie Hoecherl, *Kishwaukee College*
Judith Jones, *Valencia Community College*
Therese Jones, *Amarillo College*
Joanne Juedes, *University of Wisconsin–Marathon County*
Dennis Kimzey, *Rogue Community College*
Monica C. Kurth, *Scott Community College*
Sally Leski, *Holyoke Community College*
Sandra Lofstock, *St. Petersberg College–Tarpon Springs Center*
Elizabeth Morrison, *Valencia Community College*
Jan Alicia Nettler, *Holyoke Community College*
Marge Palaniuk, *United Tribes Technical College*
Scott Perkins, *Lake-Sumter Community College*
Angela Peterson, *Portland Community College*
Jane Pinnow, *University of Wisconsin–Parkside*
J. Doug Richey, *Northeast Texas Community College*
Angelo Segalla, *Orange Coast College*
Eric Sims, *Art Institute of Dallas*
Lee Ann Spahr, *Durham Technical Community College*
Annette Squires, *Palomar College*
John Strasser, *Scottsdale Community College*
June Strohm, *Pennsylvania State Community College–Dubois*
Rita Sturgeon, *San Bernardino Valley College*
Stuart Swain, *University of Maine at Machias*
Celeste M. Teluk, *D'Youville College*
Jo Anne Temple, *Texas Technical University*
Sharon Testone, *Onondaga Community College*
Marilyn Treder, *Rochester Community College*
Sven Trenholm, *Herkeimer County Community College*
Thomas Vanden Eynden, *Thomas More College*
Stephen Whittle, *Augusta State University*
Mary Lou Wogan, *Klamath Community College*

ABOUT THE AUTHORS

Alan S. Tussy

Alan Tussy teaches all levels of developmental mathematics at Citrus College in Glendora, California. He has written nine math books—a paperback series and a hardcover series. A meticulous, creative, and visionary teacher who maintains a keen focus on his students' greatest challenges, Alan Tussy is an extraordinary author, dedicated to his students' success. Alan received his Bachelor of Science degree in Mathematics from the University of Redlands and his Master of Science degree in Applied Mathematics from California State University, Los Angeles. He has taught up and down the curriculum from Prealgebra to Differential Equations. He is currently focusing on the developmental math courses. Professor Tussy is a member of the American Mathematical Association of Two-Year Colleges.

R. David Gustafson

R. David Gustafson is Professor Emeritus of Mathematics at Rock Valley College in Illinois and coauthor of several best-selling math texts, including Gustafson/Frisk's *Beginning Algebra, Intermediate Algebra, Beginning and Intermediate Algebra: A Combined Approach, College Algebra,* and the Tussy/Gustafson developmental mathematics series. His numerous professional honors include Rock Valley Teacher of the Year and Rockford's Outstanding Educator of the Year. He earned a Master of Arts from Rockford College in Illinois, as well as a Master of Science from Northern Illinois University.

Diane R. Koenig

Diane Koenig received a Bachelor of Science degree in Secondary Math Education from Illinois State University in 1980. She began her career at Rock Valley College in 1981, when she became the Math Supervisor for the newly formed Personalized Learning Center. Earning her Master's Degree in Applied Mathematics from Northern Illinois University, Ms. Koenig in 1984 had the distinction of becoming the first full-time woman mathematics faculty member at Rock Valley College. In addition to being nominated for AMATYC's Excellence in Teaching Award, Diane Koenig was chosen as the Rock Valley College Faculty of the Year by her peers in 2005, and, in 2006, she was awarded the NISOD Teaching Excellence Award as well as the Illinois Mathematics Association of Community Colleges Award for Teaching Excellence. In addition to her teaching, Ms. Koenig has been an active member of the Illinois Mathematics Association of Community Colleges (IMACC). As a member, she has served on the board of directors, on a state-level task force rewriting the course outlines for the developmental mathematics courses, and as the association's newsletter editor.

APPLICATIONS INDEX

Examples that are applications are shown with boldface page numbers.
Exercises that are applications are shown with lightface pages numbers.

Study Skills Workshop

OBJECTIVES

1. Make the Commitment
2. Prepare to Learn
3. Manage Your Time
4. Listen and Take Notes
5. Build a Support System
6. Do Your Homework
7. Prepare for the Test

© iStockphoto.com/Aldo Murillo

*S*UCCESS IN YOUR COLLEGE COURSES *requires more than just mastery of the content. The development of strong study skills and disciplined work habits plays a crucial role as well. Good note-taking, listening, test-taking, team-building, and time management skills are habits that can serve you well, not only in this course, but throughout your life and into your future career. Students often find that the approach to learning that they used for their high school classes no longer works when they reach college. In this* Study Skills Workshop, *we will discuss ways of improving and fine-tuning your study skills, providing you with the best chance for a successful college experience.*

1 Make the Commitment

Starting a new course is exciting, but it also may be a little frightening. Like any new opportunity, in order to be successful, it will require a commitment of both time and resources. You can decrease the anxiety of this commitment by having a plan to deal with these added responsibilities.

Set Your Goals for the Course.   Explore the reasons why you are taking this course. What do you hope to gain upon completion? Is this course a prerequisite for further study in mathematics? Maybe you need to complete this course in order to begin taking coursework related to your field of study. No matter what your reasons, setting goals for yourself will increase your chances of success. Establish your ultimate goal and then break it down into a series of smaller goals; it is easier to achieve a series of short-term goals rather than focusing on one larger goal.

Keep a Positive Attitude.   Since your level of effort is significantly influenced by your attitude, strive to maintain a positive mental outlook throughout the class. From time to time, remind yourself of the ways in which you will benefit from passing the course. Overcome feelings of stress or math anxiety with extra preparation, campus support services, and activities you enjoy. When you accomplish short-term goals such as studying for a specific period of time, learning a difficult concept, or completing a homework assignment, reward yourself by spending time with friends, listening to music, reading a novel, or playing a sport.

Attend Each Class.   Many students don't realize that missing even one class can have a great effect on their grade. Arriving late takes its toll as well. If you are just a few minutes late, or miss an entire class, you risk getting behind. So, keep these tips in mind.

- Arrive on time, or a little early.

- If you must miss a class, get a set of notes, the homework assignments, and any handouts that the instructor may have provided for the day that you missed.

- Study the material you missed. Take advantage of the help that comes with this textbook, such as the video examples and problem-specific tutorials.

Now Try This

1. List six ways in which you will benefit from passing this course.

2. List six short-term goals that will help you achieve your larger goal of passing this course. For example, you could set a goal to read through the entire *Study Skills Workshop* within the first 2 weeks of class or attend class regularly and on time. (**Success Tip:** Revisit this action item once you have read through all seven *Study Skills Workshop* learning objectives.)

3. List some simple ways you can reward yourself when you complete one of your short-term class goals.

4. Plan ahead! List five possible situations that could cause you to be late for class or miss a class. (Some examples are parking/traffic delays, lack of a babysitter, oversleeping, or job responsibilities.) What can you do ahead of time so that these situations won't cause you to be late or absent?

2 Prepare to Learn

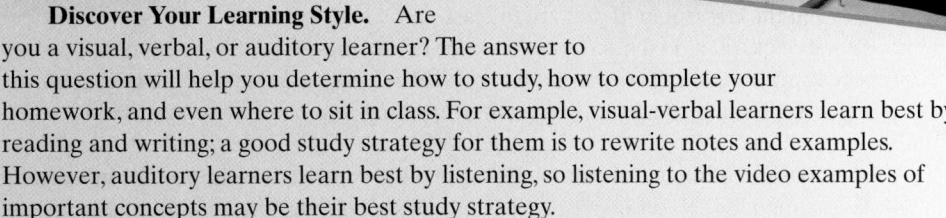

Many students believe that there are two types of people—those who are good at math and those who are not—and that this cannot be changed. This is not true! You can increase your chances for success in mathematics by taking time to prepare and taking inventory of your skills and resources.

Discover Your Learning Style. Are you a visual, verbal, or auditory learner? The answer to this question will help you determine how to study, how to complete your homework, and even where to sit in class. For example, visual-verbal learners learn best by reading and writing; a good study strategy for them is to rewrite notes and examples. However, auditory learners learn best by listening, so listening to the video examples of important concepts may be their best study strategy.

Get to Know Your Textbook and Its Resources. You have made a significant investment in your education by purchasing this book and the resources that accompany it. It has been designed with you in mind. Use as many of the features and resources as possible in ways that best fit your learning style.

Know What Is Expected. Your course syllabus maps out your instructor's expectations for the course. Read the syllabus completely and make sure you understand all that is required. If something is not clear, contact your instructor for clarification.

Organize Your Notebook. You will definitely appreciate a well-organized notebook when it comes time to study for the final exam. So let's start now! Refer to your syllabus and create a separate section in the notebook for each chapter (or unit of study) that your class will cover this term. Now, set a standard order within each section. One recommended order is to begin with your class notes, followed by your completed homework assignments, then any study sheets or handouts, and, finally, all graded quizzes and tests.

Now Try This

1. To determine what type of learner you are, take the *Learning Style Survey* at http://www.metamath.com/multiple/multiple_choice_questions.html. You may also wish to take the *Index of Learning Styles Questionnaire* at http://www.engr.ncsu.edu/learningstyles/ilsweb.html, which will help you determine your learning type and offer study suggestions by type. List what you learned from taking these surveys. How will you use this information to help you succeed in class?

2. Complete the *Study Skills Checklists* found at the end of sections 1–4 of Chapter 1 in order to become familiar with the many features that can enhance your learning experience using this book.

3. Read through the list of Student Resources found in the Preface of this book. Which ones will you use in this class?

4. Read through your syllabus and write down any questions that you would like to ask your instructor.

5. Organize your notebook using the guidelines given above. Place your syllabus at the very front of your notebook so that you can see the dates over which the material will be covered and for easy reference throughout the course.

3 | Manage Your Time

Now that you understand the importance of attending class, how will you make time to study what you have learned while attending? Much like learning to play the piano, math skills are best learned by practicing a little every day.

Make the Time.   In general, 2 hours of independent study time is recommended for every hour in the classroom. If you are in class 3 hours per week, plan on 6 hours per week for reviewing your notes and completing your homework. It is best to schedule this time over the length of a week rather than to try to cram everything into one or two marathon study days.

Prioritize and Make a Calendar.   Because daily practice is so important in learning math, it is a good idea to set up a calendar that lists all of your time commitments, as well as the time you will need to set aside for studying and doing your homework. Consider how you spend your time each week and prioritize your tasks by importance. During the school term, you may need to reduce or even eliminate certain nonessential tasks in order to meet your goals for the term.

Maximize Your Study Efforts.   Using the information you learned from determining your learning style, set up your blocks of study time so that you get the most out of these sessions. Do you study best in groups or do you need to study alone to get anything done? Do you learn best when you schedule your study time in 30-minute time blocks or do you need at least an hour before the information kicks in? Consider your learning style to set up a schedule that truly suits your needs.

Avoid Distractions.   Between texting and social networking, we have so many opportunities for distraction and procrastination. On top of these, there are the distractions of TV, video games, and friends stopping by to hang out. Once you have set your schedule, honor your study times by turning off any electronic devices and letting your voicemail take messages for you. After this time, you can reward yourself by returning phone calls and messages or spending time with friends after the pressure of studying has been lifted.

Now Try This

1. Keep track of how you spend your time for a week. Rate each activity on a scale from 1 (not important) to 5 (very important). Are there any activities that you need to reduce or eliminate in order to have enough time to study this term?

2. List three ways that you learn best according to your learning style. How can you use this information when setting up your study schedule?

3. Download the *Weekly Planner Form* from www.cengage.com/math/tussy and complete your schedule. If you prefer, you may set up a schedule in Google Calendar (calendar.google.com), www.rememberthemilk.com, your cell, or your email system. Many of these have the ability to set up useful reminders and to-do lists in addition to a weekly schedule.

4. List three ways in which you are most often distracted. What can you do to avoid these distractions during your scheduled study times?

4 Listen and Take Notes

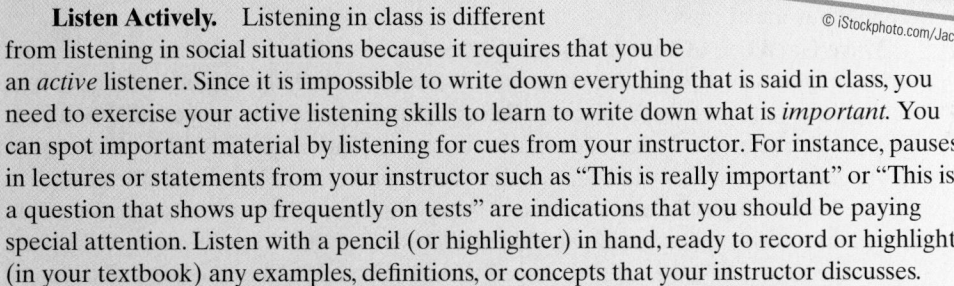

Make good use of your class time by listening and taking notes. Because your instructor will be giving explanations and examples that may not be found in your textbook, as well as other information about your course (test dates, homework assignments, and so on), it is important that you keep a written record of what was said in class.

© iStockphoto.com/Jacob Wackerhausen

Listen Actively.   Listening in class is different from listening in social situations because it requires that you be an *active* listener. Since it is impossible to write down everything that is said in class, you need to exercise your active listening skills to learn to write down what is *important*. You can spot important material by listening for cues from your instructor. For instance, pauses in lectures or statements from your instructor such as "This is really important" or "This is a question that shows up frequently on tests" are indications that you should be paying special attention. Listen with a pencil (or highlighter) in hand, ready to record or highlight (in your textbook) any examples, definitions, or concepts that your instructor discusses.

Take Notes You Can Use.   Don't worry about making your notes really neat. After class you can rework them into a format that is more useful to you. However, you should organize your notes as much as possible as you write them. Copy the examples your instructor uses in class. Circle or star any key concepts or definitions that your instructor mentions while explaining the example. Later, your homework problems will look a lot like the examples given in class, so be sure to copy each of the steps in detail.

Listen with an Open Mind.   Even if there are concepts presented that you feel you already know, keep tuned in to the presentation of the material and look for a deeper understanding of the material. If the material being presented is something that has been difficult for you in the past, listen with an open mind; your new instructor may have a fresh presentation that works for you.

Avoid Classroom Distractions.   Some of the same things that can distract you from your study time can distract you, and others, during class. Because of this, be sure to turn off your cell phone during class. If you take notes on a laptop, log out of your email and social networking sites during class. In addition to these distractions, avoid getting into side conversations with other students. Even if you feel you were only distracted for a few moments, you may have missed important verbal or body language cues about an upcoming exam or hints that will aid in your understanding of a concept.

Now Try This

1. Before your next class, refer to your syllabus and read the section(s) that will be covered. Make a list of the terms that you predict your instructor will think are most important.

2. During your next class, bring your textbook and keep it open to the sections being covered. If your instructor mentions a definition, concept, or example that is found in your text, highlight it.

3. Find at least one classmate with whom you can review notes. Make an appointment to compare your class notes as soon as possible after the class. Did you find differences in your notes?

4. Go to www.cengage.com/math/tussy and read the *Reworking Your Notes* handout. Complete the action items given in this document.

5 Build a Support System

© iStockphoto.com/Chris Schmidt

Have you ever had the experience where you understand everything that your instructor is saying in class, only to go home and try a homework problem and be completely stumped? This is a common complaint among math students. The key to being a successful math student is to take care of these problems before you go on to tackle new material. That is why you should know what resources are available outside of class.

Make Good Use of Your Instructor's Office Hours.   The purpose of your instructor's office hours is to be available to help students with questions. Usually these hours are listed in your syllabus and no appointment is needed. When you visit your instructor, have a list of questions and try to pinpoint exactly where in the process you are getting stuck. This will help your instructor answer your questions efficiently.

Use Your Campus Tutoring Services.   Many colleges offer tutorial services for free. Sometimes tutorial assistance is available in a lab setting where you are able to drop in at your convenience. In some cases, you need to make an appointment to see a tutor in advance. Make sure to seek help as soon as you recognize the need, and come to see your tutor with a list of identified problems.

Form a Study Group.   Study groups are groups of classmates who meet outside of class to discuss homework problems or study for tests. Get the most out of your study group by following these guidelines:

- Keep the group small—a maximum of four committed students. Set a regularly scheduled meeting day, time, and place.

- Find a place to meet where you can talk and spread out your work.

- Members should attempt all homework problems before meeting.

- All members should contribute to the discussion.

- When you meet, practice verbalizing and explaining problems and concepts to each other. The best way to really learn a topic is by teaching it to someone else.

Now Try This

1. Refer to your syllabus. Highlight your instructor's office hours and location. Next, pay a visit to your instructor during office hours this week and introduce yourself. (**Success Tip:** Program your instructor's office phone number and email address into your cell phone or email contact list.)

2. Locate your campus tutoring center or math lab. Write down the office hours, phone number, and location on your syllabus. Drop by or give them a call and find out how to go about making an appointment with a tutor.

3. Find two to three classmates who are available to meet at a time that fits your schedule. Plan to meet 2 days before your next homework assignment is due and follow the guidelines given above. After your group has met, evaluate how well it worked. Is there anything that the group can do to make it better next time you meet?

4. Download the *Support System Worksheet* at www.cengage.com/math/tussy. Complete the information and keep it at the front of your notebook following your syllabus.

6 Do Your Homework

Attending class and taking notes are important, but the only way that you are really going to learn mathematics is by completing your homework. Sitting in class and listening to lectures will help you to place concepts in short-term memory, but in order to do well on tests and in future math classes, you want to put these concepts in long-term memory. When completed regularly, homework assignments will help with this.

Give Yourself Enough Time.   In Objective 3, you made a study schedule, setting aside 2 hours for study and homework for every hour that you spend in class. If you are not keeping this schedule, make changes to ensure that you can spend enough time outside of class to learn new material.

Review Your Notes and the Worked Examples from Your Text.   In Objective 4, you learned how to take useful notes. Before you begin your homework, review or rework your notes. Then, read the sections in your textbook that relate to your homework problems, paying special attention to the worked examples. With a pencil in hand, work the *Self Check* and *Now Try* problems that are listed next to the examples in your text. Using the worked example as a guide, solve these problems and try to understand each step. As you read through your notes and your text, keep a list of anything that you don't understand.

Now Try Your Homework Problems.   Once you have reviewed your notes and the textbook worked examples, you should be able to successfully manage the bulk of your homework assignment easily. When working on your homework, keep your textbook and notes close by for reference. If you have trouble with a homework question, look through your textbook and notes to see if you can identify an example that is similar to the homework question. See if you can apply the same steps to your homework problem. If there are places where you get stuck, add these to your list of questions.

Get Answers to Your Questions.   At least one day before your assignment is due, seek help with the questions you have been listing. You can contact a classmate for assistance, make an appointment with a tutor, or visit your instructor during office hours.

Now Try This

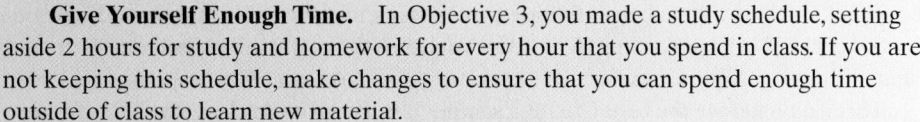

1. Review your study schedule. Are you following it? If not, what changes can you make to adhere to the rule of 2 hours of homework and study for every hour of class?

2. Find five homework problems that are similar to the worked examples in your textbook. Were there any homework problems in your assignment that didn't have a worked example that was similar? (**Success Tip:** Look for the *Now Try* and *Guided Practice* features for help linking problems to worked examples.)

3. As suggested in this Objective, make a list of questions while completing your homework. Visit your tutor or your instructor with your list of questions and ask one of them to work through these problems with you.

4. Go to www.cengage.com/math/tussy and read the *Study and Memory Techniques* handout. List the techniques that will be most helpful to you in your math course.

7 Prepare for the Test

Image copyright Cristian M, 2009. Used under license from Shutterstock.com

Taking a test does not need to be an unpleasant experience. Use your time management, organization, and these test-taking strategies to make this a learning experience and improve your score.

Make Time to Prepare.   Schedule at least four daily 1-hour sessions to prepare specifically for your test.

Four days before the test: Create your own study sheet using your reworked notes. Imagine you could bring one $8\frac{1}{2} \times 11$ sheet of paper to your test. What would you write on that sheet? Include all the key definitions, rules, steps, and formulas that were discussed in class or covered in your reading. Whenever you have the opportunity, pull out your study sheet and review your test material.

Three days before the test: Create a sample test using the in-class examples from your notes and reading material. As you review and work these examples, make sure you understand how each example relates to the rules or definitions on your study sheet. While working through these examples, you may find that you forgot a concept that should be on your study sheet. Update your study sheet and continue to review it.

Two days before the test: Use the *Chapter Test* from your textbook or create one by matching problems from your text to the example types from your sample test. Now, with your book closed, take a timed trial test. When you are done, check your answers. Make a list of the topics that were difficult for you and review or add these to your study sheet.

One day before the test: Review your study sheet once more, paying special attention to the material that was difficult for you when you took your practice test the day before. Be sure you have all the materials that you will need for your test laid out ahead of time (two sharpened pencils, a good eraser, possibly a calculator or protractor, and so on). The most important thing you can do today is get a good night's rest.

Test day: Review your study sheet, if you have time. Focus on how well you have prepared and take a moment to relax. When taking your test, complete the problems that you are sure of first. Skip the problems that you don't understand right away, and return to them later. Bring a watch or make sure there will be some kind of time-keeping device in your test room so that you can keep track of your time. Try not to spend too much time on any one problem.

Now Try This

1. Create a study schedule using the guidelines given above.

2. Read the *Preparing for a Test* handout at www.cengage.com/math/tussy.

3. Read the *Taking the Test* handout at www.cengage.com/math/tussy.

4. After your test has been returned and scored, read the *Analyzing Your Test Results* handout at www.cengage.com/math/tussy.

5. Take time to reflect on your homework and study habits after you have received your test score. What actions are working well for you? What do you need to improve?

6. To prepare for your final exam, read the *Preparing for Your Final Exam* handout at www.cengage.com/math/tussy. Complete the action items given in this document.

An Introduction to Algebra

© 2009 Jupiterimages

from *Campus to Careers*

Physician Assistant

Physician assistants practice medicine under the direction of doctors and surgeons. They are trained to diagnose, treat, and suggest preventative health care measures as directed by their supervising physician. Working as members of a health care team, they take medical histories, examine and treat patients, order and read laboratory tests and x-rays, and make diagnoses.

In **Problem 78** of **Study Set 1.4,** you will see how physician assistants use signed numbers to help assess a patient's risk of contracting heart disease.

JOB TITLE:
Physician Assistant

EDUCATION: Most programs require 2 or more years of study leading to a master's degree.

JOB OUTLOOK: Excellent. Jobs are expected to grow much faster than average for all occupations through the year 2016.

ANNUAL EARNINGS: Median salary: $74,160

FOR MORE INFORMATION:
www.bls.gov/oco/ocos081.htm

Objectives

1 Read tables and graphs.

2 Use the basic vocabulary and notation of algebra.

3 Identify algebraic expressions and equations.

4 Use equations to construct tables of data.

SECTION 1.1
The Language of Algebra

© Andersen Ross/Getty Images

Algebra is the result of contributions from many cultures over thousands of years. The word *algebra* comes from the title of the book *Ihm Al-jabr wa'l muqābalah*, written by the Arabian mathematician al-Khwarizmi around A.D. 800. Using the vocabulary and notation of algebra, we can mathematically **model** many situations in the real world. In this section, we begin to explore the language of algebra by introducing some of its basic components.

1 Read tables and graphs.

Two-column **tables** are often used to describe numerical relationships. For example, the table below lists the number of bicycle tires a production planner must order when a given number of bicycles are to be manufactured. For a production run of, say, 300 bikes, we locate 300 in the left-hand column and then scan across the table to see that the company must order 600 tires.

The information in the table can be presented in a **bar graph** as shown below. The **horizontal axis** labeled "Number of bicycles to be manufactured" has been scaled in units of 100 bicycles. The **vertical axis,** labeled "Number of tires to order," is scaled in units of 100 tires. The bars directly over each of the production amounts extend to a height indicating the corresponding number of tires to order. For example, if 200 bikes are to be manufactured, the height of the bar indicates that 400 tires should be ordered.

Bicycles to be manufactured	Tires to order
100	200
200	400
300	600
400	800

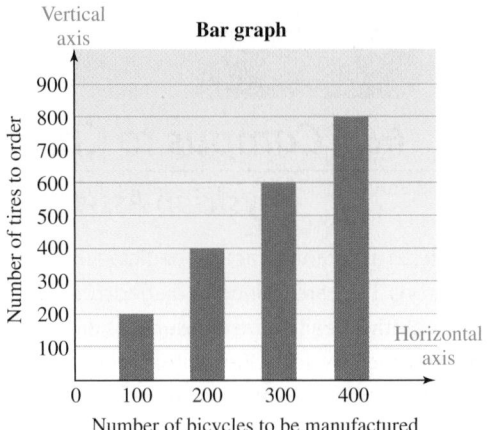

> **The Language of Algebra** *Horizontal* is a form of the word *horizon*. Think of the sun setting over the *horizon*. For *vertical*, think of vertical blinds. They are usually used as window coverings for large window areas and run up and down.

Another way to present the information is with a **line graph.** Instead of using a bar to denote the number of tires to order for a production run of a given size, we use a dot drawn at the correct height. After drawing the four data points for 100, 200, 300, and 400 bicycles, we connect them with line segments to create the following line graph.

Line graph

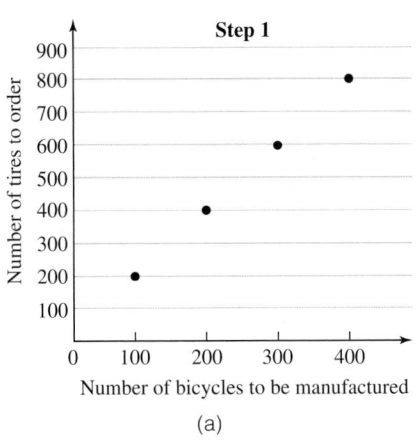

Step 1

(a)

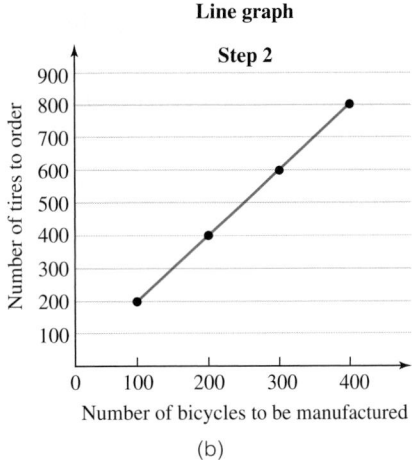

Step 2

(b)

The line graph not only presents all the information contained in the table and the bar graph, it also provides additional information that they do not. We can use the line graph to find the number of tires to order for a production run of a size not shown in the table or the bar graph.

EXAMPLE 1 Use the line graph to find the number of tires needed when 250 bicycles are to be manufactured.

Strategy We will start on the horizontal axis at 250. Then we will scan up to the line, and over, to read the number of tires to order on the vertical axis.

WHY We start on the horizontal axis because that scale gives the number of bicycles to be manufactured. We scan up and over to the vertical axis because that scale gives the number of tires to order.

Solution

First, locate 250 (between 200 and 300) on the horizontal axis. Then draw a line straight up to intersect the graph. (See the figure below.) From the point of intersection, draw a horizontal line to the left that intersects the vertical axis. We see that the number of tires to order is 500.

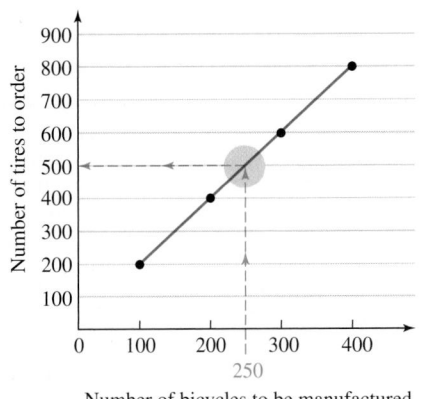

2 Use the basic vocabulary and notation of algebra.

From the table, the bar graph, and the line graph, we see that there is a relationship between the number of tires to order and the number of bicycles to be manufactured. Using words, we can express this relationship as follows:

"The number of tires to order is two times the number of bicycles to be manufactured."

Since the word **product** is used to indicate the answer to a multiplication, we can restate the relationship this way:

"The number of tires to order is the *product* of 2 and the number of bicycles to be manufactured."

To indicate other arithmetic operations, we will use the following words.

- A **sum** is the result of an addition: The sum of 5 and 6 is equal to 11.
- A **difference** is the result of a subtraction: The difference of 3 and 2 is equal to 1.
- A **quotient** is the result of a division: The quotient of 6 and 3 is equal to 2.

Many symbols used in arithmetic are also used in algebra. For example, a + symbol is used to indicate addition, and a − symbol is used to indicate subtraction, and an = symbol means *is equal to*. Because the letter x is often used in algebra and could be confused with the multiplication symbol ×, we usually write multiplication using a **raised dot** or **parentheses.**

Symbols Used for Multiplication

×	times symbol	$6 \times 4 = 24$
·	raised dot	$6 \cdot 4 = 24$
( )	parentheses	$(6)4 = 24$ or $6(4) = 24$ or $(6)(4) = 24$

There are a few ways to indicate division. In algebra, the symbol most often used to indicate division is the *fraction bar.*

Symbols Used for Division

÷	division symbol	$24 \div 4 = 6$
$)$	long division	$4\overline{)24}$ with 6 on top
—	fraction bar	$\dfrac{24}{4} = 6$

Self Check 2

Express the following statement in words.

$$22 \cdot 11 = 242$$

Now Try Problem 49

Self Check 2 Answer
The product of 22 and 11 is equal to 242.

EXAMPLE 2   Express each statement in words, using one of the words *sum, product, difference,* or *quotient.*   **a.** $22 \div 11 = 2$ **b.** $22 + 11 = 33$

Strategy We will look at the symbols used in each statement to see whether addition, subtraction, multiplication, or division is indicated.

WHY The word we should use (*sum, product, difference,* or *quotient*) depends on the arithmetic operation we have to describe.

Solution

a. The quotient of 22 and 11 is equal to 2.

b. The sum of 22 and 11 is equal to 33.

Teaching Example 2 Express each statement in words, using one of the words *sum, difference, product,* or *quotient.*
a. $7 \cdot 5 = 35$
b. $26 - 15 = 11$
Answers:
a. The product of 7 and 5 is equal to 35.
b. The difference of 26 and 15 is equal to 11.

3 Identify algebraic expressions and equations.

Another way to describe the tires–to–bicycles relationship uses *variables*. **Variables** are letters (or symbols) that stand for numbers. If we let the letter b represent the number of bicycles to be manufactured, then the number of tires to order is two times b, written $2b$. In the notation, the number 2 is an example of a **constant** because it does not change value.

> ***The Language of Algebra***   Since the number of bicycles to be manufactured can *vary,* or change, it is represented using a *variable.*

When multiplying a variable by a number, or a variable by another variable, we can omit the symbol for multiplication. For example,

$2b$ means $2 \cdot b$ xy means $x \cdot y$ $8abc$ means $8 \cdot a \cdot b \cdot c$

We call $2b$, xy, and $8abc$ *algebraic expressions.*

Algebraic Expressions

Variables and/or numbers can be combined with the operations of addition, subtraction, multiplication, and division to create **algebraic expressions.**

Here are some other examples of algebraic expressions.

$4a + 7$ This expression is a combination of the numbers 4 and 7, the variable a, and the operations of multiplication and addition.

$\dfrac{10 - y}{3}$ This expression is a combination of the numbers 10 and 3, the variable y, and the operations of subtraction and division.

$15mn(2m)$ This expression is a combination of the numbers 15 and 2, the variables m and n, and the operation of multiplication.

> ***The Language of Algebra***   We often refer to *algebraic expressions* as simply *expressions.*

In the bicycle manufacturing example, if we let the letter t stand for the number of tires to order, we can translate the **verbal model** to mathematical symbols.

The number of tires to order	is	two	times	the number of bicycles to be manufactured
t	$=$	2	$\cdot$	b

The statement $t = 2 \cdot b$, or more simply, $t = 2b$, is called an *equation*. An **equation** is a mathematical sentence that contains an $=$ symbol. The $=$ symbol indicates that the expressions on either side of it have the same value. Other examples of equations are

$3 + 5 = 8$ $x + 5 = 20$ $17 - 2r = 14 + 3r$ $p = 100 - d$

> **The Language of Algebra**   The equal symbol = can be represented by verbs such as:
>
>   *is*   *are*   *gives*   *yields*
>
> The symbol ≠ is read as *"is not equal to."*

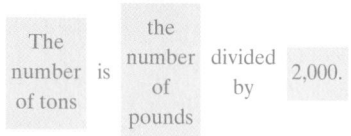
EXAMPLE 3   Translate the verbal model into an equation.

| The number of decades | is | the number of years | divided by | 10. |

Strategy We will represent the unknown quantities using variables and we will use symbols to represent the words *is* and *divided by*.

WHY To translate a verbal (word) model into an equation means to write it using mathematical symbols.

Solution

We can represent the two unknown quantities using variables: Let d = the number of decades and y = the number of years. Then we have:

| The number of decades | is | the number of years | divided by | 10. |
| d | $=$ | y | $\div$ | 10 |

If we write the division using a fraction bar, then the verbal model translates to the equation $d = \frac{y}{10}$. ∎

In the bicycle-manufacturing example, using the equation $t = 2b$ to describe the relationship has one major advantage over the other methods we have discussed. It can be used to determine the number of tires needed for a production run of *any* size.

EXAMPLE 4   Use the equation $t = 2b$ to find the number of tires needed for a production run of 178 bicycles.

Strategy In $t = 2b$, we will replace b with 178. Then we will multiply 178 by 2 to obtain the value of t.

WHY The equation $t = 2b$ indicates that the number of tires is found by multiplying the number of bicycles by 2.

Solution

$t = 2b$	This is the describing equation.
$t = 2(\mathbf{178})$	Replace b, which stands for the number of bicycles, with 178. Use parentheses to show the multiplication.
$t = 356$	Perform the multiplication: $2(178) = 356$.

To manufacture 178 bicycles, 356 tires will be needed.

> **The Language of Algebra** To *substitute* means to put or use in place of another, as with a *substitute* teacher. In Example 4, we substitute 178 for b.

4 Use equations to construct tables of data.

Equations such as $t = 2b$, which express a relationship between two or more variables, are called **formulas.** Formulas are used in many fields, such as economics, biology, nursing, and construction. In the next example, we will see that the results found using the formula $t = 2b$ can be presented in table form.

EXAMPLE 5   Find the number of tires to order for production runs of 233 and 852 bicycles. Present the results in a table.

Strategy In the formula $t = 2b$, we will replace b with 233 and then with 852.

WHY We need to find the number of tires to order for two different-sized production runs.

Solution

Step 1 We begin by constructing a two-column table with the appropriate column headings. The size of each production run (233 and 852) is entered in the left-hand column of the table.

Bicycles to be manufactured b	Tires to order t
233	
852	

Step 2 We use the formula $t = 2b$ to find the number of tires needed if 233 and 852 bicycles are to be manufactured.

$t = 2b$

$t = 2(233)$ Replace b with 233.

$t = 466$

$t = 2b$

$t = 2(852)$ Replace b with 852.

$t = 1{,}704$

Step 3 We enter these results in the right-hand column of the table: 466 tires for 233 bicycles to be manufactured and 1,704 tires for 852 bicycles to be manufactured.

Bicycles to be manufactured b	Tires to order t
233	466
852	1,704

Now Try Problem 64

> **Self Check 5**
>
> Find the number of tires needed for production runs of 87 and 487 bicycles. Present the results in a table.
>
> **Self Check 5 Answers**
>
> | Bicycles to be manufactured b | Tires to order t |
> |---|---|
> | 87 | 174 |
> | 487 | 974 |
>
> **Teaching Example 5** Find the number of tires to order for production runs of 53 and 121 bicycles. Present the results in a table.
> *Answer:*
>
> | Bicycles b | Tires t |
> |---|---|
> | 53 | 106 |
> | 121 | 242 |

ANSWERS TO SELF CHECKS

1. 700 **2.** The product of 22 and 11 is equal to 242. **3.** $u = 500 - p$ **4.** 1,208

5.

Bicycles to be manufactured b	Tires to order t
87	174
487	974

STUDY SKILLS CHECKLIST

Get to Know Your Textbook

Congratulations. You now own a state-of-the-art textbook that has been written especially for you. The following checklist will help you become familiar with the organization of the book. Place a check mark ☑ in each box after you answer the question.

☐ Turn to the **Table of Contents** on page v. How many chapters does the book have?

☐ Each chapter of the book is divided into **sections.** How many sections are there in Chapter 1, which begins on page 1?

☐ **Learning Objectives** are listed at the start of each section. How many objectives are there for Section 1.6, which begins on page 58?

☐ Each section ends with a **Study Set.** How many problems are there in Study Set 1.5, which begins on page 56?

☐ Each chapter has a **Chapter Summary & Review.** Which column of the Chapter Summary found on page 106 contains examples?

☐ How many review problems are there for Section 1.1 in the **Chapter Summary & Review,** which begins on page 106?

☐ Each chapter has a **Chapter Test.** How many problems are there in the Chapter 1 Test, which begins on page 116?

☐ Each chapter beginning with Chapter 2 ends with a **Cumulative Review.** What chapters are covered by the Cumulative Review, which begins on page 383?

Answers: 9, 9, 4, 86, the right column, 12, 42, 1–4

SECTION 1.1   STUDY SET

▌VOCABULARY

Fill in the blanks.

1. The answer to an addition problem is called a _sum_. The answer to a subtraction problem is called a _difference_.

▶ 2. The answer to a multiplication problem is called a _product_. The answer to a division problem is called a _quotient_.

3. _Variables_ are letters or symbols that stand for numbers.

▶ 4. Variables and numbers can be combined with the operations of addition, subtraction, multiplication, and division to create algebraic _expressions_.

▶ 5. An _equation_ is a mathematical sentence that contains an = symbol.

6. An equation, such as $t = 2b$, which expresses a relationship between two or more variables, is called a _formula_.

7. In the illustration shown in Exercise 8, a _line_ graph is shown.

8. In the illustration below, the _horizontal_ axis of the graph has been scaled in units of 1 second. The _vertical_ axis of the graph has been scaled in units of 50 feet.

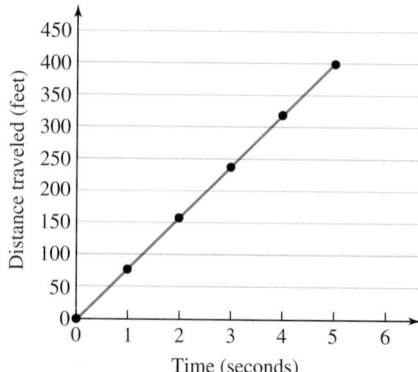

▌CONCEPTS

Classify each item as either an algebraic expression or an equation.

9. $18 + m = 23$
   equation

▶ 10. $18 + m$
   algebraic expression

▶ Selected exercises available online at
www.webassign.net/brookscole

11. $y - 1$
algebraic expression

▶ **12.** $y - 1 = 2$
equation

13. $30x$ algebraic expression

14. $t = 16b$ equation

15. $r = \dfrac{2}{3}$
equation

▶ **16.** $\dfrac{c - 7}{5}$
algebraic expression

17. a. What operations does the expression $5x - 16$ contain? multiplication, subtraction

b. What variable does the expression contain? x

▶ **18. a.** What operations does the expression $\dfrac{12 + t}{25}$ contain? addition, division

b. What variable does the expression contain? t

19. a. What operations does the equation $m + 1 = 20 - m$ contain? addition, subtraction

b. What variable does it contain? m

▶ **20. a.** What operations does the equation $y + 14 = 5(6)$ contain? addition, multiplication

b. What variable does it contain? y

21. TRAFFIC SAFETY As the railroad crossing guard drops, the measure of angle 1 (denoted ∠1) increases, while the measure of ∠2 decreases. At any instant, the sum of the measures of the two angles is 90°.

a. Complete the table.

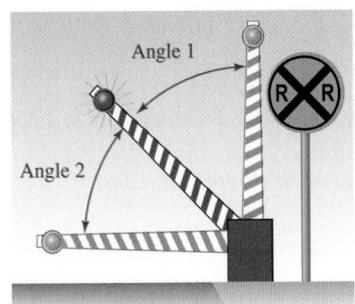

∠1	∠2
0°	90°
30°	60°
45°	45°
60°	30°
90°	0°

b. Use the data in the table to construct a line graph for values of ∠1 from 0° to 90°.

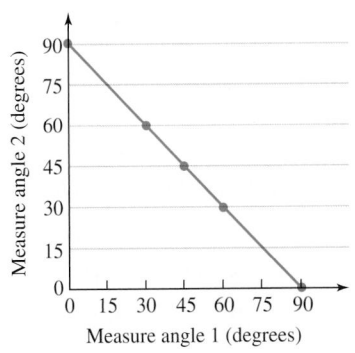

22. KEYBOARDS As the legs of the keyboard stand are widened, the measure of angle 1 (denoted ∠1) will increase, and, in turn, the measure of ∠2 will decrease. For any position, the sum of the measures of the two angles is 180°.

a. Complete the table.

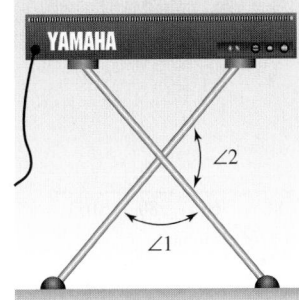

∠1	∠2
50°	130°
60°	120°
70°	110°
80°	100°
90°	90°

b. Use the data in the table to construct a line graph for values of ∠1 from 50° to 90°.

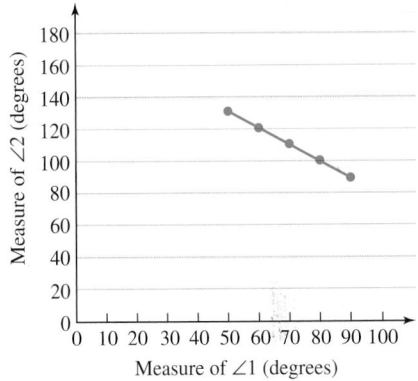

23. a. Explain what the dashed lines help us find in the graph shown below. They help us determine that 15-year-old machinery is worth $35,000.

b. As the machinery ages, what happens to its value? It decreases.

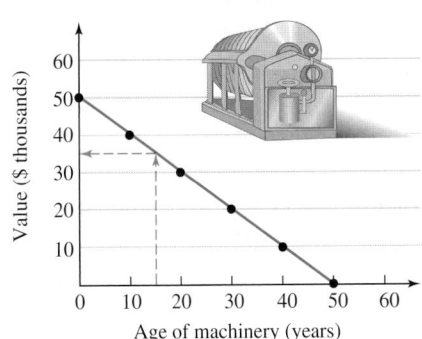

24. a. Use the following line graph to find the income received from 30, 50, and 70 customers. $250, $350, $450

   b. As the number of customers increases, what happens to the income? It increases.

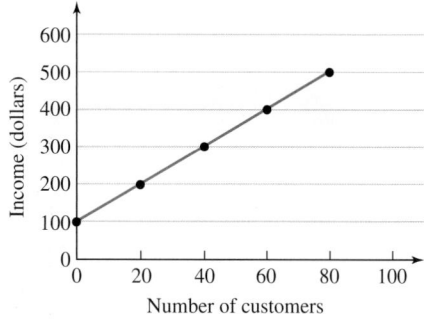

Write each multiplication in two other ways. First, using a raised dot · and then using parentheses ( ).

25. 5×6 5 · 6, 5(6)   **26.** 4×7 4 · 7, 4(7)

27. 34×75 34 · 75, 34(75)   **28.** 90×12 90 · 12, 90(12)

Write each expression without using a multiplication symbol.

▶ **29.** $4 \cdot x$ 4x   **30.** $5 \cdot y$ 5y

31. $3 \cdot r \cdot t$ 3rt   **32.** $22 \cdot q \cdot s$ 22qs

33. $l \cdot w$ lw   **34.** $b \cdot h$ bh

▶ **35.** $P \cdot r \cdot t$ Prt   **36.** $l \cdot w \cdot h$ lwh

▶ **37.** $2(w)$ 2w   **38.** $2(l)$ 2l

39. $(x)(y)$ xy   **40.** $(r)(t)$ rt

Write each division using a fraction bar.

41. $32 \div x$ $\frac{32}{x}$ ▶ **42.** $y \div 15$ $\frac{y}{15}$

43. $30\overline{)90}$ $\frac{90}{30}$ **44.** $20\overline{)80}$ $\frac{80}{20}$

Use the line graph in Example 1 to find the number of tires needed to make the following number of bicycles.
See Example 1.

▶ **45.** 125 bicycles 250   **46.** 400 bicycles 800

47. 100 bicycles 200   **48.** 200 bicycles 400

Express each statement using one of the words **sum, difference, product,** *or* **quotient.** *See Example 2.*

49. $18(24) = 432$ ▶ **50.** $45 \cdot 12 = 540$
The product of 18 and 24   The product of 45 and 12
is equal to 432.   is equal to 540.

▶ **51.** $11 - 9 = 2$ ▶ **52.** $65 + 89 = 154$
The difference of   The sum of 65 and 89
11 and 9 is equal to 2.   is equal to 154.

53. $2x = 1$ ▶ **54.** $16t = 9$
The product of   The product of 16 and t is
2 and x is equal to 1.   equal to 9.

55. $\dfrac{66}{11} = 6$ ▶ **56.** $12 \div 3 = 4$
The quotient of   The quotient of 12 and 3 is
66 and 11 is equal to 6.   equal to 4.

Translate each verbal model into an equation. (Hint: You will need to use variables. Answers may vary, depending on the variables chosen.) See Example 3.

▶ **57.**

| The sale price | is | $100 | minus | the discount. | $p = 100 - d$ |

58.

| The cost of dining out | equals | the cost of the meal | plus | $7 for parking. |

$c = m + 7$

59.

| 7 | times | the age of a dog in years | gives | the dog's equivalent human age. | $7d = h$ |

60.

| The number of centuries | is | the number of years | divided by | 100. |

$c = \dfrac{y}{100}$

Use the given equation to complete each table. See Examples 4 and 5.

▶ **61.** $d = 360 + L$

Lunch time (L) minutes	School day (d) minutes
30	390
40	400
45	405

▶ **62.** $b = 1,024k$

Kilobytes (k)	Bytes (b)
1	1,024
5	5,120
10	10,240

▶ **63.** $t = 1,500 - d$

Deductions (d)	Take-home pay (t)
200	1,300
300	1,200
400	1,100

▶ **64.** $w = \dfrac{s}{12}$

Inches of snow (s)	Inches of water (w)
12	1
24	2
72	6

TRY IT YOURSELF

Translate each verbal model into an equation. Answers may vary, depending on the variables chosen.

▶ **65.** The amount of sand that should be used is the product of 3 and the amount of cement used. $s = 3c$

▶ **66.** The number of waiters needed is the quotient of the number of customers and 10. $w = \frac{c}{10}$

▶ **67.** The weight of the truck is the sum of the weight of the engine and 1,200. $w = e + 1,200$

▶ **68.** The number of classes that are still open is the difference of 150 and the number of classes that are closed. $n = 150 - c$

▶ **69.** The profit is the difference of the revenue and 600. $p = r - 600$

▶ **70.** The distance is the product of the rate and 3. $d = 3r$

▶ **71.** The quotient of the number of laps run and 4 is the number of miles run. $\frac{l}{4} = m$

▶ **72.** The sum of the tax and 35 is the total cost. $t + 35 = c$

Use the data in the table to complete each formula.

73. $d = \dfrac{e}{\boxed{12}}$

Eggs e	Dozen d
24	2
36	3
48	4

74. $p = \boxed{2}\,c$

Canoes c	Paddles p
6	12
7	14
8	16

▶ **75.** $I = \boxed{2}\,c$

Couples c	Individuals I
20	40
100	200
200	400

76. $t = \dfrac{p}{\boxed{5}}$

Players p	Teams t
5	1
10	2
15	3

APPLICATIONS

77. CHAIR PRODUCTION Use the diagram to complete the six formulas that planners could use to order the necessary number of legs l, arms a, seats S, backs b, arm pads p, and screws s for a production run of c chairs.

$l = \boxed{4}\,c$ $b = \boxed{c}$

$a = \boxed{2}\,c$ $p = \boxed{2}\,c$

$S = \boxed{c}$ $s = \boxed{20}\,c$

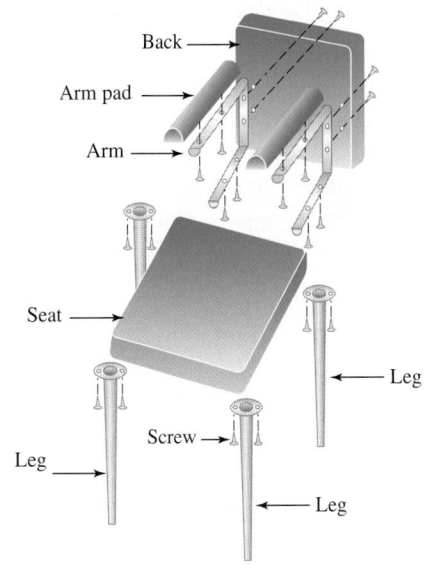

Back

Arm pad

Arm

Seat

Leg

Screw

Leg

Leg

▶ **78.** STAIRCASE PRODUCTION Complete the four formulas that could be used by the job superintendent to order the necessary number of staircase parts for a tract of h homes, each of which will have a staircase as shown.

$$b = \boxed{16}\, h \qquad r = \boxed{2}\, h$$
$$p = \boxed{3}\, h \qquad t = \boxed{8}\, h$$

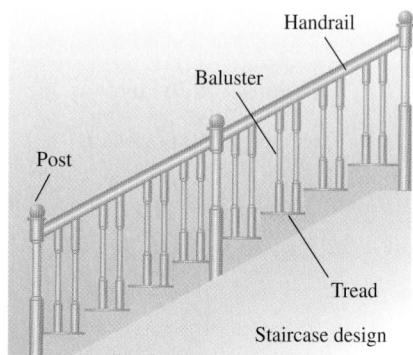

Staircase design

79. FACEBOOK The following table shows the number of Facebook subscribers (in millions) by selected countries for July 2008. Graph the data on the given axis using a bar graph.

Country	Number of subscribers (in millions)
Austria	3
Canada	10
Chile	2
Colombia	2
Norway	1
U.K.	11
U.S.A	28

Source: www.nickburcher.com

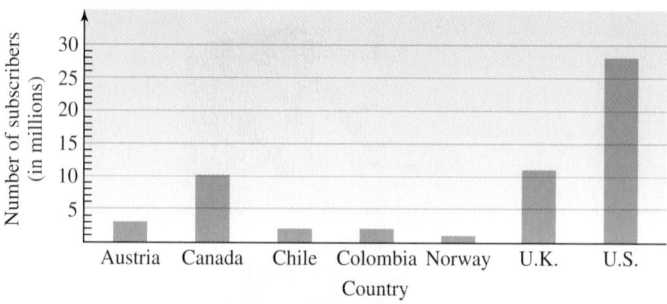

80. U.S. CRIME STATISTICS Property crimes include burglary, theft, and motor vehicle theft. Graph the property crime rates listed in the table using a line graph.

Year	Victimizations per 1,000 households
1994	310
1996	266
1998	217
2000	178
2002	159
2004	161
2006	161

Source: Bureau of Justice Statistics

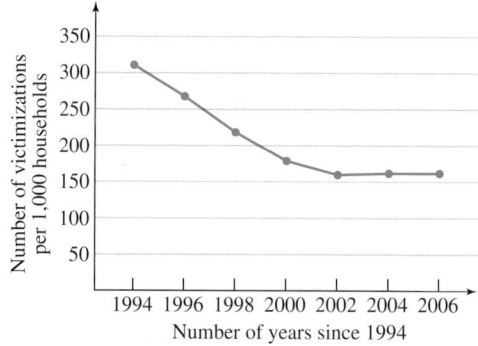

WRITING

▶ **81.** Many people misuse the word *equation* when discussing mathematics. What is an equation? Give an example.

▶ **82.** Explain the difference between an algebraic expression and an equation. Give an example of each.

83. Which do you think is more informative, a bar graph or a line graph? Explain your reasoning.

84. Create a bar graph that shows, on average, how many hours of television you watch each day of the week. Let Sunday be day 1, Monday day 2, and so on.

Fractions

Objectives

1 Factor and prime factor natural numbers.

2 Recognize special fraction forms.

3 Multiply and divide fractions.

4 Build equivalent fractions.

5 Simplify fractions.

6 Add and subtract fractions.

7 Simplify answers.

8 Compute with mixed numbers.

In arithmetic, we add, subtract, multiply, and divide **natural numbers:** 1, 2, 3, 4, 5, and so on. Assuming that you have mastered those skills, we will now review the arithmetic of fractions.

1 **Factor and prime factor natural numbers.**

To compute with fractions, we need to know how to *factor* natural numbers. To **factor** a number means to express it as a product of two or more numbers. For example, some ways to factor 12 are

$$1 \cdot 12, \quad 6 \cdot 2, \quad 4 \cdot 3, \quad \text{and} \quad 2 \cdot 2 \cdot 3$$

The numbers 1, 2, 3, 4, 6, and 12 that were used to write the products are called *factors* of 12. In general, a **factor** is a number being multiplied.

> **The Language of Algebra** When we say "factor 8," we are using the word *factor* as a verb. When we say "2 is a *factor* of 12," we are using the word *factor* as a noun.

Sometimes a number has only two factors, itself and 1. We call such numbers *prime numbers.*

> **Prime Numbers and Composite Numbers**
>
> A **prime number** is a natural number greater than 1 that has only itself and 1 as factors. The first ten prime numbers are 2, 3, 5, 7, 11, 13, 17, 19, 23, and 29.
>
> A **composite number** is a natural number, greater than 1, that is not prime. The first ten composite numbers are 4, 6, 8, 9, 10, 12, 14, 15, 16, and 18.

Every composite number can be factored into the product of two or more prime numbers. This product of these prime numbers is called its **prime factorization.**

EXAMPLE 1 Find the prime factorization of 210.

Strategy We will use a series of steps to express 210 as a product of only prime numbers.

WHY To *prime factor* a number means to write it as a product of prime numbers.

Solution

First, write 210 as the product of two natural numbers other than 1.

$$210 = \mathbf{10 \cdot 21} \quad \text{The resulting prime factorization will be the same no matter which two factors of 210 you begin with.}$$

Neither 10 nor 21 are prime numbers, so we factor each of them.

$$210 = \mathbf{2 \cdot 5 \cdot 3 \cdot 7} \quad \text{Factor 10 as } 2 \cdot 5 \text{ and factor 21 as } 3 \cdot 7.$$

Writing the factors in ascending order, the **prime-factored form** of 210 is $2 \cdot 3 \cdot 5 \cdot 7$.

Self Check 1

Find the prime factorization of 189. $189 = 3 \cdot 3 \cdot 3 \cdot 7$

Now Try **Problem 15**

Teaching Example 1 Find the prime factorization of 104.
Answer:
$2 \cdot 2 \cdot 2 \cdot 13$

Two other methods for prime factoring 210 are shown below.

Factor tree   **Division ladder**

Work downward.
Factor each number as
a product of two
numbers (other than 1
and itself) until all
factors are prime.
Circle prime numbers as
they appear at the end
of a branch.

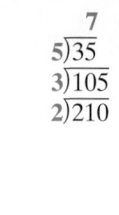

Work upward.
Perform repeated division
until the final quotient is
a prime number. It is
helpful to start with the
smallest prime, 2, as a
trial divisor. Then, in
order, try larger primes
as divisors: 3, 5, 7, 11,
and so on.

Either way, the factorization is $2 \cdot 3 \cdot 5 \cdot 7$. To check it, multiply the prime factors. The product should be 210.

The Language of Algebra   Prime factors are often written in *ascending* order. To *ascend* means to move upward.

Success Tip   A whole number is divisible by

- 2 if it ends in 0, 2, 4, 6, or 8
- 3 if the sum of the digits is divisible by 3
- 5 if it ends in 0 or 5
- 10 if it ends in 0

---

2 Recognize special fraction forms.

In a fraction, the number above the **fraction bar** is called the **numerator,** and the number below is called the **denominator.**

Fraction bar → $\dfrac{5}{6}$ ← Numerator
← Denominator

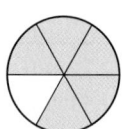

Fractions can describe the number of equal parts of a whole. For example, consider the circle with 5 of 6 equal parts colored red. We say that $\frac{5}{6}$ (five-sixths) of the circle is shaded.

The Language of Algebra   The word *fraction* comes from the Latin word *fractio* meaning "breaking in pieces."

Fractions are also used to indicate division. For example, $\frac{8}{2}$ indicates that the numerator, 8, is to be divided by the denominator, 2:

$$\frac{8}{2} = 8 \div 2 = 4$$ We know that $\frac{8}{2} = 4$ because of its related multiplication statement: $2 \cdot 4 = 8$.

If the numerator and denominator of a fraction are the same nonzero number, the fraction indicates division of a number by itself, and the result is 1. Each of the following fractions is, therefore, a **form of 1.**

$$1 = \frac{1}{1} = \frac{2}{2} = \frac{3}{3} = \frac{4}{4} = \frac{5}{5} = \frac{6}{6} = \frac{7}{7} = \frac{8}{8} = \frac{9}{9} = \dots$$

If a denominator is 1, the fraction indicates division by 1, and the result is simply the numerator. For example, $\frac{5}{1} = 5$ and $\frac{24}{1} = 24$.

Special Fraction Forms

For any nonzero number a,

$$\frac{a}{a} = 1 \quad \text{and} \quad \frac{a}{1} = a$$

---

3 Multiply and divide fractions.

The rule for multiplying fractions can be expressed in words and in symbols as follows.

Multiplying Fractions

To multiply two fractions, multiply the numerators and multiply the denominators.

For any two fractions $\frac{a}{b}$ and $\frac{c}{d}$,

$$\frac{a}{b} \cdot \frac{c}{d} = \frac{a \cdot c}{b \cdot d}$$

EXAMPLE 2

Multiply: $\dfrac{7}{8} \cdot \dfrac{3}{5}$

Strategy To find the product, we will multiply the numerators, 7 and 3, and multiply the denominators, 8 and 5.

WHY This is the rule for multiplying two fractions.

Solution

$$\frac{7}{8} \cdot \frac{3}{5} = \frac{7 \cdot 3}{8 \cdot 5} \quad \begin{array}{l}\text{Multiply the numerators.}\\ \text{Multiply the denominators.}\end{array}$$

$$= \frac{21}{40}$$

Self Check 2

Multiply: $\dfrac{5}{9} \cdot \dfrac{2}{3}$ $\frac{10}{27}$

Now Try **Problem 27**

Teaching Example 2 Multiply: $\frac{12}{25} \cdot \frac{10}{3}$
Answer:
$\frac{8}{5}$

One number is called the **reciprocal** of another if their product is 1. To find the reciprocal of a fraction, we invert its numerator and denominator.

$\frac{3}{4}$ is the reciprocal of $\frac{4}{3}$, because $\frac{3}{4} \cdot \frac{4}{3} = \frac{12}{12} = 1$.

$\frac{1}{10}$ is the reciprocal of 10, because $\frac{1}{10} \cdot 10 = \frac{10}{10} = 1$.

Success Tip Every number, except **0**, has a reciprocal. Zero has no reciprocal, because the product of 0 and a number cannot be 1.

We use reciprocals to divide fractions.

Dividing Fractions

To divide two fractions, multiply the first fraction by the reciprocal of the second.

For any two fractions $\frac{a}{b}$ and $\frac{c}{d}$, where $c \neq 0$,

$$\frac{a}{b} \div \frac{c}{d} = \frac{a}{b} \cdot \frac{d}{c}$$

Self Check 3

Divide: $\frac{6}{25} \div \frac{1}{2}$ $\frac{12}{25}$

Now Try **Problem 31**

Teaching Example 3 Divide: $\frac{6}{5} \div \frac{2}{15}$
Answer:
9

EXAMPLE 3   Divide: $\dfrac{1}{3} \div \dfrac{4}{5}$

Strategy We will multiply the first fraction, $\frac{1}{3}$, by the reciprocal of the second fraction, $\frac{4}{5}$.

WHY This is the rule for dividing two fractions.

Solution

$$\frac{1}{3} \div \frac{4}{5} = \frac{1}{3} \cdot \frac{5}{4} \qquad \text{Multiply } \tfrac{1}{3} \text{ by the reciprocal of } \tfrac{4}{5}. \text{ The reciprocal of } \tfrac{4}{5} \text{ is } \tfrac{5}{4}.$$

$$= \frac{1 \cdot 5}{3 \cdot 4} \qquad \begin{array}{l}\text{Multiply the numerators.}\\ \text{Multiply the denominators.}\end{array}$$

$$= \frac{5}{12}$$

---

4 Build equivalent fractions.

The two rectangles on the right are the same size. The first rectangle is divided into 10 equal parts. Since 6 of those parts are red, $\frac{6}{10}$ of the figure is shaded.

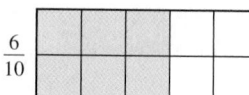

The second rectangle is divided into 5 equal parts. Since 3 of those parts are red, $\frac{3}{5}$ of the figure is shaded. We can conclude that $\frac{6}{10} = \frac{3}{5}$ because $\frac{6}{10}$ and $\frac{3}{5}$ represent the same shaded part of the rectangle. We say that $\frac{6}{10}$ and $\frac{3}{5}$ are *equivalent fractions*.

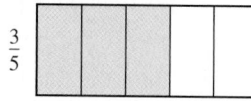

Equivalent Fractions

Two fractions are **equivalent** if they represent the same number.

Writing a fraction as an equivalent fraction with a larger denominator is called **building** the fraction. To build a fraction, we multiply it by a form of 1. Since any number multiplied by 1 remains the same (identical), 1 is called the **multiplicative identity element.**

Multiplication Property of 1

The product of 1 and any number is that number.

For any number a,

$$1 \cdot a = a \qquad \text{and} \qquad a \cdot 1 = a$$

EXAMPLE 4   Write $\dfrac{3}{5}$ as an equivalent fraction with a denominator of 35.

Strategy We will compare the given denominator to the required denominator and ask, "By what must we multiply 5 to get 35?"

WHY The answer to that question helps us determine the form of 1 to be used to build an equivalent fraction.

Solution
We need to multiply the denominator of $\frac{3}{5}$ by 7 to obtain a denominator of 35. It follows that $\frac{7}{7}$ should be the form of 1 that is used to build $\frac{3}{5}$. Multiplying $\frac{3}{5}$ by $\frac{7}{7}$ changes its appearance but does not change its value, because we are multiplying it by 1.

$$\frac{3}{5} = \frac{3}{5} \cdot \frac{7}{7} \qquad \frac{7}{7} = 1$$

$$= \frac{3 \cdot 7}{5 \cdot 7} \qquad \text{Multiply the numerators.}$$
$$\qquad\qquad \text{Multiply the denominators.}$$

$$= \frac{21}{35}$$

To build an equivalent fraction in Example 4, we multiplied $\frac{3}{5}$ by 1 in the form of $\frac{7}{7}$. As a result of that step, the numerator and the denominator of $\frac{3}{5}$ were multiplied by 7.

Step 1 $\dfrac{3}{5} = \dfrac{3}{5} \cdot \dfrac{7}{7}$

Step 2 $\quad = \dfrac{3 \cdot 7}{5 \cdot 7}$ The numerator is multiplied by 7.
The denominator is multiplied by 7.

Step 3 $\quad = \dfrac{21}{35}$ The result is a fraction equivalent to $\frac{3}{5}$.

This process illustrates an important property of fractions.

The Fundamental Property of Fractions

If the numerator and denominator of a fraction are multiplied by the same nonzero number, the resulting fraction is equivalent to the original fraction.

If $\frac{a}{b}$ is a fraction and c is a nonzero number,

$$\frac{a}{b} = \frac{ac}{bc}$$

Since multiplying the numerator and denominator of a fraction by the same nonzero number produces an equivalent fraction, your instructor may allow you to begin your solution to Example 4 at Step 2.

Building Fractions

To build a fraction, multiply it by 1 in the form of $\frac{c}{c}$, where c is any nonzero number.

Self Check 4
Write $\frac{5}{8}$ as an equivalent fraction with a denominator of 24. $\frac{15}{24}$

Now Try Problem 35

Teaching Example 4 Write $\frac{8}{11}$ as an equivalent fraction with a denominator of 66.
Answer:
$\frac{48}{66}$

5 Simplify fractions.

Every fraction can be written in infinitely many equivalent forms. For example, some equivalent forms of $\frac{10}{15}$ are:

$$\frac{2}{3} = \frac{4}{6} = \frac{6}{9} = \frac{8}{12} = \mathbf{\frac{10}{15}} = \frac{12}{18} = \frac{14}{21} = \frac{16}{24} = \frac{18}{27} = \frac{20}{30} = \cdots$$

> **The Language of Algebra** The word *infinitely* is a form of the word *infinite*, which means endless.

Of all of the equivalent forms in which we can write a fraction, we often need to determine the one that is in *simplest form*.

> ### Simplest Form of a Fraction
>
> A fraction is in **simplest form,** or **lowest terms,** when the numerator and denominator have no common factors other than 1.

To **simplify a fraction,** we write it in simplest form by removing a factor equal to 1. For example, to simplify $\frac{10}{15}$, we note that the greatest factor common to the numerator and denominator is 5 and proceed as follows:

$$\frac{10}{15} = \frac{2 \cdot 5}{3 \cdot 5} \qquad \text{Factor 10 and 15.}$$

$$= \frac{2}{3} \cdot \frac{5}{5} \qquad \text{Use the rule for multiplying fractions in reverse: write } \frac{2\cdot5}{3\cdot5} \text{ as the product of two fractions, } \frac{2}{3} \text{ and } \frac{5}{5}.$$

$$= \frac{2}{3} \cdot 1 \qquad \text{A nonzero number divided by itself is equal to 1: } \frac{5}{5} = 1.$$

$$= \frac{2}{3} \qquad \text{Use the multiplication property of 1: any number multiplied by 1 remains the same.}$$

To simplify $\frac{10}{15}$, we removed a factor equal to 1 in the form of $\frac{5}{5}$. The result, $\frac{2}{3}$, is equivalent to $\frac{10}{15}$.

We can easily identify the greatest common factor of the numerator and the denominator of a fraction if we write them in prime-factored form.

Self Check 5

Simplify each fraction, if possible:

a. $\frac{24}{56}$ $\frac{3}{7}$ **b.** $\frac{16}{125}$ in simplest form

Now Try Problem 45

Teaching Example 5 Simplify, if possible:
a. $\frac{39}{54}$ **b.** $\frac{8}{27}$
Answers:
a. $\frac{13}{18}$
b. in simplest form

EXAMPLE 5

Simplify each fraction, if possible: **a.** $\dfrac{63}{42}$ **b.** $\dfrac{33}{40}$

Strategy We will begin by prime factoring the numerator and denominator of the fraction. Then, to simplify it, we will remove a factor equal to 1.

WHY We need to make sure that the numerator and denominator have no common factors other than 1. If that is the case, then the fraction is in *simplest form.*

Solution

a. After prime factoring 63 and 42, we see that the greatest common factor of the numerator and the denominator is $3 \cdot 7 = 21$.

$$\frac{63}{42} = \frac{3 \cdot 3 \cdot 7}{2 \cdot 3 \cdot 7} \qquad \text{Write 63 and 42 in prime-factored form.}$$

$$= \frac{3}{2} \cdot \frac{3 \cdot 7}{3 \cdot 7} \qquad \text{Write } \frac{3\cdot3\cdot7}{2\cdot3\cdot7} \text{ as the product of two fractions, } \frac{3}{2} \text{ and } \frac{3\cdot7}{3\cdot7}.$$

$$= \frac{3}{2} \cdot 1 \qquad \text{A nonzero number divided by itself is equal to 1: } \frac{3 \cdot 7}{3 \cdot 7} = 1.$$

$$= \frac{3}{2} \qquad \text{Any number multiplied by 1 remains the same.}$$

b. Prime factor 33 and 40.

$$\frac{33}{40} = \frac{3 \cdot 11}{2 \cdot 2 \cdot 2 \cdot 5}$$

Since the numerator and the denominator have no common factors other than 1, the fraction $\frac{33}{40}$ is in simplest form (lowest terms).

The Language of Algebra   What do Calvin Klein, Queen Latifah, and Tom Hanks have in common? They all attended a community college. The word *common* means shared by two or more. In this section, we will work with *common* factors and *common* denominators.

To streamline the simplifying process, we can replace pairs of factors common to the numerator and denominator with the equivalent fraction $\frac{1}{1}$.

EXAMPLE 6   Simplify: $\dfrac{90}{105}$

Strategy We will begin by prime factoring the numerator, 90, and denominator, 105. Then we will look for any factors common to the numerator and denominator and remove them.

WHY When the numerator and/or denominator of a fraction are large numbers, such as 90 and 105, writing their prime factorizations is helpful in identifying any common factors.

Solution

$$\frac{90}{105} = \frac{2 \cdot 3 \cdot 3 \cdot 5}{3 \cdot 5 \cdot 7} \qquad \text{Write 90 and 105 in prime-factored form.}$$

$$= \frac{2 \cdot \overset{1}{\cancel{3}} \cdot 3 \cdot \overset{1}{\cancel{5}}}{\underset{1}{\cancel{3}} \cdot \underset{1}{\cancel{5}} \cdot 7} \qquad \begin{array}{l}\text{Slashes and 1's are used to show that } \frac{3}{3} \text{ and } \frac{5}{5} \text{ are replaced by the} \\ \text{equivalent fraction } \frac{1}{1}. \text{ A factor equal to 1 in the form of } \frac{3 \cdot 5}{3 \cdot 5} = \frac{15}{15} \\ \text{was removed.}\end{array}$$

$$= \frac{6}{7} \qquad \begin{array}{l}\text{Multiply the remaining factors in the numerator: } 2 \cdot 1 \cdot 3 \cdot 1 = 6. \\ \text{Multiply the remaining factors in the denominator: } 1 \cdot 1 \cdot 7 = 7.\end{array}$$

We can use the following steps to simplify a fraction.

Self Check 6

Simplify: $\dfrac{126}{70}$ $\frac{9}{5}$

Now Try **Problem 53**

Teaching Example 6 Simplify: $\frac{180}{315}$
Answer:
$\frac{4}{7}$

Simplifying Fractions

1. Factor (or prime factor) the numerator and denominator to determine their common factors.

2. Remove factors equal to 1 by replacing each pair of factors common to the numerator and denominator with the equivalent fraction $\frac{1}{1}$.

3. Multiply the remaining factors in the numerator and in the denominator.

We have seen that the Fundamental Property of Fractions can be used to build equivalent fractions. If the sides of the equation $\frac{a}{b} = \frac{ac}{bc}$ are reversed, it can also be used to simplify fractions.

The Fundamental Property of Fractions

If the numerator and denominator of a fraction are divided by the same nonzero number, the resulting fraction is equivalent to the original fraction.

If $\frac{a}{b}$ is a fraction and c is a nonzero number,

$$\frac{ac}{bc} = \frac{a}{b}$$

Caution!   When all common factors of the numerator and/or the denominator of a fraction are removed, forgetting to write 1's above the slashes can lead to a common mistake.

Correct	Incorrect
$\dfrac{15}{45} = \dfrac{\overset{1}{3} \cdot \overset{1}{5}}{\underset{1}{3} \cdot 3 \cdot \underset{1}{5}} = \dfrac{1}{3}$	$\dfrac{15}{45} = \dfrac{\cancel{3} \cdot \cancel{5}}{3 \cdot 3 \cdot \cancel{5}} = \dfrac{0}{3} = 0$

6 Add and subtract fractions.

In algebra as in everyday life, we can only add or subtract objects that are similar. For example, we can add dollars to dollars, but we cannot add dollars to oranges. This concept is important when adding fractions.

Consider the problem $\frac{2}{5} + \frac{1}{5}$. When we write it in words, it is apparent we are adding similar objects.

two-**fifths**   +   one-**fifth**
$\underset{\text{Similar objects}}{\uparrow \underline{\qquad\qquad\qquad} \uparrow}$

Because the denominators of $\frac{2}{5}$ and $\frac{1}{5}$ are the same, we say that they have a **common denominator.**

Adding and Subtracting Fractions That Have the Same Denominator

To add (or subtract) fractions that have the same denominator, add (or subtract) their numerators and write the sum (or difference) over the common denominator.

For any fractions $\frac{a}{d}$ and $\frac{b}{d}$,

$$\frac{a}{d} + \frac{b}{d} = \frac{a + b}{d} \qquad \text{and} \qquad \frac{a}{d} - \frac{b}{d} = \frac{a - b}{d}$$

For example,

$$\frac{2}{5} + \frac{1}{5} = \frac{2 + 1}{5} = \frac{3}{5} \qquad \text{and} \qquad \frac{18}{23} - \frac{9}{23} = \frac{18 - 9}{23} = \frac{9}{23}$$

Caution!   We **do not** add fractions by adding the numerators and adding the denominators!

$$\frac{2}{5} + \frac{1}{5} = \frac{2+1}{5+5} = \frac{3}{10}$$

The same caution applies when subtracting fractions.

Now we consider the problem $\frac{2}{5} + \frac{1}{3}$. Since the denominators are not the same, we cannot add these fractions in their present form.

two-**fifths**   +   one-**third**

└── *Not similar objects* ──┘

To add (or subtract) fractions with different denominators, we express them as equivalent fractions that have a common denominator. The smallest common denominator, called the **least** or **lowest common denominator,** is usually the easiest common denominator to use.

Least Common Denominator (LCD)

The **least** or **lowest common denominator (LCD)** for a set of fractions is the smallest number each denominator will divide exactly (divide with no remainder).

Success Tip   To determine the LCD of two fractions, list the multiples of one of the denominators. The first number in the list that is exactly divisible by the other denominator is their LCD. For $\frac{2}{5}$ and $\frac{1}{3}$, the multiples of the first denominator, 5, are

5, 10, ⑮, 20, 25, …

Since 15 is the first number in the list that is exactly divisible by the second denominator, 3, the LCD is 15.

The denominators of $\frac{2}{5}$ and $\frac{1}{3}$ are 5 and 3. The numbers 5 and 3 divide many numbers exactly (30, 45, and 60, to name a few), but the smallest number that they divide exactly is 15. Thus, 15 is the LCD for $\frac{2}{5}$ and $\frac{1}{3}$.

To find $\frac{2}{5} + \frac{1}{3}$, we find equivalent fractions that have denominators of 15 and we use the rule for adding fractions.

$$\frac{2}{5} + \frac{1}{3} = \frac{2}{5} \cdot \frac{3}{3} + \frac{1}{3} \cdot \frac{5}{5} \qquad \text{Multiply } \tfrac{2}{5} \text{ by 1 in the form of } \tfrac{3}{3}. \text{ Multiply } \tfrac{1}{3} \text{ by 1 in the form of } \tfrac{5}{5}.$$

$$= \frac{2 \cdot 3}{5 \cdot 3} + \frac{1 \cdot 5}{3 \cdot 5} \qquad \begin{array}{l}\text{Multiply the numerators.}\\ \text{Multiply the denominators.}\end{array}$$

$$= \frac{6}{15} + \frac{5}{15} \qquad \text{Note that the denominators are now the same.}$$

$$= \frac{6 + 5}{15} \qquad \text{Add the numerators.}$$
$$\qquad\qquad\qquad \text{Write the sum over the common denominator.}$$
$$= \frac{11}{15}$$

When adding (or subtracting) fractions with unlike denominators, the least common denominator is not always obvious. Prime factorization is helpful in determining the LCD.

Finding the LCD Using Prime Factorization

1. Prime factor each denominator.

2. The LCD is a product of prime factors, where each factor is used the greatest number of times it appears in any one factorization found in step 1.

Self Check 7

Subtract: $\frac{11}{48} - \frac{7}{40} \quad \frac{13}{240}$

Now Try **Problem 65**

Teaching Example 7 Subtract: $\frac{5}{12} - \frac{4}{21}$
Answer:
$\frac{19}{84}$

EXAMPLE 7   Subtract: $\dfrac{3}{10} - \dfrac{5}{28}$

Strategy We will begin by expressing each fraction as an equivalent fraction that has the LCD for its denominator. Then we will use the rule for subtracting fractions with *like* denominators.

WHY To add or subtract fractions, the fractions must have like denominators.

Solution

To find the LCD, we find the prime factorization of both denominators and use each prime factor the *greatest* number of times it appears in any one factorization:

$$\left.\begin{array}{l} 10 = 2 \cdot 5 \\ 28 = 2 \cdot 2 \cdot 7 \end{array}\right\} \text{LCD} = 2 \cdot 2 \cdot 5 \cdot 7 = 140$$

2 appears twice in the factorization of 28.
5 appears once in the factorization of 10.
7 appears once in the factorization of 28.

Since 140 is the smallest number that 10 and 28 divide exactly, we write $\frac{3}{10}$ and $\frac{5}{28}$ as fractions with the LCD 140.

$$\frac{3}{10} - \frac{5}{28} = \frac{3}{10} \cdot \frac{\mathbf{14}}{\mathbf{14}} - \frac{5}{28} \cdot \frac{\mathbf{5}}{\mathbf{5}} \qquad \begin{array}{l}\text{We must multiply 10 by 14 to obtain 140.} \\ \text{We must multiply 28 by 5 to obtain 140.}\end{array}$$

$$= \frac{3 \cdot \mathbf{14}}{10 \cdot \mathbf{14}} - \frac{5 \cdot \mathbf{5}}{28 \cdot \mathbf{5}} \qquad \begin{array}{l}\text{Multiply the numerators.} \\ \text{Multiply the denominators.}\end{array}$$

$$= \frac{42}{140} - \frac{25}{140} \qquad \text{Note that the denominators are now the same.}$$

$$= \frac{42 - 25}{140} \qquad \begin{array}{l}\text{Subtract the numerators.} \\ \text{Write the difference over the common denominator.}\end{array}$$

$$= \frac{17}{140}$$

We can use the following steps to add or subtract fractions with different denominators.

Adding and Subtracting Fractions That Have Different Denominators

1. Find the LCD.
2. Rewrite each fraction as an equivalent fraction with the LCD as the denominator. To do so, build each fraction using a form of 1 that involves any factors needed to obtain the LCD.
3. Add or subtract the numerators and write the sum or difference over the LCD.
4. Simplify the result, if possible.

7 Simplify answers.

When adding, subtracting, multiplying, or dividing fractions, remember to express the answer in simplest form.

EXAMPLE 8   Perform the operations and simplify:

a. $45\left(\dfrac{4}{9}\right)$ **b.** $\dfrac{5}{12} + \dfrac{3}{2} - \dfrac{1}{4}$

Strategy We will perform the indicated operations and then make sure that the answer is in simplest form (lowest terms).

WHY Fractional answers should always be given in simplest form.

> **Caution!** Remember that an LCD is **not needed** when multiplying or dividing fractions.

Solution

a. $45\left(\dfrac{4}{9}\right) = \dfrac{45}{1}\left(\dfrac{4}{9}\right)$ Write 45 as a fraction: $45 = \dfrac{45}{1}$.

$= \dfrac{45 \cdot 4}{1 \cdot 9}$ Multiply the numerators.
Multiply the denominators.

$= \dfrac{5 \cdot \overset{1}{\cancel{9}} \cdot 4}{1 \cdot \underset{1}{\cancel{9}}}$ To simplify the result, factor 45 as $5 \cdot 9$. Then remove the common factor 9 of the numerator and denominator.

$= 20$ Multiply the remaining factors in the numerator. Multiply the remaining factors in the denominator. Simplify: $\dfrac{20}{1} = 20$.

b. Since the smallest number that 12, 2, and 4 divide exactly is 12, the LCD is 12.

$\dfrac{5}{12} + \dfrac{3}{2} - \dfrac{1}{4} = \dfrac{5}{12} + \dfrac{3}{2} \cdot \dfrac{6}{6} - \dfrac{1}{4} \cdot \dfrac{3}{3}$ $\dfrac{5}{12}$ already has a denominator of 12. Build $\dfrac{3}{2}$ and $\dfrac{1}{4}$ so that their denominators are 12.

$= \dfrac{5}{12} + \dfrac{3 \cdot 6}{2 \cdot 6} - \dfrac{1 \cdot 3}{4 \cdot 3}$ Multiply the numerators.
Multiply the denominators.

$= \dfrac{5}{12} + \dfrac{18}{12} - \dfrac{3}{12}$ The denominators are now the same.

$= \dfrac{20}{12}$ Add the numerators, 5 and 18, to get 23. From that sum, subtract 3. Write that result, 20, over the common denominator.

$$= \frac{\overset{1}{4} \cdot 5}{3 \cdot \underset{1}{4}}$$

To simplify $\frac{20}{12}$, factor 20 and 12, using their greatest common factor, 4. Then remove $\frac{4}{4} = 1$.

$$= \frac{5}{3}$$

THINK IT THROUGH   *Budgeting*

"Working with a personal budget puts you in control of your money. It can also help you achieve your savings goals."

Leigh Roberts in Business Times

In the article "Budget Basics for College Graduates," Janet Bodnar offers financial guidance to new college grads beginning a job. The circle graph below shows her spending guidelines presented as a fraction of one's monthly take-home pay. How much does she recommend should be spent on each budget item if a person takes home $2,100 a month?

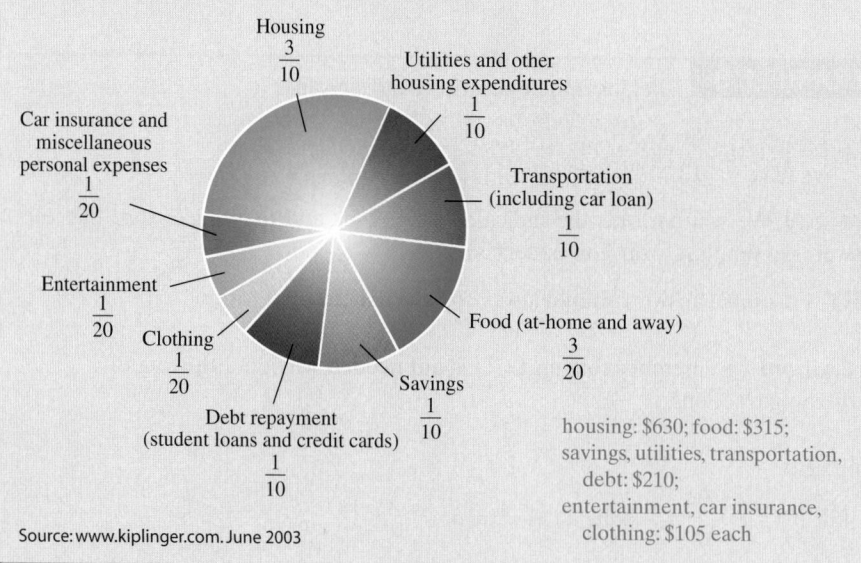

Source: www.kiplinger.com. June 2003

housing: $630; food: $315; savings, utilities, transportation, debt: $210; entertainment, car insurance, clothing: $105 each

---

8   Compute with mixed numbers.

A **mixed number** represents the sum of a whole number and a fraction. For example, $5\frac{3}{4}$ means $5 + \frac{3}{4}$.

EXAMPLE 9   Divide: $5\dfrac{3}{4} \div 2$

Strategy We begin by writing the mixed number $5\frac{3}{4}$ and the whole number 2 as fractions. Then we use the rule for dividing two fractions.

WHY To multiply (or divide) with mixed numbers, we first write them as fractions, and then multiply (or divide) as usual.

Solution

$$5\frac{3}{4} \div 2 = \frac{23}{4} \div \frac{2}{1}$$

Write $5\frac{3}{4}$ as an improper fraction by multiplying its whole-number part by the denominator: $5 \cdot 4 = 20$. Then add the numerator to that product: $3 + 20 = 23$. Finally, write the result, 23, over the denominator 4. Write 2 as a fraction: $2 = \frac{2}{1}$.

$$= \frac{23}{4} \cdot \frac{1}{2}$$ Multiply by the reciprocal of $\frac{2}{1}$, which is $\frac{1}{2}$.

$$= \frac{23}{8}$$ Multiply the numerators.
Multiply the denominators.

$$= 2\frac{7}{8}$$ Write $\frac{23}{8}$ as a mixed number by dividing the numerator, 23, by the denominator, 8. The quotient, 2, is the whole-number part; the remainder, 7, over the divisor, 8, is the fractional part.

The Language of Algebra   Fractions such as $\frac{23}{4}$, with a numerator greater than or equal to the denominator, are called **improper fractions.** In algebra, such fractions are often preferable to their equivalent mixed number form.

EXAMPLE 10   *Freeway Signs*   How far apart are the Downtown San Diego and Sea World Drive exits?

Strategy   We can find the distance between exits by finding the difference in the mileages on the freeway sign: $6\frac{1}{2} - 1\frac{3}{4}$.

WHY   The word *difference* indicates subtraction.

Solution

$$
\begin{array}{r}
6\frac{1}{2} = \ \ 6\frac{2}{4} = \ 5\frac{2}{4} + \frac{4}{4} = \ \ 5\frac{6}{4} \\
-1\frac{3}{4} = -1\frac{3}{4} = -1\frac{3}{4} \qquad\quad = \ -1\frac{3}{4} \\
\hline
4\frac{3}{4}
\end{array}
$$

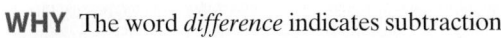

Using vertical form, express $\frac{1}{2}$ as an equivalent fraction with denominator 4. Then, borrow 1 in the form of $\frac{4}{4}$ from 6 to subtract the fractional parts of the mixed numbers.

The Downtown San Diego and Sea World Drive exits are $4\frac{3}{4}$ miles apart.

Self Check 10
Subtract: $5\frac{1}{3} - 3\frac{3}{4}$ $1\frac{7}{12}$
Now Try   Problem 79

Teaching Example 10   Subtract:
$6\frac{1}{4} - 1\frac{2}{3}$
Answer:
$4\frac{7}{12}$

Success Tip   Example 10 could also be solved by writing the mixed numbers $6\frac{1}{2}$ and $1\frac{3}{4}$ as improper fractions and subtracting them.

ANSWERS TO SELF CHECKS

1. $189 = 3 \cdot 3 \cdot 3 \cdot 7$ **2.** $\frac{10}{27}$ **3.** $\frac{12}{25}$ **4.** $\frac{15}{24}$ **5. a.** $\frac{3}{7}$ **b.** In simplest form   **6.** $\frac{9}{5}$ **7.** $\frac{13}{240}$
8. a. 28   **b.** $\frac{4}{5}$ **9.** $\frac{81}{8} = 10\frac{1}{8}$ **10.** $1\frac{7}{12}$

STUDY SKILLS CHECKLIST

Learning from the Worked Examples

The following checklist will help you become familiar with the example structure in this book. Place a check mark in each box after you answer the question.

☐ Each section of the book contains worked **Examples** that are numbered. How many worked examples are there in Section 1.3, which begins on page 29?

☐ Each worked example contains a **Strategy.** Fill in the blanks to complete the following strategy for Example 6 on page 36: We will _simplify_ _the_ _expression_ on each side and then compare the values.

☐ Each Strategy statement is followed by an explanation of **Why** that approach is used. Fill in the blanks to complete the following Why for Example 6 on page 36: Simplifying the sides helps us determine _which_ _symbol_ _to_ _use_.

☐ Each worked example has a **Solution.** How many lettered parts are there to the Solution in Example 6 on page 36?

☐ Each example uses magenta **Author notes** to explain the steps of the solution. Fill in the blanks to complete the second author note in the solution of Example 8 on page 23: Multiply the _numerators_.

☐ After reading a worked example, you should work the **Self Check** problem. How many Self Check problems are there for Example 8 on page 23?

☐ At the end of each section, you will find the **Answers to Self Checks.** What is the answer to Self-Check problem 4 on page 25?

☐ After completing a Self Check problem, you can **Now Try** similar problems in the Study Sets. For Example 10 on page 25, which Study Set problem is suggested?

Answers: 6, simplify the expression, which symbol to use, 2, numerators, 2, $\frac{15}{24}$, 79

SECTION 1.2 STUDY SET

VOCABULARY

Fill in the blanks.

1. A factor is a number being _multiplied_.

2. Numbers that have only 1 and themselves as factors, such as 23, 37, and 41, are called _prime_ numbers.

3. When we write 60 as $2 \cdot 2 \cdot 3 \cdot 5$, we say that we have written 60 in _prime-factored_ form.

4. The _numerator_ of the fraction $\frac{3}{4}$ is 3, and the _denominator_ is 4.

5. Two fractions that represent the same number, such as $\frac{1}{2}$ and $\frac{2}{4}$, are called _equivalent_ fractions.

6. $\frac{2}{3}$ is the _reciprocal_ of $\frac{3}{2}$, because their product is 1.

7. The _least or lowest_ common denominator for a set of fractions is the smallest number each denominator will divide exactly.

▶ 8. The _mixed_ number $7\frac{1}{3}$ represents the sum of a whole number and a fraction: $7 + \frac{1}{3}$.

CONCEPTS

Complete each fact about fractions.

▶ 9. a. $\dfrac{a}{a} = \boxed{1}$ b. $\dfrac{a}{1} = \boxed{a}$

c. $\dfrac{a}{b} \cdot \dfrac{c}{d} = \boxed{\dfrac{a \cdot c}{b \cdot d}}$ d. $\dfrac{a}{b} \div \dfrac{c}{d} = \boxed{\dfrac{a \cdot d}{b \cdot c}}$

e. $\dfrac{a}{d} + \dfrac{b}{d} = \boxed{\dfrac{a + b}{d}}$ f. $\dfrac{a}{d} - \dfrac{b}{d} = \boxed{\dfrac{a - b}{d}}$

10. What two equivalent fractions are shown? $\frac{4}{12} = \frac{1}{3}$

11. Complete each statement.

a. To simplify a fraction, we remove factors equal to $\boxed{1}$ in the form of $\frac{2}{2}, \frac{3}{3}$, or $\frac{4}{4}$, and so on.

b. To build a fraction, we multiply it by $\boxed{1}$ in the form of $\frac{2}{2}, \frac{3}{3}$, or $\frac{4}{4}$, and so on.

12. What is the LCD for fractions having denominators of 24 and 36? 72

51. $\frac{26}{39}$ $\frac{2}{3}$	52. $\frac{72}{64}$ $\frac{9}{8}$
▶ 53. $\frac{36}{225}$ $\frac{4}{25}$	54. $\frac{175}{490}$ $\frac{5}{14}$

NOTATION

Fill in the blanks.

13. a. Multiply $\frac{5}{6}$ by a form of 1 to build an equivalent fraction with denominator 30.

b. Remove common factors to simplify $\frac{12}{42}$.

$$\frac{12}{42} = \frac{2 \cdot \boxed{2} \cdot 3}{2 \cdot 3 \cdot \boxed{7}} = \frac{2}{7}$$

$$\frac{5}{6} \cdot \frac{5}{5} = \frac{25}{30}$$

▶ **14. a.** Write $2\frac{15}{16}$ as an improper fraction. $\frac{47}{16}$

b. Write $\frac{49}{12}$ as a mixed number. $4\frac{1}{12}$

GUIDED PRACTICE

Find the prime factorization of each number. **See Example 1.**

▶ **15.** 75 $3 \cdot 5 \cdot 5$ **16.** 20 $2 \cdot 2 \cdot 5$

17. 28 $2 \cdot 2 \cdot 7$ **18.** 54 $2 \cdot 3 \cdot 3 \cdot 3$

▶ **19.** 81 $3 \cdot 3 \cdot 3 \cdot 3$ **20.** 125 $5 \cdot 5 \cdot 5$

21. 117 $3 \cdot 3 \cdot 13$ **22.** 147 $3 \cdot 7 \cdot 7$

23. 220 $2 \cdot 2 \cdot 5 \cdot 11$ **24.** 270 $2 \cdot 3 \cdot 3 \cdot 3 \cdot 5$

25. 1,254 $2 \cdot 3 \cdot 11 \cdot 19$ **26.** 1,144 $2 \cdot 2 \cdot 2 \cdot 11 \cdot 13$

Perform each operation. **See Examples 2 and 3.**

27. $\frac{5}{6} \cdot \frac{1}{8}$ $\frac{5}{48}$ ▶ **28.** $\frac{2}{3} \cdot \frac{1}{5}$ $\frac{2}{15}$

▶ **29.** $\frac{7}{11} \cdot \frac{3}{5}$ $\frac{21}{55}$ **30.** $\frac{13}{9} \cdot \frac{2}{3}$ $\frac{26}{27}$

31. $\frac{3}{4} \div \frac{2}{5}$ $\frac{15}{8}$ ▶ **32.** $\frac{7}{8} \div \frac{6}{13}$ $\frac{91}{48}$

33. $\frac{6}{5} \div \frac{5}{7}$ $\frac{42}{25}$ **34.** $\frac{4}{3} \div \frac{3}{2}$ $\frac{8}{9}$

Build each fraction or whole number to an equivalent fraction with the indicated denominator. **See Example 4.**

▶ **35.** $\frac{1}{3}$, denominator 9 $\frac{3}{9}$ **36.** $\frac{3}{8}$, denominator 24 $\frac{9}{24}$

▶ **37.** $\frac{4}{9}$, denominator 54 $\frac{24}{54}$ **38.** $\frac{9}{16}$, denominator 64 $\frac{36}{64}$

39. 7, denominator 5 $\frac{35}{5}$ **40.** 12, denominator 3 $\frac{36}{3}$

41. 5, denominator 7 $\frac{35}{7}$ **42.** 6, denominator 8 $\frac{48}{8}$

Simplify each fraction, if possible. **See Examples 5 and 6.**

43. $\frac{6}{18}$ $\frac{1}{3}$ **44.** $\frac{6}{9}$ $\frac{2}{3}$

▶ **45.** $\frac{24}{28}$ $\frac{6}{7}$ **46.** $\frac{35}{14}$ $\frac{5}{2}$

47. $\frac{15}{40}$ $\frac{3}{8}$ **48.** $\frac{22}{77}$ $\frac{2}{7}$

▶ **49.** $\frac{33}{56}$ lowest terms   **50.** $\frac{26}{21}$ lowest terms

Perform the operations and, if possible, simplify. **See Objective 6 and Example 7.**

55. $\frac{3}{5} + \frac{3}{5}$ $\frac{6}{5}$ **56.** $\frac{4}{9} - \frac{1}{9}$ $\frac{1}{3}$

▶ **57.** $\frac{6}{7} - \frac{2}{7}$ $\frac{4}{7}$ ▶ **58.** $\frac{5}{13} + \frac{6}{13}$ $\frac{11}{13}$

59. $\frac{1}{6} + \frac{1}{24}$ $\frac{5}{24}$ **60.** $\frac{17}{25} - \frac{2}{5}$ $\frac{7}{25}$

61. $\frac{7}{10} - \frac{1}{14}$ $\frac{22}{35}$ **62.** $\frac{9}{8} - \frac{5}{6}$ $\frac{7}{24}$

63. $\frac{2}{15} + \frac{7}{9}$ $\frac{41}{45}$ **64.** $\frac{7}{25} + \frac{3}{10}$ $\frac{29}{50}$

65. $\frac{21}{56} - \frac{9}{40}$ $\frac{3}{20}$ **66.** $\frac{13}{24} - \frac{3}{40}$ $\frac{7}{15}$

Perform the operations and, if possible, simplify. **See Example 8.**

67. $16\left(\frac{3}{2}\right)$ 24   ▶ **68.** $30\left(\frac{5}{6}\right)$ 25

69. $18\left(\frac{2}{9}\right)$ 4   **70.** $14\left(\frac{3}{7}\right)$ 6

71. $\frac{2}{3} - \frac{1}{6} + \frac{5}{18}$ $\frac{7}{9}$ ▶ **72.** $\frac{3}{5} - \frac{7}{10} + \frac{7}{20}$ $\frac{1}{4}$

73. $\frac{5}{12} + \frac{1}{3} - \frac{2}{5}$ $\frac{7}{20}$ **74.** $\frac{7}{15} + \frac{1}{5} - \frac{4}{9}$ $\frac{2}{9}$

Perform the operations and, if possible, simplify. **See Examples 9 and 10.**

75. $4\frac{2}{3} \cdot 7$ $32\frac{2}{3}$ **76.** $7 \cdot 1\frac{3}{28}$ $7\frac{3}{4}$

77. $8 \div 3\frac{1}{5}$ $2\frac{1}{2}$ ▶ **78.** $15 \div 3\frac{1}{3}$ $4\frac{1}{2}$

▶ **79.** $8\frac{2}{9} - 7\frac{2}{3}$ $\frac{5}{9}$ **80.** $3\frac{4}{5} - 3\frac{1}{10}$ $\frac{7}{10}$

81. $3\frac{3}{16} + 2\frac{5}{24}$ $5\frac{19}{48}$ ▶ **82.** $15\frac{5}{6} + 11\frac{5}{8}$ $27\frac{11}{24}$

TRY IT YOURSELF

Perform the operations and, if possible, simplify.

83. $\frac{3}{5} + \frac{2}{3}$ $\frac{19}{15}$ **84.** $\frac{4}{3} + \frac{7}{2}$ $\frac{29}{6}$

85. $21\left(\frac{10}{3}\right)$ 70   **86.** $28\left(\frac{4}{7}\right)$ 16

87. $6 \cdot 2\frac{7}{24}$ $13\frac{3}{4}$ **88.** $3\frac{1}{2} \cdot \frac{1}{5}$ $\frac{7}{10}$

89. $\dfrac{2}{3} - \dfrac{1}{4} + \dfrac{1}{12}$ $\frac{1}{2}$

90. $\dfrac{3}{7} - \dfrac{2}{5} + \dfrac{2}{35}$ $\frac{3}{35}$

91. $\dfrac{21}{35} \div \dfrac{3}{14}$ $\frac{14}{5}$

92. $\dfrac{23}{25} \div \dfrac{46}{5}$ $\frac{1}{10}$

93. $\dfrac{4}{3}\left(\dfrac{6}{5}\right)$ $\frac{8}{5}$

94. $\dfrac{21}{8}\left(\dfrac{2}{15}\right)$ $\frac{7}{20}$

95. $\dfrac{4}{63} + \dfrac{1}{45}$ $\frac{3}{35}$

▶ **96.** $\dfrac{5}{18} + \dfrac{1}{99}$ $\frac{19}{66}$

97. $3 - \dfrac{3}{4}$ $\frac{9}{4}$

98. $4 - \dfrac{7}{3}$ $\frac{5}{3}$

99. $\dfrac{1}{2} \cdot \dfrac{3}{5}$ $\frac{3}{10}$

▶ **100.** $\dfrac{3}{4} \cdot \dfrac{5}{7}$ $\frac{15}{28}$

101. $3\dfrac{1}{3} \div 1\dfrac{5}{6}$ $1\frac{9}{11}$

102. $2\dfrac{1}{2} \div 1\dfrac{5}{8}$ $1\frac{7}{13}$

103. $\dfrac{11}{21} - \dfrac{8}{21}$ $\frac{1}{7}$

104. $\dfrac{19}{35} - \dfrac{12}{35}$ $\frac{1}{5}$

APPLICATIONS

105. FORESTRY A ranger cut down a pine tree and measured the widths of the outer two growth rings.

  a. What was the growth over this 2-year period? $\frac{7}{32}$ in.

  b. What is the difference in the widths of the rings? $\frac{3}{32}$ in.

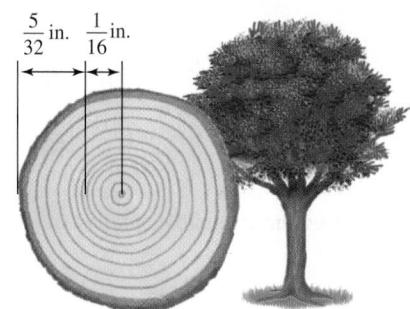

$\frac{5}{32}$ in. $\frac{1}{16}$ in.

▶ **106. HARDWARE** To secure the bracket to the stock, a bolt and a nut are used. How long should the threaded part of the bolt be? $7\frac{9}{16}$ in.

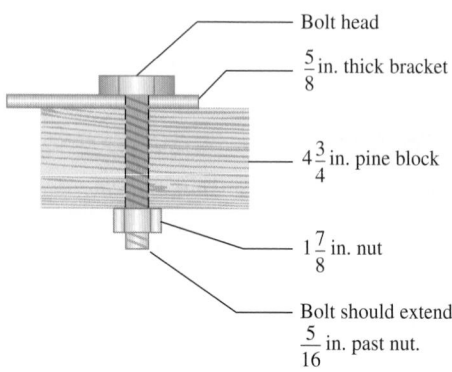

— Bolt head

— $\frac{5}{8}$ in. thick bracket

— $4\frac{3}{4}$ in. pine block

— $1\frac{7}{8}$ in. nut

— Bolt should extend $\frac{5}{16}$ in. past nut.

▶ **107. COOKING** How much butter is left in a $10\frac{1}{2}$-pound tub of butter if $4\frac{3}{4}$ pounds are used to make a wedding cake? $5\frac{3}{4}$ lb

108. CALORIES A company advertises that its mints contain only $3\frac{1}{2}$ calories a piece. What is the calorie intake if you eat an entire package of 20 mints? 70 calories

109. FRAMES How many inches of molding are needed to make the square picture frame? $40\frac{1}{2}$ in.

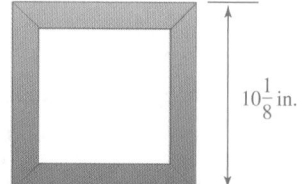

$10\frac{1}{8}$ in.

▶ **110. DECORATING** The materials used to make a pillow are shown. Examine the inventory list to decide how many pillows can be manufactured in one production run with the materials in stock. 147

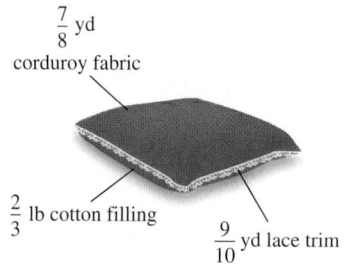

$\frac{7}{8}$ yd corduroy fabric

$\frac{2}{3}$ lb cotton filling

$\frac{9}{10}$ yd lace trim

Factory Inventory List	
Materials	**Amount in stock**
Lace trim	135 yd
Corduroy fabric	154 yd
Cotton filling	98 lb

WRITING

111. Explain how to add two fractions having unlike denominators.

▶ **112.** To multiply two fractions, must they have like denominators? Explain.

113. What are equivalent fractions?

114. Explain the error in the following addition.

$$\dfrac{4}{3} + \dfrac{3}{2} = \dfrac{4 + 3}{3 + 2} = \dfrac{7}{5}$$

REVIEW

Use the formula to complete each table.

115. $T = 15g$

Number of gears (g)	Number of teeth (T)
10	150
12	180

▶ **116.** $p = r - 200$

Revenue (r)	Profit (p)
1,000	800
5,000	4,800

SECTION 1.3
The Real Numbers

Objectives

1. Define the set of integers.

2. Graph sets of numbers on the number line.

3. Define the set of rational numbers.

4. Define the set of irrational numbers.

5. Define the set of real numbers.

6. Find the absolute value of a real number.

We have discussed the set of whole numbers, natural numbers, and the set of prime numbers. In this section, we define other sets of numbers and show that they are part of a larger collection of numbers called **real numbers.**

1 Define the set of integers.

In the table, we see the low temperatures for Rockford during the first week of January. In the left column, we have used the numbers 1, 2, 3, 4, 5, 6, and 7 to denote the calendar days of the month. This collection of numbers is called a **set,** and the members (or **elements**) of the set can be listed within **braces** { }.

{1, 2, 3, 4, 5, 6, 7}

Day of the month	Low temperature (°F)
1	4
2	−5
3	−6
4	0
5	3
6	6
7	6

Each of the numbers 1, 2, 3, 4, 5, 6, and 7 is a member of a basic set of numbers called the **natural numbers,** the numbers that we use for counting.

Natural Numbers

The set of **natural numbers** is {1, 2, 3, 4, 5, 6, 7, 8, 9, 10,…}.

The Language of Algebra The symbol … is called an *ellipsis* and indicates the pattern continues forever.

The natural numbers together with 0 make up another important set of numbers called the **whole numbers.**

Whole Numbers

The set of **whole numbers** is {0, 1, 2, 3, 4, 5, 6, 7, 8, 9, 10,…}.

Caution! Since every natural number is a whole number, we say that the set of natural numbers is a **subset** of the set of whole numbers. However, not all whole numbers are natural numbers. Note that 0 is a whole number but not a natural number.

The table above contains positive and negative temperatures. For example, on the second day of the month, the low temperature was −5° (read as "negative 5 degrees"), and it means 5° below zero. On the fifth day, the low temperature was 3° (3° above zero). The numbers used to represent the temperatures listed in the table are members of a set of numbers called the **integers.**

Integers

The set of **integers** is {…, −4, −3, −2, −1, 0, 1, 2, 3, 4,…}.

> **Caution!** Since every whole number is an integer, we say that the set of whole numbers is a *subset* of the set of integers. The natural numbers are also a subset of the integers. However, not all integers are whole numbers, nor are they all natural numbers. For example, the integer -2 is neither a whole number nor a natural number.

2 Graph sets of numbers on the number line.

We can illustrate sets of numbers with the **number line.** Like a ruler, the number line is straight and has uniform markings, as in the number line below. The arrowheads indicate that the number line continues forever to the left and to the right. Numbers to the right of 0 have values that are greater than 0; they are called **positive numbers.** Numbers to the left of 0 have values that are less than 0; they are called **negative numbers.** The number 0 is neither positive nor negative.

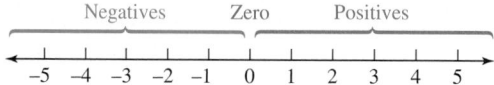

Positive numbers can be written with or without a $+$ sign. For example, $2 = +2$. Negative numbers are always written with a $-$ sign. They can be used to describe amounts that are less than 0, such as a checking account that is \$75 overdrawn ($-\$75$), an elevation of 200 feet below sea level (-200 ft), and a loss of 8 points (-8).

Using a process known as **graphing,** a single number or a set of numbers can be represented on a number line. The **graph of a number** is the point on the number line that corresponds to that number. *To graph a number* means to locate its position on the number line and then to highlight it by using a heavy dot.

EXAMPLE 1   Graph the integers between -4 and 5.

Strategy We will identify the integers between -4 and 5 and locate their positions on the number line. We will then draw a bold dot for each number and label them.

WHY To *graph a number* means to make a drawing that represents the number.

Solution
The integers between -4 and 5 are -3, -2, -1, 0, 1, 2, 3, and 4. To graph each integer, we locate its position on the number line and draw a dot.

> **Success Tip** "Between" means you do not include the endpoints. "From-to" means you do include the endpoints as long as they are in the set to be graphed.

As we move to the right on the number line, the values of the numbers increase. As we move to the left, the values of the numbers decrease. In the figure, we know that 5 is greater than -3 because the graph of 5 lies to the right of the graph of -3. We also know that -3 is less than 5 because its graph lies to the left of the graph of 5.

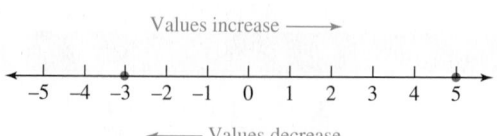

The **inequality symbol** > ("is greater than") can be used to show that 5 is greater than −3, and the inequality symbol < ("is less than") can be used to show that −3 is less than 5.

$5 > -3$ Read as "5 is greater than −3."

$-3 < 5$ Read as "−3 is less than 5."

To distinguish between these two inequality symbols, remember that each one points to the smaller of the two numbers involved.

$5 > -3$ $-3 < 5$

⌞──── Points to the smaller number. ────⌝

> ***The Language of Algebra***   To state that a number x is positive, we can write $x > 0$. To state that a number x is negative, we can write $x < 0$.

EXAMPLE 2   Use one of the symbols > or < to make each of the following statements true: **a.** −4 ▨ 4   **b.** −2 ▨ −3

Strategy To pick the correct inequality sign, we will determine the position of the graph of each number on the number line.

WHY When we compare the positions of two numbers on the number line, the number on the left is the smaller number and the number on the right is the larger.

Solution

a. Since −4 is to the left of 4 on the number line, we have $-4 < 4$.

b. Since −2 is to the right of −3 on the number line, we have $-2 > -3$. ▪

By extending the number line to include negative numbers, we can represent more situations graphically. In the figure to the right, the line graph illustrates the low temperatures listed in the table on page 29. The vertical axis is scaled in units of two degrees Fahrenheit, and temperatures below zero (negative temperatures) are graphed. For example, for the third day of the month, the low was −6°F.

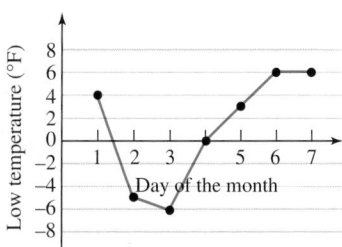

Self Check 2

Use one of the symbols > or < to make each of the following statements true:
a. 1 ▨ −1 >
b. −5 ▨ −4 <

Now Try Problems 55 and 57

Teaching Example 2 Use one of the symbols > or < to make each of the following statements true:
a. −3 ▨ −1   **b.** −2 ▨ −5
Answers:
a. <   **b.** >

3 **Define the set of rational numbers.**

In this course, we will work with positive and negative fractions. For example, the time it takes a motorist to complete the commute home might be $\frac{3}{4}$ of an hour, or a surveyor might indicate that a building's foundation has fallen below finished grade by expressing its elevation as $-\frac{7}{8}$ of an inch.

We will also work with positive and negative mixed numbers. For example, a piece of fabric might be $12\frac{2}{3}$ yards long, or the time before a rocket launch might be expressed as "$-5\frac{1}{2}$ minutes and counting."

Fractions and mixed numbers belong to the set of **rational numbers,** so named because *rational* numbers can be written as the *ratio* (or quotient) of two integers. This means that rational numbers can be written in the fractional form:

$\dfrac{\text{integer}}{\text{integer}}$ The numerator can be any integer.

The denominator can be any integer except 0.

Fractions such as $\frac{3}{4}$ and $\frac{25}{12}$ are rational numbers, because they have an integer numerator and a nonzero integer denominator. We can use the fact that

$$-\frac{a}{b} = \frac{-a}{b} = \frac{a}{-b}, \quad \text{where } b \neq 0$$

to show that negative fractions are rational numbers. For example, $-\frac{7}{8}$ is a rational number because it can be written as $\frac{-7}{8}$ or as $\frac{7}{-8}$. Positive and negative mixed numbers such as $12\frac{2}{3}$ and $-5\frac{1}{2}$ are also rational numbers because they can be written as the ratios of two integers.

$$12\frac{2}{3} = \frac{38}{3} \quad \text{and} \quad -5\frac{1}{2} = \frac{-11}{2}$$

Many numerical quantities are expressed in decimal notation. For example, a candy bar might cost $0.89, or a dragster might travel at 203.156 mph, or the first-quarter loss of a business might be $-$2.7 million. Since these terminating decimals can be written as ratios of two integers, they are rational numbers.

$$0.89 = \frac{89}{100} \qquad 203.156 = 203\frac{156}{1,000} = \frac{203,156}{1,000} \qquad -2.7 = -2\frac{7}{10} = \frac{-27}{10}$$

To find the *decimal equivalent* for a fraction, we divide its numerator by its denominator. For example, to write $\frac{3}{4}$ as an equivalent decimal, we proceed as follows:

$$
\begin{array}{r}
0.75 \\
4\overline{)3.0} \\
-2\,8 \\
\hline
20 \\
20 \\
\hline
0
\end{array}
$$

Decimals such as $0.33333\ldots$ and $2.161616\ldots$ are repeating decimals and can also be represented using **overbar** notation. $0.33333\ldots = 0.\overline{3}$ and $2.1616\ldots = 2.\overline{16}$. You have seen that $0.33333\ldots = \frac{1}{3}$. It can be shown that $2.161616\ldots = 2\frac{16}{99} = \frac{214}{99}$. In fact, *any* repeating decimal can be expressed as a ratio of two integers. For this reason, repeating decimals are also rational numbers.

> **Success Tip** All terminating and repeating decimals are rational numbers.

The set of rational numbers is too extensive to be listed in the same way that we have listed other sets in this section. Instead, we use **set-builder notation** to describe it.

The Set of Rational Numbers

$$\left\{ \frac{a}{b} \,\middle|\, a \text{ and } b \text{ are integers and } b \neq 0 \right\}$$

Read as "the set of all numbers of the form $\frac{a}{b}$, where a and b represent integers and $b \neq 0$."

4 Define the set of irrational numbers.

The square root of 2 $\left(\text{denoted } \sqrt{2}\right)$ is the number that, when multiplied by itself, gives 2. That is, $\sqrt{2} \cdot \sqrt{2} = 2$. In illustration (a) on the next page, the anchor wire is the diagonal of a square with sides that are 1 yard in length. It can be shown that the length of the wire is $\sqrt{2}$ yards.

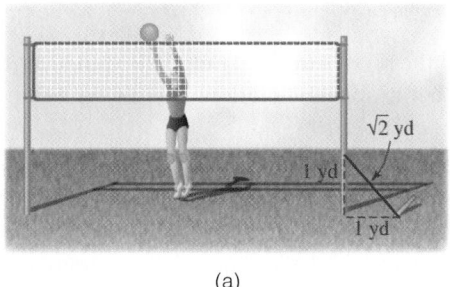

(a)   (b)

The number represented by the Greek letter π (read as "pi") is often used in geometry. In illustration (b), the distance around the hula hoop (circumference) is found by multiplying the diameter of the hoop by π.

Expressed in decimal form,

$$\sqrt{2} = 1.414213562\ldots \quad \text{and} \quad \pi = 3.141592654\ldots$$

> **The Language of Algebra**   Since π is irrational, its decimal representation has an infinite number of decimal places that do not repeat a block of digits. In 2002, a University of Tokyo mathematician used a super computer to calculate π to over one trillion decimal places.

These **nonterminating, nonrepeating decimals** cannot be written as the ratio of two integers. Therefore, $\sqrt{2}$ and π are *not* rational numbers—they are called **irrational numbers.**

Irrational Numbers

An **irrational number** is a nonterminating, nonrepeating decimal.

Other examples of irrational numbers are $\sqrt{89}$, $-\sqrt{5}$, $-\pi$, and 3π (this means $3 \cdot \pi$). When doing calculations with irrational numbers, we often approximate them.

Using Your CALCULATOR   Approximating Irrational Numbers

We can use the square root key $\boxed{\sqrt{}}$ on a calculator to approximate $\boxed{\sqrt{2}}$. To approximate π, we use the $\boxed{\pi}$ key. With a scientific calculator that is reverse entry, we enter these numbers and press these keys.

2 $\boxed{\sqrt{}}$ $\boxed{\text{1.414213562}}$

$\boxed{\pi}$ (you may have to use a $\boxed{\text{2nd}}$ or $\boxed{\text{Shift}}$ key first.) $\boxed{\text{3.141592654}}$

We see that $\sqrt{2} \approx 1.414213562$. The symbol $\approx$ means "is approximately equal to." Rounded to the nearest hundredth, $\sqrt{2} \approx 1.41$. Rounded to the nearest thousandth, $\pi \approx 3.142$.

To approximate $\sqrt{2}$ and π using a graphing calculator or direct-entry scientific calculator, we enter these numbers and press these keys.

$\boxed{\text{2nd}}\ \boxed{\sqrt{}}\ \boxed{2}\ \boxed{)}\ \boxed{\text{ENTER}}$

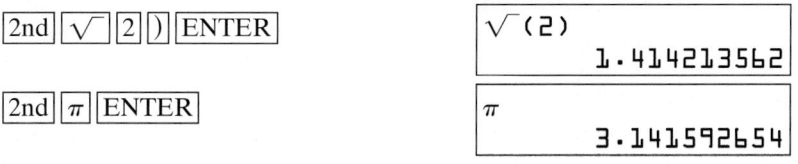

$\boxed{\text{2nd}}\ \boxed{\pi}\ \boxed{\text{ENTER}}$

5 **Define the set of real numbers.**

The set of rational numbers together with the set of irrational numbers form the set of **real numbers.** That is, a real number is either rational or irrational. All of the numbers that we have discussed in this section are real numbers.

> ### The Real Numbers
>
> A **real number** is any number that is either a rational or an irrational number.

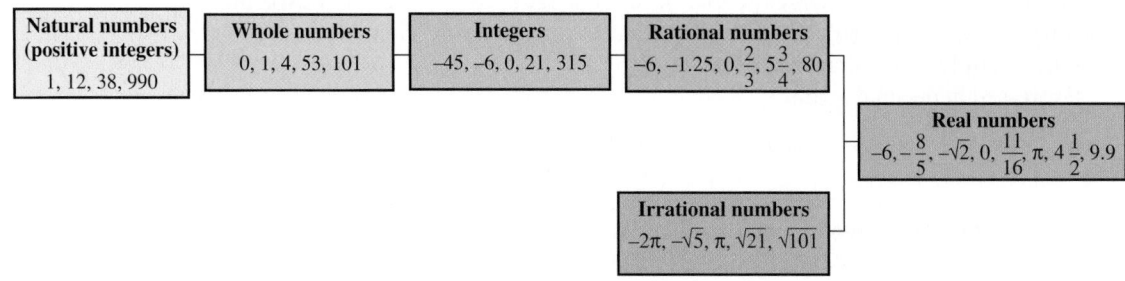

The diagram above shows how the sets of numbers introduced in this section are related. Note that a number can belong to more than one set. For example, -6 is an integer, a rational number, and a real number.

EXAMPLE 3   Determine which numbers in the following set are natural numbers, whole numbers, integers, rational numbers, irrational numbers, and real numbers: $\left\{-3.4, \tfrac{2}{5}, 0, -6, 1\tfrac{3}{4}, \pi, 16\right\}$.

Strategy We will start by scanning the set to see if there are natural numbers. Then we will scan the set for each of the other types of real numbers listed.

WHY It is easier to look for numbers that belong to one of the specified sets at a time.

Solution

Natural numbers: 16

Whole numbers: $0, 16$

Integers: $0, -6, 16$

Rational numbers: $-3.4, \tfrac{2}{5}, 0, -6, 1\tfrac{3}{4}, 16$ *Rational numbers can be expressed as a ratio of two integers:* $-3.4 = \tfrac{-34}{10}$, $0 = \tfrac{0}{1}$, $-6 = \tfrac{-6}{1}$, $1\tfrac{3}{4} = \tfrac{7}{4}$, *and* $16 = \tfrac{16}{1}$.

Irrational numbers: π

Real numbers: $-3.4, \tfrac{2}{5}, 0, -6, 1\tfrac{3}{4}, \pi, 16$

The set of real numbers corresponds to all points on a number line. One and only one point on the number line corresponds to each real number.

EXAMPLE 4   Graph each number in the set $\left\{-3.25, -\tfrac{1}{5}, \sqrt{5}, 3\tfrac{7}{8}, 0.666\ldots, -\tfrac{3}{2}\right\}$ on the number line.

Strategy We will find decimal approximations for the fractions and irrational numbers.

WHY Decimal approximations help locate the position of the graph of such numbers. ▼

Solution
We locate the position of each number on the number line and then draw a heavy dot. Recall that $0.25 = \frac{1}{4}$, so $-3.25 = -3\frac{1}{4}$. In mixed-number form, $-\frac{3}{2} = -1\frac{1}{2}$.

Using a calculator, we see that $\sqrt{5} \approx 2.2$. The repeating decimal $0.666\ldots$ is $\frac{2}{3}$.

6   Find the absolute value of a real number.

On the number line, -4 and 4 are both a distance of 4 away from 0. Because of this, we say that -4 and 4 are **opposites.**

Opposites

Two numbers represented by points on a number line that are the same distance away from 0, but on opposite sides of it, are called **opposites.**

To write the opposite of a number, a $-$ symbol can be used. For example, the opposite of 6 can be written as -6. The opposite of 0 is 0, so $-0 = 0$. Since the opposite of -6 is 6, we have $-(-6) = 6$. In general, if a represents any real number,

$$-(-a) = a$$

The **absolute value** of a number gives the distance between the number and 0 on the number line. To indicate absolute value, a number is inserted between two vertical bars. For the example, we would write $|-4| = 4$. This notation is read as "The absolute value of negative 4 is 4," and it tells us that the distance between -4 and 0 is 4 units. We also see that $|4| = 4$.

Absolute Value

The **absolute value** of a number is the distance on the number line between the number and 0.

Success Tip   Since absolute value expresses distance, the absolute value of a number is always positive or zero—never negative.

EXAMPLE 5   Find each absolute value: **a.** $|18|$ **b.** $\left|-\frac{7}{8}\right|$ **c.** $|0|$

Strategy We will find the distance that the number within the absolute value bars is from 0.

WHY The absolute value of a number is the distance between 0 and the number on a number line.

Now Try **Problem 72**

Teaching Example 5 Find each absolute value:
a. $|-\pi|$ **b.** $|5|$ **c.** $\left|\sqrt{3}\right|$ **d.** $-\left|-2\right|$
Answers:
a. π **b.** 5 **c.** $\sqrt{3}$ **d.** -2

Solution
a. Since 18 is a distance of 18 from 0 on the number line, $|18| = 18$.
b. Since $-\frac{7}{8}$ is a distance of $\frac{7}{8}$ from 0 on the number line, $\left|-\frac{7}{8}\right| = \frac{7}{8}$.
c. Since 0 is a distance of 0 from 0 on the number line, $|0| = 0$.

Self Check 6

Insert one of the symbols $>$, $<$, or $=$ in each blank:
a. $-(-7)$ ___ 12 $<$
b. $3\frac{3}{4}$ ___ $\left|-\frac{5}{4}\right|$ $>$

Now Try **Problems 75 and 77**

Teaching Example 6 Insert one of the symbols $>$, $<$, or $=$ in each blank:
a. 15 ___ $-(-16)$
b. $-\left|-\frac{2}{3}\right|$ ___ π
c. $-(-4)$ ___ 4
Answers:
a. $<$
b. $<$
c. $=$

EXAMPLE 6 Insert one of the symbols $>$, $<$, or $=$ in each blank:
a. $-(-3.9)$ ___ 3 **b.** $-\left|-\frac{4}{5}\right|$ ___ $\left|\sqrt{5}\right|$

Strategy We will simplify the expression on each side and then compare the values.

WHY Simplifying the sides helps us determine which symbol to use.

Solution
a. $-(-3.9) > 3$, because $-(-3.9) = 3.9$.
b. $-\left|-\frac{4}{5}\right| < \left|\sqrt{5}\right|$, because $-\left|-\frac{4}{5}\right| = -\frac{4}{5}$, and $\left|\sqrt{5}\right| = \sqrt{5} \approx 2.2$.

ANSWERS TO SELF CHECKS

1.

2. a. $>$ **b.** $<$ **3.** natural numbers: 45; whole numbers: 45; integers: 45, -2; rational numbers: 0.4, $-\frac{2}{7}$, 45, -2, $\frac{13}{4}$; irrational numbers: $\sqrt{2}$; real numbers: 0.4, $\sqrt{2}$, $-\frac{2}{7}$, 45, -2, $\frac{13}{4}$ **4.**

5. a. 100 **b.** 4.7 **c.** $\sqrt{2}$ **6. a.** $<$ **b.** $>$

STUDY SKILLS CHECKLIST

Getting the Most from the Study Sets

The following checklist will help you become familiar with the Study Sets in this book. Place a check mark in each box after you answer the question.

☐ Answers to the odd numbered **Study Set** problems are located in the appendix on page A-7. On what page do the answers to Study Set 1.2 appear?

☐ Each Study Set begins with **Vocabulary** problems. How many Vocabulary problems appear in Study Set 1.2, which begins on page 26?

☐ Following the Vocabulary problems, you will see **Concepts.** How many Concepts problems appear in Study Set 1.2?

☐ Following the Concepts problems, you will see **Notation** problems. How many Notation problems appear in Study Set 1.2?

☐ After the Notation problems, **Guided Practice** problems are given, which are linked to similar examples within the section. How many Guided Practice problems appear in Study Set 1.2?

☐ After the Guided Practice problems, **Try It Yourself** problems are given and can be used to help you prepare for quizzes. How many Try It Yourself problems appear in Study Set 1.2?

☐ Following the Try It Yourself problems, you will see **Applications.** How many Applications problems appear in Study Set 1.2?

☐ After completing the Application problems, a few **Writing** problems are given. How many Writing problems appear in Study Set 1.2?

☐ Lastly, each Study Set ends with a few **Review** problems. How many Review problems appear in Study Set 1.2?

Answer: A-7, 8, 4, 2, 68, 22, 6, 4, 2

SECTION 1.3 STUDY SET

VOCABULARY

Fill in the blanks.

1. The set of __natural__ numbers is $\{1, 2, 3, 4, 5, \ldots\}$.

2. The set of __whole__ numbers is $\{0, 1, 2, 3, 4, 5, \ldots\}$.

3. The set of __integers__ is $\{\ldots, -2, -1, 0, 1, 2, \ldots\}$.

4. Numbers less than zero are __negative__, and numbers greater than zero are __positive__.

5. The symbols $<$ and $>$ are __inequality__ symbols.

6. A __rational__ number can be written as a quotient (ratio) of two integers.

7. In __set-builder__ notation, the set of rational numbers is written as $\left\{\dfrac{a}{b} \,\middle|\, a \text{ and } b \text{ are integers and } b \neq 0\right\}$.

8. An irrational number is a nonterminating, nonrepeating __decimal__.

▶ 9. An __irrational__ number cannot be expressed as a quotient (ratio) of two integers.

▶ 10. All numbers that can be represented by points on the number line are called __real__ numbers.

11. Two numbers represented by points on the number line that are the same distance away from 0, but on opposite sides of it, are called __opposites__.

12. The __absolute value__ of a real number is the distance on the number line between the number and 0.

CONCEPTS

13. Show that each of the following numbers is a rational number by expressing it as a fraction with an integer in its numerator and a nonzero integer in its denominator: $6, -9, -\frac{7}{8}, 3\frac{1}{2}, -0.3, 2.83$.
   $\frac{6}{1}, \frac{-9}{1}, \frac{-7}{8}, \frac{7}{2}, \frac{-3}{10}, \frac{283}{100}$

▶ 14. Represent each situation using a signed number.

   a. A loss of $15 million $-\$15$ million

   b. A rainfall total 0.75 inch below average -0.75 in.

   c. A score $12\frac{1}{2}$ points under the standard $-12\frac{1}{2}$ points

   d. A building foundation $\frac{5}{16}$ inch above grade $+\frac{5}{16}$ in.

15. What numbers are a distance of 8 away from 5 on the number line? 13 and -3

16. Suppose the variable m stands for a negative number. Use an inequality to state this fact. $m < 0$

17. The variables a and b represent real numbers. Use an inequality symbol, $<$ or $>$, to make each statement true.

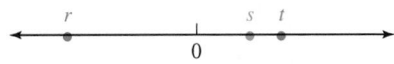

   a. $a < b$ **b.** $b > a$

   c. $b > 0$ and $a < 0$

18. **a.** Write the statement $-6 < -5$ using an inequality symbol that points in the other direction. $-5 > -6$

   b. Write the statement $16 > -25$ using an inequality symbol that points in the other direction. $-25 < 16$

19. What is the length of the diagonal of the square shown below? $\sqrt{2}$ in.

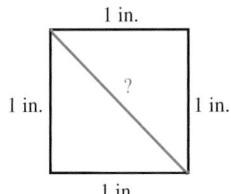

20. The following diagram can be used to show how the natural numbers, whole numbers, integers, rational numbers, and irrational numbers make up the set of real numbers. If the natural numbers are represented as shown, label each of the other sets.

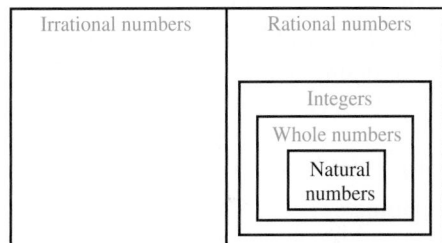

Determine whether each statement is true or false.

▶ 21. **a.** Every whole number is an integer. true

   b. Every integer is a natural number. false

   c. Every integer is a whole number. false

   d. Irrational numbers are nonterminating, nonrepeating decimals. true

▶ 22. **a.** Irrational numbers are real numbers. true

   b. Every whole number is a rational number. true

   c. Every rational number can be written as a fraction. true

   d. Every rational number is a whole number. false

▶ 23. If we begin with the number -4 and find its opposite, and then find the opposite of that result, what number do we obtain? -4

▶ 24. Which number graphed below has the largest absolute value? r

Approximate each irrational number to the nearest thousandth.

25. $\sqrt{5}$ 2.236   26. $\sqrt{19}$ 4.359

27. $\sqrt{99}$ 9.950   ▶ 28. $\sqrt{42}$ 6.481

29. π 3.142   ▶ **30.** 2π 6.283

31. $\dfrac{\pi}{2}$ 1.571   **32.** $\dfrac{\pi}{6}$ 0.524

NOTATION

Fill in the blanks.

33. $\sqrt{5}$ is read "the __square__ __root__ of 5."

34. $|-15|$ is read "the __absolute__ __value__ of -15."

35. The symbol $\approx$ means __is approximately equal to__ .

36. The symbols { }, called __braces__ , are used when writing a set.

For exercises 37 and 38, write each fraction as a decimal. Determine whether the result is a terminating or nonterminating decimal.

37. a. $\dfrac{2}{3}$ 0.666..., nonterminating   **b.** $\dfrac{4}{5}$ 0.8, terminating

38. a. $\dfrac{5}{8}$ 0.625, terminating   **b.** $\dfrac{5}{11}$ 0.454545..., nonterminating

39. The symbols $<, >, \leq,$ and $\geq$ are called __inequalities__ .

40. The symbol ... is called an __ellipsis__ and it indicates that a set follows an established pattern that continues forever.

Write each expression in simpler form.

41. The opposite of 5 -5 **42.** The opposite of -9 9

43. The opposite of $-\dfrac{7}{8}$ $\dfrac{7}{8}$ **44.** The opposite of 6.56 -6.56

45. $-(-10)$ 10   **46.** $-(-1)$ 1

47. $-(-2.3)$ 2.3   **48.** $-\left(-\dfrac{3}{4}\right)$ $\dfrac{3}{4}$

49. The opposite of the absolute value of 3 -3

50. $-|-5|$ -5

GUIDED PRACTICE

Graph the integers between the given numbers. **See Example 1.**

▶ **51.** -3 and 6

52. -1 and 7

53. -6 and 8

54. -3 and 5

Insert one of the symbols $>, <,$ or $=$ in the blank to make the statement true. **See Example 2.**

55. 5 $>$ -4 **56.** -11 $<$ -9

57. -2 $>$ -4 ▶ **58.** 0 $<$ 32

59. $|3.4|$ $>$ $\sqrt{10}$ ▶ **60.** 0.08 $>$ 0.079

61. $-|-1.1|$ $<$ -1 **62.** $-(-5.5)$ $=$ $-\left(-5\dfrac{1}{2}\right)$

Determine which numbers in the set are natural numbers, whole numbers, integers, rational numbers, irrational numbers, and real numbers. **See Example 3.**

▶ **63.** $\left\{-\dfrac{5}{6},\ \ 35.99,\ \ 0,\ \ 4\dfrac{3}{8},\ \ \sqrt{2},\ \ -50,\ \ \dfrac{17}{5}\right\}$

natural: none; whole: 0; integers: 0, -50; rational: $-\dfrac{5}{6}$, 35.99, 0, $4\dfrac{3}{8}$, -50, $\dfrac{17}{5}$; irrational: $\sqrt{2}$; real: all

▶ **64.** $\left\{-0.001,\ \ 10\dfrac{1}{2},\ \ 6,\ \ \pi,\ \ \sqrt{7},\ \ -23,\ \ -5.6\right\}$

natural: 6; whole: 6; integers: 6, -23; rational: -0.001, $10\dfrac{1}{2}$, 6, -23, -5.6; irrational: π, $\sqrt{7}$; real: all

65. $\left\{-\pi,\ \ 0,\ \ 1\dfrac{3}{5},\ \ 8,\ \ \pi,\ \ \sqrt{11},\ \ -3,\ \ 2.6,\ \ 2\right\}$

natural: 2, 8; whole: 0, 2, 8; integers: 0, 8, -3, 2; rational: 0, $1\dfrac{3}{5}$, 8, -3, 2.6, 2; irrational: $-\pi$, π, $\sqrt{11}$; real: all

66. $\left\{3\dfrac{5}{6},\ \ 9,\ \ \sqrt{3},\ \ 0.00023,\ \ -2.7,\ \ 0,\ \ -3\right\}$

natural: 9; whole: 0, 9; integers: 9, 0, -3; rational: $3\dfrac{5}{6}$, 9, 0.00023, -2.7, 0, -3; irrational: $\sqrt{3}$; real: all

Graph each set of numbers on the number line. **See Example 4.**

▶ **67.** $\left\{-\pi,\ \ 4.25,\ \ -1\dfrac{1}{2},\ \ -0.333...,\ \ \sqrt{2},\ \ -\dfrac{35}{8},\ \ 3\right\}$

68. $\left\{\pi,\ -2\dfrac{1}{8},\ \ 2.75,\ \ -\sqrt{17},\ \ \dfrac{17}{4},\ \ -0.666...,\ \ -3\right\}$

69. $\left\{-3\dfrac{5}{8},\ \ 2,\ \ \sqrt{3},\ \ \dfrac{17}{5},\ \ 0.333...,\ \ 5\right\}$

70. $\left\{-1\dfrac{7}{9},\ \ 3.5,\ \ -\sqrt{11},\ \ \dfrac{9}{4},\ \ 1.666...,\ \ 4\right\}$

Evaluate each expression. **See Example 5.**

71. $|-17|$ 17   ▶ **72.** $\left|-\dfrac{3}{5}\right|$ $\dfrac{3}{5}$

73. $-|-2.5|$ -2.5 **74.** $-|\pi|$ $-\pi$

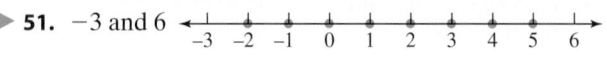

Insert one of the symbols >, <, or = in the blank to make the statement true. **See Example 6.**

75. $-|-2|$ $=$ -2

76. $-\left|-\dfrac{2}{3}\right|$ $<$ $\dfrac{3}{4}$

77. $-\left|\dfrac{5}{6}\right|$ $>$ -2

78. $-\left|-\dfrac{3}{4}\right|$ $<$ $\dfrac{3}{4}$

79. $-\left(-\dfrac{5}{8}\right)$ $>$ $-\left(-\dfrac{3}{8}\right)$

80. $-19\dfrac{2}{3}$ $<$ $-19\dfrac{1}{3}$

81. $\left|-\dfrac{15}{2}\right|$ $=$ 7.5

82. $\sqrt{2}$ $<$ π

83. $\dfrac{99}{100}$ $=$ 0.99

84. $|2|$ $>$ $-|-2|$

85. $0.333\ldots$ $>$ 0.3

86. $\left|-2\dfrac{2}{3}\right|$ $>$ $-\left(-\dfrac{3}{2}\right)$

87. $-(-1)$ $>$ $\left|-\dfrac{15}{16}\right|$

88. $-0.666\ldots$ $<$ 0

89. $-(-1)$ $<$ $\left|-\dfrac{19}{13}\right|$

90. $-0.666\ldots$ $>$ -1.34

APPLICATIONS

91. BANKING In the table below, which numbers are natural numbers, whole numbers, integers, rational numbers, irrational numbers, and real numbers?

Type of account	Principal	Rate	Time (years)	Interest
Checking	$135.75	0.0275	$\dfrac{31}{365}$	$0.32
Savings	$5,000	0.06	$2\dfrac{1}{2}$	$750

natural, whole, integers: 750, 5,000; rational: all; irrational: none; real: all

92. DRAFTING The following drawing shows the dimensions of an aluminum bracket.

   a. Which numbers shown are natural numbers, whole numbers, integers, rational numbers, irrational numbers, and real numbers? natural, whole, integers: 9; rational: 9, $\frac{15}{16}$, $3\frac{1}{8}$, 1.765; irrational: 2π, 3π, $\sqrt{89}$; real: all

   b. Approximate all the irrational numbers in the drawing to the nearest thousandth.
   $3\pi \approx 9.425$, $2\pi \approx 6.283$, $\sqrt{89} \approx 9.434$

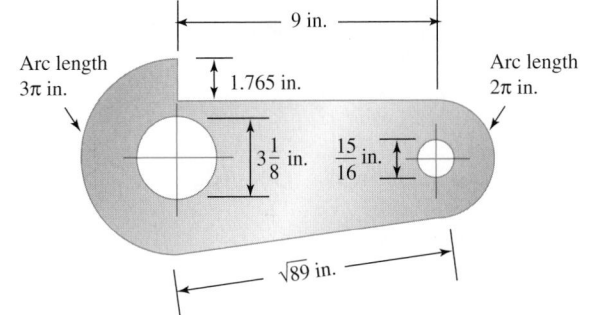

93. TRADE Each year from 1991 through 2007, the United States imported more goods and services from Japan than it exported to Japan. This caused trade deficits, which are represented by negative numbers on the graph.

   a. In which year was the deficit the worst? Express that deficit using a signed number.
   2006, −$88 billion

   b. In which year was the deficit the smallest? Estimate that deficit using a signed number.
   1991, −$43 billion

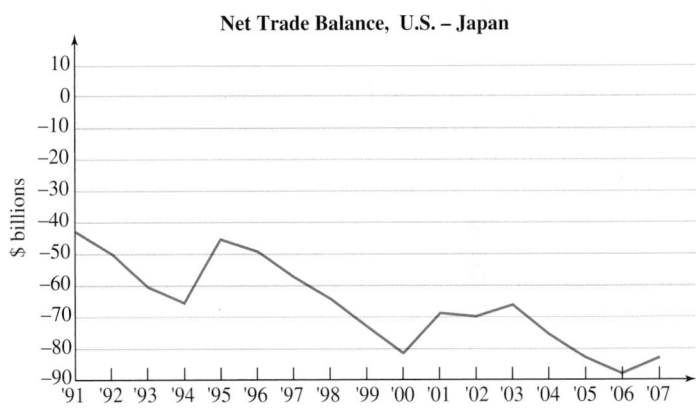

Net Trade Balance, U.S. – Japan

Source: U.S. Bureau of the Census

94. U.S. BUDGET A budget *deficit* is a negative number that indicates the government spent more money than it took in that year. A budget *surplus* is a positive number that indicates the government took in more money than it spent that year. Refer to the graph.

   a. In which year was the federal budget deficit the worst? Estimate that deficit using a signed number.
   2004, −$410 billion

   b. In which years was the federal budget surplus the greatest? Estimate that surplus.
   2000, $240 billion

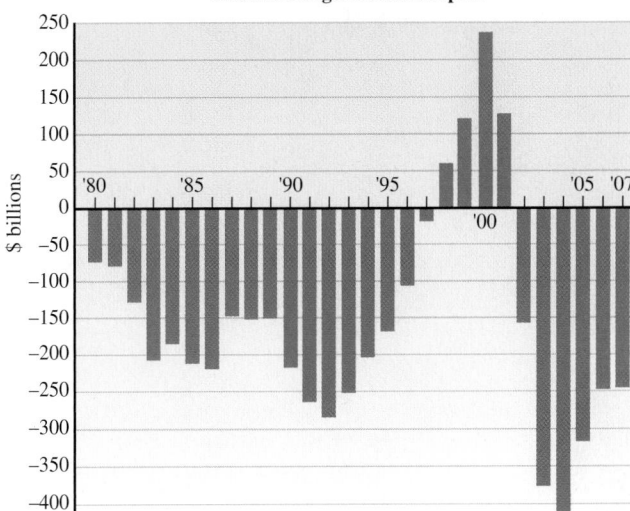

Federal Budget Deficit/Surplus

Source: U.S. Bureau of the Census

95. TIRES The distance a tire rolls in one revolution can be found by computing the circumference of the circular tire using the formula $C = \pi d$, where d is the diameter of the tire. How far will the tire in the illustration roll in one revolution? Answer to the nearest tenth of an inch. 81.7 in.

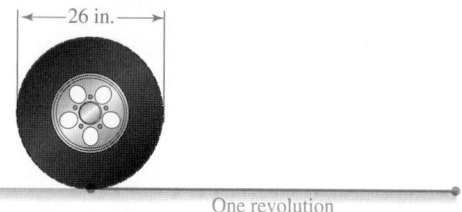

26 in.

One revolution

96. HULA HOOPS The length of plastic pipe needed to form a hula hoop can be found by computing the circumference of the circular hula hoop using the formula $C = \pi d$, where d is its diameter. Find the length of pipe needed to form the hula hoop in the illustration. Answer to the nearest tenth of an inch. 106.8 in.

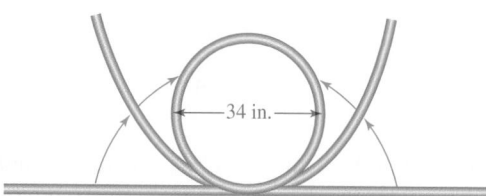

34 in.

A length of pipe is bent to form a hula hoop.

97. ARCHERY Which arrow landed farther from the target? How does the concept of absolute value apply here? Arrow 1, $|-6| > |5|$

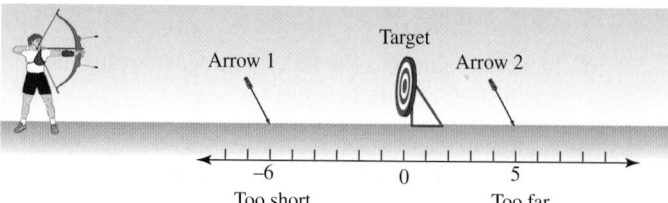

Arrow 1   Target   Arrow 2

−6   0   5

Too short   Too far

98. Refer to the historical time line.

MAYA CIVILIZATION

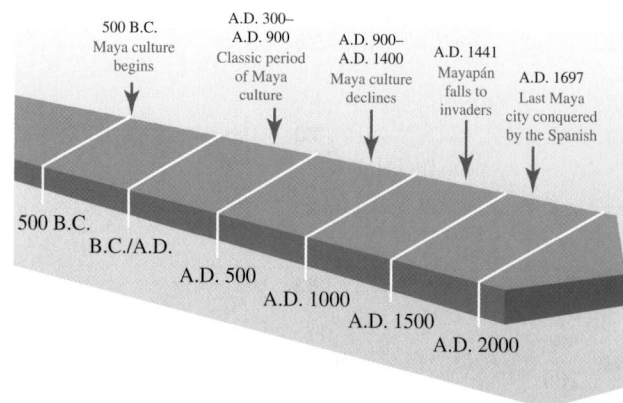

500 B.C. Maya culture begins

A.D. 300– A.D. 900 Classic period of Maya culture

A.D. 900– A.D. 1400 Maya culture declines

A.D. 1441 Mayapán falls to invaders

A.D. 1697 Last Maya city conquered by the Spanish

500 B.C.

B.C./A.D.

A.D. 500

A.D. 1000

A.D. 1500

A.D. 2000

a. What basic unit was used to scale the time line? 500 years

b. On the time line, what symbolism is used to represent zero? B.C./A.D.

c. On the time line, which numbers could be thought of as positive and which could be thought of as negative? pos: A.D.; neg: B.C.

d. Express the dates for the Maya civilization using positive and negative numbers. −500 to 1697

WRITING

99. Explain the difference between a rational and an irrational number.

100. Can two different numbers have the same absolute value? Explain.

101. Give two examples each of fractions, mixed numbers, decimals, and negative numbers that you use in your everyday life.

102. In writing courses, students are warned not to use double negatives in their compositions. Identify the double negative in the following sentence. Then rewrite the sentence so that it conveys the same idea without using a double negative. "No one didn't turn in the homework."

REVIEW

103. Simplify: $\dfrac{24}{54}$ $\frac{4}{9}$

104. Prime factor 60. $2 \cdot 2 \cdot 3 \cdot 5$

105. Mulitply: $\dfrac{3}{4}\left(\dfrac{8}{5}\right)$ $\frac{6}{5}$

106. Divide: $5\dfrac{2}{3} \div 2\dfrac{5}{9}$ $2\frac{5}{23}$

107. Add: $\dfrac{3}{10} + \dfrac{2}{15}$ $\frac{13}{30}$

108. Write $\dfrac{4}{25}$ as a decimal. 0.16

109. Write $\dfrac{3}{8}$ as a decimal. 0.375

110. Add: $\dfrac{5}{7} + \dfrac{3}{7}$ $\frac{8}{7}$

Objectives

1 Find the sum of two real numbers with the same sign.

2 Find the sum of two real numbers with different signs.

3 Use properties of addition.

Recall that all points on the number line represent the set of real numbers. Real numbers that are greater than zero are *positive real numbers*. See the number line below. Positive numbers can be written with or without a + sign. For example, 2 = +2 and 4.75 = +4.75. Real numbers that are less than zero are *negative real numbers*. They must be written with a − sign. For example, *negative* 2 = −2 and *negative* 4.75 = −4.75. Positive and negative numbers are called **signed numbers.**

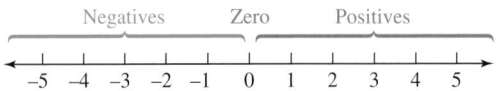

Caution! Zero is neither positive nor negative.

We can use signed numbers to describe many situations. Words such as *gain, above, up, to the right,* and *in the future* indicate positive numbers. Words such as *loss, below, down, to the left,* and *in the past* indicate negative numbers.

In words	In symbols	Meaning
16 degrees above 0	+16°	positive sixteen degrees
30 seconds after liftoff	30 sec	positive thirty seconds
$10.50 overdrawn	−$10.50	negative ten dollars and fifty cents
$5\frac{1}{2}$ feet below sea level	$-5\frac{1}{2}$ ft	negative five and one-half feet

In the figure to the right, signed numbers are used to denote the 2008 quarterly profits and losses of the Barnes & Noble Corporation. The first-quarter profit of $115 million and the third-quarter profit of $15 million are represented by the positive numbers 115 and 15. The second-quarter loss of $2 million and the fourth-quarter loss of $18 million are represented by the negative numbers −2 and −18. To find Barnes & Noble's 2008 net income, we must add these positive and negative numbers.

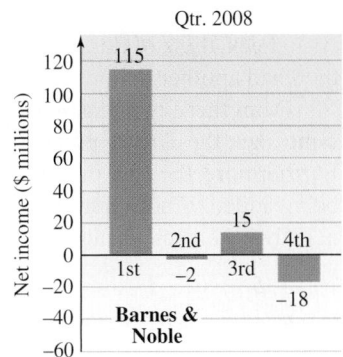

Source: *Wall Street Journal*

Net income = 115 + (−2) + 15 + (−18)

In this section, we will discuss how to perform such additions. We will also introduce a rule that is helpful when subtracting signed numbers.

1 Find the sum of two real numbers with the same sign.

We can use a number line to explain the addition of signed numbers. For example, the number line on the next page shows the steps that are used to compute 5 + 2. We begin at the **origin** (the zero point) and draw an arrow 5 units long, pointing to the right; this represents 5. From that point, we draw an arrow 2 units long, also pointing to the right; this represents 2. We end up at 7; therefore, 5 + 2 = 7.

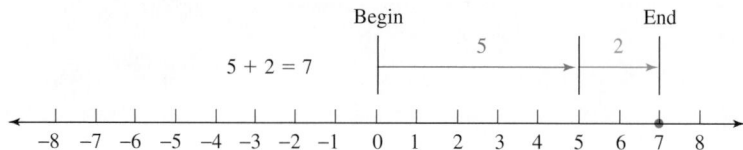

The Language of Algebra   The names of the parts of an addition fact are

Addend   Addend   Sum
↓   ↓   ↓
5   +   2   =   7

To compute $-5 + (-2)$ on a number line, we begin at the origin and draw an arrow 5 units long, pointing to the left; this represents -5. From there, we draw an arrow 2 units long, also pointing to the left; this represents -2. We end up at -7, as shown below. Therefore, $-5 + (-2) = -7$.

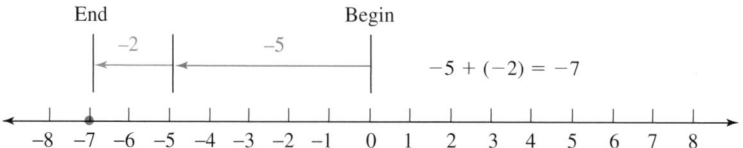

Caution!   To avoid confusion, we write negative numbers within parentheses to separate the negative sign $-$ from the addition symbol $+$. $-5 + (-2)$

As a check, think of this problem in terms of money. If you had a debt of $5, (-5),$ and then had another debt of $2, (-2),$ you would have a debt of $7, (-7).$

From these two examples, we observe that when we add two numbers with the same sign, the arrows point in the same direction and they build upon each other. Furthermore, the answer that they point to has the same sign as the numbers that are being added. If both numbers are positive, their sum is positive. If both numbers are negative, their sum is negative.

$$5 \;+\; 2 \;=\; 7 \qquad \text{and} \qquad -5 \;+\; (-2) \;=\; -7$$

positive + positive = positive   negative + negative = negative

These observations suggest the following rule.

Adding Two Real Numbers with the Same (Like) Sign

To add two real numbers with the same (like) sign, add their absolute values and attach their common sign to the sum.

Success Tip   The sum of two positive numbers is always positive. The sum of two negative numbers is always negative.

EXAMPLE 1   Find the sum: $-25 + (-18)$

Strategy We will use the rule for adding two real numbers that have the same sign.

WHY We use that rule because the addition involves two negative numbers.

Solution

Since both numbers are negative, the answer is negative.

$$-25 + (-18) = -43$$ Add their absolute values, 25 and 18, to get 43. Attach their common sign (which is a − sign) to 43.

The Language of Algebra   Two negative numbers, as well as two positive numbers, are said to have *like* signs.

Self Check 1

Find the sum: $-45 + (-12)$

Now Try **Problem 27**

Self Check 1 Answers
-57

Teaching Example 1 Find the sum:
$-16 + (-21)$
Answer:
-37

2 Find the sum of two real numbers with different signs.

To compute $5 + (-2)$ on the number line, we begin at the origin and draw an arrow 5 units long, pointing to the right; this represents 5. From there, we draw an arrow 2 units long, pointing to the left; this represents -2. We end up at 3, as shown below. Therefore, $5 + (-2) = 3$. In terms of money, if you had \$5 $(+5)$, and lost \$2 (-2), you would have \$3 $(+3)$ left.

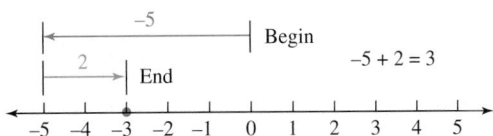

To compute $-5 + 2$ on the number line, we start at the origin and draw an arrow 5 units long, pointing to the left; this represents -5. From there, we draw an arrow 2 units long, pointing to the right; this represents 2. We end up at -3, as shown below. Therefore, $-5 + 2 = -3$. In terms of money, if you owed a friend \$5 (-5), and paid back \$2 $(+2)$, you would still owe your friend \$3 (-3).

The Language of Algebra   A positive number and a negative number are said to have *unlike* or *different* signs.

From these two examples, we observe that when we add two numbers with different signs, the arrows point in opposite directions. Furthermore, the longer arrow determines the sign of the answer. If the longer arrow represents a positive number, the sum is positive. If the longer arrow represents a negative number, the sum is negative.

$$5 \ + \ (-2) \ = \ 3 \qquad \text{and} \qquad -5 \ + \ 2 \ = \ -3$$
positive + negative = positive   negative + positive = negative

These observations suggest the following rule.

Adding Two Real Numbers with Different (Unlike) Signs

To add two real numbers with different (unlike) signs, subtract their absolute values (the smaller from the larger). To this result, attach the sign of the number with the larger absolute value.

Self Check 2

Add:
a. $63 + (-87)$ -24
b. $-6.27 + 8$ 1.73
c. $-\dfrac{1}{10} + \dfrac{1}{2}$ $\dfrac{2}{5}$

Now Try **Problem 34**

Teaching Example 2 Add:
a. $-10 + 32$
b. $-3.98 + 2.17$
c. $-\frac{1}{5} + \left(\frac{3}{5}\right)$
Answers:
a. 22 **b.** -1.81 **c.** $\frac{2}{5}$

EXAMPLE 2

Add: **a.** $-17 + 32$ **b.** $5.4 + (-7.7)$ **c.** $\dfrac{3}{25} + \left(-\dfrac{19}{25}\right)$

Strategy We will use the rule for adding two real numbers with different signs.

WHY We use that rule because we are asked to add a positive and a negative number.

Solution

a. Since 32 has the larger absolute value, the answer is positive.

$$-17 + 32 = 15 \quad \text{Subtract their absolute values, 17 from 32, to get 15.}$$

b. Since -7.7 has the larger absolute value, the answer is negative.

$$5.4 + (-7.7) = -2.3 \quad \begin{array}{l}\text{Subtract their absolute values, 5.4 from 7.7, to get 2.3.}\\ \text{Attach a } - \text{ sign.}\end{array}$$

c. Since the fractions have the same denominator, we add the numerators and keep the common denominator.

$$\dfrac{3}{25} + \left(-\dfrac{19}{25}\right) = \dfrac{3}{25} + \left(\dfrac{-19}{25}\right) \quad \text{Write } -\tfrac{19}{25} \text{ as } \tfrac{-19}{25}. \left(\text{Recall: } -\tfrac{a}{b} = \tfrac{-a}{b}.\right)$$

$$= -\dfrac{16}{25} \quad \begin{array}{l}\text{Add the numerators: } 3 + (-19) = -16. \text{ Write}\\ \text{the sum over the common denominator 25,}\\ \text{putting the } - \text{ sign in front of the fraction.}\end{array}$$

Success Tip The sum of two numbers with different signs may be positive or negative. The sign of the sum is the sign of the number with the greater absolute value.

Using Your CALCULATOR   The Sign Change Key

A reverse entry scientific calculator can be used to add positive and negative numbers. For example, to do the addition $-31 + 15 + (-4) + 29$, we do not have to do anything special to enter the positive numbers. To enter negative 31 and negative 4, we must press the *opposite* or *sign change key* $\boxed{+/-}$ after entering 31 and after entering 4.

$31 \boxed{+/-} \boxed{+} 15 \boxed{+} 4 \boxed{+/-} \boxed{+} 29 \boxed{=}$ $\boxed{\qquad\qquad 9}$

Using a graphing calculator or direct-entry scientific calculator, we enter a negative number by first pressing the *negation* key $\boxed{(-)}$. To perform the addition, we enter these numbers and press these keys.

$\boxed{(-)} \ 31 \ \boxed{+} \ 15 \ \boxed{+} \ \boxed{(-)} \ 4 \ \boxed{+} \ 29 \ \boxed{\text{ENTER}}$

$$\boxed{\begin{array}{r}-31 + 15 + -4 + 29\\ 9\end{array}}$$

As before, the sum is 9.

EXAMPLE 3   Find the 2008 net income of the Barnes & Noble Corporation from the data given in the graph on page 41.

Strategy We will add the signed numbers that represent the quarterly profits and losses.

WHY The 2008 net income is the sum of the quarterly profits/losses that year.

Solution
To find the annual net income, we add the 2008 quarterly profits and losses, performing the additions as they occur from left to right.

$$115 + (-2) + 15 + (-18) = 113 + 15 + (-18) \quad 115 + (-2) = 113$$
$$= 128 + (-18) \quad 113 + 15 = 128$$
$$= 110$$

In 2008, Barnes & Noble's net income was $110 million.

Self Check 3

Add: $-7 + 13 + (-5) + 10$ 11

Now Try **Problem 35**

Teaching Example 3 Find the net income of the Barnes & Noble Corporation for the 3rd and 4th quarters.
Answer:
$-$3 million

3   Use properties of addition.

The **commutative property of addition** states that two real numbers can be added in either order to get the same result. For example, when adding the numbers 10 and -25, we see that

$$10 + (-25) = -15 \quad \text{and} \quad -25 + 10 = -15$$

To state the *commutative property of addition* concisely, we use variables.

The Commutative Property of Addition

Changing the order when adding does not affect the answer.

For any real numbers a and b,

$$a + b = b + a$$

The Language of Algebra   *Commutative* is a form of the word *commute*, meaning to go back and forth. *Commuter* trains take people to and from work.

To find the sum of three numbers, we first add two of them and then add the third to that result. In the following example, we add $-3 + 7 + 5$ in two ways. To show this, we will use grouping symbols ( ), called **parentheses**. Standard practice requires that we perform the operations within parentheses first.

Method 1: Group -3 and 7

$$(-3 + 7) + 5 = 4 + 5 \quad \text{Because of the parentheses, add } -3 \text{ and 7 first to get 4.}$$
$$= 9 \quad \text{Then add 4 and 5.}$$

Method 2: Group 7 and 5

$$-3 + (7 + 5) = -3 + 12 \quad \text{Because of the parentheses, add 7 and 5 first to get 12.}$$
$$= 9 \quad \text{Then add } -3 \text{ and 12.}$$

Either way, the sum is 9. This illustrates that it doesn't matter how we *group* or *associate* numbers in addition—we get the same result. This property is called the **associative property of addition.**

The Associative Property of Addition

Changing the grouping when adding does not affect the answer.

For any real numbers a, b, and c,

$$(a + b) + c = a + (b + c)$$

The Language of Algebra *Associative* is a form of the word *associate,* meaning to join a group. The NBA (National Basketball *Association*) is a group of professional basketball teams.

Self Check 4

Find the contestant's net gain or loss after the first two questions.

Now Try Problem 43

Self Check 4 Answers
−$100

Teaching Example 4 Find the contestant's net gain or loss after the first three questions.
Answer:
$200

EXAMPLE 4 *Game Shows* A contestant on "Jeopardy!" answered the first question correctly to win $100, missed the second question to lose $200, answered the third question correctly to win $300, and answered the fourth question incorrectly to lose $400. Find her net gain or loss after four questions.

Strategy We will add the amounts won and lost after the four questions she had answered.

WHY The net gain or loss after four questions is the sum of the signed amounts from each question.

Solution
"To win $100" can be represented by 100. "To lose $200" can be represented by −200. "To win $300" can be represented by 300, and "to lose $400" can be represented by −400. Her net gain or loss is the sum of these four numbers. We can find the sum by performing the additions from left to right. An alternate method, which uses the commutative and associative properties of addition, is to add the positives, then add the negatives, and add those results.

$$100 + (-200) + 300 + (-400)$$

$$= 100 + 300 + (-200) + (-400) \qquad \text{Reorder the numbers.}$$

$$= (100 + 300) + [(-200) + (-400)] \qquad \text{Group the positives together. Group the negatives together using brackets [ ].}$$

$$= 400 + (-600) \qquad \text{Add the positives. Add the negatives.}$$

$$= -200$$

After four questions, she had a net loss of $200.

Whenever we add zero to a number, the number remains the same. For example,

$$0 + 8 = 8, \qquad 2.3 + 0 = 2.3, \qquad \text{and} \qquad -16 + 0 = -16$$

These examples illustrate the **addition property of zero.** Since any number added to 0 remains the same, 0 is called the **identity element** for addition.

Addition Property of Zero (Identity Property of Addition)

When 0 is added to any real number, the result is the same real number.

For any real number a,

$$a + 0 = a \quad \text{and} \quad 0 + a = a$$

The Language of Algebra   *Identity* is a form of the word *identical*, meaning the same. You have probably seen *identical* twins.

Recall that two numbers that are the same distance away from the origin, but on opposite sides of it, are called **opposites** or **additive inverses**. For example, 10 is the additive inverse of -10, and -10 is the additive inverse of 10. Whenever we add opposites or additive inverses, the result is 0.

$$10 + (-10) = 0, \quad -\frac{4}{5} + \frac{4}{5} = 0, \quad 56.8 + (-56.8) = 0$$

Addition Property of Opposites (Inverse Property of Addition)

The sum of a real number and its opposite (additive inverse) is 0.

For any real number a,

$$a + (-a) = 0$$

THINK IT THROUGH   *Calculating Sleep Debt*

"College students sleep an average of six to seven hours a night, down from seven to seven and a half in the 1980s."

National Sleep Foundation Alert, April 21, 2004

Because of our demanding schedules, many of us don't get enough sleep. According to the National Sleep Foundation, sleep deprivation is a common problem among college students. As a result, we build up a *sleep debt*. For example, if you require 8 hours of sleep a night, but only get 7, your sleep debt is -1 hour. It is possible to make up sleep if your sleep debt is not too great. It takes about two hours of weekend sleep to make up for every lost hour of sleep during the week.

How many hours of sleep do you need each night to feel refreshed in the morning? To see whether you get the necessary sleep during the week, complete the following log. On Friday, determine whether you have a sleep debt. Then calculate how many extra hours you need to sleep on the weekend to make up for the sleep debt.

	Bedtime	Awaken	Hours slept	Sleep debt
Sunday night				
Monday night				
Tuesday night				
Wednesday night				
Thursday night				
			Total sleep debt:	

ANSWERS TO SELF CHECKS

1. -57 **2. a.** -24 **b.** 1.73   **c.** $\frac{2}{5}$ **3.** 11   **4.** $-\$100$

STUDY SKILLS CHECKLIST

Get the Most from Your Textbook

The following checklist will help you become familiar with some useful features in this book. Place a check mark in each box after you answer the question.

☐ Locate the **Definition** for *Absolute Value* on page 35 and the steps for *Simplifying Fractions* on page 19. What color are these boxes?

☐ Find the **Caution** box, the **Success Tip** box, and the **Language of Algebra** box on page 42. What color is used to identify these boxes?

☐ Each chapter begins with **From Campus to Careers** (see page 1). Chapter 1 gives information on how to become a physician assistant. On what page does a related problem appear in Study Set 1.4?

☐ Locate the **Study Skills Workshop** at the beginning of your text beginning on page S-1. How many Objectives appear in the Study Skills Workshop?

Answers: green, red, 49, 7

SECTION 1.4   STUDY SET

VOCABULARY

Fill in the blanks.

1. Real numbers that are greater than zero are called __positive__ real numbers. Real numbers that are less than zero are called __negative__ real numbers.

▶ 2. The only real number that is neither positive nor negative is __zero__.

3. The __commutative__ property of addition states that two numbers can be added in either order to get the same result.

4. The grouping symbols ( ) are called __parentheses__.

5. The property that allows us to group numbers in addition in any way we want is called the __associative__ property of addition.

▶ 6. Whenever we add __opposites__, or additive __inverses__, the result is 0.

CONCEPTS

Use the following number line to find each sum.

7. $2 + 3$ 5
8. $-3 + (-2)$ -5
9. $4 + (-3)$ 1
10. $-5 + 3$ -2

$$\underset{-5 \quad -4 \quad -3 \quad -2 \quad -1 \quad 0 \quad 1 \quad 2 \quad 3 \quad 4 \quad 5}{\longleftarrow\!\!\mid\!\!\mid\!\!\mid\!\!\mid\!\!\mid\!\!\mid\!\!\mid\!\!\mid\!\!\mid\!\!\mid\!\!\mid\!\!\longrightarrow}$$

Fill in the blanks.

11. To add two real numbers with the same sign, __add__ their absolute values and attach their common sign to the sum.

12. To add two real numbers with different signs, __subtract__ their absolute values, the __smaller__ from the __larger__, and attach the sign of the number with the __larger__ absolute value.

Use the commutative property of addition to complete each statement.

13. $-5 + 1 = $ __$1 + (-5)$__
14. $15 + (-80.5) = $ __$-80.5 + 15$__
15. $-20 + (4 + 20) = -20 + $ __$(20 + 4)$__
16. $(5 + 7) + 9 = $ __$(7 + 5)$__ $+ 9$

Use the associative property of addition to complete each statement.

17. $(-6 + 2) + 8 = $ __$-6 + (2 + 8)$__
18. $-7 + (7 + 3) = $ __$(-7 + 7) + 3$__
19. $-96 + (4 + 200) = $ __$(-96 + 4) + 200$__
20. $(-9 + 4) + 15 = $ __$-9 + (4 + 15)$__
21. What is the opposite of 7? -7
22. What is the opposite of -15? 15
23. What is the opposite of $-\dfrac{1}{2}$? $\dfrac{1}{2}$
24. What is the opposite of $\dfrac{2}{3}$? $-\dfrac{2}{3}$

NOTATION

Complete each solution.

25. $(-13 + 6) + 4 = $ __-13__ $+ (6 + 4)$
$$= -13 + \boxed{10}$$
$$= -3$$

▶ 26. $-9 + (9 + 43) = ($ __-9__ $+ 9) + 43$
$$= \boxed{0} + 43$$
$$= 43$$

▶ Selected exercises available online at
www.webassign.net/brookscole

GUIDED PRACTICE

Find each sum. See Example 1.

▶ **27.** $-65 + (-12)$ -77 **28.** $-21 + (-12)$ -33

29. $-4.1 + (-5.7)$ -9.8 ▶ **30.** $-2.5 + (-1.7)$ -4.2

Find each sum. See Example 2.

31. $6 + (-8)$ -2 **32.** $4 + (-3)$ 1

33. $15 + (-11)$ 4 ▶ **34.** $27 + (-30)$ -3

Find each sum. See Example 3.

35. $8 + (-5) + 13$ 16 ▶ **36.** $17 + (-12) + (-23)$ -18

37. $21 + (-27) + (-9)$ -15 ▶ **38.** $-32 + 12 + 17$ -3

39. $-27 + (-3) + (-13) + 22$ -21

40. $53 + (-27) + (-32) + (-7)$ -13

▶ **41.** $57 + (-47) + (-64) + 113$ 59

42. $32 + (-44) + (-37) + (-52)$ -101

Use the associative property of addition to find each sum. See Example 4.

43. $-99 + (99 + 215)$ ▶ **44.** $67 + (-67 + 127)$
     215 127

45. $(-4 + 15) + (-15)$ ▶ **46.** $(-18 + 37) + (-37)$
     -4 -18

TRY IT YOURSELF

Find each sum.

47. $5 + (-5)$ 0 **48.** $-2.2 + 2.2$ 0

49. $0 + (-6)$ -6 **50.** $-\dfrac{15}{16} + 0$ $-\dfrac{15}{16}$

51. $-\dfrac{3}{4} + \dfrac{3}{4}$ 0 **52.** $19 + (-19)$ 0

53. $-6 + 8$ 2 **54.** $75 + (-13)$ 62

55. $300 + (-335)$ -35 **56.** $240 + (-340)$ -100

57. $-10.5 + 2.3$ -8.2 **58.** $-2.1 + 0.4$ -1.7

59. $-9.1 + (-11)$ -20.1 ▶ **60.** $-6.7 + (-7.1)$ -13.8

61. $-\dfrac{9}{16} + \dfrac{7}{16}$ $-\dfrac{1}{8}$ **62.** $-\dfrac{3}{4} + \dfrac{1}{4}$ $-\dfrac{1}{2}$

63. $-20 + (-16 + 10)$ -26 **64.** $-13 + (-16 + 4)$ -25

65. $-\dfrac{1}{4} + \dfrac{2}{3}$ $\dfrac{5}{12}$ **66.** $\dfrac{3}{16} + \left(-\dfrac{1}{2}\right)$ $-\dfrac{5}{16}$

67. $4.125 + (-7.341)$ -3.216 **68.** $3,718 + (-5,237)$ $-1,519$

69. $735 + (-462)$ 273 **70.** $837 + (-429)$ 408

71. $-5,235 + (-17,235)$ $-22,470$

72. $32.137 + (-34.36) + (-32.137)$ -34.36

73. $736 + 67 + (-736)$ 67

74. $-237.37 + (-315.07) + (-27.4)$ -579.84

▶ **75.** $-587.77 + (-1,732.13) + 687.39$ $-1,632.51$

76. $-37.57 + 85.02 + (-77.1)$ -29.65

APPLICATIONS

77. MILITARY SCIENCE During a battle, an army retreated 1,500 meters, regrouped, and advanced 2,400 meters. The next day, it advanced another 1,250 meters. Find the army's net gain.   2,150 m

▶ **78.** MEDICAL QUESTIONNAIRES Find the point total for the six risk factors (in blue) on the medical questionnaire. Then use the table to determine the patient's risk of contracting heart disease in the next 10 years.   4%

from Campus to Careers
Physician Assistant

© 2009 Jupiterimages

Age		Total Cholesterol	
Age 35	Points −4	Reading 280	Points 3

Cholesterol		Blood Pressure	
HDL 62	Points −3	Systolic/Diastolic 124/100	Points 3

Diabetic		Smoker	
	Points		Points
Yes	4	Yes	2

10-Year Heart Disease Risk			
Total Points	Risk	Total Points	Risk
−2 or less	1%	5	4%
−1 to 1	2%	6	6%
2 to 3	3%	7	6%
4	4%	8	7%

Source: National Heart, Lung, and Blood Institute

79. GOLF The illustration on the next page shows the top four finishers from the 1997 Masters Golf Tournament. The scores for each round are related to *par*, the number of strokes an experienced golfer would take to complete the course. A score of −2, for example, indicates that the golfer used two strokes less than par to complete the course. A score of +5 indicates the golfer used five strokes more than par.

   a. Determine the tournament total for each golfer.

b. Tiger Woods won by the largest margin in the history of the Masters. Find the margin. 12 strokes

Leaderboard

	Round				
	1	2	3	4	Total
Tiger Woods	−2	−6	−7	−3	−18
Tom Kite	+5	−3	−6	−2	−6
Tommy Tolles	0	0	0	−5	−5
Tom Watson	+3	−4	−3	0	−4

▶ **80.** CREDIT CARDS Refer to the monthly statement. What is the new balance? $1,242.86

Previous Balance	New Purchases, Fees, Advances & Debts	Payments & Credits	New Balance
3,660.66	1,408.78	3,826.58	

04/21/09 Billing Date	05/16/09 Date Payment Due	9,100 Credit Line

81. THE OLYMPICS The ancient Greek Olympian Games, which eventually evolved into the modern Olympic Games, were first held in 776 B.C. How many years after this did the 1996 Olympic Games in Atlanta, Georgia, take place? 2,772

▶ **82.** SUBMARINES A submarine was cruising at a depth of 1,250 feet. The captain gave the order to climb 550 feet. Relative to sea level, find the new depth of the sub. −700 ft

▶ **83.** STOCK EXCHANGE Many newspapers publish daily summaries of the stock market's activity. The last entry on the line for June 12 indicates that one share of Walt Disney Co. stock lost $0.81 in value that day. How much did the value of a share of Disney stock rise or fall over the 5-day period shown? It fell $0.38.

June 12	43.88	23.38	Disney	.21	0.5	87	−43	40.75	−.81
June 13	43.88	23.38	Disney	.21	0.5	86	−15	40.19	−.56
June 14	43.88	23.38	Disney	.21	0.5	87	−50	41.00	+.81
June 15	43.88	23.38	Disney	.21	0.5	89	−28	41.81	+.81
June 16	43.88	23.38	Disney				−15	41.19	−.63

Based on data from the *Los Angeles Times*

▶ **84.** POLITICS What will be the effect on state government if the following ballot initiative passes? a gain of $2.2 million

212 Campaign Spending Limits	YES ☐ NO ☐
Limits contributions to $200 in state campaigns. Fiscal impact: Costs of $4.5 million for implementation and enforcement. Increases state revenue by $6.7 million by eliminating tax deductions for lobbying.	

85. MOVIE LOSSES According to the *Numbers Box Office Data* website, the movie *Stealth*, released in 2005 by Sony Pictures, cost about $176,350,000 to produce, promote, and distribute. It reportedly earned just $76,700,000 worldwide. Use a signed number to express the loss suffered by Sony Pictures. −$99,650,000

86. SAHARA DESERT From 1980 to 1990, a satellite was used to trace the expansion and contraction of the southern boundary of the Sahara Desert in Africa. If movement southward is represented with a negative number and movement northward with a positive number, use the data in the table to determine the net movement of the Sahara Desert boundary over the 10-year period. southward, 132 km

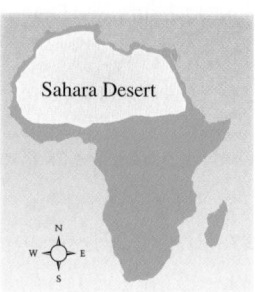

Data from A. Dolgoff, Physical Geology (D.C. Heath, 1996, p.496)

Years	Distance/direction
1980–1984	240 km/south
1984–1985	110 km/north
1985–1986	30 km/north
1986–1987	55 km/south
1987–1988	100 km/north
1988–1990	77 km/south

Source: Based on data from A. Dolgoffs *Physical Geology* (Heath, 1996), p. 496

▶ **87.** BANKING On February 1, Marta had $1,704.29 in a checking account. During the month, she made deposits of $713.87 and $1,245.57, wrote checks for $813.45, $937.49, and $1,532.79, and had a total of $500 in ATM withdrawals. Find her checking account balance at the end of the month. −$120 (overdrawn $120)

88. CARD GAMES In the second hand of a card game, Gonzalo was the winner and earned 50 points. Matt and Hydecki had to deduct the value of each of the cards left in their hands from their running point totals. Use the following information to update the score sheet on the next page. (Face cards are counted as 10 points and aces as 1 point.)

Matt   Hydecki

Running point total	Hand 1	Hand 2
Matt	+50	+29
Gonzalo	−15	+35
Hydecki	−2	−23

▶ **89. PROFITS AND LOSSES** The 2007 quarterly profits and losses of Ford Motor Company are shown in the table. Losses are denoted with parentheses. Calculate the company's total net income for 2007. −$2,723 million

Quarter	1st	2nd	3rd	4th
Net income ($ million)	(−282)	750	(−380)	(−2,811)

Source: www.ford.com

▶ **90. POLITICS** Six months before an election, the incumbent trailed the challenger by 18 points. To overtake her opponent, the incumbent decided to use a four-part strategy. Each part of the plan is shown in the next column, with the expected point gain. With these gains, will the incumbent overtake the challenger on election day? no

- TV ads   +10
- Voter mailing   +3
- Union endorsement +2
- Telephone calls   +1

WRITING

91. Explain why the sum of two positive numbers is always positive and why the sum of two negative numbers is always negative.

92. Explain why we need to subtract the absolute value when we add two real numbers with different signs.

REVIEW

93. True or false: Every real number can be expressed as a decimal. true

▶ **94.** True or false: Irrational numbers are nonterminating, nonrepeating decimals. true

95. What two numbers are a distance of 6 away from −3 on the number line? −9 and 3

▶ **96.** Graph: $\left\{-2.5, \ \sqrt{5}, \ \frac{11}{3}, \ -0.333\ldots, \ 0.75\right\}$

SECTION 1.5
Subtracting Real Numbers

Objectives
1 Use the definition of subtraction.

2 Solve application problems using subtraction.

1 Use the definition of subtraction.

The minus symbol − is used to indicate subtraction. However, this symbol is also used in many other ways, depending on where it appears in an expression.

$4 - 9$ This is read "4 minus 9."

-3 This is usually read "negative three." It can also be read as "the additive inverse of three" or "the opposite of three."

$-(-2)$ This is usually read as "the opposite of negative two" or "the additive inverse of negative 2."

In the expression $-(-2)$, parentheses help us write the opposite of a negative number. To simplify this expression we find the opposite of the number in the parentheses.

$-(-2) = 2$ Read this equation as "the opposite of negative two is two."

The above equation suggests the following rule.

Opposite of an Opposite

The opposite of the opposite of a number is that number. In symbols:

$-(-a) = a$ Read as "the opposite of the opposite of a is a."

EXAMPLE 1 Simplify each expression:
a. $-(-45)$ **b.** $-(-h)$ **c.** $-|-10|$

Strategy To simplify each expression, we will use the concept of opposite.

WHY In each case, the outermost $-$ symbol is read as "the opposite."

Solution

a. The number within the parentheses is -45. Its opposite is 45. Therefore, $-(-45) = 45$.

b. The opposite of the opposite of h is h. Therefore, $-(-h) = h$.

c. The notation $-|-10|$ means "the opposite of the absolute value of negative ten." Since $|-10| = 10$, we have:

$$-|-10| = -10$$ The absolute value bars do not affect the $-$ symbol outside them. Therefore, the result is negative.

The subtraction $5 - 2$ can be thought of as taking 2 away from 5. We can use the number line below to illustrate this. Beginning at the origin, we draw an arrow of length 5 units pointing to the right. From that point, we move back 2 units to the left. The result, 3, is called the **difference.**

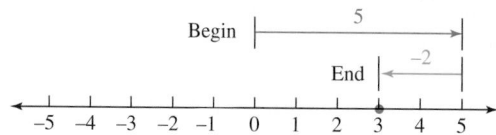

The figure above looks like the illustration for the addition problem $5 + (-2)$. In the problem $5 - 2$, we subtracted 2 from 5. In the problem $5 + (-2)$, we added -2 (which is the opposite of 2) to 5. In each case, the result is 3.

Subtracting 2 from 5   is the same as   adding the opposite of 2 to 5.

$$5 - 2 = 3 \qquad\qquad 5 + (-2) = 3$$

The results are the same.

This observation suggests the following rule.

Subtracting Real Numbers

To subtract two real numbers, add the first number to the opposite (additive inverse) of the number to be subtracted.

For any real numbers a and b,

$$a - b = a + (-b)$$

This rule indicates that *subtraction is the same as adding the opposite of the number to be subtracted.* We won't need this rule for every subtraction. For example, $5 - 2$ is obviously 3. However, for more complicated subtractions such as $-8 - (-3)$, the subtraction rule will be helpful.

$$-8 - (-3) = -8 + 3$$ To subtract -3, add the opposite of -3, which is 3.
$$= -5$$ Perform the addition.

> **The Language of Algebra**   When we change a number to its opposite, we say we have *changed* (or *reversed*) its sign.

EXAMPLE 2

Subtract: **a.** $-13 - 18$ **b.** $-45 - (-27)$ **c.** $\dfrac{1}{4} - \left(-\dfrac{1}{8}\right)$

Strategy   To find each difference, we will use the rule for subtraction: add the first number to the opposite of the second number.

WHY   Changing the problem to the addition of the opposite of the second number lessens the chance of making an error.

Solution

a. In $-13 - 18$, the number to be subtracted is 18.

$$-13 - 18 = -13 + (-18)$$ To subtract 18, add the opposite of 18, which is -18.

$$= -31$$ Add their absolute values, 13 and 18, to get 31. Keep their common sign.

b. In $-45 - (-27)$, the number to be subtracted is -27.

$$-45 - (-27) = -45 + 27$$ To subtract -27, add the opposite of -27, which is 27.

$$= -18$$ Subtract their absolute values, 27 from 45, to get 18. Use the sign of the number with the greater absolute value, which is -45.

c. The lowest common denominator (LCD) for the fractions is 8.

$$\dfrac{1}{4} - \left(-\dfrac{1}{8}\right) = \dfrac{2}{8} - \left(-\dfrac{1}{8}\right)$$ Express $\dfrac{1}{4}$ in terms of eighths: $\dfrac{1}{4} = \dfrac{2}{8}$.

$$= \dfrac{2}{8} + \dfrac{1}{8}$$ The number to be subtracted is $-\dfrac{1}{8}$. Add the opposite of $-\dfrac{1}{8}$, which is $\dfrac{1}{8}$.

$$= \dfrac{3}{8}$$ Add the numerators: $2 + 1 = 3$. Write the sum over the common denominator, 8.

> **The Language of Algebra**   The rule for subtracting real numbers is often stated as:
>
> *Subtracting a number is the same as adding its opposite.*

EXAMPLE 3

a. Subtract 0.5 from 4.6   **b.** Subtract 4.6 from 0.5

Strategy   We will translate each phrase to mathematical symbols and then perform the subtraction. We must be careful when translating the instruction to subtract one number *from* another number.

WHY   The order of the numbers in each word phrase must be reversed when we translate it to mathematical symbols.

Self Check 2

Subtract:

a. $-32 - 25$ -57

b. $1.7 - (-1.2)$ 2.9

c. $-\dfrac{1}{2} - \dfrac{1}{8}$ $-\dfrac{5}{8}$

***Now Try* Problem 20**

Teaching Example 2 Subtract:
a. $-9 - 11$
b. $2.6 - (-5.3)$
c. $-\dfrac{1}{3} - \left(\dfrac{1}{6}\right)$
Answers:
a. -20 **b.** 7.9 **c.** $-\dfrac{1}{2}$

Self Check 3

a. Subtract 2.2 from 4.9 2.7

b. Subtract 4.9 from 2.2 -2.7

***Now Try* Problem 27**

Teaching Example 3
a. Subtract 2.1 from 4.1
b. Subtract 4.1 from 2.1
Answers:
a. 2   **b.** -2

Solution

a. The number to be subtracted is 0.5.

Subtract 0.5 from 4.6

$4.6 - 0.5 = 4.1$ To translate, reverse the order in which 0.5 and 4.6 appear in the sentence.

b. The number to be subtracted is 4.6.

Subtract 4.6 from 0.5

$0.5 - 4.6 = 0.5 + (-4.6)$ To translate, reverse the order in which 4.6 and 0.5 appear in the sentence. Add the opposite of 4.6.

$= -4.1$

Caution! Notice from parts a and b that $4.6 - 0.5 \neq 0.5 - 4.6$. This result illustrates an important fact: Subtraction is *not* commutative. When subtracting two numbers, it is important that we write them in the correct order, because, in general, $a - b \neq b - a$.

EXAMPLE 4   Perform the operations: $-9 - 15 + 20 - (-6)$

Strategy This expression contains addition and subtraction. We will write each subtraction as addition of the opposite and then evaluate the expression.

WHY It is easy to make an error when subtracting signed numbers. We will probably be more accurate if we write each subtraction as addition of the opposite.

Solution
$$-9 - 15 + 20 - (-6) = -9 + (-15) + 20 + 6$$
$$= -24 + 26 \qquad \text{Add the negatives. Add the positives. Add the results.}$$
$$= 2$$

2 **Solve application problems using subtraction.**

Subtraction finds the *difference* between two numbers. When we find the difference between the maximum value and the minimum value of a collection of measurements, we are finding the **range** of the values.

EXAMPLE 5   *U.S. Temperatures*   The record high temperature in the United States was 134°F in Death Valley, California, on July 10, 1913. The record low was $-80°F$ at Prospect Creek, Alaska, on January 23, 1971. Find the temperature range for these extremes.

Strategy We will subtract the lowest temperature from the highest temperature.

WHY The *range* of a collection of data indicates the spread of the data. It is the difference between the largest and smallest values.

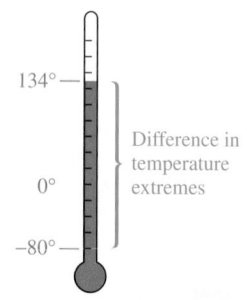

Solution
$$134 - (-80) = 134 + 80 \qquad \text{134° is the higher temperature and } -80° \text{ is the lower.}$$
$$= 214$$

The temperature range for these extremes is 214°F.

Using Your CALCULATOR   U.S. Temperature Extremes

To find the difference between the temperatures in Example 5, we can use a calculator.

We can subtract positive and negative real numbers using a reverse-entry scientific calculator. To find $134 - (-80)$, we enter these numbers and press these keys.

134 $\boxed{-}$ 80 $\boxed{+/-}$ $\boxed{=}$ $\boxed{\qquad\qquad 214}$

If we use a graphing calculator or a direct-entry scientific calculator, we enter these numbers and press these keys.

134 $\boxed{-}$ $\boxed{(-)}$ 80 $\boxed{\text{ENTER}}$ $\boxed{\begin{array}{r} 134 - {}^-80 \\ 214 \end{array}}$

The difference in the record high and low temperatures is 214°F, as we found in Example 5.

EXAMPLE 6   *Water Levels*   In one

week, the water level in a storage tank went from 16 feet above normal to 14 feet below normal. Find the change in the water level.

Strategy We can represent a water level above normal using a positive number and a water level below normal using a negative number. To find the change in the water level, we will subtract.

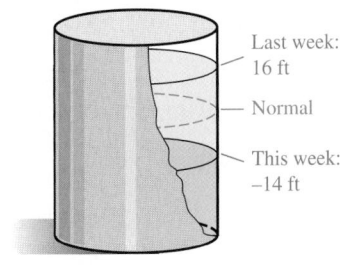

Last week: 16 ft
— Normal
This week: −14 ft

WHY In general, *to find the change in a quantity, we subtract the earlier value from the later value.*

Solution

$$-14 - 16 = -14 + (-16) \qquad \text{The earlier water level, 16, is subtracted from the later water level, −14.}$$

$$= -30$$

The negative result indicates that the water level fell 30 feet that week.

> **Caution!** When applying the subtraction rule, *do not* change the first number:
>
> $$\downarrow \qquad\quad \downarrow$$
> $$-14 - 16 = -14 + (-16)$$

ANSWERS TO SELF CHECKS

1. a. 1 **b.** y **c.** -500 **2. a.** -57 **b.** 2.9 **c.** $-\frac{5}{8}$ **3. a.** 2.7 **b.** -2.7 **4.** -8
5. 41°F **6.** -11 ft

SECTION 1.5   STUDY SET

VOCABULARY

Fill in the blanks.

1. __Subtraction__ finds the difference between two numbers.
2. In a subtraction, the result is called the __difference__.
3. To subtract *b* from *a*, add the __opposite__ of *b* to *a*.
4. The difference between the maximum and the minimum values of a collection of measurements is called the __range__ of the values.

CONCEPTS

Fill in the blanks.

5. $-(-a) =$ __a__
6. To subtract two real numbers, change the __subtraction__ to addition and take the opposite of the second number: $a - b = a + (-b)$.

NOTATION

Fill in the blanks.

7. The expression -7 is read as __negative__ 7.
8. The expression $-(-5)$ is read as the __opposite__ of -5.

GUIDED PRACTICE

Simplify each expression. **See Example 1.**

9. $-(-15)$ _15_
10. $-(-p)$ _p_
11. $-|7|$ _−7_
12. $-|-25|$ _−25_

Find each difference. **See Example 2.**

13. $8 - (-3)$ _11_
14. $17 - (-21)$ _38_
15. $-12 - 9$ _−21_
16. $-25 - 17$ _−42_
17. $-19 - (-17)$ _−2_
18. $-30 - (-11)$ _−19_
19. $-1.5 - 0.8$ _−2.3_
20. $-1.5 - (-0.8)$ _−0.7_
21. $-\dfrac{1}{8} - \dfrac{3}{8}$ _$-\frac{1}{2}$_
22. $-\dfrac{3}{4} - \dfrac{1}{4}$ _−1_
23. $-\dfrac{9}{16} - \left(-\dfrac{1}{4}\right)$ _$-\frac{5}{16}$_
24. $-\dfrac{1}{2} - \left(-\dfrac{1}{4}\right)$ _$-\frac{1}{4}$_

Find each difference. **See Example 3.**

25. Subtract -5 from 17. _22_
26. Subtract 45 from -50. _−95_
27. Subtract 1.2 from -1.3. _−2.5_
28. Subtract -1.1 from -2. _−0.9_

Perform the operations. **See Example 4.**

29. $8 - 9 - 10$ _−11_
30. $1 - 2 - 3$ _−4_
31. $-25 - (-50) - 75$ _−50_
32. $-33 - (-22) - 44$ _−55_

33. $-6 + 8 - (-1) - 10$ _−7_
34. $-4 + 5 - (-3) - 13$ _−9_
35. $61 - (-62) + (-64) - 60$ _−1_
36. $93 - (-92) + (-94) - 95$ _−4_

TRY IT YOURSELF

Perform the operations.

37. $2.8 - (-1.8)$ _4.6_
38. $4.7 - (-1.9)$ _6.6_
39. $-44 - 44$ _−88_
40. $-33 - 33$ _−66_
41. $0 - (-12)$ _12_
42. $0 - 12$ _−12_
43. $-25 - (-25)$ _0_
44. $13 - (-13)$ _26_
45. $0 - 4$ _−4_
46. $0 - (-3)$ _3_
47. $8,713 - (-3,753)$ _12,466_
48. $-2,727 - 1,208$ _−3,935_
49. $-27,357.875 - 17,213.376$ _−44,571.251_
50. $-45,307.039 - (-27,592.47)$ _−17,714.569_
51. $-62 - 71 - (-37) + 99$ _3_
52. $-17 - 32 - (-85) - 51$ _−15_
53. Subtract 47.5 from 0. _−47.5_
54. Subtract 30.3 from 0. _−30.3_
55. Subtract 5 from -7. _−12_
56. Subtract -7 from 5. _12_
57. Subtract -137 from 12. _149_
58. Subtract 512 from -47. _−559_
59. Subtract $-\dfrac{1}{3}$ from $\dfrac{5}{3}$. _2_
60. Subtract $\dfrac{2}{5}$ from $\dfrac{4}{5}$. _$\frac{2}{5}$_
61. $-\dfrac{5}{6} - \dfrac{3}{4}$ _$-\frac{19}{12}$_
62. $-\dfrac{3}{7} - \dfrac{2}{5}$ _$-\frac{29}{35}$_
63. $-\dfrac{3}{5} - \dfrac{2}{15}$ _$-\frac{11}{15}$_
64. $-\dfrac{4}{11} - \dfrac{1}{2}$ _$-\frac{19}{22}$_

APPLICATIONS

65. TEMPERATURE RECORDS Find the difference between the record high temperature of 108°F set in 1926 and the record low of -52°F set in 1979 for New York State. _160°F_
66. LIE DETECTORS A burglar scored -18 on a lie detector test, a score that indicates deception. However, on a second test, he scored $+3$, a score that is inconclusive. Find the difference in the scores. _21_
67. LAND ELEVATIONS The elevation of Death Valley, California, is 282 feet below sea level. The elevation of the Dead Sea in Israel is 1,312 feet below sea level. Find the difference in their elevations. _1,030 ft_

68. THE SUNSHINE STATE Florida's record high temperature of 109°F was set in 1931, and the record low of −2°F was set in 1899. What is the range of these temperature extremes? 111°F

▶ **69.** EYESIGHT Nearsightedness, the condition where near objects are clear and far objects are blurry, is measured using negative numbers. Farsightedness, the condition where far objects are clear and near objects are blurry, is measured using positive numbers. Find the range in the measurements shown. 6.85

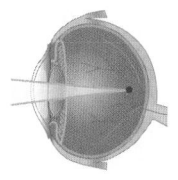

Nearsighted	Farsighted
−2.5	+4.35

▶ **70.** LAW ENFORCEMENT A burglar scored −15 on a lie detector test, a score that indicates deception. However, on a second test, he scored +2, a score that is inconclusive. Find the change in the scores. 17

71. RACING To improve handling, drivers often adjust the angle of the wheels of their car. When the wheel leans out, the degree measure is considered positive. When the wheel leans in, the degree measure is considered negative. Find the change in the position of the wheel shown. −5.75°

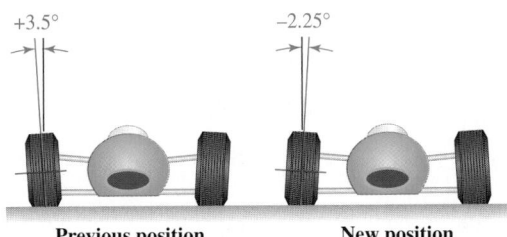

Previous position	New position
Lean outward	Lean inward

72. U.S. JOBS The table lists the three occupations that are predicted to have the largest job declines from 2004–2014. Complete the column labeled "Change."

Number of jobs			
Occupation	**2004**	**2014**	**Change**
Farmers/ranchers	1,065,000	910,000	−155,000
Stock clerks	1,566,000	1,451,000	−115,000
Sewing machine operators	256,000	163,000	−93,000

Source: Bureau of Labor Statistics

73. GEOGRAPHY The elevation of Denver, Colorado, is 5,183 feet above sea level. The elevation of New Orleans, Louisiana, is 6 feet below sea level. Find the difference in their elevations. 5,189 ft

▶ **74.** CARD GAMES Gonzalo won the second round of a card game and earned 50 points. Matt and Hydecki had to deduct the value of each of the cards left in their hands from their score on the first round. Use this information to update the score sheet below. Then find the range in Gonzalo and Hydecki's score. (Face cards are counted as 10 points, aces as 1 point, and all others have the value of the number printed on the card.) 66 points

Matt   Hydecki

Running point total	Round 1	Round 2
Matt	+54	+33
Gonzalo	−12	+38
Hydecki	−7	−28

75. FOREIGN POLICY In 2004, Congress forgave $4.1 billion of Iraqi debt owed to the United States. Before that, Iraq's total debt was estimated to be $120.2 billion.

  a. Which expression below can be used to find Iraq's total debt after getting debt relief from the United States? iii

 i. $120.2 + 4.1$ **ii.** $120.2 − (−4.1)$

 iii. $−120.2 − (−4.1)$ **iv.** $−120.2 − 4.1$

  b. Find Iraq's total debt after getting the debt relief. −$116.1 billion

▶ **76.** HISTORY Plato, a famous Greek philosopher, died in 347 B.C. at the age of 81. When was he born? 428 B.C.

77. NASCAR Complete the table below to determine how many points the third, fourth, and fifth place finishers were behind the leader.

2006 final driver standings			
Rank	**Driver**	**Points**	**Points behind leader**
1	Jimmie Johnson	6,475	. . .
2	Matt Kenseth	6,419	−56
3	Denny Hamlin	6,407	−68
4	Kevin Harvick	6,397	−78
5	Dale Earnhardt, Jr	6,328	−147

78. GAUGES With the engine off, the ammeter on a car reads 0. If the headlights, which draw a current of 7 amps, and the radio, which draws a current of 6 amps, are both turned on, what will be the new reading? −13

WRITING

79. Is subtracting 2 from 10 the same as subtracting 10 from 2? Explain.

80. Explain why we can subtract by adding the opposite.

81. Explain what it means when we say that *subtraction is not commutative.*

82. Is having a debt of $100 forgiven the same as having a gain of $100? Explain.

REVIEW

83. Find the prime factorization of 30. $2 \cdot 3 \cdot 5$

84. True or false: $-4 > -5$ true

85. Use the associative property of addition to simplify $-18 + (18 + 89)$. 89

86. Multiply: $(4.5)(2.3)$ 10.35

Objectives

1 Multiply signed numbers.

2 Use properties of multiplication.

3 Divide signed numbers.

4 Use properties of division.

SECTION **1.6**

Multiplying and Dividing Real Numbers; Multiplication and Division Properties

In this course, you will often need to multiply or divide positive and negative numbers. For example,

- If the temperature drops 3° per hour for 4 hours, we can find the total drop in temperature by performing the multiplication $4(-3)$.

- If the temperature uniformly drops 15° over a 5-hour period, we can find the number of degrees it drops each hour by performing the division $\frac{-15}{5}$.

In this section, we will show how to perform such multiplications and divisions.

1 Multiply signed numbers.

Multiplication represents repeated addition. For example, $4(3)$ equals the sum of four 3's.

$$4(3) = 3 + 3 + 3 + 3$$
$$= 12$$

This example illustrates that *the product of two positive numbers is positive.*

To develop a rule for multiplying a positive number and a negative number, we will find $4(-3)$, which is equal to the sum of four -3's.

$$4(-3) = -3 + (-3) + (-3) + (-3)$$
$$= -6 + (-3) + (-3) \qquad \text{Work from left to right.}$$
$$= -9 + (-3)$$
$$= -12 \qquad \text{The result is negative.}$$

In terms of money, if you lose $3 four times, you have lost a total of $12, which is denoted as −$12.

This example illustrates that *the product of a positive number and a negative number is negative.*

Multiplying Two Numbers That Have Different (Unlike) Signs

To multiply a positive number and a negative number, multiply their absolute values. Then make the final answer negative.

EXAMPLE 1   Multiply: **a.** $-5(7)$ **b.** $8(-12)$ **c.** $-15 \cdot 25$

Strategy To find each product, we will use the rule for multiplying two real numbers with different signs.

WHY In each part, we are asked to multiply a positive number and a negative number.

Solution

a. $-5(7) = -35$ Multiply the absolute values, 5 and 7, to get 35. Since one factor is negative and the other is positive, the answer is negative.

b. $8(-12) = -96$ Multiply the absolute values, 8 and 12, to get 96. Make the answer negative.

c. $-15 \cdot 25 = -375$ Multiply the absolute values, 15 and 25, to get 375. Make the answer negative.

Success Tip The product of two numbers with unlike signs is *always* negative.

Self Check 1

Multiply:
a. $20(-30)$ -600
b. $-0.4 \cdot 2$ -0.8

Now Try **Problem 25**

Teaching Example 1 Multiply:
a. $(-5)(2)$ **b.** $4(-3)$
c. $-2 \cdot 5$
Answers:
a. -10 **b.** -12 **c.** -10

To develop a rule for multiplying two negative numbers, we will find $-4(-3)$. Examine the following pattern, in which we multiply -4 and a series of factors that decrease by 1. After finding the first four products, we graph them on a number line, as shown.

This factor decreases by 1 as you read down the column.   Look for a pattern here.

$$-4(3) = -12$$
$$-4(2) = -8$$
$$-4(1) = -4$$
$$-4(0) = 0$$
$$-4(-1) = ?$$
$$-4(-2) = ?$$
$$-4(-3) = ?$$

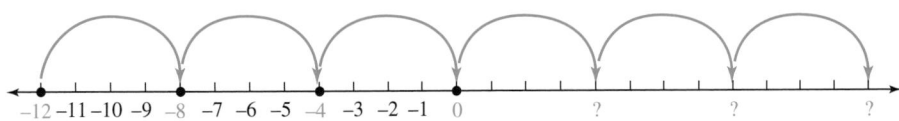

From the pattern, we see that the product increases by 4 each time. Thus,

$$-4(-1) = 4, \qquad -4(-2) = 8, \qquad \text{and} \qquad -4(-3) = 12$$

In terms of money, losing four debts of \$3 is the same as gaining \$12: $-4(-\$3) = \$12$.

These results illustrate that *the product of two negative numbers is positive.*

> ### Multiplying Two Numbers That Have the Same (Like) Signs
>
> To multiply two numbers that have the same sign, multiply their absolute values. The final answer is positive.

Self Check 2

Multiply:

a. $-15(-8)$ 120

b. $-\dfrac{1}{4}\left(-\dfrac{1}{3}\right)$ $\frac{1}{12}$

Now Try Problem 35

Teaching Example 2 Multiply:
a. $-2.3(-1.1)$
b. $-3(-7)$
c. $\left(-\frac{2}{3}\right)\left(-\frac{15}{4}\right)$
Answers:
a. 2.53
b. 21
c. $\frac{5}{2}$

EXAMPLE 2 Multiply: **a.** $-5(-6)$ **b.** $\left(-\frac{1}{2}\right)\left(-\frac{5}{8}\right)$

Strategy To find each product, we will use the rule for multiplying two real numbers with the same sign.

WHY In each part, we are asked to multiply two negative numbers.

Solution

a. $-5(-6) = 30$ Multiply the absolute values, 5 and 6, to get 30. Since both factors are negative, the product is positive.

b. $\left(-\dfrac{1}{2}\right)\left(-\dfrac{5}{8}\right) = \dfrac{5}{16}$ Multiply the absolute values, $\frac{1}{2}$ and $\frac{5}{8}$, to get $\frac{5}{16}$. The product is positive.

> **Success Tip** The product of two numbers with like signs is *always* positive.

Using Your CALCULATOR   Bank Promotions

To attract business, a bank gave a clock radio to each customer who opened a checking account. The radios cost the bank $12.75 each, and 230 new accounts were opened. Each of the 230 radios was given away at a cost of $12.75, which can be expressed as -12.75. To find how much money the promotion cost the bank, we need to find the product of 230 and -12.75.

We can multiply positive and negative numbers with a reverse-entry scientific calculator. To find the product $(230)(-12.75)$, we enter these numbers and press these keys.

230 $\boxed{\times}$ 12.75 $\boxed{+/-}$ $\boxed{=}$ $\boxed{-2932.5}$

Using a graphing calculator or a direct-entry scientific calculator, we enter the following sequence:

230 $\boxed{\times}$ $\boxed{(-)}$ 12.75 $\boxed{\text{ENTER}}$ $\boxed{\begin{array}{r} 230*-12.75 \\ -2932.5 \end{array}}$

The promotion cost the bank $2,932.50.

2 Use properties of multiplication.

A special property of multiplication is that two real numbers can be multiplied in either order to get the same result. For example, when multiplying -6 and 5, we see that

$$-6(5) = -30 \quad \text{and} \quad 5(-6) = -30$$

This property is called the **commutative property of multiplication.**

The Commutative Property of Multiplication

Changing the order when multiplying does not affect the answer.

For any real numbers a and b,

$$ab = ba$$

To find the product of three numbers, we first multiply two of them, and then we multiply the third by that result. In the following example, we multiply $-3 \cdot 7 \cdot 5$ in two ways. We will use parentheses ( ) to show this. Recall that we perform the operations within parentheses first.

Method 1: Group -3 and 7

$$(-3 \cdot 7)5 = (-21)5 \quad \text{Because of the parentheses, multiply } -3 \text{ and 7 first.}$$
$$= -105 \quad \text{Then multiply } -21 \text{ and 5.}$$

Method 2: Group 7 and 5

$$-3(7 \cdot 5) = -3(35) \quad \text{Because of the parentheses, multiply 7 and 5 first.}$$
$$= -105 \quad \text{Then multiply } -3 \text{ and 35.}$$

Either way, the product is -105, which suggests that it doesn't matter how we *group* or *associate* numbers in multiplication. This property is called the **associative property of multiplication.**

The Associative Property of Multiplication

Changing the grouping when multiplying does not affect the answer.

For any real numbers a, b, and c,

$$(ab)c = a(bc)$$

Success Tip   The commutative and associative properties of multiplication are very similar to those of addition. The only change is the operation is now multiplication.

EXAMPLE 3   Multiply: **a.** $-5(-37)(2)$ **b.** $2(-3)(-2)(-3)$

Strategy We will use the commutative and associative properties of multiplication to rewrite the product. Then we will apply the rules for multiplying signed numbers.

WHY Reordering and regrouping the factors make the computations easier so we are less likely to make an error.

Solution

Using the commutative and associative properties of multiplication, we can reorder and regroup the factors to simplify the computations.

a. $-5(-37)(2) = -10(-37)$ Think of the problem as $-5(2)(-37)$, and then multiply -5 and 2 in your head.

$$= 370 \quad \text{The product of two negative numbers is positive.}$$

b. $2(-3)(-2)(-3) = -6(6)$ Multiply the first two factors, and then multiply the last two factors.

$$= -36 \quad \text{The product of two numbers with unlike signs is negative.}$$

Whenever we multiply a number and 0, the product is 0. For example,

$$0 \cdot 8 = 0, \qquad 6.5(0) = 0, \qquad \text{and} \qquad 0(-12) = 0$$

Self Check 3

Multiply:
a. $-25(-3)(-4)$ -300
b. $-1(-2)(-3)(-3)$ 18

Now Try **Problem 38**

Teaching Example 3 Multiply:
a. $4(-3)(-2)$
b. $5(-2)(-1)(-4)$
Answers:
a. 24
b. -40

We also see that whenever we multiply a number by 1, the number remains the same. For example,

$$6 \cdot 1 = 6, \qquad 4.53(1) = 4.53, \qquad \text{and} \qquad 1(-9) = -9$$

These examples illustrate the **multiplication properties of 0 and 1.** Since any number multiplied by 1 remains the same (is identical), the number 1 is called the **identity element** for multiplication.

Multiplication Properties of 0 and 1

The product of 0 and any real number is 0. The product of 1 and any real number is that number.

For any real number a,

$$a \cdot 0 = 0 \qquad \text{and} \qquad 0 \cdot a = 0$$
$$a \cdot 1 = a \qquad \text{and} \qquad 1 \cdot a = a$$

Recall that if the product of two numbers is 1, the numbers are **reciprocals.** The numbers are also called **multiplicative inverses** of each other. For example, because $8 \cdot \frac{1}{8} = 1$, the numbers 8 and $\frac{1}{8}$ are reciprocals (or multiplicative inverses). Likewise, $-\frac{3}{4}$ and $-\frac{4}{3}$ are multiplicative inverses because $-\frac{3}{4}\left(-\frac{4}{3}\right) = 1$. All real numbers, except 0, have reciprocals (multiplicative inverses).

Multiplicative Inverses or Reciprocals (Inverse Property of Multiplication)

The product of any nonzero real number and its multiplicative inverse (reciprocal) is 1.

For any nonzero real number a,

$$a\left(\frac{1}{a}\right) = 1$$

Caution!   Do not change the sign of a number when finding its reciprocal.

---

3 **Divide signed numbers.**

Every division fact containing three numbers can be written as an equivalent multiplication fact containing the same three numbers. For example,

$$\frac{15}{5} = 3 \qquad \text{because} \qquad 5(3) = 15$$

We will use this relationship between multiplication and division to develop the rules for dividing signed numbers. From the example $\frac{15}{5} = 3$, we see that *the quotient of two positive numbers is positive.*

To determine the quotient of two negative numbers, we consider the division $\frac{-15}{-5} = ?$. We can do the division by examining its related multiplication fact: $-5(?) = -15$. To find the number that should replace the question mark, we use the rules for multiplying signed numbers discussed earlier in this section.

	Multiplication fact	**Division fact**	
This must be positive 3 if the product is to be negative 15.	$-5(?) = -15$	$\dfrac{-15}{-5} = 3$	*So the quotient is positive 3.*

From this example, we see that *the quotient of two negative numbers is positive.*

To determine the quotient of a positive number and a negative number, we consider $\frac{15}{-5} = ?$ and its equivalent multiplication fact $-5(?) = 15$.

	Multiplication fact	**Division fact**	
This must be negative 3 if the product is to be positive 15.	$-5(?) = 15$	$\dfrac{15}{-5} = -3$	*So the quotient is negative 3.*

From this example, we see that *the quotient of a positive number and a negative number is negative.*

To determine the quotient of a negative number and a positive number, we consider $\frac{-15}{5} = ?$ and its equivalent multiplication fact $5(?) = -15$.

	Multiplication fact	**Division fact**	
This must be negative 3 if the product is to be negative 15.	$5(?) = -15$	$\dfrac{-15}{5} = -3$	*So the quotient is negative 3.*

From this example, we see that *the quotient of a negative number and a positive number is negative.*

We can now summarize the results from the previous discussion. Note that the rules for division are similar to those for multiplication.

Dividing Two Real Numbers

To divide two real numbers, divide their absolute values.

1. The quotient of two numbers with the same (like) signs is positive.
2. The quotient of two numbers with different (unlike) signs is negative.

EXAMPLE 4 Divide: **a.** $\dfrac{66}{11}$ **b.** $\dfrac{-81}{-9}$ **c.** $\dfrac{-45}{9}$ **d.** $\dfrac{28}{-7}$

Strategy To find the quotients, we will use the rules for dividing signed numbers.

WHY The signs of the numbers that we are dividing determine the sign of the result.

Solution
To divide numbers with like signs, we find the quotient of their absolute values and make the quotient positive.

a. $\dfrac{66}{11} = 6$ *Divide the absolute values, 66 by 11, to get 6. The answer is positive.*

b. $\dfrac{-81}{-9} = 9$ *Divide the absolute values, 81 by 9, to get 9. The answer is positive.*

Self Check 4

Divide:

a. $\dfrac{48}{12}$ *4*

b. $\dfrac{-63}{-9}$ *7*

c. $\dfrac{40}{-8}$ *−5*

d. $\dfrac{-49}{7}$ *−7*

Now Try Problem 45

To divide numbers with unlike signs, we find the quotient of their absolute values and make the quotient negative.

c. $\dfrac{-45}{9} = -5$ Divide the absolute values, 45 by 9, to get 5. The answer is negative.

d. $\dfrac{28}{-7} = -4$ Divide the absolute values, 28 by 7, to get 4. The answer is negative.

4   Use properties of division.

The examples

$$\frac{12}{1} = 12, \qquad \frac{-80}{1} = -80, \qquad \text{and} \qquad \frac{7.75}{1} = 7.75$$

illustrate that *any number divided by 1 is the number itself.* The examples

$$\frac{35}{35} = 1, \qquad \frac{-4}{-4} = 1, \qquad \text{and} \qquad \frac{0.9}{0.9} = 1$$

illustrate that *any number (except 0) divided by itself is 1.*

Division Properties

Any real number divided by 1 is the number itself. Any number (except 0) divided by itself is 1.

For any real number a,

$$\frac{a}{1} = a \qquad \text{and} \qquad \frac{a}{a} = 1, \quad \text{where } a \neq 0$$

We will now consider three types of division that involve zero. In the first case, we will examine a division of zero; in the second, a division by zero; in the third case, a division of zero by zero.

Division statement	Related multiplication statement		Result
$\dfrac{0}{2} = ?$	$2(?) = 0$	This must be 0 if the product is to be 0.	$\dfrac{0}{2} = 0$
$\dfrac{2}{0} = ?$	$0(?) = 2$	There is no number that gives 2 when multiplied by 0.	There is no quotient.
$\dfrac{0}{0} = ?$	$0(?) = 0$	Any number times 0 is 0.	Any number can be the quotient.

We see that $\frac{0}{2} = 0$. Since $\frac{2}{0}$ does not have a quotient, we say that division of 2 by 0 is *undefined.* Since $\frac{0}{0}$ can be any number, we say that $\frac{0}{0}$ is *indeterminate.* These results suggest the following division facts.

Division Involving 0

1. If a represents a nonzero number, $\dfrac{0}{a} = 0$.

2. If a represents a nonzero number, $\dfrac{a}{0}$ is undefined.

3. $\dfrac{0}{0}$ is indeterminate.

The Language of Algebra When we say a division by 0, like $\frac{5}{0}$, is *undefined,* we mean that $\frac{5}{0}$ does not represent a number.

Using Your CALCULATOR Depreciation of a House

Over a 17.5-year period, the value of a \$124,930 house fell at a uniform rate to \$97,105. To find how much the house depreciated per year, we must first find the change in its value by subtracting \$124,930 from \$97,105. To compute this difference, we enter these numbers and press these keys on a scientific calculator.

97105 $\boxed{-}$ 124930 $\boxed{=}$ $\qquad\qquad\qquad$ $\boxed{-27825}$

-27825 represents a drop in value of \$27,825. Since this depreciation occurred in 17.5 years, we divide $-27,825$ by 17.5 to find the amount of depreciation per year. With $-27,825$ on the display, we then enter these numbers and press these keys.

$\boxed{\div}$ 17.5 $\boxed{=}$ $\qquad\qquad\qquad$ $\boxed{-1590}$

If we use a graphing or direct-entry calculator, we enter these numbers and press these keys.

97105 $\boxed{-}$ 124930 $\boxed{\text{ENTER}}$ $\boxed{\div}$ 17.5 $\boxed{\text{ENTER}}$

```
97105 - 124930
             -27825
Ans/17.5
             -1590
```

The amount of depreciation per year was \$1,590.

EXAMPLE 5

Divide, if possible: **a.** $\dfrac{0}{13}$ **b.** $\dfrac{-13}{0}$ **c.** $\dfrac{7}{7}$ **d.** $\dfrac{9}{1}$

Strategy We will determine the appropriate division property to use for each quotient.

WHY Each of these expressions is a special case of division.

Solution

a. $\dfrac{0}{13}$ is division of 0 by a nonzero number. $\dfrac{0}{13} = 0$ *Because 13(0) = 0*

b. Since $\dfrac{-13}{0}$ involves division by zero, the division is undefined.

c. $\dfrac{7}{7} = 1$ *Because 7(1) = 7*

d. $\dfrac{9}{1} = 9$ *Because 1(9) = 9*

Self Check 5

Find each quotient, if possible:

a. $\dfrac{4}{0}$ undefined **b.** $\dfrac{0}{17}$ 0

c. $\dfrac{12}{12}$ 1

Now Try **Problems 49 and 51**

Teaching Example 5
a. $\frac{0}{4}$ **b.** $\frac{-3}{0}$ **c.** $\frac{-5}{-5}$
Answers:
a. 0 **b.** undefined **c.** 1

SECTION 1.6 STUDY SET

VOCABULARY

Fill in the blanks.

1. The answer to a multiplication is called a <u>product</u>.
   The answer to a division is called a <u>quotient</u>.

2. The numbers -4 and -6 are said to have <u>like</u> signs.
   The numbers -10 and 12 are said to have <u>unlike</u> signs.

3. The <u>commutative</u> property of multiplication states
   that two numbers can be multiplied in either order to
   get the same result.

4. The statement $(ab)c = a(bc)$ expresses the
   <u>associative</u> property of multiplication.

5. Division of a nonzero number by zero is <u>undefined</u>.

▶ 6. If the product of two numbers is 1, the numbers are
   called <u>reciprocals</u> or <u>multiplicative</u> inverses.

CONCEPTS

Fill in the blanks.

7. The expression $-5 + (-5) + (-5) + (-5)$ can be
   represented by the multiplication statement $4(-5)$.

8. The quotient of two numbers with <u>unlike</u> signs is
   negative.

9. The product of two negative numbers is <u>positive</u>.

▶ 10. The product of zero and any number is 0.

11. The product of 1 and any number is that number.

12. The division fact $\frac{25}{-5} = -5$ is related to the
    multiplication fact $-5(-5) = 25$.

13. **a.** If we multiply two different numbers and the
    answer is 0, what is true about one of the
    numbers?
    One of the numbers is 0.

    b. If we multiply two different numbers and the
    answer is 1, what is true about the numbers?
    They are reciprocals (multiplicative inverses).

14. **a.** If we divide two nonzero numbers and the answer
    is 1, what is true about the numbers?
    The numbers are the same.

    b. If we divide two numbers and the answer is 0,
    what is true about the numbers? The number being
    divided is 0, the number we are dividing by is not 0.

15. Which property justifies each statement?

    a. $-5(2 \cdot 17) = (-5 \cdot 2)17$
    associative property of multiplication

b. $5\left(\frac{1}{5}\right) = 1$
multiplicative inverse

c. $-5 \cdot 2 = 2(-5)$
commutative property of multiplication

d. $-5(1) = -5$
multiplication property of 1

16. **a.** Find $-1(8)$. In general, what is the result when a
    number is multiplied by -1
    -8, the opposite of that number

    b. Find $\frac{8}{-1}$. In general, what is the result when a
    number is divided by -1?
    -8, the opposite of that number

*POS stands for a positive number and NEG stands for a negative
number. Determine the sign of each result, if possible.*

17. **a.** POS · NEG NEG **b.** POS + NEG not possible
    to tell

    c. POS − NEG POS **d.** $\dfrac{POS}{NEG}$ NEG

18. **a.** NEG · NEG POS **b.** NEG + NEG NEG

    c. NEG − NEG **d.** $\dfrac{NEG}{NEG}$ POS
    not possible to tell

19. What is wrong with the following statement?
    A negative and a positive is a negative.
    If we are
    multiplying or
    dividing, this is true. If we are adding, the sum of a negative number and a positive

20. Give the opposite (additive inverse) and the
    reciprocal (multiplicative inverse) of each number.
    number could
    be positive.
    For example,
    $-6 + 7 = 1$.

    a. 2 $-2, \frac{1}{2}$ **b.** $-\dfrac{4}{5}$ $\frac{4}{5}, -\frac{5}{4}$

    c. 1.75 $-1.75, \frac{4}{7}$ **d.** -5 $5, -\frac{1}{5}$

21. When a calculator was used to compute $16 \div 0$, the
    message shown appeared on the display screen.
    Explain what the message means. Since division by
    0 is undefined, the
    calculator was
    unable to perform
    the division.

    ```
    Error
    ```

22. **a.** Is 80 divided by -5 the same as -5 divided by 80? no

    b. Is 80 times -5 the same as -5 times 80? yes

▶ Selected exercises available online at
www.webassign.net/brookscole

NOTATION

Complete each solution.

23. $(-37 \cdot 5)2 = -37(\boxed{5} \cdot 2)$
$= -37(\boxed{10})$
$= -370$

▶ **24.** $-20(5 \cdot 79) = (\boxed{-20} \cdot 5) \cdot 79$
$= \boxed{-100} \cdot 79$
$= -7{,}900$

GUIDED PRACTICE

Perform each multiplication. See Example 1.

▶ **25.** $12(-5)$ -60 **26.** $(-9)(11)$ -99

27. $-6 \cdot 4$ -24 ▶ **28.** $-8 \cdot 9$ -72

29. $-20(40)$ -800 **30.** $-10(10)$ -100

31. $(6)(-9)$ -54 **32.** $(8)(-7)$ -56

Perform each multiplication. See Example 2.

▶ **33.** $(-6)(-6)$ 36 **34.** $(-1)(-1)$ 1

▶ **35.** $-\dfrac{1}{2}\left(-\dfrac{3}{4}\right)$ $\dfrac{3}{8}$ **36.** $-\dfrac{1}{3}\left(-\dfrac{5}{16}\right)$ $\dfrac{5}{48}$

Multiply. See Example 3.

▶ **37.** $3(-4)(-5)$ 60 ▶ **38.** $(-2)(-4)(-5)$ -40

39. $(-0.4)(0.3)(-0.7)$ 0.084 **40.** $0.5(-0.3)(-0.4)$ 0.06

Perform each division, if possible. See Example 4.

▶ **41.** $\dfrac{-6}{-2}$ 3 **42.** $\dfrac{-36}{9}$ -4

▶ **43.** $\dfrac{4}{-2}$ -2 **44.** $\dfrac{-9}{3}$ -3

▶ **45.** $\dfrac{80}{-20}$ -4 **46.** $\dfrac{-66}{33}$ -2

47. $\dfrac{17}{-17}$ -1 **48.** $\dfrac{-24}{24}$ -1

Perform each division, if possible. See Example 5.

49. $\dfrac{0}{150}$ 0 ▶ **50.** $\dfrac{225}{0}$ undefined

51. $\dfrac{-17}{0}$ undefined **52.** $\dfrac{0}{-12}$ 0

TRY IT YOURSELF

Perform each operation.

53. $-5.2 \cdot 100$ -520 ▶ **54.** $-1.17 \cdot 1{,}000$ $-1{,}170$

55. $0(-22)$ 0 **56.** $-8 \cdot 0$ 0

57. $-3(-4)(0)$ 0 ▶ **58.** $15(0)(-22)$ 0

59. $(-2)(-3)(-4)(-5)$ 120 **60.** $(-3)(-4)(5)(-6)$ -360

61. $(-23.5)(47.2)$ $-1{,}109.2$ **62.** $(-435.7)(-37.8)$ $16{,}469.46$

63. $(-6.37)(-7.2)(-9.1)$ ▶ **64.** $(5.2)(-8.2)(7.75)$ -330.46
-417.3624

65. $-0.6(-4)$ 2.4 **66.** $-0.7(-8)$ 5.6

67. $1.2(-0.4)$ -0.48 **68.** $0(-0.2)$ 0

69. $-1\dfrac{1}{4}\left(-\dfrac{3}{4}\right)$ $\dfrac{15}{16}$ **70.** $-1\dfrac{1}{8}\left(-\dfrac{3}{8}\right)$ $\dfrac{27}{64}$

71. $\dfrac{204.6}{-37.2}$ -5.5 **72.** $\dfrac{-30.56625}{-4.875}$ 6.27

73. $\dfrac{-110}{-110}$ 1 ▶ **74.** $\dfrac{-200}{-200}$ 1

75. $\dfrac{-160}{40}$ -4 **76.** $\dfrac{-250}{-50}$ 5

77. $\dfrac{320}{-16}$ -20 ▶ **78.** $\dfrac{-180}{36}$ -5

79. $\dfrac{0.5}{-100}$ -0.005 **80.** $\dfrac{-1.7}{10}$ -0.17

81. $-\dfrac{1}{3} \div \dfrac{4}{5}$ $-\dfrac{5}{12}$ **82.** $-\dfrac{1}{8} \div \dfrac{2}{3}$ $-\dfrac{3}{16}$

83. $-\dfrac{3}{16} \div \left(-\dfrac{2}{3}\right)$ $\dfrac{9}{32}$ **84.** $-\dfrac{3}{25} \div \left(-\dfrac{2}{3}\right)$ $\dfrac{9}{50}$

85. $-30 \div (-3)$ 10 **86.** $-12 \div (-2)$ 6

87. $-42 \div 7$ -6 **88.** $72 \div (-8)$ -9

Use the associative property of multiplication to help find the product.

89. $-5(2 \cdot 67)$ -670 **90.** $\left(-\dfrac{5}{16} \cdot \dfrac{1}{7}\right)7$ $-\dfrac{5}{16}$

91. $(-7 \cdot 8) \cdot 5$ -280 **92.** $(-8 \cdot 7)3$ -168

APPLICATIONS

▶ **93.** TEMPERATURE CHANGE In a lab, the temperature of a fluid was decreased 6° per hour for 12 hours. What signed number indicates the change in temperature? $-72°$

▶ **94.** BACTERIAL GROWTH To warm a bacterial culture, biologists programmed a heating pad under the culture to increase the temperature 4° every hour for 6 hours. What signed number indicates the change in the temperature of the pad? $+24°$

95. FLUID TEMPERATURE In a lab, the temperature of a fluid was decreased 5° per hour for 14 hours. What signed number indicates the drop in temperature? $-70°$

▶ **96.** REAL ESTATE A house has depreciated $1,250 each year for 8 years. What signed number indicates its change in value over that time period? $-\$10{,}000$

▶ **97.** ASTRONOMY The temperature on Pluto gets as low as $-386°$F. This is twice as low as the lowest temperature reached on Jupiter. What is the lowest temperature on Jupiter? $-193°$F

▶ **98.** CAR RADIATORS The instructions on the back of a container of antifreeze state, "A 50/50 mixture of antifreeze and water protects against freeze-ups down to −34°F, while a 60/40 mix protects against freeze-ups down to one and one-half times that temperature." To what temperature does the 60/40 mixture protect? −51°F

99. ACCOUNTING For 2004, the net income for Martha Stewart Living Omnimedia, Inc., was about −$60,000,000. The company's losses for 2005 were even worse, by a factor of about 1.25. What signed number indicates the company's net income that year? −$75,000,000

▶ **100.** AIRLINES In the 2005 income statement for Delta Airlines, numbers within parentheses represent a loss. Complete the statement given these facts. The second and fourth quarter *losses* were approximately the same and totaled $2,200 million. The third quarter loss was about $\frac{1}{3}$ of the first quarter loss. −$1,100, −$400, −$1,100

DELTA INCOME STATEMENT				2005
All amounts in millions of dollars	1st Qtr (1,200)	2nd Qtr (?)	3rd Qtr (?)	4th Qtr (?)

Source: Yahoo! Finance

101. THE *QUEEN MARY* The ocean liner *Queen Mary* was commissioned in 1936 and cost $22,500,000 to build. In 1967, the ship was purchased by the city of Long Beach, California for $3,450,000 and now serves as a hotel and convention center. What signed number indicates the annual average depreciation of the *Queen Mary* over the 31-year period from 1936 to 1967? Round to the nearest dollar. −$614,516

▶ **102.** COMPUTER SPREADSHEETS The formula = A1*B1*C1 in cell D1 of the spreadsheet instructs the computer to multiply the values in cells A1, B1, and C1 and to print the result *in place of the formula* in cell D1. What values will the computer print in cells D1, D2, and D3? 340, −9,240, −40,800

⌄ File	Edit	View	Insert	Format	Tools	Data	Window
	A		B		C		D
1	4		−5		−17		= A1*B1*C1
2	22		−30		14		= A2*B2*C2
3	−60		−20		−34		= A3*B3*C3
4							
5							

103. PHYSICS An oscilloscope is an instrument that displays electrical signals, which appear as wavy lines on a fluorescent screen. By switching the magnification setting (MAGNIFN.) to × 2, for example, the "height" of the peak and the "depth" of the valley of a graph will be doubled. Use signed numbers to indicate the peak height and the valley depth for each setting of the magnification dial.

a. normal 5, −10 **b.** × 0.5 2.5, −5

c. × 1.5 7.5, −15 **d.** × 2 10, −20

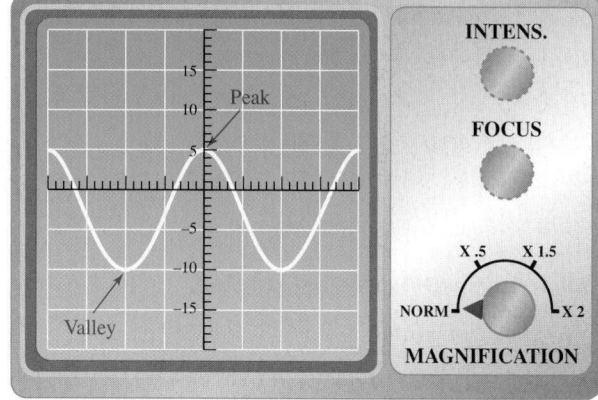

▶ **104.** LIGHT Water acts as a selective filter of light. As shown in the illustration below, red light waves penetrate water only to a depth of about 5 meters. How many times deeper does

a. yellow light penetrate than red light?
6 times deeper

b. green light penetrate than orange light?
4 times deeper

c. blue light penetrate than yellow light?
2.5 times deeper

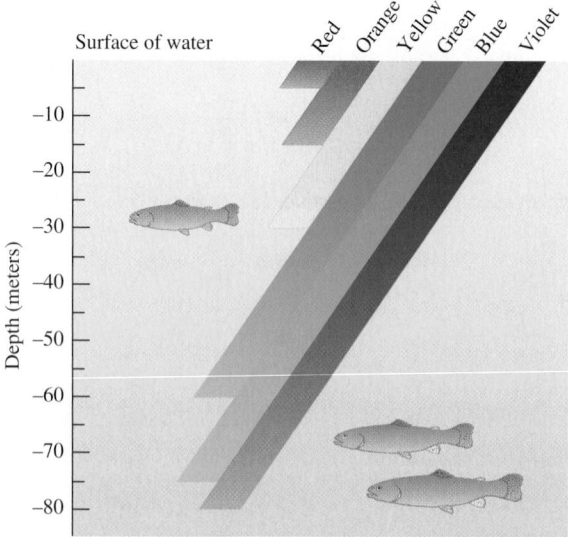

WRITING

105. Explain how you would decide whether the product of several numbers is positive or negative.

▶ **106.** If the product of five numbers is negative, how many of them could be negative? Explain.

REVIEW

107. Is every integer a rational number? yes

▶ **108.** Write the subtraction statement $-3 - (-5)$ as addition of the opposite. $-3 + 5$

109. Find $\frac{1}{2} + \frac{1}{4} + \frac{1}{3}$ and express the result as a decimal.
1.083

110. Describe the balance in a checking account that is overdrawn $65 using a signed number.
$-\$65$

111. Find: $0.475(1,000)$
475

112. Give two examples of irrational numbers.
$\sqrt{2}, \pi$ (answers may vary)

SECTION **1.7**

Exponents and Order of Operations

Objectives

1 Evaluate exponential expressions.

2 Use the order of operations rules.

3 Evaluate expressions with no grouping symbols.

4 Evaluate expressions containing grouping symbols.

5 Find the mean (average).

In this course, we will perform six operations with real numbers: addition, subtraction, multiplication, division, raising to a power, and finding a root. Quite often, we will have to **evaluate** (find the value of) expressions containing more than one operation. In that case, we need to know the order in which the operations are to be performed. That is a topic of this section.

1 Evaluate exponential expressions.

In the expression $3 \cdot 3 \cdot 3 \cdot 3 \cdot 3$, the number 3 is used as a factor 5 times. We call 3 a *repeated factor*. To express a repeated factor, we can use an **exponent.**

Exponent and Base

An **exponent** is used to indicate repeated multiplication. It tells how many times the **base** is used as a factor.

$$\underbrace{3 \cdot 3 \cdot 3 \cdot 3 \cdot 3}_{\text{Five repeated factors of 3.}} = 3^{\overset{\text{The exponent is 5.}}{5}}$$

The base is 3.

In the **exponential expression** a^n, a is the base, and n is the exponent. The expression a^n is called a **power of a.** Some examples of powers are

5^2 Read as "5 to the second power" or "5 squared."

9^3 Read as "9 to the third power" or "9 cubed."

$(-2)^5$ Read as "−2 to the fifth power."

The Language of Algebra 5^2 represents the area of a square with sides 5 units long. 4^3 represents the volume of a cube with sides 4 units long.

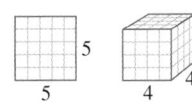

Self Check 1

Write each expression using exponents:
a. $(12)(12)(12)(12)(12)(12)$ 12^6
b. $2 \cdot 9 \cdot 9 \cdot 9$ $2 \cdot 9^3$
c. fifty squared 50^2
d. $(-30)(-30)(-30)$ $(-30)^3$

Now Try **Problem 23**

Teaching Example 1 Write each
expression using exponents:
a. $(-2)(-2)(-2)$ b. twelve squared
Answers:
a. $(-2)^3$
b. 12^2

EXAMPLE 1   Write each expression using exponents: a. $4 \cdot 4 \cdot 4$
b. $(-5)(-5)(-5)(-5)(-5)$ c. sixteen cubed   d. $8 \cdot 8 \cdot 15 \cdot 15 \cdot 15 \cdot 15$

Strategy We will count the number of repeated factors in each expression.

WHY An exponent can be used to represent repeated multiplication.

Solution

a. The factor 4 is repeated 3 times. We can represent this repeated multiplication
with an exponential expression having a base of 4 and an exponent of 3:
$4 \cdot 4 \cdot 4 = 4^3$.

b. The factor -5 is repeated 5 times: $(-5)(-5)(-5)(-5)(-5) = (-5)^5$.

c. Sixteen cubed can be written as 16^3.

d. $8 \cdot 8 \cdot 15 \cdot 15 \cdot 15 \cdot 15 = 8^2 \cdot 15^4$

In the next example, we use exponents to rewrite expressions involving repeated
variable factors.

Self Check 2

Write each product using
exponents:
a. $y \cdot y \cdot y \cdot y$ y^4
b. $12 \cdot b \cdot b \cdot b \cdot c$ $12b^3c$

Now Try **Problem 27**

Teaching Example 2 Write each product using exponents:
a. $xxxxx$ b. $xxyyyzzzz$
Answers:
a. x^5 b. $x^2y^3z^4$

EXAMPLE 2   Write each product using exponents:
a. $a \cdot a \cdot a \cdot a \cdot a \cdot a$ b. $4 \cdot \pi \cdot r \cdot r$

Strategy We will count the number of repeated factors in each expression.

WHY An exponent can be used to represent repeated multiplication.

Solution

a. $a \cdot a \cdot a \cdot a \cdot a \cdot a = a^6$ *a is repeated as a factor 6 times.*

b. $4 \cdot \pi \cdot r \cdot r = 4\pi r^2$ *r is repeated as a factor 2 times.*

Self Check 3

Find each power:
a. 2^5 32
b. $(-6)^2$ 36
c. $(-5)^3$ -125

Now Try **Problem 35**

Teaching Example 3 Find each power:
a. 3^2 b. $(-2)^5$ c. $(-5)^4$
Answers:
a. 9 b. -32 c. 625

EXAMPLE 3   Find each power: a. 5^3 b. 10^1 c. $(-3)^4$ d. $(-3)^5$

Strategy We will identify the base to determine the repeated factor and identify the
exponent to determine the number of times the factor is repeated. Then we will
multiply to evaluate the expression.

WHY Exponents represent repeated multiplication.

Solution
We write the base as a factor the number of times indicated by the exponent. Then
we perform the multiplication.

a. $5^3 = 5 \cdot 5 \cdot 5 = 125$ *The base is 5, the exponent is 3.*

b. $10^1 = 10$ *The base is 10, the exponent is 1.*

c. $(-3)^4 = (-3)(-3)(-3)(-3)$ *Write -3 as a factor 4 times.*

$= 9(-3)(-3)$ *Work from left to right: $(-3)(-3) = 9$.*

$= -27(-3)$ *Work from left to right: $9(-3) = -27$.*

$= 81$

d. $(-3)^5 = (-3)(-3)(-3)(-3)(-3)$ *Write -3 as a factor 5 times.*

$= 9(-3)(-3)(-3)$ *Work from left to right: $(-3)(-3) = 9$.*

$= -27(-3)(-3)$ *Work from left to right: $9(-3) = -27$.*

$= 81(-3)$ *Work from left to right: $-27(-3) = 81$.*

$= -243$

> ***Caution!*** Don't make the mistake of multiplying the base and the exponent.
>
> | Incorrect | Correct |
> |---|---|
> | $5^3 = 5 \cdot 3$ | $5^3 = 5 \cdot 5 \cdot 5$ |
> | | $= 125$ |

We can now make some observations about raising a negative number to an *even power* (2, 4, 6, 8, and so on) and raising a negative number to an *odd power* (1, 3, 5, 7, and so on). In part c of Example 3, we raised -3 to an even power, and the result was positive. In part d, we raised -3 to an odd power, and the result was negative. These results illustrate the following general rule.

Even and Odd Powers of a Negative Number

When a negative number is raised to an even power, the result is positive.

When a negative number is raised to an odd power, the result is negative.

> ***Caution!*** Although the expressions -4^2 and $(-4)^2$ look alike, they are not. In -4^2, the base is 4 and the exponent is 2. The $-$ sign in front of 4^2 means the opposite of 4^2. In $(-4)^2$, the base is -4 and the exponent is 2. When we find the value of each expression, it becomes clear that they are not equivalent.
>
> | $-4^2 = -(4 \cdot 4)$ | Write 4 as a factor 2 times. | $(-4)^2 = (-4)(-4)$ | Write -4 as a factor 2 times. |
> |---|---|---|---|
> | $= -16$ | Multiply within the parentheses. | $= 16$ | The product of two negative numbers is positive. |
>
> Different results

EXAMPLE 4 Find each power: **a.** $\left(-\frac{2}{3}\right)^3$ **b.** $(0.6)^2$ **c.** -2^6

Strategy We will write each exponential expression as a product and multiply the repeated factors.

WHY Exponents represent repeated multiplication.

Solution

a. $\left(-\frac{2}{3}\right)^3 = \left(-\frac{2}{3}\right)\left(-\frac{2}{3}\right)\left(-\frac{2}{3}\right)$ Since $-\frac{2}{3}$ is the base and 3 is the exponent, we write $-\frac{2}{3}$ as a factor 3 times.

$= \frac{4}{9}\left(-\frac{2}{3}\right)$ Multiply: $\left(-\frac{2}{3}\right)\left(-\frac{2}{3}\right) = \frac{4}{9}$.

$= -\frac{8}{27}$ Perform the multiplication.

b. $(0.6)^2 = (0.6)(0.6)$ Since 0.6 is the base and 2 is the exponent, we write 0.6 as a factor 2 times.

$= 0.36$ Perform the multiplication.

c. $-2^6 = -(2 \cdot 2 \cdot 2 \cdot 2 \cdot 2 \cdot 2)$ Since 2 is the base and 6 is the exponent, we write 2 as a factor 6 times. We use the opposite of the final value.

$= -64$ Perform the multiplication.

Self Check 4

Find each power:

a. $\left(-\frac{3}{4}\right)^3$ $-\frac{27}{64}$

b. $(-0.3)^2$ 0.09

c. -5^2 -25

Now Try Problem 37

Teaching Example 4 Find each power:

a. $\left(-\frac{2}{5}\right)^2$

b. $(-0.1)^3$

c. -3^2

Answers:

a. $\frac{4}{25}$ **b.** -0.001

c. -9

Using Your CALCULATOR   Finding a Power

On a scientific calculator, we can use the squaring key $\boxed{x^2}$ to find the square of a number, and we can use the exponential key $\boxed{y^x}$ (on some calculators labeled x^y) to raise a number to a power. For example, to evaluate 125^2 and 2^{10} using a scientific calculator, we enter these numbers and press these keys.

125 $\boxed{x^2}$ $\boxed{\qquad 15625}$

2 $\boxed{y^x}$ 10 $\boxed{=}$ $\boxed{\qquad 1024}$

Using a graphing or direct-entry calculator, we can evaluate 125^2 and 2^{10} by pressing these keys.

125 $\boxed{x^2}$ $\boxed{\text{ENTER}}$ $\boxed{\begin{array}{l} 125^2 \\ \qquad 15625 \end{array}}$

2 $\boxed{\wedge}$ 10 $\boxed{\text{ENTER}}$ $\boxed{\begin{array}{l} 2^{\wedge}10 \\ \qquad 1024 \end{array}}$

We have found that $125^2 = 15,625$ and $2^{10} = 1,024$.

---

2   Use the order of operations rules.

Suppose you have been asked to contact a friend if you see a Rolex watch for sale when you are traveling in Europe. While in Switzerland, you find the watch and send the text message shown on the left. The next day, you get the response shown on the right.

(a)   (b)

Something is wrong. The first part of the response (No price too high!) says to buy the watch at any price. The second part (No! Price too high.) says not to buy it, because it's too expensive. The placement of the exclamation point makes us read the two parts of the response differently, resulting in different meanings. When reading a mathematical statement, the same kind of confusion is possible. For example, consider the expression

$$2 + 3 \cdot 6$$

which contains two operations: addition and multiplication. We can consider doing the calculations in two ways. We can add first and then multiply. Or we can multiply first and then add. However, we get different results.

Method 1: Add first

$2 + 3 \cdot 6 = 5 \cdot 6$ Add 2 and 3 first.

$= 30$ Multiply 5 and 6.

Method 2: Multiply first

$2 + 3 \cdot 6 = 2 + 18$ Multiply 3 and 6 first.

$= 20$ Add 2 and 18.

If we don't establish a uniform order of operations, the expression $2 + 3 \cdot 6$ has two different values. To avoid this possibility, we always use the following set of priority rules.

Order of Operations

1. Perform all calculations within parentheses and other grouping symbols following the order listed in steps 2–4 below, working from the innermost pair to the outermost pair.

2. Evaluate all exponential expressions.

3. Perform all multiplications and divisions as they occur from left to right.

4. Perform all additions and subtractions as they occur from left to right.

When grouping symbols have been removed, repeat steps 2–4 to complete the calculation.

If a fraction is present, evaluate the expression above and the expression below the bar separately. Then do the division indicated by the fraction bar, if possible.

It isn't necessary to apply all of these steps in every problem. For example, the expression $2 + 3 \cdot 6$ does not contain any parentheses, and there are no exponential expressions. So we look for multiplications and divisions to perform. To evaluate $2 + 3 \cdot 6$ correctly, we proceed as follows:

$2 + 3 \cdot 6 = 2 + 18$ Multiply first: $3 \cdot 6 = 18$.

$= 20$ Add.

Therefore, the correct result when evaluating $2 + 3 \cdot 6$ is 20.

3 Evaluate expressions with no grouping symbols.

EXAMPLE 5   Evaluate: $3 \cdot 2^3 - 4$

Strategy We will scan the expression to determine what operations need to be performed. Then we will perform those operations, one at a time, following the order of operations rules.

WHY The order of operations gives us the steps needed to find the correct result.

Solution

To find the value of this expression, we must perform the operations of multiplication, raising to a power, and subtraction. The rules for the order of operations tell us to begin by evaluating the exponential expression.

$3 \cdot 2^3 - 4 = 3 \cdot 8 - 4$ Evaluate the exponential expression: $2^3 = 8$.

$= 24 - 4$ Multiply: $3 \cdot 8 = 24$.

$= 20$ Subtract.

Self Check 5

Evaluate: $2 \cdot 3^2 + 17$ 35

Now Try **Problem 43**

Teaching Example 5 Evaluate:
$4 + 3 \cdot 2^2 - 5$
Answer:
11

The Language of Algebra   Sometimes, for problems like these, the instruction *Simplify* is used instead of *Evaluate*.

Self Check 6

Evaluate: $-40 - 9 \cdot 4 + 10$ -66

Now Try Problem 49

Teaching Example 6 Evaluate:
$-10 - 5 \cdot 3 + 8$
Answer:
-17

EXAMPLE 6 Evaluate: $-30 - 4 \cdot 5 + 9$

Strategy We will scan the expression to determine what operations need to be performed. Then we will perform those operations, one at a time, following the order of operations rules.

WHY The order of operations gives us the steps needed to find the correct result.

Solution
To evaluate this expression, we must perform the operations of subtraction, multiplication, and addition. The rules for the order of operations tell us to begin with the multiplication.

$$-30 - 4 \cdot 5 + 9 = -30 - 20 + 9 \quad \text{Multiply: } 4 \cdot 5 = 20.$$
$$= -50 + 9 \quad \text{Working from left to right, subtract}$$
$$-30 - 20 = -30 + (-20) = -50.$$
$$= -41 \quad \text{Add.}$$

> **Caution!** Some students think that additions are always done before subtractions. As you saw in Example 6, this is not true. Working from left to right, we do the additions or subtractions in the order in which they occur. The same is true for multiplications and divisions.

Self Check 7

Evaluate:
$240 \div (-8)(3) - 3(-2)4$ -66

Now Try Problem 54

Teaching Example 7 Evaluate:
$120 \div (-3)(2) - 4(-1)5$
Answer:
-60

EXAMPLE 7 Evaluate: $160 \div (-4)(3) - 6(-2)3$

Strategy We will scan the expression to determine what operations need to be performed. Then we will perform those operations, one at a time, following the order of operations rules.

WHY The order of operations gives us the steps needed to find the correct result.

Solution
Although this expression contains parentheses, there are no operations to perform within them. Since there are no exponents, we perform multiplications and divisions as they occur from left to right.

$$160 \div (-4)(3) - 6(-2)3 = -40(3) - 6(-2)3 \quad \text{Divide: } 160 \div (-4) = -40.$$
$$= -120 - 6(-2)3 \quad \text{Multiply: } -40(3) = -120$$
$$= -120 - (-12)3 \quad \text{Multiply: } 6(-2) = -12.$$
$$= -120 - (-36) \quad \text{Multiply: } (-12)3 = -36.$$
$$= -120 + 36 \quad \text{Write the subtraction as}$$
$$\text{addition of the opposite.}$$
$$= -84 \quad \text{Add.}$$

> **Caution!** A common mistake is to forget to work from left to right and incorrectly perform the multiplication before the division.

4 Evaluate expressions containing grouping symbols.

Grouping symbols are mathematical punctuation marks. They help determine the order in which an expression is to be evaluated. Examples of grouping symbols are parentheses ( ), brackets [ ], absolute value symbols | |, and the fraction bar —.

EXAMPLE 8   Evaluate: $(6 - 3)^2$

Strategy We will perform the operation(s) within the parentheses first. When there is more than one operation to perform within the parentheses, we follow the order of operations rules.

WHY This is the first step of the order of operations.

Solution

This expression contains parentheses. By the rules for the order of operations, we must perform the operation within the parentheses first.

$(6 - 3)^2 = 3^2$ Subtract within the parentheses: $6 - 3 = 3$.

$ = 9$ Evaluate the exponential expression.

Self Check 8

Evaluate: $(12 - 6)^3$ 216

Now Try Problem 59

Teaching Example 8 Evaluate:
$(7 - 2)^3$
Answer:
125

EXAMPLE 9   Evaluate: $5^3 + 2(-8 - 3 \cdot 2)$

Strategy We will perform the operation(s) within the parentheses first. When there is more than one operation to perform within the parentheses, we follow the order of operations rules.

WHY This is the first step of the order of operations.

Solution

First, we perform the operations within the parentheses in the proper order.

$5^3 + 2(-8 - \mathbf{3 \cdot 2}) = 5^3 + 2(-8 - 6)$ Multiply within the parentheses: $3 \cdot 2 = 6$.

$ = 5^3 + 2(-14)$ Subtract within the parentheses: $-8 - 6 = -8 + (-6) = -14$.

$ = 125 + 2(-14)$ Evaluate the exponential expression: $5^3 = 125$.

$ = 125 + (-28)$ Multiply: $2(-14) = -28$.

$ = 97$ Add.

Self Check 9

Evaluate: $1^3 + 6(-6 - 3 \cdot 0)$

Now Try Problem 63
Self Check 9 Answers
-35

Teaching Example 9 Evaluate:
$3^2 + 4(-5 - 2 \cdot 7)$
Answer:
-67

> ***Success Tip*** Multiplication is indicated when a number is next to a parentheses or bracket.

Expressions can contain two or more pairs of grouping symbols. To evaluate the following expression, we begin by working within the innermost pair of grouping symbols. Then we work within the outermost pair.

Innermost pair
$$-4[-2 - 3(4 - 8^2)] - 2$$
Outermost pair

> ***The Language of Algebra*** When one pair of grouping symbols is inside another pair, we say that those grouping symbols are *nested*, or *embedded*.

Self Check 10

Evaluate:
$-5[2(5^2 - 15) + 4] - 10$ -130

Now Try **Problem 74**

Teaching Example 10 Evaluate:
$-3[4(2^3 - 4) - 5] + 3$
Answer:
-30

EXAMPLE 10   Evaluate: $-4[-2 - 3(4 - 8^2)] - 2$

Strategy We will work within the parentheses first and then within the brackets. At each stage, we follow the order of operations rules.

WHY By the order of operations, we must work from the *innermost* pair of grouping symbols to the *outermost*.

Solution
We work within the innermost grouping symbols (the parentheses) first.

$$-4[-2 - 3(4 - \mathbf{8^2})] - 2$$

$$= -4[-2 - 3(4 - \mathbf{64})] - 2 \qquad \text{Evaluate the exponential expression within the parentheses: } 8^2 = 64.$$

$$= -4[-2 - 3(-60)] - 2 \qquad \text{Subtract within the parentheses:}\\ 4 - 64 = 4 + (-64) = -60.$$

$$= -4[-2 - (-180)] - 2 \qquad \text{Multiply within the brackets: } 3(-60) = -180.$$

$$= -4(178) - 2 \qquad \text{Subtract within the brackets:}\\ -2 - (-180) = -2 + 180 = 178.$$

$$= -712 - 2 \qquad \text{Multiply.}$$

$$= -714 \qquad \text{Subtract: } -712 - 2 = -712 + (-2) = -714.$$

Self Check 11

Evaluate: $\dfrac{-4(-2 + 8) + 6}{8 - 5(-2)}$ -1

Now Try **Problem 75**

Teaching Example 11 Evaluate:
$\dfrac{-2(-4 + 7) + 9}{6 - 3(-7)}$
Answer:
$\dfrac{1}{9}$

EXAMPLE 11   Evaluate: $\dfrac{-3(3 + 2) + 5}{17 - 3(-4)}$

Strategy We will evaluate the expression above and the expression below the fraction bar separately. Then we will simplify the fraction, if possible.

WHY Fraction bars are grouping symbols. They group the numerator and denominator. The expression could be written as $[-3(3 + 2) + 5] \div [17 - 3(-4)]$.

Solution
We simplify the numerator and the denominator separately.

$$\frac{-3(\mathbf{3 + 2}) + 5}{17 - 3(-4)} = \frac{-3(\mathbf{5}) + 5}{17 - (\mathbf{-12})} \qquad \text{In the numerator, add within the parentheses. In the denominator, multiply.}$$

$$= \frac{-15 + 5}{17 + 12} \qquad \text{In the numerator, multiply. In the denominator, write the subtraction as addition of the opposite of } -12, \text{ which is } 12.$$

$$= \frac{-10}{29} \qquad \text{Perform the additions.}$$

$$= -\frac{10}{29} \qquad \text{Write the } - \text{ sign in front of the fraction:}\\ \frac{-10}{29} = -\frac{10}{29}.$$

> ***Success Tip*** The order of operations are built in to most calculators. A left parenthesis key **(** and a right parenthesis key **)** should be used when grouping symbols, including a fraction bar, are in the problem.

Self Check 12

Evaluate: $10^3 + 3|24 - 25|$ $1{,}003$

Now Try **Problem 86**

EXAMPLE 12   Evaluate: $10|9 - 15| - 2^5$

Strategy The absolute value bars are grouping symbols. We will perform the calculation within them first.

WHY By the order of operations, we must perform all calculations within parentheses and other grouping symbols (such as absolute value bars) first.

Solution

Since the absolute value bars are grouping symbols, we perform the calculation within them first.

$$10|9 - 15| - 2^5 = 10|-6| - 2^5 \qquad \text{Subtract: } 9 - 15 = 9 + (-15) = -6.$$

$$= 10(6) - 2^5 \qquad 10|-6| \text{ means 10 times } |-6|. \text{ Find the absolute value: } |-6| = 6.$$

$$= 10(6) - 32 \qquad \text{Evaluate the exponential expression: } 2^5 = 32.$$

$$= 60 - 32 \qquad \text{Multiply.}$$

$$= 28$$

> **Caution!** When a number is next to an absolute value symbol, multiplication is indicated.

Teaching Example 12 Evaluate:
$4^2|6 - 8| - 12 \div 3(4)$
Answer:
16

5 Find the mean (average).

The **arithmetic mean** (or **average**) of a set of numbers is a value around which the values of the numbers are grouped.

Finding an Arithmetic Mean

To find the **mean** of a set of values, divide the sum of the values by the number of values.

EXAMPLE 13 *Hotel Reservations*

In an effort to improve customer service, a hotel electronically recorded the number of times the reservation desk telephone rang before it was answered by a receptionist. The results of the week-long survey are shown in the table. Find the average number of times the phone rang before a receptionist answered.

Number of rings	Number of calls
1	11
2	46
3	45
4	28
5	20

Strategy First, we will determine the total number of times the reservation desk telephone rang during the week. Then we will divide that result by the total number of calls received.

WHY To find the *average* value of a set of values, we divide the sum of the values by the number of values.

Solution

To find the total number of rings, we multiply each *number of rings* (1, 2, 3, 4, and 5 rings) by the respective number of occurrences and add those subtotals.

Total number of rings $= 11(1) + 46(2) + 45(3) + 28(4) + 20(5)$

The total number of calls received was $11 + 46 + 45 + 28 + 20$. To find the average, we divide the total number of rings by the total number of calls.

Self Check 13

On an evaluation, students are to mark 1 for *strongly agree,* 2 for *agree,* 3 for *disagree,* and 4 for *strongly disagree.* If on a question 17 students marked 1, 5 students marked 2, and 2 students marked 4, find the average response for this question on the survey. 1.46

***Now Try* Problem 133**

Teaching Example 13 For a recent survey, the responses of 1 = satisfied, 2 = no opinion, and 3 = dissatisfied were recorded. The results are shown in the table. Find the average rating of satisfaction for these responses.

Survey options	Number of responses
1	15
2	1
3	4

Answer:
1.45

$$\text{Average} = \frac{11(1) + 46(2) + 45(3) + 28(4) + 20(5)}{11 + 46 + 45 + 28 + 20}$$

In the numerator, do the multiplications. In the denominator, do the additions.

$$= \frac{11 + 92 + 135 + 112 + 100}{150}$$

$$= \frac{450}{150}$$

Do the addition.

$$= 3$$

Simplify the fraction.

The average number of times the phone rang before it was answered was 3.

ANSWERS TO SELF CHECKS

1. a. 12^6 **b.** $2 \cdot 9^3$ **c.** 50^2 **d.** $(-30)^3$ **2. a.** y^4 **b.** $12b^3c$ **3. a.** 32 **b.** 36 **c.** -125
4. a. $\frac{-27}{64}$ **b.** 0.09 **c.** -25 **5.** 35 **6.** -66 **7.** -66 **8.** 216 **9.** -35 **10.** -130
11. -1 **12.** $1,003$ **13.** 1.46

SECTION 1.7   STUDY SET

VOCABULARY

Fill in the blanks.

1. In the exponential expression 3^2, 3 is the <u>base</u>, and 2 is the <u>exponent</u>.

2. 10^2 can be read as ten <u>squared</u>, and 10^3 can be read as ten <u>cubed</u>.

3. 7^5 is the fifth <u>power</u> of seven.

▶ **4.** An <u>exponent</u> is used to represent repeated multiplication.

5. The rules for the <u>order</u> of operations guarantee that an evaluation of a numerical expression will result in a single answer.

6. The arithmetic <u>mean</u> or average of a set of numbers is a value around which the values of the numbers are grouped.

CONCEPTS

7. Given: $4 + 5 \cdot 6$

  a. What operations does this expression contain? addition and multiplication

  b. Evaluate the expression in two different ways, and state the two possible results. 54, 34

  c. Which result from part b is correct, and why? 34, multiplication is to be done before addition.

8. a. What repeated multiplication does 5^3 represent? $5 \cdot 5 \cdot 5$

  b. Write a multiplication statement in which the factor x is repeated 4 times. Then write the expression in simpler form using an exponent.
$x \cdot x \cdot x \cdot x = x^4$

  c. How can we represent the repeated addition $3 + 3 + 3 + 3 + 3$ in a simpler form? 5(3)

9. a. How is the mean (or average) of a set of scores found? Divide the sum of the scores by the number of scores.

  b. Find the average of $75, 81, 47$, and 53. 64

10. In the expression $-8 + 2[15 - (-6 + 1)]$, which grouping symbols are innermost and which are outermost? innermost: parentheses, outermost: brackets

11. a. What operations does the expression $12 + 5^2(-3)$ contain? addition, power, multiplication

  b. In what order should they be performed? power, multiplication, addition

12. a. What operations does the expression $20 - (-2)^2 + 3(-1)$ contain? subtraction, power, addition, multiplication

  b. In what order should they be performed? power, multiplication, subtraction, addition

13. Consider the expression $\frac{36 - 4(7)}{2(10 - 8)}$. In the numerator, what operation should be done first? In the denominator, what operation should be done first? multiplication, subtraction

14. Explain the differences in evaluating $4 \cdot 2^2$ and $(4 \cdot 2)^2$.
In $4 \cdot 2^2$, find the power, then multiply. In $(4 \cdot 2)^2$, multiply, then find the power.

▶ Selected exercises available online at **www.webassign.net/brookscole**

15. To evaluate each expression, what operation should be performed first?

   a. $-80 - 3 + 5 - 2^2$ power

   b. $-80 - (3 + 5) - 2^2$ addition

   c. $-80 + 3 + (5 - 2)^2$ subtraction

▶ **16.** To evaluate each expression, what operation should be performed first?

   a. $(65 - 3)^3$ subtraction

   b. $65 - 3^3$ power

   c. $6(5) - (3)^3$ power

▌ NOTATION

17. Write an exponential expression with a base of 12 and an exponent of 6. 12^6

18. Give the name of each grouping symbol: ( ), [ ], | |, and —. parentheses, brackets, absolute value symbols, fraction bar

Complete each evaluation.

19. $50 + 6 \cdot 3^2 = 50 + 6 \cdot \boxed{9}$
$$= 50 + \boxed{54}$$
$$= 104$$

▶ **20.** $-100 - (25 - 8 \cdot 2) = -100 - (25 - \boxed{16})$
$$= -100 - \boxed{9}$$
$$= -109$$

21. $-19 - 2[(1 + 2) \cdot 3] = -19 - 2[\boxed{3} \cdot 3]$
$$= -19 - 2(\boxed{9})$$
$$= -19 - \boxed{18}$$
$$= -37$$

22. $\dfrac{46 - 2^3}{-3(5) - 4} = \dfrac{46 - \boxed{8}}{\boxed{-15} - 4}$
$$= \dfrac{38}{-19}$$
$$= -2$$

▌ GUIDED PRACTICE

Write each product using exponents. **See Example 1.**

23. $3 \cdot 3 \cdot 3 \cdot 3$ 3^4

24. $(-7)(-7)(-7)(-7)(-7)(-7)$ $(-7)^6$

25. $10 \cdot 10 \cdot 12 \cdot 12 \cdot 12$ $10^2 \cdot 12^3$

▶ **26.** $5(5)(5)(11)(11)$ $5^3 \cdot 11^2$

Write each product using exponents. **See Example 2.**

27. $8 \cdot \pi \cdot r \cdot r \cdot r$ $8\pi r^3$ ▶ **28.** $4 \cdot \pi \cdot r \cdot r$ $4\pi r^2$

29. $6(x)(x)(y)(y)(y)$ $6x^2y^3$ **30.** $76 \cdot s \cdot s \cdot s \cdot s \cdot t$ $76s^4t$

Find each power. **See Examples 3–4.**

31. 7^2 49   **32.** 11^3 1,331

33. $(-6)^2$ 36   **34.** $(-4)^4$ 256

▶ **35.** $(-2)^3$ -8 **36.** -5^3 -125

37. $\left(-\dfrac{2}{5}\right)^3$ $-\dfrac{8}{125}$ **38.** $\left(-\dfrac{1}{4}\right)^3$ $-\dfrac{1}{64}$

39. $(-0.4)^2$ 0.16   **40.** $(-0.5)^2$ 0.25

41. -6^2 -36 **42.** -4^4 -256

Evaluate each expression. **See Example 5.**

▶ **43.** $3 \cdot 8^2 - 5$ 187   **44.** $3 \cdot 4^2 - 8$ 40

45. $3 - 5 \cdot 4^2$ -77 **46.** $-4 \cdot 6^2 + 5$ -139

Evaluate each expression. **See Examples 6–7.**

47. $8 \cdot 5 - 4 \div 2$ 38   ▶ **48.** $9 \cdot 5 - 6 \div 3$ 43

49. $100 - 8(10) + 60$ 80   **50.** $50 - 2(5) - 7$ 33

51. $-22 - 15(-3)$ 23   **52.** $-33 - 8(-10)$ 47

53. $-2(9) - 2(5)$ -28 **54.** $18 \div 9(-2) - 4(-3)$ 8

55. $5^2 + 13^2$ 194   ▶ **56.** $3^3 - 2^3$ 19

57. $2 \cdot 3^2 + 5 \cdot 2^3$ 58   **58.** $4 \cdot 2^5 - 3 \cdot 5^2$ 53

Evaluate each expression. **See Example 8.**

59. $(-5 - 2)^2$ 49   **60.** $(-3 - 5)^2$ 64

61. $(12 - 2)^3$ 1,000   ▶ **62.** $(10 - 3)^2$ 49

Evaluate each expression. **See Example 9.**

63. $175 - 2 \cdot 3^4$ 13   **64.** $75 - 3 \cdot 1^2$ 72

▶ **65.** $200 - (-6 + 5)^3$ 201   **66.** $19 - (-45 + 41)^3$ 83

67. $-6(130 - 4^3)$ -396 **68.** $-5(150 - 3^3)$ -615

69. $5 \cdot 2^2 \cdot 4 - 30$ 50   **70.** $2 + (3 \cdot 2^2 \cdot 4)$ 50

Evaluate each expression. **See Example 10.**

▶ **71.** $-3[5^2 - (7 - 3)^2]$ -27 **72.** $3 - [3^3 + (3 - 1)^3]$ -32

73. $5 + (4^2 - 2^3)^2$ 69   ▶ **74.** $(-5)^3[4(2^3 - 3^2)]^2$ $-2,000$

Evaluate each expression. **See Example 11.**

▶ **75.** $\dfrac{5 \cdot 50 - 160}{-9}$ -10 **76.** $\dfrac{5(68 - 32)}{-9}$ -20

77. $\dfrac{(4^3 - 10) + (-4)}{5^2 - (-4)(-5)}$ 10   **78.** $\dfrac{(6 - 5)^4 - (-21)}{(-9)(-3) - 4^2}$ 2

79. $\dfrac{72 - (2 - 2 \cdot 1)}{10^2 - (90 + 2^2)}$ 12   ▶ **80.** $\dfrac{13^2 - 5^2}{-3(5 - 9)}$ 12

81. $\dfrac{40 \div 2 - 5 \cdot 2}{3^2 - (-1)}$ 1   **82.** $\dfrac{(5 - 2)^2 - (2 - (-1))}{5 \cdot 2 + (-7)}$ 2

Evaluate each expression. **See Example 12.**

83. $-2|4 - 8|$ -8 **84.** $-5|1 - 8|$ -35

85. $|7 - 8(4 - 7)|$ 31   ▶ **86.** $|9 - 5(1 - 8)|$ 44

87. $\dfrac{|6 - 4| + 2| - 4|}{26 - 2^4}$ 1   **88.** $\dfrac{4|9 - 7| + | - 7|}{3^2 - 2^2}$ 3

▶ **89.** $\dfrac{(3 + 5)^2 + | - 2|}{-2(5 - 8)}$ 11   **90.** $\dfrac{| - 25| - 8(-5)}{2^4 - 29}$ -5

TRY IT YOURSELF

Evaluate each expression.

91. $-(-6)^4$ $-1{,}296$ **92.** $-(-7)^2$ -49

93. $-4(6 + 5)$ -44 **94.** $-3(5 - 4)$ -3

95. $4^2 - (-2)^2$ 12 **96.** $3 + (-5)^2$ 28

97. $12 + 2\left(-\dfrac{9}{3}\right) - (-2)$ 8

98. $2 + 3\left(-\dfrac{25}{5}\right) - (-4)$ -9

99. $1(2)(3)(-4)$ -24 **100.** $3(4)(5)(-6)$ -360

101. $[6(5) - 5(5)]4$ 20 **102.** $5[9(2) - 2(8)]$ 10

103. $(17 - 5 \cdot 2)^3$ 343 ▶ **104.** $(4 + 2 \cdot 3)^4$ $10{,}000$

105. $-5(-2)^3(3)^2$ 360 **106.** $-3(-2)^5(2)^2$ 384

107. $-2\left(\dfrac{15}{-5}\right) - \dfrac{6}{2} + 9$ 12 **108.** $-6\left(\dfrac{25}{-5}\right) - \dfrac{36}{9} + 1$ 27

109. $5(10 + 2) - 1$ 59 **110.** $14 + 3(7 - 5)$ 20

111. $64 - 6[15 + (-3)3]$ 28 ▶ **112.** $4 + 2[26 + 5(-3)]$ 26

113. $(-2)^3\left(\dfrac{-6}{2}\right)(-1)$ -24 **114.** $(-3)^3\left(\dfrac{-4}{2}\right)(-1)$ -54

115. $\dfrac{-7 - 3^2}{2 \cdot 4}$ -2 ▶ **116.** $\dfrac{-5 - 3^3}{2^3}$ -4

117. $\dfrac{1}{2}\left(\dfrac{1}{8}\right) + \left(-\dfrac{1}{4}\right)^2$ $\dfrac{1}{8}$ **118.** $-\dfrac{1}{9}\left(\dfrac{1}{4}\right) + \left(-\dfrac{1}{6}\right)^2$ 0

119. $3 + 2[-1 - 4(5)]$ -39

120. $4 + 2[-7 - 3(9)]$ -64

121. $-(2 \cdot 3 - 4)^3$ -8 **122.** $-(3 \cdot 5 - 2 \cdot 6)^2$ -9

123. $\dfrac{2[-4 - 2(3 - 1)]}{3(-3)(-2)}$ $-\dfrac{8}{9}$

124. $\dfrac{3[-9 + 2(7 - 3)]}{(5 - 8)(7 - 9)}$ $-\dfrac{1}{2}$

125. $-\left(\dfrac{40 - 1^3 - 2^4}{3(2 + 5) + 2}\right)$ -1 ▶ **126.** $-\left(\dfrac{8^2 - 10}{2(3)(4) - 5(3)}\right)$ -6

127. $\dfrac{3(3{,}246 - 1{,}111)}{561 - 546}$ 427

128. $54^3 - 16^4 + 19(3)$ $91{,}985$

129. $(23.1)^2 - (14.7)(-61)^3$ $3{,}337{,}154.31$

130. $12 - 7\left(-\dfrac{85.684}{34.55}\right)^3$ 118.770944

APPLICATIONS

▶ **131.** LIGHT The illustration shows that the light energy that passes through the first unit of area, 1 yard away from the bulb, spreads out as it travels away from the source. How much area does that light energy cover 2 yards, 3 yards, and 4 yards from the bulb? Express each answer using exponents.
2^2 square units, 3^2 square units, 4^2 square units

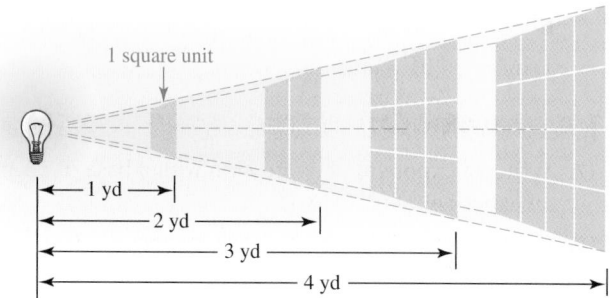

▶ **132.** CHAIN LETTERS A store owner sent two friends a letter advertising her store's low prices. The ad closed with the following request: "Please send a copy of this letter to two of your friends."

a. Assume that all those receiving letters respond and that everyone in the chain receives just one letter. Complete the table.

b. How many letters will be circulated in the tenth level of the mailing? $2^{10} = 1{,}024$

Level	Numbers of letters circulated
1st	$2 = 2^1$
2nd	$4 = 2^2$
3rd	$8 = 2^3$
4th	$16 = 2^4$

▶ **133.** AUTO INSURANCE See the premium comparison in the table. What is the average 6-month insurance premium? $\$2{,}106$

Allstate	$2,672	Mercury	$1,370
Auto Club	$1,680	State Farm	$2,737
Farmers	$2,485	20th Century	$1,692

Criteria: Six-month premium. Husband, 45, drives a 1995 Explorer, 12,000 annual miles. Wife, 43, drives a 1996 Dodge Caravan, 12,000 annual miles. Son, 17, is an occasional operator. All have clean driving records.

▶ **134.** SWEEPS WEEK During sweeps week, television networks make a special effort to gain viewers by showing unusually flashy programming. Use the information in the illustration on the next page to determine the average daily gain (or loss) of ratings points by a network for the 7-day sweeps period.
a gain of 0.6 of a rating point

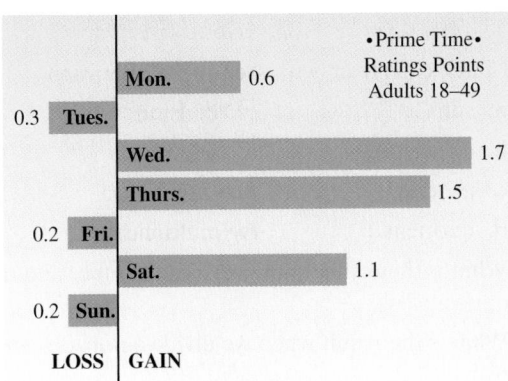

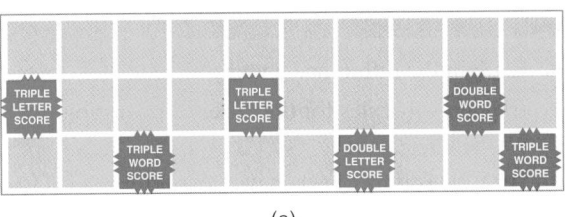

(a)

$$Q_{10} \quad U_1 \quad A_1 \quad R_1 \quad T_1 \quad Z_{10} \quad Y_4$$

(b)

▶ **135. YOUTUBE VIDEO CONTEST** A video contest is to be part of a promotional kickoff for a new sports drink. The prizes to be awarded are shown.

> **YouTube Video Contest**
>
> **Grand prize: Disney World vacation plus $2,500**
>
> Four 1st place prizes of $500
> Thirty-five 2nd place prizes of $150
> Eighty-five 3rd place prizes of $25

  a. How much money will be awarded in the promotion? $11,875

  b. What is the average cash prize? $95

▶ **136. ENERGY USAGE** Refer to the illustration below. Find the average number of therms of natural gas used per month. Then draw a dashed line across the graph showing the average. 31.5 therms

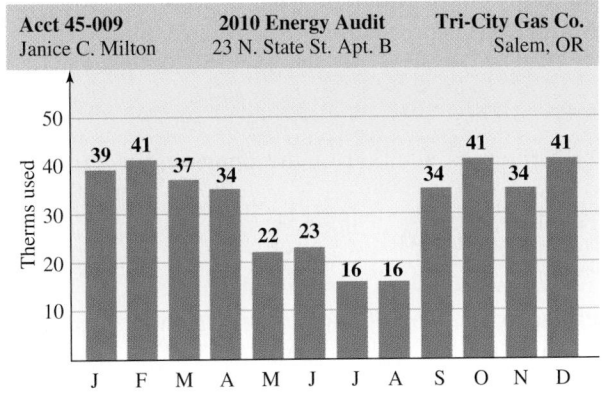

▶ **137. SCRABBLE** Illustration (a) in the next column shows a portion of the game board before and illustration (b) shows it after the word *QUARTZY* is played. Determine the score. (The number on each tile gives the point value of the letter.)
$3(10 + 1 + 1 + 1 + 1 + 2 \cdot 10 + 4) = 114$

▶ **138. WRAPPING GIFTS** How much ribbon is needed to wrap the package shown if 15 inches of ribbon are needed to make the bow? 81 in.

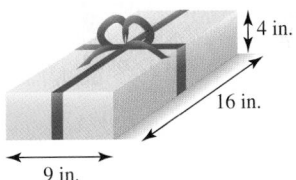

139. SPREADSHEETS This spreadsheet contains data collected by a chemist. For each row, the sum of the values in columns A and B is to be subtracted from the product of 6 and the value in column C. That result is then to be divided by 12 and entered in column D. Use this information to complete the spreadsheet.

	A	B	C	D
1	20	4	8	2
2	9	3	16	7
3	1	5	11	5

140. DOG SHOWS The final score for each dog competing in a toy breeds competition is computed by dividing the sum of the judges' marks, after the highest and lowest have been dropped, by 6. See the table.

  a. What was their order of finish? pomeranian, terrier, pekingese

  b. Did any judge rate all the dogs the same? yes, judge 6

Judge	1	2	3	4	5	6	7	8
Terrier	14	11	11	10	12	12	13	13
Pekingese	10	9	8	11	11	12	9	10
Pomeranian	15	14	13	11	14	12	10	14

141. Explain the difference between 2^3 and 3^2.

142. Explain why rules for the order of operations are necessary.

143. What does it mean when we say perform all additions and subtractions *as they occur from left to right?*

▶ **144.** In what settings do you encounter or use the concept of arithmetic mean (average) in your everyday life?

145. Match each term with the proper operation.

   a. sum ii   **i.** division

   b. difference iii   **ii.** addition

   c. product iv   **iii.** subtraction

   d. quotient i   **iv.** multiplication

▶ **146.** What is the result when we add a number and its opposite? 0

147. What is the result when we divide a nonzero number by itself? 1

148. What is wrong with the following statement? Subtraction is the same as adding.

Subtraction is the same as adding the opposite.

Objectives

1 Identify terms and coefficients of terms.

2 Write word phrases as algebraic expressions.

3 Analyze problems to determine hidden operations.

4 Evaluate algebraic expressions.

SECTION 1.8

Algebraic Expressions

Since problems in algebra are often presented in words, the ability to interpret what you read is important. In this section, we will introduce several strategies that will help you translate English words into mathematical symbols.

1 Identify terms and coefficients of terms.

Recall that variables and/or numbers can be combined with the operations of arithmetic to create **algebraic expressions.** Addition symbols separate expressions into parts called *terms.* For example, the expression $x + 8$ has two terms.

$$x \quad + \quad 8$$
First term   Second term

Since subtraction can be written as addition of the opposite, the expression $a^2 - 3a - 9$ has three terms.

$$a^2 - 3a - 9 = \quad a^2 \quad + \quad (-3a) \quad + \quad (-9)$$
                  First term   Second term   Third term

In general, a **term** is a product or quotient of numbers and/or variables. A single number or variable is also a term. Examples of terms are:

$$4, \quad y, \quad 6r, \quad -w^3, \quad 3.7x^5, \quad \frac{3}{n}, \quad -15ab^2$$

> **The Language of Algebra** By the commutative property of multiplication, $r6 = 6r$ and $-15b^2a = -15ab^2$. However, we usually write the numerical factor first and the variable factors in alphabetical order.

The numerical factor of a term is called the **coefficient** of the term. For instance, the term $6r$ has a coefficient of 6 because $6r = 6 \cdot r$. The coefficient of $-15ab^2$ is -15 because $-15ab^2 = -15 \cdot ab^2$. More examples are shown.

A term such as 4, that consists of a single number, is called a **constant term.**

Term	Coefficient	
$8y^2$	8	
$-0.9pq$	-0.9	
$\frac{3}{4}b$	$\frac{3}{4}$	This term could be written $\frac{3b}{4}$.
$-\frac{x}{6}$	$-\frac{1}{6}$	Because $-\frac{x}{6} = -\frac{1x}{6} = -\frac{1}{6} \cdot x$
x	1	Because $x = 1x$
$-t$	-1	Because $-t = -1t$
27	27	

> **The Language of Algebra** Terms such as x and y have *implied* coefficients of 1. *Implied* means suggested without being precisely expressed.

EXAMPLE 1 Identify the coefficient of each term in the following expression: $7x^2 - x + 6$

Strategy We will begin by writing the subtraction as addition of the opposite. Then we will determine the numerical factor of each term.

WHY Addition symbols separate expressions into terms.

Solution

If we write $7x^2 - x + 6$ as $7x^2 + (-x) + 6$, we see that it has three terms: $7x^2$, $-x$, and 6. The numerical factor of each term is its coefficient.

The coefficient of $7x^2$ is **7** because $7x^2$ means $\mathbf{7} \cdot x^2$.

The coefficient of $-x$ is $\mathbf{-1}$ because $-x$ means $\mathbf{-1} \cdot x$.

The coefficient of the constant 6 is 6.

It is important to be able to distinguish between the *terms* of an expression and the *factors* of a term.

EXAMPLE 2 Is m used as a *factor* or a *term* in each expression?

a. $m + 6$ **b.** $8m$

Strategy We will begin by determining whether m is involved in an addition or a multiplication.

WHY Addition symbols separate expressions into *terms*. A *factor* is a number being multiplied.

Solution

a. Since m is added to 6, m is a term of $m + 6$.

b. Since m is multiplied by 8, m is a factor of $8m$.

2 Write word phrases as algebraic expressions.

In the following tables, we list some words and phrases that are used to indicate addition, subtraction, multiplication, and division, and we show how they can be translated to form algebraic expressions.

Addition

The phrase	Translates to
the sum of *a* and 8	$a + 8$
4 plus *c*	$4 + c$
16 added to *m*	$m + 16$
4 more than *t*	$t + 4$
20 greater than *F*	$F + 20$
T increased by *r*	$T + r$
exceeds *y* by 35	$y + 35$

Subtraction

The phrase	Translates to
the difference of 23 and *P*	$23 - P$
550 minus *h*	$550 - h$
18 less than *w*	$w - 18$
7 decreased by *j*	$7 - j$
M reduced by *x*	$M - x$
12 subtracted from *L*	$L - 12$
5 less *f*	$5 - f$

> *Caution!*   Be careful when translating subtraction. Order is important. For example, when translating the phrase "18 less than *w*," the terms are reversed.
>
> 18 less than *w*
>
> $w - 18$

Multiplication

The phrase	Translates to
the product of 4 and *x*	$4x$
20 times *B*	$20B$
twice *r*	$2r$
triple the profit *P*	$3P$
$\frac{3}{4}$ of *m*	$\frac{3}{4}m$

Division

The phrase	Translates to
the quotient of *R* and 19	$\frac{R}{19}$
s divided by *d*	$\frac{s}{d}$
the ratio of *c* to *d*	$\frac{c}{d}$
k split into 4 equal parts	$\frac{k}{4}$

> *Caution!*   The phrase *greater than* is used to indicate addition. The phrase *is greater than* refers to the symbol $>$. Similarly, the phrase *less than* indicates subtraction, and the phrase *is less than* refers to the symbol $<$.

EXAMPLE 3   Write each phrase as an algebraic expression.

a. The sum of the length *l* and the width 20

b. 5 less than the capacity *c*

c. The product of the weight *w* and 2,000, increased by 300

Strategy We will read each phrase and pay close attention to key words that can be translated to mathematical operations. We will refer to the tables as a guide if needed.

WHY Key phrases can be translated to mathematical symbols.

Solution
a. Key word: *sum*   **Translation:** add

The phrase translates to $l + 20$.

b. Key phrase: *less than*   **Translation:** subtract

The capacity c is to be made less, so we subtract 5 from it: $c - 5$.

c. Key word: *product*   **Translation:** multiply

Key phrase: *increased by*   **Translation:** add

The weight w is to be multiplied by 2,000, and then 300 is to be added to the product: $2,000w + 300$.

When solving problems, we often begin by letting a variable stand for an unknown quantity.

EXAMPLE 4   *Food Preparation*   A butcher trims 4 ounces of fat from a roast that originally weighed x ounces. Write an algebraic expression that represents the weight of the roast after it is trimmed.

Strategy We will start by letting x represent the original weight of the roast. Then we will look for a key word or phrase to write an expression that represents the trimmed weight of the roast.

WHY The weight after trimming is related to the original weight of the roast.

Solution

We let $x =$ the original weight of the roast (in ounces).

Key word: *trimmed*   **Translation:** subtract

After 4 ounces of fat have been trimmed, the weight of the roast is $(x - 4)$ ounces.

EXAMPLE 5   *Competitive Swimming*   The swimming pool to the right is x feet wide. If it is to be sectioned into 8 equally wide swimming lanes, write an algebraic expression that represents the width of each lane.

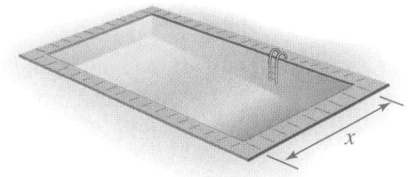

Strategy We start by letting x represent the width of the swimming pool. Then we will look for key words or phrases to write an expression that represents the width of each lane.

WHY The width of each lane is related to the width of the pool.

Solution

We let $x =$ the width of the swimming pool (in feet).

Key phrase: *sectioned into 8 equally wide lanes*   **Translation:** divide

The width of each lane is $\dfrac{x}{8}$ feet.

When we are solving problems, the variable to be used is rarely specified. We must decide what the unknown quantities are and how they will be represented using variables. The following examples illustrate how to approach these situations.

Self Check 6

A candy bar has twice the number of calories as a serving of pears. Write an expression that represents the number of calories in a candy bar.

Now Try Problem 47

Self Check 6 Answers

x = the number of calories in a serving of pears, $2x$ = the number of calories in a candy bar

Teaching Example 6 A delivery of x cases of pies, each containing 8 pies, is made to a fundraiser. Write an expression for the number of pies delivered to the fundraiser.
Answer:
x = the number of cases of pies
$8x$ = the number of pies

EXAMPLE 6 *Collectibles* The value of a collectible doll is three times that of an antique toy truck. Write an expression that represents the value of the doll.

Strategy We start by letting x represent the value of the toy truck. Then we will look for key words or phrases to write an expression that represents the value of the antique doll.

WHY The value of the doll is related to the value of the toy truck.

Solution
There are two unknown quantities. Since the doll's value is related to the truck's value, we will let x = the value of the toy truck in dollars.

  Key phrase: 3 *times*   **Translation:** multiply by 3

The value of the doll is $\$3x$.

> **Caution!**   A variable is used to represent an unknown number. Therefore, in Example 6, it would be incorrect to write, "Let x = toy truck," because the truck is not a number. We need to write, "Let x = the *value* of the toy truck."

Self Check 7

Part of a $900 donation to a college went to the scholarship fund, the rest to the building fund. Choose a variable to represent the amount donated to one of the funds. Then write an expression that represents the amount donated to the other fund.

Now Try Problem 52

Self Check 7 Answers

s = amount donated to scholarship fund in dollars, $900 - s$ = amount donated to building fund

Teaching Example 7 Part of a $2000 investment is to be invested in an account paying $3\frac{1}{2}\%$, and the rest in an account paying 4%. Choose a variable to represent the amount invested at $3\frac{1}{2}\%$. Write an expression that represents the amount invested at 4%.
Answer: x = amount invested at $3\frac{1}{2}\%$, $2000 - x$ = amount invested at 4%

EXAMPLE 7 *Painting* A 10-inch-long paintbrush has two parts: a handle and bristles. Choose a variable to represent the length of one of the parts. Then write an expression to represent the length of the other part.

Strategy There are two approaches. We can let h = the length of the handle or we can let b = the length of the bristles.

WHY Both the length of the handle and the length of the bristles are unknown, however we do know the entire length of the paintbrush.

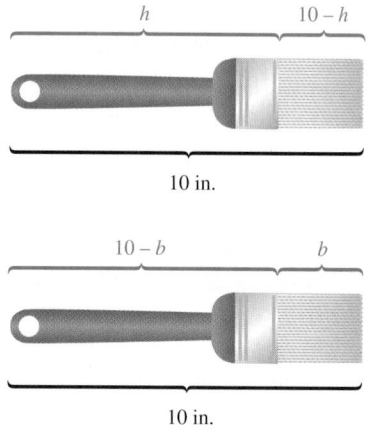

Solution
Refer to the drawing on the top. If we let h = the length of the handle (in inches), then the length of the bristles is $10 - h$.

   Now refer to the drawing on the bottom. If we let b = the length of the bristles (in inches), then the length of the handle is $10 - b$.

Self Check 8

The number of votes received by the incumbent in an election was 55 fewer than three times the number the challenger received. Write an expression that represents the number of votes received by the incumbent.

Now Try Problem 53

EXAMPLE 8 *Student Enrollments* In the second semester, student enrollment in a retraining program at a college was 32 more than twice that of the first semester. Write an expression that represents the student enrollment in the second semester.

Strategy We start by letting x represent the enrollment in the first semester. Then we will look for a key word or phrase to write an expression to represent the second-semester enrollment.

WHY The second-semester enrollment is related to the first-semester enrollment. ▼

Solution

Since the second-semester enrollment is expressed in terms of the first-semester enrollment, we let x = the enrollment in the first semester.

Key phrase: *more than*   **Translation:** add

Key word: *twice*   **Translation:** multiply by 2

The enrollment for the second semester is $2x + 32$. ∎

3 Analyze problems to determine hidden operations.

When analyzing problems, we aren't always given key words or key phrases to help establish what mathematical operation to use. Sometimes a careful reading of the problem is needed to determine the hidden operations.

EXAMPLE 9 *Disney Theme Parks* Disneyland, located in Anaheim, California, was in operation 16 years before the opening of Walt Disney World, in Orlando, Florida. Euro Disney, in Paris, France, was constructed 21 years after Disney World. Use algebraic expressions to express the ages (in years) of each of these Disney attractions.

Strategy We start by letting x represent the age of Disney World.

WHY The ages of Disneyland and Euro Disney are related to the age of Disney World.

Solution

The ages of Disneyland and Euro Disney are both related to the age of Walt Disney World. Therefore, we will let x = the age of Walt Disney World.

In carefully reading the problem, we find that Disneyland was built 16 years *before* Disney World, so its age is more than that of Disney World.

Key phrase: *more than*   **Translation:** add

In years, the age of Disneyland is $x + 16$. Euro Disney was built 21 years *after* Disney World, so its age is less than that of Disney World.

Key phrase: *less than*   **Translation:** subtract

In years, the age of Euro Disney is $x - 21$. The results are summarized in the table.

Attraction	Age
Disneyland	$x + 16$
Disney World	x
Euro Disney	$x - 21$

EXAMPLE 10 How many months are in x years?

Strategy There are no key words, so we must carefully analyze the problem to write an expression that represents the number of months in x years. We will begin by considering some specific cases.

WHY When no key words are present, it is helpful to work with specifics to get a better understanding of the relationship between the two quantities.

Solution

Let's calculate the number of months in 1 year, 2 years, and 3 years. When we write the results in a table, a pattern is apparent.

Self Check 9

Kayla worked 5 more hours preparing her tax return than she did on her daughter's return. Kayla's son's return took her 2 more hours to prepare than her daughter's. Write an expression to represent the hours she spent on each return.

Now Try **Problem 57**

Self Check 10

Complete the table. How many days is h hours?

Number of hours	Number of days
24	1
48	2
72	3
h	$\frac{h}{24}$

Now Try **Problem 59**

Teaching Example 10 How many seconds are in *x* minutes?
Answer:
60*x*

Number of years	Number of months
1	12
2	24
3	36
x	12*x*

We multiply the number of years
by 12 to find the number of months.

Therefore, if $x =$ the number of years, the number of months is $12 \cdot x$ or $12x$.

Some problems deal with quantities that have value. In these problems, we must distinguish between *the number of* and *the value of* the unknown quantity. For example, to find the value of 3 quarters, we multiply the number of quarters by the value (in cents) of one quarter. Therefore, the value of 3 quarters is $3 \cdot 25$ cents $= 75$ cents.

The same distinction must be made if the number is unknown. For example, the value of *n* nickels is not *n* cents. The value of *n* nickels is $n \cdot 5$ cents $= (5n)$ cents. For problems of this type, we will use the relationship

Number $\cdot$ value $=$ total value

Self Check 11

Find the value of
a. six fifty-dollar savings bonds
b. *t* one-hundred-dollar savings bonds
c. $x - 4$ one-thousand-dollar savings bonds

Now Try **Problem 62**
Self Check 11 Answers
a. \$300   **b.** \$100*t*   **c.** \$1,000$(x - 4)$

Teaching Example 11 Find the value of
a. 7 nickels
b. *t* \$50 bills
c. $x + 3$ \$20 bills
Answers:
a. 35¢   **b.** \$50*t*
c. \$20$(x + 3)$

EXAMPLE 11   Find the total value of
a. five dimes   **b.** *q* quarters   **c.** $x + 1$ half-dollars

Strategy We will find the total value (in cents) of each collection of coins by multiplying the number of coins by the value of one coin.

WHY Number $\cdot$ value $=$ total value

Solution
To find the total value (in cents) of each collection of coins, we multiply the number of coins by the value (in cents) of one coin, as shown in the table.

Type of Coin	Number	$\cdot$ Value	$=$ Total Value
Dime	5	10	50
Quarter	*q*	25	25*q*	← $q \cdot 25$ is written 25*q*.
Half-dollar	$x + 1$	50	$50(x + 1)$

4 Evaluate algebraic expressions.

To **evaluate an algebraic expression,** we replace each variable with a given number value. (When we replace a variable with a number, we say we are **substituting** for the variable.) Then we do the necessary calculations following the rules for the order of operations. For example, to evaluate $x^2 - 2x + 1$ for $x = 3$, we begin by substituting 3 for *x*.

$$
\begin{aligned}
x^2 - 2x + 1 &= 3^2 - 2(3) + 1 && \text{Substitute 3 for x.} \\
&= 9 - 2(3) + 1 && \text{Evaluate the exponential expression: } 3^2 = 9. \\
&= 9 - 6 + 1 && \text{Perform the multiplication: } 2(3) = 6. \\
&= 4 && \text{Working left to right, perform the subtraction and} \\
& && \text{then the addition.}
\end{aligned}
$$

We say that 4 is the **value** of this expression when $x = 3$.

> *Caution!*   When replacing a variable with its numerical value, use parentheses around the replacement number to avoid possible misinterpretation. For example, when substituting 5 for x in $2x + 1$, we show the multiplication using parentheses: $2(5) + 1$. If we don't show the multiplication, we could misread the expression as $25 + 1$.

EXAMPLE 12   Evaluate each expression for $x = 3$ and $y = -4$:
a. $-y$ **b.** $-3(y + x^2)$

Strategy We will replace x with 3 and y with -4 and then evaluate the expression using the order of operations.

WHY To evaluate an expression means to find its numerical value, once we know the values of the variable(s).

Solution

a. $-y = -(-4)$ Substitute -4 for y.

$\quad\ \ = 4$ The opposite of -4 is 4.

b. $-3(y + x^2) = -3(-4 + 3^2)$ Substitute 3 for x and -4 for y.

$\qquad\qquad\ \ = -3(-4 + 9)$ Work within the parentheses first. Evaluate the exponential expression.

$\qquad\qquad\ \ = -3(5)$ Perform the addition within the parentheses.

$\qquad\qquad\ \ = -15$

EXAMPLE 13   *Temperature Conversion* The expression $\frac{9C + 160}{5}$ converts a temperature in degrees Celsius (represented by C) to a temperature in degrees Fahrenheit. Convert $-170°C$, the coldest temperature on the moon, to degrees Fahrenheit.

Strategy We will replace C in the expression with -170 and evaluate it using the order of operations.

WHY The expression evaluated at $C = -170$ converts $-170°C$ to degrees Fahrenheit.

Solution
To convert $-170°C$ to degrees Fahrenheit, we evaluate the algebraic expression for $C = -170$.

$$\frac{9C + 160}{5} = \frac{9(-170) + 160}{5}\quad \text{Substitute } -170 \text{ for } C.$$

$$= \frac{-1{,}530 + 160}{5}\quad \text{Perform the multiplication.}$$

$$= \frac{-1{,}370}{5}\quad \text{Perform the addition.}$$

$$= -274\quad \text{Perform the division.}$$

In degrees Fahrenheit, the coldest temperature on the moon is $-274°$.

Self Check 12

Evaluate each expression for $x = -2$ and $y = 3$:   **a.** $-x$ **b.** $5(x - y)$

***Now Try* Problem 63**

Self Check 12 Answers
a. 2   b. -25

Teaching Example 12 Evaluate: $-5(3y + 2x^2)$ when $x = -3$ and $y = 2$.
Answer:
-120

Self Check 13

On January 22, 1943, the temperature in Spearfish, South Dakota changed from $-20°C$ to $7.2°C$ in two minutes. Convert $-20°C$ to degrees Fahrenheit.

***Now Try* Problem 75**

Self Check 13 Answer
$-4°F$

Teaching Example 13 Convert $7.2°C$ to degrees Fahrenheit.
Answer:
$44.96°F$

Using Your CALCULATOR   Evaluating Algebraic Expressions

The rotating drum of a clothes dryer is a cylinder. To find the capacity of the dryer, we can find its volume by evaluating the algebraic expression $\pi r^2 h$, where r represents the radius and h represents the height of the drum. (Here, the cylinder is lying on its side.) If we substitute 13.5 for r and 20 for h, we obtain $\pi(13.5)^2(20)$. Using a scientific calculator, we can evaluate the expression by entering these numbers and pressing these keys.

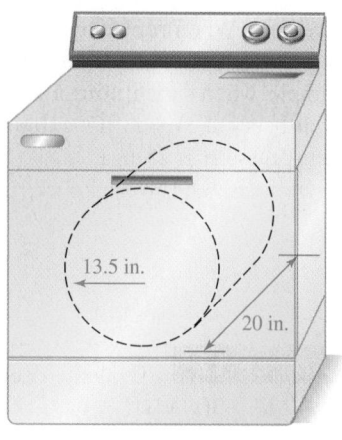

13.5 in.

20 in.

$$\boxed{\pi} \; \boxed{\times} \; 13.5 \; \boxed{x^2} \; \boxed{\times} \; 20 \; \boxed{=} \qquad\qquad \boxed{\texttt{11451.10522}}$$

Using a graphing or direct-entry calculator, we can evaluate the expression by entering these numbers and pressing these keys.

$$\boxed{\text{2nd}} \; \boxed{\pi} \; \boxed{\times} \; 13.5 \; \boxed{x^2} \; \boxed{\times} \; 20 \; \boxed{\text{ENTER}}$$

$$\boxed{\begin{array}{l} \pi * 13.5^2 * 20 \\ \qquad\qquad\qquad 11451.10522 \end{array}}$$

To the nearest cubic inch, the capacity of the dryer is 11,451 in.^{3}.

Self Check 14

In Example 14, suppose the initial velocity is 112 feet per second, so the height of the rocket is given by $112t - 16t^2$. Complete the table to find out how many seconds after launch it would hit the ground. 7 sec

t	$112t - 16t^2$
1	96
3	192
5	160
7	0

Now Try Problem 82

Teaching Example 14 Suppose the initial velocity is 160 feet per second, so the height of the rocket is given by the expression $160t - 16t^2$. Complete the table to find out how many seconds after launch it would hit the ground.

t	$160t - 16t^2$
1	144
5	400
10	0

Answer: 10 seconds

EXAMPLE 14   *Rocketry*   If a toy rocket is shot into the air with an initial velocity of 80 feet per second, its height (in feet) after t seconds in flight is given by the algebraic expression

$$80t - 16t^2$$

How many seconds after the launch will it hit the ground?

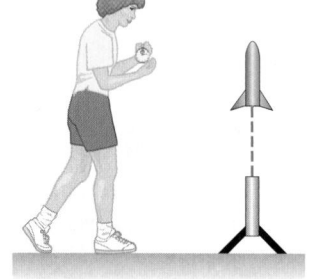

Strategy We will substitute positive values for t, the time in flight, until we find the one that gives a height of 0.

WHY When the toy rocket is on the ground, its height above the ground is 0.

Solution
We can substitute positive values for t, the time in flight, until we find the one that gives a height of 0. At that time, the rocket will be on the ground. We will begin by finding the height after the rocket has been in flight for 1 second ($t = 1$) and record the result in a table.

$$80t - 16t^2 = 80(1) - 16(1)^2 \qquad \text{Substitute 1 for } t.$$
$$= 64$$

After 1 second in flight, the height of the rocket is 64 feet. We continue to pick more values of t until we find out when the height is 0.

As we evaluate $80t - 16t^2$ for various values of t, we can show the results in a **table of values.** In the column headed "t," we list each value of the variable to be used in the evaluations. In the column headed "$80t - 16t^2$," we write the result of each evaluation.

t	$80t - 16t^2$
1	64
2	96
3	96
4	64
5	0

Evaluate for $t = 2$:
$80t - 16t^2 = 80(2) - 16(2)^2 = 96$
Evaluate for $t = 3$:
$80t - 16t^2 = 80(3) - 16(3)^2 = 96$
Evaluate for $t = 4$:
$80t - 16t^2 = 80(4) - 16(4)^2 = 64$
Evaluate for $t = 5$:
$80t - 16t^2 = 80(5) - 16(5)^2 = 0$

Since the height of the rocket is 0 when $t = 5$, the rocket will hit the ground in 5 seconds.

The two columns of a table of values are sometimes headed with the terms **input** and **output,** as shown. The t-values are the inputs into the expression $80t - 16t^2$, and the resulting values are thought of as the outputs.

Input	Output
1	64
2	96
3	96
4	64
5	0

ANSWERS TO SELF CHECKS

1. $1, -12, 3, -4$ **2. a.** factor **b.** term **3. a.** $t - 80$ **b.** $\frac{2}{3}T$ **c.** $2a - 15$
4. $m + 15$ minutes **5.** $\frac{x}{2}$ hours **6.** x = the number of calories in a serving of pears,
$2x$ = the number of calories in a candy bar **7.** s = amount donated to scholarship fund in
dollars, $900 - s$ = amount donated to building fund **8.** x = the number of votes received
by the challenger, $3x - 55$ = the number of votes received by the incumbent
9. Daughter's: x, Kayla's: $x + 5$, son's: $x + 2$ **10.** $1, 2, 3; \frac{h}{24}$ **11. a.** \$300 **b.** \$100t
c. \$1,000$(x - 4)$ **12. a.** 2 **b.** -25 **13.** $-4°F$ **14.** 7 sec (the heights are $96, 192, 160$,
and 0)

SECTION 1.8   STUDY SET

◼ VOCABULARY

Fill in the blanks.

1. To __evaluate__ an algebraic expression, we substitute the values for the variables and then apply the rules for the order of operations.

2. Variables and/or numbers can be combined with the operation symbols of addition, subtraction, multiplication, and division to create algebraic __expressions__.

3. $2x + 5$ is an example of an algebraic __expression__, whereas $2x + 5 = 7$ is an example of an __equation__.

▶ **4.** When we evaluate an algebraic expression, such as $5x - 8$, for several values of x, we can keep track of the results in an input/output __table__.

◼ CONCEPTS

5. Write two algebraic expressions that contain the variable x and the numbers 6 and 20.
$6 + 20x, \frac{6 - x}{20}$ (answers may vary)

6. a. Complete the table to determine how many days are in w weeks.

Number of weeks	Number of days
1	7
2	14
3	21
w	7w

▶ Selected exercises available online at
www.webassign.net/brookscole

b. Complete the table to answer this question: *s* seconds is how many minutes?

Number of seconds	Number of minutes
60	1
120	2
180	3
s	$\frac{s}{60}$

7. When evaluating $3x - 6$ for $x = 4$, what misunderstanding can occur if we don't write parentheses around 4 when it is substituted for the variable? We would obtain $34 - 6$; it looks like 34, not 3(4).

▶ **8.** If the knife shown is 12 inches long, write an expression for the length of the blade. $(12 - h)$ in.

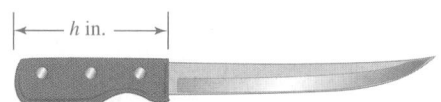

9. a. In the illustration, the weight of the van is 500 pounds less than twice the weight of the car. If the car weighs *x* pounds, write an expression that represents the weight of the van. $2x - 500$

b. If the actual weight of the car is 2,000 pounds, what is the weight of the van? 3,500 lb

▶ **10.** See the illustration.

a. If we let $b =$ the length of the beam, write an expression for the length of the pipe. $b - 15$

b. If we let $p =$ the length of the pipe, write an expression for the length of the beam. $p + 15$

15 ft

11. Complete the table.

Type of coin	Number ·	Value in cents =	Total value in cents
Nickel	6	5	30
Dime	*d*	10	10*d*
Half dollar	$x + 5$	50	$50(x + 5)$

12. If $x = -9$, find the value of

a. $-x$ 9   **b.** $-(-x)$ -9

c. $-x^2$ -81 **d.** $(-x)^2$ 81

NOTATION

Complete each evaluation.

13. Evaluate the expression $9a - a^2$ for $a = 5$.

$$9a - a^2 = 9(\boxed{5}) - (\boxed{5})^2$$
$$= 9(5) - \boxed{25}$$
$$= \boxed{45} - 25$$
$$= 20$$

▶ **14.** Evaluate $\frac{4x^2 - 3y}{9(x - y)}$ when $x = 4$ and $y = -3$.

$$\frac{4x^2 - 3\boxed{y}}{9(x - \boxed{y})} = \frac{4(4)^2 - 3(\boxed{-3})}{9[4 - (\boxed{-3})]}$$
$$= \frac{4(\boxed{16}) - 3(\boxed{-3})}{9(\boxed{7})}$$
$$= \frac{(\boxed{64}) - (\boxed{-9})}{\boxed{63}}$$
$$= \frac{73}{63}$$

GUIDED PRACTICE

Identify the coefficient of each term in the expression. **See Example 1.**

15. $4x^2 - 5x + 7$ $4, -5, 7$ ▶ **16.** $-8x^2 + 3x - 2$ $-8, 3, -2$

17. $9x^2 - 4x$ $9, -4$ **18.** $-5x^2 + 6$ $-5, 6$

Is n used as a factor or a term in each expression? **See Example 2.**

19. $n - 4$ term   **20.** $3n - 4$ factor

▶ **21.** $-5n^2 - 4n + 3$ factor   **22.** $5m^2 + n$ term

Write each phrase as an algebraic expression. If no variable is given, use x as the variable. **See Example 3.**

▶ **23.** The sum of the length *l* and 15 $l + 15$

24. The difference of a number and 10 $x - 10$

25. The product of a number and 50 $50x$

▶ **26.** Three-fourths of the population *p* $\frac{3}{4}p$

27. The ratio of the amount won *w* and lost *l* $\frac{w}{l}$

28. The tax *t* added to *c* $c + t$

29. *P* increased by *p* $P + p$

30. 21 less than the total height *h* $h - 21$

31. The square of *k* minus 2,005 $k^2 - 2,005$

▶ **32.** *s* subtracted from *S* $S - s$

33. *J* reduced by 500 $J - 500$

34. Twice the attendance *a* $2a$

35. 1,000 split *n* equal ways $\frac{1,000}{n}$

36. Exceeds the cost *c* by 25,000 $c + 25,000$

37. 90 more than the current price p $\quad p + 90$

▶ **38.** 64 divided by the cube of y $\quad \frac{64}{y^3}$

Write an algebraic expression that represents each quantity.
See Example 4.

▶ **39.** A model's skirt is x inches long. The designer then lets the hem down 2 inches. How can we express the length (in inches) of the altered skirt? $\quad (x + 2)$ in.

40. A caterer always prepares food for 10 more people than the order specifies. If p people are to attend a reception, write an expression for the number of people she should prepare for. $\quad p + 10$

41. Last year a club sold x candy bars for a fundraiser. This year they want to sell 150 more than last year. Write an expression for the number of candy bars they want to sell this year. $\quad x + 150$

▶ **42.** The tag on a new pair of 36-inch-long jeans warns that after washing, they will shrink x inches in length. Express the length (in inches) of the jeans after they are washed. $\quad (36 - x)$ in.

Write an algebraic expression that represents each quantity.
See Example 5.

43. A soft-drink manufacturer produced c cans of cola during the morning shift. Write an expression for how many six-packs of cola can be assembled from the morning shift's production. $\quad \frac{c}{6}$

44. A student has a paper to type that contains x words. If the student can type 60 words per minute, write an expression for the number of minutes it will take for her to type the paper. $\quad \frac{x}{60}$

▶ **45.** A walking path is x feet wide and is striped down the middle. Write an expression for the width of each lane of the path. $\quad \frac{x}{2}$

46. Tickets to a musical cost a total of $\$t$ for 5 tickets. Write an expression for the cost of one ticket to the musical. $\quad \frac{t}{5}$

Write an algebraic expression that represents each quantity.
See Example 6.

47. A caravan of b cars, each carrying 5 people, traveled to the state capital for a political rally. Express how many people were in the car caravan. $\quad 5b$

▶ **48.** Tickets to a circus cost $\$5$ each. Express how much tickets will cost for a family of x people if they also pay for two of their neighbors. $\quad \$5(x + 2)$

49. A rectangle is twice as long as it is wide. If the rectangle's width is w, write an expression for the length. $\quad 2w$

50. If each egg is worth e¢, express the value (in cents) of a dozen eggs. $\quad 12e$¢

Write an algebraic expression that represents each quantity.
See Examples 7–8.

51. A 12-foot board is to be cut into two pieces. Choose a variable to represent the length of one piece. Then write an expression that represents the other piece. $\quad x$ ft, $(12 - x)$ ft

52. Part of a $\$10,000$ investment is to be invested in an account paying 2% interest, and the rest in an account paying 3%. Choose a variable to represent the amount invested at 2%. Then write an expression that represents the amount invested at 3%. $\quad \$x, \$(10{,}000 - x)$

▶ **53.** The number of runners in a marathon this year is 25 more than twice the number that participated last year. Write an expression that represents the number of marathon runners this year. $\quad 2x + 25$

54. In the second year of operation, a bakery sold 31 more than three times the number of cakes it sold the first year. Write an expression that represents the number of cakes the bakery sold the second year of operation. $\quad 3x + 31$

Write an algebraic expression that represents each quantity.
See Example 9.

55. IBM was founded 80 years before Apple Computer. Dell Computer Corporation was founded 9 years after Apple.

  a. Let x represent the age (in years) of one of the companies. Write algebraic expressions to represent the ages (in years) of the other two companies.
  x = age of Apple, $x + 80$ = age of IBM, $x - 9$ = age of Dell

  b. On April 1, 2008, Apple Computer Company was 32 years old. How old were the other two companies then?
  IBM: 112 years, Dell: 23 years

▶ **56.** Abraham Lincoln was inaugurated 60 years after Thomas Jefferson. Barack Obama was inaugurated 208 years after Jefferson. Write algebraic expressions to represent the year of inauguration of each of these presidents.
Jefferson: x, Lincoln: $x + 60$, Obama $x + 208$

57. Florida became a state 27 years after Illinois. California became a state 32 years after Illinois. Write algebraic expressions to represent the year of statehood of each of these states.
Illinois: x, Florida: $x + 27$, California: $x + 32$

58. Minnesota became a state 13 years after Texas. Arizona became a state 67 years after Texas. Write algebraic expressions to represent the year of statehood of each of these states.
Texas: x, Minnesota: $x + 13$, Arizona: $x + 67$

Write an algebraic expression that represents each quantity.
See Examples 10–11.

59. How many minutes are there in

  a. 5 hours 300

  b. h hours? $60h$

▶ **60.** A woman watches television x hours a day. Express the number of hours she watches TV

  a. in a week $7x$

  b. in a year $365x$

61. a. How many feet are in y yards? $3y$

  b. How many yards are in f feet? $\frac{f}{3}$

▶ **62.** A sales clerk earns \$$x$ an hour. How much does he earn in

  a. an 8-hour day? $\$8x$

  b. a 40-hour week? $\$40x$

Evaluate each expression, for $x = 3$, $y = -2$, and $z = -4$.
See Example 12.

63. $(3 + x)y$ -12

▶ **64.** $(4 + z)y$ 0

65. $3y^2 - 6y - 4$ 20

66. $-z^2 - z - 12$ -24

67. $(4x)^2 + 3y^2$ 156

68. $4x^2 + (3y)^2$ 72

69. $(x + y)^2 - |z + y|$ -5

70. $[(z - 1)(z + 1)]^2$ 225

71. $-\dfrac{2x + y^3}{y + 2z}$ $-\frac{1}{5}$

▶ **72.** $-\dfrac{2z^2 - y}{2x - y^2}$ -17

73. $\dfrac{yz + 4x}{2z + y}$ -2

74. $\dfrac{5y + z}{z - x}$ 2

Evaluate each formula for the given values. See Example 13.

▶ **75.** $b^2 - 4ac$ for $a = -1$, $b = 5$, and $c = -2$ 17

76. $a^2 + 2ab + b^2$ for $a = -5$ and $b = -1$ 36

77. $\dfrac{n}{2}[2a + (n - 1)d]$ for $n = 10$, $a = -4$, and $d = 6$ 230

78. $\dfrac{a(1 - r^n)}{1 - r}$ for $a = -5$, $r = 2$, and $n = 3$ -35

Complete each table. See Example 14.

79.

x	$x^3 - 1$
0	-1
-1	-2
-3	-28

80.

g	$g^2 - 7g + 1$
0	1
7	1
-10	171

▶ **81.**

s	$\dfrac{5s + 36}{s}$
1	41
6	11
-12	2

82.

a	$2,500a + a^3$
2	5,008
4	10,064
-5	$-12,625$

83.

Input x	Output $2x - \dfrac{x}{2}$
100	150
-300	-450

84.

Input x	Output $\dfrac{x}{3} + \dfrac{x}{4}$
12	7
-36	-21

85.

x	$(x + 1)(x + 5)$
-1	0
-5	0
-6	5

86.

x	$\dfrac{1}{x + 8}$
-7	1
-9	-1
-8	undefined

TRY IT YOURSELF

Translate each phrase into an algebraic expression.

87. The total of 35, h, and 300 $35 + h + 300$

88. x decreased by 17 $x - 17$

▶ **89.** 680 fewer than the entire population p $p - 680$

90. Triple the number of expected participants x $3x$

91. The product of d and 4, decreased by 15 $4d - 15$

92. Forty-five more than the quotient of y and 6 $\frac{y}{6} + 45$

93. Twice the sum of 200 and t $2(200 + t)$

▶ **94.** The square of the quantity 14 less than x $(x - 14)^2$

95. The absolute value of the difference of a and 2 $|a - 2|$

▶ **96.** The absolute value of a, decreased by 2 $|a| - 2$

97. Four more than twice x $2x + 4$

98. Five less than twice w $2w - 5$

APPLICATIONS

▶ **99.** ROCKETRY The algebraic expression $64t - 16t^2$ gives the height of a toy rocket (in feet) t seconds after being launched. Find the height of the rocket for each of the times shown in the table.

t	h
0	0
1	48
2	64
3	48
4	0

100. GROWING SOD To determine the number of square feet of sod *remaining* in a field after filling an order, the manager of a sod farm uses the expression $20,000 - 3s$ (where s is the number of 1-foot-by-3-foot strips the customer has ordered). To sod a soccer field, a city orders 7,000 strips of sod. Evaluate the expression for this value of s and explain the result.
$-1,000$, the sod farm is short 1,000 ft^2 needed to fill the city's order.

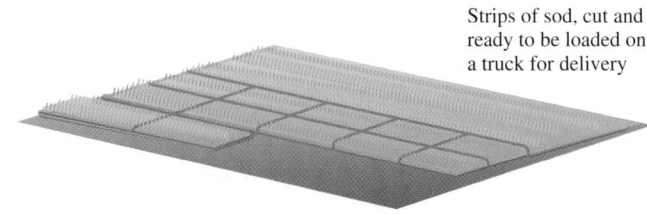

Strips of sod, cut and ready to be loaded on a truck for delivery

▶ **101. ANTIFREEZE** The expression

$$\frac{5(F - 32)}{9}$$

converts a temperature in degrees Fahrenheit (given as F) to degrees Celsius. Convert the temperatures listed on the container of antifreeze below to degrees Celsius. Round to the nearest degree. $-37°C, -64°C$

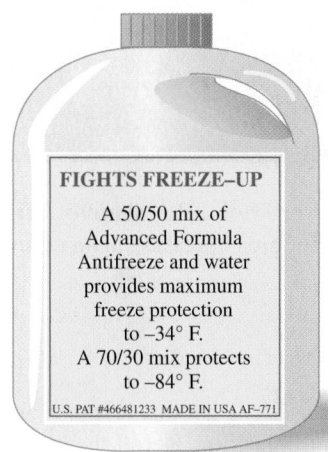

FIGHTS FREEZE–UP

A 50/50 mix of Advanced Formula Antifreeze and water provides maximum freeze protection to –34° F.
A 70/30 mix protects to –84° F.

U.S. PAT #466481233 MADE IN USA AF–771

▶ **102. TEMPERATURE ON MARS** On Mars, maximum summer temperatures can reach 20°C. However, daily temperatures average $-33°C$. Convert each of these temperatures to degrees Fahrenheit. See Example 13 (page 89). Round to the nearest degree. $68°F, -27°F$

▶ **103. TOOLS** The utility knife blade shown is in the shape of a trapezoid. Find the area of the front face of the blade. The expression $\frac{1}{2}h(b + d)$ gives the area of a trapazoid. $1\frac{23}{64}$ in.²

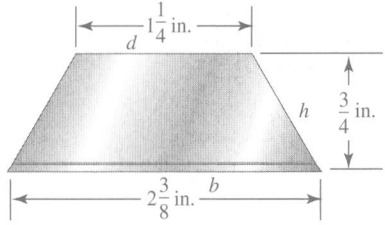

▶ **104. TRUMPET MUTES** The expression

$$\pi[b^2 + d^2 + (b + d)s]$$

can be used to find the total surface area of the trumpet mute shown. Evaluate the expression for the given dimensions to find the number of square inches of cardboard (to the nearest tenth) used to make the mute. 77.8 in.²

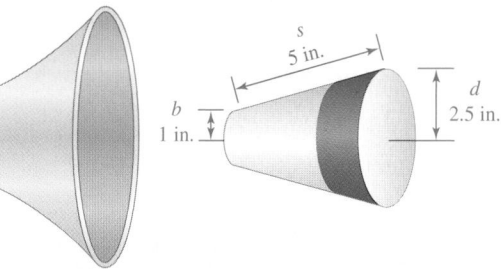

▶ **105. LANDSCAPING** A grass strip is to be planted around a tree, as shown. Find the number of square feet of sod to order by evaluating the expression $\pi(R^2 - r^2)$. Round to the nearest square foot. 235 ft²

▶ **106. ENERGY CONSERVATION** A fiberglass blanket wrapped around a water heater helps prevent heat loss. Find the number of square feet of heater surface the blanket covers by evaluating the algebraic expression $2\pi rh$, where r is the radius and h is the height. Round to the nearest square foot. 69 ft²

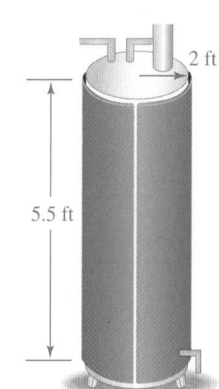

107. What is an algebraic expression? Give some examples.

108. What is a variable? How are variables used in this section?

109. In this section, we substituted a number for a variable. List some other uses of the word *substitute* that you encounter in everyday life.

▶ **110.** Explain why d dimes are not worth d cents.

REVIEW

111. Simplify: -0 0

112. Is the statement $-5 > -4$ true or false? false

113. Evaluate: $\left|-\frac{2}{3}\right|$ $\frac{2}{3}$

114. Evaluate: $2^3 \cdot 3^2$ 72

115. Write $c \cdot c \cdot c \cdot c$ in exponential form. c^4

116. Evaluate: $15 + 2[15 - (12 - 10)]$ 41

117. Find the mean (average) of the three test scores 84, 93, and 72. 83

▶ **118.** Fill in the blanks: In the multiplication statement $5 \cdot x = 5x$, 5 and x are called __factors__, and $5x$ is called the __product__.

Objectives

1 Simplify products.

2 Use the distributive property.

3 Identify like terms.

4 Combine like terms.

SECTION **1.9**

Simplifying Algebraic Expressions Using Properties of Real Numbers

In algebra, we often simplify algebraic expressions. To **simplify an algebraic expression,** we use properties of algebra to write the expression in an equivalent, less complicated form.

1 Simplify products.

Two properties that are often used to simplify algebraic expressions are the associative and commutative properties of multiplication. Recall that the associative property of multiplication enables us to change the *grouping of factors* involved in a multiplication. The commutative property of multiplication enables us to change the *order of the factors.*

As an example, let's consider the expression $8(4x)$ and simplify it as follows:

$$8(4x) = 8 \cdot (4 \cdot x) \quad \text{4x = 4 · x}$$

$$= (8 \cdot 4) \cdot x \quad \text{Use the associative property of multiplication to group 4 with 8 instead of with x.}$$

$$= 32x \quad \text{Perform the multiplication within the parentheses: 8 · 4 = 32.}$$

Since $8(4x) = 32x$, we say that $8(4x)$ simplifies to $32x$. To verify that $8(4x)$ and $32x$ are **equivalent expressions** (represent the same number), we can evaluate each expression for several choices of x. For each value of x, the results should be the same.

If $x = 10$		**If $x = -3$**	
$8(4x) = 8[4(10)]$	$32x = 32(10)$	$8(4x) = 8[4(-3)]$	$32x = 32(-3)$
$= 8(40)$	$= 320$	$= 8(-12)$	$= -96$
$= 320$		$= -96$	

Self Check 1

Simplify each expression:

a. $9 \cdot 6s$ **b.** $8\left(\frac{7}{8}h\right)$
c. $21p(-3q)$ **d.** $-4(6m)(-2m)$

EXAMPLE 1 Simplify each expression:

a. $15a(-7)$ **b.** $5\left(\frac{4}{5}x\right)$ **c.** $-5r(-6s)$ **d.** $3(7p)(-5p)$

Strategy We will use the commutative and associative properties of multiplication to reorder and regroup the factors.

WHY We want to group the numerical factors of the expression together so that we can find their product.

Solution

a. $15a(-7) = 15(-7)a$ Use the commutative property of multiplication to change the order of the factors.

$\quad\quad\quad = -105a$ Working left to right, perform the multiplications.

b. $5\left(\dfrac{4}{5}x\right) = \left(5 \cdot \dfrac{4}{5}\right)x$ Use the associative property of multiplication to group the numbers.

$\quad\quad\quad = 4x$ Multiply: $5 \cdot \dfrac{4}{5} = \dfrac{5}{1} \cdot \dfrac{4}{5} = \dfrac{\overset{1}{\cancel{5}} \cdot 4}{1 \cdot \cancel{5}} = 4.$

c. We note that the expression contains two variables.

$-5r(-6s) = [-5(-6)][r \cdot s]$ Use the commutative and associative properties of multiplication to group the numbers and group the variables.

$\quad\quad\quad = 30rs$ Perform the multiplications within the brackets: $-5(-6) = 30$ and $r \cdot s = rs.$

d. $3(7p)(-5p) = [3(7)(-5)](p \cdot p)$ Use the commutative and associative properties of multiplication to change the order and to regroup the factors.

$\quad\quad\quad = -105p^2$ Perform the multiplication within the grouping symbols: $3(7)(-5) = -105$ and $p \cdot p = p^2.$ ■

> **Success Tip** By the commutative property of multiplication, we can change the order of the factors.

Now Try **Problem 33**
Self Check 1 Answers
a. $54s$ **b.** $7h$ **c.** $-63pq$ **d.** $48m^2$

Teaching Example 1 Simplify each expression:
a. $3 \cdot 4x$
b. $\frac{1}{2}(6x)$
c. $5x(-2y)$
d. $-3(-4x)(2y)$
Answers:
a. $12x$ **b.** $3x$
c. $-10xy$ **d.** $24xy$

2 Use the distributive property.

To introduce the **distributive property,** we will consider the expression $4(5 + 3)$, which can be evaluated in two ways.

Method 1. Rules for the order of operations: We compute the sum within the parentheses first.

$\quad 4(5 + 3) = 4(8)$ Perform the addition within the parentheses first.

$\quad\quad\quad = 32$ Perform the multiplication.

Method 2. The distributive property: We multiply both 5 and 3 by 4, and then we add the results.

$\quad 4(5 + 3) = 4(5) + 4(3)$ Distribute the multiplication by 4.

$\quad\quad\quad = 20 + 12$ Perform the multiplications.

$\quad\quad\quad = 32$ Perform the addition.

Notice that each method gives a result of 32.

We can interpret the distributive property geometrically. The figure on the next page shows three rectangles that are divided into squares. Since the area of the rectangle on the left-hand side of the equals sign can be found by multiplying its width by its length, its area is $4(5 + 3)$ square units. We can evaluate this expression, or we can count squares; either way, we see that the area is 32 square units.

The area shown on the right-hand side is the sum of the areas of two rectangles: $4(5) + 4(3)$. Either by evaluating this expression or by counting squares, we see that this area is also 32 square units. Therefore,

$$4(5 + 3) = 4(5) + 4(3)$$

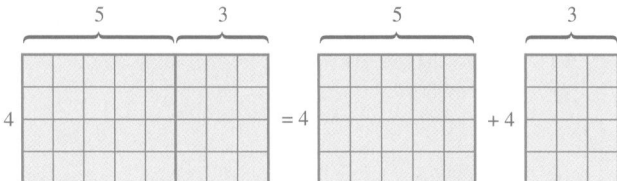

The following figure shows the general case where the width is a and the length is $b + c$.

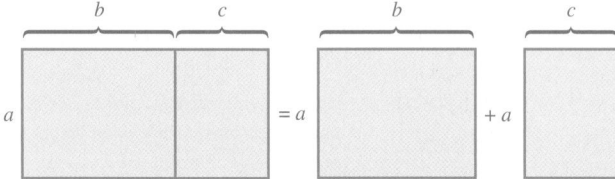

Using the figure as a basis, we can now state the distributive property in symbols.

The Distributive Property

For any real numbers, a, b, and c,

$$a(b + c) = ab + ac$$

Since subtraction is the same as adding the opposite, the distributive property also holds for subtraction.

The Distributive Property

For any real numbers, a, b, and c,

$$a(b - c) = ab - ac$$

To illustrate one use of the distributive property, let's consider the expression $5(x + 2)$. Since we are not given the value of x, we cannot add x and 2 within the parentheses. However, we can distribute the multiplication by the factor of 5 that is outside the parentheses to x and to 2 and add those products.

$$5(x + 2) = 5(x) + 5(2) \qquad \text{Distribute the multiplication by 5.}$$
$$= 5x + 10 \qquad \text{Perform the multiplications.}$$

Caution!   Since the expression $5(x + 2)$ contains parentheses, some students are tempted to perform the addition within the parentheses first. However, we cannot add x and 2, because we do not know the value of x. Instead, we should multiply $x + 2$ by 5, which requires the use of the distributive property.

EXAMPLE 2   Multiply: **a.** $3(x - 8)$ **b.** $-12(a + 1)$ **c.** $-6(-3y - 8)$

Strategy We will use the distributive property to multiply each term within the parentheses by the factor outside the parentheses.

WHY In each case, we cannot simplify the expression within the parentheses.

Solution

a. $3(x - 8) = 3(x) - 3(8)$ Distribute the multiplication by 3.

   $\qquad\qquad = 3x - 24$ Perform the multiplications.

b. $-12(a + 1) = -12(a) + (-12)(1)$ Distribute the multiplication by -12.

   $\qquad\qquad\quad = -12a + (-12)$ Perform the multiplications.

   $\qquad\qquad\quad = -12a - 12$ Write the addition of -12 as subtraction of 12.

c. $-6(-3y - 8) = -6(-3y) - (-6)(8)$ Distribute the multiplication by -6.

   $\qquad\qquad\quad = 18y - (-48)$ Perform the multiplications.

   $\qquad\qquad\quad = 18y + 48$ Add the opposite of -48, which is 48.

Caution! A common mistake is to forget to distribute the multiplication over each of the terms within the parentheses.

$3(3b - 4) = 9b - 4$

Caution! The fact that an expression contains parentheses does not necessarily mean that the distributive property can be applied. For example, the distributive property does not apply to the expressions:

$6(5x)$ or $6(-7 \cdot y)$ Here a product is multiplied by 6. Simplifying, we have $6(5x) = 30x$ and $6(-7 \cdot y) = -42y$.

However, the distributive property does apply to the expressions:

$6(5 + x)$ or $6(-7 - y)$ Here a sum and a difference are multiplied by 6. Distributing the 6, we have $6(5 + x) = 30 + 6x$ and $6(-7 - y) = -42 - 6y$.

To use the distributive property to simplify $-(x + 10)$, we note that the negative sign in front of the parentheses represents -1.

The $-$ sign represents -1.

$-(x + 10) = -1(x + 10)$

$\qquad\quad = -1(x) + (-1)(10)$ Distribute the multiplication by -1.

$\qquad\quad = -x + (-10)$ Multiply: $-1(x) = -x$ and $(-1)(10) = -10$.

$\qquad\quad = -x - 10$ Write the addition of -10 as a subtraction.

EXAMPLE 3   Simplify: $-(-12 - 3p)$

Strategy We will use the distributive property to multiply each term within the parentheses by -1.

WHY The "$-$" symbol outside the parentheses represents a factor of -1.

Self Check 2

Multiply:

a. $5(p + 2)$ $5p + 10$

b. $4(t - 1)$ $4t - 4$

c. $-8(2x - 4)$ $-16x + 32$

Now Try Problem 39

Teaching Example 2 Multiply:
a. $7(a - 2)$ **b.** $-5(m + 7)$
c. $-4(2x - 5)$
Answers:
a. $7a - 14$ **b.** $-5m - 35$
c. $-8x + 20$

Self Check 3

Simplify: $-(-5x + 18)$ $5x - 18$
Now Try Problem 49

Teaching Example 3 Simplify:
$-(-4a - 5)$
Answer: $4a + 5$

Solution

$-(-12 - 3p)$

$$
\begin{aligned}
&= -\mathbf{1}(-12 - 3p) && \text{Change the } - \text{ sign in front of the parentheses to } -1.\\
&= -\mathbf{1}(-12) - (-\mathbf{1})(3p) && \text{Distribute the multiplication by } -1.\\
&= 12 - (-3p) && \text{Multiply: } -1(-12) = 12 \text{ and } (-1)(3p) = -3p.\\
&= 12 + 3p && \text{To subtract } -3p, \text{ add the opposite of } -3p, \text{ which}\\
&&& \text{is } 3p.
\end{aligned}
$$

> **Success Tip**   Notice that distributing the multiplication by -1 changes the sign of each term within the parentheses.

Since multiplication is commutative, we can write the distributive property in the following forms.

$$(b + c)a = ba + ca \qquad\qquad (b - c)a = ba - ca$$

Self Check 4

Multiply: $(-6x - 24y)\dfrac{1}{3}$

Now Try   Problem 54

Self Check 4 Answers

$-2x - 8y$

Teaching Example 4 Multiply:
$(4x - 3)(2)$
Answer:
$8x - 6$

EXAMPLE 4   Multiply: $(6x + 4y)\dfrac{1}{2}$

Strategy We will use the distributive property to multiply each term within the parentheses by the factor outside the parentheses.

WHY In each case, we cannot simplify the expression within the parentheses.

Solution

$$
(6x + 4y)\frac{1}{2} = (6x)\frac{1}{2} + (4y)\frac{1}{2} \qquad \text{Distribute the multiplication by } \tfrac{1}{2}.
$$

$$
= 3x + 2y \qquad\qquad \text{Multiply: } (6x)\tfrac{1}{2} = \left(6 \cdot \tfrac{1}{2}\right)x = 3x \text{ and}
$$
$$
(4y)\tfrac{1}{2} = \left(4 \cdot \tfrac{1}{2}\right)y = 2y.
$$

The distributive property can be extended to situations in which there are more than two terms within parentheses.

> ### The Extended Distributive Property
>
> For any real numbers, a, b, and c,
>
> $$a(b + c + d) = ab + ac + ad \quad \text{and} \quad a(b - c - d) = ab - ac - ad$$

Self Check 5

Multiply: $-0.7(2r + 5s - 8)$

Now Try   Problem 57

Self Check 5 Answers

$-1.4r - 3.5s + 5.6$

Teaching Example 5 Multiply:
$-0.4(3m - 2n + 5)$
Answer:
$-1.2m + 0.8n - 2$

EXAMPLE 5   Multiply: $-0.3(3a - 4b + 7)$

Strategy We will use the distributive property to multiply each term within the parentheses by the factor outside the parentheses.

WHY We cannot simplify the expression within the parentheses.

Solution

$-0.3(3a - 4b + 7)$

$$
= -\mathbf{0.3}(3a) - (-\mathbf{0.3})(4b) + (-\mathbf{0.3})(7) \qquad \text{Distribute the multiplication by } -0.3.
$$

$$
= -0.9a - (-1.2b) + (-2.1) \qquad\qquad \text{Perform the three multiplications.}
$$

$$= -0.9a + 1.2b + (-2.1)$$

To substract $-1.2b$, add its opposite, which is $1.2b$.

$$= -0.9a + 1.2b - 2.1$$

Write the addition of -2.1 as a subtraction.

3 Identify like terms.

The expression $5p + 7q - 3p + 12$, which can be written $5p + 7q + (-3p) + 12$, contains four terms, $5p$, $7q$, $-3p$, and 12. Since the variable of $5p$ and $-3p$ are the same, we say that these terms are **like** or **similar terms.**

Like Terms (Similar Terms)

Like terms (or **similar terms**) are terms with exactly the same variables raised to exactly the same powers. Any numbers (called **constants**) in an expression are considered to be like terms.

Like terms	**Unlike terms**
$4x$ and $7x$	$4x$ and $3y$
↓ ↓	↓ ↓
Same variable	Different variables
$-10p^2$, $25p^2$, and $150p^2$	$15p$ and $23p^2$
Same variable to the same power	Different exponents on the variable p

---

Caution!   It is important to be able to distinguish between a *term* of an expression and a *factor* of a term. Terms are separated by + symbols. Factors are numbers and/or variables that are multiplied together. For example, x is a term of the expression $18 + x$, because x and 18 are separated by a + symbol. In the expression $18x + 9$, x is a factor of the term $18x$, because x and 18 are multiplied together.

EXAMPLE 6   List like terms:
a. $7r + 5 + 3r$ **b.** $x^4 - 6x^2 - 5$ **c.** $-7m + 7 - 2 + m$

Strategy First we will identify each term of the expression. Then we will look for terms that contain the same variable factors raised to exactly the same powers.

WHY If terms contain the same variables raised to the same powers, they are like terms.

Solution

a. $7r + 5 + 3r$ contains the like terms $7r$ and $3r$.

b. $x^4 - 6x^2 - 5$ contains no like terms.

c. $-7m + 7 - 2 + m$ contains two pairs of like terms: $-7m$ and m are like terms, and the constants, 7 and -2, are like terms.

4 Combine like terms.

To add (or subtract) objects, they must have the same units. For example, we can add dollars to dollars and inches to inches, but we cannot add dollars to inches. The same is true when we work with terms of an algebraic expression. They can be added or subtracted only when they are like terms.

This expression can be simplified, because it contains like terms.

$$3x + 4x$$

Like terms
The variable parts are identical.

This expression cannot be simplified, because its terms are not like terms.

$$3x + 4y$$

Unlike terms
The variable parts are not identical.

To simplify an expression containing like terms, we use the distributive property. For example, we can simplify $3x + 4x$ as follows:

$$3x + 4x = (3 + 4)x \qquad \text{Use the distributive property.}$$
$$= 7x \qquad\qquad \text{Perform the addition within the parentheses: } 3 + 4 = 7.$$

We have simplified the expression $3x + 4x$ by **combining like terms.** The result is the equivalent expression $7x$. This example suggests the following general rule.

Combining Like Terms

To add or subtract like terms, combine their coefficients and keep the same variables with the same exponents.

Self Check 7

Simplify by combining like terms:
a. $5n + (-8n)$ $-3n$
b. $-1.2a^3 + 1.4a^3$ $0.2a^3$

Now Try **Problem 65**

Teaching Example 7 Simplify by combining like terms:
a. $-3x - 5x$
b. $2x^3 + 5x^3$
Answers:
a. $-8x$
b. $7x^3$

EXAMPLE 7   Simplify by combining like terms:
a. $-8p + (-12p)$ **b.** $0.5s^2 - 0.3s^2$

Strategy We will use the distributive property in reverse to add (or subtract) the coefficients of the like terms. We will keep the variable factors raised to the same powers.

WHY To *combine like terms* means to add or subtract the like terms in an expression.

Solution

a. $-8p + (-12p) = -20p$ Add the coefficients of the like terms: $-8 + (-12) = -20$. Keep the variable p.

b. $0.5s^2 - 0.3s^2 = 0.2s^2$ Subtract: $0.5 - 0.3 = 0.2$. Keep the variable part s^2.

Self Check 8

Simplify: $8R + 7r - 14R - 21r$

Now Try **Problem 71**
Self Check 8 Answers
$-6R - 14r$

Teaching Example 8 Simplify:
$5D + 3d - 7D + d$
Answer:
$-2D + 4d$

EXAMPLE 8   Simplify: $7P - 8p - 12P + 25p$

Strategy We will use the commutative property of addition to write the like terms next to each other. Keep in mind that an uppercase P and a lower case p are different variables.

WHY To *simplify* an expression we use properties of real numbers to write an equivalent expression in simpler form.

Solution
The uppercase P and the lowercase p are different variables. We can use the commutative property of addition to write like terms next to each other.

$$7P - 8p - 12P + 25p$$
$$= 7P + (-8p) + (-12P) + 25p \qquad \text{Rewrite each subtraction as the addition of the opposite.}$$
$$= 7P + (-12P) + (-8p) + 25p \qquad \text{Use the commutative property of addition to write the like terms together.}$$
$$= -5P + 17p \qquad\qquad \text{Combine like terms: } 7P + (-12P) = -5P \text{ and } -8p + 25p = 17p.$$

The expression in Example 8 contained two sets of like terms, and we rearranged the terms so that like terms were next to each other. With practice, you will be able to combine like terms without having to write them next to each other.

EXAMPLE 9 Simplify: $4(x + 5) - 3(2x - 4)$

Strategy First we will use the distributive property to remove the parentheses. Then we will identify any like terms and combine them.

WHY To *simplify* an expression we use properties of real numbers, such as the distributive property, to write an equivalent expression in simpler form.

Solution

$4(x + 5) - 3(2x - 4)$

$= 4x + 20 - 6x + 12$ Use the distributive property twice.

$= -2x + 32$ Combine like terms: $4x - 6x = -2x$ and $20 + 12 = 32$.

ANSWERS TO SELF CHECKS

1. a. $54s$ **b.** $7h$ **c.** $-63pq$ **d.** $48m^2$ **2. a.** $5p + 10$ **b.** $4t - 4$ **c.** $-16x + 32$
3. $5x - 18$ **4.** $-2x - 8y$ **5.** $-1.4r - 3.5s + 5.6$ **6. a.** $-2y$ and $7y$
b. $-5pq$ and $-2pq$ **7. a.** $-3n$ **b.** $0.2a^3$ **8.** $-6R - 14r$ **9.** $3y + 32$

SECTION 1.9 STUDY SET

VOCABULARY

Fill in the blanks.

1. To __simplify__ the expression $5(6x)$ means to write it in the simpler form $5(6x) = 30x$.

2. $5(6x)$ and $30x$ are __equivalent__ expressions because for each value of x, they represent the same number.

▶ 3. To perform the multiplication $2(x + 8)$, we use the __distributive__ property to remove parentheses.

4. Terms such as $7x^2$ and $5x^2$, which have the same variables raised to exactly the same powers, are called __like__ terms.

CONCEPTS

5. What property does the equation $a(b + c) = ab + ac$ illustrate? *distributive property*

6. The illustration shows an application of the distributive property. Fill in the blanks.

$2\left(\boxed{3} + \boxed{4} \right) = 2\left(\boxed{3} \right) + 2\left(\boxed{4} \right)$

$2(3 + 4)$ = $2(3)$ + $2(4)$

Fill in the blanks.

7. $a(b + c + d) = $ __$ab + ac + ad$__

8. **a.** $2(x + 4) = 2x \boxed{+} 8$
   b. $2(x - 4) = 2x \boxed{-} 8$

9. **a.** $2(-x + 4) = -2x \boxed{+} 8$
   b. $2(-x - 4) = -2x \boxed{-} 8$

10. **a.** $-2(x + 4) = -2x \boxed{-} 8$
    b. $-2(x - 4) = -2x \boxed{+} 8$

11. **a.** $-2(-x + 4) = 2x \boxed{-} 8$
    b. $-2(-x - 4) = 2x \boxed{+} 8$

▶ 12. To add or subtract like terms, combine their __coefficients__ and keep the same variables and __exponents__.

13. A board was cut into two pieces, as shown. Add the lengths of the two pieces. How long was the original board? $x + 20 - x = 20, 20$ ft

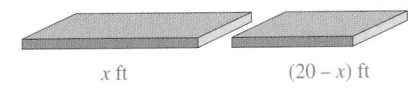

x ft $(20 - x)$ ft

---

14. Let x = the number of miles driven on the first day of a 2-day driving trip. Translate the verbal model to mathematical symbols, and simplify by combining like terms. $x + x + 100 = 2x + 100$

The miles driven one day	plus	100 miles more than the miles driven on day 1.

15. Two angles are called **complementary angles** when the sum of their measures is 90°. Add the measures of the angles in illustration (a). Are they complementary angles? yes

16. Two angles are called **supplementary angles** if the sum of their measures is 180°. Add the measures of the angles in illustration (b). Are they supplementary angles? yes

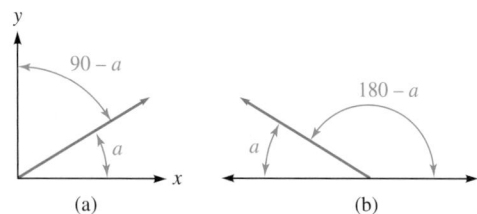

(a)   (b)

All angle measures are in degrees.

Simplify each expression, if possible.

▶ **17.** $5(2x)$ and $5 + 2x$ $10x$, can't be simplified

▶ **18.** $6(-7x)$ and $6 - 7x$ $-42x$, can't be simplified

▶ **19.** $2(3x)(3)$ and $2 + 3x + 3$ $18x, 3x + 5$

▶ **20.** $-3(2x)(4)$ and $5 - 3x + 2$ $-24x, -3x + 7$

NOTATION

Complete each solution.

21. $7(a + 2) = \boxed{7} \cdot a + \boxed{7} \cdot 2$
$= 7a + \boxed{14}$

22. $6(b - 5) + 12b + 7 = 6\left(\boxed{b}\right) - 6\left(\boxed{5}\right) + 12b + 7$
$= 6b - \boxed{30} + 12b + 7$
$= 6b + \boxed{12}b - \boxed{30} + 7$
$= \boxed{18}b - 23$

23. a. Are $2K$ and $3k$ like terms? no

b. Are $-d$ and d like terms? yes

24. Fill in the blank: $-(x + 10) = -\boxed{1}(x + 10)$

25. Write each expression using fewer symbols.

a. $5x - (-1)$ $5x + 1$ **b.** $16t + (-6)$ $16t - 6$

26. In the table in the next column, a student's answers to five problems are compared to the answers in the back of the book. Are the answers equivalent?

Student's answer	Book's answer	Equivalent?
$10x$	$10 + x$	no
$3 + y$	$y + 3$	yes
$5 - 8a$	$8a - 5$	no
$3(x) + 4$	$3(x + 4)$	no
$2x$	x^2	no

GUIDED PRACTICE

Simplify each expression. **See Example 1.**

27. $9(7m)$ $63m$

28. $12n(8)$ $96n$

29. $5(-7q)$ $-35q$

▶ **30.** $-7(5t)$ $-35t$

31. $12\left(\dfrac{5}{12}x\right)$ $5x$

32. $15\left(-\dfrac{4}{15}w\right)$ $-4w$

33. $(-5p)(-4b)$ $20bp$

▶ **34.** $(-7d)(-7c)$ $49cd$

35. $-5(4r)(-2r)$ $40r^2$

36. $7t(-4t)(-2)$ $56t^2$

37. $8q(-2q)(-3)$ $48q^2$

38. $-3m(-5m)(-2m)$ $-30m^3$

Multiply. **See Example 2.**

39. $5(x + 3)$ $5x + 15$

▶ **40.** $4(x + 2)$ $4x + 8$

▶ **41.** $-2(b - 1)$ $-2b + 2$

▶ **42.** $-7(p - 5)$ $-7p + 35$

43. $8(3t - 2)$ $24t - 16$

44. $9(2q + 1)$ $18q + 9$

45. $3(-5t - 4)$ $-15t - 12$

▶ **46.** $2(5x - 4)$ $10x - 8$

Multiply. **See Example 3.**

47. $-(r - 10)$ $-r + 10$

48. $-(h + 4)$ $-h - 4$

49. $-(x - 7)$ $-x + 7$

▶ **50.** $-(y + 1)$ $-y - 1$

Multiply. **See Example 4.**

51. $(3w - 6)\left(-\dfrac{2}{3}\right)$ $-2w + 4$

52. $(2y - 8)\dfrac{1}{2}$ $y - 4$

53. $(9x - 3y)\dfrac{2}{3}$ $6x - 2y$

▶ **54.** $(4p + 3q)\dfrac{3}{4}$ $3p + \dfrac{9}{4}q$

Multiply. **See Example 5.**

55. $17(2x - y + 2)$ $34x - 17y + 34$

▶ **56.** $-12(3a + 2b - 1)$ $-36a - 24b + 12$

57. $-0.1(-14 + 3p - t)$ $1.4 - 0.3p + 0.1t$

58. $-1.5(-x - y + 5)$ $1.5x + 1.5y - 7.5$

List all like terms, if any. **See Example 6.**

59. $8p + 7 - 5p$ $8p, -5p$

▶ **60.** $-7m - 3m + 5m$ $-7m, -3m, 5m$

61. $a^4 + 5a^2 - 7$ no like terms

62. $6q^2 + 3q - 5q^2 - 2q$ $6q^2$ and $-5q^2$, $3q$ and $-2q$

Simplify each expression by combining like terms. See Example 7.

63. $3x + 17x$ $20x$
64. $12y - 15y$ $-3y$
65. $8x^2 - 5x^2$ $3x^2$
66. $17x^2 + 3x^2$ $20x^2$
67. $-4x + 4x$ 0
68. $-16y + 16y$ 0
69. $-7b + 7b$ 0
70. $-2c + 2c$ 0

Simplify each expression by combining like terms. See Example 8.

71. $1.8h - 0.7h + p - 3p$ $1.1h - 2p$
72. $-5.7m + 4.3m + 3n - 1.2n$ $-1.4m + 1.8n$
73. $a + a + b$ $2a + b$
74. $-t - t - T - T$ $-2t - 2T$
75. $3x + 5x - 7x + 3y$ $x + 3y$
76. $-x + 3y + 2y$ $-x + 5y$
77. $-13x^2 + 2x^2 - 5y^2 + 2y^2$ $-11x^2 - 3y^2$
78. $-8x^3 - x^3 + 3y + 5y$ $-9x^3 + 8y$

Simplify each expression by combining like terms. See Example 9.

79. $(a + 2) - (a - b)$
$b + 2$
80. $3z + 2(Z - z) + Z$
$3Z + z$
81. $x(x + 3) - 3x^2$
$-2x^2 + 3x$
82. $2x + x(x - 3)$
$x^2 - x$
83. $-(c + 7) - 2(c - 3)$
$-3c - 1$
84. $-(z + 2) + 5(3 - z)$
$-6z + 13$
85. $-(c - 6) + 3(c + 1)$
$2c + 9$
86. $-2(m - 1) - 4(-2 + m)$
$-6m + 10$

TRY IT YOURSELF

Simplify.

87. $0.4(x - 4)$ $0.4x - 1.6$
88. $-2.2(2q + 1)$ $-4.4q - 2.2$
89. $2x + 4(X - x) + 3X$ $7X - 2x$
90. $3p - 6(p + z) + p$ $-2p - 6z$
91. $0 - 3x$ $-3x$
92. $0 - 4a$ $-4a$
93. $0 - (-t)$ t
94. $0 - (-2y)$ $2y$
95. $\dfrac{3}{5}t + \dfrac{1}{5}t$ $\dfrac{4}{5}t$
96. $\dfrac{3}{16}x - \dfrac{5}{16}x$ $-\dfrac{1}{8}x$
97. $(2y - 1)6$ $12y - 6$
98. $(3w - 5)5$ $15w - 25$
99. $3(y - 3) + 4(y + 1)$ $7y - 5$
100. $-5(a - 2) - 4(a + 1)$ $-9a + 6$
101. $8\left(\dfrac{3}{4}y\right)$ $6y$
102. $27\left(\dfrac{2}{3}x\right)$ $18x$
103. $-0.2r - (-0.6r)$ $0.4r$
104. $-1.1m - (-2.4m)$ $1.3m$
105. $2z + 5(z - 3)$ $7z - 15$
106. $12(m + 11) - 11$ $12m + 121$

APPLICATIONS

107. THE AMERICAN RED CROSS In 1891, Clara Barton founded the Red Cross. Its symbol is a white flag bearing a red cross. If each side of the cross in the illustration has length x, write an algebraic expression for the perimeter (the total distance around the outside) of the cross. $12x$

108. BILLIARDS Billiard tables vary in size, but all tables are twice as long as they are wide.

   a. If the following billiard table is x feet wide, write an expression involving x that represents its length. $2x$ ft

   b. Write an expression for the perimeter of the table. $6x$ ft

x ft

109. PING-PONG Write an expression for the perimeter of the table shown in the illustration. $(4x + 8)$ ft

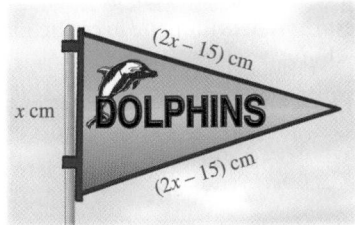

x ft $(x + 4)$ ft

110. SEWING Write an expression for the length of the blue trim needed to outline a pennant with the given side lengths. $(5x - 30)$ cm

$(2x - 15)$ cm

x cm   **DOLPHINS**

$(2x - 15)$ cm

WRITING

111. Explain why the distributive property applies to $2(3 + x)$ but not to $2(3x)$.

112. Explain why $3x^2y$ and $5x^2y$ are like terms, and explain why $3x^2y$ and $5xy^2$ are not like terms.

113. Distinguish between a *factor* and a *term* of an algebraic expression. Give examples.

▶ **114.** Describe how to combine like terms.

Teaching Guide: Refer to the Instructor's Resource Binder to find activities, worksheets on key concepts, more examples, instruction tips, overheads, and assessments.

REVIEW

Evaluate each expression for $x = -3$, $y = -5$, and $z = 0$.

115. $x^2z(y^3 - z)$　0

▶ **116.** $|y^3 - z|$　125

117. $\dfrac{x - y^2}{2y - 1 + x}$　2

118. $\dfrac{2y + 1}{x} - x$　6

CHAPTER 1　SUMMARY AND REVIEW

SECTION 1.1　The Language of Algebra

DEFINITIONS AND CONCEPTS	EXAMPLES
Tables, bar graphs, and **line graphs** are used to describe numerical relationships.	See pages 2–3 for examples of tables and graphs.
The result of an addition is called a **sum.** The result of a subtraction is called a **difference.** The result of a multiplication is called a **product.** The result of a division is called a **quotient.**	$6 + 12 = 18$ Sum $21 - 17 = 4$ Difference $8 \times 13 = 104$ Product $\dfrac{35}{7} = 5$ Quotient
An **equation** is a mathematical sentence that contains an $=$ symbol. **Variables** are letters used to stand for numbers. Variables and/or numbers can be combined with the operations of arithmetic to create **algebraic expressions.** Equations that express a known relationship between two or more variables are called **formulas.**	Equations: $3x + 4 = 12$ and $\frac{t}{9} = 12$ Variables: x, a, and y Expressions: $5y + 2$, $\frac{12x}{5}$, and $a(b - 3)$ Formula: $A = lw$ (The formula for the area of a rectangle)

REVIEW EXERCISES

Consider the following line graph that shows the number of cars parked in a mall parking structure from 6 P.M. to 12 midnight on a Saturday.

1. How many cars were in the parking structure at 11 P.M.? 100

2. At what time did the parking structure have 500 cars in it? 7 P.M.

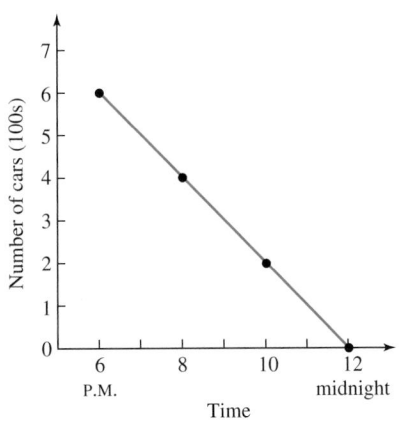

Express each statement in words.

3. $15 - 3 = 12$
The difference of 15 and 3 is 12.

4. $15 + 3 = 18$
The sum of 15 and 3 is 18.

5. $15 \div 3 = 5$
The quotient of 15 and 3 is 5.

6. $15 \cdot 3 = 45$
The product of 15 and 3 is 45.

Classify each item as either an algebraic expression or an equation.

7. $5 = 2x + 3$
equation

8. $2x + 3$
algebraic expression

9. $\dfrac{t + 6}{12}$
algebraic expression

10. $P = 2l + 2w$
equation

11. Use the formula $n = b + 5$ to complete the table.

Number of brackets (b)	Number of nails (n)
5	10
10	15
20	25

12. Use the data in the table to write a formula that mathematically describes the relationship between the two quantities, then state the relationship in words.

$f = 50c$, the total fees are the product of 50 and the number of children. (Answers may vary depending on the variables chosen.)

Number of children	Total fees (dollars)
1	50
2	100
4	200

SECTION 1.2   Fractions

DEFINITIONS AND CONCEPTS	EXAMPLES
A **prime number** is a natural number greater than 1 that is only divisible by itself and 1.	Prime numbers: $\{2, 3, 5, 7, 11, 13, 17, \ldots\}$
A **composite number** is a natural number greater than 1 that is not prime.	Composite numbers: $\{4, 6, 8, 9, 10, 12, 14, 15, \ldots\}$
Every composite number can be factored as a product of two or more prime numbers.	$15 = 3 \cdot 5, \quad 35 = 5 \cdot 7, \quad 30 = 2 \cdot 3 \cdot 5$
To **multiply two fractions,** multiply their numerators and multiply their denominators.	Multiply: $\dfrac{5}{8} \cdot \dfrac{3}{4} = \dfrac{15}{32}$
One number is the **reciprocal** of another if their product is 1.	The reciprocal of $\dfrac{7}{11}$ is $\dfrac{11}{7}$ because $\dfrac{7}{11} \cdot \dfrac{11}{7} = 1$.
To **divide two fractions,** multiply the first fraction by the reciprocal of the second fraction.	Divide: $\dfrac{4}{7} \div \dfrac{5}{8} = \dfrac{4}{7} \cdot \dfrac{8}{5} = \dfrac{32}{35}$
Multiplication property of 1: the product of 1 and any number is that number.	$1 \cdot 9 = 9 \quad$ and $\quad \dfrac{4}{7} \cdot 1 = \dfrac{4}{7}$

To **build a fraction,** multiply it by a form of 1 such as $\dfrac{2}{2}, \dfrac{3}{3}, \dfrac{4}{4}, \cdots$	Write $\dfrac{3}{7}$ as an equivalent fraction with a denominator of 35. $\dfrac{3}{7} = \dfrac{3}{7} \cdot \dfrac{5}{5} = \dfrac{15}{35}$
To **simplify a fraction,** remove pairs of factors common to the numerator and the denominator. A fraction is in **simplest form,** or **lowest terms,** when the numerator and denominator have no common factors other than 1.	Simplify: $\dfrac{39}{52} = \dfrac{3 \cdot \overset{1}{\cancel{13}}}{4 \cdot \cancel{13}} = \dfrac{3}{4} \quad \frac{13}{13} = 1$ ${\scriptstyle 1}$
To find the **least common denominator (LCD)** of two fractions, prime factor each denominator and find the product of the prime factors, using each factor the greatest number of times it appears in any one factorization.	Find the LCD of $\dfrac{2}{9}$ and $\dfrac{5}{6}$. $\left.\begin{array}{l} 9 = 3 \cdot 3 \\ 6 = 2 \cdot 3 \end{array}\right\} \text{LCD} = \mathbf{2 \cdot 3 \cdot 3}$
To **add (or subtract) fractions with the same denominator,** add (or subtract) the numerators and keep the common denominator. To **add (or subtract) fractions with unlike denominators,** write each fraction as an equivalent fraction with a denominator that is the LCD. Then add (or subtract) the numerators and keep the common denominator.	Add: $\dfrac{5}{12} + \dfrac{7}{8} = \dfrac{5}{12} \cdot \dfrac{2}{2} + \dfrac{7}{8} \cdot \dfrac{3}{3}$ *The LCD is 24. Build each fraction.* $ = \dfrac{10}{24} + \dfrac{21}{24}$ *The denominators are now the same.* $ = \dfrac{31}{24}$ *The result does not simplify.*

REVIEW EXERCISES

13. Write 24 as the product of two factors. $2 \cdot 12, 3 \cdot 8$
(answers may vary)

14. Write 24 as the product of three factors. $2 \cdot 2 \cdot 6$
(answers may vary)

Give the prime factorization of each number, if possible.

15. 54 $2 \cdot 3^3$

16. 147 $3 \cdot 7^2$

17. 385 $5 \cdot 7 \cdot 11$

18. 41 prime

Simplify each fraction to lowest terms.

19. $\dfrac{20}{35}$ $\dfrac{4}{7}$

20. $\dfrac{24}{18}$ $\dfrac{4}{3}$

Build each fraction or whole number to an equivalent fraction with the indicated denominator.

21. $\dfrac{5}{8}$, denominator 64 $\dfrac{40}{64}$

22. 12, denominator 3 $\dfrac{36}{3}$

Perform each operation.

23. $\dfrac{16}{35} \cdot \dfrac{25}{48}$ $\dfrac{5}{21}$

24. $5\dfrac{3}{5}\left(1\dfrac{11}{14}\right)$ 10

25. $\dfrac{1}{3} \div \dfrac{15}{16}$ $\dfrac{16}{45}$

26. $16\dfrac{1}{4} \div 5$ $3\dfrac{1}{4}$

27. $\dfrac{17}{25} - \dfrac{7}{25}$ $\dfrac{2}{5}$

28. $\dfrac{17}{12} + \dfrac{7}{12}$ 2

29. MACHINE SHOPS How much must be milled off the $\dfrac{17}{24}$-inch-thick steel rod so that the collar will slip over it? $\dfrac{17}{96}$ in.

$\dfrac{17}{32}$ in.

$\dfrac{17}{24}$ in.

Steel rod

Perform each operation.

30. $\dfrac{8}{11} - \dfrac{1}{2}$ $\dfrac{5}{22}$

31. $\dfrac{1}{4} + \dfrac{2}{3}$ $\dfrac{11}{12}$

32. $61\dfrac{7}{8} + 19\dfrac{2}{3}$ $81\dfrac{13}{24}$

33. $34\dfrac{1}{9} - 13\dfrac{5}{6}$ $20\dfrac{5}{18}$

SECTION 1.3   The Real Numbers

DEFINITIONS AND CONCEPTS	EXAMPLES
Set of numbers: **Natural numbers** **Whole numbers** **Integers**	Natural numbers: $\{1, 2, 3, 4, 5, 6, \ldots\}$ Whole numbers: $\{0, 1, 2, 3, 4, 5, 6, \ldots\}$ Integers: $\{\ldots, -3, -2, -1, 0, 1, 2, 3, \ldots\}$
Inequality symbols $>$ "is greater than" $<$ "is less than" A **rational number** is any number that can be written as a fraction with an integer numerator and a nonzero integer denominator. Rational numbers are either *terminating* or *repeating* decimals.	$11 > 8$ $4 < 7$ Rational numbers: 3, $\dfrac{2}{3}$, 0.75, 0, $0.\overline{25}$
An **irrational number** is a nonterminating, nonrepeating decimal. Irrational numbers cannot be written as the ratio of two integers. A **real number** is any number that is either a rational or an irrational number. Two numbers represented by points on a number line that are the same distance away from 0, but on opposite sides of it, are called **opposites.**	Irrational numbers: $\sqrt{3} = 1.732050808\ldots$, $\pi = 3.141592654\ldots$ Real numbers: 3, $\dfrac{2}{3}$, 0.75, 0, $0.\overline{25}$, $\sqrt{3}$, π Opposites: 6 and -6
The **absolute value** of a number is the distance on the number line between the number and 0.	$|8| = 8$, $|-7.5| = 7.5$, $\left|-\dfrac{5}{8}\right| = \dfrac{5}{8}$

REVIEW EXERCISES

34. Which number is a whole number but not a natural number? 0

Represent each of these situations with a signed number.

35. A budget deficit of $65 billion $-\$65$ billion

36. 206 feet below sea level -206 ft

Use one of the symbols $>$ or $<$ to make each statement true.

37. $0 < 5$

38. $-12 > -13$

Show that each of the following numbers is a rational number by expressing it as a fraction.

39. $5 \quad \dfrac{5}{1}$

40. $-12 \quad \dfrac{-12}{1}$

41. $0.7 \quad \dfrac{7}{10}$

42. $4\dfrac{2}{3} \quad \dfrac{14}{3}$

43. Graph each member of the set
$$\left\{\pi, 0.333\ldots, 3.75, -\dfrac{17}{4}, \dfrac{7}{8}, -2\right\}$$
on the number line.

44. Use a calculator to approximate $\sqrt{2}$ to the nearest hundredth. $\sqrt{2} \approx 1.41$

Determine whether each statement is true or false.

45. All integers are whole numbers. false

46. π is a rational number. false

47. The set of real numbers corresponds to all points on the number line. true

48. A real number is either rational or irrational. true

49. Determine which numbers in the given set are natural numbers, whole numbers, integers, rational numbers, irrational numbers, and real numbers.

$$\left\{ -\tfrac{4}{5}, \ 99.99, \ 0, \ \sqrt{2}, \ -12, \ 4\tfrac{1}{2}, \ 0.666\ldots, \ 8 \right\}$$

natural: 8; whole: 0, 8; integers: 0, −12, 8; rational: $-\tfrac{4}{5}$, 99.99, 0, −12, $4\tfrac{1}{2}$, 0.666 . . . , 8; irrational: $\sqrt{2}$; real: all

Write the expression in simplest form.

50. $-\left(-\dfrac{9}{16}\right)$ $\dfrac{9}{16}$

51. -0 0

Insert one of the symbols >, <, or = in the blank to make each statement true.

52. $|-6|$ > $|5|$

53. -9 > $-|-10|$

SECTION 1.4 Adding Real Numbers; Properties of Addition

DEFINITIONS AND CONCEPTS	EXAMPLES
To **add two real numbers with like signs,** add their absolute values and attach their common sign to the sum.	Add: $3 + 5 = 8$ Add: $-5 + (-11) = -16$
To **add two real numbers with unlike signs,** subtract their absolute values, the smaller from the larger. To that result, attach the sign of the number with the larger absolute value.	Add: $-8 + 6 = -2$ Add: $18 + (-3) = 15$
The **commutative property of addition:** $a + b = b + a$	$3 + 8 = 8 + 3$ Reorder
The **associative property of addition:** $(a + b) + c = a + (b + c)$	$(3 + 5) + 9 = 3 + (5 + 9)$ Regroup

REVIEW EXERCISES

Add.

54. $12 + 33$ 45

55. $-45 + (-37)$ −82

56. $-15 + 37$ 22

57. $25 + (-13)$ 12

58. $12 + (-8) + (-15)$ −11

59. $-25 + (-14) + 35$ −4

60. $-9.9 + (-2.4)$ −12.3

61. $\dfrac{5}{16} + \left(-\dfrac{1}{2}\right)$ $-\dfrac{3}{16}$

62. $35 + (-13) + (-17) + 6$ 11

63. $-21 + (-11) + 32 + (-45)$ −45

Determine what property of addition guarantees that the quantities are equal.

64. $-2 + 5 = 5 + (-2)$ commutative property of addition

65. $(-2 + 5) + 1 = -2 + (5 + 1)$ associative property of addition

---

SECTION 1.5 Subtracting Real Numbers

DEFINITIONS AND CONCEPTS	EXAMPLES
To *subtract* real numbers, add the opposite: $a - b = a + (-b)$	Subtract: $8 - 5 = 8 + (-5) = 3$

REVIEW EXERCISES

Subtract.

66. $45 - 64$ −19

67. $-17 - 32$ −49

68. $-27 - (-12)$ −15

69. $3.6 - (-2.1)$ 5.7

70. ASTRONOMY *Magnitude* is a term used in astronomy to designate the brightness of celestial objects as viewed from Earth. Smaller magnitudes are associated with brighter objects, and larger magnitudes refer to fainter objects. For each of the following pairs of objects, by how many magnitudes do their brightnesses differ?

  a. A full moon and the sun 14

  b. The star Beta Crucis and a full moon 13.78

Object	Magnitude
Sun	−26.5
Full moon	−12.5
Beta Crucis	1.28

Source: Based on data from Abell, Morrison, and Wolf, *Exploration of the Universe* (Saunders, 1987)

71. GEOGRAPHY The tallest peak on Earth is Mt. Everest, at 29,028 feet. The greatest ocean depth is the Mariana Trench, at −36,205 feet. Find the difference in the two elevations. 65,233 ft

---

SECTION 1.6 Multiplying and Dividing Real Numbers; Multiplication and Division Properties

DEFINITIONS AND CONCEPTS	EXAMPLES
To **multiply two real numbers,** multiply their absolute values.	
1. The product of two real numbers with **like signs** is positive.	Multiply: $3(5) = 15$ and $(-3)(-5) = 15$
2. The product of two real numbers with **unlike signs** is negative.	Multiply: $3(-5) = -15$ and $(-3)(5) = -15$
The commutative property of multiplication: $$ab = ba$$ **The associative property of multiplication:** $$(ab)c = a(bc)$$	$3(-4) = (-4)(3) = -12$ $[3(-4)](-5) = 3[(-4)(-5)] = 60$
To **divide two real numbers,** divide their absolute values.	
1. The quotient of two real numbers with **like signs** is positive.	Divide: $\dfrac{15}{3} = 5$ and $\dfrac{-15}{-3} = 5$
2. The quotient of two real numbers with **unlike signs** is negative.	Divide: $\dfrac{-15}{3} = -5$ and $\dfrac{15}{-3} = -5$
Division of zero by a nonzero number is 0.	Divide: $\dfrac{0}{5} = 0$
Division by zero is undefined.	Divide: $\dfrac{5}{0}$ is undefined

REVIEW EXERCISES

Multiply.

72. $-8 \cdot 7$ −56

73. $(-9)(-6)$ 54

74. $2(-3)(-2)$ 12

75. $(-3)(4)(2)$ −24

76. $(-3)(-4)(-2)$ −24

77. $(-4)(-1)(-3)(-3)$ 36

78. $-1.2(-5.3)$ 6.36

79. $0.002(-1,000)$ −2

80. $-\dfrac{2}{3}\left(\dfrac{1}{5}\right)$ $-\dfrac{2}{15}$

81. $2\dfrac{1}{4}\left(-\dfrac{1}{3}\right)$ $-\dfrac{3}{4}$

Determine what property of multiplication guarantees that the quantities are equal.

82. $(2 \cdot 3)5 = 2(3 \cdot 5)$ associative property of multiplication

83. $(-5)(-6) = (-6)(-5)$ commutative property of multiplication

84. What is the additive inverse of -3? 3

85. What is the multiplicative inverse of -3? $-\dfrac{1}{3}$

Perform each division, if possible.

86. $\dfrac{88}{44}$ 2

87. $\dfrac{-100}{25}$ -4

88. $\dfrac{-81}{-27}$ 3

89. $\dfrac{0}{37}$ 0

90. $-\dfrac{3}{5} \div \dfrac{1}{2}$ $-\dfrac{6}{5}$

91. $\dfrac{-60}{0}$ undefined

92. $\dfrac{-4.5}{1}$ -4.5

93. $\dfrac{-5}{-5}$ 1

94. MAGNIFICATION

a. Find the high and low reading that is displayed on the screen of the emissions-testing device shown.   high: 2, low: -3

b. The picture on the screen can be magnified by switching a setting on the monitor. Find the new high and low if every value is doubled.   high: 4, low: -6

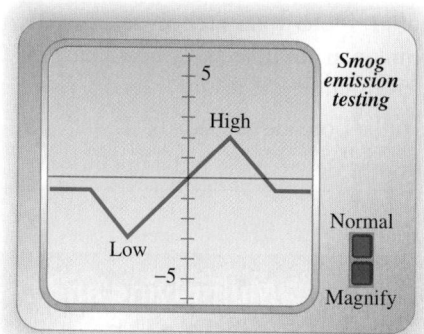

DEFINITIONS AND CONCEPTS	EXAMPLES
An **exponent** is used to represent repeated multiplication. In the **exponential expression** a^n, a is the **base** and n is the **exponent.**	In 5^4, 5 is the base, 4 is the exponent, thus, $$5^4 = 5 \cdot 5 \cdot 5 \cdot 5 = 625$$
Order of operations: 1. Perform all calculations within grouping symbols, working from the innermost pair to the outermost pair, in the following order: 2. Evaluate all exponential expressions. 3. Perform all multiplications and divisions, working from left to right. 4. Perform all additions and subtractions, working from left to right. If the expression does not contain grouping symbols, begin with step 2. In a fraction, simplify the numerator and denominator separately. Then simplify the fraction, if possible.	To simplify $3 + 2[4 - (5^2 + 1)]$, proceed as follows: $3 + 2[4 - (5^2 + 1)]$ $= 3 + 2[4 - (\mathbf{25} + 1)]$ Work within the parentheses and evaluate the exponential expression. $= 3 + 2[4 - 26]$ Add within the parentheses. $= 3 + 2[-22]$ Subtract within the brackets. $= 3 - 44$ Multiply. $= -41$ Subtract.
The **mean (or average)** is a value around which number values are grouped. $$\text{Mean} = \frac{\text{sum of values}}{\text{number of values}}$$	To find the mean of 11, 46, 46, 45, and 22, evaluate: $$\text{Mean} = \frac{11 + 46 + 46 + 45 + 22}{5} = \frac{170}{5} = 34$$

REVIEW EXERCISES

Write each expression using exponents.

95. $8 \cdot 8 \cdot 8 \cdot 8 \cdot 8$ 8^5

96. $5 \cdot 5 \cdot 5 \cdot 9 \cdot 9$ $5^3 \cdot 9^2$

97. $a(a)(a)(a)$ a^4

98. $9 \cdot \pi \cdot r \cdot r$ $9\pi r^2$

99. $x \cdot x \cdot x \cdot y \cdot y \cdot y \cdot y$ $x^3 y^4$

100. the sixth power of one 1^6

Evaluate each expression.

101. 9^2 81

102. 2 cubed 8

103. 2^5 32

104. 50^1 50

Evaluate each expression.

105. $24 - 3(6)(4)$ -48

106. $-(6 - 3)^2$ -9

107. $4^3 + 2(-6 - 2 \cdot 2)$ 44

108. $10 - 5[-3 - 2(5 - 7^2)] - 5$ -420

109. $\dfrac{-4(4 + 2) - 4}{|-18 - 4(5)|}$ $-\dfrac{14}{19}$

110. $(-3)^3\left(\dfrac{-8}{2}\right) + 5$ 113

111. $\dfrac{|-35| - 2(-7)}{2^4 - 23}$ -7

112. $-9^2 + (-9)^2$ 0

113. WALK-A-THONS Use the data in the table to find the average (mean) donation to a charity walk-a-thon. $\$20$

Donation	Number received
$5	20
$10	65
$20	25
$50	5
$100	10

SECTION 1.8   Algebraic Expressions

DEFINITIONS AND CONCEPTS	EXAMPLES
Addition symbols separate algebraic expressions into *terms*. In a term, the numerical factor is called the *coefficient*.	Since $a^2 + 3a - 5$ can be written as $a^2 + 3a + (-5)$, it has three terms. The coefficient of a^2 is 1, the coefficient of $3a$ is 3, and the coefficient of -5 is -5.
In order to describe numerical relationships, we need to translate the words of a problem into mathematical symbols. Sometimes we must rely on common sense and insight to find **hidden operations.**	5 *more than* x can be expressed as $x + 5$. 25 *less than twice* y can be expressed as $2y - 25$. *One-half of* c can be expressed as $\frac{1}{2}c$.
Number · value = total value	The value of 5 dimes is $5 \cdot 10$ cents = 50 cents.
When we replace the variable, or variables, in an algebraic expression with specific numbers and then apply the rules for the order of operations, we are **evaluating the algebraic expression.**	To evaluate $\dfrac{x + y}{x - y}$ for $x = 7$ and $y = 2$, substitute 7 for x and 2 for y and simplify. $$\dfrac{x + y}{x - y} = \dfrac{7 + 2}{7 - 2} = \dfrac{9}{5}$$

REVIEW EXERCISES

Write each phrase as an algebraic expression.

114. 25 more than the height h $h + 25$

115. 15 less than the cutoff score s $s - 15$

116. $\dfrac{1}{2}$ of the time t $\frac{1}{2}t$

117. the product of 6 and x $6x$

118. See the illustration.

a. If we let n = the length of the nail in inches, write an algebraic expression for the length of the bolt (in inches). $(n + 4)$ in.

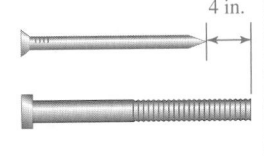

4 in.

b. If we let b = the length of the bolt in inches, write an algebraic expression for the length of the nail (in inches). $(b - 4)$ in.

119. Complete the table.

Type of coin	Number	Value (¢)	Total value (¢)
Nickel	6	5	30
Dime	d	10	$10d$

120. Complete the table.

x	$20x - x^3$
0	0
1	19
-4	-16

Evaluate each algebraic expression for the given value(s) of the variable(s).

121. $7x^2 - \dfrac{x}{2}$ for $x = 4$ 110

122. $b^2 - 4ac$ for $b = -10$, $a = 3$, and $c = 5$ 40

123. $2(24 - 2c)^3$ for $c = 9$ 432

124. $\dfrac{x + y}{-x - z}$ for $x = 19$, $y = 17$, and $z = -18$ -36

125. Find the volume, to the nearest tenth of a cubic inch, of the ice cream waffle cone by evaluating the algebraic expression

$$\frac{\pi r^2 h}{3}$$ 17.7 in.^{3}

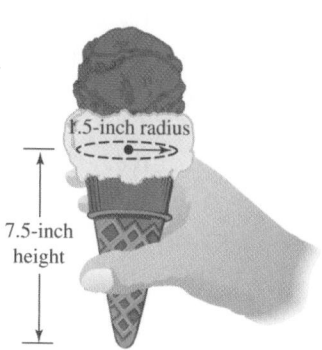

1.5-inch radius

7.5-inch height

SECTION 1.9   Simplifying Algebraic Expressions Using Properties of Real Numbers

DEFINITIONS AND CONCEPTS	EXAMPLES
We often use the *commutative property of multiplication* to reorder factors and the *associative property of multiplication* to regroup factors when **simplifying expressions.**	Simplify: $-5(3y) = (-5 \cdot 3)y = -15y$ Simplify: $-45b\left(\dfrac{5}{9}\right) = -45\left(\dfrac{5}{9}b\right) = \left(-45 \cdot \dfrac{5}{9}\right)b = -25b$
The **distributive property** can be used to remove parentheses: $a(b + c) = ab + ac$ $a(b - c) = ab - ac$ $a(b + c + d) = ab + ac + ad$	Multiply: $7(x + 3) = 7 \cdot x + 7 \cdot 3 = 7x + 21$ Multiply: $-0.2(4m - 5n - 7)$ $\quad = -0.2(4m) - (-0.2)(5n) - (-0.2)(7)$ $\quad = -0.8m + n + 1.4$
Like terms are terms with exactly the same variables raised to exactly the same powers.	$3x$ and $-5x$ are like terms. $-4t^3$ and $6t^4$ are unlike terms because they have different exponents. $0.5xyz$ and $3.7xy$ are unlike terms because they have different variables.
Simplifying the sum or difference of like terms is called **combining like terms.** Like terms are combined by adding or subtracting the coefficients of the terms and keeping the same variables with the same exponents.	Simplify: $4a + 2a = 6a$ Think $(4 + 2)a = 6a$. Simplify: $5p^2 + p - p^2 - 9p = 4p^2 - 8p$ Think $(5 - 1)p^2 = 4p^2$ and $(1 - 9)p = -8p$. Simplify: $2(k - 1) - 3(k + 2) = 2k - 2 - 3k - 6 = -k - 8$

REVIEW EXERCISES

Simplify each expression.

126. $-4(7w)$ $-28w$

127. $3(-2x)(-4)$ $24x$

128. $0.4(5.2f)$ $2.08f$

129. $\dfrac{7}{2} \cdot \dfrac{2}{7} r$ r

Multiply.

130. $5(x + 3)$
   $5x + 15$

131. $-(2x + 3 - y)$
   $-2x - 3 + y$

132. $\dfrac{3}{4}(4c - 8)$

   $3c - 6$

133. $-2(-3c - 7)(2.1)$
   $12.6c + 29.4$

Simplify each expression by combining like terms.

134. $8p + 5p - 4p$
   $9p$

135. $-5m + 2 - 2m - 2$
   $-7m$

136. $n + n + n + n$
   $4n$

137. $5(p - 2) - 2(3p + 4)$
   $-p - 18$

138. $55.7k^2 - 55.6k^2$ $0.1k^2$

139. $8a^2 + 4a^2 + 2a - 4a^2 - 2a - 1$ $8a^2 - 1$

140. $\dfrac{3}{5}w - \left(-\dfrac{2}{5}w\right)$ w

Write an equivalent expression for the given expression using fewer symbols.

141. $1x$ x

142. $-1x$ $-x$

143. $4x - (-1)$ $4x + 1$

144. $4x + (-1)$ $4x - 1$

1. Fill in the blanks.

   a. Two fractions, such as $\dfrac{3}{4}$ and $\dfrac{6}{8}$, that represent the same number are called __equivalent__ fractions.

   b. The result of an addition is called a __sum__.

   c. -5 is the __opposite__ of 5 because $-5 + 5 = 0$.

The following graph shows the cost to hire a security guard. Use the graph to answer Exercises 2 and 3.

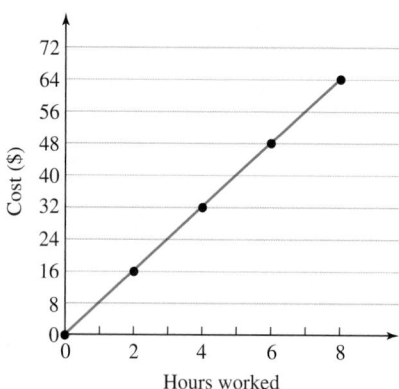

2. What will it cost to hire a security guard for 3 hours? $24

3. If a school was billed $40 for hiring a security guard for a dance, for how long did the guard work? 5 hr

4. Use the formula $f = \dfrac{a}{5}$ to complete the table.

Area in square miles (a)	Number of fire stations (f)
15	3
100	20
350	70

5. Give the prime factorization of 180.
$2 \cdot 2 \cdot 3 \cdot 3 \cdot 5 = 2^2 \cdot 3^2 \cdot 5$

6. Simplify: $\dfrac{42}{105}$ $\dfrac{2}{5}$

7. Write $\dfrac{5}{7}$ as an equivalent fraction with a denominator of 42. $\dfrac{30}{42}$

8. SHOPPING Refer to the illustration. What is the cost of the amount of fruit on the scale? $3.57

Oranges
84 cents a pound

9. Divide: $\dfrac{15}{16} \div \dfrac{5}{8}$
$\dfrac{3}{2} = 1\dfrac{1}{2}$

10. Subtract: $\dfrac{11}{12} - \dfrac{2}{9}$
$\dfrac{25}{36}$

11. Add: $11\dfrac{2}{3} + 8\dfrac{2}{5}$ $20\dfrac{1}{15}$

12. Multiply: $0.49 \cdot 100$ 49

13. QUALITY CONTROL An electronics company has strict specifications for silicon chips used in a computer. The company will install only chips that are within 0.05 centimeters of the specified thickness. The following table gives that specification for two types of chip. Fill in the blanks to complete the chart.

Chip type	Thickness specification	Acceptable range Low	Acceptable range High
A	0.78 cm	0.73	0.83
B	0.643 cm	0.593	0.693

14. Write $\dfrac{5}{6}$ as a decimal. $0.8\overline{3}$

15. Graph each member of the set on the number line.
$$\left\{ -1\tfrac{1}{4},\ \ \sqrt{2},\ \ -3.75,\ \ \dfrac{7}{2},\ \ 0.5,\ \ -3 \right\}$$

16. Determine whether each statement is true or false.

   a. Every integer is a rational number. true

   b. Every rational number is an integer. false

   c. π is an irrational number. true

   d. 0 is a whole number. true

17. Describe the set of real numbers. The set of real numbers
corresponds to all points on a number line. A real number is any
number that is either a rational number or an irrational
number.

18. Insert $>$ or $<$ in the blank to make each statement
true.

  a. $-2 \; > \; -3$

  b. $-|-7| \; < \; 8$

  c. $|-4| \; < \; -(-5)$

  d. $\left|-\dfrac{7}{8}\right| \; > \; 0.5$

19. TELEVISION During sweeps week, networks try to
gain viewers by showing their most exciting episodes.
Use the data to determine the average daily gain (or
loss) of ratings points by a network for the 7-day
sweeps period. 0.6

Day	Mon.	Tues.	Wed.	Thurs.	Fri.	Sat.	Sun.
Point loss/gain	0.6	−0.3	1.7	1.5	−0.2	1.1	−0.2

20. Add: $(-6) + 8 + (-4)$ −2

21. Add: $-\dfrac{1}{2} + \dfrac{7}{8}$ $\dfrac{3}{8}$

22. Subtract: $-10 - (-4)$ −6

23. Multiply: $(-2)(-3)(-5)$ −30

24. Divide: $\dfrac{-22}{-11}$ 2

25. Perform each operation.

  a. $0(-3)$ 0   **b.** $\dfrac{0}{-3}$ 0

  c. $0 + (-3)$ −3   **d.** $3 + (-3)$ 0

26. What property of real numbers is illustrated?

  a. $(-12 + 97) + 3 = -12 + (97 + 3)$
    associative property of addition

  b. $5 \cdot 2 = 2 \cdot 5$
    commutative property of multiplication

27. Rewrite each product using exponents.

  a. $9(9)(9)(9)(9)$ 9^5

  b. $3 \cdot x \cdot x \cdot z \cdot z \cdot z$ $3x^2z^3$

28. Evaluate: $8 + 2 \cdot 3^4$ 170

29. Evaluate: $9^2 - 3[45 - 3(6 + 4)]$ 36

30. Evaluate: $\dfrac{3(40 - 2^3)}{-2(6 - 4)^2}$ −12

31. Evaluate $3(x - y) - 5(x + y)$ for $x = 2$ and $y = -5$.
36

32. Complete the table.

x	$2x - \dfrac{30}{x}$
5	4
10	17
−30	−59

33. A band recorded x songs for an album. Technicians
had to delete two songs from the album because of
poor sound quality. Express the number of songs on
the album using an algebraic expression. $x - 2 =$ number of songs on the CD

34. What is the value of q quarters in cents? $25q$ cents

35. Explain the difference between an expression and an
equation. Give an example of each. An equation is a
mathematical sentence that contains an = sign. An expression
does not contain an = sign.

36. Explain this statement: $a - b = a + (-b)$ Subtraction
is the same as addition of the opposite.

Simplify each expression.

37. $5(-4x)$ −20x   **38.** $-8(-7t)(4)$ 224t

39. $\dfrac{4}{5}(15a + 5) - 16a$ −4a + 4

40. $-1.1d^2 - 3.8d^2 - d^2$ −5.9d²

41. $9x^2 + 2(7x - 3) - 9(x^2 - 1)$ 14x + 3

42. Write an expression that represents the perimeter of
the rectangle. $(18x + 6)$ ft

5x feet

(4x + 3) feet

Equations, Inequalities, and Problem Solving

© Jeremy Hardie/The Image Bank/Getty Images

from *Campus to Careers*

Automotive Service Technician

Anyone whose car has ever broken down appreciates the talents of automotive service technicians. To work on today's high-tech cars and trucks, a person needs strong diagnostic and problem-solving skills. Courses in automotive repair, electronics, physics, chemistry, English, computers, and mathematics provide a good educational background for a career as a service technician.

Service technicians must be knowledgeable about the repair and maintenance of automobiles and the fuels that power them. In **Problem 75** of **Study Set 2.4,** you will see how the octane ratings of three familiar grades of gasoline, unleaded, unleaded plus, and premium, are calculated using a formula.

JOB TITLE:
Automotive Service Technician

EDUCATION: Strongly recommended formal training at a vocational school or community college.

JOB OUTLOOK: Demand for technicians will grow as the number of vehicles in operation increases.

ANNUAL EARNINGS: $37,000 to $47,000

FOR MORE INFORMATION:
www.bls.gov/oco/ocos181.htm

Objectives

1. Determine whether a number is a solution.
2. Use the addition property of equality.
3. Use the subtraction property of equality.
4. Use the multiplication property of equality.
5. Use the division property of equality.

SECTION 2.1
Solving Equations Using Properties of Equality

In this section, we introduce four fundamental properties of equality that are used to solve equations.

1 Determine whether a number is a solution.

An **equation** is a statement indicating that two expressions are equal. An example is $x + 5 = 15$. The equal symbol $=$ separates the equation into two parts: The expression $x + 5$ is the **left side** and 15 is the **right side.** The letter x is the **variable** (or the **unknown**). The sides of an equation can be reversed, so we can write $x + 5 = 15$ or $15 = x + 5$.

- An equation can be true: $6 + 3 = 9$
- An equation can be false: $2 + 4 = 7$
- An equation can be neither true nor false. For example, $x + 5 = 15$ is neither true nor false because we don't know what number x represents.

An equation that contains a variable is made true or false by substituting a number for the variable. If we substitute 10 for x in $x + 5 = 15$, the resulting equation is true: $10 + 5 = 15$. If we substitute 1 for x, the resulting equation is false: $1 + 5 = 15$. A number that makes an equation true when substituted for the variable is called a **solution** and it is said to **satisfy** the equation. Therefore, 10 is a solution of $x + 5 = 15$, and 1 is not. The **solution set** of an equation is the set of all numbers that make the equation true.

> **The Language of Algebra** It is important to know the difference between an equation and an expression. An equation contains an $=$ symbol and an expression does not.

Self Check 1

Is 25 a solution of
$10 - x = 35 - 2x$? yes
Now Try Problem 19

Teaching Example 1 Is -2 a solution
of $4x - 2 = 3x - 4$?
Answer:
yes

EXAMPLE 1 Is 9 a solution of $3y - 1 = 2y + 7$?

Strategy We will substitute 9 for each y in the equation and evaluate the expression on the left side and the expression on the right side separately.

WHY If a true statement results, 9 is a solution of the equation. If we obtain a false statement, 9 is not a solution.

Solution

Evaluate the expression on the left side.

$$3y - 1 = 2y + 7$$
$$3(9) - 1 \stackrel{?}{=} 2(9) + 7$$
$$27 - 1 \stackrel{?}{=} 18 + 7$$
$$26 = 25$$

Evaluate the expression on the right side.

Since $26 = 25$ is false, 9 is not a solution of $3y - 1 = 2y + 7$.

2 Use the addition property of equality.

To **solve an equation** means to find all values of the variable that make the equation true. We can develop an understanding of how to solve equations by referring to the scales shown on the next page.

The first scale represents the equation $x - 2 = 3$. The scale is in balance because the weights on the left side and right side are equal. To find x, we must add 2 to the left side. To keep the scale in balance, we must also add 2 to the right side. After doing this, we see that x grams is balanced by 5 grams. Therefore, x must be 5. We say that we have solved the equation $x - 2 = 3$ and that the solution is 5.

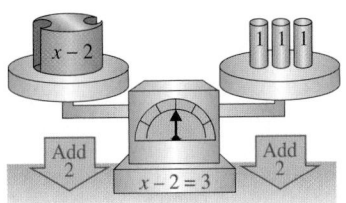

In this example, we solved $x - 2 = 3$ by transforming it to a simpler *equivalent equation*, $x = 5$.

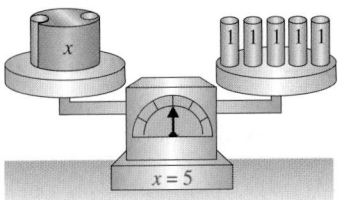

Equivalent Equations

Equations with the same solutions are called **equivalent equations.**

The procedure that we used suggests the following property of equality.

Addition Property of Equality

Adding the same number to both sides of an equation does not change its solution.

For any real numbers a, b, and c,

if $a = b$, then $a + c = b + c$

When we use this property, the resulting equation is *equivalent to the original one.* We will now show how it is used to solve $x - 2 = 3$ algebraically.

EXAMPLE 2   Solve: $x - 2 = 3$

Strategy We will use a property of equality to isolate the variable on one side of the equation.

WHY To solve the original equation, we want to find a simpler equivalent equation of the form $x = $ **a number**, whose solution is obvious.

Solution
We will use the addition property of equality to isolate x on the left side of the equation. We can undo the subtraction of 2 by adding 2 to both sides.

$$x - 2 = 3 \qquad \text{This is the equation to solve.}$$
$$x - 2 + 2 = 3 + 2 \qquad \text{Add 2 to both sides.}$$
$$x + 0 = 5 \qquad \text{The sum of a number and its opposite is zero: } -2 + 2 = 0.$$
$$x = 5 \qquad \text{When 0 is added to a number, the result is the same number.}$$

Since 5 is obviously the solution of the equivalent equation $x = 5$, the solution of the original equation, $x - 2 = 3$, is also 5. To check this result, we substitute 5 for x in the original equation and simplify.

Self Check 2

Solve: $n - 16 = 33$ 49

Now Try **Problem 37**

Teaching Example 2 Solve:
$x - 5 = -1$
Answer:
4

$$x - 2 = 3$$
$$5 - 2 \overset{?}{=} 3 \quad \text{Substitute 5 for } x.$$
$$3 = 3 \quad \text{True}$$

Since the statement is true, 5 is the solution. A more formal way to present this result is to write the solution within braces as a solution set: {5}.

The Language of Algebra We solve equations by writing a series of steps that result in an equivalent equation of the form

$$x = a \text{ number}$$

or

$$a \text{ number} = x$$

We say the variable is *isolated* on one side of the equation. *Isolated* means alone or by itself.

Self Check 3

Solve: **a.** $-5 = b - 38$ ₃₃

b. $-20 + n = 29$ ₄₉

Now Try Problems 39 and 43

Teaching Example 3 Solve:
$-3 = a - 9$
Answer:
6

EXAMPLE 3 Solve: **a.** $-19 = y - 7$ **b.** $-27 + y = -3$

Strategy We will use a property of equality to isolate the variable on one side of the equation.

WHY To solve the original equation, we want to find a simpler equivalent equation of the form $y = $ **a number** or **a number** $= y$, whose solution is obvious.

Solution

a. To isolate y on the right side, we use the addition property of equality. We can undo the subtraction of 7 by adding 7 to both sides.

$$-19 = y - 7 \qquad \text{This is the equation to solve.}$$
$$-19 + 7 = y - 7 + 7 \qquad \text{Add 7 to both sides.}$$
$$-12 = y \qquad \begin{array}{l}\text{The sum of a number and its opposite is zero:}\\ -7 + 7 = 0.\end{array}$$

Check: $\quad -19 = y - 7 \qquad \text{This is the original equation.}$
$$-19 \overset{?}{=} -12 - 7 \qquad \text{Substitute } -12 \text{ for } y.$$
$$-19 = -19 \qquad \text{True}$$

Since the statement is true, the solution is -12. The solution set is $\{-12\}$.

b. To isolate y, we use the addition property of equality. We can eliminate -27 on the left side by adding its opposite (additive inverse) to both sides.

$$-27 + y = -3 \qquad \text{The equation to solve.}$$
$$-27 + y + 27 = -3 + 27 \qquad \text{Add 27 to both sides.}$$
$$y = 24 \qquad \begin{array}{l}\text{The sum of a number and its opposite is zero:}\\ -27 + 27 = 0.\end{array}$$

Check: $\quad -27 + y = -3 \qquad \text{This is the original equation.}$
$$-27 + 24 \overset{?}{=} -3 \qquad \text{Substitute 24 for } y.$$
$$-3 = -3 \qquad \text{True}$$

The solution is 24. The solution set is {24}.

> **Caution!**   After checking a result, be careful when stating your conclusion. Here, it would be incorrect to say:
>
>   The solution is −3.
>
> The number we were checking was 24, not −3.

3   Use the subtraction property of equality.

Since any subtraction can be written as an addition by adding the opposite of the number to be subtracted, the following property is an extension of the addition property of equality.

Subtraction Property of Equality

Subtracting the same number from both sides of an equation does not change its solution.

For any real numbers a, b, and c,

  if $a = b$, then $a - c = b - c$

When we use this property, the resulting equation is equivalent to the original one.

EXAMPLE 4   Solve: **a.** $x + \dfrac{1}{8} = \dfrac{7}{4}$ **b.** $54.9 + x = 45.2$

Strategy   We will use a property of equality to isolate the variable on one side of the equation.

WHY   To solve the original equation, we want to find a simpler equivalent equation of the form $x = \textbf{a number}$, whose solution is obvious.

Solution

a. To isolate x, we use the subtraction property of equality. We can undo the addition of $\frac{1}{8}$ by subtracting $\frac{1}{8}$ from both sides.

$$x + \frac{1}{8} = \frac{7}{4} \qquad \text{This is the equation to solve.}$$

$$x + \frac{1}{8} - \frac{1}{8} = \frac{7}{4} - \frac{1}{8} \qquad \text{Subtract } \tfrac{1}{8} \text{ from both sides.}$$

$$x = \frac{7}{4} - \frac{1}{8} \qquad \text{On the left side, } \tfrac{1}{8} - \tfrac{1}{8} = 0.$$

$$x = \frac{7}{4} \cdot \frac{2}{2} - \frac{1}{8} \qquad \text{Build } \tfrac{7}{4} \text{ so that it has a denominator of 8.}$$

$$x = \frac{14}{8} - \frac{1}{8} \qquad \text{Multiply the numerators and multiply the denominators.}$$

$$x = \frac{13}{8} \qquad \text{Subtract the numerators. Write the result over the common denominator 8.}$$

Verify that $\frac{13}{8}$ is the solution by substituting it for x in the original equation and simplifying.

Self Check 4

Solve: **a.** $x + \dfrac{4}{15} = \dfrac{11}{5}$ $\frac{29}{15}$

b. $0.7 + a = 0.2$ -0.5

Now Try   **Problems 49 and 51**

Teaching Example 4 Solve:

a. $x + \dfrac{1}{3} = \dfrac{3}{4}$

b. $36.25 + x = 48.36$

Answers:

a. $\dfrac{5}{12}$ **b.** 12.11

b. To isolate x, we use the subtraction property of equality. We can undo the addition of 54.9 by subtracting 54.9 from both sides.

$$54.9 + x = 45.2 \qquad \text{This is the equation to solve.}$$
$$54.9 + x - \mathbf{54.9} = 45.2 - \mathbf{54.9} \qquad \text{Subtract 54.9 from both sides.}$$
$$x = -9.7 \qquad \text{On the left side, } 54.9 - 54.9 = 0.$$

Check:
$$54.9 + x = 45.2 \qquad \text{This is the original equation.}$$
$$54.9 + (\mathbf{-9.7}) \overset{?}{=} 45.2 \qquad \text{Substitute } -9.7 \text{ for } x.$$
$$45.2 = 45.2 \qquad \text{True}$$

The solution is -9.7. The solution set is $\{-9.7\}$.

4 Use the multiplication property of equality.

The first scale shown below represents the equation $\frac{x}{3} = 25$. The scale is in balance because the weights on the left side and right side are equal. To find x, we must triple (multiply by 3) the weight on the left side. To keep the scale in balance, we must also triple the weight on the right side. After doing this, we see that x is balanced by 75. Therefore, x must be 75.

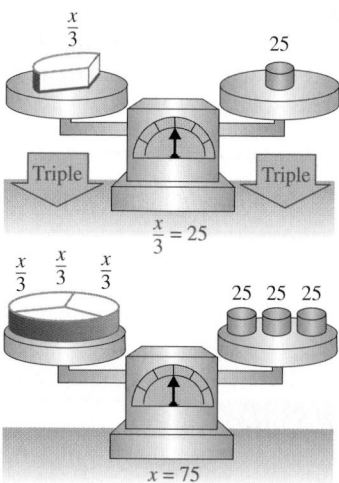

The procedure that we used suggests the following property of equality.

Multiplication Property of Equality

Multiplying both sides of an equation by the same nonzero number does not change its solution.

For any real numbers a, b, and c, where c is not 0,

   if $a = b$, then $ca = cb$

When we use this property, the resulting equation is equivalent to the original one. We will now show how it is used to solve $\frac{x}{3} = 25$ algebraically.

Self Check 5

Solve: $\frac{b}{24} = 3$ 72

Now Try Problem 53

Teaching Example 5 Solve: $\frac{y}{4} = 12$
Answer:
48

EXAMPLE 5 Solve: $\dfrac{x}{3} = 25$

Strategy We will use a property of equality to isolate the variable on one side of the equation.

WHY To solve the original equation, we want to find a simpler equivalent equation of the form $x = \textbf{a number}$, whose solution is obvious.

Solution

To isolate x, we use the multiplication property of equality. We can undo the division by 3 by multiplying both sides by 3.

$$\frac{x}{3} = 25 \qquad \text{This is the equation to solve.}$$

$$3 \cdot \frac{x}{3} = 3 \cdot 25 \qquad \text{Multiply both sides by 3.}$$

$$\frac{3x}{3} = 75 \qquad \text{Do the multiplications.}$$

$1x = 75$ Simplify $\frac{3x}{3}$ by removing the common factor of 3 in the numerator and denominator: $\frac{3}{3} = 1$.

$x = 75$ The coefficient 1 need not be written since 1x = x.

If we substitute 75 for x in $\frac{x}{3} = 25$, we obtain the true statement $25 = 25$. This verifies that 75 is the solution. The solution set is $\{75\}$.

Since the product of a number and its reciprocal (or multiplicative inverse) is 1, we can solve equations such as $\frac{2}{3}x = 6$, where the coefficient of the variable term is a fraction, as follows.

EXAMPLE 6

Solve: **a.** $\frac{2}{3}x = 6$ **b.** $-\frac{5}{4}x = 3$

Strategy We will use a property of equality to isolate the variable on one side of the equation.

WHY To solve the original equation, we want to find a simpler equivalent equation of the form $x = \textbf{a number}$, whose solution is obvious.

Solution

a. Since the coefficient of x is $\frac{2}{3}$, we can isolate x by multiplying both sides of the equation by the reciprocal of $\frac{2}{3}$, which is $\frac{3}{2}$.

$$\frac{2}{3}x = 6 \qquad \text{This is the equation to solve.}$$

$$\frac{3}{2} \cdot \frac{2}{3}x = \frac{3}{2} \cdot 6 \qquad \text{To undo the multiplication by } \tfrac{2}{3}, \text{ multiply both sides by the reciprocal of } \tfrac{2}{3}.$$

$$\left(\frac{3}{2} \cdot \frac{2}{3}\right)x = \frac{3}{2} \cdot 6 \qquad \text{Use the associative property of multiplication to group } \tfrac{3}{2} \text{ and } \tfrac{2}{3}.$$

$$1x = 9 \qquad \text{On the left, } \tfrac{3}{2} \cdot \tfrac{2}{3} = 1. \text{ On the right, } \tfrac{3}{2} \cdot 6 = \tfrac{18}{2} = 9.$$

$$x = 9 \qquad \text{The coefficient 1 need not be written since 1x = x.}$$

Check: $\frac{2}{3}x = 6$ This is the original equation.

$$\frac{2}{3}(9) \stackrel{?}{=} 6 \qquad \text{Substitute 9 for x in the original equation.}$$

$$6 = 6 \qquad \text{On the left side, } \tfrac{2}{3}(9) = \tfrac{18}{3} = 6.$$

Since the statement is true, 9 is the solution. The solution set is $\{9\}$.

The Language of Algebra Variable terms with fractional coefficients can be written in two ways. For example:

$$\frac{2x}{3} = \frac{2}{3}x \qquad \text{and} \qquad -\frac{5a}{4} = -\frac{5}{4}a$$

b. To isolate x, we multiply both sides by the reciprocal of $-\frac{5}{4}$, which is $-\frac{4}{5}$.

Self Check 6

Solve: **a.** $\frac{7}{2}x = 21$ 6

b. $-\frac{3}{8}b = 2$ $-\frac{16}{3}$

Now Try Problems 61 and 67

Teaching Example 6 Solve:

a. $\frac{5}{6}x = 10$

b. $-\frac{2}{3}x = 5$

Answers:

a. 12   **b.** $-\frac{15}{2}$

$$-\frac{5}{4}x = 3 \qquad \text{This is the equation to solve.}$$

$$-\frac{4}{5}\left(-\frac{5}{4}x\right) = -\frac{4}{5}(3) \qquad \begin{array}{l}\text{To undo the multiplication by } -\frac{5}{4}, \text{ multiply both sides by} \\ \text{the reciprocal of } -\frac{5}{4}.\end{array}$$

$$1x = -\frac{12}{5} \qquad \begin{array}{l}\text{On the left side, } -\frac{4}{5}\left(-\frac{5}{4}\right) = 1. \\ \text{On the right side, } -\frac{4}{5}(3) = -\frac{12}{5}.\end{array}$$

$$x = -\frac{12}{5} \qquad \text{The coefficient 1 need not be written since } 1x = x.$$

The solution is $-\frac{12}{5}$. Verify that this is correct by checking.   ∎

5 Use the division property of equality.

Since any division can be rewritten as a multiplication by multiplying by the reciprocal, the following property is a natural extension of the multiplication property.

Division Property of Equality

Dividing both sides of an equation by the same nonzero number does not change its solution.

For any real numbers a, b, and c, where c is not 0,

$$\text{if } a = b, \text{ then } \frac{a}{c} = \frac{b}{c}$$

When we use this property, the resulting equation is equivalent to the original one.

EXAMPLE 7   Solve: **a.** $2t = 80$ **b.** $-6.02 = -8.6t$

Strategy We will use a property of equality to isolate the variable on one side of the equation.

WHY To solve the original equation, we want to find a simpler equivalent equation of the form $t = \textbf{a number}$ or $\textbf{a number} = t$, whose solution is obvious.

Solution

a. To isolate t on the left side, we use the division property of equality. We can undo the multiplication by 2 by dividing both sides of the equation by 2.

$$2t = 80 \qquad \text{This is the equation to solve.}$$

$$\frac{2t}{2} = \frac{80}{2} \qquad \text{Use the division property of equality: Divide both sides by 2.}$$

$$1t = 40 \qquad \begin{array}{l}\text{Simplify } \frac{2t}{2} \text{ by removing the common factor of 2 in the numerator and} \\ \text{denominator: } \frac{2}{2} = 1.\end{array}$$

$$t = 40 \qquad \text{The product of 1 and any number is that number: } 1t = t.$$

If we substitute 40 for t in $2t = 80$, we obtain the true statement $80 = 80$. This verifies that 40 is the solution. The solution set is $\{40\}$.

The Language of Algebra   Since division by 2 is the same as multiplication by $\frac{1}{2}$, we can also solve $2t = 80$ using the multiplication property of equality. We could also isolate t by multiplying both sides by the *multiplicative inverse* of 2, which is $\frac{1}{2}$:

$$\frac{1}{2} \cdot 2t = \frac{1}{2} \cdot 80$$

b. To isolate t on the right side, we use the division property of equality. We can undo the multiplication by -8.6 by dividing both sides by -8.6.

$$-6.02 = -8.6t \qquad \text{This is the equation to solve.}$$

$$\frac{-6.02}{-8.6} = \frac{-8.6t}{-8.6} \qquad \text{Use the division property of equality: Divide both sides by } -8.6.$$

$$0.7 = t \qquad \text{Do the division: } 8.6\overline{)6.02}. \text{ The quotient of two negative numbers}$$
$$\text{is positive.}$$

The solution is 0.7. Verify that this is correct by checking. ∎

Success Tip   It is usually easier to multiply on each side if the coefficient of the variable term is a *fraction,* and divide on each side if the coefficient is an *integer* or *decimal.*

EXAMPLE 8   Solve: $-x = 3$

Strategy   The variable x is not isolated, because there is a $-$ sign in front of it. Since the term $-x$ has an understood coefficient of -1, the equation can be written as $-1x = 3$. We need to select a property of equality and use it to isolate the variable on one side of the equation.

WHY   To find the solution of the original equation, we want to find a simpler equivalent equation of the form $x = $ **a number**, whose solution is obvious.

Solution
To isolate x, we can either multiply or divide both sides by -1.

Multiply both sides by -1**:**		*Divide both sides by* -1**:**	
$-x = 3$	The equation to solve	$-x = 3$	The equation to solve
$-1x = 3$	Write: $-x = -1x$	$-1x = 3$	Write: $-x = -1x$
$(-1)(-1x) = (-1)3$		$\dfrac{-1x}{-1} = \dfrac{3}{-1}$	
$1x = -3$		$1x = -3$	On the left side, $\frac{-1}{-1} = 1.$
$x = -3$	$1x = x$	$x = -3$	$1x = x$

$$\text{\textbf{Check:}} \qquad -x = 3 \qquad \text{This is the original equation.}$$

$$-(-3) \stackrel{?}{=} 3 \qquad \text{Substitute } -3 \text{ for } x.$$

$$3 = 3 \qquad \text{On the left side, the opposite of } -3 \text{ is } 3.$$

Since the statement is true, -3 is the solution. The solution set is $\{-3\}$. ∎

Self Check 8

Solve: $-h = -12$ 12

Now Try   Problem 81

Teaching Example 8 Solve: $-a = -3$
Answer:
3

SECTION 2.1   STUDY SET

VOCABULARY

Fill in the blanks.

1. An _equation_ , such as $x + 1 = 7$, is a statement indicating that two expressions are equal.

2. Any number that makes an equation true when substituted for the variable is said to _satisfy_ the equation. Such numbers are called _solutions_.

▶ **3.** To _solve_ an equation means to find all values of the variable that make the equation true.

4. To solve an equation, we _isolate_ the variable on one side of the equal symbol.

5. Equations with the same solutions are called _equivalent_ equations.

6. To _check_ the solution of an equation, we substitute the value for the variable in the original equation and determine whether the result is a true statement.

CONCEPTS

7. Given $x + 6 = 12$:

   a. What is the left side of the equation? $x + 6$

   b. Is this equation true, false, or neither? neither

   c. Is 5 the solution? no

   d. Does 6 satisfy the equation? yes

▶ **8.** For each equation, determine what operation is performed on the variable. Then explain how to undo that operation to isolate the variable.

   a. $x - 8 = 24$ subtraction of 8; add 8

   b. $x + 8 = 24$ addition of 8; subtract 8 or add -8

   c. $\dfrac{x}{8} = 24$ division by 8; multiply by 8

   d. $8x = 24$ multiplication by 8; divide by 8 or multiply by $\frac{1}{8}$

9. Complete the following properties of equality.

   a. If $a = b$, then

   $$a + c = b + \boxed{c} \text{ and } a - c = b - \boxed{c}$$

   b. If $a = b$, then $ca = \boxed{c}\, b$ and $\dfrac{a}{c} = \dfrac{b}{\boxed{c}}$ $(c \neq 0)$

▶ **10. a.** To solve $\dfrac{h}{10} = 20$, do we multiply both sides of the equation by 10 or 20? 10

   b. To solve $4k = 16$, do we subtract 4 from both sides of the equation or divide both sides by 4?
   divide both sides by 4

11. Simplify each expression.

   a. $x + 7 - 7$ x

   b. $y - 2 + 2$ y

   c. $\dfrac{5t}{5}$ t

   d. $6 \cdot \dfrac{h}{6}$ h

12. a. To solve $-\frac{4}{5}x = 8$, we can multiply both sides by the reciprocal of $-\frac{4}{5}$. What is the reciprocal of $-\frac{4}{5}$? $-\frac{5}{4}$

   b. What is $-\frac{5}{4}\left(-\frac{4}{5}\right)$? 1

NOTATION

Complete each solution to solve the equation.

13.
$$x - 5 = 45$$
$$x - 5 + \boxed{5} = 45 + \boxed{5}$$
$$x = \boxed{50}$$

   Check:
   $$x - 5 = 45$$
   $$\boxed{50} - 5 \overset{?}{=} 45$$
   $$45 = 45 \text{ True}$$
   $\boxed{50}$ is the solution.

14.
$$8x = 40$$
$$\frac{8x}{\boxed{8}} = \frac{40}{\boxed{8}}$$
$$x = \boxed{5}$$

   Check:
   $$8x = 40$$
   $$8\left(\boxed{5}\right) \overset{?}{=} 40$$
   $$\boxed{40} = 40 \text{ True}$$
   $\boxed{5}$ is the solution.

15. a. What does the symbol $\overset{?}{=}$ mean? is possibly equal to

   ▶ **b.** If you solve an equation and obtain $50 = x$, can you write $x = 50$? yes

16. Fill in the blank: $-x = \boxed{-1}\, x$

GUIDED PRACTICE

Check to determine whether the given number is a solution of the equation. See Example 1.

17. $6, x + 12 = 28$
   no

▶ **18.** $110, x - 50 = 60$
   yes

19. $-8, 2b + 3 = -15$
   no

▶ **20.** $-2, 5t - 4 = -16$
   no

21. $5, 0.5x = 2.9$
   no

22. $3.5, 1.2 + x = 4.7$
   yes

23. $-6, 33 - \dfrac{x}{2} = 30$
   no

▶ **24.** $-8, \dfrac{x}{4} + 98 = 100$
   no

25. $-2, |c - 8| = 10$
   yes

▶ **26.** $-45, |30 - r| = 15$
   no

27. $12, 3x - 2 = 4x - 5$
   no

▶ **28.** $5, 5y + 8 = 3y - 2$
   no

29. $-3, x^2 - x - 6 = 0$
   no

30. $-2, y^2 + 5y - 3 = 0$
   no

31. $1, \dfrac{2}{a + 1} + 5 = \dfrac{12}{a + 1}$ yes

▶ **32.** $4, \dfrac{2t}{t - 2} - \dfrac{4}{t - 2} = 1$ no

33. $\frac{3}{4}, x - \frac{1}{8} = \frac{5}{8}$ yes **34.** $\frac{7}{3}, -4 = a + \frac{5}{3}$ no

35. $-3, (x - 4)(x + 3) = 0$ yes

36. $5, (2x + 1)(x - 5) = 0$ yes

Use a property of equality to solve each equation. Then check the result. **See Examples 2–4.**

37. $a - 5 = 66$ 71 **▶ 38.** $x - 34 = 19$ 53

39. $9 = p - 9$ 18 **40.** $3 = j - 88$ 91

41. $x - 1.6 = -2.5$ −0.9 **42.** $y - 1.2 = -1.3$ −0.1

43. $-3 + a = 0$ 3 **44.** $-1 + m = 0$ 1

45. $d - \frac{1}{9} = \frac{7}{9}$ $\frac{8}{9}$ **46.** $\frac{7}{15} = b - \frac{1}{15}$ $\frac{8}{15}$

47. $x + 7 = 10$ 3 **48.** $y + 15 = 24$ 9

49. $s + \frac{1}{5} = \frac{4}{25}$ $-\frac{1}{25}$ **▶ 50.** $\frac{1}{6} = h + \frac{4}{3}$ $-\frac{7}{6}$

51. $3.5 + f = 1.2$ −2.3 **52.** $9.4 + h = 8.1$ −1.3

Use a property of equality to solve each equation. Then check the result. **See Example 5.**

53. $\frac{x}{15} = 3$ 45 **▶ 54.** $\frac{y}{7} = 12$ 84

55. $0 = \frac{v}{11}$ 0 **56.** $\frac{d}{49} = 0$ 0

57. $\frac{d}{-7} = -3$ 21 **58.** $\frac{c}{-2} = -11$ 22

59. $\frac{y}{0.6} = -4.4$ −2.64 **▶ 60.** $\frac{y}{0.8} = -2.9$ −2.32

Use a property of equality to solve each equation. Then check the result. **See Example 6.**

61. $\frac{4}{5}t = 16$ 20 **62.** $\frac{11}{15}y = 22$ 30

63. $\frac{2}{3}c = 10$ 15 **▶ 64.** $\frac{9}{7}d = 81$ 63

65. $-\frac{7}{2}r = 21$ −6 **66.** $-\frac{4}{5}s = 36$ −45

67. $-\frac{5}{4}h = -5$ 4 **68.** $-\frac{3}{8}t = -3$ 8

Use a property of equality to solve each equation. Then check the result. **See Example 7.**

▶ 69. $4x = 16$ 4 **70.** $5y = 45$ 9

71. $63 = 9c$ 7 **▶ 72.** $40 = 5t$ 8

73. $23b = 23$ 1 **▶ 74.** $16 = 16h$ 1

75. $-8h = 48$ −6 **76.** $-9a = 72$ −8

77. $-100 = -5g$ 20 **78.** $-80 = -5w$ 16

▶ 79. $-3.4y = -1.7$ 0.5 **80.** $-2.1x = -1.26$ 0.6

Use a property of equality to solve each equation. Then check the result. **See Example 8.**

81. $-x = 18$ −18 **▶ 82.** $-y = 50$ −50

83. $-n = \frac{4}{21}$ $-\frac{4}{21}$ **84.** $-w = \frac{11}{16}$ $-\frac{11}{16}$

TRY IT YOURSELF

Solve each equation. Then check the result.

85. $8.9 = -4.1 + t$ 13 **▶ 86.** $7.7 = -3.2 + s$ 10.9

87. $-2.5 = -m$ 2.5 **88.** $-1.8 = -b$ 1.8

89. $-\frac{9}{8}x = 3$ $-\frac{8}{3}$ **90.** $-\frac{14}{3}c = 7$ $-\frac{3}{2}$

91. $\frac{3}{4} = d + \frac{1}{10}$ $\frac{13}{20}$ **92.** $\frac{5}{9} = r + \frac{1}{6}$ $\frac{7}{18}$

93. $-15x = -60$ 4 **▶ 94.** $-14x = -84$ 6

95. $-10 = n - 5$ −5 **▶ 96.** $-8 = t - 2$ −6

97. $\frac{h}{-40} = 5$ −200 **▶ 98.** $\frac{x}{-7} = 12$ −84

99. $a - 93 = 2$ 95 **100.** $18 = x - 3$ 21

APPLICATIONS

101. SYNTHESIZERS To find the unknown angle measure, which is represented by x, solve the equation $x + 115 = 180$. 65°

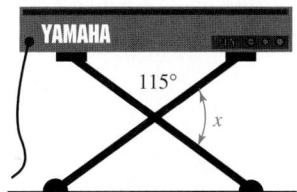

102. STOP SIGNS To find the measure of one angle of the stop sign, which is represented by x, solve the equation $8x = 1,080$. 135°

103. SHARING THE WINNING TICKET When a 2006 Florida Lotto Jackpot was won by a group of 16 nurses employed at a Southwest Florida Medical Center, each received $375,000. To find the amount of the jackpot, which is represented by x, solve the equation $\frac{x}{16} = 375,000$. $6,000,000

104. TENNIS Billie Jean King won 40 Grand Slam tennis titles in her career. This is 14 less than the all-time leader, Martina Navratilova. To find the number of titles won by Navratilova, which is represented by x, solve the equation $40 = x - 14$. 54

WRITING

105. What does it mean to solve an equation?

106. When solving an equation, we *isolate* the variable on one side of the equation. Write a sentence in which the word *isolate* is used in a different context.

107. Explain the error in the following work.

Solve: $x + 2 = 40$
~~$x + 2 - 2 = 40$~~
$x = 40$

▶ **108.** After solving an equation, how do we check the result?

REVIEW

109. Evaluate $-9 - 3x$ for $x = -3$. ₀

110. Evaluate: $-5^2 + (-5)^2$ ₀

111. Translate to symbols: Subtract x from 45 $45 - x$

▶ **112.** Evaluate: $\dfrac{2^3 + 3(5 - 3)}{15 - 4 \cdot 2}$ ₂

Objectives

1 Use more than one property of equality to solve equations.

2 Simplify expressions to solve equations.

3 Clear equations of fractions and decimals.

4 Identify identities and contradictions.

SECTION 2.2
More about Solving Equations

We have solved simple equations by using properties of equality. We will now expand our equation-solving skills by considering more complicated equations. We want to develop a general strategy that can be used to solve any kind of *linear equation in one variable*.

> ### Linear Equation in One Variable
>
> A **linear equation in one variable** can be written in the form
>
> $$ax + b = c$$
>
> where a, b and c are real numbers and $a \neq 0$.

1 Use more than one property of equality to solve equations.

Sometimes we must use several properties of equality to solve an equation. For example, on the left side of $2x + 6 = 10$, the variable x is multiplied by 2, and then 6 is added to that product. To isolate x, we use the order of operations rules in reverse. First, we undo the addition of 6, and then we undo the multiplication by 2.

$2x + 6 = 10$	This is the equation to solve.
$2x + 6 - 6 = 10 - 6$	To undo the addition of 6, subtract 6 from both sides.
$2x = 4$	Do the subtractions.
$\dfrac{2x}{2} = \dfrac{4}{2}$	To undo the multiplication by 2, divide both sides by 2.
$x = 2$	Do the divisions.

The solution is 2.

> ***The Language of Algebra*** We subtract 6 from both sides to isolate the *variable term*, $2x$. Then we divide both sides by 2 to isolate the *variable*, x.

Self Check 1

Solve: $8x - 13 = 43$ ₇

Now Try **Problem 15**

Teaching Example 1 Solve:
$-15x + 3 = 48$
Answer:
-3

EXAMPLE 1   Solve: $-12x + 5 = 17$

Strategy First we will use a property of equality to isolate the *variable term* on one side of the equation. Then we will use a second property of equality to isolate the *variable* itself.

WHY To solve the original equation, we want to find a simpler equivalent equation of the form $x = $ **a number**, whose solution is obvious.

Solution

- To isolate the variable term, $-12x$, we subtract 5 from both sides to undo the addition of 5.
- To isolate the variable, x, we divide both sides by -12 to undo the multiplication by -12.

$$-12x + 5 = 17 \qquad \text{This is the equation to solve.}$$

$$-12x + 5 - 5 = 17 - 5 \qquad \text{Use the subtraction property of equality: Subtract 5 from both sides to isolate the variable term } -12x.$$

$$-12x = 12 \qquad \text{Do the subtractions: } 5 - 5 = 0 \text{ and } 17 - 5 = 12.$$

$$\frac{-12x}{-12} = \frac{12}{-12} \qquad \text{Use the division property of equality: Divide both sides by } -12 \text{ to isolate } x.$$

$$x = -1 \qquad \text{Do the divisions.}$$

Check:
$$-12x + 5 = 17 \qquad \text{This is the original equation.}$$

$$-12(-1) + 5 \stackrel{?}{=} 17 \qquad \text{Substitute } -1 \text{ for } x.$$

$$12 + 5 \stackrel{?}{=} 17 \qquad \text{Do the multiplication on the left side.}$$

$$17 = 17 \qquad \text{True}$$

The solution is -1. The solution set is $\{-1\}$.

> **Caution!** When checking solutions, always use the original equation.

EXAMPLE 2

Solve: $\dfrac{5}{8}m - 2 = -12$

Strategy We will use properties of equality to isolate the variable on one side of the equation.

WHY To solve the original equation, we want to find a simpler equivalent equation of the form $m = $ **a number**, whose solution is obvious.

Solution

We note that the coefficient of m is $\frac{5}{8}$ and proceed as follows.

- To isolate the variable term $\frac{5}{8}m$, we add 2 to both sides to undo the subtraction of 2.
- To isolate the variable, m, we multiply both sides by $\frac{8}{5}$ to undo the multiplication by $\frac{5}{8}$.

$$\frac{5}{8}m - 2 = -12 \qquad \text{This is the equation to solve.}$$

$$\frac{5}{8}m - 2 + 2 = -12 + 2 \qquad \text{Use the addition property of equality: Add 2 to both sides to isolate the variable term } \frac{5}{8}m.$$

$$\frac{5}{8}m = -10 \qquad \text{Do the additions: } -2 + 2 = 0 \text{ and } -12 + 2 = -10.$$

$$\frac{8}{5}\left(\frac{5}{8}m\right) = \frac{8}{5}(-10) \qquad \text{Use the multiplication property of equality: Multiply both sides by } \frac{8}{5} \left(\text{which is the reciprocal of } \frac{5}{8}\right) \text{ to isolate } m.$$

$$m = -16 \qquad \text{On the left side: } \frac{8}{5}\left(\frac{5}{8}\right) = 1 \text{ and } 1m = m. \text{ On the right side: } \frac{8}{5}(-10) = -\frac{8 \cdot 2 \cdot \overset{1}{\cancel{5}}}{\underset{1}{\cancel{5}}} = -16.$$

The solution is -16. Verify this by substituting -16 into the original equation. The solution set is $\{-16\}$.

Self Check 2

Solve: $\dfrac{7}{12}a - 6 = -27$ $\quad -36$

Now Try **Problem 21**

Teaching Example 2 Solve:
$\frac{4}{7}a - 5 = 7$
Answer:
21

EXAMPLE 3   Solve: $-0.2 = -0.8 - y$

Strategy First, we will use a property of equality to isolate the variable term on one side of the equation. Then we will use a second property of equality to isolate the variable itself.

WHY To solve the original equation, we want to find a simpler equivalent equation of the form **a number** $= y$, whose solution is obvious.

Solution
To isolate the variable term $-y$ on the right side, we eliminate -0.8 by adding 0.8 to both sides.

$$-0.2 = -0.8 - y \qquad \text{This is the equation to solve.}$$
$$-0.2 + \mathbf{0.8} = -0.8 - y + \mathbf{0.8} \qquad \text{Add 0.8 to both sides to isolate } -y.$$
$$0.6 = -y \qquad \text{Do the additions.}$$

Since the term $-y$ has an understood coefficient of -1, the equation can be written as $0.6 = -1y$. To isolate y, we can either multiply both sides or divide both sides by -1. If we choose to divide both sides by -1, we proceed as follows.

$$0.6 = -1y$$
$$\frac{0.6}{-1} = \frac{-1y}{-1} \qquad \text{To undo the multiplication by } -1, \text{ divide both sides by } -1.$$
$$-0.6 = y$$

The solution is -0.6. Verify this by substituting -0.6 into the original equation. ∎

2 Simplify expressions to solve equations.

When solving equations, we should simplify the expressions that make up the left and right sides before applying any properties of equality. Often, that involves removing parentheses and/or combining like terms.

EXAMPLE 4   Solve: **a.** $3(k + 1) - 5k = 0$ **b.** $8a - 2(a - 7) = 68$

Strategy We will use the distributive property along with the process of combining like terms to simplify the left side of each equation.

WHY It's best to simplify each side of an equation before using a property of equality.

Solution

a. $3(k + 1) - 5k = 0$ This is the equation to solve.

$\qquad 3k + 3 - 5k = 0$ Distribute the multiplication by 3.

$\qquad\qquad -2k + 3 = 0$ Combine like terms: $3k - 5k = -2k$.

$\qquad -2k + 3 - 3 = 0 - 3$ To undo the addition of 3, subtract 3 from both sides. This isolates the variable term $-2k$.

$\qquad\qquad\qquad -2k = -3$ Do the subtractions: $3 - 3 = 0$ and $0 - 3 = -3$

$\qquad\qquad\quad \dfrac{-2k}{-2} = \dfrac{-3}{-2}$ To undo the multiplication by -2, divide both sides by -2. This isolates the variable k.

$\qquad\qquad\qquad\quad k = \dfrac{3}{2}$ Simplify: $\frac{-3}{-2} = \frac{3}{2}$.

Check: $3(k + 1) - 5k = 0$ This is the original equation.

$$3\left(\frac{3}{2} + 1\right) - 5\left(\frac{3}{2}\right) \stackrel{?}{=} 0$$ Substitute $\frac{3}{2}$ for k.

$$3\left(\frac{5}{2}\right) - 5\left(\frac{3}{2}\right) \stackrel{?}{=} 0$$ Do the addition within the parentheses. Think of 1 as $\frac{2}{2}$ and then add: $\frac{3}{2} + \frac{2}{2} = \frac{5}{2}$.

$$\frac{15}{2} - \frac{15}{2} \stackrel{?}{=} 0$$ Do the multiplications.

$$0 = 0$$ True

The solution is $\frac{3}{2}$ and the solution set is $\left\{\frac{3}{2}\right\}$.

> **Caution!** To check a result, we evaluate each side of the equation following the order of operations rules.

b. $8a - 2(a - 7) = 68$ This is the equation to solve.

$8a - 2a + 14 = 68$ Distribute the multiplication by -2.

$6a + 14 = 68$ Combine like terms: $8a - 2a = 6a$.

$6a + 14 - 14 = 68 - 14$ To undo the addition of 14, subtract 14 from both sides. This isolates the variable term 6a.

$6a = 54$ Do the subtractions.

$$\frac{6a}{6} = \frac{54}{6}$$ To undo the multiplication by 6, divide both sides by 6. This isolates the variable a.

$a = 9$ Do the divisions.

The solution is 9. Verify this by substituting 9 into the original equation. ∎

When solving an equation, if variables appear on both sides, we can use the addition (or subtraction) property of equality to get all variable terms on one side and all constant terms on the other.

EXAMPLE 5   Solve: $3x - 15 = 4x + 36$

Strategy There are variable terms ($3x$ and $4x$) on both sides of the equation. We will eliminate $3x$ from the left side of the equation by subtracting $3x$ from both sides.

WHY To solve for x, all the terms containing x must be on the same side of the equation.

Solution

$3x - 15 = 4x + 36$ This is the equation to solve.

$3x - 15 - 3x = 4x + 36 - 3x$ Subtract 3x from both sides to isolate the variable term on the right side.

$-15 = x + 36$ Combine like terms: $3x - 3x = 0$ and $4x - 3x = x$.

$-15 - 36 = x + 36 - 36$ To undo the addition of 36, subtract 36 from both sides.

$-51 = x$ Do the subtractions.

Self Check 5

Solve: $30 + 6n = 4n - 2$ -16

***Now Try* Problem 57**

Teaching Example 5 Solve:
$5x - 4 = 6x + 10$
Answer:
-14

Check:
$$3x - 15 = 4x + 36 \qquad \text{The original equation.}$$
$$3(-51) - 15 \stackrel{?}{=} 4(-51) + 36 \qquad \text{Substitute } -51 \text{ for } x.$$
$$-153 - 15 \stackrel{?}{=} -204 + 36 \qquad \text{Do the multiplications.}$$
$$-168 = -168 \qquad \text{True}$$

The solution is -51 and the solution set is $\{-51\}$.

3 Clear equations of fractions and decimals.

Equations are usually easier to solve if they don't involve fractions. We can use the multiplication property of equality to clear an equation of fractions by multiplying both sides of the equation by the least common denominator.

Self Check 6

Solve: $\frac{1}{4}x + \frac{1}{2} = -\frac{1}{8}$ $-\frac{5}{2}$

Now Try Problem 63

Teaching Example 6 Solve:
$\frac{1}{10}x + \frac{4}{5} = \frac{1}{2}$
Answer:
-3

EXAMPLE 6 Solve: $\dfrac{1}{6}x + \dfrac{5}{2} = \dfrac{1}{3}$

Strategy To clear the equations of fractions, we will multiply both sides by their LCD.

WHY It's easier to solve an equation that involves only integers.

Solution

$$\frac{1}{6}x + \frac{5}{2} = \frac{1}{3} \qquad \text{This is the equation to solve.}$$

$$6\left(\frac{1}{6}x + \frac{5}{2}\right) = 6\left(\frac{1}{3}\right) \qquad \begin{array}{l}\text{Multiply both sides by the LCD of } \frac{1}{6}, \frac{5}{2}, \text{ and } \frac{1}{3}, \text{ which is} \\ \text{6. Don't forget the parentheses.}\end{array}$$

$$6\left(\frac{1}{6}x\right) + 6\left(\frac{5}{2}\right) = 6\left(\frac{1}{3}\right) \qquad \text{On the left side, distribute the multiplication by 6.}$$

$$x + 15 = 2 \qquad \begin{array}{l}\text{Do each multiplication: } 6\left(\frac{1}{6}\right) = 1, 6\left(\frac{5}{2}\right) = \frac{30}{2} = 15, \text{ and} \\ 6\left(\frac{1}{3}\right) = \frac{6}{3} = 2.\end{array}$$

$$x + 15 - 15 = 2 - 15 \qquad \begin{array}{l}\text{To undo the addition of 15, subtract 15 from both} \\ \text{sides.}\end{array}$$

$$x = -13$$

Check the solution by substituting -13 for x in $\frac{1}{6}x + \frac{5}{2} = \frac{1}{3}$.

> **Caution!** Before multiplying both sides of an equation by the LCD, enclose the left and right sides with parentheses or brackets.
>
> $$\left(\frac{1}{6}x + \frac{5}{2}\right) = \left(\frac{1}{3}\right)$$

If an equation contains decimals, it is often convenient to multiply both sides by a power of 10 to change the decimals in the equation to integers.

Self Check 7

Solve:
$(15,000 - x)\,0.08x + 0.07$
$= 1,110$ $6,000$

Now Try Problem 71

EXAMPLE 7 Solve: $0.04(12) + 0.01x = 0.02(12 + x)$

Strategy To clear the equations of decimals, we will multiply both sides by a carefully chosen power of 10.

WHY It's easier to solve an equation that involves only integers.

Solution

The equation contains the decimals 0.04, 0.01, and 0.02. Since the greatest number of decimal places in any one of these numbers is two, we multiply both sides of the equation by 10^2 or 100. This changes 0.04 to 4, and 0.01 to 1, and 0.02 to 2.

$$0.04(12) + 0.01x = 0.02(12 + x)$$

$$100[0.04(12) + 0.01x] = 100[0.02(12 + x)]$$

Multiply both sides by 100. Don't forget the brackets.

$$100 \cdot 0.04(12) + 100 \cdot 0.01x = 100 \cdot 0.02(12 + x)$$

Distribute the multiplication by 100.

$$4(12) + 1x = 2(12 + x)$$

Multiply each decimal by 100 by moving its decimal point 2 places to the right.

$$48 + x = 24 + 2x$$

Distribute the multiplication by 2.

$$48 + x - 24 - x = 24 + 2x - 24 - x$$

Subtract 24 and x from both sides.

$$24 = x$$

Simplify each side.

$$x = 24$$

The solution is 24. Check by substituting 24 for x in the original equation. ∎

The previous examples suggest the following strategy for solving equations. It is important to note that not every step is needed to solve every equation.

Strategy for Solving Linear Equations in One Variable

1. **Clear the equation of fractions or decimals:** Multiply both sides by the LCD to clear fractions or multiply both sides by a power of 10 to clear decimals.

2. **Simplify each side of the equation:** Use the distributive property to remove parentheses, and then combine like terms on each side.

3. **Isolate the variable term on one side:** Add (or subtract) to get the variable term on one side of the equation and a number on the other using the addition (or subtraction) property of equality.

4. **Isolate the variable:** Multiply (or divide) to isolate the variable using the multiplication (or division) property of equality.

5. **Check the result:** Substitute the possible solution for the variable in the *original* equation to see if a true statement results.

EXAMPLE 8

Solve: $\dfrac{7m + 5}{5} = -4m + 1$

Strategy We will follow the steps of the equation-solving strategy to solve the equation.

WHY This is the most efficient way to solve a linear equation in one variable.

Solution

$$\frac{7m + 5}{5} = -4m + 1$$

This is the equation to solve.

Step 1 $5\left(\dfrac{7m + 5}{5}\right) = 5(-4m + 1)$

Clear the equation of the fraction by multiplying both sides by 5.

Teaching Example 7 Solve:
$0.03(15) + 0.03x = 0.04(5 + x)$
Answer:
25

Self Check 8

Solve: $6c + 2 = \dfrac{18 - c}{9}$ 0

Now Try Problem 79

Teaching Example 8 Solve:
$\dfrac{4x + 9}{2} = 3x + 1$
Answer:
$\dfrac{7}{2}$

Step 2 $7m + 5 = -20m + 5$

On the left side, remove the common factor 5 in the numerator and denominator. On the right side, distribute the multiplication by 5.

Step 3 $7m + 5 + 20m = -20m + 5 + 20m$

To eliminate the term $-20m$ on the right side, add $20m$ to both sides.

$27m + 5 = 5$

Combine like terms:
$7m + 20m = 27m$ and
$-20m + 20m = 0$.

$27m + 5 - 5 = 5 - 5$

To isolate the term $27m$, undo the addition of 5 by subtracting 5 from both sides.

$27m = 0$

Do the subtractions.

Step 4 $\dfrac{27m}{27} = \dfrac{0}{27}$

To isolate m, undo the multiplication by 27 by dividing both sides by 27.

$m = 0$

0 divided by any nonzero number is 0.

Step 5 Substitute 0 for m in $\frac{7m + 5}{5} = -4m + 1$ to check that the solution is 0. ∎

> *Caution!* Remember that when you multiply one side of an equation by a nonzero number, you must multiply the other side of the equation by the same number.

4 Identify identities and contradictions.

Each of the equations in Examples 1 through 8 had exactly one solution. However, some equations have no solutions while others have infinitely many solutions.

A linear equation in one variable that is true for all values of the variable is an **identity.** One example is the equation

$x + x = 2x$ If we substitute -10 for x, we get the true statement $-20 = -20$. If we substitute 7 for x, we get $14 = 14$, and so on.

Since we can replace x with any number and the equation will be true, all real numbers are solutions of $x + x = 2x$. This equation has infinitely many solutions. Its solution set is written as {all real numbers}.

An equation that is not true for any values of its variable is called a **contradiction.** One example is

$x = x + 1$ No number is 1 greater than itself.

Since $x = x + 1$ has no solutions, its solution set is the **empty set,** or **null set,** and is written as $\varnothing$.

Self Check 9

Solve:
$3(x + 5) - 4(x + 4) = -x - 1$

Now Try Problem 87

Self Check 9 Answer
All real numbers; the equation is an identity

EXAMPLE 9   Solve: $3(x + 8) + 5x = 2(12 + 4x)$

Strategy We will follow the steps of the equation-solving strategy to solve the equation.

WHY This is the most efficient way to solve a linear equation in one variable.

Solution

$3(x + 8) + 5x = 2(12 + 4x)$ This is the equation to solve.

$3x + 24 + 5x = 24 + 8x$ Distribute the multiplication by 3 and by 2.

$8x + 24 = 24 + 8x$	Combine like terms: $3x + 5x = 8x$. Note that the sides of the equation are identical.
$8x - 8x + 24 = 24 + 8x - 8x$	To eliminate the term $8x$ on the right side, subtract $8x$ from both sides.
$24 = 24$	Combine like terms on both sides: $8x - 8x = 0$.

In this case, the terms involving x drop out and the result is true. This means that any number substituted for x in the original equation will give a true statement. Therefore, *all real numbers* are solutions and this equation is an identity.

> **Success Tip**   Note that at the step $8x + 24 = 24 + 8x$ we know that the equation is an identity.

EXAMPLE 10   Solve: $3(d + 7) - d = 2(d + 10)$

Strategy We will follow the steps of the equation-solving strategy to solve the equation.

WHY This is the most efficient way to solve a linear equation in one variable.

Solution

$3(d + 7) - d = 2(d + 10)$	This is the equation to solve.
$3d + 21 - d = 2d + 20$	Distribute the multiplication by 3 and by 2.
$2d + 21 = 2d + 20$	Combine like terms: $3d - d = 2d$.
$2d + 21 - 2d = 2d + 20 - 2d$	To eliminate the term $2d$ on the right side, subtract $2d$ from both sides.
$21 = 20$	Combine like terms on both sides: $2d - 2d = 0$.

In this case, the terms involving d drop out and the result is false. This means that any number that is substituted for d in the original equation will give a false statement. Since this equation has *no solution,* it is a contradiction.

> **The Language of Algebra**   *Contradiction* is a form of the word *contradict,* meaning conflicting ideas. During a trial, evidence might be introduced that *contradicts* the testimony of a witness.

Teaching Example 9 Solve:
$4(x - 3) + 3x = 12(x - 1) - 5x$
Answer:
All real numbers, the equation is an identity.

Self Check 10
Solve:
$-4(c - 3) + 2c = 2(10 - c)$
Now Try Problem 89
Self Check 10 Answer
No solution; the equation is a contradiction

Teaching Example 10 Solve:
$3(y + 2) - 2y = 4(y - 3) - 3y$
Answer:
No solution, the equation is a contradiction.

ANSWERS TO SELF CHECKS

1. 7   **2.** -36 **3.** -3.9 **4. a.** 1   **b.** -11 **5.** -16 **6.** $-\frac{5}{2}$ **7.** 6,000   **8.** 0   **9.** All real numbers; the equation is an identity   **10.** No solution; the equation is a contradiction

---

SECTION 2.2   STUDY SET

▌ VOCABULARY

Fill in the blanks.

1. $3x + 8 = 10$ is an example of a linear ___equation___ in one variable.

▶ Selected exercises available online at
www.webassign.net/brookscole

2. To solve $\frac{s}{3} + \frac{1}{4} = -\frac{1}{2}$, we can ___clear___ the equation of the fractions by multiplying both sides by 12.

3. A linear equation in one variable that is true for all values of the variable is an ___identity___ .

4. An equation that is not true for any values of its variable is called a ___contradiction___ .

CONCEPTS

Fill in the blanks.

5. To solve $3x - 5 = 1$, we first undo the <u>subtraction</u> of 5 by adding 5 to both sides. Then we undo the <u>multiplication</u> by 3 by dividing both sides by 3.

▶ **6.** To solve $\frac{x}{2} + 3 = 5$, we can undo the <u>addition</u> of 3 by subtracting 3 from both sides. Then we can undo the <u>division</u> by 2 by multiplying both sides by 2.

7. a. Combine like terms on the left side of $6x - 8 - 8x = -24$. $-2x - 8 = -24$

   b. Distribute and then combine like terms on the right side of $-20 = 4(3x - 4) - 9x$. $-20 = 3x - 16$

8. Is -2 a solution of the equation?

   a. $6x + 5 = 7$ No   **b.** $8(x + 3) = 8$ Yes

9. Multiply.

   ▶ **a.** $20\left(\frac{3}{5}x\right)$ 12x   **b.** $100 \cdot 0.02x$ 2x

10. By what must you multiply both sides of $\frac{2}{3} - \frac{1}{2}b = -\frac{4}{3}$ to clear it of fractions? 6

11. By what must you multiply both sides of $0.7x + 0.3(x - 1) = 0.5x$ to clear it of decimals? 10

12. a. Simplify: $3x + 5 - x$ 2x + 5

   b. Solve: $3x + 5 = 9$ $\frac{4}{3}$

   c. Evaluate $3x + 5 - x$ for $x = 9$. 23

   d. Check: Is -1 a solution of $3x + 5 - x = 9$? No

NOTATION

Complete the solution.

13. Solve:
$$2x - 7 = 21$$
$$2x - 7 \boxed{+7} = 21 \boxed{+7}$$
$$2x = 28$$
$$\frac{2x}{2} = \frac{28}{2}$$
$$x = 14$$

Check:
$$2x - 7 = 21$$
$$2(\boxed{14}) - 7 \stackrel{?}{=} 21$$
$$\boxed{28} - 7 \stackrel{?}{=} 21$$
$$\boxed{21} = 21$$

$\boxed{14}$ is the solution.

14. A student multiplied both sides of $\frac{3}{4}t + \frac{5}{8} = \frac{1}{2}t$ by 8 to clear it of fractions, as shown below. Explain his error in showing this step. $8\left(\frac{3}{4}t + \frac{5}{8}\right) = 8 \cdot \frac{1}{2}t$

$$8 \cdot \frac{3}{4}t + \frac{5}{8} = 8 \cdot \frac{1}{2}t$$

GUIDED PRACTICE

Solve each equation and check the result. See Examples 1–2.

▶ **15.** $2x + 5 = 17$ 6   **16.** $3x - 5 = 13$ 6

17. $5q - 2 = 23$ 5   **18.** $4p + 3 = 43$ 10

19. $-33 = 5t + 2$ -7 **20.** $-55 = 3w + 5$ -20

21. $\frac{5}{6}k - 5 = 10$ 18   ▶ **22.** $\frac{2}{5}c - 12 = 2$ 35

23. $-\frac{7}{16}h + 28 = 21$ 16   **24.** $-\frac{5}{8}h + 25 = 15$ 16

25. $\frac{t}{3} + 2 = 6$ 12   **26.** $\frac{x}{5} - 5 = -12$ -35

27. $-3p + 7 = -3$ $\frac{10}{3}$ ▶ **28.** $-2r + 8 = -1$ $\frac{9}{2}$

29. $-5 - 2d = 0$ $-\frac{5}{2}$ **30.** $-8 - 3c = 0$ $-\frac{8}{3}$

31. $2(-3) + 4y = 14$ 5   ▶ **32.** $4(-1) + 3y = 8$ 4

33. $0.7 - 4y = 1.7$ -0.25 **34.** $0.3 - 2x = -0.9$ 0.6

Solve each equation and check the result. See Example 3.

▶ **35.** $1.2 - x = -1.7$ 2.9   **36.** $0.6 = 4.1 - x$ 3.5

37. $-6 - y = -2$ -4 **38.** $-1 - h = -9$ 8

Solve each equation and check the result. See Example 4.

39. $3(2y - 2) - y = 5$ $\frac{11}{5}$ **40.** $2(-3a + 2) + a = 2$ $\frac{2}{5}$

41. $4(5b) + 2(6b - 1) = -34$ -1

42. $9(x + 11) + 5(13 - x) = 0$ -41

43. $-(4 - m) = -10$ -6 ▶ **44.** $-(6 - t) = -12$ -6

45. $10.08 = 4(0.5x + 2.5)$ 0.04   ▶ **46.** $-3.28 = 8(1.5y - 0.5)$ 0.06

47. $6a - 3(3a - 4) = 30$ -6 **48.** $16y - 8(3y - 2) = -24$ 5

▶ **49.** $-(19 - 3s) - (8s + 1) = 35$ -11

50. $2(3x) - 5(3x + 1) = 58$ -7

Solve each equation and check the result. See Example 5.

51. $5x = 4x + 7$ 7   **52.** $3x = 2x + 2$ 2

53. $8y + 44 = 4y$ -11 **54.** $9y + 36 = 6y$ -12

55. $60r - 50 = 15r - 5$ 1   **56.** $100f - 75 = 50f + 75$ 3

57. $8y - 2 = 4y + 16$ $\frac{9}{2}$ ▶ **58.** $7 + 3w = 4 + 9w$ $\frac{1}{2}$

59. $2 - 3(x - 5) = 4(x - 1)$ 3

60. $2 - (4x + 7) = 3 + 2(x + 2)$ -2

61. $3(A + 2) = 2(A - 7)$ -20

▶ **62.** $9(T - 1) = 6(T + 2) - T$ $\frac{21}{4}$

Solve each equation and check the result. See Example 6.

63. $\frac{1}{8}y - \frac{1}{2} = \frac{1}{4}$ 6   **64.** $\frac{1}{15}x - \frac{4}{5} = \frac{2}{3}$ 22

65. $\frac{1}{3} = \frac{5}{6}x + \frac{2}{9}$ $\frac{2}{15}$ **66.** $\frac{2}{3} = -\frac{2}{3}x + \frac{3}{4}$ $\frac{1}{8}$

▶ **67.** $\frac{1}{6}y + \frac{1}{4}y = -1$ $-\frac{12}{5}$ **68.** $\frac{1}{3}x + \frac{1}{4}x = -2$ $-\frac{24}{7}$

69. $\frac{2}{3}y + 2 = \frac{1}{5} + y$ $\frac{27}{5}$ ▶ **70.** $\frac{2}{5}x + 1 = \frac{1}{3} + x$ $\frac{10}{9}$

Solve each equation and check the result. **See Example 7.**

71. $0.06(s + 9) - 1.24 = -0.08s$ 5

72. $0.08(x + 50) - 0.16x = 0.04(50)$ 25

73. $0.09(t + 50) + 0.15t = 52.5$ 200

74. $0.08(x - 100) = 44.5 - 0.07x$ 350

75. $0.06(a + 200) + 0.1a = 172$ 1,000

76. $0.03x + 0.05(6,000 - x) = 280$ 1,000

77. $0.4b - 0.1(b - 100) = 70$ 200

▶ **78.** $0.105x + 0.06(20,000 - x) = 1,740$ 12,000

Solve each equation and check the result. **See Example 8.**

79. $\frac{10 - 5s}{3} = s$ $\frac{5}{4}$ **80.** $\frac{40 - 8s}{5} = -2s$ -20

81. $\frac{7t - 9}{16} = t$ -1 ▶ **82.** $\frac{11r + 68}{3} = -3$ -7

83. $\frac{5(1 - x)}{6} = -x + 1$ 1   ▶ **84.** $\frac{3(14 - u)}{8} = -3u + 6$ $\frac{2}{7}$

85. $\frac{3(d - 8)}{4} = \frac{2(d + 1)}{3}$ ▶ **86.** $\frac{3(c - 2)}{2} = \frac{2(2c + 3)}{5}$

   80   6

Solve each equation, if possible. **See Examples 9–10.**

87. $8x + 3(2 - x) = 5x + 6$ all real numbers

▶ **88.** $5(x + 2) = 5x - 2$ no solution

89. $-3(s + 2) = -2(s + 4) - s$ no solution

▶ **90.** $21(b - 1) + 3 = 3(7b - 6)$ all real numbers

91. $2(3z + 4) = 2(3z - 2) + 13$ no solution

92. $x + 7 = \frac{2x + 6}{2} + 4$ all real numbers

93. $4(y - 3) - y = 3(y - 4)$ all real numbers

94. $5(x + 3) - 3x = 2(x + 8)$ no solution

TRY IT YOURSELF

Solve each equation, if possible. Check the result.

95. $3x - 8 - 4x - 7x = -2 - 8$ $\frac{1}{4}$

96. $-6t - 7t - 5t - 1 = 12 - 3$ $-\frac{5}{9}$

97. $0.05a + 0.01(90) = 0.02(a + 90)$ 30

98. $0.03x + 0.05(2,000 - x) = 99.5$ 25

▶ **99.** $\frac{3(b + 2)}{2} = \frac{4b - 10}{4}$ -11

100. $\frac{2(5a - 7)}{4} = \frac{9(a - 1)}{3}$
   -1

101. $4(a - 3) = -2(a - 6) + 6a$
   no solution

102. $9(t + 2) = -6(t - 3) + 15t$
   all real numbers

103. $10 - 2y = 8$ **104.** $7 - 7x = -21$
   1   4

105. $2n - \frac{3}{4}n = \frac{1}{2}n + \frac{13}{3}$ **106.** $\frac{5}{6}n + 3n = -\frac{1}{3}n - \frac{11}{9}$
   $\frac{52}{9}$ $-\frac{22}{75}$

107. $-\frac{2}{3}z + 4 = 8$ **108.** $-\frac{7}{5}x + 9 = -5$
   -6 10

109. $-2(9 - 3s) - (5s + 2) = -25$
   -5

110. $4(x - 5) - 3(12 - x) = 7$
   9

WRITING

111. To solve $3x - 4 = 5x + 1$, one student began by subtracting $3x$ from both sides. Another student solved the same equation by first subtracting $5x$ from both sides. Will the students get the same solution? Explain why or why not.

▶ **112.** What does it mean to clear an equation such as $\frac{1}{4} + \frac{1}{2}x = \frac{3}{8}$ of the fractions?

113. Explain the error in the following solution.

   Solve: $2x + 4 = 30$

   $\frac{2x}{2} + 4 = \frac{30}{2}$

   $x + 4 = 15$

   $x + 4 - 4 = 15 - 4$

   $x = 11$

114. Write an equation that is an identity. Explain why every real number is a solution.

REVIEW

Name the property that is used.

115. $x \cdot 9 = 9x$
   commutative property of multiplication

116. $4 \cdot \frac{1}{4} = 1$
   multiplicative inverse property

117. $(x + 1) + 2 = x + (1 + 2)$
   associative property of addition

118. $2(30y) = (2 \cdot 30)y$
   associative property of multiplication

Objectives

1 Change percents to decimals and decimals to percents.

2 Solve percent problems by direct translation.

3 Solve applied percent problems.

4 Find percent of increase and decrease.

5 Solve discount and commission problems.

SECTION 2.3
Applications of Percent

In this section, we will use translation skills from Chapter 1 and equation-solving skills from Chapter 2 to solve problems involving percents.

1 Change percents to decimals and decimals to percents.

The word **percent** means parts per one hundred. We can think of the percent symbol % as representing a denominator of 100. Thus, $93\% = \frac{93}{100}$. Since the fraction $\frac{93}{100}$ is equal to the decimal 0.93, it is also true that $93\% = 0.93$.

When solving percent problems, we must often convert percents to decimals and decimals to percents. To change a percent to a decimal, we *divide by 100 by moving the decimal point 2 places to the left and dropping the % symbol.* For example,

$$31\% = 31.0\% = 0.31$$

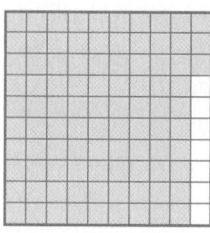

93% or $\frac{93}{100}$ or 0.93 of the figure is shaded.

To change a decimal to a percent, we *multiply the decimal by 100 by moving the decimal point 2 places to the right, and inserting a % symbol.* For example,

$$0.678 = 67.8\%$$

2 Solve percent problems by direct translation.

There are three basic types of percent problems. Examples of these are:

Type 1   What number is 8% of 215?

Type 2   102 is 21.3% of what number?

Type 3   31 is what percent of 500?

Every percent problem has three parts: the *amount,* the *percent,* and the *base.* For example, in the question *What number is 8% of 215?,* the words "what number" represent the **amount,** 8% represents the **percent,** and 215 represents the **base.** In these problems, the word "is" means "is equal to," and the word "of" means "multiplication."

What number	is	8%	of	215?
↓	↓	↓	↓	↓
Amount	**=**	**Percent**	**·**	**base**

EXAMPLE 1   What number is 8% of 215?

Strategy We will translate the words of this problem into an equation and then solve the equation.

WHY The variable in the translation equation represents the unknown number that we are asked to find.

Solution

In this problem, the phrase "what number" represents the amount, 8% is the percent, and 215 is the base.

What number   is   8%   of   215?

$$x \quad = \quad 0.08 \quad \cdot \quad 215$$

Change the percent to a decimal:
8% = 0.08.

$$x \quad = \quad 17.2$$

Do the multiplication.

Thus, 8% of 215 is 17.2.

To check, we note that 17.2 out of 215 is $\frac{17.2}{215} = 0.08 = 8\%$.

The Language of Algebra   Translate the word

- *is* to an equal symbol =
- *of* to multiplication
- *what* to a variable

We will illustrate the other two types of percent problems with application problems.

3 Solve applied percent problems.

One method for solving applied percent problems is to use the given facts to write a **percent sentence** of the form

_____ is _____ % of _____ ?

We enter the appropriate numbers in two of the blanks and the words "what" or "what number" in the remaining blank. As before, we translate the words into an equation and solve it.

EXAMPLE 2   *Aging Populations*

By the year 2075, the U.S. Bureau of the Census predicts that about 102 million residents will be age 65 or older. The **circle graph** (or **pie chart**) indicates that age group will make up 21.3% of the population. If this prediction is correct, find the population of the United States in 2075. (Round to the nearest million.)

Projection of the 2075 U.S. Population by Age

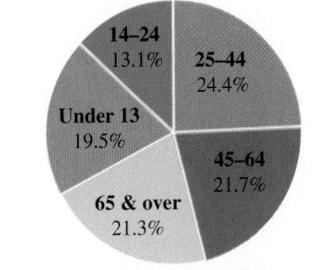

Source: U.S. Bureau of the Census (2000).

Strategy To find the predicted U.S. population in 2075, we will translate the words of the problem into an equation and then solve the equation.

WHY The variable in the translation equation represents the unknown population in 2075 that we are asked to find.

Solution

In this problem, 102 is the amount, 21.3% is the percent, and the words "what number" represent the base. The units are in millions.

102	is	21.3%	of	what number?
↓	↓	↓	↓	↓
102	=	0.213	·	x

$$\frac{102}{\mathbf{0.213}} = \frac{0.213x}{\mathbf{0.213}} \quad \text{To undo the multiplication by 0.213, divide both sides by 0.213.}$$

$$478.9 \approx x \qquad \text{Do the divisions.}$$

$$479 \approx x \qquad \text{Round 478.9 to the nearest million.}$$

The U.S. population is predicted to be about 479 million in the year 2075. We can check using estimation: 102 million out of a population of 479 million is approximately $\frac{100 \text{ million}}{500 \text{ million}}$, or $\frac{1}{5}$, which is 20%. Since this is close to 21.3%, the answer 479 seems reasonable. ■

We pay many types of taxes in our daily lives, such as sales tax, gasoline tax, income tax, and Social Security tax. **Tax rates** are usually expressed as percents.

EXAMPLE 3   *Taxes*   A maid makes $500 a week. One of the deductions from her weekly paycheck is a Social Security tax of $31. Find her Social Security tax rate.

Strategy To find the tax rate, we will translate the words of the problem into an equation and then solve the equation.

WHY The variable in the translation equation represents the unknown tax rate that we are asked to find.

Solution

31	is	what percent	of	500?
↓	↓	↓	↓	↓
31	=	x	·	500

31 is the amount, x is the percent, and 500 is the base.

$$\frac{31}{500} = \frac{500x}{500} \quad \text{To undo the multiplication by 500, divide both sides by 500.}$$

$$0.062 = x \qquad \text{Do the divisions.}$$

$$6.2\% = x \qquad \text{Change the decimal 0.062 to a percent.}$$

The Social Security tax rate is 6.2%

We can use estimation to check: $31 out of $500 is about $\frac{30}{500}$ or $\frac{6}{100}$, which is 6%. Since this is close to 6.2%, the answer seems reasonable. ■

4 Find percent of increase and decrease.

Percents are often used to describe how a quantity has changed. For example, a health care provider might increase the cost of medical insurance by 3%, or a police department might decrease the number of officers assigned to street patrols by 10%. To describe such changes, we use **percent of increase** or **percent of decrease**.

EXAMPLE 4   *Identity Theft*   The Federal Trade Commission receives complaints involving the theft of someone's identity information, such as a credit card, Social Security number, or cell phone account. Refer to the data in the table. What was the percent of increase in the number of complaints from 2001 to 2005? (Round to the nearest percent.)

IDENTITY THEFT
Data Clearinghouse

Year	2001	2005
Number of Complaints	86,000	256,000

Strategy First, we will subtract to find the *amount of increase* in the number of complaints. Then we will translate the words of the problem into an equation and solve it.

WHY A percent of increase problem involves finding the *percent of change,* and the change in a quantity is found using subtraction.

Solution

To find the *amount of increase,* we subtract the earlier value, 86,000, from the later value, 256,000.

$$256,000 - 86,000 = 170,000$$

We know that an increase of 170,000 is some unknown percent of the number of complaints in 2001, which was 86,000.

170,000	is	what percent	of	86,000?
↓	↓	↓	↓	↓
170,000	=	x	·	86,000

170,000 is the amount, x is the percent, and 86,000 is the base.

$$\frac{170,000}{86,000} = \frac{86,000x}{86,000}$$ To undo the multiplication by 86,000, divide both sides by 86,000.

$$1.977 \approx x$$ Do the divisions.

$$197.7\% \approx x$$ Change 1.977 to a percent.

Rounding 197.7% to the nearest percent, we find that the number of identity theft complaints increased by about 198% from 2001 to 2005.

A 200% increase would be double the number of complaints: 2(86,000) = 172,000. It seems reasonable that 170,000 complaints is a 198% increase.

> **Caution!** The percent of increase (or decrease) is a percent of the *original* number, that is, the number before the change occurred.

5 **Solve discount and commission problems.**

When the price of an item is reduced, we call the amount of the reduction a **discount.** If a discount is expressed as a percent, it is called the **rate of discount.**

Self Check 4

In 2004, there were 247,000 complaints of identity theft. Find the percent increase from 2004 to 2005. (Round to the nearest percent.) 4%

Now Try Problem 43

Teaching Example 4 In 2003 the tuition and fees at 4-year public colleges averaged $4694 per year. In 2008 the tuition and fees had increased to $6585. What was the percent increase in the tuition and fees for 4-year public colleges from 2003 to 2008? (Round to the nearest percent.) (Source: collegeboard.com)
Answer:
40%

EXAMPLE 5   *Health Club Discounts*   A 30% discount on a 1-year membership for a fitness center amounted to a $90 savings. Find the cost of a 1-year membership before the discount.

Strategy We will translate the words of the problem into an equation and then solve the equation.

WHY The variable in the translation equation represents the unknown cost of a 1-year membership before the discount that we are asked to find.

Solution
We are told that $90 is 30% of some unknown membership cost.

$$90 \quad \text{is} \quad 30\% \quad \text{of} \quad \text{what number?}$$

$$90 \quad = \quad 0.30 \quad \cdot \quad x \qquad \text{90 is the amount, 30\% is the percent, and } x \text{ is the base.}$$

$$\frac{90}{0.30} = \frac{0.30x}{0.30} \qquad \text{To undo the multiplication by 0.30, divide both sides by 0.30.}$$

$$300 = x \qquad \text{Do the divisions.}$$

A one-year membership cost $300 before the discount.

Instead of working for a salary or at an hourly rate, many salespeople are paid on **commission.** An employee who is paid a commission is paid a percent of the goods or services that he or she sells. We call that percent the **rate of commission.**

EXAMPLE 6   *Commissions*   A real estate agent earned $14,025 for selling a house. If she received a $5\frac{1}{2}$% commission, what was the selling price?

Strategy We will translate the words of the problem into an equation and then solve the equation.

WHY The variable in the translation equation represents the unknown selling price of the house that we are asked to find.

Solution
We are told that $14,025 is $5\frac{1}{2}$% of some unknown selling price of a house.

$$\$14,025 \quad \text{is} \quad 5.5\% \quad \text{of} \quad \text{what number?} \qquad \text{Write } 5\tfrac{1}{2}\% \text{ as 5.5\%.}$$

$$14,025 \quad = \quad 0.055 \quad \cdot \quad x \qquad \text{14,025 is the amount, 5.5\% is the percent, and } x \text{ is the base.}$$

$$\frac{14,025}{0.055} = \frac{0.055x}{0.055} \qquad \text{To undo the multiplication by 0.055, divide both sides by 0.055.}$$

$$255,000 = x \qquad \text{Do the divisions.}$$

The selling price of the house was $255,000.

ANSWERS TO SELF CHECKS

1. 2.24   **2.** 570 million   **3.** 1.45%   **4.** 4%   **5.** $120   **6.** $350

THINK IT THROUGH　*Percent of Increases in College Costs*

"The vast majority of Americans continue to believe that getting a college education is more important than it was in the past, that the country can never have too many college graduates, and that we should not allow the price of a higher education to exclude qualified and motivated students from getting a college education."

"Public Attitudes on Higher Education: A Trend Analysis, 1993–2003" (Feb. 2004) published by The National Center for Public Policy and Higher Education.

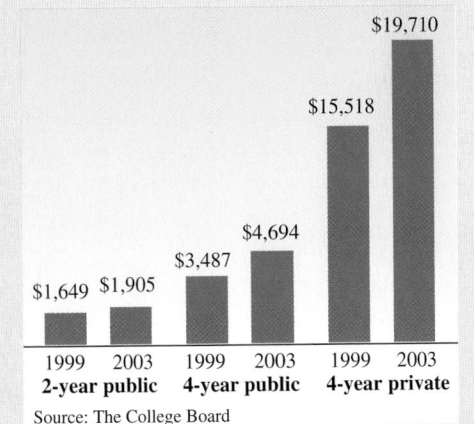

Source: The College Board

Like most everything else, college costs continue to rise. The illustration shows how tuition and fees at 2-year public, 4-year public, and 4-year private institutions have increased from 1999 to 2003. Find the percent of increase in tuition and fees for each type of institution. Round to the nearest one percent. 16%; 35%; 27%

SECTION 2.3　STUDY SET

VOCABULARY

Fill in the blanks.

1. <u>Percent</u> means parts per one hundred.

2. In the statement "10 is 50% of 20," 10 is the <u>amount</u>, 50% is the percent, and 20 is the <u>base</u>.

▶ 3. In percent questions, the word *of* means <u>multiplication</u>, and <u>is</u> means equals.

4. An employee who is paid a <u>commission</u> is paid a percent of the goods or services that he or she sells.

CONCEPTS

5. Represent the amount of the figure that is shaded using a fraction, a decimal, and a percent. $\frac{51}{100}$, 0.51, 51%

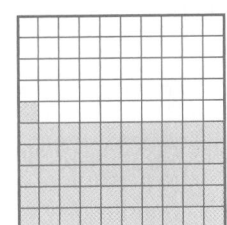

6. Fill in the blank: To solve a percent problem, we translate the words of the problem into an <u>equation</u> and solve it.

7.

High School Sports Programs Girls' Water Polo—Number of Participants	
2001	**2005**
14,792	17,241

Source: National Federation of State High School Associations

a. Find the *amount* of increase in participation. 2,449

b. Fill in blanks to find the percent of increase in participation: <u>2,449</u> is <u>what</u> % of <u>14,792</u> ?

8. Fill in the blanks using the words *percent, amount,* and *base.*

Amount	=	percent	·	base

9. Translate each sentence into an equation. **Do not solve.**

▶ a. 12 is 40% of what number? $12 = 0.40 \cdot x$

b. 99 is what percent of 200? $99 = x \cdot 200$

c. What is 66% of 3? $x = 0.66 \cdot 3$

10. Use estimation to determine if each statement is reasonable.

a. 18 is 48% of 93. no

b. 47 is 6% of 206. no

▶ Selected exercises available online at **www.webassign.net/brookscole**

NOTATION

11. Change each percent to a decimal.

   a. 35% 0.35   **b.** 8.5% 0.085

   c. 150% 1.5   **d.** $2\frac{3}{4}$% 0.0275

▶ **12.** Change each decimal to a percent.

   a. 0.9 90%   **b.** 9 900%

   c. 0.999 99.9%

GUIDED PRACTICE

See Examples 1–3.

13. What number is 48% of 650? 312

▶ **14.** What number is 60% of 200? 120

15. 78 is what percent of 300? 26%

▶ **16.** 143 is what percent of 325? 44%

17. 75 is 25% of what number? 300

▶ **18.** 78 is 6% of what number? 1,300

19. What number is 92.4% of 50? 46.2

▶ **20.** What number is 2.8% of 220? 6.16

21. 0.42 is what percent of 16.8? 2.5%

▶ **22.** 199.92 is what percent of 2,352? 8.5%

23. 128.1 is 8.75% of what number? 1,464

▶ **24.** 1.12 is 140% of what number? 0.8

APPLICATIONS

25. ANTISEPTICS
Use the facts on the
label to determine
the amount of pure
hydrogen peroxide
in the bottle. 0.48 oz

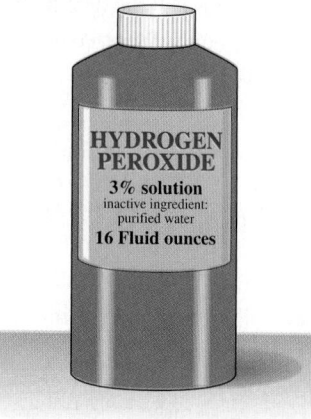

26. DINING OUT Refer to the sales receipt in the next
column. Compute the 15% tip (*rounded up* to the
nearest dollar). Then find the total cost of the meal.
$12.00, $87.18

27. U.S. FEDERAL BUDGET The circle graph shows
how the government spent $2,500 billion in 2005.
How much was spent on

   a. Social Security/Medicare? $925 billion

   b. Defense/Veterans? $600 billion

Based on 2006 Federal Income Tax Form 1040

28. TAX TABLES Use the table to compute the amount
of federal income tax to be paid on an income of
$39,909. $6,642.25

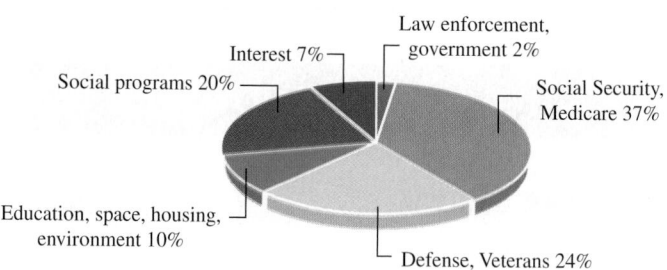

If your income is over—	But not over—	Your income tax is—	of the amount over—
$0	$7,300	.... 10%	$0
7,300	29,700	$730.00 + 15%	7,300
29,700	71,950	4,090.00 + 25%	29,700

▶ **29.** PAYPAL Many e-commerce businesses use PayPal
to perform payment processing for them. For certain
transactions, merchants are charged a fee of 2.9% of
the selling price of the item plus $0.30. What would
PayPal charge an online art store to collect payment
on a painting selling for $350? $10.45

▶ **30.** eBAY When a student sold an Xbox on eBay for
$153, she was charged a two-part final value fee:
5.25% of the first $25 of the selling price plus 3.25%
of the remainder of the selling price over $25. Find
the fee to sell the Xbox on eBay. $1.31 + $4.16 = $5.47

31. **PRICE GUARANTEES** Home Club offers a "10% Plus" guarantee: If the customer finds the same item selling for less somewhere else, he or she receives the difference in price plus 10% of the difference. A woman bought miniblinds at the Home Club for $120 but later saw the same blinds on sale for $98 at another store. How much can she expect to be reimbursed? $24.20

32. **ROOM TAXES** A guest at the San Antonio Hilton Airport Hotel paid $180 for a room plus a 9% city room tax, a $1\frac{3}{4}$% county room tax, and a 6% state room tax. Find the total amount of tax that the guest paid on the room. $30.15

33. **COMPUTER MEMORY** The *My Computer* screen on a student's computer is shown. What percent of the memory on the hard drive Local Disk (C:) of his computer is used? What percent is free? (GB stands for gigabytes.) 60%, 40%

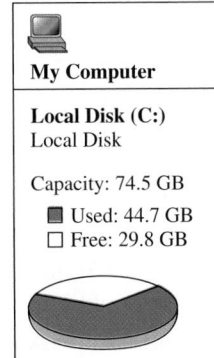

34. **GENEALOGY** Through an extensive computer search, a genealogist determined that worldwide, 180 out of every 10 million people had his last name. What percent is this? 0.0018%

35. **DENTISTRY** Refer to the dental record. What percent of the patient's teeth have fillings? Round to the nearest percent. 19%

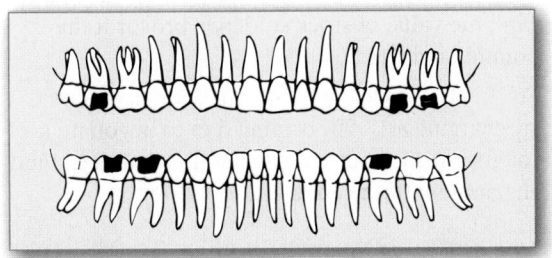

36. **TEST SCORES** The score 175/200 was written by an algebra instructor at the top of a student's test paper. Write the test score as a percent. 87.5%

37. **DMV WRITTEN TEST** To obtain a learner's permit to drive in Nevada, a score of 80% (or better) on a 50-question multiple-choice test is required. If a teenager answered 33 questions correctly, did he pass the test? no (66%)

38. **iPODS** The settings menu screen of an Apple iPod is shown in the next column. What percent of the memory capacity is still available? Round to the nearest percent. (GB stands for gigabytes.) 56%

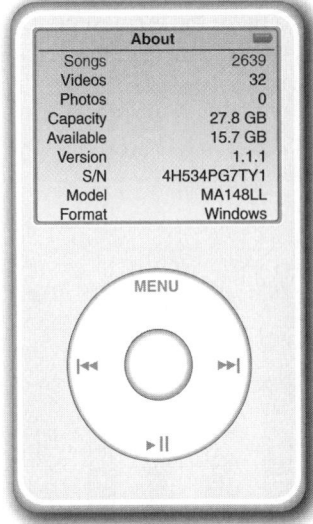

39. **CHILD CARE** After the first day of registration, 84 children had been enrolled in a day care center. That represented 70% of the available slots. Find the maximum number of children the center could enroll. 120

40. **RACING PROGRAMS** One month before a stock car race, the sale of ads for the official race program was slow. Only 12 pages, or just 30% of the available pages, had been sold. Find the total number of pages devoted to advertising in the program. 40

41. **NUTRITION** The Nutrition Facts label from a can of clam chowder is shown.

    a. Find the number of grams of saturated fat in one serving. What percent of a person's recommended daily intake is this? 5 g, 25%

    b. Determine the recommended number of grams of saturated fat that a person should consume daily. 20 g

Nutrition Facts

Serving Size 1 cup (240mL)
Servings Per Container about 2

Amount per serving		
Calories 240	Calories from Fat 140	
		% Daily Value*
Total Fat 15 g		23%
Saturated Fat 5 g		25%
Cholesterol 10 mg		3%
Sodium 980 mg		41%
Total Carbohydrate 21 g		7%
Dietary Fiber 2 g		8%
Sugars 1 g		
Protein 7 g		

42. **COMMERCIALS** Jared Fogle credits his tremendous weight loss to exercise and a diet of low-fat Subway sandwiches. His current weight (about 187 pounds) is 44% of his maximum weight (reached in March of 1998). What did he weigh then? 425 lb

▶ **43. EXPORTS** According to the graph, between what two years was there the greatest percent decrease in U.S. exports to Mexico? Find the percent of decrease. 2000–2001, about 9%

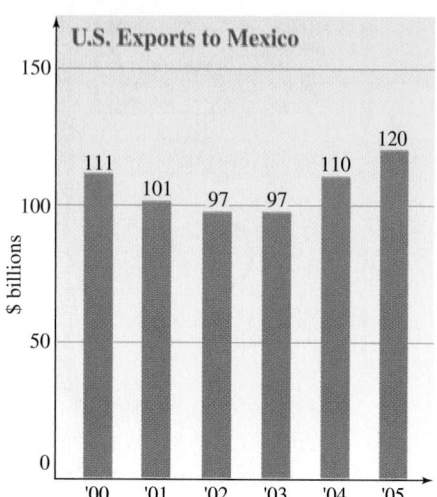

U.S. Exports to Mexico

Based on data from www.census.gov/foreign-trade

▶ **44. AUCTIONS** A pearl necklace of former First Lady Jacqueline Kennedy Onassis, originally valued at $700, was sold at auction in 1996 for $211,500. Find the percent of increase in the value of the necklace. (Round to the nearest percent.) 30,114%

45. INSURANCE COSTS A college student's good grades earned her a student discount on her car insurance premium. Find the percent of decrease to the nearest percent if her annual premium was lowered from $1,050 to $925. 12%

▶ **46. U.S. LIFE EXPECTANCY** Use the following life expectancy data for 1900 and 2004 to find the percent of increase for males and for females. Round to the nearest percent. males: 62%, females: 66%

	Years of life expected at birth	
	Male	**Female**
1900	46.3	48.3
2004	75.2	80.4

Source: National Vital Statistics Reports

47. TALK RADIO Refer to the table and find the percent increase in the number of news/talk radio stations from 2004 to 2005. Round to the nearest percent. 3%

Number of U.S. news/talk radio stations	
2004: 1,282	**2005:** 1,324

Source: *The World Almanac, 2006*

48. FOOD LABELS To be labeled "Reduced Fat," foods must contain at least 25% less fat per serving than the regular product. One serving of the original Jif peanut butter has 16 grams of fat per serving. The new Jif Reduced Fat product contains 12 grams of fat per serving. Does it meet the labeling requirement? 25% decrease, yes

▶ **49. TV SHOPPING** Jan bought a toy from the QVC home shopping network that was discounted 20%. If she saved $15, what was the original price of the toy? $75

▶ **50. DISCOUNTS** A 12% discount on a watch saved a shopper $48. Find the price of the watch before the discount. $400

51. SALES The price of a certain model patio set was reduced 35% because it was being discontinued. A shopper purchased two of them and saved a total of $210. Find the price of a patio set before the discount. $300

52. TV SALES The price of a plasma screen television was reduced $800 because it was used as a floor model. If this was a 40% savings, find the original price of the TV. $2,000

53. REAL ESTATE The $3\frac{1}{2}$% commission paid to a real estate agent on the sale of a condominium earned her $3,325. Find the selling price of the condo. $95,000

54. CONSIGNMENT An art gallery agreed to sell an artist's sculpture for a commission of 45%. What must be the selling price of the sculpture if the gallery would like to make $13,500? $30,000

▶ **55. STOCKBROKERS** A stockbroker charges a 2.5% commission to sell shares of a stock for a client. Find the value of stock sold by a broker if the commission was $640. $25,600

▶ **56. AGENTS** An agent made one million dollars by charging a 12.5% commission to negotiate a long-term contract for a professional athlete. Find the amount of the contract. $8,000,000

▌WRITING

57. Explain the error:

What is 5% of 8?

$x = 5 \cdot 8$

$x = 40$

40 is 5% of 8.

▶ **58.** Write a real-life situation that could be described by "9 is what percent of 20?"

59. Explain why 150% of a number is more than the number.

60. Why is the problem "What is 9% of 100?" easy to solve?

❙ REVIEW

61. Divide: $-\frac{16}{25} \div \left(-\frac{4}{15}\right)$ $\frac{12}{5} = 2\frac{2}{5}$

▶ **62.** What two numbers are a distance of 8 away from 4 on the number line?   12 and -4

63. Is -34 a solution of $x + 15 = -49$?   no

64. Evaluate: $2 + 3[24 - 2(2 - 5)]$ 92

SECTION 2.4
Formulas

Objectives

1   Use formulas from business.

2   Use formulas from science.

3   Use formulas from geometry.

4   Solve for a specified variable.

A **formula** is an equation that states a relationship between two or more variables. Formulas are used in fields such as business, science, and geometry.

1   Use formulas from business.

A formula for retail price: To make a profit, a merchant must sell an item for more than he or she paid for it. The price at which the merchant sells the product, called the **retail price,** is the *sum* of what the item cost the merchant plus the **markup.** Using r to represent the retail price, c the cost, and m the markup, we can write this formula as

$r = c + m$ Retail price = cost + markup

A formula for profit: The **profit** a business makes is the *difference* between the **revenue** (the money it takes in) and the cost. Using p to represent the profit, r the revenue, and c the cost, we can write this formula as

$p = r - c$ Profit = revenue − cost

If we are given the values of all but one of the variables in a formula, we can use our equation-solving skills to find the value of the remaining variable.

EXAMPLE 1   *Films*   Estimates are that 20th Century Fox made a $309 million profit on the movie *Star Wars: Revenge of the Sith.* If the studio received $424 million in worldwide box office revenue, find the cost to make and distribute the film. (Source: www.the-numbers.com, August 2006)

Strategy   To find the cost to make and distribute the film, we will substitute the given values in the formula $p = r - c$ and solve for c.

WHY   The variable c represents the unknown cost.

Solution
The movie made $309 million (the profit p) and the studio took in $424 million (the revenue r). To find the cost c, we proceed as follows.

$$p = r - c \qquad \text{This is the formula for profit.}$$

$$309 = 424 - c \qquad \text{Substitute 309 for } p \text{ and 424 for } r.$$

$$309 - 424 = 424 - c - 424 \qquad \text{To eliminate 424 on the right side, subtract 424 from both sides.}$$

❙ Self Check 1

A PTA spaghetti dinner made a profit of $275.50. If the cost to host the dinner was $1,235, how much revenue did it generate?

Now Try Problem 11
Self Check 1 Answer
$1,510.50

Teaching Example 1   A music department sold fruit for a fundraiser. If the fruit cost the music department $5,632, and they made $2,115 profit, how much revenue did the fruit sale generate?
Answer:
$7,747

© Lucasfilm Ltd./Photofest

$$-115 = -c \qquad \text{Do the subtractions.}$$

$$\frac{-115}{-1} = \frac{-c}{-1} \qquad \text{To solve for } c, \text{ divide (or multiply) both sides by } -1.$$

$$115 = c \qquad \text{The units are millions of dollars.}$$

It cost $115 million to make and distribute the film.

A formula for simple interest: When money is borrowed, the lender expects to be paid back the amount of the loan plus an additional charge for the use of the money, called **interest.** When money is deposited in a bank, the depositor is paid for the use of the money. The money the deposit earns is also called interest.

Interest is computed in two ways: either as **simple interest** or as **compound interest.** Simple interest is the *product* of the principal (the amount of money that is invested, deposited, or borrowed), the annual interest rate, and the length of time in years. Using I to represent the simple interest, P the principal, r the annual interest rate, and t the time in years, we can write this formula as

$$I = Prt \qquad \text{Interest} = \text{principal} \cdot \text{rate} \cdot \text{time}$$

> **The Language of Algebra**   The word *annual* means occurring once a year. An *annual* interest rate is the interest rate paid per year.

Self Check 2

A father loaned his daughter $12,200 at a 2% annual simple interest rate for a down payment on a house. If the interest on the loan amounted to $610, for how long was the loan? 2.5 yr

Now Try Problem 15

Teaching Example 2 A student saving for college invested $5,000. After one year she received a check for $137.50 in interest. Find the interest rate her money earned that year.
Answer:
2.75%

EXAMPLE 2   *Retirement Income*   One year after investing $15,000, a retired couple received a check for $1,125 in interest. Find the interest rate their money earned that year.

Strategy To find the interest rate, we will substitute the given values in the formula $I = Prt$ and solve for r.

WHY The variable r represents the unknown interest rate.

Solution

The couple invested $15,000 (the principal P) for 1 year (the time t) and made $1,125 (the interest I). To find the annual interest rate r, we proceed as follows.

$$I = Prt \qquad \text{This is the formula for simple interest.}$$

$$1{,}125 = 15{,}000r(1) \qquad \text{Substitute 1,125 for } I, 15{,}000 \text{ for } P, \text{ and 1 for } t.$$

$$1{,}125 = 15{,}000r \qquad \text{Simplify the right side.}$$

$$\frac{1{,}125}{15{,}000} = \frac{15{,}000r}{15{,}000} \qquad \text{To solve for } r, \text{ undo the multiplication by 15,000 by dividing both sides by 15,000.}$$

$$0.075 = r \qquad \text{Do the divisions.}$$

$$7.5\% = r \qquad \text{To write 0.075 as a percent, multiply 0.075 by 100 by moving the decimal point two places to the right and inserting a \% symbol.}$$

The couple received an annual rate of 7.5% that year on their investment. We can display the facts of the problem in a table.

	P	$\cdot \ r$	$\cdot \ t =$	I
Investment	15,000	0.075	1	1,125

> **Caution!**   When using the formula $I = Prt$, always write the interest rate r (which is given as a percent) as a decimal (or fraction) before performing any calculations.

2 Use formulas from science.

A formula for distance traveled: If we know the average rate (of speed) at which we will be traveling and the time we will be traveling at that rate, we can find the distance traveled. Using d to represent the distance, r the average rate, and t the time, we can write this formula as

$$d = rt \quad \text{Distance = rate} \cdot \text{time}$$

EXAMPLE 3   ***Whales***   As they migrate from the Bering Sea to Baja California, gray whales swim for about 20 hours each day, covering a distance of approximately 70 miles. Estimate their average swimming rate in miles per hour (mph).

Strategy   To find the swimming rate, we will substitute the given values in the formula $d = rt$ and solve for r.

WHY   The variable r represents the unknown average swimming rate.

Solution
The whales swam 70 miles (the distance d) in 20 hours (the time t). To find their average swimming rate r, we proceed as follows.

$d = rt$	This is the formula for distance traveled.
$70 = r(20)$	Substitute 70 for d and 20 for t.
$\dfrac{70}{20} = \dfrac{20r}{20}$	To solve for r, undo the multiplication by 20 by dividing both sides by 20.
$3.5 = r$	Do the divisions.

The whales' average swimming rate is 3.5 mph. The facts of the problem can be shown in a table.

	r	t	$= d$
Gray whale	3.5	20	70

A formula for converting temperatures: In the American system, temperature is measured on the Fahrenheit scale. The Celsius scale is used to measure temperature in the metric system. The formula that relates a Fahrenheit temperature F to a Celsius temperature C is:

$$C = \frac{5}{9}(F - 32)$$

EXAMPLE 4   Convert the temperature shown on the City Savings sign to degrees Fahrenheit.

Strategy   To find the temperature in degrees Fahrenheit, we will substitute the given Celsius temperature in the formula $C = \frac{5}{9}(F - 32)$ and solve for F.

CITY SAVINGS
TEMP 30°C

WHY The variable F represents the unknown temperature in degrees Fahrenheit.

Solution

The temperature in degrees Celsius is 30°. To find the temperature in degrees Fahrenheit F, we proceed as follows.

$$C = \frac{5}{9}(F - 32)$$ This is the formula for temperature conversion.

$$30 = \frac{5}{9}(F - 32)$$ Substitute 30 for C, the Celsius temperature.

$$\frac{9}{5} \cdot 30 = \frac{9}{5} \cdot \frac{5}{9}(F - 32)$$ To undo the multiplication by $\frac{5}{9}$, multiply both sides by the reciprocal of $\frac{5}{9}$.

$$54 = F - 32$$ Do the multiplications.

$$54 + 32 = F - 32 + 32$$ To isolate F, undo the subtraction of 32 by adding 32 to both sides.

$$86 = F$$

30°C is equivalent to 86°F.

---

3 Use formulas from geometry.

To find the **perimeter** of a plane (two-dimensional, flat) geometric figure, such as a rectangle or triangle, we find the distance around the figure by computing the sum of the lengths of its sides. Perimeter is measured in American units, such as inches, feet, yards, and in metric units such as millimeters, meters, and kilometers.

> **Perimeter Formulas**
>
> $P = 2l + 2w$ (rectangle)
> $P = 4s$ (square)
> $P = a + b + c$ (triangle)

> **The Language of Algebra**   When you hear the word *perimeter*, think of the distance around the "rim" of a flat figure.

EXAMPLE 5   *Flags*   The largest flag ever flown was an American flag that had a perimeter of 1,520 feet and a length of 505 feet. It was hoisted on cables across Hoover Dam to celebrate the 1996 Olympic Torch Relay. Find the width of the flag.

505 ft

Strategy To find the width of the flag, we will substitute the given values in the formula $P = 2l + 2w$ and solve for w.

WHY The variable w represents the unknown width of the flag.

Solution

The perimeter P of the rectangular-shaped flag is 1,520 ft and the length l is 505 ft. To find the width w, we proceed as follows.

$$P = 2l + 2w$$ This is the formula for the perimeter of a rectangle.

$$1{,}520 = 2(505) + 2w$$ Substitute 1,520 for P and 505 for l.

$$1{,}520 = 1{,}010 + 2w$$ Do the multiplication.

$$510 = 2w$$ To undo the addition of 1,010, subtract 1,010 from both sides.

$$255 = w$$ To isolate w, undo the multiplication by 2 by dividing both sides by 2.

The width of the flag is 255 feet. If its length is 505 feet and its width is 255 feet, its perimeter is $2(505) + 2(255) = 1{,}010 + 510 = 1{,}520$ feet, as given. ■

The **area** of a plane (two-dimensional, flat) geometric figure is the amount of surface that it encloses. Area is measured in square units, such as square inches, square feet, square yards, and square meters (written as in.², ft², yd², and m², respectively).

Area Formulas

$A = lw$ (rectangle)

$A = s^2$ (square)

$A = \dfrac{1}{2}bh$ (triangle)

$A = \dfrac{1}{2}h(B + b)$ (trapezoid)

Circle Formulas

$D = 2r$ (diameter)

$r = \dfrac{1}{2}D$ (radius)

$C = 2\pi r = \pi D$ (circumference)

$A = \pi r^2$ (area)

EXAMPLE 6   **a.** What is the circumference of a circle with diameter 14 feet? Round to the nearest tenth of a foot.   **b.** What is the area of the circle? Round to the nearest tenth of a square foot.

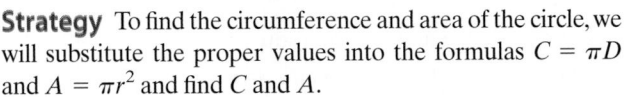
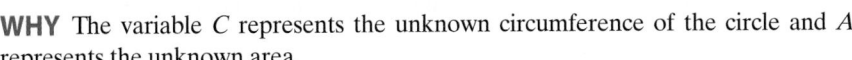

Strategy To find the circumference and area of the circle, we will substitute the proper values into the formulas $C = \pi D$ and $A = \pi r^2$ and find C and A.

WHY The variable C represents the unknown circumference of the circle and A represents the unknown area.

Solution

a. Recall that the circumference of a circle is the distance around it. To find the circumference C of a circle with diameter D equal to 14 ft, we proceed as follows.

$$C = \pi D$$ This is the formula for the circumference of a circle. πD means $\pi \cdot D$.

$$C = \pi(14)$$ Substitute 14 for D, the diameter of the circle.

$$= 14\pi$$ The exact circumference of the circle is 14π.

Self Check 6

Find the circumference of a circle with a radius of 10 inches. Round to the nearest hundredth of an inch.   62.83 in.

Now Try **Problem 28**

Teaching Example 6 If the diameter of a circle is 18 cm, find:
a. the circumference
b. the area
Answers:
a. 18π cm ≈ 56.5 cm
b. 81π cm² ≈ 254.5 cm²

$$\approx 43.98229715$$ *To use a scientific calculator to approximate the circumference, enter $\boxed{\pi}$ $\boxed{\times}$ 14 $\boxed{=}$. If you do not have a calculator, use 3.14 as an approximation of π. (Answers may vary slightly depending on which approximation of π is used.)*

The circumference is exactly 14π ft. Rounded to the nearest tenth, this is 44.0 ft.

b. The radius r of the circle is one-half the diameter, or 7 feet. To find the area A of the circle, we proceed as follows.

$A = \pi r^2$	*This is the formula for the area of a circle. πr^2 means $\pi \cdot r^2$.*
$A = \pi(7)^2$	*Substitute 7 for r, the radius of the circle.*
$= 49\pi$	*Evaluate the exponential expression: $7^2 = 49$. The exact area is 49π ft^2.*
≈ 153.93804	*To use a calculator to approximate the area, enter 49 $\boxed{\times}$ $\boxed{\pi}$ $\boxed{=}$.*

The area is exactly 49π ft^2. To the nearest tenth, the area is 153.9 ft^2.

Caution!   When an approximation of π is used in a calculation, it produces an approximate answer. Remember to use an *is approximately equal to* symbol $\approx$ in your solution to show that.

The **volume** of a three-dimensional geometric solid is the amount of space it encloses. Volume is measured in cubic units, such as cubic inches, cubic feet, and cubic meters (written as in.^{3}, ft^3, and m^3, respectively). Several volume formulas are given at the top of page 155.

Self Check 7

Find the volume of a cone whose base has a radius of 12 meters and whose height is 9 meters. Round to the nearest tenth of a cubic meter. Use the formula $V = \frac{1}{3}\pi r^2 h$. *1,357.2 m^3*

***Now Try* Problem 29**

Teaching Example 7 Find the volume of a cylinder with a diameter of 10 in. and a height of 15 in.
Answer:
375π in.$^3 \approx 1178$ in.^{3}

EXAMPLE 7   Find the volume of the cylinder. Round to the nearest tenth of a cubic centimeter.

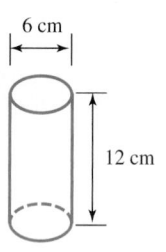

6 cm

12 cm

Strategy To find the volume of the cylinder, we will substitute the proper values into the formula $V = \pi r^2 h$ and find V.

WHY The variable V represents the unknown volume.

Solution
Since the radius of a circle is one-half its diameter, the radius r of the circular base of the cylinder is $\frac{1}{2}(6 \text{ cm}) = 3$ cm. The height h of the cylinder is 12 cm. To find volume V of the cylinder, we proceed as follows.

$V = \pi r^2 h$	*This is the formula for the volume of a cylinder. $\pi r^2 h$ means $\pi \cdot r^2 \cdot h$.*
$V = \pi(3)^2(12)$	*Substitute 3 for r and 12 for h.*
$= \pi(9)(12)$	*Evaluate the exponential expression.*
$= 108\pi$	*Multiply. The exact volume is 108π cm^3.*
≈ 339.2920066	*Use a calculator to approximate the volume.*

To the nearest tenth, the volume is 339.3 cubic centimeters. This can be written as 339.3 cm^3.

Volume Formulas

$V = lwh$ (rectangular solid) $V = \pi r^2 h$ (cylinder)

$V = s^3$ (cube)

$V = \dfrac{4}{3}\pi r^3$ (sphere)

$V = \dfrac{1}{3}\pi r^2 h$ (cone)

$V = \frac{1}{3}Bh$* (pyramid)

*Where B is the area of the base.

4 Solve for a specified variable.

Suppose a shopper wishes to calculate the markup m on several items, knowing their retail price r and their cost c to the merchant. It would take a lot of time to substitute values for r and c into the formula for retail price $r = c + m$ and then repeatedly solve for m. A better way is to solve the formula for m first, substitute values for r and c, and then compute m directly.

To **solve a formula for a specified variable** means to isolate that variable on one side of the equation, with all other variables and constants on the opposite side.

EXAMPLE 8   Solve the formula for retail price, $r = c + m$ for m.

Strategy To solve for m, we will focus on it as if it is the only variable in the equation. We will use a strategy similar to that used to solve linear equations in one variable to isolate m on one side. (See page 135 if you need to review the strategy.)

WHY We can solve the formula as if it were an equation in one variable because all the other variables are treated as if they were numbers (constants).

Solution

To solve for m, we will isolate m on this side of the equation.

$$r = c + m$$

$$r - c = c + m - c \qquad \text{To isolate } m, \text{ undo the addition of } c \text{ by subtracting } c \text{ from both sides.}$$

$$r - c = m \qquad \text{Simplify the right side: } c - c = 0.$$

$$m = r - c \qquad \text{Reverse the sides of the equation so that } m \text{ is on the left.}$$

> **The Language of Algebra**   We say that the formula is *solved for m* because m is alone on one side of the equation and the other side does not contain m.

EXAMPLE 9   Solve $A = \frac{1}{2}bh$ for b.

Strategy To solve for b, we will treat b as the only variable in the equation and use properties of equality to isolate it on one side. We will treat the other variables as if they were numbers (constants).

WHY To solve for a specified variable means to isolate it on one side of the equation.

Solution
We use the same steps to solve an equation for a specified variable that we use to solve equations with only one variable.

Self Check 8
Solve the formula for profit, $p = r - c$, for r. $r = p + c$

Now Try Problem 31

Teaching Example 8 Solve $P = a + b + c$ for a.
Answer:
$a = P - b - c$

Self Check 9
Solve $A = \frac{1}{2}r^2 a$ for a. $a = \frac{2A}{r^2}$

Now Try Problem 37

Teaching Example 9 Solve: $V = \frac{1}{3}Bh$ for h.
Answer:
$h = \frac{3V}{B}$

To solve for b, we will isolate b on this side of the equation.

$$A = \frac{1}{2}bh$$

$$2 \cdot A = 2 \cdot \frac{1}{2}bh \qquad \text{To clear the equation of the fraction, multiply both sides by 2.}$$

$$2A = bh \qquad \text{Simplify.}$$

$$\frac{2A}{h} = \frac{bh}{h} \qquad \text{To isolate } b \text{, undo the multiplication by } h \text{ by dividing both sides by } h.$$

$$\frac{2A}{h} = b \qquad \text{On the right side, remove the common factor of } h: \frac{\overset{1}{bh}}{\underset{1}{h}} = b.$$

$$b = \frac{2A}{h} \qquad \text{Reverse the sides of the equation so that } b \text{ is on the left.}$$

Self Check 10

Solve $P = 2l + 2w$ for w.

Now Try Problem 45

Self Check 10 Answer

$w = \frac{P - 2l}{2}$

Teaching Example 10 Solve:
$h = vt - 16t^2$ for v.
Answer:
$v = \frac{h + 16t^2}{t}$

EXAMPLE 10   Solve $P = 2l + 2w$ for l.

Strategy To solve for l, we will treat l as the only variable in the equation and use properties of equality to isolate it on one side. We will treat the other variables as if they were numbers (constants).

WHY To solve for a specified variable means to isolate it on one side of the equation.

Solution

To solve for l, we will isolate l on this side of the equation.

$$P = 2l + 2w$$

$$P - 2w = 2l + 2w - 2w \qquad \text{To undo the addition of } 2w \text{, subtract } 2w \text{ from both sides.}$$

$$P - 2w = 2l \qquad \text{Combine like terms: } 2w - 2w = 0.$$

$$\frac{P - 2w}{2} = \frac{2l}{2} \qquad \text{To isolate } l \text{, undo the multiplication by 2 by dividing both sides by 2.}$$

$$\frac{P - 2w}{2} = l \qquad \text{Simplify the right side.}$$

We can write the result as $l = \frac{P - 2w}{2}$.

Caution!   Do not try to simplify the result this way:

$$l = \frac{P - \overset{1}{2w}}{\underset{1}{2}}$$

This step is incorrect because 2 is not a factor of the entire numerator.

Self Check 11

Solve $x + 3y = 12$ for y.

Now Try Problem 47

Self Check 11 Answer

$y = 4 - \frac{1}{3}x$ or $y = -\frac{1}{3}x + 4$

Teaching Example 11 Solve
$5x + 3y = 9$ for y.
Answer:
$y = -\frac{5}{3}x + 3$

EXAMPLE 11   In Chapter 3, we will work with equations that involve the variables x and y, such as $3x + 2y = 4$. Solve this equation for y.

Strategy To solve for y, we will treat y as the only variable in the equation and use properties of equality to isolate it on one side.

WHY To solve for a specified variable means to isolate it on one side of the equation.

Solution

To solve for y, we will isolate y on this side of the equation.

$$3x + 2y = 4$$

$$3x + 2y - 3x = 4 - 3x$$ To eliminate 3x on the left side, subtract 3x from both sides.

$$2y = 4 - 3x$$ Combine like terms: $3x - 3x = 0$.

$$\frac{2y}{2} = \frac{4 - 3x}{2}$$ To isolate y, undo the multiplication by 2 by dividing both sides by 2.

$$y = \frac{4}{2} - \frac{3x}{2}$$ Write $\frac{4 - 3x}{2}$ as the difference of two fractions with like denominators, $\frac{4}{2}$ and $\frac{3x}{2}$.

$$y = 2 - \frac{3}{2}x$$ Simplify: $\frac{4}{2} = 2$. Write $\frac{3x}{2}$ as $\frac{3}{2}x$.

$$y = -\frac{3}{2}x + 2$$ On the right side, write the x term first.

Success Tip   When solving for a specified variable, there is often more than one way to express the result.

EXAMPLE 12   Solve $V = \pi r^2 h$ for r^2.

Strategy To solve for r^2, we will treat it as the only variable expression in the equation and isolate it on one side.

WHY To solve for a specified variable means to isolate it on one side of the equation.

Solution

To solve for r^2, we will isolate r^2 on this side of the equation.

$$V = \pi r^2 h$$

$$\frac{V}{\pi h} = \frac{\pi r^2 h}{\pi h}$$ $\pi r^2 h$ means $\pi \cdot r^2 \cdot h$. To isolate r^2, undo the multiplication by π and h on the right side by dividing both sides by πh.

$$\frac{V}{\pi h} = r^2$$ On the right side, remove the common factors of π and h: $\frac{\overset{1}{\pi} r^2 \overset{1}{h}}{\underset{1}{\pi} \underset{1}{h}} = r^2$.

$$r^2 = \frac{V}{\pi h}$$ Reverse the sides of the equation so that r^2 is on the left.

Self Check 12

Solve $V = lwh$ for w. $w = \frac{V}{lh}$

Now Try Problem 55

Teaching Example 12 Solve:
$V = \frac{1}{3}\pi r^2 h$ for r^2.
Answer:
$r^2 = \frac{3V}{\pi h}$

ANSWERS TO SELF CHECKS

1. $1,510.50 **2.** 2.5 yr **3.** 1.25 min **4.** −283°F **5.** 230 ft **6.** 62.83 in. **7.** 1,357.2 m^3
8. $r = p + c$ **9.** $a = \frac{2A}{r^2}$ **10.** $w = \frac{P - 2l}{2}$ **11.** $y = 4 - \frac{1}{3}x$ or $y = -\frac{1}{3}x + 4$ **12.** $w = \frac{V}{lh}$

SECTION 2.4   STUDY SET

VOCABULARY

Fill in the blanks.

1. A __formula__ is an equation that is used to state a known relationship between two or more variables.

2. The distance around a plane geometric figure is called its __perimeter__, and the amount of surface that it encloses is called its __area__.

▶ **3.** The __volume__ of a three-dimensional geometric solid is the amount of space it encloses.

▶ Selected exercises available online at
www.webassign.net/brookscole

4. The formula $a = P - b - c$ is <u>solved</u> for a because a is isolated on one side of the equation and the other side does not contain a.

CONCEPTS

5. Use variables to write the formula relating:

   a. Time, distance, rate $d = rt$

   b. Markup, retail price, cost $r = c + m$

   c. Costs, revenue, profit $p = r - c$

   d. Interest rate, time, interest, principal $I = Prt$

▶ **6.** Complete the table.

	Principal ·	rate ·	time =	interest
Account 1	$2,500	5%	2 yr	$250
Account 2	$15,000	4.8%	1 yr	$720

7. Complete the table to find how far light and sound travel in 60 seconds. (*Hint:* mi/sec means miles per second.)

	Rate	· time =	distance
Light	186,282 mi/sec	60 sec	11,176,920 mi
Sound	1,088 ft/sec	60 sec	65,280 ft

8. Determine which concept (perimeter, area, or volume) should be used to find each of the following. Then determine which unit of measurement, ft, ft^2, or ft^3, would be appropriate.

   a. The amount of storage in a freezer   volume, ft^3

   b. The amount of ground covered by a sleeping bag lying on the floor   area, ft^2

   c. The distance around a dance floor   perimeter, ft

NOTATION

Complete the solution.

9. Solve $Ax + By = C$ for y.

$$Ax + By = C$$
$$Ax + By - \boxed{Ax} = C - \boxed{Ax}$$
$$By = C - Ax$$
$$\frac{By}{\boxed{B}} = \frac{C - Ax}{\boxed{B}}$$
$$y = \frac{C - Ax}{\boxed{B}}$$

10. a. Approximate 98π to the nearest hundredth.   307.88

   b. In the formula $V = \pi r^2 h$, what does r represent? What does h represent?
   the radius of the cylinder, the height of the cylinder

   c. What does 45°C mean?
   45 degrees Celsius

   d. What does 15°F mean?
   15 degrees Fahrenheit

GUIDED PRACTICE

Use a formula to solve each problem. See Example 1.

11. HOLLYWOOD As of 2006, the movie *Titanic* had brought in $1,835 million worldwide and made a gross profit of $1,595 million. What did it cost to make the movie? $240 million

12. VALENTINE'S DAY Find the markup on a dozen roses if a florist buys them wholesale for $12.95 and sells them for $47.50. $34.55

13. SERVICE CLUBS After expenses of $55.15 were paid, a Rotary Club donated $875.85 in proceeds from a pancake breakfast to a local health clinic. How much did the pancake breakfast gross? $931

▶ **14.** NEW CARS The factory invoice for a minivan shows that the dealer paid $16,264.55 for the vehicle. If the sticker price of the van is $18,202, how much over factory invoice is the sticker price? $1,937.45

See Example 2.

▶ **15.** ENTREPRENEURS To start a mobile dog-grooming service, a woman borrowed $2,500. If the loan was for 2 years and the amount of interest was $175, what simple interest rate was she charged? 3.5%

16. SAVINGS A man deposited $5,000 in a credit union paying 6% simple interest. How long will the money have to be left on deposit to earn $6,000 in interest? 20 yr

17. LOANS A student borrowed some money from his father at 2% simple interest to buy a car. If he paid his father $360 in interest after 3 years, how much did he borrow? $6,000

▶ **18.** BANKING Three years after opening an account that paid simple interest of 6.45% annually, a depositor withdrew the $3,483 in interest earned. How much money was left in the account? $18,000

See Example 3.

19. SWIMMING In 1930, a man swam down the Mississippi River from Minneapolis to New Orleans, a total of 1,826 miles. He was in the water for 742 hours. To the nearest tenth, what was his average swimming rate? 2.5 mph

▶ **20.** PARADES Rose Parade floats travel down the 5.5-mile-long parade route at a rate of 2.5 mph. How long will it take a float to complete the route if there are no delays? 2.2 hr

21. HOT-AIR BALLOONS If a hot-air balloon travels at an average of 37 mph, how long will it take to fly 166.5 miles? 4.5 hours

22. AIR TRAVEL An airplane flew from Chicago to San Francisco in 3.75 hours. If the cities are 1,950 miles apart, what was the average speed of the plane? 520 mph

See Example 4.

23. FRYING FOODS One of the most popular cookbooks in U.S. history, *The Joy of Cooking*, recommends frying foods at $365°F$ for best results. Convert this to degrees Celsius. $185°C$

24. FREEZING POINTS Saltwater has a much lower freezing point than freshwater does. For saltwater that is as saturated as much it can possibly get (23.3% salt by weight), the freezing point is $-5.8°F$. Convert this to degrees Celsius. $-21°C$

▶ **25.** BIOLOGY Cryobiologists freeze living matter to preserve it for future use. They can work with temperatures as low as $-270°C$. Change this to degrees Fahrenheit. $-454°F$

26. METALLURGY Change $2{,}212°C$, the temperature at which silver boils, to degrees Fahrenheit. Round to the nearest degree. $4{,}014°F$

See Examples 5–7. *If you do not have a calculator, use 3.14 as an approximation of π. Answers may vary slightly depending on which approximation of π is used.*

27. ENERGY SAVINGS One hundred inches of foam weather stripping tape was placed around the perimeter of a rectangular-shaped window. If the length of the window is 30 inches, what is its width? 20 in.

▶ **28.** RUGS Find the amount of floor area covered by a circular throw rug that has a radius of 15 inches. Round to the nearest square inch. 707 in.^{2}

29. STRAWS Find the volume of a 150 millimeter-long drinking straw that has an inside diameter of 4 millimeters. Round to the nearest cubic millimeter. $1{,}885$ mm^3

30. RUBBER BANDS The world's largest rubber band ball is $5\frac{1}{2}$ ft tall and was made in 2006 by Steve Milton of Eugene, Oregon. Find the volume of the ball. Round to the nearest cubic foot. (*Hint:* The formula for the volume of a sphere is $V = \frac{4}{3}\pi r^3$.) 87 ft^3

Solve each formula for the specified variable. See Example 8.

31. $r = c + m$ for c
$c = r - m$

▶ **32.** $p = r - c$ for c
$c = r - p$

33. $P = a + b + c$ for b
$b = P - a - c$

34. $a + b + c = 180$ for a
$a = 180 - b - c$

Solve each formula for the specified variable. See Example 9.

35. $E = IR$ for R
$R = \frac{E}{I}$

36. $d = rt$ for t
$t = \frac{d}{r}$

37. $V = lwh$ for l
$l = \frac{V}{wh}$

38. $I = Prt$ for r
$r = \frac{I}{Pt}$

39. $C = 2\pi r$ for r
$r = \frac{C}{2\pi}$

40. $V = \pi r^2 h$ for h
$h = \frac{V}{\pi r^2}$

41. $V = \frac{1}{3}Bh$ for h
$h = \frac{3V}{B}$

42. $C = \frac{1}{7}Rt$ for R
$R = \frac{7C}{t}$

43. $w = \frac{s}{f}$ for f
$f = \frac{s}{w}$

▶ **44.** $P = \frac{ab}{c}$ for c
$c = \frac{ab}{P}$

Solve each formula for the specified variable. See Examples 10 and 11.

45. $T = 2r + 2t$ for r
$r = \frac{T - 2t}{2}$

46. $y = mx + b$ for x
$x = \frac{y - b}{m}$

47. $Ax + By = C$ for x
$x = \frac{C - By}{A}$

▶ **48.** $A = P + Prt$ for t
$t = \frac{A - P}{Pr}$

49. $K = \frac{1}{2}mv^2$ for m
$m = \frac{2K}{v^2}$

▶ **50.** $V = \frac{1}{3}\pi r^2 h$ for h
$h = \frac{3V}{\pi r^2}$

51. $A = \frac{a + b + c}{3}$ for c
$c = 3A - a - b$

52. $x = \frac{a + b}{2}$ for b
$b = 2x - a$

53. $2E = \frac{T - t}{9}$ for t
$t = T - 18E$

▶ **54.** $D = \frac{C - s}{n}$ for s
$s = C - Dn$

Solve each equation for the specified variable (or expression). See Example 12.

55. $s = 4\pi r^2$ for r^2
$r^2 = \frac{s}{4\pi}$

▶ **56.** $E = mc^2$ for c^2
$c^2 = \frac{E}{m}$

57. $Kg = \frac{wv^2}{2}$ for v^2
$v^2 = \frac{2Kg}{w}$

58. $c^2 = a^2 + b^2$ for a^2
$a^2 = c^2 - b^2$

TRY IT YOURSELF

Solve each equation for the specified variable (or expression).

59. $V = \frac{4}{3}\pi r^3$ for r^3
$r^3 = \frac{3V}{4\pi}$

60. $A = \frac{\pi r^2 S}{360}$ for r^2
$r^2 = \frac{360A}{\pi S}$

▶ **61.** $\frac{M}{2} - 9.9 = 2.1B$ for M
$M = 4.2B + 19.8$

62. $\frac{G}{0.5} + 16r = -8t$ for G
$G = -4t - 8r$

63. $S = 2\pi rh + 2\pi r^2$ for h
$h = \frac{S - 2\pi r^2}{2\pi r}$

64. $c = bn + 16t^2$ for t^2
$t^2 = \frac{c - bn}{16}$

65. $3x + y = 9$ for y
$y = -3x + 9$

66. $-5x + y = 4$ for y
$y = 5x + 4$

67. $-x + 3y = 9$ for y
$y = \frac{1}{3}x + 3$

68. $5y - x = 25$ for y
$y = \frac{1}{5}x + 5$

69. $4y + 16 = -3x$ for y
$y = -\frac{3}{4}x - 4$

70. $6y + 12 = -5x$ for y
$y = -\frac{5}{6}x - 2$

71. $A = \frac{1}{2}h(b + d)$ for b
$b = \frac{2A}{h} - d$ or $b = \frac{2A - hd}{h}$

72. $C = \frac{1}{4}s(t - d)$ for t
$t = \frac{4C + sd}{s}$ or $t = \frac{4C}{s} + d$

73. $\frac{7}{8}c + w = 9$ for c
$c = \frac{72 - 8w}{7}$

▶ **74.** $\frac{3}{4}m - t = 5b$ for m
$m = \frac{20b + 4t}{3}$

APPLICATIONS

75. If your automobile engine is making a knocking sound, a service technician will probably tell you that the octane rating of the gasoline that you are using is too low. Octane rating numbers are printed on the yellow decals on gas pumps. The formula used to calculate them is

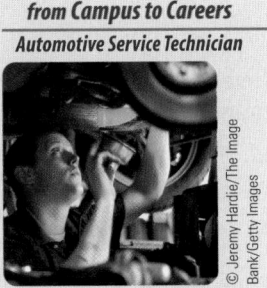
from Campus to Careers
Automotive Service Technician

© Jeremy Hardie/The Image Bank/Getty Images

$$\text{Pump octane number} = \frac{(R + M)}{2}$$

where R is the *research octane number,* which is determined with a test engine running at a low speed and M is the *motor octane number,* which is determined with a test engine running at a higher speed. Calculate the octane rating for the following three grades of gasoline.

Gasoline grade	R	M	Octane rating
Unleaded	92	82	87
Unleaded plus	95	83	89
Premium	97	85	91

76. PROPERTIES OF WATER The boiling point and the freezing point of water are to be given in both degrees Celsius and degrees Fahrenheit on the thermometer. Find the missing degree measures. 212°F, 0°C

Fahrenheit   **Celsius**

? —   — Boils: 100°

Freezes: 32° —   — ?

77. AVON PRODUCTS Complete the financial statement.

Income statement (dollar amounts in millions)	Quarter ending Sep 04	Quarter ending Sep 05
Revenue	1,806.2	1,886.0
Cost of goods sold	1,543.4	1,638.9
Operating profit	262.8	247.1

Source: Avon Products, Inc.

78. CREDIT CARDS The finance charge that a student pays on his credit card is 19.8% APR (annual percentage rate). Determine the finance charges (interest) the student would have to pay if the account's average balance for the year was $2,500. $495

79. CAMPERS The perimeter of the window of the camper shell is 140 in. Find the length of one of the shorter sides of the window. 14 in.

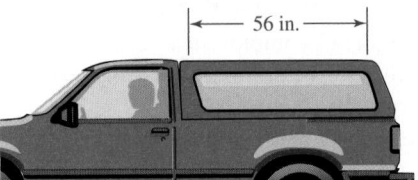
← 56 in. →

80. FLAGS The flag of Eritrea, a country in east Africa, is shown. The perimeter of the flag is 160 inches.

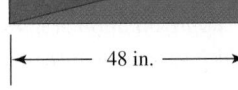
← 48 in. →

a. What is the width of the flag? 32 in.

b. What is the area of the red triangular region of the flag? 768 in.²

81. KITES 650 in.² of nylon cloth were used to make the kite shown. If its height is 26 inches, what is the wingspan? 50 in.

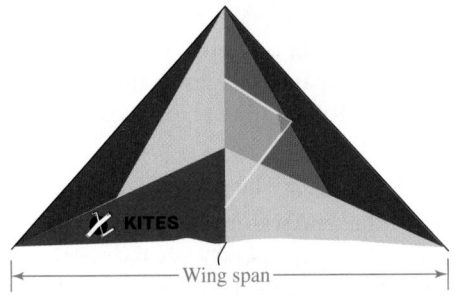
KITES
|— Wing span —|

82. MEMORIALS The Vietnam Veterans Memorial is a black granite wall recognizing the more than 58,000 Americans who lost their lives or remain missing. Find the total area of the two triangular-shaped surfaces on which the names are inscribed. 2,450 ft²

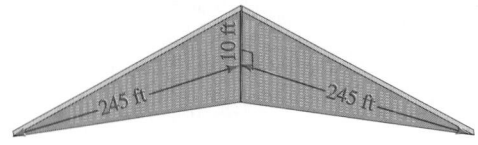
10 ft
245 ft   245 ft

83. WHEELCHAIRS Find the diameter of the rear wheel and the radius of the front wheel. 25 in., 2.5 in.

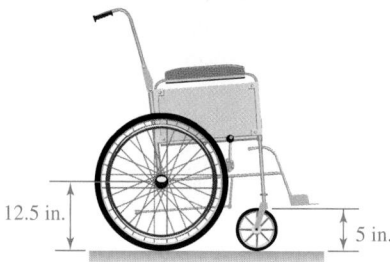

84. ARCHERY The diameter of a standard archery target used in the Olympics is 48.8 inches. Find the area of the target. Round to the nearest square inch. 1,870 in.²

85. BULLS-EYE See Exercise 84. The diameter of the center yellow ring of a standard archery target is 4.8 inches. What is the area of the bulls-eye? Round to the nearest tenth of a square inch. 18.1 in.²

86. GEOGRAPHY The circumference of the Earth is about 25,000 miles. Find its diameter to the nearest mile. 7,958 mi

87. HORSES A horse trots in a circle around its trainer at the end of a 28-foot-long rope. Find the area of the circle that is swept out. Round to the nearest square foot. 2,463 ft²

88. YO-YOS How far does a yo-yo travel during one revolution of the "around the world" trick if the length of the string is 21 inches? about 132 in.

89. WORLD HISTORY The Inca Empire (1438–1533) was centered in what is now called Peru. A special feature of Inca architecture was the trapezoid-shaped windows and doorways. A standard Inca window was 70 cm (centimeters) high, 50 cm at the base and 40 cm at the top. Find the area of a window opening. (*Hint:* The formula for the area of a trapezoid is $A = \frac{1}{2}$(height)(upperbase + lowerbase).) 3,150 cm²

90. HAMSTER HABITATS Find the amount of space in the tube. About 85 in.³

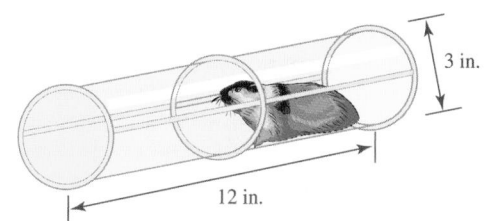

91. TIRES The road surface footprint of a sport truck tire is approximately rectangular. If the area of the footprint is 45 in.², about how wide is the tire? 6 in.

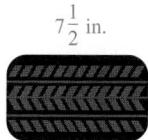

$7\frac{1}{2}$ in.

92. SOFTBALL The strike zone in fast-pitch softball is between the batter's armpit and the top of her knees, as shown. If the area of the strike zone for this batter is 442 in.², what is the width of home plate? 17 in.

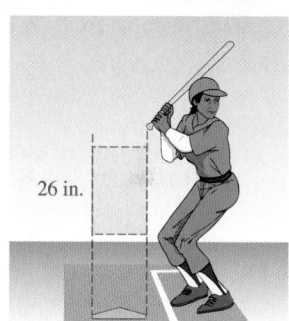

26 in.

93. FIREWOOD The cord of wood shown occupies a volume of 128 ft³. How long is the stack? 8 ft

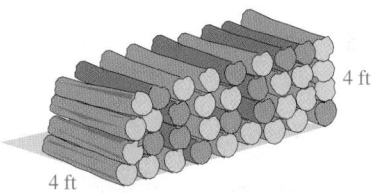

4 ft

4 ft

94. TEEPEES The teepees constructed by the Blackfoot Indians were cone-shaped tents about 10 feet high and about 15 feet across at the ground. Estimate the volume of a teepee with these dimensions, to the nearest cubic foot. 589 ft³

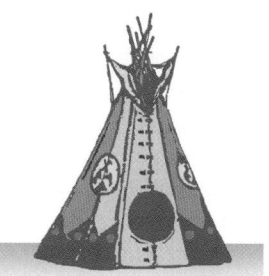

95. IGLOOS During long journeys, some Canadian Eskimos built winter houses of snow blocks stacked in the dome shape shown. Estimate the volume of an igloo having an interior height of 5.5 feet to the nearest cubic foot. 348 ft^3

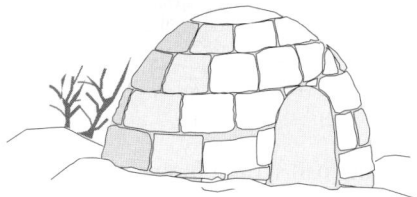

▶ **96.** PYRAMIDS The Great Pyramid at Giza in northern Egypt is one of the most famous works of architecture in the world. Find its volume to the nearest cubic foot. $85,503,750 \text{ ft}^3$

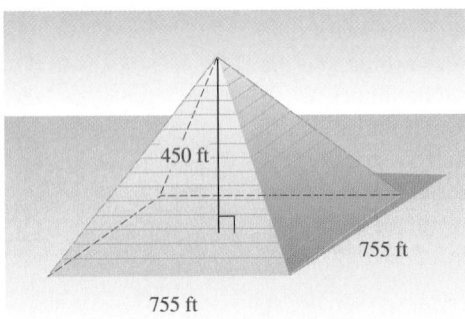

450 ft

755 ft

755 ft

97. COOKING If the fish shown in the illustration is 18 inches long, what is the area of the grill? Round to the nearest square inch. 254 in.^2

▶ **98.** SKATEBOARDING Refer to the illustration in the next column. A half-pipe ramp is in the shape of a semicircle with a radius of 8 feet. To the nearest tenth of a foot, what is the length of the arc that the rider travels on the ramp? 25.1 ft

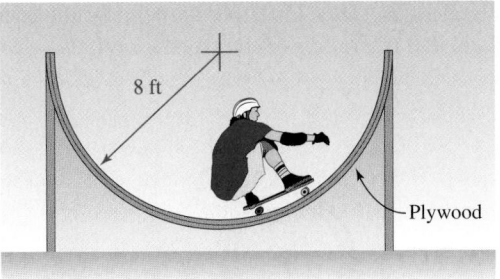

8 ft

Plywood

99. PULLEYS The approximate length L of a belt joining two pulleys of radii r and R feet with centers D feet apart is given by the formula $L = 2D + 3.25(r + R)$. Solve the formula for D. $D = \frac{L - 3.25r - 3.25R}{2}$

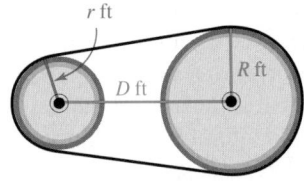

r ft

D ft

R ft

100. THERMODYNAMICS The Gibbs free-energy function is given by $G = U - TS + pV$. Solve this formula for the pressure p. $p = \frac{G - U + TS}{V}$

WRITING

101. After solving $A = B + C + D$ for B, a student compared her answer with that at the back of the textbook. Could this problem have two different-looking answers? Explain why or why not.

Student's answer: $B = A - C - D$

Book's answer: $B = A - D - C$

102. A student solved $x + 5c = 3c + a$ for c. His answer was $c = \frac{3c + a - x}{5}$ for c. Explain why the equation is not solved for c.

103. Explain the difference between what perimeter measures and what area measures.

104. Explain the error made below.

$$y = \frac{\overset{1}{\cancel{3x + 2}}}{\underset{1}{\cancel{2}}}$$

REVIEW

105. Find 82% of 168. 137.76

106. 29.05 is what percent of 415? 7%

107. What percent of 200 is 30? 15%

▶ **108.** A woman bought a coat for $98.95 and some gloves for $7.95. If the sales tax was 6%, how much did the purchase cost her? $113.31

SECTION 2.5
Problem Solving

In this section, you will see that algebra is a powerful tool that can be used to solve a wide variety of real-world problems.

1 Apply the steps of a problem-solving strategy.

To become a good problem solver, you need a plan to follow, such as the following five-step strategy.

> **The Language of Algebra** A **strategy** is a careful plan or method. For example, a businessman might develop a new advertising *strategy* to increase sales or a long distance runner might have a *strategy* to win a marathon.

Strategy for Problem Solving

1. **Analyze the problem** by reading it carefully. What information is given? What are you asked to find? What vocabulary is given? Often, a diagram or table will help you visualize the facts of the problem.

2. **Form an equation** by picking a variable to represent the numerical value to be found. Then express all other unknown quantities as expressions involving that variable. Key words or phrases can be helpful. Finally, translate the words of the problem into an equation.

3. **Solve the equation.**

4. **State the conclusion** using a complete sentence. Be sure to include the units (such as feet, seconds, or pounds) in your answer.

5. **Check the result** using the original wording of the problem, not the equation that was formed in step 2.

EXAMPLE 1 *California Coastline*

The first part of California's magnificent 17-Mile Drive begins at the Pacific Grove entrance and continues to Seal Rock. It is 1 mile longer than the second part of the drive, which extends from Seal Rock to the Lone Cypress. The final part of the tour winds through the Monterey Peninsula, eventually returning to the entrance. This part of the drive is 1 mile longer than four times the length of the second part. How long is each part of 17-Mile Drive?

© Visions of America, LLC/Alamy

Analyze The drive is composed of three parts. We need to find the length of each part. We can straighten out the winding 17-Mile Drive and model it with a line segment.

Self Check 1

The Mountain-Bay State Park Bike Trail in Northeast Wisconsin is 76 miles long. A couple rode the trail in four days. Each day they rode 2 miles more than the previous day. How many miles did they ride each day?

Now Try **Problem 16**

Self Check 1 Answer
16 mi, 18 mi, 20 mi, and 22 mi

Teaching Example 1 A mountain climber wants to cut a 213 foot rope into three pieces. If each piece is to be 2 feet longer than the previous one, how long is each piece?
Answer:
69 ft, 71 ft, and 73 ft

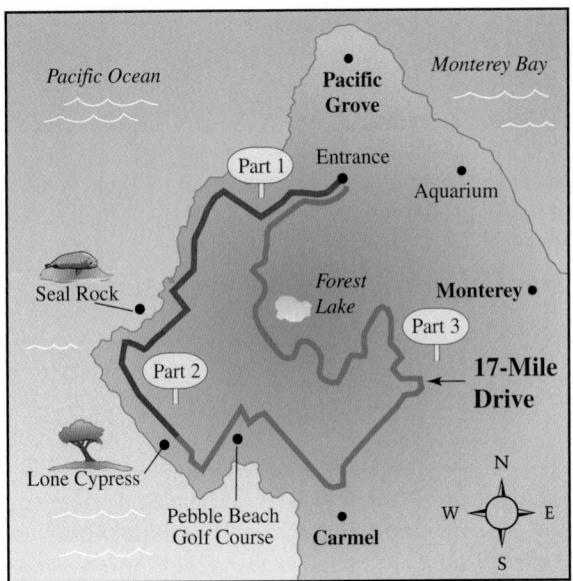

Form Since the lengths of the first part and of the third part of the drive are related to the length of the second part, we will let x represent the length of that part. We then express the other lengths in terms of x. Let

$$x = \text{the length of the second part of the drive}$$
$$x + 1 = \text{the length of the first part of the drive}$$
$$4x + 1 = \text{the length of the third part of the drive}$$

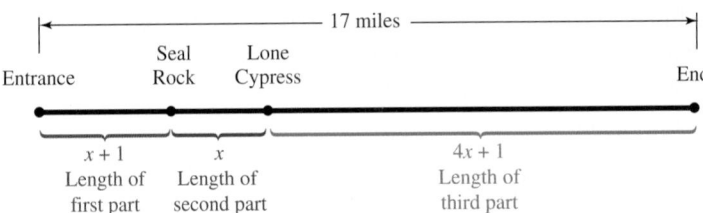

The sum of the lengths of the three parts must be 17 miles.

The length of part 1	plus	the length of part 2	plus	the length of part 3	equals	the total length.
$x + 1$	$+$	x	$+$	$4x + 1$	$=$	17

Solve

$$x + 1 + x + 4x + 1 = 17$$

$$6x + 2 = 17 \qquad \text{Combine like terms: } x + x + 4x = 6x \text{ and } 1 + 1 = 2.$$

$$6x = 15 \qquad \text{To undo the addition of 2, subtract 2 from both sides.}$$

$$\frac{6x}{6} = \frac{15}{6} \qquad \text{To isolate } x, \text{ undo the multiplication by 6 by dividing both sides by 6.}$$

$$x = 2.5 \qquad \text{Do the divisions.}$$

Recall that x represents the length of the second part of the drive. To find the lengths of the first and third parts, we evaluate $x + 1$ and $4x + 1$ for $x = 2.5$.

First part of drive   *Third part of drive*

$$x + 1 = \mathbf{2.5} + 1 \qquad 4x + 1 = 4(\mathbf{2.5}) + 1 \qquad \text{Substitute 2.5 for } x.$$

$$= 3.5 \qquad\qquad\qquad = 11$$

State The first part of the drive is 3.5 miles long, the second part is 2.5 miles long, and the third part is 11 miles long.

Check Since 3.5 mi + 2.5 mi + 11 mi = 17 mi, the answers check. ∎

EXAMPLE 2 *Computer Logos* A trucking company had their logo embroidered on the front of baseball caps. They were charged $8.90 per hat plus a one-time setup fee of $25. If the project cost $559, how many hats were embroidered?

Analyze

- It cost $8.90 to have a logo embroidered on a hat.
- The setup charge was $25.
- The project cost $559.
- We are to find the number of hats that were embroidered.

Form Let x = the number of hats that were embroidered. If x hats are embroidered, at a cost of $8.90 per hat, the cost to embroider all of the hats is $x \cdot \$8.90$ or $\$8.90x$. Now we translate the words of the problem into an equation.

The cost to embroider on hat	times	the number of hats	plus	the setup charge	equals	the total cost.
8.90	·	x	+	25	=	559

Solve

$$8.90x + 25 = 559$$

$$8.90x = 534 \qquad \text{To undo the addition of 25, subtract 25 from both sides.}$$

$$\frac{8.90x}{8.90} = \frac{534}{8.90} \qquad \text{To isolate x, undo the multiplication by 8.90 by dividing both sides by 8.90.}$$

$$x = 60 \qquad \text{Do the divisions.}$$

State The company had 60 hats embroidered.

Check The cost to embroider 60 hats is 60($8.90) = $534. When the $25 setup charge is added, we get $534 + $25 = $559. The answer checks. ∎

> **Success Tip** The *Form* step is often the hardest. To help, write a **verbal model** of the situation (shown here in blue) and then translate it into an equation.

EXAMPLE 3 *Auctions* A classic car owner is going to sell his 1960 Chevy Impala at an auction. He wants to make $46,000 after paying an 8% commission to the auctioneer. For what selling price (called the "hammer price") will the car owner make this amount of money?

Analyze When the commission is subtracted from the selling price of the car, the owner wants to have $46,000 left.

Form Let x = the selling price of the car. The amount of the commission is 8% of x, or $0.08x$. Now we translate the words of the problem to an equation.

The selling price of the car	minus	the auctioneer's commission	should be	$46,000.
x	−	0.08x	=	46,000

Self Check 2

A school club had their motto screenprinted on the front of T-shirts. They were charged $5 per shirt plus a one-time setup fee of $20. If the project cost $255, how many T-shirts were printed? 47

Now Try Problem 21

Teaching Example 2 A youth soccer league had shirts printed up for each of the players. They were charged $18 per shirt plus a one time setup fee of $20. If the total due was $4232, how many shirts were printed?
Answer:
234

Self Check 3

A farmer is going to sell one of his Black Angus cattle at an auction and would like to make $2,597 after paying a 6% commission to the auctioneer. For what selling price will the farmer make this amount of money? $2,762.77

Now Try Problem 27

Teaching Example 3 A homeowner is planning on selling his home. He wants to get $240,975 after paying a $5\frac{1}{2}$% commission. What selling price is needed to meet his requirement?
Answer: $255,000

Solve

$$x - 0.08x = 46{,}000$$

$$0.92x = 46{,}000 \qquad \text{Combine like terms: } 1.00x - 0.08x = 0.92x.$$

$$\frac{0.92x}{0.92} = \frac{46{,}000}{0.92} \qquad \text{To isolate } x, \text{ undo the multiplication by 0.92 by dividing both sides by 0.92.}$$

$$x = 50{,}000 \qquad \text{Do the divisions.}$$

State The owner will make $46,000 if the car sells for $50,000.

Check An 8% commission on $50,000 is $0.08(\$50{,}000) = \$4{,}000$. The owner will keep $\$50{,}000 - \$4{,}000 = \$46{,}000$. The answer checks.

2 Solve consecutive integer problems.

Integers that follow one another, such as 15 and 16, are called **consecutive integers.** They are 1 unit apart. **Consecutive even integers** are even integers that differ by 2 units, such as 12 and 14. Similarly, **consecutive odd integers** differ by 2 units, such as 9 and 11. When solving consecutive integer problems, if we let $x =$ the first integer, then

- two consecutive integers are x and $x + 1$
- two consecutive even integers are x and $x + 2$
- two consecutive odd integers are x and $x + 2$

Self Check 4

The definitions of the words *little* and *lobby* are on back-to-back pages in a dictionary. If the sum of the page numbers is 1,159, on what page can the definition of *little* be found? 579

Now Try **Problem 33**

Teaching Example 4 The birth years of the three children in a family are consecutive even integers. The sum of the integers is 5982. Find the year of each child's birth.
Answer:
1992, 1994, 1996

EXAMPLE 4   ***U.S. History*** The year George Washington was chosen president and the year the Bill of Rights went into effect are consecutive odd integers whose sum is 3,580. Find the years.

Analyze We need to find two consecutive odd integers whose sum is 3,580. From history, we know that Washington was elected president first and the Bill of Rights went into effect later.

Form Let $x =$ the first odd integer (the date when Washington was chosen president). The next odd integer is 2 *greater than* x, therefore $x + 2 =$ the next larger odd integer (the date when the Bill of Rights went into effect).

The first odd integer	plus	the second odd integer	is	3,580.
x	$+$	$x + 2$	$=$	$3{,}580$

Solve

$$x + x + 2 = 3{,}580$$

$$2x + 2 = 3{,}580 \qquad \text{Combine like terms: } x + x = 2x.$$

$$2x = 3{,}578 \qquad \text{To undo the addition of 2, subtract 2 from both sides.}$$

$$x = 1{,}789 \qquad \text{To isolate } x, \text{ undo the multiplication by 2 by dividing both sides by 2.}$$

State George Washington was chosen president in the year 1789. The Bill of Rights went into effect in $1789 + 2 = 1791$.

Check 1789 and 1791 are consecutive odd integers whose sum is $1789 + 1791 = 3{,}580$. The answers check.

> ***The Language of Algebra*** *Consecutive* means following one after the other in order. Elton John holds the record for the most *consecutive* years with a song on the Top 50 music chart: 31 years (1970 to 2000).

3 Solve geometry problems.

EXAMPLE 5 *Crime Scenes* Police used 400 feet of yellow tape to fence off a rectangular-shaped lot for an investigation. Fifty less feet of tape was used for each width as for each length. Find the dimensions of the lot.

Analyze Since the yellow tape surrounded the lot, the concept of perimeter applies. Recall that the formula for the perimeter of a rectangle is $P = 2l + 2w$. We also know that the width of the lot is 50 feet less than the length.

Form Since the width of the lot is given in terms of the length, we let l = the length of the lot. Then $l - 50$ = the width. Using the perimeter formula, we have:

2	times	the length	plus	2	times	the width	is	the perimeter.
2	·	l	+	2	·	$(l - 50)$	=	400

Solve

$2l + 2(l - 50) = 400$ Write the parentheses so that the entire expression $l - 50$ is multiplied by 2.

$2l + 2l - 100 = 400$ Distribute the multiplication by 2.

$4l - 100 = 400$ Combine like terms: $2l + 2l = 4l$.

$4l = 500$ To undo the subtraction of 100, add 100 to both sides.

$l = 125$ To isolate l, undo the multiplication by 4 by dividing both sides by 4.

State The length of the lot is 125 feet and width is $125 - 50 = 75$ feet.

Check The width (75 feet) is 50 less than the length (125 feet). The perimeter of the lot is $2(125) + 2(75) = 250 + 150 = 400$ feet. The answers check.

EXAMPLE 6 *Isosceles Triangles* If the vertex angle of an isosceles triangle is 56°, find the measure of each base angle.

Analyze An **isosceles triangle** has two sides of equal length, which meet to form the **vertex angle.** In this case, the measurement of the vertex angle is 56°. We can sketch the triangle as shown. The **base angles** opposite the equal sides are also equal. We need to find their measure.

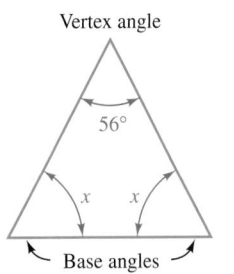

Vertex angle

56°

x x

Base angles

Form If we let x = the measure of one base angle, the measure of the other base angle is also x. Since the sum of the angles of any triangle is 180°, the sum of the base angles and the vertex angle is 180°. We can use this fact to form the equation.

One base angle	plus	the other base angle	plus	the vertex angle	is	180°.
x	+	x	+	56	=	180

Solve

$$x + x + 56 = 180$$
$$2x + 56 = 180 \quad \text{Combine like terms: } x + x = 2x.$$
$$2x = 124 \quad \text{To undo the addition of 56, subtract 56 from both sides.}$$
$$x = 62 \quad \text{To isolate } x \text{, undo the multiplication by 2 by dividing both sides by 2.}$$

State The measure of each base angle is 62°.

Check Since 62° + 62° + 56° = 180°, the answer checks.

ANSWERS TO SELF CHECKS

1. 16 mi, 18 mi, 20 mi, 22 mi   **2.** 47   **3.** $2,762.77   **4.** 579   **5.** 5 ft by 11 ft   **6.** 12 cm, 12 cm

---

SECTION 2.5 STUDY SET

VOCABULARY

Fill in the blanks.

1. Integers that follow one another, such as 7 and 8, are called _consecutive_ integers.

▶ 2. An _isosceles_ triangle is a triangle with two sides of the same length.

3. The equal sides of an isosceles triangle meet to form the _vertex_ angle. The angles opposite the equal sides are called _base_ angles, and they have equal measures.

4. When asked to find the dimensions of a rectangle, we are to find its _length_ and _width_.

CONCEPTS

▶ 5. A 17-foot pipe is cut into three sections. The longest section is three times as long as the shortest, and the middle-sized section is 2 feet longer than the shortest. Complete the diagram.

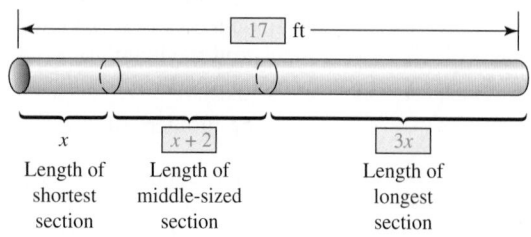

x	$x + 2$	$3x$
Length of shortest section	Length of middle-sized section	Length of longest section

6. It costs $28 per hour to rent a trailer. Write an expression that represents the cost to rent the trailer for x hours. $28x$

7. A realtor is paid a 3% commission on the sale of a house. Write an expression that represents the amount of the commission if a house sells for $\$x$. $\$0.03x$

8. The perimeter of the rectangle is 15 feet. Fill in the blanks: $2\left(5x-1 \right) + 2x = 15$

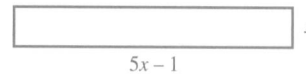

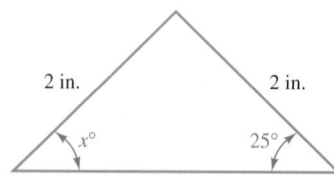

9. What is the sum of the measures of the angles of any triangle? 180°

10. What is x? 25

NOTATION

11. **a.** If x represents an integer, write an expression for the next largest integer. $x + 1$

▶ Selected exercises available online at
www.webassign.net/brookscole

b. If x represents an odd integer, write an expression for the next largest odd integer. $x + 2$

12. What does 45° mean? 45 degrees

▌ GUIDED PRACTICE

See Examples 1–3.

13. A 12-foot board has been cut into two sections, one twice as long as the other. How long is each section? 4 ft, 8 ft

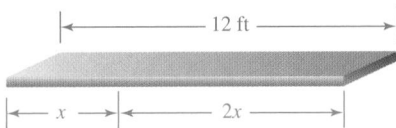

14. The robotic arm will extend a total distance of 18 feet. Find the length of each section. 5 ft, 9 ft, 4 ft

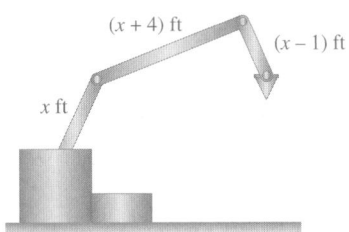

15. NATIONAL PARKS The Natchez Trace Parkway is a historical 444-mile route from Natchez, Mississippi, to Nashville, Tennessee. A couple drove the Trace in four days. Each day they drove 6 miles more than the previous day. How many miles did they drive each day? 102 mi, 108 mi, 114 mi, 120 mi

16. TOURING A rock group plans to travel for a total of 38 weeks, making three concert stops. They will be in Japan for 4 more weeks than they will be in Australia. Their stay in Sweden will be 2 weeks shorter than that in Australia. How many weeks will they be in each country? Australia: 12 wk, Japan: 16 wk, Sweden: 10 wk

17. SOLAR HEATING Refer to the illustration in the next column. One solar panel is 3.4 feet wider than the other. Find the width of each panel. 7.3 ft, 10.7 ft

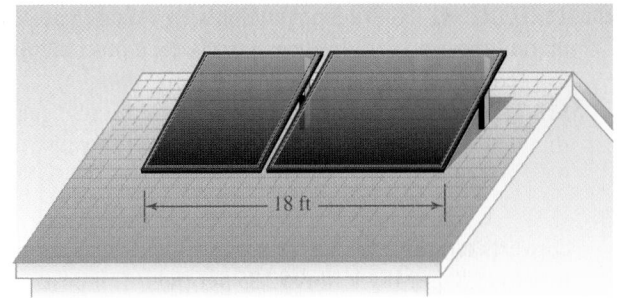

18. ACCOUNTING Determine the 2005 income of Abercrombie & Fitch Company for each quarter from the data in the graph. in millions of dollars: $40, $57, $72, $165

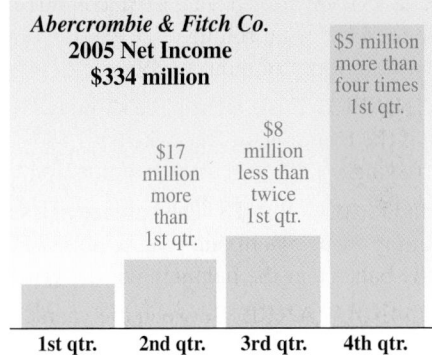

19. COUNTING CALORIES A slice of pie with a scoop of ice cream has 850 calories. The calories in the pie alone are 100 more than twice the calories in the ice cream alone. How many calories are in each food? 250 calories in ice cream, 600 calories in pie

20. WASTE DISPOSAL Two tanks hold a total of 45 gallons of a toxic solvent. One tank holds 6 gallons more than twice the amount in the other. How many gallons does each tank hold? 13 gal, 32 gal

21. CONCERTS The fee to rent a concert hall is $2,250 plus $150 per hour to pay for the support staff. For how many hours can an orchestra rent the hall and stay within a budget of $3,300? 7

22. TRUCK MECHANICS An engine repair cost a truck owner $1,185 in parts and labor. If the parts were $690 and the mechanic charged $45 per hour, how many hours did the repair take? 11

23. FIELD TRIPS It costs a school $65 a day plus $0.25 per mile to rent a 15-passenger van. If the van is rented for two days, how many miles can be driven on a $275 budget? 580

24. DECORATIONS A party supply store charges a set-up fee of $80 plus 35¢ per balloon to make a balloon arch. A business has $150 to spend on decorations for their grand opening. How many balloons can they have in the arch? (*Hint:* 35¢ = $0.35.) 200

▶ **25.** TUTORING High school students enrolling in a private tutoring program must first take a placement test (cost $25) before receiving tutoring (cost $18.75 per hour). If a family has set aside $400 to get their child extra help, how many hours of tutoring can they afford? 20

▶ **26.** DATA CONVERSION The *Books2Bytes* service converts old print books to Microsoft Word electronic files for $20 per book plus $2.25 per page. If it cost $1,201.25 to convert a novel, how many pages did the novel have? 525

▶ **27.** CATTLE AUCTIONS A cattle rancher is going to sell one of his prize bulls at an auction and would like to make $45,500 after paying a 9% commission to the auctioneer. For what selling price will the rancher make this amount of money? $50,000

28. LISTING PRICE At what price should a home be listed if the owner wants to make $567,000 on its sale after paying a 5.5% real estate commission? $600,000

29. SAVINGS ACCOUNTS The balance in a savings account grew by 5% in one year, to $5,512.50. What was the balance at the beginning of the year? $5,250

▶ **30.** AUTO INSURANCE Between the years 2000 and 2006, the average cost for auto insurance nationwide grew 27%, to $867. What was the average cost in 2000? Round to the nearest dollar. $683

***Consecutive integer problems* See Example 4.**

31. SOCCER Ronaldo of Brazil and Gerd Mueller of Germany rank 1 and 2, respectively, with the most goals scored in World Cup play. The number of goals Ronaldo and Mueller have scored are consecutive integers that total 29. Find the number of goals scored by each man. Ronaldo: 15, Mueller: 14

32. DICTIONARIES The definitions of the words *job* and *join* are on back-to-back pages in a dictionary. If the sum of those page numbers is 1,411, on what page can the definition of *job* be found? 705

▶ **33.** TV HISTORY *Friends* and *Leave It to Beaver* are two of the most popular television shows of all time. The number of episodes of each show are consecutive even integers whose sum is 470. If there are more episodes of *Friends,* how many episodes of each were there? *Friends:* 236, *Leave It to Beaver:* 234

▶ **34.** VACATIONS The table in the next column shows the average number of vacation days an employed adult receives for selected countries. Complete the table. (The numbers of days are listed in descending order.)

Average number of vacation days per year	
Country	**Days**
Italy	42
France	37
Germany	35
U.S.	13

Consecutive odd integers whose sum is 72.

Source: *The World Almanac,* 2006

35. CELEBRITY BIRTHDAYS Elvis Presley, George Foreman, and Kirstie Alley have birthdays (in that order) on consecutive even-numbered days in January. The sum of the calendar dates of their birthdays is 30. Find each birthday. Jan. 8, 10, 12

▶ **36.** LOCKS The three numbers of the combination for a lock are consecutive integers, and their sum is 81. Find the combination. 26, 27, 28

***Geometry problems* See Examples 5–6.**

▶ **37.** TENNIS The perimeter of a regulation singles tennis court is 210 feet and the length is 3 feet less than three times the width. What are the dimensions of the court? width: 27 ft, length: 78 ft

38. SWIMMING POOLS The seawater Orthlieb Pool in Casablanca, Morocco, is the largest swimming pool in the world. With a perimeter of 1,110 meters, this rectangular-shaped pool is 30 meters longer than 6 times its width. Find its dimensions. 75 m by 480 m

▶ **39.** ART The *Mona Lisa* was completed by Leonardo da Vinci in 1506. The length of the picture is 11.75 inches shorter than twice the width. If the perimeter of the picture is 102.5 inches, find its dimensions. 21 in. by 30.25 in.

© Réunion des Musées Nationaux/Art Resource, NY

▶ **40.** NEW YORK CITY Central Park, which lies in the middle of Manhattan, is rectangular-shaped and has a 6-mile perimeter. The length is 5 times the width. What are the dimensions of the park? width: 0.5 mi, length: 2.5 mi

41. ENGINEERING A truss is in the form of an isosceles triangle. Each of the two equal sides is 4 feet shorter than the third side. If the perimeter is 25 feet, find the lengths of the sides. 7 ft, 7 ft, 11 ft

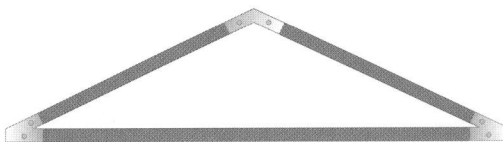

▶ **42. FIRST AID** A sling is in the shape of an isosceles triangle with a perimeter of 144 inches. The longest side of the sling is 18 inches longer than either of the other two sides. Find the lengths of each side. 60 in., 42 in., 42 in.

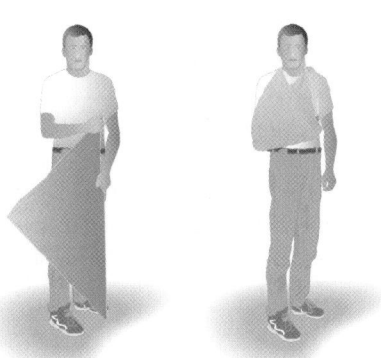

▶ **43. TV TOWERS** The two guy wires supporting a tower form an isosceles triangle with the ground. Each of the base angles of the triangle is 4 times the third angle (the vertex angle). Find the measure of the vertex angle. 20°

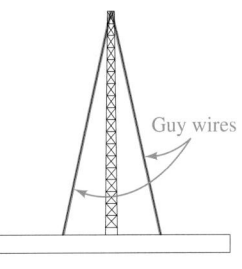

Guy wires

▶ **44. CLOTHESLINES** A pair of damp jeans are hung in the middle of a clothesline to dry. Find $x°$, the angle that the clothesline makes with the horizontal. 11°

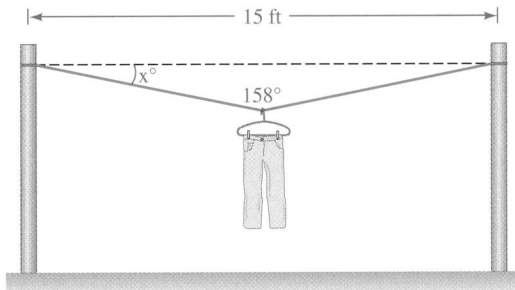

15 ft

$x°$

158°

▶ **45. MOUNTAIN BICYCLES** For the bicycle frame shown in the next column, the angle that the horizontal crossbar makes with the seat support is 15° less than twice the angle at the steering column. The angle at the pedal gear is 25° more than the angle at the steering column. Find these three angle measures. 42.5°, 70°, 67.5°

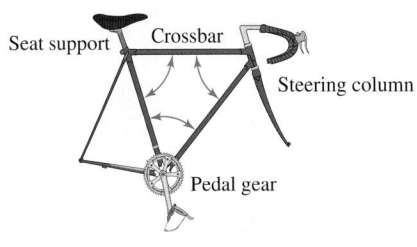

Seat support Crossbar

Steering column

Pedal gear

▶ **46. TRIANGLES** The measure of ∠1 (read as angle 1) of a triangle is one-half that of ∠2. The measure of ∠3 is equal to the sum of the measures of ∠1 and ∠2. Find each angle measure. 30°, 60°, 90°

▶ **47. COMPLEMENTARY ANGLES** Two angles are called *complementary angles* when the sum of their measures is 90°. Find the measures of the complementary angles shown in the illustration. 22°, 68°

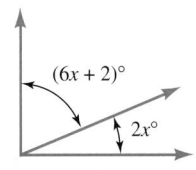

$(6x + 2)°$

$2x°$

▶ **48. SUPPLEMENTARY ANGLES** Two angles are called *supplementary angles* when the sum of their measures is 180°. Find the measures of the supplementary angles shown in the illustration. 40°, 140°

$(4x + 40)°$

$(x + 15)°$

WRITING

49. Create a geometry problem that could be answered by solving the equation $2w + 2(w + 5) = 26$.

50. What information do you need to know to answer the following question?

A business rented a copy machine for $85 per month plus 4¢ for every copy made. How many copies can be made each month?

51. Make a list of words and phrases that translate to an equal symbol =.

52. Define the word *strategy*.

REVIEW

Solve.

53. $\frac{5}{8}x = -15$ −24

54. $\frac{12x + 24}{13} = 36$ 37

55. $\frac{3}{4}y = \frac{2}{5}y - \frac{3}{2}y - 2$ $-\frac{40}{37}$

56. $6 + 4(1 - x) = 3(x + 1)$ 1

57. $4.2(y - 4) - 0.6y = -13.2$ 1

58. $16 - 8(b + 4) = 24b + 64$ $-\frac{5}{2}$

Objectives

1. Solve investment problems.

2. Solve uniform motion problems.

3. Solve liquid mixture problems.

4. Solve dry mixture problems.

5. Solve number-value problems.

SECTION **2.6**

More about Problem Solving

In this section, we will solve problems that involve money, motion, and mixtures. Tables are a helpful way to organize the information given in these problems.

1   Solve investment problems.

To find the amount of *simple interest* I an investment earns, we use the formula $I = Prt$, where P is the principal (the amount invested), r is the annual interest rate, and t is the time in years.

Self Check 1

A student invested $4,200 in certificates of deposit, one at 2% and the other at 3%. Find the amount invested at each rate if the first year combined interest income from the two investments was $102.

Now Try Problem 17

Self Check 1 Answer
$2,400 at 2%, $1,800 at 3%

Teaching Example 1 A professor has $15,000 to invest for 1 year, some at 8% and the rest at 7%. If she will earn $1,110 from these investments, how much did she invest at each rate?
Answer:
$6,000 at 8%, $9,000 at 7%

EXAMPLE 1   ***Paying Tuition***   A college student invested the $12,000 inheritance he received and decided to use the annual interest earned to pay his tuition cost of $945. The highest rate offered by a bank at that time was 6% annual simple interest. At this rate, he could not earn the needed $945, so he invested some of the money in a riskier, but more profitable, investment offering a 9% return. How much did he invest at each rate?

Analyze   We know that $12,000 was invested for 1 year at two rates: 6% and 9%. We are asked to find the amount invested at each rate so that the total return would be $945.

Form   Let $x =$ the amount invested at 6%. Then $12,000 - x =$ the amount invested at 9%. To organize the facts of the problem, we enter the principal, rate, time, and interest earned in a table.

Step 1: List each investment in a row of the table.

Bank				
Riskier investment				

Step 2: Label the columns using $I = Prt$ reversed and also write Total:.

	P	$\cdot\ r\ \cdot$	$t=$	I
Bank				
Riskier investment				
				Total:

Step 3: Enter the rates, times, and total interest.

	P	$\cdot\ r\ \cdot$	$t=$	I
Bank		0.06	1	
Riskier investment		0.09	1	
				Total: **945**

Step 4: Enter each unknown principal.

	P	· r	· t =	I
Bank	x	0.06	1	
Riskier investment	**12,000 − x**	0.09	1	
				Total: 945

Step 5: In the last column, multiply P, r, and t to obtain expressions for the interest earned.

	P	· r	· t =	I	
Bank	x	0.06	1	**0.06x**	← This is x · 0.06 · 1.
Riskier investment	12,000 − x	0.09	1	**0.09(12,000 − x)**	←
				Total: 945	

Use the information in this
column to form an equation.

This is (12,000 − x) · 0.09 · 1.

The interest earned at 6%	plus	the interest earned at 9%	equals	the total interest.
0.06x	+	[0.09(12,000 − x)]	=	945

Solve

$$0.06x + 0.09(12{,}000 - x) = 945$$

$$100[0.06x + 0.09(12{,}000 - x)] = 100(945)$$ Multiply both sides by 100 to clear the equation of decimals.

$$100(0.06x) + 100(0.09)(12{,}000 - x) = 100(945)$$ Distribute the multiplication by 100.

$$6x + 9(12{,}000 - x) = 94{,}500$$ Do the multiplications by 100.

$$6x + 108{,}000 - 9x = 94{,}500$$ Use the distributive property.

$$-3x + 108{,}000 = 94{,}500$$ Combine like terms.

$$-3x = -13{,}500$$ Subtract 108,000 from both sides.

$$x = 4{,}500$$ To isolate x, divide both sides by −3.

State The student invested $4,500 at 6% and $12,000 − $4,500 = $7,500 at 9%.

Check The first investment earned 0.06($4,500), or $270. The second earned 0.09($7,500), or $675. Since the total return was $270 + $675 = $945, the answers check.

2   Solve uniform motion problems.

If we know the rate r at which we will be traveling and the time t we will be traveling at that rate, we can find the distance d traveled by using the formula $d = rt$.

Self Check 2

Two search-and-rescue teams leave base at the same time looking for a lost boy. The first team, on foot, heads north at 2 mph, and the other, on horseback, heads south at 4 mph. How long will it take them to search a distance of 21 miles between them? 3.5 hr

Now Try **Problem 27**

Teaching Example 2 A car leaves Rockford traveling toward Wausau at the rate of 55 mph. At the same time, another car leaves Wausau traveling toward Rockford at the rate of 50 mph. How long will it take them to meet if the cities are 157.5 miles apart?
Answer:
$1\frac{1}{2}$ hr

EXAMPLE 2   *Rescues at Sea*   A cargo ship, heading into port, radios the Coast Guard that it is experiencing engine trouble and that its speed has dropped to 3 knots (this is 3 sea miles per hour). Immediately, a Coast Guard cutter leaves port and speeds at a rate of 25 knots directly toward the disabled ship, which is 56 sea miles away. How long will it take the Coast Guard to reach the ship? (Sea miles are also called nautical miles.)

Analyze We know the *rate* of each ship (25 knots and 3 knots), and we know that they must close a *distance* of 56 sea miles between them. We don't know the *time* it will take to do this.

Form Let t = the time it takes the Coast Guard to reach the cargo ship. During the rescue, the ships don't travel at the same rate, but they do travel for the same amount of time. Therefore, t also represents the travel time for the cargo ship.

   We enter the rates, the variable t for each time, and the total distance traveled by the ships (56 sea miles) in the table. To fill in the last column, we use the formula $r \cdot t = d$ twice to find an expression for each distance traveled: $25 \cdot t = 25t$ and $3 \cdot t = 3t$.

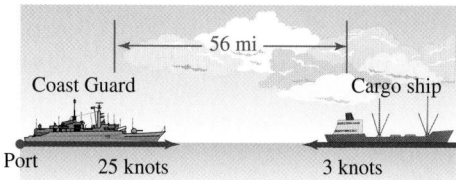

	r	$\cdot$	t	=	d
Coast Guard cutter	25		t		$25t$
Cargo ship	3		t		$3t$
				Total:	56

Multiply $r \cdot t$ to obtain an expression for each distance traveled.

Use the information in this column to form an equation.

The distance the cutter travels	plus	the distance the ship travels	equals	the original distance between the ships.
$25t$	$+$	$3t$	$=$	56

Solve

$$25t + 3t = 56$$

$$28t = 56 \qquad \text{Combine like terms: } 25t + 3t = 28t.$$

$$t = \frac{56}{28} \qquad \text{To isolate } t, \text{ divide both sides by 28.}$$

$$t = 2 \qquad \text{Do the division.}$$

State The ships will meet in 2 hours.

Check In 2 hours, the Coast Guard cutter travels $25 \cdot 2 = 50$ sea miles, and the cargo ship travels $3 \cdot 2 = 6$ sea miles. Together, they travel $50 + 6 = 56$ sea miles. Since this is the original distance between the ships, the answer checks.

> ***Success Tip***   A sketch is helpful when solving uniform motion problems.

EXAMPLE 3 *Concert Tours* While on tour, a country music star travels by bus. Her musical equipment is carried in a truck. How long will it take her bus, traveling 60 mph, to overtake the truck, traveling at 45 mph, if the truck had a $1\frac{1}{2}$-hour head start to her next concert location?

Analyze We know the rate of each vehicle (60 mph and 45 mph) and that the truck began the trip $1\frac{1}{2}$ or 1.5 hours earlier than the bus. We need to determine how long it will take the bus to catch up to the truck.

Form Let t = the time it takes the bus to overtake the truck. With a 1.5-hour head start, the truck is on the road longer than the bus. Therefore, $t + 1.5$ = the truck's travel time.

We enter each rate and time in the table, and use the formula $r \cdot t = d$ twice to fill in the distance column.

60 mph   45 mph

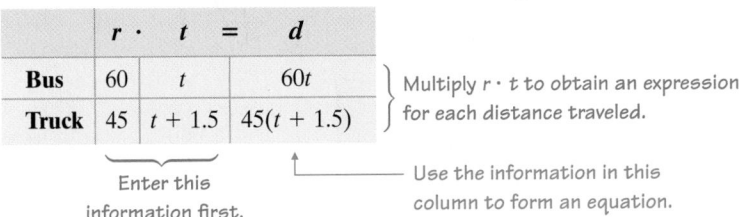

	r	$\cdot$	t	$=$	d
Bus	60		t		$60t$
Truck	45		$t + 1.5$		$45(t + 1.5)$

} Multiply $r \cdot t$ to obtain an expression for each distance traveled.

Enter this information first.

Use the information in this column to form an equation.

When the bus overtakes the truck, they will have traveled the same distance.

The distance traveled by the bus	is the same as	the distance traveled by the truck.
$60t$	$=$	$45(t + 1.5)$

Solve

$60t = 45(t + 1.5)$

$60t = 45t + 67.5$ Distribute the multiplication by 45: $45(1.5) = 67.5$.

$15t = 67.5$ Subtract $45t$ from both sides: $60t - 45t = 15t$.

$t = 4.5$ To isolate t, divide both sides by 15: $\frac{67.5}{15} = 4.5$.

State The bus will overtake the truck in 4.5 or $4\frac{1}{2}$ hours.

Check In 4.5 hours, the bus travels $60(4.5) = 270$ miles. The truck travels for $1.5 + 4.5 = 6$ hours at 45 mph, which is $45(6) = 270$ miles. Since the distance traveled are the same, the answer checks.

Success Tip We used 1.5 hrs for the head start because it is easier to solve $60t = 45(t + 1.5)$ than $60t = 45\left(t + 1\frac{1}{2}\right)$.

Self Check 3

A car leaves a vacation spot traveling at 50 mph. Half an hour later, their friends leave the same spot in a second car traveling at 60 mph. How long will it take the second car to catch up with their friends? 2.5 hr

Now Try Problem 31

Teaching Example 3 A bus carrying a group of campers leaves Normal, Illinois, traveling at a rate of 45 miles per hour. Half an hour later a car leaves Normal traveling at 65 miles per hour with camping gear that the campers forgot. How long will it take the car to catch the bus?
Answer:
1.625 hr or ≈ 1 hr, 38 min

Self Check 4

How many gallons of a 3% salt solution must be mixed with a 7% salt solution to obtain 25 gallons of a 5.4% salt solution? 10 gal

Now Try **Problem 39**

Teaching Example 4 Cream is approximately 22% butterfat. How many gallons of cream must be mixed with milk testing at 2% butterfat to get 20 gallons of milk containing 4% butterfat?
Answer:
2 gal

3 Solve liquid mixture problems.

We now discuss how to solve mixture problems. In the first type, a liquid mixture of a desired strength is made from two solutions with different concentrations.

EXAMPLE 4 *Mixing Solutions* A chemistry experiment calls for a 30% sulfuric acid solution. If the lab supply room has only 50% and 20% sulfuric acid solutions, how much of each should be mixed to obtain 12 liters of a 30% acid solution?

Analyze The 50% solution is too strong and the 20% solution is too weak. We must find how much of each should be combined to obtain 12 liters of a 30% solution.

Form If x = the number of liters of the 50% solution used in the mixture, the remaining $(12 - x)$ liters must be the 20% solution. The amount of pure sulfuric acid in each solution is given by

Amount of solution · strength of the solution = amount of pure sulfuric acid

A table and sketch are helpful in organizing the facts of the problem.

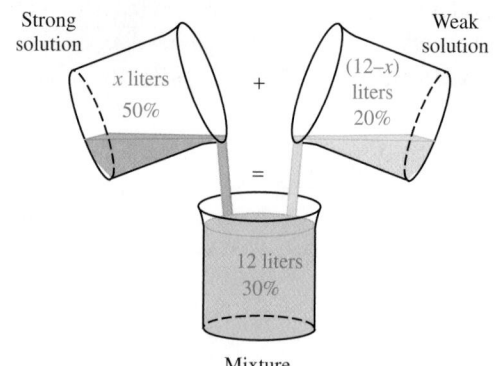

	Amount ·	Strength =	Amount of pure sulfuric acid
Strong	x	0.50	$0.50x$
Weak	$12 - x$	0.20	$0.20(12 - x)$
Mixture	12	0.30	$12(0.30)$

Multiply amount · strength three times to fill in this column.

Enter this information first.

Use the information in this column to form an equation.

The sulfuric acid in the 50% solution	plus	the sulfuric acid in the 20% solution	equals	the sulfuric acid in the mixture.
$0.50x$	$+$	$0.20(12 - x)$	$=$	$12(0.30)$

Solve

$$0.50x + 0.20(12 - x) = 12(0.30)$$
$$0.5x + 2.4 - 0.2x = 3.6 \qquad \text{Distribute the multiplication by 0.20.}$$
$$0.3x + 2.4 = 3.6 \qquad \text{Combine like terms: } 0.5x - 0.2x = 0.3x.$$
$$0.3x = 1.2 \qquad \text{Subtract 2.4 from both sides.}$$
$$x = 4 \qquad \text{To isolate } x, \text{ undo the multiplication by 0.3 by}$$
$$\text{dividing both sides by 0.3: } \frac{1.2}{0.3} = 4.$$

State 4 liters of 50% solution and $12 - 4 = 8$ liters of 20% solution should be used.

Check The amount of acid in 4 liters of the 50% solution is $0.50(4) = 2.0$ liters and the amount of acid in 8 liters of the 20% solution is $0.20(8) = 1.6$ liters. Thus, the amount of acid in these two solutions is $2.0 + 1.6 = 3.6$ liters. The amount of acid in 12 liters of the 30% mixture is also $0.30(12) = 3.6$ liters. Since the amounts of acid are equal, the answers check.

> **Success Tip**   The strength *(concentration)* of a mixture is always between the strengths of the two solutions used to make it.

4   Solve dry mixture problems.

In another type of mixture problem, a dry mixture of a specified value is created from two differently priced ingredients.

EXAMPLE 5   *Snack Foods*   Because cashews priced at $9 per pound were not selling, a produce clerk decided to combine them with less expensive peanuts and sell the mixture for $7 per pound. How many pounds of peanuts, selling at $6 per pound, should be mixed with 50 pounds of cashews to obtain such a mixture?

Analyze We need to determine how many pounds of peanuts to mix with 50 pounds of cashews to obtain a mixture worth $7 per pound.

Form Let $x =$ the number of pounds of peanuts to use in the mixture. Since 50 pounds of cashews will be combined with the peanuts, the mixture will weigh $50 + x$ pounds. The value of the mixture and of each of its ingredients is given by

$$\textbf{Amount} \cdot \textbf{the price} = \textbf{the total value}$$

We can organize the facts of the problem in a table.

	Amount ·	**Price** =	**Total value**
Peanuts	x	6	$6x$
Cashews	50	9	450
Mixture	$50 + x$	7	$7(50 + x)$

Multiply amount · price three times to fill in this column.

Enter this information first.

Use the information in this column to form an equation.

The value of the peanuts	plus	the value of the cashews	equals	the value of the mixture.
$6x$	$+$	450	$=$	$7(50 + x)$

Solve

$6x + 450 = 7(50 + x)$

$6x + 450 = 350 + 7x$ Distribute the multiplication by 7.

$450 = 350 + x$ To eliminate the term 6x on the left side, subtract 6x from both sides: 7x − 6x = x.

$100 = x$ To isolate x, subtract 350 from both sides.

State 100 pounds of peanuts should be used in the mixture.

Check The value of 100 pounds of peanuts, at $6 per pound, is 100(6) = $600 and the value of 50 pounds of cashews, at $9 per pound, 50(9) = $450. Thus, the value of these two amounts is $1,050. Since the value of 150 pounds of the mixture, at $7 per pound, is also 150(7) = $1,050, the answer checks. ∎

5 Solve number-value problems.

When problems deal with collections of different items having different values, we must distinguish between the *number of* and the *value of* the items. For these problems, we will use the fact that

$$\text{Number} \cdot \text{value} = \text{total value}$$

EXAMPLE 6   *Dining Area Improvements* A restaurant owner needs to purchase some tables, chairs, and dinner plates for the dining area of her establishment. She plans to buy four chairs and four plates for each new table. She also plans to buy 20 additional plates in case of breakage. If a table costs $100, a chair $50, and a plate $5, how many of each can she buy if she takes out a loan for $6,500 to pay for the new items?

Analyze We know the *value* of each item: Tables cost $100, chairs cost $50, and plates cost $5 each. We need to find the *number* of tables, chairs, and plates she can purchase for $6,500.

Form The number of chairs and plates she needs depends on the number of tables she buys. So we let t = the number of tables to be purchased. Since every table requires four chairs and four plates, she needs to order $4t$ chairs. Because 20 additional plates are needed, she should order $(4t + 20)$ plates. We can organize the facts of the problem in a table.

	Number ·	Value =	Total value
Tables	t	100	$100t$
Chairs	$4t$	50	$50(4t)$
Plates	$4t + 20$	5	$5(4t + 20)$
			Total: 6,500

Multiply number · value three times to fill in this column.

Enter this information first.

Use the information in this column to form an equation.

The value of the tables	plus	the value of the chairs	plus	the value of the plates	equals	the value of the purchase.
$100t$	+	$50(4t)$	+	$5(4t + 20)$	=	6,500

Solve

$$100t + 50(4t) + 5(4t + 20) = 6,500$$

$$100t + 200t + 20t + 100 = 6,500 \quad \text{Do the multiplications and distribute.}$$

$$320t + 100 = 6,500 \quad \text{Combine like terms:} \atop 100t + 200t + 20t = 320t.$$

$$320t = 6,400 \quad \text{Subtract 100 from both sides.}$$

$$t = 20 \quad \text{To isolate } t, \text{ divide both sides by 320.}$$

To find the number of chairs and plates to buy, we evaluate $4t$ and $4t + 20$ for $t = 20$.

Chairs: $4t = 4(20)$ **Plates:** $4t + 20 = 4(20) + 20$ Substitute 20 for *t*.
              $= 80$ $= 100$

State The owner needs to buy 20 tables, 80 chairs, and 100 plates.

Check The total value of 20 tables is $20(\$100) = \$2{,}000$, the total value of 80 chairs is $80(\$50) = \$4{,}000$, and the total value of 100 plates is $100(\$5) = \$500$. Because the total purchase is $\$2{,}000 + \$4{,}000 + \$500 = \$6{,}500$, the answers check.

ANSWERS TO SELF CHECKS

1. \$2,400 at 2%, \$1,800 at 3%   **2.** 3.5 hr   **3.** 2.5 hr   **4.** 10 gal   **5.** 40 lb
6. 12 iPods, 4 skins, 24 cards

SECTION 2.6 STUDY SET

VOCABULARY

Fill in the blanks.

1. Problems that involve depositing money are called __investment__ problems, and problems that involve moving vehicles are called uniform __motion__ problems.

2. Problems that involve combining ingredients are called __mixture__ problems, and problems that involve collections of different items having different values are called __number-value__ problems.

CONCEPTS

3. Complete the *principal column* given that part of \$30,000 is invested in stocks and the rest in art.
$30{,}000 - x$

	P	$\cdot$	r	$\cdot$	$t =$	I
Stocks	x					
Art	?					

4. A man made two investments that earned a combined annual interest of \$280. Complete the table and then form an equation for this investment problem.
$0.04x + 0.06(6{,}000 - x) = 280$

	P	$\cdot$	r	$\cdot t =$	I
Bank	x		0.04	1	$0.04x$
Stocks	$6{,}000 - x$		0.06	1	$0.06(6{,}000 - x)$
					Total: 280

▶ Selected exercises available online at
www.webassign.net/brookscole

5. Complete the *rate column* given that the eastbound plane flew 150 mph slower than the westbound plane.
$r - 150$

	r	$\cdot$	$t = d$
West	r		
East	?		

6. a. Complete the *time column* given that a runner wants to overtake a walker and the walker had a $\frac{1}{2}$-hour head start. $t + 0.5$

	r	$\cdot$	$t = d$
Runner		t	
Walker		?	

b. Complete the *time column* given that part of a 6-hour drive was in fog and the other part was in clear conditions. $6 - t$

	r	$\cdot$	$t = d$
Foggy		t	
Clear		?	

7. A husband and wife drive in opposite directions to work. Their drives last the same amount of time and their workplaces are 80 miles apart. Complete the table and then form an equation for this distance problem. $35t + 45t = 80$

	r	$\cdot$	$t = d$
Husband	35	t	$35t$
Wife	45	t	$45t$
			Total: 80

8. a. How many gallons of acetic acid are there in barrel 2? (See the figure on the next page.) 16.8 gal

b. Suppose the contents of the two barrels are poured into an empty third barrel. How many gallons of liquid will the third barrel contain? $x + 42$

c. Estimate the strength of the solution in the third barrel: 15%, 35%, or 60% acid? 35%

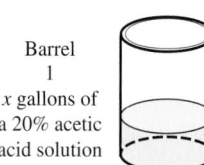 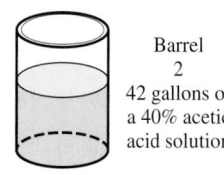

Barrel 1
x gallons of a 20% acetic acid solution

Barrel 2
42 gallons of a 40% acetic acid solution

9. a. Two antifreeze solutions are combined to form a mixture. Complete the table and then form an equation for this mixture problem.
$0.50(6) + 0.25x = 0.30(6 + x)$

	Amount ·	Strength =	Pure antifreeze
Strong	6	0.50	0.50(6)
Weak	x	0.25	0.25x
Mixture	6 + x	0.30	0.30(6 + x)

b. Two oil-and-vinegar salad dressings are combined to make a new mixture. Complete the table and then form an equation for this mixture problem.
$0.06x + 0.03(10 - x) = 0.05(10)$

	Amount ·	Strength =	Pure vinegar
Strong	x	0.06	0.06x
Weak	10 − x	0.03	0.03(10 − x)
Mixture	10	0.05	0.05(10)

10. The value of all the nylon brushes that a paint store carries is $670. Complete the table and then form an equation for this number-value problem.
$8x + 5x + 7(x + 10) = 670$

	Number ·	Value =	Total value
1-inch	2x	4	8x
2-inch	x	5	5x
3-inch	x + 10	7	7(x + 10)
			Total: 670

NOTATION

▶ **11.** Write 6% and 15.2% in decimal form. 0.06, 0.152

12. By what power of 10 should each decimal be multiplied to make it a whole number?

a. 0.08 100   **b.** 0.162 1,000

GUIDED PRACTICE

Solve each equation. See Example 1.

13. $0.18x + 0.45(12 - x) = 0.36(12)$ 4

14. $0.12x + 0.20(4 - x) = 0.6$ 2.5

15. $0.08x + 0.07(15,000 - x) = 1,110$ 6,000

▶ **16.** $0.108x + 0.07(16,000 - x) = 1,500$ 10,000

APPLICATIONS

Investment problems. See Example 1.

▶ **17.** CORPORATE INVESTMENTS The financial board of a corporation invested $25,000 overseas, part at 4% and part at 7% annual interest. Find the amount invested at each rate if the first-year combined income from the two investments was $1,300. $15,000 at 4%, $10,000 at 7%

18. LOANS A credit union loaned out $50,000, part at an annual rate of 5% and the rest at an annual rate of 8%. They collected combined simple interest of $3,400 from the loans that year. How much was loaned out at each rate? $20,000 at 5%, $30,000 at 8%

19. OLD COINS A salesperson used her $3,500 year-end bonus to purchase some old coins, with hopes of earning 15% annual interest on the gold coins and 12% annual interest on the silver coins. If she saw return on her investment of $480 the first year, how much did she invest in each type of coin? silver: $1,500, gold: $2,000

20. HIGH-RISK COMPANIES An investment club used funds totaling $200,000 to invest in a bio-tech company and in an ethanol plant, with hopes of earning 11% and 14% annual interest, respectively. Their hunch paid off. The club made a total of $24,250 interest the first year. How much was invested at each rate? $125,000 at 11%, $75,000 at 14%

▶ **21.** RETIREMENT A professor wants to supplement her pension with investment interest. If she invests $28,000 at 6% interest, how much would she have to invest at 7% to achieve a goal of $3,500 per year in supplemental income? $26,000

22. EXTRA INCOME An investor wants to receive $1,000 annually from two investments. He has put $4,500 in a money market account paying 4% annual interest. How much should he invest in a stock fund that pays 10% annual interest to achieve his goal? $8,200

23. 1099 FORMS The form on the next page shows the interest income Terrell Washington earned in 2008 from two savings accounts. He deposited a total of $15,000 at the first of that year, and made no further deposits or withdrawals. How much money did he deposit in account 822 and in account 721? 822: $9,000, 721: $6,000

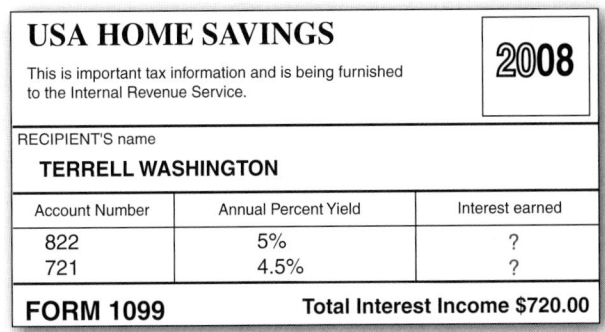

USA HOME SAVINGS   **2008**

This is important tax information and is being furnished to the Internal Revenue Service.

RECIPIENT'S name
TERRELL WASHINGTON

Account Number	Annual Percent Yield	Interest earned
822	5%	?
721	4.5%	?

FORM 1099   **Total Interest Income $720.00**

▶ **24. INVESTMENT PLANS** A financial planner recommends a plan for a client who has $65,000 to invest. (See the chart.) At the end of the presentation, the client asks, "How much will be invested at each rate?" Answer this question using the given information. $42,200 at 12%, $22,800 at 6.2%

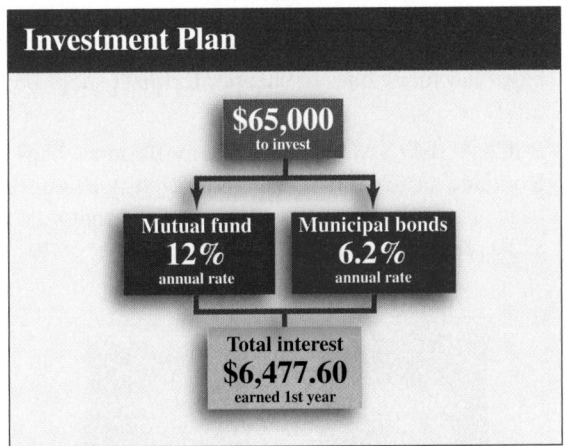

Investment Plan

$65,000
to invest

Mutual fund
12%
annual rate

Municipal bonds
6.2%
annual rate

Total interest
$6,477.60
earned 1st year

▶ **25. INVESTMENTS** Equal amounts are invested in each of three accounts paying 7%, 8%, and 10.5% annually. If one year's combined interest income is $1,249.50, how much is invested in each account? $4,900

26. PERSONAL LOANS Maggy lent her brother some money at 2% annual interest. She lent her sister twice as much money at half of the interest rate. In one year, Maggy collected combined interest of $200 from her brother and sister. How much did she lend each of them? brother: $5,000, sister: $10,000

Uniform motion problems. **See Examples 2–3.**

27. TORNADOES During a storm, two teams of scientists leave a university at the same time in vans to search for tornadoes. The first team travels east at 20 mph and the second travels west at 25 mph. If their radios have a range of up to 90 miles, how long will it be before they lose radio contact? (See the next column.) 2 hr

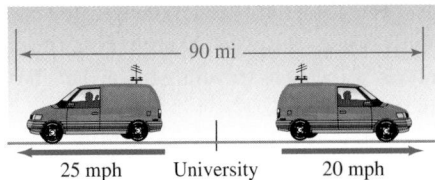

90 mi

25 mph   University   20 mph

▶ **28. UNMANNED AIRCRAFT** Two remotely controlled unmanned aircraft are launched in opposite directions. One flies east at 78 mph and the other west at 82 mph. How long will it take the aircraft to fly a combined distance of 560 miles? 3.5 hr

29. HELLO/GOODBYE A husband and wife work different shifts at the same plant. When the husband leaves from work to make the 20-mile trip home, the wife leaves their home and drives to work. They travel on the same road. The husband's driving rate is 45 mph and the wife's is 35 mph. How long into their drives can they wave at each other when passing on the road? $\frac{1}{4}$ hr = 15 min

30. AIR TRAFFIC CONTROL An airliner leaves Berlin, Germany, headed for Montreal, Canada, flying at an average speed of 450 mph. At the same time, an airliner leaves Montreal headed for Berlin, averaging 500 mph. If the airports are 3,800 miles apart, when will the air traffic controllers have to make the pilots aware that the planes are passing each other? 4 hr into the flights

▶ **31. CYCLING** A cyclist leaves his training base for a morning workout, riding at the rate of 18 mph. One and one-half hours later, his support staff leaves the base in a car going 45 mph in the same direction. How long will it take the support staff to catch up with the cyclist? 1 hr

32. PARENTING How long will it take a mother, running at 4 feet per second, to catch up with her toddler, running down the sidewalk at 2 feet per second, if the child had a 5-second head start? 5 sec

33. ROAD TRIPS A car averaged 40 mph for part of a trip and 50 mph for the remainder. If the 5-hour trip covered 210 miles, for how long did the car average 40 mph? 4 hr

34. CROSS-TRAINING An athlete runs up a set of stadium stairs at a rate of 2 stairs per second, immediately turns around, and then descends the same stairs at a rate of 3 stairs per second. If the workout takes 90 seconds, how long does it take him to run up the stairs? 54 sec

35. WINTER DRIVING A trucker drove for 4 hours before he encountered icy road conditions. He reduced his speed by 20 mph and continued driving for 3 more hours. Find his average speed during the first part of the trip if the entire trip was 325 miles. 55 mph

▶ **36.** SPEED OF TRAINS Two trains are 330 miles apart, and their speeds differ by 20 mph. Find the speed of each train if they are traveling toward each other and will meet in 3 hours. 65 mph, 45 mph

Liquid mixture problems. **See Example 4.**

▶ **37.** SALT SOLUTIONS How many gallons of a 3% salt solution must be mixed with 50 gallons of a 7% solution to obtain a 5% solution? 50 gal

38. PHOTOGRAPHY A photographer wishes to mix 2 liters of a 5% acetic acid solution with a 10% solution to get a 7% solution. How many liters of 10% solution must be added? $1\frac{1}{3}$ liters

▶ **39.** MAKING CHEESE To make low-fat cottage cheese, milk containing 4% butterfat is mixed with milk containing 1% butterfat to obtain 15 gallons of a mixture containing 2% butterfat. How many gallons of each milk must be used? 4%: 5 gal, 1%: 10 gal

40. ANTIFREEZE How many quarts of a 10% antifreeze solution must be mixed with 16 quarts of a 40% antifreeze solution to make a 30% solution? 8 quarts

▶ **41.** PRINTING A printer has ink that is 8% cobalt blue color and ink that is 22% cobalt blue color. How many ounces of each ink are needed to make 1 gallon (64 ounces) of ink that is 15% cobalt blue color? 32 ounces of 8%, 32 ounces of 22%

42. FLOOD DAMAGE One website recommends a 6% chlorine bleach–water solution to remove mildew. A chemical lab has 3% and 15% chlorine bleach–water solutions in stock. How many gallons of each should be mixed to obtain 100 gallons of the mildew spray? 75 gallons of 3%, 25 gallons of 15%

43. INTERIOR DECORATING The colors on the paint chip card below are created by adding different amounts of orange tint to a white latex base. How many gallons of Desert Sunrise should be mixed with 1 gallon of Bright Pumpkin to obtain Cool Cantaloupe? 6 gal

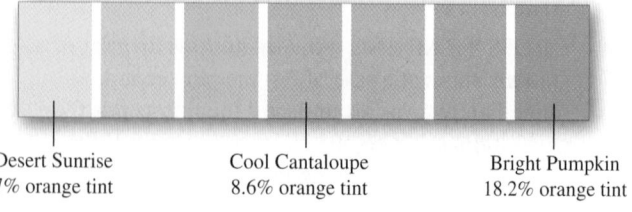

Desert Sunrise
7% orange tint

Cool Cantaloupe
8.6% orange tint

Bright Pumpkin
18.2% orange tint

▶ **44.** ANTISEPTICS A nurse wants to add water to 30 ounces of a 10% solution of benzalkonium chloride to dilute it to an 8% solution. How much water must she add? (*Hint:* Water is 0% benzalkonium chloride.) 7.5 oz

Dry mixture problems

▶ **45.** LAWN SEED A store sells bluegrass seed for $6 per pound and ryegrass seed for $3 per pound. How much ryegrass must be mixed with 100 pounds of bluegrass to obtain a blend that will sell for $5 per pound? 50 lb

46. COFFEE BLENDS A store sells regular coffee for $8 a pound and gourmet coffee for $14 a pound. To get rid of 40 pounds of the gourmet coffee, a shopkeeper makes a blend to put on sale for $10 a pound. How many pounds of regular coffee should he use? 80 lb

47. RAISINS How many scoops of natural seedless raisins costing $3.45 per scoop must be mixed with 20 scoops of golden seedless raisins costing $2.55 per scoop to obtain a mixture costing $3 per scoop? 20 scoops

▶ **48.** FERTILIZER Fertilizer with weed control costing $38 per 50-pound bag is to be mixed with a less expensive fertilizer costing $6 per 50-pound bag to make 16 bags of fertilizer that can be sold for $28 per bag. How many bags of cheaper fertilizer should be used? 5 bags

49. PACKAGED SALAD How many 10-ounce bags of Romaine lettuce must be mixed with fifty 10-ounce bags of Iceberg lettuce to obtain a blend that sells for $2.50 per ten-ounce bag? 15

Price: $2.20   Price: $3.50

50. MIXING CANDY Lemon drops worth $3.80 per pound are to be mixed with jelly beans that cost $2.40 per pound to make 100 pounds of a mixture worth $2.96 per pound. How many pounds of each candy should be used? 40 lb lemon drops, 60 lb jelly beans

▶ **51.** BRONZE A pound of tin is worth $1 more than a pound of copper. Four pounds of tin are mixed with 6 pounds of copper to make bronze that sells for $3.65 per pound. How much is a pound of tin worth? $4.25

▶ **52.** SNACK FOODS A bag of peanuts is worth $.30 less than a bag of cashews. Equal amounts of peanuts and cashews are used to make 40 bags of a mixture that sells for $1.05 per bag. How much is a bag of cashews worth? $1.20

Number-value problems. See Example 6.

▶ **53.** RENTALS The owners of an apartment building rent equal numbers of 1-, 2-, and 3-bedroom units. The monthly rent for a 1-bedroom is $550, a 2-bedroom is $700, and a 3-bedroom is $900. If the total monthly income is $36,550, how many of each type of unit are there? 17

54. WAREHOUSING A store warehouses 40 more portables than big-screen TV sets, and 15 more consoles than big-screen sets. The monthly storage cost for a portable is $1.50, a console is $4.00, and a big-screen is $7.50. If storage for all the televisions costs $276 per month, how many big-screen sets are in stock? 12

▶ **55.** SOFTWARE Three software applications are priced as shown. Spreadsheet and database programs sold in equal numbers, but 15 more word processing applications were sold than the other two combined. If the three applications generated sales of $72,000, how many spreadsheets were sold? 90

Software	Price
Spreadsheet	$150
Database	$195
Word processing	$210

▶ **56.** INVENTORIES With summer approaching, the number of air conditioners sold is expected to be double that of stoves and refrigerators combined. Stoves sell for $350, refrigerators for $450, and air conditioners for $500, and sales of $56,000 are expected. If stoves and refrigerators sell in equal numbers, how many of each appliance should be stocked? 20 stoves, 20 refrigerators, 80 air conditioners

57. PIGGY BANKS When a child emptied his coin bank, he had a collection of pennies, nickels, and dimes. There were 20 more pennies than dimes and the number of nickels was triple the number of dimes. If the coins had a value of $5.40, how many of each type coin were in the bank? 40 pennies, 20 dimes, 60 nickels

▶ **58.** WISHING WELLS A scuba diver, hired by an amusement park, collected $121 in nickels, dimes, and quarters at the bottom of a wishing well. There were 500 nickels, and 90 more quarters than dimes. How many quarters and dimes were thrown into the wishing well? dimes: 210, quarters: 300

▶ **59.** BASKETBALL Epiphanny Prince, of New York, scores 113 points in a high school game on February 1, 2006, breaking a national prep record that was held by Cheryl Miller. Prince made 46 more 2-point baskets than 3-point baskets, and only 1 free throw. How many 2-point and 3-point baskets did she make? 2-pointers: 50, 3-pointers: 4

▶ **60.** MUSEUM TOURS The admission prices for the Coca-Cola Museum in Atlanta are shown. A family purchased 3 more children's tickets than adult tickets, and 1 less senior ticket than adult tickets. The total cost of the tickets was $73. How many of each type of ticket did they purchase? adult: 3, senior: 2, child: 6

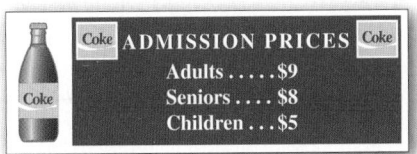

ADMISSION PRICES
Adults $9
Seniors $8
Children . . . $5

WRITING

61. Create a mixture problem of your own, and solve it.

▶ **62.** Is it possible to mix a 10% sugar solution with a 20% sugar solution to get a 30% sugar solution? Explain.

REVIEW

Multiply.

63. $-25(2x - 5)$ $-50x + 125$ **64.** $-12(3a + 4b - 32)$ $-36a - 48b + 384$

65. $-(3x - 3)$ $-3x + 3$ ▶ **66.** $\dfrac{1}{2}(4b - 8)$ $2b - 4$

67. $(4y - 4)4$ $16y - 16$ **68.** $3(5t + 1)2$ $30t + 6$

Solving Inequalities

Objectives

1 Determine whether a number is a solution of an inequality.

2 Graph solution sets and use interval notation.

3 Solve linear inequalities.

4 Solve compound inequalities.

5 Solve inequality applications.

In our daily lives, we often speak of one value being *greater than* or *less than* another. For example, a sick child might have a temperature *greater than* 98.6°F or a granola bar might contain *less than* 2 grams of fat.

In mathematics, we use *inequalities* to show that one expression is greater than or is less than another expression.

1 Determine whether a number is a solution of an inequality.

An **inequality** is a statement that contains one or more of the following symbols.

Inequality Symbols

$<$ is less than	$>$ is greater than	$\neq$ is not equal to
$\leq$ is less than or equal to	$\geq$ is greater than or equal to	

An inequality can be true, false, or neither true nor false. For example,

- $9 \geq 9$ is true because $9 = 9$.
- $37 < 24$ is false.
- $x + 1 > 5$ is neither true nor false because we don't know what number x represents.

An inequality that contains a variable can be made true or false depending on the number that is substituted for the variable. If we substitute 10 for x in $x + 1 > 5$, the resulting inequality is true: $\mathbf{10} + 1 > 5$. If we substitute 1 for x, the resulting inequality is false: $1 + 1 > 5$. A number that makes an inequality true is called a **solution** of the inequality, and we say that the number *satisfies* the inequality. Thus, 10 is a solution of $x + 1 > 5$ and 1 is not.

> ***The Language of Algebra*** Because $<$ requires one number to be strictly less than another number and $>$ requires one number to be strictly greater than another number, $<$ and $>$ are called *strict inequalities*.

In this section, we will find the solutions of *linear inequalities in one variable*.

Linear Inequality in One Variable

A **linear inequality in one variable** can be written in one of the following forms where a, b, and c are real numbers and $a \neq 0$.

$$ax + b > c \qquad ax + b \geq c \qquad ax + b < c \qquad ax + b \leq c$$

Self Check 1

Is 2 a solution of $3x - 1 \geq 0$? yes

Now Try Problem 13

Teaching Example 1 Is -3 a solution of $4x + 5 \leq -6$?
Answer:
yes

EXAMPLE 1 Is 9 a solution of $2x + 4 \leq 21$?

Strategy We will substitute 9 for x and evaluate the expression on the left side.

WHY If a true statement results, 9 is a solution of the inequality. If we obtain a false statement, 9 is not a solution.

Solution

$$2x + 4 \leq 21$$
$$2(\mathbf{9}) + 4 \overset{?}{\leq} 21 \qquad \text{Substitute 9 for x. Read } \overset{?}{\leq} \text{ as "is possibly less than or equal to."}$$
$$18 + 4 \overset{?}{\leq} 21$$
$$22 \leq 21 \qquad \text{This inequality is false.}$$

The statement $22 \leq 21$ is false because neither $22 < 21$ nor $22 = 21$ is true. Therefore, 9 is not a solution. ∎

2 Graph solution sets and use interval notation.

The **solution set** of an inequality is the set of all numbers that make the inequality true. Some solution sets are easy to determine. For example, if we replace the variable in $x > -3$ with a number greater than -3, the resulting inequality will be true. Because there are infinitely many real numbers greater than -3, it follows that $x > -3$ has infinitely many solutions. Since there are too many solutions to list, we use **set-builder notation** to describe the solutions set.

$\{x \mid x > -3\}$ Read as "the set of all x such that x is greater than −3."

We can illustrate the solution set by **graphing the inequality** on a number line. To graph $x > -3$, a **parenthesis** or **open circle** is drawn on the endpoint −3 to indicate that −3 is not part of the graph. Then we shade all of the points on the number line to the right of −3. The right arrowhead is also shaded to show that the solutions continue forever to the right.

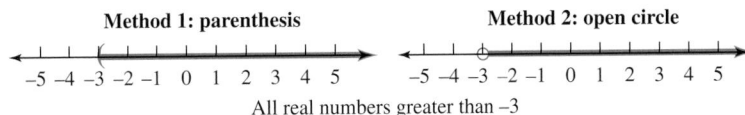

All real numbers greater than −3

The graph of $x > -3$ is an example of an **interval** on the number line. We can write intervals in a compact form called **interval notation.**

The interval notation that represents the graph of $x > -3$ is $(-3, \infty)$. As on the number line, a left parenthesis is written next to −3 to indicate that −3 is not included in the interval. The **positive infinity symbol** ∞ that follows indicates that the interval continues without end to the right. With this notation, *a parenthesis is always used next to an infinity symbol.*

The illustration below shows the relationship between the symbols used to graph an interval and the corresponding interval notation. If we begin at −3 and move to the right, the shaded arrowhead on the graph indicates that the interval approaches positive infinity ∞.

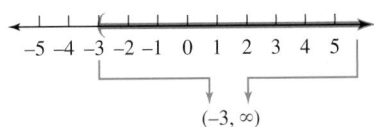

We now have three ways to describe the solution set of an inequality.

Set-builder notation   ***Number line graph***   *Interval notation*

$\{x \mid x > -3\}$ (number line graph) $(-3, \infty)$

Success Tip The *infinity* symbol ∞ does not represent a number. It indicates that an interval extends to the right without end.

EXAMPLE 2   Graph: $x \leq 2$

Strategy We need to determine which real numbers, when substituted for x, would make $x \leq 2$ a true statement.

WHY To graph $x \leq 2$ means to draw a "picture" of all of the values of x that make the inequality true.

Self Check 2

Graph: $x \geq 0$ $[0, \infty)$

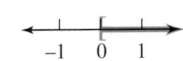

Now Try Problem 17

Teaching Example 2 Graph: $x > -1$
Answer:

Solution

If we replace x with a number less than or equal to 2, the resulting inequality will be true. To graph the solution set, a **bracket** or a **closed circle** is drawn at the endpoint 2 to indicate that 2 is part of the graph. Then we shade all of the points on the number line to the left of 2 and the left arrowhead.

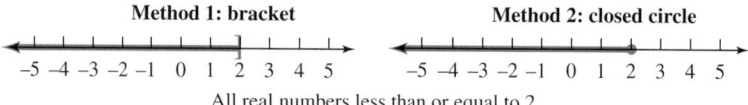

All real numbers less than or equal to 2

The interval is written as $(-\infty, 2]$. The right bracket indicates that 2 is included in the interval. The **negative infinity symbol** $-\infty$ shows that the interval continues forever to the left. The illustration below shows the relationship between the symbols used to graph the interval and the corresponding interval notation.

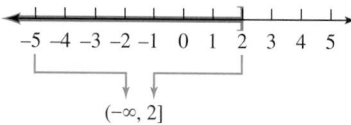

3   Solve linear inequalities.

To **solve an inequality** means to find all values of the variable that make the inequality true. As with equations, there are properties that we can use to solve inequalities.

Addition and Subtraction Properties of Inequality

Adding the same number to, or subtracting the same number from, both sides of an inequality does not change its solutions.

For any real numbers a, b, and c,

  If $a < b$, then $a + c < b + c$.
  If $a < b$, then $a - c < b - c$.

Similar statements can be made for the symbols $\leq$, $>$, and $\geq$.

After applying one of these properties, the resulting inequality is equivalent to the original one. **Equivalent inequalities** have the same solution set.

Like equations, inequalities are solved by isolating the variable on one side.

Self Check 3

Solve $x - 3 < -2$. Write the solution set in interval notation and graph it. $(-\infty, 1)$

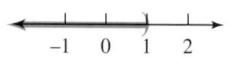

Now Try **Problem 25**

Teaching Example 3 Solve $x - 5 \leq 3$.
Write the answer in interval notation.
Answer:
$x \leq 8$, $(-\infty, 8]$

EXAMPLE 3   Solve $x + 3 > 2$. Write the solution set in interval notation and graph it.

Strategy We will use a property of inequality to isolate the variable on one side.

WHY To solve the original inequality, we want to find a simpler equivalent inequality of the form $x >$ **a number** or $x <$ **a number**, whose solution is obvious.

Solution

We will use the subtraction property of inequality to isolate x on the left side of the inequality. We can undo the addition of 3 by subtracting 3 from both sides.

$$x + 3 > 2 \qquad \text{This is the inequality to solve.}$$
$$x + 3 - 3 > 2 - 3 \qquad \text{Subtract 3 from both sides.}$$
$$x > -1$$

All real numbers greater than -1 are solutions of $x + 3 > 2$. The solution set can be written in set-builder notation as $\{x \mid x > -1\}$ and in interval notation as $(-1, \infty)$. The graph of the solution set is shown below.

Since there are infinitely many solutions, we cannot check all of them.

As an informal check, we can pick some numbers in the graph, say 0 and 30, substitute each number for x in the original inequality, and see whether true statements result.

Check:

$$x + 3 > 2 \qquad\qquad\qquad x + 3 > 2$$
$$0 + 3 \overset{?}{>} 2 \quad \text{Substitute 0 for x.} \qquad 30 + 3 \overset{?}{>} 2 \quad \text{Substitute 30 for x.}$$
$$3 > 2 \quad \text{True} \qquad\qquad\qquad 33 > 2 \quad \text{True}$$

The solution set appears to be correct. ∎

Caution! Since we use parentheses and brackets in interval notation, we will use them to graph inequalities. Note that parentheses, not brackets, are written next to ∞ and $-\infty$ because there is no endpoint.

$$(-3, \infty) \qquad (-\infty, 2]$$

As with equations, there are properties for multiplying and dividing both sides of an inequality by the same number. To develop what is called *the multiplication property of inequality,* we consider the true statement $2 < 5$. If both sides are multiplied by a positive number, such as 3, another true inequality results.

$$2 < 5 \qquad \text{This inequality is true.}$$
$$3 \cdot 2 < 3 \cdot 5 \qquad \text{Multiply both sides by 3.}$$
$$6 < 15 \qquad \text{This inequality is true.}$$

However, if we multiply both sides of $2 < 5$ by a negative number, such as -3, the direction of the inequality symbol is reversed to produce another true inequality.

$$2 < 5 \qquad \text{This inequality is true.}$$
$$-3 \cdot 2 > -3 \cdot 5 \qquad \text{Multiply both sides by } -3 \text{ and reverse the direction of the inequality.}$$
$$-6 > -15 \qquad \text{This inequality is true.}$$

The inequality $-6 > -15$ is true because -6 is to the right of -15 on the number line.

Dividing both sides of an inequality by the same negative number also requires that the direction of the inequality symbol be reversed.

$$-4 < 6 \qquad \text{This inequality is true.}$$
$$\frac{-4}{-2} > \frac{6}{-2} \qquad \text{Divide both sides by } -2 \text{ and change } < \text{ to } >.$$
$$2 > -3 \qquad \text{This inequality is true.}$$

These examples illustrate the multiplication and division properties of inequality.

Multiplication and Division Properties of Inequality

Multiplying or dividing both sides of an inequality by the same positive number does not change its solutions.

For any real numbers a, b, and c, where c is positive,

$$\text{If } a < b, \quad \text{then } ac < bc. \qquad \text{If } a < b, \quad \text{then } \frac{a}{c} < \frac{b}{c}.$$

If we multiply or divide both sides of an inequality by a negative number, the direction of the inequality symbol must be reversed for the inequalities to have the same solutions.

For any real numbers a, b, and c, where c is negative,

$$\text{If } a < b, \quad \text{then } ac > bc. \qquad \text{If } a < b, \text{ then } \frac{a}{c} > \frac{b}{c}.$$

Similar statements can be made for the symbols $\leq$, $>$, and $\geq$.

Self Check 4

Solve each inequality. Write the solution set in interval notation and graph it.

a. $-\dfrac{h}{20} \leq 10$ $[-200, \infty)$

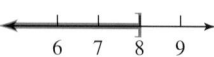

b. $-12a > -144$ $(-\infty, 12)$

Now Try Problems 31 and 33

Teaching Example 4 Solve each inequality. Write the solution set in interval notation and graph it.
a. $-\frac{5}{3}x \geq 10$
b. $-6x < 12$
Answers:
a. $x \leq -6$, $(-\infty, -6]$
b. $x > -2$, $(-2, \infty)$

EXAMPLE 4   Solve each inequality. Write the solution set in interval notation and graph it. **a.** $-\dfrac{3}{2}t \geq -12$ **b.** $-5t < 55$

Strategy We will use a property of inequality to isolate the variable on one side.

WHY To solve the original inequality, we want to find a simpler equivalent inequality, whose solution is obvious.

Solution

a. To undo the multiplication by $-\frac{3}{2}$, we multiply both sides by the reciprocal, which is $-\frac{2}{3}$.

$$-\frac{3}{2}t \geq -12 \qquad \text{This is the inequality to solve.}$$

$$-\frac{2}{3}\left(-\frac{3}{2}t\right) \leq -\frac{2}{3}(-12) \qquad \begin{array}{l}\text{Multiply both sides by } -\frac{2}{3}. \text{ Since we are multiplying} \\ \text{both sides by a negative number, reverse the direction} \\ \text{of the inequality.}\end{array}$$

$$t \leq 8 \qquad \text{Do the multiplications.}$$

The solution set is $(-\infty, 8]$ and it is graphed as shown.

b. To undo the multiplication by -5, we divide both sides by -5.

$$-5t < 55 \qquad \text{This is the inequality to solve.}$$

$$\frac{-5t}{-5} > \frac{55}{-5} \qquad \begin{array}{l}\text{To isolate } t, \text{ undo the multiplication by } -5 \text{ by dividing both sides by} \\ -5. \text{ Since we are dividing both sides by a negative number, reverse} \\ \text{the direction of the inequality.}\end{array}$$

$$t > -11$$

The solution set is $(-11, \infty)$ and it is graphed as shown.

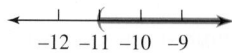

EXAMPLE 5   Solve $-5 > 3x + 7$. Write the solution set in interval notation and graph it.

Strategy First we will use a property of inequality to isolate the *variable term* on one side. Then we will use a second property of inequality to isolate the *variable* itself.

WHY To solve the original inequality, we want to find a simpler equivalent inequality of the form $x >$ **a number** or $x <$ **a number**, whose solution is obvious.

Solution

$-5 > 3x + 7$	This is the inequality to solve.
$-5 - 7 > 3x + 7 - 7$	To isolate the variable term, 3x, undo the addition of 7 by subtracting 7 from both sides.
$-12 > 3x$	Do the subtractions.
$\dfrac{-12}{3} > \dfrac{3x}{3}$	To isolate x, undo the multiplication by 3 by dividing both sides by 3.
$-4 > x$	Do the divisions.

To determine the solution set, it is useful to rewrite the inequality $-4 > x$ in an equivalent form with the variable on the left side. If -4 is greater than x, it follows that x must be less than -4.

$$x < -4$$

The solution set is $(-\infty, -4)$, whose graph is shown below.

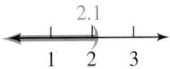

EXAMPLE 6   Solve $5.1 - 3k < 19.5$. Write the solution set in interval notation and graph it.

Strategy We will use properties of inequality to isolate the variable on one side.

WHY To solve the original inequality, we want to find a simpler equivalent inequality of the form $k >$ **a number** or $k <$ **a number**, whose solution is obvious.

Solution

$5.1 - 3k < 19.5$	This is the inequality to solve.
$5.1 - 3k - \mathbf{5.1} < 19.5 - \mathbf{5.1}$	To isolate $-3k$ on the left side, subtract 5.1 from both sides.
$-3k < 14.4$	Do the subtractions.
$\dfrac{-3k}{-3} > \dfrac{14.4}{-3}$	To isolate k, undo the multiplication by -3 by dividing both sides by -3 and reverse the direction of the $<$ symbol.
$k > -4.8$	Do the divisions.

The solution set is $(-4.8, \infty)$, whose graph is shown below.

The equation solving strategy on page 163 can be applied to inequalities. However, when solving inequalities, we must remember to *change the direction of the inequality symbol when multiplying or dividing both sides by a negative number.*

Self Check 5

Solve $-13 < 2r - 7$. Write the solution set in interval notation and graph it. $(-3, \infty)$

Now Try Problem 39

Teaching Example 5 Solve
$3 > 4x + 11$. Write the solution set in interval notation and graph it.
Answer:
$x < -2$, $(-\infty, -2)$

Self Check 6

Solve $-9n + 1.8 > -17.1$. Write the solution set in interval notation and graph it. $(-\infty, 2.1)$

Now Try Problem 47

Teaching Example 6 Solve
$-4.2 - 2x < 3.6$. Write the solution set in interval notation and graph it.
Answer:
$x > -3.9$, $(-3.9, \infty)$

Self Check 7

Solve $5(b - 2) \geq -(b - 3) + 2b$. Write the solution set in interval notation and graph it. $\left[\frac{13}{4}, \infty\right)$

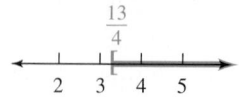

Now Try Problem 53

Teaching Example 7 Solve $4(x - 2) < 2(x + 1) + x$. Write the solution set in interval notation and graph it.
Answer:
$x < 10, (-\infty, 10)$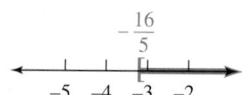

EXAMPLE 7   Solve $8(y + 1) \geq 2(y - 4) + y$. Write the solution set in interval notation and graph it.

Strategy We will follow the steps of the equation-solving strategy (adapted to inequalities) to solve the inequality.

WHY This is the most efficient way to solve a linear inequality in one variable.

Solution

$8(y + 1) \geq 2(y - 4) + y$	This is the inequality to solve.
$8y + 8 \geq 2y - 8 + y$	Distribute the multiplication by 8 and by 2.
$8y + 8 \geq 3y - 8$	Combine like terms: $2y + y = 3y$.
$8y + 8 - 3y \geq 3y - 8 - 3y$	To eliminate $3y$ from the right side, subtract $3y$ from both sides.
$5y + 8 \geq -8$	Combine like terms on both sides.
$5y + 8 - 8 \geq -8 - 8$	To isolate $5y$, undo the addition of 8 by subtracting 8 from both sides.
$5y \geq -16$	Do the subtractions.
$\dfrac{5y}{5} \geq \dfrac{-16}{5}$	To isolate y, undo the multiplication by 5 by dividing both sides by 5. Do not reverse the direction of the $\geq$ symbol.
$y \geq -\dfrac{16}{5}$	

The solution set is $\left[-\frac{16}{5}, \infty\right)$. To graph it, we note that $-\frac{16}{5} = -3\frac{1}{5}$.

4 Solve compound inequalities.

Two inequalities can be combined into a **compound inequality** to show that an expression lies between two fixed values. For example, $-2 < x < 3$ is a combination of

$$-2 < x \qquad \text{and} \qquad x < 3$$

It indicates that x is greater than -2 and that x is also less than 3. The solution set of $-2 < x < 3$ consists of all numbers that lie between -2 and 3, and we write it as $(-2, 3)$. The graph of the compound inequality is shown below.

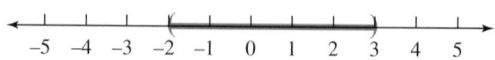

Self Check 8

Graph $-2 \leq x < 1$ and write the solution set in interval notation.

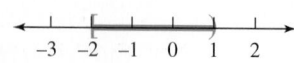

Now Try Problem 61
Self Check 8 Answer
$[-2, 1)$

EXAMPLE 8   Graph: $-4 \leq x < 0$

Strategy We need to determine which real numbers, when substituted for x, would make $-4 \leq x < 0$ a true statement.

WHY To graph $-4 \leq x < 0$ means to draw a "picture" of all of the values of x that make the compound inequality true.

Solution

If we replace the variable in $-4 \leq x < 0$ with a number between -4 and 0, including -4, the resulting compound inequality will be true. Therefore, the solution set is the interval $[-4, 0)$. To graph the interval, we draw a bracket at -4, a parenthesis at 0, and shade in between.

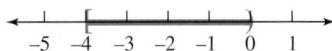

To check, we pick a number in the graph, such as -2, and see whether it satisfies the inequality. Since $-4 \leq -2 < 0$ is true, the answer appears to be correct. ◼

Success Tip Note that the two inequality symbols in $-4 \leq x < 0$ point in the same direction and point to the smaller number.

To solve compound inequalities, we isolate the variable in the middle part of the inequality. To do this, we apply the properties of inequality to all *three* parts of the inequality.

EXAMPLE 9 Solve $-4 < 2(x - 1) \leq 4$. Write the solution set in interval notation and graph it.

Strategy We will use properties of inequality to isolate the variable by itself as the middle part of the inequality.

WHY To solve the original inequality, we want to find a simpler equivalent inequality of the form **a number $< x \leq$ a number**, whose solution is obvious.

Solution

$$-4 < 2(x - 1) \leq 4 \qquad \text{This is the compound inequality to solve.}$$

$$-4 < 2x - 2 \leq 4 \qquad \text{Distribute the multiplication by 2.}$$

$$-4 + 2 < 2x - 2 + 2 \leq 4 + 2 \qquad \text{To isolate } 2x, \text{ undo the subtraction of 2 by adding 2 to all three parts.}$$

$$-2 < 2x \leq 6 \qquad \text{Do the additions.}$$

$$\frac{-2}{2} < \frac{2x}{2} \leq \frac{6}{2} \qquad \text{To isolate } x, \text{ we undo the multiplication by 2 by dividing all three parts by 2.}$$

$$-1 < x \leq 3 \qquad \text{Do the divisions.}$$

The solution set is $(-1, 3]$ and its graph is shown.

Success Tip Think of interval notation as a way to tell someone how to draw the graph, from left to right, giving them only a "start" and a "stop" instruction.

---

5 Solve inequality applications.

When solving problems, phrases such as "not more than," or "should exceed" suggest that the problem involves an inequality rather than an equation.

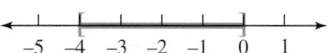

> ***The Language of Algebra***   Some phrases that suggest an inequality are:
>
> surpass: $>$ at least: $\geq$
>
> not exceed: $\leq$ at most: $\leq$
>
> between: ▨ $<$ ▨ $<$ ▨

EXAMPLE 10   *Grades*   A student has scores of 72%, 74%, and 78% on three exams. What percent score does he need on the last exam to earn a grade of no less than B (80%)?

Analyze We know three scores. We are to find what the student must score on the last exam to earn a grade of B or higher.

Form an Inequality We can let $x =$ the score on the fourth (and last) exam. To find the average grade, we add the four scores and divide by 4. To earn a grade of *no less than* B, the student's average must be *greater than or equal to* 80%.

The average of the four grades	must be no less than	80.
$\dfrac{72 + 74 + 78 + x}{4}$	$\geq$	80

Solve

$$\frac{224 + x}{4} \geq 80 \qquad \text{Combine like terms in the numerator: } 72 + 74 + 78 = 224.$$

$$4\left(\frac{224 + x}{4}\right) \geq 4(80) \qquad \text{To clear the inequality of the fraction, multiply both sides by 4.}$$

$$224 + x \geq 320 \qquad \text{Simplify each side.}$$

$$x \geq 96 \qquad \text{To isolate } x, \text{ undo the addition of 224 by subtracting 224 from both sides.}$$

State To earn a B, the student must score 96% or better on the last exam. Assuming the student cannot score higher than 100% on the exam, the solution set is written as [96, 100]. The graph is shown below.

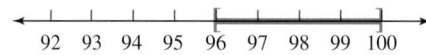

Check Pick some numbers in the interval, and verify that the average of the four scores will be 80% or greater.

ANSWERS TO SELF CHECKS

1. Yes   **2.** $[0, \infty)$ ←———[———→ (−1 0 1)   **3.** $(-\infty, 1)$ ←———)———→ (−1 0 1 2)

4. a. $[-200, \infty)$ ←—[———→ (−200 0 200)   **b.** $(-\infty, 12)$ ←———]—→ (10 11 12 13)

5. $(-3, \infty)$ ←—(———→ (−4 −3 −2 −1)   **6.** $(-\infty, 2.1)$ ←———)—→ (1 2.1 2 3)

7. $\left[\frac{13}{4}, \infty\right)$ ←—[———→ (2 3 4 5), $\frac{13}{4}$ **8.** $[-2, 1)$ ←—[———)—→ (−3 −2 −1 0 1 2)

9. $[-4, 0]$ ←—[———]—→ (−5 −4 −3 −2 −1 0 1)   **10.** 84%

SECTION 2.7 STUDY SET

VOCABULARY

Fill in the blanks.

1. An _inequality_ is a statement that contains one of the symbols: $>$, $\geq$, $<$, or $\leq$.

2. To _solve_ an inequality means to find all the values of the variable that make the inequality true.

3. The solution set of $x > 2$ can be expressed in _interval_ notation as $(2, \infty)$.

4. The inequality $-4 < x \leq 10$ is an example of a _compound_ inequality.

CONCEPTS

Fill in the blanks.

5. **a.** Adding the _same_ number to both sides of an inequality does not change the solutions.

   b. Multiplying or dividing both sides of an inequality by the same _positive_ number does not change the solutions.

   c. If we multiply or divide both sides of an inequality by a _negative_ number, the direction of the inequality symbol must be reversed for the inequalities to have the same solutions.

6. To solve $-4 \leq 2x + 1 < 3$, properties of inequality are applied to all _three_ parts of the inequality.

7. Rewrite the inequality $32 < x$ in an equivalent form with the variable on the left side. $x > 32$

8. The solution set of an inequality is graphed below. Which of the four numbers, 3, -3, 2, and 4.5, when substituted for the variable in that inequality, would make it true? $3, 4.5$

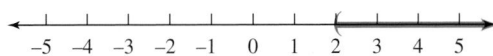

NOTATION

9. Write each symbol.

   a. is less than or equal to $\leq$

   b. infinity ∞

   c. bracket $[$ or $]$

   d. is greater than $>$

▶ 10. Consider the graph of the interval $[4, 8)$.

   a. Is the endpoint 4 included or not included in the graph? included

   b. Is the endpoint 8 included or not included in the graph? not included

▶ Selected exercises available online at
www.webassign.net/brookscole

Complete the solution to solve each inequality.

11. $4x - 5 \geq 7$

$4x - 5 + \boxed{5} \geq 7 + \boxed{5}$

$4x \geq \boxed{12}$

$\dfrac{4x}{4} \geq \dfrac{12}{4}$

$x \geq 3$ Solution set: $\left[\,\boxed{3}\,, \infty\right)$

12. $-6x > 12$

$\dfrac{-6x}{\boxed{-6}} \boxed{<} \dfrac{12}{-6}$

$x < \boxed{-2}$ Solution set: $\left(\boxed{-\infty}, -2\right)$

GUIDED PRACTICE

See Example 1.

13. Determine whether each number is a solution of $3x - 2 > 5$.

   a. 5 yes   **b.** -4 no

▶ 14. Determine whether each number is a solution of $3x + 7 < 4x - 2$.

   a. 12 yes   **b.** 9 no

15. Determine whether each number is a solution of $-5(x - 1) \geq 2x + 12$.

   a. 1 no   **b.** -1 yes

16. Determine whether each number is a solution of $\frac{4}{5}a \geq -2$.

   a. $-\dfrac{5}{4}$ yes   **b.** -15 no

Graph each inequality and describe the graph using interval notation. **See Example 2.**

17. $x < 5$ $(-\infty, 5)$

18. $x \geq -2$ $[-2, \infty)$

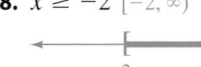

19. $-3 < x \leq 1$ $(-3, 1]$

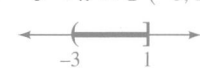

20. $-4 \leq x \leq 2$ $[-4, 2]$

Write the inequality that is represented by each graph. Then describe the graph using interval notation.

▶ 21.  $x < -1, (-\infty, -1)$

22. $x \geq 2, [2, \infty)$

23. $-7 < x \le 2, (-7, 2]$

24. $4 < x \le 6, (4, 6]$

Solve each inequality. Write the solution set in interval notation and graph it. **See Examples 3–4.**

▶ 25. $x + 2 > 5$
$(3, \infty)$

26. $x + 5 \ge 2$
$[-3, \infty)$

27. $g - 30 \ge -20$
$[10, \infty)$

28. $h - 18 \le -3$
$(-\infty, 15]$

29. $8h < 48$
$(-\infty, 6)$

30. $2t > 22$
$(11, \infty)$

31. $-\dfrac{3}{16}x \ge -9$
$(-\infty, 48]$

32. $-\dfrac{7}{8}x \le 21$
$[-24, \infty)$

▶ 33. $-3y \le -6$
$[2, \infty)$

34. $-6y \ge -6$
$(-\infty, 1]$

35. $\dfrac{2}{3}x \ge 2$
$[3, \infty)$

▶ 36. $\dfrac{3}{4}x < 3$
$(-\infty, 4)$

Solve each inequality. Write the solution set in interval notation and graph it. **See Examples 5–6.**

37. $9x + 1 > 64$
$(7, \infty)$

38. $4x + 8 < 32$
$(-\infty, 6)$

39. $0.5 \ge 2x - 0.3$
$(-\infty, 0.4]$

▶ 40. $0.8 > 7x - 0.04$
$(-\infty, 0.12)$

41. $\dfrac{x}{8} - (-9) \ge 11$
$[16, \infty)$

42. $\dfrac{x}{6} - (-12) > 14$
$(12, \infty)$

43. $\dfrac{m}{-42} - 1 > -1$
$(-\infty, 0)$

44. $\dfrac{a}{-25} + 3 < 3$
$(0, \infty)$

45. $-x - 3 \le 7$
$[-10, \infty)$

46. $-x - 9 > 3$
$(-\infty, -12)$

47. $-3x - 7 > -1$
$(-\infty, -2)$

▶ 48. $-5x + 7 \le 12$
$[-1, \infty)$

Solve each inequality. Write the solution set in interval notation and graph it. **See Example 7.**

49. $9a + 4 > 5a - 16$
$(-5, \infty)$

50. $8t + 1 < 4t - 19$
$(-\infty, -5)$

51. $0.4x \le 0.1x + 0.45$
$(-\infty, 1.5]$

52. $0.9s \le 0.3s + 0.54$
$(-\infty, 0.9]$

53. $8(5 - x) \le 10(8 - x)$
$(-\infty, 20]$

▶ 54. $17(3 - x) \ge 3 - 13x$
$(-\infty, 12]$

55. $8x + 4 > -(3x - 4)$
$(0, \infty)$

▶ 56. $7x + 6 \ge -(x - 6)$
$[0, \infty)$

57. $\dfrac{1}{2} + \dfrac{n}{5} > \dfrac{3}{4}$
$\left(\dfrac{5}{4}, \infty\right)$

58. $\dfrac{1}{3} + \dfrac{c}{5} > -\dfrac{3}{2}$
$\left(-\dfrac{55}{6}, \infty\right)$

59. $\dfrac{6x + 1}{4} \le x + 1$
$\left(-\infty, \dfrac{3}{2}\right]$

▶ 60. $\dfrac{3x - 10}{5} \le x + 4$
$[-15, \infty)$

Solve each compound inequality. Write the solution set in interval notation and graph it. **See Examples 8–9.**

61. $2 < x - 5 < 5$
$(7, 10)$

62. $-8 < t - 8 < 8$
$(0, 16)$

63. $0 \le x + 10 \le 10$
$[-10, 0]$

64. $-9 \le x + 8 < 1$
$[-17, -7)$

65. $-3 \le \dfrac{c}{2} \le 5$
$[-6, 10]$

▶ 66. $-12 < \dfrac{b}{3} < 0$
$(-36, 0)$

67. $3 \leq 2x - 1 < 5$
$[2, 3)$

68. $4 < 3x - 5 \leq 7$
$(3, 4]$

69. $-9 < 6x + 9 \leq 45$
$(-3, 6]$

70. $-30 \leq 10d + 20 < 90$
$[-5, 7)$

▶ **71.** $6 < -2(x - 1) < 12$
$(-5, -2)$

72. $4 \leq -4(x - 2) < 20$
$(-3, 1]$

TRY IT YOURSELF

Solve each inequality or compound inequality. Write the solution set in interval notation and graph it.

73. $6 - x \leq 3(x - 1)$
$\left[\frac{9}{4}, \infty\right)$

74. $3(3 - x) \geq 6 + x$
$\left(-\infty, \frac{3}{4}\right]$

75. $\dfrac{y}{4} + 1 \leq -9$
$(-\infty, -40]$

76. $\dfrac{r}{8} - 7 \geq -8$
$[-8, \infty)$

77. $0 < 5(x + 2) \leq 15$
$(-2, 1]$

78. $-18 \leq 9(x - 5) < 27$
$[3, 8)$

79. $-1 \leq -\dfrac{1}{2}n$
$(-\infty, 2]$

80. $-3 \geq -\dfrac{1}{3}t$
$[9, \infty)$

81. $-m - 12 > 15$
$(-\infty, -27)$

82. $-t + 5 < 10$
$(-5, \infty)$

83. $-\dfrac{2}{3} \geq \dfrac{2y}{3} - \dfrac{3}{4}$
$\left(-\infty, \frac{1}{8}\right]$

84. $-\dfrac{2}{9} \geq \dfrac{5x}{6} - \dfrac{1}{3}$
$\left(-\infty, \frac{2}{15}\right]$

85. $9x + 13 \geq 2x + 6x$
$[-13, \infty)$

▶ **86.** $7x - 16 < 2x + 4x$
$(-\infty, 16)$

87. $7 < \dfrac{5}{3}a + (-3)$
$(6, \infty)$

▶ **88.** $5 < \dfrac{7}{2}a + (-9)$
$(4, \infty)$

89. $-8 \leq \dfrac{y}{8} - 4 \leq 2$
$[-32, 48]$

90. $6 < \dfrac{m}{16} + 7 < 8$
$(-16, 16)$

91. $-2(2x - 3) > 17$
$\left(-\infty, -\frac{11}{4}\right)$

92. $-3(x + 0.2) < 0.3$
$(-0.3, \infty)$

93. $\dfrac{5}{3}(x + 1) \geq -x + \dfrac{2}{3}$
$\left[-\frac{3}{8}, \infty\right)$

94. $\dfrac{5}{2}(7x - 15) \geq \dfrac{11}{2}x - \dfrac{3}{2}$
$[3, \infty)$

95. $2x + 9 \leq x + 8$
$(-\infty, -1]$

96. $3x + 7 \leq 4x - 2$
$[9, \infty)$

97. $-7x + 1 < -5$
$\left(\frac{6}{7}, \infty\right)$

98. $-3x - 10 \geq -5$
$\left(-\infty, -\frac{5}{3}\right]$

APPLICATIONS

▶ **99.** GRADES A student has test scores of 68%, 75%, and 79% in a government class. What must she score on the last exam to earn a B (80% or better) in the course? 98% or better

▶ **100.** OCCUPATIONAL TESTING An employment agency requires applicants average at least 70% on a battery of four job skills tests. If an applicant scored 70%, 74%, and 84% on the first three exams, what must he score on the fourth test to maintain a 70% or better average? 52% or better

101. GAS MILEAGE A car manufacturer produces three models in equal quantities. One model has an economy rating of 17 miles per gallon, and the second model is rated for 19 mpg. If government regulations require the manufacturer to have a fleet average that exceeds 21 mpg, what economy rating is required for the third model? more than 27 mpg

▶ **102.** SERVICE CHARGES When the average daily balance of a customer's checking account falls below $500 in any week, the bank assesses a $5 service charge. The table shows the daily balances of one customer. What must Friday's balance be to avoid the service charge? $869.20 or more

Day	Balance
Monday	$540.00
Tuesday	$435.50
Wednesday	$345.30
Thursday	$310.00

103. GEOMETRY The perimeter of an equilateral triangle is at most 57 feet. What could the length of a side be? (*Hint:* All three sides of an equilateral triangle are equal.) 19 ft or less

▶ **104.** GEOMETRY The perimeter of a square is no less than 68 centimeters. How long can a side be? 17 cm or more

105. COUNTER SPACE A rectangular counter is being built for the customer service department of a store. Designers have determined that the outside perimeter of the counter (shown in red) needs to exceed 30 feet. Determine the acceptable values for *x*. more than 5 ft

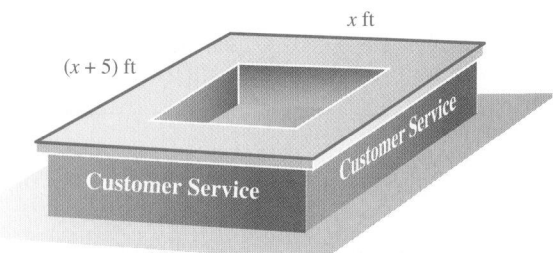

▶ **106.** NUMBER PUZZLES What numbers satisfy the condition: Four more than three times the number is at most 10? $x \leq 2$

107. GRADUATIONS It costs a student $18 to rent a cap and gown and 80 cents for each graduation announcement that she orders. If she doesn't want her spending on these graduation costs to exceed $50, how many announcements can she order? 40 or less

108. TELEPHONES A cellular telephone company has currently enrolled 36,000 customers in a new calling plan. If an average of 1,200 people are signing up for the plan each day, in how many days will the company surpass their goal of having 150,000 customers enrolled? 96 days

109. WINDOWS An architect needs to design a triangular-shaped bathroom window that has an area no greater than 100 in.². If the base of the window must be 16 inches long, what window heights will meet this condition? 12.5 in. or less

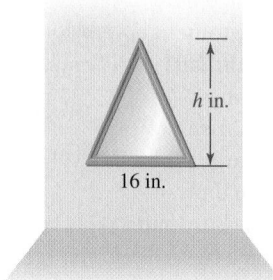

▶ **110.** ROOM TEMPERATURES To hold the temperature of a room between 19° and 22° Celsius, what Fahrenheit temperatures must be maintained? $\left(Hint:\text{ Use the formula }C = \frac{5}{9}(F - 32).\right)$ $66.2° < F < 71.6°$

111. INFANTS The graph is used to classify the weight of a baby boy from birth to 1 year. Estimate the weight range for boys in the following classifications, using a compound inequality:

a. 10 months old, "heavy" $26\text{ lb} \leq w \leq 31\text{ lb}$

b. 5 months old, "light" $12\text{ lb} \leq w \leq 14\text{ lb}$

c. 8 months old, "average" $18.5\text{ lb} \leq w \leq 20.5\text{ lb}$

d. 3 months old, "moderately light" $11\text{ lb} \leq w \leq 13\text{ lb}$

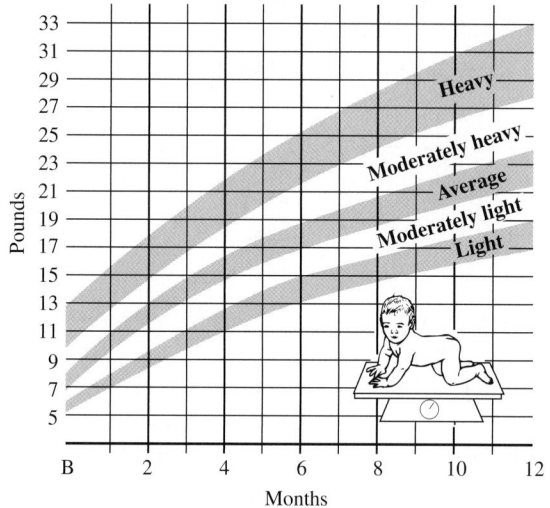

Source: Based on data from *Better Homes and Gardens Baby Book* (Meredith Corp., 1969)

▶ **112.** NUMBER PUZZLES What *whole* numbers satisfy the condition: Twice the number decreased by 1 is between 50 and 60? 26, 27, 28, 29, 30

WRITING

113. Explain why multiplying both sides of an inequality by a negative number reverses the direction of the inequality.

▶ **114.** Explain the use of parentheses and brackets for graphing intervals.

REVIEW

Complete each table.

115.

x	$x^2 - 3$
-2	1
0	-3
3	6

116.

x	$\frac{x}{3} + 2$
-6	0
0	2
12	6

STUDY SKILLS CHECKLIST

Preparing for the Chapter 2 Test

There are common mistakes that students make when working with the topics of Chapter 2. To make sure you are prepared for your test and to help you avoid these common mistakes, study this checklist below.

☐ When solving an equation, if you multiply by the LCD to remove the fractions, remember to multiply the other side by the same number.

$$\frac{2}{3}x + \frac{1}{12} = \frac{1}{4}x$$

$$12\left(\frac{2}{3}x + \frac{1}{12}\right) = 12\left(\frac{1}{4}x\right)$$

☐ When *solving an equation*, find a simpler equivalent equation of the form x = a number. When *simplifying expressions*, remove the parentheses and combine like terms.

☐ Do not try to divide by the coefficient of the variable until that term is isolated.

$$-3x + 9 = 16$$
$$-3x + 9 - 9 = 16 - 9$$
$$-3x = 7$$
$$\frac{-3x}{-3} = \frac{7}{-3}$$
$$x = -\frac{7}{3}$$

☐ When solving inequalities, remember to *change the direction of the inequality symbol when multiplying or dividing both sides by a negative number.*

Teaching Guide: Refer to the Instructor's Resource Binder to find activities, worksheets on key concepts, more examples, instruction tips, overheads, and assessments.

CHAPTER 2   SUMMARY AND REVIEW

SECTION 2.1   Solving Equations Using Properties of Equality

DEFINITIONS AND CONCEPTS	EXAMPLES
An **equation** is a statement indicating that two expressions are equal. The equal symbol = separates an equation into two parts: the left side and the right side.	$2x + 4 = 10$ $-5(a + 4) = -11a$ $\frac{3}{2}t + 6 = t - \frac{1}{3}$
A number that makes an equation a true statement when substituted for the variable is called a **solution** of the equation.	Determine whether 2 is a solution of $x + 4 = 3x$. ***Check:*** $\quad x + 4 = 3x$ $\qquad\qquad 2 + 4 \stackrel{?}{=} 3(2) \quad$ Substitute 2 for each x. $\qquad\qquad\quad 6 = 6 \qquad$ True Since the resulting statement is true, 2 is a solution.
Equivalent equations have the same solutions.	$x - 2 = 6$ and $x = 8$ are equivalent equations because they have the same solution, 8.

To **solve an equation** isolate the variable on one side of the equation by undoing the operations performed on it using properties of equality.

Addition (Subtraction) property of equality: If the same number is added to (or subtracted from) both sides of an equation, the result is an equivalent equation.	Solve: $x - 5 = 7$ Solve: $c + 9 = 16$ $x - 5 + 5 = 7 + 5$ $c + 9 - 9 = 16 - 9$ $x = 12$ $c = 7$
Multiplication (Division) property of equality: If both sides of an equation are multiplied (or divided) by the same nonzero number, the result is an equivalent equation.	Solve: $\dfrac{1}{3}m = 2$ Solve: $10y = 50$ $3\left(\dfrac{1}{3}m\right) = 3(2)$ $\dfrac{10y}{10} = \dfrac{50}{10}$ $m = 6$ $y = 5$

REVIEW EXERCISES

Determine whether the given number is a solution of the equation.

1. 84, $x - 34 = 50$ yes

2. 3, $5y + 2 = 12$ no

3. -30, $\dfrac{x}{5} = 6$ no

4. 2, $a^2 - a - 1 = 0$ no

5. -3, $5b - 2 = 3b - 8$ yes

6. 1, $\dfrac{2}{y + 1} = \dfrac{12}{y + 1} - 5$ yes

Fill in the blanks.

7. An _equation_ is a statement indicating that two expressions are equal.

8. To solve $x - 8 = 10$ means to find all the values of the variable that make the equation a _true_ statement.

Solve each equation and check the result.

9. $x - 9 = 12$ 21

10. $-y = -32$ 32

11. $a + 3.7 = -16.9$ -20.6

12. $100 = -7 + r$ 107

13. $120 = 5c$ 24

14. $t - \dfrac{1}{2} = \dfrac{3}{2}$ 2

15. $\dfrac{4}{3}t = -12$ -9

16. $3 = \dfrac{q}{-2.6}$ -7.8

17. $6b = 0$ 0

18. $\dfrac{15}{16}s = -3$ $-\frac{16}{5}$

SECTION 2.2   More about Solving Equations

DEFINITIONS AND CONCEPTS	EXAMPLES	
A five-step **strategy for solving linear equations:**	Solve: $2(y + 2) + 4y = 11 - y$	
1. *Clear* the equation of fractions or decimals.	$2y + 4 + 4y = 11 - y$	Distribute the multiplication by 2.
2. *Simplify* each side. Use the distributive property and combine like terms when necessary.	$6y + 4 = 11 - y$	Combine like terms: $2y + 4y = 6y$.
3. *Isolate the variable term.* Use the addition and subtraction properties of equality.	$6y + 4 + y = 11 - y + y$	To eliminate $-y$ on the right, add y to both sides.
	$7y + 4 = 11$	Combine like terms.
	$7y + 4 - 4 = 11 - 4$	To isolate the variable term $7y$, subtract 4 from both sides.
4. *Isolate the variable.* Use the multiplication and division properties of equality.	$7y = 7$	Simplify each side of the equation.
5. *Check* the result in the original equation.	$\dfrac{7y}{7} = \dfrac{7}{7}$	To isolate y, divide both sides by 7.
	$y = 1$	

To clear an equation of fractions, multiply both sides of an equation by the LCD.	To solve $\dfrac{1}{2} + \dfrac{x}{3} = \dfrac{3}{4}$, first multiply both sides by 12: $$12\left(\dfrac{1}{2} + \dfrac{x}{3}\right) = 12\left(\dfrac{3}{4}\right)$$
To clear an equation of decimals, multiply both sides by a power of 10 to change the decimals in the equation to integers.	To solve $0.5(x - 4) = 0.1x + 0.2$, first multiply both sides by 10: $$10[0.5(x - 4)] = 10(0.1x + 0.2)$$
A linear equation in one variable that is true for all values of the variable is called an **identity.**	When we solve $x + 5 + x = 2x + 5$, the variables drop out and we obtain a true statement $5 = 5$. All real numbers are solutions.
An equation that is not true for any value of its variable is called a **contradiction.**	When we solve $y + 2 = y$, the variables drop out and we obtain a false statement $2 = 0$. The equation has no solutions.

REVIEW EXERCISES

Solve each equation. Check the result.

19. $5x + 4 = 14$ 2

20. $98.6 - t = 129.2$ −30.6

21. $\dfrac{n}{5} + (-2) = 4$ 30

22. $\dfrac{b - 5}{4} = -6$ −19

23. $5(2x - 4) - 5x = 0$ 4

24. $-2(x - 5) = 5(-3x + 4) + 3$ 1

25. $\dfrac{3}{4} = \dfrac{1}{2} + \dfrac{d}{5}$ $\frac{5}{4}$

26. $\dfrac{5(7 - x)}{4} = 2x - 3$ $\frac{47}{13}$

27. $\dfrac{3(2 - c)}{2} = \dfrac{-2(2c + 3)}{5} - 6$

28. $\dfrac{b}{3} + \dfrac{11}{9} + 3b = -\dfrac{5}{6}b - \dfrac{22}{75}$

29. $0.15(x + 2) + 0.3 = 0.35x - 0.4$ 5

30. $0.5 - 0.02(y - 2) = 0.16 + 0.36y$ 1

31. $3(a + 8) = 6(a + 4) - 3a$ identity, all real numbers

32. $2(y + 10) + y = 3(y + 8)$ contradiction, no solution

SECTION 2.3   Applications of Percent

DEFINITIONS AND CONCEPTS	**EXAMPLES**
To solve **percent problems,** use the facts of the problem to write a sentence of the form: [ ] is [ ] % of [ ] ? Translate the sentence to mathematical symbols: *is* translates to an $=$ symbol and *of* means multiply. Then solve the equation.	648 is 30% of what number? $$648 = 30\% \cdot x \qquad \text{Translate.}$$ $$648 = 0.30x \qquad \text{Change 30\% to a decimal: 30\% = 0.30.}$$ $$\dfrac{648}{0.30} = x \qquad \text{To isolate } x \text{, divide both sides by 0.30.}$$ $$2{,}160 = x \qquad \text{Do the division.}$$ Thus, 648 is 30% of 2,160.
To find the **percent of increase** or **the percent of decrease,** find what percent the increase or decrease is of the original amount.	SALE PRICES To find the percent of decrease when ground beef prices are reduced from \$4.89 to \$4.59 per pound, we first find the amount of decrease: $4.89 - 4.59 = 0.30$. Then we determine what percent 0.30 is of 4.89 (the original price). 0.30 is what% of 4.89? $$0.30 = x \cdot 4.89 \qquad \text{Translate.}$$

$$0.30 = 4.89x$$

$$\frac{0.30}{4.89} = x \qquad \text{To isolate x, divide both sides by 4.89.}$$

$$0.061349693 \approx x \qquad \text{Do the division.}$$

$$0\,0\,6.1349693\% \approx x \qquad \text{Write the decimal as a percent.}$$

To the nearest tenth of a percent, the percent of decrease is 6.1%.

REVIEW EXERCISES

33. Fill in the blanks.

   a. __Percent__ means parts per one hundred.

   b. When the price of an item is reduced, we call the amount of the reduction a __discount__.

   c. An employee who is paid a __commission__ is paid a percent of the goods or services that he or she sells.

34. 4.81 is 2.5% of what number? 192.4

35. What number is 15% of 950? 142.5

36. What percent of 410 is 49.2? 12%

37. U.S. ONLINE DATA The circle graph below shows Internet usage in the United States by the approximately 288.5 million people, ages 3 and over, in 2007. Determine the number of broadband users and the number of dial-up users. Round to the nearest tenth of one million. 139.3 million, 45.3 million

U.S. Internet Usage,* 2007

Not online 103.9 million; **36.0%**

Broadband users ? million; **48.3%**

Dial-up users ? million; **15.7%**

Source: *Advertising Age 2007 Fact Pack*

*An Internet user is defined as someone who uses the Internet at least once per month.

38. COST OF LIVING A retired trucker receives a monthly Social Security check of $764. If she is to receive a 3.5% cost-of-living increase soon, how much larger will her check be? $26.74

39. FAMILY BUDGETS It is recommended that a family pay no more than 30% of its monthly income (after taxes) on housing. If a family has an after-tax income of $1,890 per month and pays $625 in housing costs each month, are they within the recommended range? no

40. DISCOUNTS A shopper saved $148.50 on a food processor that was discounted 33%. What did it originally cost? $450

41. TUPPERWARE The hostess of a Tupperware party is paid a 25% commission on her in-home party's sales. What would the hostess earn if sales totaled $600? $150

42. COLLECTIBLES A collector of football trading cards paid $6 for a 1984 Dan Marino rookie card several years ago. If the card is now worth $100, what is the percent of increase in the card's value? (Round to the nearest percent.) 1,567%

SECTION 2.4 Formulas

DEFINITIONS AND CONCEPTS

A **formula** is an equation that states a relationship between two or more variables.

EXAMPLES

Retail price: $r = c + m$ Profit: $p = r - c$

Simple Interest: $I = Prt$ Distance: $d = rt$

Temperature: $C = \dfrac{5}{9}(F - 32)$

The **perimeter** of a plane geometric figure is the distance around it. The **area** of a plane geometric figure is the amount of surface that it encloses. The **volume** of a three-dimensional geometric solid is the amount of space it encloses.

Rectangle: $P = 2l + 2w$ Circle: $C = \pi D = 2\pi r$

$A = lw$ $A = \pi r^2$

Rectangular solid: $V = lwh$ Cylinder: $V = \pi r^2 h$

*See the inside back cover of the text for more geometric formulas.

If we are given the values of all but one of the variables in a formula, we can use our equation-solving skills to find the value of the remaining variable.

BEDDING   The area of a standard queen-size bed sheet is 9,180 in.^{2}. If the width is 102 inches, what is the length?

$A = lw$ This is the formula for the area of a rectangle.

$9,180 = 102w$ Substitute 9,180 for the area A and 102 for the width w.

$\dfrac{9,180}{102} = w$ To isolate w, divide both sides by 102.

$90 = w$ Do the division.

The length of a standard queen-size bed sheet is 90 inches.

To solve a formula for a specific variable means to isolate that variable on one side of the equation, with all other variables and constants on the opposite side. Treat the specified variable as if it is the only variable in the equation. Treat the other variables as if they were numbers (constants).

Solve the formula for the volume of a cone for h.

$V = \dfrac{1}{3}\pi r^2 h$ This is the formula for the volume of a cone.

$3(V) = 3\left(\dfrac{1}{3}\pi r^2 h\right)$ To clear the equation of the fraction, multiply both sides by 3.

$3V = \pi r^2 h$ Simplify.

$\dfrac{3V}{\pi r^2} = \dfrac{\pi r^2 h}{\pi r^2}$ To isolate h, divide both sides by πr^2.

$\dfrac{3V}{\pi r^2} = h$ or $h = \dfrac{3V}{\pi r^2}$

REVIEW EXERCISES

43. SHOPPING Find the markup on a CD player whose wholesale cost is $219 and whose retail price is $395. $176

44. RESTAURANTS One month, a restaurant had sales of $13,500 and made a profit of $1,700. Find the expenses for the month. $11,800

45. SNAILS A typical garden snail travels at an average rate of 2.5 feet per minute. How long would it take a snail to cross a 20-foot long flower bed? 8 min

46. CERTIFICATES OF DEPOSIT A $26,000 investment in a CD earned $1,170 in interest the first year. What was the annual interest rate? 4.5%

47. JEWELRY Gold melts at about 1,065°C. Change this to degrees Fahrenheit. 1,949°F

48. CAMPING

  a. Find the perimeter of the air mattress in the next column. 168 in.

  b. Find the amount of sleeping area on the top surface of the air mattress. 1,440 in.^{2}

  c. Find the approximate volume of the air mattress if it is 3 inches thick. 4,320 in.^{3}

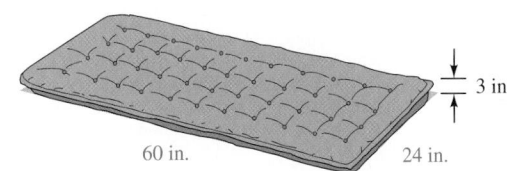

3 in.

60 in.   24 in.

49. Find the area of a triangle with a base 17 meters long and a height of 9 meters. 76.5 m^2

50. Find the area of a trapezoid with bases 11 inches and 13 inches long and a height of 12 inches. 144 in.^{2}

51. a. Find the circumference of a circle with a radius of 8 centimeters. Round to the nearest hundredth of one centimeter. 50.27 cm

  b. Find the area of the circle. Round to the nearest square centimeter. 201 cm^2

52. Find the volume of a 12-foot cylinder whose circular base has a radius of 0.5 feet. Give the result to the nearest tenth.
9.4 ft^3 (Answers may vary, depending on which approximation of π is used.)

53. Find the volume of a pyramid that has a square base, measuring 6 feet on a side, and a height of 10 feet.   120 ft³

54. HALLOWEEN After being cleaned out, a spherical-shaped pumpkin has an inside diameter of 9 inches. To the nearest hundredth, what is its volume?   381.70 in.³

Solve each formula for the specified variable.

55. $A = 2\pi rh$ for h
$h = \frac{A}{2\pi r}$

56. $A - BC = \dfrac{G - K}{3}$ for G
$G = 3A - 3BC + K$

57. $C = \dfrac{1}{4}s(t - d)$ for t
$t = \frac{4C}{s} + d$

58. $4y - 3x = 16$ for y
$y = \frac{3}{4}x + 4$

SECTION **2.5**   Problem Solving

DEFINITIONS AND CONCEPTS	EXAMPLES
To solve application problems, use the five-step problem-solving strategy. **1.** Analyze the problem. **2.** Form an equation. **3.** Solve the equation. **4.** State the conclusion. **5.** Check the result.	**INCOME TAXES** After taxes, an author kept $85,340 of her total annual earnings. If her earnings were taxed at a 15% rate, how much did she earn that year? **Analyze the Problem** The author earned some unknown amount of money. On that amount, she paid 15% in taxes. The difference between her total earnings and the taxes paid was $85,340. **Form an Equation** If we let $x =$ the author's total earnings, the amount of taxes that she paid was 15% of x or $0.15x$. We can use the words of the problem to form an equation.

Her total earnings	minus	the taxes that she paid	equals	the money that she kept.
x	$-$	$0.15x$	$=$	$85,340$

Solve the Equation

$x - 0.15x = 85,340$

$0.85x = 85,340$ Combine like terms.

$x = 100,400$ To isolate x, divide both sides by 0.85.

State the Conclusion The author earned $100,400 that year.

Check the Result The taxes were 15% of $100,400 or $15,060. If we subtract the taxes from her total earnings, we get $100,400 − $15,060 = $85,340. The answer checks.

REVIEW EXERCISES

59. SOUND SYSTEMS A 45-foot-long speaker wire is to be cut into three pieces. One piece is to be 15 feet long. Of the remaining pieces, one must be 2 feet less than 3 times the length of the other. Find the length of the shorter piece.   8 ft

60. SIGNING PETITIONS A professional signature collector is paid $50 a day plus $2.25 for each verified signature he gets from a registered voter. How many signatures are needed to earn $500 a day?   200

61. LOTTERY WINNINGS After taxes, a lottery winner was left with a lump sum of $1,800,000. If 28% of the original prize was withheld to pay federal income taxes, what was the original cash prize? $2,500,000

62. NASCAR The car numbers of drivers Bobby Labonte and Kyle Petty are consecutive odd integers whose sum is 88. If Labonte's number is the smaller, find the numbers of each car.
Labonte: 43, Petty: 45

63. ART HISTORY *American Gothic* was painted in 1930 by Grant Wood. The length of the rectangular painting is 5 inches more than the width. Find the dimensions of the painting if it has a perimeter of $109\frac{1}{2}$ inches.

24.875 in. × 29.875 in. $\left(24\frac{7}{8}\text{ in.} \times 29\frac{7}{8}\text{ in.}\right)$

© SuperStock, Inc./SuperStock

64. GEOMETRY Find the missing angle measures of the triangle. 76.5°, 76.5°

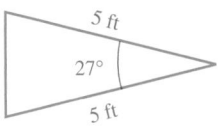

SECTION 2.6   More about Problem Solving

DEFINITIONS AND CONCEPTS	EXAMPLES

To solve application problems, use the five-step problem-solving strategy.

1. Analyze the problem.
2. Form an equation.
3. Solve the equation.
4. State the conclusion.
5. Check the result.

Tables are a helpful way to organize the facts of a problem.

TRUCKING Two trucks leave from the same place at the same time traveling in opposite directions. One travels at a rate of 60 mph and the other at 50 mph. How long will it take them to be 165 miles apart?

Analyze the Problem We know that one truck travels at 60 mph and the other at 50 mph. Together, the trucks will travel a distance of 165 miles.

Form an Equation We enter each rate in the table under the heading r. Since the trucks travel for the same length of time, say t hours, we enter t for each truck under the heading t. Since $d = r \cdot t$, the first truck will travel $60t$ miles and the second will travel $50t$ miles. We enter the distances traveled under the heading d in the table.

	r	$\cdot$ t	$=$ d
Truck 1	60	t	$60t$
Truck 2	50	t	$50t$
		Total:	165

Use the information in this column to form an equation.

The distance the first truck travels	plus	the distance the second truck travels	is	165 miles.
$60t$	$+$	$50t$	$=$	165

Solve the Equation $60t + 50t = 165$

$110t = 165$ Combine like terms.

$\dfrac{110t}{110} = \dfrac{165}{110}$ To isolate t, divide both sides by 110.

$t = 1.5$

State the Conclusion The trucks will be 165 miles apart in 1.5 hours.

Check the Result If the first truck travels 60 mph for 1.5 hours, it will go $60(1.5) = 90$ miles. If the second truck travels 50 mph for 1.5 hours, it will go $50(1.5) = 75$ miles. Since 90 miles + 75 miles = 165 miles, the result checks.

REVIEW EXERCISES

65. INVESTMENT INCOME A woman has $27,000. Part is invested for 1 year in a certificate of deposit paying 7% interest, and the remaining amount in a cash management fund paying 9%. After 1 year, the total interest on the two investments is $2,110. How much is invested at each rate? $16,000 at 7%, $11,000 at 9%

66. WALKING AND BICYCLING A bicycle path is 5 miles long. A man walks from one end at the rate of 3 mph. At the same time, a friend bicycles from the other end, traveling at 12 mph. In how many minutes will they meet? 20 min

67. AIRPLANES How long will it take a jet plane, flying at 450 mph, to overtake a propeller plane, flying at 180 mph, if the propeller plane had a $2\frac{1}{2}$-hour head start? $1\frac{2}{3}$ hr = 1 hr 40 min

68. AUTOGRAPHS Kesha collected the autographs of 8 more television celebrities than she has of movie stars. Each TV celebrity autograph is worth $75 and each movie star autograph is worth $250. If her collection is valued at $1,900, howflying many of each type of autograph does she have? TV celebrities: 12, movie stars: 4

69. MIXTURES A store manager mixes candy worth 90¢ per pound with gumdrops worth $1.50 per pound to make 20 pounds of a mixture worth $1.20 per pound. How many pounds of each kind of candy does he use? 10 lb of each

70. MILK Cream is about 22% butterfat and low-fat milk is about 2% butterfat. How many gallons of cream must be mixed with 18 gallons of low-fat milk to make whole milk that contains 4% butterfat? 2 gal

---

SECTION 2.7 Solving Inequalities

DEFINITIONS AND CONCEPTS	EXAMPLES
An **inequality** is a mathematical statement that contains an $>$, $<$, $\geq$, or $\leq$ symbol.	$3x < 8$ $\qquad \frac{1}{2}y - 4 \geq 12 \qquad 2z + 4 \leq z - 5$
A **solution of an inequality** is any number that makes the inequality true.	Determine whether 3 is a solution of $2x - 7 < 5$. $\qquad$ ***Check:*** $\quad 2x - 7 < 5$ $\qquad\qquad\qquad 2(3) - 7 \overset{?}{<} 5 \quad$ Substitute 3 for x. $\qquad\qquad\qquad\qquad -1 < 5 \quad$ True $\qquad$ Since the resulting statement is true, 3 is a solution.
We **solve inequalities** as we solve equations. However, if we multiply or divide both sides by a negative number, we must reverse the inequality symbol.	Solve: $\quad -3(z - 1) \geq -6$ $\qquad\qquad -3z + 3 \geq -6 \quad$ Distribute the multiplication by -3. $\qquad\qquad\quad -3z \geq -9 \quad$ To isolate the variable term $-3z$, subtract 3 from both sides. $\qquad\qquad \dfrac{-3z}{-3} \leq \dfrac{-9}{-3} \quad$ To isolate z, divide both sides by -3. Reverse the inequality symbol. $\qquad\qquad\qquad z \leq 3 \quad$ Do the divisions.
Interval notation can be used to describe the solution set of an inequality. A **parenthesis** indicates that a number is not in the solution set of an inequality. A **bracket** indicates that a number is included in the solution set.	In interval notation, the solution set is $(-\infty, 3]$, whose graph is shown. 0 1 2 3 4

REVIEW EXERCISES

Solve each inequality. Write the solution set in interval notation and graph it.

71. $3x + 2 < 5$ $(-\infty, 1)$

1

72. $-\dfrac{3}{4}x \geq -9$ $(-\infty, 12]$

12

73. $\dfrac{3}{4} < \dfrac{d}{5} + \dfrac{1}{2}$ $\left(\frac{5}{4}, \infty\right)$

5/4

74. $5(3 - x) \leq 3(x - 3)$
$[3, \infty)$

3

75. $\dfrac{t}{-5} - (-1.8) \geq -6.2$

$(-\infty, 40]$

40

76. $63 < 7a$ $(9, \infty)$

9

77. $8 < x + 2 < 13$ $(6, 11)$

6   11

78. $0 \leq 3 - 2x < 10$ $\left(-\frac{7}{2}, \frac{3}{2}\right]$

−7/2   3/2

79. SPORTS EQUIPMENT The acceptable weight w of Ping-Pong balls used in competition can range from 2.40 to 2.53 grams. Express this range using a compound inequality. $2.40\text{ g} \leq w \leq 2.53\text{ g}$

80. SIGNS A large office complex has a strict policy about signs. Any sign to be posted in the building must be rectangular in shape, its width must be 18 inches, and its perimeter is not to exceed 132 inches. What possible sign lengths meet these specifications? 0 in. $< l \leq 48$ in., 48 in. or less

1. Fill in the blanks.

   a. To __solve__ an equation means to find all of the values of the variable that make the equation true.

   b. __Percent__ means parts per one hundred.

   c. The distance around a circle is called its __circumference__.

   d. An __inequality__ is a statement that contains one of the symbols $>$, $\geq$, $<$, or $\leq$.

   e. The __multiplication__ property of __equality__ says that multiplying both sides of an equation by the same nonzero number does not change its solution.

2. Is 3 a solution of $5y + 2 = 12$? no

Solve each equation.

3. $3h + 2 = 8$ 2

4. $\dfrac{4}{5}t = -4$ -5

5. $-22 = -x$ 22

6. $\dfrac{11b - 11}{5} = 3b - 2$ $-\frac{1}{4}$

7. $0.8(x - 1,000) + 1.3 = 2.9 + 0.2x$ 1,336

8. $2(y - 7) - 3y = -(y - 3) - 17$ all real numbers (an identity)

9. $\dfrac{m}{2} - \dfrac{1}{3} = \dfrac{1}{4} + \dfrac{m}{6}$ $\frac{7}{4}$

10. $9 - 5(2x + 10) = -1$ -4

11. $24t = -6(8 - 4t)$ no solution (a contradiction)

12. $6a + (-7) = 3a - 7 + 2a$ 0

13. What is 15.2% of 80? 12.16

14. DOWN PAYMENTS To buy a house, a woman was required to make a down payment of $11,400. What did the house sell for if this was 15% of the purchase price? $76,000

15. BODY TEMPERATURES Suppose a person's body temperature rises from 98.6°F to a dangerous 105°F. What is the percent increase? Round to the nearest percent. 6%

16. COMMISSIONS An appliance store salesperson receives a commission of 5% of the price of every item that she sells. What will she make if she sells a $599.99 refrigerator? $30

17. GRAND OPENINGS On its first night of business, a pizza parlor brought in $445. The owner estimated his profits that night to be $150. What were the costs? $295

18. Find the Celsius temperature reading if the Fahrenheit reading is 14°. -10°C

19. PETS The spherical fishbowl is three-quarters full of water. To the nearest cubic inch, find the volume of water in the bowl. (*Hint:* The volume of a sphere is given by $V = \frac{4}{3}\pi r^3$.) 393 in.³

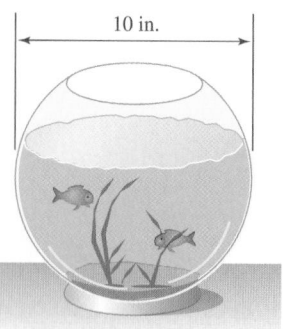

10 in.

20. Solve $A = P + Prt$ for r. $r = \frac{A - P}{Pt}$

21. IRONS Estimate the area of the soleplate of the iron. 20 in.^{2}

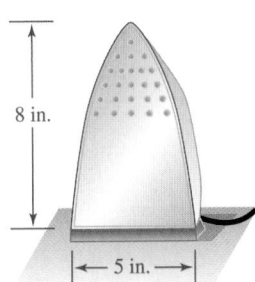

8 in.

5 in.

22. TELEVISION In a typical 30-minute block of time on TV, the number of programming minutes are 2 less than three times the number of minutes of commercials. How many minutes of programming and commercials are there? 22 min, 8 min

23. HOME SALES A condominium owner cleared $114,600 on the sale of his condo, after paying a 4.5% real estate commission. What was the selling price? $120,000

24. COLORADO The state of Colorado is approximately rectangular-shaped with a perimeter of 1,320 miles. Find the length (east to west) and width (north to south), if the length is 100 miles longer than the width. 380 mi, 280 mi

25. TEA How many pounds of green tea, worth $40 a pound, should be mixed with herbal tea, worth $50 a pound, to produce 20 pounds of a blend worth $42 a pound? green: 16 lb, herbal: 4 lb

26. READING A bookmark is inserted between two page numbers whose sum is 825. What are the page numbers? 412, 413

27. TRAVEL TIMES A car leaves Rockford, Illinois, at the rate of 65 mph, bound for Madison, Wisconsin. At the same time, a truck leaves Madison at the rate of 55 mph, bound for Rockford. If the cities are 72 miles apart, how long will it take for the car and the truck to meet? $\frac{3}{5}$ hr or 36 min

28. PICKLES To make pickles, fresh cucumbers are soaked in a salt water solution called *brine*. How many liters of a 2% brine solution must be added to 30 liters of a 10% brine solution to dilute it to an 8% solution? 10 liters

29. GEOMETRY If the vertex angle of an isosceles triangle is 44°, find the measure of each base angle. 68°

30. INVESTMENTS Part of $13,750 is invested at 9% annual interest, and the rest is invested at 8%. After one year, the accounts paid $1,185 in interest. How much was invested at the lower rate? $5,250

Solve each inequality. Write the solution set in interval notation and graph it.

31. $-8x - 20 \leq 4$
$[-3, \infty)$

−3

32. $-8.1 > \dfrac{t}{2} + (-11.3)$
$(-\infty, 6.4)$

6.4

33. $-12 \leq 2(x + 1) < 10$ $[-7, 4)$

−7   4

34. AWARDS A city honors its citizen of the year with a framed certificate. An artist charges $15 for the frame and 75 cents per word for writing out the proclamation. If a city regulation does not allow gifts in excess of $150, what is the maximum number of words that can be written on the certificate? 180 words

1. Classify each of the following as an equation or an expression. [Section 1.1]

   a. $4m - 3 + 2m$ **b.** $4m = 3 + 2m$

       expression   equation

2. Use the formula $t = \dfrac{w}{5}$ to complete the table. [Section 1.1]

Weight (lb)	Cooking time (hr)
15	3
20	4
25	5

3. Write each phrase as an algebraic expression. [Section 1.1]

   a. The sum of the width w and 12. $w + 12$

   b. Four less than a number n. $n - 4$

4. Give the prime factorization of 100. [Section 1.2]
   $2 \cdot 2 \cdot 5 \cdot 5 = 2^2 \cdot 5^2$

5. Simplify: $\dfrac{24}{36}$ [Section 1.2] $\dfrac{2}{3}$

6. Multiply: $\dfrac{11}{21}\left(-\dfrac{14}{33}\right)$ [Section 1.2] $-\dfrac{2}{9}$

7. COOKING A recipe calls for $\frac{3}{4}$ cup of flour, and the only measuring container you have holds $\frac{1}{8}$ of a cup. How many $\frac{1}{8}$ cups of flour would you need to add to follow the recipe? [Section 1.2] 6

8. Add: $\dfrac{4}{5} + \dfrac{2}{3}$ [Section 1.2] $\dfrac{22}{15} = 1\dfrac{7}{15}$

9. Subtract: $42\dfrac{1}{8} - 29\dfrac{2}{3}$ [Section 1.2] $12\dfrac{11}{24}$

10. Write $\dfrac{15}{16}$ as a decimal. [Section 1.3] 0.9375

11. Evaluate each expression. [Section 1.3]

   a. $|-65|$ 65   **b.** $-|-12|$ -12

12. Determine whether the statement is true or false. [Section 1.3]

   a. Every natural number is a whole number. true

   b. -3 is a rational number. true

   c. π is a rational number. false

13. Perform each operation.

   a. $-6 + (-12) + 8$ [Section 1.4] -10

   b. $-15 - (-1)$ [Section 1.5] -14

   c. $2(-32)$ [Section 1.6] -64

   d. $\dfrac{0}{35}$ [Section 1.6] 0

14. Write each product using exponents. [Section 1.7]

   a. $4 \cdot 4 \cdot 4$ 4^3 **b.** $\pi \cdot r \cdot r \cdot h$ $\pi r^2 h$

15. SICK DAYS Use the data in the table to find the average (mean) number of sick days used by this group of employees this year. [Section 1.7] 4

Name	Sick days	Name	Sick days
Chung	4	Ryba	0
Cruz	8	Nguyen	5
Damron	3	Tomaka	4
Hammond	2	Young	6

16. Complete the table. [Section 1.8]

x	$x^2 - 3$
-2	1
0	-3
3	6

Let $x = -5$, $y = 3$, and $z = 0$. Evaluate each expression. [Section 1.8]

17. $(3x - 2y)z$ 0

18. $\dfrac{x - 3y + |z|}{2 - x}$ -2

19. $x^2 - y^2 + z^2$ 16

20. $\dfrac{x}{y} + \dfrac{y + 2}{3 - z}$ 0

Simplify each expression. [Section 1.9]

21. $-8(4d)$
   $-32d$

22. $5(2x - 3y + 1)$
   $10x - 15y + 5$

23. $2x + 3x$ $5x$

24. $3a + 6a - 17a$ $-8a$

25. $q(q - 5) + 7q2$
   $8q^2 - 5q$

26. $5(t - 4) + 3t$
   $8t - 20$

Solve each equation. [Sections 2.1 and 2.2]

27. $3x - 4 = 23$ 9

28. $\dfrac{x}{5} + 3 = 7$ 20

29. $-5p + 0.7 = 3.7$ -0.6

30. $\dfrac{y - 4}{5} = 3$ 19

31. $-\dfrac{4}{5}x = 16$ -20

32. $-9(n + 2) - 2(n - 3) = 10$ -2

33. $9y - 3 = 6y$ 1

34. $\dfrac{1}{2} + \dfrac{x}{5} = \dfrac{3}{4}$ $\dfrac{5}{4}$

35. 45 is 15% of what number? [Section 2.3] 300

36. What is 35% of 250? [Section 2.3] 87.5

37. 65 is what percent of 260? [Section 2.3] 25%

38. A diner at a local restaurant received a bill for $10.75. Compute a 15% tip (rounded up to the nearest dollar). [Section 2.3] $2

39. Find the area of a rectangle with sides of 5 meters and 13 meters. [Section 2.4] 65 m²

40. Find the volume of a cone that is 10 centimeters tall and has a circular base whose diameter is 12 centimeters. Round to the nearest hundredth. [Section 2.4] 376.99 cm³

41. Solve $A = P + Prt$ for t. [Section 2.4] $t = \dfrac{A - P}{Pr}$

42. WORK Physicists say that *work* is done when an object is moved a distance d by a force F. To find the work done, we can use the formula $W = Fd$. Find the work done in lifting the bundle of newspapers onto the workbench shown in the illustration. (*Hint:* The force that must be applied to lift the newspapers is equal to the weight of the newspapers.) [Section 2.4] 37.5 ft-lb

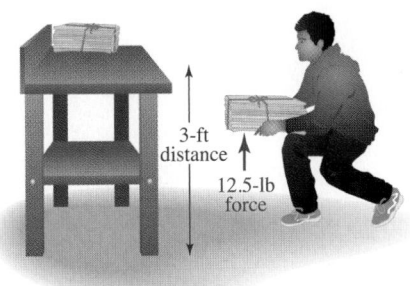

3-ft distance
12.5-lb force

43. WORK See Exercise 42. Find the weight of a 1-gallon can of paint if the amount of work done to lift it onto the workbench is 28.35 foot-pounds. [Section 2.4] 9.45 lb

44. Find the unknown angle measure represented by x. [Section 2.5] 55°, 55°

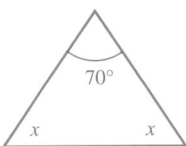

70°
x x

45. INVESTING An investment club invested part of $10,000 at 9% annual interest and the rest at 8%. If the annual income from these investments was $860, how much was invested at 8%? [Section 2.6] $4,000

46. GOLDSMITHING How many ounces of a 40% gold alloy must be mixed with 10 ounces of a 10% gold alloy to obtain an alloy that is 25% gold? [Section 2.6] 10 oz

Solve each inequality, graph the solution, and use interval notation to describe the solution. [Section 2.7]

47. $x - 4 > -6$ $x > -2, (-2, \infty)$
-2

48. $-6x \geq -12$ $x \leq 2, (-\infty, 2]$
2

49. $8x + 4 \geq 5x + 1$ $x \geq -1, [-1, \infty)$
-1

50. $-1 \leq 2x + 1 < 5$ $-1 \leq x < 2, [-1, 2)$
-1 2

Graphs, Linear Equations, and Inequalities in Two Variables; Functions

3

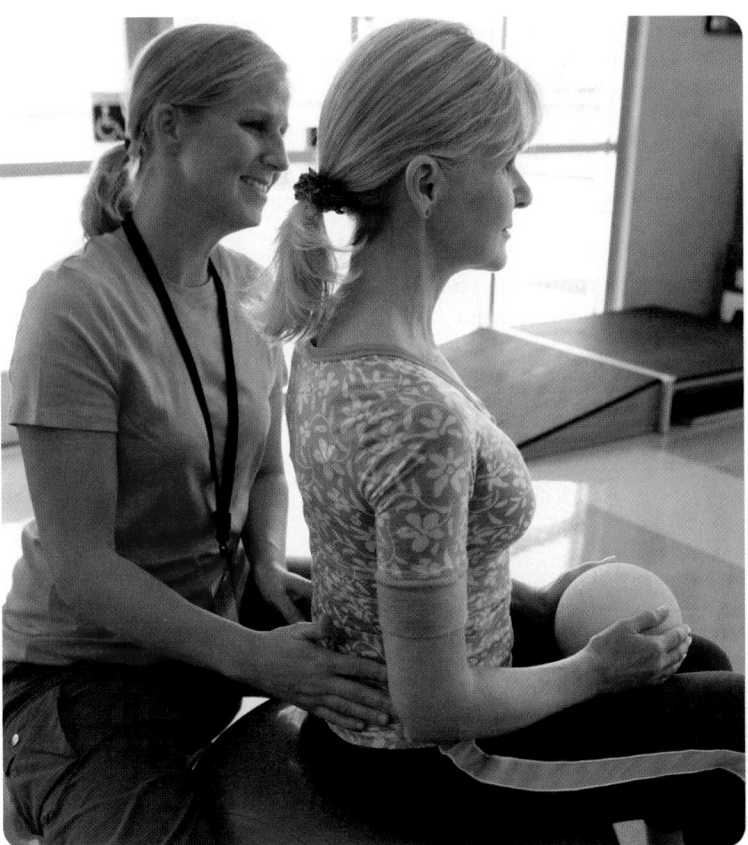

Seth Joel/Getty Images

from *Campus to Careers*

Physical Therapist

Physical therapists create treatment plans that improve a patient's ability to move, relieve pain, and prevent or lessen physical disabilities. Physical therapists use specialized equipment, wheelchairs and crutches and use their own strength to help patients work through sometimes painful exercises. Strong communication skills and a desire to help people in need are also important.

In **Problem 50** of **Study Set 3.1,** you will see how physical therapists can detect scoliosis of the human spine.

JOB TITLE:
Physical Therapist

EDUCATION: Physical therapists are required to hold at least an associates degree and must pass a state licensure test.

JOB OUTLOOK: Employment is expected to grow by 29% through the year 2016.

ANNUAL EARNINGS: In 2007, the average yearly salary for physical therapists was $71,520.

FOR MORE INFORMATION:
www.collegeboard.com/csearch/majors_careers/profiles/careers/106617.html

Objectives

1 Construct a rectangular coordinate system.

2 Plot ordered pairs and determine the coordinates of a point.

3 Graph paired data.

4 Read line graphs.

5 Read step graphs.

Graphing Using the Rectangular Coordinate System

It is often said, "A picture is worth a thousand words." In this section, we will show how numerical relationships can be described using mathematical pictures called **graphs.** We will also show how graphs are constructed and how we can obtain information from them.

1 Construct a rectangular coordinate system.

When designing the Gateway Arch in St. Louis, architects created a mathematical model called a **rectangular coordinate graph.** This graph, shown below, is drawn on a grid called a **rectangular coordinate system.** This coordinate system is also called a **Cartesian coordinate system,** after the 17th-century French mathematician René Descartes.

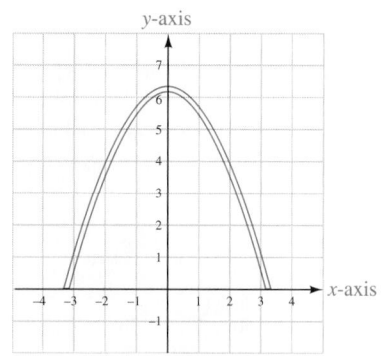

Scale: 1 unit = 100 ft

A rectangular coordinate system is formed by two perpendicular number lines. The horizontal number line is called the **x-axis,** and the vertical number line is called the **y-axis.** On the x-axis, the positive direction is to the right. On the y-axis, the positive direction is upward. The scale on each axis should fit the data. For example, the axes of the graph of the arch are scaled in units of 100 feet.

> **Success Tip**   If no scale is indicated on the axes, we assume that the axes are scaled in units of 1.

The point where the axes intersect is called the **origin.** This is the zero point on each axis. The axes form a **coordinate plane,** and they divide it into four regions called **quadrants,** which are numbered counterclockwise using Roman numerals as shown to the right. The axes are not considered to be in any quadrant.

Each point in a coordinate plane can be identified by an **ordered pair** of real numbers x and y written in the form (x, y).

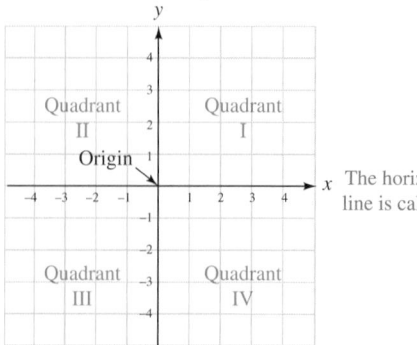

The first number, x, in the pair is called the **x-coordinate,** and the second number, y, is called the **y-coordinate.** The numbers in the pair are called the **coordinates** of the point. Some examples of such pairs are $(3, -4)$, $\left(-1, \frac{3}{2}\right)$, and $(0, 2.5)$.

$$(3, -4)$$

↑   ↑

The x-coordinate The y-coordinate
is listed first.   is listed second.

> **Caution!** Do not be confused by this new use of parentheses. The notation $(3, -4)$ represents a point on the coordinate plane, whereas $3(-4)$ indicates multiplication. Also, don't confuse the ordered pair with interval notation.

2 Plot ordered pairs and determine the coordinates of a point.

The process of locating a point in the coordinate plane is called **graphing** or **plotting** the point. In the figure to the right, we use two blue arrows to show how to graph the point with coordinates of $(3, -4)$. Since the x-coordinate, 3, is positive, we start at the origin and move 3 units to the *right* along the x-axis. Since the y-coordinate, -4, is negative, we then move *down* 4 units and draw a dot. The graph of $(3, -4)$ lies in quadrant IV.

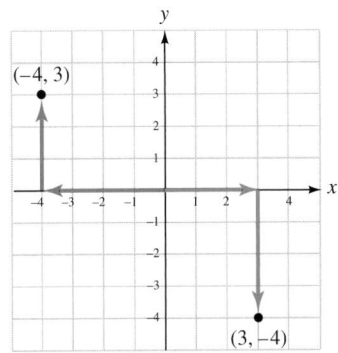

Two red arrows are used to show how to plot the point $(-4, 3)$. We start at the origin, move 4 units to the *left* along the x-axis, and then move *up* 3 units and draw a dot. The graph of $(-4, 3)$ lies in quadrant II.

> **The Language of Algebra** Note that the point with coordinates $(3, -4)$ is not the same as the point with coordinates $(-4, 3)$. Since the order of the coordinates of a point is important, we call the pairs **ordered pairs.**

In the figure to the right, we see that the points $(-4, 0)$, $(0, 0)$, and $(2, 0)$ lie on the x-axis. In fact, all points with a y-coordinate of zero will lie on the x-axis. We also see that the points $(0, -3)$, $(0, 0)$, and $(0, 3)$ lie on the y-axis. All points with an x-coordinate of zero lie on the y-axis. We can also see that the coordinates of the origin are $(0, 0)$.

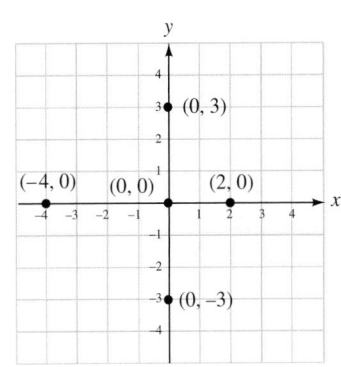

Self Check 1

Plot the points:
a. $(2, -2)$ **b.** $(-4, 0)$
c. $\left(1.5, \frac{5}{2}\right)$ **d.** $(0, 5)$

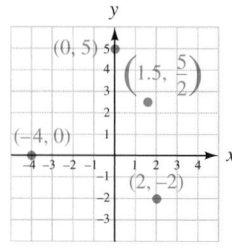

Now Try **Problem 21**

Teaching Example 1 Plot each point. Then state the quadrant in which it lies or the axis on which it lies.
a. $(4, -5)$ **b.** $\left(-2, -\frac{5}{2}\right)$ **c.** $(4, 0)$
Answers:
a. QIV **b.** QIII **c.** *x*-axis

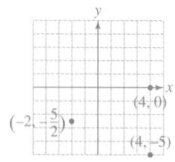

EXAMPLE 1 Plot each point. Then state the quadrant in which it lies or the axis on which it lies. **a.** $(-2, 3)$ **b.** $\left(-1, -\frac{3}{2}\right)$ **c.** $(0, 2.5)$ **d.** $(4, 2)$

Strategy We will start at the origin and move the corresponding number of units right or left for the *x*-coordinate, then move the corresponding number of units up or down for the *y*-coordinate, to locate the point. Draw a dot at the point.

WHY The coordinates of a point determine its location on the coordinate plane.

Solution

a. Since the *x*-coordinate, -2, is negative, we start at the origin and move 2 units to the *left* along the *x*-axis. Since the *y*-coordinate, 3, is positive, we then move *up* 3 units and draw a dot. The point lies in quadrant II.

b. To plot $\left(-1, -\frac{3}{2}\right)$, we begin at the origin and move 1 unit to the *left* and $\frac{3}{2}\left(\text{or } 1\frac{1}{2}\right)$ units *down*. The point lies in quadrant III.

c. To graph $(0, 2.5)$, we begin at the origin and do not move right or left, because the *x*-coordinate is 0. Since the *y*-coordinate is positive, we move 2.5 units *up*. The point lies on the *y*-axis.

d. To graph $(4, 2)$, we begin at the origin and move 4 units to the *right* and 2 units *up*. The point lies in quadrant I.

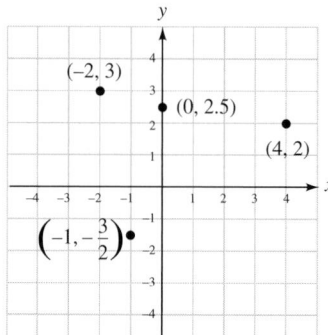

Self Check 2

Find the coordinates of each point in figure (b).

Now Try **Problem 25**

Self Check 2 Answer
$A(0, 4)$, $B(4, -3)$, $C(-2, -5)$, $D(-4, 2)$

Teaching Example 2 Find the coordinates of points A, B, C, D, and E.
Answers:
$A(4, 1)$, $B(2, -3)$, $C(-3, 0)$, $D(-2, -4)$, $E(-1, 4)$

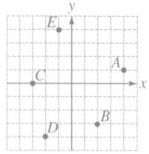

EXAMPLE 2 Find the coordinates of points A, B, C, D, and E plotted in figure (a) below.

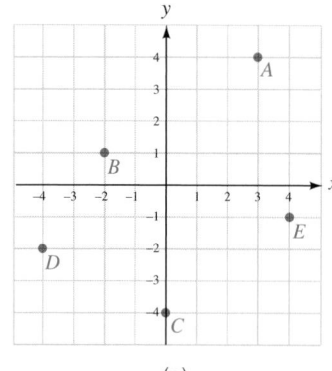

(a)

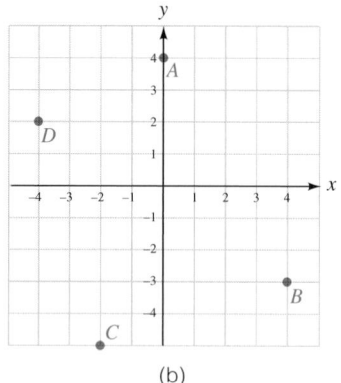

(b)

Strategy We will start at the origin and count to the right or left on the *x*-axis, and then up or down to reach each point.

WHY The right or left movement gives the *x*-coordinate and the up or down movement gives the *y*-coordinate of the point.

Solution

To find the coordinates of point A, we start at the origin, move 3 units to the right on the *x*-axis, and then 4 units up. The coordinates of point A are $(3, 4)$. The coordinates of the other points are found in the same manner: $B(-2, 1)$, $C(0, -4)$, $D(-4, -2)$, $E(4, -1)$.

3 Graph paired data.

Every day, we deal with quantities that are related:

- The time it takes to cook a turkey depends on the weight of the turkey.
- Our weight depends on how much we eat.
- The amount of water in a tub depends on how long the water has been running.

We can use graphs to visualize such relationships. For example, suppose we know the number of gallons of water that are in a tub at several time intervals after the water has been turned on. We can list that information in a **table.**

The information in the table can be used to construct a graph that shows the relationship between the amount of water in the tub and the time the water has been running. Since the amount of water in the tub depends on the time, we will associate *time* with the *x*-axis and *amount of water* with the *y*-axis.

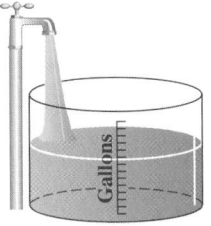

At various times, the amount of water in the tub was measured and recorded in the table.

Time (min)	Water in tub (gal)	
0	0	→ (0, 0)
1	8	→ (1, 8)
3	24	→ (3, 24)
4	32	→ (4, 32)

↑ x-coordinate ↑ y-coordinate

The data in the table can be expressed as ordered pairs (x, y).

To construct the graph below we plot the four ordered pairs and draw a straight line through the resulting data points. The *y*-axis is scaled in larger units (4 gallons) because the data range from 0 to 32 gallons.

From the graph, we can see that the amount of water in the tub steadily increases as the water is allowed to run. We can also use the graph to make observations about the amount of water in the tub at other times. For example, the dashed line on the graph shows that in 5 minutes, the tub will contain 40 gallons of water.

x	y	(x, y)
0	0	(0, 0)
1	8	(1, 8)
3	24	(3, 24)
4	32	(4, 32)

The data can be listed in a table with headings x, y, and (x, y).

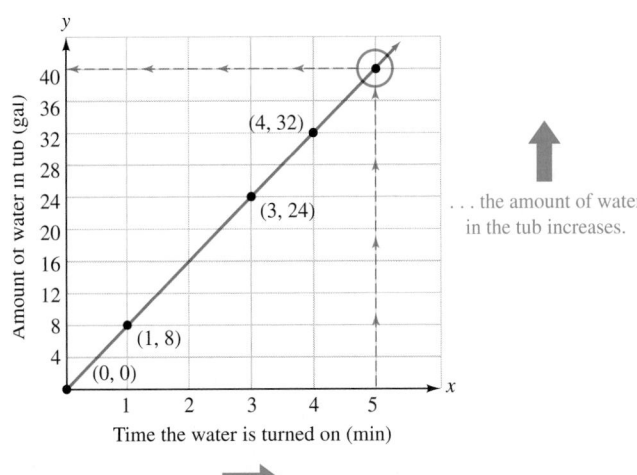

. . . the amount of water in the tub increases.

As the time increases . . .

4 Read line graphs.

Since graphs are a popular way to present information, the ability to read and interpret them is very important.

EXAMPLE 3   *TV Shows*   The graph shows the number of people in an audience before, during, and after the taping of a television show. On the *x*-axis, zero represents the time when taping began. Use the graph to answer the following questions and complete the table.

a. How many people were in the audience when taping began?

b. What was the size of the audience 10 minutes before taping began?

c. At what times were there exactly 100 people in the audience?

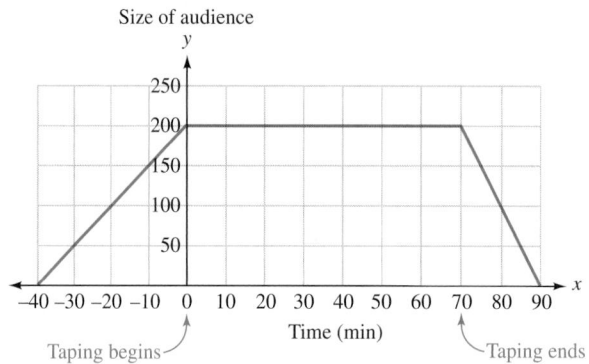

Strategy We will use an ordered pair of the form (*time, size of audience*) to describe each situation mentioned in parts a, b, and c.

WHY The coordinates of specific points on the graph can be used to answer each of these questions.

Solution

a. The time when taping began is represented by 0 on the *x*-axis. The point on the graph directly above 0 is (0, **200**). The *y*-coordinate indicates that 200 people were in the audience when the taping began. We enter this result in the table at the right.

Time (min)	Size of audience
x	*y*
0	200
−10	150
−20	100
80	100

b. Ten minutes before taping began is represented by −10 on the *x*-axis. The point on the graph directly above −10 is (−10, **150**). The *y*-coordinate indicates that 150 people were in the audience 10 minutes before the taping began. We enter this result in the table.

c. We can draw a horizontal line passing through 100 on the *y*-axis. Since this line intersects the graph twice, at (−**20**, 100) and at (**80**, 100), there are two times when 100 people were in the audience. The *x*-coordinates of the points tell us those times: 20 minutes before taping began and 80 minutes after. Enter these results in the table.

5 Read step graphs.

The graph below shows the cost of renting a trailer for different periods of time. For example, the cost of renting the trailer for 4 days is $60, which is the *y*-coordinate of the point (4, 60). The cost of renting the trailer for a period lasting over 4 and up to 5 days jumps to $70. Since the jumps in cost form steps in the graph, we call this graph a **step graph.**

EXAMPLE 4 Use the information in the figure to answer the following questions. Write the results in a table.

a. Find the cost of renting the trailer for 2 days.

b. Find the cost of renting the trailer for $5\frac{1}{2}$ days.

c. How long can you rent the trailer if you have $50?

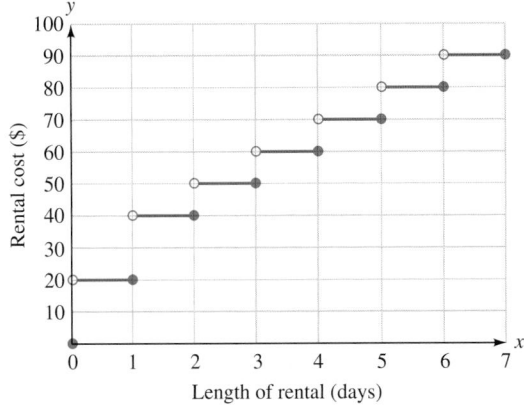

Strategy We will use an ordered pair of the form (*days, rental cost*) to describe each situation mentioned in parts a, b, and c.

WHY The coordinates of specific points on the graph can be used to answer each of these questions.

Solution

a. The solid dot at the end of each step indicates the rental cost for 1, 2, 3, 4, 5, 6, or 7 days. Each open circle indicates that that point is not on the graph. We locate 2 days on the *x*-axis and move up to locate the point on the graph directly above the 2. Since the point has coordinates (2, **40**), a 2-day rental would cost $40. We enter this result in the table below.

b. We locate $5\frac{1}{2}$ days on the *x*-axis and move straight up to locate the point with coordinates $\left(5\frac{1}{2}, \mathbf{80}\right)$, which indicates that a $5\frac{1}{2}$-day rental would cost $80. We then enter this result in the table.

c. We draw a horizontal line through the point labeled 50 on the *y*-axis. Since this line intersects one step in the graph, we can look down to the *x*-axis to find the *x*-values that correspond to a *y*-value of 50. From the graph, we see that the trailer can be rented for more than 2 and up to 3 days for $50. The point has coordinates (**3**, 50). Enter the results in the table.

Length of rental (days) *x*	Cost (dollars) *y*
2	40
$5\frac{1}{2}$	80
3	50

Self Check 4

Use the information in the figure of Example 4 to answer the following:

a. Find the cost of renting the trailer for 1 day. $20

b. Find the cost of renting the trailer for $4\frac{1}{2}$ days. $70

c. How long can you rent the trailer if you have $40? 2 days

Now Try **Problems 41 and 43**

Teaching Example 4 Use the information in the figure to answer the following questions.

a. Find the cost of renting the trailer for 6 days.

b. Find the cost of renting the trailer for $2\frac{1}{2}$ days.

c. How long can you rent the trailer if you have $70?

Answers:

a. $80   **b.** $50   **c.** 5 days

ANSWERS TO SELF CHECKS

1.

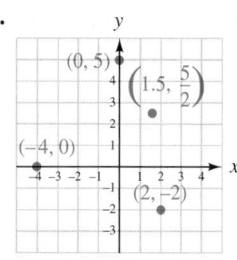

2. $A(0, 4)$, $B(4, -3)$, $C(-2, -5)$, $D(-4, 2)$
3. **a.** 30 min before and 85 min after taping began **b.** 200 **c.** 20 min **4. a.** $20 **b.** $70 **c.** 2 days

---

SECTION 3.1 STUDY SET

VOCABULARY

Fill in the blanks.

1. The point with coordinates $(4, 2)$ can be graphed on a __rectangular__ coordinate system.

2. On the rectangular coordinate system, the horizontal number line is called the __x-axis__ and the vertical number line is called the __y-axis__.

3. On the rectangular coordinate system, the point $(0, 0)$ where the axes cross is called the __origin__.

4. On the rectangular coordinate system, the axes form the __coordinate__ plane.

▶ 5. The *x*- and *y*-axes divide the coordinate plane into four regions called __quadrants__.

6. The pair of numbers $(-1, -5)$ is called an __ordered__ pair.

▶ 7. In the ordered pair $\left(-\frac{3}{2}, -5\right)$, $-\frac{3}{2}$ is called the __x-coordinate__ and -5 is called the __y-coordinate__.

▶ 8. The process of locating the position of a point on a coordinate plane is called __graphing or plotting__ the point.

CONCEPTS

Fill in the blanks.

▶ 9. To plot the point with coordinates $(-5, 4.5)$, we start at the __origin__ and move 5 units to the __left__ and then move 4.5 units __up__.

▶ 10. To plot the point with coordinates $\left(6, -\frac{3}{2}\right)$, we start at the __origin__ and move 6 units to the __right__ and then move $\frac{3}{2}$ units __down__.

11. Do $(3, 2)$ and $(2, 3)$ represent the same point? no

12. In the ordered pair $(4, 5)$, is the number 4 associated with the horizontal or the vertical axis? horizontal

▶ 13. In which quadrant do points with a negative *x*-coordinate and a positive *y*-coordinate lie? quadrant II

▶ *Selected exercises available online at* **www.webassign.net/brookscole**

▶ 14. In which quadrant do points with a positive *x*-coordinate and a negative *y*-coordinate lie? quadrant IV

▶ 15. In the following illustration, fill in the missing coordinate of each highlighted point on the graph of the circle.

a. $\left(4, \boxed{3}\right)$

b. $\left(3, \boxed{-4}\right)$

c. $\left(5, \boxed{0}\right)$

d. $\left(-3, \boxed{-4}\right)$

e. $\left(-5, \boxed{0}\right)$

f. $\left(0, \boxed{5}\right)$

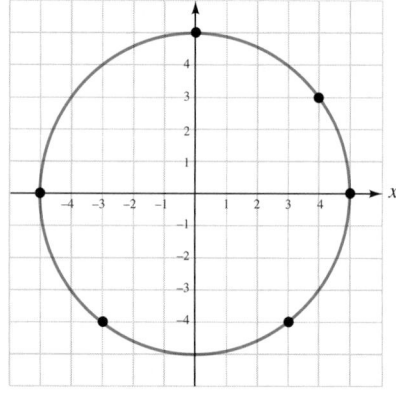

▶ 16. In the following illustration, fill in the missing coordinate of each point on the graph of the line.

a. $\left(-4, \boxed{3}\right)$

b. $\left(\boxed{2}, 0\right)$

c. $\left(\boxed{-2}, 2\right)$

d. $\left(4, \boxed{-1}\right)$

e. $\left(\boxed{0}, 1\right)$

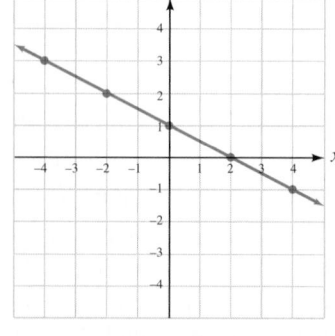

NOTATION

17. Explain the difference between $(3, 5)$, $3(5)$, and $5(3 + 5)$.

$(3, 5)$ is an ordered pair, $3(5)$ indicates multiplication, and $5(3 + 5)$ is an expression containing grouping symbols.

18. In the table, which column contains values associated with the vertical axis of a graph? the 2nd column

x	y
2	0
5	−2
−1	−$\frac{1}{2}$

19. Do these ordered pairs name the same point?

$$\left(2.5, -\tfrac{7}{2}\right), \left(2\tfrac{1}{2}, -3.5\right), \left(2.5, -3\tfrac{1}{2}\right) \text{ yes}$$

▶ **20.** Do these ordered pairs name the same point?

$$\left(-1.25, 4\right), \left(-1\tfrac{1}{4}, 4.0\right), \left(-\tfrac{5}{4}, 4\right) \text{ yes}$$

GUIDED PRACTICE

Plot each point on the grid provided. **See Example 1.**

▶ **21.** $(-3, 4)$
$(4, 3.5)$
$\left(-2, -\tfrac{5}{2}\right)$

22. $(0, -4)$
$\left(\tfrac{3}{2}, 0\right)$
$(3, -4)$

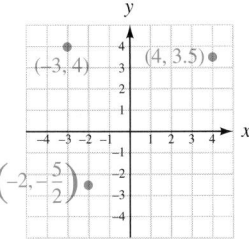
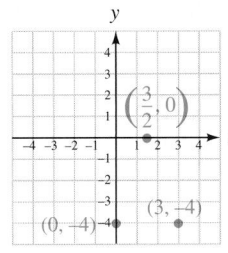

23. $(4, 4)$
$(0.5, -3)$
$(-4, -4)$

24. $(0, 0)$
$(0, 3)$
$(-2, 0)$
$(0, -1)$

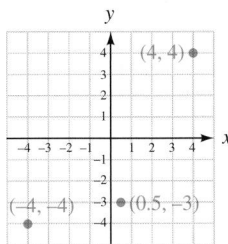
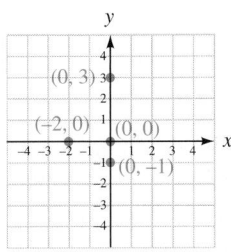

Refer to the illustration and determine the coordinates of each point. **See Example 2.**

▶ **25.** A $(2, 3)$
26. B $(-3, 4)$
27. C $(-3, -4)$
28. D $(4, -4)$
29. E $(0, 0)$
30. F $(4, 0)$
31. G $(-4, 0)$
32. H $\left(\tfrac{3}{2}, -\tfrac{5}{2}\right)$

The graph in the illustration gives the heart rate of a woman before, during, and after an aerobic workout. Use the graph to answer problems 33–40. **See Example 3.**

▶ **33.** What information does the point $(-10, 60)$ give us?
10 min before the workout, her heart rate was 60 beats/min.

34. After beginning her workout, how long did it take the woman to reach her training-zone heart rate?
10 min

35. What was the woman's heart rate half an hour after beginning the workout?
150 beats/min

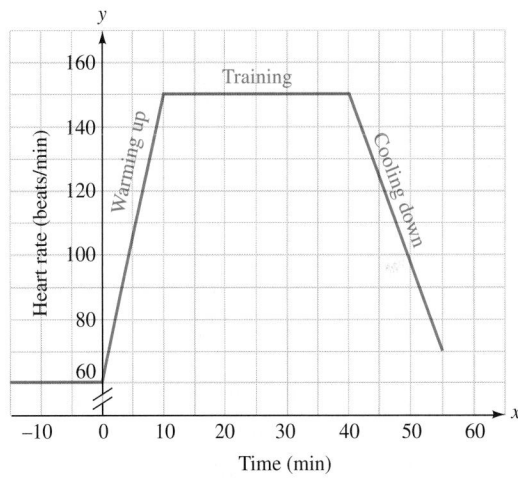

36. For how long did the woman work out at her training zone? 30 min

37. At what time was her heart rate 100 beats per minute? approximately 5 min and 50 min after starting

38. How long was her cool-down period? 15 min

39. What was the difference in the woman's heart rate before the workout and after the cool-down period? 10 beats/min faster after cool-down

40. What was her approximate heart rate 8 minutes after beginning? about 135 beats/min

The graph in the illustration on the next page gives the charges for renting a video for certain lengths of time. Use the graph to answer problems 41–44. **See Example 4.**

▶ **41.** Find the charge for a 1-day rental. $2

42. Find the charge for a 2-day rental. $4

43. What is the charge if a tape is kept for 5 days? $7

44. What is the charge if a tape is kept for a week? $9

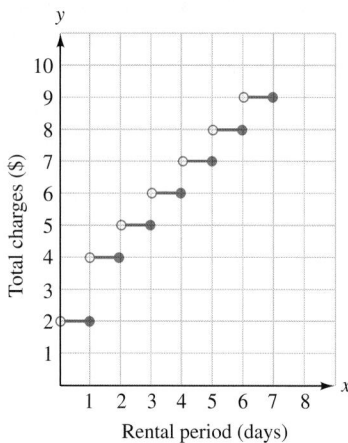

APPLICATIONS

45. BRIDGE CONSTRUCTION Find the coordinates of each rivet, weld, and anchor. rivets: $(-6, 0), (-2, 0), (2, 0), (6, 0)$; welds: $(-4, 3), (0, 3), (4, 3)$; anchors: $(-6, -3), (6, -3)$

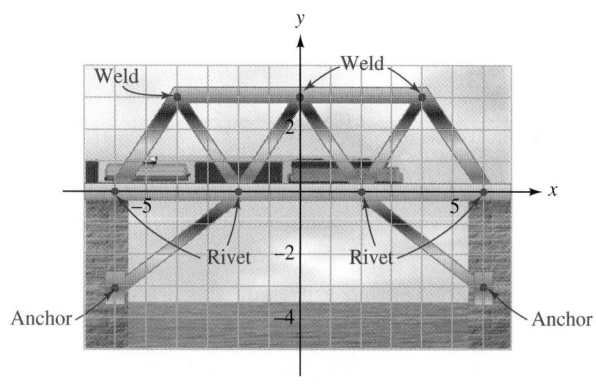

Scale: 1 unit = 8 ft

▶ **46. GOLF** A golfer is videotaped and then has her swing displayed on a computer monitor so that it can be analyzed. Give the coordinates of the points that are highlighted in red. $(6, 10), (-7, 4.5), (-5, 11)$

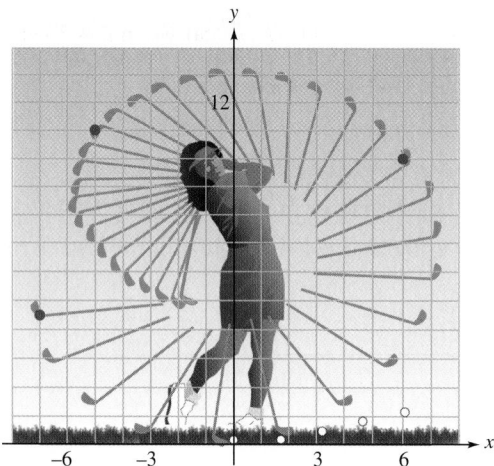

▶ **47. GAMES** In the game Battleship, the player uses coordinates to drop depth charges from a battleship to hit a hidden submarine. What coordinates should be used to make three hits on the exposed submarine shown? Express each answer in the form (letter, number). $(G, 2), (G, 3), (G, 4)$

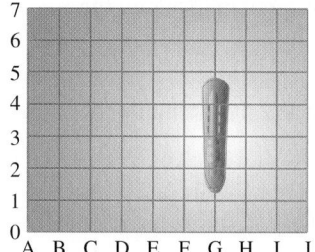

48. MAPS Use coordinates of the form (number, letter) to locate each position on the following map: Rockford, Forreston, Harvard, and the intersection of state Highway 251 and U.S. Highway 30. Rockford $(5, B)$, Forreston $(2, C)$, Harvard $(7, A)$, intersection $(5, E)$

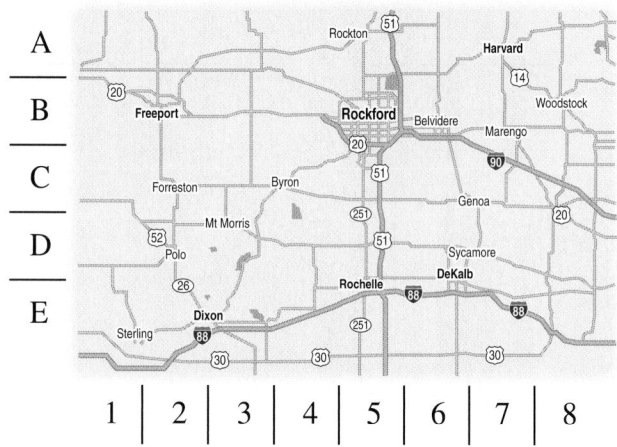

▶ **49. WATER PRESSURE** The graph shows how the path of a stream of water changes when the hose is held at two different angles.

  a. At which angle does the stream of water shoot up higher? How much higher? $60°, 4$ ft

  b. At which angle does the stream of water shoot out farther? How much farther? $30°, 4$ ft

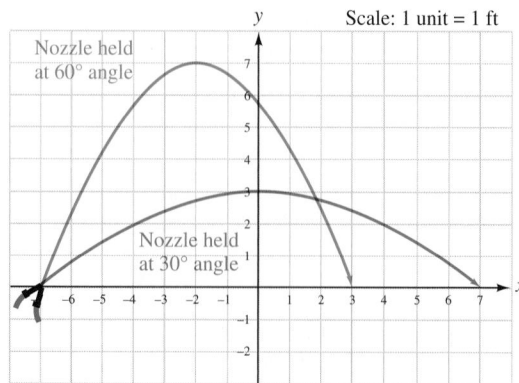

50. MEDICINE Scoliosis is a lateral curvature of the spine that can be detected when a grid is superimposed over an X-ray. In the illustration, find the coordinates of the center points of the indicated vertebrae. Note that T3 means the third thoracic vertebra, L4 means the fourth lumbar vertebra, and so on.

from Campus to Careers

Seth Joel/Getty Images

T3(2, 21), T6(3, 16), T9(3, 10), T11(2.5, 6.5), L1(1, 2.5), L2(0, 0), L4(−1, −5), L5(0, −8)

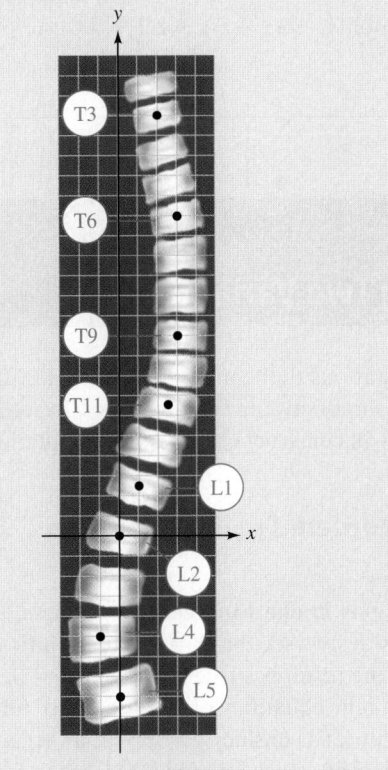

Scale: 1 unit = 0.5 in.

51. DENTISTRY Dentists describe teeth as being located in one of four quadrants as shown below:

   a. How many teeth are located in the upper left quadrant? 8

   b. Why would the upper left quadrant appear on the right in the illustration?
   It represents the patient's left side.

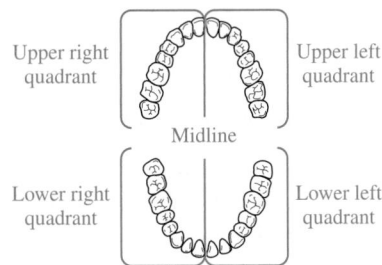

Upper right quadrant   Upper left quadrant

Midline

Lower right quadrant   Lower left quadrant

52. GAS MILEAGE The following table gives the number of miles (*y*) that a truck can be driven on *x* gallons of gasoline. Plot the ordered pairs and draw a line connecting the points.

x	y
2	10
3	15
5	25

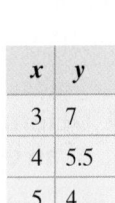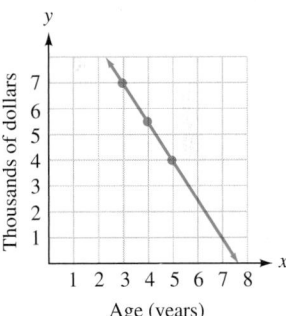

Distance (mi)

Gasoline used (gal)

   a. Estimate how far the truck can go on 7 gallons of gasoline. 35 mi

   b. How many gallons of gas are needed to travel a distance of 20 miles? 4 gal

   c. How far can the truck go on 6.5 gallons of gasoline? 32.5 mi

53. VALUE OF A CAR The following table shows the value *y* (in thousands of dollars) of a car that is *x* years old. Plot the ordered pairs and draw a line connecting the points.

x	y
3	7
4	5.5
5	4

Thousands of dollars

Age (years)

   a. What does the point (3, 7) on the graph tell you? A 3-year-old car is worth $7,000.

   b. Estimate the value of the car when it is 7 years old. $1,000

   c. After how many years will the car be worth $2,500? 6

54. BOATING The table on the next page shows the cost to rent a sailboat for a given number of hours. Plot the data in the table as ordered pairs. Then draw a line through the points.

   a. How much will it cost to rent the boat for 3 hours? $25

b. For how long can the boat be rented for $60? 10 hr

Rental time (hr)	Cost ($)
2	20
4	30
6	40

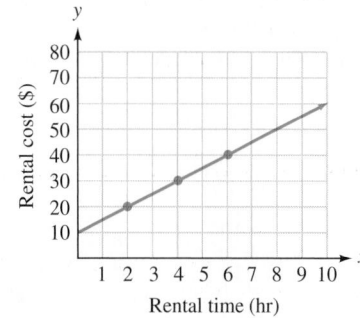

Rental cost ($)

Rental time (hr)

▶ **57.** Explain how to plot the point $(-2, 5)$.
▶ **58.** Explain why the coordinates of the origin are $(0, 0)$.

WRITING

55. Explain why the point $(-3, 3)$ is not the same as the point $(3, -3)$.

56. Explain what is meant when we say that the rectangular coordinate graph of the St. Louis Gateway Arch is made up of *infinitely many* points.

REVIEW

59. Evaluate: $-3 - 3(-5)$ 12
▶ **60.** Evaluate: $(-5)^2 + (-5)$ 20
61. What is the opposite of -8? 8
62. Simplify: $|-1 - 9|$ 10
63. Solve: $-4x + 7 = -21$ 7
64. Solve $P = 2l + 2w$ for w. $w = \dfrac{P - 2l}{2}$
65. Evaluate $(x + 1)(x + y)^2$ for $x = -2$ and $y = -5$. -49
66. Simplify: $-6(x - 3) - 2(1 - x)$ $-4x + 16$

Objectives

1. Determine whether an ordered pair is a solution of an equation.
2. Complete ordered-pair solutions of equations.
3. Construct a table of solutions.
4. Graph equations by plotting points.
5. Graph equations that use different variables.

SECTION 3.2

Equations Containing Two Variables

In this section, we will discuss equations that contain two variables. These equations are often used to describe relationships between two quantities. To see a mathematical picture of these relationships, we will construct graphs of their equations.

1 Determine whether an ordered pair is a solution of an equation.

We have previously solved **equations in one variable.** For example, $x - 4 = 3$ is an equation in x. If we add 4 to both sides, we see that $x = 7$ is the solution. To check this, we replace x with 7 and note that the result is a true statement: $3 = 3$.

In this chapter, we extend our equation-solving skills to find solutions of **equations in two variables.** To begin, let's consider $y = x - 1$, an equation in x and y.

A solution of $y = x - 1$ is a pair of values, one for x and one for y, that make the equation true. For example, suppose x is 5 and y is 4. Then we have:

$$y = x - 1 \quad \text{This is the original equation.}$$

$$4 \overset{?}{=} 5 - 1 \quad \text{Substitute 5 for x and 4 for y.}$$

$$4 = 4 \quad \text{True}$$

Since $4 = 4$ is a true statement, the ordered pair $(5, 4)$ is a solution, and we say that $(5, 4)$ **satisfies** the equation. In general, a *solution of an equation in two variables* is an ordered pair of numbers that makes the equation a true statement.

EXAMPLE 1   Is the ordered pair $(-1, -3)$ a solution of $y = x - 1$?

Strategy We will substitute -1 for x and -3 for y and see whether the resulting equation is true.

WHY An ordered pair is a *solution* of $y = x - 1$ if replacing the variables with the values of the ordered pair results in a true statement.

Solution

$$y = x - 1 \qquad \text{This is the original equation.}$$
$$-3 \stackrel{?}{=} -1 - 1 \qquad \text{Substitute } -1 \text{ for } x \text{ and } -3 \text{ for } y.$$
$$-3 = -2 \qquad \text{Perform the subtraction: } -1 - 1 = -2. \text{ False}$$

Since $-3 = -2$ is a false statement, $(-1, -3)$ is not a solution of $y = x - 1$. ∎

EXAMPLE 2   Is the ordered pair $(-6, 36)$ a solution of $y = x^2$?

Strategy We will substitute -6 for x and 36 for y and see whether the resulting equation is true.

WHY An ordered pair is a *solution* of $y = x^2$ if replacing the variables with the values of the ordered pair results in a true statement.

Solution

We substitute -6 for x and 36 for y and see whether the resulting equation is a true statement.

$$y = x^2 \qquad \text{This is the original equation.}$$
$$36 \stackrel{?}{=} (-6)^2 \qquad \text{Substitute } -6 \text{ for } x \text{ and } 36 \text{ for } y.$$
$$36 = 36 \qquad \text{Find the power: } (-6)^2 = 36. \text{ True}$$

Since the equation $36 = 36$ is true, $(-6, 36)$ is a solution of $y = x^2$. ∎

Self Check 2

Is $(-2, 5)$ a solution of $y = x^2$? no

Now Try **Problem 19**

Teaching Example 2 Is $(7, 14)$ a solution of $y = x^2$?
Answer:
no

> **Language of Algebra**   Equations in two variables often involve the variables x and y. However, other letters can be used. For example, $a - 3b = 6$ and $n = 2m + 1$ are equations in two variables.

2 Complete ordered-pair solutions of equations.

If only one of the values of an ordered-pair solution is known, we can substitute it into the equation to determine the other value.

EXAMPLE 3   Complete the solution $(-4, \ \square)$ of the equation $y = -x + 2$.

Strategy We will substitute the known x-coordinate of the solution into the given equation.

WHY We can use the resulting equation in one variable to find the unknown y-coordinate of the solution.

Solution

In the ordered pair $(-4, \ \square)$, the x-value is -4; the y-value is not known. To find y, we substitute -4 for x in the equation and evaluate the right side.

$$y = -x + 2 \qquad \text{This is the original equation.}$$
$$y = -(-4) + 2 \qquad \text{Substitute } -4 \text{ for } x.$$
$$y = 4 + 2 \qquad \text{The opposite of } -4 \text{ is } 4.$$
$$y = 6 \qquad \text{This is the missing } y\text{-coordinate of the solution.}$$

The completed ordered pair is $(-4, 6)$.

Self Check 3

Complete the solution $(-3, \ \square)$ of the equation $y = 2x - 4$. $(-3, -10)$

Now Try **Problem 26**

Teaching Example 3 Complete the solution $(2, \_)$ of the equation $y = 2x - 4$
Answer:
$(2, 0)$

3 Construct a table of solutions.

To find a solution of an equation in x and y, we can select a number, substitute it for x, and find the corresponding value of y. For example, to find a solution of the equation $y = x - 1$, we can let $x = -4$ (called the **input value**), substitute -4 for x, and solve for y (called the **output value**).

$y = x - 1$	This is the original equation.	
$y = -4 - 1$	Substitute the input -4 for x.	
$y = -5$	The output is -5.	

$y = x - 1$		
x	y	(x, y)
-4	-5	$(-4, -5)$

The ordered pair $(-4, -5)$ is a solution. We list this ordered pair in red in the **table of solutions** (or **table of values**).

To find another solution of $y = x - 1$, we select another value of x, say -2, and find the corresponding y-value.

$y = x - 1$	This is the original equation.	
$y = -2 - 1$	Substitute the input -2 for x.	
$y = -3$	The output is -3.	

$y = x - 1$		
x	y	(x, y)
-4	-5	$(-4, -5)$
-2	-3	$(-2, -3)$

A second solution is $(-2, -3)$, and we list it in the table of solutions.

If we let $x = 0$, we can find a third ordered pair that satisfies $y = x - 1$.

$y = x - 1$	This is the original equation.	
$y = 0 - 1$	Substitute the input 0 for x.	
$y = -1$	The output is -1.	

$y = x - 1$		
x	y	(x, y)
-4	-5	$(-4, -5)$
-2	-3	$(-2, -3)$
0	-1	$(0, -1)$

A third solution is $(0, -1)$, which we also add to the table of solutions.

If we let $x = 2$, we can find a fourth solution.

$y = x - 1$	This is the original equation.	
$y = 2 - 1$	Substitute the input 2 for x.	
$y = 1$	The output is 1.	

$y = x - 1$		
x	y	(x, y)
-4	-5	$(-4, -5)$
-2	-3	$(-2, -3)$
0	-1	$(0, -1)$
2	1	$(2, 1)$

A fourth solution is $(2, 1)$, and we add it to the table of solutions.

If we let $x = 4$, we have

$y = x - 1$	This is the original equation.	
$y = 4 - 1$	Substitute the input 4 for x.	
$y = 3$	The output is 3.	

A fifth solution is $(4, 3)$.

Since we can choose any real number for x, and since any choice of x will give a corresponding value of y, it is apparent that the equation $y = x - 1$ has *infinitely many solutions*. We have found five of them: $(-4, -5)$, $(-2, -3)$, $(0, -1)$, $(2, 1)$, and $(4, 3)$.

$y = x - 1$		
x	y	(x, y)
-4	-5	$(-4, -5)$
-2	-3	$(-2, -3)$
0	-1	$(0, -1)$
2	1	$(2, 1)$
4	3	$(4, 3)$

4 Graph equations by plotting points.

To graph the equation $y = x - 1$, we plot the ordered pairs listed in the table of solutions on a rectangular coordinate system, as shown in figure (a). We can see that the five points lie on a line.

We then draw a line through the points, because the graph of any solution of $y = x - 1$ will lie on this line. The arrowheads show that the line continues forever in both directions. The line is a picture of all the solutions of the equation $y = x - 1$. This line is called the **graph of the equation.** See figure (b).

$y = x - 1$		
x	y	(x, y)
-4	-5	$(-4, -5)$
-2	-3	$(-2, -3)$
0	-1	$(0, -1)$
2	1	$(2, 1)$
4	3	$(4, 3)$

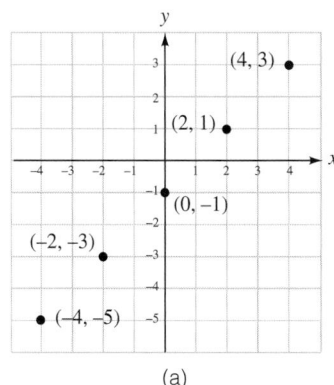

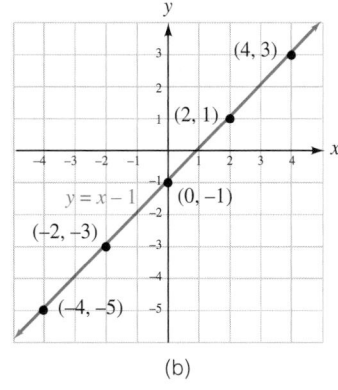

(a)   (b)

To graph an equation in x and y, we follow these steps.

Graphing an Equation in x and y

1. Make a table of solutions containing several ordered pairs of numbers (x, y) that satisfy the equation. Do this by picking values for x and finding the corresponding values for y.
2. Plot each ordered pair on a rectangular coordinate system.
3. Carefully draw a line or smooth curve through the points.

Since we will usually choose a number for x and then find the corresponding value of y, the value of y depends on x. For this reason, we call y the **dependent variable** and x the **independent variable.** The value of the independent variable is the input value, and the value of the dependent variable is the output value.

EXAMPLE 4   Graph: $y = -2x - 2$

Strategy We will find several solutions of the equation, plot them on a rectangular coordinate system, and then draw a graph passing through the points.

WHY To *graph* an equation in two variables means to make a drawing that represents all of its solutions.

Solution
To make a table of solutions, we choose numbers for x and find the corresponding values of y. If $x = -3$, we have

$y = -2x - 2$ This is the original equation.

$y = -2(-3) - 2$ Substitute -3 for x.

$y = 6 - 2$ Perform the multiplication: $-2(-3) = 6$.

$y = 4$ Perform the subtraction.

Self Check 4

Graph: $y = -3x + 1$

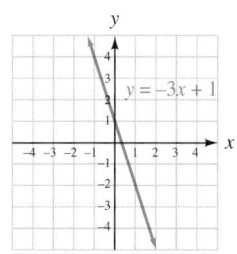

Now Try Problem 33

Teaching Example 4 Graph
$y = -x + 2$.
Answer:

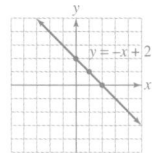

Thus, $x = -3$ and $y = 4$ is a solution. In a similar manner, we find the corresponding y-values for x-values of $-2, -1, 0,$ and 1 and record the results in the table of solutions. After plotting the ordered pairs, we draw a line through the points to get the graph shown.

$y = -2x - 2$		
x	y	(x, y)
-3	4	$(-3, 4)$
-2	2	$(-2, 2)$
-1	0	$(-1, 0)$
0	-2	$(0, -2)$
1	-4	$(1, -4)$

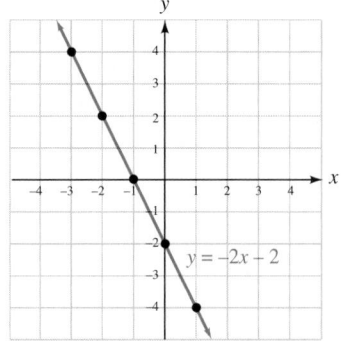

Self Check 5

Graph $y = x^2 - 2$ and compare the result to the graph of $y = x^2$. What do you notice?

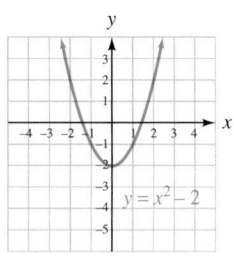

Now Try **Problem 37**

Self Check 5 Answer
The graph has the same shape, but is 2 units lower.

Teaching Example 5 Graph $y = x^2 + 3$ and compare the result to the graph of $y = x^2$. What do you notice?
Answer:
The graph has the same shape, but 3 units higher.

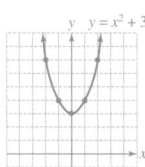

EXAMPLE 5   Graph: $y = x^2$

Strategy We will find several solutions of the equation, plot them on a rectangular coordinate system, and then draw a graph passing through the points.

WHY To *graph* an equation in two variables means to make a drawing that represents all of its solutions.

Solution
To make a table of solutions, we will choose numbers for x and find the corresponding values of y. If $x = -3$, we have

$$y = x^2 \qquad \text{This is the original equation.}$$
$$y = (-3)^2 \qquad \text{Substitute the input } -3 \text{ for } x.$$
$$y = 9 \qquad \text{The output is 9.}$$

Thus, $x = -3$ and $y = 9$ is a solution. In a similar manner, we find the corresponding y-values for x-values of $-2, -1, 0, 1, 2,$ and 3. If we plot the ordered pairs listed in the table and join the points with a smooth curve, we get the graph shown in the figure, which is called a **parabola.**

$y = x^2$		
x	y	(x, y)
-3	9	$(-3, 9)$
-2	4	$(-2, 4)$
-1	1	$(-1, 1)$
0	0	$(0, 0)$
1	1	$(1, 1)$
2	4	$(2, 4)$
3	9	$(3, 9)$

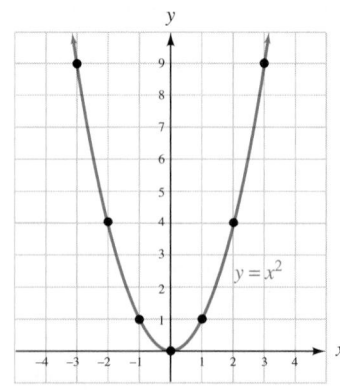

Success Tip   When selecting x-values for a table of solutions, a rule of thumb is to choose some negative numbers, some positive numbers, and 0. When $x = 0$, the computations to find y are usually quite simple.

EXAMPLE 6 Graph: $y = |x|$

Strategy We will find several solutions of the equation, plot them on a rectangular coordinate system, and then draw a graph passing through the points.

WHY To *graph* an equation in two variables means to make a drawing that represents all of its solutions.

Solution
To make a table of solutions, we will choose numbers for x and find the corresponding values of y. If $x = -5$, we have

$y = |x|$ This is the original equation.

$y = |-5|$ Substitute the input -5 for x.

$y = 5$ The output is 5.

The ordered pair $(-5, 5)$ satisfies the equation. This pair and several others that satisfy the equation are listed in the table of solutions in the figure. If we plot the ordered pairs in the table, we see that they lie in a "V" shape. We join the points to complete the graph shown in the figure.

$y = |x|$		
x	y	(x, y)
-5	5	$(-5, 5)$
-4	4	$(-4, 4)$
-3	3	$(-3, 3)$
-2	2	$(-2, 2)$
-1	1	$(-1, 1)$
0	0	$(0, 0)$
1	1	$(1, 1)$
2	2	$(2, 2)$
3	3	$(3, 3)$

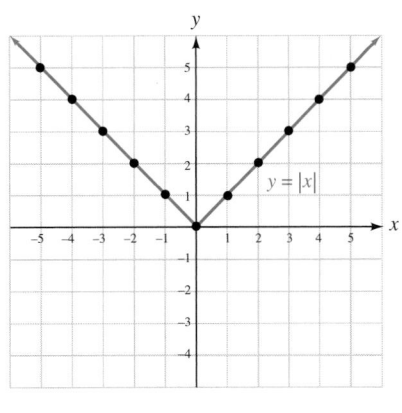

EXAMPLE 7 Graph: $y = x^3$

Strategy We will find several solutions of the equation, plot them on a rectangular coordinate system, and then draw a graph passing through the points.

WHY To *graph* an equation in two variables means to make a drawing that represents all of its solutions.

Solution
If we let $x = -2$, we have

$y = x^3$ This is the original equation.

$y = (-2)^3$ Substitute the input -2 for x.

$y = -8$ The output is -8.

The ordered pair $(-2, -8)$ satisfies the equation. This ordered pair and several others that satisfy the equation are listed in the table of solutions in the figure on the next page. Plotting the ordered pairs and joining them with a smooth curve gives us the graph shown in the figure.

Self Check 6

Graph $y = |x| + 2$ and compare the result to the graph of $y = |x|$. What do you notice?

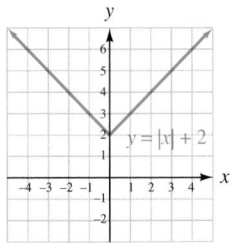

Now Try **Problem 43**
Self Check 6 Answer
The graph has the same shape, but is 2 units higher.

Teaching Example 6 Graph $y = |x| - 1$ and compare the result to the graph of $y = |x|$. What do you notice?
Answer:
The graph has the same shape, but 1 unit lower.

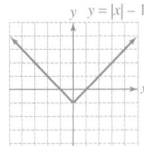

Self Check 7

Graph $y = (x - 2)^3$ and compare the result to the graph of $y = x^3$. What do you notice?

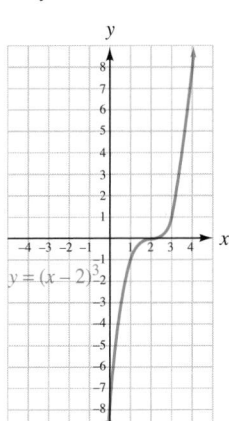

Now Try **Problem 45**
Self Check 7 Answer
The graph has the same shape but is 2 units to the right.

Teaching Example 7 Graph $y = (x + 1)^3$ and compare the result to the graph of $y = x^3$. What do you notice?

Answer:

The graph has the same shape but is 1 unit to the left.

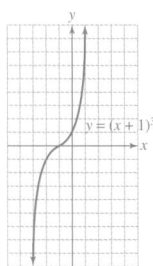

$y = x^3$		
x	y	(x, y)
-2	-8	$(-2, -8)$
-1	-1	$(-1, -1)$
0	0	$(0, 0)$
1	1	$(1, 1)$
2	8	$(2, 8)$

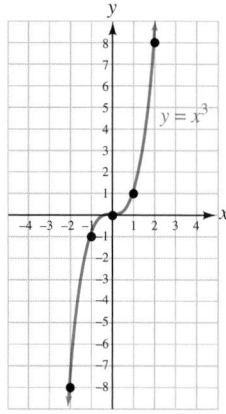

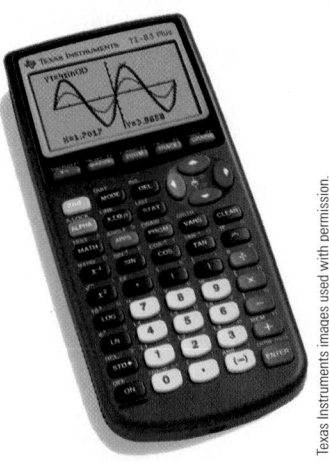

Using Your CALCULATOR Using a Graphing Calculator to Graph an Equation

We have graphed equations by making tables of solutions and plotting points. The task of graphing is much easier when we use a graphing calculator. The instructions in this discussion will be general in nature. For specific details about your calculator, please consult your owner's manual.

The viewing window

All graphing calculators have a viewing **window,** used to display graphs. The **standard window** has settings of

$$\text{Xmin} = -10, \quad \text{Xmax} = 10, \quad \text{Ymin} = -10, \quad \text{and} \quad \text{Ymax} = 10$$

which indicate that the minimum x- and y-coordinates used in the graph will be -10 and that the maximum x- and y-coordinates will be 10.

Graphing an equation

To graph the equation $y = x - 1$ using a graphing calculator, we press the $\boxed{Y =}$ key and enter the right-hand side of the equation after the symbol Y_1. The display will show the equation

$$Y_1 = x - 1$$

Then we press the $\boxed{\text{GRAPH}}$ key to produce the graph in figure (a) shown on the next page.

Next, we will graph the equation $y = |x - 4|$. Since absolute values are always nonnegative, the minimum y-value is zero. To obtain a reasonable viewing window, we press the $\boxed{\text{WINDOW}}$ key and set the Ymin value slightly lower, at Ymin $= -3$. We set Ymax to be 10 units greater than Ymin, at Ymax $= 7$. The minimum value of y occurs when $x = 4$. To center the graph in the viewing window, we set the Xmin and Xmax values 5 units to the left and right of 4. Therefore, Xmin $= -1$ and Xmax $= 9$.

After entering the right-hand side of the equation, we obtain the graph in figure (b) shown on the next page. Consult your owner's manual to learn how to enter an absolute value.

(continued)

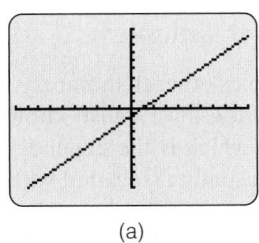
(a)

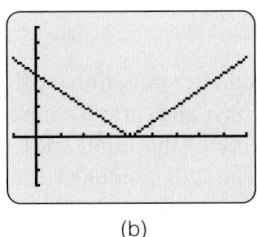
(b)

Changing the viewing window:

The choice of viewing windows is extremely important when graphing equations. To show this, let's graph $y = x^2 - 25$ with x-values from -1 to 6 and y-values from -5 to 5.

To graph this equation, we set the x and y window values and enter the right-hand side of the equation. The display will show

$$Y_1 = x^2 - 25$$

Then we press the $\boxed{\text{GRAPH}}$ key to produce the graph shown in figure (c). Although the graph appears to be a straight line, it is not. Actually, we are seeing only part of a parabola. If we pick a viewing window with x-values of -6 to 6 and y-values of -30 to 2, as in figure (d), we can see that the graph is a parabola.

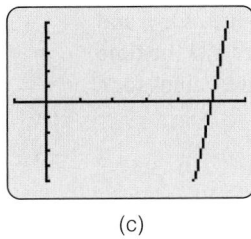
(c)

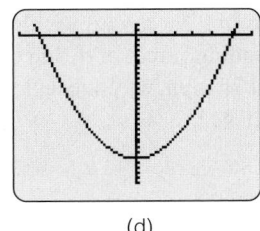
(d)

Use a graphing calculator to graph each equation. Use a viewing window of
x = −5 to 5 and y = −5 to 5.

1. $y = 2.1x - 1.1$

2. $y = 1.12x^2 - 1$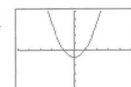

3. $y = |x + 0.7|$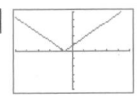

4. $y = 0.1x^3 + 1$

Graph each equation in a viewing window of x = −4 to 4 and y = −4 to 4.
Each graph is not what it first appears to be. Pick a better viewing window and
find a better representation of the true graph.

5. $y = -x^3 - 8.2$

6. $y = -|x - 4.01|$

7. $y = x^2 + 5.9$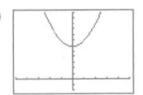

8. $y = -x + 7.95$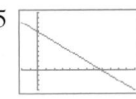

5 Graph equations that use different variables.

We will often encounter equations with variables other than x and y. When we make tables of solutions and graph these equations, we must know which is the independent variable (the input values) and which is the dependent variable (the output values). The independent variable is usually associated with the horizontal axis of the coordinate system, and the dependent variable is usually associated with the vertical axis.

Self Check 8

If the maximum speed limit on a rural highway is 55 mph, the formula for the distance traveled in t time is $d = 55t$. Graph the equation.

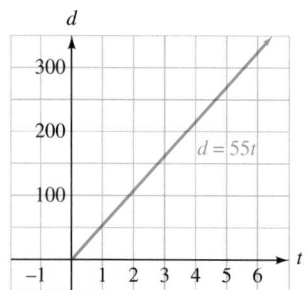

Now Try Problem 49

Teaching Example 8 If the maximum speed limit on a U.S. interstate highway is 65 mph, the formula for the distance traveled in t time is $d = 65t$. Graph the equation.
Answer:

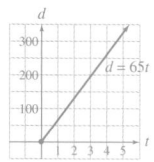

EXAMPLE 8   *Speed Limits*   In some states, the maximum speed limit on a U.S. interstate highway is 75 mph. The distance covered by a vehicle traveling at 75 mph depends on the time the vehicle travels at that speed. This relationship is described by the equation $d = 75t$, where d represents the distance (in miles) and t represents the time (in hours). Graph the equation.

Strategy We will find several solutions of the equation, plot them on a rectangular coordinate system, and then draw a graph passing through the points.

WHY We can use the graph to estimate the distance traveled (in miles) after traveling an amount of time at 75 mph.

Solution

Since d depends on t in the equation $d = 75t$, t is the independent variable (the input) and d is the dependent variable (the output). Therefore, we choose values for t and find the corresponding values of d. Since t represents the time spent traveling at 75 mph, we choose no negative values for t.
    If $t = 0$, we have

$d = 75t$ This is the original equation.
$d = 75(0)$ Substitute the input 0 for t.
$d = 0$ Perform the multiplication.

The pair $t = 0$ and $d = 0$, or $(0, 0)$, is a solution. This ordered pair and others that satisfy the equation are listed in the table of solutions shown below. If we plot the ordered pairs and draw a line through them, we obtain the graph shown in the figure. From the graph, we see (as expected) that the distance covered steadily increases as the traveling time increases.

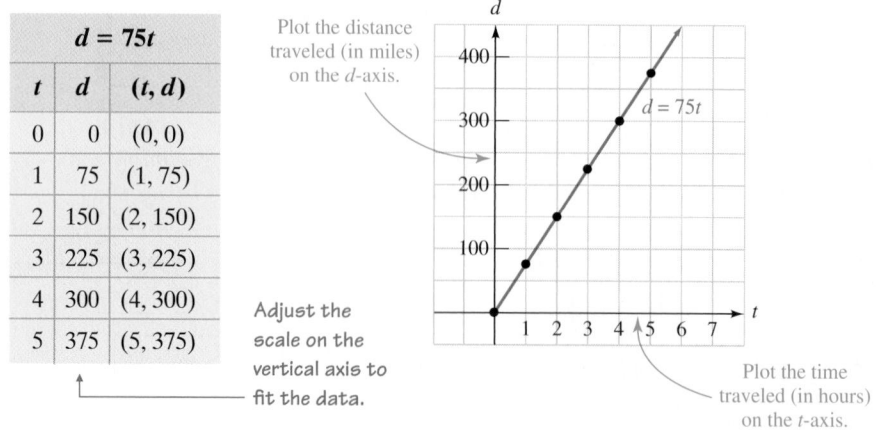

ANSWERS TO SELF CHECKS

1. yes **2.** no **3.** $(-3, -10)$

4.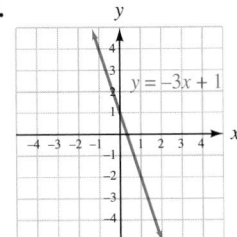

5.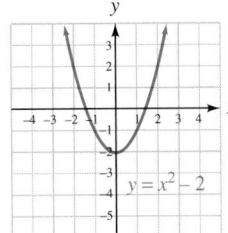

6.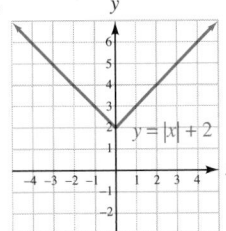

7.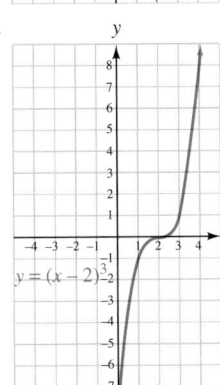

8.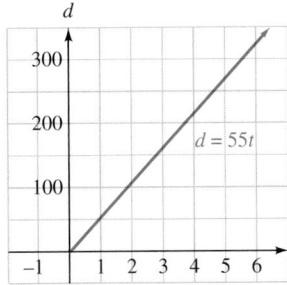

SECTION **3.2**   STUDY SET

VOCABULARY

Fill in the blanks.

1. The equation $7 = -2x + 5$ is an equation in __one__ variable. The equation $y = x + 1$ is an equation in __two__ variables, x and y.

▶ **2.** An ordered pair is a __solution__ of an equation if the numbers in the ordered pair satisfy the equation.

3. When constructing a __table__ of solutions, the values of x are the input values and the values of y are the __output__ values.

4. In equations containing the variables x and y, x is called the independent __variable__ and y is called the __dependent__ variable.

CONCEPTS

5. Consider the equation: $y = -2x + 6$

   a. How many variables does the equation contain? 2

   b. Does the ordered pair $(4, -2)$ satisfy the equation? yes

   c. Is $(-3, 12)$ a solution of the equation? yes

   d. How many solutions does this equation have? infinitely many

6. To graph an equation, five solutions were found, they were plotted (in black), and a straight line was drawn through them, as shown. From the graph, determine three other solutions of the equation.

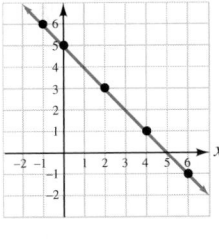

$(1, 4), (3, 2), (5, 0)$ (answers may vary)

7. Fill in the blanks: The graph of $y = -x + 5$ is shown in Problem 6. Every point on the graph represents an ordered-pair __solution__ of $y = -x + 5$, and every ordered-pair solution is a __point__ on the graph.

▶ **8.** Consider the graph of an equation shown below.

   a. If the coordinates of point M are substituted into the equation, is the result a true or false statement? true

   b. If the coordinates of point N are substituted into the equation, is the result a true or false statement? false

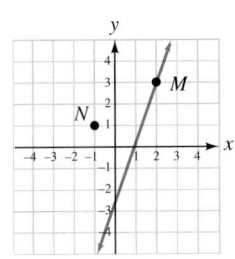

▶ Selected exercises available at
www.webassign.net/brookscole

9. Complete the table.

$y = x^3$	
x (inputs)	**y (outputs)**
0	0
−1	−1
−2	−8
1	1
2	8

10. What is wrong with the graph of $y = x - 3$ shown below?

The line is too short, and arrowheads are not drawn on both ends of the line.

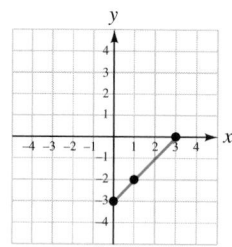

11. To graph $y = -x + 1$, a student constructed a table of solutions and plotted the ordered pairs as shown. Instead of drawing a crooked line through the points, what should he have done?

He should have checked his computations. At least one of his "solutions" is wrong.

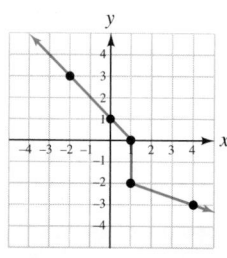

12. To graph $y = x^2 - 4$, a table of solutions is constructed and a graph is drawn, as shown. Explain the error made here.

$y = x^2 - 4$		
x	**y**	**(x, y)**
0	−4	(0, −4)
2	0	(2, 0)

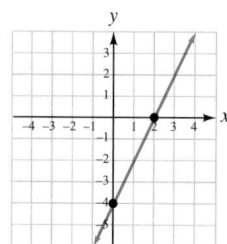

Not enough ordered pairs were found—the correct graph is a parabola.

13. Explain the error with the graph of $y = x^2$ shown in the illustration.

A smooth curve should be drawn through the points.

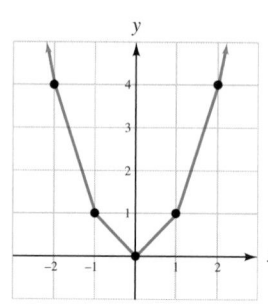

14. Several solutions of an equation are listed in the table of solutions. When graphing them, with what variable should the horizontal and vertical axes of the graph be labeled? horizontal: t, vertical: s

t	s	(t, s)
0	4	(0, 4)
1	5	(1, 5)
2	10	(2, 10)

NOTATION

Complete each solution.

15. Verify that $(-2, 6)$ satisfies $y = -x + 4$.

$$y = -x + 4$$
$$6 \overset{?}{=} -\left(\boxed{-2}\right) + 4$$
$$6 \overset{?}{=} \boxed{2} + 4$$
$$6 = 6$$

▶ **16.** For the equation $y = |x - 2|$, if $x = -3$, find y.

$$y = |x - 2|$$
$$y = \left|\boxed{-3} - 2\right|$$
$$y = \left|\boxed{-5}\right|$$
$$y = 5$$

GUIDED PRACTICE

Determine whether the ordered pair satisfies the equation. See Examples 1–2.

▶ **17.** $y = 2x - 4$, $(4, 4)$
yes

18. $y = -3x + 1$, $(2, -4)$
no

19. $y = x^2$, $(8, 48)$
no

20. $y = -x^2 + 2$, $(1, 1)$
yes

21. $y = |x - 2|$, $(4, -3)$
no

22. $y = |x + 3|$, $(0, 3)$
yes

23. $y = x^3 + 1$, $(-2, -7)$
yes

24. $y = -x^3 - 1$, $(1, -2)$
yes

Complete the solution of each equation. See Example 3.

▶ **25.** $y = 3x - 4$, $(1, ?)$ $(1, -1)$

26. $y = \frac{1}{2}x - 3$, $(2, ?)$ $(2, -2)$

27. $y = -5x + 3$, $(-3, ?)$ $(-3, 18)$

28. $y = -\frac{2}{5}x - 1$, $(-5, ?)$ $(-5, 1)$

Complete each table. See Objective 3.

29.

$y = x - 3$	
x	**y**
0	−3
1	−2
−2	−5

▶ **30.**

$y = |x - 3|$	
x	**y**
0	3
−1	4
3	0

31.

$y = x^2 - 3$	
Input	**Output**
0	−3
2	1
−2	1

▶ **32.**

$y = x + 1$	
Input	**Output**
0	1
2	3
−1	0

Construct a table of solutions and graph each equation.
See Example 4.

33. $y = 2x - 3$

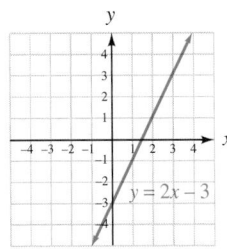

▶ **34.** $y = 3x + 1$

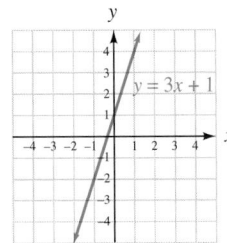

▶ **35.** $y = -2x + 1$

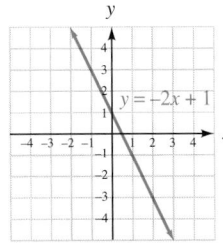

36. $y = -3x + 2$

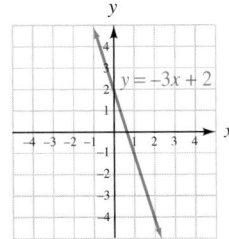

Construct a table of solutions and graph each equation.
Compare the result to the graph of $y = x^2$. See Example 5.

37. $y = x^2 + 1$
1 unit higher

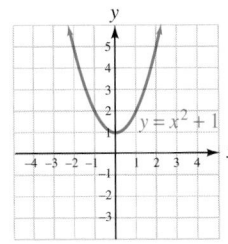

▶ **38.** $y = -x^2$
It is turned upside down.

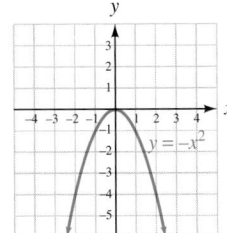

39. $y = (x - 2)^2$
2 units to the right

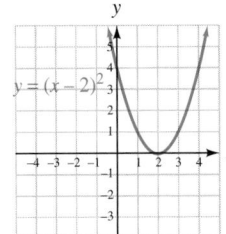

▶ **40.** $y = (x + 2)^2$
2 units to the left

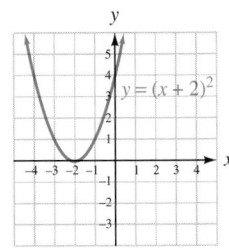

Construct a table of solutions and graph each equation.
Compare the result to the graph of $y = |x|$. See Example 6.

41. $y = -|x|$
It is turned upside down.

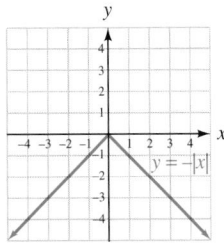

▶ **42.** $y = |x| - 2$
2 units lower

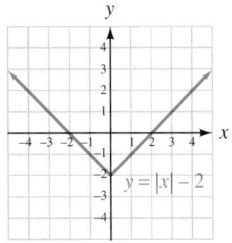

43. $y = |x + 2|$
2 units to the left

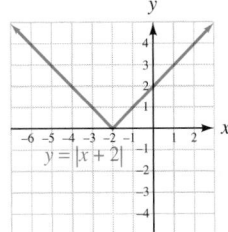

▶ **44.** $y = |x - 2|$
2 units to the right

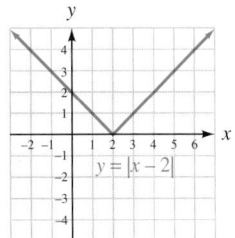

Construct a table of solutions and graph each equation.
Compare the result to the graph of $y = x^3$. See Example 7.

45. $y = -x^3$
It is turned upside down.

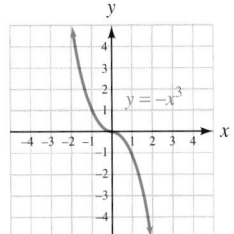

▶ **46.** $y = x^3 + 2$
2 units higher

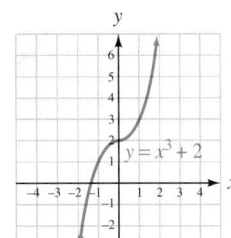

47. $y = x^3 - 2$
2 units lower

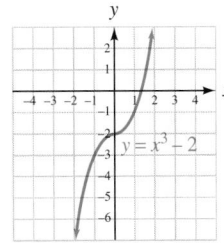

▶ **48.** $y = (x + 2)^3$
2 units to the left

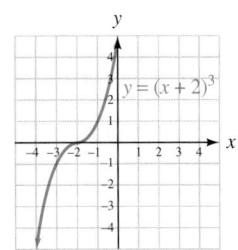

APPLICATIONS

See Example 8.

49. BILLIARDS The path traveled by the black 8 ball is described by the equations $y = 2x - 4$ and $y = -2x + 12$. Construct a table of solutions for $y = 2x - 4$ using the x-values 1, 2, and 4. Do the same for $y = -2x + 12$ using the x-values 4, 6, and 8. Then graph the path of the 8 ball.

x	1	2	4	4	6	8
y	-2	0	4	4	0	-4

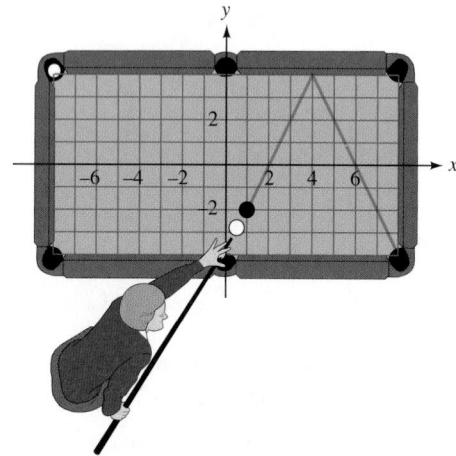

50. TABLE TENNIS The illustration shows the path traveled by a Ping-Pong ball as it bounces off the table. Use the information in the illustration to complete the table.

x	-7	-3	1	3	5
y	2	0	2	3	4

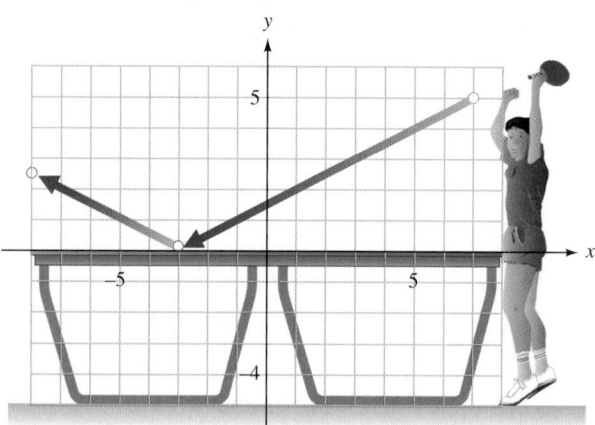

51. SUSPENSION BRIDGES The suspension cables of a bridge hang in the shape of a parabola, as shown in the next column. Use the information in the illustration to complete the table.

x	0	2	4	-2	-4
y	0	1	4	1	4

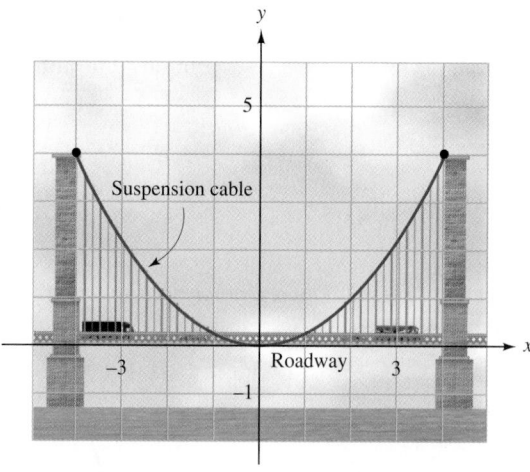

52. FIRE BOATS A stream of water from a high-pressure hose on a fire boat travels in the shape of a parabola. Use the information in the graph to complete the table.

x	1	2	3	4
y	3	4	3	0

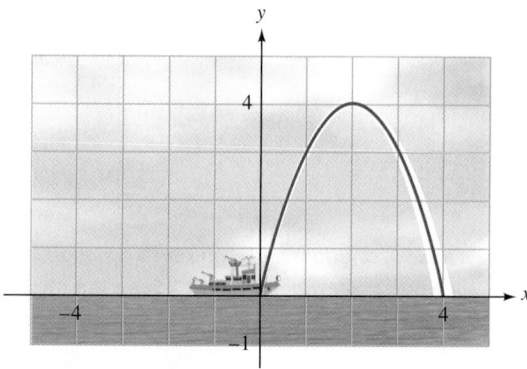

53. MANUFACTURING The graph on the next page shows the relationship between the length l (in inches) of a machine bolt and the cost C (in cents) to manufacture it.

a. What information does the point (2, 8) on the graph give us?
It costs 8¢ to make a 2-in. bolt.

b. How much does it cost to make a 7-inch bolt?
12¢

c. What length bolt is the least expensive to make?
a 4-in. bolt

d. Describe how the cost changes as the length of the bolt increases. It decreases as the length increases to 4 in., then increases as the length increases to 7 in.

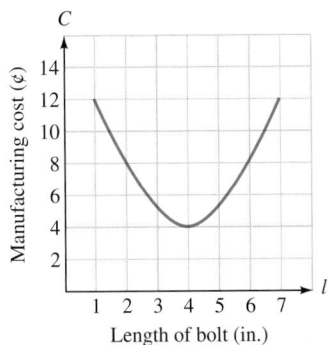

Length of bolt (in.)

54. SOFTBALL The following graph shows the relationship between the distance d (in feet) traveled by a batted softball and the height h (in feet) it attains.

a. What information does the point $(40, 40)$ on the graph give us?
After the ball has traveled 40 ft, its height is 40 ft.

b. At what distance from home plate does the ball reach its maximum height?
100 ft

c. Where will the ball land?
200 ft from home plate

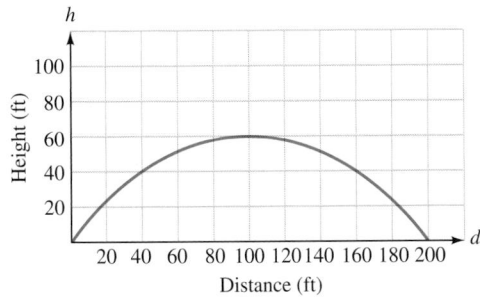

Distance (ft)

55. MARKET VALUE OF A HOUSE The following graph shows the relationship between the market value v of a house and the time t since it was purchased.

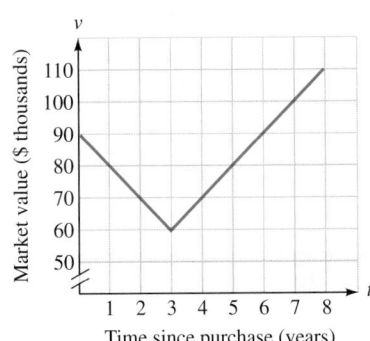

Time since purchase (years)

a. What was the purchase price of the house? $90,000

b. When did the value of the house reach its lowest point? the 3rd yr after being bought

c. When did the value of the house begin to surpass the purchase price? after the 6th yr

d. Describe how the market value of the house changed over the 8-year period.
It decreased in value for 3 yr to a low of $60,000, then increased in value for 5 yr to a high of $110,000.

56. POLITICAL SURVEYS The following graph shows the relationship between the percent P of those surveyed who rated their senator's job performance as satisfactory or better and the time t she had been in office.

a. When did her job performance rating reach a maximum? the 8th month after being elected

b. When was her job performance rating at or above the 60% mark? between the 4th and 12th months

c. Describe how her job performance rating changed over the 12-month period.
After the election, it increased for 8 mo to a high of 70%. Then it decreased for 4 mo.

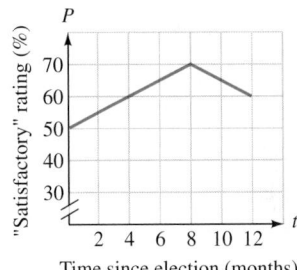

Time since election (months)

WRITING

57. What is a table of solutions?

58. To graph an equation in two variables, how many solutions of the equation must be found?

59. Give an example of an equation in one variable and an equation in two variables. How do their solutions differ?

60. When we say that $(-2, -6)$ is a solution of $y = x - 4$, what do we mean?

61. On a quiz, students were asked to graph $y = 3x - 1$. One student made the table of solutions on the left. Another student made the one on the right. Which table is incorrect? Or could they both be correct? Explain.

x	y	(x, y)
0	−1	$(0, -1)$
2	5	$(2, 5)$
3	8	$(3, 8)$
4	11	$(4, 11)$
5	14	$(5, 14)$

x	y	(x, y)
−2	−7	$(-2, -7)$
−1	−4	$(-1, -4)$
1	2	$(1, 2)$
−3	−10	$(-3, -10)$
2	5	$(2, 5)$

62. What does it mean when we say that an equation in two variables has infinitely many solutions?

REVIEW

63. Solve: $\dfrac{x}{8} = -12$ -96

64. Combine like terms: $3t - 4T + 5T - 6t$ $-3t + T$

65. Is $\dfrac{x + 5}{6}$ an expression or an equation? an expression

66. What formula is used to find the perimeter of a rectangle? $P = 2l + 2w$

67. What number is 0.5% of 250? 1.25

68. Solve: $-3x + 5 > -7$ $x < 4$

69. Find: $-2.5 - (-2.6)$ 0.1

▶ **70.** Evaluate: $(-5)^3$ -125

Objectives

1 Identify linear equations.

2 Complete ordered-pair solutions of linear equations.

3 Graph linear equations by plotting points.

4 Graph linear equations by the intercept method.

5 Identify and graph horizontal and vertical lines.

6 Use graphs of linear equations to solve applied problems.

SECTION 3.3
Graphing Linear Equations

1 Identify linear equations.

We have previously graphed the equations shown below. The graph of the equation $y = x - 1$ is a line, and we call it a **linear equation.** Since the graphs of $y = x^2$, $y = |x|$, and $y = x^3$ are *not* lines, they are **nonlinear equations.**

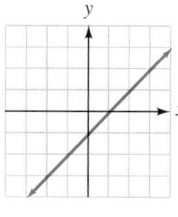

$y = x - 1$
Linear equation
(a)

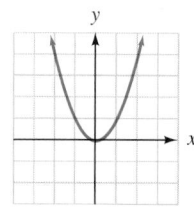

$y = x^2$
Nonlinear equation
(b)

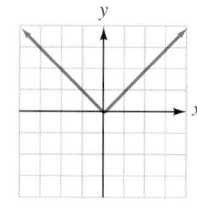

$y = |x|$
Nonlinear equation
(c)

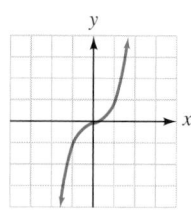

$y = x^3$
Nonlinear equation
(d)

In this section, we will discuss how to graph linear equations and show how to use their graphs to solve problems.

Any equation, such as $y = x - 1$, whose graph is a straight line is called a **linear equation in x and y.** Some other examples of linear equations are

$$y = \frac{1}{2}x + 2, \quad 3x - 2y = 8, \quad 5y - x + 2 = 0, \quad y = 4, \quad \text{and} \quad x = -3$$

A linear equation in x and y is any equation that can be written in a special form, called **general** (or **standard**) form.

General Form of a Linear Equation

If A, B, and C represent real numbers, the equation

$$Ax + By = C \text{ (both } A \text{ and } B \text{ are not zero)}$$

is called the **general form** (or **standard form**) of the equation of a line.

Whenever possible, we will write the general form $Ax + By = C$ so that A, B, and C are integers and $A \geq 0$. Note that in a linear equation in x and y, the exponents on x and y are 1.

EXAMPLE 1 Which of the following equations are linear equations?

a. $3x = 1 - 2y$ **b.** $y = x^3 + 1$ **c.** $y = -\frac{1}{2}x$

Strategy We will try to write each equation in general form $Ax + By = C$. We will also note the exponents on x and y.

WHY If we can write an equation in general form $Ax + By = C$, it is a linear equation. If the exponents on x or y are not 1, the equation is nonlinear.

Solution

a. Since the equation $3x = 1 - 2y$ can be written in $Ax + By = C$ form, it is a linear equation.

$$3x = 1 - 2y \qquad \text{This is the original equation.}$$
$$3x + 2y = 1 - 2y + 2y \qquad \text{Add } 2y \text{ to both sides.}$$
$$3x + 2y = 1 \qquad \text{Simplify the right-hand side: } -2y + 2y = 0.$$

Here $A = 3$, $B = 2$, and $C = 1$.

b. Since the exponent on x in $y = x^3 + 1$ is 3, the equation is a nonlinear equation.

c. Since the equation $y = -\frac{1}{2}x$ can be written in $Ax + By = C$ form, it is a linear equation.

$$y = -\frac{1}{2}x \qquad \text{This is the original equation.}$$
$$-2(y) = -2\left(-\frac{1}{2}x\right) \qquad \begin{array}{l}\text{Multiply both sides by } -2 \text{ so that the coefficient}\\ \text{of } x \text{ will be 1.}\end{array}$$
$$-2y = x \qquad \text{Simplify the right-hand side: } -2\left(-\frac{1}{2}\right) = 1.$$
$$0 = x + 2y \qquad \text{Add } 2y \text{ to both sides.}$$
$$x + 2y = 0 \qquad \text{Write the equation in general form.}$$

Here $A = 1$, $B = 2$, and $C = 0$.

2 Complete ordered-pair solutions of linear equations.

To find solutions of linear equations, we substitute arbitrary values for one variable and solve for the other.

EXAMPLE 2 Complete the table of solutions for $3x + 2y = 5$.

Strategy In each case we will substitute the known coordinate of the solution into the given equation.

WHY We can solve the resulting equation in one variable to find the unknown coordinate of the solution.

Solution

In the first row, we are given an x-value of 7. To find the corresponding y-value, we substitute 7 for x and solve for y.

x	y	(x, y)
7		(7,)
	4	(, 4)

$$3x + 2y = 5 \qquad \text{This is the original equation.}$$
$$3(7) + 2y = 5 \qquad \text{Substitute 7 for } x.$$
$$21 + 2y = 5 \qquad \text{Perform the multiplication: } 3(7) = 21.$$
$$2y = -16 \qquad \text{Subtract 21 from both sides: } 5 - 21 = -16.$$
$$y = -8 \qquad \text{Divide both sides by 2.}$$

Self Check 1

Which of the following are linear equations and which are nonlinear?

a. $y = |x|$ nonlinear

b. $-x = 6 - y$ linear

c. $y = x$ linear

Now Try **Problems 38 and 40**

Teaching Example 1 Which of the following are linear equations and which are nonlinear?
a. $y = 2x + 3$
b. $3x = -y + 7$
c. $y = |x| + 3$
Answers:
a. linear   **b.** linear   **c.** nonlinear

Self Check 2

Complete the table of solutions for $3x + 2y = 5$.

x	y	(x, y)
3	-2	(3, -2)
5	-5	(5, -5)

Now Try **Problem 42**

Teaching Example 2 Complete the table of solutions for $2x - 5y = 10$.

x	y	(x, y)
10	2	(10, 2)
5	0	(5, 0)

A solution of $3x + 2y = 5$ is $(7, -8)$.

In the second row, we are given a y-value of 4. To find the corresponding x-value, we substitute 4 for y and solve for x.

$3x + 2y = 5$ This is the original equation.

$3x + 2(4) = 5$ Substitute 4 for y.

$3x + 8 = 5$ Perform the multiplication: $2(4) = 8$.

$3x = -3$ Subtract 8 from both sides: $5 - 8 = -3$.

$x = -1$ Divide both sides by 3.

Another solution is $(-1, 4)$. The completed table is shown on the right.

x	y	(x, y)
7	-8	$(7, -8)$
-1	4	$(-1, 4)$

3   Graph linear equations by plotting points.

It is impossible to list the infinitely many solutions of a linear equation. However, to show all of its solutions, we can draw a mathematical "picture" of them. We call this picture the *graph of the equation*.

Graphing Linear Equations

1. Find three pairs (x, y) that satisfy the equation by picking arbitrary numbers for x and finding the corresponding values of y.

2. Plot each resulting pair (x, y) on a rectangular coordinate system. If the three points do not lie on a straight line, check your computations.

3. Draw the straight line passing through the points.

Self Check 3

Graph $y = -3x + 2$ and compare the result to the graph of $y = -3x$. What do you notice?

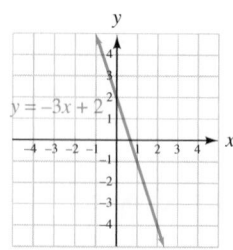

Now Try Problem 45

Self Check 3 Answer
It is a line 2 units above the graph of $y = -3x$.

EXAMPLE 3   Graph: $y = -3x$

Strategy We will find three solutions of the equations, plot them on a rectangular coordinate system, and then draw a straight line passing through the points.

WHY To *graph* a linear equation in two variables means to make a drawing that represents all of its solutions.

Solution

To find three ordered pairs that satisfy the equation, we begin by choosing three x-values: -2, 0, and 2.

If $x = -2$	**If $x = 0$**	**If $x = 2$**
$y = -3x$	$y = -3x$	$y = -3x$
$y = -3(-2)$	$y = -3(0)$	$y = -3(2)$
$y = 6$	$y = 0$	$y = -6$

We enter the results in a table of solutions, plot the points, and draw a straight line through the points. The graph appears on the next page.

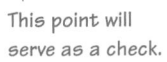

$y = -3x$		
x	y	(x, y)
-2	6	$(-2, 6)$
0	0	$(0, 0)$
2	-6	$(2, -6)$

↑
This point will
serve as a check.

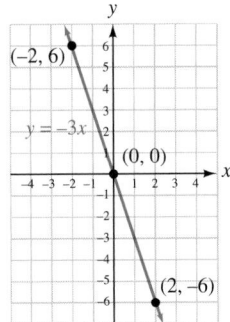

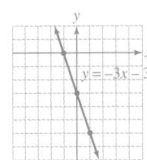

Success Tip   Since two points determine a line, only two points are needed to graph a linear equation. However, we will often plot a third point as a check. If the three points do not lie on a straight line, then at least one of them is in error.

When graphing linear equations, it is often easier to find solutions of the equation if it is first solved for y.

EXAMPLE 4   Graph: $2y = 4 - x$

Strategy We will use properties of equality to solve the given equation for y. Then we will use the point-plotting method of this section to graph the resulting equivalent equation.

WHY The calculations to find several solutions of a linear equation in two variables are usually easier when the equation is solved for y.

Solution
To solve for y, we undo the multiplication of 2 by dividing both sides by 2.

$$2y = 4 - x$$

$$\frac{2y}{2} = \frac{4}{2} - \frac{x}{2} \qquad \text{On the right-hand side, dividing each term by 2 is equivalent to dividing the entire side by 2: } \frac{4-x}{2} = \frac{4}{2} - \frac{x}{2}.$$

$$y = 2 - \frac{x}{2} \qquad \text{Simplify: } \frac{4}{2} = 2$$

Since each value of x will be divided by 2, we will choose values of x that are divisible by 2. Three such choices are -4, 0, and 4. If $x = -4$, we have

$$y = 2 - \frac{x}{2}$$

$$y = 2 - \frac{-4}{2} \qquad \text{Substitute } -4 \text{ for } x.$$

$$y = 2 - (-2) \quad \text{Divide: } \frac{-4}{2} = -2$$

$$y = 4 \qquad\qquad \text{Perform the subtraction.}$$

A solution is $(-4, 4)$. This pair and two others satisfying the equation are shown in the table on the next page. If we plot the points and draw a straight line through them, we will obtain the graph also shown on the next page.

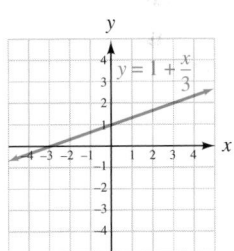
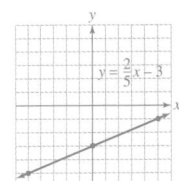

$y = 2 - \frac{x}{2}$		
x	y	(x, y)
-4	4	$(-4, 4)$
0	2	$(0, 2)$
4	0	$(4, 0)$

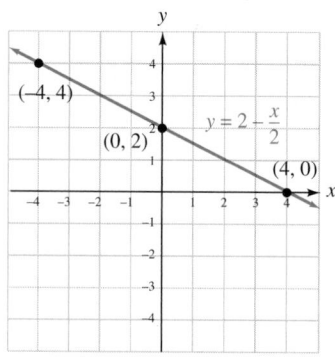

4 Graph linear equations by the intercept method.

In the figure to the right, the graph of $3x + 4y = 12$ intersects the y-axis at the point $(0, 3)$; we call this point the **y-intercept** of the graph. Since the graph intersects the x-axis at $(4, 0)$, the point $(4, 0)$ is the **x-intercept.**

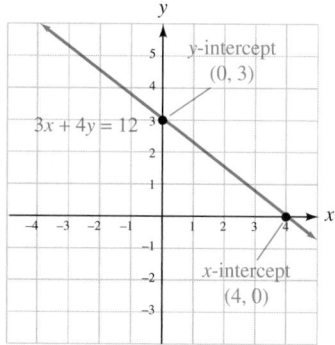

In general, we have the following definitions.

---

y- and x-intercepts

The **y-intercept** of a line is the point $(0, b)$ where the line intersects the y-axis. To find b, substitute 0 for x in the equation of the line and solve for y.

The **x-intercept** of a line is the point $(a, 0)$ where the line intersects the x-axis. To find a, substitute 0 for y in the equation of the line and solve for x.

Plotting the x- and y-intercepts of a graph and drawing a straight line through them is called the **intercept method of graphing a line.** This method is useful when graphing equations written in general form $Ax + By = C$.

Self Check 5

Graph $4x + 3y = 6$ using the intercept method.

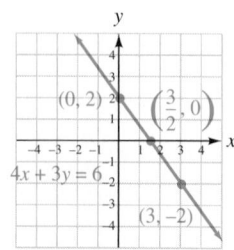

Now Try Problem 59

EXAMPLE 5   Graph: $3x - 2y = 8$

Strategy We will let $y = 0$ to find the x-intercept of the graph. We will then let $x = 0$ to find the y-intercept.

WHY Since two points determine a line, the y-intercept and the x-intercept are enough information to graph this linear equation.

Solution
x-intercept: $y = 0$

$$3x - 2y = 8$$
$$3x - 2(0) = 8 \qquad \text{Substitute 0 for } y.$$
$$3x = 8 \qquad \text{Simplify the left-hand side: } 2(0) = 0.$$
$$x = \frac{8}{3} \qquad \text{Divide both sides by 3.}$$

The x-intercept is $\left(\frac{8}{3}, 0\right)$, which can be written $\left(2\frac{2}{3}, 0\right)$. This ordered pair is entered in the table below.

y-intercept: x = 0.

$$3x - 2y = 8$$
$$3(0) - 2y = 8 \quad \text{Substitute 0 for } x.$$
$$-2y = 8 \quad \text{Simplify the left-hand side: } 3(0) = 0.$$
$$y = -4 \quad \text{Divide both sides by } -2.$$

The y-intercept is $(0, -4)$. It is entered in the table below. As a check, we find one more point on the line. If $x = 4$, then $y = 2$. We plot these three points and draw a straight line through them. The graph of $3x - 2y = 8$ is shown in the figure.

$3x - 2y = 8$		
x	y	(x, y)
$\frac{8}{3} = 2\frac{2}{3}$	0	$\left(2\frac{2}{3}, 0\right)$
0	-4	$(0, -4)$
4	2	$(4, 2)$

↑
This point serves
as a check.

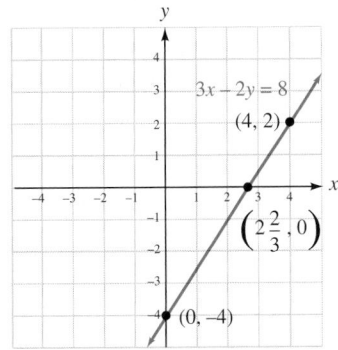

Teaching Example 5 Graph $2x - 3y = 6$ using the intercept method.
Answer:

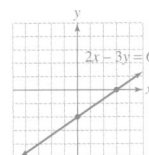

5 **Identify and graph horizontal and vertical lines.**

Equations such as $y = 4$ and $x = -3$ are linear equations, because they can be written in the general form $Ax + By = C$. For example, $y = 4$ is equivalent to $0x + 1y = 4$ and $x = -3$ is equivalent to $1x + 0y = -3$. We now discuss how to graph these types of linear equations.

EXAMPLE 6   Graph: $y = 4$

Strategy To find three ordered-pair solutions of this equation to plot, we will select three values for x and use 4 for y each time.

WHY The given equation requires that $y = 4$.

Solution
We can write the equation in general form as $0x + y = 4$. Since the coefficient of x is 0, the numbers chosen for x have no effect on y. The value of y is always 4. For example, if $x = 2$, we have

$$0x + y = 4 \quad \text{This is the original equation, } y = 4, \text{ written in general form.}$$
$$0(2) + y = 4 \quad \text{Substitute 2 for } x.$$
$$y = 4 \quad \text{Simplify the left side.}$$

The table of solutions shown on the next page contains three ordered pairs that satisfy the equation $y = 4$. If we plot the points and draw a straight line through them, the result is a horizontal line. The y-intercept is $(0, 4)$, and there is no x-intercept.

Self Check 6
Graph: $y = -2$

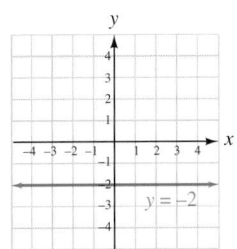

Now Try Problem 62

Teaching Example 6 Graph: $y = -3$
Answer:

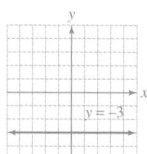

$y = 4$		
x	y	(x, y)
2	4	$(2, 4)$
-1	4	$(-1, 4)$
-3	4	$(-3, 4)$

↑
Note that each
y-coordinate is 4.

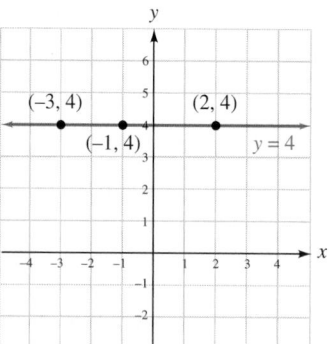

Self Check 7

Graph: $x = 4$

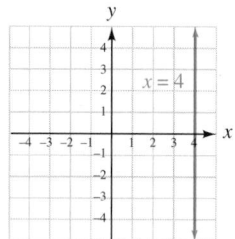

Now Try **Problem 64**

Teaching Example 7 Graph: $x = 2$
Answer:

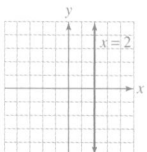

EXAMPLE 7   Graph: $x = -3$

Strategy To find three ordered-pair solutions of this equation to plot, we will select -3 for x each time and use three different values for y.

WHY The given equation requires that $x = -3$.

Solution
We can write the equation in general form as $x + 0y = -3$. Since the coefficient of y is 0, the numbers chosen for y have no effect on x. The value of x is always -3. For example, if $y = -2$, we have

$$x + 0y = -3 \quad \text{This is the original equation written in general form.}$$
$$x + 0(-2) = -3 \quad \text{Substitute } -2 \text{ for } y.$$
$$x = -3 \quad \text{Simplify the left side.}$$

The table of solutions shown below contains three ordered pairs that satisfy the equation $x = -3$. If we plot the points and draw a line through them, the result is a vertical line. The x-intercept is $(-3, 0)$, and there is no y-intercept.

$x = -3$		
x	y	(x, y)
-3	-2	$(-3, -2)$
-3	0	$(-3, 0)$
-3	3	$(-3, 3)$

↑
Note that each
x-coordinate is −3.

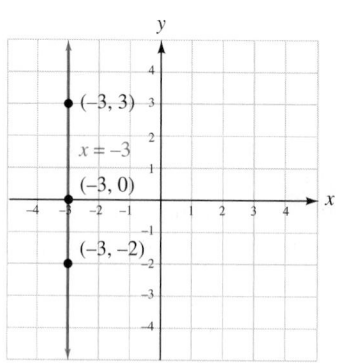

From the results of Examples 6 and 7, we have the following facts.

Equations of Horizontal and Vertical Lines

The equation $y = b$ represents the horizontal line that intersects the y-axis at $(0, b)$. If $b = 0$, the line is the x-axis.

The equation $x = a$ represents the vertical line that intersects the x-axis at $(a, 0)$. If $a = 0$, the line is the y-axis.

6 Use graphs of linear equations to solve applied problems.

EXAMPLE 8 *Birthday Parties* A restaurant offers a party package that includes food, drinks, cake, and party favors for a cost of $25 plus $3 per child. Write a linear equation that will give the cost for a party of any size, and then graph the equation.

Strategy We will form an equation and use the plotting points method to graph the equation.

WHY The graph is a picture of all the solutions of the equation.

Solution
We can let c represent the cost of the party. The cost c is the sum of the basic charge of $25 and the cost per child times the number of children attending. If the number of children attending is n, at $3 per child, the total cost for the children is $3n$.

The cost	is	the basic $25 charge	plus	$3	times	the number of children.
c	$=$	25	$+$	3	$\cdot$	n

For the equation $c = 25 + 3n$, the independent variable (input) is n, the number of children. The dependent variable (output) is c, the cost of the party. We will find three points on the graph of the equation by choosing n-values of 0, 5, and 10 and finding the corresponding c-values. The results are shown in the table.

If $n = 0$
$c = 25 + 3(0)$
$c = 25$

If $n = 5$
$c = 25 + 3(5)$
$c = 25 + 15$
$c = 40$

If $n = 10$
$c = 25 + 3(10)$
$c = 25 + 30$
$c = 55$

$c = 25 + 3n$	
n	c
0	25
5	40
10	55

Next, we graph the points and draw a line through them. We don't draw an arrowhead on the left, because it doesn't make sense to have a negative number of children attend a party. Note that the c-axis is scaled in units of $5 to accommodate costs ranging from $0 to $65. We can use the graph to determine the cost of a party of any size. For example, to find the cost of a party with 8 children, we locate 8 on the horizontal axis and then move up to find a point on the graph directly above the 8. Since the coordinates of that point are (8, 49), the cost for 8 children would be $49.

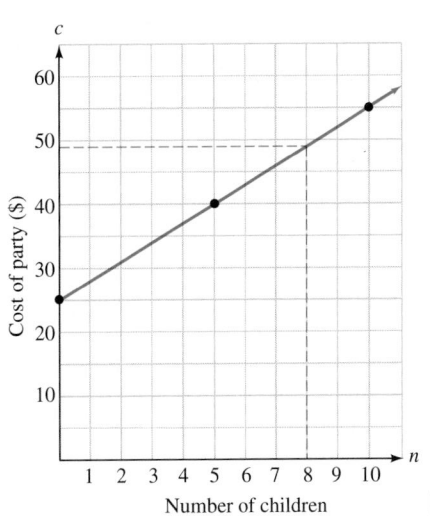

Self Check 8

A laser tag business offers a party package that includes invitations, a party room, and 2 rounds of laser tag. The cost is $15 plus $10 per child. Write a linear equation that will give the cost for a party of any size, and then graph the equation. $c = 15 + 10n$

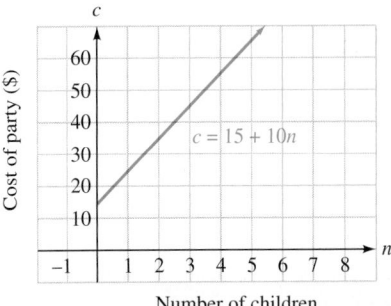

Now Try Problem 62

Teaching Example 8 The cost of embroidered hats is $25 for a setup fee and $15 per hat with the embroidered company logo. Write a linear equation that will give the cost for an order of any number of hats, and then graph the equation.
Answer:
$c = 25 + 15n$

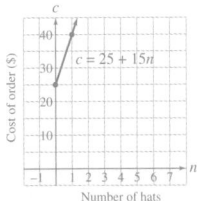

ANSWERS TO SELF CHECKS

1. a. nonlinear **b.** linear   **c.** linear   **2.** $(3, -2), (5, -5)$

3. 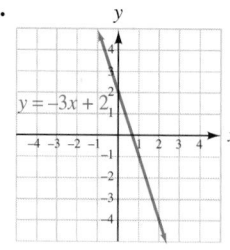   **4.** 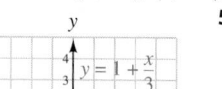   **5.**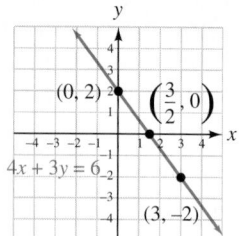

6. 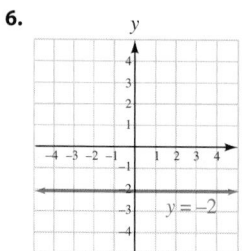   **7.** 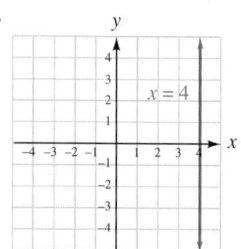   **8.**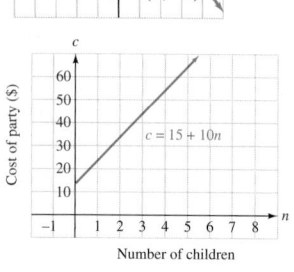

SECTION 3.3   STUDY SET

VOCABULARY

Fill in the blanks.

1. An equation whose graph is a line and whose variables are to the first power is called a __linear__ equation.

2. The equation $Ax + By = C$ is the __standard or general__ form of the equation of a line.

3. The __y-intercept__ of a line is the point $(0, b)$ where the line intersects the y-axis.

▶ **4.** The __x-intercept__ of a line is the point $(a, 0)$ where the line intersects the x-axis.

CONCEPTS

Fill in the blanks.

5. To find the y-intercept of the graph of a linear equation, let __x__ = 0 and solve for __y__.

6. To find the x-intercept of the graph of a linear equation, let __y__ = 0 and solve for __x__.

7. Lines parallel to the y-axis are __vertical__ lines.

▶ **8.** Lines parallel to the x-axis are __horizontal__ lines.

9. What is another name for the line $x = 0$? the y-axis

10. What is another name for the line $y = 0$? the x-axis

Find the power of each variable in Problems 11–13.

11. $y = 2x - 6$ y: 1st power, x: 1st power

12. $y = x^2 - 6$ y: 1st power, x: 2nd power

13. $y = x^3 + 2$ y: 1st power, x: 3rd power

14. In a linear equation in x and y, what are the exponents on x and y? 1

Consider the graph of a linear equation shown below.

15. Why will the coordinates of point A yield a true statement when substituted into the equation? because A is on the line

16. Why will the coordinates of point B yield a false statement when substituted into the equation?

because B is not on the line

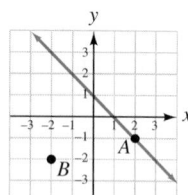

17. A student found three solutions of a linear equation and plotted them as shown. What conclusion can he make?

He made a mistake. The points should lie on a straight line.

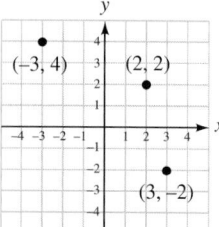

18. How many solutions are there for a linear equation in two variables? infinitely many

▶ Selected exercises available online at
www.webassign.net/brookscole

19. Give the *x*-intercept of the graph on the right. $(-3, 0)$

20. Give the *y*-intercept of the graph on the right. $(0, -1)$

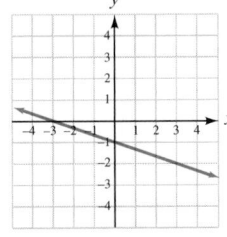

21. On the coordinate system below, draw the graph of a line with no *x*-intercept. Answers will vary.

22. On the coordinate system below, draw the graph of a line with no *y*-intercept. Answers will vary.

23. On the coordinate system below, draw a line with an *x*-intercept of $(2, 0)$. Answers will vary.

24. On the coordinate system to the right, draw a line with a *y*-intercept of $\left(0, -\dfrac{5}{2}\right)$.
Answers will vary.

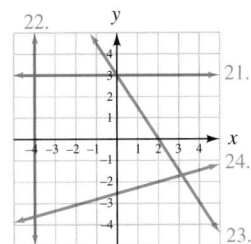

▌NOTATION

Write each equation in general form.

25. $4x = y + 6$
$4x - y = 6$

26. $2y = x$
$x - 2y = 0$

27. $x - 9 = -3y$
$x + 3y = 9$

28. $x = 12$
$x + 0y = 12$

Solve each equation for y.

29. $x + y = 8$
$y = 8 - x$

30. $2x - y = 8$
$y = 2x - 8$

31. $3x + \dfrac{y}{2} = 4$
$y = -6x + 8$

32. $y - 2 = 0$
$y = 2$

▌GUIDED PRACTICE

Classify each of the following as the graph of a linear equation or of a nonlinear equation. See Objective 1.

33.

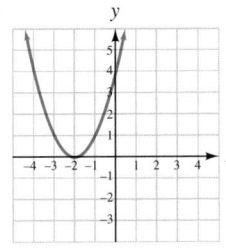

nonlinear

34.

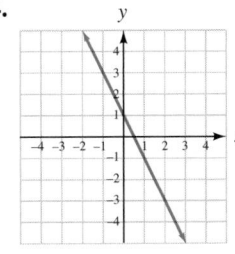

linear

35.

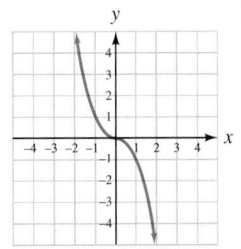

nonlinear

36. ▶

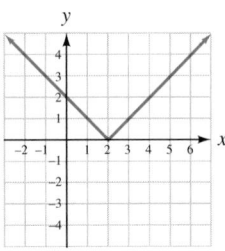

nonlinear

Classify each equation as linear or nonlinear. See Example 1.

37. $y = x^3$ nonlinear

38. $2x + 3y = 6$ linear

39. $y = -2$ linear

▶ **40.** $y = |x + 2|$ nonlinear

Complete each table of solutions. See Example 2.

41. $5y = 2x + 10$

x	y
10	6
−5	0
5	4

42. $2x + 4y = 24$

x	y
4	4
−2	7
−4	8

43. $x - 2y = 4$

x	y
0	−2
4	0
1	$-\dfrac{3}{2}$

▶ **44.** $5x - y = 3$

x	y
0	−3
$\dfrac{3}{5}$	0
1	2

Find three solutions of the equation and draw its graph. See Example 3.

45. $y = -x + 2$

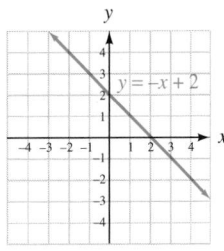

▶ **46.** $y = -x - 1$

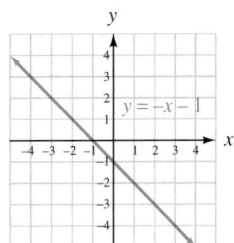

47. $y = 2x + 1$

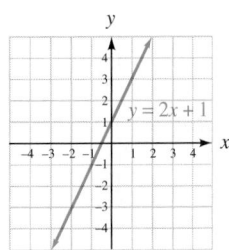

48. $y = 3x - 2$

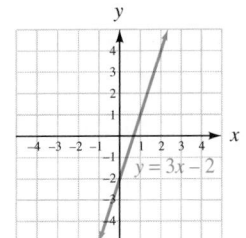

49. $y = x$ ▶ **50.** $y = 3x$

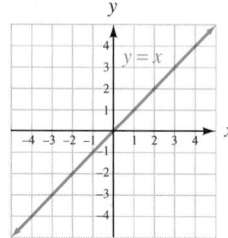   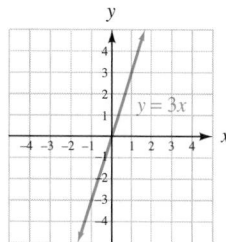

51. $y = -3x$ ▶ **52.** $y = -2x$

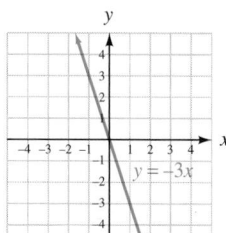   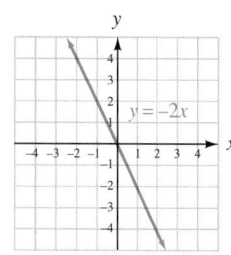

Solve each equation for y, find three solutions of the equation, and then draw its graph. **See Example 4.**

53. $2y = 4x - 6$ ▶ **54.** $3y = 6x - 3$

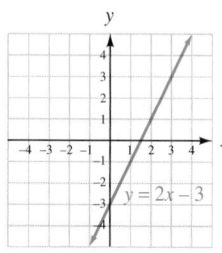   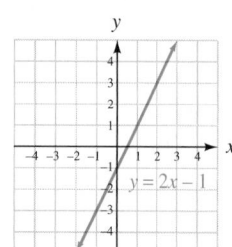

55. $2y = x - 4$ ▶ **56.** $4y = x + 16$

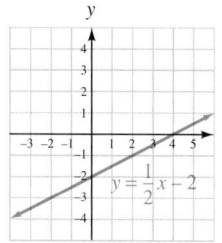   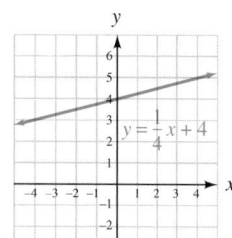

Graph each equation using the intercept method.
See Example 5.

57. $2y - 2x = 6$ ▶ **58.** $3x - 3y = 9$

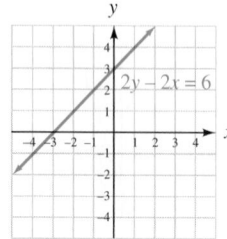   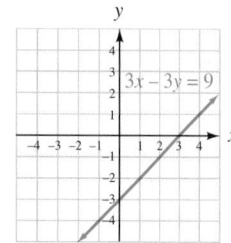

59. $4x + 5y = 20$ ▶ **60.** $3x + y = -3$

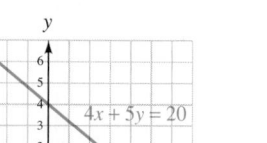   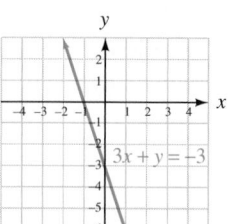

Graph each equation. **See Examples 6–7.**

61. $y = 4$ ▶ **62.** $y = -3$

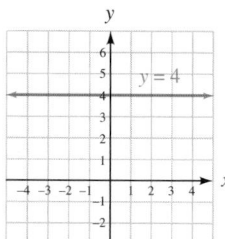   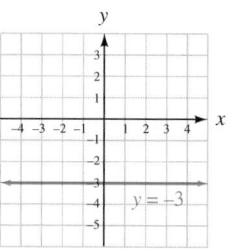

63. $x = -2$ ▶ **64.** $x = 5$

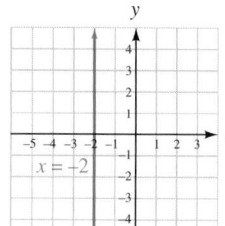   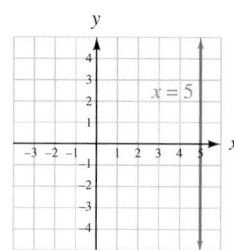

TRY IT YOURSELF

Graph each equation.

65. $15y + 5x = -15$ **66.** $8x + 4y = -24$

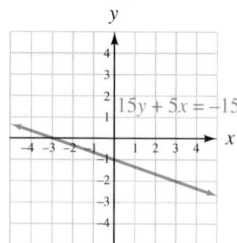   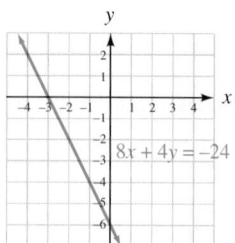

67. $3x + 4y = 8$ ▶ **68.** $2x + 3y = 9$

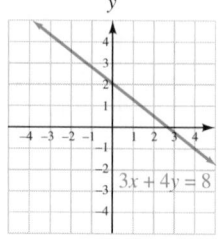   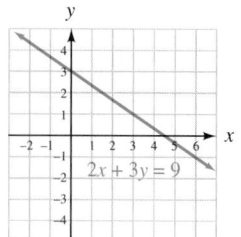

69. $y = \dfrac{x}{3}$

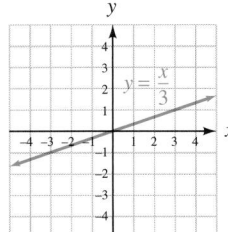

▶ **70.** $y = -\dfrac{x}{3} - 1$

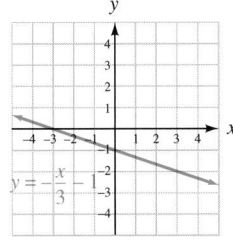

71. $-4y + 9x = -9$

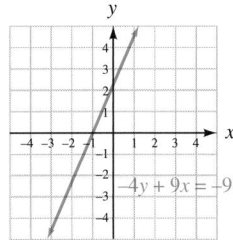

72. $-4y + 5x = -15$

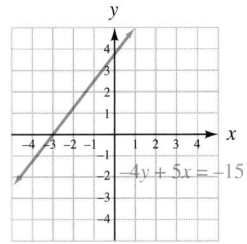

▶ **73.** $3x + 4y = 12$

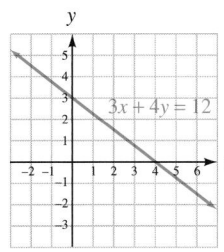

▶ **74.** $4x - 3y = 12$

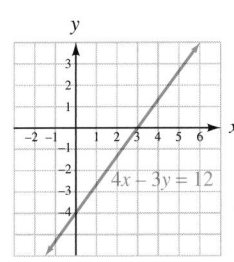

75. $y = -\dfrac{1}{2}$

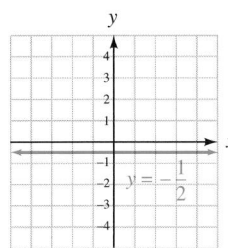

▶ **76.** $y = \dfrac{5}{2}$

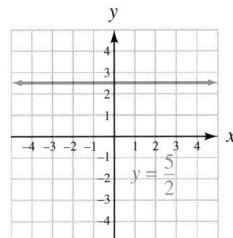

▶ **77.** $x = \dfrac{4}{3}$

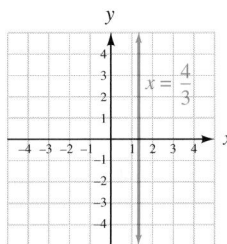

78. $x = -\dfrac{5}{3}$

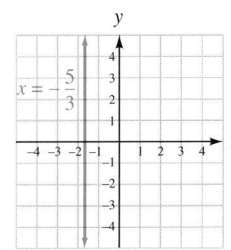

79. $y = -\dfrac{3}{2}x + 2$

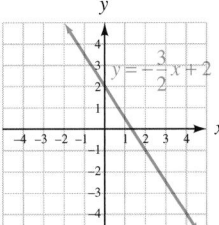

80. $y = \dfrac{2}{3}x - 2$

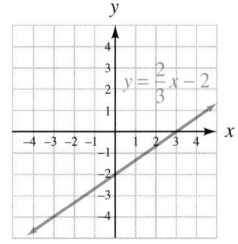

81. $2y + x = -2$

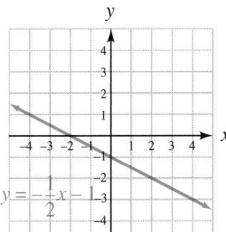

▶ **82.** $4y + 2x = -8$

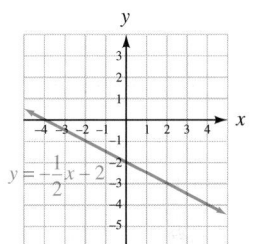

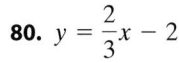
APPLICATIONS

▶ **83.** EDUCATION COSTS Each semester, a college charges a services fee of $50 plus $25 for each unit taken by a student.

   a. Write a linear equation that gives the total enrollment cost c for a student taking u units. $c = 50 + 25u$

   b. Complete the table of solutions below and graph the equation.

   c. Use the graph to find the total cost for a student taking 18 units the first semester and 12 units the second semester. $850

   d. What does the y-intercept of the line tell you? The service fee is $50.

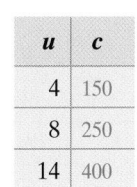 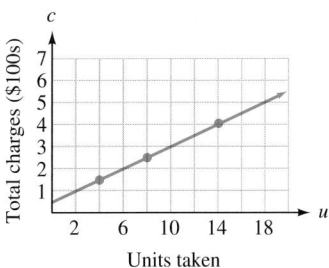

u	c
4	150
8	250
14	400

▶ **84.** GROUP RATES To promote the sale of tickets for a cruise to Alaska, a travel agency reduces the regular ticket price of $3,000 by $5 for each individual traveling in the group.

   a. Write a linear equation that would find the ticket price t for the cruise if a group of p people travel together. $t = 3{,}000 - 5p$

   b. Complete the table of solutions on the next page and graph the equation.

c. As the size of the group increases, what happens to the ticket price? It decreases.

d. Use the graph to determine the cost of an individual ticket if a group of 25 will be traveling together. $2,875

p	t
10	2,950
30	2,850
60	2,700

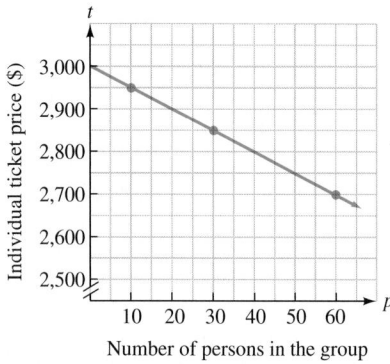

Number of persons in the group

85. PHYSIOLOGY Physiologists have found that a woman's height h (in inches) can be approximated using the linear equation $h = 3.9r + 28.9$, where r represents the length of her radius bone in inches.

a. Complete the table of solutions. Round to the nearest tenth and then graph the equation.

b. Complete this sentence: From the graph, we see that the longer the radius bone, the ...
taller the woman is.

c. From the graph, estimate the height of a woman whose radius bone is 7.5 inches long. 58 in.

r	h
7	56.2
8.5	62.1
9	64.0

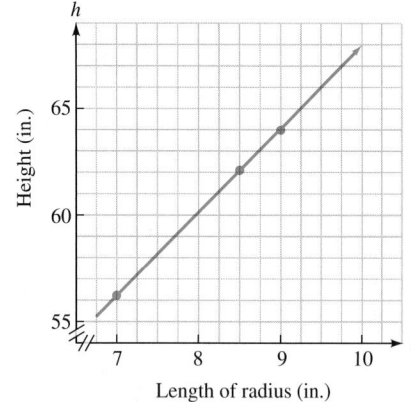

Length of radius (in.)

86. RESEARCH EXPERIMENTS A psychology major found that the time t (in seconds) that it took a white rat to complete a maze was related to the number of trials n the rat had been given. The resulting equation was $t = 25 - 0.25n$.

a. Complete the table of solutions and graph the equation.

b. Complete this sentence: From the graph, we see that the more trials the rat had, the ...
less time it took it to complete the maze.

c. From the graph, estimate the time it will take the rat to complete the maze on its 32nd trial. 17 sec

n	t
4	24
12	22
16	21

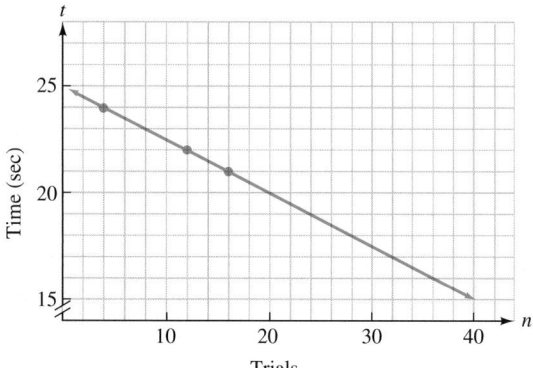

Trials

WRITING

87. A linear equation and a graph are two ways of mathematically describing a relationship between two quantities. Which do you think is more informative and why?

88. From geometry, we know that two points determine a line. Explain why it is a good practice when graphing linear equations to find and plot three points instead of just two.

89. How can we tell by looking at an equation whether its graph will be a straight line?

90. Can the x-intercept and the y-intercept of a line be the same point? Explain.

REVIEW

91. Simplify: $-(-5 - 4c)$ $5 + 4c$

92. Write the set of integers. $\{\dots, -3, -2, -1, 0, 1, 2, 3, \dots\}$

93. Solve: $\dfrac{x + 6}{2} = 1$ -4

94. Evaluate: $-2^2 + 2^2$ 0

95. Write a formula that relates profit, revenue, and costs. profit = revenue − costs

96. Find the volume, to the nearest tenth, of a sphere with radius 6 feet. 904.8 ft^3

97. Evaluate: $1 + 2[-3 - 4(2 - 8^2)]$ 491

98. Evaluate $\dfrac{x + y}{x - y}$ for $x = -2$ and $y = -4$. -3

SECTION 3.4

Rate of Change and the Slope of a Line

Since our world is one of constant change, we must be able to describe change so that we can plan for the future. In this section, we will show how to describe the amount of change of one quantity in relation to the amount of change of another quantity by finding a **rate of change.**

1 Find rates of change.

The line graph in figure (a) below shows the number of business permits issued each month by a city over a 12-month period. From the shape of the graph, we can see that the number of permits issued *increased* each month.

For situations such as the one graphed in (a), it is often useful to calculate a rate of increase (called a **rate of change**). We do so by finding the **ratio** of the change in the number of business permits issued each month to the number of months over which that change took place.

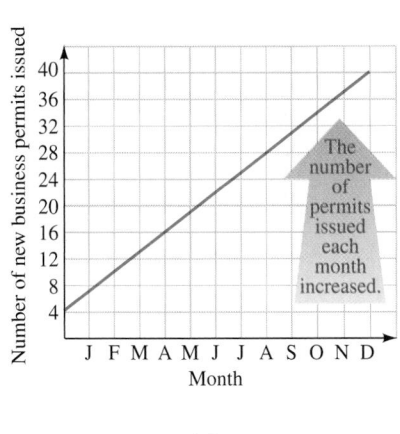

(a)

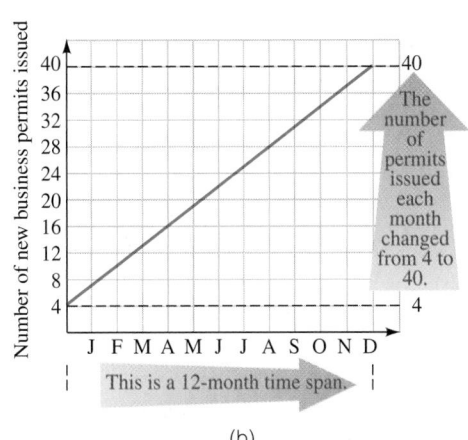

(b)

Ratios and Rates

A **ratio** is the quotient of two numbers or the quotient of two quantities with the same units. In symbols, if a and b represent two numbers, the ratio of a to b is $\frac{a}{b}$. Ratios that are used to compare quantities with different units are called **rates.**

In figure (b), we see that the number of permits issued prior to the month of January was 4. By the end of the year, the number of permits issued during the month of December was 40. This is a change of $40 - 4$, or 36, over a 12-month period. So we have

$$\text{Rate of change} = \frac{\text{change in number of permits issued each month}}{\text{change in time}} \qquad \textit{The rate of change is a ratio.}$$

$$= \frac{36 \text{ permits}}{12 \text{ months}}$$

$$= \frac{\overset{1}{\cancel{12}} \cdot 3 \text{ permits}}{\underset{1}{\cancel{12}} \text{ months}}$$

Factor 36 as 12 · 3 and remove the common factor of 12.

$$= \frac{3 \text{ permits}}{1 \text{ month}}$$

The number of business permits being issued increased at a rate of 3 per month, denoted as 3 permits/month.

> **The Language of Algebra** The preposition *per* means for each, or for every. When we say the rate of change is 3 permits *per* month, we mean 3 permits for each month.

Self Check 1

Find the rate of change in the number of subscribers over the second 5-year period. Write the rate in simplest form.

Now Try **Problem 25**
Self Check 1 Answer
40 subscribers/year

Teaching Example 1 Find the rate of change in the number of subscribers over the third 5-year period.
Answer:
−20 subscribers/year

EXAMPLE 1   The graph shows the number of subscribers to a newspaper. Find the rate of change in the number of subscribers over the first 5-year period. Write the rate in simplest form.

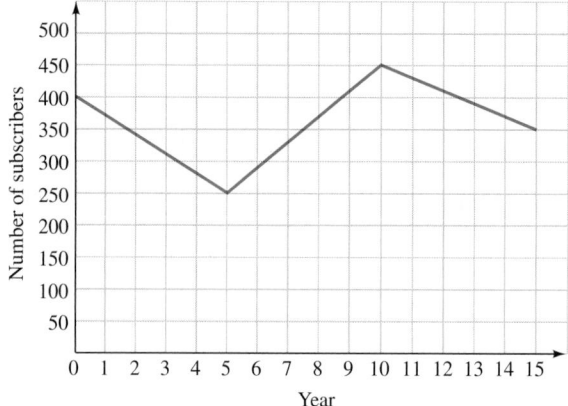

Strategy We will form a ratio of the change in the number of subscribers over the change in the time.

WHY The rate of change is given by this ratio.

Solution

$$\text{Rate of change} = \frac{\text{change in number of subscribers}}{\text{change in time}}$$

Set up the ratio.

$$= \frac{(250 - 400) \text{ subscribers}}{(5 - 0) \text{ years}}$$

Subtract the later number of subscribers from the earlier number of subscribers.

$$= \frac{-150 \text{ subscribers}}{5 \text{ years}}$$

$250 - 400 = -150$

$$= \frac{-30 \cdot \overset{1}{\cancel{5}} \text{ subscribers}}{\underset{1}{\cancel{5}} \text{ years}}$$

Factor −150 as −30 · 5 and divide out the common factor of 5.

$$= \frac{-30 \text{ subscribers}}{1 \text{ year}}$$

The number of subscribers for the first 5 years *decreased* by 30 per year, as indicated by the negative sign in the result. We can write this as −30 subscribers/year. ∎

2   Find the slope of a line from its graph.

The **slope of a nonvertical line** is a number that measures the line's steepness. We can calculate the slope by picking two points on the line and writing the ratio of the vertical change (called the **rise**) to the corresponding horizontal change (called the **run**) as we move from one point to the other. As an example, we will find the slope of the line that was used to describe the number of building permits issued and show that it gives the rate of change.

In the following figure, the line passes through points $P(0, 4)$ and $Q(12, 40)$. Moving along the line from point P to point Q causes the value of y to change from $y = 4$ to $y = 40$, an increase of $40 - 4 = 36$ units. We say that the *rise* is 36.

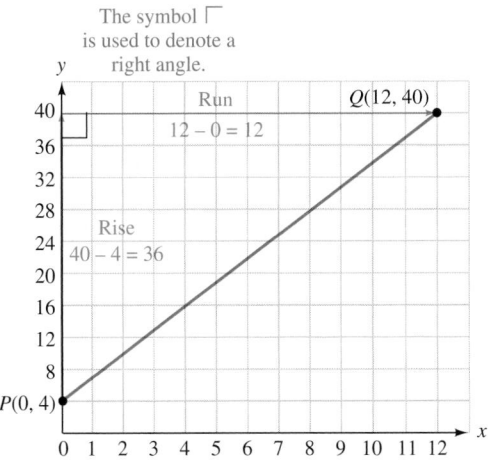

Moving from point P to point Q, the value of x increases from $x = 0$ to $x = 12$, an increase of $12 - 0 = 12$ units. We say that the *run* is 12. The slope of a line, usually denoted with the letter m, is defined to be the ratio of the change in y to the change in x.

$$m = \frac{\text{change in } y\text{-values}}{\text{change in } x\text{-values}}$$ Slope is a ratio.

$$= \frac{40 - 4}{12 - 0}$$ To find the change in y (the rise), subtract the y-values.
To find the change in x (the run), subtract the x-values.

$$= \frac{36}{12}$$ Perform the subtractions.

$$= 3$$ Perform the division.

This is the same value we obtained when we found the rate of change of the number of business permits issued over the 12-month period. Therefore, by finding the slope of the line, we found a rate of change.

EXAMPLE 2   Find the slope of the line shown in figure (a).

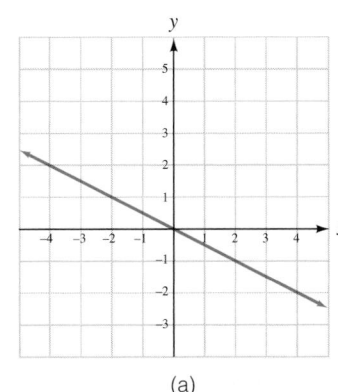

(a)

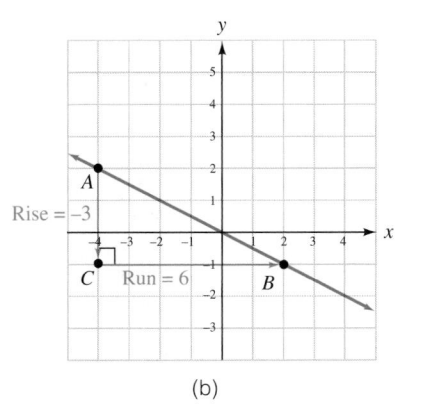

(b)

Self Check 2

Find the slope of the line using two points different from those used in Example 2. $-\frac{1}{2}$

Now Try Problem 27

Teaching Example 2 Find the slope of the line shown using $(-2, 1)$ and $(4, -2)$.
Answer:
The slope of the line is $-\frac{1}{2}$.

Strategy We will pick two points on the line, construct a slope triangle, and find the rise and the run. Then we will write the ratio of the rise to the run.

WHY The slope of a line is the ratio of the rise to the run.

Solution

We begin by choosing two points on the line—call them *A* and *B*—as shown in figure (b). One way to move from point *A* to point *B* is to start at point *A* and count *downward* 3 grid squares. Because this movement is downward, the rise is −3. Then, moving right, we count 6 grid squares to reach *B*. This indicates a run of 6. To find the slope of the line, we write a ratio of rise to run in simplified form. Usually the letter *m* is used to denote slope, so we have

$$m = \frac{\text{rise}}{\text{run}}$$ The slope of a line is the ratio of the rise to the run.

$$m = \frac{-3}{6}$$ From the slope triangle, the rise is −3 and the run is 6.

$$m = -\frac{1}{2}$$ Simplify the fraction.

The slope of the line is $-\frac{1}{2}$.

Success Tip The answers from Example 2 and the Self Check illustrate an important fact about slope: *The same value for the slope of a line will result no matter which two points on the line are used to determine the rise and the run.*

---

3 Find the slope of a line given two points.

We can generalize the graphic method for finding slope to develop a slope formula. To begin, we select points *P* and *Q* on the line shown in the figure below. To distinguish between the coordinates of these points, we use **subscript notation.** Point *P* has coordinates (x_1, y_1), which are read as "*x* sub 1 and *y* sub 1." Point *Q* has coordinates (x_2, y_2), which are read as "*x* sub 2 and *y* sub 2."

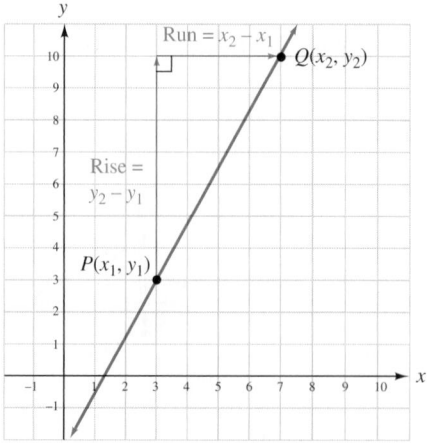

As we move from P to Q, the rise is the difference of the y-coordinates: $y_2 - y_1$. We call this difference the **change in y.** The run is the difference of the x-coordinates: $x_2 - x_1$. This difference is called the **change in x.** Since the slope is the ratio $\frac{\text{rise}}{\text{run}}$, we have the following formula for calculating slope.

Slope of a Nonvertical Line

The **slope** of a nonvertical line passing through points (x_1, y_1) and (x_2, y_2) is

$$m = \frac{\text{vertical change}}{\text{horizontal change}} = \frac{\text{rise}}{\text{run}} = \frac{\text{change in } y}{\text{change in } x} = \frac{y_2 - y_1}{x_2 - x_1} \qquad \text{if } x_2 \neq x_1$$

EXAMPLE 3   Find the slope of the line passing through $(1, 2)$ and $(3, 8)$.

Strategy   We will use the slope formula to find the slope of the line.

WHY   We know the coordinates of two points on the line.

Solution

When using the slope formula, it makes no difference which point you call (x_1, y_1) and which point you call (x_2, y_2). If we let (x_1, y_1) be $(1, 2)$ and (x_2, y_2) be $(3, 8)$, then

$$m = \frac{y_2 - y_1}{x_2 - x_1} \qquad \text{This is the slope formula.}$$

$$m = \frac{8 - 2}{3 - 1} \qquad \text{Substitute 8 for } y_2, 2 \text{ for } y_1, 3 \text{ for } x_2, \text{ and 1 for } x_1.$$

$$m = \frac{6}{2} \qquad \text{Do the subtractions.}$$

$$m = 3 \qquad \text{Simplify. Think of this as a } \frac{3}{1} \text{ rise-to-run ratio.}$$

The slope of the line is 3. The graph of the line, including the slope triangle, is shown here. Note that we obtain the same value for the slope if we let $(x_1, y_1) = (3, 8)$ and $(x_2, y_2) = (1, 2)$.

$$m = \frac{y_2 - y_1}{x_2 - x_1} = \frac{2 - 8}{1 - 3} = \frac{-6}{-2} = 3$$

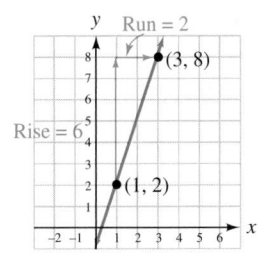

Self Check 3

Find the slope of the line passing through $(2, 1)$ and $(4, 11)$. 5

Now Try **Problem 33**

Teaching Example 3 Find the slope of the line passing through $(-2, -1)$ and $(5, 1)$.
Answer:
$\frac{2}{7}$

Caution!   When finding the slope of a line, always subtract the y-values and the x-values in the same order. Otherwise your answer will have the wrong sign:

$$m \neq \frac{y_2 - y_1}{x_1 - x_2} \qquad \text{and} \qquad m \neq \frac{y_1 - y_2}{x_2 - x_1}$$

THINK IT THROUGH   *Average Rate of Tuition Increase*

"Whatever happens in the future to the economy, whether up or down or more of the same, all current predictions point to a continuing rise over the coming decade in the cost of college education."

Daniel Silver in Show Me the Money, *News-Tribune*

The line graphed below approximates the average cost of tuition and fees at U.S. public two-year academic institutions for the years 1990–2003. Find the average rate of increase in cost over this time period by finding the slope of the line. $65 per year

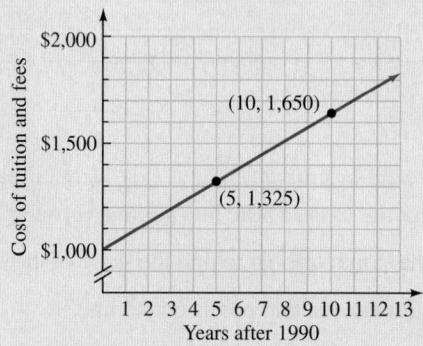

Source: The College Board

Self Check 4

Find the slope of the line that passes through $(-1, -2)$ and $(1, -7)$. $-\frac{5}{2}$

Now Try **Problem 39**

Teaching Example 4 Find the slope of the line that passes through $(3, -7)$ and $(1, -1)$.
Answer:
-3

EXAMPLE 4   Find the slope of the line that passes through $(-2, 4)$ and $(5, -6)$ and draw its graph.

Strategy We will use the slope formula to find the slope of the line.

WHY We know the coordinates of two points on the line.

Solution

Since we know the coordinates of two points on the line, we can find its slope. If (x_1, y_1) is $(-2, 4)$ and (x_2, y_2) is $(5, -6)$, then

$$x_1 = -2 \quad \text{and} \quad x_2 = 5$$
$$y_1 = 4 \qquad\qquad y_2 = -6$$

$$m = \frac{y_2 - y_1}{x_2 - x_1} \qquad \text{This is the slope formula.}$$

$$m = \frac{-6 - 4}{5 - (-2)} \qquad \text{Substitute } -6 \text{ for } y_2, 4 \text{ for } y_1, 5 \text{ for } x_2, \text{ and } -2 \text{ for } x_1.$$

$$m = -\frac{10}{7} \qquad \begin{array}{l}\text{Simplify the numerator: } -6 - 4 = -10.\\ \text{Simplify the denominator: } 5 - (-2) = 7.\end{array}$$

The slope of the line is $-\frac{10}{7}$. The figure below shows the graph of the line. Note that the line falls from left to right—a fact that is indicated by its negative slope.

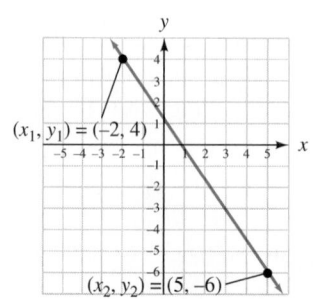

4 Recognize positive and negative slope.

In Example 3, the slope of the line was positive (3). In Example 4, the slope of the line was negative $\left(-\frac{10}{7}\right)$. In general, lines that rise from left to right have a positive slope, and lines that fall from left to right have a negative slope, as shown below.

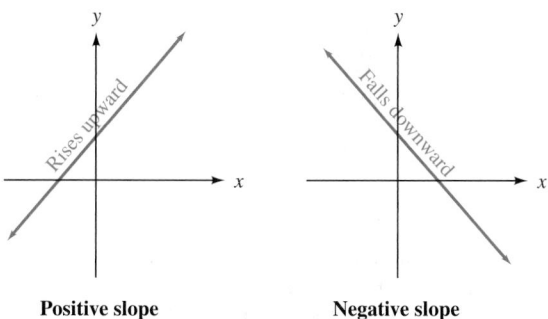

Positive slope   **Negative slope**

5 Find slopes of horizontal and vertical lines.

In the next two examples, we will calculate the slope of a horizontal line and show that a vertical line has no defined slope.

EXAMPLE 5 Find the slope of the line $y = 3$.

Strategy We will find the coordinates of two points on the line.

WHY We can then use the slope formula to find the slope of the line.

Solution

To find the slope of the line $y = 3$, we need to know two points on the line. Graph the horizontal line $y = 3$ and label two points on the line: $(-2, 3)$ and $(3, 3)$.

If (x_1, y_1) is $(-2, 3)$ and (x_2, y_2) is $(3, 3)$, we have

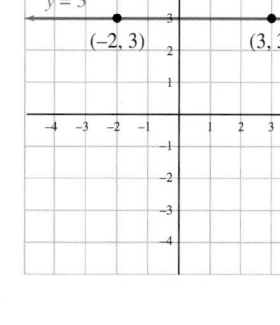

$$m = \frac{y_2 - y_1}{x_2 - x_1} \qquad \text{This is the slope formula.}$$

$$m = \frac{3 - 3}{3 - (-2)} \qquad \text{Substitute 3 for } y_2, \text{ 3 for } y_1, \text{ 3 for } x_2, \text{ and } -2 \text{ for } x_1.$$

$$m = \frac{0}{5} \qquad \text{Simplify the numerator and the denominator.}$$

$$m = 0$$

The slope of the line $y = 3$ is 0.

The y-coordinates of any two points on any horizontal line will be the same, and the x-values will be different. Thus, the numerator of $\frac{y_2 - y_1}{x_2 - x_1}$ will always be zero, and the denominator will always be nonzero. Therefore, the slope of a horizontal line is zero.

EXAMPLE 6 If possible, find the slope of the line $x = -2$.

Strategy We will find the coordinates of two points on the line.

WHY We can then use the slope formula to find the slope of the line, if it exists.

Self Check 5

Find the slope of the line $y = -2$. 0

Now Try **Problem 45**

Teaching Example 5 Find the slope of the line $y = -4$.
Answer:
0

Self Check 6

Find the slope of $x = 5$. undefined

Now Try **Problem 47**

Solution

To find the slope of the line $x = -2$, we need to know two points on the line. We graph the vertical line $x = -2$ and label two points on the line: $(-2, -1)$ and $(-2, 3)$.

If (x_1, y_1) is $(-2, -1)$ and (x_2, y_2) is $(-2, 3)$, we have

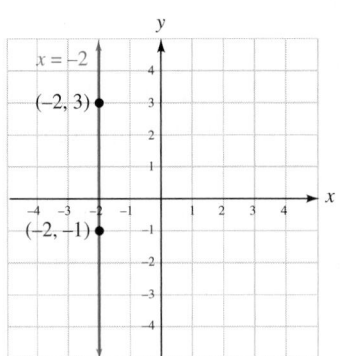

$$m = \frac{y_2 - y_1}{x_2 - x_1}$$ This is the slope formula.

$$m = \frac{3 - (-1)}{-2 - (-2)}$$ Substitute 3 for y_2, -1 for y_1, -2 for x_2, and -2 for x_1.

$$m = \frac{4}{0}$$ Simplify the numerator and the denominator.

Since division by zero is undefined, $\frac{4}{0}$ has no meaning. The slope of the line $x = -2$ is undefined.

The y-values of any two points on a vertical line will be different, and the x-values will be the same. Thus, the numerator of $\frac{y_2 - y_1}{x_2 - x_1}$ will always be nonzero, and the denominator will always be zero. Therefore, the slope of a vertical line is undefined.

We now summarize the results from Examples 5 and 6.

Slopes of Horizontal and Vertical Lines

Horizontal lines (lines with equations of the form $y = b$) have a slope of 0.

Vertical lines (lines with equations of the form $x = a$) have undefined slope.

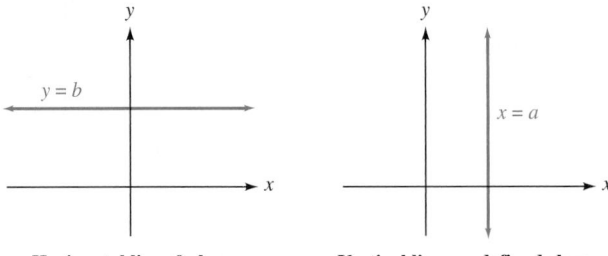

Horizontal line: 0 slope   **Vertical line: undefined slope**

6 Use slope to graph a line.

We can graph a line whenever we know the coordinates of one point on the line and the slope of the line. For example, to graph the line that passes through $P(2, 4)$ and has a slope of 3, we first plot $P(2, 4)$, as in the figure. We can express the slope of 3 as a fraction: $3 = \frac{3}{1}$. Therefore, the line *rises* 3 units for every 1 unit it *runs* to the right. We can find a second point on the line by starting at $P(2, 4)$ and moving 3 units up (rise) and 1 unit to the right (run). This brings us to a point that we will call Q with coordinates $(2 + 1, 4 + 3)$ or $(3, 7)$. The required line passes through points P and Q.

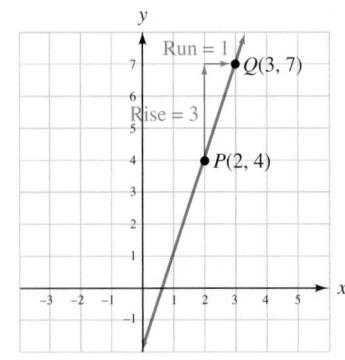

EXAMPLE 7   Graph the line that passes through the point $(-3, 4)$ with slope $-\frac{2}{5}$.

Strategy   We will plot the given point and identify the rise and the run of the slope. Then we will start at the plotted point and find a second point on the line by forming a slope triangle.

WHY   Once we locate two points on the line, we can draw the graph of the line.

Solution

We plot the point $(-3, 4)$ as shown in the figure to the right. Then, after writing the slope $-\frac{2}{5}$ as $\frac{-2}{5}$, we see that the *rise* is -2 and the *run* is 5. From the point $(-3, 4)$, we can find a second point on the line by moving 2 units down (rise) and then 5 units right (run). (A rise of -2 means to move down 2 units.) This brings us to the point with coordinates of $(2, 2)$. We then draw a line that passes through the two points.

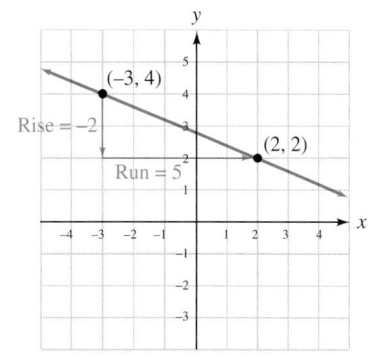

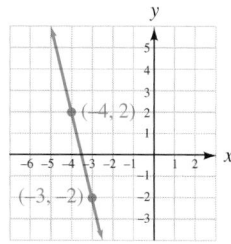
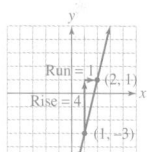
7   Determine whether lines are parallel or perpendicular using slope.

Two lines that lie in the same plane but do not intersect are called **parallel lines.** Parallel lines have the same slope and different y-intercepts. For example, the lines graphed in figure (a) are parallel because they both have slope $-\frac{2}{3}$.

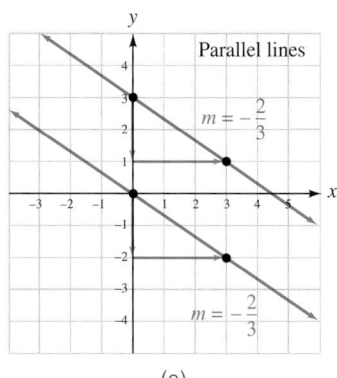

(a)

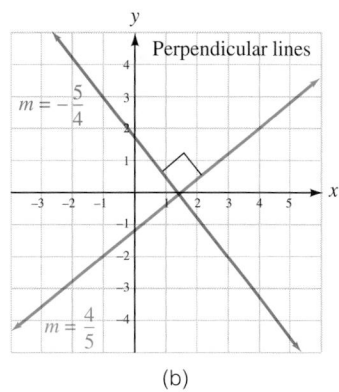

(b)

Lines that intersect to form four right angles (angles with measure $90°$) are called **perpendicular lines.** If the product of the slopes of two lines is -1, the lines are perpendicular. This means that the slopes are **negative** (or **opposite**) **reciprocals.** In figure (b), we know that the lines with slopes $\frac{4}{5}$ and $-\frac{5}{4}$ are perpendicular because

$$\frac{4}{5}\left(-\frac{5}{4}\right) = -\frac{20}{20} = -1 \qquad \text{$\frac{4}{5}$ and $-\frac{5}{4}$ are negative reciprocals.}$$

Slopes of Parallel and Perpendicular Lines

1. Two lines with the same slope are parallel.

2. Two lines are perpendicular if the product of the slopes is -1; that is, if their slopes are negative reciprocals.

3. Any horizontal line and any vertical line are perpendicular.

Self Check 8

Determine whether the line that passes through $(2, 1)$ and $(6, 8)$ and the line that passes through $(-1, 0)$ and $(4, 7)$ are parallel, perpendicular, or neither.   neither

Now Try Problems 57 and 59

Teaching Example 8 Determine whether the line that passes through $(1, 4)$ and $(5, -2)$ and the line that passes through $(6, 2)$ and $(9, 4)$ are parallel, perpendicular, or neither.
Answer:
perpendicular

EXAMPLE 8   Determine whether the line that passes through $(7, -9)$ and $(10, 2)$ and the line that passes through $(0, 1)$ and $(3, 12)$ are parallel, perpendicular, or neither.

Strategy We will use the slope formula to find the slope of each line.

WHY If the slopes are equal, the lines are parallel. If the slopes are negative reciprocals, the lines are perpendicular. Otherwise, the lines are neither parallel nor perpendicular.

Solution
To calculate the slope of each line, we use the slope formula.

The line through $(7, -9)$ and $(10, 2)$:   *The line through $(0, 1)$ and $(3, 12)$:*

$$m = \frac{y_2 - y_1}{x_2 - x_1} = \frac{2 - (-9)}{10 - 7} = \frac{11}{3} \qquad m = \frac{y_2 - y_1}{x_2 - x_1} = \frac{12 - 1}{3 - 0} = \frac{11}{3}$$

Since the slopes are the same, the lines are parallel.

Self Check 9

Find the slope of a line perpendicular to the line passing through $(-4, 1)$ and $(9, 5)$. $-\frac{13}{4}$

Now Try Problem 67

Teaching Example 9 Find the slope of a line perpendicular to the line passing through $(-3, 4)$ and $(5, 7)$.
Answer:
$-\frac{8}{3}$

EXAMPLE 9   Find the slope of a line perpendicular to the line passing through $(1, -4)$ and $(8, 4)$.

Strategy We will use the slope formula to find the slope of the line passing through $(1, -4)$ and $(8, 4)$.

WHY We can then form the negative reciprocal of the result to produce the slope of a line perpendicular to the given line.

Solution
The slope of the line that passes through $(1, -4)$ and $(8, 4)$ is

$$m = \frac{y_2 - y_1}{x_2 - x_1} = \frac{4 - (-4)}{8 - 1} = \frac{8}{7}$$

The slope of a line perpendicular to the given line has slope that is the negative (or opposite) reciprocal of $\frac{8}{7}$, which is $-\frac{7}{8}$.

ANSWERS TO SELF CHECKS

1. 40 subscribers/year   **2.** $-\frac{1}{2}$ **3.** 5   **4.** $-\frac{5}{2}$ **5.** 0   **6.** undefined

7.   **8.** neither   **9.** $-\frac{13}{4}$

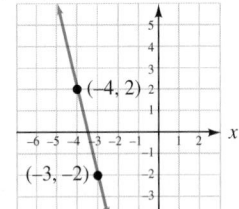

SECTION 3.4   STUDY SET

VOCABULARY

Fill in the blanks.

1. A __ratio__ is the quotient of two numbers.

2. Ratios used to compare quantities with different units are called __rates__.

3. The __slope__ of a line is defined to be the ratio of the change in y to the change in x.

4. The vertical change between two points on a coordinate system is often called the _rise_.

5. The horizontal change between two points on a coordinate system is often called the _run_.

▶ **6.** $m = \dfrac{\text{vertical change}}{\text{horizontal change}} = \dfrac{rise}{run} = \dfrac{\text{change in } y}{\text{change in } x}$

7. Two lines that lie in the same plane but do not intersect are called _parallel_ lines.

8. The rate of _change_ of a linear relationship can be found by finding the slope of the graph of the line.

CONCEPTS

Fill in the blanks.

9. _Horizontal_ lines have a slope of 0.

10. Vertical lines have _undefined_ slope.

▶ **11.** A line with positive slope _rises_ from left to right.

▶ **12.** A line with negative slope _falls_ from left to right.

In the following illustration, which line has

▶ **13.** a positive slope? l_2

▶ **14.** a negative slope? l_1

▶ **15.** zero slope? l_4

▶ **16.** undefined slope? l_3

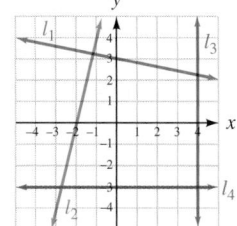

Consider the graph of the line in the following illustration:

17. Find its slope using points A and B. $\frac{1}{2}$

18. Find its slope using points B and C. $\frac{1}{2}$

19. Find its slope using points A and C. $\frac{1}{2}$

20. What observation is suggested by your answers to parts a, b, and c?
When finding the slope of a line, any two points on the line give the same result.

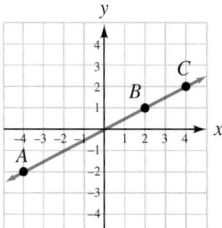

21. The following table shows the coordinates of two points on a line. Use the information to determine the slope of the graph of the line. -1

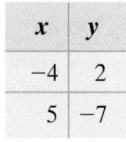

x	y
−4	2
5	−7

22. GROWTH RATES Use the graph to find the rate of change of a boy's height during the time shown. 3 in./yr

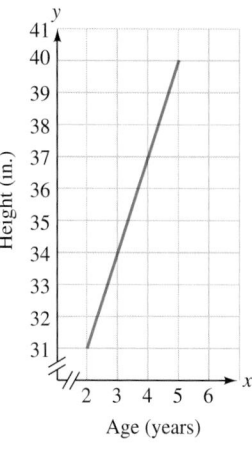

NOTATION

▶ **23.** Write the formula used to find the slope of the line passing through (x_1, y_1) and (x_2, y_2). $m = \dfrac{y_2 - y_1}{x_2 - x_1}$

▶ **24.** Explain the difference between y^2 and y_2.
y^2 means $y \cdot y$ and y_2 means y sub 2.

GUIDED PRACTICE

Find the slope of each line. See Examples 1–2.

25.

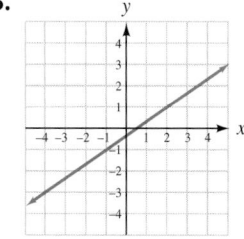

$m = \dfrac{2}{3}$

26.

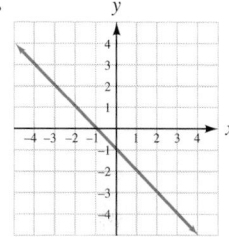

$m = -1$

27.

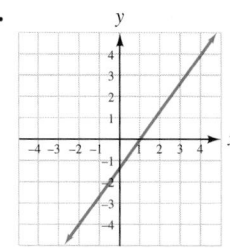

$m = \dfrac{4}{3}$

28.

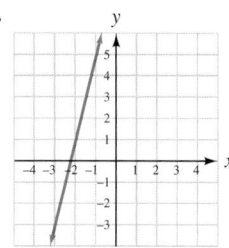

$m = 4$

▶ **29.**

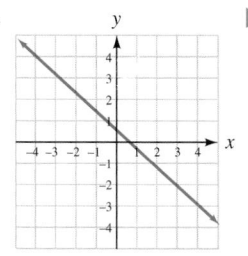

$m = -\dfrac{7}{8}$

▶ **30.**

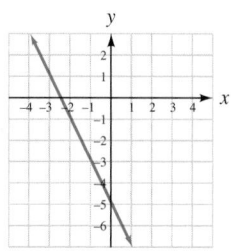

$m = -2$

31.
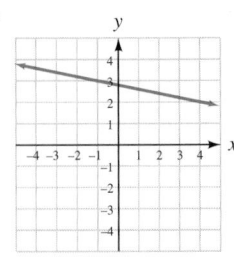
$m = -\frac{1}{5}$

32.
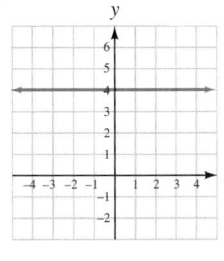
$m = 0$

Find the slope of the line passing through the given points, when possible. **See Examples 3–4.**

33. $(2, 4)$ and $(1, 3)$
1

▶ **34.** $(1, 3)$ and $(2, 5)$
2

35. $(3, 4)$ and $(2, 7)$
-3

▶ **36.** $(3, 6)$ and $(5, 2)$
-2

37. $(0, 0)$ and $(4, 5)$
$\frac{5}{4}$

38. $(4, 3)$ and $(7, 8)$
$\frac{5}{3}$

39. $(-3, 5)$ and $(-5, 6)$
$-\frac{1}{2}$

▶ **40.** $(6, -2)$ and $(-3, 2)$
$-\frac{4}{9}$

41. $(5, 7)$ and $(-4, 7)$
0

▶ **42.** $(-1, -12)$ and $(6, -12)$
0

43. $(8, -4)$ and $(8, -3)$
undefined

▶ **44.** $(-2, 8)$ and $(-2, 15)$
undefined

Find the slope of each line, if possible. **See Examples 5–6.**

▶ **45.** $y = 5$ 0

46. $x = -5$ undefined

▶ **47.** $x = 4$ undefined

48. $y = -7$ 0

Graph the line that passes through the given point and has the given slope. **See Example 7.**

49. $(0, 0), m = -4$

50. $(0, 0), m = 5$

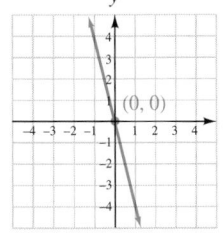

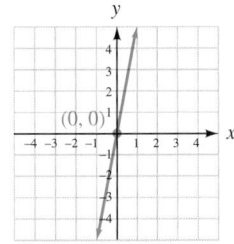

51. $(-3, -3), m = -\dfrac{3}{2}$

▶ **52.** $(-2, -1), m = \dfrac{4}{3}$

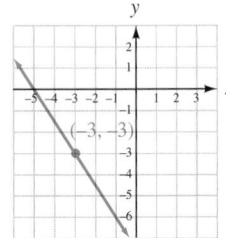

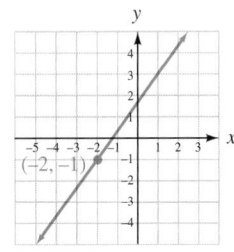

53. $(-5, 1), m = 0$

54. $(0, 3)$, undefined slope

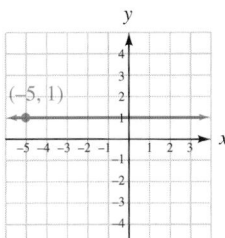

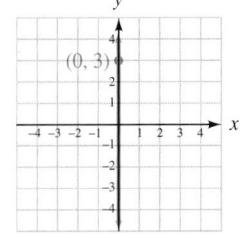

▶ **55.** $(-1, -4)$, undefined slope

56. $(-3, -2), m = 0$

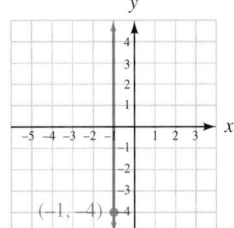

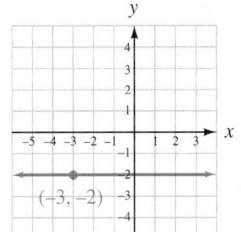

Determine whether the lines through each pair of points are parallel, perpendicular, or neither. **See Example 8.**

▶ **57.** $(5, 3)$ and $(1, 4)$
$(-3, -4)$ and $(1, -5)$
parallel

58. $(2, 4)$ and $(-1, -1)$
$(8, 0)$ and $(11, 5)$
parallel

▶ **59.** $(-4, -2)$ and $(2, -3)$
$(7, 1)$ and $(8, 7)$
perpendicular

60. $(-2, 4)$ and $(6, -7)$
$(-6, 4)$ and $(5, 12)$
perpendicular

61. $(2, 2)$ and $(4, -3)$
$(-3, 4)$ and $(-1, 9)$
neither

62. $(-1, -3)$ and $(2, 4)$
$(5, 2)$ and $(8, -5)$
neither

63. $(4, 2)$ and $(5, -3)$
$(-5, 3)$ and $(-2, 9)$
neither

64. $(8, -3)$ and $(8, -8)$
$(11, 3)$ and $(22, 3)$
perpendicular

Find the slope of a line perpendicular to the line passing through the given two points. **See Example 9.**

▶ **65.** $(0, 0)$ and $(5, -9)$ $\frac{5}{9}$

66. $(0, 0)$ and $(5, 12)$ $-\frac{5}{12}$

67. $(-1, 7)$ and $(1, 10)$ $-\frac{2}{3}$

68. $(-7, 6)$ and $(0, 4)$ $\frac{7}{2}$

▌ APPLICATIONS

▶ **69.** POOL DESIGN Find the slope of the bottom of the swimming pool as it drops off from the shallow end to the deep end, as shown. $-\frac{2}{5}$

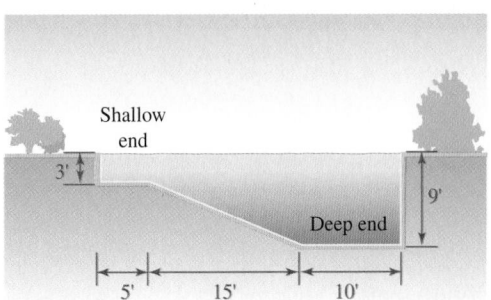

70. DRAINAGE To measure the amount of fall (slope) of a concrete patio slab, a 10-foot-long 2-by-4, a 1-foot ruler, and a level were used. Find the amount of fall in the slab. Explain what it means. $\frac{1}{40}$, 1-in. fall for every 40 in. of horizontal run

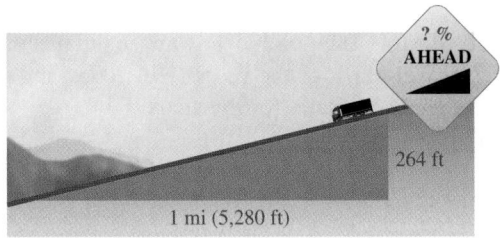

Patio slab

71. GRADE OF A ROAD The vertical fall of the road shown is 264 feet for a horizontal run of 1 mile. Find the slope of the decline and use that fact to complete the roadside warning sign for truckers. (*Hint:* 1 mile = 5,280 feet.) $\frac{1}{20}$, 5%

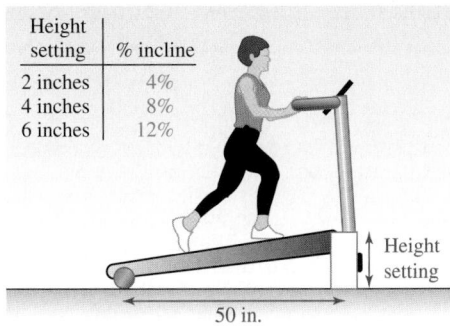

? %
AHEAD

264 ft

1 mi (5,280 ft)

72. TREADMILLS For each height setting listed in the table, find the resulting slope of the jogging surface of the treadmill below. Express each incline as a percent.

Height setting	% incline
2 inches	4%
4 inches	8%
6 inches	12%

Height setting

50 in.

73. ACCESSIBILITY The illustration in the next column shows two designs to make the upper level of a stadium wheelchair-accessible.

  a. Find the slope of the ramp in design 1. $\frac{1}{8}$

  b. Find the slopes of the ramps in design 2. $\frac{1}{12}$

c. Give one advantage and one drawback of each design. 1: less expensive, steeper; 2: not as steep, more expensive

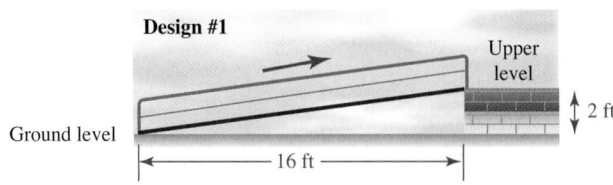

Design #1
Ground level
Upper level
2 ft
16 ft

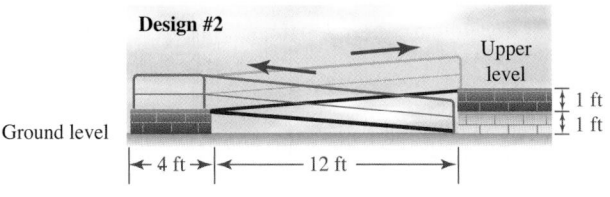

Design #2
Ground level
Upper level
1 ft
1 ft
4 ft
12 ft

74. IRRIGATION The following graph shows the number of gallons of water remaining in a reservoir as water is discharged from it to irrigate a field. Find the rate of change in the number of gallons of water for the time the field was being irrigated. −875 gal/hr

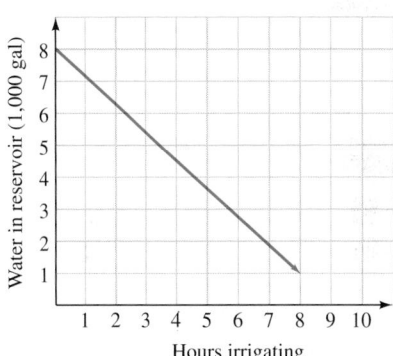

Water in reservoir (1,000 gal)

Hours irrigating

75. DEPRECIATION The following graph shows how the value of some sound equipment decreased over the years. Find the rate of change of its value during this time. −$2,500/year

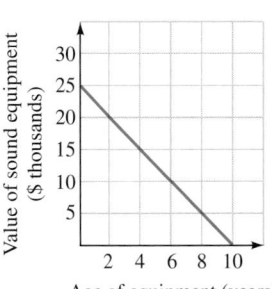

Value of sound equipment ($ thousands)

Age of equipment (years)

76. ARCHITECTURE Locate the coordinates of the peak of the roof if it is to have a pitch of $\frac{2}{5}$ and the roof line is to pass through the two points in black. (10, 10)

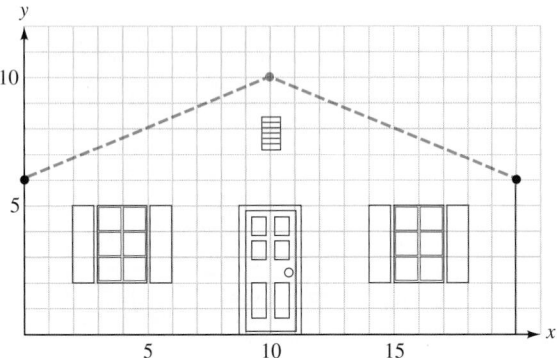

77. ENGINE OUTPUT Use the graph below to find the rate of change in the horsepower (hp) produced by an automobile engine for engine speeds in the range of 2,400 − 4,800 revolutions per minute (rpm). 3 hp/40 rpm

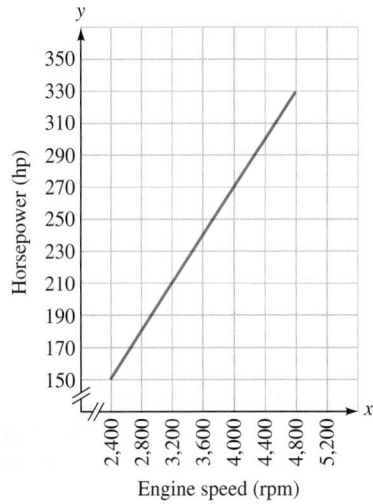

78. COMMERCIAL JETS Examine the graph and consider trips of more than 7,000 miles by a Boeing 777. Use a rate of change to estimate how the maximum payload decreases as the distance traveled increases. −15 lb/mi

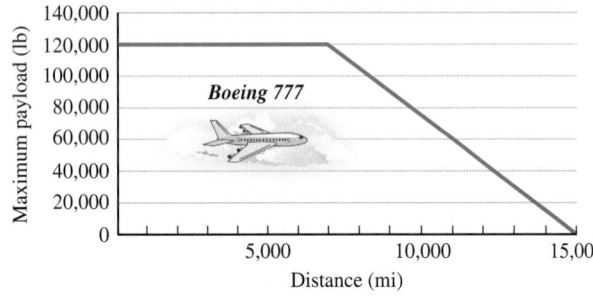

Based on data from Lawrence Livermore National Laboratory and *Los Angeles Times* (October 22, 1998).

79. MILK PRODUCTION The following graph approximates the amount of milk produced per cow in the United States for the years 1996–2005. Find the rate of change. 380 lb/yr

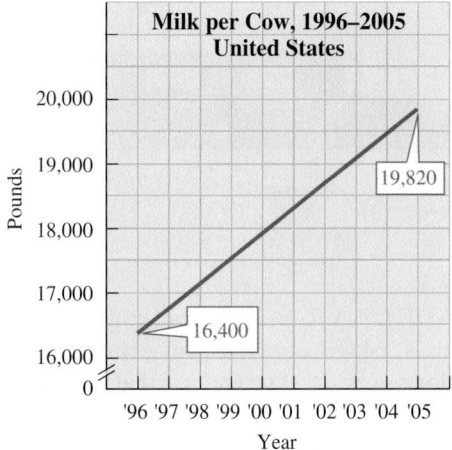

Source: United States Department of Agriculture

80. WAL-MART The graph below approximates the net sales of Wal-Mart for the years 1991–2006. Find the rate of change in sales for the years

    a. 1991–1998 $11 billion per year

    b. 1998–2006 $25 billion per year

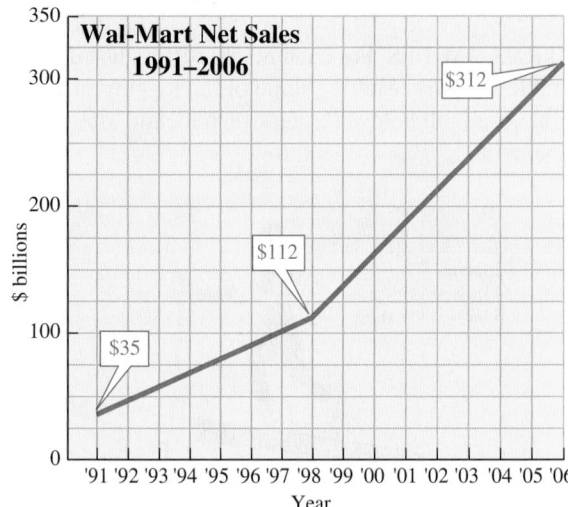

Based on data from the Wal-Mart 2006 Financial Summary

▌ WRITING

81. Explain why the slope of a vertical line is undefined.

82. How do we distinguish between a line with positive slope and a line with negative slope?

83. Give an example of a rate of change that government officials might be interested in knowing so they can plan for the future needs of our country.

84. Explain the difference between a rate of change that is positive and one that is negative. Give an example of each.

85. In what quadrant does the point $(-3, 6)$ lie? quadrant II

▶ **86.** What is the name given the point $(0, 0)$? origin

87. Is $(-1, -2)$ a solution of $y = x^2 + 1$? no

88. What basic shape does the graph of the equation $y = |x - 2|$ have? V-shape

89. Is the equation $y = 2x + 2$ linear or nonlinear? linear

▶ **90.** Solve: $-3x \leq 15$ $x \geq -5$

SECTION 3.5

Slope–Intercept Form

Objectives

1 Use slope–intercept form to identify the slope and y-intercept of a line.

2 Write a linear equation in slope–intercept form.

3 Use the slope and y-intercept to graph a linear equation.

4 Recognize parallel and perpendicular lines.

5 Use slope–intercept form to write an equation to model data.

Of all the ways in which a linear equation can be written, one form, called *slope–intercept form,* is probably the most useful. When an equation is written in this form, two important features of its graph are evident.

1 Use slope–intercept form to identify the slope and y-intercept of a line.

The graph of $y = -\frac{2}{3}x + 4$ shown in the figure enables us to see that the slope of the line is $-\frac{2}{3}$ and that the y-intercept is $(0, 4)$.

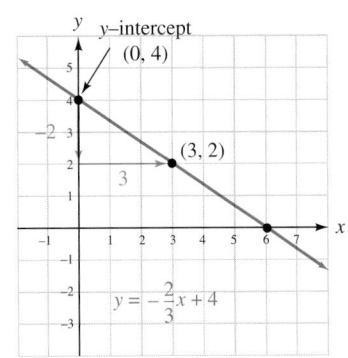

$y = -\frac{2}{3}x + 4$		
x	y	(x, y)
0	4	$(0, 4)$
3	2	$(3, 2)$

To find the slope of the line, we pick two points on the line, $(0, 4)$ and $(3, 2)$; draw a slope triangle; and count grid squares:

$$\text{slope} = \frac{\text{rise}}{\text{run}} = \frac{-2}{3} = -\frac{2}{3}$$

From the equation and the graph, we can make two observations:

- The graph crosses the y-axis at 4. This is the same as the constant term in $y = -\frac{2}{3}x + 4$

- The slope of the line is $-\frac{2}{3}$. This is the same as the coefficient of x in $y = -\frac{2}{3}x + 4$

$$y = -\frac{2}{3}x + 4$$

The slope of the line. is $-\frac{2}{3}$.   The y-intercept is $(0, 4)$.

These observations suggest the following form of an equation of a line.

Slope-Intercept Form of the Equation of a Line

If a linear equation is written in the form

$$y = mx + b$$

the graph of the equation is a line with slope m and y-intercept $(0, b)$.

Find the slope and the
y-intercept:
a. $y = -5x - 1$ $m = -5, (0, -1)$

b. $y = \dfrac{7}{8}x$ $m = \frac{7}{8}, (0, 0)$

c. $y = 5 - \dfrac{x}{3}$ $m = -\frac{1}{3}, (0, 5)$

Now Try Problems 33 and 36

Teaching Example 1 Find the slope
and the y-intercept:
a. $y = 7x + 3$
b. $y = \frac{3}{5}x$
c. $y = 6 - \frac{2x}{3}$
Answers:
a. $m = 7, (0, 3)$
b. $m = \frac{3}{5}, (0, 0)$
c. $m = -\frac{2}{3}, (0, 6)$

EXAMPLE 1   Find the slope and the y-intercept of the graph of each equation:

a. $y = 6x - 2$ **b.** $y = -\dfrac{5}{4}x$ **c.** $y = \dfrac{x}{2} + 6$

Strategy We will write each equation in slope–intercept form, $y = mx + b$.

WHY When the linear equations are written in slope–intercept form, the slope and
the y-intercept of their graphs become apparent.

Solution
a. If we write the subtraction as the addition of the opposite, the equation will be
in $y = mx + b$ form:

$$y = 6x + (-2)$$

Since $m = 6$ and $b = -2$, the slope of the line is 6 and the y-intercept is
$(0, -2)$.

b. Writing $y = -\frac{5}{4}x$ in slope–intercept form, we have

$$y = -\dfrac{5}{4}x + 0$$

Since $m = -\frac{5}{4}$ and $b = 0$, the slope of the line is $-\frac{5}{4}$ and the y-intercept is
$(0, 0)$.

c. Since $\dfrac{x}{2}$ means $\dfrac{1}{2}x$, we can rewrite $y = \dfrac{x}{2} + 6$ as

$$y = \dfrac{1}{2}x + 6$$

We see that $m = \frac{1}{2}$ and $b = 6$, so the slope of the line is $\frac{1}{2}$ and the y-intercept is
$(0, 6)$.

> **Caution!**   If a linear equation is written in the form $y = mx + b$, the slope of
> the graph is the *coefficient* of x, not the term involving x. For example, it would
> be incorrect to say that the graph of $y = 5x + 1$ has a slope of $m = 5x$. Its
> graph has slope $m = 5$.

THINK IT THROUGH   *Prospects for a Teaching Career*

**"While student enrollments are rising rapidly, more than a million veteran teachers
are nearing retirement. Experts predict that overall we will need more than 2
million new teachers in the next decade."**
National Education Association, 2004

Have you ever thought about becoming a teacher? There will be plenty of
openings in the future, especially for mathematics and science teachers. The
equation

$$y = 865x + 11,100$$

approximates the average beginning teacher salary y, where x is the number of
years after 1980. Graph the equation. What information about beginning
teacher salaries is given by the slope of the line? By the y-intercept? What is
the predicted average beginning teacher salary 5 years from now? *(Source:
American Federation of Teachers)*

The rate of increase in beginning
teacher salary is $865 per year. In 1980,
the average beginning teacher salary
was $11,100.

2 Write a linear equation in slope–intercept form.

The equation of any nonvertical line can be written in slope–intercept form. To do so, we apply the properties of equality to solve the equation for y.

EXAMPLE 2   Find the slope and the y-intercept of the line determined by $6x - 3y = 9$.

Strategy We will use the properties of equality to write each equation in slope–intercept form, $y = mx + b$.

WHY When the linear equations are written in slope–intercept form, the slope and the y-intercept of their graphs become apparent.

Solution
To find the slope and the y-intercept of the line, we write the equation in slope–intercept form by solving for y.

$$6x - 3y = 9$$

$$-3y = -6x + 9 \qquad \text{Subtract 6x from both sides.}$$

$$\frac{-3y}{-3} = \frac{-6x}{-3} + \frac{9}{-3} \qquad \begin{array}{l}\text{To undo the multiplication by }-3\text{, divide both sides by }-3.\\ \text{On the right-hand side, dividing each term by }-3\text{ is}\\ \text{equivalent to dividing the entire side by }-3\text{:}\\ \frac{-6x+9}{-3} = \frac{-6x}{-3} + \frac{9}{-3}\end{array}$$

$$y = 2x - 3 \qquad \text{Perform the divisions. Here, } m = 2 \text{ and } b = -3.$$

From the equation, we see that the slope is 2 and the y-intercept is $(0, -3)$. ∎

3 Use the slope and y-intercept to graph a linear equation.

To graph $y = 2x - 3$, we plot the y-intercept $(0, -3)$, as shown. Since the slope is $\frac{\text{rise}}{\text{run}} = 2 = \frac{2}{1}$, the line rises 2 units for every unit it moves to the right. If we begin at $(0, -3)$ and move 2 units up (rise) and then 1 unit to the right (run), we locate the point $(1, -1)$, which is a second point on the line. We then draw a line through $(0, -3)$ and $(1, -1)$.

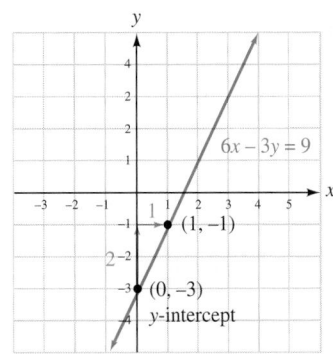

4 Recognize parallel and perpendicular lines.

The slope–intercept form enables us to quickly identify parallel and perpendicular lines.

EXAMPLE 3   Determine whether the graphs of $y = -\frac{2}{3}x$ and $y = -\frac{2}{3}x + 3$ are parallel, perpendicular, or neither.

Strategy We will find the slope of each line and compare the slopes.

WHY If the slopes are equal, the lines are parallel. If the slopes are negative reciprocals, the lines are perpendicular. Otherwise, the lines are neither parallel nor perpendicular.

Solution
The graph of $y = -\frac{2}{3}x$ is a line with slope $-\frac{2}{3}$. The graph of $y = -\frac{2}{3}x + 3$ is a line with slope of $-\frac{2}{3}$. Since the slopes $-\frac{2}{3}$ and $-\frac{2}{3}$ are the same, the lines are parallel. ∎

Self Check 2

Find the slope and the y-intercept of the line determined by $8x - 2y = -2$. $m = 4, (0, 1)$

Now Try Problem 41

Teaching Example 2 Find the slope and the y-intercept of the line determined by $10x - 2y = 6$.
Answer:
$m = 5, (0, -3)$

Self Check 3

Determine whether the graphs of $y = -\frac{3}{2}x + 1$ and $y = \frac{3}{2}x + 4$ are parallel, perpendicular, or neither. neither

Now Try Problems 45 and 46

Teaching Example 3 Determine whether the graphs of $y = \frac{1}{5}x + 2$ and $y = -5x + 9$ are parallel, perpendicular, or neither.
Answer:
perpendicular

Self Check 4

Determine whether the graphs of $y = 4x + 6$ and $x - 4y = -8$ are parallel, perpendicular, or neither. neither

Now Try Problem 49

Teaching Example 4 Are the graphs of $2x + 3y = 6$ and $6y = -4x + 7$ parallel, perpendicular, or neither?
Answer:
parallel

EXAMPLE 4 Are the graphs of $y = -5x + 6$ and $x - 5y = -10$ parallel, perpendicular, or neither?

Strategy We will find the slope of each line and then compare the slopes.

WHY If the slopes are equal, the lines are parallel. If the slopes are negative reciprocals, the lines are perpendicular. Otherwise, the lines are neither parallel nor perpendicular.

Solution
The graph of $y = -5x + 6$ is a line with slope -5. To find the slope of the graph of $x - 5y = -10$, we will write the equation in slope–intercept form.

$$x - 5y = -10$$

$$-5y = -x - 10 \qquad \text{To eliminate } x \text{ from the left side, subtract } x \text{ from both sides.}$$

$$\frac{-5y}{-5} = \frac{-x}{-5} - \frac{10}{-5} \qquad \text{To isolate } y, \text{ undo the multiplication by } -5 \text{ by dividing both sides by } -5.$$

$$y = \frac{x}{5} + 2 \qquad m = \frac{1}{5} \text{ because } \frac{x}{5} = \frac{1}{5}x.$$

The graph of $y = \frac{x}{5} + 2$ is a line with slope $\frac{1}{5}$. Since the slopes -5 and $\frac{1}{5}$ are negative reciprocals, the lines are perpendicular. This is verified by the fact that the product of their slopes is -1.

$$-5\left(\frac{1}{5}\right) = -\frac{5}{5} = -1$$

Success Tip Graphs are not necessary to determine if two lines are parallel, perpendicular, or neither. We simply examine the slopes of the lines.

---

5 Use slope–intercept form to write an equation to model data.

If we are given the slope and y-intercept of a line, we can write its equation, as in the next example.

Self Check 5

To encourage larger orders, a screen printing service offers a $0.02 per shirt discount from the normal cost of $15 per shirt. Write a linear equation that determines the per shirt cost c of a shirt if n shirts are ordered.

Now Try Problem 77
Self Check 5 Answer
$c = -0.02n + 15$

Teaching Example 5 To promote group sales for an Alaskan cruise, a travel agency reduces the regular ticket price of $4,500 by $5 for each person traveling in the group. Write a linear equation that determines the per-person cost c of the cruise, if p people travel together.
Answer:
$c = -5p + 4500$

EXAMPLE 5 *Limo Service* On weekends, a limousine service charges a fee of $100, plus 50¢ per mile, for the rental of a stretch limo. Write a linear equation that describes the relationship between the rental cost and the number of miles driven. Graph the result.

Strategy We will determine the slope and the y-intercept of the graph of the equation from the given facts about the limo service.

WHY If we know the slope and y-intercept, we can use the slope–intercept form, $y = mx + b$, to write the equation to model the situation.

Solution
To write an equation describing this relationship, we will let x represent the number of miles driven and y represent the cost (in dollars). We can make two observations:

- The cost increases by 50¢ or $0.50 for each mile driven. This is the *rate of change* of the rental cost to miles driven, and it will be the *slope* of the graph of the equation. Thus, $m = 0.50$.
- The basic fee is $100. Before driving any miles (that is, when $x = 0$), the cost y is 100. The ordered pair $(0, 100)$ will be the y-intercept of the graph of the equation. So we know that $b = 100$.

We substitute 0.50 for m and 100 for b in the slope–intercept form to get

$y = 0.50x + 100$ *Here the cost y depends on x, the number of miles driven.*
    ↑   ↑
$m = 0.50$ $b = 100$

To graph $y = 0.50x + 100$, we plot its y-intercept, $(0, 100)$. Since the slope is $0.50 = \frac{50}{100} = \frac{5}{10}$, we can start at $(0, 100)$ and locate a second point on the line by moving 5 units up (rise) and then 10 units to the right (run). This point will have coordinates $(0 + 10, 100 + 5)$ or $(10, 105)$. We draw a straight line through these two points to get a graph that illustrates the relationship between the rental cost and the number of miles driven. We draw the graph only in quadrant I, because the number of miles driven is always positive.

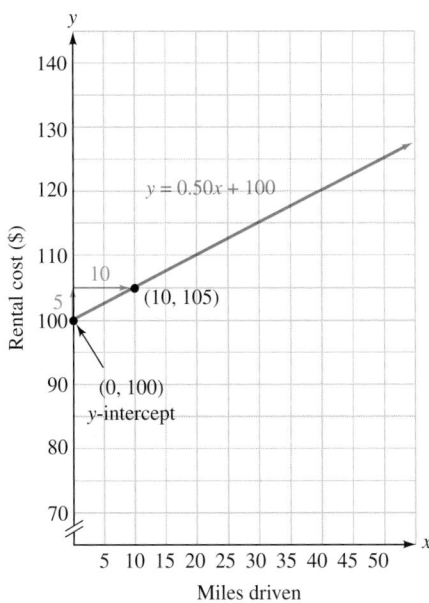

ANSWERS TO SELF CHECKS

1. a. $m = -5, (0, -1)$ **b.** $m = \frac{7}{8}, (0, 0)$ **c.** $m = -\frac{1}{3}, (0, 5)$ **2.** $m = 4, (0, 1)$
3. neither **4.** neither **5.** $c = -0.02n + 15$

SECTION **3.5** STUDY SET

VOCABULARY

Fill in the blanks.

1. The equation $y = mx + b$ is called the ___slope–intercept___ form for the equation of a line.

2. ___Parallel___ lines do not intersect. ___Perpendicular___ lines meet at right angles.

CONCEPTS

3. The graph of the linear equation $y = mx + b$ has a ___y-intercept___ of $(0, b)$ and a ___slope___ of m.

4. The numbers $\frac{5}{6}$ and $-\frac{6}{5}$ are negative ___reciprocals___ because their product is -1.

Determine whether each equation is in slope-intercept form.

5. $7x + 4y = 2$ no   **6.** $5y = 2x - 3$ no

7. $y = 6x + 1$ yes   **8.** $x = 4y - 8$ no

Determine the slope of the graph of each equation.

9. $y = \dfrac{-2x}{3} - 2$ $-\frac{2}{3}$ **10.** $y = \dfrac{x}{4} + 1$ $\frac{1}{4}$

11. $y = 2 - 8x$ -8 **12.** $y = 3x$ 3

13. $y = x$ 1 **14.** $y = -x$ -1

See the illustration.

15. What is the slope of the line? $-\frac{1}{2}$

16. What is the y-intercept of the line? $(0, -4)$

17. Write the equation of the line. $y = -\frac{1}{2}x - 4$

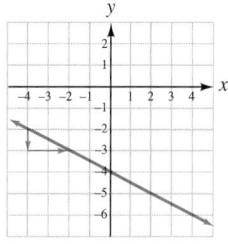

See the illustration.

18. What is the slope of the line? $\frac{5}{4}$

19. What is the y-intercept of the line? $(0, 0)$

20. Write the equation of the line. $y = \frac{5}{4}x$

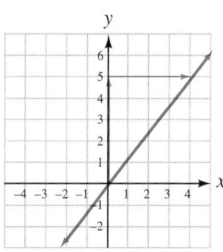

In the illustration, the slope of line l_1 is 2.

21. Determine the slope of line l_2. $-\frac{1}{2}$

22. Determine the slope of line l_3. 2

23. Determine the slope of line l_4. $-\frac{1}{2}$

24. Which lines have the same y-intercept? l_1 and l_2

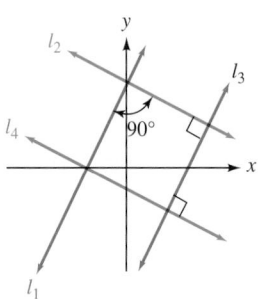

25. Determine the y-intercept of line l_1 in the illustration. $(0, 0)$

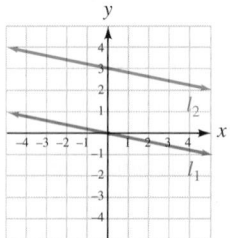

26. What do lines l_1 and l_2 have in common? How are they different? same slope, different y-intercepts

Without graphing, determine whether the graphs of each pair of lines are parallel, perpendicular, or neither.

27. $y = 0.5x - 3$, $y = \frac{1}{2}x + 3$ parallel

28. $y = 0.75x$, $y = -\frac{4}{3}x + 2$ perpendicular

29. $y = -x$, $y = -2x$ neither

30. $y = \frac{2}{3}x - 4$, $y = -\frac{3}{2}x + 4$ perpendicular

NOTATION

Complete each solution by solving the equation for y. Then find the slope and the y-intercept of its graph.

31. $6x - 2y = 10$

$6x - \boxed{6x} - 2y = -6x + 10$

$-2y = \boxed{-6x} + 10$

$\dfrac{-2y}{-2} = \dfrac{-6x}{-2} + \dfrac{10}{-2}$

$y = \boxed{3x} - 5$

The slope is $\boxed{3}$ and the y-intercept is $\boxed{(0, -5)}$.

▶ **32.** $2x + 5y = 15$

$2x + 5y - \boxed{2x} = \boxed{-2x} + 15$

$\boxed{5y} = -2x + 15$

$\dfrac{5y}{\boxed{5}} = \dfrac{-2x}{\boxed{5}} + \dfrac{15}{\boxed{5}}$

$y = -\dfrac{2}{5}x + 3$

The slope is $\boxed{-\frac{2}{5}}$ and the y-intercept is $\boxed{(0, 3)}$.

GUIDED PRACTICE

Find the slope and the y-intercept of the graph of each equation. See Examples 1–2.

▶ **33.** $y = 4x + 2$
  $4, (0, 2)$

34. $y = -4x - 2$
  $-4, (0, -2)$

35. $y = \dfrac{x}{4} - \dfrac{1}{2}$
  $\frac{1}{4}, \left(0, -\frac{1}{2}\right)$

36. $y = \frac{1}{2}x + 6$
  $\frac{1}{2}, (0, 6)$

37. $4x - 2 = y$
  $4, (0, -2)$

▶ **38.** $6 - x = y$
  $-1, (0, 6)$

39. $6y = x - 6$
  $\frac{1}{6}, (0, -1)$

▶ **40.** $6x - 1 = y$
  $6, (0, -1)$

41. $4x - 3y = 12$
  $\frac{4}{3}, (0, -4)$

42. $2x + 3y = 6$
  $-\frac{2}{3}, (0, 2)$

43. $10x - 5y = 12$
  $2, \left(0, -\frac{12}{5}\right)$

44. $7x + 4y = 16$
  $-\frac{7}{4}, (0, 4)$

For each pair of equations, determine whether their graphs are parallel, perpendicular, or neither. **See Examples 3–4.**

45. $y = 6x + 8$

$y = 6x$
parallel

46. $y = 3x - 15$

$y = -\dfrac{1}{3}x + 4$
perpendicular

47. $y = x$

$y = -x$
perpendicular

48. $y = \dfrac{1}{2}x - \dfrac{4}{5}$

$y = 0.5x + 3$
parallel

49. $y = -2x - 9$

$2x - y = 9$
neither

50. $y = \dfrac{3}{4}x + 1$

$4x - 3y = 15$
neither

51. $x - y = 12$

$-2x + 2y = -23$
parallel

52. $x = 9$

$y = 8$
perpendicular

TRY IT YOURSELF

Find the slope and the y-intercept of the graph of each equation.

53. $x + y = 8$
$-1, (0, 8)$

54. $x - y = -30$
$1, (0, 30)$

55. $2x + 3y = 6$
$-\dfrac{2}{3}, (0, 2)$

56. $3x - 5y = 15$
$\dfrac{3}{5}, (0, -3)$

57. $3y - 13 = 0$
$0, \left(0, \dfrac{13}{3}\right)$

58. $-5y - 2 = 0$
$0, \left(0, -\dfrac{2}{5}\right)$

59. $y = -5x$
$-5, (0, 0)$

60. $y = 14x$
$14, (0, 0)$

Write an equation of the line with the given slope and y-intercept. Then graph it.

61. $m = 5, (0, -3)$
$y = 5x - 3$

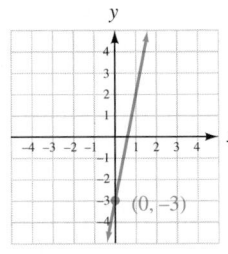

62. $m = -2, (0, 1)$
$y = -2x + 1$

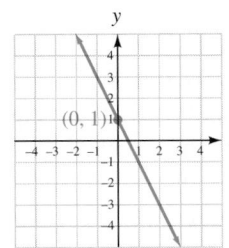

63. $m = \dfrac{1}{4}, (0, -2)$
$y = \dfrac{1}{4}x - 2$

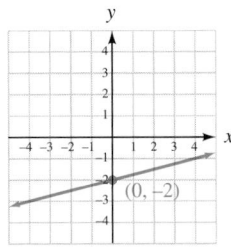

64. $m = \dfrac{1}{3}, (0, -5)$
$y = \dfrac{1}{3}x - 5$

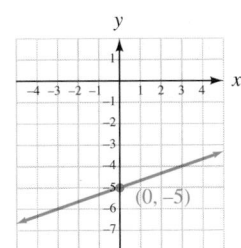

65. $m = -3, (0, 6)$
$y = -3x + 6$

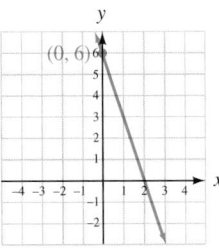

66. $m = 2, (0, 1)$
$y = 2x + 1$

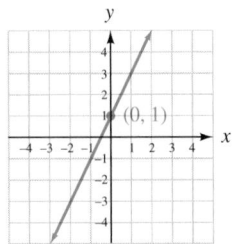

67. $m = -\dfrac{8}{3}, (0, 5)$
$y = -\dfrac{8}{3}x + 5$

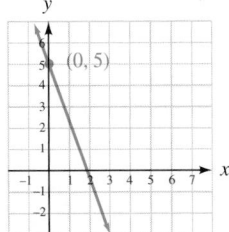

68. $m = -\dfrac{7}{6}, (0, 2)$
$y = -\dfrac{7}{6}x + 2$

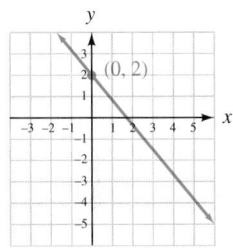

Find the slope and the y-intercept of the graph of each equation. Then graph it.

69. $y = 3x + 3$

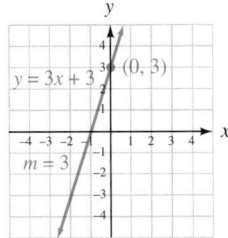

70. $y = -3x + 5$

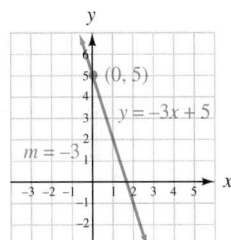

71. $y = -\dfrac{x}{2} + 2$

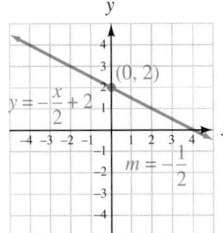

72. $y = \dfrac{x}{3}$

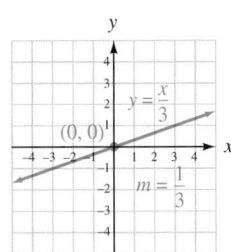

73. $3x + 4y = 16$

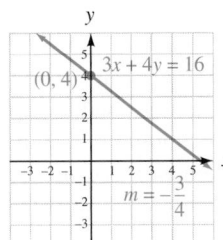

74. $2x + 3y = 9$

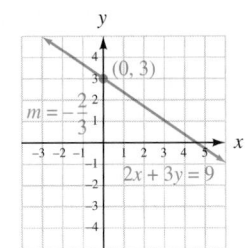

75. $10x - 5y = 5$ ▶ **76.** $4x - 2y = 6$

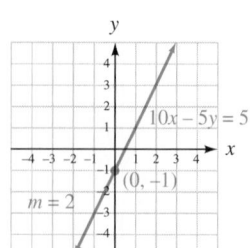   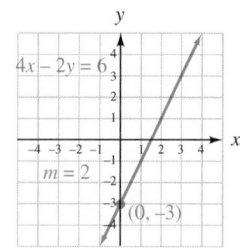

APPLICATIONS

See Example 5.

▶ **77.** PRODUCTION COSTS A television production company charges a basic fee of $5,000 and then $2,000 an hour when filming a commercial.

   a. Write a linear equation that describes the relationship between the total production costs y and the hours of filming x. $y = 2,000x + 5,000$

   b. Use your answer to part a to find the production costs if a commercial required 8 hours of filming. $21,000

▶ **78.** COLLEGE FEES Each semester, students enrolling at a community college must pay tuition costs of $20 per unit as well as a $40 student services fee.

   a. Write a linear equation that gives the total fees y to be paid by a student enrolling at the college and taking x units. $y = 20x + 40$

   b. Use your answer to part a to find the enrollment cost for a student taking 12 units. $280

▶ **79.** CHEMISTRY EXPERIMENT The following illustration shows a portion of a student's chemistry lab manual. Use the information to write a linear equation relating the temperature y (in degrees Fahrenheit) of the compound to the time x (in minutes) elapsed during the lab procedure. $y = 5x - 10$

> Chem. Lab #1   Aug. 13
>
> **Step 1:** Removed compound
> from freezer @ –10° F.
>
> **Step 2:** Used heating unit
> to raise temperature
> of compound 5° F
> every minute.

▶ **80.** INCOME PROPERTY Use the information in the newspaper advertisement in the next column to write a linear equation that gives the amount of income y (in dollars) the apartment owner will receive when the unit is rented for x months. $y = 500x + 250$

APARTMENT FOR RENT

1 bedroom/1 bath,
with garage
$500 per month +
$250 nonrefundable
security fee.

▶ **81.** SALAD BAR For lunch, a delicatessen offers a "Salad and Soda" special where customers serve themselves at a well-stocked salad bar. The cost is $1.00 for the drink and 20¢ an ounce for the salad.

   a. Write a linear equation that will find the cost y of a lunch when a salad weighing x ounces is purchased. $y = 0.20x + 1.00$

   b. Graph the equation using the grid below.

   c. How would the graph from part b change if the delicatessen began charging $2.00 for the drink? same slope, different y-intercept

   d. How would the graph from part b change if the cost of the salad changed to 30¢ an ounce? same y-intercept, steeper slope

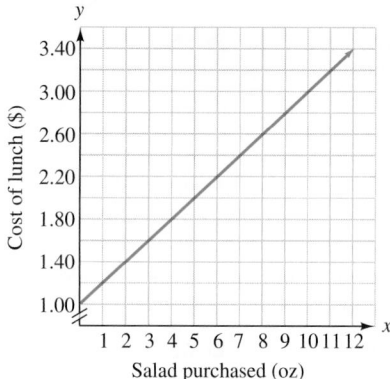

▶ **82.** SEWING COSTS A tailor charges a basic fee of $20 plus $2.50 per letter to sew an athlete's name on the back of a jacket.

   a. Write a linear equation that will find the cost y to have a name containing x letters sewn on the back of a jacket. $y = 2.50x + 20$

   b. Graph the equation on the grid on the next page.

   c. Suppose the tailor raises the basic fee to $30. On your graph from part b, draw the new graph showing the increased cost.

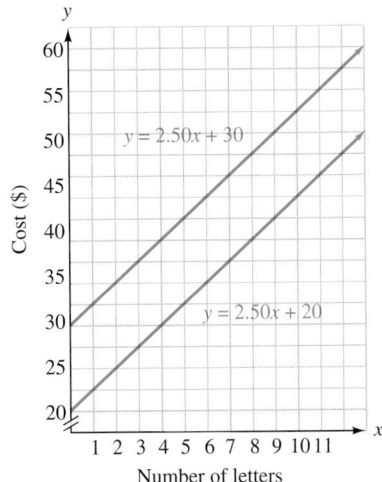

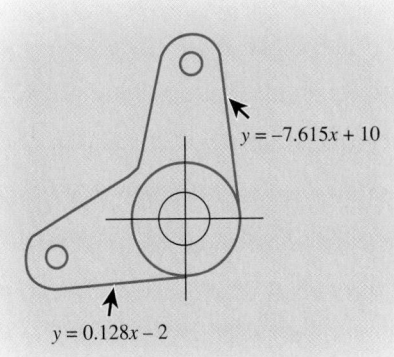

▶ **83. EMPLOYMENT SERVICE** A policy statement of LIZCO, Inc., is shown below. Suppose a secretary had to pay an employment service $500 to get placed in a new job at LIZCO. Write a linear equation that tells the secretary the actual cost y of the employment service to her x months after being hired.

$y = -20x + 500$

> **Policy no. 23452**– A new hire will be reimbursed by LIZCO for any employment service fees paid by the employee at the rate of $20 per month.

▶ **84. COMPUTER DRAFTING** The illustration in the next column shows a computer-generated drawing of an automobile engine mount. When the designer clicks the mouse on a line of the drawing, the computer finds the equation of the line. Determine whether the two lines selected in the drawing are perpendicular. not quite: $(0.128)(-7.615) = -0.97472 \neq -1$

WRITING

85. Explain the advantages of writing the equation of a line in slope–intercept form ($y = mx + b$) as opposed to general form ($Ax + By = C$).

86. Why is $y = mx + b$ called the slope–intercept form of the equation of a line?

▶ **87.** What is the minimum number of points needed to draw the graph of a line? Explain why.

88. List some examples of parallel and perpendicular lines that you see in your daily life.

REVIEW

89. Find the slope of the line passing through the points $(6, -2)$ and $(-6, 1)$. $-\frac{1}{4}$

90. Is $(3, -7)$ a solution of $y = 3x - 2$? no

91. Evaluate: $-4 - (-4)$ 0

▶ **92.** Solve: $2(x - 3) = 3x$ -6

93. To evaluate $[-2(4 - 8) + 4^2]$, which operation should be performed first? subtraction

94. Translate to mathematical symbols: four less than twice the price p. $2p - 4$

95. What percent of 6 is 1.5? 25%

96. Is -6.75 a solution of $x + 1 > -9$? yes

SECTION **3.6**
Point–Slope Form; Writing Linear Equations

Objectives

1 Use point–slope form to write an equation of a line.

2 Write an equation of a line given two points on the line.

3 Write equations of horizontal and vertical lines.

4 Write linear equations that model data.

If we know the slope of a line and its y-intercept, we can use the slope–intercept form to write the equation of the line. The question that now arises is, can any point on a line be used in combination with its slope to write its equation? In this section we will answer this question.

1 Use point–slope form to write an equation of a line.

Refer to the line graphed on the next page with slope 3 and passing through the point $(2, 1)$. If we pick another point on the line, (x, y), we can find the slope of the line by using the coordinates of points $(2, 1)$ and (x, y). Using the slope formula, we have

$$\frac{y_2 - y_1}{x_2 - x_1} = m \qquad \text{This is the slope formula.}$$

$$\frac{y - 1}{x - 2} = m \qquad \text{Substitute } y \text{ for } y_2, 1 \text{ for } y_1, x \text{ for}$$

$$x_2, \text{ and } 2 \text{ for } x_1.$$

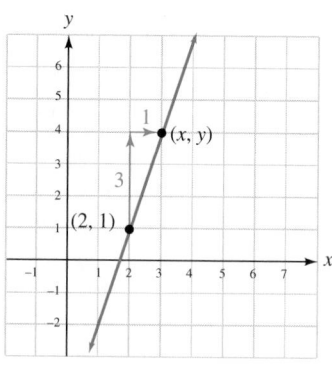

Since the slope of the line is given to be 3, we can substitute 3 for m in the previous equation.

$$\frac{y - 1}{x - 2} = m$$

$$\frac{y - 1}{x - 2} = 3$$

We then multiply both sides by $x - 2$ to get

$$\frac{y - 1}{x - 2}(x - 2) = 3(x - 2) \qquad \text{Clear the equation of the fraction.}$$

$$y - 1 = 3(x - 2) \qquad \text{Simplify the left-hand side.}$$

The resulting equation displays the slope of the line and the coordinates of one point on the line:

$$\overset{\text{Slope of}}{\underset{\text{the line}}{\downarrow}}$$

$$y - 1 = 3(x - 2)$$

$$\underset{\substack{\text{y-coordinate} \\ \text{of the point}}}{\uparrow} \qquad \underset{\substack{\text{x-coordinate} \\ \text{of the point}}}{\uparrow}$$

In general, suppose we know that the slope of a line is m and that the line passes through the point (x_1, y_1). Then if (x, y) is any other point on the line, we can use the definition of slope to write

$$\frac{y - y_1}{x - x_1} = m$$

If we multiply both sides by $x - x_1$, we have

$$y - y_1 = m(x - x_1)$$

This form of a linear equation is called the **point–slope form.** It can be used to write the equation of a line when the slope and one point on the line are known.

Point–Slope Form of the Equation of a Line

If a line with slope m passes through the point (x_1, y_1), the equation of the line is

$$y - y_1 = m(x - x_1)$$

EXAMPLE 1 Write an equation of a line that has a slope of -3 and passes through $(-1, 5)$. Write the answer in slope–intercept form.

Strategy We will use the point–slope form, $y - y_1 = m(x - x_1)$, to write an equation of the line.

WHY We are given the slope of the line and the coordinates of a point that it passes through.

Solution

$$
\begin{aligned}
y - y_1 &= m(x - x_1) && \text{This is the point–slope form.} \\
y - 5 &= -3[x - (-1)] && \text{Substitute } -3 \text{ for } m, -1 \text{ for } x_1, \text{ and 5 for } y_1. \\
y - 5 &= -3(x + 1) && \text{Simplify within the brackets.}
\end{aligned}
$$

We can write this result in slope–intercept form, as follows:

$$
\begin{aligned}
y - 5 &= -3x - 3 && \text{Distribute the multiplication by } -3. \\
y &= -3x + 2 && \text{To undo the subtraction of 5, add 5 to both sides: } -3 + 5 = 2.
\end{aligned}
$$

In slope–intercept form, the equation is $y = -3x + 2$.

Self Check 1

Write an equation of a line that has a slope of -2 and passes through $(4, -3)$. Write the answer in slope–intercept form. $y = -2x + 5$

Now Try Problems 25 and 31

Teaching Example 1 Write an equation of a line that has slope of $\frac{1}{2}$ and passes through $(-6, 1)$. Write the answer in slope–intercept form.
Answer:
$y = \frac{1}{2}x + 4$

2 Write an equation of a line given two points on the line.

In the next example, we will show that it is possible to write the equation of a line when we know the coordinates of two points on the line.

EXAMPLE 2 Write an equation of the line passing through $(4, 0)$ and $(6, -8)$.

Strategy We will use the point–slope form, $y - y_1 = m(x - x_1)$, to write an equation of the line.

WHY We can calculate the slope of the line using the coordinates of the two points given and the slope formula. We also know the coordinates of a point that the line passes through (we can choose either point).

Solution
First we find the slope of the line that passes through $(4, 0)$ and $(6, -8)$.

$$
\begin{aligned}
m &= \frac{y_2 - y_1}{x_2 - x_1} && \text{This is the slope formula.} \\
&= \frac{-8 - 0}{6 - 4} && \text{Substitute } -8 \text{ for } y_2, 0 \text{ for } y_1, 6 \text{ for } x_2, \text{ and 4 for } x_1. \\
&= \frac{-8}{2} && \text{Simplify.} \\
&= -4
\end{aligned}
$$

Since the line passes through both $(4, 0)$ and $(6, -8)$, we can choose either point and substitute its coordinates into the point–slope form. If we choose $(4, 0)$, we substitute 4 for x_1, 0 for y_1, and -4 for m and proceed as follows.

$$
\begin{aligned}
y - y_1 &= m(x - x_1) && \text{This is the point–slope form.} \\
y - 0 &= -4(x - 4) && \text{Substitute } -4 \text{ for } m, 4 \text{ for } x_1, \text{ and 0 for } y_1. \\
y &= -4x + 16 && \text{Distribute the multiplication by } -4.
\end{aligned}
$$

The equation of the line is $y = -4x + 16$.

Self Check 2

Write an equation of the line passing through $(0, -3)$ and $(2, 1)$. $y = 2x - 3$

Now Try Problems 33 and 38

Teaching Example 2 Write an equation of the line passing through $(5, 3)$ and $(4, -3)$.
Answer:
$y = 6x - 27$

> **Success Tip**   In Example 2, either of the given points can be used as (x_1, y_1) when writing the point–slope equation. The results will be the same. We usually choose the point whose coordinates make the computations the easiest.

3   Write equations of horizontal and vertical lines.

We have graphed horizontal and vertical lines. We will now discuss how to write their equations.

Self Check 3

Write an equation of each line.
a. a horizontal line passing through (3, 2) $y = 2$
b. a vertical line passing through (−1, −3) $x = -1$

Now Try Problems 41 and 44

Teaching Example 3 Write an equation of each line:
a. a horizontal line passing through (2, −7)
b. a vertical line passing through (5, 3)
Answers:
a. $y = -7$
b. $x = 5$

EXAMPLE 3   Write an equation of each line and then graph it.   **a.** a horizontal line passing through $(-2, -4)$ **b.** a vertical line passing through $(1, 3)$.

Strategy We will use the appropriate form, either $y = b$ or $x = a$, to write an equation of each line.

WHY These are the standard forms for the equations of a horizontal and a vertical line.

Solution

a. The equation of a horizontal line can be written in the form $y = b$. Since the y-coordinate of $(-2, -4)$ is -4, the equation of the line is $y = -4$. The graph is shown in the figure.

b. The equation of a vertical line can be written in the form $x = a$. Since the x-coordinate of $(1, 3)$ is 1, the equation of the line is $x = 1$. The graph is shown in the figure.

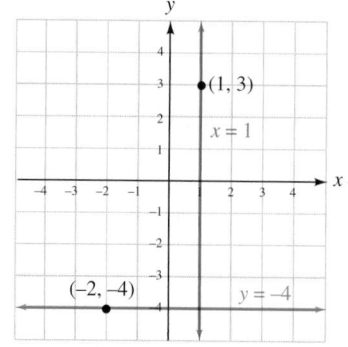

4   Write linear equations that model data.

Self Check 4

Celsius and Fahrenheit measures of temperature are not the same. There is, however, a linear relationship between the two. Degrees Fahrenheit increases by 9° for each 5° increase in Celsius. If a 212° Fahrenheit temperature measure is the same as 100° Celsius, write a linear equation that relates Fahrenheit measure to Celsius measure.

Now Try Problem 73
Self Check 4 Answer
$F = \frac{9}{5}C + 32$

EXAMPLE 4   *Temperature Drop*   A refrigeration unit lowers the temperature in a railroad car 6°F every 5 minutes. One day, the temperature in a car was 76°F after the cooler had run for 10 minutes. Find a linear equation that describes the relationship between the time the cooler has been running and the temperature in the car.

Graph the equation and use it to find the temperature in the car before the cooler was turned on and the temperature in the car after the cooler had run for 25 minutes.

Strategy We will determine the slope and a point of the graph from the given facts about the refrigeration unit.

WHY If we know the slope and a point, we can use the point–slope form, $y - y_1 = m(x - x_1)$, to write the equation to model the situation.

Solution

We will let x represent the time, in minutes, that the cooler was running, and y will represent the air temperature in the car. We can make two observations:

- With the cooler on, the temperature in the railroad car drops 6° every 5 minutes. The rate of change of $-\frac{6}{5}$ degrees per minute is the slope of the graph of the linear equation that we want to find. Thus, $m = -\frac{6}{5}$.

- We know that after the cooler had been running for 10 minutes ($x = 10$), the temperature in the car was 76° ($y = 76$). We can express these facts with the ordered pair (10, 76). This is a point on the graph of the linear equation.

To write the linear equation, we substitute $-\frac{6}{5}$ for m, 10 for x_1, and 76 for y_1, into the point–slope form of the equation of a line.

$y - y_1 = m(x - x_1)$	This is the point–slope form.
$y - 76 = -\dfrac{6}{5}(x - 10)$	Substitute: $m = -\frac{6}{5}$, $x_1 = 10$, and $y_1 = 76$.
$y - 76 = -\dfrac{6}{5}x - \left(-\dfrac{6}{5}\right)10$	Distribute the multiplication by $-\frac{6}{5}$.
$y - 76 = -\dfrac{6}{5}x - (-12)$	Multiply: $\left(-\frac{6}{5}\right)10 = \left(-\frac{6}{5}\right)\frac{10}{1} = -12$.
$y - 76 = -\dfrac{6}{5}x + 12$	On the right-hand side, change the subtraction to the addition of the opposite.
$y - 76 + 76 = -\dfrac{6}{5}x + 12 + 76$	To undo the subtraction of 76, add 76 to both sides.
$y = -\dfrac{6}{5}x + 88$	Perform the additions.

The graph of $y = -\frac{6}{5}x + 88$ is shown. From the graph, we see that the temperature in the railroad car before the cooler was turned on was 88°F. This is given by the y-intercept of the graph, (0, 88). If we locate 25 on the x-axis and move straight up to intersect the graph, we will see that the temperature in the car was 58°F. This shows that after the cooler ran for 25 minutes, the temperature was about 58°F.

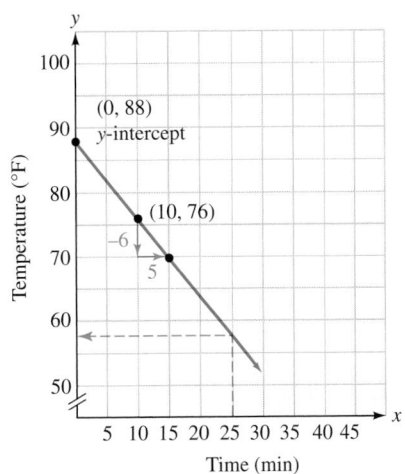

Teaching Example 4 The length (in inches) of a man's foot is not his shoe size. There is, however, a linear relationship between the two. Shoe size increases by 3 sizes for each 1-inch increase in foot length. If a man's shoe size 5 fits a 9-inch-long foot, write a linear equation that relates shoe size y to foot length x.
Answer:
$y = 3x - 22$

EXAMPLE 5 *Market Research* A company that makes a breakfast cereal has found that the number of discount coupons redeemed for its product is linearly related to the coupon's value. In one advertising campaign, 10,000 of the "10¢ off" coupons were redeemed. In another campaign, 45,000 of the "50¢ off" coupons were redeemed. How many coupons can the company expect to be redeemed if it issues a "35¢ off" coupon?

Strategy We will determine two points of the graph of the equation from the given facts about the coupon.

WHY If we know two points, we can use the point–slope form, $y - y_1 = m(x - x_1)$, to write the equation to model the situation.

Self Check 5

Orders for awards to be given to math team members were placed on two separate occasions. The first order of 32 awards cost $172 and the second order of 5 awards cost $37. Assuming no price change, write an equation of the line that would give the cost for an order of any number of awards. $c = 5n + 12$

Now Try Problem 65

Teaching Example 5 A youth soccer league places an order for 273 trophies and pays $1663. Near the end of the season, they place a second order for 13 trophies and pay $103. If there is no price change, write an equation of the line that would give the cost for an order of any number of trophies.
Answer:
$c = 6n + 25$

Solution

If we let x represent the value of a coupon and y represent the number of coupons that will be redeemed, ordered pairs will have the form

(coupon value, number redeemed)

Two points on the graph of the equation are (10, 10,000) and (50, 45,000). These points are plotted on the graph shown to the right. To write the equation of the line passing through the points, we first find the slope of the line.

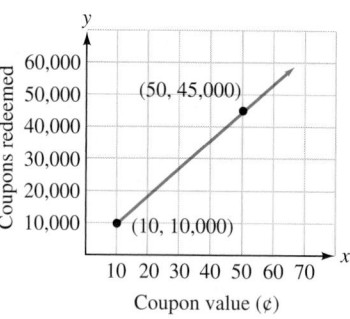

$$m = \frac{y_2 - y_1}{x_2 - x_1} \qquad \text{This is the slope formula.}$$

$$= \frac{45{,}000 - 10{,}000}{50 - 10} \qquad \text{Substitute 45,000 for } y_2, \text{ 10,000 for } y_1, \text{ 50 for } x_2, \text{ and 10 for } x_1.$$

$$= \frac{35{,}000}{40}$$

$$= 875$$

We then substitute 875 for m and the coordinates of one known point—say, (10, 10,000)—into the point–slope form of the equation of a line and proceed as follows.

$$y - y_1 = m(x - x_1) \qquad \text{This is the point–slope form.}$$

$$y - 10{,}000 = 875(x - 10) \qquad \text{Substitute for } m, x_1, \text{ and } y_1.$$

$$y - 10{,}000 = 875x - 8{,}750 \qquad \text{Distribute the multiplication by 875.}$$

$$y = 875x + 1{,}250 \qquad \text{Add 10,000 to both sides.}$$

To find the expected number of coupons that will be redeemed, we substitute the value of the coupon, 35¢, into the equation $y = 875x + 1{,}250$ and find y.

$$y = 875x + 1{,}250$$

$$y = 875(35) + 1{,}250 \qquad \text{Substitute 35 for } x.$$

$$y = 30{,}625 + 1{,}250 \qquad \text{Perform the multiplication.}$$

$$y = 31{,}875$$

The company can expect 31,875 of the 35¢ coupons to be redeemed.

ANSWERS TO SELF CHECKS

1. $y = -2x + 5$ **2.** $y = 2x - 3$ **3. a.** $y = 2$ **b.** $x = -1$ **4.** $F = \frac{9}{5}C + 32$
5. $c = 5n + 12$

SECTION 3.6   STUDY SET

■ VOCABULARY

Fill in the blanks.

▶ **1.** $y - y_1 = m(x - x_1)$ is called the __point–slope__ form of the equation of a line.

2. In the following illustration, point P has an __x-coordinate__ of 2 and a __y-coordinate__ of -1.

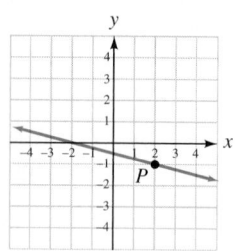

▶ Selected exercises available online at
www.webassign.net/brookscole

CONCEPTS

3. The linear equation $y = 2x - 3$ is written in *slope–intercept* form. What are the slope and the y-intercept of the graph of this line?

The slope is 2. The y-intercept is $(0, -3)$.

4. The linear equation $y - 4 = 6(x - 5)$ is written in *point–slope* form. What is the slope of the graph of this equation and what point does it pass through?

The slope is 6. The graph passes through $(5, 4)$.

5. In what form is the equation $y - 4 = 2(x - 5)$ written?

point–slope form

6. In what form is the equation $y = 2x + 15$ written?

slope–intercept form

Refer to the illustration shown below.

7. Find two points on the line whose coordinates are integers. $(-4, -2), (3, 2)$

8. Determine the slope of the line. $\frac{4}{7}$

9. Use the results of Problems 7 and 8 to write the equation of the line in point–slope form.

$y + 2 = \frac{4}{7}(x + 4)$ or
$y - 2 = \frac{4}{7}(x - 3)$

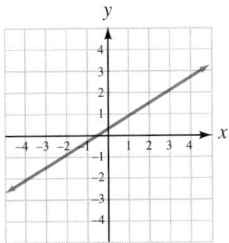

10. Is it true that the equations

$$y - 1 = 2(x - 2), \quad y = 2x - 3, \quad \text{and} \quad 2x - y = 3$$

all describe the same line? yes

In each case, is enough information given to write an equation of the line?

11. The line passes through $(2, -7)$. no

12. The slope of the line is $-\frac{3}{4}$. no

13. The line has the following table of solutions: yes

x	y
2	3
-3	-6

14. The line is horizontal. no

15. The line is vertical and passes through $(-1, 1)$. yes

16. The line has the following table of solutions: no

x	y
4	5

NOTATION

Complete each solution to write a point–slope equation in slope–intercept form.

17.
$$y - 2 = -3(x - 4)$$
$$y - 2 = \boxed{-3x} + \boxed{12}$$
$$y - 2 + \boxed{2} = -3x + 12 + \boxed{2}$$
$$y = -3x + 14$$

18.
$$y + 2 = \frac{1}{2}(x + 2)$$
$$y + 2 = \boxed{\frac{1}{2}x} + \boxed{1}$$
$$y + 2 - \boxed{2} = \frac{1}{2}x + 1 - \boxed{2}$$
$$y = \frac{1}{2}x - 1$$

19. Complete the solution to write the slope–intercept equation of the line with slope -2 that passes through the point $(-1, 5)$.

$$y - y_1 = m(x - x_1)$$
$$y - \boxed{5} = -2\left[x - \left(\boxed{-1}\right)\right]$$
$$y - 5 = \boxed{-2x} - 2$$
$$y = -2x + 3$$

▶ **20.** Complete the solution to write the slope–intercept equation of the line with slope 4 that passes through the point $(0, 3)$.

$$y - y_1 = m(x - x_1)$$
$$y - \boxed{3} = 4\left(x - \boxed{0}\right)$$
$$y - 3 = \boxed{4x}$$
$$y = 4x + 3$$

GUIDED PRACTICE

Use the point–slope form to write an equation of the line with the given slope and point. **See Objective 1.**

21. $m = 3$, passes through $(2, 1)$ $\ y - 1 = 3(x - 2)$

▶ **22.** $m = 2$, passes through $(4, 3)$ $\ y - 3 = 2(x - 4)$

23. $m = -\frac{4}{5}$, passes through $(-5, -1)$ $\ y + 1 = -\frac{4}{5}(x + 5)$

▶ **24.** $m = -\frac{7}{8}$, passes through $(-2, -9)$ $\ y + 9 = -\frac{7}{8}(x + 2)$

Use the point–slope form to first write an equation of the line with the given slope and point. Write the result in slope–intercept form. **See Example 1.**

25. $m = \dfrac{1}{5}$, passes through $(10, 1)$ $y = \frac{1}{5}x - 1$

▶ **26.** $m = \dfrac{1}{4}$, passes through $(8, 1)$ $y = \frac{1}{4}x - 1$

27. $m = -5$, passes through $(-9, 8)$ $y = -5x - 37$

▶ **28.** $m = -4$, passes through $(-2, 10)$ $y = -4x + 2$

29. $m = -\dfrac{4}{3}$,

x	y
6	−4

$y = -\frac{4}{3}x + 4$

30. $m = -\dfrac{3}{2}$,

x	y
−2	1

$y = -\frac{3}{2}x - 2$

31. $m = -\dfrac{2}{3}$, passes through $(3, 0)$ $y = -\frac{2}{3}x + 2$

32. $m = -\dfrac{2}{5}$, passes through $(15, 0)$ $y = -\frac{2}{5}x + 6$

Write an equation of the line that passes through the two given points. Write the result in slope–intercept form. **See Example 2.**

33. $(1, 7)$ and $(-2, 1)$ $y = 2x + 5$

▶ **34.** $(-2, 2)$ and $(2, -8)$ $y = -\frac{5}{2}x - 3$

35. $(5, 1)$ and $(-5, 0)$ $y = \frac{1}{10}x + \frac{1}{2}$

▶ **36.** $(-3, 0)$ and $(3, 1)$ $y = \frac{1}{6}x + \frac{1}{2}$

37. $(5, 5)$ and $(7, 5)$ $y = 5$

38. $(-2, 1)$ and $(-2, 15)$ $x = -2$

39.

x	y
−4	3
2	0

$y = -\frac{1}{2}x + 1$

40.

x	y
−1	−4
1	−2

$y = x - 3$

Write an equation of the line with the given characteristics. **See Example 3.**

41. Vertical, passes through $(4, 5)$ $x = 4$

▶ **42.** Vertical, passes through $(-2, -5)$ $x = -2$

43. Horizontal, passes through $(4, 5)$ $y = 5$

▶ **44.** Horizontal, passes through $(-2, -5)$ $y = -5$

Find the equation of the line with the following characteristics. Write the equation in slope–intercept form, if possible.

45. $m = 8$, passes through $(0, 4)$ $y = 8x + 4$

▶ **46.** $m = 6$, passes through $(0, -4)$ $y = 6x - 4$

47. $m = -3$, passes through the origin $y = -3x$

48. $m = -1$, passes through the origin $y = -x$

49. Passes through $(-8, 2)$ and $(-8, 17)$ $x = -8$

50. Vertical, passes through $(-3, 7)$ $x = -3$

51. Vertical, passes through $(12, -23)$ $x = 12$

52. Slope 7 and y-intercept $(0, 0)$ $y = 7x$

53. Slope 3 and y-intercept $(0, 4)$ $y = 3x + 4$

54. Passes through $(-2, -1)$ and $(-1, -5)$ $y = -4x - 9$

55. Passes through $(-3, 6)$ and $(-1, -4)$ $y = -5x - 9$

56. x-intercept $(7, 0)$ and y-intercept $(0, -2)$ $y = \frac{2}{7}x - 2$

57. x-intercept $(-3, 0)$ and y-intercept $(0, 7)$ $y = \frac{7}{3}x + 7$

58. Slope $\dfrac{1}{10}$, passes through the origin $y = \frac{1}{10}x$

59. Slope $\dfrac{9}{8}$, passes through the origin $y = \frac{9}{8}x$

60. Undefined slope, passes through $\left(-\dfrac{1}{8}, 12\right)$ $x = -\frac{1}{8}$

61. Undefined slope, passes through $\left(\dfrac{2}{5}, -\dfrac{5}{6}\right)$ $x = \frac{2}{5}$

62. Horizontal, passes through $(-8, 12)$ $y = 12$

63. Horizontal, passes through $(9, -32)$ $y = -32$

64. Slope $\dfrac{2}{3}$, x-intercept $(4, 0)$ $y = \frac{2}{3}x - \frac{8}{3}$

▶ **65.** TOXIC CLEANUP Three months after cleanup began at a dump site, 800 cubic yards of toxic waste had yet to be removed. Two months later, that number had been lowered to 720 cubic yards.

   a. Write a linear equation that mathematically describes the linear relationship between the length of time x (in months) the cleanup crew has been working and the number of cubic yards y of toxic waste remaining. $y = -40x + 920$

   b. Use your answer to part a to predict the number of cubic yards of waste that will still be on the site 1 year after the cleanup project began. 440 yd³

▶ **66.** DEPRECIATION To lower its corporate income tax, accountants of a large company depreciated a word processing system over several years using a linear model, as shown in the worksheet on the next page.

   a. Use the information in the worksheet to write a linear equation relating the years since the system was purchased x and its value y, in dollars. $y = -15,000x + 90,000$

b. Find the purchase price of the system by substituting $x = 0$ into your answer from part a. $90,000

Tax Worksheet

Method of depreciation: *Linear*

Property	Years after purchase	Value
Word processing system	2	$60,000
"	4	$30,000

67. POLE VAULTING Find the equations of the lines that describe the positions of the pole for parts 1, 3, and 4 of the jump. Write the equations in slope–intercept form, if possible.
$y = -\frac{2}{5}x + 4, \ y = -7x + 70, \ x = 10$

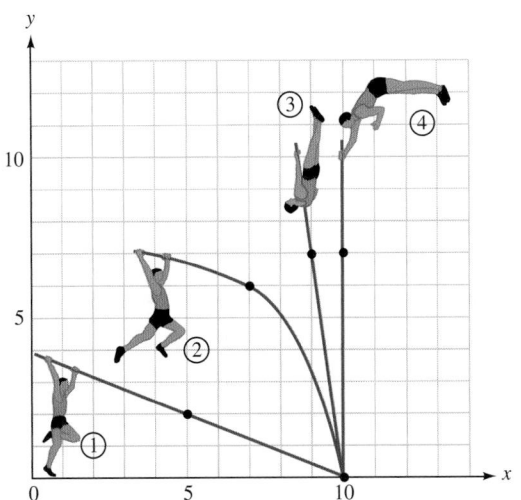

68. FREEWAY DESIGN The graph below shows the route of a proposed freeway.

a. Give the coordinates of the points where the proposed freeway will join Interstate 25 and Highway 40. $(-3, -4), (6, 2)$

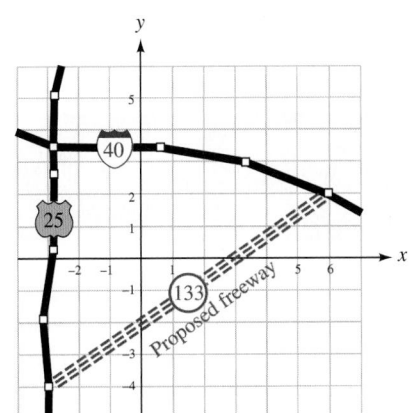

b. Write the equation of the line that mathematically describes the route of the proposed freeway. Answer in slope–intercept form. $y = \frac{2}{3}x - 2$

69. COUNSELING In the first year of her practice, a family counselor saw 75 clients. In the second year, the number of clients grew to 105. If a linear trend continues, write an equation that gives the number of clients c the counselor will have t years after beginning her practice. $c = 30t + 45$

70. GOT MILK The diagram below shows the amount of milk that an average American drank in one year for the years 1980–2004. A straight line can be used to model these data.

a. Use the highlighted two points on the line to find its equation. Write the equation in slope–intercept form. $y = -\frac{3}{10}x + \frac{283}{10}$

b. Use your answer to part a to predict the amount of milk that an average American will drink in 2020. 16.3 gal

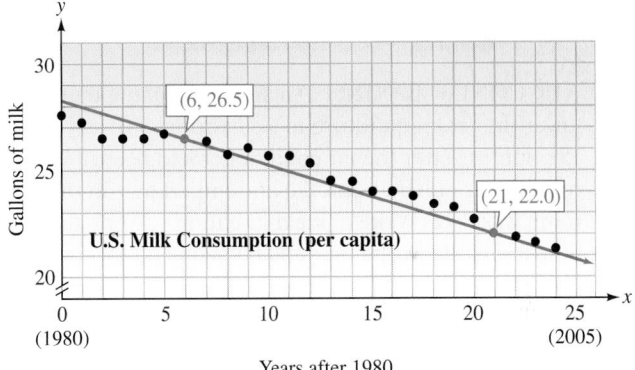

Source: United States Department of Agriculture

71. CONVERTING TEMPERATURES The relationship between Fahrenheit temperature, F, and Celsius temperature, C, is linear.

a. Use the data in the illustration below to write two ordered pairs of the form (C, F). $(0, 32), (100, 212)$

b. Use your answer to part a to write a linear equation relating the Fahrenheit and Celsius scales. $F = \frac{9}{5}C + 32$

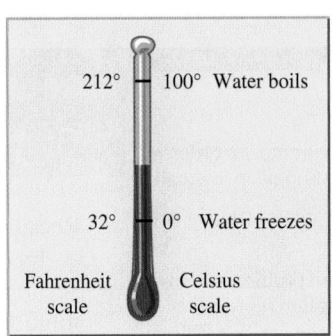

▶ **72.** TRAMPOLINES The relationship between the circumference of a circle and its radius is linear. For example, the length l of the protective pad that wraps around a trampoline is related to the radius r of the trampoline. Use the data in the illustration to write a linear equation that approximates the length of pad needed for any trampoline radius. $l = 6.25r + 0.25$

Radius (ft)	Approximate length of padding (ft)
3	19
7	44

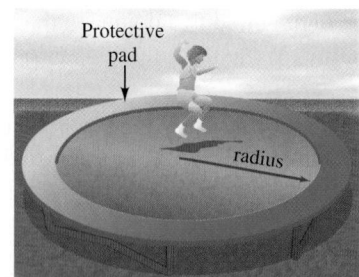

▶ **73.** AIR-CONDITIONING An air-conditioning unit can lower the air temperature in a classroom 4° every 15 minutes. After the air conditioner had been running for half an hour, the air temperature in the room was 75°F. Write a linear equation relating the time in minutes x the unit had been on and the temperature y of the classroom. (*Hint:* How many minutes are there in half an hour?) $y = -\frac{4}{15}x + 83$

▶ **74.** AUTOMATION An automated production line uses distilled water at a rate of 300 gallons every 2 hours to make shampoo. After the line had run for 7 hours, planners noted that 2,500 gallons of distilled water remained in the storage tank. Write a linear equation relating the time in hours x since the production line began and the number of gallons y of distilled water in the storage tank. $y = -150x + 3,550$

WRITING

75. Why is $y - y_1 = m(x - x_1)$ called the point–slope form of the equation of a line?

▶ **76.** If we know two points that a line passes through, we can write its equation. Explain how to do this.

77. If we know the slope of a line and a point it passes through, we can write its equation. Explain how to do this.

▶ **78.** Think of several points on the graph of the horizontal line $y = 4$. What do the points have in common? How do they differ?

REVIEW

79. Find the slope of the line passing through the points $(2, 4)$ and $(-6, 8)$. $-\frac{1}{2}$

80. Is the graph of $y = x^2$ a straight line? no

81. Find the area of a circle with a diameter of 12 feet. Round to the nearest tenth. 113.1 ft^2

82. If a 15-foot board is cut into two pieces and we let x represent the length of one piece (in feet), write an expression for the length of the other piece. $(15 - x)$ ft

83. Evaluate: $(-1)^5$ -1

▶ **84.** Solve: $\dfrac{x - 3}{4} = -4$ -13

85. What is the coefficient of the second term of $-4x^2 + 6x - 13$? 6

86. Simplify: $(-2p)(-5)(4x)$ $40px$

Objectives

1 Determine whether an ordered pair is a solution of an inequality.

2 Graph a linear inequality in two variables.

3 Solve applied problems involving linear inequalities in two variables.

SECTION **3.7**

Graphing Linear Inequalities

Recall that an **inequality** is a statement that contains one of the symbols $<$, $\le$, $>$, or $\ge$. Inequalities in one variable, such as $x - 5 < 2$ and $3x + 4 > 2x$, were solved in Section 2.7. Because they have an infinite number of solutions, we represented their solution sets graphically, by shading intervals on a number line.

We now extend that concept to linear inequalities *in two variables,* as we introduce a procedure that is used to graph their solution sets.

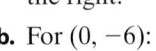 **Determine whether an ordered pair is a solution of an inequality.**

If the $=$ symbol in a linear equation in two variables is replaced with an inequality symbol, we have a **linear inequality in two variables.** Some examples are

$$2x - y > -3, \qquad y < 3, \qquad x + 4y \geq 6, \qquad \text{and} \qquad x \leq -2$$

As with linear equations, an ordered pair (x, y) is **a solution of an inequality** in x and y if a true statement results when the variables in the inequality are replaced by the coordinates of the ordered pair.

EXAMPLE 1 Determine whether each ordered pair is a solution of $x - y \leq 5$. Then graph each solution: **a.** $(4, 2)$ **b.** $(0, -6)$ **c.** $(1, -4)$

Strategy We will substitute each ordered pair of coordinates into the inequality.

WHY If the resulting statement is true, the ordered pair is a solution.

Solution

a. For $(4, 2)$:

$$x - y \leq 5 \qquad \text{This is the original inequality.}$$
$$4 - 2 \overset{?}{\leq} 5 \qquad \text{Replace 4 for } x \text{ and 2 for } y.$$
$$2 \leq 5 \qquad \text{This is true.}$$

Because $2 \leq 5$ is true, $(4, 2)$ is a solution of $x - y \leq 5$. We say that $(4, 2)$ *satisfies* the inequality. This solution is graphed as shown on the right.

b. For $(0, -6)$:

$$x - y \leq 5 \qquad \text{This is the original inequality.}$$
$$0 - (-6) \overset{?}{\leq} 5 \qquad \text{Replace 0 for } x \text{ and } -6 \text{ for } y.$$
$$6 \leq 5 \qquad \text{This is false.}$$

Because $6 \leq 5$ is false, $(0, -6)$ is not a solution.

c. For $(1, -4)$:

$$x - y \leq 5 \qquad \text{This is the original inequality.}$$
$$1 - (-4) \overset{?}{\leq} 5 \qquad \text{Replace 1 for } x \text{ and } -4 \text{ for } y.$$
$$5 \leq 5 \qquad \text{This is true.}$$

Because $5 \leq 5$ is true, $(1, -4)$ is a solution, and we graph it as shown.

Self Check 1

Using the inequality in Example 1, determine whether each ordered pair is a solution.
a. $(8, 2)$ not a solution
b. $(4, -1)$ solution
c. $(-2, 4)$ solution
d. $(-3, -5)$ solution

Now Try **Problem 33**

Teaching Example 1 Using the inequality in Example 1, determine whether each ordered pair is a solution.
a. $(-2, 1)$
b. $(0, 0)$
c. $(9, -1)$
Answers:
a. solution **b.** solution
c. not a solution

In Example 1, we graphed two solutions of the inequality $x - y \leq 5$. Since there are infinitely many more ordered pairs (x, y) that make the inequality true, it would not be reasonable to plot them. Fortunately, there is an easier way to show all of the solutions.

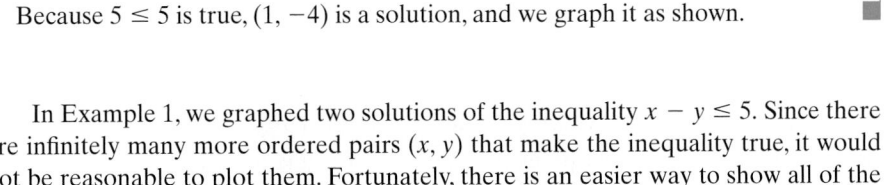 **Graph a linear inequality in two variables.**

The graph of $x - y = 5$ is a line consisting of the points whose coordinates satisfy the equation. The graph of the inequality $x - y \leq 5$ is not a line, but an area bounded by a line, called a **half-plane.** The half-plane consists of the points whose coordinates satisfy the inequality, and we use a two-step procedure to find them.

Self Check 2

Graph: $2x + y \leq 4$

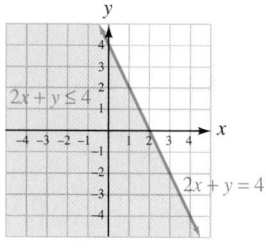

Now Try Problem 37

Teaching Example 2 Graph:
$3x - y \leq 6$
Answer:

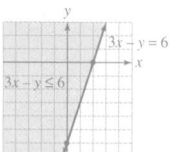

EXAMPLE 2   Graph: $x - y \leq 5$

Strategy We will graph the related *equation* $x - y = 5$ to establish a boundary line between two regions of the coordinate plane. Then we will determine which region contains points whose coordinates satisfy the given inequality.

WHY The graph of a linear inequality in two variables is a region of the coordinate plane on one side of the boundary line.

Solution

Since the inequality symbol $\leq$ includes an equals sign, the graph of $x - y \leq 5$ includes the graph of $x - y = 5$.

Step 1 Graph the equation $x - y = 5$ using the intercept method, as shown in figure (a).

$x - y = 5$		
x	y	(x, y)
0	−5	$(0, -5)$
5	0	$(5, 0)$
6	1	$(6, 1)$

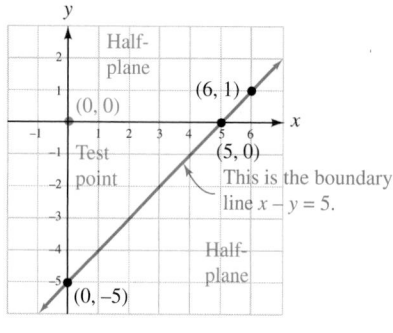

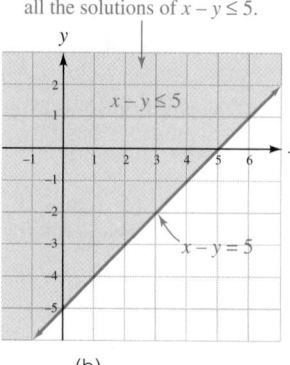

This shaded half-plane and the solid boundary represent all the solutions of $x - y \leq 5$.

(a)   (b)

Step 2 Since the inequality $x - y \leq 5$ allows $x - y$ to be less than 5, the coordinates of points other than those shown on the boundary satisfy the inequality. For example, the coordinates of the origin $(0, 0)$ satisfy the inequality. We can verify this by letting x and y be zero in the given inequality:

$$x - y \leq 5$$
$$0 - 0 \overset{?}{\leq} 5 \quad \text{Substitute 0 for x and 0 for y.}$$
$$0 \leq 5$$

Because $0 \leq 5$, the coordinates of the origin satisfy the original inequality. In fact, the coordinates of every point on the *same side* of the line as the origin satisfy the inequality. The graph of $x - y \leq 5$ is the half-plane that is shaded in figure (b). Since the **boundary line** $x - y = 5$ is included, we draw it with a solid line. ∎

EXAMPLE 3   Graph: $x + y \geq 3$

Strategy We will graph the related *equation* $x + y = 3$ to establish a boundary line between two regions of the coordinate plane. Then we will determine which region contains points whose coordinates satisfy the given inequality.

WHY The graph of a linear inequality in two variables is a region of the coordinate plane on one side of the boundary line.

Solution

To graph the inequality $x + y \geq 3$, we graph the boundary line whose equation is $x + y = 3$. Since the graph of $x + y \geq 3$ includes the line $x + y = 3$, we draw the boundary with a solid line. See figure (a) below. Note that it divides the coordinate plane into two half-planes.

To decide which half-plane to shade, we substitute the coordinates of some point that lies on one side of the boundary line into the inequality. If we use the origin $(0, 0)$ for the **test point,** we have

$$x + y \geq 3$$
$$0 + 0 \geq 3 \quad \text{Substitute 0 for x and 0 for y.}$$
$$0 \geq 3 \quad \text{This is false.}$$

Since $0 \geq 3$ is a false statement, the origin is not in the graph. In fact, the coordinates of *every* point on the origin's side of the boundary line will not satisfy the inequality. However, every point on the other side of the boundary line will satisfy the inequality. We shade that half-plane. The graph of $x + y \geq 3$ is the half-plane that appears in color in figure (b).

$x + y = 3$		
x	y	(x, y)
0	3	$(0, 3)$
3	0	$(3, 0)$
1	2	$(1, 2)$

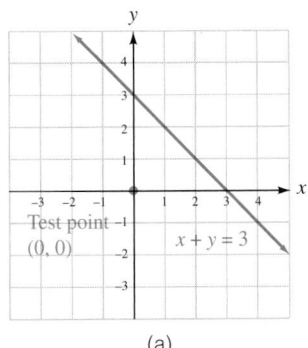

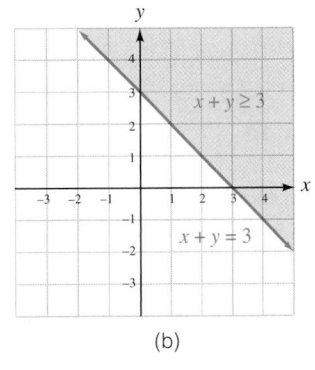

(a)   (b)

EXAMPLE 4   Graph: $y > 2x$

Strategy We will graph the related *equation* $y = 2x$ to establish a boundary line between two regions of the coordinate plane. Then we will determine which region contains points whose coordinates satisfy the given inequality.

WHY The graph of a linear inequality in two variables is a region of the coordinate plane on one side of the boundary line.

Solution

To find the boundary line, we graph $y = 2x$. Since the symbol $>$ does not include an equals sign, the points on the graph of $y = 2x$ are not part of the graph of $y > 2x$. We draw the boundary line as a dashed line to show this. See figure (a) on the next page.

To determine which half-plane to shade, we substitute the coordinates of some point that lies on one side of the boundary line into $y > 2x$. Since the origin is on the boundary, we cannot use it as a test point. The point $(2, 0)$, for example, is not on the boundary line. To see whether $(2, 0)$ satisfies $y > 2x$, we substitute 2 for x and 0 for y in the inequality.

$$y > 2x$$
$$0 > 2(2) \quad \text{Substitute 2 for x and 0 for y.}$$
$$0 > 4 \quad \text{This is false.}$$

Self Check 3

Graph: $x - y \leq -2$

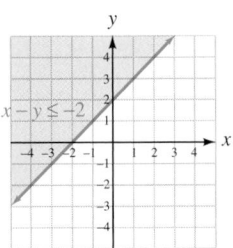

Now Try **Problem 39**

Teaching Example 3 Graph: $2x + y \geq 2$
Answer:

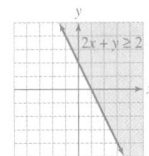

Self Check 4

Graph: $y < 3x$

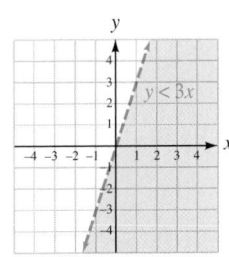

Now Try **Problem 42**

Teaching Example 4 Graph: $y > -\frac{1}{2}x$
Answer:

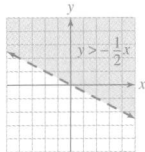

Since $0 > 4$ is a false statement, the point $(2, 0)$ does not satisfy the inequality, and is not on the side of the dashed line we wish to shade. Instead, we shade the other side of the boundary line. The graph of the solution set of $y > 2x$ is shown in figure (b).

y = 2x		
x	**y**	**(x, y)**
0	0	(0, 0)
−1	−2	(−1, −2)
1	2	(1, 2)

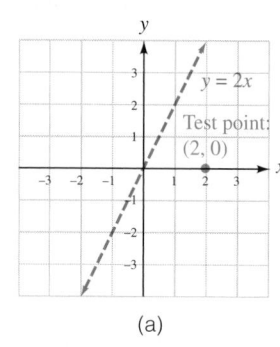

(a)

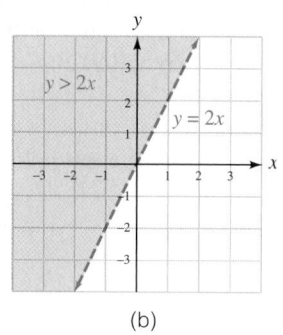

(b)

Self Check 5

Graph: $2x - y < 4$

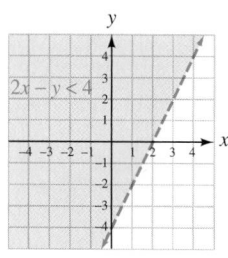

Now Try Problem 45

Teaching Example 5 Graph:
$4x + 2y < 6$
Answer:

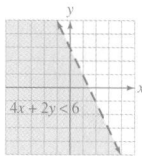

EXAMPLE 5   Graph: $x + 2y < 6$

Strategy We will graph the related *equation* $x + 2y = 6$ to establish a boundary line between two regions of the coordinate plane. Then we will determine which region contains points whose coordinates satisfy the given inequality.

WHY The graph of a linear inequality in two variables is a region of the coordinate plane on one side of the boundary line.

Solution
We find the boundary by graphing the equation $x + 2y = 6$. We draw the boundary as a dashed line to show that it is not part of the solution. We then choose a test point not on the boundary and see whether its coordinates satisfy $x + 2y < 6$. The origin is a convenient choice.

$$x + 2y < 6$$
$$0 + 2(0) < 6 \quad \text{Substitute 0 for x and 0 for y.}$$
$$0 < 6 \quad \text{This is true.}$$

Since $0 < 6$ is a true statement, we shade the side of the line that includes the origin. The graph is shown in the illustration.

x + 2y = 6		
x	**y**	**(x, y)**
0	3	(0, 3)
6	0	(6, 0)
4	1	(4, 1)

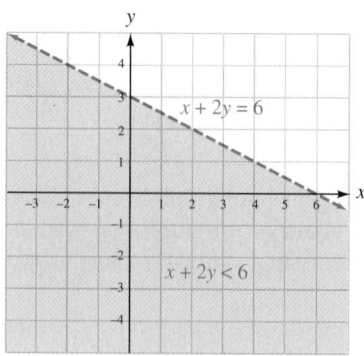

EXAMPLE 6   Graph: $y \geq 0$

Strategy We will graph the related *equation* $y = 0$ to establish a boundary line between two regions of the coordinate plane. Then we will determine which region contains points whose coordinates satisfy the given inequality.

WHY The graph of a linear inequality in two variables is a region of the coordinate plane on one side of the boundary line.

Solution

We find the boundary by graphing the equation $y = 0$. We draw the boundary as a solid line to show that it is part of the solution. We then choose a test point not on the boundary and see whether its coordinates satisfy $y \geq 0$. The point $(0, 1)$ is a convenient choice.

$$y \geq 0$$
$$1 \geq 0 \quad \text{Substitute 1 for } y.$$

Since $1 \geq 0$ is a true statement, we shade the side of the line that includes $(0, 1)$. The graph is shown below.

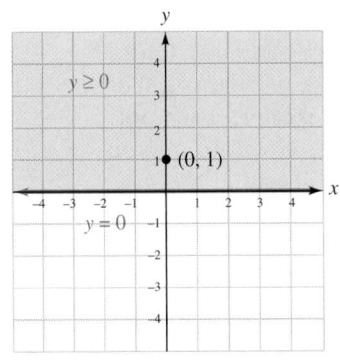

$y = 0$		
x	y	(x, y)
1	0	$(1, 0)$
2	0	$(2, 0)$
3	0	$(3, 0)$

The following is a summary of the procedure for graphing linear inequalities.

Graphing Linear Inequalities in Two Variables

1. Replace the inequality symbol with an equal symbol $=$ and graph the boundary line of the region. If the inequality allows the possibility of equality (the symbol is either $\leq$ or $\geq$), draw the boundary line as a solid line. If equality is not allowed ($<$ or $>$), draw the boundary line as a dashed line.

2. Pick a test point that is on one side of the boundary line. (Use the origin if possible.) Replace x and y in the inequality with the coordinates of that point. If the inequality is satisfied, shade the side that contains that point. If the inequality is not satisfied, shade the other side of the boundary.

---

3 Solve applied problems involving linear inequalities in two variables.

When solving applied problems, phrases such as *at least, at most,* and *should not exceed* indicate that an inequality should be used.

EXAMPLE 7   *Earning Money*   Carlos has two jobs, one paying \$10 per hour and one paying \$12 per hour. He must earn at least \$240 per week to pay his expenses while attending college. Write an inequality that shows the ways he can schedule his time to achieve his goal.

Strategy We will form an inequality using the facts about the two jobs Carlos has. Then we will graph the solution of the inequality.

Self Check 6

Graph: $x \geq 2$

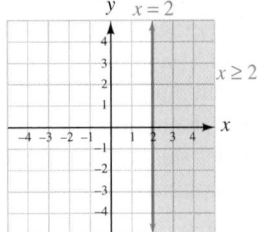

Now Try Problem 51

Teaching Example 6 Graph: $x < -3$
Answer:

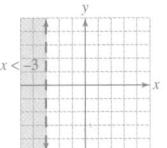

Self Check 7

Brianna and Ashley pool their resources to purchase some songs and movies on iTunes. If songs cost $1 and movies cost $4, write an inequality to represent the number of songs and movies they can buy if they have a combined spending amount of $25. $x + 4y \leq 25$

Now Try Problem 73

Teaching Example 7 Carly is going to purchase some CDs and some DVDs. If each CD costs $12 and each DVD costs $20, write an inequality to represent the number of CDs and DVDs she can buy if she wants to spend $60 or less.
Answer:
$12x + 20y \leq 60$

WHY The graph of a linear inequality in two variables gives the ways Carlos can schedule his time to achieve his goal.

Solution

If we let x represent the number of hours Carlos works on the first job and y the number of hours he works on the second job, we have

The hourly rate on the first job	times	the hours worked on the first job	plus	the hourly rate on the second job	times	the hours worked on the second job	is at least	$240.
10	·	x	+	12	·	y	≥	240

The graph of the inequality $10x + 12y \geq 240$ is shown in the figure to the right. Any point in the shaded region indicates a possible way Carlos can schedule his time and earn $240 or more per week. For example, if he works 20 hours on the first job and 10 hours on the second job, he will earn

$$\$10(20) + \$12(10) = \$200 + \$120$$
$$= \$320$$

Since Carlos cannot work a negative number of hours, a graph showing negative values of x or y would have no meaning.

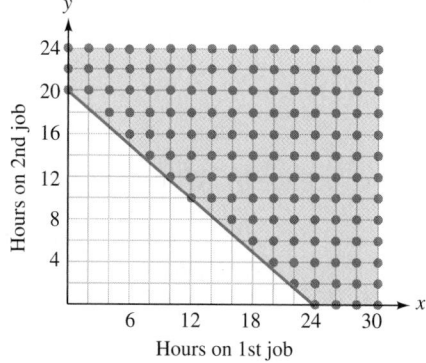

ANSWERS TO SELF CHECKS

1. a. not a solution **b.** solution **c.** solution **d.** solution

2.

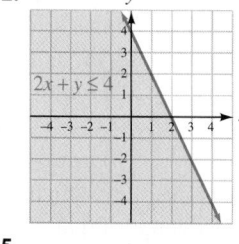

3.

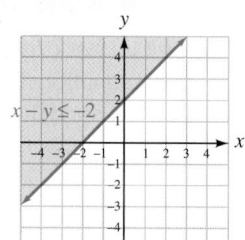

4.

5.

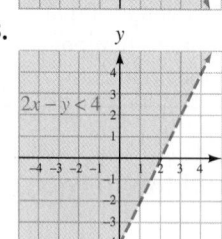

6.

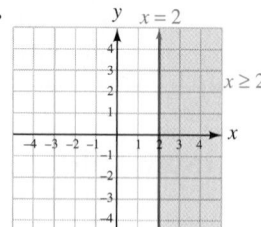

7. $x + 4y \leq 25$

SECTION 3.7   STUDY SET

▌ VOCABULARY

Fill in the blanks.

1. $2x - y \leq 4$ is a linear ___inequality___ in x and y.

2. In the illustration on the next page, the line $2x - y = 4$ divides the rectangular coordinate system into two ___half-planes___.

▶ Selected exercises available online at
www.webassign.net/brookscole

3. In the illustration, the graph of the line $2x - y = 4$ is the <u>boundary</u> line.

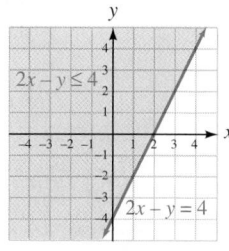

4. When graphing a linear inequality, we determine which half-plane to shade by substituting the coordinates of a <u>test point</u> into the inequality.

CONCEPTS

Determine whether each ordered pair is a solution of $5x - 3y \leq 0$.

5. $(1, 1)$ yes   **6.** $(-2, -3)$ no

7. $(0, 0)$ yes   **8.** $\left(\dfrac{1}{5}, \dfrac{4}{3}\right)$ no

Determine whether each ordered pair is a solution of $x + 4y < -1$.

9. $(3, 1)$ no   **10.** $(-2, 0)$ yes

11. $(-0.5, 0.2)$ no   **12.** $\left(-2, \dfrac{1}{4}\right)$ no

Determine whether the graph of each linear inequality includes the boundary line. When graphed, is the boundary line solid or dashed?

13. $y > -x$ no, dashed   **14.** $5x - 3y \leq -2$ yes, solid

The graph of a linear inequality is shown below. Determine whether each point satisfies the inequality.

15. $(1, -3)$ no
16. $(-2, -1)$ yes
17. $(2, 3)$ yes
18. $(3, -4)$ no

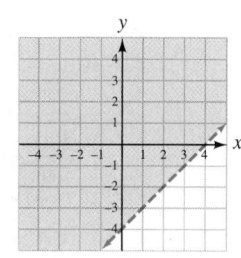

The graph of a linear inequality is shown below. Determine whether each point satisfies the inequality.

19. $(2, 1)$ yes
20. $(-2, -4)$ no
21. $(4, -2)$ no
22. $(-3, 4)$ yes

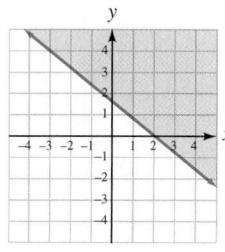

23. The boundary line for the graph of a linear inequality is shown. Why can't the origin be used as a test point to determine which side to shade?
The test point must be on one side of the boundary.

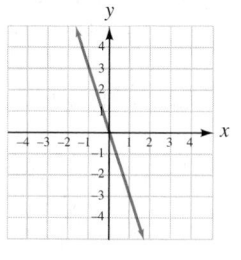

24. To determine how many pallets (x) and barrels (y) a delivery truck can hold, a dispatcher refers to the loading sheet on the right. Can a truck make a delivery of 4 pallets and 10 barrels in one trip? no

Truck Loading Sheet
(acceptable load combinations)

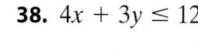

NOTATION

Write the meaning of each symbol.

25. $\leq$ is less than or equal to   **26.** $>$ is greater than

27. $<$ is less than   **28.** $\geq$ is greater than or equal to

GUIDED PRACTICE

Determine whether each ordered pair is a solution of the given inequality. **See Example 1.**

▶ **29.** $2x + y > 6, (3, 2)$ yes   **30.** $4x - 2y \geq -6, (-2, 1)$ no

▶ **31.** $-5x - 8y < 8, (-8, 4)$ no   **32.** $x + 3y > 14; (-3, 8)$ yes

33. $4x - y \leq 0, \left(\dfrac{1}{2}, 1\right)$ no   **34.** $9x - y \leq 2, \left(\dfrac{1}{3}, 1\right)$ yes

35. $-5x + 2y > -4, (0.8, 0.6)$ yes
36. $6x - 2y < -7, (-0.2, 1.5)$ no

Complete each graph by shading the correct side of the boundary. **See Examples 2–3.**

▶ **37.** $x + y \leq 1$ **38.** $4x + 3y \leq 12$

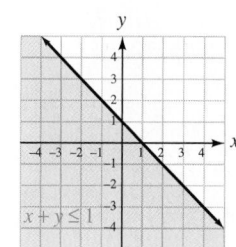

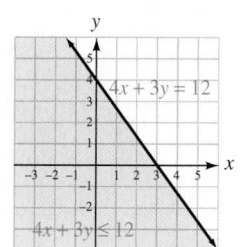

39. $x - 2y \geq 4$

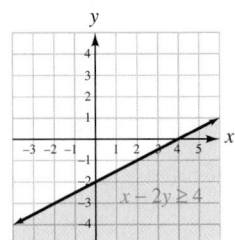

40. $y + 9x \geq 3$

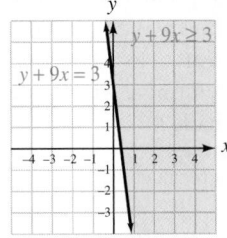

Graph each inequality. See Example 4.

41. $y > x - 3$

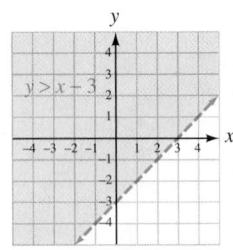

▶ **42.** $y > 3x$

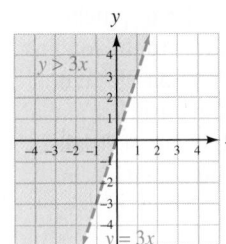

43. $y \leq x + 2$

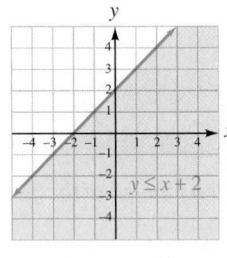

44. $y \geq 2x$

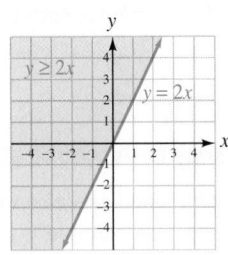

Graph each inequality. See Example 5.

45. $2y - x < 8$

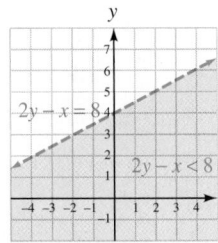

46. $3x + 2y > 12$

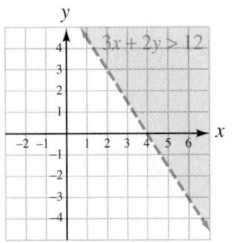

▶ **47.** $2x + y > 2$

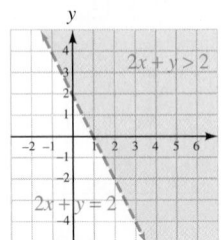

48. $7x - 2y < 21$

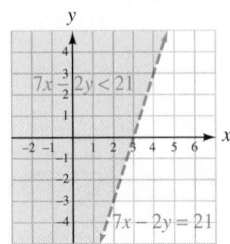

Graph each inequality. See Example 6.

49. $x < 2$

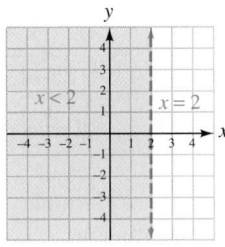

▶ **50.** $y > -3$

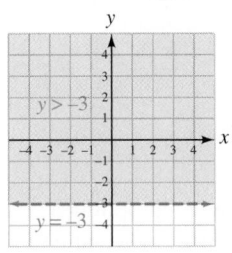

51. $y \leq 1$

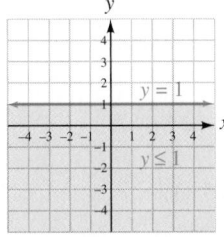

▶ **52.** $x \geq -4$

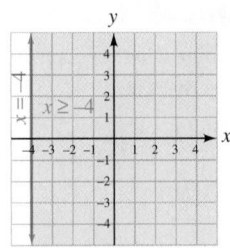

TRY IT YOURSELF

Graph each inequality.

53. $y - x \geq 0$

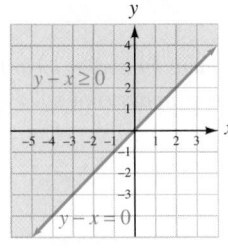

54. $y + x < 0$

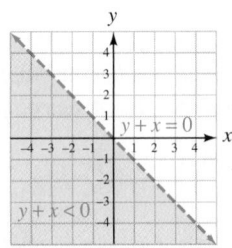

55. $y \geq 3 - x$

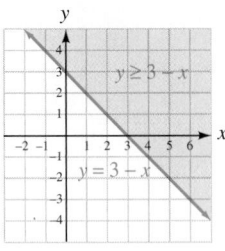

56. $y < 2 - x$

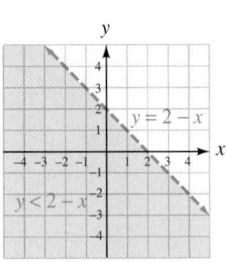

57. $y < 2 - 3x$

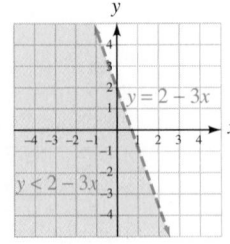

58. $y \geq 5 - 2x$

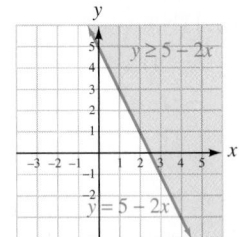

59. $y > 2x - 4$ **60.** $y \le 4x$

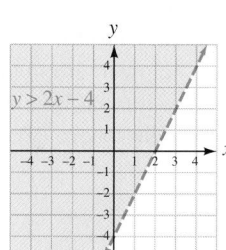   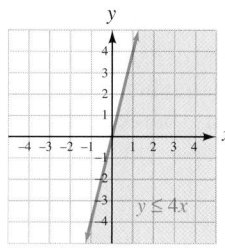

61. $y + 2x < 0$ **62.** $3x - 2y > 6$

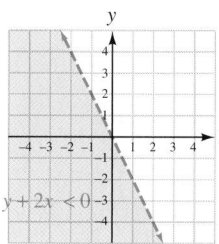   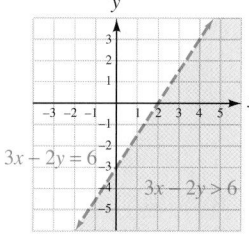

63. $3x - 4y > 12$ **64.** $5x + 4y \ge 20$

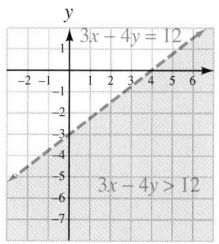   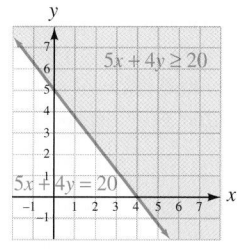

65. $3(x + y) + x < 6$ **66.** $2(x - y) - y \ge 4$

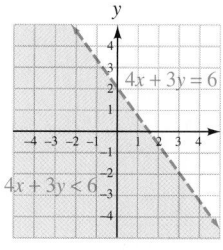   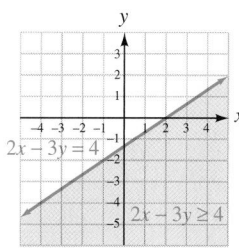

67. $4x - 3(x + 2y) \ge -6y$ **68.** $3y + 2(x + y) < 5y$

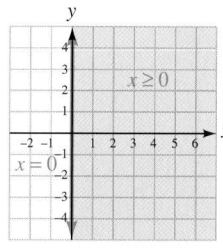   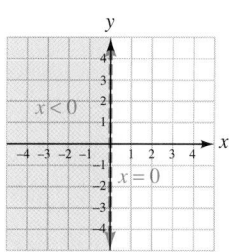

APPLICATIONS

69. NATO See the illustration in the next column. In March 1999, NATO aircraft and cruise missiles targeted Serbian military forces that were south of the 44th parallel in Yugoslavia, Montenegro, and Kosovo. Shade the geographic area that NATO was trying to rid of Serbian forces.

Based on data from *Los Angeles Times* (March 24, 1999)

70. U.S. HISTORY When he ran for president in 1844, the campaign slogan of James K. Polk was "54-40 or fight!" It meant that Polk was willing to fight Great Britain for the possession of the Oregon Territory north to the 54°40′ parallel, as shown below. In 1846, Polk accepted a compromise to establish the 49th parallel as the permanent boundary of the United States. Shade the area of land that Polk conceded to the British.

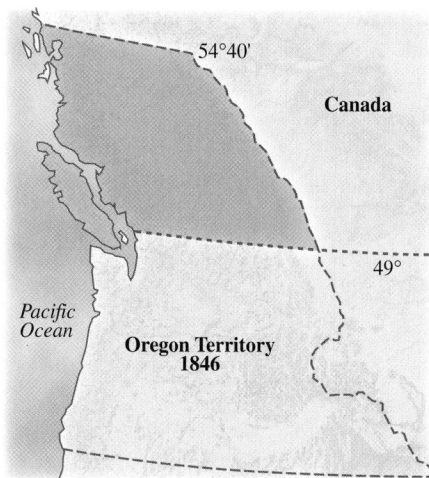

Write an inequality and graph it for nonnegative values of x and y. Then give three ordered pairs that satisfy the inequality.

71. PRODUCTION PLANNING It costs a bakery $3 to make a cake and $4 to make a pie. Production costs cannot exceed $120 per day. Use the illustration below to graph an inequality that shows the possible combinations of cakes (x) and pies (y) that can be made. $(10, 10), (20, 10), (10, 20)$

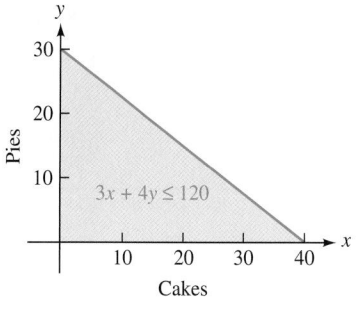

▶ **72. HIRING BABYSITTERS** Mary has a choice of two babysitters. Sitter 1 charges $6 per hour, and sitter 2 charges $7 per hour. If Mary can afford no more than $42 per week for sitters, use the illustration below to graph an inequality that shows the possible ways that she can hire sitter 1 (x) and sitter 2 (y). (2, 2), (4, 2), (3, 3)

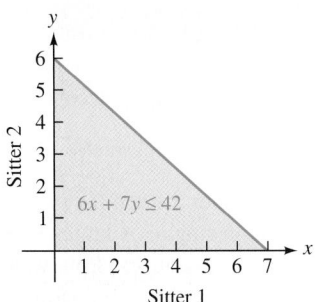

73. INVENTORIES A clothing store advertises that it maintains an inventory of at least $4,400 worth of men's jackets. If a leather jacket costs $100 and a nylon jacket costs $88, use the illustration to graph an inequality that shows the possible ways that leather jackets (x) and nylon jackets (y) can be stocked. (50, 50), (30, 40), (40, 40)

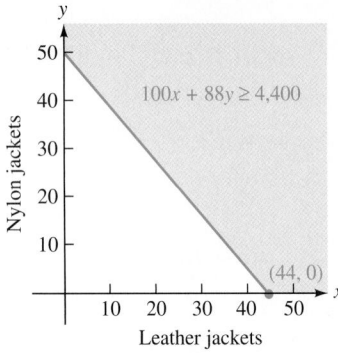

▶ **74. MAKING SPORTING GOODS** A sporting goods manufacturer allocates at least 2,400 units of production time per day to make baseballs and footballs. If it takes 20 units of time to make a baseball and 30 units of time to make a football, use the illustration to graph an inequality that shows the possible ways to schedule the production time to make baseballs (x) and footballs (y). (60, 80), (100, 60), (120, 40)

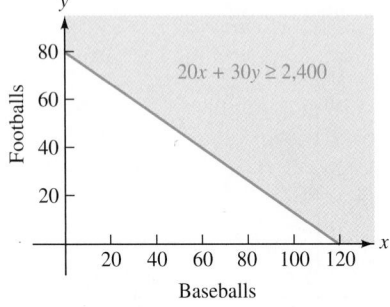

▶ **75. INVESTING** Robert has up to $8,000 to invest in two companies. If stock in Robotronics sells for $40 per share and stock in Macrocorp sells for $50 per share, use the illustration below to graph an inequality that shows the possible ways that he can buy shares of Robotronics (x) and Macrocorp (y). (80, 40), (80, 80), (120, 40)

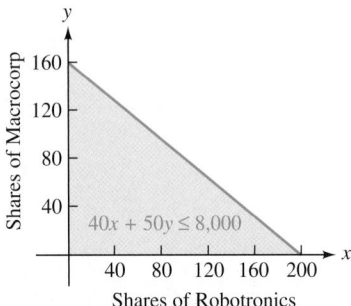

▶ **76. BASEBALL TICKETS** Tickets to the Rockford Rox baseball games cost $6 for reserved seats and $4 for general admission. If nightly receipts must average at least $10,200 to meet expenses, use the illustration to graph an inequality that shows the possible ways that the Rox can sell reserved seats (x) and general admission tickets (y). (1,200, 2,000), (1,600, 1,200), (800, 2,400)

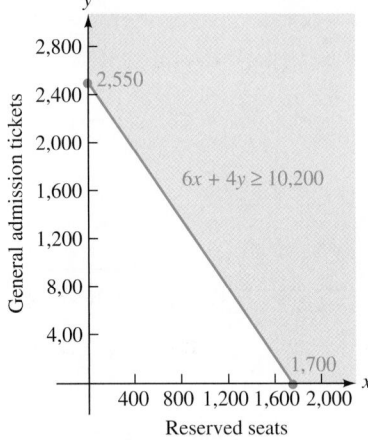

77. Explain how to find the boundary for the graph of a linear inequality in two variables.

▶ **78.** Explain how to determine which side of the boundary line to shade when graphing a linear inequality in two variables.

79. 39.75 is what percent of 265? 15%

80. Solve: $2(x - 4) \le -12$ $x \le -2$

81. Solve: $c = d\pi$ for d $d = \frac{c}{\pi}$

82. Solve: $-2x + 5 = -9$ 7

83. Write a formula relating distance, rate, and time. $d = rt$

84. What is the slope of the line $2x - 3y = 2$? $\frac{2}{3}$

85. Solve $A = P + Prt$ for t. $t = \frac{A - P}{Pr}$

▶ **86.** What is the sum of the measures of the three angles of any triangle? 180°

SECTION **3.8**

Functions

Objectives

1. Find the domain and range of a relation.

2. Identify functions and their domains and ranges.

3. Use function notation.

4. Graph functions.

5. Use the vertical line test.

In this section, we will discuss *relations* and *functions*. These two concepts are included in our study of graphing because they involve ordered pairs.

1 Find the domain and range of a relation.

The following table shows the number of medals won by American athletes at seven recent Winter Olympics.

USA Winter Olympic Medal Count

Year	1984	1988	1992	1994*	1998	2002	2006
Medals	8	6	11	13	13	34	25
	Sarajevo YUG	Calgary CAN	Albertville FRA	Lillehammer NOR	Nagano JPN	Salt Lake City USA	Turin ITA

* The Winter Olympics were moved ahead two years so that the winter and summer games would alternate every two years.

We can display the data in the table as a set of ordered pairs, where the **first component** represents the year and the **second component** represents the number of medals won by American athletes:

{(1984, 8), (1988, 6), (1992, 11), (1994, 13), (1998, 13), (2002, 34), (2006, 25)}

A set of ordered pairs, such as this, is called a **relation.** The set of all first components is called the **domain** of the relation and the set of all second components is called the **range** of a relation.

EXAMPLE 1   Find the domain and range of the relation $\{(1, 7), (4, -6), (-3, 1), (2, 7)\}$.

Strategy We will examine the first and second components of the ordered pairs.

WHY The set of first components is the domain and the set of second components is the range.

Solution

The relation $\{(1, 7), (4, -6), (-3, 1), (2, 7)\}$ has the domain $\{-3, 1, 2, 4\}$ and the range is $\{-6, 1, 7\}$. The elements of the domain and range are usually listed in increasing order, and if a value is repeated, it is listed only once.

In everyday life, we see a wide variety of situations where one quantity depends on another:

- The distance traveled by a car depends on its speed.
- The cost of renting a video depends on the number of days it is rented.
- A state's number of representatives in Congress depends on the state's population.

We will discuss many situations where one quantity depends on another according to a specific rule, called a *function*. For example, the equation $y = 2x - 3$ sets up a rule where each value of y depends on the choice of some number x. The rule is: *To find y, double the value of x and subtract* 3. In this case, y (the *dependent variable*) depends on x (the *independent variable*).

2   Identify functions and their domains and ranges.

We have previously described relationships between two quantities in different ways:

Using words

The number of tires to order	is	two	times	the number of bicycles to be manufactured.

Here words are used to state that the number of bicycle tires to order depends on the number of bicycles to be manufactured.

Using equations

$t = 1,500 - d$

This equation describes how the amount of take-home pay t depends on the amount of deductions d.

Using graphs

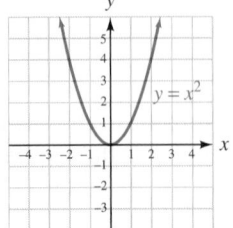

This rectangular coordinate graph shows many ordered pairs (x, y) that satisfy the equation $y = x^2$, where the value of the y-coordinate depends on the value of the x-coordinate.

Using tables

Acres	Schools
400	4
800	8
1,000	10
2,000	20

This table shows that the number of schools needed depends on the size of the housing development.

An **arrow** or **mapping diagram** can also be used to illustrate a relation. The data from the Winter Olympics example is shown below in that form.

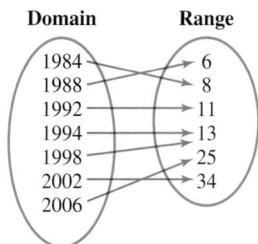

Notice that for each year, there corresponds exactly one medal count. That is, this relation assigns to each member of the domain exactly one member of the range.

Two observations can be made about these examples:

- Each one establishes a relationship between two sets of values. For example, the number of bicycle tires that must be ordered *depends* on the number of bicycles to be manufactured.
- In these relationships, each value in one set is assigned a *single* value of a second set. For example, for each number of bicycles to be manufactured, there is exactly one number of tires to order.

Relationships between two quantities that exhibit both of these characteristics are called **functions.**

Functions

A **function** is a set of ordered pairs (a relation) in which to each first component there corresponds exactly one second component.

Using the variables x and y, we can restate the previous definition as follows:

y Is a Function of *x*

For y to be a function of x, each value of x must determine exactly one value of y.

EXAMPLE 2   Determine whether the equation, table, and arrow diagram define y to be a function of x.

a. $y = 4x + 1$ **b.**

x	y
0	6
5	3
9	1
5	7
10	8

c.

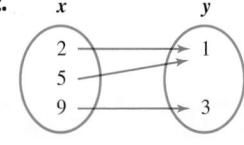

Strategy   We will check to see whether each value of x is assigned exactly one value of y.

Self Check 2

a. Does $y = 2 - x^2$ define a function? yes

b. Does the table to the right define a function? yes

x	y
2	4
1	1
0	0
−1	1
−2	4

Now Try   **Problems 29 and 31**

Teaching Example 2
a. Does $y = |x| + 1$ define a function?
b. Does the table below define a function?

x	y
−1	8
2	6
3	3
2	9
5	1

c. Does the arrow diagram define a function?

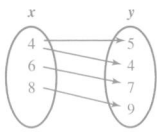

Answers:
a. yes   **b.** no   **c.** no

WHY If this is true, the equation, table, or arrow diagram defines y to be a function of x.

Solution

a. For each value of the independent variable x, we apply the rule: *Multiply x by 4 and add 1.* Since this arithmetic gives a single value of the dependent variable y, the equation defines a function.

b. Since the table assigns two different values of y, 3 and 7, to the x-value of 5, it does not define y as a function of x.

c. Each value of x is assigned to one value of y: $2 \rightarrow 1$, $5 \rightarrow 1$, $9 \rightarrow 3$. This is a function. ∎

> ***Success Tip***   The table in Self Check 2 illustrates an important fact about functions. In a function, different values of x can determine the *same* value of y. In the table, x-values of 2 and −2 determine a y-value of 4, and x-values of 1 and −1 determine a y-value of 1. Nevertheless, each value of x determines exactly one value of y, so the table does define a function.

We have seen that functions can be represented by equations in two variables. Some examples of functions are

$$y = 2x - 10, \qquad y = x^2 + 2x - 3, \qquad \text{and} \qquad s = 5 - 16t$$

For a function, the set of all possible values of the independent variable (the inputs) is called the **domain of the function.** The set of all possible values of the dependent variable (the outputs) is called the **range of the function.**

Self Check 3

Find the domain and range of the function $y = -x$.

Now Try **Problem 39**

Self Check 3 Answer
domain: all real numbers, range: all real numbers

Teaching Example 3 Find the domain and range of $y = x^2 + 1$.
Answer:
domain: all real numbers, range: all real numbers greater than or equal to 1

EXAMPLE 3   Find the domain and range of $y = |x|$.

Strategy We will determine which real numbers are allowable inputs for x for the domain. Then we will determine which real numbers are possible outputs of y for the range.

WHY The domain is the set of all possible values of the input variable, and the range is the set of all possible values of the output variable.

Solution

To find the domain of $y = |x|$, we determine which real numbers are allowable inputs for x. Since we can find the absolute value of any real number, the domain is the set of all real numbers. Since the absolute value of any real number x is greater than or equal to zero, the range of $y = |x|$ is the set of all real numbers greater than or equal to zero.

3   Use function notation.

When the variable y is a function of x, there is a special notation that we can use to denote the function.

Function Notation

The notation $y = f(x)$ denotes that y is a function of x.

The notation $y = f(x)$ is read as "y equals f of x." Note that y and $f(x)$ are two different notations for the same quantity. Thus, the equations $y = 4x + 1$ and $f(x) = 4x + 1$ represent the same relationship.

This is the variable used
to represent the input value.
$$\downarrow$$
$$f(x) = 4x + 1$$
$$\downarrow \qquad \downarrow$$

This is the   This expression shows
name of the   how to obtain an output
function.   for a given input.

Caution!   The symbol $f(x)$ denotes a function. It does not mean "f times x."
Read $f(x)$ as "f of x."

The notation $y = f(x)$ provides a compact way of representing the value of y that corresponds to some number x. For example, if $f(x) = 4x + 1$, the value of y that is determined when $x = 2$ is denoted by $f(2)$.

$$f(x) = 4x + 1 \qquad \text{This is the function.}$$
$$f(2) = 4(2) + 1 \qquad \text{Replace x with 2.}$$
$$= 8 + 1$$
$$= 9$$

Thus, $f(2) = 9$.

The letter f used in the notation $y = f(x)$ represents the word *function*. However, other letters can be used to represent functions. For example, $y = g(x)$ and $y = h(x)$ also denote functions involving the variable x.

EXAMPLE 4   For $g(x) = 3 - 2x$ and $h(x) = x^3 - 1$, find:
a. $g(3)$ **b.** $h(-2)$

Strategy We will substitute 3 for x in $3 - 2x$ and substitute -2 for x in $x^3 - 1$, and then evaluate each expression.

WHY The numbers 3 and -2, which are within the parentheses, are inputs that should be substituted for the variable x. The expression that the value of x is substituted in is determined by the name of the function.

Solution
a. To find $g(3)$, we use the function rule $g(x) = 3 - 2x$ and replace x with 3.

$$g(x) = 3 - 2x$$
$$g(3) = 3 - 2(3) \qquad \text{Substitute 3 for x.}$$
$$= 3 - 6 \qquad \text{Perform the multiplication.}$$
$$= -3$$

Thus, $g(3) = -3$.

b. To find $h(-2)$, we use the function rule $h(x) = x^3 - 1$ and replace x with -2.

$$h(x) = x^3 - 1$$
$$h(-2) = (-2)^3 - 1 \qquad \text{Substitute } -2 \text{ for x.}$$
$$= -8 - 1 \qquad \text{Evaluate the power.}$$
$$= -9$$

Thus, $h(-2) = -9$.

Self Check 4

Find $g(0)$ and $h(4)$ using the functions in Example 4. 3, 63

Now Try Problem 43

Teaching Example 4 Find $g(-4)$ and $h(2)$ using the functions in Example 4.
Answers:
a. $g(-4) = 11$ b. $h(2) = 7$

We can think of a function as a machine that takes some input x and turns it into some output $f(x)$, as shown in part (a) of the figure. The machine in part (b) turns the input value of -2 into the output value of -9, and we can write $f(-2) = -9$.

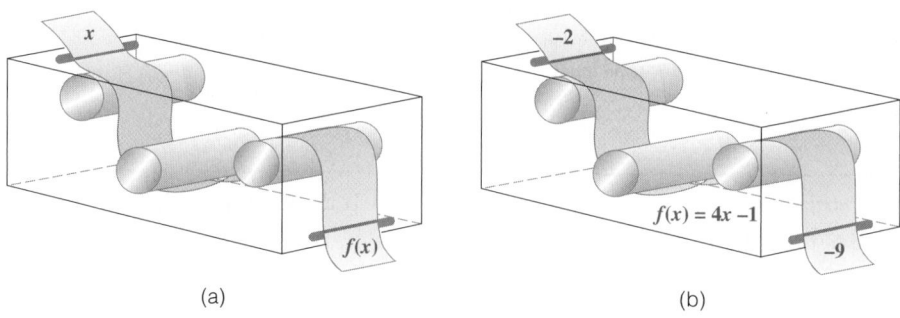

(a)   (b)

Using Your CALCULATOR Business Profits

Accountants have found that the function $f(x) = -0.000065x^2 + 12x - 278{,}000$ estimates the profit a bowling alley will make when x games are bowled per year. Suppose that management predicts that 90,000 games will be bowled in the upcoming year. The expected profit for that year can be found by evaluating $f(90{,}000)$ on a reverse-entry scientific calculator.

$$f(90{,}000) = -0.000065(90{,}000)^2 + 12(90{,}000) - 278{,}000$$

.000065 $\boxed{+\backslash-}$ $\boxed{\times}$ 90000 $\boxed{x^2}$ $\boxed{+}$ 12 $\boxed{\times}$ 90000 $\boxed{-}$ 278000 $\boxed{=}$

$$\boxed{275500}$$

To evaluate $f(90{,}000)$ with a graphing calculator or a direct-entry scientific calculator, we enter these numbers and press these keys.

$\boxed{(-)}$ .000065 $\boxed{\times}$ 90000 $\boxed{x^2}$ $\boxed{+}$ 12 $\boxed{\times}$ 90000 $\boxed{-}$ 278000 $\boxed{\text{ENTER}}$

```
-.000065*90000² +
12*90000 - 278000
            275500
```

---

4 Graph functions.

We have seen that a function such as $f(x) = 4x + 1$ assigns to each value of x a single value $f(x)$. The input-output pairs generated by a function can be written in the form $(x, f(x))$. These ordered pairs can be plotted on a rectangular coordinate system to give the graph of the function.

Self Check 5

Graph: $f(x) = -3x - 2$

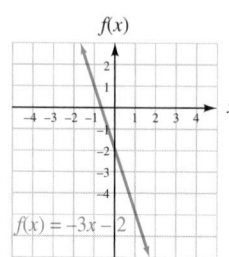

EXAMPLE 5 Graph: $f(x) = 4x + 1$

Strategy We can graph the function by creating a table of function values and plotting the corresponding ordered pairs.

WHY After drawing a line through the plotted points, we will have the graph of the function.

Solution

To make a table, we choose several values for x and find the corresponding values of $f(x)$. If x is -1, we have

$$f(x) = 4x + 1 \qquad \text{This is the function to graph.}$$
$$f(-1) = 4(-1) + 1 \qquad \text{Substitute } -1 \text{ for each } x.$$
$$= -4 + 1 \qquad \text{Evaluate the right side.}$$
$$= -3$$

Now Try Problem 45

Teaching Example 5 Graph:
$f(x) = -3x + 2$
Answer:

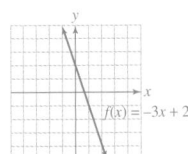

Thus, $f(-1) = -3$. This means that, when x is -1, $f(x)$ is -3, and it indicates that the ordered pair $(-1, -3)$ lies on the graph of $f(x)$.

Similarly, we find the corresponding values of $f(x)$ for x-values of 0 and 1. Then we plot the resulting ordered pairs and draw a straight line through them to get the graph of $f(x) = 4x + 1$. Since $y = f(x)$, the graph of $f(x) = 4x + 1$ is the same as the graph of the equation $y = 4x + 1$.

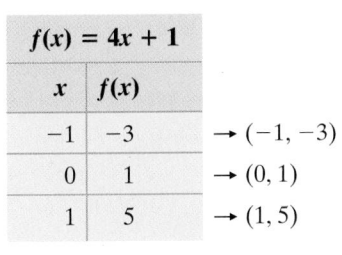

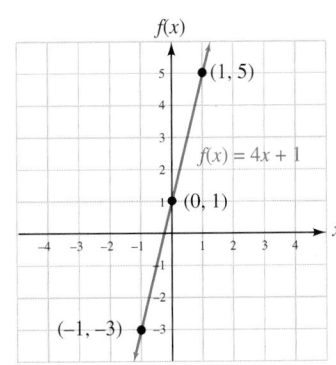

The vertical axis can be labeled y or f(x).

> **Notation**   A table of function values is similar to a table of solutions, except that the second column is usually labeled $f(x)$ instead of y.
>
>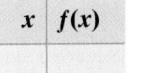

We call $f(x) = 4x + 1$ from Example 5 a **linear function** because its graph is a nonvertical line. Any linear equation, except those of the form $x = a$, can be written using function notation by writing it in slope–intercept form ($y = mx + b$) and then replacing y with $f(x)$.

EXAMPLE 6   Graph: $f(x) = |x|$

Strategy We can graph the function by creating a table of function values and plotting the corresponding ordered pairs.

WHY After drawing a "V" shape through the plotted points, we will have the graph of the function.

Solution
To create a table of function values, we choose values for x and find the corresponding values of $f(x)$. For $x = -4$ and $x = 3$, we have

$$f(x) = |x| \qquad\qquad f(x) = |x|$$
$$f(-4) = |-4| \qquad\quad f(3) = |3|$$
$$= 4 \qquad\qquad\qquad = 3$$

Thus, $f(-4) = 4$ and $f(3) = 3$.

Self Check 6
Graph: $f(x) = |x| + 2$

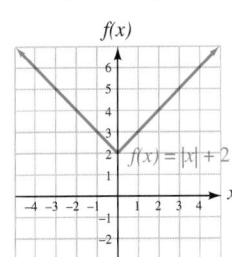

Now Try Problem 46

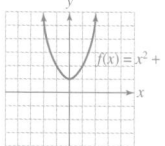

Similarly, we find the corresponding values of $f(x)$ for several other x-values. When we plot the resulting ordered pairs, we see that they lie in a "V" shape. We join the points to complete the graph as shown. We call $f(x) = |x|$ an **absolute value function.**

$f(x) = |x|$		
x	$f(x)$	
-4	4	$\rightarrow (-4, 4)$
-3	3	$\rightarrow (-3, 3)$
-2	2	$\rightarrow (-2, 2)$
-1	1	$\rightarrow (-1, 1)$
0	0	$\rightarrow (0, 0)$
1	1	$\rightarrow (1, 1)$
2	2	$\rightarrow (2, 2)$
3	3	$\rightarrow (3, 3)$
4	4	$\rightarrow (4, 4)$

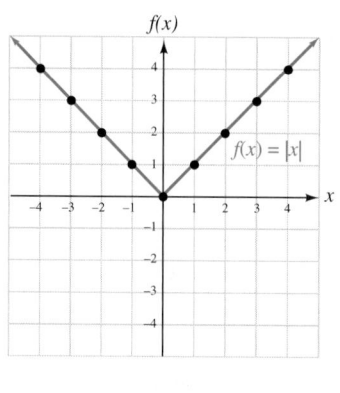

The figure below shows the graphs of four basic functions.

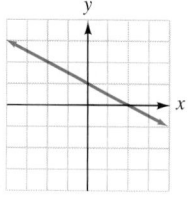

Linear function
$f(x) = mx + b$
(a)

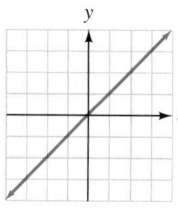

Identity function
$f(x) = x$
(b)

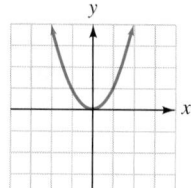

Squaring function
$f(x) = x^2$
(c)

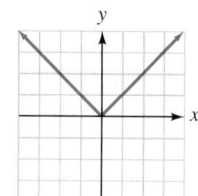

Absolute value function
$f(x) = |x|$
(d)

5 Use the vertical line test.

We can use the **vertical line test** to determine whether a given graph is the graph of a function. If any vertical line intersects a graph more than once, the graph cannot represent a function, because to one value of x, there corresponds more than one value of y. The graph in figure (a), shown in red, is not the graph of a function, because the x-value -1 determines three different y-values: 3, -1, and -4.

The graph shown in figure (b) does represent a function, because every vertical line that can be drawn intersects the graph exactly once.

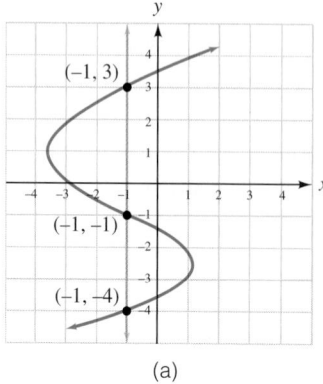

(a)

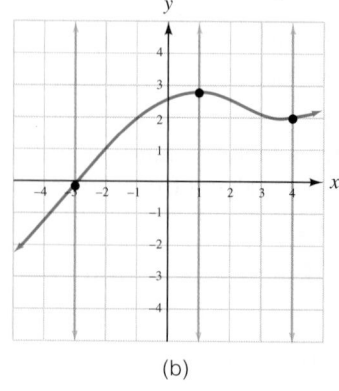

(b)

EXAMPLE 7   Determine whether each of the following is a graph of a function.

a.

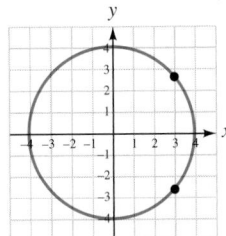

b.

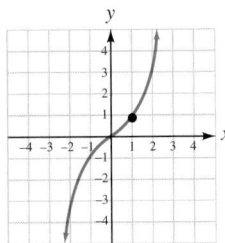

Self Check 7

Determine whether each of the following is a graph of a function.

a.   function

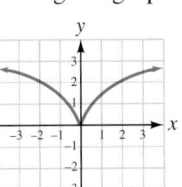

b.   not a function

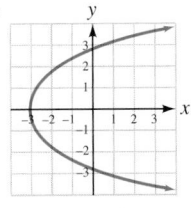

Now Try Problems 49 and 50

Teaching Example 7 Determine whether each of the following is a graph of a function.

a.   **b.**

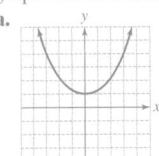 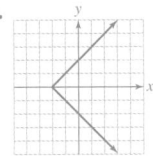

Answers:
a. function   **b.** not a function

Strategy We will check to see whether any vertical line intersects the graph more than once.

WHY If any vertical line does intersect the graph more than once, the graph is not a function.

Solution

a. This graph is not the graph of a function, because the vertical line intersects the graph at more than one point.

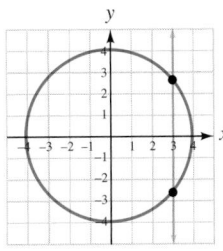

b. This graph is the graph of a function, because no vertical line will intersect the graph at more than one point.

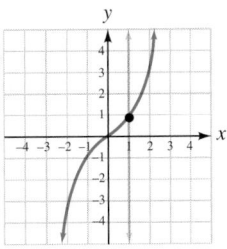

ANSWERS TO SELF CHECKS

1. domain: $\{-5, -1, 6, 8\}$, range: $\{-5, 2, 10\}$ **2. a.** yes   **b.** yes
3. domain: all real numbers, range: all real numbers   **4.** $3, 63$
5.   **6.**   **7. a.** function
                        b. not a function

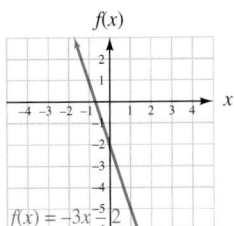

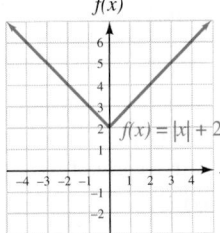

SECTION 3.8 STUDY SET

VOCABULARY

Fill in the blanks.

1. A set of ordered pairs is called a <u>relation</u>.

2. A <u>function</u> is a set of ordered pairs in which to each first component there corresponds exactly one second component.

3. In the equation $y = 2x + 8$, x is the <u>independent</u> variable.

4. In the equation $y = 2x + 8$, y is the <u>dependent</u> variable.

▶ 5. The set of all input values for a function is called the <u>domain</u>, the set of all output values is called the <u>range</u>.

6. $f(x) = 6 - 5x$ is an example of <u>function</u> notation.

CONCEPTS

Consider the function $f(x) = x^2$.

7. If positive real numbers are substituted for x, what type of numbers result? positive numbers

8. If negative real numbers are substituted for x, what type of numbers result? positive numbers

9. If 0 is substituted for x, what number results? 0

10. What are the domain and range of the function?
    D: all reals, R: real numbers greater than or equal to 0

Consider the function $g(x) = x^4$.

11. What type of numbers can be inputs in this function? What is the special name for this set?
    all real numbers, domain

12. What type of numbers will be outputs in this function? What is the special name for this set? real numbers greater than or equal to 0, range

13. Complete part b so that the statements say the same thing.

    a. In the equation $y = -5x + 1$, find the value of y when $x = -1$.

    b. In the equation $f(x) = -5x + 1$, find $f(-1)$.

▶ 14. A function can be thought of as a machine that converts inputs into outputs. Use the terms *domain*, *range*, *input*, and *output* to label the diagram of a function machine in the illustration in the next column. Then find $f(2)$. $f(2) = 4$

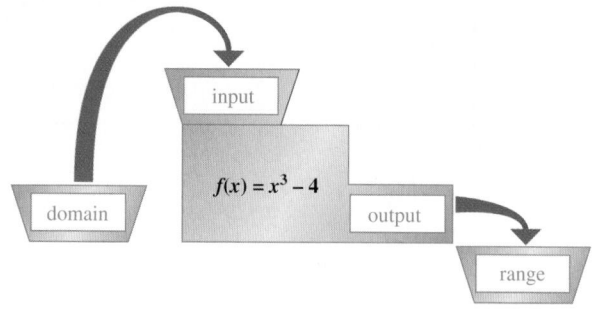

15. See the illustration.

    a. Give the coordinates of the points where the blue vertical line intersects the red graph.
       $(-2, 4), (-2, -4)$

    b. Is the red graph the graph of a function? Explain.
       No, the x-value -2 is assigned to more than one y-value (4 and -4).

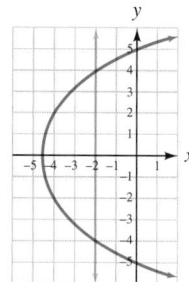

16. A student wrote the following statement about the illustration. What is wrong with his reasoning?

    When I drew a vertical line through the graph, it intersected the graph only once. By the vertical line test, the graph represents a function.

    He must determine whether *all* vertical lines that intersect the graph do so only once. This is not a graph of a function.

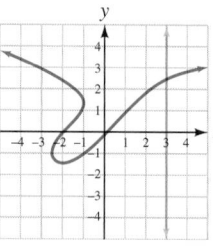

NOTATION

Fill in the blanks to make the statements true.

17. The function notation $f(4) = -5$ states that when 4 is substituted for x in function f, the result is -5. This fact can be illustrated graphically by plotting the point $\left(4, -5 \right)$.

▶ 18. $f(x) = 6 - 5x$ is read as "f <u>of</u> x is $6 - 5x$."

19. If $f(x) = 6 - 5x$, then $f(0) = 6$ is read as "f <u>of</u> zero <u>is</u> 6."

20. The equations $y = 3x + 5$ and <u>$f(x)$</u> $= 3x + 5$ are the same.

▶ Selected exercises available online at
www.webassign.net/brookscole

GUIDED PRACTICE

Find the domain and range of each relation. **See Example 1.**

21. {(6, −1), (−1, −10), (−6, 2), (8, −5)}
domain: {−6, −1, 6, 8}, range: {−10, −5, −1, 2}

22. {(11, −3), (0, 0), (4, 5), (−3, −7)}
domain: {−3, 0, 4, 11}, range: {−7, −3, 0, 5}

▶ **23.** {(0, 9), (−8, 50), (6, 9)}
domain: {−8, 0, 6}, range: {9, 50}

24. {(1, −12), (−6, 8), (5, 8)}
domain: {−6, 1, 5}, range: {−12, 8}

Determine whether each equation, table, or arrow diagram defines a function. If not, indicate an input value for which there is more than one output value. **See Example 2.**

25. $y = 2x + 10$ yes

▶ **26.** $y = x − 15$ yes

27. $y = x^2$ yes

28. $y = |x|$ yes

29. $y^2 = x$
no, (4, 2), (4, −2)

▶ **30.** $|y| = x$
no, (1, 1), (1, −1)

31.

x	y
1	7
2	15
3	23
4	16
5	8

yes

▶ **32.**

x	y
−1	1
−3	1
−5	1
−7	1
−9	1

yes

▶ **33.**

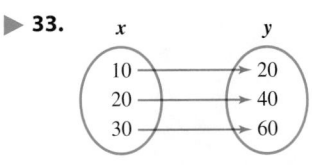

yes

34.

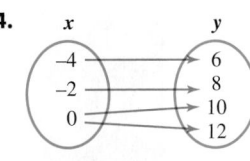

no, (0, 10), (0, 12)

35.

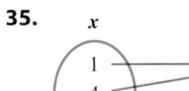

no, (4, 2), (4, 4), (4, 6)
(answers may vary)

36.

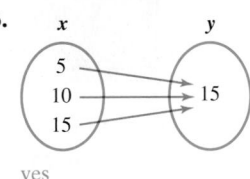

yes

Find the domain and range of each function. **See Example 3.**

37. $f(x) = x + 1$
D: all reals, R: all reals

▶ **38.** $f(x) = 3x − 2$
D: all reals, R: all reals

39. $y = x^2$
D: all reals, R: real numbers greater than or equal to 0

40. $y = −|x|$
D: all reals, R: real numbers less than or equal to 0

Find each value. **See Example 4.**

41. $f(x) = 4x − 1$
  a. $f(1)$ 3
  b. $f(−2)$ −9
  c. $f\left(\dfrac{1}{4}\right)$ 0
  d. $f(50)$ 199

▶ **42.** $g(x) = 1 − 5x$
  a. $g(0)$ 1
  b. $g(−75)$ 376
  c. $g(0.2)$ 0
  d. $g\left(−\dfrac{4}{5}\right)$ 5

43. $h(t) = 2t^2$
  a. $h(0.4)$ 0.32
  b. $h(−3)$ 18
  c. $h(1,000)$ 2,000,000
  d. $h\left(\dfrac{1}{8}\right)$ $\dfrac{1}{32}$

▶ **44.** $v(t) = 6 − t^2$
  a. $v(30)$ −894
  b. $v(6)$ −30
  c. $v(−1)$ 5
  d. $v(0.5)$ 5.75

Complete each table and graph the function. **See Examples 5–6.**

45. $f(x) = −2 − 3x$

x	f(x)
0	−2
1	−5
−1	1
−2	4

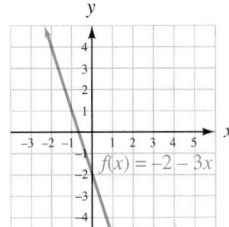

46. $h(x) = |1 − x|$

x	h(x)
0	1
1	0
2	1
3	2
−1	2
−2	3

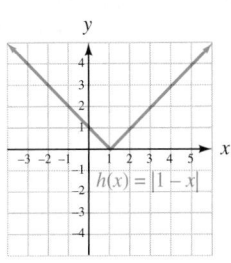

▶ **47.** $f(x) = \dfrac{1}{2}x − 2$

x	f(x)
−2	−3
0	−2
2	−1

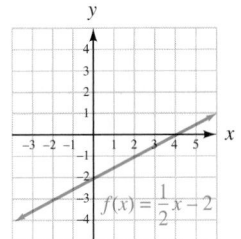

48. $f(x) = -\frac{2}{3}x + 3$

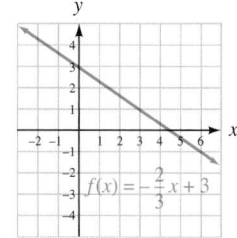

x	f(x)
0	3
3	1
6	-1

Determine whether each of the following graphs is the graph of a function. **See Example 7.**

49.

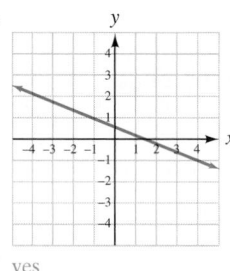

yes

▶ 50.

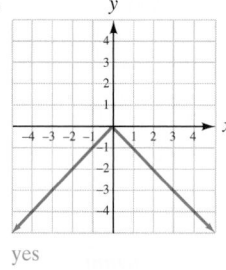

yes

▶ 51.

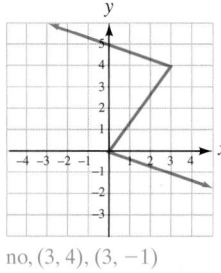

no, (3, 4), (3, -1)
(answers may vary)

▶ 52.

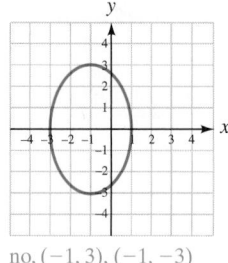

no, (-1, 3), (-1, -3)
(answers may vary)

▍ TRY IT YOURSELF

Determine whether each equation, table, or graph defines a function. If not, indicate an input value for which there is more than one output value.

53. $y = x^3$ yes

54. $y = -x$ yes

55. $x = 3$ no, (3, 1), (3, 2)

56. $y = 3$ yes

57.

x	y
-4	6
-1	0
0	-3
2	4
-1	2

no, (-1, 0), (-1, 2)

▶ 58.

x	y
30	2
30	4
30	6
30	8
30	10

no, (30, 2), (30, 4) (answers may vary)

59.

t	d
3	4
3	-4
4	3
4	-3

no, (3, 4), (3, -4) or (4, 3), (4, -3)

60.

x	y
1	1
2	2
3	3
4	4

yes

61.

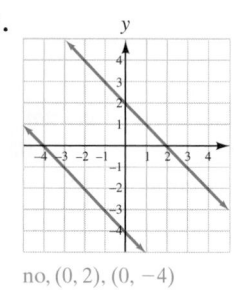

no, (0, 2), (0, -4)
(answers may vary)

62.

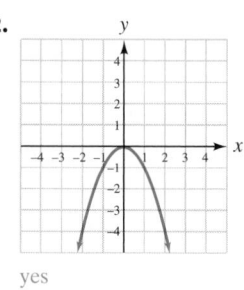

yes

63. {(3, 4), (5, 1), (6, 2)} yes

64. {(3, -2), (2, 4), (3, -1), (5, 6)} no, (3, -2), (3, -1)

▍ APPLICATIONS

▶ 65. REFLECTIONS When a beam of light hits a mirror, it is reflected off the mirror at the same angle that the incoming beam struck the mirror, as shown. What type of function could serve as a mathematical model for the path of the light beam shown here? $f(x) = |x|$

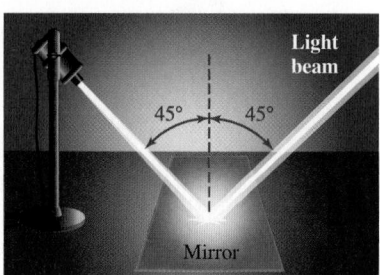

▶ 66. MATHEMATICAL MODELS The illustration below shows the path of a basketball shot taken by a player. What type of function could be used to mathematically model the path of the basketball? $f(x) = -x^2$

67. TIDES The illustration below shows the graph of a function *f*, which gives the height of the tide for a 24-hour period in Seattle, Washington. (Note that military time is used on the *x*-axis: 3 A.M. = 3, noon = 12, 3 P.M. = 15, 9 P.M. = 21, and so on.)

  a. Find the domain of the function. all real numbers from 0 through 24

  b. Find: $f(3)$ 0.5

  c. Find: $f(6)$ 1.5

  d. Estimate: $f(15)$ −1.4

  e. What information does $f(12)$ give? The low tide mark was −2.5 m.

  f. Estimate: $f(21)$ 1.6

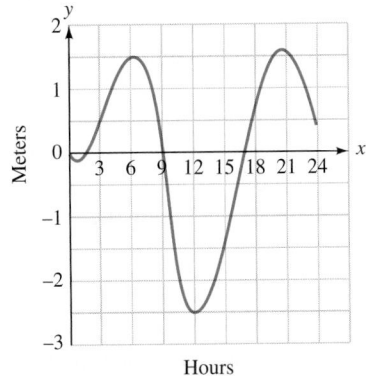

68. VACATIONING The function $C(d) = 500 + 100(d − 3)$ gives the cost in dollars to rent an RV motor home for *d* days. Find the cost of renting the motor home for a vacation that will last 7 days. $900

Rent This RV!

(3 day minimum)

69. LAWN SPRINKLERS The function $A(r) = \pi r^2$ can be used to determine the area that will be watered by a rotating sprinkler that sprays out a stream of water *r* feet. Find $A(5)$, $A(10)$, and $A(20)$. Round to the nearest tenth. 78.5 ft², 314.2 ft², 1,256.6 ft²

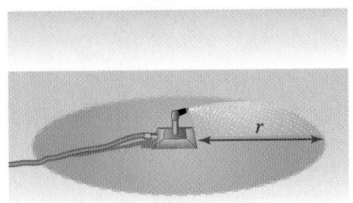

70. PARTS LIST The function

$$f(r) = 2.30 + 3.25(r + 0.40)$$

approximates the length (in feet) of the belt that joins the two pulleys shown. *r* is the radius (in feet) of the smaller pulley. Find the belt length needed for each pulley in the parts list.

Parts List		
Pulley	**r**	**Belt length**
P-45M	0.32	4.64
P-08D	0.24	4.38
P-00A	0.18	4.185
P-57X	0.38	4.835

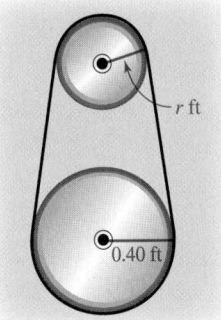

r ft

0.40 ft

WRITING

71. In the function $y = −5x + 2$, why do you think *x* is called the *independent* variable and *y* the *dependent* variable?

72. Explain what a politician meant when she said, "The speed at which the downtown area will be redeveloped is a function of the number of low-interest loans made available to the property owners."

REVIEW

73. Give the equation of the horizontal line passing through $(−3, 6)$. $y = 6$

74. Is −3 a solution of $t^2 − t + 1 = 13$? yes

75. Write the formula that relates profit, revenue, and costs. profit = revenue − costs

76. What is the word used to represent the perimeter of a circle? circumference

77. Use the distributive property to remove the parentheses in $−3(2x − 4)$. −6x + 12

78. Evaluate $r^2 − r$ for $r = −0.5$. 0.75

79. Write an expression for how many eggs there are in *d* dozen. 12d

80. On a rectangular coordinate graph, what variable is usually associated with the horizontal axis? *x*

STUDY SKILLS CHECKLIST

Preparing for the Chapter 3 Test

There are common difficulties that students have when working with the topics of Chapter 3. To make sure you are prepared for the test and to help you overcome these difficulties, study the checklist below.

☐ When finding the slope of a line, if you are given two ordered pairs, use the formula:

$$m = \frac{y_2 - y_1}{x_2 - x_1}$$ Find the slope of the line that passes through $(-2, 5)$, $(6, -1)$.

$$= \frac{-1 - 5}{6 - (-2)}$$

$$= \frac{-6}{8}$$

$$= -\frac{3}{4}$$

The slope of the line is $-\dfrac{3}{4}$.

☐ When finding the slope of a line, if you are given an equation, isolate y and the slope is the *coefficient* of x.

$$2x + 3y = 6$$

$$3y = -2x + 6 \quad \text{Subtract 2x from both sides.}$$

$$y = -\frac{2}{3}x + 2 \quad \text{Divide both sides by 3.}$$

The slope of the line is $-\dfrac{2}{3}$.

☐ Remember, the slope of a line is a ratio, and the midpoint of a line segment is a point. To find the midpoint of the line segment connecting $(-5, 4)$ and $(-2, -3)$, use

$$M\left(\frac{x_1 + x_2}{2}, \frac{y_1 + y_2}{2}\right)$$

$$M\left(\frac{-5 + -2}{2}, \frac{4 + (-3)}{2}\right)$$

$$M\left(-\frac{7}{2}, \frac{1}{2}\right)$$

☐ To graph a linear equation in two variables:

1. Find three ordered pairs that are solutions of the equation by selecting three values for x and calculating the corresponding values of y.

2. Plot these points on a rectangular coordinate system.

3. Draw a straight line passing through them.

☐ To graph a nonlinear equation in two variables:

1. Find at least *seven* ordered pairs that are solutions of the equation by selecting *seven* values for x and calculating the corresponding values of y.

2. Plot these points on a rectangular coordinate system.

3. Draw a curve passing through them.

☐ To write an equation of a line, you:

1. need the slope of the line, m.

2. need a point that line passes through (x_1, y_1).

3. input these values in the equation, $y - y_1 = m(x - x_1)$.

☐ To graph a linear inequality in two variables:

1. Graph the boundary line.

2. Pick a test point on one side of the boundary. Use the origin if possible. If the test point is a solution of the inequality, shade the side of the boundary that contains the point. If the test point is not a solution of the inequality, shade the other side.

Teaching Guide: Refer to the Instructor's Resource Binder to find activities, worksheets on key concepts, more examples, instruction tips, overheads, and assessments.

SUMMARY AND REVIEW

SECTION 3.1   Graphing Using the Rectangular Coordinate System

DEFINITIONS AND CONCEPTS

A **rectangular coordinate system** is composed of a horizontal number line called the **x-axis** and a vertical number line called the **y-axis.**

The coordinates of the **origin** are $(0, 0)$.

To plot or **graph** ordered pairs means to locate their position on a coordinate system.

The x- and y-axes divide the coordinate plane into four distinct regions, called **quadrants.**

EXAMPLES

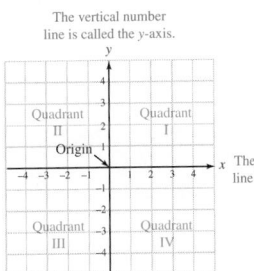

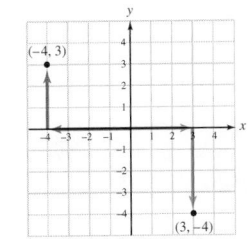

REVIEW EXERCISES

1. Graph the points with coordinates $(-1, 3)$, $(0, 1.5)$ $(-4, -4)$, $\left(2, \frac{7}{2}\right)$, and $(4, 0)$.

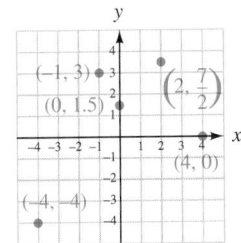

2. Use the graph in the illustration to complete the table.

x	y
3	−1
0	0
−3	1

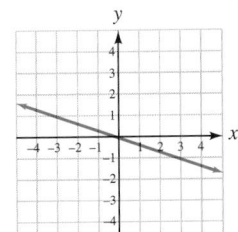

3. In what quadrant does the point $(-3, -4)$ lie? quadrant III

4. SNOWFALL The graph below gives the amount of snow on the ground at a mountain resort as measured once each day over a 7-day period.

   a. On the first day, how much snow was on the ground? 2 ft

   b. What was the difference in the amount of snow on the ground when the measurements were taken on the second and third day? 2 ft

   c. How much snow was on the ground on the sixth day? 6 ft

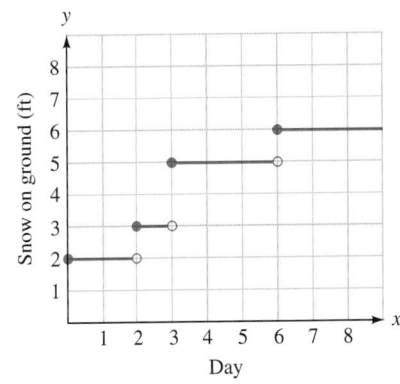

5. COLLEGE ENROLLMENTS The graph at the right gives the number of students enrolled at a college for the period from 4 weeks before to 5 weeks after the semester began.

a. What was the maximum enrollment and when did it occur? 2,500, week 2

b. How many students had enrolled 2 weeks before the semester began? 1,000

c. When was enrollment 2,250? 1st week and 5th week

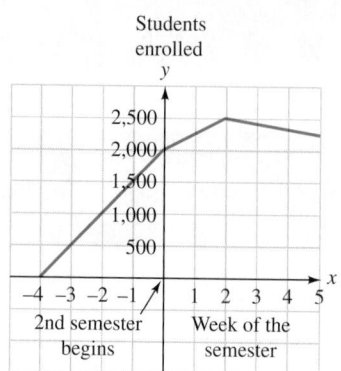

SECTION 3.2   Equations Containing Two Variables

DEFINITIONS AND CONCEPTS	EXAMPLES
An **ordered pair** is a **solution** of an equation if, after substituting the values of the ordered pair for the variables in the equation, the result is a true statement.	The ordered pair (1, 2) is a solution of $x + 2y = 5$ because the values of the ordered pair satisfy the equation: $x + 2y = 5$ $1 + 2(2) \stackrel{?}{=} 5$ $5 = 5$

Solutions of an equation can be shown in a **table of solutions**.

In an equation in x and y, x is called the **independent variable**, or **input**, and y is called the **dependent variable**, or **output**.

A table of solutions for the equation $x + 2y = 5$ includes ordered pairs that satisfy the equation. The ordered pair found above and others are shown in the table.

x	y	(x, y)
-1	3	$(-1, 3)$
1	2	$(1, 2)$
5	0	$(5, 0)$

To graph an equation in two variables:

1. Make a table of solutions that contains several solutions written as ordered pairs.

2. Plot each ordered pair.

3. Draw a line or smooth curve through the points.

To graph the equation $x + 2y = 5$, make a table of solutions, plot the points, and draw the graph as in the illustration.

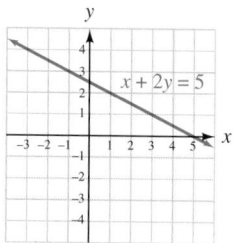

A table and a graph for the equation $y = x^2$ is shown in the illustration.

x	y	(x, y)
-2	4	$(-2, 4)$
-1	1	$(-1, 1)$
0	0	$(0, 0)$
1	1	$(1, 1)$
2	4	$(2, 4)$

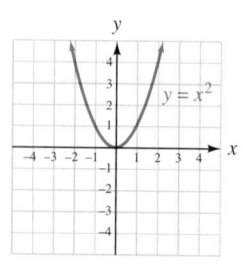

REVIEW EXERCISES

6. Determine whether $(-3, 5)$ is a solution of $y = |2 + x|$.   not a solution

7. **a.** Complete the following table of solutions and graph the equation $y = -x^3$.

x	y	(x, y)
-2	8	$(-2, 8)$
-1	1	$(-1, 1)$
0	0	$(0, 0)$
1	-1	$(1, -1)$
2	-8	$(2, -8)$

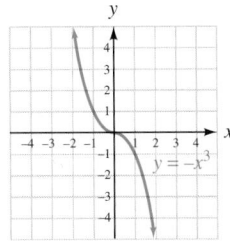

b. How would the graph of $y = -x^3 + 2$ compare to the graph of the equation given in part a?   It would be 2 units higher.

8. The graph shows the relationship between the number of oranges O an acre of land will yield if t orange trees are planted on it.

a. If $t = 70$, what is O?   9,000

b. What importance does the point $(40, 18)$ on the graph have?   It tells us that 40 trees on an acre give the highest yield, 18,000 oranges.

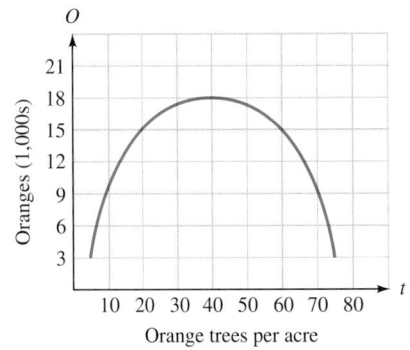

SECTION 3.3   Graphing Linear Equations

DEFINITIONS AND CONCEPTS	EXAMPLES
An equation whose graph is a straight line and whose variables are raised to the first power is called a **linear equation.**	The equations $y = -3x - 2$ and $3x + 2y = 6$ are linear equations, because their graphs are straight lines.
	The equations $y = x^2$ and $y = |x|$ are not linear equations, because the graphs of these equations are not straight lines.
The **general** or **standard form** of a linear equation is $Ax + By = C$, where A, B, and C are real numbers and A and B are not both zero.	To write the equation $y = -3x - 2$ in general or standard form, add $3x$ to both sides to get $3x + y = -2$.
To **graph a linear equation:** 1. Find three (x, y) pairs that satisfy the equation by picking three x-values and finding their corresponding y-values. 2. Plot each ordered pair. 3. Draw a straight line through the points.	A table of solutions and the graph of $3x + 2y = 6$ are shown in the illustration. 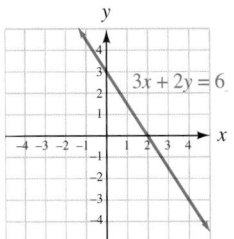
To **find the y-intercept** of a linear equation, substitute 0 for x in the equation of the line and solve for y.	The y-intercept of the line in the previous graph is $(0, 3)$.
To **find the x-intercept** of a linear equation, substitute 0 for y in the equation of the line and solve for x.	The x-intercept of the line in the previous graph is $(2, 0)$.

The table of solutions for the graph of $3x + 2y = 6$:

x	y	(x, y)
0	3	$(0, 3)$
2	0	$(2, 0)$
4	-3	$(4, -3)$

The equation $y = b$ represents the **horizontal line** that intersects the y-axis at $(0, b)$.	The graph of $y = 3$ will be a horizontal line.
The equation $x = a$ represents the **vertical line** that intersects the x-axis at $(a, 0)$.	The graph of $x = 3$ will be a vertical line.

REVIEW EXERCISES

Classify each equation as either linear or nonlinear.

9. $y = |x + 2|$ nonlinear   **10.** $3x + 4y = 12$ linear

11. $y = 2x - 3$ linear   **12.** $y = x^2 - x$ nonlinear

13. The equation $5x + 2y = 10$ is in general form; what are A, B, and C? $A = 5, B = 2, C = 10$

14. Complete the table of solutions for the equation $3x + 2y = -18$.

x	y	(x, y)
-2	-6	$(-2, -6)$
-8	3	$(-8, 3)$

15. Solve the equation $x + 2y = 6$ for y, find three solutions, and graph it.

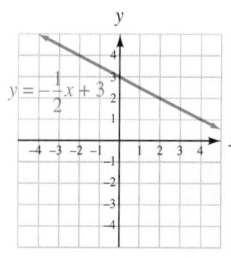

16. Graph $-4x + 2y = 8$ by finding its x- and y-intercepts.
x-intercept: $(-2, 0)$,
y-intercept: $(0, 4)$

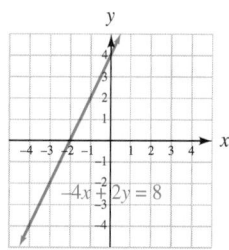

Graph each equation.

17. $y = 4$

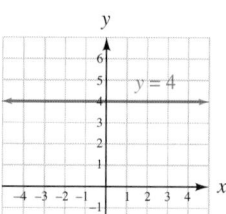

18. $x = -1$

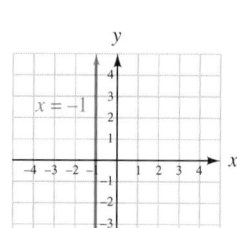

19. Since two points determine a line, only two points are needed to graph a linear equation. Why is it a good idea to plot a third point?
If the three points do not lie on a line, then at least one of them is in error.

SECTION 3.4   Rate of Change and the Slope of a Line

DEFINITIONS AND CONCEPTS	EXAMPLES
Slope of a nonvertical line: $$m = \frac{\text{change in the } y\text{-values}}{\text{change in the } x\text{-values}} = \frac{\text{rise}}{\text{run}}$$	If the change in the y-values between two points is 8 and the change in the x-values between the same two points is 5, the slope of the line is $m = \dfrac{8}{5}$.
The **slope** of a nonvertical line passing through points (x_1, y_1) and (x_2, y_2) is $$m = \frac{y_2 - y_1}{x_2 - x_1}$$	To find the slope of the line passing through the points $(-3, 2)$ and $(1, -5)$, substitute into the slope formula: $$m = \frac{y_2 - y_1}{x_2 - x_1} = \frac{-5 - 2}{1 - (-3)} = \frac{-7}{4} = -\frac{7}{4}$$

Lines that rise from left to right have a **positive slope,** and lines that fall from left to right have a **negative slope.**	In the illustration, line l_1 has a positive slope. Line l_2 has a negative slope.
Horizontal lines have **zero slope.** Vertical lines have **undefined slope.**	Line 3 in the illustration has a slope of 0. Line 4 has no defined slope. 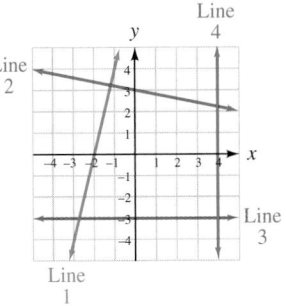

REVIEW EXERCISES

In each case, find the slope of the line.

20.

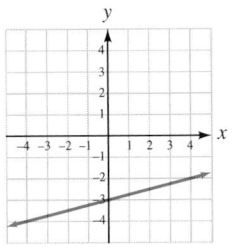

$\frac{1}{4}$

21. The line with the table of solutions shown here. -7

x	y	(x, y)
2	-3	$(2, -3)$
4	-17	$(4, -17)$

22. The line passing through the points $(2, -5)$ and $(5, -5)$. 0

23. The line passing through the points $(1, -4)$ and $(3, -7)$. $-\frac{3}{2}$

24. Graph the line that passes through $(-2, 4)$ and has slope $m = -\frac{4}{5}$.

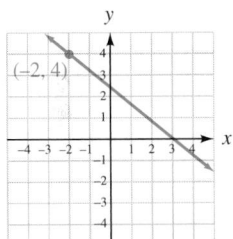

25. TOURISM The graph shows the number of international travelers to the United States in 2-year increments.

    a. Between 2000 and 2002, the largest decline in the number of visitors occurred. What was the rate of change? -4.5 million people per yr

    b. Between 1986 and 1988, the largest increase in the number of visitors occurred. What was the rate of change? 4.05 million people per yr

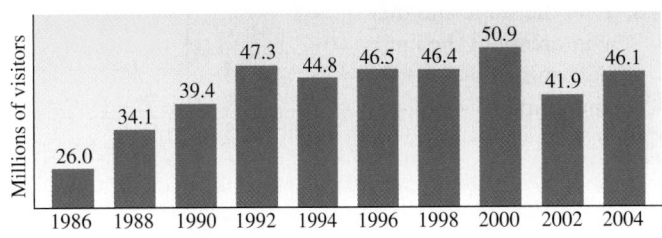

Based on data from *World Almanac* 2006.

SECTION 3.5   Slope–Intercept Form

DEFINITIONS AND CONCEPTS	EXAMPLES
If a linear equation is written in **slope–intercept form,** $$y = mx + b$$ the graph of the equation is a line with slope m and y-intercept $(0, b)$.	The slope of the graph of the equation $y = 4x - 8$ is 4. The y-intercept is the point $(0, -8)$. To find the slope and y-intercept of the graph of the equation $3x + 2y = 12$, solve the equation for y. $\qquad 3x + 2y = 12$ $\qquad\qquad 2y = -3x + 12$ Subtract 3x from both sides. $\qquad\qquad\ y = -\dfrac{3}{2}x + 6$ Divide both sides by 2. The slope is $-\dfrac{3}{2}$ and the y-intercept is $(0, 6)$.
Two lines with the same slope are **parallel.**	Since the graphs of $y = -2x + 5$ and $y = -2x + 7$ both have a slope of -2, the graphs will be parallel.
The product of the slopes of **perpendicular lines is -1.**	The graph of $y = -2x + 5$ has a slope of -2. The graph of $y = \dfrac{1}{2}x + 7$ has a slope of $\dfrac{1}{2}$. Since the product of the slopes is -1, the graphs are perpendicular.

REVIEW EXERCISES

Find the slope and the y-intercept of each line.

26. $y = \dfrac{3}{4}x - 2$ $m = \dfrac{3}{4}$, y-intercept: $(0, -2)$

27. $y = -4x$ $m = -4$, y-intercept: $(0, 0)$

28. Find the slope and the y-intercept of the line determined by $9x - 3y = 15$ and graph it.
$m = 3$, y-intercept: $(0, -5)$

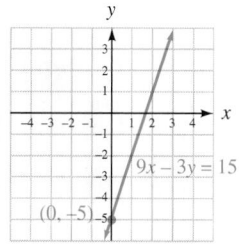

Without graphing, determine whether the graphs of the given pairs of lines would be parallel, perpendicular, or neither.

29. $\begin{cases} y = -\dfrac{2}{3}x + 6 \\ y = -\dfrac{2}{3}x - 6 \end{cases}$
parallel

30. $\begin{cases} x + 5y = -10 \\ y = 5x \end{cases}$
perpendicular

31. COPIERS A business buys a used copy machine that, when purchased, has already produced 75,000 copies.

    a. If the business plans to run 300 copies a week, write a linear equation that would find the number of copies c the machine has made in its lifetime after the business has used it for w weeks. $c = 300w + 75{,}000$

    b. Use your result to part a to predict the total number of copies that will have been made on the machine 1 year, or 52 weeks, after being purchased by the business. 90,600

SECTION 3.6   Point–Slope Form; Writing Linear Equations

DEFINITIONS AND CONCEPTS

EXAMPLES

If a line with slope m passes through the point (x_1, y_1), the equation of the line in **point–slope form** is

$$y - y_1 = m(x - x_1)$$

If a line has a slope of 5 and passes through the point $(3, 4)$, its equation in point–slope form is

$$y - 4 = 5(x - 3)$$

REVIEW EXERCISES

Write an equation of a line with the given slope that passes through the given point. Express the result in point–slope form. Then change it to slope–intercept form and graph the equation.

32. $m = 3, (1, 5)$

$y - 5 = 3(x - 1), y = 3x + 2$

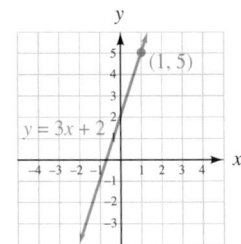

33. $m = -\dfrac{1}{2}, (-4, -1)$

$y + 1 = -\dfrac{1}{2}(x + 4), y = -\dfrac{1}{2}x - 3$

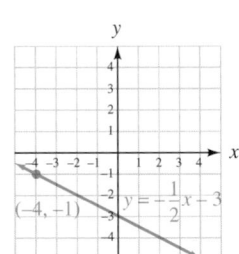

Write an equation of the line with the following characteristics. Express the result in slope–intercept form.

34. passing through $(3, 7)$ and $(-6, 1)$ $y = \frac{2}{3}x + 5$

35. horizontal, passing through $(6, -8)$ $y = -8$

36. CAR REGISTRATION   When it was 2 years old, the annual registration fee for a Dodge Caravan was \$380. When it was 4 years old, the registration fee dropped to \$310. If the relationship is linear, write an equation that gives the registration fee f in dollars for the van when it is x years old.

$f(x) = -35x + 450$

SECTION 3.7   Graphing Linear Inequalities

DEFINITIONS AND CONCEPTS

EXAMPLES

An ordered pair (x, y) is a **solution of an inequality** in x and y if a true statement results when the variables are replaced by the coordinates of the ordered pair.

To determine whether $(-2, 5)$ is a solution of $x + 3y > 6$, substitute the coordinates into the inequality and see whether a true statement results.

$$x + 3y > 6$$
$$-2 + 3(5) \overset{?}{>} 6$$
$$13 > 6 \quad \text{true}$$

Since a true statement results, $(-2, 5)$ is a solution.

To graph a linear inequality:

1. Graph the boundary line. Draw a solid line if the inequality contains an $\leq$ or an $\geq$ symbol. Draw a dashed line if the inequality contains an $<$ or an $>$ symbol.

To graph $2x - y \leq 4$, proceed as follows:

1. Graph the boundary line $2x - y = 4$ and draw it as a solid line because the inequality symbol is $\leq$.

2. Pick a test point on one side of the boundary. Use the origin if possible. Replace x and y with the coordinates of that point. If the inequality is satisfied, shade the side of the boundary that contains the point. If the inequality is not satisfied, shade the other side.

2. Test the point $(0, 0)$:

$$2x - y \le 4$$
$$2(0) - 0 \overset{?}{\le} 4$$
$$0 \le 4 \quad \text{true}$$

Since the coordinates of the test point satisfy the inequality, shade the side of a boundary that contains $(0, 0)$.

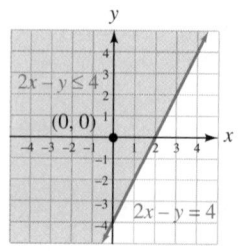

REVIEW EXERCISES

Determine whether each ordered pair is a solution of $2x - y \le -4$.

37. $(0, 5)$ yes

38. $(2, 8)$ yes

39. $(-3, -2)$ yes

40. $\left(\dfrac{1}{2}, -5\right)$ no

Graph each inequality.

41. $x - y < 5$

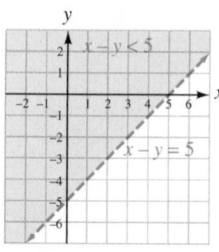

42. $2x - 3y \ge 6$

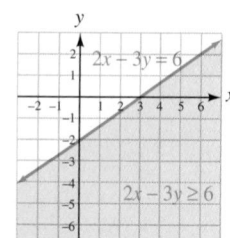

43. $y \le -2x$

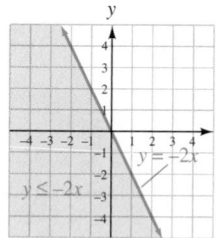

44. $y < -4$

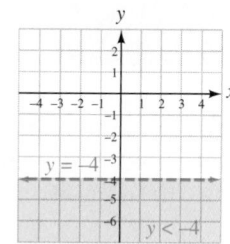

45. The graph of a linear inequality is shown in the next column. Would a true or a false statement occur if the coordinates of

a. point A were substituted into the inequality? true

b. point B were substituted into the inequality? false

c. point C were substituted into the inequality? false

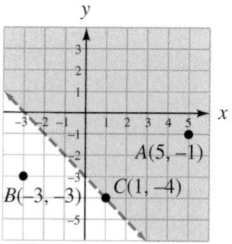

46. WORK SCHEDULES A student told her employer that during the school year, she would be available for up to 30 hours a week, working either 3- or 5-hour shifts. If x represents the number of 3-hour shifts and y represents the number of 5-hours shifts she works, the inequality $3x + 5y \le 30$ shows the possible combinations of shifts she can work. Graph the inequality and find three possible combinations. $(2, 4), (5, 3), (6, 2)$; answers will vary

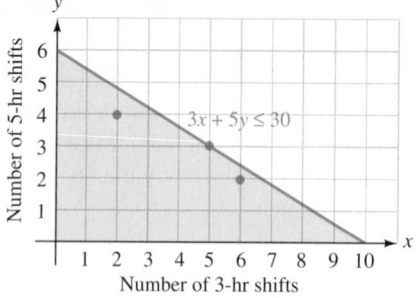

SECTION 3.8   Functions

DEFINITIONS AND CONCEPTS	EXAMPLES
A **relation** is a set of ordered pairs. The set of all **first components** is called the **domain** of the relation and the set of all **second components** is called the **range** of a relation.	The relation $\{(4, 7), (0, -3), (-3, 8), (1, 7)\}$ has the domain $\{-3, 0, 1, 4\}$ and the range is $\{-3, 7, 8\}$.
A **function** is a set of ordered pairs in which to each first component there corresponds exactly one second component.	The equation $y = |2x|$ defines a function because each value of x determines exactly one value of y. For example, if $x = 1$, then $y = 2$, and if $x = 3$, then $y = 6$.
For a function, the set of all possible values of the independent variable x (the inputs) is called the **domain.**	Since x can be any real number in the function $y = |2x|$, the domain is the set of real numbers.
The set of all possible values of the dependent variable y (the outputs) is called the **range.**	Because of the absolute value in the function $y = |2x|$, y must be either positive or 0. Thus the range is the set of all real numbers that are greater than or equal to 0.

The notation $y = f(x)$ denotes that y is a function of x.	If $f(x) = 3x + 5$, we can find $f(2)$ and $f(-3)$ as follows:

$$f(x) = 3x + 5 \qquad\qquad f(x) = 3x + 5$$
$$f(2) = 3(2) + 5 \qquad\quad f(-3) = 3(-3) + 5$$
$$= 11 \qquad\qquad\qquad = -4$$

Four basic functions are

Linear: $f(x) = mx + b$

Identity: $f(x) = x$

Squaring: $f(x) = x^2$

Absolute value: $f(x) = |x|$

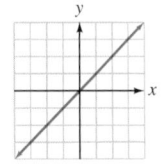
Linear function
$f(x) = mx + b$

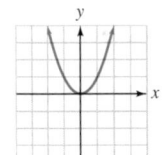
Identity function
$f(x) = x$

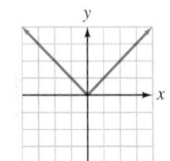
Squaring function
$f(x) = x^2$

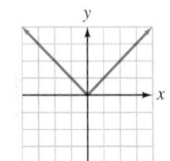
Absolute value function
$f(x) = |x|$

The vertical line test: If a vertical line intersects a graph in more than one point, the graph is not the graph of a function.

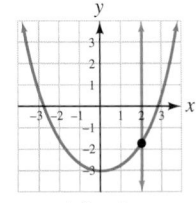

A function

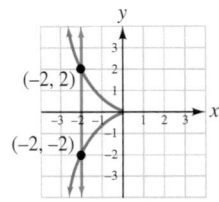
$(-2, 2)$
$(-2, -2)$
Not a function

REVIEW EXERCISES

Find the domain and range of each relation.

47. $\{(7, -3), (-5, 9), (4, 4), (0, -11)\}$
domain: $\{-5, 0, 4, 7\}$, range: $\{-11, -3, 4, 9\}$

48. $\{(2, -2), (15, -8), (-6, 9) (1, -8)\}$
domain: $\{-6, 1, 2, 15\}$, range: $\{-8, -2, 9\}$

In each case, determine whether a function is defined.

49. $y = 3x - 2$ yes   **50.** $y^2 = x$ no

51.

x	2	2	3	4	5	6
y	-2	2	3	-4	5	-6

no

52.

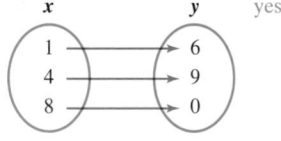

yes

Find the domain and range of each function.

53. $f(x) = x + 10$ D: all reals, R: all reals

54. $y = x^2$ D: all reals, R: real numbers greater than or equal to 0

For the function $g(x) = 1 - 6x$, find each value.

55. $g(1)$ -5 **56.** $g(-6)$ 37

57. $g(0.5)$ -2 **58.** $g\left(\dfrac{3}{2}\right)$ -8

Complete the table and graph the function.

59. $h(x) = 1 - |x|$

x	$h(x)$
0	1
1	0
2	-1
-1	0
-2	-1
-3	-2

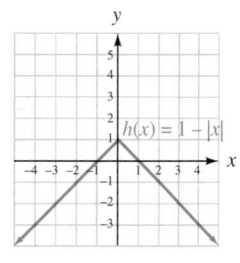

Determine whether each graph is the graph of a function.

60.

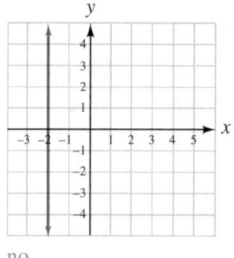

no

61.

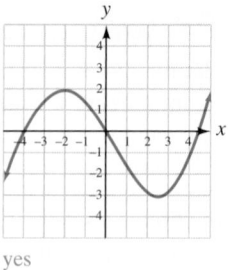

yes

62. The function $f(r) = 15.7r^2$ estimates the volume in cubic inches of a can 5 inches tall with a radius of r inches. Find the volume of the can in the illustration. Round to the nearest tenth.   1,004.8 in.^{3}

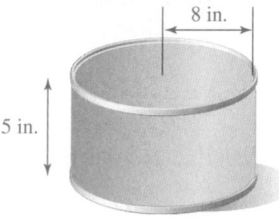

CHAPTER 3   TEST

The graph in the following illustration shows the number of dogs being boarded in a kennel over a 3-day holiday weekend. Use the graph to answer Exercises 1–4.

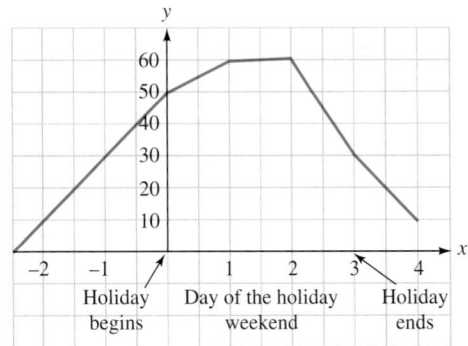

1. How many dogs were in the kennel 2 days before the holiday? 10

2. What is the maximum number of dogs that were boarded on the holiday weekend? 60

3. When were there 30 dogs in the kennel? 1 day before and the 3rd day of the holiday

4. What information does the y-intercept of the graph give? 50 dogs were in the kennel when the holiday began.

5. Graph: $y = x^2 - 4$ **6.** Graph: $8x + 4y = -24$

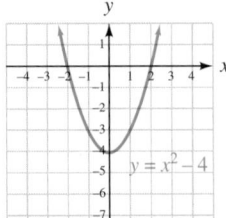 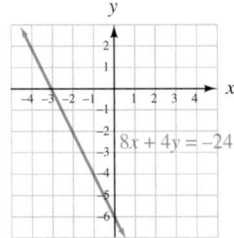

7. Is $(-3, -4)$ a solution of $3x - 4y = 7$? yes

8. Is $y = x^3$ a linear equation? no

9. What are the x- and y-intercepts of the graph of $2x - 3y = 6$? x-intercept: $(3, 0)$, y-intercept: $(0, -2)$

10. Find the slope and the y-intercept of $x + 2y = 8$. $m = -\frac{1}{2}, (0, 4)$

11. Graph: $x = -4$

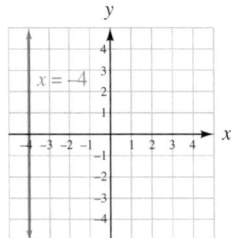

12. Graph the line passing through $(-2, -4)$ having a slope of $\frac{2}{3}$.

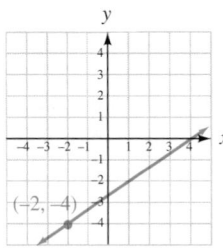

13. Find the slope of the line passing through $(-1, 3)$ and $(3, -1)$. -1

14. What is the slope of a vertical line? undefined

15. Find the slope of a line that is perpendicular to a line with slope $-\frac{7}{8}$. $\frac{8}{7}$

16. When graphed, are the lines $y = 2x + 6$ and $6x - 3y = 0$ parallel, perpendicular, or neither? parallel

Refer to the graph in the illustration below, which shows the elevation changes in a 26-mile marathon course.

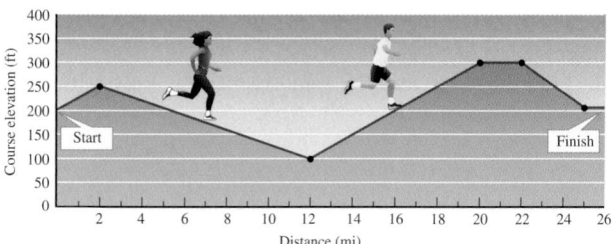

17. Find the rate of change of the decline on which the woman is running. -15 ft per mi

18. Find the rate of change of the incline on which the man is running. 25 ft per mi

19. DEPRECIATION After it is purchased, a $15,000 computer loses $1,500 in resale value every year. Write a linear equation that gives the resale value v of the computer x years after being purchased. $v = -1,500x + 15,000$

20. Write an equation of the line passing through $(-2, 5)$ and $(-3, -2)$. Answer in slope–intercept form. $y = 7x + 19$

21. Does the point with coordinates $(1, -2)$ satisfy the inequality $x - y > -2$? yes

22. Graph the inequality: $x - y > -2$

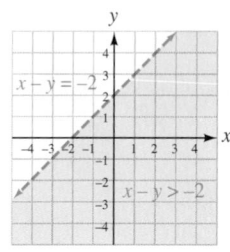

23. Find the domain and range of the relation: $\{(6, 1), (-2, 4), (7, 5), (0, 6)\}$ domain: $\{-2, 0, 6, 7\}$, range: $\{1, 4, 5, 6\}$

24. Is the circle the graph of a function? no

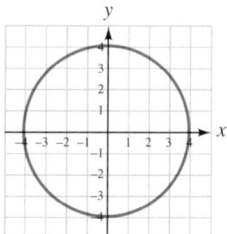

Determine whether the table, arrow diagram, or graph define y to be a function of x. If a function is defined, give its domain and range. If it does not define a function, find ordered pairs that show a value of x that corresponds to more than one value of y.

25.

x	y
1	4
2	3
3	2
4	1

yes, domain: $\{1, 2, 3, 4\}$, range: $\{1, 2, 3, 4\}$

26.

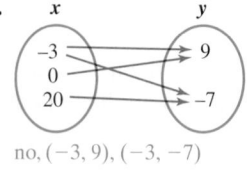

no, $(-3, 9), (-3, -7)$

27. Find the domain and range of the function $f(x) = -|x|$. D: all real numbers, R: real numbers less than or equal to 0

28. Does the equation $y = 2x - 8$ define a function? yes

29. If $f(x) = 2x - 7$, find: $f(-3)$ -13

30. If $g(x) = 3.5x^3$, find: $g(6)$ 756

CHAPTERS 1–3   CUMULATIVE REVIEW

1. Give the prime factorization of 108. [Section 1.2] $2^2 \cdot 3^3$

2. Write $\frac{1}{250}$ as a decimal. [Section 1.3] 0.004

3. Determine whether each statement is true or false. [Section 1.3]

   a. Every whole number is an integer. true

   b. Every integer is a real number. true

   c. 0 is a whole number, an integer, and a rational number. true

4. Add: $-3 + -15$ [Section 1.4] -18

Evaluate each expression. [Section 1.7]

5. $12 - 2 \cdot 3$ 6

6. $\dfrac{(6-5)^4 - (-21)}{-27 + 4^2}$ -2

7. $19 - 2[(-3.1 + 6.1) \cdot 3]$ 1

8. $64 - 6[15 - (3)3]$ 28

9. Evaluate $b^2 - 4ac$ for $a = 2$, $b = -8$, and $c = 4$. [Section 1.8] 32

10. Suppose x sheets from a 500-sheet ream of paper have been used. Write an algebraic expression to represent the number of sheets that are left. [Section 1.8] $500 - x$

Consider the algebraic expression $3x^2 - 2x + 1$. [Section 1.8]

11. How many terms does the expression have? 3

12. What is the coefficient of the second term? -2

Use the distributive property to remove parentheses.
[Section 1.9]

13. $2(x + 4)$ $2x + 8$

14. $2(x - 4)$ $2x - 8$

15. $-2(x + 4)$ $-2x - 8$

16. $-2(x - 4)$ $-2x + 8$

Simplify each expression. [Section 1.9]

17. $5a + 10 - a$ $4a + 10$

18. $-2b^2 + 6b^2$ $4b^2$

19. $(a + 2) - (a - 2)$ 4

20. $-y - y - y$ $-3y$

Solve each equation. [Sections 2.1 and 2.2]

21. $3x - 5 = 13$ 6

22. $1.2 - x = -1.7$ 2.9

23. $\dfrac{2x}{3} - 2 = 4$ 9

24. $\dfrac{y - 2}{7} = -3$ -19

25. $-3(2y - 2) - y = 5$ $\frac{1}{7}$

26. $9y - 3 = 6y$ 1

27. $\dfrac{1}{3} + \dfrac{c}{5} = -\dfrac{3}{2}$ $-\frac{55}{6}$

28. $5(x + 2) = 5x - 2$ no solution

29. AUTO SALES The five best-selling vehicles in the United States during a given year are listed in the table. Complete the table and round to the nearest tenth of one percent. [Section 2.3]

		Units sold			
Rank	Vehicle	2000	1999	1999 rank	% change
1	Ford F-Series pickup	876,716	869,001	1	+0.9
2	Chevrolet Silverado pickup	642,119	636,150	2	+0.9
3	Ford Explorer	445,157	428,772	5	+3.8
4	Toyota Camry	422,961	448,162	3	−5.6
5	Honda Accord	404,515	404,192	6	+0.1

Based on information from Reuters

30. Solve the equation $y = mx + b$ for x. [Section 2.4] $x = \frac{y - b}{m}$

31. Find the perimeter and the area of the gauze pad of the bandage shown. [Section 2.4] $3\frac{1}{8}$ in., $\frac{39}{64}$ in.^{2}

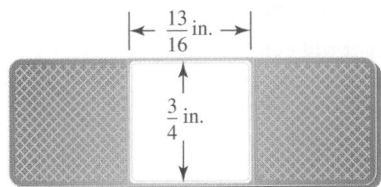

32. If the vertex of an isosceles triangle is 22°, find the measure of each base angle. [Section 2.5] 79°

33. Complete the table. [Section 2.6]

Solution	Liters	% acid	Amount of acid
50% solution	x	0.50	$0.50x$
25% solution	$13 - x$	0.25	$0.25(13 - x)$
30% mixture	13	0.30	$0.30(13)$

34. INVESTMENT A student saving for a class trip to Europe invests $2,500 in two accounts. One account pays 3% annual interest and the other riskier account pays 8%. Find the amount invested at each rate if the first year's combined interest from the two accounts was $105. [Section 2.6] $1,900 at 3%, $600 at 8%

35. ROAD TRIPS A bus, carrying the members of a marching band, and a truck, carrying their instruments, leave a high school at the same time. The bus travels at 60 mph and the truck at 50 mph. In how many hours will they be 75 miles apart? [Section 2.6] 7.5 hr

36. MIXING CANDY Candy corn worth $1.90 per pound is to be mixed with black gumdrops that cost $1.20 per pound to make 200 pounds of a mixture worth $1.48 per pound. How many pounds of each candy should be used? [Section 2.6] 80 lb candy corn, 120 lb gumdrops

Solve each inequality, graph the solution set, and write the solution in interval notation. [Section 2.7]

37. $-\dfrac{3}{16}x \geq -9$ $x \leq 48$, 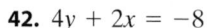, $(-\infty, 48]$

38. $8x + 4 > 3x + 4$ $x > 0$, ———(———→, $(0, \infty)$

39. MEDICATION Dosages for a certain medication are shown in the next column. Find the dosage for: [Section 3.1]

a. a 5-year-old child. 1 tsp

b. a 9-year-old child. 3 tsp

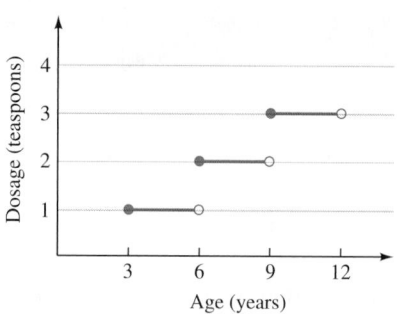

40. Is $(-2, 4)$ a solution of $y = 2x - 8$? [Section 3.2] no

Graph each equation. [Section 3.2]

41. $y = |x - 2|$ **42.** $4y + 2x = -8$

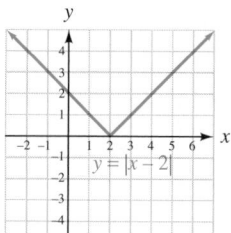   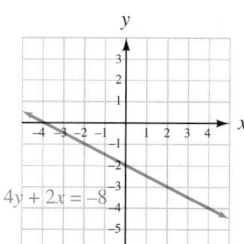

43. What is the slope of the graph of the line $y = 5$? [Section 3.4] 0

44. What is the slope of the line passing through $(-2, 4)$ and $(5, -6)$? [Section 3.4] $-\dfrac{10}{7}$

45. Find the slope and the y-intercept of the graph of the line described by $4x - 6y = -12$. [Section 3.5] $\dfrac{2}{3}$, $(0, 2)$

46. Write an equation of the line that has slope -2 and y-intercept of $(0, 1)$. [Section 3.5] $y = -2x + 1$

47. Write an equation of the line that has slope $-\dfrac{7}{8}$ and passes through $(2, -9)$. Express the answer in point–slope form. [Section 3.6] $y + 9 = -\dfrac{7}{8}(x - 2)$

48. If $f(x) = x^2 - 3x$, find $f(-2)$. [Section 3.8] 10

Solving Systems of Equations and Inequalities

4

Mark & Audrey Gibson/Jupiterimages

from *Campus to Careers*

Air Traffic Controller

The air traffic control system is a vast network of people and equipment that ensures the safe operation of commercial and private aircraft. Air traffic controllers coordinate the movement of air traffic to make certain that planes stay a safe distance apart. Their immediate concern is safety, but controllers also must direct planes efficiently to minimize delays. Some regulate airport traffic and others regulate airport arrivals and departures.

In **Problem 73** of **Study Set 4.1,** you will see one way that air traffic controllers can guard against an air collision.

JOB TITLE: Air Traffic Controller

EDUCATION: Completion of an FAA-approved program, a passing score on an FAA-authorized pre-employment test, and a thorough medical exam are required.

JOB OUTLOOK: Employment is expected to grow 10% through the year 2016.

ANNUAL EARNINGS: In 2006, salaries ranged from $86,860 to $142,210.

FOR MORE INFORMATION: www.bls.gov/oco/ocos108.htm

Objectives

1. Determine whether a given ordered pair is a solution of a system.
2. Solve systems of linear equations by graphing.
3. Use graphing to identify inconsistent systems and dependent equations.
4. Identify the number of solutions of a linear system without graphing.

SECTION **4.1**

Solving Systems of Equations by Graphing

The following illustration shows the average amounts of chicken and beef eaten per person each year in the United States from 1985 to 2005. Plotting both graphs on the same coordinate system makes it easy to compare recent trends. The point of intersection of the graphs indicates that Americans ate equal amounts of chicken and beef in 1992—about 66 pounds of each, per person.

In this section, we will use a similar graphical approach to solve systems of equations.

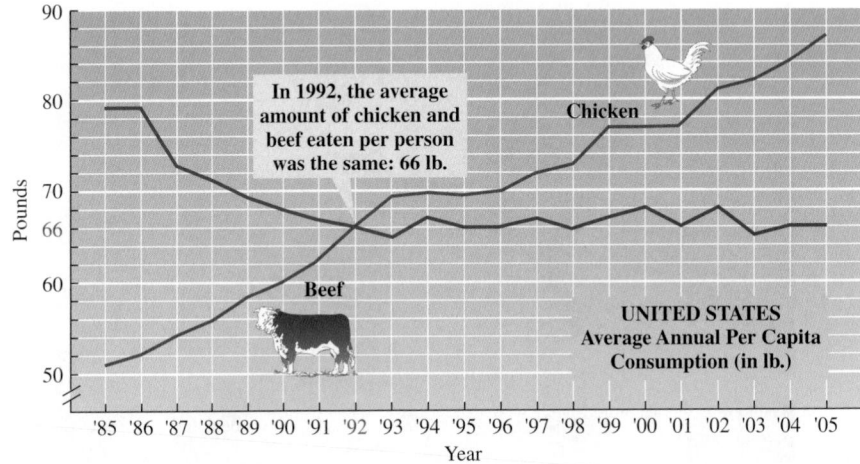

In 1992, the average amount of chicken and beef eaten per person was the same: 66 lb.

UNITED STATES
Average Annual Per Capita
Consumption (in lb.)

Source: U.S. Department of Agriculture

1 Determine whether a given ordered pair is a solution of a system.

We have previously discussed equations in two variables, such as $x + y = 3$. Because there are infinitely many pairs of numbers whose sum is 3, there are infinitely many pairs (x, y) that satisfy this equation. Some of these pairs are listed in table (a).

Now consider the equation $x - y = 1$. Because there are infinitely many pairs of numbers whose difference is 1, there are infinitely many pairs (x, y) that satisfy $x - y = 1$. Some of these pairs are listed in table (b).

$x + y = 3$		
x	y	(x, y)
0	3	$(0, 3)$
1	2	$(1, 2)$
2	1	$(2, 1)$
3	0	$(3, 0)$

(a)

$x - y = 1$		
x	y	(x, y)
0	−1	$(0, -1)$
1	0	$(1, 0)$
2	1	$(2, 1)$
3	2	$(3, 2)$

(b)

From the two tables, we see that $(2, 1)$ satisfies both equations.

When two equations with the same variables are considered simultaneously (at the same time), we say that they form a **system of equations.** Using a left brace {, we can write the equations from the previous example as a system:

$$\begin{cases} x + y = 3 \\ x - y = 1 \end{cases}$$ *Read as "the system of equations x + y = 3 and x − y = 1."*

Because the ordered pair (2, 1) satisfies both of these equations, it is called a **solution of the system.** In general, a system of linear equations can have exactly one solution, no solution, or infinitely many solutions.

> **The Language of Algebra**   We say that (2, 1) *satisfies* $x + y = 3$, because the *x*-coordinate, 2, and the *y*-coordinate, 1, make the equation true when substituted for *x* and *y*: $2 + 1 = 3$. To *satisfy* means to make content, as in *satisfy* your thirst or a *satisfied* customer.

EXAMPLE 1   Determine whether $(-2, 5)$ is a solution of each system of equations.

a. $\begin{cases} 3x + 2y = 4 \\ x - y = -7 \end{cases}$ **b.** $\begin{cases} 4y = 18 - x \\ y = 2x \end{cases}$

Strategy We will substitute the *x*- and *y*-coordinates of $(-2, 5)$ for the corresponding variables in both equations of the system.

WHY If both equations are satisfied (made true) by the *x*- and *y*-coordinates, then the ordered pair is a solution of the system.

Solution

a. Recall that in an ordered pair, the first number is the *x*-coordinate and the second number is the *y*-coordinate. To determine whether $(-2, 5)$ is a solution, we substitute -2 for *x* and 5 for *y* in each equation.

Check:

$3x + 2y = 4$ *The first equation.* $x - y = -7$ *The second equation.*

$3(-2) + 2(5) \stackrel{?}{=} 4$ $-2 - 5 \stackrel{?}{=} -7$

$-6 + 10 \stackrel{?}{=} 4$ $-7 = -7$ *True*

$4 = 4$ *True*

Since $(-2, 5)$ satisfies both equations, it is a solution of the system.

b. Again, we substitute -2 for *x* and 5 for *y* in each equation.

Check:

$4y = 18 - x$ *The first equation.* $y = 2x$ *The second equation.*

$4(5) \stackrel{?}{=} 18 - (-2)$ $5 \stackrel{?}{=} 2(-2)$

$20 \stackrel{?}{=} 18 + 2$ $5 = -4$ *False*

$20 = 20$ *True*

Although $(-2, 5)$ satisfies the first equation, it does not satisfy the second. Because it does not satisfy both equations, $(-2, 5)$ is not a solution of the system.

> **The Language of Algebra**   A system of equations is two (or more) equations that we consider *simultaneously*—at the same time. Some professional sports teams *simulcast* their games. That is, the announcer's play-by-play description is broadcast on radio and television at the same time.

Self Check 1

Determine whether $(4, -1)$ is a solution of: $\begin{cases} x - 2y = 6 \\ y = 3x - 11 \end{cases}$ no

Now Try **Problems 21 and 26**

Teaching Example 1 Determine whether $(6, -1)$ is a solution of the system of equations $\begin{cases} 2x + y = 11 \\ y = x - 7 \end{cases}$

Answer:
yes

2 Solve systems of linear equations by graphing.

To use the graphing method to solve

$$\begin{cases} x + y = 3 \\ 3x - y = 1 \end{cases}$$

we graph both equations on one set of coordinate axes using the intercept method, as shown below.

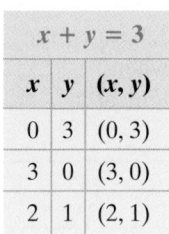
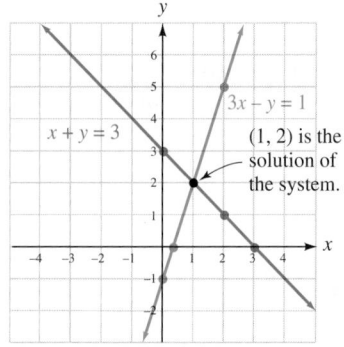

$x + y = 3$		
x	y	(x, y)
0	3	$(0, 3)$
3	0	$(3, 0)$
2	1	$(2, 1)$

$3x - y = 1$		
x	y	(x, y)
0	-1	$(0, -1)$
$\frac{1}{3}$	0	$(\frac{1}{3}, 0)$
2	5	$(2, 5)$

$(1, 2)$ is the solution of the system.

Although there are infinitely many pairs (x, y) that satisfy $x + y = 3$, and infinitely many pairs (x, y) that satisfy $3x - y = 1$, only the coordinates of the point where their graphs intersect satisfy both equations simultaneously. Thus, the solution of the system is $(1, 2)$.

To check this result, we substitute 1 for x and 2 for y in each equation and verify that the pair $(1, 2)$ satisfies each equation.

Check: **First equation**

$$x + y = 3$$
$$1 + 2 \stackrel{?}{=} 3$$
$$3 = 3 \quad \text{True}$$

Second equation

$$3x - y = 1$$
$$3(1) - 2 \stackrel{?}{=} 1$$
$$3 - 2 \stackrel{?}{=} 1$$
$$1 = 1 \quad \text{True}$$

When the graphs of two equations in a system are different lines, the equations are called **independent equations.** When a system of equations has a solution, the system is called a **consistent system.**

To solve a system of equations in two variables by graphing, we follow these steps.

The Graphing Method

1. Carefully graph each equation on the same rectangular coordinate system.

2. If the lines intersect, determine the coordinates of the point of intersection of the graphs. The ordered pair is the solution of the system.

3. Check the proposed solution in the equations of the original system.

EXAMPLE 2

Solve the system of equations by graphing: $\begin{cases} 2x + 3y = 2 \\ 3x = 2y + 16 \end{cases}$

Strategy We will graph both equations on the same coordinate system.

WHY Recall that the graph of a linear equation is a "picture" of its solutions. If both equations are graphed on the same coordinate system, we can see whether they have any common solutions.

Solution

Using the intercept method, we graph both equations on one set of coordinate axes.

Although there are infinitely many pairs (x, y) that satisfy $2x + 3y = 2$, and infinitely many pairs (x, y) that satisfy $3x = 2y + 16$, only the coordinates of the point where the graphs intersect satisfy both equations at the same time. From the graph, the solution appears to be $(4, -2)$.

$2x + 3y = 2$		
x	y	(x, y)
0	$\frac{2}{3}$	$\left(0, \frac{2}{3}\right)$
1	0	$(1, 0)$
-2	2	$(-2, 2)$

$3x = 2y + 16$		
x	y	(x, y)
0	-8	$(0, -8)$
$\frac{16}{3}$	0	$\left(\frac{16}{3}, 0\right)$
2	-5	$(2, -5)$

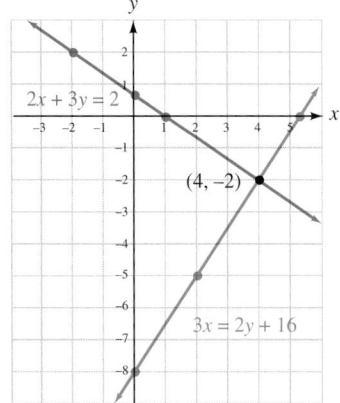

To check, we substitute 4 for x and -2 for y in each equation and verify that the pair $(4, -2)$ satisfies each equation.

Check:

$2x + 3y = 2$	This is the first equation.	$3x = 2y + 16$	This is the second equation.

$$2(4) + 3(-2) \stackrel{?}{=} 2 \qquad\qquad 3(4) \stackrel{?}{=} 2(-2) + 16$$
$$8 - 6 \stackrel{?}{=} 2 \qquad\qquad\qquad 12 \stackrel{?}{=} -4 + 16$$
$$2 = 2 \quad \text{True} \qquad\qquad 12 = 12 \qquad \text{True}$$

The equations in this system are independent equations, and the system is a consistent system of equations.

EXAMPLE 3

Solve the system of equations by graphing: $\begin{cases} -\dfrac{x}{2} - 1 = \dfrac{y}{2} \\ \dfrac{1}{3}x - \dfrac{1}{2}y = -4 \end{cases}$

Strategy We will multiply both sides of each equation by a value that will remove the fractions. Then we will graph both equations of the equivalent system on the same coordinate plane.

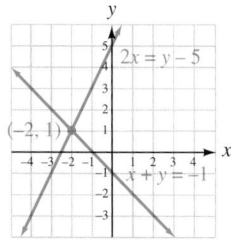
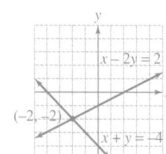

Solve the system of equations by graphing:
$$\begin{cases} -\dfrac{x}{2} = \dfrac{y}{4} \\ \dfrac{1}{4}x - \dfrac{3}{8}y = -2 \end{cases} \quad (-2, 4)$$

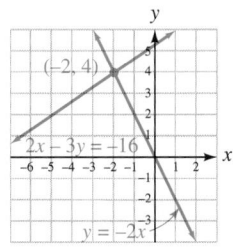

Now Try Problem 39

Teaching Example 3 Solve the system of equations by graphing:
$$\begin{cases} \frac{1}{3}x + \frac{1}{2}y = 2 \\ \frac{1}{4}x - \frac{1}{8}y = \frac{1}{2} \end{cases}$$
Answer:
$(3, 2)$

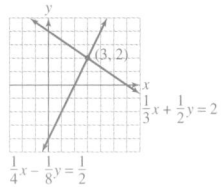

WHY Recall that the graph of a linear equation is a "picture" of its solutions. It is easier to graph equations that have integer coefficients. If both equations are graphed on the same coordinate system, we can see whether they have any common solutions.

Solution

We can multiply both sides of the first equation by 2 to clear it of fractions.

$$-\frac{x}{2} - 1 = \frac{y}{2}$$

$$2\left(-\frac{x}{2} - 1\right) = 2\left(\frac{y}{2}\right)$$

(1) $\qquad -x - 2 = y \qquad$ We will call this Equation 1.

We then multiply both sides of the second equation by 6 to clear it of fractions.

$$\frac{1}{3}x - \frac{1}{2}y = -4$$

$$6\left(\frac{1}{3}x - \frac{1}{2}y\right) = 6(-4)$$

(2) $\qquad 2x - 3y = -24 \qquad$ We will call this Equation 2.

Equations 1 and 2 form the following **equivalent system,** which has the same solutions as the original system:

$$\begin{cases} -x - 2 = y \\ 2x - 3y = -24 \end{cases}$$

We graph $-x - 2 = y$ by plotting the y-intercept $(0, -2)$ and then drawing a slope of -1. We graph $2x - 3y = -24$ using the intercept method. It appears that the point of intersection is $(-6, 4)$.

A check will show that when the coordinates of $(-6, 4)$ are substituted into the two original equations, true statements result. Therefore, the equations are independent and the system is consistent.

$$y = -x - 2$$

$$\text{So } m = -1 = \frac{-1}{1}$$

and $b = -2$.

$2x - 3y = -24$		
x	y	(x, y)
0	8	$(0, 8)$
-12	0	$(-12, 0)$
-3	6	$(-3, 6)$

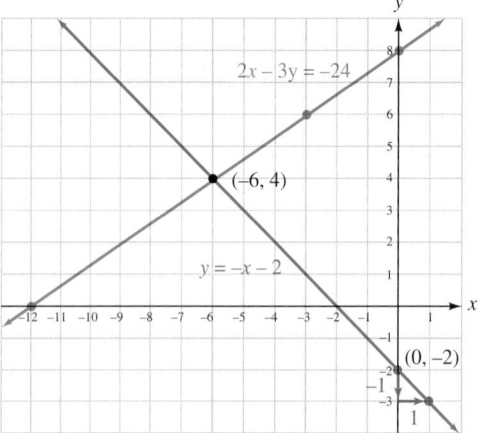

Caution! When solving a system of equations, always check your answer by substituting into the *original* equations. Do not check by substituting into the equations of an equivalent system. If an algebraic error was made while finding the equivalent system, an answer that would not satisfy the original system might appear to be correct.

THINK IT THROUGH   *Bridging the Gender Gap in Education*

"The woman of the 20th century will be the peer of man. In education, in art and science, in literature, in the home, the church, the state, everywhere she will be his acknowledged equal."

Susan B. Anthony, 1900

The following graph shows the percent of associate degrees awarded in the U.S. by gender for the years 1970–2002. Determine the point of intersection of the lines and explain its importance. (1978, 50); In 1978, 50% of the associate degrees that were awarded went to men and 50% went to women. Since then, the percent awarded to women has increased, while the percent awarded to men has decreased.

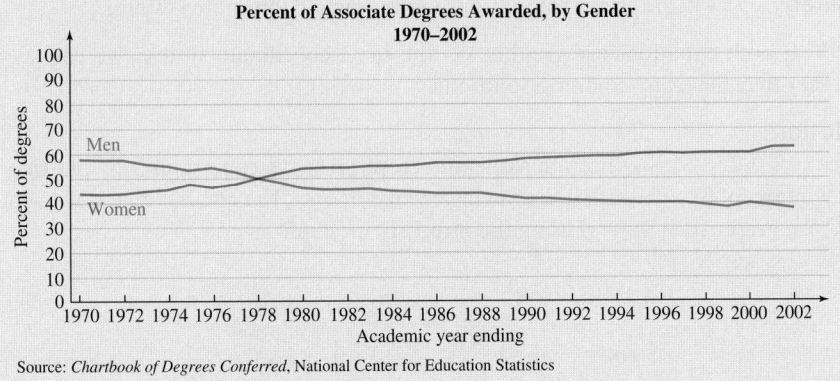

Percent of Associate Degrees Awarded, by Gender 1970–2002

Source: *Chartbook of Degrees Conferred*, National Center for Education Statistics

---

Using Your CALCULATOR   Solving Systems with a Graphing Calculator

We can use a graphing calculator to solve a system of equations, such as

$$\begin{cases} 2x + y = 12 \\ 2x - y = -2 \end{cases}.$$

However, before we can enter the equations into the calculator, we must solve them for y.

$$2x + y = 12 \qquad\qquad 2x - y = -2$$
$$y = -2x + 12 \qquad\qquad -y = -2x - 2$$
$$\qquad\qquad\qquad\qquad\quad y = 2x + 2$$

We enter the resulting equations and graph them on the same coordinate axes. If we use the standard window settings, their graphs will look like figure (a) below.

To find the solution of the system, we use the INTERSECT feature that is found on most graphing calculators. With this option, the cursor automatically moves to the point of intersection of the graphs and displays the coordinates of that point. In figure (b), we see that the solution is (2.5, 7). Consult your owner's manual for specific keystrokes to use INTERSECT.

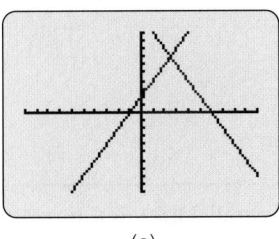   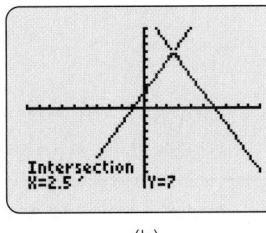

(a)   (b)

3 Use graphing to identify inconsistent systems and dependent equations.

Sometimes a system of equations has no solution. Such systems are called **inconsistent systems.**

Solve the system of equations by graphing: $\begin{cases} y = \dfrac{3}{2}x \\ 3x - 2y = 6 \end{cases}$ no solution

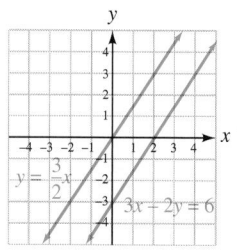

Now Try Problem 41

Teaching Example 4 Solve the system of equations by graphing:
$\begin{cases} y = \frac{1}{2}x + 1 \\ x - 2y = 4 \end{cases}$
Answer:
no solution

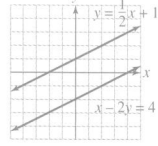

EXAMPLE 4

Solve the system of equations by graphing: $\begin{cases} y = -2x - 6 \\ 4x + 2y = 8 \end{cases}$

Strategy We will graph both equations on the same coordinate system.

WHY If both equations are graphed on the same coordinate system, we can see whether they have any common solutions.

Solution

Since $y = -2x - 6$ is written in slope–intercept form, we can graph it by plotting the y-intercept $(0, -6)$ and then drawing a slope of -2. (The rise is -2, and the run is 1.) We graph $4x + 2y = 8$ using the intercept method.

$$y = -2x - 6$$

So $m = -2 = \dfrac{-2}{1}$

and $b = -6$.

$4x + 2y = 8$		
x	y	(x, y)
0	4	$(0, 4)$
2	0	$(2, 0)$
1	2	$(1, 2)$

The system is graphed below. Since the lines in the figure are parallel, they have the same slope. We can verify this by writing the second equation in slope–intercept form and observing that the coefficients of x in each equation are equal and the y-intercepts are different, $(0, -6)$ and $(0, 4)$.

$$y = -2x - 6 \qquad 4x + 2y = 8$$
$$2y = -4x + 8$$
$$y = -2x + 4$$

Because parallel lines do not intersect, this system has no solution and is inconsistent. Since the graphs are different lines, the equations of the system are independent.

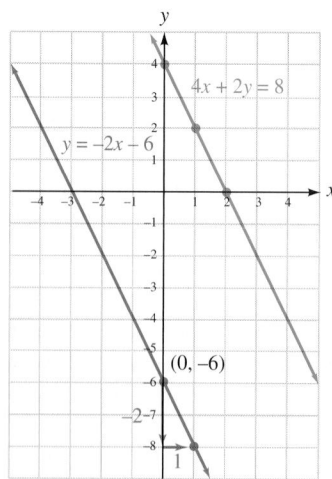

> ***Caution!*** A common error is to graph the parallel lines, but forget to answer with the words *no solution.*

Some systems of equations have infinitely many solutions, as we will see in the next example.

EXAMPLE 5

Solve the system of equations by graphing: $\begin{cases} y - 4 = 2x \\ 4x + 8 = 2y \end{cases}$

Strategy We will graph both equations on the same coordinate system.

WHY If both equations are graphed on the same coordinate system, we can see whether they have any common solutions.

Solution
We graph both equations using the intercept method.

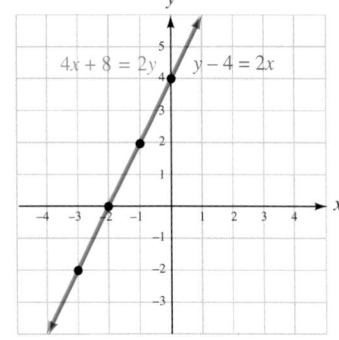

$y - 4 = 2x$		
x	y	(x, y)
0	4	$(0, 4)$
-2	0	$(-2, 0)$
-1	2	$(-1, 2)$

$4x + 8 = 2y$		
x	y	(x, y)
0	4	$(0, 4)$
-2	0	$(-2, 0)$
-3	-2	$(-3, -2)$

The lines in the figure coincide (they are the same line). Because the lines intersect at infinitely many points, the system has infinitely many solutions. From the graph, we can see that some of the solutions are $(0, 4)$, $(-1, 2)$, and $(-3, -2)$. Equations that have the same graph are called **dependent equations.** Therefore, this system is consistent and its equations are dependent. ■

There are three possible outcomes when we solve a system of two linear equations using the graphing method.

Possible graph	If the	Then
	lines are different and intersect,	the equations are independent and the system is consistent. There is one solution.
	lines are different and parallel,	the equations are independent and the system is inconsistent. There are no solutions.
	lines are the same,	the equations are dependent and the system is consistent. There are infinitely many solutions.

Self Check 5

Solve the system of equations by graphing: $\begin{cases} 6x - 2y = 4 \\ y + 2 = 3x \end{cases}$

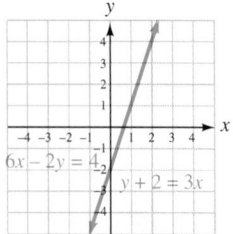

Now Try **Problem 43**

Self Check 5 Answer
infinitely many solutions

Teaching Example 5 Solve the system of equations by graphing:
$\begin{cases} x + 3y = 6 \\ y = -\frac{1}{3}x + 2 \end{cases}$
Answer:
infinitely many solutions

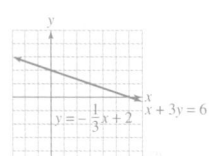

4 Identify the number of solutions of a linear system without graphing.

We can determine the number of solutions that a system of two linear equations has by writing each equation in slope–intercept form.

- If the lines have different slopes, they intersect, and the system has one solution. (See Example 2.)
- If the lines have the same slope and different y-intercepts, they are parallel, and the system has no solution. (See Example 4.)
- If the lines have the same slope and same y-intercept, they are the same line, and the system has infinitely many solutions. (See Example 5.)

Self Check 6

Without graphing, determine the number of solutions of:
$$\begin{cases} 3x + 6y = 1 \\ 2x + 4y = 0 \end{cases}$$ no solution

Now Try Problems 45 and 48

Teaching Example 6 Without graphing, determine the number of solutions of:
$$\begin{cases} 2x + y = 4 \\ 3y = -6x + 12 \end{cases}$$
Answer:
infinitely many solutions

EXAMPLE 6 Without graphing, determine the number of solutions of:
$$\begin{cases} 5x + y = 5 \\ 3x + 2y = 8 \end{cases}$$

Strategy We will write both equations in slope–intercept form.

WHY We can determine the number of solutions of a linear system by comparing the slopes and y-intercepts of the graphs of the equations.

Solution
To write each equation in slope–intercept form, we solve for y.

$5x + y = 5$ The first equation. $3x + 2y = 8$ The second equation.

$\qquad y = -5x + 5$ $\qquad 2y = -3x + 8$

$\qquad\qquad\qquad\qquad\qquad\qquad\qquad\qquad y = -\dfrac{3}{2}x + 4$

Different slopes

Since the slopes are different, the lines are neither parallel nor identical. Therefore, they will intersect at one point and the system has one solution.

ANSWERS TO SELF CHECKS

1. no   **2.** $(-2, 1)$

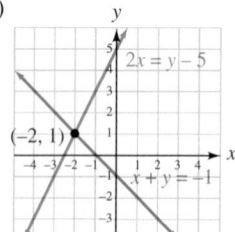

3. $(-2, 4)$

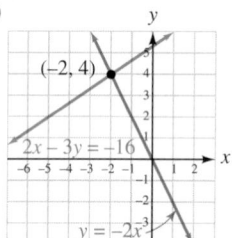

4. no solution

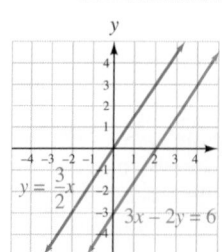

5. infinitely many solutions

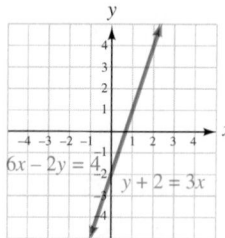

6. no solution

SECTION 4.1   STUDY SET

VOCABULARY

Fill in the blanks.

1. The pair of equations $\begin{cases} x - y = -1 \\ 2x - y = 1 \end{cases}$ is called a <u>system</u> of equations.

2. Because the ordered pair (2, 3) satisfies both equations in Problem 1, it is called a <u>solution</u> of the system of equations.

3. When the graphs of two equations in a system are different lines, the equations are called <u>independent</u> equations.

▶ 4. When a system of equations has a solution, the system is called a <u>consistent</u> system.

5. Systems of equations that have no solution are called <u>inconsistent</u> systems.

6. Equations that have the same graph are called <u>dependent</u> equations.

CONCEPTS

Refer to the following illustration. Determine whether a true or false statement would result if the coordinates of each point were substituted into the equation for the indicated line.

7. point A, line l_1 true

8. point B, line l_2 true

9. point A, line l_2 false

10. point B, line l_1 false

11. point C, line l_1 true

12. point C, line l_2 true

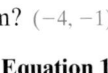

13. The following tables were created to graph the two linear equations in a system. What is the solution of the system? $(-4, -1)$

Equation 1

x	y
0	−5
−5	0
−4	−1
1	−6
2	−7

Equation 2

x	y
0	3
−3	0
−2	1
−4	−1
1	4

▶ 14. **a.** To graph $5x - 2y = 10$, we can use the intercept method. Complete the table.

x	y
0	−5
2	0

b. To graph $y = 3x - 2$, we can use the slope and y-intercept. Fill in the blanks.

slope: $3 = \dfrac{3}{1}$ y-intercept: $(0, -2)$

15. How many solutions does the system of equations graphed in the illustration have? Is the system consistent or inconsistent?

1 solution, consistent

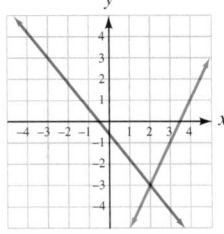

▶ 16. How many solutions does the system of equations graphed in the illustration have? Are the equations dependent or independent?

no solution, independent

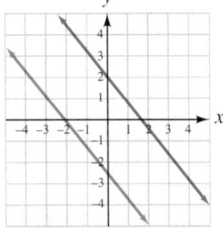

17. The solution of the system of equations graphed on the right is $\left(\frac{2}{5}, -\frac{1}{3}\right)$. Knowing this, can you see any disadvantages to the graphing method?

The method is not accurate enough to find a solution such as $\left(\frac{2}{5}, -\frac{1}{3}\right)$.

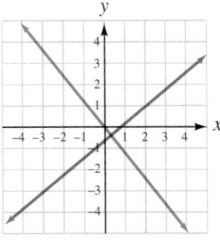

18. Draw the graphs of two linear equations so that the system has

a. one solution $(-3, -2)$.

Answers may vary.

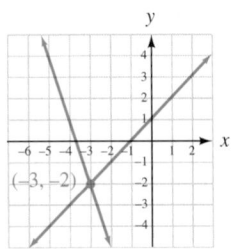

b. infinitely many solutions, three of which are $(-2, 0)$, $(1, 2)$, and $(4, 4)$.

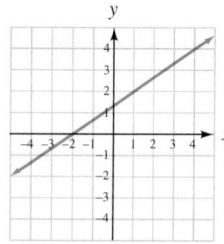

Solve each system of equations by graphing. **See Example 2.**

29. $\begin{cases} 2x + 3y = 12 \\ 2x - y = 4 \end{cases}$ $(3, 2)$ ▶ **30.** $\begin{cases} 5x + y = 5 \\ 5x + 3y = 15 \end{cases}$ $(0, 5)$

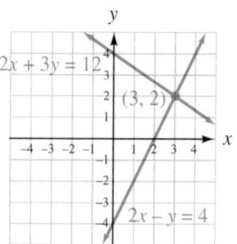
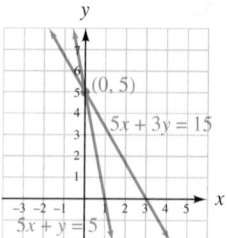

31. $\begin{cases} 3x + 2y = -8 \\ 2x - 3y = -1 \end{cases}$ $(-2, -1)$ ▶ **32.** $\begin{cases} x + 4y = -2 \\ y = -x - 5 \end{cases}$ $(-6, 1)$

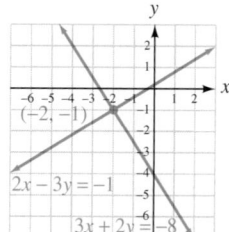
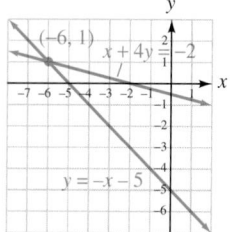

33. $\begin{cases} x + y = 2 \\ y = x - 4 \end{cases}$ $(3, -1)$ ▶ **34.** $\begin{cases} x + y = 1 \\ y = x + 5 \end{cases}$ $(-2, 3)$

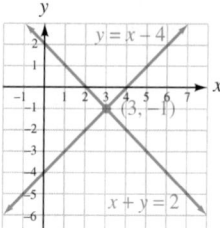
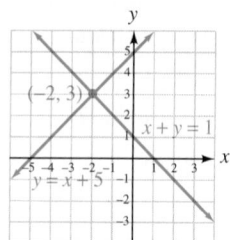

35. $\begin{cases} x = 4 \\ 2y = 12 - 4x \end{cases}$ $(4, -2)$ ▶ **36.** $\begin{cases} x = 3 \\ 3y = 6 - 2x \end{cases}$ $(3, 0)$

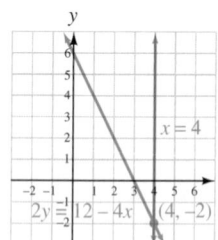
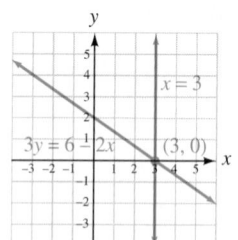

NOTATION

Clear each equation of fractions.

19. $\dfrac{1}{6}x - \dfrac{1}{3}y = \dfrac{11}{2}$

$6\left(\dfrac{1}{6}x - \dfrac{1}{3}y\right) = 6\left(\dfrac{11}{2}\right)$

$6\left(\dfrac{1}{6}x\right) - 6\left(\dfrac{1}{3}y\right) = 6\left(\dfrac{11}{2}\right)$

$x - 2y = 33$

▶ **20.** $\dfrac{3x}{5} - \dfrac{4y}{5} = -1$

$5\left(\dfrac{3x}{5} - \dfrac{4y}{5}\right) = 5(-1)$

$5\left(\dfrac{3x}{5}\right) - 5\left(\dfrac{4y}{5}\right) = 5(-1)$

$3x - 4y = -5$

GUIDED PRACTICE

Determine whether the ordered pair is a solution of the given system of equations. **See Example 1.**

21. $(1, 1)$, $\begin{cases} x + y = 2 \\ 2x - y = 1 \end{cases}$ yes

▶ **22.** $(1, 3)$, $\begin{cases} 2x + y = 5 \\ 3x - y = 0 \end{cases}$ yes

▶ **23.** $(3, -2)$, $\begin{cases} 2x + y = 4 \\ y = 1 - x \end{cases}$ yes

▶ **24.** $(-2, 4)$, $\begin{cases} 2x + 2y = 4 \\ 3y = 10 - x \end{cases}$ yes

25. $(-2, -4)$, $\begin{cases} 4x + 5y = -23 \\ -3x + 2y = 0 \end{cases}$ no

▶ **26.** $(-5, 2)$, $\begin{cases} -2x + 7y = 17 \\ 3x - 4y = -19 \end{cases}$ no

27. $\left(\dfrac{1}{2}, 3\right)$, $\begin{cases} 2x + y = 4 \\ 4x - 11 = 3y \end{cases}$ no

28. $\left(2, \dfrac{1}{3}\right)$, $\begin{cases} x - 3y = 1 \\ -2x + 6 = -6y \end{cases}$ no

Solve each system of the equations by graphing. See Example 3.

37. $\begin{cases} x + 2y = -4 \\ x - \frac{1}{2}y = 6 \end{cases}$ $(4, -4)$ ▶ **38.** $\begin{cases} \frac{2}{3}x - y = -3 \\ 3x + y = 3 \end{cases}$ $(0, 3)$

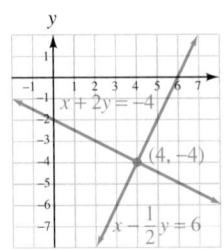 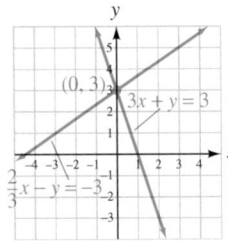

39. $\begin{cases} -\frac{3}{4}x + y = 3 \\ \frac{1}{4}x + y = -1 \end{cases}$ $(-4, 0)$ ▶ **40.** $\begin{cases} \frac{1}{3}x + y = 7 \\ \frac{2x}{3} - y = -4 \end{cases}$ $(3, 6)$

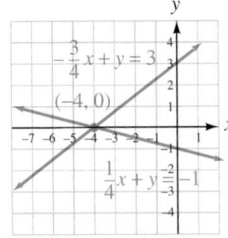 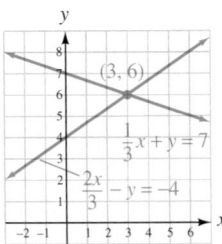

Solve each system of equations by graphing. If the equations of the system are dependent or if the system is inconsistent, so indicate. See Examples 4–5.

▶ **41.** $\begin{cases} y = -\frac{1}{3}x - 4 \\ x + 3y = 6 \end{cases}$ **42.** $\begin{cases} y = -x + 1 \\ 4x + 4y = 4 \end{cases}$

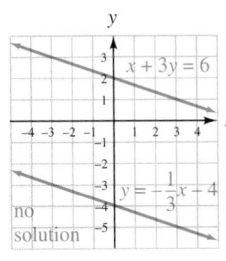 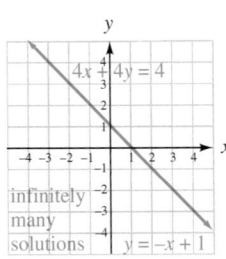

43. $\begin{cases} y = x - 1 \\ 3x - 3y = 3 \end{cases}$ **44.** $\begin{cases} y = -\frac{1}{2}x - 3 \\ x + 2y = 2 \end{cases}$

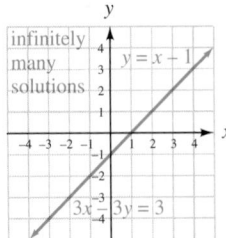 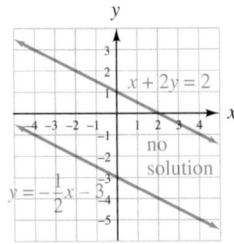

Find the slope and y-intercept of the graph of lines in each system of equations. Then, use that information to determine the number of solutions of each system. See Example 6.

45. $\begin{cases} y = 6x - 7 \\ y = -2x + 1 \end{cases}$
1 solution

▶ **46.** $\begin{cases} y = \frac{1}{2}x + 8 \\ y = 4x - 10 \end{cases}$
1 solution

47. $\begin{cases} 3x - y = -3 \\ y - 3x = 3 \end{cases}$
same line, inf. many sol.

48. $\begin{cases} x + 4y = 4 \\ 12y = 12 - 3x \end{cases}$
same line, inf. many sol.

49. $\begin{cases} x + y = 6 \\ x + y = 8 \end{cases}$
no solution

▶ **50.** $\begin{cases} 5x + y = 0 \\ 5x + y = 6 \end{cases}$
no solution

51. $\begin{cases} 6x + y = 0 \\ 2x + 2y = 0 \end{cases}$
1 solution

▶ **52.** $\begin{cases} x + y = 1 \\ 2x - 2y = 5 \end{cases}$
1 solution

TRY IT YOURSELF

Determine whether the ordered pair is a solution of the given system of equations.

53. $\left(-\frac{2}{5}, \frac{1}{4}\right)$, $\begin{cases} x - 4y = -6 \\ 8y = 10x + 12 \end{cases}$ no

54. $\left(-\frac{1}{3}, \frac{3}{4}\right)$, $\begin{cases} 3x + 4y = 2 \\ 12y = 3(2 - 3x) \end{cases}$ yes

▶ **55.** $(0.2, 0.3)$, $\begin{cases} 20x + 10y = 7 \\ 20y = 15x + 3 \end{cases}$ yes

56. $(2.5, 3.5)$, $\begin{cases} 4x - 3 = 2y \\ 4y + 1 = 6x \end{cases}$ yes

Solve each system of equations by graphing. If the equations of the system are dependent or if the system is inconsistent, so indicate.

57. $\begin{cases} 2x - 3y = -18 \\ 3x + 2y = -1 \end{cases}$
$(-3, 4)$

58. $\begin{cases} -x + 3y = -11 \\ 3x - y = 17 \end{cases}$
$(5, -2)$

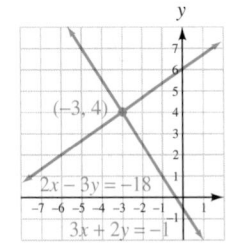 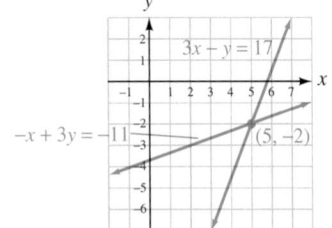

59. $\begin{cases} \frac{1}{3}x - \frac{1}{2}y = \frac{1}{6} \\ \frac{2x}{5} + \frac{y}{2} = \frac{13}{10} \end{cases}$ $(2, 1)$ **60.** $\begin{cases} \frac{3x}{4} + \frac{2y}{3} = -\frac{19}{6} \\ 3y = -x \end{cases}$ $(-6, 2)$

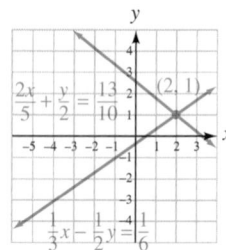 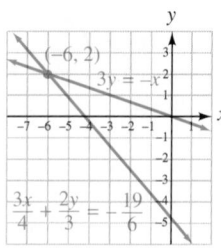

▶ 61. $\begin{cases} 3x - 6y = 18 \\ x = 2y + 3 \end{cases}$ **62.** $\begin{cases} 2y = 3x + 2 \\ \frac{3}{2}x - y = 3 \end{cases}$

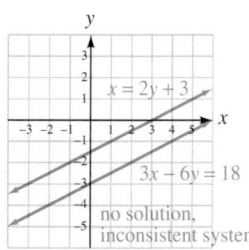 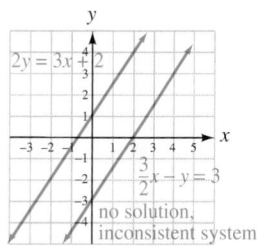

63. $\begin{cases} 4x - 2y = 8 \\ y = 2x - 4 \end{cases}$ **64.** $\begin{cases} -\frac{3}{5}x - \frac{1}{5}y = \frac{6}{5} \\ x + \frac{y}{3} = -2 \end{cases}$

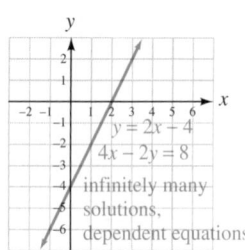 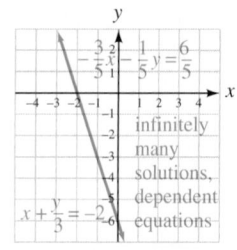
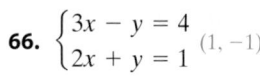

65. $\begin{cases} y = 4 - x \\ y = 2 + x \end{cases}$ $(1, 3)$ **66.** $\begin{cases} 3x - y = 4 \\ 2x + y = 1 \end{cases}$ $(1, -1)$

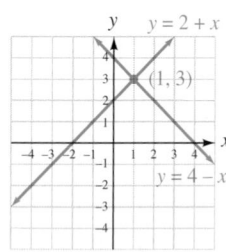 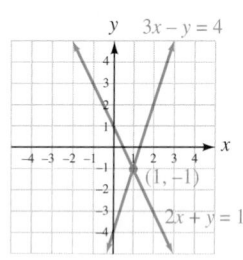
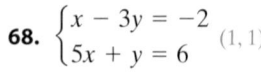

67. $\begin{cases} 6x - 2y = 5 \\ 3x = y + 10 \end{cases}$ **68.** $\begin{cases} x - 3y = -2 \\ 5x + y = 6 \end{cases}$ $(1, 1)$

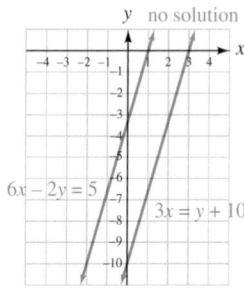 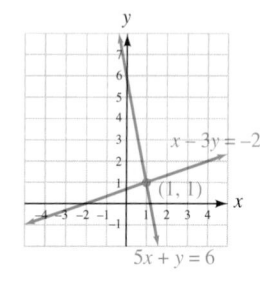

APPLICATIONS

▶ 69. TRANSPLANTS Refer to the graph.

   a. What was the relationship between the number of donors and those awaiting a transplant in 2005? Those needing a transplant outnumbered the donors.

   b. In what year were the number of donors and the number waiting for a transplant the same? Estimate the number. 1994, 4,100

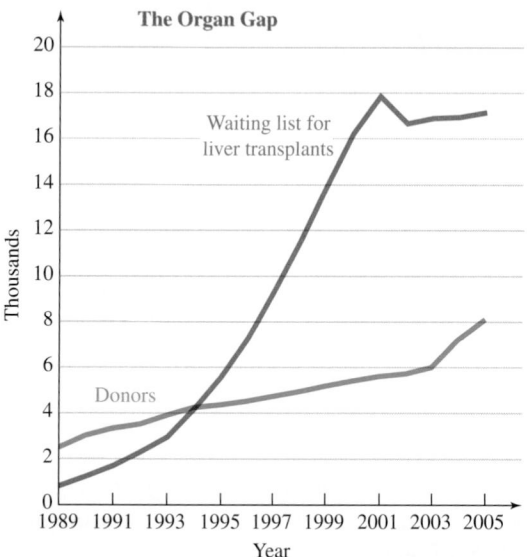

Source: Organ Procurement and Transportation Network

▶ 70. DAILY TRACKING POLLS Use the graph to answer the following.

   a. Which political candidate was ahead on October 28 and by how much? the incumbent, 7%

   b. On what day did the challenger pull even with the incumbent? November 2

   c. If the election was held November 4, who did the poll predict would win, and by how many percentage points? the challenger, 3

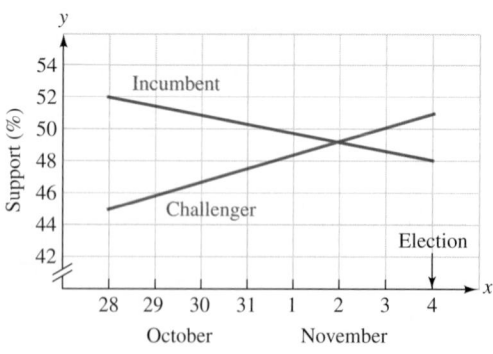

▶ 71. LATITUDE AND LONGITUDE Refer to the map on the next page.

   a. Name three American cities that lie on a latitude line of 30° north. Houston, New Orleans, St. Augustine

   b. Name three American cities that lie on a longitude line of 90° west. St. Louis, Memphis, New Orleans

c. What city lies on both lines? New Orleans

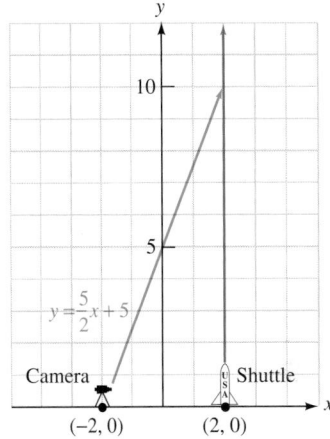

West longitude

72. ECONOMICS The following graph illustrates the law of supply and demand.

    a. Complete this sentence: As the price of an item increases, the *supply* of the item __increases__.

    b. Complete this sentence: As the price of an item increases, the *demand* for the item __decreases__.

    c. For what price will the supply equal the demand? How many items will be supplied for this price?

$6; 30,000

73. The equations describing the paths of two airplanes are $y = -\frac{1}{2}x + 3$ and $3y = 2x + 2$. Graph each equation on the radar screen shown. Is there a possibility of a mid-air collision? If so, where?
yes, (2, 2)

from Campus to Careers
Air Traffic Controller

Mark & Audrey Gibson/Jupiterimages

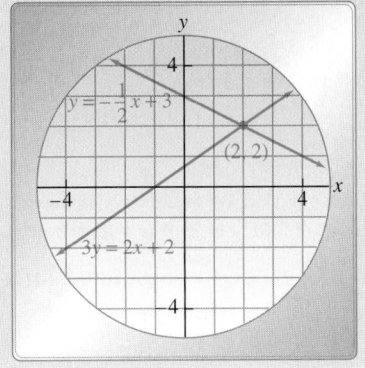

74. TV COVERAGE A television camera is located at $(-2, 0)$ and will follow the launch of a space shuttle, as shown. (Each unit in the illustration is 1 mile.) As the shuttle rises vertically on a path described by $x = 2$, the farthest the camera can tilt back is a line of sight given by $y = \frac{5}{2}x + 5$. For how many miles of the shuttle's flight will it be in view of the camera? 10 mi

$y = \frac{5}{2}x + 5$

Camera   Shuttle

$(-2, 0)$ $(2, 0)$

WRITING

75. Look up the word *simultaneous* in a dictionary and give its definition. In mathematics, what is meant by a simultaneous solution of a system of equations?

76. Suppose the solution of a system is $\left(\frac{1}{3}, -\frac{3}{5}\right)$. Do you think you would be able to find the solution using the graphing method? Explain.

REVIEW

77. Are the graphs of the lines $y = 2x - 3$ and $4x - 2y = 8$ parallel, perpendicular, or neither? parallel

78. Are the graphs of the lines $y = 5x$ and $y = -\frac{1}{5}x$ parallel, perpendicular, or neither? perpendicular

79. If $f(x) = -4x - x^2$, find $f(3)$. -21

80. In what quadrant does $(-12, 15)$ lie? quadrant II

81. Write the equation for the y-axis. $x = 0$

82. Does $(1, 2)$ lie on the line $2x + y = 4$? yes

83. What point does the line with equation $y - 2 = 7(x - 5)$ pass through? $(5, 2)$

84. Is the word *domain* associated with the inputs or the outputs of a function? inputs

Objectives

1 Solve systems of linear equations by substitution.

2 Find a substitution equation.

3 Solve systems of linear equations that contain fractions.

4 Use substitution to identify inconsistent systems and dependent equations.

SECTION 4.2

Solving Systems of Equations by Substitution

When solving a system of equations by graphing, it is often difficult to determine the exact coordinates of the point of intersection. For example, a solution of $\left(\frac{1}{16}, -\frac{3}{5}\right)$ would be almost impossible to identify. In this section, we will introduce an algebraic method that finds *exact* solutions. It is called the *substitution method*.

1 Solve systems of linear equations by substitution.

One algebraic method for solving a system of equations is the **substitution method.** It is introduced in the following example.

Self Check 1

Solve the system:
$$\begin{cases} 3x - 5y = 5 \\ x = 2y - 1 \end{cases} \quad (15, 8)$$

Now Try Problem 18

Teaching Example 1 Solve the system:
$$\begin{cases} y = 5x - 2 \\ 6x - y = 3 \end{cases}$$
Answer:
$(1, 3)$

EXAMPLE 1   Solve the system: $\begin{cases} y = 3x - 2 \\ 2x + y = 8 \end{cases}$

Strategy Note that the first equation is solved for y. Because y and $3x - 2$ are equal (represent the same value), we will substitute $3x - 2$ for y in the second equation.

WHY The objective is to obtain one equation containing only one unknown. When $3x - 2$ is substituted for y in the second equation, the result will be just that—an equation in one variable, x.

Solution

Since the right side of $y = 3x - 2$ is used to make a substitution, $y = 3x - 2$ is called the **substitution equation.**

$$\begin{cases} y = \boxed{3x - 2} \\ 2x + y = 8 \end{cases}$$

To find the solution of the system, we proceed as follows:

$$2x + y = 8 \qquad \text{This is the second equation of the system.}$$
$$2x + 3x - 2 = 8 \qquad \text{Substitute } 3x - 2 \text{ for } y.$$

The resulting equation has only one variable and can be solved for x.

$$2x + 3x - 2 = 8$$
$$5x - 2 = 8 \qquad \text{Combine like terms: } 2x + 3x = 5x.$$
$$5x = 10 \qquad \text{Add 2 to both sides.}$$
$$x = 2 \qquad \text{Divide both sides by 5. This is the } x\text{-value of the solution.}$$

We can find the y-value by substituting 2 for x in either equation of the original system. Because $y = 3x - 2$ is already solved for y, it is easier to substitute into this equation.

$$y = 3x - 2 \qquad \text{This is the first equation of the system.}$$
$$= 3(2) - 2 \qquad \text{Substitute 2 for } x.$$
$$= 6 - 2$$
$$= 4 \qquad \text{This is the } y\text{-value of the solution. We would have obtained the same result if we had substituted 2 for } x \text{ in } 2x + y = 8 \text{ and solved for } y.$$

The solution to the given system is $(2, 4)$. To check, we substitute 2 for x and 4 for y in each equation.

Check: **First equation**   **Second equation**

$$y = 3x - 2 \qquad\qquad 2x + y = 8$$

$$4 \stackrel{?}{=} 3(2) - 2 \qquad\qquad 2(2) + 4 \stackrel{?}{=} 8$$

$$4 \stackrel{?}{=} 6 - 2 \qquad\qquad 4 + 4 \stackrel{?}{=} 8$$

$$4 = 4 \quad \text{True} \qquad\qquad 8 = 8 \quad \text{True}$$

If we graphed the lines represented by the equations of the given system, they would intersect at the point $(2, 4)$. The equations of this system are independent, and the system is consistent. ∎

> *Caution!*   When using the substitution method, a common error is to find the value of one of the variables, say x, and forget to find the value of the other. Remember that a solution of a linear system of two equations is an ordered pair (x, y).

To solve a system of equations in x and y by the substitution method, we follow these steps.

The Substitution Method

1. Solve one of the equations for either x or y. If this is already done, go to step 2. (We call this equation the **substitution equation**.)

2. Substitute the expression for x or for y obtained in step 1 into the other equation and solve that equation.

3. Substitute the value of the variable found in step 2 in the substitution equation to find the value of the remaining variable.

4. Check the proposed solution in each equation of the original system. Write the solution as an ordered pair.

EXAMPLE 2

Solve the system: $\begin{cases} 2x + y = -10 \\ x = -3y \end{cases}$

Strategy We will use the substitution method to solve this system.

WHY The substitution method works well when one of the equations of the system (in this case, $x = -3y$) is solved for a variable.

Solution

Step 1 The second equation, $x = -3y$, tells us that x and $-3y$ have the same value. Therefore, we can substitute $-3y$ for x in the first equation.

$$\begin{cases} 2x + y = -10 \\ x = \boxed{-3y} \end{cases} \qquad \text{This is the substitution equation.}$$

Step 2 When we substitute $-3y$ for x in the first equation, the resulting equation contains only one variable, and it can be solved for y.

$$2x + y = -10 \qquad \text{This is the first equation of the system.}$$

$$2(-3y) + y = -10 \qquad \text{Replace } x \text{ with } -3y.$$

$$-6y + y = -10 \qquad \text{Do the multiplication.}$$

$$-5y = -10 \qquad \text{Combine like terms.}$$

$$y = 2 \qquad \text{Divide both sides by } -5.$$

Self Check 2

Solve the system:
$$\begin{cases} x = -2y \\ 3x - 2y = 8 \end{cases} \quad (2, -1)$$

Now Try Problem 21

Teaching Example 2 Solve the system:
$$\begin{cases} 3x + 40 = 8y \\ x = -4y \end{cases}$$
Answer:
$(-8, 2)$

Step 3 To find x, substitute 2 for y in the equation $x = -3y$.

$$x = -3y \quad \text{This is the second equation of the system.}$$
$$= -3(2) \quad \text{Substitute 2 for y.}$$
$$= -6$$

The solution is $(-6, 2)$.

Step 4 Verify the solution by checking it in both equations.

Check: **First equation** | **Second equation**

$$2x + y = -10 \qquad\qquad x = -3y$$
$$2(-6) + 2 \overset{?}{=} -10 \qquad\qquad -6 \overset{?}{=} -3(2)$$
$$-12 + 2 \overset{?}{=} -10 \qquad\qquad -6 = -6 \quad \text{True}$$
$$-10 = -10 \quad \text{True}$$

2 Find a substitution equation.

To find a substitution equation, solve one of the equations of the system for one of its variables. If possible, solve for a variable whose coefficient is 1 or -1 to avoid working with fractions.

Self Check 3

Solve the system:
$$\begin{cases} 2x - 3y = 13 \\ 3x + y = 3 \end{cases} \quad (2, -3)$$

Now Try Problem 26

Teaching Example 3 Solve the system:
$$\begin{cases} 3x + 4y = 11 \\ x + 2y = 5 \end{cases}$$
Answer:
$(1, 2)$

EXAMPLE 3 Solve the system: $\begin{cases} 2x + y = -5 \\ 3x + 5y = -4 \end{cases}$

Strategy Since the system does not contain an equation solved for x or y, we must choose an equation and solve it for x or y. We will solve for y in the first equation, because y has a coefficient of 1 in that equation. Then we will use the substitution method to solve the system.

WHY Solving $2x + y = -5$ for x or $3x + 5y = -4$ for x or y would involve working with cumbersome fractions.

Solution

Step 1 To find a substitution equation, solve the first equation for y.

$$2x + y = -5 \quad \text{This is the first equation of the system.}$$
$$y = -5 - 2x \quad \text{Subtract 2x from both sides to isolate y.}$$
$$\text{This is the substitution equation.}$$

Step 2 We then substitute $-5 - 2x$ for y in the second equation and solve for x.

$$3x + 5y = -4 \quad \text{This is the second equation of the system.}$$
$$3x + 5(-5 - 2x) = -4 \quad \text{Substitute } -5 - 2x \text{ for y. Don't forget to write } -5 - 2x$$
$$\text{within parentheses.}$$
$$3x - 25 - 10x = -4 \quad \text{Distribute the multiplication by 5.}$$
$$-7x - 25 = -4 \quad \text{Combine like terms: } 3x - 10x = -7x.$$
$$-7x = 21 \quad \text{Add 25 to both sides.}$$
$$x = -3 \quad \text{Divide both sides by } -7.$$

Step 3 To find y, substitute -3 for x in the equation $y = -5 - 2x$.

$$y = -5 - 2x$$
$$y = -5 - 2(-3) \quad \text{Substitute } -3 \text{ for x.}$$
$$y = -5 + 6$$
$$y = 1$$

Step 4 The solution is $(-3, 1)$. Check it in the original equations.

Systems of equations are sometimes written in variables other than x and y. For example, the system

$$\begin{cases} 3a - 3b = 5 \\ 3 - a = -2b \end{cases}$$

is written in a and b. Regardless of the variables used, the procedures used to solve the system remain the same. Unless told otherwise, list the values of the variables of a solution in alphabetical order. Here, the solution should be expressed in the form (a, b).

EXAMPLE 4 Solve the system: $\begin{cases} 3a - 3b = 5 \\ 3 - a = -2b \end{cases}$

Strategy Since the coefficient of a in the second equation is -1, we will solve that equation for a. Then we will use the substitution method to solve the system.

WHY If we solve for the variable with a numerical coefficient of -1 or 1, we can avoid having to work with fractions.

Solution

Step 1 Solve the second equation for a.

$$3 - a = -2b \qquad \text{This is the second equation of the system.}$$
$$-a = -2b - 3 \qquad \text{Subtract 3 from both sides.}$$

To obtain a on the left-hand side, we can multiply (or divide) both sides of the equation by -1.

$$-1(-a) = -1(-2b - 3) \qquad \text{Multiply both sides by } -1.$$
$$a = 2b + 3 \qquad \text{Perform the multiplications. This is the substitution equation.}$$

Step 2 We then substitute $2b + 3$ for a in the first equation and proceed as follows:

$$3a - 3b = 5 \qquad \text{This is the first equation of the system.}$$
$$3(2b + 3) - 3b = 5 \qquad \text{Substitute: } 2b + 3 \text{ for } a. \text{ Don't forget the parentheses.}$$
$$6b + 9 - 3b = 5 \qquad \text{Distribute the multiplication by 3.}$$
$$3b + 9 = 5 \qquad \text{Combine like terms: } 6b - 3b = 3b.$$
$$3b = -4 \qquad \text{Subtract 9 from both sides: } 5 - 9 = -4.$$
$$b = -\frac{4}{3} \qquad \text{Divide both sides by 3.}$$

Step 3 To find a, we substitute $-\frac{4}{3}$ for b in $a = 2b + 3$ and simplify.

$$a = 2b + 3$$
$$= 2\left(-\frac{4}{3}\right) + 3 \qquad \text{Substitute: } -\frac{4}{3} \text{ for } b.$$
$$= -\frac{8}{3} + \frac{9}{3} \qquad \text{Perform the multiplication: } 2\left(-\frac{4}{3}\right) = -\frac{8}{3}. \text{ Write 3 as } \frac{9}{3}.$$
$$= \frac{1}{3} \qquad \text{Add. This is the } a\text{-value of the solution.}$$

Step 4 The solution is $\left(\frac{1}{3}, -\frac{4}{3}\right)$. Check it in the original equations.

Self Check 4

Solve the system: $\begin{cases} 2s - t = 4 \\ 3s - 5t = 2 \end{cases}$

Now Try **Problem 29**

Self Check 4 Answer
$\left(\frac{18}{7}, \frac{8}{7}\right)$

Teaching Example 4 Solve the system:
$\begin{cases} 2a + b = 0 \\ 5a + 10b = 3 \end{cases}$
Answer:
$\left(-\frac{1}{5}, \frac{2}{5}\right)$

3 Solve systems of linear equations that contain fractions.

It is usually helpful to clear any equations of fractions and combine any like terms before performing a substitution.

EXAMPLE 5

Solve the system: $\begin{cases} \dfrac{x}{2} + \dfrac{y}{4} = -\dfrac{1}{4} \\ 2x - y = 2 + y - x \end{cases}$

Strategy We will use properties of algebra to write each equation of the system in simpler form. Then we will use the substitution method to solve the resulting equivalent system.

WHY The first equation will be easier to work with if we clear it of fractions. The second equation will be easier to work with if we eliminate the variable terms on the right side.

Solution

We begin by clearing the first equation of fractions by multiplying both sides by the LCD.

$$\frac{x}{2} + \frac{y}{4} = -\frac{1}{4}$$

$$4\left(\frac{x}{2} + \frac{y}{4}\right) = 4\left(-\frac{1}{4}\right) \quad \text{Multiply both sides by the LCD, which is 4.}$$

$$2x + y = -1$$

We can write the second equation in general form $(Ax + By = C)$ by adding x and subtracting y from both sides.

$$2x - y = 2 + y - x$$

$$2x - y + x - y = 2 + y - x + x - y$$

$$3x - 2y = 2 \quad \text{Combine like terms.}$$

The two results form the following equivalent system, which has the same solution as the original one.

(1) $\begin{cases} 2x + y = -1 \\ 3x - 2y = 2 \end{cases}$
(2)

Step 1 To solve this system, we solve Equation 1 for y.

$$2x + y = -1$$

$$2x + y - 2x = -1 - 2x \quad \text{Subtract 2x from both sides.}$$

(3) $\qquad\qquad y = -1 - 2x \quad \text{Combine like terms. This is the substitution equation.}$

Step 2 To find x, we substitute $-1 - 2x$ for y in Equation 2 and proceed as follows:

$$3x - 2y = 2$$

$$3x - 2(-1 - 2x) = 2 \quad \text{Substitute.}$$

$$3x + 2 + 4x = 2 \quad \text{Distribute the multiplication by } -2.$$

$$7x + 2 = 2 \quad \text{Combine like terms.}$$

$$7x = 0 \quad \text{Subtract 2 from both sides.}$$

$$x = 0 \quad \text{Divide both sides by 7.}$$

Step 3 To find y, we substitute 0 for x in Equation 3.

$$y = -1 - 2x$$
$$y = -1 - 2(0)$$
$$y = -1$$

Step 4 The solution is $(0, -1)$. Check it in the original equations.   ■

4 Use substitution to identify inconsistent systems and dependent equations.

In the previous section, we solved inconsistent systems and systems of dependent equations graphically. We can also solve these systems using the substitution method.

EXAMPLE 6

Solve the system: $\begin{cases} 0.01x = 0.12 - 0.04y \\ 2x = 4(3 - 2y) \end{cases}$

Strategy We will use properties of algebra to write the first equation of the system in simpler form. Then we will use the substitution method to solve the resulting equivalent system.

WHY The first equation will be easier to work with if we clear it of decimals.

Solution
We can clear the first equation of decimals by multiplying both sides by 100.

$$\begin{cases} x = 12 - 4y \\ 2x = 4(3 - 2y) \end{cases}$$

Since $x = 12 - 4y$, we can substitute $12 - 4y$ for x in the second equation and solve for y.

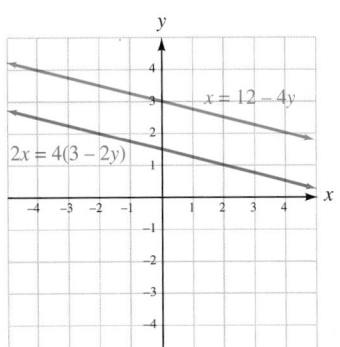

$2x = 4(3 - 2y)$	This is the second equation.
$2(12 - 4y) = 4(3 - 2y)$	Substitute.
$24 - 8y = 12 - 8y$	Distribute.
$24 \neq 12$	Add 8y to both sides.

Here, the terms involving y drop out, and a false result of $24 = 12$ is obtained. This result indicates that the equations are independent and also that the system is inconsistent. When the equations are graphed, the graphs are parallel lines. This system has no solution.

EXAMPLE 7

Solve the system: $\begin{cases} x = -3y + 6 \\ 2x + 6y = 12 \end{cases}$

Strategy We will use the substitution method to solve this system.

WHY The substitution method works well when one of the equations of the system (in this case, $x = -3y + 6$) is solved for a variable.

Solution
We can substitute $-3y + 6$ for x in the second equation and proceed as follows:

$2x + 6y = 12$	This is the second equation of the system.
$2(-3y + 6) + 6y = 12$	Substitute.

$$-6y + 12 + 6y = 12 \quad \text{Distribute the multiplication by 2.}$$
$$12 = 12 \quad \text{True}$$

Here, the terms involving y drop out, and we get $12 = 12$. This true statement indicates that the equations are dependent. When these equations are graphed, their graphs are identical.

Because any ordered pair that satisfies one equation of the system also satisfies the other, the system has infinitely many solutions. To find some, we substitute 0, 3, and 6 for x in either equation and solve for y. The pairs $(0, 2)$, $(3, 1)$, and $(6, 0)$ are some of the solutions.

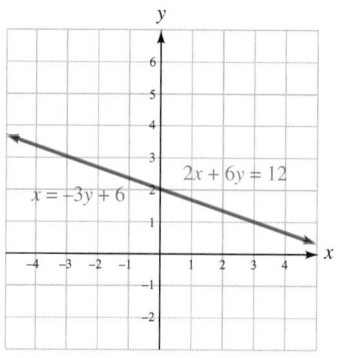

ANSWERS TO SELF CHECKS

1. $(15, 8)$ **2.** $(2, -1)$ **3.** $(2, -3)$ **4.** $\left(\frac{18}{7}, \frac{8}{7}\right)$ **5.** $(-1, 0)$ **6.** no solution
7. infinitely many solutions

SECTION 4.2   STUDY SET

VOCABULARY

Fill in the blanks.

1. We say that the equation $y = 2x + 4$ is solved for y or that y is expressed in __terms__ of x.

2. "To __check__ a solution of a system" means to see whether the coordinates of the ordered pair satisfy both equations.

3. When we write $2(x - 6)$ as $2x - 12$, we are applying the __distributive__ property.

▶ 4. In mathematics, "to __substitute__" means to replace an expression with one that is equivalent to it.

5. A dependent system has __infinitely__ many solutions.

6. In the term y, the coefficient is understood to be __1__.

CONCEPTS

7. Consider the system: $\begin{cases} 2x + 3y = 12 \\ y = 2x + 4 \end{cases}$

   a. How many variables does each equation of the system contain? 2

   b. Substitute $2x + 4$ for y in the first equation. How many variables does the resulting equation contain? 1

▶ 8. For each equation, solve for y.

   a. $y + 2 = x$ $y = x - 2$

   b. $2 + x + y = 0$ $y = -x - 2$

   c. $2 - y = x$ $y = 2 - x$

▶ Selected exercises available online at
www.webassign.net/brookscole

9. Given the equation $x - 2y = -10$,

   a. solve it for x. $x = 2y - 10$

   b. solve it for y. $y = \frac{x}{2} + 5$

   c. which variable was easier to solve for, x or y? Explain. x, it involved only one step.

10. Which variable in which equation should be solved for in step 1 of the substitution method?

   a. $\begin{cases} x - 2y = 2 \\ 2x + 3y = 11 \end{cases}$ Solve the first equation for x.

   b. $\begin{cases} 2x - 3y = 2 \\ 2x - y = 11 \end{cases}$ Solve the second equation for y.

11. a. Find the error when $x - 4$ is substituted for y.
      Parentheses must be written around $x - 4$ in line 2.

   $x + 2y = 5$ This is the first equation of the system.

   $x + 2x - 4 = 5$ Substitute for y: $y = x - 4$.

   $3x - 4 = 5$ Combine like terms.

   $3x = 9$ Add 4 to both sides.

   $x = 3$ Perform the divisions.

   b. Rework the problem to find the correct value of x. $\frac{13}{3}$

▶ 12. A student uses the substitution method to solve the system $\begin{cases} 4a + 5b = 2 \\ b = 3a - 11 \end{cases}$ and she finds that $a = 3$. What is the easiest way for her to determine the value of b?
   Substitute 3 for a in the second equation.

13. Consider the system: $\begin{cases} y = 2x \\ 3x + 2y = 6 \end{cases}$

    a. Graph the equations on the same coordinate system. Why is it difficult to determine the solution of the system?
    The coordinates of the intersection point are not integers.

    b. Solve the system by the substitution method.
    $\left(\frac{6}{7}, \frac{12}{7}\right)$

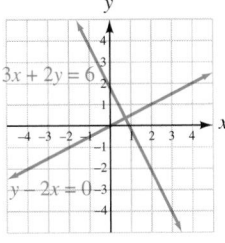

14. Suppose the equation $-2 = 1$ is obtained when a system is solved by the substitution method.

    a. Does the system have a solution? no

    b. Which of the following is a possible graph of the system? ii

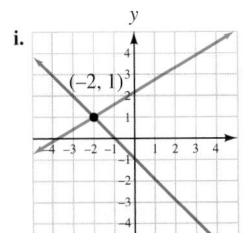
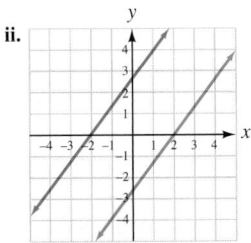

NOTATION

Complete the solution of each system.

15. Solve: $\begin{cases} y = 3x \\ x - y = 4 \end{cases}$

$$x - y = 4 \quad \text{This is the second equation.}$$
$$x - \left(\boxed{3x}\right) = 4$$
$$-2x = \boxed{4}$$
$$x = -2$$
$$y = 3x \quad \text{This is the first equation.}$$
$$y = 3\left(\boxed{-2}\right)$$
$$y = -6$$

The solution is $\boxed{(-2, -6)}$.

▶ 16. Solve: $\begin{cases} 2x + y = -5 \\ 2 - 2y = x \end{cases}$

$$2x + y = -5 \quad \text{This is the first equation.}$$
$$2\left(\boxed{2-2y}\right) + y = -5$$
$$4 - \boxed{4y} + y = -5$$
$$\boxed{4} - 3y = -5$$
$$-3y = \boxed{-9}$$
$$y = 3$$

$$2 - 2y = x \quad \text{This is the second equation.}$$
$$2 - 2\left(\boxed{3}\right) = x$$
$$2 - 6 = x$$
$$-4 = x$$

The solution is $\boxed{(-4, 3)}$.

GUIDED PRACTICE

Use the substitution method to solve each system.
See Example 1.

17. $\begin{cases} y = 2x \\ x + y = 6 \end{cases}$ $(2, 4)$

▶ 18. $\begin{cases} y = 3x \\ x + y = 4 \end{cases}$ $(1, 3)$

19. $\begin{cases} y = 2x - 6 \\ 2x + y = 6 \end{cases}$ $(3, 0)$

▶ 20. $\begin{cases} y = 2x - 9 \\ x + 3y = 8 \end{cases}$ $(5, 1)$

Use the substitution method to solve each system.
See Examples 2–3.

21. $\begin{cases} 6x - 3y = 5 \\ x = -2y \end{cases}$
$\left(\frac{2}{3}, -\frac{1}{3}\right)$

22. $\begin{cases} 5x + 10y = 3 \\ x = -\frac{1}{2}y \end{cases}$
$\left(-\frac{1}{5}, \frac{2}{5}\right)$

23. $\begin{cases} r + 3s = 9 \\ 3r + 2s = 13 \end{cases}$
$(3, 2)$

▶ 24. $\begin{cases} x - 2y = 2 \\ 2x + 3y = 11 \end{cases}$
$(4, 1)$

25. $\begin{cases} 3x + 4y = -7 \\ 2y - x = -1 \end{cases}$
$(-1, -1)$

▶ 26. $\begin{cases} 4x + 5y = -2 \\ x + 2y = -2 \end{cases}$
$(2, -2)$

27. $\begin{cases} -2x + y = 5 \\ x + 2y = -5 \end{cases}$
$(-3, -1)$

28. $\begin{cases} 2x + y = 0 \\ 3x + 2y = -1 \end{cases}$
$(1, -2)$

Use the substitution method to solve each system.
See Examples 4–5.

29. $\begin{cases} 2a = 3b - 13 \\ -b = -2a - 7 \end{cases}$
$(-2, 3)$

▶ 30. $\begin{cases} a = 3b - 1 \\ -b = -2a - 2 \end{cases}$
$(-1, 0)$

▶ 31. $\begin{cases} 5m = \frac{1}{2}n - 1 \\ \frac{1}{4}n = 10m - 1 \end{cases}$
$\left(\frac{1}{5}, 4\right)$

32. $\begin{cases} \frac{2}{3}m = 1 - 2n \\ 2(5n - m) + 11 = 0 \end{cases}$
$\left(3, -\frac{1}{2}\right)$

Use the substitution method to solve each system, if possible.
See Examples 6–7.

33. $\begin{cases} 2a + 4b = -24 \\ a = 20 - 2b \end{cases}$
no solution, inconsistent system

▶ 34. $\begin{cases} 3a + 6b = -15 \\ a = -2b - 5 \end{cases}$
infinitely many solutions, dependent equations

35. $\begin{cases} 9x = 3y + 12 \\ 4 = 3x - y \end{cases}$
infinitely many solutions, dependent equations

▶ 36. $\begin{cases} 8y = 15 - 4x \\ x + 2y = 4 \end{cases}$
no solution, inconsistent system

TRY IT YOURSELF

Use the substitution method to solve each system. If the equations of a system are dependent or if a system is inconsistent, so indicate.

37. $\begin{cases} 0.4x + 0.5y = 0.2 \\ 3x - y = 11 \end{cases}$ $(3, -2)$

38. $\begin{cases} 0.5u + 0.3v = 0.5 \\ 4u - v = 4 \end{cases}$ $(1, 0)$

39. $\begin{cases} 0.02x + 0.05y = -0.02 \\ -\frac{x}{2} = y \end{cases}$ $(4, -2)$

40. $\begin{cases} y = -\frac{x}{2} \\ 0.02x - 0.03y = -0.07 \end{cases}$ $(-2, 1)$

▶ **41.** $\begin{cases} y - x = 3x \\ 2x + 2y = 14 - y \end{cases}$ $(1, 4)$

▶ **42.** $\begin{cases} y + x = 2x + 2 \\ 6x - 4y = 21 - y \end{cases}$ $(9, 11)$

▶ **43.** $\begin{cases} 2x - y = x + y \\ -2x + 4y = 6 \end{cases}$ no solution, inconsistent system

▶ **44.** $\begin{cases} x = -3y + 6 \\ 2x + 4y = 6 + x + y \end{cases}$ infinitely many solutions, dependent equations

45. $\begin{cases} 3(x - 1) + 3 = 8 + 2y \\ 2(x + 1) = 8 + y \end{cases}$ $(4, 2)$

▶ **46.** $\begin{cases} 4(x - 2) = 19 - 5y \\ 3(x - 2) - 2y = -y \end{cases}$ $(3, 3)$

47. $\begin{cases} \frac{1}{2}x + \frac{1}{2}y = -1 \\ \frac{1}{3}x - \frac{1}{2}y = -4 \end{cases}$ $(-6, 4)$

48. $\begin{cases} \frac{2}{3}y + \frac{1}{5}z = 1 \\ \frac{1}{3}y - \frac{2}{5}z = 3 \end{cases}$ $(3, -5)$

▶ **49.** $\begin{cases} b = \frac{2}{3}a \\ 8a - 3b = 3 \end{cases}$ $\left(\frac{1}{2}, \frac{1}{3}\right)$

50. $\begin{cases} a = \frac{2}{3}b \\ 9a + 4b = 5 \end{cases}$ $\left(\frac{1}{3}, \frac{1}{2}\right)$

51. $\begin{cases} \dfrac{6x - 1}{3} - \dfrac{5}{3} = \dfrac{3y + 1}{2} \\ \dfrac{1 + 5y}{4} + \dfrac{x + 3}{4} = \dfrac{17}{2} \end{cases}$ $(5, 5)$

▶ **52.** $\begin{cases} \dfrac{5x - 2}{4} + \dfrac{1}{2} = \dfrac{3y + 2}{2} \\ \dfrac{7y + 3}{3} = \dfrac{x}{2} + \dfrac{7}{3} \end{cases}$ $(2, 1)$

APPLICATIONS

▶ **53.** **DINING** See the following breakfast menu. What substitution from the a la carte menu will the restaurant owner allow customers to make if they don't want hash browns with their country breakfast? Why? melon, because it's the same price as hash browns

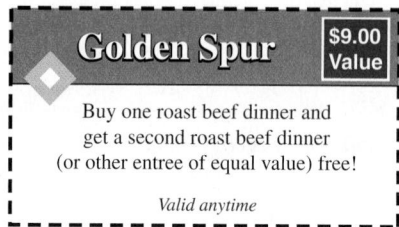

Village Vault Restaurant			
Country Breakfast		**$5.95**	
2 eggs, 3 pancakes, bacon, sausage, hash browns, coffee			
A la Carte Menu–Single Servings			
Strawberries	$1.25	Melon	$0.95
Croissant	$1.70	Orange juice	$1.65
Hash browns	$0.95	Oatmeal	$1.95
Muffin	$1.30	Ham	$1.80

▶ **54.** **DISCOUNT COUPONS** In mathematics, the substitution property states:

If a = b, then a may replace b or b may replace a in any statement.

Where on the following coupon is there an application of the substitution property? Explain. An entree of equal value may be substituted for the second roast beef dinner.

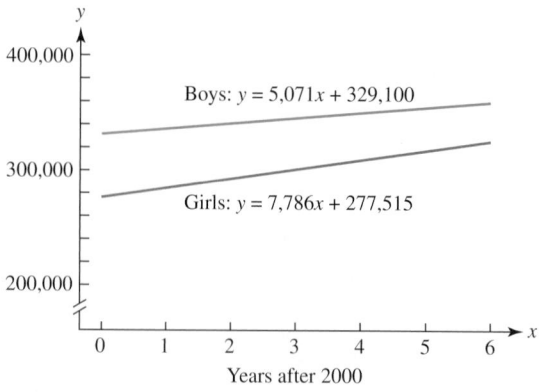

Golden Spur **$9.00 Value**

Buy one roast beef dinner and get a second roast beef dinner (or other entree of equal value) free!

Valid anytime

▶ **55.** **HIGH SCHOOL SPORTS** The equations shown model the number of boys and girls taking part in high school soccer programs. In both models, *x* is the number of years after 2000, and *y* is the number of participants. If the trends continue, the graphs will intersect. Use the substitution method to predict the year when the number of boys and girls participating in high school soccer will be the same. 2019

Boys: $y = 5{,}071x + 329{,}100$

Girls: $y = 7{,}786x + 277{,}515$

Years after 2000

Source: National Federation of State High School Associations

56. OFF ROADING The *angle of approach* indicates how steep of an incline a vehicle can drive up without damaging the front bumper. The *angle of departure* indicates a vehicle's ability to exit an incline without damaging the rear bumper. The angle of approach a and the angle of departure d for an H3 Hummer are described by the system:

$$\begin{cases} a + d = 77 \\ a = d + 3 \end{cases}$$

Use substitution to solve the system. (Each angle is measured in degrees.)

Angle of approach: 40°, angle of departure: 37°

WRITING

57. Explain how to use substitution to solve a system of equations.

58. If the equations of a system are written in general form, why is it to your advantage to solve for a variable whose coefficient is 1 when using the substitution method?

59. When solving a system, what advantages and disadvantages are there with the graphing method? With the substitution method?

▶ **60.** In this section, the substitution method for solving a system of two equations was discussed. List some other uses of the word *substitution*, or *substitute*, that you encounter in everyday life.

REVIEW

61. What is the slope of the line $y = -\frac{5}{8}x - 12$? $-\frac{5}{8}$

62. If $g(x) = -3x + 9$, find: $g(-3)$ 18

63. Find the y-intercept of $2x - 3y = 18$. $(0, -6)$

64. Write the equation of the line passing through $(-1, 5)$ with a slope of -3. $y = -3x + 2$

65. Can a circle represent the graph of a function? no

66. What is the range of the function $f(x) = |x|$?
all real numbers greater than or equal to 0

67. On what axis does $(3, 0)$ lie? x-axis

▶ **68.** On what axis does $(0, -2)$ lie? y-axis

SECTION 4.3

Solving Systems of Equations by Addition (Elimination)

Objectives

1 Solve systems of linear equations by the addition (elimination) method.

2 Use multiplication to eliminate a variable.

3 Use the addition (elimination) method to identify inconsistent systems and dependent equations.

4 Determine the most efficient method to use to solve a linear system.

In step 1 of the substitution method for solving a system of equations, we solve one equation for one of the variables. At times, this can be difficult—especially if neither variable has a coefficient of 1 or −1. In cases such as these, we can use another algebraic method called the **addition** or **elimination method** to find the exact solution of the system. This method is based on the addition property of equality: *When equal quantities are added to both sides of an equation, the results are equal.*

1 Solve systems of linear equations by the addition (elimination) method.

EXAMPLE 1 Solve the system: $\begin{cases} x + y = 8 \\ x - y = -2 \end{cases}$

Strategy Since the coefficients of the y-terms are opposites, we will add the left sides and the right sides of the given equations.

WHY When we add the equations in this way, the result will be an equation that contains only one variable, x.

Solution

Since $x - y$ and -2 are equal quantities, we can add $x - y$ to the left side and -2 to the right side of the first equation, $x + y = 8$.

Self Check 1

Solve the system:
$\begin{cases} 3x + 2y = 8 \\ -3x + 4y = -2 \end{cases}$ $(2, 1)$

Now Try Problem 15

Teaching Example 1 Solve the system:
$\begin{cases} x - 2y = 4 \\ 3x + 2y = 20 \end{cases}$
Answer:
$(6, 1)$

$$
\begin{array}{l}
\quad\;\downarrow\quad\;\downarrow\quad\;\;\downarrow \\
x + y = \;\;\;8 \\
\underline{x - y = -2} \\
2x \quad\;\; = \;\;\;6
\end{array}
$$

To add the equations, add the like terms, column by column.

Combine like terms: x + x = 2x, y + (−y) = 0, and 8 + (−2) = 6.

Write each result here.

We can then solve the resulting equation for *x*.

$$2x = 6$$

$$x = 3 \quad \text{Divide both sides by 2.}$$

To find *y*, we substitute 3 for *x* in either equation and solve it for *y*.

$$x + y = 8 \quad \text{This is the first equation of the system.}$$

$$3 + y = 8 \quad \text{Substitute 3 for x.}$$

$$y = 5 \quad \text{Subtract 3 from both sides.}$$

We check the solution by verifying that (3, 5) satisfies each equation of the system. ∎

To solve a system of equations in *x* and *y* by the addition method, we follow these steps.

The Addition (Elimination) Method

1. Write both equations of the system in general form: $Ax + By = C$.

2. If necessary, multiply one or both of the equations by nonzero quantities to make the coefficients of *x* (or the coefficients of *y*) opposites.

3. Add the equations to eliminate the terms involving *x* (or *y*).

4. Solve the equation resulting from step 3.

5. Find the value of the remaining variable by substituting the solution found in step 4 into any equation containing both variables. Or repeat steps 2–4 to eliminate the other variables.

6. Check the proposed solution in each equation of the original system. Write the solution as an ordered pair.

Self Check 2

Solve the system:
$$\begin{cases} x + 3y = 7 \\ 2x - 3y = -22 \end{cases} \quad (-5, 4)$$

Now Try **Problem 20**

Teaching Example 2 Solve the system:
$$\begin{cases} 7x - 2y = 8 \\ 3x + 2y = 12 \end{cases}$$
Answer:
(2, 3)

EXAMPLE 2

Solve the system: $\begin{cases} 5x + y = -4 \\ -5x + 2y = 7 \end{cases}$

Strategy Since the coefficients of the *x*-terms are opposites, we will add the left sides and the right sides of the given equations.

WHY When we add the equations in this way, the result will be an equation that contains only one variable, *y*.

Solution

Step 1 Both equations are in general form.

Step 2 The coefficients of *x* are opposites.

Step 3 Add the equations to eliminate *x*.

$$
\begin{array}{l}
\;\;\;5x + \;\;y = -4 \\
\underline{-5x + 2y = \;\;\;7} \\
\quad\quad\;\; 3y = \;\;\;3
\end{array}
$$

Combine like terms: 5x + (−5x) = 0, y + 2y = 3y, and −4 + 7 = 3.

Step 4 Since the result of the addition is an equation in one variable, we can solve for *y*.

$$3y = 3$$

$$y = 1 \quad \text{Divide both sides by 3.}$$

Step 5 To find x, we substitute 1 for y in either equation. If we use $5x + y = -4$, we have

$5x + y = -4$ *This is the first equation of the system.*

$5x + 1 = -4$ *Substitute 1 for y.*

$5x = -5$ *Subtract 1 from both sides.*

$x = -1$ *Divide both sides by 5.*

Step 6 Verify that $(-1, 1)$ satisfies each original equation.

2 Use multiplication to eliminate a variable.

In Example 1, the coefficients of the terms y in the first equation and $-y$ in the second equation were opposites. When we added the equations, the variable y was eliminated. For many systems, however, we are not able to immediately eliminate a variable by adding. In such cases, we use the multiplication property of equality to create coefficients of x or y that are opposites.

EXAMPLE 3 Solve the system: $\begin{cases} 3x + y = 7 \\ x + 2y = 4 \end{cases}$

Strategy We will multiply the second equation by -3 to make the coefficients of x opposites.

WHY Neither of the coefficients of x nor y are opposites in the original system.

Solution

Step 1 Both equations are in general form.

Step 2 If we add the equations as they are, neither variable will be eliminated. We must write the equations so that the coefficients of one of the variables are opposites. To eliminate x, we can multiply both sides of the second equation by -3 to get

$$\begin{cases} 3x + y = 7 \\ x + 2y = 4 \end{cases} \xrightarrow{\text{Unchanged}} \begin{cases} 3x + y = 7 \\ -3(x + 2y) = -3(4) \end{cases} \xrightarrow[\text{Simplify}]{\text{Unchanged}} \begin{cases} 3x + y = 7 \\ -3x - 6y = -12 \end{cases}$$

Multipy by -3

Step 3 The coefficients of the terms $3x$ and $-3x$ are now opposites. When the equations are added, x is eliminated.

$$\begin{array}{r} 3x + y = 7 \\ -3x - 6y = -12 \\ \hline -5y = -5 \end{array}$$

Step 4 Solve the resulting equation to find y.

$-5y = -5$

$y = 1$ *Divide both sides by -5.*

Step 5 To find x, we substitute 1 for y in the equation $x + 2y = 4$.

$x + 2y = 4$ *This is the second equation of the original system.*

$x + 2(1) = 4$ *Substitute 1 for y.*

$x + 2 = 4$ *Perform the multiplication.*

$x = 2$ *Subtract 2 from both sides.*

Step 6 Check the solution $(2, 1)$ in the original system of equations.

Self Check 3

Solve the system:

$\begin{cases} 3x - 4y = -7 \\ 2x + y = 10 \end{cases}$ $(3, 4)$

Now Try Problem 23

Teaching Example 3 Solve the system:
$\begin{cases} 5x + 2y = -9 \\ 3x + y = -5 \end{cases}$
Answer:
$(-1, -2)$

Solve the system:

$$\begin{cases} 2a + 3b = 7 \\ 5a + 2b = 1 \end{cases} \quad (-1, 3)$$

Now Try Problem 27

Teaching Example 4 Solve the system:
$$\begin{cases} 4a + 7b = -8 \\ 5a + 6b = 1 \end{cases}$$
Answer:
$(5, -4)$

EXAMPLE 4

Solve the system:
$$\begin{cases} 2a - 5b = 10 \\ 3a - 2b = -7 \end{cases}$$

Strategy We will use the addition method to solve this system.

WHY Since none of the variables has a coefficient of 1 or -1, it would be difficult to solve this system using substitution.

Solution

Step 1 Both equations are in general form $Ax + By = C$. We see that neither the coefficients of a nor b are opposites. Adding these equations as written does not eliminate a variable.

Step 2 To eliminate a, we can multiply the first equation by 3 and the second equation by -2 to get

$$\begin{array}{ccc} & \text{Multiply by 3} & \text{Simplify} \\ \begin{cases} 2a - 5b = 10 \\ 3a - 2b = -7 \end{cases} & \begin{cases} 3(2a - 5b) = 3(10) \\ -2(3a - 2b) = -2(-7) \end{cases} & \begin{cases} 6a - 15b = 30 \\ -6a + 4b = 14 \end{cases} \\ & \text{Multiply by } -2 & \text{Simplify} \end{array}$$

Step 3 When these equations are added, the terms $6a$ and $-6a$ are eliminated.

$$\begin{array}{r} 6a - 15b = 30 \\ -6a + 4b = 14 \\ \hline -11b = 44 \end{array}$$

Step 4 Solve the resulting equation to find b.

$$-11b = 44$$
$$b = -4 \quad \text{Divide both sides by } -11.$$

Step 5 To find a, we substitute -4 for b in the equation $2a - 5b = 10$.

$$\begin{array}{ll} 2a - 5b = 10 & \text{This is the first equation of the original system.} \\ 2a - 5(-4) = 10 & \text{Substitute } -4 \text{ for } b. \\ 2a + 20 = 10 & \text{Simplify.} \\ 2a = -10 & \text{Subtract 20 from both sides.} \\ a = -5 & \text{Divide both sides by 2.} \end{array}$$

Step 6 Check the solution $(-5, -4)$ in the original equations.

Solve the system:

$$\begin{cases} \dfrac{1}{3}x + \dfrac{1}{6}y = 1 \\ \dfrac{1}{2}x - \dfrac{1}{4}y = 0 \end{cases} \quad \left(\tfrac{3}{2}, 3\right)$$

Now Try Problem 29

Teaching Example 5 Solve the system:
$$\begin{cases} \frac{1}{6}x + \frac{1}{2}y = \frac{1}{3} \\ -\frac{x}{9} + y = \frac{5}{9} \end{cases}$$
Answer:
$\left(\frac{1}{4}, \frac{7}{12}\right)$

EXAMPLE 5

Solve the system:
$$\begin{cases} \dfrac{5}{6}x + \dfrac{2}{3}y = \dfrac{7}{6} \\ \dfrac{10}{7}x - \dfrac{4}{9}y = \dfrac{17}{21} \end{cases}$$

Strategy We will begin by clearing each equation of fractions. Then we will use the addition method to solve the resulting equivalent system.

WHY It is easier to create a pair of terms that are opposites if their coefficients are integers rather than fractions.

Solution

Step 1 To clear the equations of fractions, we multiply both sides of the first equation by 6 and both sides of the second equation by 63. This gives the equivalent system

(1) $\begin{cases} 5x + 4y = 7 \end{cases}$
(2) $\begin{cases} 90x - 28y = 51 \end{cases}$

Step 2 We can solve for x by eliminating the terms involving y. To do so, we multiply Equation 1 by 7.

$$\begin{cases} 5x + 4y = 7 \\ 90x - 28y = 5 \end{cases} \xrightarrow{\text{Multiply by 7}} \begin{cases} 7(5x + 4y) = 7(7) \\ 90x - 28y = 5 \end{cases} \xrightarrow{\text{Simplify}} \begin{cases} 35x + 28y = 49 \\ 90x - 28y = 51 \end{cases}$$

Unchanged   Unchanged

Step 3 Add the equations.

$$\begin{array}{r} 35x + 28y = 49 \\ 90x - 28y = 51 \\ \hline 125x \quad\quad = 100 \end{array}$$

Step 4 Solve the resulting equation for x.

$$125x = 100$$

$$x = \frac{100}{125} \quad \text{Divide both sides by 125.}$$

$$x = \frac{4}{5} \quad \text{Simplify } \tfrac{100}{125}\text{: Remove the common factor of 25.}$$

Step 5 To solve for y, we substitute $\frac{4}{5}$ for x in Equation 1 and simplify.

$$5x + 4y = 7$$

$$5\left(\frac{4}{5}\right) + 4y = 7$$

$$4 + 4y = 7 \quad \text{Simplify.}$$

$$4y = 3 \quad \text{Subtract 4 from both sides.}$$

$$y = \frac{3}{4} \quad \text{Divide both sides by 4.}$$

Step 6 Check the solution of $\left(\dfrac{4}{5}, \dfrac{3}{4}\right)$ in the original equations.

EXAMPLE 6   Solve the system: $\begin{cases} 2(2x + y) = 13 \\ 8x = 2y - 16 \end{cases}$

Strategy We will use properties of algebra to write the first equation of the system in simpler form and the second equation in general form. Then we will use the addition method to solve the resulting equivalent system.

WHY Writing the equations in general form is the first step of the addition method.

Solution

Step 1 We begin by writing each equation in $Ax + By = C$ form. For the first equation, we need only apply the distributive property. To write the second equation in general form, we subtract $2y$ from both sides.

$$2(2x + y) = 13 \qquad\qquad 8x = 2y - 16$$

$$4x + 2y = 13 \qquad 8x - 2y = 2y - 16 - 2y$$

$$8x - 2y = -16$$

The two resulting equations form the following system.

(1) $\begin{cases} 4x + 2y = 13 \\ 8x - 2y = -16 \end{cases}$
(2)

Self Check 6

Solve the system:
$\begin{cases} -3y = -5 - x \\ 3(x - y) = -11 \end{cases}$ $\left(-3, \frac{2}{3}\right)$

Now Try Problem 33

Teaching Example 6 Solve the system:
$\begin{cases} 2(4x + 11) = -12y \\ 3x = 2y + 8 \end{cases}$
Answer:
$\left(1, -\frac{5}{2}\right)$

Step 2 The coefficients of y are opposites.

Step 3 When the equations are added, the terms involving y are eliminated.

$$\begin{array}{rcr} 4x + 2y = & 13 \\ 8x - 2y = & -16 \\ \hline 12x = & -3 \end{array}$$

Step 4 Solve the resulting equation for x.

$$12x = -3$$

$$x = -\frac{1}{4} \qquad \text{Divide both sides by 12 and simplify the fraction: } -\frac{3}{12} = -\frac{1}{4}.$$

Step 5 We can use Equation 1 to find y.

$$4x + 2y = 13$$

$$4\left(-\frac{1}{4}\right) + 2y = 13 \qquad \text{Substitute } -\frac{1}{4} \text{ for } x.$$

$$-1 + 2y = 13 \qquad \text{Perform the multiplication.}$$

$$2y = 14 \qquad \text{Add 1 to both sides.}$$

$$y = 7 \qquad \text{Divide both sides by 2.}$$

Step 6 Verify that $\left(-\frac{1}{4}, 7\right)$ satisfies each original equation. ∎

3 Use the addition (elimination) method to identify inconsistent systems and dependent equations.

We have solved inconsistent systems and systems of dependent equations by substitution and by graphing. We can also solve these systems using the addition method.

Self Check 7

Solve the system:
$$\begin{cases} 2t - 7v = 5 \\ -2t + 7v = 3 \end{cases}$$ no solution

Now Try Problem 37

Teaching Example 7 Solve the system:
$$\begin{cases} 6x - 5y = 4 \\ -6x + 5y = 1 \end{cases}$$
Answer:
no solution

EXAMPLE 7

Solve the system, if possible: $\begin{cases} 3x - 2y = 8 \\ -3x + 2y = -12 \end{cases}$

Strategy We will use the addition method to solve this system.

WHY The terms $3x$ and $-3x$ are immediately eliminated.

Solution

We can add the equations to eliminate the term involving x.

$$\begin{array}{rcr} 3x - 2y = & 8 \\ -3x + 2y = & -12 \\ \hline 0 = & -4 \end{array}$$

Here the terms involving both x and y drop out, and a false result of $0 = -4$ is obtained. This indicates that the equations of the system are independent and that the system is inconsistent. This system has no solution. ∎

Self Check 8

Solve the system:
$$\begin{cases} \dfrac{3x + y}{6} = \dfrac{1}{3} \\ -0.3x - 0.1y = -0.2 \end{cases}$$

Now Try Problem 38

Self Check 8 Answer
infinitely many solutions

EXAMPLE 8

Solve the system: $\begin{cases} \dfrac{2x - 5y}{2} = \dfrac{19}{2} \\ -0.2x + 0.5y = -1.9 \end{cases}$

Strategy We will begin by clearing the equations of fractions and decimals. Then we will use the addition method to solve the resulting equivalent system.

WHY Writing the equations in general form is the first step of the addition method.

Solution

We can multiply both sides of the first equation by **2** to clear it of fractions and both sides of the second equation by **10** to clear it of decimals.

$$\begin{cases} 2\left(\dfrac{2x - 5y}{2}\right) = 2\left(\dfrac{19}{2}\right) \\ 10(-0.2x + 0.5y) = 10(-1.9) \end{cases} \xrightarrow[\text{Simplify}]{\text{Simplify}} \begin{cases} 2x - 5y = 19 \\ -2x + 5y = -19 \end{cases}$$

We add the resulting equations to get

$$\begin{array}{r} 2x - 5y = 19 \\ -2x + 5y = -19 \\ \hline 0 = 0 \end{array}$$

As in Example 7, both x and y drop out. However, this time a true result is obtained. This indicates that the equations are dependent and that the system has infinitely many solutions.

Any ordered pair that satisfies one equation also satisfies the other equation. Some solutions are $(2, -3)$, $(12, 1)$, and $\left(0, -\dfrac{19}{5}\right)$.

Teaching Example 8 Solve the system:
$$\begin{cases} \dfrac{4x - 3y}{2} = \dfrac{1}{5} \\ 0.20x - 0.15y = 0.02 \end{cases}$$
Answer:
infinitely many solutions

4 **Determine the most efficient method to use to solve a linear system.**

If no method is specified for solving a particular linear system, the following guidelines can be helpful in determining whether to use graphing, substitution, or addition.

1. If you want to show trends and see the point that the two graphs have in common, then use the **graphing method.** However, this method is not exact and can be lengthy.

2. If one of the equations is solved for one of the variables, or easily solved for one of the variables, use the **substitution method.**

3. If both equations are in general (standard) $Ax + By = C$ form, and no variable has a coefficient of 1 or -1, use the **addition method.**

4. If the coefficient of one of the variables is 1 or -1, you have a choice. You can write each equation in general (standard) $Ax + By = C$ form and use addition, or you can solve for the variable with coefficient 1 or -1 and use substitution.

Here are some examples of suggested approaches:

$$\begin{cases} 2x + 3y = 1 \\ y = 4x - 3 \end{cases} \qquad \begin{cases} 5x + 3y = 9 \\ 8x + 4y = 3 \end{cases} \qquad \begin{cases} 4x - y = -6 \\ 3x + 2y = 1 \end{cases} \qquad \begin{cases} x - 23 = 6y \\ 7x - 9y = -3 \end{cases}$$
$$\quad\text{Substitution} \qquad\qquad \text{Addition} \qquad\qquad\quad \text{Addition} \qquad\qquad\quad \text{Substitution}$$

Each method that we use to solve systems of equations has advantages and disadvantages.

ANSWERS TO SELF CHECKS

1. $(2, 1)$ **2.** $(-5, 4)$ **3.** $(3, 4)$ **4.** $(-1, 3)$ **5.** $\left(\dfrac{3}{2}, 3\right)$ **6.** $\left(-3, \dfrac{2}{3}\right)$ **7.** no solution
8. infinitely many solutions

SECTION **4.3** STUDY SET

VOCABULARY

Fill in the blanks.

1. The __coefficient__ of the term $-3x$ is -3.

▶ **2.** The __opposite__ of 4 is -4.

3. $Ax + By = C$ is the __general__ form of the equation of a line.

4. When adding the equations $\begin{array}{r} 5x - 6y = 10 \\ -3x + 6y = 24 \end{array}$ the variable y will be __eliminated__.

CONCEPTS

5. If the addition (elimination) method is to be used to solve this system, what is wrong with the form in which it is written?

$$\begin{cases} 2x - 5y = -3 \\ -2y + 3x = 10 \end{cases}$$ The second equation should be written in general form: $3x - 2y = 10$.

6. Can the system

$$\begin{cases} 2x + 5y = -13 \\ -2x - 3y = -5 \end{cases}$$ addition, the coefficients of x are opposites

be solved more easily using the addition method or the substitution method? Explain.

7. What algebraic step should be performed to clear this equation of fractions?

$$\frac{2}{3}x + 4y = -\frac{4}{5}$$ Multiply both sides by 15.

▶ **8.** If the addition method is used to solve

$$\begin{cases} 3x + 12y = 4 \\ 6x - 4y = 8 \end{cases}$$

a. By what would we multiply the first equation to eliminate x? -2

b. By what would we multiply the second equation to eliminate y? 3

9. Solve: $\begin{cases} 4x + 2y = 2 \\ 3x - 2y = 12 \end{cases}$

a. by the graphing method. $(2, -3)$

b. by the addition method. $(2, -3)$

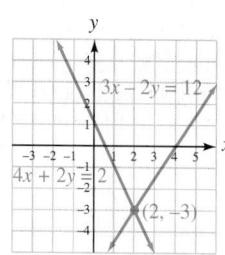

10. a. Suppose $0 = 0$ is obtained when a system is solved by the addition method. Does the system have a solution? Which of the following is a possible graph of the system? yes, ii

b. Suppose $0 = 2$ is obtained when a system is solved by the addition method. Does the system have a solution? Which of the following is a possible graph of the system? no, iii

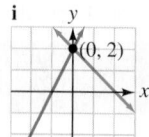
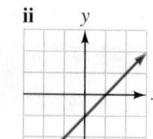
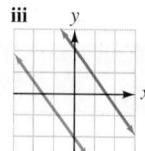

NOTATION

Complete the solution of each system.

▶ **11.** Solve: $\begin{cases} x + y = 5 \\ x - y = -3 \end{cases}$

$$\begin{aligned} x + y &= 5 \\ \underline{x - y} &= \underline{-3} \\ 2x &= 2 \\ x &= \boxed{1} \end{aligned}$$

$x + y = 5$ This is the first equation.

$\left(\boxed{1}\right) + y = 5$

$y = 4$

The solution is $(1, 4)$.

▶ **12.** Solve: $\begin{cases} x - 2y = 8 \\ -x + 5y = -17 \end{cases}$

$$\begin{aligned} x - 2y &= 8 \\ \underline{-x + 5y} &= \underline{-17} \\ 3y &= -9 \\ y &= \boxed{-3} \end{aligned}$$

$x - 2y = 8$ This is the first equation.

$x - 2\left(\boxed{-3}\right) = 8$

$x + 6 = 8$

$x = 2$

The solution is $(2, -3)$.

GUIDED PRACTICE

Use the addition (elimination) method to solve each system. See Examples 1–2.

▶ **13.** $\begin{cases} x - y = -5 \\ x + y = 1 \end{cases}$
$(-2, 3)$

▶ **14.** $\begin{cases} x + y = 1 \\ x - y = 5 \end{cases}$
$(3, -2)$

15. $\begin{cases} 2r + s = -1 \\ -2r + s = 3 \end{cases}$
$(-1, 1)$

▶ **16.** $\begin{cases} 3m + n = -6 \\ m - n = -2 \end{cases}$
$(-2, 0)$

17. $\begin{cases} 2x + y = -2 \\ -2x - 3y = -6 \end{cases}$
$(-3, 4)$

▶ **18.** $\begin{cases} 3x + 4y = 8 \\ 5x - 4y = 24 \end{cases}$
$(4, -1)$

19. $\begin{cases} 4x + 3y = 24 \\ 4x - 3y = -24 \end{cases}$
$(0, 8)$

▶ **20.** $\begin{cases} 5x - 4y = 8 \\ -5x - 4y = 8 \end{cases}$
$(0, -2)$

Use the addition (elimination) method to solve each system. See Examples 3–4.

21. $\begin{cases} x + y = 5 \\ x + 2y = 8 \end{cases}$
$(2, 3)$

▶ **22.** $\begin{cases} x + 2y = 0 \\ x - y = -3 \end{cases}$
$(-2, 1)$

23. $\begin{cases} 2x + y = 4 \\ 2x + 3y = 0 \end{cases}$
$(3, -2)$

▶ **24.** $\begin{cases} 2x + 5y = -13 \\ 2x - 3y = -5 \end{cases}$
$(-4, -1)$

25. $\begin{cases} 3x - 5y = -29 \\ 3x + 4y = 34 \end{cases}$
$(2, 7)$

▶ **26.** $\begin{cases} 3x - 5y = 16 \\ 4x + 5y = 33 \end{cases}$
$(7, 1)$

27. $\begin{cases} 8x - 4y = 18 \\ 3x - 2y = 8 \end{cases}$
$\left(1, -\frac{5}{2}\right)$

▶ **28.** $\begin{cases} 4x + 6y = 5 \\ 8x - 9y = 3 \end{cases}$
$\left(\frac{3}{4}, \frac{1}{3}\right)$

Use the addition (elimination) method to solve each system.
See Example 5.

29. $\begin{cases} \frac{3}{5}s + \frac{4}{5}t = 1 \\ -\frac{1}{4}s + \frac{3}{8}t = 1 \end{cases}$
$(-1, 2)$

▶ **30.** $\begin{cases} \frac{1}{2}s - \frac{1}{4}t = 1 \\ \frac{1}{3}s + t = 3 \end{cases}$
$(3, 2)$

▶ **31.** $\begin{cases} \frac{3}{5}x + y = 1 \\ \frac{4}{5}x - y = -1 \end{cases}$
$(0, 1)$

32. $\begin{cases} \frac{1}{2}x + \frac{4}{7}y = -1 \\ 5x - \frac{4}{5}y = -10 \end{cases}$
$(-2, 0)$

Use the addition (elimination) method to solve each system.
See Example 6.

33. $\begin{cases} -3(x - 2y) = -9 \\ 5x = 4y + 15 \end{cases}$
$(3, 0)$

34. $\begin{cases} -4x + 13 = -3y \\ 2(4y - 3x) = -16 \end{cases}$
$(4, 1)$

35. $\begin{cases} 4(x + 1) = 17 - 3(y - 1) \\ 2(x + 2) + 3(y - 1) = 9 \end{cases}$
$(4, 0)$

▶ **36.** $\begin{cases} 5(x - 1) = 8 - 3(y + 2) \\ 4(x + 2) - 7 = 3(2 - y) \end{cases}$
$(2, -1)$

Use the addition (elimination) method to solve each system. If
the equations of a system are dependent or if a system is
inconsistent, so indicate. **See Examples 7–8.**

37. $\begin{cases} 2a - 3b = -6 \\ 2a - 3b = 8 \end{cases}$
no solution, inconsistent system

▶ **38.** $\begin{cases} 3a - 4b = 6 \\ 2(2b + 3) = 3a \end{cases}$
infinitely many solutions, dependent equations

39. $\begin{cases} -2(x + 1) = 3y - 6 \\ 3(y + 2) = 10 - 2x \end{cases}$
infinitely many solutions, dependent equations

▶ **40.** $\begin{cases} 3x + 2y + 1 = 5 \\ 3(x - 1) = -2y - 4 \end{cases}$
no solution, inconsistent system

TRY IT YOURSELF

Solve each system, if possible.

41. $\begin{cases} 3x + 4y = 12 \\ 4x + 5y = 17 \end{cases}$
$(8, -3)$

▶ **42.** $\begin{cases} 2x + 11y = -10 \\ 5x + 4y = 22 \end{cases}$
$(6, -2)$

43. $\begin{cases} 2x + y = 10 \\ 0.1x + 0.2y = 1.0 \end{cases}$
$\left(\frac{10}{3}, \frac{10}{3}\right)$

▶ **44.** $\begin{cases} 0.3x + 0.2y = 0 \\ 2x - 3y = -13 \end{cases}$
$(-2, 3)$

45. $\begin{cases} 2x - y = 16 \\ 0.03x + 0.02y = 0.03 \end{cases}$
$(5, -6)$

▶ **46.** $\begin{cases} -5y + 2x = 4 \\ -0.02y + 0.03x = 0.04 \end{cases}$
$\left(\frac{12}{11}, -\frac{4}{11}\right)$

47. $\begin{cases} 6x + 3y = 0 \\ 5y = 2x + 12 \end{cases}$
$(-1, 2)$

▶ **48.** $\begin{cases} 0 = 4x - 3y \\ 5x = 4y - 2 \end{cases}$
$(6, 8)$

49. $\begin{cases} 3x + 12y = -12 \\ x = 3y + 10 \end{cases}$
$(4, -2)$

50. $\begin{cases} 3x + 2y = 3 \\ y = 2x - 16 \end{cases}$
$(5, -6)$

51. $\begin{cases} 4x - 8y = 36 \\ 3x - 6y = 27 \end{cases}$
infinitely many solutions

52. $\begin{cases} 2x + 4y = 15 \\ 3x = 8 - 6y \end{cases}$
no solutions

53. $\begin{cases} x = y \\ 0.1x + 0.2y = 1.0 \end{cases}$
$\left(\frac{10}{3}, \frac{10}{3}\right)$

▶ **54.** $\begin{cases} x = y \\ 0.4x - 0.8y = -0.5 \end{cases}$
$\left(\frac{5}{4}, \frac{5}{4}\right)$

55. $\begin{cases} \dfrac{m}{4} + \dfrac{m}{3} = -\dfrac{1}{12} \\ \dfrac{m}{2} - \dfrac{5n}{4} = \dfrac{7}{4} \end{cases}$
$(1, -1)$

56. $\begin{cases} \dfrac{x}{2} - \dfrac{y}{3} = -2 \\ \dfrac{x}{3} + \dfrac{2y}{3} = \dfrac{4}{3} \end{cases}$
$(-2, 3)$

APPLICATIONS

▶ **57. EDUCATION** The graph shows educational trends
during the years 1980–2004 for persons 25 years or
older. The equation $9x + 11y = 352$ approximates the
percent y that had less than high school completion.
The equation $5x - 11y = -198$ approximates the
percent y that had a Bachelor's or higher degree. Use
the addition method to determine in what year the
percents were equal. 1991

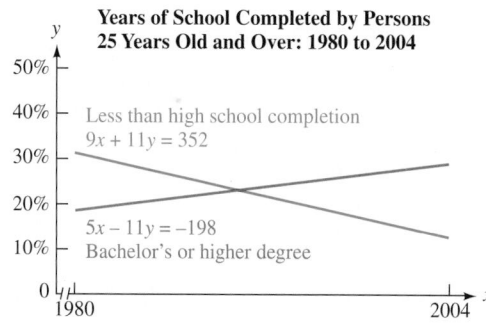

Source: U.S. Department of Commerce, Census Bureau

▶ **58. NEWSPAPERS** The graph on the next page shows
the trends in the newspaper publishing industry
during the years 1990–2004. The equation
$37x - 2y = -1{,}128$ models the number y of morning
newspapers published and $31x + y = 1{,}059$ models
the number y of evening newspapers published. In
each case, x is the number of years since 1990. Use the
addition method to determine in what year there was
an equal number of morning and evening
newspapers. 2000

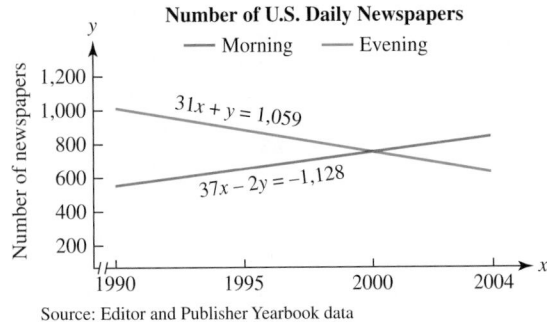

Number of U.S. Daily Newspapers

— Morning   — Evening

$31x + y = 1{,}059$

$37x - 2y = -1{,}128$

Source: Editor and Publisher Yearbook data

WRITING

59. Why is it usually to your advantage to write the equations of a system in general form before using the addition method to solve the system?

▶ **60.** How would you decide whether to use substitution or addition to solve a system of equations?

61. In this section, we discussed the addition method for solving a system of two equations. Some instructors call it the *elimination method*. Why do you think it is known by this name?

62. Explain the error in the following work.

Solve: $\begin{cases} x + y = 1 \\ x - y = 5 \end{cases}$

$$\begin{aligned} x + y &= 1 \\ x - y &= 5 \\ \hline 2x &= 6 \end{aligned}$$

$$\frac{2x}{2} = \frac{6}{2}$$

$\boxed{x = 3}$ The solution is 3.

REVIEW

63. Solve: $8(3x - 5) - 12 = 4(2x + 3)$ 4

64. Solve: $3y + \dfrac{y + 2}{2} = \dfrac{2(y + 3)}{3} + 16$ 6

65. Simplify: $x - x$ 0

66. Simplify: $3.2m - 4.4 + 2.1m + 16$ $5.3m + 11.6$

67. Find the area of a triangular-shaped sign with a base of 4 feet and a height of 3.75 feet. 7.5 ft^2

▶ **68.** Translate to mathematical symbols: *the product of the sum of x and y and the difference of x and y.*
  $(x + y)(x - y)$

69. What is 10 less than x? $x - 10$

70. Solve $y = mx + b$ for m. $m = \dfrac{y - b}{x}$

Objectives

1 Solve problems using two unknowns.

2 Use systems to solve geometry problems.

3 Use systems to solve break-point problems.

4 Use systems to solve interest problems.

5 Use systems to solve uniform motion problems.

6 Use systems to solve mixture problems.

SECTION 4.4

Problem Solving Using Systems of Equations

We have previously formed equations involving one variable to solve problems. In this section, we consider ways to solve problems using two variables and the five-step problem-solving strategy discussed in Chapter 2.

1 Solve problems using two unknowns.

We can use the following steps to solve problems involving two unknown quantities.

Problem-Solving Strategy

1. **Analyze the problem** by reading it carefully. What information is given? What are you asked to find? What vocabulary is given? Often a diagram or table will help you visualize the facts of the problem.

2. **Form two equations** by picking two different variables to represent two unknown quantities. This will give a system of two equations in two variables.

3. **Solve the system** of equations using the most convenient method: graphing, substitution, or addition.

4. **State the conclusion** using a complete sentence. Be sure to include the units (such as feet, seconds, or pounds) in your answer.

5. **Check the result** in the words of the problem.

EXAMPLE 1   *Photography*   At a school, two picture packages are available, as shown in the illustration. Find the cost of a class picture and the cost of an individual wallet-size picture.

Analyze

- Package 1 contains 1 class picture and 10 wallet-size pictures.
- Package 2 contains 2 class pictures and 15 wallet-size pictures.
- Find the cost of a class picture and the cost of a wallet-size picture.

Form   Let c = the cost of 1 class picture and w = the cost of 1 wallet-size picture. To write an equation that models the first package, we note that (in dollars) the cost of 1 class picture is c and the cost of 10 wallet-size pictures is $10 \cdot w = 10w$.

The cost of 1 class picture	plus	the cost of 10 wallet-size pictures	is	$19.
c	$+$	$10w$	$=$	19

To write an equation that models the second package, we note that (in dollars) the cost of 2 class pictures is $2 \cdot c = 2c$, and the cost of 15 wallet-size pictures is $15 \cdot w = 15w$.

The cost of 2 class pictures	plus	the cost of 15 wallet-size pictures	is	$31.
$2c$	$+$	$15w$	$=$	31

The resulting system is $\begin{cases} c + 10w = 19 \\ 2c + 15w = 31 \end{cases}$

Solve   We can use the addition method to solve this system. To eliminate c, we proceed as follows:

$$\begin{array}{rl} -2c - 20w = -38 & \text{Multiply both sides of } c + 10w = 19 \text{ by } -2. \\ \underline{2c + 15w = 31} & \\ -5w = -7 & \text{Add the equations to eliminate } c. \\ w = 1.4 & \text{Divide both sides by } -5 \text{ to isolate } w. \text{ This is the cost of a} \\ & \text{wallet-size picture.} \end{array}$$

To find c, substitute 1.4 for w in the first equation of the original system.

$$\begin{array}{rl} c + 10w = 19 & \\ c + 10(\mathbf{1.4}) = 19 & \text{Substitute 1.4 for } w. \\ c + 14 = 19 & \text{Multiply.} \\ c = 5 & \text{Subtract 14 from both sides. This is the cost of a class picture.} \end{array}$$

State   A class picture costs $5 and a wallet-size picture costs $1.40.

Check Package 1 has 1 class picture and 10 wallets: $5 + 10($1.40) = $5 + $14 = $19. Package 2 has 2 class pictures and 15 wallets: 2($5) + 15($1.40) = $10 + $21 = $31. The results check.

> **Caution!** In Example 1 we are to find two unknowns, the cost of a class picture and the cost of a wallet-size picture. Remember to give both answers in the state-the-conclusion step of the solution.

EXAMPLE 2   *Lawn Care*   An installer of underground irrigation systems wants to cut a 20-foot length of plastic tubing into two pieces. The longer piece is to be 2 feet longer than twice the shorter piece. Find the length of each piece.

Analyze Refer to the figure, which shows the pipe.

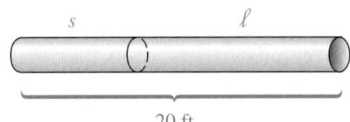

20 ft

Form We can let s = the length of the shorter piece and ℓ = the length of the longer piece.

The length of the shorter piece	plus	the length of the longer piece	is	20 feet.
s	$+$	ℓ	$=$	20

Since the longer piece is 2 feet longer than twice the shorter piece, we have

The length of the longer piece	is	2	times	the length of the shorter piece	plus	2 feet.
ℓ	$=$	2	$\cdot$	s	$+$	2

Solve We can use the substitution method to solve the system.

(1) $\begin{cases} s + \ell = 20 \\ \ell = 2s + 2 \end{cases}$
(2)

$s + 2s + 2 = 20$ Substitute $2s + 2$ for ℓ in Equation 1.

$3s + 2 = 20$ Combine like terms.

$3s = 18$ Subtract 2 from both sides.

$s = 6$ Divide both sides by 3.

The shorter piece should be 6 feet long. To find the length of the longer piece, we substitute 6 for s in Equation 2 and find ℓ.

$\ell = 2s + 2$

$= 2(6) + 2$ Substitute.

$= 12 + 2$ Simplify.

$= 14$

State The longer piece should be 14 feet long, and the shorter piece 6 feet long.

Check The sum of 6 and 14 is 20, and 14 is 2 more than twice 6. The results check.

THINK IT THROUGH *College Students and Television Viewing*

"College students watch a lot less television than other segments of the population. The typical college student watches 14.5 hours of TV a week, compared to 32 hours weekly by the average American."

Media Life, 2002

According to Nielsen Media Research, the typical high school graduate will have spent 6,000 more hours in front of a TV set than in the classroom. Combined, the television viewing and classroom time totals about 30,000 hours. Use two equations in two variables to find the number of hours spent in the classroom and the number of hours spent watching television by the typical high school graduate. 12,000 hr, 18,000 hr.

2 Use systems to solve geometry problems.

EXAMPLE 3 *Gardening* Tom has 150 feet of fencing to enclose a rectangular garden. If the garden's length is to be 5 feet less than 3 times its width, find the area of the garden.

Analyze To find the area of a rectangle, we need to know its length and width.

Form We can let ℓ = the length of the garden and w = its width, as shown in the figure. Since the perimeter of a rectangle is two lengths plus two widths, we have

2	times	the length of the garden	plus	2	times	the width of the garden	is	150 feet.
2	$\cdot$	ℓ	$+$	2	$\cdot$	w	$=$	150

Since the length is 5 feet less than 3 times the width,

The length of the garden	is	3	times	the width of the garden	minus	5 feet.
ℓ	$=$	3	$\cdot$	w	$-$	5

Solve We can use the substitution method to solve this system.

(1) $\begin{cases} 2\ell + 2w = 150 \\ \ell = 3w - 5 \end{cases}$
(2)

$2(3w - 5) + 2w = 150$ Substitute $3w - 5$ for ℓ in Equation 1.

$6w - 10 + 2w = 150$ Distribute the multiplication by 2.

$8w - 10 = 150$ Combine like terms.

$8w = 160$ Add 10 to both sides.

$w = 20$ Divide both sides by 8.

The width of the garden is 20 feet. To find the length, we substitute 20 for w in Equation 2 and simplify.

$\ell = 3w - 5$

$= 3(20) - 5$ Substitute.

$= 60 - 5$

$\ell = 55$ The length of the garden is 55 feet.

Self Check 3

In 1917, James Montgomery Flagg created the classic *I Want You* poster to help recruiting for World War I. The perimeter of the poster is 114 inches, and its length is 9 inches less than twice its width. Find the area of the poster. 770 in.²

Now Try **Problem 34**

Teaching Example 3 A pet owner wants to make a dog run from 28 feet of fencing. If the length of the dog run is to be 2 feet longer than the width, find the area that is enclosed for the pet.
Answer:
48 ft²

Now we find the area of the rectangle with dimensions 55 feet by 20 feet.

$$A = \ell w \qquad \text{This is the formula for the area of a rectangle.}$$
$$= 55 \cdot 20 \qquad \text{Substitute 55 for } \ell \text{ and 20 for } w.$$
$$A = 1{,}100$$

State The garden covers an area of 1,100 square feet.

Check Because the dimensions of the garden are 55 feet by 20 feet, the perimeter is

$$P = 2\ell + 2w$$
$$= 2(55) + 2(20) \qquad \text{Substitute 55 for } \ell \text{ and 20 for } w.$$
$$= 110 + 40$$
$$= 150$$

It is also true that 55 feet is 5 feet less than 3 times 20 feet. The results check.

3 Use systems to solve break-point problems.

© iStockphoto.com/Joerg Reimann

EXAMPLE 4   *Manufacturing*   The setup cost of a machine that mills brass plates is $750. After setup, it costs $0.25 to mill each plate. Management is considering the purchase of a larger machine that can produce the same plate at a cost of $0.20 per plate. If the setup cost of the larger machine is $1,200, how many plates would the company have to produce to make the purchase worthwhile?

Analyze We need to find the number of plates (called the **break point**) that will cost equal amounts to produce on either machine.

Form We can let c = the cost of milling p plates. If we call the machine currently being used machine 1, and the new, larger one machine 2, we can form the two equations.

The cost of making p plates on machine 1	is	the setup cost of machine 1	plus	the cost per plate on machine 1	times	the number of plates p to be made.
c	=	750	+	0.25	·	p

The cost of making p plates on machine 2	is	the setup cost of machine 2	plus	the cost per plate on machine 2	times	the number of plates p to be made.
c	=	1,200	+	0.20	·	p

Solve Since the costs are equal at the break point, we can use the substitution method to solve the system

(1) $\begin{cases} c = 750 + 0.25p \\ (2) \quad c = 1{,}200 + 0.20p \end{cases}$

$$750 + 0.25p = 1{,}200 + 0.20p \qquad \text{Substitute } 750 + 0.25p \text{ for } c \text{ in the second equation.}$$
$$0.25p = 450 + 0.20p \qquad \text{Subtract 750 from both sides.}$$
$$0.05p = 450 \qquad \text{Subtract } 0.20p \text{ from both sides.}$$
$$p = 9{,}000 \qquad \text{Divide both sides by 0.05.}$$

State If 9,000 plates are milled, the cost will be the same on either machine. If more than 9,000 plates are milled, the cost will be cheaper on the larger machine, because it mills the plates less expensively than the smaller machine.

Check We check the solution by substituting 9,000 for p in Equations 1 and 2 and verifying that 3,000 is the value of c in both cases.

If we graph the two equations, we can illustrate the break point.

Machine 1

$c = 750 + 0.25p$

p	c
0	750
1,000	1,000
5,000	2,000

Machine 2

$c = 1,200 + 0.20p$

p	c
0	1,200
4,000	2,000
12,000	3,600

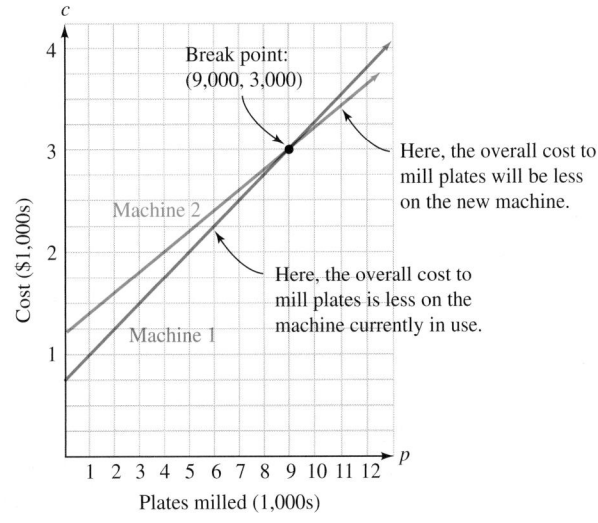

4 Use systems to solve interest problems.

EXAMPLE 5   *White-Collar Crime* Federal investigators discovered that a company secretly moved $150,000 out of the country to avoid paying corporate income tax on it. Some of the money was invested in a Swiss bank account that paid 8% interest annually. The remainder was deposited in a Cayman Islands account, paying 7% annual interest. The investigation also revealed that the combined interest earned the first year was $11,500. How much money was invested in each account?

Analyze We are told that an unknown part of the $150,000 was invested at an annual rate of 8% and the rest at 7%. Together, the accounts earned $11,500 in interest.

Form We can let x = the amount invested in the Swiss bank account and y = the amount invested in the Cayman Islands account. Because the total investment was $150,000, we have

The amount invested in the Swiss account	+	the amount invested in the Cayman Is. Account	is	$150,000.
x	+	y	=	150,000

Since the annual income on x dollars invested at 8% is $0.08x$, the income on y dollars invested at 7% is $0.07y$, and the combined income is $11,500, we have

The income on the 8% investment	+	the income on the 7% investment	is	$11,500.
$0.08x$	+	$0.07y$	=	11,500

The resulting system is

(1) $\begin{cases} x + y = 150,000 \\ 0.08x + 0.07y = 11,500 \end{cases}$
(2)

Solve To solve the system, we use the addition method to eliminate x.

$$
\begin{array}{ll}
-8x - 8y = -1,200,000 & \text{Multiply both sides of Equation 1 by } -8. \\
\underline{8x + 7y = 1,150,000} & \text{Multiply both sides of Equation 2 by 100.} \\
-y = {-50,000} & \\
y = 50,000 & \text{Multiply (or divide) both sides by } -1.
\end{array}
$$

To find x, we substitute 50,000 for y in Equation 1 and simplify.

$$
\begin{array}{ll}
x + y = 150,000 & \\
x + \mathbf{50,000} = 150,000 & \text{Substitute.} \\
x = 100,000 & \text{Subtract 50,000 from both sides.}
\end{array}
$$

State $100,000 was invested in the Swiss bank account, and $50,000 was invested in the Cayman Islands account.

Check

$$
\begin{array}{ll}
\$100,000 + \$50,000 = \$150,000 & \text{The two investments total \$150,000.} \\
0.08(\$100,000) = \$8,000 & \text{The Swiss bank account earned \$8,000.} \\
0.07(\$50,000) = \$3,500 & \text{The Cayman Islands account earned \$3,500.}
\end{array}
$$

The combined interest is $8,000 + $3,500 = $11,500. The results check.

5 Use systems to solve uniform motion problems.

Teaching Example 6 A boat traveled 20 miles downstream in 2 hours and made the return trip in 5 hours. Find the speed of the boat in still water.
Answer:
7 mph

EXAMPLE 6   *Boating* A boat traveled 30 kilometers downstream in 3 hours and made the return trip in 5 hours. Find the speed of the boat in still water.

Analyze Traveling downstream, the speed of the boat will be faster than it would be in still water. Traveling upstream, the speed of the boat will be less than it would be in still water.

Form We can let s = the speed of the boat in still water and c = the speed of the current. Then the rate of the boat going downstream is $s + c$, and its rate going upstream is $s - c$. We can organize the information as shown.

	Rate	· Time	= Distance
Downstream	$s + c$	3	$3(s + c)$
Upstream	$s - c$	5	$5(s - c)$

Since each trip is 30 miles long, the Distance column of the table gives two equations in two variables.

$$
\begin{cases}
3(s + c) = 30 \\
5(s - c) = 30
\end{cases}
$$

After using the distributive property, we have

(1) $\begin{cases} 3s + 3c = 30 \\ \end{cases}$
(2) $\begin{cases} 5s - 5c = 30 \end{cases}$

Solve To solve this system by addition, we multiply Equation 1 by 5, multiply Equation 2 by 3, add the equations, and solve for s.

$$
\begin{array}{l}
15s + 15c = 150 \\
\underline{15s - 15c = 90} \\
30s = 240 \\
s = 8 \qquad \text{Divide both sides by 30.}
\end{array}
$$

State The speed of the boat in still water is 8 kilometers per hour.

Check We leave the check to the reader.

---

6 **Use systems to solve mixture problems.**

EXAMPLE 7 *Medical Technology*

A laboratory technician has one batch of antiseptic that is 40% alcohol and a second batch that is 60% alcohol. She would like to make 8 liters of solution that is 55% alcohol. How many liters of each batch should she use?

Image copyright Yuri Arcurs, 2009. Used under license from Shutterstock.com

Analyze Some 60% solution must be added to some 40% solution to make a 55% solution.

Form We can let x = the number of liters to be used from batch 1 and y = the number of liters to be used from batch 2. We then organize the information as shown. The information provides two equations.

	Number of liters of solution	% of concentration	= Number of liters of alcohol
Batch 1	x	0.40	$0.40x$
Batch 2	y	0.60	$0.60y$
Mixture	8	0.55	$0.55(8)$

↑ One equation comes from information in this column.

↑ 40%, 60%, and 55% have been expressed as decimals.

↑ Another equation comes from information in this column.

(1) $\quad \begin{cases} x + y = 8 \end{cases}$ The number of liters of batch 1 plus the number of liters of batch 2 equals the total number of liters in the mixture.

(2) $\quad 0.40x + 0.60y = 0.55(8)$ The amount of alcohol in batch 1 plus the amount of alcohol in batch 2 equals the amount of alcohol in the mixture.

Solve We can use addition to solve this system.

$$\begin{array}{rl} -40x - 40y = -320 & \text{Multiply both sides of Equation 1 by } -40. \\ \underline{40x + 60y = 440} & \text{Multiply both sides of Equation 2 by 100.} \\ 20y = 120 & \\ y = 6 & \text{Divide both sides by 20.} \end{array}$$

To find x, we substitute 6 for y in Equation 1 and simplify.

$$\begin{array}{rl} x + y = 8 & \\ x + 6 = 8 & \text{Substitute.} \\ x = 2 & \text{Subtract 6 from both sides.} \end{array}$$

State The technician should use 2 liters of the 40% solution and 6 liters of the 60% solution.

Check The check is left to the reader.

Self Check 7

How much 1% milk must be added to 4% milk to obtain 60 liters of 2% milk? 40 liters

Now Try **Problem 43**

Teaching Example 7 How much 1% hydrocortisone cream must be mixed with 5% hydrocortisone cream to make 10 ounces of a 2% cream? *Answer:* 7.5 ounces

> **ANSWERS TO SELF CHECKS**
> **1.** team photo: $17.00, wallet: $1.50   **2.** 4 ft, 8 ft   **3.** 770 in.²   **4.** 5,000 copies
> **5.** $2,500 at 9%, $7,500 at 10%   **6.** 10 mph   **7.** 40 liters

SECTION 4.4   STUDY SET

VOCABULARY

Fill in the blanks.

1. A __variable__ is a letter that stands for a number.

▶ **2.** An __equation__ is a statement indicating that two quantities are equal.

3. $\begin{cases} a + b = 20 \\ a = 2b + 4 \end{cases}$ is a __system__ of linear equations.

4. A __solution__ of a system of linear equations satisfies both equations simultaneously.

CONCEPTS

5. For each case in the illustration, write an algebraic expression that represents the speed of the canoe in mph if its speed in still water is x mph. $x + c, x - c$

Current c mph

Current c mph

▶ **6.** See the illustration.

   a. If the contents of the two test tubes are poured into a third test tube, how much solution will the third test tube contain? (mL means milliliters.) $(x + y)$ mL

   b. Which is the best estimate of the concentration of the solution in the third test tube: 25%, 35%, or 45% acid solution? 35%

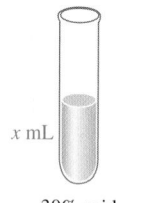
x mL
30% acid solution

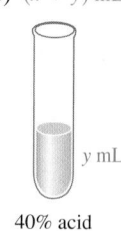
y mL
40% acid solution

7. Use the information in the table to answer the questions about two investments.

	Principal ·	Rate ·	Time =	Interest
City Bank	x	5%	1 yr	0.05x
USA Savings	y	11%	1 yr	0.11y

   a. How much money was deposited in the USA Savings account? $$y$

   b. What interest rate did the City Bank account earn? 5%

   c. Complete the table.

8. Use the information in the table to answer the questions about a plane flying in windy conditions.

	Rate ·	Time =	Distance
With	$x + y$	3 hr	450 mi
Against	$x - y$	5 hr	450 mi

   a. For how long did the plane fly against the wind? 5 hr

   b. At what rate did the plane travel when flying with the wind? $(x + y)$ mph

   c. Write two equations that could be used to solve for x and y. $3(x + y) = 450$, $5(x - y) = 450$

9. a. If a problem contains two unknowns, and if two variables are used to represent them, how many equations must be written to find the unknowns? two

   b. Name three methods that can be used to solve a system of linear equations. graphing, substitution, addition

10. Put the steps of the five-step problem-solving strategy listed below in the correct order.

   State the conclusion   Form two equations
   Analyze the problem   Check the result
   Solve the system

   analyze, form, solve, state, check

NOTATION

Write a formula that relates the given quantities.

11. length, width, area of a rectangle $A = lw$

▶ **12.** length, width, perimeter of a rectangle $P = 2l + 2w$

13. rate, time, distance traveled $d = rt$

14. principal, rate, time, interest earned $I = Prt$

Translate each verbal model into mathematical symbols. Use variables to represent any unknowns.

15. $\boxed{2}$ · $\boxed{\begin{array}{c}\text{length} \\ \text{of pool}\end{array}}$ + $\boxed{2}$ · $\boxed{\begin{array}{c}\text{width} \\ \text{of pool}\end{array}}$ $\boxed{\text{is}}$ $\boxed{\begin{array}{c}90 \\ \text{yards.}\end{array}}$

   $2l + 2w = 90$

16. $6 · [number of adults] + $2 · [number of children] is $26.

$6a + 2c = 26$

APPLICATIONS

Use two equations in two variables to solve each problem.

▶ **17.** One integer is twice another. Their sum is 96. 32, 64

▶ **18.** The sum of two integers is 38. Their difference is 12. 13, 25

▶ **19.** Three times one integer plus another integer is 29. The first integer plus twice the second is 18. 8, 5

▶ **20.** Twice one integer plus another integer is 21. The first integer plus 3 times the second is 33. 6, 9

21. TREE TRIMMING When fully extended, the arm on the tree service truck shown is 51 feet long. If the upper part of the arm is 7 feet shorter than the lower part, how long is each part of the arm? 22 ft, 29 ft

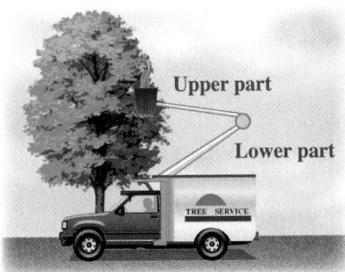

▶ **22.** TV PROGRAMMING The producer of a 30-minute TV documentary about World War I divided it into two parts. Four times as much program time was devoted to the causes of the war as to the outcome. How long is each part of the documentary? causes: 24 min, outcome: 6 min

▶ **23.** ALASKA Most of the 1,422-mile-long Alaska Highway is actually in Canada. Find the length of the highway that is in Alaska and the length that is in Canada if it is known that the difference in the lengths is 1,020 miles. 201 mi, 1,221 mi

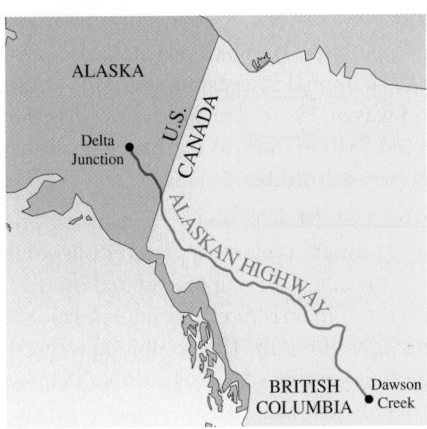

24. EXECUTIVE BRANCH The salaries of the president and vice president of the United States total $608,100 a year. If the president makes $191,900 more than the vice president, find each of their salaries. president: $400,000, vice president: $208,100

▶ **25.** CAUSES OF DEATH According to the *National Vital Statistics Reports,* in 2004, the number of Americans who died from heart disease was about 6 times the number who died from accidents. If the total number of deaths from these two causes was 763,000, how many Americans died from each cause in 2004? 109,000 from accidents, 654,000 from heart disease

▶ **26.** BUYING PAINTING SUPPLIES Two partial receipts for paint supplies are shown. How much does each gallon of paint and each brush cost? $30, $10

▶ **27.** WEDDING PICTURES A photographer sells the two wedding picture packages shown in the illustration. How much does a 10 × 14 photo cost? An 8 × 10 photo? $29.50, $21

28. BUYING TICKETS If receipts for the movie advertised below were $1,440 for an audience of 190 people, how many senior citizens attended? 115

▶ **29.** SELLING ICE CREAM At a store, ice cream cones cost $0.90 and sundaes cost $1.65. One day a total of 148 cones and sundaes were sold and the receipts totalled $180.45. How many cones were sold? 85

30. THE MARINE CORPS The Marine Corps War Memorial in Arlington, Virginia, portrays the raising of the U.S. flag on Iwo Jima during World War II. Find the measures of the two angles shown below if the measure of one of the angles is 15° less than twice the other. 65°, 115°

▶ **31.** PHYSICAL THERAPY To rehabilitate her knee, an athlete does leg extensions. Her goal is to regain a full 90° range of motion in this exercise. Use the information in the illustration to determine her current range of motion in degrees. 72°

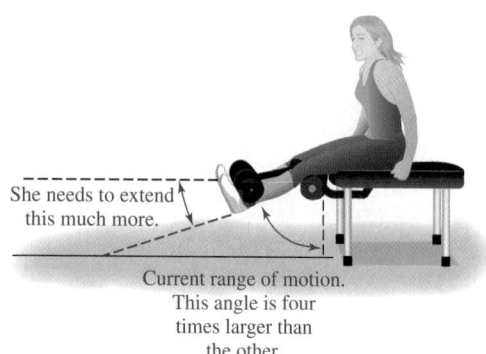

She needs to extend this much more.

Current range of motion. This angle is four times larger than the other.

32. THEATER SCREENS At an IMAX theater, the giant rectangular movie screen has a width 26 feet less than its length. If its perimeter is 332 feet, find the area of the screen. 6,720 ft²

33. ART In 1770, Thomas Gainsborough painted *The Blue Boy*. The sum of the length and width of the painting is 118 in. The difference between the length and width is 22 in. Find the length and the width of the painting.
length 70 in., width 48 in.

© Huntington Library/SuperStock

▶ **34.** GEOMETRY A 50-meter path surrounds the rectangular garden shown below. If the width of the garden is two-thirds its length, find its area. 150 m²

35. MAKING TIRES A company has two molds to form tires. One mold has a setup cost of $1,000, and the other has a setup cost of $3,000. The cost to make each tire with the first mold is $15, and the cost to make each tire with the second mold is $10.

a. Find the break point. 400 tires

b. Check your result by graphing both equations on the coordinate system in the illustration.

c. If a production run of 500 tires is planned, determine which mold should be used. the second mold

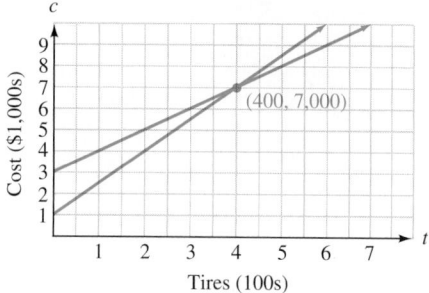

▶ **36.** CHOOSING A FURNACE A high-efficiency 90+ furnace can be purchased for $2,250 and costs an average of $412 per year to operate in Rockford, Illinois. An 80+ furnace can be purchased for only $1,715, but it costs $466 per year to operate.

a. Find the break point. about 9.9 yr

b. If you intended to live in a Rockford house for 7 years, which furnace would you choose? 80+

37. STUDENT LOANS A college used a $5,000 gift from an alumnus to make two student loans. The first was at 5% annual interest to a nursing student. The second was at 7% to a business major. If the college collected $310 in interest the first year, how much was loaned to each student? nursing: $2,000, business: $3,000

▶ **38.** FINANCIAL PLANNING In investing $6,000 of a couple's money, a financial planner put some of it into a savings account paying 6% annual interest. The rest was invested in a riskier mini-mall development plan paying 12% annually. The combined interest earned for the first year was $540. How much money was invested at each rate? 6%: $3,000, 12%: $3,000

39. THE GULF STREAM The Gulf Stream is a warm ocean current of the North Atlantic Ocean that flows northward, as shown. Heading north with the Gulf Stream, a cruise ship traveled 300 miles in 10 hours. Against the current, it took 15 hours to make the return trip. Find the speed of the current. 5 mph

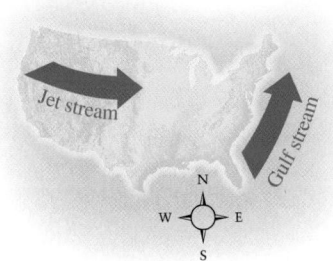

40. THE JET STREAM The jet stream is a strong wind current that flows across the United States, as shown in the illustration above. Flying with the jet stream, a plane flew 3,000 miles in 5 hours. Against the same wind, the trip took 6 hours. Find the airspeed of the plane (the speed in still air). 550 mph

41. AVIATION An airplane can fly downwind a distance of 600 miles in 2 hours. However, the return trip against the same wind takes 3 hours. Find the speed of the wind. 50 mph

42. BOATING A boat can travel 24 miles downstream in 2 hours and can make the return trip in 3 hours. Find the speed of the boat in still water. 10 mph

43. MARINE BIOLOGY A marine biologist wants to set up an aquarium containing 3% salt water. He has two tanks on hand that contain 6% and 2% salt water. How much water from each tank must he use to fill a 16-liter aquarium with a 3% saltwater mixture? 4 L 6% salt water, 12 L 2% salt water

44. COMMEMORATIVE COINS A foundry has been commissioned to make souvenir coins. The coins are to be made from an alloy that is 40% silver. The foundry has on hand two alloys, one with 50% silver content and one with a 25% silver content. How many kilograms of each alloy should be used to make 20 kilograms of the 40% silver alloy? 12 kg 50% alloy, 8 kg 25% alloy

45. MIXING NUTS A merchant wants to mix peanuts with cashews, as shown in the illustration in the next column, to get 48 pounds of mixed nuts that will be sold at $4 per pound. How many pounds of each should the merchant use? 32 lb peanuts, 16 lb cashews

46. COFFEE SALES A coffee supply store waits until the orders for its special coffee blend reach 100 pounds before making up a batch. Coffee selling for $8.75 a pound is blended with coffee selling for $3.75 a pound to make a product that sells for $6.35 a pound. How much of each type of coffee should be used to make the blend that will fill the orders? 52 lb $8.75, 48 lb $3.75

47. MARKDOWN A set of golf clubs has been marked down 40% to a sale price of $384. Let r represent the retail price and d the discount. Then use the following equations to find the original retail price. $640

Retail price	−	discount	=	sale price

Discount	=	discount rate	−	retail price

48. MARKUP A stereo system retailing at $565.50 has been marked up 45% from wholesale. Let w represent the wholesale cost and m the markup. Then use the following equations to find the wholesale cost. $390

Wholesale cost	+	markup	=	retail price

Markup	=	markup rate	·	wholesale cost

WRITING

49. When solving a problem using two variables, why isn't one equation sufficient to find the two unknown quantities?

50. Describe an everyday situation in which you might need to make a mixture.

REVIEW

Graph each inequality.

51. $x < 4$

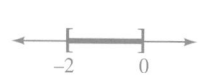

52. $x \geq -3$

53. $-1 < x \leq 2$

54. $-2 \leq x \leq 0$

Solve each equation.

55. $\dfrac{x}{5} - 4 = 2$ ₃₀ 30

56. $\dfrac{x - 5}{4} + 6 = 0$ -19

57. $3(x + 8) - 6(x + 4) = -3x$ identity

58. $2(x + 10) + x = 3(x + 8)$ no solution

Objectives

1 Solve a system of linear inequalities by graphing.

2 Use graphing to identify systems of inequalities with no solutions.

3 Solve application problems involving systems of linear inequalities.

SECTION 4.5

Solving Systems of Linear Inequalities

In Section 4.1, we solved systems of linear *equations* by the graphing method. The solution of such a system is the point of intersection of the straight lines. We now consider how to solve systems of linear *inequalities* graphically. When the solution of a linear inequality is graphed, the result is a half-plane. Therefore, we would expect to find the graphical solution of a system of inequalities by looking for the intersection, or overlap, of shaded half-planes.

1 Solve a system of linear inequalities by graphing.

Self Check 1

Graph the solutions of the system:
$$\begin{cases} x - y \leq 2 \\ x + y \geq -1 \end{cases}$$

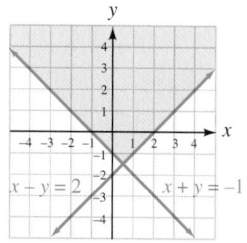

Now Try Problem 26

Teaching Example 1 Graph the solutions of the system:
$$\begin{cases} x + y \leq 3 \\ x - y \leq -1 \end{cases}$$
Answer:

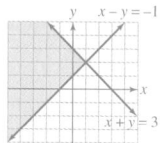

EXAMPLE 1

Graph the solutions of the system:
$$\begin{cases} x + y \geq 1 \\ x - y \geq 1 \end{cases}$$

Strategy We will graph the solutions of $x + y \geq 1$ in one color and the solutions of $x - y \geq 1$ in another color on the same coordinate system.

WHY We need to see where the graphs of the two inequalities intersect (overlap).

Solution

We first graph each inequality. For this first example, we will graph each inequality on a separate set of axes, although in practice we will draw them on the same axes.

To graph $x + y \geq 1$, we begin by graphing the boundary line $x + y = 1$. Since the inequality contains an $\geq$ symbol, the boundary is a solid line. Because the coordinates of the test point $(0, 0)$ do not satisfy $x + y \geq 1$, we shade (in red) the side of the boundary that does **not** contain $(0, 0)$. See part (a) of the figure.

To graph $x - y \geq 1$, we begin by graphing the boundary line $x - y = 1$. Since the inequality contains an $\geq$ symbol, the boundary is a solid line. Because the coordinates of the test point $(0, 0)$ do not satisfy $x - y \geq 1$, we shade (in blue) the side of the boundary that does **not** contain $(0, 0)$. See part (b) of the figure.

$x + y = 1$		
x	y	(x, y)
0	1	$(0, 1)$
1	0	$(1, 0)$
2	-1	$(2, -1)$

$x - y = 1$		
x	y	(x, y)
0	-1	$(0, -1)$
1	0	$(1, 0)$
2	1	$(2, 1)$

Shading: Check the test point (0, 0).

$x + y \geq 1$

$0 + 0 \overset{?}{\geq} 1$ Substitute

$0 \geq 1$ False

$(0, 0)$ is not a solution of $x + y \geq 1$.

Shading: Check the test point (0, 0).

$x - y \geq 1$

$0 - 0 \overset{?}{\geq} 1$ Substitute

$0 \geq 1$ False

$(0, 0)$ is not a solution of $x - y \geq 1$.

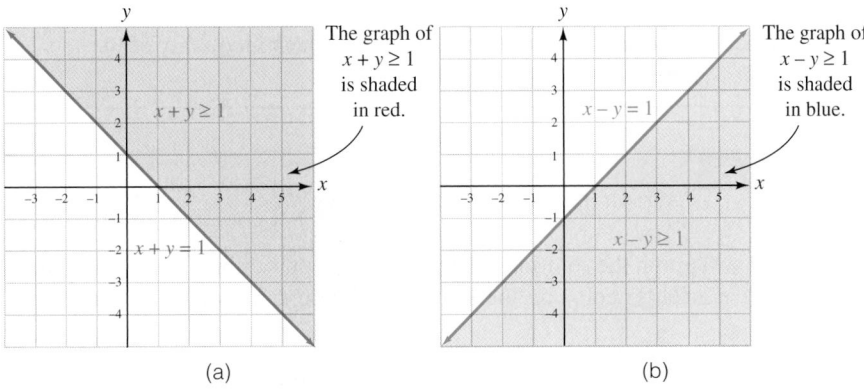

(a)   (b)

The graph of $x + y \geq 1$ is shaded in red.

The graph of $x - y \geq 1$ is shaded in blue.

In the following figure, we show the result when the inequalities $x + y \geq 1$ and $x - y \geq 1$ are graphed one at a time on the same coordinate axes. The area that is shaded twice represents the set of simultaneous solutions of the given system of inequalities. Any point in the doubly shaded region (shown in purple) has coordinates that satisfy both inequalities of the system.

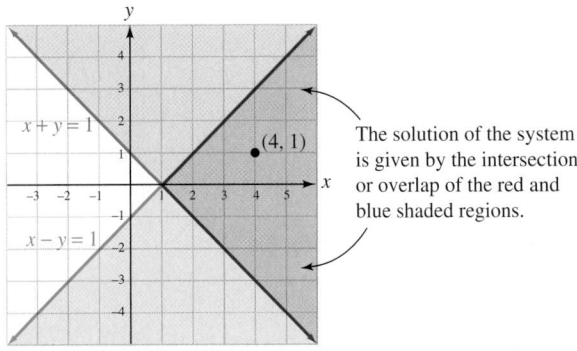

The solution of the system is given by the intersection or overlap of the red and blue shaded regions.

To see whether this is true, we can pick a point, such as $(4, 1)$, that lies in the doubly shaded region and show that its coordinates satisfy both inequalities.

Check: $x + y \geq 1$ and $x - y \geq 1$

             $4 + 1 \geq 1$ $4 - 1 \geq 1$

                $5 \geq 1$ True $3 \geq 1$ True

The resulting true statements verify that $(4, 1)$ is a solution of the system. If we pick a point that is not in the doubly shaded region, its coordinates will fail to satisfy at least one of the inequalities.

> ***The Language of Algebra***   To solve a system of linear inequalities we *superimpose* the graphs of the inequalities. That is, we place one graph on top of the other. Most cameras *superimpose* the date and time over the picture.

In general, to solve systems of linear inequalities, we will follow these steps.

> ## Solving Systems of Inequalities
>
> 1. Graph each inequality on the same rectangular coordinate system.
> 2. Use shading to highlight the intersection of the graphs (the region where the graphs overlap). The points in this region are the solutions of the system.
> 3. As an informal check, pick a test point from the region where the graphs intersect, and verify that its coordinates satisfy each inequality of the original system.

Self Check 2

Graph the solutions of the system:
$$\begin{cases} x + 3y < 3 \\ -x + 3y > 3 \end{cases}$$

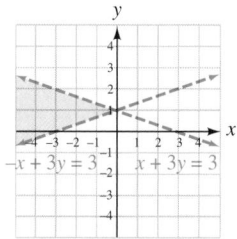

Now Try Problem 31

Teaching Example 2 Graph the solutions of the system: $\begin{cases} x + 3y < 3 \\ y > \frac{1}{3}x \end{cases}$

Answer:

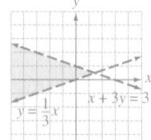

EXAMPLE 2   Graph the solutions of the system: $\begin{cases} 2x + y < 4 \\ y > 2x + 2 \end{cases}$

Strategy We will graph the solutions of $2x + y < 4$ in one color and the solutions of $y > 2x + 2$ in another color on the same coordinate system to see where the graphs intersect.

WHY The solution set of the system is the set of all points in the intersection of the two graphs.

Solution
First, we graph each inequality on one set of axes, as shown in the figure.

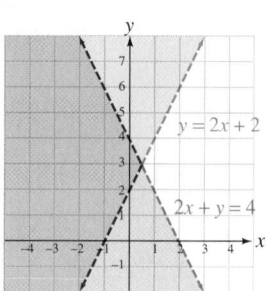

Boundary for $2x + y < 4$

$2x + y = 4$		
x	y	(x, y)
0	4	$(0, 4)$
2	0	$(2, 0)$
1	2	$(1, 2)$

Shading for $2x + y < 4$

Check the test point $(0, 0)$.

$2x + y < 4$
$2(0) + 0 \overset{?}{<} 4$ Substitute
$0 < 4$ True

Boundary for $y > 2x + 2$

$y = 2x + 2$

So $m = 2 = \dfrac{2}{1}$

and $b = 2$.

Shading for $y > 2x + 2$

Check the test point $(0, 0)$.

$y > 2x + 2$
$0 \overset{?}{>} 2(0) + 2$
$0 > 2$ False

We note that

- The graph of $2x + y < 4$ includes all points below the boundary line $2x + y = 4$. Since the boundary is not included, we draw it as a dashed line.

- The graph of $y > 2x + 2$ includes all points above the boundary line $y = 2x + 2$. Since the boundary is not included, we draw it as a dashed line.

The area that is shaded twice (the region in purple) is the solution of the given system of inequalities. Any point in the doubly shaded region has coordinates that will satisfy both inequalities of the system.

Pick a point in the doubly shaded region and show that it satisfies both inequalities.

EXAMPLE 3

Graph the solutions of the system: $\begin{cases} x \le 2 \\ y > 3 \end{cases}$

Strategy We will graph the solutions of $x \le 2$ in one color and the solutions of $y > 3$ in another color on the same coordinate system to see where the graphs intersect.

WHY The solution set of the system is the set of all points in the intersection of the two graphs.

Solution
We graph each inequality on one set of axes, as shown in the figure.

Boundary for $x \le 2$

$x = 2$

x	y	(x, y)
2	0	(2, 0)
2	2	(2, 2)
2	4	(2, 4)

Boundary for $y > 3$

$y = 3$

x	y	(x, y)
0	3	(0, 3)
1	3	(1, 3)
4	3	(4, 3)

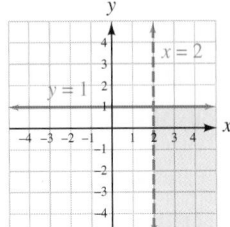

Shading for $x \le 2$

Shading for $y > 3$

Check the test point (0, 0).

$x \le 2$
$0 \overset{?}{\le} 2$ True

Check the test point (0, 0).

$y > 3$
$0 \overset{?}{>} 3$ False

We note that

- The graph of $x \le 2$ includes all points to the left of the boundary line $x = 2$. Since the boundary is included, we draw it as a solid line.
- The graph $y > 3$ includes all points above the boundary line $y = 3$. Since the boundary is not included, we draw it as a dashed line.

The area that is shaded twice is the solution of the given system of inequalities. Any point in the doubly shaded region (purple) has coordinates that will satisfy both inequalities of the system. Pick a point in the doubly shaded region and show that this is true.

Self Check 3

Graph the solutions of the system:
$\begin{cases} y \le 1 \\ x > 2 \end{cases}$

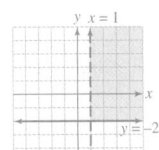

Now Try Problem 34

Teaching Example 3 Graph the solutions of the system: $\begin{cases} y \ge -2 \\ x > 1 \end{cases}$

Answer:

2 Use graphing to identify systems of inequalities with no solutions.

EXAMPLE 4

Graph the solutions of the system: $\begin{cases} y < 3x - 1 \\ y \ge 3x + 1 \end{cases}$

Strategy We will graph the solutions of $y < 3x - 1$ in one color and the solutions of $y \ge 3x + 1$ in another color on the same coordinate system to see where or if the graphs intersect.

WHY The solution set of the system is the set of all points in the intersection of the two graphs.

Self Check 4

Graph the solutions of the system:
$\begin{cases} y \ge -\dfrac{1}{2}x + 1 \\ y < -\dfrac{1}{2}x - 1 \end{cases}$ no solution

(continued)

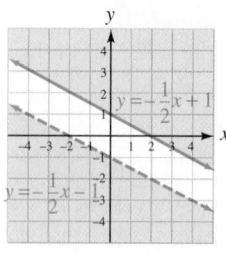

Now Try Problem 37

Teaching Example 4 Graph the solution of the system: $\begin{cases} y \leq -x + 1 \\ y > -x + 3 \end{cases}$

Answer:
no solutions

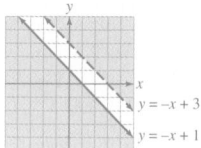

Solution

We graph each inequality as shown in the figure and make the following observations:

- The graph of $y < 3x - 1$ includes all points below the dashed line $y = 3x - 1$.
- The graph of $y \geq 3x + 1$ includes all points on and above the solid line $y = 3x + 1$.

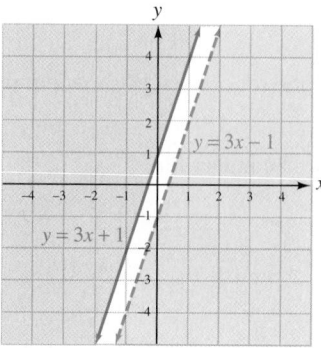

Because the graphs of these inequalities do not intersect, the solution set is empty. There are no solutions.

Graph the solutions of the system:
$\begin{cases} x \leq 1 \\ y \leq 2 \\ 2x - y \leq 4 \end{cases}$

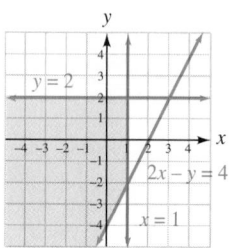

Now Try Problem 39

Teaching Example 5 Graph the solutions of the system: $\begin{cases} x \leq 3 \\ y \leq 5 \\ 2x - 3y \leq 6 \end{cases}$

Answer:

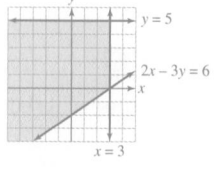

EXAMPLE 5

Graph the solutions of the system: $\begin{cases} x \geq 0 \\ y \geq 0 \\ x + 2y \leq 6 \end{cases}$

Strategy We will graph the solutions of $x \geq 0$, $y \geq 0$, and $x + 2y \leq 6$ on the same coordinate system to see where all three graphs intersect (overlap).

WHY The solution set of the system is the set of all points in the intersection of the three graphs.

Solution

We graph each inequality as shown in the figure and make the following observations:

- The graph of $x \geq 0$ includes all points on the y-axis and to the right.
- The graph of $y \geq 0$ includes all points on the x-axis and above.
- The graph of $x + 2y \leq 6$ includes all points on the line $x + 2y = 6$ and below.

The solution is the region that is shaded three times. This includes triangle OPQ and the triangular region it encloses.

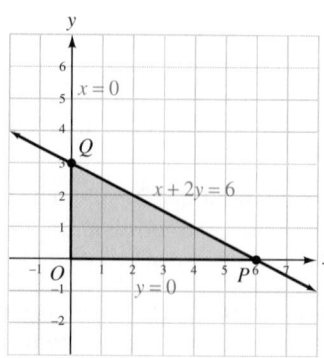

3 Solve application problems involving systems of linear inequalities.

EXAMPLE 6   *Landscaping*

A homeowner budgets from $300 to $600 for trees and bushes to land-scape his yard. After shopping around, he finds that good trees cost $150 and mature bushes cost $75. What combinations of trees and bushes can he afford to buy?

Analyze

- The homeowner wants to spend *at least* $300 but *not more than* $600 for trees and bushes.
- Trees cost $150 each and bushes cost $75 each.
- What combination of trees and bushes can he buy?

Form We can let x represent the number of trees purchased and y the number of bushes purchased. We then form the following system of inequalities:

The cost of a tree	times	the number of trees purchased	plus	the cost of a bush	times	the number of bushes purchased	should at least be	$300.
$150	·	x	+	$75	·	y	≥	$300

The cost of a tree	times	the number of trees purchased	plus	the cost of a bush	times	the number of bushes purchased	should not be more than	$600.
$150	·	x	+	$75	·	y	≤	$600

Solve We graph the system

$$\begin{cases} 150x + 75y \geq 300 \\ 150x + 75y \leq 600 \end{cases}$$

as shown in the figure.

State The coordinates of each point shown in the graph give a possible combination of the number of trees (x) and the number of bushes (y) that can be purchased. These possibilities are

$(0, 4), (0, 5), (0, 6), (0, 7), (0, 8)$

$(1, 2), (1, 3), (1, 4), (1, 5), (1, 6)$

$(2, 0), (2, 1), (2, 2), (2, 3), (2, 4)$

$(3, 0), (3, 1), (3, 2), (4, 0)$

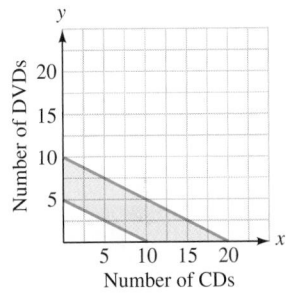

Only these points can be used, because the homeowner cannot buy a portion of a tree or a bush.

Check Suppose the homeowner picks a combination of 2 trees and 4 bushes, as represented by $(2, 4)$. Show that this point satisfies both inequalities of the system.

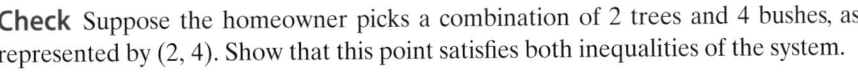

Self Check 6

BUYING CDs AND DVDs An electronics store sells CDs for $10 and DVDs for $20. Carly wants to spend at least $100 but no more than $200 on ($x$) CDs and ($y$) DVDs. What combinations of CDs and DVDs can she afford to buy?

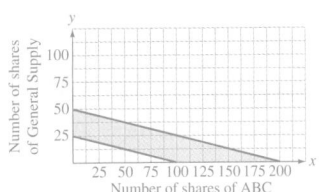

Now Try Problem 51

Self Check 6 Answer

Any ordered pair in the shaded region with whole number coordinates.

Teaching Example 6 BUYING STOCKS Marcia has at least $500 but no more than $1,000 to invest in stocks from two companies. Each share of ABC stock costs $5 per share, and each share of General Supply cost $20 per share. What combination of shares of ABC and General Supply can she afford to buy?

Answer:

Any ordered pair in the shaded region with whole number coordinates.

ANSWERS TO SELF CHECKS

1.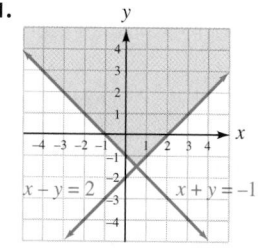

2.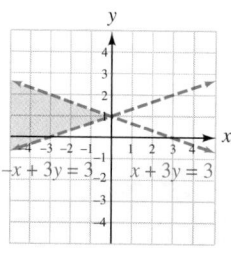

3.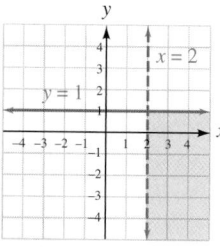

4.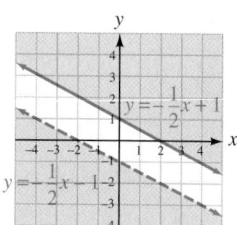

5.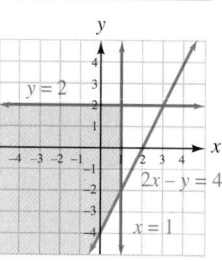

6. Any ordered pairs in the shaded region with whole number coordinates.

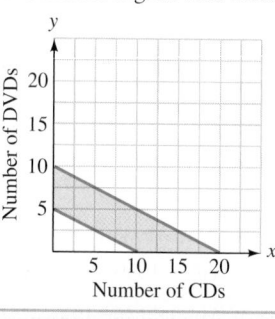

SECTION 4.5   STUDY SET

VOCABULARY

Fill in the blanks.

1. $\begin{cases} x + y > 2 \\ x + y < 4 \end{cases}$ is a system of linear ___inequalities___.

2. The ___solution___ of a system of linear inequalities is all the ordered pairs that make all inequalities of the system true at the same time.

3. Any point in the doubly ___shaded___ region of the graph of the solution of a system of two linear inequalities has coordinates that satisfy both inequalities of the system.

▶ 4. To graph a linear inequality such as $x + y > 2$, first graph the boundary. Then pick a test ___point___ to determine which half-plane to shade.

CONCEPTS

In the illustration, the solution of linear inequality 1 was shaded in red, and the solution of linear inequality 2 was shaded in blue. The overlap of the red and the blue regions is shown in purple. Determine whether a true or a false statement results when the coordinates of the given point are substituted into the given inequality.

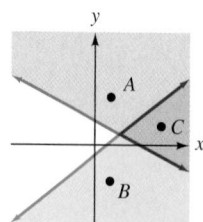

▶ 5. *A*, inequality 1 true   ▶ 6. *A*, inequality 2 false

7. *B*, inequality 1 false   8. *B*, inequality 2 true

9. *C*, inequality 1 true   10. *C*, inequality 2 true

Match each equation, inequality, or system with the graph of its solution.

11. $x + y = 2$ ii   12. $x + y \geq 2$ iii

13. $\begin{cases} x + y = 2 \\ x - y = 2 \end{cases}$ iv   14. $\begin{cases} x + y \geq 2 \\ x - y \leq 2 \end{cases}$ i

i 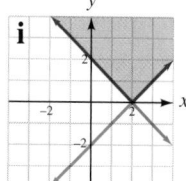   **ii**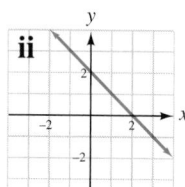

iii 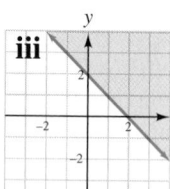   **iv**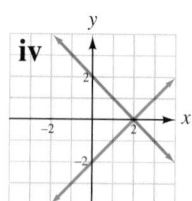

The graph of the solution of a system of two linear inequalities is shown. Determine whether each point is a part of the solution set.

▶ 15. $(4, -2)$ yes

▶ 16. $(1, 3)$ no

▶ 17. the origin no

18. $(3, 2)$ yes

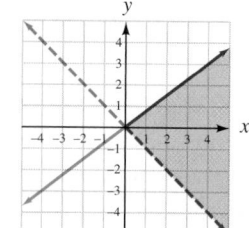

▶ Selected exercises available online at
www.webassign.net/brookscole

19. Use a system of inequalities to describe the shaded region in the illustration. $\begin{cases} x \le -2 \\ y > 2 \end{cases}$

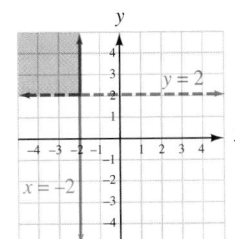

NOTATION

20. Fill in the blank: The graph of the solution of a system of linear inequalities shown can be described as the triangle $\underline{ABC}$ and the triangular region it encloses.

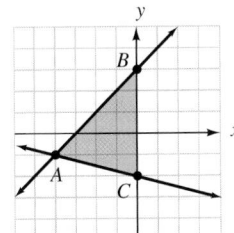

Represent each phrase using either $>$, $<$, $\ge$, *or* $\le$.

▶ **21.** is not more than $\le$ ▶ **22.** must be at least $\ge$

▶ **23.** should not surpass $\le$ ▶ **24.** cannot go below $\ge$

GUIDED PRACTICE

Graph the solutions of each system of inequalities.
See Example 1.

25. $\begin{cases} 3x + 4y \ge -7 \\ 2x - 3y \ge 1 \end{cases}$ **26.** $\begin{cases} 2x - 4y \ge -6 \\ 3x + y \ge 5 \end{cases}$

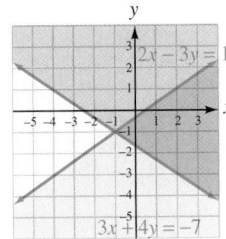 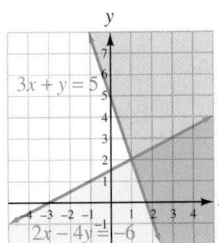

▶ **27.** $\begin{cases} x + 2y \le 3 \\ 2x - y \ge 1 \end{cases}$ ▶ **28.** $\begin{cases} 2x + y \ge 3 \\ x - 2y \le -1 \end{cases}$

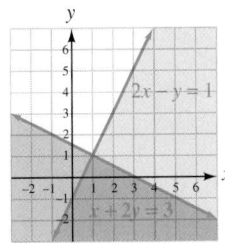 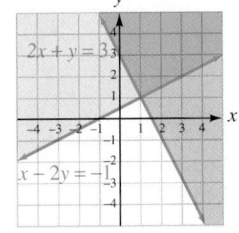

Graph the solutions of each system of inequalities.
See Example 2.

29. $\begin{cases} x + y < -1 \\ x - y > -1 \end{cases}$ ▶ **30.** $\begin{cases} x + y > 2 \\ x - y < -2 \end{cases}$

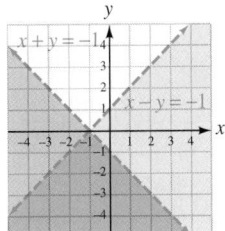 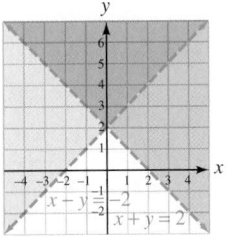

31. $\begin{cases} 2x - 3y \le 0 \\ y \ge x - 1 \end{cases}$ ▶ **32.** $\begin{cases} y > 2x - 4 \\ y \ge -x - 1 \end{cases}$

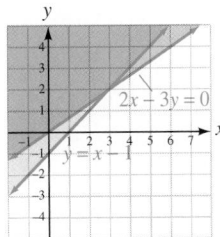 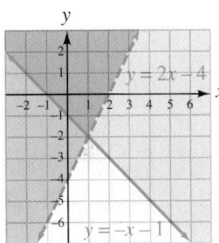

Graph the solutions of each system of inequalities.
See Example 3.

▶ **33.** $\begin{cases} x > 2 \\ y \le 3 \end{cases}$ ▶ **34.** $\begin{cases} x \ge -1 \\ y > -2 \end{cases}$

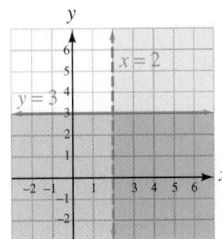 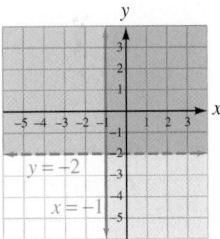

35. $\begin{cases} x > 0 \\ y > 0 \end{cases}$ ▶ **36.** $\begin{cases} x \le 0 \\ y < 0 \end{cases}$

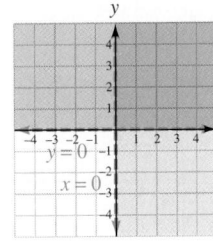 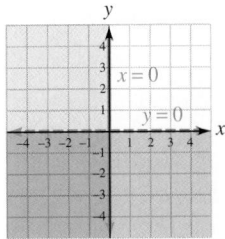

Graph the solutions of each system of inequalities, when possible. See Examples 4–5.

37. $\begin{cases} y < -x + 1 \\ y > -x + 3 \end{cases}$ ▶ **38.** $\begin{cases} 3x + y < -2 \\ y > 3(1 - x) \end{cases}$

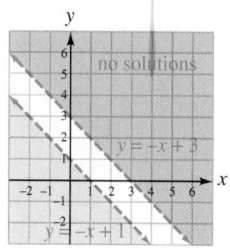 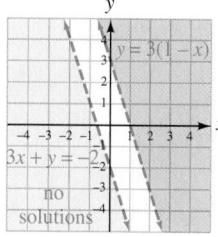

39. $\begin{cases} x \geq 0 \\ y \geq 0 \\ x + y \leq 3 \end{cases}$ ▶ **40.** $\begin{cases} x - y \leq 6 \\ x + 2y \leq 6 \\ x \geq 0 \end{cases}$

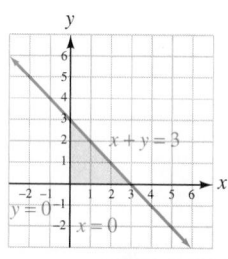 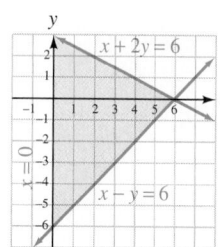

TRY IT YOURSELF

Graph the solutions of each system of inequalities.

▶ **41.** $\begin{cases} 2x + y < 7 \\ y > 2(1 - x) \end{cases}$ **42.** $\begin{cases} 2x + y \geq 6 \\ y \leq 2(2x - 3) \end{cases}$

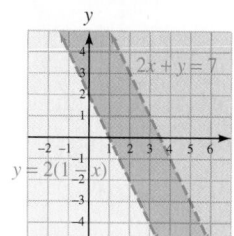 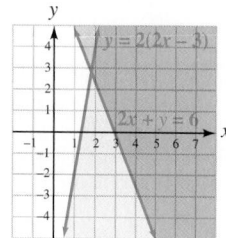

▶ **43.** $\begin{cases} 3x + y \leq 1 \\ 4x - y > -8 \end{cases}$ ▶ **44.** $\begin{cases} 2x - 3y < 0 \\ 2x + 3y \geq 12 \end{cases}$

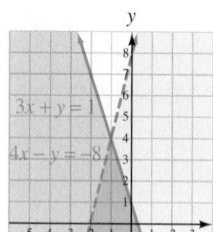 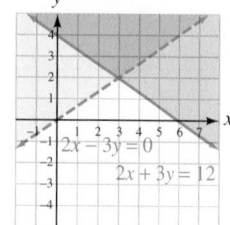

45. $\begin{cases} 3x - y \leq -4 \\ 3y > -2(x + 5) \end{cases}$ ▶ **46.** $\begin{cases} y > -x + 2 \\ y < -x + 4 \end{cases}$

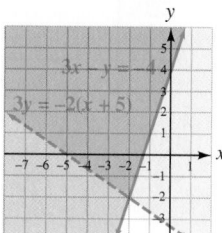 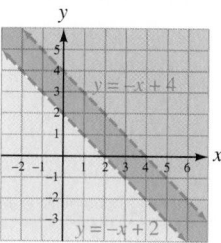

▶ **47.** $\begin{cases} \frac{x}{2} + \frac{y}{3} \geq 2 \\ \frac{x}{2} - \frac{y}{2} < -1 \end{cases}$ **48.** $\begin{cases} \frac{x}{3} - \frac{y}{2} < -3 \\ \frac{x}{3} + \frac{y}{2} > -1 \end{cases}$

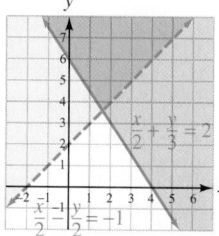 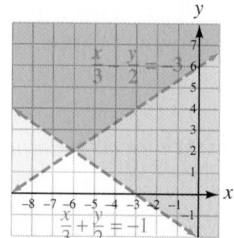

APPLICATIONS

49. BIRDS OF PREY Parts a and b of the illustration show the individual fields of vision for each eye of an owl. In part c, shade the area where the fields of vision overlap—that is, the area that is seen by both eyes.

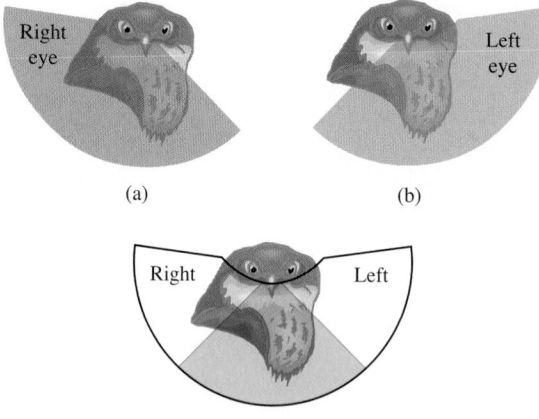

(a)   (b)

(c)

50. EARTH SCIENCE Shade the area of Earth's surface that is north of the Tropic of Capricorn and south of the Tropic of Cancer.

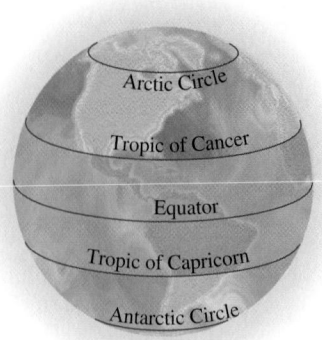

In Exercises 51–56, graph each system of inequalities and give two possible solutions.

▶ **51.** BUYING COMPACT DISCS Melodic Music has compact discs on sale for either $10 or $15. If a customer wants to spend at least $30 but no more than $60 on CDs, use the illustration to graph a system of inequalities showing the possible combinations of $10 CDs ($x$) and $15 CDs ($y$) that the customer can buy.

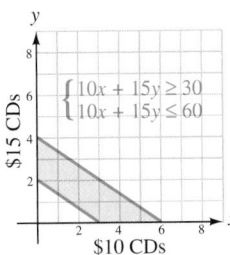

1 $10 CD and 2 $15 CDs, 4 $10 CDs and 1 $15 CD, answers vary

▶ **52.** BUYING BOATS Dry Boatworks wholesales aluminum boats for $800 and fiberglass boats for $600. Northland Marina wants to make a purchase totaling at least $2,400, but no more than $4,800. Use the illustration to graph a system of inequalities showing the possible combinations of aluminum boats (x) and fiberglass boats (y) that can be ordered.

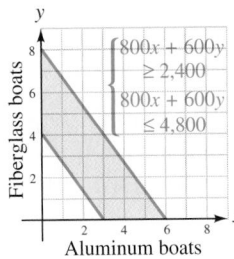

4 alum. and 1 glass, 1 alum. and 4 glass, answers vary

▶ **53.** BUYING FURNITURE A distributor wholesales desk chairs for $150 and side chairs for $100. Best Furniture wants its order to total no more than $900; Best also wants to order more side chairs than desk chairs. Use the illustration to graph a system of inequalities showing the possible combinations of desk chairs (x) and side chairs (y) that can be ordered.

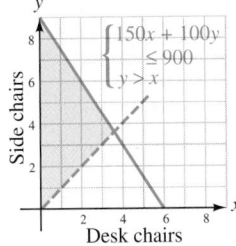

2 desk chairs and 4 side chairs, 1 desk chair and 5 side chairs, answers vary

▶ **54.** ORDERING FURNACE EQUIPMENT J. Bolden Heating Company wants to order no more than $2,000 worth of electronic air cleaners and humidifiers from a wholesaler that charges $500 for air cleaners and $200 for humidifiers. If Bolden wants more humidifiers than air cleaners, use the illustration to graph a system of inequalities showing the possible combinations of air cleaners (x) and humidifiers (y) that can be ordered.

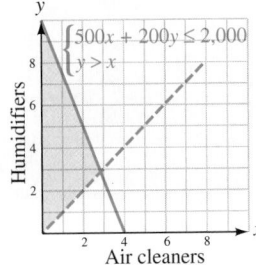

1 air cleaner and 2 humidifiers, 2 air cleaners and 3 humidifiers, answers vary

▶ **55.** PESTICIDES To eradicate a fruit fly infestation, helicopters sprayed an area of a city that can be described by $y \geq -2x + 1$ (within the city limits). Two weeks later, more spraying was ordered over the area described by $y \geq \frac{1}{4}x - 4$ (within the city limits). In the illustration, show the part of the city that was sprayed twice.

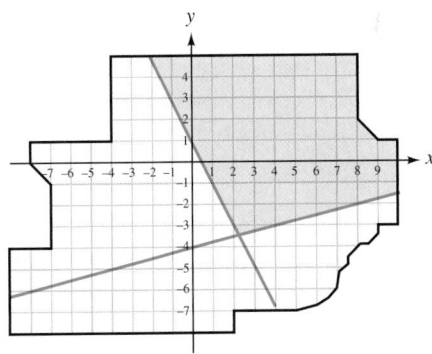

▶ **56.** REDEVELOPMENT Refer to the following diagram. A government agency has declared an area of a city east of First Street, north of Second Avenue, south of Sixth Avenue, and west of Fifth Street as eligible for federal redevelopment funds. Describe this area of the city mathematically using a system of four inequalities, if the corner of Central Avenue and Main Street is considered the origin.

$$\begin{cases} x > 1 \\ x < 5 \\ y > 2 \\ y < 6 \end{cases}$$

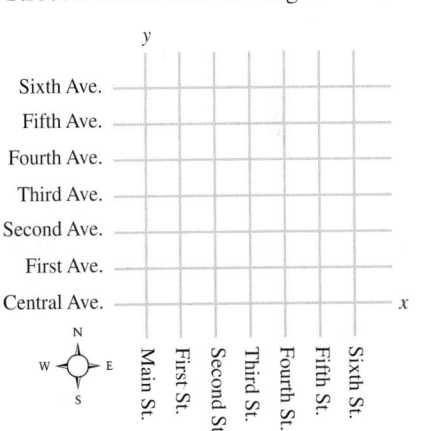

WRITING

57. Explain how to use graphing to solve a system of inequalities.

▶ **58.** Explain when a system of inequalities will have no solutions.

59. Describe how the graphs of the solutions of these systems are similar and how they differ.

$$\begin{cases} x + y = 4 \\ x - y = 4 \end{cases} \quad \text{and} \quad \begin{cases} x + y \geq 4 \\ x - y \geq 4 \end{cases}$$

▶ **60.** When a solution of a system of linear inequalities is graphed, what does the shading represent?

REVIEW

Complete each table.

61. $y = 2x^2$

x	y
8	128
−2	8

▶ **62.** $t = -|s + 2|$

s	t
−3	−1
−10	−8

63. $f(x) = 4 + x^3$

Input	Output
0	4
−3	−23

64. $g(x) = 2x - x^2$

x	$g(x)$
5	−15
−5	−35

STUDY SKILLS CHECKLIST

PREPARING FOR THE CHAPTER 4 TEST

In Chapter 4 you learned three methods to solve a system of linear equations. You also learned how to graph the solutions of a system of linear inequalities. As you prepare for the exam over this material, make sure you also review the following checklist.

☐ To check a proposed solution of a system of equations, be sure the coordinates of the ordered pair satisfies *both* equations.

Is $(3, -2)$ a solution of the system $\begin{cases} 3x + 4y = 1 \\ x + 2y = -1 \end{cases}$?

$3(3) + 4(-2) \stackrel{?}{=} 1$ Substitute 3 for x and −2 for y.

$9 - 8 \stackrel{?}{=} 1$

$1 \stackrel{?}{=} 1$ True

$3 + 2(-2) \stackrel{?}{=} -1$ Substitute 3 for x and −2 for y.

$3 - 4 \stackrel{?}{=} -1$

$-1 \stackrel{?}{=} -1$ True

Yes, $(3, -2)$ is a solution of the system.

☐ When solving a system of equations by graphing, you must determine the coordinates of the point in intersection of the graphs. That ordered pair is the solution of the system.

☐ When using the substitution or the addition (elimination) method, remember to find the value of *both* the variables.

For the system of linear equations $\begin{cases} x = 2y - 3 \\ x + 4y = 3 \end{cases}$, the y-coordinate of the solution is $y = 1$.

To find the x-value, substitute 1 for y in either equation:

$x = 2y - 3$

$x = 2(1) - 3$

$x = 2 - 3$

$x = -1$

The solution is $(-1, 1)$.

Teaching Guide: Refer to the Instructor's Resource Binder to find activities, worksheets on key concepts, more examples, instruction tips, overheads, and assessments.

CHAPTER 4   SUMMARY AND REVIEW

SECTION 4.1   Solving Systems of Equations by Graphing

DEFINITIONS AND CONCEPTS	EXAMPLES
When two equations are considered at the same time, we say that they form a **system of equations.**	Is $(4, 3)$ a solution of the system $\begin{cases} x + y = 7 \\ x - y = 5 \end{cases}$?

A **solution of a system** of equations in two variables is an ordered pair that satisfies both equations of the system.

To answer this question, we substitute 4 for x and 3 for y in each equation.

$$x + y = 7 \qquad\qquad x - y = 5$$
$$4 + 3 \overset{?}{=} 7 \qquad\qquad 4 - 3 \overset{?}{=} 5$$
$$7 = 7 \quad \text{True} \qquad\qquad 1 = 5 \quad \text{False}$$

Although $(4, 3)$ satisfies the first equation, it does not satisfy the second. Because it does not satisfy both equations, it is not a solution of the system.

To **solve a system graphically:**

1. Graph each equation on the same rectangular coordinate system.

2. If the lines intersect, determine the coordinates of the point of intersection of the graphs. This ordered pair is the solution.

3. Check the proposed solution in each equation of the original system.

Use graphing to solve the system: $\begin{cases} y = -2x + 3 \\ x - 2y = 4 \end{cases}$

Step 1 Graph each equation as shown below.

$$y = -2x + 3$$
$$m = \frac{-2}{1}$$
$$b = 3$$

x - 2y = 4	
x	**y**
0	-2
4	0

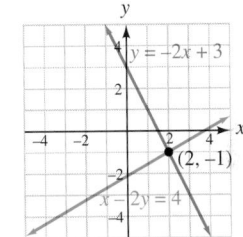

Step 2 It appears that the graphs intersect at the point $(2, -1)$. To verify that this is the solution of the system, substitute 2 for x and -1 for y in each equation.

Step 3 Check

$$x - 2y = 4 \qquad\qquad y = -2x + 3$$
$$2 - 2(-1) \overset{?}{=} 4 \qquad\qquad -1 \overset{?}{=} -2(2) + 3$$
$$4 = 4 \quad \text{True} \qquad\qquad -1 = -1 \qquad \text{True}$$

Since $(2, -1)$ makes both equations true, it is the solution of the system.

A system of equations that has at least one solution is called a **consistent system.** If the graphs of the equations of the system are parallel lines, the system has no solution and is called an **inconsistent system.**

Equations with different graphs are called **independent equations.** If the graphs of the equations in a system are the same line, the system has infinitely many solutions. The equations are called **dependent equations.**

We can determine the **number of solutions** that a system of two linear equations has by writing each equation in slope-intercept form, $y = mx + b$, and comparing the slopes and y-intercepts.

There are three possible outcomes when solving a system of two linear equations by graphing.

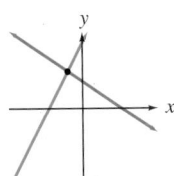
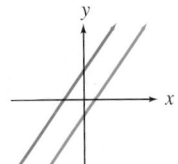
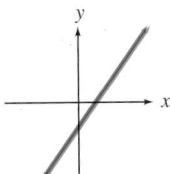

Consistent system
Independent equations
- Exactly one solution
- The lines have different slopes.

Inconsistent system
Independent equations
- No solution
- The lines have the same slope but different y-intercepts.

Consistent system
Dependent equations
- Infinitely many solutions
- The lines have the same slope and same y-intercept.

REVIEW EXERCISES

Determine whether the ordered pair is a solution of the system.

1. $(2, -3)$, $\begin{cases} 3x - 2y = 12 \\ 2x + 3y = -5 \end{cases}$ yes

2. $\left(\dfrac{7}{2}, -\dfrac{2}{3}\right)$, $\begin{cases} 4x - 6y = 18 \\ \dfrac{x}{3} + \dfrac{y}{2} = \dfrac{5}{6} \end{cases}$ yes

3. COMPARING STOCKS   Refer to the graph below. Estimate the date when Kmart stock and Sears stock sold for the same amount per share. Estimate the price per share at which they were selling on that date.   approximately March, about $42 per share

Source: *USA Today*

Use the graphing method to solve each system. If the equations of a system are dependent or if a system is inconsistent, so indicate.

4. $\begin{cases} x + y = 7 \\ 2x - y = 5 \end{cases}$

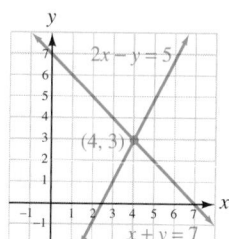

5. $\begin{cases} y = -\dfrac{x}{3} \\ 2x + y = 5 \end{cases}$

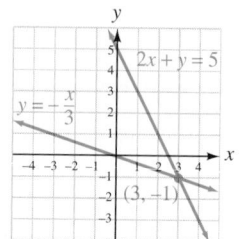

6. $\begin{cases} 3x + 6y = 6 \\ x + 2y = 2 \end{cases}$

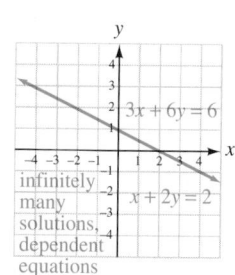

infinitely many solutions, dependent equations

7. $\begin{cases} 6x + 3y = 12 \\ 2x + y = 2 \end{cases}$

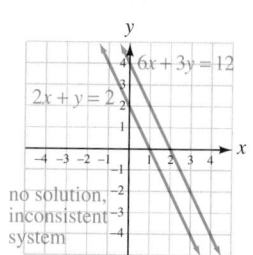

no solution, inconsistent system

SECTION 4.2   Solving Systems of Equations by Substitution

DEFINITIONS AND CONCEPTS	EXAMPLES

DEFINITIONS AND CONCEPTS

To solve a system of equations in x and y by the **substitution method:**

1. Solve one of the equations for either x or y. If this is already done, go to step 2. (We call this equation the **substitution equation.**)

2. Substitute the expression for x or for y obtained in step 1 into the other equation, and solve that equation.

3. Substitute the value of the variable found in step 2 in any equation to find the value of the remaining variable.

4. Check the proposed solution in the original equations. Write the solution as an ordered pair.

EXAMPLES

To solve the system $\begin{cases} x + 2y = -4 \\ 3x - 2y = 12 \end{cases}$ by substitution, begin by solving the first equation for x.

$$x + 2y = -4$$

(1) $x = -2y - 4$ Subtract 2y from both sides. This is the substitution equation.

Then substitute the result for x in the second equation, and solve for y.

$$3x - 2y = 12 \quad \text{This is the second equation.}$$
$$3(-2y - 4) - 2y = 12 \quad \text{Substitute } -2y - 4 \text{ for } x.$$
$$-6y - 12 - 2y = 12 \quad \text{Remove parentheses.}$$
$$-8y = 24 \quad \text{Combine terms and add 12 to both sides.}$$
$$y = -3 \quad \text{Divide both sides by } -8.$$

To find x, substitute -3 for y in Equation 1.

$$x = -2y - 4 \quad \text{This is Equation 1.}$$
$$x = -2(-3) - 4 \quad \text{Substitute } -3 \text{ for } y.$$
$$x = 2 \quad \text{Simplify.}$$

The solution $(2, -3)$ was checked in the previous section.

REVIEW EXERCISES

Use the substitution method to solve each system.

8. $\begin{cases} x = y \\ 5x - 4y = 3 \end{cases}$
$(3, 3)$

9. $\begin{cases} y = 15 - 3x \\ 7y + 3x = 15 \end{cases}$
$(5, 0)$

10. $\begin{cases} 0.2x + 0.2y = 0.6 \\ 3x = 2 - y \end{cases}$
$\left(-\frac{1}{2}, \frac{7}{2}\right)$

11. $\begin{cases} 6(r + 2) = s - 1 \\ r - 5s = -7 \end{cases}$
$(-2, 1)$

12. $\begin{cases} 9x + 3y = 5 \\ 3x + y = \dfrac{5}{3} \end{cases}$
infinitely many solutions, dependent equations

13. $\begin{cases} \dfrac{x}{6} + \dfrac{y}{10} = 3 \\ \dfrac{5x}{16} - \dfrac{3y}{16} = \dfrac{15}{8} \end{cases}$
$(12, 10)$

14. In solving a system using the substitution method, suppose you obtain the result of $8 = 9$.

  a. How many solutions does the system have? no solutions

  b. Describe the graph of the system. two parallel lines

  c. What term is used to describe the system? inconsistent system

---

SECTION 4.3 Solving Systems of Equations by Addition (Elimination)

DEFINITIONS AND CONCEPTS	EXAMPLES
To solve a system of equations using the **addition (elimination) method:** 1. Write each equation in general $Ax + By = C$ form. 2. Multiply one (or both) equation by nonzero quantities to make the coefficients of x (or y) opposites. 3. Add the equations to eliminate the terms involving x (or y). 4. Solve the equation obtained in step 3. 5. Find the value of the other variable by substituting the value of the variable found in step 4 into any equation containing both variables. 6. Check the solution in the original equations.	To solve the system $\begin{cases} x + 2y = -4 \\ 3x - 2y = 12 \end{cases}$ by addition (elimination), note that both equations are in $Ax + By = C$ form. Since the coefficients of y are opposites, add the equations to eliminate the variable y. $\begin{aligned} x + 2y &= -4 \\ 3x - 2y &= 12 \\ \hline 4x &= 8 \end{aligned}$ $x = 2$ Divide both sides by 4. Then multiply both sides of the first equation by -3 and add the equations to eliminate the variable x. $\begin{aligned} -3x - 6y &= 12 \\ 3x - 2y &= 12 \\ \hline -8y &= 24 \end{aligned}$ $y = -3$ Divide both sides by -8. The solution $(2, -3)$ was checked in Section 4.1. You could also find y by substitution. To find y, we substitute 2 for x in equation 1. $\begin{aligned} x + 2y &= -4 \\ 2 + 2y &= -4 \\ 2y &= -6 \\ \dfrac{2y}{2} &= \dfrac{-6}{2} \\ y &= -3 \end{aligned}$

REVIEW EXERCISES

Solve each system using the addition (elimination) method.

15. $\begin{cases} 2x + y = 1 \\ 5x - y = 20 \end{cases}$
$(3, -5)$

16. $\begin{cases} x + 8y = 7 \\ x - 4y = 1 \end{cases}$
$\left(3, \frac{1}{2}\right)$

17. $\begin{cases} 5a + b = 2 \\ 3a + 2b = 11 \end{cases}$
$(-1, 7)$

18. $\begin{cases} 11x + 3y = 27 \\ 8x + 4y = 36 \end{cases}$
$(0, 9)$

19. $\begin{cases} 9x + 3y = 15 \\ 3x = 5 - y \end{cases}$
infinitely many
solutions, dependent
equations

20. $\begin{cases} \dfrac{x}{3} + \dfrac{y + 2}{2} = 1 \\ \dfrac{x + 8}{8} + \dfrac{y - 3}{3} = 0 \end{cases}$
$(0, 0)$

21. $\begin{cases} 0.02x + 0.05y = 0 \\ 0.3x - 0.2y = -1.9 \end{cases}$
$(-5, 2)$

22. $\begin{cases} -\dfrac{1}{4}x = 1 - \dfrac{2}{3}y \\ 6(x - 3y) + 2y = 5 \end{cases}$
no solution, inconsistent
system

For each system, determine which method, substitution or addition (elimination), would be easier to use to solve the system and explain why.

23. $\begin{cases} 6x + 2y = 5 \\ 3x - 3y = -4 \end{cases}$
Addition, no variables
have a coefficient of
1 or −1.

24. $\begin{cases} x = 5 - 7y \\ 3x - 3y = -4 \end{cases}$
Substitution, equation 1 is
solved for x.

SECTION 4.4   Problem Solving Using Systems of Equations

DEFINITIONS AND CONCEPTS

To solve problems involving two unknown quantities:

1. **Analyze** the facts of the problem. Make a table or diagram if it is helpful.

2. **Form two equations** by picking two different variables to represent the two unknown quantities.

3. **Solve the system** of equations using the most convenient method: graphing, substitution, or addition.

4. **State the conclusion** using a complete sentence.

5. **Check the results.**

EXAMPLES

A plumber plans to cut a 12-foot pipe into two pieces so that one piece is to be 4 feet longer than the other.

Analyze To find the length of each piece, let l represent the length of the longer piece and s represent the length of the shorter piece. Since the sum of the lengths is to be 20 feet, you have

Form

The length of the longer piece	plus	the length of the shorter piece	is	20 feet.
l	$+$	s	$=$	20

Since the longer piece is to be 4 feet longer than the shorter piece, we have

The length of the longer piece	is	the length of the shorter piece	plus	4 feet.
l	$=$	s	$+$	4

Solve To find l and s, solve the system $\begin{cases} l + s = 20 \\ l = s + 4 \end{cases}$ as follows

$s + 4 + s = 20$ Substitute $s + 4$ in the second equation for l in the first equation.

$2s + 4 = 20$ Combine like terms.

$2s = 16$ Subtract 4 from both sides.

$s = 8$ Divide both sides by 2.

State The shorter piece should be 8 feet long. Because the longer piece is to be 4 feet longer, the longer piece should be 12 feet long.

Check This result checks because the sum of 8 and 12 is 20, and 12 is 4 greater than 8.

REVIEW EXERCISES

Use two equations in two variables to solve each problem.

25. CAUSES OF DEATH The number of Americans dying from heart disease is about 4.5 times more than the number dying from a stroke. If the total number of deaths from these causes in 1 year was 880,000, how many deaths were attributed to each? stroke: 160,000, heart disease: 720,000

26. PAINTING EQUIPMENT When fully extended, the ladder shown is 35 feet in length. If the extension is 7 feet shorter than the base, how long is each part of the ladder? base: 21 ft, extension: 14 ft

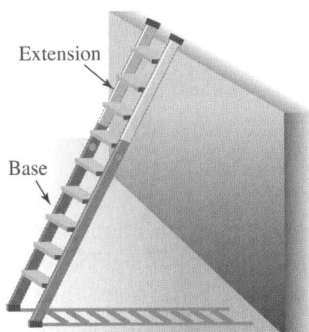

Extension

Base

27. CRASH INVESTIGATIONS In an effort to protect evidence, investigators used 420 yards of yellow "Police Line—Do Not Cross" tape to seal off a large rectangular-shaped area around an airplane crash site. How much area will the investigators have to search if the width of the rectangle is three-fourths of the length? 10,800 yd²

28. ENDORSEMENTS A company selling a home juicing machine is contemplating hiring either an athlete or an actor to serve as the spokesperson for the product. The terms of each contract would be as follows:

Celebrity	Base pay	Commission per item sold
Athlete	$30,000	$5
Actor	$20,000	$10

a. For each celebrity, write an equation giving the money (y) the celebrity would earn if x juicers were sold. $y = 5x + 30,000$, $y = 10x + 20,000$

b. For what number of juicers would the athlete and the actor earn the same amount? 2,000

c. Using the illustration, graph the equations from part a. The company expects to sell over 3,000 juicers. Which celebrity would cost the company the least money to serve as a spokesperson? the athlete

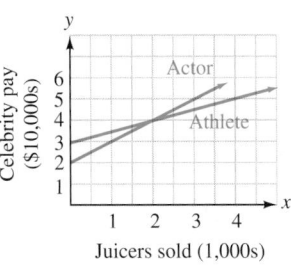

29. CANDY STORES A merchant wants to mix gummy worms worth $3 per pound and gummy bears worth $1.50 per pound to make 30 pounds of a mixture worth $2.10 per pound. How many pounds of each should he use? 12 lb worms, 18 lb bears

30. BOATING It takes a motorboat 4 hours to travel 56 miles down a river, and 3 hours longer to make the return trip. Find the speed of the current. 3 mph

31. SHOPPING Packages containing 2 bottles of contact lens cleaner and 3 bottles of soaking solution cost $63.40, and packages containing 3 bottles of cleaner and 2 bottles of soaking solution cost $69.60. Find the cost of a bottle of cleaner and a bottle of soaking solution. $16.40, $10.20

32. INVESTING Carlos invested part of $3,000 in a 10% certificate account and the rest in a 6% passbook account. The total annual interest from both accounts is $270. How much did he invest at 6%? $750

33. ANTIFREEZE How much of a 40% antifreeze solution must a mechanic mix with a 70% antifreeze solution if he needs 20 gallons of a 50% antifreeze solution? $13\frac{1}{3}$ gal 40%, $6\frac{2}{3}$ gal 70%

SECTION **4.5**   **Solving Systems of Linear Inequalities**

DEFINITIONS AND CONCEPTS

EXAMPLE

Solving a system of linear inequalities by graphing:

1. Graph each inequality on the same rectangular coordinate system.

2. Use shading to highlight the intersection of the graphs. The points in this region are the solutions of the system.

3. As an informal check, pick a test point from the region where the graphs intersect and verify that its coordinates satisfy each inequality of the original system.

To solve the system $\begin{cases} x + y \geq 1 \\ x - y \geq 1 \end{cases}$, refer to Example 1 on page 364.

REVIEW EXERCISES

Solve each system of inequalities.

34. $\begin{cases} 5x + 3y < 15 \\ 3x - y > 3 \end{cases}$

35. $\begin{cases} x \geq 3y \\ y > 3x \end{cases}$

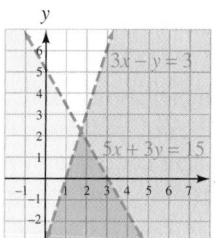

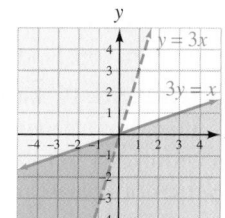

36. GIFT SHOPPING A grandmother wants to spend at least $40 but no more than $60 on school clothes for her grandson. If T-shirts sell for $10 and pants sell for $20, write a system of inequalities that describes the possible combinations of T-shirts (x) and pants (y) she can buy. Graph the system in the illustration. Give two possible solutions.

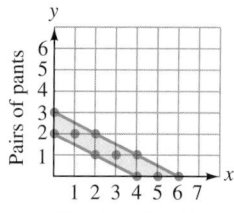

$10x + 20y \geq 40$, $10x + 20y \leq 60$; (3, 1): 3 shirts and 1 pair of pants; (1, 2): 1 shirt and 2 pairs of pants (answers may vary)

CHAPTER 4   TEST

Determine whether the given ordered pair is a solution of the given system.

1. $(5, 3)$, $\begin{cases} 3x + 2y = 21 \\ x + y = 8 \end{cases}$ yes

2. $(-2, -1)$, $\begin{cases} 4x + y = -9 \\ 2x - 3y = -7 \end{cases}$ no

3. Solve the system by graphing: $\begin{cases} 3x + y = 7 \\ x - 2y = 0 \end{cases}$ $(2, 1)$

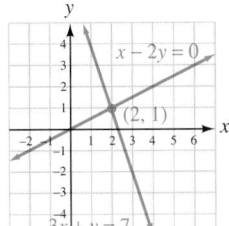

4. To solve a system of two linear equations in x and y, a student used a graphing calculator. From the calculator display shown, determine whether the system has a solution. Explain your answer.

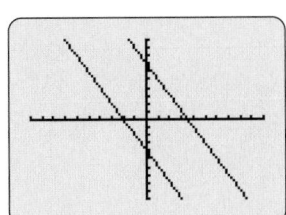

The lines appear to be parallel. Since the lines do not intersect, the system does not have a solution.

Solve each system by substitution.

5. $\begin{cases} y = x - 1 \\ 2x + y = -7 \end{cases}$ $(-2, -3)$

6. $\begin{cases} 3a + 4b = -7 \\ 2b - a = -1 \end{cases}$ $(-1, -1)$

Solve each system by addition (elimination).

7. $\begin{cases} 3x - y = 2 \\ 2x + y = 8 \end{cases}$ $(2, 4)$

8. $\begin{cases} 4x + 3y = -3 \\ -3x = -4y + 21 \end{cases}$ $(-3, 3)$

Classify each system as consistent or inconsistent, and classify the equations as dependent or independent.

9. $\begin{cases} x + y = 4 \\ x + y = 6 \end{cases}$

inconsistent, independent equations

10. $\begin{cases} \dfrac{x}{3} + y = 4 \\ x + 3y = 12 \end{cases}$

consistent, dependent equations

11. Which method would be most efficient to solve the following system?

$$\begin{cases} 5x - 3y = 5 \\ 3x + 3y = 3 \end{cases}$$

Explain your answer. (You do not need to solve the system.)

Addition method; the coefficients of y are already opposites.

12. FINANCIAL PLANNING A woman invested
some money at 8% and some at 9%. The interest for
1 year on the combined investment of $10,000 was
$840. How much was invested at 9%? Use a system
of equations in two variables to solve this
problem. $4,000

*Refer to the following illustration to answer problems 14 and 15.
The graph shows two different ways in which a salesperson can
be paid according to the number of items he or she sells.*

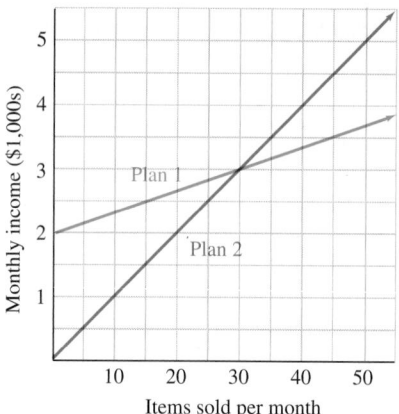

13. Solve the system by graphing: $\begin{cases} 2x + 3y \le 6 \\ x \ge 2 \end{cases}$

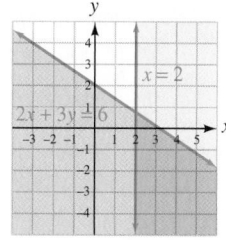

14. What is the point of intersection of the graphs?
Explain its significance.
(30, 3); if 30 items are sold, the salesperson gets paid the same
by both plans, $3,000.

15. If a salesperson expects to sell more than 30 items per
month, which plan is more profitable? Plan 2

1. **SPORTS CARS** The graph shows the Porsche vehicle sales in the United States for the years 1986–2005.

   a. In what year were sales the lowest?
   [Section 1.1] 1993

   b. In what year were sales the greatest?
   [Section 1.1] 2005

Porsche vehicle sales in U.S.

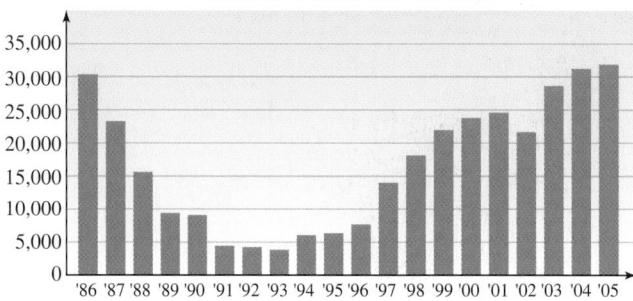

Source: Porsche Cars North America

2. Give the prime factorization of 100. [Section 1.2] $2^2 \cdot 5^2$

3. Divide: $\dfrac{3}{4} \div \dfrac{6}{5}$ [Section 1.2] $\frac{5}{8}$

4. Subtract: $\dfrac{7}{10} - \dfrac{1}{14}$ [Section 1.2] $\frac{22}{35}$

5. Is π a rational or irrational number?
   [Section 1.3] irrational

6. Graph each member of the set on the number line.
   [Section 1.3]

   $$\left\{ -2\frac{1}{4},\ \sqrt{2},\ -1.75,\ \frac{7}{2},\ 0.5 \right\}$$

7. Write $\dfrac{2}{3}$ as a decimal. [Section 1.3] $0.\overline{6}$

8. What property of real numbers is illustrated?
   [Section 1.6] associative property of multiplication

   $$3(2x) = (3 \cdot 2)x$$

Evaluate each expression.

9. $-3^2 + |4^2 - 5^2|$ [Section 1.7] 0

10. $(4 - 5)^{20}$ [Section 1.7] 1

11. $\dfrac{-3 - (-7)}{2^2 - 3}$ [Section 1.7] 4

12. $12 - 2[1 - (-8 + 2)]$ [Section 1.7] -2

13. **RACING** Suppose a driver has completed x laps of a 250-lap race. Write an expression for how many more laps he must make to finish the race.
    [Section 1.8] $250 - x$

14. What is the value of d dimes? [Section 1.8] $10d$ cents

Simplify each expression.

15. $13r - 12r$ [Section 1.9] r

16. $27\left(\dfrac{2}{3}x\right)$ [Section 1.9] $18x$

17. $4(d - 3) - (d - 1)$ [Section 1.9] $3d - 11$

18. $(13c - 3)(-6)$ [Section 1.9] $-78c + 18$

Solve each equation. Check each result.

19. $3(x - 5) + 2 = 2x$ [Section 2.2] 13

20. $\dfrac{x - 5}{3} - 5 = 7$ [Section 2.2] 41

21. $\dfrac{2}{5}x + 1 = \dfrac{1}{3} + x$ [Section 2.2] $\frac{10}{9}$

22. $-\dfrac{5}{8}h = 15$ [Section 2.2] -24

23. **GYMNASTICS** After the first day of registration, 119 children had been enrolled in a Gymboree class. That represented 85% of the available slots. Find the maximum number of children the center could enroll.
    [Section 2.3] 140

24. Solve $A = \dfrac{1}{2}h(b + B)$ for h. [Section 2.4] $h = \frac{2A}{b + B}$

25. **MIXING CANDY** The owner of a candy store wants to make a 30-pound mixture of two candies to sell for $4 per pound. If red licorice bits sell for $3.80 per pound and lemon gumdrops sell for $4.40 per pound, how many pounds of each should be used?
    [Section 2.6] 20 lb of $3.80 candy, 10 lb of $4.40 candy

26. Solve $8(4 + x) > 10(6 + x)$. Write the solution set in interval notation and graph it. [Section 2.7] $(-\infty, -14)$

    -14

27. In what quadrant does $(-3.5, 6)$ lie? [Section 3.1] II

28. Is $(-2, 8)$ a solution of $y = -2x + 3$? [Section 3.2] no

Graph each equation.

29. $x = 4$ [Section 3.3] **30.** $4x - 3y = 12$ [Section 3.3]

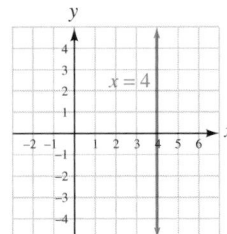
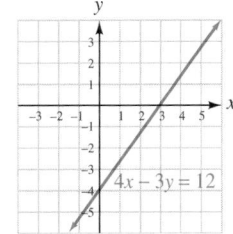

Find the slope of the line with the given properties.

31. Passing through $(-2, 4)$ and $(6, 8)$ [Section 3.4] $\frac{1}{2}$

32. A line that is horizontal [Section 3.4] 0

33. An equation of $2x - 3y = 12$ [Section 3.5] $\frac{2}{3}$

34. Are the graphs of the lines parallel or perpendicular?
[Section 3.5] perpendicular

$$y = -\frac{3}{4}x + \frac{15}{4} \qquad 4x - 3y = 25$$

Find an equation of the line with the following properties. Write the equation in slope–intercept form.

35. Slope $= \frac{2}{3}$, y-intercept $= (0, 5)$ [Section 3.5]

$y = \frac{2}{3}x + 5$

36. Passing through $(-2, 4)$ and $(6, 10)$ [Section 3.6]

$y = \frac{3}{4}x + \frac{11}{2}$

37. A horizontal line passing through $(2, 4)$ [Section 3.6]

$y = 4$

38. Graph: $y < \frac{x}{3} - 1$ [Section 3.7]

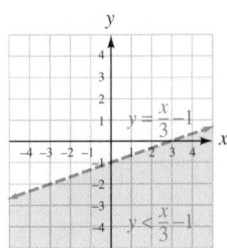

39. If $f(x) = -2x^2 - 3x^3$, find $f(-1)$. [Section 3.8] 1

40. Is this the graph of a function? [Section 3.8] no

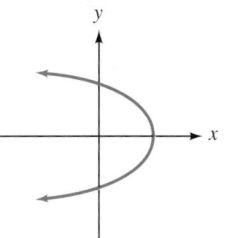

Solve each system by graphing.

41. $\begin{cases} x + 4y = -2 \\ y = -x - 5 \end{cases}$ [Section 4.1] $(-6, 1)$

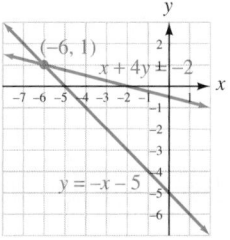

42. $\begin{cases} 2x - 3y < 0 \\ y > x - 1 \end{cases}$ [Section 4.5]

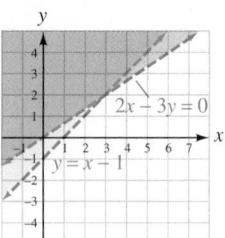

43. Solve $\begin{cases} x - 2y = 2 \\ 2x + 3y = 11 \end{cases}$ by substitution.

[Section 4.2] $(4, 1)$

44. NUTRITION The table shows per serving nutritional information for egg noodles and rice pilaf. How many servings of each food should be eaten to consume exactly 22 grams of protein and 21 grams of fat? [Section 4.4] noodles: 2 servings, rice: 3 servings

	Protein (g)	Fat (g)
Egg noodles	5	3
Rice pilaf	4	5

Exponents and Polynomials

© Robert E. Daemmrich/Getty Images

from *Campus to Careers*

Police Officer

People depend on the police to protect their lives and property. The job can be dangerous because police officers must arrest suspects and respond to emergencies. The daily activities of police officers can vary greatly depending on their specialty, such as patrol officer, game warden, or detective. Regardless of their duties, they must write reports and maintain records that will be needed if they testify in court.

In **Problem 80** of **Study Set 5.4,** you will see how police officers can compute the stopping distance of a car.

JOB TITLE:
Police Officer

EDUCATION: For many departments, two years of college or a college degree may be required. Physical education courses are helpful. Foreign language skills are desirable.

JOB OUTLOOK: Excellent—employment opportunities are expected to grow 11 percent through 2016.

ANNUAL EARNINGS: Median annual salary in 2007 was $50,330. Earnings often exceed their salary because of payments for overtime.

FOR MORE INFORMATION:
www.bls.gov/oco/ocos160.htm

Objectives

1 Identify bases and exponents.

2 Multiply exponential expressions that have like bases.

3 Divide exponential expressions that have like bases.

4 Raise exponential expressions to a power.

5 Find powers of products and quotients.

SECTION **5.1**

Natural-Number Exponents; Rules for Exponents

In this section, we will use the definition of exponent to develop some rules for simplifying expressions that contain exponents.

1 Identify bases and exponents.

We have used natural-number exponents to indicate repeated multiplication. For example,

$$9^2 = 9 \cdot 9 = 81 \qquad \text{Write 9 as a factor 2 times.}$$
$$7^3 = 7 \cdot 7 \cdot 7 = 343 \qquad \text{Write 7 as a factor 3 times.}$$
$$(-2)^4 = (-2)(-2)(-2)(-2) = 16 \qquad \text{Write } -2 \text{ as a factor 4 times.}$$
$$-2^4 = -(2 \cdot 2 \cdot 2 \cdot 2) = -16 \qquad \text{The } - \text{ sign in front of } 2^4 \text{ means the opposite of } 2^4.$$

These examples illustrate a definition for x^n, where n is a natural number.

Natural-Number Exponents

A natural-number exponent tells how many times its base is to be used as a factor. For any number x and any natural number n,

$$x^n = \overbrace{x \cdot x \cdot x \cdot \,\cdots\, \cdot x}^{n \text{ factors of } x}$$

In the **exponential expression** x^n, x is called the **base** and n is called the **exponent.** The entire expression is called a **power of x.**

$$\text{base} \rightarrow x^n \leftarrow \text{exponent}$$

If an exponent is a natural number, it tells how many times its base is to be used as a factor. An exponent of 1 indicates that its base is to be used one time as a factor, an exponent of 2 indicates that its base is to be used two times as a factor, and so on. The base of an exponential expression can be a number, a variable, or a combination of numbers and variables.

$$x^1 = x \qquad (y + 1)^2 = (y + 1)(y + 1) \qquad (-5s)^3 = (-5s)(-5s)(-5s)$$

Self Check 1

Identify the base and the exponent:

a. $5x^4$ base: x, exponent: 4
b. $(5x)^4$ base: $5x$, exponent: 4

Now Try Problems **25, 26, and 31**

Teaching Example 1 Identify the base and the exponent in each expression:
a. 12^3 **b.** $7x^{10}$
c. -4^3 **d.** $(7x)^9$
Answers:
a. base: 12, exponent: 3
b. base: x, exponent: 10
c. base: 4, exponent: 3
d. base: $7x$, exponent: 9

EXAMPLE 1   Identify the base and the exponent in each expression:

a. 7^6 **b.** $4x^3$ **c.** $-x^5$ **d.** $(2x)^4$

Strategy To identify the base and exponent, we will look for the exponent first. Then we will look for the base. We will report the base first, then the exponent.

WHY The exponent is the small raised number. The base is the number or variable directly in front of the exponent, unless there are parentheses.

Solution

a. In 7^6, the base is 7 and the exponent is 6.

b. $4x^3$ means $4 \cdot x^3$. The base is x and the exponent is 3.

c. $-x^5$ means $-1 \cdot x^5$. The base is x and the exponent is 5.

d. Because of the parentheses in $(2x)^4$, the base is $2x$ and the exponent is 4.

EXAMPLE 2   Write each expression in an equivalent form using an exponent:

a. $\dfrac{x}{5} \cdot \dfrac{x}{5} \cdot \dfrac{x}{5} \cdot \dfrac{x}{5}$ **b.** $4 \cdot y \cdot y \cdot y \cdot y \cdot y$

Strategy We will look for repeated factors and count the number of times each appears.

WHY We can use an exponent to represent repeated multiplication.

Solution

a. Since there are four repeated factors of $\dfrac{x}{5}$ in $\dfrac{x}{5} \cdot \dfrac{x}{5} \cdot \dfrac{x}{5} \cdot \dfrac{x}{5}$, the expression can be

written as $\left(\dfrac{x}{5}\right)^4$.

b. Since there are 5 repeated factors of y, the expression can be written $4y^5$. ∎

2 Multiply exponential expressions that have like bases.

To develop a rule for multiplying exponential expressions that have the same base, we consider the product $x^2 \cdot x^3$. Since the expression x^2 means that x is to be used as a factor two times, and the expression x^3 means that x is to be used as a factor three times, we have

$$x^2 \cdot x^3 = \overbrace{x \cdot x}^{2 \text{ factors of } x} \cdot \overbrace{x \cdot x \cdot x}^{3 \text{ factors of } x}$$

$$= \overbrace{x \cdot x \cdot x \cdot x \cdot x}^{5 \text{ factors of } x}$$

$$= x^5$$

This example suggests the following rule:

Product Rule for Exponents

To multiply two exponential expressions that have the same base, keep the common base and add the exponents. If m and n represent natural numbers, then

$$x^m x^n = x^{m+n}$$

EXAMPLE 3   Simplify each expression:

a. $9^5(9^6)$ **b.** $x^3 \cdot x^4$ **c.** $y^2 y^4 y$ **d.** $(c^2 d^3)(c^4 d^5)$ **e.** $(a + b)^4 (a + b)^3$

Strategy We will identify exponential expressions that have the same base in each product. Then we will use the product rule for exponents to simplify the expression.

WHY The product rule for exponents is used to multiply exponential expressions that have the same base.

Solution

a. To simplify $9^5(9^6)$ means to write it in an equivalent form using one base and one exponent.

$$9^5(9^6) = 9^{5+6} \quad \text{Use the product rule for exponents: Keep the common base, which is 9, and add the exponents.}$$

$$= 9^{11} \quad \text{Perform the addition. Since } 9^{11} \text{ is a very large number, we will leave it in this form. We won't evaluate it.}$$

Self Check 2

Write as an exponential expression: $(a + b)(a + b)$ $(a + b)(a + b)(a + b)(a + b)$

Now Try Problems 33, 38, and 44

Self Check 2 Answer

$(a + b)^6$

Teaching Example 2 Write each expression in an equivalent form using an exponent:
a. $3x \cdot 3x \cdot 3x \cdot 3x$
b. $3 \cdot x \cdot x \cdot x \cdot x$
Answers:
a. $(3x)^4$ **b.** $3x^4$

Self Check 3

Simplify:
a. $7^8(7^7)$ 7^{15}
b. $z \cdot z^3$ z^4
c. $x^2 x^3 x^6$ x^{11}
d. $(s^4 t^3)(s^4 t^4)$ $s^8 t^7$
e. $(r + s)^2 (r + s)^5$ $(r + s)^7$

Now Try Problems 45, 50, 57, and 60

Teaching Example 3 Simplify:
a. $5^3(5^6)$ **b.** $a^3 \cdot a$ **c.** $y^2 y^3 y^5$
d. $(x^3 y^2)(x^4 y^3)$ **e.** $(a + b)^2 (a + b)^4$
Answers:
a. 5^9 **b.** a^4 **c.** y^{10}
d. $x^7 y^5$ **e.** $(a + b)^6$

b. $x^3 \cdot x^4 = x^{3+4}$ Keep the common base x and add the exponents.

$\quad\quad = x^7$ Perform the addition.

c. $y^2y^4y = y^{2+4}y$ Working from left to right, keep the common base y and add the exponents.

$\quad\quad = y^6y$ Perform the addition.

$\quad\quad = y^{6+1}$ Keep the common base and add the exponents.

$\quad\quad = y^7$ Perform the addition.

d. $(c^2d^3)(c^4d^5) = c^2d^3c^4d^5$ Use the associative property of multiplication.

$\quad\quad = c^2c^4d^3d^5$ Change the order of the factors.

$\quad\quad = c^{2+4}d^{3+5}$ Keep the common base c and add the exponents. Keep the common base d and add the exponents.

$\quad\quad = c^6d^8$ Perform the additions.

e. $(a + b)^4(a + b)^3 = (a + b)^{4+3}$ Keep the common base $(a + b)$ and add the exponents.

$\quad\quad = (a + b)^7$ Perform the addition.

Caution!   We cannot use the product rule to simplify expressions like $3^2 \cdot 2^3$, where the bases are not the same. However, we can simplify this expression by doing the arithmetic: $3^2 \cdot 2^3 = 9 \cdot 8 = 72$.

THINK IT THROUGH   *PIN Code Choices*

"According to a Student Monitor LLC survey, ATM debit card ownership among college students has almost doubled from 30 percent to 57 percent in the past four years."

BYU Newsletter, Oct 2002

In 2002, there were 13.9 billion ATM transactions in the United States. On average, that's more than 38 million a day! Before each transaction, the card owner is required to enter his or her PIN (personal identification number). When an ATM card is issued, many financial institutions have the applicant select a four-digit PIN. There are 10 possible choices for the first digit of the PIN, 10 possible choices for the second digit, and so on. Write the total number of possible choices of a PIN as an exponential expression. Then evaluate the expression. $10^4 = 10,000$

---

3 **Divide exponential expressions that have like bases.**

To develop a rule for dividing exponential expressions that have the same base, we now consider the fraction

$$\frac{4^5}{4^2}$$

where the exponent in the numerator is greater than the exponent in the denominator.

We can simplify this fraction as follows:

$$\frac{4^5}{4^2} = \frac{4 \cdot 4 \cdot 4 \cdot 4 \cdot 4}{4 \cdot 4}$$ Write each expression without using exponents.

$$= \frac{\overset{1}{\cancel{4}} \cdot \overset{1}{\cancel{4}} \cdot 4 \cdot 4 \cdot 4}{\underset{1}{\cancel{4}} \cdot \underset{1}{\cancel{4}}}$$ Remove the common factors of 4.

$$= 4^3$$

We can quickly find this result if we keep the common base 4, and subtract the exponents on 4^5 and 4^2.

$$\frac{4^5}{4^2} = 4^{5-2} = 4^3$$

This example suggests another rule for exponents.

Quotient Rule for Exponents

To divide exponential expressions that have the same base, keep the common base and subtract the exponents. If m and n represent natural numbers, $m > n$, and $x \neq 0$, then

$$\frac{x^m}{x^n} = x^{m-n}$$

EXAMPLE 4   Simplify. Assume that there are no divisions by 0.

a. $\dfrac{20^{16}}{20^9}$ **b.** $\dfrac{x^4}{x^3}$ **c.** $\dfrac{a^3 b^8}{a b^5}$

Strategy We will identify exponential expressions that have the same base in each quotient. Then we will use the quotient rule for exponents to simplify the expression.

WHY The quotient rule for exponents is used to divide exponential expressions that have the same base.

Solution

a. To simplify $\dfrac{20^{16}}{20^9}$ means to write it in an equivalent form using one base and one exponent.

$$\frac{20^{16}}{20^9} = 20^{16-9}$$ Use the quotient rule for exponents: Keep the common base, which is 20, and subtract the exponents.

$$= 20^7$$ Perform the subtraction.

b. $\dfrac{x^4}{x^3} = x^{4-3}$ Keep the common base x and subtract the exponents.

$$= x^1$$ Perform the subtraction.

$$= x$$

c. $\dfrac{a^3 b^8}{a b^5} = \dfrac{a^3}{a} \cdot \dfrac{b^8}{b^5}$ Group the like bases together. Write a as a^1.

$$= a^{3-1} b^{8-5}$$ Keep the common base a and subtract the exponents. Keep the common base b and subtract the exponents.

$$= a^2 b^3$$ Perform the subtractions.

Self Check 4

Simplify:

a. $\dfrac{55^{30}}{55^5}$ 55^{25}

b. $\dfrac{a^5}{a^3}$ a^2

c. $\dfrac{b^{15} c^4}{b^4 c}$ $b^{11} c^3$

Now Try Problems 62, 65, and 70

Teaching Example 4 Simplify:

a. $\dfrac{13^{11}}{13^2}$ **b.** $\dfrac{x^8}{x^2}$ **c.** $\dfrac{y^4 z^9}{y z^7}$

Answers:

a. 13^9 **b.** x^6 **c.** $y^3 z^2$

> **Caution!** Don't make the mistake of dividing the bases when using the quotient rule. Keep the *same* base and subtract the *exponents*.
>
> $$\frac{20^{16}}{20^9} \neq 1^7$$

EXAMPLE 5   Simplify: $\dfrac{a^3 a^5 a^7}{a^4 a}$

Strategy We will use the product rule and quotient rule to write an equivalent expression using one base and one exponent.

WHY The expression involves multiplication and division of exponential expressions that have the same base.

Solution

We use the product rule for exponents to simplify the numerator and denominator separately and proceed as follows.

$$\frac{a^3 a^5 a^7}{a^4 a} = \frac{a^{15}}{a^5}$$ In the numerator, keep the common base a and add the exponents. In the denominator, keep the common base a and add the exponents.

$$= a^{15-5}$$ Use the quotient rule for exponents: Keep the common base a and subtract the exponents.

$$= a^{10}$$ Perform the subtraction.

> **Success Tip** Sometimes more than one rule for exponents is needed to simplify an expression.

It is important to pay close attention to the operation between the exponential expressions and then use the appropriate rules. To add or subtract exponential expressions, they must be like terms. To multiply or divide exponential expressions, only the bases need to be the same.

$x^2 + x^3$ The operation is addition and these are not like terms because the exponents are different. We cannot simplify the expression any further.

$x^4 + x^4 = 2x^4$ The operation is addition and these are like terms. We can simplify the expression by adding the numerical coefficients and keeping the variable expression.

$x^7 \cdot x^3 = x^{10}$ The operation is multiplication and the bases are the same. We keep the base and add the exponents.

$\dfrac{x^4}{x^3} = x$ The operation is division and the bases are the same. We keep the base and subtract the exponents. An exponent of 1 need not be written.

4   **Raise exponential expressions to a power.**

To find another rule for exponents, we consider the expression $(x^3)^4$, which can be written as $x^3 \cdot x^3 \cdot x^3 \cdot x^3$. Because each of the four factors of x^3 contains three factors of x, there are $4 \cdot 3$ (or 12) factors of x. This product can be written as x^{12}.

$$(x^3)^4 = x^3 \cdot x^3 \cdot x^3 \cdot x^3$$

$$= \overbrace{x \cdot x \cdot x}^{x^3} \cdot \underbrace{x \cdot x \cdot x}_{x^3} \cdot \underbrace{x \cdot x \cdot x}_{x^3} \cdot \underbrace{x \cdot x \cdot x}_{x^3}$$

12 factors of x

$$= x^{12}$$

We can quickly find this result if we keep the base of x and multiply the exponents.

$$(x^3)^4 = x^{3 \cdot 4} = x^{12}$$

This illustrates the following rule for exponents:

Power Rule for Exponents

To raise an exponential expression to a power, keep the base and multiply the exponents. If m and n represent natural numbers, then

$$(x^m)^n = x^{m \cdot n} \qquad \text{or, more simply,} \qquad (x^m)^n = x^{mn}$$

EXAMPLE 6   Simplify each expression: **a.** $(2^3)^7$ **b.** $(z^8)^8$

Strategy In each case, we want to write an equivalent expression using one base and one exponent. We will use the power rule for exponents to do this.

WHY Each expression is a power of a power.

Solution

a. To simplify $(2^3)^7$ means to write it in an equivalent form using one base and one exponent.

$$(2^3)^7 = 2^{3 \cdot 7} \quad \text{Keep the base of 2 and multiply the exponents.}$$

$$= 2^{21} \quad \text{Perform the multiplication.}$$

b. $(z^8)^8 = z^{8 \cdot 8} \quad \text{Keep the base and multiply the exponents.}$

$$= z^{64} \quad \text{Perform the multiplication.}$$

Self Check 6

Simplify each expression:
a. $(5^4)^6$ 5^{24}
b. $(y^5)^2$ y^{10}

Now Try Problems 78 and 84

Teaching Example 6 Simplify:
a. $(7^3)^2$ **b.** $(a^4)^5$
Answers:
a. 7^6 **b.** a^{20}

EXAMPLE 7   Simplify each expression: **a.** $(x^2x^5)^2$ **b.** $(z^2)^4(z^3)^3$

Strategy In each case, we want to write an equivalent expression using one base and one exponent. We will use the product and power rules for exponents to do this.

WHY The expressions involve products and powers of exponential expressions that have the same base.

Solution

a. We begin by using the product rule for exponents. Then we use the power rule.

$$(x^2x^5)^2 = (x^7)^2 \quad \text{Within the parentheses, keep the base } x \text{ and add the exponents.}$$

$$= x^{14} \quad \text{Keep the base } x \text{ and multiply the exponents.}$$

Self Check 7

Simplify each expression:
a. $(a^4a^3)^3$ a^{21}
b. $(a^3)^3(a^4)^2$ a^{17}

Now Try Problems 86 and 90

Teaching Example 7 Simplify each expression:
a. $(r^2r^3)^4$ **b.** $(b^2)^5(b^3)^2$
Answers:
a. r^{20} **b.** b^{16}

b. We begin by using the power rule for exponents twice. Then we use the product rule.

$$(z^2)^4(z^3)^3 = z^8 z^9 \qquad \text{For each power of } z \text{ raised to a power, keep the base } z \text{ and multiply the exponents.}$$

$$= z^{17} \qquad \text{Keep the base } z \text{ and add the exponents.}$$

5 Find powers of products and quotients.

To develop two more rules for exponents, we consider the expression $(2x)^3$, which is a *power of the product* of 2 and x, and the expression $\left(\frac{2}{x}\right)^3$, which is a *power of the quotient* of 2 and x.

$$(2x)^3 = (2x)(2x)(2x) \qquad \left(\frac{2}{x}\right)^3 = \left(\frac{2}{x}\right)\left(\frac{2}{x}\right)\left(\frac{2}{x}\right) \qquad \text{Assume } x \neq 0$$

$$= (2 \cdot 2 \cdot 2)(x \cdot x \cdot x) \qquad = \frac{2 \cdot 2 \cdot 2}{x \cdot x \cdot x} \qquad \text{Multiply the numerators.}$$
$$\qquad\qquad\qquad\qquad\qquad\qquad\qquad\qquad \text{Multiply the denominators.}$$

$$= 2^3 x^3$$
$$= 8x^3 \qquad\qquad\qquad\qquad\quad = \frac{2^3}{x^3}$$

$$\qquad\qquad\qquad\qquad\qquad\qquad\quad = \frac{8}{x^3} \qquad \text{Evaluate: } 2^3 = 8.$$

These examples illustrate the following rules for exponents:

Powers of a Product and a Quotient

To raise a product to a power, we raise each factor of the product to that power. To raise a fraction to a power, we raise both the numerator and the denominator to that power. If n represents a natural number, then

$$(xy)^n = x^n y^n \qquad \text{and if} \qquad y \neq 0, \qquad \text{then} \qquad \left(\frac{x}{y}\right)^n = \frac{x^n}{y^n}$$

Self Check 8

Simplify:
a. $(2t)^4$ $\quad 16t^4$
b. $(c^3 d^4)^6$ $\quad c^{18} d^{24}$
c. $(-3ab^5)^3$ $\quad -27a^3 b^{15}$

Now Try Problems 94, 96, and 99

Teaching Example 8 Simplify:
a. $(5x)^3$ **b.** $(a^4 b^3)^3$ **c.** $(-4a^5 b^3)^2$
Answers:
a. $125x^3$ **b.** $a^{12}b^9$ **c.** $16a^{10}b^6$

EXAMPLE 8 Simplify: **a.** $(3c)^3$ **b.** $(x^2 y^3)^5$ **c.** $(-2a^3 b)^2$

Strategy We will use the power of a product rule for exponents to write the simplified expression.

WHY Within each set of parentheses is a product, and each of those products is raised to a power.

Solution

a. Since $3c$ is the product of 3 and c, the expression $(3c)^3$ is a power of a product.

$$(3c)^3 = 3^3 c^3 \qquad \text{Use the power rule for products: Raise each factor of the product } 3c \text{ to the 3rd power.}$$

$$= 27c^3 \qquad \text{Evaluate: } 3^3 = 27.$$

b. $(x^2 y^3)^5 = (x^2)^5 (y^3)^5 \qquad \text{Raise each factor of the product } x^2 y^3 \text{ to the 5th power.}$

$$= x^{10} y^{15} \qquad \text{For each power of a power, keep the base and multiply the exponents.}$$

c. $(-2a^3 b)^2 = (-2)^2 (a^3)^2 b^2 \qquad \text{Raise each of the three factors of the product } -2a^3 b \text{ to the 2nd power.}$

$$= 4a^6 b^2 \qquad \text{Evaluate: } (-2)^2 = 4. \text{ Keep the base } a \text{ and multiply the exponents.}$$

EXAMPLE 9   Simplify: $\dfrac{(a^3b^4)^2}{ab^5}$

Strategy We will use the power of a product rule and the quotient rule for exponents to write the simplified expression.

WHY The expression involves a power of a product and a quotient of exponential expressions that have the same base.

Solution

$$\dfrac{(a^3b^4)^2}{ab^5} = \dfrac{(a^3)^2(b^4)^2}{ab^5} \qquad \text{In the numerator, raise each factor within the parentheses to the 2nd power.}$$

$$= \dfrac{a^6b^8}{ab^5} \qquad \text{In the numerator, for each power of a power, keep the base and multiply the exponents.}$$

$$= a^{6-1}b^{8-5} \qquad \text{Keep each of the bases, } a \text{ and } b, \text{ and subtract the exponents.}$$

$$= a^5b^3 \qquad \text{Perform the subtractions.}$$

Self Check 9

Simplify: $\dfrac{(c^4d^5)^3}{c^2d^3}$ $c^{10}d^{12}$

Now Try Problem 101

Teaching Example 9 Simplify:
$\dfrac{(5x^3y^4)^2}{x^2y^3}$
Answer:
$25x^4y^5$

EXAMPLE 10   Simplify: **a.** $\left(\dfrac{4}{k}\right)^3$ **b.** $\left(\dfrac{3x^2}{2y^3}\right)^5$

Strategy In each case, we will use the power of a quotient rule for exponents to simplify the expression.

WHY Each expression is a quotient raised to a power.

Solution

a. Since $\dfrac{4}{k}$ is the quotient of 4 and k, the expresion $\left(\dfrac{4}{k}\right)^3$ is a power of a quotient.

$$\left(\dfrac{4}{k}\right)^3 = \dfrac{4^3}{k^3} \qquad \text{Use the power rule for quotients: Raise the numerator and denominator to the 3rd power.}$$

$$= \dfrac{64}{k^3} \qquad \text{Evaluate: } 4^3 = 64.$$

b. $\left(\dfrac{3x^2}{2y^3}\right)^5 = \dfrac{(3x^2)^5}{(2y^3)^5} \qquad \text{Raise the numerator and the denominator to the 5th power.}$

$$= \dfrac{3^5(x^2)^5}{2^5(y^3)^5} \qquad \text{In the numerator and denominator, raise each factor within the parentheses to the 5th power.}$$

$$= \dfrac{243x^{10}}{32y^{15}} \qquad \text{Evaluate } 3^5 \text{ and } 2^5. \text{ For each power of a power, keep the base and multiply the exponents.}$$

Self Check 10

Simplify:

a. $\left(\dfrac{x}{7}\right)^3$ $\dfrac{x^3}{343}$

b. $\left(\dfrac{2x^3}{3y^2}\right)^4$ $\dfrac{16x^{12}}{81y^8}$

Now Try Problems 106 and 107

Teaching Example 10 Simplify:
a. $\left(\dfrac{a}{3}\right)^4$ **b.** $\left(\dfrac{5x^3}{3y^4}\right)^3$
Answers:
a. $\dfrac{a^4}{81}$ **b.** $\dfrac{125x^9}{27y^{12}}$

EXAMPLE 11   Simplify: $\dfrac{(5b)^9}{(5b)^6}$

Strategy We will use the quotient rule for exponents and then the power of a product rule.

WHY The expression involves division of exponential expressions that have the same base, $5b$.

Solution

$$\dfrac{(5b)^9}{(5b)^6} = (5b)^{9-6} \qquad \text{Keep the common base } 5b, \text{ and subtract the exponents.}$$

$$= (5b)^3 \qquad \text{Perform the subtraction.}$$

$$= 5^3b^3 \qquad \text{Raise each factor within the parentheses to the 3rd power.}$$

$$= 125b^3 \qquad \text{Evaluate: } 5^3 = 125.$$

Self Check 11

Simplify: $\dfrac{(-2h)^{20}}{(-2h)^{14}}$ $64h^6$

Now Try Problem 109

Teaching Example 11 Simplify: $\dfrac{(3x)^5}{(3x)^2}$
Answer:
$27x^3$

The rules for natural-number exponents are summarized below.

Rules for Exponents

If n represents a natural number, then

$$x^n = \overbrace{x \cdot x \cdot x \cdot \,\cdots\, \cdot x}^{n \text{ factors of } x}$$

If m and n represent natural numbers and there are no divisions by zero, then

Exponent of 1	**Product Rule**	**Quotient Rule**
$x^1 = x$	$x^m x^n = x^{m+n}$	$\dfrac{x^m}{x^n} = x^{m-n}$

Power Rule	**Power of a Product**	**Power of a Quotient**
$(x^m)^n = x^{mn}$	$(xy)^n = x^n y^n$	$\left(\dfrac{x}{y}\right)^n = \dfrac{x^n}{y^n}$

ANSWERS TO SELF CHECKS

1. a. base: x, exponent: 4   **b.** base: $5x$, exponent: 4   **2.** $(a + b)^6$ **3. a.** 7^{15} **b.** z^4
c. x^{11} **d.** $s^8 t^7$ **e.** $(r + s)^7$ **4. a.** 55^{25} **b.** a^2 **c.** $b^{11}c^3$ **5.** b **6. a.** 5^{24} **b.** y^{10}
7. a. a^{21} **b.** a^{17} **8. a.** $16t^4$ **b.** $c^{18}d^{24}$ **c.** $-27a^3b^{15}$ **9.** $c^{10}d^{12}$ **10. a.** $\frac{x^3}{343}$ **b.** $\frac{16x^{12}}{81y^8}$
11. $64h^6$

SECTION 5.1   STUDY SET

VOCABULARY

Fill in the blanks.

1. The _base_ of the exponential expression $(-5)^3$ is -5. The _exponent_ is 3.

▶ 2. The exponential expression x^4 represents a repeated multiplication where x is to be written as a _factor_ four times.

3. x^n is called a _power_ of x.

4. The expression $(2x^2 b)^5$ is a power of a _product_, and $\left(\dfrac{2x^2}{b}\right)^5$ is a power of a _quotient_.

CONCEPTS

Fill in the blanks.

5. $(3x)^4$ means $3x \cdot 3x \cdot 3x \cdot 3x$

6. Using an exponent, $(-5y)(-5y)(-5y)$ can be written as $(-5y)^3$.

▶ 7. $x^m x^n = x^{m+n}$ ▶ 8. $(xy)^n = x^n y^n$

▶ 9. $\left(\dfrac{a}{b}\right)^n = \dfrac{a^n}{b^n}$ ▶ 10. $(a^b)^c = a^{bc}$

▶ Selected exercises available online at
www.webassign.net/brookscole

▶ 11. $\dfrac{x^m}{x^n} = x^{m-n}$ ▶ 12. $x = x^1$

13. $(x^m)^n = x^{mn}$ 14. $(t^3)^2 = t^3 \cdot t^3$

15. Write a power of a product that has two factors. $(3x^2)^6$ (answers may vary)

16. Write a power of a quotient. $\left(\dfrac{3a^3}{b}\right)^2$ (answers may vary)

17. To simplify $(2y^3 z^2)^4$, how many factors within the parentheses must be raised to the fourth power? 3

18. To simplify $\left(\dfrac{y^3}{z^2}\right)^4$ what two expressions must be raised to the fourth power? y^3 and z^2

NOTATION

Complete each solution.

19. $(x^4 x^2)^3 = \left(x^6\right)^3$
$ = x^{18}$

▶ 20. $\dfrac{a^3 a^4}{a^2} = \dfrac{a^7}{a^2}$
$\phantom{\dfrac{a^3 a^4}{a^2}} = a^{7-2}$
$\phantom{\dfrac{a^3 a^4}{a^2}} = a^5$

Evaluate each expression.

21. $(-4)^2$ 16

▶ **22.** $(-5)^2$ 25

23. -4^2 -16

▶ **24.** -5^2 -25

❚ GUIDED PRACTICE

Identify the base and the exponent in each expression.
See Example 1.

25. 4^3
    base 4, exponent 3

26. $(-8)^2$
    base -8, exponent 2

27. x^5
    base x, exponent 5

28. $\left(\dfrac{5}{x}\right)^3$
    base $\dfrac{5}{x}$, exponent 3

29. $(-3x)^2$
    base $-3x$, exponent 2

▶ **30.** $-x^4$
    base x, exponent 4

31. $-\dfrac{1}{3}y^6$
    base y, exponent 6

▶ **32.** $3.14r^4$
    base r, exponent 4

Write each expression in an equivalent form using an exponent.
See Example 2.

33. $\dfrac{a}{3} \cdot \dfrac{a}{3} \cdot \dfrac{a}{3}$
    $\left(\dfrac{a}{3}\right)^3$

34. $\dfrac{y}{4} \cdot \dfrac{y}{4} \cdot \dfrac{y}{4} \cdot \dfrac{y}{4}$
    $\left(\dfrac{y}{4}\right)^4$

35. $-\dfrac{b}{6} \cdot \dfrac{b}{6} \cdot \dfrac{b}{6} \cdot \dfrac{b}{6} \cdot \dfrac{b}{6}$
    $-\left(\dfrac{b}{6}\right)^5$

▶ **36.** $-\dfrac{c}{5} \cdot \dfrac{c}{5} \cdot \dfrac{c}{5}$
    $-\left(\dfrac{c}{5}\right)^3$

37. $6 \cdot x \cdot x \cdot x \cdot x \cdot x$ $6x^5$

38. $-3 \cdot y \cdot y \cdot y$ $-3y^3$

39. $(4t)(4t)(4t)(4t)$ $(4t)^4$

40. $(-5u)(-5u)$ $(-5u)^2$

41. $-4 \cdot t \cdot t \cdot t$ $-4t^3$

42. $-5 \cdot u \cdot u$ $-5u^2$

43. $(x + y)(x + y)$ $(x + y)^2$

44. $(a + b)(a + b)(a + b)(a + b)$ $(a + b)^4$

Simplify each expression. See Example 3.

45. $12^3 \cdot 12^4$ 12^7

▶ **46.** $3^4 \cdot 3^6$ 3^{10}

47. $(2^3)(2^2)$ 2^5

48. $(5^5)(5^3)$ 5^8

▶ **49.** $a^3 \cdot a^3$ a^6

50. $m^7 \cdot m^7$ m^{14}

51. x^4x^3 x^7

52. y^5y^2 y^7

53. a^3aa^5 a^9

54. b^2b^3b b^6

55. $y^3(y^2y^4)$ y^9

▶ **56.** $(y^4y)y^6$ y^{11}

57. $(a^2b^3)(a^3b^3)$ a^5b^6

58. $(u^3v^5)(u^4v^5)$ u^7v^{10}

59. $(m + n)^2(m + n)^3$ $(m + n)^5$

60. $(c - d)^3(c - d)^4$ $(c - d)^7$

Simplify each expression. Assume there are no divisions by 0.
See Example 4.

61. $\dfrac{8^{12}}{8^4}$ 8^8

62. $\dfrac{10^4}{10^2}$ 10^2

63. $\dfrac{12^{15}}{12^{12}}$ 12^3

64. $\dfrac{15^{17}}{15^{10}}$ 15^7

65. $\dfrac{x^{15}}{x^3}$ x^{12}

▶ **66.** $\dfrac{y^6}{y^3}$ y^3

67. $\dfrac{c^{10}}{c^9}$ c

68. $\dfrac{h^{20}}{h^{10}}$ h^{10}

69. $\dfrac{x^2y^8}{xy^4}$ xy^4

70. $\dfrac{p^3q^8}{p^2q^6}$ pq^2

71. $\dfrac{c^3d^7}{cd}$ c^2d^6

▶ **72.** $\dfrac{r^8s^9}{rs}$ r^7s^8

Simplify each expression. Assume there are no divisions by 0.
See Example 5.

73. $\dfrac{m^2m^5m^7}{m^2m}$ m^{11}

74. $\dfrac{p^3p^4p^5}{p^2p^6}$ p^4

75. $\dfrac{a^2a^3a^4}{a^4a^4}$ a

▶ **76.** $\dfrac{aa^2a^6}{a^2a^3}$ a^4

Simplify each expression. See Example 6.

77. $(3^2)^4$ 3^8

▶ **78.** $(4^3)^3$ 4^9

79. $(2^3)^5$ 2^{15}

80. $(5^4)^2$ 5^8

81. $(y^5)^3$ y^{15}

82. $(b^3)^6$ b^{18}

83. $(m^{50})^{10}$ m^{500}

84. $(n^{25})^4$ n^{100}

Simplify each expression. See Example 7.

85. $(x^2x^3)^5$ x^{25}

86. $(y^3y^4)^4$ y^{28}

87. $(b^3b^4)^2$ b^{14}

▶ **88.** $(m^4m^2)^3$ m^{18}

89. $(y^3)^2(y^2)^4$ y^{14}

90. $(b^4)^3(b^2)^2$ b^{16}

91. $(p^2)^3(p^3)^3$ p^{15}

92. $(q^4)^2(q^2)^3$ q^{14}

Simplify each expression. See Example 8.

93. $(4p^3)^3$ $64p^9$

94. $(3n^2)^4$ $81n^8$

▶ **95.** $(a^3b^2)^3$ a^9b^6

96. $(r^3s^2)^2$ r^6s^4

97. $(p^2q^4)^2$ p^4q^8

98. $(r^3s^5)^3$ r^9s^{15}

▶ **99.** $(-2r^2s^3)^3$ $-8r^6s^9$

100. $(-3x^2y^4)^2$ $9x^4y^8$

Simplify each expression. See Example 9.

101. $\dfrac{(x^2y^3)^2}{xy^2}$ x^3y^4

102. $\dfrac{(a^3b^4)^3}{a^3b^4}$ a^6b^8

103. $\dfrac{(p^5q^2)^3}{p^{10}q^4}$ p^5q^2

▶ **104.** $\dfrac{(m^5n^2)^3}{m^{12}n^3}$ m^3n^3

Simplify each expression. See Example 10.

105. $\left(\dfrac{a}{b}\right)^3$ $\dfrac{a^3}{b^3}$

▶ **106.** $\left(\dfrac{r}{s}\right)^4$ $\dfrac{r^4}{s^4}$

107. $\left(\dfrac{2x^2}{y^3}\right)^5$ $\dfrac{32x^{10}}{y^{15}}$

108. $\left(\dfrac{3u^4}{2v^2}\right)^6$ $\dfrac{729u^{24}}{64v^{12}}$

Simplify each expression. **See Example 11.**

109. $\dfrac{(3z)^5}{(3z)^2}$ $27z^3$

110. $\dfrac{(2t)^{10}}{(2t)^5}$ $32t^5$

111. $\dfrac{(6k)^7}{(6k)^4}$ $216k^3$

▶ **112.** $\dfrac{(-3a)^{12}}{(-3a)^{10}}$ $9a^2$

TRY IT YOURSELF

Simplify each expression. Assume there are no divisions by 0.

113. $xy^2 \cdot x^2 y$ $x^3 y^3$

114. $s^8 t^2 s^2 t^7$ $s^{10} t^9$

115. $(3zz^2 z^3)^5$ $243z^{30}$

116. $(4t^3 t^6 t^2)^2$ $16t^{22}$

117. $(x^5)^2 (x^7)^3$ x^{31}

118. $(y^3 y)^2 (y^2)^2$ y^{12}

119. $(uv)^4$ $u^4 v^4$

120. $(xy)^3$ $x^3 y^3$

121. $\left(\dfrac{-2a}{b}\right)^5$ $-\dfrac{32a^5}{b^5}$

122. $\left(\dfrac{-2t}{3}\right)^4$ $\dfrac{16t^4}{81}$

123. $\dfrac{(a^2 b)^{15}}{(a^2 b)^9}$ $a^{12} b^6$

124. $\dfrac{(s^2 t^3)^4}{(s^2 t^3)^2}$ $s^4 t^6$

125. $\dfrac{(ab^2)^3}{(ab)^2}$ ab^4

126. $\dfrac{(m^3 n^4)^3}{(mn^2)^3}$ $m^6 n^6$

127. $\dfrac{(r^4 s^3)^4}{(rs^3)^3}$ $r^{13} s^3$

▶ **128.** $\dfrac{(x^2 y^5)^5}{(x^3 y)^2}$ $x^4 y^{23}$

129. $\left(\dfrac{y^3 y}{2yy^2}\right)^3$ $\dfrac{y^3}{8}$

130. $\left(\dfrac{2y^3 y}{yy^2}\right)^3$ $8y^3$

131. $\left(\dfrac{3t^3 t^4 t^5}{4t^2 t^6}\right)^3$ $\dfrac{27t^{12}}{64}$

132. $\left(\dfrac{4t^3 t^4 t^5}{3t^2 t^6}\right)^3$ $\dfrac{64t^{12}}{27}$

133. $\left(\dfrac{t^2}{2}\right)\left(\dfrac{t^2}{2}\right)\left(\dfrac{t^2}{2}\right)$ $\dfrac{t^6}{8}$

134. $c \cdot c \cdot c \cdot d \cdot d$ $c^3 d^2$

135. $(cd^4)(cd)$ $c^2 d^5$

136. $ab^3 c^4 \cdot ab^4 c^2$ $a^2 b^7 c^6$

137. $\dfrac{y^3 y^4}{yy^2}$ y^4

▶ **138.** $\dfrac{b^4 b^5}{b^2 b^3}$ b^4

APPLICATIONS

Find each area or volume. You may leave π in your answer. Refer to the area and volume formulas in Section 2.4.

▶ **139.** a^{10} mi^2

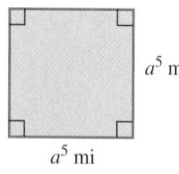

a^5 mi

a^5 mi

140. $16y^6 \pi$ yd^2

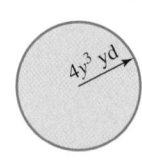

$4y^3$ yd

141. x^9 m^3

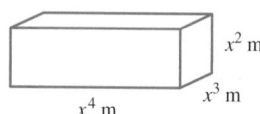

x^2 m

x^3 m

x^4 m

▶ **142.** x^{21} cm^3

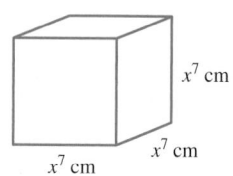

x^7 cm

x^7 cm

x^7 cm

143. ART HISTORY Leonardo da Vinci's drawing relating a human figure to a square and a circle is shown.

   a. Find an expression that represents the area of the square if the man's height is $5x$ feet. $25x^2$ ft^2

   b. Find an expression that represents the area of the circle if the distance from his waist to his feet is $3x$ feet. Leave π in your answer. $9\pi x^2$ ft^2

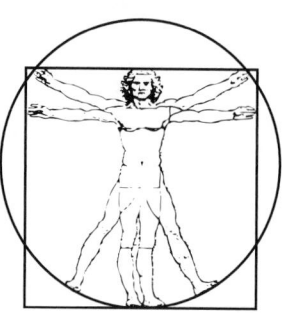

▶ **144.** PACKAGING Use the illustration to find the volume of the bowling ball and the cardboard box it is packaged in. You may leave π in your answer. $36\pi x^3$ in.^{3}, $216x^3$ in.^{3}

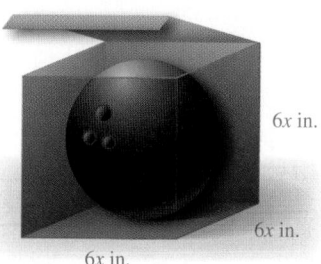

6x in.

6x in.

6x in.

▶ **145.** BOUNCING BALLS A ball is dropped from a height of 32 feet. Each rebound is one-half of its previous height.

   a. Draw a diagram of the path of the ball, showing four bounces.

   b. Explain why the expressions $32\left(\frac{1}{2}\right)$, $32\left(\frac{1}{2}\right)^2$, $32\left(\frac{1}{2}\right)^3$, and $32\left(\frac{1}{2}\right)^4$ represent the height of the ball on the first, second, third, and fourth bounces, respectively. Find the heights of the first four bounces. 16 ft, 8 ft, 4 ft, 2 ft

▶ **146.** HAVING BABIES The probability that a couple will have n baby boys in a row is given by the formula $\left(\frac{1}{2}\right)^n$. Find the probability that a couple will have four baby boys in a row. $\frac{1}{16}$

▶ **147.** COMPUTERS Text is stored by computers using a sequence of eight 0's and 1's. Such a sequence is called a **byte**. An example of a byte is 10101110.

   a. Write four other bytes, all ending in 1.
11000001, 11010001, 11001101, 11000011
(answers may vary)

b. Each of the eight digits of a byte can be chosen in *two* ways (either 0 or 1). The total number of different bytes can be represented by an exponential expression with base 2. What is it? 2^8

Image copyright hcss5, 2009. Used under license from Shutterstock.com

▶ **148. INVESTING** Guess the answer to the following problem. Then use a calculator to find the correct answer. Were you close?

   If the value of 1¢ is to double every day, what will the penny be worth after 31 days? $21,474,836.48

▌ WRITING

149. Explain the mistake.

$$2^3 \cdot 2^2 = 4^5$$
$$= 1{,}024$$

150. Are the expressions $2x^3$ and $(2x)^3$ equivalent? Explain.

151. Is the operation of raising to a power commutative? That is, is $a^b = b^a$? Explain.

▶ **152.** When a number is raised to a power, is the result always larger than the original number? Support your answer with some examples.

▌ REVIEW

Match each equation with its graph below.

153. $y = 2x - 1$ *c*   **154.** $y = 3x - 1$ *a*

155. $y = 3$ *d*   ▶ **156.** $x = 3$ *b*

a.

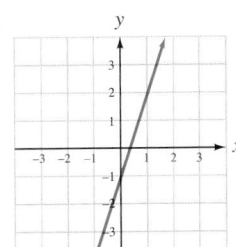

b.

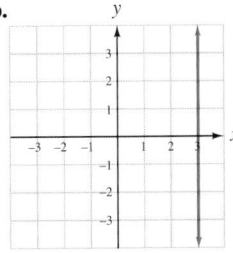

c.

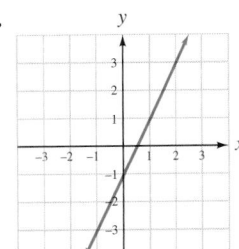

d.

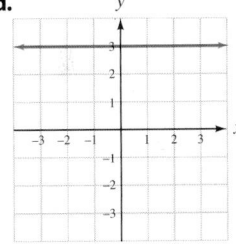

SECTION 5.2

Zero and Negative Integer Exponents

Objectives

1 Use the zero exponent rule.

2 Use the negative integer exponent rule.

3 Use exponent rules to write equivalent expressions with positive exponents.

4 Use all exponent rules to simplify expressions.

5 Use exponent rules with variable exponents.

In the previous section, we discussed natural-number exponents. We now extend the discussion to include exponents that are zero and exponents that are negative integers.

1 Use the zero exponent rule.

When we discussed the quotient rule for exponents in the previous section, the exponent in the numerator was always greater than the exponent in the denominator. We now consider what happens when the exponents are equal. To develop the definition of a zero exponent, we will simplify the expression $\frac{5^3}{5^3}$ in two ways and compare the results. If we use the quotient rule for exponents, where the exponents in the numerator and denominator are equal, we obtain 5^0. However, by removing the common factors of 5, we obtain 1.

$$\frac{5^3}{5^3} = 5^{3-3} = \mathbf{5^0} \qquad \frac{5^3}{5^3} = \frac{\overset{1}{\cancel{5}} \cdot \overset{1}{\cancel{5}} \cdot \overset{1}{\cancel{5}}}{\underset{1}{\cancel{5}} \cdot \underset{1}{\cancel{5}} \cdot \underset{1}{\cancel{5}}} = \mathbf{1}$$

These must be equal.

For this reason, we conclude that $5^0 = 1$. This example suggests the following rule.

Zero Exponents

Any nonzero real number raised to the 0 power is 1. For any nonzero real number x,

$$x^0 = 1$$

Self Check 1

Write each expression without using exponents:
a. $(-0.115)^0$ 1
b. $-5a^0 b$ $-5b$

Now Try Problems 21, 23, and 24

Teaching Example 1 Write each expression without using exponents:
a. 30^0 **b.** $5y^0$ **c.** $(5y)^0$
Answers:
a. 1 **b.** 5 **c.** 1

EXAMPLE 1   Write each expression without using exponents:

a. $\left(\dfrac{1}{13}\right)^0$ **b.** $3x^0$ **c.** $(3x)^0$

Strategy We will note the base and exponent in each case. Since each expression has an exponent that is zero, we will use the zero-exponent rule.

WHY If an expression contains a nonzero base raised to the 0 power, we can replace it with 1.

Solution

a. $\left(\dfrac{1}{13}\right)^0 = 1$ The base is $\frac{1}{13}$; the exponent is 0.

b. $3x^0 = 3(1)$ The base is x; the exponent is 0.

$\qquad = 3$

c. $(3x)^0 = 1$ The base is $3x$; the exponent is 0.

Parts b and c point out that $3x^0 \neq (3x)^0$.

Caution!   Remember, the base is only that which is directly in front of the exponent unless there are parentheses. For $3x^0$, the base is x and the exponent is 0. For $(3x)^0$, the base is $3x$ and the exponent 0.

---

2 Use the negative integer exponent rule.

To develop the definition of a negative exponent, we will simplify the expression $\dfrac{6^2}{6^5}$
in two ways. If we use the quotient rule for exponents, where the exponent in the numerator is less than the exponent in the denominator, we obtain 6^{-3}. However, by removing the common factors of 6, we obtain $\dfrac{1}{6^3}$.

$$\frac{6^2}{6^5} = 6^{2-5} = 6^{-3} \qquad \frac{6^2}{6^5} = \frac{\overset{1}{\cancel{6}} \cdot \overset{1}{\cancel{6}}}{\underset{1}{\cancel{6}} \cdot \underset{1}{\cancel{6}} \cdot 6 \cdot 6 \cdot 6} = \frac{1}{6^3}$$

These must be equal.

For this reason, we conclude that $6^{-3} = \dfrac{1}{6^3}$. In general, we have the following rule.

Negative Exponents

If x represents any nonzero number and n represents a natural number, then

$$x^{-n} = \frac{1}{x^n}$$

In words, x^{-n} is the reciprocal of x^n.

The definition of a negative exponent states that another way to write x^{-n} is to write its reciprocal, changing the sign of the exponent. We can use this definition to write expressions that contain negative exponents as expressions without negative exponents.

The Language of Algebra   The *negative integers* are: $-1, -2, -3, -4, -5, \ldots$

EXAMPLE 2   Simplify by using the definition of negative exponents: **a.** 3^{-5} **b.** $(-2)^{-3}$

Strategy Since each expression has an exponent that is negative, we will use the negative exponent rule.

WHY This rule enables us to write an exponential expression that has a negative exponent in an equivalent form using a positive exponent.

Solution

a. $3^{-5} = \dfrac{1}{3^5}$ Write the reciprocal of 3^{-5} and change the exponent from -5 to 5.

$\qquad = \dfrac{1}{243}$ Evaluate 3^5.

b. $(-2)^{-3} = \dfrac{1}{(-2)^3}$ Write the reciprocal of $(-2)^{-3}$ and change the exponent from -3 to 3.

$\qquad\quad = -\dfrac{1}{8}$ Evaluate $(-2)^3$.

Caution!   A negative exponent does not indicate a negative number. It indicates a reciprocal. For example:

$$4^{-2} = \frac{1}{4^2} = \frac{1}{16} \qquad 4^{-2} \neq -16 \qquad 4^{-2} \neq -\frac{1}{4^2}$$

Self Check 2
Simplify by using the definition of negative exponents:
a. 4^{-4} $\frac{1}{256}$
b. $(-5)^{-3}$ $-\frac{1}{125}$

Now Try Problems 28 and 30

Teaching Example 2 Simplify by using the definition of negative exponents:
a. 5^{-2} **b.** $(-3)^{-4}$
Answers:
a. $\frac{1}{25}$ **b.** $\frac{1}{81}$

---

3 Use exponent rules to write equivalent expressions with positive exponents.

Negative exponents can appear in the numerator and/or the denominator of a fraction. To develop rules for such situations, we consider the following example.

$$\frac{a^{-4}}{b^{-3}} = \frac{\dfrac{1}{a^4}}{\dfrac{1}{b^3}} = \frac{1}{a^4} \div \frac{1}{b^3} = \frac{1}{a^4} \cdot \frac{b^3}{1} = \frac{b^3}{a^4}$$

We can obtain this result in a simpler way. In $\frac{a^{-4}}{b^{-3}}$, we can move a^{-4} from the numerator to the denominator and change the sign of the exponent, and we can move b^{-3} from the denominator to the numerator and change the sign of the exponent.

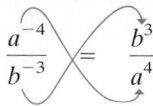

$$\frac{a^{-4}}{b^{-3}} = \frac{b^3}{a^4}$$

> ***The Language of Algebra*** *Factors* of a numerator or denominator may be moved *across the fraction bar* if we change the sign of their exponent.

This example suggests the following rules.

> ### Changing from Negative to Positive Exponents
>
> A factor can be moved from the denominator to the numerator or from the numerator to the denominator of a fraction if the sign of its exponent is changed.
>
> For any nonzero real numbers x and y, and any integers m and n,
>
> $$\frac{1}{x^{-n}} = x^n \qquad \text{and} \qquad \frac{x^{-m}}{y^{-n}} = \frac{y^n}{x^m}$$

These rules streamline the process when simplifying fractions involving negative exponents.

Self Check 3

Simplify by using the definition of negative exponents:

a. $\dfrac{1}{9^{-1}}$ 9

b. $\dfrac{8^{-2}}{7^{-1}}$ $\dfrac{7}{64}$

Now Try **Problems 32 and 34**

Teaching Example 3 Simplify by using the definition of negative exponents:

a. $\dfrac{1}{7^{-2}}$ **b.** $\dfrac{4^{-2}}{11^{-1}}$

Answers:

a. 49   **b.** $\dfrac{11}{16}$

EXAMPLE 3   Simplify by using the definition of negative exponents:

a. $\dfrac{1}{5^{-2}}$ **b.** $\dfrac{2^{-3}}{3^{-4}}$

Strategy Since the exponents are negative numbers, we will use the negative exponent rule.

WHY It is usually easier to simplify exponential expressions if the exponents are positive.

Solution

a. $\dfrac{1}{5^{-2}} = 5^2$ Move 5^{-2} to the numerator and change the sign of the exponent.

     $= 25$ Evaluate 5^2.

b. $\dfrac{2^{-3}}{3^{-4}} = \dfrac{3^4}{2^3}$ Move 2^{-3} to the denominator and change the sign of the exponent. Move 3^{-4} to the numerator and change the sign of the exponent.

     $= \dfrac{81}{8}$ Evaluate $3^4 = 81$ and $2^3 = 8$.

EXAMPLE 4   Simplify by using the definition of negative exponents. Assume that no denominators are zero.

a. x^{-4} **b.** $\dfrac{x^{-3}}{y^{-7}}$ **c.** $(-2x)^{-2}$ **d.** $-2x^{-2}$

Strategy We will note the base and exponent in each case. Since each expression has exponents that are negative numbers, we will use the negative exponent rule.

WHY The negative exponent rule enables us to write an exponential expression that has negative exponents in an equivalent form using positive exponents.

Solution

a. $x^{-4} = \dfrac{1}{x^4}$

b. $\dfrac{x^{-3}}{y^{-7}} = \dfrac{y^7}{x^3}$

c. $(-2x)^{-2} = \dfrac{1}{(-2x)^2}$

$\qquad\quad = \dfrac{1}{4x^2}$

d. $-2x^{-2} = -2\left(\dfrac{1}{x^2}\right)$

$\qquad\qquad = -\dfrac{2}{x^2}$

When a fraction base is raised to a negative power, we can use rules for exponents to change the sign of the exponent. For example,

$$\left(\dfrac{x}{y}\right)^{-2} = \dfrac{x^{-2}}{y^{-2}} = \dfrac{y^2}{x^2} = \left(\dfrac{y}{x}\right)^2$$

The exponent is the opposite of -2.
The base is the reciprocal of $\frac{x}{y}$.

This example suggests the following rule.

Negative Exponents and Reciprocals

A fraction raised to a power is equal to the reciprocal of the fraction raised to the opposite power.

For any nonzero real numbers x and y, and any integer n,

$$\left(\dfrac{x}{y}\right)^{-n} = \left(\dfrac{y}{x}\right)^n$$

EXAMPLE 5 Write $\left(\dfrac{5}{16}\right)^{-1}$ without using exponents.

Strategy We will use the negative exponent and reciprocal rule.

WHY The expression involves a fraction base to a negative exponent. It is often easier to simplify exponential expressions if the exponents are positive.

Solution

$\left(\dfrac{5}{16}\right)^{-1} = \left(\dfrac{16}{5}\right)^1$ The base is $\frac{5}{16}$ and the exponent is -1. Write the reciprocal of the base and change the sign of the exponent.

$\qquad\qquad = \dfrac{16^1}{5^1}$ To raise a fraction to a power, we raise both the numerator and the denominator to that power.

$\qquad\qquad = \dfrac{16}{5}$

---

4 Use all exponent rules to simplify expressions.

The rules for exponents involving products, powers, and quotients are also true for zero and negative exponents.

Self Check 4

Simplify by using the definition of negative exponents:

a. a^{-5} **b.** $\dfrac{r^{-4}}{s^{-5}}$ **c.** $3y^{-3}$

Now Try Problems 36, 38, 40, and 42

Self Check 4 Answers

a. $\dfrac{1}{a^5}$ **b.** $\dfrac{s^5}{r^4}$ **c.** $\dfrac{3}{y^3}$

Teaching Example 4 Simplify by using the definition of negative exponents:

a. b^{-1} **b.** $\dfrac{a^{-3}}{b^{-4}}$

c. $(-3b)^{-2}$ **d.** $-3b^{-2}$

Answers:

a. $\dfrac{1}{b}$ **b.** $\dfrac{b^4}{a^3}$ **c.** $\dfrac{1}{9b^2}$ **d.** $\dfrac{-3}{b^2}$

Self Check 5

Write $\left(\dfrac{3}{7}\right)^{-2}$ without using exponents. $\dfrac{49}{9}$

Now Try Problem 44

Teaching Example 5 Write $\left(\dfrac{2}{3}\right)^{-3}$ without using exponents.

Answer:

$\dfrac{27}{8}$

Summary of Exponent Rules

If m and n represent integers and there are no divisions by zero, then

Product rule	*Power rule*	*Power of a product*
$x^m \cdot x^n = x^{m+n}$	$(x^m)^n = x^{mn}$	$(xy)^n = x^n y^n$

Quotient rule	*Power of a quotient*	*Exponents of 0 and 1*
$\dfrac{x^m}{x^n} = x^{m-n}$	$\left(\dfrac{x}{y}\right)^n = \dfrac{x^n}{y^n}$	$x^0 = 1$ and $x^1 = x$

Negative exponent	*Negative exponents appearing in fractions*
$x^{-n} = \dfrac{1}{x^n}$	$\dfrac{1}{x^{-n}} = x^n$ $\dfrac{x^{-m}}{y^{-n}} = \dfrac{y^n}{x^m}$ $\left(\dfrac{x}{y}\right)^{-n} = \left(\dfrac{y}{x}\right)^n$

The rules for exponents are used to simplify expressions involving products, quotients, and powers. In general, an expression involving exponents is simplified when

- Each base occurs only once
- There are no parentheses
- There are no negative or zero exponents

Self Check 6

Simplify and write the result without using negative exponents:

a. $(x^4)^{-3}$ $\frac{1}{x^{12}}$

b. $\dfrac{a^4}{a^8}$ $\frac{1}{a^4}$

c. $\dfrac{a^{-4}a^{-5}}{a^{-3}}$ $\frac{1}{a^6}$

Now Try Problems 48, 50, 52, and 54

Teaching Example 6 Simplify and write the result without using negative exponents:

a. $(x^{-2})^4$ **b.** $\dfrac{x^4}{x^6}$ **c.** $(x^5x^2)^{-2}$

d. $\dfrac{a^{-3}a^{-6}}{a^{-7}}$

Answers:

a. $\dfrac{1}{x^8}$ **b.** $\dfrac{1}{x^2}$ **c.** $\dfrac{1}{x^{14}}$ **d.** $\dfrac{1}{a^2}$

EXAMPLE 6   Simplify and write the result without using negative exponents. Assume that no denominators are zero.

a. $(x^{-3})^2$ **b.** $\dfrac{x^3}{x^7}$ **c.** $(x^3x^2)^{-3}$ **d.** $\dfrac{y^{-4}y^{-3}}{y^{-20}}$

Strategy In each case, we want to use the exponent rules to write an equivalent expression that uses each base with a positive exponent only once.

WHY The expressions are not in simplest form. In each case either the bases occur as a factor more than once, there are parentheses, or there are negative exponents.

Solution

a. $(x^{-3})^2 = x^{-6}$ Use the power rule. Keep the base and multiply the exponents.

$\qquad = \dfrac{1}{x^6}$ Write the reciprocal of x^{-6} and change the sign of the exponent.

b. $\dfrac{x^3}{x^7} = x^{3-7}$ Use the quotient rule. Keep the base and subtract the exponents.

$\qquad = x^{-4}$ Do the subtraction: $3 - 7 = -4$.

$\qquad = \dfrac{1}{x^4}$ Write the reciprocal of x^{-4} and change the sign of the exponent.

c. $(x^3x^2)^{-3} = (x^5)^{-3}$ Use the product rule. Keep the base and add the exponents.

$\qquad = x^{-15}$ Use the power rule. Keep the base and multiply the exponents.

$\qquad = \dfrac{1}{x^{15}}$ Write the reciprocal of x^{-15} and change the sign of the exponent.

d. $\dfrac{y^{-4}y^{-3}}{y^{-20}} = \dfrac{y^{-7}}{y^{-20}}$ Use the product rule in the numerator.

$\qquad = y^{-7-(-20)}$ Use the quotient rule.

$\qquad = y^{13}$ Do the subtraction: $-7 - (-20) = -7 + 20 = 13$.

EXAMPLE 7 Simplify and write the answer without negative exponents. Assume no denominators are zero.

a. $\dfrac{12a^3b^4}{4a^5b^2}$ **b.** $\left(-\dfrac{x^3y^2}{xy^{-3}}\right)^{-2}$

Strategy In each case, we want to use the exponent rules to write an equivalent expression that uses each base with a positive exponent only once.

WHY The expressions are not in simplest form. In each case, either the bases occur as factors more than once, there are parentheses, or there are negative exponents.

Solution

a. $\dfrac{12a^3b^4}{4a^5b^2} = 3a^{3-5}b^{4-2}$ *Simplify the numerical coefficients. Use the quotient rule twice.*

$\quad = 3a^{-2}b^2$ *Do the subtractions.*

$\quad = \dfrac{3b^2}{a^2}$ *Move a^{-2} to the denominator and change the sign of the exponent.*

b. $\left(-\dfrac{x^3y^2}{xy^{-3}}\right)^{-2} = \left(-\dfrac{xy^{-3}}{x^3y^2}\right)^2$ *Write the reciprocal of the base and change the sign of the exponent.*

$\quad = (-x^{1-3}y^{-3-2})^2$ *Use the quotient rule for exponents twice.*

$\quad = (-x^{-2}y^{-5})^2$ *Do the subtractions.*

$\quad = x^{-4}y^{-10}$ *Raise each factor to the second power.*

$\quad = \dfrac{1}{x^4y^{10}}$ *Move x^{-4} and y^{-10} to the denominator and change the sign of the exponents.*

5 Use exponent rules with variable exponents.

We can apply the rules for exponents to simplify expressions involving variable exponents.

EXAMPLE 8 Simplify. Assume that there are no divisions by 0.

a. $\dfrac{6^n}{6^n}$ **b.** $x^{2m}x^{3m}$ **c.** $\dfrac{y^{2m}}{y^{4m}}$

Strategy We will use the rules for exponents and the rules for adding, subtracting, and multiplying variable expressions.

WHY The exponents are variables.

Solution

a. $\dfrac{6^n}{6^n} = 6^{n-n}$ *Keep the common base and subtract the exponents.*

$\quad = 6^0$ *Combine like terms: $n - n = 0$.*

$\quad = 1$ *Evaluate: $6^0 = 1$.*

b. $x^{2m}x^{3m} = x^{2m+3m}$ *Keep the common base and add the exponents.*

$\quad = x^{5m}$ *Combine like terms: $2m + 3m = 5m$.*

c. $\dfrac{y^{2m}}{y^{4m}} = y^{2m-4m}$ *Keep the base and subtract the exponents.*

$\quad = y^{-2m}$ *Combine like terms: $2m - 4m = -2m$.*

$\quad = \dfrac{1}{y^{2m}}$ *Write the reciprocal of y^{-2m} and change the exponent to $2m$.*

Self Check 7

Simplify and write the result without using negative exponents:

a. $\dfrac{20x^5y^3}{15x^2y^8}$ $\dfrac{4x^3}{3y^5}$

b. $\left(\dfrac{x^5y^3}{xy^{-3}}\right)^{-3}$ $\dfrac{1}{x^{12}y^{18}}$

Now Try Problems 56 and 58

Teaching Example 7
a. $\dfrac{15a^7b^3}{25ab^{10}}$ **b.** $\left(\dfrac{a^3b^{-2}}{a^2b^2}\right)^{-4}$
Answers:
a. $\dfrac{3a^6}{5b^7}$ **b.** $\dfrac{b^{16}}{a^4}$

Self Check 8

Simplify each expression:

a. $\dfrac{7^m}{7^m}$ 1

b. $z^{3n}z^{2n}$ z^{5n}

c. $\dfrac{z^{3n}}{z^{5n}}$ $\dfrac{1}{z^{2n}}$

Now Try Problems 60, 62, 66, and 68

Teaching Example 8 Simplify each expression:
a. $\dfrac{5^{2n}}{5^n}$ **b.** $x^{3b}x^{5b}$ **c.** $\dfrac{y^{5b}}{y^{2b}}$ **d.** $\dfrac{x^{4n}}{x^{9n}}$
Answers:
a. 5^n **b.** x^{8b} **c.** y^{3b} **d.** $\dfrac{1}{x^{5n}}$

Using Your CALCULATOR   Finding Present Value

As a gift for their newborn grandson, the grandparents want to deposit enough money in the bank now so that when he turns 18, the young man will have a college fund of $20,000 waiting for him. How much should they deposit now if the money will earn 6% annually?

To find how much money P must be invested at an annual rate i (expressed as a decimal) to have $\$A$ in n years, we use the formula $P = A(1 + i)^{-n}$. If we substitute 20,000 for A, 0.06 (6%) for i, and 18 for n, we have

$$P = A(1 + i)^{-n} \qquad \text{\textit{P is called the present value.}}$$
$$P = 20{,}000(1 + 0.06)^{-18}$$

To find P with a reverse-entry calculator, we enter these numbers and press these keys.

$$(\ 1 \ + \ .06 \ ) \ \boxed{y^x} \ 18 \ \boxed{+/-} \ \times \ 20000 \ \boxed{=} \qquad \boxed{7006.875823}$$

To evaluate the expression with a graphing or a direct-entry calculator, we use the following keystrokes.

$$20000 \ \boxed{\times} \ (\ 1 \ \boxed{+} \ .06 \ ) \ \boxed{\wedge} \ \boxed{(-)} \ 18 \ \boxed{\text{ENTER}}$$

```
20000 × (1 + .06)^ - 1
8
                 7006.875823
```

They must invest approximately $7,006.88 to have $20,000 in 18 years.

ANSWERS TO SELF CHECKS

1. a. 1 **b.** $-5b$ **2. a.** $\frac{1}{256}$ **b.** $-\frac{1}{125}$ **3. a.** 9 **b.** $\frac{7}{64}$ **4. a.** $\frac{1}{a^5}$ **b.** $\frac{s^5}{r^4}$ **c.** $\frac{3}{y^3}$ **5.** $\frac{49}{9}$

6. a. $\frac{1}{x^{12}}$ **b.** $\frac{1}{a^4}$ **c.** $\frac{1}{a^6}$ **7. a.** $\frac{4x^3}{3y^5}$ **b.** $\frac{1}{x^{12}y^{18}}$ **8. a.** 1 **b.** z^{5n} **c.** $\frac{1}{z^{2n}}$

SECTION 5.2   STUDY SET

VOCABULARY

Fill in the blanks.

1. In the exponential expression 8^{-3}, 8 is the <u>base</u> and -3 is the <u>exponent</u> .

▶ **2.** In the exponential expression 5^{-1}, the exponent is a <u>negative</u> integer.

3. Another way to write 2^{-3} is to write its <u>reciprocal</u> and to change the sign of the exponent: $2^{-3} = \dfrac{1}{2^3}$.

▶ **4.** In the expression 6^m, the <u>exponent</u> is a variable.

CONCEPTS

5. In parts a and b, fill in the blanks as you simplify the fraction in two different ways. Then complete the sentence in part c.

a. $\dfrac{6^4}{6^4} = 6^{\,4-4}$ **b.** $\dfrac{6^4}{6^4} = \dfrac{6 \cdot 6 \cdot 6 \cdot 6}{6 \cdot 6 \cdot 6 \cdot 6}$
$\qquad\quad = 6^{\,0} \qquad\qquad\qquad = 1$

c. So we define 6^0 to be 1 , and, in general, if x is any nonzero real number, then $x^0 =$ 1 .

6. In parts a and b, fill in the blanks as you simplify the fraction in two different ways. Then complete the sentence in part c.

a. $\dfrac{8^3}{8^5} = 8^{\,3-5}$ **b.** $\dfrac{8^3}{8^5} = \dfrac{8 \cdot 8 \cdot 8}{8 \cdot 8 \cdot 8 \cdot 8 \cdot 8}$
$\qquad\quad = 8^{\,-2} \qquad\qquad\qquad = \dfrac{1}{8^2}$

c. We define 8^{-2} to be $\dfrac{1}{8^2}$, and, in general, if x is any nonzero real number, then $x^{-n} =$ $\dfrac{1}{x^n}$.

▶ Selected exercises available online at
www.webassign.net/brookscole

Complete each table.

7.

x	3^x
2	9
1	3
0	1
−1	$\frac{1}{3}$
−2	$\frac{1}{9}$

▶ **8.**

x	4^x
2	16
1	4
0	1
−1	$\frac{1}{4}$
−2	$\frac{1}{16}$

▶ **9.**

x	$(-9)^x$
2	81
1	−9
0	1
−1	$-\frac{1}{9}$
−2	$\frac{1}{81}$

10.

x	$(-5)^x$
2	25
1	−5
0	1
−1	$-\frac{1}{5}$
−2	$\frac{1}{25}$

Use the graph to determine the missing y-coordinates in the table and express each y-coordinate as a power of 2.

11.

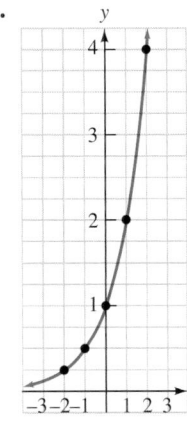

x	y	y as a power of 2
2	4	2^2
1	2	2^1
0	1	2^0
−1	$\frac{1}{2}$	2^{-1}
−2	$\frac{1}{4}$	2^{-2}

12.

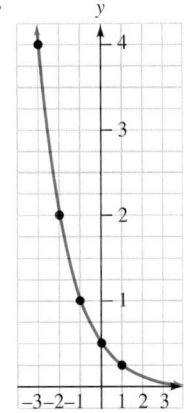

x	y	y as a power of 2
1	$\frac{1}{4}$	2^{-2}
0	$\frac{1}{2}$	2^{-1}
−1	1	2^0
−2	2	2^1
−3	4	2^2

NOTATION

Complete each solution.

13. $(y^5y^3)^{-5} = \left(y^8\right)^{-5}$

$\qquad = y^{-40}$

$\qquad = \dfrac{1}{y^{40}}$

14. $\left(\dfrac{a^2b^3}{a^{-3}b}\right)^{-3} = \left(a^{2-(-3)}b^{3-1}\right)^{-3}$

$\qquad = \left(a^5 b^2\right)^{-3}$

$\qquad = \dfrac{1}{(a^5b^2)^3}$

$\qquad = \dfrac{1}{a^{15}b^6}$

15. In the expression $3x^{-2}$, what is the base and what is the exponent? base x, exponent -2

16. In the expression $-3x^{-2}$, what is the base and what is the exponent? base x, exponent -2

17. Determine the base and the exponent and evaluate each expression.

a. -4^2 4, 2, −16

b. 4^{-2} 4, −2, $\frac{1}{16}$

c. -4^{-2} 4, −2, $-\frac{1}{16}$

▶ **18.** Determine the base and the exponent and evaluate each expression.

a. $(-7)^2$ −7, 2, 49

b. $(-7)^{-2}$ −7, −2, $\frac{1}{49}$

c. -7^{-2} 7, −2, $-\frac{1}{49}$

GUIDED PRACTICE

Write each expression without using exponents. See Example 1.

19. 7^0 1

▶ **20.** 9^0 1

21. $\left(\dfrac{1}{4}\right)^0$ 1

22. $\left(\dfrac{3}{8}\right)^0$ 1

▶ **23.** $2x^0$ 2

24. $(2x)^0$ 1

25. $(-x)^0$ 1

▶ **26.** $-x^0$ −1

Simplify each expression by using the definition of negative exponents. See Example 2.

27. 12^{-2} $\frac{1}{144}$

28. 11^{-2} $\frac{1}{121}$

▶ **29.** $(-4)^{-1}$ $-\frac{1}{4}$

30. $(-8)^{-2}$ $\frac{1}{64}$

Simplify each expression by using the definition of negative exponents. See Example 3.

31. $\dfrac{1}{5^{-3}}$ 125

▶ **32.** $\dfrac{1}{3^{-3}}$ 27

33. $\dfrac{2^{-4}}{3^{-1}}$ $\frac{3}{16}$

▶ **34.** $\dfrac{7^{-2}}{2^{-3}}$ $\frac{8}{49}$

Write each expression without using negative exponents. See Example 4.

35. x^{-2} $\frac{1}{x^2}$

36. y^{-3} $\frac{1}{y^3}$

37. $\dfrac{a^{-2}}{b^{-3}}$ $\frac{b^3}{a^2}$

▶ **38.** $\dfrac{m^{-7}}{n^{-5}}$ $\frac{n^5}{m^7}$

39. $(-4y)^{-2}$ $\frac{1}{16y^2}$

40. $(-5d)^{-3}$ $-\frac{1}{125d^3}$

▶ **41.** $-2b^{-5}$ $-\frac{2}{b^5}$

42. $-3c^{-4}$ $-\frac{3}{c^4}$

Write each expression without using exponents. See Example 5.

43. $\left(\dfrac{7}{8}\right)^{-1}$ $\frac{8}{7}$

▶ **44.** $\left(\dfrac{16}{5}\right)^{-1}$ $\frac{5}{16}$

45. $\left(\dfrac{3}{4}\right)^{-2}$ $\frac{16}{9}$

46. $\left(\dfrac{2}{3}\right)^{-2}$ $\frac{9}{4}$

Write each expression without using negative exponents.
See Example 6.

47. $(a^{-4})^3$ $\frac{1}{a^{12}}$

48. $(b^{-3})^5$ $\frac{1}{b^{15}}$

49. $\dfrac{a^3}{a^8}$ $\frac{1}{a^5}$

▶ **50.** $\dfrac{t^5}{t^{12}}$ $\frac{1}{t^7}$

51. $(ab^2)^{-3}$ $\frac{1}{a^3b^6}$

52. $(m^2n^3)^{-2}$ $\frac{1}{m^4n^6}$

53. $\dfrac{y^{-4}y^{-3}}{y^{-10}}$ y^3

54. $\dfrac{x^{-4}x^{-5}}{x^{-8}x^{-4}}$ x^3

Write each expression without using negative exponents.
See Example 7.

55. $\dfrac{15p^2q^3}{5p^3q^2}$ $\frac{3q}{p}$

56. $\dfrac{27m^3n^5}{6m^5n^3}$ $\frac{9n^2}{2m^2}$

57. $\left(\dfrac{a^2b^5}{a^2b^{-2}}\right)^{-2}$ $\frac{1}{b^{14}}$

▶ **58.** $\left(\dfrac{a^3b^{-2}}{a^2b^3}\right)^{-3}$ $\frac{b^{15}}{a^3}$

Simplify each expression. Assume that there are no divisions by 0. See Example 8.

59. $\dfrac{7^n}{7^n}$ 1

60. $\dfrac{8^p}{8^p}$ 1

61. $x^{2m}x^m$ x^{3m}

62. $y^{3m}y^{2m}$ y^{5m}

63. $u^{2m}u^{-3m}$ $\frac{1}{u^m}$

▶ **64.** $r^{5m}r^{-6m}$ $\frac{1}{r^m}$

65. $\dfrac{y^{3m}}{y^{2m}}$ y^m

66. $\dfrac{z^{4m}}{z^{2m}}$ z^{2m}

67. $\dfrac{x^{3n}}{x^{6n}}$ $\frac{1}{x^{3n}}$

68. $\dfrac{x^m}{x^{5m}}$ $\frac{1}{x^{4m}}$

TRY IT YOURSELF

Write each answer without using parentheses or negative exponents.

69. $\left(\dfrac{a^2b^3}{ab^4}\right)^0$ 1

70. $\dfrac{2}{3}\left(\dfrac{xyz}{x^2y}\right)^0$ $\frac{2}{3}$

71. $\dfrac{5}{2x^0}$ $\frac{5}{2}$

72. $\dfrac{4}{3a^0}$ $\frac{4}{3}$

73. -4^{-3} $-\frac{1}{64}$

74. -6^{-3} $-\frac{1}{216}$

75. $-(-4)^{-3}$ $\frac{1}{64}$

▶ **76.** $-(-4)^{-2}$ $-\frac{1}{16}$

77. $\dfrac{y^4y^3}{y^4y^{-2}}$ y^5

78. $\dfrac{x^{12}x^{-7}}{x^3x^4}$ $\frac{1}{x^2}$

79. $\dfrac{1}{c^{-5}}$ c^5

80. $\dfrac{3}{a^{-7}}$ $3a^7$

81. $\dfrac{3^{-2}}{2^{-3}}$ $\frac{8}{9}$

82. $\dfrac{5^{-3}}{3^{-4}}$ $\frac{81}{125}$

83. $(2y)^{-4}$ $\frac{1}{16y^4}$

84. $(-3x)^{-1}$ $-\frac{1}{3x}$

85. $2^5 \cdot 2^{-2}$ 8

▶ **86.** $10^2 \cdot 10^{-4}$ $\frac{1}{100}$

87. $4^{-3} \cdot 4^{-2} \cdot 4^5$ 1

▶ **88.** $3^{-4} \cdot 3^5 \cdot 3^{-3}$ $\frac{1}{9}$

89. $\dfrac{3^5 \cdot 3^{-2}}{3^3}$ 1

90. $\dfrac{6^2 \cdot 6^{-3}}{6^{-2}}$ 6

91. $\dfrac{y^4}{y^5}$ $\frac{1}{y}$

▶ **92.** $\dfrac{t^7}{t^{10}}$ $\frac{1}{t^3}$

93. $\dfrac{(r^2)^3}{(r^3)^4}$ $\frac{1}{r^6}$

94. $\dfrac{(b^3)^4}{(b^5)^4}$ $\frac{1}{b^8}$

95. $\dfrac{10a^4a^{-2}}{5a^2a^0}$ 2

96. $\dfrac{9b^0b^3}{3b^{-3}b^4}$ $3b^2$

97. $(ab^2)^{-2}$ $\frac{1}{a^2b^4}$

98. $(c^2d^3)^{-2}$ $\frac{1}{c^4d^6}$

99. $(x^2y)^{-3}$ $\frac{1}{x^6y^3}$

100. $(-xy^2)^{-4}$ $\frac{1}{x^4y^8}$

101. $(x^{-4}x^3)^3$ $\frac{1}{x^3}$

102. $(y^{-2}y)^3$ $\frac{1}{y^3}$

103. $(a^{-2}b^3)^{-4}$ $\frac{a^8}{b^{12}}$

104. $(y^{-3}z^5)^{-6}$ $\frac{y^{18}}{z^{30}}$

105. $(-2x^3y^{-2})^{-5}$ $-\frac{y^{10}}{32x^{15}}$

106. $(-3u^{-2}v^3)^{-3}$ $-\frac{u^6}{27v^9}$

107. $\left(\dfrac{a^3}{a^{-4}}\right)^2$ a^{14}

▶ **108.** $\left(\dfrac{a^4}{a^{-3}}\right)^3$ a^{21}

109. $\left(\dfrac{4x^2}{3x^{-5}}\right)^4$ $\frac{256x^{28}}{81}$

110. $\left(\dfrac{-3r^4r^{-3}}{r^{-3}r^7}\right)^3$ $-\frac{27}{r^9}$

111. $\left(\dfrac{12y^3z^{-2}}{3y^{-4}z^3}\right)^2$ $\frac{16y^{14}}{z^{10}}$

112. $\left(\dfrac{6xy^3}{3x^{-1}y}\right)^3$ $8x^6y^6$

APPLICATIONS

▶ **113.** THE DECIMAL NUMERATION SYSTEM
Decimal numbers are written by putting digits into place-value columns that are separated by a decimal point. Express the place value of each of the columns shown using a power of 10.
$10^2, 10^1, 10^0, 10^{-1}, 10^{-2}, 10^{-3}, 10^{-4}$

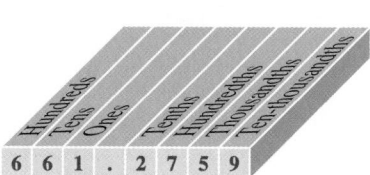

Hundreds	Tens	Ones		Tenths	Hundredths	Thousandths	Ten-thousandths
6	6	1	.	2	7	5	9

▶ **114.** UNIT COMPARISONS Consider the relative sizes of the items listed in the table. In the column titled "measurement," write the most appropriate number from the following list. Each number is used only once.

10^0 meter 10^{-1} meter 10^{-2} meter
10^{-3} meter 10^{-4} meter 10^{-5} meter

Item	Measurement (m)
Thickness of a dime	10^{-3}
Height of a bathroom sink	10^0
Length of a pencil eraser	10^{-2}
Thickness of soap bubble film	10^{-5}
Width of a video cassette	10^{-1}
Thickness of a piece of paper	10^{-4}

▶ **115. RETIREMENT YEARS** How much money should a young married couple invest now at an 8% annual rate if they want to have $100,000 in the bank when they reach retirement age in 40 years? (See the Using Your Calculator box in this section for the formula.) approximately $4,603

▶ **116. BIOLOGY** During bacterial reproduction, the time required for a population to double is called the **generation time.** If b bacteria are introduced into a medium, then after the generation time has elapsed, there will be $2b$ bacteria. After n generations, there will be $b \cdot 2^n$ bacteria. Explain what this expression represents when $n = 0$.
It gives the initial number of bacteria b.

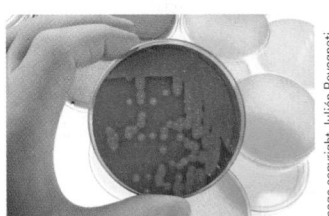

Image copyright Julián Rovagnati, 2009. Used under license from Shutterstock.com

REVIEW

119. IQ TESTS An IQ (intelligence quotient) is a score derived from the formula
$$IQ = \frac{\text{mental age}}{\text{chronological age}} \cdot 100$$

Find the mental age of a 10-year-old girl if she has an IQ of 135. 13.5 yr

120. DIVING When you are under water, the pressure in your ears is given by the formula
$$\text{Pressure} = \text{depth} \cdot \text{density of water}$$

Find the density of water (in lb/ft^3) if, at a depth of 9 feet, the pressure on your eardrum is 561.6 lb/ft^2. 62.4 lb/ft^3

121. Write the equation of the line having slope $\frac{3}{4}$ and y-intercept -5. $y = \frac{3}{4}x - 5$

▶ **122.** Find $f(-6)$ if $f(x) = x^2 - 3x + 1$. 55

SECTION 5.3

Scientific Notation

Objectives

1 Define scientific notation.

2 Write numbers in scientific notation.

3 Convert from scientific notation to standard notation.

4 Perform computations with scientific notation.

Scientists often deal with extremely large and extremely small numbers. Two examples are shown below.

The distance from Earth to the sun is approximately 150,000,000 kilometers.

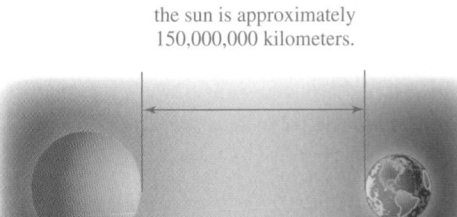

The influenza virus, which causes "flu" symptoms of cough, sore throat, headache, and congestion, has a diameter of 0.00000256 inch.

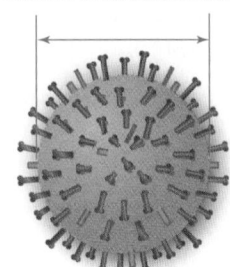

The large number of zeros in 150,000,000 and 0.00000256 makes them difficult to read and hard to remember. In this section, we will discuss a notation that will make such numbers easier to use.

1 Define scientific notation.

Scientific notation provides a compact way of writing large numbers, such as 5,213,000,000,000, and small numbers, such as 0.000000000000914.

> **Scientific Notation**
>
> A number is written in **scientific notation** when it is written as the product of a number between 1 (including 1) and 10, denoted N, and an integer power of 10, denoted n. In symbols, scientific notation has the form $N \times 10^n$.

These numbers are written in scientific notation:

$$3.9 \times 10^6, \qquad 2.24 \times 10^{-4}, \qquad \text{and} \qquad 9.875 \times 10^{22}$$

Every number written in scientific notation has the following form:

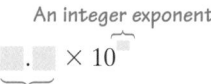

An integer exponent

$$\underbrace{\blacksquare.\blacksquare}_{\text{A decimal between 1 and 10}} \times 10^{\frown}$$

2 Write numbers in scientific notation.

To write a number in scientific notation ($N \times 10^n$), we first determine N then n.

Self Check 1

The distance from Earth to the sun is approximately 93,000,000 miles. Write this number in scientific notation. 9.3×10^7

Now Try Problem 20

Teaching Example 1 Change to scientific notation: 2,340,000,000
Answer:
2.34×10^9

EXAMPLE 1   Change to scientific notation: 150,000,000

Strategy We will write the number as a product of a number between 1 and 10 and a power of 10.

WHY Numbers written in scientific notation have the form $N \times 10^n$.

Solution
We note that 1.5 lies between 1 and 10. To obtain 150,000,000, the decimal point in 1.5 must be moved eight places to the right.

$$1 . 5\, 0\, 0\, 0\, 0\, 0\, 0\, 0$$
$$\underbrace{\qquad\qquad\qquad}_{\text{8 places to the right}}$$

Because multiplying a number by 10 moves the decimal point one place to the right, we can accomplish this by multiplying 1.5 by 10 eight times. We can show the multiplication of 1.5 by 10 eight times using the notation 10^8. Thus, 150,000,000 written in scientific notation is 1.5×10^8.

Self Check 2

The *Salmonella* bacterium, which causes food poisoning, is 0.00009055 inch long. Write this number in scientific notation. 9.055×10^{-5}

Now Try Problem 26

Teaching Example 2 Change 0.000000057 to scientific notation.
Answer:
5.7×10^{-8}

EXAMPLE 2   Change to scientific notation: 0.00000256

Strategy We will write the number as a product of a number between 1 and 10 and a power of 10.

WHY Numbers written in scientific notation have the form $N \times 10^n$.

Solution
We note that 2.56 is between 1 and 10. To obtain 0.00000256, the decimal point in 2.56 must be moved six places to the left.

$$0\, 0\, 0\, 0\, 0\, 2 . 56$$
$$\underbrace{\qquad\qquad}_{\text{6 places to the left}}$$

We can accomplish this by dividing 2.56 by 10^6, which is equivalent to multiplying 2.56 by $\frac{1}{10^6}$ (or by 10^{-6}). Thus, 0.00000256 written in scientific notation is 2.56×10^{-6}.

EXAMPLE 3   Write in scientific notation: **a.** 235,000   **b.** 0.0000073

Strategy We will write each number as a product of a number between 1 and 10 and a power of 10.

WHY Numbers written in scientific notation have the form $N \times 10^n$.

Solution

a. $235{,}000 = 2.35 \times 10^5$ Because $2.35 \times 10^5 = 235{,}000$ and 2.35 is between 1 and 10

b. $0.0000073 = 7.3 \times 10^{-6}$ Because $7.3 \times 10^{-6} = 0.0000073$ and 7.3 is between 1 and 10

> **Sucess Tip** From Examples 1, 2, and 3, we see that in scientific notation, a positive exponent is used when writing a number that is greater than 10. A negative exponent is used when writing a number that is between 0 and 1.

Using Your CALCULATOR   Calculators and Scientific Notation

When displaying a very large or a very small number as an answer, most scientific calculators express it in scientific notation. To show this, we will find the values of $(453.46)^5$ and $(0.0005)^{12}$. We enter these numbers and press these keys.

453.46 $\boxed{y^x}$ 5 $\boxed{=}$ $\boxed{1.917321395 \quad {}^{13}}$

.0005 $\boxed{y^x}$ 12 $\boxed{=}$ $\boxed{2.44140625 \quad {}^{-40}}$

Since the answers in standard notation require more space than the calculator display has, the calculator gives each result in scientific notation. The first display represents $1.917321395 \times 10^{13}$, and the second represents $2.44140625 \times 10^{-40}$.

If we evaluate the same two expressions using a graphing or direct-entry calculator, we see that the letter E is used when displaying a number in scientific notation.

453.46 $\boxed{\wedge}$ 5 $\boxed{\text{ENTER}}$ $\boxed{\begin{array}{l} 453.46{}^{\wedge}5 \\ 1.917321395\text{E}13 \end{array}}$

.0005 $\boxed{\wedge}$ 12 $\boxed{\text{ENTER}}$ $\boxed{\begin{array}{l} .0005{}^{\wedge}12 \\ 2.44140625\text{E}-40 \end{array}}$

> **Caution!** When reading an answer such as $\boxed{1.917321395 \ {}^{13}}$ off the calculator, be careful to write $1.917321395 \times 10^{13}$, not $1.917321395 \ {}^{13}$.

EXAMPLE 4   Write in scientific notation: 432.0×10^5

Strategy We will write the number as a product of a number between 1 and 10 and a power of 10.

WHY Numbers written in scientific notation have the form $N \times 10^n$.

Solution

The number 432.0×10^5 is not written in scientific notation, because 432.0 is not a number between 1 and 10. To write this number in scientific notation, we proceed as follows:

$$432.0 \times 10^5 = 4.32 \times 10^2 \times 10^5 \qquad \text{Write 432.0 in scientific notation.}$$
$$= 4.32 \times 10^7 \qquad \qquad 10^2 \times 10^5 = 10^{2+5} = 10^7.$$

Self Check 3

Write in scientific notation:
a. 17,500 1.75×10^4
b. 0.657 6.57×10^{-1}

Now Try Problems 27 and 29

Teaching Example 3 Write in scientific notation
a. 0.000042   **b.** 5,367,000,000
Answers:
a. 4.2×10^{-5} **b.** 5.367×10^9

Self Check 4

Write in scientific notation:
85×10^{-3} 8.5×10^{-2}

Now Try Problem 40

Teaching Example 4 Write 0.026×10^5 in scientific notation.
Answer:
2.6×10^3

3 Convert from scientific notation to standard notation.

We can change a number written in scientific notation to **standard notation.** For example, to write 9.3×10^7 in standard notation, we multiply 9.3 by 10^7.

$$9.3 \times 10^7 = 9.3 \times 10,000,000 \quad \text{10^7 is equal to 1 followed by 7 zeros.}$$
$$= 93,000,000$$

The following numbers are written in both scientific and standard notation. In each case, the exponent gives the number of places that the decimal point moves, and the sign of the exponent indicates the direction that it moves.

$$5.32 \times 10^5 = 5\,3\,2\,0\,0\,0 . \qquad \text{The decimal point moves 5 places to the right.}$$
$$8.95 \times 10^{-4} = 0\,.\,0\,0\,0\,8\,9\,5 \qquad \text{The decimal point moves 4 places to the left.}$$
$$9.77 \times 10^0 = 9.77 \qquad \text{There is no movement of the decimal point.}$$

The following summarizes our observations.

Converting from Scientific to Standard Notation

1. If the exponent on 10 is positive, move the decimal point the same number of places to the right as the exponent.

2. If the exponent on 10 is negative, move the decimal point the same number of places to the left as the absolute value of the exponent.

Self Check 5

Convert to standard notation:
a. 4.76×10^5 476,000
b. 9.8×10^{-3} 0.0098
Now Try Problems 50 and 52

Teaching Example 5 Convert to standard notation:
a. 2.47×10^{-5} **b.** 7.142×10^7
Answers:
a. 0.0000247
b. 71,420,000

EXAMPLE 5   Convert to standard notation: **a.** 3.4×10^5 **b.** 2.1×10^{-4}

Strategy We will identify the exponent on the 10 and consider its sign.

WHY The exponent gives the number of decimal places that we should move the decimal point. The sign of the exponent indicates whether it should be moved to the right or the left.

Solution

a. $3.4 \times 10^5 = 3.4 \times 100,000$
$$= 340,000$$

b. $2.1 \times 10^{-4} = 2.1 \times \dfrac{1}{10^4}$
$$= 2.1 \times \dfrac{1}{10,000}$$
$$= 2.1 \times 0.0001$$
$$= 0.00021$$

4 Perform computations with scientific notation.

Another advantage of scientific notation becomes apparent when we evaluate products or quotients that contain very large or very small numbers.

Self Check 6

Use scientific notation to evaluate:
(2,540,000,000,000) (0.00041)

Now Try Problem 55
Self Check 6 Answer
1.0414×10^9

EXAMPLE 6   *Astronomy*   Except for the sun, the nearest star visible to the naked eye from most parts of the United States is Sirius. Light from Sirius reaches Earth in about 70,000 hours. If light travels at approximately 670,000,000 mph, how far from Earth is Sirius?

NASA

Strategy We will use the formula $d = rt$ to find the distance from Sirius to Earth.

WHY We know the *rate* at which light travels and the *time* it takes to travel from Sirius to Earth. We want to know the distance.

Solution
We are given the rate at which light travels (670,000,000 mph) and the time it takes the light to travel from Sirius to Earth (70,000 hr). We can find the distance the light travels using the formula $d = rt$.

$$d = rt$$
$$d = 670,000,000(70,000) \qquad \text{Substitute 670,000,000 for } r \text{ and 70,000 for } t.$$
$$= (6.7 \times 10^8)(7.0 \times 10^4) \qquad \text{Write each number in scientific notation.}$$
$$= (6.7 \cdot 7.0) \times (10^8 \cdot 10^4) \qquad \text{Group the numbers together and the powers of 10 together.}$$
$$= (6.7 \cdot 7.0) \times 10^{8+4} \qquad \text{Keep the base and add the exponents.}$$
$$= 46.9 \times 10^{12} \qquad \text{Perform the multiplication. Perform the addition.}$$

We note that 46.9 is not between 0 and 1, so 46.9×10^{12} is not written in scientific notation. To answer in scientific notation, we proceed as follows.

$$= 4.69 \times 10^1 \times 10^{12} \qquad \text{Write 46.9 in scientific notation as } 4.69 \times 10^1.$$
$$= 4.69 \times 10^{13} \qquad \text{Keep the base of 10 and add the exponents.}$$

Sirius is approximately 4.69×10^{13} or 46,900,000,000,000 miles from Earth. ■

THINK IT THROUGH   *Science Majors and Space Travel*

"The number of U.S. college students earning degrees in science, technology, engineering, and math has fallen over the last 15 years. What a better way to hook our children than with a new space exploration plan?"

Patricia Arnold, Space Foundation, 2004

It has been almost 40 years since a U.S. astronaut last walked on the moon. Many educators feel that manned flights to the moon and Mars would ignite a passion for space and science studies among young people. However, the minimum distance Mars is from Earth is 135 times further than the moon is from Earth. Traveling such a long way poses many problems. If the average distance from Earth to the moon is about 2.4×10^5 miles, what is the distance between Earth and Mars? Express the result in scientific notation. 3.24×10^7 mi.

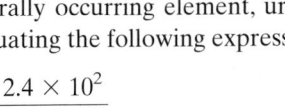 **EXAMPLE 7**   *Atoms* Scientific notation is used in chemistry. As an example, we can approximate the weight (in grams) of one atom of the heaviest naturally occurring element, uranium, by evaluating the following expression.

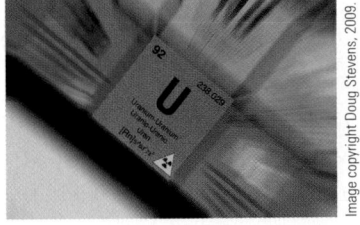

Image copyright Doug Stevens, 2009. Used under license from Shutterstock.com

$$\frac{2.4 \times 10^2}{6.0 \times 10^{23}}$$

Strategy We will divide the numbers and the powers of 10 separately.

WHY We can use the quotient rule for exponents to simplify the calculations.

Solution
$$\frac{2.4 \times 10^2}{6.0 \times 10^{23}} = \frac{2.4}{6.0} \times \frac{10^2}{10^{23}} \qquad \text{Divide the numbers and the powers of 10 separately.}$$

$$= \frac{2.4}{6.0} \times 10^{2-23} \qquad \text{For the powers of 10, keep the base and subtract the exponents.}$$

Teaching Example 6 Use scientific notation to evaluate:
(0.0000024) (5,310,000,000,000)
Answer:
1.2744×10^7 or 12,744,000

Self Check 7

Find the approximate weight (in grams) of one atom of gold by evaluating: $\dfrac{1.98 \times 10^2}{6.0 \times 10^{23}}$

Now Try Problem 58
Self Check 7 Answer
3.3×10^{-22} g

Teaching Example 7 Evaluate:
$$\frac{5.2 \times 10^{15}}{4.0 \times 10^6}$$
Answer:
1.3×10^9

$$= 0.4 \times 10^{-21} \quad \text{Perform the division. Then subtract the exponents.}$$
$$= 4.0 \times 10^{-1} \times 10^{-21} \quad \text{Write 0.4 in scientific notation as } 4.0 \times 10^{-1}.$$
$$= 4.0 \times 10^{-22} \quad \text{Keep the base and add the exponents.}$$

One atom of uranium weighs 4.0×10^{-22} gram. Written in standard notation, this is 0.000000000000000000000004 g.

Using Your CALCULATOR   Entering Numbers in Scientific Notation

We can evaluate the expression from Example 7 by entering the numbers written in scientific notation, using the $\boxed{\text{EE}}$ key on a scientific calculator.

2.4 $\boxed{\text{EE}}$ 2 $\boxed{\div}$ 6 $\boxed{\text{EE}}$ 23 $\boxed{=}$ $\boxed{\text{4.}\quad^{-22}}$

The result shown in the display means 4.0×10^{-22}.

If we use a graphing calculator, the keystrokes are similar.

2.4 $\boxed{\text{2nd}}$ $\boxed{\text{EE}}$ 2 $\boxed{\div}$ 6 $\boxed{\text{2nd}}$ $\boxed{\text{EE}}$ 23 $\boxed{\text{ENTER}}$

$\boxed{\begin{array}{r}\text{2.4E2/6E23}\\ \text{4 E } - \text{22}\end{array}}$

ANSWERS TO SELF CHECKS

1. 9.3×10^7 **2.** 9.055×10^{-5} **3. a.** 1.75×10^4 **b.** 6.57×10^{-1} **4.** 8.5×10^{-2}
5. a. $476{,}000$ **b.** 0.0098 **6.** 1.0414×10^9 **7.** 3.3×10^{-22} g

---

SECTION 5.3   STUDY SET

▌VOCABULARY

Fill in the blanks.

1. A number is written in __scientific__ notation when it is written as the product of a number between 1 (including 1) and 10 and an integer power of 10.

▶ **2.** The number 125,000 is written in __standard__ notation.

▌CONCEPTS

Fill in the blanks by writing the number in standard notation.

3. $2.5 \times 10^2 = $ __250__   **4.** $2.5 \times 10^{-2} = $ __0.025__

5. $2.5 \times 10^{-5} = $ __0.000025__   **6.** $2.5 \times 10^5 = $ __250,000__

Fill in the blanks with a power of 10.

7. $387{,}000 = 3.87 \times$ __10^5__   **8.** $38.7 = 3.87 \times$ __10^1__

9. $0.00387 = 3.87 \times$ __10^{-3}__   **10.** $0.000387 = 3.87 \times$ __10^{-4}__

11. When we multiply a decimal by 10^5, the decimal point moves __5__ places to the __right__.

12. When we multiply a decimal by 10^{-7}, the decimal point moves __7__ places to the __left__.

13. Dividing a decimal by 10^4 is equivalent to multiplying it by __10^{-4}__.

14. Multiplying a decimal by 10^0 does not move the decimal point, because $10^0 = $ __1__.

15. When a real number greater than 10 is written in scientific notation, the exponent on 10 is a __positive__ number.

▶ **16.** When a real number between 0 and 1 is written in scientific notation, the exponent on 10 is a __negative__ number.

▌NOTATION

Complete each solution.

17. Write in scientific notation: 63.7×10^5

$$63.7 \times 10^5 = \underline{6.37 \times 10^1} \times 10^5$$
$$= 6.37 \times 10^{\underline{1}+5}$$
$$= 6.37 \times 10^6$$

▶ **18.** Simplify: $\dfrac{64{,}000}{0.00004}$

$$\frac{64{,}000}{0.00004} = \frac{6.4 \times \underline{10^4}}{4 \times \underline{10^{-5}}}$$
$$= \frac{6.4}{\underline{4}} \times \frac{10^4}{10^{-5}}$$
$$= 1.6 \times 10^{\underline{4}-(-5)}$$
$$= 1.6 \times 10^9$$

▶ Selected exercises available online at
www.webassign.net/brookscole

GUIDED PRACTICE

Write each number in scientific notation. See Example 1.

19. 23,000 2.3×10^4 **20.** 4,750 4.75×10^3

21. 625,000 6.25×10^5 ▶ **22.** 320,000 3.2×10^5

Write each answer in scientific notation. See Example 2.

23. 0.062 6.2×10^{-2} **24.** 0.75 7.5×10^{-1}

25. 0.00073 7.3×10^{-4} ▶ **26.** 0.000057 5.7×10^{-5}

Write each number in scientific notation. See Example 3.

27. 543,000 5.43×10^5 **28.** 17,000,000 1.7×10^7

29. 0.00000875 8.75×10^{-6} **30.** 0.000002 2×10^{-6}

31. 1,700,000 1.7×10^6 ▶ **32.** 290,000 2.9×10^5

33. 909,000,000 9.09×10^8 **34.** 7,007,000,000 7.007×10^9

35. 0.00502 5.02×10^{-3} **36.** 0.0000081 8.1×10^{-6}

37. 0.0000051 5.1×10^{-6} ▶ **38.** 0.04 4.0×10^{-2}

Write each number in scientific notation. See Example 4.

39. 42.5×10^2 4.25×10^3 ▶ **40.** 25.2×10^{-3} 2.52×10^{-2}

41. 0.25×10^{-2} 2.5×10^{-3} ▶ **42.** 0.3×10^3 3.0×10^2

43. 201.8×10^{15} 2.018×10^{17} **44.** 154.3×10^{17} 1.543×10^{19}

▶ **45.** 0.073×10^{-3} 7.3×10^{-5} **46.** 0.0017×10^{-4} 1.7×10^{-7}

Write each number in standard notation. See Example 5.

47. 2.3×10^2 230   ▶ **48.** 3.75×10^4 37,500

49. 8.12×10^5 812,000   **50.** 1.2×10^3 1,200

51. 1.15×10^{-3} 0.00115   ▶ **52.** 4.9×10^{-2} 0.049

53. 9.76×10^{-4} 0.000976   ▶ **54.** 7.63×10^{-5} 0.0000763

Use scientific notation and the rules for exponents to simplify each expression. Give all answers in standard notation. See Examples 6–7.

55. $(3.4 \times 10^2)(2.1 \times 10^3)$ **56.** $(4.1 \times 10^{-3})(3.4 \times 10^4)$
714,000   139.4

57. $\dfrac{9.3 \times 10^2}{3.1 \times 10^{-2}}$ 30,000   ▶ **58.** $\dfrac{7.2 \times 10^6}{1.2 \times 10^8}$ 0.06

TRY IT YOURSELF

Simplify if necessary, then write the answer in standard notation.

59. 25×10^6 25,000,000   ▶ **60.** 0.07×10^3 70

61. 0.51×10^{-3} 0.00051   **62.** 2.37×10^{-4} 0.000237

▶ **63.** 617×10^{-2} 6.17   **64.** $5,280 \times 10^{-3}$ 5.280

65. 0.699×10^3 699   **66.** 0.012×10^4 120

67. $\dfrac{0.00000129}{0.0003}$ 0.0043   **68.** $\dfrac{169,000,000,000}{26,000,000}$ 6,500

69. $\dfrac{96,000}{(12,000)(0.00004)}$ ▶ **70.** $\dfrac{(0.48)(14,400,000)}{96,000,000}$
200,000   0.072

71. $(456.4)^6$
9,038,030,748,000,000

72. $(0.053)^4$
0.000007890481

73. $(0.009)^{-6}$
1,881,676,423,000

74. 225^{-3}
0.0000000877914952

75. $\left(\dfrac{1}{3}\right)^{-25}$
847,288,609,400

76. $\left(\dfrac{8}{5}\right)^{50}$
16,069,380,440

APPLICATIONS

77. ASTRONOMY The distance from Earth to Alpha Centauri (the nearest star outside our solar system) is about 25,700,000,000,000 miles. Express this number in scientific notation. 2.57×10^{13} mi

78. SPEED OF SOUND The speed of sound in air is 33,100 centimeters per second. Express this number in scientific notation. 3.31×10^4 cm/sec

79. GEOGRAPHY The largest ocean in the world is the Pacific Ocean, which covers 6.38×10^7 square miles. Express this number in standard notation. 63,800,000 mi^2

▶ **80.** ATOMS The number of atoms in 1 gram of iron is approximately 1.08×10^{22}. Express this number in standard notation. 10,800,000,000,000,000,000,000

81. LENGTH OF A METER One meter is approximately 0.00622 mile. Use scientific notation to express this number. 6.22×10^{-3} mi

82. ANGSTROM One angstrom is 1.0×10^{-7} millimeter. Express this number in standard notation. 0.0000001 mm

83. WAVELENGTHS Transmitters, vacuum tubes, and lights emit energy that can be modeled as a wave, as shown. Examples of the most common types of electromagnetic waves are given in the table. List the wavelengths in order from shortest to longest. g, x, u, v, i, m, r

This distance between the two crests of the wave is called the wavelength.

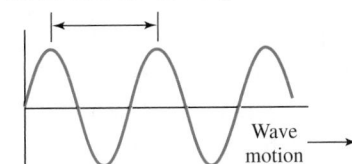

Wave motion

Type	Use	Wavelength (m)
visible light	lighting	9.3×10^{-6}
infrared	photography	3.7×10^{-5}
x-ray	medical	2.3×10^{-11}
radio wave	communication	3.0×10^2
gamma ray	treating cancer	8.9×10^{-14}
microwave	cooking	1.1×10^{-2}
ultraviolet	sun lamp	6.1×10^{-8}

▶ **84.** SPACE EXPLORATION On July 4, 1997, the *Pathfinder*, carrying the rover vehicle called Sojourner, landed on Mars to perform a scientific investigation of the planet. The distance from Mars to Earth is approximately 3.5×10^7 miles. Use scientific notation to express this distance in feet. (*Hint:* 5,280 feet = 1 mile.) 1.848×10^{11} ft

Space Frontiers/Hulton Archive/Getty Images

▶ **85.** PROTONS The mass of one proton is approximately 1.7×10^{-24} gram. Use scientific notation to express the mass of 1 million protons. 1.7×10^{-18} g

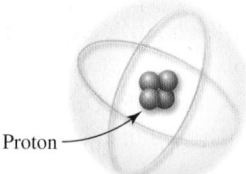

Proton

▶ **86.** SPEED OF SOUND The speed of sound in air is approximately 3.3×10^4 centimeters per second. Use scientific notation to express this speed in kilometers per second. (*Hint:* 100 centimeters = 1 meter and 1,000 meters = 1 kilometer.) 3.3×10^{-1} km/sec

▶ **87.** LIGHT YEARS One light year is about 5.87×10^{12} miles. Use scientific notation to express this distance in feet. (*Hint:* 5,280 feet = 1 mile.) 3.099363×10^{16} ft

▶ **88.** OIL RESERVES In 2006, Saudi Arabia had crude oil reserves of about 2.643×10^{11} barrels. A barrel contains 42 gallons of oil. Use scientific notation to express Saudi Arabia oil reserves in gallons. (Source: infoplease) 1.11006×10^{13} gal

89. INSURED DEPOSITS In 2006, the total insured deposits in U.S. banks and savings and loans was approximately 6.4×10^{12} dollars. If this money was invested at 4% simple annual interest, how much would it earn in 1 year? Use scientific notation to express the answer. (Source: Federal Deposit Insurance Corporation.) 2.56×10^{11} dollars

▶ **90.** CURRENCY In 2006, the number of $20 bills in circulation was approximately 5.96×10^9. Find the total value of the currency. Use scientific notation to express the answer. (Source: The Federal Reserve.) 1.192×10^{11} dollars

▶ **91.** THE MILITARY The graph shows the number of U.S. troops for several years. Estimate each of the following and express your answers in scientific and standard notation.

   a. The number of troops in 1993 1.7×10^6, 1,700,000
   b. The largest numbers of troops during these years 1986: 2.05×10^6, 2,050,000

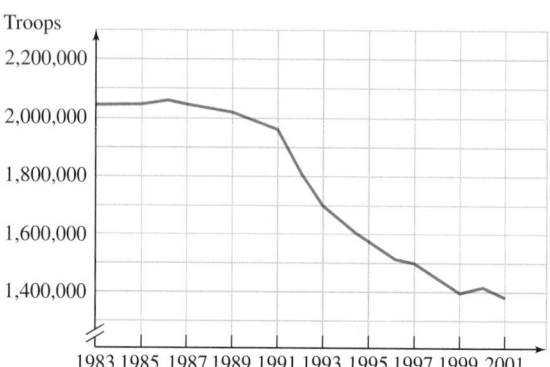

Based on data from the U.S. Department of Defense

92. SUPERCOMPUTERS In 2006, the world's fastest computer was IBM's BlueGene/L System. If it could make 2.81×10^{14} calculations in one second, how many could it make in one minute? Give the answer in scientific notation. 1.686×10^{16}

© Kimberly White/Reuters/Corbis

▌ WRITING

93. In what situations would scientific notation be more convenient than standard notation?

▶ **94.** To multiply a number by a power of 10, we move the decimal point. Which way, and how far? Explain.

95. 2.3×10^{-3} contains a negative sign but represents a positive number. Explain.

▶ **96.** Is this a true statement? $2.0 \times 10^3 = 2 \times 10^3$ Explain.

▌ REVIEW

97. If $y = -1$, find the value of $-5y^{55}$. 5

▶ **98.** What is the y-intercept of the graph of $y = -3x - 5$? $(0, -5)$

Determine which property of real numbers justifies each statement.

99. $5 + z = z + 5$ commutative property of addition

100. $7(u + 3) = 7u + 7 \cdot 3$ distributive property

Solve each equation.

101. $3(x - 4) - 6 = 0$ 6

102. $8(3x - 5) - 4(2x + 3) = 12$ 4

SECTION 5.4

Polynomials

Objectives

1 Know the vocabulary for polynomials.

2 Evaluate polynomials.

In arithmetic, we learned how to add, subtract, multiply, divide, and find powers of numbers. In algebra, we will learn how to perform these operations on *polynomials*. In this section, we will introduce polynomials, classify them into groups, define their degrees, and show how to evaluate them at specific values of their variables.

1 Know the vocabulary for polynomials.

Recall that a **term** is a number or a product of a number and one or more variables, which may be raised to powers. Examples of terms are

$$3x, \qquad -4y^2, \qquad \frac{1}{2}a^2b^3, \qquad t, \qquad \text{and} \qquad 25$$

The **numerical coefficients,** or simply **coefficients,** of the first four of these terms are $3, -4, \frac{1}{2}$, and 1, respectively. Because $25 = 25x^0$, 25 is considered to be the numerical coefficient of the term 25.

Polynomials

A **polynomial** is a term or a sum of terms in which all variables have whole-number exponents. No variable appears in a denominator.

Here are some examples of polynomials:

$$3x + 2, \qquad 4y^2 - 2y - 3, \qquad -8xy^2, \qquad \text{and} \qquad a^3 + 3a^2b + 3ab^2 + b^3$$

The polynomial $3x + 2$ has two terms, $3x$ and 2, and we say it is a **polynomial in one variable,** *x.* A single number is called a **constant,** and so its last term, 2, is called the **constant term.**

Since $4y^2 - 2y - 3$ can be written as $4y^2 + (-2y) + (-3)$, it is the sum of three terms, $4y^2, -2y$, and -3. It is written in **decreasing** or **descending powers** of y, because the powers on y decrease from left to right.

$-8xy^2$ is a polynomial with just one term. We say that it is a **polynomial in two variables,** *x* **and** *y.*

The four-term polynomial $a^3 + 3a^2b + 3ab^2 + b^3$ is written in descending powers of a and **ascending powers** of b.

Caution! The expression $2x^3 - 3x^{-2} + 5$ is not a polynomial, because the second term contains a variable with an exponent that is not a whole number. Similarly, $y^2 - \frac{7}{y}$ is not a polynomial, because $\frac{7}{y}$ has a variable in the denominator.

Self Check 1

Determine whether each expression is a polynomial:
a. $3x^{-4} + 2x^2 - 3$ no
b. $7.5p^3 - 4p^2 - 3p + 4$ yes

Now Try Problems 17 and 18

Teaching Example 1 Determine whether each expression is a polynomial:

a. $\dfrac{5}{x} + 4x^2 - 3$

b. $\dfrac{1}{2}x^2 + 2x - 7$

Answers:
a. no **b.** yes

EXAMPLE 1 Determine whether each expression is a polynomial.

a. $x^2 + 2x + 1$ **b.** $3a^{-1} - 2a - 3$ **c.** $\dfrac{1}{2}x^3 - 2.3x$ **d.** $\dfrac{p + 3}{p - 1}$

Strategy We will note the exponents on the variable bases. We will also identify each denominator.

WHY The expression is a polynomial when all the variables have whole number exponents and no variable appears in a denominator of a fraction.

Solution

a. $x^2 + 2x + 1$ is a polynomial.

b. $3a^{-1} - 2a - 3$ is not a polynomial. In the first term, the exponent on the variable is not a whole number.

c. $\dfrac{1}{2}x^3 - 2.3x$ is a polynomial, because it can be written as the sum $\dfrac{1}{2}x^3 + (-2.3x)$.

d. $\dfrac{p + 3}{p - 1}$ is not a polynomial. For a polynomial, variables cannot be in the denominator of a fraction.

A polynomial with one term is called a **monomial.** A polynomial with two terms is called a **binomial.** A polynomial with three terms is called a **trinomial.** Here are some examples.

Monomials	Binomials	Trinomials
$-6x$	$3u^3 - 4u^2$	$-5t^2 + 4t + 3$
$5x^2y$	$18a^2b + 4ab$	$27x^3 - 6x - 2$
29	$-29z^{17} - 1$	$a^2 + 2ab + b^2$

Self Check 2

Classify each polynomial as a monomial, a binomial, or a trinomial:

a. $5x$ monomial
b. $-5x^2 + 2x - 0.5$ trinomial
c. $16x^2 - 9y^2$ binomial

Now Try Problems 26, 29, and 33

Teaching Example 2 Classify each polynomial as a monomial, a binomial, or a trinomial:
a. $3x^5 - 2x^2 + 1$ **b.** $5xy^2$
c. $2x^3 + 3y^4$
Answers:
a. trinomial **b.** monomial
c. binomial

EXAMPLE 2 Classify each polynomial as a monomial, a binomial, or a trinomial:

a. $5.2x^4 + 3.1x$ **b.** $7g^4 - 5g^3 - 2$ **c.** $-5x^2y^3$

Strategy We will count the number of terms in each polynomial.

WHY The number of terms determines the type of polynomial.

Solution

a. The polynomial $5.2x^4 + 3.1x$ has two terms, $5.2x^4$ and $3.1x$, so it is a binomial.

b. The polynomial $7g^4 - 5g^3 - 2$ has three terms, $7g^4$, $-5g^3$, and -2, so it is a trinomial.

c. The polynomial $-5x^2y^3$ has one term, so it is a monomial.

> **Success Tip** Recall that terms are separated by $+$ or $-$ symbols and the numerical coefficient is the numerical factor of the term.

The monomial $7x^6$ is called a **monomial of sixth degree** or a **monomial of degree 6,** because the variable x occurs as a factor six times. The monomial $3x^3y^4$ is a monomial of seventh degree, because the variables x and y occur as factors a total of seven times. Here are some more examples:

$\qquad 2.7a$ is a monomial of degree 1.

$\qquad -2x^3$ is a monomial of degree 3.

$\qquad 47x^2y^3$ is a monomial of degree 5.

$\qquad 8$ is a monomial of degree 0, because $8 = 8x^0$.

These examples illustrate the following definition.

Degree of a Monomial

If a represents a nonzero constant, the **degree of the monomial** ax^n is n.

The **degree of a monomial** in several variables is the sum of the exponents on those variables.

Caution! Note that the degree of ax^n is not defined when $a = 0$. Since $ax^n = 0$ when $a = 0$, the constant 0 has no defined degree.

Because each term of a polynomial is a monomial, we define the degree of a polynomial by considering the degrees of each of its terms.

Degree of a Polynomial

The **degree of a polynomial** is determined by the term with the largest degree.

Here are some examples:

- $x^2 + 2x$ is a binomial of degree 2, because the degree of its first term is 2 and the degree of its second term is less than 2.
- $1 + d^3 - 3d^2$ is a trinomial of degree 3, because the degree of its second term is 3 and the degree of each of its other terms is less than 3.
- $25y^{13} - 15y^8z^{10} - 32y^{10}z^8 + 4$ is a polynomial of degree 18, because its second and third terms are of degree 18. Its other terms have degree less than 18.

EXAMPLE 3   Find the degree of each polynomial:

a. $-4x^3 - 5x^2 + 3x$ **b.** $1.6w - 1.6$ **c.** $-17a^2b^3 + 12ab^6$

Strategy We will find the degree of each term and compare them.

WHY The degree of the polynomial is the same as the highest-degree term.

Solution

a. The trinomial $-4x^3 - 5x^2 + 3x$ has terms of degree 3, 2, and 1. Therefore, its degree is 3.

b. The first term of $1.6w - 1.6$ has degree 1 and the second term has degree 0, so the binomial has degree 1.

c. The degree of the first term of $-17a^2b^3 + 12ab^6$ is 5 and the degree of the second term is 7, so the binomial has degree 7.

Self Check 3

Find the degree of each polynomial:
a. $15p^3 - 15p^2 - 3p + 4$ 3
b. $-14st^4 + 12s^3t$ 5

Now Try Problems 39 and 44

Teaching Example 3 Find the degree of each polynomial:
a. $5x^3y + 2xy^7 - 4xy^5z^3$ **b.** $4 + 7x^3$
Answers:
a. 9 **b.** 3

If written in descending powers of the variable, the **lead term** of a polynomial is the term of highest degree. For example, the leading term of $-4x^3 - 5x^2 + 3x$ is $-4x^3$. The coefficient of the leading term (in this case, -4) is called the **lead coefficient.**

2   Evaluate polynomials.

Each of the equations below defines a function, because each input x-value determines exactly one output value. Since the right-hand side of each equation is a polynomial, these functions are called **polynomial functions.**

$$f(x) = \underbrace{6x + 4} \qquad g(x) = \underbrace{3x^2 + 4x - 5} \qquad h(x) = \underbrace{-x^3 + x^2 - 2x + 3}$$

This polynomial has two terms. Its degree is 1. This polynomial has three terms. Its degree is 2. This polynomial has four terms. Its degree is 3.

To *evaluate a polynomial function* for a specific value, we replace the variable in the defining equation with the input value. Then we simplify the resulting expression to find the output. For example, suppose we wish to evaluate the polynomial function $f(x) = 6x + 4$ for $x = 1$. Then $f(1)$ represents the value of $f(x) = 6x + 4$ when $x = 1$. We find $f(1)$ as follows.

$$\begin{aligned} f(x) &= 6x + 4 && \text{This is the given function.} \\ f(\mathbf{1}) &= 6(\mathbf{1}) + 4 && \text{Substitute 1 for } x. \text{ The number 1 is the input.} \\ &= 6 + 4 && \text{Perform the multiplication.} \\ &= 10 && \text{Perform the addition. 10 is the output.} \end{aligned}$$

Thus, $f(1) = 10$.

Self Check 4

Consider the function $h(x) = -x^3 + x - 2x + 3$
Find:
a. $h(0)$ 3
b. $h(-3)$ 33

Now Try Problems 52 and 60

Teaching Example 4 Consider the function $h(x) = -x^2 + 5x - 1$
Find:
a. $h(-3)$ **b.** $h(4)$
Answers:
a. -25
b. 3

EXAMPLE 4   Consider the function $g(x) = 3x^2 + 4x - 5$. Find:
a. $g(0)$ **b.** $g(-2)$

Strategy We will substitute the value in the parentheses on the left-hand side of the equation for the letter on the right-hand side. Then we will follow the rules for the order of operations to simplify the right-hand side.

WHY To *evaluate a polynomial* means to find its numerical value, once we know the value of the variable.

Solution

a. $\begin{aligned} g(x) &= 3x^2 + 4x - 5 && \text{This is the given function.} \\ g(\mathbf{0}) &= 3(\mathbf{0})^2 + 4(\mathbf{0}) - 5 && \text{To find } g(0), \text{ substitute 0 for } x. \\ &= 3(0) + 4(0) - 5 && \text{Evaluate the power.} \\ &= 0 + 0 - 5 && \text{Perform the multiplications.} \\ g(0) &= -5 \end{aligned}$

b. $\begin{aligned} g(x) &= 3x^2 + 4x - 5 && \text{This is the given function.} \\ g(\mathbf{-2}) &= 3(\mathbf{-2})^2 + 4(\mathbf{-2}) - 5 && \text{To find } g(-2), \text{ substitute } -2 \text{ for } x. \\ &= 3(4) + 4(-2) - 5 && \text{Evaluate the power.} \\ &= 12 + (-8) - 5 && \text{Perform the multiplications.} \\ g(-2) &= -1 \end{aligned}$

Self Check 5

Find the number of cans used in a display having a square base formed by 5 cans per side. 55

Now Try Problem 80

EXAMPLE 5   *Supermarket Displays* The polynomial function $f(c) = \dfrac{1}{3}c^3 + \dfrac{1}{2}c^2 + \dfrac{1}{6}c$ gives the number of cans used in a display shaped like a square pyramid, having a square base formed by c cans per side. Find the number of cans of soup used in the display shown in the figure.

Strategy We will count the number of cans along one side of the square base of the display. Then we will evaluate the function at that number.

WHY The function gives the number of cans in the display based on the number of cans along one side of the square base.

Teaching Example 5 Find the number of cans used in a display having a square base formed by 7 cans per side.
Answer:
140

Solution
Since each side of the square base of the display is formed by 4 cans, $c = 4$. We can find the number of cans used in the display by finding $f(4)$.

$$f(c) = \frac{1}{3}c^3 + \frac{1}{2}c^2 + \frac{1}{6}c \qquad \text{This is the given function.}$$

$$f(4) = \frac{1}{3}(4)^3 + \frac{1}{2}(4)^2 + \frac{1}{6}(4) \qquad \text{Substitute 4 for } c.$$

$$= \frac{1}{3}(64) + \frac{1}{2}(16) + \frac{1}{6}(4) \qquad \text{Find the powers.}$$

$$= \frac{64}{3} + 8 + \frac{2}{3} \qquad \text{Multiply, and then simplify: } \frac{4}{6} = \frac{2}{3}.$$

$$= \frac{66}{3} + 8 \qquad \text{Add the fractions.}$$

$$= 22 + 8$$

$$= 30$$

30 cans of soup were used in the display.

ANSWERS TO SELF CHECKS

1. a. no **b.** yes **2. a.** monomial **b.** trinomial **c.** binomial **3. a.** 3 **b.** 5
4. a. 3 **b.** 33 **5.** 55

SECTION 5.4   STUDY SET

▌VOCABULARY

Fill in the blanks.

1. A _polynomial_ is a term or a sum of terms in which all variables have whole-number exponents.

2. The numerical _coefficient_ of the term $-25x^2y^3$ is -25.

3. The _degree_ of the monomial $3x^7$ is 7.

4. The degree of a polynomial is the same as the _degree_ of its term with the largest degree.

▶ 5. A _monomial_ is a polynomial with one term.

▶ 6. A _binomial_ is a polynomial with two terms.

▶ 7. A _trinomial_ is a polynomial with three terms.

▶ Selected exercises available online at
www.webassign.net/brookscole

8. For the polynomial $6x^2 + 3x - 1$, the _leading_ term is $6x^2$, and the leading _coefficient_ is 6. The _constant_ term is -1.

9. The notation $f(x)$ is read as f _of_ x.

▶ 10. $f(2)$ represents the _value_ of a function when $x = 2$.

▌CONCEPTS

Fill in the blanks.

11. $4x^3 + 7x^2 - 3x - 15$ is a polynomial in x. It is written in _decreasing or descending_ powers of x.

12. $-7 + 2y + 3y^2 - 8y^3$ is a polynomial in y. It is written in _ascending_ powers of y.

▶ **13.** Write $x - 9 + 3x^2$ in descending powers of x.
$3x^2 + x - 9$

▶ **14.** Write $-2xy + y^2 + x^2$ in descending powers of x.
$x^2 - 2xy + y^2$

NOTATION

Complete each solution.

15. If $f(x) = -2x^2 + 3x - 1$, find $f(2)$.

$$f(2) = -2\left(\boxed{2}\right)^2 + 3\left(\boxed{2}\right) - 1$$
$$= -2\left(\boxed{4}\right)^2 + \boxed{6} - 1$$
$$= -8 + 6 - \boxed{1}$$
$$= \boxed{-2} - 1$$
$$= -3$$

▶ **16.** If $f(x) = -2x^2 + 3x - 1$, find $f(-2)$.

$$f(-2) = -2\left(\boxed{-2}\right)^2 + 3\left(\boxed{-2}\right) - 1$$
$$= -2\left(\boxed{4}\right) + 3\left(\boxed{-2}\right) - 1$$
$$= \boxed{-8} + (-6) - 1$$
$$= \boxed{-14} - 1$$
$$= -15$$

GUIDED PRACTICE

Determine whether each expression is a polynomial.
See Example 1.

17. $x^3 - 5x^2 - 2$ yes   **18.** $x^{-4} - 5x$ no

▶ **19.** $\dfrac{1}{2x} + 3$ no   **20.** $x^3 - 1$ yes

21. $x^2 - y^2$ yes   **22.** $a^4 + a^3 + a^2 + a$ yes

23. $a^3 + 2a^2 - a + 2$ yes   **24.** $\dfrac{1}{x^2 + x - 7}$ no

Classify each polynomial as a monomial, a binomial, a trinomial, or none of these. **See Example 2.**

25. $3x + 7$
binomial
▶ **26.** $3y - 5$
binomial

27. $y^2 + 4y + 3$
trinomial
28. $3xy$
monomial

29. $3z^2$
monomial
30. $3x - 2x^3 + 3x - 1$
none of these

31. $t - 32$
binomial
32. $9x^2y^3z^4$
monomial

33. $s^2 - 23s + 31$
trinomial
34. $2x^3 - 5x^2 + 6x - 3$
none of these

35. $3x^5 - x^4 - 3x^3 + 7$
none of these
36. x^3
monomial

Find the degree of each polynomial. **See Example 3.**

37. $3x^4$ 4th   **38.** $3x^5$ 5th

39. $-2x^2 + 3x + 1$ 2nd   **40.** $-3x + 3x^2 - 5x^4$ 4th

41. $3x - 5$ 1st   **42.** $y^3 + 4y^2$ 3rd

43. $-5r^2s^2 - r^3s + 3$ 4th ▶ **44.** $4r^2s^3 - 5r^2s^8$ 10th

45. $x^{12} + 3x^2y^3$ 12th   ▶ **46.** $17ab^5 - 12a^3b$ 6th

47. 38 0th   **48.** -24 0th

Let $f(x) = 5x - 3$ and find each value. **See Example 4.**

49. $f(2)$ 7   ▶ **50.** $f(0)$ −3

51. $f(-1)$ −8   **52.** $f(-2)$ −13

53. $f\left(\dfrac{1}{5}\right)$ −2   **54.** $f\left(\dfrac{4}{5}\right)$ 1

55. $f(-0.9)$ −7.5   **56.** $f(-1.2)$ −9

Let $g(x) = -x^2 - 4$ and find each value.

57. $g(0)$ −4   ▶ **58.** $g(1)$ −5

59. $g(-1)$ −5   **60.** $g(-2)$ −8

Let $g(x) = -x^2 - 4$ and find each value.

61. $g(1.3)$ −5.69   ▶ **62.** $g(2.4)$ −9.76

63. $g(-13.6)$ −188.96   **64.** $g(-25.3)$ −644.09

TRY IT YOURSELF

Let $h(x) = x^3 - 2x + 3$ and find each value.

65. $h(0)$ 3   **66.** $h(3)$ 24

67. $h(-2)$ −1   ▶ **68.** $h(-1)$ 4

69. $h(0.9)$ 1.929   **70.** $h(0.4)$ 2.264

71. $h(-8.1)$ −512.241   **72.** $h(-7.7)$ −438.133

Let $f(x) = -x^4 - x^3 + x^2 + x - 1$ and find each value.

73. $f(1)$ −1   ▶ **74.** $f(-1)$ −1

75. $f(-2)$ −7   **76.** $f(2)$ −19

APPLICATIONS

▶ **77.** PACKAGING To make boxes, a manufacturer cuts equal-sized squares from each corner of a 10-inch × 12-inch piece of cardboard, and then folds up the sides. The polynomial function

$$f(x) = 4x^3 - 44x^2 + 120x$$

gives the volume (in cubic inches) of the resulting box when a square with sides x inches long is cut from each corner. Find the volume of a box if 3-inch squares are cut out. 72 in.³

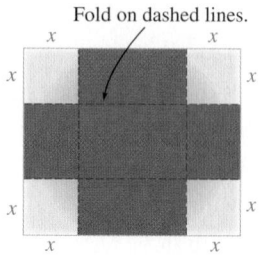
Fold on dashed lines.

78. MAXIMIZING REVENUE The revenue (in dollars) that a manufacturer of office desks receives is given by the polynomial function

$$f(d) = -0.08d^2 + 100d$$

where d is the number of desks manufactured.

a. Find the total revenue if 625 desks are manufactured. $31,250

b. Does increasing the number of desks being manufactured to 650 increase the revenue? no

79. WATER BALLOONS Some college students launched water balloons from the balcony of their dormitory on unsuspecting sunbathers. The height in feet of the balloons at a time t seconds after being launched is given by the polynomial function

$$f(t) = -16t^2 + 12t + 20$$

What was the height of the balloons 0.5 second and 1.5 seconds after being launched? 22 ft, 2 ft

80. STOPPING DISTANCE   *from Campus to Careers*
Police Officer

The number of feet that a car travels before stopping depends on the driver's reaction time and the braking distance, as shown below. For one driver, the stopping distance is given by the polynomial function

$$f(v) = 0.04v^2 + 0.9v$$

where v is the velocity of the car. Find the stopping distance when the driver is traveling at 30 mph. 63 ft

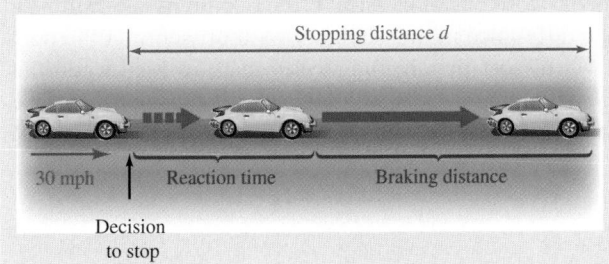

Stopping distance d

30 mph   Reaction time   Braking distance

Decision to stop

81. SUSPENSION BRIDGES The function

$$f(s) = 400 + 0.0066667s^2 - 0.0000001s^4$$

approximates the length of the cable between the two vertical towers of a suspension bridge, where s is the sag in the cable. Estimate the length of the cable of the bridge in the next column if the sag is 24.6 feet. about 404 ft

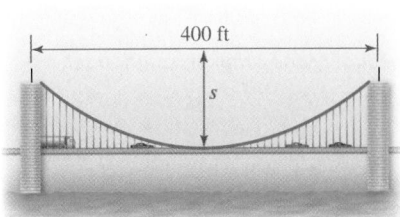

400 ft

s

82. PRODUCE DEPARTMENTS Suppose a grocer is going to set up a pyramid-shaped display of cantaloupes like that shown in the figure in Example 5. If each side of the square base of the display is made of six cantaloupes, how many will be used in the display? 91

83. DOLPHINS At a marine park, three trained dolphins jump in unison over an arching stream of water whose path can be described by the polynomial function

$$f(x) = -0.05x^2 + 2x$$

Given the takeoff points for each dolphin, how high must each dolphin jump to clear the stream of water? 18.75 ft, 20 ft, 15 ft

y

15 ft 20 ft   30 ft   Water level

Take-off points for dolphins

84. TUNNELS The arch at the entrance to a tunnel is described by the polynomial function

$$f(x) = -0.25x^2 + 23$$

What is the height of the arch at the edge of the pavement? 14 ft

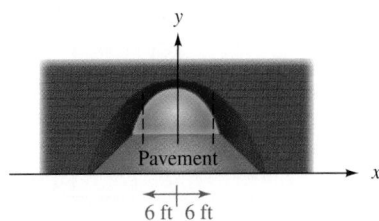

y

Pavement

x

6 ft 6 ft

WRITING

85. Describe how to determine the degree of a polynomial.

86. List some words that contain the prefixes *mono, bi,* or *tri.*

| REVIEW

Solve each inequality and graph its solution set.

87. $-4(3y + 2) \leq 28$ **88.** $-5 < 3t + 4 \leq 13$

$y \geq -3 \quad [-3, \infty)$ $-3 < t \leq 3 \quad (-3, 3]$

Write each expression without using parentheses or negative exponents.

89. $(x^2x^4)^3$ x^{18} ▶ **90.** $(a^2)^3(a^3)^2$ a^{12}

91. $\left(\dfrac{y^2y^5}{y^4}\right)^3$ y^9 **92.** $\left(\dfrac{2t^2}{t}\right)^{-4}$ $\dfrac{1}{16t^4}$

Objectives

1 Add monomials.

2 Subtract monomials.

3 Add polynomials.

4 Subtract polynomials.

5 Add and subtract multiples of polynomials.

SECTION 5.5

Adding and Subtracting Polynomials

In figure (a), the heights of the Seattle Space Needle and the Eiffel Tower in Paris are given. Using rules from arithmetic, we can find the difference in the heights of the towers by subtracting two numbers.

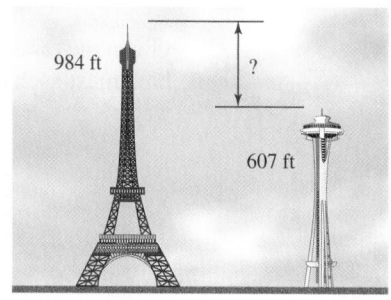

Arithmetic

$984 - 607 = 377$

The difference in height is 377 feet.

(a)

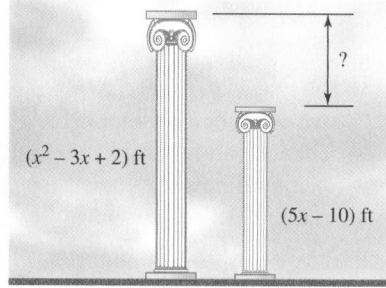

Algebra

$(x^2 - 3x + 2) - (5x - 10) = ?$

(b)

In figure (b), the heights of two types of classical Greek columns are expressed using *polynomials*. To find the difference in their heights, we must subtract the polynomials. In this section, we will discuss the algebraic rules that are used to do this. Since any subtraction can be written in terms of addition, we will consider the procedures used to add polynomials first. We begin with monomials, which are polynomials having just one term.

1 Adding monomials.

Recall that like terms have the same variables with the same exponents:

Like terms	**Unlike terms**
$-7x$ and $15x$	$-7x$ and $15a$
$4y^3$ and $16y^3$	$4y^3$ and $16y^2$
$\dfrac{1}{2}xy^2$ and $-\dfrac{1}{3}xy^2$	$\dfrac{1}{2}xy^2$ and $-\dfrac{1}{3}x^2y$

Also recall that to combine like terms, we combine their coefficients and keep the same variables with the same exponents. For example,

$$4y + 5y = (4 + 5)y \qquad \text{and} \qquad 8x^2 + x^2 = (8 + 1)x^2$$
$$= 9y \qquad\qquad\qquad\qquad\qquad = 9x^2$$

Likewise,

$$3a + 4b + 6a + 3b = 9a + 7b \quad \text{and} \quad 4cd^3 + 9cd^3 = 13cd^3$$

These examples suggest that to add like monomials, we simply combine like terms.

The Language of Algebra   Simplifying the sum or difference of like terms is called *combining like terms*.

EXAMPLE 1   Perform the following additions.

a. $4x^4 + 81x^4$ **b.** $8x^2y^2 + 6x^2y^2 + x^2y^2$ **c.** $32c^2 + 10c + 4c^2$

Strategy We will note the terms that have the same variables with the same exponents. Then we will combine their coefficients and keep the same variables with the same exponents.

WHY Only like terms can be simplified with addition.

Solution

a. $4x^4 + 81x^4 = 85x^4$ Think: $(4 + 81)x^4 = 85x^4$.

b. $8x^2y^2 + 6x^2y^2 + x^2y^2 = 15x^2y^2$ Think: $(8 + 6 + 1)x^2y^2 = 15x^2y^2$.

c. $32c^2 + 10c + 4c^2 = 32c^2 + 4c^2 + 10c$ Write the like terms together.

$\qquad\qquad\qquad\quad = 36c^2 + 10c$ Think: $(32 + 4)c^2 = 36c^2$.

Caution!   When combining like terms, the exponents on the variables *stay the same*. Don't incorrectly add the exponents.

Success Tip   When performing operations on polynomials, we usually write the terms of the solution in decreasing (or descending) powers of one variable. For instance, in Example 1, part c, the solution was written as $36c^2 + 10c$ instead of $10c + 36c^2$.

---

2 **Subtract monomials.**

To subtract one monomial from another, we add the opposite of the monomial that is to be subtracted.

EXAMPLE 2   Find each difference.

a. $8x^2 - 3x^2$ **b.** $6xy - 9xy$ **c.** $-3r - 5 - 4r$ **d.** $0.9x^2 - 1.2x - 0.5x^2 - 0.4x$

Strategy We will note the terms that have the same variables with the same exponents. Then we will combine their coefficients and keep the same variables with the same exponents.

WHY Only like terms can be simplified with subtraction.

Solution

a. $8x^2 - 3x^2 = 8x^2 + (-3x^2)$ Add the opposite of $3x^2$, which is $-3x^2$.

$\qquad\qquad\quad = 5x^2$ Combine like terms.

b. $6xy - 9xy = 6xy + (-9xy)$ Add the opposite of $9xy$, which is $-9xy$.

$\qquad\qquad = -3xy$ Combine like terms.

---

c. $-3r - 5 - 4r = -3r + (-5) + (-4r)$ Add the opposite of 5 and 4r.

$\qquad\qquad = -3r + (-4r) + (-5)$ Write like terms together.

$\qquad\qquad = -7r - 5$ Combine like terms. Write the addition of -5 as a subtraction of 5.

d. $0.9x^2 - 1.2x - 0.5x^2 - 0.4x = 0.9x^2 + (-1.2x) + (-0.5x^2) + (-0.4x)$

$\qquad\qquad\qquad\qquad = 0.9x^2 + (-0.5x^2) + (-1.2x) + (-0.4x)$

$\qquad\qquad\qquad\qquad = 0.4x^2 - 1.6x$

3 Add polynomials.

Because of the distributive property, we can remove parentheses enclosing several terms when the sign preceding the parentheses is a $+$ sign. We simply drop the parentheses.

$+(3x^2 + 3x - 2) = +1(3x^2 + 3x - 2)$

$\qquad\qquad\qquad = 1(3x^2) + 1(3x) + 1(-2)$ Distribute the multiplication by 1.

$\qquad\qquad\qquad = 3x^2 + 3x + (-2)$ Multiplicative identity property.

$\qquad\qquad\qquad = 3x^2 + 3x - 2$ Write the addition of -2 as a subtraction of 2.

We can add polynomials by removing parentheses, if necessary, and then combining any like terms that are contained within the polynomials.

Self Check 3

Add: $(2a^2 - a + 4) +$
$(5a^2 + 6a - 5)$ $7a^2 + 5a - 1$

Now Try Problem 36

Teaching Example 3 Add:
$(3c^2 - 2c - 5) + (4c^2 - 7c + 3)$
Answer:
$7c^2 - 9c - 2$

EXAMPLE 3   Add: $(3x^2 - 3x + 2) + (2x^2 + 7x - 4)$

Strategy We will reorder and write the like terms together. Then we will combine like terms.

WHY To add polynomials means to combine their like terms.

Solution

$(3x^2 - 3x + 2) + (2x^2 + 7x - 4)$

$\qquad = 3x^2 - 3x + 2 + 2x^2 + 7x - 4$ Drop the parentheses.

$\qquad = 3x^2 + 2x^2 - 3x + 7x + 2 - 4$ Write like terms together.

$\qquad = 5x^2 + 4x - 2$ Combine like terms.

Problems such as Example 3 are often written with like terms aligned vertically. We can then add the polynomials column by column.

$$\begin{array}{r} 3x^2 - 3x + 2 \\ + \underline{2x^2 + 7x - 4} \\ 5x^2 + 4x - 2 \end{array}$$

Self Check 4

Add $4q^2 - 7$ and $2q^2 - 8q + 9$ using the vertical form.

Now Try Problem 40

Self Check 4 Answer
$6q^2 - 8q + 2$

Teaching Example 4 Add $8c^2 + 2c - 1$
and $4c^2 + 5$ using the vertical form.
Answer:
$12c^2 + 2c + 4$

EXAMPLE 4   Add $4x^2 - 3$ and $3x^2 - 8x + 8$ using the vertical form.

Strategy We will write one polynomial underneath the other, aligning the like terms and drawing a horizontal line beneath them. Then we will add the like terms, column by column, and write each result under the line.

WHY *Vertical form* means to arrange the like terms in columns.

Solution

Since the first polynomial does not have an x-term, we leave a space so that the constant terms can be aligned.

$$\begin{array}{r} 4x^2 \qquad - 3 \\ + \underline{3x^2 - 8x + 8} \\ 7x^2 - 8x + 5 \end{array}$$

4 Subtract polynomials.

Because of the distributive property, we can remove parentheses enclosing several terms when the sign preceding the parentheses is a $-$ sign. We simply drop the minus sign and the parentheses, and *change the sign of every term within the parentheses.*

$$-(3x^2 + 3x - 2) = -1(3x^2 + 3x - 2)$$
$$= -1(3x^2) + (-1)(3x) + (-1)(-2)$$
$$= -3x^2 + (-3x) + 2$$
$$= -3x^2 - 3x + 2$$

This suggests that the way to subtract polynomials is to remove parentheses, change the sign of each term of the second polynomial, and combine like terms.

EXAMPLE 5 Find each difference.

a. $(3x - 4) - (5x + 7)$ **b.** $(3x^2 - 4x - 6) - (2x^2 - 6x)$
c. $(-t^3 - 2t^2 - 1) - (-t^3 - 2t^2 + 1)$

Strategy We will change the signs of the terms of the polynomial being subtracted, drop the parentheses, and collect like terms.

WHY This is the method for subtracting two polynomials.

Solution
a. $(3x - 4) - (5x + 7) = 3x - 4 - 5x - 7$ Change the sign of each term inside $(5x + 7)$ and drop the parentheses.

$$= -2x - 11$$ Combine like terms.

b. $(3x^2 - 4x - 6) - (2x^2 - 6x)$

$$= 3x^2 - 4x - 6 - 2x^2 + 6x$$ Change the sign of each term of $2x^2 - 6x$ and drop the parentheses.

$$= x^2 + 2x - 6$$ Combine like terms.

c. $(-t^3 - 2t^2 - 1) - (-t^3 - 2t^2 + 1)$

$$= -t^3 - 2t^2 - 1 + t^3 + 2t^2 - 1$$ Change the sign of each term of $-t^3 - 2t^2 + 1$ and drop the parentheses.

$$= -2$$ Combine like terms.

To subtract polynomials in vertical form, we add the opposite of the **subtrahend** (the bottom polynomial) to the **minuend** (the top polynomial).

EXAMPLE 6 Subtract $3x^2 - 2x$ from $2x^2 + 4x$.

Strategy Since $3x^2 - 2x$ is to be subtracted from $2x^2 + 4x$, we will write $3x^2 - 2x$ below $2x^2 + 4x$ in vertical form. Then we will change the signs of the terms of $3x^2 - 2x$ and add column by column.

WHY *Vertical Form* means to align the like terms in columns.

Solution

Change signs

$$\begin{array}{r} 2x^2 + 4x \\ - \ 3x^2 - 2x \end{array} \longrightarrow + \begin{array}{r} 2x^2 + 4x \\ -3x^2 + 2x \\ \hline -x^2 + 6x \end{array}$$
and add

Self Check 5
Find the difference:
$(-2a^2 + 5) - (-5a^2 - 7)$
Now Try Problems 41 and 43
Self Check 5 Answer
$3a^2 + 12$

Teaching Example 5 Find the difference:
$(-3x^2 + 5x - 7) - (x^2 - 6)$
Answer:
$-4x^2 + 5x - 1$

Self Check 6
Subtract $2p^2 + 2p - 8$ from $5p^2 - 6p + 7$. $3p^2 - 8p + 15$
Now Try Problem 45

Teaching Example 6 Subtract $-5x^2 + 2x - 1$ from $4x^2 + 6x + 7$.
Answer:
$9x^2 + 4x + 8$

EXAMPLE 7   Subtract $12a - 7$ from the sum of $6a + 5$ and $4a - 10$.

Strategy We will use brackets to show that $(12a - 7)$ is to be subtracted from the *sum* of $(6a + 5)$ and $(4a - 10)$.

WHY The key words of the problem *subtract from* and *sum* indicate mathematical operations.

Solution

$$[(6a + 5) + (4a - 10)] - (12a - 7)$$

Next, we remove the grouping symbols to obtain

$$= 6a + 5 + 4a - 10 - 12a + 7 \quad \text{Change the sign of each term in } (12a - 7).$$
$$= -2a + 2 \quad \text{Combine like terms.}$$

5 Add and subtract multiples of polynomials.

Because of the distributive property, we can remove parentheses enclosing several terms when a monomial precedes the parentheses. We simply multiply every term within the parentheses by that monomial. For example, to add $3(2x + 5)$ and $2(4x - 3)$, we proceed as follows:

$$3(2x + 5) + 2(4x - 3) = 6x + 15 + 8x - 6 \quad \text{Distribute the multiplication by 3 and by 2.}$$
$$= 6x + 8x + 15 - 6 \quad 15 + 8x = 8x + 15.$$
$$= 14x + 9 \quad \text{Combine like terms.}$$

EXAMPLE 8   Remove the parentheses and simplify.

a. $3(x^2 + 4x) + 2(x^2 - 4)$ **b.** $-8(y^2 - 2y + 3) - 4(2y^2 + y - 6)$

Strategy We will use the distributive property to remove parentheses. Then we will collect like terms.

WHY This is what it means to simplify a polynomial.

Solution

a. $3(x^2 + 4x) + 2(x^2 - 4) = 3x^2 + 12x + 2x^2 - 8 \quad \text{Use the distributive property to remove parentheses.}$

$$= 5x^2 + 12x - 8 \quad \text{Collect like terms.}$$

b. $-8(y^2 - 2y + 3) - 4(2y^2 + y - 6) = -8y^2 + 16y - 24 - 8y^2 - 4y + 24$
$$= -16y^2 + 12y$$

EXAMPLE 9   *Property Values* A house purchased for \$95,000 is expected to appreciate according to the polynomial function $f(x) = 2{,}500x + 95{,}000$, where $f(x)$ is the value of the house after x years. A second house purchased for \$125,000 is expected to appreciate according to the equation $f(x) = 4{,}500x + 125{,}000$. Find one polynomial function that will give the total value of both properties after x years.

Strategy To find the polynomial function that will give the total value of both properties, we will add the two polynomials.

WHY To *find a total* means to add.

Solution

The value of the first house after x years is given by the polynomial $2{,}500x + 95{,}000$. The value of the second house after x years is given by the polynomial $4{,}500x + 125{,}000$. The value of both houses will be the sum of these two polynomials.

$$(2{,}500x + 95{,}000) + (4{,}500x + 125{,}000) = 7{,}000x + 220{,}000$$

The total value of the properties is given by the polynomial function $f(x) = 7{,}000x + 220{,}000$.

ANSWERS TO SELF CHECKS

1. a. $35x^6$ **b.** $25pq^2$ **c.** $7a^3 + 15a$ **2. a.** $5m^3$ **b.** $-12pq - 27p$ **c.** $-2.8x^3$
3. $7a^2 + 5a - 1$ **4.** $6q^2 - 8q + 2$ **5.** $3a^2 + 12$ **6.** $3p^2 - 8p + 15$ **7.** $6q^2 - 3q$
8. $7a^2 + 4a$ **9.** $(15t + 5)$ ft

SECTION 5.5   STUDY SET

VOCABULARY

Fill in the blanks.

1. The expression $(x^2 - 3x + 2) + (x^2 - 4x)$ is the sum of two __polynomials__ .

2. The expression $(x^2 - 3x + 2) - (x^2 - 4x)$ is the __difference__ of two polynomials.

▶ **3.** __Like__ terms have the same variables and the same exponents.

4. "To add or subtract like terms" means to combine their __coefficients__ and keep the same variables with the same exponents.

CONCEPTS

Fill in the blanks.

5. To add like monomials, combine like __terms__ .

6. $a - b = a + \underline{(-b)}$

7. To add two polynomials, combine any __like__ terms contained in the polynomials.

8. To subtract two polynomials, change the __sign__ of each term in the second polynomial, and combine like terms.

9. When the sign preceding parentheses is a $-$ sign, we can remove the parentheses by dropping the sign and the parentheses, and __changing__ the sign of every term within the parentheses.

10. When a monomial precedes parentheses, we can remove the parentheses by __multiplying__ every term within the parentheses by that monomial.

11. $-(-2x^2 - 3x + 4) = \underline{2x^2 + 3x - 4}$

12. $-3(-2x^2 - 3x + 4) = \underline{6x^2 + 9x - 12}$

13. JETS Find the polynomial representing the length of the passenger jet. $(11x - 12)$ ft

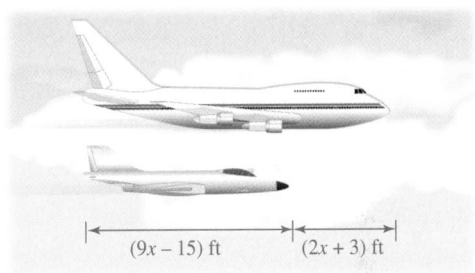

$(9x - 15)$ ft $(2x + 3)$ ft

▶ **14.** WATER SKIING Find the polynomial representing the distance of the water skier from the boat. $(9y - 4)$ m

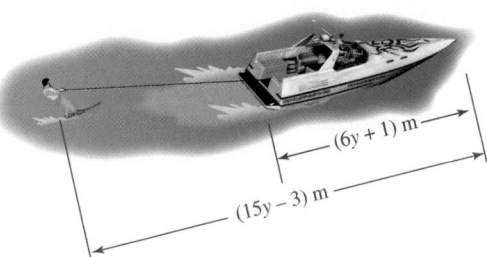

$(6y + 1)$ m

$(15y - 3)$ m

NOTATION

Complete each solution.

15. $(5x^2 + 3x) - (7x^2 - 2x)$
$$= 5x^2 + 3x - 7x^2 + 2x$$
$$= 5x^2 - 7x^2 + 3x + 2x$$
$$= -2x^2 + 5x$$

▶ **16.** $4(3x^2 - 2x) - (2x + 4)$
$$= 12x^2 - 8x - 2x - 4$$
$$= 12x^2 - 10x - 4$$

GUIDED PRACTICE

Perform the following additions. **See Example 1.**

17. $4y + 5y$ $9y$

18. $2x + 3x$ $5x$

19. $8t^2 + 4t^2$ $12t^2$

▶ **20.** $15x^2 + 10x^2$ $25x^2$

21. $4r + 3r + 7r$ $14r$

22. $2b + 7b + 3b$ $12b$

23. $4ab + 4ab + ab$ $9ab$

24. $xy + 4xy + 2xy$ $7xy$

Find each difference. **See Example 2.**

25. $7a^3 - 4a^3$ $3a^3$

26. $12ab - 5ab$ $7ab$

27. $-32u^3 - 16u^3$ $-48u^3$

▶ **28.** $-25x^3 - 7x^3$ $-32x^3$

29. $-3m - 6 - 4m$ $-7m - 6$

30. $6c - 10 - 3c - 2$ $3c - 12$

31. $0.8p^2 - 3.1p - 2.7p^2 - 1.4p$ $-1.9p^2 - 4.5p$

32. $1.7x - 3.2y - 2.5x - 7.5y$ $-0.8x - 10.7y$

Find each sum. **See Examples 3–4.**

33. $(3x + 7) + (4x - 3)$ $7x + 4$

34. $(2y - 3) + (4y + 7)$ $6y + 4$

35. $(3x^2 - 3x - 2) + (3x^2 + 4x - 3)$ $6x^2 + x - 5$

▶ **36.** $(4c^2 + 3c - 2) + (3c^2 + 4c + 2)$ $7c^2 + 7c$

37. $\quad 3x^2 + 4x + 5$
  $\underline{+2x^2 - 3x + 6}$
  $\quad 5x^2 + x + 11$

38. $\quad 2x^3 + 2x^2 - 3x + 5$
  $+\underline{3x^3 - 4x^2 - \ x - 7}$
  $\quad 5x^3 - 2x^2 - 4x - 2$

▶ **39.** $\quad 2x^3 - 3x^2 + 4x - 7$
  $+\underline{-9x^3 - 4x^2 - 5x + 6}$
  $\quad -7x^3 - 7x^2 - x - 1$

40. $\quad -3x^3 + 4x^2 - 4x + 9$
  $+\underline{\quad 2x^3 \qquad\quad + 9x - 3}$
  $\quad -x^3 + 4x^2 + 5x + 6$

Find each difference. **See Examples 5–6.**

41. $(4a + 3) - (2a - 4)$ $2a + 7$

42. $(5b - 7) - (3b - 5)$ $2b - 2$

▶ **43.** $(3a^2 - 2a + 4) - (a^2 - 3a + 7)$ $2a^2 + a - 3$

44. $(2b^2 + 3b - 5) - (2b^2 - 4b - 9)$ $7b + 4$

45. $\quad\ \ 3x^2 + 4x - 5$
  $-\underline{-2x^2 - 2x + 3}$
  $\quad\ \ 5x^2 + 6x - 8$

46. $\quad\ 3y^2 - 4y + \ 7$
  $-\underline{6y^2 - 6y - 13}$
  $\quad -3y^2 + 2y + 20$

▶ **47.** $\quad 4x^3 + 4x^2 - 3x + 10$
  $-\underline{5x^3 - 2x^2 - 4x - \ 4}$
  $\quad -x^3 + 6x^2 + x + 14$

48. $\quad\ \ 3x^3 + 4x^2 + 7x + 12$
  $-\underline{-4x^3 + 6x^2 + 9x - \ 3}$
  $\quad 7x^3 - 2x^2 - 2x + 15$

Perform the operations. **See Example 7.**

49. Find the difference when $t^3 - 2t^2 + 2$ is subtracted from the sum of $3t^3 + t^2$ and $-t^3 + 6t - 3$.
$t^3 + 3t^2 + 6t - 5$

▶ **50.** Find the difference when $-3z^3 - 4z + 7$ is subtracted from the sum of $2z^2 + 3z - 7$ and $-4z^3 - 2z - 3$.
$-z^3 + 2z^2 + 5z - 17$

51. Find the sum when $3x^2 + 4x - 7$ is added to the sum of $-2x^2 - 7x + 1$ and $-4x^2 + 8x - 1$. $-3x^2 + 5x - 7$

52. Find the difference when $32x^2 - 17x + 45$ is subtracted from the sum of $23x^2 - 12x - 7$ and $-11x^2 + 12x + 7$. $-20x^2 + 17x - 45$

Simplify each expression. **See Example 8.**

53. $2(x + 3) + 4(x - 2)$
$6x - 2$

▶ **54.** $3(y - 4) - 5(y + 3)$
$-2y - 27$

55. $-2(x^2 + 7x - 1) - 3(x^2 - 2x + 2)$
$-5x^2 - 8x - 4$

▶ **56.** $-5(y^2 - 2y - 6) + 6(2y^2 + 2y - 5)$
$7y^2 + 22y$

57. $2(2y^2 - 2y + 2) - 4(3y^2 - 4y - 1) + 4(y^2 - y - 1)$
$-4y^2 + 8y + 4$

▶ **58.** $-4(z^2 - 5z) - 5(4z^2 - 1) + 6(2z - 3)$
$-24z^2 + 32z - 13$

59. $2(ab^2 - b) - 3(a + 2ab) + (b - a + a^2b)$
$a^2b + 2ab^2 - 6ab - 4a - b$

60. $3(xy + y) - 2(x - 4 + y) + 2(y^3 + y^2)$
$2y^3 + 2y^2 + 3xy - 2x + y + 8$

TRY IT YOURSELF

Perform the operations and simplify.

61. $1.8x - 1.9x$ $-0.1x$

62. $1.7y - 2.2y$ $-0.5y$

63. $\dfrac{1}{2}st + \dfrac{3}{2}st$ $2st$

64. $\dfrac{2}{5}at + \dfrac{1}{5}at$ $\dfrac{3}{5}at$

65. $(3x)^2 - 4x^2 + 10x^2$ $15x^2$ **66.** $(2x)^4 - (3x^2)^2$ $7x^4$

67. $(2x + 3y) + (5x - 10y)$ $7x - 7y$

▶ **68.** $(5x - 8y) - (-2x + 5y)$ $7x - 13y$

69. $(-8x - 3y) - (-11x + y)$ $3x - 4y$

70. $(-4a + b) + (5a - b)$ a

71. $(2x^2 - 3x + 1) - (4x^2 - 3x + 2) + (2x^2 + 3x + 2)$
$3x + 1$

▶ **72.** $(-3z^2 - 4z + 7) + (2z^2 + 2z - 1) - (2z^2 - 3z + 7)$
$-3z^2 + z - 1$

73. $(4.52x^2 + 1.13x - 0.89) + (9.02x^2 - 7.68x + 7.04)$
$13.54x^2 - 6.55x + 6.15$

74. $(0.891a^4 - 0.442a^2 + 0.121a) - (-0.160a^4 + 0.249a^2 + 0.789a)$ $1.051a^4 - 0.691a^2 - 0.668a$

75. $2(5a + 3b - c) - 5(-2a + 4b + 4c)$ $20a - 14b - 22c$

76. $-3(4p - 3q + r) + 4(-2p - 3q - 2r)$
$-20p - 3q - 11r$

77.
$$+\begin{array}{r} -3x^2 + 4x + 25 \\ 5x^2 \quad\quad - 12 \\ \hline 2x^2 + 4x + 13 \end{array}$$

78.
$$+\begin{array}{r} -6x^3 - 4x^2 + 7 \\ -7x^3 + 9x^2 \quad\quad \\ \hline -13x^3 + 5x^2 + 7 \end{array}$$

79.
$$-\begin{array}{r} -2x^2y^2 \quad\quad + 12y^2 \\ 10x^2y^2 + 9xy - 24y^2 \\ \hline -12x^2y^2 - 9xy + 36y^2 \end{array}$$

80.
$$-\begin{array}{r} 25x^3 \quad\quad + 31xz^2 \\ 12x^3 + 27x^2z - 17xz^2 \\ \hline 13x^3 - 27x^2z + 48xz^2 \end{array}$$

Find the polynomial that represents the perimeter of each figure.

81. $(3x^2 + 6x - 2)$ yd

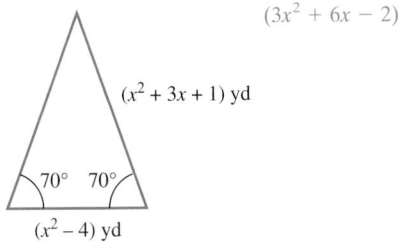

82. $(7x^2 + 5x + 6)$ mi

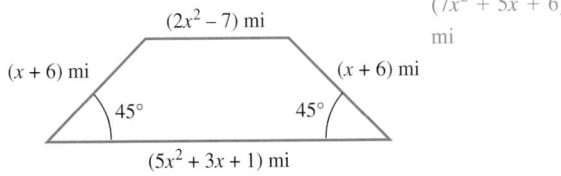

APPLICATIONS

83. GREEK ARCHITECTURE Find the difference in the heights of the columns shown in figure (b) on page 422 at the beginning of this section.
$(x^2 - 8x + 12)$ ft

84. CLASSICAL GREEK COLUMNS If the columns shown in figure (b) on page 442 at the beginning of this section were stacked one atop the other, to what height would they reach?
$(x^2 + 2x - 8)$ ft

85. AUTO MECHANICS Find the polynomial representing the length of the fan belt shown in the next column. The dimensions are in inches. Your answer will involve π. $(3x^2 + 11x + 4.5\pi)$ in.

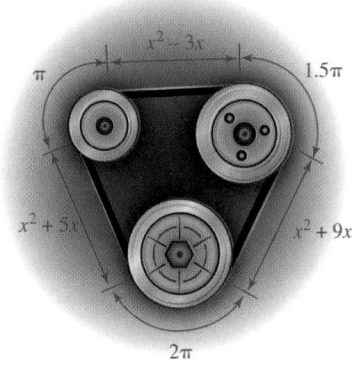

86. READING BLUEPRINTS

a. What is the difference in the length and width of the one-bedroom apartment shown below? $(6x + 5)$ ft

b. Find the perimeter of the apartment. $(4x^2 + 26)$ ft

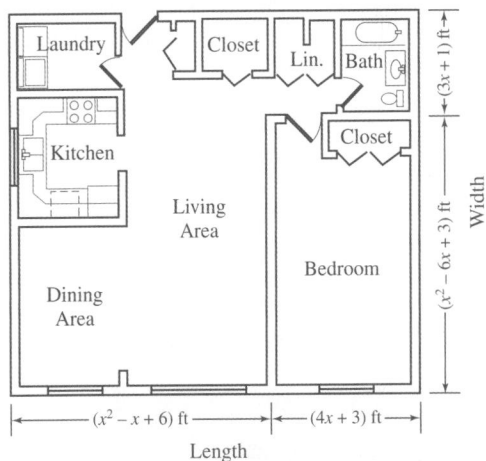

If a house is purchased for $105,000 and is expected to appreciate $900 per year, its value y after x years is given by the polynomial function $f(x) = 900x + 105,000$.

87. VALUE OF A HOUSE Find the expected value of the house in 10 years. $114,000

88. VALUE OF A HOUSE A second house is purchased for $120,000 and is expected to appreciate $1,000 per year.

a. Find a polynomial function that will give the value y of the house in x years. $f(x) = 1,000x + 120,000$

b. Find the value of this second house after 12 years. $132,000

89. VALUE OF TWO HOUSES Find one polynomial function that will give the combined value y of both houses, one from the directions and the other from problem 88, after x years. $f(x) = 1,900x + 225,000$

▶ **90.** VALUE OF TWO HOUSES Find the value of the two houses after 20 years by

    a. substituting 20 into the polynomial functions $f(x) = 900x + 105,000$ and $f(x) = 1,000x + 120,000$ and adding. $263,000

    b. substituting 20 into the result of Exercise 89. $263,000

A business purchases two computers, one for $6,600 and the other for $9,200. The first computer is expected to depreciate $1,100 per year and the second $1,700 per year.

91. VALUE OF A COMPUTER Write a polynomial function that gives the value of the first computer after x years. $f(x) = -1,100x + 6,600$

92. VALUE OF A COMPUTER Write a polynomial function that gives the value of the second computer after x years. $f(x) = -1,700x + 9,200$

93. VALUE OF TWO COMPUTERS Find one polynomial function that gives the combined value of both computers whose functions were found in Exercises 91 and 92 after x years. $f(x) = -2,800x + 15,800$

94. VALUE OF TWO COMPUTERS In two ways, find the combined value of the two computers after 3 years. $7,400

▶ **95.** NAVAL OPERATIONS Two warning flares are simultaneously fired upward from different parts of a ship. The height of the first flare is $(-16t^2 + 128t + 20)$ feet and the height of the higher-traveling second flare is $(-16t^2 + 150t + 40)$ feet, after t seconds.

    a. Find a polynomial that represents the difference in the heights of the flares. $22t + 20$

    b. In 4 seconds, the first flare reaches its peak, explodes, and lights up the sky. How much higher is the second flare at that time? 108 ft

▶ **96.** PIÑATAS Find the polynomial that represents the length of the rope used to hold up the piñata. $(2a^2 + 6a + 5)$ in.

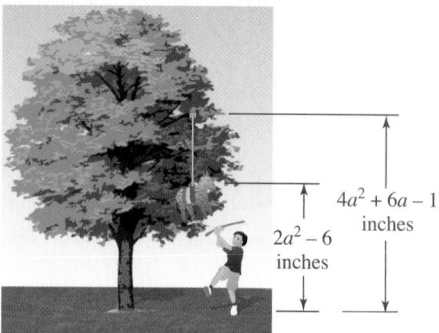

$4a^2 + 6a - 1$ inches

$2a^2 - 6$ inches

WRITING

▶ **97.** How do you recognize like terms?

▶ **98.** How do you add like terms?

99. Explain the concept that is illustrated by the statement

$$-(x^2 + 3x - 1) = -1(x^2 + 3x - 1)$$

100. Explain the mistake made in the following simplification:

$$(12x - 4) - (3x - 1) = 12x - 4 - 3x - 1$$
$$= 9x - 5$$

REVIEW

101. What is the sum of the measures of the angles of a triangle? 180°

▶ **102.** What is the sum of the measures of two complementary angles? 90°

103. Solve the inequality $-4(3x - 3) \geq -12$ and graph the solution. $x \leq 2$ $(-\infty, 2]$

104. CURLING IRONS A curling iron is plugged into a 110-volt electrical outlet and used for $\frac{1}{4}$ hour. If its resistance is 10 ohms, find the electrical power (in kilowatt hours, kwh) used by the curling iron by applying the formula:

$$\text{kwh} = \frac{(\text{volts})^2}{1,000 \cdot \text{ohms}} \cdot \text{hours}$$

0.3025 kwh

SECTION 5.6
Multiplying Polynomials

Objectives

1 Multiply monomials.

2 Multiply a polynomial by a monomial.

3 Multiply binomials.

4 Use special product formulas.

5 Multiply polynomials.

6 Multiply polynomials to solve equations.

We now discuss multiplying polynomials. We will begin with the simplest case—finding the product of two monomials.

1 Multiply monomials.

To multiply two monomials, such as $8x^2$ and $-3x^4$, we use the commutative and associative properties of multiplication to group the numerical factors and the variable factors. Then we multiply the numerical factors and multiply the variable factors.

$$8x^2(-3x^4) = 8(-3)x^2x^4$$
$$= -24x^6$$

This example suggests the following rule.

> ### Multiplying Monomials
>
> To multiply two monomials, multiply the numerical factors (the coefficients) and then multiply the variable factors.

EXAMPLE 1   Multiply:

a. $3x^4(2x^5)$ **b.** $-2a^2b^3(5ab^2)$ **c.** $-4y^5z^2(2y^3z^3)(3yz)$ **d.** $\left(\frac{3}{4}x^2y^3\right)\left(\frac{8}{3}xy^2\right)$

Strategy We will multiply the numerical factors and then multiply the variable factors.

WHY The commutative and associative properties of multiplication enable us to reorder and regroup the factors.

Solution
a. $3x^4(2x^5) = 3(2)\,x^4x^5$ Reorder the factors.

$\quad\quad = 6x^9$ Multiply the numerical factors, 3 and 2. Multiply the variable factors: $x^4x^5 = x^{4+5} = x^9$.

b. $-2a^2b^3(5ab^2) = -10a^3b^5$ Think: $-2(5) = -10$, $a^2 \cdot a = a^3$, and $b^3 \cdot b^2 = b^5$.

c. $-4y^5z^2(2y^3z^3)(3yz) = -24y^9z^6$ Think: $-4(2)(3) = -24$, $y^5 \cdot y^3 \cdot y = y^9$, and $z^2 \cdot z^3 \cdot z = z^6$.

d. $\left(\frac{3}{4}x^2y^3\right)\left(\frac{8}{3}xy^2\right) = 2x^3y^5$ Think: $\frac{3}{4}\left(\frac{8}{3}\right) = 2$, $x^2 \cdot x = x^3$, and $y^3 \cdot y^2 = y^5$.

> **Success Tip** Notice that we *multiply* the numerical coefficients. To multiply the variable factors with like bases, keep the base and *add* the exponents.

Self Check 1

Multiply:

a. $(5a^2b^3)(6a^3b^4)$ $30a^5b^7$

b. $(-15p^3q^2)(5p^3q^2)$ $-75p^6q^4$

c. $\left(\frac{2}{3}x^2y\right)(9y^2)$ $6x^2y^3$

Now Try **Problems 13 and 18**

Teaching Example 1 Multiply:
a. $(3t^4)(-2t^5)$ **b.** $\left(\frac{1}{3}a^2b^4\right)(21ab^8)$
Answers:
a. $-6t^9$ **b.** $7a^3b^{12}$

2 Multiply a polynomial by a monomial.

To find the product of a polynomial (with more than one term) and a monomial, we use the distributive property. To multiply $2x + 4$ by $5x$, for example, we proceed as follows:

$$5x(2x + 4) = 5x(2x) + 5x(4)$$ Distribute the multiplication by 5x.

$$\quad\quad = 10x^2 + 20x$$ Multiply the monomials: 5x(2x) = 10x² and 5x(4) = 20x.

This example suggests the following rule.

> ### Multiplying Polynomials by Monomials
>
> To multiply a polynomial with more than one term by a monomial, multiply each term of the polynomial by the monomial and simplify.

EXAMPLE 2

Multiply:

a. $3a^2(3a^2 - 5a)$ **b.** $-2xz^2(2x - 3z + 2z^2)$ **c.** $(2.1b^2 - 3b)(0.1b^3)$

Strategy We will multiply each term of the polynomial by the monomial.

WHY We use the distributive property to multiply a monomial and a polynomial.

Solution

a. $3a^2(3a^2 - 5a) = 3a^2(3a^2) - 3a^2(5a)$ Distribute the multiplication by $3a^2$.

$\qquad\qquad\quad = 9a^4 - 15a^3$ Multiply the monomials.

b. $-2xz^2(2x - 3z + 2z^2)$

$\quad = -2xz^2(2x) - (-2xz^2)(3z) + (-2xz^2)(2z^2)$ Use the distributive property.

$\quad = -4x^2z^2 - (-6xz^3) + (-4xz^4)$ Multiply the monomials.

$\quad = -4x^2z^2 + 6xz^3 - 4xz^4$

c. $(2.1b^2 - 3b)(0.1b^3) = 2.1b^2(0.1b^3) - 3b(0.1b^3)$ Distribute the multiplication by $0.1b^3$.

$\qquad\qquad\qquad\quad = 0.21b^5 - 0.3b^4$ Multiply the monomials.

> ***Success Tip*** $(2.1b^2 - 3b)(0.1b^3)$ could also be rewritten as $(0.1b^3)(2.1b^2 - 3b)$ using the commutative property of multiplication. Then use the distributive property to find the product $0.21b^5 - 0.3b^4$.

3 Multiply binomials.

To multiply two binomials, we must use the distributive property more than once. For example, to multiply $2a - 4$ by $3a + 5$, we proceed as follows.

$(2a - 4)(3a + 5) = (2a - 4)(3a) + (2a - 4)(5)$ Distribute the multiplication by $(2a - 4)$.

$\qquad\qquad\qquad = 3a(2a - 4) + 5(2a - 4)$ Use the commutative property of multiplication.

$\qquad\qquad\qquad = 3a(2a) - 3a(4) + 5(2a) - 5(4)$ Distribute the multiplication by $3a$ and by 5.

$\qquad\qquad\qquad = 6a^2 - 12a + 10a - 20$ Perform the multiplications.

$\qquad\qquad\qquad = 6a^2 - 2a - 20$ Combine like terms.

This example suggests the following rule.

> ### Multiplying Two Binomials
>
> To multiply two binomials, multiply each term of one binomial by each term of the other binomial and combine like terms.

EXAMPLE 3 Multiply: $(2x - y)(3x + 4y)$

Strategy We will multiply each term of $3x + 4y$ by $2x$ and $-y$.

WHY To multiply two binomials, each term of one binomial must be multiplied by each term of the other binomial.

Solution

$$
\begin{aligned}
(2x - y)(3x + 4y) &= 2x(3x + 4y) - y(3x + 4y) && \text{Multiply } 3x + 4y \text{ by } 2x \text{ and} \\
&&& \text{by } -y. \\
&= 6x^2 + 8xy - 3xy - 4y^2 && \text{Distribute the multiplication} \\
&&& \text{by } 2x. \\
&&& \text{Distribute the multiplication} \\
&&& \text{by } -y. \\
&= 6x^2 + 5xy - 4y^2 && \text{Collect like terms.}
\end{aligned}
$$

We can use a shortcut method, called the **FOIL** method, to multiply binomials. FOIL is an acronym for **F**irst terms, **O**uter terms, **I**nner terms, and **L**ast terms. To use the FOIL method to multiply $2a - 4$ by $3a + 5$, we

1. multiply the **F**irst terms $2a$ and $3a$ to obtain $6a^2$,
2. multiply the **O**uter terms $2a$ and 5 to obtain $10a$,
3. multiply the **I**nner terms -4 and $3a$ to obtain $-12a$, and
4. multiply the **L**ast terms -4 and 5 to obtain -20.

Then we simplify the resulting polynomial, if possible.

First terms   Last terms

$$
\begin{aligned}
(2a - 4)(3a + 5) &= 2a(3a) + 2a(5) + (-4)(3a) + (-4)(5) \\
&= 6a^2 + 10a - 12a - 20 && \text{Perform the} \\
&&& \text{multiplications.} \\
&= 6a^2 - 2a - 20 && \text{Combine like terms.}
\end{aligned}
$$

Inner terms

Outer terms

EXAMPLE 4 Find each product. **a.** $(x + 5)(x + 7)$ **b.** $(3x + 4)(2x - 3)$

c. $(a - 7b)(a - 4b)$ **d.** $\left(\dfrac{3}{4}r - 3s\right)\left(\dfrac{1}{2}r + 4t\right)$

Strategy We will use the FOIL method.

WHY In each case we are to find the product of two binomials, and the FOIL method is a shortcut for multiplying two binomials.

Solution

F L

$$
\begin{aligned}
\textbf{a. } (x + 5)(x + 7) &= x(x) + x(7) + 5(x) + 5(7) \\
&= x^2 + 7x + 5x + 35 && \text{Multiply the monomials.} \\
&= x^2 + 12x + 35 && \text{Combine like terms.}
\end{aligned}
$$

F L

$$
\begin{aligned}
\textbf{b. } (3x + 4)(2x - 3) &= 3x(2x) + 3x(-3) + 4(2x) + 4(-3) \\
&= 6x^2 - 9x + 8x - 12 && \text{Multiply the monomials.} \\
&= 6x^2 - x - 12 && \text{Combine like terms.}
\end{aligned}
$$

c. $(a - 7b)(a - 4b) = a(a) + a(-4b) + (-7b)(a) + (-7b)(-4b)$

$= a^2 - 4ab - 7ab + 28b^2$ Multiply the monomials.

$= a^2 - 11ab + 28b^2$ Combine like terms.

d. $\left(\dfrac{3}{4}r - 3s\right)\left(\dfrac{1}{2}r + 4t\right) = \dfrac{3}{4}r\left(\dfrac{1}{2}r\right) + \dfrac{3}{4}r(4t) - 3s\left(\dfrac{1}{2}r\right) - 3s(4t)$

$= \dfrac{3}{8}r^2 + 3rt - \dfrac{3}{2}rs - 12st$ There are no like terms.

Self Check 5

Simplify: $(x + 3)(2x - 1) + 2x(x - 1)$. $4x^2 + 3x - 3$

Now Try Problems 45 and 51

Teaching Example 5 Simplify:
$-3(2x + 5)(x - 4)$
Answer:
$-6x^2 + 9x + 60$

EXAMPLE 5 Simplify each expression.

a. $3(2x - 3)(x + 1)$ **b.** $(x + 1)(x - 2) - 3x(x + 3)$

Strategy We will use the FOIL method and the distributive property to remove the parentheses. Then we will combine like terms.

WHY To simplify an expression means to remove parentheses and combine like terms.

Solution

a. $3(2x - 3)(x + 1) = 3(2x^2 + 2x - 3x - 3)$ Multiply the binomials.

$= 3(2x^2 - x - 3)$ Combine like terms.

$= 6x^2 - 3x - 9$ Distribute the multiplication by 3.

b. $(x + 1)(x - 2) - 3x(x + 3) = x^2 - 2x + x - 2 - 3x^2 - 9x$

$= -2x^2 - 10x - 2$ Combine like terms.

---

4 Use special products formulas.

Certain products of binomials occur so frequently in algebra that it is worthwhile to learn formulas for computing them. To develop a rule to find the *square of a sum*, we consider $(x + y)^2$.

$(x + y)^2 = (x + y)(x + y)$ In $(x + y)^2$, the base is $(x + y)$ and the exponent is 2.

$= x^2 + xy + xy + y^2$ Multiply the binomials.

$= x^2 + 2xy + y^2$ Combine like terms: $xy + xy = 2xy$.

We note that the terms of this result are related to the terms of the original expression. That is, $(x + y)^2$ is equal to the square of its first term (x^2), plus twice the product of both its terms $(2xy)$, plus the square of its last term (y^2).

To develop a rule to find the *square of a difference*, we consider $(x - y)^2$.

$(x - y)^2 = (x - y)(x - y)$

$= x^2 - xy - xy + y^2$ Multiply the binomials.

$= x^2 - 2xy + y^2$ Combine like terms: $-xy - xy = -2xy$.

Again, the terms of the result are related to the terms of the original expression. When we find $(x - y)^2$, the product is composed of the square of its first term (x^2), twice the product of both its terms $(-2xy)$, and the square of its last term (y^2).

The final special product is the product of two binomials that differ only in the signs of the last terms. To develop a rule to find the product of a *sum and a difference,* we consider $(x + y)(x - y)$.

$$(x + y)(x - y) = x^2 - xy + xy - y^2 \quad \text{Multiply the binomials.}$$
$$= x^2 - y^2 \qquad\qquad \text{Combine like terms: } -xy + xy = 0.$$

The product is the square of the first term (x^2) minus the square of the second term (y^2). The expression $x^2 - y^2$ is called a **difference of two squares.**

Because these special products occur so often, it is wise to memorize their forms.

Special Products

$(x + y)^2 = x^2 + 2xy + y^2$	The square of a sum
$(x - y)^2 = x^2 - 2xy + y^2$	The square of a difference
$(x + y)(x - y) = x^2 - y^2$	The product of a sum and difference

---

EXAMPLE 6   Find: **a.** $(t + 9)^2$ **b.** $(8a - 5)^2$ **c.** $(3y + 4z)(3y - 4z)$

Strategy We will identify the special product and apply the appropriate rule.

WHY The rules for special products enables us to compute them quickly.

Solution

a. This is the square of a sum. The terms of the binomial being squared are t and 9.

$$(t + 9)^2 = \quad t^2 \quad + \quad 2(t)(9) \quad + \quad 9^2$$

$\underbrace{\qquad}$ The square of the first term, t. $\underbrace{\qquad}$ Twice the product of both terms. $\underbrace{\qquad}$ The square of the last term, 9.

$$= t^2 + 18t + 81$$

b. This is the square of a difference. The terms of the binomial being squared are $8a$ and -5.

$$(8a - 5)^2 = \quad (8a)^2 \quad - \quad 2(8a)(5) \quad + \quad 5^2$$

$\underbrace{\qquad}$ The square of the first term, $8a$. $\underbrace{\qquad}$ Twice the product of both terms. $\underbrace{\qquad}$ The square of the last term, 5.

$$= 64a^2 - 80a + 25 \quad \begin{array}{l}\text{Use the power rule for products:}\\ (8a)^2 = 8^2 a^2 = 64a^2.\end{array}$$

c. The binomials differ only in the signs of the last terms. This is the product of a sum and a difference.

$$(3y + 4z)(3y - 4z) = (3y)^2 - (4z)^2 \quad \begin{array}{l}\text{This is the square of the first term}\\ \text{minus the square of the second term.}\end{array}$$

$$= 9y^2 - 16z^2 \quad \text{Use the power rule for products twice.} \quad \blacksquare$$

Caution!   A common error when squaring a binomial is to forget the middle term of the product. For example, $(x + 2)^2 \neq x^2 + 4$ and $(x - 2)^2 \neq x^2 - 4$. Applying the special product formulas, we have $(x + 2)^2 = x^2 + 4x + 4$ and $(x - 2)^2 = x^2 - 4x + 4$.

Self Check 6

Find:

a. $(r + 6)^2$
b. $(7g - 2)^2$
c. $(5m - 9n)(5m + 9n)$

Now Try Problems 53, 56, and 57

Self Check 6 Answers
a. $r^2 + 12r + 36$
b. $49g^2 - 28g + 4$
c. $25m^2 - 81n^2$

Teaching Example 6 Find:
a. $(x + 5)^2$
b. $(2y - 3)^2$
c. $(4x + 3y)(4x - 3y)$
Answers:
a. $x^2 + 10x + 25$
b. $4y^2 - 12y + 9$
c. $16x^2 - 9y^2$

5 Multiply polynomials.

We must use the distributive property more than once to multiply a polynomial by a binomial. For example, to multiply $3x^2 + 3x - 5$ by $2x + 3$, we proceed as follows:

$$(2x + 3)(3x^2 + 3x - 5) = (2x + 3)3x^2 + (2x + 3)3x - (2x + 3)5$$
$$= 3x^2(2x + 3) + 3x(2x + 3) - 5(2x + 3)$$
$$= 6x^3 + 9x^2 + 6x^2 + 9x - 10x - 15$$
$$= 6x^3 + 15x^2 - x - 15$$

This example suggests the following rule.

Multiplying Polynomials

To multiply one polynomial by another, multiply each term of one polynomial by each term of the other polynomial and combine like terms.

It is often convenient to organize the work vertically.

EXAMPLE 7   Multiply using vertical form:

a. $(3a^2 - 4a + 7)(2a + 5)$ **b.** $(3y^2 - 5y + 4)(-4y^2 - 3)$

Strategy First, we will write one polynomial underneath the other and draw a horizontal line beneath them. Then, we will multiply each term of the upper polynomial by each term of the lower polynomial, making sure to line up like terms.

WHY *Vertical form* means to use an approach similar to that used in arithmetic to multiply two numbers.

Solution
a. Multiply:

$$\begin{array}{r} 3a^2 - 4a + 7 \\ 2a + 5 \\ \hline 15a^2 - 20a + 35 \\ 6a^3 - 8a^2 + 14a \\ \hline 6a^3 + 7a^2 - 6a + 35 \end{array}$$

Multiply $3a^2 - 4a + 7$ by 5.
Multiply $3a^2 - 4a + 7$ by 2a.
In each column, combine like terms.

b. Multiply:

$$\begin{array}{r} 3y^2 - 5y + 4 \\ -4y^2 - 3 \\ \hline -9y^2 + 15y - 12 \\ -12y^4 + 20y^3 - 16y^2 \\ \hline -12y^4 + 20y^3 - 25y^2 + 15y - 12 \end{array}$$

Multiply $3y^2 - 5y + 4$ by -3.
Multiply $3y^2 - 5y + 4$ by $-4y^2$.

When finding the product of three polynomials, we begin by multiplying any two of them, and then we multiply that result by the third polynomial.

EXAMPLE 8   Find the product: $-3a(4a + 1)(a - 7)$

Strategy We will find the product of $4a + 1$ and $a - 7$ and then multiply that result by $-3a$.

WHY It is better to find the most difficult product first. Save the simpler multiplication by $-3a$ for last.

Solution

$$-3a(4a + 1)(a - 7) = -3a(4a^2 - 28a + a - 7) \qquad \text{Multiply the two binomials.}$$
$$= -3a(4a^2 - 27a - 7) \qquad \text{Combine like terms.}$$
$$= -12a^3 + 81a^2 + 21a \qquad \text{Distribute the multiplication by } -3a.$$

Self Check 8 Answer
$-6y^3 - 14y^2 + 12y$

Teaching Example 8 Multiply:
$-3x(x - 5)(2x + 1)$
Answer:
$-6x^3 + 27x^2 + 15x$

6 Multiply polynomials to solve equations.

To solve an equation involving products of polynomials, we can do the multiplication on each side and proceed as follows.

EXAMPLE 9   Solve: $(x + 2)(x + 3) = x(x + 7)$

Strategy We will multiply the binomials on the left side of the equation and use the distributive property on the right side.

WHY The first step in solving equations is to remove parentheses.

Solution

$$(x + 2)(x + 3) = x(x + 7)$$

$$x^2 + 3x + 2x + 6 = x^2 + 7x$$
$$x^2 + 3x + 2x + 6 - x^2 = x^2 + 7x - x^2 \qquad \text{Subtract } x^2 \text{ from both sides.}$$
$$5x + 6 = 7x \qquad \text{Combine like terms: } x^2 - x^2 = 0 \text{ and } 3x + 2x = 5x.$$
$$6 = 2x \qquad \text{Subtract } 5x \text{ from both sides.}$$
$$3 = x \qquad \text{Divide both sides by 2.}$$

Check: $(x + 2)(x + 3) = x(x + 7)$
$$(3 + 2)(3 + 3) \stackrel{?}{=} 3(3 + 7) \qquad \text{Replace } x \text{ with 3.}$$
$$5(6) \stackrel{?}{=} 3(10) \qquad \text{Perform the additions within parentheses.}$$
$$30 = 30$$

Self Check 9
Solve:
$(x + 5)(x - 4) = x(x + 3)$
Now Try **Problem 71**
Self Check 9 Answer
$x = -10$

Teaching Example 9 Solve:
$x(x - 4) = (x + 2)(x - 7)$
Answer:
-14

EXAMPLE 10   *Dimensions of a Painting* A square painting is surrounded by a border 2 inches wide. If the area of the border is 96 square inches, find the dimensions of the painting.

Analyze Refer to the figure, which shows a square painting surrounded by a border 2 inches wide. We know that the area of this border is 96 square inches, and we are to find the dimensions of the painting.

Form Let $x =$ the length of a side of the square painting. Since the border is 2 inches wide, the length and the width of the outer rectangle are both $(x + 2 + 2)$ inches. Then the outer rectangle is also a square, and its dimensions are $(x + 4)$ by $(x + 4)$ inches. Since the area of a square is the product of its length and width, the area of the larger square is $(x + 4)(x + 4)$, and the area of the painting is $x \cdot x$. If we subtract the area of the painting from the area of the larger square, the difference is 96.

Self Check 10
A square painting is surrounded by a border 1 inch wide. If the area of the border is 84 square inches, find the dimensions of the painting. 20 in. by 20 in.
Now Try **Problem 114**

Teaching Example 10 A square painting is surrounded by a border 3 inches wide. If the area of the border is 216 square inches, find the dimensions of the painting.
Answer:
15 in. by 15 in.

The area of the large square	minus	the area of the square painting	is	the area of the border.
$(x + 4)(x + 4)$	$-$	$x \cdot x$	$=$	96

Solve

$(x + 4)(x + 4) - x^2 = 96$ $x \cdot x = x^2$.

$x^2 + 8x + 16 - x^2 = 96$ $(x + 4)(x + 4) = (x + 4)^2 = x^2 + 8x + 16$.

$8x + 16 = 96$ Combine like terms: $x^2 - x^2 = 0$.

$8x = 80$ Subtract 16 from both sides.

$x = 10$ Divide both sides by 8.

State The dimensions of the painting are 10 inches by 10 inches.

Check Verify that the 2-inch-wide border of a 10-inch-square painting would have an area of 96 square inches.

ANSWERS TO SELF CHECKS

1. a. $30a^5b^7$ **b.** $-75p^6q^4$ **c.** $6x^2y^3$ **2. a.** $6p^5 - 10p^4$ **b.** $-15a^3b - 10a^2b^2 + 20a^3b^2$
c. $4.5a^5b^2 - 6a^4b^2 + 3a^4b$ **3.** $35x^2 - 4xy - 4y^2$ **4. a.** $y^2 + 4y + 3$ **b.** $6a^2 + a - 2$
c. $10y^2 + 11yz - 6z^2$ **d.** $8r^2 - rs - \frac{1}{4}s^2$ **5.** $4x^2 + 3x - 3$ **6. a.** $r^2 + 12r + 36$
b. $49g^2 - 28g + 4$ **c.** $25m^2 - 81n^2$ **7. a.** $6x^3 - 8x^2 + 7x + 10$
b. $-4x^4 + 8x^3 + 8x^2 - 12x - 3$ **8.** $-6y^3 - 14y^2 + 12y$ **9.** $x = -10$
10. 20 in. by 20 in.

SECTION 5.6   STUDY SET

VOCABULARY

Fill in the blanks.

1. The expression $(2a - 4)(3a + 5)$ is the product of two <u>binomials</u>.

2. The expression $(2a - 4)(3a^2 + 5a - 1)$ is the product of a <u>binomial</u> and a <u>trinomial</u>.

▶ **3.** In the acronym FOIL, F stands for <u>first</u> terms, O for <u>outer</u> terms, I for <u>inner</u> terms, and L for <u>last</u> terms.

▶ **4.** $(x + 5)^2$ is the square of a <u>sum</u>, and $(x - 5)^2$ is the square of a <u>difference</u>.

CONCEPTS

Consider the product $(2x + 5)(3x - 4)$.

5. The product of the first terms is $6x^2$.

6. The product of the outer terms is $-8x$.

7. The product of the inner terms is $15x$.

8. The product of the last terms is -20.

▶ **9.** STAMPS Find the area of the stamp. $(6x^2 + x - 1) \text{ cm}^2$

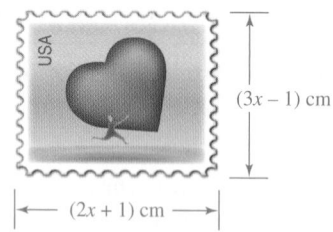

$(3x - 1)$ cm

$(2x + 1)$ cm

▶ **10.** LUGGAGE Find the volume of the garment bag shown below. $(2x^3 - 4x^2 - 6x) \text{ in.}^3$

$(2x + 2)$ in.

$(x - 3)$ in.

x in.

NOTATION

Complete each solution.

11. $7x(3x^2 - 2x + 5) = \boxed{7x}(3x^2) - \boxed{7x}(2x) + \boxed{7x}(5)$

$\qquad\qquad\qquad\quad = 21x^3 - 14x^2 + 35x$

▶ **12.** $(2x + 5)(3x - 2) = 2x(3x) - \boxed{2x}(2) + \boxed{5}(3x) - \boxed{5}(2)$

$\qquad\qquad\qquad\qquad = 6x^2 - \boxed{4x} + \boxed{15x} - 10$

$\qquad\qquad\qquad\qquad = 6x^2 + 11x - 10$

GUIDED PRACTICE

Multiply. See Example 1.

13. $(3x^2)(4x^3)$
$12x^5$

▶ **14.** $(-2a^3)(3a^2)$
$-6a^5$

▶ **15.** $(-5x^3y^6)(x^2y^2)$
$-5x^5y^8$

16. $(3x^2y)(2xy^2)$
$6x^3y^3$

17. $(x^2y^5)(x^2z^5)(-3z^3)$
$-3x^4y^5z^8$

18. $(3ab^2)(-2ab)(4ab^3)$
$-24a^3b^6$

19. $\left(\dfrac{1}{2}x^2y^3\right)\left(\dfrac{2}{3}x^3y^2\right)$ $\dfrac{1}{3}x^5y^5$

20. $\left(-\dfrac{3}{4}r^4st^2\right)(2r^2st)\left(-\dfrac{2}{3}rst\right)$ $r^7s^3t^4$

Multiply. See Example 2.

21. $-4t(t + 7)$
$-4t^2 - 28t$

22. $-8c(2c - 3)$
$-16c^2 + 24c$

▶ **23.** $6s^2(s^2 - 3s)$
$6s^4 - 18s^3$

24. $3a^3(2a^2 + 5a)$
$6a^5 + 15a^4$

25. $3y(x + 4y)$
$3xy + 12y^2$

26. $-3a^2b(a - b)$
$-3a^3b + 3a^2b^2$

▶ **27.** $2x^2(3x^2 + 4x - 7)$
$6x^4 + 8x^3 - 14x^2$

28. $3y^3(2y^2 - 7y - 8)$
$6y^5 - 21y^4 - 24y^3$

29. $2ab^2(2a + 3b - 2a^2)$
$4a^2b^2 + 6ab^3 - 4a^3b^2$

30. $-2p^2q(3p - 2q - 3pq)$
$-6p^3q + 4p^2q^2 + 6p^3q^2$

31. $(3.1p^2 - 4q)(0.2p^2)$
$0.62p^4 - 0.8p^2q$

32. $(1.5m^2 + 5.1n)(1.2m^3)$
$1.8m^5 + 6.12m^3n$

Find each product. See Examples 3–4.

33. $(a + 4)(a + 5)$
$a^2 + 9a + 20$

34. $(y - 3)(y + 5)$
$y^2 + 2y - 15$

▶ **35.** $(3x - 2)(x + 4)$
$3x^2 + 10x - 8$

36. $(t + 4)(2t - 3)$
$2t^2 + 5t - 12$

37. $(2a + 4)(3a - 5)$
$6a^2 + 2a - 20$

38. $(2b - 1)(3b + 4)$
$6b^2 + 5b - 4$

39. $(3x - 5)(2x + 1)$
$6x^2 - 7x - 5$

40. $(2y - 5)(3y + 7)$
$6y^2 - y - 35$

▶ **41.** $(2t + 3s)(3t - s)$
$6t^2 + 7st - 3s^2$

42. $(3a - 2b)(4a + b)$
$12a^2 - 5ab - 2b^2$

43. $\left(\dfrac{1}{4}t - u\right)\left(-\dfrac{1}{2}t + u\right)$

$-\dfrac{1}{8}t^2 + \dfrac{3}{4}tu - u^2$

44. $\left(-\dfrac{1}{3}t + 2s\right)\left(\dfrac{2}{3}t - 3s\right)$

$-\dfrac{2}{9}t^2 + \dfrac{7}{3}st - 6s^2$

Simplify each expression. See Example 5.

45. $4(2x + 1)(x - 2)$
$8x^2 - 12x - 8$

46. $-5(3a - 2)(2a + 3)$
$-30a^2 - 25a + 30$

47. $3a(a + b)(a - b)$
$3a^3 - 3ab^2$

▶ **48.** $-2r(r + s)(r + s)$
$-2r^3 - 4r^2s - 2rs^2$

49. $2t(t + 2) + 3t(t - 5)$ $5t^2 - 11t$

50. $3y(y + 2) + (y + 1)(y - 1)$ $4y^2 + 6y - 1$

51. $(x + y)(x - y) + x(x + y)$ $2x^2 + xy - y^2$

▶ **52.** $(3x + 4)(2x - 2) - (2x + 1)(x + 3)$ $4x^2 - 5x - 11$

Find each product. See Example 6.

▶ **53.** $(x + 4)^2$
$x^2 + 8x + 16$

54. $(a + 3)^2$
$a^2 + 6a + 9$

55. $(t - 3)^2$
$t^2 - 6t + 9$

56. $(z - 5)^2$
$z^2 - 10z + 25$

57. $(4x + 5)(4x - 5)$
$16x^2 - 25$

▶ **58.** $(5z + 1)(5z - 1)$
$25z^2 - 1$

59. $(x - 2y)^2$
$x^2 - 4xy + 4y^2$

60. $(3a + 2b)^2$
$9a^2 + 12ab + 4b^2$

Find each product. See Example 7.

61. $\begin{array}{r} x^2 - 2x + 1 \\ \underline{x + 2} \\ x^3 - 3x + 2 \end{array}$

▶ **62.** $\begin{array}{r} 5r^2 + r + 6 \\ \underline{2r - 1} \\ 10r^3 - 3r^2 + 11r - 6 \end{array}$

63. $\begin{array}{r} 4x^2 + 3x - 4 \\ \underline{3x + 2} \\ 12x^3 + 17x^2 - 6x - 8 \end{array}$

64. $\begin{array}{r} x^2 - x + 1 \\ \underline{x + 1} \\ x^3 + 1 \end{array}$

Find each product. See Example 8.

65. $3x(-2x^2)(x + 4)$
$-6x^4 - 24x^3$

66. $-2a^2(-3a^3)(3a - 2)$
$18a^6 - 12a^5$

▶ **67.** $-2x(x + 3)(2x - 3)$
$-4x^3 - 6x^2 + 18x$

68. $5x^2(2x + 3)(2x - 5)$
$20x^4 - 20x^3 - 75x^2$

Solve each equation. See Example 9.

69. $(s - 4)(s + 1) = s^2 + 5$ -3

70. $(y - 5)(y - 2) = y^2 - 4$ 2

71. $z(z + 2) = (z + 4)(z - 4)$ -8

▶ **72.** $(z + 3)(z - 3) = z(z - 3)$ 3

73. $(x + 4)(x - 4) = (x - 2)(x + 6)$ -1

74. $(y - 1)(y + 6) = (y - 3)(y - 2) + 8$ 2

75. $(a - 3)^2 = (a + 3)^2$ 0

▶ **76.** $(b + 2)^2 = (b - 1)^2$ $-\dfrac{1}{2}$

TRY IT YOURSELF

Find each product.

77. $3x(x - 2)$
$3x^2 - 6x$

78. $4y(y + 5)$
$4y^2 + 20y$

79. $-2x^2(3x^2 - x)$
$-6x^4 + 2x^3$

80. $4b^3(2b^2 - 2b)$
$8b^5 - 8b^4$

81. $3xy(x + y)$
$3x^2y + 3xy^2$

82. $-4x^2z(3x^2 - z)$
$-12x^4z + 4x^2z^2$

83. $(r + 4)(r - 4)$
$r^2 - 16$

84. $(b + 2)(b - 2)$
$b^2 - 4$

85. $(2s + 1)(2s + 1)$
$4s^2 + 4s + 1$

86. $(3t - 2)(3t - 2)$
$9t^2 - 12t + 4$

87. $(x + y)(x + z)$
$x^2 + xz + xy + yz$

88. $(a - b)(x + y)$
$ax + ay - bx - by$

89. $(x + 2)(x^2 - 2x + 3)$
$x^3 - x + 6$

▶ **90.** $(x - 5)(x^2 + 2x - 3)$
$x^3 - 3x^2 - 13x + 15$

91. $(4t + 3)(t^2 + 2t + 3)$
$4t^3 + 11t^2 + 18t + 9$

▶ **92.** $(3x + 1)(2x^2 - 3x + 1)$
$6x^3 - 7x^2 + 1$

93. $(-3x + y)(x^2 - 8xy + 16y^2)$
$-3x^3 + 25x^2y - 56xy^2 + 16y^3$

94. $(3x - y)(x^2 + 3xy - y^2)$
$3x^3 + 8x^2y - 6xy^2 + y^3$

95. $(x + 5)^2$
$x^2 + 10x + 25$

96. $(y - 6)^2$
$y^2 - 12y + 36$

97. $(2a - 3b)^2$
$4a^2 - 12ab + 9b^2$

▶ **98.** $(2x + 5y)^2$
$4x^2 + 20xy + 25y^2$

99. $(4x + 5y)^2$
$16x^2 + 40xy + 25y^2$

100. $(6p - 5q)^2$
$36p^2 - 60pq + 25q^2$

101. $2a(a + 2) - 3a(5 - a)$ $5a^2 - 11a$

102. $(3b + 4)(2b - 2) + (2b + 1)(b + 3)$ $8b^2 + 9b - 5$

APPLICATIONS

Find the area of each figure. You may leave π in your answer.

103.

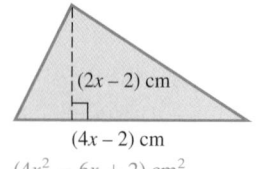

$(2x - 2)$ cm

$(4x - 2)$ cm

$(4x^2 - 6x + 2)$ cm^2

104.

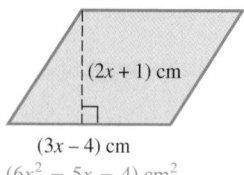

$(2x + 1)$ cm

$(3x - 4)$ cm

$(6x^2 - 5x - 4)$ cm^2

▶ **105.**

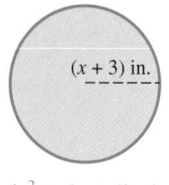

$(x + 3)$ in.

$(x^2 + 6x + 9)\pi$ in.^{2}

▶ **106.**

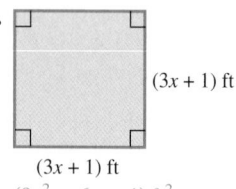

$(3x + 1)$ ft

$(3x + 1)$ ft

$(9x^2 + 6x + 1)$ ft^2

▶ **107.** TOYS Find the perimeter and the area of the screen of the Etch A Sketch.
$(24x + 14)$ cm, $(35x^2 + 43x + 12)$ cm^2

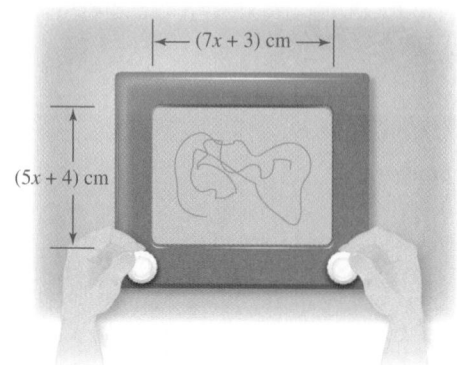

$(7x + 3)$ cm

$(5x + 4)$ cm

▶ **108.** SUNGLASSES An ellipse is an oval-shaped closed curve. The area of an ellipse is approximately 3.14*ab*, where *a* is its length and *b* is its width. Find the polynomial that approximates the total area of the elliptical-shaped lenses of the sunglasses shown.
$(6.28x^2 - 6.28)$ in.^{2}

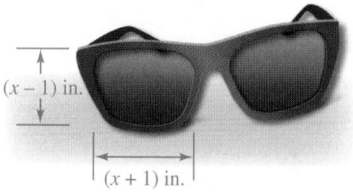

$(x - 1)$ in.

$(x + 1)$ in.

▶ **109.** GARDENING See the following illustration.

a. What is the area of the region planted with corn? tomatoes? beans? carrots? Use your answers to find the total area of the garden.
x^2 ft^2, $6x$ ft^2, $5x$ ft^2, 30 ft^2; $(x^2 + 11x + 30)$ ft^2

b. What is the length of the garden? What is its width? Use your answers to find its area.
$(x + 6)$ ft, $(x + 5)$ ft; $(x^2 + 11x + 30)$ ft^2

c. How do the answers from parts a and b for the area of the garden compare? They are the same.

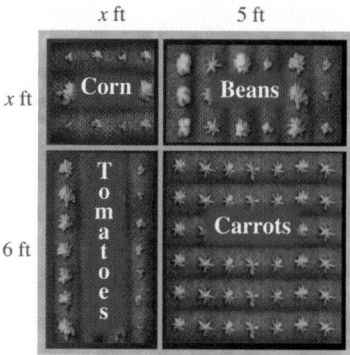

x ft   5 ft

x ft   Corn   Beans

6 ft   Tomatoes   Carrots

110. PAINTING See the illustration. To purchase the correct amount of enamel to paint these two garage doors, a painter must find their areas. Find a polynomial that gives the number of square feet to be painted. All dimensions are in feet, and the windows are squares with sides of *x* feet.
$(36x^2 + 36x + 6)$ ft^2

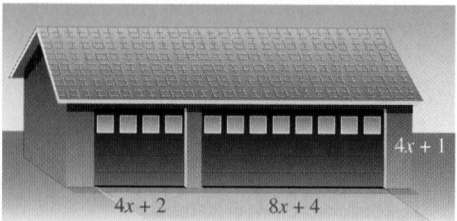

$4x + 1$

$4x + 2$ $8x + 4$

▶ **111.** INTEGER PROBLEM The difference between the squares of two consecutive positive integers is 11. Find the integers. (*Hint:* Let *x* and *x* + 1 represent the consecutive integers.) 5 and 6

112. INTEGER PROBLEM If 3 less than a certain integer is multiplied by 4 more than the integer, the product is 6 less than the square of the integer. Find the integer. 6

113. STONE-GROUND FLOUR The radius of a millstone is 3 meters greater than the radius of another, and their areas differ by 15π square meters. Find the radius of the larger millstone. 4 m

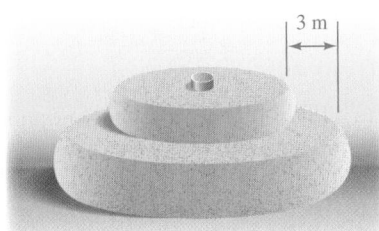

3 m

114. BOOKBINDING Two square sheets of cardboard used for making book covers differ in area by 44 square inches. An edge of the larger square is 2 inches greater than an edge of the smaller square. Find the length of an edge of the smaller square. 10 in.

115. BASEBALL In major league baseball, the distance between bases is 30 feet greater than it is in softball. The bases in major league baseball mark the corners of a square that has an area 4,500 square feet greater than for softball. Find the distance between the bases in baseball. 90 ft

116. PULLEY DESIGNS The radius of one pulley in the illustration is 1 inch greater than the radius of the second pulley, and their areas differ by 4π square inches. Find the radius of the smaller pulley. $\frac{3}{2}$ in.

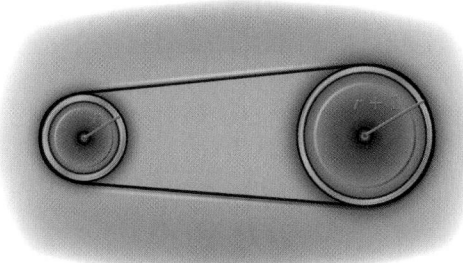

117. SIGNS Find a polynomial that represents the area of the sign. $\left(\frac{1}{2}h^2 - 2h\right)$ in.^{2}

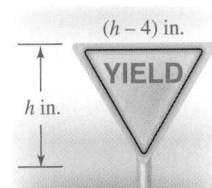

$(h-4)$ in.

YIELD

h in.

118. BASEBALL Find a polynomial that represents the amount of space within the batting cage. $(45x^3 + 12x^2 - 19x - 6)$ ft^3

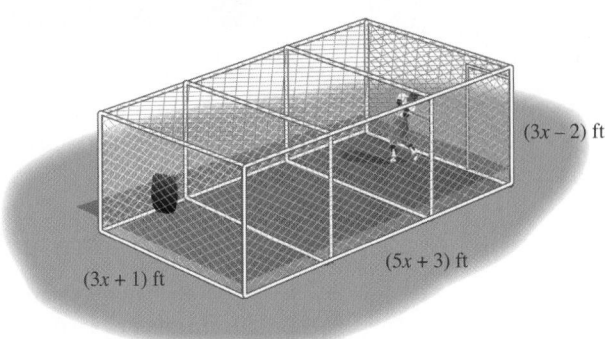

$(3x-2)$ ft

$(3x+1)$ ft

$(5x+3)$ ft

WRITING

119. Describe the steps involved in finding the product of $x + 2$ and $x - 2$.

120. Writing $(x + y)^2$ as $x^2 + y^2$ illustrates a common error. Explain.

REVIEW

Refer to the illustration.

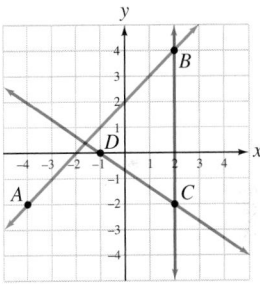

121. Find the slope of line AB. 1

122. Find the slope of line BC. no defined slope

123. Find the slope of line CD. $-\frac{2}{3}$

124. Find the slope of the x-axis. 0

125. Find the y-intercept of line AB. $(0, 2)$

126. Find the x-intercept of line AB. $(-2, 0)$

Objectives

1 Divide a monomial by a monomial.

2 Divide a polynomial by a monomial.

3 Write equivalent forms of formulas.

SECTION 5.7

Dividing Polynomials by Monomials

In this section, we will discuss how to divide polynomials by monomials. We will first divide monomials by monomials and then divide polynomials with more than one term by monomials.

1 Divide a monomial by a monomial.

Recall that to simplify a fraction, we write both its numerator and denominator as the product of several factors and then divide out all common factors:

$$\frac{4}{6} = \frac{2 \cdot 2}{2 \cdot 3} \quad \text{Factor 4 and 6.} \qquad\qquad \frac{20}{25} = \frac{4 \cdot 5}{5 \cdot 5} \quad \text{Factor 20 and 25.}$$

$$= \frac{2 \cdot \overset{1}{\cancel{2}}}{\overset{}{\cancel{2}} \cdot 3} \quad \begin{array}{l}\text{Divide out the common} \\ \text{factor of 2.}\end{array} \qquad = \frac{4 \cdot \overset{1}{\cancel{5}}}{\overset{}{\cancel{5}} \cdot 5} \quad \begin{array}{l}\text{Divide out the common} \\ \text{factor of 5.}\end{array}$$

$$= \frac{2}{3} \qquad\qquad\qquad\qquad\qquad = \frac{4}{5}$$

We can use the same method to simplify algebraic fractions that contain variables.

$$\frac{3p^2}{6p} = \frac{3 \cdot p \cdot p}{2 \cdot 3 \cdot p} \quad \text{Factor } p^2 \text{ and 6.}$$

$$= \frac{\overset{1}{\cancel{3}} \cdot \overset{1}{\cancel{p}} \cdot p}{2 \cdot \underset{1}{\cancel{3}} \cdot \underset{1}{\cancel{p}}} \quad \text{Divide out the common factors of 3 and } p.$$

$$= \frac{p}{2}$$

To divide monomials, we can use either the preceding method for simplifying arithmetic fractions or the rules for exponents.

Self Check 1

Divide: $\dfrac{-5p^2q^3}{10pq^4} \quad -\dfrac{p}{2q}$

Now Try Problems 27 and 32

Teaching Example 1 Divide:

a. $\dfrac{a^3b^2}{ab^6}$ **b.** $\dfrac{-12a^3b^5}{2a^7b^9}$

Answers:

a. $\dfrac{a^2}{b^4}$ **b.** $\dfrac{-6}{a^4b^4}$

EXAMPLE 1 Divide: **a.** $\dfrac{x^2y}{xy^2}$ **b.** $\dfrac{-8a^3b^2}{4ab^3}$

Strategy We will use the rules for simplifying fractions and/or the quotient rule for exponents.

WHY We need to make sure that the numerator and denominator have no common factors other than 1. If that is the case, then the fraction is in *simplest form*.

Solution

By simplifying fractions

a. $\dfrac{x^2y}{xy^2} = \dfrac{x \cdot x \cdot y}{x \cdot y \cdot y}$

$= \dfrac{\overset{1}{\cancel{x}} \cdot x \cdot \overset{1}{\cancel{y}}}{\underset{1}{\cancel{x}} \cdot y \cdot \underset{1}{\cancel{y}}}$

$= \dfrac{x}{y}$

Using the rules for exponents

$\dfrac{x^2y}{xy^2} = x^{2-1}y^{1-2}$

$= x^1 y^{-1}$

$= \dfrac{x}{y}$

b. $\dfrac{-8a^3b^2}{4ab^3} = \dfrac{-2 \cdot 4 \cdot a \cdot a \cdot a \cdot b \cdot b}{4 \cdot a \cdot b \cdot b \cdot b}$

$= \dfrac{-2 \cdot \overset{1}{\cancel{4}} \cdot \overset{1}{\cancel{a}} \cdot a \cdot a \cdot \overset{1}{\cancel{b}} \cdot \overset{1}{\cancel{b}}}{\underset{1}{\cancel{4}} \cdot \underset{1}{\cancel{a}} \cdot \underset{1}{\cancel{b}} \cdot b \cdot \underset{1}{\cancel{b}}}$

$= -\dfrac{2a^2}{b}$

$\dfrac{-8a^3b^2}{4ab^3} = \dfrac{-2^3 a^3 b^2}{2^2 ab^3}$

$= -2^{3-2} a^{3-1} b^{2-3}$

$= -2^1 a^2 b^{-1}$

$= -\dfrac{2a^2}{b}$

EXAMPLE 2 Simplify $\dfrac{25(s^2t^3)^2}{15(st^3)^3}$ and write the result using positive exponents only.

Strategy We will use the rules for exponents to remove the parentheses. Then we will simplify the fraction.

WHY We need to make sure that the numerator and denominator have no common factors other than 1. If that is the case, then the fraction is in *simplest form*.

Solution

$\dfrac{25(s^2t^3)^2}{15(st^3)^3} = \dfrac{25s^4t^6}{15s^3t^9}$ Use the power rules for exponents: $(xy)^n = x^n y^n$ and $(x^m)^n = x^{mn}$.

$= \dfrac{5 \cdot 5 \cdot s^{4-3} t^{6-9}}{5 \cdot 3}$ Factor 25 and 15. Use the quotient rule for exponents: $\dfrac{x^m}{x^n} = x^{m-n}$.

$= \dfrac{5 \cdot \overset{1}{\cancel{5}} \cdot s^1 t^{-3}}{\underset{1}{\cancel{5}} \cdot 3}$ Divide out the common factors of 5. Perform the subtractions.

$= \dfrac{5s}{3t^3}$ Use the negative integer exponent rule: $t^{-3} = \dfrac{1}{t^3}$.

Self Check 2

Simplify: $\dfrac{-24(h^3p)^5}{20(h^2p^2)^3} \cdot \dfrac{6h^9}{5p}$

Now Try **Problems 35 and 40**

Teaching Example 2 Simplify:
$\dfrac{3(2x^2y^3)^3}{6(3xy^4)^2}$
Answer:
$\dfrac{4x^4y}{9}$

---

2 Divide a polynomial by a monomial.

In Section 1.2, we used the following rules to add and subtract fractions with like denominators.

Adding and Subtracting Fractions with Like Denominators

To add (or subtract) fractions with like denominators, we add (or subtract) their numerators and keep the common denominator. In symbols, if a, b, and d represent numbers, and d is not 0,

$$\dfrac{a}{d} + \dfrac{b}{d} = \dfrac{a+b}{d} \qquad \text{and} \qquad \dfrac{a}{d} - \dfrac{b}{d} = \dfrac{a-b}{d}$$

We can use this rule in reverse to divide polynomials by monomials.

Dividing a Polynomial by a Monomial

To divide a polynomial by a monomial, divide each term of the polynomial by the monomial.

If A, B and D represent monomials, where $D \neq 0$, then

$$\dfrac{A+B}{D} = \dfrac{A}{D} + \dfrac{B}{D}$$

Self Check 3

Divide: $\dfrac{4 - 8b}{4}$ $1 - 2b$

Now Try Problem 42

Teaching Example 3 Divide:
$\dfrac{10x - 15}{5}$
Answer:
$2x - 3$

EXAMPLE 3 Divide: $9x + 6$ by 3

Strategy We will set up the fraction to represent the division. Then we will divide each term of the numerator by the denominator.

WHY This is the rule for dividing a polynomial by a monomial.

Solution

$$\frac{9x + 6}{3} = \frac{9x}{3} + \frac{6}{3} \quad \text{Divide each term of the numerator by the denominator.}$$

$$= 3x + 2 \quad \text{Simplify each fraction.}$$

Self Check 4

Divide: $\dfrac{9a^2b - 6ab^2 + 3ab}{3ab}$

Now Try Problem 49
Self Check 4 Answer
$3a - 2b + 1$

Teaching Example 4 Divide:
$\dfrac{4p^2q^3 + 12p^3q - 6pq}{2pq}$
Answer:
$2pq^2 + 6p^2 - 3$

EXAMPLE 4 Divide: $\dfrac{6x^2y^2 + 4x^2y - 2xy}{2xy}$

Strategy We will divide each term of the polynomial in the numerator by the monomial in the denominator.

WHY This is the rule for dividing a polynomial by a monomial.

Solution

$$\frac{6x^2y^2 + 4x^2y - 2xy}{2xy}$$

$$= \frac{6x^2y^2}{2xy} + \frac{4x^2y}{2xy} - \frac{2xy}{2xy} \quad \text{Divide each term of the numerator by the denominator.}$$

$$= 3xy + 2x - 1 \quad \text{Simplify each fraction.}$$

Self Check 5

Divide: $\dfrac{14p^3q + pq^2 - p}{7p^2q}$

Now Try Problem 52
Self Check 5 Answer
$2p + \dfrac{q}{7p} - \dfrac{1}{7pq}$

Teaching Example 5 Divide:
$\dfrac{18x^3y^2 - 6x^2y - x}{9x^2y^2}$
Answer:
$2x - \dfrac{2}{3y} - \dfrac{1}{9xy^2}$

EXAMPLE 5 Divide: $\dfrac{12a^3b^2 - 4a^2b + a}{6a^2b^2}$

Strategy We will divide each term of the polynomial in the numerator by the monomial in the denominator.

WHY This is the rule for dividing a polynomial by a monomial.

Solution

$$\frac{12a^3b^2 - 4a^2b + a}{6a^2b^2}$$

$$= \frac{12a^3b^2}{6a^2b^2} - \frac{4a^2b}{6a^2b^2} + \frac{a}{6a^2b^2} \quad \text{Divide each term of the numerator by the denominator.}$$

$$= 2a - \frac{2}{3b} + \frac{1}{6ab^2} \quad \text{Simplify each fraction.}$$

Self Check 6

Divide: $\dfrac{(x + y)^2 - (x - y)^2}{xy}$ 4

Now Try Problem 55

EXAMPLE 6 Divide: $\dfrac{(x - y)^2 - (x + y)^2}{xy}$

Strategy We will remove the parentheses in the numerator and collect like terms. Then we will divide each term of the polynomial in the numerator by the monomial in the denominator.

WHY This is the rule for dividing a polynomial by a monomial.

Solution

$$\frac{(x-y)^2 - (x+y)^2}{xy}$$

$$= \frac{x^2 - 2xy + y^2 - (x^2 + 2xy + y^2)}{xy}$$

Use the special product rules to square the binomials in the numerator.

$$= \frac{x^2 - 2xy + y^2 - x^2 - 2xy - y^2}{xy}$$

Change the sign of each term within $(x^2 + 2xy + y^2)$.

$$= \frac{-4xy}{xy}$$

Combine like terms.

$$= -4$$

Divide out the common factors of x and y. ∎

Teaching Example 6 Divide:
$$\frac{2(x+y)^2 - (x+y)(x-y)}{xy}$$
Answer:
$$\frac{x}{y} + 4 + \frac{3y}{x}$$

3 Write equivalent forms of formulas.

The area of the trapezoid shown here is given by the formula $A = \frac{1}{2}h(B + b)$, where B and b are its bases and h is its height. To solve the formula for b, we proceed as follows.

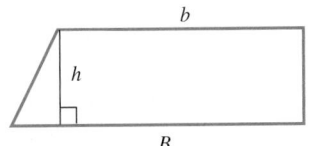

$$A = \frac{1}{2}h(B + b)$$

$$2 \cdot A = 2 \cdot \frac{1}{2}h(B + b)$$

Multiply both sides by 2 to clear the equation of the fraction.

$$2A = h(B + b)$$

Simplify: $2 \cdot \frac{1}{2} = \frac{2}{2} = 1$

$$2A = hB + hb$$

Distribute the multiplication by h.

$$2A - hB = hB + hb - hB$$

Subtract hB from both sides.

$$2A - hB = hb$$

Combine like terms: $hB - hB = 0$.

$$\frac{2A - hB}{h} = \frac{hb}{h}$$

To undo the multiplication by h, divide both sides by h.

$$\frac{2A - hB}{h} = b$$

EXAMPLE 7

Another student worked the previous problem in a different way and got a result of $b = \frac{2A}{h} - B$. Is this result correct?

Strategy We will use the rule for dividing a polynomial by a monomial on the right side of $b = \frac{2A - hB}{h}$.

WHY If the right side of $b = \frac{2A - hB}{h}$ is the same as the right side of $b = \frac{2A}{h} - B$ after applying the rule for dividing a polynomial by a monomial, then the answer is also correct.

Solution
To determine whether this result is correct, we must show that

$$\frac{2A - hB}{h} = \frac{2A}{h} - B$$

We can do this by dividing $2A - hB$ by h.

$$\frac{2A - hB}{h} = \frac{2A}{h} - \frac{hB}{h}$$

Divide each term of $2A - hB$ by the denominator, which is h.

$$= \frac{2A}{h} - B$$

Simplify the second fraction: $\frac{\overset{1}{\cancel{h}}B}{\underset{1}{\cancel{h}}} = B$.

The results are the same.

Self Check 7

Suppose another student got $b = 2A - \frac{hB}{h}$. Is this result correct? no

Now Try Problem 77

Teaching Example 7 Is $w = \frac{P - 2L}{2}$ equivalent to $w = \frac{P}{2} - L$?

Answer:
yes

SECTION 5.7   STUDY SET

VOCABULARY

Fill in the blanks.

1. A __polynomial__ is an algebraic expression that is the sum of one or more terms containing whole-number exponents.

2. A __monomial__ is a polynomial with one term.

3. A binomial is a polynomial with __two__ terms.

▶ **4.** A trinomial is a polynomial with __three__ terms.

5. $\dfrac{x^m}{x^n} = x^{m-n}$ is a rule for __exponents__ .

6. To __simplify__ a fraction, we divide out common factors of the numerator and denominator.

CONCEPTS

Fill in the blanks.

7. $\dfrac{18x + 9}{9} = \dfrac{18x}{9} + \dfrac{9x}{9}$

8. $\dfrac{30x^2 + 12x - 24}{6} = \dfrac{30x^2}{6} + \dfrac{12x}{6} - \dfrac{24}{6}$

▶ **9.** $\dfrac{x^m}{x^n} = x^{m-n}$

▶ **10.** $x^{-n} = \dfrac{1}{x^n}$

11. a. Solve the formula $d = rt$ for t. $t = \dfrac{d}{r}$

   b. Use your answer from part a to complete the table.

	r	$\cdot$ t	$= d$
Motorcycle	$2x$	$3x^2$	$6x^3$

12. a. Solve the formula $I = Prt$ for r. $r = \dfrac{I}{Pt}$

   b. Use your answer from part a to complete the table.

	P	$\cdot$ r	$\cdot$ t	$= I$
Savings account	$8x^3$	$\frac{3x^2}{2}$	$2x$	$24x^6$

13. How many nickels would have a value of $(10x + 35)$ cents? $2x + 7$

▶ **14.** How many twenty-dollar bills would have a value of $\$(60x - 100)$? $3x - 5$

NOTATION

Complete each solution.

15. $\dfrac{a^2b^3}{a^3b^2} = \dfrac{a \cdot a \cdot b \cdot b \cdot b}{a \cdot a \cdot a \cdot b \cdot b}$

$= \dfrac{\overset{1}{\cancel{a}} \cdot \overset{1}{\cancel{a}} \cdot \overset{1}{\cancel{b}} \cdot \overset{1}{\cancel{b}} \cdot b}{\underset{1}{\cancel{a}} \cdot \underset{1}{\cancel{a}} \cdot a \cdot \underset{1}{\cancel{b}} \cdot \underset{1}{\cancel{b}}}$

$= \dfrac{b}{a}$

▶ **16.** $\dfrac{6pq^2 - 9p^2q^2 + pq}{3p^2q}$

$= \dfrac{6pq^2}{3p^2q} - \dfrac{9p^2q^2}{3p^2q} + \dfrac{pq}{3p^2q}$

$= \dfrac{6 \cdot p \cdot q \cdot q}{3 \cdot p \cdot p \cdot q} - \dfrac{3 \cdot 3 \cdot p \cdot p \cdot q \cdot q}{3 \cdot p \cdot p \cdot q} + \dfrac{p \cdot q}{3 \cdot p \cdot p \cdot q}$

$= \dfrac{2q}{p} - 3q + \dfrac{1}{3p}$

GUIDED PRACTICE

Simplify each fraction. **See Objective 1.**

17. $\dfrac{5}{15}$ $\frac{1}{3}$ **18.** $\dfrac{64}{128}$ $\frac{1}{2}$

19. $\dfrac{-125}{75}$ $-\frac{5}{3}$ **20.** $\dfrac{-98}{21}$ $-\frac{14}{3}$

21. $\dfrac{120}{160}$ $\frac{3}{4}$ ▶ **22.** $\dfrac{70}{420}$ $\frac{1}{6}$

23. $\dfrac{-3,612}{-3,612}$ 1 **24.** $\dfrac{-288}{-112}$ $\frac{18}{7}$

Perform each division. **See Example 1.**

▶ **25.** $\dfrac{x^5}{x^2}$ x^3 **26.** $\dfrac{a^{12}}{a^8}$ a^4

27. $\dfrac{r^3s^2}{rs^3}$ $\frac{r^2}{s}$ **28.** $\dfrac{y^4z^3}{y^2z^2}$ y^2z

29. $\dfrac{8x^3y^2}{4xy^3}$ $\frac{2x^2}{y}$ **30.** $\dfrac{-3y^3z}{6yz^2}$ $-\frac{y^2}{2z}$

31. $\dfrac{12u^5v}{-4u^2v^3}$ $-\frac{3u^3}{v^2}$ **32.** $\dfrac{16rst^2}{-8rst^3}$ $-\frac{2}{t}$

▶ Selected exercises available online at
www.webassign.net/brookscole

Perform each division. See Example 2.

33. $\dfrac{(a^3b^4)^3}{ab^4}$ a^8b^8

34. $\dfrac{(a^2b^3)^3}{a^6b^6}$ b^3

▶ **35.** $\dfrac{15(r^2s^3)^2}{-5(rs^5)^3}$ $-\dfrac{3r}{s^9}$

36. $\dfrac{-5(a^2b)^3}{10(ab^2)^3}$ $-\dfrac{a^3}{2b^3}$

37. $\dfrac{-32(x^3y)^3}{128(x^2y^2)^3}$ $-\dfrac{x^3}{4y^3}$

38. $\dfrac{68(a^6b^7)^2}{-96(abc^2)^3}$ $-\dfrac{17a^9b^{11}}{24c^6}$

39. $\dfrac{-(4x^3y^3)^2}{(x^2y^4)^3}$ $-\dfrac{16}{y^6}$

40. $\dfrac{(2r^3s^2)^2}{-(4r^2s^2)^2}$ $-\dfrac{r^2}{4}$

Perform each division. See Examples 3–5.

41. $\dfrac{6x + 9}{3}$ $2x + 3$

▶ **42.** $\dfrac{8x + 12y}{4}$ $2x + 3y$

43. $\dfrac{5x - 10y}{25xy}$ $\dfrac{1}{5y} - \dfrac{2}{5x}$

44. $\dfrac{2x - 32}{16x}$ $\dfrac{1}{8} - \dfrac{2}{x}$

45. $\dfrac{3x^2 + 6y^3}{3x^2y^2}$ $\dfrac{1}{y^2} + \dfrac{2y}{x^2}$

46. $\dfrac{4a^2 - 9b^2}{12ab}$ $\dfrac{a}{3b} - \dfrac{3b}{4a}$

47. $\dfrac{15a^3b^2 - 10a^2b^3}{5a^2b^2}$
$3a - 2b$

48. $\dfrac{9a^4b^3 - 16a^3b^4}{12a^2b}$
$\dfrac{3a^2b^2}{4} - \dfrac{4ab^3}{3}$

49. $\dfrac{4x - 2y + 8z}{4xy}$
$\dfrac{1}{y} - \dfrac{1}{2x} + \dfrac{2z}{xy}$

50. $\dfrac{5a^2 + 10b^2 - 15ab}{5ab}$
$\dfrac{a}{b} + \dfrac{2b}{a} - 3$

▶ **51.** $\dfrac{12x^3y^2 - 8x^2y - 4x}{4xy}$
$3x^2y - 2x - \dfrac{1}{y}$

▶ **52.** $\dfrac{12a^2b^2 - 8a^2b - 4ab}{4ab}$
$3ab - 2a - 1$

Perform each division. See Example 6.

53. $\dfrac{5x(4x - 2y)}{2y}$
$\dfrac{10x^2}{y} - 5x$

▶ **54.** $\dfrac{9y(x^2 - 3xy)}{3x^2}$
$3y^2 - \dfrac{9y^2}{x}$

55. $\dfrac{(x - y)^2 - (x + y)^2}{2xy}$
-2

56. $\dfrac{(2m - n)(3m - 2n)}{-3m^2n^2}$
$-\dfrac{2}{n^2} + \dfrac{7}{3mn} - \dfrac{2}{3m^2}$

TRY IT YOURSELF

Simplify each expression.

57. $\dfrac{-16r^3y^2}{-4r^2y^4}$ $\dfrac{4r}{y^2}$

58. $\dfrac{35xyz^2}{-7x^2yz}$ $-\dfrac{5z}{x}$

59. $\dfrac{-65rs^2t}{15r^2s^3t}$ $-\dfrac{13}{3rs}$

60. $\dfrac{112u^3z^6}{-42u^3z^6}$ $-\dfrac{8}{3}$

61. $\dfrac{x^2x^3}{xy^6}$ $\dfrac{x^4}{y^6}$

62. $\dfrac{x^2y^2}{x^2y^3}$ $\dfrac{1}{y}$

63. $\dfrac{(a^2a^3)^4}{(a^4)^3}$ a^8

64. $\dfrac{(b^3b^4)^5}{(bb^2)^2}$ b^{29}

65. $\dfrac{-25x^2y + 30xy^2 - 5xy}{-5xy}$ $5x - 6y + 1$

66. $\dfrac{-30a^2b^2 - 15a^2b - 10ab^2}{-10ab}$ $3ab + \dfrac{3a}{2} + b$

67. $\dfrac{(-2x)^3 + (3x^2)^2}{6x^2}$ $-\dfrac{4x}{3} + \dfrac{3x^2}{2}$

68. $\dfrac{(-3x^2y)^3 + (3xy^2)^3}{27x^3y^4}$ $-\dfrac{x^3}{y} + y^2$

69. $\dfrac{4x^2y^2 - 2(x^2y^2 + xy)}{2xy}$ $xy - 1$

70. $\dfrac{-5a^3b - 5a(ab^2 - a^2b)}{10a^2b^2}$ $-\dfrac{1}{2}$

71. $\dfrac{(a + b)^2 - (a - b)^2}{2ab}$ 2

72. $\dfrac{(x - y)^2 + (x + y)^2}{2x^2y^2}$ $\dfrac{1}{y^2} + \dfrac{1}{x^2}$

APPLICATIONS

▶ **73.** POOL The rack shown is used to set up the balls when beginning a game of pool. If the perimeter of the rack, in inches, is given by the polynomial $6x^2 - 3x + 9$, what is the length of one side? $(2x^2 - x + 3)$ in.

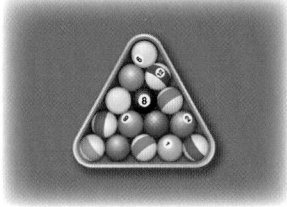

▶ **74.** CHECKERBOARDS If the perimeter (in inches) of the checkerboard is $12x^2 - 8x + 32$, find an expression that represents the length of one side. $(3x^2 - 2x + 8)$ in.

▶ **75.** AIR CONDITIONING If the volume occupied by the air conditioning unit shown is $(36x^3 - 24x^2)$ cubic feet, find an expression that represents its height. $(3x - 2)$ ft

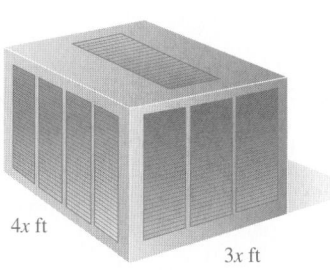

$4x$ ft

$3x$ ft

▶ **76.** MINIBLINDS The area covered by the miniblinds is $(3x^3 - 6x)$ square feet. Find an expression that represents the length of the blinds. $(x^2 - 2)$ ft

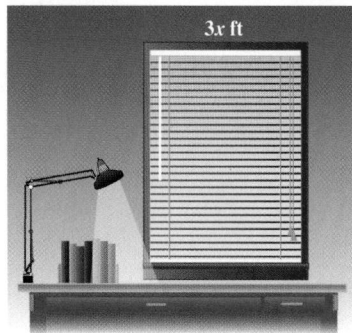

3x ft

▶ **77.** CONFIRMING FORMULAS Are these formulas the same?

$$l = \frac{P - 2w}{2} \quad \text{and} \quad l = \frac{P}{2} - w \text{ yes}$$

▶ **78.** CONFIRMING FORMULAS Are these formulas the same?

$$r = \frac{G + 2b}{2b} \quad \text{and} \quad r = \frac{G}{2b} + b \text{ no}$$

▶ **79.** ELECTRIC BILLS On an electric bill, the following two formulas are used to compute the average cost of x kwh of electricity. Are the formulas equivalent? no

$$\frac{0.08x + 5}{x} \quad \text{and} \quad 0.08x + \frac{5}{x}$$

▶ **80.** PHONE BILLS On a phone bill, the following two formulas are used to compute the average cost per minute of x minutes of phone usage. Are the formulas equivalent? yes

$$\frac{0.15x + 12}{x} \quad \text{and} \quad 0.15 + \frac{12}{x}$$

WRITING

81. Explain the error.

$$\frac{3x + 5}{5} = \frac{3x + \overset{1}{\cancel{5}}}{\underset{1}{\cancel{5}}}$$
$$= 3x$$

▶ **82.** Explain how to perform this division.

$$\frac{4x^2y + 8xy^2}{4xy}$$

REVIEW

Identify each polynomial as a monomial, a binomial, a trinomial, or none of these.

83. $5a^2b + 2ab^2$ binomial

84. $-3x^3y$ monomial

85. $-2x^3 + 3x^2 - 4x + 12$ none of these

86. $17t^2 - 15t + 27$ trinomial

87. What is the degree of the trinomial $3x^2 - 2x + 4$? 2

▶ **88.** What is the numerical coefficient of the second term of the trinomial $-7t^2 + 5t + 17$? 5

Objectives

1 Divide polynomials by polynomials.

2 Write powers in descending order.

3 Divide polynomials that are missing terms.

SECTION 5.8
Dividing Polynomials by Polynomials

In this section, we will discuss how to divide one polynomial by another.

1 Divide polynomials by polynomials.

To divide one polynomial by another, we use a method similar to long division in arithmetic. We illustrate the method with several examples.

Self Check 1

Divide $x^2 + 7x + 12$ by $x + 3$.

Now Try Problem 20

Self Check 1 Answer

$x + 4$

EXAMPLE 1 Divide $x^2 + 5x + 6$ by $x + 2$.

Strategy We will use the long division method. The dividend is $x^2 + 5x + 6$ and the divisor is $x + 2$.

WHY Since the divisor has more than one term, we must use the long division method to divide the polynomials.

Solution

We write the division using the symbol $\overline{)}$ and proceed as follows:

Step 1

$$x + 2\overline{)x^2 + 5x + 6}$$ with x above

Divide the first term of $x^2 + 5x + 6$ by the first term of $x + 2$. $\frac{x^2}{x} = x$. Write x above the division symbol.

Step 2

$$\begin{array}{r} x \\ x + 2\overline{)x^2 + 5x + 6} \\ x^2 + 2x \end{array}$$

Multiply each term in the divisor by x. Write the result, $x^2 + 2x$, under $x^2 + 5x$, and draw a line. Be sure to align like terms.

Step 3

$$\begin{array}{r} x \\ x + 2\overline{)x^2 + 5x + 6} \\ -(x^2 + 2x) \downarrow \\ \hline 3x + 6 \end{array}$$

Subtract $x^2 + 2x$ from $x^2 + 5x$. Work vertically, column by column: $x^2 - x^2 = 0$ and $5x - 2x = 3x$.

Bring down the 6.

Step 4

$$\begin{array}{r} x + 3 \\ x + 2\overline{)x^2 + 5x + 6} \\ -(x^2 + 2x) \\ \hline 3x + 6 \end{array}$$

Divide the first term of $3x + 6$ by the first term of the divisor. $\frac{3x}{x} = +3$. Write $+3$ above the division symbol to form the second term of the quotient.

Step 5

$$\begin{array}{r} x + 3 \\ x + 2\overline{)x^2 + 5x + 6} \\ x^2 + 2x + 6 \\ \hline 3x + 6 \\ 3x + 6 \\ \hline 0 \end{array}$$

Multiply each term in the divisor by 3. Write the product under $3x + 6$ and draw a line.

Step 6

$$\begin{array}{r} x + 3 \\ x + 2\overline{)x^2 + 5x + 6} \\ -(x^2 + 2x) \\ \hline 3x + 6 \\ -(3x + 6) \\ \hline 0 \end{array}$$

Subtract $3x + 6$ from $3x + 6$. Work vertically: $3x - 3x = 0$ and $6 - 6 = 0$.

This is the remainder.

The quotient is $x + 3$ and the remainder is 0.

Step 7 Check the work by verifying that $(x + 2)(x + 3)$ is $x^2 + 5x + 6$.

$$(x + 2)(x + 3) = x^2 + 3x + 2x + 6$$
$$= x^2 + 5x + 6 \qquad \text{The answer checks.}$$

The answer checks.

EXAMPLE 2

Divide: $\dfrac{6x^2 - 7x - 2}{2x - 1}$

Strategy We will use the long division method. The dividend is $6x^2 - 7x - 2$ and the divisor is $2x - 1$.

WHY Since the divisor has more than one term, we must use the long division method to divide the polynomials.

Solution

We write the division using a long division symbol $\overline{)}$ and proceed as follows:

Step 1

$$\begin{array}{r} 3x \\ 2x - 1\overline{)6x^2 - 7x - 2} \end{array}$$

Divide the first term of the dividend by the first term of the divisor. $\frac{6x^2}{2x} = 3x$. Write the $3x$ above the division symbol.

Step 2
$$\begin{array}{r} 3x \\ 2x - 1\overline{)6x^2 - 7x - 2} \\ \underline{6x^2 - 3x} \end{array}$$

Multiply each term in the divisor by 3x. Write the product under $6x^2 - 7x$ and draw a line.

Step 3
$$\begin{array}{r} 3x \\ 2x - 1\overline{)6x^2 - 7x - 2} \\ \underline{-(6x^2 - 3x)} \downarrow \\ -4x - 2 \end{array}$$

Subtract $6x^2 - 3x$ from $6x^2 - 7x$. Work vertically: $6x^2 - 6x^2 = 0$ and $-7x - (-3x) = -7x + 3x = -4x$. Bring down the -2.

Step 4
$$\begin{array}{r} 3x - 2 \\ 2x - 1\overline{)6x^2 - 7x - 2} \\ \underline{-(6x^2 - 3x)} \\ -4x - 2 \end{array}$$

Divide the first term of $-4x - 2$ by the first term of the divisor. $\frac{-4x}{2x} = -2$. Write -2 above the division symbol.

Step 5
$$\begin{array}{r} 3x - 2 \\ 2x - 1\overline{)6x^2 - 7x - 2} \\ \underline{-(6x^2 - 3x)} \\ -4x - 2 \\ \underline{-(-4x + 2)} \end{array}$$

Multiply each term in the divisor by -2. Write the product under $-4x - 2$ and draw a line.

Step 6
$$\begin{array}{r} 3x - 2 \\ 2x - 1\overline{)6x^2 - 7x - 2} \\ \underline{-(6x^2 - 3x)} \\ -4x - 2 \\ \underline{-(-4x + 2)} \\ -4 \end{array}$$

Subtract $-4x + 2$ from $-4x - 2$. Work vertically: $-4x - (-4x) = -4x + 4x = 0$ and $-2 - 2 = -4$.

Here the quotient is $3x - 2$ and the remainder is -4. It is common to write the answer as either

$$3x - 2 + \frac{-4}{2x - 1} \qquad \text{or} \qquad 3x - 2 - \frac{4}{2x - 1} \qquad \text{Quotient} + \frac{\text{remainder}}{\text{divisor}}.$$

Step 7 To check, we multiply

$$3x - 2 + \frac{-4}{2x - 1} \qquad \text{by} \qquad 2x - 1$$

The product should be the dividend.

$$(2x - 1)\left(3x - 2 + \frac{-4}{2x - 1}\right) = (2x - 1)(3x - 2) + (2x - 1)\left(\frac{-4}{2x - 1}\right)$$

$$= (2x - 1)(3x - 2) - 4$$

$$= 6x^2 - 4x - 3x + 2 - 4$$

$$= 6x^2 - 7x - 2$$

Because the result is the dividend, the answer checks.

2 Write powers in descending order.

The division method works best when the terms of the divisor and the dividend are written in descending powers of the variable. This means that the term involving the highest power of x appears first, the term involving the second-highest power of x appears second, and so on. For example, the terms in

$$3x^3 + 2x^2 - 7x + 5$$

have their exponents written in descending order.

If the powers in the dividend or divisor are not in descending order, we use the commutative property of addition to write them that way.

EXAMPLE 3   Divide: $(4x^2 + 2x^3 + 12 - 2x) \div (x + 3)$

Strategy We will write the dividend in descending powers of x and use the long division method to divide the polynomials.

WHY It is easier to carry out the division when the powers of the variables are written in descending order.

Solution
We write the dividend so that the exponents are in descending order.

$$
\begin{array}{r}
2x^2 - 2x + 4 \\
x + 3 \overline{)\, 2x^3 + 4x^2 - 2x + 12} \\
\underline{-(2x^3 + 6x^2)} \\
-2x^2 - 2x \\
\underline{-(-2x^2 - 6x)} \\
4x + 12 \\
\underline{-(4x + 12)} \\
0
\end{array}
$$

The first division: $\frac{2x^3}{x} = 2x^2$.

The second division: $\frac{-2x^2}{x} = -2x$.

The third division: $\frac{4x}{x} = 4$.

Check: $(x + 3)(2x^2 - 2x + 4) = 2x^3 - 2x^2 + 4x + 6x^2 - 6x + 12$
$$= 2x^3 + 4x^2 - 2x + 12$$

Self Check 3

Divide:
$(x^2 - 10x + 6x^3 + 4) \div (2x - 1)$

Now Try Problem 29
Self Check 3 Answer
$3x^2 + 2x - 4$

Teaching Example 3 Divide:
$(10x^3 + 12 + x^2 + 17x) \div (5x + 3)$
Answer:
$2x^2 - x + 4$

3   Divide polynomials that are missing terms.

When we write the terms of a dividend in descending powers of x, we must determine whether some powers of the variable are missing. When this happens, we should write such terms with a coefficient of 0 or leave a blank space for them.

EXAMPLE 4   Divide: $\dfrac{x^2 - 4}{x + 2}$

Strategy The dividend $x^2 - 4$ is missing an x-term. We will insert a $0x$ term as a placeholder and use the long division method.

WHY We insert placeholder terms so that like terms will be aligned in the same column when we subtract.

Solution

$$
\begin{array}{r}
x - 2 \\
x + 2 \overline{)\, x^2 + 0x - 4} \\
\underline{-(x^2 + 2x)} \\
-2x - 4 \\
\underline{-(-2x - 4)} \\
0
\end{array}
$$

The first division: $\frac{x^2}{x} = x$.

The second division: $\frac{-2x}{x} = -2$.

Check: $(x + 2)(x - 2) = x^2 - 2x + 2x - 4$
$$= x^2 - 4$$

Self Check 4

Divide: $\dfrac{x^2 - 9}{x - 3}$ $x + 3$

Now Try Problem 34

Teaching Example 4 Divide:
$\dfrac{27x^3 - 1}{3x - 1}$
Answer:
$9x^2 + 3x + 1$

ANSWERS TO SELF CHECKS

1. $x + 4$ **2.** $4x - 3 + \frac{6}{2x + 3}$ **3.** $3x^2 + 2x - 4$ **4.** $x + 3$

SECTION 5.8   STUDY SET

VOCABULARY

Fill in the blanks.

1. In the division $x + 1\overline{)x^2 + 2x + 1}$, the expression $x + 1$ is called the __divisor__ and $x^2 + 2x + 1$ is called the __dividend__.

▶ **2.** The answer to a division problem is called the __quotient__.

3. If a division does not come out even, the leftover part is called a __remainder__.

4. The powers of x in $2x^4 + 3x^3 + 4x^2 - 7x - 2$ are said to be written in __descending__ order.

CONCEPTS

Write each polynomial with the powers in descending order.

5. $4x^3 + 7x - 2x^2 + 6$ $4x^3 - 2x^2 + 7x + 6$

6. $5x^2 + 7x^3 - 3x - 9$ $7x^3 + 5x^2 - 3x - 9$

7. $9x + 2x^2 - x^3 + 6x^4$ $6x^4 - x^3 + 2x^2 + 9x$

8. $7x^5 + x^3 - x^2 + 2x^4$ $7x^5 + 2x^4 + x^3 - x^2$

Identify the missing terms in each polynomial.

9. $5x^4 + 2x^2 - 1$ $0x^3$ and $0x$

10. $-3x^5 - 2x^3 + 4x - 6$ $0x^4$ and $0x^2$

▶ **11. a.** Solve $d = rt$ for r. $r = \frac{d}{t}$

   b. Use your answer to part a and the long division method to complete the table.

	r	$\cdot$	t	$=$	d
Subway	$x - 3$		$x + 4$		$x^2 + x - 12$

▶ **12. a.** Solve $I = Prt$ for P. $P = \frac{I}{rt}$

   b. Use your answer to part a and the long division method to complete the table.

	P	$\cdot$	r	$\cdot$	t	$=$	I
Bonds	$x + 3$		$x + 4$		1		$x^2 + 7x + 12$

13. Using long division, a student found that

$$\frac{3x^2 + 8x + 4}{3x + 2} = x + 2$$

Use multiplication to see whether the result is correct.   It is correct.

14. Using long division, a student found that

$$\frac{x^2 + 4x - 21}{x - 3} = x + 7$$

Use multiplication to see whether the result is correct.   It is incorrect.

NOTATION

Complete each division.

15.
$$
\begin{array}{r}
x + 2 \\
x + 2\overline{)x^2 + 4x + 4} \\
\underline{x^2 + 2x} \\
2x + 4 \\
\underline{2x + 4} \\
0
\end{array}
$$

16.
$$
\begin{array}{r}
x^2 + x - 2 + \dfrac{7}{2x + 1} \\
2x + 1\overline{)2x^3 + 3x^2 - 3x + 5} \\
\underline{2x^3 + x^2} \\
2x^2 - 3x \\
\underline{2x^2 + x} \\
-4x + 5 \\
\underline{-4x - 2} \\
7
\end{array}
$$

GUIDED PRACTICE

Perform each division. **See Example 1.**

17. Divide $x^2 + 4x - 12$ by $x - 2$. $x + 6$

▶ **18.** Divide $x^2 - 5x + 6$ by $x - 2$. $x - 3$

19. Divide $y^2 + 13y + 12$ by $y + 1$. $y + 12$

▶ **20.** Divide $z^2 - 7z + 12$ by $z - 3$. $z - 4$

Perform each division. **See Example 2.**

21. $\dfrac{6a^2 + 5a - 6}{2a + 3}$ $3a - 2$ ▶ **22.** $\dfrac{8a^2 + 2a - 3}{2a - 1}$ $4a + 3$

23. $\dfrac{3b^2 + 11b + 6}{3b + 2}$ $b + 3$ ▶ **24.** $\dfrac{3b^2 - 5b + 2}{3b - 2}$ $b - 1$

25. $\dfrac{2x^2 + 5x + 2}{2x - 3}$ ▶ **26.** $\dfrac{3x^2 - 8x + 8}{3x - 2}$

   $x + 4 + \frac{14}{2x - 3}$ $x - 2 + \frac{4}{3x - 2}$

27. $\dfrac{4x^2 + 6x - 1}{2x + 1}$ **28.** $\dfrac{6x^2 - 11x + 2}{3x - 1}$

   $2x + 2 + \frac{-3}{2x + 1}$ $2x - 3 + \frac{-1}{3x - 1}$

*Write the terms so that the powers of x are in descending order.
Then perform each division.* See Example 3.

29. $5x + 3 \overline{)11x + 10x^2 + 3}$ $2x + 1$

▶ **30.** $2x - 7 \overline{)-x - 21 + 2x^2}$ $x + 3$

31. $4 + 2x \overline{)-10x - 28 + 2x^2}$ $x - 7$

▶ **32.** $1 + 3x \overline{)9x^2 + 1 + 6x}$ $3x + 1$

Perform each division. See Example 4.

33. $\dfrac{x^2 - 1}{x - 1}$ $x + 1$ ▶ **34.** $\dfrac{x^2 - 9}{x + 3}$ $x - 3$

35. $\dfrac{4x^2 - 9}{2x + 3}$ $2x - 3$ ▶ **36.** $\dfrac{25x^2 - 16}{5x - 4}$ $5x + 4$

TRY IT YOURSELF

Perform each division. If there is a remainder, write the answer

in quotient $+ \dfrac{\text{remainder}}{\text{divisor}}$ *form.*

37. $2x - 1 \overline{)x - 2 + 6x^2}$
   $3x + 2$

▶ **38.** $2 + x \overline{)3x + 2x^2 - 2}$
   $2x - 1$

39. $3 + x \overline{)2x^2 - 3 + 5x}$
   $2x - 1$

▶ **40.** $x - 3 \overline{)2x^2 - 3 - 5x}$
   $2x + 1$

41. $2x + 3 \overline{)2x^3 + 7x^2 + 4x - 3}$ $x^2 + 2x - 1$

▶ **42.** $2x - 1 \overline{)2x^3 - 3x^2 + 5x - 2}$ $x^2 - x + 2$

43. $3x + 2 \overline{)6x^3 + 10x^2 + 7x + 2}$ $2x^2 + 2x + 1$

▶ **44.** $4x + 3 \overline{)4x^3 - 5x^2 - 2x + 3}$ $x^2 - 2x + 1$

45. $2x + 1 \overline{)2x^3 + 3x^2 + 3x + 1}$ $x^2 + x + 1$

▶ **46.** $3x - 2 \overline{)6x^3 - x^2 + 4x - 4}$ $2x^2 + x + 2$

47. $\dfrac{x^3 + 3x^2 + 3x + 1}{x + 1}$
   $x^2 + 2x + 1$

48. $\dfrac{x^3 + 6x^2 + 12x + 8}{x + 2}$
   $x^2 + 4x + 4$

49. $\dfrac{2x^3 + 7x^2 + 4x + 3}{2x + 3}$
   $x^2 + 2x - 1 + \frac{6}{2x + 3}$

▶ **50.** $\dfrac{6x^3 + x^2 + 2x + 1}{3x - 1}$
   $2x^2 + x + 1 + \frac{2}{3x - 1}$

51. $\dfrac{2x^3 + 4x^2 - 2x + 3}{x - 2}$
   $2x^2 + 8x + 14 + \frac{31}{x - 2}$

52. $\dfrac{3y^3 - 4y^2 + 2y + 3}{y + 3}$
   $3y^2 - 13y + 41 + \frac{-120}{y + 3}$

53. $\dfrac{x^3 + 1}{x + 1}$
   $x^2 - x + 1$

54. $\dfrac{x^3 - 8}{x - 2}$
   $x^2 + 2x + 4$

▶ **55.** $\dfrac{a^3 + a}{a + 3}$
   $a^2 - 3a + 10 + \frac{-30}{a + 3}$

56. $\dfrac{y^3 - 50}{y - 5}$
   $y^2 + 5y + 25 + \frac{75}{y - 5}$

57. $3x - 4 \overline{)15x^3 - 23x^2 + 16x}$ $5x^2 - x + 4 + \frac{16}{3x - 4}$

58. $2y + 3 \overline{)21y^2 + 6y^3 - 20}$ $3y^2 + 6y - 9 + \frac{7}{2y + 3}$

APPLICATIONS

▶ **59.** FURNACE FILTERS The
area of the furnace filter
shown is $(x^2 - 2x - 24)$
square inches.

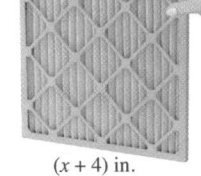

(x + 4) in.

   a. Find an expression for its
   length. $(x - 6)$ in.

   b. Find an expression for its
   perimeter. $(4x - 4)$ in.

▶ **60.** SHELF SPACE The formula $V = Bh$ gives the
volume of a cylinder where B is the area of the
base and h is the height. Find the amount of shelf
space that the container of potato chips shown
occupies if its volume is $(2x^3 - 4x - 2)$ cubic
inches. $(x^2 - x - 1)$ in.

(2x + 2) in.

$2.09

▶ **61.** COMMUNICATIONS See the illustration.
Telephone poles were installed every
$(2x - 3)$ feet along a stretch of railroad track
$(8x^3 - 6x^2 + 5x - 21)$ feet long. How many poles
were used? $4x^2 + 3x + 7$

(2x − 3) ft

▶ **62.** CONSTRUCTION COSTS Find the price per
square foot to remodel each of the three rooms listed
in the table.

Room	Remodeling cost	Area (ft²)	Cost (per ft²)
Bathroom	$(2x^2 + x - 6)$	$2x - 3$	$(x + 2)$
Bedroom	$(x^2 + 9x + 20)$	$x + 4$	$(x + 5)$
Kitchen	$(3x^3 - 9x - 6)$	$3x + 3$	$(x^2 - x - 2)$

WRITING

63. Explain how the following are related: *dividend, divisor, quotient,* and *remainder.*

▶ **64.** How would you check the results of a division?

REVIEW

Simplify each expression.

65. $(x^5x^6)^2$ x^{22}

▶ **66.** $(a^2)^3(a^3)^4$ a^{18}

67. $3(2x^2 - 4x + 5) + 2(x^2 + 3x - 7)$ $8x^2 - 6x + 1$

68. $-2(y^3 + 2y^2 - y) - 3(3y^3 + y)$ $-11y^3 - 4y^2 - y$

69. What can be said about the slopes of two parallel lines? They are the same.

70. What is the slope of a line perpendicular to a line with a slope of $\frac{3}{4}$? $-\frac{4}{3}$

STUDY SKILLS CHECKLIST

PREPARING FOR THE CHAPTER 5 TEST

While preparing for the Chapter 5 exam, it is important to keep the following in mind:

☐ When simplifying an exponential expression with negative exponents, write the reciprocal of the base and change the sign of the exponent.

$$7^{-2} = \frac{1}{7^2} = \frac{1}{49}$$

☐ Any nonzero number raised to the zero power is 1.

$$37^0 = 1, \quad 8x^0 = 8(1) = 8, \quad (-3x)^0 = 1$$

☐ To multiply a monomial to a polynomial, use the distributive property.

$$6xy^3(3xy - y^2) = 18x^2y^4 - 6xy^5$$

☐ The square of a binomial is a *trinomial.* A common error when squaring a binomial is to forget the middle term of the product.

$$(5x - 7)^2 = (5x - 7)(5x - 7)$$

$$= 25x^2 - 35x - 35x + 49$$

$$= 25x^2 - 70x + 49$$

$$\cancel{(5x - 7)^2 = 25x^2 + 49}$$

☐ To divide a polynomial by a *monomial,* do not use long division. We divide each term of the polynomial by the monomial in the denominator. Then simplify each fraction.

$$\frac{15x^2 + 3xy - 5y^2}{10xy} = \frac{15x^2}{10xy} + \frac{3xy}{10xy} - \frac{5y^2}{10xy}$$

$$= \frac{3x}{2y} + \frac{3}{10} - \frac{y}{2x}$$

☐ To divide a polynomial by a polynomial, use long division.

$$\frac{x^2 - 6x + 5}{x - 5}$$

$$\begin{array}{r} x - 1 \\ x - 5 \overline{)x^2 - 6x + 5} \\ \underline{-(x^2 - 5x)} \\ -x + 5 \\ \underline{-x + 5} \\ 0 \end{array}$$

Teaching Guide: Refer to the Instuctor's Resource Binder to find activites, worksheets on key concepts, more examples, instruction tips, overheads, and assessments.

CHAPTER 5   SUMMARY AND REVIEW

DEFINITIONS AND CONCEPTS

EXAMPLES

If n represents a natural number, then

Exponent n factors of x

$$x^n = \overbrace{x \cdot x \cdot x \cdot \cdots \cdot x}$$

Base

where x is called the **base** and n is called the **exponent.**

$5^4 = 5 \cdot 5 \cdot 5 \cdot 5 = 625$ 5 is the base, 4 is the exponent

$a^3 = a \cdot a \cdot a$ a is the base, 3 is the exponent

$(-y)^4 = (-y)(-y)(-y)(-y)$ $-y$ is the base, 4 is the exponent

$-y^4 = -y \cdot y \cdot y \cdot y$ y is the base, 4 is the exponent

---

Rules for exponents:

If m and n represent integers, then

Product rule: $x^m x^n = x^{m+n}$

Power rule: $(x^m)^n = x^{mn}$

Power of a product rule: $(xy)^n = x^n y^n$

Power of a quotient rule: $\left(\dfrac{x}{y}\right)^n = \dfrac{x^n}{y^n}$ $(y \neq 0)$

Quotient rule: $\dfrac{x^m}{x^n} = x^{m-n}$ $(x \neq 0)$

$a^3 a^4 = a^{3+4} = a^7$

$(a^3)^4 = a^{3 \cdot 4} = a^{12}$

$(ab)^3 = (ab)(ab)(ab) = a \cdot a \cdot a \cdot b \cdot b \cdot b = a^3 b^3$

$\left(\dfrac{a}{b}\right)^3 = \dfrac{a}{b} \cdot \dfrac{a}{b} \cdot \dfrac{a}{b} = \dfrac{a^3}{b^3}$

$\dfrac{a^7}{a^3} = \dfrac{a \cdot a \cdot a \cdot a \cdot \cancel{a} \cdot \cancel{a} \cdot \cancel{a}}{\cancel{a} \cdot \cancel{a} \cdot \cancel{a}} = a^{7-3} = a^4$

REVIEW EXERCISES

Write each expression without using exponents.

1. $-3x^4$ $-3 \cdot x \cdot x \cdot x \cdot x$

2. $\left(\dfrac{1}{2}pq\right)^3$ $\left(\dfrac{1}{2}pq\right)\left(\dfrac{1}{2}pq\right)\left(\dfrac{1}{2}pq\right)$

Evaluate each expression.

3. 5^3 125

4. $(-8)^2$ 64

5. -8^2 -64

6. $(5-3)^2$ 4

Simplify each expression.

7. $x^3 x^2$ x^5

8. $-3y(y^5)$ $-3y^6$

9. $(y^7)^3$ y^{21}

10. $(3x)^4$ $81x^4$

11. $b^3 b^4 b^5$ b^{12}

12. $-z^2(z^3 y^2)$ $-y^2 z^5$

13. $(-16s)^2 s$ $256s^3$

14. $(2x^2 y)^2$ $4x^4 y^2$

15. $(x^2 x^3)^3$ x^{15}

16. $\left(\dfrac{x^2 y}{xy^2}\right)^2$ $\dfrac{x^2}{y^2}$

17. $\dfrac{x^7}{x^3}$ x^4

18. $\dfrac{(5y^2 z^3)^3}{(yz)^5}$ $125yz^4$

Find the area or the volume of each figure.

19.

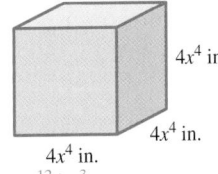

$4x^4$ in.

$4x^4$ in.

$4x^4$ in.

$64x^{12}$ in.^{3}

20.

y^2 m

y^2 m

y^4 m^2

SECTION 5.2   Zero and Negative Integer Exponents

DEFINITIONS AND CONCEPTS

EXAMPLES

Rules for exponents: For any nonzero real numbers x and y and any integers m and n,

Zero exponent: $x^0 = 1$

$$5^0 = 1 \qquad \left(\frac{a}{4}\right)^0 = 1 \qquad (x + 4)^0 = 1$$

Negative exponents: $x^{-n} = \dfrac{1}{x^n}$

$$5^{-2} = \frac{1}{5^2} = \frac{1}{25}$$

Negative to positive rules:

$$\frac{1}{x^{-n}} = x^n \qquad \frac{x^{-m}}{y^{-n}} = \frac{y^n}{x^m}$$

$$\frac{1}{5^{-2}} = 5^2 = 25 \qquad \frac{4^{-3}}{5^{-2}} = \frac{5^2}{4^3} = \frac{25}{64}$$

Negative exponents and reciprocals:

$$\left(\frac{x}{y}\right)^{-n} = \left(\frac{y}{x}\right)^n$$

$$\left(\frac{2}{3}\right)^{-3} = \left(\frac{3}{2}\right)^3 = \frac{3^3}{2^3} = \frac{27}{8}$$

REVIEW EXERCISES

Write each expression without using negative or zero exponents or parentheses.

21. x^0 1

22. $(3x^2y^2)^0$ 1

23. $(3x^0)^2$ 9

24. 10^{-3} $\frac{1}{1,000}$

25. $\left(\dfrac{3}{4}\right)^{-1}$ $\frac{4}{3}$

26. -5^{-2} $-\frac{1}{25}$

27. x^{-5} $\frac{1}{x^5}$

28. $-6y^4y^{-5}$ $-\frac{6}{y}$

29. $\dfrac{x^{-3}}{x^7}$ $\frac{1}{x^{10}}$

30. $(x^{-3}x^{-4})^{-2}$ x^{14}

31. $\left(\dfrac{x^2}{x}\right)^{-5}$ $\frac{1}{x^5}$

32. $\left(\dfrac{3z^4}{z^3}\right)^{-3}$ $\frac{1}{27z^3}$

Write each expression with a single exponent.

33. $y^{3n}y^{4n}$ y^{7n}

34. $\dfrac{z^{8c}}{z^{10c}}$ $\frac{1}{z^{2c}}$

SECTION 5.3   Scientific Notation

DEFINITIONS AND CONCEPTS

EXAMPLES

A number is written in **scientific notation** if it is written as the product of a number between 1 (including 1) and 10 and an integer power of 10.

Standard Notation	Scientific Notation
93,000,000	9.3×10^7
0.000375	3.75×10^{-4}

REVIEW EXERCISES

Write each number in scientific notation.

35. 728 7.28×10^2

36. 9,370,000 9.37×10^6

37. 0.0136 1.36×10^{-2}

38. 0.00942 9.42×10^{-3}

39. 0.018×10^{-2} 1.8×10^{-4}

40. 753×10^3 7.53×10^5

Write each number in standard notation.

41. 7.26×10^5 726,000

42. 3.91×10^{-4} 0.000391

43. 2.68×10^0 2.68

44. 5.76×10^1 57.6

Simplify each fraction by first writing each number in scientific notation. Then perform the arithmetic. Express the result in standard notation.

45. $\dfrac{(0.00012)(0.00004)}{0.00000016}$ **46.** $\dfrac{(4,800)(20,000)}{600,000}$

0.03   160

47. WORLD POPULATION In the year 2000, the world's population was estimated to be 6.08 billion. Write this number in standard notation and in scientific notation. $6,080,000,000, 6.08 \times 10^9$

48. ATOMS The illustration shows a cross section of an atom. How many nuclei, placed end to end, would it take to stretch across the atom? $1.0 \times 10^5 = 100,000$

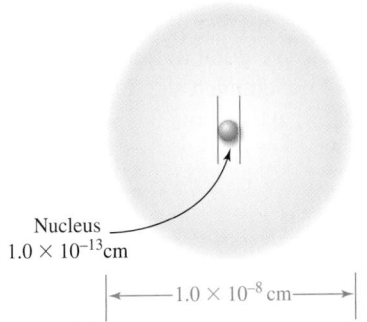

Nucleus
1.0×10^{-13}cm

$\longleftarrow$ 1.0×10^{-8} cm $\longrightarrow$

SECTION 5.4   Polynomials

DEFINITIONS AND CONCEPTS	EXAMPLES
A **polynomial** is a term or a sum of terms in which all variables have whole-number exponents. No variable appears in a denominator.	Polynomials: $3x$, $2x^2 - x + 7$, $5x^3 + 7x^4y - 3y^4$ Not polynomials: $y^2 - y^{-5}$, $4a - \dfrac{3}{a^2} + 5$
The **degree of a monomial** ax^n is n. The **degree of a monomial** in several variables is the sum of the exponents on those variables. The **degree of a polynomial** is the same as the degree of its term with the largest degree.	The polynomials above have degrees of 1, 2, and 5, respectively.
If $f(x)$ is a polynomial function in x, then $f(3)$ is the value of the function when $x = 3$.	If $f(x) = 3x^2 + x - 2$, then $f(-1) = 3(-1)^2 + (-1) - 2$ $f(2) = 3(2)^2 + 2 - 2$ $= 3(1) - 1 - 2$ $\quad = 3(4) + 2 - 2$ $= 3 - 1 - 2$ $\quad = 12 + 0$ $= 0$ $\quad = 12$

REVIEW EXERCISES

Determine whether each expression is a polynomial.

49. $x^3 - x^2 - x - 1$ yes   **50.** $x^{-2} - x^{-1} - 1$ no

51. $\dfrac{11}{y} + 4y$ no   **52.** $-16x^2y + 5xy^2$ yes

Consider the polynomial $3x^3 - x^2 + x + 10$.

53. How many terms does the polynomial have? 4

54. What is the leading term? $3x^3$

55. What is the coefficient of the second term? -1

56. What is the constant term? 10

Find the degree of each polynomial and classify it as a monomial, binomial, trinomial, or none of these.

57. $13x^7$
7th, monomial

58. $-16a^2b$
3rd, monomial

59. $5^3x + x^2$
2nd, binomial

60. $-3x^5 + x - 1$
5th, trinomial

61. $9xy^2 + 21x^3y^3$
6th, binomial

62. $4s^4 - 3s^2 + 5s + 4$
4th, none of these

Let $f(x) = 3x^2 + 2x + 1$. Find each value.

63. $f(3)$ 34   **64.** $f(0)$ 1

65. $f(-2)$ 9   **66.** $f(-0.2)$ 0.72

67. DIVING The number of inches that the woman deflects the diving board is given by the function

$$f(x) = 0.1875x^2 - 0.0078125x^3$$

where x is the number of feet that she stands from the front anchor point of the board. Find the amount of deflection if she stands on the end of the diving board, 8 feet from the anchor point. 8 in.

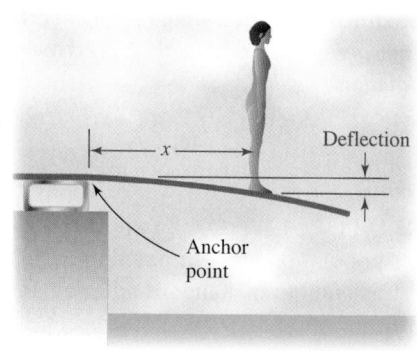

Deflection

Anchor point

SECTION 5.5 Adding and Subtracting Polynomials

DEFINITIONS AND CONCEPTS	EXAMPLES
To add (or subtract) polynomials, remove parentheses, and add (or subtract) like terms by combining the numerical coefficients and using the same variables and the same exponents.	Add: $(3x^2 + 2x - 4) + (2x^2 - 5x + 8)$ $= 3x^2 + 2x - 4 + 2x^2 - 5x + 8$ $= 3x^2 + 2x^2 + 2x - 5x - 4 + 8$ $= 5x^2 - 3x + 4$ Subtract: $(5a^2 - a + 2) - (a^2 + a - 3)$ $= 5a^2 - a + 2 - a^2 - a + 3$ $= 5a^2 - a^2 - a - a + 2 + 3$ $= 4a^2 - 2a + 5$
To add (or subtract) polynomials when a monomial precedes parentheses, we can use the distributive property to remove the parentheses and add (or subtract) the polynomials.	Simplify: $-2(4a^2 + 3a + 5) - 4(3a^2 - 7)$ $= -8a^2 - 6a - 10 - 12a^2 + 28$ Distribute the multiplication of -2 and -4. $= -8a^2 - 12a^2 - 6a - 10 + 28$ Write like terms together. $= -20a^2 - 6a + 18$ Combine like terms.

REVIEW EXERCISES

Simplify each expression.

68. $3x^6 + 5x^5 - x^6$ $2x^6 + 5x^5$

69. $x^2y^2 - 3x^2y^2$ $-2x^2y^2$

70. $(3x^2 + 2x) + (5x^2 - 8x)$ $8x^2 - 6x$

71. $3(9x^2 + 3x + 7) - 2(11x^2 - 5x + 9)$ $5x^2 + 19x + 3$

Perform the operations.

72.
$$\begin{array}{r} 2x^2 + 5x + 2 \\ +\ \ x^2 - 3x + 6 \\ \hline 4x^2 + 2x + 8 \end{array}$$

73.
$$\begin{array}{r} 20x^3 \qquad\ \ + 12x \\ -\ 12x^3 + 7x^2 - 7x \\ \hline 8x^3 - 7x^2 + 19x \end{array}$$

SECTION 5.6 Multiplying Polynomials

DEFINITIONS AND CONCEPTS	EXAMPLES
To multiply two monomials, multiply the numerical factors and then multiply the variable factors.	Multiply: $(3a^3b^2)(-2a^2b^3) = (3)(-2)a^3a^2b^2b^3$ $= -6a^5b^5$
To multiply a polynomial with more than one term by a monomial, multiply each term of the polynomial by the monomial and simplify.	Multiply: $-5a^4b(2a^2 - 3a + 2) = (-5a^4b)(2a^2) - (-5a^4b)(3a) + (-5a^4b)(2)$ $= -10a^6b + 15a^5b - 10a^4b$

To multiply two binomials, use the *FOIL* method.	Multiply: $(2a + 3b)(3a - 4b) = (2a)(3a) + (2a)(-4b) + (3b)(3a) + (3b)(-4b)$ $= 6a^2 - 8ab + 9ab - 12b^2$ $= 6a^2 + ab - 12b^2$
Special products: $(x + y)^2 = x^2 + 2xy + y^2$ $(x - y)^2 = x^2 - 2xy + y^2$ $(x + y)(x - y) = x^2 - y^2$	Multiply: $(a + 2b)^2 = a^2 + 2(a)(2b) + (2b)^2 = a^2 + 4ab + 4b^2$ $(a - 2b)^2 = a^2 + 2(a)(-2b) + (-2b)^2 = a^2 - 4ab + 4b^2$ $(a + 2b)(a - 2b) = a^2 - (2b)^2 = a^2 - 4b^2$
To multiply one polynomial by another, multiply each term of one polynomial by each term of the other polynomial, and simplify.	Multiply: $(a + 2)(a^2 + 3a - 4)$ $= a(a^2) + a(3a) + a(-4) + 2(a^2) + 2(3a) + 2(-4)$ $= a^3 + 3a^2 - 4a + 2a^2 + 6a - 8$ $= a^3 + 5a^2 + 2a - 8$

REVIEW EXERCISES

Find each product.

74. $(2x^2)(5x)$
$10x^3$

75. $(-6x^4z^3)(x^6z^2)$
$-6x^{10}z^5$

76. $(2rst)(-3r^2s^3t^4)$
$-6r^3s^4t^5$

77. $5b^3 \cdot 6b^2 \cdot 4b^6$
$120b^{11}$

78. $5(x + 3)$
$5x + 15$

79. $x^2(3x^2 - 5)$
$3x^4 - 5x^2$

80. $x^2y(y^2 - xy)$
$x^2y^3 - x^3y^2$

81. $-2y^2(y^2 - 5y)$
$-2y^4 + 10y^3$

82. $2x(3x^4)(x + 2)$
$6x^6 + 12x^5$

83. $-3x(x^2 - x + 2)$
$-3x^3 + 3x^2 - 6x$

84. $(x + 3)(x + 2)$
$x^2 + 5x + 6$

85. $(2x + 1)(x - 1)$
$2x^2 - x - 1$

86. $(3a - 3)(2a + 2)$
$6a^2 - 6$

87. $6(a - 1)(a + 1)$
$6a^2 - 6$

88. $(a - b)(2a + b)$
$2a^2 - ab - b^2$

89. $(-3x - y)(2x + y)$
$-6x^2 - 5xy - y^2$

90. $(x + 3)(x + 3)$
$x^2 + 6x + 9$

91. $(x + 5)(x - 5)$
$x^2 - 25$

92. $(a - 3)^2$
$a^2 - 6a + 9$

93. $(x + 4)^2$
$x^2 + 8x + 16$

94. $(-2y + 1)^2$
$4y^2 - 4y + 1$

95. $(y^2 + 1)(y^2 - 1)$
$y^4 - 1$

96. $(3x + 1)(x^2 + 2x + 1)$
$3x^3 + 7x^2 + 5x + 1$

97. $(2a - 3)(4a^2 + 6a + 9)$
$8a^3 - 27$

Solve each equation.

98. $x^2 + 3 = x(x + 3)$ 1

99. $x^2 + x = (x + 1)(x + 2)$ −1

100. $(x + 2)(x - 5) = (x - 4)(x - 1)$ 7

101. $(x + 5)(3x + 1) = x^2 + (2x - 1)(x - 5)$ 0

102. APPLIANCE Find the perimeter of the base, the area of the base, and the volume occupied by the dishwasher shown below.
$(6x + 10)$ in., $(2x^2 + 11x - 6)$ in.^{2}, $(6x^3 + 33x^2 - 18x)$ in.^{3}

$3x$ in.

$(x + 6)$ in.

$(2x - 1)$ in.

SECTION 5.7   Dividing Polynomials by Monomials

DEFINITIONS AND CONCEPTS	EXAMPLES
To **divide monomials,** use the method for simplifying fractions or use the rules for exponents.	$\dfrac{10}{15} = \dfrac{\cancel{5} \cdot 2}{\cancel{5} \cdot 3} = \dfrac{2}{3}$ $\dfrac{12a^2b^3}{8a^4b^2} = \dfrac{3 \cdot \cancel{4} \cdot \cancel{a} \cdot \cancel{a} \cdot b \cdot \cancel{b} \cdot \cancel{b}}{2 \cdot \cancel{4} \cdot \cancel{a} \cdot \cancel{a} \cdot a \cdot a \cdot \cancel{b} \cdot \cancel{b}} = \dfrac{3b}{2a^2}$ Remove common factors.

To **divide a polynomial by a monomial,** divide each term of the numerator by the denominator.

$$\frac{6a^2b + 8ab^2}{2ab} = \frac{6a^2b}{2ab} + \frac{8ab^2}{2ab} \qquad \text{Divide each term of the polynomial in the numerator by the demominator, 2ab.}$$

$$= \frac{3 \cdot 2 \cdot a \cdot \cancel{a} \cdot \cancel{b}}{2 \cdot \cancel{a} \cdot \cancel{b}} + \frac{4 \cdot 2 \cdot \cancel{a} \cdot b \cdot \cancel{b}}{2 \cdot \cancel{a} \cdot \cancel{b}} = 3a + 4b$$

REVIEW EXERCISES

Simplify each expression.

103. $\dfrac{-14x^2y}{21xy^3}$ $\dfrac{2x}{3y^2}$

104. $\dfrac{(x^2)^2}{xx^4}$ $\dfrac{1}{x}$

107. $\dfrac{15a^2b + 20ab^2 - 25ab}{5ab}$ $3a + 4b - 5$

108. $\dfrac{(x + y)^2 + (x - y)^2}{-2xy}$ $-\dfrac{x}{y} - \dfrac{y}{x}$

Perform each division. All variables represent positive numbers.

105. $\dfrac{8x + 6}{2}$ $4x + 3$

106. $\dfrac{14xy - 21x}{7xy}$ $2 - \dfrac{3}{y}$

109. SAVINGS BONDS How many $50 savings bonds would have a total value of $($50x + 250$)? $x + 5$

SECTION 5.8 Dividing Polynomials by Polynomials

DEFINITIONS AND CONCEPTS	EXAMPLES
Long division is used to **divide one polynomial by another.** When a division has a remainder, write the answer in the form $$\text{Quotient} + \frac{\text{remainder}}{\text{divisor}}$$	Divide: $$\begin{array}{r} x + 2 + \frac{1}{x+1} \\ x + 1 \overline{)x^2 + 3x + 3} \\ \underline{-(x^2 + x)} \\ 2x + 3 \\ \underline{-(2x + 2)} \\ 1 \end{array}$$ The first division: $\frac{x^2}{x} = x$. The second division: $\frac{2x}{x} = 2$.
The division method works best when the exponents of the terms of the divisor and the dividend are **written in descending order.**	$a + b\overline{)a^2 - 2b^2 - ab} \longrightarrow \begin{array}{r} a - 2b \\ a + b\overline{)a^2 - ab - 2b^2} \\ \underline{-(a^2 + ab)} \\ -2ab - 2b^2 \\ \underline{-(-2ab - 2b^2)} \\ 0 \end{array}$ The first division: $\frac{a^2}{a} = a$. The second division: $\frac{-2ab}{a} = -2b$.
When the dividend has **missing terms,** write it with a coefficient of zero or leave a blank space.	$4x + 1\overline{)16x^2 - 1} \longrightarrow \begin{array}{r} 4x - 1 \\ 4x + 1\overline{)16x^2 + 0x - 1} \\ \underline{-(16x^2 + 4x)} \\ -4x - 1 \\ \underline{-(-4x - 1)} \\ 0 \end{array}$ The first division: $\frac{16x^2}{4x} = 4x$. The second division: $\frac{-4x}{4x} = -1$.

REVIEW EXERCISES

Perform each division.

110. $x + 2\overline{)x^2 + 3x + 5}$ $x + 1 + \dfrac{3}{x+2}$

111. $x - 1\overline{)x^2 - 6x + 5}$ $x - 5$

112. $\dfrac{2x^2 + 3 + 7x}{x + 3}$ $2x + 1$

113. $\dfrac{3x^2 + 14x - 2}{3x - 1}$ $x + 5 + \dfrac{3}{3x - 1}$

114. $2x - 1\overline{)6x^3 + x^2 + 1}$ $3x^2 + 2x + 1 + \dfrac{2}{2x-1}$

115. $3x + 1\overline{)-13x - 4 + 9x^3}$ $3x^2 - x - 4$

116. Use multiplication to show that the answer when dividing $3y^2 + 11y + 6$ by $y + 3$ is $3y + 2$.

117. ZOOLOGY The distance in inches traveled by a certain type of snail in $(2x - 1)$ minutes is given by the polynomial $8x^2 + 2x - 3$. At what rate did the snail travel? $(4x + 3)$ in./min

CHAPTER 5   TEST

1. Use exponents to rewrite $2xxxyyyy$. $2x^3y^4$

2. Evaluate: $(3 + 5)^2$ 64

Write each expression as an expression containing only one exponent.

3. $y^2(yy^3)$ y^6

4. $(2x^3)^5(x^2)^3$ $32x^{21}$

Simplify each expression. Write answers without using parentheses or negative exponents.

5. $3x^0$ 3

6. $2y^{-5}y^2$ $\frac{2}{y^3}$

7. $\dfrac{y^2}{yy^{-2}}$ y^3

8. $\left(\dfrac{a^2b^{-1}}{4a^3b^{-2}}\right)^{-3}$ $\frac{64a^3}{b^3}$

9. What is the volume of a cube that has sides of length $10y^4$ inches? $1{,}000y^{12}$ in.^{3}

10. Rewrite 4^{-2} using a positive exponent and then evaluate the result. $\frac{1}{4^2}, \frac{1}{16}$

11. ELECTRICITY One ampere (amp) corresponds to the flow of 6,250,000,000,000,000,000 electrons per second past any point in a direct current (DC) circuit. Write this number in scientific notation. 6.25×10^{18}

12. Write in standard notation: 9.3×10^{-5} 0.000093

13. Identify $3x^2 + 2$ as a monomial, binomial, or trinomial. binomial

14. Find the degree of the polynomial: $3x^2y^3 + 2x^3y - 5x^2y$ 5th degree

15. If $f(x) = x^2 + x - 2$, find: $f(-2)$ 0

16. Simplify: $(xy)^2 + 5x^2y^2 - (3x)^2y^2$ $-3x^2y^2$

25. Solve: $(a + 2)^2 = (a - 3)^2$ $\frac{1}{2}$

17. Simplify: $-6(x - y) + 2(x + y) - 3(x + 2y)$ $-7x + 2y$

26. Simplify: $\dfrac{8x^2y^3z^4}{16x^3y^2z^4}$ $\frac{y}{2x}$

18. Subtract: $\begin{array}{r} 2x^2 - 7x + 3 \\ - \underline{3x^2 - 2x - 1} \end{array}$ $-x^2 - 5x + 4$

27. Simplify: $\dfrac{6a^2 - 12b^2}{24ab}$ $\frac{a}{4b} - \frac{b}{2a}$

Find each product.

19. $(-2x^3)(2x^2y)$
$-4x^5y$

20. $3y^2(y^2 - 2y + 3)$
$3y^4 - 6y^3 + 9y^2$

28. Divide: $2x + 3\overline{)2x^2 - x - 6}$ $x - 2$

29. In your own words, explain this rule for exponents:

$$x^{-n} = \frac{1}{x^n}$$

21. $(x - 9)(x + 9)$
$x^2 - 81$

22. $(3y - 4)^2$
$9y^2 - 24y + 16$

23. $(2x - 5)(3x + 4)$
$6x^2 - 7x - 20$

24. $(2x - 3)(x^2 - 2x + 4)$
$2x^3 - 7x^2 + 14x - 12$

30. A rectangle has an area of $(x^2 - 6x + 5)$ ft^2 and a length of $(x - 1)$ feet. Show how division can be used to find the width of the rectangle. Explain your steps.
$(x - 5)$ ft

1. Use exponents to write the prime factorization of 270. [Section 1.2] $2 \cdot 3^3 \cdot 5$

2. **a.** Use the variables a and b to state the commutative property of addition. [Section 1.4] $a + b = b + a$

   b. Use the variables x, y, and z to state the associative property of multiplication. [Section 1.6] $(xy)z = x(yz)$

Evaluate each expression.

3. $3 - 4[-10 - 4(-5)]$

   [Section 1.7] -37

4. $\dfrac{|-45| - 2(-5) + 1^5}{2 \cdot 9 - 2^4}$

   [Section 1.7] 28

Simplify each expression.

5. $27\left(\dfrac{2}{3}x\right)$ [Section 1.9] $18x$

6. $3x^2 + 2x^2 - 5x^2$ [Section 1.9] 0

Solve each equation.

7. $2 - (4x + 7) = 3 + 2(x + 2)$ [Section 2.2] -2

8. $\dfrac{2}{5}y + 3 = 9$ [Section 2.2] 15

9. **CANDY SALES** The circle graph shows how $6.3 billion in seasonal candy sales for 2005 was spent. Find the candy sales for Halloween. [Section 2.3] $2.079 billion

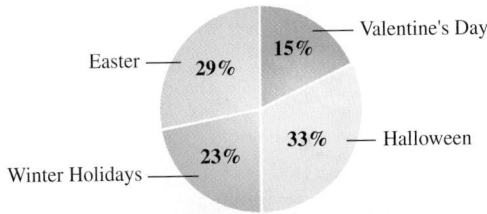

Easter — 29%   15% — Valentine's Day

23%   33% — Halloween

Winter Holidays

Source: National Confectioners Association

10. **AIR CONDITIONING** Find the volume of air contained in the duct. Round to the nearest tenth of a cubic foot. [Section 2.4] 1.2 ft^3

6 in.

6 ft

11. **ANGLE OF ELEVATION** Find x. [Section 2.5] 30

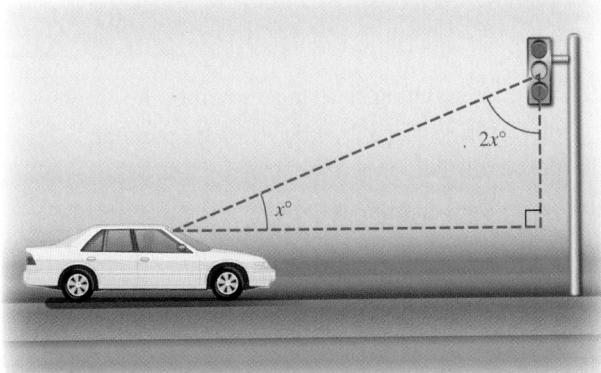

$2x°$

$x°$

12. **LIVESTOCK AUCTION** A farmer is going to sell one of her prize hogs at an auction and would like to make $6,000 after paying a 4% commission to the auctioneer. For what selling price will the farmer make this amount of money? [Section 2.5]
$6,250

13. **STOCK MARKET** An investment club invested part of $45,000 in a high-yield mutual fund that earned 12% annual simple interest. The remainder of the money was invested in Treasury bonds that earned 6.5% simple annual interest. The two investments earned $4,300 in one year. How much was invested in each account? [Section 2.6]
mutual fund: $25,000, bonds: $20,000

14. Solve $-4x + 6 > 17$ and graph the solution set. Then describe the graph using interval notation. [Section 2.7] $\left(-\infty, -\dfrac{11}{4}\right)$

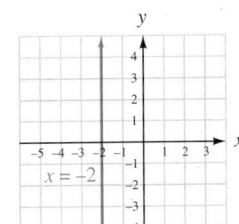

$-11/4$

Graph each equation.

15. $y = 3x$ [Section 3.2]

16. $x = -2$ [Section 3.3]

17. Find the slope of the line passing through $(6, -2)$ and $(-3, 2)$. [Section 3.4] $-\dfrac{4}{9}$

18. Find the slope and y-intercept of the line. Then write the equation of the line. [Section 3.5]

$m = 3, (0, -2); y = 3x - 2$

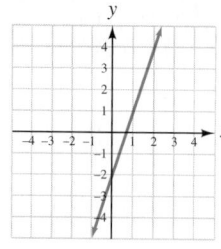

19. Without graphing, determine whether the graphs of $y = \frac{3}{2}x - 1$ and $2x + 3y = 10$ are parallel, perpendicular, or neither. [Section 3.5] perpendicular

20. Write the equation of the line that passes through $(-2, 10)$ with slope -4. Write the result in slope–intercept form. [Section 3.6] $y = -4x + 2$

21. Is $(-2, 1)$ a solution of $2x - 3y \geq -6$? [Section 3.7] no

22. If $f(x) = 2x^2 + 3x - 9$, find $f(-5)$. [Section 3.8] 26

23. Is $\left(\frac{2}{3}, -1\right)$ a solution of the system $\begin{cases} y = -3x + 1 \\ 3x + 3y = -2 \end{cases}$?

[Section 4.1] no

24. Solve the system by graphing:
$$\begin{cases} 3x + 2y = 14 \\ y = \frac{1}{4}x \end{cases}$$

[Section 4.1] $(4, 1)$

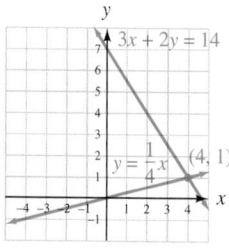

25. Solve the system $\begin{cases} 2b - 3a = 18 \\ a + 3b = 5 \end{cases}$ by substitution.

[Section 4.2] $(-4, 3)$

26. Solve the system $\begin{cases} 8s + 10t = 24 \\ 11s - 3t = -34 \end{cases}$ by addition (elimination). [Section 4.3] $(-2, 4)$

27. VACATIONS One-day passes to Universal Studios Hollywood cost a family of 5 (2 adults and 3 children) $275. A family of 6 (3 adults and 3 children) paid $336 for their one-day passes. Find the cost of an adult one-day pass and a child's one-day pass to Universal Studios. [Section 4.4] adult: $61, child: $51

28. Graph: $\begin{cases} y \leq 2x - 1 \\ x + 3y > 6 \end{cases}$

[Section 4.5]

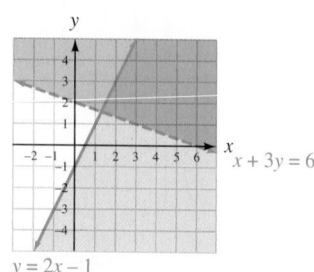

Simplify. Do not use negative exponents in the answer.

29. $(-3x^2y^4)^2$ [Section 5.1] $9x^4y^8$

30. $(v^5)^2(v^3)^4$ [Section 5.1] v^{22}

31. $ab^3c^4 \cdot ab^4c^2$ [Section 5.1] $a^2b^7c^6$

32. $\left(\frac{4t^3t^4t^5}{3t^2t^6}\right)^3$ [Section 5.1] $\frac{64t^{12}}{27}$

33. $(2y)^{-4}$ [Section 5.2] $\frac{1}{16y^4}$

34. $\frac{a^4b^0}{a^{-3}}$ [Section 5.2] a^7

35. -5^{-2} [Section 5.2] $-\frac{1}{25}$

36. $\left(\frac{a}{x}\right)^{-10}$ [Section 5.2] $\frac{x^{10}}{a^{10}}$

Write each number in scientific notation.

37. 615,000 [Section 5.3] 6.15×10^5

38. 0.0000013 [Section 5.3] 1.3×10^{-6}

39. Graph: $y = x^2$ [Section 5.4]

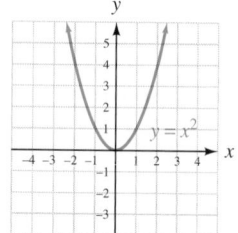

40. MUSICAL INSTRUMENTS The amount of deflection of the horizontal beam (in inches) is given by the polynomial $0.01875x^4 - 0.15x^3 + 1.2x$, where x is the distance (in feet) that the gong is hung from one end of the beam. Find the deflection if the gong is hung in the middle of the support. [Section 5.4] 1.5 in.

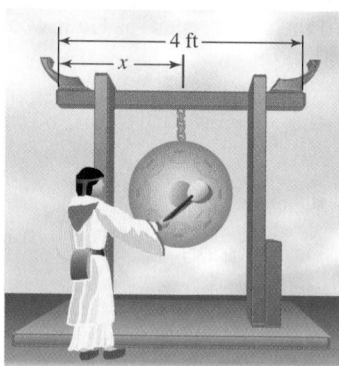

Perform the operations.

41. $(4c^2 + 3c - 2) + (3c^2 + 4c + 2)$ [Section 5.5] $7c^2 + 7c$

42. Subtract: $\quad 17x^4 - 3x^2 - 65x - 12$
$\quad\quad\quad -(23x^4 + 14x^2 + 3x - 23)$
$\quad\quad\quad \overline{-6x^4 - 17x^2 - 68x + 11}$ [Section 5.5]

43. $(2t + 3s)(3t - s)$ [Section 5.6] $6t^2 + 7st - 3s^2$

44. $3x(2x + 3)^2$ [Section 5.7] $12x^3 + 36x^2 + 27x$

45. $\frac{2x - 32}{16x}$ [Section 5.8] $\frac{1}{8} - \frac{2}{x}$

46. $5x + 3\overline{)11x + 10x^2 + 3}$ [Section 5.8] $2x + 1$

Factoring and Quadratic Equations

© 2009/Jupiterimages

from Campus to Careers

Elementary School Teacher

It has been said that a teacher takes a hand, opens a mind, and touches a heart. That is certainly true for the thousands of dedicated elementary school teachers across the country. Elementary school teachers use their training in mathematics in many ways. Besides teaching math on a daily basis, they calculate student grades, analyze test results, and order instructional materials and supplies. They use measurement and geometry for designing bulletin board displays and they construct detailed schedules so that the classroom time is used wisely.

In **Problem 28** of **Study Set 6.8,** you will determine the maximum dimensions of a bulletin board so that it meets the fire code requirements of an elementary school classroom.

JOB TITLE: Elementary School Teacher

EDUCATION: A bachelor's degree and completion of an approved teacher training program

JOB OUTLOOK: Varies from good to excellent, in some locations

ANNUAL EARNINGS: U.S. median $47,897*
*Can vary greatly by region and experience.

FOR MORE INFORMATION:
www.bls.gov/oco/ocos069.htm

Objectives

1. Find the greatest common factor of a list of terms.
2. Factor out the greatest common factor.
3. Factor by grouping.

SECTION **6.1**

The Greatest Common Factor; Factoring by Grouping

Recall that in Chapter 5 we used the distributive property to multiply a monomial and a binomial. For example,

$$4y(3y + 5) = 4y \cdot 3y + 4y \cdot 5$$
$$= 12y^2 + 20y$$

In this section, we will reverse the operation of multiplication. Given a polynomial such as $12y^2 + 20y$, we will ask, "What factors were multiplied to obtain $12y^2 + 20y$?" The process of finding the factors of a known product is called **factoring.**

Multiplication: Given the factors, we find the polynomial. $\rightarrow$

$$4y(3y + 5) = 12y^2 + 20y$$

$\leftarrow$ Factoring: Given a polynomial, we find the factors.

To **factor a polynomial** means to express it as a product of two (or more) polynomials. The first step when factoring a polynomial is to determine whether its terms have any common factors.

1 Find the greatest common factor of a list of terms.

To determine whether two or more integers have common factors, it is helpful to write them as a product of prime numbers. For example, the prime factorizations of 90 and 42 are given below.

$$90 = 2 \cdot 3 \cdot 3 \cdot 5$$
$$42 = 2 \cdot 3 \cdot 7$$

The color highlighting indicates that 90 and 42 have one prime factor of 2 and one prime factor of 3 in common. We can conclude that $2 \cdot 3 = 6$ is the largest natural number that divides 90 and 42 exactly, and we say that 6 is their *greatest common factor (GCF)*.

$$\frac{90}{6} = 15 \quad \text{and} \quad \frac{42}{6} = 7$$

The Greatest Common Factor (GCF)

The **greatest common factor (GCF)** of a list of integers is the largest common factor of those integers.

Self Check 1

Find the GCF of:
a. 45, 60, and 75   15
b. 16, 28, and 35   1

Now Try Problems 23 and 25

Teaching Example 1 Find the GCF of:
a. 36, 54, 90   **b.** 12, 15, 28
Answers:
a. 18   **b.** 1

EXAMPLE 1

Find the GCF of each list of numbers:

a. 24, 60, and 96   **b.** 6, 35, and 50

Strategy We will prime factor each number in the list. Then we will identify the common prime factors and find their product.

WHY The product of the common prime factors is the GCF of the numbers in the list.

Solution

a. The prime factors of the three numbers are shown:

$24 = 2 \cdot 2 \cdot 2 \cdot 3$ *This can be written as $2^3 \cdot 3$.*

$60 = 2 \cdot 2 \cdot 3 \cdot 5$ *This can be written as $2^2 \cdot 3 \cdot 5$.*

$96 = 2 \cdot 2 \cdot 2 \cdot 2 \cdot 2 \cdot 3$ *This can be written as $2^5 \cdot 3$.*

The highlighting shows that 24, 60, and 96 each have two factors of 2 and one factor of 3; their greatest common factor is $2 \cdot 2 \cdot 3 = 12$.

b. The prime factorization of each number is shown:

$6 = 2 \cdot 3$

$35 = 5 \cdot 7$

$50 = 2 \cdot 5 \cdot 5$

Since there are no prime factors common to 6, 35, and 50, their GCF is 1. ∎

> **Success Tip**   The exponent on any factor in a GCF is the *smallest* exponent that appears on that factor in all of the numbers under consideration.

Strategy for Finding the GCF

1. Write each coefficient as a product of prime factors.

2. Identify the numerical and variable factors common to each term.

3. Multiply the common numerical and variable factors identified in Step 2 to obtain the GCF. If there are no common factors, the GCF is 1.

EXAMPLE 2   Find the GCF of each list of terms:

a. $12x^2$ and $20x$ **b.** $9a^5b^2$, $15a^4b^2$, and $90a^3b^3$

Strategy We will prime factor each coefficient of each term in the list. Then we will identify the numerical and variable factors common to each term and find their product.

WHY The product of the common factors is the GCF of the terms in the list.

Solution

a. *Step 1* We write each coefficient, 12 and 20, as a product of prime factors. Recall that an exponent, as in x^2, indicates repeated multiplication.

$12x^2 = 2 \cdot 2 \cdot 3 \cdot x \cdot x$ *This can be written as $2^2 \cdot 3 \cdot x^2$.*

$20x = 2 \cdot 2 \cdot 5 \cdot x$ *This can be written as $2^2 \cdot 5 \cdot x$.*

Step 2 There are two common factors of 2 and one common factor of x.

Step 3 We multiply the common factors, 2, 2, and x, to obtain the GCF.

$GCF = 2 \cdot 2 \cdot x = 2^2 \cdot x = 4x$

b. *Step 1* We write the coefficients, 9, 15, and 90, as products of primes. The exponents on the variables represent repeated multiplication.

$9a^5b^2 = 3 \cdot 3 \cdot a \cdot a \cdot a \cdot a \cdot a \cdot b \cdot b$ *This can be written as $3^2 \cdot a^5 \cdot b^2$.*

$15a^4b^2 = 3 \cdot 5 \cdot a \cdot a \cdot a \cdot a \cdot b \cdot b$ *This can be written as $3 \cdot 5 \cdot a^4 \cdot b^2$.*

$90a^3b^3 = 2 \cdot 3 \cdot 3 \cdot 5 \cdot a \cdot a \cdot a \cdot b \cdot b \cdot b$ *This can be written as $2 \cdot 3^2 \cdot 5 \cdot a^3 \cdot b^3$.*

Self Check 2

Find the GCF of each list of terms:

a. $33c$ and $22c^4$ $11c$

b. $42s^3t^2$, $63s^2t^4$, and $21s^3t^3$ $21s^2t^2$

Now Try **Problems 29 and 31**

Teaching Example 2 Find the GCF of each list of terms:
a. $18y^2$ and $45y$
b. $12x^4y^6$, $18x^5y^4$, and $30x^3y^5$
Answers:
a. $9y$ **b.** $6x^3y^4$

Step 2 The highlighting shows one common factor of 3, three common factors of a, and two common factors of b.

Step 3 GCF $= 3 \cdot a \cdot a \cdot a \cdot b \cdot b = 3a^3b^2$

2 Factor out the greatest common factor.

To factor $12y^2 + 20y$, we find the GCF of $12y^2$ and $20y$ (which is $4y$) and use the distributive property in reverse: $ab + ac = a(b + c)$

$$12y^2 + 20y = 4y \cdot 3y + 4y \cdot 5 \qquad \text{Write each term of the polynomial as the product of the GCF, 4y, and one other factor.}$$

$$= 4y(3y + 5) \qquad \text{4y is a common factor of both terms.}$$

This process is called **factoring out the greatest common factor.**

Self Check 3

Factor: $18x - 24$ $6(3x - 4)$

Now Try Problem 36

Teaching Example 3 Factor: $6f + 36$
Answer:
$6(f + 6)$

EXAMPLE 3 Factor: $25 - 5m$

Strategy We will prime factor each coefficient of each term in the polynomial. Then we will write each term of the polynomial as a product of the GCF and one other factor.

WHY We can then use the distributive property to factor out the GCF.

Solution
The prime factorizations are shown:

$$\left. \begin{array}{l} 25 = \mathbf{5} \cdot 5 \\ 5m = \mathbf{5} \cdot m \end{array} \right\} \quad \text{GCF} = 5$$

We can use the distributive property in reverse to factor out the GCF.

$$25 - 5m = \mathbf{5} \cdot 5 - \mathbf{5} \cdot m \qquad \text{Factor each monomial using 5 and one other factor.}$$

$$= 5(5 - m) \qquad \text{Factor out the common factor of 5.}$$

To check, we multiply: $5(5 - m) = 5 \cdot 5 - 5 \cdot m = 25 - 5m$.

Self Check 4

Factor: $32x^2y^4 + 12x^3y^3$

Now Try Problem 45
Self Check 4 Answer
$4x^2y^3(8y + 3x)$

Teaching Example 4 Factor:
$48s^2t^2 - 84s^3t$
Answer:
$12s^2t(4t - 7s)$

EXAMPLE 4 Factor: $35a^3b^2 + 14a^2b^3$

Strategy We will prime factor each coefficient of each term in the polynomial. Then we will write each term of the polynomial as a product of the GCF and one other factor.

WHY We can then use the distributive property to factor out the GCF.

Solution
The prime factorizations of $35a^3b^2$ and $14a^2b^3$ are shown:

$$\left. \begin{array}{l} 35a^3b^2 = 5 \cdot 7 \cdot a \cdot a \cdot a \cdot b \cdot b \\ 14a^2b^3 = 2 \cdot 7 \cdot a \cdot a \cdot b \cdot b \cdot b \end{array} \right\} \quad \text{GCF} = 7 \cdot a \cdot a \cdot b \cdot b = 7a^2b^2$$

We factor out the GCF, $7a^2b^2$.

$$35a^3b^2 + 14a^2b^3 = 7a^2b^2 \cdot 5a + 7a^2b^2 \cdot 2b$$

$$= 7a^2b^2(5a + 2b) \qquad \text{Factor out the GCF } 7a^2b^2.$$

To check, we multiply: $7a^2b^2(5a + 2b) = 35a^3b^2 + 14a^2b^3$.

> **Caution!** If the GCF of the terms of a polynomial is the same as one of the terms, leave a 1 in place of that term when factoring out the GCF.

EXAMPLE 5 Factor: $4x^3y^2z - 2x^2yz + xz$

Strategy We will prime factor each coefficient of each term in the polynomial. Then we will write each term of the polynomial as a product of the GCF and one other factor.

WHY We can then use the distributive property to factor out the GCF.

Solution
The expression has three terms. We factor out the GCF, which is xz.

$$4x^3y^2z - 2x^2yz + xz = xz \cdot 4x^2y^2 - xz \cdot 2xy + xz \cdot 1$$

$$= xz(4x^2y^2 - 2xy + 1) \quad \text{Factor out the GCF } xz.$$

The last term of $4x^3y^2z - 2x^2yz + xz$ has an implied coefficient of 1. When xz is factored out, we must write this coefficient of 1, as shown in blue. To check, we multiply: $xz(4x^2y^2 - 2xy + 1) = 4x^3y^2z - 2x^2yz + xz$.

Self Check 5

Factor: $2ab^2c + 4a^2bc - ab$

Now Try **Problem 51**
Self Check 5 Answer
$ab(2bc + 4ac - 1)$

Teaching Example 5 Factor:
$14x^2y^2 - 7xy + 21x^3y$
Answer:
$7xy(2xy - 1) + 3x^2$

EXAMPLE 6 Factor: $x(x + 4) + 3(x + 4)$

Strategy We will identify the terms of the expression and find their GCF.

WHY We can then use the distributive property in reverse to factor out the GCF.

Solution
The given expression has two terms:

$$\underbrace{x(x + 4)}_{\text{The first term}} + \underbrace{3(x + 4)}_{\text{The second term}}$$

The GCF of the terms is $x + 4$, which can be factored out.

$$x(x + 4) + 3(x + 4) = x(x + 4) + 3(x + 4)$$

$$= (x + 4)(x + 3) \quad \text{Factor out the GCF } (x + 4).$$

It is often useful to factor out a common factor having a negative coefficient.

Self Check 6

Factor: $2y(y - 1) - 7(y - 1)$

Now Try **Problem 56**
Self Check 6 Answer
$(y - 1)(2y - 7)$

Teaching Example 6 Factor:
$6a(a + 7) - 5(a + 7)$
Answer:
$(a + 7)(6a - 5)$

EXAMPLE 7 Factor -1 out of $-a^3 + 2a^2 - 4$.

Strategy We will write each term of the polynomial as the product of -1 and one other factor.

WHY We can then use the distributive property in reverse to factor out the -1.

Solution
$$-a^3 + 2a^2 - 4 = (-1)a^3 + (-1)(-2a^2) + (-1)4$$

$$= -1(a^3 - 2a^2 + 4) \quad \text{Factor out } -1.$$

$$= -(a^3 - 2a^2 + 4) \quad \text{The coefficient of 1 need not be written.}$$

We check by multiplying: $-(a^3 - 2a^2 + 4) = -a^3 + 2a^2 - 4$.

Self Check 7

Factor -1 out of $-b^4 - 3b^2 + 2$.

Now Try **Problem 61**
Self Check 7 Answer
$-(b^4 + 3b^2 - 2)$

Teaching Example 7 Factor -1 out of $-x^4 - 3x^2 + 5$.
Answer:
$-(x^4 + 3x^2 - 5)$

Self Check 8

Factor out the opposite of the
GCF in $-27xy^2 - 18x^2y + 36x^2y^2$.

Now Try **Problem 66**
Self Check 8 Answer
$-9xy(3y + 2x - 4xy)$

Teaching Example 8 Factor out the
opposite of the GCF in
$-24a^3b^5 + 6a^2b - 12ab$.
Answer:
$-6ab(4a^2b^4 - a + 2)$

EXAMPLE 8   Factor out the opposite of the GCF in $-18a^2b + 6ab^2 - 12a^2b^2$.

Strategy First we will determine the GCF of the terms of the polynomial. Then
we will write each term of the polynomial as the product of the opposite of the
GCF and one other factor.

WHY We can then use the distributive property to factor out the opposite of
the GCF.

Solution

The GCF is $6ab$, the opposite of $6ab$ is $-6ab$. We write each term of the
polynomial as the product of $-6ab$ and another factor. Then we factor out $-6ab$.

$$-18a^2b + 6ab^2 - 12a^2b^2 = (-6ab)3a - (-6ab)b + (-6ab)2ab$$

$$= -6ab(3a - b + 2ab) \quad \text{Factor out } -6ab.$$

We check by multiplying: $-6ab(3a - b + 2ab) = -18a^2b + 6ab^2 - 12a^2b^2.$

> ***Success Tip***   When the first coefficient of a polynomial is negative, factor out
> the opposite of the GCF.

3 Factoring by grouping.

When a polynomial has 4 or more terms, we see if we can factor it by arranging the
terms in groups that have common factors. This method is called **factoring by grouping.**

> ### Factoring by Grouping
>
> 1. Group the terms of the polynomial so that the first two terms have a
>   common factor and the last two terms have a common factor.
> 2. Factor out the common factor from each group.
> 3. Factor out the resulting common binomial factor. If there is no common
>   binomial factor, regroup the terms of the polynomial and repeat steps 2
>   and 3.

Self Check 9

Factor: $7x - 7y + xy - y^2$

Now Try **Problem 70**
Self Check 9 Answer
$(x - y)(7 + y)$

Teaching Example 9 Factor:
$9x + 9y + xy + y^2$
Answer:
$(x + y)(9 + y)$

EXAMPLE 9   Factor: $2c - 2d + cd - d^2$

Strategy We note that there is no common factor of all four terms. Then we will
factor out a common factor from the first two terms and a common factor from
the last two terms.

WHY Often this will produce a common binomial factor that can be factored out.

Solution
Since 2 is a common factor of the first two terms and d is a common factor of the
last two terms, we have

$$2c - 2d + cd - d^2 = 2(c - d) + d(c - d) \quad \text{Factor out 2 from } 2c - 2d \text{ and } d$$
$$\text{from } cd - d^2.$$

$$= (c - d)(2 + d) \quad \text{Factor out } c - d.$$

We check by multiplying:

$$(c - d)(2 + d) = 2c + cd - 2d - d^2$$
$$= 2c - 2d + cd - d^2 \quad \text{Rearrange the terms.}$$

EXAMPLE 10   Factor: $x^2y - ax - xy + a$

Strategy We note that there is no common factor of all four terms. Then we will factor out a common factor from the first two terms and a common factor from the last two terms.

WHY Often this will produce a common binomial factor that can be factored out.

Solution

Since x is a common factor of the first two terms, we can factor it out and proceed as follows.

$$x^2y - ax - xy + a = x(xy - a) - xy + a \qquad \text{Factor out } x \text{ from } x^2y - ax.$$

If we factor -1 from $-xy + a$, a common binomial factor $(xy - a)$ appears, which we can factor out.

$$x^2y - ax - xy + a = x(xy - a) - 1(xy - a)$$
$$= (xy - a)(x - 1) \qquad \text{Factor out } (xy - a).$$

Check by multiplication.

> *Caution!*   When factoring the expressions in the previous two examples, don't think that $2(c - d) + d(c - d)$ or $x(xy - a) - 1(xy - a)$ are in factored form. For an expression to be in factored form, the result must be a product.

The next example illustrates that when factoring a polynomial, we should always look for a common factor first.

EXAMPLE 11   Factor: $10k + 10m - 2km - 2m^2$

Strategy Since all four terms have a common factor of 2, we factor it out first. Then we will factor the resulting polynomial by grouping.

WHY Factoring out the GCF first makes the factoring process easier.

Solution
$$10k + 10m - 2km - 2m^2 = 2(5k + 5m - km - m^2) \qquad \text{Factor out the GCF 2.}$$
$$= 2[5(k + m) - m(k + m)] \qquad \begin{array}{l}\text{Factor out 5 from}\\ 5k + 5m.\text{ Factor out}\\ -m\text{ from } -km - m^2.\end{array}$$
$$= 2[(k + m)(5 - m)] \qquad \text{Factor out } (k + m).$$
$$= 2(k + m)(5 - m)$$

Use multiplication to check the result.

Self Check 10

Factor: $7bt + 3ct - 7b - 3c$

Now Try **Problem 76**
Self Check 10 Answer
$(7b + 3c)(t - 1)$

Teaching Example 10 Factor:
$a^2b - ax - ab + x$
Answer:
$(ab - x)(a - 1)$

Self Check 11

Factor: $-4t - 4s - 4tz - 4sz$

Now Try **Problem 78**
Self Check 11 Answer
$-4(t + s)(1 + z)$

Teaching Example 11 Factor:
$-6x - 6y - 12ax - 12ay$
Answer:
$-6(x + y)(1 + 2a)$

ANSWERS TO SELF CHECKS

1. a. 15 **b.** 1 **2. a.** $11c$ **b.** $21s^2t^2$ **3.** $6(3x - 4)$ **4.** $4x^2y^3(8y + 3x)$
5. $ab(2bc + 4ac - 1)$ **6.** $(y - 1)(2y - 7)$ **7.** $-(b^4 + 3b^2 - 2)$
8. $-9xy(3y + 2x - 4xy)$ **9.** $(x - y)(7 + y)$ **10.** $(7b + 3c)(t - 1)$
11. $-4(t + s)(1 + z)$

SECTION 6.1   STUDY SET

VOCABULARY

Fill in the blanks.

1. The process of finding the individual factors of a known product is called <u>factoring</u>.

2. To <u>factor</u> a polynomial means to express the polynomial as a product of two (or more) polynomials.

3. The <u>prime</u> factorization of 12 is $2 \cdot 2 \cdot 3$.

4. The GCF of several integers is the <u>largest</u> common factor of those integers.

5. When we write $15x^2 - 25x$ as $5x(3x - 5)$, we say that we have <u>factored</u> <u>out</u> the greatest common factor.

6. When a polynomial has four or more terms, we can attempt to factor it by rearranging its terms in groups that have common factors. This process is called factoring by <u>grouping</u>.

CONCEPTS

Explain what is wrong with each solution.

7. Factor: $6a + 9b + 3$

$$6a + 9b + 3 = 3(2a + 3b + 0)$$
$$= 3(2a + 3b)$$

The 0 in the first line should be 1.

8. Factor out the GCF: $30a^3 - 12a^2$

$$30a^3 - 12a^2 = 6a(5a^2 - 2a)$$ The GCF is $6a^2$, not $6a$.

9. Factor: $ab + b + a + 1$.

$$ab + b + a + 1 = b(a + 1) + (a + 1)$$
$$= (a + 1)b$$

The answer should be $(a + 1)(b + 1)$.

10. What algebraic concept is illustrated in the work shown below?   factoring out the GCF

$$4 \cdot 5x + 4 \cdot 3 = 4(5x + 3)$$

11. The prime factorizations of three monomials are shown here. Find their GCF. $3x$

$$3 \cdot 3 \cdot 5 \cdot x \cdot x$$
$$2 \cdot 3 \cdot 5 \cdot x \cdot y$$
$$2 \cdot 2 \cdot 3 \cdot x \cdot y \cdot y$$

Consider the polynomial: $2k - 8 + hk - 4h$

12. Is there a common factor of all the terms?   no

13. What is the common factor of the first two terms?   2

14. What is the common factor of the last two terms? h

Complete each factorization.

15. $4a + 12 = \boxed{4}(a + 3)$

16. $r^4 + r^2 = r^2\left(\boxed{r^2} + 1\right)$

17. $4y^2 + 8y - 2xy = 2y\left(2y + \boxed{4} - \boxed{x}\right)$

18. $3x^2 - 6xy + 9xy^2 = \boxed{3x}\left(\boxed{x} - 2y + 3y^2\right)$

NOTATION

Complete each factorization.

19. Factor: $b^3 - 6b^2 + 2b - 12$

$$b^3 - 6b^2 + 2b - 12 = \boxed{b^2}(b - 6) + 2\boxed{(b-6)}$$
$$= (b - 6)\boxed{(b^2+2)}$$

▶ 20. Factor: $12b^3 - 6b^2 + 2b - 2$

$$12b^3 - 6b^2 + 2b - 2 = \boxed{2}(6b^3 - 3b^2 + b - 1)$$

21. In the expression $4x^2y + xy$, what is the coefficient of the last term?   1

22. Is the following statement true?

$$-(x^2 - 3x + 1) = -1(x^2 - 3x + 1)$$ yes

GUIDED PRACTICE

Find the GCF of each list of numbers. **See Example 1.**

23. $6, 8, 10$ 2

24. $10, 15, 25$ 5

25. $30, 45, 60$ 15

▶ 26. $78, 104, 156$ 26

Find the GCF of each list of terms. **See Example 2.**

27. $25y^3, 35y$ $5y$

28. $36a^2, 48a$ $12a$

29. $20p^2q, 40pq^2$ $20pq$

▶ 30. $36m^2n^2, 54mn$ $18mn$

31. $6t^3, 12t^2, 18t$ $6t$

32. $28r^3, 14r^2, 35r^4$ $7r^2$

33. $30a^3b^3, 45a^2b^2, 60ab$ $15ab$

34. $28u^4v^3, 35u^3v^2, 49u^2v$ $7u^2v$

Factor each expression. **See Example 3.**

35. $3x + 6$ $3(x + 2)$

▶ 36. $2y - 10$ $2(y - 5)$

37. $36 - 6x$ $6(6 - x)$

38. $48 + 12y$ $12(4 + y)$

Factor each expression. **See Example 4.**

39. $t^3 + 2t^2$ $t^2(t + 2)$

▶ 40. $b^3 - 3b^2$ $b^2(b - 3)$

41. $a^3 - a^2$ $a^2(a - 1)$

42. $r^3 + r^2$ $r^2(r + 1)$

43. $24x^2y^3 + 8xy^2$ $8xy^2(3xy + 1)$

44. $3x^2y^3 - 9x^4y^3$ $3x^2y^3(1 - 3x^2)$

45. $12uv - 18uv^2$ $6uv(2 - 3v)$

46. $14xy - 16x^2y^2$ $2xy(7 - 8xy)$

Factor each expression. **See Example 5.**

47. $12x^2 - 6 - 24a$
$6(2x^2 - 1 - 4a)$

48. $27a^2 - 9 + 45b$
$9(3a^2 - 1 + 5b)$

49. $3 + 3y - 6z$
$3(1 + y - 2z)$

▶ **50.** $2 - 4y + 8z$
$2(1 - 2y + 4z)$

51. $ab + ac - a$
$a(b + c - 1)$

52. $rs - rt + r$
$r(s - t + 1)$

53. $12r^2 - 3r + 9r^2s^2$
$3r(4r - 1 + 3rs^2)$

54. $6a - 12a^3b + 36ab$
$6a(1 - 2a^2b + 6b)$

Factor each expression. **See Example 6.**

55. $3(x + 2) - x(x + 2)$
$(x + 2)(3 - x)$

▶ **56.** $t(5 - s) + 4(5 - s)$
$(5 - s)(t + 4)$

57. $h^2(14 + r) + 2(14 + r)$
$(14 + r)(h^2 + 2)$

58. $k^2(14 + v) - 7(14 + v)$
$(14 + v)(k^2 - 7)$

Factor **−1** *out of each expression.* **See Example 7.**

59. $-a - b$
$-(a + b)$

60. $-x - 2y$
$-(x + 2y)$

61. $-3m - 4n + 1$
$-(3m + 4n - 1)$

▶ **62.** $-3r + 2s - 3$
$-(3r - 2s + 3)$

In each expression, factor out the negative of the GCF.
See Example 8.

63. $-3x^2 - 6x$ $-3x(x + 2)$

▶ **64.** $-4a^2 + 6a$ $-2a(2a - 3)$

65. $-4a^2b^3 + 12a^3b^2 + 4a^2b^2$ $-4a^2b^2(b - 3a - 1)$

66. $-25x^4y^3 + 10x^3y^3 + 30x^2y^3$ $-5x^2y^3(5x^2 - 2x - 6)$

Factor each expression. **See Example 9.**

67. $2x + 2y + ax + ay$
$(x + y)(2 + a)$

68. $bx + bz + 5x + 5z$
$(x + z)(b + 5)$

▶ **69.** $7r + 7s - kr - ks$
$(r + s)(7 - k)$

70. $9p - 9q + mp - mq$
$(p - q)(9 + m)$

71. $xr + xs + yr + ys$
$(r + s)(x + y)$

72. $pm - pn + qm - qn$
$(m - n)(p + q)$

73. $2ax + 2bx + 3a + 3b$
$(a + b)(2x + 3)$

74. $3xy + 3xz - 5y - 5z$
$(y + z)(3x - 5)$

Factor each expression completely. **See Examples 10–11.**

75. $ax^3 + bx^3 + 2ax^2y + 2bx^2y$ $x^2(a + b)(x + 2y)$

▶ **76.** $x^3y^2 - 2x^2y^2 + 3xy^2 - 6y^2$ $y^2(x - 2)(x^2 + 3)$

77. $4a^2b + 12a^2 - 8ab - 24a$ $4a(b + 3)(a - 2)$

▶ **78.** $-4abc - 4ac^2 + 2bc + 2c^2$ $-2c(b + c)(2a - 1)$

TRY IT YOURSELF

Completely factor each expression (including **−1,** *if necessary).*

79. $\pi R^2 - \pi ab$ $\pi(R^2 - ab)$

80. $\frac{1}{3}\pi R^2 h - \frac{1}{3}\pi rh$ $\frac{1}{3}\pi h(R^2 - r)$

81. $-2x + 5y$ $-(2x - 5y)$

82. $-3x + 8z$ $-(3x - 8z)$

83. $-3ab - 5ac + 9bc$
$-(3ab + 5ac - 9bc)$

84. $-6yz + 12xz - 5xy$
$-(6yz - 12xz + 5xy)$

85. $-4a^2b^2c^2 + 14a^2b^2c - 10ab^2c^2$ $-2ab^2c(2ac - 7a + 5c)$

▶ **86.** $-10x^4y^3z^2 + 8x^3y^2z - 20x^2y$ $-2x^2y(5x^2y^2z^2 - 4xyz + 10)$

87. $2ab + 2ac + 3b + 3c$ $(b + c)(2a + 3)$

88. $3ac + a + 3bc + b$ $(3c + 1)(a + b)$

89. $6x^2 - 2x - 15x + 5$ $(3x - 1)(2x - 5)$

90. $6x^2 + 2x + 9x + 3$ $(3x + 1)(2x + 3)$

91. $9mp + 3mq - 3np - nq$ $(3p + q)(3m - n)$

92. $ax + bx - a - b$ $(a + b)(x - 1)$

93. $2xy + y^2 - 2x - y$ $(2x + y)(y - 1)$

94. $2xy - 3y^2 + 2x - 3y$ $(2x - 3y)(y + 1)$

95. $8z^5 + 12z^2 - 10z^3 - 15$ $(2z^3 + 3)(4z^2 - 5)$

96. $2a^4 + 2a^3 - 4a - 4$ $(a + 1)(2a^3 - 4)$

97. $x^3y - x^2y - xy^2 + y^2$ $y(x^2 - y)(x - 1)$

▶ **98.** $2x^3z - 4x^2z + 32xz - 64z$ $2z(x - 2)(x^2 + 16)$

APPLICATIONS

▶ **99.** PICTURE FRAMING The dimensions of a family portrait and the frame in which it is mounted are shown. Write an algebraic expression that describes

   a. the area of the picture frame. $12x^3$ in.^{2}

   b. the area of the portrait. $20x^2$ in.^{2}

   c. the area of the mat used in the framing. Express the result in factored form. $4x^2(3x - 5)$ in.^{2}

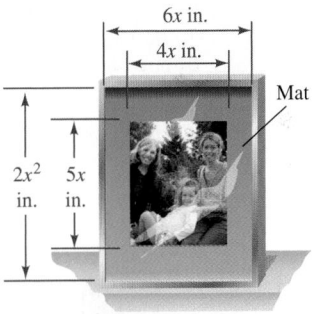

100. REARVIEW MIRRORS The dimensions of the three rearview mirrors on an automobile are given in the illustration below. Write an algebraic expression that gives

   a. the area of the rearview mirror mounted on the windshield. $6x^3$ cm^2

   b. the total area of the two side mirrors. $24x^2$ cm^2

   c. the total area of all three mirrors. Express the result in factored form. $6x^2(x + 4)$ cm^2

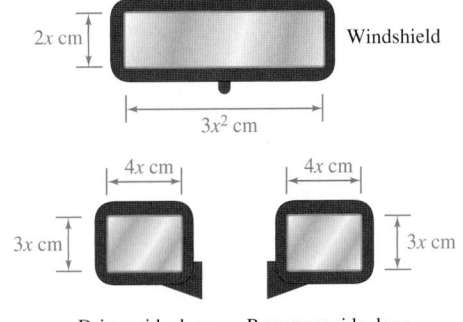

▶ **101.** COOKING See the following illustration.

   a. What is the length of a side of the square griddle, in terms of r? What is the area of the cooking surface of the griddle, in terms of r? $4r$ in., $16r^2$ in.^{2}

   b. How many square inches of the cooking surface do the pancakes cover, in terms of r? $4\pi r^2$ in.^{2}

   c. Find the amount of cooking surface that is not covered by the pancakes. Express the result in factored form. $16r^2 - 4\pi r^2 = 4r^2(4 - \pi)$ in.^{2}

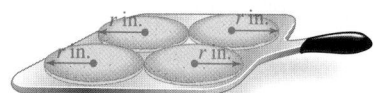

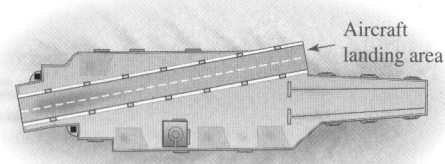

▶ **102.** AIRCRAFT CARRIERS The rectangular-shaped landing area of $(x^3 + 4x^2 + 5x + 20)$ ft^2 is shaded. The dimensions of the landing area can be found by factoring. What are the length and width of the landing area? $(x^2 + 5)$ ft, $(x + 4)$ ft.

Aircraft landing area

WRITING

103. To add $5x$ and $7x$, we combine like terms: $5x + 7x = 12x$. Explain how this is related to factoring out a common factor.

104. One student commented, "Factoring undoes the distributive property." What do you think she meant? Give an example.

105. If asked to write $ax + ay - bx - by$ in factored form, explain why $a(x + y) - b(x + y)$ is not an acceptable answer.

▶ **106.** When asked to factor $rx - sy + ry - sx$, a student wrote the expression as $rx + ry - sx - sy$. Then she factored it by grouping. Can the terms be rearranged in this manner? Explain your answer.

REVIEW

107. Simplify: $\left(\dfrac{y^3 y}{2yy^2}\right)^3$ $\dfrac{y^3}{8}$

▶ **108.** Find the slope of the line passing through the points $(3, 5)$ and $(-2, -7)$. $\dfrac{12}{5}$

109. Does the point $(3, 5)$ lie on the graph of the line $4x - y = 7$? yes

110. Simplify: $-5(3a - 2)(2a + 3)$ $-30a^2 - 25a + 30$

Objectives

1 Factor trinomials of the form $x^2 + bx + c$

2 Factor trinomials of the form $x^2 + bx + c$ after factoring out the GCF.

3 Factor trinomials of the form $x^2 + bx + c$ using the grouping method.

SECTION 6.2

Factoring Trinomials of the Form $x^2 + bx + c$

In Chapter 5, we learned how to multiply binomials. For example, to multiply $x + 2$ and $x + 3$, we proceed as follows:

$$(x + 2)(x + 3) = x^2 + 3x + 2x + 6$$
$$= x^2 + 5x + 6$$

To *factor the trinomial* $x^2 + 5x + 6$, we will reverse the multiplication process and determine what factors were multiplied to obtain $x^2 + 5x + 6$. Since the product of two binomials is often a trinomial, many trinomials factor into the product of two binomials.

Multiplication: Given the binomial factors, we find the trinomial. →

$$(x + 2)(x + 3) = x^2 + 5x + 6$$

← Factoring: Given the trinomial, we find the binomial factors.

We will now consider how to factor trinomials of the form $ax^2 + bx + c$, where a (called the **leading coefficient**) is 1.

1 Factor trinomials of the form $x^2 + bx + c$.

To develop a method for factoring trinomials, we multiply $(x + 4)$ and $(x + 5)$.

$$(x + 4)(x + 5) = x \cdot x + x \cdot 5 + 4 \cdot x + 4 \cdot 5 \quad \text{Use the FOIL method.}$$
$$= x^2 + 5x + 4x + 20$$
$$= x^2 + 9x + 20$$

First term, Middle term, Last term

The result has three terms. We can see that

- the first term, x^2, is the product of x and x,
- the last term, 20, is the product of 4 and 5, and
- the coefficient of the middle term, 9, is the sum of 4 and 5.

We can use these facts to factor trinomials with lead coefficients of 1.

EXAMPLE 1 Factor: $x^2 + 5x + 6$

Strategy We will assume that $x^2 + 5x + 6$ is the product of two binomials and we will use a systematic method to find their terms.

WHY Since the terms of $x^2 + 5x + 6$ do not have a common factor (other than 1), the only option available is to try to factor it as the product of two binomials.

Solution
Since the first term of the trinomial is x^2, the first term of each binomial factor must be x. To fill in the blanks, we must find two integers whose product is $+6$ and whose sum is $+5$.

$$x^2 + 5x + 6 = (x \quad)(x \quad) \quad \text{Because } x \cdot x \text{ will give } x^2.$$

The positive factorizations of 6 and the sum of the factors are shown in the table.

Factors of 6	Sum of the factors of 6
1(6)	$1 + 6 = 7$
2(3)	$2 + 3 = 5$

The last row contains the integers 2 and 3, whose product is 6 and whose sum is 5. To complete the factorization, we enter 2 and 3 as the second terms of the binomial factors.

$$x^2 + 5x + 6 = (x + 2)(x + 3)$$

To check the result, we verify that $(x + 2)(x + 3)$ is $x^2 + 5x + 6$.

$$(x + 2)(x + 3) = x^2 + 3x + 2x + 6 \quad \text{Use the FOIL method.}$$
$$= x^2 + 5x + 6 \quad \text{This is the original trinomial.}$$

Success Tip When factoring trinomials, the binomial factors can be written in either order. In Example 1, an equivalent factorization is $x^2 + 5x + 6 = (x + 3)(x + 2)$.

Self Check 1
Factor: $y^2 + 7y + 6$
Now Try Problem 25
Self Check 1 Answer
$(y + 1)(y + 6)$

Teaching Example 1 Factor: $a^2 + 6a + 8$
Answer: $(a + 2)(a + 4)$

Self Check 2

Factor: $p^2 - 5p + 6$

Now Try Problem 29

Self Check 2 Answer
$(p - 3)(p - 2)$

Teaching Example 2 Factor:
$x^2 - 13x + 12$
Answer:
$(x - 12)(x - 1)$

EXAMPLE 2   Factor: $y^2 - 7y + 12$

Strategy We will assume that $y^2 - 7y + 12$ is the product of two binomials and we will use a systematic method to find their terms.

WHY Since the terms of $y^2 - 7y + 12$ do not have a common factor (other than 1), the only option available is to try to factor it as the product of two binomials.

Solution

Since the first term of the trinomial is y^2, the first term of each binomial factor must be y. To fill in the blanks, we must find two integers whose product is 12 and whose sum is -7.

$$y^2 - 7y + 12 = \left(y \quad\right)\left(y \quad\right) \qquad \text{Because } y \cdot y \text{ will give } y^2.$$

The two-integer factorizations of 12 and the sums of the factors are shown in the following table.

Factors of 12	Sum of the factors of 12
1(12)	$1 + 12 = 13$
2(6)	$2 + 6 = 8$
3(4)	$3 + 4 = 7$
$-1(-12)$	$-1 + (-12) = -13$
$-2(-6)$	$-2 + (-6) = -8$
$-3(-4)$	$-3 + (-4) = -7$

The last row contains the integers -3 and -4, whose product is 12 and whose sum is -7. To complete the factorization, we enter -3 and -4 as the second terms of the binomial factors.

$$y^2 - 7y + 12 = (y - 3)(y - 4)$$

To check the result, we verify that $(y - 3)(y - 4)$ is $y^2 - 7y + 12$.

$$(y - 3)(y - 4) = y^2 - 4y - 3y + 12 \qquad \text{Use the FOIL method.}$$
$$= y^2 - 7y + 12 \qquad \text{This is the original trinomial.}$$

Self Check 3

Factor: $p^2 + 3p - 18$

Now Try Problem 34

Self Check 3 Answer
$(p + 6)(p - 3)$

Teaching Example 3 Factor:
$x^2 + 5x - 14$
Answer:
$(x + 7)(x - 2)$

EXAMPLE 3   Factor: $a^2 + 2a - 15$

Strategy We will assume that $a^2 + 2a - 15$ is the product of two binomials and we will use a systematic method to find their terms.

WHY Since the terms of $a^2 + 2a - 15$ do not have a common factor (other than 1), the only option available is to try to factor it as the product of two binomials.

Solution

Since the first term of the trinomial is a^2, the first term of each binomial factor must be a. To fill in the blanks, we must find two integers whose product is -15 and whose sum is 2.

$$a^2 + 2a - 15 = \left(a \quad\right)\left(a \quad\right) \qquad \text{Because } a \cdot a \text{ will give } a^2.$$

The possible factorizations of -15 and the sum of the factors are shown in the following table.

Factors of -15	Sum of the factors of -15
$1(-15)$	$1 + (-15) = -14$
$3(-5)$	$3 + (-5) = -2$
$5(-3)$	$5 + (-3) = 2$
$15(-1)$	$15 + (-1) = 14$

The third row contains the integers 5 and -3, whose product is -15 and whose sum is 2. To complete the factorization, we enter 5 and -3 as the second binomial factors.

$$a^2 + 2a - 15 = (a + 5)(a - 3)$$

We can check by multiplying.

$(a + 5)(a - 3) = a^2 - 3a + 5a - 15$ Use the FOIL method.
$\qquad\qquad\quad = a^2 + 2a - 15$ This is the original trinomial.

EXAMPLE 4   Factor: $z^2 - 4z - 21$

Strategy We will assume that $z^2 - 4z - 21$ is the product of two binomials and we will use a systematic method to find their terms.

WHY Since the terms of $z^2 - 4z - 21$ do not have a common factor (other than 1), the only option available is to try to factor it as the product of two binomials.

Solution
Since the first term of the trinomial is z^2, the first term of each binomial factor must be z. To fill in the blanks, we must find two integers whose product is -21 and whose sum is -4.

$$z^2 - 4y - 21 = \left(z \quad\right)\left(z \quad\right) \quad \text{Because } z \cdot z \text{ will give } z^2.$$

The factorizations of -21 and the sums of the factors are shown in the following table.

Factors of -21	Sum of the factors of -21
$1(-21)$	$1 + (-21) = -20$
$3(-7)$	$3 + (-7) = -4$
$7(-3)$	$7 + (-3) = 4$
$21(-1)$	$21 + (-1) = 20$

The second row contains the integers 3 and -7, whose product is -21 and whose sum is -4. To complete the factorization, we enter 3 and -7 as the second terms of the binomial factors.

$$z^2 - 4z - 21 = (z + 3)(z - 7)$$

We can check by multiplying.

$(z + 3)(z - 7) = z^2 - 7z + 3z - 21$ Use the FOIL method.
$\qquad\qquad\quad = z^2 - 4z - 21$ This is the original trinomial.

Self Check 4

Factor: $q^2 - 2q - 24$

Now Try **Problem 37**

Self Check 4 Answer
$(q - 6)(q + 4)$

Teaching Example 4 Factor:
$x^2 - 3x - 10$
Answer:
$(x - 5)(x + 2)$

The following sign patterns can be helpful when factoring trinomials.

Factoring Trinomials Whose Leading Coefficient Is 1

To factor $x^2 + bx + c$, find two integers whose product is c and whose sum is b.

1.   If c is positive, the integers have the same sign.

2.   If c is negative, the integers have opposite signs.

When factoring out trinomials of the form $ax^2 + bx + c$, where $a = -1$, we begin by factoring out -1.

Self Check 5

Factor: $-x^2 + 11x - 28$

Now Try **Problem 41**
Self Check 5 Answer
$-(x - 4)(x - 7)$

Teaching Example 5 Factor:
$-x^2 - 5x + 6$
Answer:
$-(x + 6)(x - 1)$

EXAMPLE 5   Factor: $-h^2 + 2h + 15$

Strategy We will factor out -1 and then factor the resulting trinomial.

WHY It is easier to factor trinomials whose leading coefficient is positive.

Solution
We factor out -1 and then factor $h^2 - 2h - 15$.

$$
\begin{aligned}
-h^2 + 2h + 15 &= -\mathbf{1}(h^2 - 2h - 15) &&\text{Factor out } -1. \\
&= -(h^2 - 2h - 15) &&\text{The 1 need not be written.} \\
&= -(h - 5)(h + 3) &&\text{Use the integers } -5 \text{ and } 3, \text{ because their} \\
&&&\text{product is } -15 \text{ and their sum is } -2.
\end{aligned}
$$

We can check by multiplying.

$$
\begin{aligned}
-(h - 5)(h + 3) &= -(h^2 + 3h - 5h - 15) &&\text{Multiply the binomials first.} \\
&= -(h^2 - 2h - 15) &&\text{Combine like terms.} \\
&= -h^2 + 2h + 15 &&\text{This is the original trinomial.} \quad\blacksquare
\end{aligned}
$$

The trinomials in the next two examples are of a form similar to $x^2 + bx + c$, and we can use the methods of this section to factor them.

Self Check 6

Factor: $s^2 + 6st - 7t^2$

Now Try **Problem 45**
Self Check 6 Answer
$(s + 7t)(s - t)$

Teaching Example 6 Factor:
$x^2 - 7xy + 12y^2$
Answer:
$(x - 4y)(x - 3y)$

EXAMPLE 6   Factor: $x^2 - 4xy - 5y^2$

Strategy We will assume that $x^2 - 4xy - 5y^2$ is the product of two binomials and we will use a systematic method to find their terms.

WHY Since the terms of $x^2 - 4xy - 5y^2$ do not have a common factor (other than 1), the only option available is to try to factor it as the product of two binomials.

Solution
The trinomial has two variables, x and y. Since the first term is x^2, the first term of each factor must be x.

$$x^2 - 4xy - 5y^2 = \left(x \quad\right)\left(x \quad\right) \qquad \text{Because } x \cdot x \text{ will give } x^2.$$

To fill in the blanks, we must find two *expressions* whose product is the last term, $-5y^2$, and that will give a middle term of $-4xy$. Two such expressions are $-5y$ and y.

$$x^2 - 4xy - 5y^2 = (x - \mathbf{5}y)(x + y)$$

Check:
$$
\begin{aligned}
(x - 5y)(x + y) &= x^2 + xy - 5xy - 5y^2 &&\text{Use the FOIL method.} \\
&= x^2 - 4xy - 5y^2 &&\text{This is the original trinomial.} \quad\blacksquare
\end{aligned}
$$

2 Factor trinomials of the form $x^2 + bx + c$ after factoring out the GCF.

If the terms of a trinomial have a common factor, the GCF should always be factored out before any of the factoring techniques of this section are used. A trinomial is **factored completely** when no factor can be factored further. Always factor completely when you are asked to factor.

EXAMPLE 7   Factor: $2x^4 + 26x^3 + 80x^2$

Strategy We will factor out the GCF, $2x^2$, first. Then we will factor the resulting trinomial.

WHY The first step in factoring any polynomial is to factor out the GCF. Factoring out the GCF first makes factoring by any method easier.

Solution
We begin by factoring out the GCF, $2x^2$.

$$2x^4 + 26x^3 + 80x^2 = \mathbf{2x^2}(x^2 + 13x + 40)$$

Next, we factor $x^2 + 13x + 40$. The integers 8 and 5 have a product of 40 and a sum of 13, so the completely factored form of the given trinomial is

$$2x^4 + 26x^3 + 80x^2 = 2x^2(x + 8)(x + 5) \qquad \text{The complete factorization must include } 2x^2.$$

Check by multiplying $2x^2$, $x + 8$, and $x + 5$.

Self Check 7
Factor: $4m^5 + 8m^4 - 32m^3$
Now Try **Problem 51**
Self Check 7 Answer
$4m^3(m + 4)(m - 2)$

Teaching Example 7 Factor:
$3x^4 - 12x^3 + 9x^2$
Answer:
$3x^2(x - 1)(x - 3)$

EXAMPLE 8   Factor completely: $-13g^2 + 36g + g^3$

Strategy We will write the terms of the trinomial in descending powers of g.

WHY It is easier to factor a trinomial if its terms are written in descending powers of one variable.

Solution
Before factoring the trinomial, we write its terms in descending powers of g.

$$\begin{aligned} -13g^2 + 36g + g^3 &= g^3 - 13g^2 + 36g \qquad \text{Rearrange the terms.} \\ &= g(g^2 - 13g + 36) \qquad \text{Factor out } g, \text{ which is the GCF.} \\ &= g(g - 9)(g - 4) \qquad \text{Factor the trinomial.} \end{aligned}$$

Check by multiplying.

Self Check 8
Factor: $-12t + t^3 + 4t^2$
Now Try **Problem 55**
Self Check 8 Answer
$t(t - 2)(t + 6)$

Teaching Example 8 Factor:
$2x^3 - 12x^2 + 10x$
Answer:
$2x(x - 1)(x - 5)$

If a trinomial cannot be factored using only integers, it is called a **prime polynomial,** or more specifically, a **prime trinomial.**

EXAMPLE 9   Factor, if possible: $x^2 + 2x + 3$

Strategy We will assume that $x^2 + 2x + 3$ is the product of two binomials and we will use a systematic method to find their terms.

WHY Since the terms of $x^2 + 2x + 3$ do not have a common factor (other than 1), the only option available is to try to factor it as the product of two binomials.

Self Check 9
Factor, if possible: $x^2 - 4x + 6$
Now Try **Problem 58**
Self Check 9 Answer
not possible; prime trinomial

Teaching Example 9 Factor:
$x^2 - 6x - 8$, if possible
Answer:
not possible; prime trinomial

Solution

To factor the trinomial, we must find two integers whose product is 3 and whose sum is 2. The possible factorizations of 3 and the sums of the factors are shown in the following table.

Factors of 3	Sum of the factors of 3
1(3)	$1 + 3 = 4$
$-1(-3)$	$-1 + (-3) = -4$

Since two integers whose product is 3 and whose sum is 2 do not exist, $x^2 + 2x + 3$ cannot be factored. It is a *prime trinomial*.

3 Factor trinomials of the form $x^2 + bx + c$ using the grouping method.

Another way to factor trinomials of the form $x^2 + bx + c$ is to write them as equivalent four-termed polynomials and factor by grouping. To factor $x^2 + 8x + 15$ using this method, we proceed as follows.

1. First, identify b as the coefficient of the x-term, and c as the last term. For trinomials of the form $x^2 + bx + c$, we call c the **key number.**

    $$\left. \begin{array}{c} x^2 + bx + c \\ \downarrow \quad\ \downarrow \\ x^2 + 8x + 15 \end{array} \right\} b = 8 \text{ and } c = 15$$

2. Now find two integers whose product is the key number, 15, and whose sum is $b = 8$. Since the integers must have a positive product and a positive sum, we consider only positive factors of 15.

Key number = 15	$b = 8$
Positive factors of 15	**Sum of the positive factors of 15**
$1 \cdot 15 = 15$	$1 + 15 = 16$
$3 \cdot 5 = 15$	$3 + 5 = 8$

    The second row of the table contains the correct pair of integers 3 and 5, whose product is the key number 15 and whose sum is $b = 8$.

3. Express the middle term, $8x$, of the trinomial as the *sum of two terms,* using the integers 3 and 5 found in step 2 as coefficients of the two terms.

    $$x^2 + 8x + 15 = x^2 + 3x + 5x + 15 \quad \text{Express 8x as 3x + 5x.}$$

4. Factor the equivalent four-term polynomial by grouping:

    $$x^2 + 3x + 5x + 15 = x(x + 3) + 5(x + 3) \quad \text{Factor x out of } x^2 + 3x \text{ and 5 out of 5x + 15.}$$

    $$= (x + 3)(x + 5) \quad \text{Factor out x + 3.}$$

    Check the factorization by multiplying.

    The grouping method is an alternative to the method for factoring trinomials discussed earlier in this section. It is especially useful when the constant term, c, has many factors.

Factoring Trinomials of the Form $x^2 + bx + c$ Using Grouping

To factor a trinomial that has a leading coefficient of 1:

1. Identify b and the key number, c.
2. Find two integers whose product is the key number and whose sum is b.
3. Express the middle term, bx, as the sum (or difference) of two terms. Enter the two numbers found in step 2 as coefficients of x in the form shown below. Then factor the equivalent four-term polynomial by grouping.

$$x^2 + \boxed{}x + \boxed{}x + c$$

The product of these numbers must
be c, and their sum must be b.

4. Check the factorization using multiplication.

EXAMPLE 10 Factor by grouping: $a^2 + a - 20$

Strategy We will express the middle term, a, of the trinomial as the difference of two carefully chosen terms.

WHY We want to produce an equivalent four-term polynomial that can be factored by grouping.

Solution
Since $a^2 + a - 20 = a^2 + 1a - 20$, we identify b as **1** and the key number c as **−20**. We must find two integers whose product is −20 and whose sum is 1. Since the integers must have a negative product, their signs must be different.

Key number = −20	$b = 1$
Factors of −20	**Sum of the factors of −20**
$1(-20) = -20$	$1 + (-20) = -19$
$2(-10) = -20$	$2 + (-10) = -8$
$4(-5) = -20$	$4 + (-5) = -1$
$5(-4) = -20$	$5 + (-4) = 1$
$10(-2) = -20$	$10 + (-2) = 8$
$20(-1) = -20$	$20 + (-1) = 19$

The fourth row of the table contains the correct pair of integers 5 and −4, whose product is −20 and whose sum is 1. They serve as the coefficients of $5a$ and $-4a$, the two terms that we use to represent the middle term, a, of the trinomial.

$$a^2 + a - 20 = a^2 + 5a - 4a - 20 \qquad \text{Express the middle term, } a, \text{ as } 5a - 4a.$$
$$= a(a + 5) - 4(a + 5) \qquad \text{Factor } a \text{ out of } a^2 + 5a \text{ and } -4 \text{ out of } -4a - 20.$$
$$= (a + 5)(a - 4) \qquad \text{Factor out } a + 5.$$

Check the factorization by multiplying.

Self Check 10

Factor by grouping:
$m^2 + m - 42$

Now Try **Problem 61**
Self Check 10 Answer
$(m + 7)(m - 6)$

Teaching Example 10 Factor by grouping: $x^2 - 15x + 14$
Answer:
$(x - 1)(x - 14)$

> **Success Tip**   We could also express the middle term as $-4a + 5a$. We obtain the same binomial factors, but in reverse order.
>
> $$a^2 - 4a + 5a - 20$$
> $$= a(a - 4) + 5(a - 4)$$
> $$= (a - 4)(a + 5)$$

Self Check 11

Factor by grouping:
$q^2 - 2qt - 24t^2$

Now Try **Problem 63**

Self Check 11 Answer
$(q + 4t)(q - 6t)$

Teaching Example 11 Factor by
grouping: $x^2 + 7xy + 12y^2$
Answer:
$(x + 3y)(x + 4y)$

EXAMPLE 11   Factor by grouping: $x^2 - 4xy - 5y^2$

Strategy We will express the middle term, $-4xy$, of the trinomial as the sum of two carefully chosen terms.

WHY We want to produce an equivalent four-term polynomial that can be factored by grouping.

Key number = −5 b = −4	
Factors	**Sum**
$-5(1) = -5$	$-5 + 1 = -4$

Solution

In $x^2 - 4xy - 5y^2$, we identify b as -4 and the key number c as -5. We must find two integers whose product is -5 and whose sum is -4. Such a pair is -5 and 1. They serve as the coefficients of $-5xy$ and $1xy$, the two terms that we use to represent the middle term, $-4xy$, of the trinomial.

$$x^2 - 4xy - 5y^2 = x^2 - 5xy + 1xy - 5y^2 \qquad \text{Express the middle term, } -4xy, \text{ as } -5xy + 1xy. \text{ (1xy } - 5xy \text{ could also be used.)}$$

$$= x(x - 5y) + y(x - 5y) \qquad \text{Factor } x \text{ out of } x^2 - 5xy \text{ and } y \text{ out of } 1xy - 5y^2.$$

$$= (x - 5y)(x + y) \qquad \text{Factor out } x - 5y.$$

Check the factorization by multiplying.

Self Check 12

Factor completely:
$3m^3 - 27m^2 + 24m$

Now Try **Problem 66**

Self Check 12 Answer
$3m(m - 8)(m - 1)$

Teaching Example 12 Factor
completely: $5x^3 + 5x^2 - 100x$
Answer:
$5x(x + 5)(x - 4)$

EXAMPLE 12   Factor completely: $2x^3 - 20x^2 + 18x$

Strategy We will factor out the GCF, $2x$, first. Then we will factor the resulting trinomial using the grouping method.

WHY The first step in factoring any polynomial is to factor out the GCF.

Solution

We begin by factoring out the GCF, $2x$, from $2x^3 - 20x^2 + 18x$.

$$2x^3 - 20x^2 + 18x = 2x(x^2 - 10x + 9)$$

Key number = 9 b = −10	
Factors	**Sum**
$-9(-1) = 9$	$-9 + (-1) = -10$

To factor $x^2 - 10x + 9$ by grouping, we must find two integers whose product is the key number 9 and whose sum is $b = -10$. Such a pair is -9 and -1.

$$x^2 - 10x + 9 = x^2 - 9x - 1x + 9 \qquad \text{Express } -10x \text{ as } -9x - 1x. \text{ (}-1x - 9x \text{ could also be used.)}$$

$$= x(x - 9) - 1(x - 9) \qquad \text{Factor } x \text{ out of } x^2 - 9x \text{ and } -1 \text{ out of } -1x + 9.$$

$$= (x - 9)(x - 1) \qquad \text{Factor out } x - 9.$$

The complete factorization of the original trinomial is

$2x^3 - 20x^2 + 18x = \mathbf{2x}(x - 9)(x - 1)$ *Don't forget to write the GCF, 2x.*

Check the factorization by multiplying.   ∎

ANSWERS TO SELF CHECKS

1. $(y + 1)(y + 6)$ **2.** $(p - 3)(p - 2)$ **3.** $(p + 6)(p - 3)$ **4.** $(q - 6)(q + 4)$
5. $-(x - 4)(x - 7)$ **6.** $(s + 7t)(s - t)$ **7.** $4m^3(m + 4)(m - 2)$ **8.** $t(t - 2)(t + 6)$
9. not possible; prime trinomial   **10.** $(m + 7)(m - 6)$ **11.** $(q + 4t)(q - 6t)$
12. $3m(m - 8)(m - 1)$

SECTION **6.2**   STUDY SET

▌ VOCABULARY

Fill in the blanks.

1. A polynomial with three terms is called a __trinomial__ .

2. In the polynomial $x^2 - x - 6$, x^2 is the __first__ term, $-x$ is the middle __term__ , and __-6__ is the last term.

3. The statement $x^2 - x - 12 = (x - 4)(x + 3)$ shows that $x^2 - x - 12$ __factors__ into the product of two binomials.

4. A trinomial is said to be factored __completely__ when no factor can be factored further.

▶ 5. A __prime__ polynomial cannot be factored by using only integer coefficients.

6. When factoring trinomials of the form $x^2 + bx + c$ by the grouping method, the number c is called the __key__ number.

▌ CONCEPTS

Fill in the blanks.

7. Two factorizations of 4 that involve only positive numbers are $4 \cdot 1$ and $2 \cdot 2$. Two factorizations of 4 that involve only negative numbers are $-4\left(-1\right)$ and $-2\left(-2\right)$.

8. Before attempting to factor a trinomial, be sure that the exponents are written in __descending__ order.

9. Before attempting to factor a trinomial into two binomials, always factor out any __common__ factors first.

10. To factor $x^2 + x - 56$, we must find two integers whose __product__ is -56 and whose __sum__ is 1.

11. Two factors of 18 whose sum is -9 are __-6__ and __-3__ .

12. Complete the table.

Factors of 8	Sum of the factors of 8
1(8)	$1 + 8 = 9$
2(4)	$2 + 4 = 6$
$-1(-8)$	$-1 + (-8) = -9$
$-2(-4)$	$-2 + (-4) = -6$

13. Complete the table.

Factors of -9	Sum of the factors of -9
1(-9)	$1 + (-9) = -8$
3(-3)	$3 + (-3) = 0$
$-1(9)$	$-1 + 9 = 8$

14. Find two integers whose:
   a. product is 10 and whose sum is 7. 5, 2
   b. product is 8 and whose sum is -6. $-2, -4$
   c. product is -6 and whose sum is 1. 3, -2
   d. product is -9 and whose sum is -8. 1, -9

15. Given: $x^2 + 8x + 15$
   a. What is the coefficient of the x^2 term? 1
   b. What is the last term? What is the coefficient of the middle term? 15, 8
   c. What two integers have a product of 15 and a sum of 8? 5, 3

16. What trinomial has the factorization of $(x + 8)(x - 2)$? $x^2 + 6x - 16$

Complete each factorization.

17. $x^2 + 3x + 2 = (x + 2)(x + 1)$

18. $y^2 + 4y + 3 = (y + 3)(y + 1)$

19. $t^2 - 9t + 14 = (t - 7)(t - 2)$

20. $c^2 - 9c + 8 = (c - 8)(c - 1)$

21. $a^2 + 6a - 16 = (a + 8)(a - 2)$

22. $x^2 - 3x - 40 = (x - 8)(x + 5)$

NOTATION

Complete each factorization.

23. $6 + 5x + x^2 = x^2 + 5x + 6$
$$= (x + 3)(x + 2)$$

▶ **24.** $-a^2 - a + 20 = -(a^2 + a - 20)$
$$= -(a + 5)(a - 4)$$

GUIDED PRACTICE

Factor each trinomial. See Example 1.

25. $z^2 + 12z + 11$
$(z + 11)(z + 1)$

▶ **26.** $x^2 + 7x + 10$
$(x + 5)(x + 2)$

27. $p^2 + 9p + 14$
$(p + 2)(p + 7)$

28. $q^2 + 11q + 24$
$(q + 3)(q + 8)$

Factor each trinomial. See Example 2.

29. $m^2 - 5m + 6$
$(m - 3)(m - 2)$

30. $n^2 - 7n + 10$
$(n - 5)(n - 2)$

31. $y^2 - 13y + 30$
$(y - 3)(y - 10)$

▶ **32.** $r^2 - 10r + 24$
$(r - 4)(r - 6)$

Factor each trinomial. See Example 3.

▶ **33.** $b^2 + 6b - 7$
$(b + 7)(b - 1)$

34. $x^2 + 5x - 24$
$(x + 8)(x - 3)$

35. $a^2 + 6a - 16$
$(a + 8)(a - 2)$

36. $b^2 + 2b - 99$
$(b + 11)(b - 9)$

Factor each trinomial. See Example 4.

▶ **37.** $a^2 - 4a - 5$
$(a - 5)(a + 1)$

▶ **38.** $t^2 - 5t - 50$
$(t - 10)(t + 5)$

39. $z^2 - 3z - 18$
$(z - 6)(z + 3)$

40. $s^2 - 2s - 120$
$(s - 12)(s + 10)$

Factor each trinomial. See Example 5.

41. $-x^2 - 7x - 10$
$-(x + 5)(x + 2)$

42. $-x^2 + 9x - 20$
$-(x - 5)(x - 4)$

43. $-t^2 - 15t + 34$
$-(t + 17)(t - 2)$

▶ **44.** $-t^2 - t + 30$
$-(t + 6)(t - 5)$

Factor each trinomial. See Example 6.

45. $x^2 + 4xy + 4y^2$
$(x + 2y)(x + 2y)$

▶ **46.** $a^2 + 10ab + 9b^2$
$(a + 9b)(a + b)$

47. $m^2 + 3mn - 10n^2$
$(m + 5n)(m - 2n)$

▶ **48.** $m^2 - mn - 12n^2$
$(m - 4n)(m + 3n)$

Factor each trinomial. See Example 7.

49. $2x^2 + 10x + 12$
$2(x + 3)(x + 2)$

▶ **50.** $3y^2 - 21y + 18$
$3(y - 6)(y - 1)$

51. $5p^3 + 25p^2 - 70p$
$5p(p + 7)(p - 2)$

52. $3m^4 - 9m^3 - 54m^2$
$3m^2(m + 3)(m - 6)$

Factor each trinomial. See Example 8.

53. $4rx + r^2 + 3x^2$
$(r + 3x)(r + x)$

54. $a^2 + 5b^2 + 6ab$
$(a + b)(a + 5b)$

▶ **55.** $-3a^2b + a^3 + 2ab^2$
$a(a - 2b)(a - b)$

56. $-13yz^2 + y^2z - 14z^3$
$z(y - 14z)(y + z)$

Factor each trinomial, if possible. See Example 9.

▶ **57.** $r^2 - 9r - 12$ prime

58. $u^2 + 10u + 15$ prime

59. $r^2 - 2rs + 4s^2$ prime

60. $m^2 + 3mn - 20n^2$ prime

Factor each trinomial by grouping. See Examples 10–12.

61. $p^2 + p - 30$
$(p + 6)(p - 5)$

62. $q^2 - 10q + 24$
$(q - 4)(q - 6)$

63. $m^2 - 3mn - 4n^2$
$(m - 4n)(m + n)$

▶ **64.** $r^2 - 2rs - 15s^2$
$(r + 3s)(r - 5s)$

65. $3x^3 - 27x^2 + 60x$
$3x(x - 4)(x - 5)$

66. $2x^3 + 4x^2 - 70x$
$2x(x + 7)(x - 5)$

67. $4y^3 - 28y^2 + 40y$
$4y(y - 5)(y - 2)$

68. $5y^3 + 45y^2 + 100y$
$5y(y + 5)(y + 4)$

TRY IT YOURSELF

Completely factor each of the following expressions. If an expression is prime, so indicate.

69. $a^2 - 10a - 39$
$(a - 13)(a + 3)$

▶ **70.** $v^2 + 9v + 15$
prime

71. $s^2 + 11s - 26$
$(s + 13)(s - 2)$

▶ **72.** $y^2 + 8y + 12$
$(y + 6)(y + 2)$

73. $r^2 - 2r + 4$
prime

74. $m^2 + 3m - 10$
$(m + 5)(m - 2)$

75. $a^2 - 4ab - 12b^2$
$(a - 6b)(a + 2b)$

▶ **76.** $p^2 + pq - 6q^2$
$(p + 3q)(p - 2q)$

77. $-r^2 + 14r - 40$
$-(r - 10)(r - 4)$

78. $-r^2 + 14r - 45$
$-(r - 9)(r - 5)$

79. $-a^2 - 4ab - 3b^2$
$-(a + 3b)(a + b)$

80. $-a^2 - 6ab - 5b^2$
$-(a + b)(a + 5b)$

81. $4 - 5x + x^2$
$(x - 4)(x - 1)$

82. $y^2 + 5 + 6y$
$(y + 5)(y + 1)$

83. $10y + 9 + y^2$
$(y + 9)(y + 1)$

▶ **84.** $x^2 - 13 - 12x$
$(x - 13)(x + 1)$

85. $-r^2 + 2 + r$
$-(r - 2)(r + 1)$

86. $u^2 - 3 + 2u$
$(u + 3)(u - 1)$

87. $-5a^2 + 25a - 30$
$-5(a - 3)(a - 2)$

▶ **88.** $-2b^2 + 20b - 18$
$-2(b - 9)(b - 1)$

89. $-4x^2y - 4x^3 + 24xy^2$
$-4x(x + 3y)(x - 2y)$

▶ **90.** $3x^2y^3 + 3x^3y^2 - 6xy^4$
$3xy^2(x + 2y)(x - y)$

Choose the correct method from Section 6.1 or 6.2 to factor completely each expression. If an expression is prime, so indicate.

91. $m^2 - m - 12$
$(m - 4)(m + 3)$

▶ **92.** $u^2 + u - 42$
$(u + 7)(u - 6)$

93. $3a^2b + 3ab^2$
$3ab(a + b)$

94. $3p^2 - 12p + 6$
$3(p^2 - 4p + 2)$

95. $-4a^2 - 8a$
$-4a(a + 2)$

96. $3p + p^2 + 3q + pq$
$(p + q)(3 + p)$

97. $-x^2 + 6xy + 7y^2$
$-(x - 7y)(x + y)$

98. $-x^2 - 10xy + 11y^2$
$-(x + 11y)(x - y)$

99. $12xy + 4x^2y - 72y$
$4y(x + 6)(x - 3)$

100. $48xy + 6xy^2 + 96x$
$6x(y + 4)(y + 4)$

101. $3ap + 2p + 3aq + 2q$
$(3a + 2)(p + q)$

102. $-9abc - 9ac^2 + 3bc + 3c^2$
$-3c(b + c)(3a - 1)$

103. $3z^2 - 15z + 12$
$3(z - 4)(z - 1)$

104. $5m^2 + 45m - 50$
$5(m + 10)(m - 1)$

▌ APPLICATIONS

▶ **105.** PETS The cage shown is used for transporting dogs. Its volume is $(x^3 + 12x^2 + 27x)$ in.³. The dimensions of the cage can be found by factoring this expression. If the cage is longer than it is tall and taller than it is wide, write expressions that represent its length, height, and width.

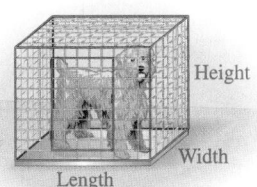

$(x + 9)$ in., $(x + 3)$ in., x in.

▶ **106.** CARPOOLING The average rate at which a carpool van travels and the distance it covers are given in the table in terms of t. Factor the expression representing the distance traveled and then complete the table.

Rate (mi/hr)	Time (hr)	Distance traveled (mi)
$t + 11$	$t + 5$	$t^2 + 16t + 55$

▌ WRITING

107. Explain what it means when we say that a trinomial is the product of two binomials. Give an example.

▶ **108.** Are $2x^2 - 12x + 16$ and $x^2 - 6x + 8$ factored in the same way? Explain why or why not.

109. When factoring $x^2 - 2x - 3$, one student got $(x - 3)(x + 1)$, and another got $(x + 1)(x - 3)$. Are both answers acceptable? Explain.

110. Explain how to use multiplication to check the factorization of a trinomial.

111. A student begins to factor a trinomial as shown below. Explain why the student is off to a bad start.

$$x^2 - 2x - 63 = (x - \quad)(x - \quad)$$

▶ **112.** Explain why the given trinomial is not factored completely.

$$3x^2 - 3x - 60 = 3(x^2 - x - 20)$$

▌ REVIEW

Graph the solution of each inequality on the number line.

113. $x - 3 > 5$

8

▶ **114.** $x + 4 \leq 3$

−1

115. $-3x - 5 \geq 4$

−3

116. $2x - 3 < 7$

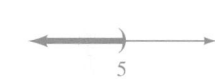
5

SECTION **6.3**

Factoring Trinomials of the Form $ax^2 + bx + c$

Objectives

1 Factor trinomials using the trial-and-check method.

2 Factor trinomials after factoring out the GCF.

3 Factor trinomials using the grouping method.

In this section, we will factor trinomials with leading coefficients other than 1, such as $2x^2 + 5x + 3$ and $6a^2 - 17a + 5$. Two methods are used to factor these trinomials. With the first method, educated guesses are made. These guesses are checked by multiplication. The correct factorization is determined by a process of elimination. The second method is an extension of factoring by grouping.

1   Factor trinomials using the trial-and-check method.

In the work below, we find the products $(2x + 1)(x + 3)$ and $(2x + 3)(x + 1)$. There are several observations that can be made when we compare the results.

$$(2x + 1)(x + 3) = 2x^2 + 6x + x + 3 \qquad (2x + 3)(x + 1) = 2x^2 + 2x + 3x + 3$$
$$= 2x^2 + 7x + 3 \qquad\qquad\qquad = 2x^2 + 5x + 3$$

In each case, the result is a trinomial, and

- the first terms are the same ($2x^2$),
- the last terms are the same (3), and
- the middle terms are different ($7x$ and $5x$).

These observations indicate that when the last terms in $(2x + 1)(x + 3)$ are interchanged to form $(2x + 3)(x + 1)$, only the middle terms of the products are different. This fact is helpful when factoring trinomials using the *trial-and-check method*.

Self Check 1

Factor: $3x^2 + 7x + 2$

Now Try **Problem 27**
Self Check 1 Answer
$(3x + 1)(x + 2)$

Teaching Example 1 Factor:
$3x^2 + 8x + 5$
Answer:
$(3x + 5)(x + 1)$

EXAMPLE 1   Factor: $2x^2 + 5x + 3$

Strategy We will assume that $2x^2 + 5x + 3$ is the product of two binomials and we will use a systematic method to find their terms.

WHY Since the terms of $2x^2 + 5x + 3$ do not have a common factor (other than 1), the only option available is to try to factor it as the product of two binomials.

Solution
Since the first term is $2x^2$, the first terms of the binomial factors must be $2x$ and x. To fill in the blanks, we must find two factors of 3 that will give a middle term of $5x$.

$$\left(2x \;\rule{1.5em}{0.8em}\;\right)\left(x \;\rule{1.5em}{0.8em}\;\right) \qquad \text{Because } 2x \cdot x \text{ will give } 2x^2.$$

Because each term of the trinomial is positive, we need only consider positive factors of the last term. Since the positive factors of 3 are 1 and 3, there are two possible factorizations.

$$(2x + 1)(x + 3) \qquad \text{or} \qquad (2x + 3)(x + 1)$$

The first possibility is incorrect: When we find the outer and inner products and combine like terms, we obtain an incorrect middle term of $7x$.

Outer: 6x

$(2x + 1)(x + 3)$ Multiply and add to find the middle term: 6x + x = 7x.

Inner: x

The second possibility is correct, because it gives a middle term of $5x$.

Outer: 2x

$(2x + 3)(x + 1)$ Multiply and add to find the middle term: 2x + 3x = 5x.

Inner: 3x

Thus,

$$2x^2 + 5x + 3 = (2x + 3)(x + 1)$$

EXAMPLE 2   Factor: $6a^2 - 17a + 5$

Strategy We will assume that $6a^2 - 17a + 5$ is the product of two binomials and we will use a systematic method to find their terms.

WHY Since the terms of $6a^2 - 17a + 5$ do not have a common factor (other than 1), the only option available is to try to factor it as the product of two binomials.

Solution
Since the first term is $6a^2$, the first terms of the binomial factors must be $6a$ and a or $3a$ and $2a$. To fill in the blanks, we must find two factors of 5 that will give a middle term of $-17a$.

$$\left(6a \quad\right)\left(a \quad\right) \quad\text{or}\quad \left(3a \quad\right)\left(2a \quad\right)$$

Because the sign of the last term is positive and the sign of the middle term is negative, we need only consider negative factors of the last term. Since the negative factors of 5 are -1 and -5, there are four possible factorizations.

$$\overset{-30a}{(6a - 1)(a - 5)} \quad -30a - a = -31a. \qquad \overset{-6a}{(6a - 5)(a - 1)} \quad -6a - 5a = -11a.$$
$$\underset{-a}{} \qquad\qquad\qquad\qquad \underset{-5a}{}$$

$$\overset{-15a}{(3a - 1)(2a - 5)} \quad -15a - 2a = -17a. \qquad \overset{-3a}{(3a - 5)(2a - 1)} \quad -3a - 10a = -13a.$$
$$\underset{-2a}{} \qquad\qquad\qquad\qquad\quad \underset{-10a}{}$$

Only the possibility shown in blue gives the correct middle term of $-17a$. Thus,

$$6a^2 - 17a + 5 = (3a - 1)(2a - 5)$$

■

EXAMPLE 3   Factor: $3y^2 - 7y - 6$

Strategy We will assume that $3y^2 - 7y - 6$ is the product of two binomials and we will use a systematic method to find their terms.

WHY Since the terms of $3y^2 - 7y - 6$ do not have a common factor (other than 1), the only option available is to try to factor it as the product of two binomials.

Solution
Since the first term is $3y^2$, the first terms of the binomial factors must be $3y$ and y.

$$\left(3y \quad\right)\left(y \quad\right) \quad\text{Because 3y} \cdot \text{y will give } 3y^2.$$

The second terms of the binomials must be two integers whose product is -6. There are four such pairs: $1(-6)$, $-1(6)$, $2(-3)$, and $-2(3)$. When these pairs are entered, and then reversed, as second terms of the binomials, there are eight possibilities to consider. Four of them can be discarded because they include a binomial whose terms have a common factor. If $3y^2 - 7y - 6$ does not have a common factor, neither can any of its binomial factors.

For the factors -1 and 6: $\overset{18y}{(3y - 1)(y + 6)} \quad\text{or}\quad \underline{(3y + 6)(y - 1)}$
$$\underset{-y}{} \qquad\qquad\qquad \text{A common factor of 3}$$
$$18y - y = 17y$$

Self Check 2

Factor: $6x^2 - 7x + 2$

Now Try **Problem 32**
Self Check 2 Answer
$(3x - 2)(2x - 1)$

Teaching Example 2 Factor:
$3x^2 - 10x + 8$
Answer:
$(3x - 4)(x - 2)$

Self Check 3

Factor: $5a^2 - 23a - 10$

Now Try **Problem 36**
Self Check 3 Answer
$(5a + 2)(a - 5)$

Teaching Example 3 Factor:
$7x^2 - 5x - 2$
Answer:
$(7x + 2)(x - 1)$

$$\overset{\displaystyle -18y}{\frown}$$

For the factors 1 and −6: $(3y + 1)(y - 6)$ or $\underline{(3y - 6)(y + 1)}$

$$\underset{\displaystyle y}{\smile}$$

$$-18y + y = -17y$$ A common factor of 3

$$\overset{\displaystyle 9y}{\frown}$$

For the factors −2 and 3: $(3y - 2)(y + 3)$ or $(3y + 3)(y - 2)$

$$\underset{\displaystyle -2y}{\smile}$$

$$9y - 2y = 7y$$ A common factor of 3

$$\overset{\displaystyle -9y}{\frown}$$

For the factors 2 and −3: $(3y + 2)(y - 3)$ or $(3y - 3)(y + 2)$

$$\underset{\displaystyle 2y}{\smile}$$

$$-9y + 2y = -7y$$ A common factor of 3

Only the possibility shown in blue gives the correct middle term of $-7y$. Thus,

$$3y^2 - 7y - 6 = (3y + 2)(y - 3)$$

Check the factorization by multiplication. ■

> **Success Tip**   If a trinomial does not have a common factor, the terms of each of its binomial factors will not have a common factor.

Self Check 4

Factor: $4x^2 + 4xy - 3y^2$

Now Try **Problem 39**
Self Check 4 Answer
$(2x + 3y)(2x - y)$

Teaching Example 4 Factor:
$6x^2 + 7xy - 20y^2$
Answer:
$(3x - 4y)(2x + 5y)$

EXAMPLE 4   Factor: $4b^2 + 8bc - 45c^2$

Strategy We will assume that $4b^2 + 8bc - 45c^2$ is the product of two binomials and we will use a systematic method to find their terms.

WHY Since the terms of $4b^2 + 8bc - 45c^2$ do not have a common factor (other than 1), the only option available is to try to factor it as the product of two binomials.

Solution
Since the first term is $4b^2$, the first terms of the factors must be $4b$ and b or $2b$ and $2b$.

$$\left(4b \;\rule{1.5em}{0.4pt}\;\right)\left(b \;\rule{1.5em}{0.4pt}\;\right) \qquad \text{or} \qquad \left(2b \;\rule{1.5em}{0.4pt}\;\right)\left(2b \;\rule{1.5em}{0.4pt}\;\right) \qquad \begin{array}{l}\text{Because } 4b \cdot b \text{ or } 2b \cdot 2b \\ \text{give } 4b^2.\end{array}$$

To fill in the blanks, we must find two factors of $-45c^2$ that will give a middle term of $8bc$.

    Since $-45c^2$ has many factors, there are many possible combinations for the last terms of the binomial factors. The signs of the factors must be different, because the last term of the trinomial is negative.

    If we pick factors of $4b$ and b for the first terms, and $-c$ and $45c$ for the last terms, the multiplication gives an incorrect middle term of $179bc$. So the factorization is incorrect.

$$\overset{\displaystyle 180bc}{\frown}$$

$$(4b - c)(b + 45c) \qquad 180bc - bc = 179bc$$

$$\underset{\displaystyle -bc}{\smile}$$

If we pick factors of $4b$ and b for the first terms and $15c$ and $-3c$ for the last terms, the multiplication gives an incorrect middle term of $3bc$.

$$-12bc$$

$$(4b + 15c)(b - 3c) \qquad -12bc + 15bc = 3bc$$

$$15bc$$

If we pick factors of $2b$ and $2b$ for the first terms and $-5c$ and $9c$ for the last terms, we have

$$18bc$$

$$(2b - 5c)(2b + 9c) \qquad 18bc - 10bc = 8bc$$

$$-10bc$$

which gives the correct middle term of $8bc$. Thus,

$$4b^2 + 8bc - 45c^2 = (2b - 5c)(2b + 9c)$$

Check by multiplication. ∎

Because some guesswork is often necessary, it is difficult to give specific rules for factoring trinomials with a lead coefficient other than 1. However, the following hints are helpful.

Factoring $ax^2 + bx + c$ $(a \ne 1)$

1. Write the trinomial in descending powers of the variable and factor out any GCF (including -1 if that is necessary to make the leading coefficient positive).

2. Attempt to write the trinomial as *the product of two binomials*. The coefficients of the first terms of each binomial factor must be factors of a, and the last terms must be factors of c.

   ```
        ┌── Factors ──┐
             of a
   ( ▢ x + ▢ )( ▢ x + ▢ )
             └── Factors ──┘
                  of c
   ```

3. If the sign of the last term of the trinomial is positive, the signs between the terms of the binomial factors are the same as the sign of the middle term. If the sign of the last term is negative, the signs between the terms of the binomial factors are opposite.

4. Try combinations of coefficients of the first terms and last terms until you find one that gives the middle term of the trinomial. If no combination works, the trinomial is prime.

5. Check the factorization by multiplying.

2 Factor trinomials after factoring out the GCF.

Self Check 5

Factor: $12y - 2y^3 - 2y^2$

Now Try Problem 43

Self Check 5 Answer
$-2y(y + 3)(y - 2)$

Teaching Example 5 Factor:
$12x - 10x^3 - 26x^2$
Answer:
$-2x(5x - 2)(x + 3)$

EXAMPLE 5 Factor: $2x^2 - 8x^3 + 3x$

Strategy We will write the trinomial in descending powers of x and factor out the common factor, $-x$.

WHY It is easier to factor trinomials that have a positive leading coefficient.

Solution
We write the trinomial in descending powers of x

$$-8x^3 + 2x^2 + 3x$$

and we factor out the negative of the GCF, which is $-x$.

$$-8x^3 + 2x^2 + 3x = -x(8x^2 - 2x - 3)$$

We must now factor $8x^2 - 2x - 3$. Its factorization has the form

$$\left(x \quad \right)\left(8x \quad \right) \quad \text{or} \quad \left(2x \quad \right)\left(4x \quad \right)$$ Because $x \cdot 8x$ or $2x \cdot 4x$ will give $8x^2$.

To fill in the blanks, we find two factors of the last term of the trinomial (-3) that will give a middle term of $-2x$. Because the sign of the last term is negative, the signs within its binomial factors will be different. If we pick factors of $2x$ and $4x$ for the first terms and 1 and -3 for the last terms, we have

$$(2x + 1)(4x - 3) \quad -6x + 4x = -2x.$$

which gives the correct middle term of $-2x$, so it is correct.

$$8x^2 - 2x - 3 = (2x + 1)(4x - 3)$$

We can now give the complete factorization.

$$-8x^3 + 2x^2 + 3x = -x(8x^2 - 2x - 3)$$
$$= -x(2x + 1)(4x - 3)$$

Check by multiplication.

3 Factor trinomials using the grouping method.

The method of factoring by grouping can be used to help factor trinomials of the form $ax^2 + bx + c$. For example, to factor $2x^2 + 5x + 3$, we proceed as follows.

1. We find the product ac: In $2x^2 + 5x + 3$, $a = 2$, $b = 5$, and $c = 3$, so $ac = 2(3) = 6$. This number is called the **key number.**

2. Next, find two numbers whose product is $ac = 6$ and whose sum is $b = 5$. Since the numbers must have a positive product and a positive sum, we consider only positive factors of 6. The correct factors are 2 and 3.

Positive factors of 6	Sum of the factors of 6
$1 \cdot 6 = 6$	$1 + 6 = 7$
$2 \cdot 3 = 6$	$2 + 3 = 5$

3. Use the factors 2 and 3 as coefficients of two terms to be placed between $2x^2$ and 3:

$$2x^2 + 5x + 3 = 2x^2 + 2x + 3x + 3$$ Express $5x$ as $2x + 3x$.

4.   Factor by grouping:

$$2x^2 + 2x + 3x + 3 = 2x(x + 1) + 3(x + 1)$$ Factor 2x out of $2x^2 + 2x$ and 3 out of $3x + 3$.

$$= (x + 1)(2x + 3)$$ Factor out $x + 1$.

So $2x^2 + 5x + 3 = (x + 1)(2x + 3)$. Verify this factorization by multiplication.

Factoring $ax^2 + bx + c$ by Grouping

1.   Write the trinomial in descending powers of the variable and factor out any GCF (including -1 if that is necessary to make the leading coefficient positive).

2.   Calculate the key number ac.

3.   Find two numbers whose product is the key number found in step 2 and whose sum is the coefficient of the middle term of the trinomial.

4.   Write the numbers in the blanks of the form shown below, and then factor the polynomial by grouping.

$$ax^2 + \boxed{}\,x + \boxed{}\,x + c$$

The product of these numbers must be ac and their sum must be b.

5.   Check the factorization using multiplication.

EXAMPLE 6   Factor: $10x^2 + 13x - 3$

Strategy We will express the middle term, $13x$, of the trinomial as the sum of two carefully chosen terms.

WHY We want to produce an equivalent four-term polynomial that can be factored by grouping.

Solution

Since $a = 10$ and $c = -3$ in the trinomial, $ac = -30$. We now find two factors of -30 whose sum is 13. Two such factors are 15 and -2. We use these factors as coefficients of two terms to be placed between $10x^2$ and -3.

$$10x^2 + 13x - 3 = 10x^2 + 15x - 2x - 3$$ Express 13x as 15x − 2x.

Finally, we factor by grouping.

$$10x^2 + 15x - 2x - 3 = 5x(2x + 3) - 1(2x + 3)$$ Factor out 5x from $10x^2 + 15x$. Factor out −1 from −2x − 3.

$$= (2x + 3)(5x - 1)$$ Factor out (2x + 3).

So $10x^2 + 13x - 3 = (2x + 3)(5x - 1)$. Check the result.

Self Check 6

Factor: $15a^2 + 17a - 4$

Now Try **Problem 51**

Self Check 6 Answer

$(3a + 4)(5a - 1)$

Teaching Example 6 Factor:
$6x^2 + 7x - 24$
Answer:
$(3x + 8)(2x - 3)$

EXAMPLE 7   Factor: $12x^5 - 17x^4 + 6x^3$

Strategy We will factor out the GCF, x^3, first. Then we will factor the resulting trinomial using the grouping method.

WHY The first step in factoring any polynomial is to factor out the GCF.

Solution

First, we factor out the GCF, which is x^3.

$$12x^5 - 17x^4 + 6x^3 = x^3(12x^2 - 17x + 6)$$

Self Check 7

Factor: $21a^4 - 13a^3 + 2a^2$

Now Try **Problem 56**

Self Check 7 Answer

$a^2(7a - 2)(3a - 1)$

Teaching Example 7 Factor:
$10x^4 - 17x^3 + 3x^2$
Answer:
$x^2(5x - 1)(2x - 3)$

To factor $12x^2 - 17x + 6$, we need to find two integers whose product is $12(6) = 72$ and whose sum is -17. Two such numbers are -8 and -9.

$$12x^2 - 17x + 6 = 12x^2 - 8x - 9x + 6 \qquad \text{Express } -17x \text{ as } -8x - 9x.$$
$$= 4x(3x - 2) - 3(3x - 2) \qquad \text{Factor out } 4x \text{ and factor out } -3.$$
$$= (3x - 2)(4x - 3) \qquad \text{Factor out } 3x - 2.$$

The complete factorization is

$$12x^5 - 17x^4 + 6x^3 = x^3(3x - 2)(4x - 3) \qquad \text{Do not forget to write the GCF, } x^3.$$

Check the result.

ANSWERS TO SELF CHECKS

1. $(3x + 1)(x + 2)$ **2.** $(3x - 2)(2x - 1)$ **3.** $(5a + 2)(a - 5)$ **4.** $(2x + 3y)(2x - y)$
5. $-2y(y + 3)(y - 2)$ **6.** $(3a + 4)(5a - 1)$ **7.** $a^2(7a - 2)(3a - 1)$

SECTION 6.3 STUDY SET

VOCABULARY

Fill in the blanks.

1. The trinomial $3x^2 - x - 12$ has a <u>leading</u> coefficient of 3. The <u>last</u> term is -12.

2. The numbers 3 and 2 are <u>factors</u> of the first term of the trinomial $6x^2 + x - 12$.

3. Consider $(x - 2)(5x - 1)$. The product of the <u>outer</u> terms is $-x$ and the product of the <u>inner</u> terms is $-10x$.

▶ **4.** When we write $2x^2 + 7x + 3$ as $(2x + 1)(x + 3)$, we say that we have <u>factored</u> the trinomial—it has been expressed as the product of two <u>binomials</u>.

5. The <u>middle</u> term of $4x^2 - 7x + 13$ is $-7x$.

6. The <u>sum</u> of the middle terms of the polynomial $4a^2 - 12a - a + 3$ is $-13a$.

7. The <u>GCF</u> of the terms of the trinomial $6b^3 - 3b^2 - 12b$ is $3b$.

8. When factoring the trinomial $ax^2 + bx + c$ by grouping, the product ac is called the <u>key</u> number.

CONCEPTS

Complete each sentence.

9.

These coefficients must be factors of 5 .

$$5x^2 + 6x - 8 = (\boxed{\ } x + \boxed{\ })(\boxed{\ } x + \boxed{\ })$$

These numbers must be factors of -8 .

▶ **10.**

The product of these coefficients must be 15 .

$$3x^2 + 16x + 5 = 3x^2 + \boxed{\ } x + \boxed{\ } x + 5$$

The sum of these coefficients must be 16 .

A trinomial has been partially factored. Complete each statement that describes the type of integers we should consider for the blanks.

11. $5y^2 - 13y + 6 = \left(5y \boxed{\ }\right)\left(y \boxed{\ }\right)$
Since the last term of the trinomial is <u>positive</u> and the middle term is <u>negative</u>, the integers must be <u>negative</u> factors of 6.

12. $5y^2 + 13y + 6 = \left(5y \boxed{\ }\right)\left(y \boxed{\ }\right)$
Since the last term of the trinomial is <u>positive</u> and the middle term is <u>positive</u>, the integers must be <u>positive</u> factors of 6.

13. $5y^2 + 7y - 6 = \left(5y \boxed{\ }\right)\left(y \boxed{\ }\right)$
Since the last term of the trinomial is <u>negative</u>, the signs of the integers will be <u>different</u>.

▶ **14.** $5y^2 - 7y - 6 = \left(5y \boxed{\ }\right)\left(y \boxed{\ }\right)$
Since the last term of the trinomial is <u>negative</u>, the signs of the integers will be <u>different</u>.

Complete each factorization.

15. $3a^2 + 13a + 4 = (3a + 1)(a + 4)$

16. $2b^2 + 7b + 6 = (2b + 3)(b + 2)$

17. $4z^2 - 13z + 3 = (z - 3)(4z - 1)$

18. $4t^2 - 4t + 1 = (2t - 1)(2t - 1)$

19. $2m^2 + 5m - 12 = (2m - 3)(m + 4)$

20. $10u^2 - 13u - 3 = (2u - 3)(5u + 1)$

A trinomial is to be factored by the grouping method. Complete each statement that describes the type of integers we should consider for the blanks.

21. $8c^2 - 11c + 3 = 8c^2 + \boxed{}c + \boxed{}c + 3$

We need to find two integers whose product is $\underline{24}$ and whose sum is $\underline{-11}$.

22. $15c^2 + 4c - 4 = 15c^2 + \boxed{}c + \boxed{}c - 4$

We need to find two integers whose product is $\underline{-60}$ and whose sum is $\underline{4}$.

Complete each step of the factorization by grouping.

23. $12t^2 + 17t + 6 = 12t^2 + \boxed{9}t + 8t + 6$

$= \boxed{3t}(4t + 3) + \boxed{2}(4t + 3)$

$= \left(\boxed{4t + 3}\right)(3t + 2)$

24. $35t^2 - 11t - 6 = 35t^2 + \boxed{10}t - 21t - 6$

$= 5t(7t + 2) - 3\left(\boxed{7t + 2}\right)$

$= \left(\boxed{7t + 2}\right)(5t - 3)$

▌ NOTATION

25. Write a trinomial of the form: $ax^2 + bx + c$

  a. where $a = 1$ $x^2 + 2x + 3$ (answers may vary)

  b. where $a \neq 1$ $2x^2 + 2x + 3$ (answers may vary)

▶ **26.** Write the terms of the trinomial $40 - t - 4t^2$ in descending powers of the variable. $-4t^2 - t + 40$

▌ GUIDED PRACTICE

Factor each trinomial. See Example 1.

27. $3a^2 + 13a + 4$
$(3a + 1)(a + 4)$

▶ **28.** $2b^2 + 7b + 6$
$(2b + 3)(b + 2)$

29. $4z^2 + 13z + 3$
$(z + 3)(4z + 1)$

30. $6y^2 + 7y + 2$
$(3y + 2)(2y + 1)$

Factor each trinomial. See Example 2.

31. $4t^2 - 4t + 1$
$(2t - 1)(2t - 1)$

32. $6x^2 - 7x + 2$
$(3x - 2)(2x - 1)$

33. $2x^2 - 3x + 1$
$(2x - 1)(x - 1)$

▶ **34.** $2y^2 - 7y + 3$
$(2y - 1)(y - 3)$

Factor each trinomial. See Example 3.

▶ **35.** $8u^2 - 2u - 15$
$(2u - 3)(4u + 5)$

36. $2x^2 - 3x - 2$
$(2x + 1)(x - 2)$

37. $12y^2 - y - 1$
$(4y + 1)(3y - 1)$

38. $10a^2 - 3a - 4$
$(5a - 4)(2a + 1)$

Factor each trinomial. See Example 4.

▶ **39.** $6r^2 + rs - 2s^2$
$(3r + 2s)(2r - s)$

40. $4a^2 - 4ab + b^2$
$(2a - b)(2a - b)$

41. $2b^2 - 5bc + 2c^2$
$(2b - c)(b - 2c)$

▶ **42.** $3m^2 + 5mn + 2n^2$
$(3m + 2n)(m + n)$

Factor each trinomial. See Example 5.

43. $4x^2 + 10x - 6$
$2(2x - 1)(x + 3)$

44. $9x^2 + 21x - 18$
$3(3x - 2)(x + 3)$

45. $-y^3 - 13y^2 - 12y$
$-y(y + 12)(y + 1)$

46. $-2xy^2 - 8xy + 24x$
$-2x(y + 6)(y - 2)$

47. $6x^3 - 15x^2 - 9x$
$3x(2x + 1)(x - 3)$

48. $9y^3 + 3y^2 - 6y$
$3y(3y - 2)(y + 1)$

49. $30r^5 + 63r^4 - 30r^3$
$3r^3(5r - 2)(2r + 5)$

▶ **50.** $6s^5 - 26s^4 - 20s^3$
$2s^3(3s + 2)(s - 5)$

Factor each trinomial by grouping. See Example 6.

51. $10y^2 - 3y - 1$
$(5y + 1)(2y - 1)$

52. $6m^2 + 19m + 3$
$(6m + 1)(m + 3)$

53. $12y^2 - 5y - 2$
$(3y - 2)(4y + 1)$

▶ **54.** $10x^2 + 21x - 10$
$(2x + 5)(5x - 2)$

Factor each trinomial by grouping. See Example 7.

55. $12y^4 + y^3 - y^2$
$y^2(3y + 1)(4y - 1)$

56. $36p^3 - 3p^2 - 18p$
$3p(4p - 3)(3p + 2)$

57. $-16m^3n - 20m^2n^2 - 6mn^3$
$-2mn(4m + 3n)(2m + n)$

▶ **58.** $-84x^4 - 100x^3y - 24x^2y^2$
$-4x^2(3x + y)(7x + 6y)$

▌ TRY IT YOURSELF

Completely factor each of the following expressions. If an expression is prime, so indicate.

▶ **59.** $4x^2 + 8x + 3$
$(2x + 3)(2x + 1)$

▶ **60.** $15t^2 - 34t + 8$
$(15t - 4)(t - 2)$

61. $7x^2 - 9x + 2$
$(7x - 2)(x - 1)$

62. $2m^2 + 5m - 10$
prime

▶ **63.** $10u^2 - 13u - 6$
prime

64. $-5t^2 - 13t - 6$
$-(5t + 3)(t + 2)$

▶ **65.** $-16y^2 - 10y - 1$
$-(8y + 1)(2y + 1)$

66. $-16m^2 + 14m - 3$
$-(8m - 3)(2m - 1)$

▶ **67.** $-16x^2 - 16x - 3$
$-(4x + 1)(4x + 3)$

68. $13x^2 + 24xy + 11y^2$
$(13x + 11y)(x + y)$

69. $4b^2 + 15bc - 4c^2$
$(4b - c)(b + 4c)$

70. $18a^2 + 31ab - 10b^2$
$(18a - 5b)(a + 2b)$

71. $12x^2 + 5xy - 3y^2$
$(4x + 3y)(3x - y)$

72. $-13x + 3x^2 - 10$
$(3x + 2)(x - 5)$

73. $-14 + 3a^2 - a$
$(3a - 7)(a + 2)$

74. $15 + 8a^2 - 26a$
$(2a - 5)(4a - 3)$

75. $16 - 40a + 25a^2$
$(5a - 4)(5a - 4)$

76. $2a^2 + 3b^2 + 5ab$
$(2a + 3b)(a + b)$

77. $11uv + 3u^2 + 6v^2$
$(3u + 2v)(u + 3v)$

78. $pq + 6p^2 - q^2$
$(3p - q)(2p + q)$

Choose the correct method from sections 6.1, 6.2, or 6.3 to factor completely each of the following expressions. If an expression is prime, so indicate.

79. $12y^2 + 12 - 25y$
$(4y - 3)(3y - 4)$

80. $18t^3 - 30t^2$
$6t^2(3t - 5)$

81. $6x^2 - 15x + 2xy - 5y$
$(3x + y)(2x - 5)$

82. $12t^2 - 1 - 4t$
$(6t + 1)(2t - 1)$

83. $6a^2 - 10 - 11a$
$(3a + 2)(2a - 5)$

84. $3x^2 + 6 + x$
prime

85. $12p^2 + 5pq - 2q^2$
$(3p + 2q)(4p - q)$

▶ **86.** $25 + 2u^2 + 3u$
prime

87. $-3a^3 - 6a^2 + 9a$
$-3a(a + 3)(a - 1)$

88. $3m^2 + 4m - 6mn - 8n$
$(m - 2n)(3m + 4)$

89. $-28u^3v^3 + 26u^2v^4 - 6uv^5$ $-2uv^3(7u - 3v)(2u - v)$

90. $9t^3 + 33t^2 - 12t$ $3t(t + 4)(3t - 1)$

91. $-16x^4y^3 + 30x^3y^4 + 4x^2y^5$ $-2x^2y^3(8x + y)(x - 2y)$

92. $22pq + 6p^2 + 12q^2$ $2(3p + 2q)(p + 3q)$

▶ **93.** $-11mn + 12m^2 + 2n^2$ $(3m - 2n)(4m - n)$

94. $-18b + 36b^3 - 3b^2$ $3b(4b - 3)(3b + 2)$

APPLICATIONS

▶ **95.** OFFICE FURNITURE The area of the desktop shown below is given by the expression $(4x^2 + 20x - 11)$ in.². Factor this expression to find the expressions that represent its length and width. Then determine the difference in the length and width of the desktop. $(2x + 11)$ in., $(2x - 1)$ in.; 12 in.

▶ **96.** STORAGE The volume of the 8-foot-wide portable storage container shown below is given by the expression $(72x^2 + 120x - 400)$ ft³. If its dimensions can be determined by factoring the expression, find the height and the length of the container. $(3x - 5)$ ft, $(3x + 10)$ ft

WRITING

97. A student begins to factor a trinomial as shown below. Explain why the student is off to a bad start.

$$3x^2 - 5x - 2 = \left(3x - \boxed{}\right)\left(x - \boxed{}\right)$$

98. Two students factor $2x^2 + 20x + 42$ and get two different answers:

$$(2x + 6)(x + 7) \quad \text{and} \quad (x + 3)(2x + 14)$$

Do both answers check? Why don't they agree? Is either answer completely correct? Explain.

99. Why is the process of factoring $6x^2 - 5x - 6$ more complicated than the process of factoring $x^2 - 5x - 6$?

▶ **100.** How can the factorization shown below be checked?

$$6x^2 - 5x - 6 = (3x + 2)(2x - 3)$$

REVIEW

101. Simplify: $(x^2x^5)^2$ x^{14}

102. Simplify: $\dfrac{(a^3b^4)^2}{ab^5}$ a^5b^3

103. Evaluate: $\dfrac{1}{2^{-3}}$ 8

104. Evaluate: 7^0 1

Objectives

1. Recognize perfect-square trinomials.

2. Factor perfect-square trinomials.

3. Factor the difference of two squares.

SECTION **6.4**

Factoring Perfect-Square Trinomials and the Difference of Two Squares

In this section, we will discuss a method that can be used to factor two types of trinomials, called *perfect-square trinomials*. We also develop techniques for factoring a type of binomial called the *difference of two squares*.

1 Recognize perfect-square trinomials.

We have seen that the square of a binomial is a trinomial. We have also seen that the special-product rules shown below can be used to quickly find the square of a sum and the square of a difference. The terms of the resulting trinomial are related to the terms of the binomial that was squared.

$$(A + B)^2 = \qquad A^2 \qquad + \qquad 2AB \qquad + \qquad B^2$$

This is the square of the first term of the binomial.

This is twice the product of the terms of the binomial.

This is the square of the last term of the binomial.

$$(A - B)^2 = \qquad A^2 \qquad - \qquad 2AB \qquad + \qquad B^2$$

Trinomials that are squares of a binomial are called **perfect-square trinomials.** Some examples are

$y^2 + 6y + 9$ — Because it is the square of $(y + 3)$: $(y + 3)^2 = y^2 + 6y + 9$

$t^2 - 14t + 49$ — Because it is the square of $(t - 7)$: $(t - 7)^2 = t^2 - 14t + 49$

$4m^2 - 20m + 25$ — Because it is the square of $(2m - 5)$: $(2m - 5)^2 = 4m^2 - 20m + 25$

EXAMPLE 1 Determine whether the following are perfect-square trinomials: **a.** $x^2 + 10x + 25$ **b.** $c^2 - 12c - 36$ **c.** $25y^2 - 30y + 9$ **d.** $4t^2 + 18t + 81$

Strategy We will compare each trinomial, term-by-term, to one of the special-product forms discussed above.

WHY If a trinomial matches one of these forms, it is a perfect-square trinomial.

Solution

a. To determine whether this is a perfect-square trinomial, we note that

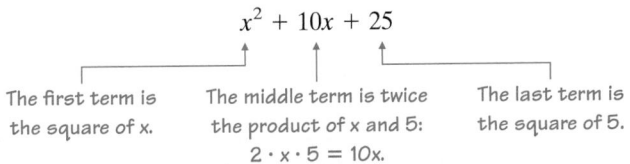

$$x^2 + 10x + 25$$

The first term is the square of x.

The middle term is twice the product of x and 5: $2 \cdot x \cdot 5 = 10x$.

The last term is the square of 5.

Thus, $x^2 + 10x + 25$ is a perfect-square trinomial.

b. To determine whether this is a perfect-square trinomial, we note that

$$c^2 - 12c - 36$$

The last term, -36, is not the square of a real number.

Since the last term is negative, $c^2 - 12c - 36$ is not a perfect-square trinomial.

c. To determine whether this is a perfect-square trinomial, we note that

$$25y^2 - 30y + 9$$

The first term is the square of 5y.

The middle term is twice the product of 5y and -3: $2(5y)(-3) = -30y$.

The last term is the square of -3.

Thus, $25y^2 - 30y + 9$ is a perfect-square trinomial.

Self Check 1

Determine whether the following are perfect-square trinomials:
a. $y^2 + 4y + 4$ yes
b. $b^2 - 6b - 9$ no
c. $4z^2 + 4z + 4$ no
d. $49x^2 - 28x + 16$ no

Now Try Problems 25, 29, and 32

Teaching Example 1 Determine whether the following are perfect-square trinomials:
a. $x^2 + 14x + 49$
b. $4x^2 - 20x + 25$
c. $x^2 - 10x - 25$
Answers:
a. yes **b.** yes **c.** no

> **The Language of Algebra**   The expressions $25y^2$ and 9 are called *perfect squares* because $25y^2 = (5y)^2$ and $9 = 3^2$.

d. To determine whether this is a perfect-square trinomial, we note that

$$4t^2 + 18t + 81$$

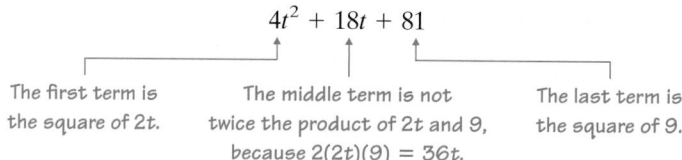

The first term is	The middle term is not	The last term is
the square of 2t.	twice the product of 2t and 9,	the square of 9.
	because 2(2t)(9) = 36t.	

Thus, $4t^2 + 18t + 81$ is not a perfect-square trinomial.   ∎

2 Factor perfect-square trinomials.

We can factor perfect-square trinomials using the methods previously discussed in Sections 6.2 and 6.3. However, in many cases, we can factor them more quickly by inspecting their terms and applying the special-product rules in reverse.

Factoring Perfect-Square Trinomials

$$A^2 + 2AB + B^2 = (A + B)^2$$ Each of these trinomials factors as the square of a binomial.

$$A^2 - 2AB + B^2 = (A - B)^2$$

When factoring perfect-square trinomials, it is helpful to know the integers that are perfect squares. The number 400, for example, is a perfect-integer square, because $400 = 20^2$.

$1 = 1^2$	$25 = 5^2$	$81 = 9^2$	$169 = 13^2$	$289 = 17^2$
$4 = 2^2$	$36 = 6^2$	$100 = 10^2$	$196 = 14^2$	$324 = 18^2$
$9 = 3^2$	$49 = 7^2$	$121 = 11^2$	$225 = 15^2$	$361 = 19^2$
$16 = 4^2$	$64 = 8^2$	$144 = 12^2$	$256 = 16^2$	$400 = 20^2$

Self Check 2

Factor:
a. $x^2 + 18x + 81$ $(x + 9)^2$
b. $16x^2 - 8xy + y^2$ $(4x - y)^2$

Now Try Problems 33 and 35

Teaching Example 2 Factor:
a. $x^2 - 22x + 121$
b. $x^2 + 16x + 64$
c. $4x^2 - 20xy + 25y^2$
Answers:
a. $(x - 11)^2$ **b.** $(x + 8)^2$
c. $(2x - 5y)^2$

EXAMPLE 2   Factor: **a.** $x^2 + 20x + 100$ **b.** $9x^2 - 30xy + 25y^2$

Strategy The terms of each trinomial do not have a common factor (other than 1). We will determine whether each is a perfect-square trinomial.

WHY If it is, we can factor it using a special-product rule in reverse.

Solution
a. $x^2 + 20x + 100$ is a perfect-square trinomial, because:

- The first term x^2 is the square of x.

- The last term 100 is the square of **10**.

- The middle term is twice the product of x and **10**: $2(x)(10) = 20x$.

To find the factorization, we match $x^2 + 20x + 100$ to the proper rule for factoring a perfect-square trinomial.

$$A^2 + 2 \quad A \quad B + B^2 = (A + B)^2$$
$$x^2 + 20x + 10^2 = x^2 + 2 \cdot x \cdot 10 + 10^2 = (x + 10)^2$$

Therefore, $x^2 + 20x + 10^2 = (x + 10)^2$. Check by finding $(x + 10)^2$.

b. $9x^2 - 30xy + 25y^2$ is a perfect-square trinomial, because:

- The first term $9x^2$ is the square of **3x**: $(3x)^2 = 9x^2$.
- The last term $25y^2$ is the square of **−5y**: $(-5y)^2 = 25y^2$.
- The middle term is twice the product of **3x** and **−5y**: $2(3x)(-5y) = -30xy$.

We can use these observations to write the trinomial in one of the special-product forms that then leads to its factorization.

$$9x^2 - 30xy + 25y^2 = (3x)^2 - 2(3x)(5y) + (-5y)^2 \quad -2(3x)(5y) = 2(3x)(-5y)$$
$$= (3x - 5y)^2$$

Therefore, $9x^2 - 30xy + 25y^2 = (3x - 5y)^2$. Check by finding $(3x - 5y)^2$. ∎

Success Tip   The sign of the middle term of a perfect-square trinomial is the same as the sign of the second term of the squared binomial.

$$A^2 + 2AB + B^2 = (A + B)^2$$
$$A^2 - 2AB + B^2 = (A - B)^2$$

EXAMPLE 3   Factor completely: $4a^3 - 4a^2 + a$

Strategy We will factor out the GCF, a, first. Then we will factor the resulting perfect-square trinomial using a special-product rule in reverse.

WHY The first step in factoring any polynomial is to factor out the GCF.

Solution
The terms of $4a^3 - 4a^2 + a$ have the common factor a, which should be factored out first. Within the parentheses, we recognize $4a^2 - 4a + 1$ as a perfect square trinomial of the form $A^2 - 2AB + B^2$, and factor it as such.

$$4a^3 - 4a^2 + a = a(4a^2 - 4a + 1) \quad \text{Factor out } a.$$
$$= a(2a - 1)^2 \quad 4a^2 = (2a)^2, 1 = (-1)^2, \text{ and } -4a = 2(2a)(-1). \blacksquare$$

Self Check 3

Factor completely:
$49x^3 - 14x^2 + x \quad x(7x - 1)^2$

Now Try **Problem 41**

Teaching Example 3 Factor
completely: $9x^3 - 6x^2 + x$
Answer:
$x(3x - 1)^2$

3 Factor the difference of two squares.

Recall the special-product rule for multiplying the sum and difference of the same two terms:

$$(A + B)(A - B) = A^2 - B^2$$

The binomial $A^2 - B^2$ is called a **difference of two squares,** because A^2 is the square of A and B^2 is the square of B. If we reverse this rule, we obtain a method for factoring a difference of two squares.

Factoring $\longrightarrow$
$$A^2 - B^2 = (A + B)(A - B)$$

This pattern is easy to remember if we think of a difference of two squares as the square of a **F**irst quantity minus the square of a **L**ast quantity.

The Language of Algebra   The expression $A^2 - B^2$ is a *difference of two squares,* whereas $(A - B)^2$ is the *square of a difference.* They are not equivalent because $(A - B)^2 \neq A^2 - B^2$.

> ### Factoring a Difference of Two Squares
>
> To factor the square of a First quantity minus the square of a Last quantity, multiply the First plus the Last by the First minus the Last.
>
> $$F^2 - L^2 = (F + L)(F - L)$$

Self Check 4

Factor, if possible:
a. $c^2 - 4$ $(c + 2)(c - 2)$
b. $121 - t^2$ $(11 + t)(11 - t)$
c. $x^2 - 24$ prime
d. $s^2 + 36$ prime

Now Try **Problems 45 and 53**

Teaching Example 4 Factor, if possible:
a. $a^2 - 121$ **b.** $25 - x^2$
c. $x^2 + 36$ **d.** $x^2 - 8$
Answers:
a. $(a + 11)(a - 11)$
b. $(5 + x)(5 - x)$
c. prime
d. prime

EXAMPLE 4   Factor, if possible:
a. $x^2 - 9$ **b.** $16 - b^2$ **c.** $n^2 - 45$ **d.** $a^2 + 81$

Strategy The terms of each binomial do not have a common factor (other than 1). The only option available is to attempt to factor each as a difference of two squares.

WHY If a binomial is a difference of two squares, we can factor it using a special-product rule in reverse.

Solution

a. $x^2 - 9$ is the difference of two squares because it can be written as $x^2 - 3^2$. We can match it to the rule for factoring a difference of two squares to find the factorization.

$$\begin{array}{ccccccc} F^2 & - & L^2 & = & (F & + & L)(F & - & L) \\ \downarrow & & \downarrow & & \downarrow & & \downarrow & & \downarrow \\ x^2 & - & 3^2 & = & (x & + & 3)(x & - & 3) \end{array} \quad \text{9 is a perfect-integer square: } 9 = 3^2.$$

Therefore, $x^2 - 9 = (x + 3)(x - 3)$.

Check by multiplying: $(x + 3)(x - 3) = x^2 - 9$.

b. $16 - b^2$ is the difference of two squares because $16 - b^2 = 4^2 - b^2$. Therefore,

$$16 - b^2 = (4 + b)(4 - b) \quad \text{16 is a perfect-integer square: } 16 = 4^2.$$

Check by multiplying.

c. Since 45 is not a perfect-integer square, $n^2 - 45$ cannot be factored using integers. It is prime.

d. $a^2 + 81$ can be written $a^2 + 9^2$, and is, therefore, the **sum of two squares.** We might attempt to factor $a^2 + 81$ as $(a + 9)(a + 9)$ or $(a - 9)(a - 9)$. However, the following checks show that neither product is $a^2 + 81$.

$$(a + 9)(a + 9) = a^2 + 18a + 81 \qquad (a - 9)(a - 9) = a^2 - 18a + 81$$

In general, the sum of two squares (with no common factor other than 1) cannot be factored using real numbers. Thus, $a^2 + 81$ is prime.

Terms containing variables such as $25x^2$ and $4y^4$ are perfect squares, because they can be written as the square of a quantity. For example:

$$25x^2 = (5x)^2 \qquad \text{and} \qquad 4y^4 = (2y^2)^2$$

Self Check 5

Factor:
a. $16y^2 - 9$ $(4y + 3)(4y - 3)$
b. $9m^2 - 64n^4$ $(3m + 8n^2)(3m - 8n^2)$

Now Try **Problems 57 and 59**

EXAMPLE 5   Factor: **a.** $25x^2 - 49$ **b.** $4y^4 - 121z^2$

Strategy In each case, the terms of the binomial do not have a common factor (other than 1). To factor them, we will write each binomial in a form that clearly shows it is a difference of two squares.

WHY We can then use a special-product rule in reverse to factor it.

Solution

a. We can write $25x^2 - 49$ in the form $(5x)^2 - 7^2$ and match it to the rule for factoring the difference of two squares:

$$F^2 \ -L^2 = (\ F \ + \ L)(\ F-L)$$
$$\downarrow \quad \downarrow \quad\quad \downarrow \quad \downarrow \quad \downarrow \quad \downarrow$$
$$(5x)^2- 7^2 = (5x \ + \ 7)(5x- 7)$$

Therefore, $25x^2 - 49 = (5x + 7)(5x - 7)$. Check by multiplying.

b. We can write $4y^4 - 121z^2$ in the form $(2y^2)^2 - (11z)^2$ and match it to the rule for factoring the difference of two squares:

$$F^2 \ - \ L^2 \ = (\ F \ + \ L \ )(\ F \ - \ L \ )$$
$$\downarrow \quad\quad \downarrow \quad\quad \downarrow \quad \downarrow \quad \downarrow \quad \downarrow$$
$$(2y^2)^2-(11z)^2 = (2y^2 \ + \ 11z)(2y^2-11z)$$

Therefore, $4y^4 - 121z^2 = (2y^2 + 11z)(2y^2 - 11z)$. Check by multiplying.

> **Success Tip** Remember that a *difference of two squares* is a binomial. Each term is a square and the terms have different signs. The powers of the variables in the terms must be even.

EXAMPLE 6   Factor completely: $8x^2 - 8$

Strategy We will factor out the GCF, 8, first. Then we will factor the resulting difference of two squares.

WHY The first step in factoring any polynomial is to factor out the GCF.

Solution

$$8x^2 - 8 = 8(x^2 - 1) \qquad \text{The GCF is 8.}$$
$$= 8(x + 1)(x - 1) \qquad \text{Think of } x^2 - 1 \text{ as } x^2 - 1^2 \text{ and factor the difference of}$$
$$\text{two squares.}$$

Check: $8(x + 1)(x - 1) = 8(x^2 - 1)$ Multiply the binomials first.
$$= 8x^2 - 8 \qquad \text{Distribute the multiplication by 8.}$$

Teaching Example 5 Factor:
a. $36a^2 - 25$
b. $9x^4 - 49y^2$
Answers:
a. $(6a + 5)(6a - 5)$
b. $(3x^2 + 7y)(3x^2 - 7y)$

Self Check 6

Factor completely: $4x^2 - 400$

Now Try **Problem 65**
Self Check 6 Answer
$4(x + 10)(x - 10)$

Teaching Example 6 Factor completely: $18x^2 - 32$
Answer:
$2(3x + 4)(3x - 4)$

ANSWERS TO SELF CHECKS

1. a. yes **b.** no **c.** no **d.** no **2. a.** $(x + 9)^2$ **b.** $(4x - y)^2$ **3.** $x(7x - 1)^2$
4. a. $(c + 2)(c - 2)$ **b.** $(11 + t)(11 - t)$ **c.** prime **d.** prime
5. a. $(4y + 3)(4y - 3)$ **b.** $(3m + 8n^2)(3m - 8n^2)$ **6.** $4(x + 10)(x - 10)$

SECTION 6.4   STUDY SET

▌VOCABULARY

Fill in the blanks.

▶ **1.** $x^2 + 6x + 9$ is a __perfect__-square trinomial because it is the square of the binomial $x + 3$.

▶ **2.** The binomial $x^2 - 25$ is called a __difference__ of two squares.

▶ Selected exercises available online at
www.webassign.net/brookscole

CONCEPTS

Fill in the blanks.

3. Consider: $25x^2 + 30x + 9$
   a. The first term is the square of $5x$.
   b. The last term is the square of 3.
   c. The middle term is twice the product of $5x$ and 3.

4. Consider: $49x^2 - 28xy + 4y^2$
   a. The first term is the square of $7x$.
   b. The last term is the square of $-2y$.
   c. The middle term is twice the product of $7x$ and $-2y$.

5. If a trinomial is the square of one quantity, plus the square of a second quantity, plus ___twice___ the product of the quantities, it factors into the square of the ___sum___ of the quantities.

6. Explain why each trinomial is not a perfect-square trinomial.
   a. $9h^2 - 6h + 7$ 7 is not a perfect square.
   b. $j^2 - 8j - 16$ The sign of the last term must be positive.
   c. $25r^2 + 20r + 16$ The middle term is not twice the product of 5r and 4.

7. List the first ten perfect integer squares. 1, 4, 9, 16, 25, 36, 49, 64, 81, 100

8. To factor the square of a First quantity minus the square of a Last quantity, we multiply the ___First___ plus the ___Last___ by the ___First___ minus the ___Last___.

9. a. $36x^2 = \left(6x\right)^2$ b. $100x^4 = \left(10x^2\right)^2$
   c. $4x^2 - 9 = \left(2x\right)^2 - \left(3\right)^2$

10. a. Three incorrect factorizations of $x^2 + 36$ are given below. Explain why each one is wrong.

    $(x + 6)(x - 6)$ $x^2 - 36$
    $(x + 6)(x + 6)$ $x^2 + 12x + 36$
    $(x - 6)(x - 6)$ $x^2 - 12x + 36$

    b. Can $x^2 + 36$ be factored using only integer coefficients? no

Complete each factorization.

11. $a^2 - 6a + 9 = \left(a - 3\right)^2$

12. $t^2 + 2t + 1 = \left(t + 1\right)^2$

13. $4x^2 + 4x + 1 = \left(2x + 1\right)^2$

14. $9y^2 - 12y + 4 = \left(3y - 2\right)^2$

15. $y^2 - 49 = \left(y + 7\right)\left(y - 7\right)$

16. $p^4 - q^2 = (p^2 + q)\left(p^2 - q\right)$

17. $t^2 - w^2 = \left(t + w\right)(t - w)$

18. $49u^2 - 64v^2 = \left(7u + 8v\right)\left(7u - 8v\right)$

NOTATION

Write each expression as a polynomial in simpler form.

19. $(3a)^2 - 2(3a)(5b) + (5b)^2$ $9a^2 - 30ab + 25b^2$
20. $(2s)^2 + 2(2s)(9t) + (9t)^2$ $4s^2 + 36st + 81t^2$
21. $(6x)^2 - (5y)^2$ $36x^2 - 25y^2$ 22. $(4x)^2 - (9y)^2$ $16x^2 - 81y^2$

Use an exponent to write each expression in simpler form.

23. $(x + 8)(x + 8)$ $(x + 8)^2$ ▶ 24. $(x - 8)(x - 8)$ $(x - 8)^2$

GUIDED PRACTICE

Determine whether the following expressions are perfect-square trinomials. **See Example 1.**

25. $x^2 + 18x + 81$ yes   26. $x^2 + 14x + 49$ yes
27. $y^2 + 2y + 4$ no   28. $y^2 + 4y + 16$ no
▶ 29. $9n^2 - 30n - 25$ no   30. $9a^2 - 48a - 64$ no
31. $4y^2 - 12y + 9$ yes   32. $9x^2 - 30x + 25$ yes

Factor each polynomial. **See Example 2.**

33. $x^2 + 6x + 9$ ▶ 34. $x^2 + 10x + 25$
    $(x + 3)^2$ $(x + 5)^2$
35. $t^2 - 20t + 100$ ▶ 36. $r^2 + 24r + 144$
    $(t - 10)^2$ $(r + 12)^2$
37. $a^2 + 2ab + b^2$ 38. $a^2 - 2ab + b^2$
    $(a + b)^2$ $(a - b)^2$
39. $16x^2 - 8xy + y^2$ ▶ 40. $25x^2 + 20xy + 4y^2$
    $(4x - y)^2$ $(5x + 2y)^2$

Factor each polynomial. **See Example 3.**

41. $y^3 - 8y^2 + 16y$ 42. $u^4 - 18u^3 + 81u^2$
    $y(y - 4)^2$ $u^2(u - 9)^2$
▶ 43. $8x^3 + 24x^2 + 18x$ 44. $108x^3 + 36x^2 + 3x$
    $2x(2x + 3)^2$ $3x(6x + 1)^2$

Factor each polynomial. If a polynomial is prime, so indicate. **See Example 4.**

45. $x^2 - 16$ ▶ 46. $x^2 - 25$
    $(x + 4)(x - 4)$ $(x + 5)(x - 5)$
47. $t^2 - 49$ 48. $m^2 - 121$
    $(t + 7)(t - 7)$ $(m + 11)(m - 11)$
49. $49 - c^2$ 50. $81 - t^2$
    $(7 + c)(7 - c)$ $(9 + t)(9 - t)$
51. $144 - 25a^2$ 52. $169 - 9t^2$
    $(12 + 5a)(12 - 5a)$ $(13 + 3t)(13 - 3t)$
53. $p^2 - 54$ 54. $q^2 - 20$
    prime   prime
55. $a^2 + b^2$ 56. $121a^2 + 144b^2$
    prime   prime

Factor each polynomial. **See Example 5.**

57. $4y^2 - 1$
$(2y + 1)(2y - 1)$

▶ **58.** $9z^2 - 1$
$(3z + 1)(3z - 1)$

59. $49a^2 - 169$
$(7a + 13)(7a - 13)$

60. $16b^2 - 225$
$(4b + 15)(4b - 15)$

61. $9x^2 - y^2$
$(3x + y)(3x - y)$

62. $4x^2 - z^2$
$(2x + z)(2x - z)$

63. $16a^2 - 25b^2$
$(4a + 5b)(4a - 5b)$

64. $36a^2 - 121b^2$
$(6a + 11b)(6a - 11b)$

Factor each polynomial. **See Example 6.**

65. $8a^2 - 32$
$8(a + 2)(a - 2)$

66. $2p^2 - 200$
$2(p + 10)(p - 10)$

67. $7 - 7a^2$
$7(1 + a)(1 - a)$

▶ **68.** $5 - 20x^2$
$5(1 + 2x)(1 - 2x)$

TRY IT YOURSELF

Factor each expression completely.

▶ **69.** $z^2 - 2z + 1$
$(z - 1)^2$

▶ **70.** $v^2 - 14v + 49$
$(v - 7)^2$

▶ **71.** $4x^2 - 4x + 1$
$(2x - 1)^2$

▶ **72.** $4x^2 - 20x + 25$
$(2x - 5)^2$

73. $a^4 - 144b^2$
$(a^2 + 12b)(a^2 - 12b)$

▶ **74.** $81y^4 - 100z^2$
$(9y^2 + 10z)(9y^2 - 10z)$

75. $t^2z^2 - 64$
$(tz + 8)(tz - 8)$

76. $900 - B^2C^2$
$(30 + BC)(30 - BC)$

77. $6x^4 - 6x^2y^2$
$6x^2(x + y)(x - y)$

▶ **78.** $4b^2y - 16c^2y$
$4y(b + 2c)(b - 2c)$

79. $a^2b^2 - 144$
$(ab + 12)(ab - 12)$

80. $20m^2 + 100m + 125$
$5(2m + 5)^2$

81. $16 - 40z + 25z^2$
$(5z - 4)^2$

82. $49p^2 + 28pq + 4q^2$
$(7p + 2q)^2$

83. $16x^2 - 40x^3 + 25x^4$
$x^2(5x - 4)^2$

84. $8a^2x^3y - 2b^2xy$
$2xy(2ax + b)(2ax - b)$

Choose the correct method from Section 6.1, 6.2, 6.3, or 6.4 to factor completely each of the following expressions:

85. $8x^2 - 32y^2$
$8(x + 2y)(x - 2y)$

86. $2a^2 - 200b^2$
$2(a + 10b)(a - 10b)$

87. $8m^2n^3 - 24mn^4$
$8mn^3(m - 3n)$

88. $3rs + 6r^2 - 18s^2$
$3(2r - 3s)(r + 2s)$

89. $x^2 + 7x + 1$
prime

90. $14t^3 - 40t^2 + 6t^4$
$2t^2(3t - 5)(t + 4)$

91. $-9x^2y^2 + 6xy - 1$
$-(3xy - 1)^2$

92. $2c^2 - 5cd - 3d^2$
$(2c + d)(c - 3d)$

93. $2ac + 4ad + bc + 2bd$
$(c + 2d)(2a + b)$

94. $10r^2 - 13r - 4$
prime

95. $6x^2 - x - 16$
prime

96. $4x^2 + 9y^2$
prime

97. $6a^3 + 35a^2 - 6a$
$a(6a - 1)(a + 6)$

98. $21t^3 - 10t^2 + t$
$t(7t - 1)(3t - 1)$

99. $70p^4q^3 - 35p^4q^2 + 49p^5q^2$ $7p^4q^2(10q - 5 + 7p)$

100. $2ab^2 + 8ab - 24a$ $2a(b + 6)(b - 2)$

101. $a^2c + a^2d^2 + bc + bd^2$ $(c + d^2)(a^2 + b)$

102. $-8p^3q^7 - 4p^2q^3$ $-4p^2q^3(2pq^4 + 1)$

APPLICATIONS

▶ **103.** GENETICS The Hardy–Weinberg equation, one of the fundamental concepts in population genetics, is

$$p^2 + 2pq + q^2 = 1$$

where p represents the frequency of a certain dominant gene and q represents the frequency of a certain recessive gene. Factor the left-hand side of the equation. $(p + q)^2$

▶ **104.** SPACE TRAVEL The surface area of the spherical part of the spacecraft shown below is given by $(36\pi r^2 - 48\pi r + 16\pi)$ m^2. Factor the expression. $4\pi(3r - 2)^2$ m^2

▶ **105.** PHYSICS The illustration shows a time-sequence picture of a falling apple. Factor the expression, which gives the distance the apple falls during the time interval from t_1 to t_2 seconds.
$0.5g(t_1 + t_2)(t_1 - t_2)$

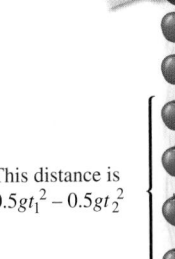

This distance is $0.5gt_1^2 - 0.5gt_2^2$

▶ **106.** DARTS A circular dart board has a series of rings around a solid center, called the bulls'-eye. To find the area of the outer black ring, we can use the formula

$$A = \pi R^2 - \pi r^2$$

Factor the expression on the right side of the equation. $\pi(R + r)(R - r)$

❙ WRITING

107. When asked to factor $x^2 - 25$, one student wrote $(x + 5)(x - 5)$, and another student wrote $(x - 5)(x + 5)$. Are both answers correct? Explain.

108. Explain the error in the factorization shown below:

$$4x^2 - 16y^2 = (2x + 4y)(2x - 4y)$$

❙ REVIEW

Perform each division.

109. $\dfrac{5x^2 + 10y^2 - 15xy}{5xy}$ $\dfrac{x}{y} + \dfrac{2y}{x} - 3$

▶ **110.** $\dfrac{-30c^2d^2 - 15c^2d - 10cd^2}{-10cd}$ $3cd + \dfrac{3c}{2} + d$

111. $2a - 1\overline{)a - 2 + 6a^2}$ $3a + 2$

112. $4b + 3\overline{)4b^3 - 5b^2 - 2b + 3}$ $b^2 - 2b + 1$

Objective

1 Factor the sum and difference of two cubes.

SECTION **6.5**

Factoring the Sum and Difference of Two Cubes

In this section we will discuss how to factor two types of binomials, called the *sum* and the *difference of two cubes.*

1 Factor the sum and difference of two cubes.

We have seen that the sum of two squares, such as $x^2 + 4$ or $25a^2 + 9b^2$, cannot be factored. However, the sum of two cubes and the difference of two cubes can be factored.

The sum of two cubes

$$x^3 + 8$$

This is x cubed.   This is 2 cubed: $2^3 = 8$.

The difference of two cubes

$$a^3 - 64b^3$$

This is a cubed.   This is 4b cubed: $(4b)^3 = 64b^3$.

To find rules for factoring the sum of two cubes and the difference of two cubes, we need to find the products shown below. Note that each term of the trinomial is multiplied by each term of the binomial.

$$(x + y)(x^2 - xy + y^2) = x^3 - x^2y + xy^2 + x^2y - xy^2 + y^3$$
$$= x^3 + y^3 \quad \text{Combine like terms: } -x^2y + x^2y = 0 \text{ and } xy^2 - xy^2 = 0.$$

> **The Language of Algebra** The expression $x^3 + y^3$ is a *sum of two cubes*, whereas $(x + y)^3$ is the *cube of a sum*. If you expand $(x + y)^3$, you will see that $(x + y)^3 \neq x^3 + y^3$.

$$(x - y)(x^2 + xy + y^2) = x^3 + x^2y + xy^2 - x^2y - xy^2 - y^3$$
$$= x^3 - y^3 \quad \text{Combine like terms.}$$

These results justify the rules for factoring the **sum and difference of two cubes.** They are easier to remember if we think of a sum (or a difference) of two cubes as the cube of a **F**irst quantity plus (or minus) the cube of the **L**ast quantity.

Factoring the Sum and Difference of Two Cubes

To factor the cube of a **F**irst quantity plus the cube of a **L**ast quantity, multiply the **F**irst plus the **L**ast by the **F**irst squared, minus the **F**irst times the **L**ast, plus the **L**ast squared.

$$F^3 + L^3 = (F + L)(F^2 - FL + L^2)$$

To factor the cube of a **F**irst quantity minus the cube of a **L**ast quantity, multiply the **F**irst minus the **L**ast by the **F**irst squared, plus the **F**irst times the **L**ast, plus the **L**ast squared.

$$F^3 - L^3 = (F - L)(F^2 + FL + L^2)$$

To factor the sum or difference of two cubes, it is helpful to know the cubes of integers from 1 to 10. The number 216, for example, is a **perfect-integer cube,** because $216 = 6^3$.

$1 = 1^3$	$27 = 3^3$	$125 = 5^3$	$343 = 7^3$	$729 = 9^3$
$8 = 2^3$	$64 = 4^3$	$216 = 6^3$	$512 = 8^3$	$1{,}000 = 10^3$

EXAMPLE 1   Factor: $x^3 + 8$

Strategy We will write $x^3 + 8$ in a form that clearly shows it is the sum of two cubes.

WHY We can then use the rule for factoring the sum of two cubes.

Solution

$x^3 + 8$ is the sum of two cubes because it can be written as $x^3 + 2^3$. We can match it to the rule for factoring the sum of two cubes to find its factorization.

$$F^3 + L^3 = (F + L)(F^2 - F \cdot L + L^2)$$

To write the trinomial factor:
· Square the first term of the binomial factor.
· Multiply the terms of the binomial factor.
· Square the last term of the binomial factor.

$$x^3 + 2^3 = (x + 2)(x^2 - x \cdot 2 + 2^2)$$
$$= (x + 2)(x^2 - 2x + 4) \quad x^2 - 2x + 4 \text{ does not factor.}$$

Therefore, $x^3 + 8 = (x + 2)(x^2 - 2x + 4)$. We can check by multiplying.

$$(x + 2)(x^2 - 2x + 4) = x^3 - 2x^2 + 4x + 2x^2 - 4x + 8$$
$$= x^3 + 8 \quad \text{This is the original binomial.}$$

Caution! A common error is to try to factor $x^2 - 2x + 4$. It is not a perfect square trinomial, because the middle term needs to be $-4x$. Furthermore, it cannot be factored by the methods of Section 6.2. It is prime.

Self Check 1

Factor: $h^3 + 27$

Now Try **Problem 17**
Self Check 1 Answer
$(h + 3)(h^2 - 3h + 9)$

Teaching Example 1 Factor: $y^3 + 125$
Answer:
$(y + 5)(y^2 - 5y + 25)$

Terms containing variables such as $64b^3$ and m^6 are also perfect cubes, because they can be written as the cube of a quantity:

$$64b^3 = (4b)^3 \qquad \text{and} \qquad m^6 = (m^2)^3$$

EXAMPLE 2   Factor: $a^3 - 64b^3$

Strategy We will write $a^3 - 64b^3$ in a form that clearly shows it is the difference of two cubes.

WHY We can then use the rule for factoring the difference of two cubes.

Solution

$a^3 - 64b^3$ is the difference of two cubes because it can be written as $a^3 - (4b)^3$. We can match it to the rule for factoring the difference of two cubes to find its factorization.

$$F^3 - L^3 = (F - L)(F^2 + F\ L + L^2)$$
$$a^3 - (4b)^3 = (a - 4b)[a^2 + a \cdot 4b + (4b)^2]$$
$$= (a - 4b)(a^2 + 4ab + 16b^2) \quad a^2 + 4ab + 16b^2 \text{ does not factor.}$$

Therefore, $a^3 - 64b^3 = (a - 4b)(a^2 + 4ab + 16b^2)$. Check by multiplying.

You should memorize the rules for factoring the sum and the difference of two cubes. Note that the right side of each rule has the form

(a binomial)(a trinomial)

and that there is a relationship between the signs that appear in these forms.

The Sum of Two Cubes   ***The Difference of Two Cubes***

$$F^3 + L^3 = (F + L)(F^2 - FL + L^2) \qquad F^3 - L^3 = (F - L)(F^2 + FL + L^2)$$

The same sign · Opposite signs · Always plus   The same sign · Opposite signs · Always plus

If the terms of a binomial have a common factor, the GCF (or the opposite of the GCF) should always be factored out first.

EXAMPLE 3   Factor: $-2t^5 + 250t^2$

Strategy We will factor out the common factor, $-2t^2$. We can then factor the resulting binomial as a difference of two cubes.

WHY The first step in factoring any polynomial is to factor out the GCF, or its opposite.

Solution

$$-2t^5 + 250t^2 = -2t^2(t^3 - 125) \qquad \text{Factor out the opposite of the GCF,} \\ -2t^2.$$

$$= -2t^2(t - 5)(t^2 + 5t + 25) \quad \text{Factor } t^3 - 125.$$

Therefore, $-2t^5 + -50t^2 = -2t^2(t - 5)(t^2 + 5t + 25)$. Check by multiplying.

ANSWERS TO SELF CHECKS

1. $(h + 3)(h^2 - 3h + 9)$ **2.** $(2c - 1)(4c^2 + 2c + 1)$ **3.** $4(c + d)(c^2 - cd + d^2)$

SECTION 6.5   STUDY SET

VOCABULARY

1. The binomial $x^3 + 27$ is called a sum of two ___cubes___ .

2. The binomial $x^3 - 8$ is called a ___difference___ of two cubes.

CONCEPTS

Fill in the blanks.

3. $F^3 + L^3 = \left(\boxed{F} + \boxed{L}\right)(F^2 - FL + L^2)$

4. $F^3 - L^3 = (F - L)\left(\boxed{F^2} + FL + \boxed{L^2}\right)$

▶ 5. $(x - 2)(x^2 + 2x + 4)$ is the factorization of what binomial? $x^3 - 8$

6. $(x + 3)(x^2 - 3x + 9)$ is the factorization of what binomial? $x^3 + 27$

7. List the first five positive perfect-integer cubes. $1, 8, 27, 64, 125$

8. Use multiplication to determine whether the factorization is correct.

$$b^3 + 64 = (b + 4)(b^2 + 4b + 16) \quad \text{no}$$

9. $27m^3 = \left(\boxed{3m}\right)^3$

10. $a^6 = \left(\boxed{a^2}\right)^3$

11. $8x^3 - 27 = \left(\boxed{2x}\right)^3 - \left(\boxed{3}\right)^3$

12. $x^3 + 64y^3 = \left(\boxed{x}\right)^3 + \left(\boxed{4y}\right)^3$

NOTATION

Complete each factorization.

13. $a^3 + 8 = (a + 2)\left(a^2 - \boxed{2a} + 4\right)$

▶ 14. $x^3 - 1 = (x - 1)\left(x^2 + \boxed{x} + 1\right)$

15. $b^3 + 27 = \left(\boxed{b + 3}\right)(b^2 - 3b + 9)$

▶ 16. $z^3 - 125 = \left(\boxed{z - 5}\right)(z^2 + 5z + 25)$

GUIDED PRACTICE

Factor each polynomial. **See Example 1.**

17. $y^3 + 1$
$(y + 1)(y^2 - y + 1)$

▶ 18. $b^3 + 125$
$(b + 5)(b^2 - 5b + 25)$

19. $y^3 + 343$
$(y + 7)(y^2 - 7y + 49)$

▶ 20. $b^3 + 216$
$(b + 6)(b^2 - 6b + 36)$

21. $a^3 + 64$
$(a + 4)(a^2 - 4a + 16)$

22. $n^3 + 1$
$(n + 1)(n^2 - n + 1)$

23. $m^3 + 512$
$(m + 8)(m^2 - 8m + 64)$

24. $t^3 + 729$
$(t + 9)(t^2 - 9t + 81)$

Factor each polynomial. **See Example 2.**

▶ 25. $x^3 - 8$
$(x - 2)(x^2 + 2x + 4)$

▶ 26. $a^3 - 27$
$(a - 3)(a^2 + 3a + 9)$

27. $z^3 - 343$
$(z - 7)(z^2 + 7z + 49)$

28. $c^3 - 1,000$
$(c - 10)(c^2 + 10c + 100)$

29. $s^3 - 8t^3$
$(s - 2t)(s^2 + 2st + 4t^2)$

▶ 30. $27a^3 - b^3$
$(3a - b)(9a^2 + 3ab + b^2)$

31. $s^3 - 64t^3$
$(s - 4t)(s^2 + 4st + 16t^2)$

▶ 32. $64x^3 - 27y^3$
$(4x - 3y)(16x^2 + 12xy + 9y^2)$

Factor each polynomial. **See Example 3.**

33. $-x^3 + 216$
$-(x - 6)(x^2 + 6x + 36)$

▶ 34. $-x^3 - 125$
$-(x + 5)(x^2 - 5x + 25)$

35. $2x^3 + 54$
$2(x + 3)(x^2 - 3x + 9)$

36. $2x^3 - 2$
$2(x - 1)(x^2 + x + 1)$

37. $64m^3x - 8n^3x$
$8x(2m - n)(4m^2 + 2mn + n^2)$

▶ 38. $16r^4 + 128rs^3$
$16r(r + 2s)(r^2 - 2rs + 4s^2)$

39. $x^4y + 216xy^4$
$xy(x + 6y)(x^2 - 6xy + 36y^2)$

40. $16a^5 - 54a^2b^3$
$2a^2(2a - 3b)(4a^2 + 6ab + 9b^2)$

TRY IT YOURSELF

Completely factor each expression.

41. $8 + x^3$
$(2 + x)(4 - 2x + x^2)$

42. $27 - y^3$
$(3 - y)(9 + 3y + y^2)$

▶ 43. $8u^3 + w^3$
$(2u + w)(4u^2 - 2uw + w^2)$

44. $a^3 + 8b^3$
$(a + 2b)(a^2 - 2ab + 4b^2)$

45. $64x^3 - 27$
$(4x - 3)(16x^2 + 12x + 9)$

46. $27x^3 + 125$
$(3x + 5)(9x^2 - 15x + 25)$

47. $a^6 - b^3$
$(a^2 - b)(a^4 + a^2b + b^2)$

▶ 48. $a^3 + b^6$
$(a + b^2)(a^2 - ab^2 + b^4)$

49. $x^9 + y^6$
$(x^3 + y^2)(x^6 - x^3y^2 + y^4)$

▶ 50. $x^3 - y^9$
$(x - y^3)(x^2 + xy^3 + y^6)$

51. $81r^4s^2 - 24rs^5$
$3rs^2(3r - 2s)(9r^2 + 6rs + 4s^2)$

52. $4m^5n + 500m^2n^4$
$4m^2n(m + 5n)(m^2 - 5mn + 25n^2)$

53. $3a^3 + 24b^3$
$3(a + 2b)(a^2 - 2ab + 4b^2)$

54. $-2x^5 + 128x^2$
$-2x^2(x - 4)(x^2 + 4x + 16)$

55. $8p^6 - 27q^6$
$(2p^2 - 3q^2)(4p^4 + 6p^2q^2 + 9q^4)$

56. $125p^3 - 64y^3$
$(5p - 4y)(25p^2 + 20py + 16y^2)$

Choose the correct method from Sections 6.1–6.5 to factor completely each of the following expressions:

57. $x^2 - 81$ $(x + 9)(x - 9)$

58. $y^2 - 625$ $(y + 25)(y - 25)$

59. $a^2 - 16$ $(a + 4)(a - 4)$

60. $b^2 - 256$ $(b + 16)(b - 16)$

61. $81r^2 - 256s^2$
$(9r + 16s)(9r - 16s)$

62. $16y^2 - 81z^2$
$(4y + 9z)(4y - 9z)$

63. $a^2(x - a) - b^2(x - a)$ 64. $at^2 - 16a$
$(x - a)(a + b)(a - b)$ $a(t + 4)(t - 4)$

65. $x^2y^2 - 2x^2 - y^2 + 2$ $(y^2 - 2)(x + 1)(x - 1)$

66. $5x^3y^3z^4 + 25x^2y^3z^2 - 35x^3y^2z^5$ $5x^2y^2z^2(xyz^2 + 5y - 7xz^3)$

67. $81p^4 - 16q^4$ $(9p^2 + 4q^2)(3p + 2q)(3p - 2q)$

68. $30a^4 + 5a^3 - 200a^2$ $5a^2(3a + 8)(2a - 5)$

69. $54x^3 + 250y^6$ $2(3x + 5y^2)(9x^2 - 15xy^2 + 25y^4)$

70. $-16x^4y^2z + 24x^5y^3z^4 - 15x^2y^3z^7$
$-x^2y^2z(16x^2 - 24x^3yz^3 + 15yz^6)$

▶ Selected exercises available online at
www.webassign.net/brookscole

▶ **71.** Explain why $x^3 - 25$ is not the difference of two cubes.

72. Explain why $x^6 - 1$ can be thought of as a difference of two squares or as a difference of two cubes.

73. Solve: $x + 20 = 4x - 1 + 2x$ $\frac{21}{5}$

74. Evaluate $2x^2 + 5x - 3$ for $x = -3$. 0

75. Is 4 a solution of $3(m - 8) + 2m = 4 - (m + 2)$? no

76. When expressed as a decimal, is $\frac{7}{9}$ a terminating or repeating decimal? repeating

---

Objective

1 Factor randomly chosen polynomials.

SECTION 6.6

A Factoring Strategy

The factoring methods discussed so far will be used in the remaining chapters to simplify expressions and solve equations. In such cases, we must determine the factoring method—it will not be specified. This section will give you practice in selecting the appropriate factoring method to use given a randomly chosen polynomial.

1 **Factor randomly chosen polynomials.**

The following strategy is helpful when factoring polynomials.

> ### Steps for Factoring a Polynomial
>
> 1. Is there a common factor? If so, factor out the GCF, or the opposite of the GCF, so that the leading coefficient is positive.
>
> 2. How many terms does the polynomial have?
>
>   If it has *two terms*, look for the following problem types:
>
>   **a.** The difference of two squares
>
>   **b.** The sum of two cubes
>
>   **c.** The difference of two cubes
>
>   If it has *three terms*, look for the following problem types:
>
>   **a.** A perfect-square trinomial
>
>   **b.** If the trinomial is not a perfect square, use the trial-and-check method or the grouping method.
>
>   If it has *four or more terms*, try to factor by grouping.
>
> 3. Can any factors be factored further? If so, factor them completely.
>
> 4. Does the factorization check? Check by multiplying.

Self Check 1

Factor: $11a^6 - 11a^2$

Now Try Problem 21

Self Check 1 Answer
$11a^2(a^2 + 1)(a + 1)(a - 1)$

Teaching Example 1 Factor: $3x^4 - 48$
Answer:
$3(x^2 + 4)(x + 2)(x - 2)$

EXAMPLE 1   Factor: $2x^4 - 162$

Strategy We will answer the four questions listed in the *Steps for Factoring a Polynomial*.

WHY The answers to these questions help us determine which factoring techniques to use.

Solution

Is there a common factor?   Yes. Factor out the GCF, which is 2.

$$2x^4 - 162 = 2(x^4 - 81)$$

How many terms does it have?   The polynomial within the parentheses, $x^4 - 81$, has two terms. It is a difference of two squares.

$$2x^4 - 162 = 2(x^4 - 81) \qquad \text{Think of } x^4 - 81 \text{ as } (x^2)^2 - 9^2.$$
$$= 2(x^2 + 9)(x^2 - 9)$$

Is it factored completely?   No. $x^2 - 9$ is also the difference of two squares and can be factored.

$$2x^4 - 162 = 2(x^4 - 81)$$
$$= 2(x^2 + 9)(x^2 - 9) \qquad \text{Think of } x^2 - 9 \text{ as } x^2 - 3^2.$$
$$= 2(x^2 + 9)(x + 3)(x - 3) \qquad x^2 + 9 \text{ is a sum of two squares and does}$$
$$\text{not factor.}$$

Therefore, $2x^4 - 162 = 2(x^2 + 9)(x + 3)(x - 3)$.

| **The Language of Algebra**   Remember that the instruction to *factor* means to *factor completely*. A polynomial is *factored completely* when no factor can be factored further.

Does it check?   Yes.

$$2(x^2 + 9)(x + 3)(x - 3) = 2(x^2 + 9)(x^2 - 9) \qquad \text{Multiply } (x + 3)(x - 3) \text{ first.}$$
$$= 2(x^4 - 81) \qquad \text{Multiply } (x^2 + 9)(x^2 - 9).$$
$$= 2x^4 - 162 \qquad \text{This is the original polynomial.} \quad \blacksquare$$

EXAMPLE 2   Factor: $-4c^5d^2 - 12c^4d^3 - 9c^3d^4$

Strategy We will answer the four questions listed in the *Steps for Factoring a Polynomial*.

WHY The answers to these questions help us determine which factoring techniques to use.

Solution
Is there a common factor?   Yes. Factor out the opposite of the GCF, $-c^3d^2$, so that the leading coefficient is positive.

$$-4c^5d^2 - 12c^4d^3 - 9c^3d^4 = -c^3d^2(4c^2 + 12cd + 9d^2)$$

How many terms does it have?   The polynomial within the parentheses has three terms. It is a perfect-square trinomial because $4c^2 = (2c)^2$, $9d^2 = (3d)^2$, and $12cd = 2 \cdot 2c \cdot 3d$.

$$-4c^5d^2 - 12c^4d^3 - 9c^3d^4 = -c^3d^2(4c^2 + 12cd + 9d^2)$$
$$= -c^3d^2(2c + 3d)^2$$

Is it factored completely?   Yes. The binomial $2c + 3d$ does not factor further.

Therefore, $-4c^5d^2 - 12c^4d^3 - 9c^3d^4 = -c^3d^2(2c + 3d)^2$.

Does it check?   Yes.

$$-c^3d^2(2c + 3d)^2 = -c^3d^2(4c^2 + 12cd + 9d^2) \qquad \text{Use a special-product rule.}$$
$$= -4c^5d^2 - 12c^4d^3 - 9c^3d^4 \qquad \text{This is the original polynomial.} \quad \blacksquare$$

EXAMPLE 3   Factor: $y^4 - 3y^3 + y - 3$

Strategy We will answer the four questions listed in the *Steps for Factoring a Polynomial*.

Self Check 2

Factor: $-32h^4 - 80h^3 - 50h^2$

Now Try **Problem 33**
Self Check 2 Answer
$-2h^2(4h + 5)^2$

Teaching Example 2 Factor:
$-3x^3y^2 + 18x^2y^2 - 27xy^2$
Answer:
$-3xy^2(x - 3)^2$

Self Check 3

Factor: $b^4 + b^3 + 8b + 8$

Now Try **Problem 37**
Self Check 3 Answer
$(b + 1)(b + 2)(b^2 - 2b + 4)$

WHY The answers to these questions help us determine which factoring techniques to use.

Solution

Is there a common factor? No. There is no common factor (other than 1).

How many terms does it have? Since the polynomial has four terms, we will try factoring by grouping.

$$y^4 - 3y^3 + y - 3 = y^3(y - 3) + 1(y - 3) \quad \text{Factor out } y^3 \text{ from } y^4 - 3y^3. \text{ Factor out 1 from } y - 3.$$

$$= (y - 3)(y^3 + 1)$$

Is it factored completely? No. We can factor $y^3 + 1$ as a sum of two cubes.

$$y^4 - 3y^3 + y - 3 = y^3(y - 3) + 1(y - 3)$$
$$= (y - 3)(y^3 + 1) \quad \text{Think of } y^3 + 1 \text{ as } y^3 + 1^3.$$
$$= (y - 3)(y + 1)(y^2 - y + 1) \quad y^2 - y + 1 \text{ does not factor further.}$$

Therefore, $y^4 - 3y^3 + y - 3 = (y - 3)(y + 1)(y^2 - y + 1)$.

Does it check? Yes.

$$(y - 3)(y + 1)(y^2 - y + 1) = (y - 3)(y^3 + 1) \quad \text{Multiply the last two factors.}$$
$$= y^4 + y - 3y^3 - 3 \quad \text{Use the FOIL method.}$$
$$= y^4 - 3y^3 + y - 3 \quad \text{This is the original polynomial.} \blacksquare$$

Self Check 4

Factor: $6m^2 - 54m + 6m^3$

Now Try Problem 45
Self Check 4 Answer
$6m(m^2 + m - 9)$

EXAMPLE 4 Factor: $32n - 4n^2 + 4n^3$

Strategy We will answer the four questions listed in the *Steps for Factoring a Polynomial*.

WHY The answers to these questions help us determine which factoring techniques to use.

Solution

Is there a common factor? Yes. When we write the terms in descending powers of n, we see that the GCF is $4n$.

$$4n^3 - 4n^2 + 32n = 4n(n^2 - n + 8)$$

How many terms does it have? The polynomial within the parentheses has three terms. It is not a perfect-square trinomial because the last term, 8, is not a perfect-integer square.

To factor the trinomial $n^2 - n + 8$, we must find two integers whose product is 8 and whose sum is -1. As we see in the table, there are no such integers. Thus, $n^2 - n + 8$ is prime.

Negative factors of 8	Sum of the negative factors of 8
$-1(-8) = 8$	$-1 + (-8) = -9$
$-2(-4) = 8$	$-2 + (-8) = -10$

Is it factored completely? Yes.

Therefore, $4n^3 - 4n^2 + 32n = 4n(n^2 - n + 8)$. Remember to write the GCF, $4n$, from the first step.

Does it check? Yes.

$$4n(n^2 - n + 8) = 4n^3 - 4n^2 + 32n \quad \text{This is the original polynomial.} \blacksquare$$

EXAMPLE 5   Factor: $3y^3 - 4y^2 - 4y$

Strategy We will answer the four questions listed in the *Steps for Factoring a Polynomial.*

WHY The answers to these questions help us determine which factoring techniques to use.

Solution

Is there a common factor?   Yes. The GCF is y.

$$3y^3 - 4y^2 - 4y = y(3y^2 - 4y - 4)$$

How many terms does it have?   The polynomial within the parentheses has three terms. It is not a perfect-square trinomial because the first term, $3y^2$, is not a perfect square.

   If we use grouping to factor $3y^2 - 4y - 4$, the key number is $ac = 3(-4) = -12$. We must find two integers whose product is -12 and whose sum is $b = -4$.

Key number $= -12$ **$b = -4$**

Factors of -12	Sum of the factors of -12
$2(-6) = -12$	$2 + (-6) = -4$

From the table, the correct pair is 2 and -6. They serve as the coefficients of $2y$ and $-6y$, the two terms that we use to represent the middle term, $-4y$, of the trinomial.

$$3y^2 - 4y - 4 = 3y^2 + 2y - 6y - 4 \qquad \text{Express } -4y \text{ as } 2y - 6y.$$
$$= y(3y + 2) - 2(3y + 2) \qquad \text{Factor } y \text{ from the first two terms and factor } -2 \text{ from the last two terms.}$$
$$= (3y + 2)(y - 2) \qquad \text{Factor out } 3y + 2.$$

The trinomial $3y^2 - 4y - 4$ factors as $(3y + 2)(y - 2)$.

Is it factored completely?   Yes. Because $3y + 2$ and $y - 2$ do not factor.

Therefore, $3y^3 - 4y^2 - 4y = y(3y + 2)(y - 2)$.   Remember to write the GCF, y, from the first step.

Does it check?   Yes.

$$y(3y + 2)(y - 2) = y(3y^2 - 4y - 4) \qquad \text{Multiply the binomials.}$$
$$= 3y^3 - 4y^2 - 4y \qquad \text{This is the original polynomial.}$$

Self Check 5

Factor: $6y^3 + 21y^2 - 12y$

Now Try **Problem 67**

Self Check 5 Answer
$3y(2y - 1)(y + 4)$

Teaching Example 5 Factor:
$12x^3 + 14x^2 - 6x$
Answer:
$2x(3x - 1)(2x + 3)$

ANSWERS TO SELF CHECKS

1. $11a^2(a^2 + 1)(a + 1)(a - 1)$ **2.** $-2h^2(4h + 5)^2$ **3.** $(b + 1)(b + 2)(b^2 - 2b + 4)$
4. $6m(m^2 + m - 9)$ **5.** $3y(2y - 1)(y + 4)$

SECTION 6.6   STUDY SET

VOCABULARY

Fill in the blanks.

1. To factor a polynomial means to express it as a ___product___ of two (or more) polynomials.

2. A polynomial is factored __completely__ when each factor is prime.

CONCEPTS

For each of the following polynomials, which factoring method would you use first?

3. $2x^5y - 4x^3y$
factor out the GCF

▶ **4.** $9b^2 + 12y - 5$
trinomial factoring

5. $x^2 + 18x + 81$
perfect-square trinomial

6. $ax + ay - x - y$
factoring by grouping

7. $x^3 + 27$
sum of two cubes

▶ **8.** $y^3 - 64$
difference of two cubes

9. $m^2 + 3mn + 2n^2$
trinomial factoring

10. $16 - 25z^2$
difference of two squares

11. What is the first question that should be asked when using the strategy of this section to factor a polynomial? Is there a common factor?

12. Use multiplication to determine whether the factorization is correct. yes

$$5c^3d^2 - 40c^2d^3 + 35cd^4 = 5cd^2(c - 7d)(c - d)$$

NOTATION

Complete each factorization.

13. $6m^3 - 28m^2 + 16m = 2m\left(3m^2 - \boxed{14m} + 8\right)$
$$= 2m(3m - 2)\left(\boxed{m} - 4\right)$$

14. $2a^3 + 3a^2 - 2a - 3$
$$= \boxed{a^2}(2a + 3) - 1\left(\boxed{2a} + 3\right)$$
$$= \left(\boxed{2a + 3}\right)(a^2 - 1)$$
$$= (2a + 3)(a + 1)\left(\boxed{a - 1}\right)$$

TRY IT YOURSELF

The following is a list of random factoring problems. Factor each expression completely. If an expression is not factorable, write "prime." See Examples 1–5.

15. $2b^2 + 8b - 24$
$2(b + 6)(b - 2)$

16. $32 - 2t^4$
$2(4 + t^2)(2 + t)(2 - t)$

17. $8p^3q^7 + 4p^2q^3$
$4p^2q^3(2pq^4 + 1)$

▶ **18.** $8m^2n^3 - 24mn^4$
$8mn^3(m - 3n)$

▶ **19.** $2 + 24y + 40y^2$
$2(2y + 1)(10y + 1)$

▶ **20.** $6r^2 + 3rs - 18s^2$
$3(2r - 3s)(r + 2s)$

▶ **21.** $8x^4 - 8$
$8(x^2 + 1)(x + 1)(x - 1)$

22. $t - 90 + t^2$
$(t + 10)(t - 9)$

23. $14c - 147 + c^2$
$(c + 21)(c - 7)$

24. $ab^2 - 4a + 3b^2 - 12$
$(a + 3)(b + 2)(b - 2)$

25. $x^2 + 7x + 1$
prime

▶ **26.** $3a^3 + 24b^3$
$3(a + 2b)(a^2 - 2ab + 4b^2)$

▶ **27.** $-2x^5 + 128x^2$
$-2x^2(x - 4)(x^2 + 4x + 16)$

28. $16 - 40z + 25z^2$
$(5z - 4)^2$

29. $a^2c + a^2d^2 + bc + bd^2$
$(c + d^2)(a^2 + b)$

▶ **30.** $6t^4 + 14t^3 - 40t^2$
$2t^2(3t - 5)(t + 4)$

31. $-9x^2y^2 + 6xy - 1$
$-(3xy - 1)^2$

▶ **32.** $x^2y^2 - 2x^2 - y^2 + 2$
$(y^2 - 2)(x + 1)(x - 1)$

33. $-20m^3 - 100m^2 - 125m$
$-5m(2m + 5)^2$

34. $5x^3y^3z^4 + 25x^2y^4z^2 - 35x^3y^2z^5$
$5x^2y^2z^2(xyz^2 + 5y^2 - 7xz^3)$

35. $2c^2 - 5cd - 3d^2$
$(2c + d)(c - 3d)$

36. $125p^3 - 64y^3$
$(5p - 4y)(25p^2 + 20py + 16y^2)$

37. $p^4 - 2p^3 - 8p + 16$
$(p - 2)^2(p^2 + 2p + 4)$

▶ **38.** $a^2 + 8a + 3$
prime

39. $a^2(x - a) - b^2(x - a)$
$(x - a)(a + b)(a - b)$

40. $70p^4q^3 - 35p^4q^2 + 49p^5q^2$
$7p^4q^2(10q - 5 + 7p)$

41. $a^2b^2 - 144$
$(ab + 12)(ab - 12)$

▶ **42.** $-16x^4y^2z + 24x^5y^3z^4 - 15x^2y^3z^7$
$-x^2y^2z(16x^2 - 24x^3yz^3 + 15yz^6)$

43. $2x^3 + 10x^2 + x + 5$
$(x + 5)(2x^2 + 1)$

44. $u^2 - 18u + 81$
$(u - 9)^2$

45. $8v^2 - 14v^3 + v^4$
$v^2(v^2 - 14v + 8)$

▶ **46.** $28 - 3m - m^2$
$-(m + 7)(m - 4)$

47. $x^4 - 13x^2 + 36$
$(x + 2)(x - 2)(x + 3)(x - 3)$

48. $81r^4 - 256$
$(9r^2 + 16)(3r + 4)(3r - 4)$

49. $8a^2x^3 - 2b^2x$
$2x(2ax + b)(2ax - b)$

▶ **50.** $12x^2 + 14x - 6$
$2(3x - 1)(2x + 3)$

51. $6x^2 - 14x + 8$
$2(3x - 4)(x - 1)$

▶ **52.** $12x^2 - 12$
$12(x + 1)(x - 1)$

53. $4x^2y^2 + 4xy^2 + y^2$
$y^2(2x + 1)^2$

54. $81r^4s^2 - 24rs^5$
$3rs^2(3r - 2s)(9r^2 + 6rs + 4s^2)$

55. $4m^5 + 500m^2$
$4m^2(m + 5)(m^2 - 5m + 25)$

56. $ae + bf + af + be$
$(a + b)(f + e)$

57. $x^4 - 2x^2 - 8$
$(x + 2)(x - 2)(x^2 + 2)$

▶ **58.** $6x^2 - x - 16$
prime

59. $4x^2 + 9y^2$
prime

60. $x^4y + 216xy^4$
$xy(x + 6y)(x^2 - 6xy + 36y^2)$

61. $16a^5 - 54a^2$
$2a^2(2a - 3)(4a^2 + 6a + 9)$

▶ **62.** $25x^2 - 16y^2$
$(5x + 4y)(5x - 4y)$

63. $27x - 27y - 27z$
$27(x - y - z)$

64. $12x^2 + 52x + 35$
$(6x + 5)(2x + 7)$

65. $xy - ty + xs - ts$
$(x - t)(y + s)$

▶ **66.** $bc + b + cd + d$
$(b + d)(c + 1)$

67. $35x^8 - 2x^7 - x^6$
$x^6(7x + 1)(5x - 1)$

▶ **68.** $x^3 - 25$
prime

69. $5(x - 2) + 10y(x - 2)$
$5(x - 2)(1 + 2y)$

70. $16x^2 - 40x^3 + 25x^4$
$x^2(5x - 4)^2$

71. $49p^2 + 28pq + 4q^2$
$(7p + 2q)^2$

▶ **72.** $x^2y^2 - 6xy - 16$
$(xy + 2)(xy - 8)$

73. $4t^2 + 36$
$4(t^2 + 9)$

74. $r^5 + 3r^3 + 2r^2 + 6$
$(r^2 + 3)(r^3 + 2)$

75. $m^2n^2 - 9m^2 + 3n^2 - 27$
$(n + 3)(n - 3)(m^2 + 3)$

76. $z^2 + 6yz^2 + 9y^2z^2$
$z^2(1 + 3y)^2$

WRITING

77. Which factoring method do you find the most difficult? Why?

78. What four questions make up the factoring strategy for polynomials discussed in this section?

79. What does it mean to factor a polynomial?

▶ **80.** How is a factorization checked?

█ REVIEW

81. Graph the real numbers $-3, 0, 2,$ and $-\frac{3}{2}$ on a number line.

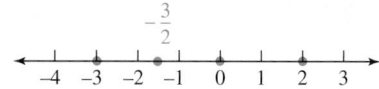

82. Graph the interval $(-2, 3]$ on a number line.

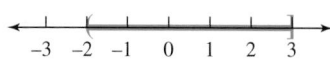

83. Graph: $y = \dfrac{1}{2}x + 1$ ▶ **84.** Graph: $y < 2 - 3x$

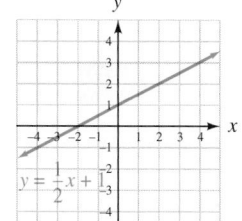 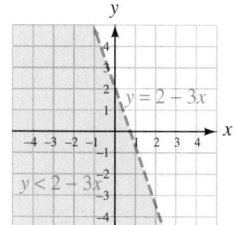

SECTION 6.7

Solving Quadratic Equations by Factoring

Objectives

1 Define quadratic equations.

2 Solve quadratic equations using the zero-factor property.

3 Solve quadratic equations by factoring.

4 Solve third-degree equations by factoring.

Equations that involve first-degree polynomials, such as $9x - 6 = 0$, are called *linear equations*. Equations that involve second-degree polynomials, such as $9x^2 - 6x = 0$, are called **quadratic equations.** In this section, we will define quadratic equations and learn how to solve many of them by factoring.

1 Define quadratic equations.

If a polynomial contains one variable with an exponent to the second (but no higher) power, it is called a **second-degree polynomial.** A quadratic, or second-degree equation, has a term in which the exponent on the variable is 2, and has no other terms of higher degree. Some examples are

$$9x^2 - 6x = 0, \qquad x^2 - 2x - 63 = 0, \qquad \text{and} \qquad 2x^2 + 3x - 2 = 0$$

Quadratic Equation

A **quadratic equation** is an equation that can be written in the **standard form**

$$ax^2 + bx + c = 0$$

where a, b, and c represent real numbers, and a is not 0.

To write a quadratic equation such as $21x = 10 - 10x^2$ in $ax^2 + bx + c = 0$ form (called **standard form**), we use the addition and subtraction properties of equality to get 0 on the right-hand side.

$$21x = 10 - 10x^2$$

$$10x^2 + 21x = 10 - 10x^2 + 10x^2 \qquad \text{Add } 10x^2 \text{ to both sides.}$$

$$10x^2 + 21x = 10 \qquad\qquad\qquad \text{Combine like terms: } -10x^2 + 10x^2 = 0.$$

$$10x^2 + 21x - 10 = 0 \qquad\qquad \text{Subtract 10 from both sides.}$$

2   Solve quadratic equations using the zero-factor property.

To **solve a quadratic equation,** we find all the values of the variable that make the equation true.

The method that we have used to solve linear equations cannot be used to solve a quadratic equation, because those techniques cannot isolate the variable on one side of the equation. However, we can often solve quadratic equations using factoring and the following property of real numbers.

The Zero-Factor Property

If a and b represent real numbers, and

$$\text{if } ab = 0, \text{ then } a = 0 \text{ or } b = 0.$$

In words, the zero-factor property states that when the product of two numbers is zero, at least one of them must be zero.

EXAMPLE 1   Solve: $(4y - 1)(y + 6) = 0$

Strategy We will set $4y - 1$ equal to 0 and $y + 6$ equal to 0 and solve each equation.

WHY The product of $4y - 1$ and $y + 6$ is equal to 0. By the zero-factor property, $4y - 1$ must equal 0, or $y + 6$ must equal 0.

Solution

The left-hand side of the equation is $(4y - 1)(y + 6)$. By the zero-factor property, one of these factors must be 0.

$$4y - 1 = 0 \quad \text{or} \quad y + 6 = 0$$

We can solve each of the linear equations.

$$4y - 1 = 0 \quad \text{or} \quad y + 6 = 0 \qquad \textit{Set each factor equal to zero.}$$

$$4y = 1 \qquad\qquad y = -6 \qquad \textit{Solve each equation.}$$

$$y = \frac{1}{4}$$

The equation has two solutions, $\frac{1}{4}$ and -6. To check, we substitute the results for y in the original equation and simplify.

For $y = \frac{1}{4}$	**For $y = -6$**
$(4y - 1)(y + 6) = 0$	$(4y - 1)(y + 6) = 0$
$\left[4\left(\dfrac{1}{4}\right) - 1\right]\left(\dfrac{1}{4} + 6\right) \overset{?}{=} 0$	$[4(-6) - 1](-6 + 6) \overset{?}{=} 0$
$(1 - 1)\left(6\dfrac{1}{4}\right) \overset{?}{=} 0$	$(-24 - 1)(0) \overset{?}{=} 0$
$0\left(6\dfrac{1}{4}\right) \overset{?}{=} 0$	$-25(0) \overset{?}{=} 0$
$0 = 0 \quad$ True	$0 = 0 \quad$ True

3   Solve quadratic equations by factoring.

In Example 1, the right-hand side of the equation was zero, and the left-hand side was in factored form, so we were able to use the zero-factor property immediately. However, to solve many quadratic equations, we must first do the factoring.

EXAMPLE 2   Solve: $9x^2 - 6x = 0$

Strategy We will factor the binomial on the left side of the equation and use the zero-factor property.

WHY To use the zero-factor property, we need one side of the equation to be factored completely and the other side to be 0.

Solution

We begin by factoring the left-hand side of the equation.

$$9x^2 - 6x = 0 \qquad \text{This is the equation to solve.}$$
$$3x(3x - 2) = 0 \qquad \text{Factor out the GCF of 3x.}$$

By the zero-factor property, we have

$$3x = 0 \qquad \text{or} \qquad 3x - 2 = 0$$

We can solve each of the linear equations to get

$$x = 0 \qquad \text{or} \qquad x = \frac{2}{3}$$

To check, we substitute the results for x in the original equation and simplify.

For $x = 0$	**For $x = \frac{2}{3}$**
$9x^2 - 6x = 0$	$9x^2 - 6x = 0$
$9(0)^2 - 6(0) \stackrel{?}{=} 0$	$9\left(\dfrac{2}{3}\right)^2 - 6\left(\dfrac{2}{3}\right) \stackrel{?}{=} 0$
$0 - 0 \stackrel{?}{=} 0$	$9\left(\dfrac{4}{9}\right) - 6\left(\dfrac{2}{3}\right) \stackrel{?}{=} 0$
$0 = 0$ True	$4 - 4 \stackrel{?}{=} 0$
	$0 = 0$ True

The solutions of $9x^2 - 6x = 0$ are 0 and $\frac{2}{3}$.

We can use the following steps to solve a quadratic equation by factoring.

Solving Quadratic Equations by Factoring

1. Write the equation in standard form: $ax^2 + bx + c = 0$ or $0 = ax^2 + bx + c$.
2. Factor completely.
3. Use the zero-factor property to set each factor equal to zero.
4. Solve each resulting linear equation.
5. Check the results in the original equation.

EXAMPLE 3   Solve: $x^2 = 9$

Strategy We will subtract 9 from both sides of the equation to get 0 on the right side. Then we will factor the resulting binomial and use the zero-factor property.

WHY To use the zero-factor property, we need one side of the equation to be factored completely and the other side to be 0.

Solution

Before we can use the zero-factor property, we must subtract 9 from both sides to make the right-hand side zero.

Self Check 2

Solve: $5x^2 + 10x = 0$ 0, −2

Now Try **Problem 22**

Teaching Example 2 Solve:
$15x^2 - 25x = 0$
Answer:
$0, \dfrac{5}{3}$

Self Check 3

Solve: $x^2 = 25$ −5, 5

Now Try **Problem 26**

Teaching Example 3 Solve: $x^2 = 16$
Answer:
4, −4

$$x^2 = 9 \qquad \text{This is the equation to solve.}$$
$$x^2 - 9 = 0 \qquad \text{Subtract 9 from both sides.}$$
$$(x + 3)(x - 3) = 0 \qquad \text{Factor the difference of two squares.}$$
$$x + 3 = 0 \quad \text{or} \quad x - 3 = 0 \qquad \text{Set each factor equal to zero.}$$
$$x = -3 \quad | \qquad x = 3 \qquad \text{Solve each linear equation.}$$

Check each possible solution by substituting it into the original equation.

For $x = -3$	**For $x = 3$**
$x^2 = 9$	$x^2 = 9$
$(-3)^2 \stackrel{?}{=} 9$	$(3)^2 \stackrel{?}{=} 9$
$9 = 9$	$9 = 9$

The solutions of $x^2 = 9$ are -3 and 3.

Self Check 4

Solve: $x^2 + 5x + 6 = 0$ $-2, -3$

Now Try **Problem 31**

Teaching Example 4 Solve:
$x^2 - 2x - 35 = 0$
Answer:
$7, -5$

EXAMPLE 4   Solve: $x^2 - 2x - 63 = 0$

Strategy We will factor the trinomial on the left side of the equation and use the zero-factor property.

WHY To use the zero-factor property, we need one side of the equation to be factored completely and the other side to be 0.

Solution

$$x^2 - 2x - 63 = 0 \qquad \text{This is the equation to solve.}$$
$$(x + 7)(x - 9) = 0 \qquad \text{Factor the trinomial } x^2 - 2x - 63.$$
$$x + 7 = 0 \quad \text{or} \quad x - 9 = 0 \qquad \text{Set each factor equal to zero.}$$
$$x = -7 \quad | \qquad x = 9 \qquad \text{Solve each linear equation.}$$

The solutions are -7 and 9. Check each one.

Self Check 5

Solve: $3x^2 - 6 = -7x$

Now Try **Problem 34**
Self Check 5 Answer
$\dfrac{2}{3}, -3$

Teaching Example 5 Solve:
$8x^2 - 15 = -2x$
Answer:
$\dfrac{5}{4}, \dfrac{-3}{2}$

EXAMPLE 5   Solve: $2x^2 + 3x = 2$

Strategy We will subtract 2 from both sides of the equation to get 0 on the right side. Then we will factor the resulting trinomial and use the zero-factor property.

WHY To use the zero-factor property, we need one side of the equation to be factored completely and the other side to be 0.

Solution
The equation is not in $ax^2 + bx + c = 0$ form. To get 0 on the right side, we proceed as follows:

$$2x^2 + 3x = 2 \qquad \text{This is the equation to solve.}$$
$$2x^2 + 3x - 2 = 0 \qquad \text{Subtract 2 from both sides so that the right-hand side is zero.}$$
$$(2x - 1)(x + 2) = 0 \qquad \text{Factor } 2x^2 + 3x - 2.$$
$$2x - 1 = 0 \quad \text{or} \quad x + 2 = 0 \qquad \text{Set each factor equal to zero.}$$
$$2x = 1 \quad | \qquad x = -2 \qquad \text{Solve each linear equation.}$$
$$x = \frac{1}{2} \quad |$$

Use a check to verify that $\frac{1}{2}$ and -2 are solutions.

EXAMPLE 6 Solve: $x(9x - 12) = -4$

Strategy To write the equation in standard form, we will distribute the multiplication by x and add 4 to both sides. Then we will factor the resulting trinomial and use the zero-factor property.

WHY To use the zero-factor property, we need one side of the equation to be factored completely and the other side to be 0.

Solution

First, we need to write the equation in the form $ax^2 + bx + c = 0$.

$$x(9x - 12) = -4 \qquad \text{This is the equation to solve.}$$
$$9x^2 - 12x = -4 \qquad \text{Distribute the multiplication by } x.$$
$$9x^2 - 12x + 4 = 0 \qquad \text{To get 0 on the right side, add 4 to both sides.}$$
$$(3x - 2)(3x - 2) = 0 \qquad \text{Factor the trinomial.}$$

$$3x - 2 = 0 \quad \text{or} \quad 3x - 2 = 0 \qquad \text{Set each factor equal to zero.}$$
$$3x = 2 \qquad\qquad 3x = 2 \qquad \text{Add 2 to both sides.}$$
$$x = \frac{2}{3} \qquad\qquad x = \frac{2}{3} \qquad \text{Divide both sides by 3.}$$

The equation has two solutions that are the same. We call $\frac{2}{3}$ a *repeated solution*. Check by substituting it into the original equation.

Self Check 6

Solve: $x(4x + 12) = -9$

Now Try Problem 38

Self Check 6 Answer
$-\frac{3}{2}, -\frac{3}{2}$

Teaching Example 6 Solve:
$3x(3x - 10) = -25$
Answer:
$\frac{5}{3}, \frac{5}{3}$

---

4 Solve third-degree equations by factoring.

EXAMPLE 7 Solve: $6x^3 + 12x = 17x^2$

Strategy This equation is not quadratic, because it contains a term involving x^3. However, we can solve it by using factoring. First we get 0 on the right side by subtracting $17x^2$ from both sides. Then we factor the polynomial on the left side and use an extension of the zero-factor property.

WHY To use the zero-factor property, we need one side of the equation to be factored completely and the other side to be 0.

Solution

$$6x^3 + 12x = 17x^2 \qquad \text{This is the equation to solve.}$$
$$6x^3 - 17x^2 + 12x = 0 \qquad \text{Subtract } 17x^2 \text{ from both sides to get 0 on the right-hand side.}$$
$$x(6x^2 - 17x + 12) = 0 \qquad \text{Factor out the GCF, } x.$$
$$x(2x - 3)(3x - 4) = 0 \qquad \text{Factor } 6x^2 - 17x + 12.$$

$$x = 0 \quad \text{or} \quad 2x - 3 = 0 \quad \text{or} \quad 3x - 4 = 0 \qquad \text{Set each factor equal to zero.}$$
$$2x = 3 \qquad\qquad 3x = 4 \qquad \text{Solve the linear equations.}$$
$$x = \frac{3}{2} \qquad\qquad x = \frac{4}{3}$$

This equation has three solutions, $0, \frac{3}{2}$, and $\frac{4}{3}$.

Self Check 7

Solve: $10x^3 + x^2 - 2x = 0$

Now Try Problem 43

Self Check 7 Answer
$0, \frac{2}{5}, -\frac{1}{2}$

Teaching Example 7 Solve:
$6x^3 - 11x^2 = 7x$
Answer:
$0, -\frac{1}{2}, \frac{7}{3}$

ANSWERS TO SELF CHECKS

1. $\frac{3}{4}, \frac{4}{5}$ **2.** $0, -2$ **3.** $-5, 5$ **4.** $-2, -3$ **5.** $\frac{2}{3}, -3$ **6.** $-\frac{3}{2}, -\frac{3}{2}$ **7.** $0, \frac{2}{5}, -\frac{1}{2}$

SECTION **6.7** STUDY SET

VOCABULARY

Fill in the blanks.

1. Any equation that can be written in the form $ax^2 + bx + c = 0$ is called a ___quadratic___ equation.

▶ 2. To ___factor___ a binomial or trinomial means to write it as a product.

CONCEPTS

Fill in the blanks.

3. When the product of two numbers is 0, at least one of them is ___0___. Symbolically, we can state this: If $ab = 0$, then $a = $ ___0___ or $b = $ ___0___.

4. We can often use ___factoring___ and the zero-factor property to solve quadratic equations.

5. To write a quadratic equation in standard form means that one side of the equation must be ___zero___ and the other side must be in the form $ax^2 + bx + c$.

6. Classify each equation as quadratic or linear.

   a. $3x^2 + 4x + 2 = 0$ b. $3x + 7 = 0$
      ___quadratic___   ___linear___

   c. $2 = -16 - 4x$ d. $-6x + 2 = x^2$
      ___linear___   ___quadratic___

7. Check to see whether the given number is a solution of the given quadratic equation.

   a. $x^2 - 4x = 0; x = 4$ ___yes___

   b. $x^2 + 2x - 4 = 0; x = -2$ ___no___

8. a. Evaluate $x^2 + 6x - 16$ for $x = 0$. ___−16___

   b. Factor: $x^2 + 6x - 16$ ___$(x - 2)(x + 8)$___

9. The equation $3x^2 - 4x + 5 = 0$ is written in $ax^2 + bx + c = 0$ form. What are a, b, and c? ___3, −4, 5___

10. a. How many solutions does the linear equation $2a + 3 = 2$ have? ___1___

   b. How many solutions does the quadratic equation $2a^2 + 3a = 2$ have? ___2___

NOTATION

Complete each solution to solve the equation.

▶ 11. $7y^2 + 14y = 0$

   ___$7y$___ $(y + 2) = 0$

   $7y = 0$ or   ___$y + 2$___ $= 0$

   $y = 0$ | $y = -2$

▶ 12. $12p^2 - p - 6 = 0$

   $\left(\;\boxed{4p}\; - 3\right)\left(3p + \boxed{2}\right) = 0$

   $\boxed{4p - 3} = 0$ or $3p + 2 = \boxed{0}$

   $4p = \boxed{3}$ $3p = \boxed{-2}$

   $p = \dfrac{3}{4}$ | $p = -\dfrac{2}{3}$

GUIDED PRACTICE

Solve each equation. See Example 1.

13. $(x - 2)(x + 3) = 0$ 14. $(x - 3)(x - 2) = 0$
    2, −3   3, 2

15. $(2s - 5)(s + 6) = 0$ 16. $(3h - 4)(h + 1) = 0$
    $\frac{5}{2}, -6$ $\frac{4}{3}, -1$

17. $x(x - 3) = 0$ 0, 3   ▶ 18. $x(x + 5) = 0$ 0, −5

19. $(x - 1)(x + 2)(x - 3) = 0$ 1, −2, 3

▶ 20. $(x + 2)(x + 3)(x - 4) = 0$ −2, −3, 4

Solve each equation. See Example 2.

21. $w^2 - 7w = 0$ 0, 7   22. $p^2 + 5p = 0$ 0, −5

23. $3x^2 + 8x = 0$ 0, $-\frac{8}{3}$ ▶ 24. $5x^2 - x = 0$ 0, $\frac{1}{5}$

Solve each equation. See Example 3.

25. $x^2 = 100$ −10, 10   26. $z^2 = 25$ −5, 5

▶ 27. $4x^2 = 81$ $-\frac{9}{2}, \frac{9}{2}$ 28. $9y^2 = 64$ $-\frac{8}{3}, \frac{8}{3}$

Solve each equation. See Example 4.

29. $x^2 - 4x - 21 = 0$ ▶ 30. $x^2 + 2x - 15 = 0$
    −3, 7   3, −5

31. $x^2 - 13x + 12 = 0$ ▶ 32. $x^2 + 7x + 6 = 0$
    12, 1   −1, −6

Solve each equation. See Example 5.

33. $4r^2 + 4r = -1$ 34. $9m^2 + 6m = -1$
    $-\frac{1}{2}, -\frac{1}{2}$ $-\frac{1}{3}, -\frac{1}{3}$

▶ 35. $-15x^2 + 2 = -7x$ 36. $-8x^2 - 10x = -3$
    $\frac{2}{3}, -\frac{1}{5}$ $\frac{1}{4}, -\frac{3}{2}$

Solve each equation. See Example 6.

37. $x(2x - 3) = 20$ 38. $x(2x - 3) = 14$
    $-\frac{5}{2}, 4$ $\frac{7}{2}, -2$

▶ 39. $(d + 1)(8d + 1) = 18d$ 40. $4h(3h + 2) = h + 12$
    $\frac{1}{8}, 1$ $-\frac{4}{3}, \frac{3}{4}$

Solve each equation. See Example 7.

41. $x^3 + 3x^2 + 2x = 0$ ▶ 42. $x^3 - 7x^2 + 10x = 0$
    0, −1, −2   0, 5, 2

43. $k^3 - 27k - 6k^2 = 0$ 44. $j^3 - 22j - 9j^2 = 0$
    0, 9, −3   0, 11, −2

TRY IT YOURSELF

Solve each equation.

45. $x(2x - 5) = 0$ $0, \frac{5}{2}$ **46.** $x(5x + 7) = 0$ $0, -\frac{7}{5}$

47. $8s^2 - 16s = 0$ $0, 2$ **48.** $15s^2 - 20s = 0$ $0, \frac{4}{3}$

49. $x^2 - 25 = 0$ $-5, 5$ ▶ **50.** $x^2 - 36 = 0$ $-6, 6$

51. $4x^2 - 1 = 0$ $-\frac{1}{2}, \frac{1}{2}$ **52.** $9y^2 - 1 = 0$ $-\frac{1}{3}, \frac{1}{3}$

53. $9y^2 - 4 = 0$ $-\frac{2}{3}, \frac{2}{3}$ ▶ **54.** $16z^2 - 25 = 0$ $-\frac{5}{4}, \frac{5}{4}$

55. $x^2 - 9x + 8 = 0$ $8, 1$ **56.** $x^2 - 14x + 45 = 0$ $9, 5$

57. $a^2 + 8a = -15$ $-3, -5$ **58.** $a^2 - a = 56$ $8, -7$

59. $2y - 8 = -y^2$ $-4, 2$ ▶ **60.** $-3y + 18 = y^2$ $3, -6$

61. $2x^2 - 5x + 2 = 0$ $\frac{1}{2}, 2$ **62.** $2x^2 + x - 3 = 0$ $-\frac{3}{2}, 1$

63. $5x^2 - 6x + 1 = 0$ $\frac{1}{5}, 1$ **64.** $6x^2 - 5x + 1 = 0$ $\frac{1}{3}, \frac{1}{2}$

65. $(x - 1)(x^2 + 5x + 6) = 0$ $1, -2, -3$

66. $(x - 2)(x^2 - 8x + 7) = 0$ $2, 7, 1$

67. $2x(3x^2 + 10x) = -6x$ $0, -3, -\frac{1}{3}$

▶ **68.** $2x^3 = 2x(x + 2)$ $0, -1, 2$

69. $x^3 + 7x^2 = x^2 - 9x$ $0, -3, -3$

70. $x^2(x + 10) = 2x(x - 8)$ $0, -4, -4$

WRITING

71. Explain the zero-factor property.

72. Find the error in the following solution:

$$x(x + 1) = 6$$
$$\cancel{x = 6 \quad \text{or} \quad x + 1 = 6}$$
$$| \qquad x = 5$$

The solutions are 6 and 5.

REVIEW

Perform the operations and simplify.

73. $5b(2b - 3) + 2b(b - 5)$ $12b^2 - 25b$

74. $3x(a + x) - 2(x + 3)$ $3ax + 3x^2 - 2x - 6$

75. $(2b - 3)(2b - 5)$ $4b^2 - 16b + 15$

76. $(a + x)(x + 3)$ $ax + 3a + x^2 + 3x$

77. $\dfrac{a + 1}{2} + \dfrac{a - 1}{2}$ a **78.** $\dfrac{x + 2}{3} - \dfrac{2x + 1}{2}$ $\dfrac{-4x + 1}{6}$

79. $3z - 2\overline{)6z^2 + 5z - 6}$ $2z + 3$

80. $2a - 1\overline{)6a^3 + a^2 + 4a - 2}$ $3a^2 + 2a + 3 + \dfrac{1}{2a - 1}$

SECTION 6.8

Applications of Quadratic Equations

In Chapter 2, we solved mixture, investment, and uniform motion problems. To model those equations, we used *linear equations* in one variable. We will now consider situations that are modeled by *quadratic equations*.

Objectives

1 Solve problems given the quadratic equation model.

2 Solve problems involving consecutive integers.

3 Solve problems involving geometric figures.

4 Solve problems involving the Pythagorean Theorem.

1 Solve problems given the quadratic equation model.

EXAMPLE 1   *Softball*   A pitcher can throw a fastball underhand at 63 feet per second (about 45 mph). If she throws a ball into the air with that velocity, its height h in feet, t seconds after being released, is given by the formula

$$h = -16t^2 + 63t + 4$$

After the ball is thrown, in how many seconds will it hit the ground?

Solution
When the ball hits the ground, its height will be 0 feet. To find the time that it will take for the ball to hit the ground, we set h equal to 0, and solve the quadratic equation for t.

$$h = -16t^2 + 63t + 4$$
$$0 = -16t^2 + 63t + 4 \qquad \text{Substitute 0 for the height } h.$$
$$0 = -(16t^2 - 63t - 4) \qquad \text{Factor out } -1.$$
$$0 = -(16t + 1)(t - 4) \qquad \text{Factor } 16t^2 - 63t - 4.$$

Self Check 1

A student uses rubber tubing to launch a water balloon from the roof of his dormitory. The height h (in feet) of the balloon, t seconds after being launched, is given by $h = -16t^2 + 48t + 64$. After how many seconds will the balloon hit the ground?   4 sec

Now Try Problem 12

Teaching Example 1 A pitcher can throw a fast ball at 79 feet per second. If she throws the ball into the air with that velocity, its height h in feet, t seconds after being released, is given by $h = -16t^2 + 79t + 5$. After the ball is thrown, in how many seconds will it hit the ground?
Answer:
5 sec

$$16t + 1 = 0 \quad \text{or} \quad t - 4 = 0 \qquad \text{Set each factor that contains a variable equal to 0.}$$

$$16t = -1 \qquad\qquad t = 4 \qquad \text{Solve each equation.}$$

$$t = -\frac{1}{16}$$

Since time cannot be negative, we discard the solution $-\frac{1}{16}$. The second solution indicates that the ball hits the ground 4 seconds after being released. Check this answer by substituting 4 for t in $h = -16t^2 + 63t + 4$. You should get $h = 0$.

2 Solve problems involving consecutive integers.

Consecutive integers are integers that follow one another, such as 15 and 16. When solving consecutive integer problems, if we let $x = $ the first integer, then:

- two consecutive integers are x and $x + 1$
- two consecutive even integers are x and $x + 2$
- two consecutive odd integers are x and $x + 2$

EXAMPLE 2   *Women's Tennis*   In the 1998 Australian Open, sisters Venus and Serena Williams played against each other for the first time as professionals. Venus was victorious over her younger sister. At that time, their ages were consecutive integers whose product was 272. How old were Venus and Serena when they met in this match?

Analyze
- Venus is older than Serena.
- Their ages were consecutive integers.
- The product of their ages was 272.
- Find Venus' and Serena's age when they played this match.

Form Let $x = $ Serena's age when she played in the 1998 Australian Open. Since their ages were consecutive integers, and since Venus is older, we let $x + 1 = $ Venus' age. The word *product* indicates multiplication.

Serena's age	times	Venus' age	was	272.
x	$\cdot$	$(x + 1)$	$=$	272

Solve

$$x(x + 1) = 272$$

$$x^2 + x = 272 \qquad \text{Distribute the multiplication by x. Note that this is a quadratic equation.}$$

$$x^2 + x - 272 = 0 \qquad \text{Subtract 272 from both sides to make the right side 0.}$$

$$(x + 17)(x - 16) = 0 \qquad \text{Factor } x^2 + x - 272. \text{ Two numbers whose product is } -272 \text{ and whose sum is 1 are 17 and } -16.$$

$$x + 17 = 0 \quad \text{or} \quad x - 16 = 0 \qquad \text{Set each factor equal to 0.}$$

$$x = -17 \quad | \quad\quad x = 16 \qquad \text{Solve each equation.}$$

Self Check 2

The product of two consecutive integers is 552. Find the integers.

Now Try **Problem 19**

Self Check 2 Answers
23 and 24

Teaching Example 2 The product of two consecutive odd integers is 255. Find the integers.
Answer:
15 and 17

State The solutions of the equation are −17 and 16. Since x represents Serena's age, and it cannot be negative, we discard −17. Thus, Serena Williams was 16 years old and Venus Williams was $16 + 1 = 17$ years old when they played against each other for the first time as professionals. ∎

> **Success Tip**   The prime factorization of 272 is helpful in determining that $272 = 17 \cdot 16$.
>
> $$16 \begin{cases} 2\,\underline{|\,272} \\ \ \ 2\,\underline{|\,136} \\ \ \ \ \ 2\,\underline{|\,68} \\ \ \ \ \ \ \ 2\,\underline{|\,34} \\ \ \ \ \ \ \ \ \ \ 17 \end{cases}$$

3   Solve problems involving geometric figures.

EXAMPLE 3   *Perimeter of a Rectangle*
Assume that the rectangle has an area of 52 square centimeters and that its length is 1 centimeter more than 3 times its width. Find the perimeter of the rectangle.

Analyze The area of the rectangle is 52 square centimeters. Recall that the formula that gives the area of a rectangle is $A = lw$. To find the perimeter of the rectangle, we need to know its length and width. We are told that its length is related to its width; the length is 1 centimeter more than 3 times the width.

Form Let w represent the width of the rectangle. Then $3w + 1$ represents its length. Because the area is 52 square centimeters, we substitute 52 for A and $3w + 1$ for l in the formula $A = lw$.

$$A = lw$$
$$52 = (3w + 1)w$$

Solve Now we solve the equation for w.

$52 = (3w + 1)w$	This is the equation to solve.
$52 = 3w^2 + w$	Distribute the multiplication by w.
$0 = 3w^2 + w - 52$	Subtract 52 from both sides to make the left-hand side zero.
$0 = (3w + 13)(w - 4)$	Factor the trinomial.
$3w + 13 = 0 \quad$ or $\quad w - 4 = 0$	Set each factor equal to zero.
$3w = -13 \qquad\qquad w = 4$	Solve each linear equation.
$w = -\dfrac{13}{3}$	

State Since the width cannot be negative, we discard the solution $-\frac{13}{3}$. Thus, the width of the rectangle is 4, and the length is given by

$$3w + 1 = 3(4) + 1 \quad \text{Substitute 4 for } w.$$
$$= 12 + 1$$
$$= 13$$

The dimensions of the rectangle are 4 centimeters by 13 centimeters. We find the perimeter by substituting 13 for l and 4 for w in the formula for the perimeter of a rectangle.

Self Check 3

A rectangle has an area of 55 square meters. Its length is 1 meter more than twice its width. Find the perimeter of the rectangle.   32 m

***Now Try* Problem 23**

Teaching Example 3 A rectangular-shaped X-ray film has an area of 80 square inches. The length is 2 inches longer than the width. Find its width and length.
Answer:
8 in., 10 in.

$$P = 2l + 2w$$
$$= 2(\mathbf{13}) + 2(\mathbf{4})$$
$$= 26 + 8$$
$$= 34$$

The perimeter of the rectangle is 34 centimeters.

Check A rectangle with dimensions of 13 centimeters by 4 centimeters does have an area of 52 square centimeters, and the length is 1 centimeter more than 3 times the width. A rectangle with these dimensions has a perimeter of 34 centimeters.

---

4 **Solve problems involving the Pythagorean Theorem.**

The next example involves a right triangle. A **right triangle** is a triangle that contains a 90° angle. The longest side of a right triangle is the **hypotenuse,** which is the side opposite the right angle. The remaining two sides are the **legs** of the triangle. The **Pythagorean theorem** provides a formula relating the lengths of the three sides of a right triangle.

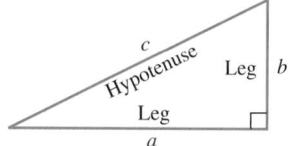

THINK IT THROUGH   *Pythagorean Triples*

"Fraternity and sorority membership nationwide is declining, down about 30% in the last decade."

Chronicle of Higher Education, 2003

The first college social fraternity, Phi Beta Kappa, was founded in 1776 on the campus of The College of William and Mary. However, secret societies have existed since ancient times, and from these roots the essence of today's fraternities and sororities have their foundation. Pythagoras, the Greek mathematician of the 6th century B.C., was the leader of a secret fraternity/sorority called the Pythagoreans. They were a community of men and women that studied mathematics, and in particular, the

"magic 3-4-5 triangle." This right triangle is special because the sum of the squares of the lengths of its legs is equal to the square of the length of its hypotenuse: $3^2 + 4^2 = 5^2$ or $9 + 16 = 25$. Today, we call a set of three natural numbers a, b, and c that satisfy $a^2 + b^2 = c^2$ a Pythagorean triple. Show that each list of numbers is a Pythagorean triple.

1. 5, 12, 13   **2.** 7, 24, 25   **3.** 8, 15, 17

4. 9, 40, 41   **5.** 11, 60, 61   **6.** 12, 35, 37

Pythagorean Theorem

If the length of the hypotenuse of a right triangle is c and the lengths of the two legs are a and b, then

$$c^2 = a^2 + b^2$$

EXAMPLE 4   *Right Triangles*   The longer leg of a right triangle is 3 units longer than the shorter leg. If the hypotenuse is 6 units longer than the shorter leg, find the lengths of the sides of the triangle.

Analyze We begin by drawing a right triangle and labeling the legs and the hypotenuse.

Form We let a = the length of the shorter leg. Then the length of the hypotenuse is $a + 6$ and the length of the longer leg is $a + 3$. By the Pythagorean theorem, we have

$\begin{pmatrix}\text{The length of}\\\text{the shorter leg}\end{pmatrix}^2$	plus	$\begin{pmatrix}\text{The length of}\\\text{the longer leg}\end{pmatrix}^2$	equals	$\begin{pmatrix}\text{The length of}\\\text{the hypotenuse}\end{pmatrix}^2$
a^2	$+$	$(a + 3)^2$	$=$	$(a + 6)^2$

Solve

$$a^2 + (a + 3)^2 = (a + 6)^2$$

$a^2 + a^2 + 6a + 9 = a^2 + 12a + 36$ Find $(a + 3)^2$ and $(a + 6)^2$.

$2a^2 + 6a + 9 = a^2 + 12a + 36$ Combine like terms on the left-hand side.

$a^2 - 6a - 27 = 0$ Subtract a^2, $12a$, and 36 from both sides to make the right-hand side 0.

Now solve the quadratic equation for a.

$$a^2 - 6a - 27 = 0$$

$(a - 9)(a + 3) = 0$ Factor.

$a - 9 = 0$ or $a + 3 = 0$ Set each factor to zero.

$a = 9$ | $a = -3$ Solve each equation.

State Since a side cannot have a negative length, we discard the solution -3. Thus, the shorter leg is 9 units long, the hypotenuse is $9 + 6 = 15$ units long, and the longer leg is $9 + 3 = 12$ units long.

Check The longer leg, with length 12, is 3 units longer than the shorter leg, with length 9. The hypotenuse, with length 15, is 6 units longer than the shorter leg. Since these lengths satisfy the Pythagorean theorem, the results check.

$$9^2 + 12^2 \stackrel{?}{=} 15^2$$

$$81 + 144 \stackrel{?}{=} 225$$

$$225 = 225$$

Self Check 4

The longer leg of a right triangle is 7 inches longer than the shorter leg. If the hypotenuse is 9 units longer than the shorter leg, find the lengths of the sides of the triangle.

Now Try **Problem 29**

Self Check 4 Answer
8 in., 15 in., and 17 in.

Teaching Example 4 The longer leg of a right triangle is 7 cm longer than the shorter leg. If the hypotenuse is 8 cm longer than the shorter side, find the lengths of the sides of the triangle.
Answer:
5 cm, 12 cm, and 13 cm

ANSWERS TO SELF CHECKS

1. 4 sec   **2.** 23 and 24   **3.** 32 m   **4.** 8 in., 15 in., and 17 in.

SECTION 6.8   STUDY SET

VOCABULARY

Fill in the blanks.

1. Integers that follow one another, such as 6 and 7, are called <u>consecutive</u> integers.

2. A <u>right</u> triangle is a triangle that contains a 90° angle.

3. The longest side of a right triangle is called the <u>hypotenuse</u>.

4. The <u>Pythagorean</u> theorem is a formula that relates the lengths of the three sides of a right triangle.

CONCEPTS

Fill in the blanks.

5. The formula for the area of a rectangle is $A = \underline{lw}$.

6. If a and b are legs of a right triangle and c is the hypotenuse, then $\underline{a^2 + b^2 = c^2}$.

NOTATION

Complete each solution.

7. $0 = -16t^2 + 32t + 48$

   $0 = \boxed{-16}(t^2 - 2t - 3)$

   $0 = -16(t - 3)(t + \boxed{1})$

   $t - 3 = \boxed{0}$ or $t + 1 = \boxed{0}$

   $t = \boxed{3}$ | $t = \boxed{-1}$

8. $6 = w(w + 1)$

   $6 = \boxed{w^2} + w$

   $0 = w^2 + w \boxed{-6}$

   $0 = \left(w \boxed{+ 3}\right)\left(w \boxed{- 2}\right)$

   $w + 3 = \boxed{0}$ or $w - 2 = \boxed{0}$

   $w = \boxed{-3}$ | $w = \boxed{2}$

APPLICATIONS

An object has been thrown straight up into the air. The formula $h = vt - 16t^2$ gives the height h of the object above the ground after t seconds, when it is thrown upward with an initial velocity v. See Example 1.

9. TIME OF FLIGHT After how many seconds will the object hit the ground if it is thrown with a velocity of 144 feet per second? 9 sec

▶ 10. TIME OF FLIGHT After how many seconds will the object hit the ground if it is thrown with a velocity of 160 feet per second? 10 sec

▶ 11. OFFICIATING Before a football game, a coin toss is used to determine which team will kick off. The height h (in feet) of a coin above the ground t seconds after being flipped up into the air is given by

$$h = -16t^2 + 22t + 3$$

How long will the coin be in the air? $\frac{3}{2} = 1.5$ sec

▶ 12. DOLPHINS The height h in feet reached by a dolphin t seconds after breaking the surface of the water is given by

$$h = -16t^2 + 32t$$

How long will it take the dolphin to jump out of the water and touch the trainer's hand? 1 sec

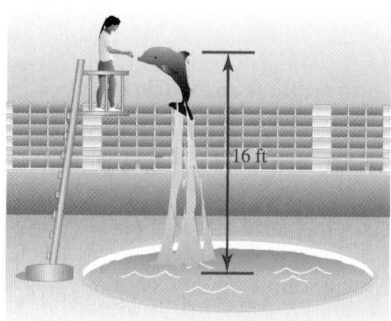

▶ 13. EXHIBITION DIVING In Acapulco, Mexico, men diving from a cliff to the water 64 feet below are a tourist attraction. A diver's height h above the water t seconds after diving is given by $h = -16t^2 + 64$. How long does a dive last? 2 sec

14. FORENSIC MEDICINE The kinetic energy E of a moving object is given by $E = \frac{1}{2}mv^2$, where m is the mass of the object (in kilograms) and v is the object's velocity (in meters per second). Kinetic energy is measured in joules. Examining the damage done to a victim, a police pathologist determines that the energy of a 3-kilogram mass at impact was 54 joules. Find the velocity at impact. (*Hint:* Multiply both sides of the equation by 2.) 6 m/s

15. CHOREOGRAPHY For the finale of a musical, 36 dancers are to assemble in a triangular-shaped series of rows, where each successive row has one more dancer than the previous row. The illustration shows the beginning of such a formation. The relationship between the number of rows r and the number of dancers d is given by

$$d = \frac{1}{2}r(r + 1)$$

Determine the number of rows in the formation. (*Hint:* Multiply both sides of the equation by 2.) 8

16. CRAFTS The illustration shows how a geometric wall hanging can be created by stretching yarn from peg to peg across a wooden ring. The relationship between the number of pegs p placed evenly around the ring and the number of yarn segments s that crisscross the ring is given by the formula

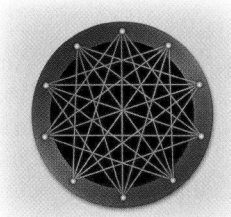

$$s = \frac{p(p - 3)}{2}$$

How many pegs are needed if the designer wants 27 segments to crisscross the ring? (*Hint:* Multiply both sides of the equation by 2.) 9

See Example 2.

17. NASCAR The car numbers of drivers Kasey Kahne and Scott Riggs are consecutive positive integers whose product is 90. If Kahne's car number is the smaller, find the number of each car. Kahne: 9, Riggs: 10

18. BASEBALL Catcher Thurman Munson and pitcher Whitey Ford are two of the sixteen New York Yankees who have had their uniform numbers retired. These numbers are consecutive integers whose product is 240. If Munson's was the smaller number, determine the uniform number of each player. Munson: 15, Ford: 16

19. CUSTOMER SERVICE At a pharmacy, customers take a number to reserve their place in line. If the product of the ticket number now being served and the next ticket number to be served is 156, what number is now being served? 12

20. HISTORY Delaware was the first state to enter the Union and Hawaii was the 50th. If we order the positions of entry for the rest of the states, we find that Kentucky entered the Union right after Vermont, and the product of their order-of-entry numbers is 210. Use the given information to complete each statement:

Kentucky was the 15 th state to enter the Union.

Vermont was the 14 th state to enter the Union.

21. PLOTTING POINTS The x- and y-coordinates of a point in Quadrant I are consecutive odd integers whose product is 143. Find the coordinates of the point. (11, 13)

22. PRESIDENTS George Washington was born on 2-22-1732. He died in 1799 at the age of 67. The month in which he died and the day of the month on which he died are consecutive even integers whose product is 168. When did Washington die? 12-14-1799

See Example 3.

23. INSULATION The area of the rectangular slab of foam insulation in the illustration is 36 square meters. Find the dimensions of the slab. 4 m by 9 m

24. FLAGS The length of the flag of Australia is twice as long as it is wide. If the area of an Australian flag is 18 ft², find its dimensions. 3 ft by 6 ft

25. SHIPPING PALLETS The length of a rectangular shipping pallet is 2 feet less than 3 times its width. Its area is 21 square feet. Find the dimensions of the pallet. 3 ft by 7 ft

26. BILLIARDS Pool tables are rectangular and their length is twice their width. Find the dimensions of a pool table if it occupies 50 ft² of floor space. 5 ft by 10 ft

27. FURNITURE A rectangular kitchen table has an area of 15 square feet. Find the dimensions of the table if its length is 2 ft longer than its width. 3 ft by 5 ft

28. Suppose you are an elementary school teacher. You want to order a rectangular bulletin board to mount on a classroom wall that has an area of 90 square feet. Fire code requirements allow for no more than 30% of a classroom wall to be covered by a bulletin board. If the length of the board to be three times as long as the width, what are the dimensions of the largest bulletin board that meets fire code? 3 ft by 9 ft

from **Campus to Careers**
Bulletin Boards

© 2009/Jupiterimages

See Example 4.

29. BOATING The inclined ramp of the boat launch shown is 8 meters longer than the rise of the ramp. The run is 7 meters longer than the rise. How long are the three sides of the ramp? 5 m, 12 m, 13 m

30. CAR REPAIRS To create some space to work under the front end of a car, a mechanic drives it up steel ramps. The ramp in the illustration is 1 foot longer than the back, and the base is 2 feet longer than the back of the ramp. Find the length of each side of the ramp. 3 ft, 4 ft, 5 ft

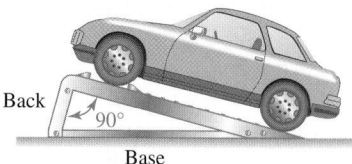

Back

90°

Base

31. GARDENING TOOLS The dimensions (in millimeters) of the teeth of a pruning saw blade are given in the illustration. Find each length. 3 mm, 4 mm, 5 mm

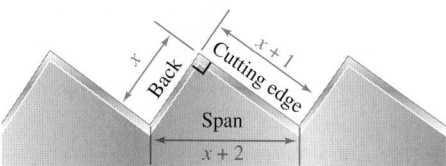

x Back Cutting edge $x + 1$

Span

$x + 2$

32. HARDWARE An aluminum brace used to support a wooden shelf has a length that is 2 inches less than twice the width of the shelf. The brace is anchored to the wall 8 inches below the shelf. Find the width of the shelf and the length of the brace. 6 in., 10 in.

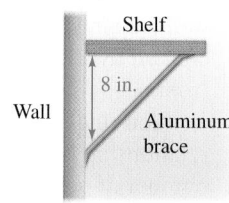

Shelf

8 in.

Wall

Aluminum brace

33. DESIGNING A TENT The length of the base of the triangular sheet of canvas above the door of a tent is 2 feet more than twice its height. The area is 30 square feet. Find the height and the length of the base of the triangle. $h = 5$ ft, $b = 12$ ft

h

34. DIMENSIONS OF A TRIANGLE The height of a triangle is 2 inches less than 5 times the length of its base. The area is 36 square inches. Find the length of the base and the height of the triangle. 4 in., 18 in.

More problems that are modeled by quadratic equations.

▶ **35.** TUBING A piece of cardboard in the shape of a parallelogram is twisted to form the tube for a roll of paper towels. The parallelogram has an area of 60 square inches. If its height h is 7 inches more than the length of the base b, what is the length of the base? (*Hint:* The formula for the area of a parallelogram is $A = bh$.) 5 in.

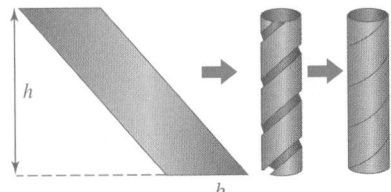

▶ **36.** SWIMMING POOL BORDERS The owners of the rectangular swimming pool in the illustration want to surround the pool with a crushed-stone border of uniform width. They have enough stone to cover 74 square meters. How wide should they make the border? (*Hint:* The area of the larger rectangle minus the area of the smaller is the area of the border.) 1 m

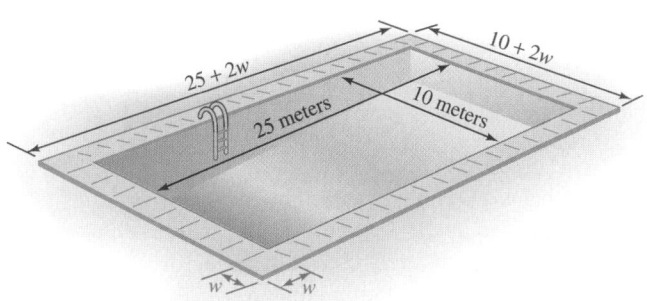

37. HOUSE CONSTRUCTION The formula for the area of a trapezoid is

$$A = \frac{h(B + b)}{2}$$

The area of the trapezoidal truss in the illustration is 24 square meters. Find the height of the trapezoid if one base is 8 meters and the other base is the same as the height. (*Hint:* Multiply both sides of the equation by 2.) 4 m

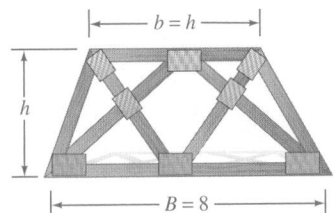

▶ **38.** VOLUME OF A PYRAMID The volume of a pyramid is given by the formula

$$V = \frac{Bh}{3}$$

where B is the area of its base and h is its height. The volume of the following pyramid is 192 cubic centimeters. Find the dimensions of its rectangular base if one edge of the base is 2 centimeters longer than the other and the height of the pyramid is 12 centimeters. 6 cm by 8 cm

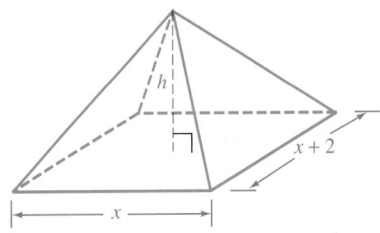

▶ **39.** THRILL RIDES At the peak of a roller coaster ride, a rider's wristwatch flew off his wrist. The height h (in feet) of the watch, t seconds after he lost it, is given by $h = -16t^2 + 64t + 80$. After how many seconds will the watch hit the ground? 5 sec

▶ **40.** PARADES A celebrity on the top of a parade float is tossing pieces of candy to children on the street below. The height h (in feet) of a piece of candy, t seconds after being thrown, is given by $h = -16t^2 + 16t + 32$. After how many seconds will the candy hit the ground? 2 sec

║ WRITING

▶ **41.** Suppose that to find the length of the base of a triangle, you write a quadratic equation and solve it to find $b = 6$ or $b = -8$. Explain why one solution should be discarded.

42. What error is apparent in the following illustration?

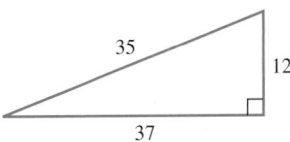

║ REVIEW

Find each special product.

43. $(5b - 2)^2$
   $25b^2 - 20b + 4$

44. $(2a + 3)^2$
   $4a^2 + 12a + 9$

45. $(s^2 + 4)^2$
   $s^4 + 8s^2 + 16$

46. $(m^2 - 1)^2$
   $m^4 - 2m^2 + 1$

47. $(9x + 6)(9x - 6)$
   $81x^2 - 36$

48. $(5b + 2c)(5b - 2c)$
   $25b^2 - 4c^2$

STUDY SKILLS CHECKLIST

Preparing for the Chapter 6 Test

In the first five sections of Chapter 6, different factoring methods were discussed. In Section 6.6, an overall factoring strategy was presented on page 506. This strategy is helpful when factoring randomly chosen polynomials. As you study the material for the test on this chapter, review the following checklist for factoring and for solving quadratic equations.

☐ Always factor out the Greatest Common Factor first. If this step is not done, it is easy to miss factorizations that need to be done to factor the expression completely.

Factor: $2x^3 - 50x$

$$2x^3 - 50x = 2x(x^2 - 25)$$ Factor out the GCF 2x.

$$= 2x(x^2 - 5^2)$$ $x^2 - 25$ is the difference of two squares.

$$= 2x(x + 5)(x - 5)$$

☐ Although $x^2 - 9x$ and $x^2 - 9$ look very similar, they have entirely different factorizations. Be sure to look closely at each term and remember the *Steps for Factoring a Polynomial* found on page 506 of this text:

$$x^2 - 9x = x(x - 9)$$ Factor out the GCF x.

$$x^2 - 9 = (x + 3)(x - 3)$$ There are no common factors. It is the difference of two squares and factors as the product of two binomials.

☐ To factor the sum or difference of two cubes, write the two terms as the base to the third power that is equivalent to the original polynomial. Then follow the rule for factoring the sum or difference of two cubes:

Factor: $x^3 + 8y^3$

$$x^3 + 8y^3 = x^3 + (2y)^3$$ This polynomial is the sum of two cubes. Write each term as a base to the third power that is equivalent to the original polynomial

$$= (x + 2y)(x^2 - x(2y) + (2y)^2)$$
$$= (x + 2y)(x^2 - 2xy + 4y^2)$$

☐ Although there is a factorization for the sum of two *cubes,* in general the sum of two squares is a prime polynomial.

$$x^3 + y^3 = (x + y)(x^2 - xy + y^2)$$
$$x^2 + y^2$$ Is a prime polynomial.

☐ It is important to remember that the instruction to factor means to factor completely. A polynomial is factored completely when no factor can be factored further.

Factor: $x^4 - 16y^4$

$$x^4 - 16y^4 = (x^2 + 4y^2)(x^2 - 4y^2)$$ Think of $x^4 - 16y^4$ as $(x^2)^2 - (4y^2)^2$.

$$= (x^2 + 4y^2)(x^2 - 4y^2)$$ Think of $x^2 - 4y^2$ as $x^2 - (2y)^2$.

$$= (x^2 + 4y^2)(x + 2y)(x - 2y)$$ $x^2 + 4y^2$ is a sum of two squares and does not factor.

☐ To solve a quadratic equation by factoring, write the equation in $ax^2 + bx + c = 0$ form, factor the polynomial completely, use the zero-factor property to set each factor equal to zero, and solve the resulting linear equations.

Solve: $x(x + 5) = 14$

$$x(x + 5) = 14$$ This is the equation to solve.

$$x^2 + 5x = 14$$ Distribute the multiplication by x.

$$x^2 + 5x - 14 = 0$$ Subtract 14 from both sides to get 0 on the right side of the equation.

$$(x + 7)(x - 2) = 0$$ Factor $x^2 + 5x - 14$.

$$x + 7 = 0 \quad \text{or} \quad x - 2 = 0$$ Set each factor equal to 0.

$$x = -7 \quad \text{or} \quad x = 2$$ Solve each linear equation.

Teaching Guide: Refer to the Instructor's Resource Binder to find activities, worksheets on key concepts, more examples, instruction tips, overheads, and assessments.

CHAPTER 6   SUMMARY AND REVIEW

SECTION 6.1   The Greatest Common Factor; Factoring by Grouping

DEFINITIONS AND CONCEPTS	EXAMPLES
The **greatest common factor** of a list of integers is the largest common factor of those integers. To **find the greatest common factor (GCF)** of several monomials: 1. Write each monomial as a product of prime factors. 2. Identify the numerical and variable factors common to each term. 3. Multiply the common numerical and variable factors identified in Step 2 to obtain the GCF. If there are no common factors, the GCF is 1.	To find the GCF of 24, 36, and 60, prime factor each number in the list: $24 = 4 \cdot 6 = 2 \cdot 2 \cdot 2 \cdot 3$ $36 = 6 \cdot 6 = 2 \cdot 3 \cdot 2 \cdot 3 = 2 \cdot 2 \cdot 3 \cdot 3$ $60 = 4 \cdot 15 = 2 \cdot 2 \cdot 3 \cdot 5$ Since 24, 36, and 60 each have two factors of 2 and one factor of 3, their greatest common factor is $2 \cdot 2 \cdot 3 = 12$. To find the GCF of $18a^2b$ and $24a^2b^2$, prime factor each monomial in the list: $18a^2b = 2 \cdot 3 \cdot 3 \cdot a \cdot a \cdot b$ $24a^2b^2 = 2 \cdot 2 \cdot 2 \cdot 3 \cdot a \cdot a \cdot b \cdot b$ Since $18a^2b$ and $24a^2b^2$ each have one factor of 2, one factor of 3, two factors of a, and one factor of b, their greatest common factor is $2 \cdot 3 \cdot a \cdot a \cdot b = 6a^2b$.
To **factor a polynomial** means to express it as a product of two (or more) polynomials.	Factor: $81 - 9x = 9(9 - x)$ Factor out the GCF of 9. $18a^2b + 24a^2b^2 = 6a^2b(3 + 4b)$ Factor out the GCF of $6a^2b$. $-15x^2y + 20xy^2 = -5xy(3x - 4y)$ Factor out the GCF of $-5xy$.
If a polynomial has four terms, try **factoring by grouping.** 1. Group the terms of the polynomial so that the first two terms have a common factor and the last two terms have a common factor. 2. Factor out the common factor from each group. 3. Factor out the resulting common binomial factor. If there is no common binomial factor, regroup the terms of the polynomial and repeat steps 2 and 3.	Factor: $a^2 + 2a + ab + 2b = a(a + 2) + b(a + 2)$ Factor out a from $a^2 + 2a$ and b from $ab + 2b$. $\quad\quad\quad\quad\quad = (a + 2)(a + b)$ Factor out $(a + 2)$.

REVIEW EXERCISES

Find the GCF of each list of numbers.

1. $35, 45$ 5

2. $45, 54$ 9

3. $12, 30, 42$ 6

4. $30, 45, 60$ 15

5. $36p^2q^2, 54pq$
$18pq$

6. $28p^4q^3, 35p^3q^2, 63p^2q$
$7p^2q$

Factor each polynomial completely.

7. $3x + 9y$ $3(x + 3y)$

8. $5ax^2 + 15a$ $5a(x^2 + 3)$

9. $7s^2 + 14s$ $7s(s + 2)$

10. $\pi ab - \pi ac$ $\pi a(b - c)$

11. $2x^3 + 4x^2 - 8x$
$2x(x^2 + 2x - 4)$

12. $x^2yz + xy^2z + xyz$
$xyz(x + y + 1)$

13. $-5ab^2 + 10a^2b - 15ab$
$-5ab(b - 2a + 3)$

14. $4(x - 2) - x(x - 2)$
$(x - 2)(4 - x)$

Factor out −1 from each polynomial.

15. $-a - 7$
$-(a + 7)$

16. $-4t^2 + 3t - 1$
$-(4t^2 - 3t + 1)$

Factor by grouping.

17. $2c + 2d + ac + ad$ $(c + d)(2 + a)$

18. $3xy + 9x - 2y - 6$ $(y + 3)(3x - 2)$

19. $2a^3 - a + 2a^2 - 1$ $(2a^2 - 1)(a + 1)$

20. $4m^2n + 12m^2 - 8mn - 24m$ $4m(n + 3)(m - 2)$

SECTION 6.2   Factoring Trinomials of the Form $x^2 + bx + c$

DEFINITIONS AND CONCEPTS	EXAMPLES
Many trinomials factor as the product of two binomials. To **factor a trinomial** of the form $x^2 + bx + c$, find two integers whose product is c, and whose sum is b. $$\left(x \quad \right)\left(x \quad \right)$$ The product of these numbers must be c and their sum must be b.	Factor: $p^2 + 7p + 12 = \left(p \quad \right)\left(p \quad \right)$ The product of these numbers must be 12 and their sum must be 7. Since $3 \cdot 4 = 12$ and $3 + 4 = 7$, we have: $$p^2 + 7p + 12 = (p + 3)(p + 4)$$
Before factoring a trinomial, write it in **descending powers** of one variable. Also, factor out −1 if that is necessary to make the **leading coefficient positive.**	Factor: $7q - q^2 - 6$ $= -q^2 + 7q - 6$ Write the terms in descending powers of q. $= -(q^2 - 7q + 6)$ Factor out −1. $= -(q - 1)(q - 6)$ Factor the trinomial.
If a trinomial cannot be factored using only integer coefficients, it is called a **prime polynomial.**	$q^2 + 2q - 5$ is a prime trinomial because there are no two integers whose product is −5 and whose sum is 2.
The GCF should always be factored out first. A trinomial is **factored completely** when it is expressed as a product of prime polynomials.	Factor: $3p^3 - 6p^2 - 24p$ $= 3p(p^2 - 2p - 8)$ Factor out $3p$. $= 3p(p + 2)(p - 4)$ Factor the trinomial.
To factor a trinomial of the form $x^2 + bx + c$ by **grouping,** write it as an equivalent four-term polynomial. $$x^2 + \underset{\rule{0pt}{0.5em}}{\quad} x + \quad x + c$$ The product of these numbers must be c, and their sum must be b.	Factor by grouping: $p^2 + 7p + 12$ Find two numbers whose product is 12 and whose sum is 7. $= p^2 + 4p + 3p + 12$ Write $7p$ as $4p + 3p$. $= p(p + 4) + 3(p + 4)$ Factor p out of $p^2 + 4p$ and 3 out of $3p + 12$. $= (p + 4)(p + 3)$ Factor out $p + 4$.

REVIEW EXERCISES

Factor each trinomial, if possible.

21. $x^2 + 2x - 24$
$(x + 6)(x - 4)$

22. $x^2 - 4x - 12$
$(x - 6)(x + 2)$

23. $n^2 - 7n + 10$
$(n - 5)(n - 2)$

24. $t^2 + 10t + 15$
prime

25. $-y^2 + 9y - 20$
$-(y - 5)(y - 4)$

26. $10y + 9 + y^2$
$(y + 9)(y + 1)$

27. $c^2 + 3cd - 10d^2$
$(c + 5d)(c - 2d)$

28. $-3mn + m^2 + 2n^2$
$(m - 2n)(m - n)$

Completely factor each trinomial.

29. $5a^2 + 45a - 50$
$5(a + 10)(a - 1)$

30. $-4x^2y - 4x^3 + 24xy^2$
$-4x(x + 3y)(x - 2y)$

Use grouping to factor each trinomial completely.

31. $p^2 + p - 20$
$(p + 5)(p - 4)$

32. $-4q^3 + 4q^2 + 24q$
$-4q(q + 2)(q - 3)$

SECTION 6.3   Factoring Trinomials of the Form $ax^2 + bx + c$

DEFINITIONS AND CONCEPTS	EXAMPLES
To use the **trial-and-check method** to factor $ax^2 + bx + c$, we must determine four integers. *The product of these numbers must be a.* $$ax^2 + bx + c = (\;\square\; x\; \square\;)(\;\square\; x\; \square\;)$$ *The product of these numbers must be c.* Use the FOIL method to check the factorization.	Factor: $2p^2 - 5p - 12$ *The product of these numbers must be 2.* $$2p^2 - 5p - 12 = (2p + 3)(1p - 4)$$ *The product of these numbers must be −12.* The numbers must also give the correct middle term when we use the FOIL method to check. To check, verify that $(2p + 3)(p - 4) = 2p^2 - 5p - 12$.
To use **grouping** to factor $ax^2 + bx + c$, write it as an equivalent four-term polynomial: $$ax^2 + bx + c = ax^2 + \boxed{}\, x + \boxed{}\, x + c$$ *The product of these numbers must be ac, and their sum must be b.* Then factor the four-term polynomial by grouping. Use the FOIL method to check your work.	Factor by grouping: $2p^2 - 5p - 12$ Find two numbers whose product is $2(-12) = -24$ and whose sum is -5. Two such numbers are -8 and 3. $\begin{aligned}&= 2p^2 - 8p + 3p - 12 &&\text{Write } -5p \text{ as } -8p + 3p.\\ &= 2p(p - 4) + 3(p - 4) &&\text{Factor the first two terms and the last}\\ &&&\text{two terms.}\\ &= (p - 4)(2p + 3) &&\text{Factor out } p - 4.\end{aligned}$ To check, verify that $(p - 4)(2p + 3) = 2p^2 - 5p - 12$.

REVIEW EXERCISES

Factor each trinomial completely, if possible.

33. $2x^2 - 5x - 3$
$(2x + 1)(x - 3)$

34. $10y^2 + 21y - 10$
$(2y + 5)(5y - 2)$

35. $-3x^2 + 14x + 5$
$-(3x + 1)(x - 5)$

36. $-9p^2 - 6p + 6p^3$
$3p(2p + 1)(p - 2)$

37. $4b^2 - 17bc + 4c^2$
$(4b - c)(b - 4c)$

38. $3y^2 + 7y - 11$
prime

Use grouping to factor each trinomial completely.

39. $12p^2 - 2 - 5p$
$(3p - 2)(4p + 1)$

40. $12q^3 - q^2 - 6q$
$q(4q - 3)(3q + 2)$

41. $-16p^2 - 24p - 4pq - 6q$ $-2(4p + q)(2p + 3)$

42. ENTERTAINING The rectangular-shaped area occupied by the table setting shown is $(12x^2 - x - 1)$ square inches. Factor the expression to find the binomials that represent the length and width of the table setting. $(4x + 1)$ in., $(3x - 1)$ in.

SECTION 6.4   Factoring Perfect-Square Trinomials and the Difference of Two Squares

DEFINITIONS AND CONCEPTS	EXAMPLES
Special product formulas can be used to factor **perfect-square trinomials.** $$A^2 + 2AB + B^2 = (A + B)^2$$ $$A^2 - 2AB + B^2 = (A - B)^2$$	Factor: $$p^2 + 8p + 16 = p^2 + 2 \cdot p \cdot 4 + 4^2 = (p + 4)^2$$ $$m^2 - 18mn + 81n^2 = m^2 - 2 \cdot m \cdot 9n + (9n)^2 = (m - 9n)^2$$
To factor the **difference of two squares,** use the formula $$\mathbf{F}^2 - \mathbf{L}^2 = (\mathbf{F} + \mathbf{L})(\mathbf{F} - \mathbf{L})$$ In general, the sum of two squares (with no common factor other than 1) cannot be factored using real numbers.	Factor: $4p^2 - 25q^2$ $$= (2p)^2 - (5q)^2$$ $$= (2p + 5q)(2p - 5q) \quad \text{This is the difference of two squares.}$$ $x^2 + 25$ and $81x^2 + 49$ are prime polynomials.

REVIEW EXERCISES

Factor each polynomial completely.

43. $x^2 + 10x + 25$
$(x + 5)^2$

44. $9y^2 - 24y + 16$
$(3y - 4)^2$

45. $-z^2 + 2z - 1$
$-(z - 1)^2$

46. $25a^2 + 20ab + 4b^2$
$(5a + 2b)^2$

Factor each polynomial completely, if possible.

47. $x^2 - 9$
$(x + 3)(x - 3)$

48. $49t^2 - 25y^2$
$(7t + 5y)(7t - 5y)$

49. $x^2y^2 - 400$
$(xy + 20)(xy - 20)$

50. $8at^2 - 32a$
$8a(t + 2)(t - 2)$

51. $4c^3 - 64c$
$4c(c + 4)(c - 4)$

52. $h^2 + 36$
prime

SECTION 6.5 Factoring the Sum and Difference of Two Cubes

DEFINITIONS AND CONCEPTS

EXAMPLES

To factor the **sum and difference of two cubes**, use the formulas

$$\mathbf{F}^3 + \mathbf{L}^3 = (\mathbf{F} + \mathbf{L})(\mathbf{F}^2 - \mathbf{FL} + \mathbf{L}^2)$$

$$\mathbf{F}^3 - \mathbf{L}^3 = (\mathbf{F} - \mathbf{L})(\mathbf{F}^2 + \mathbf{FL} + \mathbf{L}^2)$$

Factor: $p^3 + 64 = p^3 + 4^3$ *This is the sum of two cubes.*

$$= (p + 4)(p^2 - p \cdot 4 + 4^2)$$
$$= (p + 4)(p^2 - 4p + 16)$$

Factor: $m^3 - 27n^3 = m^3 - (3n)^3$ *This is the difference of two cubes.*

$$= (m - 3n)[m^2 + m \cdot (3n) + (3n)^2]$$
$$= (m - 3n)(m^2 + 3mn + 9n^2)$$

REVIEW EXERCISES

Factor each polynomial completely, if possible.

53. $h^3 + 1$
$(h + 1)(h^2 - h + 1)$

54. $125p^3 + q^3$
$(5p + q)(25p^2 - 5pq + q^2)$

55. $x^3 - 27$
$(x - 3)(x^2 + 3x + 9)$

56. $16x^5 - 54x^2y^3$
$2x^2(2x - 3y)(4x^2 + 6xy + 9y^2)$

SECTION 6.6 A Factoring Strategy

DEFINITIONS AND CONCEPTS

EXAMPLES

To **factor a random polynomial,** use the **factoring strategy** discussed in the section.

Factor: $a^5 + 8a^2 + 4a^3 + 32$

Is there a common factor other than 1?   No.

How many terms does it have?   Since the polynomial has four terms, try factoring by grouping.

$$a^5 + 8a^2 + 4a^3 + 32 = a^2(a^3 + 8) + 4(a^3 + 8)$$
$$= (a^3 + 8)(a^2 + 4)$$

Remember that the instruction to factor means to factor completely. A polynomial is factored completely when no factor can be factored further.

Is it factored completely?   No. We can factor $a^3 + 8$ as the sum of two cubes.

$$a^5 + 8a^2 + 4a^3 + 32 = a^2(a^3 + 8) + 4(a^3 + 8)$$
$$= (a^3 + 8)(a^2 + 4)$$
$$= (a + 2)(a^2 - 2a + 4)(a^2 + 4)$$

Does it check?   Check by multiplication.

REVIEW EXERCISES

Factor each polynomial completely, if possible.

57. $14y^3 + 6y^4 - 40y^2$
$2y^2(3y - 5)(y + 4)$

58. $s^2t + s^2u^2 + tv + u^2v$
$(t + u^2)(s^2 + v)$

59. $j^4 - 16$
$(j^2 + 4)(j + 2)(j - 2)$

60. $-3j^3 - 24k^3$
$-3(j + 2k)(j^2 - 2jk + 4k^2)$

61. $12w^2 - 36w + 27$
$3(2w - 3)^2$

62. $121p^2 + 36q^2$
prime

63. $15x^2y - 5xy^2 + 5xy$
$5xy(3x - y + 1)$

64. $2x^3 + 12$
$2(x^3 + 6)$

SECTION 6.7   Solving Equations by Factoring

DEFINITIONS AND CONCEPTS	EXAMPLES
A **quadratic equation** is an equation of the form $ax^2 + bx + c = 0$ $(a \neq 0)$, where a, b, and c represent real numbers.	Quadratic Equations: $x^2 - 3x - 4 = 0$ $3a^2 + 5a - 6 = 0$

The Zero-Factor Property

If a and b are real numbers, then:

    If $ab = 0$, then $a = 0$ or $b = 0$

Solve: $(4a - 3)(2a + 3) = 0$

$$4a - 3 = 0 \quad \text{or} \quad 2a + 3 = 0 \qquad \text{Set each factor equal to 0.}$$

$$4a = 3 \qquad\qquad 2a = -3 \qquad \text{Solve each equation.}$$

$$a = \frac{3}{4} \qquad\qquad a = -\frac{3}{2}$$

To use the factoring method to solve a quadratic equation:

1. Write the equation in $ax^2 + bx + c = 0$ form.
2. Factor the left side.
3. Use the *zero-factor property* (if $ab = 0$, then $a = 0$ or $b = 0$) and set each factor equal to zero.
4. Solve each resulting linear equation.
5. Check the results in the original equation.

Solve: $9p^2 - 3p = 0$

$$3p(3p - 1) = 0$$

$$3p = 0 \quad \text{or} \quad 3p - 1 = 0 \qquad \text{Set each factor equal to 0.}$$

$$p = 0 \qquad\qquad p = \frac{1}{3} \qquad \text{Solve each equation.}$$

Solve: $2a^2 + 1 = 3a$

$$2a^2 - 3a + 1 = 0$$

$$(2a - 1)(a - 1) = 0$$

$$2a - 1 = 0 \quad \text{or} \quad a - 1 = 0 \qquad \text{Set each factor equal to 0.}$$

$$a = \frac{1}{2} \qquad\qquad a = 1 \qquad \text{Solve each equation.}$$

REVIEW EXERCISES

Solve each quadratic equation by factoring.

65. $x^2 + 2x = 0$ $0, -2$ **66.** $x(x - 6) = 0$ $0, 6$ **69.** $t^2 + 4t + 4 = 0$ $-2, -2$ **70.** $2x - x^2 + 24 = 0$ $6, -4$

67. $x^2 - 9 = 0$ $-3, 3$ **68.** $a^2 - 7a + 12 = 0$ $3, 4$ **71.** $5a^2 - 6a + 1 = 0$ $\frac{1}{5}, 1$ **72.** $2p^3 = 2p(p + 2)$ $0, -1, 2$

SECTION 6.8   Applications of Quadratic Equations

DEFINITIONS AND CONCEPTS	EXAMPLES
To solve many application problems, use the **five-step problem-solving strategy:** 1. Analyze the problem. 2. Form an equation. 3. Solve the equation. 4. State the conclusion. 5. Check the result.	Find two consecutive positive integers whose product is 72. **Analyze** *Consecutive integers* are integers that follow each other. The word *product* indicates multiplication. **Form** Let $x =$ the smaller positive integer. Then $x + 1 =$ the larger integer.

The smaller integer	times	the larger integer	equals	72.
x	$\cdot$	$x + 1$	$=$	72

Solve

$$x(x + 1) = 72$$

$$x^2 + x = 72 \qquad \text{Remove parentheses.}$$

$$x^2 + x - 72 = 0 \qquad \text{Subtract 72 from both sides.}$$

$$(x + 9)(x - 8) = 0 \qquad \text{Factor the trinomial.}$$

$$x + 9 = 0 \quad \text{or} \quad x - 8 = 0 \qquad \text{Set each factor equal to 0.}$$

$$x = -9 \quad | \quad x = 8 \qquad \text{Solve each equation.}$$

State Since we are looking for a positive integer, -9 must be discarded. Thus, the smaller integer is 8. The larger integer is $x + 1 = 9$.

Check The integers 8 and 9 are consecutive positive integers and their product is 72.

The Pythagorean Theorem If the length of the hypotenuse of a right triangle is c and the lengths of the two legs are a and b, then $c^2 = a^2 + b^2$.	To show that a triangle with sides of 5, 12, and 13 units is a right triangle, we verify that $5^2 + 12^2 = 13^2$: 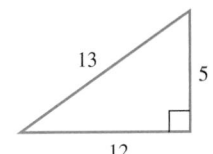 $$5^2 + 12^2 \stackrel{?}{=} 13^2$$ $$25 + 144 \stackrel{?}{=} 169$$ $$169 = 169 \quad \text{True}$$

REVIEW EXERCISES

73. BALLOONING A hot-air balloonist dropped his camera overboard while traveling at a height of 1,600 ft. The height h (in feet) of the camera t seconds after being dropped is given by $h = -16t^2 + 1,600$. In how many seconds will the camera hit the ground? 10 sec

74. Find two consecutive positive integers whose product is 42. 6 and 7

75. CONSTRUCTION The face of the triangular preformed concrete panel shown has an area of 45 square meters, and its base is 3 meters longer than twice its height. How long is its base? 15 m

76. GARDENING A rectangular flower bed occupies 27 square feet and is 3 feet longer than twice its width. Find its dimensions. 3 ft by 9 ft

77. TIGHTROPE WALKERS A circus performer intends to walk up a taut cable to a platform atop a pole, as shown. How high above the ground is the platform? 5 m

CHAPTER 6 TEST

Find the prime factorization of each number.

1. 196 $2^2 \cdot 7^2$

2. 111 $3 \cdot 37$

Factor each polynomial completely. If a polynomial cannot be factored, write "prime."

3. $4x + 16$
$4(x + 4)$

4. $30a^2b^3 - 20a^3b^2 + 5abc$
$5ab(6ab^2 - 4a^2b + c)$

5. $q^2 - 81$
$(q + 9)(q - 9)$

6. $x^2 + 9$
prime

7. $16x^4 - 81$
$(4x^2 + 9)(2x + 3)(2x - 3)$

8. $x^2 + 4x + 3$
$(x + 3)(x + 1)$

9. $-x^2 + 9x + 22$
$-(x - 11)(x + 2)$

10. $9a - 9b + ax - bx$
$(a - b)(9 + x)$

11. $2a^2 + 5a - 12$
$(2a - 3)(a + 4)$

12. $18x^2 - 60xy + 50y^2$
$2(3x - 5y)^2$

13. $x^3 + 8$
$(x + 2)(x^2 - 2x + 4)$

14. $2a^3 - 54$
$2(a - 3)(a^2 + 3a + 9)$

15. LANDSCAPING The combined area of the portions of the square lot that the sprinkler doesn't reach is given by $4r^2 - \pi r^2$, where r is the radius of the circular spray. Factor this expression. $r^2(4 - \pi)$

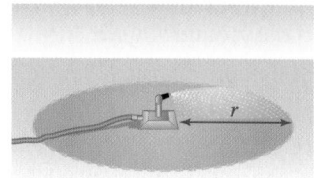

16. CHECKERS The area of the square checkerboard is $25x^2 - 40x + 16$. Find an expression that represents the length of a side. $5x - 4$

17. What is the greatest common factor of $4a^3b^2$ and $18ab^2$? $2ab^2$

26. What is a quadratic equation? Give an example.
A quadratic equation is an equation that can be written in the form $ax^2 + bx + c = 0$; $x^2 - 2x + 1 = 0$. (answers may vary)

18. Factor: $x^2 - 3x - 54$. Show a check of your answer.
$(x - 9)(x + 6)$; To check, multiply the binomials:
$(x - 9)(x + 6) = x^2 + 6x - 9x - 54 = x^2 - 3x - 54$

27. Find the length of the hypotenuse of the following right triangle. 10

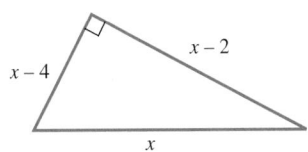

Solve each equation.

19. $(x + 3)(x - 2) = 0$
$-3, 2$

20. $x^2 - 25 = 0$
$-5, 5$

21. $6x^2 - x = 0$ $0, \frac{1}{6}$

22. $x^2 + 6x + 9 = 0$ $-3, -3$

28. If the product of two numbers is 0, what conclusion can be drawn about the numbers?
At least one of them is 0.

23. $6x^2 + x - 1 = 0$ $\frac{1}{3}, -\frac{1}{2}$

24. $x^2 + 7x = -6$ $-1, -6$

25. DRIVING SAFETY Virtually all cars have a blind spot where it is difficult for the driver to see a car behind and to the right. The area of the blind spot shown is 54 square feet. Find the width and length of the blind spot. 6 ft by 9 ft

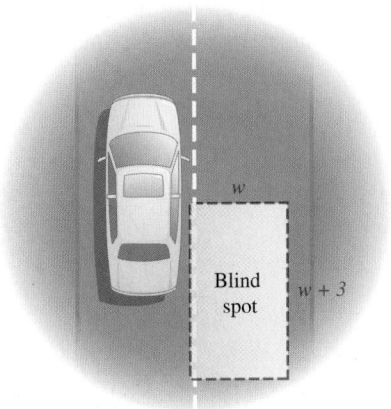

1. **HEART RATES** Refer to the graph. Determine the difference in the maximum heart beat rate for a 70-year-old as compared to someone half that age. [Section 1.1] about 35 beats/min difference

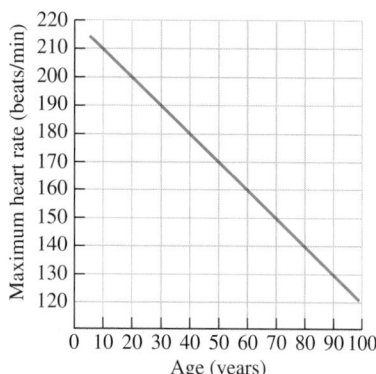

Based on data from *Cardiopulmonary Anatomy and Physiology: Essentials for Respiratory Care*, 2nd ed.

2. Find the prime factorization of 250. [Section 1.2] $2 \cdot 5^3$

3. Find the quotient: $\frac{16}{5} \div \frac{10}{3}$ [Section 1.2] $\frac{24}{25}$

4. Write $\frac{124}{125}$ as a decimal. [Section 1.3] 0.992

5. Determine whether each statement is true or false. [Section 1.3]

   a. Every integer is a whole number. false

   b. Every integer is a rational number. true

   c. π is a real number. true

6. Which division is undefined, $\frac{0}{5}$ or $\frac{5}{0}$? [Section 1.6] $\frac{5}{0}$

Evaluate each expression.

7. $3 + 2[-1 - 4(5)]$ [Section 1.7] -39

8. $\dfrac{|-25| - 2(-5)}{9 - 2^4}$ [Section 1.7] -5

9. What is -3 cubed? [Section 1.7] -27

10. What is the value of x twenty-dollar bills? [Section 1.8] $20x$

11. Evaluate $\dfrac{-x - a}{y - b}$ for $x = -2$, $y = 1$, $a = 5$, and $b = 2$. [Section 1.8] 3

12. Identify the coefficient of each term in the expression $8x^2 - x + 9$. [Section 1.8] $8, -1, 9$

Simplify each expression.

13. $-8y^2 - 5y^2 + 6$ [Section 1.9] $-13y^2 + 6$

14. $3z + 2(y - z) + y$ [Section 1.9] $3y + z$

Solve each equation.

15. $-(3a + 1) + a = 2$ [Section 2.2] $-\frac{3}{2}$

16. $2 - (4x + 7) = 3 + 2(x + 2)$ [Section 2.2] -2

17. $\dfrac{3t - 21}{2} = t - 6$ [Section 2.2] 9

18. $-\dfrac{1}{3} - \dfrac{x}{5} = \dfrac{3}{2}$ [Section 2.2] $-\frac{55}{6}$

19. **WATERMELONS** The heaviest watermelon on record weighed 270 pounds. If watermelon is 92% water by weight, what was its water weight? (Round to the nearest pound.) [Section 2.3] 248 lb

20. Find the distance traveled by a truck traveling for $5\frac{1}{2}$ hours at a rate of 60 miles per hour. [Section 2.4] 330 mi

21. What is the formula for simple interest? [Section 2.4] $I = Prt$

22. **GEOMETRY TOOLS** A compass is adjusted so that the distance between the pointed ends is 2 inches. Then a circle is drawn. What will the area of the circle be? Round to the nearest tenth of a square inch. [Section 2.4] 12.6 in.^{2}

23. Solve $A = P + Prt$ for t. [Section 2.4] $t = \frac{A - P}{Pr}$

24. HISTORY George Washington was the first president of the United States. John Adams was the second, and Thomas Jefferson was the third, and so on. Grover Cleveland was president two *different* times, as shown in the illustration. The sum of the numbers of Cleveland's presidencies is 46. Find these two numbers. [Section 2.5] 22nd president, 24th president

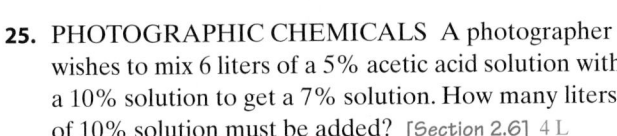

Grover Cleveland Benjamin Harrison Grover Cleveland

25. PHOTOGRAPHIC CHEMICALS A photographer wishes to mix 6 liters of a 5% acetic acid solution with a 10% solution to get a 7% solution. How many liters of 10% solution must be added? [Section 2.6] 4 L

26. Solve $-\frac{x}{2} + 4 > 5$. Write the solution set in interval notation and graph it. [Section 2.7] $(-\infty, -2)$

27. Is $(-2, 5)$ a solution of $3x + 2y = 4$? [Section 3.2] yes

28. Graph: $y = 2x - 3$
[Section 3.2]

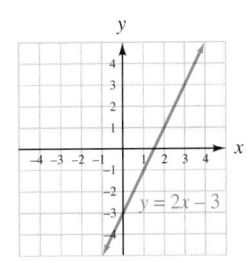

29. Is the graph of $x = 3$ a vertical or horizontal line? [Section 3.3] vertical line

30. If two lines are parallel, what can be said about their slopes? [Section 3.4] They are the same.

31. BOTTLED WATER Refer to the graph below. Determine the rate of change in the number of gallons of bottled water that the average American drank in a year for 1995 through 2005.
[Section 3.4] 1.4 gal/yr

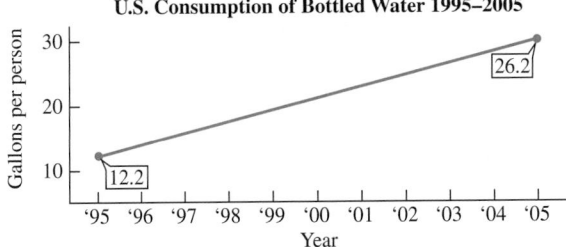

U.S. Consumption of Bottled Water 1995–2005

Source: Beverage Marketing Coproration, 2005

32. Find the slope and the y-intercept of the graph of $3x - 3y = 6$. [Section 3.5] $1, (0, -2)$

33. Graph the line passing through $(-4, 1)$ that has slope -3. [Section 3.5]

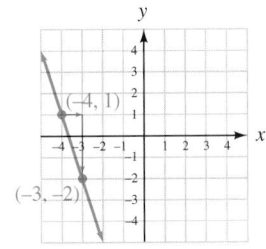

34. Find an equation of the line passing through $(-2, 5)$ and $(-3, -2)$. Write the equation in slope–intercept form. [Section 3.6] $y = 7x + 19$

35. Graph: $8x + 4y \geq -24$
[Section 3.7]

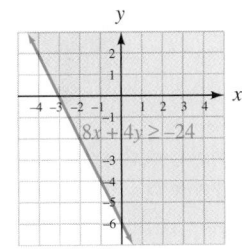

36. If $f(x) = 3x^2 - 2x + 1$, find $f(-2)$. [Section 3.8] 17

37. Is $\left(\frac{1}{2}, 1\right)$ a solution of the system $\begin{cases} 4x - y = 1 \\ 2x + y = 2 \end{cases}$?
[Section 4.1] yes

38. Solve the system $\begin{cases} 3x - 2y = 6 \\ x - y = 1 \end{cases}$ by graphing.
[Section 4.1] $(4, 3)$

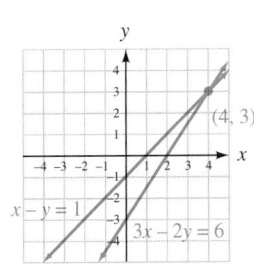

39. Solve the system $\begin{cases} y = -4x + 1 \\ 4x - y = 5 \end{cases}$ by substitution.
[Section 4.2] $\left(\frac{3}{4}, -2\right)$

40. Solve the system $\begin{cases} 5a + 3b = -8 \\ 2a + 9b = 2 \end{cases}$ by addition (elimination). [Section 4.3] $\left(-2, \frac{2}{3}\right)$

41. FUNDRAISING A Rotary Club held a city-wide recycling drive. They collected a total of 14 tons of newspaper and cardboard that earned them $356. They were paid $31 per ton for the newspaper and $18 per ton for the cardboard. How many tons of each did they collect? [Section 4.4]
newspaper: 8 tons, cardboard: 6 tons

42. Graph: $\begin{cases} 4x + 3y \geq 12 \\ y < 4 \end{cases}$ [Section 4.5]

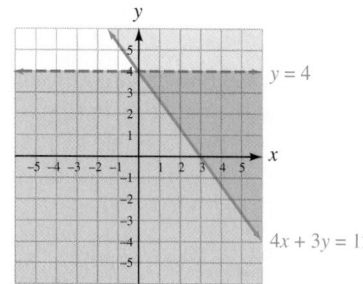

Simplify each expression. Write each answer without negative exponents.

43. $-y^2(4y^3)$ [Section 5.1]
$-4y^5$

44. $\dfrac{(x^2y^5)^5}{(x^3y)^2}$ [Section 5.1]
x^4y^{23}

45. $\left(\dfrac{b^5}{b^{-2}}\right)$ [Section 5.2] b^7

46. $2x^0$ [Section 5.2] 2

47. Write 0.00009011 in scientific notation.
[Section 5.3] 9.011×10^{-5}

48. Write 1,700,000 in scientific notation.
[Section 5.3] 1.7×10^6

49. Find the degree of $7y^3 + 4y^2 + y + 3$. [Section 5.4] 3

50. Graph: $y = x^3 + 2$
[Section 5.4]

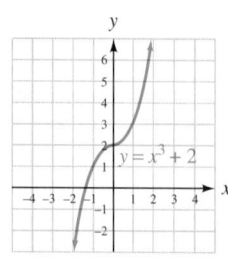

Perform the operations.

51. $(x^2 - 3x + 8) - (3x^2 + x + 3)$
[Section 5.5] $-2x^2 - 4x + 5$

52. $4b^3(2b^2 - 2b)$ [Section 5.6] $8b^5 - 8b^4$

53. $(3x - 2)(x + 4)$ [Section 5.6] $3x^2 + 10x - 8$

54. $(y - 6)^2$ [Section 5.6] $y^2 - 12y + 36$

55. $\dfrac{12a^2b^2 - 8a^2b - 4ab}{4ab}$ [Section 5.7] $3ab - 2a - 1$

56. $x - 3\overline{)2x^2 - 5x - 3}$ [Section 5.8] $2x + 1$

57. PLAYPENS Find an expression that represents the
   a. perimeter of the playpen. [Section 5.5] $(4x + 8)$ in.
   b. area of the floor of the playpen.
      [Section 5.6] $(x^2 + 4x + 3)$ in.^{2}
   c. volume of the playpen.
      [Section 5.6] $(x^3 + 4x^2 + 3x)$ in.^{3}

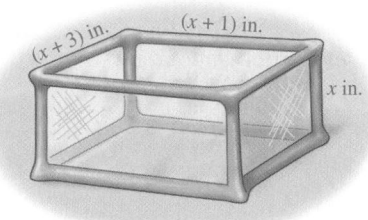

58. Find the GCF of $24x^5y^8$ and $54x^6y$. [Section 6.1] $6x^5y$

Factor completely.

59. $9b^3 - 27b^2$
   [Section 6.1]
   $9b^2(b - 3)$

60. $ax + bx + ay + by$
   [Section 6.1]
   $(x + y)(a + b)$

61. $u^2 - 3 + 2u$
   [Section 6.2]
   $(u + 3)(u - 1)$

62. $10x^2 + x - 2$
   [Section 6.3]
   $(2x + 1)(5x - 2)$

63. $4a^2 - 12a + 9$
   [Section 6.4]
   $(2a - 3)^2$

64. $9z^2 - 1$
   [Section 6.4]
   $(3z + 1)(3z - 1)$

65. $t^3 - 8$
   [Section 6.5]
   $(t - 2)(t^2 + 2t + 4)$

66. $3a^2b^2 - 6a^2 - 3b^2 + 6$
   [Section 6.6]
   $3(b^2 - 2)(a + 1)(a - 1)$

Solve each equation.

67. $15s^2 - 20s = 0$
   [Section 6.7] $0, \frac{4}{3}$

68. $2x^2 - 5x = -2$
   [Section 6.7] $\frac{1}{2}, 2$

Rational Expressions and Equations

© BananaStock/SuperStock

from *Campus to Careers*

Recreation Director

People of all ages enjoy participating in activities, such as arts and crafts, camping, sports, and the performing arts. Recreation directors plan, organize, and oversee these activities in local playgrounds, camps, community centers, religious organizations, theme parks, and tourist attractions. The job of recreation director requires mathematical skills such as budgeting, scheduling, and forecasting trends.

Problem 21 of **Study Set 7.7** involves an area of responsibility for many recreation directors—swimming pools.

JOB TITLE:
Recreation Director

EDUCATION: An associate's or bachelor's degree in parks and recreation is preferred.

JOB OUTLOOK: Employment is expected to increase by 13% through the year 2016.

ANNUAL EARNINGS: Median annual salary is $20,470, up to $35,780 or more

FOR MORE INFORMATION:
http://stats.bls.gov/oco/ocos058.htm

Objectives

1. Evaluate rational expressions.

2. Find numbers that cause a rational expression to be undefined.

3. Simplify rational expressions.

4. Simplify rational expressions that have factors that are opposites.

SECTION 7.1

Simplifying Rational Expressions

Fractions such as $\frac{1}{2}$ and $\frac{3}{4}$ that are the quotient of two integers are *rational numbers*. Fractions such as

$$\frac{3}{2y}, \qquad \frac{x}{x+2}, \qquad \text{and} \qquad \frac{5a^2 + 6ab + b^2}{25a^2 - b^2}$$

where the numerators and denominators are polynomials are called *rational expressions*.

> ### Rational Expressions
>
> A **rational expression** is an expression of the form $\frac{A}{B}$, where A and B are polynomials and B does not equal zero.

---

1 Evaluate rational expressions.

To evaluate a rational expression, we replace each variable with a given number value and simplify.

EXAMPLE 1 Evaluate $\dfrac{2x - 1}{x^2 + 1}$ for $x = -3$.

Strategy We will replace each x in the rational expression with -3. Then we will evaluate the expression following the order of operations.

WHY Recall from Chapter 1 that to *evaluate an expression* means to find its numerical value, once we know the value of its variable.

Solution

$$\frac{2x - 1}{x^2 + 1} = \frac{2(-3) - 1}{(-3)^2 + 1} \qquad \text{Substitute } -3 \text{ for } x.$$

$$= \frac{-6 - 1}{9 + 1} \qquad \begin{array}{l}\text{In the numerator, perform the multiplication. In the} \\ \text{denominator, evaluate the exponential expression.}\end{array}$$

$$= -\frac{7}{10}$$

---

2 Find numbers that cause a rational expression to be undefined.

Since rational expressions indicate division, we must make sure that the denominator of a rational expression is not equal to 0.

EXAMPLE 2 Find all real numbers for which each rational expression is undefined: **a.** $\dfrac{7x}{x - 5}$ **b.** $\dfrac{x - 1}{x^2 - x - 6}$

Strategy To find the real numbers for which each rational expression is undefined, we will find the values of the variable that make the *denominator* 0.

WHY A denominator of 0 makes a rational expression undefined, because a denominator of 0 indicates division by 0. We don't need to examine the numerator of the rational expression; it can be any value, including 0.

Solution

a. The expression $\dfrac{7x}{x-5}$ will be undefined if the denominator is zero. To find the value, we solve

$$x - 5 = 0 \quad \text{Set the denominator equal to zero.}$$
$$x = 5 \quad \text{Add 5 to both sides to solve for } x.$$

Check $\dfrac{7x}{x-5} = \dfrac{7(5)}{5-5} = \dfrac{35}{0}$

Since $\frac{35}{0}$ is undefined, the rational expression $\frac{7x}{x-5}$ is undefined for $x = 5$.

b. The expression $\dfrac{x-1}{x^2-x-6}$ will be undefined for values of x that make the denominator 0. To find these values, we solve $x^2 - x - 6 = 0$.

$$x^2 - x - 6 = 0 \qquad \text{Set the denominator of the rational expression equal to 0.}$$
$$(x - 3)(x + 2) = 0 \qquad \text{Factor the trinomial.}$$
$$x - 3 = 0 \quad \text{or} \quad x + 2 = 0 \qquad \text{Set each factor equal to 0.}$$
$$x = 3 \quad | \quad x = -2 \qquad \text{Solve each linear equation.}$$

Since the values 3 and -2 make the denominator 0, the expression is undefined for $x = 3$ or $x = -2$.

Self Check 2

Find the values for x for which each expression is undefined.

a. $\dfrac{x}{x+9}$ -9

b. $\dfrac{x+7}{x^2-25}$ 5 or -5

Now Try Problems 18 and 22

Teaching Example 2 Find the values for x for which each expression is undefined.

a. $\dfrac{3x}{x-7}$ **b.** $\dfrac{x+8}{x^2-7x+6}$

Answer:

a. 7 **b.** 1, 6

---

3   Simplify rational expressions.

To simplify a fraction we remove a factor equal to 1. This can be accomplished in two ways. For example, to simplify $\frac{6}{15}$, we proceed as follows:

Method 1

$$\frac{6}{15} = \frac{2 \cdot 3}{5 \cdot 3} \qquad \text{Factor the numerator and the denominator.}$$

$$= \frac{2}{5} \cdot \frac{3}{3} \qquad \text{From Section 1.2, we know that } \frac{a \cdot c}{b \cdot d} = \frac{a}{b} \cdot \frac{c}{d}.$$

$$= \frac{2}{5} \cdot 1 \qquad \text{A number divided by itself is equal to 1: } \frac{3}{3} = 1.$$

$$= \frac{2}{5} \qquad \text{Any number multiplied by 1 remains the same.}$$

Method 2

$$\frac{6}{15} = \frac{2 \cdot 3}{5 \cdot 3} \qquad \text{Factor the numerator and the denominator.}$$

$$= \frac{2 \cdot \overset{1}{\cancel{3}}}{5 \cdot \underset{1}{\cancel{3}}} \qquad \text{Remove } \frac{3}{3} = 1.$$

$$= \frac{2}{5} \qquad \text{Multiply to find the numerator: } 2 \cdot 1 = 2. \text{ Multiply to find the denominator: } 5 \cdot 1 = 5.$$

When all pairs of factors common to the numerator and denominator of a fraction have been removed, the fraction is **expressed in simplified form.** Since it usually requires fewer steps, we will use method 2 in the following examples. The generalization of method 2 is called the **fundamental property of fractions** and can be applied to rational expressions as well.

Fundamental Property of Fractions

If A, B, and C are polynomials, and B and C are not 0,

$$\frac{AC}{BC} = \frac{A}{B}$$

Simplifying rational expressions is similar to simplifying fractions. We write the rational expression so that the numerator and denominator have no common factors other than 1.

Simplifying Rational Expressions

1. Factor the numerator and denominator completely to determine their common factors.

2. Remove factors equal to 1 by replacing each pair of factors common to the numerator and denominator with the equivalent fraction $\frac{1}{1}$.

3. Multiply the remaining factors in the numerator and in the denominator.

Self Check 3

Simplify: $\dfrac{32a^3b^2}{24ab^4}$ $\dfrac{4a^2}{3b^2}$

Now Try Problem 39

Teaching Example 3 Simplify: $\dfrac{20x^5y^8}{15x^9y^3}$

Answer:
$\dfrac{4y^5}{3x^4}$

EXAMPLE 3 Simplify: $\dfrac{21x^2y}{14xy^2}$

Strategy We will write the numerator and denominator in factored form and then remove pairs of factors that are equal to 1.

WHY The rational expression is simplified when the numerator and denominator have no common factor other than 1.

Solution

$$\frac{21x^2y}{14xy^2} = \frac{3 \cdot 7 \cdot x \cdot x \cdot y}{2 \cdot 7 \cdot x \cdot y \cdot y} \qquad \text{Factor the numerator and denominator.}$$

$$= \frac{3 \cdot \overset{1}{\cancel{7}} \cdot \overset{1}{\cancel{x}} \cdot x \cdot \cancel{y}}{2 \cdot \underset{1}{\cancel{7}} \cdot \underset{1}{\cancel{x}} \cdot y \cdot \underset{1}{\cancel{y}}} \qquad \begin{array}{l}\text{Replace } \frac{7}{7}, \frac{x}{x}, \text{ and } \frac{y}{y} \text{ with the equivalent fraction } \frac{1}{1}.\\ \text{This removes the factor } \frac{7 \cdot x \cdot y}{7 \cdot x \cdot y}, \text{ which is equal to 1.}\end{array}$$

$$= \frac{3x}{2y} \qquad \begin{array}{l}\text{Multiply the remaining factors in the numerator and in the}\\ \text{denominator: } 3 \cdot 1 \cdot 1 \cdot x \cdot 1 = 3x \text{ and } 2 \cdot 1 \cdot 1 \cdot y \cdot 1 = 2y.\end{array}$$

To simplify rational expressions, we often make use of the factoring techniques discussed in Chapter 6.

Self Check 4

Simplify: $\dfrac{x^2 - 5x}{5x - 25}$ $\dfrac{x}{5}$

Now Try Problem 43

Teaching Example 4 Simplify:
$\dfrac{x^2 + 7x}{2x + 14}$
Answer:
$\dfrac{x}{2}$

EXAMPLE 4 Simplify: $\dfrac{x^2 + 3x}{3x + 9}$

Strategy We will begin by factoring the numerator and denominator. Then we will remove any factors common to the numerator and denominator.

WHY We need to make sure that the numerator and denominator have no common factors other than 1. When this is true, the rational expression is simplified.

Solution
We note that the terms of the numerator have a common factor of x and the terms of the denominator have a common factor of 3.

$$\frac{x^2 + 3x}{3x + 9} = \frac{x(x + 3)}{3(x + 3)} \qquad \text{Factor the numerator and the denominator.}$$

$$= \frac{x(\overset{1}{\cancel{x + 3}})}{3(\underset{1}{\cancel{x + 3}})} \qquad \text{Remove a factor equal to 1 by replacing } \frac{x + 3}{x + 3} \text{ with } \frac{1}{1}.$$

$$= \frac{x}{3} \qquad \begin{array}{l}\text{Multiply in the numerator: } x \cdot 1 = x.\\ \text{Multiply in the denominator: } 3 \cdot 1 = 3.\end{array}$$

EXAMPLE 5 Simplify: $\dfrac{x^2 + 13x + 12}{x^2 - 144}$

Strategy We will begin by factoring the numerator and denominator. Then we will remove any factors common to the numerator and denominator.

WHY We need to make sure that the numerator and denominator have no common factors other than 1. When this is true, the rational expression is simplified.

Solution
The numerator is a trinomial, and the denominator is a difference of two squares.

$$\dfrac{x^2 + 13x + 12}{x^2 - 144} = \dfrac{(x + 1)(x + 12)}{(x + 12)(x - 12)} \quad \text{Factor the numerator and the denominator.}$$

$$= \dfrac{(x + 1)\overset{1}{\cancel{(x + 12)}}}{\underset{1}{\cancel{(x + 12)}}(x - 12)} \quad \text{Remove a factor equal to 1 by replacing } \tfrac{x + 12}{x + 12} \text{ with } \tfrac{1}{1}.$$

$$= \dfrac{x + 1}{x - 12}$$

Self Check 5

Simplify: $\dfrac{3x^2 - 8x - 3}{x^2 - 9}$ $\dfrac{3x + 1}{x + 3}$

Now Try Problem 45

Teaching Example 5 Simplify:
$\dfrac{2x^2 - x - 15}{x^2 - 9}$
Answer:
$\dfrac{2x + 5}{x + 3}$

Caution! When simplifying a fraction, remember that only *factors* that are common to the *entire numerator* and the *entire denominator* can be removed. For example, consider the correct simplification

$$\dfrac{5 + 8}{5} = \dfrac{13}{5}$$

It would be incorrect to remove the common *term* of 5 in this simplification. Doing so gives an incorrect answer of 9.

$$\dfrac{5 + 8}{5} = \dfrac{\overset{1}{\cancel{5}} + 8}{\underset{1}{\cancel{5}}} = \dfrac{1 + 8}{1} = 9$$

When simplifying rational expressions, *it is incorrect to remove terms common to both the numerator and denominator.*

$$\dfrac{\overset{1}{\cancel{x}} + 5}{\underset{1}{\cancel{x}} + 6} \qquad \dfrac{a^2 - 3\overset{1}{\cancel{a}} + \overset{1}{\cancel{2}}}{\underset{1}{\cancel{a}} + \underset{1}{\cancel{2}}} \qquad \dfrac{\overset{1}{\cancel{y^2}} - 36}{\underset{1}{\cancel{y^2}} - y - 7}$$

Any number or algebraic expression divided by 1 remains unchanged. For example,

$$\dfrac{37}{1} = 37, \qquad \dfrac{5x}{1} = 5x, \qquad \text{and} \qquad \dfrac{3x + y}{1} = 3x + y$$

In general, we have the following.

Division by 1

For any real number a, $\dfrac{a}{1} = a$.

Self Check 6

Simplify: $\dfrac{a^2 + a - 2}{a - 1}$ $a + 2$

Now Try Problem 49

Teaching Example 6 Simplify:
$\dfrac{3x^3 + x^2}{3x + 1}$
Answer:
x^2

EXAMPLE 6 Simplify: $\dfrac{x^3 + x^2}{x + 1}$

Strategy We will begin by factoring the numerator and denominator. Then we will remove any factors common to the numerator and denominator.

WHY We need to make sure that the numerator and denominator have no common factors other than 1. When this is true, the rational expression is simplified.

Solution

$$\frac{x^3 + x^2}{x + 1} = \frac{x^2(x + 1)}{x + 1} \qquad \text{Factor the numerator.}$$

$$= \frac{x^2(\overset{1}{\cancel{x + 1}})}{\underset{1}{\cancel{x + 1}}} \qquad \text{Remove a factor equal to 1 by replacing } \tfrac{x + 1}{x + 1} \text{ with } \tfrac{1}{1}.$$

$$= \frac{x^2}{1}$$

$$= x^2 \qquad \text{Denominators of 1 need not be written.}$$

Self Check 7

Simplify: $\dfrac{4(x - 2) + 4}{3(x - 2) + 3}$ $\dfrac{4}{3}$

Now Try Problem 55

Teaching Example 7 Simplify:
$\dfrac{6(x - 4) + 12}{5(x - 4) + 10}$
Answer:
$\dfrac{6}{5}$

EXAMPLE 7 Simplify: $\dfrac{5(x + 3) - 5}{7(x + 3) - 7}$

Strategy We will begin by simplifying the numerator, $5(x + 3) - 5$, and the denominator, $7(x + 3) - 7$, separately. Then we will factor each result and remove any common factors.

WHY We cannot immediately remove $x + 3$ because it is not a factor of the *entire* numerator and the *entire* denominator.

Solution

$$\frac{5(x + 3) - 5}{7(x + 3) - 7} = \frac{5x + 15 - 5}{7x + 21 - 7} \qquad \begin{array}{l}\text{Use the distributive property in the numerator}\\\text{and the denominator.}\end{array}$$

$$= \frac{5x + 10}{7x + 14} \qquad \text{Combine like terms: } 15 - 5 = 10 \text{ and } 21 - 7 = 14.$$

$$= \frac{5(x + 2)}{7(x + 2)} \qquad \text{Factor the numerator and the denominator.}$$

$$= \frac{5(\overset{1}{\cancel{x + 2}})}{7(\underset{1}{\cancel{x + 2}})} \qquad \begin{array}{l}\text{Remove the common factor of } (x + 2) \text{ in the}\\\text{numerator and denominator.}\end{array}$$

$$= \frac{5}{7}$$

Self Check 8

Simplify: $\dfrac{a(a + 2) - 2(a - 1)}{a^2 + 2}$ 1

Now Try Problem 57

Teaching Example 8 Simplify:
$\dfrac{x(x + 5) - 5(x + 2)}{x^2 - 10}$
Answer:
1

EXAMPLE 8 Simplify: $\dfrac{x(x + 3) - 3(x - 1)}{x^2 + 3}$

Strategy We will begin by simplifying the numerator, $x(x + 3) - 3(x - 1)$. Then we will look for any common factors that can be removed in the numerator and the denominator.

WHY We need to make sure that the numerator and denominator have no common factors other than 1. When this is true, the rational expression is simplified.

Solution

We simplify the numerator and look for any common factors to remove in the numerator and denominator.

$$\frac{x(x + 3) - 3(x - 1)}{x^2 + 3} = \frac{x^2 + 3x - 3x + 3}{x^2 + 3}$$

Use the distributive property twice in the numerator.

$$= \frac{x^2 + 3}{x^2 + 3}$$

Combine like terms in the numerator: $3x - 3x = 0$.

$$= \frac{\overset{1}{\cancel{x^2 + 3}}}{\underset{1}{\cancel{x^2 + 3}}}$$

Remove the common factor: $\frac{x^2 + 3}{x^2 + 3} = 1$

$$= 1$$

Sometimes a fraction does not simplify. For example, to attempt to simplify

$$\frac{x^2 + x - 2}{x^2 + x}$$

we factor the numerator and the denominator.

$$\frac{x^2 + x - 2}{x^2 + x} = \frac{(x + 2)(x - 1)}{x(x + 1)}$$

Because there are no factors common to the numerator and denominator, this fraction is already in lowest terms.

4 Simplify rational expressions that have factors that are opposites.

If the terms of two polynomials are the same, except that they are opposite in sign, the polynomials are called **opposites (negatives)**. For example, the following pairs of polynomials are opposites of each other:

$x - y$	and	$-x + y$	Compare terms: x and −x; −y and y.
$2a - 1$	and	$-2a + 1$	Compare terms: 2a and −2a; −1 and 1.
$-3x^2 - 2x + 5$	and	$3x^2 + 2x - 5$	Compare terms: $-3x^2$ and $3x^2$; −2x and 2x; 5 and −5.

Example 9 shows why the quotient of two binomials that are opposites is equal to -1.

EXAMPLE 9

Simplify: $\dfrac{2a - 1}{1 - 2a}$

Strategy We will rearrange the terms of the numerator $2a - 1$, and factor out -1.

WHY This step is useful when the numerator and denominator contain factors that are opposites, such as $2a - 1$ and $1 - 2a$. It produces a common factor that can be removed.

Solution

$$\frac{2a - 1}{1 - 2a} = \frac{-1 + 2a}{1 - 2a}$$

In the numerator, think of $2a - 1$ as $2a + (-1)$. Then change the order of the terms: $2a + (-1) = -1 + 2a$.

$$= \frac{-(1 - 2a)}{1 - 2a}$$

In the numerator, factor out −1: $-1 + 2a = -(1 - 2a)$.

Self Check 9

Simplify: $\dfrac{3p - 2}{2 - 3p}$ -1

Now Try Problem 61

Teaching Example 9 Simplify: $\dfrac{5x - 3}{3 - 5x}$

Answer:
-1

$$= \frac{-(1 - 2a)}{1 - 2a} \quad \text{Remove the common factor: } \frac{1 - 2a}{1 - 2a} = 1.$$

$$= -1$$

In general, we have this important fact.

The Quotient of Opposites

The quotient of any nonzero expression and its opposite is -1.

Caution! Only apply the preceding rule to expressions that are opposites. For example, it would be incorrect to use this rule to simplify $\frac{x + 1}{1 + x}$. Since $x + 1$ equals $1 + x$ by the commutative property of addition, this is the quotient of a number and itself. The result is 1, not -1.

$$\frac{x + 1}{1 + x} = \frac{x + 1}{x + 1} = 1$$

Self Check 10

Simplify, if possible:

a. $\dfrac{m^2 - 100}{10m - m^2} \quad -\dfrac{m + 10}{m}$

b. $\dfrac{2x - 3}{2x + 3}$ does not simplify

Now Try Problem 64

Teaching Example 10 Simplify, if possible:

a. $\dfrac{a^2 - 9}{18 - 6a}$

b. $\dfrac{-x + 3}{-x - 3}$

Answers:

a. $-\dfrac{a + 3}{6}$

b. does not simplify

EXAMPLE 10

Simplify, if possible: **a.** $\dfrac{y^2 - 1}{3 - 3y}$ **b.** $\dfrac{t + 8}{t - 8}$

Strategy We will begin by factoring the numerator and denominator. Then we look for common factors, or factors that are opposites, and remove them.

WHY We need to make sure that the numerator and denominator have no common factor (or opposite factors) other than 1. When this is the case, then the rational expression is simplified.

Solution

a. $\dfrac{y^2 - 1}{3 - 3y} = \dfrac{(y + 1)(y - 1)}{3(1 - y)}$ Factor the numerator.
Factor the denominator.

$$= \frac{(y + 1)(y - 1)}{3(1 - y)}$$ Since $y - 1$ and $1 - y$ are opposites, simplify by replacing $\frac{y - 1}{1 - y}$ with the equivalent fraction $\frac{-1}{1}$. This removes the factor $\frac{y - 1}{1 - y} = -1$.

$$= \frac{-(y + 1)}{3}$$

This result may be written in several other equivalent forms.

$$\frac{-(y + 1)}{3} = -\frac{y + 1}{3}$$ The $-$ symbol in $-(y + 1)$ can be written in the front of the fraction, and the parentheses can be dropped.

$$\frac{-(y + 1)}{3} = \frac{-y - 1}{3}$$ The $-$ symbol in $-(y + 1)$ represents a factor of -1. Distribute the multiplication by -1 in the numerator.

$$\frac{-(y + 1)}{3} = \frac{y + 1}{-3}$$ The $-$ symbol in $-(y + 1)$ can be applied to the denominator. However, we don't usually use this form.

Caution! A − symbol in front of a fraction may be applied to the numerator or to the denominator, but not to both:

$$-\frac{y+1}{3} \neq \frac{-(y+1)}{-3}$$

b. The binomials $t + 8$ and $t - 8$ are not opposites because their first terms do not have opposite signs. Thus, $\frac{t+8}{t-8}$ does not simplify.

ANSWERS TO SELF CHECKS

1. −2 **2. a.** −9 **b.** 5 or −5 **3.** $\frac{4a^2}{3b^2}$ **4.** $\frac{x}{5}$ **5.** $\frac{3x+1}{x+3}$ **6.** $a+2$ **7.** $\frac{4}{3}$ **8.** 1

9. −1 **10. a.** $-\frac{m+10}{m}$ **b.** does not simplify

SECTION 7.1   STUDY SET

VOCABULARY

Fill in the blanks.

1. In a fraction, the part above the fraction bar is called the _numerator_ , and the part below is called the _denominator_ .

2. A fraction that has polynomials in its numerator and denominator, such as $\frac{x+2}{x-3}$, is called a _rational_ expression.

3. Division by 0 is _undefined_ .

▶ **4.** A fraction is in _simplified_ form when all common factors of the numerator and denominator have been removed.

5. To _simplify_ a rational expression means we remove factors common to the numerator and denominator.

6. If the terms of two polynomials are the same, except for sign, the polynomials are called _opposites_ of each other.

CONCEPTS

7. What value of x makes each rational expression undefined?

a. $\frac{x+2}{x}$ 0 **b.** $\frac{x+2}{x-6}$ 6 **c.** $\frac{x+2}{x+6}$ −6

8. In the following work, what common factor has been removed? $x + 1$

$$\frac{x^2 + 2x + 1}{x^2 + 4x + 3} = \frac{(\overset{1}{\cancel{x+1}})(x+1)}{(x+3)(\underset{1}{\cancel{x+1}})} = \frac{x+1}{x+3}$$

▶ **9.** Simplify each rational expression.

a. $\frac{x-8}{x-8}$ 1 **b.** $\frac{x-8}{8-x}$ −1 **c.** $\frac{x-8}{1}$ $x-8$

10. Explain the error in the following work.

$$\frac{x}{x+2} = \frac{\overset{1}{\cancel{x}}}{\cancel{x}+2} = \frac{1}{3}$$
$$\phantom{\frac{x}{x+2}}\quad_{1}$$

x is not a common factor of the numerator and denominator and cannot be removed.

NOTATION

Complete each solution.

11. $\dfrac{x^2 + 5x - 6}{x^2 - 1} = \dfrac{(x + \boxed{6})(x-1)}{(x+1)(x - \boxed{1})}$

$\phantom{\dfrac{x^2 + 5x - 6}{x^2 - 1}} = \dfrac{x+6}{\boxed{x+1}}$

▶ **12.** $\dfrac{5(x+2)-5}{4(x+2)-4} = \dfrac{5x+\boxed{10}-5}{4x+\boxed{8}-4}$

$\phantom{\dfrac{5(x+2)-5}{4(x+2)-4}} = \dfrac{5x+\boxed{5}}{4x+\boxed{4}}$

$\phantom{\dfrac{5(x+2)-5}{4(x+2)-4}} = \dfrac{5\,\boxed{(x+1)}}{4(x+1)}$

$\phantom{\dfrac{5(x+2)-5}{4(x+2)-4}} = \dfrac{5}{\boxed{4}}$

GUIDED PRACTICE

Evaluate each expression for $x = 6$. See Example 1.

13. $\dfrac{x-2}{x-5}$ 4 ▶ **14.** $\dfrac{3x-2}{x-2}$ 4

15. $\dfrac{-2x-3}{x^2-1}$ $-\frac{3}{7}$ ▶ **16.** $\dfrac{x^2-11}{-x-4}$ $-\frac{5}{2}$

▶ Selected exercises available online at
www.webassign.net/brookscole

Which value(s) of *x*, if any, make each rational expression undefined? See Example 2.

17. $\dfrac{15}{x-2}$ 2

18. ▶ $\dfrac{5x}{x+5}$ −5

19. $\dfrac{15x+2}{16}$ none

20. ▶ $\dfrac{x^2-4x}{25}$ none

21. $\dfrac{30}{x^2-36}$ −6, 6

22. ▶ $\dfrac{2x-15}{x^2-49}$ −7, 7

23. $\dfrac{15}{x^2+x-2}$ −2, 1

24. $\dfrac{x-20}{x^2+2x-8}$ −4, 2

Simplify each fraction. See Objective 3.

25. $\dfrac{28}{35}$ $\frac{4}{5}$

26. ▶ $\dfrac{14}{20}$ $\frac{7}{10}$

27. $\dfrac{9}{27}$ $\frac{1}{3}$

28. ▶ $\dfrac{15}{45}$ $\frac{1}{3}$

29. $-\dfrac{36}{48}$ $-\frac{3}{4}$

30. $-\dfrac{32}{40}$ $-\frac{4}{5}$

31. $-\dfrac{49}{35}$ $-\frac{7}{5}$

32. $-\dfrac{36}{52}$ $-\frac{9}{13}$

Simplify each expression. If an expression cannot be simplified, so indicate. Assume that no denominators are 0. See Examples 3–4.

33. ▶ $\dfrac{45}{9a}$ $\frac{5}{a}$

34. $\dfrac{48}{16y}$ $\frac{3}{y}$

35. $\dfrac{2x}{3x}$ $\frac{2}{3}$

36. $\dfrac{5y}{7y}$ $\frac{5}{7}$

37. $\dfrac{2x^2}{3y}$ in simplified form

38. $\dfrac{5x^2}{2y^2}$ in simplified form

39. $\dfrac{15x^2y}{5xy^2}$ $\frac{3x}{y}$

40. ▶ $\dfrac{12xz}{4xz^2}$ $\frac{3}{z}$

41. $\dfrac{6x+3}{3y}$ $\frac{2x+1}{y}$

42. $\dfrac{4x+12}{2y}$ $\frac{2x+6}{y}$

43. $\dfrac{a^2+4a}{4a+16}$ $\frac{a}{4}$

44. $\dfrac{9c-27}{bc-3b}$ $\frac{9}{b}$

Simplify each expression. Assume that no denominators are 0. See Example 5–6.

45. $\dfrac{3x^2-14x+8}{x^2-16}$ $\frac{3x-2}{x+4}$

46. $\dfrac{4x^2+22x+10}{x^2-25}$ $\frac{4x+2}{x-5}$

47. $\dfrac{x^2+3x+2}{x^2+x-2}$ $\frac{x+1}{x-1}$

48. ▶ $\dfrac{x^2+x-6}{x^2-x-2}$ $\frac{x+3}{x+1}$

49. $\dfrac{x^4-x^3}{x-1}$ x^3

50. $\dfrac{a^3+a^2}{a^2+a}$ a

51. $\dfrac{x^2+3x+2}{x^3+x^2}$ $\frac{x+2}{x^2}$

52. $\dfrac{x^2-13x+30}{x^4-3x^3}$ $\frac{x-10}{x^3}$

Simplify each expression. Assume that no denominators are 0. See Example 7–8.

53. $\dfrac{4(x+3)+4}{3(x+2)+6}$ $\frac{4}{3}$

54. $\dfrac{4+2(x-5)}{3x-5(x-2)}$ $\frac{x-3}{5-x}$

55. $\dfrac{6+2(x+2)}{3(x-2)+21}$ $\frac{2}{3}$

56. ▶ $\dfrac{-5(a+2)+15}{-12+4(a+2)}$ $-\frac{5}{4}$

57. $\dfrac{a(a+2)-2(a+1)}{2a^2-4}$ $\frac{1}{2}$

58. $\dfrac{2b(b-3)+6(b-1)}{4b^2-12}$ $\frac{1}{2}$

59. $\dfrac{x^2-9}{(2x+3)-(x+6)}$ $x+3$

60. $\dfrac{x^2+5x+4}{2(x+3)-(x+2)}$ $x+1$

Simplify each expression. Assume that no denominators are 0. See Examples 9–10.

61. $\dfrac{x-7}{7-x}$ −1

62. $\dfrac{18-d}{d-18}$ −1

63. $\dfrac{6x-30}{5-x}$ −6

64. $\dfrac{6t-42}{7-t}$ −6

65. $\dfrac{2-a}{a^2-a-2}$ $-\frac{1}{a+1}$

66. $\dfrac{4-b}{b^2-5b+4}$ $-\frac{1}{b-1}$

67. $\dfrac{a+b-c}{c-a-b}$ −1

68. ▶ $\dfrac{x-y-z}{z+y-x}$ −1

TRY IT YOURSELF

Simplify each expression. If it is already in simplified form, so indicate. Assume that no denominators are 0.

69. $\dfrac{x^2-5x}{x^3-25x}$ $\frac{1}{x+5}$

70. $\dfrac{4x}{8x+12}$ $\frac{x}{2x+3}$

71. $\dfrac{6xy}{15x^2y^3}$ $\frac{2}{5xy^2}$

72. $\dfrac{7-a}{a^2-49}$ $\frac{-1}{a+7}$

73. $\dfrac{5+5}{5z}$ $\frac{2}{z}$

74. $\dfrac{x+x}{2}$ x

75. $\dfrac{(3+4)a}{24-3}$ $\frac{a}{3}$

76. $\dfrac{(3-18)k}{25}$ $-\frac{3k}{5}$

77. $\dfrac{6x^2}{4x^2}$ $\frac{3}{2}$

78. $\dfrac{9xy}{6xy}$ $\frac{3}{2}$

79. ▶ $\dfrac{x+3}{3x+9}$ $\frac{1}{3}$

80. $\dfrac{2x+14}{x-7}$ in simplified form

81. $\dfrac{2x^2-8x}{x^2-6x+8}$ $\frac{2x}{x-2}$

82. $\dfrac{3y^2-15y}{y^2-3y-10}$ $\frac{3y}{y+2}$

83. $\dfrac{6x^2-13x+6}{3x^2+x-2}$ $\frac{2x-3}{x+1}$

84. $\dfrac{7x^2+20x-3}{3x^2+8x-3}$ $\frac{7x-1}{3x-1}$

85. $\dfrac{2x^2-8}{4x^2-7x-2}$ $\frac{2(x+2)}{4x+1}$

86. $\dfrac{3x^2-27}{2x^2-7x+3}$ $\frac{3(x+3)}{2x+1}$

87. $\dfrac{m^2-2mn+n^2}{2m^2-2n^2}$ $\frac{m-n}{2(m+n)}$

88. $\dfrac{c^2-d^2}{c^2-2cd+d^2}$ $\frac{c+d}{c-d}$

89. $\dfrac{5x^2 + 2x - 3}{6x^2 - x - 1}$ in simplified form

90. $\dfrac{3x^2 - 10x - 77}{x^2 - 4x - 21}$ $\dfrac{3x + 11}{x + 3}$

▶ **91.** $\dfrac{x^2 - 3(2x - 3)}{9 - x^2}$ $\dfrac{3 - x}{3 + x}$

92. $\dfrac{x(x - 8) + 16}{16 - x^2}$ $\dfrac{4 - x}{4 + x}$

93. $\dfrac{y - xy}{xy - x}$ in simplified form

▶ **94.** $\dfrac{x^2 + y^2}{x + y}$ in simplified form

95. $\dfrac{6a - 6b + 6c}{9a - 9b + 9c}$ $\dfrac{2}{3}$

▶ **96.** $\dfrac{3a - 3b - 6}{2a - 2b - 4}$ $\dfrac{3}{2}$

97. $\dfrac{15x - 3x^2}{25y - 5xy}$ $\dfrac{3x}{5y}$

▶ **98.** $\dfrac{xz - 2x}{yz - 2y}$ $\dfrac{x}{y}$

99. $\dfrac{12 - 3x^2}{x^2 - x - 2}$ $\dfrac{-3(x + 2)}{x + 1}$

100. $\dfrac{-5x + 10}{x^2 - 4x + 4}$ $-\dfrac{5}{x - 2}$

101. $\dfrac{x^2 - 8x + 15}{x^2 - x - 6}$ $\dfrac{x - 5}{x + 2}$

102. $\dfrac{x^2 - 6x - 7}{x^2 + 8x + 7}$ $\dfrac{x - 7}{x + 7}$

APPLICATIONS

▶ **103.** ORGAN PIPES The number of vibrations n per second of an organ pipe is given by the formula

$$n = \frac{512}{L}$$

where L is the length of the pipe in feet. How many times per second will a 6-foot pipe vibrate? $85\frac{1}{3}$

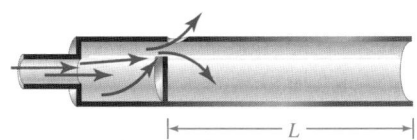

▶ **104.** WORD PROCESSORS For the word processor shown, the number of words w that can be typed on a piece of paper is given by the formula

$$w = \frac{8{,}000}{x}$$

where x is the font size used. Find the number of words that can be typed on a page for each font size choice shown. 1,000, 800, about 667, 500, about 333, about 222

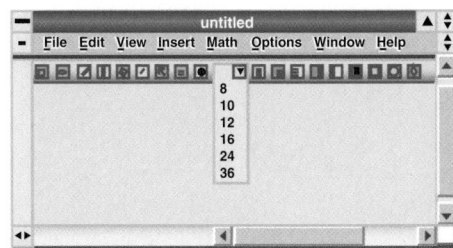

▶ **105.** ROOFING Refer to the illustration in the next column. The *pitch* of a roof is a measure of how steep or how flat the roof is. If pitch = $\frac{\text{rise}}{\text{run}}$, find the pitch of the roof of the cabin shown. Express the result in lowest terms. $\frac{x + 2}{x - 2}$

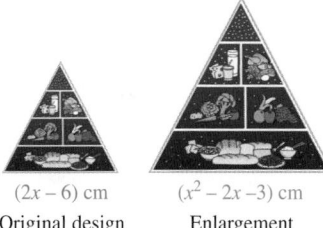

(x² + 4x + 4) ft
(x² − 4) ft

▶ **106.** GRAPHIC DESIGN A chart of the basic food groups, in the shape of an equilateral triangle, is to be enlarged and distributed to schools for display in their health classes. What is the length of a side of the original design divided by the length of a side of the enlargement? Express the result in lowest terms. $\frac{2}{x + 1}$

(2x − 6) cm   (x² − 2x − 3) cm
Original design   Enlargement

WRITING

107. Explain why $\dfrac{x - 7}{7 - x} = -1$.

108. Explain the difference between a factor and a term. Give several examples.

109. Explain the error.

$$\frac{3(\overset{1}{\cancel{x + 1}}) - x}{\underset{1}{\cancel{x + 1}}} = 3 - x$$

▶ **110.** Explain why there are no values for x for which

$$\frac{x - 7}{x^2 + 49}$$ is undefined.

REVIEW

111. State the associative property of addition using the variables a, b, and c. $(a + b) + c = a + (b + c)$

112. State the distributive property using the variables x, y, and z. $x(y + z) = xy + xz$

113. If $ab = 0$, what must be true about a or b? One of them is zero.

114. What is the product of a number and 1? the number

▶ **115.** Find the opposite of: $-\dfrac{5}{3}$ $\dfrac{5}{3}$

116. Find the cube of 2 squared. 64

Objectives

1 Multiply rational expressions.

2 Multiply a rational expression by a polynomial.

3 Divide rational expressions.

4 Convert units of measurement.

SECTION **7.2**

Multiplying and Dividing Rational Expressions

In this section, we extend the rules for multiplying and dividing numerical fractions to problems involving multiplication and division of rational expressions.

1 Multiply rational expressions.

Recall that to multiply fractions, we multiply their numerators and multiply their denominators. For example,

$$\frac{4}{7} \cdot \frac{3}{5} = \frac{4 \cdot 3}{7 \cdot 5}$$ Multiply the numerators and multiply the denominators.

$$= \frac{12}{35}$$ Perform the multiplication in the numerator: $4 \cdot 3 = 12$.
Perform the multiplication in the denominator: $7 \cdot 5 = 35$.

We use the same procedure to multiply rational expressions.

Multiplying Rational Expressions

To multiply rational expressions, multiply their numerators and their denominators. Then, if possible, factor and simplify.

For any two rational expressions, $\frac{A}{B}$ and $\frac{C}{D}$,

$$\frac{A}{B} \cdot \frac{C}{D} = \frac{AC}{BD}, \text{ where } B \text{ and } D \text{ are not zero.}$$

Self Check 1

Multiply: $\dfrac{3x}{4} \cdot \dfrac{x-3}{5}$

Now Try Problems 12, 16, and 22

Self Check 1 Answer

$\dfrac{3x(x-3)}{20}$

Teaching Example 1 Multiply:

a. $\dfrac{2x}{3} \cdot \dfrac{5}{7y^2}$

b. $\dfrac{x+3}{x} \cdot \dfrac{x+7}{x-4}$

Answers:

a. $\dfrac{10x}{21y^2}$ **b.** $\dfrac{(x+3)(x+7)}{x(x-4)}$

EXAMPLE 1

Multiply: **a.** $\dfrac{x}{3} \cdot \dfrac{2}{5}$ **b.** $\dfrac{7}{9} \cdot \dfrac{-5}{3x}$ **c.** $\dfrac{x^2}{2} \cdot \dfrac{3}{y^2}$ **d.** $\dfrac{t+1}{t} \cdot \dfrac{t-1}{t-2}$

Strategy We will use the rule for multiplying rational expressions. In the process, we must be ready to factor the numerators and denominators so that all common factors can be removed. If no common factors are present, the fraction is already in simplest form.

WHY We want to give the result in simplified form, which requires that the numerator and denominator have no common factors other than 1.

Solution

a. $\dfrac{x}{3} \cdot \dfrac{2}{5} = \dfrac{x \cdot 2}{3 \cdot 5}$

$= \dfrac{2x}{15}$

b. $\dfrac{7}{9} \cdot \dfrac{-5}{3x} = \dfrac{7(-5)}{9 \cdot 3x}$

$= \dfrac{-35}{27x}$

$= -\dfrac{35}{27x}$

c. $\dfrac{x^2}{2} \cdot \dfrac{3}{y^2} = \dfrac{x^2 \cdot 3}{2 \cdot y^2}$

$= \dfrac{3x^2}{2y^2}$

d. $\dfrac{t+1}{t} \cdot \dfrac{t-1}{t-2} = \dfrac{(t+1)(t-1)}{t(t-2)}$

EXAMPLE 2   Multiply: $\dfrac{35x^2y}{7y^2z} \cdot \dfrac{z}{5xy}$

Strategy We will use the rule for multiplying rational expressions. In the process, we must be ready to factor the numerators and denominators so that all common factors can be removed.

WHY We want to give the result in simplified form, which requires that the numerator and denominator have no common factors other than 1.

Solution

$$\dfrac{35x^2y}{7y^2z} \cdot \dfrac{z}{5xy} = \dfrac{35x^2y \cdot z}{7y^2z \cdot 5xy}$$
    Multiply the numerators and multiply the denominators.

$$= \dfrac{5 \cdot 7 \cdot x \cdot x \cdot y \cdot z}{7 \cdot y \cdot y \cdot z \cdot 5 \cdot x \cdot y}$$
    Factor $35x^2$ and factor y^2.

$$= \dfrac{\overset{1}{5} \cdot \overset{1}{7} \cdot \overset{1}{x} \cdot x \cdot \overset{1}{y} \cdot \overset{1}{z}}{\underset{1}{7} \cdot \underset{1}{y} \cdot y \cdot \underset{1}{z} \cdot \underset{1}{5} \cdot \underset{1}{x} \cdot y}$$
    Simplify by removing the common factors.

$$= \dfrac{x}{y^2}$$
    Perform the multiplications in the numerator and the denominator.

Self Check 2

Multiply: $\dfrac{a^2b^2}{2a} \cdot \dfrac{9a^3}{3b^3} \dfrac{3a^4}{2b}$

Now Try **Problem 18**

Teaching Example 2 Multiply:
$\dfrac{12a^3b^2}{3a^2c} \cdot \dfrac{c^4}{20a^2bc}$
Answer:
$\dfrac{bc^2}{5a}$

EXAMPLE 3   Multiply: $\dfrac{x^2 - x}{2x + 4} \cdot \dfrac{x + 2}{x}$

Strategy We will use the rule for multiplying rational expressions. In the process, we must be ready to factor the monomials, binomials, or trinomials in the numerators and denominators so that all common factors can be removed.

WHY We want to give the result in simplified form, which requires that the numerator and denominator have no common factors other than 1.

Solution

$$\dfrac{x^2 - x}{2x + 4} \cdot \dfrac{x + 2}{x} = \dfrac{(x^2 - x)(x + 2)}{(2x + 4)(x)}$$
    Multiply the numerators and multiply the denominators.

We now factor the numerator and denominator to see whether this product can be simplified.

$$\dfrac{x^2 - x}{2x + 4} \cdot \dfrac{x + 2}{x} = \dfrac{x(x - 1)(x + 2)}{2(x + 2)x}$$
    Factor the numerator: $(x^2 - x) = x(x - 1)$.
Factor the denominator: $(2x + 4) = 2(x + 2)$.

$$= \dfrac{\overset{1}{x}(x - 1)(\overset{1}{x + 2})}{2(\underset{1}{x + 2})\underset{1}{x}}$$
    Simplify by removing the common factors.

$$= \dfrac{x - 1}{2}$$

Self Check 3

Multiply: $\dfrac{x^2 + x}{3x + 6} \cdot \dfrac{x + 2}{x + 1} \dfrac{x}{3}$

Now Try **Problem 26**

Teaching Example 3 Multiply:
$\dfrac{x - 3}{x^2 - 3x} \cdot \dfrac{x}{x + 5}$
Answer:
$\dfrac{1}{x + 5}$

EXAMPLE 4   Multiply: $\dfrac{x^2 - 3x}{x^2 - x - 6} \cdot \dfrac{x^2 + x - 2}{x^2 - x}$

Strategy We will use the rule for multiplying rational expressions. In the process, we must be ready to factor the monomials, binomials, or trinomials in the numerators and denominators so that all common factors can be removed.

WHY We want to give the result in simplified form, which requires that the numerator and denominator have no common factors other than 1.

Self Check 4

Multiply: $\dfrac{a^2 + a}{a^2 - 4} \cdot \dfrac{a^2 - a - 2}{a^2 + 2a + 1}$

Now Try **Problem 32**
Self Check 4 Answer
$\dfrac{a}{a + 2}$

Teaching Example 4 Multiply:
$$\frac{x^2 + 5x}{x^2 - 25} \cdot \frac{x^2 - 4x - 5}{x^2 - 1}$$
Answer:
$$\frac{x}{x - 1}$$

Solution

$$\frac{x^2 - 3x}{x^2 - x - 6} \cdot \frac{x^2 + x - 2}{x^2 - x}$$

$$= \frac{(x^2 - 3x)(x^2 + x - 2)}{(x^2 - x - 6)(x^2 - x)}$$ Multiply the numerators and multiply the denominators.

$$= \frac{x(x - 3)(x + 2)(x - 1)}{(x + 2)(x - 3)x(x - 1)}$$ Factor the numerator and denominator to see whether the result can be simplified.

$$= \frac{\overset{1}{x}(\overset{1}{x - 3})(\overset{1}{x + 2})(\overset{1}{x - 1})}{(\underset{1}{x + 2})(\underset{1}{x - 3})\underset{1}{x}(\underset{1}{x - 1})}$$ Simplify by removing the common factors.

$$= 1$$

2   Multiply a rational expression by a polynomial.

Since any number divided by 1 remains unchanged, we can write any polynomial as a fraction by inserting a denominator of 1.

Self Check 5

Multiply:

a. $\dfrac{9}{7y} \cdot 7y$ 9

b. $36b\left(\dfrac{1}{6b}\right)$ 6

c. $4x\left(\dfrac{x + 3}{x}\right)$ $4x + 12$

Now Try **Problems 36 and 40**

EXAMPLE 5   Multiply: **a.** $\dfrac{4}{x} \cdot x$ **b.** $63x\left(\dfrac{1}{7x}\right)$ **c.** $5a\left(\dfrac{3a - 1}{a}\right)$

Strategy We will write each of the monomials, x, $63x$, and $5a$, as rational expressions with a denominator of 1. (Remember, any number divided by 1 remains unchanged.) Then we will use the rule for multiplying rational expressions.

WHY Writing x, $63x$, and $5a$ over 1 is helpful during the multiplication process when we multiply numerators and multiply denominators.

Teaching Example 5 Multiply:

a. $26x \cdot \dfrac{2}{13x}$ **b.** $4x\left(\dfrac{1}{12x}\right)$

c. $3x\left(\dfrac{2x - 1}{x}\right)$

Answers:

a. 4   **b.** $\dfrac{1}{3}$ **c.** $6x - 3$

Solution

a. $\dfrac{4}{x} \cdot x = \dfrac{4}{x} \cdot \dfrac{x}{1}$ Write x as a fraction: $x = \frac{x}{1}$.

$$= \frac{4 \cdot \overset{1}{x}}{\underset{1}{x} \cdot 1}$$ Multiply the fractions and remove the common factor in the numerator and denominator.

$$= 4$$ Simplify.

b. $63x\left(\dfrac{1}{7x}\right) = \dfrac{63x}{1}\left(\dfrac{1}{7x}\right)$ Write $63x$ as a fraction: $63x = \frac{63x}{1}$.

$$= \frac{63x \cdot 1}{1 \cdot 7 \cdot x}$$ Multiply the fractions.

$$= \frac{9 \cdot \overset{1}{7} \cdot \overset{1}{x} \cdot 1}{1 \cdot \underset{1}{7} \cdot \underset{1}{x}}$$ Write $63x$ in factored form as $9 \cdot 7 \cdot x$ and remove the common factors.

$$= 9$$ Simplify.

c. $5a\left(\dfrac{3a - 1}{a}\right) = \dfrac{5a}{1}\left(\dfrac{3a - 1}{a}\right)$ Write $5a$ as a fraction: $5a = \frac{5a}{1}$.

$$= \frac{5\overset{1}{a}(3a - 1)}{1 \cdot \underset{1}{a}}$$ Multiply the fractions and remove the common factor of a.

$$= 5(3a - 1)$$ Simplify.

$$= 15a - 5$$ Distribute the multiplication by 5.

EXAMPLE 6 Multiply: $\dfrac{x^2 + x}{x^2 + 8x + 7} \cdot (x + 7)$

Strategy We will write the binomial factor over 1. Then we will use the rule for multiplying rational expressions.

WHY Writing $(x + 7)$ over 1 is helpful during the multiplication process when we multiply numerators and denominators.

Solution

$\dfrac{x^2 + x}{x^2 + 8x + 7} \cdot (x + 7)$

$= \dfrac{x^2 + x}{x^2 + 8x + 7} \cdot \dfrac{x + 7}{1}$ Write $x + 7$ as a fraction with a denominator of 1.

$= \dfrac{x(x + 1)(x + 7)}{(x + 1)(x + 7)1}$ Multiply the fractions and factor where possible.

$= \dfrac{x\cancel{(x + 1)}\cancel{(x + 7)}}{\cancel{(x + 1)}\cancel{(x + 7)}1}$ Simplify by removing the common factors.

$= x$

Self Check 6

Multiply: $(a - 7) \cdot \dfrac{a^2 - a}{a^2 - 8a + 7}$

Now Try **Problem 46**

Self Check 6 Answer

a

Teaching Example 6 Multiply:

$(r + 4) \cdot \dfrac{r^2 - 5r}{r^2 - r - 20}$

Answer:

r

3 **Divide rational expressions.**

Division by a nonzero number is equivalent to multiplying by its reciprocal. Thus, to divide two fractions, we can invert the divisor (the fraction following the ÷ sign) and multiply. For example,

$\dfrac{4}{7} \div \dfrac{3}{5} = \dfrac{4}{7} \cdot \dfrac{5}{3}$ Invert $\frac{3}{5}$ and change the division to a multiplication.

$= \dfrac{20}{21}$ Multiply the numerators and denominators.

We use the same procedures to divide rational expressions.

Dividing Rational Expressions

To divide two rational expressions, multiply the first by the reciprocal of the second. Then, if possible, we factor and simplify.

For any two rational expressions $\dfrac{A}{B}$ and $\dfrac{C}{D}$, where B, C, and D are not 0,

$$\dfrac{A}{B} \div \dfrac{C}{D} = \dfrac{A}{B} \cdot \dfrac{D}{C}$$

EXAMPLE 7 Divide: **a.** $\dfrac{a}{13} \div \dfrac{17}{26}$ **b.** $-\dfrac{9x}{35y} \div \dfrac{15x^2}{14}$

Strategy We will use the rule for dividing rational expressions. After multiplying by the reciprocal, we will factor the monomials that are not prime, and remove any common factors of the numerator and denominator.

Self Check 7

Divide: $-\dfrac{8a}{3b} \div \dfrac{16a^2}{9b^2}$ $-\dfrac{3b}{2a}$

Now Try **Problems 48 and 56**

WHY We want to give the result in simplified form, which requires that the numerator and denominator have no common factor other than 1.

Solution

a. $\dfrac{a}{13} \div \dfrac{17}{26} = \dfrac{a}{13} \cdot \dfrac{26}{17}$ Invert the divisor, which is $\frac{17}{26}$, and change the division to a multiplication.

$\qquad = \dfrac{a \cdot 2 \cdot 13}{13 \cdot 17}$ Multiply the fractions and factor where possible.

$\qquad = \dfrac{a \cdot 2 \cdot \overset{1}{\cancel{13}}}{\underset{1}{\cancel{13}} \cdot 17}$ Simplify by removing the common factors.

$\qquad = \dfrac{2a}{17}$

b. $-\dfrac{9x}{35y} \div \dfrac{15x^2}{14} = -\dfrac{9x}{35y} \cdot \dfrac{14}{15x^2}$ Multiply by the reciprocal of $\frac{15x^2}{14}$.

$\qquad = -\dfrac{3 \cdot 3 \cdot x \cdot 2 \cdot 7}{5 \cdot 7 \cdot y \cdot 3 \cdot 5 \cdot x \cdot x}$ Multiply the fractions and factor where possible.

$\qquad = -\dfrac{3 \cdot \overset{1}{\cancel{3}} \cdot \overset{1}{\cancel{x}} \cdot 2 \cdot \overset{1}{\cancel{7}}}{5 \cdot \underset{1}{\cancel{7}} \cdot y \cdot \underset{1}{\cancel{3}} \cdot 5 \cdot \underset{1}{\cancel{x}} \cdot x}$ Simplify by removing the common factors.

$\qquad = -\dfrac{6}{25xy}$ Multiply the remaining factors.

Self Check 8

Divide:
$$\frac{z^2 - 1}{z^2 + 4z + 3} \div \frac{z - 1}{z^2 + 2z - 3}$$

Now Try **Problem 64**

Self Check 8 Answer
$z - 1$

EXAMPLE 8   Divide: $\dfrac{x^2 + x}{3x - 15} \div \dfrac{x^2 + 2x + 1}{6x - 30}$

Strategy We will use the rule for dividing rational expressions. After multiplying by the reciprocal, we will factor the binomials and trinomials that are not prime. Then we will remove any common factors of the numerator and denominator.

WHY We want to give the result in simplified form, which requires that the numerator and denominator have no common factor other than 1.

Solution

$\dfrac{x^2 + x}{3x - 15} \div \dfrac{x^2 + 2x + 1}{6x - 30}$

$= \dfrac{x^2 + x}{3x - 15} \cdot \dfrac{6x - 30}{x^2 + 2x + 1}$ Invert the divisor and change the division to multiplication.

$= \dfrac{x(x + 1) \cdot 2 \cdot 3(x - 5)}{3(x - 5)(x + 1)(x + 1)}$ Multiply the fractions and factor.

$= \dfrac{x\overset{1}{\cancel{(x + 1)}} \cdot 2 \cdot \overset{1}{\cancel{3}}\overset{1}{\cancel{(x - 5)}}}{\underset{1}{\cancel{3}}\underset{1}{\cancel{(x - 5)}}\underset{1}{\cancel{(x + 1)}}(x + 1)}$ Simplify by removing the common factors.

$= \dfrac{2x}{x + 1}$

To divide a rational expression by a polynomial, we write the polynomial as a fraction by inserting a denominator of 1, and then we divide the fractions.

EXAMPLE 9   Divide: $\dfrac{2x^2 - 3x - 2}{2x + 1} \div (4 - x^2)$

Strategy We begin by writing $4 - x^2$ as a rational expression by writing it over 1. Then we will use the rule for dividing rational expressions.

WHY Writing $4 - x^2$ over 1 is helpful when we invert its numerator and denominator to find its reciprocal.

Solution

$\dfrac{2x^2 - 3x - 2}{2x + 1} \div (4 - x^2)$

$= \dfrac{2x^2 - 3x - 2}{2x + 1} \div \dfrac{4 - x^2}{1}$ Write $4 - x^2$ as a fraction with a denominator of 1.

$= \dfrac{2x^2 - 3x - 2}{2x + 1} \cdot \dfrac{1}{4 - x^2}$ Invert the divisor and change the division to multiplication.

$= \dfrac{(2x + 1)(x - 2) \cdot 1}{(2x + 1)(2 + x)(2 - x)}$ Multiply the fractions and factor where possible.

$= \dfrac{\overset{1}{\cancel{(2x + 1)}}\overset{-1}{\cancel{(x - 2)}} \cdot 1}{\underset{1}{\cancel{(2x + 1)}}(2 + x)\underset{1}{\cancel{(2 - x)}}}$ Remove the common factors. The binomials $x - 2$ and $2 - x$ are opposites: $\frac{x-2}{2-x} = -1$.

$= \dfrac{-1}{2 + x}$

$= -\dfrac{1}{2 + x}$

Self Check 9

Divide: $\dfrac{a^2 - b^2}{a^2 + ab} \div (b - a)$ $-\dfrac{1}{a}$

Now Try Problem 68

Teaching Example 9 Divide:
$\dfrac{9x^2 + 3x - 2}{3x + 2} \div (1 - 9x^2)$
Answer:
$-\dfrac{1}{1 + 3x}$

---

4   Convert units of measurement.

We can use the concepts discussed in this section to make conversions from one unit of measure to another. *Unit conversion factors* play an important role in this process. A **unit conversion factor** is a fraction that has a value of 1. For example, we can use the fact that 1 square yard = 9 square feet to form two unit conversion factors:

$\dfrac{1 \text{ yd}^2}{9 \text{ ft}^2} = 1$ Read as "1 square yard per 9 square feet." $\dfrac{9 \text{ ft}^2}{1 \text{ yd}^2} = 1$ Read as "9 square feet per 1 square yard."

> **Success Tip**   Remember that unit conversion factors are equal to 1. Some examples are:
>
> $\dfrac{12 \text{ in.}}{1 \text{ ft}} = 1$ $\dfrac{60 \text{ min}}{1 \text{ hr}} = 1$

Since a unit conversion factor is equal to 1, multiplying a measurement by a unit conversion factor does not change the measurement, it only changes the units of measure.

EXAMPLE 10   *Carpeting*   A roll of carpeting is 12 feet wide and 150 feet long. Find the number of square yards of carpeting on the roll.

Strategy We will begin by determining the number of square feet of carpeting on the roll. Then we will multiply that result by a unit conversion factor.

Self Check 10

Convert 5,400 ft^2 to square yards.   600 yd^2

Now Try Problem 71

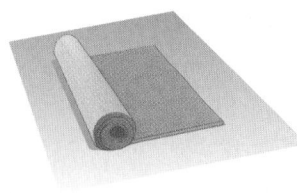

Teaching Example 10 Convert 630 square feet to square yards.
Answer:
70 yd^2

WHY A properly chosen unit conversion factor can convert the number of square feet of carpeting on the roll to the number of square yards on the roll.

Solution

When unrolled, the carpeting forms a rectangular shape with an area of $12 \cdot 150 = 1{,}800$ square feet. We will multiply 1,800 ft^2 by a unit conversion factor such that the units of ft^2 are removed and the units of yd^2 are introduced. Since $1 \text{ yd}^2 = 9 \text{ ft}^2$, we will use $\frac{1 \text{ yd}^2}{9 \text{ ft}^2}$.

$$\frac{1{,}800 \text{ ft}^2}{1 \text{ roll}} = \frac{1{,}800 \text{ ft}^2}{1 \text{ roll}} \cdot \frac{\mathbf{1 \text{ yd}^2}}{\mathbf{9 \text{ ft}^2}}$$ Multiply by a unit conversion factor that relates yd^2 to ft^2.

$$= \frac{1{,}800 \text{ ft}^2}{1 \text{ roll}} \cdot \frac{1 \text{ yd}^2}{9 \text{ ft}^2}$$ Remove the units of ft^2 that are common to the numerator and denominator.

$$= \frac{200 \text{ yd}^2}{1 \text{ roll}}$$ Divide 1,800 by 9 to get 200.

There are 200 yd^2 of carpeting on the roll.

Self Check 11

A mosquito flaps it wings about 600 times per second. How many times per minute does a mosquito flap its wings?

Now Try **Problem 75**
Self Check 11 Answer
36,000 flaps per minute

Teaching Example 11 A hummingbird can flap its wings up to 200 times per second. Express this speed in beats per minute.
Answer:
12,000 beats per minute

EXAMPLE 11 *The Speed of Light* The speed with which light moves through space is about 186,000 miles per second. Express this speed in miles per minute.

Strategy The speed of light can be expressed as $\frac{186{,}000 \text{ mi}}{1 \text{ sec}}$. We will multiply that fraction by a unit conversion factor.

WHY A properly chosen unit conversion factor can convert the number of miles traveled per second to the number of miles traveled per minute.

Solution

We will multiply $\frac{186{,}000 \text{ mi}}{1 \text{ sec}}$ by a unit conversion factor such that the units of seconds are removed and the units of minutes are introduced. Since 60 seconds = 1 minute, we will use $\frac{60 \text{ sec}}{1 \text{ min}}$.

$$\frac{186{,}000 \text{ mi}}{1 \text{ sec}} = \frac{186{,}000 \text{ mi}}{1 \text{ sec}} \cdot \frac{\mathbf{60 \text{ sec}}}{\mathbf{1 \text{ min}}}$$ Multiply by a unit conversion factor that relates seconds to minutes.

$$= \frac{186{,}000 \text{ mi}}{1 \text{ sec}} \cdot \frac{60 \text{ sec}}{1 \text{ min}}$$ Remove the units of seconds that are common to the numerator and denominator.

$$= \frac{11{,}160{,}000 \text{ mi}}{1 \text{ min}}$$ Multiply 186,000 and 60 to get 11,160,000.

The speed of light is about 11,160,000 miles per minute.

ANSWERS TO SELF CHECKS

1. $\frac{3x(x-3)}{20}$ **2.** $\frac{3a^4}{2b}$ **3.** $\frac{x}{3}$ **4.** $\frac{a}{a+2}$ **5. a.** 9 **b.** 6 **c.** $4x+12$ **6.** a **7.** $-\frac{3b}{2a}$ **8.** $z-1$
9. $-\frac{1}{a}$ **10.** 600 yd^2 **11.** 36,000 flaps per minute

---

SECTION 7.2 STUDY SET

VOCABULARY

Fill in the blanks.

▶ **1.** The __reciprocal__ of $\dfrac{3}{x+1}$ is $\dfrac{x+1}{3}$.

▶ **2.** A __unit__ conversion factor is a fraction containing units that is equal to 1, such as $\dfrac{3 \text{ ft}}{1 \text{ yd}}$.

▶ Selected exercises available online at
www.webassign.net/brookscole

CONCEPTS

Fill in the blanks.

3. To multiply rational expressions, multiply their __numerators__ and multiply their __denominators__.

4. $\dfrac{A}{B} \cdot \dfrac{C}{D} = \dfrac{AC}{BD}$

5. To divide rational expressions, multiply the first by the __reciprocal__ of the second.

6. $\dfrac{A}{B} \div \dfrac{C}{D} = \dfrac{A}{B} \cdot \dfrac{D}{C}$

7. The product of $\dfrac{x}{x+2}$ and its reciprocal $\dfrac{x+2}{x}$ is __1__.

8. Use the fact that 1 tablespoon = 3 teaspoons to write two unit conversion factors. $\dfrac{1 \text{ tablespoon}}{3 \text{ teaspoons}}$ or $\dfrac{3 \text{ teaspoons}}{1 \text{ tablespoon}}$

NOTATION

Complete each solution.

9. $\dfrac{x^2+x}{3x-6} \cdot \dfrac{x-2}{x+1} = \dfrac{(x^2+x)}{(3x-6)} \cdot \dfrac{(x-2)}{(x+1)}$

$= \dfrac{x(x+1)(x-2)}{3(x-2)(x+1)}$

$= \dfrac{x}{3}$

▶ 10. $\dfrac{x^2-x}{4x+12} \div \dfrac{x-1}{x+3} = \dfrac{x^2-x}{4x+12} \cdot \dfrac{x+3}{x-1}$

$= \dfrac{(x^2-x)(x+3)}{(4x+12)(x-1)}$

$= \dfrac{x(x-1)(x+3)}{4(x+3)(x-1)}$

$= \dfrac{x}{4}$

GUIDED PRACTICE

Perform each multiplication. Simplify answers if possible. See Examples 1–2.

11. $\dfrac{3}{y} \cdot \dfrac{y}{2}$ $\dfrac{3}{2}$

12. $\dfrac{2}{z} \cdot \dfrac{z}{3}$ $\dfrac{2}{3}$

13. $\dfrac{7z}{9z} \cdot \dfrac{-4z}{2z}$ $-\dfrac{14}{9}$

14. $\dfrac{-8}{2x} \cdot \dfrac{16x}{3x}$ $-\dfrac{64}{3x}$

15. $\dfrac{2x^2y}{3xy} \cdot \dfrac{3xy^2}{2}$ x^2y^2

▶ 16. $\dfrac{2x^2z}{z} \cdot \dfrac{5x}{z}$ $\dfrac{10x^3}{z}$

17. $\dfrac{8x^2y^2}{4x^2} \cdot \dfrac{2xy}{2y}$ $2xy^2$

18. $\dfrac{9x^2y}{3x} \cdot \dfrac{3xy}{3y}$ $3x^2y$

19. $-\dfrac{2xy}{x^2} \cdot \dfrac{3xy}{2}$ $-3y^2$

▶ 20. $-\dfrac{3x}{x^2} \cdot \dfrac{2xz}{3}$ $-2z$

21. $\dfrac{z+7}{7} \cdot \dfrac{z+2}{z}$ $\dfrac{(z+7)(z+2)}{7z}$

22. $\dfrac{a-3}{a} \cdot \dfrac{a+3}{5}$ $\dfrac{(a-3)(a+3)}{5a}$

Perform each multiplication. Simplify answers if possible. See Examples 3–4.

23. $\dfrac{x-2}{2} \cdot \dfrac{2x}{x-2}$ x

▶ 24. $\dfrac{y+3}{y} \cdot \dfrac{3y}{y+3}$ 3

25. $\dfrac{x+5}{5} \cdot \dfrac{x}{x+5}$ $\dfrac{x}{5}$

▶ 26. $\dfrac{y-9}{y+9} \cdot \dfrac{y}{9}$ $\dfrac{y(y-9)}{9(y+9)}$

27. $\dfrac{(x+1)^2}{x+1} \cdot \dfrac{x+2}{x+1}$ $x+2$

▶ 28. $\dfrac{(y-3)^2}{y-3} \cdot \dfrac{y-3}{y-3}$ $y-3$

29. $\dfrac{2x+6}{x+3} \cdot \dfrac{3}{4x}$ $\dfrac{3}{2x}$

▶ 30. $\dfrac{3y-9}{y-3} \cdot \dfrac{y}{3y^2}$ $\dfrac{1}{y}$

31. $\dfrac{x^2+x-6}{5x} \cdot \dfrac{5x-10}{x+3}$ $\dfrac{(x-2)^2}{x}$

32. $\dfrac{z^2+4z-5}{5z-5} \cdot \dfrac{5z}{z+5}$ z

33. $\dfrac{m^2-2m-3}{2m+4} \cdot \dfrac{m^2-4}{m^2+3m+2}$ $\dfrac{(m-2)(m-3)}{2(m+2)}$

34. $\dfrac{p^2-p-6}{3p-9} \cdot \dfrac{p^2-9}{p^2+6p+9}$ $\dfrac{(p+2)(p-3)}{3(p+3)}$

Perform each multiplication. Simplify answers if possible. See Examples 5–6.

35. $\dfrac{5}{m} \cdot m$ 5

36. $p \cdot \dfrac{10}{p}$ 10

37. $4d \cdot \dfrac{3}{2d}$ 6

▶ 38. $9x \cdot \dfrac{25}{3x}$ 75

39. $15x\left(\dfrac{x+1}{15x}\right)$ $x+1$

40. $30t\left(\dfrac{t-7}{30t}\right)$ $t-7$

41. $12y\left(\dfrac{y+8}{6y}\right)$ $2y+16$

42. $16x\left(\dfrac{3x+8}{4x}\right)$ $12x+32$

43. $(x+8)\dfrac{x+5}{x+8}$ $x+5$

▶ 44. $(y-2)\dfrac{y+3}{y-2}$ $y+3$

45. $(10h+90)\dfrac{h-3}{h+9}$ $10h-30$

46. $(r^2-25r)\dfrac{r+4}{r-25}$ r^2+4r

Perform each division. Simplify answers when possible. See Example 7.

47. $\dfrac{2}{y} \div \dfrac{4}{3}$ $\dfrac{3}{2y}$

48. $\dfrac{3}{a} \div \dfrac{9}{a}$ $\dfrac{27}{a^2}$

49. $\dfrac{3x}{2} \div \dfrac{x}{2}$ 3

50. $\dfrac{y}{6} \div \dfrac{2}{3y}$ $\dfrac{y^2}{4}$

51. $\dfrac{3x}{y} \div \dfrac{2x}{4}$ $\dfrac{6}{y}$

52. $\dfrac{3y}{8} \div \dfrac{2y}{4y}$ $\dfrac{3y}{4}$

53. $\dfrac{4x}{3x} \div \dfrac{2y}{9y}$ 6

54. $\dfrac{14}{7y} \div \dfrac{10}{5z}$ $\dfrac{z}{y}$

55. $-\dfrac{x^2}{3} \div \dfrac{2x}{4}$ $-\dfrac{2x}{3}$

▶ 56. $-\dfrac{z^2}{z} \div \dfrac{z}{3z}$ $-3z$

57. $\dfrac{x^2y}{3xy} \div \dfrac{xy^2}{6y}$ $\dfrac{2}{y}$

58. $\dfrac{2xz}{z} \div \dfrac{4x^2}{z^2}$ $\dfrac{z^2}{2x}$

Perform each division. Simplify answers when possible.
See Example 8.

▶ 59. $\dfrac{x^2 - 4}{3x + 6} \div \dfrac{x - 2}{x + 2}$ $\frac{x+2}{3}$

60. $\dfrac{x^2 - 9}{5x + 15} \div \dfrac{x - 3}{x + 3}$ $\frac{x+3}{5}$

61. $\dfrac{x^2 - 1}{3x - 3} \div \dfrac{x + 1}{3}$ 1

62. $\dfrac{x^2 - 16}{x - 4} \div \dfrac{3x + 12}{x}$ $\frac{x}{3}$

63. $\dfrac{x^2 - 2x - 35}{3x^2 + 27x} \div \dfrac{x^2 + 7x + 10}{6x^2 + 12x}$ $\frac{2(x-7)}{x+9}$

▶ 64. $\dfrac{x^2 - x - 6}{2x^2 + 9x + 10} \div \dfrac{x^2 - 25}{2x^2 + 15x + 25}$ $\frac{x-3}{x-5}$

65. $\dfrac{2d^2 + 8d - 42}{d - 3} \div \dfrac{2d^2 + 14d}{d^2 + 5d}$ $d + 5$

▶ 66. $\dfrac{5x^2 + 13x - 6}{x + 3} \div \dfrac{5x^2 - 17x + 6}{x - 2}$ $\frac{x-2}{x-3}$

Perform each division. Simplify answers when possible.
See Example 9.

67. $\dfrac{x^2 + 2x - 3}{x - 1} \div (9 - x^2)$ $\frac{1}{3 - x}$

68. $\dfrac{x^2 - 1}{3x - 3} \div (x + 1)$ $\frac{1}{3}$

69. $\dfrac{x^2 - 10x + 9}{x - 9} \div (x - 1)$ 1

▶ 70. $\dfrac{3m + n}{18} \div (9m^2 + 6mn + n^2)$ $\frac{1}{18(3m + n)}$

Complete each unit conversion. See Examples 10–11.

71. $\dfrac{150 \text{ yards}}{1} \cdot \dfrac{3 \text{ feet}}{1 \text{ yard}} = ?$ 450 ft

72. $\dfrac{60 \text{ inches}}{1} \cdot \dfrac{1 \text{ foot}}{12 \text{ inches}} = ?$ 5 ft

73. $\dfrac{6 \text{ pints}}{1} \cdot \dfrac{1 \text{ gallon}}{8 \text{ pints}} = ?$ $\frac{3}{4} \text{ gal}$

74. $\dfrac{4 \text{ cups}}{1} \cdot \dfrac{1 \text{ gallon}}{16 \text{ cups}} = ?$ $\frac{1}{4} \text{ gal}$

75. $\dfrac{30 \text{ miles}}{1 \text{ hour}} \cdot \dfrac{1 \text{ hour}}{60 \text{ minutes}} = ?$ $\frac{1}{2} \text{ mi per min}$

▶ 76. $\dfrac{300 \text{ meters}}{3 \text{ months}} \cdot \dfrac{12 \text{ months}}{1 \text{ year}} = ?$ $1{,}200 \text{ m per yr}$

77. $\dfrac{30 \text{ meters}}{1 \text{ second}} \cdot \dfrac{60 \text{ seconds}}{1 \text{ minute}} = ?$ $1{,}800 \text{ m per min}$

78. $\dfrac{288 \text{ inches}^2}{1} \cdot \dfrac{1 \text{ foot}^2}{144 \text{ inches}^2} = ?$ $2 \text{ ft}^2 \text{ per yr}$

TRY IT YOURSELF

Perform each operation and simplify.

79. $\dfrac{5y}{7} \cdot \dfrac{7}{5}$ y

▶ 80. $\dfrac{4x}{3y} \cdot \dfrac{3y}{7x}$ $\frac{4}{7}$

81. $\dfrac{x^2 - x}{x} \cdot \dfrac{3x - 6}{3x - 3}$ $x - 2$

▶ 82. $\dfrac{5z - 10}{z + 2} \cdot \dfrac{3}{3z - 6}$ $\frac{5}{z + 2}$

83. $\dfrac{7y - 14}{y - 2} \cdot \dfrac{x^2}{7x}$ x

84. $\dfrac{y^2 + 3y}{9} \cdot \dfrac{3x}{y + 3}$ $\frac{xy}{3}$

▶ 85. $\dfrac{b^2 - 5b + 6}{b^2 - 10b + 16} \div \dfrac{b^2 + 2b}{b^2 - 6b - 16}$ $\frac{b - 3}{b}$

86. $\dfrac{m^2 + m - 6}{m^2 - 6m + 9} \div \dfrac{m^2 - 4}{m^2 - 9}$ $\frac{(m + 3)^2}{(m - 3)(m + 2)}$

87. $\dfrac{x + 2}{3x} \div \dfrac{x + 2}{2}$ $\frac{2}{3x}$

▶ 88. $\dfrac{z - 3}{3z} \div \dfrac{z + 3}{z}$ $\frac{z - 3}{3(z + 3)}$

89. $\dfrac{(z - 2)^2}{3z^2} \div \dfrac{z - 2}{6z}$ $\frac{2(z - 2)}{z}$

90. $\dfrac{(x + 7)^2}{x + 7} \div \dfrac{(x - 3)^2}{x + 7}$ $\frac{(x + 7)^2}{(x - 3)^2}$

91. $\dfrac{(z - 7)^2}{z + 2} \div \dfrac{z(z - 7)}{5z^2}$ $\frac{5z(z - 7)}{z - 2}$

▶ 92. $\dfrac{y(y + 2)}{y^2(y - 3)} \div \dfrac{y^2(y + 2)}{(y - 3)^2}$ $\frac{y - 3}{y^3}$

93. $\dfrac{2r - 3s}{12} \div (4r^2 - 12rs + 9s^2)$ $\frac{1}{12(2r - 3s)}$

94. $\dfrac{r^2 - 11r + 18}{r - 9} \div (r - 2)$ 1

APPLICATIONS

▶ 95. INTERNATIONAL ALPHABET The symbols representing the letters A, B, C, D, E, and F in an international code used at sea are printed six to a sheet and then cut into separate cards. If each card is a square, find the area of the large printed sheet shown in the illustration. $\frac{12x^2 + 12x + 3}{2}$ in.^{2}

$\left. \right\}$ $\dfrac{2x + 1}{2}$ in.

▶ 96. PHYSICS The following table contains algebraic expressions for the rate an object travels, and the time traveled at that rate, in terms of a constant k. Complete the table.

Rate (mph)	Time (hr)	Distance (mi)
$\dfrac{k^2 + k - 6}{k - 3}$	$\dfrac{k^2 - 9}{k^2 - 4}$	$\dfrac{(k + 3)^2}{k + 2}$

WRITING

97. Explain how to multiply two fractions and how to simplify the result.

▶ 98. Explain why any mathematical expression can be written as a fraction.

99. To divide fractions, you must first know how to multiply fractions. Explain.

100. Explain how to do the division: $\dfrac{a}{b} \div \dfrac{c}{d} \div \dfrac{e}{f}$

103. $(3y)^{-4}$ $\dfrac{1}{81y^4}$

▶ **104.** $x^{3m} \cdot x^{4m}$ x^{7m}

Perform the operations and simplify.

105. $-4(y^3 - 4y^2 + 3y - 2) - 4(-2y^3 - y)$
$4y^3 + 16y^2 - 8y + 8$

106. $y - 5 \overline{)5y^3 - 3y^2 + 4y - 1}$ $5y^2 + 22y + 114 + \dfrac{569}{y - 5}$

| **REVIEW** |

Simplify each expression. Write all answers without using negative exponents.

101. $2x^3y^2(-3x^2y^4)$ $-6x^5y^6$ **102.** $\dfrac{8x^4y^5}{-2x^3y^2}$ $-4xy^3$

SECTION 7.3

Adding and Subtracting with Like Denominators; Least Common Denominators

Objectives

1 Add and subtract rational expressions that have the same denominator.

2 Find the least common denominator.

3 Build rational expressions into equivalent expressions.

In this section, we extend the rules for adding and subtracting numerical fractions to problems involving addition and subtraction of rational expressions.

1 Add and subtract rational expressions that have the same denominator.

To add (or subtract) fractions with a common denominator, we add (or subtract) their numerators and keep the common denominator. For example,

$$\frac{3}{7} + \frac{2}{7} = \frac{3 + 2}{7} \qquad \text{and} \qquad \frac{3}{7} - \frac{2}{7} = \frac{3 - 2}{7}$$

$$= \frac{5}{7} \qquad\qquad\qquad\qquad = \frac{1}{7}$$

We use the same procedure to add and subtract rational expressions with like denominators.

Adding and Subtracting Fractions with Like Denominators

If A, B, and D represent rational expressions, and D is not 0,

$$\frac{A}{D} + \frac{B}{D} = \frac{A + B}{D} \qquad \text{and} \qquad \frac{A}{D} - \frac{B}{D} = \frac{A - B}{D}$$

EXAMPLE 1

Add: **a.** $\dfrac{x}{8} + \dfrac{3x}{8}$ **b.** $\dfrac{3x + y}{5x} + \dfrac{x + y}{5x}$

Strategy Because the rational expressions have the same denominator, we will add the numerators and write the sum over the common denominator. Then, if possible, we will factor and simplify.

WHY This is the rule for adding rational expressions, such as these that have the same denominator.

Self Check 1

Add:

a. $\dfrac{x}{7} + \dfrac{4x}{7}$ $\dfrac{5x}{7}$

b. $\dfrac{3x}{7y} + \dfrac{4x}{7y}$ $\dfrac{x}{y}$

Now Try **Problems 11 and 17**

Teaching Example 1 Add:

a. $\dfrac{2x}{15} + \dfrac{3x}{15}$ b. $\dfrac{2x + y}{7x} + \dfrac{3x + 6y}{7x}$

Answers:

a. $\dfrac{x}{3}$ b. $\dfrac{5x + 7y}{7x}$

Solution

a. $\dfrac{x}{8} + \dfrac{3x}{8} = \dfrac{x + 3x}{8}$ Add the numerators and keep the common denominator.

$= \dfrac{4x}{8}$ Combine like terms: $x + 3x = 4x$.

$= \dfrac{\overset{1}{4} \cdot x}{\underset{1}{4} \cdot 2}$ Factor the numerator and denominator and remove the common factor, 4.

$= \dfrac{x}{2}$ Simplify.

b. $\dfrac{3x + y}{5x} + \dfrac{x + y}{5x} = \dfrac{3x + y + x + y}{5x}$ Add the numerators and keep the common denominator.

$= \dfrac{4x + 2y}{5x}$ Combine like terms.

Self Check 2

Add: $\dfrac{x + 4}{6x - 12} + \dfrac{x - 8}{6x - 12}$ $\dfrac{1}{3}$

Now Try **Problem 20**

Teaching Example 2 Add:

$\dfrac{4x - 3}{7x - 14} + \dfrac{2x - 9}{7x - 14}$

Answer:

$\dfrac{6}{7}$

EXAMPLE 2   Add: $\dfrac{3x + 21}{5x + 10} + \dfrac{8x + 1}{5x + 10}$

Strategy We will add the numerators and write the sum over the common denominator. Then, if possible, we will factor and simplify.

WHY This is the rule for adding rational expressions that have the same denominator.

Solution

$\dfrac{3x + 21}{5x + 10} + \dfrac{8x + 1}{5x + 10} = \dfrac{3x + 21 + 8x + 1}{5x + 10}$ Add the numerators and keep the common denominator.

$= \dfrac{11x + 22}{5x + 10}$ Combine like terms.

$= \dfrac{11(\overset{1}{\cancel{x + 2}})}{5(\underset{1}{\cancel{x + 2}})}$ Simplify the result by factoring the numerator and denominator. Remove the common factor of $x + 2$.

$= \dfrac{11}{5}$

Self Check 3

Subtract: $\dfrac{2y + 1}{y + 5} - \dfrac{y - 4}{y + 5}$ 1

Now Try **Problems 23 and 29**

EXAMPLE 3   Subtract: **a.** $\dfrac{5x}{3} - \dfrac{2x}{3}$ **b.** $\dfrac{5x + 1}{x - 3} - \dfrac{4x - 2}{x - 3}$

Strategy We will use the rule for subtracting rational expressions that have the same denominators. In part b, it is important to note that the numerator of the second fraction has *two* terms.

WHY We must make sure that the entire numerator (not just the first term) of the second fraction is subtracted.

Solution

a. $\dfrac{5x}{3} - \dfrac{2x}{3} = \dfrac{5x - 2x}{3}$

$\qquad\quad = \dfrac{3x}{3} \qquad$ Combine like terms: $5x - 2x = 3x$.

$\qquad\quad = \dfrac{x}{1} \qquad$ Remove the common factor of 3.

$\qquad\quad = x \qquad$ Denominators of 1 need not be written.

b. $\dfrac{5x + 1}{x - 3} - \dfrac{4x - 2}{x - 3} = \dfrac{5x + 1 - (4x - 2)}{x - 3} \qquad$ The second numerator, $4x - 2$, is written within parentheses to make sure that we subtract both of its terms.

$\qquad\qquad\qquad = \dfrac{5x + 1 - 4x + 2}{x - 3} \qquad$ Distribute the multiplication by -1: $-(4x - 2) = -4x + 2$.

$\qquad\qquad\qquad = \dfrac{x + 3}{x - 3} \qquad$ Combine like terms.

To add and/or subtract three or more rational expressions, we follow the rules for the order of operations.

Teaching Example 3 Subtract:

a. $\dfrac{4x}{5} - \dfrac{14x}{5}$

b. $\dfrac{6x + 3}{x + 2} - \dfrac{4x - 1}{x + 2}$

Answers:
a. $-2x$ **b.** 2

EXAMPLE 4   Simplify: $\dfrac{3x + 1}{x^2 + x + 1} - \dfrac{5x + 2}{x^2 + x + 1} + \dfrac{2x + 1}{x^2 + x + 1}$

Strategy We note that each of the denominators of the rational expressions to be added and subtracted have the same denominator. Then we will perform the additions and subtractions from left to right.

WHY We must follow the rule for adding and/or subtracting rational expressions as well as the rules for order of operations.

Solution

This example combines addition and subtraction. Unless parentheses indicate otherwise, we perform additions and subtractions from left to right.

$\dfrac{3x + 1}{x^2 + x + 1} - \dfrac{5x + 2}{x^2 + x + 1} + \dfrac{2x + 1}{x^2 + x + 1}$

$= \dfrac{3x + 1 - (5x + 2) + 2x + 1}{x^2 + x + 1} \qquad$ Combine the numerators and keep the common denominator.

$= \dfrac{3x + 1 - 5x - 2 + 2x + 1}{x^2 + x + 1} \qquad$ Distribute the multiplication by -1: $-(5x + 2) = -5x - 2$.

$= \dfrac{0}{x^2 + x + 1} \qquad$ Combine like terms.

$= 0 \qquad$ If the numerator of a fraction is zero and the denominator is not zero, the fraction's value is zero.

Self Check 4

Simplify:
$\dfrac{2a^2 - 3}{a - 5} + \dfrac{3a^2 + 2}{a - 5} - \dfrac{5a^2}{a - 5}$

Now Try Problem 35

Self Check 4 Answer

$-\dfrac{1}{a - 5}$

Teaching Example 4 Simplify:
$\dfrac{2x + 1}{x^2 + 5} + \dfrac{3x - 7}{x^2 + 5} - \dfrac{2x - 4}{x^2 + 5}$

Answer:
$\dfrac{3x - 2}{x^2 + 5}$

---

2   Find the least common denominator.

Since the denominators of the fractions in the addition $\frac{4}{7} + \frac{3}{5}$ are different, we cannot add the fractions in their present form.

$\qquad$ four-sevenths $\qquad + \qquad$ three-fifths

$\qquad\qquad\qquad$ └── Different denominators ──┘

To add these fractions, we need to express them as equivalent expressions with a common denominator. The **least common denominator (LCD)** is usually the easiest one to use. The least common denominator of several rational expressions can be found as follows:

Finding the LCD

1. Factor each denominator completely.

2. The LCD is a product that uses each different factor obtained in step 1 the greatest number of times it appears in any one factorization.

EXAMPLE 5   Find the LCD of each pair of rational expressions:

a. $\frac{11}{8x}$ and $\frac{7}{18x^2}$ **b.** $\frac{20}{x}$ and $\frac{4x}{x - 9}$

Strategy We will begin by factoring completely the denominator of each rational expression. Then we will form a product using each factor the greatest number of times it appears in any one factorization.

WHY Since the LCD must contain the factors of each denominator, we need to write each denominator in factored form.

Solution

a. $8x = 2 \cdot 2 \cdot 2 \cdot x$ Prime factor 8.

$18x^2 = 2 \cdot 3 \cdot 3 \cdot x \cdot x$ Prime factor 18. Factor x^2.

The factorizations of $8x$ and $18x^2$ contain the factors 2, 3, and x. The LCD of $\frac{11}{8x}$ and $\frac{7}{18x^2}$ should contain each factor of $8x$ and $18x^2$ the greatest number of times it appears in any one factorization.

The greatest number of times the factor 2 appears is three times.
The greatest number of times the factor 3 appears is twice.
The greatest number of times the factor x appears is twice.

$$\text{LCD} = 2 \cdot 2 \cdot 2 \cdot 3 \cdot 3 \cdot x \cdot x$$
$$= 72x^2$$

The LCD for $\frac{11}{8x}$ and $\frac{7}{18x^2}$ is $72x^2$.

Success Tip The factorizations can be written:

$$8x = 2^3 \cdot x$$
$$18x^2 = 2 \cdot 3^2 \cdot x^2$$

Note that the highest power of each factor is used to form the LCD.

$$LCD = 2^3 \cdot 3^2 \cdot x^2 = 72x^2$$

b. Since the denominators of $\frac{20}{x}$ and $\frac{4x}{x - 9}$ are completely factored, the factor x appears once and the factor $x - 9$ appears once. Thus, the LCD is $x(x - 9)$.

EXAMPLE 6   Find the LCD of each pair of rational expressions:

a. $\dfrac{x}{7x + 7}$ and $\dfrac{x - 2}{5x + 5}$ **b.** $\dfrac{6 - x}{x^2 + 8x + 16}$ and $\dfrac{15x}{x^2 - 16}$

Strategy We will begin by factoring completely each binomial and trinomial in the denominators of the rational expressions. Then we will form a product using each factor the greatest number of times it appears in any one factorization.

WHY Since the LCD must contain the factors of each denominator, we need to write each denominator in factored form.

Solution

a. Factor each denominator completely.

$$7x + 7 = 7(x + 1) \qquad \text{The GCF is 7.}$$
$$5x + 5 = 5(x + 1) \qquad \text{The GCF is 5.}$$

The factorizations of $7x + 7$ and $5x + 5$ contain the factors 7, 5, and $x + 1$. The LCD of $\frac{x}{7x+7}$ and $\frac{x-2}{5x+5}$ should contain each factor of $7x + 7$ and $5x + 5$ the greatest number of times it appears in any one factorization.

The greatest number of times the factor 7 appears is once.
The greatest number of times the factor 5 appears is once.
The greatest number of times the factor $x + 1$ appears is once.

$$\text{LCD} = 7 \cdot 5 \cdot (x + 1) = 35(x + 1)$$

Success Tip Rather than performing the multiplication, it is often better to leave an LCD in factored form:

$$\text{LCD} = 35(x + 1)$$

b. Factor each denominator completely.

$$x^2 + 8x + 16 = (x + 4)(x + 4) \qquad \text{Factor the trinomial.}$$
$$x^2 - 16 = (x + 4)(x - 4) \qquad \text{Factor the difference of two squares.}$$

The factorizations of $x^2 + 8x + 16$ and $x^2 - 16$ contain the factors $x + 4$ and $x - 4$.

The greatest number of times the factor $x + 4$ appears is twice.
The greatest number of times the factor $x - 4$ appears is once.

$$\text{LCD} = (x + 4)(x + 4)(x - 4) = (x + 4)^2(x - 4)$$

Self Check 6

Find the LCD of each pair of rational expressions:

a. $\dfrac{x^3}{x^2 - 6x}$ and $\dfrac{25x}{2x - 12}$

b. $\dfrac{m + 1}{m^2 - 9}$ and $\dfrac{6m^2}{m^2 - 6m + 9}$

Now Try **Problems 47 and 49**

Self Check 6 Answers
a. $2x(x - 6)$
b. $(m + 3)(m - 3)^2$

Teaching Example 6 Find the LCD of:
a. $\dfrac{a}{3a - 6}$ and $\dfrac{13}{5a - 10}$
b. $\dfrac{x + 5}{x^2 - 9}$ and $\dfrac{x - 7}{x^2 + 5x + 6}$
Answers:
a. $15(a - 2)$
b. $(x + 3)(x - 3)(x + 2)$

3 Build rational expressions into equivalent expressions.

Recall from Chapter 1 that writing a fraction as an equivalent fraction with a larger denominator is called **building the fraction.** For example, to write $\frac{3}{5}$ as an equivalent fraction with a denominator of 35, we multiply it by 1 in the form of $\frac{7}{7}$:

$$\frac{3}{5} = \frac{3}{5} \cdot \frac{7}{7} = \frac{21}{35} \qquad \begin{array}{l}\text{Multiply the numerators.}\\ \text{Multiply the denominators.}\end{array}$$

To add and subtract rational expressions with different denominators, we must write them as equivalent expressions having a common denominator. To do so, we build rational expressions.

> ## Building Rational Expressions
>
> To build a rational expression, multiply it by 1 in the form of $\frac{c}{c}$, where c is any nonzero number or expression.

EXAMPLE 7   Write each rational expression as an equivalent expression with the indicated denominator:

a. $\dfrac{7}{15n}$, denominator $30n^3$

b. $\dfrac{6x}{x + 4}$, denominator $(x + 4)(x - 4)$

Strategy We will begin by asking, "By what must we multiply the given denominator to get the required denominator?"

WHY The answer to that question helps us determine the form of 1 to be used to build an equivalent rational expression.

Solution

a. We need to multiply the denominator of $\frac{7}{15n}$ by $2n^2$ to obtain a denominator of $30n^3$. It follows that $\frac{2n^2}{2n^2}$ is the form of 1 that should be used to build an equivalent expression.

$$\frac{7}{15n} = \frac{7}{15n} \cdot \frac{2n^2}{2n^2} \qquad \text{Multiply the given rational expression by 1, in the form of } \tfrac{2n^2}{2n^2}.$$

$$= \frac{14n^2}{30n^3} \qquad \begin{array}{l}\text{Multiply the numerators.}\\ \text{Multiply the denominators.}\end{array}$$

b. We need to multiply the denominator of $\frac{6x}{x + 4}$ by $x - 4$ to obtain a denominator of $(x + 4)(x - 4)$. It follows that $\frac{x - 4}{x - 4}$ is the form of 1 that should be used to build an equivalent expression.

$$\frac{6x}{x + 4} = \frac{6x}{x + 4} \cdot \frac{x - 4}{x - 4} \qquad \begin{array}{l}\text{Multiply the given rational expression by 1, in the form}\\ \text{of } \tfrac{x - 4}{x - 4}.\end{array}$$

$$= \frac{6x(x - 4)}{(x + 4)(x - 4)} \qquad \begin{array}{l}\text{Multiply the numerators.}\\ \text{Multiply the denominators.}\end{array}$$

$$= \frac{6x^2 - 24x}{(x + 4)(x - 4)} \qquad \begin{array}{l}\text{In the numerator, distribute the multiplication by } 6x.\\ \text{Leave the denominator in factored form.}\end{array}$$

Success Tip To get this answer, we multiplied the factors in the numerator to obtain a polynomial in unfactored form: $6x^2 - 24x$. However, we left the denominator in factored form. This approach is beneficial in the next section when we add and subtract rational expressions with unlike denominators.

EXAMPLE 8   Write $\dfrac{x + 1}{x^2 + 6x}$ as an equivalent expression with a denominator of $x(x + 6)(x + 2)$.

Strategy We will begin by factoring the denominator of $\frac{x + 1}{x^2 + 6x}$. Then we will compare the factors of $x^2 + 6x$ to those of $x(x + 6)(x + 2)$.

WHY This comparison will enable us to answer the question, "By what must we multiply $x^2 + 6x$ to obtain $x(x + 6)(x + 2)$?"

Solution

We factor the denominator to determine what factors are missing.

$$\frac{x + 1}{x^2 + 6x} = \frac{x + 1}{x(x + 6)}$$ Factor out the GCF, x, from $x^2 + 6x$.

It is now apparent that we need to multiply the denominator by $x + 2$ to obtain a denominator of $x(x + 6)(x + 2)$. It follows that $\frac{x + 2}{x + 2}$ is the form of 1 that should be used to build an equivalent expression.

$$\frac{x + 1}{x^2 + 6x} = \frac{x + 1}{x(x + 6)} \cdot \frac{x + 2}{x + 2}$$ Multiply the given rational expression by 1, in the form of $\frac{x + 2}{x + 2}$.

$$= \frac{(x + 1)(x + 2)}{x(x + 6)(x + 2)}$$ Multiply the numerators. Multiply the denominators.

$$= \frac{x^2 + 3x + 2}{x(x + 6)(x + 2)}$$ In the numerator, use the FOIL method to multiply $(x + 1)(x + 2)$. Leave the denominator in factored form.

> **Teaching Example 8** Write $\dfrac{x + 4}{x^2 - 9x}$ as an equivalent expression with a denominator of $x(x - 9)(x + 1)$.
> *Answer:*
> $$\frac{x^2 + 5x + 4}{x(x - 9)(x + 1)}$$

> **Success Tip** When building rational expressions, write the numerator of the result as a polynomial in unfactored form. Write the denominator in factored form.

ANSWERS TO SELF CHECKS

1. a. $\frac{5x}{7}$ **b.** $\frac{x}{y}$ **2.** $\frac{1}{3}$ **3.** 1   **4.** $-\frac{1}{a - 5}$ **5. a.** $150y^3$ **b.** $a(a + 3)$ **6. a.** $2x(x - 6)$
b. $(m + 3)(m - 3)^2$ **7. a.** $\frac{21m}{60m^3}$ **b.** $\frac{2c^2 + 6c}{(c + 1)(c + 3)}$ **8.** $\frac{x^2 + 5x - 24}{x(x - 4)(x + 8)}$

SECTION 7.3   STUDY SET

VOCABULARY

Fill in the blanks.

1. The rational expressions $\dfrac{7}{6n}$ and $\dfrac{n + 1}{6n}$ have a common __denominator__ of $6n$.

2. The __LCD__ of $\dfrac{x - 8}{x + 6}$ and $\dfrac{6 - 5x}{x}$ is $x(x + 6)$.

▶ **3.** To __build__ a rational expression, multiply it by a form of 1. For example, $\dfrac{2}{n^2} \cdot \dfrac{8}{8} = \dfrac{16}{8n^2}$.

4. The expressions $\dfrac{2}{n^2}$ and $\dfrac{16}{8n^2}$ are called __equivalent__ expressions because they have the same value for all values of n, except for $n = 0$.

CONCEPTS

Fill in the blanks.

5. To add two fractions with like denominators, add their __numerators__ and keep the __common__ __denominator__.

6. To subtract two fractions with __like__ denominators, subtract their numerators and keep the common denominator.

7. To build the rational expression $\dfrac{3y}{4x}$ into $\dfrac{9y^2}{12xy}$, multiply both the numerator and the denominator by __3y__.

▶ **8.** The sum of two rational expressions is $\dfrac{4x + 4}{5(x + 1)}$. After factoring the numerator and simplifying the result, you will have __$\frac{4}{5}$__.

NOTATION

Complete each solution.

9. $\dfrac{6a - 1}{4a + 1} + \dfrac{2a + 3}{4a + 1} = \dfrac{6a - 1 + 2a + 3}{4a + 1}$

$$= \frac{8a + 2}{4a + 1}$$

$$= \frac{2(4a + 1)}{4a + 1}$$

$$= 2$$

The type of mutiplication that is used to build rational expressions is shown below. Fill in the blanks.

10. a. $\dfrac{4x}{5} \cdot \dfrac{2}{2} = \dfrac{8x}{10}$ **b.** $\dfrac{3}{t} \cdot \dfrac{t-2}{t-2} = \dfrac{3t-6}{t(t-2)}$

   c. $\dfrac{m+1}{m-3} \cdot \dfrac{m-5}{m-5} = \dfrac{m^2 - 4m - 5}{(m-3)(m-5)}$

▌ GUIDED PRACTICE

Perform each addition. Simplify answers, if possible.
See Example 1.

11. $\dfrac{x}{9} + \dfrac{2x}{9}$ $\dfrac{x}{3}$ ▶ **12.** $\dfrac{5x}{7} + \dfrac{9x}{7}$ $2x$

13. $\dfrac{2x}{y} + \dfrac{2x}{y}$ $\dfrac{4x}{y}$ **14.** $\dfrac{4y}{3x} + \dfrac{2y}{3x}$ $\dfrac{2y}{x}$

15. $\dfrac{4}{7y} + \dfrac{10}{7y}$ $\dfrac{2}{y}$ ▶ **16.** $\dfrac{x^2}{4y} + \dfrac{x^2}{4y}$ $\dfrac{x^2}{2y}$

17. $\dfrac{y+2}{10z} + \dfrac{y+4}{10z}$ $\dfrac{y+3}{5z}$ ▶ **18.** $\dfrac{x+3}{2x^2} + \dfrac{x+5}{2x^2}$ $\dfrac{x+4}{x^2}$

Perform each addition. Simplify answers, if possible.
See Example 2.

19. $\dfrac{3x-5}{x-2} + \dfrac{6x-13}{x-2}$ 9 ▶ **20.** $\dfrac{8x-7}{x+3} + \dfrac{2x+37}{x+3}$ 10

▶ **21.** $\dfrac{b}{b^2-4} + \dfrac{2}{b^2-4}$ $\dfrac{1}{b-2}$

22. $\dfrac{a}{a^2+5a+6} + \dfrac{3}{a^2+5a+6}$ $\dfrac{1}{a+2}$

Perform each subtraction. Simplify answers, if possible.
See Example 3.

23. $\dfrac{35y}{72} - \dfrac{44y}{72}$ $-\dfrac{y}{8}$ **24.** $\dfrac{13t}{99} - \dfrac{35t}{99}$ $-\dfrac{2t}{9}$

25. $\dfrac{2x}{y} - \dfrac{x}{y}$ $\dfrac{x}{y}$ ▶ **26.** $\dfrac{7y}{5t} - \dfrac{4y}{5t}$ $\dfrac{3y}{5t}$

▶ **27.** $\dfrac{7x+7}{5y} - \dfrac{2x+7}{5y}$ $\dfrac{x}{y}$ **28.** $\dfrac{3y-2}{2y+6} - \dfrac{2y-5}{2y+6}$ $\dfrac{1}{2}$

▶ **29.** $\dfrac{5x+8}{3x+15} - \dfrac{3x-2}{3x+15}$ $\dfrac{2}{3}$ **30.** $\dfrac{2c}{c^2-d^2} - \dfrac{2d}{c^2-d^2}$ $\dfrac{2}{c+d}$

Perform the operations. Simplify answers, if possible.
See Example 4.

31. $-\dfrac{x}{y} + \dfrac{2x}{y} - \dfrac{x}{y}$ 0 **32.** $\dfrac{5y}{8x} + \dfrac{4y}{8x} - \dfrac{9y}{8x}$ 0

33. $\dfrac{3x}{y+2} - \dfrac{3y}{y+2} + \dfrac{x+y}{y+2}$ $\dfrac{4x-2y}{y+2}$

▶ **34.** $\dfrac{3y}{x-5} + \dfrac{x}{x-5} - \dfrac{y-x}{x-5}$ $\dfrac{2(y+x)}{x-5}$

35. $\dfrac{2a}{a^2+2a+1} - \dfrac{3a-1}{a^2+2a+1} + \dfrac{a+2}{a^2+2a+1}$ $\dfrac{3}{a^2+2a+1}$

36. $\dfrac{b+2}{b^2-3b-2} - \dfrac{b}{b^2-3b-2} + \dfrac{b-2}{b^2-3b-2}$ $\dfrac{b}{b^2-3b-2}$

37. $\dfrac{3p+1}{p^2-3p+2} + \dfrac{2p-1}{p^2-3p+2} - \dfrac{p}{p^2-3p+2}$ $\dfrac{4p}{p^2-3p+2}$

38. $\dfrac{2q+1}{q^2-q+1} + \dfrac{q-1}{q^2-q+1} - \dfrac{3q+2}{q^2-q+1}$ $\dfrac{-2}{q^2-q+1}$

Find the LCD of each pair of rational expressions.
See Examples 5–6.

39. $\dfrac{1}{2x}, \dfrac{9}{6x}$ **40.** $\dfrac{4}{9y}, \dfrac{11}{3y}$
    $6x$ $9y$

41. $\dfrac{33}{15a^3}, \dfrac{9}{10a}$ ▶ **42.** $\dfrac{m-21}{12m^4}, \dfrac{m+1}{18m}$
    $30a^3$ $36m^4$

43. $\dfrac{8}{c}, \dfrac{8-c}{c+2}$ **44.** $\dfrac{d^2-5}{d+9}, \dfrac{d-3}{d}$
    $c(c+2)$ $d(d+9)$

45. $\dfrac{3x+1}{3x-1}, \dfrac{3x}{6x+2}$ **46.** $\dfrac{-2x}{x^2-1}, \dfrac{5x}{x+1}$
    $2(3x+1)(3x-1)$ $(x+1)(x-1)$

47. $\dfrac{b-9}{4b+8}, \dfrac{b}{6}$ **48.** $\dfrac{5m+6}{4m+12}, \dfrac{7}{6m}$
    $12(b+2)$ $12m(m+3)$

49. $\dfrac{8-b}{b^2+6b+9}, \dfrac{12b}{b^2-9}$ **50.** $\dfrac{2a+3}{a^2-4a+4}, \dfrac{a-2}{a^2-4}$
    $(b+3)^2(b-3)$ $(a-2)^2(a+2)$

Write each rational expression as an equivalent fraction with the indicated denominator. See Examples 7–8.

51. $\dfrac{25}{4}; 20x$ $\dfrac{125x}{20x}$ ▶ **52.** $\dfrac{5}{y}; y^2$ $\dfrac{5y}{y^2}$

53. $\dfrac{8}{x}; x^2y$ $\dfrac{8xy}{x^2y}$ ▶ **54.** $\dfrac{7}{y}; xy^2$ $\dfrac{7xy}{xy^2}$

55. $\dfrac{2y}{x}; x(x+1)$ $\dfrac{2xy+2y}{x(x+1)}$ **56.** $\dfrac{3x}{y}; y(y-1)$ $\dfrac{3xy-3x}{y(y-1)}$

57. $\dfrac{3x}{x+1}; (x+1)^2$ $\dfrac{3x^2+3x}{(x+1)^2}$

▶ **58.** $\dfrac{5y}{y-2}; (y-2)^2$ $\dfrac{5y^2-10y}{(y-2)^2}$

59. $\dfrac{z+2}{z^2-6z}; z(z-6)(z+1)$ $\dfrac{z^2+3z+2}{z(z-6)(z+1)}$

60. $\dfrac{y+1}{y^2+2y}; y(y+2)(y-2)$ $\dfrac{y^2-y-2}{y(y+2)(y-2)}$

61. $\dfrac{3}{2x+4}; 2x^2+6x+4$ $\dfrac{3x+3}{2(x+1)(x+2)}$

62. $\dfrac{4}{3x-3}; 3x^2+3x-6$ $\dfrac{4x+8}{3(x-1)(x+2)}$

TRY IT YOURSELF

Perform the operations. Then simplify, if possible.

63. $\dfrac{9y}{3x} - \dfrac{6y}{3x}$ $\dfrac{y}{x}$

64. $\dfrac{5r^2}{2r} - \dfrac{r^2}{2r}$ $2r$

65. $\dfrac{6x - 5}{3xy} - \dfrac{3x - 5}{3xy}$ $\dfrac{1}{y}$

66. $\dfrac{3t}{t^2 - 8t + 7} - \dfrac{3}{t^2 - 8t + 7}$ $\dfrac{3}{t - 7}$

67. $\dfrac{13x}{15} + \dfrac{12x}{15} - \dfrac{5x}{15}$ $\dfrac{4x}{3}$

68. $\dfrac{13y}{32} + \dfrac{13y}{32} - \dfrac{10y}{32}$ $\dfrac{y}{2}$

69. $\dfrac{x + 1}{x - 2} - \dfrac{2(x - 3)}{x - 2} + \dfrac{3(x + 1)}{x - 2}$ $\dfrac{2x + 10}{x - 2}$

70. $\dfrac{3xy}{x - y} - \dfrac{x(3y - x)}{x - y} - \dfrac{x(x - y)}{x - y}$ $\dfrac{xy}{x - y}$

71. $\dfrac{3t}{t^2 - 8t + 7} - \dfrac{21}{t^2 - 8t + 7}$ $\dfrac{3}{t - 1}$

72. $\dfrac{10t}{t^2 - 2t + 1} - \dfrac{10}{t^2 - 2t + 1}$ $\dfrac{10}{t - 1}$

73. $\dfrac{1}{(t - 1)(t + 1)} - \dfrac{6 - t}{(t + 1)(t - 1)}$ $\dfrac{t - 5}{(t + 1)(t - 1)}$

74. $\dfrac{5r - 27}{3r^2 - 9r} + \dfrac{4r}{3r^2 - 9r}$ $\dfrac{3}{r}$

75. $\dfrac{9a}{5a^2 + 25a} + \dfrac{a + 50}{5a^2 + 25a}$ $\dfrac{2}{a}$

76. $\dfrac{a^2 + a}{4a^2 - 8a} + \dfrac{2a^2 - 7a}{4a^2 - 8a}$ $\dfrac{3}{4}$ **77.** $\dfrac{3b^2}{b + 1} - \dfrac{-b + 2}{b + 1}$ $3b - 2$

78. $\dfrac{7}{(t - 1)(t + 1)} - \dfrac{6 - t}{(t + 1)(t - 1)}$ $\dfrac{1}{t - 1}$

APPLICATIONS

Refer to the illustration of the funnel in the next column.

▶ **79.** Find the total height of the funnel. $\frac{20x + 9}{6x^2}$ cm

▶ **80.** What is the difference between the diameter of the opening at the top of the funnel and the diameter of its spout? $\frac{16x^2 - 3}{6x^3}$ cm

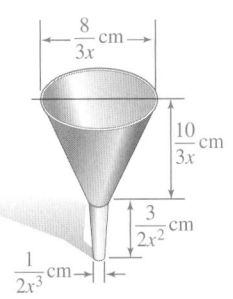

WRITING

81. Explain how to add fractions with the same denominator.

▶ **82.** Explain how to find a lowest common denominator.

Explain what is wrong with each solution.

83. $\dfrac{2x + 3}{x + 5} - \dfrac{x + 2}{x + 5} = \dfrac{2x + 3 - x + 2}{x + 5}$

$= \dfrac{x + 5}{x + 5}$

$= 1$

84. $\dfrac{5x + 4}{y} + \dfrac{x}{y} = \dfrac{5x - 4 + x}{y + y}$

$= \dfrac{6x - 4}{2y}$

$= \dfrac{2(3x - 2)}{2y}$

$= \dfrac{3x - 2}{y}$

REVIEW

Write each number in prime-factored form.

85. 49 7^2

▶ **86.** 64 2^6

87. 136 $2^3 \cdot 17$

88. 315 $3^2 \cdot 5 \cdot 7$

SECTION **7.4**

Adding and Subtracting with Unlike Denominators

Objectives

1 Add and subtract rational expressions that have unlike denominators.

2 Add and subtract rational expressions that have denominators that are opposites.

We have discussed a method for finding the least common denominator (LCD) of two rational expressions. We have also built rational expressions into equivalent expressions having a given denominator. We will now use these skills to add and subtract rational expressions with unlike denominators.

1 **Add and subtract rational expressions that have unlike denominators.**

The following steps summarize how to add (or subtract) rational expressions that have different denominators.

> ### Adding or Subtracting Rational Expressions That Have Unlike Denominators
>
> 1. Find the LCD.
> 2. Rewrite each rational expression as an equivalent expression with the LCD as the denominator. To do this, build each fraction using a form of 1 that involves any factor(s) needed to obtain the LCD.
> 3. Add (or subtract) the numerators and write the sum or difference over the LCD.
> 4. Simplify the result, if possible.

Self Check 1

Add: $\dfrac{y}{2} + \dfrac{6y}{7}$ $\dfrac{19y}{14}$

Now Try Problem 13

Teaching Example 1 Add: $\dfrac{a}{11} + \dfrac{2a}{3}$

Answer:
$\dfrac{25a}{33}$

EXAMPLE 1 Add: $\dfrac{4x}{7} + \dfrac{3x}{5}$

Strategy We will use the procedure for adding rational expressions that have unlike denominators. The first step is to determine the LCD.

WHY If we are to add (or subtract) fractions, their denominators must be the same. Since the denominators of these rational expressions are different, we cannot add them in their present form.

Solution

Step 1 The denominators are 7 and 5. The LCD is $7 \cdot 5 = 35$.

Step 2 We need to multiply the denominator of $\frac{4x}{7}$ by 5 and the denominator of $\frac{3x}{5}$ by 7 to obtain the LCD, 35. It follows that $\frac{5}{5}$ and $\frac{7}{7}$ are the forms of 1 that should be used to write the equivalent rational expressions.

$$\frac{4x}{7} + \frac{3x}{5} = \frac{4x}{7} \cdot \frac{5}{5} + \frac{3x}{5} \cdot \frac{7}{7}$$ Build the rational expressions so that each has a denominator of 35.

$$= \frac{20x}{35} + \frac{21x}{35}$$ Perform the multiplications.

Step 3 $$= \frac{20x + 21x}{35}$$ Add the numerators and keep the common denominator.

$$= \frac{41x}{35}$$ Add the numerators and keep the common denominator.

Step 4 Since 41 and 35 have no common factors, the result cannot be simplified. ∎

Self Check 2

Add: $\dfrac{3}{28z} + \dfrac{5}{21z}$ $\dfrac{29}{84z}$

Now Try Problem 19

EXAMPLE 2 Add: $\dfrac{5}{24b} + \dfrac{11}{18b}$

Strategy We will use the procedure for adding rational expressions that have unlike denominators. The first step is to determine the LCD.

WHY If we are to add (or subtract) fractions, their denominators must be the same. Since the denominators of these rational expressions are different, we cannot add them in their present form.

Solution

Step 1 To find the LCD, we form a product that uses each different factor of $24b$ and $18b$ the greatest number of times it appears in any one factorization.

$$24b = 2 \cdot 2 \cdot 2 \cdot 3 \cdot b$$
$$18b = 2 \cdot 3 \cdot 3 \cdot b$$
$$\text{LCD} = 2 \cdot 2 \cdot 2 \cdot 3 \cdot 3 \cdot b = 72b$$

Step 2 We need to multiply the denominator of $\frac{5}{24b}$ by 3 and the denominator of $\frac{11}{18b}$ by 4 to obtain the LCD, $72b$. It follows that $\frac{3}{3}$ and $\frac{4}{4}$ are the forms of 1 that should be used to write the equivalent rational expressions.

$$= \frac{5}{24b} \cdot \frac{3}{3} + \frac{11}{18b} \cdot \frac{4}{4} \qquad \textit{Build each fraction to get the common denominator.}$$

$$= \frac{15}{72b} + \frac{44}{72b} \qquad \textit{Perform the multiplications.}$$

Step 3 $\quad = \dfrac{15 + 44}{72b} \qquad \textit{Add the numerators and keep the common denominator.}$

$$= \frac{59}{72b} \qquad \textit{Add the numerators and keep the common denominator.}$$

Step 4 Since 59 and 72 have no common factors, the result cannot be simplified. ∎

EXAMPLE 3

Add: $\dfrac{x+4}{x^2} + \dfrac{x-5}{4x}$

Strategy We will use the procedure for adding rational expressions when the denominators are different. The first step is to find the LCD.

WHY Since the denominators are different, we cannot add these rational expressions in their present form.

Solution

First we find the LCD.

$$\left.\begin{array}{l} x^2 = x \cdot x \\ 4x = 2 \cdot 2 \cdot x \end{array}\right\} \quad \text{LCD} = x \cdot x \cdot 2 \cdot 2 = 4x^2$$

$$\frac{x+4}{x^2} + \frac{x-5}{4x} = \frac{x+4}{x^2} \cdot \frac{4}{4} + \frac{x-5}{4x} \cdot \frac{x}{x} \qquad \textit{Build the fractions to get the common denominator, } 4x^2.$$

$$= \frac{4x+16}{4x^2} + \frac{x^2-5x}{4x^2} \qquad \textit{Perform the multiplications.}$$

$$= \frac{4x+16+x^2-5x}{4x^2} \qquad \textit{Add the numerators and keep the common denominator.}$$

$$= \frac{x^2-x+16}{4x^2} \qquad \textit{Combine like terms.}$$

EXAMPLE 4

Subtract: $\dfrac{x}{x+1} - \dfrac{3}{x}$

Strategy We will use the procedure for subtracting rational expressions when the denominators are different. The first step is to find the LCD.

Teaching Example 4 Subtract:
$$\frac{2x}{x+5} - \frac{3}{x}$$
Answer:
$$\frac{2x^2 - 3x - 15}{x(x+5)}$$

WHY Since the denominators are different, we cannot subtract these rational expressions in their present form.

Solution

By inspection, the least common denominator is $(x+1)x$.

$$\frac{x}{x+1} - \frac{3}{x} = \frac{x}{x+1} \cdot \frac{x}{x} - \frac{3}{x} \cdot \frac{x+1}{x+1}$$ Build the fractions to get the common denominator.

$$= \frac{x(x) - 3(x+1)}{x(x+1)}$$ Subtract the numerators and keep the common denominator.

$$= \frac{x^2 - 3x - 3}{x(x+1)}$$ Perform the multiplications in the numerator.

Self Check 5

Subtract: $\dfrac{b}{b-2} - \dfrac{8}{b^2-4}$ $\dfrac{b+4}{b+2}$

Now Try Problem 35

Teaching Example 5 Subtract:
$$\frac{x}{x+3} - \frac{18}{x^2-9}$$
Answer:
$$\frac{x-6}{x-3}$$

EXAMPLE 5   Subtract: $\dfrac{a}{a-1} - \dfrac{2}{a^2-1}$

Strategy We use the procedure for subtracting rational expressions when the denominators are binomials. The first step is to find the LCD.

WHY Since the denominators are different, we cannot subtract these rational expressions in their present form.

Solution

We factor $a^2 - 1$ to see that the LCD is $(a+1)(a-1)$.

$$\frac{a}{a-1} - \frac{2}{a^2-1}$$

$$= \frac{a}{(a-1)} \cdot \frac{a+1}{a+1} - \frac{2}{(a+1)(a-1)}$$ Build the first fraction to get the LCD.

$$= \frac{a(a+1) - 2}{(a-1)(a+1)}$$ Subtract the numerators and keep the common denominator.

$$= \frac{a^2 + a - 2}{(a-1)(a+1)}$$ Distribute the multiplication by a.

$$= \frac{(a+2)\overset{1}{\cancel{(a-1)}}}{\underset{1}{\cancel{(a-1)}}(a+1)}$$ Simplify the result by factoring $a^2 + a - 2$. Remove the common factor of $a - 1$.

$$= \frac{a+2}{a+1}$$

Self Check 6

Subtract:

$$\frac{a}{a^2-2a+1} - \frac{1}{6a-6}$$ $\dfrac{5a+1}{6(a-1)^2}$

Now Try Problem 41

Teaching Example 6 Subtract:
$$\frac{x}{x^2-6x+9} - \frac{3}{2x-6}$$
Answer:
$$\frac{-x+9}{2(x-3)^2}$$

EXAMPLE 6   Subtract: $\dfrac{2a}{a^2+4a+4} - \dfrac{1}{2a+4}$

Strategy We use the procedure for subtracting rational expressions when the denominators are binomials and/or trinomials. The first step is to find the LCD.

WHY Since the denominators are different, we cannot subtract these rational expressions in their present form.

Solution

Find the least common denominator by factoring each denominator.

$$\left.\begin{array}{l} a^2 + 4a + 4 = (a+2)(a+2) \\ 2a + 4 = 2(a+2) \end{array}\right\} \quad \text{LCD} = (a+2)(a+2)2$$

We build each fraction into a new fraction with a denominator of $2(a + 2)(a + 2)$.

$$\frac{2a}{a^2 + 4a + 4} - \frac{1}{2a + 4}$$

$$= \frac{2a}{(a + 2)(a + 2)} - \frac{1}{2(a + 2)}$$ Write the denominators in factored form.

$$= \frac{2a}{(a + 2)(a + 2)} \cdot \frac{2}{2} - \frac{1}{2(a + 2)} \cdot \frac{a + 2}{a + 2}$$ Build each fraction to get a common denominator.

$$= \frac{4a - 1(a + 2)}{2(a + 2)^2}$$ Subtract the numerators and keep the common denominator. Write $(a + 2)(a + 2)$ as $(a + 2)^2$.

$$= \frac{4a - a - 2}{2(a + 2)^2}$$ Distribute the multiplication by -1.

$$= \frac{3a - 2}{2(a + 2)^2}$$ Combine like terms.

EXAMPLE 7

Add: $\dfrac{4b}{a - 5} + b$

Strategy We will begin by writing the second addend, b, as $\frac{b}{1}$ and then find the LCD.

WHY To add b to the rational expression, $\frac{4b}{a - 5}$, we must rewrite b as a rational expression.

Solution
The LCD of $\frac{4b}{a - 5}$ and $\frac{b}{1}$ is $1(a - 5)$, or simply $a - 5$. Since we must multiply the denominator of $\frac{b}{1}$ by $a - 5$ to obtain the LCD, we will use $\frac{a - 5}{a - 5}$ to write an equivalent rational expression.

$$\frac{4b}{a - 5} + b = \frac{4b}{a - 5} + \frac{b}{1} \cdot \frac{a - 5}{a - 5}$$ Build $\frac{b}{1}$ so that it has a denominator of $a - 5$.

$$= \frac{4b}{a - 5} + \frac{ab - 5b}{a - 5}$$ Multiply numerators: $b(a - 5) = ab - 5b$. Multiply denominators: $1(a - 5) = a - 5$.

$$= \frac{4b + ab - 5b}{a - 5}$$ Add the numerators. Write the sum over the common denominator.

$$= \frac{ab - b}{a - 5}$$ Combine like terms in the numerator: $4b - 5b = -b$.

Although the numerator factors as $b(a - 1)$, the numerator and denominator do not have a common factor. Therefore, the result is in simplest form.

Self Check 7

Add: $\dfrac{10y}{n + 4} + y$ $\dfrac{ny + 14y}{n + 4}$

Now Try Problem 50

Teaching Example 7 Add: $\dfrac{3x}{x - 2} + x$

Answer:
$\dfrac{x^2 + x}{x - 2}$

---

2   Add and subtract rational expressions that have denominators that are opposites.

Recall that two polynomials are **opposites** if their terms are the same but they are opposite in sign. For example, $x - 5$ and $5 - x$ are opposites. If we multiply one of these binomials by -1, the subtraction is reversed, and the result is the other binomial.

$$-1(x - 5) = -x + 5 \qquad\qquad -1(5 - x) = -5 + x$$

$$= 5 - x \quad \text{Write the expression} \qquad = x - 5 \quad \text{Write the expression}$$
$$\text{with 5 first.} \qquad\qquad\qquad \text{with x first.}$$

> ### Multiplying by −1
> When a polynomial is multiplied by -1, the result is its opposite.

Self Check 8

Subtract: $\dfrac{5}{a-b} - \dfrac{2}{b-a} \quad \dfrac{7}{a-b}$

Now Try Problem 57

Teaching Example 8 Subtract:
$\dfrac{11}{x-2} - \dfrac{5}{2-x}$
Answer:
$\dfrac{16}{x-2}$

EXAMPLE 8 Subtract: $\dfrac{3}{x-y} - \dfrac{x}{y-x}$

Strategy We note that the denominators are opposites. Either can serve as the LCD; we will choose $x-y$. To obtain a common denominator, we will multiply $\dfrac{x}{y-x}$ by $\dfrac{-1}{-1}$.

WHY When $y-x$ is multiplied by -1, the subtraction is reversed, and the result is $x-y$.

Solution
We note that the second denominator is the opposite (negative) of the first. So we can multiply the numerator and denominator of the second fraction by -1 to get

$$\frac{3}{x-y} - \frac{x}{y-x} = \frac{3}{x-y} - \frac{x}{y-x} \cdot \frac{-1}{-1} \qquad \text{Multiply numerator and denominator by } -1.$$

$$= \frac{3}{x-y} - \frac{-x}{-y+x} \qquad \begin{array}{l}\text{Distribute the multiplication by } -1\text{:}\\ -1(y-x) = -y+x.\end{array}$$

$$= \frac{3}{x-y} - \frac{-x}{x-y} \qquad \begin{array}{l}-y+x = x-y. \text{ The fractions now have}\\ \text{a common denominator of } x-y.\end{array}$$

$$= \frac{3-(-x)}{x-y} \qquad \begin{array}{l}\text{Subtract the numerators and keep the}\\ \text{common denominator.}\end{array}$$

$$= \frac{3+x}{x-y} \qquad -(-x) = x.$$

To add and/or subtract three or more rational expressions, we follow the rules for the order of operations.

Self Check 9

Perform the operations:
$\dfrac{5}{ab^2} - \dfrac{b}{a} + \dfrac{a}{b}$

Now Try Problem 63
Self Check 9 Answer
$\dfrac{5 - b^3 + a^2 b}{ab^2}$

Teaching Example 9 Perform the operations: $\dfrac{4}{xy} + \dfrac{3}{xy^2} - \dfrac{2}{x^2 y}$
Answer:
$\dfrac{4xy + 3x - 2y}{x^2 y^2}$

EXAMPLE 9 Perform the operations: $\dfrac{3}{x^2 y} + \dfrac{2}{xy} - \dfrac{1}{xy^2}$

Strategy We note that the denominators of the rational expressions to be added and subtracted do not have the same denominator. We will find the LCD of all three rational expressions, build to get equivalent rational expressions with the LCD, and then we will perform the additions and subtractions from left to right.

WHY We must follow the rule for adding and/or subtracting rational expressions as well as the rules for order of operations.

Solution
Find the least common denominator.

$$\left.\begin{array}{l} x^2 y = x \cdot x \cdot y \\ xy = x \cdot y \\ xy^2 = x \cdot y \cdot y \end{array}\right\} \quad \text{Factor each denominator.}$$

In any one of these denominators, the factor x occurs at most twice, and the factor y occurs at most twice. Thus,

$$\begin{aligned} \text{LCD} &= x \cdot x \cdot y \cdot y \\ &= x^2 y^2 \end{aligned}$$

We build each fraction into one with a denominator of x^2y^2.

$$\frac{3}{x^2y} + \frac{2}{xy} - \frac{1}{xy^2}$$

$$= \frac{3}{x \cdot x \cdot y} \cdot \frac{y}{y} + \frac{2}{x \cdot y} \cdot \frac{x \cdot y}{x \cdot y} - \frac{1}{x \cdot y \cdot y} \cdot \frac{x}{x}$$

Factor each denominator and build each fraction.

$$= \frac{3y + 2xy - x}{x^2y^2}$$

Perform the multiplications and combine the numerators. Write the result over the LCD.

ANSWERS TO SELF CHECKS

1. $\frac{19y}{14}$ **2.** $\frac{29}{84z}$ **3.** $\frac{a^2 - 10a + 18}{9a^2}$ **4.** $\frac{a^2 - 5a + 5}{a(a-1)}$ **5.** $\frac{b+4}{b+2}$ **6.** $\frac{5a+1}{6(a-1)^2}$ **7.** $\frac{ny + 14y}{n+4}$

8. $\frac{7}{a-b}$ **9.** $\frac{5 - b^3 + a^2b}{ab^2}$

SECTION 7.4   STUDY SET

VOCABULARY

1. $\frac{x}{x-7}$ and $\frac{1}{x-7}$ have _like_ denominators. $\frac{x-1}{2x+3}$ and $\frac{x}{2x-3}$ have _unlike_ denominators.

▶ **2.** Two polynomials are _opposites_ if their terms are the same, but are opposite in sign.

CONCEPTS

3. Write the denominator of $\frac{x+1}{20x^2}$ in factored form.

$2 \cdot 2 \cdot 5 \cdot x \cdot x$

4. Write the denominator of $\frac{3x^2 - 4}{x^2 + 4x - 12}$ in factored form. $(x-2)(x+6)$

5. Factor each denominator and find the LCD of $\frac{1}{12a}$ and $\frac{1}{18a^2}$. $36a^2$

6. Factor each denominator and find the LCD of $\frac{1}{x^2 - 36}$ and $\frac{1}{3x - 18}$. $3(x+6)(x-6)$

7. Find the LCD of $\frac{x-1}{x+6}$ and $\frac{1}{x+3}$. $(x+6)(x+3)$

8. Find the LCD of $\frac{x+3}{x^2-4}$ and $\frac{x-1}{x^2+2x}$. $x(x+2)(x-2)$

NOTATION

Complete each solution.

9. $\frac{2}{5} + \frac{7}{3x} = \frac{2}{5} \cdot \frac{3x}{3x} + \frac{7}{3x} \cdot \frac{5}{5}$

$$= \frac{6x}{15x} + \frac{35}{15x}$$

$$= \frac{6x + 35}{15x}$$

▶ **10.** Are the student's answers and the book's answers equivalent?

Student's answer	Book's answer	Equivalent?
$\dfrac{m^2 + 2m}{(m-1)(m-4)}$	$\dfrac{m^2 + 2m}{(m-4)(m-1)}$	yes
$\dfrac{-5x^2 - 7}{4x(x+3)}$	$\dfrac{5x^2 + 7}{4x(x+3)}$	yes
$\dfrac{-2x}{x-y}$	$-\dfrac{2x}{y-x}$	no

GUIDED PRACTICE

Add the rational expressions. Simplify the result, if possible.
See Example 1.

11. $\frac{2y}{9} + \frac{y}{3}$ $\frac{5y}{9}$

12. $\frac{7y}{6} + \frac{10y}{9}$ $\frac{41y}{18}$

▶ Selected exercises available online at
www.webassign.net/brookscole

13. $\dfrac{x}{3} + \dfrac{2x}{7}$ $\;\dfrac{13x}{21}$

14. $\dfrac{y}{4} + \dfrac{3y}{5}$ $\;\dfrac{17y}{20}$

15. $\dfrac{5a}{6} + \dfrac{5a}{3}$ $\;\dfrac{5a}{2}$

▶ **16.** $\dfrac{4x}{3} + \dfrac{x}{6}$ $\;\dfrac{3x}{2}$

17. $\dfrac{21x}{14} + \dfrac{5x}{21}$ $\;\dfrac{73x}{42}$

18. $\dfrac{8a}{15} + \dfrac{5a}{12}$ $\;\dfrac{19a}{20}$

Add the rational expressions. Simplify the result, if possible. See Example 2.

19. $\dfrac{4}{15a} + \dfrac{9}{20a}$ $\;\dfrac{43}{60a}$

20. $\dfrac{5}{14b} + \dfrac{2}{21b}$ $\;\dfrac{19}{42b}$

21. $\dfrac{6}{25p} + \dfrac{7}{15p}$ $\;\dfrac{53}{75p}$

▶ **22.** $\dfrac{3}{54q} + \dfrac{2}{63q}$ $\;\dfrac{11}{126q}$

Add the rational expressions. Simplify the result, if possible. See Example 3.

23. $\dfrac{y+2}{5y^2} + \dfrac{y+4}{15y}$ $\;\dfrac{y^2 + 7y + 6}{15y^2}$

24. $\dfrac{x+3}{x^2} + \dfrac{x+5}{2x}$ $\;\dfrac{x^2 + 7x + 6}{2x^2}$

25. $\dfrac{x-1}{x} + \dfrac{y+1}{y}$ $\;\dfrac{2xy + x - y}{xy}$

▶ **26.** $\dfrac{a+2}{b} + \dfrac{b-2}{a}$ $\;\dfrac{a^2 + 2a + b^2 - 2b}{ab}$

Subtract the rational expressions. Simplify the result, if possible. See Example 4.

27. $\dfrac{21x}{14} - \dfrac{5x}{21}$ $\;\dfrac{53x}{42}$

28. $\dfrac{8a}{15} - \dfrac{5a}{12}$ $\;\dfrac{7a}{60}$

29. $\dfrac{7}{8} - \dfrac{4}{t}$ $\;\dfrac{7t - 32}{8t}$

30. $\dfrac{5}{a} - \dfrac{3}{b}$ $\;\dfrac{5b - 3a}{ab}$

31. $\dfrac{a}{a+2} - \dfrac{2}{a}$ $\;\dfrac{a^2 - 2a - 4}{a(a+2)}$

32. $\dfrac{2n}{n-3} - \dfrac{1}{n}$ $\;\dfrac{2n^2 - n + 3}{n(n-3)}$

▶ **33.** $\dfrac{5}{d} - \dfrac{d}{d+1}$ $\;\dfrac{-d^2 + 5d + 5}{d(d+1)}$

34. $\dfrac{8}{b} - \dfrac{2b}{b-2}$ $\;\dfrac{-2b^2 + 8b - 16}{b(b-2)}$

Perform the operations. Simplify the result, if possible. See Examples 5–6.

35. $\dfrac{y}{y+1} - \dfrac{2}{y^2 - 1}$ $\;\dfrac{y-2}{y-1}$

36. $\dfrac{b}{b+2} - \dfrac{8}{b^2 - 4}$ $\;\dfrac{b-4}{b-2}$

▶ **37.** $\dfrac{d}{d^2 + 6d + 5} - \dfrac{3}{d^2 + 5d + 4}$ $\;\dfrac{d^2 + d - 15}{(d+5)(d+1)(d+4)}$

38. $\dfrac{r}{r^2 + 5r + 6} - \dfrac{2}{r^2 + 3r + 2}$ $\;\dfrac{r-3}{(r+3)(r+1)}$

39. $\dfrac{4}{s^2 + 5s + 4} + \dfrac{s}{s^2 + 2s + 1}$ $\;\dfrac{s^2 + 8s + 4}{(s+4)(s+1)^2}$

▶ **40.** $\dfrac{3}{t^2 + t - 6} + \dfrac{1}{t^2 + 3t - 10}$ $\;\dfrac{4t + 18}{(t+5)(t-2)(t-3)}$

41. $\dfrac{3b}{b^2 + 2b + 1} - \dfrac{1}{2b + 2}$ $\;\dfrac{5b - 1}{2(b+1)^2}$

42. $\dfrac{2a}{a^2 + 6a + 9} - \dfrac{5}{3a + 9}$ $\;\dfrac{a - 15}{3(a+3)^2}$

43. $\dfrac{1}{b+3} - \dfrac{1}{b^2 + 7b + 12}$ $\;\dfrac{1}{b+4}$

44. $\dfrac{1}{c+6} - \dfrac{-4}{c^2 + 8c + 12}$ $\;\dfrac{1}{c+2}$

45. $\dfrac{b}{b+1} - \dfrac{b+1}{2b+2}$ $\;\dfrac{b-1}{2(b+1)}$

46. $\dfrac{2x}{x+2} + \dfrac{x+1}{x-3}$ $\;\dfrac{3x^2 - 3x + 2}{(x-3)(x+2)}$

Perform the operations. Simplify the result, if possible. See Example 7.

47. $\dfrac{8}{x} + 6$ $\;\dfrac{6x + 8}{x}$

48. $\dfrac{2}{y} + 7$ $\;\dfrac{7y + 2}{y}$

49. $\dfrac{9}{x-4} + x$ $\;\dfrac{x^2 - 4x + 9}{x-4}$

50. $\dfrac{9}{m+4} + 9$ $\;\dfrac{9m + 45}{m+4}$

51. $b - \dfrac{3}{a^2}$ $\;\dfrac{a^2b - 3}{a^2}$

▶ **52.** $c - \dfrac{5}{3b}$ $\;\dfrac{3bc - 5}{3b}$

53. $\dfrac{x+2}{x+1} - 5$ $\;\dfrac{-4x - 3}{x+1}$ or $-\dfrac{4x+3}{x+1}$

54. $\dfrac{y+8}{y-8} - 4$ $\;\dfrac{-3y + 40}{y-8}$ or $-\dfrac{3y-40}{y-8}$

Perform the operations. Simplify the result, if possible. See Example 8.

55. $\dfrac{2}{a-b} - \dfrac{a}{b-a}$ $\;\dfrac{a+2}{a-b}$

56. $\dfrac{m}{m-n} - \dfrac{n}{n-m}$ $\;\dfrac{m+n}{m-n}$

57. $\dfrac{5}{a-4} + \dfrac{7}{4-a} - \dfrac{2}{a-4}$

58. $\dfrac{p}{p-q} + \dfrac{q}{q-p}$ $\;1$

▶ **59.** $\dfrac{2x+2}{x-2} - \dfrac{2x}{2-x}$ $\;\dfrac{4x+2}{x-2}$

60. $\dfrac{y+3}{y-1} - \dfrac{y+4}{1-y}$ $\;\dfrac{2y+7}{y-1}$

61. $\dfrac{r+2}{r^2 - 4} + \dfrac{4}{4-r^2}$ $\;\dfrac{1}{r+2}$

62. $\dfrac{h}{h^2 - 49} + \dfrac{7}{49 - h^2}$ $\;\dfrac{1}{h+7}$

Perform the operations. Simplify the result, if possible. See Example 9.

63. $\dfrac{3}{a^2b} + \dfrac{4}{ab} - \dfrac{2}{ab^2}$ $\;\dfrac{3b + 4ab - 2a}{a^2b^2}$

64. $\dfrac{2}{pq} - \dfrac{a}{pq^2} + \dfrac{b}{p^2q^2}$ $\;\dfrac{2pq - ap + b}{p^2q^2}$

65. $\dfrac{2}{x-1} + \dfrac{3}{x+1} - \dfrac{1}{x^2 - 1}$ $\;\dfrac{5x-2}{(x+1)(x-1)}$

▶ **66.** $\dfrac{3}{2y+2} - \dfrac{2}{3y+3} + \dfrac{1}{y+1}$ $\;\dfrac{11}{6(y+1)}$

67. $\dfrac{2x}{x^2 - 3x + 2} + \dfrac{2x}{x-1} - \dfrac{x}{x-2}$ $\;\dfrac{x}{x-2}$

68. $\dfrac{4a}{a-2} - \dfrac{3a}{a-3} + \dfrac{4a}{a^2 - 5a + 6}$ $\dfrac{a}{a-3}$

69. $\dfrac{2x}{x-1} + \dfrac{3x}{x+1} - \dfrac{x+3}{x^2-1}$ $\dfrac{5x+3}{x+1}$

70. $\dfrac{a}{a-1} - \dfrac{2}{a+2} + \dfrac{3(a-2)}{a^2+a-2}$ $\dfrac{a+4}{a+2}$

TRY IT YOURSELF

Perform the operations and simplify, if possible.

71. $\dfrac{2y}{5x} - \dfrac{y}{2}$
$\dfrac{4y - 5xy}{10x}$

72. $\dfrac{2}{x} - 3x$
$\dfrac{2 - 3x^2}{x}$

73. $\dfrac{7}{m^2} + \dfrac{2}{m}$
$\dfrac{7 + 2m}{m^2}$

74. $\dfrac{3}{8a} + \dfrac{11}{12a}$
$\dfrac{31}{24a}$

75. $\dfrac{4x}{3} + \dfrac{2x}{y}$
$\dfrac{4xy + 6x}{3y}$

76. $14 + \dfrac{10}{y^2}$
$\dfrac{14y^2 + 10}{y^2}$

77. $\dfrac{x}{x+1} + \dfrac{x-1}{x}$
$\dfrac{2x^2 - 1}{x(x+1)}$

78. $\dfrac{3x}{xy} + \dfrac{x+1}{y-1}$
$\dfrac{4y - 3 + xy}{y(y-1)}$

79. $\dfrac{x+5}{xy} - \dfrac{x-1}{x^2y}$
$\dfrac{x^2 + 4x + 1}{x^2y}$

80. $\dfrac{y+7}{2y} - \dfrac{y^2 + 5y + 14}{2y^2}$
$\dfrac{y-7}{y^2}$

81. $\dfrac{x}{x-2} + \dfrac{4+2x}{x^2-4}$
$\dfrac{x+2}{x-2}$

82. $\dfrac{y}{y+3} - \dfrac{2y-6}{y^2-9}$
$\dfrac{y-2}{y+3}$

▶ **83.** $\dfrac{4}{b-6} - \dfrac{b}{6-b}$
$\dfrac{b+4}{b-6}$

84. $\dfrac{t+1}{t-7} - \dfrac{t+1}{7-t}$
$\dfrac{2t+2}{t-7}$

85. $\dfrac{4x+1}{8x-12} + \dfrac{x-3}{2x-3}$
$\dfrac{8x-11}{4(2x-3)}$

86. $\dfrac{x+1}{x-1} + \dfrac{x-1}{x+1}$
$\dfrac{2x^2+2}{(x-1)(x+1)}$

87. $\dfrac{2}{a^2+4a+3} + \dfrac{1}{a+3}$
$\dfrac{1}{a+1}$

88. $\dfrac{3}{s-8} + t$
$\dfrac{st-8t+3}{s-8}$

89. $\dfrac{x+1}{2x+4} - \dfrac{x^2}{2x^2-8}$
$-\dfrac{1}{2(x-2)}$

90. $\dfrac{x+1}{x+2} - \dfrac{x^2+1}{x^2-x-6}$
$-\dfrac{2}{x-3}$

91. $\dfrac{7}{3a} + \dfrac{1}{a-2}$
$\dfrac{10a - 14}{3a(a-2)}$

92. $\dfrac{5}{9x} + \dfrac{4}{x+6}$
$\dfrac{41x + 30}{9x(x+6)}$

93. $\dfrac{3}{x+2} + \dfrac{x}{x-1} - \dfrac{3x}{x^2+x-2}$
$\dfrac{x+3}{x+2}$

94. $\dfrac{2x}{x^2-3x+2} + \dfrac{2x}{x-1} - \dfrac{x}{x-2}$
$\dfrac{x}{x-2}$

WRITING

95. Explain the error:
$$\dfrac{3}{x} + \dfrac{8}{y} = \dfrac{3+8}{x+y} = \dfrac{11}{x+y}$$

▶ **96.** Explain how to add two rational expressions with unlike denominators.

REVIEW

97. Find the slope and y-intercept of the graph of $y = 8x + 2$. $8, (0, 2)$

98. Find the slope and y-intercept of the graph of $3x + 4y = -36$. $-\dfrac{3}{4}, (0, -9)$

99. What is the slope of the graph of $y = 2$? 0

100. Is the graph of the equation $x = 0$ the x-axis or the y-axis? *y-axis*

SECTION 7.5
Simplifying Complex Fractions

Objectives

1 Simplify complex fractions using division.

2 Simplify complex fractions using the LCD.

A rational expression whose numerator and/or denominator contain fractions is called a **complex rational expression** or a **complex fraction.** The expression above the main fraction bar of a complex fraction is the numerator, and the expression below the main fraction bar is the denominator. Two examples of complex fractions are:

$$\dfrac{\dfrac{5x}{3}}{\dfrac{2x}{9}}$$ ← Numerator of complex fraction → $$\dfrac{\dfrac{1}{2} - \dfrac{1}{x}}{\dfrac{x}{3} + \dfrac{1}{5}}$$
← Main fraction bar →
← Denominator of complex fraction →

In this section, we will discuss two methods for simplifying complex fractions. To **simplify a complex fraction** means to write it in the form $\frac{A}{B}$, where A and B are polynomials that have no common factors.

1 Simplify complex fractions using division.

One method for simplifying complex fractions uses the fact that the main fraction bar indicates division.

> ### Simplifying Complex Fractions Method 1: Using Division
>
> 1. Add or subtract in the numerator and/or denominator so that the numerator is a single fraction and the denominator is a single fraction.
> 2. Perform the indicated division by multiplying the numerator of the complex fraction by the reciprocal of the denominator.
> 3. Simplify the result, if possible.

Self Check 1

Simplify: $\dfrac{\frac{7y^3}{8}}{\frac{21y^2}{20}}$ $\frac{5y}{6}$

Now Try Problem 15

Teaching Example 1 Simplify: $\dfrac{\frac{12x^2}{5}}{\frac{7x}{15}}$

Answer:
$\dfrac{36x}{7}$

EXAMPLE 1

Simplify: $\dfrac{\frac{5x^2}{3}}{\frac{2x^3}{9}}$

Strategy We will perform the division indicated by the main fraction bar using the procedure for dividing rational expressions from Section 7.2.

WHY We can skip the first step of method 1 and immediately divide because the numerator and the denominator of the complex fraction are already single fractions.

Solution

$$\dfrac{\frac{5x^2}{3}}{\frac{2x^3}{9}} = \frac{5x^2}{3} \div \frac{2x^3}{9} \qquad \text{Write the division indicated by the main fraction bar using a} \div \text{symbol.}$$

$$= \frac{5x^2}{3} \cdot \frac{9}{2x^3} \qquad \text{To divide rational expressions, multiply the first by the reciprocal of the second.}$$

$$= \frac{5x^2 \cdot 9}{3 \cdot 2x^3} \qquad \begin{array}{l}\text{Multiply the numerators.}\\ \text{Multiply the denominators.}\end{array}$$

$$= \frac{5 \cdot \overset{1}{\cancel{x}} \cdot \overset{1}{\cancel{x}} \cdot \overset{1}{\cancel{3}} \cdot 3}{\underset{1}{\cancel{3}} \cdot 2 \cdot \underset{1}{\cancel{x}} \cdot \underset{1}{\cancel{x}} \cdot x} \qquad \text{Factor 9 as } 3 \cdot 3. \text{ Then simplify by removing factors equal to 1.}$$

$$= \frac{15}{2x} \qquad \begin{array}{l}\text{Multiply the remaining factors in the numerator.}\\ \text{Multiply the remaining factors in the denominator.}\end{array}$$

Self Check 2

Simplify: $\dfrac{\frac{1}{3} + \frac{1}{x}}{\frac{x}{5} - \frac{1}{2}}$ $\frac{10(x+3)}{3x(2x-5)}$

Now Try Problem 21

EXAMPLE 2

Simplify: $\dfrac{\frac{1}{2} - \frac{1}{x}}{\frac{x}{3} + \frac{1}{5}}$

Strategy We will simplify the expressions above and below the main fraction bar separately to write $\frac{1}{2} - \frac{1}{x}$ and $\frac{x}{3} + \frac{1}{5}$ as single fractions. Then we will perform the indicated division.

WHY The numerator and the denominator of the complex fraction must be written as single fractions before dividing.

Solution

To write the numerator as a single fraction, we build $\frac{1}{2}$ and $\frac{1}{x}$ to have an LCD of $2x$, and then subtract. To write the denominator as a single fraction, we build $\frac{x}{3}$ and $\frac{1}{5}$ to have an LCD of 15, and then add.

$$\dfrac{\dfrac{1}{2} - \dfrac{1}{x}}{\dfrac{x}{3} + \dfrac{1}{5}} = \dfrac{\dfrac{1}{2}\cdot\dfrac{x}{x} - \dfrac{1}{x}\cdot\dfrac{2}{2}}{\dfrac{x}{3}\cdot\dfrac{5}{5} + \dfrac{1}{5}\cdot\dfrac{3}{3}}$$

 ← The LCD for the numerator is $2x$. Build each fraction so that each has a denominator of $2x$.

 ← The LCD for the denominator is 15. Build each fraction so that each has a denominator of 15.

$$= \dfrac{\dfrac{x}{2x} - \dfrac{2}{2x}}{\dfrac{5x}{15} + \dfrac{3}{15}}$$

Multiply the numerators and multiply the denominators.

$$= \dfrac{\dfrac{x-2}{2x}}{\dfrac{5x+3}{15}}$$

Subtract in the numerator and add in the denominator of the complex fraction.

Now that the numerator and the denominator of the complex fraction are single fractions, we perform the indicated division.

$$\dfrac{\dfrac{x-2}{2x}}{\dfrac{5x+3}{15}} = \dfrac{x-2}{2x} \div \dfrac{5x+3}{15}$$

Write the division indicated by the main fraction bar using a ÷ symbol.

$$= \dfrac{x-2}{2x} \cdot \dfrac{15}{5x+3}$$

Multiply by the reciprocal of $\frac{5x+3}{15}$.

$$= \dfrac{15(x-2)}{2x(5x+3)}$$

Multiply the numerators.
Multiply the denominators.

Since the numerator and denominator have no common factor, the result does not simplify. ■

Success Tip The result after simplifying a complex fraction can often have several equivalent forms. The result for Example 2 could be written:

$$\dfrac{15x - 30}{2x(5x+3)}$$

EXAMPLE 3

Simplify: $\dfrac{\dfrac{6}{x} + y}{\dfrac{6}{y} + x}$

Strategy We will simplify the expressions above and below the main fraction bar separately to write $\frac{6}{x} + y$ and $\frac{6}{y} + x$ as single fractions. Then we will perform the indicated division.

WHY The numerator and the denominator of the complex fraction must be written as single fractions before dividing.

Solution

To write $\frac{6}{x} + y$ as a single fraction, we build y into a fraction with a denominator of x and add. To write $\frac{6}{y} + x$ as a single fraction, we build x into a fraction with a denominator of y and add.

$$\frac{\dfrac{6}{x} + y}{\dfrac{6}{y} + x} = \frac{\dfrac{6}{x} + \dfrac{y}{1} \cdot \dfrac{x}{x}}{\dfrac{6}{y} + \dfrac{x}{1} \cdot \dfrac{y}{y}}$$

← Write y as $\frac{y}{1}$. The LCD for the numerator is x. Build $\frac{y}{1}$ so that it has a denominator of x.

← Write x as $\frac{x}{1}$. The LCD for the denominator is y. Build $\frac{x}{1}$ so that it has a denominator of y.

$$= \frac{\dfrac{6}{x} + \dfrac{xy}{x}}{\dfrac{6}{y} + \dfrac{xy}{y}}$$

Multiply in the numerator and multiply in the denominator.

$$= \frac{\dfrac{6 + xy}{x}}{\dfrac{6 + xy}{y}}$$

Add in the numerator and in the denominator of the complex fraction.

Now that the numerator and the denominator of the complex fraction are single fractions, we can perform the division.

$$\frac{\dfrac{6 + xy}{x}}{\dfrac{6 + xy}{y}} = \frac{6 + xy}{x} \div \frac{6 + xy}{y}$$

Write the division indicated by the main fraction bar using a $\div$ symbol.

$$= \frac{6 + xy}{x} \cdot \frac{y}{6 + xy}$$

Multiply by the reciprocal of $\frac{6 + xy}{y}$.

$$= \frac{y(6 + xy)}{x(6 + xy)}$$

Multiply the numerators.
Multiply the denominators.

$$= \frac{y(\overset{1}{\cancel{6 + xy}})}{x(\underset{1}{\cancel{6 + xy}})}$$

Simplify the result by removing a factor equal to 1.

$$= \frac{y}{x}$$

2 Simplify complex fractions using the LCD.

A second method for simplifying complex fractions uses the concepts of LCD and multiplication by a form of 1. The multiplication by 1 produces a simpler, equivalent expression, which will not contain fractions in its numerator or denominator.

Simplifying Complex Fractions Method 2: Multiplying by the LCD

1. Find the LCD of all fractions within the complex fraction.
2. Multiply the complex fraction by 1 in the form $\frac{\text{LCD}}{\text{LCD}}$.
3. Perform the operations in the numerator and denominator. No fractional expressions should remain within the complex fraction.
4. Simplify the result, if possible.

We will use method 2 to rework Example 2.

EXAMPLE 4

Simplify: $\dfrac{\dfrac{1}{2} - \dfrac{1}{x}}{\dfrac{x}{3} + \dfrac{1}{5}}$

Strategy Using method 1 to simplify this complex fraction, we worked with $\frac{1}{2} - \frac{1}{x}$ and $\frac{x}{3} + \frac{1}{5}$ separately. With method 2, we will use the LCD of *all four* fractions within the complex fraction.

WHY Multiplying a complex fraction by 1 in the form of $\frac{\text{LCD}}{\text{LCD}}$ clears its numerator and denominator of fractions.

Solution

The denominators of all the fractions within the complex fraction are 2, x, 3, and 5. Thus, their LCD is $2 \cdot x \cdot 3 \cdot 5 = 30x$.

We now multiply the complex fraction by a factor equal to 1, using the LCD: $\frac{30x}{30x} = 1$.

$$\dfrac{\dfrac{1}{2} - \dfrac{1}{x}}{\dfrac{x}{3} + \dfrac{1}{5}} = \dfrac{\dfrac{1}{2} - \dfrac{1}{x}}{\dfrac{x}{3} + \dfrac{1}{5}} \cdot \dfrac{30x}{30x}$$

$$= \dfrac{\left(\dfrac{1}{2} - \dfrac{1}{x}\right)30x}{\left(\dfrac{x}{3} + \dfrac{1}{5}\right)30x} \quad \begin{array}{l}\leftarrow \text{ Multiply the numerators.}\\[1.5em] \leftarrow \text{ Multiply the denominators.}\end{array}$$

$$= \dfrac{\dfrac{1}{2}(30x) - \dfrac{1}{x}(30x)}{\dfrac{x}{3}(30x) + \dfrac{1}{5}(30x)} \quad \begin{array}{l}\leftarrow \text{ In the numerator, distribute the multiplication}\\ \text{by 30x.}\\[0.8em] \leftarrow \text{ In the denominator, distribute the multiplication}\\ \text{by 30x.}\end{array}$$

$$= \dfrac{15x - 30}{10x^2 + 6x} \quad \begin{array}{l}\text{Perform each of the four multiplications by 30x.}\\ \text{Notice that no fractional expressions remain within}\\ \text{the complex fraction.}\end{array}$$

To attempt to simplify the result, factor the numerator and denominator. Since they do not have a common factor, the result is in simplest form.

$$\dfrac{15x - 30}{10x^2 + 6x} = \dfrac{15(x - 2)}{2x(5x + 3)}$$

Success Tip When simplifying a complex fraction, the same result will be obtained regardless of the method used. See Example 2.

EXAMPLE 5

Simplify: $\dfrac{\dfrac{1}{8} - \dfrac{1}{y}}{\dfrac{8 - y}{4y^2}}$

Strategy Using method 1, we would work with $\frac{1}{8} - \frac{1}{y}$ and $\frac{8 - y}{4y^2}$ separately. With method 2, we use the LCD of all three fractions within the complex fraction.

WHY Multiplying a complex fraction by 1 in the form of $\frac{\text{LCD}}{\text{LCD}}$ clears its numerator and denominator of fractions.

Self Check 4

Use method 2 to simplify:

$\dfrac{\dfrac{1}{4} - \dfrac{1}{x}}{\dfrac{x}{5} + \dfrac{1}{3}}$ $\dfrac{15(x - 4)}{4x(3x + 5)}$

Now Try Problem 44

Teaching Example 4 Simplify:

$\dfrac{\dfrac{1}{x} - \dfrac{1}{7}}{\dfrac{x}{2} + \dfrac{1}{3}}$

Answer:

$\dfrac{6(7 - x)}{7x(3x + 2)}$

Self Check 5

Simplify: $\dfrac{\dfrac{10 - n}{5n^2}}{\dfrac{1}{10} - \dfrac{1}{n}}$ $-\dfrac{2}{n}$

Now Try Problem 54

Solution

The denominators of all fractions within the complex fraction are 8, y, and $4y^2$. Therefore, the LCD is $8y^2$ and we multiply the complex fraction by a factor equal to 1, using the LCD: $\dfrac{8y^2}{8y^2} = 1$.

$$\dfrac{\dfrac{1}{8} - \dfrac{1}{y}}{\dfrac{8 - y}{4y^2}} = \dfrac{\dfrac{1}{8} - \dfrac{1}{y}}{\dfrac{8 - y}{4y^2}} \cdot \dfrac{8y^2}{8y^2}$$

$$= \dfrac{\left(\dfrac{1}{8} - \dfrac{1}{y}\right)8y^2}{\left(\dfrac{8 - y}{4y^2}\right)8y^2} \quad \begin{array}{l}\leftarrow \text{Multiply the numerators.} \\ \\ \leftarrow \text{Multiply the denominators.}\end{array}$$

$$= \dfrac{\dfrac{1}{8}(8y^2) - \dfrac{1}{y}(8y^2)}{\left(\dfrac{8 - y}{4y^2}\right)(8y^2)} \quad \text{Distribute the multiplication by } 8y^2.$$

$$= \dfrac{y^2 - 8y}{(8 - y)2} \quad \text{Perform each of the three multiplications by } 8y^2.$$

$$= \dfrac{y(\overset{-1}{\cancel{y - 8}})}{(\underset{1}{\cancel{8 - y}})2} \quad \begin{array}{l}\text{In the numerator, factor out the GCF, } y. \text{ Since } y - 8 \\ \text{and } 8 - y \text{ are opposites, simplify by replacing } \dfrac{y - 8}{8 - y} \\ \text{with } \dfrac{-1}{1}.\end{array}$$

$$= -\dfrac{y}{2}$$

EXAMPLE 6

Simplify: $\quad\dfrac{1}{1 + \dfrac{1}{x + 1}}$

Strategy Although either method can be used, we will use method 2 to simplify this complex fraction.

WHY Method 2 is often easier when the complex fraction contains a sum or difference.

Solution

The only fraction within the complex fraction has the denominator $x + 1$. Therefore, the LCD is $x + 1$. We multiply the complex fraction by a factor equal to 1, using the LCD: $\dfrac{x + 1}{x + 1} = 1$.

$$\dfrac{1}{1 + \dfrac{1}{x + 1}} = \dfrac{1}{1 + \dfrac{1}{x + 1}} \cdot \dfrac{x + 1}{x + 1}$$

$$= \dfrac{1(x + 1)}{\left(1 + \dfrac{1}{x + 1}\right)(x + 1)} \quad \begin{array}{l}\text{Multiply the numerators.} \\ \text{Multiply the denominators.}\end{array}$$

$$= \dfrac{1(x + 1)}{1(x + 1) + \dfrac{1}{x + 1}(x + 1)} \quad \begin{array}{l}\text{In the denominator, distribute the} \\ \text{multiplication by } x + 1.\end{array}$$

$$= \dfrac{x + 1}{x + 1 + 1} \quad \begin{array}{l}\text{Perform each of the three} \\ \text{multiplications by } x + 1.\end{array}$$

$$= \frac{x + 1}{x + 2}$$

Combine like terms in the denominator.

The result does not simplify.

Success Tip   Simplifying using the LCD (method 2) works well when the complex fraction has sums and/or differences in the numerator and/or denominator.

ANSWERS TO SELF CHECK

1. $\frac{5y}{6}$ **2.** $\frac{10(x + 3)}{3x(2x - 5)}$ **3.** $\frac{b}{a}$ **4.** $\frac{15(x - 4)}{4x(3x + 5)}$ **5.** $-\frac{2}{n}$ **6.** $\frac{2(x + 2)}{2x + 5}$

SECTION 7.5   STUDY SET

VOCABULARY

Fill in the blanks.

1. If a fraction has a fraction in its numerator or denominator, it is called a __complex__ __fraction__ .

▶ **2.** The denominator of the complex fraction $\dfrac{\dfrac{3}{x} + \dfrac{x}{y}}{\dfrac{1}{x} + 2}$ is

$\dfrac{1}{x} + 2$.

CONCEPTS

Fill in the blanks.

3. Method 1: To simplify a complex fraction, we write the numerator and the denominator of a complex fraction as __single__ fractions. Then perform the indicated __division__ by multiplying the numerator of the complex fraction by the __reciprocal__ of the denominator.

▶ **4.** Method 2: To simplify a complex fraction, we multiply the numerator and denominator of the complex fraction by the __LCD__ of the fractions in its numerator and denominator.

NOTATION

Complete each solution.

5. $\dfrac{\dfrac{2b - a}{ab}}{\dfrac{b + 2a}{ab}} = \dfrac{2b - a}{ab} \div \dfrac{b + 2a}{ab}$

$= \dfrac{2b - a}{ab} \cdot \dfrac{ab}{b + 2a}$

$= \dfrac{(2b - a)\,ab}{ab\,(b + 2a)}$

$= \dfrac{2b - a}{b + 2a}$

6. $\dfrac{\dfrac{2}{a} - \dfrac{1}{b}}{\dfrac{1}{a} + \dfrac{2}{b}} = \dfrac{ab\left(\dfrac{2}{a} - \dfrac{1}{b}\right)}{ab\left(\dfrac{1}{a} + \dfrac{2}{b}\right)}$

$= \dfrac{2b - a}{b + 2a}$

GUIDED PRACTICE

Simplify each complex fraction. See Example 1.

7. $\dfrac{\dfrac{2}{3}}{\dfrac{3}{4}}$ $\dfrac{8}{9}$

8. $\dfrac{\dfrac{3}{5}}{\dfrac{2}{7}}$ $\dfrac{21}{10}$

9. $\dfrac{\dfrac{4}{5}}{\dfrac{32}{15}}$ $\dfrac{3}{8}$

10. $\dfrac{\dfrac{7}{8}}{\dfrac{49}{4}}$ $\dfrac{1}{14}$

11. $\dfrac{\dfrac{x}{2}}{\dfrac{6}{5}}$ $\dfrac{5x}{12}$

12. $\dfrac{\dfrac{9}{4}}{\dfrac{7}{x}}$ $\dfrac{9x}{28}$

13. $\dfrac{\dfrac{x}{y}}{\dfrac{1}{x}}$ $\dfrac{x^2}{y}$

▶ **14.** $\dfrac{\dfrac{y}{x}}{\dfrac{x}{xy}}$ $\dfrac{y^2}{x}$

15. $\dfrac{\dfrac{5t^2}{9x^2}}{\dfrac{3t}{x^2t}}$ $\dfrac{5t^2}{27}$

16. $\dfrac{\dfrac{5w^2}{4tz}}{\dfrac{15wt}{z^2}}$ $\dfrac{wz}{12t^2}$

17. $\dfrac{\dfrac{4t - 8}{t^2}}{\dfrac{8t - 16}{t^5}}$ $\dfrac{t^3}{2}$

18. $\dfrac{\dfrac{9m - 27}{m^6}}{\dfrac{2m - 6}{m^8}}$ $\dfrac{9m^2}{2}$

▶ Selected exercises available online at **www.webassign.net/brookscole**

Simplify each complex fraction. See Example 2.

19. $\dfrac{\dfrac{1}{2} + \dfrac{3}{4}}{\dfrac{3}{2} + \dfrac{1}{4}}$ $\dfrac{5}{7}$

20. $\dfrac{\dfrac{2}{3} - \dfrac{5}{2}}{\dfrac{2}{3} - \dfrac{3}{2}}$ $\dfrac{11}{5}$

21. $\dfrac{\dfrac{3}{5} + \dfrac{1}{y}}{\dfrac{y}{3} - \dfrac{2}{5}}$ $\dfrac{9y + 15}{5y^2 - 6y}$

22. $\dfrac{\dfrac{2}{x} - \dfrac{1}{3}}{\dfrac{2}{3} + \dfrac{x}{5}}$ $\dfrac{30 - 5x}{10x + 3x^2}$

23. $\dfrac{\dfrac{1}{y} - \dfrac{5}{2}}{\dfrac{3}{y} + \dfrac{1}{2}}$ $\dfrac{2 - 5y}{6 + y}$

24. $\dfrac{\dfrac{1}{6} - \dfrac{5}{s}}{\dfrac{2}{s}}$ $\dfrac{s - 30}{12}$

25. $\dfrac{\dfrac{4}{c} - \dfrac{c}{6}}{\dfrac{2}{c}}$ $\dfrac{24 - c^2}{12}$

26. $\dfrac{\dfrac{10}{n} - \dfrac{n}{4}}{\dfrac{8}{n}}$ $\dfrac{40 - n^2}{32}$

27. $\dfrac{\dfrac{2}{s} - \dfrac{2}{s^2}}{\dfrac{4}{s^2} + \dfrac{4}{s^3}}$ $\dfrac{s^2 - s}{2s + 2}$

28. $\dfrac{\dfrac{3}{a} - \dfrac{2}{b}}{\dfrac{1}{a} + \dfrac{5}{b}}$ $\dfrac{3b - 2a}{b + 5a}$

29. $\dfrac{\dfrac{2}{a} + \dfrac{1}{b}}{\dfrac{1}{a} - \dfrac{3}{b}}$ $\dfrac{2b + a}{b - 3a}$

30. $\dfrac{\dfrac{1}{4} + \dfrac{1}{y}}{\dfrac{y}{3} - \dfrac{1}{2}}$ $\dfrac{3y + 12}{4y^2 - 6y}$

Simplify each complex fraction. See Example 3.

31. $\dfrac{\dfrac{2}{3} + 1}{\dfrac{1}{3} + 1}$ $\dfrac{5}{4}$

32. $\dfrac{\dfrac{3}{5} - 2}{\dfrac{2}{5} - 2}$ $\dfrac{7}{8}$

33. $\dfrac{\dfrac{1}{x} - 3}{\dfrac{5}{x} + 2}$ $\dfrac{1 - 3x}{5 + 2x}$

34. $\dfrac{\dfrac{1}{y} + 3}{\dfrac{3}{y} - 2}$ $\dfrac{1 + 3y}{3 - 2y}$

35. $\dfrac{\dfrac{2}{x} + 2}{\dfrac{4}{x} + 2}$ $\dfrac{1 + x}{2 + x}$

36. $\dfrac{\dfrac{3}{x} - 3}{\dfrac{9}{x} - 3}$ $\dfrac{1 - x}{3 - x}$

37. $\dfrac{\dfrac{3y}{x} - y}{y - \dfrac{y}{x}}$ $\dfrac{3 - x}{x - 1}$

38. $\dfrac{\dfrac{y}{x} + 3y}{y + \dfrac{2y}{x}}$ $\dfrac{3x + 1}{x + 2}$

39. $\dfrac{4 - \dfrac{1}{8h}}{12 + \dfrac{3}{4h}}$ $\dfrac{32h - 1}{96h + 6}$

40. $\dfrac{12 + \dfrac{1}{3b}}{12 - \dfrac{1}{b^2}}$ $\dfrac{36b^2 + b}{36b^2 - 3}$

41. $\dfrac{1 - \dfrac{9}{d^2}}{2 + \dfrac{6}{d}}$ $\dfrac{d - 3}{2d}$

42. $\dfrac{1 - \dfrac{16}{a^2}}{\dfrac{12}{a} + 3}$ $\dfrac{a - 4}{3a}$

Simplify each complex fraction by using the LCD. See Example 4.

43. $\dfrac{\dfrac{1}{6} - \dfrac{2}{x}}{\dfrac{1}{6} + \dfrac{1}{x}}$ $\dfrac{x - 12}{x + 6}$

44. $\dfrac{\dfrac{3}{4} + \dfrac{1}{y}}{\dfrac{5}{6} - \dfrac{1}{y}}$ $\dfrac{9y + 12}{10y - 12}$

45. $\dfrac{\dfrac{a}{7} - \dfrac{7}{a}}{\dfrac{1}{a} + \dfrac{1}{7}}$ $a - 7$

46. $\dfrac{\dfrac{t}{9} - \dfrac{9}{t}}{\dfrac{1}{t} + \dfrac{1}{9}}$ $t - 9$

47. $\dfrac{\dfrac{m}{n} + \dfrac{n}{m}}{\dfrac{m}{n} - \dfrac{n}{m}}$ $\dfrac{m^2 + n^2}{m^2 - n^2}$

48. $\dfrac{\dfrac{2a}{b} - \dfrac{b}{a}}{\dfrac{2a}{b} + \dfrac{b}{a}}$ $\dfrac{2a^2 - b^2}{2a^2 + b^2}$

49. $\dfrac{\dfrac{1}{4} + \dfrac{1}{y}}{\dfrac{y}{3} - \dfrac{1}{2}}$ $\dfrac{3y + 12}{4y^2 - 6y}$

50. $\dfrac{\dfrac{3}{5} + \dfrac{2}{x}}{\dfrac{1}{3} - \dfrac{4}{y}}$ $\dfrac{9xy + 30y}{5xy - 60x}$

Simplify each complex fraction by using the LCD. See Example 5.

51. $\dfrac{\dfrac{1}{c} + \dfrac{5}{4}}{\dfrac{2}{c^2}}$ $\dfrac{4c + 5c^2}{8}$

52. $\dfrac{\dfrac{1}{s} + \dfrac{10}{3}}{\dfrac{7}{s^2}}$ $\dfrac{3s + 10s^2}{21}$

53. $\dfrac{\dfrac{2}{x}}{\dfrac{2}{y} - \dfrac{4}{x}}$ $\dfrac{y}{x - 2y}$

54. $\dfrac{\dfrac{2y}{3}}{\dfrac{2y}{3} - \dfrac{8}{y}}$ $\dfrac{y^2}{y^2 - 12}$

Simplify each complex fraction by using the LCD. See Example 6.

55. $\dfrac{\dfrac{5}{x + 3}}{1 + \dfrac{1}{x + 1}}$ $\dfrac{5}{x + 4}$

56. $\dfrac{\dfrac{1}{x - 4}}{1 - \dfrac{1}{x - 4}}$ $\dfrac{1}{x - 5}$

57. $\dfrac{\dfrac{4}{x - 4}}{\dfrac{x}{x - 4} + 3}$ $\dfrac{1}{x - 3}$

58. $\dfrac{\dfrac{2}{x - 2}}{\dfrac{2}{x - 2} - 1}$ $\dfrac{2}{4 - x}$

59. $\dfrac{3 + \dfrac{3}{x - 1}}{3 - \dfrac{3}{x - 1}}$ $\dfrac{x}{x - 2}$

60. $\dfrac{2 - \dfrac{2}{x + 1}}{2 + \dfrac{2}{x + 1}}$ $\dfrac{x}{x + 2}$

61. $\dfrac{m - \dfrac{1}{2m + 1}}{1 - \dfrac{m}{2m + 1}}$ $2m - 1$

62. $\dfrac{1 - \dfrac{r}{2r + 1}}{r - \dfrac{1}{2r + 1}}$ $\dfrac{1}{2r - 1}$

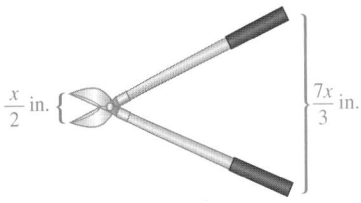

TRY IT YOURSELF

Simplify each complex fraction.

63. $\dfrac{\dfrac{3y}{x} - y}{y - \dfrac{y}{x}}$ $\dfrac{3-x}{x-1}$

64. $\dfrac{\dfrac{y}{x} + 3y}{y + \dfrac{2y}{x}}$ $\dfrac{3x+1}{x+2}$

65. $\dfrac{\dfrac{3}{x+1}}{5 + \dfrac{1}{x+1}}$ $\dfrac{3}{5x+6}$

66. $\dfrac{\dfrac{1}{x-1}}{1 - \dfrac{1}{x-1}}$ $\dfrac{1}{x-2}$

67. $\dfrac{\dfrac{3x}{3x+2}}{\dfrac{x}{3x+2} + x}$ $\dfrac{1}{x+1}$

68. $\dfrac{2 - \dfrac{5}{x}}{7 + \dfrac{2}{x}}$ $\dfrac{2x-5}{7x+2}$

69. $\dfrac{\dfrac{1}{y} + 3}{\dfrac{3}{y} - 2}$ $\dfrac{1+3y}{3-2y}$

70. $\dfrac{\dfrac{1}{x-5}}{\dfrac{2}{x-5} - 1}$ $\dfrac{1}{7-x}$

71. $\dfrac{1}{\dfrac{1}{x} + \dfrac{1}{y}}$ $\dfrac{xy}{y+x}$

72. $\dfrac{1}{\dfrac{b}{a} - \dfrac{a}{b}}$ $\dfrac{ab}{b^2-a^2}$

73. $\dfrac{\dfrac{2}{x}}{\dfrac{2}{y} - \dfrac{4}{x}}$ $\dfrac{y}{x-2y}$

74. $\dfrac{\dfrac{2y}{3}}{\dfrac{2y}{3} - \dfrac{8}{y}}$ $\dfrac{y^2}{y^2-12}$

75. $\dfrac{3 + \dfrac{3}{x-1}}{3 - \dfrac{3}{x}}$ $\dfrac{x^2}{(x-1)^2}$

76. $\dfrac{2 - \dfrac{2}{x+1}}{2 + \dfrac{2}{x}}$ $\dfrac{x^2}{(x+1)^2}$

77. $\dfrac{\dfrac{3}{x} + \dfrac{4}{x+1}}{\dfrac{2}{x+1} - \dfrac{3}{x}}$ $\dfrac{7x+3}{-x-3}$

78. $\dfrac{\dfrac{5}{y-3} - \dfrac{2}{y}}{\dfrac{1}{y} + \dfrac{2}{y-3}}$ $\dfrac{y+2}{y-1}$

79. $\dfrac{\dfrac{2}{x} - \dfrac{3}{x+1}}{\dfrac{2}{x+1} - \dfrac{3}{x}}$ $\dfrac{x-2}{x+3}$

80. $\dfrac{\dfrac{5}{y} + \dfrac{4}{y+1}}{\dfrac{4}{y} - \dfrac{5}{y+1}}$ $\dfrac{9y+5}{4-y}$

81. $\dfrac{\dfrac{1}{y^2+y} - \dfrac{1}{xy+x}}{\dfrac{1}{xy+x} - \dfrac{1}{y^2+y}}$ -1

82. $\dfrac{\dfrac{2}{b^2-1} - \dfrac{3}{ab-a}}{\dfrac{3}{ab-a} - \dfrac{2}{b^2-1}}$ -1

APPLICATIONS

83. GARDENING TOOLS In the illustration, what is the result when the opening of the cutting blades is divided by the opening of the handles? Express the result in simplest form. $\dfrac{3}{14}$

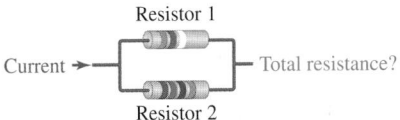

84. EARNED RUN AVERAGE The earned run average (ERA) is a statistic that gives the average number of earned runs a pitcher allows. For a softball pitcher, this is based on a six-inning game. The formula for ERA is

$$\text{ERA} = \dfrac{\dfrac{\text{earned runs}}{\text{innings pitched}}}{6}$$

Simplify the complex fraction on the right side of the equation. $\text{ERA} = \frac{6\,\cdot\,\text{earned runs}}{\text{innings pitched}}$

85. ELECTRONICS In electronic circuits, resistors oppose the flow of an electric current. To find the total resistance of a parallel combination of two resistors, we can use the formula

$$\text{Total resistance} = \dfrac{1}{\dfrac{1}{R_1} + \dfrac{1}{R_2}}$$

where R_1 is the resistance of the first resistor and R_2 is the resistance of the second. Simplify the complex fraction on the right side of the formula. $\frac{R_1 R_2}{R_2 + R_1}$

86. DATA ANALYSIS Use the data in the table to find the average measurement for the three-trial experiment. $\frac{4k}{9}$

	Trial 1	Trial 2	Trial 3
Measurement	$\dfrac{k}{2}$	$\dfrac{k}{3}$	$\dfrac{k}{2}$

WRITING

87. Explain how to use method 1 to simplify

$$\dfrac{1 + \dfrac{1}{x}}{3 - \dfrac{1}{x}}$$

88. Explain how to use method 2 to simplify the expression in Exercise 87.

Write each expression as an expression involving only one exponent.

89. $t^3 t^4 t^2$ t^9

90. $(a^0 a^2)^3$ a^6

91. $-2r(r^3)^2$ $-2r^7$

▶ **92.** $(s^3)^2(s^4)^0$ s^6

Write each expression without using parentheses or negative exponents.

93. $\left(\dfrac{3r}{4r^3}\right)^4$ $\dfrac{81}{256r^8}$

94. $\left(\dfrac{12y^{-3}}{3y^2}\right)^{-2}$ $\dfrac{y^{10}}{16}$

95. $\left(\dfrac{6r^{-2}}{2r^3}\right)^{-2}$ $\dfrac{r^{10}}{9}$

96. $\left(\dfrac{4x^3}{5x^{-3}}\right)^{-2}$ $\dfrac{25}{16x^{12}}$

Objectives

1 Solve rational equations.

2 Solve for a specified variable in a formula.

SECTION 7.6

Solving Rational Equations

In Chapter 2, we solved equations such as $\frac{1}{6}x + \frac{5}{2} = \frac{1}{3}$ by multiplying both sides by the LCD. With this approach, the equation that results is equivalent to the original equation, but easier to solve because it is cleared of fractions.

In this section, we will extend the fraction-clearing strategy to solve another type of equation, called a *rational equation*.

Rational Equations

A **rational equation** is an equation that contains one or more rational expressions.

Rational equations often have a variable in a denominator. Some examples are:

$$\frac{2}{3} = \frac{1}{3x} + \frac{3}{x} \qquad \frac{2}{x} + \frac{1}{4} = \frac{5}{2x} \qquad \frac{11x}{x-5} = 6 + \frac{55}{x-5}$$

1 Solve rational equations.

To **solve a rational equation,** we find all the values of the variable that make the equation true. Any value of the variable that makes a denominator in a rational equation equal to 0 cannot be a solution of the equation. Such a number must be rejected, because division by 0 is undefined.

The following steps can be used to solve rational equations.

Strategy for Solving Rational Equations

1. Determine which numbers cannot be solutions of the equation.
2. Multiply both sides of the equation by the LCD of all rational expressions in the equation. This clears the equation of fractions.
3. Solve the resulting equation.
4. Check all possible solutions in the original equation.

EXAMPLE 1　Solve: $\dfrac{x}{6} + \dfrac{5}{2} = \dfrac{1}{3}$

Strategy We will use the multiplication property of equality to clear this rational equation of fractions by multiplying both sides by the LCD.

WHY Equations that contain only integers are usually easier to solve than equations that contain fractions.

Solution
There are no restrictions on x, because no value of x ever makes a denominator 0. Since the denominators are 3, 6, and 2, we multiply both sides of the equation by the LCD, 6.

$$\frac{x}{6} + \frac{5}{2} = \frac{1}{3}$$

$$6\left(\frac{x}{6} + \frac{5}{2}\right) = 6\left(\frac{1}{3}\right) \qquad \text{Multiply both sides of the equation by the LCD of } \tfrac{x}{6}, \tfrac{5}{2}, \text{ and } \tfrac{1}{3}, \text{ which is 6.}$$

$$6 \cdot \frac{x}{6} + 6 \cdot \frac{5}{2} = 6 \cdot \frac{1}{3} \qquad \text{Distribute the multiplication by 6.}$$

$$x + 15 = 2 \qquad \text{Perform the multiplications.}$$

$$x + 15 - 15 = 2 - 15 \qquad \text{To undo the addition of 15, subtract 15 from both sides.}$$

$$x = -13 \qquad \text{Perform the subtractions.}$$

This method can be used to solve rational equations. It is important to note that if we multiply both sides of an equation by an expression that involves a variable, we must check the apparent solutions.

EXAMPLE 2　Solve: $\dfrac{4}{x} + 1 = \dfrac{6}{x}$

Strategy This equation contains two rational expressions that have a variable in their denominator. We begin by asking, "What value(s) of x make either denominator 0?" Then we will use the multiplication property of equality to clear this rational equation of fractions by multiplying both sides by the LCD, x.

WHY If a number makes the denominator of a rational expression 0, that number cannot be a solution of the equation because division by 0 is undefined.

Solution
To clear the equation of fractions, we multiply both sides by the LCD of $\tfrac{4}{x}$ and $\tfrac{6}{x}$, which is x.

$$\frac{4}{x} + 1 = \frac{6}{x}$$

$$x\left(\frac{4}{x} + 1\right) = x\left(\frac{6}{x}\right) \qquad \text{Write each side of the equation within parentheses, and then multiply both sides by x.}$$

$$\overset{1}{x} \cdot \frac{4}{\underset{1}{x}} + x \cdot 1 = \overset{1}{x} \cdot \frac{6}{\underset{1}{x}} \qquad \text{Distribute the multiplication by x.}$$

$$4 + x = 6 \qquad \text{Perform each multiplication.}$$

$$x = 2 \qquad \text{Subtract 4 from both sides.}$$

$$Check: \quad \frac{4}{x} + 1 = \frac{6}{x}$$

$$\frac{4}{2} + 1 \overset{?}{=} \frac{6}{2} \quad \text{Substitute 2 for } x.$$

$$2 + 1 \overset{?}{=} 3 \quad \text{Simplify.}$$

$$3 = 3$$

Self Check 3

Solve: $\dfrac{7}{6} - \dfrac{2r - 11}{r} = \dfrac{1}{r}$ 12

Now Try Problem 33

Teaching Example 3 Solve:
$-\dfrac{6}{x} = \dfrac{1}{2} - \dfrac{x-2}{x}$
Answer:
16

EXAMPLE 3 Solve: $\dfrac{22}{5} - \dfrac{3a - 1}{a} = \dfrac{8}{a}$

Strategy This equation contains two rational expressions that have a variable in their denominator. We begin by asking, "What value(s) of a make either denominator 0?" Then we will use the multiplication property of equality to clear this rational equation of fractions by multiplying both sides by the LCD, $5a$.

WHY If a number makes the denominator of a rational expression 0, that number cannot be a solution of the equation because division by 0 is undefined.

Solution

We multiply both sides by $5a$, the LCD of the rational expressions in the equation.

$$\frac{22}{5} - \frac{3a - 1}{a} = \frac{8}{a}$$

$$5a\left(\frac{22}{5} - \frac{3a - 1}{a}\right) = 5a\left(\frac{8}{a}\right) \quad \begin{array}{l}\text{Write each side of the equation within}\\\text{parentheses, and then multiply both}\\\text{sides by } 5a.\end{array}$$

$$\overset{1}{\cancel{5}} \cdot a\left(\frac{22}{\cancel{5}}\right) - 5 \cdot \overset{1}{\cancel{a}}\left(\frac{3a - 1}{\cancel{a}}\right) = 5 \cdot \overset{1}{\cancel{a}}\left(\frac{8}{\cancel{a}}\right) \quad \text{Distribute the multiplication by } 5a.$$

$$22a - 5(3a - 1) = 40 \quad \begin{array}{l}\text{Simplify. Note that } 3a - 1 \text{ must be}\\\text{written within parentheses.}\end{array}$$

$$22a - 15a + 5 = 40 \quad \text{Distribute the multiplication by } -5.$$

$$7a + 5 = 40 \quad \text{Combine like terms: } 22a - 15a = 7a.$$

$$7a = 35 \quad \text{Subtract 5 from both sides.}$$

$$a = 5 \quad \text{Divide both sides by 7.}$$

$$Check: \quad \frac{22}{5} - \frac{3a - 1}{a} = \frac{8}{a}$$

$$\frac{22}{5} - \frac{3(5) - 1}{5} \overset{?}{=} \frac{8}{5} \quad \text{Substitute 5 for } a.$$

$$\frac{22}{5} - \frac{14}{5} \overset{?}{=} \frac{8}{5}$$

$$\frac{8}{5} = \frac{8}{5}$$

Caution! After multiplying both sides by the LCD and simplifying, the equation should not contain any fractions. If it does, check for an algebraic error, or perhaps your LCD is incorrect.

EXAMPLE 4   Solve: $\dfrac{x + 2}{x + 3} + \dfrac{1}{x^2 + 2x - 3} = 1$

Strategy We will multiply both sides by the LCD of the two rational expressions in the equation. To find the LCD, we must factor the second denominator.

WHY To find the restrictions of the variable and to find the LCD, we need to write each denominator in factored form.

Solution
To find the LCD, we must factor the second denominator.

$$\frac{x + 2}{x + 3} + \frac{1}{x^2 + 2x - 3} = 1$$

$$\frac{x + 2}{x + 3} + \frac{1}{(x + 3)(x - 1)} = 1 \qquad \text{Factor } x^2 + 2x - 3.$$

We see that -3 and 1 cannot be solutions of the equation.
    To clear the equation of fractions, we multiply both sides by the LCD, which is $(x + 3)(x - 1)$.

$$(x + 3)(x - 1)\left[\frac{x + 2}{x + 3} + \frac{1}{(x + 3)(x - 1)}\right] = (x + 3)(x - 1)1$$

Next, we distribute the multiplication by $(x + 3)(x - 1)$.

$$\overset{1}{(x + 3)}(x - 1)\frac{x + 2}{\underset{1}{x + 3}} + \overset{1}{(x + 3)}\overset{1}{(x - 1)}\frac{1}{\underset{1}{(x + 3)}\underset{1}{(x - 1)}} = (x + 3)(x - 1)1$$

$$\begin{aligned}
(x - 1)(x + 2) + 1 &= (x + 3)(x - 1) && \text{Simplify.} \\
x^2 + x - 2 + 1 &= x^2 + 2x - 3 && \text{Multiply the pairs of binomials.} \\
x^2 + x - 1 &= x^2 + 2x - 3 && \text{Combine like terms.} \\
x - 1 &= 2x - 3 && \text{Subtract } x^2 \text{ from both sides.} \\
-x - 1 &= -3 && \text{Subtract } 2x \text{ from both sides.} \\
-x &= -2 && \text{Add 1 to both sides.} \\
x &= 2 && \text{Multiply (or divide) both sides by } -1.
\end{aligned}$$

Verify that 2 is a solution of the given equation.

EXAMPLE 5   Solve: $\dfrac{4}{5} + y = \dfrac{4y - 50}{5y - 25}$

Strategy We will multiply both sides by the LCD of the two rational expressions in the equation. To find the LCD, we must factor the second denominator.

WHY To find the restrictions of the variable and to find the LCD, we need to write each denominator in factored form.

Solution
To find the LCD, we must factor $5y - 25$.

$$\frac{4}{5} + y = \frac{4y - 50}{5y - 25}$$

$$\frac{4}{5} + y = \frac{4y - 50}{5(y - 5)}$$

We see that 5 cannot be a solution of the equation. To clear the equation of fractions, we multiply both sides by the LCD, which is $5(y - 5)$.

Self Check 4

Solve: $\dfrac{1}{x + 3} + \dfrac{1}{x - 3} = \dfrac{10}{x^2 - 9}$

Now Try **Problem 40**
Self Check 4 Answer
5

Teaching Example 4 Solve:
$\dfrac{3}{x - 2} = \dfrac{6x + 4}{x^2 - 2x} - \dfrac{1}{x}$
Answer:
-3

Self Check 5

Solve: $\dfrac{x - 6}{3x - 9} - \dfrac{1}{3} = \dfrac{x}{2}$ 1, 2

Now Try **Problem 47**

Teaching Example 5 Solve:
$\dfrac{x}{x - 1} - \dfrac{20}{x^2 - x} = \dfrac{-1}{x - 1}$
Answers:
$-5, 4$

$$5(y - 5)\left[\frac{4}{5} + y\right] = 5(y - 5)\left[\frac{4y - 50}{5(y - 5)}\right]$$ Multiply both sides by the LCD, which is $5(y - 5)$.

$$\overset{1}{5}(y - 5)\left(\frac{4}{5}\right) + 5(y - 5)y = \overset{1}{5}(y \overset{1}{-} 5)\left[\frac{4y - 50}{5(y - 5)}\right]$$ Distribute $5(y - 5)$.

$$4(y - 5) + 5y(y - 5) = 4y - 50$$

$$4y - 20 + 5y^2 - 25y = 4y - 50$$ Distribute 4 and 5y.

$$5y^2 - 25y - 20 = -50$$ Subtract 4y from both sides and rearrange terms.

$$5y^2 - 25y + 30 = 0$$ Add 50 to both sides.

$$y^2 - 5y + 6 = 0$$ Divide both sides by 5.

$$(y - 3)(y - 2) = 0$$ Factor $y^2 - 5y + 6$.

$$y - 3 = 0 \quad \text{or} \quad y - 2 = 0$$ Set each factor equal to zero.

$$y = 3 \quad | \quad y = 2$$ Solve each equation.

Verify that 3 and 2 satisfy the original equation.

Success Tip Don't confuse procedures. To simplify the expression $\frac{4}{5} + y$, we build each fraction to have the LCD 5, add the numerators, and write the sum over the LCD. To solve the equation $\frac{4}{5} + y = \frac{4y - 50}{5y - 25}$ we multiply both sides by the LCD $5y - 25$ to eliminate the denominators.

Self Check 6

Solve: $\dfrac{x + 5}{x - 2} = \dfrac{7}{x - 2}$

Now Try **Problem 51**

Self Check 6 Answer
2 is extraneous.

Teaching Example 6 Solve:
$\dfrac{x + 11}{x + 5} = \dfrac{6}{x + 5}$
Answer:
−5 is extraneous.

EXAMPLE 6 Solve: $\dfrac{x + 3}{x - 1} = \dfrac{4}{x - 1}$

Strategy We will multiply both sides of the equation by the LCD, $x - 1$.

WHY This will clear the equation of fractions.

Solution
To clear the equation of fractions, we multiply both sides by the LCD, which is $x - 1$.

$$\frac{x + 3}{x - 1} = \frac{4}{x - 1}$$

$$(x - 1)\frac{x + 3}{x - 1} = (x - 1)\frac{4}{x - 1}$$ Multiply both sides by x − 1.

$$x + 3 = 4$$ Simplify.

$$x = 1$$ Subtract 3 from both sides.

Because both sides were multiplied by an expression containing a variable, we must check the apparent solution.

$$\frac{x + 3}{x - 1} = \frac{4}{x - 1}$$

$$\frac{1 + 3}{1 - 1} \overset{?}{=} \frac{4}{1 - 1}$$ Substitute 1 for x.

$$\frac{4}{0} \overset{?}{=} \frac{4}{0}$$ Simplify.

We have determined that 1 makes both denominators in the original equation 0. Therefore, 1 is not a solution. Since 1 is the only possible solution, and it must be rejected, it follows that $\frac{x+3}{x-1} = \frac{4}{x-1}$ has no solution.

When solving an equation, a possible solution that does not satisfy the original equation is called an **extraneous solution.** In this example, 1 is an extraneous solution.

> ***The Language of Algebra*** Extraneous means not a vital part. Mathematicians speak of extraneous solutions. Rock groups don't want extraneous sounds (like feedback) coming from their amplifiers. Artists erase extraneous marks on their sketches.

2 Solve for a specified variable in a formula.

Many formulas are equations that contain rational expressions. To solve these formulas for a specified variable, we use the same steps, in the same order, as we do when solving rational equations having only one variable.

EXAMPLE 7 The formula $\frac{1}{r} = \frac{1}{r_1} + \frac{1}{r_2}$ is used in electronics to calculate parallel resistances. Solve it for r.

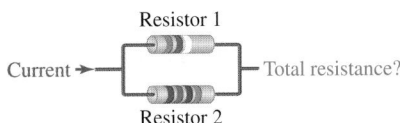

Current → □ ─ Total resistance?

Resistor 1

Resistor 2

Strategy We will begin by multiplying both sides of the equation by the LCD, rr_1r_2.

WHY This will clear the equation of fractions.

Solution

$$\frac{1}{r} = \frac{1}{r_1} + \frac{1}{r_2}$$

$$rr_1r_2\left(\frac{1}{r}\right) = rr_1r_2\left(\frac{1}{r_1} + \frac{1}{r_2}\right) \qquad \text{Multiply both sides by } rr_1r_2.$$

$$\frac{rr_1r_2}{r} = \frac{rr_1r_2}{r_1} + \frac{rr_1r_2}{r_2} \qquad \text{Distribute the multiplication by } rr_1r_2.$$

$$r_1r_2 = rr_2 + rr_1 \qquad \text{Simplify each fraction.}$$

$$r_1r_2 = r(r_2 + r_1) \qquad \text{Factor out } r.$$

$$\frac{r_1r_2}{r_2 + r_1} = r \qquad \text{To isolate } r, \text{ divide both sides by } r_2 + r_1.$$

or

$$r = \frac{r_1r_2}{r_2 + r_1}$$

Self Check 7

Solve the formula in Example 7 for r_1.

Now Try **Problem 54**

Self Check 7 Answer

$$r_1 = \frac{rr_2}{r_2 - r}$$

Teaching Example 7 Solve the formula in Example 7 for r_2.
Answer:

$$r_2 = \frac{rr_1}{r_1 - r}$$

SECTION 7.6   STUDY SET

VOCABULARY

Fill in the blanks.

1. Equations that contain one or more rational expressions, such as $\dfrac{x + 2}{x + 3} + \dfrac{1}{x^2 + 2x - 3} = 1$ are called __rational__ __equations__ .

2. To clear an equation of fractions, we multiply both sides by the __LCD__ of the fractions in the equation.

3. If you multiply both sides of an equation by an expression that involves a variable, you must __check__ the solution.

▶ 4. False solutions that result from multiplying both sides of an equation by a variable are called __extraneous__ solutions.

5. In the formula $I = Pr$, I stands for the amount of __interest__ earned in one year, P stands for the __principal__ , and r stands for the annual interest __rate__ .

6. In the formula $d = rt$, d stands for the __distance__ traveled, r is the __rate__ , and t is the __time__ .

CONCEPTS

Is 5 a solution of the following equations?

7. $\dfrac{1}{x - 1} = 1 - \dfrac{3}{x - 1}$ yes   8. $\dfrac{x}{x - 5} = 3 + \dfrac{5}{x - 5}$ no

By what should we multiply both sides of each equation to clear it of fractions?

9. $\dfrac{1}{x} + 2 = \dfrac{5}{x}$
   x

10. $\dfrac{x}{x - 2} - \dfrac{x}{x - 1} = 5$
    $(x - 2)(x - 1)$

11. A student was asked to solve a rational equation. The first step of his solution is as follows:

$$12x\left(\dfrac{5}{x} + \dfrac{2}{3}\right) = 12x\left(\dfrac{7}{4x}\right)$$

   a. What equation was he asked to solve? $\dfrac{5}{x} + \dfrac{2}{3} = \dfrac{7}{4x}$

   b. What LCD is used to clear the equation of fractions? $12x$

12. Fill in the blanks.

$$\underbrace{8x\left(\dfrac{3}{4x}\right)}_{6} = \underbrace{8x\left(\dfrac{1}{8x}\right)}_{1} + \underbrace{8x\left(\dfrac{5}{4}\right)}_{10x}$$

By what should both sides of the equation be multiplied to clear it of fractions?

13. **a.** $\dfrac{1}{y} = 20 - \dfrac{5}{y}$
        y

   b. $\dfrac{x}{x^2 - 4} = \dfrac{4}{x - 2}$
        $(x + 2)(x - 2)$

▶ 14. **a.** $\dfrac{x}{5} = \dfrac{3x}{10} + \dfrac{7}{2x}$
        $10x$

   b. $\dfrac{2x}{x - 6} = 4 + \dfrac{1}{x - 6}$
        $x - 6$

Solve: $d = rt$

15. for r $r = \dfrac{d}{t}$ 16. for t $t = \dfrac{d}{r}$

Solve: $I = Prt$

17. for r $r = \dfrac{I}{Pt}$ 18. for P $P = \dfrac{I}{rt}$

19. Complete the following table.

		r	$\cdot$	t	$=$	d
Snowmobile		r		$\dfrac{4}{r}$		4
4 × 4 truck		$r - 5$		$\dfrac{3}{r - 5}$		3

20. Complete the following table.

	P	$\cdot$	r	$\cdot$	t	$=$	I
City Savings	$\dfrac{50}{r}$		r		1		50
Credit Union	$\dfrac{75}{r - 0.02}$		$r - 0.02$		1		75

NOTATION

Complete each solution.

21.
$$\dfrac{2}{a} + \dfrac{1}{2} = \dfrac{7}{2a}$$

$$2a\left(\dfrac{2}{a} + \dfrac{1}{2}\right) = 2a\left(\dfrac{7}{2a}\right)$$

$$2a \cdot \dfrac{2}{a} + 2a \cdot \dfrac{1}{2} = 2a \cdot \dfrac{7}{2a}$$

$$4 + a = 7$$

$$4 + a - 4 = 7 - 4$$

$$a = 3$$

22.
$$\frac{3}{5} + \frac{7}{a+2} = 2$$

$$5(a+2)\left(\frac{3}{5} + \frac{7}{a+2}\right) = 5(a+2) \cdot 2$$

$$5(a+2) \cdot \frac{3}{5} + 5(a+2) \cdot \frac{7}{a+2} = 5(a+2) \cdot 2$$

$$3(a+2) + 35 = 10(a+2)$$

$$3a + 6 + 35 = 10a + 20$$

$$3a + 41 = 10a + 20$$

$$-7a = -21$$

$$a = 3$$

23. The following work shows both sides of an equation being multiplied by the LCD to clear it of fractions. What was the original equation? $\frac{3}{5} + \frac{7}{x-1} = 2$

$$5(x-1)\left(\frac{3}{5}\right) + 5(x-1)\left(\frac{7}{x-1}\right) = 5(x-1) \cdot 2$$

24. After solving a rational equation, a student checked her answer and obtained the following:

$$\frac{-1}{0} + \frac{1}{0} = 0$$

What conclusion can be drawn?
The answer is an extraneous solution.

GUIDED PRACTICE

Solve each equation and check the result. **See Example 1.**

25. $\dfrac{x}{2} + 4 = \dfrac{3x}{2}$ 4

26. $\dfrac{2y}{5} - 8 = \dfrac{4y}{5}$ -20

27. $\dfrac{x+1}{3} + \dfrac{x-1}{5} = \dfrac{2}{15}$ 0

28. $\dfrac{3x-1}{6} - \dfrac{x+3}{2} = \dfrac{3x+4}{3}$ -3

Solve each equation and check the result. **See Example 2.**

29. $\dfrac{3}{x} + 2 = 3$ 3

30. $\dfrac{2}{x} + 9 = 11$ 1

31. $\dfrac{3}{4h} + \dfrac{2}{h} = 1$ $\frac{11}{4}$

32. $\dfrac{5}{3k} + 2 = -\dfrac{1}{k}$ $-\frac{4}{3}$

Solve each equation and check the result. **See Example 3.**

33. $\dfrac{15}{4} - \dfrac{a+3}{2a} = \dfrac{10}{2a}$ 2

34. $\dfrac{7}{3} + \dfrac{a+1}{a} = \dfrac{11}{a}$ 3

35. $\dfrac{3r}{2} - \dfrac{3}{r} = \dfrac{3r}{2} + 3$ -1

36. $\dfrac{2p}{3} - \dfrac{1}{p} = \dfrac{2p-1}{3}$ 3

Solve each equation and check the result. **See Example 4.**

37. $\dfrac{2}{y+1} + 5 = \dfrac{12}{y+1}$ 1

38. $\dfrac{3}{p+6} - 2 = \dfrac{7}{p+6}$ -8

39. $\dfrac{x+4}{x+3} - \dfrac{4x}{x^2+6x+9} = 1$ 1

40. $\dfrac{1}{x^2+x-2} + \dfrac{x+1}{x+2} = 1$ 2

Solve each equation and check the result. **See Example 5.**

41. $\dfrac{a}{4} - \dfrac{4}{a} = 0$ $-4, 4$

42. $0 = \dfrac{t}{3} - \dfrac{12}{t}$ $-6, 6$

43. $\dfrac{2x}{x^2+x-2} + \dfrac{2}{x+2} = 1$ 0, 3

44. $\dfrac{4x}{x^2+2x-3} + \dfrac{3}{x+3} = 1$ 0, 5

45. $\dfrac{3}{b-1} = \dfrac{2b}{b+4}$ $4, -\dfrac{3}{2}$

46. $\dfrac{a}{a+4} = \dfrac{a-4}{6}$ $8, -2$

47. $\dfrac{b+2}{b+3} + 1 = \dfrac{-7}{b-5}$ $-2, 1$

48. $1 - \dfrac{3}{b} = \dfrac{-8b}{b^2+3b}$ $1, -9$

Solve each equation and check the result. **See Example 6.**

49. $\dfrac{2x+3}{x-2} = \dfrac{7}{x-2}$
No solution; 2 is extraneous.

50. $\dfrac{5}{a} - \dfrac{4}{a} = 8 + \dfrac{1}{a}$
No solution; 0 is extraneous.

51. $\dfrac{x}{x-5} - \dfrac{5}{x-5} = 3$
No solution; 5 is extraneous.

52. $\dfrac{3}{y-2} + 1 = \dfrac{3}{y-2}$
No solution; 2 is extraneous.

Solve each formula for the indicated variable. **See Example 7.**

53. $\dfrac{1}{a} + \dfrac{1}{b} = 1$ for a
$a = \dfrac{b}{b-1}$

54. $\dfrac{1}{a} + \dfrac{1}{b} = 1$ for b
$b = \dfrac{a}{a-1}$

55. $I = \dfrac{E}{R+r}$ for r
$r = \dfrac{E - IR}{I}$

56. $h = \dfrac{2A}{b+d}$ for A
$A = \dfrac{h(b+d)}{2}$

TRY IT YOURSELF

Solve each equation and check the result. If an equation has no solutions, so indicate.

57. $\dfrac{3}{4} + \dfrac{x}{4} = \dfrac{2x+2}{x+3}$ $1, 1$

58. $\dfrac{11}{b} + \dfrac{13}{b} = 12$ 2

59. $\dfrac{1}{3} + \dfrac{2}{x-3} = 1$ 6

60. $\dfrac{3}{5} + \dfrac{7}{x+2} = 2$ 3

61. $\dfrac{z-4}{z-3} = \dfrac{z+2}{z+1}$ 1

62. $\dfrac{a+2}{a+8} = \dfrac{a-3}{a-2}$ 4

63. $\dfrac{v}{v+2} + \dfrac{1}{v-1} = 1$ 4

64. $\dfrac{x}{x-2} = 1 + \dfrac{1}{x-3}$ 4

▶ **65.** $\dfrac{a^2}{a+2} - \dfrac{4}{a+2} = a$ No solution; -2 is extraneous.

▶ **66.** $\dfrac{z^2}{z+1} + 2 = \dfrac{1}{z+1}$ No solution; -1 is extraneous.

67. $\dfrac{7}{q^2 - q - 2} + \dfrac{1}{q+1} = \dfrac{3}{q-2}$ 1

68. $\dfrac{3}{x-1} - \dfrac{1}{x+9} = \dfrac{18}{x^2 + 8x - 9}$ -5

69. $\dfrac{u}{u-1} + \dfrac{1}{u} = \dfrac{u^2 + 1}{u^2 - u}$ 2

▶ **70.** $\dfrac{3}{x-2} + \dfrac{1}{x} = \dfrac{2(3x+2)}{x^2 - 2x}$ -3

71. $\dfrac{n}{n^2 - 9} + \dfrac{n+8}{n+3} = \dfrac{n-8}{n-3}$ 0

72. $\dfrac{7}{x-5} - \dfrac{3}{x+5} = \dfrac{40}{x^2 - 25}$ $-\dfrac{5}{2}$

▶ **73.** $\dfrac{5}{x+4} + \dfrac{1}{x+4} = x - 1$ 2, -5

74. $\dfrac{7}{x-3} + \dfrac{1}{x-3} = x - 5$ 7, 1

75. $\dfrac{3}{x+1} - \dfrac{x-2}{2} = \dfrac{x-2}{x+1}$ -4, 3

76. $\dfrac{2}{x-1} + \dfrac{x-2}{3} = \dfrac{4}{x-1}$ 4, -1

▶ **77.** $\dfrac{x-4}{x-3} + \dfrac{x-2}{x-3} = x - 3$ 5; 3 is extraneous.

78. $\dfrac{5}{4y+12} - \dfrac{3}{4} = \dfrac{5}{4y+12} - \dfrac{y}{4}$ 3; -3 is extraneous.

79. $\dfrac{x}{x-1} - \dfrac{12}{x^2 - x} = \dfrac{-1}{x-1}$ 3, -4

▶ **80.** $y + \dfrac{2}{3} = \dfrac{2y - 12}{3y - 9}$ 1, 2

Solve each formula for the indicated variable.

81. $\dfrac{a}{b} = \dfrac{c}{d}$ for d

$d = \dfrac{bc}{a}$

82. $F = \dfrac{L^2}{6d} + \dfrac{d}{2}$ for L^2

$L^2 = 6dF - 3d^2$

APPLICATIONS

83. OPTICS The focal length f of a lens is given by the formula

$$\dfrac{1}{f} = \dfrac{1}{d_1} + \dfrac{1}{d_2}$$

where d_1 is the distance from the object to the lens and d_2 is the distance from the lens to the image. Solve the formula for f. $f = \dfrac{d_1 d_2}{d_1 + d_2}$

84. OPTICS Solve the formula in Exercise 83 for d_1.
$d_1 = \dfrac{fd_2}{d_2 - f}$

85. MEDICINE Radioactive tracers are used for diagnostic work in nuclear medicine. The **effective half-life** H of a radioactive material in an organism is given by the formula

$$H = \dfrac{RB}{R + B}$$

where R is the radioactive half-life and B is the biological half-life of the tracer. Solve the formula for R. $R = \dfrac{HB}{B - H}$

▶ **86.** CHEMISTRY Charles's law describes the relationship between the volume and the temperature of a gas that is kept at a constant pressure. It states that as the temperature of the gas increases, the volume of the gas will increase:

$$\dfrac{V_1}{V_2} = \dfrac{T_1}{T_2}$$

Solve the formula for V_2. $V_2 = \dfrac{V_1 T_2}{T_1}$

WRITING

87. Why is it important to check your solutions of an equation that contains fractions with variables in the denominator?

88. Explain the difference between the procedures used to simplify $\dfrac{1}{x} + \dfrac{1}{3}$ and the procedure used to solve

$$\dfrac{1}{x} + \dfrac{1}{3} = \dfrac{1}{2}$$

REVIEW

Factor each expression.

89. $x^2 + 4x$
$x(x + 4)$

▶ **90.** $x^2 - 16y^2$
$(x + 4y)(x - 4y)$

91. $2x^2 + x - 3$
$(2x + 3)(x - 1)$

92. $6a^2 - 5a - 6$
$(3a + 2)(2a - 3)$

93. $x^4 - 16$
$(x^2 + 4)(x + 2)(x - 2)$

94. $4x^2 + 10x - 6$
$2(x + 3)(2x - 1)$

SECTION 7.7
Problem Solving Using Rational Equations

Objectives

1 Solve number problems.

2 Solve shared-work problems.

3 Solve uniform motion problems.

4 Solve investment problems.

1 Solve number problems.

We will now use the five-step problem-solving strategy to solve application problems. We begin with an example in which we find an unknown number.

EXAMPLE 1 *A Number Problem* If the same number is added to both the numerator and the denominator of the fraction $\frac{3}{5}$, the result is $\frac{4}{5}$. Find the number.

Analyze We are asked to find a number. If we add it to both the numerator and the denominator of $\frac{3}{5}$, we will get $\frac{4}{5}$.

Form Let $n =$ the unknown number and add n to both the numerator and the denominator of $\frac{3}{5}$. Then set the result equal to $\frac{4}{5}$ to get the equation

$$\frac{3+n}{5+n} = \frac{4}{5}$$

Solve To solve the equation, we proceed as follows:

$$\frac{3+n}{5+n} = \frac{4}{5}$$

$$5(5+n)\frac{3+n}{5+n} = 5(5+n)\frac{4}{5} \qquad \text{Multiply both sides by } 5(5+n), \text{ which is the LCD of the fractions appearing in the equation.}$$

$$5(3+n) = (5+n)4 \qquad \text{Simplify.}$$

$$15 + 5n = 20 + 4n \qquad \text{Distribute the multiplications by 5 and by 4.}$$

$$15 + n = 20 \qquad \text{Subtract } 4n \text{ from both sides.}$$

$$n = 5 \qquad \text{Subtract 15 from both sides.}$$

State The number is 5.

Check When we add 5 to both the numerator and denominator of $\frac{3}{5}$, we get

$$\frac{3+5}{5+5} = \frac{8}{10} = \frac{4}{5}$$

The result checks.

Self Check 1

If the same number is added to both the numerator and denominator of the fraction $\frac{7}{9}$, the result is $\frac{8}{9}$. Find the number. 9

Now Try Problem 11

Teaching Example 1 If the same number is added to both the numerator and denominator of the fraction $\frac{9}{11}$, the result is $\frac{10}{11}$. Find the number.
Answer:
11

2 Solve shared-work problems.

We can use rational equations to model shared-work problems. In this case, we assume that the work is being performed at a constant rate by all of those involved.

EXAMPLE 2 *Filling an Oil Tank* An inlet pipe can fill an oil tank in 7 days, and a second inlet pipe can fill the same tank in 9 days. If both pipes are used, how long will it take to fill the tank?

Analyze The key is to determine what each pipe can do in 1 day. If we add what the first pipe can do in 1 day to what the second pipe can do in 1 day, the sum is what they can do in 1 day, working together.

Self Check 2

A school secretary can prepare a mass mailing of an informational flyer in 6 hours. A student worker would take 8 hours to prepare the mailing. How long will it take to prepare the mailing if they work together? $3\frac{3}{7}$ hr

Now Try **Problem 21**

Teaching Example 2 A caterer can prepare cream puffs for an event in 4 hours. Her employee can prepare the same number of cream puffs in 7 hours. How long will it take them to make the dessert if they work together?
Answer:
$2\frac{6}{11}$ hr

Since the first pipe can fill the tank in 7 days, it can do $\frac{1}{7}$ of the job in 1 day. Since the second pipe can fill the tank in 9 days, it can do $\frac{1}{9}$ of the job in 1 day. If it takes x days for both pipes to fill the tank, together they can do $\frac{1}{x}$ of the job in 1 day.

Form Let x = the number of days it will take to fill the tank if both inlet pipes are used. Then form the equation.

What the first inlet pipe can do in 1 day	plus	what the second inlet pipe can do in 1 day	equals	what they can do together in 1 day.
$\dfrac{1}{7}$	$+$	$\dfrac{1}{9}$	$=$	$\dfrac{1}{x}$

Solve To solve the equation, we proceed as follows:

$$\frac{1}{7} + \frac{1}{9} = \frac{1}{x}$$

$$63x\left(\frac{1}{7} + \frac{1}{9}\right) = 63x\left(\frac{1}{x}\right) \quad \text{Multiply both sides by 63x, which is the LCD, to clear the equation of fractions.}$$

$$63x\left(\frac{1}{7}\right) + 63x\left(\frac{1}{9}\right) = 63x\left(\frac{1}{x}\right) \quad \text{Distribute the multiplication by 63x.}$$

$$9x + 7x = 63$$

$$16x = 63 \quad \text{Combine like terms.}$$

$$x = \frac{63}{16} \quad \text{Divide both sides by 16.}$$

State If both inlet pipes are used, it will take $\frac{63}{16}$ or $3\frac{15}{16}$ days to fill the tank.

Check In $\frac{63}{16}$ days, the first pipe fills $\frac{1}{7}\left(\frac{63}{16}\right)$ of the tank and the second pipe fills $\frac{1}{9}\left(\frac{63}{16}\right)$ of the tank. The sum of these efforts, $\frac{9}{16} + \frac{7}{16}$, is equal to one full tank.

3 **Solve uniform motion problems.**

Self Check 3

A cyclist can ride 24 miles in the same amount of time that her friend can walk 8 miles. If the cyclist travels 8 mph faster than the walker, find the speed of the walker. 4 mph

Now Try **Problem 29**

© Digital Vision/Alamy

EXAMPLE 3   *Track and Field*   A coach can run 10 miles in the same amount of time as his best student-athlete can run 12 miles. If the student can run 1 mile per hour faster than the coach, how fast can the student run?

Analyze We can use the formula $d = rt$, where d is the distance traveled, r is the rate, and t is the time. If we solve this formula for t, we obtain

$$t = \frac{d}{r}$$

Form It will take $\frac{10}{r}$ hours for the coach to run 10 miles at some unknown rate of r mph. It will take $\frac{12}{r+1}$ hours for the student to run 12 miles at some unknown rate of $(r + 1)$ mph. We can organize the information of the problem in a table, as shown below.

	r	$\cdot$ t	$= d$
Student	$r + 1$	$\dfrac{12}{r+1}$	12
Coach	r	$\dfrac{10}{r}$	10

The time it takes the student to run 12 miles	equals	the time it takes the coach to run 10 miles.

$$\frac{12}{r+1} = \frac{10}{r}$$

Solve We can solve the equation as follows:

$$\frac{12}{r+1} = \frac{10}{r}$$

$$\overset{1}{r(\cancel{r+1})}\frac{12}{\cancel{r+1}} = \overset{1}{\cancel{r}(r+1)}\frac{10}{\cancel{r}} \qquad \text{Multiply both sides by } r(r+1).$$

$$12r = 10(r+1) \qquad \text{Simplify.}$$

$$12r = 10r + 10 \qquad \text{Distribute the multiplication by 10.}$$

$$2r = 10 \qquad \text{Subtract 10r from both sides.}$$

$$r = 5 \qquad \text{Divide both sides by 2.}$$

State The coach can run 5 mph. The student, running 1 mph faster, can run 6 mph.

Check Verify that these results check.

---

4 **Solve investment problems.**

EXAMPLE 4 **Banking** At one bank, a sum of money invested for 1 year will earn $96 interest. If invested in bonds, that money would earn $108, because the interest rate paid by the bonds is 1% greater than that paid by the bank. Find the bank's rate.

Analyze This interest problem is based on the formula $I = Prt$, where I is the interest, P is the principal (the amount invested), r is the annual rate of interest and t is the time in years. If we solve this formula for P, we obtain

$$P = \frac{I}{rt}$$

Form If we let r = the bank's rate of interest, then $r + 0.01$ = the rate paid by the bonds. If a person earns $96 interest at a bank at some unknown rate r, the principal invested was $\frac{96}{r(1)}$. If a person earns $108 interest in bonds at some unknown rate $(r + 0.01)$, the principal invested was $\frac{108}{(r+0.01)(1)}$. We can organize the information of the problem in a table, as shown below.

	Principal ·	Rate	· Time =	Interest
Bank	$\dfrac{96}{r(1)}$	r	1	96
Bonds	$\dfrac{108}{(r+0.01)1}$	$r + 0.01$	1	108

Because the same principal would be invested in either account, we can set up the following equation:

$$\frac{96}{r(1)} = \frac{108}{(r+0.01)1} \quad \text{or} \quad \frac{96}{r} = \frac{108}{r+0.01}$$

Teaching Example 3 Cyclists in the Tour de France can ride 50 miles in the same time the average cyclist can travel 24 miles. If the average cyclist's rate is 13 mph slower than the Tour de France competitors, how fast does the average cyclist ride?
Answer:
12 mph

Self Check 4
An amount of money invested for one year in a certificate of deposit will earn $210. The same amount of money in a savings account will earn $70. If the certificate of deposit's interest rate is 2% more than the savings account's rate, find the interest rate of the savings account. 1%

Now Try **Problem 41**

Teaching Example 4 An amount of money invested for one year in bonds will earn $120. At a bank, that same amount of money will only earn $75 interest, because the interest rate paid by the bank is 3% less than that paid by the bonds. Find the rate of interest paid by each investment.
Answer:
bond 8%, bank 5%

Solve We can solve the equation as follows:

$$\frac{96}{r} = \frac{108}{r + 0.01}$$

$$\overset{1}{\cancel{r}}(r + 0.01) \cdot \frac{96}{\underset{1}{\cancel{r}}} = r\overset{1}{\cancel{(r + 0.01)}} \cdot \frac{108}{\underset{1}{\cancel{r + 0.01}}} \qquad \text{Multiply both sides by } r(r + 0.01).$$

$$96(r + 0.01) = 108r \qquad \text{Simplify.}$$

$$96r + 0.96 = 108r \qquad \text{Distribute the multiplication by 96.}$$

$$0.96 = 12r \qquad \text{Subtract } 96r \text{ from both sides.}$$

$$0.08 = r \qquad \text{Divide both sides by 12.}$$

State The bank's interest rate is 0.08, or 8%. The bonds pay 9% interest, a rate 1% greater than that paid by the bank.

Check Verify that these rates check.

ANSWERS TO SELF CHECKS

1. 9   **2.** $3\frac{3}{7}$ hr   **3.** 4 mph   **4.** 1%

SECTION 7.7   STUDY SET

VOCABULARY

Fill in the blanks.

1. Problems that involve people or things completing jobs are called shared-<u>work</u> problems.
2. Problems that involve moving vehicles are called uniform <u>motion</u> problems.
3. Problems that involve depositing money are called <u>investment</u> problems.
4. The amount of money in an account is called the <u>principal</u>.

CONCEPTS

5. Write the formula that relates distance, rate, and time. $d = rt$
6. Write the formula that relates interest, principal, rate, and time. $I = Prt$

NOTATION

7. Write $\frac{55}{9}$ days as a mixed number. $6\frac{1}{9}$ days
8. Write $32\frac{2}{5}$ days as an improper fraction. $\frac{162}{5}$
9. Write 9% as a decimal. 0.09
10. Write 0.035 as a percent. 3.5%

GUIDED PRACTICE

Solve each number problem. **See Example 1.**

▶ **11.** If the same number is added to both the numerator and the denominator of $\frac{2}{5}$, the result is $\frac{2}{3}$. Find the number. 4

▶ **12.** If the same number is subtracted from both the numerator and the denominator of $\frac{11}{13}$, the result is $\frac{3}{4}$. Find the number. 5

▶ **13.** If the denominator of $\frac{3}{4}$ is increased by a number and the numerator of the fraction is doubled, the result is 1. Find the number. 2

▶ **14.** If a number is added to the numerator of $\frac{7}{8}$ and the same number is subtracted from the denominator, the result is 2. Find the number. 3

▶ **15.** If a number is added to the numerator of $\frac{3}{4}$ and twice the number is added to the denominator, the result is $\frac{4}{7}$. Find the number. 5

▶ **16.** If a number is added to the numerator of $\frac{5}{7}$ and twice the number is subtracted from the denominator, the result is 8. Find the number. 3

▶ **17.** The sum of a number and its reciprocal is $\frac{13}{6}$. Find the number and its reciprocal. $\frac{2}{3}, \frac{3}{2}$

18. The sum of the reciprocals of two consecutive even integers is $\frac{7}{24}$. Find the integers. (*Hint:* Let x = the first integer and $x + 2$ = the second integer.) 6, 8

APPLICATIONS

See Example 1.

19. COOKING If the same number is added to both the numerator and the denominator of the amount of butter used in the following recipe, the result is the amount of brown sugar to be used. Find the number. 8

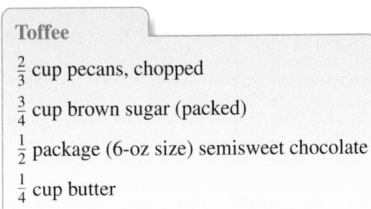

> **Toffee**
> $\frac{2}{3}$ cup pecans, chopped
> $\frac{3}{4}$ cup brown sugar (packed)
> $\frac{1}{2}$ package (6-oz size) semisweet chocolate
> $\frac{1}{4}$ cup butter

20. TAPE MEASURES If the same number is added to both the numerator and the denominator of the first measurement, the result is the second measurement. Find the number. 8

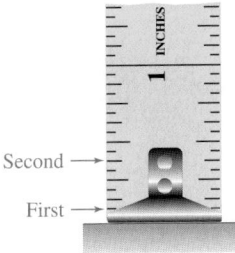

Second →
First →

See Example 2.

21. Suppose you are a recreation director at a summer camp. The water in the camp swimming pool was drained out for the winter and it is now time to refill the pool. One pipe can fill the empty pool in 12 hours and another can fill the empty pool in 18 hours. Suppose both pipes are opened at 8:00 A.M. and you have scheduled a swimming activity for 2:00 P.M. that day. Will the pool be filled by then?

from Campus to Careers
Recreation Director

© BananaStock/SuperStock

No; after the pipes are opened, the swimming is scheduled to take place in 6 hours. It takes 7.2 hr (7 hr 12 min) to fill the pool.

22. ROOFING HOUSES A homeowner estimates that it will take him 7 days to roof his house. A professional roofer estimates that he could roof the house in 4 days. How long will it take if the homeowner helps the roofer? $2\frac{6}{11}$ days

23. HOLIDAY DECORATING One crew can put up holiday decorations in the mall in 8 hours. If a slower crew can put up the decorations in 10 hours, how long will it take if both crews work together? $4\frac{4}{9}$ hr

24. GROUNDSKEEPING It takes a groundskeeper 45 minutes to prepare a softball field for a game. If it takes his assistant 55 minutes to prepare the same field, how long will it take if they work together? 24.75 min = $24\frac{3}{4}$ min

25. FILLING POOLS One inlet pipe can fill an empty pool in 4 hours, and a drain can empty the pool in 8 hours. How long will it take the pipe to fill the pool if the drain is left open? 8 hr

26. SEWAGE TREATMENT A sludge pool is filled by two inlet pipes. One pipe can fill the pool in 15 days, and the other can fill it in 21 days. However, if no sewage is added, continuous waste removal will empty the pool in 36 days. How long will it take the two inlet pipes to fill an empty sludge pool? $11\frac{61}{109}$ days

27. GRADING PAPERS On average, it takes a teacher 30 minutes to grade a set of quizzes. If it takes her aide twice as long to grade the quizzes, how long will it take if they work together? 20 min

28. DOG KENNELS It takes the owner of a dog kennel 6 hours to clean all of the cages. If it takes her assistant 2 hours longer, how long will it take if they work together? $3\frac{3}{7}$ hr

See Example 3.

29. TOUR DE FRANCE Maurice Garin of France won the first Tour de France road race in 1903. In 2005, American Lance Armstrong won his seventh consecutive Tour de France. His average speed in 2005 was 10 mph faster than Garin's in 1903. In the time it took Garin to ride 80 miles, Armstrong could have ridden 130 miles. Find the average speed of each cyclist. Garin: 16 mph; Armstrong: 26 mph

30. PHYSICAL FITNESS A woman can bike 28 miles in the same time it takes her to walk 8 miles. If she can bike 10 mph faster than she can walk, how fast can she walk? 4 mph

31. PACKAGING FRUIT The illustration shows how apples are processed for market. Although the second conveyor belt is shorter, an apple spends the same amount of time on each belt because the second conveyor belt moves 1 foot per second slower than the first. Determine the speed of each conveyor belt. first: $1\frac{1}{2}$ ft per sec, second: $\frac{1}{2}$ ft per sec

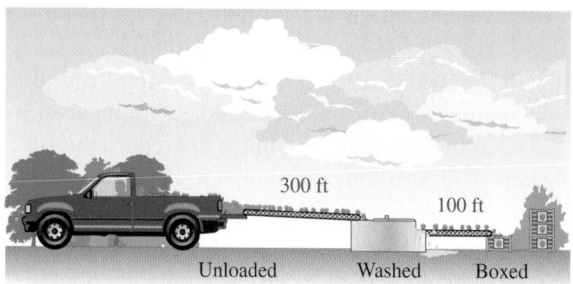

32. COMPARING TRAVEL A plane can fly 300 miles in the same time as it takes a car to go 120 miles. If the car travels 90 mph slower than the plane, find the speed of the plane. 150 mph

33. BIRDS IN FLIGHT On average, a Canada goose can fly 10 mph faster than a great blue heron. In the same time that a Canada goose can fly 120 miles, a heron can fly 80 miles. Find the flying speed of each bird. Canada goose: 30 mph, great blue heron: 20 mph

34. MUSCLE CARS The top speed of a Dodge Charger SRT8 is 33 mph less than the top speed of a Chevrolet Corvette Z06. At top speeds, a Corvette can travel 6 miles in the same time that a Charger can travel 5 miles. Find the speed of each car.
Charger: 165 mph, Corvette: 198 mph

35. TRAVEL TIMES A company president flew 680 miles one way in the corporate jet but returned in a smaller plane that could fly only half as fast. If the total travel time was 6 hours, find the speed of each plane. 340 mph, 170 mph

36. TRAVEL TIMES A car can travel 280 miles in the same time as a truck can travel 240 miles. If the car travels at a speed that is 10 mph more than the speed of the truck, find the speeds of the car and the truck. car: 70 mph, truck 60 mph

37. WIND SPEED When a plane flies downwind, the wind pushes the plane so that its speed is the *sum* of the speed of the plane in still air and the speed of the wind. Traveling upwind, the wind pushes against the plane so that its speed is the *difference* of the speed of the plane in still air and the speed of the wind. Suppose a plane that can travel 255 mph in still air can travel 300 miles downward in the same time as it takes to travel 210 miles upwind. Complete the following table and find the speed of the wind, represented by x.

	Rate	· Time	= Distance
Downwind	$255 + x$	$\frac{300}{255 + x}$	300
Upwind	$255 - x$	$\frac{210}{255 - x}$	210

38. BOATING A boat that travels 18 mph in still water can travel 22 miles downstream in the same time as it takes to travel 14 miles upstream. Find the speed of the current in the river. 4 mph

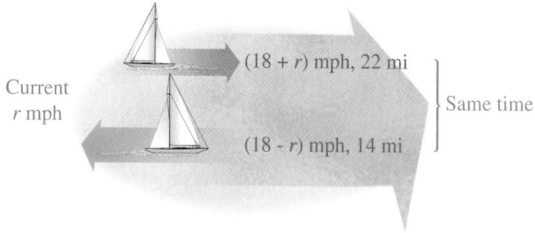

39. RIVER TOURS A river boat tour begins by going 60 miles upstream against a 5-mph current. There, the boat turns around and returns with the current. What still-water speed should the captain use to complete the tour in 5 hours? 25 mph

40. BOAT TRAVEL A boat can cruise at 12 mph in still water. If it cruises 6 miles upstream on the Mississippi River in the same amount of time it cruises 10 miles downstream, find the current in that portion of the river. 3 mph

See Example 4.

41. COMPARING INVESTMENTS Two certificates of deposit (CDs) pay interest at rates that differ by 1%. Money invested for one year in the first CD earns $175 interest. The same principal invested in the second CD earns $200. Find the two rates of interest. 7%, 8%

42. COMPARING INTEREST RATES Two bond funds pay interest at rates that differ by 2%. Money invested for one year in the first fund earns $315 interest. The same amount invested in the second fund earns $385. Find the lower rate of interest. 9%

43. SHARING COSTS Several office workers bought a $35 gift for their boss. If there had been two more employees to contribute, everyone's cost would have been $2 less. How many workers contributed to the gift? 5

▶ **44.** SALES A dealer bought some radios for a total of $1,200. She gave away 6 radios as gifts, sold the rest for $10 more than she paid for each radio, and broke even. How many radios did she buy? 30

45. SALES A bookstore can purchase several calculators for a total cost of $120. If each calculator cost $1 less, the bookstore could purchase 10 additional calculators at the same total cost. How many calculators can be purchased at the regular price? 30

▶ **46.** FURNACE REPAIR A repairman purchased several furnace-blower motors for a total cost of $210. If his cost per motor had been $5 less, he could have purchased one additional motor. How many motors did he buy at the regular rate? 6

▌ WRITING

In Example 2, one inlet pipe could fill an oil tank in 7 days, and another could fill the same tank in 9 days. We were asked to find how long it would take if both pipes were used. Explain why each of the approaches in Problems 47–49 is incorrect.

47. The time it would take to fill the tank is the *sum* of the lengths of time it takes each pipe to fill the tank:

$$7 \text{ days} + 9 \text{ days} = 16 \text{ days}.$$

48. The time it would take to fill the tank is the *difference* in the lengths of time it takes each pipe to fill the tank:

$$9 \text{ days} - 7 \text{ days} = 2 \text{ days}.$$

49. The time it would take to fill the tank is the *average* of the lengths of time it takes each pipe to fill the tank:

$$\frac{7 \text{ days} + 9 \text{ days}}{2} = \frac{16 \text{ days}}{2} = 8 \text{ days}$$

▶ **50.** Write a shared-work problem that can be modeled by the equation $\frac{x}{3} + \frac{x}{4} = 1$.

▌ REVIEW

51. Solve using substitution: $\begin{cases} x + y = 4 \\ y = 3x \end{cases}$ (1, 3)

52. Solve using addition (elimination): $\begin{cases} 5x - 4y = 19 \\ 3x + 2y = 7 \end{cases}$
(3, −1)

53. Use a check to determine whether $\frac{21}{5}$ is a solution of $x + 20 = 4x - 1 + 2x$. yes

▶ **54.** Solve: $4x^2 + 8x = 0$ 0, −2

55. Evaluate $2x^2 + 5x - 3$ for $x = -3$. 0

56. Solve $T - R = ma$ for R. $R = T - ma$

SECTION 7.8

Proportions and Similar Triangles

Objectives

1 Write ratios and rates in simplest form.

2 Solve proportions.

3 Use proportions to solve problems.

4 Use proportions to solve problems that involve similar triangles.

In this section, we will discuss a problem-solving tool called a *proportion*. A proportion is a type of rational equation that involves two *ratios* or two *rates*.

1 Write ratios and rates in simplest form.

Ratios enable us to compare numerical quantities.

- To prepare fuel for a lawnmower, gasoline must be mixed with oil in the ratio of 50 to 1.
- To make 14-karat jewelry, gold is mixed with other metals in the ratio of 14 to 10.
- In the stock market, winning stocks might outnumber losing stocks in the ratio of 7 to 4.

Ratios

A **ratio** is the quotient of two numbers or the quotient of two quantities that have the same units.

There are three common ways to write a ratio: as a fraction, with the word *to*, or with a colon. For example, the ratio comparing the number of winning stocks to the number of losing stocks mentioned earlier can be written as

$$\frac{7}{4}, \qquad 7 \text{ to } 4, \qquad \text{or} \qquad 7{:}4$$

Each of these forms can be read as "the ratio of 7 to 4."

Self Check 1

Translate each phrase into a ratio written in fractional form:
a. The ratio of 15 to 2 $\frac{15}{2}$
b. 12 hours to 2 days $\frac{1}{4}$

Now Try **Problems 19 and 25**

Teaching Example 1 Translate each phrase into a ratio written in fractional form:
a. The ratio of 12 to 27
b. 154 cm to 2 m
Answers:
a. $\frac{12}{27}$ **b.** $\frac{77}{100}$

EXAMPLE 1   Translate each phrase into a ratio written in fractional form:

a. The ratio of 5 to 9   **b.** 12 ounces to 2 pounds

Strategy To translate, we need to identify the number (or quantity) before the word *to* and the number (or quantity) after it.

WHY The number before the word *to* is the numerator of the ratio and the number after it is the denominator.

Solution

a. The ratio of 5 to 9 is written $\frac{5}{9}$.

b. To write a ratio of two quantities with the same units, we must express 2 pounds in terms of ounces. Since 1 pound = 16 ounces, 2 pounds = 32 ounces. The ratio of 12 ounces to 32 ounces can be simplified so that no units appear in the final form.

$$\frac{12 \text{ ounces}}{32 \text{ ounces}} = \frac{3 \cdot \overset{1}{4} \text{ ounces}}{\underset{1}{4} \cdot \overset{1}{8} \text{ ounces}} = \frac{3}{8}$$

The Language of Algebra   A ratio that is the quotient of two quantities having the same units should be simplified so that no units appear in the final answer.

When quotients are used to compare quantities with different units, they are called *rates*. For example, if the 495-mile drive from New Orleans to Dallas takes 9 hours, the average rate of speed is the quotient of the miles driven to the length of time the trip takes.

$$\text{Average rate of speed} = \frac{495 \text{ miles}}{9 \text{ hours}} = \frac{55 \text{ miles}}{1 \text{ hour}} \qquad \frac{495}{9} = \frac{\overset{1}{9} \cdot 55}{\underset{1}{9} \cdot 1} = \frac{55}{1}.$$

Rates

A **rate** is a quotient of two quantities that have different units.

THINK IT THROUGH   *Student Loan Calculations*

"A consistent majority of students who borrow to pay for their higher education believe they could not have gone to college without student loans. Over 70% agree that student loans were very or extremely important in allowing them access to education after high school."

National Student Loan Survey, 2002

Many student loan programs calculate a *debt-to-income ratio* to assist them in determining whether the borrower has sufficient income to repay the loan. A debt-to-income ratio compares an applicant's monthly debt payments (mortgages, credit cards, auto loans, etc.) to their gross monthly income. Most education lenders require borrower debt-to-income ratios of $\frac{2}{5}$ or less, according to the Nellie Mae Debt Management Edvisor. Calculate the debt-to-income ratio for each loan applicant shown below. Then determine whether it makes them eligible for a student loan.

	Applicant #1	Applicant #2	Applicant #3
Monthly debt payments	$250	$1,000	$1,200
Gross monthly income	$1,000	$2,000	$3,000
Debt-to-income ratio	$\frac{1}{4}$	$\frac{1}{2}$	$\frac{2}{5}$
Is the ratio $\leq \frac{2}{5}$?	yes	no	yes

2   Solve proportions.

Consider the following table, in which we are given the costs of various numbers of gallons of gasoline.

Number of gallons	Cost
2	$3.72
5	$9.30
8	$14.88
12	$22.32
20	$37.20

If we compare the costs to the numbers of gallons purchased, we see that they are equal. In this example, each quotient represents the cost of 1 gallon of gasoline, which is $1.86.

$$\frac{\$3.72}{2} = \$1.86, \qquad \frac{\$9.30}{5} = \$1.86, \qquad \frac{\$14.88}{8} = \$1.86,$$

$$\frac{\$22.32}{12} = \$1.86, \qquad \text{and} \qquad \frac{\$37.20}{20} = \$1.86$$

When two ratios or rates $\left(\text{such as } \frac{\$3.72}{2} \text{ and } \frac{\$9.30}{5}\right)$ are equal, they form a *proportion*.

Proportions

A **proportion** is a mathematical statement that two ratios or two rates are equal.

Some examples of proportions are

$$\frac{1}{2} = \frac{3}{6}, \qquad \frac{3 \text{ waiters}}{7 \text{ tables}} = \frac{9 \text{ waiters}}{21 \text{ tables}}, \qquad \text{and} \qquad \frac{a}{b} = \frac{c}{d}$$

- The proportion $\frac{1}{2} = \frac{3}{6}$ can be read as "1 is to 2 as 3 is to 6."
- The proportion $\frac{3 \text{ waiters}}{7 \text{ tables}} = \frac{9 \text{ waiters}}{21 \text{ tables}}$ can be read as "3 waiters is to 7 tables as 9 waiters is to 21 tables."
- The proportion $\frac{a}{b} = \frac{c}{d}$ can be read as "a is to b as c is to d."

In the proportion $\frac{a}{b} = \frac{c}{d}$, a and d are called the **extremes,** and b and c are called the **means.** We can show that the product of the extremes (ad) is equal to the product of the means (bc) by multiplying both sides of the proportion by bd and observing that $ad = bc$.

$$\frac{a}{b} = \frac{c}{d}$$

$$\overset{1}{\cancel{bd}} \cdot \frac{a}{\underset{1}{\cancel{b}}} = \overset{1}{\cancel{bd}} \cdot \frac{c}{\underset{1}{\cancel{d}}} \qquad \text{To clear the equation of fractions, multiply both sides by the LCD, which is } bd.$$

$$ad = bc \qquad \text{Perform each multiplication and simplify.}$$

Since $ad = bc$, the product of the extremes equals the product of the means.

The Fundamental Property of Proportions

In a proportion, the product of the extremes is equal to the product of the means. If $\frac{a}{b} = \frac{c}{d}$, then $ad = bc$, and if $ad = bc$, then $\frac{a}{b} = \frac{c}{d}$.

To determine whether an equation is a proportion, we can check to see whether the product of the extremes is equal to the product of the means.

Self Check 2

Determine whether the equation

is a proportion: $\dfrac{6}{13} = \dfrac{24}{53}$ no

Now Try Problems 34 and 35

Teaching Example 2 Determine
whether each equation is a proportion:
a. $\dfrac{7}{13} = \dfrac{5}{9}$ **b.** $\dfrac{5}{12} = \dfrac{20}{48}$
Answers:
a. no **b.** yes

EXAMPLE 2 Determine whether each equation is a proportion:
a. $\dfrac{3}{7} = \dfrac{9}{21}$ **b.** $\dfrac{8}{3} = \dfrac{13}{5}$

Strategy We will check to see whether the product of the extremes is equal to the product of the means.

WHY If the product of the extremes equals the product of the means, the equation is a proportion. If the cross products are not equal, the equation is not a proportion.

Solution

In each case, we check to see whether the product of the extremes is equal to the product of the means.

a. The product of the extremes is $3 \cdot 21 = 63$. The product of the means is

$7 \cdot 9 = 63$. Since the products are equal, the equation is a proportion: $\frac{3}{7} = \frac{9}{21}$.

$$3 \cdot 21 = 63 \qquad 7 \cdot 9 = 63$$

$$\frac{3}{7} \diagdown = \diagup \frac{9}{21} \qquad \text{The product of the extremes and the product of the means are also known as cross products.}$$

b. The product of the extremes is $8 \cdot 5 = 40$. The product of the means is $3 \cdot 13 = 39$. Since the cross products are not equal, the equation is not a proportion: $\frac{8}{3} \neq \frac{13}{5}$.

$8 \cdot 5 = 40$ $3 \cdot 13 = 39$

$$\frac{8}{3} \cancel{=} \frac{13}{5}$$ One cross product is 40 and the other is 39.

Suppose that we know three terms in the proportion

$$\frac{x}{5} = \frac{24}{20}$$

To find the unknown term, we can multiply both sides of the equation by 20 to clear it of fractions, and then solve for x. However, with proportions, it is often easier to simply compute the cross products, set them equal, and solve for the variable.

$$\frac{x}{5} = \frac{24}{20}$$

$20 \cdot x = 5 \cdot 24$ In a proportion, the product of the extremes equals the product of the means.

$20x = 120$ Perform the multiplication: $5 \cdot 24 = 120$.

$\dfrac{20x}{20} = \dfrac{120}{20}$ To undo the multiplication by 20, divide both sides by 20.

$x = 6$ Perform the divisions.

Thus, x is 6. To check this result, we substitute 6 for x in $\frac{x}{5} = \frac{24}{20}$ and find the cross products.

$$\frac{6}{5} \stackrel{?}{=} \frac{24}{20}$$ $6 \cdot 20 = 120$
   $5 \cdot 24 = 120$

Since the cross products are equal, this is a proportion. The result, 6, is correct.

EXAMPLE 3   Solve: $\dfrac{12}{18} = \dfrac{3}{x}$

Strategy To solve for x, we will set the cross products equal.

WHY Since the equation is a proportion, the product of the means equals the product of the extremes.

Solution

$$\frac{12}{18} = \frac{3}{x}$$

$12 \cdot x = 18 \cdot 3$ In a proportion, the product of the extremes equals the product of the means.

$12x = 54$ Multiply: $18 \cdot 3 = 54$.

$\dfrac{12x}{12} = \dfrac{54}{12}$ To undo the multiplication by 12, divide both sides by 12.

$x = \dfrac{9}{2}$ Simplify: $\frac{54}{12} = \frac{9 \cdot \cancel{6}^{\,1}}{\cancel{6}_{\,1} \cdot 2} = \frac{9}{2}$.

Thus, x is $\frac{9}{2}$. Check the result.

Self Check 3

Solve: $\dfrac{15}{x} = \dfrac{25}{40}$ 24

Now Try **Problem 40**

Teaching Example 3 Solve: $\dfrac{15}{6} = \dfrac{10}{x}$

Answer:
4

> **Success Tip** Since proportions are rational equations, they can also be solved by multiplying both sides by the LCD. Here an alternate approach is to multiply both sides by $18x$.

Caution! Remember that a cross product is the product of the means or extremes of a *proportion*. For example, it would be incorrect to try to compute cross products to solve the rational equation $\frac{12}{18} = \frac{3}{x} + \frac{1}{2}$. The right-hand side is not a ratio, so the equation is *not* a proportion.

Using Your CALCULATOR **Solving Proportions with a Calculator**

To solve the proportion $\dfrac{3.5}{7.2} = \dfrac{x}{15.84}$ with a calculator, we can proceed as follows.

$$\frac{3.5}{7.2} = \frac{x}{15.84}$$

$$\frac{3.5(15.84)}{7.2} = x \qquad \text{To undo the division by 15.84 and isolate } x, \text{ multiply both sides of the equation by 15.84.}$$

We can find x by entering these numbers into a scientific calculator.

3.5 $\boxed{\times}$ 15.84 $\boxed{\div}$ 7.2 $\boxed{=}$ $\qquad$ $\boxed{ 7.7}$

Using a graphing calculator, we enter these numbers and press these keys.

3.5 $\boxed{\times}$ 15.84 $\boxed{\div}$ 7.2 $\boxed{\text{ENTER}}$ $\qquad$ $\boxed{\begin{array}{l} 3.5*15.84/7.2 \\ 7.7 \end{array}}$

Thus, x is 7.7.

Self Check 4

Solve: $\dfrac{3x - 1}{2} = \dfrac{12.5}{5}$ 2

Now Try **Problem 49**

Teaching Example 4 Solve:
$\dfrac{3a + 2}{5} = -\dfrac{1}{5}$
Answer:
-1

EXAMPLE 4 Solve: $\dfrac{2a + 1}{4} = \dfrac{10}{8}$

Strategy To solve for a, we will set the cross products equal.

WHY Since the equation is a proportion, the product of the means equals the product of the extremes.

Solution
$$\frac{2a + 1}{4} = \frac{10}{8}$$

$$8(2a + 1) = 40 \qquad \text{In a proportion, the product of the extremes equals the product of the means.}$$

$$16a + 8 = 40 \qquad \text{Distribute the multiplication by 8.}$$

$$16a + 8 - 8 = 40 - 8 \qquad \text{To undo the addition of 8, subtract 8 from both sides.}$$

$$16a = 32 \qquad \text{Combine like terms.}$$

$$\frac{16a}{16} = \frac{32}{16} \qquad \text{To undo the multiplication by 16, divide both sides by 16.}$$

$$a = 2 \qquad \text{Perform the divisions.}$$

Thus, a is 2. Check the result.

Self Check 5

Solve: $\dfrac{6}{c} = \dfrac{c - 1}{5}$ $-5, 6$

Now Try **Problem 53**

Teaching Example 5 Solve: $\dfrac{x}{5} = \dfrac{3}{x + 14}$
Answer: $-15, 1$

EXAMPLE 5 Solve: $\dfrac{a}{2} = \dfrac{4}{a - 2}$

Strategy To solve for a, we will set the cross products equal.

WHY Since this equation is a proportion, the product of the means equals the product of the extremes.

Solution

$$\frac{a}{2} = \frac{4}{a-2}$$ This is the given proportion.

$$a(a-2) = 2 \cdot 4$$ Find each cross product and set them equal. Don't forget to write the parentheses.

$$a^2 - 2a = 8$$ On the left hand side, distribute the multiplication by a. This is a quadratic equation.

$$a^2 - 2a - 8 = 0$$ To get 0 on the right side of the equation, subtract 8 from both sides.

$$(a+2)(a-4) = 0$$ Factor $a^2 - 2a - 8$.

$$a + 2 = 0 \quad \text{or} \quad a - 4 = 0$$ Set each factor equal to 0.

$$a = -2 \quad | \quad a = 4$$ Solve each equation.

The solutions are -2 and 4. Verify this using a check.

3 Use proportions to solve problems.

We can use proportions to solve many real-world problems. If we are given a ratio (or rate) comparing two quantities, the words of the problem can be translated to a proportion, and we can solve it to find the unknown.

EXAMPLE 6   *Grocery Shopping*   If 6 apples cost $1.38, how much will 16 apples cost?

Analyze We know the cost of 6 apples; we are to find the cost of 16 apples.

Form Let c = the cost of 16 apples. If we compare the number of apples to their cost, we know that the two rates are equal.

> *6 apples is to $1.38 as 16 apples is to $c.*

Number of apples $\rightarrow$ $\dfrac{6}{1.38} = \dfrac{16}{c}$ $\leftarrow$ Number of apples
Cost of the apples $\rightarrow$ $\phantom{\dfrac{6}{1.38}}$ $\leftarrow$ Cost of the apples

Solve

$$6 \cdot c = 1.38(16)$$ In a proportion, the product of the extremes equals the product of the means.

$$6c = 22.08$$ Perform the multiplication: 1.38(16) = 22.08.

$$\frac{6c}{6} = \frac{22.08}{6}$$ To undo the multiplication by 6, divide both sides by 6.

$$c = 3.68$$ Divide: $\frac{22.08}{6} = 3.68$.

State Sixteen apples will cost $3.68.

Check If 16 apples are bought, this is about 3 times as many as 6 apples, which cost $1.38. If we multiply $1.38 by 3, we get an estimate of the cost of 16 apples: $1.38 \cdot 3 = $4.14. The result, $3.68, seems reasonable.

In Example 6, we could have compared the cost of the apples to the number of apples: $1.38 is to 6 apples as $c is to 16 apples. This would have led to the proportion

Cost of the apples $\rightarrow$ $\dfrac{1.38}{6} = \dfrac{c}{16}$ $\leftarrow$ Cost of the apples
Number of apples $\rightarrow$ $\phantom{\dfrac{1.38}{6}}$ $\leftarrow$ Number of apples

If we solve this proportion for c, we will obtain the same result: $c = 3.68$.

Self Check 6

If 9 tickets to a concert cost $112.50, how much will 15 tickets cost? $187.50

Now Try Problem 77

© iStockphoto.com/Alex Potemkin

Teaching Example 6 If 6 tickets to a Broadway show cost $345, how much do 11 tickets cost?
Answer:
$632.50

> *Caution!* When solving problems using proportions, we must make sure that the units of both numerators are the same and the units of both denominators are the same. In Example 6, it would be incorrect to write
>
> Cost of the apples → $\dfrac{1.38}{6} = \dfrac{16}{c}$ ← Number of apples
> Number of apples → $\phantom{\dfrac{1.38}{6} = \dfrac{16}{c}}$ ← Cost of the apples

Self Check 7

The scale for a blueprint indicates $\frac{1}{4}$ inch on the print is equivalent to 1 foot for the actual building. If the width of the building on the print is 7.5 inches, what is the width of the actual building? 30 ft

Now Try **Problem 90**

Teaching Example 7 An N scale model railroad car is 4.75 inches long. If the N scale is 1 to 160, how long is the real railroad car, in inches and in feet?
Answer:
760 in., $63\frac{1}{3}$ ft

EXAMPLE 7 *Scale Models*

A **scale** is a ratio (or rate) that compares the size of a model, drawing, or map to the size of an actual object. The scale shown in the figure indicates that 1 inch on the model carousel is equivalent to 160 inches on the actual carousel. How wide should the model be if the actual carousel is 35 feet wide?

Carousel ratio
1 inch:160 inches

Analyze We are asked to determine the width of the miniature carousel, if a ratio of 1 inch to 160 inches is used. We would like the width of the model to be given in inches, not feet, so we will express the 35-foot width of the actual carousel as $35 \cdot 12 = 420$ inches.

Form Let w = the width of the model. The ratios of the dimensions of the model to the corresponding dimensions of the actual carousel are equal.

1 inch is to 160 inches as w inches is to 420 inches.

model → $\dfrac{1}{160} = \dfrac{w}{420}$ ← model
actual → $\phantom{\dfrac{1}{160} = \dfrac{w}{420}}$ ← actual

Solve

$420 = 160w$ In a proportion, the product of the extremes is equal to the product of the means.

$\dfrac{420}{160} = \dfrac{160w}{160}$ To undo the multiplication by 160, divide both sides by 160.

$2.625 = w$ Do the division: $\frac{420}{160} = 2.625$.

State The width of the miniature carousel should be 2.625 in., or $2\frac{5}{8}$ in.

Check A width of $2\frac{5}{8}$ in. is approximately 3 in. When we write the ratio of the model's approximate width to the width of the actual carousel, we get $\frac{3}{420} = \frac{1}{140}$, which is about $\frac{1}{160}$. The answer seems reasonable.

Self Check 8

How many cups of sugar will be needed to make several cakes that will require a total of 25 cups of flour? $12\frac{1}{2}$

Now Try **Problem 83**

EXAMPLE 8 *Baking* A recipe for rhubarb cake calls for $1\frac{1}{4}$ cups of sugar for every $2\frac{1}{2}$ cups of flour. How many cups of flour are needed if the baker intends to use 3 cups of sugar?

Analyze The baker needs to maintain the same ratio between the amounts of sugar and flour as is called for in the original recipe.

Form Let f = the number of cups of flour to be mixed with the 3 cups of sugar. The ratios of the cups of sugar to the cups of flour are equal.

$1\frac{1}{4}$ *cups sugar is to* $2\frac{1}{2}$ *cups flour as 3 cups sugar is to f cups flour.*

$$\text{Cups sugar} \rightarrow \quad \frac{1\frac{1}{4}}{2\frac{1}{2}} = \frac{3}{f} \quad \leftarrow \text{Cups sugar}$$
$$\text{Cups flour} \rightarrow \qquad \qquad \leftarrow \text{Cups flour}$$

Solve

$$\frac{1.25}{2.5} = \frac{3}{f} \qquad \text{Change the fractions to decimals.}$$

$$1.25f = 2.5 \cdot 3 \qquad \text{In a proportion, the product of the extremes equals the product of the means.}$$

$$1.25f = 7.5 \qquad \text{Perform the multiplication: } 2.5 \cdot 3 = 7.5.$$

$$\frac{1.25f}{\mathbf{1.25}} = \frac{7.5}{\mathbf{1.25}} \qquad \text{To undo the multiplication by 1.25, divide both sides by 1.25.}$$

$$f = 6 \qquad \text{Divide: } \frac{7.5}{1.25} = 6.$$

State   The baker should use 6 cups of flour.

Check   The recipe calls for about 2 cups of flour for about 1 cup of sugar. If 3 cups of sugar are used, 6 cups of flour seems reasonable.

Teaching Example 8   Refer to Example 8.
How many cups of sugar will be needed to make several cakes that require a total of 30 cups of flour?
Answer:
15

4   Use proportions to solve problems that involve similar triangles.

If two angles of one triangle have the same measures as two angles of a second triangle, the triangles have the same shape. Triangles with the same shape are called **similar triangles.** In the figure, $\triangle ABC \sim \triangle DEF$. (Read the symbol $\sim$ as "is similar to.")

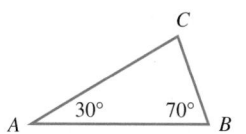 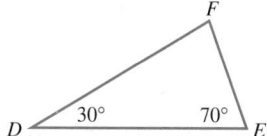

Property of Similar Triangles

If two triangles are **similar,** all pairs of corresponding sides are in proportion.

In the similar triangles shown in the figure above, the following proportions are true.

$$\frac{AB}{DE} = \frac{BC}{EF}, \qquad \frac{BC}{EF} = \frac{CA}{FD}, \qquad \text{and} \qquad \frac{CA}{FD} = \frac{AB}{DE} \qquad \text{Read AB as "the length of segment AB."}$$

EXAMPLE 9   *Finding the Height of a Tree*   A tree casts a shadow 18 feet long at the same time as a woman 5 feet tall casts a shadow 1.5 feet long. Find the height of the tree.

Analyze   The figure shows the similar triangles determined by the tree and its shadow and the woman and her shadow. Since the triangles are similar, the lengths

Self Check 9

Find the height of the tree in Example 9 if the woman is 5 feet 6 inches tall and her shadow is 1.5 feet long.   66 ft

Now Try   Problem 97

of their corresponding sides are in proportion. We can use this fact to find the height of the tree.

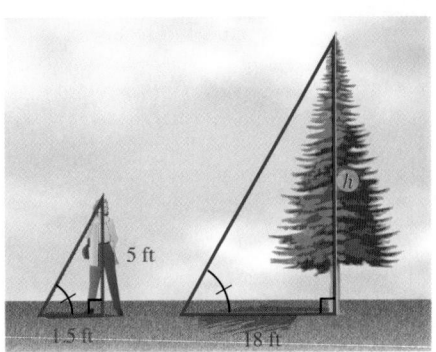

Each triangle has a right angle. Since the sun's rays strike the ground at the same angle, the angles highlighted with a tick mark have the same measure. Therefore, two angles of the smaller triangle have the same measures as two angles of the larger triangle; the triangles are similar.

Form If we let h = the height of the tree, we can find h by solving the following proportion.

$$\frac{h}{5} = \frac{18}{1.5} \qquad \frac{\text{Height of the tree}}{\text{Height of the woman}} = \frac{\text{Length of shadow of the tree}}{\text{Length of shadow of the woman}}$$

Solve

$$1.5h = 5(18) \qquad \text{In a proportion, the product of the extremes equals the product of the means.}$$

$$1.5h = 90 \qquad \text{Perform the multiplication.}$$

$$\frac{1.5h}{\mathbf{1.5}} = \frac{90}{\mathbf{1.5}} \qquad \text{To undo the multiplication by 1.5, divide both sides by 1.5.}$$

$$h = 60 \qquad \text{Divide: } \frac{90}{1.5} = 60.$$

State The tree is 60 feet tall.

Check $\frac{18}{1.5} = 12$ and $\frac{60}{5} = 12$. The ratios are the same. The result checks.

ANSWERS TO SELF CHECKS

1. a. $\frac{15}{2}$ **b.** $\frac{1}{4}$ **2.** no **3.** 24 **4.** 2 **5.** $-5, 6$ **6.** \$187.50 **7.** 30 ft **8.** $12\frac{1}{2}$ **9.** 66 ft

---

SECTION 7.8   STUDY SET

VOCABULARY

Fill in the blanks.

1. A _ratio_ of two numbers is the quotient of two quantities with the same units.

2. A _rate_ is a quotient of two quantities that have different units.

▶ **3.** A _proportion_ is a mathematical statement that two ratios or two rates are equal.

4. In the proportion $\frac{a}{b} = \frac{c}{d}$, a and d are called the _extremes_ of the proportion.

5. In the proportion $\frac{a}{b} = \frac{c}{d}$, b and c are called the _means_ of the proportion.

▶ **6.** The product of the extremes and the product of the means of a proportion are also known as _cross_ products.

7. If two triangles have the same _shape_, they are said to be *similar*.

8. If two triangles are _similar_, their corresponding sides are in proportion.

CONCEPTS

Fill in the blanks.

9. WEST AFRICA Write the ratio (in fractional form) of the number of red stripes to the number of white stripes on the flag of Liberia. $\frac{6}{5}$

▶ 10. The equation $\frac{a}{b} = \frac{c}{d}$ is a proportion if the cross product __ad__ is equal to the cross product __bc__.

▶ 11. Is 45 a solution of $\frac{5}{3} = \frac{75}{x}$? yes

12. Consider: $\frac{2}{3} = \frac{x}{15}$

   a. Solve the proportion by multiplying both sides by the LCD. 10

   b. Solve the proportion by setting the cross products equal. 10

13. MINIATURES A high-wheeler bicycle is shown below. A model of it is to be made using a scale of 2 inches to 15 inches. The following proportion was set up to determine the height of the front wheel of the model. Explain the error.

$$\frac{2}{15} \;\cancel{=}\; \frac{48}{h} \quad \text{The ratio on the right side should be } \frac{h}{48}.$$

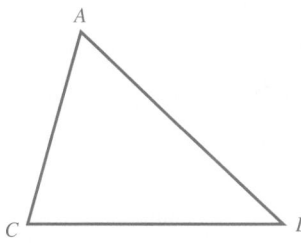

48 in.

▶ 14. Two similar triangles are shown below. Fill in the blanks to make the proportions true.

$$\frac{AB}{DE} = \frac{BC}{EF} \qquad \frac{BC}{EF} = \frac{CA}{FD} \qquad \frac{CA}{FD} = \frac{AB}{DE}$$

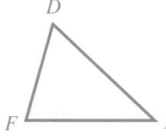

NOTATION

Complete each solution.

15. Solve for x: $\frac{12}{18} = \frac{x}{24}$

$$12 \cdot 24 = 18 \cdot x$$
$$288 = 18x$$
$$\frac{288}{18} = \frac{18x}{18}$$
$$16 = x$$

▶ 16. Solve for x: $\frac{14}{x} = \frac{49}{17.5}$

$$14 \cdot 17.5 = 49x$$
$$245 = 49x$$
$$\frac{245}{49} = \frac{49x}{49}$$
$$5 = x$$

17. We read "$\triangle ABC$" as "__triangle__ ABC."

18. The symbol $\sim$ is read as "__is similar to__."

GUIDED PRACTICE

Translate each ratio into a ratio in simplest form. **See Example 1.**

19. 4 boxes to 15 boxes $\frac{4}{15}$ ▶ 20. 2 miles to 9 miles $\frac{2}{9}$

21. 18 watts to 24 watts $\frac{3}{4}$ 22. 11 cans to 121 cans $\frac{1}{11}$

23. 30 days to 24 days $\frac{5}{4}$ 24. 45 people to 30 people $\frac{3}{2}$

25. 90 minutes to 3 hours $\frac{1}{2}$ 26. 20 inches to 2 feet $\frac{5}{6}$

27. 8 quarts to 4 gallons $\frac{1}{2}$ 28. 6 feet to 12 yards $\frac{1}{6}$

29. 6,000 feet to 1 mile $\frac{25}{22}$ 30. 5 tons to 4,000 pounds $\frac{5}{2}$
   (*Hint:* 1 mi = 5,280 ft) (*Hint:* 1 ton = 2,000 lb)

Determine whether each equation is a proportion. **See Example 2.**

31. $\frac{9}{7} = \frac{81}{70}$ no 32. $\frac{5}{2} = \frac{20}{8}$ yes

33. $\frac{7}{3} = \frac{14}{6}$ yes ▶ 34. $\frac{13}{19} = \frac{65}{95}$ yes

35. $\frac{9}{19} = \frac{38}{80}$ no 36. $\frac{40}{29} = \frac{29}{22}$ no

37. $\frac{10.4}{3.6} = \frac{41.6}{14.4}$ yes 38. $\frac{13.23}{3.45} = \frac{39.96}{11.35}$ no

Solve each proportion. **See Example 3.**

39. $\frac{2}{3} = \frac{x}{6}$ 4 ▶ 40. $\frac{3}{6} = \frac{x}{8}$ 4

41. $\frac{5}{10} = \frac{3}{c}$ 6 ▶ 42. $\frac{7}{14} = \frac{2}{x}$ 4

Solve each proportion. See Example 4.

43. $\dfrac{x+1}{5} = \dfrac{3}{15}$ 0

44. $\dfrac{x-1}{7} = \dfrac{2}{21}$ $\dfrac{5}{3}$

45. $\dfrac{x+3}{12} = \dfrac{-7}{6}$ −17

46. $\dfrac{x+7}{-4} = \dfrac{1}{4}$ −8

47. $\dfrac{13}{4-x} = \dfrac{26}{11}$ $-\dfrac{3}{2}$

48. $\dfrac{17}{5-x} = \dfrac{34}{13}$ $-\dfrac{3}{2}$

49. $\dfrac{14}{3} = \dfrac{2x+1}{18}$ $\dfrac{83}{2}$

50. $\dfrac{9}{54} = \dfrac{2x-1}{18}$ 2

Solve each proportion. See Example 5.

51. $\dfrac{y}{4} = \dfrac{4}{y}$ 4, −4

52. $\dfrac{2}{3x} = \dfrac{6x}{36}$ 2, −2

53. $\dfrac{2}{c} = \dfrac{c-3}{2}$ 4, −1

54. $\dfrac{b-5}{3} = \dfrac{2}{b}$ 6, −1

55. $\dfrac{a-4}{a} = \dfrac{15}{a+4}$ −1, 16

56. $\dfrac{s}{s-5} = \dfrac{s+5}{24}$ −1, 25

57. $\dfrac{t+3}{t+5} = \dfrac{-1}{2t}$ $-\dfrac{5}{2}$, −1

58. $\dfrac{5h}{14h+3} = \dfrac{1}{h}$ $-\dfrac{1}{5}$, 3

TRY IT YOURSELF

Solve each proportion.

59. $\dfrac{6}{x} = \dfrac{8}{4}$ 3

60. $\dfrac{4}{x} = \dfrac{2}{8}$ 16

61. $\dfrac{x}{3} = \dfrac{9}{3}$ 9

62. $\dfrac{x}{2} = \dfrac{18}{6}$ 6

63. $\dfrac{2}{x+6} = \dfrac{-2x}{5}$ −5, −1

64. $\dfrac{x-1}{x+1} = \dfrac{2}{3x}$ $-\dfrac{1}{3}$, 2

65. $\dfrac{x+1}{4} = \dfrac{3x}{8}$ 2

66. $\dfrac{x-1}{9} = \dfrac{2x}{3}$ $-\dfrac{1}{5}$

67. $\dfrac{3}{4x} = \dfrac{x-4}{x+\dfrac{5}{3}}$ $-\dfrac{1}{4}$, 5

68. $\dfrac{3}{x-1} = \dfrac{x}{4}$ 4, −3

69. $\dfrac{y-4}{y+1} = \dfrac{y+3}{y+6}$ $-\dfrac{27}{2}$

70. $\dfrac{r-6}{r-8} = \dfrac{r+1}{r-4}$ $\dfrac{32}{3}$

71. $\dfrac{c}{10} = \dfrac{10}{c}$ −10, 10

72. $\dfrac{-6}{r} = \dfrac{r}{-6}$ −6, 6

73. $\dfrac{m}{3} = \dfrac{4}{m+1}$ −4, 3

74. $\dfrac{n}{2} = \dfrac{5}{n+3}$ −5, 2

75. $\dfrac{3}{3b+4} = \dfrac{2}{5b-6}$ $\dfrac{26}{9}$

76. $\dfrac{2}{4d-1} = \dfrac{3}{2d+1}$ $\dfrac{5}{8}$

APPLICATIONS

Set up and solve a proportion. Use a calculator if it is helpful. See Examples 6–8.

77. GROCERY SHOPPING If 3 pints of yogurt cost $1, how much will 51 pints cost? $17

78. SHOPPING FOR CLOTHES If shirts are on sale at two for $25, how much will five shirts cost? $62.50

79. ADVERTISING In 2008, a 30-second TV ad during the Super Bowl telecast cost $2.2 million. At this rate, what was the cost of a 45-second ad? $3.3 million

80. COOKING A recipe for spaghetti sauce requires four 16-ounce bottles of ketchup to make 2 gallons of sauce. How many bottles of ketchup are needed to make 10 gallons of sauce? 20

81. MIXING PERFUME A perfume is to be mixed in the ratio of 3 drops of pure essence to 7 drops of alcohol. How many drops of pure essence should be mixed with 56 drops of alcohol? 24

82. CPR A first aid handbook states that when performing cardiopulmonary resuscitation on an adult, the ratio of chest compressions to breaths should be 30:2. If 210 compressions were administered to an adult patient, how many breaths should have been given? 14

83. COOKING A recipe for wild rice soup is shown. Find the amounts of chicken broth, rice, and flour needed to make 15 servings. $7\frac{1}{2}$, $1\frac{2}{3}$, 5

> **Wild Rice Soup**
>
> *A sumptuous side dish with a nutty flavor*
>
> | | |
> |---|---|
> | 3 cups chicken broth | 1 cup light cream |
> | $\frac{2}{3}$ cup uncooked rice | 2 tablespoons flour |
> | $\frac{1}{4}$ cup sliced onions | $\frac{1}{8}$ teaspoon pepper |
> | $\frac{1}{2}$ cup shredded carrots | Serves: 6 |

84. QUALITY CONTROL In a manufacturing process, 95% of the parts made are to be within specifications. How many defective parts would be expected in a run of 940 pieces? 47

85. QUALITY CONTROL Out of a sample of 500 men's shirts, 17 were rejected because of crooked collars. How many crooked collars would you expect to find in a run of 15,000 shirts? 510

86. GAS CONSUMPTION If a car can travel 42 miles on 1 gallon of gas, how much gas is needed to travel 315 miles? $7\frac{1}{2}$ gal

87. HIP-HOP According to the *Guinness Book of World Records,* Rebel X.D. of Chicago rapped 674 syllables in 54.9 seconds. At this rate, how many syllables could he rap in 1 minute? Round to the nearest syllable. 737

88. BANKRUPTCY After filing for bankruptcy, a company was able to pay its creditors only 15 cents on the dollar. If the company owed a lumberyard $9,712, how much could the lumberyard expect to be paid? $1,456.80

89. COMPUTING A PAYCHECK Billie earns $412 for a 40-hour week. If she missed 10 hours of work last week, how much did she get paid? $309

90. MODEL RAILROADS A model railroad engine is 9 inches long. If the scale is 87 feet to 1 foot, how long is a real engine? 65 ft, 3 in.

91. MODEL RAILROADS A model railroad caboose is 3.5 inches long. If the scale is 169 feet to 1 foot, how long is a real caboose? 49 ft, $3\frac{1}{2}$ in.

92. NUTRITION The following table shows the nutritional facts about a 10-oz chocolate milkshake sold by a fast-food restaurant. Use the information to complete the table for the 16-oz shake. Round to the nearest unit when an answer is not exact.

	Calories	Fat (gm)	Protein (gm)
10-oz chocolate milkshake	355	8	9
16-oz chocolate milkshake	568	13	14

93. DRIVER'S LICENSES Of the 50 states, Alabama has one of the largest ratios of licensed drivers to residents. If the ratio is 800:1,000 and Alabama's population is 4,500,000, how many residents of that state have a driver's license? 3,600,000

94. MIXING FUEL The instructions on a can of oil intended to be added to lawnmower gasoline read as follows:

Recommended	Gasoline	Oil
50 to 1	6 gal	16 oz

Are the instructions correct? (*Hint:* There are 128 ounces in 1 gallon.) not exactly, but close

95. PHOTO ENLARGEMENT In the illustration, the 3-by-5 photograph is to be blown up to the larger size. Find *x*. $3\frac{3}{4}$ in.

5 in. $6\frac{1}{4}$ in.

3 in.   *x* in.

96. BLUEPRINTS The scale for the blueprint shown in the next column tells the reader that a $\frac{1}{4}$-inch length $\left(\frac{1}{4}''\right)$ on the drawing corresponds to an actual size of 1 foot (1'0"). Suppose the length of the kitchen is $2\frac{1}{2}$ inches on the drawing. How long is the actual kitchen? 10 ft

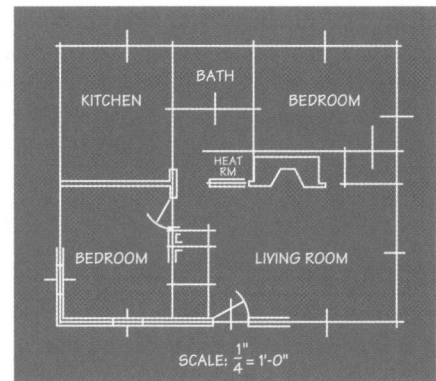

SCALE: $\frac{1}{4}''$ = 1'-0"

Use similar triangles to solve each problem. **See Example 9.**

97. HEIGHT OF A TREE A tree casts a shadow of 26 feet at the same time as a 6-foot man casts a shadow of 4 feet. Find the height of the tree. 39 ft

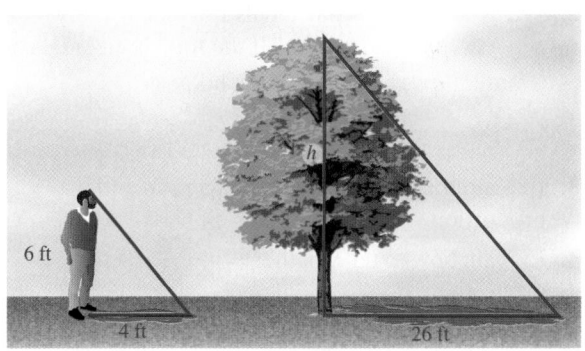

6 ft   *h*

4 ft   26 ft

98. HEIGHT OF A BUILDING A man places a mirror on the ground and sees the reflection of the top of a building, as shown. The two triangles in the illustration are similar. Find the height, *h*, of the building. 25 ft

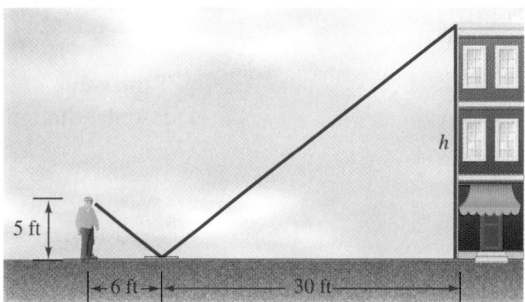

5 ft   *h*

6 ft   30 ft

99. WIDTH OF A RIVER Use the dimensions in the illustration to find *w*, the width of the river. (The two triangles in the illustration are similar.) $46\frac{7}{8}$ ft

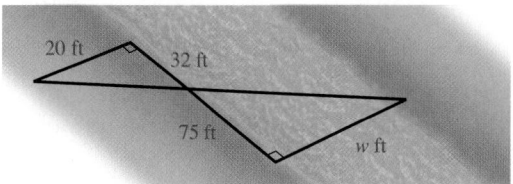

20 ft   32 ft

75 ft   *w* ft

▶ **100.** FLIGHT PATHS The airplane shown below ascends 100 feet as it flies a horizontal distance of 1,000 feet. How much altitude will it gain as it flies a horizontal distance of 1 mile? (*Hint:* 5,280 feet = 1 mile.) 528 ft

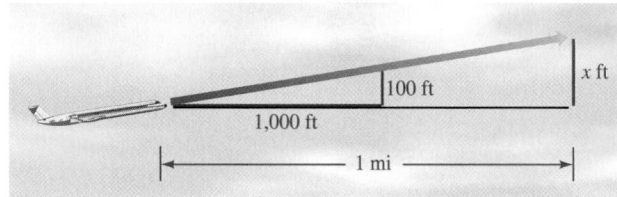

101. FLIGHT PATHS An airplane descends 1,350 feet as it flies a horizontal distance of 1 mile. How much altitude is lost as it flies a horizontal distance of 5 miles? 6,750 ft

▶ **102.** SKI RUNS A ski course falls 100 feet in every 300 feet of horizontal run. If the total horizontal run is $\frac{1}{2}$ mile, find the height of the hill. 880 ft

▌WRITING

103. Explain the difference between a ratio and a proportion.

▶ **104.** Explain how to tell whether $\frac{3.2}{3.7} = \frac{5.44}{6.29}$ is a proportion.

105. Explain why the concept of cross products cannot be used to solve the equation

$$\frac{x}{3} - \frac{3x}{4} = \frac{1}{12}$$

106. Write a problem about a situation you encounter in your daily life that could be solved by using a proportion.

▌REVIEW

107. Change $\frac{9}{10}$ to a percent. 90%

▶ **108.** Change $33\frac{1}{3}\%$ to a fraction. $\frac{1}{3}$

109. Find 30% of 1,600. 480

▶ **110.** SHOPPING Maria bought a dress for 25% off the original price of $98. How much did the dress cost? $73.50

111. Find the slope of the line passing through $(-2, -2)$ and $(-12, -8)$. $\frac{3}{5}$

112. What are the slope and the y-intercept of the graph of $y = 2x - 3$? 2, (0, −3)

Objectives

1 Solve direct variation problems.

2 Solve inverse variation problems.

SECTION 7.9

Variation

If the value of one quantity depends on the value of another quantity, we can often describe that relationship using the language of variation:

- The sales tax on an item varies with the price.
- The intensity of light varies with the distance from its source.
- The pressure exerted by water on an object varies with the depth of the object beneath the surface.

In this section, we will discuss two types of variation, and we will see how to represent them algebraically using equations.

1 Solve direct variation problems.

One type of variation, called **direct variation,** is represented by an equation of the form $y = kx$, where k is a constant (a number). Two variables are said to *vary directly* if one is a constant multiple of the other.

Direct Variation

The words *y varies directly with x* mean that

$$y = kx$$

for some constant k, called the **constant of variation.**

EXAMPLE 1   Suppose *y* varies directly as *x*. If $y = 12$ when $x = 4$, find *y* when $x = 6$.

Strategy We will use the equation $y = kx$ to solve this problem.

WHY The words *varies directly* indicate that we should use the direct variation equation $y = kx$.

Solution
We can use the given pair of values of *x* and *y* to determine the constant of variation *k*.

$y = kx$ This is the equation that models direct variation.

$12 = k(4)$ Substitute 4 for *x* and 12 for *y*.

$3 = k$ To isolate *k* on the right side, divide both sides by 4. This is the constant of variation.

Since $y = kx$ and $k = 3$, we have $y = 3x$.
We can use $y = 3x$ to find other pairs of values of *x* and *y*. When $x = 6$, we see that

$y = 3(6) = 18$ Substitute 6 for *x*.

Thus, when $x = 6$, the value of *y* is 18.

> **Success Tip**   If we divide both sides of $y = kx$ by *x*, we obtain $\frac{y}{x} = k$. Thus, for the direct variation model, *k* is simply the quotient of one pair of values of *x* and *y*.

Scientists have found that the distance a spring will stretch varies directly with the force applied to it. The more force applied to the spring, the more it will stretch. If *d* represents the distance stretched and *f* represents the force applied, this relationship can be expressed by the equation

$d = kf$ where *k* is the constant of variation

Suppose that a 150-pound weight stretches a spring 18 inches. (See the figure to the right.) We can find the constant of variation for the spring by substituting 150 for *f* and 18 for *d* in the equation $d = kf$ and solving for *k*:

Unstretched spring

Stretched spring

18 in.

150-lb force

$d = kf$

$18 = k(150)$

$\dfrac{18}{150} = k$ Divide both sides by 150 to isolate *k*.

$\dfrac{3}{25} = k$ Simplify the fraction: $\dfrac{18}{150} = \dfrac{\overset{1}{\cancel{6}} \cdot 3}{\underset{1}{\cancel{6}} \cdot 25} = \dfrac{3}{25}$.

Self Check 1

Suppose *y* varies directly as *x*. If $y = 24$ when $x = 3$, find *y* when $x = 5$. 40

Now Try **Problem 29**

Teaching Example 1 Suppose *d* varies directly with *m*. If $d = 18$ when $m = 6$, find *d* when $m = 8$.
Answer:
24

Therefore, the equation describing the relationship between the distance the spring will stretch and the amount of force applied to it is $d = \frac{3}{25}f$. To find the distance that the same spring will stretch when a 50-pound weight is attached, we proceed as follows:

$$d = \frac{3}{25}f \qquad \text{This is the equation describing the direct variation.}$$

$$d = \frac{3}{25}(50) \qquad \text{Substitute 50 for } f.$$

$$d = 6 \qquad \text{Perform the multiplication.}$$

The spring will stretch 6 inches when a 50-pound weight is attached.

The table shows some other possible values for f and d as determined by the equation $d = \frac{3}{25}f$. When these ordered pairs are graphed and a straight line is drawn through them, it is apparent that as the force f applied to a spring increases, the distance d it stretches increases. Furthermore, the slope of the graph is $\frac{3}{25}$, the constant of variation.

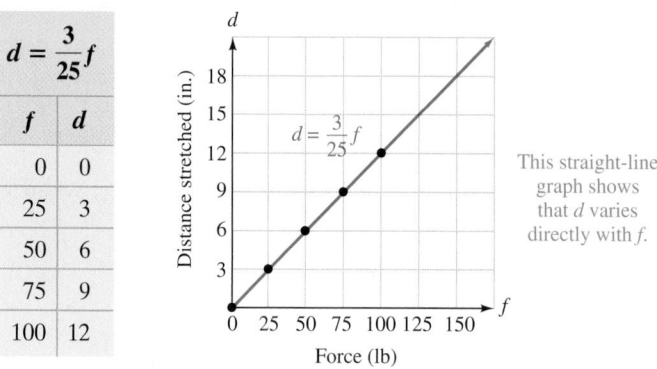

$d = \frac{3}{25}f$	
f	d
0	0
25	3
50	6
75	9
100	12

This straight-line graph shows that d varies directly with f.

Success Tip   The value of k is for this specific example. Another spring made out of a different type of steel will more than likely have a different value of k.

We can use the following steps to solve variation problems.

Strategy for Solving Variation Problems

1. Translate the verbal model into an equation.

2. Substitute the first set of values into the equation from step 1 to determine the value of k.

3. Substitute the value of k into the equation from step 1.

4. Substitute the remaining set of values into the equation from step 3 and solve for the unknown variable.

Self Check 2

The cost of a bus ticket varies directly with the number of miles traveled. If a ticket for a 180-mile trip cost $45, what would a ticket for a 1,500-mile trip cost? $375

EXAMPLE 2   *Geology*   The weight of an object on Earth varies directly with its weight on the moon. If a rock weighs 5 pounds on the moon and 30 pounds on Earth, what would be the weight on Earth of a larger rock weighing 26 pounds on the moon?

Strategy We will follow the strategy for solving a direct variation problem.

WHY In the words of the problem, the phrase *varies directly* indicates that a direct variation model should be used.

Solution

Step 1 We let e represent the weight of the object on Earth and m the weight of the object on the moon. Translating the words *weight on Earth varies directly with weight on the moon,* we get the equation

$$e = km$$

Step 2 To find the constant of variation, k, we substitute 30 for e and 5 for m.

$$e = km$$
$$30 = k(5)$$
$$6 = k \qquad \text{To undo the multiplication by 5, divide both sides by 5.}$$

Step 3 The equation describing the relationship between the weight of an object on Earth and on the moon is

$$e = 6m$$

Step 4 We can find the weight of the larger rock on Earth by substituting 26 for m in the equation from step 3.

$$e = 6m$$
$$e = 6(26)$$
$$e = 156$$

The rock would weigh 156 pounds on Earth.

2 Solve inverse variation problems.

Another type of variation, called **inverse variation,** is represented by an equation of the form $y = \frac{k}{x}$, where k is a constant. Two variables are said to *vary inversely* if one is a constant multiple of the reciprocal of the other.

Inverse Variation

The words *y varies inversely with x* mean that

$$y = \frac{k}{x}$$

for some constant k, called the **constant of variation.**

EXAMPLE 3   Suppose y varies inversely as x. If $y = 5$ when $x = 20$, find y when $x = 50$.

Strategy We will use the equation $y = \frac{k}{x}$ to solve this problem.

WHY The words *varies inversely* indicate that we should use the inverse variation equation $y = \frac{k}{x}$.

Solution

We can use the given pair of values of x and y to determine the constant of variation, k, in $y = \frac{k}{x}$.

Now Try Problem 45

Teaching Example 2 The cost of a piece of material varies directly with the number of yards purchased. If a $1\frac{1}{2}$-yard piece of material cost $9, how much will a 12-yard piece of the same material cost?
Answer:
$72

Self Check 3

Suppose y varies inversely as x. If $y = 25$ when $x = 3$, find y when $x = 15$. 5

Now Try Problem 37

Teaching Example 3 Suppose w varies inversely with z. If $w = 12$ when $z = 8$, find w when $z = 6$.
Answer:
16

$$y = \frac{k}{x} \qquad \text{This is the equation that models inverse variation.}$$

$$5 = \frac{k}{20} \qquad \text{Substitute 20 for x and 5 for y.}$$

$$20 \cdot 5 = k \qquad \text{To isolate k on the right side, multiply both sides by 20.}$$

$$100 = k \qquad \text{This is the constant of variation.}$$

Since $y = \frac{k}{x}$ and $k = 100$, we have

$$y = \frac{100}{x}$$

We can use $y = \frac{100}{x}$ to find other pairs of values of x and y. When $x = 50$, we see that

$$y = \frac{100}{50} = 2 \qquad \text{Substitute 50 for x.}$$

Thus, when $x = 50$, the value of y is 2. ∎

Suppose that the time (in hours) it takes to paint a house varies inversely with the size of the painting crew. As the number of painters increases, the time that it takes to paint the house decreases. If n represents the number of painters and t represents the time it takes to paint the house, this relationship can be expressed by the equation

$$t = \frac{k}{n} \qquad \text{where } k \text{ is the constant of variation}$$

If we know that a crew of 8 can paint the house in 12 hours, we can find the constant of variation by substituting 8 for n and 12 for t in the equation $t = \frac{k}{n}$ and solving for k:

$$t = \frac{k}{n}$$

$$12 = \frac{k}{8}$$

$$12 \cdot 8 = k \qquad \text{Multiply both sides by 8 to isolate k.}$$

$$96 = k$$

The equation describing the relationship between the size of the painting crew and the time it takes to paint the house is $t = \frac{96}{n}$. We can use this equation to find the time it will take a crew of any size to paint the house. For example, to find the time it would take a 4-person crew, we substitute 4 for n in the equation $t = \frac{96}{n}$.

$$t = \frac{96}{n} \qquad \text{This is the equation describing the inverse variation.}$$

$$t = \frac{96}{4} \qquad \text{Substitute 4 for n.}$$

$$t = 24$$

It would take a 4-person crew 24 hours to paint the house.

The table shows some possible values for n and t as determined by the equation $t = \frac{96}{n}$. When these ordered pairs are graphed and a smooth curve is drawn through them, it is clear that as the number of painters n increases, the time t decreases.

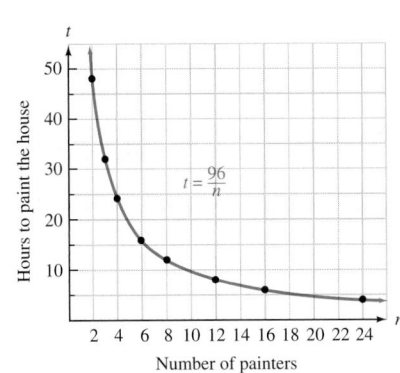

$t = \dfrac{96}{n}$	
n	**t**
2	48
3	32
4	24
6	16
8	12
12	8
16	6
24	4

This curved graph shows that *t* varies inversely with *n*.

EXAMPLE 4　　*Gas Laws*　The volume occupied by a gas varies inversely with the pressure placed on it. That is, the volume decreases as the pressure increases. If a gas occupies a volume of 15 cubic inches when placed under 4 pounds per square inch (psi) of pressure, how much pressure is needed to compress the gas into a volume of 10 cubic inches?

Strategy We will follow the strategy for solving an inverse variation problem.

WHY In the words of the problem, the phrase *varies inversely* indicates that an inverse variation model should be used.

Solution

Step 1 We let V represent the volume occupied by the gas and p represent the pressure. Translating the words *volume occupied by a gas varies inversely with the pressure*, we get the equation

$$V = \frac{k}{p}$$

Step 2 To find the constant of variation, k, we substitute 15 for V and 4 for p.

$$V = \frac{k}{p}$$

$$15 = \frac{k}{4}$$

$$60 = k \qquad \text{Multiply both sides by 4.}$$

Step 3 The equation describing the relationship between the volume occupied by the gas and the pressure placed on it is

$$V = \frac{60}{p}$$

Step 4 We can now find the pressure needed to compress the gas into a volume of 10 cubic inches by substituting 10 for V in the equation and solving for p.

$$V = \frac{60}{p}$$

$$10 = \frac{60}{p}$$

Self Check 4

How much pressure is needed to compress the gas in Example 4 into a volume of 8 cubic inches? 7.5 psi

Now Try Problem 49

Teaching Example 4 How much pressure is needed to compress the gas in Example 4 into a volume of 12 cubic inches?
Answer:
5 psi

$$10p = 60 \qquad \text{To clear the equation of the fraction, multiply both sides by } p.$$

$$p = 6 \qquad \text{To undo the multiplication by 10, divide both sides by 10.}$$

It will take 6 psi of pressure to compress the gas into a volume of 10 cubic inches. ■

THINK IT THROUGH *Study Time vs. Effectiveness*

"Above all, review regularly and plan to study ahead, so that the night before an exam, all you do is review material. Avoid all-nighters!"

Improve Your Studying Skills, Counseling Service at The University of North Carolina, Chapel Hill

Each graph below shows a direct or inverse relationship between two components of the educational process as found by researchers in *An Analysis of the Study Time* (Orlando J. Olivares, Department of Psychology, Bridgewater State College, 2002). For each graph, explain why you agree or disagree with the findings.

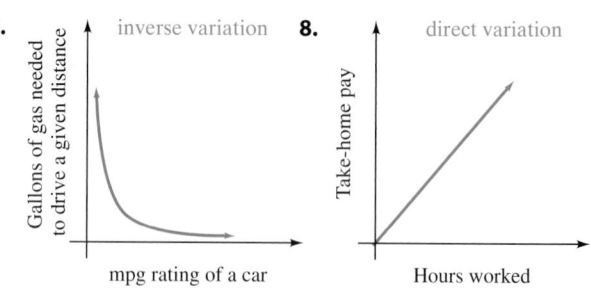

ANSWERS TO SELF CHECKS

1. 40   **2.** $375   **3.** 5   **4.** 7.5 psi

SECTION 7.9 STUDY SET

VOCABULARY

Fill in the blanks.

▶ **1.** The equation $y = kx$ defines __direct__ variation.

▶ **2.** The equation $y = \frac{k}{x}$ defines __inverse__ variation.

3. In $y = kx$, the __constant__ of variation is k.

4. In $y = \dfrac{k}{x}$, the constant of variation is __k__.

CONCEPTS

Determine whether each graph represents direct variation or inverse variation.

5. direct variation   **6.** inverse variation

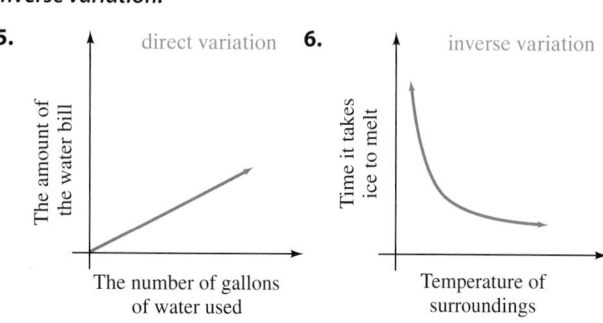

7. inverse variation   **8.** direct variation

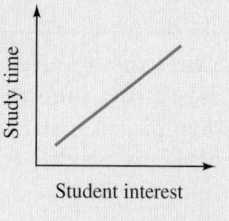 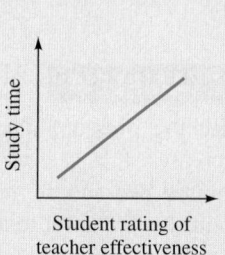

9. Translate the following sentence into mathematical symbols: $h = ka$

| A farmer's harvest, h | varies directly | with the number of acres planted, a. |

10. If the constant of variation for Problem 9 is $k = 10,000$, what will happen to the size of the harvest as the number of acres planted increases?
It will increase.

▶ Selected exercises available online at
www.webassign.net/brookscole

11. Express the following relationship with an equation:

The number of gallons g of paint needed to paint a room varies directly with the number of square feet f to be painted. $g = kf$

12. Express the following relationship with an equation:

The amount of sales tax t varies directly with the purchase price p of a new car. $t = kp$

13. Translate the following sentence into mathematical symbols: $t = \frac{k}{s}$

The time t in hours it takes a commuter to drive from her home to her office	varies inversely	with her average speed s (in mph).

14. If the constant of variation for Problem 13 is $k = 30$, what will happen to the time her commute takes her as her average speed increases? It will decrease.

15. Express this relationship using an equation: The number of hot dogs n that a street vendor sells varies inversely with the price p that he charges. $n = \frac{k}{p}$

16. a. If y varies directly with x and $k > 0$, what happens to y as x increases? It increases.

   b. If y varies inversely with x and $k > 0$, what happens to y as x increases? It decreases.

17. Assume that y varies inversely with x and $y = \frac{k}{x}$. If $y = 15$ when $x = 10$, find k. 150

▶ **18.** Assume that c varies inversely with d and $c = \frac{k}{d}$. If $c = 9$ when $d = 5$, find k. 45

NOTATION

Determine whether the equation defines direct variation.

▶ **19.** $y = kx$ yes ▶ **20.** $y = k + x$ no

▶ **21.** $y = \frac{k}{x}$ no ▶ **22.** $m = kc$ yes

Determine whether each equation defines inverse variation.

23. $y = kx$ no **24.** $y = \frac{k}{x}$ yes

25. $d = \frac{k}{g}$ yes **26.** $y = \frac{x}{k}$ no

Complete each solution.

27. Find f if $d = 21$ and $k = \frac{7}{5}$.

$$d = kf$$

$$21 = \boxed{\frac{7}{5}} f$$

$$\boxed{\frac{5}{7}} \cdot 21 = \boxed{\frac{5}{7}} \cdot \frac{7}{5} f$$

$$15 = f$$

▶ **28.** Find f if $d = 20$ and $k = 0.75$.

$$d = \frac{k}{f}$$

$$\boxed{20} = \frac{0.75}{f}$$

$$\boxed{f} \cdot 20 = \boxed{f} \cdot \frac{0.75}{f}$$

$$20f = \boxed{0.75}$$

$$f = \frac{0.75}{\boxed{20}}$$

$$f = 0.0375$$

GUIDED PRACTICE

Solve each direct variation problem. **See Examples 1–2.**

▶ **29.** y varies directly with x. If $y = 10$ when $x = 2$, find y when $x = 7$. 35

▶ **30.** r varies directly with s. If $r = 21$ when $s = 6$, find r when $s = 12$. 42

31. l varies directly with m. If $l = 50$ when $m = 200$, find l when $m = 25$. 6.25

▶ **32.** x and y vary directly. If $x = 30$ when $y = 2$, find y when $x = 45$. 3

▶ **33.** n_1 and n_2 vary directly. If $n_1 = 315$ when $n_2 = 3$, find n_2 when $n_1 = 10.5$. 0.1

34. d is directly proportional to t. If $d = 21$ when $t = 6$, find d when $t = 4$. 14

35. t varies directly with s. If $t = 21$ when $s = 6$, find k. $\frac{7}{2}$

36. y varies directly with x. If $y = 10$ when $x = 2$, find k. 5

Solve each inverse variation problem. **See Examples 3–4.**

▶ **37.** y varies inversely with x. If $y = 8$ when $x = 1$, find y when $x = 8$. 1

▶ **38.** r varies inversely with s. If $r = 40$ when $s = 10$, find r when $s = 15$. $\frac{80}{3}$

39. a varies inversely with t. If $a = 600$ when $t = 300$, find a when $t = 15$. 12,000

40. t_1 and t_2 vary inversely. If $t_1 = 4$ when $t_2 = 5$, find t_2 when $t_1 = 3\frac{1}{3}$. 6

▶ **41.** a and r vary inversely. If $a = 9$ when $r = 7$, find r when $a = \frac{1}{9}$. 567

42. q is inversely proportional to s. If $q = 6$ when $s = 9$, find q when $s = 24$. $\frac{9}{4}$

43. a varies inversely with b^3. If $a = 4$ when $b = 2$, find a when $b = 3$. $\frac{32}{27}$

44. s varies inversely with t^2. If $s = 180$ when $t = 3$, find s when $t = 9$. 20

APPLICATIONS

Solve each direct variation problem. **See Example 2.**

45. DRIVING The distance that a car can travel without refueling varies directly with the number of gallons of gasoline in the tank. If a car can go 360 miles on a full tank of gas (15 gallons), how far can it go on 7 gallons? 168 mi

46. GRAVITY The force of gravity acting on an object varies directly with the mass of the object. The force on a mass of 5 kilograms is 49 newtons. What is the force acting on a mass of 12 kilograms? 117.6 newtons

47. DOSAGES The recommended dose (in milligrams) of Demerol, a preoperative medication given to children, varies directly with the child's weight (in pounds). If the proper dosage for a child weighing 30 pounds is 18 milligrams, find the proper dosage for a child weighing 45 pounds. 27 mg

48. MEDICATIONS To fight ear infections in children, doctors often prescribe Ceclor. The recommended dose in milligrams varies directly with the child's body weight in pounds. If the proper dosage for a 20-pound child is 124 milligrams, find the proper dosage for a 28-pound child. 173.6 mg

Solve each direct variation problem. **See Example 4.**

49. TRAVELING The time it takes a car to travel a certain distance varies inversely with its rate of speed. If a certain trip takes 3 hours at 50 mph, how long will the trip take at 60 mph? $2\frac{1}{2}$ hr

50. GEOMETRY For a fixed area, the length of a rectangle is inversely proportional to its width. A rectangle has a width of 12 feet and a length of 20 feet. If its length is increased to 12.5 feet, find the width that will maintain the same area. 19.2 ft

51. ELECTRICITY The current in an electric circuit varies inversely with the resistance. If the current in the circuit shown is 30 amps when the resistance is 4 ohms, what will the current be for a resistance of 15 ohms? 8 amps

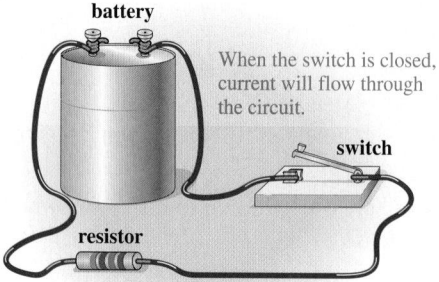

52. FARMING The length of time a given number of bushels of corn will last when feeding cattle varies inversely with the number of animals. If a certain number of bushels will feed 25 cows for 10 days, how long will the feed last for 10 cows? 25 days

TRY IT YOURSELF

Use a calculator to help solve each variation problem.

53. g varies directly with t. If $g = 3{,}616$ when $t = 8{,}000$, find g when $t = 2{,}405$. 1,087.06

54. b varies inversely with c. If $b = 0.45$ when $c = 1.6$, find b when $c = 80$. 0.009

55. p varies inversely with q. If $p = 55$ when $q = 2.5$, find p when $q = 100$. 1.375

56. m varies directly with n. If $m = 4{,}560$ when $n = 950$, find m when $n = 725$. 3,480

57. PULLEYS The speeds, in revolutions per minute (rpm), of two pulleys connected by a belt are inversely proportional to their diameters. If a pulley 24 inches in diameter, making 120 revolutions per minute, is belted to a second pulley 16 inches in diameter, how many rpm does the smaller pulley make? 180

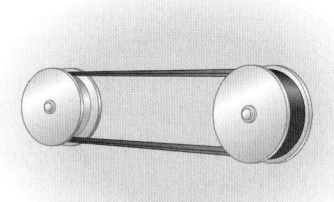

58. CIDER For the following, the number of inches of stick cinnamon to use varies directly with the number of servings of spiced cider to be made. How many inches of stick cinnamon are needed to make 36 servings? 27

Hot Spiced Cider

8 cups apple cider or apple juice
$\frac{1}{4}$ to $\frac{1}{2}$ cup packed brown sugar
6 inches stick cinnamon
1 teaspoon whole allspice
1 teaspoon whole cloves
8 thin orange wedges or slices (optional)
8 whole cloves (optional)   **Makes 8 servings**

59. LUNAR GRAVITY Refer to the illustration on the next page. The weight of an object on the moon varies directly with its weight on Earth. If 6 pounds on Earth weighs 1 pound on the moon, what would the scale register if the astronaut were weighed on the moon? 55 lb

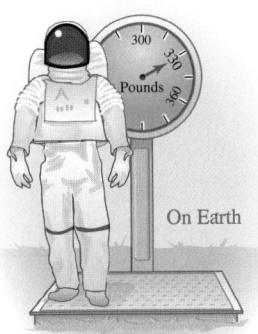

On Earth

▶ **60. SEESAWS** When a seesaw is balanced, the distance (in feet) each person is from the fulcrum is inversely proportional to that person's weight. Use the information in the illustration to determine how far away from the fulcrum that Brandon is sitting. 6 ft

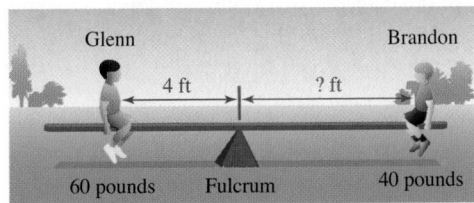

Glenn   Brandon

4 ft   ? ft

60 pounds   Fulcrum   40 pounds

61. HOOKE'S LAW The distance that a spring will stretch varies directly with the force applied to it. Suppose that a 15-kilogram weight stretches a spring 24 centimeters. Find the distance that the same spring will stretch when a 25-kilogram weight is used. 40 cm

▶ **62. ARCHITECTURE** The total numbers of windows needed in the construction of an apartment building varies directly with the number of floors. If a 4-story building requires 176 windows, how many windows will an 11-story building require? 484

▶ **63. COMPUTING PRESSURES** If the temperature of a gas is constant, the volume occupied varies inversely with the pressure. If a gas occupies a volume of 40 cubic meters under a pressure of 8 atmospheres, find the volume when the pressure is changed to 6 atmospheres. $53\frac{1}{3}$ m³

▶ **64. DEPRECIATION** Assume that the value of a machine varies inversely with its age. If a drill press is worth \$300 when it is 2 years old, find its value when it is 6 years old. How much has the machine depreciated over that 4-year period? \$100, \$200

WRITING

65. Give two examples of quantities that vary directly and two that do not.

▶ **66.** What is the difference between direct variation and inverse variation?

▶ **67.** What is a constant of variation?

Is there a direct variation or an inverse variation between each pair of quantities? Explain why.

68. The time it takes to type a term paper and the speed at which you type.

69. The time it takes to type a term paper (working at a constant rate) and the length of the term paper.

70. The time it takes to type a term paper and the amount of time you did research.

REVIEW

Solve each equation.

71. $x^2 - 5x - 6 = 0$ $-1, 6$

72. $x^2 - 25 = 0$ $5, -5$

73. $(t + 2)(t^2 + 7t + 12) = 0$ $-2, -3, -4$

▶ **74.** $2(y - 4) = -y^2$ $2, -4$

75. $y^3 - y^2 = 0$ $0, 0, 1$

76. $5a^3 - 125a = 0$ $0, 5, -5$

77. $(x^2 - 1)(x^2 - 4) = 0$ $1, -1, 2, -2$

78. $6t^3 + 35t^2 = 6t$ $0, -6, \frac{1}{6}$

STUDY SKILLS CHECKLIST

Preparing for the Chapter 7 Test

There are several common mistakes that students make when working with the topics of Chapter 7. To make sure you are prepared for your test, study this checklist of common mistakes below.

☐ When simplifying fractions that have more than one term in the numerator and/or the denominator, you must factor the numerator and denominator using the factoring strategies from Chapter 6. When you have completely factored the numerator and denominator, remove all common factors.

$$\frac{a^2 - 3a - 10}{a^2 - 25} = \frac{\overset{1}{\cancel{(a-5)}}(a+2)}{\underset{1}{\cancel{(a-5)}}(a+5)} = \frac{a+2}{a+5}$$

☐ To multiply fractions, you do not need a common denominator. Simply factor across the numerators and factor across the denominators and remove common factors.

$$\frac{x^2 - x}{x^2 - 1} \cdot \frac{x^2 - x - 2}{x - 2} = \frac{x\overset{1}{\cancel{(x-1)}}\overset{1}{\cancel{(x-2)}}(x+1)}{\underset{1}{\cancel{(x+1)}}\underset{1}{\cancel{(x-1)}}\underset{1}{\cancel{(x-2)}}} = x$$

☐ To divide fractions, make sure to multiply the first fraction by the reciprocal of the *second* fraction.

$$\frac{4a^2}{3b^2} \div \frac{8a^2}{3b} = \frac{4a^2}{3b^2} \cdot \frac{3b}{8a^2} = \frac{4 \cdot a^2 \cdot 3 \cdot b}{3 \cdot b^2 \cdot 2 \cdot 4 \cdot a^2} = \frac{1}{2b}$$

☐ When adding or subtracting fractions, you must have a common denominator. Then you add or subtract across the numerator and *keep the common denominator.*

$$\frac{2}{x+5} + \frac{6}{x} = \frac{2x}{x(x+5)} + \frac{6(x+5)}{x(x+5)}$$
$$= \frac{2x + 6x + 30}{x(x+5)} = \frac{8x + 30}{x(x+5)}$$

☐ When subtracting a fraction with more than one term in the numerator, make sure you distribute the negative through the entire numerator being subtracted.

$$\frac{5x+7}{x(x-2)} - \frac{3x-5}{x(x-2)} = \frac{5x + 7 - (3x-5)}{x(x-2)}$$
$$= \frac{5x + 7 - 3x + 5}{x(x-2)} = \frac{2x + 12}{x(x-2)}$$

☐ When *solving equations* that involve rational expressions, you can remove the fractions by multiplying both sides by the LCD of the entire equation. When working with *rational expressions,* you must work with the fractions that are in the expression.

Teaching Guide: Refer to the Instructor's Resource Binder to find activities, worksheets on key concepts, more examples, instruction tips, overheads, and assessments.

CHAPTER 7   SUMMARY AND REVIEW

SECTION 7.1   Simplifying Rational Expressions

DEFINITIONS AND CONCEPTS	EXAMPLES
A **rational expression** is an expression of the form $\frac{A}{B}$, where A and B are polynomials and $B \neq 0$.	**Rational expressions:** $\frac{8}{7t}, \quad \frac{a}{a-3}, \quad \text{and} \quad \frac{4x^2 - 16x}{x^2 - 6x + 8}$

To **evaluate a rational expression,** substitute the values of its variables and simplify.	Evaluate $\dfrac{3x + 1}{x - 2}$ for $x = 5$.
	$\dfrac{3x + 1}{x - 2} = \dfrac{3(5) + 1}{5 - 2} = \dfrac{16}{3}$ Substitute 5 for x.
To find the real numbers for which a **rational expression is undefined,** find the values of the variable that make the denominator 0.	For which real numbers is $\dfrac{11}{2x - 3}$ undefined?
	$2x - 3 = 0$ Set the denominator equal to 0 and solve for x.
	$2x = 3$
	$x = \dfrac{3}{2}$ The expression is undefined for $x = \dfrac{3}{2}$.
Fundamental property of fractions: If A, B, and C are polynomials and B and C are not 0, $$\dfrac{AC}{BC} = \dfrac{A}{B}$$	$\dfrac{3a}{ab} = \dfrac{3 \cdot \overset{1}{\cancel{a}}}{b \cdot \underset{1}{\cancel{a}}} = \dfrac{3}{b}$ $\dfrac{4t^3}{bst^2} = \dfrac{4t \cdot \overset{1}{\cancel{t^2}}}{bs \cdot \underset{1}{\cancel{t^2}}} = \dfrac{4t}{5s}$
To **simplify a rational expression:** 1. Factor the numerator and denominator completely. 2. Remove all factors equal to 1. 3. Multiply the remaining factors in the numerator and denominator.	$\dfrac{x^2 - 4}{x^2 - 7x + 10} = \dfrac{(x + 2)\overset{1}{\cancel{(x - 2)}}}{(x - 5)\underset{1}{\cancel{(x - 2)}}}$ Factor and simplify.
	$= \dfrac{x + 2}{x - 5}$
The quotient of any nonzero expression and its opposite is -1.	$\dfrac{2t - 3}{3 - 2t} = -1$ Because $2t - 3$ and $3 - 2t$ are opposites.

REVIEW EXERCISES

1. Evaluate $\dfrac{x^2 - 1}{x - 5}$ for $x = -2$. $-\dfrac{3}{7}$

2. Find the values of x for which the rational expression $\dfrac{x - 1}{x^2 - 16}$ is undefined. $4, -4$

Write each fraction in simplest form. If it is already in simplest form, so indicate.

3. $\dfrac{10}{25}$ $\dfrac{2}{5}$

4. $-\dfrac{12}{18}$ $-\dfrac{2}{3}$

Simplify each rational expression, if possible . Assume that no denominators are 0.

5. $\dfrac{3x^2}{6x^3}$ $\dfrac{1}{2x}$

6. $\dfrac{5xy^2}{2x^2y^2}$ $\dfrac{5}{2x}$

7. $\dfrac{x^2}{x^2 + x}$ $\dfrac{x}{x + 1}$

8. $\dfrac{a^2 - 4}{a + 2}$ $a - 2$

9. $\dfrac{3p - 2}{2 - 3p}$ -1

10. $\dfrac{8 - x}{x^2 - 5x - 24}$ $-\dfrac{1}{x + 3}$

11. $\dfrac{2x^2 - 16x}{2x^2 - 18x + 16}$ $\dfrac{x}{x - 1}$

12. $\dfrac{x^2 + x - 2}{x^2 - x - 2}$ in simplest form

13. Explain the error in the following work:

$\dfrac{x + 1}{x} = \dfrac{\overset{1}{\cancel{x}} + 1}{\underset{1}{\cancel{x}}} = \dfrac{2}{1}$ x is not a common factor of the numerator and the denominator.

14. Simplify: $\dfrac{4(t + 3) + 8}{3(t + 3) + 6}$ $\dfrac{4}{3}$

SECTION 7.2 Multiplying and Dividing Rational Expressions

DEFINITIONS AND CONCEPTS	EXAMPLES
To **multiply rational expressions,** multiply their numerators and multiply their denominators. $$\frac{A}{B}\cdot\frac{C}{D}=\frac{AC}{BD}\text{ where }B, D\neq 0$$	$$\frac{4b}{b+2}\cdot\frac{7}{b}=\frac{4b\cdot 7}{(b+2)b}\quad\text{Multiply the numerators. Multiply the denominators.}$$ $$=\frac{4\overset{1}{b}\cdot 7}{(b+2)\underset{1}{b}}\quad\text{Simplify by removing the common factors.}$$ $$=\frac{28}{b+2}$$
To write the **reciprocal** of a rational expression, invert its numerator and denominator.	The reciprocal of $\dfrac{c}{c-7}$ is $\dfrac{c-7}{c}$.
To **divide rational expressions,** multiply the first expression by the reciprocal of the second. $$\frac{A}{B}\div\frac{C}{D}=\frac{A}{B}\cdot\frac{D}{C}\text{ where }B, C, D\neq 0$$	$$\frac{t}{t+1}\div\frac{8}{t^2+t}=\frac{t}{t+1}\cdot\frac{t^2+t}{8}$$ $$=\frac{t\cdot t(\overset{1}{t+1})}{(\underset{1}{t+1})\cdot 8}\quad\text{Factor and simplify.}$$ $$=\frac{t^2}{8}$$
A **unit conversion factor** is a fraction containing units that has a value of 1.	$$\frac{1\text{ yd}^2}{9\text{ ft}^2}=1\quad\text{and}\quad\frac{1\text{ mi}}{5{,}280\text{ ft}}=1$$

REVIEW EXERCISES

Perform each multiplication and simplify.

15. $\dfrac{3xy}{2x}\cdot\dfrac{4x}{2y^2}$ $\dfrac{3x}{y}$

16. $56x\left(\dfrac{12}{7x}\right)$ 96

17. $\dfrac{x^2-1}{x^2+2x}\cdot\dfrac{x}{x+1}$ $\dfrac{x-1}{x+2}$

18. $\dfrac{x^2+x}{3x-15}\cdot\dfrac{6x-30}{x^2+2x+1}$ $\dfrac{2x}{x+1}$

Perform each division and simplify.

19. $\dfrac{3x^2}{5x^2y}\div\dfrac{6x}{15xy^2}$ $\dfrac{3y}{2}$

20. $\dfrac{x^2+5x}{x^2+4x-5}\div\dfrac{x^2}{x-1}$ $\dfrac{1}{x}$

21. $\dfrac{x^2-x-6}{2x-1}\div\dfrac{x^2-2x-3}{2x^2+x-1}$ $x+2$

22. Simplify: $(b+2)\div\dfrac{b^2-4}{b+2}$ $\dfrac{b+2}{b-2}$

Determine whether each fraction is a unit conversion factor

23. $\dfrac{1\text{ ft}}{12\text{ in.}}$ yes

24. $\dfrac{60\text{ min}}{1\text{ day}}$ no

25. $\dfrac{1\text{ gal}}{4\text{ qt}}$ yes

26. TRAFFIC SIGNS Convert the speed limit on the sign to miles per minute.
$0.\overline{3}$ mi/min

SPEED LIMIT **20** mph

SECTION 7.3 Adding and Subtracting with Like Denominators; Least Common Denominators

DEFINITIONS AND CONCEPTS

EXAMPLES

To **add (or subtract) rational expressions** that have the same denominator, add (or subtract) their numerators and write the sum (or difference) over their common denominator.

$$\frac{A}{D} + \frac{B}{D} = \frac{A + B}{D} \text{ where } D \neq 0$$

$$\frac{A}{D} - \frac{B}{D} = \frac{A - B}{D} \text{ where } D \neq 0$$

Add: $\dfrac{2b}{3b - 9} + \dfrac{b}{3b - 9} = \dfrac{2b + b}{3b - 9}$

$$= \frac{\overset{1}{3b}}{\underset{1}{3(b - 3)}} \quad \text{Factor and simplify.}$$

$$= \frac{b}{b - 3}$$

Subtract: $\dfrac{x + 1}{x} - \dfrac{x - 1}{x} = \dfrac{x + 1 - (x - 1)}{x}$ Don't forget the parentheses.

$$= \frac{x + 1 - x + 1}{x}$$

$$= \frac{2}{x}$$

To find the **LCD** of several rational expressions, factor each denominator. Then form a product using each different factor the greatest number of times it appears in any one factorization.

Find the LCD of $\dfrac{3}{x^3 - x^2}$ and $\dfrac{x}{x^2 - 1}$.

$$\left.\begin{array}{l} x^3 - x^2 = x \cdot x \cdot (x - 1) \\ x^2 - 1 = (x + 1)(x - 1) \end{array}\right\} \text{LCD} = x \cdot x \cdot (x - 1)(x + 1)$$

To **build an equivalent rational expression,** multiply the given expression by 1 written in the form $\frac{c}{c}$, where $c \neq 0$.

$$\frac{7}{4t} = \frac{7}{4t} \cdot \frac{3t}{3t}$$

$$= \frac{21t}{12t^2}$$

$$\frac{x + 1}{x - 7} = \frac{x + 1}{x - 7} \cdot \frac{x - 1}{x - 1}$$

$$= \frac{(x + 1)(x - 1)}{(x - 7)(x - 1)}$$

$$= \frac{x^2 - 1}{x^2 - 8x + 7}$$

REVIEW EXERCISES

Perform each operation. Simplify all answers.

27. $\dfrac{13}{15d} - \dfrac{8}{15d}$ $\frac{1}{3d}$

28. $\dfrac{x}{x + y} + \dfrac{y}{x + y}$ 1

29. $\dfrac{3x}{x - 7} - \dfrac{x - 2}{x - 7}$ $\frac{2x + 2}{x - 7}$

30. $\dfrac{a}{a^2 - 2a - 8} + \dfrac{2}{a^2 - 2a - 8}$ $\frac{1}{a - 4}$

Find the LCD of each pair of rational expressions.

31. $\dfrac{12}{x}, \dfrac{1}{9}$ $9x$

32. $\dfrac{1}{2x^3}, \dfrac{5}{8x}$ $8x^3$

33. $\dfrac{7}{m}, \dfrac{m + 2}{m - 8}$ $m(m - 8)$

34. $\dfrac{x}{5x + 1}, \dfrac{5x}{5x - 1}$ $(5x + 1)(5x - 1)$

35. $\dfrac{6 - a}{a^2 - 25}, \dfrac{a^2}{a - 5}$ $(a + 5)(a - 5)$

36. $\dfrac{4t + 25}{t^2 + 10t + 25}, \dfrac{t^2 - 7}{2t^2 + 17t + 35}$ $(2t + 7)(t + 5)^2$

Build each rational expression into an equivalent rational expression having the denominator shown in red.

37. $\dfrac{9}{a}, 7a$ $\frac{63}{7a}$

38. $\dfrac{2y + 1}{x - 9}, x(x - 9)$ $\frac{2xy + x}{x(x - 9)}$

39. $\dfrac{b + 7}{3b - 15}, 6(b - 5)$ $\frac{2b + 14}{6(b - 5)}$

40. $\dfrac{9r}{r^2 + 6r + 5}, (r + 1)(r - 4)(r + 5)$ $\frac{9r^2 - 36r}{(r + 1)(r - 4)(r + 5)}$

SECTION 7.4   **Adding and Subtracting with Unlike Denominators**

DEFINITIONS AND CONCEPTS	EXAMPLES
To **add (or subtract) rational expressions** with unlike denominators: 1. Find the LCD. 2. Write each rational expression as an equivalent expression whose denominator is the LCD. 3. Add (or subtract) the numerators and write the sum (or difference) over the LCD. 4. Simplify the resulting rational expression, if possible.	Add: $\dfrac{4x}{x} + \dfrac{2}{x-1} = \dfrac{4x}{x} \cdot \dfrac{x-1}{x-1} + \dfrac{2}{x-1} \cdot \dfrac{x}{x}$ The LCD is $x(x-1)$. $= \dfrac{4x(x-1)}{x(x-1)} + \dfrac{2x}{x(x-1)}$ $= \dfrac{4x^2 - 4x + 2x}{x(x-1)}$ Distribute the multiplication by 4x. $= \dfrac{4x^2 - 2x}{x(x-1)}$ Combine like terms. $= \dfrac{2\overset{1}{x}(2x-1)}{\underset{1}{x}(x-1)}$ Factor and simplify. $= \dfrac{2(2x-1)}{x-1}$
When a polynomial is multiplied by -1, the result is its opposite. This fact is used when adding (or subtracting) rational expressions whose **denominators are opposites**.	$\dfrac{c}{c-4} - \dfrac{1}{4-c} = \dfrac{c}{c-4} - \dfrac{1}{4-c} \cdot \dfrac{-1}{-1}$ $= \dfrac{c}{c-4} - \dfrac{-1}{c-4}$ $-1(4-c) = c-4$ $= \dfrac{c+1}{c-4}$ $-(-1) = +1$

REVIEW EXERCISES

Perform each operation. Simplify all answers.

41. $\dfrac{1}{7} - \dfrac{1}{c}$

$\dfrac{c-7}{7c}$

42. $\dfrac{x}{x-1} + \dfrac{1}{x}$

$\dfrac{x^2 + x - 1}{x(x-1)}$

43. $\dfrac{2t+2}{t^2 + 2t + 1} - \dfrac{1}{t+1}$

$\dfrac{1}{t+1}$

44. $\dfrac{x+2}{2x} - \dfrac{2-x}{x^2}$

$\dfrac{x^2 + 4x - 4}{2x^2}$

45. $\dfrac{x}{x+2} + \dfrac{3}{x} - \dfrac{4}{x^2 + 2x}$

$\dfrac{x+1}{x}$

46. $\dfrac{6}{b-1} - \dfrac{b}{1-b}$

$\dfrac{b+6}{b-1}$

47. A student added two rational expressions and obtained $\dfrac{-5n^3 - 7}{3n(n+6)}$. Another student obtained $-\dfrac{5n^3 + 7}{3n(n+6)}$. Are the answers equivalent?   yes

48. VIDEO CAMERAS Find the perimeter and the area of the LED screen of the camera.

$\dfrac{14x + 28}{(x+6)(x-1)}$ units, $\dfrac{12}{(x+6)(x-1)}$ square units

SECTION 7.5   Simplifying Complex Fractions

DEFINITIONS AND CONCEPTS	EXAMPLES
Complex fractions contain fractions in their numerators and/or their denominators.	Complex fractions: $\dfrac{\dfrac{2}{t}}{\dfrac{5}{4t}}$ and $\dfrac{\dfrac{3}{m}+\dfrac{m}{4}}{\dfrac{m}{2}}$

To simplify a complex fraction:

Method 1

Write the numerator and denominator of the complex fraction as a single rational expression and perform the indicated division and simplify.

Simplify: $\dfrac{\dfrac{3}{m}+\dfrac{m}{2}}{\dfrac{m}{4}} = \dfrac{\dfrac{3}{m}\cdot\dfrac{2}{2}+\dfrac{m}{2}\cdot\dfrac{m}{m}}{\dfrac{m}{4}}$ In the numerator, build to have an LCD of $2m$.

$= \dfrac{\dfrac{6}{2m}+\dfrac{m^2}{2m}}{\dfrac{m}{4}}$ The main fraction bar indicates division.

$= \dfrac{\dfrac{6+m^2}{2m}}{\dfrac{m}{4}}$ Add the fractions in the numerator.

$= \dfrac{6+m^2}{2m}\cdot\dfrac{4}{m}$ Multiply by the reciprocal of $\dfrac{m}{4}$.

$= \dfrac{(6+m^2)\cdot\overset{1}{2}\cdot 2}{2\cdot m\cdot m}$ Factor and simplify.
$\hspace{2cm}\underset{1}{}$

$= \dfrac{12+2m^2}{m^2}$ Distribute the multiplication by 2.

Method 2

Determine the LCD of the rational expressions in the complex fraction and multiply the complex fraction by 1, written in the form $\frac{\text{LCD}}{\text{LCD}}$. Then simplify, if possible.

Simplify: $\dfrac{\dfrac{3}{m}+\dfrac{m}{2}}{\dfrac{m}{4}} = \dfrac{\dfrac{3}{m}+\dfrac{m}{2}}{\dfrac{m}{4}}\cdot\dfrac{4m}{4m}$ The LCD for all the rational expressions is $4m$.

$= \dfrac{\dfrac{3}{m}\cdot 4m+\dfrac{m}{2}\cdot 4m}{\dfrac{m}{4}\cdot 4m}$ In the numerator, distribute the multiplication by $4m$.

$= \dfrac{12+2m^2}{m^2}$ Perform each multiplication by $4m$.

REVIEW EXERCISES

Simplify each complex fraction.

49. $\dfrac{\dfrac{3}{2}}{\dfrac{2}{3}}$ $\dfrac{9}{4}$

50. $\dfrac{\dfrac{3}{2}+1}{\dfrac{2}{3}+1}$ $\dfrac{3}{2}$

51. $\dfrac{\dfrac{n^4}{30}}{\dfrac{7n}{15}}$ $\dfrac{n^3}{14}$

52. $\dfrac{\dfrac{r^2-81}{18s^2}}{\dfrac{4r-36}{9s}}$ $\dfrac{r+9}{8s}$

53. $\dfrac{\dfrac{1}{y}+1}{\dfrac{1}{y}-1}$ $\dfrac{1+y}{1-y}$

54. $\dfrac{1+\dfrac{3}{x}}{2-\dfrac{1}{x^2}}$ $\dfrac{x(x+3)}{2x^2-1}$

55. $\dfrac{\dfrac{2}{x-1}+\dfrac{x-1}{x+1}}{\dfrac{1}{x^2-1}}$ x^2+3

56. $\dfrac{\dfrac{1}{x^2y}-\dfrac{5}{xy}}{\dfrac{3}{xy}-\dfrac{7}{xy^2}}$ $\dfrac{y-5xy}{3xy-7x}$

SECTION 7.6   Solving Rational Equations

DEFINITIONS AND CONCEPTS	EXAMPLES

To **solve a rational equation,** use these steps:

1. Determine which numbers cannot be solutions.

2. Clear the equation of fractions by multiplying both sides of the equation by the LCD of the rational expressions contained in the equation.

3. Solve the resulting equation.

4. Check all possible solutions in the *original* equation. An apparent solution that does not satisfy the original equation is called an **extraneous solution.**

$$\frac{y}{y-2} - 1 = \frac{1}{y}$$

Since no denominator can be 0, $y \neq 2$ and $y \neq 0$.

$$y(y-2)\left[\frac{y}{y-2} - 1\right] = y(y-2)\left(\frac{1}{y}\right)$$

The LCD is $y(y-2)$.

$$y(y-2)\left(\frac{y}{y-2}\right) - y(y-2)(1) = y(y-2)\left(\frac{1}{y}\right)$$

Distribute and simplify.

$$y \cdot y - y(y-2) = (y-2) \cdot 1$$

$$y^2 - y^2 + 2y = y - 2$$

Remove parentheses.

$$2y = y - 2$$

Combine like terms.

$$y = -2$$

REVIEW EXERCISES

Solve each equation and check all answers.

57. $\dfrac{3}{x} = \dfrac{2}{x-1}$ 3

58. $\dfrac{a}{a-5} = 3 + \dfrac{5}{a-5}$ no solution, 5 is extraneous

59. $\dfrac{2}{3t} + \dfrac{1}{t} = \dfrac{5}{9}$ 3

60. $a = \dfrac{3a-50}{4a-24} - \dfrac{3}{4}$ 2, 4

61. $\dfrac{4}{x+2} - \dfrac{3}{x+3} = \dfrac{6}{x^2+5x+6}$ 0

62. $\dfrac{3}{x+1} - \dfrac{x-2}{2} = \dfrac{x-2}{x+1}$ −4, 3

63. Solve for y: $\dfrac{1}{x} = \dfrac{1}{y} + \dfrac{1}{z}$ $y = \dfrac{xz}{z-x}$

64. **ENGINEERING** The efficiency E of a Carnot engine is given by the following formula. Solve it for T_1.

$$E = 1 - \frac{T_2}{T_1}   \qquad T_1 = \frac{T_2}{1-E}$$

SECTION 7.7   Problem Solving Using Rational Equations

DEFINITIONS AND CONCEPTS	EXAMPLES

To solve applications problems, follow these steps:

1. Analyze the problem.

2. Form an equation.

3. Solve the equation.

4. State the conclusion.

5. Check the result.

WASHING CARS Working alone, Carlos can wash the family car in 30 minutes. Victor, his brother, can wash the same car in 20 minutes. How long will it take them if they work together?

Analyze Since Carlos can wash the car in 30 minutes, he can wash $\frac{1}{30}$ of the car in one minute. Since Victor can wash the car in 20 minutes, he can wash $\frac{1}{20}$ of the car in one minute. If $x =$ the number of minutes it will take them working together, they can wash $\frac{1}{x}$ of the car in one minute.

Form

What Carlos can do in one minute	plus	what Victor can do in one minute	equals	what they can do together in one minute.
$\dfrac{1}{30}$	$+$	$\dfrac{1}{20}$	$=$	$\dfrac{1}{x}$

Solve

$$\frac{1}{30} + \frac{1}{20} = \frac{1}{x}$$

$$60x\left(\frac{1}{30} + \frac{1}{20}\right) = 60x\left(\frac{1}{x}\right) \qquad \text{Multiply both sides by the LCD, 60x.}$$

$$2x + 3x = 60 \qquad \text{Do the multiplications.}$$

$$5x = 60 \qquad \text{Combine like terms.}$$

$$x = 12 \qquad \text{Divide both sides by 5.}$$

State Working together, it will take 12 minutes to wash the car.

Check The check is left to the student.

Uniform motion problems: Distance = rate · time	See Example 3 in Section 7.7.
Investment problems: Interest = principal · rate · time	See Example 4 in Section 7.7.

REVIEW EXERCISES

65. NUMBER PROBLEM If a number is subtracted from the denominator of $\frac{4}{5}$ and twice as much is added to the numerator, the result is 5. Find the number. 3

66. HOUSE CLEANING If a maid can clean a house in 4 hours, how much of the house does she clean in 1 hour? $\frac{1}{4}$

67. PAINTING HOUSES If a homeowner can paint a house in 14 days and a professional painter can paint it in 10 days, how long will it take if they work together? $5\frac{5}{6}$ days

68. EXERCISE A woman can bicycle 30 miles in the same time that it takes her to jog 10 miles. If she can ride 10 mph faster than she can jog, how fast can she jog? 5 mph

69. WIND SPEED A plane flies 400 miles downwind in the same amount of time as it takes to travel 320 miles upwind. If the plane can fly at 360 mph in still air, find the velocity of the wind. 40 mph

70. INVESTMENTS In one year, a student earned $100 interest on money she deposited at a savings and loan. She later learned that the money would have earned $120 if she had deposited it at a credit union, because the credit union paid 1% more interest at the time. Find the rate she received from the savings and loan. 5%

SECTION 7.8   Proportions and Similar Triangles

DEFINITIONS AND CONCEPTS	EXAMPLES
A **ratio** is the quotient of two numbers or two numbers with the same units. A **rate** is the quotient of two quantities with different units.	Ratios: $\dfrac{2}{3}$, $\dfrac{1}{50}$, and $2:3$ Rates: $\dfrac{4\ oz}{6\ lb}$, $\dfrac{525\ mi}{15\ hr}$, $\dfrac{\$1.95}{2\ lb}$
A **proportion** is a statement that two ratios or two rates are equal. In the proportion $\dfrac{a}{b} = \dfrac{c}{d}$, a and d are the **extremes,** and b and c are the **means.**	Proportions: $\dfrac{4}{9} = \dfrac{28}{63}$ Extremes: 4 and 63; $4 \cdot 63 = 252$ Means: 9 and 28; $9 \cdot 28 = 252$.
In any proportion, the product of the extremes is equal to the product of the means. **To solve a proportion,** set the product of the extremes equal to the product of the means and solve the resulting equation.	Solve the proportion: $\dfrac{3}{2} = \dfrac{x}{10}$ $\dfrac{3}{2} = \dfrac{x}{10}$ $3 \cdot 10 = 2 \cdot x$ The product of the extremes is equal to the product of the means. $30 = 2x$ $15 = x$ Solve for x.
The measures of corresponding sides of **similar triangles** are in proportion.	In these similar triangles: $\dfrac{a}{d} = \dfrac{b}{e} = \dfrac{c}{f}$ 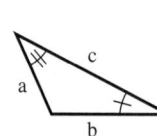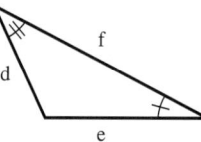

REVIEW EXERCISES

71. Find the ratio of the number of teeth of the larger gear to the number of teeth of the smaller gear? $\frac{3}{2}$

72. Determine whether $\frac{4}{7} = \frac{20}{34}$ is a proportion. no

Solve each proportion.

73. $\dfrac{3}{x} = \dfrac{6}{9}$ $\frac{9}{2}$

74. $\dfrac{x}{3} = \dfrac{x}{5}$ 0

75. $\dfrac{x-2}{5} = \dfrac{x}{7}$ 7

76. $\dfrac{2x}{x+4} = \dfrac{3}{x-1}$ $4, -\frac{3}{2}$

77. DENTISTRY The diagram in the illustration was displayed in a dentist's office. According to the diagram, if the dentist has 340 adult patients, how many will develop gum disease? 255

3 out of 4 adults will develop gum disease.

78. A telephone pole casts a shadow 12 feet long at the same time that a man 6 feet tall casts a shadow of 3.6 feet. How tall is the pole? 20 ft

SECTION 7.9   Variation

DEFINITIONS AND CONCEPTS	EXAMPLES
Direct variation: As one variable gets larger, the other gets larger as described by the equation $y = kx$, where k is the **constant of variation.**	The time t it takes to order at a fast-food drive-through *varies directly* with the number n of cars in line: $t = kn$.
Inverse variation: As one variable gets larger, the other gets smaller as described by the equation $y = \frac{k}{x}$ where k is a constant.	The time t it takes to read a book *varies inversely* with the reader's reading rate r: $t = \frac{k}{r}$.
Strategy for Solving Variation Problems: 1. Translate the verbal model into an equation. 2. Substitute a pair of values to find k. 3. Substitute the value of k into the variation equation. 4. Substitute the remaining given value into the equation from step 3 and answer the question.	Suppose d varies inversely with h. If $d = 5$ when $h = 4$, find d when $h = 10$. 1. The words *d varies inversely with h* translate into $d = \frac{k}{h}$. 2. If we substitute 5 for d and 4 for h, we have $$5 = \frac{k}{4} \quad \text{or} \quad k = 20$$ 3. Since $k = 20$, the inverse variation equation is $d = \frac{20}{h}$. 4. To answer the final question, substitute 10 for h. $$d = \frac{20}{10} = 2$$

REVIEW EXERCISES

Change each verbal model into a variation equation.

79. PHYSICAL FITNESS The number of calories c burned while jogging varies directly as the time t spent jogging. $c = kt$

80. GUITARS The frequency f of a vibrating string varies inversely with the length of the string. $f = \frac{k}{L}$

Solve each variation problem.

81. PROFIT The profit made by a strawberry farm varies directly with the number of baskets of strawberries sold. If a profit of $500 was made from the sale of 750 baskets, find the profit if 1,250 baskets are sold. $833.33

82. ELECTRICITY For a fixed voltage, the current in an electrical circuit varies inversely with the resistance in the circuit. If a certain circuit has a current of $2\frac{1}{2}$ amps when the resistance is 150 ohms, find the current in the circuit when the resistance is doubled. 1.25 amps

83. Give an example of two quantities that vary directly. answers vary

84. Does the graph illustrate direct or inverse variation? inverse variation

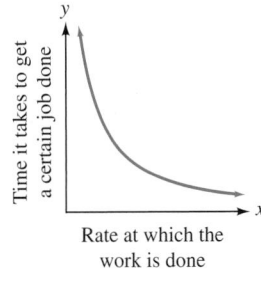

CHAPTER 7   TEST

1. Find the values of x for which $\dfrac{x}{x^2 + x - 6}$ is undefined. $-3, 2$

2. Simplify: $\dfrac{48x^2y}{54xy^2}$ $\dfrac{8x}{9y}$

3. Simplify: $\dfrac{2x^2 - x - 3}{4x^2 - 9}$ $\dfrac{x+1}{2x+3}$

4. Simplify: $\dfrac{3(x+2) - 3}{2x + 3 - (x+2)}$ 3

5. Multiply and simplify: $-\dfrac{12x^2y}{15xy} \cdot \dfrac{25y^2}{16x}$ $-\dfrac{5y^2}{4}$

6. Multiply and simplify: $\dfrac{x^2 + 3x + 2}{3x + 9} \cdot \dfrac{x + 3}{x^2 - 4}$ $\dfrac{x+1}{3(x-2)}$

7. Divide and simplify: $\dfrac{8x^2}{25x} \div \dfrac{16x^2}{30x}$ $\dfrac{3}{5}$

8. Divide and simplify: $\dfrac{x - x^2}{3x^2 + 6x} \div \dfrac{3x - 3}{3x^3 + 6x^2}$ $-\dfrac{x^2}{3}$

9. Simplify: $\dfrac{x^2 + x}{x - 1} \cdot \dfrac{x^2 - 1}{x^2 - 2x} \div \dfrac{x^2 + 2x + 1}{x^2 - 4}$ $x + 2$

10. Add: $\dfrac{5x - 4}{x - 1} + \dfrac{5x + 3}{x - 1}$ $\dfrac{10x - 1}{x - 1}$

11. Subtract: $\dfrac{3y + 7}{2y + 3} - \dfrac{3(y - 2)}{2y + 3}$ $\dfrac{13}{2y + 3}$

12. Add: $\dfrac{x + 1}{x} + \dfrac{x - 1}{x + 1}$ $\dfrac{2x^2 + x + 1}{x(x + 1)}$

13. Subtract: $\dfrac{a + 3}{a - 1} - \dfrac{a + 4}{1 - a}$ $\dfrac{2a + 7}{a - 1}$

14. Subtract: $\dfrac{2n}{5m} - \dfrac{n}{2}$ $\dfrac{4n - 5mn}{10m}$

15. Simplify: $\dfrac{1 + \dfrac{y}{x}}{\dfrac{y}{x} - 1}$ $\dfrac{x + y}{y - x}$ **16.** Solve: $\dfrac{1}{3} + \dfrac{4}{3y} = \dfrac{5}{y}$ 11

17. Solve: $\dfrac{7}{q^2 - q - 2} + \dfrac{1}{q + 1} = \dfrac{3}{q - 2}$ 1

18. Solve: $\dfrac{2}{3} = \dfrac{2c - 12}{3c - 9} - c$ $1, 2$

19. Solve: $\dfrac{9n}{n - 6} = 3 + \dfrac{54}{n - 6}$ no solution, 6 is extraneous

20. Solve for B: $H = \dfrac{RB}{R + B}$ $B = \dfrac{HR}{R - H}$

21. Is $\dfrac{3}{5} = \dfrac{51}{85}$ a proportion?   yes

22. Solve the proportion: $\dfrac{y}{y - 1} = \dfrac{y - 2}{y}$ $\dfrac{2}{3}$

23. HEALTH RISKS A medical newsletter states that a healthy waist-to-hip ratio for men is 19:20 or less. Does the patient shown below fall within the healthy range? yes

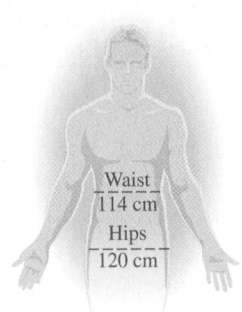

Waist
114 cm

Hips
120 cm

24. FLIGHT PATHS A plane drops 575 feet as it flies a horizontal distance of $\frac{1}{2}$ mile, as shown below. How much altitude will it lose as it flies a horizontal distance of 7 miles? 8,050 ft

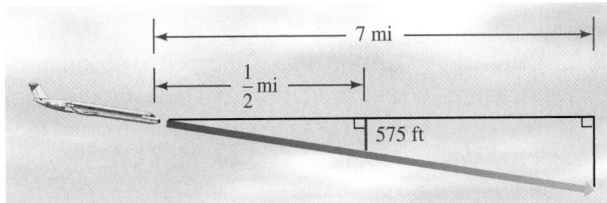

7 mi

$\frac{1}{2}$ mi

575 ft

25. POGO STICKS The force required to compress a spring varies directly with the change in the length of the spring. If a force of 130 pounds compresses the spring on the pogo stick 6.5 inches, how much force is required to compress the spring 5 inches? 100 lb

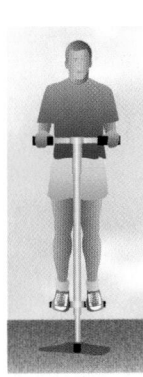

26. If i varies inversely with d, find the constant of variation if $i = 100$ when $d = 2$. 200

27. CLEANING HIGHWAYS One highway worker can pick up all the trash on a strip of highway in 7 hours, and his helper can pick up the trash in 9 hours. How long will it take them if they work together? $3\frac{15}{16}$ hr

28. BOATING A boat can motor 28 miles downstream in the same amount of time as it can motor 18 miles upstream. Find the speed of the current if the boat can motor at 23 mph in still water. 5 mph

29. Explain why we can remove the 5's in $\frac{5x}{5}$ and why we can't remove them in $\frac{5+x}{5}$.
We can remove only common factors, as in the first expression. We can't remove common terms, as in the second expression.

30. Explain what it means to clear the following equation of fractions.

$$\frac{u}{u-1} + \frac{1}{u} = \frac{u^2+1}{u^2-u}$$

Why is this a helpful first step in solving the equation?
We multiply both sides of the equation by the LCD of the rational expressions appearing in the equation. The resulting equation is easier to solve.

CHAPTERS 1–7 CUMULATIVE REVIEW

1. Evaluate: $9^2 - 3[45 - 3(6 - 4)]$ [Section 1.7] −36

2. **PAIN RELIEVERS** For a 12-month period, Tylenol had sales of \$567,600,000. Use the information in the illustration to determine the total amount of money spent on pain-relieving tablets for that 12-month period. [Section 2.3] \$2,580,000,000

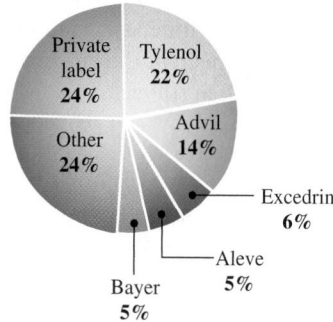

3. Find the average (mean) test score of a student in a history class with scores of 80, 73, 61, 73, and 98. [Section 1.7] 77

4. What is the value in cents of x 43¢ stamps? [Section 1.8] $43x$¢

5. Solve: $\dfrac{3}{4} = \dfrac{1}{2} + \dfrac{x}{5}$ [Section 2.2] $\dfrac{5}{4}$

6. Change 40°C to degrees Fahrenheit. [Section 2.4] 104°F

7. Find the volume of a pyramid that has a square base, measuring 6 feet on a side, and whose height is 20 feet. [Section 2.4] 240 ft³

8. Determine whether each statement is true or false.
   a. Every integer is a whole number. [Section 1.3] false
   b. 0 is not a rational number. [Section 1.3] false
   c. π is an irrational number. [Section 1.3] true
   d. The set of integers is the set of whole numbers and their opposites. [Section 1.3] true

9. Solve: $2 - 3(x - 5) = 4(x - 1)$ [Section 2.2] 3

10. Simplify: $8(c + 7) - 2(c - 3)$ [Section 2.2] $6c + 62$

11. Solve $A - c = 2B + r$ for B. [Section 2.4]
$$B = \frac{A - c - r}{2}$$

12. Solve $7x + 2 \geq 4x - 1$ and graph the solution. Then describe the graph using interval notation. [Section 2.7] $x \geq -1, [-1, \infty)$

13. Solve: $\dfrac{4}{5}d = -4$ [Section 2.2] −5

14. **BLENDING TEA** One grade of tea (worth \$3.20 per pound) is to be mixed with another grade (worth \$2 per pound) to make 20 pounds of a mixture that will be worth \$2.72 per pound. How much of each grade of tea must be used? [Section 2.6] 12 lb of the \$3.20 tea and 8 lb of the \$2 tea

15. **SPEED OF A PLANE** Two planes are 6,000 miles apart, and their speeds differ by 200 mph. If they travel toward each other and meet in 5 hours, find the speed of the slower plane. [Section 2.6] 500 mph

16. Graph: $y = 2x - 3$ [Section 3.3]

17. Graph: $y = (x + 2)^3$ [Section 3.2]

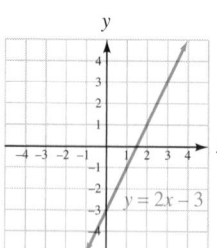

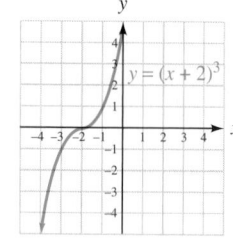

18. Find the slope of the line passing through $(-1, 3)$ and $(3, -1)$. [Section 3.4] −1

19. Write the equation of a line that has slope 3 and passes through the point $(1, 5)$. [Section 3.6]
$y = 3x + 2$

20. Graph: $3x - 2y = 6$ **21.** Graph: $y = \dfrac{5}{2}$

[Section 3.3]   [Section 3.3]

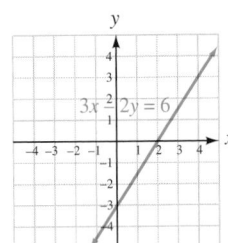   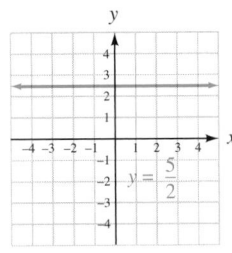

22. What is the slope of a line perpendicular to the line $y = -\dfrac{7}{8}x - 6$? [Section 3.5] $\frac{8}{7}$

23. Is this the graph of a function? [Section 3.8] no

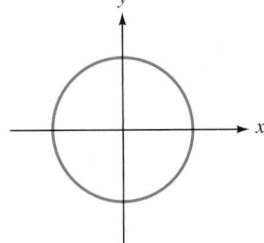

24. CUTTING STEEL The following graph shows the amount of wear (in mm) on a cutting blade for a given length of a cut (in m). Find the rate of change in the length of the cutting blade. [Section 3.4] 0.008 mm/m

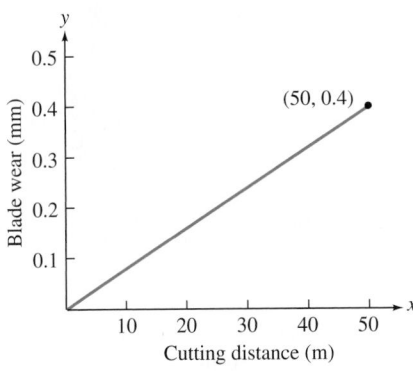
Cutting distance (m)

25. Find $f(-4)$ if $f(x) = \dfrac{x^2 - 2x}{2}$. [Section 3.8] 12

26. Evaluate: -5^2 [Section 5.1] -25

Simplify each expression. Write each answer without using negative exponents.

27. x^4x^3 [Section 5.1] x^7 **28.** $(x^2x^3)^5$ [Section 5.1] x^{25}

29. $\left(\dfrac{y^3y}{2yy^2}\right)^3$ [Section 5.1]   **30.** $\left(\dfrac{-2a}{b}\right)^5$ [Section 5.1]

$\dfrac{y^3}{8}$ $-\dfrac{32a^5}{b^5}$

31. $(a^{-2}b^3)^{-4}$ [Section 5.2]   **32.** $\dfrac{9b^0b^3}{3b^{-3}b^4}$ [Section 5.2]

$\dfrac{a^8}{b^{12}}$ $3b^2$

33. Write 290,000 in scientific notation.
[Section 5.3] 2.9×10^5

34. What is the degree of the polynomial $5x^3 - 4x + 16$?
[Section 5.4] 3

Perform the operations.

35. $(3x^2 - 3x - 2) + (3x^2 + 4x - 3)$
[Section 5.5] $6x^2 + x - 5$

36. $(2x^2y^3)(3x^3y^2)$ [Section 5.6] $6x^5y^5$

37. $(2y - 5)(3y + 7)$ [Section 5.6] $6y^2 - y - 35$

38. $-4x^2z(3x^2 - z)$ [Section 5.6] $-12x^4z + 4x^2z^2$

39. $\dfrac{6x + 9}{3}$ [Section 5.7]   **40.** $\dfrac{15(r^2s^3)^2}{-5(rs^5)^3}$ [Section 5.7]

$2x + 3$ $-\dfrac{3r}{s^9}$

41. LICENSE PLATES The number of different license plates of the form three digits followed by three letters, as shown, is $10 \cdot 10 \cdot 10 \cdot 26 \cdot 26 \cdot 26$. Write this expression using exponents. Then evaluate it.
[Section 5.1] $10^3 \cdot 26^3; 17,576,000$

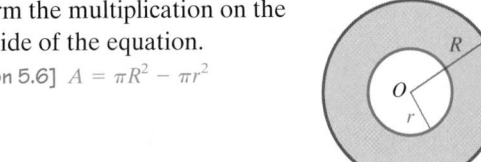

42. CONCENTRIC CIRCLES The area of the ring between the two concentric circles of radius r and R is given by the formula

$$A = \pi(R + r)(R - r)$$

Perform the multiplication on the right side of the equation.
[Section 5.6] $A = \pi R^2 - \pi r^2$

Factor each polynomial completely, if possible.

43. $k^3t - 3k^2t$ [Section 6.1] $k^2t(k - 3)$

44. $ax + bx + az + bz$ [Section 6.1] $(a + b)(x + z)$

45. $2a^2 - 200b^2$ [Section 6.4] $2(a + 10b)(a - 10b)$

46. $b^3 + 125$ [Section 6.5] $(b + 5)(b^2 - 5b + 25)$

47. $u^2 - 18u + 81$ [Section 6.4] $(u - 9)^2$

48. $6x^2 - 63 - 13x$ [Section 6.3] $(2x - 9)(3x + 7)$

49. $-r^2 + 2 + r$ [Section 6.3] $-(r - 2)(r + 1)$

50. $u^2 + 10u + 15$ [Section 6.2] prime

Solve each equation by factoring.

51. $5x^2 + x = 0$ [Section 6.7] $0, -\frac{1}{5}$

52. $6x^2 - 5x = -1$ [Section 6.7] $\frac{1}{3}, \frac{1}{2}$

53. COOKING The electric griddle shown has a cooking surface of 160 square inches. Find the length and the width of the griddle. [Section 6.8] 10 in., 16 in.

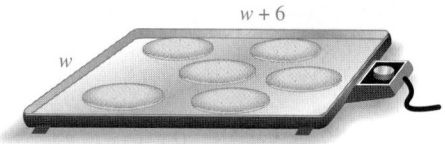

$w + 6$

w

54. For what values of x is the rational expression
$\dfrac{3x^2}{x^2 - 25}$ undefined? [Section 7.1] $5, -5$

Perform the operations and simplify, if possible.

55. $\dfrac{x^2 - 16}{x - 4} \div \dfrac{3x + 12}{x}$ [Section 7.2] $\frac{x}{3}$

56. $\dfrac{4}{x - 3} + \dfrac{5}{3 - x}$ [Section 7.4] $-\dfrac{1}{x - 3}$

57. $\dfrac{2 - \dfrac{2}{x + 1}}{2 + \dfrac{2}{x}}$ [Section 7.5] $\dfrac{x^2}{(x + 1)^2}$

58. $\dfrac{4a}{a - 2} - \dfrac{3a}{a - 3} + \dfrac{4a}{a^2 - 5a + 6}$ [Section 7.4] $\dfrac{a}{a - 3}$

Solve each equation.

59. $\dfrac{7}{5x} - \dfrac{1}{2} = \dfrac{5}{6x} + \dfrac{1}{3}$ [Section 7.6] $\dfrac{17}{25}$

60. $\dfrac{3}{5} + \dfrac{7}{x + 2} = 2$ [Section 7.6] 3

61. COMPUTING INTEREST For a fixed rate and principal, the interest earned in a bank account paying simple interest varies directly with the length of time the principal is left on deposit. If an investment earns $700 in 2 years, how much will it earn in 7 years? [Section 7.7] $2,450

62. HEIGHT OF A TREE A tree casts a shadow of 29 feet at the same time as a vertical yardstick casts a shadow of 2.5 feet. Find the height of the tree. [Section 7.8] 34.8 ft

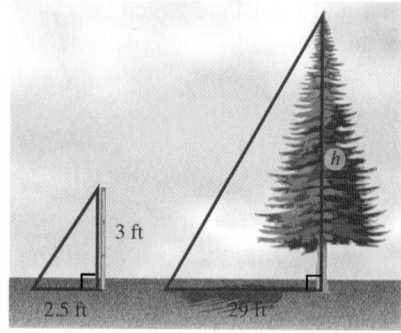

h

3 ft

2.5 ft   29 ft

63. DRAINING A TANK If one outlet pipe can drain a tank in 24 hours, and another pipe can drain the tank in 36 hours, how long will it take for both pipes to drain the tank? [Section 7.7] $14\frac{2}{5}$ hr

64. Explain what it means for two variables to vary inversely. [Section 7.9]
One variable is a constant multiple of the reciprocal of the other; $y = \frac{k}{x}$.

Roots and Radicals

Ira Block/Getty Images

from *Campus to Careers*

Archaeologists

Archaeologists examine and recover material evidence including the ruins of buildings, tools, pottery, and other objects remaining from past human cultures. They use these items to determine the history, customs, and living habits of earlier civilizations. Many archaeologists specialize in a particular region of the world. They may work under rugged conditions, and their work may involve strenuous physical exertion.

In **Problem 81** of **Study Set 8.1,** you will see how archaeologists can use the Pythagorean theorem to help them determine how far they are from base camp.

JOB TITLE: Archaeologist

EDUCATION: Graduates with a master's degree in archaeology usually are qualified for positions outside of colleges and universities. A Ph.D. degree may be required for higher-level positions. Training in statistics and mathematics is essential for many archaeologists.

JOB OUTLOOK: Excellent. Jobs are expected to grow 15% from 2006-2016, which is about as fast as average.

ANNUAL EARNINGS: In 2006, the median annual earnings for archaeologists working in various capacities were $49,930.

FOR MORE INFORMATION: www.bls.gov/oco/oco/ocos054.htm

Objectives

1 Find square roots of perfect squares.

2 Approximate irrational square roots.

3 Graph the square root function.

4 Use the Pythagorean theorem to solve problems.

SECTION **8.1**

Square Roots

To find the area A of the square shown in the figure, we multiply its length by its width.

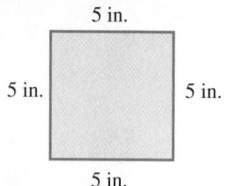

5 in.

5 in.   5 in.

5 in.

$$A = l \cdot w$$
$$A = 5 \cdot 5$$
$$ = 25$$

The area is 25 square inches.

We have seen that the product $5 \cdot 5$ can be denoted by the exponential expression 5^2, where 5 is raised to the second power. Whenever we raise a number to the second power, we are squaring it, or finding its **square.** This example illustrates that the formula for the area of a square with sides of length s is $A = s^2$.

Here are some more squares of numbers:

- The square of 3 is 9, because $3^2 = 9$.
- The square of -3 is 9, because $(-3)^2 = 9$.
- The square of 12 is 144, because $12^2 = 144$.
- The square of -12 is 144, because $(-12)^2 = 144$.
- The square of $\frac{1}{8}$ is $\frac{1}{64}$, because $\left(\frac{1}{8}\right)^2 = \frac{1}{8} \cdot \frac{1}{8} = \frac{1}{64}$.
- The square of $-\frac{1}{8}$ is $\frac{1}{64}$, because $\left(-\frac{1}{8}\right)^2 = \left(-\frac{1}{8}\right)\left(-\frac{1}{8}\right) = \frac{1}{64}$.
- The square of 0 is 0, because $0^2 = 0$.

In this section, we reverse the squaring process and find *square roots* of numbers.

1 Find square roots of perfect squares.

Suppose we know that the area of the square shown in the figure is 36 square inches. To find the length of each side, we substitute 36 for A in the formula $A = s^2$ and solve for s.

s in.

s in. $A = 36$ in.^{2} s in.

s in.

$$A = s^2$$
$$36 = s^2$$

To solve for s, we must find a positive number whose square is 36. Since 6 is such a number, the sides of the square are 6 inches long. The number 6 is called a *square root* of 36, because 6 is the positive number that we square to get 36.

Here are some more square roots of numbers:

- 3 is a square root of 9, because $3^2 = 9$.
- -3 is a square root of 9, because $(-3)^2 = 9$.
- 12 is a square root of 144, because $12^2 = 144$.
- -12 is a square root of 144, because $(-12)^2 = 144$.
- $\frac{1}{8}$ is a square root of $\frac{1}{64}$, because $\left(\frac{1}{8}\right)^2 = \left(\frac{1}{8}\right)\left(\frac{1}{8}\right) = \frac{1}{64}$.
- $-\frac{1}{8}$ is a square root of $\frac{1}{64}$, because $\left(-\frac{1}{8}\right)^2 = \left(-\frac{1}{8}\right)\left(-\frac{1}{8}\right) = \frac{1}{64}$.
- 0 is a square root of 0, because $0^2 = 0$.

In general, we have the following definition.

Square Root

The number b is a **square root** of a if $b^2 = a$.

All positive numbers have two square roots, one positive and one negative. The two square roots of 9 are 3 and -3, and the two square roots of 144 are 12 and -12. The number 0 is the only number that has one square root, which is 0.

The **principal square root** of a positive number is its positive square root. Although 3 and -3 are both square roots of 9, only 3 is the principal square root. The symbol $\sqrt{}$, called a **radical symbol,** is used to represent the principal square root of a number, and $-\sqrt{}$ is used to represent the negative square root of a number. For example, $\sqrt{9} = 3$ and $-\sqrt{9} = -3$. Likewise, $\sqrt{144} = 12$ and $-\sqrt{144} = -12$.

Principal Square Root

If a is positive, the expression $\sqrt{a}$ represents the **principal** (or positive) **square root** of a.

The principal square root of 0 is 0: $\sqrt{0} = 0$.

The expression under a radical symbol is called the **radicand.** In $\sqrt{9}$, the number 9 is the radicand, and the entire symbol $\sqrt{9}$ is called a **radical.** We read $\sqrt{9}$ as either "the square root of 9" or as "radical 9."

An algebraic expression containing a radical is called a **radical expression.** In this chapter, we will consider radical expressions such as

$$\sqrt{49}, \quad \frac{5}{\sqrt{3}}, \quad -2\sqrt{x+1}, \quad \text{and} \quad \sqrt{28y^2} - 2y\sqrt{63}$$

EXAMPLE 1 Find each square root:

a. $\sqrt{16}$ **b.** $\sqrt{1}$ **c.** $\sqrt{0.36}$ **d.** $\sqrt{\dfrac{4}{9}}$ **e.** $-\sqrt{225}$

Strategy In each case, we will determine the positive number, when squared, that produces the radicand.

WHY The radical symbol $\sqrt{}$ indicates that the positive square root (principal square root) of the number under it should be found.

Solution

a. $\sqrt{16} = 4$ Ask: What positive number, when squared, is 16? The answer is 4.

b. $\sqrt{1} = 1$ Ask: What positive number, when squared, is 1? The answer is 1.

c. $\sqrt{0.36} = 0.6$ Ask: What positive number, when squared, is 0.36? The answer is 0.6.

d. $\sqrt{\dfrac{4}{9}} = \dfrac{2}{3}$ Ask: What positive number, when squared, is $\frac{4}{9}$? The answer is $\frac{2}{3}$.

e. $-\sqrt{225}$ is the opposite of the square root of 225. Since $\sqrt{225} = 15$, we have
$-\sqrt{225} = -15$ $-\sqrt{225} = -1 \cdot \sqrt{225} = -1 \cdot 15 = -15.$ ∎

Square roots of certain numbers, such as 7, are hard to compute by hand. However, we can approximate $\sqrt{7}$ with a calculator.

Self Check 1

Find each square root:

a. $\sqrt{121}$ 11

b. $-\sqrt{49}$ -7

c. $\sqrt{0.64}$ 0.8

d. $\sqrt{256}$ 16

e. $\sqrt{\dfrac{1}{25}}$ $\frac{1}{5}$

f. $\sqrt{\dfrac{9}{49}}$ $\frac{3}{7}$

Now Try Problems 25, 29, and 32

Teaching Example 1 Find each square root:

a. $\sqrt{49}$ **b.** $-\sqrt{144}$

c. $\sqrt{0.81}$ **d.** $\sqrt{\dfrac{25}{49}}$

e. $\sqrt{0}$

Answers:

a. 7 **b.** -12

c. 0.9 **d.** $\frac{5}{7}$

e. 0

2 Approximate irrational square roots.

To find the principal square root of 7, we can enter 7 into a scientific calculator and press the $\sqrt{x}$ key. The approximate value of $\sqrt{7}$ will appear on the display.

$$\sqrt{7} \approx 2.6457513 \qquad \text{Read} \approx \text{as "is approximately equal to."}$$

Since $\sqrt{7}$ represents the number that, when squared, gives 7, we would expect squares of approximations of $\sqrt{7}$ to be close to 7.

- Rounded to one decimal place, $\sqrt{7} \approx 2.6$ and $(2.6)^2 = 6.76$.
- Rounded to two decimal places, $\sqrt{7} \approx 2.65$ and $(2.65)^2 = 7.0225$.
- Rounded to three decimal places, $\sqrt{7} \approx 2.646$ and $(2.646)^2 = 7.001316$.

Using Your **CALCULATOR**   **Freeway Road Sign**

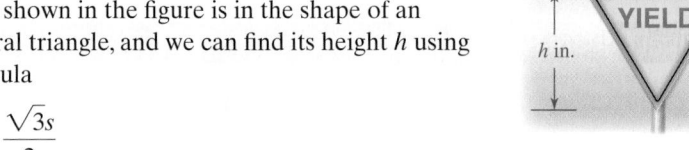

The sign shown in the figure is in the shape of an equilateral triangle, and we can find its height h using the formula

$$h = \frac{\sqrt{3}s}{2}$$

where s is the length of a side of the triangle. In this case, $s = 24$ inches, so we have

$$h = \frac{\sqrt{3}(24)}{2} \qquad \sqrt{3}(24) \text{ means } \sqrt{3} \cdot 24.$$

To evaluate this expression with a reverse-entry scientific calculator, we enter these numbers and press these keys.

$3 \;\boxed{\sqrt{x}}\; \boxed{\times}\; 24 \;\boxed{\div}\; 2 \;\boxed{=}$ $\boxed{\text{20.784609}}$

To evaluate this expression using a direct-entry or graphing calculator, we press these keys.

$\boxed{\text{2nd}}\; \boxed{\sqrt{}}\; 3 \;\boxed{)}\; \boxed{\times}\; 24 \;\boxed{\div}\; 2 \;\boxed{\text{ENTER}}$ $\boxed{\begin{array}{l}\sqrt{}(3)*24/2 \\ \qquad\qquad 20.78460969\end{array}}$

The height of the sign is approximately 21 inches.

THINK IT THROUGH   *Traffic Accidents*

"The U.S. Surgeon General reports that life expectancy has improved in the U.S. over the past 75 years for every age group except one: the death rate for 15- to 24-year-olds is higher today than it was 20 years ago. The leading cause of death is drunk/drugged driving."

Mothers Against Drunk Driving, MADD

Accident investigators often determine a vehicle's speed prior to braking from the length of the skid marks that it leaves on the street. To do this, they use the formula $s = \sqrt{30Df}$, where s is the speed of the vehicle in mph, D is the skid distance in feet, and f is the drag factor for the road surface. Estimate the speed of each vehicle prior to braking given the following conditions. Round to the nearest mile per hour.

1. Length of skid marks: 71 ft
   Road surface: asphalt, $f = 0.75$
   40 mph

2. Length of skid marks: 133 ft
   Road surface: concrete, $f = 0.90$
   60 mph

EXAMPLE 2 *Period of a Pendulum* The *period of a pendulum* is the time required for the pendulum to swing back and forth to complete one cycle. (See the figure.) The period (in seconds) of a pendulum having length L (in feet) is approximated by the function

$$f(L) = 1.11\sqrt{L} \quad \text{Read } 1.11\sqrt{L} \text{ as "1.11 times } \sqrt{L}\text{."}$$

Find the period of a pendulum that is 5 feet long.

Strategy We will substitute 5 for L in the formula, use a calculator to approximate $\sqrt{5}$ and multiply that value by 1.11.

WHY $1.11\sqrt{L}$ means $1.11 \cdot \sqrt{L}$.

Solution
We substitute 5 for L in the formula and multiply using a calculator.

$$f(L) = 1.11\sqrt{L}$$
$$f(5) = 1.11\sqrt{5} \quad 1.11\sqrt{5} \text{ means } 1.11 \cdot \sqrt{5}.$$
$$\approx 2.482035455$$

The period is approximately 2.5 seconds.

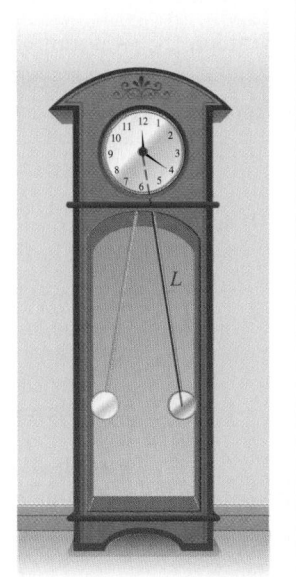

Whole numbers such as 4, 9, 16, and 49 are called **integer squares,** because each one is the square of an integer. The square root of any integer square is an integer and therefore a rational number:

$$\sqrt{4} = 2, \quad \sqrt{9} = 3, \quad \sqrt{16} = 4, \quad \text{and} \quad \sqrt{49} = 7$$

The square root of any whole number that is not an integer square is an **irrational number.** For example, $\sqrt{7}$ is an irrational number. Recall that the set of rational numbers and the set of irrational numbers together make up the set of real numbers.

EXAMPLE 3 Classify each square root as rational, irrational, or not a real number: **a.** $\sqrt{55}$ **b.** $\sqrt{-81}$ **c.** $-\sqrt{400}$

Strategy We need to determine whether the radicand is positive or negative and whether it is a perfect square.

WHY If a positive number is a perfect square, its square root is rational. If a positive number is not a perfect square, its square root is irrational. The square root of a negative number is not a real number.

Solution
a. Since 55 is positive, but not a perfect square, $\sqrt{55}$ is an irrational number. If we use a calculator and round to two decimal places, we find that $\sqrt{55} \approx 7.42$.

b. $\sqrt{-81}$ is not a real number because it is the square root of a negative number.

c. Since $400 = (20)^2$, it is a perfect square and $-\sqrt{400}$ is rational: $-\sqrt{400} = -20$.

Self Check 2

Find the period of a pendulum that is 3 feet long. about 1.9 sec

Now Try Problem 38

Teaching Example 2 Find the period of a pendulum that is 6 feet long.
Answer:
about 2.7 sec

Self Check 3

Classify each square root as rational, irrational, or not a real number:

a. $\sqrt{-6}$ **b.** $-\sqrt{37}$ **c.** $\sqrt{\frac{16}{9}}$

Now Try Problem 43
Self Check 3 Answers
a. not a real number   b. irrational
c. rational

Teaching Example 3 Classify each square root as rational, irrational, or not a real number:
a. $\sqrt{-36}$ **b.** $-\sqrt{25}$ **c.** $\sqrt{12}$
Answers:
a. not a real number   b. rational
c. irrational

> *Caution!*   Square roots of negative numbers are not real numbers. For example, $\sqrt{-4}$ is nonreal, because the square of no real number is -4. The number $\sqrt{-4}$ is an example from a set of numbers called **imaginary numbers.** Remember: *The square root of a negative number is not a real number.*

If we attempt to evaluate $\sqrt{-4}$ using a calculator, an error message like the ones shown below will be displayed.

Scientific calculator   Graphing calculator

In this chapter, we will assume that *all radicands under the square root symbols are either positive or zero.* Thus, all square roots will be real numbers.

3 Graph the square root function.

Since there is one principal square root for every nonnegative real number x, the equation $f(x) = \sqrt{x}$ determines a square root function. For example, the value that is determined by $f(x) = \sqrt{x}$ when $x = 4$ is denoted by $f(4)$, and we have $f(4) = \sqrt{4} = 2$.

To graph this function, we make a table of values and plot each ordered pair. Then, from the origin, we draw a smooth curve that passes through the points. In the table, we chose five values for x: 0, 1, 4, 9, and 16, that are integer squares. This made computing $f(x)$ quite simple. The graph appears in the figure below.

$f(x) = \sqrt{x}$		
x	$f(x)$	$(x, f(x))$
0	0	$(0, 0)$
1	1	$(1, 1)$
4	2	$(4, 2)$
9	3	$(9, 3)$
16	4	$(16, 4)$

Values to be input into $\sqrt{x}$ Output values   Ordered pairs to plot

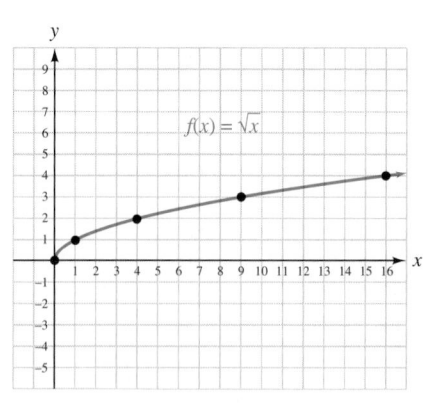

4 Use the Pythagorean theorem to solve problems.

The longest side of a right triangle is the **hypotenuse,** which is the side opposite the right angle. The remaining two sides are the **legs** of the triangle. See the figure to the right. Recall that the **Pythagorean theorem** provides a formula relating the lengths of the three sides of a right triangle.

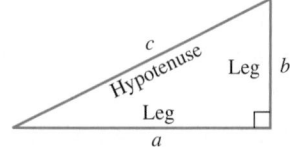

The Pythagorean Theorem

If the length of the hypotenuse of a right triangle is c and the lengths of the two legs are a and b,

$$c^2 = a^2 + b^2$$

Since the lengths of the sides of a triangle are positive numbers, we can use the **square root property of equality** and the Pythagorean theorem to find the length of the third side of any right triangle when the measures of two sides are given.

Square Root Property of Equality

If a and b represent positive numbers, and if $a = b$,

$$\sqrt{a} = \sqrt{b}$$

EXAMPLE 4 *Picture Frames* After gluing together two pieces of picture frame, the maker checks her work by making a diagonal measurement. (See the figure below.) If the sides of the frame form a right angle, what measurement should the maker read on the yardstick?

Analyze The 15- and 20-inch sides of the frame in the figure are the legs of a right triangle, and the diagonal measurement is the hypotenuse. We need to find the length of the diagonal using the Pythagorean theorem.

Form We can use the Pythagorean theorem to form an equation. We substitute 15 for a, 20 for b, and let c represent the length of the hypotenuse.

Solve

$c^2 = a^2 + b^2$ This is the Pythagorean theorem.

$c^2 = 15^2 + 20^2$ Substitute 15 for a and 20 for b.

$c^2 = 225 + 400$ $15^2 = 225$ and $20^2 = 400$.

$c^2 = 625$ Perform the addition: $225 + 400 = 625$.

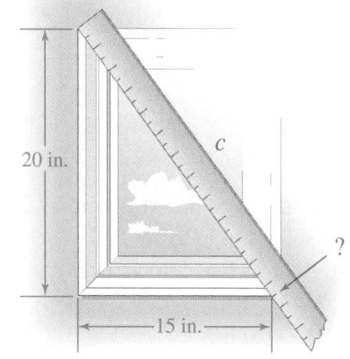

20 in.

15 in.

c

?

To find c, we must find a number that, when squared, is 625. There are two such numbers, one positive and one negative. They are called the *square roots* of 625. Since c represents the length of the hypotenuse, c cannot be negative. Thus, we need only determine the positive square root of 625.

$c^2 = 625$ This is the equation to solve.

$\sqrt{c^2} = \sqrt{625}$ To find c, we undo the operation performed on it by taking the positive square root of both sides. Recall that a radical symbol $\sqrt{}$ is used to indicate the positive square root of a number.

$c = 25$ $\sqrt{c^2} = c$ because $(c)^2 = c^2$, and $\sqrt{625} = 25$ because $25^2 = 625$.

State The diagonal distance should measure 25 inches. If it does not, the sides of the frame do not form a right angle.

Check If the diagonal is 25 inches, we have $15^2 + 20^2 = 225 + 400 = 625$, which is 25^2. The answer, 25, checks.

> **Success Tip** When using the Pythagorean theorem $c^2 = a^2 + b^2$, we can let a represent the length of either leg of the right triangle in question. We then let b represent the length of the other leg. The variable c must always represent the length of the hypotenuse.

Self Check 5

A support line for a 6-foot badminton pole is 10 feet long. How far from the base of the pole should the line be anchored so that the pole and the ground form a right angle?   8 ft

Now Try **Problem 83**

Teaching Example 5 A carpenter is using an 8-foot angle brace to support a 6-foot-wide balcony. How far below the balcony should the end of the brace be attached so that the balcony makes a right angle with the building? (Round to nearest tenth.)
Answer:
5.3 ft

EXAMPLE 5 *Building a High Ropes Adventure Course* The builder of a high ropes course wants to use a 25-foot cable to stabilize the vertical pole shown in the figure. To be safe, the ground anchor stake must be farther than 18 feet from the base of the pole. Is the cable long enough to use?

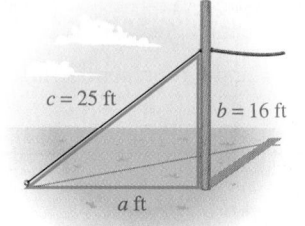

Analyze The pole should make a right angle with the ground, with the cable being the hypotenuse.

Form We can use the Pythagorean theorem to form an equation. We substitute 16 for b, 25 for c, and let a represent the distance from the pole to the stake.

Solve We use the Pythagorean theorem, with $b = 16$ and $c = 25$, to find a.

$$c^2 = a^2 + b^2$$
$$25^2 = a^2 + 16^2 \quad \text{Substitute 25 for } c \text{ and 16 for } b.$$
$$625 = a^2 + 256 \quad 25^2 = 625 \text{ and } 16^2 = 256.$$
$$369 = a^2 \quad \text{To isolate } a^2, \text{ subtract 256 from both sides.}$$
$$\sqrt{369} = \sqrt{a^2} \quad \text{To find } a, \text{ we undo the operation that is performed on it (squaring) by taking the positive square root of both sides.}$$
$$19.209373 \approx a \quad \text{Use a calculator to approximate } \sqrt{369}.$$

State Since the anchor stake will be more than 18 feet from the base, the 25-foot cable is long enough to use.

Check If the stake is about 19.209373 feet from the base of the pole, we have $(19.209373)^2 + (16)^2 \approx 369 + 256 = 625$, which is 25^2. Since 19.209373 feet is more than 18 feet, the answer checks.

Self Check 6

A 13-foot ladder rests against the side of a building. If the ladder reaches 12 feet up the wall, how far from the building is the base of the ladder?   5 ft

Now Try **Problem 75**

EXAMPLE 6 *Reach of a Ladder* A 26-foot ladder rests against the side of a building. If the base of the ladder is 10 feet from the wall, how far up the building will the ladder reach?

Analyze The wall, the ground, and the ladder form a right triangle, as shown in the figure. In this triangle, the hypotenuse is 26 feet, and one of the legs is the base-to-wall distance of 10 feet. We can let $x =$ the length of the other leg, which is the distance that the ladder will reach up the wall.

Form We use the Pythagorean theorem to form the equation.

The hypotenuse squared	is	one leg squared	plus	the other leg squared.
26^2	$=$	10^2	$+$	x^2

Solve

$$26^2 = 10^2 + x^2$$
$$676 = 100 + x^2 \qquad 26^2 = 676 \text{ and } 10^2 = 100.$$
$$676 - 100 = x^2 \qquad \text{To isolate } x^2, \text{ subtract 100 from both sides.}$$
$$576 = x^2 \qquad 676 - 100 = 576.$$
$$\sqrt{576} = \sqrt{x^2} \qquad \text{Take the positive square root of both sides.}$$
$$24 = x \qquad \sqrt{576} = 24 \text{ because } 24^2 = 576.$$

State The ladder will reach 24 feet up the side of the building.

Check If the ladder reaches 24 feet up the side of the building, we have $10^2 + 24^2 = 100 + 576 = 676$, which is 26^2. The answer, 24, checks.

EXAMPLE 7 *Roof Design* The gable end of the roof shown in the figure is an isosceles right triangle with a span of 48 feet. Find the distance from the eaves to the peak.

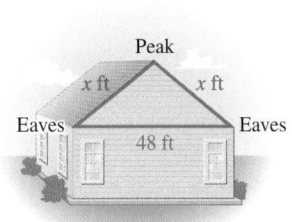

Analyze The two equal sides of the isosceles triangle are the two legs of the right triangle, and the span of 48 feet is the length of the hypotenuse. We can let x = the length of each leg, which is the distance from eaves to peak.

Form We use the Pythagorean theorem to form the equation.

The hypotenuse squared	is	one leg squared	plus	the other leg squared.
48^2	$=$	x^2	$+$	x^2

Solve

$$48^2 = x^2 + x^2$$
$$2{,}304 = 2x^2 \qquad 48^2 = 2{,}304 \text{ and } x^2 + x^2 = 2x^2.$$
$$1{,}152 = x^2 \qquad \text{To isolate } x^2, \text{ divide both sides by 2.}$$
$$\sqrt{1{,}152} = \sqrt{x^2} \qquad \text{Take the positive square root of both sides.}$$
$$33.9411255 \approx x \qquad \text{Use a calculator to approximate } \sqrt{1{,}152}.$$

State The eaves-to-peak distance of the roof is approximately 34 feet.

Check If the eaves-to-peak distance is approximately 34 feet, we have $34^2 + 34^2 = 1{,}156 + 1{,}156 = 2{,}312$, which is approximately 48^2. The answer, 34, seems reasonable.

ANSWERS TO SELF CHECKS

1. a. 11 **b.** -7 **c.** 0.8 **d.** 16 **e.** $\frac{1}{5}$ **f.** $\frac{3}{7}$ **2.** about 1.9 sec **3. a.** not a real number **b.** irrational **c.** rational **4.** 5 ft **5.** 8 ft **6.** 5 ft **7.** about 18.4 cm

SECTION **8.1** STUDY SET

VOCABULARY

Fill in the blanks.

1. b is a _square_ root of a if $b^2 = a$.

2. The symbol $\sqrt{}$ is called a _radical_ symbol.

3. The principal square root of a positive number is a _positive_ number.

▶ 4. The number under the radical sign is called the _radicand_.

5. If a triangle has a right angle, it is called a _right_ triangle.

6. The longest side of a right triangle is called the _hypotenuse_, and the other two sides are called _legs_.

CONCEPTS

Fill in the blanks.

7. The number 25 has _two_ square roots. They are _5_ and _−5_.

8. $\sqrt{-11}$ is not a _real_ number.

9. If the length of the hypotenuse of a right triangle is c and the legs are a and b, then $c^2 = $ _$a^2 + b^2$_.

10. The hypotenuse squared is one leg _squared_ plus the other leg _squared_.

11. If a and b are positive numbers and $a = b$, then $\sqrt{a} = $ _$\sqrt{b}$_.

▶ 12. 2 is a square _root_ of 4, because $2^2 = 4$.

13. To isolate x, what step should be used to undo the operation performed on it? (Assume that x is a positive number.)

   a. $2x = 16$ Divide both sides by 2.

   b. $x^2 = 16$ Take the positive square root of both sides.

🔲 14. Graph each number on the number line.

$$\left\{ \sqrt{16},\ -\sqrt{\frac{9}{4}},\ \sqrt{1.8},\ \sqrt{6},\ -\sqrt{23} \right\}$$

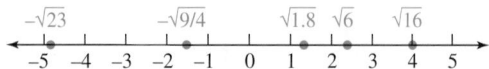

15. Complete the table. Do not use a calculator.

x	$\sqrt{x}$
0	0
$\dfrac{1}{81}$	$\dfrac{1}{9}$
0.16	0.4
36	6
400	20

16. If $f(x) = \sqrt{x}$, find each value. **Do not use a calculator.**

   a. $f(81)$ 9   b. $f(1)$ 1   c. $f(0.25)$ 0.5

   d. $f\left(\dfrac{1}{121}\right)$ $\dfrac{1}{11}$ e. $f(900)$ 30

17. a. Use the dashed lines in the following graph to approximate $\sqrt{5}$. $\sqrt{5} \approx 2.2$

   b. Use the graph to approximate $\sqrt{3}$ and $\sqrt{8}$.
   $\sqrt{3} \approx 1.7,\ \sqrt{8} \approx 2.8$

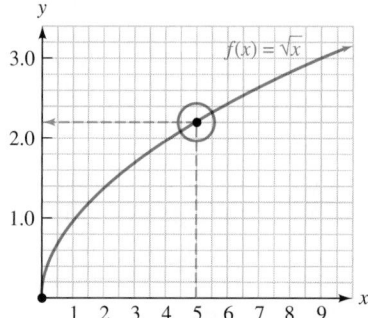

18. A calculator was used to find $\sqrt{-16}$. Explain the message shown on the calculator display.

   There is an error: $\sqrt{-16}$ is not a real number.

NOTATION

Complete each solution.

▶ 19. If the legs of a right triangle measure 5 and 12 centimeters, find the length of the hypotenuse.

$$c^2 = a^2 + b^2$$
$$c^2 = 5^2 + 12^2$$
$$c^2 = 25 + 144$$
$$c^2 = 169$$
$$\sqrt{c^2} = \sqrt{169}$$
$$c = 13$$

20. If the hypotenuse of a right triangle measures 25 centimeters and one leg measures 24 centimeters, find the length of the other leg.

$$c^2 = a^2 + b^2$$
$$25^2 = 24^2 + b^2$$
$$625 = 576 + b^2$$
$$49 = b^2$$
$$\sqrt{49} = \sqrt{b}$$
$$7 = b$$

21. Is the statement $-\sqrt{9} = \sqrt{-9}$ true or false? Explain your answer.

False; $-\sqrt{9} = -3$, $\sqrt{-9}$ is not a real number.

22. Consider the statement $\sqrt{26} \approx 5.1$. Explain why an $\approx$ symbol is used instead of an $=$ symbol.

Since $(5.1)^2$ is 26.01, rather than exactly 26, we write $\sqrt{26} \approx 5.1$.

GUIDED PRACTICE

Find each square root without using a calculator. **See Example 1.**

23. $\sqrt{25}$ 5
24. $\sqrt{49}$ 7
25. $\sqrt{196}$ 14
26. $\sqrt{169}$ 13
27. $-\sqrt{81}$ −9
28. $-\sqrt{36}$ −6
29. $\sqrt{1.21}$ 1.1
30. $\sqrt{1.69}$ 1.3
31. $\sqrt{\dfrac{9}{256}}$ $\dfrac{3}{16}$
32. $\sqrt{\dfrac{4}{225}}$ $\dfrac{2}{15}$
33. $-\sqrt{289}$ −17
34. $-\sqrt{324}$ −18

Use a calculator to evaluate each expression to three decimal places. **See Objective 2.**

35. $\sqrt{2}$ 1.414
36. $\sqrt{3}$ 1.732
37. $\sqrt{11}$ 3.317
38. $\sqrt{53}$ 7.280
39. $\sqrt{95}$ 9.747
40. $\sqrt{99}$ 9.950
41. $\sqrt{428}$ 20.688
42. $\sqrt{844}$ 29.052

Determine whether each number in each set is rational, irrational, or imaginary. **See Example 3.**

43. $\left\{\sqrt{9}, \sqrt{17}\right\}$
$\sqrt{9}$ rational, $\sqrt{17}$ irrational

44. $\left\{-\sqrt{5}, \sqrt{0}\right\}$
$-\sqrt{5}$ irrational, $\sqrt{0}$ rational

45. $\left\{\sqrt{49}, \sqrt{-49}\right\}$
$\sqrt{49}$ rational, $\sqrt{-49}$ imaginary

46. $\left\{\sqrt{-100}, -\sqrt{225}\right\}$
$\sqrt{-100}$ imaginary, $-\sqrt{225}$ rational

Complete the table and graph the function. **See Objective 3.**

47. $f(x) = 1 + \sqrt{x}$

x	f(x)
0	1
1	2
4	3
9	4
16	5

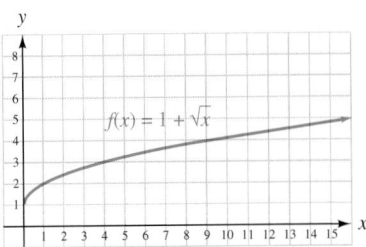

48. $f(x) = -1 + \sqrt{x}$

x	f(x)
0	−1
1	0
4	1
9	2
16	3

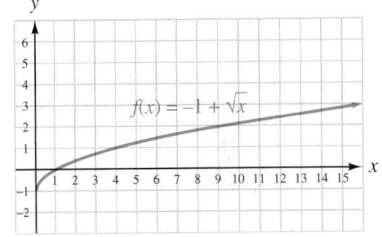

49. $f(x) = -\sqrt{x}$

x	f(x)
0	0
1	−1
4	−2
9	−3
16	−4

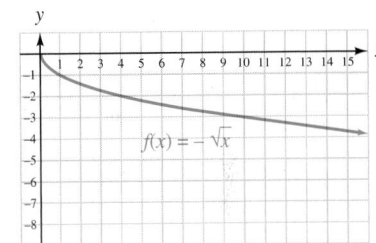

50. $f(x) = 1 - \sqrt{x}$

x	f(x)
0	1
1	0
4	−1
9	−2
16	−3

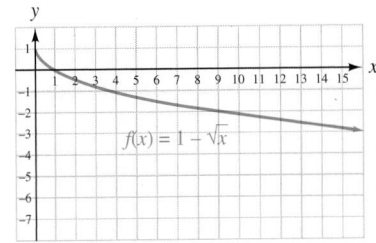

Refer to the following right triangle and find the length of the unknown side. **See Example 4.**

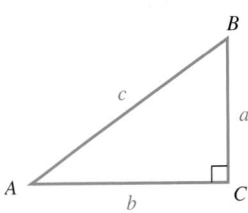

51. Find c if $a = 4$ and $b = 3$. 5

▶ **52.** Find c if $a = 5$ and $b = 12$. 13

53. Find b if $a = 15$ and $c = 17$. 8

▶ **54.** Find b if $a = 21$ and $c = 29$. 20

TRY IT YOURSELF

 Find each square root. You may use a calculator.

55. $-\sqrt{2,500}$ −50   **56.** $-\sqrt{625}$ −25

57. $\sqrt{3,600}$ 60   ▶ **58.** $\sqrt{1,600}$ 40

59. $-\sqrt{9,876}$ −99.378   **60.** $-\sqrt{3,619}$ −60.158

61. $\sqrt{21.35}$ 4.621   **62.** $\sqrt{13.78}$ 3.712

63. $\sqrt{0.3588}$ 0.599   **64.** $\sqrt{0.9999}$ 1.000

65. $-\sqrt{0.8372}$ −0.915   **66.** $-\sqrt{0.4279}$ −0.654

67. $2\sqrt{3}$ 3.464   ▶ **68.** $3\sqrt{2}$ 4.243

69. $\dfrac{2 + \sqrt{3}}{2}$ 1.866   **70.** $\dfrac{2 - \sqrt{3}}{2}$ 0.134

Refer to the right triangle on the previous page for Problems 51–54 and find the length of the unknown side.

▶ **71.** Find a if $b = 16$ and $c = 34$. 30

▶ **72.** Find a if $b = 45$ and $c = 53$. 28

73. Find b if $c = 125$ and $a = 44$. 117

74. Find c if $a = 176$ and $b = 57$. 185

APPLICATIONS

Use a calculator to help solve each problem. If an answer is not exact, give it to the nearest tenth. **See Examples 2–7.**

75. ADJUSTING A LADDER 20-foot ladder reaches a window 16 feet above the ground. How far from the wall is the base of the ladder? 12 ft

▶ **76.** LINE OF SIGHT A movie viewer in a car parked at a drive-in theater sits 600 feet from the base of the vertical screen. What is the line-of-sight distance for the viewer to the middle of the screen, which is 35 feet above the base? 601.0 ft

77. QUALITY CONTROL How can a tool manufacturer use the Pythagorean theorem to verify that the two sides of the carpenter's square shown meet to form a 90° angle?
The diagonal measurement should be $\sqrt{16^2 + 30^2} = 34$ in.

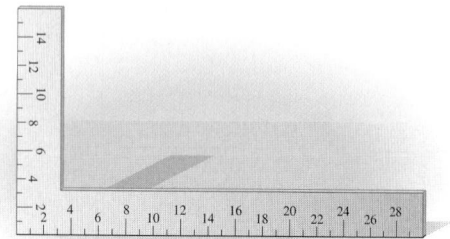

▶ **78.** GARDENING A rectangular garden has sides of 28 and 45 feet. Find the length of a path that extends from one corner to the opposite corner. 53 ft

79. BASEBALL A baseball diamond is a square, with each side 90 feet long, as shown. How far is it from home plate to second base? 127.3 ft

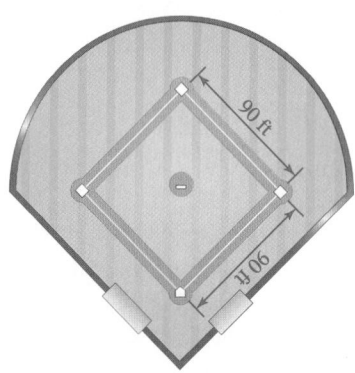

▶ **80.** TELEVISION The size of a television screen is the diagonal distance from the upper left to the lower right corner. What is the size of the screen shown? 27.0 in.

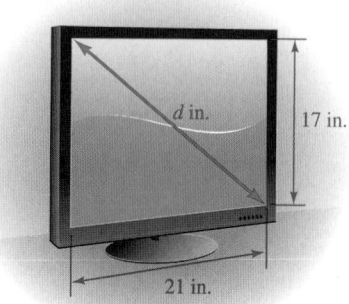

81. FINDING LOCATION **from Campus to Careers** / **Archaeologist** A team of archaeologists travels 4.2 miles east and then 4.0 miles north of their base camp to explore some ancient ruins. "As the crow flies," how far from their base camp are they? 5.8 mi

▶ **82.** SHORTCUTS Instead of walking on the sidewalk, students take a diagonal shortcut across the rectangular vacant lot shown. How much distance do they save? 44 ft

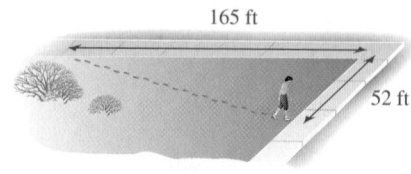

165 ft   52 ft

83. FOOTBALL On first down and ten, a quarterback tells his tight end to go out 6 yards, cut 45° to the right, and run 6 yards, as shown. The tight end follows instructions, catches a pass, and is tackled immediately.

   a. Find x. $\sqrt{18}$ yd ≈ 4.2 yd

   b. Does he gain the necessary 10 yards for a first down? yes

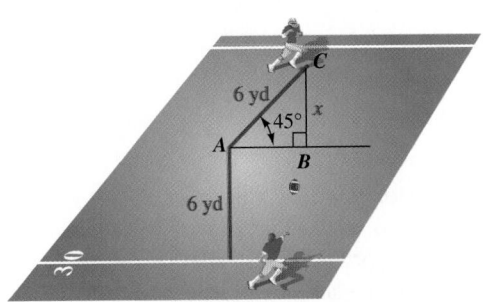

▶ **84. GEOMETRY** The legs of a right triangle are equal, and the hypotenuse is 2.82843 units long. Find the length of each leg. 2.0 units

85. WRESTLING The sides of a square wrestling ring are 18 feet long. Find the distance from one corner to the opposite corner. 25.5 ft

▶ **86. PERIMETER OF A SQUARE** The diagonal of a square is 3 feet long. Find its perimeter. 8.5 ft

87. HEIGHT OF A TRIANGLE Find the area of the isosceles triangle shown. 240 in.²

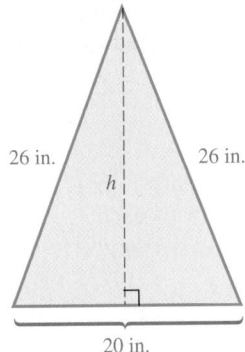

26 in.   26 in.

h

20 in.

▶ **88. INTERIOR DECORATING** The following square table is covered by a circular tablecloth. If the sides of the table are 2 feet long, find the area of the tablecloth. 6.3 ft²

2 ft
2 ft   2 ft
2 ft

89. DRAFTING Refer to the illustration in the next column. Among the tools used in drafting are 30–60–90 and 45–45–90 triangles.

a. Find the length of the hypotenuse of the 45–45–90 triangle if it is $\sqrt{2}$ times as long as a leg. 8.5 in.

b. Find the length of the side opposite the 60° angle of the other triangle if it is $\dfrac{\sqrt{3}}{2}$ times as long as the hypotenuse. 7.8 in.

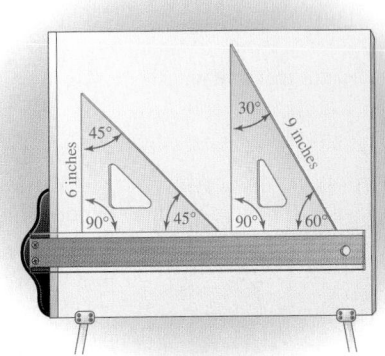

▶ **90. ORGAN PIPES** The design for a set of brass pipes for a church organ is shown. Find the length of each pipe (to the nearest tenth of a foot), and then find the total length of pipe needed to construct this set. 2, 2.8, 3.5, 4, 4.5, 4.9, 5.3, 5.7, and 6 ft; 38.7 ft

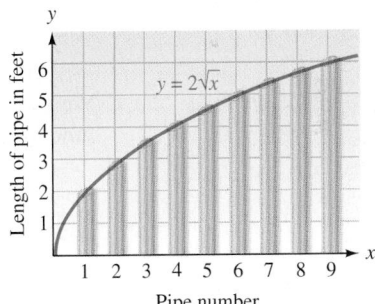

WRITING

91. Explain why the square root of a negative number cannot be a real number.

92. Explain the Pythagorean theorem.

93. Suppose you are told that $\sqrt{10}$ ≈ 3.16. Explain how another key on your calculator (besides the square root key $\sqrt{}$) could be used to see whether this is a reasonable approximation.

▶ **94.** Explain the difference between the *square* of a number and the *square root* of a number.

REVIEW

95. Add: $(3s^2 - 3s - 2) + (3s^2 + 4s - 3)$ $6s^2 + s - 5$

▶ **96.** Subtract: $(3c^2 - 2c + 4) - (c^2 - 3c + 7)$ $2c^2 + c - 3$

97. Multiply: $(3x - 2)(x + 4)$ $3x^2 + 10x - 8$

▶ **98.** Divide $x^2 + 13x + 12$ by $x + 1$. $x + 12$

Objectives

1 Find cube roots of perfect cubes.

2 Approximate irrational cube roots.

3 Graph the cube root function.

4 Find higher-order roots.

5 Simplify radicands that contain variables.

SECTION 8.2

Higher-Order Roots; Radicands That Contain Variables

To find the volume V of the cube shown in the figure, we multiply its length, width, and height.

$$V = l \cdot w \cdot h$$
$$V = 5 \cdot 5 \cdot 5$$
$$= 125$$

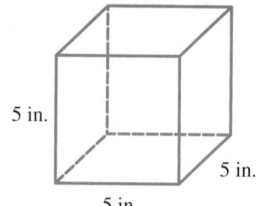

5 in.

5 in.

5 in.

The volume is 125 cubic inches.

We have seen that $5 \cdot 5 \cdot 5$ can be denoted by the exponential expression 5^3, where 5 is raised to the third power. Whenever we raise a number to the third power, we are cubing it, or finding its **cube.** This example illustrates that the formula for the volume of a cube with each side of length s is $V = s^3$.

Here are some more cubes of numbers:

- The cube of 3 is 27, because $3^3 = 27$.
- The cube of -3 is -27, because $(-3)^3 = -27$.
- The cube of 12 is 1,728, because $12^3 = 1,728$.
- The cube of -12 is $-1,728$, because $(-12)^3 = -1,728$.
- The cube of $\frac{1}{4}$ is $\frac{1}{64}$, because $\left(\frac{1}{4}\right)^3 = \frac{1}{4} \cdot \frac{1}{4} \cdot \frac{1}{4} = \frac{1}{64}$.
- The cube of $-\frac{1}{4}$ is $-\frac{1}{64}$, because $\left(-\frac{1}{4}\right)^3 = \left(-\frac{1}{4}\right)\left(-\frac{1}{4}\right)\left(-\frac{1}{4}\right) = -\frac{1}{64}$.
- The cube of 0 is 0, because $0^3 = 0$.

In this section, we will reverse the cubing process and find **cube roots** of numbers. We will also consider fourth roots, fifth roots, and so on. After graphing the cube root function, we will work with radical expressions having radicands containing variables.

1 **Find the cube roots of perfect cubes.**

Suppose we know that the volume of the cube shown in the figure is 216 cubic inches. To find the length of each side, we substitute 216 for V in the formula $V = s^3$ and solve for s.

$$V = s^3$$
$$\mathbf{216} = s^3$$

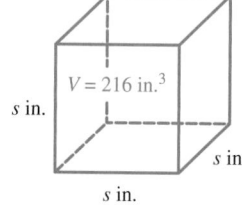

$V = 216$ in.^{3}

s in.

s in.

s in.

To solve for s, we must find a number whose cube is 216. Since 6 is such a number, the sides of the cube are 6 inches long. The number 6 is called a *cube root* of 216, because $6^3 = 216$.

Here are more examples of cube roots:

- 3 is a cube root of 27, because $3^3 = 27$.
- -3 is a cube root of -27, because $(-3)^3 = -27$.
- 12 is a cube root of 1,728, because $12^3 = 1,728$.
- -12 is a cube root of $-1,728$, because $(-12)^3 = -1,728$.
- $\frac{1}{4}$ is a cube root of $\frac{1}{64}$, because $\left(\frac{1}{4}\right)^3 = \left(\frac{1}{4}\right)\left(\frac{1}{4}\right)\left(\frac{1}{4}\right) = \frac{1}{64}$.
- $-\frac{1}{4}$ is a cube root of $-\frac{1}{64}$, because $\left(-\frac{1}{4}\right)^3 = \left(-\frac{1}{4}\right)\left(-\frac{1}{4}\right)\left(-\frac{1}{4}\right) = -\frac{1}{64}$.
- 0 is a cube root of 0, because $0^3 = 0$.

In general, we have the following definition.

Cube Root

The number b is a **cube root** of a if $b^3 = a$.

All real numbers have one real cube root. As the preceding examples show, a positive number has a positive cube root, a negative number has a negative cube root, and the cube root of 0 is 0.

Cube Root Notation

The cube root of a is denoted by $\sqrt[3]{a}$. By definition,

$$\sqrt[3]{a} = b \qquad \text{if} \qquad b^3 = a$$

EXAMPLE 1   Find each cube root:
a. $\sqrt[3]{8}$ **b.** $\sqrt[3]{343}$ **c.** $\sqrt[3]{-8}$ **d.** $\sqrt[3]{-125}$ **e.** $-\sqrt[3]{1000}$

Strategy In each case, we will determine what number, when cubed, produces the radicand.

WHY The symbol $\sqrt[3]{}$ indicates that the cube root of the number written under it should be found.

Solution
a. $\sqrt[3]{8} = 2$, because $2^3 = 8$.

b. $\sqrt[3]{343} = 7$, because $7^3 = 343$.

c. $\sqrt[3]{-8} = -2$, because $(-2)^3 = -8$.

d. $\sqrt[3]{-125} = -5$, because $(-5)^3 = -125$.

e. $-\sqrt[3]{1,000}$ is the opposite of the cube root of 1,000. Since $\sqrt[3]{1,000}$ is 10, we have
$-\sqrt[3]{1,000} = -10$. $-\sqrt[3]{1,000} = -1 \cdot \sqrt[3]{1,000} = -1 \cdot 10 = -10.$

EXAMPLE 2   Find each cube root: **a.** $\sqrt[3]{\dfrac{1}{8}}$ **b.** $\sqrt[3]{-\dfrac{125}{27}}$

Strategy We will determine what number, when cubed, produces the radicand.

WHY The symbol $\sqrt[3]{}$ indicates that the cube root of the number written under it should be found.

Solution
a. $\sqrt[3]{\dfrac{1}{8}} = \dfrac{1}{2}$, because $\left(\dfrac{1}{2}\right)^3 = \dfrac{1}{2} \cdot \dfrac{1}{2} \cdot \dfrac{1}{2} = \dfrac{1}{8}$.

b. $\sqrt[3]{-\dfrac{125}{27}} = -\dfrac{5}{3}$, because $\left(-\dfrac{5}{3}\right)^3 = \left(-\dfrac{5}{3}\right)\left(-\dfrac{5}{3}\right)\left(-\dfrac{5}{3}\right) = -\dfrac{125}{27}$.

Cube roots of numbers such as 7 are hard to compute by hand. However, we can approximate $\sqrt[3]{7}$ with a calculator.

2 Approximate irrational cube roots.

To find $\sqrt[3]{7}$, we can enter 7 into a reverse-entry scientific calculator, press the root key $\sqrt[x]{y}$, enter 3, and press the = key. The approximate value of $\sqrt[3]{7}$ will appear on the calculator's display.

$$\sqrt[3]{7} \approx 1.912931183$$

Self Check 1

Find each cube root:
a. $\sqrt[3]{64}$ 4
b. $\sqrt[3]{-64}$ −4
c. $\sqrt[3]{216}$ 6
d. $-\sqrt[3]{125}$ −5

Now Try Problems 17 and 21

Teaching Example 1
Find each cube root:
a. $\sqrt[3]{512}$ **b.** $\sqrt[3]{-512}$
c. $-\sqrt[3]{8}$ **d.** $\sqrt[3]{-1}$
Answers:
a. 8 **b.** −8
c. −2 **d.** −1

Self Check 2

Find each cube root:
a. $\sqrt[3]{\dfrac{1}{27}}$ $\frac{1}{3}$

b. $\sqrt[3]{-\dfrac{8}{125}}$ $-\frac{2}{5}$

Now Try Problem 26

Teaching Example 2 Find each cube root:
a. $\sqrt[3]{\dfrac{1}{125}}$ **b.** $\sqrt[3]{-\dfrac{8}{27}}$
Answers:
a. $\dfrac{1}{5}$ **b.** $-\dfrac{2}{3}$

If your calculator doesn't have a $\sqrt[x]{y}$ key, you can use the y^x key. We will see later that $\sqrt[3]{7} = 7^{1/3}$. To find the value of $7^{1/3}$, we enter 7 into the calculator and press these keys:

$$7\ y^x\ (\ 1 \div 3\ ) =$$

The display will read 1.912931183.

Since $\sqrt[3]{7}$ represents the number that, when cubed, gives 7, we would expect cubes of approximations of $\sqrt[3]{7}$ to be close to 7.

- Rounded to one decimal place, $\sqrt[3]{7} \approx 1.9$, and $(1.9)^3 = 6.859$.
- Rounded to two decimal places, $\sqrt[3]{7} \approx 1.91$, and $(1.91)^3 = 6.967871$.
- Rounded to three decimal places, $\sqrt[3]{7} \approx 1.913$, and $(1.913)^3 = 7.000755497$.

Numbers such as 8, -27, -64, and 125 are called **integer cubes,** because each one is the cube of an integer. The cube root of any integer cube is an integer and therefore a rational number:

$$\sqrt[3]{8} = 2, \qquad \sqrt[3]{-27} = -3, \qquad \sqrt[3]{-64} = -4, \qquad \text{and} \qquad \sqrt[3]{125} = 5$$

Cube roots of integers such as 7 and -10, which are not integer cubes, are irrational numbers. For example, $\sqrt[3]{7}$ and $\sqrt[3]{-10}$ are irrational numbers.

> **Caution!**   Recall that the square root of a negative number (for example, $\sqrt{-27}$) is not a real number, because no real number squared is equal to a negative number. However, the cube root of a negative number is a real number. For example, $\sqrt[3]{-27} = -3$, because $(-3)^3 = (-3)(-3)(-3) = -27$.

3 Graph the cube root function.

Since every real number has one real-number cube root, there is a cube root function $f(x) = \sqrt[3]{x}$. For example, the value that is determined by $f(x) = \sqrt[3]{x}$ when $x = -8$ is denoted as $f(-8)$, and we have $f(-8) = \sqrt[3]{-8} = -2$.

To graph this function, we substitute numbers for x, compute $f(x)$, plot the resulting ordered pairs, and draw a smooth curve through the points as shown in the figure. In the table, we chose five values for x: -8, -1, 0, 1, and 8, which are integer cubes. This made computing $f(x)$ quite simple.

$f(x) = \sqrt[3]{x}$		
x	$f(x)$	$(x, f(x))$
-8	-2	$(-8, -2)$
-1	-1	$(-1, -1)$
0	0	$(0, 0)$
1	1	$(1, 1)$
8	2	$(8, 2)$

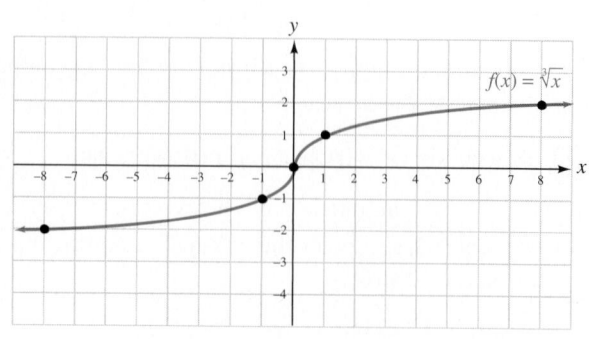

Using Your CALCULATOR Radius of a Water Tank

Engineers want to design a spherical tank that will hold 33,500 cubic feet of water, as shown in the figure. They know that the formula for the radius r of a sphere with volume V is given by the formula

$$r = \sqrt[3]{\frac{3V}{4\pi}} \quad \text{Where } \pi = 3.14159\ldots.$$

To use a reverse-entry scientific calculator to find the radius r, we substitute 33,500 for V and enter these numbers and press these keys.

3 ☒ 33500 ☒ ⦗ 4 ☒ π ⦘ ☒ $\sqrt[x]{y}$ 3 ☒   [19.99794636]

To evaluate this expression using a direct-entry or graphing calculator, we press the [MATH] key. In this mode, arrow down [▼] to highlight the option $\sqrt[3]{\ }$ and [ENTER]. Then we press the following keys.

3 ☒ 33500 ☒ ⦗⦗ 4 ☒ [2nd] π ⦘ ⦘ [ENTER]

```
3√(3*33500/(4*π)
)
        19.99794636
```

Since the result is 19.99794636, the engineers should design a tank with a radius of 20 feet.

4 Find higher-order roots.

Just as there are square roots and cube roots, there are also fourth roots, fifth roots, sixth roots, and so on. In general, we have the following definition.

> The **nth root of a** is denoted by $\sqrt[n]{a}$, and
>
> $$\sqrt[n]{a} = b \quad \text{if} \quad b^n = a$$
>
> The number n is called the **index** of the radical. If n is an even natural number, a must be positive or zero, and b must be positive.

In the square root symbol $\sqrt{\ }$, the unwritten index is understood to be 2.

$$\sqrt{a} = \sqrt[2]{a}$$

EXAMPLE 3 Find each root: **a.** $\sqrt[4]{81}$ **b.** $\sqrt[5]{32}$ **c.** $\sqrt[5]{-32}$ **d.** $\sqrt[4]{-81}$

Strategy We will determine what number, when raised to the power of the index, produces the radicand.

WHY The index of the radical sign indicates the root of the number written under it that should be found.

Solution
a. $\sqrt[4]{81} = 3$, because $3^4 = 81$. **b.** $\sqrt[5]{32} = 2$, because $2^5 = 32$.

c. $\sqrt[5]{-32} = -2$, because $(-2)^5 = -32$.

d. $\sqrt[4]{-81}$ is not a real number, because no real number raised to the fourth power is -81.

Self Check 3

Find each root:

a. $\sqrt[4]{16}$ 2

b. $\sqrt[5]{243}$ 3

c. $\sqrt[5]{-1,024}$ -4

Now Try Problems 37 and 43

Teaching Example 3 Find each root:
a. $\sqrt[6]{64}$ **b.** $\sqrt[5]{-243}$ **c.** $\sqrt[4]{-625}$
Answers:
a. 2 **b.** -3 **c.** not real

Self Check 4

Find each root:

a. $\sqrt[4]{\dfrac{1}{16}}$ $\dfrac{1}{2}$

b. $\sqrt[5]{-\dfrac{243}{32}}$ $-\dfrac{3}{2}$

Now Try Problem 46

Teaching Example 4 Find each root:

a. $\sqrt[4]{\dfrac{1}{625}}$ **b.** $\sqrt[5]{-\dfrac{100{,}000}{243}}$

Answers:

a. $\dfrac{1}{5}$ **b.** $-\dfrac{10}{3}$

EXAMPLE 4   Find each root: **a.** $\sqrt[4]{\dfrac{1}{81}}$ **b.** $\sqrt[5]{-\dfrac{32}{243}}$

Strategy We will determine what number, when raised to the power of the index, produces the radicand.

WHY The index of the radical sign indicates the root of the number written under it that should be found.

Solution

a. $\sqrt[4]{\dfrac{1}{81}} = \dfrac{1}{3}$, because $\left(\dfrac{1}{3}\right)^4 = \dfrac{1}{81}$.

b. $\sqrt[5]{-\dfrac{32}{243}} = -\dfrac{2}{3}$, because $\left(-\dfrac{2}{3}\right)^5 = -\dfrac{32}{243}$.

---

5 Simplify radicands that contain variables.

When n is even and $x \geq 0$, we say that the radical $\sqrt[n]{x}$ represents an **even root**. We can find even roots of many quantities that contain variables, provided that these variables represent positive numbers or zero.

Self Check 5

Find each root. Assume that each variable represents a positive number.

a. $\sqrt{a^4}$ a^2

b. $\sqrt{m^6 n^8}$ $m^3 n^4$

Now Try Problems 51 and 58

Teaching Example 5 Find each root. Assume all variables represent a positive number.

a. $\sqrt{x^8}$ **b.** $\sqrt{x^{10} y^6}$

Answers:

a. x^4 **b.** $x^5 y^3$

EXAMPLE 5   Find each root. Assume that each variable represents a positive number. **a.** $\sqrt{x^2}$ **b.** $\sqrt{x^4}$ **c.** $\sqrt{x^4 y^2}$

Strategy In each case, we will determine what variable expression, when raised to the second power, produces the radicand.

WHY The radical symbol $\sqrt{}$ indicates that the positive square root (principal square root) of the expression written under it should be found.

Solution

a. $\sqrt{x^2} = x$, because $(x)^2 = x^2$. **b.** $\sqrt{x^4} = x^2$, because $(x^2)^2 = x^4$.

c. $\sqrt{x^4 y^2} = x^2 y$, because $(x^2 y)^2 = x^4 y^2$.

When n is odd, we say that the radical expression $\sqrt[n]{x}$ represents an **odd root.**

Self Check 6

Find each root:

a. $\sqrt[3]{64 p^6}$ $4p^2$

b. $\sqrt[3]{-27 p^9}$ $-3p^3$

c. $\sqrt[5]{\dfrac{1}{32} n^{15}}$ $\dfrac{1}{2} n^3$

Now Try Problems 65 and 69

Teaching Example 6 Find each root:

a. $\sqrt[4]{16 x^8}$ **b.** $\sqrt[3]{-125 p^9}$

c. $\sqrt[4]{81 x^8 y^{12}}$

Answers:

a. $2x^2$ **b.** $-5p^3$ **c.** $3x^2 y^3$

EXAMPLE 6   Find each root: **a.** $\sqrt[3]{8y^3}$ **b.** $\sqrt[3]{64 x^6}$ **c.** $\sqrt[5]{32 x^{10}}$

Strategy In each case, we will determine what expression, when raised to the power of the index, produces the radicand.

WHY The index of the radical sign indicates the root of the number written under it that should be found.

Solution

a. $\sqrt[3]{8y^3} = 2y$, because $(2y)^3 = 8y^3$. **b.** $\sqrt[3]{64 x^6} = 4x^2$, because $(4x^2)^3 = 64 x^6$.

c. $\sqrt[5]{32 x^{10}} = 2x^2$, because $(2x^2)^5 = 32 x^{10}$.

ANSWERS TO SELF CHECKS

1. a. 4 **b.** -4 **c.** 6 **d.** -5 **2. a.** $\dfrac{1}{3}$ **b.** $-\dfrac{2}{5}$ **3. a.** 2 **b.** 3 **c.** -4 **4. a.** $\dfrac{1}{2}$ **b.** $-\dfrac{3}{2}$

5. a. a^2 **b.** $m^3 n^4$ **6. a.** $4p^2$ **b.** $-3p^3$ **c.** $\dfrac{1}{2} n^3$

SECTION 8.2   STUDY SET

VOCABULARY

Fill in the blanks.

1. If $p^3 = q$, p is called a __cube__ root of q.

2. If $p^4 = q$, p is called a __fourth__ root of q.

3. We denote the cube root __function__ with the notation $f(x) = \sqrt[3]{x}$.

▶ **4.** If the index of a radical is an even number, the root is called an __even__ root.

CONCEPTS

Fill in the blanks.

5. -3 is a cube __root__ of -27, because $(-3)^3 = -27$.

▶ **6.** $\sqrt[3]{a} = b$ if b^3 = a.

7. $\sqrt[3]{-216} = -6$, because $\left(-6 \right)^3 = -216$.

8. $\sqrt[5]{32x^5} = 2x$, because $(2x)^5 = 32x^5$.

9. Find each value, if possible.

   a. $\sqrt{-125}$ not a real number

   b. $\sqrt[3]{-125}$ -5

10. Graph each number on the number line.
$$\left\{ \sqrt[3]{16},\ -\sqrt[4]{100},\ \sqrt[3]{-1.8},\ \sqrt[4]{0.6} \right\}$$

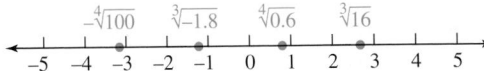

11. If $f(x) = \sqrt[3]{x}$, find each value. **Do not use a calculator.**

   a. $f(1)$ 1

   b. $f\left(-\dfrac{1}{27} \right)$ $-\dfrac{1}{3}$

   c. $f(125)$ 5

   d. $f(0.008)$ 0.2

   c. $f(1,000)$ 10

12. a. Use the dashed lines in the following graph to approximate $\sqrt[3]{5}$. $\sqrt[3]{5} \approx 1.7$

   b. Use the graph to approximate $\sqrt[3]{4}$ and $\sqrt[3]{-6}$.
   $\sqrt[3]{4} \approx 1.6$; $\sqrt[3]{-6} \approx -1.8$

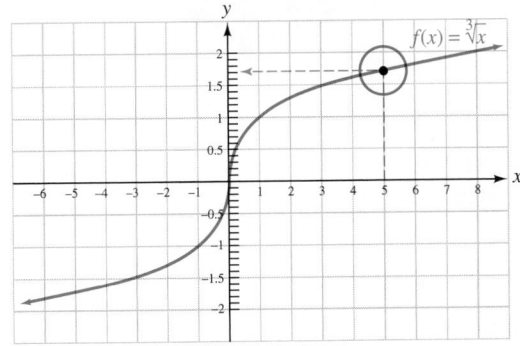

NOTATION

Fill in the blanks.

▶ **13.** In the notation $\sqrt[3]{x^6}$, 3 is called the __index__ and x^6 is called the __radicand__.

▶ **14.** $\sqrt{}$ is called a __radical__ symbol.

15. The "understood" index of the radical expression $\sqrt{55}$ is __2__.

16. In reading $f(x) = \sqrt[3]{x}$, we say "f __of__ x equals the cube root __of__ x."

GUIDED PRACTICE

Find each value without using a calculator. **See Examples 1–2.**

17. $\sqrt[3]{125}$ 5   **18.** $\sqrt[3]{27}$ 3

19. $\sqrt[3]{0}$ 0   **20.** $\sqrt[3]{1}$ 1

▶ **21.** $\sqrt[3]{-8}$ -2 **22.** $-\sqrt[3]{1}$ -1

23. $-\sqrt[3]{27}$ -3 ▶ **24.** $\sqrt[3]{-27}$ -3

25. $\sqrt[3]{\dfrac{1}{125}}$ $\dfrac{1}{5}$ ▶ **26.** $\sqrt[3]{-\dfrac{1}{1,000}}$ $-\dfrac{1}{10}$

27. $-\sqrt[3]{-1}$ 1   ▶ **28.** $-\sqrt[3]{-27}$ 3

Use a calculator to find each cube root to the nearest hundredth. **See Objective 2.**

29. $\sqrt[3]{32,100}$ 31.78   ▶ **30.** $\sqrt[3]{-25,713}$ -29.52

31. $\sqrt[3]{-0.11324}$ -0.48 **32.** $\sqrt[3]{0.875}$ 0.96

Complete the table and graph the function. **See Objective 3.**

33. $f(x) = \sqrt[3]{x} + 1$

x	$f(x)$
-8	-1
-1	0
0	1
1	2
8	3

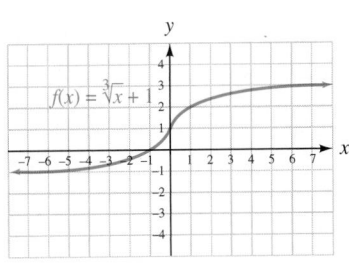

▶ **34.** $f(x) = \sqrt[4]{x}$

x	$f(x)$
0	0
1	1
16	2

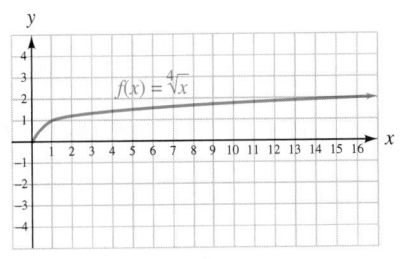

35. $f(x) = -\sqrt[3]{x}$

x	f(x)
−8	2
−1	1
0	0
1	−1
8	−2

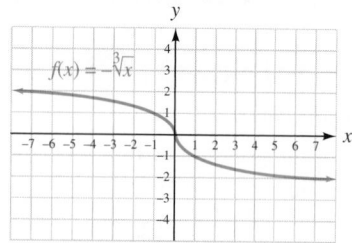

$f(x) = -\sqrt[3]{x}$

▶ 36. $f(x) = \sqrt[4]{x} - 1$

x	f(x)
0	−1
1	0
16	1

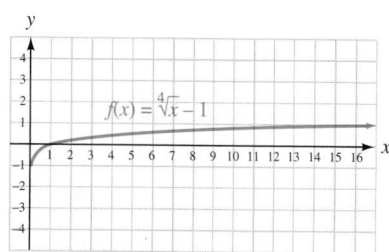

$f(x) = \sqrt[4]{x} - 1$

Find each value without using a calculator. See Examples 3–4.

37. $\sqrt[4]{625}$ 5

▶ 38. $\sqrt[4]{81}$ 3

39. $-\sqrt[5]{32}$ −2

40. $-\sqrt[5]{243}$ −3

41. $\sqrt[6]{1}$ 1

42. $\sqrt[6]{0}$ 0

▶ 43. $\sqrt[5]{-243}$ −3

▶ 44. $\sqrt[7]{-1}$ −1

▶ 45. $\sqrt[4]{\dfrac{1}{256}}$ $\dfrac{1}{4}$

46. $\sqrt[4]{\dfrac{16}{81}}$ $\dfrac{2}{3}$

47. $\sqrt[5]{-\dfrac{1}{32}}$ $-\dfrac{1}{2}$

48. $\sqrt[5]{\dfrac{243}{100,000}}$ $\dfrac{3}{10}$

Find each root. All variables represent positive numbers.
See Example 5.

49. $\sqrt{y^2}$ y

50. $\sqrt{y^4}$ y^2

51. $\sqrt{x^6}$ x^3

▶ 52. $\sqrt{b^8}$ b^4

53. $\sqrt{x^{10}}$ x^5

54. $\sqrt{y^{12}}$ y^6

55. $\sqrt{4z^2}$ 2z

▶ 56. $\sqrt{9t^6}$ $3t^3$

57. $-\sqrt{x^4y^2}$ $-x^2y$

58. $-\sqrt{x^2y^4}$ $-xy^2$

59. $\sqrt{36z^{36}}$ $6z^{18}$

60. $\sqrt{64y^{64}}$ $8y^{32}$

61. $-\sqrt{625z^2}$ −25z

62. $-\sqrt{729x^8}$ $-27x^4$

63. $-\sqrt{144x^6}$ $-12x^3$

64. $-\sqrt{49x^8y^{12}}$ $-7x^4y^6$

Find each root. See Example 6.

65. $\sqrt[3]{y^6}$ y^2

66. $\sqrt[3]{c^3}$ c

67. $\sqrt[3]{27y^3}$ 3y

▶ 68. $\sqrt[3]{-p^6q^3}$ $-p^2q$

69. $\sqrt[5]{f^5}$ f

70. $\sqrt[5]{y^{20}}$ y^4

71. $\sqrt[5]{-32t^{10}}$ $-2t^2$

72. $\sqrt[5]{\dfrac{z^{15}}{32}}$ $z^{3/2}$

TRY IT YOURSELF

Find each root.

73. $-\sqrt[3]{64}$ −4

▶ 74. $-\sqrt[3]{343}$ −7

75. $\sqrt[3]{729}$ 9

76. $\sqrt[3]{512}$ 8

77. $\sqrt[3]{1,000}$ 10

78. $-\sqrt{0.04y^2}$ −0.2y

79. $-\sqrt{0.81b^6}$ $-0.9b^3$

80. $-\sqrt{25x^4z^{12}}$ $-5x^2z^6$

81. $-\sqrt{100a^6b^4}$ $-10a^3b^2$

82. $\sqrt[3]{64y^6}$ $4y^2$

83. $\sqrt[3]{-r^{12}t^6}$ $-r^4t^2$

84. $\sqrt[4]{x^4}$ x

85. $\sqrt[4]{x^8}$ x^2

86. $\sqrt[3]{125}$ 5

87. $\sqrt[5]{-\dfrac{x^{10}}{32}}$ $-\dfrac{x^2}{2}$

88. $\sqrt[5]{\dfrac{x^{15}y^{10}}{100,000}}$ $\dfrac{x^3y^2}{10}$

Use a calculator to find each root to the nearest hundredth.

89. $\sqrt[4]{125}$ 3.34

90. $\sqrt[5]{12,450}$ 6.59

91. $\sqrt[5]{-6,000}$ −5.70

92. $\sqrt[6]{0.5}$ 0.89

APPLICATIONS

Use a calculator to help solve each problem. Give your answers to the nearest hundredth.

▶ 93. PACKAGING A cubical box has a volume of 2 cubic feet. Substitute 2 for V in the formula $V = s^3$ and solve for s to find the length of each side of the box. 1.26 ft

▶ 94. HOT-AIR BALLOONS If the hot-air balloon shown is in the shape of a sphere, what is its radius? (*Hint:* See the Using Your Calculator feature in this section.) 15.30 ft

$V = 15,000$ cubic ft

▶ 95. WINDMILLS The power generated by a windmill is related to the speed of the wind by the formula

$$S = \sqrt[3]{\dfrac{P}{0.02}}$$

where S is the speed of the wind (in mph) and P is the power (in watts). Find the speed of the wind when the windmill is producing 400 watts of power. 27.14 mph

▶ **96. ASTRONOMY** In the early 17th century, Johannes Kepler, a German astronomer, discovered that a planet's mean distance R from the sun (in millions of miles) is related to the time T (in years) it takes the planet to orbit the sun by the formula

$$R = 93\sqrt[3]{\frac{T^2}{1.002}}$$

Use the information in the illustration to find R for Mercury, Earth, and Jupiter.
Mercury: 35.89, Earth: 92.94, Jupiter: 483.34

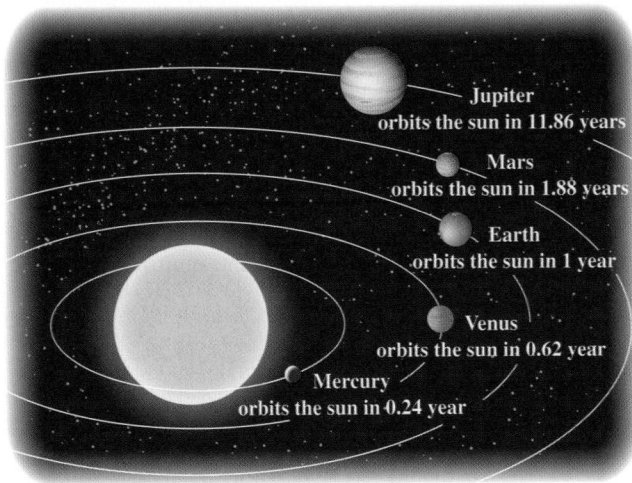

▶ **97. DEPRECIATION** The formula

$$r = 1 - \sqrt[n]{\frac{S}{C}}$$

gives the annual depreciation rate r (in percent) of an item that had an original cost of C dollars and has a useful life of n years and a salvage value of S dollars. Use the information in the illustration in the next column to find the annual depreciation rate for the new piece of sound equipment. $33\frac{1}{3}\%$

OFFICE MEMO

To: Purchasing Dept.
From: Bob Kinsell, Engineering Dept. BK
Re: New sound board

We recommend you purchase the new Sony sound board @ $81K. This equipment does become obsolete quickly but we figure we can use it for 4 yrs. A college would probably buy it from us then. I bet we could get around $16K for it.

▶ **98. SAVINGS ACCOUNTS** The interest rate r (in percent) earned by a savings account after n compoundings is given by the formula

$$\sqrt[n]{\frac{V}{P}} - 1 = r$$

where V is the current value and P is the original principal. What interest rate r was paid on an account in which a deposit of $1,000 grew to $1,338.23 after five compoundings? 6.00%

WRITING

99. Explain why a negative number can have a real number for its cube root yet cannot have a real number for its fourth root.

▶ **100.** To find $\sqrt[3]{15}$, we can use the $\sqrt[n]{x}$ key on a calculator to obtain 2.466212074. Explain how a key other than $\sqrt[n]{x}$ can be used to check the validity of this result.

REVIEW

Simplify each expression.

101. $m^5 m^2$ m^7 **102.** $(-5x^3)(-5x)$ $25x^4$

103. $(3^2)^4$ 3^8 or 9^4 **104.** $r^3 r r^5$ r^9

105. $(x^2 x^3)^5$ x^{25} ▶ **106.** $(3aa^2a^3)^5$ $243a^{30}$

107. $4x^3(6x^5)$ $24x^8$ **108.** $-2x(5x^2)$ $-10x^3$

SECTION 8.3

Simplifying Radical Expressions

Square dancing is an American folk dance in which four couples, arranged in a square, perform various moves. The figure shows a group as they move around a square.

Objectives

1 Use the product rule to simplify radicals.

2 Use prime factorization to simplify radicals.

3 Simplify radicals of variable expressions.

4 Use the quotient rule to simplify radicals.

If the square shown in the figure has an area of 12 square yards, the length of a side is $\sqrt{12}$ yards. We can use the formula for the area of a square and the concept of square root to show that this is so.

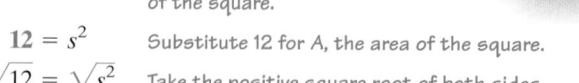

$A = s^2$ *s is the length of a side of the square.*

$12 = s^2$ *Substitute 12 for A, the area of the square.*

$\sqrt{12} = \sqrt{s^2}$ *Take the positive square root of both sides.*

$\sqrt{12} = s$ *The length of a side of the square is $\sqrt{12}$ yards.*

The form in which we express the length of a side of the square depends on the situation. If an approximation is acceptable, we can use a calculator to find that $\sqrt{12} \approx 3.464101615$, and we can then round to a specified degree of accuracy. For example, to the nearest tenth, each side is 3.5 yards long.

If the situation calls for the *exact* length, we must use a radical expression. As you will see in this section, it is common practice to write a radical expression such as $\sqrt{12}$ in *simplified form*. To simplify radicals, we will use the multiplication and division properties of radicals.

1 **Use the product rule to simplify radicals.**

We introduce the first of two properties of radicals with the following examples:

Square root of a product   Product of square roots

$\sqrt{4 \cdot 25} = \sqrt{100}$ and $\sqrt{4}\sqrt{25} = 2 \cdot 5$ *Read as "the square root of 4 times the square root of 25."*

$= 10$ $= 10$

In each case, the answer is 10. Thus, $\sqrt{4 \cdot 25} = \sqrt{4}\sqrt{25}$. Likewise,

$\sqrt{9 \cdot 16} = \sqrt{144}$ and $\sqrt{9}\sqrt{16} = 3 \cdot 4$

$= 12$ $= 12$

In each case, the answer is 12. Thus, $\sqrt{9 \cdot 16} = \sqrt{9}\sqrt{16}$. These results illustrate the **product rule for square roots.**

The Product Rule for Square Roots

For any nonnegative real numbers a and b,

$$\sqrt{a \cdot b} = \sqrt{a}\sqrt{b}$$

In words, *the square root of the product of two nonnegative numbers is equal to the product of their square roots.*

A square root radical is in **simplified form** when each of the following statements is true.

Simplified Form of a Square Root

1. Except for 1, the radicand has no perfect-square factors.
2. No fraction appears in a radicand.
3. No radical appears in the denominator.

We can use the multiplication property of radicals to simplify square roots whose radicands have perfect-square factors. For example, we can simplify $\sqrt{12}$ as follows:

$$\sqrt{12} = \sqrt{4 \cdot 3} \qquad \text{Factor 12 as } 4 \cdot 3.$$

$$= \sqrt{4}\sqrt{3} \qquad \text{The square root of } 4 \cdot 3 \text{ is equal to the square root of 4 times the square root of 3.}$$

$$= 2\sqrt{3} \qquad \text{Write } \sqrt{4} \text{ as 2. Read as "2 times the square root of 3" or as "2 radical 3."}$$

The square in the figure, which we considered in the introduction to this section, has a side length of $\sqrt{12}$ yards. We now see that the *exact* length of a side can be expressed in simplified form as $2\sqrt{3}$ yards.

To simplify more difficult square roots, it is helpful to know the **natural-number perfect squares.** For example, 81 is a perfect square, because it is the square of 9: $9^2 = 81$. The first 20 natural-number perfect squares are

1, 4, 9, 16, 25, 36, 49, 64, 81, 100, 121, 144, 169, 196, 225, 256, 289, 324, 361, 400

EXAMPLE 1   Simplify: $\sqrt{27}$

Strategy We will factor 27 as $9 \cdot 3$ and then use the product rule for square roots to simplify the radical expression.

WHY Factoring the radicand in this way leads to a square root of a perfect square that we can easily evaluate.

Solution

$$\sqrt{27} = \sqrt{9 \cdot 3}$$

$$= \sqrt{9}\sqrt{3} \qquad \text{The square root of a product is equal to the product of their square roots.}$$

$$= 3\sqrt{3} \qquad \text{Find the square root of the perfect-square factor: } \sqrt{9} = 3.$$

As a check, recall that $\sqrt{27}$ is the number that, when squared, gives 27. If $3\sqrt{3} = \sqrt{27}$, then $\left(3\sqrt{3}\right)^2$ should be equal to 27.

$$\left(3\sqrt{3}\right)^2 = (3)^2\left(\sqrt{3}\right)^2 \qquad \text{Use the power of a product rule for exponents: Raise each factor of the product } 3\sqrt{3} \text{ to the second power.}$$

$$= 9(3) \qquad \sqrt{3}, \text{ when squared, gives 3.}$$

$$= 27$$

The Language of Algebra   The instructions *simplify* and *approximate* do not mean the same thing.

Simplify: $\sqrt{12} = 2\sqrt{3}$ (exact)   *Approximate:* $\sqrt{12} \approx 3.464$ (not exact)

EXAMPLE 2   Simplify: $\sqrt{600}$

Strategy We will factor 600 as $100 \cdot 6$ and then use the product rule for square roots to simplify the radical expression.

WHY We want to choose the factorization of 600 that contains the biggest perfect-square factor, which is 100.

Solution

$$\sqrt{600} = \sqrt{100 \cdot 6}$$

$$= \sqrt{100}\sqrt{6} \qquad \text{The square root of a product is equal to the product of their square roots.}$$

$$= 10\sqrt{6} \qquad \text{Find the square root of the perfect-square factor: } \sqrt{100} = 10.$$

Check the result.

Self Check 1

Simplify: $\sqrt{28}$ $2\sqrt{7}$

Now Try **Problem 21**

Teaching Example 1 Simplify: $\sqrt{242}$
Answer:
$11\sqrt{2}$

Self Check 2

Simplify: $\sqrt{500}$ $10\sqrt{5}$

Now Try **Problem 23**

Teaching Example 2 Simplify: $\sqrt{162}$
Answer:
$9\sqrt{2}$

2 **Use prime factorization to simplify radicals.**

When simplifying square roots, prime factorization can be useful in finding the greatest perfect-square factor of the radicand.

EXAMPLE 3 Simplify, if possible: **a.** $\sqrt{150}$ **b.** $\sqrt{95}$

Strategy In each case, the greatest perfect-square factor of the radicand (if there is one) is not obvious. Another approach is to find the prime factorization of the radicand and look for pairs of like factors.

WHY Identifying a pair of like factors of the radicand leads to a square root of a perfect square that we can easily evaluate.

Solution

a. $\sqrt{150} = \sqrt{2 \cdot 3 \cdot 5 \cdot 5}$ Write 150 in prime-factored form.

$\qquad = \sqrt{2 \cdot 3}\sqrt{5 \cdot 5}$ Group the pair of like factors together and use the product rule for square roots.

$\qquad = \sqrt{6} \cdot 5$ Evaluate the square root of the perfect square: $\sqrt{5 \cdot 5} = \sqrt{25} = 5$.

$\qquad = 5\sqrt{6}$ Write the factor 5 first. This way, no misunderstanding can occur about exactly what is under the radical symbol.

b. We prime factor 95 to get $95 = 5 \cdot 19$. Since the factorization does not contain a pair of like factors, 95 does not have a perfect-square factor. It follows that $\sqrt{95}$ cannot be simplified.

> *Caution!* As we see in part b, some radical expressions cannot be simplified because the radicand does not have a perfect-square factor.

3 **Simplify radicals of variable expressions.**

Variable expressions can also be perfect squares. For example, x^2, x^4, x^6, and x^8 are perfect squares because

$$x^2 = (x)^2, \qquad x^4 = (x^2)^2, \qquad x^6 = (x^3)^2, \qquad \text{and} \qquad x^8 = (x^4)^2$$

Perfect squares like these are used to simplify square roots involving variable radicands.

EXAMPLE 4 Simplify: $\sqrt{x^3}$

Strategy We will factor x^3 as $x^2 \cdot x$ and then use the product rule for square roots to simplify the radical expression.

WHY Factoring the radicand in this way leads to the square root of a perfect square that can be easily simplified.

Solution

$\sqrt{x^3} = \sqrt{x^2 \cdot x}$

$\qquad = \sqrt{x^2}\sqrt{x}$ The square root of a product is equal to the product of their square roots.

$\qquad = x\sqrt{x}$ Find the square root of the perfect-square factor: $\sqrt{x^2} = x$.

As a check, recall that $\sqrt{x^3}$, when squared, gives x^3. If $x\sqrt{x} = \sqrt{x^3}$, then $\left(x\sqrt{x}\right)^2$ should be equal to x^3.

$$\left(x\sqrt{x}\right)^2 = (x)^2\left(\sqrt{x}\right)^2 \quad \text{Raise each factor of the product } x\sqrt{x} \text{ to the 2nd power.}$$
$$= x^2(x) \qquad \sqrt{x}\text{, when squared, gives } x.$$
$$= x^3 \qquad \text{Keep the base } x \text{ and add the exponents.}$$

EXAMPLE 5   Simplify: $-7\sqrt{8m}$

Strategy We will write $\sqrt{8m}$ in simplified form and then multiply the result by -7.

WHY The expression $-7\sqrt{8m}$ means $-7 \cdot \sqrt{8m}$.

Solution
By inspection, we see that the radicand, $8m$, has a perfect-square factor of 4. We can write $8m$ in factored form as $4 \cdot 2m$.

$$-7\sqrt{8m} = -7\sqrt{4 \cdot 2m}$$
$$= -7\sqrt{4}\sqrt{2m} \quad \text{The square root of a product is equal to the product of}$$
$$\text{their square roots.}$$
$$= -7(2)\sqrt{2m} \quad \text{Find the square root of the perfect-square factor:}$$
$$\sqrt{4} = 2.$$
$$= -14\sqrt{2m} \quad \text{Multiply: } -7(2) = -14.$$

Self Check 5

Simplify: $-2\sqrt{50c}$ $-10\sqrt{2c}$

Now Try **Problem 42**

Teaching Example 5 *Simplify:*
$-2\sqrt{75x}$
Answer:
$-10\sqrt{3x}$

Caution! When writing radical expressions such as $-14\sqrt{2m}$, be sure to extend the radical symbol completely over $2m$, because the expressions $-14\sqrt{2m}$ and $-14\sqrt{2}m$ are not the same. Similar care should be taken when writing expressions such as $\sqrt{3}x$. To avoid any misinterpretation, $\sqrt{3}x$ can be written as $x\sqrt{3}$.

EXAMPLE 6   Simplify: $\sqrt{72x^3}$

Strategy We will determine the greatest perfect-square factor of the numerical part and the greatest perfect-square factor of the variable part of the radicand separately.

WHY It is easier to determine the greatest perfect-square factor of the entire radicand if we consider the numerical and variable factors separately.

Solution
We factor $72x^3$ into two factors, one of which is the greatest perfect square that divides $72x^3$. Since the greatest perfect square that divides $72x^3$ is $36x^2$, such a factorization is $72x^3 = 36x^2 \cdot 2x$. We now use the multiplication property of radicals to get

$$\sqrt{72x^3} = \sqrt{36x^2 \cdot 2x}$$
$$= \sqrt{36x^2}\sqrt{2x} \quad \text{The square root of a product is equal to the product of}$$
$$\text{their square roots.}$$
$$= 6x\sqrt{2x} \quad \text{Find the square root of the perfect-square factor:}$$
$$\sqrt{36x^2} = 6x.$$

Self Check 6

Simplify: $\sqrt{48y^3}$ $4y\sqrt{3y}$

Now Try **Problem 46**

Teaching Example 6 *Simplify:* $\sqrt{45x^5}$
Answer:
$3x^2\sqrt{5x}$

EXAMPLE 7   Simplify: $3a\sqrt{288a^4b^7}$

Strategy We will write $\sqrt{288a^4b^7}$ in simplified form and then multiply the result by $3a$.

WHY The expression $3a\sqrt{288a^4b^7}$ means $3a \cdot \sqrt{288a^4b^7}$.

Solution

To simplify $\sqrt{288a^4b^7}$, we look for the greatest perfect square that divides $288a^4b^7$. Because

- 144 is the greatest perfect square that divides 288,
- a^4 is the greatest perfect square that divides a^4, and
- b^6 is the greatest perfect square that divides b^7,

the factor $144a^4b^6$ is the greatest perfect square that divides $288a^4b^7$.

We can now use the multiplication property of radicals to simplify the radical.

$$3a\sqrt{288a^4b^7} = 3a\sqrt{144a^4b^6 \cdot 2b}$$

$$= 3a\sqrt{144a^4b^6}\sqrt{2b} \qquad \text{The square root of a product is equal to the product of their square roots.}$$

$$= 3a(12a^2b^3)\sqrt{2b} \qquad \sqrt{144a^4b^6} = 12a^2b^3.$$

$$= 36a^3b^3\sqrt{2b} \qquad \text{Multiply: } 3a(12a^2b^3) = 36a^3b^3.$$

Caution! The multiplication property of radicals applies to the square root of the product of two numbers. There is no such property for sums or differences. To illustrate this, we consider these correct simplifications:

$$\sqrt{9 + 16} = \sqrt{25} = 5 \qquad \text{and} \qquad \sqrt{25 - 16} = \sqrt{9} = 3$$

It is incorrect to write

$$\sqrt{9 + 16} = \sqrt{9} + \sqrt{16} \qquad \text{or} \qquad \sqrt{25 - 16} = \sqrt{25} - \sqrt{16}$$
$$= 3 + 4 \qquad\qquad\qquad\qquad = 5 - 4$$
$$= 7 \qquad\qquad\qquad\qquad\quad = 1$$

Thus, $\sqrt{a + b} \neq \sqrt{a} + \sqrt{b}$ and $\sqrt{a - b} \neq \sqrt{a} - \sqrt{b}$.

---

4 Use the quotient rule to simplify radicals.

To introduce the second property of radicals, we consider these examples.

$$\sqrt{\frac{100}{25}} = \sqrt{4} \qquad \text{and} \qquad \frac{\sqrt{100}}{\sqrt{25}} = \frac{10}{5} \qquad \text{Read as "the square root of 100 divided by the square root of 25."}$$

$$= 2 \qquad\qquad\qquad\qquad = 2$$

Since the answer is 2 in each case,

$$\sqrt{\frac{100}{25}} = \frac{\sqrt{100}}{\sqrt{25}}$$

Likewise,

$$\sqrt{\frac{36}{4}} = \sqrt{9} \qquad \text{and} \qquad \frac{\sqrt{36}}{\sqrt{4}} = \frac{6}{2}$$

$$= 3 \qquad\qquad\qquad\qquad = 3$$

Since the answer is 3 in each case,

$$\sqrt{\frac{36}{4}} = \frac{\sqrt{36}}{\sqrt{4}}$$

These results illustrate the *quotient rule for radicals*.

The Quotient Rule for Radicals

For any positive real numbers a and b,

$$\sqrt{\frac{a}{b}} = \frac{\sqrt{a}}{\sqrt{b}}$$

In words, *the square root of the quotient of two numbers is the quotient of their square roots*.

We can use the division property of radicals to simplify radicals that have fractions in their radicands. For example,

$$\sqrt{\frac{59}{49}} = \frac{\sqrt{59}}{\sqrt{49}}$$

$$= \frac{\sqrt{59}}{7} \qquad \sqrt{49} = 7.$$

EXAMPLE 8   Simplify: $\sqrt{\dfrac{108}{25}}$

Strategy The square root is not in simplified form because the radicand contains a fraction. To write the radical expression in simplified form, we use the quotient rule for square roots.

WHY Writing the expression in $\frac{\sqrt{a}}{\sqrt{b}}$ form leads to a square root of a perfect square in the denominator that we can easily evaluate.

Solution

$$\sqrt{\frac{108}{25}} = \frac{\sqrt{108}}{\sqrt{25}} \qquad \text{The square root of a quotient is equal to the quotient of their square roots.}$$

$$= \frac{\sqrt{36 \cdot 3}}{5} \qquad \text{Factor 108 using the largest perfect-square factor of 108, which is 36. Write } \sqrt{25} \text{ as 5.}$$

$$= \frac{\sqrt{36}\sqrt{3}}{5} \qquad \text{The square root of a product is equal to the product of their square roots.}$$

$$= \frac{6\sqrt{3}}{5} \qquad \text{This result can also be written as } \frac{6}{5}\sqrt{3}.$$

Self Check 8

Simplify: $\sqrt{\dfrac{20}{81}}$ $\dfrac{2\sqrt{5}}{9}$

Now Try **Problem 54**

Teaching Example 8 Simplify: $\sqrt{\dfrac{75}{49}}$

Answer:

$\dfrac{5\sqrt{3}}{7}$

EXAMPLE 9   Simplify: $\sqrt{\dfrac{44x^3}{9xy^2}}$

Strategy Because the radicand is a rational expression, we will remove common factors before using the quotient rule for square roots.

WHY After simplifying the rational radicand, our hope is that the numerator and/or the denominator of the resulting rational expression is a perfect square.

Self Check 9

Simplify: $\sqrt{\dfrac{99b^3}{16a^2b}}$ $\dfrac{3b\sqrt{11}}{4a}$

Now Try **Problem 58**

Solution

$$\sqrt{\dfrac{44x^3}{9xy^2}} = \sqrt{\dfrac{44x^2}{9y^2}}$$

Simplify the fraction by removing the common factor of

x: $\dfrac{44x^3}{9xy} = \dfrac{44x^2\overset{1}{\cancel{x}}}{9\cancel{x}y^2} = \dfrac{44x^2}{9y^2}$.

$$= \dfrac{\sqrt{44x^2}}{\sqrt{9y^2}}$$

The square root of a quotient is equal to the quotient of their square roots.

$$= \dfrac{\sqrt{4x^2}\sqrt{11}}{\sqrt{9y^2}}$$

Factor $44x^2$ as $4x^2 \cdot 11$. The square root of a product is equal to the product of their square roots.

$$= \dfrac{2x\sqrt{11}}{3y}$$

$\sqrt{4x^2} = 2x$ and $\sqrt{9y^2} = 3y$.

The multiplication and division properties of radicals are also true for cube roots and higher. To simplify cube roots, we must know the following natural-number **perfect cubes:**

$$8, 27, 64, 125, 216, 343, 512, 729, 1{,}000$$

Properties of Radicals

For any real numbers a and b,

$$\sqrt[3]{ab} = \sqrt[3]{a}\sqrt[3]{b} \qquad \sqrt[3]{\dfrac{a}{b}} = \dfrac{\sqrt[3]{a}}{\sqrt[3]{b}}, \quad \text{provided } b \neq 0.$$

EXAMPLE 10 Simplify: $\sqrt[3]{54}$

Strategy We will factor 54 as $27 \cdot 2$ and then use the product rule for radicals to simplify the radical expression.

WHY Factoring the radicand in this way leads to a cube root of a perfect cube that we can easily evaluate.

Solution
The greatest perfect cube that divides 54 is 27.

$$\sqrt[3]{54} = \sqrt[3]{27 \cdot 2} \qquad \text{Factor 54: } 54 = 27 \cdot 2.$$

$$= \sqrt[3]{27}\sqrt[3]{2} \qquad \text{The cube root of a product is equal to the product of their cube roots.}$$

$$= 3\sqrt[3]{2} \qquad \text{Find the cube root of the perfect-cube factor: } \sqrt[3]{27} = 3.$$

As a check, we note that $\sqrt[3]{54}$ is the number that, when cubed, gives 54. If $3\sqrt[3]{2} = \sqrt[3]{54}$, then $\left(3\sqrt[3]{2}\right)^3$ will be equal to 54.

$$\left(3\sqrt[3]{2}\right)^3 = (3)^3\left(\sqrt[3]{2}\right)^3 \qquad \text{Raise each factor of the product } 3\sqrt[3]{2} \text{ to the third power.}$$

$$= 27(2) \qquad \sqrt[3]{2}, \text{ when cubed, gives 2.}$$

$$= 54$$

Variable expressions can also be perfect cubes. For example, x^3, x^6, x^9, and x^{12} are perfect cubes because

$$x^3 = (x)^3, \qquad x^6 = (x^2)^3, \qquad x^9 = (x^3)^3, \qquad \text{and} \qquad x^{12} = (x^4)^3$$

Perfect cubes like these are used to simplify cube roots involving variable radicands.

EXAMPLE 11   Simplify: **a.** $\sqrt[3]{16x^3y^4}$ **b.** $\sqrt[3]{\dfrac{64n^4}{27m^3}}$

Strategy   In the first case, we will factor the radicand so one factor is the greatest possible perfect cube, use the product rule for radicals, and then simplify. We will use the quotient rule for radicals for the second case.

WHY   Factoring the radicand in this way leads to a cube root of a perfect cube that we can easily evaluate.

Solution

a. We factor $16x^3y^4$ into two factors, one of which is the greatest perfect cube that divides $16x^3y^4$. Since $8x^3y^3$ is the greatest perfect cube that divides $16x^3y^4$, the factorization is $16x^3y^4 = 8x^3y^3 \cdot 2y$.

$$\sqrt[3]{16x^3y^4} = \sqrt[3]{8x^3y^3 \cdot 2y}$$

$$= \sqrt[3]{8x^3y^3}\,\sqrt[3]{2y} \qquad \text{The cube root of a product is equal to the product of the cube roots.}$$

$$= 2xy\sqrt[3]{2y} \qquad \text{Find the cube root of the perfect-cube factor: } \sqrt[3]{8x^3y^3} = 2xy.$$

b. $\sqrt[3]{\dfrac{64n^4}{27m^3}} = \dfrac{\sqrt[3]{64n^4}}{\sqrt[3]{27m^3}}$ The cube root of a quotient is equal to the quotient of the cube roots.

$$= \dfrac{\sqrt[3]{64n^3}\,\sqrt[3]{n}}{3m} \qquad \text{In the numerator, use the multiplication property of radicals. In the denominator, } \sqrt[3]{27m^3} = 3m.$$

$$= \dfrac{4n\sqrt[3]{n}}{3m} \qquad \sqrt[3]{64n^3} = 4n.$$

ANSWERS TO SELF CHECKS

1. $2\sqrt{7}$ **2.** $10\sqrt{5}$ **3. a.** $2\sqrt{35}$ **b.** cannot be simplified   **4.** $y^2\sqrt{y}$ **5.** $-10\sqrt{2c}$
6. $4y\sqrt{3y}$ **7.** $15p^2q^3\sqrt{7p}$ **8.** $\dfrac{2\sqrt{5}}{9}$ **9.** $\dfrac{3b\sqrt{11}}{4a}$ **10.** $5\sqrt[3]{2}$ **11. a.** $3ab\sqrt[3]{2b^2}$ **b.** $\dfrac{3q\sqrt[3]{q^2}}{4p}$

SECTION 8.3   STUDY SET

VOCABULARY

Fill in the blanks.

1. Squares of integers such as 4, 9, and 16 are called <u>perfect</u> squares.

2. Cubes of integers such as 8, 27, and 64 are called perfect <u>cubes</u>.

3. "To <u>simplify</u> $\sqrt{8}$" means to write it as $2\sqrt{2}$.

4. The word *product* is associated with the operation of multiplication and the word *quotient* with <u>division</u>.

CONCEPTS

5. Fill in the blanks.

   a. The square root of the product of two positive numbers is equal to the <u>product</u> of their square roots. In symbols,

$$\sqrt{ab} = \sqrt{a}\sqrt{b}$$

   b. The square root of the quotient of two positive numbers is equal to the <u>quotient</u> of their square roots. In symbols

$$\sqrt{\dfrac{a}{b}} = \dfrac{\sqrt{a}}{\sqrt{b}}$$

6. Which of the perfect squares 1, 4, 9, 16, 25, 36, 49, 64, 81, and 100 is the *largest* factor of the given number?

   a. 20 4   **b.** 45 9

   c. 72 36   **d.** 98 49

What is wrong with each simplification?

7. $\sqrt{20} = \sqrt{16 + 4}$
$= \sqrt{16} + \sqrt{4}$ Line 2 is not true. There is no addition
$= 4 + 2$ property of radicals.
$= 6$

8. $\sqrt{27} = \sqrt{36 - 9}$
$= \sqrt{36} - \sqrt{9}$ Line 2 is not true. There is no subtrac-
$= 6 - 3$ tion property of radicals.
$= 3$

9. A crossword puzzle in a newspaper occupies an area of 28 square inches. See the illustration below.

  a. Express the exact length of a side of the square-shaped puzzle in simplified radical form. $2\sqrt{7}$ in.

  b. What is the length of a side to the nearest tenth of an inch? 5.3 in.

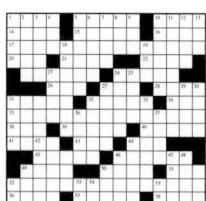

▶ **10.** See the illustration.

  a. Find the exact length of a side of the cube written in simplified radical form? $2\sqrt[3]{5}$ ft

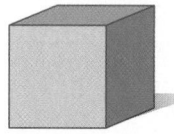

Volume = 40 ft³

  b. What is the length of a side to the nearest tenth of a foot? 3.4 ft

Evaluate the expression $\sqrt{b^2 - 4ac}$ for the given values. Perform the operations within the radical and simplify the radical.

11. $a = 5, b = 10, c = 3$
$2\sqrt{10}$

12. $a = 2, b = 6, c = 1$
$2\sqrt{7}$

13. $a = -1, b = 6, c = 9$
$6\sqrt{2}$

14. $a = 1, b = -2, c = -11$
$4\sqrt{3}$

NOTATION

Complete each solution.

15. $\sqrt{80a^3b^2} = \sqrt{16 \cdot \boxed{5} \cdot a^2 \cdot a \cdot b^2}$
$= \sqrt{16a^2b^2 \cdot \boxed{5a}}$
$= \sqrt{\boxed{16a^2b^2}}\sqrt{5a}$
$= 4ab\sqrt{5a}$

16. $\sqrt[3]{\dfrac{27a^4b^2}{64}} = \dfrac{\sqrt[3]{27a^4b^2}}{\boxed{\sqrt[3]{64}}}$

$= \dfrac{\sqrt[3]{27a^3 \cdot \boxed{ab^2}}}{\sqrt[3]{64}}$

$= \dfrac{\sqrt[3]{\boxed{27a^3}}\,\sqrt[3]{ab^2}}{\sqrt[3]{64}}$

$= \dfrac{3a\sqrt[3]{ab^2}}{4}$

17. What operation is indicated between the two radicals in the expression $\sqrt{4}\sqrt{3}$? multiplication

18. Fill in each blank to make a true statement.
  a. $16x^2 = \left(\boxed{4x}\right)^2$ **b.** $27a^3b^6 = \left(\boxed{3ab^2}\right)^3$

19. Write each expression in a better form.
  a. $\sqrt{5} \cdot 2$ $2\sqrt{5}$ **b.** $\sqrt{7}a$ $a\sqrt{7}$
  c. $9\sqrt{x^2}\sqrt{6}$ $9x\sqrt{6}$ **d.** $\sqrt{y} \cdot \sqrt{25z^4}$ $5z^2\sqrt{y}$

20. **a.** Explain the difference between $\sqrt{5}x$ and $\sqrt{5x}$. $\sqrt{5x} = \sqrt{5 \cdot x}$; $\sqrt{5}x = \sqrt{5} \cdot x$

  b. Why is it better to write $\sqrt{5}x$ as $x\sqrt{5}$?
    $\sqrt{5}x$ could be mistaken for $\sqrt{5x}$.

GUIDED PRACTICE

Simplify each square root. See Examples 1–2.

21. $\sqrt{20}$ $2\sqrt{5}$ ▶ **22.** $\sqrt{18}$ $3\sqrt{2}$

▶ **23.** $\sqrt{50}$ $5\sqrt{2}$ ▶ **24.** $\sqrt{75}$ $5\sqrt{3}$

Use prime factorization to simplify each square root. See Example 3.

25. $\sqrt{45}$ $3\sqrt{5}$ ▶ **26.** $\sqrt{54}$ $3\sqrt{6}$

27. $\sqrt{98}$ $7\sqrt{2}$ **28.** $\sqrt{147}$ $7\sqrt{3}$

29. $\sqrt{48}$ $4\sqrt{3}$ **30.** $\sqrt{128}$ $8\sqrt{2}$

31. $\sqrt{200}$ $10\sqrt{2}$ ▶ **32.** $\sqrt{300}$ $10\sqrt{3}$

Simplify each square root. Assume that all variables represent positive numbers. See Examples 4–5.

33. $\sqrt{n^3}$ $n\sqrt{n}$ ▶ **34.** $\sqrt{x^5}$ $x^2\sqrt{x}$

35. $\sqrt{5a^5}$ $a^2\sqrt{5a}$ **36.** $\sqrt{7b^7}$ $b^3\sqrt{7b}$

37. $\sqrt{4k}$ $2\sqrt{k}$ ▶ **38.** $\sqrt{9p}$ $3\sqrt{p}$

39. $\sqrt{12x}$ $2\sqrt{3x}$ **40.** $\sqrt{20y}$ $2\sqrt{5y}$

41. $-6\sqrt{75t}$ $-30\sqrt{3t}$ ▶ **42.** $-2\sqrt{24s}$ $-4\sqrt{6s}$

43. $128\sqrt{8c}$ $256\sqrt{2c}$ **44.** $11\sqrt{242d}$ $121\sqrt{2d}$

Simplify each square root. Assume that all variables represent positive numbers. See Examples 6–7.

45. $\sqrt{25x^3}$ $5x\sqrt{x}$

▶ **46.** $\sqrt{36y^3}$ $6y\sqrt{y}$

47. $\sqrt{192a^3}$ $8a\sqrt{3a}$

48. $\sqrt{88t^5}$ $2t^2\sqrt{22t}$

49. $2x\sqrt{9x^4y^3}$ $6x^3y\sqrt{y}$

▶ **50.** $3y\sqrt{32xy^2}$ $12y^2\sqrt{2x}$

51. $12x\sqrt{16x^2y^3}$ $48x^2y\sqrt{y}$

52. $-4y^3\sqrt{72x^3y^3}$ $-24xy^4\sqrt{2xy}$

Write each quotient as the quotient of two radicals and simplify. See Examples 8–9.

53. $\sqrt{\dfrac{25}{9}}$ $\dfrac{5}{3}$

▶ **54.** $\sqrt{\dfrac{36}{49}}$ $\dfrac{6}{7}$

55. $\sqrt{\dfrac{81}{64}}$ $\dfrac{9}{8}$

56. $\sqrt{\dfrac{121}{144}}$ $\dfrac{11}{12}$

57. $\sqrt{\dfrac{72x^3}{y^2}}$ $\dfrac{6x\sqrt{2x}}{y}$

58. $\sqrt{\dfrac{108b^2}{d^4}}$ $\dfrac{6b\sqrt{3}}{d^2}$

59. $\sqrt{\dfrac{125n^5}{64n}}$ $\dfrac{5n^2\sqrt{5}}{8}$

▶ **60.** $\sqrt{\dfrac{72q^7}{25q^3}}$ $\dfrac{6q^2\sqrt{2}}{5}$

Simplify each cube root. See Examples 10–11.

61. $\sqrt[3]{24}$ $2\sqrt[3]{3}$

▶ **62.** $\sqrt[3]{32}$ $2\sqrt[3]{4}$

63. $\sqrt[3]{-128}$ $-4\sqrt[3]{2}$

64. $\sqrt[3]{-250}$ $-5\sqrt[3]{2}$

65. $\sqrt[3]{8x^3}$ $2x$

66. $\sqrt[3]{-64x^5}$ $-4x\sqrt[3]{x^2}$

67. $\sqrt[3]{54x^3z^6}$ $3xz^2\sqrt[3]{2}$

▶ **68.** $\sqrt[3]{-24x^3y^5}$ $-2xy\sqrt[3]{3y^2}$

69. $\sqrt[3]{\dfrac{27m^2}{8n^6}}$ $\dfrac{3\sqrt[3]{m^2}}{2n^2}$

70. $\sqrt[3]{\dfrac{125t^9}{27s^6}}$ $\dfrac{5t^3}{3s^2}$

71. $\sqrt[3]{\dfrac{r^4s^5}{1,000t^3}}$ $\dfrac{rs\sqrt[3]{rs^2}}{10t}$

72. $\sqrt[3]{\dfrac{54m^4n^3}{r^3s^6}}$ $\dfrac{3mn\sqrt[3]{2m}}{rs^2}$

TRY IT YOURSELF

Simplify each radical. Assume that all variables represent positive numbers.

73. $\sqrt{250}$ $5\sqrt{10}$

74. $\sqrt{1,000}$ $10\sqrt{10}$

75. $2\sqrt{24}$ $4\sqrt{6}$

76. $3\sqrt{32}$ $12\sqrt{2}$

77. $-2\sqrt{28}$ $-4\sqrt{7}$

78. $-3\sqrt{72}$ $-18\sqrt{2}$

79. $\sqrt{a^2b}$ $a\sqrt{b}$

80. $\sqrt{rs^4}$ $s^2\sqrt{r}$

81. $\dfrac{1}{5}x^2y\sqrt{50x^2y^2}$ $x^3y^2\sqrt{2}$

82. $\dfrac{1}{5}x^5y\sqrt{75x^3y^2}$ $x^6y^2\sqrt{3x}$

83. $-\dfrac{2}{5}\sqrt{80mn^4}$ $-\dfrac{8n^2\sqrt{5m}}{5}$

84. $\dfrac{5}{6}\sqrt{180ab^6}$ $5b^3\sqrt{5a}$

85. $\sqrt{\dfrac{26}{25}}$ $\dfrac{\sqrt{26}}{5}$

86. $\sqrt{\dfrac{17}{169}}$ $\dfrac{\sqrt{17}}{13}$

87. $-\sqrt{\dfrac{20}{49}}$ $-\dfrac{2\sqrt{5}}{7}$

88. $-\sqrt{\dfrac{50}{9}}$ $-\dfrac{5\sqrt{2}}{3}$

89. $\sqrt{\dfrac{48}{81}}$ $\dfrac{4\sqrt{3}}{9}$

▶ **90.** $\sqrt{\dfrac{27}{64}}$ $\dfrac{3\sqrt{3}}{8}$

91. $\sqrt{\dfrac{32}{25}}$ $\dfrac{4\sqrt{2}}{5}$

92. $\sqrt{\dfrac{75}{16}}$ $\dfrac{5\sqrt{3}}{4}$

▶ **93.** $\sqrt[3]{27x^3}$ $3x$

▶ **94.** $\sqrt[3]{-16x^4}$ $-2x\sqrt[3]{2x}$

95. $\sqrt[3]{-81x^2y^3}$ $-3y\sqrt[3]{3x^2}$

96. $\sqrt[3]{81y^2z^3}$ $3z\sqrt[3]{3y^2}$

97. $\sqrt{\dfrac{128m^3n^5}{81mn^7}}$ $\dfrac{8m\sqrt{2}}{9n}$

98. $\sqrt{\dfrac{75p^3q^2}{p^5q^4}}$ $\dfrac{5\sqrt{3}}{pq}$

99. $\sqrt{\dfrac{12r^7s^7}{r^5s^2}}$ $2rs^2\sqrt{3s}$

100. $\sqrt{\dfrac{m^2n^9}{100mn^3}}$ $\dfrac{n^3\sqrt{m}}{10}$

APPLICATIONS

Use a calculator to help solve each problem.

▶ **101.** AMUSEMENT PARK RIDES The illustration shows a pirate ship ride. The time (in seconds) it takes to swing from one extreme to the other is given by

$$t = \pi\sqrt{\dfrac{L}{32}}$$

a. Find t and express it in simplified radical form. Leave π in your answer. $\dfrac{3\pi\sqrt{3}}{4}$ sec

b. Express your answer to part a as a decimal. Round to the nearest tenth of a second. 4.1 sec

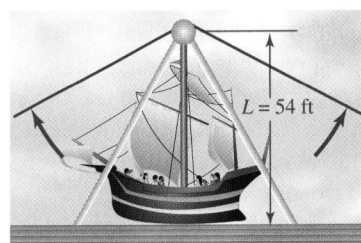

$L = 54$ ft

▶ **102.** HERB GARDENS Refer to the illustration on the next page. The perimeter of the herb garden is given by

$$p = 2\pi\sqrt{\dfrac{a^2+b^2}{2}}$$

a. Find the length of fencing (in meters) needed to enclose the garden. Express the result in simplified radical form. Leave π in your answer. $10\pi\sqrt{2}$ m

b. Express the result from part a as a decimal. Round to the nearest tenth of a meter. 44.4 m

b. Express the result from part a as a decimal. Round to the nearest hundredth of a mile. 4.47 mi

c. How much longer is the proposed entrance as compared to the direct route into the campground? about 2.47 mi

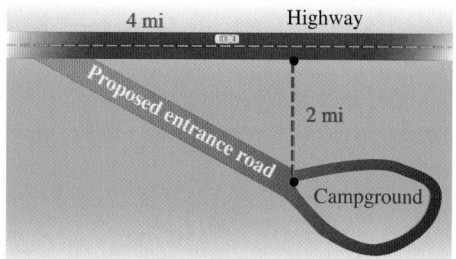

▶ **103.** ARCHAEOLOGY Framed grids, made up of 20 cm × 20 cm squares, are often used to record the location of artifacts found during an excavation.

a. Use the Pythagorean theorem to determine the *exact* distance between a piece of pottery found at point *A* and a cooking utensil found at point *B*. $60\sqrt{2}$ cm

b. Approximate the distance to the nearest tenth of a centimeter. 84.9 cm

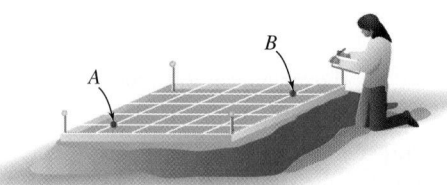

▶ **104.** ENVIRONMENTAL PROTECTION Refer to the illustration in the next column. A new campground is to be constructed 2 miles from a major highway. The proposed entrance, although longer than the direct route, bypasses a grove of old-growth redwood trees.

a. Use the Pythagorean theorem to find the length of the proposed entrance road. Express the result as a radical in simplified form. $2\sqrt{5}$ mi

| **WRITING** |

105. State the multiplication property of radicals.

▶ **106.** When comparing $\sqrt{8}$ and $2\sqrt{2}$, why is $2\sqrt{2}$ called simplified radical form?

| **REVIEW** |

107. Multiply: $(-2a^3)(3a^2)$ $-6a^5$

108. Find the slope of the line passing through $(-6, 0)$ and $(0, -4)$. $-\frac{2}{3}$

109. Write the equation of the line passing through $(0, 3)$ with slope -2. $y = -2x + 3$

▶ **110.** Solve: $-x = -5$ 5

111. Solve: $-x > -5$ $x < 5$ ◄━━━━━)━━━━► $(-\infty, 5)$
                                          5

112. Find the slope of a line perpendicular to a line with a slope of 2. $-\frac{1}{2}$

Objectives

1 Add or subtract square roots.

2 Simplify square roots in a sum or difference.

3 Simplify cube roots in a sum or difference.

SECTION **8.4**

Adding and Subtracting Radical Expressions

We have discussed how to add and subtract like terms. In this section, we will discuss how to add and subtract expressions that contain like radicals.

1 Add or subtract square roots.

When adding monomials, we can often combine *like terms*. For example,

$$3x + 5x = (3 + 5)x \qquad \text{Use the distributive property.}$$
$$= 8x \qquad \text{Perform the addition.}$$

> *Caution!* The expression $3x + 5y$ cannot be simplified, because $3x$ and $5y$ are not like terms.

It is often possible to combine terms that contain *like radicals*.

Like Radicals

Radicals are called **like radicals** when they have the same index and the same radicand.

<table>
<tr><th>Like radicals</th><th>Unlike radicals</th></tr>
<tr><td>$3\sqrt{2}$ and $5\sqrt{2}$</td><td>$3\sqrt{2}$ and $5\sqrt{3}$</td></tr>
<tr><td>The same index and the same radicand</td><td>The same index but different radicands</td></tr>
<tr><td>$5x\sqrt{3y}$ and $-2x\sqrt{3y}$</td><td>$5x\sqrt[3]{3y}$ and $-2x\sqrt{3y}$</td></tr>
<tr><td>The same index and the same radicand</td><td>The same radicands but a different index</td></tr>
</table>

Expressions that contain like radicals can be combined by addition and subtraction. For example, we have

$$3\sqrt{2} + 5\sqrt{2} = (3 + 5)\sqrt{2} \qquad \text{Use the distributive property.}$$

$$= 8\sqrt{2} \qquad \text{Perform the addition.}$$

Likewise, we can simplify the expression $5x\sqrt{3y} - 2x\sqrt{3y}$.

$$5x\sqrt{3y} - 2x\sqrt{3y} = (5x - 2x)\sqrt{3y} \qquad \text{Use the distributive property.}$$

$$= 3x\sqrt{3y} \qquad \text{Perform the subtraction: } 5x - 2x = 3x.$$

> *Caution!* The expression $3\sqrt{2} + 5\sqrt{3}$ cannot be simplified, because the radicals are unlike. For the same reason, we cannot simplify $5x\sqrt[3]{3y} - 2x\sqrt{3y}$.

EXAMPLE 1 Simplify: **a.** $\sqrt{6} + 6 + 5\sqrt{6}$ **b.** $-2\sqrt{m} - 3\sqrt{m}$

Strategy First, we will see if the radicands of the square roots are the same. If they are, we can use the distributive property in reverse to add (or subtract) like radicals.

WHY We must check the radicands first because only square roots with the same radicand can be added or subtracted.

Solution

a. The expression contains three terms: $\sqrt{6}$, 6, and $5\sqrt{6}$. The first and third terms have like radicals, and they can be combined.

$$\sqrt{6} + 6 + 5\sqrt{6} = 6 + \left(1\sqrt{6} + 5\sqrt{6}\right) \qquad \begin{array}{l}\text{Group the expressions with like} \\ \text{radicals. Write } \sqrt{6} \text{ as } 1\sqrt{6}.\end{array}$$

$$= 6 + (1 + 5)\sqrt{6} \qquad \text{Use the distributive property.}$$

$$= 6 + 6\sqrt{6} \qquad \text{Perform the addition.}$$

Note that 6 and $6\sqrt{6}$ do not contain like radicals and cannot be combined.

b. The expressions $-2\sqrt{m}$ and $-3\sqrt{m}$ contain like radicals. We can combine them.

$$-2\sqrt{m} - 3\sqrt{m} = (-2 - 3)\sqrt{m} \qquad \text{Use the distributive property.}$$

$$= -5\sqrt{m} \qquad \text{Perform the subtraction: } -2 - 3 = -5.$$

Self Check 1

Simplify:

a. $\sqrt{7} + 7 + 7\sqrt{7}$ $7 + 8\sqrt{7}$

b. $24\sqrt{m} - 25\sqrt{m}$ $-\sqrt{m}$

Now Try Problem 19

Teaching Example 1 Simplify:
a. $4\sqrt{2} + 7 + \sqrt{2}$
b. $9\sqrt{x} - \sqrt{x}$
Answers:
a. $7 + 5\sqrt{2}$ b. $8\sqrt{x}$

2 Simplify square roots in a sum or difference.

If a sum or difference involves radicals that are unlike, make sure each one is written in simplified form. After doing so, like radicals may result that can be combined.

EXAMPLE 2 Simplify: $3\sqrt{18} + 5\sqrt{8}$

Strategy We will simplify the radicals in each term of the expression. Then we will see if there are like radicals that can be combined.

WHY Only like radicals can be combined.

Solution

The radical $\sqrt{18}$ is not in simplified form, because 18 has a perfect-square factor of 9. The radical $\sqrt{8}$ is not in simplified form either, because 8 has a perfect-square factor of 4. To simplify the radicals and add the expressions, we proceed as follows.

$$3\sqrt{18} + 5\sqrt{8} = 3\sqrt{9 \cdot 2} + 5\sqrt{4 \cdot 2} \qquad \text{Factor 18 and 8 using perfect-square factors.}$$

$$= 3\sqrt{9}\sqrt{2} + 5\sqrt{4}\sqrt{2} \qquad \text{The square root of a product is equal to the product of their square roots.}$$

$$= 3(3)\sqrt{2} + 5(2)\sqrt{2} \qquad \sqrt{9} = 3 \text{ and } \sqrt{4} = 2.$$

$$= 9\sqrt{2} + 10\sqrt{2} \qquad \text{Multiply: } 3(3) = 9 \text{ and } 5(2) = 10.$$

$$= 19\sqrt{2} \qquad \text{To combine like radicals, combine their coefficients: } 9 + 10 = 19.$$

EXAMPLE 3 Simplify: $\sqrt{44x^2y} + x\sqrt{99y}$

Strategy Since the radicals in each part are unlike radicals, we cannot add them in their current form. However, we will simplify the radicals in each term and hope that like radicals result.

WHY Only like radicals can be combined.

Solution

$$\sqrt{44x^2y} + x\sqrt{99y}$$

$$= \sqrt{4x^2 \cdot 11y} + x\sqrt{9 \cdot 11y} \qquad \text{Factor } 44x^2y \text{ and } 99y.$$

$$= \sqrt{4x^2}\sqrt{11y} + x\sqrt{9}\sqrt{11y} \qquad \text{The square root of a product is equal to the product of their square roots.}$$

$$= 2x\sqrt{11y} + 3x\sqrt{11y} \qquad \text{Simplify: } \sqrt{4x^2} = 2x \text{ and } \sqrt{9} = 3.$$

$$= 5x\sqrt{11y} \qquad \text{To combine like radicals, combine their coefficients: } 2x + 3x = 5x.$$

EXAMPLE 4 Simplify: $\sqrt{28x^2y} - 2\sqrt{63y^3}$

Strategy Since the radicals are unlike radicals, we cannot subtract them in their current form. However, we will simplify the radicals in each term and hope that like radicals result.

WHY Only like radicals can be combined.

Solution

$$\sqrt{28x^2y} - 2\sqrt{63y^3}$$

$$= \sqrt{4x^2 \cdot 7y} - 2\sqrt{9y^2 \cdot 7y} \qquad \text{Factor } 28x^2y \text{ and } 63y^3.$$

$$= \sqrt{4x^2}\sqrt{7y} - 2\sqrt{9y^2}\sqrt{7y}$$ The square root of a product is equal to the product of their square roots.

$$= 2x\sqrt{7y} - 2(3y)\sqrt{7y}$$ $\sqrt{4x^2} = 2x$ and $\sqrt{9y^2} = 3y$.

$$= 2x\sqrt{7y} - 6y\sqrt{7y}$$

Since $2x$ and $6y$ are not like terms and therefore cannot be subtracted, the expression does not simplify further.

EXAMPLE 5 Simplify: $\sqrt{27xy} + \sqrt{20xy}$

Strategy Since the radicals are unlike radicals, we cannot add them in their current form. However, we will simplify the radicals in each term and hope that like radicals result.

WHY Only like radicals can be combined.

Solution

$$\sqrt{27xy} + \sqrt{20xy} = \sqrt{9 \cdot 3xy} + \sqrt{4 \cdot 5xy}$$ Factor 27xy and 20xy.

$$= \sqrt{9}\sqrt{3xy} + \sqrt{4}\sqrt{5xy}$$ The square root of a product is equal to the product of their square roots.

$$= 3\sqrt{3xy} + 2\sqrt{5xy}$$ $\sqrt{9} = 3$ and $\sqrt{4} = 2$.

Since the terms have unlike radicals, the expression does not simplify further.

EXAMPLE 6 Simplify: $\sqrt{8x} + \sqrt{3y} - \sqrt{50x} + \sqrt{27y}$

Strategy Since the radicals are unlike radicals, we cannot add or subtract them in their current form. However, we will simplify the radicals in each term and hope that like radicals result.

WHY Only like radicals can be combined.

Solution

$$\sqrt{8x} + \sqrt{3y} - \sqrt{50x} + \sqrt{27y}$$

$$= \sqrt{4 \cdot 2x} + \sqrt{3y} - \sqrt{25 \cdot 2x} + \sqrt{9 \cdot 3y}$$ Factor 8x, 50x, and 27y.

$$= \sqrt{4}\sqrt{2x} + \sqrt{3y} - \sqrt{25}\sqrt{2x} + \sqrt{9}\sqrt{3y}$$

$$= 2\sqrt{2x} + \sqrt{3y} - 5\sqrt{2x} + 3\sqrt{3y}$$

$$= -3\sqrt{2x} + 4\sqrt{3y}$$ Combine like radicals: $2 - 5 = -3$ and $1 + 3 = 4$.

---

3 **Simplify cube roots in a sum or difference.**

We can extend the concepts used to combine square roots to radicals with higher order.

EXAMPLE 7 Simplify: $\sqrt[3]{81x^4} - x\sqrt[3]{24x}$

Strategy Since the radicals are unlike radicals, we cannot add them in their current form. However, we will simplify the radicals in each term and hope that like radicals result.

WHY Only like radicals can be combined.

Teaching Example 7 Simplify:
$a\sqrt[3]{54a} + \sqrt[3]{16a^4}$
Answer:
$5a\sqrt[3]{2a}$

Solution
We simplify each radical and then combine like radicals.

$$\sqrt[3]{81x^4} - x\sqrt[3]{24x} = \sqrt[3]{27x^3 \cdot 3x} - x\sqrt[3]{8 \cdot 3x} \qquad \text{Factor } 81x^4 \text{ and } 24x.$$

$$= \sqrt[3]{27x^3}\sqrt[3]{3x} - x\sqrt[3]{8}\sqrt[3]{3x}$$

$$= 3x\sqrt[3]{3x} - 2x\sqrt[3]{3x}$$

$$= x\sqrt[3]{3x} \qquad \text{Combine like radicals:}$$
$$3x - 2x = x.$$

ANSWERS TO SELF CHECKS

1. a. $7 + 8\sqrt{7}$ **b.** $-\sqrt{m}$ **2.** $14\sqrt{2}$ **3.** $5y\sqrt{3x}$ **4.** $2n\sqrt{5m} - 4m\sqrt{5m}$
5. $5\sqrt{3ab} + 6\sqrt{2ab}$ **6.** $-6\sqrt{2x} + 4\sqrt{5y}$ **7.** $5a\sqrt[3]{3a}$

SECTION 8.4 STUDY SET

VOCABULARY

Fill in the blanks.

1. Like __radicals__ , such as $2\sqrt{3}$ and $5\sqrt{3}$, have the same index and the same radicand.

▶ **2.** Like __terms__ , such as $2x$ and $5x$, have the same variables with the same exponents.

3. When $\sqrt{8}$ and $\sqrt{18}$ are written in __simplified__ form, the results are the like radicals $2\sqrt{2}$ and $3\sqrt{2}$.

4. The expression $3\sqrt{2} + \sqrt{8} - 2$ contains three __terms__ .

CONCEPTS

Determine whether the expressions contain like radicals.

5. $5\sqrt{2}$ and $2\sqrt{3}$ no **6.** $7\sqrt{3x}$ and $3\sqrt{3x}$ yes
7. $125\sqrt[3]{13a}$ and $-\sqrt[3]{13a}$ **8.** $-17\sqrt[4]{5x}$ and $25\sqrt[3]{5x}$
yes   no

What is wrong with the following work?

9. $7\sqrt{5} - 3\sqrt{2} = 4\sqrt{3}$
Because the radicals don't have the same radicand, they can't be combined.

10. $12\sqrt{7} + 20\sqrt{11} = 32\sqrt{18}$
Because the radicals don't have the same radicand, they can't be combined.

11. $7 - 3\sqrt{2} = 4\sqrt{2}$
Because the terms are not like terms, they cannot be combined.

12. $12 + 20\sqrt{11} = 32\sqrt{11}$
Because the terms are not like terms, they cannot be combined.

Complete each table.

13.

x	$\sqrt{x} + \sqrt{3}$
3	$2\sqrt{3}$
12	$3\sqrt{3}$
27	$4\sqrt{3}$
48	$5\sqrt{3}$

▶ **14.**

x	$3\sqrt{x} - \sqrt{2}$
2	$2\sqrt{2}$
8	$5\sqrt{2}$
18	$8\sqrt{2}$
32	$11\sqrt{2}$

NOTATION

Complete each solution.

15. $9\sqrt{5} - 3\sqrt{20} = 9\sqrt{5} - 3\sqrt{4 \cdot 5}$

$$= 9\sqrt{5} - 3\sqrt{4}\sqrt{5}$$

$$= 9\sqrt{5} - 3 \cdot 2\sqrt{5}$$

$$= 9\sqrt{5} - 6\sqrt{5}$$

$$= 3\sqrt{5}$$

▶ **16.** $3\sqrt{80} + 4\sqrt{125} = 3\sqrt{16 \cdot 5} + 4\sqrt{25 \cdot 5}$

$$= 3\sqrt{16} \cdot \sqrt{5} + 4\sqrt{25} \cdot \sqrt{5}$$

$$= 3(4)\sqrt{5} + 4(5)\sqrt{5}$$

$$= 12\sqrt{5} + 20\sqrt{5}$$

$$= 32\sqrt{5}$$

▶ Selected exercises available online at
www.webassign.net/brookscole

GUIDED PRACTICE

Simplify each expression. All variables represent positive numbers. **See Example 1.**

17. $5\sqrt{7} + 4\sqrt{7}$
$9\sqrt{7}$

▶ **18.** $3\sqrt{10} + 4\sqrt{10}$
$7\sqrt{10}$

19. $5 + 3\sqrt{3} + 3\sqrt{3}$
$5 + 6\sqrt{3}$

▶ **20.** $\sqrt{5} + 2 + 3\sqrt{5}$
$2 + 4\sqrt{5}$

▶ **21.** $\sqrt{x} - 4\sqrt{x}$
$-3\sqrt{x}$

22. $\sqrt{t} - 9\sqrt{t}$
$-8\sqrt{t}$

23. $-1 + 2\sqrt{r} - 3\sqrt{r}$
$-1 - \sqrt{r}$

▶ **24.** $-8 - 5\sqrt{c} + 4\sqrt{c}$
$-8 - \sqrt{c}$

Simplify each expression. **See Example 2.**

25. $\sqrt{12} + \sqrt{27}$
$5\sqrt{3}$

▶ **26.** $\sqrt{20} + \sqrt{45}$
$5\sqrt{5}$

▶ **27.** $\sqrt{18} - \sqrt{8}$
$\sqrt{2}$

▶ **28.** $\sqrt{32} - \sqrt{18}$
$\sqrt{2}$

29. $2\sqrt{45} + 2\sqrt{80}$
$14\sqrt{5}$

▶ **30.** $3\sqrt{80} + 3\sqrt{125}$
$27\sqrt{5}$

▶ **31.** $\sqrt{20} + \sqrt{45} + \sqrt{80}$
$9\sqrt{5}$

32. $\sqrt{48} + \sqrt{27} + \sqrt{75}$
$12\sqrt{3}$

33. $\sqrt{200} - \sqrt{75} + \sqrt{48}$
$10\sqrt{2} - \sqrt{3}$

34. $\sqrt{20} + \sqrt{80} - \sqrt{125}$
$\sqrt{5}$

35. $8\sqrt{6} - 5\sqrt{2} - 3\sqrt{6}$
$5\sqrt{6} - 5\sqrt{2}$

▶ **36.** $3\sqrt{2} - 3\sqrt{15} - 4\sqrt{15}$
$3\sqrt{2} - 7\sqrt{15}$

Simplify each expression. All variables represent positive numbers. **See Examples 3–5.**

37. $\sqrt{2x^2} + \sqrt{8x^2}$
$3x\sqrt{2}$

38. $\sqrt{2d^3} + \sqrt{8d^3}$
$3d\sqrt{2d}$

▶ **39.** $\sqrt{49xy^3} + y\sqrt{xy}$
$8y\sqrt{xy}$

40. $\sqrt{20a^2b} + a\sqrt{180b}$
$8a\sqrt{5b}$

41. $5\sqrt{2ab^2} - b\sqrt{98a}$
$-2b\sqrt{2a}$

42. $3\sqrt{9b^5} - 2b\sqrt{b^3}$
$7b^2\sqrt{2b}$

43. $\sqrt{32x^5} - \sqrt{18x^5}$
$x^2\sqrt{2x}$

44. $\sqrt{3a^3} - a\sqrt{12a}$
$-a\sqrt{3a}$

45. $\sqrt{18x^2y} - \sqrt{27x^2y}$
$3x\sqrt{2y} - 3x\sqrt{3y}$

46. $\sqrt{3xy^2} - \sqrt{12x^2y}$
$y\sqrt{3x} - 2x\sqrt{3y}$

47. $\sqrt{18ab} + \sqrt{27ab}$
$3\sqrt{2ab} + 3\sqrt{3ab}$

▶ **48.** $\sqrt{180x} + \sqrt{252y}$
$6\sqrt{5x} + 6\sqrt{7y}$

Simplify each expression. All variables represent positive numbers. **See Example 6.**

49. $\sqrt{48} - \sqrt{8} + \sqrt{27} - \sqrt{32}$ $7\sqrt{3} - 6\sqrt{2}$

50. $\sqrt{162} + \sqrt{50} - \sqrt{75} - \sqrt{108}$ $14\sqrt{2} - 11\sqrt{3}$

51. $5\sqrt{x} + 4\sqrt{4y} - 13\sqrt{x} + 2\sqrt{9y}$ $-8\sqrt{x} + 14\sqrt{y}$

▶ **52.** $\sqrt{4a} + \sqrt{25b} - 2\sqrt{9a} + 5\sqrt{16b}$ $-4\sqrt{a} + 25\sqrt{b}$

Simplify each expression. **See Example 7.**

53. $\sqrt[3]{3} + \sqrt[3]{3}$
$2\sqrt[3]{3}$

54. $\sqrt[3]{2} + 5\sqrt[3]{2}$
$6\sqrt[3]{2}$

55. $2\sqrt[3]{x} - 3\sqrt[3]{x}$
$-\sqrt[3]{x}$

▶ **56.** $4\sqrt[3]{s} - 5\sqrt[3]{s}$
$-\sqrt[3]{s}$

57. $\sqrt[3]{8x^5} + \sqrt[3]{27x^8}$
$2x\sqrt[3]{x^2} + 3x^2\sqrt[3]{x^2}$

58. $\sqrt[3]{192x^4y^5} - \sqrt[3]{24x^4y^5}$
$2xy\sqrt[3]{3xy^2}$

59. $\sqrt[3]{24a^5b^4} + \sqrt[3]{81a^5b^4}$
$5ab\sqrt[3]{3a^2b}$

▶ **60.** $\sqrt[3]{135x^7y^4} - \sqrt[3]{40x^7y^4}$
$x^2y\sqrt[3]{5xy}$

TRY IT YOURSELF

61. $2\sqrt{80} - 3\sqrt{125}$
$-7\sqrt{5}$

▶ **62.** $3\sqrt{245} - 2\sqrt{180}$
$9\sqrt{5}$

▶ **63.** $2\sqrt{28} + 7\sqrt{63}$
$25\sqrt{7}$

64. $\sqrt{12} - \sqrt{48}$
$-2\sqrt{3}$

65. $\sqrt{48} - \sqrt{75}$
$-\sqrt{3}$

66. $\sqrt{288} - 3\sqrt{200}$
$-18\sqrt{2}$

67. $\sqrt[3]{32} + \sqrt[3]{108}$
$5\sqrt[3]{4}$

68. $\sqrt[3]{40} + \sqrt[3]{125}$
$2\sqrt[3]{5} + 5$

69. $\sqrt[3]{3,000} - \sqrt[3]{192}$
$6\sqrt[3]{3}$

70. $\sqrt[3]{x^4} - \sqrt[3]{x^7}$
$x\sqrt[3]{x} - x^2\sqrt[3]{x}$

71. $\sqrt{80} - \sqrt{245}$
$-3\sqrt{5}$

72. $2\sqrt{28} + 2\sqrt{112}$
$12\sqrt{7}$

73. $4\sqrt{63} + 6\sqrt{112}$
$36\sqrt{7}$

74. $\sqrt{24} + \sqrt{150} + \sqrt{240}$
$7\sqrt{6} + 4\sqrt{15}$

▶ **75.** $3\sqrt{54b^2} + 5\sqrt{24b^2}$
$19b\sqrt{6}$

76. $3\sqrt{24x^4y^3} + 2\sqrt{54x^4y^3}$
$12x^2y\sqrt{6y}$

77. $\sqrt[3]{24} - \sqrt[3]{81}$
$-\sqrt[3]{3}$

78. $\sqrt[3]{81} - \sqrt[3]{24}$
$\sqrt[3]{3}$

▶ **79.** $\sqrt{28} + \sqrt{63} + \sqrt{18}$
$5\sqrt{7} + 3\sqrt{2}$

80. $\sqrt{27xy^3} - \sqrt{48xy^3}$
$-y\sqrt{3xy}$

81. $\sqrt[3]{16} + \sqrt[3]{54}$
$5\sqrt[3]{2}$

82. $\sqrt[3]{56a^4b^5} + \sqrt[3]{7a^4b^5}$
$3ab\sqrt[3]{7ab^2}$

83. $y\sqrt{490y} - 2\sqrt{360y^3}$
$-5y\sqrt{10y}$

84. $\sqrt{20x^3y} + \sqrt{45x^5y^3} - \sqrt{80x^7y^5}$
$2x\sqrt{5xy} + 3x^2y\sqrt{5xy} - 4x^3y^2\sqrt{5xy}$

85. $x\sqrt{48xy^2} - y\sqrt{27x^3} + \sqrt{75x^3y^2}$
$6xy\sqrt{3x}$

86. $\sqrt{72p^2q} + \sqrt{54p} - p\sqrt{50q}$
$p\sqrt{2q} + 3\sqrt{6p}$

APPLICATIONS

87. ANATOMY Find the length of the patient's arm in the illustration if he lets it fall to his side. $18\sqrt{3}$ in.

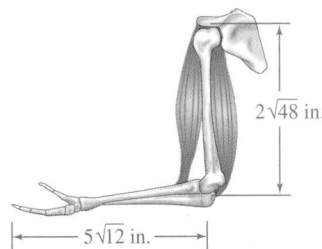

$2\sqrt{48}$ in.

$5\sqrt{12}$ in.

88. PLAYGROUND EQUIPMENT Find the total length of pipe necessary to construct the frame of the swing set shown below. $(16 + 24\sqrt{5})$ ft

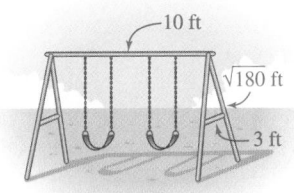

10 ft

$\sqrt{180}$ ft

3 ft

89. BLUEPRINTS Find the length of the motor on the machine shown below. $27\sqrt{2}$ cm

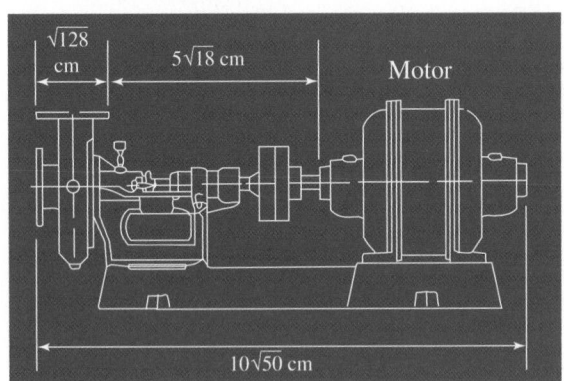

$\sqrt{128}$ cm

$5\sqrt{18}$ cm

Motor

$10\sqrt{50}$ cm

90. TENTS The length of a center support pole for the tents shown in the next column is given by the formula

$$l = 0.5s\sqrt{3}$$

where s is the length of the side of the tent. Find the total length of the four poles needed for the parents' and children's tents. $10\sqrt{3}$ ft

$s = 9$ ft

Parents' tent

$s = 4$ ft

Children's tent

91. FENCING Find the number of feet of fencing needed to enclose the swimming pool complex shown below. $133\sqrt{6}$ ft

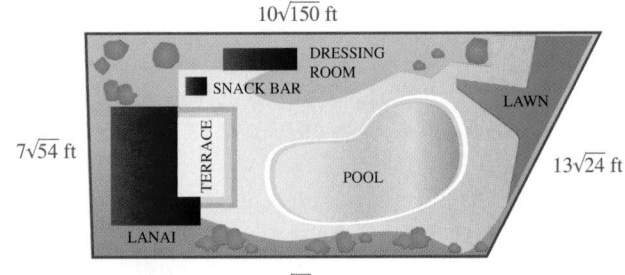

$10\sqrt{150}$ ft

DRESSING ROOM

SNACK BAR

LAWN

$7\sqrt{54}$ ft

TERRACE

POOL

$13\sqrt{24}$ ft

LANAI

$9\sqrt{96}$ ft

92. HARDWARE Find the difference in the lengths of the arms of the door-closing device shown below. $4\sqrt{3}$ in.

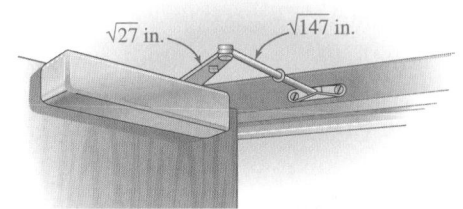

$\sqrt{27}$ in.

$\sqrt{147}$ in.

WRITING

93. Explain why $\sqrt{3} + \sqrt{2}$ cannot be combined.

94. Explain why $\sqrt{4x}$ and $\sqrt[3]{4x}$ cannot be combined.

REVIEW

Simplify each expression. Write each answer without using negative exponents.

95. 3^{-2} $\frac{1}{9}$

96. $\frac{1}{3^{-2}}$ 9

97. -3^2 -9

98. -3^{-2} $-\frac{1}{9}$

99. x^{-3} $\frac{1}{x^3}$

100. $\frac{1}{x^{-3}}$ x^3

101. 3^0 1

102. x^0 1

SECTION 8.5
Multiplying and Dividing Radical Expressions

Objectives

1 Multiply radical expressions.

2 Find powers of square roots.

3 Multiply radical expressions with more than one term.

4 Divide radical expressions.

5 Rationalize denominators.

In this section, we will discuss the methods used to multiply and divide radical expressions.

1 Multiply radical expressions.

Recall that the *product of the square roots of two nonnegative numbers is equal to the square root of the product of those numbers.* For example,

$$\sqrt{2}\sqrt{8} = \sqrt{2 \cdot 8} \qquad \sqrt{3}\sqrt{27} = \sqrt{3 \cdot 27} \qquad \sqrt{x}\sqrt{x^3} = \sqrt{x \cdot x^3}$$
$$= \sqrt{16} \qquad\qquad\qquad = \sqrt{81} \qquad\qquad\qquad = \sqrt{x^4}$$
$$= 4 \qquad\qquad\qquad\quad = 9 \qquad\qquad\qquad\quad = x^2$$

Likewise, the *product of the cube roots of two numbers is equal to the cube root of the product of those numbers.* For example,

$$\sqrt[3]{2}\sqrt[3]{4} = \sqrt[3]{2 \cdot 4} \qquad \sqrt[3]{4}\sqrt[3]{16} = \sqrt[3]{4 \cdot 16} \qquad \sqrt[3]{3x^2}\sqrt[3]{9x} = \sqrt[3]{3x^2 \cdot 9x}$$
$$= \sqrt[3]{8} \qquad\qquad\qquad = \sqrt[3]{64} \qquad\qquad\qquad = \sqrt[3]{27x^3}$$
$$= 2 \qquad\qquad\qquad\quad = 4 \qquad\qquad\qquad\quad = 3x$$

These examples illustrate that radical expressions with the same index can be multiplied.

The Product Rule for Radicals

For any nonnegative real numbers a and b,

$$\sqrt{a} \cdot \sqrt{b} = \sqrt{a \cdot b} \qquad \text{and} \qquad \sqrt[n]{a} \cdot \sqrt[n]{b} = \sqrt[n]{ab}$$

EXAMPLE 1   Multiply and then simplify, if possible:
a. $\sqrt{3}\sqrt{2}$ **b.** $\sqrt{6}\sqrt{8}$ **c.** $\sqrt[3]{4}\sqrt[3]{10}$

Strategy To multiply the radicals, we will multiply their radicands and write the product within the radical. Then, we will simplify the result if possible.

WHY The product of the radicals with the same index is the radical of the product of those numbers.

Solution

a. $\sqrt{3}\sqrt{2} = \sqrt{3 \cdot 2}$ The product of the square roots of two numbers is equal to the square root of the product of those numbers.

$\qquad = \sqrt{6}$ Perform the multiplication within the radical.

b. $\sqrt{6}\sqrt{8} = \sqrt{6 \cdot 8}$ The product of two square roots is equal to the square root of the product.

$\qquad = \sqrt{48}$ Perform the multiplication within the radical. Note that this radical can be simplified.

$\qquad = \sqrt{16}\sqrt{3}$ Factor 48 as $16 \cdot 3$.

$\qquad = 4\sqrt{3}$ $\sqrt{16} = 4$.

Self Check 1

Multiply and then simplify, if possible:

a. $\sqrt{5}\sqrt{3}$ $\sqrt{15}$

b. $\sqrt{8}\sqrt{9}$ $6\sqrt{2}$

c. $\sqrt[3]{6}\sqrt[3]{9}$ $3\sqrt[3]{2}$

Now Try Problems 22, 26, and 29

Teaching Example 1 Multiply and then simplify, if possible:

a. $\sqrt{7}\sqrt{5}$

b. $\sqrt{15}\sqrt{10}$

c. $\sqrt[3]{9}\sqrt[3]{12}$

Answers:

a. $\sqrt{35}$

b. $5\sqrt{6}$

c. $3\sqrt[3]{4}$

c. $\sqrt[3]{4}\sqrt[3]{10} = \sqrt[3]{4 \cdot 10}$ *The product of two cube roots is equal to the cube root of the product.*

$\phantom{c. \sqrt[3]{4}\sqrt[3]{10}} = \sqrt[3]{40}$ *Perform the multiplication within the radical.*

$\phantom{c. \sqrt[3]{4}\sqrt[3]{10}} = \sqrt[3]{8}\sqrt[3]{5}$ $\sqrt[3]{40} = \sqrt[3]{8 \cdot 5} = \sqrt[3]{8}\sqrt[3]{5}.$

$\phantom{c. \sqrt[3]{4}\sqrt[3]{10}} = 2\sqrt[3]{5}$ $\sqrt[3]{8} = 2.$ ∎

To multiply radical expressions having only one term, we multiply the coefficients and multiply the radicals separately and then simplify the result, when possible.

Self Check 2

Multiply and simplify if possible:
a. $\left(2\sqrt{2x}\right)\left(-3\sqrt{3x}\right)$ *−6x√6*
b. $\left(5\sqrt[3]{2}\right)\left(2\sqrt[3]{4}\right)$ *20*

Now Try **Problems 34 and 38**

Teaching Example 2 Multiply and
simplify if possible:
a. $\left(5\sqrt{3a}\right)\left(-4\sqrt{11a}\right)$
b. $\left(2\sqrt[3]{49}\right)\left(3\sqrt[3]{7}\right)$
Answers:
a. $-20a\sqrt{33}$ **b.** 42

EXAMPLE 2   Multiply and simplify if possible:
a. $3\sqrt{6} \cdot 4\sqrt{3}$ **b.** $-2\sqrt[3]{7x} \cdot 6\sqrt[3]{49x^2}$

Strategy We will use the commutative and associative properties to multiply the coefficients and the radicals separately. Then we will simplify the result if possible.

WHY This is the rule for multiplying radical expressions that have only one term.

Solution

a. $3\sqrt{6} \cdot 4\sqrt{3} = 3(4)\sqrt{6}\sqrt{3}$ *Write the coefficients together and the radicals together.*

$\phantom{3\sqrt{6} \cdot 4\sqrt{3}} = 12\sqrt{18}$ *Multiply the coefficients and multiply the radicals.*

$\phantom{3\sqrt{6} \cdot 4\sqrt{3}} = 12\sqrt{9}\sqrt{2}$ $\sqrt{18} = \sqrt{9 \cdot 2} = \sqrt{9}\sqrt{2}.$

$\phantom{3\sqrt{6} \cdot 4\sqrt{3}} = 12(3)\sqrt{2}$ $\sqrt{9} = 3.$

$\phantom{3\sqrt{6} \cdot 4\sqrt{3}} = 36\sqrt{2}$ *Perform the multiplication: 12(3) = 36.*

b. $-2\sqrt[3]{7x} \cdot 6\sqrt[3]{49x^2} = -2(6)\sqrt[3]{7x}\sqrt[3]{49x^2}$ *Write the coefficients together and the radicals together.*

$\phantom{-2\sqrt[3]{7x} \cdot 6\sqrt[3]{49x^2}} = -12\sqrt[3]{7x \cdot 49x^2}$ *Multiply the coefficients and multiply the radicals.*

$\phantom{-2\sqrt[3]{7x} \cdot 6\sqrt[3]{49x^2}} = -12\sqrt[3]{343x^3}$ *Perform the multiplication within the radical.*

$\phantom{-2\sqrt[3]{7x} \cdot 6\sqrt[3]{49x^2}} = -12(7x)$ $\sqrt[3]{343x^3} = 7x.$

$\phantom{-2\sqrt[3]{7x} \cdot 6\sqrt[3]{49x^2}} = -84x$ *Multiply.* ∎

2 Find powers of square roots.

By definition, when the square root of a positive number is squared, the result is that positive number.

Success Tip Since $\left(\sqrt{a}\right)^2 = \sqrt{a} \cdot \sqrt{a}$, it also follows that $\sqrt{a} \cdot \sqrt{a} = a$, if a is a positive real number.

Self Check 3

Find: $\left(6\sqrt{3}\right)^2$ *108*

Now Try **Problems 44 and 48**

Teaching Example 3 Find: $\left(-5\sqrt{2}\right)^2$
Answer: 50

EXAMPLE 3   Find: $\left(2\sqrt{5}\right)^2$

Strategy We will use the rule $\left(\sqrt{a}\right)^2 = a$ to find each power.

WHY Each expression involves the square of the square root of a positive number. ▼

Solution

Recall that a power is used to indicate repeated multiplication.

$$\left(2\sqrt{5}\right)^2 = (2)^2\left(\sqrt{5}\right)^2 \qquad \text{Raise each factor to the second power.}$$

$$= 4 \cdot 5 \qquad\qquad \text{Simplify: } 2^2 = 4 \text{ and } \left(\sqrt{5}\right)^2 = 5.$$

$$= 20$$

3 Multiply radical expressions with more than one term.

Recall that to multiply a polynomial by a monomial, we use the distributive property. We use the same technique to multiply a radical expression that has two or more terms by a radical expression that has only one term.

EXAMPLE 4 Multiply and simplify if possible:

a. $\sqrt{2x}\left(\sqrt{6x} + \sqrt{8x}\right)$ **b.** $\sqrt[3]{3}\left(\sqrt[3]{9} - 2\right)$

Strategy As with polynomials, we will multiply each term within the parentheses by the term outside the parentheses.

WHY This is an application of the distributive property.

Solution

a. $\sqrt{2x}\left(\sqrt{6x} + \sqrt{8x}\right) = \sqrt{2x}\sqrt{6x} + \sqrt{2x}\sqrt{8x}$ 　Distribute the multiplication by $\sqrt{2x}$.

$$= \sqrt{12x^2} + \sqrt{16x^2} \qquad \begin{array}{l}\text{The product of two square roots}\\ \text{is equal to the square root of}\\ \text{the product.}\end{array}$$

$$= \sqrt{4x^2 \cdot 3} + \sqrt{16x^2} \qquad \text{Factor } 12x^2 \text{ as } 4x^2 \cdot 3.$$

$$= \sqrt{4x^2}\sqrt{3} + \sqrt{16x^2} \qquad \begin{array}{l}\text{The square root of a product is}\\ \text{equal to the product of the}\\ \text{square roots.}\end{array}$$

$$= 2x\sqrt{3} + 4x \qquad\qquad \sqrt{4x^2} = 2x \text{ and } \sqrt{16x^2} = 4x.$$

b. $\sqrt[3]{3}\left(\sqrt[3]{9} - 2\right) = \sqrt[3]{3}\sqrt[3]{9} - 2\sqrt[3]{3}$ 　Distribute the multiplication by $\sqrt[3]{3}$.

$$= \sqrt[3]{27} - 2\sqrt[3]{3} \qquad \begin{array}{l}\text{The product of two cube roots is equal to the}\\ \text{cube root of the product.}\end{array}$$

$$= 3 - 2\sqrt[3]{3} \qquad \sqrt[3]{27} = 3.$$

To multiply two binomials, we multiply each term of one binomial by each term of the other binomial and simplify. We multiply two radical expressions, each having two terms, in the same way.

EXAMPLE 5 Multiply: $\left(\sqrt{3x} + 1\right)\left(\sqrt{3x} + 2\right)$

Strategy We will multiply each term within the first set of parentheses by each term within the second set of parentheses. Then, we will simplify the result, if possible.

WHY This is an application of the FOIL method for multiplying two term expressions.

Solution

$$\left(\sqrt{3x} + 1\right)\left(\sqrt{3x} + 2\right)$$

$$= \sqrt{3x}\sqrt{3x} + 2\sqrt{3x} + \sqrt{3x} + 2 \qquad \text{Use the FOIL method.}$$

$$= \sqrt{3x}\sqrt{3x} + 3\sqrt{3x} + 2 \qquad \text{Combine like radicals.}$$

$$= 3x + 3\sqrt{3x} + 2 \qquad \sqrt{3x}\sqrt{3x} = \left(\sqrt{3x}\right)^2 = 3x.$$

Self Check 6

Multiply:
$\left(\sqrt{5} + \sqrt{11}\right)\left(\sqrt{5} - \sqrt{11}\right)$ -6

Now Try Problem 70

Teaching Example 6 Multiply:
$\left(\sqrt{11} - \sqrt{2}\right)\left(\sqrt{11} + \sqrt{2}\right)$
Answer:
9

EXAMPLE 6 Multiply: $\left(\sqrt{7} + \sqrt{2}\right)\left(\sqrt{7} - \sqrt{2}\right)$

Strategy We will multiply each term within the first set of parentheses by each term within the second set of parentheses. Then, we will simplify the result, if possible.

WHY This is an application of the FOIL method for multiplying two term expressions.

Solution
Recall that the product of two binomials that differ only in sign between the terms is the square of the first term minus the square of the second term: $(x + y)(x - y) = x^2 - y^2$. We can use this special product formula to multiply the radical expressions.

$$\left(\sqrt{7} + \sqrt{2}\right)\left(\sqrt{7} - \sqrt{2}\right) = \left(\sqrt{7}\right)^2 - \left(\sqrt{2}\right)^2$$

$$= 7 - 2$$

$$= 5$$

> *Caution!* Note that the answers to Example 6 and Self Check 6 did not contain any radicals. This will be the case whenever we find the product of radical expressions (containing *square* roots) of this form, which differ only in the sign between the terms.

Self Check 7

Multiply:
$\left(\sqrt[3]{3x} + 1\right)\left(\sqrt[3]{9x^2} - 2\right)$

Now Try Problem 74
Self Check 7 Answer
$3x - 2\sqrt[3]{3x} + \sqrt[3]{9x^2} - 2$

Teaching Example 7
$\left(\sqrt[3]{25x} + 4\right)\left(\sqrt[3]{5x^2} - 2\right)$
Answer:
$5x - 2\sqrt[3]{25x} + 4\sqrt[3]{5x^2} - 8$

EXAMPLE 7 Multiply: $\left(\sqrt[3]{4x} - 3\right)\left(\sqrt[3]{2x^2} + 1\right)$

Strategy We will multiply each term within the first set of parentheses by each term within the second set of parentheses. Then, we will simplify the result, if possible.

WHY This is an application of the FOIL method for multiplying two term expressions.

Solution

$$\left(\sqrt[3]{4x} - 3\right)\left(\sqrt[3]{2x^2} + 1\right)$$

$$= \sqrt[3]{4x}\sqrt[3]{2x^2} + \sqrt[3]{4x} - 3\sqrt[3]{2x^2} - 3 \qquad \text{Use the FOIL method.}$$

$$= \sqrt[3]{8x^3} + \sqrt[3]{4x} - 3\sqrt[3]{2x^2} - 3 \qquad \text{The product of two cube roots is equal to the cube root of the product.}$$

$$= 2x + \sqrt[3]{4x} - 3\sqrt[3]{2x^2} - 3 \qquad \sqrt[3]{8x^3} = 2x.$$

4 Divide radical expressions.

To divide radical expressions, we use the division property of radicals. For example, to divide $\sqrt{108}$ by $\sqrt{36}$, we proceed as follows:

$$\frac{\sqrt{108}}{\sqrt{36}} = \sqrt{\frac{108}{36}}$$ The quotient of two square roots is the square root of the quotient.

$$= \sqrt{3}$$ Perform the division within the radical: $108 \div 36 = 3$.

EXAMPLE 8   Divide: $\dfrac{\sqrt{22a^2}}{\sqrt{99a^4}}$

Strategy To divide the square roots, we will divide the radicands and write the quotient within a square root symbol. Then, we will simplify the result, if possible.

WHY Since each denominator contains a square root, these expressions are not in simplified form.

Solution

$$\frac{\sqrt{22a^2}}{\sqrt{99a^4}} = \sqrt{\frac{22a^2}{99a^4}}$$

$$= \sqrt{\frac{2}{9a^2}}$$ Simplify the radicand: $\frac{22a^2}{99a^4} = \frac{\overset{1}{\cancel{11}} \cdot 2 \cdot \overset{1}{\cancel{a^2}}}{\underset{1}{\cancel{11}} \cdot 9 \cdot \underset{1}{\cancel{a^2}} \cdot a^2} = \frac{2}{9a^2}$.

$$= \frac{\sqrt{2}}{\sqrt{9a^2}}$$ The square root of a quotient is equal to the quotient of their square roots.

$$= \frac{\sqrt{2}}{3a}$$ $\sqrt{9a^2} = 3a$.

Self Check 8

Divide: $\dfrac{\sqrt{30y^9}}{\sqrt{160y^5}}$ $\dfrac{y^2\sqrt{3}}{4}$

Now Try Problems 80 and 84

Teaching Example 8 Divide: $\dfrac{\sqrt{15x^{11}}}{\sqrt{125x^{17}}}$

Answer:

$\dfrac{\sqrt{3}}{5x^3}$

---

5 Rationalize denominators.

The length of a diagonal of one of the square tiles shown in the figure is 1 foot. Using the Pythagorean theorem, it can be shown that the length of a side of a tile is $\dfrac{1}{\sqrt{2}}$ feet. Because the expression $\dfrac{1}{\sqrt{2}}$ contains a radical in its denominator, it is not in simplified form. Since it is often easier to work with a radical expression if the denominator does not contain a radical, we now consider how to change the denominator from a radical that represents an irrational number to a rational number. The process is called **rationalizing the denominator.**

To rationalize the denominator of $\dfrac{1}{\sqrt{2}}$, we multiply by 1 in the form $\dfrac{\sqrt{2}}{\sqrt{2}}$.

$$\frac{1}{\sqrt{2}} = \frac{1}{\sqrt{2}} \cdot \frac{\sqrt{2}}{\sqrt{2}} \qquad \text{Multiply by 1 in the form } \frac{\sqrt{2}}{\sqrt{2}}.$$

$$= \frac{\sqrt{2}}{2} \qquad \text{In the numerator, } 1\sqrt{2} = \sqrt{2}. \text{ In the denominator,}$$
$$\sqrt{2}\sqrt{2} = \left(\sqrt{2}\right)^2 = 2. \text{ The denominator is now a rational number.}$$

The length of a side of a patio tile is $\dfrac{1}{\sqrt{2}} = \dfrac{\sqrt{2}}{2}$ feet.

This example suggests the following procedure for rationalizing denominators.

Rationalizing Denominators

To **rationalize a square root denominator,** multiply the numerator and denominator of the given fraction by the square root that makes a perfect-square radicand in the denominator.

To **rationalize a cube root denominator,** multiply the numerator and denominator of the given fraction by the cube root that makes a perfect-cube radicand in the denominator.

Self Check 9

Rationalize each denominator:

a. $\sqrt{\dfrac{2}{7}} \qquad \dfrac{\sqrt{14}}{7}$

b. $\dfrac{5}{\sqrt[3]{5}} \qquad \sqrt[3]{25}$

Now Try Problems 87 and 90

Teaching Example 9 Rationalize each denominator:

a. $\sqrt{\dfrac{11}{5}}$ **b.** $\dfrac{5}{\sqrt[3]{4}}$

Answers:

a. $\dfrac{\sqrt{55}}{5}$ **b.** $\dfrac{5\sqrt[3]{2}}{2}$

EXAMPLE 9

Rationalize each denominator: **a.** $\sqrt{\dfrac{5}{3}}$ **b.** $\dfrac{2}{\sqrt[3]{3}}$

Strategy In each case, we will rationalize the denominator.

WHY The expression will then be in simplest form.

Solution

a. The expression $\sqrt{\dfrac{5}{3}}$ is not in simplified form, because the radicand is a fraction. To write it in simplified form, we use the division property of radicals. Then we use the fundamental property of fractions to rationalize the denominator by multiplying the numerator and the denominator by $\sqrt{3}$.

$$\sqrt{\frac{5}{3}} = \frac{\sqrt{5}}{\sqrt{3}} \qquad \text{The square root of a quotient is the quotient of the square roots. Note that the denominator is the irrational number } \sqrt{3}.$$

$$= \frac{\sqrt{5}}{\sqrt{3}} \cdot \frac{\sqrt{3}}{\sqrt{3}} \qquad \text{To build an equivalent fraction, multiply by } \frac{\sqrt{3}}{\sqrt{3}} = 1.$$

$$= \frac{\sqrt{15}}{3} \qquad \text{In the numerator, do the multiplication. Simplify in the denominator: } \sqrt{3}\sqrt{3} = \left(\sqrt{3}\right)^2 = 3.$$

b. The denominator contains a cube root. We multiply by the smallest factor that gives an integer cube radicand in the denominator. Since $\sqrt[3]{3}\sqrt[3]{9} = \sqrt[3]{27}$ and 27 is a perfect integer cube, we multiply the numerator and denominator by $\sqrt[3]{9}$ and simplify.

$$\frac{2}{\sqrt[3]{3}} = \frac{2}{\sqrt[3]{3}} \cdot \frac{\sqrt[3]{9}}{\sqrt[3]{9}} \qquad \text{To build an equivalent fraction, multiply by } \frac{\sqrt[3]{9}}{\sqrt[3]{9}} = 1.$$

$$= \frac{2\sqrt[3]{9}}{\sqrt[3]{27}} \qquad \text{Multiply: } \sqrt[3]{3}\sqrt[3]{9} = \sqrt[3]{27}.$$

$$= \frac{2\sqrt[3]{9}}{3} \qquad \sqrt[3]{27} = 3. \text{ The denominator is now a rational number.}$$

EXAMPLE 10

Rationalize the denominator and simplify: $\dfrac{5\sqrt{y}}{\sqrt{20x}}$

Strategy We will start by multiplying the numerator and denominator by the smallest factor that will force a perfect square under the square root in the denominator. Then we will simplify the fraction if possible.

WHY We can then evaluate the square root in the denominator.

Solution

To rationalize the denominator, we don't need to multiply the numerator and denominator by $\sqrt{20x}$. To keep the numbers small, we can multiply by $\sqrt{5x}$, because $5x \cdot 20x = 100x^2$, which is a perfect square.

$$\dfrac{5\sqrt{y}}{\sqrt{20x}} = \dfrac{5\sqrt{y}}{\sqrt{20x}} \cdot \dfrac{\sqrt{5x}}{\sqrt{5x}} \qquad \text{To build an equivalent fraction, multiply by } \tfrac{\sqrt{5x}}{\sqrt{5x}} = 1.$$

$$= \dfrac{5\sqrt{5xy}}{\sqrt{100x^2}} \qquad \sqrt{y}\sqrt{5x} = \sqrt{5xy} \text{ and } \sqrt{20x}\sqrt{5x} = \sqrt{100x^2}.$$

$$= \dfrac{5\sqrt{5xy}}{10x} \qquad \sqrt{100x^2} = 10x.$$

$$= \dfrac{\overset{1}{5}\sqrt{5xy}}{\underset{1}{5} \cdot 2x} \qquad \text{Factor 10x and remove a common factor of 5.}$$

$$= \dfrac{\sqrt{5xy}}{2x} \qquad \tfrac{5}{5} = 1.$$

At times, we will encounter fractions such as $\dfrac{2}{\sqrt{3}-1}$, whose denominator has two terms. Note that $\sqrt{3}-1$ is an irrational number. Because $\sqrt{3}-1$ has two terms, multiplying it by $\sqrt{3}$ will not make it a rational number. The key to rationalizing this denominator is to multiply the numerator and denominator by $\sqrt{3}+1$, because the product $(\sqrt{3}+1)(\sqrt{3}-1)$ has no radicals. Radical expressions such as $\sqrt{3}+1$ and $\sqrt{3}-1$ are called **conjugates** of each other.

EXAMPLE 11

Rationalize the denominator and simplify: $\dfrac{2}{\sqrt{3}-1}$

Strategy We will rationalize the denominator by multiplying the numerator and denominator by the conjugate of the denominator.

WHY Since the product of a radical expression and its conjugate contains no radicals, this step clears the denominator of radicals.

Solution

$$\dfrac{2}{\sqrt{3}-1} = \dfrac{2(\sqrt{3}+1)}{(\sqrt{3}-1)(\sqrt{3}+1)} \qquad \begin{array}{l}\text{Multiply the numerator and denominator by the}\\ \text{conjugate of the denominator, which is } \sqrt{3}+1.\end{array}$$

$$= \dfrac{2(\sqrt{3}+1)}{3-1} \qquad \begin{array}{l}\text{Use a special product formula:}\\ (\sqrt{3}-1)(\sqrt{3}+1) = 3-1.\end{array}$$

$$= \dfrac{2(\sqrt{3}+1)}{2} \qquad \begin{array}{l}\text{Subtract. The denominator is now a rational}\\ \text{number.}\end{array}$$

$$= \sqrt{3}+1 \qquad \begin{array}{l}\text{Simplify the fraction by removing the common}\\ \text{factor of 2 in the numerator and denominator.}\end{array}$$

Self Check 10

Rationalize the denominator and simplify: $\dfrac{6\sqrt{z}}{\sqrt{50y}} \quad \dfrac{3\sqrt{2yz}}{5y}$

Now Try **Problem 96**

Teaching Example 10 Rationalize the denominator and simplify: $\dfrac{10\sqrt{a}}{\sqrt{18b}}$

Answer:

$\dfrac{5\sqrt{2ab}}{3b}$

Self Check 11

Rationalize the denominator and simplify: $\dfrac{3}{\sqrt{2}+1} \quad 3(\sqrt{2}-1)$

Now Try **Problem 98**

Teaching Example 11 Rationalize the denominator and simplify: $\dfrac{14}{3+\sqrt{2}}$

Answer:

$2(3-\sqrt{2})$

Self Check 12

Rationalize the denominator and

simplify: $\dfrac{\sqrt{x} - 1}{\sqrt{x} + 1}$ $\dfrac{x - 2\sqrt{x} + 1}{x - 1}$

Now Try Problem 102

Teaching Example 12 Rationalize the

denominator and simplify: $\dfrac{3\sqrt{x} - 2}{3\sqrt{x} + 2}$

Answer:

$\dfrac{9x - 12\sqrt{x} + 4}{9x - 4}$

EXAMPLE 12

Rationalize the denominator and simplify: $\dfrac{\sqrt{x} + 1}{\sqrt{x} - 1}$

Strategy We will rationalize the denominator by multiplying the numerator and denominator by the conjugate of the denominator.

WHY Since the product of a radical expression and its conjugate contains no radicals, this step clears the denominator of radicals.

Solution

We multiply the numerator and denominator by the conjugate of the denominator, which is $\sqrt{x} + 1$.

$$\frac{\sqrt{x} + 1}{\sqrt{x} - 1} = \frac{\left(\sqrt{x} + 1\right)\left(\sqrt{x} + 1\right)}{\left(\sqrt{x} - 1\right)\left(\sqrt{x} + 1\right)}$$ Multiply the numerator and denominator by $\sqrt{x} + 1$.

$$= \frac{\sqrt{x}\sqrt{x} + \sqrt{x}(1) + 1\left(\sqrt{x}\right) + 1}{\sqrt{x}\sqrt{x} + \sqrt{x}(1) - 1\left(\sqrt{x}\right) - 1}$$ Perform the multiplications.

$$= \frac{x + 2\sqrt{x} + 1}{x - 1}$$ $\sqrt{x}\sqrt{x} = \left(\sqrt{x}\right)^2 = x$. Combine like radicals.

ANSWERS TO SELF CHECKS

1. a. $\sqrt{15}$ **b.** $6\sqrt{2}$ **c.** $3\sqrt[3]{2}$ **2. a.** $-6x\sqrt{6}$ **b.** 20 **3.** 108 **4. a.** $9\sqrt{2} - 3$
b. $3\sqrt[3]{2x} - 2x$ **5.** $5a + \sqrt{5a} - 6$ **6.** -6 **7.** $3x - 2\sqrt[3]{3x} + \sqrt[3]{9x^2} - 2$ **8.** $\dfrac{y^2\sqrt{3}}{4}$
9. a. $\dfrac{\sqrt{14}}{7}$ **b.** $\sqrt[3]{25}$ **10.** $\dfrac{3\sqrt{2yz}}{5y}$ **11.** $3\left(\sqrt{2} - 1\right)$ **12.** $\dfrac{x - 2\sqrt{x} + 1}{x - 1}$

SECTION 8.5 STUDY SET

VOCABULARY

Fill in the blanks.

1. In the radical expression $3\sqrt{7}$, the number 3 is the <u>coefficient</u> of the radical.

▶ 2. Radical expressions with the same <u>index</u> can be multiplied.

3. The method of changing a radical denominator of a fraction into a rational number is called <u>rationalizing</u> the denominator.

▶ 4. $3 + \sqrt{2}$ is the <u>conjugate</u> of $3 - \sqrt{2}$.

CONCEPTS

Fill in the blanks.

5. $\sqrt{a} \cdot \sqrt{b} = \sqrt{a \cdot b}$ ▶ 6. $\sqrt{\dfrac{a}{b}} = \dfrac{\sqrt{a}}{\sqrt{b}}$

7. To rationalize the denominator of $\dfrac{x}{\sqrt{x} + 1}$, multiply the numerator and denominator by $\sqrt{x} - 1$.

8. To multiply $2\sqrt{x}$ and $6\sqrt{x}$, we first multiply the <u>coefficients</u>, then multiply the <u>radicals</u>, and simplify the result.

Perform each operation, if possible.

9. $\sqrt{2} + \sqrt{3}$ not possible   10. $\sqrt{2} \cdot \sqrt{3}$ $\sqrt{6}$

11. $\sqrt{2} - \sqrt{3}$ not possible   12. $\dfrac{\sqrt{2}}{\sqrt{3}}$ $\dfrac{\sqrt{6}}{3}$

13. $\sqrt{2} + 3\sqrt{2}$ $4\sqrt{2}$ 14. $\sqrt{2} \cdot 3\sqrt{2}$ 6

15. $\sqrt{2} - 3\sqrt{2}$ $-2\sqrt{2}$ 16. $\dfrac{\sqrt{2}}{3\sqrt{2}}$ $\dfrac{1}{3}$

Find each special product.

17. $\left(\sqrt{6} + \sqrt{3}\right)\left(\sqrt{6} - \sqrt{3}\right)$ 3

18. $\left(\sqrt{a} + \sqrt{7}\right)\left(\sqrt{a} - \sqrt{7}\right)$ $a - 7$

▶ Selected exercises available online at
www.webassign.net/brookscole

NOTATION

Complete each solution.

19. $\left(\sqrt{x} + \sqrt{2}\right)\left(\sqrt{x} - 3\sqrt{2}\right)$

$$= \sqrt{x}\,\sqrt{x} - \sqrt{x}\left(3\sqrt{2}\right) + \sqrt{2}\,\sqrt{x} - \sqrt{2}\left(3\sqrt{2}\right)$$

$$= x - 3\sqrt{2x} + \sqrt{2x} - 3\sqrt{2}\sqrt{2}$$

$$= x - 2\sqrt{2x} - 3(2)$$

$$= x - 2\sqrt{2x} - 6$$

▶ 20. $\dfrac{x}{\sqrt{x} - 2} = \dfrac{x\left(\sqrt{x} + 2\right)}{\left(\sqrt{x} - 2\right)\left(\sqrt{x} + 2\right)}$

$$= \dfrac{x\left(\sqrt{x} + 2\right)}{\left(\sqrt{x}\right)^2 - 2^2}$$

$$= \dfrac{x\sqrt{x} + 2x}{x - 4}$$

GUIDED PRACTICE

Perform each multiplication. See Example 1.

21. $\sqrt{7}\sqrt{3}$ $\sqrt{21}$

▶ 22. $\sqrt{2}\sqrt{11}$ $\sqrt{22}$

23. $\sqrt{5}\sqrt{7}$ $\sqrt{35}$

24. $\sqrt{7}\sqrt{6}$ $\sqrt{42}$

25. $\sqrt{2}\sqrt{8}$ 4

▶ 26. $\sqrt{27}\sqrt{3}$ 9

27. $\sqrt{8}\sqrt{7}$ $2\sqrt{14}$

28. $\sqrt{6}\sqrt{8}$ $4\sqrt{3}$

29. $\sqrt[3]{6}\sqrt[3]{4}$ $2\sqrt[3]{3}$

30. $\sqrt[3]{10}\sqrt[3]{200}$ $10\sqrt[3]{2}$

31. $\sqrt[3]{7}\sqrt[3]{98}$ $7\sqrt[3]{2}$

32. $\sqrt[3]{16}\sqrt[3]{54}$ $6\sqrt[3]{4}$

Perform each multiplication. See Example 2.

33. $\left(-5\sqrt{6}\right)\left(4\sqrt{3}\right)$ $-60\sqrt{2}$

34. $\left(6\sqrt{3}\right)\left(-7\sqrt{2}\right)$ $-42\sqrt{6}$

35. $\left(4\sqrt{x}\right)\left(-2\sqrt{x}\right)$ $-8x$

▶ 36. $\left(3\sqrt{y}\right)\left(15\sqrt{y}\right)$ $45y$

37. $\left(2\sqrt[3]{4}\right)\left(3\sqrt[3]{3}\right)$ $6\sqrt[3]{12}$

38. $\left(-3\sqrt[3]{3}\right)\left(\sqrt[3]{5}\right)$ $-3\sqrt[3]{15}$

39. $\left(-3\sqrt[3]{5a}\right)\left(2\sqrt[3]{25a^2}\right)$ $-30a$

40. $\left(2\sqrt[3]{4b^2}\right)\left(4\sqrt[3]{16b^4}\right)$ $32b^2$

Find each power. See Example 3.

41. $\left(\sqrt{5}\right)^2$ 5

▶ 42. $\left(\sqrt{11}\right)^2$ 11

43. $\left(2\sqrt{3}\right)^2$ 12

44. $\left(-3\sqrt{5}\right)^2$ 45

45. $\left(-\sqrt[3]{9}\right)^3$ -9

▶ 46. $\left(\sqrt[3]{3}\right)^3$ 3

47. $\left(2\sqrt[3]{9}\right)^3$ 72

48. $-2\left(-\sqrt[3]{3}\right)^3$ 6

Perform each multiplication. All variables represent positive numbers. See Example 4.

49. $\sqrt{2}\left(\sqrt{2} + 1\right)$ $2 + \sqrt{2}$

▶ 50. $\sqrt{5}\left(\sqrt{5} + 2\right)$ $5 + 2\sqrt{5}$

51. $2\sqrt{2}\left(\sqrt{8} - 1\right)$ $8 - 2\sqrt{2}$

52. $\sqrt{3}\left(\sqrt{6} + 1\right)$ $3\sqrt{2} + \sqrt{3}$

53. $\sqrt{x}\left(\sqrt{3x} - 2\right)$ $x\sqrt{3} - 2\sqrt{x}$

54. $\sqrt{y}\left(\sqrt{y} + 5\right)$ $y + 5\sqrt{y}$

55. $2\sqrt{x}\left(\sqrt{9x} + 3\right)$ $6x + 6\sqrt{x}$

56. $3\sqrt{z}\left(\sqrt{4z} - \sqrt{z}\right)$ $3z$

57. $\sqrt[3]{7}\left(\sqrt[3]{49} - 2\right)$ $7 - 2\sqrt[3]{7}$

58. $\sqrt[3]{5}\left(\sqrt[3]{25} + 3\right)$ $5 + 3\sqrt[3]{5}$

59. $\sqrt[3]{2x}\left(\sqrt[3]{27x^2} + 3\right)$ $3x\sqrt[3]{2} + 3\sqrt[3]{2x}$

60. $\sqrt[3]{6a^2}\left(\sqrt[3]{36a} - 5\right)$ $6a - 5\sqrt[3]{6a^2}$

Perform each multiplication. All variables represent positive numbers. See Examples 5–6.

61. $\left(\sqrt{2b} + 2\right)\left(\sqrt{2b} - 1\right)$ $2b + \sqrt{2b} - 2$

62. $\left(\sqrt{3p} - 5\right)\left(\sqrt{3p} - 2\right)$ $3p - 7\sqrt{3p} + 10$

63. $\left(2 + \sqrt{3t}\right)\left(3 - \sqrt{3t}\right)$ $6 + \sqrt{3t} - 3t$

64. $\left(5 - \sqrt{2q}\right)\left(2 + \sqrt{2q}\right)$ $10 + 3\sqrt{2q} - 2q$

65. $\left(\sqrt{2x} + 3\right)\left(\sqrt{8x} - 6\right)$ $4x - 18$

66. $\left(\sqrt{5y} - 3\right)\left(\sqrt{20y} + 6\right)$ $10y - 18$

67. $\left(\sqrt{2} + 1\right)\left(\sqrt{2} - 1\right)$ 1

▶ 68. $\left(\sqrt{3} - 1\right)\left(\sqrt{3} + 1\right)$ 2

69. $\left(\sqrt{5} + 3\right)\left(\sqrt{5} - 3\right)$ -4

70. $\left(\sqrt{7} - 2\right)\left(\sqrt{7} + 2\right)$ 3

71. $\left(\sqrt{x} + 2\right)\left(\sqrt{x} - 2\right)$ $x - 4$

72. $\left(\sqrt{p} + 3\right)\left(\sqrt{p} - 3\right)$ $p - 9$

Perform each multiplication. See Example 7.

73. $\left(\sqrt[3]{2} + 1\right)\left(\sqrt[3]{2} + 3\right)$ $\sqrt[3]{4} + 4\sqrt[3]{2} + 3$

▶ 74. $\left(\sqrt[3]{5} - 2\right)\left(\sqrt[3]{5} - 1\right)$ $\sqrt[3]{25} - 3\sqrt[3]{5} + 2$

75. $\left(\sqrt[3]{4y} + 3\right)\left(\sqrt[3]{2y^2} - 1\right)$ $2y - \sqrt[3]{4y} + 3\sqrt[3]{2y^2} - 3$

76. $\left(\sqrt[3]{3c} - 2\right)\left(\sqrt[3]{9c^2} + 2\right)$ $3c + 2\sqrt[3]{3c} - 2\sqrt[3]{9c^2} - 4$

Perform each division. Assume that all variables represent positive numbers. See Example 8.

77. $\dfrac{\sqrt{12x^3}}{\sqrt{27x}}$ $\dfrac{2x}{3}$

78. $\dfrac{\sqrt{32}}{\sqrt{98x^2}}$ $\dfrac{4}{7x}$

79. $\dfrac{\sqrt{18x}}{\sqrt{25x}}$ $\dfrac{3\sqrt{2}}{5}$

▶ 80. $\dfrac{\sqrt{27x}}{\sqrt{75x}}$ $\dfrac{3}{5}$

81. $\dfrac{\sqrt{196x}}{\sqrt{49x^3}}$ $\dfrac{2}{x}$

82. $\dfrac{\sqrt{50}}{\sqrt{98z^2}}$ $\dfrac{5}{7z}$

83. $\dfrac{\sqrt[3]{16x^6}}{\sqrt[3]{54x^3}}$ $\dfrac{2x}{3}$

84. $\dfrac{\sqrt[3]{128a^6}}{\sqrt[3]{16a^3}}$ $2a$

Rationalize each denominator and simplify. All variables represent positive numbers. See Example 9.

85. $\dfrac{1}{\sqrt{3}}$ $\dfrac{\sqrt{3}}{3}$

86. $\dfrac{1}{\sqrt{5}}$ $\dfrac{\sqrt{5}}{5}$

87. $\sqrt{\dfrac{13}{7}}$ $\dfrac{\sqrt{91}}{7}$

▶ 88. $\sqrt{\dfrac{3}{11}}$ $\dfrac{\sqrt{33}}{11}$

89. $\dfrac{5}{\sqrt[3]{5}}$ $\sqrt[3]{25}$

90. $\dfrac{7}{\sqrt[3]{7}}$ $\sqrt[3]{49}$

91. $\dfrac{4}{\sqrt[3]{4}}$ $2\sqrt[3]{2}$

92. $\dfrac{7}{\sqrt[3]{10}}$ $\dfrac{7\sqrt[3]{100}}{10}$

Rationalize each denominator and simplify. All variables represent positive numbers. **See Example 10.**

93. $\dfrac{12}{\sqrt{y}}$ $\dfrac{12\sqrt{y}}{y}$

94. $\dfrac{\sqrt{9y}}{\sqrt{2x}}$ $\dfrac{3\sqrt{2xy}}{2x}$

95. $\dfrac{4\sqrt{a}}{\sqrt{20b}}$ $\dfrac{2\sqrt{5ab}}{5b}$

▶ **96.** $\dfrac{6\sqrt{m}}{\sqrt{72n}}$ $\dfrac{\sqrt{2mn}}{2n}$

Rationalize each denominator and simplify. **See Example 11.**

97. $\dfrac{3}{\sqrt{3}-1}$ $\dfrac{3\sqrt{3}+3}{2}$

98. $\dfrac{3}{\sqrt{5}-2}$ $3\sqrt{5}+6$

99. $\dfrac{3}{\sqrt{7}+2}$ $\sqrt{7}-2$

▶ **100.** $\dfrac{5}{\sqrt{8}+3}$ $15-10\sqrt{2}$

Rationalize each denominator and simplify. Assume that all variables are positive. **See Example 12.**

▶ **101.** $\dfrac{\sqrt{x}+2}{\sqrt{x}-2}$ $\dfrac{x+4\sqrt{x}+4}{x-4}$

102. $\dfrac{\sqrt{x}-3}{\sqrt{x}+3}$ $\dfrac{x-6\sqrt{x}+9}{x-9}$

103. $\dfrac{\sqrt{2a}+1}{\sqrt{2a}-2}$ $\dfrac{2a+3\sqrt{2a}+2}{2a-4}$

104. $\dfrac{\sqrt{3b}+2}{\sqrt{3b}-1}$ $\dfrac{3b+3\sqrt{3b}+2}{3b-1}$

| TRY IT YOURSELF

Perform the operations and simplify, if possible.

105. $\left(3\sqrt{6}\right)^2$ 54

106. $\left(-7\sqrt{2}\right)^2$ 98

107. $3\sqrt{2}\sqrt{x}$ $3\sqrt{2x}$

108. $4\sqrt{3x}\sqrt{5y}$ $4\sqrt{15xy}$

109. $\sqrt{8x}\sqrt{2x^3}$ $4x^2$

▶ **110.** $\sqrt{27y}\sqrt{3y^3}$ $9y^2$

111. $3\sqrt{3x}\left(\sqrt{27x}-1\right)$ $27x-3\sqrt{3x}$

112. $\sqrt{2a}\left(\sqrt{6a}-2\right)$ $2a\sqrt{3}-2\sqrt{2a}$

113. $\left(2\sqrt{7}-x\right)\left(3\sqrt{2}+x\right)$ $6\sqrt{14}+2x\sqrt{7}-3x\sqrt{2}-x^2$

▶ **114.** $\left(4\sqrt{2}-\sqrt{x}\right)\left(\sqrt{x}+2\sqrt{3}\right)$ $4\sqrt{2x}+8\sqrt{6}-x-2\sqrt{3x}$

115. $\left(\sqrt{6}+1\right)^2$ $7+2\sqrt{6}$

▶ **116.** $\left(3-\sqrt{3}\right)^2$ $12-6\sqrt{3}$

117. $\dfrac{9}{\sqrt{27}}$ $\sqrt{3}$

▶ **118.** $\dfrac{4}{\sqrt{20}}$ $\dfrac{2\sqrt{5}}{5}$

119. $\dfrac{3}{\sqrt{32x}}$ $\dfrac{3\sqrt{2x}}{8x}$

120. $\dfrac{5}{\sqrt{18y}}$ $\dfrac{5\sqrt{2y}}{6y}$

121. $\sqrt{\dfrac{12}{5}}$ $\dfrac{2\sqrt{15}}{5}$

122. $\sqrt{\dfrac{24}{7}}$ $\dfrac{2\sqrt{42}}{7}$

123. $\sqrt[3]{4}\left(\sqrt[3]{16}-1\right)$ $4-\sqrt[3]{4}$

124. $\sqrt[3]{5a}\left(\sqrt[3]{25a}+\sqrt[3]{a^2}\right)$ $5\sqrt[3]{a^2}+a\sqrt[3]{5}$

125. $\dfrac{12}{3-\sqrt{3}}$ $6+2\sqrt{3}$

126. $\dfrac{10}{5-\sqrt{5}}$ $\dfrac{5+\sqrt{5}}{2}$

127. $\dfrac{x}{\sqrt{3}+\sqrt{2}}$ $x\sqrt{3}-x\sqrt{2}$

128. $\dfrac{a}{\sqrt{3}-\sqrt{2}}$ $a\sqrt{3}+a\sqrt{2}$

129. $\dfrac{\sqrt[3]{5}}{\sqrt[3]{2}}$ $\dfrac{\sqrt[3]{20}}{2}$

130. $\dfrac{\sqrt[3]{2}}{\sqrt[3]{5}}$ $\dfrac{\sqrt[3]{50}}{5}$

131. $\dfrac{\sqrt{y}+3}{\sqrt{y}-3}$ $\dfrac{y+6\sqrt{y}+9}{y-9}$

132. $\dfrac{\sqrt{t}-1}{\sqrt{t}+4}$ $\dfrac{t-5\sqrt{t}+4}{t-16}$

| APPLICATIONS

▶ **133.** LAWNMOWERS See the illustration below, which shows the blade of a rotary lawnmower. Use the formula for the area of a circle, $A = \pi r^2$, to find the area of lawn covered by one rotation of the blade. Leave π in the answer. 108π in.²

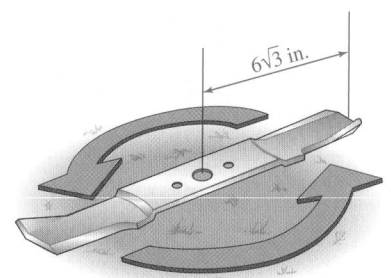

▶ **134.** AWARDS PLATFORMS Find the total number of cubic feet of concrete needed to construct the Olympic Games awards platforms shown below. $24\sqrt{2}$ ft³

▶ **135.** AIR HOCKEY Find the area of the playing surface of the air hockey game in the illustration. $1,800\sqrt{2}$ in.²

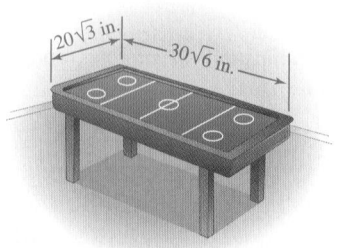

▶ **136. PROJECTOR SCREENS** To find the length l of a rectangle, we can use the formula

$$l = \frac{A}{w}$$

where A is the area of the rectangle and w is its width. Find the length of the screen shown below if its area is 54 square feet. $\frac{9\sqrt{3}}{2}$ ft

2√12 ft

▶ **137. COSTUME DESIGNS** The pattern for one panel of an 1870s English dress is printed on the 1 in. × 1 in. grid shown below. Find the number of square inches of fabric in the trapezoidal-shaped panel. (*Hint:* Use the Pythagorean theorem to determine the lengths of the sides.) 90 in.²

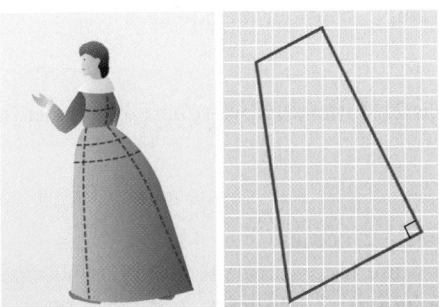

▶ **138. SET DESIGNS** The director of a stage play requested bright down lighting over the portion of the set shown below. Find the area of the rectangle. (*Hint:* Use the Pythagorean theorem to determine the lengths of the sides.) 34 ft²

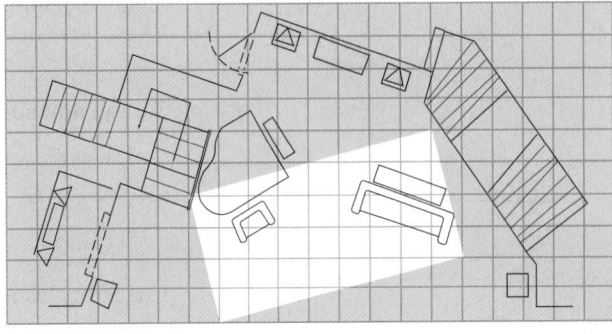

WRITING

139. When rationalizing the denominator of $\frac{5}{\sqrt{6}}$, why must we multiply both the numerator and denominator by $\sqrt{6}$?

▶ **140.** A calculator is used to find decimal approximations for the expressions $\frac{2}{\sqrt{6}}$ and $\frac{\sqrt{6}}{3}$. In each case, the calculator display reads 0.816496581. Explain why the results are the same.

REVIEW

141. Is -2 a solution of $3x - 7 = 5x + 1$? no

142. To evaluate the expression $2 - (-3 + 4)^2$, which operation should be performed first? addition

143. The graph of a straight line rises from left to right. Is the slope of the line positive or negative? positive

144. Multiply: $(x - 4)(x + 4)$ $x^2 - 16$

SECTION 8.6

Solving Radical Equations; the Distance Formula

Objectives

1. Use the squaring property of equality.
2. Check possible solutions.
3. Solve equations containing one square root.
4. Solve radical equations by squaring a binomial.
5. Solve equations containing two square roots.
6. Solve equations containing cube roots.
7. The distance formula.
8. Solve problems modeled by a radical equation.

Many situations can be modeled mathematically by equations that contain radicals. In this section, we will develop techniques to solve such equations.

1 Use the squaring property of equality.

The equation $\sqrt{x} = 6$ is called a **radical equation**, because it contains a radical expression with a variable radicand. To solve this equation, we isolate x by undoing the operation performed on it. Recall that $\sqrt{x}$ represents the number that, when squared, gives x. Therefore, if we *square* $\sqrt{x}$, we will obtain x.

$$\left(\sqrt{x}\right)^2 = x$$

Using this observation, we can eliminate the radical on the left-hand side of $\sqrt{x} = 6$ by squaring that side. Intuition tells us that we should also square the right-hand side. This is a valid step, because *if two numbers are equal, their squares are equal.*

Squaring Property of Equality

For any real numbers a and b if $a = b$, then $a^2 = b^2$.

We can now solve $\sqrt{x} = 6$ by applying the squaring property of equality.

$\sqrt{x} = 6$ This is the equation to solve.

$\left(\sqrt{x}\right)^2 = (6)^2$ Square both sides of the equation to eliminate the radical.

$x = 36$ Simplify each side: $\left(\sqrt{x}\right)^2 = x$ and $(6)^2 = 36$.

Checking this result, we have

$\sqrt{x} = 6$

$\sqrt{36} \overset{?}{=} 6$ Substitute 36 for x.

$6 = 6$ Simplify the left-hand side: $\sqrt{36} = 6$.

Since we obtain a true statement, 36 is the solution.

2 Check possible solutions.

If we square both sides of an equation, the resulting equation may not have the same solutions as the original one. For example, consider the equation

$x = 2$

The only solution of this equation is 2. However, if we square both sides, we obtain $(x)^2 = 2^2$, which simplifies to

$x^2 = 4$

This new equation has solutions 2 and -2, because $2^2 = 4$ and $(-2)^2 = 4$.

The equations $x = 2$ and $x^2 = 4$ are not equivalent equations because they do not have the same solutions. The solution -2 satisfies $x^2 = 4$ but it does not satisfy $x = 2$. We see that squaring both sides of an equation can produce an equation with solutions that don't satisfy the original one. We call such numbers *extraneous solutions*. Therefore, we must check each possible solution in the original equation.

3 Solve equations containing one square root.

To solve an equation containing square root radicals, we follow these steps.

Solving Radical Equations

1. Isolate a radical term on one side of the equation.

2. Square both sides of the equation and solve the resulting equation.

3. Check the possible solutions in the original equation. Discard any extraneous solutions. This step is required.

Self Check 1

Solve: $\sqrt{x-4} = 9$ ₈₅

EXAMPLE 1   Solve: $\sqrt{x+2} = 3$

Strategy We will square both sides of the equation.

WHY The radical is already on a side by itself. Squaring both sides will clear the equation of the square root.

Solution

Since this might produce an equation with more solutions than the original one, we must check each solution.

$$\sqrt{x + 2} = 3$$

$$\left(\sqrt{x + 2}\right)^2 = (3)^2 \qquad \text{Square both sides.}$$

$$x + 2 = 9 \qquad \left(\sqrt{x+2}\right)^2 = x + 2 \text{ and } 3^2 = 9.$$

$$x = 7 \qquad \text{Subtract 2 from both sides.}$$

We check by substituting 7 for x in the original equation.

$$\sqrt{x + 2} = 3$$

$$\sqrt{7 + 2} \overset{?}{=} 3 \qquad \text{Substitute 7 for x.}$$

$$\sqrt{9} \overset{?}{=} 3 \qquad \text{Perform the addition within the radical symbol.}$$

$$3 = 3$$

Since a true statement results, 7 is the solution.

EXAMPLE 2   Solve: $\sqrt{5x + 1} + 7 = 3$

Strategy Since 7 is a term outside the square root symbol, there are two terms on the left side of the equation. To isolate the radical, we will subtract 7 from both sides.

WHY This will put the equation in a form where we can square both sides to clear the radical.

Solution

We isolate the radical on one side and proceed as follows:

$$\sqrt{5x + 1} + 7 = 3$$

$$\sqrt{5x + 1} = -4 \qquad \text{Subtract 7 from both sides.}$$

$$\left(\sqrt{5x + 1}\right)^2 = (-4)^2 \qquad \text{Square both sides to eliminate the radical.}$$

$$5x + 1 = 16 \qquad \left(\sqrt{5x+1}\right)^2 = 5x + 1 \text{ and } (-4)^2 = 16.$$

$$5x = 15 \qquad \text{Subtract 1 from both sides.}$$

$$x = 3 \qquad \text{Divide both sides by 5.}$$

We check by substituting 3 for x in the original equation.

$$\sqrt{5x + 1} + 7 = 3$$

$$\sqrt{5(3) + 1} + 7 \overset{?}{=} 3 \qquad \text{Substitute 3 for x.}$$

$$\sqrt{16} + 7 \overset{?}{=} 3 \qquad \text{Evaluate the expression within the radical symbol.}$$

$$4 + 7 \overset{?}{=} 3$$

$$11 \neq 3$$

Since $11 \neq 3$, 3 is not a solution. In fact, the equation has no solution. This was apparent in step 2 of the solution. There is no real number x that could make the nonnegative number $\sqrt{5x + 1}$ equal to -4.

Example 2 shows that squaring both sides of an equation can lead to possible solutions that do not satisfy the original equation. We call such numbers **extraneous solutions.** In Example 2, 3 is an extraneous solution of $\sqrt{5x + 1} + 7 = 3$.

Now Try Problem 27

Teaching Example 1 Solve:
$\sqrt{x - 10} = 6$
Answer:
46

Self Check 2

Solve: $\sqrt{3x - 2} + 6 = 1$

Now Try Problem 32
Self Check 2 Answer
no solution

Teaching Example 2 Solve:
$\sqrt{2x + 1} + 5 = 2$
Answer:
no solution

4 Solve radical equations by squaring a binomial.

Self Check 3

Solve:
$b + 4 = \sqrt{b^2 + 6b + 12}$ −2

Now Try **Problem 36**

Teaching Example 3 Solve:
$x - 3 = \sqrt{x^2 - 7x + 15}$
Answer:
6

EXAMPLE 3 Solve: $a + 2 = \sqrt{a^2 + 3a + 3}$

Strategy We will square both sides to clear the equation of the radical.

WHY The radical is by itself on one side of the equation.

Solution

The radical is isolated on the right-hand side, so we proceed by squaring both sides to eliminate it.

$$a + 2 = \sqrt{a^2 + 3a + 3}$$

$$(a + 2)^2 = \left(\sqrt{a^2 + 3a + 3}\right)^2 \qquad \text{Square both sides.}$$

$$a^2 + 4a + 4 = a^2 + 3a + 3 \qquad \begin{array}{l}\text{Use a special product formula:}\\(a + 2)^2 = a^2 + 4a + 4.\\\left(\sqrt{a^2 + 3a + 3}\right)^2 = a^2 + 3a + 3.\end{array}$$

$$a^2 + 4a + 4 - a^2 = a^2 + 3a + 3 - a^2 \qquad \begin{array}{l}\text{To eliminate } a^2, \text{ subtract } a^2 \text{ from both}\\\text{sides.}\end{array}$$

$$4a + 4 = 3a + 3 \qquad \text{Combine like terms: } a^2 - a^2 = 0.$$

$$a + 4 = 3 \qquad \text{Subtract } 3a \text{ from both sides.}$$

$$a = -1 \qquad \text{Subtract 4 from both sides.}$$

We check by substituting -1 for a in the original equation.

$$a + 2 = \sqrt{a^2 + 3a + 3}$$

$$-1 + 2 \overset{?}{=} \sqrt{(-1)^2 + 3(-1) + 3} \qquad \text{Substitute } -1 \text{ for } a.$$

$$1 \overset{?}{=} \sqrt{1 - 3 + 3} \qquad \begin{array}{l}\text{Within the radical symbol, first find the power,}\\\text{then perform the multiplication.}\end{array}$$

$$1 \overset{?}{=} \sqrt{1} \qquad \text{Simplify within the radical symbol.}$$

$$1 = 1$$

The solution is -1.

Sometimes, after clearing an equation of a radical, the result is a quadratic equation.

Self Check 4

Solve: $\sqrt{x + 4} - x = -2$ 5

Now Try **Problem 46**

Teaching Example 4 Solve:
$\sqrt{x - 2} - x = -4$
Answer:
6, 3 is extraneous

EXAMPLE 4 Solve: $\sqrt{3 - x} - x = -3$

Strategy We will add x to both sides of the equation to get the radical alone on one side of the equation.

WHY This will put the equation in a form where we can square both sides to clear the radical.

Solution

$$\sqrt{3 - x} - x = -3$$

$$\sqrt{3 - x} = x - 3 \qquad \text{Add } x \text{ to both sides.}$$

We then square both sides to clear the equation of the radical.

$$\left(\sqrt{3 - x}\right)^2 = (x - 3)^2 \qquad \text{Square both sides.}$$

$$3 - x = (x - 3)(x - 3) \qquad \text{The second power indicates two factors of } x - 3.$$

$$3 - x = x^2 - 6x + 9 \qquad \text{Multiply the binomials.}$$

To solve the resulting quadratic equation, we write it in standard form so that the left-hand side is 0.

$$3 = x^2 - 5x + 9 \qquad \text{Add x to both sides.}$$
$$0 = x^2 - 5x + 6 \qquad \text{Subtract 3 from both sides.}$$
$$0 = (x - 3)(x - 2) \qquad \text{Factor } x^2 - 5x + 6.$$
$$x - 3 = 0 \quad \text{or} \quad x - 2 = 0 \qquad \text{Set each factor equal to 0.}$$
$$x = 3 \quad | \qquad x = 2 \qquad \text{Solve each equation.}$$

There are two possible solutions to check in the original equation.

For x = 3

$$\sqrt{3 - x} - x = -3$$
$$\sqrt{3 - 3} - 3 \stackrel{?}{=} -3$$
$$\sqrt{0} - 3 \stackrel{?}{=} -3$$
$$0 - 3 \stackrel{?}{=} -3$$
$$-3 = -3$$

For x = 2

$$\sqrt{3 - x} - x = -3$$
$$\sqrt{3 - 2} - 2 \stackrel{?}{=} -3$$
$$\sqrt{1} - 2 \stackrel{?}{=} -3$$
$$1 - 2 \stackrel{?}{=} -3$$
$$-1 \neq -3$$

Since a true statement results when 3 is substituted for x, 3 is a solution. Since a false statement results when 2 is substituted for x, 2 is an extraneous solution.

5 Solve equations containing two square roots.

In the next example, the equation contains two square roots.

EXAMPLE 5 Solve: $\sqrt{x + 12} = 3\sqrt{x + 4}$

Strategy We will square both sides to clear the equation of both radicals.

WHY We can immediately square both sides since each square root term is by itself on one side of the equation. This step will clear the equation of both radicals.

Solution

$$\sqrt{x + 12} = 3\sqrt{x + 4}$$
$$\left(\sqrt{x + 12}\right)^2 = \left(3\sqrt{x + 4}\right)^2 \qquad \text{Square both sides.}$$
$$x + 12 = 9(x + 4) \qquad \begin{array}{l}\left(\sqrt{x + 12}\right)^2 = x + 12. \\ \left(3\sqrt{x + 4}\right)^2 = 3^2\left(\sqrt{x + 4}\right)^2 = 9(x + 4).\end{array}$$
$$x + 12 = 9x + 36 \qquad \text{Distribute the multiplication by 9.}$$
$$-8x = 24 \qquad \text{Subtract 9x and 12 from both sides.}$$
$$x = -3 \qquad \text{Divide both sides by } -8.$$

We check the solution by substituting -3 for x in the original equation.

$$\sqrt{x + 12} = 3\sqrt{x + 4}$$
$$\sqrt{-3 + 12} \stackrel{?}{=} 3\sqrt{-3 + 4} \qquad \text{Substitute } -3 \text{ for x.}$$
$$\sqrt{9} \stackrel{?}{=} 3\sqrt{1} \qquad \text{Simplify within the radical symbols.}$$
$$3 = 3$$

The solution is -3.

Self Check 5

Solve: $\sqrt{x - 4} = 2\sqrt{x - 16}$ 20

Now Try **Problem 48**

Teaching Example 5 Solve:
$3\sqrt{x - 2} = \sqrt{4x - 3}$
Answer:
3

6 Solve equations containing cube roots.

In the next example, we cube both sides of an equation to eliminate a cube root.

EXAMPLE 6   Solve: $\sqrt[3]{2x + 10} = 2$

Strategy We will cube both sides of the equation.

WHY This will clear the equation of the cube root.

Solution

$$\sqrt[3]{2x + 10} = 2$$

$$\left(\sqrt[3]{2x + 10}\right)^3 = (2)^3 \qquad \text{Cube both sides.}$$

$$2x + 10 = 8 \qquad \left(\sqrt[3]{2x + 10}\right)^3 = 2x + 10 \text{ and } (2)^3 = 8.$$

$$2x = -2 \qquad \text{Subtract 10 from both sides.}$$

$$x = -1 \qquad \text{Divide both sides by 2.}$$

Check the result.

7   The distance formula.

We can use the Pythagorean theorem to derive a formula for finding the distance between two points $P(x_1, y_1)$ and $Q(x_2, y_2)$ on a rectangular coordinate system. The distance d between points P and Q is the length of the hypotenuse of the triangle. The two legs have lengths $x_2 - x_1$ and $y_2 - y_1$.

By the Pythagorean theorem, we have

$$d^2 = (x_2 - x_1)^2 + (y_2 - y_1)^2$$

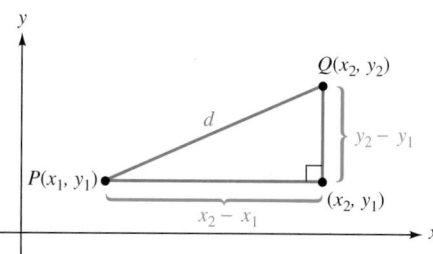

We can take the positive square root of both sides of this equation to get the **distance formula.**

$$d = \sqrt{(x_2 - x_1)^2 + (y_2 - y_1)^2}$$

The Distance Formula

The distance d between the points with coordinates (x_1, y_1) and (x_2, y_2) is given by

$$d = \sqrt{(x_2 - x_1)^2 + (y_2 - y_1)^2}$$

EXAMPLE 7   Find the distance between the points $(1, 2)$ and $(4, 6)$.

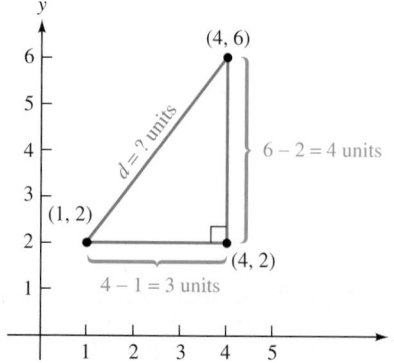

Strategy We will substitute the coordinates into the distance formula and solve for d.

WHY In the formula, d represents the distance between the points.

Solution
We use the distance formula and substitute 1 for x_1, 2 for y_1, 4 for x_2, and 6 for y_2. Then we evaluate the expression under the radical symbol.

$$d = \sqrt{(x_2 - x_1)^2 + (y_2 - y_1)^2}$$

$$= \sqrt{(4 - 1)^2 + (6 - 2)^2} \qquad \text{Substitute.}$$

$$= \sqrt{3^2 + 4^2} \qquad \text{Perform the subtractions within the parentheses first.}$$

$$= \sqrt{9 + 16} \qquad \text{Evaluate the powers.}$$

$$= \sqrt{25} \qquad \text{Perform the addition.}$$

$$= 5 \qquad \text{Find the square root.}$$

The distance between the points is 5 units. ∎

EXAMPLE 8   Find the distance between the points $(-4, 5)$ and $(3, -1)$.

Strategy We will substitute the coordinates into the distance formula and solve for d.

WHY In the formula, d represents the distance between the points.

Solution
We use the distance formula and substitute -4 for x_1, 5 for y_1, 3 for x_2, and -1 for y_2.

$$d = \sqrt{(x_2 - x_1)^2 + (y_2 - y_1)^2}$$

$$= \sqrt{[3 - (-4)]^2 + (-1 - 5)^2} \qquad \text{Substitute.}$$

$$= \sqrt{7^2 + (-6)^2} \qquad \text{Perform the subtractions.}$$

$$= \sqrt{49 + 36} \qquad \text{Evaluate the powers.}$$

$$= \sqrt{85} \qquad \text{Perform the addition.}$$

$$\approx 9.219544457 \qquad \text{Use a calculator.}$$

The distance between the points is exactly $\sqrt{85}$ or approximately 9.22 units. ∎

Self Check 8

Find the distance between the points $(-1, 2)$ and $(-6, 4)$.

Now Try **Problem 64**

Self Check 8 Answer

$\sqrt{29} \approx 5.39$

Teaching Example 8 Find the distance between $(2, -5)$ and $(-2, 6)$.
Answer:
$\sqrt{137} \approx 11.70$

---

8 Solve problems modeled by a radical equation.

Radical equations can be used to model many real life equations.

EXAMPLE 9   *Height of a Bridge* The distance d (in feet) that an object will fall in t seconds is given by the formula

$$t = \sqrt{\frac{d}{16}}$$

To find the height of the bridge shown in the figure on the next page, a man drops a stone into the water. If it takes the stone 3 seconds to hit the water, how high is the bridge?

Self Check 9

If it takes 4 seconds for the stone in Example 9 to hit the water, how high is the bridge? 256 ft

Now Try **Problem 91**

Strategy We will substitute 3 for t in the formula and solve for d.

WHY Since the coin fell for 3 seconds, $t = 3$. The height of the bridge above the water is the same as the distance d that the coin fell.

Solution
We substitute 3 for t in the formula and solve for d.

$$t = \sqrt{\frac{d}{16}}$$

$$3 = \sqrt{\frac{d}{16}} \qquad \text{Substitute 3 for } t.$$

$$(3)^2 = \left(\sqrt{\frac{d}{16}}\right)^2 \qquad \text{Square both sides to eliminate the radical.}$$

$$9 = \frac{d}{16} \qquad 3^2 = 9 \text{ and } \left(\sqrt{\tfrac{d}{16}}\right)^2 = \tfrac{d}{16}.$$

$$144 = d \qquad \text{Multiply both sides by 16.}$$

The bridge is 144 feet above the water. Check this result in the original equation. ■

> **ANSWERS TO SELF CHECKS**
> **1.** 85 **2.** no solution **3.** -2 **4.** 5 **5.** 20 **6.** 10 **7.** 10 **8.** $\sqrt{29} \approx 5.39$ **9.** 256 ft

---

SECTION 8.6 STUDY SET

VOCABULARY

Fill in the blanks.

1. A __radical__ equation contains one or more radical expressions with a variable radicand.

2. To __isolate__ the radical expression in $\sqrt{x} + 1 = 10$ means to get $\sqrt{x}$ by itself on one side of the equation.

3. A false solution that occurs when you square both sides of an equation is called an __extraneous__ solution.

▶ 4. The squaring property of equality states that if two numbers are equal, their __squares__ are equal.

CONCEPTS

Fill in the blanks.

5. The squaring property of equality states that

If $a = b$, then $a^2 = \boxed{b^2}$.

6. The distance formula states that

$$d = \boxed{\sqrt{(x_2 - x_1)^2 + (y_2 - y_1)^2}}$$

▶ Selected exercises available online at **www.webassign.net/brookscole**

To isolate x, what step should be used to undo the operation performed on it? (Assume that x is a positive number.)

7. $x^2 = 4$ Take the positive square root of both sides.

8. $\sqrt{x} = 4$ Square both sides.

Simplify each expression.

▶ 9. $\left(\sqrt{x}\right)^2$ x

▶ 10. $\left(\sqrt{x-1}\right)^2$ $x - 1$

▶ 11. $\left(2\sqrt{x}\right)^2$ $4x$

▶ 12. $\left(2\sqrt{x} - 1\right)^2$ $4x - 4\sqrt{x} + 1$

▶ 13. $\left(\sqrt{2x}\right)^2$ $2x$

▶ 14. $\left(\sqrt[3]{x}\right)^3$ x

What is wrong with each solution?

15.
$$\sqrt{x - 2} = 3$$
$$\left(\sqrt{x - 2}\right)^2 = 3$$
$$x - 2 = 3$$
$$x = 5$$

On the second line, both sides of the equation were not squared—only the left-hand side.

16.   ~~$2 = \sqrt{x - 9}$~~

~~$(2)^2 = \left(\sqrt{x - 9}\right)^2$~~

~~$4 = x - 9$~~

~~$-5 = x$~~

~~$x = -5$~~

On the third line, 9 wasn't added to *both* sides.

17.   ~~$\sqrt{a + 2} - 5 = 4$~~

~~$\left(\sqrt{a + 2} - 5\right)^2 = 4^2$~~

~~$a + 2 - 25 = 16$~~

~~$a - 23 = 16$~~

~~$a = 39$~~

On the second line, $\sqrt{a + 2}$ wasn't isolated before squaring both sides. Also, $\left(\sqrt{a + 2} - 5\right)^2 \ne a + 2 - 25$.

18.   ~~$\sqrt[3]{x + 1} = -2$~~

~~$\left(\sqrt[3]{x + 1}\right)^2 = (-2)^2$~~

~~$x + 1 = 4$~~

~~$x = 3$~~

On the second line, both sides should be cubed.

19. a. On the graph below, plot the points $A(-4, 6)$, $B(4, 0)$, $C(1, -4)$, and $D(-7, 2)$.

b. Draw figure $ABCD$. What type of geometric figure is it? rectangle

c. Find the length of each side of the figure. *AB*: 10, *BC*: 5, *CD*: 10, *DA*: 5

d. Find the perimeter of the figure. 30 units

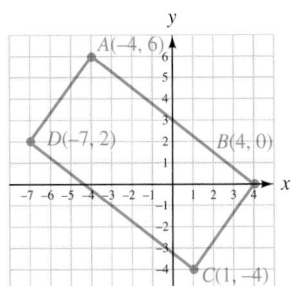

20. a. What type of geometric figure is figure $ABCD$ shown in the following illustration? trapezoid

b. Give the coordinates of points A, B, C, and D. $(-2, 5), (2, 5), (8, -3), (-8, -3)$

c. Find the length of each side of the figure. *AB*: 4, *BC*: 10, *CD*: 16, *DA*: 10

d. Find the area of the figure. 80 square units

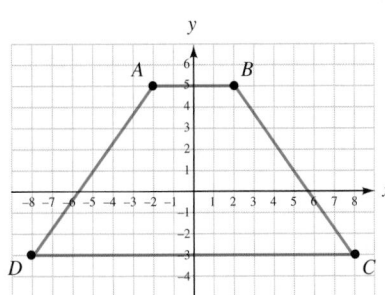

NOTATION

Complete each solution.

21. Solve: $\sqrt{x - 3} = 5$

$\left(\sqrt{x - 3}\right)^2 = 5^2$

$x - 3 = 25$

$x = 28$

▶ **22.** Solve: $\sqrt{2x - 18} = \sqrt{x - 1}$

$\left(\sqrt{2x - 18}\right)^2 = \left(\sqrt{x - 1}\right)^2$

$2x - 18 = x - 1$

$x - 18 = -1$

$x = 17$

GUIDED PRACTICE

Solve each equation and check all solutions. **See Example 1.**

23. $\sqrt{x} = 3$ 9

▶ **24.** $\sqrt{x} = 5$ 25

25. $\sqrt{2a} = 4$ 8

▶ **26.** $\sqrt{3a} = 9$ 27

▶ **27.** $\sqrt{x + 3} = 2$ 1

▶ **28.** $\sqrt{x - 2} = 3$ 11

29. $\sqrt{6 + 2x} = 4$ 5

▶ **30.** $\sqrt{5 - T} = 10$ −95

Solve each equation and check all solutions. **See Example 2.**

31. $\sqrt{3 - T} + 2 = 0$
no solution

32. $\sqrt{7 + 2x} + 4 = 0$
no solution

▶ **33.** $\sqrt{r + 6} = 2$
no solution

34. $\sqrt{r + 5} = 4$
no solution

Solve each equation and check all solutions. **See Example 3.**

35. $x - 3 = \sqrt{x^2 - 15}$
4

36. $v - 2 = \sqrt{v^2 - 16}$
5

37. $x - 1 = \sqrt{x^2 - 4x + 9}$
4

▶ **38.** $\sqrt{15 - 3t} = t - 5$
5

39. $3d = \sqrt{9d^2 - 2d + 8}$
4

40. $\sqrt{4m^2 + 6m + 6} = -2m$
−1

41. $y - 9 = \sqrt{y - 3}$
12

42. $m - 9 = \sqrt{m - 7}$
11

Solve each equation and check all solutions. **See Example 4.**

43. $b = \sqrt{2b - 2} + 1$
1, 3

▶ **44.** $c = \sqrt{5c + 1} - 1$
0, 3

45. $\sqrt{24 + 10n} - n = 4$
−2, 4

46. $\sqrt{7 + 6y} - y = 2$
−1, 3

Solve each equation and check all solutions. **See Example 5.**

47. $\sqrt{3t - 9} = \sqrt{t + 1}$
5

▶ **48.** $\sqrt{a - 3} = \sqrt{2a - 8}$
5

49. $\sqrt{10 - 3x} = \sqrt{2x + 20}$
−2

50. $\sqrt{1 - 2x} = \sqrt{x + 10}$
−3

Solve each equation and check all solutions. **See Example 6.**

51. $\sqrt[3]{x} = 7$ 343

52. $\sqrt[3]{x} = -9$ −729

53. $\sqrt[3]{x - 1} = 4$ 65

54. $\sqrt[3]{2x + 5} = 3$ 11

55. $\sqrt[3]{\frac{1}{2}x - 3} = 2$ 22

56. $\sqrt[3]{x + 4} = 1$ −3

57. $\sqrt[3]{7n - 1} + 1 = 4$ 4

58. $\sqrt[3]{12m + 4} + 2 = 6$ 5

Find the distance between the two points. If an answer contains a radical, give an exact answer and an approximate answer to two decimal places. **See Examples 7–8.**

59. $(3, -4)$ and $(0, 0)$
5

60. $(0, 0)$ and $(-6, 8)$
10

61. $(2, 4)$ and $(5, 9)$
$\sqrt{34}, 5.83$

62. $(5, 9)$ and $(9, 13)$
$4\sqrt{2}, 5.66$

63. $(-2, -8)$ and $(3, 4)$
13

64. $(-5, -2)$ and $(7, 3)$
13

65. $(6, 8)$ and $(12, 16)$
10

66. $(10, 4)$ and $(2, -2)$
10

TRY IT YOURSELF

Solve each equation. Assume that all variables are positive.

67. $-\sqrt{x} = -5$
25

68. $-\sqrt{x} = -12$
144

69. $10 - \sqrt{s} = 7$
9

70. $-4 = 6 - \sqrt{s}$
100

71. $\sqrt{5x - 5} - 5 = 0$
6

72. $\sqrt{6x + 19} - 7 = 0$
5

73. $\sqrt{x + 3} + 5 = 12$
46

74. $\sqrt{x - 5} - 3 = 4$
54

75. $\sqrt{3c - 8} - \sqrt{c} = 0$
4

76. $\sqrt{2x} - \sqrt{x + 8} = 0$
8

77. $\sqrt{9t^2 + 4t + 20} = -3t$
−5

78. $\sqrt{1 - 8s} = s + 4$
−1

79. $\sqrt{3x + 3} = 3\sqrt{x - 1}$
2

80. $2\sqrt{4x + 5} = 5\sqrt{x + 4}$
no solution

81. $2\sqrt{3x + 4} = \sqrt{5x + 9}$
−1

82. $\sqrt{3x + 6} = 2\sqrt{2x - 11}$
10

83. $\sqrt{y + 3} = y - 3$
6, 1 is extraneous

84. $\sqrt{p - 4} + 2 = \sqrt{p}$
4

85. $\sqrt{3x + 1} + 1 = x$
5, 0 is extraneous

86. $\sqrt{4x + 1} + 1 = x$
6, 0 is extraneous

87. $\sqrt[3]{7a - 1} + 1 = 4$
4

88. $\sqrt[3]{12x + 4} - 2 = 2$
5

Find the distance between the two points.

89. $(-2, 3)$ and $(4, -5)$ 10

90. $(-2, -8)$ and $(3, 4)$ 13

APPLICATIONS

91. NIAGARA FALLS The distance s (in feet) that an object will fall in t seconds is given by the formula

$$t = \frac{\sqrt{s}}{4}$$

The time it took a stuntman to go over Niagara Falls in a barrel was 3.25 seconds. Substitute 3.25 for t and solve the equation for s to find the height of the waterfall. 169 ft

92. THE WASHINGTON MONUMENT Gabby Street, a baseball player of the 1920s, was known for once catching a ball dropped from the top of the Washington Monument. If the ball fell for slightly less than 6 seconds before it was caught, find the approximate height of the monument. (*Hint:* See Exercise 91.) about 576 ft

93. PENDULUMS The time t (in seconds) required for a pendulum of length L feet to swing through one back-and-forth cycle, called its **period,** is given by the formula

$$t = 1.11\sqrt{L}$$

The Foucault pendulum in Chicago's Museum of Science and Industry is used to demonstrate the rotation of the Earth. The pendulum completes one cycle in 8.91 seconds. To the nearest tenth of a foot, how long is the pendulum? 64.4 ft

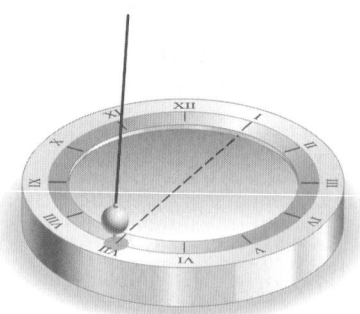

94. POWER USAGE The current I (in amperes), the resistance R (in ohms), and the power P (in watts) are related by the formula

$$I = \sqrt{\frac{P}{R}}$$

Find the power (to the nearest watt) used by a space heater that draws 7 amps when the resistance is 10.2 ohms. 500 watts

95. ROAD SAFETY The formula $s = k\sqrt{d}$ relates the speed s (in mph) of a car and the distance d of the skid when a driver hits the brakes. On wet pavement, $k = 3.24$. How far will a car skid if it is going 55 mph? about 288 ft

96. ROAD SAFETY How far will the car in Exercise 95 skid if it is traveling on dry pavement? On dry pavement, $k = 5.34$. about 106 ft

97. SATELLITE ORBITS Refer to the illustration in the next column. The orbital speed s of an Earth satellite is related to its distance r from Earth's center by the formula

$$\sqrt{r} = \frac{2.029 \times 10^7}{s}$$

If the satellite's orbital speed is 7×10^3 meters per second, find its altitude a (in meters) above Earth's surface. about 2×10^6 m

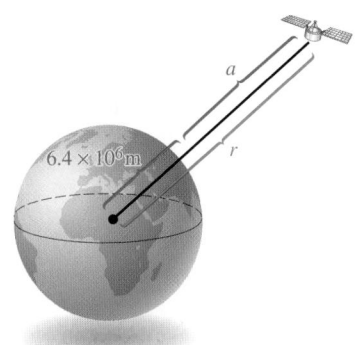

a. position 1? $\sqrt{2} \approx 1.4$ units

b. position 2? $\sqrt{10} \approx 3.2$ units

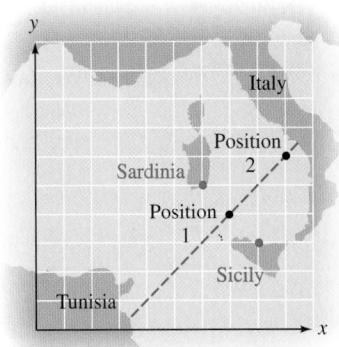

▶ **98. HIGHWAY DESIGNS** A highway curve banked at 8° will accommodate traffic traveling at speed s (in mph) if the radius of the curve is r (feet), according to the equation $s = 1.45\sqrt{r}$. If highway engineers expect traffic to travel at 65 mph, to the nearest foot, what radius should they specify? 2,010 ft

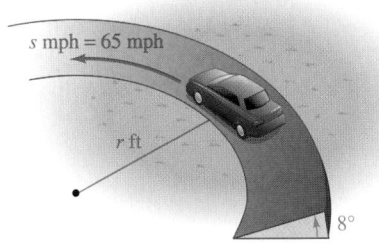

▶ **102. DECK DESIGN** The plans for a patio deck shown below call for three redwood support braces directly under the hot tub. Find the length of each support. Round to the nearest tenth of a foot.
brace 1: 4.2 units, brace 2: 6.7 units, brace 3: 2.2 units

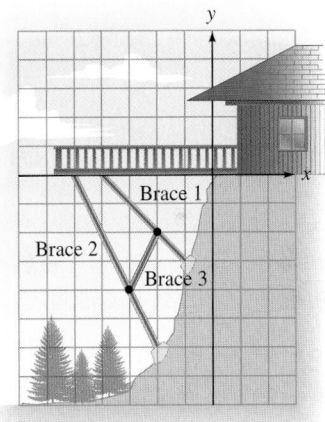

▶ **99. GEOMETRY** The radius of a cone with volume V and height h is given by the formula

$$r = \sqrt{\frac{3V}{\pi h}}$$

Solve the equation for V. $V = \frac{\pi r^2 h}{3}$

100. WINDMILLS The power produced by a certain windmill is related to the speed of the wind by the formula

$$s = \sqrt[3]{\frac{P}{0.02}}$$

where P is the power (in watts) and s is the speed of the wind (in mph). How much power will the windmill produce if the wind is blowing at 30 mph? 540 watts

▶ **101. NAVIGATION** An oil tanker is to travel from Tunisia to Italy, as shown in the next column. The captain wants to travel a course that is always the same distance from a point on the coast of Sardinia as it is from a point on the coast of Sicily. How far will the tanker be from these points when it reaches

WRITING

103. Explain why a check is necessary when solving radical equations.

▶ **104.** How would you know, without solving it, that the equation $\sqrt{x + 2} = -4$ has no solution?

REVIEW

Perform the operations.

105. $(3x^2 + 2x) + (5x^2 - 8x)$ $8x^2 - 6x$

106. $(7a^2 + 2a - 5) - (3a^2 - 2a + 1)$ $4a^2 + 4a - 6$

107. $(x + 3)(x + 3)$ $x^2 + 6x + 9$

108. $x - 1\overline{)x^2 - 6x + 5}$ $x - 5$

109. $(5x - 2)^2$ $25x^2 - 20x + 4$

▶ **110.** $(3y - 7)^2$ $9y^2 - 42y + 49$

Objectives

1 Evaluate expressions of the form $a^{1/n}$.

2 Evaluate expressions of the form $a^{m/n}$.

3 Apply rules of exponents.

SECTION **8.7**

Rational Exponents

We have seen that a positive integer exponent indicates the number of times that a base is to be used as a factor in a product. For example, x^4 means that x is to be used as a factor four times.

$$\overbrace{x^4 = x \cdot x \cdot x \cdot x}^{4 \text{ factors of } x}$$

Also, recall the following rules for exponents.

Rules for Exponents

If m and n represent natural numbers and there are no divisions by zero, then

$$x^m x^n = x^{m+n} \qquad (x^m)^n = x^{mn} \qquad (xy)^n = x^n y^n \qquad \left(\frac{x}{y}\right)^n = \frac{x^n}{y^n}$$

$$x^0 = 1 \qquad x^{-n} = \frac{1}{x^n} \qquad \frac{x^m}{x^n} = x^{m-n}$$

In this section, we will extend the definition and rules for exponents to cover fractional exponents.

1 **Evaluate expressions of the form $a^{1/n}$.**

It is possible to raise numbers to fractional powers. To give meaning to **rational (or fractional) exponents,** we consider $\sqrt{7}$. Because $\sqrt{7}$ is the positive number whose square is 7, we have

$$\left(\sqrt{7}\right)^2 = 7$$

We now consider the symbol $7^{1/2}$. If fractional exponents are to follow the same rules as integer exponents, the square of $7^{1/2}$ must be 7, because

$$(7^{1/2})^2 = 7^{(1/2)2} \qquad \text{Keep the base 7 and multiply the exponents.}$$
$$= 7^1 \qquad \tfrac{1}{2} \cdot 2 = 1.$$
$$= 7$$

The Language of Algebra Rational exponents are also called *fractional exponents.*

Since $(7^{1/2})^2$ and $\left(\sqrt{7}\right)^2$ are both equal to 7, we define $7^{1/2}$ to be $\sqrt{7}$. Similarly, we make these definitions.

$$7^{1/3} = \sqrt[3]{7}$$
$$7^{1/7} = \sqrt[7]{7}$$

and so on. In general, we have the following definition.

Definition of $a^{a/n}$

If n represents a positive integer greater than 1 and $\sqrt[n]{a}$ represents a real number, then

$$a^{1/n} = \sqrt[n]{a}$$

EXAMPLE 1   Simplify: **a.** $64^{1/2}$ **b.** $64^{1/3}$ **c.** $(-64)^{1/3}$

Strategy We will identify the base and the exponent of the exponential expression so that we can write the exponential expression in equivalent radical form.

WHY We know how to evaluate radicals.

Solution

a. $64^{1/2} = \sqrt{64} = 8$ *The denominator of the fractional exponent is 2. Therefore, we find the square root of the base, 64.*

b. $64^{1/3} = \sqrt[3]{64} = 4$ *The denominator of the fractional exponent is 3. Therefore, we find the cube root of the base, 64.*

c. $(-64)^{1/3} = \sqrt[3]{-64} = -4$ *The denominator of the fractional exponent is 3. Therefore, we find the cube root of the base, −64.*

Self Check 1

Simplify:
a. $81^{1/2}$ 9
b. $125^{1/3}$ 5
c. $(-27)^{1/3}$ −3
Now Try **Problems 22, 28, and 29**

Teaching Example 1 Simplify:
a. $25^{1/2}$
b. $8^{1/3}$
c. $-27^{1/3}$
Answers:
a. 5 b. 2 c. −3

---

2 Evaluate expressions of the form $a^{m/n}$.

We can extend the definition of $a^{1/n}$ to cover fractional exponents for which the numerator is not 1. For example, because $4^{3/2}$ can be written as $(4^{1/2})^3$, we have

$$4^{3/2} = (4^{1/2})^3 = \left(\sqrt{4}\right)^3 = 2^3 = 8$$

Because $4^{3/2}$ can also be written as $(4^3)^{1/2}$, we have

$$4^{3/2} = (4^3)^{1/2} = 64^{1/2} = \sqrt{64} = 8$$

In general, $a^{m/n}$ can be written as $(a^{1/n})^m$ or as $(a^m)^{1/n}$. Since $(a^{1/n})^m = \left(\sqrt[n]{a}\right)^m$, and $(a^m)^{1/n} = \sqrt[n]{a^m}$, we make the following definition.

The Definition of $a^{m/n}$

If m and n represent positive integers ($n \neq 1$) and $\sqrt[n]{a}$ represents a real number, then

$$a^{m/n} = \sqrt[n]{a^m} = \left(\sqrt[n]{a}\right)^m$$

EXAMPLE 2   Simplify: **a.** $8^{2/3}$ **b.** $(27)^{4/3}$

Strategy We will identify the base and the exponent of the exponential expression so that we can write the exponential expression in equivalent radical form.

WHY We know how to evaluate radicals.

Solution

a. $8^{2/3} = \left(\sqrt[3]{8}\right)^2$

$\qquad = 2^2$

$\qquad = 4$

b. $(27)^{4/3} = \left(\sqrt[3]{27}\right)^4$

$\qquad = (3)^4$

$\qquad = 81$

Self Check 2

Simplify:
a. $16^{3/2}$ 64
b. $(8)^{4/3}$ 16
Now Try **Problems 34 and 40**

Teaching Example 2 Simplify:
a. $81^{3/4}$ b. $(125)^{2/3}$
Answers:
a. 27 b. 25

> **Success Tip**   The work in Example 2 suggests that in order to avoid large numbers, it is usually easier to take the root of the base first and then find the power.

Self Check 3

Simplify:
a. $-100^{3/2}$ $-1{,}000$
b. $(-8)^{2/3}$ 4

Now Try Problem 47

Teaching Example 3 Simplify:
a. $(-64)^{2/3}$ **b.** $(-27)^{2/3}$
Answers:
a. 16   **b.** 9

EXAMPLE 3   Simplify: **a.** $(-125)^{4/3}$ **b.** $-9^{5/2}$ **c.** $-25^{3/2}$

Strategy We will identify the base and the exponent of the exponential expression so that we can write the exponential expression in equivalent radical form.

WHY We know how to evaluate radicals.

Solution

a. $(-125)^{4/3} = \left(\sqrt[3]{-125}\right)^4$
$= (-5)^4$
$= 625$

b. $-9^{5/2} = -\left(\sqrt{9}\right)^5$
$= -(3)^5$
$= -243$

c. $-25^{3/2} = -\left(\sqrt{25}\right)^3$
$= -(5)^3$
$= -125$

Using Your CALCULATOR   **Fractional Exponents**

To use a reverse-entry scientific calculator to evaluate an exponential expression containing a fractional exponent, we can use the $\boxed{y^x}$ key. For example, to evaluate $6^{-2/3}$, we enter these numbers and press these keys.

6 $\boxed{y^x}$ $\boxed{(}$ 2 $\boxed{+/-}$ $\boxed{\div}$ 3 $\boxed{)}$ $\boxed{=}$ $\boxed{\text{0.302853432}}$

So $6^{-2/3} \approx 0.302853432$.

To use a direct-entry or graphing calculator to evaluate $6^{-2/3}$, we press the following keys.

6 $\boxed{\wedge}$ $\boxed{(}$ $\boxed{(-)}$ 2 $\boxed{\div}$ 3 $\boxed{)}$ $\boxed{\text{ENTER}}$ $\boxed{\begin{array}{l}\text{6}^{\wedge}(\text{-2/3})\\ \quad\text{.3028534321}\end{array}}$

---

3 Apply rules of exponents.

Because of the way in which $a^{1/n}$ and $a^{m/n}$ are defined, the familiar rules for exponents are valid for rational exponents. The following example illustrates the use of each rule.

Self Check 4

Simplify:
a. $5^{1/3}5^{1/3}$ **b.** $(5^{1/3})^4$
c. $(3x)^{1/5}$ **d.** $\dfrac{5^{3/7}}{5^{2/7}}$
e. $\left(\dfrac{2}{3}\right)^{2/3}$ **f.** $5^{-2/7}$
g. $(12^{1/2})^0$

Now Try Problems 50, 58, and 62

Self Check 4 Answers
a. $5^{2/3}$ **b.** $5^{4/3}$ **c.** $3^{1/5}x^{1/5}$ **d.** $5^{1/7}$
e. $\dfrac{2^{2/3}}{3^{2/3}}$ **f.** $\dfrac{1}{5^{2/7}}$ **g.** 1

EXAMPLE 4   Simplify: **a.** $4^{2/5}\,4^{1/5}$ **b.** $(5^{2/3})^{1/2}$ **c.** $(3x)^{2/3}$
d. $\dfrac{4^{3/5}}{4^{2/5}}$ **e.** $\left(\dfrac{3}{2}\right)^{2/5}$ **f.** $4^{-2/3}$ **g.** $(5^{1/3})^0$

Strategy In each case, we will identify the correct rule of exponents to be applied.

WHY The rules for exponents are also valid for fractional exponents.

Solution

a. $4^{2/5}4^{1/5} = 4^{2/5+1/5} = 4^{3/5}$ $\quad x^m x^n = x^{m+n}$.

b. $(5^{2/3})^{1/2} = 5^{(2/3)(1/2)} = 5^{1/3}$ $\quad (x^m)^n = x^{m\cdot n}$.

c. $(3x)^{2/3} = 3^{2/3}x^{2/3}$ $\quad (xy)^m = x^m y^m$.

d. $\dfrac{4^{3/5}}{4^{2/5}} = 4^{3/5-2/5} = 4^{1/5}$ $\dfrac{x^m}{x^n} = x^{m-n}.$

e. $\left(\dfrac{3}{2}\right)^{2/5} = \dfrac{3^{2/5}}{2^{2/5}}$ $\left(\dfrac{x}{y}\right)^n = \dfrac{x^n}{y^n}.$

f. $4^{-2/3} = \dfrac{1}{4^{2/3}}$ $x^{-n} = \dfrac{1}{x^n}.$

g. $(5^{1/3})^0 = 1$ $x^0 = 1.$

We can use the rules for exponents to simplify expressions containing rational exponents.

EXAMPLE 5   Simplify. All variables represent positive numbers:
a. $64^{-2/3}$ **b.** $(x^2)^{1/2}$ **c.** $(x^6y^4)^{1/2}$ **d.** $(27x^{12})^{-1/3}$

Strategy In each case, we will identify the correct rule of exponents to be applied.

WHY The rules for exponents are also valid for fractional exponents.

Solution

a. $64^{-2/3} = \dfrac{1}{64^{2/3}}$

$= \dfrac{1}{(64^{1/3})^2}$

$= \dfrac{1}{4^2}$

$= \dfrac{1}{16}$

b. $(x^2)^{1/2} = x^{2(1/2)}$

$= x^1$

$= x$

c. $(x^6y^4)^{1/2} = x^{6(1/2)}y^{4(1/2)}$

$= x^3y^2$

d. $(27x^{12})^{-1/3} = \dfrac{1}{(27x^{12})^{1/3}}$

$= \dfrac{1}{27^{1/3}x^{12(1/3)}}$

$= \dfrac{1}{3x^4}$

EXAMPLE 6   Simplify: **a.** $x^{1/3}x^{1/2}$ **b.** $\dfrac{3x^{2/3}}{6x^{1/5}}$ **c.** $\dfrac{2x^{-1/2}}{x^{3/4}}$

Strategy In each case, we will identify the correct rule of exponents to be applied.

WHY The rules for exponents are also valid for fractional exponents.

Solution
a. $x^{1/3}x^{1/2} = x^{2/6}x^{3/6}$ *Get a common denominator for the fractional exponents.*

$= x^{5/6}$ *Keep the base x and add the exponents.*

b. $\dfrac{3x^{2/3}}{6x^{1/5}} = \dfrac{3x^{10/15}}{6x^{3/15}}$ *Get a common denominator for the fractional exponents.*

$= \dfrac{1}{2}x^{10/15-3/15}$ *Simplify $\frac{3}{6}$. Keep the base x and subtract the exponents.*

$= \dfrac{1}{2}x^{7/15}$

c. $\dfrac{2x^{-1/2}}{x^{3/4}} = \dfrac{2x^{-2/4}}{x^{3/4}}$ Get a common denominator for the fractional exponents.

$= 2x^{-2/4-3/4}$ Keep the base x and subtract the exponents.

$= 2x^{-5/4}$ Simplify.

$= \dfrac{2}{x^{5/4}}$ $x^{-5/4} = \dfrac{1}{x^{5/4}}.$

ANSWERS TO SELF CHECKS

1. a. 9 **b.** 5 **c.** -3 **2. a.** 64 **b.** 16 **3. a.** $-1{,}000$ **b.** 4 **4. a.** $5^{2/3}$ **b.** $5^{4/3}$
c. $3^{1/5}x^{1/5}$ **d.** $5^{1/7}$ **e.** $\dfrac{2^{2/3}}{3^{2/3}}$ **f.** $\dfrac{1}{5^{2/7}}$ **g.** 1 **5. a.** $\dfrac{1}{125}$ **b.** x **c.** $\dfrac{1}{x^4 y^6}$ **6. a.** $x^{7/6}$ **b.** $\dfrac{1}{2}x^{5/12}$

SECTION 8.7   STUDY SET

VOCABULARY

Fill in the blanks.

1. A fractional exponent is also called a ___rational___ exponent.

▶ **2.** In the expression $27^{1/3}$, 27 is called the ___base___ and the exponent is $\underset{3}{\overset{1}{}}$.

CONCEPTS

Complete each rule for exponents.

3. $x^m x^n = $ x^{m+n} ▶ **4.** $(x^m)^n = $ x^{mn}

5. $\left(\dfrac{x}{y}\right)^n = $ $\dfrac{x^n}{y^n}$ **6.** $x^0 = $ 1

7. $x^{-n} = $ $\dfrac{1}{x^n}$ **8.** $\dfrac{x^m}{x^n} = $ x^{m-n}

9. $x^{1/n} = $ $\sqrt[n]{x}$ **10.** $x^{m/n} = $ $\sqrt[n]{x^m}$ or $\left(\sqrt[n]{x}\right)^m$

11. Write $\sqrt{5}$ using a fractional exponent. $5^{1/2}$

12. Write $5^{1/3}$ using a radical. $\sqrt[3]{5}$

13. Write $8^{4/3}$ using a radical. $\left(\sqrt[3]{8}\right)^4$ or $\sqrt[3]{8^4}$

14. Write $\left(\sqrt{8}\right)^3$ using a fractional exponent. $8^{3/2}$

15. Complete the table.   **16.** Complete the table.

x	$x^{1/2}$
0	0
1	1
4	2
9	3

x	$x^{1/3}$
0	0
-1	-1
-8	-2
8	2

▶ Selected exercises available at
www.webassign.net/brookscole

17. Graph each number on the number line.
$\{8^{1/3}, 17^{1/2}, 2^{3/2}, -5^{2/3}\}$

18. Graph each number on the number line.
$\{4^{-1/2}, 64^{-2/3}, (-8)^{-1/3}\}$

NOTATION

Complete each solution.

19. $(-216)^{4/3} = \left(\sqrt[3]{(-216)}\right)^4$

$= \left(-6\right)^4$

$= 1{,}296$

▶ **20.** $\dfrac{3x^{-2/3}}{x^{3/4}} = \dfrac{3x^{-8/12}}{x^{9/12}}$

$= 3x^{-8/12 - 9/12}$

$= 3x^{-17/12}$

$= \dfrac{3}{x^{17/12}}$

GUIDED PRACTICE

Simplify each expression. See Example 1.

▶ **21.** $81^{1/2}$ 9 **22.** $100^{1/2}$ 10

23. $-144^{1/2}$ -12 ▶ **24.** $-400^{1/2}$ -20

▶ **25.** $\left(\dfrac{4}{49}\right)^{1/2}$ $\dfrac{2}{7}$ ▶ **26.** $\left(\dfrac{9}{64}\right)^{1/2}$ $\dfrac{3}{8}$

27. $27^{1/3}$ 3 **28.** $8^{1/3}$ 2

29. $-125^{1/3}$ -5 **30.** $-1,000^{1/3}$ -10

31. $\left(\dfrac{27}{64}\right)^{1/3}$ $\dfrac{3}{4}$ ▶ **32.** $\left(\dfrac{64}{125}\right)^{1/3}$ $\dfrac{4}{5}$

Simplify each expression. See Example 2.

33. $8^{4/3}$ 16 ▶ **34.** $27^{2/3}$ 9

35. $81^{3/2}$ 729 ▶ **36.** $16^{3/2}$ 64

▶ **37.** $25^{3/2}$ 125 **38.** $4^{5/2}$ 32

39. $125^{4/3}$ 625 **40.** $8^{4/3}$ 16

41. $1,000^{2/3}$ 100 **42.** $27^{4/3}$ 81

43. $\left(\dfrac{8}{27}\right)^{2/3}$ $\dfrac{4}{9}$ **44.** $\left(\dfrac{49}{64}\right)^{3/2}$ $\dfrac{343}{512}$

Simplify each expression. See Example 3.

45. $(-8)^{2/3}$ 4 **46.** $(-125)^{2/3}$ 25

47. $(-1,000)^{2/3}$ 100 ▶ **48.** $(-216)^{4/3}$ $1,296$

Simplify each expression. See Example 4.

49. $6^{3/5}6^{2/5}$ 6 ▶ **50.** $3^{4/7}3^{3/7}$ 3

51. $5^{2/3}5^{4/3}$ 25 ▶ **52.** $2^{7/8}2^{9/8}$ 4

53. $(7^{2/5})^{5/2}$ 7 ▶ **54.** $(8^{1/3})^3$ 8

55. $(5^{2/7})^7$ 25 **56.** $(3^{3/8})^8$ 27

57. $(2x)^{1/2}$ $2^{1/2}x^{1/2}$ **58.** $(5a)^{3/2}$ $5^{3/2}a^{3/2}$

59. $\dfrac{8^{3/2}}{8^{1/2}}$ 8 **60.** $\dfrac{11^{9/7}}{11^{2/7}}$ 11

61. $\dfrac{5^{11/3}}{5^{2/3}}$ 125 **62.** $\dfrac{27^{13/15}}{27^{8/15}}$ 3

63. $\left(\dfrac{5}{2}\right)^{2/3}$ $\dfrac{5^{2/3}}{2^{2/3}}$ **64.** $\left(\dfrac{3}{7}\right)^{3/2}$ $\dfrac{3^{3/2}}{7^{3/2}}$

Simplify each expression. Write your answers without using negative exponents. See Example 5.

65. $4^{-1/2}$ $\dfrac{1}{2}$ **66.** $8^{-1/3}$ $\dfrac{1}{2}$

67. $27^{-2/3}$ $\dfrac{1}{9}$ **68.** $36^{-3/2}$ $\dfrac{1}{216}$

69. $(m^{1/2})^2$ m ▶ **70.** $(x^9)^{1/3}$ x^3

71. $(x^{12}y^6)^{1/3}$ x^4y^2 **72.** $(x^{18}y^{10})^{1/2}$ x^9y^5

73. $16^{-3/2}$ $\dfrac{1}{64}$ **74.** $100^{-5/2}$ $\dfrac{1}{100,000}$

75. $(-27a^9)^{-4/3}$ $\dfrac{1}{81a^{12}}$ **76.** $(-8b^3)^{-4/3}$ $\dfrac{1}{16b^4}$

Simplify each expression. All variables represent positive numbers. See Example 6.

77. $x^{5/6}x^{7/6}$ x^2 **78.** $x^{2/3}x^{7/3}$ x^3

79. $y^{4/7}y^{10/7}$ y^2 ▶ **80.** $y^{5/11}y^{6/11}$ y

81. $\dfrac{x^{3/5}}{x^{1/5}}$ $x^{2/5}$ **82.** $\dfrac{x^{4/3}}{x^{2/3}}$ $x^{2/3}$

83. $\dfrac{2a^{-1/2}}{a^{1/4}}$ $\dfrac{2}{a^{3/4}}$ **84.** $\dfrac{5b^{-2/3}}{b^{5/6}}$ $\dfrac{5}{b^{3/2}}$

85. $\left(\dfrac{1}{4}\right)^{1/2}$ $\dfrac{1}{2}$ ▶ **86.** $\left(\dfrac{1}{25}\right)^{1/2}$ $\dfrac{1}{5}$

87. $(-8)^{1/3}$ -2 **88.** $(-125)^{1/3}$ -5

89. $64^{4/3}$ 256 **90.** $64^{3/2}$ 512

91. $(-343)^{2/3}$ 49 **92.** $(-512)^{4/3}$ $4,096$

93. $\dfrac{x^{1/7}x^{3/7}}{x^{2/7}}$ $x^{2/7}$ **94.** $\dfrac{x^{5/6}x^{5/6}}{x^{7/6}}$ $x^{1/2}$

95. $x^{2/3}x^{3/4}$ $x^{17/12}$ **96.** $a^{3/5}a^{1/2}$ $a^{11/10}$

97. $(b^{1/2})^{3/5}$ $b^{3/10}$ **98.** $(x^{2/5})^{4/7}$ $x^{8/35}$

99. $\dfrac{t^{2/3}}{t^{2/5}}$ $t^{4/15}$ **100.** $\dfrac{p^{3/4}}{p^{1/3}}$ $p^{5/12}$

101. $\dfrac{4b^{-3/2}}{b^{3/4}}$ $\dfrac{4}{b^{9/4}}$ **102.** $\dfrac{p^{-2/3}}{6p^{3/2}}$ $\dfrac{1}{6p^{13/6}}$

103. $\left(\dfrac{x^{4/5}}{x^{2/15}}\right)^3$ x^2 **104.** $\left(\dfrac{y^{2/3}}{y^{1/5}}\right)^{15}$ y^7

If an answer is not exact, round to the nearest tenth.

▶ **105.** SPEAKERS The formula $A = V^{2/3}$ can be used to find the area A of one face of a cube if its volume V is known. Find the amount of floor space on the dance floor taken up by the speakers shown below if each speaker is a cube with a volume of 2,744 cubic inches. 392 in.^{2}

▶ **106.** MEDICAL TESTS Before a series of X-rays are taken, a patient is injected with a special contrast mixture that highlights obstructions in his blood vessels. The amount of the original dose of contrast material remaining in the patient's bloodstream h hours after it is injected is given by $h^{-3/2}$. How much of the contrast material remains in the patient's bloodstream 4 hours after the injection? $\frac{1}{8}$ of the dose

▶ **107. HOLIDAY DECORATING** Find the length s of each string of colored lights used to decorate an evergreen tree in the manner shown below if $s = (r^2 + h^2)^{1/2}$. 26 ft

$h = 24$ ft

s

$r = 10$ ft

▶ **108. VISIBILITY** The distance d in miles a person in an airplane can see to the horizon on a clear day is given by the formula $d = 1.22a^{1/2}$, where a is the altitude of the plane in feet. Find d in the illustration. 231.5 mi

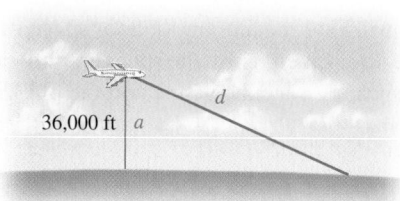

d

36,000 ft | a

▶ **109. TOY DESIGNS** Knowing the volume V of a sphere, we can find its radius r using the formula

$$r = \left(\frac{3V}{4\pi}\right)^{1/3}$$

If the volume occupied by a ball is 2π cubic inches, find its radius. 1.1 in.

▶ **110. EXERCISE EQUIPMENT** Find the length l of the incline bench in the illustration, using the formula $l = (a^2 + b^2)^{1/2}$. 78.5 in.

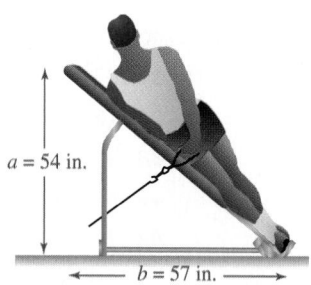

$a = 54$ in.

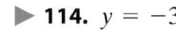
$b = 57$ in.

WRITING

▶ **111.** What is a rational exponent? Give several examples.

▶ **112.** Explain this statement: *In the expression $16^{3/2}$, the number 3/2 requires that two operations be performed on 16.*

REVIEW

Graph each equation.

113. $x = 3$ ▶ **114.** $y = -3$

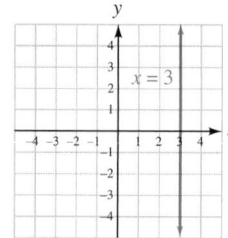

$x = 3$

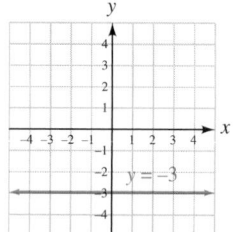

$y = -3$

115. $-2x + y = 4$ **116.** $4x - y = 4$

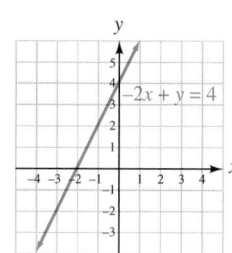

$-2x + y = 4$

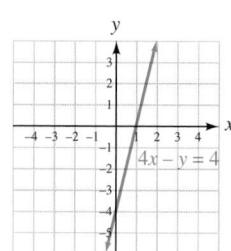

$4x - y = 4$

STUDY SKILLS CHECKLIST

Preparing for the Chapter 8 Test

There are several common mistakes that students make when working with the topics of Chapter 8. To make sure you are prepared for the test over this material, read the list below to help you avoid these mistakes.

☐ When adding or subtracting radicals expressions, you must have *like radicals*. Like radicals are radical expressions in which the index and the radicand are the same.

$5\sqrt{3} + 2\sqrt{3} = 7\sqrt{3}$ — Both have the same index and radicand. Add the coefficients of the terms and keep the same radical.

$5\sqrt{3} + 2\sqrt{7}$ cannot be combined. — The operation is addition but the radicals are not like radicals. The expression is in simplest form.

$$5\sqrt{18} + 2\sqrt{50} = 5\sqrt{9 \cdot 2} + 2\sqrt{25 \cdot 2}$$ — Write 18 as 18 = 9 · 2. Write 50 as 50 = 25 · 2.

$$= 5\sqrt{9} \cdot \sqrt{2} + 2\sqrt{25} \cdot \sqrt{2}$$ — The square root of a product is equal to the product of the square roots.

$$= 5 \cdot 3 \cdot \sqrt{2} + 2 \cdot 5 \cdot \sqrt{2}$$ — Evaluate $\sqrt{9} = 3$ and $\sqrt{25} = 5$.

$$= 15\sqrt{2} + 10\sqrt{2}$$ — Multiply 5 · 3 = 15 and 2 · 5 = 10.

$$= 25\sqrt{2}$$ — Both radicals have the same index and the same radicand. To combine them, add the coefficients and keep the radical.

☐ To multiply the radicals, only the index has to be the same. Use the product rule for radicals to carry out the multiplication. Be sure to simplify all answers.

$$3\sqrt{15}\left(2\sqrt{10}\right) = 3 \cdot 2\sqrt{15} \cdot \sqrt{10}$$ — Multiply the integer factors, 3 and 2, and multiply the radicals.

$$= 6\sqrt{150}$$ — Use the product rule for radicals.

$$= 6\sqrt{25}\sqrt{6}$$

$$= 6(5)\sqrt{6}$$

$$= 30\sqrt{6}$$

☐ To multiply radical expressions with more than one term, we use the distributive property.

$$3\sqrt{5}\left(2\sqrt{15} - 6\sqrt{10}\right) = 3\sqrt{5} \cdot 2\sqrt{15} - 3\sqrt{5} \cdot 6\sqrt{10}$$

$$= 6\sqrt{75} - 18\sqrt{50}$$

$$= 6\sqrt{3 \cdot 5 \cdot 5} - 18\sqrt{2 \cdot 5 \cdot 5}$$

$$= 6 \cdot 5\sqrt{3} - 18 \cdot 5\sqrt{2}$$

$$= 30\sqrt{3} - 90\sqrt{2}$$

☐ When solving radical equations, isolate the radical on one side of the equation before raising both sides to the power that matches the index.

☐ Even if you are certain that no algebraic mistakes were made when solving a radical equation, you must still check your solutions. Raising both sides to a power can introduce extraneous solutions that must be discarded.

Teaching Guide: Refer to the Instructor's Resource Binder to find activities, worksheets on key concepts, more examples, instruction tips, overheads, and assessments.

CHAPTER **8**   SUMMARY AND REVIEW

SECTION **8.1**   **Square Roots**

DEFINITIONS AND CONCEPTS	EXAMPLES
The number b is a **square root** of a if $b^2 = a$.	3 is a square root of 9 because $3^2 = 9$. $\dfrac{1}{2}$ is a square root of $\dfrac{1}{4}$ because $\left(\dfrac{1}{2}\right)^2 = \dfrac{1}{4}$.
If a is positive, the expression $\sqrt{a}$ represents the **principal** (or **positive**) **square root** of a. The principal square root of 0 is 0.	$\sqrt{16} = 4$: 4 is the principal square root of 16. $\sqrt{\dfrac{9}{25}} = \dfrac{3}{5}$: $\dfrac{3}{5}$ is the principal square root of $\dfrac{9}{25}$. $\sqrt{0} = 0$: 0 is the principal square root of 0.
The expression within a **radical symbol** $\sqrt{}$ is called the **radicand**.	In the expression $\sqrt{16}$, 16 is the radicand. In the expression $\sqrt{\dfrac{9}{25}}$, $\dfrac{9}{25}$ is the radicand.
If a positive number is not a **perfect square**, its square root is irrational. Square roots of negative numbers are called **imaginary numbers**.	$\sqrt{11}$ is an irrational number. $\sqrt{-5}$ is an imaginary number.
The function $f(x) = \sqrt{x}$ is called the **square root function**.	Evaluate $f(x) = \sqrt{x}$ for $x = 9$ and $x = 16$. $f(9) = \sqrt{9} = 3 \qquad f(16) = \sqrt{16} = 4$
If a and b are positive numbers, and $a = b$, then $\sqrt{a} = \sqrt{b}$. **The Pythagorean theorem:** If the length of the hypotenuse of a right triangle is c and the lengths of the two legs are a and b, then $c^2 = a^2 + b^2$.	If $h^2 = 169$, then $\sqrt{h^2} = \sqrt{169}$ or $h = 13$. To find the hypotenuse h of a right triangle with sides of 5 and 12 inches, use the Pythagorean theorem: $h^2 = 5^2 + 12^2 = 25 + 144 = 169$ Since $h^2 = 169$, $h = \sqrt{169} = 13$.

REVIEW EXERCISES

Fill in the blank:

1. 4 is a <u> square </u> root of 16, because $4^2 = 16$.

2. $\dfrac{1}{3}$ is a square root of $\dfrac{1}{9}$, because $\underline{\left(\dfrac{1}{3}\right)^2 = \dfrac{1}{9}}$.

Find each square root. Do not use a calculator.

3. $\sqrt{25}$ 5

4. $\sqrt{49}$ 7

5. $-\sqrt{144}$ -12

6. $-\sqrt{\dfrac{16}{81}}$ $-\dfrac{4}{9}$

7. $\sqrt{900}$ 30

8. $-\sqrt{0.64}$ -0.8

9. $\sqrt{1}$ 1

10. $\sqrt{0}$ 0

⊞ *Use a calculator to approximate each expression to three decimal places.*

11. $\sqrt{21}$ 4.583

12. $-\sqrt{15}$ -3.873

13. $2\sqrt{7}$ 5.292

14. $\sqrt{751.9}$ 27.421

15. Determine whether each number is rational, irrational, or imaginary. Which is not a real number? $\left\{\sqrt{-2}, \sqrt{68}, \sqrt{81}, \sqrt{3}\right\}$

$\sqrt{-2}$: imaginary, $\sqrt{68}$: irrational, $\sqrt{81}$: rational, $\sqrt{3}$: irrational, $\sqrt{-2}$ is not real

Complete the table of values for each function and then graph it.

16. $f(x) = \sqrt{x}$

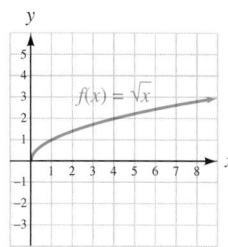

x	f(x)
0	0
1	1
4	2
9	3

17. $f(x) = 2 - \sqrt{x}$

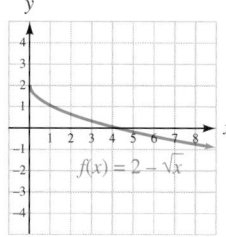

x	f(x)
0	2
1	1
4	0
9	−1

Refer to the right triangle shown.

18. Find c where $a = 21$ and $b = 28$. 35

19. Find b where $a = 1$ and $c = \sqrt{2}$. 1

20. Find a where $b = 5$ and $c = 6$. $\sqrt{11}$

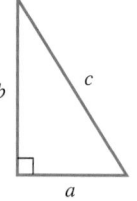

⊞ **21.** THEATER SEATING For the theater seats shown, how much higher is the seat at the top of the incline compared to the one at the bottom? 5 ft

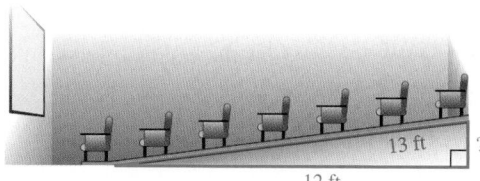

13 ft   ?

12 ft

22. ROAD SIGNS To find the maximum velocity a car can safely travel around a curve without skidding, we can use the formula $v = \sqrt{2.5r}$, where v is the velocity in mph and r is the radius of the curve in feet. How should the road sign in the illustration be labeled if it is to be posted in front of a curve with a radius of 360 feet? 30 mph

? mph

SECTION 8.2   Higher-Order Roots; Radicands That Contain Variables

DEFINITIONS AND CONCEPTS	EXAMPLES
The number b is a **cube root** of a if $b^3 = a$.	4 is a cube root of 64 because $4^3 = 64$. $\dfrac{1}{5}$ is a cube root of $\dfrac{1}{125}$ because $\left(\dfrac{1}{5}\right)^3 = \dfrac{1}{125}$.
The cube root of a is denoted by $\sqrt[3]{a}$, and by definition, $\quad \sqrt[3]{a} = b$ if $b^3 = a$.	$\sqrt[3]{343} = 7$ because $7^3 = 343$. $\sqrt[3]{\dfrac{8}{125}} = \dfrac{2}{5}$ because $\left(\dfrac{2}{5}\right)^3 = \dfrac{8}{125}$.

The function $f(x) = \sqrt[3]{x}$ is called the **cube root function**.	Evaluate $f(x) = \sqrt[3]{x}$ for $x = 27$ and $x = -64$. $$f(27) = \sqrt[3]{27} = 3 \qquad f(-64) = \sqrt[3]{-64} = -4$$
The number b is an **nth root of a** if $b^n = a$.	3 is a fourth root of 81 because $3^4 = 81$.
In $\sqrt[n]{a}$, the number n is called the **index** of the radical.	$\frac{1}{3}$ is a fifth root of $\frac{1}{243}$ because $\left(\frac{1}{3}\right)^5 = \frac{1}{243}$. The index of $\sqrt[5]{24x}$ is 5. The index of $\sqrt[6]{32ab}$ is 6.
When n is even, we say that the radical $\sqrt[n]{x}$ is an **even root**. When n is odd, $\sqrt[n]{x}$ is an **odd root**. $\sqrt{a} = \sqrt[2]{a}$	$\sqrt{24}$ and $\sqrt[4]{32a^3}$ are even roots. $\sqrt[3]{45mn}$ and $\sqrt[5]{100pq}$ are odd roots. $\sqrt{9}$ means $\sqrt[2]{9}$

REVIEW EXERCISES

Fill in the blanks.

23. $\sqrt[3]{125} = 5$, because $5^3 = 125$; 5 is called the ___cube___ root of 125.

24. $\frac{1}{3}$ is a cube root of $\frac{1}{27}$, because $\left(\frac{1}{3}\right)^3 = \frac{1}{27}$.

Find each root. Do not use a calculator.

25. $\sqrt[3]{-27}$ -3

26. $-\sqrt[3]{125}$ -5

27. $\sqrt[4]{81}$ 3

28. $\sqrt[5]{32}$ 2

29. $\sqrt[5]{0}$ 0

30. $\sqrt[3]{-1}$ -1

31. $\sqrt[3]{\frac{1}{64}}$ $\frac{1}{4}$

32. $\sqrt[3]{1}$ 1

Use a calculator to find each root to three decimal places.

33. $\sqrt[3]{16}$ 2.520

34. $\sqrt[3]{-102.35}$ -4.678

35. $\sqrt[4]{6}$ 1.565

36. $\sqrt[5]{34{,}500}$ 8.083

Find each root. Each variable represents a positive number.

37. $\sqrt{x^2}$ x

38. $\sqrt{4b^2}$ $2b$

39. $\sqrt{x^4y^4}$ x^2y^2

40. $-\sqrt{y^{12}}$ $-y^6$

41. $\sqrt[3]{x^3}$ x

42. $\sqrt[3]{y^6}$ y^2

43. $\sqrt[3]{27x^3}$ $3x$

44. $\sqrt[3]{-r^{12}}$ $-r^4$

45. DICE Find the length of an edge of one of the dice shown if each one has a volume of 1,728 cubic millimeters. 12 mm

46. If the volume of a cube is 2,744 in.³, find the length of one side. 14 in.

SECTION 8.3 Simplifying Radical Expressions

DEFINITIONS AND CONCEPTS	EXAMPLES
The **product rule for square roots:** For any nonnegative real numbers a and b, $$\sqrt{ab} = \sqrt{a}\sqrt{b}$$	Simplify: $$\sqrt{50x^7} = \sqrt{25x^6 \cdot 2x}$$ $$= \sqrt{25x^6} \cdot \sqrt{2x}$$ $$= 5x^3\sqrt{2x}$$

Simplified form of a square root:

1. Except for 1, the radicand has no perfect-square factors.

2. No fraction appears in the radicand.

3. No radical appears in the denominator.

The following square roots are not in simplified form:

$\sqrt{32}$ because 32 has a perfect-square factor of 16.

$\sqrt{\dfrac{1}{2}}$ because the radicand is a fraction.

$\dfrac{1}{\sqrt{2}}$ because a radical appears in a denominator.

The **quotient rule of square roots:** For any positive real numbers a and b,

$$\sqrt{\dfrac{a}{b}} = \dfrac{\sqrt{a}}{\sqrt{b}} \text{ where } b \neq 0$$

Simplify:

$$\sqrt{\dfrac{7}{16}} = \dfrac{\sqrt{7}}{\sqrt{16}} = \dfrac{\sqrt{7}}{4}$$

Simplify:

$$\sqrt{\dfrac{32x}{25}} = \dfrac{\sqrt{32x}}{\sqrt{25}} = \dfrac{\sqrt{32x}}{5}$$

Properties of radicals:

$$\sqrt[3]{ab} = \sqrt[3]{a}\sqrt[3]{b} \qquad \sqrt[3]{\dfrac{a}{b}} = \dfrac{\sqrt[3]{a}}{\sqrt[3]{b}} \quad (b \neq 0)$$

Simplify:

$$\begin{aligned}\sqrt[3]{16} &= \sqrt[3]{8 \cdot 2} \\ &= \sqrt[3]{8} \cdot \sqrt[3]{2} \\ &= 2\sqrt[3]{2}\end{aligned}$$

Simplify:

$$\begin{aligned}\sqrt[3]{\dfrac{11}{27}} &= \dfrac{\sqrt[3]{11}}{\sqrt[3]{27}} \\ &= \dfrac{\sqrt[3]{11}}{3}\end{aligned}$$

REVIEW EXERCISES

Simplify each expression. All variables represent positive numbers.

47. $\sqrt{32}$ $4\sqrt{2}$

48. $\sqrt{500}$ $10\sqrt{5}$

49. $\sqrt{80x^2}$ $4x\sqrt{5}$

50. $-2\sqrt{63}$ $-6\sqrt{7}$

51. $-\sqrt{250t^3}$ $-5t\sqrt{10t}$

52. $-\sqrt{700z^5}$ $-10z^2\sqrt{7z}$

53. $\sqrt{200x^2y}$ $10x\sqrt{2y}$

54. $\dfrac{1}{5}\sqrt{75y^4}$ $y^2\sqrt{3}$

55. $\sqrt[3]{8x^2y^3}$ $2y\sqrt[3]{x^2}$

56. $\sqrt[3]{250x^4y^3}$ $5xy\sqrt[3]{2x}$

Simplify each expression. All variables represent positive numbers.

57. $\sqrt{\dfrac{16}{25}}$ $\dfrac{4}{5}$

58. $\sqrt{\dfrac{60}{49}}$ $\dfrac{2\sqrt{15}}{7}$

59. $\sqrt[3]{\dfrac{1{,}000}{27}}$ $\dfrac{10}{3}$

60. $\sqrt{\dfrac{242x^4}{169x^2}}$ $\dfrac{11x\sqrt{2}}{13}$

Refer to the sit-up board shown in the illustration.

61. Find its length. Express the answer in simplified radical form. $2\sqrt{10}$ ft

62. Express your result to part a as a decimal approximation rounded to the nearest tenth. 6.3 ft

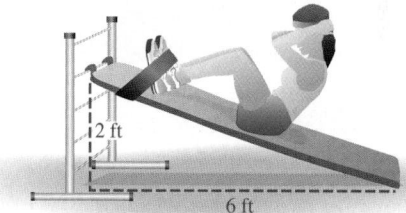

2 ft

6 ft

SECTION 8.4 Adding and Subtracting Radical Expressions

DEFINITIONS AND CONCEPTS	EXAMPLES
Square root radicals are called **like radicals** when they have the same radicand.	Like radicals: $4\sqrt{2}$ and $5\sqrt{2}$ Unlike radicals: $3\sqrt{6}$ and $7\sqrt{3}$ *The same radicand* *Different radicands*

Radical expressions can be added or subtracted if they contain like radicals. To **combine like radicals** we use the distributive property in reverse.	Add: $3\sqrt{7} + 5\sqrt{7} = (3 + 5)\sqrt{7}$ $= 8\sqrt{7}$ Subtract: $8\sqrt{2y} - 2\sqrt{2y} = (8 - 2)\sqrt{2y}$ $= 6\sqrt{2y}$
If a sum or difference involves unlike radicals, make sure that each one is written in simplified form. After doing so, like radicals may result that can be combined.	Add: $\sqrt{12} + \sqrt{75} = \sqrt{4}\sqrt{3} + \sqrt{25}\sqrt{3}$ *Simplify $\sqrt{12}$ and $\sqrt{75}$.* $= 2\sqrt{3} + 5\sqrt{3}$ $= 7\sqrt{3}$ *Combine like radicals.*

REVIEW EXERCISES

Perform the operations. All variables represent positive numbers.

63. $\sqrt{2} + \sqrt{8} - \sqrt{18}$
    0

64. $\sqrt{3} + 4 + \sqrt{27} - 7$
    $-3 + 4\sqrt{3}$

65. $5\sqrt{28} - 3\sqrt{63}$
    $\sqrt{7}$

66. $3y\sqrt{5xy^3} - y^2\sqrt{20xy}$
    $y^2\sqrt{5xy}$

67. $\sqrt[3]{16} + \sqrt[3]{54}$
    $5\sqrt[3]{2}$

68. $\sqrt[3]{2,000x^3} - \sqrt[3]{128x^3}$
    $6x\sqrt[3]{2}$

69. Explain why we cannot add $3\sqrt{5}$ and $5\sqrt{3}$.
    They do not contain like radicals; the radicands are different.

70. GARDENING Find the difference in the lengths of the two wires used to secure the tree shown. $13\sqrt{5}$ in.

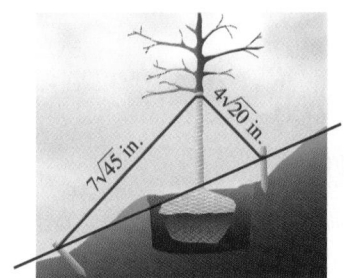

SECTION 8.5 **Multiplying and Dividing Radical Expressions**

DEFINITIONS AND CONCEPTS	EXAMPLES
The **product rule for radicals:** For any nonnegative real numbers a and b: $\sqrt{a}\sqrt{b} = \sqrt{ab}$ $\sqrt[3]{a}\sqrt[3]{b} = \sqrt[3]{ab}$	Multiply: $\sqrt{2}\sqrt{8} = \sqrt{2 \cdot 8} = \sqrt{16} = 4$ $\sqrt[3]{3}\sqrt[3]{9} = \sqrt[3]{3 \cdot 9} = \sqrt[3]{27} = 3$
To multiply radical expressions containing only one term, first multiply the coefficients, then multiply the radicals separately, and simplify the result.	Multiply: $3\sqrt{8} \cdot 3\sqrt{2} = 3 \cdot 3\sqrt{8}\sqrt{2}$ $= 9\sqrt{8 \cdot 2}$ $= 9\sqrt{16}$ $= 9(4)$ $= 36$
To multiply two binomials, multiply each term of one binomial by each term of the other binomial and simplify.	Multiply: $\left(\sqrt{5x} + 2\right)\left(\sqrt{5x} - 1\right)$ $= \sqrt{5x}\sqrt{5x} - (1)\sqrt{5x} + 2\sqrt{5x} - 2$ $= 5x + \sqrt{5x} - 2$

If the denominator of a fraction is a square root, **rationalize** the denominator by multiplying the numerator and denominator by some appropriate square root that makes a perfect-square radicand in the denominator.	Rationalize the denominator. $$\frac{x}{\sqrt{5}} = \frac{x\sqrt{5}}{\sqrt{5}\sqrt{5}} = \frac{x\sqrt{5}}{5}$$
If the denominator of a fraction is a cube root, **rationalize** the denominator by multiplying the numerator and denominator by the cube root that makes a perfect cube radicand in the denominator.	$$\frac{2}{\sqrt[3]{25}} = \frac{2}{\sqrt[3]{25}} \cdot \frac{\sqrt[3]{5}}{\sqrt[3]{5}} = \frac{2\sqrt[3]{5}}{5}$$
If the denominator of a fraction contains two terms with square roots, multiply the numerator and denominator by the **conjugate** of the denominator.	$$\frac{x}{\sqrt{x}-2} = \frac{x\left(\sqrt{x}+2\right)}{\left(\sqrt{x}-2\right)\left(\sqrt{x}+2\right)} = \frac{x\left(\sqrt{x}+2\right)}{x-4}$$

REVIEW EXERCISES

Perform the operations.

71. $\sqrt{2}\sqrt{3}$
$\sqrt{6}$

72. $\left(-5\sqrt{5}\right)\left(-2\sqrt{2}\right)$
$10\sqrt{10}$

73. $\left(3\sqrt{3x}\right)\left(4\sqrt{6x}\right)$
$36x\sqrt{2}$

74. $\left(\sqrt{15}+3x\right)^2$
$15 + 6x\sqrt{15} + 9x^2$

75. $\sqrt{2}\left(\sqrt{8}-\sqrt{18}\right)$ -2

76. $\left(\sqrt{3}+\sqrt{5}\right)\left(\sqrt{3}-\sqrt{5}\right)$ -2

77. $\left(\sqrt[3]{4}\right)\left(2\sqrt[3]{4}\right)$
$4\sqrt[3]{2}$

78. $\left(\sqrt[3]{3}+2\right)\left(\sqrt[3]{3}-1\right)$
$\sqrt[3]{9}+\sqrt[3]{3}-2$

Rationalize each denominator.

79. $\dfrac{1}{\sqrt{7}}$ $\dfrac{\sqrt{7}}{7}$

80. $\sqrt{\dfrac{3}{7}}$ $\dfrac{\sqrt{21}}{7}$

81. $\dfrac{\sqrt{9}}{\sqrt{18}}$ $\dfrac{\sqrt{2}}{2}$

82. $\dfrac{\sqrt{c}-4}{\sqrt{c}+4}$ $\dfrac{c-8\sqrt{c}+16}{c-16}$

83. $\dfrac{7}{\sqrt{2}+1}$ $7\sqrt{2}-7$

84. $\dfrac{8}{\sqrt[3]{16}}$ $2\sqrt[3]{4}$

The illustration shows the amount of surface area of a rug suctioned by a vacuum nozzle attachment.

$5\sqrt{3}$ in. $2\sqrt{6}$ in.

85. Find the perimeter and area of this section of rug. Express the answers in simplified radical form. $\left(4\sqrt{6}+10\sqrt{3}\right)$ in.; $30\sqrt{2}$ in.^{2}

86. Express your results to Problem 85 as decimal approximations to the nearest tenth. 27.1 in., 42.4 in.^{2}

SECTION 8.6   Solving Radical Equations; the Distance Formula

DEFINITIONS AND CONCEPTS	EXAMPLES
The squaring property of equality: If $a = b$, then $a^2 = b^2$.	If $\sqrt{x} = 6$, then $\left(\sqrt{x}\right)^2 = (6)^2$ or $x = 36$.

To solve equations containing square roots:

1. Isolate the radical term on one side of the equation.
2. Square both sides and solve the resulting equation.
3. Check the solution. Discard any **extraneous solutions.**

Solve:

$$\sqrt{x - 2} + 1 = 5$$

$\sqrt{x - 2} = 4$ To isolate the radical, subtract 1 from both sides.

$\left(\sqrt{x - 2}\right)^2 = (4)^2$ Square both sides.

$x - 2 = 16$

$x = 18$ Add 2 to both sides.

Check: $\sqrt{x - 2} + 1 = 5$ The original equation.

$\sqrt{18 - 2} + 1 \stackrel{?}{=} 5$ Substitute 18 for x.

$\sqrt{16} + 1 \stackrel{?}{=} 5$ Evaluate the left side.

$4 + 1 \stackrel{?}{=} 5$

$5 = 5$ True

The distance formula:

$$d = \sqrt{(x_2 - x_1)^2 + (y_2 - y_1)^2}$$

To find the distance between the points $(2, -3)$ and $(5, -7)$, substitute into the distance formula:

$$d = \sqrt{(x_2 - x_1)^2 + (y_2 - y_1)^2}$$

$d = \sqrt{(5 - 2)^2 + [(-7 - (-3)]^2}$ Substitute.

$= \sqrt{3^2 + (-4)^2}$ $5 - 2 = 3, -7 - (-3) = -4$

$= \sqrt{9 + 16}$ Evaluate the powers.

$= \sqrt{25}$ Perform the addition.

$= 5$ Find the square root.

REVIEW EXERCISES

Simplify each expression. All variables represent positive numbers.

87. $\left(\sqrt{x}\right)^2$ x

88. $\left(\sqrt[3]{x}\right)^3$ x

89. $\left(2\sqrt{t}\right)^2$ $4t$

90. $\left(\sqrt{e - 1}\right)^2$ $e - 1$

Solve each equation and check all solutions.

91. $\sqrt{x} = 9$
  81

92. $\sqrt{3x + 4} + 5 = 3$
  no solution

93. $\sqrt{24 + 10y} = y + 4$
  $-2, 4$

94. $\sqrt{2(r + 4)} = 2\sqrt{r}$
  4

95. $\sqrt{p^2 - 3} = p + 3$
  -2

96. $\sqrt[3]{x - 1} = 3$
  28

Find the distance between the points. If an answer contains a radical, round to the nearest hundredth.

97. $(-7, 12), (-4, 8)$
  5

98. $(-15, -3), (-10, -16)$
  13.93

99. FERRIS WHEELS The distance d in feet that an object will fall in t seconds is given by the formula

$$t = \sqrt{\frac{d}{16}}$$

If a person drops a coin from the top of a Ferris wheel and it takes 2 seconds to hit the ground, how tall is the Ferris wheel?   64 ft

SECTION 8.7   Rational Exponents

DEFINITIONS AND CONCEPTS	EXAMPLES
To evaluate exponential expressions involving fractional exponents, use the **rules for rational exponents** to write the expressions in an equivalent radical form. $x^{1/n} = \sqrt[n]{x}$ $x^{m/n} = \sqrt[n]{x^m} = \left(\sqrt[n]{x}\right)^m$ $x^{-m/n} = \dfrac{1}{x^{m/n}}$	Evaluate: $8^{1/3} = \sqrt[3]{8} = 2$ Simplify: $(16x^2)^{1/2} = \sqrt{16x^2} = 4x$ Simplify: $(8x^6)^{1/3} = \sqrt[3]{8x^6} = 2x^2$ Simplify: $(-64)^{4/3} = \left(\sqrt[3]{-64}\right)^4 = (-4)^4 = 256$ Simplify: $(27x^3)^{2/3} = [(27x^3)^{1/3}]^2 = (3x)^2 = 9x^2$ Simplify: $125^{-2/3} = \dfrac{1}{125^{2/3}}$ $= \dfrac{1}{(125^{1/3})^2}$ $= \dfrac{1}{(5)^2}$ $= \dfrac{1}{25}$
The rules for exponents can be used to simplify expressions involving rational exponents.	Simplify: $7^{1/9}7^{4/9} = 7^{1/9+4/9} = 7^{5/9}$

REVIEW EXERCISES

Simplify each expression. Write answers without using negative exponents.

100. $49^{1/2}$ 7

101. $(-1,000)^{1/3}$ -10

102. $36^{3/2}$ 216

103. $\left(\dfrac{8}{27}\right)^{2/3}$ $\dfrac{4}{9}$

104. $4^{-3/2}$ $\dfrac{1}{8}$

105. $8^{2/3}8^{4/3}$ 64

106. $(3^{2/3})^3$ 9

107. $(a^4b^8)^{-1/2}$ $\dfrac{1}{a^2b^4}$

108. $x^{1/3}x^{2/5}$ $x^{11/15}$

109. $\dfrac{t^{3/4}}{t^{2/3}}$ $t^{1/12}$

110. $\dfrac{x^{2/5}x^{1/5}}{x^{-2/5}}$ x

111. $\dfrac{x^{17/7}}{x^{3/7}}$ x^2

112. Graph each number on the number line: $\{4^{-1/2}, 12^{1/2}, 9^{1/3}, -2^{2/3}\}$.

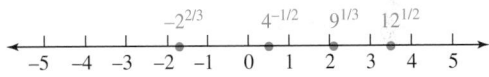

113. DENTISTRY The fractional amount of painkiller remaining in the system of a patient h hours after the original dose was injected into her gums is given by $h^{-3/2}$. How much of the original dose is in the patient's system 16 hours after the injection?

$\frac{1}{64}$ of the original dose

114. Explain why $(-4)^{1/2}$ is not a real number.

$(-4)^{1/2} = \sqrt{-4}$; there is no real number that, when squared, gives -4.

CHAPTER **8**   TEST

Simplify each radical.

1. $\sqrt{100}$ 10

2. $-\sqrt{\dfrac{400}{9}}$ $-\dfrac{20}{3}$

3. $\sqrt[3]{-27}$ -3

4. $\sqrt{\dfrac{50}{49}}$ $\dfrac{5\sqrt{2}}{7}$

5. Evaluate $\sqrt{b^2 - 4ac}$ for $a = 2$, $b = 10$, and $c = 6$. Round to the nearest tenth. 7.2

6. A 26-foot ladder reaches a point on a wall 24 feet above the ground. How far from the wall is the ladder's base? 10 ft

Simplify each expression. Assume that x and y represent positive numbers.

7. $\sqrt{4x^2}$ $2x$

8. $\sqrt{54x^3}$ $3x\sqrt{6x}$

9. $\sqrt{\dfrac{18x^2y^3}{2xy}}$ $3y\sqrt{x}$

10. $\sqrt[3]{x^6y^3}$ x^2y

Suppose a square has an area of 24 square yards.

11. Express the length of a side of the square in simplified radical form. $2\sqrt{6}$ yd

12. Round the length of a side of the square to the nearest tenth. 4.9 yd

Perform each operation and simplify.

13. $\sqrt{12} + \sqrt{27}$ $5\sqrt{3}$

14. $\sqrt{8x^3} - x\sqrt{18x}$ $-x\sqrt{2x}$

15. $\left(-2\sqrt{8x}\right)\left(3\sqrt{12x}\right)$ $-24x\sqrt{6}$

16. $\sqrt{3}\left(\sqrt{8} + \sqrt{6}\right)$ $2\sqrt{6} + 3\sqrt{2}$

17. $\left(\sqrt{2} + \sqrt{3}\right)\left(\sqrt{2} - \sqrt{3}\right)$ -1

18. $\left(2\sqrt{x} + 2\right)\left(\sqrt{x} - 3\right)$ $2x - 4\sqrt{x} - 6$

19. SEWING A corner of fabric is folded over to form a collar and stitched down as shown below. From the dimensions given in the figure, determine the exact number of inches of stitching that must be made. Then give an approximation to one decimal place. (All measurements are in inches.) $\left(6\sqrt{2} + 2\sqrt{10}\right)$ in., 14.8 in.

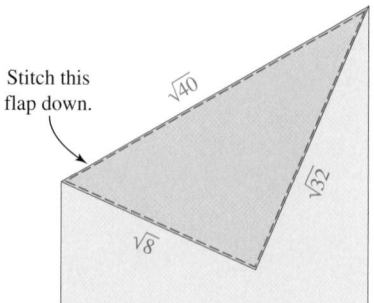

Stitch this flap down.

$\sqrt{40}$

$\sqrt{32}$

$\sqrt{8}$

Rationalize each denominator.

20. $\dfrac{2}{\sqrt{2}}$ $\sqrt{2}$

21. $\dfrac{\sqrt{3x}}{\sqrt{x}+2}$ $\dfrac{x\sqrt{3}-2\sqrt{3x}}{x-4}$

Solve each equation.

22. $\sqrt{x}=15$
225

23. $\sqrt{2-x}-2=6$
−62

24. $\sqrt{3x+9}=2\sqrt{x+1}$
5

25. $x-1=\sqrt{x-1}$
2, 1

26. $\sqrt{3a+4}+2=0$
no solution

27. $\sqrt[3]{x-2}=3$
29

28. Find the distance between points $(-2,-3)$ and $(-8,5)$.   10

29. Complete the table and graph the function. Round to the nearest tenth when necessary.

$f(x)=\sqrt{x}$	
x	$f(x)$
0	0
1	1
2	1.4
4	2
6	2.4
9	3

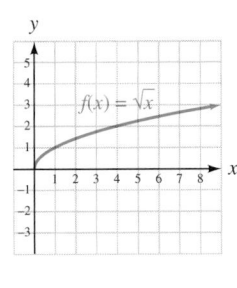

30. Is 0 a solution of the radical equation $\sqrt{3x+1}=x-1$? Explain your answer.
No; when 0 is substituted for x, the result is not a true statement: $1 \neq -1$.

31. Explain why we cannot perform the subtraction $4\sqrt{3}-7\sqrt{2}$.
The terms do not contain like radicals—the radicands are different.

32. CARPENTRY In the illustration below, a carpenter is using a tape measure to see whether the wall he just put up is perfectly square with the floor. Explain what mathematical concept he is applying. If the wall is positioned correctly, what should the measurement on the tape read?   the Pythagorean theorem; 5 ft

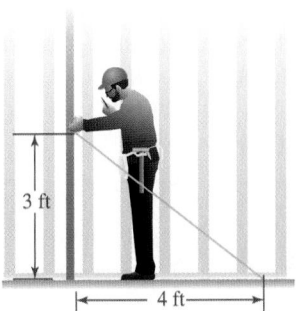

33. Explain why $\sqrt{-9}$ is not a real number.
There is no real number that, when squared, gives −9.

Simplify each expression.

34. $121^{1/2}$ 11

35. $p^{2/3}p^{4/3}$ p^2

CHAPTERS 1–8   CUMULATIVE REVIEW

1. Determine whether each statement is true or false.

   a. All whole numbers are integers. [Section 1.3] true

   b. π is a rational number. [Section 1.3] false

   c. A real number is either rational or irrational. [Section 1.3] true

2. Evaluate: $\dfrac{-3(3 + 2)^2 - (-5)}{17 - 3|-4|}$ [Section 1.7] −14

3. BACKPACKS Pediatricians advise that children should not carry more than 20% of their own body weight in backpacks. According to this warning, how much weight can a fifth-grade girl who weighs 85 pounds safely carry in her backpack?
   [Section 2.3] 17 lb

4. SCIENCE The illustration below shows the recent budgets for the National Science Foundation. Determine the percent change for the 1996 budget as compared to the 1995 budget. Round to the nearest tenth of a percent. [Section 2.3] −1.8%

In billions		% change
1992	$2.55	8.7%
1993	$2.75	8.0%
1994	$2.99	8.6%
1995	$3.27	9.5%
1996	$3.21	?
1997	$3.30	2.9%
1998	$3.43	3.9%
1999	$3.67	7.1%
2000	$3.91	6.5%

Based on data from the National Science Foundation

5. Simplify: $3p - 6(p + z) + p$ [Section 2.2] $-2p - 6z$

6. Solve: $2 - (4x + 7) = 3 + 2(x + 2)$ [Section 2.2] −2

7. Solve $3 - 3x \geq 6 + x$, graph the solution, and use interval notation to describe the solution.
   [Section 2.7] $x \leq -\frac{3}{4}, \left(-\infty, -\frac{3}{4}\right]$

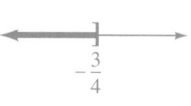

8. Solve $0 \leq \dfrac{4 - x}{3} < 2$, graph the solution, and use interval notation to describe the solution.
   [Section 2.7] $-2 < x \leq 4, (-2, 4]$

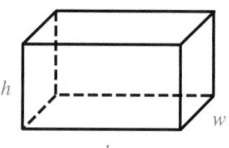

9. SEARCH AND RESCUE Two search and rescue teams leave base at the same time, looking for a lost boy. The first team, on foot, heads north at 2 mph and the other, on horseback, south at 4 mph. How long will it take them to search a distance of 21 miles between them? [Section 2.6] 3.5 hr

10. BLENDING COFFEES A store sells regular coffee for $4 a pound and gourmet coffee for $7 a pound. Using 40 pounds of the gourmet coffee, the owner makes a blend to put on sale for $5 a pound. How many pounds of regular coffee should he use?
    [Section 2.6] 80

11. SURFACE AREA The total surface area A of a box with dimensions l, w, and h is given by the formula

    $A = 2lw + 2wh + 2lh$

    If $A = 202$ square inches, $l = 9$ inches, and $w = 5$ inches, find h. [Section 2.4] 4 in.

Graph each equation or inequality.

12. $3x - 4y = 12$

    [Section 3.3]

13. $y = \dfrac{1}{2}x$

    [Section 3.3]

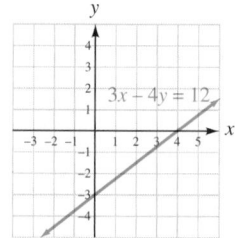

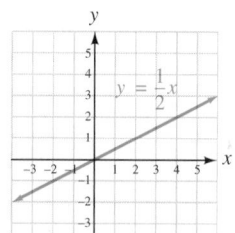

14. $x = 5$
[Section 3.3]

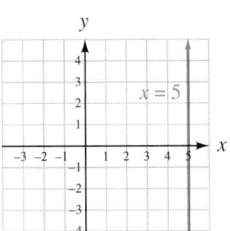

15. $3x + 4y \leq 12$
[Section 3.7]

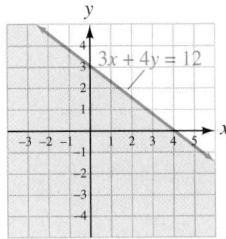

16. Write an equation of the line passing through $(-2, 5)$ and $(4, 8)$. Express the result in slope–intercept form.
[Section 3.6] $y = \frac{x}{2} + 6$

17. Find the slope of the line defined by each equation.
   a. $y = 3x - 7$ [Section 3.5] 3
   b. $2x + 3y = -10$ [Section 3.5] $-\frac{2}{3}$

18. What is true about the slopes of two
   a. parallel lines? [Section 3.4] They are the same.
   b. perpendicular lines? [Section 3.4] They are negative reciprocals.

19. SHOPPING On the graph, the line approximates the growth in retail sales for U.S. shopping centers during the years 1994–2002. Find the rate of increase in sales by finding the slope of the line.
[Section 3.4] $52 billion per yr

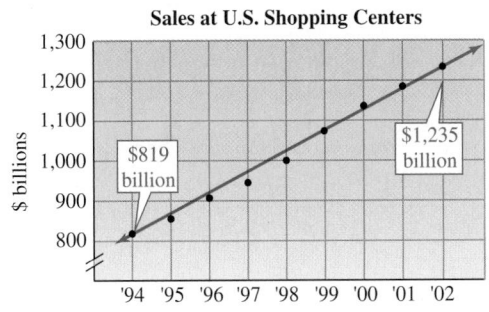

Sales at U.S. Shopping Centers

Based on data from International Council of Shopping Centers

20. If $f(x) = x^3 - x + 5$, find $f(-2)$. [Section 3.8] -1

21. Complete the table and graph the function. Then give the domain and range of the function. [Section 3.8]

$f(x) = \lvert 1 - x \rvert$	
x	$f(x)$
0	1
1	0
2	1
3	2
-1	2
-2	3

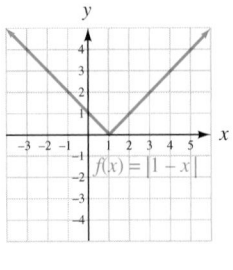

D: all reals, R: all real numbers greater than or equal to 0

22. BOATING The following graph shows the vertical distance from a point on the tip of a propeller to the centerline as the propeller spins. Is this the graph of a function? [Section 3.8] yes

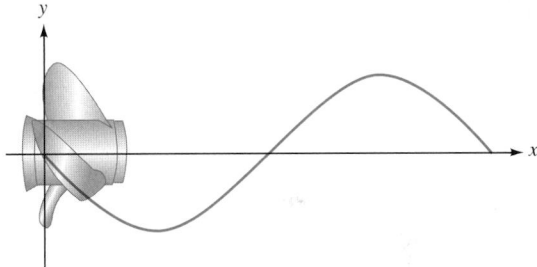

Simplify each expression. Write each answer without using parentheses or negative exponents.

23. $(x^5)^2(x^7)^3$
[Section 5.1] x^{31}

24. $\left(\dfrac{a^3 b}{c^4}\right)^5$
[Section 5.1] $\dfrac{a^{15} b^5}{c^{20}}$

25. $4^{-3} \cdot 4^{-2} \cdot 4^5$
[Section 5.2] 1

26. $(a^{-2} b^3)^{-4}$
[Section 5.2] $\dfrac{a^8}{b^{12}}$

27. ASTRONOMY The **parsec,** a unit of distance used in astronomy, is 3×10^{16} meters. The distance to Betelgeuse, a star in the constellation Orion, is 1.6×10^2 parsecs. Use scientific notation to express this distance in meters. [Section 5.3] 4.8×10^{18} m

28. NCAA MEN'S BASKETBALL The following graph shows the University of Connecticut's lead or deficit during the second half of the 1999 championship game with Duke University.

a. How many x-intercepts does the graph have? Explain their importance. [Section 3.1]
   3; they indicate that the game was tied 3 times in the second half.

b. Give the coordinates of the highest point and the lowest point on the graph. What is the importance of each? [Section 3.1]
   $(11, 6)$; in the second half, UConn had its largest lead (6 points) after 11 min had elapsed. $(4, -5)$; in the second half, UConn faced its largest deficit (5 points) after 4 min had elapsed.

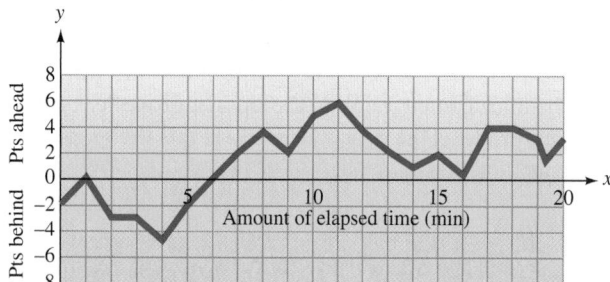

Perform the operations.

29. $(r^4 st^2)(2r^2 st)(rst)$
   [Section 5.1]
   $2r^7 s^3 t^4$

30. $(-3t + 2s)(2t - 3s)$
   [Section 5.6]
   $-6t^2 + 13st - 6s^2$

31. $(3a^2 - 2a + 4) - (a^2 - 3a + 7)$ [Section 5.5]
   $2a^2 + a - 3$

32. $(y - 6)^2$ [Section 5.6] $y^2 - 12y + 36$

33. $\dfrac{4x - 3y + 8z}{4xy}$ [Section 5.7] $\dfrac{1}{y} - \dfrac{3}{4x} + \dfrac{2z}{xy}$

34. $2 + x \overline{)3x + 2x^2 - 2}$ [Section 5.8] $2x - 1$

Factor each expression completely.

35. $3x^2 y - 6xy^2$
   [Section 6.1]
   $3xy(x - 2y)$

36. $2x^2 + 2xy - 3x - 3y$
   [Section 6.1]
   $(x + y)(2x - 3)$

37. $25p^4 - 16q^2$
   [Section 6.4]
   $(5p^2 + 4q)(5p^2 - 4q)$

38. $3x^3 - 243x$
   [Section 6.4]
   $3x(x + 9)(x - 9)$

39. $x^2 - 11x - 12$
   [Section 6.2]
   $(x - 12)(x + 1)$

40. $a^3 + 8b^3$
   [Section 6.5]
   $(a + 2b)(a^2 - 2ab + 4b^2)$

41. $6a^2 - 7a - 20$
   [Section 6.3]
   $(3a + 4)(2a - 5)$

42. $16m^2 - 20m - 6$
   [Section 6.3]
   $2(4m + 1)(2m - 3)$

Solve each equation.

43. $x^2 + 3x + 2 = 0$
   [Section 6.7]
   $-1, -2$

44. $5x^2 = 10x$
   [Section 6.7]
   $0, 2$

45. $6x^2 - x - 2 = 0$
   [Section 6.7]
   $\dfrac{2}{3}, -\dfrac{1}{2}$

46. $2y^2 = 12 - 5y$
   [Section 6.7]
   $\dfrac{3}{2}, -4$

47. CHILDREN'S STICKERS This rectangular-shaped sticker has an area of 20 cm². The width is 1 cm shorter than the length. Find the length of the sticker. [Section 6.8] 5 cm

48. For what value of x is $\dfrac{4x}{x - 6}$ undefined? [Section 7.1] 6

Simplify each expression.

49. $\dfrac{x^2 + 2x + 1}{x^2 - 1}$ [Section 7.1]
   $\dfrac{x + 1}{x - 1}$

50. $-\dfrac{15a^2}{25a^3}$ [Section 7.1]
   $-\dfrac{3}{5a}$

Perform the operation(s) and simplify when possible.

51. $\dfrac{p^2 - p - 6}{3p - 9} \div \dfrac{p^2 + 6p + 9}{p^2 - 9}$ [Section 7.2] $\dfrac{(p + 2)(p - 3)}{3(p + 3)}$

52. $\dfrac{x^2 y^2}{cd} \cdot \dfrac{d^2}{c^2 x}$ [Section 7.2] $\dfrac{xy^2 d}{c^3}$

53. $\dfrac{x + 2}{x + 5} - \dfrac{x - 3}{x + 7}$ [Section 7.4] $\dfrac{7x + 29}{(x + 5)(x + 7)}$

54. $\dfrac{3x}{x + 2} + \dfrac{5x}{x + 2} - \dfrac{7x - 2}{x + 2}$ [Section 7.3] 1

55. $\dfrac{3a}{2b} - \dfrac{2b}{3a}$ [Section 7.4]

$\dfrac{9a^2 - 4b^2}{6ab}$

56. $\dfrac{\dfrac{1}{x} + \dfrac{1}{y}}{\dfrac{1}{x} - \dfrac{1}{y}}$ [Section 7.5]

$\dfrac{y + x}{y - x}$

Solve each equation.

57. $\dfrac{4}{a} = \dfrac{6}{a} - 1$ [Section 7.6] 2

58. $\dfrac{a + 2}{a + 3} - 1 = \dfrac{-1}{a^2 + 2a - 3}$ [Section 7.6] 2

59. Solve the formula $\dfrac{1}{r} = \dfrac{1}{r_1} + \dfrac{1}{r_2}$ for r.

[Section 7.6] $r = \dfrac{r_1 r_2}{r_2 + r_1}$

60. ONLINE SALES A company found that, on average, it made 9 online sales transactions for every 500 hits on its Internet website. If the company's website had 360,000 hits in one year, how many sales transactions did it have that year? [Section 7.8] 6,480

61. Assume that y varies inversely with x. If $y = 8$ when $x = 2$, find y when $x = 8$. [Section 7.9] 2

62. FILLING A POOL An inlet pipe can fill an empty swimming pool in 5 hours, and another inlet pipe can fill the pool in 4 hours. How long will it take both pipes to fill the pool? [Section 7.7] $2\frac{2}{9}$ hr

Solve each system of equations. If the equations of a system are dependent or if a system is inconsistent, so indicate.

63. $\begin{cases} x = y + 4 \\ 2x + y = 5 \end{cases}$

[Section 4.2] $(3, -1)$

64. $\begin{cases} \frac{3}{5}s + \frac{1}{5}t = 1 \\ \frac{1}{4}s + \frac{3}{8}t = 1 \end{cases}$

[Section 4.3] $(1, 2)$

65. FINANCIAL PLANNING In investing $6,000 of a couple's money, a financial planner put some of it into a savings account paying 6% annual interest. The rest was invested in a riskier mini-mall development plan paying 12% annually. The combined interest earned for the first year was $540. How much money was invested at each rate? Use two variables to solve this problem. [Section 4.4] 6%: $3,000, 12%: $3,000

66. Graph the solution of: $\begin{cases} 3x + 2y \geq 6 \\ x + 3y \leq 6 \end{cases}$ [Section 4.5]

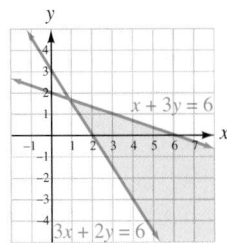

Simplify each expression. All variables represent positive numbers.

67. $\sqrt{\dfrac{49}{225}}$ [Section 8.1] $\frac{7}{15}$

68. $-\sqrt[3]{-27}$ [Section 8.2] 3

69. $-12x\sqrt{16x^2y^3}$ [Section 8.3] $-48x^2y\sqrt{y}$

70. $\sqrt{48} - \sqrt{8} + \sqrt{27} - \sqrt{32}$ [Section 8.4] $7\sqrt{3} - 6\sqrt{2}$

71. $\left(\sqrt{y} - 4\right)\left(\sqrt{y} - 5\right)$ [Section 8.5] $y - 9\sqrt{y} + 20$

72. $\left(-5\sqrt{6}\right)\left(4\sqrt{3}\right)$ [Section 8.5] $-60\sqrt{2}$

73. $\dfrac{4}{\sqrt{20}}$ [Section 8.5] $\dfrac{2\sqrt{5}}{5}$

74. $\dfrac{\sqrt{x} - 3}{\sqrt{x} + 3}$ [Section 8.5] $\dfrac{x - 6\sqrt{x} + 9}{x - 9}$

75. Solve: $\sqrt{6x + 19} - 5 = 2$ [Section 8.6] 5

76. CARGO SPACE How wide a piece of plywood can be stored diagonally in the back of the van shown? [Section 8.1] 73 in.

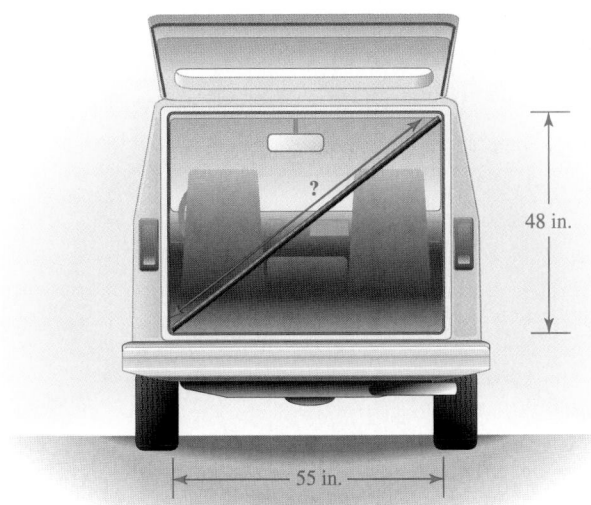

Quadratic Equations

© iStockphoto.com/Chris Schmidt

from *Campus to Careers*

Graphic Designer

Graphic designers combine their artistic talents with their mathematical skills to create attractive advertisements, photography, packaging, and websites. They perform arithmetic computations with fractions and decimals to determine proper font sizes and page margins. They apply algebraic concepts such as graphing and equation solving to plan page layouts. They also use formulas to create production schedules and calculate costs.

Graphic designers often begin a project with the final product in mind and work backwards to determine the specifics. In **Problem 70** of **Study Set 9.3,** you will do just that. Given the area of a triangular-shaped poster, you are to find the length of its base and its height by writing and then solving a quadratic equation.

JOB TITLE: Graphic Designer

EDUCATION: A bachelor's degree is required for most entry-level positions.

JOB OUTLOOK: Employment is expected to increase between 9% and 17% through the year 2014.

ANNUAL EARNINGS: Median annual salary for entry-level designers is $32,000 and for staff level designers is $42,500.

FOR MORE INFORMATION: www.bls.gov/oco/ocos090.htm

SECTION **9.1**

Solving Quadratic Equations: The Square Root Property

Recall that a **quadratic equation** can be written in the form $ax^2 + bx + c = 0$, where a, b, and c represent real numbers and $a \neq 0$. Some examples are

$$x^2 - x - 6 = 0, \quad 4x^2 + 4x + 1 = 0, \quad \text{and} \quad x^2 - 16 = 0$$

We have solved quadratic equations like these using factoring in combination with the zero-factor property. To review this method, let's solve $x^2 - 16 = 0$.

$$x^2 - 16 = 0$$
$$(x + 4)(x - 4) = 0 \qquad \text{Factor the difference of two squares.}$$
$$x + 4 = 0 \quad \text{or} \quad x - 4 = 0 \qquad \text{Set each factor equal to 0.}$$
$$x = -4 \quad | \quad x = 4 \qquad \text{Solve each equation.}$$

The solutions are -4 and 4.

1 Use the square root property to solve equations of the form $x^2 = c$.

We will now solve $x^2 - 16 = 0$ in another way. This time, we will ignore the zero-factor property condition that requires 0 on one side of the equation. Instead, we will add 16 to both sides to isolate x^2.

$$x^2 - 16 = 0$$
$$x^2 = 16 \qquad \text{Add 16 to both sides.}$$

We see that x must be a number whose square is 16. Therefore, x must be a square root of 16. Since every positive number has two square roots, one positive and one negative, we have

$$x = \sqrt{16} \quad \text{or} \quad x = -\sqrt{16}$$
$$x = 4 \quad | \quad x = -4$$

As with the factor method, we find that the solutions of $x^2 - 16 = 0$ are 4 and -4. This approach illustrates how the following *square root property* can be used to solve certain types of quadratic equations.

The Square Root Property of Equations

For any nonnegative real number c, if $x^2 = c$, then

$$x = \sqrt{c} \quad \text{or} \quad x = -\sqrt{c}$$

We can write the conclusion of the square root property in more compact form, called **double-sign notation:**

$$x = \pm\sqrt{c} \qquad \text{Read as "x is equal to the positive or negative square root of c."}$$

EXAMPLE 1   Solve: **a.** $x^2 - 5 = 0$ **b.** $x^2 = 12$ **c.** $3a^2 + 1 = 11$
d. $n^2 = -4$

Strategy We will use properties of equality to isolate the *squared term* on one side of the equation. Then we will use the square root property to isolate the variable itself.

WHY To solve the original equation, we want to find a simpler equivalent equation of the form $x = \pm$ **a number,** whose solutions are obvious.

Solution

a. We can use the addition property of equality to isolate x^2.

$$x^2 - 5 = 0 \qquad \text{This is the equation to solve.}$$
$$x^2 = 5 \qquad \text{Add 5 to both sides.}$$

Now we use the square root property to isolate x.

$$x = \sqrt{5} \qquad \text{or} \qquad x = -\sqrt{5}$$
$$x = \pm\sqrt{5} \qquad \text{Use double-sign notation.}$$

The check for $\sqrt{5}$:   **The check for $-\sqrt{5}$:**
$$x^2 - 5 = 0 \qquad\qquad x^2 - 5 = 0$$
$$\left(\sqrt{5}\right)^2 - 5 \stackrel{?}{=} 0 \qquad\qquad \left(-\sqrt{5}\right)^2 - 5 \stackrel{?}{=} 0$$
$$5 - 5 \stackrel{?}{=} 0 \qquad\qquad 5 - 5 \stackrel{?}{=} 0$$
$$0 = 0 \quad \text{True} \qquad\qquad 0 = 0 \quad \text{True}$$

Since each statement is true, the solutions are $\sqrt{5}$ and $-\sqrt{5}$, or $\pm\sqrt{5}$. The solution set is written as $\left\{-\sqrt{5}, \sqrt{5}\right\}$ or $\left\{\pm\sqrt{5}\right\}$.

b. Since x^2 is already isolated, we simply apply the square root property.

$$x^2 = 12 \qquad \text{This is the equation to solve.}$$
$$x = \sqrt{12} \quad \text{or} \quad x = -\sqrt{12} \qquad \text{To isolate x, use the square root property.}$$
$$x = \pm\sqrt{12} \qquad \text{Use double-sign notation.}$$
$$x = \pm 2\sqrt{3} \qquad \begin{array}{l}\text{Simplify the radical:}\\ \sqrt{12} = \sqrt{4\cdot 3} = \sqrt{4}\sqrt{3} = 2\sqrt{3}.\end{array}$$

Verify that $2\sqrt{3}$ and $-2\sqrt{3}$ are solutions by checking each in the original equation.

Caution! When using the square root property to solve an equation, always write the $\pm$ symbol, or you will lose one of the solutions.

c. $3a^2 + 1 = 11$ \qquad This is the equation to solve.
$$3a^2 = 10 \qquad \text{To isolate the term } 3a^2, \text{ subtract 1 from both sides.}$$
$$a^2 = \frac{10}{3} \qquad \text{To isolate } a^2, \text{ divide both sides by 3.}$$
$$a = \pm\sqrt{\frac{10}{3}} \qquad \begin{array}{l}\text{To isolate } a, \text{ use the square root property: } a = \sqrt{\frac{10}{3}} \text{ or}\\ a = -\sqrt{\frac{10}{3}}. \text{ Use double-sign notation.}\end{array}$$

To rationalize the denominator of the result, we proceed as follows:

$$x = \pm\sqrt{\frac{10}{3}} = \pm\frac{\sqrt{10}}{\sqrt{3}} \cdot \frac{\sqrt{3}}{\sqrt{3}} = \pm\frac{\sqrt{30}}{3}$$

Verify that $\frac{\sqrt{30}}{3}$ and $-\frac{\sqrt{30}}{3}$ are solutions by checking each in the original equation.

Self Check 1

Solve: **a.** $x^2 - 21 = 0$
b. $b^2 = 54$ **c.** $5m^2 - 1 = 6$
d. $x^2 = -25$

Now Try **Problems 23, 25, 31, and 33**

Self Check 1 Answers

a. $\pm\sqrt{21}$ **b.** $\pm 3\sqrt{6}$ **c.** $\pm\frac{\sqrt{35}}{5}$

d. no real-number solutions

Teaching Example 1 Solve:
a. $x^2 - 15 = 0$
b. $x^2 = 18$
c. $5a^2 + 4 = 21$
d. $y^2 = -25$
Answers:
a. $\pm\sqrt{15}$ **b.** $\pm 3\sqrt{2}$ **c.** $\pm\frac{\sqrt{85}}{5}$
d. no real solutions

The Language of Algebra The *exact* solutions are $\pm \frac{\sqrt{30}}{3}$. To the nearest hundredth, the *approximate* solutions are ± 1.83.

d. $n^2 = -4$ This is the equation to solve.

$n = \pm \sqrt{-4}$ Use the square root property.

Since the square root of -4 is not a real number, the equation has no real-number solutions.

2 Use the square root property to solve equations of the form $(ax + b)^2 = c$.

We can extend the square root property to solve equations that involve the square of a binomial.

EXAMPLE 2   Solve: **a.** $(x - 3)^2 = 36$ **b.** $(x + 1)^2 = 50$ **c.** $(2s - 4)^2 = 7$

Strategy Instead of a variable squared on the left side of the equation, we have a quantity squared. We still use the square root property to solve each equation.

WHY We want to eliminate the square on the binomial, so that we can eventually isolate the variable on one side of the equation.

Solution

a. $(x - 3)^2 = 36$ This is the equation to solve.

$x - 3 = \sqrt{36}$ or $x - 3 = -\sqrt{36}$ Use the square root property.

$x - 3 = \pm\sqrt{36}$ Use double-sign notation.

$x - 3 = \pm 6$ Evaluate: $\sqrt{36} = 6$.

$x = 3 \pm 6$ To isolate x, add 3 to both sides. It is standard practice to write the 3 in front of the $\pm$ symbol.

We read 3 ± 6 as "3 plus or minus 6." To find the solutions, we perform the calculation using a plus symbol $+$ and then using a minus symbol $-$.

$x = 3 + 6$ or $x = 3 - 6$

$x = 9$ | $x = -3$

The check for 9:   **The check for −3:**

$(x - 3)^2 = 36$ $(x - 3)^2 = 36$

$(9 - 3)^2 \stackrel{?}{=} 36$ $(-3 - 3)^2 \stackrel{?}{=} 36$

$(6)^2 \stackrel{?}{=} 36$ $(-6)^2 \stackrel{?}{=} 36$

$36 = 36$ True $36 = 36$ True

The solutions are 9 and -3.

Caution! It might be tempting to square the binomial on the left side of $(x - 3)^2 = 36$. However, that causes unnecessary, additional steps to be used to solve the equation in another way.

$(x - 3)^2 = 36$

$x^2 - 6x + 9 = 36$

b. $(x + 1)^2 = 50$ This is the equation to solve.

$\qquad x + 1 = \pm\sqrt{50}$ By the square root property, x + 1 = $\sqrt{50}$ or
$\qquad\qquad\qquad\qquad$ x + 1 = $-\sqrt{50}$. Use double-sign notation.

$\qquad x + 1 = \pm 5\sqrt{2}$ $\sqrt{50} = \sqrt{25 \cdot 2} = \sqrt{25}\sqrt{2} = 5\sqrt{2}$.

$\qquad\qquad x = -1 \pm 5\sqrt{2}$ To isolate x, subtract 1 from both sides (or add −1 to both
$\qquad\qquad\qquad\qquad$ sides). It is standard practice to write the −1 in front of the
$\qquad\qquad\qquad\qquad$ ± symbol.

Use a check to verify that the solutions are $-1 + 5\sqrt{2}$ and $-1 - 5\sqrt{2}$.

c. $(2s - 4)^2 = 7$ This is the equation to solve.

$\qquad 2s - 4 = \pm\sqrt{7}$ By the square root property, 2s − 4 = $\sqrt{7}$ or
$\qquad\qquad\qquad\qquad$ 2s − 4 = $-\sqrt{7}$. Use double-sign notation.

$\qquad\qquad 2s = 4 \pm \sqrt{7}$ To isolate the variable term 2s, add 4 to both sides.

$\qquad\qquad s = \dfrac{4 \pm \sqrt{7}}{2}$ To isolate s, divide both sides by 2.

> *Caution!* Since 2 is not a common factor of the entire numerator, it would be incorrect to simplify the solutions as shown:
>
> $$s = \dfrac{\overset{2}{\cancel{4}} \pm \sqrt{7}}{\underset{1}{\cancel{2}}}$$

Use a check to verify that the solutions are $\dfrac{4 + \sqrt{7}}{2}$ and $\dfrac{4 - \sqrt{7}}{2}$. ∎

> *Caution!* Equations like $(x - 3)^2 = -16$ and $(5y + 6)^2 = -4$ have no real-number solutions because no real number squared is negative.

If one side of the equation factors as the square of a binomial, we can use the methods of Example 2 to solve the equation.

EXAMPLE 3   Solve: $x^2 + 16x + 64 = 2$

Strategy We will attempt to factor the trinomial on the left side of the equation. Our hope is that it factors as the square of a binomial.

WHY If the equation can be written in the form $(ax + b)^2 = c$, we can use the square root property to solve it.

> *The Language of Algebra* Recall that trinomials that are squares of binomials are called **perfect-square trinomials.**

Solution
Since $x^2 + 16x + 64 = x^2 + 2 \cdot x \cdot 8 + 8^2$, it is a perfect-square trinomial and factors as $(x + 8)^2$.

$\qquad x^2 + 16x + 64 = 2$ This is the equation to solve.

$\qquad\qquad (x + 8)^2 = 2$ Factor the perfect-square trinomial $x^2 + 16x + 64$.

$\qquad\qquad x + 8 = \pm\sqrt{2}$ By the square root property, x + 8 = $\sqrt{2}$ or
$\qquad\qquad\qquad\qquad$ x + 8 = $-\sqrt{2}$. Use double-sign notation.

$\qquad\qquad x = -8 \pm \sqrt{2}$ To isolate x, subtract 8 from both sides.

Self Check 3

Solve: $x^2 - 14x + 49 = 11$

***Now Try* Problem 47**

Self Check 3 Answer

$7 \pm \sqrt{11}$

Teaching Example 3 Solve:
$x^2 - 10x + 25 = 7$
Answer:
$5 \pm \sqrt{7}$

As an informal check, we can use a calculator to approximate $-8 + \sqrt{2}$ and $-8 - \sqrt{2}$. Then we can substitute each approximation into the original equation.

> **Success Tip**   To check, we must substitute $-8 + \sqrt{2}$ and then $-8 - \sqrt{2}$ for x in $x^2 + 16x + 64 = 2$. Those calculations would be difficult by hand. Instead, we can perform an informal check using approximations of the possible solutions.

The check for $-8 + \sqrt{2} \approx -6.6$**:**	***The check for*** $-8 - \sqrt{2} \approx -9.4$**:**
$x^2 + 16x + 64 = 2$	$x^2 + 16x + 64 = 2$
$(-6.6)^2 + 16(-6.6) + 64 \stackrel{?}{=} 2$	$(-9.4)^2 + 16(-9.4) + 64 \stackrel{?}{=} 2$
$1.96 \approx 2$	$1.96 \approx 2$

In each case, the sides are approximately equal. This suggests that the results, $-8 + \sqrt{2}$ and $-8 - \sqrt{2}$, are reasonable.

3 Solve problems modeled by quadratic equations.

The equation solving methods discussed in this section can be used to solve a variety of real-world applications that are modeled by quadratic equations.

EXAMPLE 4   *Movie Stunts*   In a scene for an action movie, a stuntwoman falls from the top of a 95-foot-tall building into a 10-foot-tall airbag directly below her on the ground. The formula $d = 16t^2$ gives the distance d in feet that she falls in t seconds. For how many seconds will she fall before making contact with the airbag?

95 ft

10 ft

Solution
The woman will fall a distance of $95 - 10 = 85$ feet before making contact with the airbag. To find the number of seconds that the fall will last, we substitute 85 for d in the formula and solve for t, the time.

$$d = 16t^2 \qquad \text{This is the formula that models the situation.}$$

$$85 = 16t^2 \qquad \text{Substitute 85 for } d, \text{ the distance in feet, that the stuntwoman falls.}$$

The resulting quadratic equation is easily solved by the square root property.

$$\frac{85}{16} = t^2 \qquad \text{To isolate } t^2, \text{ divide both sides by 16.}$$

$$\pm\sqrt{\frac{85}{16}} = t \qquad \text{To isolate } t, \text{ use the square root property. Use double-sign notation.}$$

$$\pm\frac{\sqrt{85}}{\sqrt{16}} = t \qquad \text{Use the quotient rule for square roots: The square root of a quotient is the quotient of square roots.}$$

$$\pm\frac{\sqrt{85}}{4} = t \qquad \text{Evaluate: } \sqrt{16} = 4. \text{ Since } 85 = 5 \cdot 17, \text{ we cannot simplify } \sqrt{85}.$$

The stuntwoman will fall for $\frac{\sqrt{85}}{4}$ seconds (approximately 2.3 seconds) before making contact with the airbag. We discard the other solution, $-\frac{\sqrt{85}}{4}$, because a negative time does not make sense in this example.

ANSWERS TO SELF CHECKS

1. a. $\pm\sqrt{21}$ **b.** $\pm3\sqrt{6}$ **c.** $\pm\frac{\sqrt{35}}{5}$ **d.** no real-number solutions **2. a.** $10, -6$
b. $-3 \pm 7\sqrt{2}$ **c.** $\frac{1 \pm \sqrt{3}}{3}$ **3.** $7 \pm \sqrt{11}$ **4.** $\sqrt{3}$ sec ≈ 1.7 sec

SECTION 9.1   STUDY SET

VOCABULARY

Fill in the blanks.

1. $x^2 - 15 = 0$ is an example of a __quadratic__ equation.

2. $x^2 + 6x + 9$ is a perfect __square__ trinomial because
   $x^2 + 6x + 9 = (x + 3)^2$.

CONCEPTS

Fill in the blanks.

3. The square root property of equations: If $x^2 = c$, then
   $x = \boxed{\sqrt{c}}$ or $x = \boxed{-\sqrt{c}}$.

4. **a.** If $x^2 = 5$, then $x = \pm \boxed{\sqrt{5}}$.

   b. If $(x - 2)^2 = 7$, then $x - 2 = \pm \boxed{\sqrt{7}}$.

▶ 5. Use a property of equality to isolate the variable on
   the left side of the equation.

   a. $x + 9 = \pm\sqrt{2}$ $\quad x = -9 \pm \sqrt{2}$

   b. $6x = 3 \pm \sqrt{2}$ $\quad x = \frac{3 \pm \sqrt{2}}{6}$

6. Rationalize the denominator: $x = \pm\sqrt{\frac{7}{2}}$ $\quad x = \pm\frac{\sqrt{14}}{2}$

7. Is $2\sqrt{5}$ a solution of $x^2 = 20$? yes

8. Is -4 a solution of $(x - 1)^2 = 25$? yes

NOTATION

9. Write the statement $x = \sqrt{6}$ or $x = -\sqrt{6}$ using
   a $\pm$ symbol (double-sign notation). $x = \pm\sqrt{6}$

10. Fill in the blanks: $2 \pm \sqrt{3}$ is read as "Two __plus__ or
    __minus__ the square root of three."

GUIDED PRACTICE

Use the square root property to solve each equation, if possible.
See Example 1.

11. $x^2 - 36 = 0$ ± 6 ▶ 12. $x^2 - 4 = 0$ ± 2

13. $b^2 - 9 = 0$ ± 3 14. $a^2 - 25 = 0$ ± 5

15. $x^2 = \dfrac{49}{16}$ $\pm\frac{7}{4}$ 16. $x^2 = \dfrac{81}{121}$ $\pm\frac{9}{11}$

17. $4x^2 = 400$ ± 10 18. $3m^2 = 27$ ± 3

▶ 19. $5x^2 = 125$ ± 5 ▶ 20. $4x^2 = 16$ ± 2

▶ 21. $x^2 - 6 = 0$ $\pm\sqrt{6}$ 22. $x^2 - 7 = 0$ $\pm\sqrt{7}$

23. $b^2 - 17 = 0$ $\pm\sqrt{17}$ 24. $a^2 - 26 = 0$ $\pm\sqrt{26}$

25. $m^2 = 20$ $\pm 2\sqrt{5}$ 26. $n^2 = 32$ $\pm 4\sqrt{2}$

▶ 27. $t^2 = 72$ $\pm 6\sqrt{2}$ 28. $n^2 = 75$ $\pm 5\sqrt{3}$

29. $2x^2 + 8 = 23$ $\pm\frac{\sqrt{30}}{2}$ 30. $3m^2 + 5 = 18$ $\pm\frac{\sqrt{39}}{3}$

31. $6r^2 - 3 = 4$ $\pm\frac{\sqrt{42}}{6}$ ▶ 32. $2w^2 - 9 = 12$ $\pm\frac{\sqrt{42}}{2}$

33. $x^2 = -81$ ▶ 34. $y^2 = -100$
   no real-number solutions   no real-number solutions

Use the square root property to solve each equation.
See Example 2.

35. $(x + 1)^2 = 25$ ▶ 36. $(x - 1)^2 = 49$
   $-6, 4$ $-6, 8$

37. $(x + 2)^2 = 81$ ▶ 38. $(x + 3)^2 = 16$
   $7, -11$ $1, -7$

39. $(x - 2)^2 = 8$ 40. $(x + 2)^2 = 50$
   $2 \pm 2\sqrt{2}$ $-2 \pm 5\sqrt{2}$

41. $(s + 9)^2 = 63$ ▶ 42. $(t - 11)^2 = 45$
   $-9 \pm 3\sqrt{7}$ $11 \pm 3\sqrt{5}$

43. $(3x + 1)^2 - 18 = 0$ 44. $(6y + 5)^2 - 72 = 0$
   $\frac{-1 \pm 3\sqrt{2}}{3}$ $\frac{-5 \pm 6\sqrt{2}}{6}$

▶ 45. $(5c - 10)^2 - 6 = 0$ 46. $(4n + 8)^2 - 17 = 0$
   $\frac{10 \pm \sqrt{6}}{5}$ $\frac{-8 \pm \sqrt{17}}{4}$

Use the square root property to solve each equation.
See Example 3.

47. $x^2 + 2x + 1 = 10$ 48. $x^2 + 8x + 16 = 6$
   $-1 \pm \sqrt{10}$ $-4 \pm \sqrt{6}$

49. $x^2 - 18x + 81 = 7$ 50. $x^2 - 14x + 49 = 19$
   $9 \pm \sqrt{7}$ $7 \pm \sqrt{19}$

▶ 51. $a^2 - 6a + 9 = 40$ ▶ 52. $b^2 - 10b + 25 = 90$
   $3 \pm 2\sqrt{10}$ $5 \pm 3\sqrt{10}$

53. $m^2 + 4m + 4 = 75$ ▶ 54. $m^2 + 16m + 64 = 80$
   $-2 \pm 5\sqrt{3}$ $-8 \pm 4\sqrt{5}$

TRY IT YOURSELF

Use the square root property to solve each equation, if possible.

55. $(x + 12)^2 = 27$ 56. $(m + 1)^2 = 32$
   $-12 \pm 3\sqrt{3}$ $-1 \pm 4\sqrt{2}$

57. $m^2 = 98$ 58. $n^2 = 99$
   $\pm 7\sqrt{2}$ $\pm 3\sqrt{11}$

59. $b^2 - 12b + 36 = 2$ 60. $a^2 - 18a + 81 = 5$
   $6 \pm \sqrt{2}$ $9 \pm \sqrt{5}$

▶ Selected exercises available online at
www.webassign.net/brookscole

▶ **61.** $(y - 15)^2 - 8 = 0$
$15 \pm 2\sqrt{2}$

62. $(y - 5)^2 - 12 = 0$
$5 \pm 2\sqrt{3}$

▶ **63.** $t^2 = \dfrac{1}{144}$
$\pm \dfrac{1}{12}$

64. $d^2 = \dfrac{1}{9}$
$\pm \dfrac{1}{3}$

65. $4(t - 7)^2 - 12 = 0$
$7 \pm \sqrt{3}$

66. $2(t - 6)^2 - 22 = 0$
$6 \pm \sqrt{11}$

67. $h^2 + 25 = 0$
no real-number solutions

68. $4r^2 + 16 = 0$
no real-number solutions

69. $5x^2 + 1 = 18$
$\pm \dfrac{\sqrt{85}}{5}$

70. $7x^2 + 3 = 6$
$\pm \dfrac{\sqrt{21}}{7}$

71. $x^2 - 14 = 0$
$\pm \sqrt{14}$

72. $x^2 - 46 = 0$
$\pm \sqrt{46}$

73. $(8y + 9)^2 = 44$
$\dfrac{-9 + 2\sqrt{11}}{8}$

▶ **74.** $(6y + 13)^2 = 99$
$\dfrac{-13 + 3\sqrt{11}}{6}$

APPLICATIONS

▶ **75.** LIGHTHOUSES The 144-foot-tall Tybee Island Lighthouse is located near Savannah, Georgia. If an object is dropped from the top of the lighthouse, how long would it take for it to hit the ground? (*Hint:* refer to Example 4.) 3 sec

76. SKYSCRAPERS A downtown office building on the north side of the Chicago River is 784 feet tall. If an object is dropped from the top of the building, how long would it take for it to hit the ground? (*Hint:* refer to Example 4.) 7 sec

▶ **77.** SCIENCE HISTORY Legend has it that Galileo Galilei (1564–1642) dropped two objects having different weights from the leaning tower of Pisa in order to prove that they fall at the same rate. If a steel ball is dropped from the lowest side of the tower, and falls 183 feet, how long will it take to hit the ground? Round to the nearest tenth of a second. (*Hint:* refer to Example 4.) 3.4 sec

© Scala/Art Resource, NY

© Hideo Kurihari/Alamy

78. STUDYING MICROGRAVITY NASA's Glenn Research Center in Cleveland, Ohio, has a 435-foot drop tower that begins on the surface and descends into Earth like a mineshaft. How long will it take a sealed container to fall 435 feet? Round to the nearest tenth of a second. (*Hint:* refer to Example 4.) 5.2 sec

79. DAREDEVILS In 1873, Henry Bellini combined a tightrope walk with a leap into the Niagara River below, where he was picked up by a boat. If the rope was 200 feet above the water, for how many seconds did he fall before hitting the water? Round to the nearest tenth of a second. (*Hint:* refer to Example 4.) 3.5 sec

▶ **80.** ROLLER COASTERS Soaring to a height of 420 feet, the *Top Thrill Dragster* at Cedar Point Amusement Park in Sandusky, Ohio, is one of the tallest and fastest roller coasters in the world. If a rider accidentally dropped a camera as the coaster reached its highest point, how long would it take the camera to hit the ground? Round to the nearest tenth. (*Hint:* refer to Example 4.) 5.1 sec

81. PRO WRESTLING A WWE (World Wrestling Entertainment) ring is square in shape and has an area of 400 ft^2. Find the length of a side of the ring. (*Hint:* Use the formula for the area of a square, $A = s^2$.) 20 ft

▶ **82.** CHESS A tournament chessboard is square in shape and has an area of 441 in.^{2}. Find the length of a side of the board. (*Hint:* Use the formula for the area of a square, $A = s^2$.) 21 in.

WRITING

83. Explain why the equation $x^2 + 16 = 0$ has no real-number solutions.

84. Explain why the notation $6 \pm \sqrt{2}$ represents two real numbers.

85. Explain the error in the following work.
Solve: $x^2 = 7$
$$\cancel{x = \sqrt{7}}$$

86. Explain the error in the following work.
Solve: $x^2 = 28$
$$\cancel{x = \pm\sqrt{28}}$$
$$x = 2 \pm \sqrt{7}$$

REVIEW

Solve each equation.

87. $\sqrt{5x - 6} = 2$ 2

88. $\sqrt{6x + 1} + 2 = 7$ 4

89. $2\sqrt{x} = \sqrt{5x - 16}$
16

90. $\sqrt{22y + 86} = y + 9$
5, −1

Objectives

1 Complete the square to write perfect-square trinomials.

2 Solve quadratic equations with leading coefficients of 1 by completing the square.

3 Solve quadratic equations with leading coefficients other than 1 by completing the square.

SECTION 9.2

Solving Quadratic Equations: Completing the Square

In Section 9.1, we used the square root property to solve equations such as $(x - 3)^2 = 36$ and $(x + 1)^2 = 50$, whose left side is a binomial squared and right side is a constant. We also solved equations such as $x^2 + 16x + 64 = 2$ in a similar way by first factoring the perfect-square trinomial on the left side.

In this section, we will discuss a procedure that enables us to solve quadratic equations such as $x^2 + 4x = -3$, whose left side is not a perfect-square trinomial. To make the left side a perfect-square trinomial we will use a procedure called *completing the square.*

1 Complete the square to write perfect-square trinomials.

Consider the following perfect-square trinomials and their factored forms.

$$x^2 + 2bx + b^2 = (x + b)^2 \qquad \text{and} \qquad x^2 - 2bx + b^2 = (x - b)^2$$

In each of these perfect-square trinomials, the third term is the square of one-half of the coefficient of x.

- In $x^2 + 2bx + b^2$, the coefficient of x is $2b$. If we find $\frac{1}{2} \cdot 2b$, which is b, and square it, we get the third term, b^2.
- In $x^2 - 2bx + b^2$, the coefficient of x is $-2b$. If we find $\frac{1}{2}(-2b)$, which is $-b$, and square it, we get the third term: $(-b)^2 = b^2$.

We can use these observations to change certain binomials into perfect-square trinomials. For example, to change $x^2 + 12x$ into a perfect-square trinomial, we find one-half of the coefficient of x, square the result, and add the square to $x^2 + 12x$.

$$x^2 + 12x + \square$$

First, find one-half of the coefficient of x.

Finally, add the square to the binomial to create a trinomial.

$$\frac{1}{2} \cdot 12 = 6 \qquad 6^2 = 36$$

Then square the result.

We obtain the perfect-square trinomial $x^2 + 12x + 36$ that factors as $(x + 6)^2$. By adding 36 to $x^2 + 12x$, we **completed the square** on $x^2 + 12x$.

Completing the Square

To complete the square on $x^2 + bx$, add the square of one-half of the coefficient of x:

$$x^2 + bx + \left(\frac{1}{2}b\right)^2$$

EXAMPLE 1 Complete the square and factor the resulting perfect-square trinomial: **a.** $x^2 + 4x$ **b.** $x^2 - 6x$ **c.** $x^2 - 5x$

Strategy In each case, we will add the square of one-half the coefficient of x to the given binomial.

WHY Adding such a term will change the binomial into a perfect-square trinomial that will factor.

Self Check 1

Complete the square and factor the resulting perfect-square trinomial:
a. $y^2 + 6y$
b. $y^2 - 8y$
c. $y^2 + 3y$

Now Try **Problems 18, 19, and 21**

Self Check 1 Answers

a. $y^2 + 6y + 9 = (y + 3)^2$

b. $y^2 - 8y + 16 = (y - 4)^2$

c. $y^2 + 3y + \frac{9}{4} = \left(y + \frac{3}{2}\right)^2$

Teaching Example 1 Complete the square and factor the resulting perfect-square trinomial:

a. $x^2 + 10x$

b. $y^2 - 14y$

c. $a^2 + 7a$

Answers:

a. $x^2 + 10x + 25 = (x + 5)^2$

b. $y^2 - 14y + 49 = (y - 7)^2$

c. $a^2 + 7a + \frac{49}{4} = \left(a + \frac{7}{2}\right)^2$

Solution

a. Since the coefficient of x is 4, we add the square of one-half of 4.

$$x^2 + 4x + \left[\frac{1}{2}(4)\right]^2 = x^2 + 4x + (2)^2 \qquad \tfrac{1}{2}(4) = 2.$$

$$= x^2 + 4x + 4 \qquad \text{Square 2 to get 4.}$$

This perfect-square trinomial factors as $(x + 2)^2$.

b. Since the coefficient of x is -6, we add the square of one-half of -6.

$$x^2 - 6x + \left[\frac{1}{2}(-6)\right]^2 = x^2 - 6x + (-3)^2 \qquad \tfrac{1}{2}(-6) = -3.$$

$$= x^2 - 6x + 9 \qquad \text{Square } -3 \text{ to get 9.}$$

This perfect-square trinomial factors as $(x - 3)^2$.

c. Since the coefficient of x is -5, we add the square of one-half of -5.

$$x^2 - 5x + \left[\frac{1}{2}(-5)\right]^2 = x^2 - 5x + \left(-\frac{5}{2}\right)^2 \qquad \tfrac{1}{2}(-5) = -\tfrac{5}{2}.$$

$$= x^2 - 5x + \frac{25}{4} \qquad \text{Square } -\tfrac{5}{2} \text{ to get } \tfrac{25}{4}.$$

This perfect-square trinomial factors as $\left(x - \frac{5}{2}\right)^2$. ■

2 **Solve quadratic equations with leading coefficients of 1 by completing the square.**

If the quadratic equation $ax^2 + bx + c = 0$ has a leading coefficient of 1, it's easy to solve by completing the square.

Self Check 2

Solve: $x^2 + 5x = 3$

Approximate the solutions to the nearest hundredth.

Now Try **Problem 33**

Self Check 2 Answers

$\frac{-5 \pm \sqrt{37}}{2}$; $0.54, -5.54$

Teaching Example 2 Solve:

$x^2 - 9x = 5$

Answer:

$\frac{9 \pm \sqrt{101}}{2}$; $-0.52, 9.52$

EXAMPLE 2   Solve: $x^2 - 7x = 2$

Strategy We will use the addition property of equality and add the square of one-half of the coefficient of x to both sides of the equation.

WHY This will create a perfect-square trinomial on the left side that will factor as the square of a binomial. Then we can use the square root property to solve for x.

Solution

$$x^2 - 7x = 2 \qquad \text{This is the equation to solve.}$$

$$x^2 - 7x + \left[\frac{1}{2}(-7)\right]^2 = 2 + \left[\frac{1}{2}(-7)\right]^2 \qquad \begin{array}{l}\text{Since the coefficient of } x \text{ is } -7, \text{ add the} \\ \text{square of one-half of } -7 \text{ to both sides.}\end{array}$$

$$x^2 - 7x + \frac{49}{4} = 2 + \frac{49}{4} \qquad \tfrac{1}{2}(-7) = -\tfrac{7}{2}. \text{ Then square } -\tfrac{7}{2} \text{ to get } \tfrac{49}{4}.$$

$$\left(x - \frac{7}{2}\right)^2 = \frac{8}{4} + \frac{49}{4} \qquad \text{Factor the left-hand side. Write 2 as } \tfrac{8}{4}.$$

$$\left(x - \frac{7}{2}\right)^2 = \frac{57}{4} \qquad \begin{array}{l}\text{The fractions have a common} \\ \text{denominator. Add them.}\end{array}$$

$$x - \frac{7}{2} = \pm\sqrt{\frac{57}{4}} \qquad \begin{array}{l}\text{Use the square root method to solve for} \\ x - \tfrac{7}{2}.\end{array}$$

$$x - \frac{7}{2} = \pm\frac{\sqrt{57}}{2} \qquad \sqrt{\tfrac{57}{4}} = \tfrac{\sqrt{57}}{\sqrt{4}} = \tfrac{\sqrt{57}}{2}.$$

$$x = \frac{7}{2} \pm \frac{\sqrt{57}}{2} \qquad \text{Add } \frac{7}{2} \text{ to both sides.}$$

$$x = \frac{7 \pm \sqrt{57}}{2} \qquad \text{Since the fractions have a common denominator of 2, we can combine them.}$$

The solutions are $\frac{7 \pm \sqrt{57}}{2}$. If we approximate the solutions to the nearest hundredth, we have

$$\frac{7 + \sqrt{57}}{2} \approx 7.27 \qquad \frac{7 - \sqrt{57}}{2} \approx -0.27$$

EXAMPLE 3 Solve $x^2 + 4x - 13 = 0$. Give each answer to the nearest hundredth.

Strategy We will use the addition property of equality and add 13 to both sides. Then we will proceed as in Example 2.

WHY To prepare to complete the square, we need to isolate the variable terms, x^2 and $4x$, on the left side of the equation and the constant term on the right.

Solution
Since the coefficient of x^2 is 1, we can complete the square as follows:

$$x^2 + 4x - 13 = 0 \qquad \text{This is the equation to solve.}$$

$$x^2 + 4x = 13 \qquad \text{Add 13 to both sides so that the constant term is on the right-hand side.}$$

We then find one-half of the coefficient of x, square it, and add the result to both sides to make the left-hand side a perfect-square trinomial.

$$x^2 + 4x + \left[\frac{1}{2}(4)\right]^2 = 13 + \left[\frac{1}{2}(4)\right]^2 \qquad \text{Since the coefficient of x is 4, add the square of one-half of 4 to both sides.}$$

$$x^2 + 4x + 4 = 13 + 4 \qquad \frac{1}{2}(4) = 2. \text{ Then square 2 to get 4.}$$

$$(x + 2)^2 = 17 \qquad \text{Factor } x^2 + 4x + 4 \text{ and simplify.}$$

$$x + 2 = \pm\sqrt{17} \qquad \text{Use the square root method to solve for } x + 2.$$

$$x = -2 \pm \sqrt{17} \qquad \text{Subtract 2 from both sides to isolate x. Write } -2 \text{ in front of the radical.}$$

We can use a calculator to approximate each solution.

$$x = -2 + \sqrt{17} \qquad \text{or} \quad x = -2 - \sqrt{17}$$

$$x \approx -2 + 4.123105626 \qquad x \approx -2 - 4.123105626$$

$$x \approx 2.12 \qquad x \approx -6.12$$

3 Solve quadratic equations with leading coefficients other than 1 by completing the square.

If the quadratic equation $ax^2 + bx + c = 0$ has a leading coefficient other than 1, we can make the leading coefficient 1 by dividing both sides of the equation by a.

EXAMPLE 4 Solve: $4x^2 + 4x - 3 = 0$

Strategy We will use the addition property of equality to get the variable terms on one side of the equation and the constant term on the other. Then we will use the division property of equality and divide both sides by 4 so that the coefficient of x^2 is 1.

Self Check 3
Solve $x^2 + 10x - 4 = 0$. Give each answer to the nearest hundredth. $-5 \pm \sqrt{29}; 0.39, -10.39$

Now Try **Problem 41**

Teaching Example 3 Solve by completing the square. Give each answer to the nearest hundredth.
$x^2 - 12x - 3 = 0$
Answer:
$6 \pm \sqrt{39}; -0.24, 12.24$

Self Check 4
Solve: $2x^2 - 5x - 3 = 0$ $3, -\frac{1}{2}$

Now Try **Problem 46**

Teaching Example 4 Solve:
$3x^2 - 24x + 21 = 0$
Answers: 1, 7

WHY This will create a leading coefficient of 1 so that we can complete the square to solve the equation.

Solution

$$4x^2 + 4x - 3 = 0 \qquad \text{This is the equation to solve.}$$

$$x^2 + x - \frac{3}{4} = 0 \qquad \text{Divide both sides by 4: } \tfrac{4x^2}{4} + \tfrac{4x}{4} - \tfrac{3}{4} = \tfrac{0}{4}.$$

$$x^2 + x = \frac{3}{4} \qquad \text{Add } \tfrac{3}{4} \text{ to both sides so that the constant term is on the right-hand side.}$$

$$x^2 + 1x + \left[\frac{1}{2}(1)\right]^2 = \frac{3}{4} + \left[\frac{1}{2}(1)\right]^2 \qquad \text{Since the coefficient of x is 1, add the square of one-half of 1 to both sides.}$$

$$x^2 + x + \frac{1}{4} = \frac{3}{4} + \frac{1}{4} \qquad \tfrac{1}{2}(1) = \tfrac{1}{2}. \text{ Then square } \tfrac{1}{2} \text{ to get } \tfrac{1}{4}.$$

$$\left(x + \frac{1}{2}\right)^2 = 1 \qquad \text{Factor the trinomial. Add the fractions.}$$

$$x + \frac{1}{2} = \pm 1 \qquad \text{Solve for } x + \tfrac{1}{2} \text{ using the square root method.}$$

$$x = -\frac{1}{2} \pm 1 \qquad \text{Subtract } \tfrac{1}{2} \text{ from both sides to isolate x.}$$

$$x = -\frac{1}{2} + 1 \quad \text{or} \quad x = -\frac{1}{2} - 1$$

$$x = \frac{1}{2} \qquad\qquad\quad x = -\frac{3}{2}$$

The solutions are $\frac{1}{2}$ and $-\frac{3}{2}$. Check each one.

Success Tip In Example 4, you may have noticed that $4x^2 + 4x - 3$ can be factored. Therefore, we could have solved $4x^2 + 4x - 3 = 0$ by factoring. This example illustrates an important fact: Completing the square can be used to solve any quadratic equation.

The previous examples illustrate that to solve a quadratic equation by completing the square, we follow these steps.

Completing the Square to Solve a Quadratic Equation in x

1. If the coefficient of x^2 is 1, go to step 2. If it is not 1, make it 1 by dividing both sides of the equation by the coefficient of x^2.

2. Get all variable terms on one side of the equation and constants on the other side.

3. Complete the square by finding one-half of the coefficient of x, squaring the result, and adding the square to both sides of the equation.

4. Factor the perfect-square trinomial as the square of a binomial.

5. Solve the resulting equation using the square root property.

6. Check your answers in the original equation.

EXAMPLE 5   Solve: $2x^2 - 2 = 4x$

Strategy We will use the addition and subtraction properties of equality to get the variable terms on one side of the equation and the constant term on the other. Then we will use the division property of equality and divide both sides by 2 so that the coefficient of x^2 is 1.

WHY This will create a leading coefficient of 1 so that we can complete the square to solve the equation.

Solution

$$2x^2 - 2 = 4x \qquad \text{This is the equation to solve.}$$

$$2x^2 - 4x - 2 = 0 \qquad \text{Subtract 4x from both sides to get 0 on the right-hand side.}$$

(1) $x^2 - 2x - 1 = 0 \qquad \text{Divide both sides by 2: } \frac{2x^2}{2} - \frac{4x}{2} - \frac{2}{2} = \frac{0}{2}.$

Since Equation 1 cannot be solved by factoring, we complete the square.

$$x^2 - 2x = 1 \qquad \text{Add 1 to both sides.}$$

$$x^2 - 2x + \left[\frac{1}{2}(-2)\right]^2 = 1 + \left[\frac{1}{2}(-2)\right]^2 \qquad \begin{array}{l}\text{Since the coefficient of x is } -2, \text{ add the}\\ \text{square of one-half of } -2 \text{ to both sides.}\end{array}$$

$$x^2 - 2x + 1 = 1 + 1 \qquad \tfrac{1}{2}(-2) = -1. \text{ Then square } -1 \text{ to get 1.}$$

$$(x - 1)^2 = 2 \qquad \text{Factor the trinomial and simplify.}$$

$$x - 1 = \pm\sqrt{2} \qquad \begin{array}{l}\text{Use the square root method to solve}\\ \text{for x} - 1.\end{array}$$

$$x = 1 \pm \sqrt{2} \qquad \text{Add 1 to both sides.}$$

The solutions are $1 \pm \sqrt{2}$. Check each one.

> *Caution!* A common error is to add a constant to one side of an equation to complete the square and forget to add it to the other side.

EXAMPLE 6   Solve by completing the square: $4x^2 - 3 = 24x$

Strategy We will use the addition and subtraction properties of equality to get the variable terms on one side of the equation and the constant term on the other. Then we will use the division property of equality and divide both sides by 4 so that the coefficient of x^2 is 1.

WHY This will create a leading coefficient of 1 so that we can complete the square to solve the equation.

Solution

$$4x^2 - 3 = 24x \qquad \text{This is the equation to solve.}$$

$$4x^2 - 24x = 3 \qquad \begin{array}{l}\text{To have both variable terms on the left side, subtract}\\ \text{24x from both sides. To have the constant term on the}\\ \text{right, add 3 to both sides.}\end{array}$$

$$x^2 - 6x = \frac{3}{4} \qquad \begin{array}{l}\text{To make the coefficient of the } x^2 \text{ term 1, divide both}\\ \text{sides by 4: } \frac{4x^2}{4} - \frac{24x}{4} = \frac{3}{4}.\end{array}$$

$$x^2 - 6x + 9 = \frac{3}{4} + 9 \qquad \begin{array}{l}\text{Complete the square: } \tfrac{1}{2}(-6) = -3 \text{ and } (-3)^2 = 9.\\ \text{Add 9 to both sides.}\end{array}$$

$$(x - 3)^2 = \frac{39}{4} \qquad \begin{array}{l}\text{On the left side, factor. On the right side, express 9 as}\\ \frac{36}{4} \text{ and add to } \frac{3}{4} \text{ to get } \frac{39}{4}.\end{array}$$

$$x - 3 = \pm\sqrt{\frac{39}{4}} \qquad \text{Use the square root property.}$$

$$x - 3 = \pm \frac{\sqrt{39}}{2} \qquad \text{Use the quotient rule to simplify: } \sqrt{\frac{39}{4}} = \frac{\sqrt{39}}{\sqrt{4}} = \frac{\sqrt{39}}{2}.$$

$$x = 3 \pm \frac{\sqrt{39}}{2} \qquad \text{To isolate } x, \text{ add 3 to both sides.}$$

$$x = \frac{6}{2} \pm \frac{\sqrt{39}}{2} \qquad \text{To write the solutions in compact form, express 3 as a}$$
$$\text{fraction with denominator 2: } 3 = \frac{3}{1} \cdot \frac{2}{2} = \frac{6}{2}.$$

$$x = \frac{6 \pm \sqrt{39}}{2} \qquad \text{Write the sum (and difference) over the common}$$
$$\text{denominator 2.}$$

The exact solutions are $\frac{6 \pm \sqrt{39}}{2}$. Check each one in the original equation. We can approximate the solutions using a calculator. To the nearest hundredth, we have

$$\frac{6 + \sqrt{39}}{2} \approx 6.12 \qquad \frac{6 - \sqrt{39}}{2} \approx -0.12$$

ANSWERS TO SELF CHECKS

1. **a.** $y^2 + 6y + 9 = (y + 3)^2$ **b.** $y^2 - 8y + 16 = (y - 4)^2$ **c.** $y^2 + 3y + \frac{9}{4} = \left(y + \frac{3}{2}\right)^2$

2. $\frac{-5 \pm \sqrt{37}}{2}$; $0.54, -5.54$ **3.** $-5 \pm \sqrt{29}$; $0.39, -10.39$ **4.** $3, -\frac{1}{2}$ **5.** $3 \pm \sqrt{5}$

6. $\frac{8 \pm \sqrt{65}}{2}$; $8.03, -0.03$

SECTION 9.2 STUDY SET

VOCABULARY

Fill in the blanks.

1. Since $x^2 + 12x + 36 = (x + 6)^2$, we call the trinomial a perfect-<u>square</u> trinomial.

▶ 2. When we add 9 to $x^2 + 6x$, we say that we have completed the <u>square</u> on $x^2 + 6x$.

3. The <u>leading</u> coefficient of $5x^2 - 4x + 8 = 0$ is 5 and the <u>constant</u> term is 8.

4. If the polynomial in the equation $ax^2 + bx + c = 0$ doesn't factor, we can solve the equation by <u>completing</u> the square.

CONCEPTS

Fill in the blanks.

5. Find one-half of the given number and then square the result.

   a. 6 9   **b.** -12 36

   c. 3 $\frac{9}{4}$ **d.** -5 $\frac{25}{4}$

6. To complete the square on $x^2 + 8x$, we add the <u>square</u> of one-half of 8, which is 16.

▶ 7. To complete the square on $x^2 - 10x$, we add the square of <u>one-half</u> of -10, which is 25.

8. The solutions of $x^2 = c$, where $c > 0$, are $\boxed{\sqrt{c}}$ and $\boxed{-\sqrt{c}}$.

9. If $(x - 2)^2 = 7$, then $x - 2 = \pm \boxed{\sqrt{7}}$.

10. What is the first step if we solve $x^2 - 2x = 35$

   a. by the factoring method? Subtract 35 from both sides.

   b. by completing the square? Add 1 to both sides.

11. Why can't $x^2 - 2x - 1 = 0$ be solved by the factoring method? $x^2 - 2x - 1$ doesn't factor

12. Find the result when both sides of $2x^2 + 4x - 8 = 0$ are divided by 2. $x^2 + 2x - 4 = 0$

NOTATION

Complete each solution to solve the equation.

13. $(y - 1)^2 = 9$

$y - 1 = \boxed{\sqrt{9}}$ or $y - 1 = -\sqrt{9}$

$\boxed{y - 1} = 3$ $\qquad$ $y - 1 = \boxed{-3}$

$y = 4$ $\qquad$ $y = -2$

▶ Selected exercises available online at
www.webassign.net/brookscole

14. $y^2 + 2y - 3 = 0$

$$y^2 + 2y = \boxed{3}$$
$$y^2 + 2y + 1 = 3 + \boxed{1}$$
$$(y + 1)^2 = \boxed{4}$$
$$\boxed{y + 1} = \sqrt{4} \quad \text{or} \quad y + 1 = -\sqrt{4}$$
$$y + 1 = \boxed{2} \quad \Big| \quad \boxed{y + 1} = -2$$
$$y = 1 \quad \Big| \quad y = -3$$

15. a. In solving a quadratic equation, a student obtains $x = \pm\sqrt{10}$. How many solutions are represented by this notation? List them. two; $\sqrt{10}, -\sqrt{10}$

b. In solving a quadratic equation, a student obtains $x = 8 \pm \sqrt{3}$. List each solution separately. Round each one to the nearest hundredth.
$8 + \sqrt{3}, 8 - \sqrt{3}; 9.73, 6.27$

▶ **16.** Solve $x + 1 = \pm\sqrt{2}$ for x. $-1 \pm \sqrt{2}$

GUIDED PRACTICE

Complete the square and factor the perfect-square trinomial.
See Example 1.

17. $x^2 + 2x$
$x^2 + 2x + 1 = (x + 1)^2$

▶ **18.** $x^2 + 12$
$x^2 + 12x + 36 = (x + 6)^2$

▶ **19.** $x^2 - 4x$
$x^2 - 4x + 4 = (x - 2)^2$

▶ **20.** $x^2 - 14x$
$x^2 - 14x + 49 = (x - 7)^2$

21. $x^2 + 7x$
$x^2 + 7x + \frac{49}{4} = \left(x + \frac{7}{2}\right)^2$

22. $x^2 + 21x$
$x^2 + 21x + \frac{441}{4} = \left(x + \frac{21}{2}\right)^2$

23. $x^2 + x$
$x^2 + x + \frac{1}{4} = \left(x + \frac{1}{2}\right)^2$

24. $x^2 - x$
$x^2 - x + \frac{1}{4} = \left(x - \frac{1}{2}\right)^2$

25. $a^2 - 3a$
$a^2 - 3a + \frac{9}{4} = \left(a - \frac{3}{2}\right)^2$

26. $b^2 - 13b$
$b^2 - 13b + \frac{169}{4} = \left(b - \frac{13}{2}\right)^2$

27. $b^2 + \frac{2}{3}b$
$b^2 + \frac{2}{3}b + \frac{1}{9} = \left(b + \frac{1}{3}\right)^2$

28. $c^2 - \frac{5}{2}c$
$c^2 - \frac{5}{2}c + \frac{25}{16} = \left(c - \frac{5}{4}\right)^2$

Solve each equation by completing the square. See Example 2.

29. $g^2 + 5g = 6$ $1, -6$　　**30.** $s^2 + 5s = 14$ $2, -7$

31. $x^2 + 6x = -8$ $-2, -4$　▶ **32.** $x^2 + 8x = -12$ $-2, -6$

33. $a^2 + 4a = 5$ $-5, 1$　　**34.** $y^2 + 6y = 7$ $-7, 1$

35. $h^2 - 2h = 15$ $-3, 5$　　**36.** $k^2 - 8k = -12$ $2, 6$

Solve each equation by completing the square. Give the exact solutions, and then round them to the nearest hundredth.
See Example 3.

▶ **37.** $x^2 + 8x - 6 = 0$
$-4 \pm \sqrt{22}; 0.69, -8.69$

38. $x^2 + 6x - 2 = 0$
$-3 \pm \sqrt{11}; 0.32, -6.32$

▶ **39.** $x^2 + 6x + 4 = 0$
$-3 \pm \sqrt{5}; -0.76, -5.24$

▶ **40.** $x^2 + 8x + 6 = 0$
$-4 \pm \sqrt{10}; -0.84, -7.16$

41. $x^2 + 4x + 1 = 0$
$-2 \pm \sqrt{3}; -0.27, -3.73$

42. $x^2 + 6x + 2 = 0$
$-3 \pm \sqrt{7}; -0.35, -5.65$

43. $x^2 - 2x - 4 = 0$
$1 \pm \sqrt{5}; 3.24, -1.24$

▶ **44.** $x^2 - 4x - 2 = 0$
$2 \pm \sqrt{6}; 4.45, -0.45$

Solve each equation by completing the square. See Example 4.

45. $3x^2 + 5x - 2 = 0$
$\frac{1}{3}, -2$

▶ **46.** $4x^2 + 4x - 3 = 0$
$\frac{3}{2}, -\frac{1}{2}$

47. $6x^2 - 5x - 6 = 0$
$\frac{3}{2}, -\frac{2}{3}$

48. $10x^2 + 21x - 10 = 0$
$\frac{2}{5}, -\frac{5}{2}$

Solve each equation by completing the square. See Example 5.

49. $x^2 = 4x + 3$
$2 \pm \sqrt{7}$

▶ **50.** $x^2 = 6x - 3$
$3 \pm \sqrt{6}$

51. $4x^2 + 4x + 1 = 20$
$\frac{-1 \pm 2\sqrt{5}}{2}$

52. $9x^2 = 8 - 12x$
$\frac{-2 \pm 2\sqrt{3}}{3}$

Solve each equation by completing the square. Give the solutions to the nearest hundredth. See Example 6.

53. $t^2 - 2t - 4 = 0$
$3.24, -1.24$

54. $m^2 - 4m - 2 = 0$
$4.45, -0.45$

55. $2t^2 = -6t - 1$
$-0.18, -2.82$

▶ **56.** $3p^2 = -4p + 3$
$0.54, -1.87$

57. $4x^2 + 4x + 1 = 20$
$-2.74, 1.74$

58. $9x^2 = 8 - 12x$
$0.49, -1.82$

59. $3q^2 - 4 = -2q$
$0.87, -1.54$

60. $2y^2 + 3 = 10y$
$4.68, 0.32$

TRY IT YOURSELF

Solve each equation by completing the square.

61. $2x^2 = 4 - 2x$
$1, -2$

62. $3q^2 = 3q + 6$
$2, -1$

63. $k^2 - 8k + 12 = 0$
$2, 6$

64. $p^2 - 4p + 3 = 0$
$3, 1$

65. $x^2 - 2x = 15$
$5, -3$

▶ **66.** $x^2 - 2x = 8$
$4, -2$

67. $3x^2 + 9x + 6 = 0$
$-1, -2$

68. $3d^2 + 48 = -24d$
$-4, -4$

69. $2x^2 = 3x + 2$
$2, -\frac{1}{2}$

70. $3x^2 = 2 - 5x$
$-2, \frac{1}{3}$

71. $4x^2 = 2 - 7x$
$-2, \frac{1}{4}$

72. $2x^2 = 5x + 3$
$3, -\frac{1}{2}$

73. $4x^2 - 24x - 13 = 0$
$\frac{13}{2}, -\frac{1}{2}$

74. $4d^2 - 16d - 9 = 0$
$\frac{9}{2}, -\frac{1}{2}$

75. $4a^2 - 9a + 1 = 0$
$\frac{9 \pm \sqrt{65}}{8}$

76. $4a^2 - 11a + 1 = 0$
$\frac{11 \pm \sqrt{105}}{8}$

77. $2x^2 + 6x = 8$
$1, -4$

78. $3x^2 - 6x = 9$
$3, -1$

79. $6x^2 - 6 = 5x$
$\frac{3}{2}, -\frac{2}{3}$

80. $6x^2 - 4 = 5x$
$\frac{4}{3}, -\frac{1}{2}$

81. $x^2 + 3x - \frac{1}{2} = -2$
$\frac{-3 \pm \sqrt{3}}{2}$

82. $x^2 + x = 3x - \frac{2}{3}$
$\frac{3 \pm \sqrt{3}}{3}$

APPLICATIONS

▶ **83.** CAROUSELS In 1999, the city of Lancaster, Pennsylvania, considered installing a classic Dentzel carousel in an abandoned downtown building. After learning that the circular-shaped carousel would occupy 2,376 square feet of floor space and that it was 26 feet high, the proposal was determined to be impractical because of the large remodeling costs. Find the diameter of the carousel to the nearest foot. 55 ft

▶ **84.** ESCAPE VELOCITY The speed at which a rocket must be fired for it to leave the Earth's gravitational attraction is called the **escape velocity.** If the escape velocity v_e, in mph, is given by

$$\frac{v_e^2}{2g} = R$$

where $g = 78,545$ and $R = 3,960$, find v_e. Round to the nearest mi/hr. 24,941 mi/hr

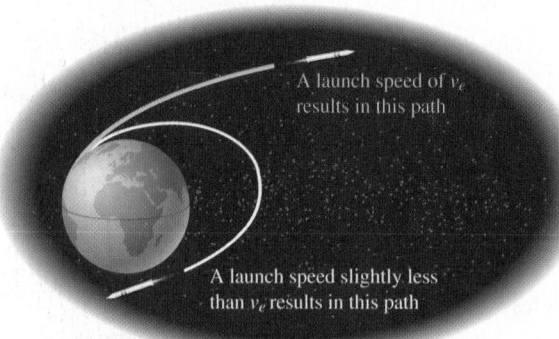

A launch speed of v_e results in this path

A launch speed slightly less than v_e results in this path

▶ **85.** BICYCLE SAFETY See the illustration in the next column. A bicycle training program for children uses a figure-8 course to help them improve their balance and steering. The course is laid out over a paved area covering 800 square feet. Find its dimensions. 20 ft by 40 ft

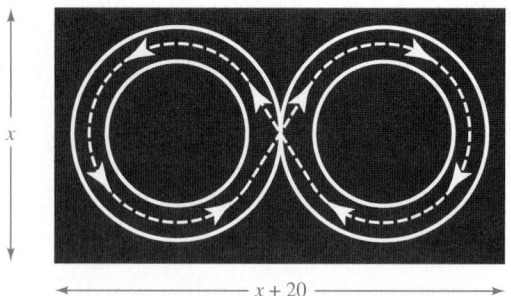

x

$x + 20$

▶ **86.** BADMINTON The badminton court shown below occupies 880 square feet of the floor space of a gymnasium. If its length is 4 feet more than twice its width, find its dimensions. 20 ft by 44 ft

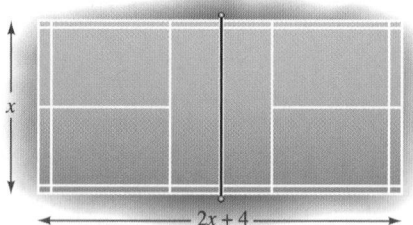

x

$2x + 4$

WRITING

87. Explain how to complete the square on $x^2 - 5x$.

88. Explain the error in the following work.

$$x^2 = 28$$
$$x = \pm\sqrt{28}$$
$$x = 2 \pm \sqrt{7}$$

The 2 was incorrectly moved in front of the $\pm$ symbol. The correct answer is $\pm 2\sqrt{7}$.

89. Rounded to the nearest hundredth, one solution of the equation $x^2 + 4x + 1 = 0$ is -0.27. Use your calculator to check it. How could it be a solution if it doesn't make the left-hand side zero? Explain.

▶ **90.** Give an example of a perfect-square trinomial. Why do you think the word *perfect* is used to describe it?

REVIEW

Perform each operation.

91. $(y - 1)^2$ $y^2 - 2y + 1$ **92.** $(z + 2)^2$ $z^2 + 4z + 4$

93. $(x + y)^2$ $x^2 + 2xy + y^2$ **94.** $(a - b)^2$ $a^2 - 2ab + b^2$

95. $(2z)^2$ $4z^2$ ▶ **96.** $(xy)^2$ x^2y^2

Solving Quadratic Equations: The Quadratic Formula

Objectives

1 Use the quadratic formula to solve quadratic equations.

2 Identify quadratic equations with no real-number solutions.

3 Determine the most efficient method to solve a quadratic equation.

4 Solve problems modeled by quadratic equations.

We can solve any quadratic equation by completing the square, but the work is often lengthy and involved. In this section, we will develop a formula, called the *quadratic formula,* that will enable us to solve quadratic equations with much less effort.

1 Use the quadratic formula to solve quadratic equations.

We can solve the **general quadratic equation** $ax^2 + bx + c = 0$, where $a \neq 0$, by completing the square.

$$ax^2 + bx + c = 0$$

$$\frac{ax^2}{a} + \frac{bx}{a} + \frac{c}{a} = \frac{0}{a} \qquad \text{Divide both sides by } a \text{ so that the coefficient of } x^2 \text{ is 1.}$$

$$x^2 + \frac{b}{a}x + \frac{c}{a} = 0 \qquad \text{Simplify } \frac{\overset{1}{\cancel{a}x^2}}{\underset{1}{\cancel{a}}} = x^2. \text{ Write } \frac{bx}{a} \text{ as } \frac{b}{a}x.$$

$$x^2 + \frac{b}{a}x = -\frac{c}{a} \qquad \text{Subtract } \frac{c}{a} \text{ from both sides.}$$

Since the coefficient of x is $\dfrac{b}{a}$, we can complete the square on $x^2 + \dfrac{b}{a}x$ by adding

$$\left(\frac{1}{2} \cdot \frac{b}{a}\right)^2, \qquad \text{which is} \qquad \frac{b^2}{4a^2}$$

to both sides:

$$x^2 + \frac{b}{a}x + \frac{b^2}{4a^2} = \frac{b^2}{4a^2} - \frac{c}{a}$$

After factoring the perfect-square trinomial on the left-hand side, we have

$$\left(x + \frac{b}{2a}\right)\left(x + \frac{b}{2a}\right) = \frac{b^2}{4a^2} - \frac{4ac}{4aa} \qquad \text{The lowest common denominator on the right-hand side is } 4a^2. \text{ Build the second fraction.}$$

$$\left(x + \frac{b}{2a}\right)^2 = \frac{b^2 - 4ac}{4a^2} \qquad \text{Subtract the numerators and write the difference over the common denominator.}$$

The resulting equation can be solved by the square root method to obtain

$$x + \frac{b}{2a} = \sqrt{\frac{b^2 - 4ac}{4a^2}} \qquad \text{or} \qquad x + \frac{b}{2a} = -\sqrt{\frac{b^2 - 4ac}{4a^2}}$$

$$x + \frac{b}{2a} = \frac{\sqrt{b^2 - 4ac}}{\sqrt{4a^2}} \qquad\qquad x + \frac{b}{2a} = -\frac{\sqrt{b^2 - 4ac}}{\sqrt{4a^2}}$$

$$x = -\frac{b}{2a} + \frac{\sqrt{b^2 - 4ac}}{2a} \qquad\qquad x = -\frac{b}{2a} - \frac{\sqrt{b^2 - 4ac}}{2a}$$

$$x = \frac{-b + \sqrt{b^2 - 4ac}}{2a} \qquad\qquad x = \frac{-b - \sqrt{b^2 - 4ac}}{2a}$$

These solutions are usually written in one formula called the **quadratic formula.**

The Quadratic Formula

The solutions of the quadratic equation $ax^2 + bx + c = 0$ are

$$x = \frac{-b \pm \sqrt{b^2 - 4ac}}{2a} \quad \text{where } a \neq 0$$

Caution! When you write the quadratic formula, draw the fraction bar so that it includes the complete numerator. Do not write

$$x = -b \pm \frac{\sqrt{b^2 - 4ac}}{2a}$$

Self Check 1

Solve: $x^2 + 6x + 5 = 0$ $\quad$ $-1, -5$

Now Try Problem 29

Teaching Example 1 Solve:
$x^2 + 13x + 12 = 0$
Answer:
$-1, -12$

EXAMPLE 1 Solve: $x^2 + 5x + 6 = 0$

Strategy We will compare the given equation to the general quadratic equation $ax^2 + bx + c = 0$ to identify a, b, and c.

WHY To use the quadratic formula, we need to know what numbers to substitute for a, b, and c in $x = \dfrac{-b \pm \sqrt{b^2 - 4ac}}{2a}$.

Solution

The equation is written in $ax^2 + bx + c = 0$ form with $a = 1$, $b = 5$, and $c = 6$.

$$1x^2 + 5x + 6 = 0$$
$$\uparrow \qquad \uparrow \qquad \uparrow$$
$$ax^2 + bx + c = 0$$

To find the solutions, we substitute these values into the quadratic formula and evaluate the right-hand side.

$$x = \frac{-b \pm \sqrt{b^2 - 4ac}}{2a} \qquad \text{This is the quadratic formula.}$$

$$= \frac{-5 \pm \sqrt{5^2 - 4(1)(6)}}{2(1)} \qquad \text{Substitute 1 for } a, 5 \text{ for } b, \text{ and 6 for } c.$$

$$= \frac{-5 \pm \sqrt{25 - 24}}{2} \qquad \text{Evaluate the power and multiply within the radical symbol.}$$

$$= \frac{-5 \pm \sqrt{1}}{2} \qquad \text{Perform the subtraction within the radical symbol.}$$

$$x = \frac{-5 \pm 1}{2} \qquad \sqrt{1} = 1.$$

This notation represents two solutions. We simplify them separately, first using the $+$ sign and then using the $-$ sign.

$$x = \frac{-5 + 1}{2} \quad \text{or} \quad x = \frac{-5 - 1}{2}$$

$$x = \frac{-4}{2} \qquad\qquad x = \frac{-6}{2}$$

$$x = -2 \qquad\qquad\quad x = -3$$

The solutions are -2 and -3.

> **Success Tip** In Example 1, you may have noticed that we could have solved $x^2 + 5x + 6 = 0$ by factoring.

EXAMPLE 2   Solve: $2x^2 = 5x + 3$

Strategy We will use the subtraction property of equality to get 0 on the right side of the equation. Then we will compare the resulting equation to the general quadratic equation $ax^2 + bx + c = 0$ to identify a, b, and c.

WHY To use the quadratic formula, we need to know what numbers to substitute for a, b, and c in $x = \dfrac{-b \pm \sqrt{b^2 - 4ac}}{2a}$.

Solution

$$2x^2 = 5x + 3 \qquad \text{This is the equation to solve.}$$
$$2x^2 - 5x - 3 = 0 \qquad \text{Subtract 5x and 3 from both sides.}$$

In this equation, $a = 2$, $b = -5$, and $c = -3$. To find the solutions, we substitute these values into the quadratic formula and evaluate the right-hand side.

$$x = \frac{-b \pm \sqrt{b^2 - 4ac}}{2a} \qquad \text{This is the quadratic formula.}$$

$$= \frac{-(-5) \pm \sqrt{(-5)^2 - 4(2)(-3)}}{2(2)} \qquad \text{Substitute 2 for } a, -5 \text{ for } b, \text{ and } -3 \text{ for } c.$$

$$= \frac{5 \pm \sqrt{25 - (-24)}}{4} \qquad \begin{array}{l} -(-5) = 5. \text{ Evaluate the power and} \\ \text{multiply within the radical symbol.} \end{array}$$

$$= \frac{5 \pm \sqrt{49}}{4} \qquad \begin{array}{l} \text{Perform the subtraction within the radical} \\ \text{symbol: } 25 - (-24) = 25 + 24 = 49. \end{array}$$

$$= \frac{5 \pm 7}{4} \qquad \sqrt{49} = 7.$$

Thus,

$$x = \frac{5 + 7}{4} \quad \text{or} \quad x = \frac{5 - 7}{4}$$

$$x = \frac{12}{4} \qquad\qquad x = \frac{-2}{4}$$

$$x = 3 \qquad\qquad\quad x = -\frac{1}{2}$$

The solutions are 3 and $-\frac{1}{2}$. Check each one in the original equation.

EXAMPLE 3   Solve $3x^2 = 2x + 4$. Round each solution to the nearest hundredth.

Strategy We will use the subtraction property of equality to get 0 on the right side of the equation. Then we will compare the resulting equation to the general quadratic equation $ax^2 + bx + c = 0$ to identify a, b, and c.

WHY To use the quadratic formula, we need to know what numbers to substitute for a, b, and c in $x = \dfrac{-b \pm \sqrt{b^2 - 4ac}}{2a}$.

Solution

We begin by writing the given equation in $ax^2 + bx + c = 0$ form.

Self Check 2

Solve: $4x^2 - 11x = 3$ $3, -\frac{1}{4}$

Now Try Problem 33

Teaching Example 2 Solve:
$5x^2 = -2x + 3$
Answer:
$-1, \frac{3}{5}$

Self Check 3

Solve $2x^2 - 1 = 2x$. Round each solution to the nearest hundredth.

Now Try Problem 37

Self Check 3 Answer
$\frac{1 + \sqrt{3}}{2} \approx 1.37, \frac{1 - \sqrt{3}}{2} \approx -0.37$

Teaching Example 3 Solve:
$3x^2 - 1 = 5x$. Round each solution to the nearest hundredth.
Answer:
$\frac{5 + \sqrt{37}}{6} \approx 1.85, \frac{5 - \sqrt{37}}{6} \approx -0.18$

$$3x^2 = 2x + 4 \qquad \text{This is the equation to solve.}$$

$$3x^2 - 2x - 4 = 0 \qquad \text{Subtract 2x and 4 from both sides.}$$

In this equation, $a = 3$, $b = -2$, and $c = -4$. To find the solutions, we substitute these values into the quadratic formula and evaluate the right-hand side.

$$x = \frac{-b \pm \sqrt{b^2 - 4ac}}{2a} \qquad \text{This is the quadratic formula.}$$

$$= \frac{-(-2) \pm \sqrt{(-2)^2 - 4(3)(-4)}}{2(3)} \qquad \text{Substitute 3 for } a, -2 \text{ for } b, \text{ and } -4 \text{ for } c.$$

$$= \frac{2 \pm \sqrt{4 + 48}}{6} \qquad \begin{array}{l}-(-2) = 2. \text{ Simplify within the radical} \\ \text{symbol.}\end{array}$$

$$= \frac{2 \pm \sqrt{52}}{6} \qquad \begin{array}{l}\text{Perform the addition within the radical} \\ \text{symbol.}\end{array}$$

$$= \frac{2 \pm 2\sqrt{13}}{6} \qquad \sqrt{52} = \sqrt{4 \cdot 13} = 2\sqrt{13}.$$

$$= \frac{\overset{1}{\cancel{2}}\left(1 \pm \sqrt{13}\right)}{\underset{1}{2} \cdot 3} \qquad \begin{array}{l}\text{In the numerator, factor out 2:} \\ 2 \pm 2\sqrt{13} = 2(1 \pm \sqrt{13}). \text{ Write 6 as } 2 \cdot 3. \\ \text{Then remove the common factor of 2.}\end{array}$$

$$x = \frac{1 \pm \sqrt{13}}{3} \qquad \text{Simplify.}$$

The solutions are $\frac{1 \pm \sqrt{13}}{3}$. We can use a calculator to approximate each of them. To the nearest hundredth,

$$\frac{1 + \sqrt{13}}{3} \approx 1.54 \qquad \frac{1 - \sqrt{13}}{3} \approx -0.87$$

2 Identify quadratic equations with no real-number solutions.

The next example shows that some quadratic equations have no real-number solutions.

Self Check 4

Does the equation

$$2x^2 + x + 1 = 0$$

have any real-number solutions? no

Now Try Problem 41

Teaching Example 4 Does the equation
$4x^2 - 3x + 2 = 0$
have any real-number solutions?
Answer:
no

EXAMPLE 4   Does the equation $x^2 + 2x + 5 = 0$ have any real-number solutions?

Strategy We will compare the given equation to the general quadratic equation $ax^2 + bx + c = 0$ to identify a, b, and c.

WHY To use the quadratic formula, we need to know what numbers to substitute for a, b, and c in $x = \dfrac{-b \pm \sqrt{b^2 - 4ac}}{2a}$.

Solution
In this equation $a = 1$, $b = 2$, and $c = 5$. We substitute these values into the quadratic formula.

$$x = \frac{-b \pm \sqrt{b^2 - 4ac}}{2a} \qquad \text{This is the quadratic formula.}$$

$$= \frac{-2 \pm \sqrt{2^2 - 4(1)(5)}}{2(1)} \qquad \text{Substitute 1 for } a, 2 \text{ for } b, \text{ and } 5 \text{ for } c.$$

$$= \frac{-2 \pm \sqrt{4 - 20}}{2} \qquad \begin{array}{l}\text{Evaluate the power and multiply within the radical} \\ \text{symbol.}\end{array}$$

$$x = \frac{-2 \pm \sqrt{-16}}{2} \qquad \begin{array}{l}\text{Perform the subtraction within the radical symbol. The} \\ \text{result is a negative number, } -16.\end{array}$$

Since $\sqrt{-16}$ is not a real number, there are no real-number solutions.

3 Determine the most efficient method to solve a quadratic equation.

We have discussed four methods that are used to solve quadratic equations. The following table shows some advantages and disadvantages of each method.

Method	Advantages	Disadvantages	Examples
Factoring and the zero-factor property	It can be very fast. When each factor is set equal to 0, the resulting equations are usually easy to solve.	Some polynomials may be difficult to factor and others impossible.	$x^2 - 2x - 24 = 0$ $4a^2 + a = 0$
Square root property	It is the fastest way to solve equations of the form $ax^2 = n$ or $(ax + b)^2 = n$, where n is a number.	It only applies to equations that are in these forms.	$x^2 = 27$ $(2y + 3)^2 = 25$
Completing the square*	It can be used to solve any quadratic equation. It works well with equations of the form $x^2 + bx = n$, where b is even.	It involves more steps than the other methods. The algebra can be cumbersome if the leading coefficient is not 1.	$t^2 - 14t = 9$ $x^2 + 4x + 1 = 0$
Quadratic formula	It can be used to solve any quadratic equation.	It involves several computations where sign errors can be made. Often the result must be simplified.	$x^2 + 3x - 33 = 0$ $4s^2 - 10s + 5 = 0$

*The quadratic formula is just a condensed version of completing the square and is usually easier to use. However, you need to know how to complete the square because it is used in more advanced mathematics courses.

To determine the most efficient method for a given equation, we can use the following strategy.

Strategy for Solving Quadratic Equations

1. See whether the equation is in a form such that the **square root method** is easily applied.

2. See whether the equation is in a form such that the **completing the square method** is easily applied.

3. If neither Step 1 nor Step 2 is reasonable, write the equation in $ax^2 + bx + c = 0$ form.

4. See whether the equation can be solved using the **factoring method.**

5. If you can't factor, solve the equation by the **quadratic formula.**

---

4 Solve problems modeled by quadratic equations.

The equation solving methods discussed in this section can be used to solve a variety of real-world applications that are modeled by quadratic equations.

A rectangular garden is 4 feet longer than it is wide. If the garden has an area of 96 square feet, find the garden's length and width. width: 8 ft, length: 12 ft

Now Try Problem 69

Teaching Example 5 An architect needs to design a triangular-shaped window that has an area of 100 in.² If the height is 10 in. less than the base, find the base and height.
Answer:
base: 20 in., height: 10 in.

EXAMPLE 5   *Sailing* The height of a triangular sail is 4 feet more than the length of the base. If the sail has an area of 30 square feet, find the length of its base and the height.

$b + 4$

b

Analyze
- The height of the sail is 4 feet more than the length of the base.
- The area of the sail is 30 ft².
- Find the length of the base and height of the sail.

Form If we let b = the length of the base in feet of the triangular sail, then $b + 4 =$ the height in feet. We can use the formula for the area of a triangle, $A = \frac{1}{2}bh$, to form an equation.

$\frac{1}{2}$	times	the length of the base	times	the height	equals	the area of the triangle.
$\frac{1}{2}$	$\cdot$	b	$\cdot$	$(b + 4)$	$=$	30

> *Success Tip* It is usually easier to clear quadratic equations of fractions before attempting to solve them.

Solve

$$\frac{1}{2}b(b + 4) = 30$$

$b(b + 4) = 60$ To clear the equation of the fraction, multiply both sides by 2.

$b^2 + 4b = 60$ Distribute the multiplication by b.

Since the coefficient of the b-term is the even number 4, this equation can be solved quickly by completing the square.

$$b^2 + 4b = 60$$

$b^2 + 4b + 4 = 60 + 4$ Complete the square: $\frac{1}{2}(4) = 2$ and $(2)^2 = 4$. Add 4 to both sides.

$(b + 2)^2 = 64$ On the left side, factor the perfect-square trinomial. On the right, add.

$b + 2 = \pm\sqrt{64}$ Use the square root property.

$b = -2 \pm 8$ To isolate b, subtract 2 from both sides. Evaluate: $\sqrt{64} = 8$.

$b = -2 + 8$ or $b = -2 - 8$ To find the solutions, perform the calculation using a + symbol and then using a − symbol.

$b = 6$ $b = -10$ Discard the solution −10. The length of the base cannot be negative.

State The length of the base of the sail is 6 feet. Since the height is given by $b + 4$, the height of the sail is $6 + 4 = 10$ feet.

Check A height of 10 feet is 4 feet more than the length of the base, which is 6 feet. Also, the area of the triangle is $\frac{1}{2}(6)(10) = 30$ ft². The results check.

EXAMPLE 6   *Televisions*   A television's screen size is measured diagonally. For the 42-inch plasma television shown in the illustration, the screen's height is 16 inches less than its length. What are the height and length of the screen?

Analyze   A sketch of the screen shows that two adjacent sides and the diagonal form a right triangle. The length of the hypotenuse is 42 inches.

Form   If we let l = the length of the screen in inches, then $l - 16$ represents the height of the screen in inches. We can use the Pythagorean theorem to form an equation.

$a^2 + b^2 = c^2$	This is the Pythagorean theorem.
$l^2 + (l - 16)^2 = 42^2$	Substitute l for a, $l - 16$ for b, and 42 for c.
$l^2 + l^2 - 32l + 256 = 1,764$	Find $(l - 16)^2$ and 42^2.
$2l^2 - 32l - 1,508 = 0$	To get 0 on the right side of the equation, subtract 1,764 from both sides.
$l^2 - 16l - 754 = 0$	Divide both sides of the equation by 2: $\frac{2l^2}{2} - \frac{32l}{2} - \frac{1,508}{2} = \frac{0}{2}$.

Solve   Because of the large constant term, -754, we will not attempt to solve this quadratic equation by factoring. Instead, we will use the quadratic formula, with $a = 1$, $b = -16$, and $c = -754$.

$l = \dfrac{-b \pm \sqrt{b^2 - 4ac}}{2a}$	In the quadratic formula, replace x with l.
$l = \dfrac{-(-16) \pm \sqrt{(-16)^2 - 4(1)(-754)}}{2(1)}$	Substitute 1 for a, -16 for b, and -754 for c.
$l = \dfrac{16 \pm \sqrt{256 - (-3,016)}}{2}$	Evaluate the power and multiply within the radical. Multiply in the denominator.
$l = \dfrac{16 \pm \sqrt{3,272}}{2}$	Subtract within the radical.

We can use a calculator to approximate each one to the nearest tenth. The negative solution is discarded because the length of the screen cannot be negative.

$$\frac{16 + \sqrt{3,272}}{2} \approx 36.6 \quad \text{or} \quad \frac{16 - \sqrt{3,272}}{2} \approx -20.6$$

State   The length of the television screen is approximately 36.6 inches. Since the height is $l - 16$, the height is approximately $36.6 - 16$ or 20.6 inches.

Check   The sum of the squares of the lengths of the sides is $(36.6)^2 + (20.6)^2 = 1,763.92$. The square of the length of the hypotenuse is $42^2 = 1,764$. Since these are approximately equal, the results seem reasonable.

> **ANSWERS TO SELF CHECKS**
> **1.** $-1, -5$ **2.** $3, -\frac{1}{4}$ **3.** $\frac{1+\sqrt{3}}{2} \approx 1.37, \frac{1-\sqrt{3}}{2} \approx -0.37$ **4.** no
> **5.** width: 8 ft, height: 12 ft **6.** width: 8.40 in., length: 12.90 in.

SECTION **9.3**   STUDY SET

▌VOCABULARY

Fill in the blanks.

1. To _solve_ a quadratic equation means to find all the values of the variable that make the equation true.

▶ 2. $\sqrt{-16}$ is not a _real_ number.

3. The general _quadratic_ equation is $ax^2 + bx + c = 0$.

4. The formula $x = \dfrac{-b \pm \sqrt{b^2 - 4ac}}{2a}$ is called the
   quadratic formula.

▌CONCEPTS

Fill in the blanks.

5. In the quadratic equation $ax^2 + bx + c = 0, a \ne 0$.

▶ 6. Before we can determine a, b, and c for $x = 3x^2 - 1$, we must write the equation in _quadratic_ (general) form.

7. In the quadratic equation $3x^2 - 5 = 0$, $a = 3$, $b = 0$, and $c = -5$

8. In the quadratic equation $-4x^2 + 8x = 0$, $a = -4$, $b = 8$, and $c = 0$

9. The formula for the area of a rectangle is $A = lw$, and the formula for the area of a triangle is $A = \frac{1}{2}bh$.

10. If a, b, and c are three sides of a right triangle and c is the hypotenuse, then $c^2 = a^2 + b^2$.

11. In evaluating the numerator of $\dfrac{-5 \pm \sqrt{5^2 - 4(2)(1)}}{2(2)}$
    what operation should be performed first? Evaluate 5^2

12. Consider the expression $\dfrac{3 \pm 6\sqrt{2}}{3}$

    a. How many terms does the numerator contain? 2
    b. What common factor do the terms have? 3
    c. Simplify the expression. $1 \pm 2\sqrt{2}$

13. A student used the quadratic formula to solve an equation and obtained $x = \dfrac{-3 \pm \sqrt{15}}{2}$

    a. How many solutions does the equation have? 2
    b. What are they exactly? $\frac{-3 + \sqrt{15}}{2}, \frac{-3 - \sqrt{15}}{2}$
    c. Approximate them to the nearest hundredth. $0.44, -3.44$

14. The solutions of a quadratic equation are $x = 2 \pm \sqrt{3}$. Graph them on the number line.

▌NOTATION

Complete each solution.

15. Solve: $x^2 - 5x - 6 = 0$

$$x = \frac{-b \pm \sqrt{b^2 - 4ac}}{2a}$$
$$= \frac{-(-5) \pm \sqrt{(-5)^2 - 4(1)(-6)}}{2(1)}$$
$$= \frac{5 \pm \sqrt{25 + 24}}{2}$$
$$= \frac{5 \pm \sqrt{49}}{2}$$
$$x = \frac{5 \pm 7}{2}$$
$$x = \frac{5 + 7}{2} = 6 \quad \text{or} \quad x = \frac{5 - 7}{2} = -1$$

16. Solve: $3x^2 + 2x - 2 = 0$

$$x = \frac{-b \pm \sqrt{b^2 - 4ac}}{2a}$$
$$= \frac{-2 \pm \sqrt{2^2 - 4(3)(-2)}}{2(3)}$$
$$= \frac{-2 \pm \sqrt{4 + 24}}{6}$$
$$= \frac{-2 \pm \sqrt{28}}{6}$$
$$= \frac{-2 \pm 2\sqrt{7}}{6}$$
$$= \frac{2(-1 \pm \sqrt{7})}{2 \cdot 3}$$
$$x = \frac{-1 \pm \sqrt{7}}{3}$$

▶ Selected exercises available online at
www.webassign.net/brookscole

17. What is wrong with the following work?

Solve: $x^2 + 4x - 5 = 0$

$$x = -4 \pm \frac{\sqrt{16 - 4(1)(-5)}}{2}$$

The fraction bar is not extended to underline the complete numerator.

▶ **18.** In reading $\dfrac{-b \pm \sqrt{b^2 - 4ac}}{2a}$ we say, "the
<u>opposite (negative)</u> of b, plus or minus the <u>square</u>
root of b squared minus 4 <u>times</u> a times c,
all <u>over</u> $2a$."

GUIDED PRACTICE

*Change each equation into quadratic form, if necessary, and find
the values of a, b, and c.* **Do not solve the equation.**
See Example 1.

19. $x^2 + 4x + 3 = 0$
$a = 1, b = 4, c = 3$

▶ **20.** $x^2 - x - 4 = 0$
$a = 1, b = -1, c = -4$

21. $3x^2 - 2x + 7 = 0$
$a = 3, b = -2, c = 7$

▶ **22.** $4x^2 + 7x - 3 = 0$
$a = 4, b = 7, c = -3$

23. $4y^2 = 2y - 1$
$a = 4, b = -2, c = 1$

▶ **24.** $2x = 3x^2 + 4$
$a = 3, b = -2, c = 4$

25. $x(3x - 5) = 2$
$a = 3, b = -5, c = -2$

▶ **26.** $y(5y + 10) = 8$
$a = 5, b = 10, c = -8$

Use the quadratic formula to find all real solutions.
See Example 1.

27. $x^2 - 5x + 6 = 0$
$2, 3$

▶ **28.** $x^2 + 5x + 4 = 0$
$-1, -4$

29. $x^2 + 7x + 12 = 0$
$-3, -4$

30. $x^2 - x - 12 = 0$
$-3, 4$

Use the quadratic formula to find all real solutions.
See Example 2.

31. $2x^2 - x = 1$
$1, -\frac{1}{2}$

▶ **32.** $2x^2 + 3x = 2$
$-2, \frac{1}{2}$

33. $3x^2 + 2 = -5x$
$-1, -\frac{2}{3}$

34. $3x^2 + 1 = 4x$
$1, \frac{1}{3}$

*Use the quadratic formula to find all real solutions. Round each
solution to the nearest hundredth.* **See Example 3.**

35. $x^2 - 2x - 1 = 0$
$1 \pm \sqrt{2}; -0.41, 2.41$

▶ **36.** $b^2 = 18$
$\pm 3\sqrt{2}; \pm 4.24$

37. $2x^2 + x = 5$
$\frac{-1 \pm \sqrt{41}}{4}; -1.85, 1.35$

38. $3x^2 - x = 1$
$\frac{1 \pm \sqrt{13}}{6}; -0.43, 0.77$

*Does each equation have any real-number solutions. If so, find
them.* **See Example 4.**

39. $3m^2 - 2m + 5 = 0$
no

▶ **40.** $4n^2 + 12n - 3 = 0$
yes, $\frac{-3 \pm 2\sqrt{3}}{2}$

41. $2d^2 + 8d + 5 = 0$
yes, $\frac{-4 \pm \sqrt{6}}{2}$

42. $9c^2 - 2c + 4 = 0$
no

*Use the most convenient method to find all real solutions. If a
solution contains a radical, give the exact solution and then
approximate it to the nearest hundredth.* **See Objective 3.**

43. $(2y - 1)^2 = 25$
$-2, 3$

44. $m^2 + 14m + 49 = 0$
$-7, -7$

45. $2x^2 - x + 2 = 0$
no real solutions

46. $x^2 + 2x + 7 = 0$
no real solutions

47. $x^2 - 2x - 35 = 0$
$-5, 7$

▶ **48.** $x^2 + 5x + 3 = 0$
$\frac{-5 \pm \sqrt{13}}{2}; -4.30, -0.70$

49. $4c^2 + 16c = 0$
$-4, 0$

50. $t^2 - 1 = 0$
± 1

51. $18 = 3y^2$
$\pm \sqrt{6}; \pm 2.45$

52. $25x - 50x^2 = 0$
$0, \frac{1}{2}$

TRY IT YOURSELF

Determine a, b, and c.

53. $7(x^2 + 3) = -14x$ $a = 7, b = 14, c = 21$

54. $(2a + 3)(a - 2) = (a + 1)(a - 1)$ $a = 1, b = -1, c = -5$

Use the quadratic formula to find all real solutions.

55. $4x^2 + 4x - 3 = 0$
$\frac{1}{2}, -\frac{3}{2}$

56. $4x^2 + 3x - 1 = 0$
$\frac{1}{4}, -1$

57. $x^2 + 3x + 1 = 0$
$\frac{-3 \pm \sqrt{5}}{2}$

▶ **58.** $x^2 + 3x - 2 = 0$
$\frac{-3 \pm \sqrt{17}}{2}$

59. $3x^2 - x = 3$
$\frac{1 \pm \sqrt{37}}{6}$

▶ **60.** $5x^2 = 3x + 1$
$\frac{3 \pm \sqrt{29}}{10}$

61. $x^2 + 5 = 2x$
no real solutions

62. $2x^2 + 3x = -3$
no real solutions

63. $x^2 = 1 - 2x$
$-1 \pm \sqrt{2}$

▶ **64.** $x^2 = 4 + 2x$
$1 \pm \sqrt{5}$

65. $3x^2 = 6x + 2$
$\frac{3 \pm \sqrt{15}}{3}$

66. $3x^2 = -8x - 2$
$\frac{-4 \pm \sqrt{10}}{3}$

Solve each equation. Round each solution to the nearest tenth.

67. $2.4x^2 - 9.5x + 6.2 = 0$
$0.8, 3.1$

▶ **68.** $-1.7x^2 + 0.5x + 0.9 = 0$
$-0.6, 0.9$

APPLICATIONS

69. HEIGHT OF A TRIANGLE The triangle shown has
an area of 30 square inches. Find its height. 6 in.

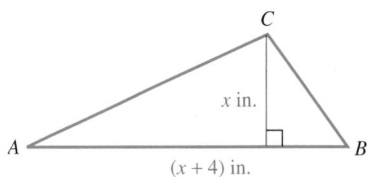

▶ **70.** A poster that shows former UCLA basketball coach John Wooden's Pyramid of Success has an area of 80 square inches. The base of the triangular-shaped poster is 6 inches longer than the height. Find the length of the base and the height of the poster. 16 in., 10 in.

from Campus to Careers
Graphic Designer

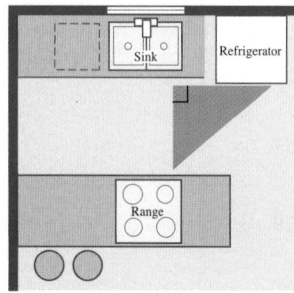

▶ **71.** KITCHEN FLOOR PLANS To minimize the number of steps that a cook must take when preparing meals, designers carefully plan the *kitchen work triangle* (the area between the sink, refrigerator, and range). The one leg of the work triangle shown is 2 feet longer than the other leg, and the area covered is 24 ft². Find the length of each leg of the triangle. 6 ft, 8 ft

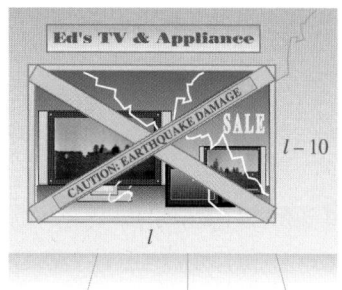

72. EARTHQUAKES After an earthquake, a store owner nailed a 50-inch-long board across a broken window. Find the height and length of the window if the height is 10 inches less than the length. 30 in., 40 in.

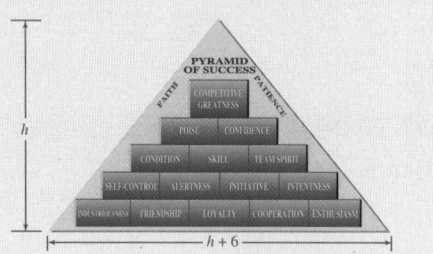
$l - 10$
l

73. FLAGS According to the *Guinness Book of World Records 1998,* the largest flag flown from a flagpole was a Brazilian national flag, a rectangle having an area of 3,102 ft². If the flag is 19 feet longer than it is wide, find its width and length. 47 ft by 66 ft

▶ **74.** COMICS See the illustration. A comic strip occupies 96 square centimeters of space in a newspaper. The length of the rectangular space is 4 centimeters more than twice its width. Find its dimensions. 6 cm by 16 cm

75. COMMUNITY GARDENS See the illustration. Residents of a community can work their own 16 ft × 24 ft plot of city-owned land if they agree to the following stipulations:

- The area of the garden cannot exceed 180 square feet.
- A path of uniform width must be maintained around the garden.

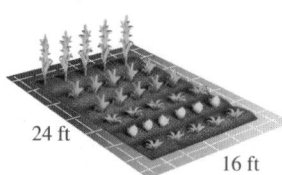
24 ft
16 ft

Find the dimensions of the largest possible garden. 10 ft by 18 ft

▶ **76.** DECKING The owner of the pool shown below wants to surround it with a concrete deck of uniform width (shown in gray). If he can afford 368 square feet of decking, how wide can he make the deck? 4 ft

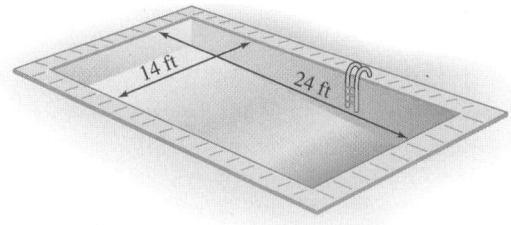
14 ft
24 ft

▶ **77.** FALLING OBJECTS A tourist drops a penny from the observation deck of a skyscraper 1,377 feet above the ground. How long will it take for the penny to hit the ground? (*Hint:* Refer to Example 4 in Section 9.1.) about 9.3 sec

78. ABACUS The Chinese abacus shown consists of a frame, parallel wires, and beads that are moved to perform arithmetic computations. If the frame is 21 centimeters wider than it is high, find its dimensions. 15 cm by 36 cm

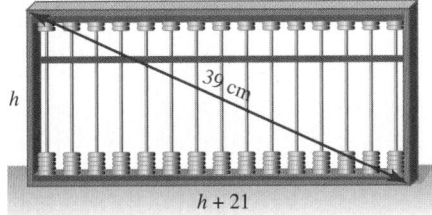

79. SIDEWALKS A 170-meter-long sidewalk from the mathematics building M to the student center C is shown in red in the illustration. However, students prefer to walk directly from M to C. How long are the two segments of the existing sidewalk? 50 m and 120 m

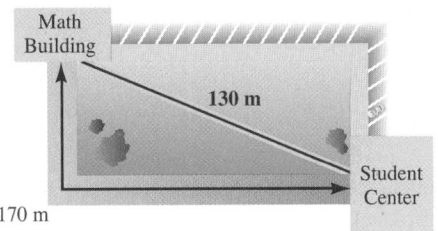

80. NAVIGATION Two boats leave port at the same time, one sailing east and one sailing south. If one boat sails 10 nautical miles more than the other and they are then 50 nautical miles apart, how far does each boat sail? 30 and 40 nautical mi

81. NAVIGATION One plane heads west from an airport, flying at 200 mph. One hour later, a second plane heads north from the same airport, flying at the same speed. When will the planes be 1,000 miles apart? 3 hr after the second plane takes off

82. INVESTING We can use the formula $A = P(1 + r)^2$ to find the amount A that P will become when invested at an annual rate of $r\%$ for 2 years. What interest rate is needed to make \$5,000 grow to \$5,724.50 in 2 years? 7%

83. INVESTING What interest rate is needed to make \$7,000 grow to \$8,470 in 2 years? (See Exercise 82.) 10%

84. MANUFACTURING A firm has found that its revenue for manufacturing and selling x television sets is given by the formula $R = -\frac{1}{6}x^2 + 450x$. How much revenue will be earned by manufacturing 600 television sets? \$210,000

85. RETAILING When a wholesaler sells n CD players, his revenue R is given by the formula $R = 150n - \frac{1}{2}n^2$. How many players would he have to sell to receive \$11,250? (*Hint:* Multiply both sides of the equation by -2.) 150

86. METAL FABRICATION A square piece of tin, 12 inches on a side, is to have four equal squares cut from its corners, as shown. If the edges are then to be folded up to make a box with a floor area of 64 square inches, find the depth of the box. 2 in.

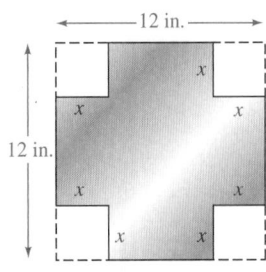

87. MAKING GUTTERS A piece of sheet metal, 18 inches wide, is bent to form the gutter shown. If the cross-sectional area is 36 square inches, find the depth of the gutter. 3 in. or 6 in.

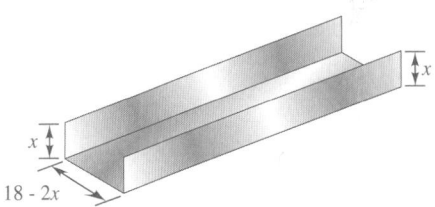

WRITING

88. Do you agree with the following statement? Explain your answer.

The quadratic formula is the easiest method to use to solve quadratic equations.

89. Explain the meaning of the $\pm$ symbol.

90. Use the quadratic formula to solve $x^2 - 2x - 4 = 0$. What is an exact solution, and what is an approximate solution of this equation? Explain the difference.

91. Rewrite in words:

$$x = \frac{-b \pm \sqrt{b^2 - 4ac}}{2a}$$

REVIEW

Solve each equation for the indicated variable.

92. $A = p + prt$, for r $r = \frac{A - p}{pt}$

93. $F = \dfrac{GMm}{d^2}$, for M $M = \frac{Fd^2}{Gm}$

Write an equation of the line that has the given properties in slope–intercept form.

94. Slope of $\frac{3}{5}$ and passing through $(0, 12)$ $y = \frac{3}{5}x + 12$

95. Passes through $(6, 8)$ and the origin $y = \frac{4}{3}x$

Simplify each expression.

96. $\sqrt{80}$ $4\sqrt{5}$

97. $2\sqrt{x^3y^2}$ $2xy\sqrt{x}$

Rationalize each denominator and simplify.

98. $\dfrac{x}{\sqrt{7x}}$ $\frac{\sqrt{7x}}{7}$

99. $\dfrac{\sqrt{x} + 2}{\sqrt{x} - 2}$ $\frac{x + 4\sqrt{x} + 4}{x - 4}$

Objectives

1. Understand the vocabulary used to describe parabolas.
2. Find the intercepts of a parabola.
3. Determine the vertex of a parabola.
4. Graph equations of the form $y = ax^2 + bx + c$.
5. Solve quadratic equations graphically.

SECTION 9.4

Graphing Quadratic Equations

In this section, we will combine our graphing skills with our equation-solving skills to graph *quadratic equations in two variables.*

1 Understand the vocabulary used to describe parabolas.

Equations that can be written in the form $y = ax^2 + bx + c$, where $a \neq 0$, are called **quadratic equations in two variables.** Some examples are

$$y = x^2 - 2x - 3 \qquad y = -2x^2 - 8x - 8 \qquad y = x^2 + x$$

In Section 3.2, we graphed $y = x^2$, a quadratic equation in two variables. To do this, we constructed a table of solutions, plotted points, and joined them with a smooth curve, called a **parabola.** The parabola opens upward, and the lowest point on the graph, called the **vertex,** is the point $(0, 0)$. If we fold the graph paper along the y-axis, the two sides of the parabola match. We say that the graph is *symmetric about the y-axis* and we call the y-axis the **axis of symmetry.**

> **The Language of Algebra**   An *axis of symmetry* (or *line of symmetry*) divides a parabola into two matching sides. The sides are said to be *mirror images* of each other.

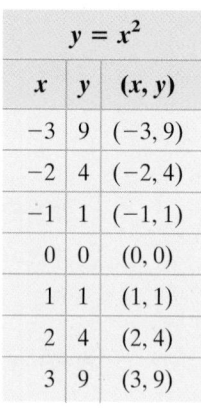

$y = x^2$		
x	y	(x, y)
-3	9	$(-3, 9)$
-2	4	$(-2, 4)$
-1	1	$(-1, 1)$
0	0	$(0, 0)$
1	1	$(1, 1)$
2	4	$(2, 4)$
3	9	$(3, 9)$

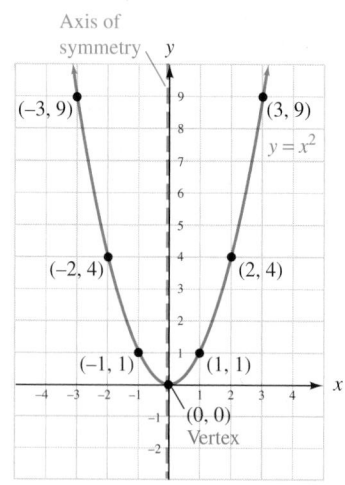

Using the same steps, we can also graph $y = -x^2 + 2$, another quadratic equation in two variables. The resulting parabola opens downward, and the **vertex** (in this case, the highest point on the graph) is the point $(0, 2)$. The axis of symmetry is the y-axis.

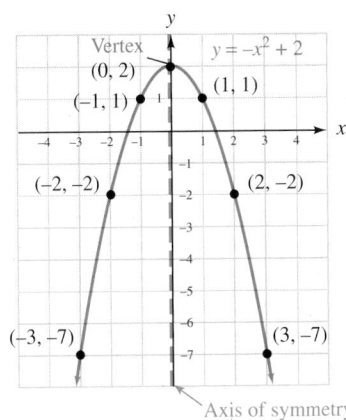

$y = -x^2 + 2$		
x	y	(x, y)
-3	-7	$(-3, -7)$
-2	-2	$(-2, -2)$
-1	1	$(-1, 1)$
0	2	$(0, 2)$
1	1	$(1, 1)$
2	-2	$(2, -2)$
3	-7	$(3, -7)$

For the equation $y = x^2$, the coefficient of the x^2 term is the positive number 1. For $y = -x^2 + 2$, the coefficient of the x^2 term is the negative number -1. These observations suggest the following fact.

Graphs of Quadratic Equations

The graph of $y = ax^2 + bx + c$, where $a \neq 0$, is a parabola. It opens upward when $a > 0$ and downward when $a < 0$.

The Language of Algebra In the equation $y = ax^2 + bx + c$, each value of x determines exactly one value of y. Therefore, the equation defines y to be a function of x and we could write $f(x) = ax^2 + bx + c$. Your instructor may ask you to use the vocabulary and notation of functions throughout this section.

Parabolic shapes can be seen in a wide variety of real-world settings. These shapes can be modeled by quadratic equations in two variables.

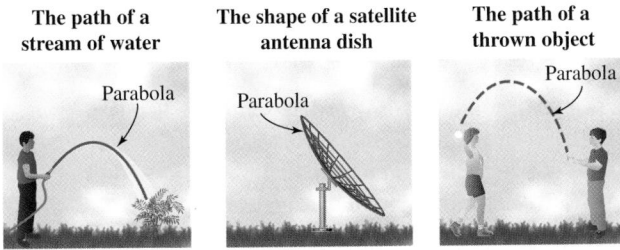

The path of a stream of water

Parabola

The shape of a satellite antenna dish

Parabola

The path of a thrown object

Parabola

The Language of Algebra The word *parabolic* (pronounced $par \cdot a \cdot BOL \cdot ic$) means having the form of a parabola. For example, the light bulb in most flashlights is surrounded by a *parabolic* reflecting mirror.

---

2 Find the intercepts of a parabola.

When graphing quadratic equations, it is helpful to know the x- and y-intercepts of the parabola. To find the intercepts of a parabola, we use the same steps that we used to find the intercepts of the graphs of linear equations.

Finding Intercepts
To find the y-intercept, substitute 0 for x in the given equation and solve for y.
To find the x-intercepts, substitute 0 for y in the given equation and solve for x.

EXAMPLE 1 Find the y- and x-intercepts of the graph of $y = x^2 - 2x - 3$.

Strategy To find the y-intercept of the graph, we will let $x = 0$ and find y. To find the x-intercepts of the graph, we will let $y = 0$ and solve the resulting equation for x.

WHY A point on the y-axis has an x-coordinate of 0. A point on the x-axis has a y-coordinate of 0.

Solution
We let $x = 0$ and evaluate the right side to find the y-intercept.

$$y = x^2 - 2x - 3 \qquad \text{This is the given equation.}$$
$$y = 0^2 - 2(0) - 3 \qquad \text{Substitute 0 for } x.$$
$$y = -3 \qquad \text{Evaluate the right side.}$$

The y-intercept is $(0, -3)$. We note that the y-coordinate of the y-intercept is the same as the value of the constant term c on the right side of $y = x^2 - 2x - 3$.

Next, we let $y = 0$ and solve the resulting quadratic equation to find the x-intercepts.

$$y = x^2 - 2x - 3 \qquad \text{This is the given equation.}$$
$$0 = x^2 - 2x - 3 \qquad \text{Substitute 0 for } y.$$
$$0 = (x - 3)(x + 1) \qquad \text{Factor the trinomial.}$$
$$x - 3 = 0 \quad \text{or} \quad x + 1 = 0 \qquad \text{Set each factor equal to 0.}$$
$$x = 3 \quad | \qquad x = -1$$

Since there are two solutions, the graph has two x-intercepts: $(3, 0)$ and $(-1, 0)$. ∎

3 Determine the vertex of a parabola.

It is usually easier to graph a quadratic equation when we know the coordinates of the vertex of its graph. Because of symmetry, if a parabola has two x-intercepts, the x-coordinate of the vertex is exactly midway between them. We can use this fact to derive a formula to find the vertex of a parabola.

In general, if a parabola has two x-intercepts, they can be found by solving $0 = ax^2 + bx + c$ for x. We can use the quadratic formula to find the solutions. They are

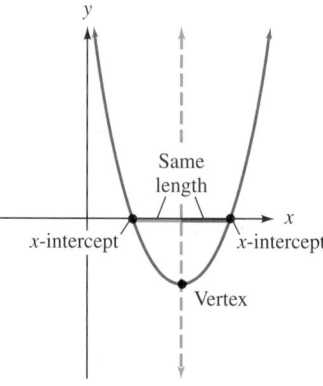

$$x = \frac{-b - \sqrt{b^2 - 4ac}}{2a} \qquad \text{and} \qquad x = \frac{-b + \sqrt{b^2 - 4ac}}{2a}$$

Thus, the parabola's x-intercepts are $\left(\frac{-b - \sqrt{b^2 - 4ac}}{2a}, 0\right)$ and $\left(\frac{-b + \sqrt{b^2 - 4ac}}{2a}, 0\right)$.

Since the x-value of the vertex of a parabola is halfway between the two x-intercepts, we can find this value by finding the average, or $\frac{1}{2}$ of the sum of the x-coordinates of the x-intercepts.

$$x = \frac{1}{2}\left(\frac{-b - \sqrt{b^2 - 4ac}}{2a} + \frac{-b + \sqrt{b^2 - 4ac}}{2a}\right)$$

$$x = \frac{1}{2}\left(\frac{-b - \sqrt{b^2 - 4ac} + (-b) + \sqrt{b^2 - 4ac}}{2a}\right) \qquad \text{Add the numerators and keep the common denominator.}$$

$$x = \frac{1}{2}\left(\frac{-2b}{2a}\right) \qquad -b + (-b) = -2b.\ -\sqrt{b^2-4ac} + \sqrt{b^2 - 4ac} = 0.$$

$$x = \frac{-b}{2a} \qquad \text{Simplify.}$$

This result is true even if the graph has no x-intercepts.

Finding the Vertex of a Parabola

The graph of the quadratic equation $y = ax^2 + bx + c$ is a parabola whose vertex has an x-coordinate of $\frac{-b}{2a}$. To find the y-coordinate of the vertex, substitute $\frac{-b}{2a}$ for x into the equation and find y.

EXAMPLE 2   Find the vertex of the graph of $y = x^2 - 2x - 3$.

Strategy We will compare the given equation to the general form $y = ax^2 + bx + c$ to identify a and b.

WHY To use the vertex formula, we need to know a and b.

Solution
From the following diagram, we see that $a = 1$, $b = -2$, and $c = -3$.

$$y = 1x^2 - 2x - 3$$
$$\uparrow \qquad \uparrow \qquad \uparrow$$
$$y = ax^2 + bx + c$$

To find the x-coordinate of the vertex, we substitute the values for a and b into the formula $x = \frac{-b}{2a}$.

$$x = \frac{-b}{2a} = \frac{-(-2)}{2(1)} = 1$$

The x-coordinate of the vertex is 1. To find the y-coordinate, we substitute 1 for x in the original equation.

$$y = x^2 - 2x - 3 \qquad \text{This is the given equation.}$$
$$y = 1^2 - 2(1) - 3 \qquad \text{Substitute 1 for } x.$$
$$y = -4 \qquad \text{Evaluate the right side.}$$

The vertex of the parabola is $(1, -4)$. ■

Success Tip   An easy way to remember the vertex formula is to note that $x = \frac{-b}{2a}$ is part of the quadratic formula:

$$x = \frac{-b \pm \sqrt{b^2 - 4ac}}{2a}$$

Self Check 2

Find the vertex of the graph of $y = x^2 + 6x + 8$. $(-3, -1)$

Now Try Problem 21

Teaching Example 2 Find the vertex of the graph of $y = x^2 - 6x + 5$.
Answer:
$(3, -4)$

4 Graph equations of the form $y = ax^2 + bx + c$.

Much can be determined about the graph of $y = ax^2 + bx + c$ from the coefficients a, b, and c. We can use this information to help graph the equation.

Graphing a Quadratic Equation $y = ax^2 + bx + c$

1. **Test for opening upward/downward** Determine whether the parabola opens upward or downward. If $a > 0$, the graph opens upward. If $a < 0$, the graph opens downward.

2. **Find the vertex/axis of symmetry** The x-coordinate of the vertex of the parabola is $x = \frac{-b}{2a}$. To find the y-coordinate, substitute $\frac{-b}{2a}$ for x into the equation and find y. The axis of symmetry is the vertical line passing through the vertex.

3. **Find the intercepts** To find the y-intercept, substitute 0 for x in the given equation and solve for y. The result will be c. Thus, the y-intercept is $(0, c)$.
   To find the x-intercepts (if any), substitute 0 for y and solve the resulting quadratic equation $ax^2 + bx + c = 0$. If no real-number solutions exist, the graph has no x-intercepts.

4. **Plotting points/using symmetry** To find two more points on the graph, select a convenient value for x and find the corresponding value of y. Plot that point and its mirror image on the opposite side of the axis of symmetry.

5. **Draw the parabola** Draw a smooth curve through the located points.

Self Check 3

Use your results from Self Checks 1 and 2 to help graph:
$y = x^2 + 6x + 8$

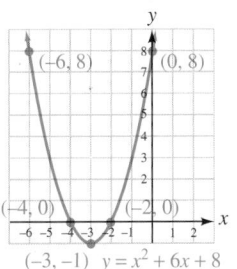

(−6, 8)   (0, 8)
(−4, 0)   (−2, 0)
(−3, −1) $y = x^2 + 6x + 8$

Now Try **Problem 25**

Teaching Example 3 Graph:
$y = x^2 - 6x + 5$
Answer:

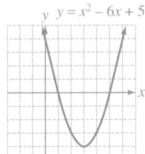

$y = x^2 - 6x + 5$

EXAMPLE 3   Graph: $y = x^2 - 2x - 3$

Strategy We will use the five-step procedure described above to sketch the graph of the equation.

WHY This strategy is usually faster than making a table of solutions and plotting points.

Solution
Upward/downward: The equation is in the form $y = ax^2 + bx + c$, with $a = 1$, $b = -2$, and $c = -3$. Since $a > 0$, the parabola opens upward.

Vertex/axis of symmetry: In Example 2, we found that the vertex of the graph is $(1, -4)$. The axis of symmetry will be the vertical line passing through $(1, -4)$. See figure (a) on the next page.

Intercepts: In Example 1, we found that the y-intercept is $(0, -3)$ and x-intercepts are $(3, 0)$ and $(-1, 0)$.
   If the point $(0, -3)$, which is 1 unit to the left of the axis of symmetry, is on the graph, the point $(2, -3)$, which is 1 unit to the right of the axis of symmetry, is also on the graph. See figure (a) on the next page.

Plotting points/using symmetry: It would be helpful to locate two more points on the graph. To find a solution of $y = x^2 - 2x - 3$, we select a convenient value for x, say -2, and find the corresponding value of y.

$$y = x^2 - 2x - 3 \qquad \text{This is the equation to graph.}$$
$$y = (-2)^2 - 2(-2) - 3 \qquad \text{Substitute } -2 \text{ for } x.$$
$$y = 5 \qquad \text{Evaluate the right side.}$$

Thus, the point $(-2, 5)$ lies on the parabola. If the point $(-2, 5)$, which is 3 units to the left of the axis of symmetry, is on the graph, the point $(4, 5)$, which is 3 units to the right of the axis of symmetry, is also on the graph. See figure (a).

$y = x^2 - 2x - 3$		
x	y	(x, y)
-2	5	$(-2, 5)$

Draw a smooth curve through the points: The completed graph of $y = x^2 - 2x - 3$ is shown in figure (b).

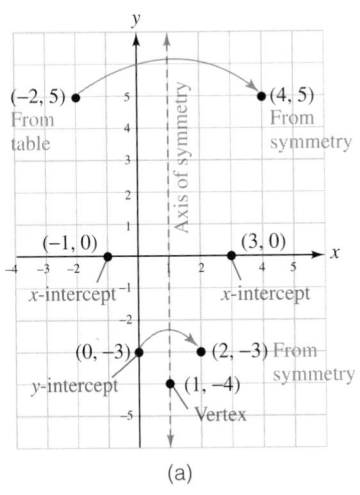
(a)

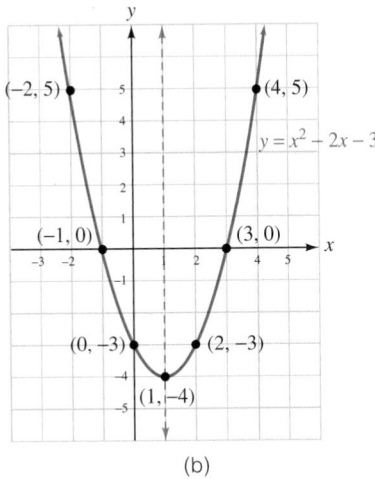
(b)

Success Tip The most important point to find when graphing a quadratic equation in two variables is the vertex.

EXAMPLE 4   Graph: $y = -2x^2 - 8x - 8$

Strategy We will follow the five-step procedure to sketch the graph of the equation.

WHY This strategy is usually faster than making a table of solutions and plotting points.

Solution

Upward/downward: The equation is in the form $y = ax^2 + bx + c$, with $a = -2$, $b = -8$, and $c = -8$. Since $a < 0$, the parabola opens downward.

Vertex/axis of symmetry: To find the x-coordinate of the vertex, we substitute -2 for a and -8 for b into the formula $x = \frac{-b}{2a}$.

$$x = \frac{-b}{2a} = \frac{-(-8)}{2(-2)} = -2$$

The x-coordinate of the vertex is -2. To find the y-coordinate, we substitute -2 for x in the original equation and find y.

$y = -2x^2 - 8x - 8$ This is the equation to graph.

$y = -2(-2)^2 - 8(-2) - 8$ Substitute -2 for x.

$y = 0$ Evaluate the right side.

The vertex of the parabola is the point $(-2, 0)$. The axis of symmetry is the vertical line passing through $(-2, 0)$. See figure (a) on the next page.

Self Check 4
Graph: $y = -2x^2 + 4x - 2$

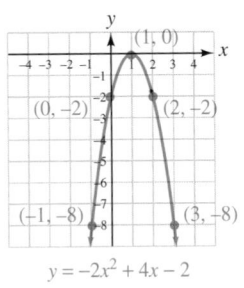

$y = -2x^2 + 4x - 2$

Now Try Problem 29

Teaching Example 4
Graph: $y = -\frac{1}{2}x^2 + 2x + 2$
Answer:

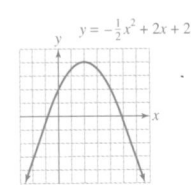

Intercepts: Since $c = -8$, the y-intercept of the parabola is $(0, -8)$. The point $(-4, -8)$, which is 2 units to the left of the axis of symmetry, must also be on the graph. See figure (a).

To find the x-intercepts, we let $y = 0$ and solve the resulting quadratic equation.

$y = -2x^2 - 8x - 8$	This is the equation to graph.
$0 = -2x^2 - 8x - 8$	Substitute 0 for y.
$0 = x^2 + 4x + 4$	Divide both sides by -2: $\frac{0}{-2} = \frac{-2x^2}{-2} - \frac{8x}{-2} - \frac{8}{-2}$.
$0 = (x + 2)(x + 2)$	Factor the trinomial.
$x + 2 = 0 \quad$ or $\quad x + 2 = 0$	Set each factor equal to 0.
$x = -2 \quad | \quad x = -2$	

Since the solutions are the same, the graph has only one x-intercept: $(-2, 0)$. This point is the vertex of the parabola and has already been plotted.

Plotting points/using symmetry: It would be helpful to know two more points on the graph. To find a solution of $y = -2x^2 - 8x - 8$, we select a convenient value for x, say -3, and find the corresponding value for y.

$y = -2x^2 - 8x - 8$		
x	y	(x, y)
-3	-2	$(-3, -2)$

$y = -2x^2 - 8x - 8$	This is the equation to graph.
$y = -2(-3)^2 - 8(-3) - 8$	Substitute -3 for x.
$y = -2$	Evaluate the right side.

Thus, the point $(-3, -2)$ lies on the parabola. We plot $(-3, -2)$ and then use symmetry to determine that $(-1, -2)$ is also on the graph. See figure (a).

Draw a smooth curve through the points: The completed graph of $y = -2x^2 - 8x - 8$ is shown in figure (b) below.

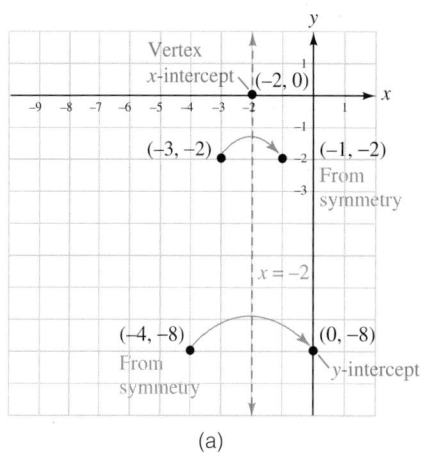

(a)

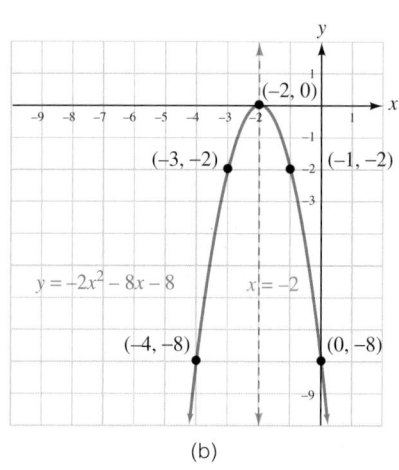

(b)

EXAMPLE 5   Graph: $y = x^2 + 2x - 2$

Strategy We will follow the five-step procedure to sketch the graph of the equation.

WHY This strategy is usually faster than making a table of solutions and plotting points.

Solution

Upward/downward: The equation is in the form $y = ax^2 + bx + c$, with $a = 1$, $b = 2$, and $c = -2$. Since $a > 0$, the parabola opens upward.

Vertex/axis of symmetry: To find the x-coordinate of the vertex, we substitute 1 for a and 2 for b into the formula $x = \frac{-b}{2a}$.

$$x = \frac{-b}{2a} = \frac{-2}{2(1)} = -1$$

The x-coordinate of the vertex is -1. To find the y-coordinate, we substitute -1 for x in the original equation and find y.

$y = x^2 + 2x - 2$	This is the equation to graph.
$y = (-1)^2 + 2(-1) - 2$	Substitute -1 for x.
$y = -3$	Evaluate the right side.

The vertex of the parabola is the point $(-1, -3)$. The axis of symmetry is the vertical line passing through $(-1, -3)$. See figure (a) on the next page.

Intercepts: Since $c = -2$, the y-intercept of the parabola is $(0, -2)$. The point $(-2, -2)$, which is one unit to the left of the axis of symmetry, must also be on the graph. See figure (a) on the next page.

To find the x-intercepts, we let $y = 0$ and solve the resulting quadratic equation.

$y = x^2 + 2x - 2$	This is the equation to graph.
$0 = x^2 + 2x - 2$	Substitute 0 for y.

Since $x^2 + 2x - 2$ does not factor, we will use the quadratic formula to solve for x.

$x = \dfrac{-2 \pm \sqrt{2^2 - 4(1)(-2)}}{2(1)}$	In the quadratic formula, substitute 1 for a, 2 for b, and -2 for c.
$x = \dfrac{-2 \pm \sqrt{12}}{2}$	Evaluate the right side.
$x = \dfrac{-2 \pm 2\sqrt{3}}{2}$	Simplify the radical: $\sqrt{12} = \sqrt{4 \cdot 3} = 2\sqrt{3}$.
$x = \dfrac{\overset{1}{\cancel{2}}\left(-1 \pm \sqrt{3}\right)}{\underset{1}{\cancel{2}}}$	Factor out the GCF, 2, from the terms in the numerator. Then simplify by removing the common factor of 2 in the numerator and denominator.
$x = -1 \pm \sqrt{3}$	

The x-intercepts of the graph are $\left(-1 + \sqrt{3}, 0\right)$ and $\left(-1 - \sqrt{3}, 0\right)$. To help to locate their position on the graph, we can use a calculator to approximate the two irrational numbers. See figure (a) on the next page.

$$-1 + \sqrt{3} \approx 0.7 \quad \text{and} \quad -1 - \sqrt{3} \approx -2.7$$

Plotting points/using symmetry: To find two more points on the graph, we let $x = 2$, substitute 2 for x in $y = x^2 + 2x - 2$, and find that y is 6. We plot $(2, 6)$ and then use symmetry to determine that $(-4, 6)$ is also on the graph. See figure (a) on the next page.

$y = x^2 + 2x - 2$		
x	y	(x, y)
2	6	$(2, 6)$

Draw a smooth curve through the points: The completed graph of $y = x^2 + 2x - 2$ is shown in figure (b) on the next page.

Self Check 5

Graph: $y = x^2 - 4x - 3$

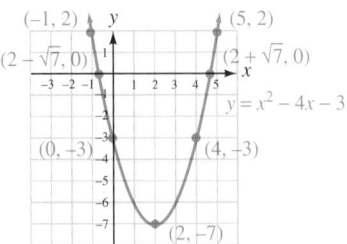

Now Try **Problem 43**

Teaching Example 5 Graph:
$y = -x^2 + 2x + 3$
Answer:

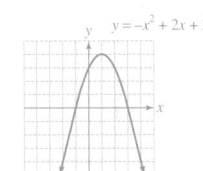

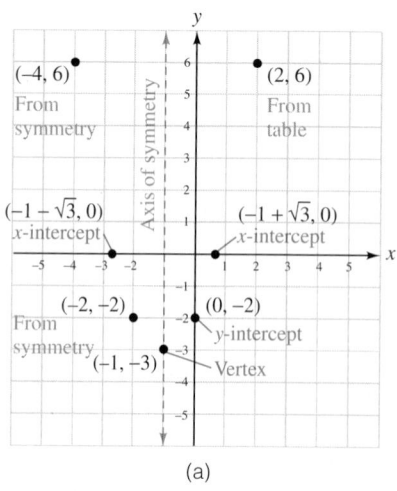

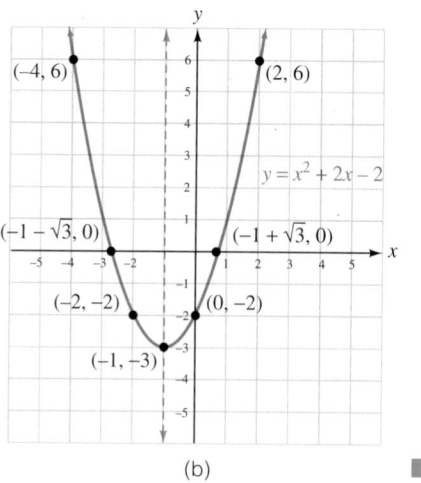

(a)   (b)

> **Success Tip**   To plot the x-intercepts, we use the approximations $(0.7, 0)$ and $(-2.7, 0)$ to locate their position on the x-axis. However, we label the points on the graph using the exact values: $\left(-1 + \sqrt{3}, 0\right)$ and $\left(-1 - \sqrt{3}, 0\right)$.

5 Solve quadratic equations graphically.

The number of distinct x-intercepts of the graph of $y = ax^2 + bx + c$ is the same as the number of distinct real-number solutions of $ax^2 + bx + c = 0$. For example, the graph of $y = x^2 + x - 2$ in figure (a) below has two x-intercepts, and $x^2 + x - 2 = 0$ has two real-number solutions. In figure (b), the graph has one x-intercept, and the corresponding equation has one real-number solution. In figure (c), the graph does not have an x-intercept, and the corresponding equation does not have any real-number solutions. Note that the solutions of each equation are given by the x-coordinates of the x-intercepts of each respective graph.

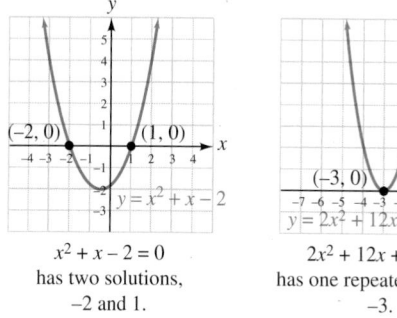

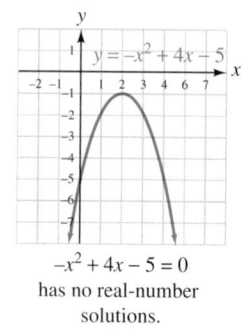

$x^2 + x - 2 = 0$	$2x^2 + 12x + 18 = 0$	$-x^2 + 4x - 5 = 0$
has two solutions,	has one repeated solution,	has no real-number
-2 and 1.	-3.	solutions.
(a)	(b)	(c)

ANSWERS TO SELF CHECKS

1. y-intercept: $(0, 8)$; x-intercepts: $(-2, 0)$, $(-4, 0)$ **2.** $(-3, -1)$

3.

4.

5.

SECTION 9.4   STUDY SET

VOCABULARY

Fill in the blanks.

▶ **1.** $y = 3x^2 + 5x - 1$ is a _quadratic_ equation in two variables. Its graph is a cup-shaped figure called a _parabola_ .

▶ **2.** The lowest point on a parabola that opens upward, and the highest point on a parabola that opens downward, is called the _vertex_ of the parabola.

3. Points where a parabola intersects the x-axis are called the x-_intercepts_ of the graph and the point where a parabola intersects the y-axis is called the y-_intercept_ of the graph.

4. The vertical line that splits the graph of a parabola into two identical parts is called the axis of _symmetry_ .

CONCEPTS

Fill in the blanks.

5. The graph of $y = ax^2 + bx + c$ opens downward when $a \; < \; 0$ and upward when $a > \; 0$.

▶ **6.** The graph of $y = ax^2 + bx + c$ is a parabola whose vertex has an x-coordinate given by $\frac{-b}{2a}$.

7. a. To find the y-intercepts of a graph, substitute 0 for x in the given equation and solve for y.

   b. To find the x-intercepts of a graph, substitute 0 for y in the given equation and solve for x .

▶ **8.**

$y = x^2 - 3x - 1$		
x	y	(x, y)
3	-1	$(3, -1)$

9. a. What do we call the curve shown in the graph? parabola

   b. What are the x-intercepts of the graph? $(1, 0), (3, 0)$

   c. What is the y-intercept of the graph? $(0, -3)$

   d. What is the vertex? $(2, 1)$

   e. Draw the axis of symmetry on the graph. It is a vertical line through $(2, 1)$.

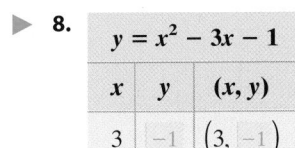

10. Does the graph of each quadratic equation open upward or downward?

   a. $y = 2x^2 + 5x - 1$ upward   **b.** $y = -6x^2 - 3x + 5$ downward

11. The vertex of a parabola is $(1, -3)$, its y-intercept is $(0, -2)$, and it passes through the point $(3, 1)$. Draw the axis of symmetry and use it to help determine two other points on the parabola. $(2, -2), (-1, 1)$

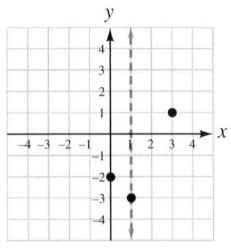

12. Sketch the graph of a quadratic equation using the given facts about its graph.

   • Opens upward
   • Vertex: $(3, -1)$
   • y-intercept: $(0, 8)$
   • x-intercepts: $(2, 0), (4, 0)$

x	y	(x, y)
1	3	$(1, 3)$

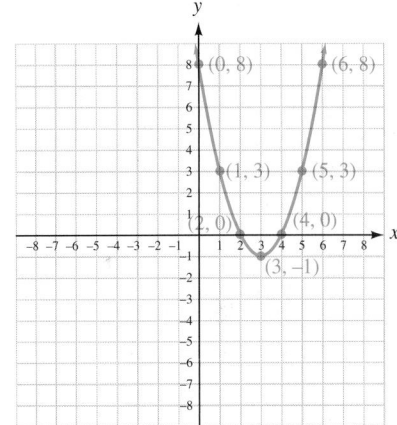

13. Examine the graph of $y = x^2 + 2x - 3$. How many real-number solutions does the equation $x^2 + 2x - 3 = 0$ have? Find them. two; $-3, 1$

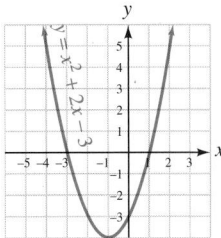

14. Examine the graph of $y = x^2 + 4x + 4$. How many real-number solutions does the equation $x^2 + 4x + 4 = 0$ have? Find them.

one repeated solution, -2

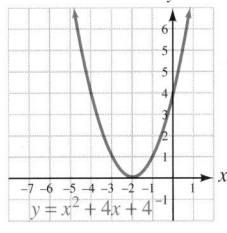

NOTATION

15. Consider the equation $y = 2x^2 + 4x - 8$.

 a. What are a, b, and c? $2, 4, -8$

 b. Find $\frac{-b}{2a}$. -1

▶ **16.** Evaluate: $\frac{-(-12)}{2(-3)}$ -2

GUIDED PRACTICE

Find the y- and x-intercepts of the graph of the quadratic equation. See Example 1.

17. $y = x^2 - 6x + 8$
$(0, 8);\ (4, 0),\ (2, 0)$

▶ **18.** $y = 2x^2 - 4x$
$(0, 0);\ (0, 0),\ (2, 0))$

19. $y = -x^2 - 10x - 21$
$(0, -21);\ (-3, 0),\ (-7, 0)$

▶ **20.** $y = 3x^2 + 6x - 9$
$(0, -9);\ (-3, 0),\ (1, 0)$

Find the vertex of the graph of each quadratic equation. See Example 2.

▶ **21.** $y = 2x^2 - 4x + 1$
$(1, -1)$

▶ **22.** $y = 2x^2 + 8x - 4$
$(-2, -12)$

23. $y = -x^2 + 6x - 8$
$(3, 1)$

▶ **24.** $y = -x^2 - 2x - 1$
$(-1, 0)$

Graph each quadratic equation by finding the vertex, the x- and y-intercepts, and the axis of symmetry of its graph. See Examples 3 and 4.

25. $y = x^2 + 2x - 3$

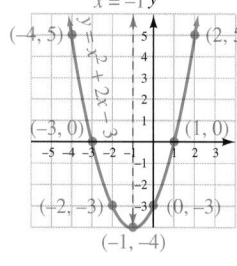

26. $y = x^2 + 6x + 5$

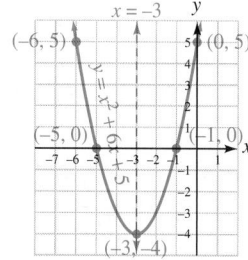

▶ **27.** $y = 2x^2 + 8x + 6$

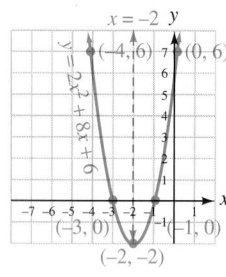

28. $y = 3x^2 - 12x + 9$

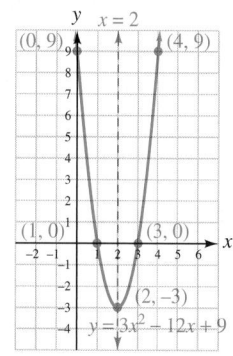

29. $y = -x^2 + 2x + 3$

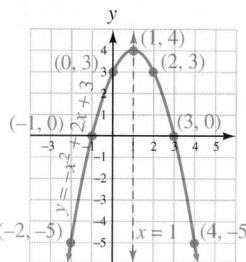

▶ **30.** $y = -2x^2 + 4x$

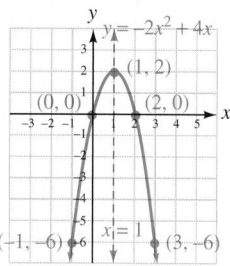
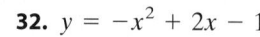

31. $y = -x^2 + 5x - 4$

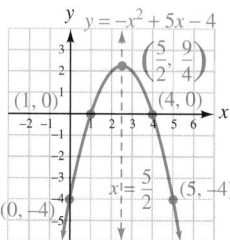

32. $y = -x^2 + 2x - 1$

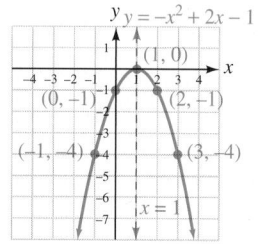

33. $y = x^2 - 2x$

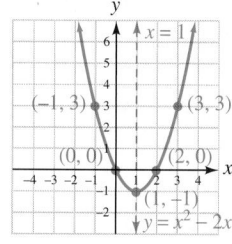

34. $y = x^2 + x$

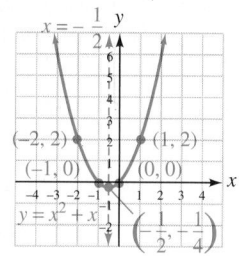
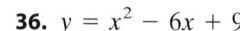

35. $y = x^2 + 4x + 4$

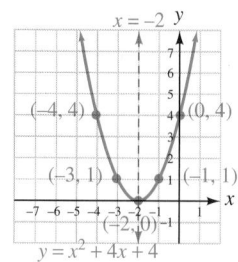

36. $y = x^2 - 6x + 9$

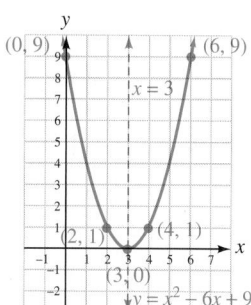

37. $y = -x^2 - 4x$

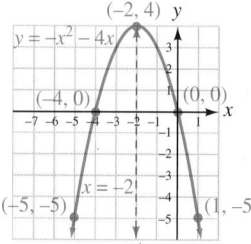

38. $y = -x^2 + 2x$

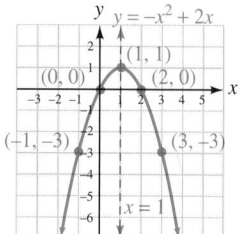

39. $y = 2x^2 + 3x - 2$

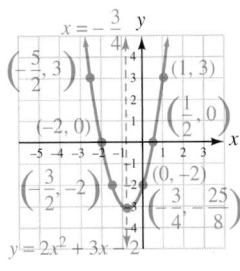

40. $y = 3x^2 - 7x + 2$

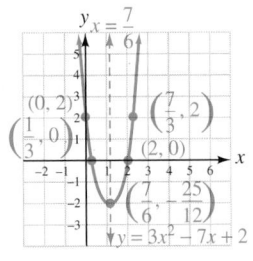

41. $y = 4x^2 - 12x + 9$ ▶ **42.** $y = -x^2 - 2x - 1$

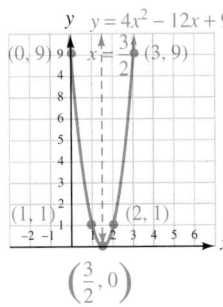

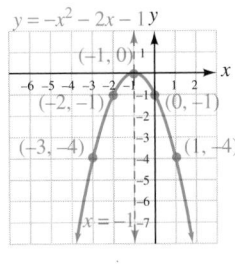

Graph each quadratic equation by finding the vertex, the x- and y-intercepts, and the axis of symmetry of its graph.
See Example 5.

43. $y = x^2 - 4x - 1$

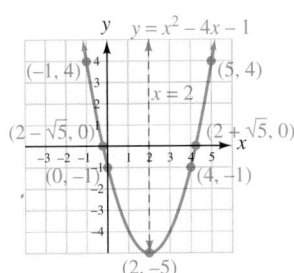

▶ **44.** $y = x^2 + 2x - 5$

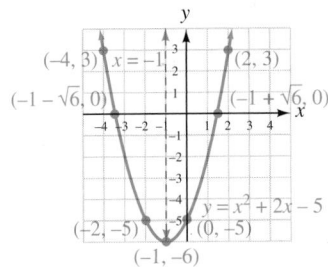

45. $y = -x^2 - 2x + 2$

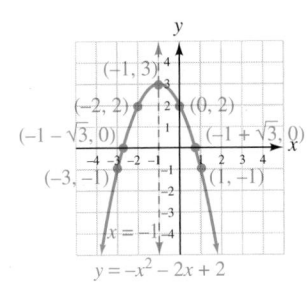

46. $y = -x^2 - 4x + 3$

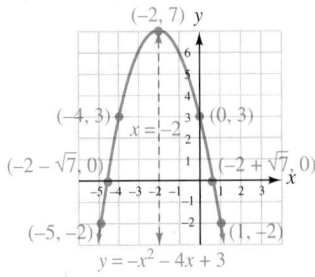

47. $y = -x^2 - 6x - 4$

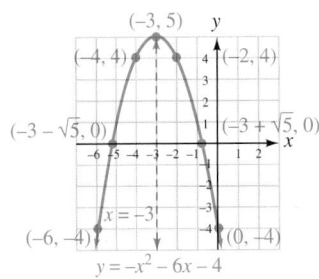

48. $y = x^2 - 6x + 4$

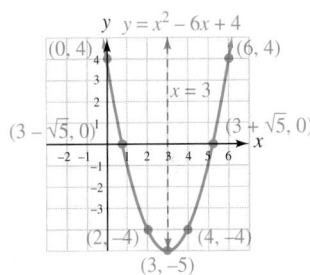

▶ **49.** $y = x^2 - 6x + 10$

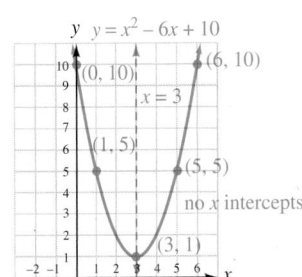

50. $y = x^2 - 2x + 4$

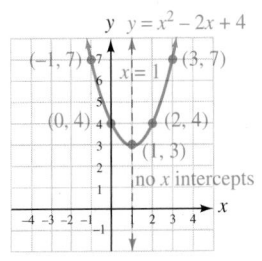

APPLICATIONS

51. BIOLOGY Draw an axis of symmetry over the sketch of the butterfly.
It is a vertical line through the body of the butterfly.

52. CROSSWORD PUZZLES Darken the appropriate squares to the right of the dashed blue line so that the puzzle has symmetry with respect to that line.

axis of symmetry

▶ **53. COST ANALYSIS** A company has found that when it assembles x carburetors in a production run, the manufacturing cost of y per carburetor is given by the graph below. What important piece of information does the vertex give?
The cost to manufacture a carburetor is lowest ($100) for a production run of 30 units.

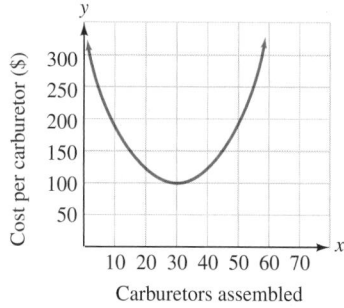

Carburetors assembled

▶ **54. HEALTH DEPARTMENT** The number of cases of flu seen by doctors at a county health clinic each week during a 10-week period is described by the graph. Write a brief summary report about the flu outbreak. What important piece of information does the vertex give?
The most cases of flu (25) were reported the fifth week.

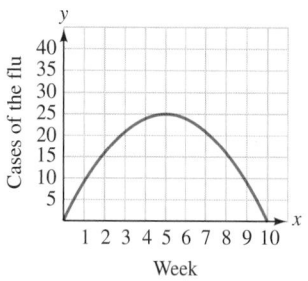

Week

▶ **55. TRAMPOLINES** The graph in the next column shows how far a trampolinist is from the ground (in relation to time) as she bounds into the air and then falls back down to the trampoline.

   a. How many feet above the ground is she $\frac{1}{2}$ second after bounding upward?   14 ft

b. When is she 9 feet above the ground?
0.25 sec and 1.75 sec

c. What is the maximum number of feet above the ground she gets? When does this occur?
18 ft; 1.0 sec

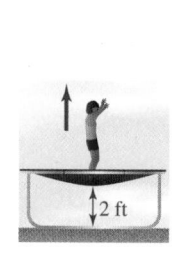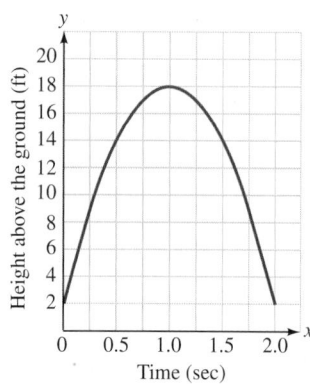

Time (sec)

▶ **56. TRACK AND FIELD** Sketch the parabolic path traveled by the long-jumper's center of gravity from the take-off board to the landing. Let the x-axis represent the ground.

Take-off board ◀———— 22 ft ————▶ Landing

WRITING

▶ **57.** A mirror is held against the y-axis of the graph of a quadratic equation. What fact about parabolas does this illustrate?

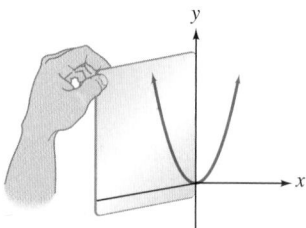

▶ **58.** Use the example of a stream of water from a drinking fountain to explain the concept of the vertex of a parabola.

59. Explain why the y-intercept of the graph of the quadratic equation $y = ax^2 + bx + c$ is $(0, c)$.

▶ **60.** Explain how to determine from its equation whether the graph of a parabola opens upward or downward.

61. Is it possible for the graph of a parabola with equation of the form $y = ax^2 + bx + c$ not to have a y-intercept? Explain.

62. Sketch the graphs of parabolas with zero, one, and two x-intercepts. Can the graph of a quadratic equation of the form $y = ax^2 + bx + c$ have more than two x-intercepts? Explain why or why not.

REVIEW

Simplify each expression.

63. $\sqrt{8} - \sqrt{50} + \sqrt{72}$ **64.** $\left(4\sqrt{x}\right)\left(-2\sqrt{x}\right)$
$3\sqrt{2}$ $-8x$

65. $3\sqrt{z}\left(\sqrt{4z} - \sqrt{z}\right)$ **66.** $\sqrt[3]{27y^3z^6}$
$3z$ $3yz^2$

SECTION 9.5
Complex Numbers

Objectives

1 Express square roots of negative numbers in terms of i.

2 Write complex numbers in $a + bi$ form.

3 Add and subtract complex numbers.

4 Multiply and divide complex numbers.

5 Solve quadratic equations with complex-number solutions.

Earlier in this chapter, we saw that some quadratic equations do not have real-number solutions. When we used the square root property or the quadratic formula to solve them, we encountered the square root of a negative number.

Section 9.1   Example 1d

Solve: $n^2 = -4$

$n = \pm\sqrt{-4}$

No real-number solutions

Section 9.3   Example 4

Solve: $x^2 + 2x + 5 = 0$

$$x = \frac{-2 \pm \sqrt{-16}}{2}$$

No real-number solutions

To solve such equations, we must define the square root of a negative number.

1 Express square roots of negative numbers in terms of *i*.

Recall that the square root of a negative number is not a real number. However, an expanded number system, called the *complex number system,* has been devised to give meaning to expressions such as $\sqrt{-4}$ and $\sqrt{-16}$. To define complex numbers, we use a new type of number that is denoted by the letter i.

The Number *i*

The **imaginary number** i is defined as

$$i = \sqrt{-1}$$

From the definition, it follows that $i^2 = -1$.

We can use extensions of the product and quotient rules for radicals to write the square root of a negative number as the product of a real number and i.

EXAMPLE 1   Write each expression in terms of i:

a. $\sqrt{-4}$ **b.** $\sqrt{-16}$ **c.** $-\sqrt{-48}$ **d.** $\sqrt{-\dfrac{54}{25}}$

Strategy We will write each radicand as the product of -1 and a positive number. Then we will apply the appropriate rules for radicals.

WHY We want our work to produce a factor of $\sqrt{-1}$ so that we can replace it with i.

Self Check 1

Write each expression in terms of i:

a. $\sqrt{-81}$ $9i$

b. $-\sqrt{-11}$ $-i\sqrt{11}$

c. $\sqrt{-28}$ $2i\sqrt{7}$

d. $\sqrt{-\dfrac{27}{100}}$ $\dfrac{3i\sqrt{3}}{10}$

Now Try Problems 13, 17, and 23

Teaching Example 1 Write each expression in terms of i:
a. $\sqrt{-49}$
b. $\sqrt{-17}$
c. $-\sqrt{-12}$
d. $\sqrt{-\frac{60}{49}}$
Answers:
a. $7i$ b. $i\sqrt{17}$ c. $-2i\sqrt{3}$ d. $\frac{2\sqrt{15}}{7}i$

Solution

After factoring the radicand, use the product rule for radicals.

a. $\sqrt{-4} = \sqrt{-1 \cdot 4} = \sqrt{-1}\sqrt{4} = i \cdot 2 = 2i$ $\qquad$ Replace $\sqrt{-1}$ with i.

b. $\sqrt{-16} = \sqrt{-1 \cdot 16} = \sqrt{-1}\sqrt{16} = i\sqrt{16} = 4i$ $\qquad$ Replace $\sqrt{-1}$ with i.

c. $-\sqrt{-48} = -\sqrt{-1 \cdot 16 \cdot 3} = -\sqrt{-1}\sqrt{16}\sqrt{3} = -i \cdot 4 \cdot \sqrt{3} = -4i\sqrt{3}$ or $-4\sqrt{3}i$

d. After factoring the radicand, use the product and quotient rules for radicals.

$$\sqrt{-\frac{54}{25}} = \sqrt{-1 \cdot \frac{54}{25}} = \frac{\sqrt{-1 \cdot 54}}{\sqrt{25}} = \frac{\sqrt{-1}\sqrt{9}\sqrt{6}}{\sqrt{25}} = \frac{3i\sqrt{6}}{5} \text{ or } \frac{3\sqrt{6}}{5}i$$

> **Success Tip**   Since it is easy to confuse $\sqrt{23}i$ with $\sqrt{23i}$, we write i first so that it is clear that the i is not within the radical symbol. However, both $\sqrt{23}i$ and $i\sqrt{23}$ are correct.

2   **Write complex numbers in $a + bi$ form.**

The imaginary number i is used to define *complex numbers*.

Complex Numbers

A **complex number** is any number that can be written in the form $a + bi$, where a and b are real numbers and $i = \sqrt{-1}$.

Complex numbers of the form $a + bi$, where $b \neq 0$ are also called **imaginary numbers**. Complex numbers of the form bi are also called **pure imaginary numbers.**

For a complex number written in the standard form $a + bi$, we call the real number a the **real part** and the real number b the **imaginary part.**

Self Check 2

Write each number in the form $a + bi$:
a. -18 $-18 + 0i$
b. $\sqrt{-36}$ $0 + 6i$
c. $1 + \sqrt{-24}$ $1 + 2i\sqrt{6}$

Now Try Problems 25 and 29

Teaching Example 2 Write each number in the form $a + bi$:
a. 15 b. $\sqrt{-81}$
c. $3 - \sqrt{-63}$
Answers:
a. $15 + 0i$ b. $0 + 9i$
c. $3 - 3i\sqrt{7}$

EXAMPLE 2   Write each number in the form $a + bi$:
a. 6 **b.** $\sqrt{-16}$ **c.** $-8 + \sqrt{-45}$

Strategy To write each number in the form $a + bi$, we will determine a and bi.

WHY The standard form $a + bi$ of a complex number is composed of two parts, the real part a and the imaginary part b.

Solution

a. $6 = 6 + 0i$ The real part is 6 and the imaginary part is 0.

b. To simplify $\sqrt{-16}$, we need to write $\sqrt{-16}$ in terms of i:

$$\sqrt{-16} = \sqrt{-1}\sqrt{16} = 4i$$

Thus, $\sqrt{-16} = 0 + 4i$.   The real part is 0 and the imaginary part is 4.

c. To simplify $-8 + \sqrt{-45}$, we need to write $\sqrt{-45}$ in terms of i:

$$\sqrt{-45} = \sqrt{-1}\sqrt{45} = \sqrt{-1}\sqrt{9}\sqrt{5} = 3i\sqrt{5}$$

Thus, $-8 + \sqrt{-45} = -8 + 3i\sqrt{5}$.   The real part is -8 and the imaginary part is $3\sqrt{5}$.

The following illustration shows the relationship between the real numbers, the imaginary numbers, and the complex numbers.

Complex numbers

Real numbers				Imaginary numbers		
-6	$\frac{5}{16}$	-1.75	π	$9 + 7i$	$-2i$	$\frac{1}{4} - \frac{3}{4}i$
48	0	$-\sqrt{10}$	$-\frac{7}{2}$	$0.56i$	$6 + i\sqrt{3}$	

3 Add and subtract complex numbers.

Adding and subtracting complex numbers is similar to adding and subtracting polynomials.

Addition and Subtraction of Complex Numbers

1. To add complex numbers, add their real parts and add their imaginary parts.
2. To subtract complex numbers, add the opposite of the complex number being subtracted.

EXAMPLE 3 Find each sum or difference:
a. $(5 + 2i) + (1 + 8i)$ **b.** $(-6 - 5i) - (3 - 4i)$ **c.** $11i + (-2 + 6i)$

Strategy To add the complex numbers, we will add their real parts and add their imaginary parts. To subtract the complex numbers, we will add the opposite of the complex number to be subtracted.

WHY We perform the indicated operations as if the complex numbers were polynomials with i as a variable.

Solution
a. $(5 + 2i) + (1 + 8i) = (5 + 1) + (2 + 8)i$

The sum of the imaginary parts.
The sum of the real parts.

$$= 6 + 10i$$

Add

b. $(-6 - 5i) - (3 - 4i) = (-6 - 5i) + (-3 + 4i)$ To find the opposite, change the sign of each term of $3 - 4i$.

the opposite

$$= [-6 + (-3)] + (-5 + 4)i$$ Add the real parts. Add the imaginary parts.

$$= -9 - i$$

c. $11i + (-2 + 6i) = -2 + (11 + 6)i$ Add the imaginary parts.
$$= -2 + 17i$$

Self Check 3

Find the sum or difference. Write each result in the form $a + bi$:
a. $(3 - 5i) + (-2 + 6i)$ $1 + i$
b. $(-4 - i) - (-1 - 6i)$ $-3 + 5i$
c. $9 + (16 - 4i)$ $25 - 4i$

Now Try Problems 33 and 35

Teaching Example 3 Find each sum or difference:
a. $(6 + 4i) + (2 + 3i)$
b. $(-5 - 2i) - (7 - 4i)$
c. $16i + (-3 + 7i)$
Answers:
a. $8 + 7i$
b. $-12 + 2i$
c. $-3 + 23i$

Success Tip i is not a variable, but it is helpful to think of it as one when adding, subtracting, and multiplying. For example:

$$4i + 3i = 7i$$
$$8i - 6i = 2i$$
$$i \cdot i = i^2$$

4 Multiply and divide complex numbers.

Multiplying complex numbers is similar to multiplying polynomials.

EXAMPLE 4   Find each product:

a. $5i(4 - i)$ **b.** $(2 + 5i)(6 + 4i)$ **c.** $(3 + 5i)(3 - 5i)$

Strategy We will use the distributive property or the FOIL method to find the products.

WHY We perform the indicated operations as if the complex numbers were polynomials with i as a variable.

Solution

a. $5i(4 - i) = 5i \cdot 4 - 5i \cdot i$ Distribute the multiplication by 5i.

$\qquad\qquad = 20i - 5i^2$

$\qquad\qquad = 20i - 5(-1)$ Replace i^2 with -1.

$\qquad\qquad = 20i + 5$

$\qquad\qquad = 5 + 20i$ Write the result in the form $a + bi$.

                       F   O   I   L

b. $(2 + 5i)(6 + 4i) = 12 + 8i + 30i + 20i^2$ Use the FOIL method.

$\qquad\qquad\qquad\quad = 12 + 38i + 20(-1)$ $8i + 30i = 38i$. Replace i^2 with -1.

$\qquad\qquad\qquad\quad = 12 + 38i - 20$

$\qquad\qquad\qquad\quad = -8 + 38i$ Subtract: $12 - 20 = -8$.

                       F   O   I   L

c. $(3 + 5i)(3 - 5i) = 9 - 15i + 15i - 25i^2$ Use the FOIL method.

$\qquad\qquad\qquad\quad = 9 - 25(-1)$ Add: $-15i + 15i = 0$. Replace i^2 with -1.

$\qquad\qquad\qquad\quad = 9 + 25$

$\qquad\qquad\qquad\quad = 34$

Written in the form $a + bi$, the product is $34 + 0i$.

In Example 4c, we saw that the product of the imaginary numbers $3 + 5i$ and $3 - 5i$ is the real number 34. We call $3 + 5i$ and $3 - 5i$ *complex conjugates* of each other.

Complex Conjugates

The complex numbers $a + bi$ and $a - bi$ are called **complex conjugates.**

For example,

- $7 + 4i$ and $7 - 4i$ are complex conjugates.
- $5 - i$ and $5 + i$ are complex conjugates.
- $-6i$ and $6i$ are complex conjugates, because $-6i = 0 - 6i$ and $6i = 0 + 6i$.

Success Tip   To find the conjugate of a complex number, write it in $a + bi$ form and change the sign between the real and imaginary parts from + to − or from − to +.

In general, the product of the complex number $a + bi$ and its complex conjugate $a - bi$ is the real number $a^2 + b^2$, as the following work shows:

$$
\begin{aligned}
\overbrace{(a + bi)(a - bi)} &= a^2 - abi + abi - b^2i^2 \quad &\text{Use the FOIL method.} \\
&= a^2 - b^2(-1) \quad &\text{Add: } -abi + abi = 0.\ \text{Replace } i^2 \text{ with } -1. \\
&= a^2 + b^2
\end{aligned}
$$

We can use this fact when dividing by a complex number. The process that we use is similar to rationalizing two-term denominators.

EXAMPLE 5

Write each quotient in the form $a + bi$:   **a.** $\dfrac{6}{7 - 4i}$ **b.** $\dfrac{3 - i}{2 + i}$

Strategy We will build each fraction by multiplying it by a form of 1 that uses the conjugate of the denominator.

WHY This step produces a real number in the denominator so that the result can then be written in the form $a + bi$.

Solution

a. We want to build a fraction equivalent to $\dfrac{6}{7 - 4i}$ that does not have i in the denominator. To make the denominator, $7 - 4i$, a real number, we need to multiply it by its complex conjugate, $7 + 4i$. It follows that $\dfrac{7 + 4i}{7 + 4i}$ should be the form of 1 that is used to build $\dfrac{6}{7 - 4i}$.

$$
\begin{aligned}
\frac{6}{7 - 4i} &= \frac{6}{7 - 4i} \cdot \frac{7 + 4i}{7 + 4i} \quad &\text{To build an equivalent fraction, multiply by } \tfrac{7 + 4i}{7 + 4i} = 1. \\[2mm]
&= \frac{42 + 24i}{49 - 16i^2} \quad &\substack{\text{To multiply the numerators, distribute the} \\ \text{multiplication by 6.} \\ \text{To multiply the denominators, find } (7 - 4i)(7 + 4i).} \\[2mm]
&= \frac{42 + 24i}{49 - 16(-1)} \quad &\substack{\text{Replace } i^2 \text{ with } -1.\ \text{The denominator no longer} \\ \text{contains } i.} \\[2mm]
&= \frac{42 + 24i}{49 + 16} \quad &\text{Simplify the denominator.} \\[2mm]
&= \frac{42 + 24i}{65} \quad &\substack{\text{This notation represents the sum of two fractions} \\ \text{that have the common denominator 65: } \tfrac{42}{65} \text{ and } \tfrac{24i}{65}.} \\[2mm]
&= \frac{42}{65} + \frac{24}{65}i \quad &\text{Write the result in the form } a + bi.
\end{aligned}
$$

b. We can make the denominator of $\dfrac{3 - i}{2 + i}$ a real number by multiplying it by the complex conjugate of $2 + i$, which is $2 - i$.

$$
\begin{aligned}
\frac{3 - i}{2 + i} &= \frac{3 - i}{2 + i} \cdot \frac{2 - i}{2 - i} \quad &\text{To build an equivalent fraction, multiply by } \tfrac{2 - i}{2 - i} = 1. \\[2mm]
&= \frac{6 - 3i - 2i + i^2}{4 - i^2} \quad &\substack{\text{To multiply the numerators, find } (3 - i)(2 - i).\ \text{To} \\ \text{multiply the denominators, find } (2 + i)(2 - i).} \\[2mm]
&= \frac{6 - 5i + (-1)}{4 - (-1)} \quad &\substack{\text{Replace } i^2 \text{ with } -1.\ \text{The denominator no longer} \\ \text{contains } i.} \\[2mm]
&= \frac{5 - 5i}{5} \quad &\text{Simplify the numerator and the denominator.} \\[2mm]
&= \frac{5}{5} - \frac{5i}{5} \quad &\substack{\text{Write each term of the numerator over the} \\ \text{denominator, 5.}} \\[2mm]
&= 1 - i \quad &\text{Simplify each fraction.}
\end{aligned}
$$

Self Check 5

Write each quotient in the form $a + bi$:

a. $\dfrac{5}{4 - i}$ $\tfrac{20}{17} + \tfrac{5}{17}i$

b. $\dfrac{5 - 3i}{4 + 2i}$ $\tfrac{7}{10} - \tfrac{11}{10}i$

Now Try Problems 49 and 53

Teaching Example 5 Write each quotient in the form $a + bi$:

a. $\dfrac{10}{3 - 4i}$ b. $\dfrac{5 + i}{3 - i}$

Answers:

a. $\tfrac{6}{5} + \tfrac{8}{5}i$ b. $\tfrac{7}{5} + \tfrac{4}{5}i$

> **Caution!** A common mistake is to replace i with -1. Remember, $i \neq -1$. By definition, $i = \sqrt{-1}$ and $i^2 = -1$.

As the results of Example 5 show, we use the following rule to divide complex numbers.

Division of Complex Numbers

To divide complex numbers, multiply the numerator and denominator by the complex conjugate of the denominator.

5 Solve quadratic equations with complex-number solutions.

We have seen that certain quadratic equations do not have real-number solutions. In the complex number system, all quadratic equations have solutions. We can write their solutions in the form $a + bi$.

Self Check 6

Solve each equation. Express the solutions in the form $a + bi$:

a. $x^2 + 121 = 0$ $0 \pm 11i$

b. $(d - 3)^2 = -48$ $3 \pm 4i\sqrt{3}$

Now Try Problems 57 and 63

Teaching Example 6 Solve each equation. Express the solutions in the form $a + bi$:

a. $x^2 + 36 = 0$

b. $(x - 5)^2 = -18$

Answers:

a. $0 \pm 6i$ **b.** $5 \pm 3i\sqrt{2}$

EXAMPLE 6 Solve each equation. Express the solutions in the form $a + bi$:

a. $x^2 + 25 = 0$ **b.** $(y - 3)^2 = -54$

Strategy We will use the square root property to solve each equation.

WHY It is the fastest way to solve equations of this form.

Solution

a. $x^2 + 25 = 0$ This is the equation to solve.

$\qquad x^2 = -25$ To isolate x^2, subtract 25 from both sides.

$\qquad x = \pm\sqrt{-25}$ Use the square root property. Note that the radicand is negative.

$\qquad x = \pm 5i$ Write $\sqrt{-25}$ in terms of i: $\sqrt{-25} = \sqrt{-1}\sqrt{25} = 5i$.

To express the solutions in the form $a + bi$, we must write 0 for the real part, a. Thus, the solutions are $0 + 5i$ and $0 - 5i$, or more simply, $0 \pm 5i$.

b. $(y - 3)^2 = -54$ This is the equation to solve.

$\qquad y - 3 = \pm\sqrt{-54}$ Use the square root property. Note that the radicand is negative.

$\qquad y - 3 = \pm 3i\sqrt{6}$ Write $\sqrt{-54}$ in terms of i: $\sqrt{-54} = \sqrt{-1}\sqrt{9}\sqrt{6} = 3i\sqrt{6}$.

$\qquad y = 3 \pm 3i\sqrt{6}$ To isolate y, add 3 to both sides.

The solutions are $3 + 3i\sqrt{6}$ and $3 - 3i\sqrt{6}$, or more simply, $3 \pm 3i\sqrt{6}$.

Self Check 7

Solve $a^2 + 2a + 3 = 0$. Express the solutions in the form $a + bi$. $-1 \pm i\sqrt{2}$

Now Try Problem 65

Teaching Example 7 Solve: $3z^2 - 4z + 2 = 0$. Express the solutions in the form $a + bi$.

Answer:

$\frac{2}{3} \pm \frac{\sqrt{2}}{3}i$

EXAMPLE 7 Solve $4t^2 - 6t + 3 = 0$. Express the solutions in the form $a + bi$.

Strategy We use the quadratic formula to solve the equation.

WHY $4t^2 - 6t + 3$ does not factor.

Solution

$$t = \frac{-b \pm \sqrt{b^2 - 4ac}}{2a}$$ In the quadratic formula, replace x with t.

$$t = \frac{-(-6) \pm \sqrt{(-6)^2 - 4(4)(3)}}{2(4)}$$ Substitute 4 for a, −6 for b, and 3 for c.

$$t = \frac{6 \pm \sqrt{36 - 48}}{8}$$ Evaluate the power and multiply within the radical.
Multiply in the denominator.

$$t = \frac{6 \pm \sqrt{-12}}{8}$$ Subtract within the radical: $36 - 48$. Note that the radicand is negative.

$$t = \frac{6 \pm 2i\sqrt{3}}{8}$$ Write $\sqrt{-12}$ in terms of i:
$\sqrt{-12} = \sqrt{-1}\sqrt{12} = \sqrt{-1}\sqrt{4}\sqrt{3} = 2i\sqrt{3}$

$$t = \frac{\overset{1}{\cancel{2}}\left(3 \pm i\sqrt{3}\right)}{\underset{1}{2 \cdot 4}}$$ Factor out the GCF 2 from $6 \pm 2i\sqrt{3}$ and factor 8 as $2 \cdot 4$. Then remove the common factor 2: $\frac{2}{2} = 1$.

$$t = \frac{3 \pm i\sqrt{3}}{4}$$ This notation represents the sum and difference of two fractions that have the common denominator 4: $\frac{3}{4}$ and $\frac{i\sqrt{3}}{4}$.

Writing each result as a complex number in the form $a + bi$, the solutions are

$$\frac{3}{4} + \frac{\sqrt{3}}{4}i \quad \text{and} \quad \frac{3}{4} - \frac{\sqrt{3}}{4}i \quad \text{or more simply} \quad \frac{3}{4} \pm \frac{\sqrt{3}}{4}i$$

ANSWERS TO SELF CHECKS

1. a. $9i$ **b.** $-i\sqrt{11}$ **c.** $2i\sqrt{7}$ **d.** $\frac{3i\sqrt{3}}{10}$ **2. a.** $-18 + 0i$ **b.** $0 + 6i$ **c.** $1 + 2i\sqrt{6}$
3. a. $1 + i$ **b.** $-3 + 5i$ **c.** $25 - 4i$ **4. a.** $36 + 12i$ **b.** $7 - 22i$ **c.** $40 + 0i$
5. a. $\frac{20}{17} + \frac{5}{17}i$ **b.** $\frac{7}{10} - \frac{11}{10}i$ **6. a.** $0 \pm 10i$ **b.** $3 \pm 4i\sqrt{3}$ **7.** $-1 \pm i\sqrt{2}$

SECTION 9.5   STUDY SET

VOCABULARY

Fill in the blanks.

▶ **1.** $9 + 2i$ is an example of a __complex__ number. The __real__ part is 9 and the __imaginary__ part is 2.

2. The __imaginary__ number i is used to define complex numbers.

CONCEPTS

Fill in the blanks.

3. a. $i = \boxed{\sqrt{-1}}$ **b.** $i \cdot i = i^2 = \boxed{-1}$

4. $\sqrt{-25} = \sqrt{\boxed{-1} \cdot 25} = \boxed{\sqrt{-1}}\sqrt{25} = 5\boxed{i}$

5. a. $5i + 3i = \boxed{8i}$ **b.** $5i - 3i = \boxed{2i}$

▶ **6.** The product of any complex number and its complex conjugate is a __real__ number.

7. To write the quotient $\frac{2 - 3i}{6 - i}$ as a complex number in standard form, we multiply it by $\boxed{\frac{6 + i}{6 + i}}$.

▶ **8.** $\dfrac{3 \pm \sqrt{-4}}{5} = \dfrac{3 \pm \boxed{2i}}{5}$

9. Determine whether each statement is true or false.

a. Every real number is a complex number. true

b. $2 + 7i$ is an imaginary number. true

c. $\sqrt{-16}$ is a real number. false

d. In the complex number system, all quadratic equations have solutions. true

10. Give the complex conjugate of each number.

a. $2 - 9i$ $2 + 9i$ **b.** $-8 + i$ $-8 - i$

c. $4i$ $0 - 4i$ **d.** $-11i$ $0 + 11i$

NOTATION

11. Write each expression so it is clear that i is not within the radical symbol.

a. $\sqrt{7}i$ $i\sqrt{7}$ **b.** $2\sqrt{3}i$ $2i\sqrt{3}$

▶ **12.** Write $\frac{3 - 4i}{5}$ in the form $a + bi$. $\frac{3}{5} - \frac{4}{5}i$

▶ Selected exercises available online at
www.webassign.net/brookscole

GUIDED PRACTICE

Write each expression in terms of i. See Example 1.

13. $\sqrt{-9}$
$3i$

14. $\sqrt{-4}$
$2i$

15. $\sqrt{-7}$
$i\sqrt{7}$ or $\sqrt{7}i$

16. $\sqrt{-11}$
$i\sqrt{11}$ or $\sqrt{11}i$

17. $\sqrt{-24}$
$2i\sqrt{6}$ or $2\sqrt{6}i$

18. $\sqrt{-28}$
$2i\sqrt{7}$ or $2\sqrt{7}i$

19. $-\sqrt{-32}$
$-4i\sqrt{2}$ or $-4\sqrt{2}i$

20. $-\sqrt{-72}$
$-6i\sqrt{2}$ or $-6\sqrt{2}i$

21. $5\sqrt{-81}$
$45i$

22. $6\sqrt{-49}$
$42i$

23. $\sqrt{-\dfrac{25}{9}}$
$\frac{5}{3}i$

24. $\sqrt{-\dfrac{121}{144}}$
$\frac{11}{12}i$

Write each number in the form a + bi. See Example 2.

25. 12 $12 + 0i$

26. -27 $-27 + 0i$

27. $\sqrt{-100}$ $0 + 10i$

28. $\sqrt{-64}$ $0 + 8i$

29. $6 + \sqrt{-16}$ $6 + 4i$

30. $14 + \sqrt{-25}$ $14 + 5i$

31. $-9 - \sqrt{-49}$ $-9 - 7i$

32. $-45 - \sqrt{-36}$ $-45 - 6i$

Perform the operations. Write all answers in the form a + bi. See Example 3.

33. $(3 + 4i) + (5 - 6i)$
$8 - 2i$

34. $(5 + 3i) - (6 - 9i)$
$-1 + 12i$

35. $(7 - 3i) - (4 + 2i)$
$3 - 5i$

36. $(8 + 3i) + (-7 - 2i)$
$1 + i$

37. $(14 - 4i) - 9i$
$14 - 13i$

38. $(20 - 5i) - 17i$
$20 - 22i$

39. $15 + (-3 - 9i)$
$12 - 9i$

40. $-25 + (18 - 9i)$
$-7 - 9i$

Perform the operations. Write all answers in the form a + bi. See Example 4.

41. $3(2 - i)$
$6 - 3i$

42. $9(-4 - 4i)$
$-36 - 36i$

43. $-5i(5 - 5i)$
$-25 - 25i$

44. $2i(7 + 2i)$
$-4 + 14i$

45. $(3 - 2i)(2 + 3i)$
$12 + 5i$

46. $(3 - i)(2 + 3i)$
$9 + 7i$

47. $(4 + i)(3 - i)$
$13 - i$

48. $(1 - 5i)(1 - 4i)$
$-19 - 9i$

Write each quotient in the form a + bi. See Example 5.

49. $\dfrac{5}{2 - i}$ $2 + i$

50. $\dfrac{26}{3 - 2i}$ $6 + 4i$

51. $\dfrac{-4i}{7 - 2i}$ $\frac{8}{53} - \frac{28}{53}i$

52. $\dfrac{5i}{6 + 2i}$ $\frac{1}{4} + \frac{3}{4}i$

53. $\dfrac{2 + 3i}{2 - 3i}$ $-\frac{5}{13} + \frac{12}{13}i$

54. $\dfrac{2 - 5i}{2 + 5i}$ $-\frac{21}{29} - \frac{20}{29}i$

55. $\dfrac{4 - 3i}{7 - i}$ $\frac{31}{50} - \frac{17}{50}i$

56. $\dfrac{4 + i}{4 - i}$ $\frac{15}{17} + \frac{8}{17}i$

Solve each equation. Write all solutions in the form a + bi. See Example 6.

57. $x^2 + 9 = 0$
$0 \pm 3i$

58. $x^2 + 100 = 0$
$0 \pm 10i$

59. $d^2 + 8 = 0$
$0 \pm 2i\sqrt{2}$

60. $a^2 + 27 = 0$
$0 \pm 3i\sqrt{3}$

61. $(x + 3)^2 = -1$
$-3 \pm i$

62. $(x + 2)^2 = -25$
$-2 \pm 5i$

63. $(x - 11)^2 = -75$
$11 \pm 5i\sqrt{3}$

64. $(x - 22)^2 = -18$
$22 \pm 3i\sqrt{2}$

Solve each equation. Write all solutions in the form a + bi. See Example 7.

65. $x^2 - 3x + 4 = 0$
$\frac{3}{2} \pm \frac{\sqrt{7}}{2}i$

66. $y^2 + y + 3 = 0$
$-\frac{1}{2} \pm \frac{\sqrt{11}}{2}i$

67. $2x^2 + x + 1 = 0$
$-\frac{1}{4} \pm \frac{\sqrt{7}}{4}i$

68. $2x^2 + 3x + 3 = 0$
$-\frac{3}{4} \pm \frac{\sqrt{15}}{4}i$

TRY IT YOURSELF

Perform the operations. Write all answers in the form a + bi.

69. $\dfrac{3}{5 + i}$
$\frac{15}{26} - \frac{3}{26}i$

70. $\dfrac{-4}{7 - 2i}$
$-\frac{28}{53} - \frac{8}{53}i$

71. $(6 - i) + (9 + 3i)$
$15 + 2i$

72. $(5 - 4i) + (3 + 2i)$
$8 - 2i$

73. $(-3 - 8i) - (-3 - 9i)$
$0 + i$

74. $(-1 - 8i) - (-1 - 7i)$
$0 - i$

75. $(2 + i)(2 + 3i)$
$1 + 8i$

76. $2i(7 + 2i)$
$-4 + 14i$

77. $\dfrac{3 - 2i}{3 + 2i}$
$\frac{5}{13} - \frac{12}{13}i$

78. $\dfrac{3 + 2i}{3 + i}$
$\frac{11}{10} + \frac{3}{10}i$

79. $(10 - 9i) + (-1 + i)$
$9 - 8i$

80. $(32 - 3i) + (-44 + 15i)$
$-12 + 12i$

81. $-4(3 + 4i)$
$-12 - 16i$

82. $-7(5 - 3i)$
$-35 + 21i$

83. $(2 + i)^2$
$3 + 4i$

84. $(3 - 2i)^2$
$5 - 12i$

Solve each equation. Write all solutions in the form a + bi.

85. $2x^2 + x = -5$
$-\frac{1}{4} \pm \frac{\sqrt{39}}{4}i$

86. $4x^2 = -7x - 4$
$-\frac{7}{8} \pm \frac{\sqrt{15}}{8}i$

87. $(x - 4)^2 = -45$
$4 \pm 3i\sqrt{5}$

88. $(x - 9)^2 = -80$
$9 \pm 4i\sqrt{5}$

89. $b^2 + 2b + 2 = 0$
$-1 \pm i$

90. $t^2 - 2t + 6 = 0$
$1 \pm i\sqrt{5}$

91. $x^2 = -36$
$0 \pm 6i$

92. $x^2 = -49$
$0 \pm 7i$

93. $x^2 = -\dfrac{16}{9}$
$0 \pm \frac{4}{3}i$

94. $x^2 = -\dfrac{25}{4}$
$0 \pm \frac{5}{2}i$

95. $3x^2 + 2x + 1 = 0$
$-\frac{1}{3} \pm \frac{\sqrt{2}}{3}i$

▶ **96.** $3x^2 - 4x + 2 = 0$
$\frac{2}{3} \pm \frac{\sqrt{2}}{3}i$

▌ APPLICATIONS

▶ **97.** ELECTRICITY In an AC (alternating current) circuit, if two sections are connected in series and have the same current in each section, the voltage is given by $V = V_1 + V_2$. Find the total voltage in a given circuit if the voltages in the individual sections are $V_1 = 10.31 - 5.97i$ and $V_2 = 8.14 + 3.79i$. $18.45 - 2.18i$

▶ **98.** ELECTRONICS The impedance Z in an AC (alternating current) circuit is a measure of how much the circuit impedes (hinders) the flow of current through it. The impedance is related to the voltage V and the current I by the formula

$$V = IZ$$

If a circuit has a current of $(0.5 + 2.0i)$ amps and an impedance of $(0.4 - 3.0i)$ ohms, find the voltage.
$6.2 - 0.7i$

▌ WRITING

99. What unusual situation discussed at the beginning of this section illustrated the need to define the square root of a negative number?

▶ **100.** Explain the difference between the opposite of a complex number and its conjugate.

101. What is an imaginary number?

102. In this section, we have seen that $i^2 = -1$. From your previous experience in this course, what is unusual about that fact?

▌ REVIEW

Rationalize the denominator.

103. $\dfrac{1}{\sqrt{7}}$ $\frac{\sqrt{7}}{7}$

104. $\dfrac{\sqrt{3}}{\sqrt{10}}$ $\frac{\sqrt{30}}{10}$

105. $\dfrac{8}{\sqrt{x} - 2}$ $\frac{8\sqrt{x} + 16}{x - 4}$

106. $\dfrac{\sqrt{3}}{5 + \sqrt{x}}$ $\frac{5\sqrt{3} - \sqrt{3x}}{25 - x}$

Preparing for the Chapter 9 Test

The material in Chapter 9 focused on quadratic equations, graphing quadratic equations, and complex numbers. Be sure to review the following checklist in addition to your other studying as you prepare for the exam over this material

☐ When solving a quadratic equation using the factoring method, one side of the equation must be 0. Example:

Solve:

$$x^2 = 9x \quad \text{This is the equation to solve.}$$

$$x^2 - 9x = 0 \quad \text{Subtract 9x from both sides to get 0 on the right side.}$$

$$x(x - 9) = 0 \quad \text{Factor the right side.}$$

$$x = 0 \quad \text{or} \quad x - 9 = 0 \quad \text{Set each factor equal to 0.}$$

$$x = 9 \quad \text{Solve each linear equation.}$$

☐ When using the square root property to solve a quadratic equation, always write the ± sign. Example:

Solve:

$$x^2 - 7 = 0 \quad \text{This is the equation to solve.}$$

$$x^2 = 7 \quad \text{Add 7 from both sides to isolate the } x^2 \text{ term.}$$

$$\sqrt{x^2} = \pm\sqrt{7} \quad \text{Use the square root property and remember the ±.}$$

$$x = \pm\sqrt{7} \quad \text{Simplify the left side of the equation.}$$

☐ We can find the vertex of the graph of a quadratic equation in two variables by completing the square or by using the fact that the x-coordinate of the vertex is $x = \frac{-b}{2a}$. To find the y-coordinate of the vertex, substitute $x = \frac{-b}{2a}$ for x into the equation and find y.

☐ When solving a quadratic equation using the completing the square method, make sure the coefficient of the x^2 term is 1 before you complete the square. If it is not 1, you must divide both sides of the equation by the coefficient of the x^2 to make it 1. Example:

Solve by completing the square.

$$2x^2 - 12x = 6 \quad \text{This is the equation to solve.}$$

$$x^2 - 6x = 3 \quad \text{Divide both sides by 2 to make the coefficient of the } x^2 \text{ term 1.}$$

$$x^2 - 6x + 9 = 3 + 9 \quad \text{Complete the square on the right side by } \frac{1}{2}(-6) = -3, (-3)^2 = 9, \text{ add 9 to both sides.}$$

$$(x - 3)^2 = 12 \quad \text{Factor the left side and simplify the right side of the equation.}$$

$$\sqrt{(x - 3)^2} = \pm\sqrt{12} \quad \text{Use the square root property and remember the ±.}$$

$$x - 3 = \pm 2\sqrt{3} \quad \text{Simplify the left and right sides of the equation.}$$

$$x = 3 \pm 2\sqrt{3} \quad \text{Isolate x by adding 3 to both sides of the equation.}$$

☐ Adding, subtracting, and multiplying complex numbers is similar to these operations with polynomials. Remember to replace i^2 with -1 when simplifying the expression.

Teaching Guide: Refer to the Instructor's Resource Binder to find activities, worksheets on key concepts, more examples, instruction tips, overheads, and assessments.

SECTION 9.1   **Solving Quadratic Equations: The Square Root Property**

DEFINITIONS AND CONCEPTS

We can use the **square root property** to solve equations of the form $x^2 = c$, where $c > 0$. The two solutions are

$$x = \sqrt{c} \quad \text{or} \quad x = -\sqrt{c}$$

We can write $x = \sqrt{c}$ or $x = -\sqrt{c}$ in more compact form using **double-sign notation:**

$$x = \pm\sqrt{c}$$

EXAMPLES

Solve: $x^2 = 27$

$\quad x = \sqrt{27} \quad \text{or} \quad x = -\sqrt{27}$ Use the square root property.

$\qquad\qquad x = \pm\sqrt{27}$ Use double-sign notation.

$\qquad\qquad x = \pm 3\sqrt{3}$ Simplify: $\sqrt{27} = \sqrt{9 \cdot 3} = \sqrt{9} \cdot \sqrt{3} = 3\sqrt{3}$.

Solve: $(x - 3)^2 = 5$

$\quad x - 3 = \pm\sqrt{5}$ Use the square root property and double-sign notation.

$\qquad x = 3 \pm \sqrt{5}$ To isolate x, add 3 to both sides.

The exact solutions are $3 + \sqrt{5}$ and $3 - \sqrt{5}$. If we approximate the solutions to the nearest hundredth, we have

$$3 + \sqrt{5} \approx 3 + 2.236067978 \approx 5.24 \quad \text{Use a calculator.}$$
$$3 - \sqrt{5} \approx 3 - 2.236067978 \approx 0.76$$

Solve: $x^2 - 22x + 121 = 25$

$\qquad (x - 11)^2 = 25$ Factor the perfect-square trinomial.

$\qquad x - 11 = \pm\sqrt{25}$ Use the square root property.

$\qquad\qquad x = 11 \pm 5$ Add 11 to both sides and simplify $\sqrt{25}$.

$x = 11 + 5 \quad \text{or} \quad x = 11 - 5$

$x = 16 \quad\quad\quad\quad x = 6$

REVIEW EXERCISES

Use the square root property to solve each equation.

1. $x^2 = 64$
± 8

2. $t^2 - 8 = 0$
$\pm 2\sqrt{2}$

3. $2x^2 - 1 = 149$
$\pm 5\sqrt{3}$

4. $(x - 1)^2 = 25$
$-4, 6$

5. $(9x - 8)^2 = 40$
$\frac{8 \pm 2\sqrt{10}}{9}$

6. $4(x - 2)^2 - 9 = 0$
$\frac{7}{2}, \frac{1}{2}$

7. $p^2 - 20p + 100 = 9$
$13, 7$

8. $9m^2 + 6m + 1 = 6$
$\frac{-1 \pm \sqrt{6}}{3}$

Use the square root property to find all real-number solutions of each equation. Round each solution to the nearest hundredth.

9. $x^2 = 12$
± 3.46

10. $(x - 1)^2 = 55$
$-6.42, 8.42$

11. $m^2 + 36 = 0$
no real-number solutions

12. $(2x - 3)^2 = -8$
no real-number solutions

13. **CLIFF DIVERS** The La Quebrada Cliff Divers of Acapulco, Mexico, perform daily for the public by diving 148 feet from ocean-side cliffs into the sea below. Find the length of time of a dive. Round to the nearest one tenth of one second. (*Hint:* Use the formula $d = 16t^2$.) 3.0 sec

14. **RUBIK'S CUBE** The area of one of the square faces of a Rubik's cube is $\frac{81}{16}$ in.^{2}. Find the length of one side of a Rubik's cube. Express your answer as a mixed number. (*Hint:* Use the formula for the area of a square, $A = s^2$.) $2\frac{1}{4}$ in.

© Klaus Hackenberg/zefa/Corbis

SECTION 9.2 Solving Quadratic Equations: Completing the Square

DEFINITIONS AND CONCEPTS	EXAMPLES
To **complete the square** on $x^2 + bx$, add the square of one-half of the coefficient of x. $$x^2 + bx + \left(\frac{1}{2}b\right)^2$$	Complete the square on $x^2 + 12x$ and factor the resulting perfect-square trinomial. $x^2 + 12x + 36$ The coefficient of x is 12. To complete the square: $\frac{1}{2} \cdot 12 = 6$ and $6^2 = 36$. Add 36 to the binomial. This trinomial factors as $(x + 6)^2$. We can check using multiplication.
To **solve a quadratic equation in x by completing the square:** 1. If necessary, divide both sides of the equation by the coefficient of x^2 to make its coefficient 1. 2. Get all variable terms on one side of the equation and all constants on the other side. 3. Complete the square by finding one-half of the coefficient of x, squaring the result, and adding the square to both sides of the equation. 4. Factor the perfect-square trinomial. 5. Solve the resulting equation by using the square root property. 6. Check your answers in the original equation.	Solve: $3x^2 - 12x + 6 = 0$ $\dfrac{3x^2}{3} - \dfrac{12}{3}x + \dfrac{6}{3} = 0$ To make the leading coefficient 1, divide both sides by 3. $x^2 - 4x + 2 = 0$ Do the divisions. $x^2 - 4x = -2$ Subtract 2 from both sides so that the constant term, -2, is on the right side. $x^2 - 4x + 4 = -2 + 4$ The coefficient of x is -4. To complete the square: $\frac{1}{2}(-4) = -2$ and $(-2)^2 = 4$. Add 4 to both sides. $(x - 2)^2 = 2$ Factor the perfect-square trinomial on the left side. Add on the right side. $x - 2 = \pm\sqrt{2}$ Use the square root property. $x = 2 \pm \sqrt{2}$ To isolate x, add 2 to both sides. The solutions are $2 + \sqrt{2}$ and $2 - \sqrt{2}$. We can approximate each solution. To the nearest one hundredth $2 + \sqrt{2} \approx 3.41 \quad 2 - \sqrt{2} \approx 0.59$

REVIEW EXERCISES

Complete the square to make each expression a perfect-square trinomial. Then factor.

15. $x^2 + 4x$
$x^2 + 4x + 4 = (x + 2)^2$

16. $t^2 - 5t$
$t^2 - 5t + \frac{25}{4} = \left(t - \frac{5}{2}\right)^2$

19. $x^2 + 2x = 5$
$-1 \pm \sqrt{6}$

20. $4x^2 - 16x = 7$
$\frac{4 \pm \sqrt{23}}{2}$

21. $2x^2 - 2x - 1 = 0$
$\frac{1 \pm \sqrt{3}}{2}$

22. $3x^2 + 5x + 2 = 0$
$-1, -\frac{2}{3}$

Solve each quadratic equation by completing the square.

17. $x^2 - 8x + 15 = 0$
3, 5

18. $x^2 = -5x + 14$
2, -7

Solve each quadratic equation by completing the square. Round each solution to the nearest hundredth.

23. $x^2 + 4x + 1 = 0$
$-0.27, -3.73$

24. $x^2 - 7x = 5$
$-0.65, 7.65$

SECTION 9.3   Solving Quadratic Equations: The Quadratic Formula

DEFINITIONS AND CONCEPTS	EXAMPLES

To **solve a quadratic equation in x using the quadratic formula:**

1. Write the equation in standard form:

$$ax^2 + bx + c = 0$$

2. Identify a, b, and c.

3. Substitute the values for a, b, and c in the quadratic formula

$$x = \frac{-b \pm \sqrt{b^2 - 4ac}}{2a}$$

and evaluate the right side to obtain the solutions.

Use the quadratic formula to solve: $3x^2 - 2x = 2$

$$3x^2 - 2x - 2 = 0 \quad \text{To get 0 on the right side, subtract 2 from both sides.}$$

Here, $a = 3$, $b = -2$, and $c = -2$.

$$x = \frac{-b \pm \sqrt{b^2 - 4ac}}{2a} \quad \text{This is the quadratic formula.}$$

$$x = \frac{-(-2) \pm \sqrt{(-2)^2 - 4(3)(-2)}}{2(3)} \quad \text{Substitute 3 for } a, -2 \text{ for } b, \text{ and } -2 \text{ for } c.$$

$$x = \frac{2 \pm \sqrt{4 - (-24)}}{6} \quad \text{Evaluate within the radical. Multiply in the denominator.}$$

$$x = \frac{2 \pm \sqrt{28}}{6} \quad \begin{array}{l}\text{Add the opposite:}\\ 4 - (-24) = 4 + 24 = 28.\end{array}$$

$$x = \frac{2 \pm 2\sqrt{7}}{6} \quad \begin{array}{l}\text{Simplify:}\\ \sqrt{28} = \sqrt{4}\sqrt{7} = 2\sqrt{7}.\end{array}$$

$$x = \frac{\overset{1}{\cancel{2}}\left(1 \pm \sqrt{7}\right)}{\underset{1}{\cancel{2}} \cdot 3} \quad \begin{array}{l}\text{Factor out the GCF, 2, in the numerator. In the denominator, factor 6. Remove the common factor, 2.}\end{array}$$

$$x = \frac{1 \pm \sqrt{7}}{3} \quad \text{The solutions are } \frac{1 \pm \sqrt{7}}{3}.$$

A **strategy for solving quadratic equations** is given on page 739.

A suggested method for solving each quadratic equation is given.

Factor method	*Square root property*
$x^2 - 3x - 18 = 0$	$(x - 1)^2 = 18$

Complete the square	*Quadratic formula*
$x^2 + 6x - 11 = 0$	$3x^2 - 9x + 1 = 0$

$\uparrow$
even coefficient

REVIEW EXERCISES

Write each equation in $ax^2 + bx + c = 0$ form and find $a, b,$ and c.

25. $x^2 + 2x = -5$ $x^2 + 2x + 5 = 0; 1, 2, 5$

26. $6x^2 = 2x + 1$ $6x^2 - 2x - 1 = 0; 6, -2, -1$

Use the quadratic formula to find all real-number solutions of each equation.

27. $x^2 - 2x - 15 = 0$ $5, -3$ **28.** $6x^2 = 7x + 3$ $\frac{3}{2}, -\frac{1}{3}$

29. $p^2 - 4 = 2p$ $1 \pm \sqrt{5}$ **30.** $x^2 + 7 = 6x$ $3 \pm \sqrt{2}$

31. $3x^2 + 3x = 1$ $\frac{-3 \pm \sqrt{21}}{6}$ **32.** $5x^2 + x = 1$ $\frac{-1 \pm \sqrt{21}}{10}$

33. $7x^2 - x + 2 = 0$

no real-number solutions

34. $2x^2 + 6x = 5$

$\frac{-3 \pm \sqrt{19}}{2}$

Use the most efficient method to find all real-number solutions of each equation.

35. $4x^2 + 16x = 0$ $0, -4$ **36.** $(y + 3)^2 = 16$ $1, -7$

37. $3g^2 - 81 = 0$ $\pm 3\sqrt{3}$ **38.** $3x^2 - 6x = -1$ $\frac{3 \pm \sqrt{6}}{3}$

39. $2x^2 + 2x - 5 = 0$ **40.** $a^2 = 4a - 4$

$\frac{-1 \pm \sqrt{11}}{2}$ 2

41. $(2x - 5)^2 = 64$ **42.** $a^2 - 2a + 5 = 0$

$\frac{13}{2}, -\frac{3}{2}$ no real-number solutions

43. Use the quadratic formula to solve $3x^2 + 2x - 2 = 0$. Give the solutions in exact form and then rounded to the nearest hundredth. $\frac{-1 \pm \sqrt{7}}{3}$; $-1.22, 0.55$

44. SECURITY GATES The length of the frame for an iron gate is 14 feet longer than the width. A diagonal cross brace is 26 feet long. Find the width and length of the gate frame. 10 ft, 24 ft

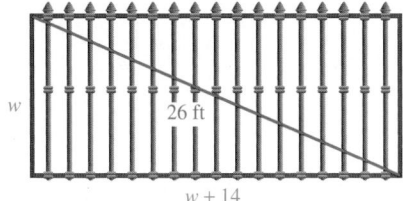

45. THE GRAND CANYON The depth of the Grand Canyon at the South Rim is almost one mile. Suppose a visitor standing on the rim tosses a rock upward over the canyon. The time t (in seconds) that it takes for the rock to hit the bottom of the canyon can be found by solving the quadratic equation $0 = -16t^2 + 8t + 5,040$. Find t. 18 sec

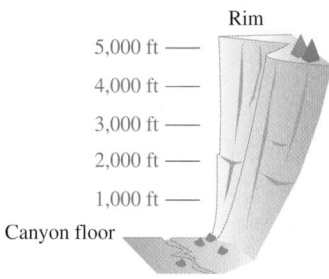

Rim

5,000 ft —
4,000 ft —
3,000 ft —
2,000 ft —
1,000 ft —

Canyon floor

46. GEOMETRY The triangle shown has an area of 24 square inches. Find its height. 6 in.

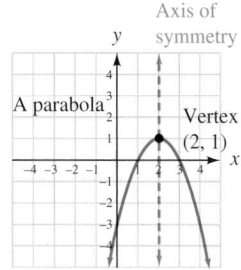

SECTION 9.4   Graphing Quadratic Equations

DEFINITIONS AND CONCEPTS	EXAMPLES
The **vertex** of a parabola is the lowest (or highest) point on the parabola. A vertical line through the vertex of a parabola that opens upward or downward is called its **axis of symmetry**.	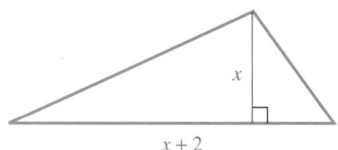

Graph: $y = x^2 + 6x + 8$

Equations that can be written in the form $y = ax^2 + bx + c$, where $a \neq 0$, are called **quadratic equations in two variables**.

The graph of $y = ax^2 + bx + c$ is a **parabola**. Much can be determined about the graph from the coefficients a, b, and c.

The parabola opens **upward** when $a > 0$ and downward when $a < 0$.

Upward/downward: The equation is in the form $y = ax^2 + bx + c$, with $a = 1$, $b = 6$, and $c = 8$. Since $a > 0$, the parabola opens upward.

Vertex/axis of symmetry: The x-coordinate of the vertex is

$$\frac{-b}{2a} = \frac{-6}{2(1)} = -3$$

The x-coordinate of the **vertex** of the parabola is $x = \frac{-b}{2a}$. To find the y-coordinate of the vertex, substitute $\frac{-b}{2a}$ for x in the equation of the parabola and find y.

To find the **y-intercept**, substitute 0 for x in the given equation and solve for y. To find the **x-intercepts,** substitute 0 for y in the given equation and solve for x.

The number of distinct x-intercepts of the graph of a quadratic equation $y = ax^2 + bx + c$ is the same as the number of distinct **real-number solutions** of $ax^2 + bx + c = 0$.

The y-coordinate of the vertex is:

$$y = x^2 + 6x + 8 \qquad \text{\textit{The equation to graph.}}$$
$$y = (-3)^2 + 6(-3) + 8$$
$$y = 9 - 18 + 8$$
$$y = -1$$

The vertex of the parabola is $(-3, -1)$.

Intercepts: Since $c = 8$, the y-intercept of the parabola is $(0, 8)$. The point $(-6, 8)$, which is 3 units to the left of the axis of symmetry, must also be on the graph.

To find the x-intercepts of the graph of $y = x^2 + 6x + 8$, we set $y = 0$ and solve for x.

$$0 = x^2 + 6x + 8$$
$$0 = (x + 4)(x + 2)$$
$$x + 4 = 0 \quad \text{or} \quad x + 2 = 0$$
$$x = -4 \quad | \quad x = -2$$

The x-intercepts of the graph are $(-4, 0)$ and $(-2, 0)$.

Plotting points/using symmetry: To locate two more points on the graph, we let $x = -1$ and find the corresponding value of y.

$$y = (-1)^2 + 6(-1) + 8 = 3$$

Thus, the point $(-1, 3)$ lies on the parabola. We use symmetry to determine that $(-5, 3)$ is also on the graph.

Draw a smooth curve through the points: The completed graph of $y = x^2 + 6x + 8$ is shown here.

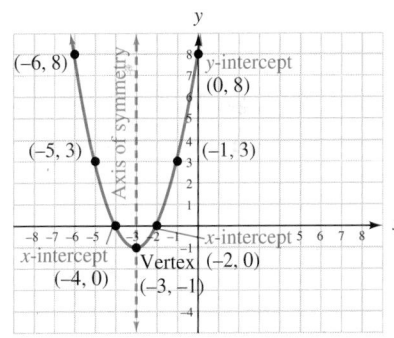

Since the graph of $y = x^2 + 6x + 8$ (shown above) has two x-intercepts, $(-4, 0)$ and $(-2, 0)$, the equation $x^2 + 6x + 8 = 0$ has two distinct real-number solutions, -4 and -2.

REVIEW EXERCISES

47. Refer to the figure.

    a. What are the x-intercepts of the parabola? $(-3, 0), (1, 0)$

    b. What is the y-intercept of the parabola? $(0, -3)$

    c. What is the vertex of the parabola? $(-1, -4)$

    d. Draw the axis of symmetry of the parabola on the graph. a vertical line through $(-1, -4)$

48. The point $(0, -3)$ lies on the parabola graphed above. Use symmetry to determine the coordinates of another point that lies on the parabola. $(-2, -3)$

Find the vertex of the graph of each quadratic equation and tell in which direction the parabola opens. Do not draw the graph.

49. $y = 2x^2 - 4x + 7$
    (1, 5), upward

50. $y = -3x^2 + 18x - 11$
    (3, 16), downward

Find the x- and y-intercepts of the graph of each quadratic equation.

51. $y = x^2 + 6x + 5$
　　$(-5, 0), (-1, 0); (0, 5)$

52. $y = x^2 + 2x + 3$
　　no x-intercepts; (0, 3)

Graph each quadratic equation by finding the vertex, the x- and y-intercepts, and the axis of symmetry of its graph.

53. $y = x^2 + 2x - 3$

54. $y = -2x^2 + 4x - 2$

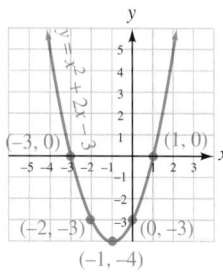

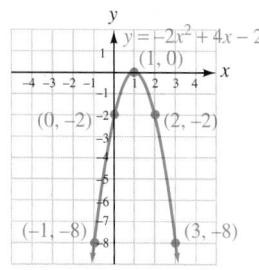

55. $y = -x^2 - 2x + 5$

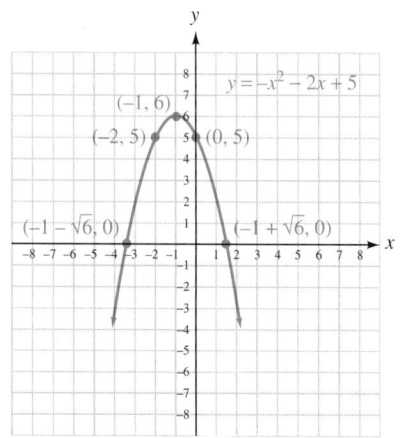

56. $y = x^2 + 4x - 1$

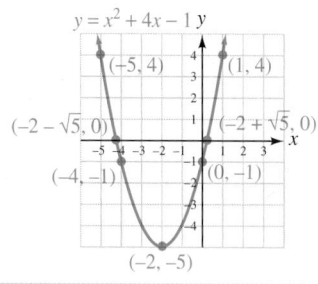

57. The graphs of three quadratic equations in two variables are shown. Fill in the blanks.

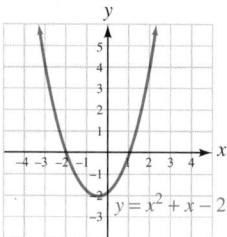

$x^2 + x - 2 = 0$ has ⬚2⬚ real-number solution(s). Give the solution(s): ⬚-2, 1⬚

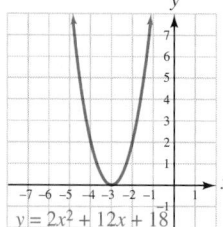

$2x^2 + 12x + 18 = 0$ has ⬚1⬚ repeated real-number solution. Give the solution(s): ⬚-3⬚

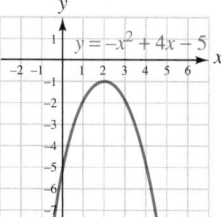

$-x^2 + 4x - 5 = 0$ has ⬚no⬚ real-number solution(s).

58. MANUFACTURING What important information can be obtained from the vertex of the parabola in the graph below?

The maximum profit of $16,000 is obtained from the sale of 400 units.

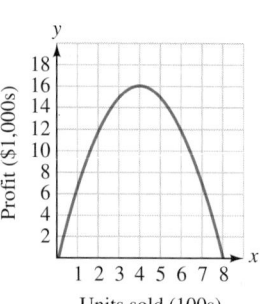

SECTION 9.5   Complex Numbers

DEFINITIONS AND CONCEPTS	EXAMPLES
The **imaginary number** i is defined as $$i = \sqrt{-1}$$ From the definition, it follows that $i^2 = -1$.	Write each expression in terms of i: $$\sqrt{-100} = \sqrt{-1 \cdot 100} \qquad \sqrt{-75} = \sqrt{-1 \cdot 75}$$ $$= \sqrt{-1}\sqrt{100} \qquad = \sqrt{-1}\sqrt{75}$$ $$= i \cdot 10 \qquad = i\sqrt{25}\sqrt{3}$$ $$= 10i \qquad = 5i\sqrt{3} \quad \text{or} \quad 5\sqrt{3}i$$
A **complex number** is any number that can be written in the form $a + bi$, where a and b are real numbers and $i = \sqrt{-1}$. We call a the **real part** and b the **imaginary part.** If $b \neq 0$, $a + bi$ is also an **imaginary number.**	Show that each number is a complex number by writing it in the form $a + bi$. $$10 = 10 + 0i \quad \text{10 is the real part and 0 is the imaginary part.}$$ $$5i = 0 + 5i \quad \text{0 is the real part and 5 is the imaginary part.}$$ $$-2 - \sqrt{-16} = -2 - 4i \quad \text{−2 is the real part and −4 is the imaginary part.}$$
Adding and subtracting complex numbers is similar to adding and subtracting polynomials. To **add two complex numbers,** add their real parts and add their imaginary parts.	Add: $$(3 - 4i) + (5 + 7i) = (3 + 5) + (-4 + 7)i \quad \text{Add the real parts. Add the imaginary parts.}$$ $$= 8 + 3i$$
To **subtract two complex numbers,** add the opposite of the complex number being subtracted.	Subtract: $$(3 - 4i) - (5 + 7i) = (3 - 4i) + (-5 - 7i) \quad \text{Add the opposite of } 5 + 7i.$$ $$= (3 - 5) + [-4 + (-7)]i \quad \text{Add the real parts. Add the imaginary parts.}$$ $$= -2 - 11i$$
Multiplying complex numbers is similar to multiplying polynomials.	Find each product: $$7i(4 - 9i) = 28i - 63i^2 \qquad (2 + 3i)(4 - 3i) = 8 - 6i + 12i - 9i^2$$ $$= 28i - 63(-1) \qquad\qquad = 8 + 6i - 9(-1)$$ $$= 28i + 63 \qquad\qquad = 8 + 6i + 9$$ $$= 63 + 28i \qquad\qquad = 17 + 6i$$
The complex numbers $a + bi$ and $a - bi$ are called **complex conjugates.**	The complex numbers $4 - 3i$ and $4 + 3i$ are complex conjugates.

To write the **quotient of two complex numbers** in the form $a + bi$, multiply the numerator and denominator by the complex conjugate of the denominator. The process is similar to rationalizing two-term denominators.

Write each quotient in the form $a + bi$:

$$\frac{6}{4 - 3i} = \frac{6}{4 - 3i} \cdot \frac{4 + 3i}{4 + 3i}$$

$$= \frac{24 + 18i}{16 - 9i^2}$$

$$= \frac{24 + 18i}{16 - 9(-1)}$$

$$= \frac{24 + 18i}{16 + 9}$$

$$= \frac{24 + 18i}{25}$$

$$= \frac{24}{25} + \frac{18}{25}i$$

$$\frac{2 + i}{1 + i} = \frac{2 + i}{1 + i} \cdot \frac{1 - i}{1 - i}$$

$$= \frac{2 - 2i + i - i^2}{1 - i^2}$$

$$= \frac{2 - i - (-1)}{1 - (-1)}$$

$$= \frac{3 - i}{2}$$

$$= \frac{3}{2} - \frac{1}{2}i$$

Some quadratic equations have **complex solutions that are imaginary numbers.**

Use the quadratic formula to solve: $p^2 + p + 3 = 0$

Here, $a = 1$, $b = 1$, and $c = 3$.

$$p = \frac{-b \pm \sqrt{b^2 - 4ac}}{2a}$$ In the quadratic forumla, replace x with p.

$$p = \frac{-1 \pm \sqrt{1^2 - 4(1)(3)}}{2(1)}$$ Substitute 1 for a, 1 for b, and 3 for c.

$$p = \frac{-1 \pm \sqrt{-11}}{2}$$ Evaluate the power and multiply within the radical. Multiply in the denominator.

$$p = \frac{-1 \pm i\sqrt{11}}{2}$$ Write $\sqrt{-11}$ in terms of i.

$$p = -\frac{1}{2} \pm \frac{\sqrt{11}}{2}i$$ Write the solutions in the form a + bi.

REVIEW EXERCISES

Write each expression in terms of i.

59. $\sqrt{-25}$ 5i

60. $\sqrt{-18}$ $3i\sqrt{2}$

61. $-\sqrt{-49}$ $-7i$

62. $\sqrt{-\dfrac{9}{64}}$ $\frac{3}{8}i$

63. Complete the diagram.

Complex numbers	
Real numbers	Imaginary numbers

64. Determine whether each statement is true or false.

  a. Every real number is a complex number. true

  b. $3 - 4i$ is an imaginary number. true

  c. $\sqrt{-4}$ is a real number. false

  d. i is a real number. false

Give the complex conjugate of each number.

65. $3 + 6i$ $3 - 6i$

66. $-1 - 7i$ $-1 + 7i$

67. $19i$ $0 - 19i$

68. $-i$ $0 + i$

Perform the operations. Write all answers in the form $a + bi$.

69. $(3 + 4i) + (5 - 6i)$
   $8 - 2i$

70. $(7 - 3i) - (4 + 2i)$
   $3 - 5i$

71. $3i(2 - i)$
   $3 + 6i$

72. $(2 + 3i)(3 - i)$
   $9 + 7i$

73. $\dfrac{2 + 3i}{2 - 3i}$
   $-\frac{5}{13} + \frac{12}{13}i$

74. $\dfrac{3}{5 + i}$
   $\frac{15}{26} - \frac{3}{26}i$

Solve each equation. Write all solutions in the form $a + bi$.

75. $x^2 + 9 = 0$
   $0 \pm 3i$

76. $3x^2 = -16$
   $0 \pm \frac{4\sqrt{3}}{3}i$

77. $(p - 2)^2 = -24$
   $2 \pm 2i\sqrt{6}$

78. $(q + 3)^2 = -54$
   $-3 \pm 3i\sqrt{6}$

79. $x^2 + 2x = -2$
   $-1 \pm i$

80. $2x^2 - 3x + 2 = 0$
   $\frac{3}{4} \pm \frac{\sqrt{7}}{4}i$

CHAPTER 9 TEST

1. Fill in the blanks.

   a. A _complex_ number is any number that can be written in the form $a + bi$, where a and b are real numbers and $i = \sqrt{-1}$.

   b. The graph of the equation $y = x^2$ is a cup-shaped figure called a _parabola_.

   c. A _quadratic_ equation can be written in the form $ax^2 + bx + c = 0$, where a, b, and c represent real numbers and $a \neq 0$.

   d. For $7 + 8i$, the real part is 7 and the _imaginary_ part is 8.

   e. The _leading_ coefficient of $3x^2 + 8x - 9$ is 3.

2. Write the statement $x = \sqrt{5}$ or $x = -\sqrt{5}$ using double-sign notation. $x = \pm\sqrt{5}$

Solve each equation by the square root method.

3. $x^2 = 17$ $\pm\sqrt{17}$

4. $(x - 2)^2 = 3$ $2 \pm \sqrt{3}$

5. $4y^2 - 25 = 0$ $\pm\frac{5}{2}$

6. $x^2 + 16x + 64 = 24$ $-8 \pm 2\sqrt{6}$

7. Explain why the equation $m^2 + 49 = 0$ has no real-number solutions.
   $m = \pm\sqrt{-49}$ and $\sqrt{-49}$ is not a real number.

8. ARCHERY The area of a circular archery target is 5,026 cm². What is the radius of the target? Round to the nearest centimeter. 40 cm

Complete the square and factor the resulting perfect-square trinomial.

9. $x^2 - 14x$ $x^2 - 14x + 49 = (x - 7)^2$

10. $a^2 - \frac{5}{3}a$ $a^2 - \frac{5}{3}a + \frac{25}{36} = \left(a - \frac{5}{6}\right)^2$

11. Complete the square to solve $a^2 + 2a - 4 = 0$. Give the exact solutions and then round them to the nearest hundredth. $-1 \pm \sqrt{5}$; $-3.24, 1.24$

12. Complete the square to solve: $2x^2 = 3x + 2$ $2, -\frac{1}{2}$

Use the quadratic formula to solve each equation.

13. $2x^2 - 5x - 12 = 0$ $-\frac{3}{2}, 4$

14. $5x^2 + 11x = -3$ $\frac{-11 \pm \sqrt{61}}{10}$

15. Solve $3x^2 - 2x - 2 = 0$ using the quadratic formula. Give the exact solutions, and then approximate them to the nearest hundredth. $\frac{1 \pm \sqrt{7}}{3}$; $-0.55, 1.22$

16. NEW YORK CITY The rectangular Samsung sign in Times Square is a full-color LED screen that has an area of 2,665 ft². Its length is 17 feet less than twice its width. Find the width and length of the sign. 41 ft, 65 ft

© Hugh Sitton/Getty Images

Use the most efficient method to solve each equation.

17. $x^2 - 4x = -2$ $2 \pm \sqrt{2}$ **18.** $(3b + 1)^2 = 16$ $1, -\frac{5}{3}$

19. $u^2 - 24 = 0$
$\pm 2\sqrt{6}$

20. $3x^2 + 2x + 1 = 0$
$-\frac{1}{3} \pm \frac{\sqrt{2}}{3}i$ or $\frac{-1 \pm i\sqrt{2}}{3}$

21. ADVERTISING When a business runs x advertisements per week on television, the number y of air conditioners it sells is given by the graph. What important information can be obtained from the vertex?

The most air conditioners sold in a week (18) occurred when 3 ads were run.

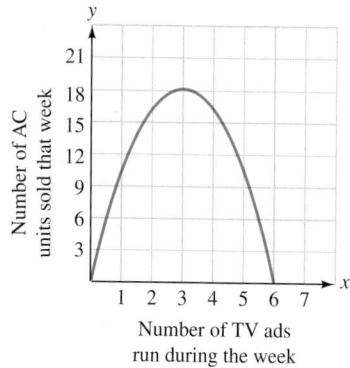

Graph each quadratic equation by finding the vertex, the x- and y-intercepts, and the axis of symmetry of its graph.

23. $y = x^2 + 6x + 5$

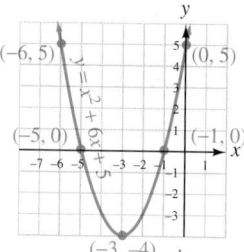

24. $y = -x^2 + 6x - 7$

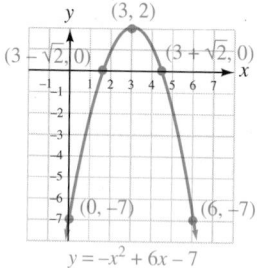

Write each expression in terms of i.

25. $\sqrt{-100}$ $10i$

26. $-\sqrt{-18}$ $-3i\sqrt{2}$

Perform the operations. Write all answers in the form $a + bi$.

27. $(8 + 3i) + (-7 - 2i)$
$1 + i$

28. $(5 + 3i) - (6 - 9i)$
$-1 + 12i$

29. $(2 - 4i)(3 + 2i)$
$14 - 8i$

30. $\dfrac{3 - 2i}{3 + 2i}$
$\frac{5}{13} - \frac{12}{13}i$

22. Fill in the blanks: The graph of $y = ax^2 + bx + c$ opens downward when $a < 0$ and upward when $a > 0$.

CHAPTERS 1–9   CUMULATIVE REVIEW

1. Determine whether each statement is true or false. [Section 1.3]

   a. Every rational number can be written as a ratio of two integers. true

   b. The set of real numbers corresponds to all points on the number line. true

   c. The whole numbers and their opposites form the set of integers. true

2. **DRIVING SAFETY** In cold-weather climates, salt is spread on roads to keep snow and ice from bonding to the pavement. This allows snowplows to remove accumulated snow quickly. According to the graph, when is the accident rate the highest? [Section 1.4] 2 hours before salt is spread

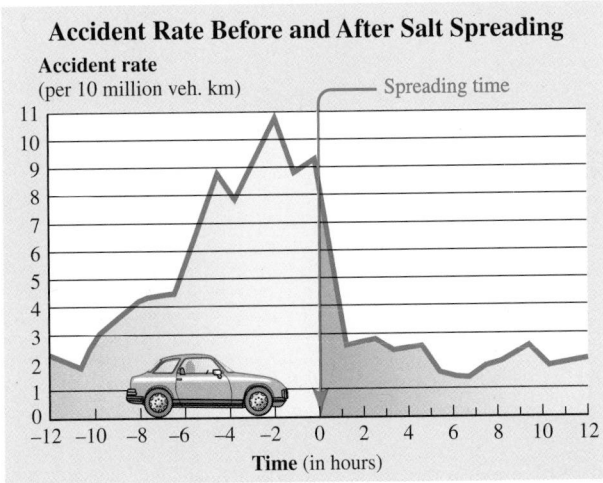

Accident Rate Before and After Salt Spreading

Based on data from the Salt Institute

3. Evaluate: $-4 + 2[-7 - 3(-9)]$ [Section 1.7] 36

4. Evaluate: $\left|\frac{4}{5} \cdot 10 - 12\right|$ [Section 1.7] 4

5. Evaluate $(x - a)^2 + (y - b)^2$ for $x = -2$, $y = 1$, $a = 5$, and $b = -3$. [Section 1.8] 65

6. Simplify: $3p - 6(p - 9) + p$ [Section 1.9] $-2p + 54$

7. Solve $\frac{5}{6}k = 10$ and check the result. [Section 2.1] 12

8. Solve $-(3a + 1) + a = 2$ and check the result. [Section 2.2] $-\frac{3}{2}$

9. **LOOSE CHANGE** The Coinstar machines that are in many grocery stores count unsorted coins and print out a voucher that can be exchanged for cash at the checkout stand. However, to use this service, a processing fee is charged. If a boy turned in a jar of coins worth $50 and received a voucher for $45.55, what was the processing fee (expressed as a percent) charged by Coinstar? [Section 2.3] 8.9%

10. Solve $T = 2r + 2t$ for r. [Section 2.4] $r = \frac{T - 2t}{2}$

11. **SELLING A HOME** At what price should a home be listed if the owner wants to make $330,000 on its sale after paying a 4% real estate commission? [Section 2.5] $343,750

12. **BUSINESS LOANS** Last year, a women's professional organization made two small-business loans totaling $28,000 to young women beginning their own businesses. The money was lent at 7% and 10% simple interest rates. If the annual income the organization received from these loans was $2,560, what was each loan amount? [Section 2.6] $8,000 at 7%, $20,000 at 10%

13. Solve $5x + 7 < 2x + 1$ and graph the solution set. Then use interval notation to describe the solution. [Section 2.7] $(-\infty, -2)$

14. Is $(-5, -3)$ a solution of $2x - 3y = -1$? [Section 3.1] yes

Graph each equation or inequality.

15. $y = -x + 2$ [Section 3.2]

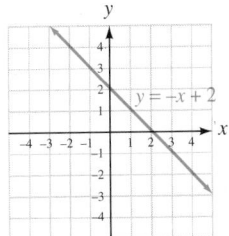

16. $2y - 2x = 6$ [Section 3.3]

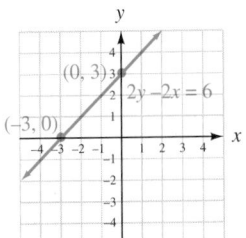

17. $y = -3$
[Section 3.3]

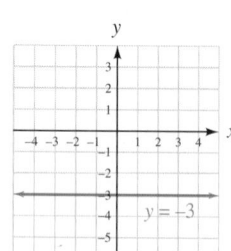

18. $y < 3x$
[Section 3.7]

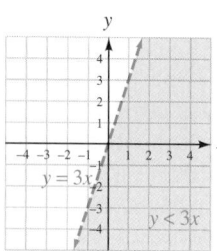

19. Find the slope of the line passing through $(-2, -2)$ and $(-12, -8)$. [Section 3.4] $\frac{3}{5}$

20. TV NEWS The graph in red approximates the evening news viewership on all networks for the years 1995–2005. Find the rate of decrease over this period of time. [Section 3.4] a decrease of 750,000 viewers per year

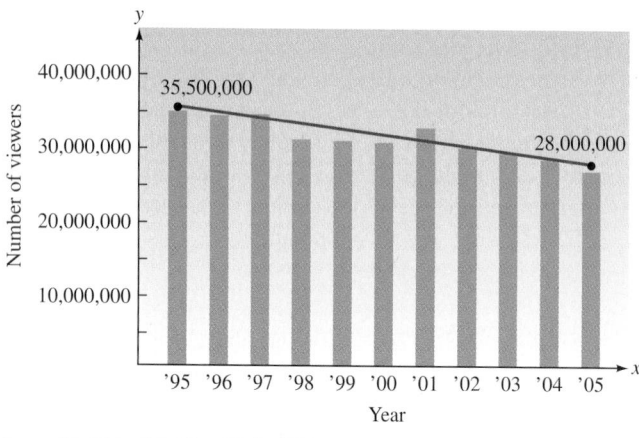

Source: The State of the News Media, 2006

21. What is the slope of the line defined by $4x + 5y = 6$?
[Section 3.5] $-\frac{4}{5}$

22. Write the equation of the line whose graph has slope -2 and y-intercept $(0, 1)$. [Section 3.5] $y = -2x + 1$

23. Are the graphs of $y = 4x + 9$ and $x + 4y = -10$ parallel, perpendicular, or neither?
[Section 3.5] perpendicular

24. Write the equation of the line whose graph has slope $\frac{1}{4}$ and passes through the point $(8, 1)$. Write the equation in slope–intercept form.
[Section 3.6] $y = \frac{1}{4}x - 1$

25. Graph the line passing through $(-2, -1)$ and having slope $\frac{4}{3}$. [Section 3.6]

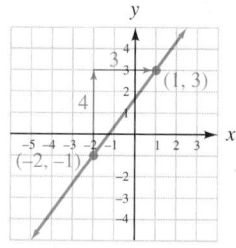

26. If $f(x) = 3x^2 + 3x - 8$, find $f(-1)$. [Section 3.8] -8

27. Find the domain and range of the relation:
$\{(1, 8), (4, -3), (-4, 2), (5, 8)\}$ [Section 3.8]
domain: $\{-4, 1, 4, 5\}$, range: $\{-3, 2, 8\}$

28. Is this the graph of a function? [Section 3.8] yes

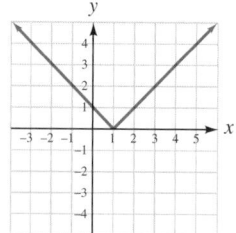

29. Solve using the graphing method. [Section 4.1] $(-2, 3)$
$$\begin{cases} x + y = 1 \\ y = x + 5 \end{cases}$$

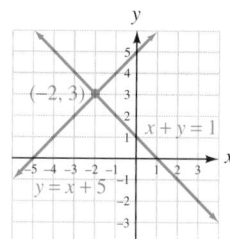

30. Solve using the substitution method.
$$\begin{cases} y = 2x + 5 \\ x + 2y = -5 \end{cases}$$ [Section 4.2] $(-3, -1)$

31. Solve using the elimination (addition) method.
$$\begin{cases} \frac{3}{5}s + \frac{4}{5}t = 1 \\ -\frac{1}{4}s + \frac{3}{8}t = 1 \end{cases}$$ [Section 4.3] $(-1, 2)$

32. AVIATION With the wind, a plane can fly 3,000 miles in 5 hours. Against the wind, the trip takes 6 hours. Find the airspeed of the plane (the speed in still air). Use two variables to solve this problem.
[Section 4.4] 550 mph

33. MIXING CANDY How many pounds of each candy must be mixed to obtain 48 pounds of candy that would be worth $4.50 per pound? Use two variables to solve this problem. [Section 4.4]

36 lb of hard candy, 12 lb soft candy

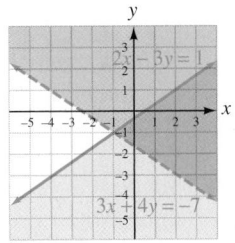

34. Solve the system of linear inequalities.

$$\begin{cases} 3x + 4y > -7 \\ 2x - 3y \geq 1 \end{cases}$$

[Section 4.5]

Simplify each expression. Write each answer without using parentheses or negative exponents.

35. $y^3(y^2y^4)$ [Section 5.1] y^9 **36.** $\left(\dfrac{b^2}{3a}\right)^3$ [Section 5.1] $\dfrac{b^6}{27a^3}$

37. $\dfrac{10a^4a^{-2}}{5a^2a^0}$ [Section 5.2] 2

38. $\left(\dfrac{21x^{-2}y^2z^{-2}}{7x^3y^{-1}}\right)^{-2}$ [Section 5.2] $\dfrac{x^{10}z^4}{9y^6}$

39. FIVE-CARD POKER The odds against being dealt the hand shown are about 2.6×10^6 to 1. Express 2.6×10^6 using standard notation. [Section 5.3] 2,600,000

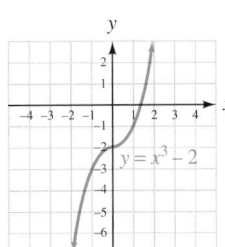

40. Write 0.00073 in scientific notation. [Section 5.3] 7.3×10^{-4}

41. Graph: $y = x^3 - 2$ [Section 5.4]

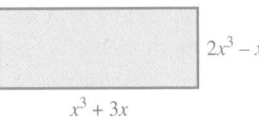

42. Write a polynomial that represents the perimeter of the rectangle. [Section 5.5] $6x^3 + 4x$

($2x^3 - x$ and $x^3 + 3x$ shown on rectangle)

Perform the operations.

43. $4(4x^3 + 2x^2 - 3x - 8) - 5(2x^3 - 3x + 8)$ [Section 5.5] $6x^3 + 8x^2 + 3x - 72$

44. $(-2a^3)(3a^2)$ [Section 5.6] $-6a^5$

45. $(2b - 1)(3b + 4)$ [Section 5.6] $6b^2 + 5b - 4$

46. $(3x + y)(2x^2 - 3xy + y^2)$ [Section 5.6] $6x^3 - 7x^2y + y^3$

47. $(2x + 5y)^2$ [Section 5.7] $4x^2 + 20xy + 25y^2$

48. $(9m^2 - 1)(9m^2 + 1)$ [Section 5.7] $81m^4 - 1$

49. $\dfrac{12a^3b - 9a^2b^2 + 3ab}{6a^2b}$ [Section 5.8] $2a - \frac{3}{2}b + \frac{1}{2a}$

50. $x - 3\overline{)2x^2 - 3 - 5x}$ [Section 5.8] $2x + 1$

Factor each expression completely.

51. $6a^2 - 12a^3b + 36ab$ [Section 6.1] $6a(a - 2a^2b + 6b)$

52. $2x + 2y + ax + ay$ [Section 6.1] $(x + y)(2 + a)$

53. $x^2 - 6x - 16$ [Section 6.2] $(x + 2)(x - 8)$

54. $30y^5 + 63y^4 - 30y^3$ [Section 6.3] $3y^3(5y - 2)(2y + 5)$

55. $t^4 - 16$ [Section 6.4] $(t^2 + 4)(t + 2)(t - 2)$

56. $b^3 + 125$ [Section 6.5] $(b + 5)(b^2 - 5b + 25)$

Solve each equation by factoring.

57. $3x^2 + 8x = 0$ [Section 6.7] $0, -\frac{8}{3}$

58. $15x^2 - 2 = 7x$ [Section 6.7] $\frac{2}{3}, -\frac{1}{5}$

59. HEIGHT OF A TRIANGLE The triangle shown has an area of 22.5 square inches. Find its height.
[Section 6.8] 5 in.

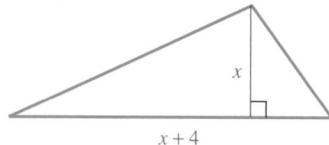

x

$x + 4$

60. For what value is $\frac{x}{x + 8}$ undefined? [Section 7.1] -8

Simplify each expression.

61. $\frac{3x^2 - 27}{x^2 + 3x - 18}$
[Section 7.1] $\frac{3(x + 3)}{x + 6}$

62. $\frac{a - 15}{15 - a}$
[Section 7.1] -1

Perform the operations and simplify when possible.

63. $\frac{x^2 - x - 6}{2x^2 + 9x + 10} \div \frac{x^2 - 25}{2x^2 + 15x + 25}$ [Section 7.2] $\frac{x - 3}{x - 5}$

64. $\frac{1}{s^2 - 4s - 5} + \frac{s}{s^2 - 4s - 5}$ [Section 7.3] $\frac{1}{s - 5}$

65. $\frac{x + 5}{xy} - \frac{x - 1}{x^2 y}$
[Section 7.4] $\frac{x^2 + 4x + 1}{x^2 y}$

66. $\frac{x}{x - 2} + \frac{3x}{x^2 - 4}$
[Section 7.4] $\frac{x^2 + 5x}{x^2 - 4}$

Simplify each complex fraction.

67. $\dfrac{\dfrac{9m - 27}{m^6}}{\dfrac{2m - 6}{m^8}}$
[Section 7.5] $\frac{9m^2}{2}$

68. $\dfrac{\dfrac{5}{y} + \dfrac{4}{y + 1}}{\dfrac{4}{y} - \dfrac{5}{y + 1}}$
[Section 7.5] $\frac{9y + 5}{4 - y}$

Solve each equation.

69. $\frac{2p}{3} - \frac{1}{p} = \frac{2p - 1}{3}$ [Section 7.6] 3

70. $\frac{7}{q^2 - q - 2} + \frac{1}{q + 1} = \frac{3}{q - 2}$ [Section 7.6] 1

71. Solve the formula $\frac{1}{a} + \frac{1}{b} = 1$ for a.
[Section 7.6] $a = \frac{b}{b - 1}$

72. ROOFING A homeowner estimates that it will take him 7 days to roof his house. A professional roofer estimates that he can roof the house in 4 days. How long will it take if the homeowner helps the roofer?
[Section 7.7] $2\frac{6}{11}$ days

73. LOSING WEIGHT If a person cuts his or her daily calorie intake by 100, it will take 350 days for that person to lose 10 pounds. How long will it take for the person to lose 25 pounds? [Section 7.8] 875 days

74. $\triangle ABC$ and $\triangle DEC$ are similar triangles. Find x.
[Section 7.8] 39

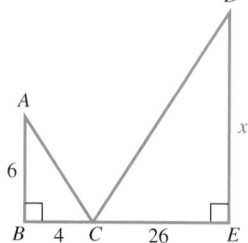

75. Suppose w varies directly as x. If $w = 1.2$ when $x = 4$, find w when $x = 30$. [Section 7.9] 9

76. GEARS The speed of a gear varies inversely with the number of teeth. If a gear with 10 teeth makes 3 revolutions per second, how many revolutions per second will a gear with 25 teeth make?
[Section 7.9] 1.2 rpm

Simplify each radical expression. All variables represent positive numbers.

77. $\sqrt{100x^2}$
[Section 8.1] $10x$

78. $-\sqrt{18b^3}$
[Section 8.2] $-3b\sqrt{2b}$

Perform the indicated operation.

79. $3\sqrt{24} + \sqrt{54}$
[Section 8.3] $9\sqrt{6}$

80. $\left(\sqrt{2} + 1\right)\left(\sqrt{2} - 3\right)$
[Section 8.4] $-1 - 2\sqrt{2}$

Rationalize the denominator.

81. $\frac{8}{\sqrt{10}}$ [Section 8.4]
$\frac{4\sqrt{10}}{5}$

82. $\frac{\sqrt{2}}{3 - \sqrt{a}}$ [Section 8.4]
$\frac{3\sqrt{2} + \sqrt{2a}}{9 - a}$

Solve each equation.

83. $\sqrt{6x + 1} + 2 = 7$
[Section 8.5] 4

84. $\sqrt{3t + 7} = t + 3$
[Section 8.5] $-2, -1$

Simplify each radical expression. All variables represent positive numbers.

85. $\sqrt[3]{\dfrac{27m^3}{8n^6}}$ [Section 8.6] $\frac{3m}{2n^2}$ **86.** $\sqrt[4]{16}$ [Section 8.6] 2

Evaluate each expression.

87. $25^{3/2}$ [Section 8.6]
125

88. $(-8)^{-4/3}$ [Section 8.6]
$\frac{1}{16}$

Solve each equation.

89. $t^2 = 75$

[Section 9.1] $\pm 5\sqrt{3}$

90. $(6y + 5)^2 - 72 = 0$

[Section 9.1] $\frac{-5 \pm 6\sqrt{2}}{6}$

91. STORAGE CUBES The diagonal distance across the face of each of the stacking cubes is 15 inches. What is the height of the entire storage arrangement? Round to the nearest tenth of an inch.
[Section 9.1] 21.2 in.

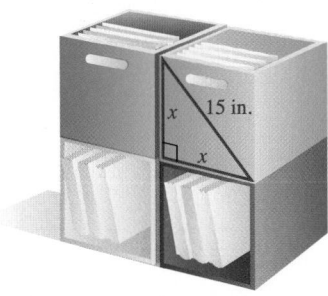

92. Solve $x^2 + 8x + 12 = 0$ by completing the square.
[Section 9.2] $-2, -6$

93. Solve $4x^2 - x - 2 = 0$ using the quadratic formula. Give the exact solutions, and then approximate each to the nearest hundredth. [Section 9.3]
$\frac{1 \pm \sqrt{33}}{8}$; $-0.59, 0.84$

94. QUILTS According to the *Guinness Book of World Records 1998*, the world's largest quilt was made by the Seniors' Association of Saskatchewan, Canada, in 1994. If the length of the rectangular quilt is 11 feet less than twice its width and it has an area of 12,865 ft², find its width and length.
[Section 9.3] 83 ft × 155 ft

95. Graph the quadratic equation $y = 2x^2 + 8x + 6$. Find the vertex, the x- and y-intercepts, and the axis of symmetry of the graph.
[Section 9.4]

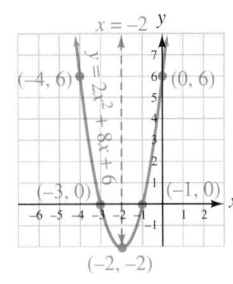

96. POWER OUTPUT The graph shows the power output (in horsepower, hp) of a certain engine for various engine speeds (in revolutions per minute, rpm). For what engine speed does the power output reach a maximum? [Section 9.4] 4,000 rpm

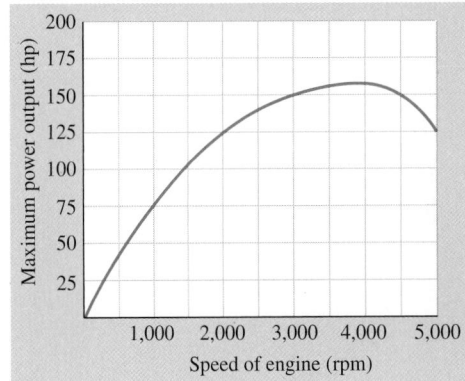

Write each expression in terms of i.

97. $\sqrt{-49}$ [Section 9.5]
$7i$

98. $\sqrt{-54}$ [Section 9.5]
$3i\sqrt{6}$

Perform the operations. Express each answer in the form a + bi.

99. $(2 + 3i) - (1 - 2i)$
[Section 9.5] $1 + 5i$

100. $(7 - 4i) + (9 + 2i)$
[Section 9.5] $16 - 2i$

101. $(3 - 2i)(4 - 3i)$

[Section 9.5] $6 - 17i$

102. $\dfrac{3 - i}{2 + i}$

[Section 9.5] $1 - i$

Solve each equation. Express the solutions in the form a + bi.

103. $x^2 + 16 = 0$
[Section 9.5] $0 \pm 4i$

104. $x^2 - 4x = -5$
[Section 9.5] $2 \pm i$

Statistics

Statistics is a branch of mathematics that deals with the analysis of numerical data. In statistics, three types of averages are commonly used as measures of central tendency of a distribution of numbers: the *mean,* the *median,* and the *mode.*

In this appendix, you will learn about:

1 The mean

2 The median

3 The mode

1 The mean

We have previously discussed the mean of a distribution.

The Mean

The mean of several values is the sum of those values divided by the number of values.

$$\text{Mean} = \frac{\text{sum of the values}}{\text{number of values}}$$

EXAMPLE 1 *Physiology* As part of a class project, a student measured 10 people's reaction time to a visual stimulus. Their reaction times (in seconds) were

$$0.36, 0.24, 0.23, 0.41, 0.28, 0.25, 0.20, 0.28, 0.39, 0.26$$

Find the mean reaction time.

Strategy We will add the values and divide by the number of values.

WHY This is the formula for finding the mean of several values.

Solution

$$\text{Mean} = \frac{0.36 + 0.24 + 0.23 + 0.41 + 0.28 + 0.25 + 0.20 + 0.28 + 0.39 + 0.26}{10}$$

$$= \frac{2.9}{10}$$

$$= 0.29$$

The mean reaction time is 0.29 second.

Self Check 1

Find the mean of 2.3, 4.1, 5.2, 6.3, 3.7, 5.1, 4.6, 5.3 4.575

Now Try **Problem 6**

Teaching Example 1 Find the mean of 4.1, 2.3, 2.8, 4.0, 5.3, 3.2, 4.2, 5.2, 4.9
Answer:
4

EXAMPLE 2 *Banking* When the mean (average) daily balance of a checking account falls below $500 in any week, the customer must pay a $20 service charge. What minimum balance must a customer have on Friday to avoid a service charge? See the table on the next page.

GRADING To receive a grade of A in math, Lindsey must have a mean (average) of at least 80 on five exams. On the first four exams, she received scores of 94, 97, 80, and 87. What is the lowest score she can get on her final exam and still earn an A? 92

Now Try **Problem 1**

Teaching Example 2 GRADING To get a grade of C in algebra, Taylor must have a mean (average) of at least 70 on six exams. On the first five exams, Taylor's scores were 77, 71, 62, 66, and 73. What is the lowest score he can get on the last exam and still get a C?
Answer:
71

Security savings bank		
Day	**Date**	**Daily balance**
Mon	5/09	$670.70
Tues	5/10	$540.19
Wed	5/11	−$60.39
Thurs	5/12	$475.65
Fri	5/13	

Analyze We can find the mean (average) daily balance for the week by adding the daily balances and dividing by 5. If the mean is $500 or more, there will be no service charge.

Form We can let x = the minimum balance needed on Friday and translate the words into mathematical symbols.

The sum of the five daily balances	divided by	5	is	$500.

$$\frac{670.70 + 540.19 + (-60.39) + 475.65 + x}{5} = 500$$

Solve

$$\frac{670.70 + 540.19 + (-60.39) + 475.65 + x}{5} = 500$$

$$\frac{1{,}626.15 + x}{5} = 500 \qquad \text{Simplify the numerator.}$$

$$5\left(\frac{1{,}626.15 + x}{5}\right) = 5(500) \qquad \text{Multiply both sides by 5.}$$

$$1{,}626.15 + x = 2{,}500$$

$$x = 873.85 \qquad \text{Subtract 1,626.15 from both sides.}$$

State On Friday, the account balance must be at least $873.85 to avoid a service charge.

Check Check the result by adding the five daily balances and dividing by 5.

2 The median

The Median

The **median** of several values is the middle value. To find the median of several values,

1. Arrange the values in increasing order.
2. If there are an odd number of values, choose the middle value.
3. If there are an even number of values, add the middle two values and divide by 2.

EXAMPLE 3   *Finding the Median*   In Example 1, the following values were the reaction times of ten people to a visual stimulus.

$$0.36, 0.24, 0.23, 0.41, 0.28, 0.25, 0.20, 0.28, 0.39, 0.26$$

Find the median of these values.

Strategy We will put the values in increasing order. Then, since there is an even number of values, we will add the middle two values and divide by two.

WHY These are the steps to find the median of an even number of values.

Solution
To find the median, we first arrange the values in increasing order:

$$0.20, 0.23, 0.24, 0.25, 0.26, 0.28, 0.28, 0.36, 0.39, 0.41$$

Because there are an even number of values, the median will be the sum of the middle two values, 0.26 and 0.28, divided by 2. Thus, the median is

$$\text{Median} = \frac{0.26 + 0.28}{2} = 0.27$$

The median reaction time is 0.27 second.

Self Check 3

For the values in Self Check 1, find the median. 4.85

Now Try Problem 4

Teaching Example 3 For the values in Teaching Example 1, find the median
Answer:
4.1

3 **The mode**

The Mode

The **mode** of several values is the value that occurs most often.

EXAMPLE 4   *Finding the Mode*   Find the mode of the following values.

$$0.36, 0.24, 0.23, 0.41, 0.28, 0.25, 0.20, 0.28, 0.39, 0.26$$

Strategy We will count the number of times each value occurs.

WHY The mode is the value that occurs most often.

Solution
Since the value 0.28 occurs most often, it is the mode.

Self Check 4

Find the mode of 12, 16, 13, 13, 12, 15, 14, 13 13

Now Try Problem 5

Teaching Example 4 Find the mode of 1.3, 2.7, 1.4, 3.2, 1.4, 5.2, 1.4, 2.1
Answer:
1.4

If two different numbers in a distribution tie for occurring most often, there are two modes, and the distribution is called **bimodal.**

Although the mean is probably the most common measure of average, the median and the mode are frequently used. For example, workers' salaries are usually compared to the median (average) salary. To say that the modal (average) shoe size is 10 means that a shoe size of 10 occurs more often than any other shoe size.

APPENDIX 1 — STUDY SET

PRACTICE

In Exercises 1–3, use the following distribution of values: 7, 5, 9, 10, 8, 6, 6, 7, 9, 12, 9.

1. Find the mean. 8
2. Find the median. 8
3. Find the mode. 9

In Exercises 4–6, use the following distribution of values: 8, 12, 23, 12, 10, 16, 26, 12, 14, 8, 16, 23.

4. Find the median. 13
5. Find the mode. 12
6. Find the mean. 15
7. Find the mean, median, and mode of the following values: 24, 27, 30, 27, 31, 30, and 27. 28, 27, 27
8. Find the mean, median, and mode of the following golf scores: 85, 87, 88, 82, 85, 91, 88, and 88. 86.75, 87.5, 88

APPLICATIONS

9. FOOTBALL The gains and losses made by a running back on seven plays were −8 yd, 2 yd, −6 yd, 6 yd, 4 yd, −7 yd, and −5 yd. Find his average (mean) yards per carry. −2 yd
10. SALES If a clerk had the sales shown below for one week, find the mean of her daily sales. $1,211

Monday	$1,525
Tuesday	$ 785
Wednesday	$1,628
Thursday	$1,214
Friday	$ 917
Saturday	$1,197

11. VIRUSES The following table gives the approximate lengths (in centimicrons) of the viruses that cause five common diseases. Find the mean length of the viruses. 74.5 centimicrons

Polia	2.5
Influenza	105.1
Pharyngitis	74.9
Chicken pox	137.4
Yellow fever	52.6

12. SALARIES Ten workers in a small business have monthly salaries of $2,500, $1,750, $2,415, $3,240, $2,790, $3,240, $2,650, $2,415, $2,415, and $2,650. Find the average (mean) salary. $2,606.50
13. JOB TESTING To be accepted into a police training program, a recruit must have an average (mean) score of 85 on a battery of four tests. If a candidate scored 78 on the oral test, 91 on the physical test, and 87 on the psychological test, what is the lowest score she can obtain on the written test and be accepted into the program? 84
14. GAS MILEAGE Mileage estimates for four cars owned by a small business are shown in the table. If the business buys a fifth car, what must its mileage average be so that the five-car fleet averages 20.8 mpg? 24.5 mpg

Model	City mileage (mpg)
Chevrolet Lumina	20.3
Jeep Cherokee	14.1
Ford Contour	28.2
Dodge Caravan	16.9

15. SPORT FISHING The weights (in pounds) of the trophy fish caught one week in Catfish Lake were 4, 7, 4, 3, 3, 5, 6, 9, 4, 5, 8, 13, 4, 5, 4, 6, and 9. Find the median and modal averages of the fish caught. 5 lb, 4 lb
16. SALARIES Find the median and mode of the 10 salaries given in Exercise 12. $2,575, $2,415
17. FUEL EFFICIENCY The ten most fuel-efficient cars in 2002, based on manufacturer's estimated city and highway average miles per gallon (mpg), are shown in the table on the next page. Find the mean, median, and mode of the city mileages estimates. mean 43, median 42, mode 42

Model	mpg city/hwy
Honda Insight	61/68
Toyota Prius	52/45
Honda Civic Hybrid	47/51
VW Jetta Wagon	42/50
VW Golf	42/49
VW Jetta Sedan	42/49
VW Beetle	42/49
Honda Civic Coupe	36/44
Toyota Echo	34/41
Chevy Prizm	32/41

Source: edmonds.com

18. FUEL EFFICIENCY Use the data in the table for Problem 17 to find the median and mode of the highway mileage estimates. median 49, mode: 49

WRITING

19. Explain why the mean of two numbers is halfway between the numbers.

20. Can the mean, median, and mode of a distribution be the same number? Explain.

21. Must the mean, median, and mode of a distribution be the same number? Explain.

22. Can the mode of a distribution be greater than the mean? Explain.

Roots and Powers

n	n^2	$\sqrt{n}$	n^3	$\sqrt[3]{n}$	n	n^2	$\sqrt{n}$	n^3	$\sqrt[3]{n}$
1	1	1.000	1	1.000	51	2,601	7.141	132,651	3.708
2	4	1.414	8	1.260	52	2,704	7.211	140,608	3.733
3	9	1.732	27	1.442	53	2,809	7.280	148,877	3.756
4	16	2.000	64	1.587	54	2,916	7.348	157,464	3.780
5	25	2.236	125	1.710	55	3,025	7.416	166,375	3.803
6	36	2.449	216	1.817	56	3,136	7.483	175,616	3.826
7	49	2.646	343	1.913	57	3,249	7.550	185,193	3.849
8	64	2.828	512	2.000	58	3,364	7.616	195,112	3.871
9	81	3.000	729	2.080	59	3,481	7.681	205,379	3.893
10	100	3.162	1,000	2.154	60	3,600	7.746	216,000	3.915
11	121	3.317	1,331	2.224	61	3,721	7.810	226,981	3.936
12	144	3.464	1,728	2.289	62	3,844	7.874	238,328	3.958
13	169	3.606	2,197	2.351	63	3,969	7.937	250,047	3.979
14	196	3.742	2,744	2.410	64	4,096	8.000	262,144	4.000
15	225	3.873	3,375	2.466	65	4,225	8.062	274,625	4.021
16	256	4.000	4,096	2.520	66	4,356	8.124	287,496	4.041
17	289	4.123	4,913	2.571	67	4,489	8.185	300,763	4.062
18	324	4.243	5,832	2.621	68	4,624	8.246	314,432	4.082
19	361	4.359	6,859	2.668	69	4,761	8.307	328,509	4.102
20	400	4.472	8,000	2.714	70	4,900	8.367	343,000	4.121
21	441	4.583	9,261	2.759	71	5,041	8.426	357,911	4.141
22	484	4.690	10,648	2.802	72	5,184	8.485	373,248	4.160
23	529	4.796	12,167	2.844	73	5,329	8.544	389,017	4.179
24	576	4.899	13,824	2.884	74	5,476	8.602	405,224	4.198
25	625	5.000	15,625	2.924	75	5,625	8.660	421,875	4.217
26	676	5.099	17,576	2.962	76	5,776	8.718	438,976	4.236
27	729	5.196	19,683	3.000	77	5,929	8.775	456,533	4.254
28	784	5.292	21,952	3.037	78	6,084	8.832	474,552	4.273
29	841	5.385	24,389	3.072	79	6,241	8.888	493,039	4.291
30	900	5.477	27,000	3.107	80	6,400	8.944	512,000	4.309
31	961	5.568	29,791	3.141	81	6,561	9.000	531,441	4.327
32	1,024	5.657	32,768	3.175	82	6,724	9.055	551,368	4.344
33	1,089	5.745	35,937	3.208	83	6,889	9.110	571,787	4.362
34	1,156	5.831	39,304	3.240	84	7,056	9.165	592,704	4.380
35	1,225	5.916	42,875	3.271	85	7,225	9.220	614,125	4.397
36	1,296	6.000	46,656	3.302	86	7,396	9.274	636,056	4.414
37	1,369	6.083	50,653	3.332	87	7,569	9.327	658,503	4.431
38	1,444	6.164	54,872	3.362	88	7,744	9.381	681,472	4.448
39	1,521	6.245	59,319	3.391	89	7,921	9.434	704,969	4.465
40	1,600	6.325	64,000	3.420	90	8,100	9.487	729,000	4.481
41	1,681	6.403	68,921	3.448	91	8,281	9.539	753,571	4.498
42	1,764	6.481	74,088	3.476	92	8,464	9.592	778,688	4.514
43	1,849	6.557	79,507	3.503	93	8,649	9.644	804,357	4.531
44	1,936	6.633	85,184	3.530	94	8,836	9.695	830,584	4.547
45	2,025	6.708	91,125	3.557	95	9,025	9.747	857,375	4.563
46	2,116	6.782	97,336	3.583	96	9,216	9.798	884,736	4.579
47	2,209	6.856	103,823	3.609	97	9,409	9.849	912,673	4.595
48	2,304	6.928	110,592	3.634	98	9,604	9.899	941,192	4.610
49	2,401	7.000	117,649	3.659	99	9,801	9.950	970,299	4.626
50	2,500	7.071	125,000	3.684	100	10,000	10.000	1,000,000	4.642

INDEX

to work. I'm never allowed to take a vacation. Monday through Friday, I work from 8:15 in the morning to 8:15 or 8:30 at night. I get one hour for lunch. Saturday I work from 8 A.M. to 4 or 5 P.M., with no break. I am very hungry by the time I leave work. I'm never paid anything extra if I work more hours.

Elena:

If there's something the matter with the stitching, we have to sew them by hand to fix them. So only when we finish with all the repairs can we leave. We can't leave earlier because they won't give us our IDs. If we get to work five minutes late, they deduct 10 pesos from our pay. Sometimes if we arrive late they won't let us into the factory until 9 A.M., and they deduct 30 or more pesos for this.

Carolina:

We don't have any safety equipment besides mouth covers and aprons; nothing for our hands or eyes, and there aren't any machine guards either. If we lose scissors or other equipment, they make us pay for it.

Luz:

Supervisors yelled at us and pressured us. Once a supervisor threw pants at me and yelled at me because the stitches weren't exactly the same on 30 pairs of pants. I had to re-do these pants before I left as punishment. . . . We had to contribute 3 pesos a month to buy soap, Pine Sol and Ajax to clean the bathroom. Then they assign us to take turns cleaning the bathroom after we've finished our work for the day, because there's no one who works there to clean the bathrooms. They don't have toilet paper in the bathrooms, we have to bring it from home. We're only supposed to go to the bathroom once a day. . . . (NICWJ, 1998)

It is important not only to recognize women's contribution to the global economy, but to take steps to avoid their exploitation as well.

Questions

- The text calls women "often the most exploited of workers." At the same time, it mentions that women often choose to work outside the home. How can you reconcile these two seemingly contradictory remarks? What drives women to work in exploitative jobs?
- How can exploited workers get pay raises or increased benefits? What tactics might they use? What role does gender play in salary negotiations?
- Compare the photographs with the quotes from the workers. Do the words and the images create different impressions? How? Why?

equipment, transoceanic shipping and domestic trucking, advertising and merchandising, retail floor space—and, of course, the profits of Toys "R" Us and other retailers.

Although manufacturing in the global commodity chain typically takes place in peripheral countries, an exception to this trend has developed. Low-wage, low-profit factories known as sweatshops are today reappearing in core countries, sometimes for the first time in half a century or more. A sweatshop is a small factory that has numerous violations of wage, health, and safety laws. In New York City and Los Angeles, for example, more than 100,000 workers labor in tiny garment factories that make many of the brands of clothing you can buy in major department stores. Many laborers work for less than minimum wage, in buildings described by government officials as firetraps.

The private experience of these workers is shaped by larger social forces. First, garment workers in New York and Los Angeles are in direct competition with workers in the Caribbean and Mexico, where wages are a tenth as much as in the United States. If workers in New York and Los Angeles want to keep their jobs, they are often forced to settle for sweatshop wages and conditions. Otherwise, the work will be moved to another country. Second, most garment workers are immigrants, many lacking proper papers. If they complain about their working conditions, they will lose their jobs and possibly be deported.

The global economy has brought sweatshops back to the United States, a country where they were largely unknown for more than half a century. The global economy has also provided the immigrants to work in them.

State-Centered Theories

Some of the most recent explanations of successful economic development emphasize the role of state policy in promoting growth. Differing sharply from market-oriented theories, **state-centered theories** argue that appropriate government policies do not interfere with economic development but rather can play a key role in bringing it about. A large body of research now suggests that in some regions of the world, such as East Asia, successful economic development has been state led. Even the World Bank, long a strong proponent of free-market theories of development, has changed its thinking about the role of the state. In its 1997 report *The State in a Changing World,* the World Bank concludes that without an effective state, "sustainable development, both economic and social, is impossible" (World Bank, 1997).

Strong governments contributed in various ways to economic growth in the East Asian NIEs during the 1980s and 1990s (Appelbaum and Henderson, 1992; Amsden, Kochanowicz, and Taylor, 1994; Evans, 1995; Cumings, 1997; World Bank, 1997):

1. **East Asian governments have sometimes aggressively acted to ensure political stability, while keeping labor costs low.** They have accomplished this by acts of repression, such as outlawing trade unions, banning strikes, jailing labor leaders, and, in general, silencing the voices of workers. The governments of Taiwan, South Korea, and Singapore in particular have engaged in such practices.

2. **East Asian governments have frequently sought to steer economic development in desired directions.** For example, state agencies have often provided cheap loans and tax breaks to businesses that invest in industries favored by the government. Sometimes this strategy has backfired, resulting in bad loans held by the government (one of the causes of the region's economic problems during the late 1990s). Some governments have prevented businesses from investing their profits in other countries, forcing them to invest in economic growth at home. Sometimes governments have owned and therefore controlled key industries.

3. **East Asian governments have often been heavily involved in social programs such as low-cost housing and universal education.** The world's largest public housing systems (outside of socialist or formerly socialist countries) have been in Hong Kong and Singapore, where government subsidies keep rents extremely low. As a result, workers don't require high wages to pay for their housing, so they can compete better with American and European workers in the emerging global labor market. In Singapore, which has an extremely strong central government, well-funded public education and training help to provide workers with the skills they need to compete effectively in the emerging global labor market. The Singaporean government also requires businesses and individual citizens alike to save a large percentage of their income for investment in future growth.

Evaluating Global Theories of Inequality

Each of these four sets of theories of global inequality just discussed has its strengths and weaknesses. Together they enable us to better understand the causes and cures for global inequality.

1. **Market-oriented theories** recommend the adoption of modern capitalist institutions to promote economic development, as the recent example of East Asia attests.

They further argue that countries can develop economically only if they open their borders to trade, and they can cite evidence in support of this argument. But market-oriented theories also fail to take into account the various economic ties between poor countries and wealthy ones—ties that can impede economic growth under some conditions and enhance it under others. They tend to blame low-income countries themselves for their poverty rather than looking to the influence of outside factors, such as the business operations of more powerful nations. Market-oriented theories also ignore the ways government can work with the private sector to spur economic development. Finally, they fail to explain why some countries manage to take off economically while others remain grounded in poverty and underdevelopment.

2. **Dependency theories** address the market-oriented theories' neglect in considering poor countries' ties with wealthy countries by focusing on how wealthy nations have economically exploited poor ones. However, although dependency theories help to account for much of the economic backwardness in Latin America and Africa, they are unable to explain the occasional success story among such low-income countries as Brazil, Argentina, and Mexico or the rapidly expanding economies of East Asia. In fact, some countries once in the low-income category have risen economically even in the presence of multinational corporations. Even some former colonies, such as Hong Kong and Singapore, both once dependent on Great Britain, count among the success stories.

3. **World-systems theory** seeks to overcome the shortcomings of both market-oriented and dependency theories by analyzing the world economy as a whole. Rather than beginning with individual countries, world-systems theorists look at the complex global web of political and economic relationships that influence development and inequality in poor and rich nations alike. Within the world-systems framework, the concept of *global commodity chains* takes this notion one step further, focusing on global businesses and their activities rather than relationships between countries. World-systems theory is thus well suited to understanding the global economy at a time when businesses are increasingly free to set up operations anywhere, acquiring an economic importance that rivals that of many countries. Yet this is also a weakness of the commodity chains approach: It tends to emphasize the importance of business decisions over other factors, such as the role that both workers and governments play in shaping a country's economy (Amsden, 1989; Deyo, 1989; Evans, 1995; Cumings, 1997).

4. **State-centered theories** stress the governmental role in fostering economic growth. They thus offer a useful alternative to both the prevailing market-oriented theories, with their emphasis on states as economic hindrances, and dependency theories, which view states as allies of global business elites in exploiting poor countries. When combined with the other theories—particularly world-systems theory—state-centered theories can explain the radical changes now transforming the world economy.

Why Global Economic Inequality Matters to You

Today the social and economic forces leading to a single global capitalist economy appear to be irresistible. The principal challenge to this outcome—socialism—came to an end with the collapse of the Soviet Union in 1991. The largest remaining socialist country in the world today, the People's Republic of China, is rapidly adopting many capitalist economic institutions and is the fastest-growing economy in the world. It is too soon to tell how far the future leaders of China will move down the capitalist road. Will they eventually adopt a complete market-oriented economy or some combination of state controls and capitalist institutions? Yet most China experts agree on one thing: When China, with its 1.2 billion people, fully enters the global capitalist system, it will have an impact felt around the world. China has an enormous work force, much of which is well trained and educated and now receives extremely low wages—less than one-twentieth as much as comparable U.S. workers. Such a work force will be extremely competitive in a global economy and will force wages down from London to Los Angeles.

What does rapid globalization mean for the future of global inequality? No sociologist knows for certain, but many possible scenarios exist. In one, our world might be dominated by large, global corporations, with workers everywhere competing with one another at a global wage. Such a scenario might predict falling wages for large numbers of people in today's high-income countries and rising wages for a few in low-income countries. There might be a general leveling out of average income around the world, although at a level much lower than that currently enjoyed in the United States and other industrialized nations. In this scenario, the polarization between the haves and the have-nots within countries would grow, as the whole world would be increasingly divided into those who benefit from the global economy and those who do not. Such polarization could fuel conflict between ethnic

Sociology in South Africa

[***]

[***] Sociologists can be caught between their commitment to open debate in the university (and pressures to publish their work in professional journals) and the discipline imposed by involvement in outside organizations. The tendency has been to resolve this contradiction by either retreating into the safer haven of professional sociology or by making your primary loyalty to public sociology. In the latter case, professional sociology simply provides the base for the public sociologist to create a different world outside the university, populated by activists and public intellectuals.

This was the path taken by the two leading public sociologists during the apartheid period, Richard Turner and David Webster. Both were to pay the ultimate price for their public roles when they were assassinated by the apartheid police, Turner on the 8th January 1978 and Webster on the 1st May 1989. Although neither was employed in departments of sociology (Turner was in political science and Webster in social anthropology) they are exemplars of social scientists that deliberately and permanently shifted their orientation to public sociology.

The main themes of Turner's ideas are set out in a remarkable book published in 1972, *The Eye of the Needle*, in which he stressed the capacity of people to change the world in which they live while at the same time providing them with a vision of a future South Africa based on participatory democracy. Most importantly, Turner placed heavy emphasis on the significance of black workers in the economy. He believed that it was through collective organization, especially trade unions, that black people could exercise some control over their lives and influence the direction of change in South Africa.

I chose a different path from that of Turner by trying to resolve the contradiction between the professional and public roles by institutionalizing the link between these two types of sociology

inside the university. The key institutional innovation was the creation of a research program, the Sociology of Work Programme (SWOP), in 1983, linking high-quality academic research on the world of work with a broad range of actors within the world of work. In 1988 I became head of the Department of Sociology at the University of the Witwatersrand, where I was able to cement the links between the University based research entity and teaching program with movements outside the University.

[***]

[***] Once you engage in participatory research relations with outside organizations where you jointly identify the problem to be studied, share ideas on how best to conduct the study,

and report back on the results, a number of problems emerge. In particular it can lead to attempts to suppress uncomfortable research findings. Our research program experienced this when we investigated how the system of migrant labor created a market for prostitution and a potential AIDS pandemic. We needed to negotiate carefully with our research partners before coming to an agreement to publish these unwelcome facts on the devastating social consequences of migrant labor.

[***]

The research we undertook on AIDS in 1989 "percolated" into the consciousness of union officials and, with the support of sympathetic individuals in the union, they overturned accustomed patterns of thought. It helped clarify the union agenda leading this union to become the first to take up AIDS in a systematic way. But this does not mean that the public sociologist wields a lot of power.

[***]

The production of social knowledge is a political process. [***] This was brought home sharply to our researchers quite early on in the development of our research program, when we embarked on research among underground gold miners around issues of health and safety. We were able to show that even so-called "unskilled workers" exercised a range of tacit skills, tricks of the trade essential to production, but received no formal acknowledgment. Workers, we argued, were able to anticipate rock falls underground. We called the project Talking Rocks.

[***] The powerful employers' association, the Chamber of Mines, systematically attempted to discredit the research, arguing that it was their prerogative to decide who worked where, and it was only their university-accredited rock scientists that had the knowledge to predict rock falls. In the event, one of the first pieces of legislation to be passed by the new democratic government was an amendent to the Mine Health

and Safety Act to allow mine workers to refuse to work in dangerous conditions.

The importance of by whom and how scientific knowledge is accredited is a crucial issue for the public sociologist. It is necessary to engage directly with the discipline and attempt to shape the production of knowledge in the arenas where the discipline is shaped, the professional associations, the journals, and the textbooks.

[***]

SOURCE: Edward Webster, "Sociology in South Africa: Its Past, Present and Future," *Society in Transition* 35, no. 1 (2004): 27–41.

EDWARD WEBSTER is a professor of sociology and the Director of the Sociology of Work Unit at the University of the Witwatersrand, Johannesburg, South Africa. He is the author of Trade Unions and Democratisation in South Africa 1985–1996 *with G. Adler,* Cast in a Racial Mould—Labor Process and Trade Unionism in the Foundries, Essays in Southern African Labour History, *and* Change, Reform and Economic Growth in South Africa. *He is a founder of the* South African Labour Bulletin, *and is currently a secretary of the Research Committee on Labor Movements for the International Sociological Association.*

groups and even nations, as those suffering from economic globalization would blame others for their plight (Hirst and Thompson, 1992; Wagar, 1992).

On the other hand, a global economy could mean greater opportunity for everyone, as the benefits of modern technology stimulate worldwide economic growth. According to this more optimistic scenario, the more successful East Asian NIEs, such as Hong Kong, Taiwan, South Korea, and Singapore, are only a sign of things to come. Other NIEs such as Malaysia and Thailand will soon follow, along with China, Indonesia, Vietnam, and other Asian countries. India, the world's second most populous country, already boasts a middle class of around 200 million people, about a quarter of its total population (although roughly the same number live in poverty) (Kulkarni, 1993).

A countervailing trend, however, is the technology gap that divides rich and poor countries, which today appears to be widening, making it even more difficult for poor countries to catch up. The global technology gap is a result of the disparity in wealth between nations, but it also reinforces those disparities, widening the gap between rich and poor countries. Poor countries cannot easily afford modern technology—yet, in the absence of modern technology, they face major barriers to overcoming poverty. They are caught in a vicious downward spiral from which it is difficult to escape.

Jeffrey Sachs, director of the Center for International Development and professor of international trade at Harvard University, and a prominent adviser to many East European and developing countries, claims that the world is divided into three classes: technology innovators, technology adopters, and the technologically disconnected (Sachs, 2000).

Technology innovators are those regions that provide nearly all of the world's technological inventions; they account for no more than 15 percent of the world's population. *Technology adopters* are those regions that are able to adopt technologies invented elsewhere, applying them to production and consumption; they account for 50 percent of the world's population. Finally, the *technologically disconnected* are those regions that neither innovate nor adopt technologies developed elsewhere; they account for 35 percent of the world's population. Note that Sachs speaks of regions rather than countries: In today's increasingly borderless world, technology use (or exclusion) does not always respect national frontiers. For example, Sachs notes that technologically disconnected regions include "southern Mexico and pockets of tropical Central America; the Andean countries; most of tropical Brazil; tropical sub-Saharan Africa; most of the former Soviet Union aside from the areas nearest to European and Asian markets; landlocked parts of Asia such as the Ganges valley states of India; landlocked Laos and Cambodia; and the deep-interior states of China" (2000). These impoverished regions lack

access to markets or major ocean trading routes. They are caught in what Sachs terms a "poverty trap," plagued by "tropical infectious disease, low agricultural productivity and environmental degradation—all requiring technological solutions beyond their means" (2000).

Innovation requires a critical mass of ideas and technology to become self-sustaining. That is why the technological innovation in the United States tends to be concentrated in regions rich in universities and high-tech firms: for example, California's "Silicon Valley," which grew up around Stanford University and other educational and research institutions located south of San Francisco. Poor countries are ill equipped to develop such high-tech regions. Sachs calculates that forty-eight tropical or partly tropical countries, whose combined population totaled 750 million, accounted for only forty-seven of the fifty-one thousand U.S. patents granted to foreign inventors in 1997. Most poor countries lack even a science adviser to their government. Moreover, these countries are too poor to import computers, cell phones, fax machines, computerized factory machinery, or other kinds of high technology. Nor can they afford to license technology from the foreign companies that hold the patents.

What can be done to overcome the technological abyss that divides rich and poor countries? Sachs calls on wealthy, high-technology countries to provide much greater financial and technical assistance to poor countries than they now do. For example, lethal infectious diseases such as malaria, measles, and diarrhea claim million of lives each year in poor countries. The modern medical technology necessary to eradicate these illnesses would cost only $10 billion a year—less than $15 from every person who lives in a high-income country, if the cost were shared equally.

Sachs urges the governments of wealthy countries, along with international lending institutions, to provide loans and grants for scientific and technological development. Sachs notes that very little money is available to support research and development in poor countries. The World Bank, a major source of funding for development projects in poor countries, spends only $60 million a year supporting tropical, agricultural, or health research and development. By way of comparison, Merck, the giant pharmaceutical corporation, spends thirty-five times that much ($2.1 billion) for research and development for its own products. Even universities in wealthy nations could play a role, establishing overseas research and training institutes that would foster collaborative research projects. From computers and the Internet to biotechnology, the "wealth of nations" increasingly depends on modern information technology. As long as major regions of the world remain technologically disconnected, it seems unlikely that global poverty will be eradicated.

In the most optimistic view, the republics of the former Soviet Union, as well as the formerly socialist countries of Eastern Europe, will eventually advance into the ranks of the high-income countries. Economic growth will spread to Latin America, Africa, and the rest of the world. Because capitalism requires that workers be mobile, the remaining caste societies around the world will be replaced by class-based societies. These societies will experience enhanced opportunities for upward mobility.

What is the future of global inequality? It is difficult to be entirely optimistic for now. Global economic growth has slowed, and many of the once promising economies of Asia now seem to be in trouble. The Russian economy, in its move from socialism to capitalism, has encountered many pitfalls, leaving many Russians much poorer than ever. It remains to be seen whether the countries of the world will learn from one another and work together to create better lives for their peoples. What is certain is that the past quarter century has witnessed a global economic transformation of unprecedented magnitude. The effects of this transformation in the next quarter century will leave few lives on the planet untouched.

Study Outline

www.wwnorton.com/giddens5

Differences Between Countries

- The countries of the world can be stratified according to their per-person gross national product. Forty percent of the world's population live in low-income countries, compared with only 16 percent in high-income countries.
- An estimated 1.3 billion people in the world, or nearly one in four people, live in poverty today, an increase since the early 1980s. Many are the victims of discrimination based on race, ethnicity, or tribal affiliation.
- In general, people in high-income countries enjoy a far higher standard of living than their counterparts in low-income countries. They are likely to have more food to eat, less likely to starve or suffer from malnutrition, and likely to live longer. They are far more likely to be literate and educated and therefore have higher-skilled, higher-paying jobs. Additionally, they are less likely to have large families, and their children are much less likely to die in infancy of malnutrition or childhood diseases.

Can Poor Countries Become Rich?

- Such newly industrializing economies as Hong Kong, Singapore, Taiwan, and South Korea have experienced explosive economic growth since the mid-1970s. This growth is due partly to historical circumstances, to a lesser degree to the cultural characteristics of these countries, and most important, to the central role played by their governments. Whether this growth will continue is now in question, given the economic difficulties some of these countries currently face.

Theories of Global Inequality

- *Market-oriented theories of global inequality*, such as *modernization theory*, claim that cultural and institutional barriers to develop-ment explain the poverty of low-income societies. In this view, to eliminate poverty, fatalistic attitudes must be overcome, government meddling in economic affairs ended, and a high rate of savings and investment encouraged.
- *Dependency theories* claim that global poverty is the result of the exploitation of poor countries by wealthy ones. *Dependent development theory* argues that even though the economic fate of poor countries is ultimately determined by wealthy ones, some development is possible within dependent capitalistic relations.
- *World-systems theory* argues that the capitalist world system as a whole—not just individual countries—must be understood if we hope to make sense of global inequality. World-systems theory focuses on the relationships of *core, peripheral,* and *semiperipheral countries* in the global economy; long-term trends in the global economy; and *global commodity chains* that erase national borders.
- *State-centered theories* emphasize the role that governments can play in fostering economic development. These theories draw on the experience of the rapidly growing East Asian newly industrializing economies as an example.

The Future of Global Inequality

- No one can say for sure whether global inequality will increase or decrease in the future. It is possible that some leveling out of wages will occur worldwide, as wages decline in wealthy countries and rise in poor countries. It is also possible that all countries will someday prosper as the result of a unified global economy.

Key Concepts

colonialism (p. 263)
core country (p. 264)
dependent development (p. 263)
dependency theory (p. 263)

Review Questions

1. Which of the following is considered a high-income country?
   a. Singapore
   b. United States
   c. Taiwan
   d. All of the above

2. Most famine and hunger today are the result of:
   a. natural and social forces.
   b. natural force only.
   c. social force only.
   d. wars.

3. Economic growth in East Asia has its costs. These include:
   a. violent repression of labor and civil rights.
   b. terrible factory conditions.
   c. the exploitation of an increasingly female work force.
   d. all of the above.

4. Which country has the highest rate of economic growth?
   a. United States
   b. Canada
   c. China
   d. Brazil

5. Which theory argues that the world capitalist economic system must be understood as a single unit, not in terms of individual countries?
   a. State-centered development theory
   b. Modernization theory
   c. Dependency theory
   d. World-systems theory

6. Which theory argues that the poverty of low-income countries stems from their exploitation by wealthy countries and the multinational corporations that are based in wealthy countries?
   a. State-centered development theory
   b. Modernization theory
   c. Dependency theory
   d. World-systems theory

7. Of the estimated 26 million people worldwide infected with HIV/AIDS, what percent live in developing countries?
   a. 5 percent
   b. 35 percent

c. 75 percent
   d. 95 percent

8. What is the relationship between income and fertility at the national level?
   a. Positive
   b. Negative
   c. No relationship
   d. Can be either positive or negative

9. What percent of the world's population lives in poverty?
   a. About 75 percent
   b. About 50 percent
   c. About 25 percent
   d. About 10 percent

10. _____ claims that cultural and institutional barriers to development explain the poverty of low-income societies.
    a. Dependency development theory
    b. Modernization theory
    c. Dependency theory
    d. World-systems theory

Thinking Sociologically Exercises

1. Concisely review the four theories offered in this chapter that explain why there are gaps between nations' economic developments and resulting global inequality: market-oriented theory, dependency theory, world-systems theory, and state-centered theories. Briefly discuss the distinctive characteristics of each theory and how each differs from the others. Which theory do you feel offers the most explanatory power to addressing economic developmental gaps?

2. This chapter states that global economic inequality has personal relevance and importance to people in advanced, affluent economies. Briefly review this argument. Explain carefully whether you were persuaded by it or not.

Data Exercises

www.wwnorton.com/giddens5
Keyword: Data9

- The nations of the world are not all equal when it comes to national wealth, but have you ever stopped to think about why such inequalities exist? Or what consequences these differences have in terms of patterns of consumption and social development? The data exercise for this chapter will give you an opportunity to learn more about global inequalities and to evaluate the different theoretical perspectives on global stratification.

Gender Differences: Nature versus Nurture

Think about whether differences between women and men are the result of biological differences or social and cultural influences.

Forms of Gender Inequality

Recognize that gender differences are a part of our social structure and create inequalities between women and men. Learn the forms these inequalities take, particularly in the workplace, the family, the educational system, the political system, and as violence against women.

Gender Inequality in Global Perspective

Understand the ways in which women around the world experience economic and political inequality.

Analyzing Gender Inequality

Think about various explanations for gender inequality and apply them to a real-life example. Learn some feminist theories about how to achieve gender equality.

Why Gender Inequality Matters

CHAPTER TEN

GENDER INEQUALITY

round midnight one cold night in December, a little before the end of the second shift, Andrea Ellington is standing by the Coke machine in the workers' lounge, cleaning out her oversized pocketbook. She empties its contents, which begin with a gold plastic makeup bag, a wallet, and a bunch of monthly bills. "I gotta go wake my five-year-old daughter up at my mother's house," she says as she opens the makeup bag. "Then I go to the other baby-sitter and get my baby twins. Then I take them home and they've gotta go back to sleep, try to go back to sleep. By the time my daughter gets back to sleep, it's time for her to get back up again" (Interview by the authors).

An African American woman of twenty-three, Andrea Ellington has three children to support on a low-rung clerical salary of $20,000 per year. She has been working at a Chicago law firm for four years; she had taken the job believing that with hard work, eventually she could advance enough to move her family out of public housing, her foremost goal.

Most of the five hundred or so employees in the law office where she works are not attorneys but "support staff," who work in one of many departments at the center of the floors, surrounded by plush attorneys' offices on the perimeter. The Network Center where she types is solely a nighttime word-processing department, with shifts from 4 P.M. to midnight and midnight to 8 A.M. The people who work as word processors are all women. They sit at computer terminals in one of four clusters separated by gray partitions. Almost all of these women who work at night are also rearing children during the day. Most live far from the law firm's gleaming downtown building.

Balancing the commitments of work and family is not only a challenge in terms of time but also money. Raising three children on her modest income, Andrea lives from paycheck to paycheck. She seeks out extra work to help her get by with her everyday responsibilities. As she says, "[working] overtime has helped me pay bills on time, buy clothes for my children, and buy food that I normally have had to wait until each paycheck to get." As a result of Andrea's persistence, her supervisor assigned her to work an extra eight hours of overtime per week, on Sundays. Andrea came to work for the first two Sundays and then began missing her weekend assignments when she couldn't find a baby-sitter for her three children. When her supervisor learned of the absences, she canceled the overtime.

Many people who encounter someone like Andrea Ellington might make certain assumptions about her life. They might assume, for example, that a disproportionate number of women become typists and word processors because it is natural for women to have certain kinds of occupations, including secretarial jobs. They might also assume that mothers should be responsible for taking care of children. Finally, they might assume that Andrea's poverty and low position in society are a result of her natural abilities. It is the job of sociology to analyze these assumptions and allow us to take a much wider view of our society and people like Andrea. Sociology allows us to understand why women are likely to work in low-paying clerical jobs, why women are likely to spend more time on child care, and why women on the whole are less powerful in society than men. Explaining the differences and inequalities between women and men in a society is now one of the most central topics in sociology.

In this chapter, we will explore a sociological approach to gender differences and gender inequality. Gender is a way for society to divide people into two categories: "men" and "women." According to this socially created division, men and women have different identities and social roles. In other words, men and women are expected to think and act in certain different ways. Since in almost all societies, men's roles are valued more than are women's roles, gender also serves as a social status. Men and women are not only different, but also unequal in terms of power, prestige, and wealth. Despite the advances that many women have made in the United States and other Western societies, this remains true today. Sociologists are interested in explaining not only how society differentiates between women and men, but also how these differences serve as the basis for social inequalities (Chafetz, 1990). Some sociologists are also concerned about the ways in which women can achieve positions of equality in society.

In this chapter, we will first look at the origins of gender differences, assessing the debate over the role of biological versus social influences on the formation of gender roles. We will also look to other cultures for evidence on this debate. We will then review the various forms of gender inequality that exist in American society. In this section, we will focus on the prominent social institutions of the workplace, the family, the educational system, and the political system. We will also examine how women are so often the targets of sexual violence. Next, we will examine how economic and political inequality affects women all over the world. We will review the various forms of feminism and assess prospects for future change toward a gender equal society. We will then analyze some theories of gender inequality and apply them to the circumstances of Andrea's life. We conclude the chapter by looking at the role of women around the world as we enter the twenty-first century.

Gender Differences: Nature versus Nurture

We begin by inquiring into the origins of the differences between boys and girls, men and women. The nature-nurture debate, noted earlier in Chapter 3, appears again with some force here. Scholars are divided about the degree to which inborn biological characteristics have an enduring impact on our gender identities as "feminine" or "masculine" and the social roles based on those identities. The debate is really about how much learning there is. No one any longer supposes that our behavior is instinctive in the sense in which the sexual activity of many lower animals—like the celebrated birds and bees—is instinctive. Some scholars, however, allow more prominence than others to social influences in analyzing gender differences.

Before we review these competing theories, we need to make an important distinction between sex and gender. While **sex** refers to physical differences of the body, **gender** concerns the psychological, social, and cultural differences between males and females. The distinction between sex and gender is fundamental, since many differences between males and females are not biological in origin.

The Role of Biology

How much are differences in the behavior of women and men the result of sex rather than gender? In other words, how much are they the result of biological differences? The opinions of researchers are divided. Some hold that innate differences of behavior between women and men appear in some form in all cultures and that the findings of sociobiology point strongly in this direction. Such researchers are likely to draw attention to the fact, for example, that in almost all cultures, men rather than women take part in hunting and warfare. Surely, they argue, this indicates that men possess biologically based tendencies toward aggression that women lack. In looking at the case of the word processors, they might point out that typing is a more passive occupation than being a bicycle messenger (an equivalent job category within the firm), which requires more physical strength and aggressiveness in traffic.

Most sociologists are unconvinced by these arguments. The level of aggressiveness of men, they say, varies widely among different cultures, and women are expected to be more passive or gentle in some cultures than in others (Elshtain, 1981). Theories of "natural difference" are often grounded in data on animal behavior, critics point out, rather than in anthropological or historical evidence about human behavior, which reveals variation over time and place. In the majority of cultures, most women spend a significant part of their lives caring for children and therefore cannot readily take part in hunting or war.

Although the hypothesis that biological factors determine behavior patterns in men and women cannot be dismissed out of hand, nearly a century of research to identify the physiological origins of such an influence has been unsuccessful. There is no evidence of the mechanisms that would link such biological forces with the complex social behaviors exhibited by human men and women (Connell, 1987). Theories that see individuals as complying with some kind of innate predisposition neglect the vital role of social interaction in shaping human behavior.

What does the evidence show? One possible source of information is the differences in hormonal makeup between the sexes. Some have claimed that the male sex hormone, testosterone, is associated with the male propensity to violence (Rutter and Giller, 1984). Research has indicated, for instance, that if male monkeys are castrated at birth, they become less aggressive; conversely, female monkeys given testosterone will become more aggressive than normal females. However, it has also been found that providing monkeys with opportunities to dominate others actually increases the testosterone level. Aggressive behavior may thus affect the production of the hormone, rather than the hormone's causing increased aggression.

Another possible source of evidence is direct observations of animal behavior. Writers who connect male aggression with biological influences often stress male aggressiveness among the higher animals. If we look at the behavior of chimpanzees, they say, male animals are invariably more aggressive than females. Yet there are in fact large differences between types of animals. Among gibbons, for instance, there are few noticeable differences in aggression between the sexes. Moreover, many

Many children's toys may promote gender stereotyping.

female apes or monkeys are highly aggressive in some situations, such as when their young are threatened.

Another source of information comes from the experience of identical twins. Identical twins derive from a single egg and have *exactly the same* genetic makeup. In one particular case, one of a pair of identical male twins was seriously injured while being circumcised, and the decision was made to reconstruct his genitals as a female. He was thereafter raised as a girl. The twins at six years old demonstrated typical male and female traits as found in Western culture. The little girl enjoyed playing with other girls, helped with the housework, and wanted to get married when she grew up. The boy preferred the company of other boys, his favorite toys were cars and trucks, and he wanted to become a firefighter or police officer.

For some time, this case was treated as a conclusive demonstration of the overriding influence of social learning on gender differences. However, when the girl was a teenager, she was interviewed during a television program, and the interview showed that she felt some unease about her gender identity, even perhaps that she was "really" a boy after all. She had by then learned of her unusual background, and this knowledge may very well have been responsible for this altered perception of herself (Ryan, 1985).

Gender Socialization

Another route to take in understanding the origins of gender differences is the study of **gender socialization**, the learning of gender roles with the help of social agencies such as the family and the media (see also Chapter 4). Such an approach makes a distinction between biological sex and social gender—an infant is born with the first and develops the second. Through contact with various agencies of socialization, both primary and secondary, children gradually internalize the social norms and expectations that are seen to correspond with their sex. Gender differences are not biologically determined; they are culturally produced. According to this view, gender inequalities result because men and women are socialized into different roles.

Theories of gender socialization have been favored by functionalists, who see boys and girls as learning "sex roles" and the male and female identities—masculinity and femininity—that accompany them. They are guided in this process by positive and negative *sanctions*, socially applied forces that reward or restrain behavior. For example, a small boy could be positively sanctioned in his behavior ("What a brave boy you are!") or be the recipient of negative sanction ("Boys don't play with dolls"). These positive and negative reinforcements aid boys and girls in learning and conforming to expected sex roles. If an individual develops gender practices that do not correspond with his or her biological sex—that is, he or she is deviant—the explanation is seen to reside in inadequate or irregular socialization. According to this functionalist view, socializing agencies contribute to the maintenance of social order by overseeing the smooth gender socialization of new generations.

This rigid interpretation of sex roles and socialization has been criticized on a number of fronts. Many writers argue that gender socialization is not an inherently smooth process; different agencies such as the family, schools, and peer groups may be at odds with one another. Moreover, socialization theories ignore the ability of individuals to reject, or modify, the social expectations surrounding sex roles.

It is important to remember that humans are not passive objects or unquestioning recipients of gender programming, as some sociologists have suggested. People are active agents who create and modify roles for themselves. Although we should be skeptical of any wholesale adoption of the sex roles approach, many studies have shown that to some degree gender identities *are* a result of social influences.

In order to understand this argument, let's take a look at the following two scenes. Two newborn infants lie in the nursery of a hospital maternity ward. One, a male baby, is wrapped in a blue blanket, the other, a female, is in a pink blanket. Both babies are only a few hours old and are being seen by their grandparents for the first time. The conversation between one pair of grandparents runs along these lines:

Grandma A: *There he is—our first grandchild, and a boy.*
Grandpa A: *Hey, isn't he a hefty little fellow? Look at that fist he's making. He's going to be a regular little fighter, that guy is.* (Grandpa A smiles and throws out a boxing jab to his grandson.) *At-a-boy!*
Grandma A: *I think he looks like you. He has your strong chin. Oh, look, he's starting to cry.*

Grandpa A: *Yeah—just listen to that set of lungs. He's going to be some boy.*
Grandma A: *Poor thing—he's still crying.*
Grandpa A: *It's okay. It's good for him. He's exercising and it will develop his lungs.*
Grandma A: *Let's go and congratulate the parents. I know they're thrilled about little Fred. They wanted a boy first.*
Grandpa A: *Yeah, and they were sure it would be a boy too, what with all that kicking and thumping going on even before he got here.*

When they depart to congratulate the parents, the grandparents of the other child arrive. The dialogue between them goes like this:

Grandma B: *There she is . . . the only one with a pink bow taped to her head. Isn't she darling.*
Grandpa B: *Yeah—isn't she little. Look at how tiny her fingers are. Oh, look—she's trying to make a fist.*
Grandma B: *Isn't she sweet . . . you know, I think she looks a little like me.*
Grandpa B: *Yeah, she sorta does. She has your chin.*
Grandma B: *Oh, look, she's starting to cry.*
Grandpa B: *Maybe we better call the nurse to pick her up or change her or something.*
Grandma B: *Yes, let's. Poor little girl.* (To the baby) *There, there, we'll try to help you.*
Grandpa B: *Let's find the nurse. I don't like to see her cry . . .*
Grandma B: *Hmm. I wonder when they will have their next one. I know Fred would like a son, but little Fredericka is well and healthy. After all, that's what really matters.*
Grandpa B: *They're young yet. They have time for more kids. I'm thankful too that she's healthy.*
Grandma B: *I don't think they were surprised when it was a girl anyway . . . she was carrying so low.* (Walum, 1977)

The contrast between the two sets of conversations sounds so exaggerated that it is tempting to think they were made up. In fact, they are composed of transcripts of actual dialogue recorded in a maternity ward. The very first question usually asked of a parent—in Western culture at least—is, "Is it a boy or a girl?" Our images of others are fundamentally structured around gender identity. In turn, social and cultural expectations for each gender create expectations about the roles and identities one should assume.

People create gender through social interactions with others, such as family members, friends, and colleagues. As we just saw, this process begins at birth when doctors, nurses, and family members—the first to see an infant—assign the person to a gender category on the basis of physical characteristics. Babies are immediately dressed in a way that marks the sex category: "parents don't want to be constantly asked if their child is a boy or a girl" (Lorber, 1994). Once the child is marked as male or female, everyone who interacts with the child will treat it in accordance with its gender. They do so on the basis of the society's assumptions, which lead people to treat women and men differently, even as opposites (Renzetti and Curran, 1995).

Clearly, gender socialization is very powerful, and challenges to it can be upsetting. Once a gender is "assigned," society expects individuals to act like "females" and "males." It is in the practices of everyday life that these expectations are fulfilled and reproduced (Bourdieu, 1990; Lorber, 1994).

The Social Construction of Gender

In recent years, socialization and gender role theories have been criticized by a growing number of sociologists. Rather than seeing sex as biologically determined and gender as culturally learned, they argue that we should view *both* sex and gender as socially constructed products. Not only is gender a purely social creation that lacks a fixed essence, but the human body itself is subject to social forces that shape and alter it in various ways.

According to such a perspective, writers who focus on gender roles and role learning implicitly accept that there *is* a biological basis to gender differences. In the socialization approach, a biological distinction between the sexes provides a framework that becomes culturally elaborated in society itself. In contrast to this, theorists who believe in the **social construction of gender** reject all biological bases for gender differences. Gender identities emerge, they argue, in relation to perceived sex differences in society and in turn help to shape those differences. For example, a society in which ideas of masculinity are characterized by physical strength and tough attitudes will encourage men to cultivate a specific body image and set of mannerisms. In other words, gender identities and sex differences are inextricably linked within individual human bodies (Connell, 1987; Butler, 1989; Scott and Morgan, 1993).

Gender Identity in Everyday Life

Our conceptions of gender identity are formed so early in life that as adults we mainly take them for granted. Yet gender is more than learning to act like a girl or boy. Gender differences are something we live with every day.

In other words, gender as a physical concept does not exist; we all, as some sociologists put it, "do gender" in our daily interactions with others (West and Zimmerman, 1987). For instance, Jan Morris, the celebrated travel writer, used to be a man. As James Morris, she was a member of the British expedition, led by Sir Edmund Hillary, that successfully climbed Mount Everest. She was, in fact, a very "manly" man—a race

This photo (top), dated November 30, 1952, shows George Jorgensen before his sex change. After he was discharged from the U.S. Army he traveled to Copenhagen, Denmark, where he had a sex change operation. After the operation he changed his name to Christine. Christine Jorgensen (bottom), returning from a nightclub engagement in Cuba in 1953.

car driver and an athlete. Yet she had always felt herself to be a woman in a male body. So she underwent a sex-change operation and lived the rest of her life as a woman.

Jan Morris had to learn how to do gender when she discovered how differently she was expected to behave as a woman, rather than as a man. As she says, there is "no aspect of existence" that is not gendered. But she did not notice this until she changed her sex.

> It amuses me to consider, for instance, when I am taken out to lunch by one of my more urbane men friends, that not so many years ago th[e] waiter would have treated *me* as he is now treating *him*. Then he would have greeted me with respectful seriousness. Now he unfolds my napkin with a playful flourish, as if to humor me. Then he would have taken my order with grave concern, now he expects me to say something frivolous (and I do). (Morris, 1974)

The subtle ways in which we do gender are so much a part of our lives that we don't notice them until they are missing or radically altered.

This differentiation between the roles and identities that society creates for men and women occurs not only in face-to-face interaction, but is also part of society's institutions, such as the economy, political system, educational system, religions, and family forms. Because gender is so pervasive in structuring social life, gender statuses must be clearly differentiated if society is to function in an orderly manner. However, gender differentiation can also be the basis for inequalities between men and women (Lorber, 1994; West and Fenstermaker, 1995).

Findings from Other Cultures

If gender differences were mostly the result of biology, then we could expect that gender roles would not vary much from culture to culture. However, one set of findings that helps show gender roles are in fact socially constructed comes from anthropologists, who have studied gender in other times and cultures.

NEW GUINEA

In her classic New Guinea study, *Sex and Temperament in Three Primitive Societies*, Margaret Mead (1963) observed wide variability among gender role prescriptions—and such marked differences from those in the United States—that any claims to the universality of gender roles had to be rejected. Mead studied three separate tribes in New Guinea, which var-ied widely in their gender roles. In Arapesh society, both males and females generally had characteristics and behaviors that would typically be associated with the Western female role. Both sexes among the Arapesh were passive, gentle, unaggressive, and emotionally responsive to the needs of others. In contrast, Mead found that in another New Guinea group, the Mundugumor, both the males and females were characteristically aggressive, suspicious, and, from a Western observer's perspective, excessively cruel, especially toward children. In both cultures, however, men and women were expected to behave very similarly.

Mead then studied the Tchambuli tribe of New Guinea. The gender roles of the males and females were almost exactly reversed from the roles traditionally assigned to males and females in Western society. Mead reported in her autobiography that "among the Tchambuli the expected relations between men and women reversed those that are characteristic of our own culture. For it was Tchambuli women who were brisk and hearty, who managed the business affairs of life, and worked comfortably in large cooperative groups" (1972).

The children also exhibited these characteristics. Girls were considered the brightest and most competent and displayed "the most curiosity and the freest expression of intelligence." The Tchambuli boys "were already caught up in the rivalrous, catty, and individually competitive life of the men" (Mead, 1972). Mead also reported that while the women managed the affairs of the family, the men were engaged differently: "Down by the lake shore in ceremonial houses the men carved and painted, gossiped and had temper tantrums, and played out their rivalries" (1972).

THE !KUNG

Another example can be found among the !Kung of the Kalahari desert. Although "men hunt and women gather" in this society, a vast majority of its food comes from the gathering activities of women (see Draper, as cited in Renzetti, 2000). Indeed, !Kung women are respected for their specialized knowledge of the bush: "Successful gathering over the years requires the ability to discriminate among hundreds of edible and inedible species of plants at various stages in their life cycle" (Draper, 1975). In addition, women return from their gathering expeditions armed not only with food for the community but also with valuable information for hunters. Draper noted that "women are skilled in reading the signs of the bush, and they take careful note of animal tracks, their age, and the direction of movement. . . . In general, the men take advantage of women's reconnaissance and query them routinely on the evidence of game movements, the location of water and the like" (1975).

Due to the non-confrontational parenting practices of the !Kung, who oppose violent conflict and physical punishment, children learn that aggressive behavior will not be tolerated by either men or women. The !Kung do have specific sex roles, but it is very common for both men and women to engage in child care. Whereas in the United States it is still common for boys and girls to have very distinct upbringings, this is not true in the !Kung society (See Draper, as cited in Renzetti, 2000).

SUDHEST ISLAND

Recent anthropological evidence continues to contradict the idea that gender inequality is universal. The anthropologist Maria Lepowsky of the University of Wisconsin did ethnographic research with the people of Sudhest Island, 200 miles south of Papua, New Guinea in the South Pacific. After living with them for two years, she concluded that the inhabitants of the island, the Vanatinai society, "offers any adult, regardless of sex or kin group, the opportunity of excelling at prestigious activities" (Lepowsky, 1990, as cited in Renzetti, 2000). Men even participate in child care. On the other hand, even here she did not find absolute equality: Women tend to sweep up pig excrement whereas men hunt wild boar.

MULTIPLE GENDERS

The understanding that only two genders (i.e. male and female) exist is not true among all societies. The Spaniards who came to both North and South America in the seventeenth century noticed men in the native tribes who had taken on the mannerisms of women, as well as women who occupied male roles. Indeed, many citizens of the United States who are intolerant of same-sex marriage are surprised to learn that Native Americans have a long tradition in which men enact female roles and women enact male roles, and which allows same-sex marriage. This practice has now been documented by anthropologists in over 155 Native American tribes.

A person occupying an opposite gender role is called a *berdache*. But many scholars are unhappy with this term because its derivation does not come from the Native American cultures themselves (it derives from Persia), and some believe it has a negative connotation, not unlike "faggot." Others argue that it is more often a substitute for lover or boyfriend (Roscoe, 2000). In any event, some anthropologists have tried to replace *berdache* with "two-spirit." In fact, "two-spirit" has become a contemporary label used by Native Americans who are gay, lesbian, bisexual, and transgendered.

A *we'wha* (or *berdache*) of the Zuni people of New Mexico.

Berdaches are not the counterpart of transsexuals or transvestites in the United States, however. Roscoe (1991) has studied Zuni *berdaches* and noted that although *berdaches* technically do "cross-dress," their cross-dressing is routine, public, and without erotic motives. Moreover, *berdaches* are not necessarily homosexual; rather, some are heterosexual, some homosexual, and others sexually oriented toward other *berdaches*.

In one society, Roscoe found that both males and females have characteristics typically associated with the female role in the West. In another group, both males and females are aggressive. In both cultures, men and women are expected to behave similarly. These findings demonstrate that culture—not biology—is at the root of gender differences. There was a time in the development of feminist approaches when gender roles and gender socialization were the dominant concepts in understanding why women tended to cluster in particular occupations.

In recent years, however, sociologists have noted that while society teaches people to assume certain "masculine" or "feminine" gender roles, such an approach does not tell us where these gender roles come from or how they can be changed. For this, we need to look at the way that gender is built into the institutions of society (Lorber, 1994). For example, we need to know how the schools Andrea attended and the law firm Andrea works in operate to establish "patterns of expectations" that lead people to assume certain roles (Lorber, 1994).

Forms of Gender Inequality

Anthropologists and historians have found that most groups, collectives, and societies throughout history differentiate between women's and men's societal roles. Although there are considerable variations in the respective roles of women and men in different cultures, there are few instances of a society in which women are more powerful than men. Women everywhere are primarily concerned with child rearing and the maintenance of the home, while political and military activities tend to be resoundingly male. Nowhere in the world do men have primary responsibility for the rearing of children. Conversely, there are few if any cultures in which women are charged with the main responsibility for the herding of large animals, the hunting of large game, deep-sea fishing, or plow agriculture (Brown, 1977). Just because women and men perform different tasks or have different responsibilities in societies does not necessarily mean that women are unequal to men. However, if the work and activities of women and men are valued differently, then the division of labor between them can become the basis for unequal gender relations. In modern societies, the division of labor between the sexes has become less clear cut than it was in premodern cultures, but men still outnumber women in all spheres of power and influence.

Male dominance in a society is usually referred to as **patriarchy**. Although men are favored in almost all of the world's societies, the degree of patriarchy varies. In the United States, women have made tremendous progress, but several forms of gender inequality still exist.

Sociologists define **gender inequality** as the difference in the status, power, and prestige women and men have in

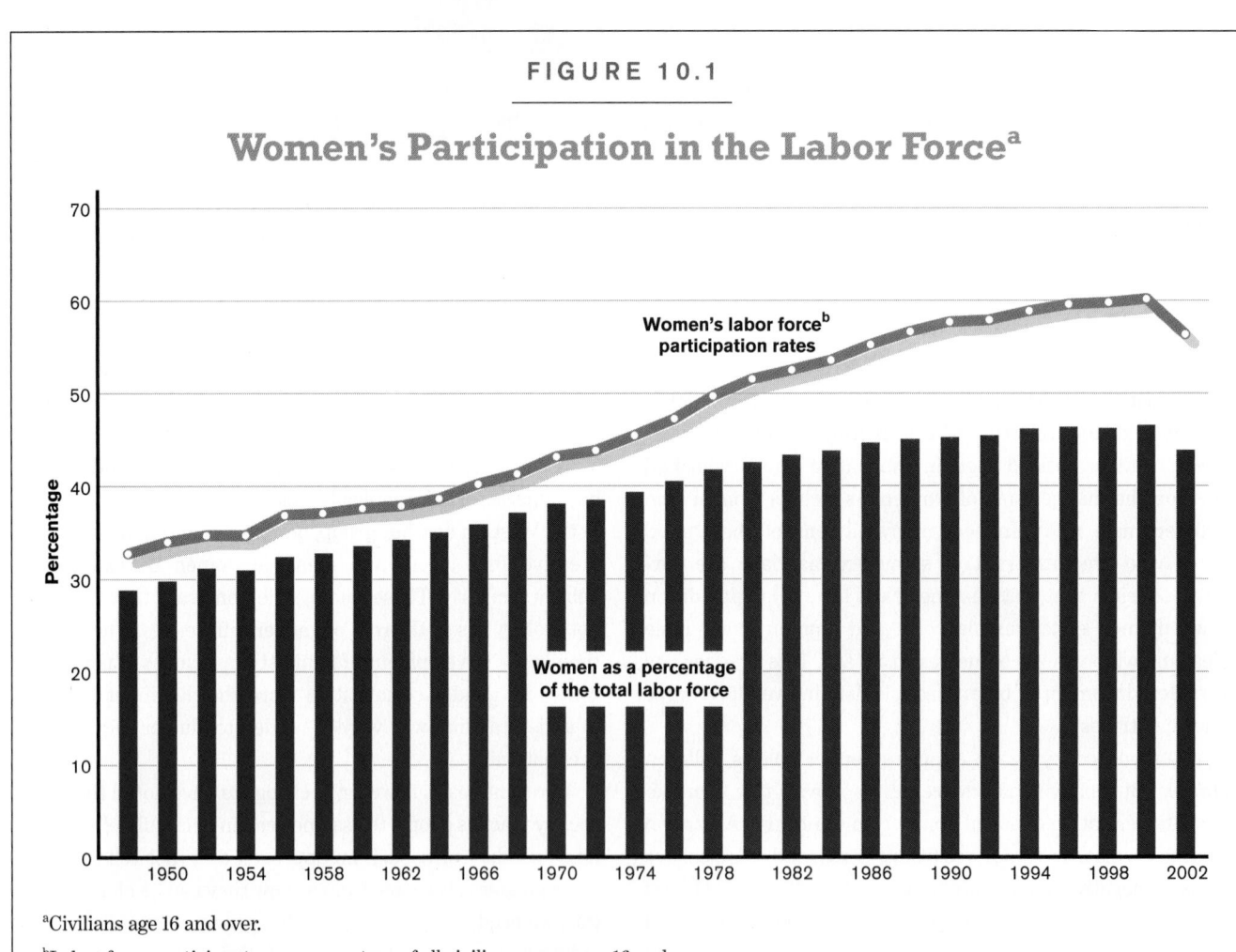

FIGURE 10.1

Women's Participation in the Labor Force[a]

Women's labor force[b] participation rates

Women as a percentage of the total labor force

[a]Civilians age 16 and over.

[b]Labor force participants as a percentage of all civilian women age 16 and over.

SOURCE: U.S. Bureau of Labor Statistics, "Household Data, Annual Averages," Tables 1 and 2, www.bls.gov/cps/cpsaat1.pdf and www.bls.gov/cps/cpsaat2.pdf.

groups, collectives, and societies. In thinking about gender inequality between men and women, we can ask the following questions: Do women and men have equal access to valued societal resources—for example, food, money, power, and time? Second, do women and men have similar life options? Third, are women's and men's roles and activities valued similarly? We will turn to look at the various forms of gender inequality in the workplace, in the home, in education systems, and in politics, as well as in the violence practiced on women. As you read through this section, keep the above questions in mind.

Women and the Workplace

Rates of employment of women outside the home, for all classes, were quite low until well into the twentieth century. Even as late as 1910 in the United States, more than a third of gainfully employed women were maids or house servants. The female labor force consisted mainly of young, single women and children. When women or girls worked in factories or offices, employers often sent their wages straight home to their parents. When they married, they withdrew from the labor force.

Since then, women's participation in the paid labor force has risen more or less continuously, especially in the past fifty years (see Figure 10.1). In 1996, 59 percent of women age sixteen and older were in the labor force. In contrast, 38 percent of working-age women were in the labor force in 1960. An even greater change in the rate of labor-force participation has occurred among married mothers of young children. In 1978, only 14 percent of married women with preschool-age children (under six years old) worked full time year round, yet this figure increased to 35 percent by 1998 (see Figure 10.2) (Cohen and Bianchi, 1999).

How can we explain this increase? One force behind women's increased entry into the labor force was the increase in demand, since 1940, for clerical and service workers like Andrea, as the U.S. economy expanded and changed (Oppenheimer, 1970). From 1940 until the mid- to late 1960s, labor-force activity increased among women who were past their prime child-rearing years. During the 1970s and 1980s, as the marriage age rose, fertility declined, and women's educational attainment increased,

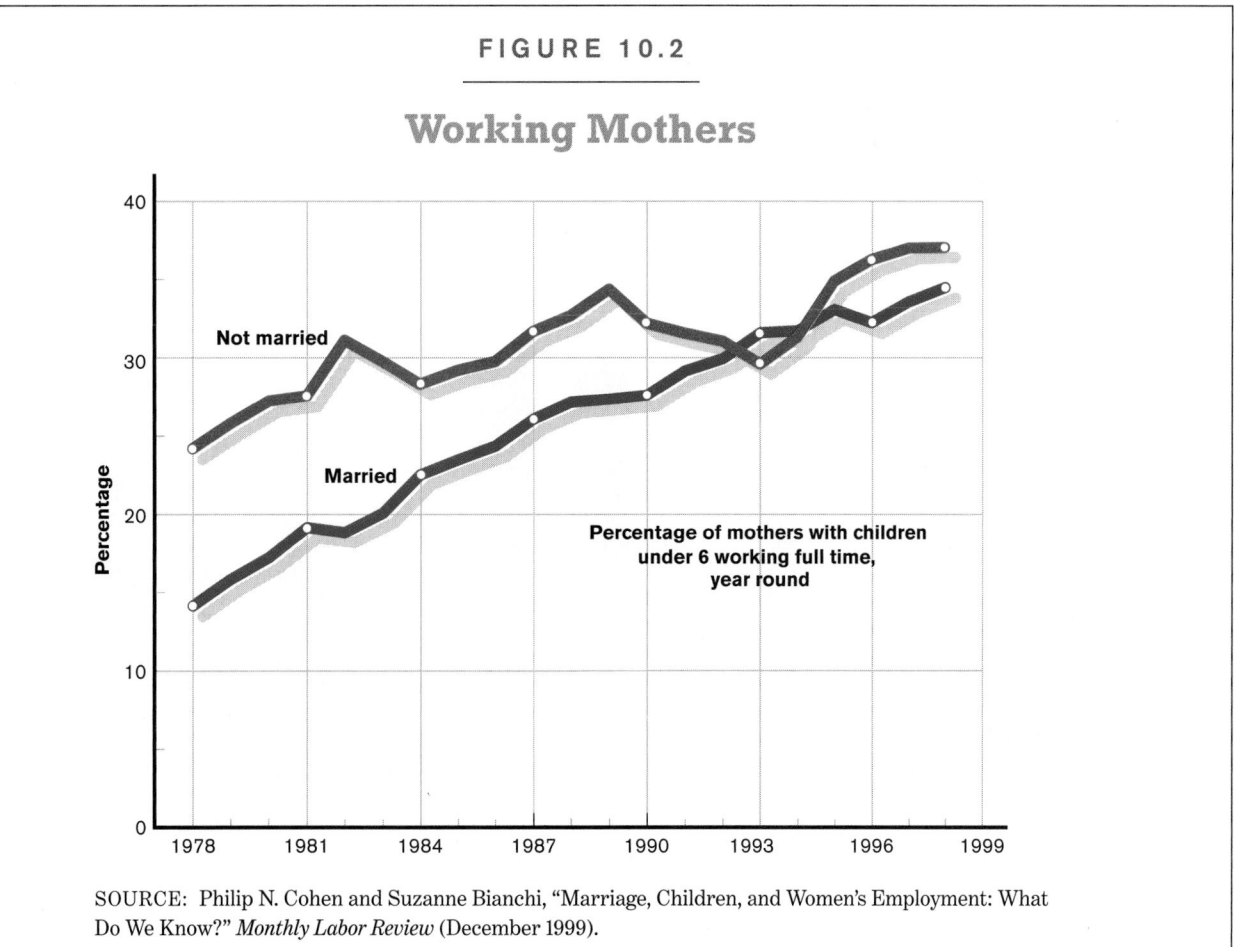

FIGURE 10.2

Working Mothers

SOURCE: Philip N. Cohen and Suzanne Bianchi, "Marriage, Children, and Women's Employment: What Do We Know?" *Monthly Labor Review* (December 1999).

the growth in labor force participation spread to younger women. Many women now postpone family formation to complete their education and establish themselves in the labor force. Despite family obligations, today a majority of women of all educational levels now work outside the home during their child-rearing years (Spain and Bianchi, 1996).

Inequalities at Work

Until recently, women workers were overwhelmingly concentrated in routine, poorly paid occupations. The fate of the occupation of clerk (office worker) provides a good illustration. In 1850 in the United States, clerks held responsible positions, requiring accountancy skills and carrying managerial responsibilities; fewer than 1 percent were women. The twentieth century saw a general mechanization of office work (starting with the introduction of the typewriter in the late nineteenth century), accompanied by a marked downgrading of the status of clerk—together with a related occupation, secretary—into a routine, low-paid occupation. Women filled these occupations

as the pay and prestige of such jobs declined. Today, most secretaries and clerks are women.

Studies of particular types of occupations have shown how **gender typing** occurs in the workplace. Expanding areas of work of a lower-level kind, such as secretarial positions or retail sales, draw in a substantial proportion of women. These jobs are poorly paid and hold few career prospects. Men with good educational qualifications aspire to something higher, while others choose blue-collar work. Once an occupation has become gender typed—once it is seen as mainly a "woman's job"—inertia sets in. Job hierarchies are

built around the assumption that men will occupy superior positions, while a stream of women will flow through subordinate jobs. Employers are guided in future hiring decisions by gender labels. And the very conditions of most female jobs lead to adaptive responses on the part of women—low job commitment, few career ambitions, high turnover, seeking alternative rewards in social relations—which fortify the image of women as suitable for only lower-level jobs. (Lowe, 1987)

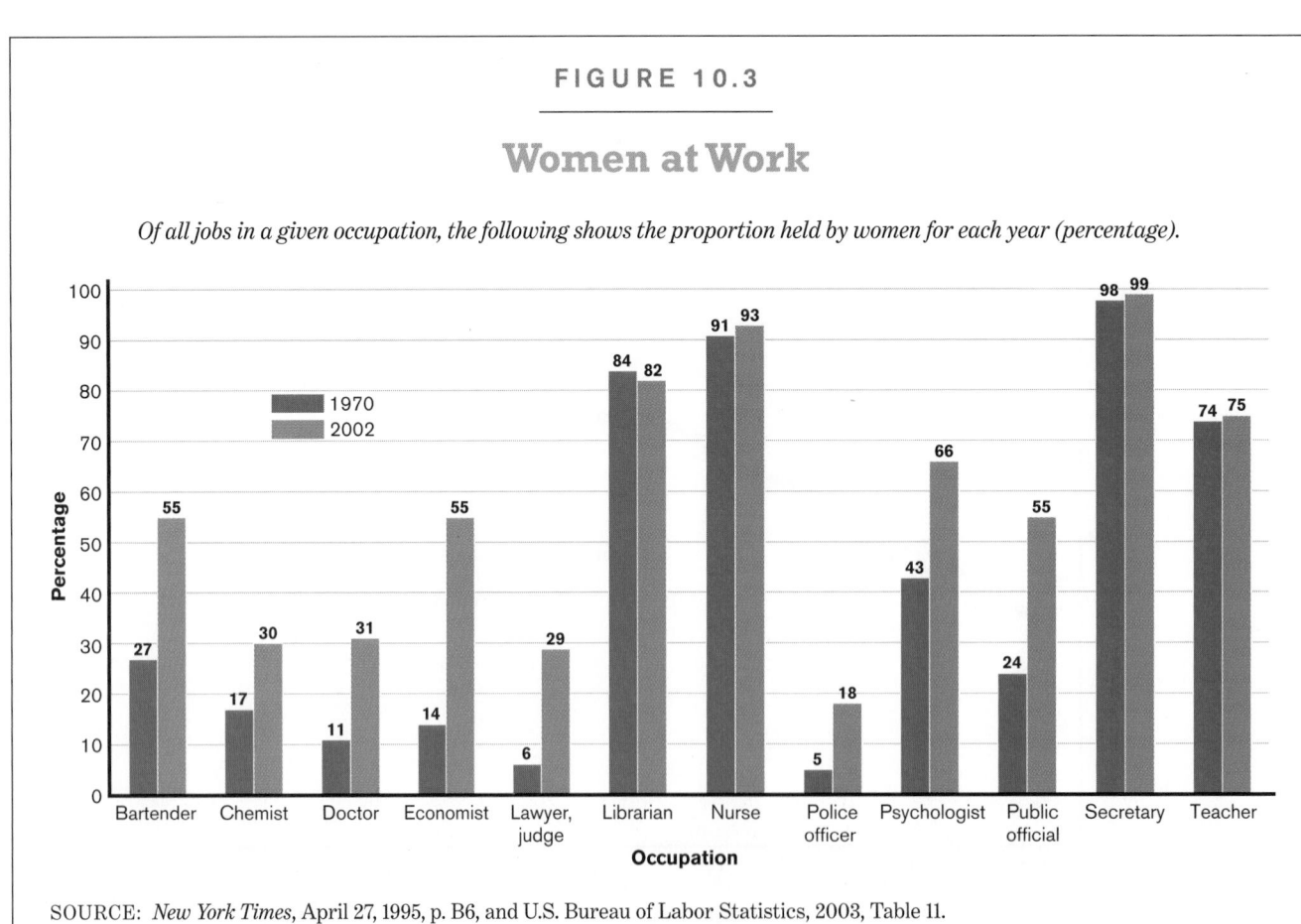

FIGURE 10.3

Women at Work

Of all jobs in a given occupation, the following shows the proportion held by women for each year (percentage).

SOURCE: *New York Times*, April 27, 1995, p. B6, and U.S. Bureau of Labor Statistics, 2003, Table 11.

These social conditions often tend to reinforce outlooks produced by early gender socialization. Women may grow up believing that they should put their husband's career before their own. (Men also are frequently brought up to believe the same thing.)

Women have recently made some inroads into occupations once defined as "men's jobs" (see Figure 10.3). By the 1990s, women constituted a majority of workers in previously male-dominated professions such as accounting, journalism, psychology, public service, and bartending. In fields such as law, medicine, and engineering, their proportion has risen substantially since 1970. In 2003, a woman was more likely to be in a managerial or professional job than a clerical or service position.

Another important economic trend of the past thirty years was the narrowing of the gender gap in earnings. Between 1970 and 2002, the ratio of women's to men's earnings among full-time, year-round workers increased from 62 to 78 percent (see Table 10.1). Moreover, this ratio increased among all races and ethnic groups. During the 1980s, women's hourly wages as a percentage of men's increased from 64 to 79 percent, weekly earnings rose from 63 to 75 percent, and the ratio of annual earnings among all workers (not just those working full time) increased from 46 to 61 percent (Spain and Bianchi, 1996). Despite the lessening of the gender gap in pay, men still earn substantially more than women (see Figure 10.4). Several competing theories have been offered by economists and sociologists to explain this gap.

The Gender Pay Gap: The Sociological Debate

The "gender gap" in pay is a widely recognized fact. Even as recently as 2002, women who worked full time year round (i.e., more than thirty-five hours per week for fifty-two weeks per year) earned only 78 percent as much as men. What could account for this discrepancy?

Sex segregation or gender typing is viewed by many sociologists as a cause of the "gender gap" in earnings. Sex segregation refers to the fact that men and women are concentrated in different occupations. For instance, in 1989, jobs that were over 80 percent female included secretary, child-care worker, hairdresser, cashier, bookkeeper, telephone operator, receptionist, typist, elementary school teacher, librarian, and nurse. Jobs that were over 80 percent male included doctor, lawyer, dentist, taxi driver, plumber, electrician, carpenter, firefighter, auto mechanic, machinist, and truck driver (Reskin and Padavic, 1994).

TABLE 10.1

Women's Earnings Compared with Men's

Although the earnings gap between women and men is narrowing, it remains substantial. It is also significant that since the early 1990s, the gap has remained fairly constant. Analysts wonder whether this is temporary or permanent. The table shows what women earned for each dollar earned by men.

YEAR	EARNINGS RATIO
1970	.62
1980	.64
1990	.71
1991	.74
1992	.75
1993	.76
1994	.76
1995	.75
1996	.75
1997	.74
1998	.76
1999	.76
2000	.76
2001	.76
2002	.78

SOURCE: U.S. Bureau of Labor Statistics, "Women's Earnings Up Relative to Men's in 2002," www.bls.gov/opub/ted/2003/apr/wk3/art03.htm.

In 1990, many women still worked in primarily female occupations. Of the 56 million women in the labor force in 1990, one third worked in just ten of the 503 detailed occupations recognized in the U.S. Census. These top ten occupations included secretary, elementary school teacher, cashier, registered nurse, bookkeeper, nurse's aide, and waitress. Men were more evenly distributed across the 503 census occupational groups; only 25 percent worked in the top ten occupations (versus 33 percent of women).

The reason that sex segregation is problematic is that the gender composition of a job is associated with the pay received for that job. This finding has emerged in numerous studies. An analysis of 1980 census data (England, 1992) showed that both women and men are directly disadvantaged

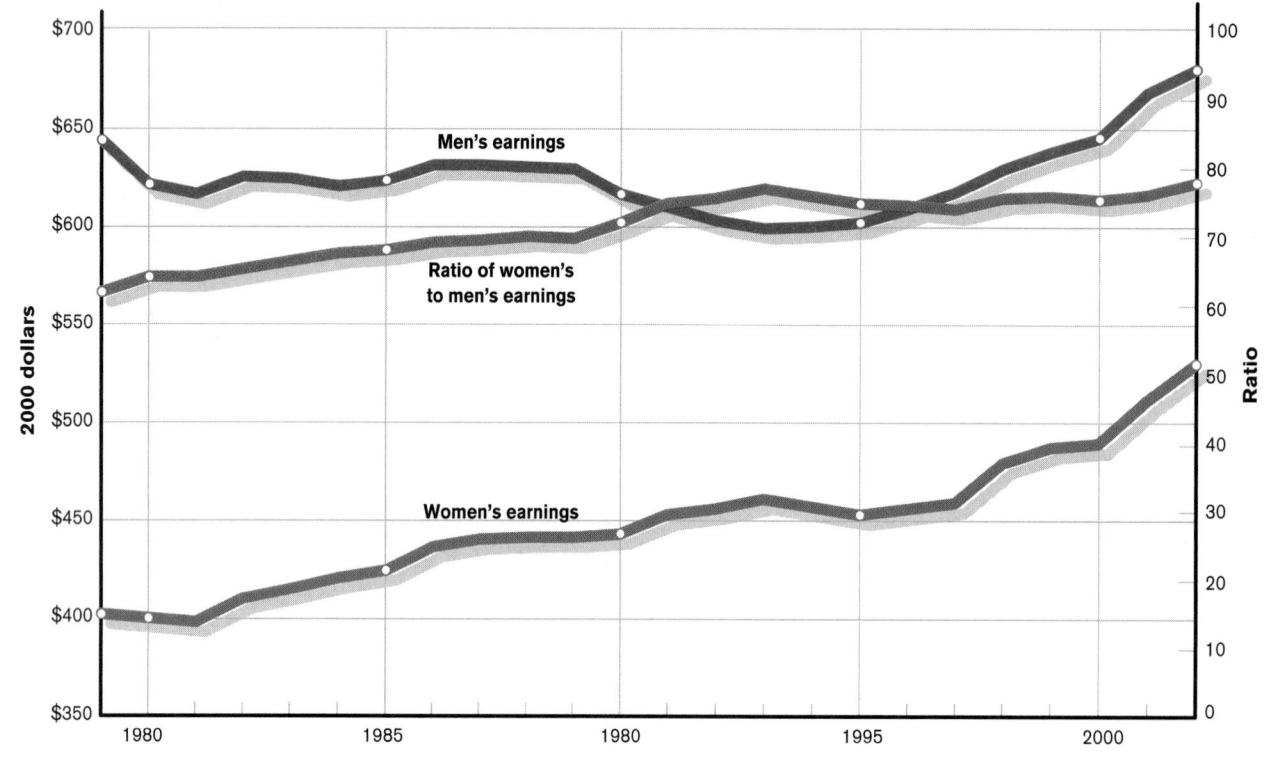

FIGURE 10.4

The Gender Pay Gap

This figure, in which weekly earnings are shown in constant 2000 dollars, illustrates what has been happening to the gender pay gap over time. After narrowing gradually for years, it widened a little after 1993, when men's inflation-adjusted earnings were increasing slightly and women's were not.

SOURCE: U.S. Bureau of Labor Statistics, "Household Data Annual Averages" Table 37, "Median weekly earnings of full-time wage and salary workers by selected characteristics," www.bls.gov/cps/cpsaat37.pdf.

by employment in an occupation that is predominantly female. Even "after adjusting for cognitive, social, and physical skill demands, amenities, disamenities, demands for effort, and industrial and organization characteristics, jobs pay less if they contain a higher proportion of females" (England, 1992).

Although an Equal Pay Act was established in 1963, it has done little to eradicate pay differences attributable to gender. The Equal Pay Act requires employers to provide equal pay to workers in the *same job*. Consequently, the gender gap in pay hasn't been remedied since the 1963 act because men and women often do not work at the same jobs. As long as employers segregate men and women into separate jobs, the best hope for narrowing the pay gap is to establish a pay-equity policy, meaning that pay policies remunerate workers on the basis of the worth of their work and not the sex, race, or other personal characteristics of the majority of workers in a job (Stryker, 1996). Comparable-worth policies would be one such strategy.

However, economists and sociologists differ in their explanations of *how* occupational segregation leads to a gender gap in pay. Economists typically focus on the occupational choices women make, while sociologists tend to focus on the constraints women face. Specifically, many economists—as well as employers and public-policy makers—endorse a **human capital theory** explanation. Human capital theory, developed by Gary Becker (1964), argues that individuals make investments in their own "human capital" in order to increase their productivity and earnings. "Human capital" includes formal schooling, on-the-job training, and work experience. Those who invest more in their own human capital are considered more productive and consequently are paid higher wages.

This theory has been specifically applied to explain gender differences in earnings. Human capital theorists reason that women intentionally select occupations that are easy to move in and out of, while still providing moderately good incomes. Central to this argument is the assumption that women's primary allegiance is to home and family; thus they seek undemanding dead-end jobs that require little personal investment in training or skills acquisition so that they can better tend to their household responsibilities. When women leave the labor force to rear children, the skills they have deteriorate and they suffer a wage penalty when they reenter. Moreover, employers may also choose to "invest" less in women workers because they believe women will work less continuously than men and that consequently they will not realize the return on investment in women workers that they will in male workers.

Feminist sociologists critique human capital theory on several grounds. First, they dispute the claim that women freely "choose" certain occupations. The forces blocking women from freely choosing a career may be indirect or direct. For instance, childhood socialization promoting "traditional" gender roles often indirectly limits women's career choices; girls may choose occupations such as teaching or nursing, which are viewed as compatible with "feminine" traits such as warmth or nurturance. More direct obstacles to women's career choices come in the form of discriminatory bosses, coworkers, and customers. Workplace "gatekeepers" have been shown to prohibit women from entering certain occupations. For example, State Farm Insurance was successfully sued in 1992 for sex discrimination; the firm was forced to provide back pay to 814 women who were denied jobs as insurance agents because of their sex.

Sociologists further argue that human capital theory neglects power differentials between men and women in the workplace and society. Numerous studies reveal that even when men and women are in the same job, men are paid more.

Women's work is devalued by society and by employers, and thus women are rewarded less for performing their work. Moreover, women's relative powerlessness prevents them from redefining the work they do as "skilled." As long as jobs predominantly filled by women, such as caring for children and the elderly, are viewed as "unskilled," wages in women's jobs will remain low.

These competing explanations have very different implications for the future. According to human capital theory, the gender gap in pay could disappear if women and men received equal amounts of education and workplace training and if they took equal responsibility for family commitments, such as child care. If feminist sociologists are correct in arguing that women's work is devalued, a drastic change in gender ideology must occur if men and women are to become equally rewarded for their participation in the workplace.

COMPARABLE WORTH

Comparable worth is a policy that compares pay levels of jobs held disproportionately by women with pay levels of jobs held disproportionately by men and tries to adjust pay so that the women and men who work in female-dominated jobs are not penalized. The policy presumes that jobs can be ranked objectively according to skill, effort, responsibility, and working conditions. After such a ranking, pay is adjusted so that equivalently ranked male- and female-dominated jobs receive equivalent pay (Hartmann et al., 1985).

Although comparable worth policies may help to reduce the gender gap in pay, only a handful of U.S. states have instituted comparable worth policies for public sector employees (Blum, 1991). One reason that comparable worth policies have not been implemented is that they raise multiple technical, political, and economic issues. Perhaps most important is the issue of job evaluation, or the technical process that reduces male- and female-dominated jobs to an underlying common denominator of skill, effort, responsibility, and working conditions so as to compare and rank them independent of the race and gender of job incumbents (Stryker, 1996). Effective implementation requires that job evaluations be free from gender bias. However, substantial research shows that gender-neutral assessments of jobs and required job skills are very difficult. Once men and women know which jobs are predominantly male and which are predominantly female, they tend to attribute to them the job content that best fits with gender stereotypes (Steinberg, 1990).

Opposition to comparable-worth policies has been offered by both economists and feminists. Some economists worry that comparable worth is inflationary and will cause wage losses and unemployment for some (disproportionately women) because of benefits enacted for others. Feminists counter that comparable worth reinforces gender stereotyping rather than breaking down gender barriers at work (Blum, 1991).

Whether or not comparable worth policies are enacted, the surrounding debates show that what jobs society values are determined not by their market or societal worth but by power relations (Blum, 1991).

THE GLASS CEILING AND THE GLASS ESCALATOR

Although women are increasingly entering "traditionally male" jobs, their entry into such jobs may not necessarily be accompanied by increases in pay—and increases in occupational mobility—due to the "**glass ceiling**." The glass ceiling is a promotion barrier that prevents a woman's upward mobility within an organization. The glass ceiling is particularly problematic for women who work in male-dominated occupations and the professions. Women's progress is blocked not by virtue of innate inability or lack of basic qualifications, but by not having the sponsorship of well-placed, powerful senior colleagues to articulate their value to the organization or profession (Alvarez et al., 1996). As a result, women tend to progress until mid-level management positions, but they do not, in proportionate numbers, move beyond mid-management ranks.

One explanation for women's blocked mobility is based on gender stereotypes. Research shows that college-educated white males in professional jobs tend to identify potential leaders as people who are like themselves. Women are thus assessed negatively because they deviate from this norm or standard (Cleveland, 1996).

What about men who work in female-dominated professions? Do they also face subtle obstacles to promotion? On the contrary, the sociologist Christine Williams (1992) has observed that a **"glass escalator"** pushes these men to the top of their corporate ladders. Williams found that employers singled out male workers in traditionally female jobs, such as nurse, librarian, elementary school teacher, and social worker, and promoted them to top administrative jobs in disproportionately high numbers. "Often, despite their intentions, they face invisible pressures to move up in their professions. Like being on a moving escalator, they have to work to stay in place," writes Williams (1992). These pressures may take posi-

Sociologist Christine Williams asserts that men in female-dominated professions, such as this elementary school teacher, are routinely promoted to top administrative positions and face constant pressure to advance.

tive forms, such as close mentoring and encouragement from supervisors, or they may be the result of prejudicial attitudes of those outside the profession, such as clients who prefer to work with male rather than female executives. Some of the men in Williams's study faced unwelcome pressure to accept promotions, such as a male children's librarian who received negative evaluations for "not shooting high enough" in his career aspirations.

SEXUAL HARASSMENT IN THE WORKPLACE

Sexual harassment is unwanted or repeated sexual advances, remarks, or behavior that are offensive to the recipient and cause discomfort or interference with job performance. Power imbalances facilitate harassment; even though women can and do sexually harass subordinates, because men usually hold positions of authority, it is more common for men to harass women (Reskin and Padavic, 1994).

The U.S. courts have identified two types of sexual harassment. One is the quid pro quo, in which a supervisor demands sexual acts from a worker as a job condition or promises work-related benefits in exchange for sexual acts. The other is the "hostile work environment," in which a pattern of sexual language, lewd posters, or sexual advances makes a worker so uncomfortable that it is difficult for her to do her job (Reskin and Padavic, 1994).

Recognition of sexual harassment, and women's willingness to report it, has increased substantially since the testimony of Anita Hill to the Senate Judiciary Committee during the confirmation hearings for Clarence Thomas's 1991 nomination to the U.S. Supreme Court. Although Thomas was ultimately confirmed as a U.S. Supreme Court justice, Hill's recounting of his harassment raised public awareness of the seriousness of the problem and encouraged more women to report harassment incidents (see Figure 10.5). In the first six months of 1992 alone, the number of workplace harassment complaints increased by more than 50 percent (Gross, 1992). In 1992 overall, workers filed over 10,000 complaints of sexual harassment with the Equal Employment Opportunity Commission (Equal Employment Opportunity Commission, 1993).

Despite this increased awareness, sociologists have observed that "the great majority of women who are abused by behavior that fits legal definitions of sexual harassment—and who are traumatized by the experience—do not label what has happened to them as sexual harassment" (Paludi and Barickman, 1991).

Women's reluctance to report may be due to the following factors: (1) many still do not recognize that sexual harassment is an actionable offense; (2) victims may be reluctant to come forward with complaints, fearing that they will not be be-

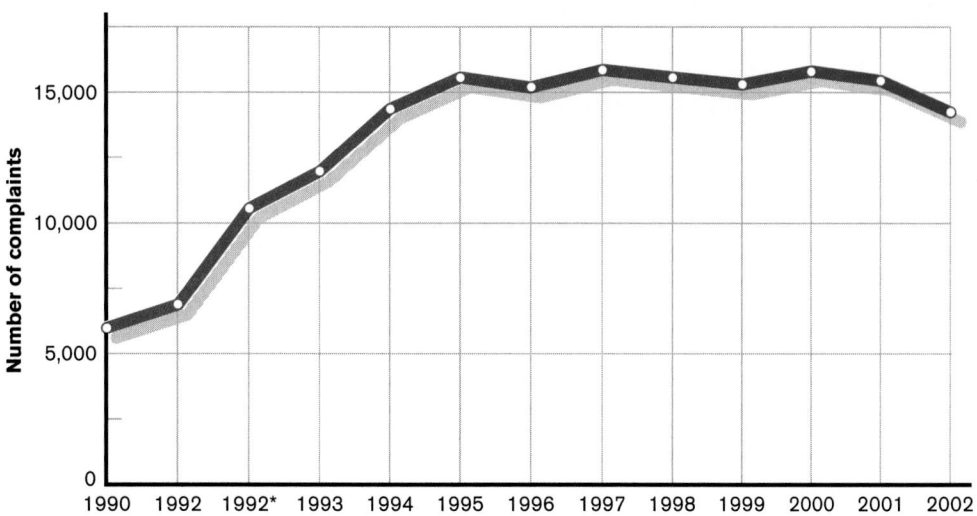

FIGURE 10.5

Increase in Sexual Harassment Complaints in the United States, 1990–2002

*Following Anita Hill's testimony before the Senate.

SOURCE: Equal Employment Opportunity Commission, "Sexual Harassment Charges, EEOC & FEPA combined: FY 1992–FY 2002."

lieved, that their charges will not be taken seriously, or that they will be subject to reprisals; (3) it may be difficult to differentiate between harassment and joking on the job (Giuffre and Williams, 1994).

In 1998, the U.S. Supreme Court decided that the Civil Rights Act outlaws harassment between members of the same sex. The case involved a Louisiana man who was forced to quit his job on an offshore oil rig because he had been repeatedly grabbed, ridiculed, and threatened by two male supervisors. Justice Antonin Scalia ruled neither "roughhousing" among men, nor "flirtations" between men and women, nor even some types of "verbal or physical harassment" is illegal. Nonetheless, he determined, when sexual harassment is so "severely hostile or abusive" that it prevents workers from doing their jobs, it violates the Civil Rights Act—regardless of whether the offender and the person who is harassed are of the same or the opposite sex (Savage, 1998).

The Family and Gender Issues

BALANCING WORK AND CHILD CARE

One of the major factors affecting women's careers is the male perception that for female employees, work comes sec-

ond to having children. One study carried out in Britain investigated the views of managers interviewing female applicants for positions as technical staff in the health services. The researchers found that the interviewers always asked the women about whether or not they had, or intended to have, children (this is now illegal in the United States). They virtually never followed this practice with male applicants. When asked why, two themes ran through their answers: Women with children may require extra time off for school holidays or if a child falls sick, and responsibility for child care is a mother's problem rather than a parental one.

Some managers thought their questions indicated an attitude of "caring" toward female employees. But most saw such a line of questioning as part of their task in assessing how far a female applicant would prove a reliable colleague. Thus, one manager remarked:

It's a bit of a personal question, I appreciate that, but I think it's something that has to be considered. It's something that can't happen to a man really, but I suppose in a sense it's unfair—it's not equal opportunity because the man could never find himself having a family as such. (Homans, 1987)

Can men and women truly share equal responsibility for their children or will women always be regarded as the primary caretakers?

Although men cannot biologically "have a family" in the sense of bearing children, they can be fully involved in and responsible for child care. Such a possibility was not taken into account by any of the managers studied. The same attitudes were held about the promotion of women. Women were seen as likely to interrupt their careers to care for young children, no matter how senior a position they might have reached. The few women in this study who held senior management positions were all without children, and several of those who planned to have children in the future said they intended to leave their jobs and would perhaps retrain for other positions subsequently.

How should we interpret these findings? Are women's job opportunities hampered mainly by male prejudices? Some managers expressed the view that women with children should *not* work, but should occupy themselves with child care and the home. Most, however, accepted the principle that women should have the same career opportunities as men. The bias in their attitudes had less to do with the workplace itself than with the domestic responsibilities of parenting. So long as most of the population take it for granted that parenting cannot be shared on an equal basis by both women and men, the problems facing women employees will persist. It will remain a fact of life, as one of the managers put it, that women are disadvantaged, compared with men, in their career opportunities.

In her book *Working Women Don't Have Wives* (1994), Terri Apter argues that women find themselves struggling with two contradictory forces. They want and need economic independence but at the same time want to be mothers to their children. Both goals are reasonable, but while men with wives who take prime responsibility for domestic work can achieve them, women cannot do likewise. Greater flexibility in working life is one partial solution. Much more difficult is getting men to alter their attitudes.

HOUSEWORK

Although there have been revolutionary changes in women's status in recent decades in the United States, including the entry of women into male-dominated professions, one area of work has lagged far behind: housework. Because of the increase of married women in the workforce and the resulting change in status, it was presumed that men would contribute more to housework. On the whole, this has not been the case. Although men now do more housework than they did three decades ago (about one to two hours more per week) and women do slightly less, the balance is still unequal (Shelton and John, 1993). Sociologists calculate that working women perform fifteen more hours of housework per week than their husbands, in effect a "second shift" of work (Hochschild, 1989; Shelton, 1992). The UN estimates that women in the United States work 6 percent more than men, a majority of which is spent in non-market activities (UN, 2003). These figures do not include time spent on child care, which if factored in would increase the gap. The UN has estimated that if all of the non-market work of women was accounted for, the official estimate of the size of the world economy would be $11 trillion higher (UN, 1995). Findings like these have led Arlie Hochschild to call the state of relations between women and men a "stalled revolution" (1989). Why does housework remain women's work? This question has been the focus of a good deal of research in recent years.

Some sociologists have suggested that this phenomenon is best explained as a result of economic forces: Household work is exchanged for economic support. Because women earn less than men, they are more likely to remain economically dependent on their husbands and thus perform the bulk of the housework. Until the earnings gap is narrowed, women will likely remain in their dependent position. Hochschild has suggested that women are thus doubly oppressed by men: once during the "first shift" and again during the "second shift." But although this dependency model contributes to our understanding of the gendered aspects of housework, it breaks down when applied to situations where the wife earns more than her husband. For instance, of the husbands that Hochschild studied who earned less than their wives, none shared in the housework.

Some sociologists have approached the problem from a symbolic interactionist perspective, asking how the performance or nonperformance of housework is related to the gender roles created by society. For example, through interviews and participant observation, Hochschild found that the assignment of household tasks falls clearly along gendered lines. Wives do most of the daily chores, such as cooking and routine cleaning, while husbands tend to take on more occasional tasks, such as mowing the lawn or doing home repairs. The major difference between these two types of tasks is the amount of control the individual has over when they do the work. The jobs women do in the home are those that tend to bind them to a fixed schedule, whereas men's household tasks are done less regularly and are more discretionary.

The sociologist Marjorie Devault looked at how the caring activities within a household are socially constructed as women's work in her book *Feeding the Family* (1991). She argues that women perform the bulk of the housework because the family "incorporates a strong and relatively enduring association of caring activity with the woman's position in the household." Even in households where men contribute, an egalitarian division of household labor between spouses is greatly impeded when the couple have children—children require constant attention, and their care schedules are often unpredictable. Mothers overwhelmingly spend more time with child-rearing tasks than do fathers (Shelton, 1992).

Sociologists argue that underlying this inequitable distribution of tasks is the implicit understanding that men and women are responsible for, and should operate in, different spheres. Men are expected to be providers, while women are expected to tend to their families—even if they are breadwinners as well as mothers. Expectations like this reinforce traditional gender roles learned during childhood socialization. By reproducing these roles in everyday life, men and women "do gender" and reinforce gender as a means for society to differentiate between men and women.

Education and Unequal Treatment in the Classroom

Sociologists have found that schools help foster gender differences in outlook and behavior. Although this has become less common today, regulations that compelled girls to wear dresses or skirts in school formed one of the most obvious ways in which gender typing occurred. The consequences went beyond mere appearance. As a result of the clothes they had to wear, girls lacked the freedom to sit casually, to join in rough-and-tumble games, or sometimes to run as fast as they were able. Although the strict enforcement of styles of school dress has become quite rare, differences in informal styles of dress still persist, influencing gender behavior in school. School reading texts also help to perpetuate gender images. Although this too is changing, storybooks in elementary school often portray boys showing initiative and independence, while girls, if they appear at all, are portrayed as more passive and

shown watching their brothers. Stories written especially for girls often have an element of adventure in them, but this usually takes the form of intrigues or mysteries in a domestic or school setting. Boys' adventure stories are more wide ranging, having heroes who travel off to distant places or who in other ways are sturdily independent (Statham, 1986).

In general, people interact differently with men and women, and boys and girls (Lorber, 1994). This is apparent even in the classrooms of elementary schools. Studies document that teachers interact differently—and often inequitably—with their male and female students. These interactions differ in at least two ways: the frequency of teacher-student interactions and the content of those interactions. Both of the patterns are based on—and perpetuate—traditional assumptions about male and female behavior and traits.

One study shows that regardless of the sex of the teacher, male students interact more with their teachers than female students do. Boys receive more teacher attention and instructional time than girls do. This is due in part to the fact that boys are more demanding than girls (AAUW, 1992). Another study reported that boys are eight times more likely to call out answers in class, thus grabbing their teachers' attention. This research also shows that even when boys do not voluntarily participate in class, teachers are more likely to solicit information from them than from girls. However, when girls try to bring attention to themselves by calling out in class without raising their hands, they were reprimanded by comments such as "In this class, we don't shout out answers, we raise our hands" (Sadker and Sadker, 1994).

Sociologists have also found that the content of student-teacher interactions differs depending on the sex of the students. After observing elementary school teachers and students over many years, researchers found that teachers provided boys with assistance in working out the correct answers whereas they simply gave girls the correct answers and did not engage them in the problem-solving process. In addition, teachers posed more academic challenges to boys, encouraging them to think through their answers in order to arrive at the best possible response (Sadker and Sadker, 1994).

Boys were also disadvantaged in several ways, however. Because of their rowdy behavior, they were more often scolded and punished than the girl students. Moreover, boys outnumber girls in special education programs by startling percentages. Sociologists have argued that school personnel may be mislabeling boys' behavioral problems as learning disabilities.

This differential treatment of boys and girls perpetuates stereotypic gender-role behavior. Girls are trained to be quiet, well behaved, and to turn to others for answers, while boys are encouraged to be inquisitive, outspoken, active problem solvers. Female children from ethnic minorities are in some respects doubly disadvantaged. A study of what it was like to

Masculinity and School Shootings

In a small New York City public school where I worked as a social worker and mediator, I saw gang wars and kids tormenting other kids. When boys harassed and teased others, there was one insult that I heard frequently, the one that was considered the worst of all: "You look gay."

Boys found early that being sensitive, respectful, and kind would earn them no respect. Instead they learned not to back down from a fight or apologize for a mistake, and to defend their honor against any slight, with violence if necessary, no matter how risky the situation nor how minor the offense. The reaction was similar whether or not the targets of this abuse actually identified themselves as gay or straight. This is also what happened in the horrific school shootings that shocked the nation between 1996 and 2003.

After opening fire at his school in 1997, Kentucky student Michael Carneal explained that he was tired of being called a "faggot"; he wanted to kill the "popular preppie students" he blamed for his mistreatment. In 1999, at Columbine High School in Colorado, Eric Harris's manifesto, found after his suicide and shooting with Dylan Klebold, declared their actions a response to being ridiculed and teased. Members of their social group, the Trench Coat Mafia, said Harris and Klebold were harassed initially because they were smart; other boys often attacked them and called them homosexuals. In all, fifteen boys retaliated against such abuse between 1996 and 2003; boys, ages eleven to eighteen, killed thirty-five people and wounded 102 others in thirteen major non-gang-related school shootings (Klein, 2003).

Why did these boys kill? And what do their cases have in common with teenagers who murdered in other major school shootings and the violence I saw in New York City schools? Popular theories include lax gun control laws, media violence, parents, and deviant kids. My firsthand observation of teasing in schools, however, provides sociological insights through a gender lens, and adds an important missing puzzle piece, without which none of these other theories can explain what had happened.

Though the details differ, two common threads run through the horrific school shootings. First, classmates consistently described school shooters as "different": skinny, lanky, chubby, or scrawny (Klein, 2003). Second, all of the teenage killers apparently thought that teasing was enough of a reason to kill.

The pattern is devastating: Boys who appeared less masculine in traditional terms turned to extreme violence. Like the boys I worked with in New York City public schools, the killers had been taught from a young age to defend their "manhood" when teased, to fight to win, and to show the other "who's the man." That's what these killers thought they accomplished: "proving" their masculinity.

How could these students have come to hold such destructive beliefs? Many sociologists have made important contributions toward understanding masculinity and, ultimately, school violence. R. W. Connell (1995) argues that boys feel pressured to achieve *hegemonic masculinity*, which he defines as the form of masculinity that a given society legitimizes most. Men are pressured to embody stereotypical masculine traits such as being unemotional, tough, authoritative, and controlling, if they wish to gain status in a competitive masculinities hierarchy. Thus the boys who killed had been demonized, harassed, and ostracized by "preps and jocks" who accrued status by picking on them. This is consistent with Max Weber's contention that a given status group maintains its cohesion and gains influence through its ability to distance itself from other groups in society and ultimately dominate them (Klein, 2005). Even so, prestige holders must fight to maintain their positions. Popular students often feel compelled to continue to win competitions so they can maintain their social status and differentiate themselves from unpopular kids. Otherwise, they risk a quick loss of power (Klein, 2005).

The sociology of gender can also explain why other students and adults overlooked the killers' threats. In *Slow Motion: Changing Masculinities, Changing Men*, Lynne Segal (1990) argues that homophobia is a means to keep all men in line by oppressing gay men and expressing contempt for men who display emotional qualities associated with femininity. Boys are taught to despise the "feminine enemy within themselves" and to try to destroy any person that draws attention to these rejected aspects of their personality (Klein and Chancer, 2000). Significantly, many of the shooters specifically killed their ex-girlfriends—for instance, in Mississippi, Kentucky, and Arkansas—lashing out against the blow to their manhood suffered as a result of the break-up, and demonstrating another way to differentiate from and express hostility toward femininity. By associating themselves with violent retaliation, they sought to gain greater masculinity status.

These sociological insights suggest ways to prevent future school shootings. If someone had paid attention—perhaps as a result of the insight that sociology offers—warning signs might have been noticed and saved lives. Ending the bullying of "different" boys is not just a matter of punishing bad behavior. It involves providing alternatives to winning social approval through violent demonstrations of power. Parents, counselors, school faculty, and fellow students need sociologists' help to develop new ways to support positive social dynamics, and a clearer understanding of how to avoid condoning destructive behavior, for instance, gay-baiting, bullying, and retaliatory threats that conform to expectations that "boys will be boys." At the same time, male role models among faculty, parents, and student peers should encourage academic success and community participation, not just athletics, competition, and power. These new models of manhood could go far to ameliorate school violence.

This approach has been effective in the New York City public schools where I worked for eleven years as a conflict resolution and mediation coordinator, a teacher, a social worker, and an administrator. I conducted mediation sessions between boys, raised the problem at faculty meetings, and addressed the issue as a community social problem in school assemblies. Students who were picked on talked about what it was like to be teased, and in this setting, other students found the strength to support them and to shout out their support for a more respectful school environment. Boys and girls alike

talked about the importance of being kind, respectful, and sensitive regardless of their gender or sexual identity. In this context, students expressed the importance of apologizing, acknowledging mistakes, and resolving differences peacefully. After these interventions, the school had significantly fewer fights than other schools in the same area.

My experiences show how effectively sociologists can use their recommendations to change the way society thinks about problems like the gay-baiting that makes so many young boys miserable and drives some of them to violence. By analyzing problems that are common in society, identifying previously invisible causes, and helping devise new solutions, sociology provides the tools for creating more peaceful and inclusive communities.

JESSIE KLEIN is a professor at City University of New York/Lehman College in the Department of Sociology and Social Work; her recommendations regarding school violence prevention have appeared in USA Today *and the* New York Times *in addition to many scholarly journals and books. She worked at five New York City public schools: Bayard Rustin High School for the Humanities, Stuyvesant High School, Richard R. Greene High School for Teaching, Norman Thomas High School, and Humanities Preparatory Academy.*

be a black female pupil in a white school reported that unlike the boys, the black girls were initially enthusiastic about school but altered their attitudes because of the difficulties they encountered. Even when the girls were quite small, aged seven or eight, teachers would disperse them if they were standing chatting in a group on the playground—in contrast to their treatment of the white children, whose similar behavior was tolerated. Once treated as "troublemakers," they rapidly became so (Bryan, Dadzie, and Scafe, 1987).

Gender Inequality in Politics

Women are playing an increasingly important role in U.S. politics, although they are still far from achieving full equality. Before 1993, there were only two women in the U.S. Senate (out of one hundred Senate members), and twenty-nine in the U.S. House of Representatives (out of 435). Less than a decade later—in 2001—there were a record thirteen women in the Senate and fifty-nine in the House. Currently, there are fourteen women Senators but sixty-eight Representatives (U.S. House of Representatives, 2005). Women in 2003 held a little more than 22 percent of all seats in state legislatures, five times as many as they held in 1969, but only nine governorships (out of fifty) (CAWP, 2001; NGA, 2003). The U.S. Supreme Court had its first woman justice appointed in 1981, and its second twelve years later. It was not until 1984 that a woman was nominated as the vice presidential candidate of either major party, neither of which has ever nominated a woman for the presidency.

Typically, the more local the political office, the more likely it is to be occupied by a woman. Men outnumber women in politics at all levels, but women are often elected members of city and county governing boards and as mayors. In most states, women are less likely to be found as representatives to state government than as representatives at the local level, but even women elected at the state level are more common than women representatives to Congress. The reason is partly that local politics is often part-time work, particularly in smaller cities and towns. Local politics can thus be good "women's work," offering low pay, part-time employment, flexible hours, and the absence of a clear career path. The farther from home the political office, the more likely it is to be regarded as "man's work," providing a living wage, full-time employment, and a lifetime career.

Violence Against Women

Violence directed against women is found in many societies, including the United States. One out of three women has been beaten, coerced into sex, or abused in some other way—most often by someone she knows, including her husband or a male relative (UNFPA, 2003). More women are injured as a result of beatings by spouses than by any other cause, a problem that is ignored by most governments (Human Rights Watch, 1995). In Japan, three out of five women report having been sexually or physically abused by a partner. In India, an estimated twenty thousand brides were killed between 1990 and 1995—usually by being burned alive—for bringing an inadequate dowry to their husbands' families (Wright, 1995). Between 100 and 130 million girls and women worldwide have been subjected to "genital mutilation" (see Global Map 10.1), while an equal number are "missing," partly as the result of female infanticide in cultures where boys are more highly valued than girls.

In the United States, many scholars argue that the increased depiction of violence in movies, on television, and elsewhere in American popular culture contributes to a climate in which women are often victimized. The most common manifestation of violence against women is rape, although stalking and sexual harassment increasingly are seen as a form of psychological (if not physical) violence as well.

RAPE

Rape can be sociologically defined as the forcing of nonconsensual vaginal, oral, or anal intercourse. Sociologists Paulene Bart and Patricia O'Brien (Bart and O'Brien, 1985), who studied different forms of sexual relationships between men and women, offer the following classification:

- CONSENSUAL SEX: Intercourse that is desired equally by both partners.
- ALTRUISTIC SEX: One partner (usually female) "goes along" because she feels sorry for or guilty toward her partner.
- COMPLIANT SEX: One partner (usually female) goes along because she feels that the consequences of refusal would be worse than assenting to sex.
- RAPE: One partner (usually female) is forced, often by actual or threatened violence, to have sex against her will (see also Brownmiller, 1986).

As one researcher observed, between consensual sex and rape lies "a continuum of pressure, threat, coercion, and force" (Kelly, 1987). Common to all forms of rape is the lack of consent: At least in principle, "no" means "no" when it comes to sexual relations in most courts of law in the United States. Virtually all rapes are committed by men against women, although men rape other men in prisons and other all-male institutional environments.

Estimated Percentage of Female Population That Has Undergone Genital Mutilation, Selected African Countries, 1999

Map of Africa with selected countries labeled with estimated percentage of female population that has undergone genital mutilation:

- Tunisia
- Morocco
- Algeria
- Libya
- Egypt 97%
- Western Sahara
- Mauritania 25%
- Mali 94%
- Niger 5%
- Chad 60%
- Sudan 89%
- Eritrea 95%
- Djibouti 98%
- Somalia 98%
- Ethiopia 85%
- Senegal 20%
- Gambia 80%
- Guinea 50%
- Cote D'Ivoire 43%
- Burkina Faso 70%
- Nigeria 50%
- Central African Republic 43%
- Cameroon 20%
- Guinea Bissau 50%
- Sierra Leone 90%
- Liberia 60%
- Togo 50%
- Ghana 30%
- Benin 50%
- Equatorial Guinea
- Gabon
- Congo 5%
- Rwanda
- Uganda 5%
- Kenya 38%
- Dem. Rep. Of Congo
- Burundi
- Tanzania 18%
- Angola
- Zambia
- Malawi
- Zimbabwe
- Mozambique
- Namibia
- Botswana
- Madagascar
- Swaziland
- South Africa
- Lesotho
- Red Sea

SOURCE: UN, 2000.

Rape is an act of violence, rather than a purely sexual act. It is often carefully planned rather than performed on the spur of the moment to satisfy some uncontrollable sexual desire. Many rapes involve beatings, knifings, and even murder. Even when rape leaves no physical wounds, it is a highly traumatic violation of a woman's person that leaves long-lasting psychological scars.

It is difficult to know with accuracy how many rapes actually occur, since most rapes go unreported. One comprehensive study of American sexual behavior found that 22 percent of the women surveyed reported having been forced into a sexual encounter. Yet the same study found that only 3 percent of the men admitted to having forced a woman into having sex, a discrepancy the study's authors attribute to different perceptions between men and women regarding what constitutes forced sex (Laumann et al., 1994). Based on its semiannual survey of nearly 100,000 Americans, the U.S. Department of Justice estimates that in 2002, there were 148,040 sexual assaults on women, 57,270 attempted rapes, and 116,760 rapes. The total number of sexual assaults, attempted rapes, and rapes (322,060) was nearly 25 percent lower than in 1999—part of an overall decrease in violent crimes since 1994. In fact, criminal victimizations, which include rape and sexual assault, are at their lowest point since 1973 (U.S. Department of Justice, 2003).

Most rapes are committed by relatives (fathers or stepfathers, brothers, uncles), partners, or acquaintances. Among college students, most rapes are likely to be committed by boyfriends, former boyfriends, or classmates. The National College Women Sexual Victimization Study (NCWSV), a national survey of 4,446 women attending two- or four-year colleges or universities, presents a chilling picture of violence against women on campuses across the country (Fisher, Cullen, and Turner, 2000). The study, which was conducted during spring semester 1997, asked college women about their experience with rape, attempted rape, coerced sex, unwanted sexual contact, and stalking during the 1996–1997 school year. Overall, since the beginning of the school year, 1.7 percent had been the victim of a completed rape, and 1.1 percent of an attempted rape. Since students were typically interviewed seven months into the academic year, the authors estimate that over the entire academic year nearly 5 percent of the women in the sample would have fallen victim to a rape or attempted rape. Over the typical five years of a college career, this suggests that between a fifth and a quarter of all women attending college would fall victim to rape or attempted rape—some 2.2 million women.

Moreover, fully a tenth of the female students surveyed had been raped prior to the study period (which began in the fall of 1996), and a tenth had been the victims of attempted rape. The study also found that for both completed and attempted rapes, nine out of ten offenders were known to the victim. Fifty-five

percent of rape victims used physical force in an effort to thwart the rape, as did 69 percent of attempted rape victims.

The incidence of other forms of victimization reported in the study was substantially higher than that of rape. Nearly one out of six female students reported being the target of attempted or completed sexual coercion or unwanted sexual contact during the current academic year, half involving the use or threat of physical force. More than a third reported that they had experienced a threatened, attempted, or completed unwanted sexual assault at some time during their lives. And about one out of every eight reported having been stalked at some time during the current year, almost always by someone they knew—typically a former boyfriend or classmate. Stalking, it was reported, was emotionally traumatizing and in 15 percent of the incidents involved actual or threatened physical harm.

The conclusions of the study are worth quoting at length:

> To summarize, the national-level survey of 4,446 college women suggests that many students will encounter sexist and harassing comments, will likely receive an obscene phone call, and will have a good chance of being stalked or of enduring some form of coerced sexual contact. During any given academic year, 2.8 percent of women will experience a completed and/or attempted rape. . . . Furthermore, the level of rape and other types of victimization found in the survey becomes an increasing concern when the victimization figures are projected over a full year, a full college career, and the full population of women at one college or at colleges across the Nation. . . . Although exceptions exist, most sexual victimizations occur when college women are alone with a man they know, at night, and in the privacy of a residence. (Fisher, Cullen, and Turner, 2000)

WHY ARE WOMEN SO OFTEN THE TARGETS OF SEXUAL VIOLENCE?

Some scholars claim that men are socialized to regard women as sex objects and that this at least in part explains the high levels of victimization women reported to the National College Women Sexual Victimization Study (Griffin, 1979; Dworkin, 1981, 1987). Susan Brownmiller (1986), for example, claims that the constant threat of rape contributes to a "rape culture," one that is the result of male socialization that reinforces male domination by fostering a state of continual fear in women. One aspect of a "rape culture" is male socialization to a sense of sexual entitlement, which may encourage sexual conquest and promote insensitivity to the difference between consensual and nonconsensual sex (Scully, 1990). From seemingly innocent high school locker-room jokes, to television commercials and magazine ads that depict women as sexually inviting, mindless bodies, to television and movie images equating masculinity with the conquest of women, many men grow up learning to believe that women exist for their pleasure. Under such circumstances, it is argued, rape is all too "normal" (Wolf, 1992).

The fact that "acquaintance rapes" occur suggests that at least some men are likely to feel entitled to sexual access if they already know the woman. A survey of nearly 270,000 first-year college students reported that 55 percent of male students agreed with the statement: "If two people really like each other, it's all right for them to have sex even if they've known each other only for a very short time." Only 31 percent of female students were in agreement, suggesting a rather large gender gap concerning notions of sexual entitlement (ACE, 2001). Another national study of first-year college students found that one out of five males felt they were entitled to have sex if the women "led them on" (Higher Education Research Institute, 1990), while a national survey reported that 43 percent of all men believed that a woman is partly to blame if she is raped after changing her mind about having sex (Yankelovich, 1991). When a man goes out on a date with sexual conquest on his mind, he may force his attentions on an unwilling partner, overcoming her resistance through the use of alcohol, persistence, or both. While such an act may not be legally defined as rape, it would be experienced as such by many women.

Because men are socialized to feel a sense of sexual entitlement to women, rapes are most common when men believe that norms condemning rape somehow do not apply and so they are free to act as they choose. Rapes are thus common in times of war. Japanese soldiers raped as many as twenty thousand women when they conquered the city of Nanking in China in 1937 (Chang and Kirby, 1997). Although this is one of the best-known modern cases of mass rape by conquering troops, war-related rapes are as old as human history. Followers of Rome's legendary founder, Romulus, were reputed to have captured Sabine women in order to populate Rome—an act that was glamorized in the famous sixteenth-century sculpture *The Rape of the Sabines*. American soldiers committed rapes during the Civil War and the Vietnam War.

Rape is often an explicit military strategy: During World War II, for example, Japanese soldiers forced as many as two hundred thousand young women and girls to serve as "comfort women" for Japanese troops. These women—mainly Korean, but also taken from other Asian countries conquered by the Japanese—were forced to work as sex slaves in military brothels throughout the Pacific. Many died in captivity, often of despair. A large number committed suicide (Stetz and Oh, 2001). Rape was widely used as a Serbian strategy in the recent wars

This sixteenth century sculpture by Giambologna, entitled *The Rape of the Sabines*, depicts the legend in which soldiers following Romulus, the mythical founder of Rome, captured and raped Sabine women in order to populate Rome.

in Kosovo and Bosnia. By systematically raping and impregnating Muslim women, the Serbian forces hoped to humiliate the Muslim population into fleeing their homelands (Allen, 1996).

Gender Inequality in Global Perspective

Women the world over experience economic and political inequality. Although the United States has made major strides during the past quarter century in achieving greater gender inequality, it is by no means the world's leader in this effort.

Economic Inequality

Worldwide, women now make up more than a third of the world's paid workforce in all regions except northern Africa and western Asia (UN, 2000). Women around the world work in the lowest-wage jobs and are likely to make less than men doing similar work—although there is some evidence that the wage gap is slowly decreasing, at least in industrialized countries (ILO, 1995). Because women work a "second shift" the world over, women also work longer hours than men in most countries. A recent United Nations report found that women in the United States worked on average 25 minutes each day more than men—a difference that was considerably smaller than that in Austria (45 minutes) or Italy (103 minutes).

Access to knowledge about birth control enables women to choose to exercise greater control over childbearing, so that many are able to work outside the home. Education also encourages women to seek financial independence from men. More women are getting college degrees and professional jobs than even before. Women make up about half of all college students in the economically developed countries of the industrial world and nearly half in Latin America, although in much of Africa and Asia, they are much less likely to go to college. Women's ability to achieve specialized education in science, engineering, business, and government has been limited, even with increased access to secondary and advanced education in much of the world.

Women remain in the poorest-paying industrial and service-sector jobs in all countries, and in the less industrialized nations, they are concentrated in the declining agricultural sector. The feminization of the global work force has brought with it the increased exploitation of young, uneducated, largely rural women around the world. These women labor under conditions that are often unsafe and unhealthy, at low pay and with nonexistent job security.

Yet at the same time, even poor-paying factory jobs may enable some women to achieve a measure of economic independence and power. In China, for example, as many as 40 to 50 million young women have left their home villages in search of factory jobs in large cities. Such "working sisters" earn and save more than their brothers, a fact that has raised their economic status in Chinese society, where women have traditionally been valued less than men. As one Chinese scholar explains, "A whole generation has learned that women have value and girls have choice. When they have a girl, they will feel differently toward her than their parents and grandparents did" (Farley, 1998). There is some indication that

women's changing economic role has changed their self-concept as well. More rural Chinese women are divorcing their husbands now that they can better afford to end unhappy marriages. And in a society where the oppressiveness of life as a woman contributes to one of the highest female suicide rates in the world, fewer women appear to be taking their own lives (Farley, 1998; Rosenthal, 1999).

At the other end of the occupational spectrum, a recent study by the International Labor Organization concludes that women throughout the world still encounter a "glass ceiling" that restricts their movement into the top positions. Even though women have made progress in moving into managerial and professional positions, globally they still hold only 2 to 3 percent of the top corporate jobs, and those who do make it to the top typically earn less than men. In Japan, for example, women are especially likely to face barriers to upper-level positions: When college-educated Japanese women interview for managerial jobs, they are typically assigned to noncareer secretarial work. As many as 40 percent of Japanese companies hire no women college graduates for management-level positions (French, 2001a). On the other hand, in Australia, Canada, Thailand, and the United States women own more than 30 percent of all businesses (ILO, 2003). Female participation in senior management has reached nearly 22 percent in the Netherlands, 21 percent in Canada, and over 36 percent in Hungary. In some developing countries, progress has been even greater: In Chile, for example, 27 percent of senior managers are women; in Singapore, 37 percent (ILO, 1997, 2003a).

Political Inequality

Women play an increasing role in politics throughout the world. In Japan, for example, where women have traditionally faced significant barriers to achieving equality with men, five women were recently appointed to cabinet-level positions by Junichiro Koizumi, the reform-minded prime minister who took office in spring 2001—one in the key position of foreign minister (French, 2001b). Yet of 188 countries that belong to the United Nations, only nine are presently headed by women. Since World War II, thirty-eight countries have been headed by women; the United States is not among them.

As of mid-2001, women made up only 14 percent of the combined membership of the national legislatures throughout the world. Only in the Scandinavian countries of Sweden, Finland, Norway, and Denmark do women make up a significant part of parliament (39 percent); in the Arab states, it is only 5 percent. The U.S. Congress is 13.8 percent female, placing the United States fifty-third out of 173 countries for which data exist. Women are most likely to hold seats in national legislatures in countries where women's rights are a strong cultural value.

United Nations Gender Empowerment Rankings: The Top 10 Countries Plus the United States

RANK	COUNTRY	SEATS IN PARLIAMENT HELD BY WOMEN (%)	FEMALE ADMINISTRATORS AND MANAGERS (%)	FEMALE PROFESSIONAL AND TECHNICAL WORKERS (%)
1	Norway	36.4	25	49
2	Iceland	34.9	27	53
3	Sweden	42.7	29	49
4	Denmark	38	23	50
5	Finland	36.5	27	56
6	Netherlands	32.9	27	46
7	Canada	23.6	35	53
8	Germany	31	27	50
9	New Zealand	30.8	38	54
10	Australia	26.5	26	48
11	United States	13.8	45	54

SOURCE: UNDP, 2002.

These are likely to be countries where women have long had the right to vote and are well represented in the professions. They are also likely to be countries that have strong socialist parties that play a role in government (Kenworthy and Malami, 1999).

The United Nations ranks countries according to a measure of "gender empowerment," which is based on such factors as seats in the national legislature held by women, female administrators and managers (as a percentage of total administrators and managers), female professional and technical workers (as a percentage of total professional and technical workers), and the ratio of women's to men's earned income. By this measure, the United States ranks twelfth—behind the Scandinavian and other northern European countries and Canada and New Zealand (see Table 10.2).

Analyzing Gender Inequality

Sociologists have tried to explain why gender inequalities exist. One plausible explanation for gender inequality is relatively sim-

ple. Women give birth to and care for children. The helplessness of the human infant demands that such care be intensive and prolonged—hence the centrality of "mothering" to women's experience (as emphasized by Chodorow; see Chapter 4). Because of their role as mothers, women are absorbed primarily in domestic activities. Women become what the French novelist and social critic Simone de Beauvoir (1974; orig. 1949) called "the second sex," because of their exclusion from the more "public" activities in which men are free to engage. Men are not dominant over women as a result of superior physical strength or any special intellectual powers, but because prior to the development of birth control, women were at the mercy of their biological constitution. Constant childbirth and continuous caring for infants made them dependent on males for material provision (Firestone, 1971; Mitchell, 1975).

The prevailing division of labor between the sexes has led to men and women assuming unequal positions in terms of power, prestige, and wealth. Despite the advances that women have made in countries around the world, gender differences continue to serve as the basis for social inequalities. Investigating and accounting for gender inequality has become a central concern of sociologists. Many theoretical perspectives have been advanced to explain men's enduring dominance over women—in the realm of economics, politics, the family, and elsewhere. In this section, we will review the main theoretical approaches to explaining the nature of gender inequality at the level of society.

Functionalist Approaches

As we saw in Chapter 1, the functional approach sees society as a system of interlinked parts that, when in balance, operate smoothly to produce social solidarity. Thus, functionalist and functionalist-inspired perspectives on gender seek to show that gender differences contribute to social stability and integration. Though such views once commanded great support, they have been heavily criticized for neglecting social tensions at the expense of consensus and for promulgating a conservative view of the social world.

Writers who subscribe to the natural differences school of thought tend to argue that the division of labor between men and women is biologically based. Women and men perform those tasks for which they are biologically best suited. Thus, the anthropologist George Murdock saw it as both practical and convenient that women should concentrate on domestic and family responsibilities while men work outside the home. On the basis of a cross-cultural study of more than two hundred societies, Murdock concluded that the sexual division of labor is present in all cultures (1949). Although this is not the result of biological programming, it is the most logical basis for the organization of society.

Talcott Parsons, a leading functionalist thinker, concerned himself with the role of the family in industrial societies (Parsons and Bales, 1955). He was particularly interested in the socialization of children and believed that stable, supportive families are the key to successful socialization. In Parsons's view, the family operates most efficiently with a clear-cut sexual division of labor in which females act in *expressive* roles, providing care and security to children and offering them emotional support, and men perform *instrumental* roles—namely, being the breadwinner in the family. Because of the stressful nature of this role, women's expressive and nurturing tendencies should also be used to stabilize and comfort men. This complementary division of labor, springing from a biological distinction between the sexes, would ensure the solidarity of the family according to Parsons.

Another functionalist perspective on child rearing was advanced by John Bowlby (1953), who argued that the mother is crucial to the primary socialization of children. If the mother is absent or if a child is separated from the mother at a young age—a state referred to as *maternal deprivation*—the child runs a high risk of being inadequately socialized. This can lead to serious social and psychological difficulties later in life, including

antisocial and psychopathic tendencies. Bowlby argued that a child's well-being and mental health can be best guaranteed through a close, personal and continuous relationship with its mother. He did concede that an absent mother can be replaced by a mother substitute, but suggested that such a substitute should also be a woman—leaving little doubt about his view that the mothering role is a distinctly female one. Bowlby's maternal deprivation thesis has been used by some to argue that working mothers are neglectful of their children.

Feminists have sharply criticized claims of a biological basis to the sexual division of labor, arguing that there is nothing natural or inevitable about the allocation of tasks in society. Women are not prevented from pursuing occupations on the basis of any biological features; rather, humans are socialized into roles that are culturally expected of them.

There is a steady stream of evidence to suggest that the maternal deprivation thesis is questionable—studies have shown that children's educational performance and personal development are in fact enhanced when both parents are employed at least part of the time outside the home. Parsons's view on the "expressive" female has similarly been attacked by feminists and other sociologists who see his views as condoning the subordination of women in the home. There is no basis to the belief that the "expressive" female is necessary for the smooth operation of the family—rather, it is a role that is promoted largely for the convenience of men.

In addition, cross-cultural studies show that even though most societies distinguish between men's and women's roles, the degree to which they differentiate tasks as exclusively male or female and assign different tasks and responsibilities to women and men can vary greatly (Coltrane, 1992). The degree to which certain tasks can be shared between women and men, and even how open groups and societies are to women performing men's activities and roles, differs across cultures and across time. Finally, cultures and societies have assigned different values to women and men and differ in the degree to which men are seen as "naturally" dominant over women. Thus, gender inequalities do not seem to be fixed or static. The division of labor based on gender and the devaluation of women relative to men have taken different forms and shapes throughout history.

Biological determinists see differences based on gender and gender inequalities as inevitable and unchangeable because they are consequences of biological necessities—not of social processes. Social constructionists disagree with biological determinists about where to find the sources of gender inequality and whether there is a potential for change: Sociological approaches look at society rather than at nature to explain why gender inequalities exist and how they can change. According to many sociologists, the key to understanding gender inequality is looking at a society's gendered division of labor and the value that society assigns to men's and women's roles (Coltrane, 1992; Collins et al., 1993; Dunn et al., 1993; Baxter and Kane, 1995; Chafetz, 1997). It is also important to recognize that gender inequality is also tied to issues of race and class (Collins, 1990).

Feminist Approaches

The feminist movement has given rise to a large body of theory that attempts to explain gender inequalities and set forth agendas for overcoming those inequalities. **Feminist theories** in relation to gender inequality contrast markedly with one another. Feminist writers are all concerned with women's unequal position in society, but their explanations for it vary substantially. Competing schools of feminism have sought to explain gender inequalities through a variety of deeply embedded social processes, such as sexism, patriarchy, capitalism, and racism. In the following sections, we will look at the arguments behind three main feminist perspectives—liberal, radical, and black feminism.

LIBERAL FEMINISM

Liberal feminism looks for explanations of gender inequalities in social and cultural attitudes. Unlike radical feminists, liberal feminists do not see women's subordination as part of a larger system or structure. Instead, they draw attention to many separate factors that contribute to inequalities between men and women. For example, liberal feminists are concerned with sexism and discrimination against women in the workplace, educational institutions, and the media. They tend to focus their energies on establishing and protecting equal opportunities for women through legislation and other democratic means. Legal advances such as the Equal Pay Act and the Sex Discrimination Act were actively supported by liberal feminists, who argued that enshrining equality in law is important to eliminating discrimination against women. Liberal feminists seek to work through the existing system to bring about reforms in a gradual way. In this respect, they are more moderate in their aims and methods than radical feminists, who call for an overthrow of the existing system.

While liberal feminists have contributed greatly to the advancement of women over the past century, critics charge that they are unsuccessful in dealing with the root cause of gender inequality and do not acknowledge the systemic nature of women's oppression in society. They say that by focusing on the independent deprivations that women suffer—sexism, discrimination, the "glass ceiling," unequal pay—liberal feminists draw only a partial picture of gender inequality. Radical feminists accuse liberal feminists of encouraging women to accept an unequal society and its competitive character.

RADICAL FEMINISM

At the heart of **radical feminism** is the belief that men are responsible for and benefit from the exploitation of women. The analysis of patriarchy—the systematic domination of females by males—is of central concern to this branch of feminism. Patriarchy is viewed as a universal phenomenon that has existed across time and cultures. Radical feminists often concentrate on the family as one of the primary sources of women's oppression in society. They argue that men exploit women by relying on the free domestic labor that women provide in the home and that as a group, men also deny women access to positions of power and influence in society.

Radical feminists differ in their interpretations of the basis of patriarchy, but most agree that it involves the appropriation of women's bodies and sexuality in some form. Shulamith Firestone (1971), an early radical feminist writer, argues that men control women's roles in reproduction and child rearing. Because women are biologically able to give birth to children, they become dependent materially on men for protection and livelihood. This "biological inequality" is socially organized in the nuclear family. Firestone speaks of a "sex class" to describe women's social position and argues that women can be emancipated only through the abolition of the family and the power relations that characterize it.

Other radical feminists point to male violence against women as central to male supremacy. According to such a view, domestic violence, rape, and sexual harassment are all part of the systematic oppression of women, rather than isolated cases with their own psychological or criminal roots. Even interactions in daily life—such as nonverbal communication, patterns of listening and interrupting, and women's sense of comfort in public—contribute to gender inequality. Moreover, the argument goes, popular conceptions of beauty and sexuality are imposed by men on women in order to produce a certain type of femininity. For example, social and cultural norms emphasizing a slim body and a caring, nurturing attitude toward men help to perpetuate women's subordination. The objectification of women through the media, fashion, and advertising turns women into sexual objects whose main role is to please and entertain men.

Radical feminists do not believe that women can be liberated from sexual oppression through reforms or gradual change. Because patriarchy is a systemic phenomenon, they argue, gender equality can only be attained by overthrowing the patriarchal order.

The use of patriarchy as a concept for explaining gender inequality has been popular with many feminist theorists. In asserting that "the personal is political," radical feminists have drawn widespread attention to the many linked dimensions of women's oppression. Their emphasis on male violence and the objectification of women has brought these issues into the heart of mainstream debates about women's subordination.

Many objections can be raised, however, to radical feminist views. The main one, perhaps, is that the concept of patriarchy as it has been used is inadequate as a general explanation for women's oppression. Radical feminists have tended to claim that patriarchy has existed throughout history and across cultures—that it is a universal phenomenon. Critics argue, however, that such a conception of patriarchy does not leave room for historical or cultural variations. It also ignores the important influence that race, class, or ethnicity may have on the nature of women's subordination. In other words, it is not possible to see patriarchy as a universal phenomenon; doing so risks *biological reductionism*—attributing all the complexities of gender inequality to a simple distinction between men and women.

BLACK FEMINISM

Do the versions of feminism outlined above apply equally to the experiences of both white and nonwhite women? Many black feminists and feminists from developing countries claim they do not. They argue that ethnic divisions among women are not considered by the main feminist schools of thought, which are oriented to the dilemmas of white, predominantly middle-class women living in industrialized societies. It is not valid, they claim, to generalize theories about women's subordination as a whole from the experience of a specific group of women. Moreover, the very idea that there is a unified form of gender oppression that is experienced equally by all women is problematic.

Dissatisfaction with existing forms of feminism has led to the emergence of a **black feminism** that concentrates on the particular problems facing black women. In the foreword to her personal memoirs, the African American feminist Bell Hooks argues:

Many feminist thinkers writing and talking about girlhood right now like to suggest that black girls have better self-esteem than their white counterparts. The measurement of this difference is often that black girls are more assertive, speak more, appear more confident. Yet in traditional southern-based black life, it was and is expected of girls to be articulate, to hold ourselves with dignity. Our parents and teachers were always urging us to stand up right and speak clearly. These traits were meant to uplift the race. They were not necessarily traits associated with building female self-esteem. An outspoken girl

might still feel that she was worthless because her skin was not light enough or her hair wasn't the right texture. These are the variables that white researchers often do not consider when they measure the self-esteem of black females with a yardstick that was designed based on values emerging from white experience. (Hooks, 1996)

Black feminist writings tend to emphasize history—aspects of the past that inform the current problems facing black women. The writings of African American feminists emphasize the influence of the powerful legacy of slavery, segregation, and the civil rights movement on gender inequalities in the black community. They point out that early black suffragettes supported the campaign for women's rights but realized that the question of race could not be ignored: Black women were discriminated against on the basis of their race *and* gender. In recent years, black women have not been central to the women's liberation movement in part because "womanhood" dominated their identities much less than concepts of race did.

Hooks has argued that explanatory frameworks favored by white feminists—for example, the view of the family as a mainstay of patriarchy—may not be applicable in black communities, where the family represents a main point of solidarity against racism. In other words, the oppression of black women may be found in different locations from that of white women.

Black feminists contend, therefore, that any theory of gender equality that does not take racism into account cannot be expected to explain black women's oppression adequately. Class dimensions are another factor that cannot be neglected in the case of many black women. Some black feminists have held that the strength of black feminist theory is its focus on the interplay among race, class, and gender concerns. Black

Surrounded by minority women at the Houston Civic Center, Coretta Scott King speaks about the resolution on minority women's rights that won the support of the National Women's Conference in 1977. The minority resolution, proposed by representatives of many races, declared that minority women suffered discrimination based on both race and sex.

women are multiply disadvantaged, they argue, on the basis of their color, their sex, *and* their class position. When these three factors interact, they reinforce and intensify each other (Brewer, 1993).

Using Sociology to Understand Andrea's Life

We have reviewed how sociologists analyze gender inequality, but let us think about how these ideas might help us illuminate the life of Andrea Ellington, whom we met at the beginning of the chapter. Andrea, a young black woman working the night shift as a word processor at an elite law firm, grew up in a poor neighborhood on the South Side of Chicago and today has three children to raise on her own.

To Andrea and women in similar life circumstances, the difficult conditions in which they find themselves may seem natural because of their sex. In other words, people may think it is natural for Andrea to be responsible for her children or to work as a word processor because she is a woman. Others might be inclined to consider whether her life circumstances are all her own doing, the result of bad personal choices regarding childbearing and the decision not to be married. Part of the job of someone who thinks like a sociologist is to ask whether such explanations are convincing given what is known about gender inequality.

In conducting the exercise of thinking about Andrea's life, we also have a chance to employ one of the key insights of contemporary feminist theory in sociology: that gender does not operate by itself, but comes together with race and class. This "coming together" is known as the intersection of gender, race, and class.

ANDREA'S JOB

The forms of gender inequality in the workplace, as discussed earlier, show that Andrea's experience as a clerical worker in the law firm is typical for women. Jobs for women have been created primarily in the service sector of the economy. Today, word processing and secretarial work are predominantly women's occupations, with the characteristics of lower pay, a high degree of sex segregation, and few possibilities for promotion. Typical of jobs that have been created in the past thirty years, Andrea's job has nonstandard working hours—she works the night shift.

Although nothing about the biological differences between the sexes would lead more women than men to work as word processors, societal forces tend to encourage women to aspire to such jobs. To begin with, many business colleges in Chicago advertise their secretarial programs with photographs of women, and many firms would rather hire women for their secretarial and word processing positions. Such positions have traditionally been, after all, jobs that service the clerical needs of the upper class of workers, many of whom are still men. An analysis of gender inequality would look closely at the way that people learn roles associated with gender—both the word processors and the people who do the hiring at firms. But it would also look at how those perceptions of difference become part of the structure of the organization, thereby reinforcing even more inequality.

Andrea's problems as a low-wage worker are those of many other persons similarly situated. Women are usually found at the lower end of the job ladder. One reason is that unlike jobs in male-dominated areas, women's occupations tend to be dead-end jobs with fewer possibilities for promotion. Andrea's position on the lower end of the pay scale may be due to her age and her lower level of experience in the job, which would be equivalent to that of a poor, similarly under-educated white woman her age. However, another barrier she encounters is due to her race. Within occupations dominated by women there can also be hierarchies according to class and/or race (Collins 1990; Brewer, 1993). Thus, someone studying gender inequality might look at the intersection of race, class, and gender to ask whether white women working as support staff at many law firms tend to have better-paying secretarial jobs, while black women might have word-processing positions with lower pay—a plausible possibility given the circumstances at the firm where Andrea works.

Finally, we need to examine broad global economic trends. We need to look at what kinds of jobs women can get in the present economy, which is influenced by processes of globalization and economic restructuring. Thus, the mere integration of women into the labor market does not necessarily mean more gender equality in general. Differences based on class and race between women have increased because of specific economic processes (Brewer, 1993).

ANDREA'S FAMILY

Contemporary political debates on "welfare" in the United States have heavily focused on marriage as the solution to the financial problems Andrea faces. The idea behind these political discussions is that if black single mothers would only get married, they would not be poor and would not need public assistance in the form of housing and health care.

It is further argued that women like Andrea must bear personal responsibility for having children out of wedlock.

A sociological analysis could begin by accepting the assumption that Andrea bears some personal responsibility for having children out of wedlock, while also trying to understand

Andrea's Dream

When journalists and sociologists seek to understand race relations, they seldom look closely at highly organized business offices. In trying to account for the disaffection, resistance and rebellious stances of the black poor, they think about the significance of Malcolm X caps, gangsta rap songs and the videotapes of Rodney King's struggles to rise from the pavement. When they want to understand urban poverty, they gravitate toward housing projects and street corners, carryouts and pool halls, and the vast arrays of institutions that comprise ghettos themselves.

Such an exclusive focus overlooks another less sensational story. During the [past few decades], while manufacturing declined, there was a rise in the financial and service sectors. A vast number of Chicago adults like Andrea Ellington participate in the larger society mainly through their work in the labor market that supports law firms, accounting firms and other high-level services.

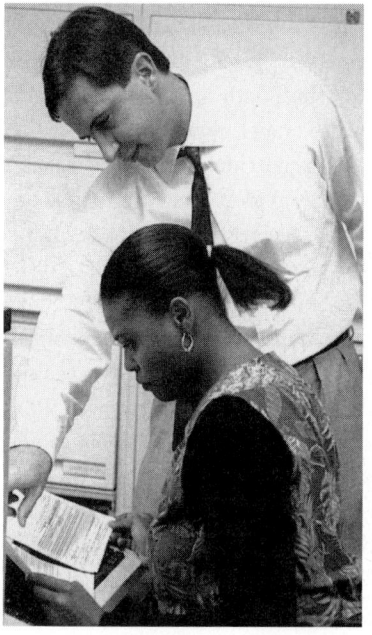

Though in the past Andrea Ellington had worked overtime at [her law firm] when she needed extra money, recently there hadn't been much extra work in the Network Center, and the supervisor was allocating overtime more carefully. When Andrea could no longer get overtime assignments, she requested a number of cash advances from the personnel director at [the firm] so she could pay her bills on time. Then she wrote a memo to her supervisor, who worked the day shift, asking for more overtime:

"I don't know if the personnel director has brought this to your attention but in the past few weeks I have been requesting cash advances. The reasons are very personal but I did go over a few with him as to why I had been requesting the cash advances. He mentioned to me last Friday that he sympathizes with my situation but he also made very good and valuable sense that the firm is not a bank and should not be responsible for my management of money.

"One of the reasons I started requesting cash advances is because the Center no longer had overtime available because of budget reasons. I understand this, but I also recall you say-

ing that if anyone wants to work overtime he or she should come directly to you. Well, I really depended on the overtime that was available and if there is in any way possible that I can get overtime I would appreciate it greatly. . . . I want to apologize for any inconvenience that I have put upon the firm and especially toward the personnel director. My intent was not to abuse the privilege of cash advances. Please give me a call at home or respond with a memo so that maybe we can discuss this issue further."

The supervisor looked upon Andrea's letter as an act of "incredible conscientiousness." As she put it, "It seemed that she wanted to make sure she didn't overstep her bounds, yet she was coming to us with a problem and trying to solve it in a practical way. I felt that we had to try."

Later that day, the supervisor assigned Andrea to work an extra eight hours of overtime per week, on Sunday. Andrea came to work for the first two Sundays, and then began missing her weekend assignments when she couldn't find a baby-sitter for Lauren, Cubie, and Corey, her three children. When her supervisor learned of her absences, she canceled the overtime.

Andrea wrote again in response to that decision:

"This memo is in regards to the cancellation of overtime hours regarding the litigation project. I really counted on the overtime tremendously and it has been a big help in ways you can't imagine. I know my financial situation is not a priority or a concern of the firm's, but I really need to work the extra hours to get by for an everyday living. . . .

"This overtime has help me pay bills on time, buy cloths for my children, and buy food that I would normally have had to wait until each pay check to get. If the decision was made due to budget reasons by the firm then I have no choice but to try to do the best with what I have, but if you have any information on anyone looking for part-time help or know any agencies that hire for part-time, please inform me as soon as possible on anything you might know of.". . .

[Andrea is again given overtime, and again misses it because she cannot find reliable child care. She goes to see her supervisor.]

"Well, you cut out my overtime. I really need that overtime."

"I'm very sorry, Andrea," the supervisor responded.

"Maybe I can just come in an hour instead of the four hours I was coming in or whatever."

"No."

"Because it was really helping me out there."

The supervisor didn't know what to say. She looked up stonily from her desk.

Andrea says it took everything in her power not to break down and cry. "You know, I just don't make much money for what I do. I know I'm the lowest paid person in the Network Center."

"How do you know?" the supervisor asked.

"That does not matter," Andrea answered. "I just need the money. Because I'm really not making what I should be making in the first place. So at least allow me to have the overtime."

"You're making a decent living," her supervisor said.

There was silence.

Andrea went on. "I might be a paycheck away from being homeless. Thank you."

SOURCE: Mitchell Duneier, "Andrea's Dream: A Single Parent's Fight for Independence," series, *Chicago Tribune*, December 1994, pp. 3–4, 13–15.

Questions

- Andrea belongs to several historically disadvantaged sociological groups: women, single mothers, African Americans, and the poor. In what ways might her problems at work and at home relate to her membership in these groups?
- Andrea is trying to raise a family and to keep her job. How and why do these two goals seem to contradict each other?

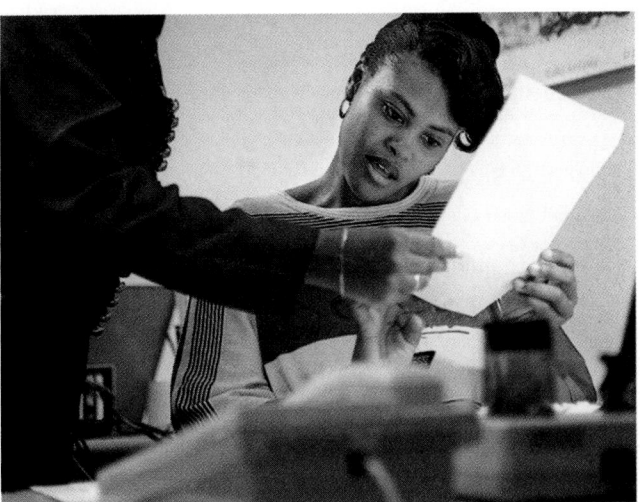

The International Women's Movement

Do you have any interest in joining the women's movement? Every year countless American college students are inspired by feminism and enlist in the fight for such causes as reproductive rights, equal pay, or the preservation of welfare benefits for poor women. In today's increasingly globalized world, there is a good chance that those who become active in the U.S. women's movement will come into contact with women pursuing other feminist struggles overseas.

The women's movement, of course, is not simply an American or Western European phenomenon. In China, for example, women are working to secure "equal rights, employment, women's role in production, and women's participation in politics" (Zhang and Xu, 1995). In South Africa, women played a pivotal role in the battle against apartheid and are fighting in the post-apartheid era to improve "the material conditions of the oppressed majority; those who have been denied access to education, decent homes, health facilities, and jobs" (Kemp et al., 1995). In Peru, activists have been working for decades to give women a greater "opportunity to participate in public life" (Blondet, 1995), while "in Russia, women's protest was responsible for blocking the passage of legislation that the Russian parliament considered in 1992 that encouraged women to stay home and perform 'socially necessary labor'" (Basu, 1995).

Although participants in women's movements have, for many years, cultivated ties to activists in other countries, the number and importance of such contacts has increased with

the societal conditions that lead so many poor women to make that choice. Here we can see again that there is a link between race, class, and gender. Studies of urban labor markets (Wilson, 1987) have demonstrated that the loss of jobs for poor black men in the inner city has made marriage less attractive to many black women. Why, the reasoning goes, should women get married to men who don't have jobs? This increases women's independence from men to some degree, so that women do not necessarily have to marry the fathers of their children (Huber, 1992).

In addition to the impact of this societal force on women like Andrea, there is likely also the influence of social norms. When many other women are influenced by the same structural barriers to meeting men with jobs, it comes to seem quite logical to those women to have children on their own. In these circumstances, we can begin to comprehend how women like Andrea make the choice to have children out of wedlock. The loss of jobs that might make self-support for black men possible also makes it more difficult for them to fulfill their obligations to provide child support. One reason Andrea does not have enough money to pay her bills and to attain her dream to move out of the housing project she lives in is that she has not received enough money from the father of her children.

ANDREA'S CHALLENGES IN COMBINING WORK AND FAMILY

The most prominent example of how gender inequalities in the workplace are intertwined with inequalities arising from women's roles as mothers is seen in Andrea's negotiations with her employer about overtime.

Since Andrea did not earn enough money from her low-paying job, she asked her boss if she could work extra hours. When the boss scheduled these extra projects on a Sunday, Andrea was unable to find reliable child care. Because she missed work on several occasions, the boss canceled the extra projects.

globalization. A prime forum for the establishment of cross-national contacts has been the United Nation's Conference on Women, held four times since 1975. Approximately fifty thousand people—of which more than two-thirds were women—attended the most recent conference, held in Beijing, China, in 1995. Delegates from 181 nations were in attendance, along with representatives from thousands of nongovernmental organizations (UN Chronicle, 1995). Seeking ways to "ensure women's equal access to economic resources including land, credit, science and technology, vocational training, information, communication and markets," conference participants spent ten days listening to presentations on the state of women worldwide, debating ways to improve their condition, and building professional and personal ties to one another. Mallika Dutt, one of the attendees, recently wrote in the journal *Feminist Studies* that "for most women from the United States, Beijing was an eye-opening, humbling, and transformative experience. U.S. women were startled by the sophisticated analysis and well-organized and powerful voices of women from other parts of the world" (1996). At the same time, according to Dutt, many of the conference participants left Beijing with a "sense of global solidarity, pride, and affirmation" (1996).

The Platform for Action finally agreed to by the conference participants called on the countries of the world to address such issues as:

The persistent and increasing burden of poverty on women;

Violence against women;

The effects of armed or other kinds of conflict on women;

Inequality between men and women in the sharing of power and decision-making;

Stereotyping of women;

Gender inequalities in the management of natural resources;

Persistent discrimination against and violation of the rights of the girl child.

Must women's movements have an international orientation to be effective? Are women's interests essentially the same throughout the world? What might feminism mean to women in the developing world? These and many other questions are being hotly debated as the process of globalization continues apace.

Subsequently, this boss assumed that Andrea wasn't able to work overtime and, therefore, refused to offer her extra projects. This, in turn, had an effect on how Andrea felt about her job, a process that lowers occupational aspirations (Huber, 1990).

It is quite understandable how a reasonable employer would draw such a conclusion about Andrea. Yet, a sociological approach would ask whether these incidents are due to a problem with Andrea or with the system of child care. If the system were different, is it possible that women like Andrea would appear much more responsible?

Someone aware of gender inequality would look at the way the gender division of labor in our society places the burden of child raising on mothers. In the United States, child care is not a public responsibility, nor is it seen as the responsibility of the employer. Andrea's boss feels that it is Andrea's task to find child care, even on a Sunday. And yet, since the wages of her job are low, she needs that overtime to earn enough money to support her children and to move out of the housing project.

The ways in which societies organize the care of children, elderly, and disabled people profoundly shape gender relations. For example, if there is little public support for child care, then parents have to find caregivers for their children when they are working outside the home. Moreover, in societies that view child care primarily as the task of women, yet attach little value to this task, mothers in the workplace are disadvantaged. In contrast, if society valued taking care of children as an important contribution for future generations, Andrea might get financial support for taking care of her children herself; or, if taking care of children was not a low-paying job but was supported by employers and government, Andrea might find a good-quality child-care center open on a Sunday.

Andrea's mother usually takes care of Andrea's daughter. We can see how child care can be informally organized across generations of women. Research on African American communities demonstrates that black women used to be tied into kinships, neighborhoods, and other networks of women who shared child raising responsibilities. But these structures of shared motherhood have been crumbling (Collins, 1990; Brewer, 1993; Glenn, 1994).

Why Gender Inequality Matters

A Chinese saying holds that "women hold up half the sky." In fact, as we have seen in this chapter, women typically hold up far more than half: As the world moves into the twenty-first century, women have become a central part of the world's paid workforce, while at the same time maintaining their traditional responsibilities for home and family.

China was the site of the 1995 United Nations' Fourth World Conference on Women, where some 35,000 people, representing 180 governments and 7,000 women's organizations, discussed the problems of women worldwide. The conference, held in the capital city of Beijing, grappled with a central problem women face the world over: What happens when a country's traditional cultural beliefs conflict with modern notions of women's rights? Globalization has not only brought factories and television to nearly every place on the planet, but has also exposed people throughout the world to ideas about equality and democracy. The modern women's movement has become a global champion of universal rights for women.

The Beijing Women's Conference's final action platform was clear: When cultural traditions conflict with women's rights, women's rights should take precedence. The platform called for women's right to control their own reproduction and sexuality, as well as to inherit wealth and property—two rights that women are denied in many countries. It concluded that no society can truly hope to better the lives if its citizens until it fosters gender equality:

The advancement of women and the achievement of equality between women and men are a matter of human rights and a condition for social justice and should not be seen in isolation as a women's issue. They are the only way to build a sustainable, just and developed society. Empowerment of women and equality between women and men are prerequisites for achieving political, social, economic, cultural and environmental security among all peoples. (Beijing Women's Conference, 1995)

Five years after the Beijing conference, a special session of the United Nations General Assembly reaffirmed these principles, challenging the world's governments to realize the conference's goals. Noting that women occupied only 13 percent of parliament seats worldwide, the UN called for a global increase in women's political power. The Women's Environment and Development Organization, A New York–based women's advocacy group, was more specific in its statement to the UN: It pushed for equal representation of women in cabinet ministries and legislative bodies by 2005. The goal was set not only to benefit women, but to benefit society as a whole. In the view of the organization's executive director, increased women's representation would help shift a country's policies to "real-life concerns," as is seen in Scandinavia, where women are well represented in all levels of government: "Their commitment to the social safety net, to [an] expansive childcare system, to helping women and men balance work and family needs, I think, reflects women's experiences" (Hogan, 2000).

The feminization of labor has altered the world economy. Will the feminization of politics do the same for global governance? The shift to a greater role for women in economics and politics may well signal a shift to greater equality for all people—not only for women but also for minority people, including sexual minorities—the world over.

Study Outline

www.wwnorton.com/giddens5

Gender Differences: Nature versus Nurture

• *Sex* in the sense of physical difference is distinct from *gender* (masculine and feminine), which concerns cultural and psychological differences. It is no simple matter to determine which observable differences are due to biology (sex) and which are socially constructed (gender). Arguments from animal behavior are usually ambiguous. Some researchers claim, for instance, that hormones explain such differences as greater male aggressiveness, but it may just as easily be the case that aggressive behavior causes changes in hormone levels. Studies of gender differences from a variety of human societies have shown no conclusive evidence that gender is biologically determined; rather, biological differences seem to provide a means of marking or differentiating social roles.

- Studies of parent-infant interactions reveal that boys and girls are treated differently right from birth; the same features and behaviors are interpreted as either "masculine" or "feminine" depending on the parents' expectations.

Forms of Gender Inequality

- *Patriarchy* refers to male dominance over women. There are few known societies that are not patriarchal, although the degree and character of inequalities between the sexes varies considerably across cultures. In the United States, women have made considerable progress yet are still unequal in many ways.
- Women's participation in the paid labor force has risen steadily, especially married women's and especially in expanding areas of the economy. Many women, however, are poorly paid and have dim career prospects. Even women who are successful in the corporate world face discrimination in the form of deeply held cultural expectations about the proper role of women in society.
- The increasing number of women in the labor force has had a big impact on family responsibilities like child care and housework. Though men are contributing more to these responsibilities, women still shoulder the bulk of the work. For working women, these household obligations constitute a "second shift."
- The ways schools are organized and how classes are taught have tended to sustain *gender inequalities*. Rules specifying distinct dress for girls and boys encourages sex typing, as do the texts containing established gender images. There is evidence that teachers treat girls and boys differently, and there is a long history of specialized subjects for separate sexes.

Violence Against Women

- Violence perpetrated by men against women is found in many societies—in the form of spousal abuse, rape, and sexual harassment, for example. The most common manifestation of violence against women is *rape*, which is the forcing of nonconsensual intercourse. Some scholars argue that women are often the targets of sexual violence because men are socialized to see women as sex objects and to feel a sense of sexual entitlement to women.

Gender Inequality Throughout the World

- Women throughout the world work in the lowest-wage jobs, and are likely to make less than men doing similar work—although there is some evidence that the wage gap is decreasing slowly, at least in industrialized countries. In developing countries, women are likely to experience exploitative job conditions. Yet at the same time, their enhanced economic role has sometimes resulted in increased economic independence and greater social status.

- Worldwide, women do not share the same political power as men, although thirty-eight countries have been headed by a woman since World War II. The United States is about average among countries in terms of women's representation in the national legislature, but has never had a woman president.
- *Gender* is one of the most important dimensions of inequality, although it was neglected in the study of stratification for a long time. Although there are few societies in which women have more wealth and status than men, there are significant variations in how women's and men's roles are valued within a society. Sociologists have argued that gender inequalities are not fixed. They have also drawn attention to the links between gender inequality and race and class.

Theories of Gender Inequality

- In explaining gender inequality, functionalists have emphasized that gender differences and the sexual division of labor contribute to social stability and integration. Feminist approaches reject the idea that gender inequality is somehow natural. Liberal feminists have explained gender inequality in terms of social and cultural attitudes, such as sexism and discrimination. Radical feminists argue that men are responsible for the exploitation of women through patriarchy—the systematic domination of females by males. Black feminists have seen factors such as class and ethnicity, in addition to gender, as essential for understanding the oppression experienced by nonwhite women.

Key Concepts

black feminism (p. 304)
comparable worth (p. 289)
feminist theories (p. 303)
gender (p. 278)
gender inequality (p. 284)
gender socialization (p. 279)
gender typing (p. 286)
"glass ceiling" (p. 289)
"glass escalator" (p. 290)
human capital theory (p. 288)
liberal feminism (p. 303)
patriarchy (p. 284)
radical feminism (p. 303)
rape (p. 296)
sex (p. 278)
sexual harassment (p. 290)
social construction of gender (p. 281)

Review Questions

1. What's the difference between sex and gender?
   a. Sex refers to the physical differences in the body, whereas gender concerns the psychological, social, and cultural differences between males and females.
   b. Sex is what couples do to conceive, whereas gender is an attribute of their baby.
   c. A culture's understanding of gender determines what types of physical intimacy constitute sex.
   d. There is none. In sociology, as in everyday life, the terms are interchangeable.

2. What is the "glass ceiling"?
   a. It is the "old-boy network" in firms that helps men get ahead by making clear what management expects. Men can see through the "glass ceiling" but women cannot.
   b. It is an invisible barrier that prevents women from achieving the highest positions in a firm, usually because they do not have the sponsorship of a senior manager.
   c. It refers to the earnings gap between white women and women of color.
   d. It is an invisible barrier that prevents women from being hired in the first place because managers expect most women to leave the firm sooner or later to have a family.

3. What is patriarchy?
   a. The name given to societies in which property is passed down by the male lineage.
   b. The name given to societies in which Eastern Orthodoxy is the main religion.
   c. The name given to societies in which women are treated as property.
   d. The name given to male dominance in a society.

4. Which of the following passages best describes women's movement into the labor force?
   a. From 1940 until the mid- to late 1960s, women's participation in the labor force was led by older women, past their childbearing years. From that point on, as women's educational achievements began to catch up with men's, labor force participation spread to younger women.
   b. From 1940 until the mid-1960s, women's participation in the labor force was led by men who wanted their wives to contribute to their household finances. From that point on, as women's educational achievements began to catch up with men's, labor force participation spread to young, unmarried women.
   c. From 1940 until the middle to late 1960s, women's participation in the labor force was led by younger women who were more willing to confront traditional conceptions of women's role in the home. From that point on, as the hold of traditional conceptions weakened, older women followed their younger sisters into the labor force.
   d. None of the above.

5. What is the "second shift"?
   a. The first shift was women's movement into the workforce. The second shift is women's movement into the professions.
   b. The first shift was the movement into the workforce of older women with grown-up children. The second shift was the movement into the work force of younger women with small children.
   c. The first shift is overcoming traditional male conceptions that a woman's natural role is in the home. The second shift is overcoming male reluctance to treat women as equals in the workplace.
   d. The first shift is a woman's day at work. The second shift is the extra responsibility she bears for housework when she gets home.

6. In which country has the women's movement played an important role in improving women's status?
   a. China
   b. Peru
   c. South Africa
   d. All of the above.

7. What does it mean for men and women to "do gender"?
   a. To "do gender" means to follow traditional conceptions of the responsibilities of men and women in everyday life and to reinforce the idea that gender is a natural means for society to differentiate itself.
   b. To "do gender" means to challenge traditional conceptions of the responsibilities of men and women in everyday life and to attack the idea that gender is a natural means for society to differentiate itself.
   c. To "do gender" means to take the traditional role of the opposite gender (men acting as women and women as men).
   d. To "do gender" refers to the process by which children learn about traditional conceptions of gender roles.

8. Paludi and Barickman found that most women who were abused by behavior that fits legal definitions of sexual harassment
   a. filed legal complaints.
   b. did not label what had happened to them as sexual harassment.
   c. filed legal complaints but withdrew their cases.
   d. got compensation from their offenders.

9. Most schoolteachers are women. In classroom discussions,
   a. female teachers are more likely to solicit information from boys than from girls.
   b. female teachers are more likely to solicit information from girls than from boys.
   c. female teachers are no more likely to solicit information from boys than from girls.
   d. this has not been studied.

10. According to Firestone and Mitchell, before the development of birth control, why were men dominant over women?
    a. Men have superior physical strength.
    b. Men controlled women's fertility.
    c. Women depended on men for material provision due to constant childbirth and continuous caring for infants.
    d. All of the above.

Thinking Sociologically Exercises

1. What does cross-cultural evidence from tribal societies in New Guinea, Africa, and North America suggest about the differences in gender roles? Explain.
2. Why are minority women likely to think very differently about gender inequality than white women? Explain.

Data Exercises

www.wwnorton.com/giddens5
Keyword: Data10

- While women in the United States still have a ways to go before they can claim full equality, women in many other nations continue to face extreme disadvantages relative to men. Completing the data exercise for Chapter 10, you will learn more about women's lives in other countries and make global comparisons about women's social status.

Race and Ethnicity: Key Concepts

Learn the cultural bases of race and ethnicity and how racial and ethnic differences create sharp divisions. Learn the leading psychological theories and sociological interpretations of prejudice and discrimination.

Ethnic Relations

Recognize the importance of the historical roots, particularly in the expansion of Western colonialism, of ethnic conflict. Understand the different models for a multiethnic society.

Global Migration

Understand global migration patterns and their impact.

Ethnic Relations in the United States

Familiarize yourself with the history and social dimensions of ethnic relations in America.

Racial and Ethnic Inequality

Learn the forms of inequality experienced by different racial and ethnic groups in the United States. See that the history of prejudice and discrimination against ethnic minorities has created conditions of hardship for many but that some have succeeded despite societal barriers.

CHAPTER ELEVEN

ETHNICITY AND RACE

maureen, a forty-five-year-old black woman who was born in the Caribbean, came to England at the age of twelve with her family. She is the Social Services Manager for Home Care in Leicester, a city located ninety miles north of London in the East Midlands. She has three brothers and ten nieces and nephews. All of her brothers have established families with white English women. She describes six of her nieces and nephews as "dual heritage." Yet she also believes that these children of multiracial heritage will be classified as "black" by those outside the family. Here she sums her view of one of her white sisters-in-law whom she respects: "I feel—she very much wants the child to have a black identity. So, every Sunday she would bring [my niece] up to my mum's house so that she knows her black family. If you say 'Do this for her hair,' she'd be religiously doing it. And she's asked for advice about her hair. And you'd see her plaiting it. And her hair is always so pretty." Maureen and her other black Caribbean family members consider her niece to be "racially" black although she has a white birth mother. They recognize that in spite of having a white mother, this girl will be classified as black because of her physical appearance, and thus she should be trained to identify herself as a black. The labor required of Maureen's white sister-in-law demonstrates how "race," like ethnicity, is learned. They are "socially constructed."

In 1991, according to the UK census 50 percent of UK-born black men had selected a white partner (Modood et al., 1997). The sociologist France Winddance Twine has found in her research among black-white multiracial families in the United States and the United Kingdom (some of her subjects are pictured on p. 310) that some parents train their children to develop what she terms **"racial literacy"** skills in order to help them cope with racial hierarchies and to integrate multiple ethnic identities. Twine defines one dimension of racial literacy as a form of antiracist training which the parents of African-descent children employ to teach their children to recognize the forms of racism that they might encounter (2003). Twine found that there were gaps between how parents viewed their children racially, their children's own racial self-identification, and how they were socially classified outside the home. For example, there were shifts and intense struggles among parents, extended family members, and teachers over a child's racial and ethnic classification (Twine, 1991, 1997, 2004). Twine's research, as well as others, illustrates how difficult it is to easily define the conditions of racial and ethnic group membership for some individuals of multiracial heritage. In recent decades a number of sociologists have turned their attention to this problem of multiracial identity and racial classification schemes. They have argued that a "static measure of race" is not useful for individuals of multiracial heritage who may assert different identities in different social contexts (Harris, 2003; Harris and Sim, 2000; Goldstein and Morning, 2000).

Race and Ethnicity: Key Concepts

In your daily life, you have no doubt used the terms *race* and *ethnicity* many times, but do you know what they mean? In fact, defining these terms is very difficult, but what is most important is that you begin by dispensing with what you think you know. Do not think of race and ethnicity as completely different phenomena.

Ethnicity refers to cultural practices and outlooks of a given community that have emerged historically and tend to set people apart. Members of ethnic groups see themselves as culturally distinct from other groups in a society and are seen by those other groups to be so in return. Different characteristics may serve to distinguish ethnic groups from one another, but the most common are some combination of language, history, religious faith, and ancestry—real or imagined—and styles of dress or adornment. Some examples of ethnic groups in the United States would include Irish Americans, Jewish Americans, Italian Americans, Cuban Americans, and Japanese Americans. Ethnic differences are learned.

The difference between race and ethnicity is not as clear cut as some people think. When you think of it, everything that has been said here about ethnicity would apply very well

to Maureen's mixed-race nieces above. Their black relatives and white mother are teaching them many cultural practices that people associate with being black—from how to braid their hair to how to respond to racism. So does this mean that race is really a kind of ethnicity?

In a way it is, but race has certain defining characteristics that make it different from ethnicity. At certain historical moments, ethnic differences take on two additional characteristics. First, some ethnic differences become the basis of stigmas that cannot be removed by conversion or assimilation. Second, these stigmas become the basis of extreme hierarchy.

The mixed-race children with white mothers and black relatives in England look black to many people. Some aspects of their blackness, such as learning to braid their hair from relatives and friends, are cultural practices akin to ethnicity. Yet what makes their blackness into race is the fact that in the United Kingdom, dark skin color has historically been stigmatized, as in the United States. And this stigma has laid the foundation for extreme hierarchy in England, as in the United States.

Race, then, can be understood as a classification system that assigns individuals and groups to categories that are ranked or hierarchical. But there are no clear-cut "races," only a range of physical variations among human beings. Differences in physical type among groups of human beings arise from population inbreeding, which varies according to the degree of contact among different social or cultural groups. Human population groups are a continuum. The genetic diversity *within* populations that share visible physical traits is as great as the diversity *between* them. Racial distinctions are more than ways of describing human differences—they are also important factors in the reproduction of patterns of power and inequality within society.

The process by which understandings of race are used to classify individuals or groups of people is called **racialization**. Historically, racialization meant that certain groups of people came to be labeled as constituting distinct biological groups on the basis of naturally occurring physical features. From the fifteenth century onward, as Europeans came into increased contact with people from different regions of the world, they attempted to systematize knowledge by categorizing and explaining both natural and social phenomena. Non-European populations were "racialized" in opposition to the European "white race." In some instances this racialization took on codified institutional forms, as in the case of slavery in the former British, French, and Spanish colonies in the Americas, slavery in the United States, and the establishment of apartheid in South Africa after World War II (1948). More commonly, however, everyday political, educational, legal, and other institutions become racialized through legislation. In the United States after the civil rights movement, de facto racial segregation and racial

Celebrating the Chinese New Year with performances and decorations is not just a picturesque event every year in Soho, but an important symbol of cultural continuity for London's Chinese community.

hierarchies persisted even after state-sanctioned segregation was dismantled. Within a racialized system, an individual's social life and his or her life chances—including education, employment, incarceration, housing, health care, and legal representation are all shaped and constrained by the racial assignments and racial hierarchies in that system.

In recent years, sociologists who study ethnicity in the United States have come to understand that larger forces that give rise to ethnic-group collective consciousness have declined. For example, people who are Jewish or Irish no longer face the kind of housing discrimination that led them to cluster in particular neighborhoods prior to World War II. In addition, intermarriage between members of different religious groups and European and Asian groups has increased substantially. In the face of such changing conditions, sociologists have noted that ethnic identity, at least in the United States, has less of an impact on the everyday lives of the members of these social groups, unless they choose an ethnic label. As a result, ethnicity is now a choice of whether to be ethnic at all. More and more people must also make a choice about which ethnicity to be (Gans, 1979; Waters, 1990). Because of this phenomenon, sociologists refer to *situational ethnicity* and *symbolic ethnicity*.

Situational ethnicity is a concept that illustrates one of the ways in which ethnic and racial identification is socially constructed. Some people of multiracial ancestry may choose to assert or not to reveal a salient aspect of their identity or heritage in particular situations, such as applying for a job in which certain racial groups predominate. They may not report an identity at other times when it could lead to discrimination. This shows that larger political forces, such as the categories devised by governments, affect the identity people display.

Symbolic ethnicity occurs when members of an ethnic group assimilate into the larger culture, perhaps moving away from the old neighborhood to the suburbs where a smaller percentage of people are engaged in ethnic practices. Such people might only participate in ethnic customs on symbolic occasions such as Saint Patrick's Day or at Passover, when they attend a seder. During the rest of the year, their ethnic identity might not be very salient at all.

Whereas ethnicity is primarily a symbolic option for white Americans, race is not always such a choice for non-whites. And, although it is sometimes a choice for people of "mixed race" whose racial characteristics are ambiguous, for members of many racial groups it is not a choice. One sociologist who has studied how many Americans think about their ancestry and backgrounds has written that "the social and political consequences of being Asian or Hispanic or black are not symbolic for the most part, or voluntary. They are real and often hurtful" (Waters, 1990). Minority group status can have many negative consequences for its members. One such negative consequence is segregation (discussed later in this chapter).

Despite the increase in the number of people in the United States self-identifying as multiracial, many North Americans continue to believe, mistakenly, that race is a natural category and that human beings can be neatly separated into biologically distinct "races." This is a legacy of European colonialization and scientific racism. During the sixteenth century, Europeans began to classify animals, people, and the material culture that they collected as they explored the world. Racial classification schemes were invented during a period when Europeans were conquering territories and expanding. The Swedish botanist Carolus Linnaeus is considered the founder

Four schoolboys represent the "racial scale" in South Africa; black, Indian, half-caste, and white.

of scientific taxonomy. In 1735, he published what is recognized as the first version of a modern classification scheme of human populations. Linnaeus included humans in a larger classification scheme with relations to apes and monkeys. He grouped human beings into four basic varieties—Europaeus, Americanus, Asiaticus, and Africanus. At this time it was believed that human beings descended from a common original ancestor. Physical features, behaviors, and psychological traits were correlated. Linnaeus assumed that each species had qualities of behavior or temperament that were innate and could not be altered. He acquired much of his data from the writings, descriptions, commentaries, and beliefs of plantation owners, missionaries, slave traders, explorers, and travelers. Thus his scientific data were shaped by the prejudices and power that Europeans had over the people whom they conquered (Smedley, 1993).

Racial Categories

Census categories today reflect political constituencies and power relations. The categories used on the census have not remained consistent over time and have changed. In 1970 the Hispanic category was added to the United States census. Other racial categories have been removed such as "mulatto," which last appeared on the 1920 Census. The question of why some racial groups and ethnic groups appear and disappear from the census challenges the notion that racial groups are based on simple biological differences.

After a three-year study, a governmental task force proposed that the Office of Management and Budget (OMB) allow for the addition of a multiracial category to the 2000 U.S. Census. This recommendation came after a coalition of individuals of multiracial heritage and advocacy groups across the nation lobbied the OMB. For the first time the census allowed individuals to check more than one racial category if they desired. The debate surrounding the possible addition of a multiracial category reveals the degree to which Americans continue to hold beliefs that racial groups are "natural," even though in reality these groups reflect political relations among people descended from groups that were conquered and colonized. Racial and ethnic groups in the United States, as in other nations, are stratified. The U.S. Bureau of the Census distinguishes four races (American Indian/Alaska Native, Asian and Pacific Islander, black, and white), but too many exceptions and inconsistencies in the classifications have been found to make any of them workable without great controversy.

Racism and Antiracism

Both racism and antiracism are fairly new terms. Racism did not come into use until the 1930s and antiracism is a concept that emerged in the twentieth century but did not appear in regular usage until the 1960s. Both terms can be defined in many ways because there are different definitions of what constitutes racism in different national contexts.

RACISM

Some see **racism** as a system of domination that operates in social processes and social institutions; others see it as operating in the individual consciousness. Racism can refer to explicit beliefs in racial supremacy such as the systems established in Nazi Germany, before the civil rights movement in the United States, and in South Africa under apartheid.

Yet many have argued that racism is more than simply the ideas held by a small number of bigoted individuals. Rather, racism is embedded in the very structure and operation of society. The idea of **institutional racism** suggests that racism pervades all of society's structures in a systematic manner. According to this view, institutions such as the police, the health-care industry, and the educational system all promote policies that favor certain groups while discriminating against others.

The idea of institutional racism was developed in the United States in the late 1960s by black power activists (Stokeley Carmichael and Charles Hamilton) and taken up by civil rights campaigners who believed that white supremacy structured all social relations and that racism was the foundation of the very fabric of U.S. society, rather than merely representing the opinions of a small minority. In subsequent years, the existence of institutional racism came to be widely accepted and openly acknowledged in many settings. A 1990s investigation into the practices of the Los Angeles Police Department, in light of the beating of Rodney King, found that institutional racism is pervasive within the police force and the criminal justice system. A similar case occurred more recently in New York City, when police officers shot and killed an unarmed African man from Guinea, Amadou Diallo. In culture and the arts, institutional racism has been demonstrated to exist in Hollywood films, television broadcasting (negative or limited portrayals of racial and ethnic minorities in programming), and the international modeling industry (industry-wide bias against fashion models who appear to be of non-European ancestry and/or mixed race).

FROM "OLD RACISM" TO "NEW RACISM"

Just as the concept of biological race has been discredited, old-style "biological" racism based on differences in physical traits is rarely openly expressed in society today. The end of state-sanctioned segregation in the United States and the collapse of apartheid in South Africa in 1994 were important turning points in the rejection of biological racism. In both of these cases, racist attitudes were proclaimed by directly associating physical traits with biological inferiority. Such blatantly racist ideas are rarely heard today, except in the cases of violent hate crimes or the platforms of certain extremist groups. But racist attitudes have not disappeared from modern societies. Rather, as some scholars argue, they have been replaced by a more sophisticated "new racism" (or cultural racism), which uses the idea of cultural differences to exclude certain groups (Barker, 1981).

Those who argue that a "new racism" has emerged claim that cultural arguments are now employed instead of biological ones in order to support discrimination against certain segments of the population. According to this view, hierarchies of superiority and inferiority are constructed according to the values of the majority culture. Those groups that stand apart from the majority can be marginalized or vilified for their refusal to assimilate. It is alleged that new racism has a clear political dimension. The fact that racism is increasingly based on cultural rather than biological grounds has led some scholars to suggest that we live in an age of "multiple racisms," where discrimination is experienced differently across segments of the population (Modood et al., 1997).

ANTIRACISM

Antiracism is a concept that emerged in the twentieth century but did not appear in regular usage until the 1960s. It has been defined by Alistair Bonnett (2000) as

> forms of thought and/or practice that seek to confront, eradicate and/or ameliorate racism. Antiracism implies the ability to identify a phenomenon—racism—and to do something about it. Different forms of antiracism exist because there are different definitions of what constitutes racism in different national contexts.

Opposition to racism has been embraced by some governments as a way to protect their political interests and prove themselves worthy of power. Affirmative-action programs, which are a form of antiracism, vary tremendously in different national contexts. In other national contexts, as in India and Malaysia, antiracism has been employed as a component of national identity and a symbol of national allegiance (Bonnett, 2000). For example, in the aftermath of the race riots in Kuala Lumpur between Malays and Chinese in May of 1969, the Malaysian government implemented affirmation-action programs. These affirmative action programs were introduced under the New Economic Policy Act (NEP) and established a quota in which 40 percent of jobs in most industries were set aside for Malays and a target of 30 percent was established for Malay ownership of commercial and industrial enterprises. Another measure, the Constitution Amendment Bill, gave the government the power to require universities to lower their qualification entrance requirements for Malay students (Nesiah, 1997). Another example of antiracism is the affirmative-action program established in India to provide constitutional safeguards for what are known as the scheduled castes and tribes. Articles 330 and 332 of the Indian Constitution reserve a percentage of the legislative seats in the Lower Parliament for members of these groups. These quotas constitute a form of affirmative action that is much stronger and more radical in its goals than are programs in the United States.

Sociologists have only recently begun to place an analysis of antiracism, particularly white antiracism, at the center of analysis. The sociologist Becky Thompson interviewed white antiracists all over the United States to understand their political trajectories and how they formed an antiracist constituency and community after World War II (2001). Many students of sociology today consider themselves to be antiracists, though many sociologists still believe that the science of society should be kept separate from personal politics.

Psychological Interpretations of Prejudice and Discrimination

Psychological theories can help us understand the nature of prejudiced and racist attitudes and also why ethnic differences matter so much to people.

PREJUDICE, DISCRIMINATION, AND RACISM

The concept of race is modern, but prejudice and discrimination have been widespread in human history, and we must first clearly distinguish between them. **Prejudice** refers to opinions or attitudes held by members of one group toward another. A prejudiced person's preconceived views are often based on hearsay rather than on direct evidence, and are resistant to change even in the face of new information. People may harbor favorable prejudices about groups with which they identify and negative prejudices against others. Someone who is prejudiced against a particular group will refuse to give it a fair hearing.

Discrimination refers to *actual behavior* toward another group. It can be seen in activities that distribute rewards and benefits unequally based on membership in the dominant ethnic groups. It involves excluding or restricting members of specific racial or ethnic groups from opportunities that are available to other groups. For example, blacks have been excluded and continue to be underrepresented in entire job categories despite the increase of education among blacks and the emergence of an educated black middle class. Discrimination does not necessarily derive directly from prejudice. For example, white home buyers might steer away from purchasing properties in predominantly black neighborhoods, not because of attitudes of hostility they might feel toward African Americans, but because of worries about declining property values. Prejudiced attitudes in this case influence discrimination, but in an indirect fashion.

STEREOTYPES AND SCAPEGOATS

Prejudice operates mainly through the use of **stereotyping**, which means thinking in terms of fixed and inflexible categories. Stereotyping is often closely linked to the psychological mechanism of **displacement**, in which feelings of hostility or anger are directed against objects that are not the real origin of those feelings. People vent their antagonism against **scapegoats**, others who are blamed for problems that are not their fault. The term *scapegoat* originated with the ancient Hebrews, who each year ritually loaded all their sins onto a goat, which was then chased into the wilderness. Scapegoating is common when two deprived ethnic groups come into competition with one another for economic rewards. People who direct racial attacks against African Americans, for example, are often in a similar economic position to them. They blame blacks for grievances whose real causes lie elsewhere.

Scapegoating is normally directed against groups that are distinctive and relatively powerless, because they make an easy target. Protestants, Catholics, Jews, Italians, racial minorities, and others have played the unwilling role of scapegoat at various times throughout Western history. Scapegoating frequently involves *projection*, the unconscious attribution to others of one's own desires or characteristics. For example, research has consistently demonstrated that when the members of a dominant group practice violence against a minority and exploit it sexually, they are likely to believe that the minority group itself displays these traits of sexual violence. For instance, in the United States before the civil rights movement, some white men's bizarre ideas about the lustful nature of African American men probably originated in their own frustrations, since sexual access to white women was limited by the formal nature of courtship. Similarly, in apartheid South Africa, the belief that black males were exceptionally potent sexually and that black women were promiscuous was widespread among whites. Black males were thought to be sexually dangerous to white women—but in fact, virtually all criminal sexual contact was initiated by white men against black women (Simpson and Yinger, 1986).

MINORITY GROUPS

The term *minority group* as used in everyday life can be quite confusing. This is because the term refers to political power and is not simply a numerical distinction. There are many minorities in a statistical sense, such as people having red hair or weighing more than two hundred fifty pounds, but these are not minorities according to the sociological concept. In sociology, members of a **minority group** are disadvantaged as compared with the dominant group (a group possessing more wealth, power, and prestige) and have some sense of group solidarity, of belonging together. The experience of being subject to prejudice and discrimination usually heightens feelings of common loyalty and interests.

Members of minority groups, such as Spanish-speakers in the United States, often tend to see themselves as a people separated or distinct from the majority. Minority groups are sometimes, but not always, physically and socially isolated from the larger community. Although they tend to be concentrated in certain neighborhoods, cities, or regions of a country, their children may often intermarry with members of the dominant group. People who belong to minority groups sometimes (for example, Jews) actively promote endogamy (marriage within the group) in order to keep alive their cultural distinctiveness.

The idea of a "minority group" is more confusing today than ever before. Some groups that were once clearly identified as minorities, such as Asians and Jews, now have more resources, intermarry at greater rates, and experience less discrimination than they did when they were originally conceived of as minority groups. This highlights the fact that the concept of a minority group is really about disadvantage, rather than a numerical distinction. Perhaps in the future it would be more meaningful for sociologists to use the terms *dominant* and *disadvantaged* to avoid these misunderstandings but these new terms would be fraught with their own problems! For now, sociologists continue to use the term *minority group*, so it is best for the student to be aware of its definitions and ambiguities as a concept.

Ethnic Relations

In an age of globalization and rapid social change, the rich benefits and complex challenges of ethnic diversity are confronting a growing number of states. International migration is accelerating with the further integration of the global economy; the movement and mixing of human populations seems sure to intensify in years to come. Meanwhile, ethnic tensions and conflicts continue to flare in societies around the world, threatening to lead to the disintegration of some multiethnic states and hinting at protracted violence in others. How can ethnic diversity be accommodated and the outbreak of ethnic conflict averted? Within multiethnic societies what should be the relation between ethnic minority groups and the majority population? There are four primary models of ethnic integration that have been adopted by multiethnic societies in relation to these challenges: assimilation, the "melting pot," pluralism, and multiculturalism. These will be discussed shortly.

To fully analyze ethnic relations in current times, we must first take a historical and comparative perspective. It is impossible to understand ethnic divisions today without giving prime place to the impact of the expansion of Western colonialism on the rest of the world (see Figure 11.1). Global migratory movements resulting from colonialism helped to create ethnic divisions by placing different peoples in close proximity. We will now delve into this history in more detail.

Ethnic Antagonism: A Historical Perspective

From the fifteenth century onward, Europeans began to venture into previously uncharted seas and unexplored land masses, pursuing the aims of exploration and trade but also conquering and subduing native peoples. They poured out by

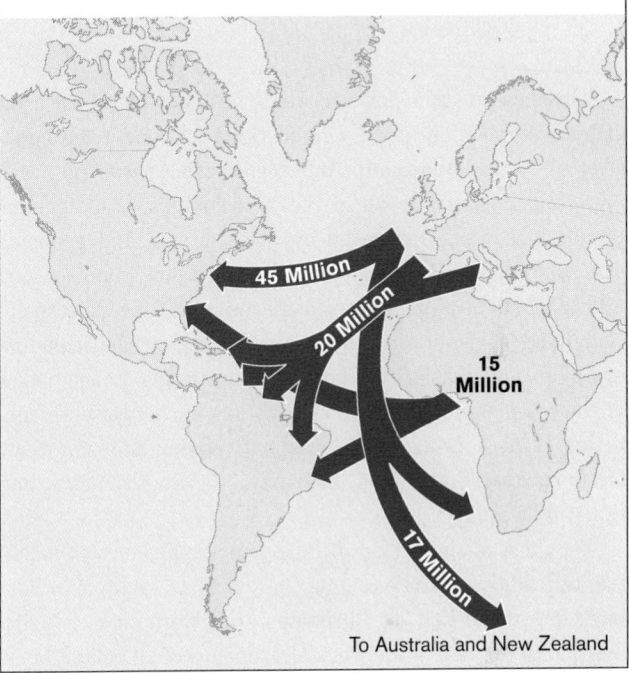

FIGURE 11.1

Colonization and Ethnicity

This map shows the massive movement of peoples from Europe who colonized the Americas, South Africa, Australia, and New Zealand, resulting in the ethnic composition of populations there today. People from Africa were brought to the Americas to be slaves.

the millions from Europe to settle in these new areas. In the shape of the slave trade, they also occasioned a large-scale movement of people from Africa to the Americas. The following are the extraordinary shifts in population that have occurred over the past 350 years or so:

1. **Europe to North America.** From the seventeenth century to the present, some 45 million people have emigrated from Europe to what is now the United States and Canada. About 200 million in North America today can trace their ancestry to this migration.

2. **Europe to Central and South America.** About 20 million people from Europe, mostly from Spain, Portugal, and Italy, migrated to Central and South America. Some 50 million in these areas today are of European ancestry.

3. **Europe to Africa and Australasia.** Approximately 17 million people in these continents are of European ancestry. In Africa, the majority emigrated to the state of

South Africa, which was colonized mainly by the British and the Dutch.

4. **Africa to the Americas.** Starting in the sixteenth century, about 10 million blacks were unwillingly transported to the North and South American continents. Under a million arrived in the sixteenth century; some 1.3 million in the seventeenth century; 6 million in the eighteenth century; and 2 million in the nineteenth century. Black Africans were brought to the Americas in chains to serve as slaves; families and whole communities were destroyed in the process.

These population flows formed the basis of the current ethnic composition of the United States, Canada, the countries of Central and South America, South Africa, Australia, and New Zealand. In all of these societies, the indigenous populations were decimated by disease, war, and genocide and subjected to European rule. They are now impoverished ethnic minorities. Since the Europeans were from diverse national and ethnic origins, they transplanted various ethnic hierarchies and divisions to their new homelands. At the height of the colonial era, in the nineteenth and early twentieth centuries, Europeans also ruled over native populations in many other regions: South Asia, East Asia, the South Pacific, and the Middle East.

For most of the period of European expansion, ethnocentric attitudes were rife among the colonists, many of whom were convinced that, as Christians, they were on a civilizing mission to the rest of the world. Europeans of all political persuasions believed themselves to be superior to the peoples they colonized and conquered. The fact that many of those peoples possessed technologies, agricultural skills, and knowledge that the Europeans embraced and incorporated (for example, the civil service system in India) is not so relevant, since the Europeans possessed the power to institutionalize their interpretation. The early period of colonization coincided with the rise of scientific racism, and ever since then, the legacy of European colonization has generated ethnic divisions that have occupied a central place in regional and global conflicts. In particular, racist views distinguishing the descendants of Europeans from those of Africans became central to European racist attitudes.

The Rise of Racism

Why has racism flourished? There are several reasons. The first reason for the rise of modern racism lies in the exploitative relations that Europeans established with the peoples they encountered and conquered. The slave trade could not have been carried on had Europeans not constructed a belief system that allowed them to justify their actions by convincing themselves that Africans belonged to an inferior, even subhuman race. Racism helped justify colonial rule over nonwhite peoples and denied them the rights of political participation that were being won by whites in their European homelands. The relations between whites and nonwhites varied according to different patterns of colonial settlement—and were influenced as well by cultural differences among Europeans themselves.

Second, an opposition between the colors white and black as cultural symbols was deeply rooted in European culture. White had long been associated with purity, black with evil (there is nothing natural about this symbolism; in some other cultures, it is reversed). The symbol of blackness held negative meanings *before* the West came into extensive contact with black peoples. These symbolic meanings tended to infuse the Europeans' reactions to blacks when they were first encountered on African shores. The sense that there was a radical difference between black and white peoples combined with the "heathenism" of the Africans led many Europeans to regard blacks with disdain and fear. As a seventeenth-century observer expressed it, blacks "in color as in condition are little other than Devils incarnate" (Jordan, 1968). Although the more extreme expressions of such attitudes have disappeared today, it is difficult not to believe that elements of this black-white cultural symbolism remain widespread.

A third important factor leading to modern racism was simply the invention and diffusion of the concept of race itself. Racist attitudes have been known to exist for hundreds of years. In China of 300 B.C.E., for example, we find recorded descriptions of barbarian peoples "who greatly resemble monkeys from whom they are descended." But the notion of race as a cluster of inherited characteristics comes from European thought of the eighteenth and nineteenth centuries. Count Joseph Arthur de Gobineau (1816–1882), who is sometimes called the father of modern racism, proposed ideas that became influential in many circles. According to de Gobineau, three races exist: white, black, and yellow. The white race possesses superior intelligence, morality, and will power, and these inherited qualities underlie the spread of Western influence across the world. The blacks are the least capable, marked by an animal nature, a lack of morality, and emotional instability.

The ideas of de Gobineau and others who proposed similar views were presented as supposedly scientific theories. The notion of the superiority of the white race, although completely without value factually, remains a key element of white racism. It is an explicit element, for example, in the ideology of the Ku Klux Klan, and it was the basis of **apartheid** (separate racial development) in South Africa.

A young girl joins members of the Ku Klux Klan at a demonstration against the Martin Luther King Day holiday in Pulaski, Tennessee.

Ethnic Conflict

The most extreme and devastating form of group relations in human history involves **genocide**, the systematic, planned destruction of a racial, political, or cultural group. The most horrific recent instance of brutal destructiveness against such a group was the massacre of 6 million Jews in the German concentration camps during World War II. The Holocaust is not the only example of mass genocide in the twentieth century. Between 1915 and 1923 over a million Armenians were killed by the Ottoman Turkish government. In the late 1970s 2 million Cambodians died in the Khmer Rouge's killing fields. During the 1990s, in the African country of Rwanda, hundreds of thousands of the minority Tutsis were massacred by the dominant Hutu group. And in the former Yugoslavia, Bosnian and Kosovar Muslims were summarily executed by the Serb majority.

The conflicts in the former Yugoslavia have involved attempts at **ethnic cleansing**, the creation of ethnically homogeneous areas through the mass expulsion of other ethnic populations. Croatia, for example, has become an independent "monoethnic" state after a costly war in which thousands of Serbs were expelled from the country. The war—which broke out in Bosnia in 1992 among Serbs, Croats, and Muslims—involved the ethnic cleansing of the Bosnian Muslim population at the hands of the Serbs. Thousands of Muslim men were

forced into internment camps and a campaign of systematic rape was carried out against Muslim women. The war in Kosovo in 1999 was prompted by charges that Serbian forces were ethnically cleansing the Kosovar Albanian (Muslim) population from the province.

In both Bosnia and Kosovo, ethnic conflict became internationalized. Hundreds of thousands of refugees spilled over into neighboring areas, further destabilizing the region. Western states intervened both diplomatically and militarily to protect the human rights of ethnic groups who had become targets of ethnic cleansing. In the short term, such interventions succeeded in quelling the systematic violence. Yet they have had unintended consequences as well. The fragile peace in Bosnia has been maintained, but only through the presence of peacekeeping troops and the partitioning of the country into separate ethnic enclaves. In Kosovo a process of reverse ethnic cleansing ensued after the NATO bombing campaign. Ethnic Albanian Kosovars began to drive the local Serb population out of Kosovo; the presence of UN-led "KFOR" troops has been inadequate to prevent ethnic tensions from reigniting.

Ethnic cleansing involves the forced relocation of ethnic populations through targeted violence, harassment, threats, and campaigns of terror.

It has been noted that violent conflicts around the globe are increasingly based on ethnic divisions. Only a tiny proportion of wars now occur between states; the vast majority are civil wars with ethnic dimensions. In a world of increasing interdependence and competition, international factors become even more important in shaping ethnic relations, while the effects of internal ethnic conflicts are felt well outside national borders. As we have seen, ethnic conflicts attract international attention and have sometimes provoked physical intervention. International war crimes tribunals have been convened to investigate and try those responsible for the ethnic cleansing and genocide in the former Yugoslavia and Rwanda. Responding to and preventing ethnic conflict has become one of the key challenges facing both individual states and international political structures. Although ethnic tensions are often experienced, interpreted, and described at the local level, they are increasingly taking on national and international dimensions.

In other areas of the world, exploitation of minority groups has been an ugly part of many countries' histories. The concept of group closure has been institutionalized in the form of **segregation**, a practice whereby racial and ethnic groups are kept physically separate by law, thereby maintaining the superior position of the dominant group. For instance, in apartheid-era South Africa, laws forced blacks to live separately from whites and forbade sexual relations among races. In the United States, African Americans have also experienced legal forms of segregation. In 1967 the Supreme Court ruled in the case of *Loving v. Virginia* that the prohibition of interracial marriage violated the right to privacy. At that time racial intermarriage was still a crime in most southern states. Interracial marriage had been criminalized for more than two hundred seventy years in every state except Alaska and Hawaii. Economic and social segregation was enforced by law, for instance those requiring blacks and whites to use separate public bathrooms. Even today, segregated residential areas still exist in many cities, leading some to claim that an American system of apartheid has developed (Massey and Denton, 1993).

Models of Ethnic Integration

For many years, the two most common positive models of political ethnic harmony in the United States were those of as-

similation and the melting pot (see Figure 11.2). **Assimilation** meant that new immigrant groups would assume the attitudes and language of the dominant white community. The idea of the **melting pot** was different—it meant merging different cultures and outlooks by stirring them all together. A newer model of ethnic relations is **pluralism**, in which ethnic cultures are given full validity to exist separately, yet participate in the larger society's economic and political life. A recent outgrowth of pluralism is **multiculturalism**, in which ethnic groups exist separately and *equally*. It does seem at least possible to create a society in which ethnic groups are separate but equal, as is demonstrated by Switzerland, where French, German, and Italian groups coexist in the same society. But this situation is unusual, and it seems unlikely that the United States could come close to mirroring this achievement in the near future.

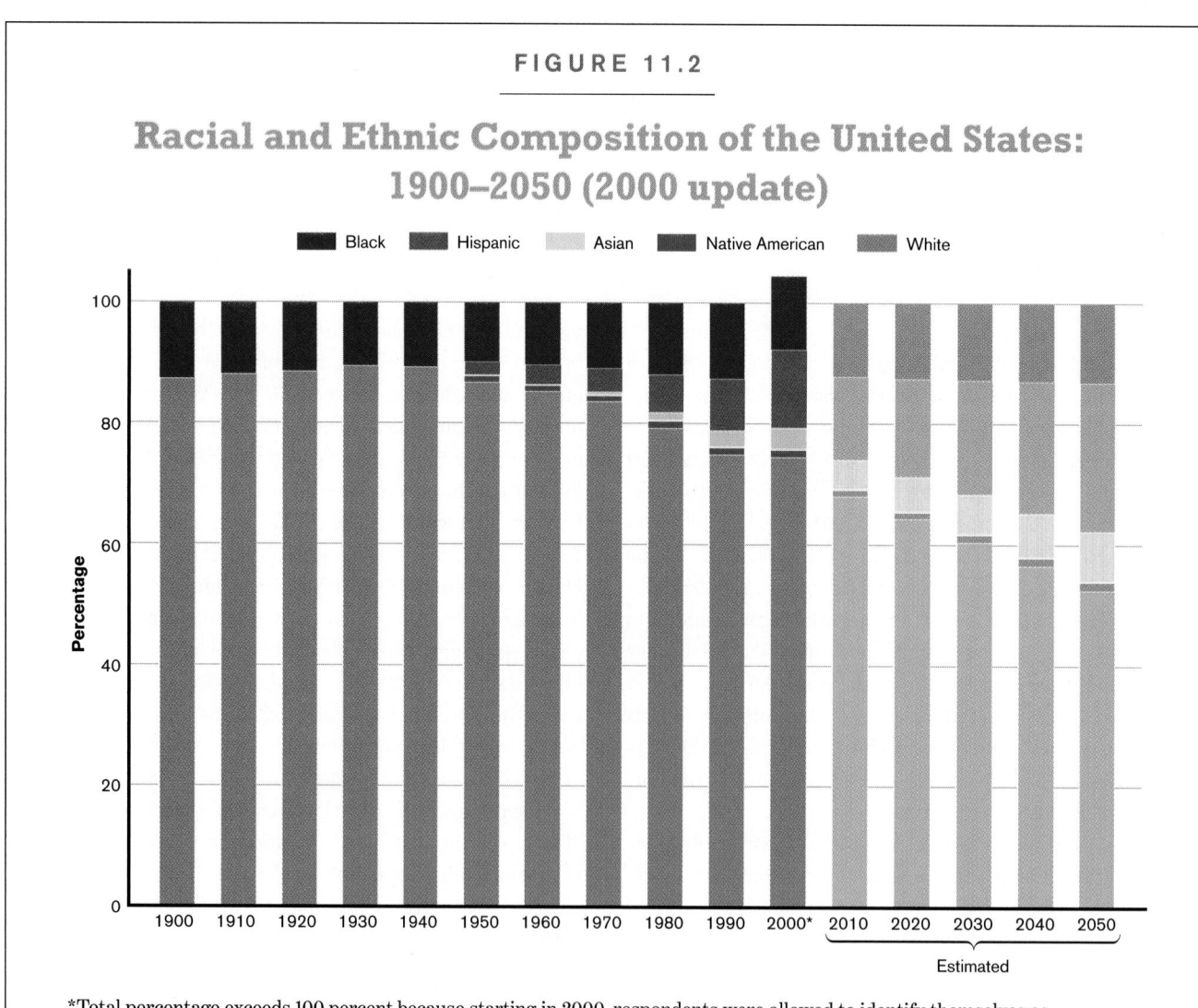

FIGURE 11.2

Racial and Ethnic Composition of the United States: 1900–2050 (2000 update)

*Total percentage exceeds 100 percent because starting in 2000, respondents were allowed to identify themselves as belonging to more than one race category.

SOURCE: U.S. Bureau of the Census, Factfinder, 2004, http://factfinder.census.gov/home/saff/main.html?_lang=en.

Global Migration

Today floods of refugees and emigrants move restlessly across different regions of the globe, either trying to escape from such conflicts or fleeing poverty in search of a better life. Often they reach a new country only to find they are resented by people who some generations ago were immigrants themselves. Sometimes there are reversals, as has happened in Southern California and other areas of the United States along the Mexican border. Much of what is now California was once part of Mexico. Today, some Mexican Americans might say, the new waves of Mexican immigrants are reclaiming what used to be their heritage. Except that most of the existing groups in California don't quite see things this way.

Aborigines from all over Pitjabjantjaira Country gather to protest and protect their land from mining/mineral development.

MIGRATORY MOVEMENTS

Although migration is not a new phenomenon, it is one that seems to be accelerating as part of the process of global integration. Worldwide migration patterns can be seen as one reflection of the rapidly changing economic, political, and cultural ties among countries. It has been estimated that the world's migrant population in 1990 was more than 80 million people, 20 million of whom were refugees. This number appears likely to continue increasing in the twenty-first century, prompting some scholars to label this the "age of migration" (Castles and Miller, 1993).

Immigration, the movement of people into a country to settle, and **emigration**, the process by which people leave a country to settle in another, combine to produce global migration patterns linking countries of origin and countries of destination. Migratory movements add to ethnic and cultural diversity in many societies and help to shape demographic, economic, and social dynamics. The intensification of global migration since World War II, and particularly over the last two decades, has transformed immigration into an important political issue in many countries. Rising immigration rates in many Western societies have challenged commonly held notions of national identity and have forced a reexamination of concepts of citizenship.

Scholars have identified four models of migration to describe the main global population movements since 1945. The *classic model* of migration applies to countries such as Canada, the United States, and Australia, which have developed as nations of immigrants. In such cases, immigration has been largely encouraged and the promise of citizenship has been extended to newcomers, although restrictions and quotas help to limit the annual intake of immigrants. The *colonial model* of immigration, pursued by countries such as France and the United Kingdom, tends to favor immigrants from former colonies over those from other countries. The large number of immigrants from former British colonies in Britain reflects this tendency.

Countries such as Germany, Switzerland, and Belgium have followed a third policy—the *guest workers model*. Under such a scheme, immigrants are admitted into the country on a temporary basis, often in order to fulfill demands within the labor market, but do not receive citizenship rights even after long periods of settlement. Finally, *illegal models* of immigration are becoming increasingly common due to tightening immigration laws in many industrialized countries. Immigrants who are able to gain entry into a country either secretly or under a nonimmigration pretense are often able to live illegally outside the realm of official society. Examples of this can be seen in the large number of Mexican illegal aliens in many southern American states or in the growing international business of smuggling refugees across national borders.

What are the forces behind global migration and how are they changing as a result of globalization? Many early theories about migration focused on so-called push and pull factors. *Push factors* referred to dynamics within a country of origin that forced people to emigrate, such as war, famine, political oppression, or population pressures. *Pull factors*, by contrast, were those features of destination countries that attracted immigrants: prosperous labor markets, better overall living conditions, and lower population density, for example, could "pull" immigrants from other regions.

More recently, push and pull theories of migration have been criticized for offering overly simplistic explanations of a complex and multifaceted process. Instead scholars of migration are increasingly looking at global migration patterns as systems that are produced through interactions between macro-level and micro-level processes. This idea may sound complicated, but it is actually quite simple. Macro-level factors refer to overarching issues such as the political situation in an area, the laws and regulations controlling immigration and emigration, or changes in the international economy. Micro-level factors, on the other hand, are concerned with the resources, knowledge, and understandings that the migrant populations themselves possess.

The intersection of macro and micro processes can be seen in the case of Germany's large Turkish immigrant community. On the macro level are factors such as Germany's economic need for labor, its policy of accepting foreign "guest workers," and the state of the Turkish economy, which prevents many Turks from earning at the level they would wish. At the micro level are the informal networks and channels of mutual support within the Turkish community in Germany and the strong links to family and friends who have remained in Turkey. Among potential Turkish migrants, knowledge about Germany and "social capital"—human or community resources that can be drawn on—help to make Germany one of the most popular destination countries. Supporters of the migration systems approach emphasize that no one factor can explain the process of migration. Rather, each particular migratory movement, like that between Turkey and Germany, is the product of an interaction of macro- and micro-level processes.

In examining recent trends in global migration, Stephen Castles and Mark Miller (1993) have identified four tendencies that they claim will characterize migration patterns in coming years:

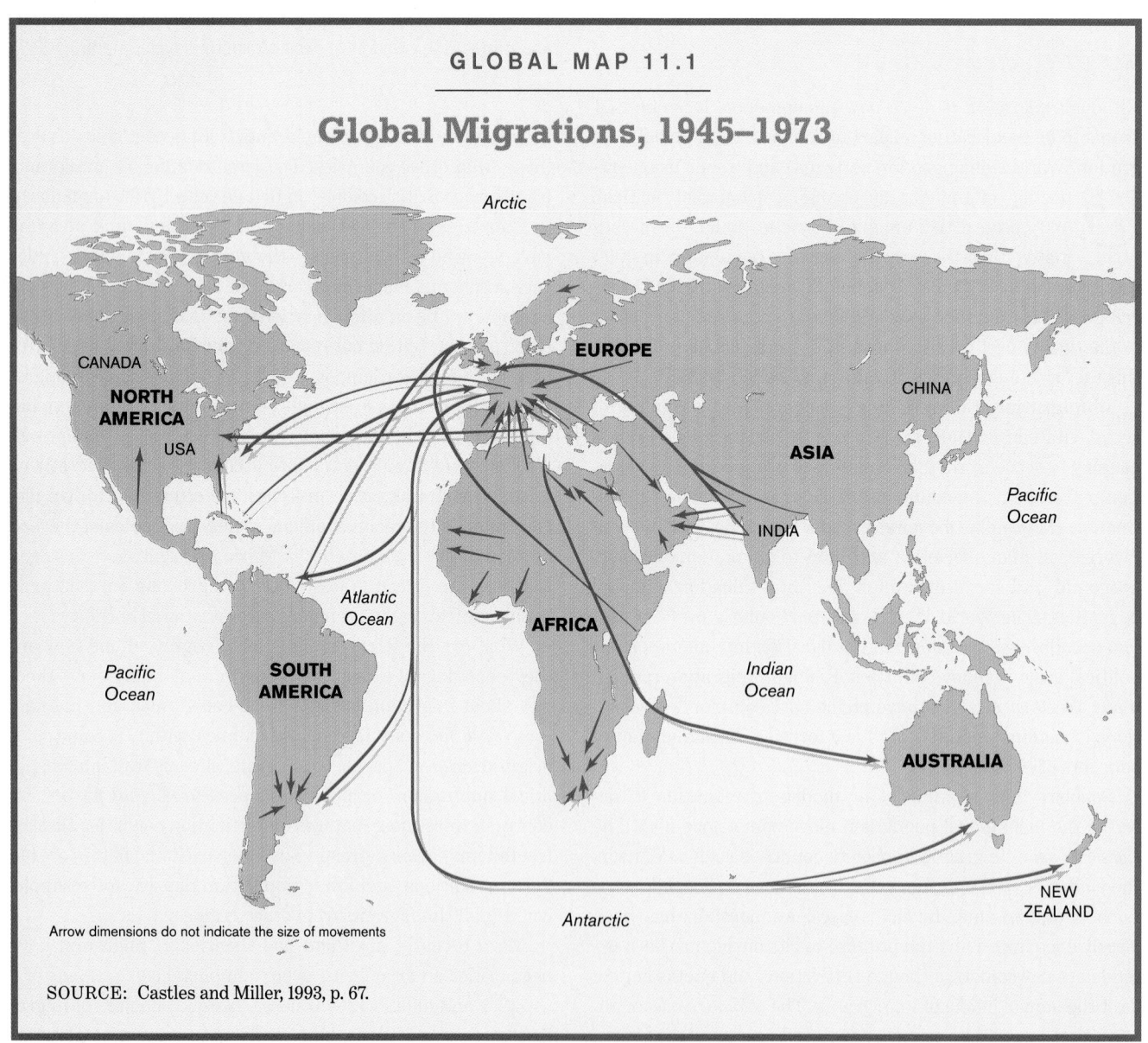

GLOBAL MAP 11.1

Global Migrations, 1945–1973

Arrow dimensions do not indicate the size of movements

SOURCE: Castles and Miller, 1993, p. 67.

- ACCELERATION. Migration across borders is occurring in greater numbers than ever before.
- DIVERSIFICATION. Most countries now receive immigrants of many different types, in contrast with earlier times when particular forms of immigration, such as labor immigration or refugees, were predominant.
- GLOBALIZATION. Migration has become more global in nature, involving a greater number of countries as both senders and recipients (see Global Maps 11.1 and 11.2).
- FEMINIZATION. A growing number of migrants are women, making contemporary migration much less male dominated than in previous times. The increase in female migrants is closely related to changes in the global labor market, including the growing demand for domestic workers, the expansion of sex tourism and

"trafficking" in women and the "mail-order brides" phenomenon.

GLOBAL DIASPORAS

Another way to understand global migration patterns is through the study of diasporas. The term **diaspora** refers to the dispersal of an ethnic population from an original homeland into foreign areas, often in a forced manner or under traumatic circumstances. References are often made to the Jewish and African diasporas to describe the way in which these populations have become redistributed across the globe as a result of slavery and genocide. Although members of a diaspora are by definition scattered apart geographically, they are held together by factors such as shared

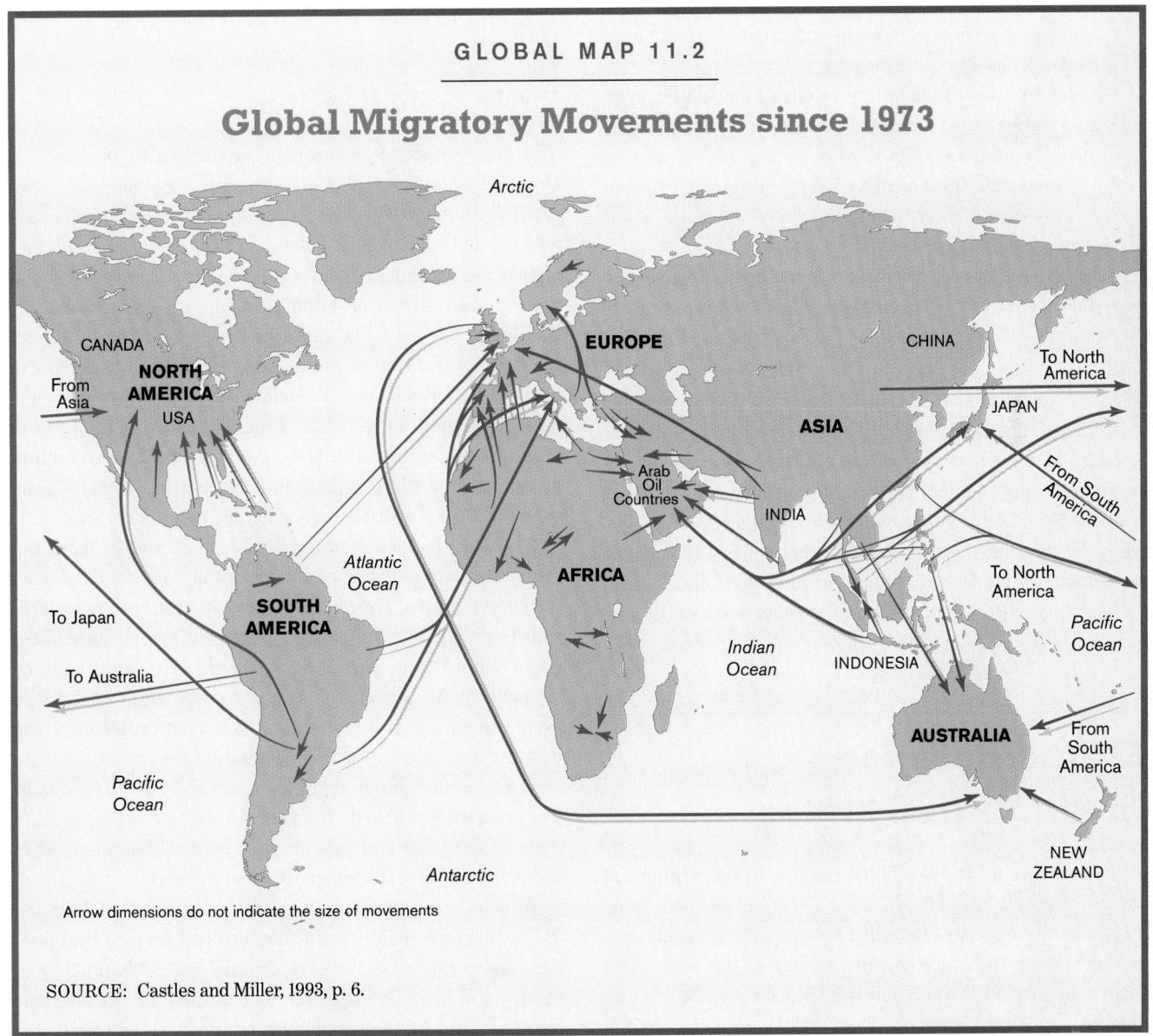

GLOBAL MAP 11.2

Global Migratory Movements since 1973

Arrow dimensions do not indicate the size of movements

SOURCE: Castles and Miller, 1993, p. 6.

history, a collective memory of the original homeland, or a common ethnic identity that is nurtured and preserved.

Robin Cohen has argued that diasporas occur in a number of diverse forms, although the most commonly cited examples are those that occurred involuntarily as a result of persecution and violence. In *Global Diasporas* (1997), Cohen adopts a historical approach and identifies five different categories of diasporas according to the forces underlying the original population dispersion: *victim* (e.g., African, Jewish, and Armenian), *imperial* (British), *labor* (Indian), *trade* (Chinese), and *cultural* (Caribbean). In certain of these cases, such as that of the Chinese, large-scale population movements occurred on a voluntary basis, not as a result of a defining traumatic event.

Despite the diversity of forms, however, all diasporas share certain key features. Cohen suggests that all diasporas meet the following criteria:

- a forced or voluntary movement from an original homeland to a new region or regions;
- a shared memory about the original homeland, a commitment to its preservation, and a belief in the possibility of eventual return;
- a strong ethnic identity sustained over time and distance;
- a sense of solidarity with members of the same ethnic group also living in areas of the diaspora;
- a degree of tension in relation to the host societies; and
- the potential for valuable and creative contributions to pluralistic host societies.

Some scholars have accused Cohen of trying to simplify complex and distinctive migration experiences into a narrow typology, by associating categories of diasporas with particular ethnic groups. Others argue that his conceptualization of diaspora is not sufficiently precise for the analysis he undertakes. Yet despite these critiques, Cohen's study is valuable for demonstrating that diasporas are not static but instead are ongoing processes of maintaining collective identity and preserving ethnic culture in a rapidly globalizing world.

Ethnic Relations in the United States

We concentrate for the rest of the chapter on the origins and nature of ethnic diversity in the United States (see Table 11.1)—and its consequences, which have often been highly contentious. More than most other societies in the world, this country is peopled almost entirely by immigrants. Only a tiny minority, less than 1 percent, of the population today are Na-tive Americans, those whom Christopher Columbus, erroneously supposing he had arrived in India, called Indians.

Before the American Revolution, British, French, and Dutch settlers established colonies in what is now the United States. Some descendants of the French colonists are still to be found in parts of Louisiana. Millions of slaves were brought over from Africa to North America. Huge waves of European, Russian, Asian, and Latin American immigrants have washed across the country at different periods since then. The United States is one of the most *ethnically diverse* countries on the face of the globe. In this section we will pay particular attention to the divisions that have separated whites and nonwhite minority groups, such as African Americans and Hispanic Americans. The emphasis is on *struggle*. Members of these groups have made repeated efforts to defend the integrity of their cultures and advance their social position in the face of persistent prejudice and discrimination from the wider social environment.

Early Colonization

The first European colonists in what was to become the United States were actually of quite homogeneous background. At the time of the Declaration of Independence, the majority of the colonial population was of British descent, and almost everyone was Protestant. Settlers from outside the British Isles were at first admitted only with reluctance, but the desire for economic expansion meant having to attract immigrants from other areas. Most came from countries in northwest Europe, such as Holland, Germany, and Sweden; such migration into North America dates initially from around 1820. In the century following, about 33 million immigrants entered the United States. No migrant movement on such a scale has ever been documented before or since.

The early waves of immigrants came mostly from the same countries of origin as the groups already established in the United States. They left Europe to escape economic hardship and religious and political oppression, and because of the opportunities to acquire land as the drive westward gained momentum. As a result of successive potato famines that had produced widespread starvation, 1.5 million people migrated from Ireland, settling for the most part in the coastal areas, in contrast to most other immigrants from rural backgrounds. The Irish were primarily from rural areas and accustomed to a life of hardship and despair, and most of them settled in urban industrial areas where they sought work.

A major new influx of immigrants arrived in the 1880s and 1890s, this time mainly from southern and eastern Europe—the Austro-Hungarian empire, Russia, and Italy. Each successive group of immigrants was subject to considerable discrimination on the part of people previously established in

TABLE 11.1

Racial and Ethnic Populations in the United States, 2002

RACE OR ETHNICITY	POPULATION	PERCENTAGE OF TOTAL POPULATION[a]	POPULATION ESTIMATE	SHARE OF TOTAL POPULATION
Total U.S. population			280,540,330	100.00
RACE				
One race	274,595,678	97.6	274,034,883	97.68
White (including Hispanics)	211,460,626	75.1	212,541,793	75.76
White alone (non-Hispanic)			191,238,314	68.17
Black or African American	34,658,190	12.3	33,768,036	12.04
American Indian and Alaska Native	2,475,956	0.9	1,959,347	0.70
Asian	10,242,998	3.6	11,213,133	4.00
Asian Indian	1,678,765	0.6	2,069,584	0.74
Chinese (except Taiwanese)	2,432,585	0.9	2,670,887	0.95
Filipino	1,850,314	0.7	2,013,117	0.72
Japanese	796,700	0.3	802,330	0.29
Korean	1,076,872	0.4	1,147,968	0.41
Vietnamese	1,122,528	0.4	1,169,772	0.42
Other Asian	1,285,234	0.5	1,339,475	0.48
Native Hawaiian and Other Pacific Islander	398,835	0.1	365,474	0.13
Native Hawaiian	140,652	0.0	149,559	0.05
Guamanian or Chamorro	58,240	0.0	61,215	0.02
Samoan	91,029	0.0	63,687	0.02
Other Pacific Islander	108,914	0.0	91,013	0.03
Hispanic or Latino (of any race)	35,305,818	12.5	37,872,475	13.50
Mexican	20,640,711	7.3	23,999,836	8.55
Puerto Rican	3,406,178	1.2	3,608,309	1.29
Cuban	1,241,685	0.4	1,357,744	0.48
Other Hispanic or Latino	10,017,244	3.6	8,906,586	3.17
Some other race	15,359,073	5.5	14,187,100	5.06
Two or more races	6,826,228	2.4	6,505,447	2.32

[a]Percentages do not total 100 percent because Hispanics or Latinos can be of any race.

SOURCE: U.S. Bureau of the Census, "Census 2000 Summary File 1," www.census.gov/Press-Release/www/2001/sumfile1.html.

the country. Negative views of the Irish, for example, emphasized their supposedly low level of intelligence and drunken behavior. Job vacancies often specifically stated, "No Irish need apply." But as they were concentrated within the cities, the Irish Americans were able to organize to protect their interests and gained a strong influence over political life. The Italians and Polish, when they reached America, were in turn discriminated against by the Irish.

Asian immigrants first arrived in the United States in large numbers in the late nineteenth century, encouraged by employers who needed cheap labor in the developing industries of the West. Some two hundred thousand Chinese emigrated in this period. Most were men, who came with the idea of saving money to send back to their families in China, anticipating that they would also later return there. Bitter conflicts broke out between white workers and the Chinese when employment

Paddy's Ladder to Wealth is a Free Country An unflattering picture of an Irish immigrant on a ladder holding a brick carrier.

opportunities diminished. The Chinese Exclusion Act, passed in 1882, cut down further immigration to a trickle until after World War II.

Japanese immigrants began to arrive not long after the ending of Chinese immigration. They were also subject to great hostility from whites. Opposition to Japanese immigration intensified in the early part of the twentieth century, leading to strict limits, or *quotas*, being placed on the numbers allowed to enter the United States.

Most immigrant groups in the early twentieth century settled in urban areas and engaged in the developing industrial economy. They also tended to cluster in ethnic neighborhoods of their own. Chinatowns, Little Italys, and other clearly defined areas became features of most large cities. The very size of the influx provoked backlash from the Anglo-Saxon sections of the population. During the 1920s, new immigration quotas were set up, which discriminated against new arrivals from southern and eastern Europe. Many immigrants found the conditions of life in their new land little better and sometimes worse than the areas from which they originated. Eva Morawska, the author of a historical study of immigrants journeying from east central Europe to Johnstown, Pennsylvania, observes:

The ambivalence and heart-rending uncertainty that accompanied the immigrants when they made their decision to cross the ocean to try their luck in America

became further sharpened in this country by feelings of bewilderment and nostalgia, and by disillusionment with the reality of the "Promised Land" as compared with the dreams they had harbored in Europe. To a number of East Central Europeans, the arrival in Johnstown was bitterly disappointing. The town was soiled and the air filled with soot and fumes from the furnace chimneys. "My disappointment was unspeakable," recalls an eighty-four-year-old Galician, "when after a twelve-day journey I saw the city of Johnstown: squalid and ugly, with those congested shabby houses, blackened with soot from the factory chimneys—this was the America I saw." (Morawska, 1986)

The immigrants may have gained greater religious and political freedom in their new home, but they met with prejudice and discrimination if their ways of life differed from those of the dominant Anglo-Saxon community. The large flow of immigration and competition for jobs allowed employers to compel workers to accept very long working days, low levels of pay, and unhealthy working conditions. Since new immigrants were commonly used as strike breakers (people hired to replace striking workers), conflicts between them and established groups were frequent. In spite of these conditions, the economy was rapidly growing, and a substantial proportion of immigrant workers in the end managed to improve their standards of living.

Immigration to the United States: The Sociological Debate

The United States is often euphemistically referred to as a "melting pot," or a nation of immigrants. The cultural and social landscape of the United States is viewed as an amalgam of diverse cultures, due largely to our nation's history as a refuge for immigrants. Today, however, policy makers and social scientists are embroiled in a dispute over the social and economic costs of immigration. Do new immigrants help or hinder the United States' economy?

Before addressing both sides of this debate, it is important to understand the current state of immigration to the United States. During the early 1990s, the United States admitted more than 800,000 legal immigrants each year, and an additional 300,000 entered and stayed in the country illegally. Unlike the major wave of immigration that occurred at the turn of the century, fewer than 10 percent of immigrants admitted into the United States in the last two decades were of European origin. In fact, between 1989 and 1993, more than half of all immigrants entering the United States came from just four countries: Mexico, the Philippines, Vietnam, and El Salvador. This change in the composition of immigrants is generally attributed to two government acts: the 1965 Immigration and Nationality Act Amendments, which abolished preference for northern and western European immigrants and gave preference to "family reunification"—rather than occupational skills—as a reason for accepting immigrants, and the 1986 Immigration Reform and Control Act, which provided amnesty for many illegal immigrants.

Consequently, many of the debates surrounding immigration focus on new immigrants' ability to secure employment and achieve economic self-sufficiency. In his 1994 essay "The Economics of Immigration," the economist George Borjas argued that since the 1980s, the United States has attracted "lower quality" immigrants, who have less education and few marketable job skills. Moreover, these new immigrants are less skilled than both natives (i.e., persons born in the United States) and earlier migrants; thus they are more reliant on government assistance for survival. Borjas's estimates show that 21 percent of immigrant households participate in some means-tested social assistance program such as Medicaid or food stamps, as compared with 14 percent of native households. Because recent immigrants are often unable to find gainful employment in the short term, economic assimilation is quite slow; Borjas estimated that recent immigrants will likely earn 20 percent less than native-born Americans for most of their working lives.

Borjas also was concerned about the effect of immigrants on natives' economic prospects. He argued that large-scale migration of less-skilled workers has done harm to the economic opportunities of less-skilled natives—particularly African Americans. This occurs because immigrants increase the number of workers in the economy; they create additional competition in the labor market, and thus wages of the least skilled workers fall.

Although Borjas described a bleak scenario, other economists and policy analysts argue that recent immigration has either a positive effect or no influence on the U.S. economy. Economist Julian Simon has written several books, including *The Ultimate Resource* (1981) and *The Economic Consequences of Immigration* (1989), that argue that immigrants provide a windfall to the U.S. economy by joining the labor force and paying into the federal revenue system for their whole lives. By the time they retire and collect government benefits such as Social Security and Medicare, their children will be covering these costs by working and paying into the tax system. Simon's arguments, however, are based on the assumption that immigrants earn the same wages and are as employable as natives—an assumption refuted by Borjas's research.

Simon also argues that immigrants are a cultural asset to the United States. In fact, he claims that "the notion of wanting to keep out immigrants in order to keep our institutions and our values pure is prejudice" (quoted in Brimelow, 1995). Moreover, Simon argues that human beings have the intelligence to adapt to their surroundings and that the more immigrants that come to the United States, the larger pool of potential innovators and problem solvers our nation will have.

Studies conducted by Simon and the Urban Institute, a nonprofit research organization, acknowledge that although some recent immigrants may benefit from federally funded programs such as welfare, these costs are often quite short term. Immigrant children who benefit from the U.S. educational system go on to become productive, tax-paying workers.

Assessing the fiscal costs of immigration proves difficult, however. Although much of the public debate focuses on the costs of providing services to illegal immigrants, actual statistics documenting the number of illegal immigrants are difficult to obtain and verify. Moreover, few policy analysts can predict whether U.S. immigration policy—or the characteristics of immigrants themselves—will change drastically in the future.

African Americans in the United States

By 1780, there were nearly 4 million slaves in the American South. Since there was little incentive for them to work, physical punishment was often resorted to. Slaves who ran away were hunted with dogs and on their capture were manacled, sometimes branded with their master's mark, and occasionally even castrated. Slaves had virtually no rights in law whatsoever. But they did not passively accept the conditions their masters imposed on them. The struggles of slaves against their oppressive conditions sometimes took the form of direct opposition or disobedience to orders, and occasionally outright rebellion (although collective slave revolts were more common in the Caribbean than in the United States). On a more subtle level, their response took the form of a cultural creativity—a mixing of aspects of African cultures, Christian ideals, and cultural threads woven from their new environments. Some of the art forms they developed, as in music— for example, the invention of jazz—were genuinely new.

Feelings of hostility toward blacks on the part of the white population were in some respects more strongly developed in states where slavery had never been known than in the South itself. The celebrated French political observer Alexis de Tocqueville noted in 1835, "The prejudice of race appears to be stronger in the states that have abolished slavery than in

Immigrant America

If globalization is understood as the emergence of new patterns of interconnection among the world's peoples and cultures, then surely one of the most significant aspects of globalization is the changing racial and ethnic composition of Western societies. In the United States, shifting patterns of immigration since the end of World War II have altered the demographic structure of many regions, affecting social and cultural life in ways that can hardly be overstated. Although the United States has always been a nation of immigrants (with the obvious exception of Native Americans), most of those who arrived here prior to the early 1960s were European. Throughout the nineteenth and early twentieth centuries, vast numbers of people from Ireland, Italy, Germany, Russia, and other European and east European countries flocked to America in search of a new life, giving a distinctive European bent to American culture. (Of course, until 1808, another significant group of immigrants—Africans—came not because America was a land of opportunity, but because they had been enslaved.) In part because of changes in immigration policy, however, most of those admitted since 1965 have been Asian or Hispanic. In 1993, for example, of the approximately 900,000 immigrants who were legally admitted to the United States, more than 350,000 came from Asia and more than 300,000 were from Latin America. There are also an estimated 4.5 to 5 million illegal immigrants living in the United States, many of whom are Hispanic. As a result, as

of 1990, 42 percent of U.S. residents who were foreign born were from Latin America, while 25 percent were from Asia. In contrast, in 1900 almost 85 percent of the foreign born were European (Duignan and Gann, 1998).

those where it still exists; and nowhere is it so intolerant as in those states where servitude has never been known" (Tocqueville, 1969). Moral rejection of slavery seems to have been confined to a few more educated groups. The main factors underlying the Civil War were political and economic; most northern leaders were more interested in sustaining the Union than in abolishing slavery, although this was the eventual outcome of the conflict. The formal abolition of slavery changed the real conditions of life for African Americans in the South relatively little. The "black codes"—laws limiting the rights of blacks—placed restrictions on the behavior of the former slaves and punished their transgressions in much the same way as under slavery. Acts were also passed legalizing segregation of blacks from whites in public

places. One kind of slavery was thus replaced by another, based on social, political, and economic discrimination.

INTERNAL MIGRATION FROM SOUTH TO NORTH

Industrial development in the North, combined with the mechanization of agriculture in the South, produced a progressive movement of African Americans northward from the turn of the century on. In 1900, more than 90 percent of African Americans lived in the South, mostly in rural areas. Today, less than half of the black population remains in the South; three quarters now live in northern urban areas. African Americans used to be farm laborers and domestic

Most of these new immigrants have settled in six "port-of-entry" states: California, New York, Texas, Illinois, New Jersey, and Massachusetts. These states are attractive to new immigrants not necessarily because of the job opportunities they afford, but because they house large immigrant communities into which newcomers are welcomed (Frey and Liaw, 1998). As the flow of Asian and Hispanic immigration continues, and as some nonimmigrants respond by moving to regions of the country with smaller immigrant populations, the percentage of residents of port-of-entry states who are white will continue to drop. California was approximately 52 percent white in 1996; by 2010, this number is expected to fall to 40 percent (Maharidge, 1996). "Other states will follow," Dale Maharidge writes in the book *The Coming White Minority* (1996), "Texas sometime around 2015, and in later years Arizona, New York, Nevada, New Jersey, and Maryland. By 2050 the nation will be almost half nonwhite."

The effect of these demographic changes on everyday social life has been profound. Take California as an example. In California's urban centers, residents fully expect street scenes to be multiethnic in character and would be shocked to visit a state like Wisconsin, where the vast majority of public interactions take place between whites. In some California communities, store and street signs are printed in Spanish or Chinese or Vietnamese, as well as in English. Interracial marriages are on the rise, ethnic restaurants have proliferated, and the schools are filled with nonwhite children. In fact, nonwhites make up two thirds of the undergraduate population at the University of California at Berkeley, where Asian students are on the verge of predominating.

Unfortunately, these changes have exacerbated social tensions. Many white Californians have retreated into prosperous suburban enclaves and have grown resentful of immigrants

and nonwhites. Because rates of voter turnout are higher for whites than for other racial groups in the state and because whites control a significant share of the state's wealth, they have managed to pass a number of laws that seek to preserve opportunities for the "coming white minority." Proposition 187, for example, passed in 1994, denied vital public services to illegal immigrants. More recently, the regents of the University of California, in a highly controversial move, decided to abolish affirmative action for the entire nine-campus state university system. Were these decisions based on solid economic and philosophical rationales—the perception that California taxpayers were shouldering too much of the economic burden of illegal immigration or the sense that affirmative action constitutes "reverse discrimination" against whites—or were they motivated principally by xenophobia, the fear of those different from oneself? Whatever the answer, there can be little doubt but that immigration—an important aspect of globalization—is changing the face of American society.

servants, but over a period of little more than two generations, they have become mainly urban, industrial, and service-economy workers. But African Americans have not become assimilated into the wider society in the way in which the successive groups of white immigrants were. They have for the most part been unable to break free from the conditions of neighborhood segregation and poverty that other immigrants faced on arrival. Together with those of Anglo-Saxon origin, African Americans have lived in the United States far longer than most other immigrant groups. What was a transitional experience for most of the later, white immigrants has become a seemingly permanent experience for blacks. In the majority of cities, both South and North, blacks and whites live in separate neighborhoods and are educated in different

schools. It has been estimated that 80 percent of either blacks or whites would have to move in order to desegregate housing fully in the average American city.

THE CIVIL RIGHTS MOVEMENT

Struggles by minority groups to achieve equal rights and opportunities have for a long while been a part of the United States. In contrast to other racial and ethnic minorities, blacks and Native Americans have largely been denied opportunities for self-advancement. The National Association for the Advancement of Colored People (NAACP) and the National Urban League, founded in 1909 and 1910 respectively, fought for black civil rights, but began to have some real effect only

Martin Luther King, Jr. addresses a large crowd at a civil rights march on Washington in 1963. Born in 1929, King was a Baptist minister, civil rights leader, and winner of the 1964 Nobel Peace Prize. He was assassinated by James Earl Ray in 1968.

after World War II, when the NAACP instituted a campaign against segregated public education. This struggle came to a head when the organization sued five school boards, challenging the concept of separate but equal schooling that then prevailed. In 1954, in *Brown v. Board of Education of Topeka, Kansas*, the U.S. Supreme Court unanimously decided that "separate educational facilities are inherently unequal."

This decision became the platform for struggles for civil rights from the 1950s to the 1970s. The strength of the resistance from many whites persuaded black leaders that mass militancy was necessary to give civil rights any real substance. In 1955, a black woman, Rosa Parks, was arrested in Montgomery, Alabama, for declining to give up her seat on a bus to a white man. As a result, almost the entire African American population of the city, led by a Baptist minister, Martin Luther King, Jr., boycotted the transportation system for 381 days. Eventually the city was forced to abolish segregation in public transportation.

Further boycotts and sit-ins followed, with the object of desegregating other public facilities. The marches and demonstrations began to achieve a mass following from blacks and white sympathizers. In 1963, a quarter of a million civil rights supporters staged a march on Washington and cheered as King announced, "We will not be satisfied until justice rolls down like the waters and righteousness like a mighty stream." In 1964, the Civil Rights Act was passed by Congress and signed into law by President Lyndon B. Johnson, comprehensively banning discrimination in public facilities, education, employment, and any agency receiving government funds. Further bills in follow-

ing years were aimed at ensuring that African Americans became fully registered voters and outlawed discrimination in housing.

Attempts to implement the new civil rights legislation continued to meet with ferocious resistance from opponents. Civil rights marchers were insulted and beaten up, and some lost their lives. But in spite of barriers that hampered the full realization of its provisions, the Civil Rights Act proved to be fundamentally important. Its principles applied not just to African Americans but to anyone subject to discrimination, including other ethnic groups and women. It served as the starting point for a range of movements asserting the rights of oppressed groups.

How successful has the civil rights movement been? On one hand, a substantial black middle class has emerged over the last three to four decades. And many African Americans—such as the writer Toni Morrison, the literary scholar Henry Louis Gates, Secretary of State Condoleezza Rice, media mogul Oprah Winfrey, and basketball player Michael Jordan—have achieved positions of power and influence in the wider society. On the other hand, a large number of African Americans, making up an underclass, live trapped in the ghettos. Scholars have debated whether the existence of the black underclass has resulted primarily from economic disadvantage or dependency on the welfare system. We will examine the forms of inequality that African Americans and other minority groups continue to experience later in this chapter.

Latinos in the United States

The wars of conquest that created the boundaries of the contemporary United States were not only directed against the Native American population but also against Mexico. The territory that later became California, Nevada, Arizona, New Mexico, and Utah, along with a quarter of a million Mexicans—was taken by the United States in 1848 as a result of the American war with Mexico. The terms Mexican American and *Chicano* include the descendants of these people, together with subsequent immigrants from Mexico. The term *Latino* refers to anyone from Spanish-speaking regions living in the United States.

The three main groups of Latinos in the United States are Mexican Americans (around 20.6 million), Puerto Ricans (3.4 million), and Cubans (1.2 million). A further 10 million Spanish-speaking residents are from countries in Central and South America. The Latino population, as mentioned earlier, is increasing at an extraordinary rate—53 percent between 1980 and 1990 and 58 percent between 1990 and 2000—mainly as a result of the large-scale flow of new immigrants from across the Mexican border. Latino residents now slightly outnumber African Americans.

MEXICAN AMERICANS

Mexican Americans continue to reside mainly in California, Texas, and the remaining southwestern states, although there are substantial groups in the midwest and in northern cities. The majority have come to work at low-paying jobs. In the post–World War II period up to the early 1960s, Mexican workers were admitted without much restriction. This was succeeded by a phase in which numbers were limited and efforts made to deport those who had entered illegally. Illegal immigrants today continue to flood across the border. Large numbers are intercepted and sent back each year by immigration officials, but most simply try again, and it is estimated that four times as many escape officials as are stopped.

Since Mexico is a relatively poor country existing alongside the much wealthier United States, it seems unlikely that this flow of people northward will diminish in the near future. Illegal immigrants can be employed more cheaply than indigenous workers, and they are prepared to perform jobs that most of the rest of the population would not accept. Legislation was passed by Congress in 1986 making it possible for illegal immigrants who had lived in the United States for at least five years to claim legal residence.

Many Mexican Americans resist assimilation into the dominant English-speaking culture and, in common with other ethnic groups, have increasingly begun to display pride in their own cultural identity within the United States.

PUERTO RICANS AND CUBANS

Puerto Rico was acquired by the United States through war, and Puerto Ricans have been American citizens since 1917. The island is poor, and many of its inhabitants have migrated to the mainland United States to improve their conditions of life. Puerto Ricans originally settled in New York City, but since the 1960s, they have moved elsewhere. A reverse migration of Puerto Ricans began in the 1970s; more have left the mainland than have arrived since that date. One of the most important issues facing Puerto Rican activists is the political destiny of their homeland. Puerto Rico is at present a commonwealth, not a full state within the United States. For years, Puerto Ricans have been divided about whether the island should retain its present status, opt for independence, or attempt to become the fifty-first state of the Union.

A third Latino group in the United States, the Cubans, differs from the two others in key respects. Half a million Cubans fled communism following the rise of Fidel Castro in 1959, and the majority settled in Florida. Unlike other Latino immigrants, they were mainly educated people from white-collar and professional backgrounds. They have managed to thrive within the United States, many finding positions comparable to those they abandoned in Cuba. As a group, Cubans have the highest family income of all Latinos.

A further wave of Cuban immigrants, from less affluent origins, arrived in 1980. Lacking the qualifications held by the first wave, these people tend to live in circumstances closer to the rest of the Latino communities in the United States. Both sets of Cuban immigrants are mainly political refugees rather than economic migrants. The later immigrants to a large extent have become the "working class" for the earlier immigrants. They are paid low wages, but Cuban employers tend to take them on in preference to other ethnic groups. In Miami, nearly one third of all businesses are owned by Cubans, and 75 percent of the labor force in construction is Cuban.

The Asian Connection

About 3.6 percent of the population of the United States is of Asian origin—10.2 million people. Chinese, Japanese, and Filipinos (immigrants from the Philippines) form the largest groups. But now there are also significant numbers of Asian Indians, Pakistanis, Koreans, and Vietnamese living in America. And as a result of the war in Vietnam, some 350,000 refugees from that country entered the United States in the 1970s.

Most of the early Chinese immigrants settled in California, where they were employed mainly in heavy industries such as mining and railroad construction. The retreat of the Chinese into distinct Chinatowns was not primarily their choice, but was made necessary by the hostility they faced. Since Chinese immigration was ended by law in 1882, the Chinese remained largely isolated from the wider society, at least until recently.

The early Japanese immigrants also settled in California and the other Pacific states. During World War II, following the attack on Pearl Harbor by Japan, all Japanese Americans in the United States were made to report to "relocation centers," which were effectively concentration camps, surrounded by barbed wire and gun turrets. In spite of the fact that most of these people were American citizens, they were compelled to live in the hastily established camps for the duration of the war. Paradoxically, this situation eventually led to their greater integration within the wider society, since, following the war, Japanese Americans did not return to the separate neighborhoods in which they had previously lived. They have become extremely successful in reaching high levels of education and income, marginally outstripping whites. The rate of intermarriage of Japanese Americans with whites is now nearly 50 percent.

Life On the Work Line

Seven days a week—early mornings to mid-afternoons—men from south of the border, mostly from Mexico, hang out in work lines on Queens Boulevard or Roosevelt Avenue. They wait for cars, vans, or trucks belonging to small business owners, contractors, and construction companies who are looking for cheap day-labor. It took six years for Miguel to graduate from being one of the guys on the line to being one of the guys with the boss in the vehicle, picking who works and who doesn't. In between caring for their three kids, Miguel's wife, Marianna, practices aroma and herbal cleansings. They shared their story of [***] migration and survival as undocumented "aliens" from their one-room basement apartment next to the Grand Central Expressway.

[***]

MARIANNA: We went to Tijuana to get away from our mothers—but we ended up with his crazy cousin. A twenty-eight-year-old man married to a sixty-eight-year-old woman. Nothing but a liar and a thief, his cousin. I kept saying "Miguel, let's go north, to New York. We can stay with my father. Make enough to live good and send money home to our families." But Miguel was so macho about the United States.

MIGUEL: I always thought, why would I go to the United States? Just so they could humiliate me for cheap labor. *Never!* [***] The high school I went to was a Socialist school. Always in my mind the United States was an evil place.

Miguel called a cousin who gave him the name of a coyote who could take them across the border.

[***]

MIGUEL: He takes us to a town closer to the border where he has other people waiting to cross. At one o'clock in the morning we leave in a Camaro with California plates. We were three men in a trunk big enough for only one man, [***] I was curled up sideways in the trunk. Another guy was curled up the other way. The third one went across the two of us. [***]

MARIANNA: I was in the backseat with the baby, three other women and two other little girls—all squashed together and a big cloth over everything. I was worried my baby was going to suffocate under the blanket. El Sabrás [the coyote] finally said "Okay, you can uncover the baby, but don't let him look up."

[***]

MIGUEL: The car stops and the trunk door opens. [***] Two hours in the trunk and we could barely stand. Even if your

whole body is numb, you have to make sure not to look suspicious because INS knows the look of people walking out of trunks.

[***]

MIGUEL: We spent whatever money we had left flying from L.A. to New York so Marianna could be near her father and sister. Everyone else in the airplane was white. They were staring at us with our nerves all at an end. Probably they were thinking, look, they are *mojaditos* [slang for Mexicans who cross; literally "the wet ones"]. My father-in-law forgot he was supposed to pick us up at JFK Airport. We're waiting in the cold for a long time, putting quarters in phone booths.

[***]

MIGUEL: Most of the jobs I've had here I got from the work line on Roosevelt Avenue. In the beginning they were day jobs, doing yard work, washing cars, passing out fliers, installing air conditioners. Sometimes the jobs are more steady: busboy, dishwasher, mechanic's assistant, selling carpets.

Work lines are like survival. The one who runs the fastest gets the job. We could be six or seven of us standing around, talking. When a van pulls up, you stop what you're doing and run. If they need two painters, you say you're a painter. If they need a mover, you're a mover. The guy working for the boss looking for people is an instant employment agency. *"You, you, and you come with me."* I'm that guy now. I'm working for a guy who's Turkish and it's easier for him to have me do it, because a lot of Mexican guys don't want to go with an Arab or a Chinese or a Greek.

We ask, "After everything that you've been through, was it worth it, coming to the United States?"

MARIANNA: I pray that my husband will get a job with better pay and that my children have a chance to study and have a good head so they don't become little bums. That's what they learn over here. Children are out by themselves without their parents' permission. Many of them are in gangs. They should be in their homes studying or with their family. Even if they are drawing on the walls, at least they're in their homes. More than anything I want my son, Lalo, to have the opportunity to study. It is better for him here in the U.S., even if it is not better for us.

SOURCE: Warren Lehrer and Judith Sloan, *Crossing the BLVD* (New York: W. W. Norton, 2003).

Following the passing of a new immigration act in 1965, large-scale immigration of Asians into the United States again took place. Foreign-born Chinese Americans today outnumber those brought up in the United States. The newly arrived Chinese have avoided the Chinatowns in which the long-established Chinese have tended to remain, mostly moving into other neighborhoods.

Racial and Ethnic Inequality

A 1996 *New York Times* headline proclaimed "Quality of Life Is Up for Many Blacks" (Holmes, 1996). The following year, the same paper reported that "New Reports Say Minorities Benefit in Fiscal Recovery" (Holmes, 1997). Since the civil rights movement of the 1960s, has real progress been made? On the one hand, an increasing number of blacks joined the middle class by acquiring college degrees, professional jobs, and new homes. On the other hand, blacks are far more likely than whites to live in poverty and be socially isolated from good schools and economic opportunity. Also, large numbers of immigrants came to the United States throughout the 1980s and 1990s to find new economic opportunity. Yet some of these groups, particularly immigrants from Mexico, have among the lowest levels of educational achievement and live in dire poverty. For the most part, sociologists agree on the facts about racial and ethnic inequality. There is, however, a disagreement among sociologists about how these facts should be interpreted. Are improving economic conditions for minority groups part of a long-term process or were they temporary reflections of the booming 1990s economy? Is racial and ethnic inequality primarily the result of a person's racial or ethnic background or does it reflect a person's class position? In other words, is a black American, for example, more likely to live in poverty because of racial discrimination or because of the lower-class status that many blacks hold? In this section, we will first examine the facts: how racial and ethnic inequality is reflected in terms of educational and occupational attainment, income, health, residential segregation, and political power. We will then look at the divergent social statuses found within the largest racial and ethnic groups. We will conclude by looking at how sociologists have sought to explain racial inequality.

Educational Attainment

Differences between blacks and whites in levels of educational attainment have decreased, but these seem more the result of long-established trends rather than the direct outcome of the struggles of the 1960s. After steadily improving their levels of educational attainment for the last fifty years, young African Americans are for the first time close to whites in terms of finishing high school. The number of blacks over the age of twenty-five with high school degrees has increased from about 20 percent in 1960 to 78.5 percent in 2000. By contrast, about 85 percent of whites have completed high school (see Figure 11.3). Some analysts see this development as a hopeful sign and an indicator that young blacks need not live a life of hopelessness and despair. But not all signs have been positive. While more blacks are attending college now than in the 1960s, a much higher proportion of whites than blacks graduate from college today. In today's global economy and job market, which value college degrees, the result is a wide disparity in incomes between whites and blacks (see below). As sociologist Christopher Jencks remarked, "You have a situation where the black kids coming out of high school are better qualified, but the number of jobs that they are qualified for is actually shrinking" (quoted in Holmes, 1997).

Another negative trend with potentially far-reaching consequences is the large gap in educational attainment between Hispanics and both whites and blacks. Hispanics have by far the highest high school dropout rate of any group in the United States. While rates of college attendance and success in graduation have gradually improved for other groups, the rate for Hispanics has held relatively steady since the mid-1980s. Only about 10 percent hold a college degree. It is possible that these poor results can be attributed to the large number of poorly educated immigrants from Latin America who have come to the United States in the last two decades. Many of these immigrants have poor English language skills and their children encounter difficulties in schools. One study found, however, that even among Mexican Americans whose families have lived in the United States for three generations or more, there has been a decline in educational attainment (Bean et al., 1994). For these Hispanics with low levels of education and poor language skills, living in the United States has been "the American nightmare, not the American dream" (Holmes, 1997).

Employment and Income

As a result of the increase in educational attainment, blacks now hold a slightly higher proportion of managerial and professional jobs than in 1960, though still not in proportion to their overall numbers. In 1998, out of the approximately 39 million managerial or professional positions in the United States, whites held about 34 million (about 87 percent), African Americans just under 3 million (about 7.5 percent), and Hispanics just under 2 million (about 5 percent). During that same year, black men

FIGURE 11.3

Educational Attainment (for persons 25 years old and over)

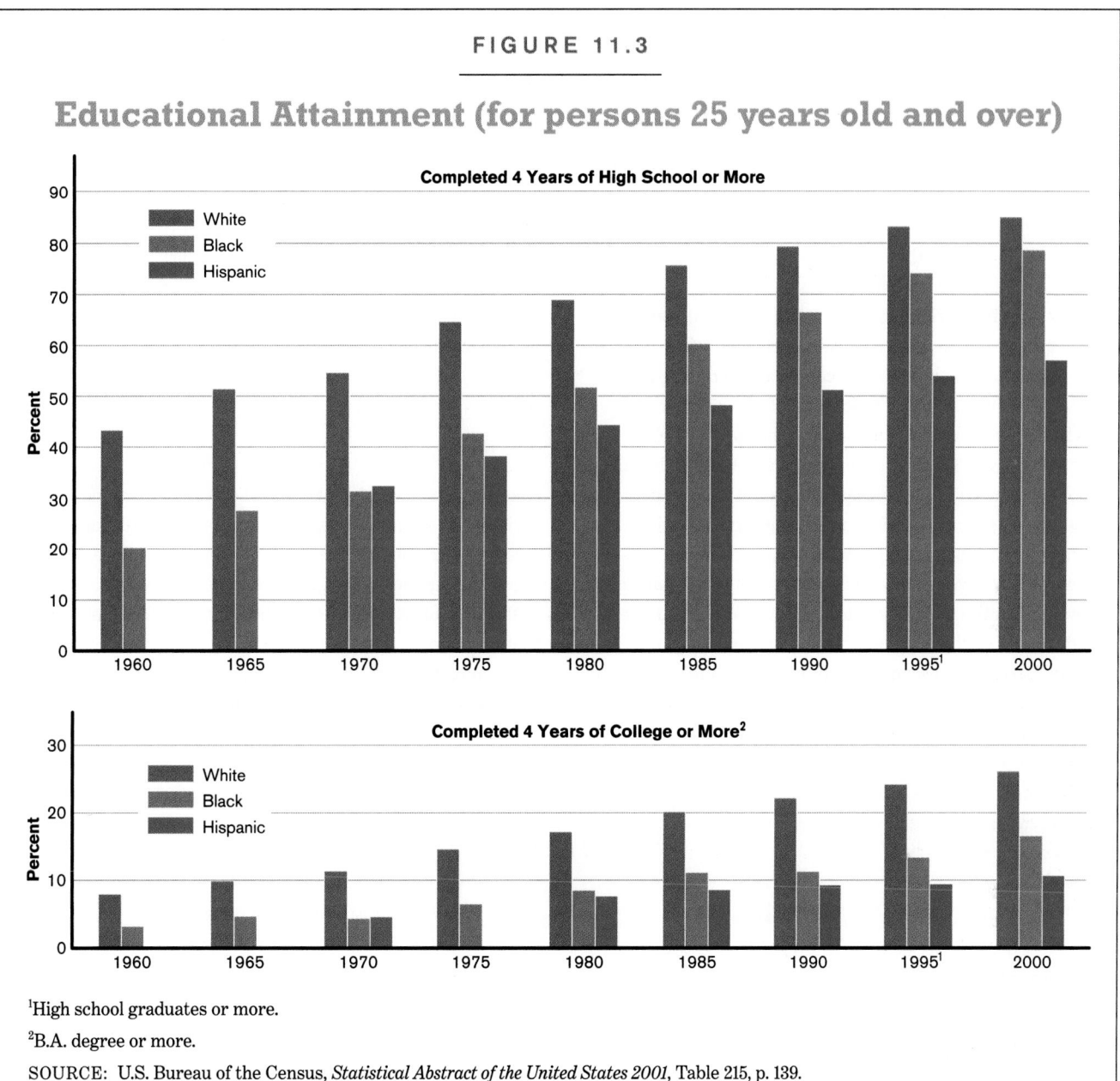

¹High school graduates or more.

²B.A. degree or more.

SOURCE: U.S. Bureau of the Census, *Statistical Abstract of the United States 2001*, Table 215, p. 139.

were about twice as likely as whites to be service workers and about one and one half times as likely to hold a blue-collar job.

The unemployment rate of black and Hispanic men outstrips that of whites by the same degree today as was the case in the early 1960s. Twice as many black and Hispanic men as white men are registered as unemployed (in 1998, 4 percent for whites versus about 8 percent for both blacks and Hispanics). There has also been some debate about whether employment opportunities for minorities have improved or worsened. Statistics on unemployment don't adequately measure economic opportunity, since they measure only those known to be looking for work. A higher proportion of blacks and Hispanics

have simply opted out of the occupational system, neither working nor looking for work. They have become disillusioned by the frustration of searching for employment that is not there. Unemployment figures also do not reflect the increasing numbers of young men from minority groups who have been incarcerated (see also Chapter 7). Finally, although many new jobs were created during the economic boom of the 1990s, most of them available to those without a college degree were in lower-paying service occupations. As we just saw, blacks and Hispanics are underrepresented among college graduates.

Nevertheless, the disparities between the earnings of blacks and whites are gradually diminishing. As measured in terms of weekly income, black men now earn 76 percent of the level of pay of whites. In 1959, the proportion was only 49 percent. In terms of household family income (adjusted for inflation), blacks are the only social group to have seen an improvement during the 1990s. By 1995, poverty rates for African Americans had fallen to their lowest rates since the government started tracking the figure in 1955 and continued to improve for the rest of the decade. Milton Morris, who tracks trends among African Americans, claimed "I think that this is a short period of really very substantial and significant gains. . . . [V]ery few people have been paying serious attention. And yet when you do, you see that by virtually every measure of well-being, African-Americans have been on a significant uptrend during the 90s" (quoted in Holmes, 1996). These signs of improvement appear to be felt by African Americans across the country. One Jersey City resident said "In my area, I see things getting better all the time. It used to be like hell, groups always on the corner, cussing and fighting, ripping and raiding, shooting each other. It calmed down a whole hell of a lot" (quoted in Holmes, 1996).

Some scholars have warned, however, that these gains could be reversed as the economy falters. They also pointed out that though there has been considerable improvement, large gaps between African Americans and whites still exist in terms of the attainment of college degrees, infant mortality, poverty rates, and household income (see Figure 11.4). Finally, though the eco-

nomic status of blacks appears to have improved, prospects for Hispanics have stagnated or worsened over the same time period. Between 1989 and 1995, Hispanic household incomes (adjusted for inflation) decreased by about 10 percent. For the first time ever, the poverty rate of Hispanics surpassed that of African Americans. The large influx of immigrants, who tend to be poor, has caused some of the decline in average income, but even among Hispanics born in the United States, income levels declined as well. As one Latino group leader commented, "Most Hispanic residents are caught in jobs like gardener, nanny, and restaurant worker that will never pay well and from which they will never advance" (quoted in Goldberg, 1997).

Health

Jake Najman recently surveyed the evidence linking health to racial and economic inequalities. He also considered what strategies might best be used to improve the health of the poorer groups in society. After studying data for a number of different countries, including the United States, he concluded that for people in the poorest 20 percent, as measured in terms of income, the death rates were 1.5–2.5 times those of the highest 20 percent of income earners. In the United States, the rate of infant mortality for the poorest 20 percent was four times

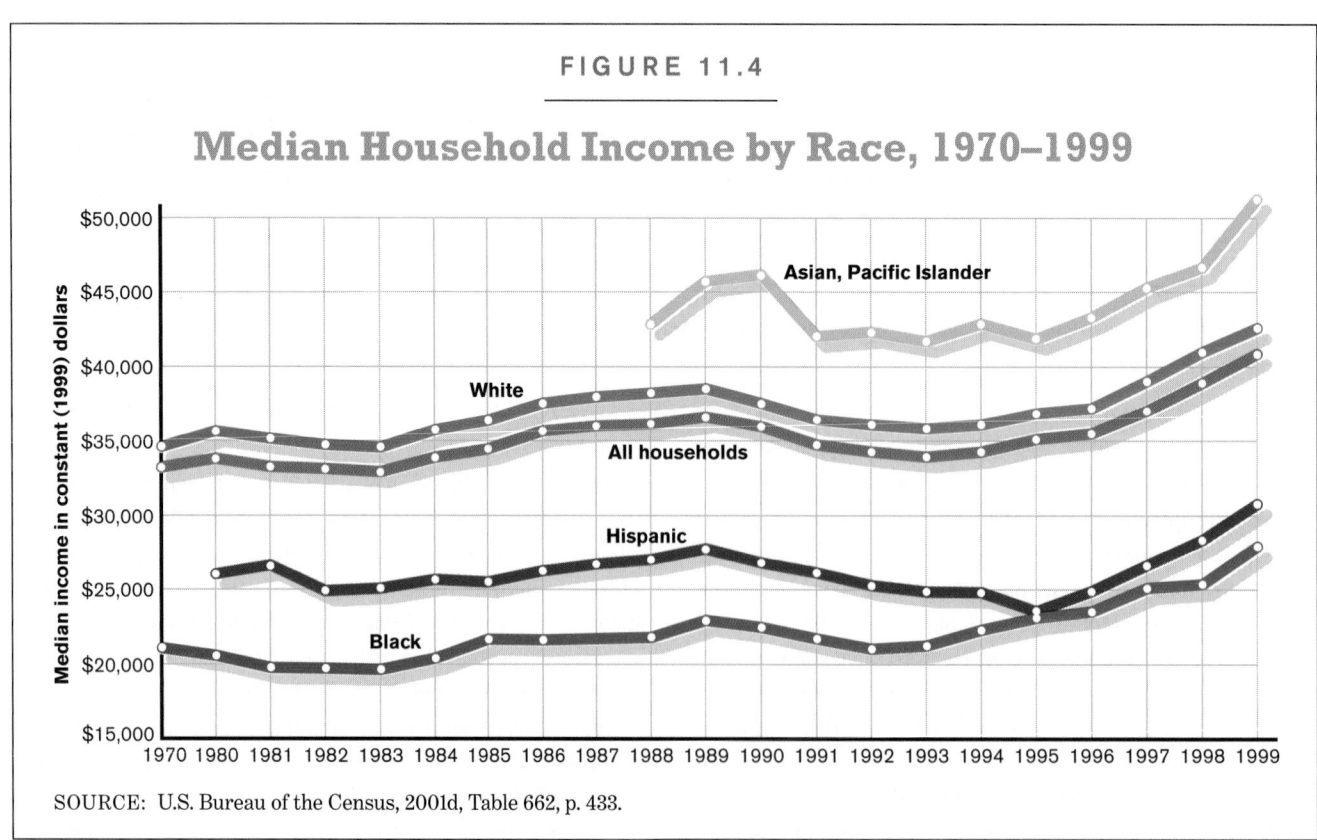

FIGURE 11.4

Median Household Income by Race, 1970–1999

SOURCE: U.S. Bureau of the Census, 2001d, Table 662, p. 433.

higher than for the wealthiest 20 percent. When differences were measured between whites and African Americans in the United States, rather than only in terms of income, the contrast in infant mortality rates was even higher—five times higher for blacks than for whites. The contrast is also becoming greater rather than less. The same is true of life expectancy—the average age to which individuals at birth can expect to live. In 1984, whites on average could expect to live 5.6 years more than African Americans. By 1996, this had increased to 6.5 years and could increase to 8.2 by 2010.

How might the influence of poverty and race on health be countered? Extensive programs of health education and disease prevention are one possibility. But such programs tend to work better among more prosperous, well-educated groups and in any case usually produce only small changes in behavior. Increased accessibility to health services would help, but probably to a limited degree. The only really effective policy option, it is argued, would be to attack poverty itself, so as to reduce the income gap between rich and poor (Najman, 1993).

Residential Segregation

Neighborhood segregation seems to have declined little over the past quarter century. Studies show that discriminatory practices between black and white clients in the housing market continue (Lake, 1981). Black and white children now attend the same schools in most rural areas of the South and in many of the smaller- and medium-size cities throughout the country. Most black college students now also go to the same colleges and universities as whites, instead of the traditional all-black institutions (Bullock, 1984). Yet in the larger cities a high level of educational segregation persists as a result of the continuing movement of whites to suburbs or rural environs.

In *American Apartheid* (1993), Douglas Massey and Nancy A. Denton argue that the history of racial segregation and its specific urban form, the black ghetto, are responsible for the perpetuation of black poverty and the continued polarization of black and white.

The persistence of segregation, they say, is not a result of impersonal market forces. Even many middle-class blacks still find themselves segregated from the white society. For them, as for poor blacks, this becomes a self-perpetuating cycle. Affluent blacks who could afford to live in comfortable, predominantly white neighborhoods may deliberately choose not to, because of the struggle for acceptance they know they would face. The black ghetto, the authors conclude, was constructed through a series of well-defined institutional practices of racial discrimination—private behavior and public policies by which whites sought to contain growing urban black populations. Until policy makers, social scientists, and private citizens rec-

ognize the crucial role of such institutional discrimination in perpetuating urban poverty and racial injustice, the United States will remain a deeply divided and troubled society.

Political Power

Blacks have made some gains in holding local elective offices; the number of black public officials has increased from forty in 1960 to over eight thousand today. The numbers of black mayors and judges have increased appreciably. Blacks have been voted into every major political office, except president and vice president, including areas where white voters predominate. In 1992, after congressional districts were reshaped to give minority candidates more opportunity, a record number of African Americans and Latinos were elected to Congress. Yet these changes are still relatively small scale. Black officials still make up only about 2 percent of the elective offices in the United States. Most of these are in relatively minor local positions. The share of representation that Latinos and African Americans have in Congress is not equal to their overall size in American society. Following the defeat of Senator Carol Moseley-Braun in 1998, the U.S. Senate had no black or Latino members.

Gender and Race

The status of minority women in the United States is especially plagued by inequalities (see Figure 11.5). Gender and race discrimination combined make it particularly difficult for these women to escape conditions of poverty. They share the legacy of past discrimination against members of minority groups and women in general. Until about twenty-five years ago, most minority women worked in low-paying occupations such as household work or farmwork or low-wage manufacturing jobs. Changes in the law and gains in education have allowed for more minority women to enter white-collar professions, and their economic and occupational status has improved. By 1987, the average African American female college graduate earned 90 percent of the average for white female college graduates. But in general, female college graduates earn less than men with only high school educations. And white male high school dropouts, on average, earn more than black female college graduates (Rhode, 1990; Higginbotham, 1992).

However unequal the status and pay of minority women, these women play a critical role in their communities. They are often the major or sole wage earners in their families. Yet their incomes are not always sufficient to maintain a family. About half of all families headed by African American or Latino women live at poverty levels.

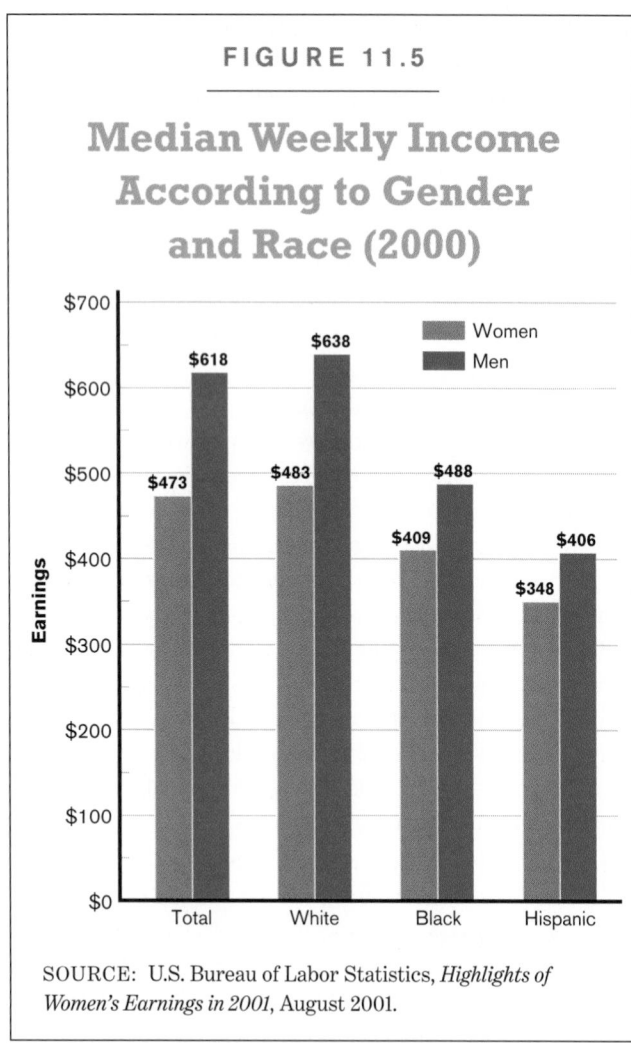

FIGURE 11.5

Median Weekly Income According to Gender and Race (2000)

Women
Men

Earnings

Total: $473 (Women), $618 (Men)
White: $483 (Women), $638 (Men)
Black: $409 (Women), $488 (Men)
Hispanic: $348 (Women), $406 (Men)

SOURCE: U.S. Bureau of Labor Statistics, *Highlights of Women's Earnings in 2001*, August 2001.

Divergent Fortunes

When we survey the development and current position of the major ethnic groups in America, one conclusion that emerges is that they have achieved varying levels of success. Whereas successive waves of European immigrants managed to overcome most of the prejudice and discrimination they originally faced and become assimilated into the wider society, other groups have not. These latter groups include two minorities that have lived in North America for centuries, Native Americans and African Americans, as well as Mexicans, Puerto Ricans, and to some extent Chinese.

THE ECONOMIC DIVIDE WITHIN THE AFRICAN AMERICAN COMMUNITY

The situation of blacks is the most conspicuous case of divergent fortunes. After more than two centuries of continuous presence on the North American subcontinent, longer than

any other group except for Native Americans and the European settlers, blacks are in the worst situation, with the sole exception of Native Americans, of any ethnic group in the United States. The reasons for this lie in the historical backdrop of slavery and its residue in the long years of struggle that it took to free African Americans from open prejudice and discrimination.

It seems probable that a division has opened up between the minority of blacks who have obtained white-collar, managerial, or professional jobs—who form a small black middle class—and the majority whose living conditions have not improved. In 1960, most of the nonmanual-labor jobs open to blacks were those serving the black community—a small proportion of blacks could work as teachers, social workers, or less often, lawyers or doctors. No more than some 13 percent of blacks held white-collar jobs, contrasted to 44 percent of whites. Since that date, however, there have been significant changes. Between 1960 and 1970, the percentage of blacks in white-collar occupations doubled—although this level of growth slowed markedly in the 1980s. This increase was greater than that for the half century previous to 1960.

Bart Landry carried out a systematic study of the growing black middle class (1988). He surveyed white-collar blacks and whites in twenty-one metropolitan areas across the country and also analyzed government statistics from the early 1980s. Landry found that middle-class blacks were much better off, and much more numerous, than their predecessors twenty years before (see also Jacoby, 1998). Opportunities have opened up partly through changes in legislation brought into being as a result of the civil rights movement. However, the population of blacks in middle-class jobs remains well below that of whites, and their average incomes are less.

THE ASIAN SUCCESS STORY

Unlike African Americans, other minority groups have outlasted the open prejudice and discrimination they once faced. The intense hostility once held toward the Irish, for instance, is now mostly a distant memory. Feelings of prejudice and antagonism still exist between people of Irish and Italian backgrounds in Boston and New York, and from both groups toward Jews. For the most part, however, such feelings are much less pronounced than in former times and are not widely expressed in practices of discrimination.

The changing fate of Asians in the United States is especially remarkable. Until about half a century ago, the level of prejudice and discrimination experienced by the Chinese and Japanese in North America was greater than for any other group of nonblack immigrants. Since that time, Asian Americans have achieved a steadily increasing prosperity and no longer face the same levels of antagonism from the white community. The median income of Asian Americans is now actually higher than that of whites.

This statistic conceals some big discrepancies between and within different Asian groups; there are still many Asian Americans, including those whose families have resided in the United States for generations, who live in poverty. However, the turnaround in the fortunes of Asian Americans, on the whole, is so impressive that some have referred to the Asian American "success story" as a prime example of what minorities can achieve in the United States.

LATINOS: A TALE OF TWO CITIES

Miami and Los Angeles both have large Latino populations. In Los Angeles, the large majority of Latinos are well down the ladder of privilege and power. But although both cities experience ethnic tensions, in Miami, Latinos have achieved a position of economic and political prominence not found elsewhere.

In *City on the Edge*, Alejandro Portes and Alex Stepik describe the ethnic transformation of Miami over recent years. In 1980, whites were already in a minority in the city, at 48 percent of the population. African Americans made up 17 percent, and those of Spanish origin, 35 percent. In that year, as Portes and Stepik put it, "the city abandoned, once and for all, the image of a sunny tourist destination and faced that of an uncertain bridge between two worlds" (1993). The reason was a large influx of Cuban immigrants. Struggles developed among the new immigrants, whites, and blacks; black leaders accused the Cubans of taking their jobs.

These struggles continue today. In Miami, those of Cuban origin have often moved into positions of considerable influence. Some Cubans have become very successful in business and have become more wealthy than the "old" white families that once ran the city. They haven't been assimilated into the white community but maintain their own customs, institutions, and language. Miami is now a place of "parallel structures" existing alongside one another, each including powerful and wealthy people, not integrated into one unified group. There is much tension, but some Anglo and Cuban politicians now speak of Miami as the capital of the Caribbean—a city not only part of the United States, but looking also to the other societies, mostly developing countries, surrounding it.

Los Angeles points to the Pacific Rim—to what some analysts see as the future center of economic power, linking the West Coast of North America with Japan and the newly industrializing countries of Hong Kong, Taiwan, South Korea, and perhaps China. Immigrants from all of these countries have recently arrived in Los Angeles. At the same time, millions of Latinos have now settled in the city.

Los Angeles has been referred to as "the capital of the Third World" because of its large Latino and Asian popula-
tions. The city already contained the largest group of Mexicans in the United States in the 1920s. Then, as now, it was Mexicans who performed most of the menial jobs. Then, as now, most Anglos "were at once aware that this was the case," and "yet they would act as if these people, once they had finished working, went home not to the Old Plaza or, as now, to East L.A., but to another planet" (Rieff, 1991).

Some optimistic observers have suggested that Los Angeles in the twenty-first century will combine Asian family loyalty, Hispanic industriousness, and Anglo-Saxon respect for individual liberty. Is such a vision possible? It would certainly take some profound social changes even to come close. Los Angeles is an ethnic mosaic that symbolizes the increasing diversity of American society as a whole. Will the Hispanic population of the city be able to achieve economic success similar to the Cubans in Miami? Will there exist separate but equal Hispanic communities in Los Angeles as well as in other U.S. cities in the future? How will such successes, if they happen, affect the black urban poor? These are all at the moment open questions, to which no one can give certain answers.

Understanding Racial Inequality

What distinguishes less fortunate groups such as African Americans and Mexican Americans is not just that they are nonwhite, but that they were originally present in America as *colonized peoples* rather than willing immigrants. In a classic analysis, Robert Blauner (1972) suggested that a sharp distinction should be drawn between groups who journeyed voluntarily to settle in the new land and those who were incorporated into the society through force or violence. Native Americans are part of American society as a result of military conquest; African Americans were transported in the slave trade; Puerto Rico was colonized as a result of war; and Mexicans were originally incorporated as a result of the conquest of the Southwest by the United States in the nineteenth century. These groups have consistently been the target of racism, which both reflects and perpetuates their separation from other ethnic communities.

But, given that this has been the case for most of American history, what explains the growth of the black middle class? William Julius Wilson (1978; see also Wilson et al., 1987) has argued that race is of diminishing importance in explaining inequalities between whites and blacks. In his view, these inequalities are now based on class rather than skin color. The old racist barriers are crumbling. What remain are inequalities similar to those affecting all lower-class groups.

Wilson's work has proved controversial. His book was awarded a prize by the American Sociological Association, but the Association of Black Sociologists passed a resolution

The Cost of Slavery

[Writing columns and opinion pieces for local and national newspapers is one of the traditional ways that sociologists engage a wider public audience. In this *New York Times* article, Dalton Conley weighs in on the debate over reparations for slavery with his own sociological perspective.]

Marching across the South in 1865, Union soldiers seized up to 900,000 acres of "abandoned property." Some radical Northerners hoped to use this land to provide freed slaves with the now-legendary "40 acres and a mule" as restitution for slavery. Their hopes were obviously dashed. But the argument for reparations lives on nearly 140 years later.

While few doubt that slavery was a great wrong, the challenge before us is how to make things right through financial restitution. But just how would we devise a practical formula to determine who gets what?

Most assessments start with the notion of payment for lost wages. One researcher took 1860s prices for slaves as an esti-mate of their labor value and applied compound interest. The result: $2 trillion to $4 trillion. Six generations after slavery's demise, such approaches present serious difficulties. There are issues of what to do with whites (and blacks) who immigrated here after slavery ended. What about descendants of blacks who lived freely during the antebellum period? Does someone who is born to a white parent and a black parent cancel out? It would take Solomon to solve this.

Perhaps the issue needs to be looked at differently. One way is to recognize slavery as an institution upon which America's wealth was built. If we take this view, it is not important whether a white family arrived in 1700 or in 1965. If you wear cotton blue jeans, if you take out an insurance policy, if you buy from anyone who has a connection to the industries that were built on chattel labor, then you have benefited from slavery. Likewise, if you are black—regardless of when your ancestors arrived—you live with slavery's stigma.

Extending the reparations argument this broadly frees one to move beyond the issue of lost wages and seek out other factors on which to base a formula. If there were one statistic that captured the persistence of racial inequality, it would be net worth.

The typical white family enjoys a net worth that is more than eight times that of its black counterpart, according to the economist Edward Wolff. Even at equivalent income levels, gaps remain large. Among families earning less than $15,000 a year, the median African American family has a net worth of zero, while the corresponding white family has $10,000 in equity. The typical white family earning $40,000 annually has a nest egg of around $80,000. Its black counterpart has about half that amount.

This equity inequity is partly the result of the head start whites enjoy in accumulating and passing on assets. Some economists estimate that up to 80 percent of lifetime wealth accumulation results from gifts from earlier generations, ranging from the down payment on a home to a bequest by a parent. If the government used such net-worth inequality as a basis, and then factored in measures like population size, it could address reparations by transferring about 13 percent of white household wealth to blacks. A two-adult black family would receive an average reparation of about $35,000.

What would be the effect of wealth redistribution on such a vast scale? My own research—using national data to follow black and white adolescents into adulthood—shows that when

we compare families with the same net worth, blacks are more likely to finish high school than whites and are equally likely to complete a bachelor's degree. Racial differences in welfare rates disappear. Thus, one generation after reparations were paid, racial gaps in education should close—eliminating the need for affirmative action.

The unpopularity of this radical plan would no doubt be unprecedented. There are also no guarantees that reparations would be a magic bullet for lingering racial problems. That said, it remains vital, especially during Black History Month, to explore formulas and keep the reparations debate alive. It is important because each resulting dollar amount implies a theory of race, history and equal opportunity. That includes the figure implicit in our current policy—zero—which rests on the most absurd assumption of all: that slavery didn't matter.

SOURCE: Dalton Conley, "The Cost of Slavery," *New York Times,* February 15, 2003.

DALTON CONLEY, *associate professor of sociology and director of the Center for Advanced Social Science Research at New York University, is author of* Being Black, Living in the Red: Race, Wealth and Social Policy in America *and* Honky.

stating that the book "omits significant data regarding the continuing discrimination against blacks at all class levels." "It is the consensus of this organization," the resolution continues, "that this book denies the overwhelming evidence regarding the significance of race and the literature that speaks to the contrary." The resolution criticized the view that the circumstances of blacks have substantially improved or even that racism has declined significantly. Most of the changes, it was argued, have been relatively minor, and racism has only become less vocal since the 1964 Civil Rights Act, rather than diminishing in any substantial sense (quoted in Pinkney, 1984).

Yet Wilson had made it clear in his book that the living conditions of poor blacks were deteriorating. In Wilson's view, his critics have almost completely ignored this aspect of his work. He has since extended his analysis of the most deprived sectors of the black population. Middle-class blacks today tend no longer to live in ghetto neighborhoods. Their exodus has led to an even higher concentration of the disadvantaged in these areas than previously was the case. Wilson recognizes that racism plays a part in this situation of the disadvantaged but points out that other class-related and economic factors are at least equally important—in particular, the very high rate of unemployment and welfare dependency characteristic of the poorest neighborhoods. Wilson's argument is not so much that racism as such has declined, but that it has declined in its *significance* for blacks. Other forms of discrimination based more on economic and class-based disadvantages are as important.

Are racial inequalities to be explained primarily in terms of class? It is true that racial divisions provide a means of social closure, whereby economic resources can be monopolized by privileged class groups. But the argument that racial inequality should be explained primarily in terms of class domination, however, has never been a satisfactory one. Ethnic discrimination, particularly of a racial kind, is partly independent of class differences: the one cannot be separated from the other. This still seems to remain true in the United States today.

For instance, opinion surveys show a general decline in hostile attitudes toward blacks over the past thirty years among white Americans (Schuman, Steel, and Bobo, 1985; Bobo and Kluegel, 1991). The overall level of prejudice seems to be diminishing fairly markedly. David Wellman has argued, however, that the concept of prejudice only captures the more open and individual forms of hostile attitudes toward ethnic minorities. Racism can also be expressed in more subtle ways—in terms of beliefs that, regardless of the intentions involved, defend the position of privileged groups. Many sociologists, according to Wellman, have underestimated the true incidence of racism, because they have looked only at its more obvious manifestations. Most studies have investigated prejudice using surveys; but these do not get at the less obvious, complex aspects of people's views about such emotive topics as ethnicity and race.

Wellman sought to illuminate these complex aspects of racism by means of in-depth interviews with 105 white Americans of varying backgrounds. Most of those he interviewed said that they believed that everyone is equal and that they held no hostility toward blacks. Their beliefs and attitudes did not show the rigidities characteristic of prejudice and stereotypical thinking. Yet their views about contexts of social life (such as education, housing, or jobs) in which black rights threatened their own position were effectively antiblack. Their opposition to change was expressed in ways that did not directly express racial antagonism. People would say, for instance, "I'm not opposed to blacks; but if they come into the neighborhood house prices will be affected"—or, as one individual put it, "I favor anything that doesn't affect me personally" (Wellman, 1987).

These attitudes can still underlie quite rigid institutional patterns of discrimination. Ethnic inequalities are structured into existing social institutions, and patterns of behavior having no immediate connection to ethnicity can serve to reinforce them. Rights and opportunities are not the same thing. Even if it were true that every member of the population accepted that members of all ethnic groups have the same civil rights, major inequalities would persist. There are many examples that demonstrate this. A black person who wishes to obtain a bank loan in order to be able to make home improvements finds it hard to borrow money. The bank might use purely "objective" measures in reaching such decisions, based on the likelihood of the loan repayments being successfully made. Nevertheless, the effect of this institutional racism is the perpetuation of ethnic discrimination (Massey and Denton, 1993).

In sum, although both individual and institutional racism seem to be declining in the United States, the differences between white and nonwhite ethnic groups are long enduring (Ringer, 1985; Conley, 1999). Moreover, the relative success of white ethnics has been to some degree purchased at the expense of nonwhites. A combination of continued white immigration and white racism, up to at least the World War II period, served to keep nonwhites out of the better-paid occupations, forcing them into the least-skilled, most marginal sectors of the economy. With the slowing down of white immigration, this situation is changing, although some newly arrived groups, like the Cubans in Miami, seem to be repeating the process.

Study Outline

www.wwnorton.com/giddens5

Race and Ethnicity: Key Concepts

- Ethnic groups have common cultural characteristics that separate them from others within a given population. Ethnic differences are wholly learned, although they are sometimes depicted as "natural."
- *Race* refers to physical characteristics, such as skin color, that are treated by members of a community or society as socially significant—as signaling distinct cultural characteristics. Many popular beliefs about race are mythical. There are no distinct characteristics by means of which human beings can be allocated to different races.
- *Racism* is prejudice based on socially significant physical distinctions. A racist is someone who believes that some individuals are superior, or inferior, to others as a result of racial differences.
- *Displacement* and *scapegoating* are psychological mechanisms associated with *prejudice* and *discrimination*. In displacement, feelings of hostility become directed against objects that are not the real origin of these anxieties. People project their anxieties and insecurities onto scapegoats. Prejudice involves holding preconceived views about an individual or group; discrimination refers to actual behavior that deprives members of a group of opportunities open to others. Prejudice usually involves *stereotypical thinking*—thinking in terms of fixed and inflexible categories.

Ethnic Relations

- Four models of possible future developments in race and ethnic relations can be distinguished—the first stressing Anglo-conformity, or *assimilation*, the second the *melting pot*, the third *pluralism*, and the fourth *multiculturalism*. In recent years there has been a tendency to emphasize the fourth of these avenues, whereby different ethnic identities are accepted as equal and separate within the context of the overall national culture.

Global Migration

- Beginning in the fifteenth century, global migratory movements resulting from exploration, colonialism, and slavery created multi-ethnic populations in various regions of the world and therefore ethnic and racial antagonism. Today, migration appears to be on the rise as part of the process of globalization.

Ethnic Relations in the United States

- A remarkable diversity of ethnic minorities is found in the United States today, each group having its own distinctive cultural characteristics. Some of the most important minority communities nu-

merically, after blacks, are Native Americans, Mexican Americans, Puerto Ricans, Cubans, Chinese, and Japanese.
- An important distinction must be drawn between those minorities that came to America as willing immigrants and the colonized peoples who either were here already (Native Americans, Mexican Americans) or were brought by force (African Americans) and who were generally incorporated by violence. Racism targeted at these latter groups has been most persistent and most destructive. Gender discrimination compounds the difficulties facing women of color; about half of African American and Latino families that depend primarily on women's incomes live in poverty.

Key Concepts

antiracism (p. 319)
apartheid (p. 322)
assimilation (p. 324)
diaspora (p. 327)
discrimination (p. 320)
displacement (p. 320)
emigration (p. 325)
ethnic cleansing (p. 323)
ethnicity (p. 316)
genocide (p. 323)
immigration (p. 325)
institutional racism (p. 318)
melting pot (p. 324)
minority group (p. 320)
multiculturalism (p. 324)
pluralism (p. 324)
prejudice (p. 320)
race (p. 316)
"racial literacy" (p. 316)
racialization (p. 316)
racism (p. 318)
scapegoat (p. 320)
segregation (p. 323)
situational ethnicity (p. 317)
stereotype (p. 320)
symbolic ethnicity (p. 317)

Review Questions

1. What is ethnicity?
   a. The physical manifestation of racial difference
   b. Any biologically grounded features of a group of people
   c. Any group outside the white, English-speaking majority
   d. The cultural practices and outlooks of a given community that have emerged historically and tend to set people apart

2. Why has racism flourished in modern societies?
   a. Because there was a symbolic distinction between white and black (denoting good and bad) in European cultures before European explorers went to Africa
   b. Because of the dissemination of the idea of race and the ideologies that developed around it
   c. Because of the relations of exploitation that Europeans established with Africans
   d. All of the above

3. What is the "master status"?
   a. A feature like skin color that dominates our perception, often overriding in our minds a person's other characteristics
   b. Our socioeconomic standing
   c. A feature such as skin color that dominates a person's perception of him- or herself, often overriding all other factors in the way a person sees him- or herself
   d. Our gender and/or sexual orientation

4. Which of the following is not one of the models of global population movements since 1945?
   a. Classic model
   b. Colonial model
   c. Guest worker model
   d. Refugee model

5. By the late 1990s, which of the following groups in U.S. society had the highest rate of poverty?
   a. Whites
   b. African Americans
   c. Hispanics
   d. Asian Americans

6. What's the difference between biological racism and cultural racism (new racism)?
   a. Biological racism is the belief that some groups are inferior because their members are biologically inferior, whereas cultural racism is the belief that some groups are inferior because they have a dysfunctional culture.
   b. Biological racism is the official ideology of a political party or social movement that supports the dominance of a majority group, such as white supremacist organizations, while cultural racism is a commonplace superstition, such as the widespread but ill-founded belief that the predominance of blacks in certain American sports reflects so-called racial advantages.
   c. Biological racism is the belief that there are absolute differences between groups, whereas cultural racism is the belief that there are only relative differences.
   d. Biological racism is the belief that some groups are inferior because they have dysfunctional genes, whereas cultural racism is the belief that some groups are inferior because their members have inherently weaker cognitive abilities.

7. What is the difference between the assimilation and melting-pot models of integrating new ethnic groups into the dominant society?
   a. The assimilation model refers to the new group adopting the norms and values of the dominant society, whereas the melting-pot model refers to the merging and blending of dominant and ethnic cultures.
   b. The assimilation model refers to members of the new group becoming citizens of the host nation, whereas the melting-pot model refers to members of the new group remaining guest workers and having only the legal rights afforded to those on work visas.
   c. The assimilation model refers to members of the new group learning the language of the host nation and dispersing to the suburbs, whereas the melting-pot model refers to members of the new group sticking to their own language and concentrating in particular urban neighborhoods.
   d. The assimilation model refers to the experience of twentieth-century immigrants to the United States, whereas the melting-pot model refers to the experience of nineteenth-century immigrants.

8. Which of the following groups have *not* been the victim of scapegoating in Western history?
   a. Blacks
   b. Chinese
   c. White Protestants
   d. All have been victims at one time or another.

9. What is the difference between situational ethnicity and symbolic ethnicity?
   a. Situational ethnicity is secular, whereas symbolic ethnicity is religious.
   b. Situational ethnicity occurs when people choose to assert their ethnic background for social or economic advantage, whereas symbolic ethnicity occurs when people choose to participate in the most important religious holidays or parades of their ethnic group while ignoring their ethnicity for most of the year.
   c. Situational ethnicity is transitory, whereas symbolic ethnicity is permanent.
   d. Situational ethnicity occurs when people choose to participate in the most important religious holidays or parades of their ethnic group while ignoring their ethnicity for most of the year, whereas symbolic ethnicity occurs when people choose to assert their ethnic background for social or economic advantage.

10. How much difference did the formal abolition of slavery in the United States make to the condition of blacks?
    a. An enormous amount—they were no longer enslaved and were able to move in great numbers to seek manufacturing jobs in the northern cities.
    b. A good deal—their legal situation improved, and the formal rights they won formed the basis of the civil rights movement a century later.
    c. Relatively little—acts were soon passed legalizing the segregation of blacks and whites in public places.
    d. None—all of the conditions of slavery were replicated under sharecropping.

Thinking Sociologically Essay Questions

1. Review the discussion of the assimilation of different American minorities, then write a short essay comparing the different assimilation experiences of Asians and Latinos. In your essay identify the criteria for assimilation and discuss which group has assimilated most readily. Then explain the sociological reasons for the difference in assimilation between these two groups.

2. Does affirmative action still have a future in the United States? On the one hand, increasing numbers of African Americans have joined the middle class by earning college degrees, professional jobs, and new homes. Yet blacks are still far more likely than whites to live in poverty, to attend poor schools, and to lack economic opportunity. Given these differences and other contrasts mentioned in the text, do we still need affirmative action?

Data Exercises

www.wwnorton.com/giddens5
Keyword: Data11

- The American Indian and Alaska Native populations have often been described as the most disadvantaged racial minorities in the United States, and images of this population are often stereotypical. The data exercise for this chapter provides you with an opportunity to look beyond the stereotypes and learn more about the contemporary status of the American Indian and Alaska Native populations.

The Graying of U.S. Society

Learn some basic facts about the increase in the proportion of the U.S. population that is becoming elderly.

How Do People Age?

Understand that aging is a combination of biological, psychological, and sociological processes.

Growing Old: Competing Sociological Explanations

Consider the various theories of aging, particularly those that focus on how society shapes the social roles of the elderly and emphasize aspects of age stratification.

Aging in the United States

Evaluate the experience of growing old in the United States.

The Politics of Aging

Understand and analyze the politics of generational equity.

Globalization: The Graying of the World Population

Assess the social issues of graying on a global level.

CHAPTER TWELVE

AGING

When Fenya Crown decided to run the Los Angeles marathon, she was seventy years old. That was twenty-one years ago. Since that time, she has completed eight of the 26.2-mile races, most recently the Rome, Italy, marathon in March 2001. The ninety-one-year-old great-grandmother, who has recovered from three bouts with breast cancer during the past decade, has completed marathons from New York to Shanghai. Born in Ukraine in 1913, Crown emigrated to the United States, where she worked for many years as a dress designer in New York City's garment district.

Like Crown, Rose Freedman also worked as a young woman in the New York City garment industry. Although she never ran a marathon, she nonetheless possessed the endurance to work twelve-to-fourteen-hour days as a seamstress in the city's garment factories. In 1911, at age eighteen, Freedman was working in the Triangle Shirtwaist Factory when fire swept through the building. She survived by racing up several floors to the factory's roof and then leaping to the safety of another building. Most of her coworkers—young female Jewish and Italian immigrants—were not so lucky: within thirty minutes, 500 were injured and 146 dead. The Triangle fire spurred the unionization of the garment industry and left Freedman with indelible memories of the disaster. She continued to speak out against abuses in the garment industry until her death in February 2001—at age 107.

John Glenn was seventy-seven years old when he completed a ten-day research mission in orbit aboard the space shuttle Discovery in the fall of 1998. This was not Glenn's first venture into space. Thirty-two years earlier, the longtime Democratic U.S. senator from Ohio was the first American astronaut in space, when he completed three orbits around the earth as part of America's fledgling space program. The purpose of Glenn's most recent trip was to study the effects of aging in the weightless environment of space. Glenn, who exercises daily and lifts weights, is in excellent shape. As expressed by NASA administrator Daniel Goldin, Glenn was "poised to show the world that senior citizens have the right stuff."

More and more Americans are leading longer, healthier, and more productive lives than ever before. In 2000, there were nearly 4.2 million Americans eighty-five or older, including some 52,000 over one hundred years old (U.S. Census, 2000). Growing old can be a fulfilling and rewarding experience, as it was with the people just described. Or it can be filled with physical distress and social isolation. For most elderly Americans, the experience of aging lies somewhere in between.

In this chapter, we shall examine the nature of aging in U.S. society, exploring what it means to grow old in a world that is rapidly changing. We begin with a brief snapshot of how the American population is growing older, before examining biological, psychological, and social aspects of aging. We then look at the ways in which people adapt to growing old, at least in the eyes of sociologists. This will lead us to a discussion of aging in the United States, focusing on some of the special challenges and problems that the elderly face. We also discuss political issues surrounding the aging of the American population, issues that assume increasing importance given the growing numbers of elderly people. We conclude with a discussion of the graying of the world population and what it can mean for you.

The Graying of U.S. Society

The world's population is getting older.

About two thousand years ago, the average newborn Roman baby could expect to live to the ripe old age of twenty-two. In fact, for most of human history the average life expectancy at birth was less than twenty years, with most people failing to survive the first few years of life. The average baby born into the world today can expect to live to be sixty-five, although there is enormous variation depending on where the baby is born—from an average life expectancy of eighty in Japan to one of thirty-eight in Sierra Leone (Weiss, 1997). These changes are due to many factors. Modern agriculture, sanitation systems, epidemic control, and medicine

have all contributed to a decline in mortality throughout the world. In most societies today, fewer children die in infancy, and more adults survive to become elderly.

The U.S. population, like other industrial societies, is aging even faster than the preindustrial societies of the world. Thanks to better nutrition and health care, people are living longer. They are also having fewer children. As a result, the median age of the population is rising. In 1850, half the population were younger than nineteen, and half were older. Today, half are over thirty-five; by the middle of the century, half will be over forty (see Figure 12.1).

As a result, the United States and other industrial societies are said to be **graying**, that is, experiencing an increase in the proportion of the population becoming elderly. "Graying" is the result of two long-term trends in industrial societies: the tendency of families to have fewer children (discussed in Chapter 15) and the fact that people are living longer. The average life expectancy at birth for all Americans increased from forty-seven years for someone born in 1900 to seventy-seven years for someone born today (see Figure 12.2). The average U.S. male born today can expect to live to about seventy-four; for females, the figure is nearly eighty. Most of these gains occurred in the first half of the twentieth century and were largely due to the improved chances for survival among the young. Although relatively few people made it to age sixty-five in the year 1900, most of those who did could expect to live to age seventy-seven, almost as long as most of those people who make it to sixty-five today can expect to live—to eighty-two (U.S. Bureau of the Census, 1996a).

Because of the graying of the American population, there are today nearly 35 million Americans older than sixty-five, a figure forecast to reach 80 million people by the year 2030 (U.S. Census, 2000; Treas, 1995). According to U.S. Census estimates, 25 percent of all people reaching age sixty-five today will live to be ninety. By the middle of this century, that figure is expected to rise to 42 percent. According to some projections, by that time there may be as many as a million living Americans who have celebrated their one-hundredth birthday (Weiss, 1997).

These trends have enormous importance for the future of American society. In a culture that often worships eternal youth, what will happen when a quarter of the population is over sixty-five?

How Do People Age?

In examining the nature of aging we will draw on studies of **social gerontology**, a discipline concerned with the study of the

FIGURE 12.1

Median Age, U.S. Population, 1850–2050

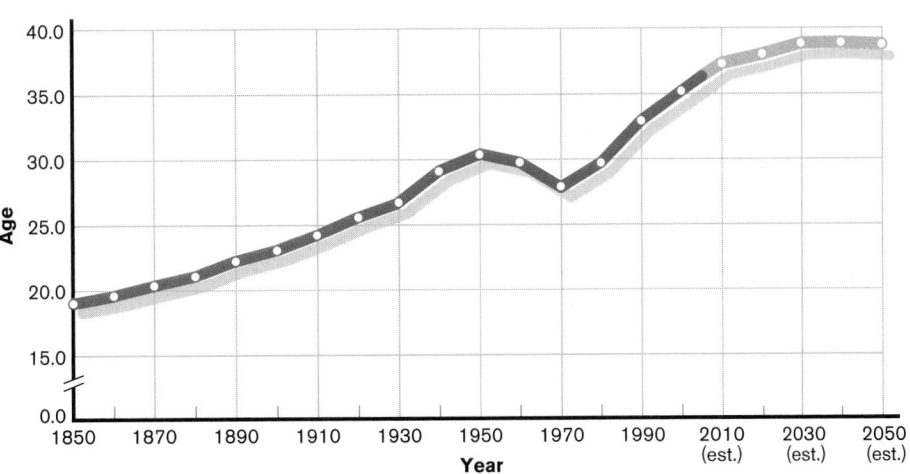

SOURCE: U.S. Bureau of the Census, "National Population Projections," 2002, www.census.gov/
population/www/projections/natproj.html.

FIGURE 12.2

Average Life Expectancy at Birth for Males and Females, 1900–2001 in the United States

SOURCE: Centers for Disease Control and Prevention, "Life Expectancy at Birth, at 65 years
of age, according to race and sex: United States, selected years 1900–2001," Table 27, 2002,
www.cdc.gov/nchs/data/hus/tables/2003/03hus0273.pdf.

social aspects of aging. Studying aging is a bit like examining a moving target: As people grow older, society itself changes at the same time, and so does the very meaning of being "old" (Riley, Foner, and Waring, 1988). For Americans born in the first quarter of the twentieth century, a high school education was regarded as more than sufficient for most available jobs, and most people did not expect to live much past their mid-fifties—and then only at the cost of suffering a variety of disabilities. Today those very same people find themselves in their seventies and eighties; many are relatively healthy, unwilling to disengage from work and social life, and in need of more schooling than they ever dreamed would be necessary.

What does it mean to age? **Aging** can be sociologically defined as the combination of biological, psychological, and social processes that affect people as they grow older (Abeles and Riley, 1987; Riley, Foner, and Waring, 1988; Atchley, 2000). These three processes suggest the metaphor of three different, although interrelated, developmental "clocks": (1) a biological one, which refers to the physical body; (2) a psychological one, which refers to the mind and mental capabilities; and (3) a social one, which refers to cultural norms, values, and role expectations having to do with age. There is an enormous range of variation in all three of these processes, as will be shown below. Our notions about the meaning of age are rapidly changing, both because recent research is dispelling many myths about aging and because advances in nutrition and health have enabled many people to live longer, healthier lives than ever before.

Biological Aging

The biological effects of aging are well established, although the exact chronological age at which they occur varies greatly from individual to individual, depending on genetics, lifestyle, and luck. In general, for men and women alike, biological aging typically means:

- declining vision, as the eye lens loses its elasticity (small type is the bane of most people over fifty);
- hearing loss, first of higher-pitched tones, then of lower-pitched ones;
- wrinkles, as the skin's underlying structure becomes more and more brittle (billions of dollars invested in skin lotion and increasingly common surgical face lifts only delay the inevitable);
- a decline of muscle mass and an accompanying accumulation of fat, especially around the middle (eating habits that were offset by exercise when you were twenty-five come back to haunt you when you are fifty); and
- a drop in cardiovascular efficiency, as less oxygen can be inhaled and utilized during exercise (lifelong runners

who ran six-minute miles at age thirty are happy to break eight-minute miles once they turn sixty).

The normal processes of aging cannot be avoided, but they can be partly compensated for and offset by good health, proper diet and nutrition, and a reasonable amount of exercise (John, 1988). Lifestyle can make a significant health difference for people of all ages. For many people, the physical changes of aging do not significantly prevent them from leading active, independent lives well into their eighties. Some scientists have even argued that with a proper lifestyle and advances in medical technology, more and more people will be able to live relatively illness-free lives until they reach their biological maximum, experiencing only a brief period of sickness just before death (Fries, 1980). Eventually, of course, the biological clock runs out for everyone. About ninety to one hundred years seems to be the upper end of the genetically determined age distribution for most human beings, although some have argued that it may be as high as 120 (Fries, 1980; Rusting, 1992; Treas, 1995; Atchley, 2000).

Even though the majority of older Americans suffer no significant physical impairment and remain physically active, unfortunate stereotypes about the "weak and frail elderly" continue to exist (Heise, 1987). These stereotypes have more to do with the social than the biological meaning of aging in U.S. culture, which is preoccupied with youthfulness and fears of growing old and dying.

Psychological Aging

The psychological effects of aging are much less well established than the physical effects. Even though such things as memory, learning, intelligence, skills, and motivation to learn are widely assumed to decline with age, research into the psychology of aging suggests a much more complicated process (Schaie, 1984; Birren and Cunningham, 1985). Memory and learning ability, for example, do not decline significantly until very late in life for most people, although the speed with which one recalls or analyzes information may slow somewhat, giving the false impression of mental impairment. For most elderly people whose lives are stimulating and rich, such mental abilities as motivation to learn, clarity of thought, and problem-solving capacity do not appear to decline significantly until the late eighties (Baltes and Schaie, 1977; Schaie, 1979; Abeles and Riley, 1987; Schooler, 1987; Cutler and Grams, 1988; Atchley, 2000).

Even **Alzheimer's disease**, the progressive deterioration of brain cells which is the primary cause of dementia in old age, is relatively rare in noninstitutionalized persons under seventy-five, although it may afflict as many as half of all people over eighty-five. Former president Ronald Reagan is perhaps the most famous example of someone who suffered from Alzheimer's (Treas, 1995).

Social Aging

Social age consists of the norms, values, and roles that are culturally associated with a particular chronological age. Ideas about social age differ from one society to another and, at least in modern industrial societies, change over time as well. Societies such as Japan and China have traditionally revered elderly people, regarding them as a source of historical memory and wisdom. Societies such as the United States are more likely to dismiss them as nonproductive, dependent people who are out of step with the times—both because they are less likely to have the high-tech skills so valued by young people and because of American culture's obsession with youthfulness. In a country where the approximately 75 million once youthful "baby boomers" born in the decade after World War II are now turning fifty at the rate of one every ten seconds, a fortune is being spent on prescription drugs, plastic surgery, and home remedies that promise eternal youth. These include such things as tummy tucks and face lifts, antibaldness pills and lotions, and pills that claim to increase memory and concentration. Three weeks after it hit the market in 1998, the anti-impotence drug Viagra accounted for 94 percent of all prescription drug sales in the United States (Hotz, 1998).

Role expectations are extremely important sources of one's personal identity. Some of the roles associated with aging in American society are positive: Supreme Court justice, senior adviser, doting grandparent, religious elder, wise spiritual teacher. Other roles may be damaging, leading to lowered self-esteem and isolation. Highly stigmatizing stereotypical roles for older people in American culture include "grumpy old man" (or woman), old-fashioned "senior citizen," "spinster," and mentally confused "doddering old man." In fact, like all people, the elderly do not simply passively play out assigned social roles; they actively shape and redefine them (Riley, Foner, and Waring, 1988).

Growing Old: Competing Sociological Explanations

Social gerontologists have offered a number of theories regarding the nature of aging in U.S. society. Some of the earliest theories emphasized individual adaptation to changing social roles

Some societies have traditionally revered the elderly. Here the young respect the old with an offering of tea, a traditional Chinese custom.

as a person grows older. Later theories focused on how society shapes the social roles of the elderly, often in inequitable ways, and emphasized various aspects of age stratification. The most recent theories have been more multifaceted, focusing on the ways in which the elderly actively create their lives within specific institutional contexts (Hendricks, 1992).

The First Generation of Theories: Functionalism

The earliest theories of aging reflected the functionalist approach that was dominant in sociology during the 1950s and 1960s. They emphasized how individuals adjusted to changing social roles as they aged and how those roles were useful to society. The earliest theories often assumed that aging brings with it physical and psychological decline and that changing social roles have to take this decline into account (Hendricks, 1992).

Talcott Parsons, one of the most influential functionalist theorists of the 1950s, argued that U.S. society needs to find roles for the elderly consistent with advanced age. He expressed concern that the United States, with its emphasis on youth and its avoidance of death, had failed to provide roles that adequately drew on the potential wisdom and maturity of its older citizens. Moreover, given the graying of U.S. society that was evident even in Parsons's time, he argued that this failure could well lead to older people's becoming discouraged and alienated from society. In order to achieve a "healthy maturity," Parsons (1960) argued, the elderly need to adjust psychologically to their changed circumstances, while society needs to redefine the social roles of the elderly. Old roles (such as work) have to be abandoned, while new forms of productive activity (such as volunteer service) need to be identified.

Parsons's ideas anticipated those of **disengagement theory**, the notion that it is functional for society to remove people from their traditional roles when they become elderly, thereby freeing up those roles for others (Cumming and Henry, 1961; Estes, Binney, and Culbertson, 1992). According to this perspective, given the increasing frailty, illness, and dependency of elderly people, it becomes increasingly dysfunctional for them to occupy traditional social roles they are no longer capable of adequately fulfilling. The elderly therefore should retire from their jobs, pull back from civic life, and eventually withdraw from other activities as well. Disengagement is assumed to be functional for the larger society because it opens up roles formerly filled by the elderly for younger people, who presumably will carry them out with fresh energy and new skills. Disengagement is also assumed to be functional for the elderly, because it enables them to take on less taxing roles consistent with their advancing age and declining health. A number of studies of older adults indeed report that the large majority feel good about retiring, which they claim has improved their morale and increased their happiness (Crowley, 1985; Palmore et al., 1985; Howard et al., 1986; Atchley, 2000).

Although there is obviously some truth to disengagement theory, the idea that elderly people should completely disengage from the larger society takes for granted the prevailing stereotype that old age necessarily involves frailty and dependence. As a result, no sooner did the theory appear than these very assumptions were challenged, often by some of the theory's original proponents (Cumming, 1963, 1975; Henry, 1965; Maddox, 1965, 1970; Hochschild, 1975; Hendricks, 1992). These challenges gave rise to another functionalist theory of aging, which drew conclusions quite opposite to those of disengagement theory: *activity theory*.

According to **activity theory**, elderly people who are busy and engaged, leading fulfilling and productive lives, can be functional for society. Activity theory regards aging as a normal part of human development and argues that elderly people can best serve society, as well as themselves, by remaining active as long as possible. Although there may come a time in most peoples' lives when disengagement will best serve their interests as well as society's, activity theory argues that an active individual is much more likely to remain healthy, alert, and socially useful. In this view, people should remain engaged in their work and other social roles as long as they are capable of doing so. If a time comes when a particular role becomes too difficult or taxing, then other roles can be sought—for example, volunteer work in the community.

Activity theory finds support in research showing that continued activity well into old age is associated with enhanced mental and physical health (Schaie, 1983; Rowe and Kahn, 1987; Birren and Bengston, 1988). For example, there is some evidence that continued part- or full-time employment is associated with higher morale and happiness, possibly because of the expanded friendship networks that result from continued work (Soumerai and Avorn, 1983; Conner, Dorfman, and Tompkins, 1985; Riddick, 1985; Bosse et al., 1987; Mor-Barak et al., 1992).

Critics of functionalist theories of aging argue that these theories emphasize the need for the elderly to adapt to existing conditions, either by disengaging from socially useful roles or by actively pursuing them, but that they do not question whether or not the circumstances faced by the elderly are just. In reaction another group of theorists arose—those growing out of the social conflict tradition (Hendricks, 1992).

The Second Generation of Theories: Social Conflict

Unlike their predecessors, whose emphasis was on how well the elderly could be integrated into the larger society, the second generation of theorists focused on sources of social conflict between the elderly and society (Hendricks, 1992). Much like other theorists who were studying social conflict in U.S. society during the 1970s and early 1980s, these theorists stressed the ways in which the larger social structure helped to shape the opportunities available to the elderly; unequal opportunities were seen as creating the potential for conflict.

According to this view, many of the problems of aging—such as poverty, inadequate health care, or lack of decent nursing homes—are systematically produced by the routine operation of social institutions. A capitalist society, the reasoning goes, favors those who are most economically powerful. While there are certainly some elderly people who have "made it" and are set for life, many have not—and these people must fight to get even a meager share of society's scarce resources.

Conflict theories of aging flourished during the 1980s, when a shrinking job base and cutbacks in federal spending threatened to pit different social groups against each other in the competition for scarce resources. The elderly were seen as competing with the young for increasingly scarce jobs and dwindling federal dollars. Conflict theorists further pointed out that even among the elderly, those who fared worst were women, low-income people, and minorities, in a cumulating spiral of social conflict (McKinlay, 1975; Estes, Swan, and Gerard, 1982; Estes, Zones, and Swan, 1984; Estes, 1986, 1991; Hendricks and Hendricks, 1986; Hendricks, 1992; Atchley, 2000).

The Third Generation of Theories: Self-Concept and Aging

The most recent theories reject what they regard as the one-sided emphases of both functionalism and conflict theory. They view the elderly as playing an active role in determining

Older people are informed by experience, and possess knowledge and skills that can be beneficial to young people. In turn, keeping active and maintaining close contact with young people can be vital in shaping a positive self-concept among the elderly.

their own physical and mental well-being, rather than as merely adapting to the larger society (functionalism) or as victims of the stratification system (social conflict). Circumstances such as family, work, and living situation are important sources of one's self-concept, which in turn affects one's life satisfaction. The elderly are seen as playing a significant role in shaping those circumstances (Dannefer, 1989; Hendricks, 1992; Schaie and Hendricks, 2000).

One recent research project, for example, involved a partnership between the Margaret Warner School of Education and Human Development at the University of Rochester (N.Y.) and two local nursing homes. The project was set up to study how changes in the organizational culture of the homes—as seen in such things as architecture, physical layout, and programming—can affect resident satisfaction and well-being. The objective was to increase social interaction among residents, involving them in satisfying and useful activities. In the words of the gerontologist Dale Dannefer, who headed the project, "If we expect people in nursing homes to improve their health and thrive, to remain socially engaged and make contributions to the lives of others, it should show up in measurable gains in their health and functional status" (quoted in Dickman, 1999). These recent theories also emphasize the increasing diversity among the elderly, showing how people age differently depending on their circumstances (Nelson and Dannefer, 1992). Many provide detailed ethnographic accounts of what it means to grow old in U.S. society, with concrete illustrations from elderly peoples' lives (Gubrium, 1986, 1991, 1993; Gubrium and Sankar, 1994).

Aging in the United States

The elderly make up a highly diverse category about whom few broad generalizations can be made. For one thing, the elderly reflect the diversity of U.S. society that we've made note of elsewhere in this textbook: They are rich, poor, and in between; they belong to all racial and ethnic groups; they live alone and in families of various sorts; they vary in their political values and preferences; and they are gay and lesbian as well as heterosexual. Furthermore, like other Americans, they are diverse with respect to health: While some suffer from mental and physical disabilities, most lead active, independent lives.

There are significant racial differences among the elderly. Whites, on average, live six years longer than African Americans, largely because blacks have much higher rates of poverty and therefore are more likely to suffer from inadequate health

TABLE 12.1

Percentage of Population over 65 and over 85, in Different Racial Groups, 2000

A higher percentage of whites is elderly than any other group. This is the result of lower fertility (whites have fewer children on average) and greater longevity (whites tend to live longer than most other racial and ethnic groups).

RACIAL GROUP	OVER AGE 65	OVER AGE 85
White	12.8	1.2
Black	7.8	0.8
Asian/Pacific Islander	7.3	0.6
American Indian	6.6	0.2
TOTAL	10.4	0.8

SOURCE: U.S. Bureau of the Census, 2001c.

care. As a result, a much higher percentage of whites are elderly than other racial groups (see Table 12.1). The combined effect of race and sex is substantial—white women live, on average, fifteen years longer than black men. Hispanics are graying the least, partly because this category includes many young immigrant workers with large families.

Currently, one tenth of the elderly population in the United States is foreign born. In California, New York, Hawaii, and other states that receive large numbers of immigrants, as much as one fifth of the elderly population was born outside the United States (Treas, 1995). Most elderly immigrants either do not speak English well or do not speak it at all. Integrating elderly immigrants into U.S. society poses special challenges: some are highly educated, but most are not. Many require special education and training programs. Most lack a retirement income, so that they are dependent on their families or public assistance for support. Among those who arrived in the United States after 1980, one quarter were receiving welfare in 1989, nearly four times the rate of elderly people born in this country (Treas, 1995).

Finally, as people live to increasingly older ages, the elderly are becoming diverse in terms of age itself. It is useful to distin-guish between different age categories of the elderly, such as the "**young old**" (ages sixty-five to seventy-four), the "**old old**" (ages seventy-five to eighty-four), and the "**oldest old**" (age eighty-five and older) (see Figure 12.3). The "young old" are most likely to be economically independent, healthy, active, and engaged; the "oldest old"—the fastest-growing segment of the elderly population—are most likely to encounter difficulties such as poor health, financial insecurity, isolation, and loneliness. These differences are not necessarily due only to the effects of aging. The "young-old" came of age during the post–World War II period of strong economic growth and benefited as a result: They are more likely to be educated; to have acquired wealth in the form of a home, savings, or investments; and to have had many years of stable employment. These advantages are much less likely to be enjoyed by the "oldest old," partly because their education and careers began at an earlier time, when economic conditions were not so favorable (Treas, 1995).

What is the experience of growing old in the United States? Although the elderly do face some special challenges, most elderly people lead relatively healthy, satisfying lives. Still, one national survey found a substantial discrepancy between what most Americans under sixty-five thought life would be like when they passed that milestone and the actual experiences of those who had (see Figure 12.4). In this section, we examine differences among the elderly in the United States, along with some of the common problems that they confront; in the next section, we will look at their growing political ability to do something about these problems.

Poverty

Relatively few elderly people live in poverty, although some of the very poorest people are elderly, particularly among minorities. Since older people have for the most part retired from work, their income is based primarily on **Social Security** and private retirement programs. Social Security and **Medicare** have been especially important in lifting many elderly people out of poverty. Yet people who depend solely on these two programs for income and health care coverage are likely to live modestly at best. Social Security accounts for only about 40 percent of the income of the typical retiree; most of the remainder comes from investments and private pension funds, and sometimes earnings. Low-income households in particular are likely to rely heavily on Social Security, which accounts for as much as three quarters of all income for retirees living on less than $10,000 a year (Atchley, 2000). Yet even the combination of Social Security and private pensions results in modest retirement incomes for most people (Krueger, 1995). Although almost all elderly are covered by Medicare, about 75 percent of persons between sixty-five and

FIGURE 12.3

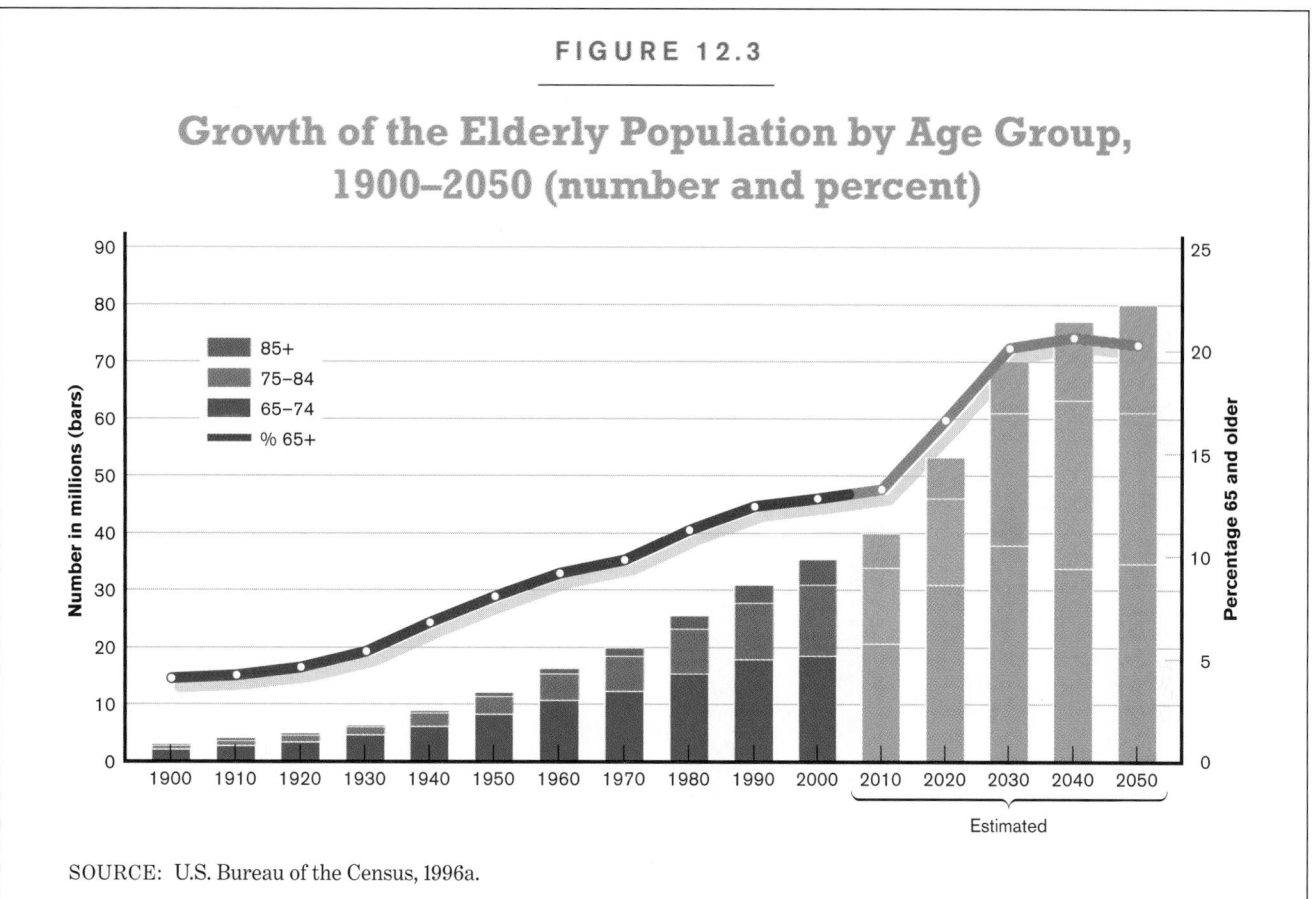

Growth of the Elderly Population by Age Group, 1900–2050 (number and percent)

SOURCE: U.S. Bureau of the Census, 1996a.

seventy-four are covered by private health insurance as well (U.S. Bureau of the Census, 1996a).

The economic conditions of the elderly have improved steadily over the past thirty years. As Figure 12.5 shows, in 1959, 35 percent of all people over sixty-five lived in poverty. That figure began to drop during President Lyndon B. Johnson's War on Poverty in the mid-1960s, when Medicare was enacted and Social Security benefits increased. By the early 1970s, poverty rates among the elderly had dropped to below 15 percent, and today they hover around 10 percent. This is two thirds the rate of poverty among children, 26 percent of whom were poor in 2001 (Proctor and Dalaker, 2002). Race appears to be much more important than age in explaining poverty among the elderly (see Figure 12.6). Among whites, only 8.1 percent of the elderly reported poverty-level incomes in 2001, compared with 21.9 percent of blacks and 21.8 percent of Hispanics (Proctor and Dalaker, 2002).

Social Isolation

One of the common stereotypes about the elderly is that they are isolated from human contact. This is not true of the ma-

jority of older people, however. Four out of five older people have living children, and the vast majority of them can rely on their children for support if necessary (AARP, 1997). More than nine out of ten adult children report believing that maintaining parental contact is important to them, including the provision of financial support if it is needed (Finley, Roberts, and Banahan, 1988). The reverse is also true: Many studies have found that elderly parents continue to provide support for their adult children, particularly during times of difficulty, such as divorce. Most elderly parents and adult children report feeling that the amount of support they receive from the other is fair. Being geographically distant from family members does not seem to be a problem either, since 85 percent of elderly people with children live close to at least one of them (Bankoff, 1983; Moss, Moss, and Moles, 1985; Greenberg and Becker, 1988; Peterson and Peterson, 1988; Bengston, Rosenthal, and Burton, 1990).

Future generations may suffer more from social isolation than do elderly people today. Changing patterns of gender relations, including increases in divorce and a decline in remarriage, may mean that an increasing proportion of elderly people will live alone (Goldscheider, 1990). A majority of such people will likely be women, given the fact that women on

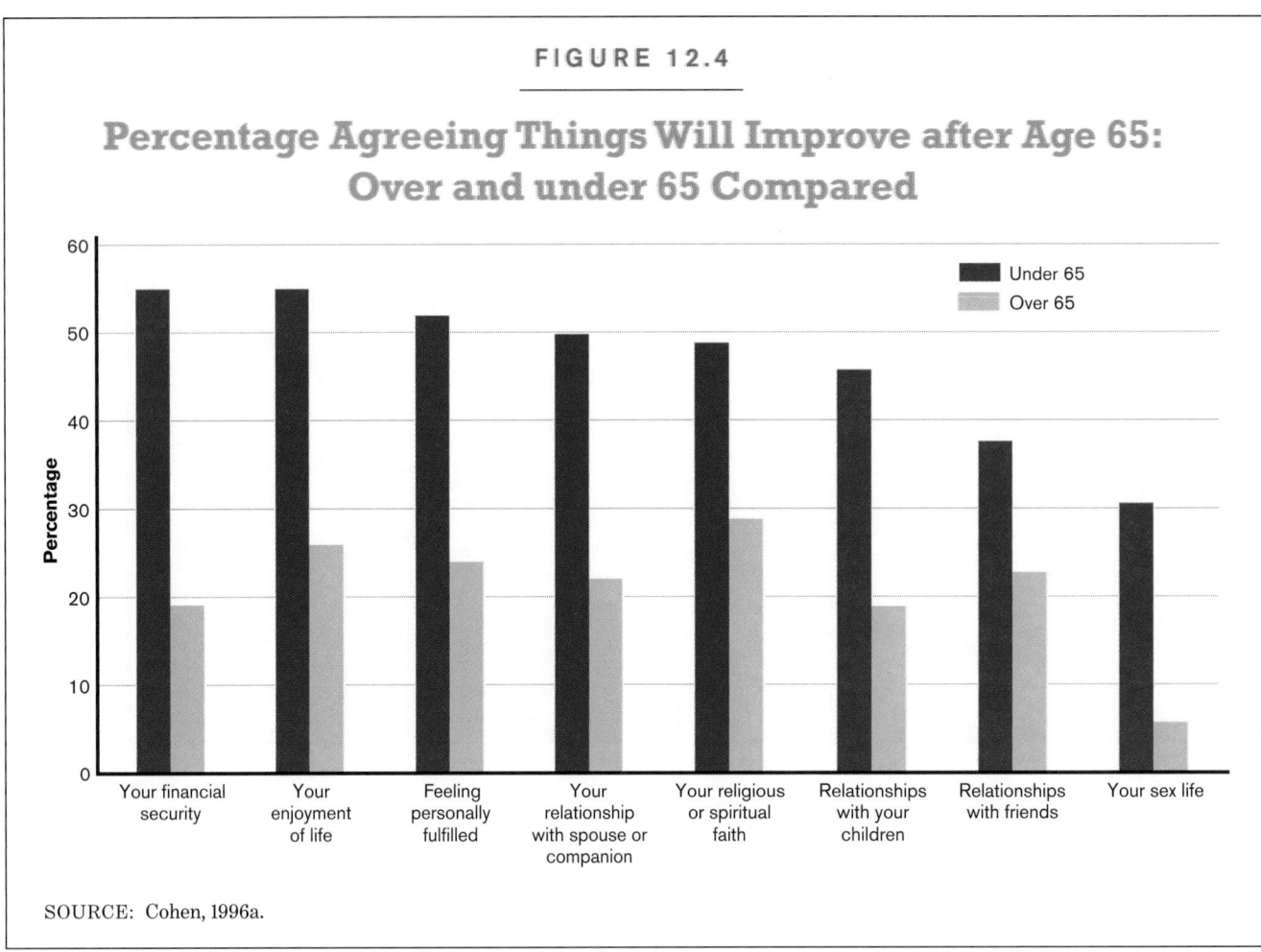

FIGURE 12.4

Percentage Agreeing Things Will Improve after Age 65: Over and under 65 Compared

Legend: ■ Under 65 ▨ Over 65

Y-axis: Percentage (0 to 60)

Categories (X-axis): Your financial security; Your enjoyment of life; Feeling personally fulfilled; Your relationship with spouse or companion; Your religious or spiritual faith; Relationships with your children; Relationships with friends; Your sex life

SOURCE: Cohen, 1996a.

average outlive men. Among people over sixty, there are only seventy-one men for every one hundred women; for those seventy or older, the number of men per one hundred women drops to sixty-two. Partly because of the dearth of older men, only about half of all women aged sixty-five to seventy-four live with a spouse or a mate, compared with nearly four out of five men in that age range. Among those over seventy-five, only a quarter of all women live with a mate; the rate for men is seventy percent (Treas, 1995).

The fact that women outlive men means that elderly women are more likely to experience problems of isolation and loneliness. These problems are compounded by cultural values that make "growing old gracefully" easier for men than for women. In U.S. culture, youth and beauty are viewed as especially desirable qualities for women. Older men, on the other hand, are more likely to be valued for their material success: Graying at the temples is a sign of distinction for a man, rather than a call for a visit to the hairdresser. As a result, elderly divorced or widowed men are much more likely to find a mate than elderly women who are living alone, since the pool of eligible mates for elderly men is more likely to include potential partners who are

many years younger. One study of fifty-nine elderly women who had lost their husbands found that some eventually managed to overcome their grief, while others never fully recovered from their husband's death (Hunter, 1990). The widows who overcame their grief tended to be much more satisfied with their social support networks than those who did not.

Prejudice

Discrimination on the basis of age is now against federal law. Nonetheless, prejudices based on false stereotypes are common. **Ageism** is prejudice and/or discrimination based on age and, like all prejudices, is fueled in part by stereotypes. The elderly are frequently seen as perpetually lonely, sad, infirm, forgetful, dependent, senile, old-fashioned, inflexible, and embittered.

There are a number of reasons for such prejudice. The previously mentioned American obsession with youthfulness, reflected in popular entertainment and advertising, leads many younger people to disparage their elders, frequently

FIGURE 12.5

Percentage of Population over 65 Living in Poverty, 1959–2001

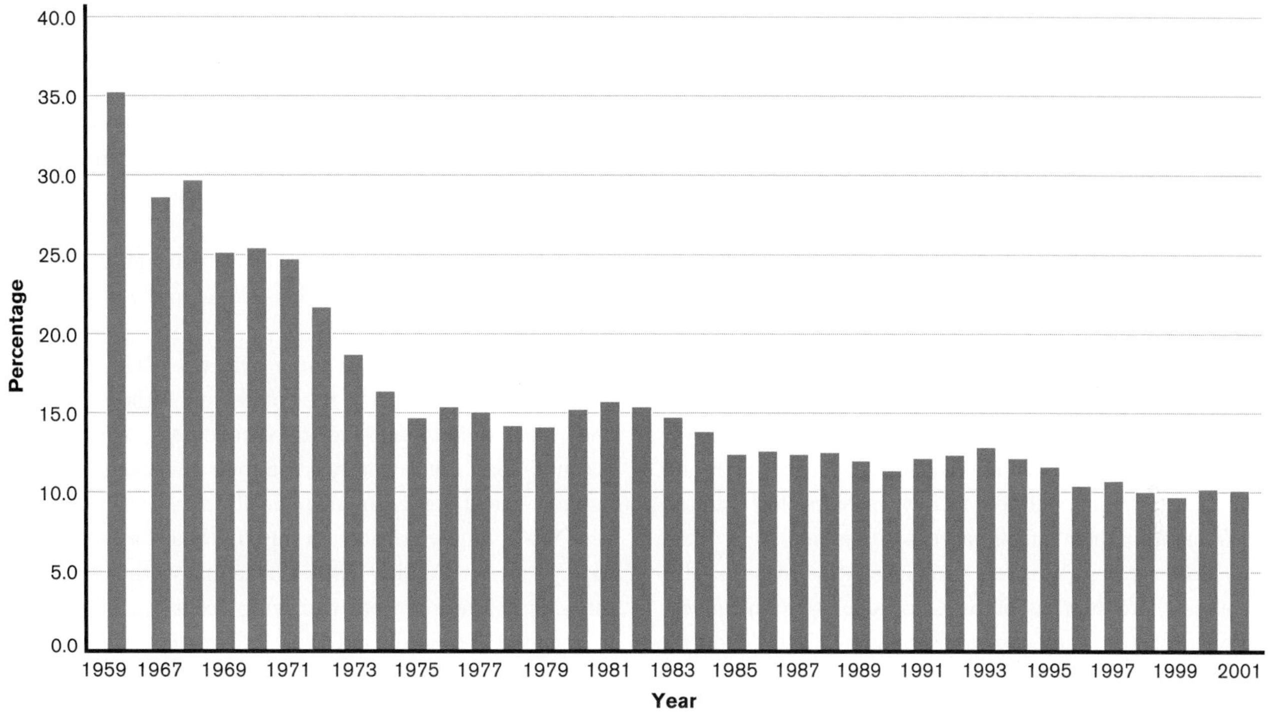

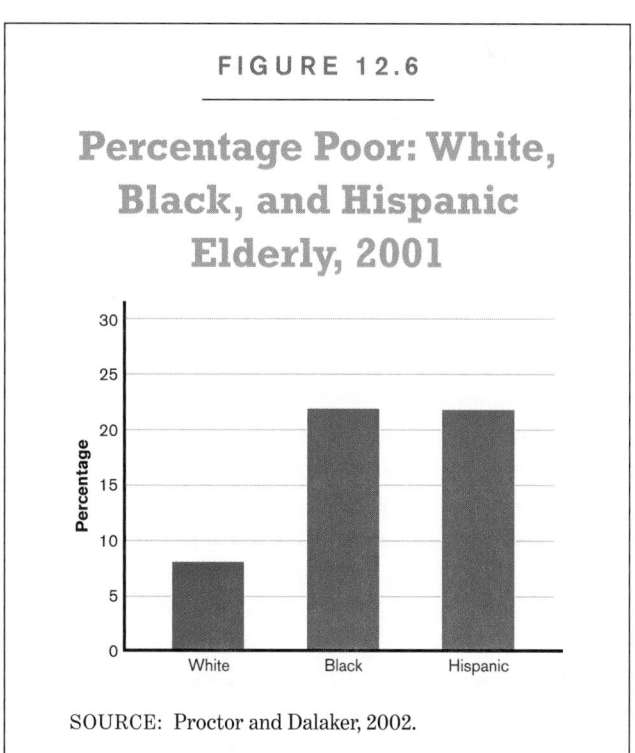

SOURCE: Proctor and Dalaker, 2002.

dismissing them as irrelevant. The new information technology undoubtedly reinforces these prejudices, since youthfulness and computer abilities seem to go hand in hand. In the fast-paced world of MTV, the Web, and dot-com businesses that seem to flourish and perish overnight, young people may come to view the elderly as anachronistic. Associated with the emphasis of youthfulness is a fear-filled avoidance of reminders of death and dying. Such fear carries over into negative attitudes toward the elderly, who serve as a constant reminder of one's mortality (Fry, 1980).

In one study (Levin, 1988), college students were shown a photograph of the same man at ages twenty-five, fifty-two, and seventy-three and were asked to rate him in terms of a variety of personality characteristics. The ratings were significantly more negative for the man depicted at age seventy-three. When he looked old in his photograph, the students were more likely to perceive him negatively, even though they knew absolutely nothing about him. The mere fact of his being elderly was sufficient to trigger a negative cultural stereotype. Widely shared cultural stereotypes of "grumpy old men" can lead to private opinions that are hurtful to older people.

FIGURE 12.6

Percentage Poor: White, Black, and Hispanic Elderly, 2001

SOURCE: Proctor and Dalaker, 2002.

Physical Abuse

Cases of elderly abuse certainly exist, but most research suggests that it is not so widespread as is commonly believed. One random survey among two thousand noninstitutionalized elderly people in the Boston area found that only about 2 percent had experienced physical violence, although these figures may be somewhat low because abuse rates may be higher among those who are unable to respond to surveys. Fewer than 1 percent reported being seriously neglected in terms of their daily needs, while about 1 percent claimed they were subject to chronic verbal aggression. These figures represent a small percentage of the elderly population. Still, they do represent eight thousand to nine thousand cases in the Boston area alone. Although elderly men reported higher rates of abuse than did elderly women, 57 percent of the abused women (compared with 6 percent of the men) reported suffering injuries (Pillemer and Finkelhor, 1988).

It is widely believed that abuse results from the anger and resentment that adult children feel when confronted with the need to care for their infirm parents (Steinmetz, 1983; King, 1984). Most studies, however, have found this to be a false stereotype. More than half of the abuse reported in the above-mentioned Boston study was perpetrated by a spouse; only a quarter of the cases occurred at the hands of an adult child (Pillemer and Finkelhor, 1988). Furthermore, in cases when a child abused an elderly parent, it was found that he or she was more likely to be financially dependent on the parent, rather than the reverse. The child may feel resentment about being dependent, while the parent may be unwilling to terminate the abusive relationship because he or she feels obligated to help the child (Pillemer, 1985).

Health Problems

The prevalence of chronic disabilities among the elderly has declined in recent years (Manton, Corder, and Stallard, 1993), and most elderly people rate their health as reasonably good and free of major disabilities. Still, elderly people obviously suffer from more health problems than most younger people, and health difficulties often increase with advancing age. In 1990, the elderly accounted for about a third of all U.S. health care expenditures (Clark, 1993). Nearly half of all noninstitutionalized persons over sixty-five report having at least some problems with arthritis, while about a third report suffering from such ailments as high blood pressure, heart disease, or hearing loss (Treas, 1995). One out of ten people diagnosed for the first time as having HIV/AIDS is over fifty and a quarter of these are over sixty; nearly three times as many people sixty and older died of AIDS in 1992 as did those under twenty

(Bennet, 1992; UN AIDS, 2002). Age-related health conditions, such as osteoporosis, create complications for the treatment of the elderly living with AIDS and accelerates the progression from HIV to AIDS (UN AIDS, 2002).

Two out of three noninstitutionalized people over seventy-five consider their health to be "good," "very good," or "excellent" compared with others their age (U.S. Bureau of the Census, 1996a). Not surprisingly, the percentage of people needing help with daily activities increases with age: Whereas only about one in ten people between the ages sixty-five and seventy-five report needing daily assistance, the figure rises to one in five for people between seventy-five and seventy-nine, and to one in three for people between eighty and eighty-four. Half of all people over eighty-five require assistance (U.S. Bureau of the Census, 1996a).

Paradoxically, there is some evidence that the fastest-growing group of elderly, the "oldest old" (those eighty-five and older), tend to enjoy relative robustness, which partially accounts for their having reached their advanced age. This is possibly one of the reasons that health care costs for a person who dies at ninety are about a third of those for a person who dies at seventy (Angier, 1995). Unlike many other Americans, the elderly are fortunate in having access to public health insurance (Medicare) and therefore medical services. The United States, however, stands virtually alone among the industrialized nations in failing to provide adequately for the complete health care of its most senior citizens (Hendricks and Hatch, 1993; Hendricks and Rosenthal, 1993).

Although some 42 million Americans lacked health insurance in 1996 (about 16 percent of the population), only 1 percent of the elderly lacked coverage (Weinberg, 1996). Ninety-six percent of the elderly are covered to some extent by Medicare. But since this program covers less than half of the total health care expenses of the elderly, nearly two out of three supplement Medicare with their own private insurance (Treas, 1995). The rising costs of private insurance, unfortunately, have made this option impossible for a growing number of the elderly. Despite Medicare, the elderly still spend nearly one fifth of their income on health care (Hess, 1990). At present, the rising costs of Medicare have made it a candidate for federal budget cuts.

When the elderly become physically unable to care for themselves, they may wind up in nursing homes. Only about one out of every twenty people over age sixty-five is in a nursing home, a figure that rises to about one out of every five among people over eighty-five (Atchley, 2000). Medicaid, the government program that provides health insurance for the poor, covers long-term supervision and nursing costs, although only when most of one's assets (except for one's home) have been used up. About three out of five elderly people in nursing homes receive assistance from Medicaid (Hudson, 1995). Since the average cost of a nursing home is now over $66,000 a year

TABLE 12.2

What Is Your Worst Fear about Growing Old?

When it comes to growing old, most Americans fear boredom and death far less than they fear winding up living in a nursing home lonely, isolated, and mentally incapacitated by Alzheimer's disease.

Living for many years in a nursing home	64%
Developing Alzheimer's disease	56%
Becoming a financial burden on others	47%
Being lonely	36%
Loss of physical attractiveness	34%
Death	28%
Having nothing to do	26%

SOURCE: Washington Post National Survey, as reported in Cohen, 1997.

(Chicago Tribune, 2003), the nonpoor elderly who require such institutionalization may find that their lifetime savings will be quickly depleted. Nursing homes have long had a reputation for austerity and loneliness. In fact, however, the quality of most has improved in recent years, both because federal programs such as Medicaid help to cover the cost of care and because of federal quality regulations.

Still, living for many years in a nursing home was the most widely cited concern about growing old, according to a recent national survey (see Table 12.2). Perhaps that is why the average length of stay in nursing homes dropped from 1,026 days in 1985 to 876 days in 2003, as more elderly people seek home care (Chicago Tribune, 2003; Dey, 1997).

Lifelong Learning

As more and more people live well beyond the age of retirement, they enter a new stage of life for which there are few socially prescribed roles (Laslett, 1991; Moen, 1995). Many people can look forward to ten or twenty years of relatively healthy living, free from the obligations of paid work and raising a family. Furthermore, the elderly will be increasingly well educated, since young people today are much more likely to have gone to college than their parents—or grandparents. This is important

for a number of reasons. Better-educated people tend to be economically comfortable in later life. They also tend to be healthier: They are better informed on health-related issues, more likely to choose a healthy lifestyle, and more likely to seek medical treatment when they require it (Treas, 1995).

These trends suggest that the elderly are much more likely to remain a part of mainstream society, rather than to become isolated. As U.S. society continues to age, it will increasingly be forced to confront a growing elderly population that is unwilling to slip quietly into years of retirement and inactivity. It is important for elderly people to maintain a readiness to learn, stimulated by participation in a wide variety of learning activities. As noted earlier, this can contribute to mental alertness, a positive psychological attitude, and even improved physical health (Dychtwald, 1990; Plett, 1990; Plett and Lester, 1991).

Some scholars have even argued that "adult education" will soon become as important as "youth education" (Brookfield, 1986). Educators have coined the terms **andragogy** to refer to adult learning (literally, the "leading of adults") and **geragogy** (the "leading of the old") to refer to older-adult learning (John, 1988). In contrast to conventional notions of teaching, adult learning methods emphasize building on the extensive life experience of older people, rather than providing them with information in a standard undergraduate-classroom format. Adult learning tends to be informal, combining the learners' concrete experience with more theoretical sorts of knowledge. It draws on the interests and concerns of adult learners, who may be unwilling to spend time studying things that seem unrelated to their central cares (John, 1988; Plett, 1990).

The Politics of Aging

Because of their growing numbers, the elderly are a potentially potent voice in Washington. The American Association for the Advancement of Retired People (**AARP**), a nonprofit organization that boasts a membership of 35 million Americans over the age of fifty, has been one highly effective advocate. Because of their high voter turnout rates, the elderly account for as much as one fifth of all voters (Treas, 1995; Atchley, 2000). This is not to suggest that the elderly all hold the same political views; on the contrary, they are as politically heterogeneous as the other groups in our society. But on issues they perceive as affecting their interests—such as retirement pensions and health care benefits—they are likely to have strong opinions. Moreover, because cuts in programs for the elderly would shift the burden of supporting them to their families, opposition to significant reductions in these programs is likely to be widespread.

Old and on Their Own

As a woman in my 90s, I have empathy for those who will come after me and live into their 100s and beyond. They will, I trust, include my grandchildren and great-grandchildren, of whom I have quite a few. I have some thoughts for those planning the quality of life to be enjoyed by this stunningly larger older population to come. The way things are going now, as I see it, the 21st century will be witness to two segments of society—the elderly and the rest of the human race. My word is: Please do not keep them apart. . . .

In a society that aims to be inclusive, why should older people be encouraged to live in a separate community? Most senior housing complexes are sterile—totally lacking the vitality that a generationally mixed community thrives on. Many people face old age just waiting to die, so society (and developers and the government) hand them a group of "activities" to keep them busy, to keep them occupied among people their own age, out of the sight of children, away from a flourishing community. Too often they have limited access to streets to walk on; shops to visit; churches, libraries, museums and other cultural centers. They are relegated to a life where they see only reflections of themselves, other old people.

Housing complexes ought to be designed for all ages, with some apartments appropriate for older people and others suited to the needs of younger people with families. Young mothers, as well as the elderly, can benefit from what is now offered in many senior complexes, like in-house restaurants, beauty parlors, libraries, and on-site nurses and doctors. And many planned "activities" can be enjoyed by all ages. A painting class, for example, is more fun when not limited to old people.

For sure, age-integrated housing will not cure the generation gap, but perhaps it is a way to help older people get over adopting judgmental attitudes toward the young—being horrified at dyed hair, baggy clothes, pierced bodies—without ever having a five-minute conversation with any of them. As for young people, it would do them no harm to live side by side with older people, to really see us day by day, recognize that we are still people, men and women who were once as young as they are, and that like us, if they are lucky, they will one day be old, too. We have a lot in common.

We are all just people, and we should be neighbors living on the same street.

SOURCE: Hila Colman, "Young and Old Thrive Side by Side," *New York Times*, August 15, 2001, p. A23.

[Robert Coles compiled his interviews with Americans over seventy-five in *Old and on Their Own*. He described his book as "trying to catch sight of some people who manage, often with

some difficulty, to *hold on*—to maintain considerably more than a semblance of their privacy, their independence, their personal sovereignty, their 'home rule,' one woman put it, delightfully, instructively. . . . Such affirmations, such declarations of determination, are no mere bombast, or frightened footnotes to the progression of disease, deformity, decay, disability, overall decline. Such spoken statements of intent as well as hope and wish cast a glow of light on lives inevitably darkened by all kinds of diminishment." Excerpts from his interviews are quoted below.]

[A seventy-five-year-old Massachusetts man said of himself:]

"You know, that's what I do, every day," he remarked, and then the description: "I'll talk to myself—out loud. If one of you psychiatrists was here, listening, you'd fill out a legal form and have me sent away for observation. I know how you guys work—someone is behaving a little strange, so you check him off as nuts! Well, being old and being sick is being nuts, in a way. You're at the edge of life; you're hurting; you never do know if you'll see another day. . . . What I do—I talk to myself. I say, 'It's Tuesday today, and you've got this long desert to hike through, hours and hours of time. So, better make the best of it.' When I hear my voice, I feel I've got company. I'm alive, and that's something."

[When Anne was eighty-one, her husband of fifty years died. She struggled with alcoholism and grief for years, until ballroom dance lessons gave her a way to remember her happy moments and find meaning in her present life.]

Dancing had become her passion. She danced at the studio, of course, and at the social functions it sponsored, but more than anywhere else, she danced at home, alone. In the kitchen, especially, with its imitation tile floor, she

glided here and there, mostly in a circle around the table where she ate. She took to singing out loud, supplying her own music to her solo performances—all the while, in her mind, conjuring up a partner: the ever-available Fred Astaire, of course, her husband Carl, and some men she knew in the past, all husbands of her (four closest) friends, and all now "gone," the word that she used when speaking of someone's departure by virtue of death.

[Laura reconsiders old age while talking to her new friend Theresa:]

"Maybe, when you get old, you lose some of your perspective. You don't only forget people's names, and dates, and chores you're meant to do, but you forget what it was once like in the country; and since you're now old, and you're not in the middle of things, all you do is hear about the bad side, from radio and from television, and if your eyes hold out, from the papers. You're not seeing a lot of the good things that are happening, because you're cut off, more and more, from them. Theresa told me, 'Watch out, Laura—you'll get more and more scared of this world, the further off you are from it!'"

SOURCE: Robert Coles, *Old and on Their Own* (New York: DoubleTake/W. W. Norton, 1997), pp. 4, 31–33, 72, 78–79, 84–85.

Questions

- How do these writings and images change your impression about the lives of older people?
- Compare the strategies used by these aging people to manage their pain and loneliness.
- Hila Colman's article describes old people as isolated from mainstream society. How do the photographs and selections from *Old and on Their Own* argue for or against her point?

The two principal governmental programs that provide financial support for the elderly are Medicare, which was instituted in 1965, and Social Security, whose benefits were increased at about the same time (the program itself was begun in 1935). The full benefits of Medicare and Social Security are available at age sixty-five, although partial benefits are available to some people a few years earlier.

Social Security and Medicare are financed by workers' payroll deductions, employer contributions, and taxes on those who are self-employed. Working Americans pay into these programs today so they can be eligible for them when they are no longer able to earn a living. By providing a degree of economic support for the elderly, such programs also make it economically possible to retire; in the absence of the economic security such programs provide, elderly people would be under greater economic pressure to continue working as long as they are physically capable.

Medicare, which pays for acute medical costs for the elderly, reached more than 40 million people in 2002, and cost $226 billion, one eighth of the federal budget (Office of the President, 2002). Because it reaches so many people, Medicare has made an enormous difference in the elderly's access to adequate health care—although at a high cost. Controversial revisions to the Medicare program in 2003 provide government subsidies for the purchase of medicines by the elderly and provide special assistance to low-income elderly. The AARP played an influential role in lobbying Congress during the debate over these changes.

Social Security provides retirement pay for all elderly persons who have worked a certain number of years during their lives and have contributed a portion of their paycheck (typically matched by their employer) into a government fund. The program disbursed $407.6 billion in 2000, and benefited 45.4 million individuals. Most of these were retirees over sixty-five, but some younger retirees and dependents of deceased workers received benefits as well. The amount of the monthly benefit one receives under Social Security depends in part on earnings before retirement. The average monthly benefit in December 2000 was $845 for retired workers, $786 for disabled workers, and $810 for nondisabled widows and widowers (U.S. Social Security Administration, 2001). Since retired women are less likely than men to have had continuous paid employment throughout their lives, their average retirement income is correspondingly lower. As these figures suggest, Social Security provides an extremely minimal level of support for the elderly—by itself, barely enough to keep them out of poverty (Belgrave, 1988; Treas, 1995; U.S. Social Security Administration, 1997a).

The elderly are likely to be at the center of one of the major political debates of this century: the extent to which the government should continue funding programs that virtu-

ally eliminated poverty among the elderly over the past thirty years. Programs such as Social Security and Medicare will become increasingly costly as more and more Americans retire. There is particular concern over whether the Social Security system will remain financially sound as retiring baby boomers collect their pensions. It is currently expected to have sufficient assets to pay full benefits until at least 2029, although if it is to avoid running out of money in the long run, changes will have to be made in the way the system is run (AARP, 1997). There have been calls to "privatize" at least part of Social Security—that is, to enable workers to invest part of their Social Security withholdings in the stock market, rather than simply paying it all into a government fund. The effectiveness of this approach depends, of course, on how well the stock market performs in the future. Although it looked promising in the 1990s when stocks were soaring, today it does not look nearly so hopeful.

Do the Elderly Get an Unfair Amount of Government Support?

The costs of providing for the elderly come largely out of taxes paid by working people. In the United States, for example, the growing ratio of the elderly to the working-age population has alarmed policy makers. They point out that for every one hundred people of working age (eighteen to sixty-four years old) in 1990, there were twenty people over sixty-five. By the year 2030, there will be thirty-six elderly people for every one hundred working-age people. A rapidly aging population will pose serious challenges to public policy throughout this century.

Do government programs adequately promote **generational equity**, the striking of a balance between the needs and interests of members of different generations? The issue of generational equity was first raised by an organization called Americans for Generational Equity (AGE), created in 1984 by Dave Durenberger, a U.S. senator from Minnesota, to challenge the notion that elderly people are entitled to Social Security benefits (Quadagno, 1989). AGE's chief criticisms were of the program's method of funding, which requires working people to contribute a portion of their earnings to a government-managed trust fund in order to pay for their retirement.

AGE argued that as the U.S. population grays, those who are working will bear an increasing burden for those who are not. AGE also argued that Social Security unfairly favors retirees over other needy groups in society. For example, AGE pointed out that retirees are sometimes wealthier than the working people whose taxes fund Social Security and that there are more than three times as many impoverished children under sixteen than impoverished people over sixty-five (10.6 million versus 3.3 million) (U.S. Census Bureau, 2004). In the early 1990s, roughly a third of the total budget for Medicaid, the federal health insurance program for the poor, was used to provide long-term health care for the elderly. The elderly, blind, and disabled made up only a quarter of all Medicaid beneficiaries, yet required 70 percent of all Medicaid spending (Quadagno, 1989; Hudson, 1995).

The difficulty arises from the fact that there are fewer and fewer working-age people to shoulder the tax burden necessary to support more and more retirees. There may come a time when a predominantly white elderly retired population is supported by taxes paid by a predominantly nonwhite working population.

Globalization: The Graying of the World Population

An "elder explosion" is sweeping the world today. The 1998 report of the United Nations Population Fund (UNFPA) notes that the sixty-five-and-older population worldwide grew by about 9 million in 1998. By 2010, the elderly population will grow by 14.5 million; by 2050, 21 million. The most rapid growth of the sixty-five-and-older group will take place in the industrialized nations of the world, where families have fewer children and people live longer than in poorer countries. In the industrialized countries, the percentage of the population that is elderly grew from 8 percent in 1950 to 14 percent in 1998, and it is projected to reach 25 percent by 2050. After the middle of the century, the developing nations will follow suit, as they experience their own elder explosion, though only in the United States and other developed nations will the elderly continue to outnumber the population under fifteen (U.S. Census, 1998).

The populations of most of the world's societies are aging as the result of a decline in both birth and death rates, although the populations of the poorer countries continue to have shorter life spans because of poverty, malnutrition, and disease (see Chapter 19). According to United Nations estimates (UNFPA, 1998), the world's average life expectancy grew from forty-six in 1950 to fifty in 1985 and will reach seventy-one by 2025. At that time, some 800 million people will be over sixty-five, nearly a threefold increase in numbers from 1990. Among the very old (those over

eighty-five), whose medical and service needs are the greatest, the number will increase by half in North America, while it will double in China and grow nearly one and a half times in West Africa (Sokolovsky, 1990). This growth will place major demands on the resources of many countries that are already too poor to support their populations adequately.

This explosion has enormous implications for social policy. Over one hundred fifty nations currently provide public assistance for people who are elderly or disabled, or for their survivors when they die. Elderly people are especially likely to require costly health care services. Their rapid growth in numbers threatens to strain the medical systems in many industrial nations, where the cost of providing health care to the elderly threatens to overwhelm government budgets.

Countries vary widely in what they are doing to cope with their growing numbers of older people. As we have seen already, the United States relies primarily on Social Security and Medicare to serve the financial and health needs of the elderly. Other industrial nations provide a much broader array of services. In Japan, for example, men and women remain active well into old age because the Japanese culture encourages this activity and because business policies often support postretirement work with the same company one worked for before retirement. A number of national laws in Japan support the employment and training of older workers, and private businesses also support retraining.

Societies that have large extended families and practice ancestor worship are more likely to treasure their elders, honoring them at public events and seeking their counsel in political matters. In countries such as Thailand, China, and Japan, reverence for ancestors remains strong (Cowgill, 1968; Falk, Falk, and Tomashevich, 1981; Glascock and Feinman, 1981; Seefeldt and Keawkungwal, 1985). Yet globalization has begun to change the treatment of the elderly throughout the world (Fry, 1980; Homes, 1983; Foner, 1984; Cowgill, 1986). As more and more people live to old age, respect for them has tended to decline. The reason is partly that their growing numbers result in a greater economic burden on their families. Additionally, as previously agrarian societies become a part of the emerging global economy, traditional ways of thinking and behaving are likely to change. When extended families are uprooted from farms and move into cities in search of factory work, their ability to support nonworking members is likely to decline. In those societies that are highly family oriented, the responsibility for supporting elderly parents and working for outside income often falls on young women. Research conducted in Taiwan, for example, has found that young girls often work a full day in a nearby factory, returning home during lunch and after work to care for infirm parents or grandparents (Cheng and Hsiung, 1992).

The combination of graying and globalization will shape the lives of elderly people throughout the world well into this century. Traditional patterns of family care will be challenged, as family-based economies continue to give way to labor on the farms and in the offices and factories of global businesses. Like the industrial nations earlier in the twentieth century, all societies will be challenged to find roles for their aging citizens. This challenge will include identifying new means of economic support, often financed by government programs. It will also entail identifying ways to incorporate rather than isolate the elderly, by drawing on their considerable reserves of experience and talents.

Study Outline

www.wwnorton.com/giddens5

Aging

- Biological, psychological, and social *aging* are not the same and may vary considerably within and across cultures. It is important not to confuse a person's *social age* with his or her chronological age.
- Physical aging is inevitable, but for most people, proper nutrition, diet, and exercise can preserve a high level of health well into old age.

The Graying of U.S. Society

- Because of low mortality and fertility rates, American society is rapidly graying, or aging. There are today some 34 million Americans older than sixty-five, a figure forecast to reach 80 million by the year 2030. The elderly are a large and rapidly growing category that is extremely diverse economically, socially, and politically.

Theories of Aging

- Functionalist theories of aging originally argued that the disengagement of the elderly from society was desirable. *Disengagement theory* held that the elderly should pull back from their traditional social roles as younger people move into them. *Activity theory*, on the other hand, soon came to emphasize the importance of being engaged and busy as a source of vitality.
- Conflict theorists of aging have focused on how the routine operation of social institutions produces various forms of inequality among the elderly.
- The most recent theories regard the elderly as capable of taking control over their own lives and playing an active role in politics and the economy.

Aging and Inequality

- Most of the elderly in U.S. society manage to lead independent lives that they report to be largely satisfying and fulfilling. Still, some suffer from poverty, social isolation, and costly medical problems, as well as from *ageism*, prejudice, and/or discrimination based on age.
- By providing the elderly with retirement income and critical health care insurance, Social Security and Medicare have helped to raise a significant number of elderly people out of poverty. There is some debate over whether these programs are overly generous to the elderly and therefore threaten *generational equity*. In fact, however, the levels of support they offer are modest. Considerable debate nonetheless exists over whether their future funding is likely to be sound.

The Politics of Aging

- The elderly are as politically and socially diverse as any group in society. But on issues that affect their interest, they are capable of exerting a great deal of uniform political pressure. Their political influence is likely to increase as their numbers grow.

Lifelong Learning

- The elderly are capable of lifelong learning, and it seems likely that as their numbers increase, so will efforts to provide *andragogy* (adult-centered education) and *geragogy* (older-adult learning) for those who want it.

Globalization and Social Change

- Globalization threatens the traditional roles of the elderly in many societies. The role of the elderly throughout the world is in a rapid state of transition.

Key Concepts

AARP (p. 363)
activity theory (p. 356)
ageism (p. 360)
aging (p. 354)
Alzheimer's disease (p. 354)
andragogy (p. 363)
conflict theory of aging (p. 356)
disengagement theory (p. 356)
generational equity (p. 366)
geragogy (p. 363)
graying (p. 352)

Medicare (p. 358)

"oldest old" (p. 358)

"old old" (p. 358)

social age (p. 355)

social gerontology (p. 352)

Social Security (p. 358)

"young old" (p. 358)

Review Questions

1. For most of human history the average life expectancy at birth was
   a. more than sixty.
   b. more than forty.
   c. less than twenty.
   d. less than fifteen.
2. The graying of the population in the United States is the result of a
   a. lower fertility rate.
   b. longer life expectancy.
   c. lower mortality rate.
   d. lower fertility rate and longer life expectancy.
3. Aging can be sociologically defined as the combination of _____ processes that affect people as they grow older.
   a. biological, psychological, and social
   b. cultural, structural, and social
   c. biological, cultural, and social
   d. psychological, cultural, and social
4. Which of the following societies has or have traditionally revered elderly people?
   a. China
   b. Japan
   c. Both China and Japan
   d. United States
5. What is the impact of globalization on the status of the elderly in the less-developed world?
   a. It is likely to increase the status of the elderly.
   b. It is likely to decrease the status of the elderly.
   c. It is likely to have no impact on the status of the elderly.
   d. No definite answer.
6. What is the central argument of the functional theory in the analysis of aging?
   a. An elderly person should never retreat from active social roles after he/she retires.
   b. Whether to retreat from one's active social roles depends on one's health condition.
   c. An elderly person should retreat from active social roles after he/she retires.
   d. An elderly person should retreat from active social roles even before he/she retires.
7. The second generation of aging theories emphasizes
   a. how well the elderly were integrated into the larger society.

b. how an elderly person can play an active role in determining his or her own physical and mental well-being.
   c. how life style and exercise improve one's health.
   d. the sources of social conflict between the elderly and society.
8. The health-care costs for a person who dies at ninety are about _____ of those for a person who dies at seventy.
   a. three times
   b. one third
   c. five times
   d. the same
9. In the industrialized countries, the percentage of the population that is elderly is projected to reach _____ by 2050.
   a. 15 percent
   b. 25 percent
   c. 35 percent
   d. 45 percent
10. According to Cohen (1997), what is the worst fear about growing old among most Americans?
    a. Living for many years in a nursing home
    b. Developing Alzheimer's disease
    c. Becoming a financial burden on others
    d. Being lonely

Thinking Sociologically Exercises

1. Briefly discuss the competing theories about growing old that are presented in this chapter. How do these theories compare with each other? Which theory do you feel is most appropriate to explain aging and why do you feel this way about it?
2. What do you think the United States could do socially and politically to alleviate the problems of aging for its elder citizens? How likely is it that your suggestions for alleviating the problems of age could be adopted into the American political process and why?

Data Exercises

www.wwnorton.com/giddens5
Keyword: Data12

• If you are a traditional age student, you've probably not given much thought to aging, but our society is aging rapidly; we are experiencing *the graying of America*. The data exercise for this chapter provides you with an opportunity to learn more about what is happening in the United States and throughout the world, and what this demographic change means for society.

The Concept of the State

Learn the basic concepts underlying modern nation-states.

Democracy

Learn about different types of democracy, how this form of government has spread around the world, some theories about power in a democracy, and some of the problems associated with modern-day democracy.

Political and Social Change

Learn some basic theories about social movements, and apply this understanding to the feminist movement in the United States. Assess the impact of globalization and technology on social movements today. Learn about nationalism and the importance of nationalist movements.

The Nation-State, National Identity, and Globalization

Evaluate whether or not globalization is weakening national identity.

CHAPTER THIRTEEN

GOVERNMENT, POLITICAL POWER, AND SOCIAL MOVEMENTS

Slobodan Milosevic—the "Butcher of the Balkans"—ruled Serbia for thirteen years, increasingly with an iron hand. A fervent Serbian nationalist, Milosevic had sought to restore Serbian control over the warring ethnic groups that had once made up the country of Yugoslavia. After the collapse of the Soviet Union, Yugoslavia—a communist republic—began to break up into a number of independent states, each one dominated by a different ethnic group. Milosevic tried to stop this process, often by brutal means.

Milosevic had risen to power by fanning the fires of nationalism, drawing on centuries-old memories of Serbian power and greatness in hopes of carving a "Greater Serbia" out of Serbia's neighboring republics. He sought to accomplish this by instilling among Serbs fear of their ethnic neighbors, which could then be used to drive other ethnic groups out of their historic homelands.

When Muslim-dominated Bosnia sought to secede from Serbian control in 1992, local Serbian militias, backed by the Serbian military, seized control by launching a reign of terror against Bosnia's Muslim population. Milosevic sought to "purify" Bosnia through "ethnic cleansing," driving Muslims out of the country by mass killings of civilians, widespread rape, and imprisonment of countless men in concentration camps. Televised images of mass graves and hundreds of thousands of Bosnian refugees galvanized world opinion, and the North Atlantic Treaty Organization (NATO) threatened military intervention.

Although peace talks eventually ended the Bosnian conflict and ousted the Serbian military, a similar conflict broke out when Kosovo sought independence in 1998, causing its Serbian minority to fear domination by the ethnic Albanian majority. Once again Milosevic called for ethnic cleansing, and once again the world was horrified by televised images of the mass murder of Bosnian men and teenage boys, with streams of terrified women and children fleeing over mountain passes. This time NATO launched a bombing campaign against Serbia itself, and Milosevic was forced to withdraw his forces from Bosnia.

Serbs were enraged by the Western intervention, and turned their anger against Milosevic. He was forced to call elections in September 2000, but refused to step down when he lost the vote. Hundreds of thousands of people took to the streets, and on October 5 he was toppled from power in a peaceful revolution. Milosevic was turned over to the United Nations and eventually stood trial for crimes against humanity in the UN International War Crimes Tribunal in the Hague, the Netherlands.

The popular uprising that overturned his regime drew on modern technology: although Milosevic controlled the country's television networks and newspapers, he couldn't control satellite TV, the distribution of videotapes, or the use of the Internet. The uprising was also made possible by Western military intervention and economic sanctions, which curbed Milosevic's military power and undermined popular support. And it drew inspiration from the rise of democratic movements throughout the world.

Democratization is one of the major political forces in the world. Like so many aspects of contemporary societies, the realm of government and politics is undergoing major changes. **Government** refers to the regular enactment of policies, decisions, and matters of state on the part of the officials within a political apparatus. **Politics** concerns the means whereby power is used to affect the scope and content of governmental activities. The sphere of the *political* may range well beyond that of government itself. Television is only one influence contributing to these changes. In this chapter, we will study the main factors affecting political life today. Many people find politics remote and uninteresting. Whether we like it or not, however, all of our lives are touched by what happens in the political sphere. Governments influence quite personal activities and, in times of war, can even order us to lay down our lives for aims they deem necessary. The sphere of government is the sphere of political power. All political life is about power: who holds it, how they achieve it, and what they do with it.

Power and Authority

As mentioned in Chapter 1, the study of power is of fundamental importance for sociology. **Power** is the ability of individuals or groups to make their own interests or concerns count, even when others resist. It sometimes involves the direct use of force, such as when Slobodan Milosevic used brutal force in an effort to seize control of Bosnia and Kosovo in an effort to create a "Greater Serbia." Power is an element in almost all social relationships, such as that between employer and employee. This chapter focuses on a narrower aspect of power, governmental power. In this form, it is almost always accompanied by ideologies, which are used to justify the actions of the powerful. For example, the Serbian government's use of force in "ethnic cleansing" was justified by an ideology of Serbian nationalism.

Authority is a government's legitimate use of power: Those subject to a government's authority consent to it. Power is thus different from authority. Contrary to what many believe, democracy is not the only type of government people consider legitimate. Dictatorships can have legitimacy as well. But as we shall see later, democracy is presently the most widespread form of government considered legitimate.

The Concept of the State

A **state** exists where there is a political apparatus of government (institutions like a parliament or congress, plus civil service officials) ruling over a given territory, whose authority is backed by a legal system and by the capacity to use military force to implement its policies. All modern states lay claim to specific territories, possess formalized codes of law, and are backed by the control of military force. **Nation-states** have come into existence at various times in different parts of the world (e.g., the United States in 1776 and the Czech Republic in 1993). Their main characteristics, however, contrast rather sharply with those of states in traditional civilizations.

Characteristics of the State

Sovereignty The territories ruled by traditional states were always poorly defined, the level of control wielded by the central government being quite weak. The notion of **sovereignty**— that a government possesses authority over an area with clear-cut borders, within which it is the supreme power—had little relevance. All nation-states, by contrast, are sovereign states.

Citizenship In traditional states, most of the population ruled by the king or emperor showed little awareness of, or interest in, those who governed them. Neither did they have any political rights or influence. Normally only the dominant classes or more affluent groups felt a sense of belonging to an overall political community. In modern societies, by contrast, most peo-

FIGURE 13.2

Business-Labor-Ideology Split in PAC, Soft, and Individual Donations to Candidates and Parties, 2002 Election Cycle

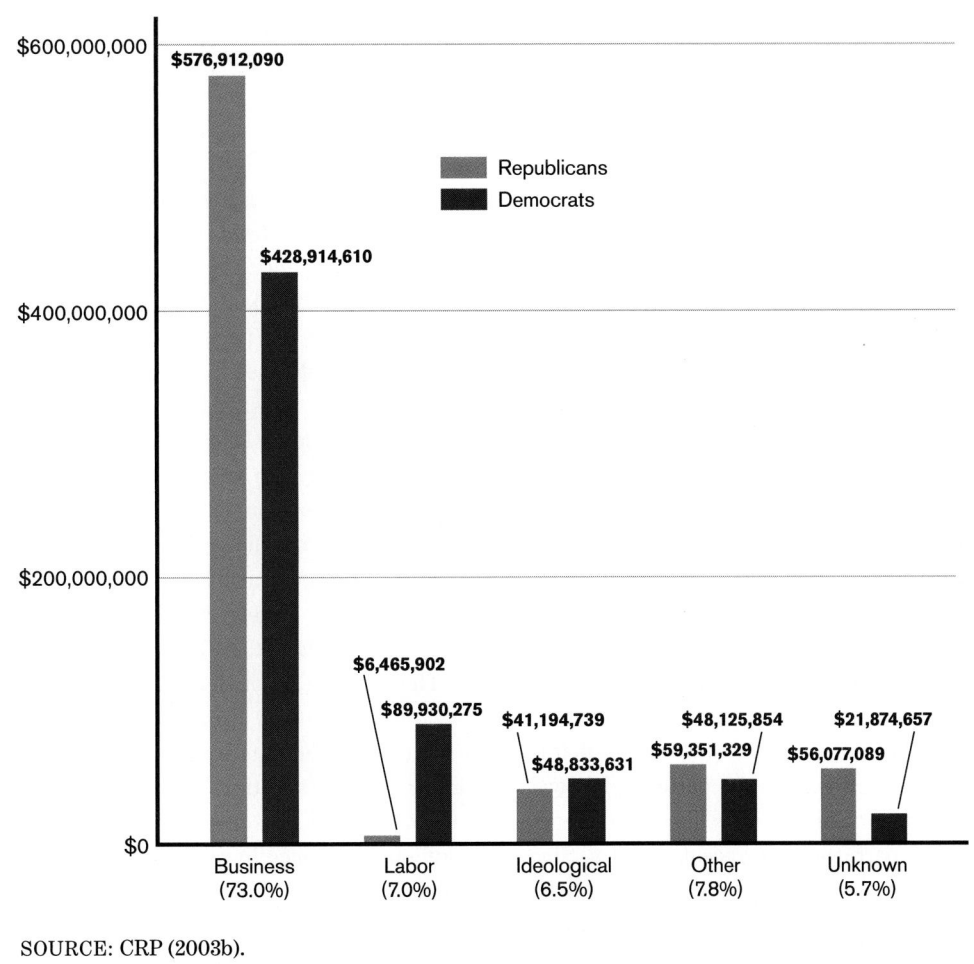

SOURCE: CRP (2003b).

Interest groups and PACs not only help elect candidates—they also influence the outcome of votes in Congress. The Medicare Reform Act of 2003, which creates a $400 billion program to extend prescription drug benefits to the elderly, was heavily pushed by the pharmaceutical industry, which since 1996 has spent more than a half a billion dollars to lobby Congress, the White House, and federal regulators, as well as to launch advertising campaigns aimed at the general public (Common Cause, 2003). Although the long-run benefit to the elderly was hotly debated by members of Congress, there is no question that drug companies will reap considerable benefit.

In 2002 Congress passed the McCain-Feingold campaign finance reform law, which severely restricted the ability to make unlimited campaign contributions. Under federal laws, some dating back a century, corporations and labor unions are prohibited from contributing to federal campaigns. Legal loopholes, however, permit unlimited "soft-money" contributions to be made to the political parties' "nonfederal accounts," supposedly destined for "party-building" activities unrelated to federal campaigns. In fact, almost all of the money finds its way back into presidential and congressional elections, reaching nearly a half a billion dollars in 2001–2002 (Common Cause, 2002b). The McCain-Feingold law, which was upheld as constitutional in a landmark Supreme Court decision in December 2003, closes the loophole. Candidates for federal elections are once again restricted to raising money from individuals—two thousand dollars per candidate, twenty-five thousand dollars to political parties. However, campaigns have already found a loophole, 527 organizations. These groups are political organizations that typically engage in campaigning and lobbying for candidates and are funded by unlimited soft money donations. They cannot coordinate their actions with any of the candidates, but they typically support one party or the other. In the 2004 presidential campaign, 527s like MoveOn.org and the Swift Vets and POWs for Truth spent nearly $400 million.

The Political Participation of Women

Voting has a special meaning for women against the background of their long struggle to obtain universal suffrage. The members of the early women's movements saw the vote both as the symbol of political freedom and as the means of achieving greater economic and social equality. In the United States, where the attempts by women to gain voting rights were more active, and often provoked violence, women's leaders underwent considerable hardships to reach this end. Even today, in many countries, women do not have the same voting rights as men.

Women's obtaining the vote has not greatly altered the nature of politics. Women's voting patterns, like those of men, are shaped by party preferences, policy options, and the choice of available candidates. The influence of women on politics cannot be assessed solely through voting patterns, however. Feminist groups have made an impact on political life independently of the franchise, particularly in recent decades. Since the early 1960s, the National Organization for Women (NOW) and other women's groups in the United States have played a significant role in the passing of equal opportunity acts and have pressed for a range of issues directly affecting women to be placed on the political agenda. Such issues include equal rights at work, the availability of abortion, changes in family and divorce laws, and lesbian rights. In 1973, women achieved a legal victory when the Supreme Court ruled in *Roe v. Wade* that women had a legal right to abortion. The 1989 Court ruling in *Webster v. Reproductive Health Services*, which placed restrictions on that right, resulted in a resurgence of involvement in the women's movement.

In most of the European countries, comparable national women's organizations have been lacking, but the "second wave" of feminism, characteristic of the 1960s and since, has brought the same issues to the center of the political stage. Although many of these matters—such as the question of whether abortion should be freely available—have proved highly controversial among women as well as men, it seems clear that many problems and concerns that particularly affect women, which previously had seemed to be "outside politics," are now central to political debates.

Yet in general, as in so many other sectors of social life, women are poorly represented among political elites. Following the 2002 midterm elections in the United States, there were fifty-nine female members in the House of Representatives in 2003, making up just under 14 percent of the total membership. This number has almost tripled since the early 1970s, but it is still not representative of the number of female citizens. In 2003 there were only thirteen women in the Senate, representing 13 percent of those sitting in the upper chamber.

What is surprising about the figures on women's involvement at the higher levels of political organizations is not this lack of representation itself, but the slowness with which things seem to be changing. In the business sector, men still monopolize the top positions, but women are now making more inroads into the strongholds of male privilege than previously. As yet at least, this does not seem to be happening in the political sphere—in spite of the fact that nearly all political parties today are nominally committed to securing equal opportunities for women and men. Since 1990, female candidates for political office have been successful *when they have run for office*. The critical factor seems to be that political parties (which are largely run by men) have not recruited as many women to run for office.

The factors that present difficulties for women's advancement in the economy also exist in the realm of politics. Rising within a political organization requires a great deal of expenditure of effort and time, which women who have major domestic burdens can rarely generate. But there may be an additional influence in political life. A high level of power is concentrated in the political area: Perhaps men are especially reluctant to abandon their dominance in such a sphere.

From considering the position of women in politics, we now broaden our scope to look at some basic ideas of political power. First, we take up the issue of who actually holds the reins of power, drawing on comparative materials to help illuminate the discussion. We then consider whether democratic governments around the world are "in crisis."

Who Rules? Theories of Democracy

DEMOCRATIC ELITISM

One of the most influential views of the nature and limits of modern democracy was set out by Max Weber and, in rather modified form, by the economist Joseph Schumpeter (1983).

The ideas they developed are sometimes referred to as the theory of **democratic elitism**.

Weber began from the assumption that direct democracy is impossible as a means of regular government in large-scale societies. This is not only for the obvious logistical reason that millions of people cannot meet to make political decisions, but because running a complex society demands *expertise*. Participatory democracy, Weber believed, can only succeed in small organizations in which the work to be carried out is fairly simple and straightforward. Where more complicated decisions have to be made, or policies worked out, even in modest-sized groups—such as a small business firm—specialized knowledge and skills are necessary. Experts have to carry out their jobs on a continuous basis; positions that require expertise cannot be subject to the regular election of people who may only have a vague knowledge of the necessary skills and information. While higher officials, responsible for overall policy decisions, are elected, there must be a large substratum of full-time bureaucratic officials who play a large part in running a country (Weber, 1979).

In Weber's view, the development of mass citizenship, which is so closely connected with the idea of general democratic participation, greatly expands the need for bureaucratic officialdom. For example, provision for welfare, health, and education demands permanent large-scale administrative systems. As Weber (1979) expresses this, "It is obvious that technically the large modern state is absolutely dependent upon a bureaucratic basis. The larger the state, and the more it is a great power, the more unconditionally this is the case."

Representative multiparty democracy, according to Weber, helps defend against both arbitrary decision making on the part of political leaders, because they are subject to popular elections, and power being completely usurped by bureaucrats, because elected officials set overall policy. But under these circumstances, the contribution of democratic institutions is less than many advocates of a more pure democracy would hope. "Rule by the people" is possible in only a very limited sense. In order to achieve power, political parties themselves must become organized in a systematic way. In short, they, too, must become bureaucratized. "Party machines" develop, which threaten the autonomy of parliaments or congresses as places in which policies are discussed and formulated. If a party with a majority representation is able to dictate policy, and if that party is itself mainly run by officials who are permanently in control, the level of democracy that has been achieved is slim indeed.

In order for democratic systems to have some degree of effectiveness, Weber argued, two conditions have to be met. First, there must be parties that represent different interests and have different outlooks. If the policies of competing parties are more or less the same, voters are denied any effective choice. Weber rejected the idea that one-party systems can be democratic in any meaningful way. Second, there must be polit-

ical leaders who have the imagination and courage necessary to escape the inertia of bureaucracy. Weber placed a great deal of emphasis on the importance of *leadership* in democracy—which is why his view is referred to as "democratic elitism." He argued that rule by elites is inevitable; the best we can hope for is that those elites effectively represent our interests and that they do so in an innovative and insightful fashion. Parliaments and congresses provide a breeding ground for capable political leaders able to counter the influence of bureaucracy and to command mass support. Weber valued multiparty democracy more for the quality of leadership it generates than for the mass participation in politics it makes possible.

Joseph Schumpeter fully agreed with Weber about the limits of mass political participation. For Schumpeter, as for Weber, democracy is more important as a method of generating effective and responsible government than as a means of providing significant power for the majority. Democracy cannot offer more than the possibility of replacing a given political leader or party by another. Democracy, Schumpeter stated, is the rule of *the politician*, not *the people*. Politicians are "dealers in votes" much as brokers are dealers in shares on the stock exchange. To achieve voting support, however, politicians must be at least minimally responsive to the demands and interests of the electorate. Only if there is some degree of competition to secure votes can arbitrary rule effectively be avoided.

PLURALIST THEORIES

The ideas of Weber and Schumpeter influenced some of the **pluralist theories of modern democracy**, although the pluralists developed their ideas somewhat differently. Pluralists accept that individual citizens can have little or no *direct* influence on political decision making. But they argue that tendencies toward the centralization of power in the hands of government officials are limited by the presence of interest groups. Competing interest groups or factions are vital to democracy because they divide up power, reducing the exclusive influence of any one group or class (Truman, 1981).

According to the pluralist view, government policies in a democracy are influenced by continual processes of bargaining among numerous groups representing different interests—business organizations, trade unions, ethnic groups, environmental organizations, religious groups, and so forth. A democratic political order is one in which there is a balance among competing interests, all having some impact on policy but none dominating the actual mechanisms of government. Elections are also influenced by this situation, for to achieve a broad enough base of support to lay claim to government, parties must be responsive to numerous diverse interest groups. The United States, it is held, is the most pluralistic of industrialized societies and, therefore, the most democratic.

Competition between diverse interest groups occurs not only at the national level but within the states and in the politics of local communities.

THE POWER ELITE

The view suggested by C. Wright Mills in his celebrated work *The Power Elite* is quite different from pluralist theories (Mills, 1956). According to Mills, in earlier periods of its history, American society did show flexibility and diversity at all levels; however, this has since changed.

Mills argues that during the course of the twentieth century a process of institutional centralization occurred in the political order, the economy, and the sphere of the military. On the political side, individual state governments used to be very powerful and were only loosely coordinated by the federal government. Political power today, Mills argues, has become tightly coordinated at the federal level. Similarly, the economy was once made up of many small units, businesses, banks, and farms across the country, but has now become dominated by a cluster of very large corporations. Finally, since World War II, the military, once kept restricted in size, has grown to a giant establishment at the heart of the country's institutions.

Not only has each of these spheres become more centralized, according to Mills, but they have become increasingly merged with one another to form a unified system of power. Those who are in the highest positions in all three institutional areas come from similar social backgrounds, have parallel interests, and often know one another on a personal basis. They have become a single **power elite** that runs the country—and, given the international position of the United States, also influences a great deal of the rest of the world.

The power elite, in Mills's portrayal, is composed mainly of white Anglo-Saxon Protestants (WASPs). Many are from wealthy families, have been to the same prestigious universities, belong to the same clubs, and sit on government committees with one another. They have closely connected concerns. Business and political leaders work together, and both have close relationships with the military through weapons contracting and the supply of goods for the armed forces. There is a great deal of movement among top positions in the three spheres. Politicians have business interests; business leaders often run for public office; higher military personnel sit on the boards of the large companies.

In opposition to pluralist interpretations, Mills argues that there are three distinct levels of power in the United States. The power elite occupies the highest level, formally and informally making the most important policy decisions affecting both the domestic arena and foreign policy. Interest groups, on which the pluralists concentrate their attention, operate at the middle levels of power, together with local government agencies. Their influence over major policy decisions is limited. At the bottom is the large mass of the population, who have virtually no influence on the decisions at all, since these are made within the closed settings in which the members of the power elite come together. The power elite spans the top of both party organizations, each party being run by individuals with similar overall interests and outlooks. Thus the choices open to voters in presidential and congressional elections are so small as to be of little consequence.

Since Mills published his study, numerous other research investigations have analyzed the social background and interconnections of leading figures in the various spheres of American society (Dye, 1986). All studies agree on the finding that the social backgrounds of those in leading positions are highly unrepresentative of the population as a whole (Domhoff, 1971, 1979, 1983, 1998).

The main argument among sociologists about the distribution of power in the United States now focuses on the relative power of government officials and of the business leaders who run large corporations. One group of scholars argues that the government is where true power lies and that business leaders are not nearly as powerful as the experts and politicians who run the government (Skocpol, 1992; Orloff, 1993; Amenta, 1998). An alternative view holds that corporate business executives and families of great wealth form a capitalist class, which has great influence over government officials and experts through lobbying, campaign contributions, the sponsorship of think tanks, and the appointment of top corporate leaders to important government positions (Domhoff, 1998). Both sides agree, however, that it is not inevitable that business leaders or government officials will always be dominant. Although an elite class—whether elected, expert, or corporate—rules America, the power of groups can change over time, leaving open the possibility that those who are now powerless could be dominant sometime in the future.

THE ROLE OF THE MILITARY

Mills's argument that the military plays a central role in the power elite was buttressed by a well-known warning from a former military hero and U.S. president, Dwight David Eisenhower. In his farewell presidential speech in 1961, Eisenhower—who was the supreme commander of the Allied forces in Europe in World War II—warned of the dangers of what he termed the "military-industrial complex." As Eisenhower bluntly put it, "The conjunction of an immense military establishment and a large arms industry is new in the American experience. In the councils of government, we must guard against the acquisition of unwarranted influence, whether

TABLE 13.1

World's Fifteen Largest Military Budgets

RANK	COUNTRY	AMOUNT (BILLIONS)	PERCENT WORLD SHARE
1	United States	$399.1	45.9
2	Russia[a]	$65.0	7.5
3	China[a]	$47.0	5.4
4	Japan	$42.6	4.9
5	United Kingdom	$38.4	4.4
6	France	$29.5	3.4
7	Germany	$24.9	2.9
8	Saudi Arabia	$21.3	2.4
9	Italy	$19.4	2.2
10	India	$15.6	1.8
11	South Korea	$14.1	1.6
12	Brazil[a]	$10.7	1.2
13	Taiwan[a]	$10.7	1.2
14	Israel	$10.6	1.2
15	Spain	$8.4	1.0
Subtotal	(top 15)	$749.7	86.1
World		$870.0	100.0

[a]Figures are for 2001–2003, depending on availability; world total estimated; expenditures used were significantly higher than budget estimates.

SOURCE: Hellman, 2003.

sought or unsought, by the military-industrial complex. The potential for the disastrous rise of misplaced power exists and will persist" (Eisenhower Library, 1961).

With the collapse of the Soviet Union in 1991, the United States has emerged as the world's unrivaled military superpower, accounting for nearly half of total military spending—more than the next fifteen countries combined (Table 13.1). In 1989, at the end of the cold war, U.S. defense spending—which had reached $300 billion in that year—began to decline slightly. But the decline was short lived. There turned out to be no "peace dividend" to spend on improving schools, repairing highways, or other domestic needs. By 2001 military spending once again topped $300 billion. It reached $400 billion in 2004, and is projected at $500 billion in 2009, for a total of $2.3 trillion in military spending over the next five years—figures that do not include the cost of military operations in Afghanistan and Iraq (CDI, 2003).

The global "war on terror," discussed below, has instead triggered yet another cycle of military spending. Eisenhower's dire warning seems no less true today than when he uttered it some fifty years ago.

Democracy in Trouble?

As liberal democracy is becoming so widespread, we might expect it to be highly successful. Yet such is not the case. Democracy almost everywhere is in some difficulty. This is not only because it is proving difficult to set up a stable democratic order in Russia and other erstwhile communist societies. Democracy is in trouble in its main countries of origin—the United States is a good example. The numbers of people voting in presidential and other elections have been in decline for some while. In surveys, many people say they don't trust politicians and regard most of them as tricksters.

Forty years ago (in 1964), confidence in government was fairly high: Nearly four out of five people answered "most of the time" or "just about always" when asked, "How much of the time do you trust the government in Washington to do the right thing?" This level of confidence then dropped steadily for the next twenty years, rising somewhat in the 1980s, then dropping to a low of one in five in 1994. Since that time the level of reported trust has increased steadily. Today—bolstered by an increased confidence in government following the attacks of September 11, 2001—a solid majority of Americans (about three out of every five) report that they trust the government "most of the time" or "just about always."

Of those expressing continuing trust in government, most vote in presidential elections; of those who lack trust, most do not vote. As we have seen, younger people have less interest in electoral politics than older generations have, although the young have a greater interest than their elders in issues like the environment (Nye, 1997). Some have argued that trends like these indicate that people are increasingly skeptical of traditional forms of authority. Connected to this has been a shift in political values in democratic nations from "scarcity values" to "post-materialist values" (Inglehart, 1997). This means that after a certain level of economic prosperity has been reached, voters become concerned less with economic issues than with the quality of their individual (as opposed to collective) lifestyles, such as the desire for meaningful work. As a result, voters are generally less interested in national politics, except for areas involving personal liberty.

The last few decades have also been a period in which, in several Western countries, the welfare state has come under attack. Rights and benefits, fought for over long periods, have been contested and cut back. Rightist parties have attempted to reduce levels of welfare expenditure in their countries. Even in states led by socialist governments, such as Spain, commitment to government provision of public resources has been restricted. One reason for this governmental retrenchment is the declining revenues available to governments as a result of the general world recession that began in the early 1970s. Yet an increasing skepticism also seems to have developed, shared not only by some governments but by many of their citizens, about the effectiveness of relying on the state for the provision of many essential goods and services. This skepticism is based on the belief that the welfare state is bureaucratic, alienating, and inefficient, and that welfare benefits can create perverse consequences that undermine what they were designed to achieve (Giddens, 1998).

Among the major industrial democracies, the United States spends the lowest portion of its total economy on government: roughly one third of its gross domestic product goes for government spending at the federal, state, and local levels. By way of comparison, Sweden devotes more than half of its GDP to government spending; the European Union, 44 percent; and all industrial countries combined, 38 percent. Americans have relatively lower taxes than other industrial democracies, but they also received lower levels of support for health care, housing, education, unemployment compensation, and social services in general. This is arguably another reason for the low levels of confidence in government, and poor voter turnout: Americans simply expect less, and get less, from their government.

Why are so many people dissatisfied with the very political system that seems to be sweeping all before it across the world? The answers, curiously, are bound up with the factors that have helped spread democracy—the impact of capitalism and the globalizing of social life. For instance, while capitalist economies have proved to generate more wealth than any other type of economic system, that wealth is unevenly distributed (see Chapter 8). And economic inequalities influence who votes, joins parties, and gets elected. Wealthy individuals and corporations back interest groups that lobby for elected officials to support their aims when deciding on legislation. Not being subject to election, interest groups are not accountable to the majority of the electorate.

Economic inequalities also create an underclass of people living in poverty. About 20 percent of the population of liberal democracies lives below the poverty line. Most Western liberal democracies establish policies to reduce poverty levels, but they vary in how much they spend to achieve that aim. Societies that spend the most to implement a complex welfare system require a higher level of taxation and a larger nonelected government bureaucracy. The question arises: How much of an economic and political price is a society willing to pay to reduce poverty, and what is the impact of this cost?

Two theories have been put forward by different authors to account for this changing political situation. One is the theory of **state overload** (Britain, 1975; Nordhaus, 1975). According to this view, governments in the twentieth century acquired more responsibilities than they could capably fund and manage, from establishing public ownership of industries, utilities, and transportation to creating extensive welfare programs. One reason for this situation is that political parties tried to woo voters by promising to provide too many benefits and services. Governments were unable to deliver on these promises because the level of state expenditure rose beyond the resources provided by tax revenues: state responsibilities were overloaded (Etzioni-Halévy, 1985).

Consequently, it is argued, voters have become skeptical about claims made by governments and political parties. The Democratic party in the United States and leftist parties elsewhere have lost some of their traditional support from lower-class groups, as it became apparent that states could no longer deliver the promised benefits. The rise of new right politics is explained as an attempt to cope with this situation by trimming back the state and encouraging private enterprise.

A rival theory, developed by Jürgen Habermas, is known as the theory of **legitimation crisis** (Habermas, 1975; Offe, 1984, 1985). According to this theory, modern governments lack the legitimacy to carry out tasks they are required to undertake, such as providing highways, public housing, and health care. People who feel that they pay most for these services through higher taxes—the more affluent—are likely to believe that they gain least from them. On the one hand, governments are asked to take more and more responsibility for providing health care for those who cannot afford it; on the other, taxpayers resist any increases in taxation or even want tax payments reduced. Governments cannot cope with the contradictory demands of lower taxes and more responsibilities, leading to decreased public support and general disillusionment about government's capabilities. According to Habermas, legitimation crises could probably be overcome if the electorate were persuaded to accept high taxation in return for a wide range of government services.

As the sociologist Daniel Bell has observed, national government is too small to respond to the big questions, such as the influence of global economic competition or the destruction of the world's environment; but it has become too big to deal with the small questions, issues that affect particular cities or regions. Governments have little power, for instance, over the activities of giant business corporations, the main actors within the global economy. A U.S. corporation may decide to shut down its production plants in America and set up a new factory in Mexico instead, in order to lower costs and compete more effectively with other corporations. The result is that thousands of American workers lose their jobs. They are likely to want the government to do something, but national governments are unable to control processes bound up with the world economy. All the government can do is try to soften the blow, for example, by providing unemployment benefits or job retraining.

At the same time that governments have shrunk in relation to global issues, they have also become more remote from the lives of most citizens. Many Americans resent that decisions affecting their lives are made by distant "power brokers" in Washington—party officials, interest groups, lobbyists, and bureaucratic officials. They believe that the government is unable to deal with important local issues as well, such as crime and homelessness. The result is that Americans' faith in government has dropped substantially. This in turn affects people's willingness to participate in the political process.

Political and Social Change

Political life is by no means carried on only within the orthodox framework of political parties, voting, and representation in legislative and governmental bodies. It often happens that groups find that their objectives or ideals cannot be achieved within, or are actively blocked by, this framework. Despite the spread of democracy described above, the persistence of authoritarian regimes in many countries—such as China, Cuba, and the former Yugoslavia—reminds us that effecting change within existing political structures is not always possible. Sometimes political and social change can only be brought about through recourse to unorthodox forms of political action.

The most dramatic and far-reaching example of unorthodox political action is **revolution**—the overthrow of an existing political order by means of a mass movement, using violence. Revolutions are tense, exciting, and fascinating events; understandably they attract great attention. Yet for all of their high drama, revolutions occur relatively infrequently. The most common type of unorthodox political activity takes place through **social movements**—collective attempts to further a common interest or secure a common goal through action outside the sphere of established institutions. A wide variety of social movements besides those leading to revolution, some enduring, some transient, have existed in modern societies. They are as evident a feature of the contemporary world as are the formal, bureaucratic organizations they often oppose. Many contemporary social movements are international in scope and rely heavily on the use of information technology in linking local campaigners to global issues.

Why Do Social Movements Occur?

Sociology arose in the late nineteenth century as part of an effort to come to grips with the massive political and economic transformations that Europe underwent on its way from the preindustrial to the modern world (Moore, 1966). Perhaps because sociology was founded in this context, sociologists have never lost their fascination with these transformations.

Since mass social movements have been so important in world history over the past two centuries, it is not surprising that a diversity of theories exists to try to account for them. Some theories were formulated early in the history of the social sciences; the most important was that of Karl Marx. Marx, who lived well before any of the social movements undertaken in the name of his ideas took place, intended his views to be taken not just as an analysis of the conditions of revolutionary change, but as a means of furthering such change. Whatever their intrinsic validity, Marx's ideas had an immense practical impact on twentieth-century social change.

We shall look at four frameworks for the study of social movements, many of which were developed in the context of revolution: economic deprivation, resource mobilization, structural strain, and fields of action.

ECONOMIC DEPRIVATION

Marx's view of social movements is based on his interpretation of human history in general (see Chapter 1). According to Marx, the development of societies is marked by periodic class conflicts that, when they become acute, tend to end in a process of revolutionary change. Class struggles derive from the *contradictions*—unresolvable tensions—in societies. The main sources of contradiction can be traced to economic changes, or changes in the forces of production. In any stable society, there is a balance between the economic structure, social relationships, and the political system. As the forces of production alter, contradiction is intensified, leading to open clashes between classes—and ultimately to revolution.

Marx applied this model both to the past development of feudalism and to what he saw as the probable future evolution of industrial capitalism. The traditional, feudal societies of Europe were based on peasant production; the producers were serfs ruled by a class of landed aristocrats and gentry. Economic changes within these societies gave rise to towns and cities, where trade and manufacture developed. This new economic system, created *within* feudal society, threatened its very basis. Rather than being founded on the traditional lord-serf relationship, the emerging economic order encouraged industrialists to produce goods for sale in open markets. The contradictions between the old feudal economy and the newly

Possibilities for Change in American Communities

Teaching and learning sociology often involves finding ways to bring the outside world into the classroom. To more meaningfully connect students to the contexts within which social change efforts occur, I have developed the "Possibilities for Change in American Communities" program at Brandeis University. The yearlong program combines two semesters of in-class work with a month of bus travel around the eastern United States. In the classroom, our goal is to present theories of social change and introduce particular movements that we will experience firsthand during our travels. We then board a bus that serves as our home on wheels for a month, carrying us to a wide range of communities where we apply and test recently acquired ideas about social movements and social change.

The point of our travel is to connect students with activists and social movement organizations, and to the local communities in which these movements operate. Our route is designed to expose the group to a broad set of communities, consistent with our overall strategy of comparatively examining the contexts in which change occurs. Frequently, our students—typically raised in urban or suburban areas around Boston, New York, Chicago, or Los Angeles—learn enduring lessons in areas that diverge most sharply from their own backgrounds. Following a meeting with a local advocacy organization in rural North Carolina, for instance, the group's leader invited us to dinner at his truck-stop restaurant on the outskirts of town. We gladly accepted, and were treated not only to a delicious meal, but also to back-room political negotiations when our host and several of his colleagues held an impromptu meeting over barbeque with the local mayor and town planner. While readings and class discussions may focus on the tight-knit, highly interdependent nature of rural and small-town social relations, such lessons have a lasting impact when we see these connections in action.

Our time spent on the road also provides an opportunity for students to engage in a range of community-based work. Our aim is not to passively study communities and organizations, but to integrate ourselves into their perspectives and activities. The groups we select are purposely wide-ranging, and include direct service, advocacy, and community organizing ventures. Over the course of a single month, we cooked and distributed meals with Food Not Bombs in Chapel Hill, North Carolina; spoke out for gun control legislation on CNN's *Talk Back Live* in Atlanta, Georgia; stuffed envelopes to support Sister Helen Prejean's Moratorium Campaign in New

Orleans; helped restore a house with Habitat for Humanity in Baton Rouge, Louisiana; lobbied our congressional representatives in Washington, DC; and helped recruit participants in the Kensington Welfare Rights Union's battle for affordable housing and health care in Philadelphia. Alongside this work, we also met with participants in past and current activist efforts, spoke with several noted social movement scholars, and visited a number of historically important sites.

To many of the people we encounter along the way, our mode of travel seems at least as interesting as our educational mission. A sleeper bus is something used mostly by bands or touring theater groups—they stand out due to their large size, lack of windows, and airbrushed artwork. Considering the space constraints, the interior is really quite comfortable, providing living and sleeping space for fifteen. Importantly, the tight living arrangement provides plenty of opportunity for us to forge our own functioning community. And combining our accommodations with our mode of transportation is exceedingly efficient, as it allows us to travel at night while we sleep. We thus spend the vast majority of our waking hours at our destinations rather than in transit.

Quite literally, the bus provides a vehicle to understand the longer-term impacts of social movement activity, linking causes to effects and the past to the present. In Jackson, Mississippi, for instance, we visited with Bob Moses and Dave Dennis, both veterans of civil rights work with the Student Non-Violent Coordinating Committee during the 1960s. For the past twenty years, both have worked to develop the Algebra Project, a math literacy program that they view as key to students' future economic access in the same way that sharecroppers' ability to vote had determined their political access a generation earlier.

Just two days before our visit to Jackson, we spent time in Selma, Alabama, the site of the 1965 "Bloody Sunday" march in which several hundred civil rights marchers were brutally beaten by police officers seeking to prevent them from crossing the Edmund Pettus Bridge to begin their fifty-mile trek to the state capitol in Montgomery. In Selma, we were able to follow the aborted march route over the Pettus Bridge and hear firsthand accounts by local participants at the nearby National Voting Rights Museum and Institute. We also canvassed Selma neighborhoods to interview longtime residents about their lives since the 1960s, and met with current Mayor

James Perkins, the first African American resident elected to that post in Selma.

By connecting to movement activists and directly experiencing the sites of social movement activity, we are able to explore more fully the long-term impact of specific events like the Selma-to-Montgomery march, and the larger civil rights movement. We also forge links to ongoing movements, gaining an on-the-ground understanding of their strategies, tactics, and day-to-day operations. These links are first put into action following our return, when students work on ambitious projects tied to our travels. From creating campus partnerships with community organizations to further their ongoing campaigns, to analyzing interview and archival data to formulate strategic plans to improve citizens' access to community resources, students continue to apply their experience and knowledge actively. Such activities provide a means to understand the dynamics of social movement activity, while creating long-term benefits both for our students and for the communities that they will be part of in the future.

DAVID CUNNINGHAM is an assistant professor in the Department of Sociology at Brandeis University. He is currently pursuing research on the political repression of protest groups and Ku Klux Klan mobilization in the civil rights-era South. He is the author of There's Something Happening Here: The New Left, the Klan, and FBI Counterintelligence, *published in 2004 by the University of California Press.*

emerging capitalist one eventually became acute, taking the form of violent conflicts between the rising capitalist class and the feudal landowners. Revolution was the outcome of this process, the most important example being the French Revolution of 1789. Through such revolutions and revolutionary changes occurring in other European societies, Marx argued, the capitalist class managed to achieve dominance.

But the coming of industrial capitalism, according to Marx, set up new contradictions, which would eventually lead to a further series of revolutions prompted by ideals of socialism or communism. Industrial capitalism, an economic order based on the private pursuit of profit and on competition between firms to sell their products, creates a gulf between a rich minority who control the industrial resources and an impoverished majority of wage workers. Workers and capitalists come into more and more intense conflict with one another. Labor movements and political parties representing the mass of the working population eventually mount a challenge to the rule of the capitalist class and overthrow the existing political system. When the position of a dominant class is particularly entrenched, Marx believed, violence is necessary to bring about the required transition. In other circumstances, this process might happen peacefully through parliamentary action; a revolution (in the sense defined above) would not be necessary.

Contrary to Marx's expectations, revolutions failed to occur in the advanced industrialized societies of the West. Why? The sociologist James Davies, a critic of Marx, pointed to periods of history when people lived in dire poverty but did not rise up in protest. Constant poverty or deprivation does not make people into revolutionaries; rather, they usually endure such conditions with resignation or mute despair. Social protest, and ultimately revolution, is more likely to occur, Davies argued, when there is an *improvement* in people's living conditions. Once standards of living have started to rise, people's levels of expectation also go up. If improvement in actual conditions subsequently slows down, propensities to revolt are created because rising expectations are frustrated (Davies, 1962).

Thus, it is not absolute deprivation that leads to protest but **relative deprivation**—the discrepancy between the lives people are forced to lead and what they think could realistically be achieved. Davies's theory is useful in understanding the connections between revolution and modern social and economic development. The influence of ideals of progress, together with expectations of economic growth, tend to induce rising hopes, which, if then frustrated, spark protest. Such protest gains further strength from the spread of ideas of equality and democratic political participation, ideas that played a basic role not only in the American Revolution of 1776 and the Russian Revolution of 1917, but also in the revolutions of 1989 in Europe.

As Charles Tilly has pointed out, however, Davies's theory does not show how and why different groups *mobilize* to seek

Relative deprivation between the peasantry and the elite in France led to the overthrow of the monarchy.

revolutionary change. Protest might well often occur against a backdrop of rising expectations; to understand how it is transformed into a mass social movement, we need to identify how groups become collectively organized to make effective political challenges.

RESOURCE MOBILIZATION

In *From Mobilization to Revolution*, Charles Tilly analyzed processes of revolutionary change in the context of broader forms of protest and violence (Tilly, 1978). He distinguished four main components of **collective action**, action taken to contest or overthrow an existing social order:

1. The *organization* of the group or groups involved. Protest movements are organized in many ways, varying from the spontaneous formation of crowds to tightly disciplined revolutionary groups. The Russian Revolution, for example, began as a small group of activists.
2. *Mobilization*, the ways in which a group acquires sufficient resources to make collective action possible. Such resources may include supplies of material goods, political support, and weaponry. Lenin was able to acquire material and moral support from a sympathetic peasantry, together with many townspeople.
3. The *common interests* of those engaging in collective action, what they see as the gains and losses likely to be achieved by their policies. Some common goals always underlie mobilization to collective action. Lenin managed to weld together a broad coalition of support because many people had a common interest in removing the existing government.

4. *Opportunity*. Chance events may occur that provide opportunities to pursue revolutionary aims. Numerous forms of collective action, including revolution, are greatly influenced by such incidental events. There was no inevitability to Lenin's success, which depended on a number of contingent factors—including success in battle. If Lenin had been killed, would there have been a revolution?

Collective action itself can simply be defined as people acting together in pursuit of interests they share—for example, gathering to demonstrate in support of their cause. Some of these people may be intensely involved, others may lend more passive or irregular support. Effective collective action, such as action that culminates in revolution, usually moves through stages 1 to 4.

Social movements, in Tilly's view, tend to develop as means of mobilizing group resources either when people have no institutionalized means of making their voices heard or when their needs are directly repressed by the state authorities. Although collective action at some point involves open confrontation with the political authorities—"taking to the streets"—only when such activity is backed by groups who are systematically organized is confrontation likely to have much impact on established patterns of power.

Typical modes of collective action and protest vary with historical and cultural circumstances. In the United States today, for example, most people are familiar with forms of demonstration like mass marches, large assemblies, and street riots, whether or not they have participated in such activities. Other types of collective protest, however, have become less common or have disappeared altogether in most modern societies (such as fights between villages, machine breaking, or lynching). Protesters can also build on examples taken from elsewhere; for instance, guerrilla movements proliferated in various parts of the world once disaffected groups learned how successful guerrilla actions can be against regular armies. And, as discussed above, a new form of collective action may be emerging—"smart-mobbing" and other forms of social protest accomplished through the Internet.

When and why does collective action become violent? After studying a large number of incidents that have occurred in Western Europe since 1800, Tilly concluded that most collective violence develops from action that is not itself initially violent. Whether violence occurs depends not so much on the nature of the activity as on other factors—in particular, how the authorities respond. A good instance is the street demonstration. The vast majority of such demonstrations take place without damage either to people or to property. A minority lead to violence and are then labeled as riots. Sometimes the authorities step in when violence has already occurred; more often, the historical record shows, they are the originators of violence. In Tilly's words, "In the modern European experience repressive forces are themselves the most consistent initiators and performers of collective violence" (1978). Moreover, when violent confrontations do occur, the agents of authority are responsible for the largest share of deaths and injuries. This is not surprising given their special access to arms and military discipline. The groups they are attempting to control, conversely, do greater damage to objects or property.

Revolutionary movements, according to Tilly, are a type of collective action that occurs in situations of what he calls **multiple sovereignty**—these occur when a government for some reason lacks full control over the areas it is supposed to administer. Multiple sovereignty can arise as a result of external war, internal political clashes, or the two combined. Whether a revolutionary takeover of power is accomplished depends on how far the ruling authorities maintain control over the armed forces, the extent of conflicts within ruling groups, and the level of organization of the protest movements trying to seize power.

Tilly's work represents one of the most sophisticated attempts to analyze collective violence and revolutionary struggles. The concepts he develops seem to have wide application, and his use of them is sensitive to the variabilities of historical time and place. How social movements are organized, the resources they are able to mobilize, the common interests of groups contending for power, and chance opportunities are all important facets of social transformation.

Tilly says little, however, about the circumstances that lead to multiple sovereignty. This is such a fundamental part of explaining revolution that it represents a serious omission. According to Theda Skocpol, Tilly assumes that social movements are guided by the conscious and deliberate pursuit of interests, and that successful processes of revolutionary change occur when people manage to realize these interests. Skocpol, by contrast, sees social movements as more ambiguous and indecisive in their objectives. Revolutions, she emphasizes, largely emerge as unintended consequences of more partial aims:

> In fact, in historical revolutions, differently situated and motivated groups have become participants in complex unfoldings of multiple conflicts. These conflicts have been powerfully shaped and limited by existing social, economic and international conditions. And they have proceeded in different ways depending upon how each revolutionary situation emerged in the first place. (1979)

Skocpol's argument seems correct when we analyze the revolutionary changes that occurred in East European societies in 1989, compared with earlier revolutionary episodes.

In addition to the above theories, which seek to explain the collective behavior that leads to revolutions, other theoretical perspectives on more general forms of collective action are also important. We will now look at two of those theories, structural strain and fields of action.

STRUCTURAL STRAIN

Neil Smelser (1963) distinguished six conditions underlying the origins of collective action in general, and social movements in particular: the presence of structurally conducive conditions, the existence of structural strain in society, the spread of generalized beliefs, the presence of precipitating factors of effective leadership, and the nature of social control directed against the social movement.

1. *Structural conduciveness* refers to the general social conditions promoting or inhibiting the formation of social movements of different types. For example, in Smelser's view, the sociopolitical system of the United States leaves open certain avenues of mobilization for protest because of the relative absence of state regulation in those areas. For example, there is no official state-sponsored religion. People are free to exercise their religious beliefs. This makes for a conducive environment in which religious movements might compete for individuals, so long as they do not transgress criminal or civil law.

2. Just because the conditions are conducive to the development of a social movement does not mean those conditions will bring them into being. There must be **structural strain**—tensions (or, in Marx's terminology, contradictions) that produce conflicting interests within societies. Uncertainties, anxieties, ambiguities, or direct clashes of goals, are expressions of such strains. Sources of strain may be quite general, or specific to particular situations. Thus sustained inequalities between ethnic groups give rise to overall tensions; these may become focused in the shape of specific conflicts when, say, blacks begin to move into a previously all-white area.

3. The third condition Smelser outlined is the spread of *generalized beliefs*. Social movements do not develop simply as responses to vaguely felt anxieties or hostilities. They are shaped by the influence of definite ideologies, which crystallize grievances and suggest courses of action that might be pursued to remedy them. Revolutionary movements, for instance, are based on ideas about why injustice occurs and how it can be alleviated by political struggle.

4. *Precipitating factors* are events or incidents that actually trigger direct action by those who become involved in the movement. In 1955, when a black woman named Rosa Parks refused to give up her seat to a white man on a bus in Montgomery, Alabama, her action helped spark the civil rights movement (see Chapter 11).

5. The first four conditions combined, Smelser argued, might occasionally lead to street disturbances or outbreaks of violence. But such incidents do not lead to the development of social movements unless there is a coordinated group that becomes mobilized for action. *Leadership* and some means of *regular communication* among participants, together with funding and material resources, are necessary for a social movement to exist.

6. Finally, the manner in which a social movement develops is strongly influenced by the *operation of social control*. The governing authorities may respond to initial protests by intervening in the conditions of conduciveness and strain that stimulated the emergence of the movement. For instance, in a situation of ethnic tension, steps might be taken to reduce ethnic inequality that generated resentment and conflict. Other important aspects of social control concern the responses of the police or armed forces. A harsh reaction might encourage further protest and help solidify the movement. Also, doubt and divisions within the police and military can be crucial in deciding the outcome of confrontations with revolutionary movements.

Smelser's model is useful for analyzing the sequences in the development of social movements, and collective action in general. According to Smelser, each stage in the sequence "adds value" to the overall outcome; also, each stage is a condition for the occurrence of the next one. But some critical comments can be made about Smelser's theory. Some social movements become strong without any particular precipitating incidents. Conversely, a series of incidents might bring home the need to establish a movement to change the circumstances that gave rise to them. Also, a movement itself might create strains, rather than develop in response to them. For example, the women's movement has actively sought to identify and combat gender inequalities where previously these had gone unquestioned. Smelser's theory treats social movements as *responses* to situations, rather than allowing that their members might spontaneously organize to achieve desired social changes. In this respect his ideas contrast with the approach developed by Alain Touraine.

FIELDS OF ACTION

Alain Touraine (1977, 1981) developed his analysis of social movements on the basis of four main ideas. The first, which he called **historicity**, explains why there are so many more movements in the modern world than there were in earlier times. In modern societies, individuals and groups know that social activism can be used to achieve social goals and reshape society.

Second, Touraine focused on the *rational objectives* of social movements. Such movements do not just come about as irrational responses to social divisions or injustices; rather, they develop from specific views and rational strategies as to how injustices can be overcome.

Third, Touraine saw a process of *interaction* in the shaping of social movements. Movements do not develop in isolation; instead, they develop in deliberate antagonism with established organizations and sometimes with other rival social movements. All social movements have interests or aims that they are *for;* all have views and ideas they are *against.* In Touraine's view, other theories of social movements (including that of Smelser) have given insufficient consideration to how the objectives of a social movement are shaped by encounters with others holding divergent positions, as well as by the ways in which they themselves influence the outlooks and action of their opponents. For instance, the objectives and outlook of the women's movement have been shaped in opposition to the male-dominated institutions that it seeks to alter. The goals and outlook of the movement have shifted in relation to its successes and failures and have also influenced the perspectives of men. These changed perspectives in turn stimulated a reorientation in women's movements, and so the process of shaping and reshaping continues.

Fourth, social movements and change occur in the context of what Touraine called "fields of action." A **field of action** refers to the connections between a social movement and the forces or influences against it. The process of mutual negotiation among antagonists in a field of action may lead to the social changes sought by the movement as well as to changes in the social movement itself and in its antagonists. In either circumstance, the movement may evaporate—or become institutionalized as a permanent organization. For example, the labor-union movements became formal organizations when they achieved the right to strike and to engage in types of bargaining acceptable to both workers and employers. These changes in both the movement and the original worker-owner relationship were forged out of earlier processes involving widespread violent confrontation on both sides. Where there are continuing sources of conflict (as in the case of the relation between unions and employers), new movements still tend to reemerge.

Touraine's analysis can also be applied to movements concerned primarily with individual change even though Touraine himself has said little about them. For instance, Alcoholics Anonymous is a movement based on medical findings about the harmful effects of alcohol on people's health and social activities. The movement itself has been shaped by its own opposition to advertising designed to encourage alcoholic drinking and by its attempt to confront the outside pressures faced by alcoholics in a society in which drinking is easily tolerated.

Feminist Movements

As we just saw, theories of revolution inevitably tend to overlap with those of social movements. Charles Tilly's emphasis on resource mobilization, for example, has been applied to social movements such as the feminist movement.

The first groups actively organized to promote women's rights date from the period immediately following the American and French Revolutions (Evans, 1977). In the 1790s, inspired by the ideals of freedom and equality for which the revolutions had been fought, several women's clubs were formed in Paris and major provincial cities. The clubs provided meeting places for women, but they also petitioned for equal rights in education, employment, and government. Marie Gouze, a leader of one of the clubs, drew up a statement entitled "Declaration of the Rights of Women," based on the "Declaration of the Rights of Man and the Citizen," the main constitutional document of the French Revolution. How could true equality be achieved, she argued, when half the population was excluded from the privileges that men share?

The response from the male revolutionary leaders was less than sympathetic—Marie Gouze was executed in 1793, charged with "having forgotten the virtues which belong to her sex." The women's clubs were subsequently dissolved by government decree. Feminist groups and women's movements have been formed repeatedly in Western countries since that date, almost always encountering hostility, and sometimes provoking violence, from the established authorities. Marie Gouze was by no means the only feminist to give her life to the cause of achieving equal rights for her sex.

In the nineteenth century, feminism became more advanced in the United States than elsewhere, and most leaders of women's movements in other countries looked to the struggles of American women as a model. In the 1840s and 1850s, American feminists were closely involved with groups devoted to the abolition of slavery. Yet, having no formal political rights (the Constitution did not give women the right to vote), women were excluded from the political lobbying through which reformers could pursue their objectives. No women were allowed to take part in a world antislavery convention held in London in 1840. This fact led the women's groups to turn more directly to considering gender inequalities. In 1848, just as their French counterparts had done a half century before, women leaders in the United States met to approve a "Declaration of Sentiments and Resolutions," modeled on the Declaration of Independence. "We hold these truths to be self-evident," it began, "that all men and women are created equal." The declaration set out a long list of the injustices to which women were subject (Hartman and Banner, 1974). However, few real gains in improving the social or political position of women were made during this period. When slavery ended, Congress ruled that only freed *male* slaves should be given the vote.

Some African American women played a part in the early development of the women's movement in the United States, although they often had to contend with hostility and racism from their white sisters. One, Sojourner Truth, spoke out against both slavery and the disenfranchisement of women, linking the two issues closely. When she forcefully and passionately addressed an antislavery rally in Indiana in the 1850s and a white man yelled at her, "I don't believe you really are a woman," she publicly bared her breasts to prove him wrong. Although Truth played a prominent part in women's struggles of the period (Hooks, 1981), other black women who tried to participate became disillusioned with the prejudice they encountered; African American feminists as a result were few in number.

One of the most important events in the early development of feminist movements in Europe was the presentation of a petition, signed by fifteen hundred women, to the British Parliament in 1866, demanding that the electoral reforms then being discussed include full voting rights for women. The petition was ignored; in response, its organizers set up the National Society for Women's Suffrage the following year. The members of the society became known as suffragettes, and throughout the remainder of the nineteenth century they continued to petition Parliament to extend voting rights to women. By the early twentieth century, the world influence of British feminism rivaled that of feminists in the United States. Frequent marches and street demonstrations were organized in both countries. An open-air meeting held in London in June 1908 attracted a crowd of half a million people. During this period, women's movements mushroomed in all the major European countries, together with Australia and New Zealand.

Emmeline Pankhurst, a leading suffragette, participated in several speaking tours of the United States, recounting the British struggles to large audiences. Two Americans who had become involved in the campaigns in Britain, Alice Paine and Harriet Stanton Blatch, organized massive marches and parades through New York and other eastern cities from 1910 onward.

By 1920, women had attained the right to vote in several Western countries (see Table 13.2). After achieving that right, though, most feminist movements in the United States and elsewhere fell into decline. Radical women tended to be absorbed into other movements, such as those combating fas-

The militant campaigner for female suffrage, Emmeline Pankhurst, and one of her daughters, are welcomed to a meeting of fellow suffragettes with banners and flowers.

cism, a political doctrine of the extreme right gaining ground in Germany, Italy, and elsewhere in the 1930s. Little was left of feminism as a distinct movement against male-dominated institutions. The achievement of equal political rights did little to extend quality to other spheres of women's lives.

THE RESURGENCE OF FEMINISM

In the late 1960s, women's movements again gained prominence (Chafe, 1974, 1977). Over the three decades since then, feminism has become a major influence in countries throughout the world, including many in the developing world. The resurgence began in the United States, influenced by the civil rights movement and by the student activism of the period. Women who were active in these causes often found themselves relegated by male activists to a traditionally subordinate role. Civil rights leaders were resistant to women's rights being included in their manifestos of equality. Hence, women's groups began to establish independent organizations concerned primarily with feminist issues.

The women's movement today in fact involves a variety of interest groups and organizations. Among the most prominent in the United States is the National Organization for Women (NOW), with more than a half million members (men as well as women, although the large majority are women). Another group is the National Women's Political Caucus (NWPC), which numbers about half the membership of NOW. Some organizations are concerned with single issues such as abortion, education, or pension rights. Yet other groups consist of women in various occupations, like the American Association of University Women.

TABLE 13.2

The Year in Which Women Achieved the Right to Vote on an Equal Basis with Men, by Country

1893	New Zealand	1946	Albania, Romania, Panama
1902	Australia	1947	Argentina, Venezuela
1906	Finland	1948	Israel, Korea
1913	Norway	1949	China, Chile
1915	Denmark, Iceland	1950	El Salvador, Ghana, India
1917	Soviet Union	1951	Nepal
1918	Canada	1952	Greece
1919	Austria, Germany, the Netherlands, Poland, Sweden, Luxembourg, Czechoslovakia	1953	Mexico
		1954	Colombia
1920	**United States**	1955	Nicaragua
1922	Ireland	1956	Egypt, Pakistan, Senegal
1928	Great Britain	1957	Lebanon
1929	Ecuador	1959	Morocco
1930	South Africa	1962	Algeria
1931	Spain, Sri Lanka, Portugal	1963	Iran, Kenya, Libya
1932	Thailand	1964	Sudan, Zambia
1934	Brazil, Cuba	1965	Afghanistan, Guatemala
1936	Costa Rica	1971	Switzerland
1937	Philippines	1977	Nigeria
1941	Indonesia	1979	Peru, Zimbabwe
1942	Dominican Republic, Uruguay		
1945	France, Hungary, Italy, Japan, Vietnam, Yugoslavia, Bolivia		

SOURCE: Lisa Tuttle, *Encyclopedia of Feminism* (New York: Facts on File, 1986).

FEMINIST MOVEMENTS: AN INTERPRETATION

The rise of women's movements over the past century can easily be interpreted in terms of the concepts set out by Charles Tilly. Social movements arise, Tilly argues, when people have no chance of making themselves heard or when they lack outlets for their aspirations. In the first phase of develop-

ment of feminist movements, in the nineteenth and early twentieth centuries, feminist leaders sought above all to *gain a voice* for women in the political process—in other words, to obtain the right to vote. In the second phase, women's movements sought to extend the gains they had achieved, fighting for economic as well as political equality for women.

In both phases, the leaders of women's movements were able to *mobilize collective resources* to place effective pressure on the governing authorities. During the early period, women activists' chief resource was mass marches and demonstrations. Later on, organizations (such as NOW) were able to fight for women's rights in a more consistent and organized way. The *common interests* to which women's group leaders have been able to appeal include the concern that women should have a role in political decision making, be able to engage in paid work if they wish, and have equal rights in divorce proceedings.

Finally, the *opportunity* of feminist activists to influence social change has been affected by a variety of factors. The outbreak of World War I, for example, helped in the aim of securing the vote: Governments fighting the war needed the support and active involvement of women in the war effort. In the second phase of the development of feminism, the civil rights movement was the spark that ignited a new wave of activism.

Social movements hold a double interest for sociologists. They provide subject matter for study, but more than this, they help shift the ways in which sociologists look at certain areas of behavior. The women's movement, for instance, is relevant to sociology not just because it provides material for research. It has identified weaknesses in established frameworks of sociological thought and developed concepts (such as that of patriarchy) that help us understand issues of gender and power. There is a continuing dialogue not only between social movements and the organizations, such as government, that they confront, but also between social movements and sociology itself.

Globalization and Social Movements

Social movements come in all shapes and sizes. Some are very small, numbering no more than a few dozen members; others may include thousands or even millions of people. Although some social movements carry on their activities within the laws of the society in which they exist, others operate as illegal or underground groups. It is characteristic of protest movements, however, that they operate near the margins of what is defined as legally permissible by governments at any particular time or place.

Social movements often arise with the aim of bringing about change on a public issue, such as expanding civil rights for a segment of the population. In response to social movements, countermovements sometimes arise in defense of the status quo. The campaign for women's right to abortion, for example, has been vociferously challenged by antiabortion ("prolife") activists, who believe that abortion should be illegal.

Often, laws or policies are altered as a result of the action of social movements. These changes in legislation can have far-ranging effects. For example, it used to be illegal for groups of workers to call their members out on strike, and striking was punished with varying degrees of severity in different countries. Eventually, however, the laws were amended, making the strike a permissible tactic of industrial conflict.

NEW SOCIAL MOVEMENTS

The last three decades have seen an explosion of social movements in countries around the globe. These various movements—ranging from the civil rights and feminist movements of the 1960s and 1970s to the antinuclear and ecological movements of the 1980s to the gay rights campaign of the 1990s—are often referred to by commentators as **new social movements**. This description seeks to differentiate contemporary social movements from those that preceded them in earlier decades. They are often concerned with the quality of private life as much as with political and economic issues, calling for large-scale changes in the way people think and act.

In other words, what makes new social movements "new" is that—unlike conventional social movements—they are not based on single-issue objectives that typically involve changes in the distribution of economic resources or power. Rather, they involve the creation of collective identities based around entire lifestyles, often calling for sweeping cultural changes. New social movements have emerged in recent years around issues such as ecology, peace, gender and sexual identity, gay and lesbian rights, women's rights, alternative medicine, and opposition to globalization.

Because new social movements involve new collective identities, they can provide a strong incentive for action. Social movements are always plagued by the "free-rider" problem—how can they motivate people to devote their time and resources, when they will benefit from the movement's success regardless of their personal involvement? With new social movements, however, participation is viewed as a moral obligation (and even a pleasure), rather than a calculated effort to achieve some specific goal. Moreover, the forms of protest chosen by new social movements are a form of "expressive logic" whereby participants make a statement about who they are: Protest is an end in itself, a way of affirming one's identity, as well as a means to achieving concrete objectives (Polletta and Jasper, 2001).

Many observers believe that new social movements are a unique product of late modern society and are profoundly different in their methods, motivations, and orientations from forms of collective action in earlier times.

The rise of new social movements in recent years is a reflection of the changing risks facing human societies. The conditions are ripe for social movements—increasingly traditional political institutions are unable to cope with the challenges before them. They find it impossible to respond creatively to the threats facing the natural environment, the potential dangers of nuclear energy and genetically modified organisms, and the powerful effects of information technology. Existing democratic political institutions cannot hope to fix these new problems. As a result, these unfolding challenges are frequently ignored or avoided until it is too late and a full-blown crisis is at hand.

The cumulative effect of these new challenges and risks is a sense that people are losing control of their lives in the midst of rapid change. Individuals feel less secure and more isolated—a combination that leads to a sense of powerlessness. By contrast, corporations, governments, and the media appear to be dominating more and more aspects of people's lives, heightening the sensation of a runaway world. There is a growing sense that left to its own logic, globalization will present ever-greater risks to citizens' lives.

Although faith in traditional politics seems to be waning, the growth of new social movements is evidence that citizens in late modern societies are not apathetic or uninterested in politics, as is sometimes claimed. Rather, there is a belief that direct action and participation is more useful than reliance on politicians and political systems. More than ever before, people are supporting social movements as a way of highlighting complex moral issues and putting them at the center of social life. In this respect, new social movements are helping to revitalize democracy in many countries. They are at the heart of a strong civic culture or **civil society**—the sphere between the state and the marketplace occupied by family, community associations, and other noneconomic institutions.

Technology and Social Movements

In recent years, two of the most influential forces in late modern societies—information technology and social movements—have come together, with astonishing results. In our current information age, social movements around the globe are able to join together in huge regional and international networks comprising nongovernmental organizations, religious and humanitarian groups, human rights associations, consumer protection advocates, environmental activists, and others who campaign in the public interest. These electronic networks now have the unprecedented ability to respond immediately to events as they occur, to gain access to and share sources of information, and to put pressure on corporations, governments, and international bodies as part of their campaigning strategies. The enormous protests against the World Trade Organization that took place in Seattle, Prague, and Genoa, for example, were organized in large part through Internet-based networks. And, as we saw earlier, Web-based organizations such as MoveOn.org played an influential role in the anti–Iraq war movement.

The Internet has been at the forefront of these changes, although mobile phones, fax machines, and satellite broadcasting have also hastened their evolution. With the press of a button, local stories are disseminated internationally. Grassroots activists from Japan to Bolivia can meet online to share informational resources, exchange experiences, and coordinate joint action.

This last dimension—the ability to coordinate international political campaigns—is the most worrisome for governments and the most inspiring to participants in social movements. In the last decade, the number of international social movements has grown steadily with the spread of the Internet. From global protests in favor of canceling Third World debt to the international campaign to ban land mines (which culminated in a Nobel Peace Prize), the Internet has proved its ability to unite campaigners across national and cultural borders. Some observers argue that the information age is witnessing a migration of power away from nation-states into new nongovernmental alliances and coalitions.

There are reasons to think that social movements have indeed been radically transformed in recent years. Manuel Castells, in *The Power of Identity* (1997), examines the cases of three social movements that, while completely dissimilar in their concerns and objectives, have all attracted international attention to their cause through the effective use of information technology. The Mexican Zapatista rebels, the American "militia" movement, the Japanese Aum Shinrikyo cult, and al Qaeda have all used media skills in order to spread their message of opposition to the effects of globalization and to express their anger at losing control over their own destinies.

According to Castells, each of these movements relies on information technologies as its organizational infrastructure. Without the Internet, for example, the Zapatista rebels would remain an isolated guerrilla movement in southern Mexico. Instead, within hours of their armed uprising in January 1994, local, national, and international support groups had emerged online to promote the cause of the rebels and to condemn the Mexican government's brutal repression of the rebellion. The Zapatistas used telecommunications, videos, and media interviews to voice their objections to trade policies, such as the North American Free Trade Agreement (NAFTA), that further exclude impoverished Indians of the Oaxaca and Chiapas areas from the benefits of globalization. Because their cause was thrust to the forefront of the online networks of social campaigners, the Zapatistas were able to force negotiations with the Mexican government and to draw international intention to the harmful effects of free trade on indigenous populations.

The Antisweatshop Movement

"We have the university by the balls," said Nati Passow, a University of Pennsylvania junior, in a meeting with his fellow antisweatshop protestors. "Whatever way we twist them is going to hurt." Passow was one of thirteen Penn students—the group later grew to include forty—occupying the university president's office around the clock in early February [2000] to protest the sweatshop conditions under which clothing bearing the U-Penn logo is made. The Penn students, along with hundreds of other members of United Students Against Sweatshops nationwide, were demanding that their university withdraw from the Fair Labor Association (FLA), an industry-backed monitoring group, and instead join the Worker Rights Consortium (WRC), an organization independent of industry influence, founded by students in close cooperation with scholars, activists and workers'-rights organizations in the global south.

At first the administration met the students with barely polite condescension. In one meeting, President Judith Rodin was accompanied by U-Penn professor Larry Gross, an earring-wearing baby boomer well known on campus for his left-wing views, who urged the protesters to have more faith in the administration and mocked the sit-in strategy, claiming he'd "been there, done that." President Rodin assured them that a task force would review the problem by February 29, and there was no way she could speed up its decision. She admonished them to "respect the process."

Watching the Penn students negotiate with this university's president, it was clear they didn't believe any of her assurances. They knew there was no reason to trust that the administration would meet one more arbitrary deadline after missing so many others—so they stayed in the office. After eight days of torture by folk-singing, acoustic guitar, recorders, tambourines and ringing cell phones, as well as a flurry of international news coverage, Judith Rodin met the protesters halfway by withdrawing from the FLA. (To students' frustration, the task force decided in early April to postpone a decision about WRC membership until later [that] spring.)

The most remarkable thing about the Penn students' action was that it wasn't an isolated or spontaneous burst of idealism. Penn's was just the first antisweatshop sit-in of the year; by mid-April students at the universities of Michigan, Wisconsin, Oregon, Iowa and Kentucky, as well as SUNY-Albany, Tulane, Purdue and Macalester had followed suit. And the sit-in wasn't the protesters' only tactic: Purdue students held an eleven-day hunger strike. The protests were a coordinated effort; members of United Students Against Sweatshops (USAS), which was founded three years ago and now has chapters at more than 200 schools, work closely with one another, a process made easier by the many listservs and Web sites that the students use to publicize actions, distribute information and help fuel turnout.

Though the largest, most successful—and before Seattle, the most visible—thread of the movement has focused on improving work conditions in the $2.5 billion collegiate apparel industry, university licensing policies have not been the only targets of recent anticorporate agitation on campus. This year, from UC-Davis to the University of Vermont, students have held globalization teach-ins, planned civil disobedience for the April IMF/World Bank meetings, protested labor policies at the Gap and launched vigorous campaigns to drive Starbucks out of university dining services. Students at Johns Hopkins and at Wesleyan held sit-ins demanding better wages for university workers. And at the end of March hundreds of students, many bearing hideously deformed papier-mâché puppets to illustrate the potential horrors of biotechnology, joined Boston's carnivalesque protest against genetic engineering.

With a *joie de vivre* that the American economic left has probably lacked since before WWI, college students are increasingly engaged in well-organized, thoughtful and morally outraged resistance to corporate power. These activists, more than any student radicals in years, passionately denounce the wealth gap, globally and in the United States, as well as the lack of democratic accountability in a world dominated by corporations. While some attend traditionally political schools like Evergreen, Michigan and Wisconsin, this movement does not revolve around usual suspects; some of this winter's most dramatic actions took place at campuses that have always been conservative, like the University of Pennsylvania, Virginia Commonwealth and Johns Hopkins. . . . It is neither too soon, nor too naïvely optimistic, to call it a movement.

SOURCE: Liza Featherstone, "The New Student Movement," *The Nation*, May 15, 2000.

Questions

- Many antisweatshop activists view their protests as a political and moral crusade. Do you agree with them that morals and politics should influence economic behavior? How does this affect your understanding of the study of sociology?
- What techniques did the students use to present their point of view? How did media coverage influence their methods of political protest?
- The students involved in these protests attend prestigious schools, for the most part. How does their membership in an elite group complicate their response to the issue of globalization and its discontents?

Nationalist Movements

Some of the most important social movements in the contemporary world are nationalist movements. The sociological thinkers of the nineteenth and early twentieth centuries displayed little interest in or concern with nationalism. Marx and Durkheim saw nationalism as above all a destructive tendency and believed that the increasing economic integration produced by modern industry would cause its rapid decline. Only Max Weber spent much time analyzing nationalism or was prepared to declare himself a nationalist. But even Weber failed to estimate the importance that nationalism and the idea of the nation would have in the twentieth century.

At the start of the twenty-first century, nationalism is not only alive, but—in some parts of the world at least—flourishing. Although the world has become more interdependent, especially over the past thirty or forty years, this interdependence has not spelled the end of nationalism. In some respects it has probably even helped to intensify it. Recent thinkers have come up with contrasting ideas about why this is so. There are also disagreements about the stage of history at which nationalism, the nation, and the nation-state came into being. Some say they have much earlier origins than others.

NATIONALISM AND MODERN SOCIETY

Perhaps the leading theorist of nationalism is Ernest Gellner (1925–1995). Gellner argues that nationalism, the nation, and the nation-state are all products of modern civilization, whose origins lie in the industrial revolution of the late eighteenth century. He claims that nationalism and the feelings or sentiments associated with it do not have deep roots in human nature—they are the products of the new large-scale society that industrialism creates. According to Gellner, nationalism as such is unknown in traditional societies, as is the idea of the nation (1983).

Several features of modern societies have led to the emergence of these phenomena. First, a modern industrial society is associated with rapid economic development and a complex division of labor. Gellner points out that modern industrialism creates the need for a much more effective system of state and government than existed before. Second, in the modern state, individuals must interact all the time with strangers, since the basis of society is no longer the local village or town, but a very much larger unit. Mass education, based on an official language taught in the schools, is the main means whereby a large-scale society can be organized and kept unified.

Gellner's theory has been criticized in more than one respect. It is a functionalist theory, critics say, that argues that education functions to produce social unity. As with the functionalist approach more generally, this view tends to underestimate the role of education in producing conflict and division. Gellner's theory does not really explain the passions that nationalism can, and often does, arouse. The power of nationalism is probably related not just to education but to its capacity to create an *identity* for people—something that individuals cannot live without.

The need for identity is certainly not just born with the emergence of modern industrial society. Critics therefore argue that Gellner is wrong to separate nationalism and the nation so strongly from premodern times. Nationalism is in some ways quite modern, but it also draws on sentiments and forms of symbolism that go back much further into the past. According to one of the best-known current scholars of nationalism, Anthony Smith, nations tend to have direct lines of continuity with earlier ethnic communities, or what he calls "ethnies." An **ethnie** is a group that shares ideas of common ancestry, a common cultural identity, and a link with a specific homeland.

Many nations, Smith points out, do have premodern continuities, and at previous periods of history there have been ethnic communities that resemble nations. The Jews, for example, have formed a distinct ethnie for more than two thousand years. At certain periods, Jews clustered in communities that had some of the characteristics of nations. But only following World War II were all of these elements brought together in the form of the nation-state of Israel. Like most other nation-states, Israel was not formed from just a single ethnie. The Palestinian minority in Israel traces its origins to a quite different ethnic background and claims that the creation of the Israeli state has displaced the Palestinians from their ancient homelands—hence their persistent tensions with Jews in Israel, the tensions between Israel and most surrounding Arab states, and the tragic violence and fighting between Palestinians and Israelis that has escalated in the new years of the twenty-first century.

Different nations have followed divergent patterns of development in relation to ethnies. In some, including most of the nations of Western Europe, a single ethnie expanded so as to push out earlier rivals. Thus, in France in the seventeenth century, several other languages were spoken and different ethnic histories were linked to them. As French became the dominant language, most of these rivals subsequently disappeared. Yet remnants of them persist in a few areas. One is the Basque country overlapping the French and Spanish frontiers. The Basque language is quite different from either French or Spanish, and the Basques claim a separate cultural history of their own. Some Basques want their own nation-state, completely separate from France and Spain. Although there has been nothing like the level of violence seen in other areas—such as East Timor, or Chechnya in southern Russia—separatist groups in the Basque country have sporadically used bombing campaigns to further their goal of independence.

NATIONS WITHOUT STATES

The persistence of well-defined ethnies within established nations leads to the phenomenon of **nations without states**. In these situations, many of the essential characteristics of the nation are present, but those who make up the nation lack an independent political community. Separatist movements such as those in Chechnya and the Basque country, as well as those in many other areas of the world—such as in Kashmir in northern India—are driven by the desire to set up an autonomous, self-governing state.

Several different types of nations without states can be recognized, depending on the relationship between the ethnie and the larger nation-state in which its exists (Guibernau, 1999):

1. In some situations, a nation-state may accept the cultural differences among its minority or minorities and allow them a certain amount of active development. Thus, in Great Britain, Scotland and Wales are recognized as having histories and cultural features partly divergent from the rest of the United Kingdom, and to some extent they have their own institutions. The majority of Scots, for instance, are Presbyterians, and Scotland has long had a separate educational system from that of England and Wales. Scotland and Wales achieved further autonomy within the United Kingdom as a whole with the setting up of a Scottish Parliament and a Welsh Assembly in 1999.

2. Some nations without states have a higher degree of autonomy. In Quebec (the French-speaking province of Canada) and Flanders (the Dutch-speaking area in the north of the Netherlands), regional political bodies have the power to make major decisions, without actually being fully independent. As in the cases mentioned under the previous point, they also contain nationalist movements agitating for complete independence.

3. On the other hand, some nations that more or less completely lack recognition from the state that contains them. In such cases, the larger nation-state uses force in order to deny recognition to the minority. The Palestinians are a clear example of such a group (although some would argue that their isolated acts of terrorism and violence against Israelis have encouraged the Israeli army's show of force). Others include the Tibetans in China and the Kurds, whose homeland overlaps parts of Turkey, Syria, Iran, and Iraq.

NATIONS AND NATIONALISM IN DEVELOPING COUNTRIES

In most of the countries of the developing world, the course followed by nationalism, the nation, and the nation-state has been different compared with the industrial societies. Most less-developed countries were once colonized by Europeans and achieved independence at some point in the second half of the twentieth century. In many of these countries, boundaries between colonial administrations were agreed upon arbitrarily in Europe and did not take into account existing economic, cultural, or ethnic divisions among the population. The colonial powers defeated or subjugated the kingdoms and tribal groupings existing on the African subcontinent, in India, and in other parts of Asia, and set up their own colonial administrations or protectorates. As a consequence, each colony was "a collection of peoples and old states, or fragments of these, brought together within the same boundaries" (Akintoye, 1976). Most colonized areas contained a mosaic of ethnies and other groups.

When former colonies achieved their independence, they often found it difficult to create a sense of nationhood and national belonging. Although nationalism played a great part in securing the independence of colonized areas, it was largely confined to small groups of activists. Nationalist ideas did not influence the majority of the population. Even today many postcolonial states are continually threatened by internal rivalries and competing claims to political authority.

The continent that was most completely colonized was Africa. Nationalist movements promoting independence in Africa following World War II sought to free the colonized areas from European domination. Once this had been achieved, the new leaders everywhere faced enormous problems in trying to create national unity. Many of the leaders in the 1950s and 1960s had been educated in Europe or the United States, and there was a vast gulf between them and their citizens, most of whom were illiterate, poor, and unfamiliar with the rights and obligations of democracy. Under colonialism, some ethnic groups had prospered more than others; these groups had different interests and goals and legitimately saw each other as enemies.

Civil wars broke out in a number of postcolonial states in Africa, such as Sudan, Zaire, and Nigeria, while ethnic rivalries and antagonisms characterized many others both in Africa and Asia. In the case of Sudan, about 40 percent of the population spoke Arabic and claimed Arabic ethnic origins. In other regions of the country, particularly in the south, Arabic was barely spoken at all. Once the nationalists took power, they set up a program for national integration based on Arabic as the national language. The attempt was only partly successful, and the stresses and strains it produced are still visible. The severe problems faced by much of the African continent are a direct result of difficulties like these.

The ongoing civil war in Sudan has displaced more than 4 million people. Some fled to southern cities, such as Juba; others trekked as far north as Khartoum and even into Ethiopia, Kenya, Uganda, Egypt, and other neighboring countries. These refugees were unable to grow food or earn money to feed themselves, and malnutrition and starvation became widespread. The lack of investment in the south also resulted in what international humanitarian organizations call a "lost generation" who lack educational opportunities, access to basic health care services, and few prospects for productive employment in the small and weak economies of the south and the north.

In summary, most states in the developing world came into being as a result of different processes of nation formation from those that occurred in the industrialized world. States were imposed externally on areas that often had no prior cultural or ethnic unity. These problems are everywhere proving difficult to overcome. Modern nations have arisen most effectively either in areas that were never fully colonized or where there was already a great deal of cultural unity—such as Japan, Korea, and Thailand.

The Nation-State, National Identity, and Globalization

In some parts of Africa, nations and nation-states are not as yet fully formed. Yet in other areas of the world, some writers are already speaking of the "end of the nation-state" in the face of globalization. According to the Japanese writer Kenichi Ohmae, as a result of globalization we increasingly live in a borderless world in which national identity is becoming weaker (1995).

How valid is this point of view? All states are certainly being affected by globalizing processes. The very rise of "nations without states" is probably bound up with globalization. As globalization progresses, people often react by reviving local identities in an effort to achieve security in a rapidly changing world. Nations have less economic power of their own than they used to have, as a result of the spread of the global marketplace.

Yet it wouldn't be accurate to say that we are witnessing the end of the nation-state. In some ways the opposite is the case. Today every country in the world is a nation-state or aspires to be one; the nation-state has become a universal political form. Until quite recently it still had rivals. For most of the twentieth century, colonized areas and empires existed alongside nation-states. It is arguable that the last empire only disappeared in 1990 with the collapse of Soviet communism. The Soviet Union was effectively at the center of an empire embracing satellite states in Eastern Europe. Now all of these have become independent nation-states, as have many areas inside what was formerly the Soviet Union. There are actually far more sovereign nations in the world today than there were twenty-five years ago.

Study Outline

www.wwnorton.com/giddens5

Government and Power

- The term *government* refers to a political apparatus in which officials enact policies and make decisions. *Politics* refers to the use of power to affect government actions.
- *Power* is the capacity to achieve one's aims even against the resistance of others, and often involves the use of force. A government is said to have *authority* when its use of power is legitimate. Such legitimacy derives from the consent of those being governed. The most common form of legitimate government is democratic, but other legitimate forms are also possible.

The Concept of the State

- A *state* is characterized by a political apparatus (government institutions), including civil service officials, ruling over a geographically defined territory, and whose authority is backed by a legal system and that has the capacity to use force to implement policies.
- All modern states have certain additional features: *sovereignty*, the idea that government has authority over a given area; *citizenship*, the idea that people have common rights and duties and are aware of their part in the state; and *nationalism*, the sense of being part of a broader, unifying political community.
- Most nation-states became centralized through the activities of monarchs who concentrated social power. Citizens initially had few rights of political participation, or none at all; such rights were achieved only through a long process of struggle that continues to this day. *Civil rights* refer to the freedoms and privileges guaranteed to individuals by law. *Political rights* ensure that citizens may participate in politics (by voting, for example). *Social rights* guarantee every individual some minimum standard of living. Social rights are the basis for the *welfare state*, which supports citizens who are unable to support themselves.

Democracy

- The term *democracy* literally means rule by the people, but this phrase can be interpreted in various ways. For instance, "the people" has often really meant "adult male property owners," while "rule" might refer to government policies, administrative decisions, or both.

- Several different forms of democracy exist, including: *participatory democracy*, also called *direct democracy*, which occurs when everyone is immediately involved in all decision making, although this can be cumbersome for larger groups; *liberal democracy*, which is a system in which citizens have a choice to vote between at least two political parties for representatives who will be entrusted with decision making; and *constitutional monarchy*, which includes a royal family whose powers are severely restricted by a constitution, which puts authority in the hands of democratically elected representatives.

Democracy in the United States

- A political party is an organization oriented toward achieving legitimate control of government through an electoral process. There is usually some connection between voting patterns and class differences. In many Western countries there has recently been a decline in allegiance to traditional parties and a growing disenchantment with the party system in general.
- Women achieved the right to vote much later than men in all countries and continue to be poorly represented among political elites. They have been influential on social and civil rights issues, and most Western countries have passed equal rights legislation over recent years.

Who Rules?

- According to Weber and Schumpeter, the level of democratic participation that can be achieved in a modern, large-scale society is limited. The rule of *power elites* is inevitable, but multiparty systems provide the possibility of choosing *who* exercises power. The *pluralist theorists* add the claim that the competition of *interest groups* limits the degree to which ruling elites are able to concentrate power in few hands.
- The number of countries with democratic governments has rapidly increased in recent years, due in large part to the effects of globalization and mass communication and to the spread of competitive capitalism. But democracy is not without its problems; people everywhere have begun to lose faith in the capacity of politicians and governments to solve problems and to manage economies, and many no longer vote.
- *Revolution* is the overthrow of an existing political order by means of a mass movement, using violence. *Social movements*, by contrast, involve a collective attempt to further common interests through collaborative action outside the sphere of established institutions. The term *new social movements* is applied to a set of social movements that have arisen in Western countries since the 1960s in response to the changing risks facing human societies. Unlike earlier social movements, new social movements are single-issue cam-

paigns oriented to nonmaterial ends and draw support from across class lines. Information technology has become a powerful organizing tool for many new social movements.

Theories of Revolution and Social Movements

- Theories of social movements and revolutions overlap. Marx argued that class struggles deriving from the *contradictions*, or unresolvable tensions within society, lead to revolutionary changes. James Davies argues that social movements occur from *relative deprivation*, a discrepancy between the lives people actually lead and what people believe to be possible. Charles Tilly analyzes revolutionary change from a broader context of *collective action*, which refers to action taken to contest or overthrow an existing social order. Collective action culminating in social movements progresses from organization, mobilization, the perception of common interests, and finally the opportunity to act. For Tilly, social movements occur in circumstances of *multiple sovereignty*, a situation in which the government lacks full control.
- Neil Smelser's theory treats social movements as responses to situations, which undergo a series of stages. Alain Touraine argues that social movements rest on *historicity*, which is the idea that people know that social activism can shape history and affect society. Social movements occur in *fields of action*, which refers to the connection between a movement and the forces acting against it.
- Social movements provide not only a subject of study for sociologists; they also challenge the established frameworks of thought of sociology (e.g., the impact of the women's movement on the study of gender).

Nationalism

- Nationalism refers to a set of symbols and beliefs that provide the sense of being part of a single political community. It emerged alongside the development of the modern state. Although the founders of sociology believed that nationalism would disappear in industrial societies, at the start of the twenty-first century it seems to be flourishing. *Nations without states* refer to cases in which a national group lacks political sovereignty over the area it claims as its own.

Key Concepts

authority (p. 372)
citizen (p. 373)
civil rights (p. 373)
civil society (p. 401)
collective action (p. 394)

communism (p. 377)

constitutional monarchy (p. 377)

democracy (p. 377)

democratic elitism (p. 387)

direct democracy (p. 377)

ethnie (p. 404)

field of action (p. 397)

government (p. 372)

historicity (p. 397)

interest group (p. 383)

legitimation crisis (p. 390)

liberal democracy (p. 377)

local nationalisms (p. 373)

multiple sovereignty (p. 395)

nation-state (p. 372)

nationalism (p. 373)

nations without states (p. 405)

new social movements (p. 400)

participatory democracy (p. 377)

pluralist theories of modern democracy (p. 387)

political rights (p. 373)

politics (p. 372)

power (p. 372)

power elite (p. 388)

relative deprivation (p. 394)

revolution (p. 391)

social movement (p. 391)

social rights (p. 373)

sovereignty (p. 372)

state (p. 372)

state overload (p. 390)

structural strain (p. 396)

welfare state (p. 373)

Review Questions

1. What is the difference between politics and government?
   a. There is none.
   b. Politics involves the exercise of power in regard to the actions of government, whereas government is concerned with the enactment of policies, decisions, and matters of state.
   c. Politics involves the government's legitimate use of power, whereas government is concerned with the way power is used to influence the state's activities.
   d. Politics involves the enactment of policies, decisions, and matters of state, whereas government is concerned with the exercise of power in regard to the actions of government.

2. What is the difference between power and authority?
   a. Power is a Marxist concept, whereas authority is a Weberian concept.
   b. Power is the ability of individuals or groups to make their interests count, even in the face of opposition from others, whereas authority is the use of power by government where the exercise of that power is seen as legitimate by those who are subject to it.
   c. Power is the ability to spend money to solve a problem, whereas authority is the respect a person is accorded by others.
   d. Power is the use of power by government where the exercise of that power is seen as legitimate by those who are subject to it, whereas authority is the ability of individuals or groups to make their interests count, even in the face of opposition from others.

3. What was Max Weber's theory of democracy?
   a. Democratic elitism
   b. Pluralism
   c. The power elite
   d. The "iron law of oligarchy"

4. What are the three rights associated with the growth of citizenship?
   a. Civil, political, and social rights
   b. Civil, voting, and welfare rights
   c. Civil, social, and economic rights
   d. Civil, human, and animal rights

5. When and why did women win the vote in most Western countries?
   a. The vote was given to women in the general wave of social reforms that followed World War II.
   b. The vote was won through the efforts of the suffragist movement and as a consequence of women's mobilization in World War I.
   c. Voting rights were accorded to women, as well as to blacks, in the Voting Rights Act of 1965.
   d. Women were allowed to vote as a result of their increased participation in the economy and their increasing economic independence from men.

6. In 1998 women made up 13 percent of the membership of the House of Representatives and 9 percent of the Senate. Why has women's participation in the higher echelons of the American political system remained so modest?
   a. Women are running for office in larger numbers than ever, but voters are not electing them to office because the majority still regard politics as a "man's game."
   b. The political parties (which are largely run by men) have not recruited many women to run for high political office.
   c. Women are being elected to lower offices, but more of them need to work their way up through the seniority system before they are given the chance to run for the House or Senate.
   d. Female candidates find it harder to raise money than male candidates.

7. In the 1990s, the United States and various governments in Europe passed immigration laws that attempt to use citizenship as a tool of social closure. What does this mean?
   a. Governments have set up immigration criteria in an effort to attract the most educated immigrants and exclude the least educated.

b. An increasing number of governments have tried to get all their citizens to register with a national identity-card system.

c. Governments have sought to exclude poor migrants from the status and benefits that full citizenship confers.

d. Conservative politicians have attempted to use immigration as a wedge to divide constituencies that would normally support their liberal or social democratic opponents.

8. What is liberal democracy and where can it be found in the modern world?

a. It is a nation-state where most adults have the right to vote and where two or more parties are involved in competitive elections. Generally, these conditions are found in the developed world, although some Third World countries have liberal democracies.

b. It is a political system that has a large established and competitive liberal or social democratic party that is in a position to effect the composition of government. Some nations—for example, Mexico and Ireland—have no liberal or social democratic party and are therefore not liberal democracies.

c. It is a nation-state whose constitution formally commits its government to the preservation of human rights. These conditions are found all over the world but are not always observed.

d. It is a political system in which there has been an alternation of power between parties. This is regarded as a crucial test of the robustness of a democracy and did not occur in some democracies in developed nations—such as Italy and Japan—before the 1980s.

9. What is the theory of relative deprivation?

a. Social movements go through four stages of collective action: organization, mobilization, dissemination of common interests, and seizing on opportunities to further the cause.

b. It is not absolute deprivation that leads to protest but comparison of present living standards with those of the upper class.

c. It is not absolute deprivation that leads to protest but relative deprivation—the discrepancy between the lives people are forced to lead and what they think could realistically be achieved.

d. It is not absolute deprivation that leads to protest but comparison of one's living standards with those of the more fortunate members of one's family.

10. Which two thinkers were responsible for "structural strain" theory and "fields of action" theory?

a. Neil Smelser and Alain Touraine
b. Mary Hartman and Lois Banner
c. Charles Tilly and Theda Skocpol
d. William Chafe and David Aberle

11. Kenichi Ohmae argues that as a result of globalization we increasingly live in a "borderless world." What does he mean by "borderless world"?

a. The world has no geographic boundary.
b. National identity is becoming weaker.
c. The Internet makes it possible to travel across national boundaries.
d. Globalization reduces the need for obtaining visas when visiting other countries.

Thinking Sociologically Exercises

1. Discuss the differences between the "pluralistic" and the "power elite" theories of democratic political processes. Which theory do you find most appropriate to describe U.S. politics in recent years?

2. Your textbook offers a variety of explanations on the formation of social movements. Briefly review the predisposing conditions for social movements and then discuss their relevance in the development of the feminist social movement in the United States.

Data Exercises

www.wwnorton.com/giddens5
Keyword: Data13

• In the data exercise for this chapter you will learn more about the patterns of political participation. Did you know that more people are registered to vote today than 30 years ago, but fewer do? As you work through the exercise think about who is opting out of participation and why they are.

PART FOUR

SOCIAL INSTITUTIONS

Social institutions are the "cement" of social life. They are the basic living arrangements that human beings work out with one another, by means of which continuity is achieved across the generations.

We begin in Chapter 14 with work and economic life. Although the nature of work varies widely both within and between societies, it is one of the most pervasively important of all human pursuits.

In Chapter 15, we look at the institutions of kinship, marriage, and the family. Although the social obligations associated with kinship vary between different types of societies, the family is everywhere the context within which the young are provided with care and protection. Marriage is more or less universally connected to the family, since it is a means of establishing new kin connections and forming a household in which children are brought up. In traditional cultures, much of the direct learning a child receives occurs within the family context. In modern societies, children spend many years of their lives in special places of instruction outside the family—schools and colleges. They also are constantly fed images and information from the mass media. Chapter 16 looks at the ways in which formal education is organized, concentrating particularly on how the educational system relates to the mass media.

The subject of Chapter 17 is religion. Although religious beliefs and practices are found in all cultures, the changes affecting religion in modern societies have been particularly acute. We analyze the nature of these changes, considering in what ways traditional types of religion still maintain their influence.

The Social Significance of Work

Assess the sociological ramifications of paid and unpaid work.

The Social Organization of Work

Understand that modern economies are based on the division of labor and economic interdependence. Learn Marx's theory of alienation. Familiarize yourself with modern systems of economic production.

The Modern Economy

See the importance of the rise of large corporations; consider particularly the global impact of transnational corporations.

The Changing Nature of Work

Learn about the impact of global economic competition on employment. Consider how work will change over the coming years.

CHAPTER FOURTEEN

WORK AND ECONOMIC LIFE

1ike many auto factories around the country, the GM assembly plant in Linden, New Jersey, confronted new challenges beginning in the 1980s (Milkman, 1997). The plant, founded in 1937 to build Cadillacs, was a top-of-the-line operation that offered blue-collar workers salaries and benefits that were among the best in any industry. The emergence of a competitive auto industry, first in Japan and later in South Korea, threatened the GM system by producing high-quality cars at a lower cost than was possible in the United States. In the mid-1980s, GM responded to these pressures by reorganizing the plant in Linden and introducing robots and organizational innovations borrowed from the Japanese, such as "just-in-time" inventory systems. The plant also switched from producing luxury vehicles to producing small cars, a shift that resulted in significant numbers of job cuts in the plant. GM negotiated a plan with the United Auto Workers' (UAW) union that offered cash payments to workers who voluntarily agreed to leave their jobs at GM.

Edward Salermo is a former GM employee who in 1987 accepted the company's offer to give up his job, after working at the plant for eight years. Salermo had grown up in Linden, and his father had worked at GM before him. He was never really happy with his job at GM—he had aspirations of finding a more challenging occupation—but was lured by the salary he could make on the production line when he was hired just out of high school. Consistent with these aspirations, Salermo took courses while he was laid off from GM during the year-long reorganization of the plant. He hoped that the electronics training he acquired would allow him to return to a spot in a more skilled position fixing the new robotics. After the plant reopened, however, GM made it clear that they would rehire Salermo only as a production worker. Salermo decided to take the buyout offer, equivalent to a year's pay, about $30,000. Salermo used the money to go back to school to study computer programming. He was hired at a new job installing business telephone systems but was laid off after a few months. He then found his current job, working on payroll for a large insurance company. While he is happier at this current job than he was at GM—it is, he reports, a much less conflictual work environment—he is attempting to further improve his prospects by attending night school to obtain an associate's degree in computer science. "If something else came along, I would take it," he remarks (Milkman, 1997).

Faced with a similar decision, Susan Roberts decided to keep her job at the newly reorganized GM plant in Linden. She was tempted to take GM's offer to leave, as she could have used the buyout money for the down payment on a house, but she did not have another job. Instead, along with three thousand of her coworkers, she returned to GM for a two-week retraining program. Much had changed in the organization of the plant. For one, workers were instructed to "build the car in the station," meaning that if they found a defect, they were to stop the line and correct the problem immediately, rather than just noting the defect for another worker to fix it somewhere down the line. For another, GM adopted the Japanese just-in-time inventory system, based on the tight coordination of parts delivered by suppliers just as they were needed, rather than stockpiling the parts in the factory. Finally, workers were encouraged to participate more in decision making and problem solving in the day-to-day operations of the plant.

Roberts was excited about many of these changes, as she felt that GM was finally taking the Japanese challenge seriously, giving the U.S. auto industry a chance of regaining its competitive edge. She was so enthusiastic about the new direction of the Linden plant that she even volunteered to take a leadership role in the newly introduced Employee Involvement Groups (EIG), an innovation that GM hoped would facilitate communication between workers and management about production and quality problems. But her enthusiasm soon waned. One reason is that Roberts discovered that stopping the line at each station to correct problems as they occurred created conflicts with workers farther down the line, who would immediately want to know why the line had stopped and become angry at the interruption. The EIG program was also a disappointment, as management was slow to implement suggestions made by workers (Milkman, 1997).

The challenges faced by workers such as Edward Salermo and Susan Roberts are illustrative of dilemmas encountered by workers in many industries since the 1970s, as the organization of work and the economy has changed. In this chapter we examine these changes and try to place them in sociological perspective.

Work may be defined as carrying out tasks that require the expenditure of mental and physical effort, which has as its objective the production of goods and services that cater to human needs. An **occupation**, or job, is work that is done in exchange for a regular wage, or salary. In all cultures, work is the basis of the economic system, or economy. The **economy** consists of institutions that provide for the production and distribution of goods and services.

The study of economic institutions is of major importance in sociology, because the economy influences all segments of society and therefore social reproduction in general. Hunting and gathering, pastoralism, agriculture, industrialism—these different ways of gaining a livelihood have a fundamental influence on the lives people lead. The distribution of goods and variations in the economic position of those who produce them also strongly influence social inequalities of all kinds. Wealth and power do not inevitably go together, but in general the privileged in terms of wealth are also among the more powerful groups in a society.

In this chapter, we will analyze the nature of work in modern societies and look at the major changes affecting economic life today. We will investigate the changing nature of industrial production, the ownership structure of large business corporations, and the changing nature of work itself. Modern industry, as has been stressed in other parts of this book, differs in a fundamental way from premodern systems of production, which were based above all on agriculture. Most people worked in the fields or cared for livestock. In modern societies, by contrast, only a tiny proportion of the population works in agriculture, and farming itself has become industrialized—it is carried on largely by means of machines rather than by human hands.

Modern industry is itself always changing—technological change is one of its main features. **Technology** refers to the harnessing of science to machinery to achieve greater productive efficiency. The nature of industrial production also changes in relation to wider social and economic influences. In this chapter, we focus on both technological and economic change, showing how these are transforming industry today.

We will also see that globalization makes a great deal of difference to our working lives; the nature of the work we do is being changed by forces of global economic competition.

The Social Significance of Work

To tackle these issues, we need to relate work to the broad contours of our society and to industrial organization as a whole. We often associate the notion of work with drudgery—with a set of tasks that we want to minimize and, if possible, escape from altogether. You may have this very thought in mind as you set out to read this chapter! Is this most people's attitude toward their work, and if so, why? We will try to find out in the following pages.

Work has more going for it than drudgery, or people would not feel so lost and disoriented when they become unemployed. How would you feel if you thought you would never get a job? In modern societies, having a job is important for maintaining self-esteem. Even where work conditions are relatively unpleasant, and the tasks involved dull, work tends to be a structuring element in people's psychological makeup and the cycle of their daily activities. Several characteristics of work are relevant here.

- MONEY. A wage or salary is the main resource many people depend on to meet their needs. Without such an income, anxieties about coping with day-to-day life tend to multiply.
- ACTIVITY LEVEL. Work often provides a basis for the acquisition and exercise of skills and capacities. Even where work is routine, it offers a structured environment in which a person's energies may be absorbed. Without it, the opportunity to exercise such skills and capacities may be reduced.
- VARIETY. Work provides access to contexts that contrast with domestic surroundings. In the working environment, even when the tasks are relatively dull, individuals may enjoy doing something different from home chores.
- TEMPORAL STRUCTURE. For people in regular employment, the day is usually organized around the rhythm of work. Although work may sometimes be oppressive, it provides a sense of direction in daily activities. Those who are out of work frequently find boredom a major problem and develop a sense of apathy about time. As one unemployed man remarked, "Time doesn't matter now as much as it used to. . . . There's so much of it" (Fryer and McKenna, 1987).
- SOCIAL CONTACTS. The work environment often provides friendships and opportunities to participate in shared activities with others. Separated from the work setting, a person's circle of possible friends and acquaintances is likely to dwindle.
- PERSONAL IDENTITY. Work is usually valued for the sense of stable social identity it offers. For men in particular, self-esteem is often bound up with the economic contribution they make to the maintenance of the household. In addition, job conditions, such as the opportunity to work in jobs that are challenging, not routinized, and not subject to close supervision, are known to affect a person's sense of self-worth (Kohn, 1977).

Against the backdrop of this formidable list, it is not difficult to see why being without work may undermine individuals' confidence in their social value.

Unpaid Work

We often tend to think of work, as the notion of being "out of work" implies, as equivalent to having a paid job, but in fact this is an oversimplified view. Nonpaid labor (such as repairing one's own car or doing one's own housework) looms large in many people's lives. Many types of work do not conform to orthodox categories of paid employment. Much of the work done in the informal economy, for example, is not recorded in any direct way in the official employment statistics. The term **informal economy** refers to transactions outside the sphere of regular employment, sometimes involving the exchange of cash for services provided, but also often involving the direct exchange of goods or services.

Someone who comes to fix the television may be paid in cash, "off the books," without any receipt being given or details of the job recorded. People may exchange pilfered or stolen goods with friends or associates in return for other favors. The informal economy includes not only "hidden" cash transactions, but many forms of *self-provisioning* that people carry on inside and outside the home. Do-it-yourself activities and household appliances and tools, for instance, provide goods and services that would otherwise have to be purchased (Gershuny and Miles, 1983).

Housework, which has traditionally mostly been carried out by women, is usually unpaid. But it is work, often very hard and exhausting work, nevertheless. Volunteer work, for charities or other organizations, has an important social role. Having a paid job is important for all the reasons listed above—but the category of "work" stretches more widely.

The Social Organization of Work

One of the most distinctive characteristics of the economic system of modern societies is the existence of a highly complex **division of labor:** Work has become divided into an enormous number of different occupations in which people specialize. In traditional societies, nonagricultural work entailed the mastery of a craft. Craft skills were learned through a lengthy period of apprenticeship, and the worker normally carried out all aspects of the production process from beginning to end. For example, a metalworker making a plow would forge the iron, shape it, and assemble the implement itself. With the rise of modern industrial production, most traditional crafts have disappeared altogether, replaced by skills that form part of more large-scale production processes. An electrician working in an industrial setting today, for instance, may inspect and repair only a few parts of one type of machine; different people will deal with the other parts and other machines.

The contrast in the division of labor between traditional and modern societies is truly extraordinary. Even in the largest traditional societies, there usually existed no more than twenty or thirty major craft trades, together with such specialized pursuits as merchant, soldier, and priest. In a modern industrial system, there are literally thousands of distinct occupations. The U.S. Census Bureau lists some twenty thousand distinct jobs in the American economy. In traditional communities, most of the population worked on farms and were economically self-sufficient. They produced their own food, clothes, and other necessities of life. One of the main features of modern societies, by contrast, is an enormous expansion of **economic interdependence**. We are all dependent on an immense number of other workers—today stretching right across the world—for the products and services that sustain our lives. With few exceptions, the vast majority of people in modern societies do not produce the food they eat, the houses in which they live, or the material goods they consume.

Taylorism and Fordism

Writing some two centuries ago, Adam Smith, one of the founders of modern economics, identified advantages that the division of labor provides in terms of increasing productivity. His most famous work, *The Wealth of Nations*, opens with a description of the division of labor in a pin factory. A person working alone could perhaps make 20 pins per day. By breaking down that worker's task into a number of simple operations, however, ten workers carrying out specialized jobs in collaboration with one another could collectively produce 48,000 pins per day. The rate of production per worker, in other words, is increased from 20 to 4,800 pins, each specialist operator producing 240 times more than when working alone.

More than a century later, these ideas reached their most developed expression in the writings of Frederick Winslow Taylor, an American management consultant. Taylor's approach to what he called "scientific management" involved the detailed study of industrial processes in order to break them down into simple operations that could be precisely timed and organized. **Taylorism**, as scientific management came to be called, was not merely an academic study. It was a system of production designed to maximize industrial output,

and it had a widespread impact not only on the organization of industrial production and technology, but also on workplace politics as well. In particular, Taylor's time and motion studies wrested control over knowledge of the production process from the worker and placed such knowledge firmly in the hands of management, eroding the basis on which craft workers maintained autonomy from their employers (Braverman, 1974). As such, Taylorism has been widely associated with the deskilling and degradation of labor.

The principles of Taylorism were appropriated by the industrialist Henry Ford. In 1908, Ford designed his first auto plant at Highland Park, Michigan, to manufacture only one product—the Model T Ford—thereby allowing the introduction of specialized tools and machinery designed for speed, precision, and simplicity of operation. One of Ford's most significant innovations was the introduction of the assembly line, said to have been inspired by Chicago slaughterhouses, in which animals were disassembled section by section on a moving conveyor belt. Each worker on Ford's assembly line was assigned a specialized task, such as fitting the left-side door handles as the car bodies moved along the line. By 1929, when production of the Model T ceased, over 15 million cars had been assembled.

Ford was among the first to realize that mass production requires mass markets. Ford reasoned that if standardized commodities such as the automobile were to be produced on an ever greater scale, the presence of consumers who were able to buy those commodities must also be ensured. In 1914, Ford took the unprecedented step of unilaterally raising wages at his Dearborn, Michigan, plant to $5 for an eight-hour day—a very generous wage at the time and one that ensured a working-class lifestyle that included owning such an automobile. As Harvey remarks, "The purpose of the five dollar, eight hour day was only in part to secure worker compliance with the discipline required to work the highly productive assembly-line system. It was coincidentally meant to provide workers with sufficient income to consume the mass-produced products the corporations were about to turn out in ever vaster quantities" (1989). Ford also enlisted the services of a small army of social workers who were sent into the homes of workers in order to educate them in the proper habits of consumption.

Fordism is the name given to designate the system of mass production tied to the cultivation of mass markets. In certain contexts, the term has a more specific meaning, referring to a historical period in the development of post–World War II capitalism in which mass production was associated with stability in labor relations and a high degree of unionization. Under Fordism, firms made long-term commitments to workers, and wages were tightly linked to productivity growth. As such, *collective bargaining agreements*—formal agreements negotiated between firms and unions that specified working conditions

One of Henry Ford's most significant innovations was the introduction of the assembly line, which allowed for mass production of the Model T.

such as wages, seniority rights, benefits, and so on—closed a virtuous circle that ensured worker consent to automated work regimes *and* sufficient demand for mass-produced commodities. The system is generally understood to have broken down in the 1970s, giving rise to greater flexibility and insecurity in working conditions.

The reasons for the demise of Fordism are complex and intensely debated. As firms in a variety of industries adopted Fordist production methods, the system encountered certain limitations. Fordism was not suitable for all industries; it could only be applied successfully to industries that produced standardized commodities for large markets. At one time, it looked as though Fordism represented the likely future of industrial production as a whole. This has not proved to be the case. Setting up mechanized production lines is enormously expensive, and once a Fordist system is established, it is quite rigid; to alter a product, for example, substantial reinvestment is needed. Fordist production is easy to copy if sufficient funding is available to set up the plant. But firms in countries in which labor power is expensive find it difficult to compete with those where wages are cheaper. This was one of the factors originally leading to the rise of the Japanese car industry (although Japanese wage levels today are no longer low) and, more recently, that of South Korea.

Work and Alienation

Karl Marx was one of the first writers to grasp that the development of modern industry would reduce many people's work to dull, uninteresting tasks. According to Marx, the division of labor alienates human beings from their work. For Marx, **alienation** refers to feelings of indifference or hostility not only to work, but to the overall framework of industrial production within a capitalist setting.

In traditional societies, he pointed out, work was often exhausting—peasant farmers sometimes had to toil from dawn to dusk. Yet peasants held a real measure of control over their work, which required much knowledge and skill. Many industrial workers, by contrast, have little control over their jobs, only contribute a fraction to the creation of the overall product, and have no influence over how or to whom it is eventually sold. Work thus appears as something alien, a task that the worker must carry out in order to earn an income but that is intrinsically unsatisfying.

Low-Trust and High-Trust Systems

Fordism and Taylorism are what some industrial sociologists call **low-trust systems**. Jobs are set by management and are geared to machines. Those who carry out the work tasks are closely supervised and are allowed little autonomy of action. Where there are many low-trust positions, the level of worker dissatisfaction and absenteeism is high, and industrial conflict is common. A **high-trust system** is one in which workers are permitted to control the pace and even the content of their work, within overall guidelines. Such systems are usually concentrated at the higher levels of industrial organizations.

Industrial Conflict

There have long been conflicts between workers and those in economic and political authority over them. Riots against conscription and high taxes and food riots at periods of harvest failure were common in urban areas of Europe in the eighteenth century. These "premodern" forms of labor conflict continued up to not much more than a century ago in some countries. For example, there were food riots in several large Italian towns in 1868 (Geary, 1981). Such traditional forms of confrontation were not just sporadic, irrational outbursts of violence: The threat or use of violence had the effect of lowering the price of grain and other essential foodstuffs (Rudé, 1964; Thompson, 1971; Booth, 1977).

Industrial conflict between workers and employers at first tended to follow these older patterns. In situations of confrontation, workers would quite often leave their places of employment and form crowds in the streets; they would make their grievances known through their unruly behavior or by engaging in acts of violence against the authorities. Workers in some parts of France in the late nineteenth century would threaten disliked employers with hanging (Holton, 1978). Use of the *strike* as a weapon, today commonly associated with organized bargaining between workers and management, developed only slowly and sporadically.

STRIKES

We can define a **strike** as a temporary stoppage of work by a group of employees in order to express a grievance or enforce a demand (Hyman, 1984). All the components of this definition are important in separating strikes from other forms of opposition and conflict. A strike is *temporary*, since workers intend to return to the same job with the same employer; where workers quit altogether, the term *strike* is not appropriate. As a *stoppage of work*, a strike is distinguishable from an overtime ban or "slowdown." A *group* of workers has to be involved, because a strike is a collective action, not the response of one individual worker. That those involved are *employees* serves to separate strikes from protests such as may be conducted by tenants or students. Finally, a strike involves seeking to make known a grievance or press a demand; workers who miss work to go to a ball game could not be said to be on strike (see Figure 14.1).

Strikes represent only one aspect or type of conflict in which workers and management may become involved. Other closely related expressions of organized conflict are lockouts (where the employers rather than the workers bring about a stoppage of work), output restrictions, and clashes in contract negotiations. Less-organized expressions of conflict may include high labor turnover, absenteeism, and interference with production machinery.

Workers choose to go out on strike for many specific reasons. They may be seeking to gain higher wages, forestall a proposed reduction in their earnings, protest against technological changes that make their work duller or lead to layoffs, or obtain greater security of employment. However, in all these circumstances the strike is essentially a mechanism of

power: a weapon of people who are relatively powerless in the workplace and whose working lives are affected by managerial decisions over which they have little or no control. It is usually a weapon of last resort, to be used when other negotiations have failed, because workers on strike either receive no income or depend on union funds, which might be limited.

Labor Unions

Although their levels of membership and the extent of their power vary widely, union organizations exist in all Western countries, which also all legally recognize the right of workers to strike in pursuit of economic objectives. Why have unions become a basic feature of Western societies? Why does union-management conflict seem to be a more or less ever-present possibility in industrial settings?

In the early development of modern industry, workers in most countries had no political rights and little influence over the conditions of work in which they found themselves. Unions developed as a means of redressing the imbalance of power between workers and employers. Whereas workers had virtually no power as individuals, through collective organization their influence was considerably increased. An employer can do without the labor of any particular worker but not without that of all or most of the workers in a factory or plant. Unions originally were mainly "defensive" organizations, providing the means whereby workers could counter the overwhelming power that employers wielded over their lives.

Workers today have voting rights in the political sphere, and there are established forms of negotiation with employers, by means of which economic benefits can be pressed for and grievances expressed. However, union influence, both at the level of the local plant and nationally, still remains primarily *veto power*. In other words, using the resources at their disposal, including the right to strike, unions can only *block* employers' policies or initiatives, not help formulate them in the first place. There are exceptions to this, for instance where unions and employers negotiate periodic contracts covering conditions of work.

The post–World War II period witnessed a dramatic reversal in the positions of unions in advanced industrial societies. In most developed countries, the period from 1950 to 1980 was a time of steady growth in **union density**, a statistic that represents the number of union members as a percentage of the number of people who could potentially be union members. Union density across the Western economies was highly variable, however. In the United States, for example, union density peaked in the late 1950s, much earlier than in Europe. Countries that reached the highest levels of union density—Belgium, Denmark, Finland, and Sweden, with more than 80 percent of

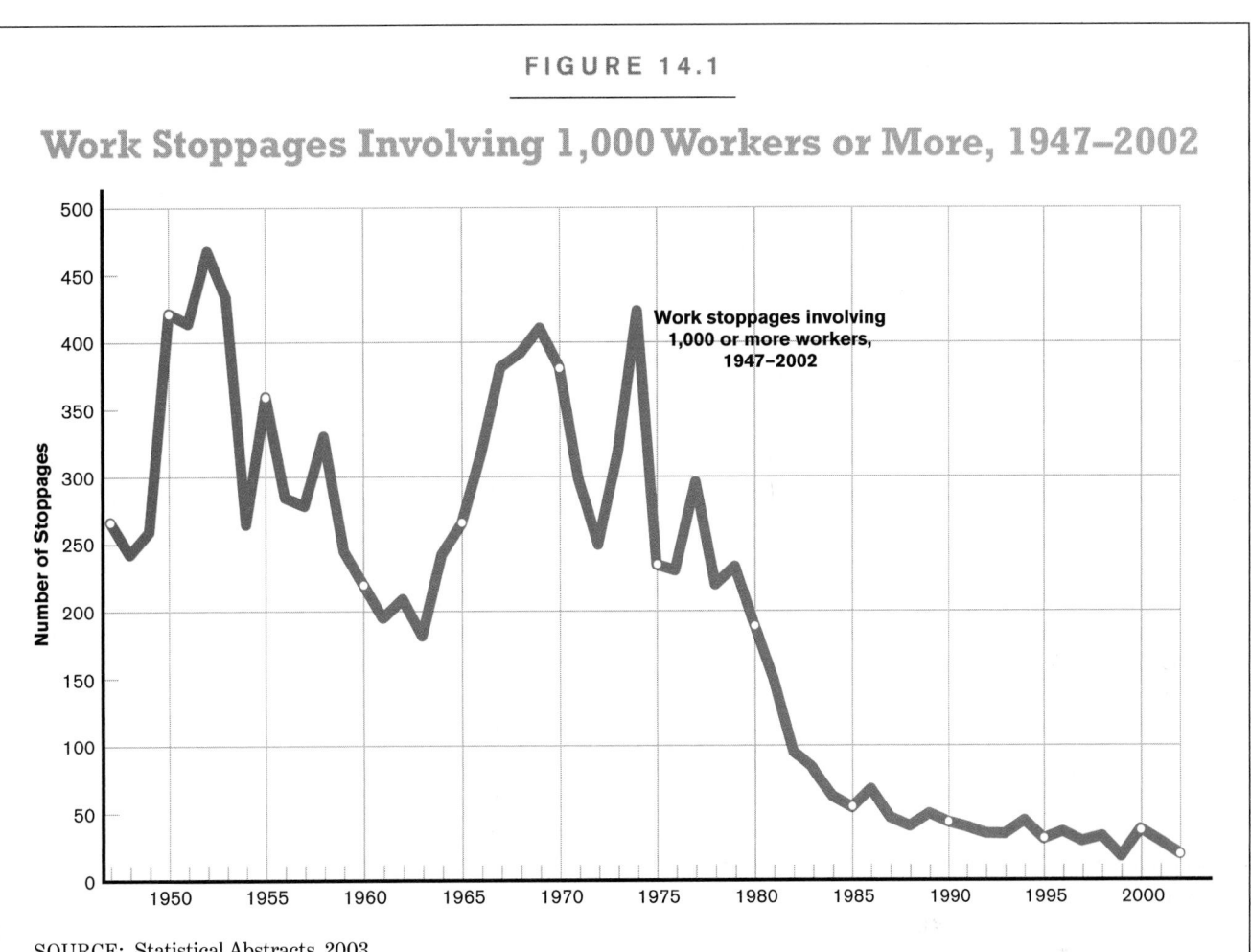

FIGURE 14.1

Work Stoppages Involving 1,000 Workers or More, 1947–2002

Number of Stoppages (y-axis: 0, 50, 100, 150, 200, 250, 300, 350, 400, 450, 500)

Work stoppages involving 1,000 or more workers, 1947–2002

(x-axis: 1950, 1955, 1960, 1965, 1970, 1975, 1980, 1985, 1990, 1995, 2000)

SOURCE: Statistical Abstracts, 2003.

all workers belonging to labor unions in 1985—shared three features in common (Western, 1977). First, strong working-class political parties created favorable conditions for labor organizing. Second, bargaining between firms and labor unions was coordinated at the national level rather than occurring in decentralized fashion at sectoral or local levels. Third, unions rather than the state directly administered unemployment insurance, ensuring that workers who lost their jobs did not leave the labor movement. Countries in which some combination but not all three of these factors were present had lower rates of union density, ranging between two-fifths and two-thirds of the working population.

After 1980, unions suffered declines across the advanced industrial countries. In the United States, the share of the work force belonging to unions declined from 23 percent in 1980 to under 13 percent in 2003 (Hirsch and Macpherson, 2004). There are several prominent explanations for the difficulties confronted by unions since 1980. Perhaps the most common is the decline of the older manufacturing industries and the rise of the service sector. Traditionally, manufacturing

has been a stronghold for labor, whereas jobs in services are resistant to unionization. However, this explanation has recently come under scrutiny. The sociologist Bruce Western (1997) argues that such an explanation cannot account for the experience of the 1970s, which was generally (although not in the United States) a good period for unions and yet was also characterized by a structural shift from manufacturing to services. Similarly, a significant share of growth in service-sector employment has occurred in social services—typically public-sector union jobs. Therefore, Western argues that declines in unionization *within* manufacturing may be more significant than declines across sectors. Explanations that are consistent with the fall in union density within as well as among industries include: the recession in world economic activity, associated with high levels of unemployment, which weakens the bargaining position of labor; the increasing intensity of international competition, particularly from Far Eastern countries where wages are often lower than in the West; and the rise to power in many countries of rightist governments that launched an aggressive assault on unions in the 1980s.

New Strategies for the Labor Movement

[***]

[***] How can labor be a leader in making the local and regional economic development policy that helps shape employer choice on competitive strategy work better for workers and the community? How can labor make that leadership part of and useful to its realization of broader political and organizing ambitions?

Like many local labor movements, Wisconsin labor has been struggling with these questions for years. And for years now, we at the Center on Wisconsin Strategy (COWS) have been working with Wisconsin's labor on a series of projects—among them the Wisconsin Regional Training Partnerships (WRTP) and Milwaukee Jobs Initiative (MJI), both centered in the Milwaukee metro area; and more recently the Jobs With a Future (JWF) project in the Madison metro area, an environment quite different from Milwaukee's—that attempt to answer them.

In different ways, all these projects are aimed simultaneously at upgrading the skills, wages, and career advancement

Joel Rogers

opportunities for workers near the bottom of the labor market; building industry competitiveness through modernization, better work force development practices, and other means; and increasing worker voice and power in firm and industry decision making. And all these projects are framed by a certain broader view of what labor needs to do to advance in today's economy—beginning with a clear definition of its role in the economy. In order to find the popular support and political cachet for its own advancement, labor has always needed to do big things for the broader society. This necessity has commonly meant solving problems that capital cannot solve on its own.

In the past, labor's signal contribution was to ensure "effective demand"—raising wage floors enough to promise investors markets for expanded production. These opportunities in turn increased the productivity of that output, which lowered the real cost of consumption goods, which could then be ever more widely purchased by better-paid workers in an unending upward spiral of living standards. But for a host of reasons, the conditions under which labor made that contribution have been undermined since the early 1970s. In proximate result, wages have stagnated or declined for most of the working population, inequality has soared, and even in that handful of industrial sectors that provided the foundation of postwar private-sector union power, that power has been drastically diminished. More immediately still, perhaps, labor has no clear function, beyond obstruction, in a fully marketized economy subject to increased competitive pressures.

This is the familiar starting point for the strategy considered here: to make labor again "part of the solution" to problems of industrial order. This time, however, we must focus as much on the supply side and framing conditions of that order (that is, the organization of production itself and the rules by which it is socially constrained) as on the demand side and the operation of internal labor markets. More specifically, labor must harness its residual strength and unique position in the economy to support

Laura Dresser

nections between the TRTP and the MJI have helped place more than 1,300 "disadvantaged" central city workers—including many former AFDC/TANF recipients—in jobs that more than doubled their previous year's earnings (from an average of $9,000 to $23,000 annually), while providing health insurance and clear opportunities for further advancement. Upon examination, this MJI/WRTP work may prove the most cost-effective job-training and welfare-to-work program in the country—in large measure because it starts with employer demand and commitment to working with the program rather than with the individual served by it—with among the highest rates of participant job retention.

[***]

a form of production—the "high road"—that is socially superior to present business practices. Such a high road would provide advantages to labor more or less immediately, but also further the interest of the broader society and even a significant share of capital itself. Specifically, labor helps to organize employers willing to take the high road to the point where they embark on it together to realize the efficiencies that come of their collective organization. In return for labor leadership, employers share some of that gain with labor—a sort of productivity bargaining, or rent-sharing, on a grand scale. This strategy also anticipates high-road employers' allying with labor against the most salient threat to them both: low-road firms and the public policies that support them. This arrangement, then, becomes the shared political program of a new "social partnership" between labor and capital: to close off the low road, to help build the high road, and to enable workers and firms now stuck on the first to be able to travel the second.

[***]

The aggregate results of the WRTP are impressive. Taken together, WRTP members have stabilized manufacturing employment in the Milwaukee metro area, and indeed contributed about 6,000 additional industrial jobs to it over the past five years. Among member firms, productivity is way up—exceeding productivity growth in nonmember firms. Once-stagnant wages are also up, and easily outpace wage growth outside the partnership. Individual firm commitment to training frontline workers is evident in direct training costs of some $20 million annually—an increase of almost that magnitude from prior levels. Direct training reaches some 6,000 workers (one-quarter of whom are people of color) each year. Because entry-level job requirements among member firms are known and broadly shared, moreover, the WRTP has been able to offer employment opportunities to those traditionally neglected in Milwaukee metro's labor market. Con-

New Directions

Looking to the future, the WRTP has several new items on its plate. Most important is replication in other sectors. With an RSA grant of its own from the U.S. Department of Labor, WRTP is creating new partnerships in construction, data networking, health care, hospitality, and transportation. While the specific needs of each industry differ, the basic steps are the same. First, steering committees of business and labor leaders have been formed in each sector, with an emphasis on coalition building and recruiting firms and unions. The next stage is that the committees develop strategic plans to meet the staffing and training needs of their industry, drawing on research and firm surveys. Pilot recruiting and training programs are then put in place and evaluated. Throughout, the fledgling partnerships are benefiting enormously from the groundwork already laid by the mature manufacturing partnership (such as ties to community colleges, public agencies, and community groups, and knowledge of public-funding streams).

[***]

SOURCE: Annett Bernhardt, Laura Dresser, and Joel Rogers, "Taking the High Road in Milwaukee: The Wisconsin Regional Training Partnership," *Working USA* 5, no. 3 (January 2002): 109.

ANNETT BERNHARDT, LAURA DRESSER, and JOEL ROGERS all work at the Center on Wisconsin Strategy (COWS), a research and policy center based at the University of Wisconsin that was instrumental in the creation of the Wisconsin Regional Training Partnership (WRTP) and still provides it with technical assistance and staffing. Bernhardt is a senior research associate at COWS; Dresser is the research director; Rogers is the director and also a professor of law, political science, and sociology at the university.

In the United States, unions face a crisis of even greater dimensions than their counterparts in most European countries. In 1983, just over 20 percent of American workers were union members—low by European standards—yet by 2001 the number of union members had dropped dramatically to just under 13 percent (U.S. Bureau of the Census, 2002). Union-protected working conditions and wages have eroded in several major industries over the past twenty-five years. Workers in the trucking, steel, and car industries have all accepted lower wages than those previously negotiated. The unions came out second best in several major strikes, perhaps the most notable example being the crushing of the air traffic controllers' union in the early 1980s. At the same time, unions have made progress in organizing outside their traditional manufacturing base, including the successful unionization of janitors in Los Angeles; teaching assistants at the University of Massachusetts, the University of California, and other institutions; and attempts to organize doctors. These new fronts in attempts to organize labor reflect the changing conditions of work in the United States toward the provision of services.

Decline in union membership and influence is something of a general phenomenon in the industrialized countries and is not to be explained wholly in terms of political pressure applied by rightist governments against the unions. Unions usually become weakened during periods when unemployment is high, as has been the case for a considerable while in many Western countries. Trends toward more flexible production tend to diminish the force of unionism, which flourishes more extensively where many people are working together in large factories.

What Do Workers Want?

An individual's quality of life depends on his or her position in the labor market. Arguably this is more true in the United States than in any other comparably developed economy. Americans spend more time at work than do citizens of other advanced industrial countries. U.S. living standards also reflect income and employment-related benefits more directly than do living standards in other comparably developed countries where governments universally guarantee paid vacation, job training, and health insurance. There is also more variability in terms of pay and work conditions in the U.S. labor market than elsewhere. Yet, in spite of the overwhelming importance of the labor market for the life conditions of working Americans, there has been relatively little investigation of how workers view the framework through which the U.S. labor market is governed. For this reason, Richard Freeman of Harvard University and Joel Rogers of the University of

This photo shows members of the Service Employees International Union picketing outside city hall in Los Angeles. The county workers, who include nurses and medical staff, library workers, and staff workers at the civic center, beaches, and harbors, are demanding raises, improved job security, and better benefits.

Wisconsin recently set out to find out what workers want with regard to the conditions under which they labor. Freeman and Rogers designed the Worker Representation and Participation Survey (WRPS) to canvass workers systematically in a wide variety of professions for their opinions about their employment and how their workplaces could be improved.

Freeman and Rogers's (1999) findings are based on a national telephone survey of twenty-four hundred workers in private sector establishments that employ twenty-five or more people. They excluded top managers, the self-employed, owners of firms or their relatives, public-sector workers, and employees in small firms. Overall, the population from which survey respondents were selected covers approximately 75 percent of all private sector workers. Freeman and Rogers's findings range across a wide variety of aspects of people's work lives, including causes of worker dissatisfaction, attitudes toward unionization, views of management, and worker knowledge of protective labor legislation. In-depth follow-up interviews were conducted with 801 workers, who were asked about their views of alternative institutional designs for American workplaces.

The overwhelming finding of Freeman and Rogers's study is that what workers want is more influence at work. American workers believe that if they had more say over how production is carried out, they would not only enjoy work more, but their firms would be more competitive, and problems would be solved more effectively. Furthermore, influence is associated with a broader range of attitudes about work: Workers satisfied with their degree of influence report that they enjoy going to work, grade employee-management relations as excellent, and trust their employer. In contrast, workers who are dissatisfied with their degree of influence tend to dislike going to work, report poor relations with management, and distrust their employers.

One of the most surprising findings of the WRPS concerns the kind of institutional arrangement that workers consider ideal for achieving greater say. Contrary to what Freeman and Rogers expected, workers prefer an organization run jointly by workers and management to one run by employees alone. Workers were also asked to choose between two hypothetical organizations, "one that management cooperated with in discussing issues, but had no power to make decisions," and "one that had more power but management opposed" (Freeman and Rogers, 1999). Sixty-three percent of all employees chose the former organization, whereas only 22 percent stated that they would prefer the latter. These results—in which workers effectively indicated that they would prefer weaker to stronger organizations, in spite of the fact that they also reported wanting more say at work—make sense in light of another question on Freeman and Rogers's survey. When asked if they thought an organization could be effective without managerial support, three quarters of all respondents indicated that they believed an employee organization could function only with management cooperation.

The Modern Economy

Modern societies are, in Marx's term, capitalistic. **Capitalism** is a way of organizing economic life that is distinguished by the following important features: private ownership of the means of production; profit as incentive; free competition for markets to sell goods, acquire cheap materials, and utilize cheap labor; and restless expansion and investment to accumulate capital. Capitalism, which began to spread with the growth of the Industrial Revolution in the early nineteenth century, is a vastly more dynamic economic system than any other that preceded it in history. Although the system has had many critics, such as Marx, it is now the most widespread form of economic organization in the world.

So far in this chapter, we have been looking at industry mostly from the perspective of occupations and employees. We have studied how patterns of work have changed and the factors influencing the development of labor unions. But we have also to concern ourselves with the nature of the business firms in which the work force is employed. (It should be recognized that many people today are employees of government organizations, although we will not consider these here.) What is happening to business corporations today, and how are they run?

Corporations and Corporate Power

Since the turn of the twentieth century, modern capitalist economies have been more and more influenced by the rise of large business **corporations**. The share of total manufacturing assets held by the two hundred largest *manufacturing* firms in the United States has increased by 0.5 percent each year from 1900 to the present day; these two hundred corporations now control over half of all manufacturing assets. The two hundred largest *financial* organizations—banks, building societies, and insurance companies—account for more than half of all financial activity. There are numerous connections between large firms. For example, financial institutions hold well over 30 percent of the shares of the largest two hundred manufacturing firms.

Of course, there still exist thousands of smaller firms and enterprises within the American economy. In these companies, the image of the **entrepreneur**—the boss who owns and runs the firm—is by no means obsolete. The large corporations are a different matter. Ever since Adolf Berle and Gardiner Means published their celebrated study *The Modern Corporation and Private Property* seventy years ago, it has been accepted that most of the largest firms are not run by those who own them (Berle and Means, 1982). In theory, the large corporations are the property of their shareholders, who have the right to make all important decisions. But Berle and Means argued that since share ownership is so dispersed, actual control has passed into the hands of the managers who run firms on a day-to-day basis. *Ownership* of the corporations is thus separated from their *control*.

Whether they are run by owners or managers, the power of the major corporations is very extensive. When one or a handful of firms dominate in a given industry, they often cooperate in setting prices rather than freely competing with one another. Thus, the giant oil companies normally follow one another's lead in the price charged for gasoline. When one firm occupies a commanding position in a given industry, it is said to be in a **monopoly** position. More common is a situation of **oligopoly**, in which a small group of giant corporations predominate. In situations of oligopoly, firms are able more or less to dictate the terms on which they buy goods and services from the smaller firms that are their suppliers.

The emergence of the global economy has contributed to a wave of mergers and acquisitions on an unprecedented scale, which have created oligopolies in industries such as communications and media. In 1998, the German auto maker Daimler-Benz purchased Chrysler for $38 billion, and Exxon purchased the oil giant Mobil for $86 billion. In 1999, AT&T acquired the media corporation MediaOne for $5 billion to create the world's largest cable company. Also in 1999, CBS purchased Viacom for $35 billion. In 2000, Britian's Vodafone Airtouch took over Germany's Mannesmann for $130 billion in the world's largest hostile takover. In that same year, Time Warner and the internet service provider America Online announced the largest merger in history—worth over $166 billion (PBS, 2003). As the global market becomes increasingly integrated, we are likely to see even more mergers and acquisitions on an even larger scale.

A number of factors have contributed to this trend, including technological advances, which have lowered global transportation and communications costs; a relaxation of regulation of corporate business activities; new and efficient ways of financing and pooling the large sums of capital needed to conduct a merger or acquisition. Yet over 70 percent of the mergers and acquisitions have been between businesses competing in the same industry (UNCTAD, 2000). This suggests that the primary aim of the recent wave of business consolidations has been to eliminate direct competition and productive overcapacity. *Overcapacity* is a problem that occurs when businesses produce more goods than the market will consume. Following the logic of supply and demand, this leads to decline in the value of the goods that they produce and to a decline in profits. Consolidation of firms is an attempt to avoid this problem. Yet it doesn't always work. In response to the declining success of AOL, Time Warner dropped AOL from its name and posted a $99 billion dollar loss for 2002 (PBS, 2003).

Types of Corporate Capitalism

There have been three general stages in the development of business corporations, although each overlaps with the others and all continue to coexist today. The first stage, characteristic of the nineteenth and early twentieth centuries, was dominated by **family capitalism**. Large firms were run either by individual entrepreneurs or by members of the same family and then passed on to their descendants. The famous corporate dynasties, such as the Rockefellers and Fords, belong in this category. These individuals and families did not just own a single large corporation, but held a diversity of economic interests and stood at the apex of economic empires.

Most of the big firms founded by entrepreneurial families have since become public companies—that is, shares of their stock are traded on the open market—and have passed into managerial control. But important elements of family capitalism remain, even within some of the largest corporations, such as the Ford Motor Company, where William Clay Ford, Jr., serves as chair of the board. Among small firms, such as local shops run by their owners, small plumbing and house-painting businesses, and so forth, family capitalism continues

to dominate. Some of these firms, such as shops that remain in the hands of the same family for two or more generations, are also dynasties on a minor scale. However, the small business sector is highly unstable, and economic failure is very common; the proportion of firms that are owned by members of the same family for extended periods of time is minuscule.

In the large corporate sector, family capitalism was increasingly succeeded by **managerial capitalism**. As managers came to have more and more influence through the growth of very large firms, the entrepreneurial families were displaced. The result has been described as the replacement of the family in the company by the company itself. The corporation emerged as a more defined economic entity. In studying the two hundred largest manufacturing corporations in the United States, Michael Allen found that in cases where profit showed a decline, family-controlled enterprises were unlikely to replace their chief executive, but manager-controlled firms did so rapidly (Allen, 1981).

There is no question that managerial capitalism has left an indelible imprint on modern society. The large corporation drives not only patterns of consumption but also the experience of employment in contemporary society—it is difficult to imagine how the work lives of many Americans would be different in the absence of large factories or corporate bureaucracies. Sociologists have identified another area in which the large corporation has left a mark on modern institutions. **Welfare capitalism** refers to a practice that sought to make the corporation—rather than the state or trade unions—the primary shelter from the uncertainties of the market in modern industrial life. Beginning at the end of the nineteenth century, large firms began to provide certain services to their employees, including child care, recreational facilities, profit-sharing plans, paid vacations, and group life and unemployment insurance. These programs often had a paternalistic bent, such as that sponsoring "home visits" for the "moral education" of employees. Viewed in less benevolent terms, a major objective of welfare capitalism was coercion, as employers deployed all manner of tactics—including violence—to avoid unionization. As such, conventional histories typically suggest that welfare capitalism met its demise in the depression years as labor unions achieved unprecedented levels of influence and as the New Deal administration began to guarantee many of the benefits provided by firms. In contrast to this standard interpretation, others argue that welfare capitalism did not die but instead went underground during the apex of the labor movement (Jacoby, 1997). In firms that avoided unionization during the period between the 1930s and 1960s—such as Kodak, Sears, and Thompson Products—welfare capitalism was modernized, shedding blatantly paternalistic aspects and routinizing benefit programs. When the union movement began to weaken after 1970, these companies offered a model to many other firms, which were now able to press their advantage against flanking unions, reasserting the role of the firm as "industrial manor" and workers as "industrial serfs."

Despite the overwhelming importance of managerial capitalism in shaping the modern economy, many scholars now see the contours of a third, different phase in the evolution of the corporation emerging. They argue that managerial capitalism has today partly ceded place to **institutional capitalism**. This term refers to the emergence of a consolidated network of business leadership, concerned not only with decision making within single firms but also with the development of corporate power beyond them. Institutional capitalism is based on the practice of corporations holding shares in other firms. In effect, interlocking boards of directors exercise control over much of the corporate landscape. This reverses the process of increasing managerial control, since the managers' shareholdings are dwarfed by the large blocks of shares owned by other corporations. One of the main reasons for the spread of institutional capitalism is the shift in patterns of investment that has occurred over the past thirty years. Rather than investing directly by buying shares in a business, individuals now invest in money market, trust, insurance, and pension funds that are controlled by large financial organizations, which in turn invest these grouped savings in industrial corporations.

The Transnational Corporations

With the intensifying of globalization, most large corporations now operate in an international economic context. When they establish branches in two or several countries, they are referred to as **transnational**, or **multinational corporations**. *Transnational* is the preferred term, indicating that these companies operate across many different national boundaries. The United Nations Committee on Trade and Development (UNCTAD) estimated that in 2002 over 650,000 transnational corporations controlled assets outside their home countries (UNCTAD, 2002).

The largest transnationals are gigantic; their wealth outstrips that of many countries. Half of the hundred largest economic units in the world today are nations; the other half are transnational corporations. The scope of these companies' operations is staggering. The combined sales of the world's largest five hundred transnational corporations totaled $13.7 trillion in 2003—nearly half (46 percent) of the value of goods and services produced by the entire world (World Bank, 2003; *Fortune,* 2003). The revenues of the largest two hundred companies rose tenfold between the mid-1970s and the 1990s, reaching $9.5 trillion in 2001. Over the past twenty years, the transnationals' activities have become increasingly global: In

1950 only three of the world's largest companies had manufacturing subsidiaries in more than twenty countries; some fifty do so today. These are still a small minority; most of the transnationals have subsidiaries in two to five countries. Altogether an estimated 850,000 affiliates of transnational corporations do business around the globe (World Bank, 2003).

One hundred ninety-two of the top five hundred transnational corporations in the world are based in the United States, contributing about 40 percent of the total global sales. The share of American companies has, however, fallen significantly since 1960, during which time Japanese companies have grown dramatically; only five Japanese corporations were included in the top two hundred in 1960, as compared with eighty-eight in 2003. Of the fifty largest Asian corporations, forty of them are Japanese (*Fortune,* 2003).

Contrary to common belief, three quarters of all foreign direct investment occurs among the industrialized countries. Of the one hundred largest corporations, one is from Mexico and none are from Latin America, Africa, the Middle East, Eastern Europe, or the former Soviet Union. The rest are all from North America, Europe, and Asia. Nevertheless, the involvements of transnationals in developing world countries are extensive, with Brazil, Mexico, and India showing the highest levels of foreign investment. The most rapid rate of increase in corporate investment by far has been in the Asian newly industrializing economies (NIEs) of Singapore, Taiwan, Hong Kong, South Korea, and Malaysia.

The reach of the transnationals over the past thirty years would not have been possible without advances in transport and communications. Air travel now allows people to move around the world at a speed that would have seemed inconceivable even sixty years ago. Technological innovations, referred to together as "containerization," have permitted the rapid movement and distribution of bulk goods around the world. The best example of containerization is the development of extremely large ocean-going vessels (superfreighters) that carry tractor trailers full of goods. These trailers can be easily loaded and sealed at the point of manufacture, loaded onto ships and moved across an ocean, than transferred onto a train or truck and delivered to a store, where the trailers are finally opened and unloaded.

Telecommunications technologies now permit more or less instantaneous communication from one part of the world to another. Satellites have been used for commercial telecommunications since 1965, when the first satellite could carry 240 telephone conversations at once. Current satellites can carry 12,000 simultaneous conversations! The larger transnationals now have their own satellite-based communications systems. The Mitsubishi Corporation, for instance, has a massive network across which 5 million words are transmitted to and from its headquarters in Tokyo each day.

Container ships are cargo ships that carry all of their load in truck-size containers. As this technique greatly accelerates the speed by which goods can be transported to and from ports, these ships now carry the majority of the world's dry cargo.

TYPES OF TRANSNATIONAL CORPORATIONS

The transnationals have assumed an increasingly important place in the world economy over the course of this century. They are of key importance in the **international division of labor**—the specialization in producing goods for the world market that divides regions into zones of industrial or agricultural production or high- or low-skilled labor (Fröbel et al., 1979; McMichael, 1996). Just as national economies have become increasingly *concentrated*—dominated by a limited number of very large companies—so has the world economy. In the case of the United States and several of the other leading industrialized countries, the firms that dominate nationally also have a very wide-ranging international presence. Many sectors of world production (such as agribusiness) are oligopolies. Over the past two or three decades, international oligopolies have developed in the automobile, microprocessor, and electronics industries, and in the production of some other goods marketed worldwide.

H. V. Perlmutter divides transnational corporations into three types. One consists of **ethnocentric transnationals**, in which company policy is set and as far as possible put into practice from a headquarters in the country of origin. Compa-

nies and plants that the parent corporation owns around the world are cultural extensions of the originating company—its practices are standardized across the globe. A second category is that of **polycentric transnationals**, whose overseas subsidiaries are managed by local firms in each country. The headquarters in the country or countries of origin of the main company establish broad guidelines within which local companies manage their own affairs. Finally, there are **geocentric transnationals**, which are international in their management structure. Managerial systems are integrated on a global basis, and higher managers are very mobile, moving from country to country as needs dictate (Perlmutter, 1972).

Planning on a World Scale

The global corporations have become the first organizations able to plan on a truly world scale. Coca-Cola ads reach billions. A few companies with developed global networks are able to shape the commercial activities of diverse nations. There are four webs of interconnecting commercial activity in the new world economy. These are what Richard Barnet and John Cavanagh call the Global Cultural Bazaar, the Global Shopping Mall, the Global Workplace, and the Global Financial Network (Barnet and Cavanagh, 1994).

The Global Cultural Bazaar is the newest of the four but already the most extensive. Global images and global dreams are diffused through movies, TV programs, music, videos, games, toys, and T-shirts, sold on a worldwide basis. All over the earth, even in the poorest developing countries, people use the same electronic devices to see or listen to the same commercially produced songs and shows.

The Global Shopping Mall is a "planetary supermarket with a dazzling spread of things to eat, drink, wear and enjoy," according to Barnet and Cavanagh. It is more exclusive than the Cultural Bazaar because the poor do not have the resources to participate—they only have the status of window shoppers. Of the 6 billion people who make up the world's population, 3.5 billion lack the cash or credit to purchase any consumer goods.

The third global web, the Global Workplace, is the increasingly complex global division of labor that affects all of us. It consists of the massive array of offices, factories, restaurants, and millions of other places where goods are produced and consumed or information is exchanged. This web is closely bound up with the Global Financial Network, which it fuels and is financed by. The Global Financial Network consists of billions of bits of information stored in computers and portrayed on computer screens. It entails almost endless currency exchanges, credit card transactions, insurance plans, and buying and selling of stocks and shares.

The Large Corporation: The Same, but Different

There are big differences between the large corporation of the early twenty-first century and its mid-twentieth-century counterpart. Many of the names are the same—General Motors, Ford, IBM, AT&T—but these have been joined by other giant firms, largely unknown in the 1950s, such as Microsoft and Intel. They all wield great power, and their top executives still inhabit the large buildings that dominate so many city centers.

But below the surface similarities between today and half a century ago, some profound transformations have taken place. The origin of these transformations lies in that process we have encountered often in this book: globalization. Over the past fifty years, the giant corporations have become more and more caught up in global competition; as a result, their internal composition, and in a way their very nature, has altered.

The former U.S. Labor Secretary Robert Reich has written:

Underneath, all is changing. America's core corporation no longer plans and implements the production of a large volume of goods and services; it no longer invests in a vast array of factories, machinery, laboratories, inventories, and other tangible assets; it no longer employs armies of production workers and middle-level managers. . . . In fact, the core corporation is no longer even American. It is, increasingly, a facade, behind which teems an array of decentralized groups and subgroups continuously contracting with similarly diffuse working units all over the world. (Reich, 1991)

The large corporation is less and less a big business than an "enterprise web"—a central organization that links smaller firms together. IBM, for example, which used to be one of the most jealously self-sufficient of all large corporations, in the 1980s and early 1990s joined with dozens of U.S.-based companies and more than eighty foreign-based firms to share strategic planning and cope with production problems.

Some corporations remain strongly bureaucratic and centered in the United States. However, most are no longer so clearly located anywhere. The old transnational corporation used to work mainly from its American headquarters, from where its overseas production plants and subsidiaries were controlled. Now, with the transformation of space and time noted earlier (Chapter 5), groups situated in any region of the world are able, via telecommunications and computer, to work with others. Nations still try to influence flows of information, resources, and money across their borders. But modern communications technologies make this more and more difficult, if not impossible. Knowledge and finances can be transferred across the world as electronic blips moving at the speed of light.

Even the production of the technology that makes the global activities of transnational corporations possible is spread out over the globe. The computer-chip manufacturer Intel has 86,200 employees, thirteen production sites, and eleven assembly sites spread over seven countries. Two thirds of its work force is located in the United States, while 11 percent is in Malaysia; 8 percent is in the Philippines; 4 percent is in Ireland; 3 percent is in Israel; 2 percent is in Costa Rica; and 1 percent is in China. Intel is the leading national exporter from Ireland, the Philippines, and Costa Rica, yet it is an "American" company (UNCTAD, 2002).

The products of the transnational companies similarly have an international character. When is something "made in America," and when not? There is no longer any clear answer. What could be more American than a Ford? Today, the answer may be a Toyota or Honda. Automobiles contain over twenty thousand different parts, and the production and the manufacture of vehicles have become a truly globalized system (see Figure 14.2). In 2002, Toyota employed over thirty-four thousand people in North America and spent over $15 billion on American parts and accessories (Toyota, 2003). The Toyota Avalon, for example, built at a production facility in Kentucky, comprises 70 percent U.S. or Canadian parts. This is a higher percentage than the Chrysler-built PT Cruiser. And GM's use of a Honda-made engine in its Saturn cars actually increased the percentage of its parts and accessories made in the United States (*Charleston Business Journal*, 2003). In fact, all of the Honda Accords sold in the United States contain 97 percent domestic parts and accessories and are assembled at one of its several North American production facilities (Honda, 2002).

On top of all of this, it is no longer clear what even constitutes an "American" car company. As mentioned earlier, in 1998, the German auto maker Daimler-Benz acquired Chrysler; Daimler-Benz also owns about 38 percent of Mitsubishi. General Motors owns 49 percent of Isuzu, 20 percent of the makers of Subaru, and 20 percent of Suzuki. Ford owns over 33 percent of Mazda and parts of Jaguar, Land Rover, and Volvo (*Charleston Business Journal*, 2003).

The Changing Nature of Work

The globalizing of economic production, together with the spread of information technology, is altering the nature of the

FIGURE 14.2

Where Does Your Car Come From?

This schematic shows how automobile parts are produced in several countries and then sent to a central plant for final production of the car.

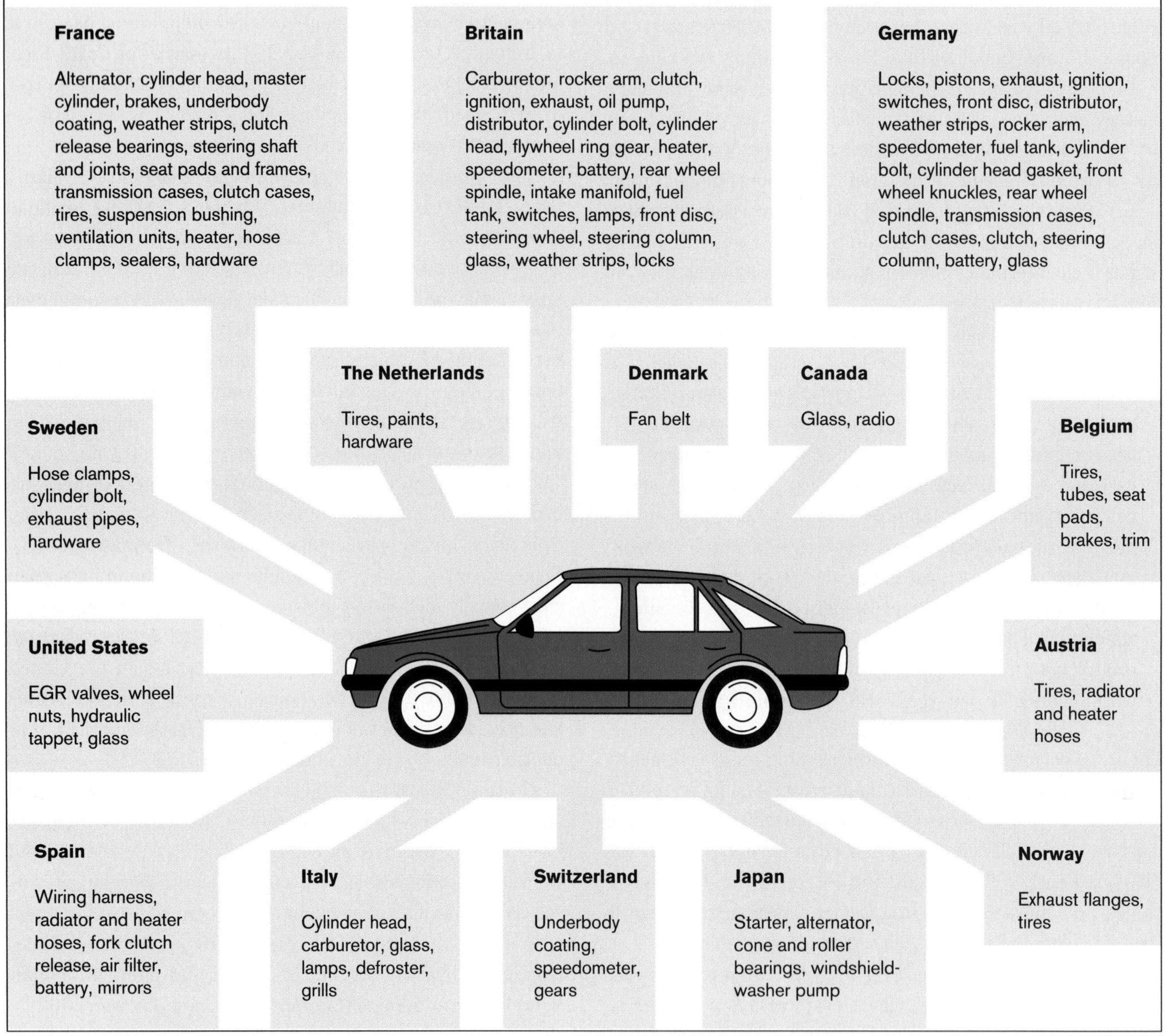

France

Alternator, cylinder head, master cylinder, brakes, underbody coating, weather strips, clutch release bearings, steering shaft and joints, seat pads and frames, transmission cases, clutch cases, tires, suspension bushing, ventilation units, heater, hose clamps, sealers, hardware

Britain

Carburetor, rocker arm, clutch, ignition, exhaust, oil pump, distributor, cylinder bolt, cylinder head, flywheel ring gear, heater, speedometer, battery, rear wheel spindle, intake manifold, fuel tank, switches, lamps, front disc, steering wheel, steering column, glass, weather strips, locks

Germany

Locks, pistons, exhaust, ignition, switches, front disc, distributor, weather strips, rocker arm, speedometer, fuel tank, cylinder bolt, cylinder head gasket, front wheel knuckles, rear wheel spindle, transmission cases, clutch cases, clutch, steering column, battery, glass

The Netherlands

Tires, paints, hardware

Denmark

Fan belt

Canada

Glass, radio

Sweden

Hose clamps, cylinder bolt, exhaust pipes, hardware

Belgium

Tires, tubes, seat pads, brakes, trim

United States

EGR valves, wheel nuts, hydraulic tappet, glass

Austria

Tires, radiator and heater hoses

Spain

Wiring harness, radiator and heater hoses, fork clutch release, air filter, battery, mirrors

Italy

Cylinder head, carburetor, glass, lamps, defroster, grills

Switzerland

Underbody coating, speedometer, gears

Japan

Starter, alternator, cone and roller bearings, windshield-washer pump

Norway

Exhaust flanges, tires

jobs most people do. As discussed earlier in Chapter 8, the proportion of people working in blue-collar jobs in industrial countries has progressively fallen. Fewer people work in factories than before. New jobs have been created in offices and in service centers such as supermarkets and airports. Many of these new jobs are filled by women.

Work and Technology

The relationship between technology and work has long been of interest to sociologists. How is our experience of work affected by the type of technology that is involved? As industrialization has progressed, technology has assumed an ever greater role at the workplace—from factory automation to the computerization of office work. The current information technology revolution has attracted renewed interest in this question. Technology can lead to greater efficiency and productivity, but how does it affect the way work is experienced by those who carry it out? For sociologists, one of the main questions is how the move to more complex systems influences the nature of work and the institutions in which it is performed.

AUTOMATION AND THE SKILL DEBATE

The concept of **automation**, or programmable machinery, was introduced in the mid-1800s, when Christopher Spencer, an American, invented the Automat, a programmable lathe that made screws, nuts, and gears. Automation has thus far affected relatively few industries, but with advances in the design of industrial robots, its impact is certain to become greater. A robot is an automatic device that can perform functions ordinarily done by human workers. The term *robot* comes from the Czech word *robota*, or serf, popularized about fifty years ago by the playwright Karel Čapek.

The majority of the robots used in industry worldwide are to be found in automobile manufacture. The usefulness of robots in production thus far is relatively limited, because their capacity to recognize different objects and manipulate awkward shapes is still at a rudimentary level. Yet it is certain that automated production will spread rapidly in coming years; robots are becoming more sophisticated, while their costs are decreasing.

The spread of automation provoked a heated debate among sociologists and experts in industrial relations over the impact of the new technology on workers, their skills, and their level of commitment to their work. In his influential *Alienation and Freedom* (1964), Robert Blauner examined the experience of workers in four different industries with varying levels of technology. Using the ideas of Durkheim and Marx, Blauner operationalized the concept of *alienation* and measured the extent to which workers in each industry experienced it in the form of powerlessness, meaninglessness, isolation, and self-estrangement. He concluded that workers on assembly lines were the most alienated of all, but that levels of alienation were somewhat lower at workplaces using automation. In other words, Blauner argued that the introduction of automation to factories was responsible for *reversing* the otherwise steady trend toward increased worker alienation. Automation helped to integrate the work force and gave workers a sense of control over their work that had been lacking with other forms of technology.

A very different thesis was set forth by Harry Braverman in the famous *Labor and Monopoly Capital* (1974). In Braverman's

eyes, automation was part of the overall "deskilling" of the industrial labor force. By imposing Taylorist organizational techniques and breaking up the labor process into specialized tasks, managers were able to exert control over the work force. In both industrial settings and modern offices, the introduction of technology contributed to this overall degradation of work by limiting the need for creative human input. Instead, all that was required was an unthinking, unreflective body capable of endlessly carrying out the same unskilled task.

A newer study sheds some more light on this debate. The sociologist Richard Sennett studied the people who worked in a bakery that had been bought by a large food conglomerate and automated with the introduction of high-tech machinery. Computerized baking radically altered the way that bread was made. Instead of using their hands to mix the ingredients and knead the dough and their noses and eyes to judge when the bread was done baking, the bakery's workers had no physical contact with the materials or the loaves of bread. In fact, the entire process was controlled and monitored via computer screen. Computers decided the temperature and baking time of the ovens. Although at times the machines produced excellent-quality bread, at other times the results were burned, blackened loaves. The workers at this bakery (it would be erroneous to call them bakers) were hired because they were skilled with computers, not because they knew how to bake bread. Ironically, these workers used very few of their computer skills. The production process involved little more than pushing buttons on a computer. In fact, one time when the computerized machinery broke down, the entire production process was halted because none of the bakery's "skilled" workers were trained or empowered to repair the problem. The workers that Sennett observed wanted to be helpful, to make things work again, but they could not, because automation had diminished their autonomy (Sennett, 1998). The introduction of computerized technology in the workplace has led to a general increase in all workers' skills, but has also led to a bifurcated work force composed of a small group of highly skilled professionals with high degrees of flexibility and autonomy in their jobs and a larger group of clerical, service, and production workers who lack autonomy in their jobs.

The skill debate is very difficult to resolve, however. Both the conceptualization and measurement of skill are problematic. As feminist researchers have argued, what constitutes "skill" is socially constructed (Steinberg, 1990). As such, conventional understandings of "skilled" work tend to reflect the social status of the typical incumbent of the job, rather than the difficulty of the task in an objective sense. The history of occupations is rife with examples of jobs in which the very same task was assigned a different skill level (and even renamed!)

once women entered the field (Reskin and Roos, 1990). The same, of course, holds for other low-status workers, such as racial minorities. Even where gender and racial biases are not in operation, skill has multiple dimensions; the same job may be downgraded on one dimension while simultaneously upgraded on another (Block, 1990). Thus, opinions as to whether automation has deskilled work depend on which dimension of skill is examined. In his comprehensive review of the skill debate, Spenner (1983) notes that studies that have examined skill in terms of the substantive complexity of tasks have tended to support the "upskilling" position, whereas those that have examined skill in terms of the autonomy and/or control exercised by the worker have tended to find that work has in fact been "deskilled" through automation (c.f., Zuboff, 1988; Vallas and Beck, 1996).

INFORMATION TECHNOLOGY

Blauner's and Braverman's opposing perspectives on the effects of automation are echoed today in debates over the impact of information technology (IT) in the workplace. Certainly there is little question that the Internet, e-mail, teleconferencing, and e-commerce are changing the way in which companies do business. But they are also affecting the way in which employees work on a daily basis. Those who take an optimistic approach, as Blauner did, argue that information technology will revolutionize the world of work by allowing new, more flexible ways of working to emerge. These opportunities will permit us to move beyond the routine and alienating aspects of industrial work into a more liberating informational age giving workers greater control over and input into the work process. Enthusiastic advocates of technological advances are sometimes referred to as "technological determinists," because they believe in the power of technology to determine the nature and shape of work itself.

Others are not convinced that information technology will bring about an entirely positive transformation of work. As Shoshana Zuboff (1988) concluded in her research into the use of IT in firms, management can choose to use IT toward very different ends. When embraced as a creative, decentralizing force, information technology can help to break down rigid hierarchies, to engage more employees in decision making and to involve workers more closely in the day-to-day affairs of the company. On the other hand, it can just as easily be used as a way to strengthen hierarchies and surveillance practices. The adoption of IT in the workplace can cut down on face-to-face interactions, block channels of accountability and transform an office into a network of self-contained and isolated modules. Such an approach sees the impact of information technology as influenced by the uses to which it is put and how those using the technology understand its role.

The spread of information technology will certainly produce exciting and heightened opportunities for some segments of the labor force. In the fields of media, advertising, and design, for example, IT both enhances creativity in the professional realm and introduces flexibility into personal work styles. It is qualified, valued employees in responsible positions for whom the vision of wired workers and telecommuting comes closest to being realized. Yet at the other end of the spectrum are thousands of low-paid, unskilled individuals working in call centers and data-entry companies. These positions, which are largely a product of the telecommunications explosion in recent years, are characterized by degrees of isolation and alienation that rival those of Braverman's deskilled workers. Employees at call centers that process travel bookings and financial transactions work according to strictly standardized formats with little or no room for employee discretion or creative input. Employees are closely monitored and their interactions with customers are tape recorded for "quality assurance." The information revolution seems to have produced a large number of routine, unskilled jobs on a par with those of the industrial economy.

Post-Fordism

Over the last three decades, flexible practices have been introduced in a number of spheres, including product development, production techniques, management style, the working environment, employee involvement, and marketing. Group production, problem-solving teams, multitasking, and niche marketing are just some of the strategies that have been adopted by companies attempting to restructure themselves under shifting conditions. Some commentators have suggested that, taken collectively, these changes represent a radical departure from the principles of Fordism; they contend that we are now operating in a period that can best be understood as post-Fordism. **Post-Fordism**, a phrase popularized by Michael Piore and Charles Sabel in *The Second Industrial Divide* (1984), describes a new era of capitalist economic production in which flexibility and innovation are maximized in order to meet market demands for diverse, customized products.

The idea of post-Fordism is somewhat problematic, however. The term is used to refer to a set of overlapping changes that are occurring not only in the realm of work and economic life, but throughout society as a whole. Some writers argue that the tendency toward post-Fordism can be seen in spheres as diverse as party politics, welfare programs, and consumer and lifestyle choices. While observers of late modern societies often point to many of the same changes, there is no consensus about the precise meaning of post-Fordism or, indeed, if this is even the best way of understanding the phenomenon we are witnessing.

Despite the confusion surrounding the term *post-Fordism*, several distinctive trends within the world of work have emerged in recent decades that seem to represent a clear departure from earlier Fordist practices. These include the decentralization of work into nonhierarchical team groups, the idea of flexible production, the increase in mass customization as a result of technological advances, the spread of global production, and the introduction of more flexible working patterns. We will now consider examples of the first four trends; the emergence of flexible working patterns will be addressed later in the chapter.

GROUP PRODUCTION

Group production—collaborative work groups in place of assembly lines—has sometimes been used in conjunction with automation as a way of reorganizing work. The underlying idea is to increase worker motivation by letting groups of workers collaborate in team production processes rather than requiring each worker to spend the whole day doing a single repetitive task, such as inserting the screws in the door handle of a car.

An example of group production is **quality circles (QCs)**, groups of between five and twenty workers who meet regularly to study and resolve production problems. Workers who belong to QCs receive extra training, enabling them to contribute technical knowledge to the discussion of production issues. QCs were initiated in the United States, taken up by a number of Japanese companies, then repopularized in the West in the 1980s. They represent a break from the assumptions of Taylorism, since they recognize that workers possess the expertise to contribute to the definition and method of the tasks they carry out.

The positive effects of group production on workers can include the acquisition of new skills, increased autonomy, reduced managerial supervision, and growing pride in the goods and services that they produce. However, studies have identified a number of negative consequences of team production. Although direct managerial authority is less apparent in a team process, other forms of monitoring exist, such as supervision by other team workers (Smith, 1997). The sociologist Laurie Graham went to work on the assembly line at a Subaru-Isuzu factory and found that peer pressure from other workers to achieve greater productivity was relentless. One coworker told her that after initially being enthusiastic about the team concept, she found that peer supervision was just a new means of management trying to work people "to death." Graham also found that Subaru-Isuzu used the group-production concept as a means to resist labor unions, their argument being that if management and workers were on the same "team," then there should be no conflict between the two. In other words, the good "team player" doesn't complain.

At the Subaru-Isuzu plant Graham worked in, demands for higher pay or reduced responsibilities were viewed as a lack of employee cooperativeness (Graham, 1995). Studies such as Graham's have led sociologists to conclude that although team-based production processes provide workers opportunities for less monotonous forms of work, systems of power and control remain the same in the workplace.

FLEXIBLE PRODUCTION

One of the most important changes in worldwide production processes over the past few years has been the introduction of computer-aided design and **flexible production**. Although Taylorism and Fordism were successful at producing mass products (that were all the same) for mass markets, they were completely unable to produce small orders of goods, let alone goods specifically made for an individual customer. Computer-aided designs, coupled to other types of computer-based technology, have altered this situation in a radical way. Stanley Davis speaks of the emergence of "mass customizing": The new technologies allow the large-scale production of items designed for particular customers. Five thousand shirts might be produced on an assembly line each day. It is now possible to customize every one of the shirts just as quickly as and at no greater expense than producing five thousand identical shirts (Davis, 1987).

Flexible production has produced benefits for consumers and the economy as a whole, but the effect on workers has not been wholly positive. Though workers do learn new skills and have less monotonous jobs, flexible production can create a whole new set of pressures for workers resulting from the need to coordinate carefully the complex production process and to quickly produce the results. Laurie Graham's study of the Subaru-Isuzu factory documented instances when workers were left waiting until the last minute for critical parts in the production process. As a result, employees were forced to work longer and more intensely to keep up with the production schedule, without additional compensation. And as we saw in Chapter 8, although the American economy was booming throughout most of the 1980s and 1990s, average pay for most workers remained quite steady. The profits of these companies mostly benefited upper management and shareholders.

TECHNOLOGY AND EVERYDAY LIFE: MASS CUSTOMIZATION

Technology such as the Internet can be used to solicit information about individual consumers and then manufacture products to their precise specifications. Enthusiastic proponents argue that mass customization offers nothing short of a

Deindustrialization

In 1929, the sociologists Robert and Helen Lynd published a book about the impact of industrialization on a midwestern city they called "Middletown." The Lynds observed that as an increasing number of relatively high-wage factory jobs became available over the years in the city's glass and automobile-parts industries, the habits and values of Middletown workers began to change. Thriftiness, for example, which had been an important feature of the workers' Protestant value system, was replaced by a consumer culture emphasizing car ownership. Similarly, those who engaged in the standardized labor of factory work came to prefer passive and standardized forms of leisure such as listening to the radio and reading popular magazines. Almost every aspect of social life in the community, the Lynds argued, including child-rearing practices, housing patterns, and political beliefs, was somehow affected by the industrial boom that had taken place in Middletown since 1890.

Were the Lynds to conduct their study today, they would find that an opposite process—*deindustrialization*—has been underway in many American cities since the 1970s. Deindustri-

alization is defined as "a systematic decline in the industrial base" (Bluestone, 1988), or as the process whereby the proportion of jobs in the manufacturing sector of the economy decreases over time. The consequences of deindustrialization are as significant as the changes noted by the Lynds almost seventy years ago.

Dell Computer has discovered a unique way to reconcile giving customers exactly what they want while maintaining a low production cost. By using the Internet to process orders, avoiding the expense of keeping a retail space, and producing only what is ordered and no more, Dell has succeeded in creating a system to rapidly produce custom-made products at an affordable price.

new industrial revolution, a development as momentous as the introduction of mass-production techniques in the previous century. Skeptics, however, are quick to point out that as currently practiced, mass customization only creates the illusion of choice—in reality, the options available to the Internet customer are no greater than those offered by a typical mail-order catalog (Collins, 2000).

The manufacturer that has taken mass customization the farthest is Dell Computer. Consumers who want to purchase a computer from the manufacturer must go online—the company does not maintain retail outlets—and navigate Dell's Web site. Customers can select the precise mix of features they desire. After the order is placed, a computer is custom built according to specifications and then shipped—typically within days. In effect, Dell has turned traditional ways of doing business upside down: Firms used to build a product first, then worry about selling it; now, mass customizers like Dell sell first and build second. Such a shift has important consequences for industry. The need to hold stocks of parts on hand—a major cost for manufacturers—has been dramatically reduced. In ad-

It is estimated that factory, store, and office closings resulted in the loss of an astonishing 38 million jobs in the United States in the 1970s (Bluestone and Harrison, 1982), with job losses continuing into the present. Hardest hit are cities in the Northeast and Upper Midwest. Manufacturing employment in Allentown, Pennsylvania, for example, decreased by almost 28 percent between 1980 and 1987, and dropped a staggering 47 percent in Gary, Indiana, during the same period (Goe, 1994). Similar changes are occurring in cities across Europe (Lash and Urry, 1987; Byrne, 1995).

Why is deindustrialization happening? Some sociologists argue that the economies of First World nations are increasingly oriented toward the production and consumption of services such as education and recreation rather than manufactured goods; this orientation may account for the relative decline of the manufacturing sector. Others attribute deindustrialization to the globalization of the economy. As manufacturing firms develop the capacity to do business overseas, they can relocate factories to countries where labor costs are low.

Whatever its causes, the effects of deindustrialization are readily apparent. First, although many laid-off industrial workers eventually find employment elsewhere, they typically wind up in low-wage service sector jobs. Deindustrialization may make downward mobility a common experience for blue-collar workers, with serious implications for their economic and psychological well-being as well as for the welfare of their families. Second, deindustrialization affects some groups of

workers to a greater extent than others. The sociologist William Julius Wilson, for example, argues that the decline in manufacturing jobs has had a particularly severe impact on African Americans, many of whom live in deindustrialized cities. The consequences of job loss for inner-city life are profound and include spiraling rates of poverty, crime, and drug use (Wilson, 1996). Third, deindustrialization may undermine the strength of left-wing influence in political parties, inasmuch as the base of their working-class support narrows.

How serious has deindustrialization been in your community? If you were doing a study today like the one done by the Lynds in the 1920s, what aspects of social life would you expect to be affected by deindustrialization?

dition, an increasing share of production is outsourced. Thus, the rapid transfer of information between manufacturers and suppliers—also facilitated by Internet technology—is essential to the successful implementation of mass customization.

GLOBAL PRODUCTION

Changes in industrial production include not only *how* products are manufactured, but, as we saw earlier with the example of an "American-made" car, *where* products are manufactured. For much of the twentieth century, the most important business organizations were large manufacturing firms that controlled both the making of goods and their final sales. Giant automobile companies such as Ford and General Motors typify this approach. Such companies employ tens of thousands of factory workers making everything from components to the final cars, which are then sold in the manufacturers' showrooms. Such manufacture-dominated production processes are organized as large bureaucracies, often controlled by a single firm.

During the past quarter century, however, another form of production has become important—one that is controlled by giant retailers. In retailer-dominated production, firms such as Wal-Mart and Kmart buy products from manufacturers, who in turn arrange to have their products made by independently owned factories. The sociologists Edna Bonacich and Richard Appelbaum, for example, show that in clothing manufacturing, most manufacturers actually employ no garment workers at all. Instead, they rely on thousands of factories around the world to make their apparel, which they then sell in department stores and other retail outlets. Clothing manufacturers do not own any of these factories and therefore are not responsible for the conditions under which the clothing is made.

Two thirds of all clothing sold in America is made in factories outside the United States, where workers are paid a fraction of U.S. wages. (In China, workers are lucky to make $40 a month.) Bonacich and Appelbaum argue that such competition has resulted in a global "race to the bottom," in which retailers and manufacturers will go anyplace on earth where they can pay the lowest wages possible. One result is that much of the clothing we buy today was likely made in sweatshops by young workers—most likely teenage girls—who get paid pennies for making clothing or athletic shoes that sell for $50, $100, or even more (Bonacich and Appelbaum, 2000).

Trends in the Occupational Structure

The occupational structure in all industrialized countries has changed very substantially since the beginning of the twentieth century (see Figure 14.3). In 1900, about three quarters of the employed population was in manual work, either farming or blue-collar work such as manufacturing. White-collar professional and service jobs were much fewer in number. By 1960, however, more people worked in white-collar professional and service jobs than in manual labor. By 1993, the occupational system had basically reversed its structure from 1900. Almost three quarters of the employed population worked in white-collar professional and service jobs, while the rest worked in blue-collar and farming jobs. In the period 2001–2004, the United States lost 2.6 million manufacturing jobs. By 2010, blue-collar work will have declined even further, with most of the increase in new jobs occurring in the service industries. As we saw in Chapter 10, over the course of the twentieth century, numerous women joined the paid labor force. In 1998, however, 42 percent of working women had service-based or clerical positions, while only 16 percent of men had these types of jobs. Likewise, 38 percent of men held blue-collar manual jobs, while only 10 percent of women were in such positions.

The reasons for the transformation of the occupational structure seem to be several. One is the continuous introduction of labor-saving machinery, culminating in the spread of information technology and computerization in industry in recent decades. Another is the rise of the manufacturing industry in other parts of the world, primarily Asia. The older industries in Western societies have experienced major job cutbacks because of their inability to compete with the more efficient Asian producers, whose labor costs are lower. As we have seen, this global economic transformation forced American companies to adopt new forms of production, which in turn forced employees to learn new skills and new occupations as manufacturing-related jobs moved to other countries. A final important trend is the decline of full-time paid employment with the same employer over a long period of time. Not only has the transformation of the global economy affected the nature of day-to-day work, it has also changed the career patterns of many workers.

THE KNOWLEDGE ECONOMY

Taking these trends into account, some observers suggest that what is occurring today is a transition to a new type of society no longer based primarily on industrialism. We are entering, they claim, a phase of development beyond the industrial era altogether. A variety of terms have been coined to describe this new social order, such as the *postindustrial society*, the *information age*, and the *"new" economy*. The term that has come into most common usage, however, is the **knowledge economy**.

A precise definition of the knowledge economy is difficult to formulate, but in general terms, it refers to an economy in which ideas, information, and forms of knowledge underpin innovation and economic growth. In a knowledge economy, much of the work force is involved not in the physical production or distribution of material goods, but in their design, development, technology, marketing, sale, and servicing. These employees

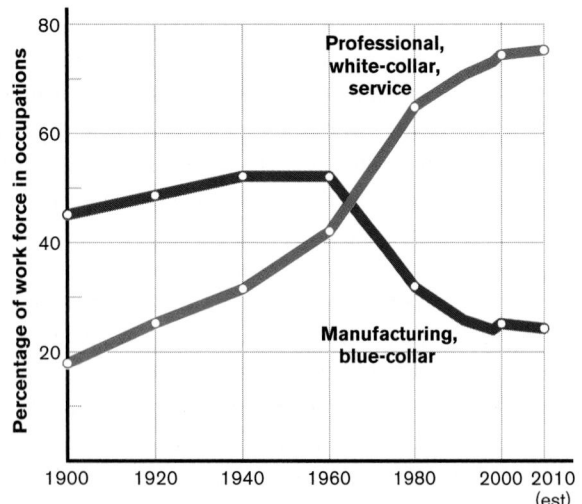

FIGURE 14.3

The Changing Occupational Structure

The United States has lost a large number of manufacturing and other blue-collar jobs in the twentieth century. Many new professional/managerial and other white-collar jobs have been created. However, a large proportion entail work in the service industries, and although these can be classified as white-collar, they resemble blue-collar jobs in terms of pay.

SOURCE: *Historical Statistics of the United States*, vol. 1; U.S. Bureau of Labor Statistics, 2000.

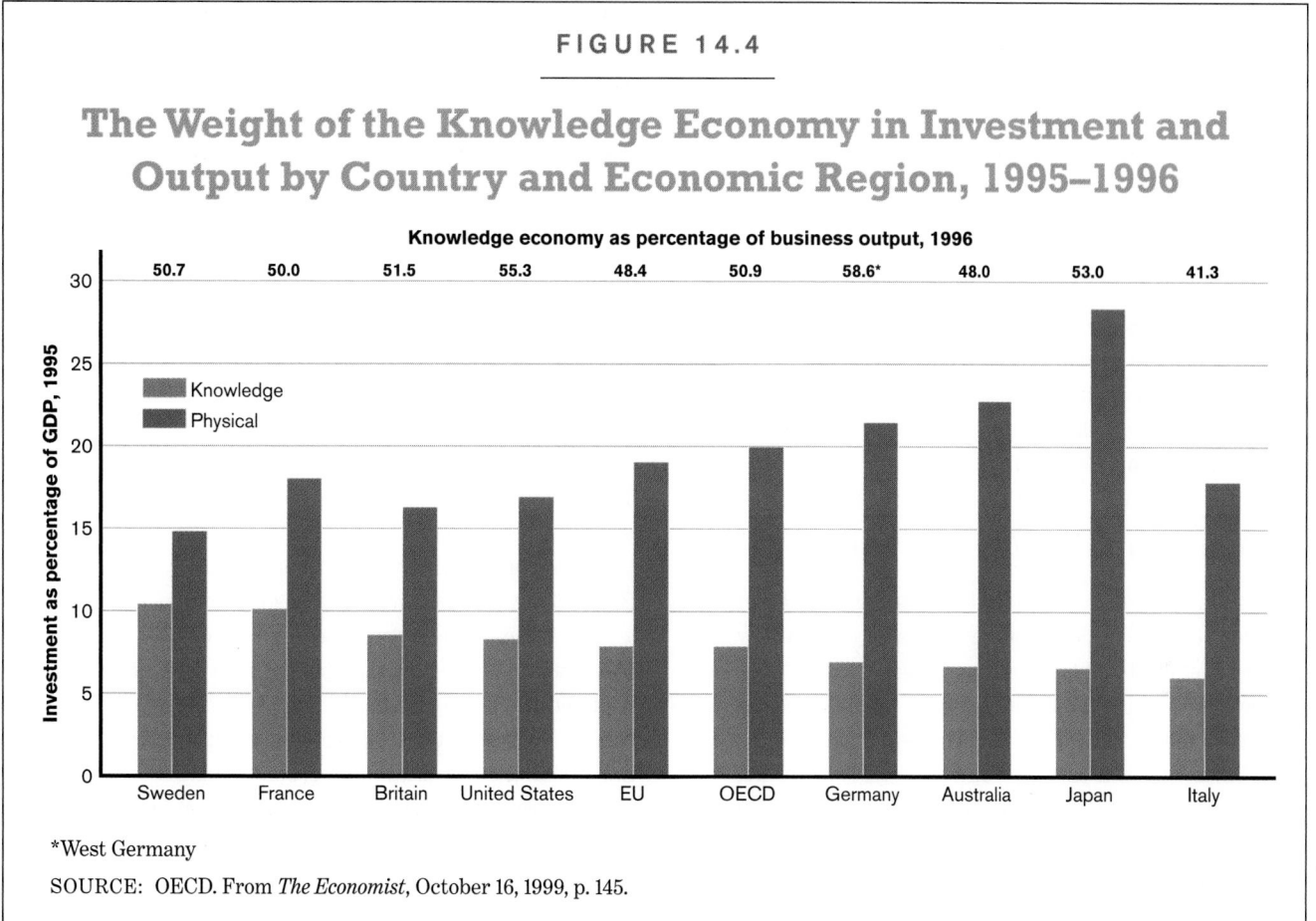

FIGURE 14.4

The Weight of the Knowledge Economy in Investment and Output by Country and Economic Region, 1995–1996

Knowledge economy as percentage of business output, 1996

Sweden	France	Britain	United States	EU	OECD	Germany	Australia	Japan	Italy
50.7	50.0	51.5	55.3	48.4	50.9	58.6*	48.0	53.0	41.3

Investment as percentage of GDP, 1995

Knowledge
Physical

*West Germany

SOURCE: OECD. From *The Economist*, October 16, 1999, p. 145.

can be termed "knowledge workers." The knowledge economy is dominated by the constant flow of information and opinions and by the powerful potentials of science and technology.

How widespread is the knowledge economy at the start of the twenty-first century? A recent study by the Organization for Economic Cooperation and Development has attempted to gauge the extent of the knowledge economy among developed nations by measuring the percentage of each country's overall business output that can be attributed to knowledge-based industries (see Figure 14.4). Knowledge-based industries are understood broadly to include high technology, education and training, research and development, and the financial and investment sector. Among OECD countries as a whole, knowledge-based industries accounted for more than half of all business output in the mid-1990s. Western Germany had a high figure of 58.6 percent, and the United States, Japan, Britain, Sweden, and France were all at or over 50 percent.

Investments into the knowledge economy—in the form of public education, spending on software development, and research and development—now make up significant part of many countries' budgets. Sweden, for example, invested 10.6

percent of its overall gross domestic product in the knowledge economy in 1995. France was a close second because of its extensive spending on public education.

THE PORTFOLIO WORKER

In the light of the impact of the knowledge economy and the demand for a "flexible" labor force, some sociologists and economists have argued that more and more people in the future will become "portfolio workers." They will have a "skill portfolio"—a number of different job skills and credentials—that they will use to move between several jobs during the course of their working lives. Only a relatively small proportion of workers will have continuous "careers" in the current sense.

Some see this move to the **portfolio worker** in a positive light: Workers will not be stuck in the same job for years on end and will be able to plan their work lives in a creative way (Handy, 1994). Others hold that "flexibility" in practice means that organizations can hire and fire more or less at will, undermining any sense of security their workers might have. Employers will only have a short-term commitment to their work forces and will be able to minimize the paying of extra benefits or pension rights.

A study of Silicon Valley, California, claims that the economic success of the area is already founded on the portfolio skills of its work force. The failure rate of firms in Silicon Valley is very high: About three hundred new companies are established every year, but an equivalent number also go bust. The work force, which has a very high proportion of professional and technical workers, has learned to adjust to this. The result, the authors say, is that talents and skills migrate rapidly from one firm to another, becoming more adaptable on the way. Technical specialists become consultants, consultants become managers, employees become venture capitalists—and back again (Bahrami and Evans, 1995).

THE CONTINGENT WORK FORCE

Another important employment trend of the past decade has been the replacement of full-time workers by part-time workers who are hired and fired on a contingency basis. Most temporary workers are hired for the least-skilled, lowest-paying jobs. But many of the "portfolio" workers whom we just discussed take jobs on a part-time basis as well. As a general rule, part-time jobs do not include the benefits associated with full-time work, such as medical insurance, paid vacation time, or retirement benefits. Because employers can save on the costs of wages and benefits, the use of part-time workers has become increasingly common. Researchers estimate that contingency workers make up between 29 and 33 percent of the American work force. This is up from 20 to 23 percent just ten years ago.

The temporary employment agency Manpower, Inc., founded in Milwaukee, Wisconsin, in 1948, has become a global leader in the provision of temporary workers. This company employed 1.9 million temps in 36 countries in 2001 and was the 182nd largest corporation in the world (Manpower, Inc., 2003). Manpower provides labor on a "flexible" basis to 95 percent of Fortune 500 companies. Clearly, temporary labor has become a critical component of the worldwide organization of work and occupations.

There has been some debate over the psychological effects of part-time work on the work force. Many temporary workers fulfill their assignments in a prompt and satisfactory manner, but others rebel against their tenuous positions by shirking their responsibilities or sabotaging their results. Some temporary workers have been observed trying to "look busy" or to work longer than necessary on rather simple tasks. Finally, contingency workers have tried to avoid emotionally intensive work that would require them to become psychologically committed to their employer.

However, some recent surveys of work indicate that part-time workers register higher levels of job satisfaction than those in full-time employment. This may be because most part-time workers are women, who have lower expectations for their careers than men or who are particularly relieved to escape from the monotony of domestic work. Yet many individuals seem to find reward precisely in the fact that they are able to balance paid work with other activities and enjoy a more varied life. Some people might choose to "peak" their lives, giving full commitment to paid work from their youth to their middle years, then perhaps changing to a second career, which would open up new interests.

Unemployment

The idea of work is actually a complex one. All of us work in many ways besides in paid employment. Cleaning the house, planting a garden, and going shopping are plainly all work. But for two centuries or more, Western society has been built around the central importance of paid work. The experience of unemployment—being unable to find a job when one wants it—is still a largely negative one. And unemployment does bring with it unfortunate effects including, sometimes, falling into poverty. Yet as we shall see, some today are arguing that we should think about the relation between being "in work" and "out of work" in a completely different way from the way we did in the recent past.

Rates of unemployment fluctuated considerably over the course of the twentieth century. In Western countries, unemployment reached a peak in the early 1930s, when some 20 percent of the work force were out of work in the United States. The economist John Maynard Keynes, who strongly influenced public policy in Europe and the United States during the post–World War II period, believed that unemployment results from consumers' lacking sufficient resources to buy goods. Governments can intervene to increase the level of demand in an economy, leading to the creation of new jobs; and the newly employed then have the income with which to buy more goods, thus creating yet more jobs for people who produce them. State management of economic life, most people came to believe, meant that high rates of unemployment belonged to the past. Commitment to full employment became part of government policy in virtually all Western societies. Until the 1970s, these policies seemed successful, and economic growth was more or less continuous.

During the 1970s and 1980s, however, Keynesianism was largely abandoned. In the face of economic globalization, governments lost the capability to control economic life as they once did. One consequence was that unemployment rates shot up in many countries.

Several factors probably explain the increase in unemployment levels in Western countries at that time. One was the rise of international competition in industries on which Western prosperity used to be founded. In 1947, 60 percent of steel production in the world was carried out in the United States. Today, the figure is only about 15 percent, whereas steel production has risen by 300 percent in Japan, Singapore, Taiwan, and Hong Kong. A second factor was the worldwide economic recession of the late 1980s, which has still not fully abated. A third reason was the increasing use of microelectronics in industry, the net effect of which has been to reduce the need for labor power. Finally, beginning in the 1970s more women sought paid employment, meaning that more people were chasing a limited number of available jobs.

During this time, rates of unemployment tended to be lower in the United States, for example, than in some European nations. This is perhaps because the sheer economic strength of the country gives it more power in world markets than smaller, more fragile economies. Alternatively, it may be that the exceptionally large service sector in the United States provides a greater source of new jobs than in countries where more of the population has traditionally been employed in manufacturing. And within countries, unemployment is not equally distributed. It varies by race or ethnic background, by age, and by industry and geographic region (see Figure 14.5). Ethnic minorities living in central cities in the United States have much higher rates of long-term unemployment than the rest of the population. A substantial proportion of young people are among the long-term unemployed, again especially among minority groups.

The Future of Work

Over the past twenty years, in all the industrialized countries except the United States, the average length of the working week has become shorter. Workers still undertake long stretches of overtime, but some governments are beginning to introduce new limits on permissible working hours. In France, for example, annual overtime is restricted to a maximum of 130 hours a year. In most countries, there is a general tendency toward shortening the average working career. More people would probably quit the labor force at sixty or earlier if they could afford to do so.

If the amount of time given over to paid employment continues to shrink, and the need to have a job becomes less central, the nature of working careers might become substantially reorganized. Job sharing or flexible working hours, which arose primarily as a result of the increasing numbers of working parents trying to balance the commitments of workplace and family, for example, might become more common. Some work analysts have suggested that sabbaticals of the university type should be extended to workers in other spheres: People would be entitled to take a year off in order to study or pursue some form of self-improvement. Perhaps more individuals will engage in "life planning," in which they arrange to work in different ways (paid, unpaid, full or part time, etc.) at different stages in their lives. Thus, some people might choose to enter the labor force in their late thirties, having followed a period of formal education in their early twenties with time devoted to

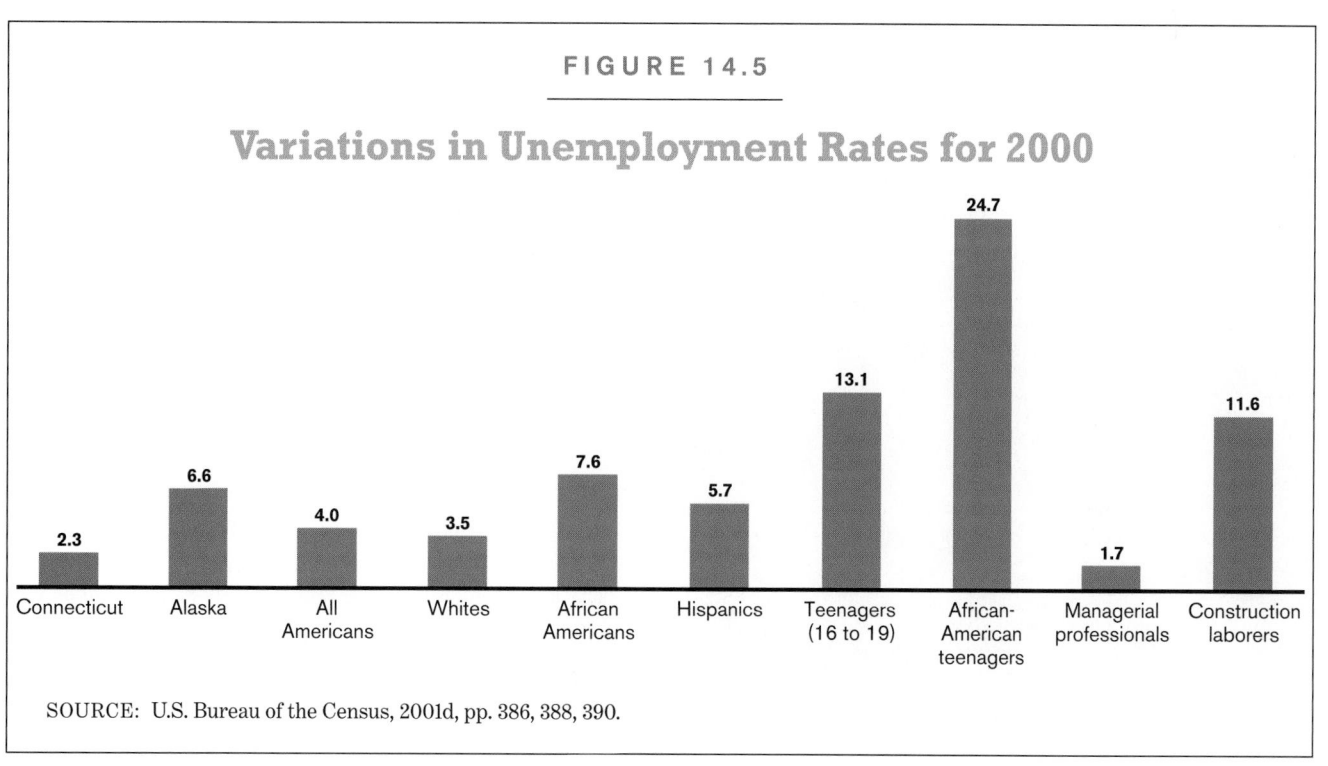

FIGURE 14.5

Variations in Unemployment Rates for 2000

Connecticut	2.3	
Alaska	6.6	
All Americans	4.0	
Whites	3.5	
African Americans	7.6	
Hispanics	5.7	
Teenagers (16 to 19)	13.1	
African-American teenagers	24.7	
Managerial professionals	1.7	
Construction laborers	11.6	

SOURCE: U.S. Bureau of the Census, 2001d, pp. 386, 388, 390.

Layoffs and Downsizing

When the last worker passed through the doors of White Furniture Company in May of 1993, hardly anyone beyond the city limits of Mebane, North Carolina, noticed. In national terms, it made little difference that 203 men and women were out of work or that a venerable, family-owned firm (the "South's oldest maker of fine furniture") had been sold to a conglomerate and now was being shut down. After all, what happened to White's is hardly unique. In the 1990s, in every walk of life and on all social levels, Americans have had to learn a new vocabulary of economic anxiety—layoff, outsourcing, buyout, off-shoring, downsizing, closing. The statistics are mind-numbing: 70,000 people laid off from General Motors in 1991; 50,000 workers from Sears and 63,000 from IBM in 1993; 40,000 from AT&T in 1996. In these times, why should we care about the closing of one furniture factory in a small southern town?

There are many reasons to care, not least that the story of White Furniture Company is a study in miniature of work—what it means when you have it, what it means when you don't. Behind the grim headlines are real men and women who, like the White workers, are devastated not just by the lack of income but by the end of a way of life based on doing a

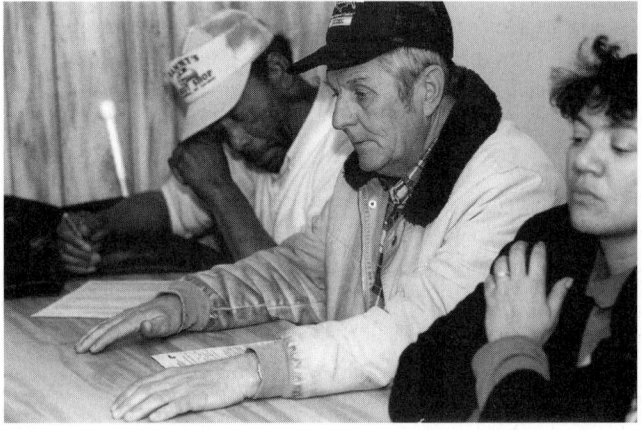

job and doing it well. The wages at White Furniture may have been low; the equipment was antiquated and the working conditions harsh—incessant noise, fumes pervading the air, the factory building cold in winter and sweltering in summer. Yet, looking back, White's workers mourn the closing of the plant and, mostly, they mourn the loss of their craft and their companions. Factory work—industrialization—had a high price tag. Now we are seeing, everywhere around us and on every social level, the dire cost of post-industrialism....

A closing doesn't happen in the melodramatic way one might expect: a door slamming shut and two hundred people out in the cold. It happens in bits and pieces, one worker at a time. At White's there was a grim logic to the layoffs. They followed production. The last piece of furniture came down the line, was worked on, and then the line closed down behind it, and the workers in that section would be let go. A few workers made one last walk-through of the plant, saying good-bye to their friends, but most just left.

The layoffs started in the kiln area where the lumber was brought in to the yard. After the lumber ran through the saws in the rough mill, those people would be let go. After the wood was glued together, the workers on the glue machine left. The piece was machined, and the next day the machine room was empty. The last piece of furniture was sanded, assembled, and then finished, with workers from each department leaving in turn. Finally, the piece went to rub and pack, where it was prepared for shipping and then boxed. The last piece on the line was ready to be sent away. And so were the last workers. You finished your job. You were called away from your department an hour or so before closing time. You sat in the personnel room and signed some papers. The personnel officer shook your hand. And then it was over.

There's a reason for laying off people in this way: it is the best way to ensure that a plant shutdown will be orderly, economical, and efficient. Yet, as many industrial psychologists have noted, people who leave their jobs like this typically feel despair, isolation, and shame. They feel oppressed by the enormity of what lies ahead for them, at the mercy of forces beyond their control. There is little sense of solidarity with other workers, either those who have gone before or those who will be laid off in the future. There is no opportunity for collective anger or organized protest. No one knows who is being laid off, when, how many, or who will be next. . . .

Despite the fact that other companies paid better, workers stayed at White's out of some combination of job satisfaction,

friendship, loyalty, desire for security, and personal pride of craft. To use a formulation that is typically reserved for middle-class rather than for blue-collar workers, they chose to stay at White's because it was a career, not just a job. White's wasn't perfect, and none of the workers says it was. Yet metaphors of death run through the comments so many of the workers make about the closing precisely because people felt that something of themselves died when White Furniture closed. . . .

[James Gilland worked at White Furniture Company from 1951 until 1992.] When you ask him about his job at White's, he answers with his philosophy of work: "Changing jobs is one of the worst things that anybody can do today as a young person. The best thing to do is to start looking when you're young and find a job that you're really interested in, one that you like, that you think you can work with. It's just like getting married. Somebody that you think you can live with the rest of your life. A job is the same way."

SOURCE: Bill Bamberger and Cathy N. Davidson, *Closing: The Life and Death of an American Factory* (New York: DoubleTake/W. W. Norton, 1998), pp. 17, 41, 72, 168.

Questions

- How is James Gilland's view of job loyalty outdated? How could it be revised to fit current hiring and firing patterns?
- Judging from the photographs, what do the impending layoffs and closing of the factory mean to the workers?
- Company buyouts and layoffs are more and more prevalent. Under these uncertain conditions, what can boost workers' morale and inspire pride in their work?

pursuits like travel. People might *opt* to work part time throughout their lives, rather than being forced to because of a lack of full-time employment opportunities.

The French sociologist André Gorz has argued that in the future paid work will play a less and less important part in people's lives. Gorz bases his views on a critical assessment of Marx's writings. Marx believed that the working class—to which more and more people would supposedly belong—would lead a revolution that would bring about a more humane type of society, in which work would be central to the satisfactions life has to offer. Although writing as a leftist, Gorz rejects this view. Rather than the working class becoming the largest grouping in society (as Marx suggested) and leading a successful revolution, it is actually shrinking. Blue-collar workers have now become a minority—and a declining minority—of the labor force.

It no longer makes much sense, in Gorz's view, to suppose that workers can take over the enterprises of which they are a part, let alone seize state power. There is no real hope of transforming the nature of paid work, because it is organized according to technical considerations that are unavoidable if an economy is to be efficient. "The point now," as Gorz puts it, "is to free oneself *from* work. . . ." (Gorz, 1982). This is particularly necessary where work is organized along Taylorist lines or is otherwise oppressive or dull.

Rising unemployment, together with the spread of part-time work, Gorz argues, has already created what he calls a "non-class of nonworkers," alongside those in stable employment. Most people, in fact, are in this "non-class," because the proportion of the population in stable paid jobs at any one time is relatively small—if we exclude the young, the retired, the ill, and homemakers, together with people who are in part-time work or unemployed. The spread of microtechnology, Gorz believes, will further reduce the numbers of full-time jobs available. The result is likely to be a swing toward rejecting the "productivist" outlook of Western society, with its emphasis on wealth, economic growth, and material goods. A diversity of lifestyles, followed outside the sphere of permanent, paid work, will be pursued by the majority of the population in coming years.

According to Gorz, we are moving toward a "dual society." In one sector, production and political administration will be organized to maximize efficiency. The other sector will be a sphere in which individuals occupy themselves with a variety of nonwork pursuits offering enjoyment or personal fulfillment.

How likely is all this to happen? It does seem possible that more and more people will become disenchanted with "productivism"—the stress on constant economic growth and the accumulation of material possessions. It is surely valuable to see unemployment not entirely in a negative light, but as offering opportunities for individuals to pursue their interests and develop their talents.

The nature of the work most people do and the role of work in our lives, like so many other aspects of the societies in which we live, are undergoing major changes. The chief reasons are global economic competition, the widespread introduction of information technology and computerization, and the large-scale entry of women into the work force.

How will work change in the future? It appears very likely that people will take a more active look at their lives than in the past, moving in and out of paid work at different points. These are only positive options, however, when they are deliberately chosen. The reality for most is that regular paid work remains the key to day-to-day survival and that unemployment is experienced as a hardship rather than an opportunity.

Study Outline

www.wwnorton.com/giddens5

The Social Significance of Work

- *Work* is the carrying out of tasks that involve the expenditure of mental and physical effort and has as its objective the production of goods and services catering to human needs. An *occupation* is work that is done in exchange for a regular wage. In all cultures work is the basis of the *economy*.

- A distinctive characteristic of the economic system of modern societies is the development of a highly complex and diverse *division of labor*. The division of labor means that work is divided into different occupations requiring specialization. One result is *economic interdependence:* We are all dependent on each other to maintain our livelihoods.

Taylorism and Fordism

- One manifestation of this division is *Taylorism*, or scientific management. Taylorism divides work into simple tasks that can be timed and organized. *Fordism* extended the principles of scientific management to mass production tied to mass markets. Fordism and Taylorism can be seen as *low-trust systems* that maximize worker alienation. A *high-trust system* allows workers control over the pace and even content of their work.

Organizations and Economic Life

- Union organizations, together with recognition of the right to *strike*, are characteristic features of economic life in all Western countries. Unions emerged as defensive organizations, concerned to provide a measure of control for workers over their conditions of labor. Today, union leaders quite often play an important role in formulating national economic policies.
- The modern economy is dominated by the large *corporations*. When one firm has a commanding influence in a given industry, it is in a *monopoly* position. When a cluster of firms wields such influence, a situation of *oligopoly* exists. Through their influence on government policy and on the consumption of goods, the giant corporations have a profound effect on people's lives.

Transnational Corporations

- Corporations have undergone profound transformations in recent years because of increasing world interdependence, or globalization. The modern corporation is increasingly an enterprise web of many smaller firms linked together, rather than a single big business.
- *Multinational* or *transnational corporations* operate across different national boundaries. The largest of them exercise tremendous economic power. Half of the one hundred largest economic units are not countries, but privately owned companies.

Automation and Group Production

- In recent years, computer-aided design and planning tools have provided the capability to develop *flexible production* systems. *Automation* involves the use of robots in the production process. *Group production*, often used with automation, establishes collaborative work groups such as the *quality circle*, in which workers actively participate in the design and implementation of production methods.

Work and Social Change

- Major changes have occurred in the occupational system during the course of the century. Particularly important has been the relative increase in non-manual occupations at the expense of manual ones. The interpretation of these changes, however, is disputed. Some speak of the arrival of the *portfolio worker*—the worker who has a "portfolio" of different skills and will be able to move readily from job to job. Such workers do exist, but for many people in the work force "flexibility" is more likely to be associated with poorly paid jobs with few career prospects.
- Unemployment has been a recurrent problem in the industrialized countries in the twentieth century. As work is a structuring element in a person's psychological makeup, the experience of unemployment is often disorienting. The impact of new technology seems likely to further increase unemployment rates.
- Major changes are currently occurring in the nature and organization of work. It seems certain that these will become even more important in the future. Nonetheless, work remains for many people the key basis of generating resources necessary to sustain a varied life.

Key Concepts

alienation (p. 417)

automation (p. 429)

capitalism (p. 423)

corporation (p. 423)

division of labor (p. 415)

economic interdependence (p. 416)

economy (p. 414)

entrepreneur (p. 423)

ethnocentric transnationals (p. 426)

family capitalism (p. 424)

flexible production (p. 431)

Fordism (p. 416)

geocentric transnationals (p. 426)

group production (p. 431)

high-trust system (p. 417)

informal economy (p. 415)

institutional capitalism (p. 425)

international division of labor (p. 426)

knowledge economy (p. 434)

low-trust system (p. 417)

managerial capitalism (p. 424)

monopoly (p. 423)

occupation (p. 414)

oligopoly (p. 423)

polycentric transnationals (p. 426)

post-Fordism (p. 430)

portfolio worker (p. 435)

quality circle (QC) (p. 431)

strike (p. 418)

Taylorism (p. 416)

technology (p. 414)

transnational/multinational corporation (p. 425)

union density (p. 418)

welfare capitalism (p. 424)

work (p. 414)

Review Questions

1. What is the overwhelming finding of Freeman and Rogers's study on "what workers want"?
   a. They want more vacation time.
   b. They want more pay.
   c. They want more influence.
   d. They want fewer working hours.

2. From a sociological perspective, women who are housewives
   a. don't have a job.
   b. want a job.
   c. do *work*, although they are not part of the paid labor force.
   d. None of the above.

3. What is the informal economy?
   a. It refers to domestic labor within the home.
   b. It refers to transactions outside the sphere of regular employment, sometimes involving the exchange of cash for services provided, but also often involving the direct exchange of goods and services.
   c. It refers to transactions between small businesses.
   d. It refers to the economy in traditional societies.

4. What is the difference between high-trust and low-trust systems of production?
   a. Low-trust systems, such as Taylorism and Fordism, are found in manufacturing and impose tough work regimes on workers. High-trust systems allow workers flexibility and autonomy in the way they perform their jobs.
   b. Low-trust systems, which feature short-term contracts and high labor turnover, are more often found in the United States, whereas high-trust systems, which feature long-term contracts and low labor turnover, are more often found in Japan.
   c. Low-trust systems are found in the employment of less-educated workers, whereas high-trust systems are found in the employment of better-educated workers.
   d. In low-trust systems, most commonly found in large-scale public bureaucracies, workers and management are suspicious and resentful of one another. In high-trust systems, most commonly found in large corporations, workers and management have learned to cooperate and see that they are basically on the same side.

5. Which of the following types of transnational corporations has managerial systems integrated on a global basis?
   a. Ethnocentric
   b. Exocentric
   c. Geocentric
   d. Polycentric

6. What is Fordism?
   a. The type of large corporation that manufactures and distributes its goods around the world.
   b. The system of flexible production that allows goods to be customized on the assembly line.
   c. The system of assembly-line mass production for mass-market consumption.
   d. The type of credit plans Ford developed that allow consumers to pay back car loans at low monthly payments over a period of years.

7. What is the definition of a strike?
   a. A spontaneous stoppage of work by a group of employees to show their employers how angry they are at the company's actions.
   b. A temporary stoppage of work by a group of employees in order to express a grievance or enforce a demand.
   c. The culmination of a series of industrial actions that usually begin with increased absenteeism, which includes a slowdown and may involve a lockout.
   d. All of the above.

8. The decline in unionization can be attributed to
   a. the recession in world economic activity.
   b. the increasing intensity of international competition.
   c. the rise to power in many countries of rightist governments that launched an aggressive assault on unions in the 1980s.
   d. All of the above.

9. What is a "portfolio worker"?
   a. An artist or a graphic designer who brings a folder full of samples of work to job interviews
   b. A worker with a "skill portfolio"—a number of different job skills and credentials—that he or she will use to move between several different jobs during the course of a career
   c. A computer expert who specializes in a particular set of software applications
   d. An investment consultant who advises people on their retirement plans

10. The majority of the robots used in industry worldwide are to be found in
    a. computer production.
    b. electronic production.
    c. automobile production.
    d. furniture production.

Thinking Sociologically Exercises

1. Explain the meaning of globalization of the modern economy. Explain how this textbook sees globalization affecting workers in Third World countries and in advanced industrial societies.

2. Discuss some of the important ways that the nature of work will change for the contemporary worker as companies apply more automation and larger-scale production processes and as oligopolies become more pervasive. Explain each of these trends and how they affect workers, both now and in the future.

Data Exercises

www.wwnorton.com/giddens5
Keyword: Data14

- Approximately how many hours do you work each week? In what ways does the kind of job or even a worker's sex affect the number of hours worked? You may think that these social factors have nothing to do with structuring the work week, but after completing the data exercise for this chapter you may be surprised by what you learn.

Theoretical Perspectives on the Family

Review the development of sociological thinking about the family and family life.

The Family in History

Learn how the family has changed over the last five hundred years.

Changes in Family Patterns Worldwide

See that although a diversity of family forms exist in different societies today, widespread changes are occurring that relate to the spread of globalization.

Marriage and the Family in the United States

Learn about patterns of marriage, childbearing, and divorce. Analyze how different these patterns are today compared with other periods.

The Dark Side of the Family

Learn about sexual abuse and violence within families.

Alternatives to Traditional Forms of Marriage and the Family

Learn some alternatives to traditional marriage and family patterns that are becoming more widespread.

The Future of the American Family: The Sociological Debate

Consider alternative responses to the question, Is the American family in a state of crisis?

CHAPTER FIFTEEN

FAMILIES AND INTIMATE RELATIONSHIPS

the theme of much of this book has been change. We live in a turbulent, difficult, and unfamiliar world today. Whether we like it or not, we all must come to terms with the mixture of opportunity and risk it presents. Nowhere is this observation more true than in the domain of personal and emotional life.

In our personal lives, we now have to deal with "relationships." When someone asks you, "How is your relationship going?" she is usually asking about a sexual involvement. But we are increasingly caught up in relationships with parents, friends, and others. The term *relationship*, as applied to personal life, came into general use only twenty or thirty years ago, as did the idea that there is a need for "commitment" in personal life.

The fact that most of us now think about these changes a great deal, whether we resist them or not, is indicative of the basic transformations that have affected our personal and emotional lives over the past few decades. A relationship is something *active*—you have to work at it. It depends on winning the trust of the other person if it is going to survive over time. Most kinds of sexual relations have become like this now, and so has marriage. Many troubles we see all around us in sexual and family life derive from this necessity to work at relationships, which is in some respects quite new. But opportunities of a positive kind come from it too.

For example, today the couple, married or unmarried, is at the core of what the family is. The couple came to be at the center of family life as the economic role of the family dwindled and love, or love and sexual attraction, became the basis of forming marriage ties. Most people in our society believe that a good relationship is based on emotional communication or intimacy. The idea of intimacy, like so many other familiar notions we've discussed in this book, sounds old but in fact is very new. In the past, marriage was never based on intimacy and emotional communication. No doubt these were important to a good marriage but not the foundation of it. For the modern couple they are. Communication is the means of establishing a good relationship in the first place, and it is the chief rationale for its continuation. A good relationship is a relationship of equals, where each party has equal rights and obligations. In such a relationship, each person has respect and wants the best for the other. Talk, or dialogue, is the basis of making the relationship work. Relationships function best if people don't hide too much from each other—there has to be mutual trust. And trust has to be worked at; it can't just be taken for granted. Finally, a good relationship is one free from arbitrary power, coercion, or violence.

The changes affecting the personal and emotional spheres go far beyond the borders of any particular country, even one as large as the United States. We find the same issues almost everywhere, differing only in degree and according to the cultural context in which they take place. In China, for example, the state is considering making a divorce more difficult to obtain. In the late 1960s, very liberal marriage laws were passed. Marriage is a working contract that can be dissolved "when husband and wife both desire it." Even if one partner objects, divorce can be granted when "mutual affection" has gone from the marriage. Only a two-week wait is required, after which the two pay $4 and are henceforth independent. The Chinese divorce rate is still low compared with that in Western countries, but it is rising rapidly—as is true in the other developing Asian societies. In Chinese cities, not only divorce, but cohabitation is becoming more frequent. In the vast Chinese countryside, by contrast, everything is different. Marriage and the family are much more traditional—in spite of the official policy of limiting childbirth through a mixture of incentives and punishment. Marriage is an arrangement between two families, fixed by the parents rather than the individuals concerned. A recent study in the province of Gansu, which has only a low level of economic development, found that 60 percent of marriages are still arranged by parents. As a Chinese saying has it: "Meet once, nod your head and marry." There is a twist in the story in modernizing China. Many of those currently divorcing in the urban centers were married in the traditional manner in the country.

In China, there is much talk of protecting the "traditional" family. In many Western countries, the debate is even more intense and divisive. Defenders of the traditional family form argue that the emphasis on relationships comes at the expense of the family as a basic institution of society. Many of these critics now speak of the breakdown of the family. If such a breakdown is occurring, it is extremely significant. The family is the meeting point of a range of trends affecting society as a whole—increasing equality between the sexes, the widespread entry of women into the labor force, changes in sexual behavior and expectations, the changing relationship between home and work. Among all the changes going on today, none is more important than those happening in our personal lives—in sexuality, emotional life, marriage, and the family. There is a global revolution going on in how we think of ourselves and how we form ties and connections with others. It is a revolution advancing unevenly in different parts of the world, with much resistance.

How do we begin to understand the nature of these changes and their impact on our lives? It's only possible to understand what is going on in our personal lives and the family as a social institution today if we know something about how people lived in the past and how people currently live in other societies. So in this chapter, after discussing various theoretical perspectives on the family, we will look at the development of marriage and the family in earlier times, before analyzing the consequences of present-day changes both in the United States and elsewhere.

Basic Concepts

We need first of all to define some basic concepts, particularly those of family, kinship, and marriage. A **family** is a group of persons directly linked by kin connections, the adult members of which assume responsibility for caring for children. **Kinship** ties are connections between individuals, established either through marriage or through the lines of descent that connect blood relatives (mothers, fathers, offspring, grandparents, etc.). **Marriage** can be defined as a socially acknowledged and approved sexual union between two adult individuals. When two people marry, they become kin to one another; the marriage bond also, however, connects together a wider range of kinspeople. Parents, brothers, sisters, and other blood relatives become relatives of the partner through marriage.

Family relationships are always recognized within wider kinship groups. In virtually all societies, we can identify what sociologists and anthropologists call the **nuclear family**, two adults living together in a household with their own or adopted children. In most traditional societies, the nuclear family was part of a larger kinship network of some type. When close relatives in addition to a married couple and children live either in the same household or in a close and continuous relationship with one another, we speak of an **extended family**. An extended family may include grandparents, brothers and their wives, sisters and their husbands, aunts, and nephews.

Whether nuclear or extended, so far as the experience of each individual is concerned, families can be divided into **families of orientation** and **families of procreation**. The first is

An extended family gathers for a photograph in Zimbabwe.

the family into which a person is born; the second is the family into which one enters as an adult and within which a new generation of children is brought up. A further important distinction concerns place of residence. In the United States, when a couple marry, they are usually expected to set up a separate household. This can be in the same area in which the bride's or groom's parents live, but may be in some different town or city altogether. In some other societies, however, everyone who marries is expected to live close to or within the same dwelling as the parents of the bride or groom. When the couple live near or with the bride's parents, the arrangement is called **matrilocal**. In a **patrilocal** pattern, the couple live near or with the parents of the groom.

In Western societies, marriage, and therefore the family, is associated with **monogamy**. It is illegal for a man or woman to be married to more than one individual at any one time. But monogamy is not the most common type of marriage in the world as a whole. In a comparison of several hundred present-day societies, George Murdock found that **polygamy**, a marriage that allows a husband or wife to have more than one spouse, was permitted in over 80 percent (Murdock, 1949). There are two types of polygamy: **polygyny**, in which a man may be married to more than one woman at the same time, and **polyandry**, much less common, in which a woman may have two or more husbands simultaneously.

Theoretical Perspectives on the Family

The study of the family and family life has been taken up differently by sociologists with contrasting approaches. Many of the perspectives adopted even a few decades ago now seem much less convincing in the light of recent research and important changes in the social world. Nevertheless it is valuable to trace briefly the evolution of sociological thinking before turning to contemporary approaches to the study of the family.

Functionalism

The functionalist perspective sees society as a set of social institutions that perform specific functions to ensure continuity and consensus. According to this perspective, the family performs important tasks that contribute to society's basic needs and helps to perpetuate social order. Sociologists working in the functionalist tradition have regarded the nuclear family as fulfilling certain specialized roles in modern societies. With the advent of industrialization, the family became less important as a unit of economic production and more focused on reproduction, child rearing, and socialization.

According to the American sociologist Talcott Parsons, the family's two main functions are *primary socialization* and *personality stabilization* (Parsons and Bales, 1955). **Primary socialization** is the process by which children learn the cultural norms of the society into which they are born. Because this happens during the early years of childhood, the family is the most important area for the development of the human personality. **Personality stabilization** refers to the role that the family plays in assisting adult family members emotionally. Marriage between adult men and women is the arrangement through which adult personalities are supported and kept healthy. In industrial society, the role of the family in stabilizing adult personalities is said to be critical. This is because the nuclear family is often distanced from its extended kin and is unable to draw on larger kinship ties as families could prior to industrialization.

Parsons regarded the nuclear family as the unit best equipped to handle the demands of industrial society. In the "conventional family," one adult can work outside the home while the second adult cares for the home and children. In practical terms, this specialization of roles within the nuclear family involved the husband adopting the "instrumental" role as breadwinner and the wife assuming the "affective," emotional role in domestic settings.

In our present age, Parsons's view of the family comes across as inadequate and outdated. Functionalist theories of the family have come under heavy criticism for justifying the domestic division of labor between men and women as something natural and unproblematic. Yet viewed in their own historical context, the theories are somewhat more understandable. The immediate post–World War II years saw women returning to their traditional domestic roles and men reassuming positions as sole breadwinners. We can criticize functionalist views of the family on other grounds, however. In emphasizing the importance of the family in performing certain functions, both theorists neglect the role that other social institutions—such as government, media, and schools—play in socializing children. The theories also neglect variations in family forms that do not correspond to the model of the nuclear family. Families that did not conform to the white, suburban, middle-class "ideal" were seen as deviant.

Feminist Approaches

For many people, the family provides a vital source of solace and comfort, love and companionship. Yet it can also be a locus for exploitation, loneliness, and profound inequality. Feminism has had a great impact on sociology by challenging the vision of the family as a harmonious and egalitarian realm. In 1965, one of the first dissenting voices was that of the American feminist Betty Friedan, who wrote of "the problem with no name"—the isolation and boredom that gripped many suburban American housewives who felt relegated to an endless cycle of child care and housework. Others followed, exploring the phenomenon of the "captive wife" (Gavron, 1966) and the damaging effects of "suffocating" family settings on interpersonal relationships (Laing, 1971).

During the 1970s and 1980s, feminist perspectives dominated most debates and research on the family. If previously the sociology of the family had focused on family structures, the historical development of the nuclear and extended family, and the importance of kinship ties, feminism succeeded in directing attention inside families to examine the experiences of women in the domestic sphere. Many feminist writers have questioned the vision of the family as a cooperative unit based on common interests and mutual support. They have sought to show that the presence of unequal power relationships within the family means that certain family members tend to benefit more than others.

Feminist writings have emphasized a broad spectrum of topics, but three main themes are of particular importance. One of the central concerns is the *domestic division of labor*—the way in which tasks are allocated among members of a household. Among feminists, there are differing opinions about the historical emergence of this division. While some feminists see it as an outcome of industrial capitalism, others claim that it is linked to patriarchy and thus predates industrialization. There is reason to believe that a domestic division of labor existed prior to industrialization, but it seems clear that capitalist production brought about a much sharper distinction between the domestic and work realms. This process resulted in the crystallization of "male spheres" and "female spheres" and power relationships that are felt to this day. Until recently, the *male breadwinner* model has been widespread in most industrialized societies.

Feminist sociologists have undertaken studies on the way domestic tasks, such as child care and housework, are shared between men and women. They have investigated the validity of claims such as that of the "symmetrical family" (Young and Willmott, 1973)—the belief that, over time, families are becoming more egalitarian in the distribution of roles and responsibilities. Findings have shown that women continue to bear the main responsibility for domestic tasks and enjoy less leisure time than men, despite the fact that more women are working in paid employment outside the home than ever before (Hochschild, 1989; Gershuny et al., 1994; Sullivan, 1997). Pursuing a related theme, some sociologists have examined the contrasting realms of paid and unpaid work, focusing on the contribution that women's unpaid domestic labor makes to the overall economy (Oakley, 1974). Others have investigated the way in which resources are distributed among family members and the patterns of access to and control over household finances (Pahl, 1989).

Second, feminists have drawn attention to the *unequal power relationships* that exist within many families. One topic that has received increased attention as a result of this is the phenomenon of domestic violence. Wife battering, marital rape, incest, and the sexual abuse of children have all received more public attention as a result of feminists' claims that the violent and abusive sides of family life have long been ignored in both academic contexts and legal and policy circles. Feminist sociologists have sought to understand how the family serves as an arena for gender oppression and even physical abuse.

The study of *caring activities* is a third area in which feminists have made important contributions. This is a broad realm that encompasses a variety of processes, from attending to a family member who is ill to looking after an elderly relative over a long period of time. Sometimes caring means simply being attuned to someone else's psychological well-being—several feminist writers have been interested in "emotion work" within relationships. Not only do women tend to shoulder concrete tasks such as cleaning and child care, but they also invest large amounts of emotional labor in maintaining personal relationships (Duncombe and Marsden, 1993). While caring activities are grounded in love and deep emotion, they are also a form of work that demands an ability to listen, perceive, negotiate, and act creatively.

New Perspectives in the Sociology of the Family

Theoretical and empirical studies conducted from a feminist perspective during the last few decades have generated increased interest in the family among both academics and the general population. Terms such as the *second shift*—referring to women's dual roles at work and at home—have entered our everyday vocabulary. But because they often focused on specific issues within the domestic realm, feminist studies of the family did not always reflect larger trends and influences taking place outside the home.

In the past decade, an important body of sociological literature on the family has emerged that draws on feminist perspectives but is not strictly informed by them. Of primary concern are the larger transformations that are taking place in family forms—the formation and dissolution of families and households and the evolving expectations within individuals' personal relationships. The rise in divorce and single parenting, the emergence of "reconstituted families" and gay families, and the popularity of cohabitation are all subjects of concern. Yet these transformations cannot be understood apart from the larger changes occurring in our late modern age. Attention must be paid to the shifts occurring at the societal, and even global, level if we are to grasp the link between personal transformations and larger patterns of change.

The Family in History

Sociologists once thought that prior to the modern period, the predominant form of family in western Europe was of the extended type. Research has shown this view to be mistaken. The nuclear family seems long to have been preeminent. Premodern household size was larger than it is today, but the difference is not especially great. In the United States, for example, throughout the seventeenth, eighteenth, and nineteenth centuries, the average household size was 4.75 persons. The current average is 2.59 (U.S. Bureau of the Census, 2000). Since the earlier figure includes domestic servants, the difference in family size is small. Extended family groups were more important in eastern Europe and Russia.

Children in the premodern United States and Europe were often working—helping their parents on the farm—from seven or eight years of age. Those who did not remain in the family enterprise frequently left the parental household at an early age to do domestic work in the houses of others or to follow apprenticeships. Children who went away to work in other households would rarely see their parents again.

Other factors made family groups then even more impermanent than they are now, in spite of the high rates of divorce in current times. Rates of mortality (numbers of deaths per thousand of the population in any one year) for people of all ages were much higher. A quarter or more of all infants in early modern Europe did not survive beyond the first year of life (in contrast to well under 1 percent today), and women frequently died in childbirth. The death of children or of one or both spouses often dislocated or shattered family relations.

The Development of Family Life

The historical sociologist Lawrence Stone has charted some of the changes leading from premodern to modern forms of family life in Europe. Stone distinguished three phases in the development of the family from the 1500s to the 1800s. In the early part of this period, the main family form was a type of nuclear family that lived in fairly small households but maintained deeply embedded relationships within the community, including with other kin. This family structure was not clearly separated from the community. According to Stone (although some historians have challenged this), the family at that time was not a major focus of emotional attachment or dependence for its members. People didn't experience, or look for, the emotional intimacies we associate with family life today. Sex within marriage was not regarded as a source of pleasure but as a necessity to propagate children.

Individual freedom of choice in marriage and other matters of family life were subordinated to the interests of parents, other kin, or the community. Outside aristocratic circles, where it was sometimes actively encouraged, erotic or romantic love was regarded by moralists and theologians as a sickness. As Stone puts it, the family during this period "was an open-ended, low-keyed, unemotional, authoritarian institution. . . . It was also very short-lived, being frequently dissolved by the death of the husband or wife or the death or very early departure from the home of the children" (Stone, 1980).

This type of family was succeeded by a transitional form that lasted from the early seventeenth century to the beginning of the eighteenth. This later type was largely confined to the upper reaches of society but was nevertheless very important, because from it spread attitudes that have since become almost universal. The nuclear family became a more separate entity, distinct from ties to other kin and to the local community. There was a growing stress on the importance of marital and parental love, although there was also an increase in the authoritarian power of fathers.

In the third phase, the type of family system we are most familiar with in the West today gradually evolved. This family is a group tied by close emotional bonds, enjoying a high degree of domestic privacy and preoccupied with the rearing of children. It is marked by the rise of **affective individualism**, the formation of marriage ties on the basis of personal selection, guided by sexual attraction or romantic love. Sexual aspects of love began to be glorified within marriage instead of in extramarital relationships. The family became geared to consumption rather than production, as a result of the increasing

Balancing Family and Work

How many hours each week did your parents spend doing paid work when you were growing up? Did their commitment to work affect the way you or your siblings were raised? One of the ways globalization has affected family life in the United States is by increasing the amount of time that people spend each week at work. While there is some disagreement among researchers as to whether Americans, on average, are putting in more hours at work now than they did in the past, many sociologists give credence to the findings of the economist Juliet Schor, author of the 1992 book *The Overworked American.* Schor argues that workers today spend on average 164 more hours each year at work than they did twenty years ago. Workers are also taking less vacation time than they did previously. Perhaps more significant, the percentage of mothers who are working full time has increased dramatically since the end of World War II. In fact, in a comprehensive study of the multiple roles that modern women occupy, Daphne Spain and Suzanne Bianchi (1996) found that the group of women that saw the most dramatic increase in labor force participation in the United States were married women with young children. Taken together, these facts suggest that parents today have less time available to spend with their children than was the

spread of workplaces separate from the home. Women became associated with domesticity and men with being the breadwinners. Originating among more affluent groups, this family type became more or less universal in Western countries with the spread of industrialization.

In premodern Europe marriage usually began as a property arrangement, was in its middle mostly about raising children, and only in the end was about love. Few couples in fact married "for love," but many grew to love each other in time as they jointly managed their household, reared their offspring, and shared life's experiences. Nearly all surviving epitaphs to spouses evince profound affection. By contrast, in most of the modern West, marriage *begins* being about love, in its middle is still mostly about raising children (if there are children), and in the end is—often—about property, by which point love is absent or a distant memory (Boswell, 1995).

"The Way We Never Were": Myths of the Traditional Family

Many people in current times feel that family life is being undermined. They contrast what they see as the decline of the family with more traditional forms of family life. Was the family of the past as peaceful and harmonious as many people recall it, or is this a simply idealized fiction? As Stephanie Coontz points out in her book *The Way We Never Were* (1992), as with other visions of a golden age of the past, the rosy light shed on the "traditional family" dissolves when we look back to previous times to see what things really were like.

Many admire the colonial family of early days as a disciplined, stable family. However, colonial families suffered from the same disintegrative forces as their counterparts in Europe. Especially high death rates meant that the average

case in decades past. As a result, there has been a significant increase in the percentage of children enrolled in day-care programs—and, some would argue, a palpable increase in tension and stress within families as more of the day-to-day parental role is offloaded onto child-care providers.

In her book *The Time Bind* (1997), sociologist Arlie Hochschild suggests that these developments may be related to globalization. Globalization, of course, is not responsible for the gains women have made in securing positions in the paid labor force. Nevertheless, some corporations, according to Hochschild, have responded to the pressures of global competition by encouraging their salaried employees to put in longer hours at work, thus increasing levels of productivity. Why would employees willingly agree to spend so much time at their jobs—often considerably more than forty hours each week—when they are not paid to do so, when they know that such a commitment disrupts their family life, and in an age when computerization has greatly improved workplace efficiency? Shouldn't technological progress allow workers to spend more time with their families rather than less? Hochschild's answer to this question is that some corporations rely on the power of workplace norms to elicit a greater time commitment from their workers. New employees are socialized into a corporate culture in which working long hours is seen as a badge of dedication and professionalism. Employees, seeking status and the approval of their peers and supervisors, become motivated to put as much time into work as possible and to make sure that those around them know precisely how much time they spend working. In some cases, such a corporate culture has arisen unintentionally, as workers respond to the threat of corporate

downsizing by redoubling their commitment to the organization. In other cases—as with the corporation Hochschild studied—executives have consciously sought to shape the culture of the organization, reminding employees through handbooks, speeches, and newsletters that working more than forty hours a week is the mark of a "good" worker.

Although globalization has touched all the nations of the world, its effects on work time seem to vary by country. In France and Germany, for example, workers—sometimes acting through unions, sometimes making their power known at the voting booth—have rejected corporate calls for a longer workweek, and are instead pressuring employers to reduce the workweek and to grant longer vacations. Do Europeans simply value family and leisure time more than Americans? Or would American workers be making the same demands if unions were stronger in this country?

length of marriages was less than twelve years, and more than half of all children saw the death of at least one parent by the time they were twenty-one. The admired discipline of the colonial family was rooted in the strict authority of parents over their children. The way in which this authority was exercised would be considered exceedingly harsh by today's standards.

If we consider the Victorian family of the 1850s, the ideal family still eludes us. In this period, wives were more or less forcibly confined to the home. According to Victorian morality, women were supposed to be strictly virtuous, while men were sexually licentious: Many visited prostitutes and paid regular visits to brothels. In fact, wives and husbands often had little to do with one another, communicating only through their children. Moreover, domesticity wasn't even an option for poorer groups of this period. African American slaves in the South lived and worked frequently in the most appalling

conditions. In the factories and workshops of the North, white families worked long hours with little time for home life. Child labor was also rampant in these groups.

Our most recent memory draws us to the 1950s as the time of the ideal American family. This was a period when women worked only in the home, while men were responsible for earning the family wage. Yet large numbers of women didn't actually *want* to retreat to a purely domestic role and felt miserable and trapped in it. Women had held paid jobs during World War II as part of the war effort. They lost these jobs when men returned from the war. Moreover, men were still emotionally removed from their wives and often observed a strong sexual double standard, seeking sexual adventures for themselves but setting strict codes for their spouses.

Betty Friedan's best-selling book *The Feminine Mystique* first appeared in 1963, but its research referred to the 1950s.

Friedan struck a chord in the hearts of thousands of women when she spoke of the "problem with no name": the oppressive nature of a domestic life bound up with child care, domestic drudgery, and a husband who only occasionally put in an appearance and with whom little emotional communication was possible. Even more severe than the oppressive home life endured by many women was the alcoholism and violence suffered within many families during a time period when society was not prepared to fully confront these issues.

Let's now look directly at the changes affecting personal life, marriage, and the family in the world today. There is no doubt that some of these changes are profound and far-reaching. But interpreting their likely implications, particularly in the United States, means taking account of just how unrealistic it is to contrast what is happening now with a fictional or mythical view of the traditional family.

Changes in Family Patterns Worldwide

There is a diversity of family forms today in different societies across the world. In some areas, such as more remote regions in Asia, Africa, and the Pacific Rim, traditional family systems are little altered. In most developing countries, however, widespread changes are occurring. The origins of these changes are complex, but several factors can be picked out as especially important. One is the spread of Western culture. Western ideals of romantic love, for example, have spread to societies in which they were previously unknown. Another factor is the development of centralized government in areas previously composed of autonomous smaller societies. People's lives become influenced by their involvement in a national political system; moreover, governments make active attempts to alter traditional ways of behavior. Because of the problem of rapidly expanding population growth, states frequently introduce programs advocating smaller families, the use of contraception, and so forth.

A further influence is the large-scale migration from rural to urban areas. Often men go to work in towns or cities, leaving family members in the home village. Alternatively, a nuclear-family group will move as a unit to the city. In both cases, traditional family forms and kinship systems may become weakened. Finally, and perhaps most important, employment opportunities away from the land and in such organizations as government bureaucracies, mines, plantations, and—where they exist—industrial firms tend to have disruptive consequences for family systems previously centered on landed production in the local community.

In general, these changes are creating a worldwide movement toward the predominance of the nuclear family, breaking down extended-family systems and other types of kinship groups. This was first documented by William J. Goode in his book *World Revolution in Family Patterns* (1963) and has been borne out by subsequent research.

Directions of Change

The most important changes occurring worldwide are the following:

1. Clans and other kin groups are declining in their influence.
2. There is a general trend toward the free choice of a spouse.
3. The rights of women are becoming more widely recognized, in respect to both the initiation of marriage and decision making within the family.
4. Kin marriages are becoming less common.
5. Higher levels of sexual freedom are developing in societies that were very restrictive.
6. There is a general trend toward the extension of children's rights.

In many countries, especially Western industrial societies, the nuclear family has been the preeminent family form. However, as mentioned earlier, in some societies extended families have been and still are the norm and traditional family practices continue. Moreover, there are differences in the speed at which change is occurring, and there are reversals and countertrends. A study in the Philippines, for example, found a higher proportion of extended families in urban areas than in surrounding rural regions. These had not just developed from traditional extended-family households but represented something new. Leaving the rural areas, cousins, nephews, and nieces went to live with their relatives in the cities to take advantage of the employment opportunities available there. Parallel examples have also been noted elsewhere in the world (Strinner, 1979), including some industrialized nations. Certain regions of Poland, for instance, show evidence of a rejuvenation of the extended family. A good number of industrial workers in Poland have farms that they tend part time. In the cities, grandparents move in with their children's family, run the household, and bring up the grandchildren, while the younger generation is engaged in outside employment (Turowski, 1977).

Given the ethnically diverse character of the United States, there are considerable variations in family and marriage within the country. Some of the most striking include differences between white and African American family patterns, and we need to consider why this is so. We will then move on to examine divorce, remarriage, and stepparenting in relation to contemporary patterns of family life.

Marriage and the Family in the United States

The United States has long been characterized by high marriage rates. Nearly every American adult eventually marries; almost 95 percent of adults in their early fifties today are or have previously been married. The age at which first marriages are contracted has risen, however, over the past twenty years (it was also high at the turn of the century, declining in the 1922–1950 period). There are several explanations for this trend in the last several decades toward later marriage. Some researchers contend that increases in cohabitation among younger people account for the decreases (or delays) in marriage among this group. Young people are cohabiting before or instead of marrying. Others argue that increases in postsecondary school enrollment, especially among women, are partially responsible for delays in marriage. Similarly, women's increased participation in the labor force often leads to delays in marriage as women work to establish their careers before marrying and starting a family (Oppenheimer, 1988). Labor force participation also increases economic independence among women. By earning their own income, many women no longer need a male breadwinner in their home. The flip side of the economic independence argument is the idea that the deterioration of men's economic position since the late 1980s has made them less attractive mates and less ready to marry. Some researchers have used this idea—the marriageable men hypothesis—to explain the especially low marriage rates among blacks: Because black men have suffered the worst economic conditions in the last few decades, they might be viewed by black women as particularly poor marriage candidates. Finally, some researchers believe that modernization and a secular change in attitudes promote individualism and make marriage less important than it once was. The true reason for the decline in marriage is most likely some combination of the above explanations. But we must be careful how we make our comparisons. Although some have argued that the trend since 1970 toward later marriage is a break from tradition, it actually is close to the age of first marriage for the period 1890–1940. To say that people today are postponing marriage is true only if we compare ourselves with the 1950s generation. It might be more accurate to say that the 1950s generation married at an unusually young age.

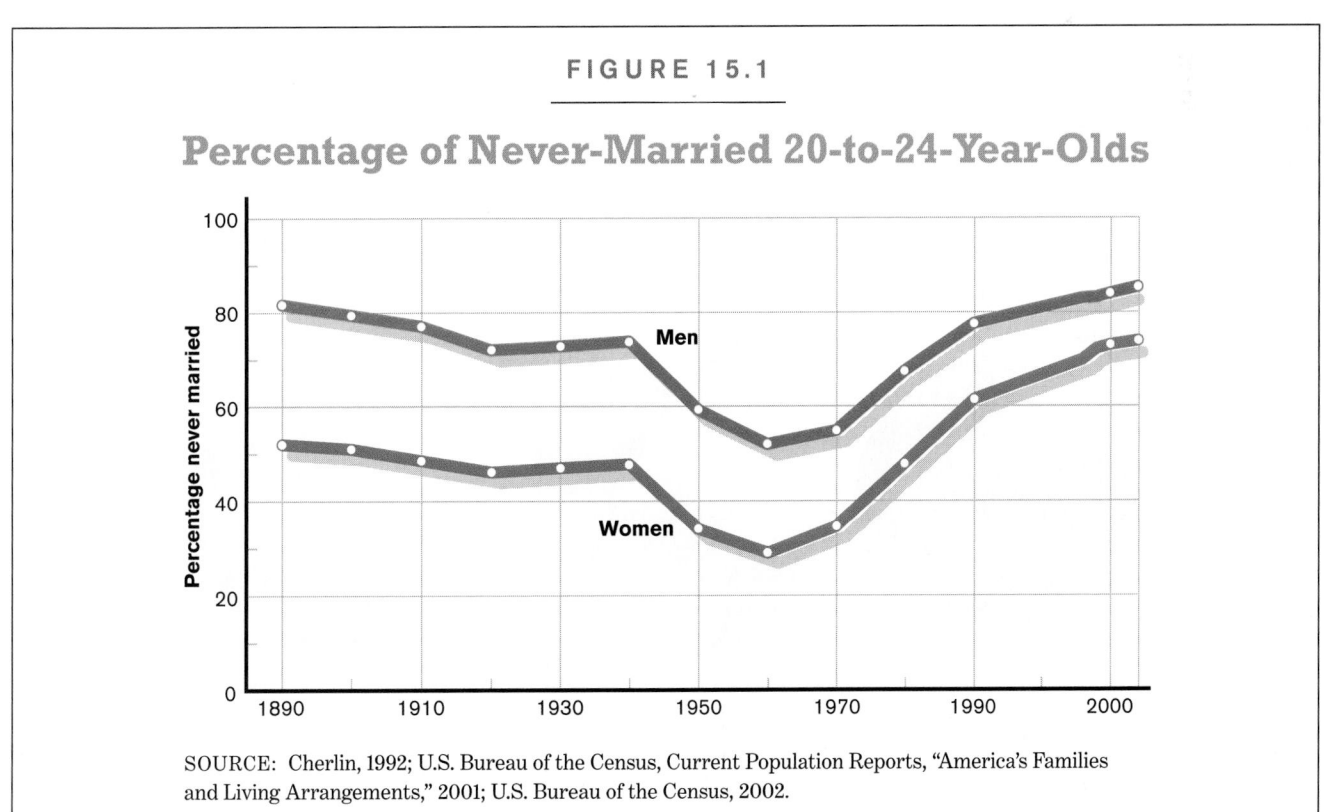

FIGURE 15.1

Percentage of Never-Married 20-to-24-Year-Olds

SOURCE: Cherlin, 1992; U.S. Bureau of the Census, Current Population Reports, "America's Families and Living Arrangements," 2001; U.S. Bureau of the Census, 2002.

In 1960, the average age of first marriages was 22.8 for men and 20.3 for women. The comparable ages in 2000 were 26.8 for men and 25.1 for women. Another way of measuring the relations between age and first marriage is to look at the numbers of people who remain unmarried before a certain age (see Figure 15.1). Thus, in 1960, just 28 percent of women aged less than 24 years had never married. In 2002, that proportion was 74 percent. The U.S. census now incorporates a category of "unmarried couples sharing the same household." As this practice of cohabitation is new, it is not easy to make direct comparisons with preceding years. Nonetheless, we can accurately estimate that the number of couples among younger age groups who live together without being married has risen steeply (see Figure 15.2) from 11 percent around 1970 to 44 percent in the early 1980s and probably about 50 percent today (Cherlin, 1999). By age thirty about 50 percent of women will have cohabitated outside marriage (National Center for Health Statistics, 2002).

No one knows for certain how the trend toward cohabitation will develop in the future. We can get some guidance from what has happened in other industrial countries. In France, cohabiting relationships are more widespread than in the United States and tend to be of longer duration. A survey in that country published in the late 1980s found that over half of cohabiting couples "did not think about marriage." Cohabitation, in other words, leads to marriage only for a minority; for most people, it is a phase of life in which partners want to leave their options open (Cherlin, 1992). We will return to the topic of cohabitation as an alternative to marriage later in this chapter.

An extraordinary increase in the proportion of people living alone in the United States has also taken place over recent years—a phenomenon that partly reflects the high levels of marital separation and divorce. More than one in every four households now consists of one person, a rise of 44 percent since 1960. There has been a particularly sharp rise in the proportion of individuals living alone in the twenty-four-to-forty-four age bracket.

Some people still suppose that the average American family is made up of a husband who works in paid employment and a wife who looks after the home, living together with their two children. This is very different from the real situation: Only about 25 percent of children live in households that fit this picture. One reason is the rising rates of divorce: A substantial proportion of the population live either in single-parent households or in stepfamilies, or both. Another is the high proportion of women who work. Dual-career marriages and single-parent families are now the norm (see Figure 15.3). The majority of married women working outside the home also care for a child or children. Although many working women are concentrated in jobs with poor or nonexistent promotion prospects, the standard of living of many American couples is dependent on the

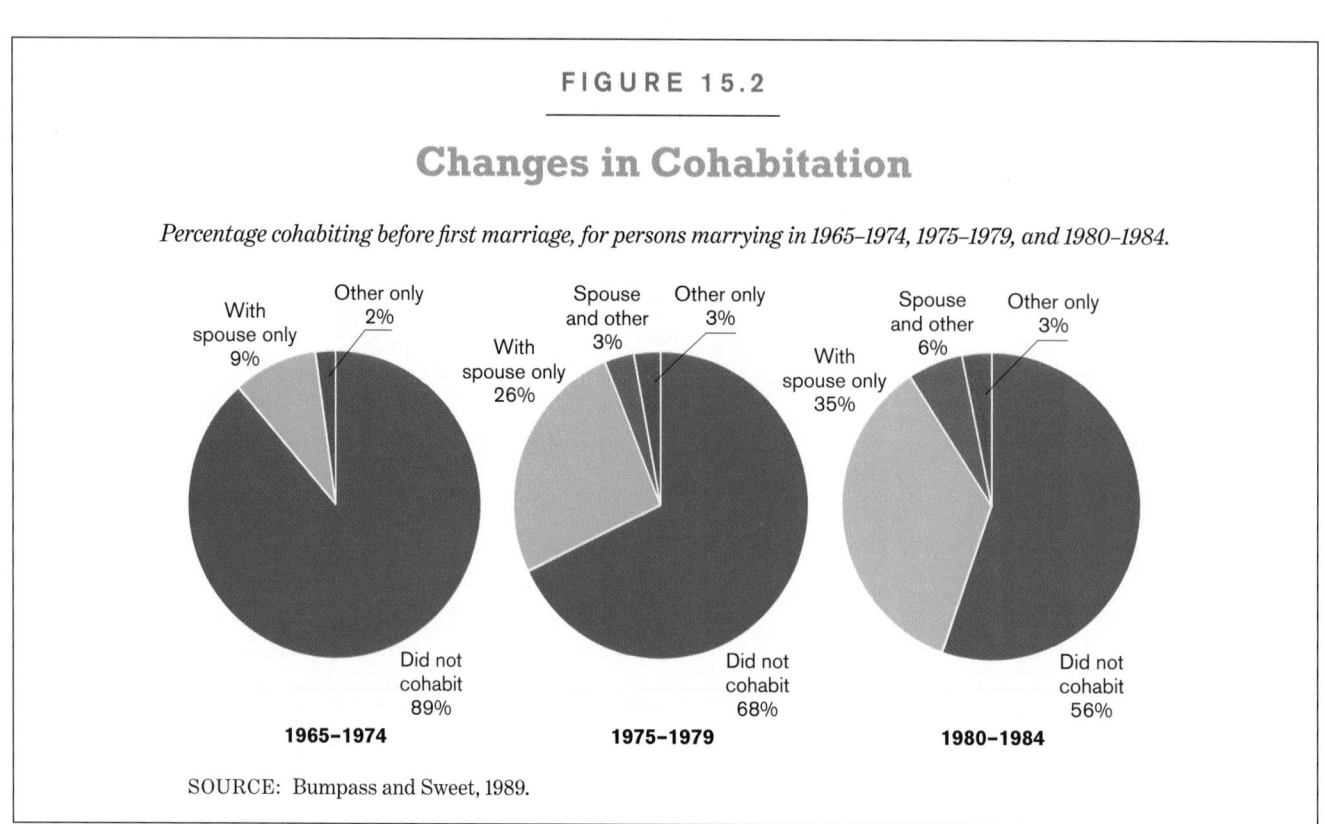

FIGURE 15.2

Changes in Cohabitation

Percentage cohabiting before first marriage, for persons marrying in 1965–1974, 1975–1979, and 1980–1984.

1965–1974
With spouse only 9%
Other only 2%
Did not cohabit 89%

1975–1979
With spouse only 26%
Spouse and other 3%
Other only 3%
Did not cohabit 68%

1980–1984
With spouse only 35%
Spouse and other 6%
Other only 3%
Did not cohabit 56%

SOURCE: Bumpass and Sweet, 1989.

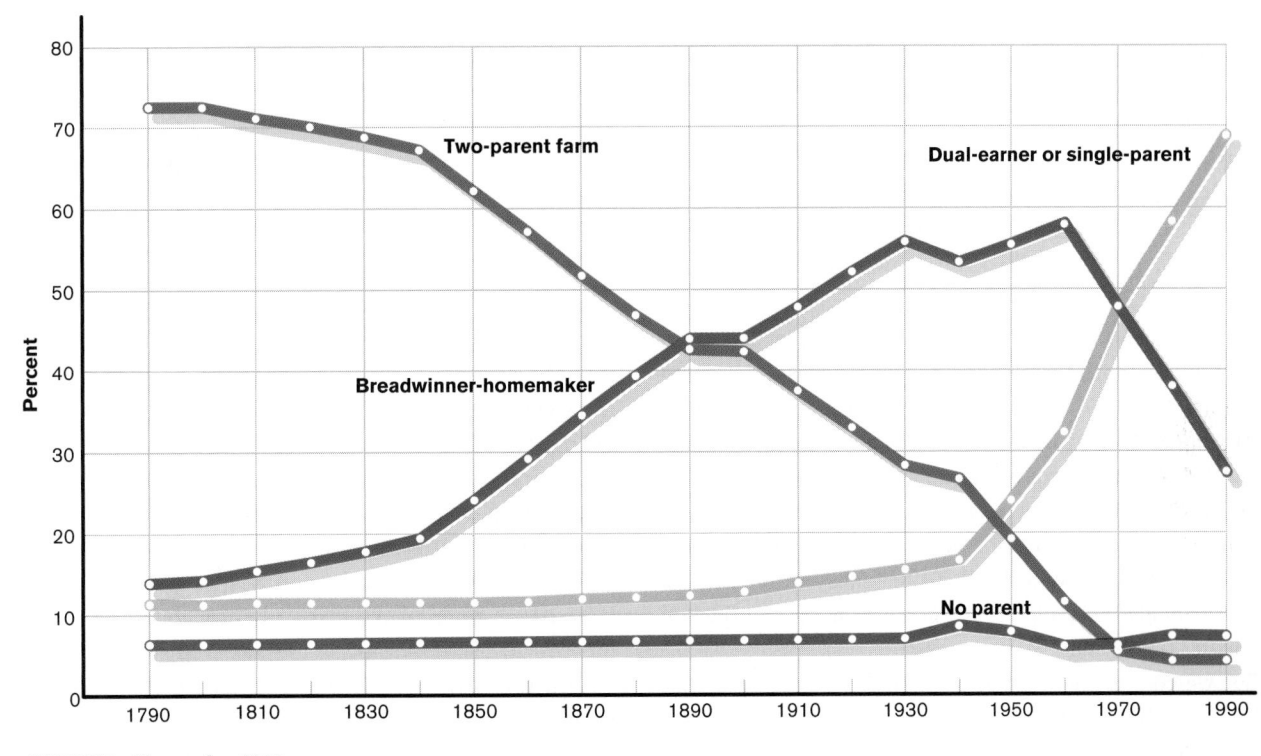

FIGURE 15.3

The Changing Structure of American Families with Children

Percentage of American children 17 and younger living in each of four types of families, 1790–1990.

Two-parent farm

Dual-earner or single-parent

Breadwinner-homemaker

No parent

SOURCE: Hernandez, 1993.

income contributed by the wife, as well as on the unpaid work she undertakes in the home (see also Chapter 14).

There are also some large differences in patterns of child-bearing between parents in the 1950s and later generations. The birthrate rose sharply just after World War II and again during the 1950s. Women in the 1950s had their first child earlier in their lives than has been true of the later generations, and subsequent children were born closer together. Since the late 1960s, the average age at which women have their first child has progressively risen. And women are leaving larger gaps between children. In 1976, only 20 percent of births were to women aged over thirty. By 2000, this proportion had grown to 38 percent.

African American Families

As mentioned earlier, there are important differences in white and black family patterns. One of the most striking is that far fewer African American women aged twenty-five to forty-four are married and living with a husband than white women in the same age group. This fact has given rise to heated disputes about the nature of African American families in the United States.

More than thirty years ago, Senator Daniel Patrick Moynihan described black families as "disorganized" and caught up in a "tangle of pathology" (Moynihan, 1965). Moynihan, among others, looked back at the history of the black family for reasons. The early development of African American family patterns was largely governed by the conditions imposed by slavery. The circumstances of slavery prevented blacks from maintaining the cultural customs of their societies of origin. Members of similar African tribal groups were deliberately dispersed to different plantations. Some owners treated their slaves considerately, fostering the development of family life. Others, however, regarded their slaves as little better than livestock and inherently promiscuous, and therefore believed marriage formalities to be unnecessary.

But slavery was not the only historical factor contributing to contemporary problems. Following emancipation, new cultural experiences and structural factors came to wreak havoc on black families. Among these were continued yet new forms of discrimination against African Americans, changes in the economy such as the development of sharecropping in the South after the Civil War, and the migration of black families from the South to northern cities in the early decades of the twentieth century (Jones, 1986).

However, the divergence between black and white family patterns has become much greater since the 1960s, when Moynihan's study was published, and it seems probable that we have to look mainly to present-day influences to explain them. In 2002, 79 percent of white families included a married couple, as compared to 46 percent of black families (U.S. Census, 2000). In 1960, 21 percent of African American families were headed by females; among white families, the proportion was 8 percent. By 2002, the proportion for black families had risen to more than 48 percent, while that for white families was under 18 percent (see Figure 15.4) (U.S. Census, 2002). Female-headed families are more prominently represented among poorer blacks. African Americans in poor urban neighborhoods have experienced little rise in living conditions over the past two decades: Many are confined to low-wage jobs or are more or less permanently unemployed. In these circumstances, there is little to foster continuity in marital relationships.

But we should not see the situation of African American families purely in a negative light. The director of the National Urban League, a black organization, titled a research report produced in the 1970s "The Strengths of Black Families." These families, the report claimed, show characteristics that promote stability, including strong and adaptable kin ties. Extended kinship networks are important among poor blacks—much more significant, relative to marital ties, than in most white communities. A mother heading a one-parent family is likely to have a close and supportive network of relatives to depend on. This contradicts the idea that black single parents and their children form unstable families. A far higher proportion of female-headed families among African Americans have other relatives living with them than do white families headed by females.

Historical evidence also reveals that black-white differences in family structure (especially female headship and children living with parents) are not contemporary phenomena but existed at the turn of the twentieth century. Some of the historical differences (black women being more likely to be heads of households and their children less likely to be living with them) are due to higher black male mortality rates. However, some of the differences at the turn of the century and even today may be explained by cultural/historical factors such as the emphasis on extended kin ties in sub-Saharan Africa—some suggest they may rival conjugal ties—and the institution of fosterage in West Africa whereby families sent their children to live with other relatives for a variety of reasons (Morgan et al., 1993).

In her book *Lifelines* (1983), Joyce Aschenbrenner provides a comprehensive portrayal of extended kin relationships in African American families. Aschenbrenner gained a new perspective on both white and black family types in the United States as a result of fieldwork she had earlier carried out in Pakistan. From the point of view of the Pakistanis, the white family in the United States seemed weak and "disorganized." They could not understand how a mere couple, let alone a single parent, could bring up children. They viewed with abhorrence the practice of hiring a stranger to baby-sit while the parents went out. Where were the uncles and grandparents? Why weren't a woman's brothers on hand to lend assistance if she was left on her own to bring up her children? The way they thought of the family was closer to the situation of African American families rather than to the usual family structure among whites.

Discussions of the black family, Aschenbrenner suggests, have focused too strongly on the marriage relationship. This emphasis is in line with the overriding importance of marriage in American society, but this relationship does not necessarily form the structure of the African American family. In most societies that include extended families, relationships such as mother-daughter, father-son, or brother-sister may be more socially significant than that between husband and wife (Aschenbrenner, 1983).

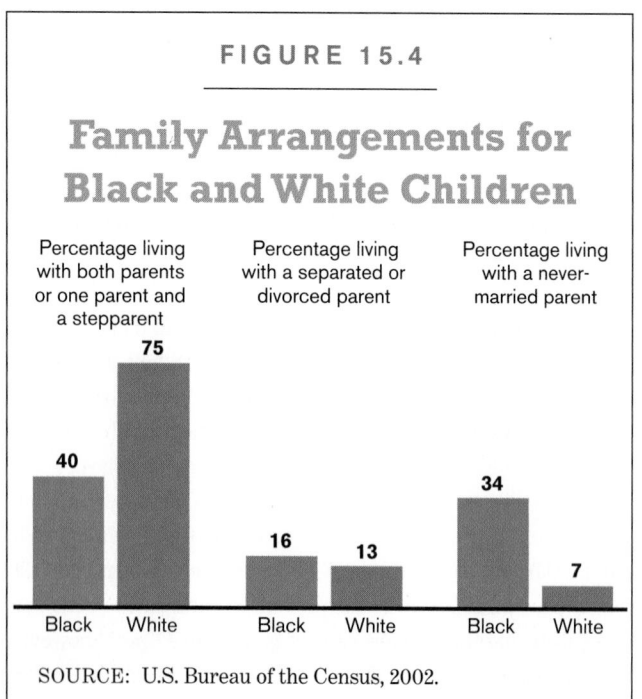

FIGURE 15.4

Family Arrangements for Black and White Children

Percentage living with both parents or one parent and a stepparent

Percentage living with a separated or divorced parent

Percentage living with a never-married parent

40	75	16	13	34	7
Black	White	Black	White	Black	White

SOURCE: U.S. Bureau of the Census, 2002.

Latino Families

As in many other areas, Hispanics are very heterogeneous when it comes to family patterns. Mexicans, Puerto Ricans, and Cubans are three of the largest Hispanic subgroups. In the U.S. census of 1990, Mexicans were the largest Hispanic group—over 58 percent of the whole Hispanic population. Puerto Ricans constituted nearly 10 percent down from 12 percent in 1990, Cubans were just 3.5 percent, and the rest of the Hispanic population was made up of much smaller groups from many Latin American nations (U.S. Census, 2000a).

Mexican American families are characterized by multigenerational households and a high birthrate. Economically, Mexican American families are more well off than Puerto Rican families but less well off than Cuban families. Defying cultural stereotypes of a Mexican American home with a male breadwinner and female homemaker, more than half of all Mexican American women are in the labor force (Ortiz, 1995). Still, ethnographic research indicates that this is due to necessity rather than desire. Many Mexican American families suggest that the breadwinner-homemaker model would be their preference but that they are constrained by finances (Hurtado, 1995).

Although Puerto Rico is a U.S. commonwealth, Puerto Ricans are still considered part of the umbrella category of Hispanics. However, because of their status as U.S. citizens, Puerto Ricans can and do move about freely between Puerto Rico and the mainland without the difficulties often encountered by immigrants. Researchers have shown that when barriers to immigration are high, only the most able (physically, financially, etc.) members of a society will be able to leave their homeland and move to another country. Because Puerto Ricans do not face as many barriers, even the least able can manage the migration process. The economic upshot of unrestricted migration for Puerto Ricans is that they are the most economically disadvantaged of all the major Hispanic groups.

Puerto Rican families are also characterized by a higher percentage of children born to unmarried mothers than any other Hispanic group—second only to African Americans (Cherlin, 1999). However, consensual unions—cohabiting relationships in which couples consider themselves married but are not legally married—are often the context for births to unmarried mothers. Nancy Landale and Kelly Fennelly (1992) conducted a study of the marital experiences of Puerto Rican women and found that many of these women lived in consensual unions. They suggest that Puerto Ricans respond to tough economic times by forming consensual unions as the next best option to what is often a much more expensive legal marriage.

Cuban American families are the most prosperous of all the Hispanic groups but still less prosperous than whites. Most Cuban Americans have settled in the Miami area and have formed immigrant enclaves in which they rely on other Cubans for their business and social needs (e.g., banking, schools, shopping, etc.). The relative wealth of Cuban Americans is driven largely by family business ownership. In terms of childbearing, Cuban Americans have lower levels of fertility than non-Hispanic whites and equally low levels of nonmarital fertility.

Asian American Families

One of the primary features of the Asian American family is that of dependence on the extended family. In many Asian cultures, family concerns are almost always a priority over individual concerns. Family interdependence also helps Asian Americans prosper financially. Asian American family and friend networks often pool money to help their members start a business or buy a house. This help is reciprocated as the recently endowed family member then contributes to the others. The result is a median family income for Asian Americans that is *higher* than that of the median for non-Hispanic whites.

There is a less detailed body of research on differences among Asian American subgroups than is the case with Hispanic subgroups. However, some fertility differences have been established. Chinese American and Japanese American women have much lower fertility rates than do any other racial/ethnic group. Chinese, Japanese, and Filipino families have lower levels of nonmarital fertility than all other racial/ethnic groups, including non-Hispanic whites. Low levels of nonmarital fertility combined with low levels of divorce for most Asian American groups demonstrate the emphasis on marriage as the appropriate forum for family formation and maintenance.

Native American Families

Kinship ties are also very important in Native American families. As Cherlin (1999) notes, "kinship networks constitute tribal organization; kinship ties confer identity" for Native Americans. However, fewer than half of all Native Americans live on or near tribal lands, so for those who live in cities or away from reservations, kin ties may be less prominent. Furthermore, Native Americans have higher rates of intermarriage than any other racial/ethnic group. In fact, in 1990, less than half of all married Native Americans were married to other Native Americans (Sandefur and Liebler, 1997).

The Native American fertility experience is similar to that of African Americans. Native American women have a high fertility rate and a high percentage of nonmarital fertility. Over half of all Native American women giving birth in 1990 were not married (U.S. National Center for Health Statistics, 1993). Sandefur and Liebler (1997) also report a high divorce rate for Native Americans.

Divorce and Separation

The past thirty years have seen major increases in rates of divorce, together with a relaxation of previously held attitudes of disapproval of divorce. For centuries in the West, marriage was regarded as virtually indissoluble. Divorces were granted only in limited situations, such as nonconsummation of a marriage. Yet today most countries have moved rapidly toward making divorce more easily available.

Divorce rates, calculated by looking at the number of divorces per thousand married men or women per year, have fluctuated in the United States in different periods (Figure 15.5). They rose, for example, following World War II, then dropped off before climbing to much higher levels. The divorce rate increased steeply from the 1960s to the late 1970s, reaching a peak in 1980 (thereafter declining somewhat). It used to be common for divorced women to move back to their parents' homes after separation; today, most set up their own households.

Divorce exerts an enormous impact on the lives of children. Since 1970, more than 1 million American children per year have been affected by divorce. In one calculation, about one half of children born in 1980 became members of a one-parent family at some stage in their lives. Since two thirds of women and three fourths of men who are divorced eventually remarry, most of these children nonetheless grew up in a family environment. Only just over 2 percent of children under fourteen in the United States today are not living with either parent. The remarriage figures are substantially lower for African Americans. Only 32 percent of black women and 55 percent of black men who divorce remarry within ten years. Black children are half as likely as white children to be living with both parents or one parent and a stepparent (37 percent versus 76 percent) (Cherlin, 1992).

Lenore Weitzman (1985) has argued that no-fault divorce laws have helped to recast the psychological context of divorce positively (reducing some of the hostility it once generated), but they have had strong negative consequences for the economic position of women. Laws that were designed to be gender-neutral have had the unintended consequence of depriving divorced women of the financial protections that the old laws provided. Women are expected to be as capable as men of supporting themselves after divorce. Yet because most women's careers are still secondary to their work as

FIGURE 15.5

Divorce Rates in the United States

SOURCE: Cherlin, 1999.

homemakers, they may lack the qualifications and earning power of men. The living standards of divorced women and their children on average fell by 27 percent in the first year following the divorce settlement. The average standard of living of divorced men, by contrast, *rose* by 10 percent. Most court judgments left the former husband with a high proportion of his income intact; therefore, he had more to spend on his own needs than while he was married (Peterson, 1996).

REASONS FOR DIVORCE

Divorce rates are obviously not a direct index of marital unhappiness. For one thing, they do not include people who are separated but have not been legally divorced. Moreover, people who are unhappily married may choose to stay together—because they believe in the sanctity of marriage, they are wary about the consequences they will suffer in the case of a breakup, or they wish to remain with one another for the sake of the children.

Why has divorce become much more common over recent years? There are several reasons, which involve the wider changes going on in modern societies and in social institutions. As mentioned before, changes in the law have made divorce easier. Additionally, except for a small proportion of wealthy people, marriage today no longer has much connection with the desire to perpetuate property and status from generation to generation. As women become more economically independent, marriage is less of a necessary economic partnership. Greater overall prosperity means that it is easier to establish a separate household in case of marital disaffection (Lee, 1982). The fact that little stigma now attaches to divorce is in some part the result of these developments but adds momentum to them also. A further important factor is the growing tendency to evaluate marriage in terms of the levels of personal satisfaction it offers. Rising rates of divorce do not seem to indicate a deep dissatisfaction with marriage as such, but an increased determination to make it a rewarding and satisfying relationship (Cherlin, 1990).

Other factors that show a positive correlation to the likelihood of divorce are related to an individual's life cycle. They include:

- parental divorce (people whose parents divorce are more likely to divorce);
- premarital cohabitation (people who cohabitate before marriage have a higher divorce rate);
- premarital childbearing (people who marry after having children are more likely to divorce);
- marriage at an early age (people who marry as teenagers have a higher divorce rate);

- a childless marriage (couples without children are more likely to divorce); and
- low incomes (divorce is more likely among couples with low incomes) (White, 1990).

THE EXPERIENCE OF DIVORCE

It is extremely difficult to draw up a balance sheet of the social advantages and costs of high levels of divorce. More tolerant attitudes toward divorce mean that couples can terminate an unrewarding relationship without incurring social ostracism. On the other hand, marriage breakup is almost always emotionally stressful and may create financial hardship, especially for women.

In her study *Uncoupling*, Diane Vaughan (1986) carried out a series of interviews with 103 recently separated or divorced people (mainly from middle-class backgrounds) to chart the process of transition from living together to living apart. The notion of "uncoupling" refers to how people make the transition from intimate relationships to living alone. She found that in many cases, before the actual physical parting, there was a "social separation"—at least one of the partners developed a new life pattern, becoming interested in new pursuits and making new friends, in contexts in which the other was not included. This usually meant keeping secrets from the other—especially, of course, when a relationship with a lover was involved.

According to Vaughan's research, uncoupling is often unintentional in its beginnings. One individual—whom she calls the "initiator"—becomes more dissatisfied with the relationship than the other. The initiator creates a "territory" independent of the activities in which the couple engage together. For some time before this, the initiator may have been trying unsuccessfully to change the partner, to get him to behave in more acceptable ways, foster shared interests, and so forth. At some point, the initiator feels that this attempt has been a failure and that the relationship is fundamentally flawed. From then on, she becomes preoccupied with the ways in which the relationship or the partner is defective. Vaughan suggested that this is the opposite of the process of falling in love, when an individual focuses on the attractive features of the other and ignores those that may be more dubious.

DIVORCE AND CHILDREN

The effects of divorce on children are difficult to gauge. How contentious the relationship is between the parents prior to separation, the ages of the children at the time, whether or not there are brothers or sisters, the availability of grandparents and other relatives, the children's relationship with their individual parents, and how frequently they continue to see both parents

The American Family

Kansas

As divorce has increased, remarriage and stepparenting have become common family arrangements in both rural and urban America. For children and adults involved in "blended" families, the transition can be both challenging and rewarding. A family in rural Kansas has created friendships and connections that are extended to all of its family members. Six years ago two young girls participated in the wedding of their mother and new stepfather. Since then, the girls have helped to raise their half-brother and to support the family cattle and soybean business. The girls' biological father (a valued parent and friend) is also an active part of the family, visiting frequently, joining celebrations, and involving the girls with their paternal relatives.

"Living here in the Flint Hills country on a farm/ranch, we are involved in 4H, and all school activities. Grandparents, aunts, uncles, and cousins are also a big part of our lives. I feel very fortunate to be a part of this wonderful family. I guess we forget, or just don't think of ourselves as being 'blended,' just a family that enjoys, works, listens, and loves each other to the fullest. The girls are lucky that they have two dads that love and take care of them. I feel this has a great deal to do with our family doing so well together. The two dads do not compete to outdo the other or put the other down. They are both there for the girls and the girls' needs. I think the girls enjoy having a little brother, although being the baby with two older sisters and old parents, he is as spoiled as we can get him, which means he can become a real pain from time to time. But we all love him so much, it's hard to be firm when his smile melts us all."

—Mom, Rural Kansas

South Dakota

Fostering children is a universally understood and commonly practiced Lakota Sioux custom. According to tradition, children in need of help are embraced as family members and foster families are highly regarded within the community. On the Rosebud Sioux Reservation in South Dakota, two sisters and a daughter have taken to heart the Lakota understanding of family and opened their doors to foster children for over twenty years. All of the children (placed by state and private foster agencies) are loved, provided for, celebrated and respected as precious members of the larger community circle.

"Being a 'foster' parent is something that came really naturally to me. Having grown up in a Lakota family, I have a large extended family. I saw so many people come and go through

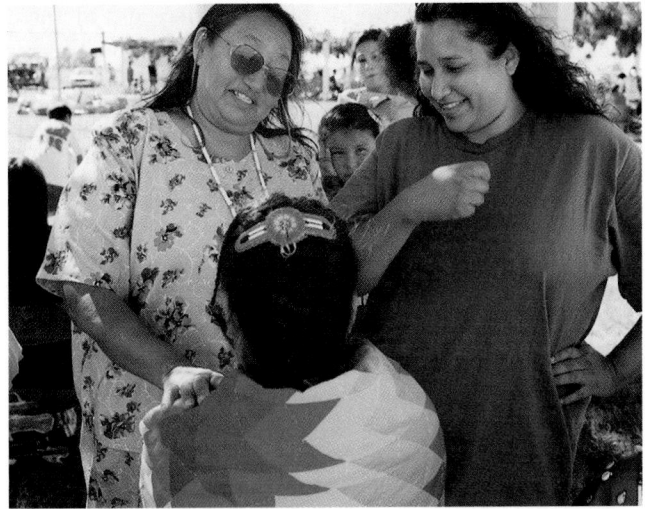

my grandmother's and my mother's house. It didn't matter if they were blood or not, their doors were always open. So I think this is why it was so easy for me to open my home to others. I never really thought about becoming a foster parent. Even before we were officially licensed, we cared for other kids in our home. I married my husband in 1987, when I was nineteen years old, and we got custody of his younger brothers and sisters in the next spring. So, I was nineteen taking care of a sixteen, thirteen, and eleven year old. It was hard, but I had my mom and family to help us. When the kids started to graduate and move on with their lives, the house felt empty, but there is always someone else who needs a family to love and support them. I don't like the word 'foster' because it puts separation between us and the kids. My own kids are happy to have more brothers and sisters. We are a family, and the kids are my kids. You know what they say; the more the merrier. Don't get me wrong; everything isn't always rosy, but you get

past the rough seas, and into calm waters. Even though the older ones are adults and have their own lives, they still come home when they need to or call when they are having a hard time. And we will always be there for all of them."

—Mom, Rosebud Sioux Reservation, South Dakota

Ohio

With the divorce rate estimated to be as high as 50 percent, single parent families are one of the largest and fastest growing family types in America. (In 1997, over one quarter of children lived with only one parent.) Raising the youngest three of his six adopted children, a single parent father in Cleveland cooks, cleans, and cares for his kids between working full-time shifts as an inner city police officer.

"Children are the heart of any family and mine are my heart. Most men think it's a woman's job to raise children, but it's not. I work, clean house, cook and help the kids with homework, and if one of the kids is sick, it's me that takes them to the hospital and sits at their bedside. Whether the times are good or bad, it's dad to the rescue."

—Dad, Cleveland, Ohio

SOURCE: Courteney Coolidge, "American Families: Beyond the White Picket Fence," a photo project, available at http://10families.com.

Questions

- How would you define "family," based on the three examples above?
- In terms of lifestyle and function, what are the differences between these families and the nuclear family?

can all affect the process of adjustment. Since children whose parents are unhappy with each other but stay together may also be affected, assessing the consequences of divorce for children is doubly problematic.

Research indicates that children often suffer a period of marked emotional anxiety following the separation of their parents. Judith Wallerstein and Joan Kelly studied 131 children of sixty families in Marin County, California, following the separation of the parents. They contacted the children at the time of the divorce, a year and a half after, and five years after. According to the authors, almost all the children experienced intense emotional disturbance at the time of the divorce. Preschool-age children were confused and frightened, tending to blame themselves for the separation. Older children were better able to understand their parents' motives for divorce but frequently worried about its effects on their future and expressed sharp feelings of anger. At the end of the five-year period, however, the researchers found that two thirds were coping reasonably well with their home lives and their commitments outside. A third remained dissatisfied with their lives, were subject to depression, and expressed feelings of loneliness, even in cases where the parent with whom they were living had remarried (Wallerstein and Kelly, 1980).

Wallerstein continued her study of this same group of children, following 116 of the original 131 into young adulthood with interviews at the end of ten-year and fifteen-year periods. The interviews revealed that these children brought memories and feelings of their parents' divorce into their own romantic relationships. Almost all felt that they had suffered in some way from their parents' mistakes. Not surprisingly, most of them shared a hope for something their parents had failed to achieve—a good, committed marriage based on love and faithfulness. Nearly half the group entered adulthood as "worried, underachieving, self-deprecating, and sometimes angry young men and women." Although many of them got married themselves, the legacy of their parents' divorce lived with them. Those who appeared to manage the best were often helped by supportive relationships with one or both parents (Wallerstein and Blakeslee, 1989).

We cannot say, of course, how the children might have fared if their parents had stayed together. The parents and children studied all came from an affluent white area and might or might not be representative of the wider population. Moreover, the families were self-selected: They had approached counselors seeking help. Those who actively seek counseling might be less (or more) able to cope with separation than those who do not.

A more recent study found that the majority of persons whose parents had divorced did not have serious mental health problems. They did find small differences in mental health between those whose parents divorced and those whose parents stayed together (favoring those whose parents stayed together), but much of this difference in mental health had been identified in children at age seven, before any of the families experienced divorce (Cherlin et al., 1998). The most prominent sociologist of the family in the United States, Andrew Cherlin, has argued that the general effects of divorce on children are:

- Almost all children experience an initial period of intense emotional upset after their parents separate.
- Most resume normal development without serious problems within about two years after the separation.
- A minority of children experience some long-term problems as a result of the breakup that may persist into adulthood (Cherlin, 1999).

Remarriage and Stepparenting

Before 1900, the large majority of all marriages in the United States were first marriages. Most remarriages involved at least one widowed person. With the progressive rise in the divorce rate, the level of remarriage also began to climb, and in an increasing proportion of remarriages, at least one person was divorced.

Today, thirty-five out of every one hundred marriages involve at least one previously married person. Up to age thirty-five, the majority of remarriages are between divorced people. After that age, the proportion of remarriages with widows or widowers rises. By age fifty-five, the proportion of such remarriages is larger than those following divorce.

Odd though it might seem, the best way to maximize the chances of marriage, for both sexes, is to have been married previously. People who have been married and divorced are more likely to marry again than single people in similar age groups are to marry for the first time. At all age levels, divorced men are more likely to remarry than divorced women. Two in every three divorced women remarry, but three in every four divorced men eventually marry again. Many divorced individuals also choose to cohabitate instead of remarry. In statistical terms, at least, remarriages are less successful than first marriages: rates of divorce are higher.

This does not mean that second marriages are doomed to fail. People who have been divorced may have higher expectations of marriage than those who remain married to their first spouses. Hence, they may be more ready to dissolve new marriages than those only married once. The second marriages that endure are usually more satisfying, on average, than the first.

A **stepfamily** may be defined as a family in which at least one of the adults is a stepparent. Many who remarry become stepparents of children who regularly visit rather than live in the same household. By this definition, the number of stepfamilies is much greater than shown in available official statistics, since these usually refer only to families with whom stepchildren live. Stepfamilies bring into being kin ties that resemble those of some traditional societies but that are new in Western countries. Children may now have two "mothers" and two "fathers"—their natural parents and their stepparents. Some stepfamilies regard all the children and close relatives from previous marriages as part of the family. If we consider that at least some of the grandparents may be part of the family as well, the result is a situation of some complexity.

Certain particular difficulties tend to arise in stepfamilies. In the first place, there usually exists a biological parent living elsewhere whose influence over the child or children is likely to remain powerful. Cooperative relations between divorced individuals often become strained when one or both remarry. Take as an illustration the case of a woman with two children who marries a man also with two children, all six living together. If the "outside" parents demand the same times of visitation as previously, the tensions that arise from welding such a newly established family together are likely to be intense. It may prove impossible to have the new family all together on weekends.

Stepfamilies merge children from different backgrounds, who may have varying expectations in the family milieu. Since most stepchildren belong to two households, the possibilities of clashes of habits and outlooks are considerable. There are few established norms defining the relationship between stepparent and stepchild. Should a child call a new stepparent by name, or is "Dad" or "Mom" more appropriate? Should the stepparent play the same part in disciplining the children as the natural parent? How should a stepparent treat the new spouse of her previous partner when the children are picked up?

Research on family-structure effects on children shows that girls experience more detrimental outcomes from stepfamily living, whereas boys demonstrate more negative outcomes from single-parent family living. The more negative effects for boys may be because single-parent family living generally means living with a mother only, and thus the male role model is absent. Girls are more likely to bond with their mothers in this type of family. A remarriage that introduces a stepfather may cause girls to feel that their close relationship with their mother is threatened. It is speculated that this is why girls living in stepfamilies experience more negative outcomes.

Members of stepfamilies are finding their own ways of adjusting to the relatively uncharted circumstances in which they find themselves. Perhaps the most appropriate conclusion to be drawn is that while marriages are broken up by divorce, families on the whole are not. Especially where children are involved, ties persist.

Single-Parent Households

Single-parent households have become increasingly common. As a result of the increase in divorce rates and births before marriage, about one half of all children spend some time in their lives in a single-parent family (Furstenberg and Cherlin, 1991). The vast majority are headed by women, since the mother usually obtains custody of the children following a divorce (in a small proportion of single-parent households, the individual, again almost always a woman, has never been married). There are over 12 million single-parent households in the United States today, and the number may continue to increase (see Figure 15.6). Such households comprise one in five of all families with dependent children. On average, they are among the poorest groups in contemporary society. Many single parents, whether they have ever been married or not, still face social disapproval as well as economic insecurity. Earlier and more judgmental terms such as *deserted wives, fatherless families,* and *broken homes* are tending to disappear, however.

The category of single-parent household is an internally diverse one. For instance, more than half of widowed mothers are homeowners, but the vast majority of never-married single mothers live in rented accommodations. Single parenthood tends to be a changing state, and its boundaries are rather blurred. In the case of a person who is widowed, the break is obviously clear cut—although even here a person might have effectively been living on his or her own for some while if the partner was hospitalized prior to death. About 60 percent of single-parent households today, however, are brought about by separation or divorce. In such cases, individuals may live together sporadically over a quite lengthy period. As one single mother remarks:

> I think it takes a time to come to terms with being a single mother. In my case I've only accepted what I am in the past year. I suppose before I always thought that we might get back together but when he got married I had to give up. I felt very bad at the time, but now I think it was the best thing that could have happened because it made me come to terms with my life. (Quoted in Crow and Hardey, 1992)

Most people do not wish to be single parents, but a growing minority choose to become so—who set out to have a child or children without the support of a spouse or partner. "Single

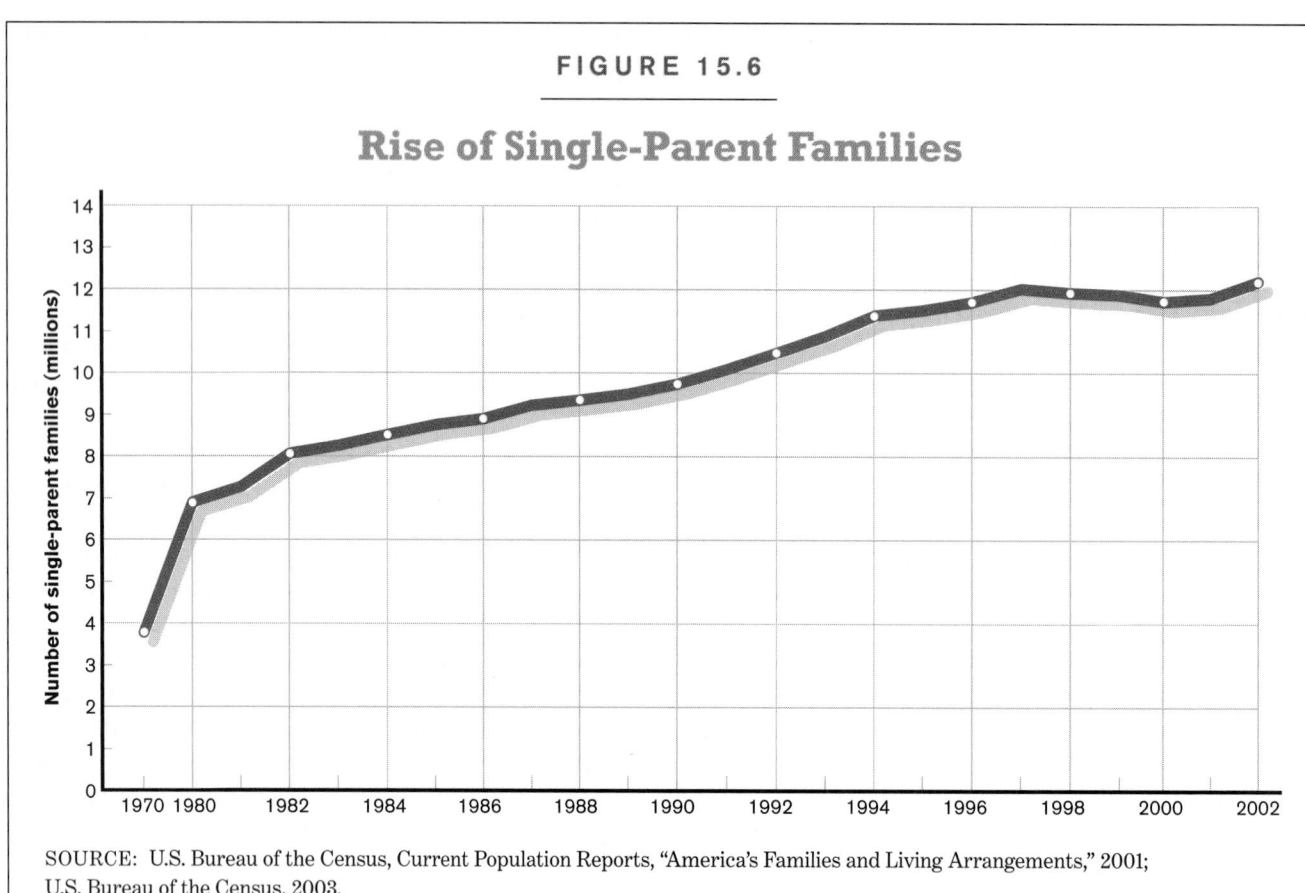

FIGURE 15.6

Rise of Single-Parent Families

SOURCE: U.S. Bureau of the Census, Current Population Reports, "America's Families and Living Arrangements," 2001; U.S. Bureau of the Census, 2003.

mothers by choice" is an apt description of some parents, normally those who possess sufficient resources to manage satisfactorily as a single-parent household. For the majority of unmarried or never-married mothers, however, the reality is different: There is a high correlation between the rate of births outside marriage and indicators of poverty and social deprivation. As we saw earlier, these influences are very important in explaining the high proportion of single-parent households among families of African American background in the United States.

A debate exists among sociologists about the impact on children of growing up with a single parent. The most exhaustive set of studies carried out to date, by Sara McLanahan and Gary Sandefur, rejects the claim that children raised by only one parent do just as well as children raised by both parents. A large part of the reason is economic—the sudden drop in income associated with divorce. But about half of the disadvantage comes from inadequate parental attention and lack of social ties. Separation or divorce weakens the connection between child and father, as well as the link between the child and the father's network of friends and acquaintances. On the basis of wide empirical research, the authors conclude it is a myth that there are

usually strong support networks or extended family ties available to single mothers (McLanahan and Sandefur, 1994).

The Dark Side of the Family

Since family or kin relations are part of almost everyone's experience, family life encompasses virtually the whole range of emotional experience. Family relationships—between wife and husband, parents and children, brothers and sisters, or more distant relatives—can be warm and fulfilling. But they can equally be full of the most extreme tension, driving people to despair or imbuing them with a deep sense of anxiety and guilt. The dark side of family life is extensive and belies the rosy images of family harmony frequently depicted in TV commercials and programs. It can take many forms. Among the most devastating in their consequences, however, are the incestuous abuse of children and domestic violence.

Family Violence

Violence within families is primarily a male domain. The two broad categories of family violence are child abuse and spousal abuse. Because of the sensitive and private nature of violence within families, it is difficult to obtain national data on levels of domestic violence. Data on child abuse is particularly sparse because of the cognitive development and ethical issues involved in studying child subjects.

Child Abuse

Although there are many variations on what constitutes child abuse, the most common definition is serious physical harm (trauma, sexual abuse with injury, or willful malnutrition) with intent to injure. One national study of married or cohabiting adults indicates that about 2 percent of respondent adults abused their children in 1985 (Straus and Gelles, 1986). More recent statistics are based on national surveys of child welfare professionals. These surveys miss children who are not seen by professionals or reported to state agencies. However, they remain the most current source of information on child abuse. In the 1993 National Incidence Study of Child Abuse and Neglect (NIS), almost half of all substantiated cases of child abuse and neglect fell into the neglect category (47 percent). Physical abuse was the next most common violation (25 percent), followed by sexual abuse (15 percent) (Sedlak and Broadhurst, 1996). The most recent statistics based on the National Child Abuse and Neglect Reporting System indicate that in 2001 there were more than 900,000 reported child victims of abuse or neglect. Of these, more than half of all victims (57.2 percent) suffered neglect, 18.6 percent suffered physical abuse, and 9.6 percent were sexually abused (U.S. Department of Health and Human Services, 2003). The number of reported cases of child abuse has stayed the same since 1998. The rate of neglect has increased from 54 percent while the occurrence of physical abuse has dropped from 23 percent and the occurrence of sexual abuse has dropped from 12 percent (U.S. Department of Health and Human Services, 1998; 2003). The highest child victimization rates were for the zero-to-three age group. These studies also show that child abuse is more likely to occur in low-income families and single-parent families.

Spousal Abuse

A 1985 study by Straus and his colleagues found that spousal violence has occurred at least once in the past year in 16 percent of all marriages and at some point in the marriage in 28 percent of all marriages. This does not, however, distinguish between severe acts, such as beating up and threatening with or using a gun or knife, and less severe acts of violence, such as slapping, pushing, grabbing, or shoving one's spouse. When the authors disaggregated this number, they found that approximately 3 percent of all husbands admitted to perpetrating at least one act of severe violence on their spouse in the last year, and this is likely to be an underestimate.

The national survey by Straus and his colleagues also uncovers a finding that is somewhat contrary to most people's beliefs about spousal violence: They find that women reported perpetrating about the same amount of violent acts as men. This lies in stark contrast to much of the literature based on crime statistics, hospital records, and shelter administrative records. These sources all indicate that spousal violence is almost exclusively man-on-woman violence.

Michael Johnson (1995) was able to untangle these inconsistencies. Johnson recognized that the data that were generating such conflicting findings were collected from two very different samples. In the shelter samples, respondents are generally women who were severely beaten by their husbands or partners. The severity of their situation drew them to a shelter. On the other hand, those responding to a national survey are generally living in their homes and have the time, energy, or wherewithal to complete a survey. It is unlikely that individuals who are experiencing extreme violence in the home would respond to a national survey. Furthermore, it is unlikely that those who experience less severe kinds of violence (e.g., slapping) will end up in a domestic violence shelter. Therefore, these are two very different groups of people.

Johnson argued that the spousal abuse in the two samples was also different in character. He referred to the extreme abuse experienced by many in the shelter samples as "patriarchal terrorism." This type of violence is perpetuated by feelings of power and control. The type of violence reported in national surveys is referred to as "common couple violence." This type of violence is generally reactionary to a specific incident and is not rooted in power or control.

SOCIAL CLASS

Although, no social class is immune to spousal abuse, several studies indicate that it is more common among low-income couples (Cherlin, 1999). Three decades ago, William Goode suggested that low-income men may be more prone to violence because they have few other means to control their wives, such as through having a higher income or education than their wives (Goode, 1971). In addition, the high levels of stress induced by poverty and unemployment may lead to more violence within families. In support of these assertions, Gelles and Cornell (1990) found that unemployed men are nearly twice as likely as employed men to assault their wives.

Alternatives to Traditional Forms of Marriage and the Family

Cohabitation

Cohabitation—in which a couple lives together in a sexual relationship without being married—has become increasingly widespread in most Western societies. Until a few decades ago, cohabitation was generally regarded as somewhat scandalous. As we saw earlier in the chapter, however, during the 1980s the number of unmarried men and women sharing a household went up sharply. Cohabitation has become widespread among college and university students, although they were not the initiators of this trend, as many people believe. Bumpass, Sweet, and Cherlin (1991) found that the cohabitation phenomenon started with lower-educated groups in the 1950s. The college-educated population has always had and continues to have lower rates of cohabitation than those who do not go to college. The fact that those who are less educated were initiators in the trend toward cohabitation indicates that

for this group, cohabitation may serve as a substitute for marriage, which may involve economic constraints.

While for some cohabitation may be a substitute for marriage, for many it is viewed as a stage in the process of relationship building that precedes marriage. Young people come to live together usually by drifting into it, rather than through calculated planning. A couple who are already having a sexual relationship spend more and more time together, eventually giving up one of their individual homes. The close connection between cohabitation and marriage for many is indicated in Figure 15.7, which shows that the most important reason for cohabitating for both women and men is so that "couples can be sure they are compatible before marriage."

Most cohabiting couples either marry or stop living together, although the chances of a cohabitating union transitioning to a first marriage is related to a number of socioeconomic factors. For instance, the probability that the first cohabitation will become a marriage within five years is 75 percent for white women, but only 61 percent for Hispanic women and 48 percent for black women. Similarly, the likelihood of a first marriage resulting from cohabitation is positively associated with higher education, the absence of children during cohabitation, higher family income. It is also more likely in communities with low male unemployment rates (Bramlett

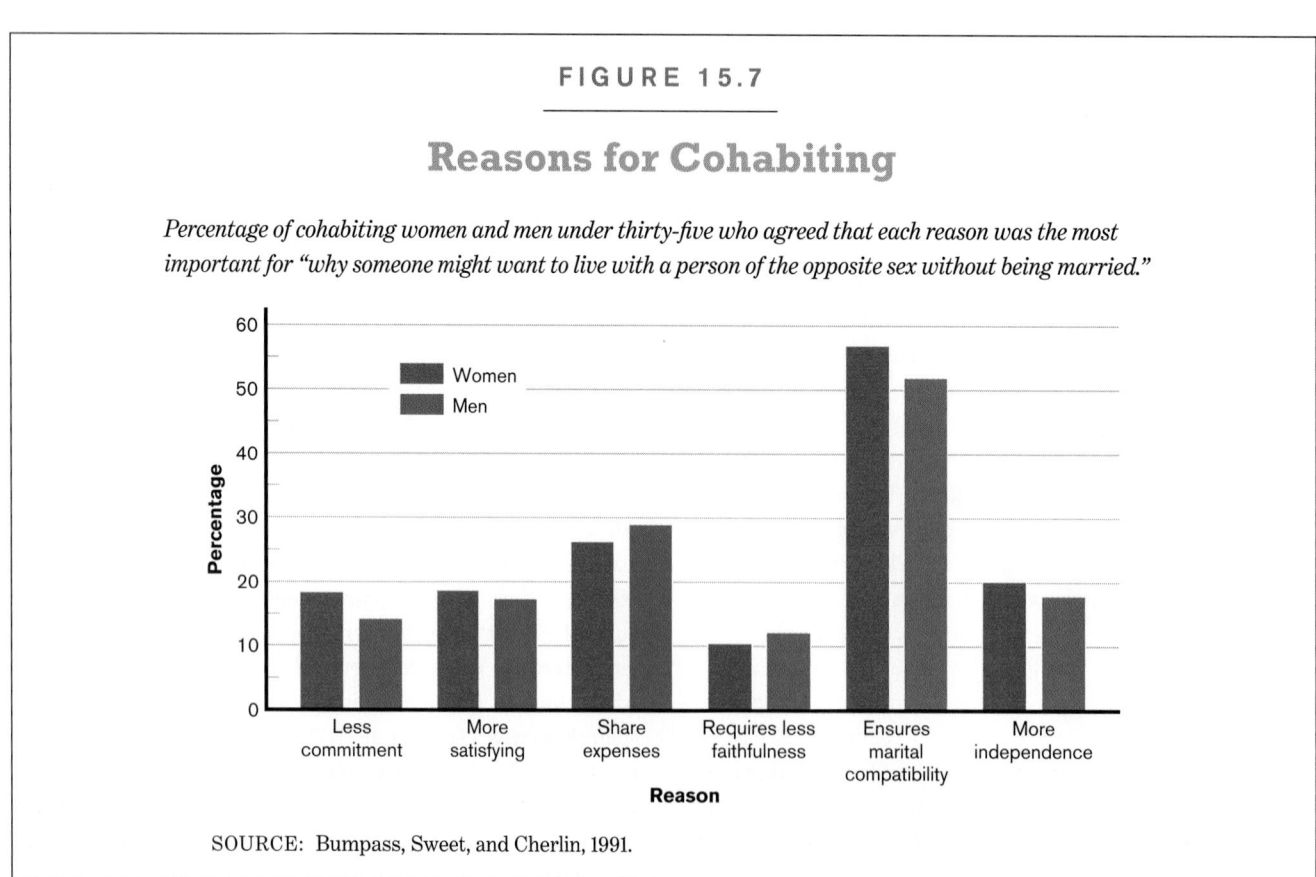

FIGURE 15.7

Reasons for Cohabiting

Percentage of cohabiting women and men under thirty-five who agreed that each reason was the most important for "why someone might want to live with a person of the opposite sex without being married."

SOURCE: Bumpass, Sweet, and Cherlin, 1991.

and Mosher, 2002). Although many view cohabitation as a precursor to marriage, for a large number of people, it does not end in marriage. Only about 35 percent of cohabitors married their partners within three years of starting to live together. Increasingly, we are seeing evidence that cohabitation is not necessarily a "stage in the process" between dating and marriage, but rather it may be an end in itself for an increasing number of cohabitors.

Evidence provided by Judith Seltzer cautions that although cohabitation is often viewed as a "trial marriage," an increasing proportion of cohabiting unions are not leading to marriage. Over the past decade, the rate of childbearing within cohabiting unions has increased by 25 percent (Seltzer, 2000). At the same time, the percentage of all children born to unmarried parents has increased from about 18 percent in 1980 to over 33 percent in 2000 (National Center for Health Statistics, 2000a). Cohabiting couples are the source of much of this increase. In the early 1980s, 29 percent of all nonmarital births were to those in cohabiting unions. A decade later this was up to 39 percent. Finally, in the past, couples who got pregnant before they were married often married before the birth of the baby. Currently, only 11 percent of single women who have a pregnancy that results in a live birth are married by the time the child is born. Although the percentage of those who marry before the birth of a child that was conceived while the couple was single has declined, there has been an increase in the rate at which unmarried women begin cohabiting with their partner once they find out they are pregnant. Currently, 11 percent of single women who have a pregnancy that results in a live birth begin cohabiting by the time the baby is born. Thus, equal percentages of couples now marry and begin cohabiting to "legitimate" a pregnancy.

Recent research, however, has shown that cohabitation is less stable than marriage. Where the likelihood of a first marriage ending in separation or divorce within five years is 20 percent, there is a 49 percent chance that a premarital cohabitation will break up within five years. Similarly, after ten years, the probability of a first marriage ending is 33 percent, compared with 62 percent for cohabitations (National Center for Health Statistics, 2002).

The United States is certainly not alone in the increasing prevalence of cohabitation. Many European countries are experiencing similar, and in some cases much greater, proportions of unions beginning with cohabitation rather than marriage. The Nordic countries of Denmark, Sweden, and Finland, along with France, show particularly high rates of cohabitation. However, unions in the southern European countries of Spain, Greece, and Italy—along with Ireland and Portugal—still largely begin with marriage.

As cohabitation becomes increasingly common as a first union and among those who have been married and now are

Evelyn Rivera's family (her son Mark, nephew Sal, and lesbian partner Debbie Rodriguez) is just one example of the changing idea of the "typical" American family.

divorced, children are spending more and more time in cohabiting unions. Recent research by Larry Bumpass and Hsien-Hen Lu (2000) finds that about two fifths of all children spend some time living with their mother and a cohabiting partner and that approximately one third of the time children spend with unmarried mothers is actually spent in cohabitation. Clearly, the lives of children are increasingly embedded in families formed by cohabitation. The effects of this alternative family form on children will only become apparent as these children age.

Gay-Parent Families

Many homosexual men and women now live in stable relationships as couples, and there is a movement afoot to legally recognize these unions as marriages. Four recent decisions, three in the United States and one in Canada, demonstrate the current pulse of this movement.

In November 1998, voters in Hawaii decided to approve a state constitutional amendment to limit legal marriages to one man and one woman. Before the issue was put to the electorate, the Hawaii Supreme Court was closer than ever before to legalizing gay marriage. In fact, in 1993 the state's supreme court ruled that restricting marriage to heterosexual couples was sex discrimination, and the court asked the state of Hawaii to show a compelling reason for the restriction. Many legal observers believe the court would have ruled for gay marriage if not for the vote on the constitutional amendment.

In May 1999, the Supreme Court of Canada ruled that same-sex couples are entitled to equal legal treatment as married couples. That is, same-sex partners are entitled to the same benefits as married partners under Ontario's Family Law Act.

Weighing In on the Gay Marriage Debate

[***]

Virtual Objectivity

Under contemporary conditions of mass communication, the movers, shakers, and makers of public opinion and policy do not merely welcome, but actively seek relevant research data and analysis from sociologists. However, the operative and slippery word here is "relevant." Partisans engaged in public policy controversies deploy social science data selectively on all sides of any issue. [***]

[***]

Since the publication in 2001 of an article I co-authored about research on the effects of lesbian parenthood, I have become one of the social science spin-sters courted by gay marital and parent rights suitors as well as by the mainstream media to perform family sociology in transnational media and court cases. In the process, I have lost some of the innocence I once sustained about the progressive potential of public sociology.

[***]

In July 2001, I naively agreed to a live-broadcast appearance on *The O'Reilly Factor*, a confrontational, reactionary infotainment program on the Fox network. While I sat alone staring into a camera in a Los Angeles studio, a satellite hookup relayed O'Reilly's disembodied voice from across the continent. O'Reilly fired leading questions at me crafted to elicit two desired sound bites—that gay parents produce gay children and that liberal scholars, constrained by "PC" dogma, have suppressed this finding. When I balked at this script and attempted to correct O'Reilly's distorted interpretations of

my published views, he abruptly terminated the interview, and my microphone went dead. In this instance, I was literally "silenced" for refusing to provide the virtual social science data that supported O'Reilly's *a priori* views. [***]

Sound-bite social science cannot accommodate complexity, nuance, ambiguity, or uncertainty—the fundamental features of critical reason and intellectual inquiry. [***]

[***]

[***] News stories need a "hook," and no scholar gets to control the spin by which her work is represented. Unsurprisingly, therefore, most of the print stories reporting about our study featured the controversial issues of gender and sexual differences. Typical and influential in this regard, a Reuters wire service story, published days after our article appeared,

led by overstating our analysis of gender nonconformity and of the defensive way in which prior researchers had reported such findings:

> USC sociologists Judith Stacey and Timothy Biblarz examined 21 studies on the subject [of the effects of parental sexual orientation] dating back to 1980 and found that children of lesbians and gays are more likely to depart from traditional gender roles than children of heterosexual couples. In an interview on Friday, Biblarz said that the study found that information on the subject had previously been stifled and the differences played down. (Tippit 2001)

"Stifled," however, was the reporter's term, not Biblarz's, and our article did not claim that the children ARE more likely to depart from or conform to anything; only that there were good theoretical reasons to expect this and that a few studies reported findings in this direction. It seems likely that Reuters's comparatively sober print formulation of the two sound-bites that O'Reilly failed to elicit from me during my brief appearance on his program actually generated my invitation to appear there in the first place.

[***]

To my surprise and satisfaction, the most dramatic departure form the sound-bite treatment of our gay parenting study proved also to be the most influential. "A Rainbow of Differences in Gays' Children," announced a serious and nuanced story in the Science section of the *New York Times* by a reporter endowed with sufficient lead time, resources, responsibility and skills to read and discuss the research with me in some depth. Because of the prestige and influence of the venue, this story initiated a second, even broader round of public notice and courtship by international media, community organizations, social services, and legal rights and advocacy projects. Soon I found myself discussing research regularly with journalists and with social and legal activists pursuing same-sex marriage, gay adoption, and "second-parent" adoption rights in the course of public opinion as well as law.

[***]

Having been too frequently seduced and abandoned, stood up, manipulated, and misunderstood by public suitors, I find myself a more jaded, wary social science spin-ster. I am learning to screen the character and credentials of my companions with greater care, to select reasonably safe public venues in which to meet, to negotiate the terms and limits of our encounters, and to temper my expectations about the prospects for success. Yet, if I have learned to adopt an ambivalent posture toward my public sociology prospects, nonetheless, when courted with sensitivity, I dare to continue to spin.

SOURCE: Judith Stacey, "Marital Suitors Court Social Science Spinsters: The Unwittingly Conservative Effects of Public Sociology." *Social Problems* 51, no. 1: 131–145. © 2004, The Society for the Study of Social Problems, Inc. All rights reserved. Used by permission.

JUDITH STACEY is professor of sociology at New York University. She is the author of In the Name of the Family: Rethinking Family Values in a Postmodern Age, Brave New Families: Stories of Domestic Upheaval in Late Twentieth-Century America, *and* Patriarchy and Socialist Revolution in China *as well as numerous articles. Her areas of research are gender, family, sexuality, feminist and queer theory, and ethnography.*

Maria Castillo (left) and Georjina Graciano hold their marriage license at City Hall in San Francisco, California, on February 16, 2004. The mayor of San Francisco, Gavin Newsom, ignited a passionate nationwide debate in February 2004 by allowing 4,037 same-sex couples to wed over a four-week period before the California high court annulled the marriages.

The Canada case was initiated when a lesbian filed for spousal support from her ex-partner. Initially, the Family Law Act had permitted only partners of the opposite sex to make a claim for spousal support after a breakup. The court therefore decided to first resolve the constitutional issue of whether same-sex couples have a right to seek spousal support. The Supreme Court's decision was that the Family Law Act's restriction to opposite-sex partners was unconstitutional.

An even more recent decision on the issue of same-sex couples came in July 2000, when the Vermont legislature voted to allow same-sex partners to register their "civil unions" with town clerks. The move allows same-sex couples access to all the state-granted rights, privileges, and responsibilities of marriage. Though this was a big victory for gay and lesbian marriage advocates, the measure falls short of calling the partnerships "marriage" and instead opts for "civil unions." Also, it is still unclear if a civil union in Vermont will be recognized in other states.

Most recently, in November 2003, the Massachusetts Supreme Court ruled that the state constitution does not forbid gays and lesbians to marry and gave the Massachusetts State Legislature six months to rewrite the state's marriage laws to permit gay marriages. This decision in part encouraged the mayor of San Francisco, Gavin Newsom, to start issuing marriage licenses to gay and lesbian couples. Mayor Newsom has argued that the state referendum, passed in 2000 and which defined marriage as between a man and a woman, violates the state constitution, which prevents discrimination against any social group. This prompted an immediate response from California's governor, Arnold Schwarzenegger, to order the state attorney general to halt the action, and for President George W. Bush to publicly endorse a constitutional amendment "defining and protecting marriage as a union of a man and woman as husband and wife" (CNN, 2004). (The president did not call for a ban on civil unions between homosexuals, which would be left up to the states to determine.)

Although the ultimate outcome—whether these marriages will be respected by state law—is yet to be determined, these events clearly demonstrate the growing social movement toward legalizing gay marriages.

Beyond civil unions or marriages, same-sex couples are forming families with children. Relaxation of previously intolerant attitudes toward homosexuality has been accompanied by a growing tendency for courts to allocate custody of children to mothers living in gay relationships. Techniques of artificial insemination mean that gay women may have children and become gay-parent families without any heterosexual contact. Moreover, only two of the fifty U.S. states—Florida and New Hampshire—have laws preventing lesbians and gay men from adopting children.

Staying Single

Several factors have combined to increase the numbers of people living alone in modern Western societies. One is a trend toward later marriages—people now marry on average about three years later than was the case in 1960; another is the rising rate of divorce. Yet another is the growing number of old people in the population whose partners have died. Being single means different things at different periods of the life cycle. A larger proportion of people in their twenties are unmarried than used to be the case. By their mid-thirties, however, only a small minority of men and women have never been married. The majority of single people aged thirty to fifty are divorced and "in between" marriages. Most single people over fifty are widowed.

More than ever before, young people are leaving home simply to start an independent life rather than to get married (which had been one of the most common paths out of the home in the past). Hence it seems that the trend of "staying single" or living on one's own may be part of the societal trend toward valuing independence at the expense of family life.

Still, most people (over 90 percent) ultimately marry, so although independence or "staying single" may be an increasingly common path out of the parental home, a large majority of these people will eventually marry (Goldschneider and Goldschneider, 1999).

The Future of the American Family: The Sociological Debate

Is the American family in a state of crisis? Or are family arrangements simply changing to keep pace with rapid economic, technological, and social changes in the United States? Sociologists David Popenoe and Judith Stacey offer very different perspectives on the "future of the family." Popenoe, a Rutgers University professor, argues that the family has changed for the worse since 1960. In the last forty-plus years, divorce, nonmarital births, and cohabitation rates have increased, while marriage and marital fertility rates have decreased. These trends, taken together, are at the root of countless social ills, including child poverty, adolescent pregnancy, substance abuse, and juvenile crime. Increasing rates of divorce and nonmarital births have created millions of female-headed households and have consequently removed men from the child-rearing process. Popenoe argues that this is harmful for children (1993, 1996).

Stacey, a professor at New York University, counters that the traditional American family of the 1950s—praised by Popenoe and conservative politicians as the panacea for all social problems—is a dated and oppressive institution. According to Stacey, the "breadwinner-father and child-rearing-mother" family, defined by Stacey as the "modern family," perpetuated the "segregation of the sexes by extracting men from, and consigning white married women to, an increasingly privatized domestic domain." The "modern family" has been replaced by many new family forms. These new forms, which Stacey has named the "postmodern family," include single mothers, blended families, cohabiting couples, lesbian and gay partners, communes, and two-worker families. The postmodern family is not inferior to the traditional two-parent family. To the contrary, it is well suited to meet the challenges of the current economy and is an appropriate setting for raising children: Children need capable, loving caretakers—regardless of their gender, marital status, or sexual orientation, argues Stacey.

Popenoe agrees with Stacey's claim that children need capable, loving caretakers, yet maintains that "on the whole, two parents—a father and a mother—are better for a child than one parent." Why? Popenoe claims that biological fathers make "distinctive, irreplaceable contributions" to their children's welfare. Fathers offer a strong male role model to sons, they play the role of disciplinarian for trouble-prone children, they provide their daughters with a male perspective on heterosexual relationships, and, through their unique "play" styles, they teach their children about teamwork, competition, independence, self-fulfillment, self-control, and regulation of one's emotions. Mothers, alternatively, teach their children about communion, or the feeling of being connected to others. Both needs must be met and can be achieved only through the gender-differentiated parenting of a mother and father, argues Popenoe.

Stacey retorts that the "postmodern family" is better suited to meet the challenges of the current "postmodern economy." In the postmodern economy, employment has shifted from heavy industries to nonunionized clerical, service, and new industrial sectors. The loss of union-protected jobs means that men no longer earn enough to support a wife and children. At the same time, demand for clerical and service labor, escalating consumption standards, increases in women's educational attainment, and the persistence of high divorce rates has given more and more women reason to seek paid employment outside the home.

Stacey also takes issue with media rhetoric and claims by conservatives such as Popenoe that elevate the married, two-parent family as the ideal family form. Their condemnation of other family forms is particularly harmful to the millions of children who live with gay or lesbian parents. Rather than condemning nontraditional family forms, Stacey reasons that family sociologists and policy makers should instead develop strategies to mitigate the harmful effects of divorce and single parenthood on children. She suggests that restructuring work schedules and benefit policies to accommodate familial responsibilities; redistributing work opportunities to reduce unemployment rates; enacting comparable-worth standards of pay equity to enable women as well as men to earn a family wage; providing universal health, prenatal, and child care, and sex education; and rectifying the economic inequities of divorce would be much more admirable efforts. These child-friendly efforts, she argues, are truly "pro-family" (Stacey, 1990, 1993, 1996).

Popenoe's policy recommendations are based on the claim that "marriage must be reestablished as a strong social institution." How? He argues that employers should reduce the practice of relocating married couples with children and should provide more generous parental leave. He also supports a two-tiered system of divorce law. Marriages without minor children would be relatively easy to dissolve, but marriages with young children would be dissolvable only by mutual agreement or on grounds that clearly involve a wrong by one party against the other.

Study Outline

Kinship, Family, and Marriage: Key Concepts

- *Kinship, family*, and *marriage* are closely related terms of key significance for sociology and anthropology. Kinship comprises either genetic ties or ties initiated by marriage. A family is a group of kin having responsibility for the upbringing of children. Marriage is a union of two persons living together in a socially approved sexual relationship.

- A *nuclear family* refers to a household in which a married couple or single parent lives with their own or adopted children. Where kin in addition to parents and children live in the same household or are involved in close and continuous relationships, we speak of the existence of an *extended family*.

- In Western societies, marriage, and therefore the family, is associated with *monogamy* (a culturally approved sexual relationship between one man and one woman). Many other cultures tolerate or encourage *polygamy*, in which an individual may be married to two or more spouses at the same time. *Polygyny*, in which a man may marry more than one wife, is far more common than *polyandry*, in which a woman may have more than one husband.

The Family in History

- The modern Western family, which features close emotional bonds, domestic privacy, and a preoccupation with child rearing, is also characterized by *affective individualism*, meaning that marriage partners are usually selected on the basis of romantic love. This is now the norm, but it was not always so. In premodern Europe, parents, extended family members, or even landlords decided on marriage partners, basing their choices largely on social or economic considerations.

- There are many types of families in the world, but there is a trend toward the Western norm of the nuclear family. Some reasons for this trend include: the Western ideal of romantic love, the growth of urbanization and of centralized governments, and employment in organizations outside traditional family influence.

Changes in Family Patterns

- There have been major changes in patterns of family life in the United States during the post–World War II period: A high percentage of women are in the paid labor force, there are rising rates of divorce, and substantial proportions of the population are either in single-parent households or are living with stepfamilies. *Cohabitation* (in which a couple lives together in a sexual relationship outside of marriage) has become increasingly common in many industrial countries.

- Family life is by no means always a picture of harmony and happiness. The "dark side" of the family is found in the patterns of abuse and family violence that often occur within it. Although no social class is immune to spousal abuse, studies do indicate that it is more common among low-income couples.

- Cohabitation and homosexuality have become more common in recent years. It seems certain that alternative forms of social and sexual relationships to those prevalent in the past will flourish still further. Yet marriage and the family remain firmly established institutions.

Key Concepts

affective individualism (p. 449)
cohabitation (p. 466)
extended family (p. 446)
family (p. 446)
family of orientation (p. 446)
family of procreation (p. 446)
kinship (p. 446)
marriage (p. 446)
matrilocal family (p. 447)
monogamy (p. 447)
nuclear family (p. 446)
patrilocal family (p. 447)
personality stabilization (p. 447)
polyandry (p. 447)
polygamy (p. 447)
polygyny (p. 447)
primary socialization (p. 447)
stepfamily (p. 463)

Review Questions

1. The process by which children learn the cultural norms of the society in which they are born is called
   a. personality stabilization.
   b. primary socialization.
   c. secondary socialization.
   d. personality socialization.
2. Cherlin (1999) and Goode (1971) found that spousal abuse is more common among
   a. high-income couples.
   b. middle-income couples.
   c. low-income couples.
   d. both high- and middle-income couples.
3. What's the difference between families of orientation and families of procreation?

a. Families of orientation are childless couples and families of procreation are couples with children.

b. A family of orientation is the family into which a person is born, whereas a family of procreation is the family into which a person enters as an adult and within which their children are raised.

c. Families of orientation are gay couples and families of procreation are straight couples.

d. A family of orientation is the family into which a person enters as an adult and within which children are raised; whereas a family of procreation is the family into which a person is born.

4. According to Cherlin's research on the effects of divorce on children,

a. almost all children experience an initial period of calmness.

b. a majority of children experience some long-term problems as a result of the breakup that may persist into adulthood.

c. most people whose parents divorced did not experience serious mental problems.

d. most children resume normal development without serious problems within about six months of separation.

5. What is the "absent father"?

a. The term refers to the period from the late 1930s through the 1940s when fathers rarely saw their children because of war service.

b. The term refers to the period from the 1950s through the 1970s when fathers were the family's only breadwinner and would only see their children in the evening and on weekends.

c. The term refers to the period from the 1970s until today and it refers to fathers who, as a result of separation and divorce, either have infrequent contact with their children or lose touch with them all together.

d. All of the above.

6. About half the babies in Sweden are born to unmarried mothers. Nineteen out of twenty of these are born in households with a father, but many will grow up without their own fathers at home, as half of all Swedish marriages end in divorce and unmarried parents split up three times more often than married ones. What kind of social and economic problems are caused by these figures?

a. Many. Sweden has exactly the same experience as the United States as a result of its high divorce rate.

b. Some, but fewer than in the United States. There is a greater social taboo against becoming a "deadbeat dad" in the more socialistic climate of Sweden.

c. Very few. In Sweden, generous welfare benefits mean that single-parent families do not slip into poverty.

d. None whatsoever.

7. Which one of the following is *not* true regarding the important changes in families occurring worldwide?

a. There is a general trend toward the free choice of a spouse.

b. The rights of women are becoming more widely recognized.

c. Kin marriages are becoming more common.

d. Higher levels of sexual freedom are developing in societies that were very restrictive.

8. Which theoretical perspective is interested in the experience of women in the domestic sphere?

a. Functionalism

b. Symbolic interactionism

c. Feminism

d. None of the above.

9. What percent of American families is made up of a husband who works in paid employment and a wife who looks after the home, living together with their two children?

a. 15 percent

b. 25 percent

c. 35 percent

d. 45 percent

10. Research on the effects of family structure on children shows that

a. girls experience less detrimental outcomes from stepfamily living than boys.

b. girls experience more detrimental outcomes from stepfamily living than boys.

c. both girls and boys experience the same detrimental outcomes from stepfamily living.

d. stepfamily living has no detrimental outcomes for either boys or girls.

Thinking Sociologically Exercises

1. Using this textbook's presentation, compare the structures and lifestyles between contempory white non-Hispanic, Asian American, Latino, and African American families.

2. Increases in cohabitation and single-parent households suggest that marriage may be beginning to fall by the wayside in our contemporary society. However, this chapter claims that marriage and the family remain firmly established institutions in our society. Explain the rising patterns of cohabitation and single-parent households and show how these seemingly paradoxical trends can be reconciled with the claims offered by this textbook.

Data Exercises

www.wwnorton.com/giddens5
Keyword: Data15

- The data exercise for Chapter 15 focuses on recent changes in marriage and family patterns within the United States. It is designed to give you an opportunity to analyze survey data and learn more about what's been happening with these important social institutions.

The Development of Schooling

Know how and why systems of mass education emerged in the United States.

Education and Inequality

Become familiar with the most important research on whether education reduces or perpetuates inequality. Learn the social and cultural influences on educational achievement.

Education and Literacy in the Developing World

Know some basic facts about the education system and literacy rates of developing countries.

Communication and the Mass Media

Recognize the important impact of the mass media on society and learn some important theories about that impact.

Technological Change, Media, and Education

See the ways in which technological change is transforming the mass media and education.

CHAPTER SIXTEEN

EDUCATION AND THE MASS MEDIA

imagine being in the shoes—or the wooden clogs—of Jean-Paul Didion, a peasant boy growing up in a French farming community two centuries ago. In 1750, Jean-Paul is fourteen years old. He cannot read or write, but this is not uncommon; only a few of the adults in his village have the ability to decipher more than the odd word or two of written texts. There are some schools in nearby districts run by monks and nuns, but these are completely removed from Jean-Paul's experience. He has never known anyone well who attended school, save the local priest. For eight or nine years, Jean-Paul has been spending most of his days helping with domestic tasks and working in the fields. The older he gets, the longer each day he is expected to share in the back-breaking chores demanded by the intensive tilling of his father's plot of land.

Jean-Paul is likely never to leave the area in which he was born and may spend virtually the whole of his life within the confines of the village and surrounding fields, only occasionally traveling to other local villages and towns. He may have to wait until he is in his late fifties before inheriting his father's plot of land, sharing control of it with his younger brothers. Jean-Paul is aware that he is "French," that his country is ruled over by Louis XV, and that there is a wider world beyond even France itself. But he only has a vague awareness even of "France" as a distinct political entity. There is no such thing as "news," nor any regular means by which information about events elsewhere reaches him. What he knows of the wider world comes from stories and tales he has heard told by adults and by visiting travelers. Like others in his community, he only learns about major events—such as the death of the king—days, weeks, or sometimes months after they have occurred.

Although in modern terms Jean-Paul is uneducated, he is far from ignorant. He has a sensitive and developed understanding of the family and children, having had to care for those younger than him since he was very young. He is already highly knowledgeable about the land, methods of crop production, and ways of preserving and storing food. His mastery of local customs and traditions is profound, and he can turn his hand to many different tasks over and above agricultural cultivation, such as weaving or basket making.

Jean-Paul is an invented figure, but the above description portrays the typical experience of a boy growing up in preindustrial Europe. Compare this with our situation today. In the industrialized countries, virtually everyone can read and write—that is, people are *literate*. We have all gone through a process of formal schooling. We are all aware of the common characteristics we share with other members of the same society and have at least some sort of knowledge of its geographical and political position in the world and of its past history. Our lives are influenced at all ages beyond infancy by information we pick up through books, newspapers, magazines, radio, and television, in short, the various *media*. We live in a media-saturated world. The printed word and electronic communication, combined with the formal teaching provided by schools and colleges, have become fundamental to our way of life. This being so, schooling and the media extend the process of socialization, which we took up earlier in Chapter 4. There, we focused on early influences, especially parent-infant interaction, but we only touched briefly on schooling and the media.

In this chapter, two themes dominate: education and media as socializing processes and education and media as sources of power. First, we will show how present-day education developed and analyze its socializing influence, which at times complements, and at others competes with, the family. We will also look at education in relation to social inequality and consider how far the educational system serves to encourage or to reduce such inequality. We then move to studying the nature of modern mass media.

The Development of Schooling

The term *school* has its origins in a Greek word meaning "leisure," or "recreation." In premodern societies, schooling existed for the few who had the time and resources available to pursue the cultivation of the arts and philosophy. For some,

their engagement with schooling was like taking up a hobby. For others, like religious leaders or priests, schooling was a way of gaining skills and thus increasing their ability to interpret sacred texts. But for the vast majority of people, growing up meant learning by example the same social habits and work skills as their elders. Learning was a family affair—there were no schools at all for the mass of the population. Since children often started to help with domestic duties and farming work at a very young age, they rapidly became full-fledged members of the community.

Education in its modern form, the instruction of pupils within specially constructed school premises, gradually emerged in the first few years of the nineteenth century, when primary schools began to be constructed in Europe and the United States. One main reason for the rise of large educational systems was the process of industrialization, with its ensuing expansion of cities.

Education and Industrialization

Until the first few decades of the nineteenth century, most of the world's population had no schooling whatsoever. But as the industrial economy rapidly expanded, there was a great demand for specialized schooling that could produce an educated, capable work force. As occupations became more differentiated and were increasingly located away from the home, it was impossible for work skills to be passed on directly from parents to children.

As educational systems became universal, more and more people were exposed to abstract learning (of subjects like math, science, history, literature, and so on), rather than to the practical transmission of specific skills. In a modern society, people have to be furnished with basic skills—such as reading, writing, and calculating—and a general knowledge of their physical, social, and economic environment, but it is also important that they know how to learn, so that they are able to master new, sometimes very technical, forms of information. An advanced society also needs pure research and insights with no immediate practical value to push out the boundaries of knowledge.

In the modern age, education and qualifications became an important stepping stone into job opportunities and careers. Schools and universities not only broaden people's minds and perspectives, but are expected to prepare new generations of citizens for participation in economic life. The right balance between a generalist education and specific work skills is a difficult one at which to arrive. Specialized forms of technical, vocational, and professional training often supplement pupils' liberal education and facilitate the transition from school to work. Internships and work experience schemes, for example, allow young people to develop specific knowledge applicable to their future careers.

Although many teachers in schools and universities seek above all to provide a well-rounded education, policy makers and employers are concerned to ensure that education and training programs coincide with a country's economic profile and employment demands. Yet in times of rapid economic and technical change, there is not always a smooth match between the priorities of the educational system and the availability of professional opportunities. The rapid expansion of a country's health-care system, for example, would dramatically increase the demand for trained health professionals, laboratory technicians, capable administrators, and computer systems analysts familiar with public-health issues. Industry-wide changes in factory-floor production technology would require a work force with a set of skills that might be in short supply.

Sociological Theories

Sociologists have debated why formal systems of schooling developed in modern societies by studying the social functions that schools provide. For example, some have argued that mass education promotes feelings of nationalism and aided the development of national societies, constituted of citizens from different regions who would know the same history and speak a common language (Ramirez and Boli, 1987). Marxist sociologists have argued that the expansion of education was brought about by employer's need for certain personality characteristics in their workers—self-discipline, dependability, punctuality, obedience, and the like—which are all taught in schools (Bowles and Gintis, 1976). Another influential perspective comes from the sociologist Randall Collins, who has argued that the primary social function of mass education derives from the need for diplomas and degrees to determine one's credentials for a job, even if the work involved has nothing to do with the education one has received. Over time, the practice of credentialism results in demands for higher credentials, which require higher levels of educational attainment. Jobs, such as sales representative, that thirty years ago would have required a high school diploma now require a college degree. Since educational attainment is closely related to class position, credentialism reinforces the class structure within a society (Collins, 1971, 1979).

Education and Inequality

The expansion of education has always been closely linked to the ideals of democracy. Reformers value education for its own sake—for the opportunity it provides for individuals to develop their capabilities. Yet education has also consistently been seen as a means of equalization. Access to universal education, it has been argued, could help reduce disparities of wealth and power. Are educational opportunities equal for everyone? Has education in fact proved to be a great equalizer? Much research has been devoted to answering these questions.

"Savage Inequalities"

Between 1988 and 1990, the journalist Jonathan Kozol studied schools in about thirty neighborhoods around the United States. There was no special logic to the way he chose the schools, except that he went where he happened to know teachers, principals, or ministers. What startled him most was the segregation within these schools and the inequalities among them. Kozol brought these terrible conditions to the attention of the American people in his book *Savage Inequalities*, which became a bestseller (Kozol, 1991).

In his passionate opening chapter, he first took readers to East St. Louis, Illinois, a city that is 98 percent black, had no regular trash collection, and few jobs. Three quarters of its residents were living on welfare at the time. City residents were forced to use their backyards as garbage dumps, which attracted a plague of flies and rats during the hot summer months. One resident told Kozol about "rats as big as puppies" that lived in his mother's yard. City residents also contended with pollution fumes from two major chemical plants in the city. Another public health problem resulted from raw sewage, which regularly backed up into people's homes. East St. Louis also had some of the sickest children in the United States, with extremely high rates of infant death, asthma, and poor nutrition and extremely low rates of immunization. Only 55 percent of the children had been fully immunized for polio, diphtheria, measles, and whooping cough. Among the city's other social problems were crime, dilapidated housing, poor health care, and lack of education.

Kozol showed how the problems of the city often spilled over into the schools, in this case literally. Over the course of two weeks, raw sewage backed up into the school on three occasions, each time requiring the evacuation of students and the cancellation of classes. But the city's problems also negatively affected the school on a daily basis. Teachers often had to hold classes without chalk or paper. One teacher commented on the school's poor conditions by saying, "Our problems are severe. I don't even know where to begin. I have no materials with the exception of a single textbook given to each child. If I bring in anything else—books or tapes or magazines—I bring it in myself. The high school has no VCRs. They are such a crucial tool. So many good things run on public television. I can't make use of anything I see unless I unhook my VCR and bring it into school. The AV equipment in the school is so old that we are pressured not to use it." Comments from students reflected the same concerns. "I don't go to physics class, because my lab has no equipment," said one student. Another added, "The type-writers in my typing class don't work." A third said, "I wanted to study Latin but we don't have Latin in this school." Only 55 percent of the students in this high school ultimately graduate, about one third of whom go on to college.

Kozol also wrote about the other end of the inequality spectrum, taking readers into a wealthy suburban school in Westchester County outside of New York City. This school had 96 computers for the 546 students. Most studied a foreign language (including Latin) for four or five years. Two thirds of the senior class were enrolled in an advanced placement (AP) class. Kozol visited an AP class to ask students about their perceptions of inequalities within the educational system. Students at this school were well aware of the economic advantages that they enjoyed at both home and school. With regard to their views about students less well-off than themselves, the general consensus was that equal spending among schools was a worthy goal but it would probably make little difference since poor students lack motivation and would fail because of other problems. These students also realized that equalizing spending could have adverse affects on their school. As one student said, "If you equalize the money, someone's got to be shortchanged. I don't doubt that [poor] children are getting a bad deal. But do we want everyone to get a mediocre education?"

It is impossible to read these descriptions of life in East St. Louis and Westchester County without believing that the extremes of wealth and poverty in the public schools are being exposed. Yet, many sociologists have argued that although Kozol's book is a moving portrait, it provides an inaccurate view of educational inequality. Why would Kozol's research not be compelling? There are several reasons, including the unsystematic way that he chose the schools that he studied. But the most important criticism of his work is that sociological research has shown that student achievement varies much more within schools than among schools—the proportions are about 80 percent to 20 percent. This means that differences among schools are not the main sources of inequality in achievement, even though Kozol's study may provoke outrage over these inequalities. This fact does not mean that Kozol was wrong—there are schools at both extremes—but these are not the kinds of extremes that account for most educational inequality in America. Let's now look more closely at the work that sociologists have done to understand this complex relationship between education and inequality.

Sociological research addressing equal educational opportunities falls into two categories: research assessing "between school effects" and research assessing "within school effects." "Between school effects" refer to inequalities among children

The problem of schools falling into disrepair is a chronic one in poverty-stricken areas all over the country. Dilapidated schools like this one in the South Bronx lack funding for even the most basic necessities and, once they have fallen into a state of ruin, there is no money to undertake necessary repairs.

who go to different schools, asking—for example—whether students who attend schools with more resources end up ahead in the socioeconomic system. "Within school effects" are differences among students in the same school, asking—for example—if dividing students into honors or remedial classes leads to later disparities in educational attainment, occupational prestige, and wealth.

Coleman's Study of "Between School Effects" in American Education

The study of "between school effects" has been the focus of sociological research on the educational system for the past three decades. One of the classic investigations of educational inequality was undertaken in the United States in the 1960s.

As part of the Civil Rights Act of 1964, the commissioner of education was required to prepare a report on educational inequalities resulting from differences of ethnic background, religion, and national origin. James Coleman, a sociologist, was appointed director of the research program. The outcome was a study, published in 1966, based on one of the most extensive research projects ever carried out in sociology.

Information was collected on more than half a million pupils who were given a range of achievement tests assessing verbal and nonverbal abilities, reading levels, and mathematical skills. Sixty thousand teachers also completed forms providing data for about four thousand schools. The report found that a large majority of children went to schools that effectively segregated black from white. Almost 80 percent of schools attended by white students contained only 10 percent or less African American students. White and Asian American students scored higher on achievement tests than did blacks and other ethnic minority students. Coleman had supposed his results would also show mainly African American schools to have worse facilities, larger classes, and more inferior buildings than schools that were predominantly white. But surprisingly, the results showed far fewer differences of this type than had been anticipated.

Coleman therefore concluded that the material resources provided in schools made little difference to educational performance; the decisive influence was the children's backgrounds. In Coleman's words, "Inequalities imposed on children by their home, neighborhood, and peer environment are carried along to become the inequalities with which they confront adult life at the end of school" (Coleman et al., 1966). There was, however, some evidence that students from deprived backgrounds who formed close friendships with those from more favorable circumstances were likely to be more successful educationally.

Not long after Coleman's study, Christopher Jencks produced an equally celebrated work that reviewed empirical evidence accumulated on education and inequality up to the end of the 1960s (Jencks et al., 1972). Jencks reaffirmed two of Coleman's conclusions: (1) that educational and occupational attainment are governed mainly by family background and nonschool factors, and (2) that on their own, educational reforms can produce only minor effects on existing inequalities. Jencks's work has been criticized on methodological grounds, but his overall conclusions remain persuasive. Subsequent research has tended to confirm them.

Tracking and "Within School Effects"

The practice of **tracking**—dividing students into groups that receive different instruction on the basis of assumed similarities in ability or attainment—is common in American schools. In some schools, students are tracked only for certain subjects; in others, for all subjects. Sociologists have long believed that tracking is entirely negative in its effects. The conventional wisdom has been that tracking partly explains why schooling seems to have little effect on existing social inequalities, since being placed in a particular track labels a student as either able or otherwise. As we have seen in the case of labeling and deviance, once attached, such labels are hard to break away from. Children from more privileged backgrounds, in which academic work is encouraged, are likely to find themselves in the higher tracks early on—and by and large stay there (see Figure 16.1).

Jeannie Oakes (1985) studied tracking in twenty-five junior and senior high schools, both large and small and in both urban and rural areas. But she concentrated on differences

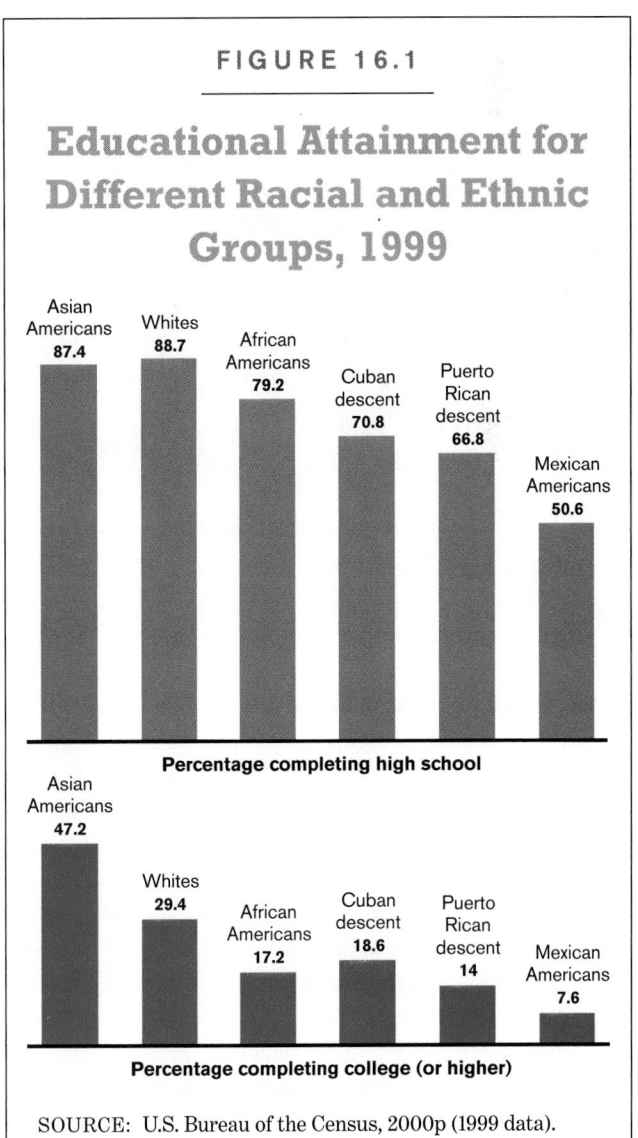

FIGURE 16.1

Educational Attainment for Different Racial and Ethnic Groups, 1999

Asian Americans 87.4
Whites 88.7
African Americans 79.2
Cuban descent 70.8
Puerto Rican descent 66.8
Mexican Americans 50.6

Percentage completing high school

Asian Americans 47.2
Whites 29.4
African Americans 17.2
Cuban descent 18.6
Puerto Rican descent 14
Mexican Americans 7.6

Percentage completing college (or higher)

SOURCE: U.S. Bureau of the Census, 2000p (1999 data).

The Internationalization of Education

How many foreign students are enrolled in your sociology course? How many foreign students are there at your university? In 1943, approximately 8,000 foreign students were enrolled in American colleges and universities. By 2000, this number had skyrocketed to more than 515,000 (U.S. Census, 2002). Although the American university system as a whole grew considerably during this period, such that 515,000 students represented only 3.3 percent of total 2000 student enrollment, it is clear that foreign students are flocking to the United States in record numbers. Most foreign students

today come from Asia—China, Japan, Taiwan, India, and South Korea all send sizeable contingents of students abroad. The United States takes in more foreign students than any other country, and there are six times as many foreign students in the United States as there are American students overseas. What do foreign students in the United States study? At the undergraduate level, more than 20 percent focus on business and management, 16 percent study engineering, and 8 percent concentrate on science (U.S. Census, 2002). More than 20 percent of foreign graduate students study engineering (Lambert, 1995).

Some scholars regard the exchange of international students as a vital component of globalization. Foreign students, in addition to serving as global "carriers" of specialized technical and scientific knowledge, have an important cultural role to play in the globalizing process. Cross-national understandings are enhanced and xenophobic and isolationist attitudes are minimized as native students in host countries develop social ties to their foreign classmates and as foreign students return to their country of origin with an appreciation for the cultural mores of the nation in which they have studied.

Yet there is considerable debate in the United States about what is sometimes called the "internationalization of education." On most college campuses, it is not hard to find disgruntled students who complain that given the competitive nature

within schools rather than between them. She found that although several schools claimed they did not track students, virtually all of them had mechanisms for sorting students into groups that seemed to be alike in ability and achievement, to make teaching easier. In other words, they employed tracking but did not choose to use the term *tracking* itself. Even where tracking only existed in this informal fashion, she found strong labels developing—high ability, low achieving, slow, average, and so on. Individual students in these groups came to be defined by teachers, other students, and themselves in terms of such labels. A student in a "high-achieving" group was considered a high-achieving *person*—smart and quick. Pupils in a "low-achieving" group came to be seen as slow, below average —or, in more forthright terms, as dummies, sweathogs, or ya-

hoos. What is the impact of tracking on students in the "low" group? A subsequent study by Oakes found that these students received a poorer education in terms of the quality of courses, teachers, and textbooks made available to them (Oakes, 1990). Moreover, the negative impact of tracking affected mostly African American, Latino, and poor students.

The usual reason given for tracking is that bright children learn more quickly and effectively in a group of others who are equally able and that clever students are held back if placed in mixed groups. Surveying the evidence, Oakes attempted to show that these assumptions are wrong. The results of later research investigations are not wholly consistent, but a pathbreaking study by the sociologist Adam Gamoran and his colleagues concluded that Oakes was partially correct in her

of the U.S. higher education system, the influx of foreign students deprives deserving Americans of educational opportunities. Moreover, although more than two thirds of foreign students receive nothing in the way of scholarships, some top-notch foreign students *are* given financial inducements to attend American schools. The outcry against this practice has been loudest at public universities, which receive support from tax revenue. Critics charge that U.S. taxpayers should not shoulder the financial burden for educating foreign students whose families have not paid U.S. taxes and who are likely to return home after earning their degrees.

Supporters of international education find such arguments unconvincing. Some Americans may lose out to foreign students in the competition for slots at prestigious universities, but this is a small price to pay for the economic, political, and cultural benefits the United States receives from having educated millions of foreign business executives, policy makers, scientists, and professionals over the years—many of whom became sympathetically disposed to the United States as a result of their experiences here. And although some foreign students receive scholarships from American universities, most are supported by their parents. In fact, it is estimated that foreign students pump hundreds of millions of dollars each year into the U.S. economy. Rather than curtail the number of foreign students admitted to American universities, supporters of international education suggest that even more should be done to encourage the exchange of students. On the one hand, greater effort should be made to recruit foreign students, to help them select the university and program that will best meet their needs, and to provide them with a positive social and educational experience while they are in the United States. On the other hand, more Americans should be encouraged to study abroad. American students are notorious for

having poor foreign-language skills and for knowing little about global geography, much less about the cultures of other nations. This ignorance puts the United States at a disadvantage relative to other countries as the world becomes increasingly globalized; encouraging Americans to study overseas may be the best way to inculcate a global worldview.

Should there be a greater focus on international education in American colleges and universities? Should the international exchange of students be expanded? These are among the issues that educational institutions are forced to confront in the context of globalization.

arguments. They agreed with Oakes's conclusions that tracking reinforces previously existing inequalities for average or poor students but countered her argument by asserting that tracking does have positive benefits for "advanced" students (Gamoran et al., 1995). The debate about the effects of tracking is sure to continue as scholars continue to analyze more data.

The Social Reproduction of Inequality

The educational system provides more than formal instruction: It socializes children to get along with each other, teaches basic skills, and transmits elements of culture such as language and values. Sociologists have looked at education as a form of social reproduction, a concept discussed in Chapter 1 and elsewhere. In the context of education, social reproduction refers to the ways in which schools help perpetuate social and economic inequalities across the generations. It also directs our attention to the means whereby schools influence the learning of values, attitudes, and habits via the hidden curriculum.

The concept of the **hidden curriculum** addresses the fact that much of what is learned in school has nothing directly to do with the formal content of lessons. Schools, by the nature of the discipline and regimentation they entail, tend to teach students "passive consumption"—an uncritical acceptance of the existing social order. These lessons are not consciously taught;

they are implicit in school procedures and organization. The hidden curriculum teaches children that their role in life is "to know their place and to sit still with it" (Illich, 1983). Children spend long hours in school, and as Illich stresses, they learn a great deal more in the school context than is contained in the lessons they are actually taught. Children get an early taste of what the world of work will be like, learning that they are expected to be punctual and apply themselves diligently to the tasks that those in authority set for them.

Schools also reinforce variations in cultural values and outlooks picked up in early life. As we saw earlier in Chapter 8, the French sociologist Pierre Bourdieu calls this process the transmission of **cultural capital** (Bourdieu, 1984, 1988), whereby the cultural advantages that coming from a "good home" confers are capital, which succeeding generations inherit from one another, thus perpetuating inequalities (see Figure 16.2).

Another influential theory on the question of how schools reproduce social inequality was introduced by Samuel Bowles and Herbert Gintis. Modern education, they propose, is a response to the economic needs of industrial capitalism. Schools help to provide the technical and social skills required by industrial enterprise, and they instill discipline and respect for authority into the labor force.

Authority relations in school, which are hierarchical and place strong emphasis on obedience, directly parallel those dominating the workplace. The rewards and punishments held out in school also replicate those found in the world of work. Schools help to motivate some individuals toward "achievement" and "success," while discouraging others, who find their way into low-paying jobs.

Bowles and Gintis accept that the development of mass education has had many beneficial consequences. Illiteracy rates are low compared with premodern times, and schooling provides access to learning experiences that are intrinsically self-fulfilling. Yet because education has expanded mainly as a response to economic needs, the school system falls far short of what enlightened reformers had hoped from it. That is, schooling has not become the "great equalizer"; rather, schools merely produce for many the feelings of powerlessness that continue throughout their experience in industrial settings. The ideals of personal development central to education can only be achieved if people have the capability to control the conditions of their own life and to develop their talents and abilities of self-expression. Under the current system, schools "are destined to legitimate inequality, limit personal development to forms compatible with submission to arbitrary author-

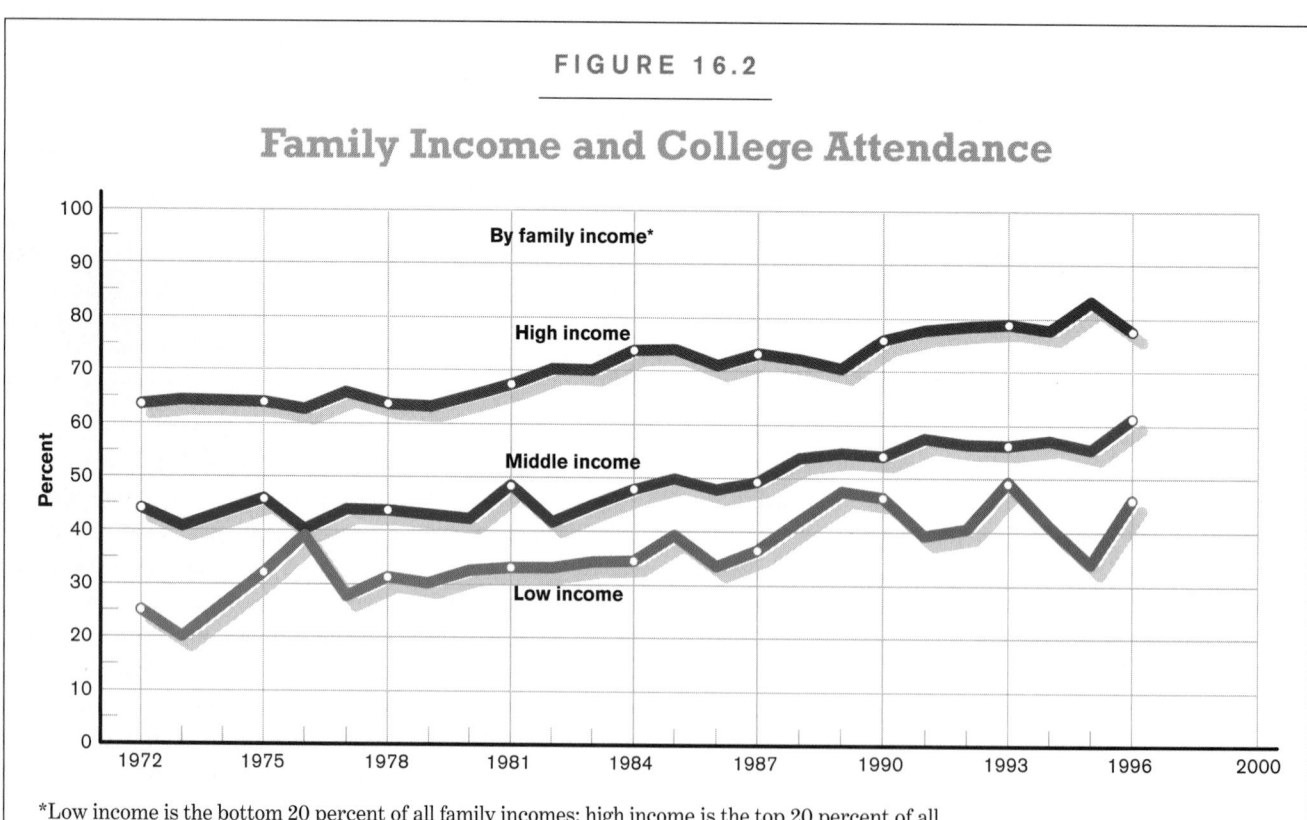

FIGURE 16.2

Family Income and College Attendance

By family income*

High income

Middle income

Low income

*Low income is the bottom 20 percent of all family incomes; high income is the top 20 percent of all family incomes; middle income is the 60 percent in between.

SOURCE: U.S. Bureau of the Census, 2000d.

ity, and aid in the process whereby youth are resigned to their fate" (Bowles and Gintis, 1976). If there were greater democracy in the workplace and more equality in society at large, Bowles and Gintis argue, a system of education could be developed that would provide for greater individual fulfillment.

Intelligence and Inequality

Suppose differences in educational attainment, and in subsequent occupations and incomes, directly reflected differential intelligence. In such circumstances, it might be argued, there is in fact equality of opportunity in the school system, for people find a level equivalent to their innate potential.

WHAT IS INTELLIGENCE?

For years, psychologists, geneticists, statisticians, and others have debated whether there exists a single human capability that can be called **intelligence** and, if so, whether it rests on innately determined differences. Intelligence is difficult to define because, as the term is usually employed, it covers qualities that may be unrelated to one another. We might suppose, for example, that the "purest" form of intelligence is the ability to solve abstract mathematical puzzles. However, people who are very good at such puzzles sometimes show low capabilities in other areas, such as history or art. Since the concept has proved so resistant to accepted definition, some psychologists have proposed (and many educators have by default accepted) that intelligence should simply be regarded as "what **IQ (intelligence quotient)** tests measure." Most IQ tests consist of a mixture of conceptual and computational problems. The tests are constructed so that the average score is 100 points: Anyone scoring below is thus labeled "below-average intelligence," and anyone scoring above is "above-average intelligence." In spite of the fundamental difficulty in measuring intelligence, IQ tests are widely used in research studies, as well as in schools and businesses.

IQ AND GENETIC FACTORS: THE SOCIOLOGICAL DEBATE

Scores on IQ tests do in fact correlate highly with academic performance (which is not surprising, since IQ tests were originally developed to predict success at school). They therefore also correlate closely with social, economic, and ethnic differences, since these are associated with variations in levels of educational attainment. White students score better, on average, than African Americans or members of other disadvantaged minorities. An article published by Arthur Jensen in 1967 caused a furor by attributing IQ differences between blacks and whites in part to genetic variations (Jensen, 1967, 1979).

More recently, the psychologist Richard J. Herrnstein and the sociologist Charles Murray have reopened the debate about IQ and education in a controversial way. They argue in their book *The Bell Curve: Intelligence and Class Structure in American Life* (1994) that the accumulated evidence linking IQ to genetic inheritance has now become overwhelming. The significant differences in intelligence among various racial and ethnic groups, they say, must in part be explained in terms of heredity. According to Herrnstein and Murray, the available evidence strongly indicates that some ethnic groups on average have higher IQs than other groups. Asian Americans, particularly Japanese Americans and Chinese Americans, on average possess higher IQs than whites, although the difference is not large. The average IQs of Asians and whites, however, are substantially higher than those of blacks. Summarizing the findings of 156 studies, Herrnstein and Murray find an average difference of sixteen IQ points between these two racial groups. The authors argue that such differences in inherited intelligence contribute in an important way to social divisions in American society. The smarter an individual is, the greater the chance that she will rise in the social scale. Those at the top are there partly because they are smarter than the rest of the population—from which it follows that those at the bottom remain there because, on average, they are not as smart.

Herrnstein and Murray's claim created a great deal of controversy and raised the ire and indignation of countless liberals, social scientists, and members of the African American community. Although Herrnstein and Murray's claims may be seen as racist and reprehensible, is this sufficient reason to attack their work? Or are their conclusions based on faulty social research? The answer to both questions is a resounding yes. A team of sociologists at the University of California at Berkeley have reanalyzed much of the data that Herrnstein and Murray based their conclusions on and came up with quite different findings.

In the original analysis, Herrnstein and Murray analyzed data from the National Longitudinal Study of Youth (NLSY), a survey of more than ten thousand young Americans who were interviewed multiple times over more than a decade. As part of this study, subjects were given the Armed Forces Qualifying Test (AFQT), a short test that assesses IQ. Herrnstein and Murray then conducted statistical analyses, which used the AFQT score to predict a variety of outcomes. They concluded that having a high IQ was the best predictor of later economic success and that low IQ was the best predictor of poverty later in life.

The Berkeley sociologists, in their 1996 book *Inequality by Design: Cracking the Bell Curve Myth* (Fischer et al., 1996), countered that the AFQT does not necessarily measure intelligence, but only how much a person has learned in school. Moreover, they found that intelligence is only one factor among several that predict how well people do in life. Social

What If We Ended Social Promotion?

[In 1998], I chaired a study of appropriate uses of testing for the National Research Council. The NRC panel was a diverse group of fifteen scholars from all over the country. We wrote our report, "High Stakes: Testing for Tracking, Promotion and Graduation," in response to a congressional mandate. The study was prompted by the Clinton administration's proposal, in 1997, for voluntary national tests of fourth grade reading and eighth grade math. The panel took no position about the value of voluntary national testing for its stated purposes—to tell American students, parents, and teachers how well they are doing relative to high national standards—but we recommended strongly against such tests' use for any

high-stakes purpose. The report, published [in 1999], has a lot of useful information about proper test use, and I commend it to readers. One of the strongest recommendations is that "accountability for educational outcomes should be a shared responsibility of states, school districts, public officials, educators, parents, and students. High standards cannot be established and maintained merely by imposing them on students."

Early in its work, the NRC panel decided to consider whether good tests could serve bad purposes. Thus, we evaluated the consequences of high-stakes educational decisions that may be based, at least in part, on test scores. In particular, we found—as American schools presently operate—that decisions to place students in typical lower-level tracks and decisions to hold students back to repeat the same grade are not educationally sound. Those decisions hurt students, and good tests will not improve them. This is not to say that all forms of tracking are bad for students, or that all grade retention is necessarily bad for students. Our findings were based on the actual and typical, not the ideal. But research evidence based on actual experience should inform new policies.

[***]

We should know that a new policy works before we try it out on a large scale. In its plan to end social promotion, the administration appears to have mixed a number of fine and credible proposals for educational reform with an enforcement provision—flunking kids by the carload lot—about which the great mass of evidence is strongly negative. And this policy [would] hurt poor and minority children most of all.

Students who have been held back typically do not catch up; in fact, low-performing students learn more if they are promoted—even without remedial help—than if they are held back. One reason for this is that the elementary and secondary school curriculum does not change radically from one grade to the next; there is a lot of review and overlap. Another is that it is simply boring to repeat exactly the same material.

Students who have been held back are much more likely to drop out before completing high school. That effect often occurs many years after a student is held back in grade and thus is invisible—without careful longitudinal study—to those who make the retention decision. The teachers and administrators who make decisions to hold children back do not have to live with the long-term consequences of their decisions.

[***]

There is one more critical point on which the National Research Council report provides strong evidence: We do not practice social promotion in the United States now, and we have not practiced it for many years. Our statistics are not very good; neither the federal government nor most states collect the right data, but we do know a few things.

Age at entry to first grade has increased since 1970. At that time, almost all six-year-olds were in the first grade (about 4 percent of six-year-old boys and 8 percent of six-year-old girls were enrolled below the first grade). In 1996, 18 percent of six-year-olds were enrolled below the first grade. Part of that change is due to holding children back in kindergarten.

Many students are held back during elementary and secondary school. Nationally, among children who entered school in the late 1980s, 21 percent were enrolled below the usual grade at ages six to eight; 28 percent were below the usual grade at ages nine to eleven; 31 percent at ages twelve to fourteen; and this rose to 36 percent at ages fifteen to seventeen. Not counting kindergarten and the later grades of high school, this means that at least 15 percent of children—and probably 20 percent—have been held back at some time in their childhood.

Worse yet, minorities and poor children are the most likely to be held back. Black, Hispanic, and white children enter first grade at just about the same ages, but between entry and adolescence, about 10 percent of white girls fall behind in grade, while 25 percent to 30 percent of minority children fall behind. By ages fifteen to seventeen, 45 percent to 50 percent of black and Hispanic youths are below the expected grade levels for their ages.

Holding students back—flunking them—has a much greater impact on minority and poor youths than on majority, middle-class children. It decreases educational opportunity, and it makes opportunities less equal among groups. For thirty-five years, American education has aimed to reduce social inequality. While much remains to be done, we have made major gains—narrowing differences in test scores in the 1970s and 1980s and reducing the dropout difference between majority and minority children. If we start holding back ever larger numbers of children, we are likely to reverse the progress of the past four decades.

SOURCE: Robert M. Hauser, "What If We Ended Social Promotion?" *Education Week*, April 7, 1999.

ROBERT M. HAUSER is the Vilas research professor of sociology in the Center for Demography at the University of Wisconsin-Madison. He is the editor, with Jay P. Heubert, of the National Research Council's report "High Stakes: Testing for Tracking, Promotion, and Graduation" (National Academy Press, 1999).

factors including education, gender, community conditions, marital status, current economic conditions, and—perhaps most important—parents' socioeconomic status better predict one's occupational and economic success. In the original analysis, Herrnstein and Murray measured parents' socioeconomic status by taking an average of mother's education, father's education, father's occupation, and family income.

The Berkeley sociologists recognized that each of these four factors matters differently in predicting a child's occupational outcomes and thus weighted the four components differently. Their analysis showed that the effects of socioeconomic background on a young adult's risk of later poverty were substantially greater than Herrnstein and Murray had originally found. The Berkeley sociologists also recognized that IQ is closely associated with one's level of education. They reanalyzed the NLSY data, taking into consideration the individuals' level of education and found that Herrnstein and Murray drastically overestimated the effects of IQ on a person's later achievements.

The relationship between race and intelligence is also best explained by social rather than biological causes, according to the Berkeley sociologists. All societies have oppressed ethnic groups. Low status, often coupled with discrimination and mistreatment, leads to socioeconomic deprivation, group segregation, and a stigma of inferiority. The combination of these forces often prevents racial minorities from obtaining education, and consequently, their scores on standardized intelligence tests are lower.

The average lower IQ score of African Americans in the United States is remarkably similar to that of deprived ethnic minorities in other countries—such as the "untouchables" in India (who are at the very bottom of the caste system), the Maori in New Zealand, and the *burakumin* of Japan. Children in these groups score an average of 10 to 15 IQ points below children belonging to the ethnic majority. The *burakumin*—descendants of people who in the eighteenth century, as a result of local wars, were dispossessed from their land and became outcasts and vagrants—are a particularly interesting example. They are not in any way physically distinct from other Japanese, although they have suffered from prejudice and discrimination for centuries. In this case, the difference in average IQ results cannot derive from genetic variations since there are no genetic differences between them and the majority population; yet the IQ difference is as thoroughly fixed as that between blacks and whites. *Burakumin* children in America, where they are treated like other Japanese, do as well on IQ tests as other Japanese.

Such observations strongly suggest that the IQ variations between African Americans and whites in the United States result from social and cultural differences. This conclusion receives further support from a comparative study of fourteen nations (including the United States) showing that average IQ scores have risen substantially over the past half century for the population as a whole (Coleman, 1987). IQ tests are regularly updated. When old and new versions of the tests are given to the same group of people, they score significantly higher on the old tests. Present-day children taking IQ tests from the 1930s outscored 1930s groups by an average of 15 points—just the kind of average difference that currently separates blacks and whites. Children today are not innately superior in intelligence to their parents or grandparents; the shift presumably derives from increasing prosperity and social advantages. The average social and economic gap between whites and African Americans is at least as great as that between the different generations and is sufficient to explain the variation in IQ scores. Although there may be genetic variations between individuals that influence scores on IQ tests, these have no overall connection to racial differences.

Educational Reform in the United States

Research done by sociologists has played a big role in reforming the educational system. The object of James Coleman's research, commissioned as part of the 1964 Civil Rights Act, was not solely academic; it was undertaken to influence policy. And influence policy it certainly did. On the basis of the act, it was decided in the courts that segregated schools violated the rights of minority pupils. But rather than attacking the origins of educational inequalities directly, as Christopher Jencks's later work suggested was necessary, the courts decided that the schools in each district should achieve a similar racial balance. Thus began the practice of busing students to other schools.

Busing provoked a great deal of opposition, particularly from parents and children in white areas, and led to episodes of violence at the gates of schools where the children were bused in from other neighborhoods. White children paraded with placards reading: "We don't want them!" Busing in fact met with a good deal of success, reducing levels of school segregation quite steeply, particularly in the South. But busing has also produced a number of unintended consequences. Some white parents reacted to busing by either putting their children into private schools or moving to mainly white suburbs where busing wasn't practiced. As a result, in the cities, some schools are virtually as segregated as the old schools were in the past. Busing, however, was only one factor prompting the white flight to the suburbs. Whites also left as a reaction to urban decay: to escape city crowding, housing problems, and rising rates of crime.

In 1970 a U.S. judge in North Carolina ordered that black students be bused to white schools and that white students be bused to black schools. It was hoped that this crosstown "school busing" would end the *de facto* segregation of public schools caused by white students living in predominantly white neighborhoods and black students living in predominantly black neighborhoods.

While busing is less prominent today as an issue, another problem regarding the American educational system has become an important focus of research: functional illiteracy. Most of the population can read and write at a very basic level, but one in every five adults is functionally illiterate—when they leave school, they can't read or write at the fourth-grade level (U.S. Department of Education, 1993). Of course, the United States is a country of immigrants, who when they arrive may not be able to read and write and who may also have trouble with English. But this doesn't explain why America lags behind most other industrial countries in terms of its level of functional illiteracy, because many people affected are not recent immigrants at all.

What is to be done? Some educationists have argued that the most important change that needs to be made is to improve the quality of teaching, either by increasing teachers' pay or by introducing performance-related pay scales, with higher salaries going to the teachers who are most effective in the classroom. Others have proposed giving schools more control over their budgets (a reform that has been carried out in Britain). The idea is that more responsibility for and control over budgeting decisions will create a greater drive to im-

prove the school. Further proposals include the refunding of federal programs such as Head Start to ensure healthy early child development and thus save millions of dollars in later costs. Another proposal that has gained numerous supporters in recent years is that public education should be privatized.

PRIVATIZATION

Widespread concern about the crisis in education has opened the door for *public-private partnerships* aimed at injecting private sector know-how into failing public schools. In 1994, then Present Bill Clinton signed into law the Goals 2000: Educate America Act, which authorized states to use federal funds for experiments with school privatization. Local school districts can choose to contract out specific educational services—or the entire school administration—to private companies without losing federal funding. In the past decade, a number of U.S. school districts—including large urban systems such as those in Hartford, Baltimore, and Minneapolis—have invited for-profit educational companies to run their school systems.

Supporters of school privatization argue that state and federal education authorities have shown that they are unable to improve the nation's schools. The educational system, they argue, is wasteful and bureaucratic; it spends a disproportionate amount of its funding on noninstructional administrative costs. Because of their top-heavy nature, it is nearly impossible for school systems to be flexible and innovative. Incompetent teachers are difficult to remove because of the strength of teacher unions.

What backers of school privatization claim can solve these problems is a strong dose of private-sector ideology: competition, experimentation, and incentive. For-profit companies can run school systems more efficiently and produce better outcomes by applying private sector logic. Good teachers would be attracted to teaching—and retained—by performance-based pay schemes, while underperforming teachers could be removed more easily. Competition within and between schools would lead to higher levels of innovation; privatized schools would have more liberty to institutionalize the results of successful experiments.

One of the leading players in the U.S. market for privatized education is the Edison Project, an educational company that manages a chain of eighty public schools in sixteen different states. The verdict on whether the Edison Project is improving educational outcomes in its schools is mixed, and the company itself has been heavily criticized on a number of fronts, including for poor financial management. Critics have been quick to point out that the Edison Project's vision for schools is little more than a slick repackaging of well-known practices from public education, such as cooperative learning and pupil-centered teaching (Molnar, 1996). The company requires that

Thomas Jefferson High School

The route to [New York City's] Thomas Jefferson High School for the students who commute on the L train is littered with broken glass and garbage. Jefferson High serves students from 53 different housing projects, which is notable because the violence is almost entirely territory related. There are only two white and no Asian students at the school, and the Hispanic students mix easily with the Caribbean and black students.

Of a senior class of about 400, that began with 600 freshmen, a mere 92 students were expected to graduate. Of those 92, 20 hopefuls didn't make it. But what became most fascinating to me was not the oppressive atmosphere but the unimaginable resilience of the students and faculty against what are truly horrendous odds. I photographed the self-esteem and leadership classes, the conflict resolution workshops, peer mediation sessions, and the range of support groups—the programs that combat the violent tendencies of the community.

Mr. Heath's bilingual class was silent as the students read their report cards. Jefferson falls short of what is considered a pitiful citywide average of seniors who graduate, 51.5 percent.

In the 1993–1994 school year, [***] only 34.4 percent of the senior class graduated. Andre Hamilton, a senior, is about to get promoted to shift manager [at Taco Bell]. "Me and my friend we just get together every day and talk about how we can't wait to break out."

"You never know what the weekend might have brought," says one student. "You can't even be sure who'll come back to school after the weekend." In 1993 East New York had the highest homicide rate in the country—140 dead in the summer alone. The Seventy-fifth Precinct had T-shirts made that read, "You give us 22 minutes, we'll give you a homicide." With sixty-one surveillance monitors and twice the security officers of any other New York City high school, Jefferson, dubbed "Homicide High," at times feels more like a cell block than an academic institution. [Still,] Marion Johnson, like many students, stays after school rather than go home. "Someone actually wrote in my junior high yearbook, 'If you're going to Jeff, don't get shot.'"

Anyone will tell you racism is not the issue. Gangs assemble in the various housing projects. Eddy Denis worried about

being jumped by the guys in the Alabama projects when he came to Jefferson as a freshman. But he has had no incidents to speak of, and told me, "Jefferson is just a school . . . not a bad school."

SOURCE: Alex Tehrani, "Thomas Jefferson High School," in *25 and Under*, ed. Alice Rose George (New York: DoubleTake/W. W. Norton, 1997).

Questions

- What aspects of education does Jefferson High fail to provide?
- What is the influence of race and class at Jefferson High?
- How does constant surveillance and police presence affect or interact with education?

all students in Edison schools have a computer at home—and assists those families that cannot afford them—but it is less clear how this enthusiasm for technology is linked into the curriculum in a meaningful way. Opponents of school privatization argue that companies such as the Edison Project are less serious about reforming education and reducing inequalities than about promoting education reform as a lucrative market for wealthy investors.

The crisis in American schools won't be solved in the short term, and it won't be solved by educational reforms alone, no matter how thoroughgoing. The lesson of sociological research is that inequalities and barriers in educational opportunity reflect wider social divisions and tensions. While the United States remains wracked by racial tensions and the polarization between decaying cities and affluent suburbs persists, the crisis in the school system is likely to prove difficult to turn around.

Education and Literacy in the Developing World

Literacy is the "baseline" of education. Without it, schooling cannot proceed. We take it for granted in the West that the majority of people are literate, but as has been mentioned, this is only a recent development in Western history, and in previous times no more than a tiny proportion of the population had any literacy skills.

Today, over 35 percent of the population of developing countries is still illiterate (see Global Map 16.1). The Indian government has estimated the number of illiterate people in that country alone to be over 285 million, a number that exceeds the total population of the United States. Even if the provision of primary education increased to match the level of population growth, illiteracy would not be markedly reduced for years, because a high proportion of those who cannot read or write are adults. The absolute number of illiterate people is actually rising (Coombs, 1985). According to UNESCO estimates, the total grew from 569 million in 1970 to 625 million in 1980 to 826 million in 2003 (UNESCO, 2003).

Although countries have instituted literacy programs, these have made only a small contribution to a problem of large-scale dimensions. Television, radio, and the other electronic media can be used, where they are available, to skip the stage of learning literacy skills and convey educational programs directly to adults. But educational programs are usually less popular than commercialized entertainment.

During the period of colonialism, colonial governments regarded education with some trepidation. Until the twentieth century, most believed indigenous populations to be too primitive to be worth educating. Later, education was seen as a way of making local elites responsive to European interests and ways of life. But to some extent, the result was to foment discontent and rebellion, since the majority of those who led anticolonial and nationalist movements were from educated elites who had attended schools or colleges in Europe. They were able to compare first hand the democratic institutions of the European countries with the absence of democracy in their lands of origin.

The education that the colonizers introduced usually pertained to Europe, not the colonial areas themselves. Educated Africans in the British colonies knew about the kings and queens of England, read Shakespeare, Milton, and the English poets, but knew next to nothing about their own countries' histories or past cultural achievements. Policies of educational reform since the end of colonialism have not completely altered the situation even today.

Partly as a result of the legacy of colonial education, which was not directed toward the majority of the population, the educational system in many developing countries is top heavy: Higher education is disproportionately developed, relative to primary and secondary education. The result is a correspondingly overqualified group who, having attended colleges and universities, cannot find white-collar or professional jobs. Given the low level of industrial development, most of the better-paid positions are in government, and there are not enough of those to go around.

In recent years, some developing countries, recognizing the shortcomings of the curricula inherited from colonialism, have tried to redirect their educational programs toward the rural poor. They have had limited success, because usually there is insufficient funding to pay for the scale of the necessary innovations. As a result, countries such as India have begun programs of self-help education. Communities draw on existing resources without creating demands for high levels of finance. Those who can read and write and who perhaps possess job skills are encouraged to take others on as apprentices, whom they coach in their spare time.

Communication and the Mass Media

The modern world depends on the continuous communication or interaction between people widely separated from one another. If we were not so dependent on "communication across distance," schooling would be less necessary. In traditional cultures—as that of Jean-Paul Didion in France, the example with which we opened the chapter—most knowledge was what the anthropologist Clifford Geertz has called **local knowledge** (Geertz, 1983). Traditions were passed on through the local community, and although general cultural ideas gradually spread across large areas, processes of cultural diffusion were long, drawn out, slow, and inconsistent. Today, we live in "the whole world" in a way that would have been quite inconceivable to Jean-Paul Didion, or anyone else living in cultures of the past.

We learn a great deal about the world from formal schooling. But we also learn much from the various communication media, which operate outside the context of schools. All of us are aware of situations and events that happen thousands of miles away—electronic communication makes such awareness almost instantaneous. Changes in the spread of information, and in information technologies, are as much a part of the development of modern societies as any aspect of industrial production (Kern, 1983). During the twentieth century, rapid transportation and electronic communication such as the Internet greatly intensified the global diffusion of information.

The **mass media**—newspapers, magazines, movies, compact discs, digital video discs, TV, and the Internet—are often associated with entertainment and therefore are seen as rather marginal to most people's lives. Such a view is quite misleading. Mass communications enter our social activities at many different points. For instance, a bank account is no longer a pile of money kept in a safe, but is a series of digits printed on an account sheet and stored in a computer, and monetary transactions are now mainly performed through the exchange of information between computers. Anyone who uses a credit card is connected with a very complex system of electronically stored and transmitted information, which has now become the very basis of modern financial accounting. Today, many people use the Internet to buy CDs and books.

Even "recreational" media such as newspapers or TV have a wide-ranging influence over our experience. This is not just because they affect our attitudes in specific ways, but because they are the *means of access* to the knowledge on which many social activities depend. Voting in national elections, for example, would be quite different if information about current political events, candidates, and parties were not generally available. Even those who are largely uninterested in politics and have little knowledge of the personalities involved have some awareness of national and international events, such as former President Bill Clinton's impeachment trial. Only a complete hermit would be entirely detached from the "news events" that impinge to some degree on the consciousness of all of us—and we could suspect that a modern hermit might very well own a transistor radio!

The Sociological Study of the Mass Media

How do we go about studying the influence of the mass media on our lives? A basic concept needed here is that of **communication,** which means the transfer of information from one person, context, or group to another. We saw in Chapter 6 that the communication and storage of information has been fundamental to the development of modern societies. Sociologically speaking, therefore, we need to put the rise of the mass media and popular culture in the context of the basic trends analyzed earlier.

There are close connections between the rise of the media and the development of modern systems of mass education. The two can only be properly understood sociologically in relation to one another. The German social thinker Jürgen Habermas offers a useful concept to describe this connection when he speaks of the emergence of a **public sphere** with the early development of the industrial societies. The public sphere is a sphere of communication, where public opinion is formed and attitudes shaped. In earlier forms of society, most communication was local and simply carried through speech, the ordinary daily talk of neighbors and friends in village communities. A rudimentary public sphere developed in early civilizations, well before the emergence of industrial societies. But it was very restricted, because only small groups were literate—could read and write. Moreover, written documents had to be laboriously prepared by hand, so there weren't many in circulation. From about the sixteenth century onward in Europe, as the new technology of printing spread and levels of literacy grew, the public sphere began to expand. The first local newspapers appeared in the mid-1700s. Mass-circulation newspapers followed about a century later, to be joined in our century by the electronic media of radio, TV, and other forms.

Learning to read and write and mastering other forms of knowledge is necessary for us to play a part in this developing wider society of communication. In the industrialized countries today, most people can read and write, but in historical terms, this is a recent development, dating back no more than a hundred years. The sorts of outlooks and knowledge acquired in school allow us to participate in the public sphere—to be able to read newspapers and magazines, for example. But the mass media might often also crosscut the goals of formal schooling. For instance, perhaps literacy and other educational skills are beginning to slump now that television and other forms of electronic media play such a large part in our lives. It isn't obvious, after all, that being able to do well at Nintendo games helps much with school achievement. The increasing influence of television is probably the single most important development in the media over the past forty years. Television is as important as books, magazines, and newspapers in the

Adult Literacy Rates Worldwide
(15 years and older)

Percentage literate

- High
- Medium
- Low

SOURCE: United Nations, *Human Development Report*, 2003 (2001 data).

expansion of indirect forms of communication characteristic of modern societies. It frames the ways in which we interpret and respond to the social world by helping to order our experience of it. Assumptions built in to the overall character of TV production and distribution may perhaps be more significant than whatever particular programs are shown. If current trends continue, by age eighteen, the average child born today will have spent more time watching TV than doing any other activity save sleeping. Virtually every industrialized household now possesses a television set. In the United States, the average set is switched on between five and six hours a day, and much the same is true in the European countries (Goodhardt, Ehrenberg, and Collins, 1987).

Theories of the Mass Media's Influence on Society

THE GLOBAL VILLAGE

One influential early theorist of the mass media was the Canadian author Marshall McLuhan. According to McLuhan, "the medium is the message" (1964). That is to say, the nature of the media found in a society influences its structure much more than the content, or the messages, that the media convey. Television, for instance, is a very different medium from the printed book. It is electronic, visual, and composed of fluid images. A society in which television plays a basic role is one in which everyday life is experienced differently from one that only has print. Thus the TV news conveys global information instantaneously to millions of people. The electronic media, McLuhan thought, are creating what he called a **global village**—people throughout the world see major news items unfold and hence participate in the same events as one another. Millions of people in different countries, for example, knew about Princess Diana's life, her problems with the British royal family, and her death in an automobile accident in Paris.

Jean Baudrillard, whose ideas we will look at in this section, has been strongly influenced by the ideas of McLuhan. We turn first, however, to the theories of the German sociologist and philosopher Jürgen Habermas.

JURGEN HABERMAS: THE PUBLIC SPHERE

The German philosopher and sociologist Jürgen Habermas is linked to the "Frankfurt School" of social thought. The Frankfurt School was a group of authors inspired by Marx who nevertheless believed that Marx's views needed radical revision to bring them up to date. Among other things, they believed that Marx had not given enough attention to the influence of culture in modern capitalist society.

The Frankfurt School made extensive study of what they called the "culture industry," meaning the entertainment industries of film, TV, popular music, radio, newspapers, and magazines. They argued that the spread of the culture industry, with its undemanding and standardized products, undermines the capacity of individuals for critical and independent thought. Art disappears, swamped by commercialization— "Mozart's Greatest Hits."

Habermas has taken up some of these themes, but developed them in a different way. He analyzes the development of media from the early eighteenth century up to the present moment, tracing out the emergence—and subsequent decay—of the public sphere (Habermas, 1989).

The public sphere, according to Habermas, developed first in the salons and coffeehouses of London, Paris, and other European cities. People met in such salons to discuss issues of the moment, using as a means for such debate the news sheets and newspapers that had just begun to emerge. Political debate became a matter of particular importance. Although only small numbers of the population were involved, Habermas argues that the salons were vital to the early development of democracy, for they introduced the idea of resolving political problems through public discussion. The public sphere—at least in principle—involves individuals coming together as equals in a forum for public debate.

However, the promise offered by the early development of the public sphere, Habermas concludes, has not been fully realized. Democratic debate in modern societies is stifled by the development of the culture industry. The development of the mass media and mass entertainment causes the public sphere to become largely a sham. Politics is stage managed in government and the media, while commercial interests triumph over those of the public. Public opinion is not formed through open, rational discussion, but through manipulation and control—as, for example, in advertising.

JEAN BAUDRILLARD: THE WORLD OF HYPERREALITY

One of the most influential current theorists of media is the French author Jean Baudrillard. Baudrillard regards the impact of modern mass media as being quite different from and much more profound than that of any other technology. The coming of the mass media, particularly electronic media such as television, has transformed the very nature of our lives. Television does not just "represent" the world to us, it increasingly defines what the world in which we live actually *is*.

During the O. J. Simpson trial six television channels broadcast the court proceedings simultaneously. This excess of exposure, where televised events seem more real than the actual events, is an example of Baudrillard's concept of "hyperreality."

Consider as an example the O.J. Simpson trial, a celebrated court case that unfolded in Los Angeles in 1994–1995. Simpson originally became famous as an American football star, but later became known around the world as a result of appearing in several popular films, including the *Naked Gun* series. He was accused of the murder of his wife, Nicole, and after a very long trial was acquitted (although subsequently Simpson was found guilty in a civil suit filed by the families of Nicole Brown Simpson and the man who was murdered with her, Ronald Goldman). The criminal trial was televised live and was watched in many countries, including Britain. In America, six television channels covered the trial on a continuous basis.

The trial did not just happen in the courtroom. It was a televisual event linking millions of viewers and commentators in the media. The trial is an illustration of what Baudrillard calls **hyperreality**. There is no longer a "reality" (the events in the courtroom), which television allows us to see. The "reality" is actually the string of images on the TV screens of the world, which defined the trial as a global event.

Just before the outbreak of hostilities in the Persian Gulf in 1991, Baudrillard wrote a newspaper article entitled "The Gulf War Cannot Happen." When war was declared and a bloody conflict took place it might seem obvious that Baudrillard had been wrong. Not a bit of it. After the end of the war, Bau-drillard wrote a second article, "The Gulf War Did Not Happen." What did he mean? He meant that the war was not like other wars that have happened in history. It was a war of the media age, a televisual spectacle, in which, along with other viewers throughout the world, George Bush and Saddam Hussein watched the coverage by CNN to see what was actually "happening." Baudrillard argues that in an age where the mass media are everywhere, in effect a new reality—hyperreality—is created, composed of the intermingling of people's behavior and media images.

JOHN THOMPSON: THE MEDIA AND MODERN SOCIETY

Drawing in some part on the writings of Habermas, John Thompson has analyzed the relation between the media and the development of industrial societies (Thompson, 1990, 1995). From early forms of print through to electronic communication, Thompson argues, the media have played a central role in the development of modern institutions. Thompson believes that the main founders of sociology—including Marx, Weber, and Durkheim—gave too little attention to the role of media in shaping even the early development of modern society.

Thompson's theory of the media depends on a distinction among three types of interaction. Face-to-face interaction, such as people talking at a party, is rich in clues that individuals use to make sense of what others say. **Mediated interaction** involves the use of a media technology—paper, electrical connections, electronic impulses. Characteristic of mediated interaction is that it is stretched out in time and space—it goes well beyond the contexts of ordinary face-to-face interaction. Mediated interaction takes place between individuals in a direct way—for instance, two people talking on the telephone—but there isn't the same variety of clues as when people are face to face.

A third type of interaction is **mediated quasi-interaction**. This refers to the sort of social relations created by the mass media. Such interaction is stretched across time and space, but it doesn't link individuals directly: hence the term *quasi-interaction*. The two previous types are "dialogical": Individuals communicate in a direct way. Mediated quasi-interaction is "monological": A TV program, for example, is a one-way form of communication. People watching the program may discuss it, and perhaps address some remarks to the TV set—but, of course, it doesn't answer back.

Thompson's point is not that the third type comes to dominate the other two—essentially the view taken by Baudrillard—but rather that all three types intermingle in our lives today. The mass media, Thompson suggests, change the balance between the public and the private in our lives. Contrary to what

TROUBLETOWN

BY LLOYD DANGLE

ALL I NEED TO KNOW IN LIFE I LEARN FROM LITTLE **SYMBOLIC MEDIA TIDBITS!**...

BLACKS BELIEVE O.J.!

A HETEROSEXUAL COUPLE WAS ASKED TO LEAVE A **GAY BAR** FOR EXCESSIVE PUBLIC KISSING & GROPING!

CONCLUSION: **THEY** DISCRIMINATE **TOO!** THIS MAKES OUR INTOLERANCE COMPLETELY JUSTIFIABLE.

A SIX-YEAR-OLD BOY WAS CHARGED WITH SEXUAL HARASSMENT FOR KISSING A FEMALE CLASSMATE!

HA! I KNEW SEXUAL HARASSMENT WAS JUST A THING DREAMED-UP BY CRAZY, OVER-SENSITIVE FEMINISTS!

McDONALDS WAS ONCE SUED BY A PERSON WHO SPILLED HOT COFFEE ON HERSELF!

ANY COMPLAINT AGAINST A CORPORATION IS A FRIVOLOUS EXTORTION ATTEMPT!

A MURDER WAS COMMITTED IN FLORIDA OR TEXAS BY SOMEONE WHO WAS **OUT ON PAROLE!!**

ALL CRIMES SHOULD CARRY MANDATORY LIFE SENTENCES— AT THE **VERY LEAST!**

SHOPLIFTING DEATH ROW

CELL BLOCK C

PARKING VIOLATIONS

THEY'RE BITE-SIZED, EASY TO REMEMBER, AND THE OUTRAGE LASTS FOR DAYS! SYMBOLIC MEDIA TIDBITS ARE MY KEY TO ENLIGHTENMENT!

CHILD BEAUTY QUEENS!

Habermas says, much more comes into the public domain than before, and this leads quite often to debate and controversy.

An example would be former President Bill Clinton's televised testimony about his affair with Monica Lewinsky. Viewers learned a great deal about the president's private business, perhaps more details than they cared to know. At the time, Clinton's affairs were widely discussed by many Americans. The media's reporting of the affair also sparked debate about the division between the private and public, not only in newspapers and on television, but in homes, bars, offices, and Internet chat rooms across the country.

GLOBALIZATION AND MEDIA IMPERIALISM

If today we all live in "one world," it is in large part a result of the international scope of the communications media. Anyone who switches on the TV set and watches "the world news" ordinarily gets what the description suggests: a presentation of events that occurred that day or shortly before in many different parts of the world. Television programs are sold to large international markets, and hundreds of millions of people watch them. Like other aspects of the global society, the development of a **world information order**—an international system for the production, distribution, and consumption of information—has been uneven and reflects the divisions between the developed societies and developing countries.

The paramount position of the industrialized countries, above all the United States, in the production and diffusion of media has led many observers to speak of *media imperialism*. A cultural empire, it is argued, has been established. Developing countries are held to be especially vulnerable, because they lack the resources to maintain their own cultural independence.

Via the electronic media, Western cultural products have certainly become widely diffused across the globe. Pico Iyer speaks of "video nights in Katmandu," of frequenting discos in Bali (Iyer, 1989). American videos are commonplace in the Islamic republic of Iran, as are audiotapes of Western popular music, brought in on the black market (Sreberny-Mohammadi, 1992). Not only more popular entertainment forms are at issue, however. Control of the world's news by the major Western agencies, it has been suggested, means the predominance of a First World outlook in the information conveyed. Thus, it has been claimed that attention is given to the developing world in news broadcasts mainly in times of disaster, crisis, or military confrontation, and that the daily files of other types of news kept on the industrialized world are not maintained for developing world coverage.

Herbert Schiller has claimed that control of global communications by U.S. firms has to be seen in relation to various factors. He argues that American TV and radio networks have fallen increasingly under the influence of the federal government and particularly the Department of Defense. He points out that RCA, which until 1986 owned the NBC television and radio networks, is also a leading defense subcontractor to the Pentagon. American television exports, coupled with advertising, propagate a commercialized culture that corrodes local forms of cultural expression. Even where governments prohibit commercial broadcasting within their borders, radio and television from surrounding countries can often be directly received.

Schiller argues that although Americans were the first to be affected by the "corporate-message cocoon . . . [W]hat is now happening is the creation and global extension of a new total corporate informational-cultural environment" (Schiller, 1989). Since U.S. corporations and culture are globally dominant, they have "overwhelmed a good part of the world," such that "American cultural domination . . . sets the boundaries for national discourse" (Schiller, 1991).

Technological Change, Media, and Education

Although we have concentrated so far on newspapers, television, and other parts of the "culture industry," we should not think of the media of communication only in those terms. Particularly as influenced by the computer, the media are affecting what we do in many other areas as well.

The Internet

By the early 1990s, many experts in the computer and technology industries were conceding that the reign of the personal computer was over. It was becoming increasingly clear to them that the future lay not with the individual computer but with a global system of interconnected computers—the *Internet*. Although many computer users may not have realized it at the time, the PC was quickly to become little more than a point of access to events happening elsewhere—events happening on a network stretching across the planet, a network that is not owned by any individual or company.

ORIGINS OF THE INTERNET

The Internet has come about in a spontaneous way. It is the product of an undivided world—a world after the fall of the Berlin Wall. Yet its first origins were in the cold war period that preceded 1989. The Internet had its beginnings in the Pentagon, the headquarters of the American military. It was established in 1969 and was first named the ARPA net, after the Pentagon's Advanced Research Projects Agency. The aim was limited. The ARPA sought to allow scientists working on military contracts in different parts of America to pool their resources and to share the expensive equipment they were using. Almost as an afterthought, its originators thought up a way of sending messages, too. Thus electronic mail—e-mail—was born.

Until the early 1980s, the Pentagon Internet consisted of five hundred computers, all located in military laboratories and university computer science departments. Other people in universities then started catching on and began using the system for their own purposes. By 1987 the Internet had expanded to include twenty-eight thousand host computers, at many different universities and research labs.

For several years, the Internet remained confined to universities. With the spread of home-based personal computers, however, it began to move outside—and then entered a period of explosive growth. By the year 2002, 58.5 percent of households owned computers, and nearly 127 million adult Americans actively logged on to the Internet each month (U.S. Bureau of the Census, 2001; Cyberatlas, 2003). The spread of commercial Internet service providers (ISPs) that offer dial-up access through modems has fueled the growing proportion of households with online capabilities. Online services, electronic bulletin boards, chat rooms, and software libraries were uploaded onto the Internet by a bewildering variety of people,

no longer situated just in North America, but all over the world. Corporations also got in on the act. In 1994, companies overtook universities as the dominant users of the network.

Access to the Internet is highly uneven. In 1998, 88 percent of the world's Internet users lived in the developed world. North America accounted for more than 50 percent of all users, although it contains only 5 percent of the total world population. By 2002, however, the share of Internet users located in North America had dropped to under 33 percent, indicating the rise of Internet usage worldwide. The United States has the highest levels of computer ownership and online access. More than 182 million Americans use the Internet; in Germany there are over 40 million Internet users, and Britain boasts more than 35 million. In Japan, a country where the Internet craze arrived somewhat late, more than 44 percent of the population (56 million people) used the Internet in 2002 (Cyberatlas, 2003). These numbers are expected to grow rapidly in the coming years.

THE IMPACT OF THE INTERNET

In a world of quite stunning technological change, no one can be sure what the future holds. Many see the Internet as exemplifying the new global order emerging at the close of the twentieth century. Users of the Internet live in "cyberspace." **Cyberspace** means the space of interaction formed by the global network of computers that compose the Internet. In cyberspace, much as Baudrillard might say, we are no longer people but instead are messages on each other's screens. Apart from e-mail, where users usually identify themselves, no one on the Internet can be sure of who anyone else really is, whether they are male or female, or where they are in the world.

The spread of the Internet across the globe has raised important questions for sociologists. The Internet is transforming the contours of daily life—blurring the boundaries between the global and the local, presenting new channels for communication and interaction, and allowing more and more everyday tasks to be carried out online. Yet at the same time as it provides exciting new opportunities to explore the social world, the Internet also threatens to undermine human relationships and communities. Although the information age is still in its early stages, many sociologists are already debating the complex implications of the Internet for late modern societies.

Opinions on the effects of the Internet on social interaction fall into two broad categories. On the one hand are those observers who see the online world as fostering new forms of electronic relationships that either enhance or supplement existing face-to-face interactions. While traveling or working abroad, individuals can use the Internet to communicate regularly with friends and relatives at home. Distance and separation become more tolerable. The Internet also allows the formation of new types of relationships: Anonymous online users can meet in chat rooms and discuss topics of mutual interest. These cyber contacts sometimes evolve into fully fledged electronic friendships or even result in face-to-face meetings. Many Internet users become part of lively online communities that are qualitatively different from those they inhabit in the physical world. Scholars who see the Internet as a positive addition to human interaction argue that it expands and enriches people's social networks.

Not everyone takes such an enthusiastic stance, however. As people spend more and more time communicating online and handling their daily tasks in cyberspace, it may be that they spend less time interacting with one another in the physical world. Some sociologists fear that the spread of Internet technology will lead to increased social isolation and atomization. They argue that one effect of increasing Internet access in households is that people are spending less quality time with their families and friends. The Internet is encroaching on domestic life as the lines between work and home are blurred: Many employees continue to work at home after hours—checking e-mail or finishing tasks that they were unable to complete during the day. Human contact is reduced, personal relationships suffer, traditional forms of entertainment such as the theater and books fall by the wayside, and the fabric of social life is weakened.

How are we to evaluate these contrasting positions? Most certainly there are elements of truth on both sides of the debate. The Internet is undoubtedly broadening our horizons and presents unprecedented opportunities for making contact with others. Yet the frenzied pace at which it is expanding also presents challenges and threats to traditional forms of human interaction. Will the Internet radically transform society into a fragmented, impersonal realm where humans rarely venture out of their homes and lose their ability to communicate? It seems unlikely. About fifty years ago very similar fears were expressed as television burst on the media scene. In *The Lonely Crowd* (1961), an influential sociological analysis of American society in the 1950s, David Riesman and his colleagues expressed concern about the effects of TV on family and community life. Some of their fears were justified, but television and the mass media have also enriched the social world in many ways.

Just like television before it, the Internet has aroused both hopes and fears. Will we lose our identities in cyberspace? Will computerized technology dominate us rather than the reverse? Will human beings retreat into an antisocial online world? The answer to each of these questions, fortunately, almost certainly is no. For example, people don't use video conferencing if they can get together with others in an ordinary way. Business executives have far more forms of electronic communication avail-able to them than ever before. At the same time, the number of face-to-face business conferences has shot up.

Education and New Communications Technology

The spread of information technology looks set to influence education in a number of different ways, some of which may perhaps be quite fundamental. The new technologies are affecting the nature of work, replacing some types of human work by machines. The sheer pace of technological change is creating a much more rapid turnover of jobs than once was the case. Education can no longer be regarded as a stage of preparation before an individual enters work. As technology changes, necessary skills change, and even if education is seen from a purely vocational point of view—as providing skills relevant to work—most observers agree that lifelong exposure to education will be needed in the future.

TECHNOLOGIES OF EDUCATION

The rise of education in its modern sense was connected with a number of other major changes happening in the nineteenth century. One was the development of the school. One might naively think that there was a demand for education and that schools and universities were set up to meet that demand. But that was not how things happened. Schools arose, as Michel Foucault has shown, as part of the administrative apparatus of the modern state. The "hidden curriculum" was about discipline and about the control of children.

A second influence was the development of printing and the arrival of "book culture." The mass distribution of books, newspapers, and other printed media was as distinctive a feature of the development of industrial society as were machines and factories. Education developed to provide skills of literacy and computation giving access to the world of printed media. Nothing is more characteristic of the school than the schoolbook or textbook.

In the eyes of many, all this is set to change with the growing use of computers and multimedia technologies in education. It has been said that "around 70–80 percent of telecommunications trials conducted in the emerging multimedia technologies around the world involve education or at least have an education component" (quoted in Kenway et al., 1995).

As in many other areas of contemporary social life, markets and information technology are major influences on educational change. The commercializing and marketizing of education also reflect such pressures. Schools are being reengineered in much the same way as business corporations.

Many of those likely to enter the education field will be organizations whose relation to schooling was previously marginal or nonexistent. They include cable companies, software houses, telecommunication groups, filmmakers, and equipment suppliers. Their influence will not be limited to schools or universities. They are already forming part of what has been called "edutainment"—a sort of parallel education industry linked to the software industry in general, to museums, science parks, and heritage areas.

EDUCATION AND THE TECHNOLOGY GAP

Whether the new technologies will have the radical implications for education that some claim is still an open question. Critics have pointed out that, even if they do have major effects, these may act to reinforce educational inequalities. **Information poverty** might be added to the material deprivations that currently have such an effect on schooling. The sheer pace of technological change and the demand of employers for computer-literate workers may mean that those who are technologically competent "leapfrog" over people who have little experience with computers.

Some already fear the emergence of a "computer underclass" within Western societies. Although developed countries have the highest levels of computer and Internet usage in the world, there are stark inequalities in computer use within those societies. Many schools and colleges are suffering from underfunding and long-standing neglect; even if these institutions become beneficiaries of schemes that distribute secondhand computer hardware to schools, they must gain the technical expertise and ability to teach information technology skills to pupils. Because the market for computer specialists is so strong, many schools are struggling to attract and keep information technology teachers, who can earn far greater incomes in the private sector.

Yet the technology gap within Western societies appears minor compared to the digital divide separating Western classrooms from their counterparts in the developing world. As the global economy becomes increasingly knowledge based, there is a real danger that poorer countries will become even more marginalized because of the gap between the information rich and the information poor.

According to the UNDP *Human Development Report* (1999), Internet access has become the new line of demarcation between the rich and the poor. South Asia, with 23 percent of the world's total population, has less than 1 percent of world Internet users. In Africa, there are a mere seven Internet hosts per 1 million people. A high proportion of these are located in South Africa, by far the most developed and prosperous African nation.

Information technology enthusiasts argue that computers need not result in greater national and global inequalities—that their very strength lies in their ability to draw people together and to open up new opportunities. Schools in Asia and Africa that are lacking textbooks and qualified teachers can benefit from the Internet, it is claimed. Distance-learning programs and collaboration with colleagues overseas could be the key to overcoming poverty and disadvantage. When technology is put in the hands of smart, creative people, they argue, the potential is limitless.

Technology can be breathtaking and open important doors, but it has to be recognized that there is no such thing as an easy "techno-fix." Underdeveloped regions struggling with mass illiteracy and lacking telephone lines and electricity need an improved educational infrastructure before they can truly benefit from distance-learning programs. The Internet cannot be substituted for direct contact between teachers and pupils under these conditions.

Lifelong Learning

New technologies and the rise of the knowledge economy are transforming traditional ideas about work and education. The sheer pace of technological change is creating a much more rapid turnover of jobs than once was the case. Training and the attainment of qualifications are now occurring throughout people's lives, rather than just once early in life. Mid-career professionals are choosing to update their skills through continuing education programs and Internet-based learning. Many employers now allow workers to participate in on-the-job training as a way of enhancing loyalty and improving the company skills base.

As our society continues to transform, the traditional beliefs and institutions that underpin it are also undergoing change. The idea of education—implying the structured transmission of knowledge within a formal institution—is giving way to a broader notion of learning that takes place in a diversity of settings. The shift from education to learning is not an inconsequential one. Learners are active, curious social actors who can derive insights from a multiplicity of sources, not just within an institutional setting. Emphasis on learning acknowledges that skills and knowledge can be gained through all types of encounters—with friends and neighbors, at seminars and museums, in conversations at the local Starbucks, through the Internet and other media, and so forth.

The shift in emphasis toward *lifelong learning* can already be seen within schools themselves, where there are a growing number of opportunities for pupils to learn *outside* the confines of the classroom. The boundaries between schools and the outside world are breaking down, not only via cyberspace, but in the physical world as well. "Service learning," for example, has become a mainstay of many American secondary schools. As part of their graduation requirements, pupils devote a certain amount of time to volunteer work in the community. Partnerships with local businesses have also become commonplace in the United States, fostering interaction and mentor relationships between adult professionals and pupils.

Lifelong learning should and must play a role in the move toward a knowledge society. Not only is it essential to a well-trained, motivated work force, but learning should also be seen in relation to wider human values. Learning is both a means and an end to the development of a rounded and autonomous self-education in the service of self-development and self-understanding. There is nothing utopian in this idea; indeed it reflects the humanistic ideals of education developed by educational philosophers. An example already in existence are lifelong learning programs for the elderly, which provide retired people with the opportunity to educate themselves as they choose, developing whatever interests they care to follow.

Study Outline

www.wwnorton.com/giddens5

The Development of Schooling

- Education in its modern form, involving the instruction of pupils within specially designated school premises, began to emerge with the spread of printed materials and higher levels of literacy. Knowledge could be retained, reproduced, and consumed by more people in more places. With industrialization, work became more specialized, and knowledge was increasingly acquired in more abstract rather than practical ways—the skills of reading, writing, and calculating.

Education and Inequality

- The expansion of education in the twentieth century has been closely tied to perceived needs for a literate and disciplined work force. Although reformers have seen education for all as a means of reducing inequalities, its impact in this respect is fairly limited. Education tends to express and reaffirm existing inequalities more than it acts to change them.
- The formal school curriculum is only one part of a more general process of social reproduction influenced by many informal aspects of learning, education, and school settings. The *hidden curriculum* plays a significant role in such reproduction.
- Because *intelligence* is difficult to define, there has been a great deal of controversy about the subject. Some argue that genes determine one's *IQ;* others believe that social influences determine it. The weight of the evidence appears to be on the side of those arguing for social and cultural influences. A major controversy about IQ has developed as a result of the book *The Bell Curve*. The book claims that races differ in terms of their average level of inherited intelligence. Critics reject this thesis completely.

Communication and the Mass Media

- The *mass media* have come to play a fundamental role in modern society. The mass media are media of communication—newspapers, magazines, television, radio, movies, videos, CDs, DVDs, and other forms—that reach mass audiences. The influence of the mass media on our lives is profound. The media not only provide entertainment, but provide and shape much of the information that we utilize in our daily lives.
- A range of different theories of media and popular culture have been developed. McLuhan argued that media influence society more in terms of how they communicate than what they communicate. In McLuhan's words, "the medium is the message": TV, for example, influences people's behavior and attitudes because it is so different in nature from other media, such as newspapers or books.
- Other important theorists include Habermas, Baudrillard, and Thompson. Habermas points to the role of the media in creating a *public sphere*—a sphere of public opinion and public debate. Baudrillard has been strongly influenced by McLuhan. He believes that new media, particularly television, actually change the "reality" we experience. Thompson argues that the mass media have created a new form of social interaction—*mediated quasi-interaction*—that is more limited, narrow, and one-way than everyday social interaction.

Technological Change, Media, and Education

- The sense today of inhabiting one world is in large part a result of the international scope of media of communication. A *world information order*—an international system of the production, distribution, and consumption of informational goods—has come into being. Given the paramount position of the industrial countries in the world information order, many believe that the developing countries are subject to a new form of media imperialism.

- Recent years have seen the emergence of multimedia, linked to the development of the Internet. *Multimedia* refers to the combination on a single medium of what used to be different media needing different technologies, so that a CD-ROM, for example, can carry both visuals and sound and be played on a computer. Many claims have been made about the likely social effects of these developments, but it is still too early to judge how far these will be borne out.

Key Concepts

communication (p. 491)
cultural capital (p. 482)
cyberspace (p. 497)
global village (p. 494)
hidden curriculum (p. 481)
hyperreality (p. 495)
information poverty (p. 499)
intelligence (p. 483)
IQ (intelligence quotient) (p. 483)
local knowledge (p. 491)
mass media (p. 491)
mediated interaction (p. 495)
mediated quasi-interaction (p. 495)
public sphere (p. 491)
tracking (p. 479)
world information order (p. 496)

Review Questions

1. What is the "hidden curriculum"?
   a. The "tricks of the trade" that enable teachers to keep discipline in class, sustain student interest, and impart instruction.
   b. The effects of school procedures and organization on students. The hidden curriculum teaches students to know their place and to sit still.
   c. The strategies that students use to make otherwise dull classes interesting.
   d. The political agenda that is seen to animate education: for conservatives it is the liberal obsession with political correctness and multiculturalism; for liberals it is the conservative obsession with standardized testing and the moral character of education.

2. What is "social reproduction"?
   a. The way schools educate each succeeding generation.
   b. The ways schools help perpetuate social and economic inequalities across the generations.
   c. The combined effect of the formal and hidden curricula on student character.
   d. The ways schools handle sex education.

3. What is the main argument against the idea—popularized by Herrnstein and Murray's book *The Bell Curve*—that systematic differences in IQ test scores between whites and blacks are the result of genetic differences?
   a. White and Asian Americans are just better test takers.
   b. Ethnic minorities in many societies score lower on standardized intelligence tests than ethnic majorities because their subordinate position in society gives them fewer educational opportunities and results in their having less confidence and experiencing greater stress in testing situations.
   c. There is no such thing as the core intelligence that Herrnstein and Murray claim IQ tests measure.
   d. Blacks are steadily closing the IQ gap with whites.

4. What is "media imperialism"?
   a. The ability of the United States to disseminate Western values through the dominance of Hollywood and American television, and through the agenda of Western news organizations.
   b. The monopoly position of large media conglomerates such as AOL/Time Warner and Fox Communications.
   c. The predominance of media—particularly television— in our private lives.
   d. None of the above.

5. What was the main conclusion of the landmark studies of educational inequality carried out in the 1960s by James Coleman and Christopher Jencks?
   a. Educational and occupational attainment are governed mainly by family background and nonschool factors.
   b. Outside the poorest areas, black schools are often as well funded as white schools.
   c. Reform of the educational system is essentially useless without reform of society.
   d. Intelligence is largely a product not of heredity but of the environment and, in particular, the actions of parents.

6. What is shown by sociological research on the impact of tracking in schools?
   a. Tracking does not benefit students, but it does make it easier for teachers to manage classes.
   b. Tracking ameliorates previously existing inequalities for advanced students but has no benefit for average or poor students.
   c. Tracking reinforces previously existing inequalities for average or poor students, but it does have benefits for advanced students.
   d. Tracking works best where there is a proper system of promotion and relegation of good and bad students.

7. What is "cultural capital"?
   a. The total monetary value of all the cultural artifacts—books, videos, CDs—in a home.
   b. The cultural advantages conferred on children who come from a good home.
   c. The city—not necessarily the political capital—with the most prestigious cultural institutions in a country, such as New York City for the United States.
   d. The economic and political clout wielded by the cultural industries.

8. What did Baudrillard mean when he argued that the "Gulf War did not happen"?
   a. There was no war as it is conventionally understood because the bombing campaign by the U.S. Air Force had obliterated the enemy before the army engaged them.
   b. President George Bush made the whole thing up to increase his popularity.
   c. The war was a hyperreal event and existed only in the public imagination and not on the ground in the Persian Gulf.
   d. In an age where the mass media pervade our lives, a new reality—hyperreality—is created, composed of the intermingling of people's behavior and media images.

9. What does Thompson mean by "mediated quasi-interaction" and how is it related to face-to-face and mediated interaction?
   a. It is the type of interaction created by the mass media: It is monological, or one-way, communication, from broadcaster to viewer. Thompson argued that all three types of interaction intermingle in our lives today.
   b. It is the type of interaction created by daytime chat shows that focus on issues in viewers' personal lives. It is that type of intimacy created by the public exposure of private troubles.
   c. It is the type of interaction created by telephones and cell phones, where the voice is heard and communication takes place in real time, as opposed to the mediated type of interaction in letters and e-mail.
   d. It is the type of interaction created by the mass media. Echoing Baudrillard, Thompson argued that it has come to predominate over mediated and face-to-face interactions in our private lives.

10. One main reason for the rise of large educational systems was the process of
    a. medical innovation.
    b. stock market expansion.
    c. industrialization.
    d. computer innovation.

Thinking Sociologically Exercises

1. From your reading of this chapter, describe what might be the principal advantages and disadvantages of having children go to private versus public schools in the United States at this time. Assess whether privatization of our public schools would help to improve them.

2. Back in 1964, Marshall McLuhan argued that the developments of radio and television helped to produce a global village. Carefully explain what he meant by the term *global village* and its importance. Explain how the advent of the Internet and cell phones will be likely to extend the concept of the global village further and faster than ever before.

Data Exercises

www.wwnorton.com/giddens5
Keyword: Data16

- The data exercise for this chapter provides you with an opportunity to explore the link between a parent's educational attainment and that of his child. Before you begin, think about your own life. What are your own educational goals? In what ways did your parents' educational achievements influence your decisions about what kind of education and how much education to pursue?

The Sociological Study of Religion

Learn the elements that make up a religion.

Theories of Religion

Know the sociological approaches to religion developed by Marx, Durkheim, and Weber, as well as the contemporary debate over secularization and the religious economy approach.

Types of Religious Organizations

Learn the various ways religious communities are organized and how they have become institutionalized.

Gender and Religion

Recognize the changes taking place in the interrelationships between gender and religion.

World Religions

Familiarize yourself with the various forms religion takes in traditional and modern societies.

Religion in the United States

Learn about the sociological dimensions of religion in the United States, including the rise of fundamentalism and the electronic church.

Globalization and Religion

Recognize how the globalization of religion is reflected in religious activism in poor countries and the rise of religious nationalist movements.

CHAPTER SEVENTEEN

RELIGION IN MODERN SOCIETY

O n September 11, 2001, a well-organized group of nineteen men, equipped with box cutters, a rudimentary knowledge of how to pilot commercial jet aircraft, and fervent religious conviction, forever changed our world.

American Airlines Flight 11 and United Flight 175, both bound for Los Angeles from Boston, were hijacked shortly after takeoff and flown into the twin towers of New York City's World Trade Center. American Airlines Flight 77, en route from Washington's Dulles airport to Los Angeles was hijacked over Kansas and flown back to Washington, where it plummeted into the Pentagon. A fourth plane, United Airlines Flight 93, bound for San Francisco from Newark, crashed into a field in Pennsylvania, most likely because heroic passengers overpowered the hijackers before it could reach the White House or the Capitol.

The hijacking was organized by al Qaeda, a global network of religious extremists dedicated to restoring their version of traditional Islamic rule. Al Qaeda had already unleashed violent attacks before September 11. These included two 1998 car bombings of the U.S. embassies in Kenya and Tanzania that killed several hundred people and injured more than five thousand, and an attack on the U.S. destroyer *Cole* in 2000. The organization had also planned to blow up a dozen trans-Pacific U.S. commercial flights on a single day in 1995, a plot that was thwarted when one of the perpetrators was caught in the Philippines.

The September 11 attacks were unprecedented in U.S. history, claiming nearly three thousand lives. The images of passenger planes exploding into the twin skyscrapers, the buildings' fiery collapse, and the resulting human devastation were seared into the memories of countless people around the world who witnessed the event, over and over again, on television. As a result of the attacks, one of the largest governmental reorganizations in the past century occurred with the creation of the cabinet-level Department of Homeland Security. And a global "war on terror" was launched, first against the rulers of Afghanistan (where al Qaeda was headquartered), then against Iraq, whose repressive leader, Saddam Hussein, was said to pose a danger to global security.

Yet September 11 was not the first religiously motivated attack on U.S. soil. On April 19, 1995, a truck laden with two tons of explosive materials destroyed a government office building in Oklahoma City. One hundred sixty-eight people died, including nineteen children from the building's day-care center. More than five hundred were injured. The blast—at the time the worst terrorist attack in U.S. history—was immediately blamed on Islamic extremists. A number of men of Middle Eastern appearance were rounded up for questioning, until it became clear that the bombing was not the work of foreign terrorists. Rather, it was completely home grown, planned and executed by American religious extremists who believed in a racially pure version of Protestantism. Timothy McVeigh, who was eventually convicted of the bombing and executed, was a twenty-seven-year-old ex-Army sergeant who had served in the Gulf War. He was also connected with the Christian Identity movement, a loosely knit group of religious extremists who shared a hatred for racial minorities, Jews, and the U.S. government. Like al Qaeda, the Christian Identity movement claimed to base its beliefs in Scripture and was dedicated to the use of violence to achieve its objectives.

What explains the rise of militant, often violent religious movements in the modern world? Under what conditions does religion unite communities, and under what conditions does it divide them? To study these issues, we will ask what religion actually is and look at some of the different forms that religious beliefs and practices take. We will also analyze the various types of religious organizations. As in many of the other chapters in this book, the emphasis is on social change. Religious concerns today can be properly understood only in relation to social changes that have affected the position of religion in the wider world.

The study of religion is a challenging enterprise that places special demands on the sociological imagination. In analyzing religious practices, we must be sensitive to ideals that inspire profound conviction in believers, yet at the same time take a balanced view of them. We must confront ideas that seek the eternal while recognizing that religious groups also promote quite mundane goals, such as acquiring money or followers. We need to recognize the diversity of religious beliefs and modes of conduct, but also probe the nature of religion as a general phenomenon.

The Sociological Study of Religion

Religion is one of the oldest human institutions. Cave drawings suggest that religious beliefs and practices existed more than forty thousand years ago. According to anthropologists, there have probably been about one hundred thousand religions throughout human history (Hadden, 1997a). Sociologists define **religion** as a cultural system of commonly shared beliefs and rituals that provides a sense of ultimate meaning and purpose by creating an idea of reality that is sacred, all-encompassing, and supernatural (Durkheim, 1965, orig. 1912; Berger, 1967; Wuthnow, 1988). There are three key elements in this definition:

1. Religion is a form of culture. You will recall from Chapter 3 that *culture* consists of the shared beliefs, values, norms, and material conditions that create a common identity among a group of people. Religion shares all of these characteristics.
2. Religion involves beliefs that take the form of ritualized practices. All religions thus have a behavioral aspect—special activities in which believers take part and that identify them as members of the religious community.
3. Perhaps most important, religion provides a sense of purpose—a feeling that life is ultimately meaningful. It does so by explaining coherently and compellingly what transcends or overshadows everyday life, in ways that other aspects of culture (such as an educational system or a belief in democracy) typically cannot (Geertz, 1973; Wuthnow, 1988).

What is absent from the sociological definition of religion is as important as what is included: Nowhere is there mention of God. We often think of **theism**—a belief in one or more supernatural deities (the term originates from the Greek word for god)—as basic to religion, but this is not necessarily the case. As we shall see later, some religions, such as Buddhism, believe in the existence of spiritual forces rather than a particular god.

How Sociologists Think About Religion

When sociologists study religion, they do so as sociologists and not as believers (or disbelievers) in any particular faith. This stance has several implications for the sociological study of religion:

1. **Sociologists are not concerned with whether religious beliefs are true or false.** From a sociological perspective, religions are regarded not as being decreed by God but as being socially constructed by human beings. As a result, sociologists put aside their personal beliefs when they study religion. They are concerned with the human rather than the divine aspects of religion. Sociologists ask: How is the religion organized? What are its principal beliefs and values? How is it related to the larger society? What explains its success or failure in recruiting and retaining believers? The question of whether a particular belief is "good" or "true," however important it may be to the believers of the religion under study, is not something that sociologists are able to address as sociologists. (As individuals, they may have strong opinions on the matter, but one hopes that as sociologists they can keep these opinions from biasing their research.)

2. **Sociologists are especially concerned with the social organization of religion.** Religions are among the most important institutions in society. They are a primary source of the deepest-seated norms and values. At the same time, religions are typically practiced through an enormous variety of social forms. Within Christianity and Judaism, for example, religious practice often occurs in formal organizations, such as churches or synagogues. Yet this is not necessarily true of such Asian religions as Hinduism and Buddhism, where religious practices are likely to occur in the home, as well as temples or some other natural setting. The sociology of religion is concerned with how different religious institutions and organizations actually function. The earliest European religions were often indistinguishable from the larger society, as religious beliefs and practices were incorporated into daily life. This is still true in many parts of the world today. In modern industrial society, however, religions have become established in separate, often bureaucratic, organizations, and so sociologists focus on the organizations through which religions must operate in order to survive (Hammond, 1992). As we will see below, this institutionalization has even led some sociologists to view religions in the United States and Europe as similar to business organizations, competing with each other for members (Warner, 1993).

3. **Sociologists often view religions as a major source of social solidarity.** To the extent that religions provide their believers with a common set of norms and values, they are an important source of social solidarity. Religious beliefs, rituals, and bonds help to create a "moral community" in which all members know how to behave toward one another (Wuthnow, 1988). If a single religion dominates a society, the religion may be an important source of social stability. If a society's members adhere to numerous competing religions, however, religious differences may lead to destabilizing social conflicts. Recent examples of religious conflict within a society include struggles among Sikhs, Hindus, and Muslims in India; clashes between Muslims and Christians in Bosnia and other parts of the former Yugoslavia; and "hate crimes" against Jews, Muslims, and other religious minorities in the United States.

4. **Sociologists tend to explain the appeal of religion in terms of social forces rather than in terms of purely personal, spiritual, or psychological factors.** For many people, religious beliefs are a deeply personal experience, involving a deep sense of connection with forces that transcend everyday reality. Sociologists do not question the depth of such feelings and experiences, but they are unlikely to limit themselves to a purely spiritual explanation of religious commitment. A person may claim that he or she became religious when God suddenly appeared in a vision, but sociologists are likely to look for more earthly explanations. Some researchers argue that people often "get religion" when their fundamental sense of a social order is threatened by economic hardship, loneliness, loss or grief, physical suffering, or poor health (Berger, 1967; Schwartz, 1970; Glock, 1976; Stark and Bainbridge, 1980). In explaining the appeal of religious movements, sociologists are more likely to focus on the problems of the social order than on the psychological response of the individual.

What Do Sociologists of Religion Study?

Several types of social forces are likely to be of special interest to sociologists of religion. We will discuss these in greater detail throughout this chapter.

First, sociologists sometimes focus on the ways in which religious fervor results from a crisis in prevailing beliefs. Such a crisis occurred in the United States during the 1960s, when the challenges to the status quo included opposition to the Vietnam war, the civil rights movement, social movements among racial and ethnic minorities, and the youth-oriented counterculture. As a result, unusually large numbers of people were attracted to religious teachers, ranging from Indian gurus to fundamentalist preachers, who offered everything from meditation and yoga to astrology and New Age religions (Wuthnow, 1988).

Second, sociologists study how competition among religious organizations leads some to thrive and others to perish.

This study has led to an increased interest in the organizational dynamics of religious groups (Stark and Bainbridge, 1987; Finke and Stark, 1988, 1992; Roof and McKinney, 1990; Hammond, 1992).

Finally, sociologists are concerned with the relationship among religion, ethnic identity, and politics. This is seen in the resurgence of ethnically based religion in pluralist societies such as the United States, as well as in the rise of religious nationalism throughout the world (Merkyl and Smart, 1983; Lawrence, 1989; Sahliyeh, 1990; Juergensmeyer, 1993; see the discussion below of religious nationalism).

Theories of Religion

Sociological approaches to religion are still strongly influenced by the ideas of Marx, Durkheim, and Weber. None of the three was religious himself, and all believed that religion would become less and less significant in modern times. Each argued that religion was fundamentally an illusion: The very diversity of religions and their obvious connection to different societies and regions of the world made the claims by their advocates inherently implausible. An individual born into an Australian society of hunters and gatherers would plainly hold different religious beliefs from someone born into the caste system of India or the Catholic Church of medieval Europe.

Marx: Religion and Inequality

In spite of the influence of his views on the subject, Karl Marx never studied religion in any detail. His thinking on religion was mostly derived from the writings of Ludwig Feuerbach, who believed that through a process he called **alienation,** human beings tend to attribute their own culturally created values and norms to alien, or separate, beings (i.e., divine forces or gods), because they do not understand their own history. Thus, the story of the Ten Commandments given to Moses by God is a mythical version of the origins of the moral precepts that govern the lives of Jewish and Christian believers.

Marx accepted the view that religion represents human self-alienation. In a famous phrase, Marx declared that religion was the "opium of the people." Religion defers happiness and rewards to the afterlife, he said, teaching the resigned acceptance of existing conditions in the earthly life. Attention is thus diverted away from inequalities and injustices in this world by the promise of what is to come in the next. Religion contains a strong ideological element: Religious belief can often provide justifications for those in power. For example,

"The meek shall inherit the earth" suggests attitudes of humility and nonresistance to oppression.

Durkheim: Religion and Functionalism

In contrast to Marx, Émile Durkheim spent a good part of his intellectual career studying religion, concentrating particularly on totemism as practiced by Australian aboriginal societies. *The Elementary Forms of the Religious Life,* first published in 1912, is perhaps the most influential single study in the sociology of religion (1965). Durkheim connected religion not with social inequalities or power, but with the overall nature of the institutions of a society. His argument was that totemism represented religion in its most "elementary" form—hence the title of his book.

Durkheim defined religion in terms of a distinction between the sacred and the profane. **Sacred** objects and symbols, he held, are treated as apart from the routine, utilitarian aspects of day-to-day existence—the realm of the **profane.** A totem (an animal or plant believed to have particular symbolic significance), Durkheim argued, is a sacred object, regarded with veneration and surrounded by ritual activities. These ceremonies and rituals, in Durkheim's view, are essential to binding the members of groups together.

Durkheim's theory of religion is a good example of the functionalist tradition of thought in sociology. To analyze the function of a social behavior or social institution like religion is to study the contribution it makes to the continuation of a group, community, or society. According to Durkheim, religion has the function of cohering a society by ensuring that people meet regularly to affirm common beliefs and values.

Weber: The World Religions and Social Change

Durkheim based his arguments on a restricted range of examples, even though he claimed his ideas applied to religion in general. Max Weber, by contrast, embarked on a massive study of religions worldwide. No scholar before or since has undertaken a task of the scope Weber attempted.

Weber's writings on religion differ from those of Durkheim because they concentrate on the connection between religion and social change, something to which Durkheim gave little direct attention. They also contrast with those of Marx, because Weber argued that religion was not necessarily a conservative force; on the contrary, religiously inspired movements have often produced dramatic social transformations. Thus, Protestantism, particularly Puritanism, according to Weber, was the source of the capitalistic outlook found in the modern West. The early entrepreneurs were mostly Calvinists. Their drive to succeed, which helped initiate Western economic development, was originally prompted by a desire to serve God. Material success was a sign of divine favor.

Weber conceived of his research on the world religions as a single project. His discussion of the impact of Protestantism on the development of the West was connected to a comprehensive attempt to understand the influence of religion on social and economic life in various cultures. After analyzing the Eastern religions, Weber concluded that they provided insuperable barriers to the development of industrial capitalism such as took place in the West. This was not because the non-Western civilizations were backward; they were simply oriented toward different values, such as escape from the toils of the material world, from those that came to predominate in Europe.

In traditional China and India, Weber pointed out, there was at certain periods a significant development of commerce, manufacture, and urbanism. But these did not generate the radical patterns of social change involved in the rise of industrial capitalism in the West. Religion was a major influence inhibiting such change. Consider, for example, Hinduism. Hinduism is what Weber called an "other-worldly" religion. That is to say, its highest values stress escape from the toils of the material world to a higher plane of spiritual existence. The religious feelings and motivations produced by Hinduism do not focus on controlling or shaping the material world. On the contrary, Hinduism sees material reality as a veil hiding the true spiritual concerns to which humankind should be oriented. Confucianism also acts to direct activity away from economic "progress," as this came to be understood in the West. Confucianism emphasizes harmony with the world, rather than promoting an active mastery of it. Although China was for a long while the most powerful and culturally most developed civilization in the world, its dominant religious values acted as a brake on a stronger commitment to economic development.

Weber regarded Christianity as a *salvation religion*. According to such religions, human beings can be "saved" if they are converted to the beliefs of the religion and follow its moral tenets. The notions of "sin" and of being rescued from sinfulness by God's grace are important here. They generate a tension and an emotional dynamism essentially absent from the Eastern religions. Salvation religions have a "revolutionary" aspect. Whereas the religions of the East cultivate an attitude of passivity or acceptance within the believer, Christianity demands a constant struggle against sin and so can stimulate revolt against the existing order. Religious leaders—such as Luther or Calvin—have arisen who reinterpret existing doctrines in such a way as to challenge the extant power structure.

Critical Assessment of the Classical View

Marx, Durkheim, and Weber each identified some important general characteristics of religion, and in some ways their views complement one another. Marx was right to claim that religion often has ideological implications, serving to justify the interests of ruling groups at the expense of others. There are innumerable instances of this in history. For example, the European missionaries who sought to convert "heathen" peoples to Christian beliefs were no doubt sincere in their efforts. Yet their teachings in large part reinforced the destruction of traditional cultures and the imposition of white domination. Almost all Christian denominations tolerated, or endorsed, slavery in the United States and other parts of the world into the nineteenth century. Doctrines were developed proclaiming slavery to be based on divine law, disobedient slaves being guilty of an offense against God as well as their masters (Stampp, 1956).

Yet Weber was certainly correct to emphasize the unsettling and often revolutionary impact of religious ideals on the established social order. In spite of the churches' early support for slavery in the United States, church leaders later played a key role in fighting to abolish the institution. Religious beliefs have prompted social movements seeking to overthrow unjust systems of authority; for instance, religious sentiments played a prominent part in the civil rights movements of the 1960s. Religion has also generated social change through wars fought for religious motives.

These divisive influences of religion, so prominent in history, find little mention in Durkheim's work. Durkheim emphasized above all the role of religion in promoting social cohesion. Yet it is not difficult to redirect his ideas toward explaining religious division, conflict, and change as well as solidarity. After all, much of the strength of feeling that may be generated *against* other religious groups derives from the commitment to religious values generated *within* each community of believers.

Among the most valuable points of Durkheim's writings is his stress on ritual and ceremony. All religions comprise regular assemblies of believers, at which ritual prescriptions are observed. As Durkheim rightly points out, ritual activities also mark the major transitions of life—birth, entry to adulthood (rituals associated with puberty are found in many cultures), marriage, and death (Van Gennep, 1977).

Finally, Marx, Durkheim, and Weber's theories on religion were based on their studies of societies in which a single religion predominated. As a consequence, it seemed reasonable for them to examine the relationship between a predominant religion and the society as a whole. However, in the past fifty years this classical view has been challenged by some U.S. sociologists. Because of their own experience in a society that is highly tolerant of religious diversity, these theorists have focused on

The Spread of New Age Religions

If you pick up a local newspaper in any U.S. city and turn to the classifieds section, you are likely to find a number of listings relating to spirituality and the New Age movement. You have no doubt seen advertisements like these before: "A course in miracles. Personal coaching by the hour." "Soul purpose, past lives, intuitive healing." "Under the guidance of a Living Spiritual Teacher, you can be guided to take the next step in your spiritual unfoldment." These ads appeal to those who feel strong spiritual yearnings, who have a sense that their lives are not going quite the way they should, and who have become disenchanted with well-established religions. While some of the advertisements are clearly attempts to profit from the willingness of some to believe anything they are told, most participants in the New Age movement see themselves as being on a sincere spiritual quest for self-enlightenment. The religious studies scholar Paul Heelas, in his 1996 book *The New Age Movement,* describes the New Age movement that has sprung up in response to this spiritual demand as having three essential characteristics: "It explains why life—as conventionally experienced—is not what it should be; it provides an account of what it is to find perfection; and it provides the means for obtaining salvation."

By most estimates, the number of people interested in such concerns is growing. Meditation groups, psychic fairs, spirituality discussion groups, training sessions designed to help participants reach their "true" spiritual potential, tarot card readings, books on spirituality and psychological self-help—all have proliferated since the 1960s.

religious pluralism rather than on religious domination. Not surprisingly, their conclusions differ substantially from the earlier views as advanced in different ways by Marx, Durkheim, and Weber, each of whom regarded religion as closely bound up with the larger society. Religion was believed to reflect and reinforce society's values, or at least the values of those who were most powerful; to provide an important source of solidarity and social stability; and to be an important engine of social change. According to this view, religion is threatened by the rise of **secular thinking,** that is, worldly thinking, particularly as seen in the rise of science, technology, and rational thought in general.

The classical theories of religion argued that the key problem facing religions in the modern world is **secularization,** or a rise in worldly thinking and a simultaneous decline in the influence of religion. Secularization is typically accompanied by a decrease in religious belief and involvement and results in a weakening of the social and political power of religious organizations. Peter Berger (1967) has described religion in premod-

ern societies as a "sacred canopy" that covers all aspects of life and is therefore seldom questioned. In modern society, however, the sacred canopy is more like a quilt, a patchwork of numerous different religious and secular belief systems. When beliefs are compared and contrasted, it becomes increasingly difficult to sustain the idea that there is any single true faith. According to this view, secularization is the likely result.

Secularization: The Sociological Debate

The debate over secularization is one of the most complex areas in the sociology of religion. In the most basic terms, the disagreement is between supporters of the secularization thesis—who agree with sociology's founders and see religion as diminishing in power and importance in the modern world—

From the perspective of the sociology of religion, we can ask a number of questions about these developments. To what extent do these diverse phenomena form part of a coherent whole? What sociological factors account for the current popularity of the New Age movement? In what ways does the New Age movement differ from traditional forms of religiosity?

With respect to the last of these questions, one unique feature of the New Age movement is its eclecticism. Religions, of course, have always borrowed from one another. But most religions—no matter how much they adapt to current social and moral conditions—place a heavy emphasis on maintaining religious tradition. The faithful are often required by religious authorities to believe in the essential dogmas held by previous generations of worshipers. New Agers, however, tend to deny that there is much value in clinging to well-defined religious traditions. Instead, they see it as important, that individuals pick and choose those spiritual beliefs and practices that suit them best. Heelas writes: "Much of the New Age would appear to be quite radically detraditionalized (rejecting voices of authority associated with established orders)." Individuals, New Agers believe, should learn to listen to their intuition or "inner voice" to help them select the spiritual practices and make the life choices that are right for them.

The social organization of the New Age movement is entirely consistent with this philosophy. The movement consists of thousands of different groups, varying tremendously in size, with each group oriented around a different eclectic appropriation of the world's spiritual traditions. Many groups borrow

heavily from Eastern spirituality—from Tibetan Buddhism, for example. Others incorporate certain Native American traditions. Still others combine these with elements of Christianity. There is an almost infinite number of permutations.

What does this have to do with globalization? New Agers insist that they should be free to borrow any spiritual practices that are right for them. Why, they ask, should Tibetan Buddhism be reserved for Tibetans, or Native American rituals for Native Americans? Without wishing to rob these groups of their rich cultural heritage, New Agers firmly believe that the geographic borders of nation-states are entirely irrelevant to spirituality. Their eclecticism is truly global, and, primarily through books and travel, they scour the world in search of meaningful forms of spirituality. If the differences between nation-states begin to fade in a globalized world, New Agers may well embody the growing penetration of globalization into the religious realm.

and opponents of the concept, who argue that religion remains a significant force, albeit often in new and unfamiliar forms.

Secularization is a complex sociological concept in part because there is little consensus about how the process should be measured. Moreover, many sociologists employ definitions of religion that do not coincide: Whereas some argue that religion is best understood in terms of the traditional church, others argue that a much broader view must be taken to include dimensions such as personal spirituality and deep commitment to certain values. These differences in perception will necessarily influence arguments for or against secularization.

We can evaluate secularization according to a number of aspects or dimensions. Some of them are objective in nature, such as the *level of membership* of religious organizations. Statistics and official records can show how many people belong to a church or other religious body and are active in attending services or other ceremonies. As we will see, with the exception of the United States, the industrialized countries have all

experienced considerable secularization according to this index. The pattern of religious decline seen in Britain is found in most of Western Europe, including Catholic countries such as France or Italy. More Italians than French attend church regularly and participate in the major rituals (such as Easter Communion), but the overall pattern of declining religious observance is similar in both cases.

A second dimension of secularization concerns how far churches and other religious organizations maintain their *social influence, wealth,* and *prestige.* In earlier times, religious organizations could wield considerable influence over governments and social agencies and commanded high respect in the community. How much is this still the case? The answer to the question is clear. Even if we confine ourselves to the present century, we see that religious organizations have progressively lost much of the social and political influence they previously had, particularly in the advanced industrial nations, although there are some exceptions. Church leaders can no longer automatically expect to be influential with the powerful. Although some established churches remain very wealthy by any standards, and new religious movements may rapidly build up fortunes, the material circumstances of many long-standing religious organizations are insecure. Churches and temples have to be sold off or are in a state of disrepair, and entire dioceses have considered filing for bankruptcy.

The third dimension of secularization concerns beliefs and values. We can call this the dimension of *religiosity*. Levels of church-going and the degree of social influence of churches are obviously not necessarily a direct expression of the beliefs or ideals people hold. Many who have religious beliefs do not regularly attend services or take part in public ceremonies; conversely, regularity of such attendance or participation does not always imply the holding of strong religious views—people may attend out of habit or because it is expected of them in their community.

As in the other dimensions of secularization, we need an accurate understanding of the past to see how far religiosity has declined today. Supporters of the secularization thesis argue that in the past, religion was far more important to people's daily lives than it is today. The church was at the heart of local affairs and was a strong influence on family and personal life. Yet critics of the thesis contest this idea, arguing that just because people attended church more regularly does not necessarily prove that they were more religious. In many traditional societies, including medieval Europe, commitment to religious belief was less strong and less important in day-to-day life than might be supposed. Research into English history, for example, shows that lukewarm commitment to religious beliefs was common among the ordinary people. Religious skeptics seem to have been found in most cultures, particularly in the larger traditional societies (Ginzburg, 1980).

Yet there can be no doubt at all that the hold of religious ideas today is weaker than was generally the case in the traditional world—particularly if we include under the term *religion* the whole range of the supernatural in which people believed. Most of us simply no longer experience our environment as permeated by divine or spiritual entities. Some of the major tensions in the world today—such as those afflicting the Middle East and the Balkans or the violence perpetrated by Osama bin Laden and the al Qaeda terrorist network—derive primarily, or in some part, from religious differences. But the majority of conflicts and wars are now mainly secular in nature—concerned with divergent political goals or material interests.

Contemporary Approaches: "Religious Economy"

One of the most recent and influential approaches to the sociology of religion is tailored to societies such as the United States, which offer many different faiths from which to pick and choose. Taking their cue from economic theory, sociologists who favor the **religious economy** approach argue that religions can be fruitfully understood as organizations in competition with each other for followers (Stark and Bainbridge, 1987; Finke and Stark, 1988, 1992; Roof and McKinney, 1990; Hammond, 1992; Warner, 1993; Moore, 1994).

Like contemporary economists who study businesses, these sociologists argue that competition is preferable to monopoly when it comes to ensuring religious vitality. This position is exactly opposite to those of the classical theorists. Marx, Durkheim, and Weber assumed that religion weakens when challenged by different religious or secular viewpoints, whereas the religious economists argue that competition increases the overall level of religious involvement in modern society. Religious economists believe this is true for two reasons. First, competition makes each religious group try that much harder to win followers. Second, the presence of numerous religions means that there is likely to be something for just about everyone. In a culturally diverse society such as the United States, a single religion will probably appeal to only a limited range of followers, whereas the presence of Indian gurus and fundamentalist preachers, in addition to mainline churches, is likely to encourage a high level of religious participation.

This analysis is adapted from the business world, in which competition presumably encourages the emergence of highly specialized products that appeal to the very specific markets. In fact, religious economists borrow the language of business in describing the conditions that lead to the success or failure of a particular religious organization. According to Roger Finke and Rodney Stark (1992), a successful religious group must be well organized for competition, have eloquent preachers who are effective "sales reps" in spreading the word, offer beliefs and rituals that are packaged as an appealing product, and develop effective marketing techniques. Religion, in this view, is a business much like any other. Television evangelists, whom we shall consider below, have been especially good businesspeople in selling their religious products.

Thus religious economists such as Finke and Stark do not see competition as undermining religious beliefs and thus contributing to secularization. Rather, they argue that modern religion is constantly renewing itself through active marketing and recruitment. Although a growing body of research supports the notion that competition is good for religion (Stark and Bainbridge, 1980, 1985; Finke and Stark, 1992), not all research comes to this conclusion (Land, Deane, and Blau, 1991).

The religious-economy approach overestimates the extent to which people rationally pick and choose among different religions, as if they were shopping around for a new car or a pair of shoes. Among deeply committed believers, particularly in societies that lack religious pluralism, it is not obvious that religion is a matter of rational choice. In such societies, even when people are allowed to choose among different religions, most are likely to practice their childhood religion without ever questioning whether or not there are more appealing alternatives. Even in the United States, where the religious-economy approach originated, sociologists may overlook the spiritual aspects of religion if they simply assume that religious buyers are always on spiritual shopping sprees. Wade Clark Roof's study (1993) of fourteen hundred baby boomers found that a third had remained loyal to their childhood faith, while another third had continued to profess their childhood beliefs although they no longer belonged to a religious organization. Thus only a third were actively looking around for a new religion, making the sorts of choices presumed by the religious economy approach.

Types of Religious Organizations

The sociology of religion has concerned itself with non-European religions since its origins in the writings of Durkheim and Weber. Nonetheless, there has frequently been a tendency to view all religions through concepts and theories that grew out of the European experience. For example, notions such as *denomination* or *sect* presuppose the existence of formally organized religious institutions; they are of questionable utility in the study of religions that emphasize ongoing spiritual practice as a part of daily life or that pursue the complete integration of religion with civic and political life. In recent years, there has been an effort to create a more comparative sociology of religion, one that seeks to understand religious traditions from within their own frames of reference (Wilson, 1982; Smart, 1989; Juergensmeyer, 1993; Van der Veer, 1994).

Early theorists such as Max Weber (1963, orig. 1921), Ernst Troeltsch (1931), and Richard Niebuhr (1929) described religious organizations as falling along a continuum, based on the degree to which they are well established and conventional: Churches lie at one end (they are conventional and well established), cults lie at the other (they are neither), and sects fall somewhere in the middle. These distinctions were based on the study of European and U.S. religions. There is much debate over how well they apply to the non-Christian world.

Today, sociologists are aware that the terms *sect* and *cult* have negative connotations, something they wish to avoid. For this reason, contemporary sociologists of religion sometimes use the phrase *new religious movements* to characterize novel religious organizations that lack the respectability that comes with being well established for a long period of time (Hexham and Poewe, 1997; Hadden, 1997b).

Churches and Sects

Churches are large, established religious bodies; one example is the Roman Catholic Church. They normally have a formal, bureaucratic structure, with a hierarchy of religious officials. Churches often represent the conservative face of religion, since they are integrated within the existing institutional order. Most of their adherents are born into and grow up with the church.

Sects are smaller, less highly organized groups of committed believers, usually set up in protest against an established church, as Calvinism and Methodism were initially. Sects aim at discovering and following the "true way" and either try to change the surrounding society or withdraw from it into communities of their own, a process known as *revival*. The members of sects regard established churches as corrupt. Many sects have few or no officials, and all members are regarded as equal participants. For the most part, people are not born into sects, but actively join them in order to further commitments in which they believe.

Denominations and Cults

A **denomination** is a sect that has cooled down and become an institutionalized body rather than an activist protest group. Sects that survive over any period of time inevitably become denominations. Thus, Calvinism and Methodism were sects during their early period of formation, when they generated great fervor among their members; but over the years, they have become more established. (Calvinists today are called Presbyterians.) Denominations are recognized as legitimate by churches and exist alongside them, often cooperating harmoniously with them.

Cults resemble sects, but their emphases are different. Cults are the most loosely knit and transient of all religious organizations. They are composed of individuals who reject what they see as the values of the outside society, unlike sects, which try to revive an established church. They are a form of religious innovation, rather than revival. Their focus is on individual experience, bringing like-minded people together. Like sects, cults often form around the influence of an inspirational leader.

Cults are likely to be in a high degree of tension with the larger society. A tragic example occurred in 1993 when eighty members of the Branch Davidian religious cult (including nineteen children) burned to death in their Waco, Texas compound

Megachurches as Minitowns

Patty Anderson and her husband, Gary, found faith where they least expected it—he on the free-throw line and she swathed in sweats in an aerobics class.

It happened at the 50,000-square-foot activities center of the Southeast Christian Church [in Louisville, Kentucky,] where pumping iron and praising the Lord go hand and hand. Amenities at the gym include 16 basketball courts and a Cybex health club, free to churchgoers, where the music is Christian and the rules ban cursing even during the crunch.

"I really had no intention of being part of a church," recalled Gary Anderson, a physiology professor at the University of Louisville School of Medicine. But hoops at this 22,000-member megachurch led him to the sanctuary. And after three years, he said, like a slam dunk, "the sermons sunk in."

Southeast Christian is an example of a new breed of megachurch—a full-service "24/7" sprawling village, which offers many of the conveniences and trappings of secular life wrapped around a spiritual core. It is possible to eat, shop, go to school, bank, work out, scale a rock-climbing wall and pray there, all without leaving the grounds.

These churches are becoming civic in a way unimaginable since the thirteenth century and its cathedral towns. No longer simply places to worship, they have become part resort, part mall, part extended family and part town square.

[***]

The churches reflect a desire by congregants for a "universe where everything from the temperature to the theology is safely controlled," [one professor] said. "They don't have to worry about finding schools, social networks or a place to eat. It's all prepackaged."

[***]

"People are looking at churches with a similar cost-benefit analysis they'd give to any other consumer purchase," [a megachurch consultant added]. "There is little brand loyalty. Many are looking for the newest and the greatest."

Dave Stone, the associate minister of Southeast, calls his church, which is open daily from 5:30 A.M. to 11 P.M. , "a refueling station."

"If we can get people to come to our gym," he explained, "it's only a matter of time before we can get them to visit our sanctuary."

The church was deliberately designed like a mall. (The sanctuary is the anchor tenant.) Hallways 20 feet wide with curves enhance "people flow," said Jack Coffee, a church elder and chairman of the building committee. Preschoolers frolic at a Disneyesque play land, with mazes. There is an education wing for Bible classes, a concert-hall-size atrium with glass elevators, crisscrossing escalators and giant monitors that itemize the day's offerings: meetings to help smokers quit, a cross-trainers minimarathon and pat the Bible classes for six-month-olds.

Such amenities are typically paid for by the congregation with three-year capital campaigns, on top of the church's operating budget, which is often financed with tithes, said Malcolm P. Graham, president of Cargill Associates' church division, a fund-raising consultant. A study by the Hartford Institute for Religion Research at the Hartford Seminary finds the average annual income for a megachurch is $4.6 million a year. Annual contributions to Southeast Christian are more than $20 million.

Southeast Christian churchgoers speak of a 22,000-person family, and visitors are regaled with statistics: the coffeepot that serves 5,000 cups an hour, the 403 toilets. Southeast's size has spawned the invention of the Greenlee Communion Dispensing Machine, designed by Wilfred Greenlee, 79, a congregant. It can fill 40 communion cups in 2 seconds.

[***]

Not incidentally, it gives the congregants who flock to church for more than 80 activities each evening—like children's theater and adult computer classes—an excuse to stick around. "If you have to go home for dinner, you don't come back out," [a pastor said].

But some scholars and municipalities are troubled by the civic expansion of 24/7 churches. They are becoming "a parallel universe that's Christianized," in the words of Dr. Scott Thumma, a sociologist of religion at the Hartford Institute.

Dr. Wade Clark Roof, a professor of religion and society at the University of California at Santa Barbara, said he worried that full-service churches are "the religious version of the gated community."

"It's an attempt to create a world where you're dealing with like-minded people," he said. "You lose the dialogue with the larger culture."

[***]

SOURCE: Patricia Leigh Brown, "Megachurches as Minitowns," *New York Times,* May 9, 2002, pp. F1–F6.

Questions

- How might Marx, Durkheim, and Weber each analyze the development of megachurches?
- Are megachurches evidence in favor of the religious economy approach to the sociology of religion?
- In your view, what do megachurches reveal about American society? Are congregants seeking social solidarity or trying to isolate themselves from the rest of society?

during an assault by federal officials that ended a lengthy armed standoff. Federal officials maintain that the cult members were virtual prisoners of their charismatic leader, David Koresh, who was allegedly stockpiling illegal weapons, practicing polygyny, and having sex with some of the children. Controversy remains over whether the fire was ordered by Koresh, who reportedly preferred mass suicide to surrender, or whether the actions of the federal authorities caused the tragedy (Tabor and Gallagher, 1995). In 1997, thirty-nine members of Heaven's Gate, a cult whose members believed that they were destined for a "higher level," took their lives in order to ascend to a spaceship they believed lurked behind the Hale-Bopp comet (See Chapter 6).

Like sects, cults flourish when there is a breakdown in well-established and widespread societal belief systems. This is happening throughout the world today, in places as diverse as Japan, India, and the United States. When such a breakdown occurs, cults may originate within the society itself, or they may be "imported" from outside. In the United States, examples of homegrown, or indigenous, cults include New Age religions based on such things as spiritualism, astrology, and religious practices adapted from Asian or Native American cultures. Examples of imported cults include the Reverend Sun Myung Moon's Unification Church ("Moonies"), which originated in South Korea, and transcendental meditation.

It should be obvious that what is a cult in one country may well be an established religious practice in another. When Indian gurus (religious teachers) bring their beliefs into the United States, what might be considered an established religion in India is regarded as a cult in the United States. Christianity began as an indigenous cult in ancient Jerusalem, and in many Asian countries today Evangelical Protestantism is regarded as a cult imported from the United States. Thus, cults should not be thought of as "weird." A leading sociologist of religion, Jeffrey K. Hadden, points out that all the approximately one hundred thousand religions that humans have devised were once new; most if not all were initially despised cults from the standpoint of respectable religious belief of the times (Hadden, 1997a). Jesus was crucified because his ideas were so threatening to the established order of the Roman-dominated religious establishment of ancient Judaea.

Religious Movements

Religious movements represent a subtype of social movement in general. A religious movement is an association of people who join together to spread a new religion or to promote a new interpretation of an existing religion. Religious movements are larger than sects and less exclusivist in their membership—although like churches and sects, movements and sects (or cults) are not always clearly distinct from each other. In fact, all sects and cults can be classified as religious movements. Examples of religious movements include the groups that originally founded and spread Christianity in the first century, the Lutheran movement that split Christianity in Europe about fifteen hundred years afterward, and the groups involved in the more recent Islamic revolution (discussed in more detail later in the chapter).

Religious movements tend to pass through certain definite phases of development. In the first phase, the movement usually derives its life and cohesion from a powerful leader. Max Weber classified such leaders as **charismatic,** that is, having inspirational qualities capable of capturing the imagination and devotion of a mass of followers. (Charismatic leaders in Weber's formulation could include political as well as religious figures—revolutionary China's Mao Zedong for example, as well as Jesus and Muhammad.) The leaders of religious movements are usually critical of the religious establishment and seek to proclaim a new message. In their early years, religious movements are fluid; they do not have an established authority system. Their members are normally in direct contact with the charismatic leader, and together they spread the new teachings.

The second phase of development occurs following the death of the leader. Rarely does a new charismatic leader arise from the masses, so this phase is crucial. The movement is now faced with what Weber termed the "routinization of charisma." To survive, it has to create formalized rules and procedures, since it can no longer depend on the central role of the leader in organizing the followers. Many movements fade away when their leaders die or lose their influence. A movement that survives and takes on a permanent character becomes a church. In other words, it becomes a formal organization of believers with an established authority system and established symbols and rituals. The church might itself at some later point become the origin of other movements that question its teachings and either set themselves up in opposition or break away completely.

New Religious Movements

Although traditional churches have been experiencing a decline in membership in recent decades, other forms of religious activity have been on the rise. Sociologists use the term **new religious movements** to refer collectively to the broad range of religious and spiritual groups, cults, and sects that have emerged in Western countries, including the United States, alongside mainstream religions. New religious movements encompass an enormous diversity of groups, from spiritual and self-help groups within the New Age movement to exclusive sects such as the "Hare Krishnas" (International Society for Krishna Consciousness).

Many new religious movements are derived from mainstream religious traditions, such as Hinduism, Christianity, and Buddhism, while others have emerged from traditions that were almost unknown in the West until recently. Some new religious movements are essentially new creations of the charismatic leaders who head their activities. This is the case with the Unification Church, led by the Reverend Sun Myung Moon. Membership in new religious movements mostly consists of converts rather than individuals brought up in a particular faith. Members more often than not are well educated and from middle-class backgrounds.

Since World War II, the United States has witnessed a far greater proliferation of religious movements than at any previous time in its history, including an unprecedented series of mergers of and divisions among denominations. Most have been short lived, but a few have achieved remarkable followings.

Various theories to explain the popularity of new religious movements have been advanced. Some observers argue that they should be seen as a response to the process of liberalization and secularization within society and even within traditional churches. People who feel that traditional religions have become ritualistic and devoid of spiritual meaning may find comfort and a greater sense of community in smaller, less impersonal new religious movements.

Others have pointed to new religious movements as an outcome of rapid social change (Wilson, 1982). As traditional social norms are disrupted, people search for both explanations and reassurance. The rise of groups and sects that emphasize personal spirituality, for example, suggest that many individuals feel a need to reconnect with their own values of beliefs in the face of instability and uncertainty.

A further factor may be that new religious movements appeal to people who feel alienated from mainstream society. The collective, communal approaches of sects and cults, some authors argue, can offer support and a sense of belonging. For example, middle-class youth are not marginalized from society in a material sense, but they may feel isolated emotionally and spiritually. Membership in a cult can help to overcome this feeling of alienation (Wallis, 1984).

New religious movements can be understood as falling into three broad categories: *world-affirming, world-rejecting,* and *world-accommodating* movements. Each is based on the relationship of the individual group to the larger social world.

WORLD-AFFIRMING MOVEMENTS

World-affirming movements are more akin to self-help or therapy groups than to conventional religious groups. These movements often lack rituals, churches, and formal theologies, turning their focus on members' spiritual well-being. As the name suggests, world-affirming movements do not reject the outside world or its values. Rather, they seek to enhance their followers' abilities to perform and succeed in that world by unlocking human potential.

The Church of Scientology is one such group. Founded by L. Ron Hubbard, the Church of Scientology has grown from its original base in California to include a large membership in countries around the world. Scientologists believe we are all spiritual beings but have neglected our spiritual nature. Through training that makes them aware of their real spiritual capacities, people can recover forgotten supernatural powers, clear their minds, and reveal their full potential.

Many strands of the so-called **New Age movement** fall under the category of world-affirming movements. The New Age movement emerged from the counterculture of the 1960s and 1970s and encompasses a broad spectrum of beliefs, practices, and ways of life. Pagan teachings (Celtic, Druidic, Native American, and others), shamanism, forms of Asian mysticism, Wiccan rituals, and Zen meditation are only a few of the activities that are thought of as New Age.

On the surface, the mysticism of the New Age movement appears to stand in stark contrast to the modern societies in which it is favored. Followers of New Age movements seek out and develop alternative ways of life in order to cope with the challenges of modernity. Yet New Age activities should not be interpreted as simply a radical break with the present. They should also be seen as part of a larger cultural trajectory that *exemplifies* aspects of mainstream culture. In late modern societies, individuals possess unparalleled degrees of autonomy and freedom to chart their own lives. In this respect, the aims of the New Age movement coincide closely with the modern age: People are encouraged to move beyond traditional values and expectations and to live their lives actively and reflectively.

WORLD-REJECTING MOVEMENTS

As opposed to world-affirming groups, **world-rejecting movements** are highly critical of the outside world. They often demand significant lifestyle changes from their followers—members may be expected to live ascetically, to change their dress or hairstyle, or to follow a certain diet. World-rejecting movements are frequently exclusive, in contrast to world-affirming movements, which tend to be inclusive in nature. Some world-rejecting movements display characteristics of **total institutions;** members are expected to subsume their individual identities in that of the group, to adhere to strict ethical codes or rules, and to withdraw from activity in the outside world.

Most of the world-rejecting movements place far more demands on their members, in terms of time and commitment, than do older established religions. Some groups have been known to use the technique of "love bombing" to gain the individual's total adherence. A potential convert is overwhelmed by attention and constant displays of instant affection until he or she is drawn emotionally into the group. Some new movements, in fact, have been accused of brainwashing their adherents—seeking to control their minds in such a way as to rob them of the capacity for independent decision making.

Many world-rejecting cults and sects have come under the intense scrutiny of state authorities, the media, and the public. Certain extreme cases of world-rejecting cults have attracted much concern. For example, the Japanese group Aum Shinrikyo released deadly sarin gas into the Tokyo subway system in 1995, injuring thousands of morning commuters. In the United States, the Branch Davidian cult, based in Waco, Texas, became embroiled in a deadly confrontation with federal authorities in 1993 after accusations of child abuse and weapons stockpiling.

WORLD-ACCOMMODATING MOVEMENTS

The third type of new religious movement is the one most like traditional religions. **World-accommodating movements** tend to emphasize the importance of inner religious life over more worldly concerns. Members of such groups seek to reclaim the spiritual purity that they believe has been lost in traditional religious settings. Where followers of world-rejecting and world-affirming groups often alter their lifestyles in accordance with their religious activity, many adherents of world-accommodating movements carry on in their everyday lives and careers with little visible change. One example of a world-accommodating movement is Pentecostalism. Pentecostalists believe that the Holy Spirit can be heard through individuals who are granted the gift of "speaking in tongues."

NEW RELIGIOUS MOVEMENTS AND SECULARIZATION

The enduring popularity of new religious movements presents another challenge to the secularization thesis. Opponents of the thesis point to the diversity and dynamism of new religious movements and argue that religion and spirituality remain a central facet of modern life. As traditional religions lose their hold, religion is not disappearing, but is being channeled in new directions. Not all scholars agree, however. Proponents of the idea of secularization point out that these movements remain peripheral to society as a whole, even if they make a profound impact on the lives of their individual followers. New religious movements are fragmented and relatively unorganized; they also suffer from high turnover rates as people are attracted to a movement for some time and then move on to something new. Compared to a serious religious commitment, they argue, participation in a new religious movement appears little more than a hobby or lifestyle choice.

Gender and Religion

Churches and denominations resemble other institutions in social life in that women have been mostly excluded from power. This is clear in Christianity, but it is also characteristic of virtually all the major religions. In the following sections, we shall examine some of the interrelations of religion and gender. The issue is an important one, because this is an area in which significant changes are taking place.

Religious Images

In Christianity, although Mary, the mother of Jesus, is sometimes treated as if she had divine qualities, God is "the Father," a male figure, and Jesus took the human shape of a man. Genesis, the first book of the Bible, reveals that woman was created from a rib taken from man. These facts have not gone unnoticed by women's movements. A hundred years ago, Elizabeth Cady Stanton published a series of commentaries on the Scriptures, entitled *The Woman's Bible*. In her view, the deity had created women and men as beings of equal value, and the Bible should fully reflect this fact. Its "masculinist" character, she believed, reflected not the authentic word of God, but the fact that the Bible was written by men. In 1870, the Church of England established a Revising Committee to revise and update the biblical texts; but as Stanton pointed out, the committee contained not a single woman. She asserted that there was no reason to suppose that God is a man, since it was clear in the Scriptures that all human beings were fashioned in the image of God. When a colleague opened a women's rights conference with a prayer to "God, our Mother," there was a virulent reaction from the church authorities. Yet Stanton pressed ahead, organizing a Women's Revising Committee in America, composed of twenty-three women, to advise her in preparing *The Woman's Bible,* which was published in 1895.

In some Buddhist orders, especially Mahayana Buddhism, women are represented in a favorable light. But on the whole, Buddhism, like Christianity, is "an overwhelmingly male-created institution dominated by a patriarchal power structure," in which the feminine is mostly "associated with the secular, powerless, profane, and imperfect" (Paul, 1985). The contrasting pictures of women that appear in the Buddhist texts no doubt mirror the ambiguous attitudes of men toward women in the secular world: Women are portrayed as wise, maternal, and gentle yet also as mysterious, polluting, and destructive, threatening evil.

The Role of Women in Religious Organizations

In both Buddhism and (later) Christianity, women were allowed to express strong religious convictions by choosing to become nuns. The first orders for women were probably established as early as the twelfth century; their membership remained small until the 1800s. At that time, many women took religious vows in order to become teachers and nurses, since these occupations were largely controlled by the religious orders. All along, however, female religious orders remained subject to a male hierarchy, and this subjugation was reinforced by some elaborate rituals. For example, all nuns were regarded as "brides of Christ." Until changes were made in some orders in the 1950s and 1960s, "marriage" ceremonies were carried out, during the course of which the novice would cut her hair, receive her religious name, and sometimes be given a wedding ring. After several years, a novice took a vow of perpetual profession, after which she was required to receive dispensation if she chose to leave.

Women's orders today show a considerable diversity in their beliefs and modes of life. In some convents, sisters still dress in full traditional habit and live together in communities removed from the secular world. In other convents, by contrast, the nuns wear ordinary dress and may live in apartments or houses. Traditional restrictions such as not talking to others at certain periods of the day or walking with the hands folded and hidden under the habit are rarely evident.

In spite of such liberalization, women have filled only inferior positions in religious organizations. This situation is changing, in line with changes affecting women in society generally. In recent years, women's groups have pressed to achieve equal status in religious orders. Increasingly, the Catholic and Episcopalian churches are under strong pressure to allow women an equal voice in their hierarchies. Yet in 1977, the Sacred Congregation for the Doctrine of the Faith in Rome declared formally that women could not be admitted to the Catholic priesthood; the reason given was that Jesus had not called a woman to be one of his disciples. Ten years later, 1987 was officially designated as the "Year of the Madonna," in which women were advised to recall their traditional role as wives and mothers. The barriers to Catholic women in the hierarchy of the church thus remain formidable. In a letter published in May 1994, Pope John Paul II reaffirmed the Roman Catholic Church's ban on the ordination of women. The letter stated: "Wherefore, in order that all

Women are playing an increasingly important role as religious leaders today. Laura Geller is the senior rabbi at Temple Emmanuel in Beverly Hills, one of the country's largest synagogues. When she was ordained in 1976, Geller was only the third female rabbi in the United States; she was the first to become the head rabbi at a major synagogue.

doubt may be removed regarding a matter of great importance . . . I declare that the Church has no authority to confer priestly ordination on women and that this judgment is to be definitively held by all the Church's faithful."

The Episcopal Church has been more open and has allowed women into its priesthood since 1976. Altogether, women have been ordained as ministers in about half of the Protestant denominations in the United States, including the Presbyterian Church (U.S.A.), the Evangelical Lutheran Church in America, the African Methodist Episcopal Church, and the United Methodist Church. And except within Orthodox Judaism, women in the United States can become rabbis.

Women and Islam

Before a militant group of Islamic nationalists called the Taliban took over Afghanistan, Shafiqa Habibi's face was known throughout the country: She was Afghanistan's most popular television news anchor. But during the Taliban's rule, she spent her time at home doing chores, her face hidden from public view. When she dared to venture out of her house, none of her body was visible, since it had to be covered by a tentlike garment with a screen sewn into the fabric over her face to hide her eyes but allow some ability to see out (Filkin, 1998).

Shafiqa Habibi's experience was shared by all Afghan women. The Taliban's extreme Islamic beliefs, which were denounced by Iran and other neighboring Muslim nations, forbade women to work outside the home, attend school, or appear in public without covering their bodies from head to toe. Women who were seen in public with any man who was not their husband or relative were brutally beaten and sometimes killed. Since the overthrow of the Taliban in 2001, women have begun to regain their rights in Afghanistan, at least in the capital city of Kabul. But throughout much of the rest of the country, where there has been little effective U.S. military presence, local religious leaders, including the Taliban, have begun to make a comeback, and women are afraid to exercise their legal rights publicly, for fear of retribution—if not immediately, then when the U.S. military finally withdraws from the country.

World Religions

Although there are thousands of different religions throughout the world, three of them—Christianity, Islam, and Hinduism—are embraced by nearly three quarters of the people on earth (see Table 17.1 and Global Map 17.1).

Christianity

With its estimated 2.1 billion followers—roughly a third of the world's population—Christianity encompasses enormously divergent denominations, sects, and cults. Common to all of these is the belief that Jesus of Nazareth was the Christ (Messiah, or "anointed one") foretold in the Hebrew Bible. Christianity is a form of **monotheism**—belief in a single all-knowing, all-powerful God—although in most Christian faiths God is also regarded as a trinity embracing a heavenly Father, his Son the Savior, and his sustaining Holy Spirit.

When Christianity originally emerged in Palestine some two thousand years ago, it was a persecuted sect outside mainstream Jewish and Roman religious practices. Yet, within four centuries, Christianity had become the official religion of the Roman empire. In the eleventh century, Christianity divided into the Eastern Orthodox Church (based in Turkey) and the Catholic Church (based in Rome). A second great split occurred within the Catholic branch in the sixteenth century, when the Protestant Reformation gave rise to numerous divergent Protestant denominations, sects, and cults. Protestants tend to emphasize a direct relationship between the individual and God, each person being responsible for his or her own salvation. Catholics, on the other hand, emphasize the importance of the church hierarchy as the means to salvation, the pope in Rome being the highest earthly authority.

Christianity was spread through conquest and missionary work. The European colonization of much of Africa, Asia, and North and South America that began in the fifteenth century brought with it Christian teachings, churches, and large-scale conversion of native peoples. Today it has become the largest religion in the world, including about a billion Catholics and nearly half a billion Protestants. In some places, converts were marginal people from the impoverished classes, for whom Christianity was a means of social mobility. Only in Asia are Christians a small minority (9 percent), largely because countries like Japan and China successfully resisted most colonization and the Christianization that went along with it.

In recent years, there has been a substantial increase in the efforts of Protestant evangelical groups to convert people throughout the world, making significant inroads in traditionally Catholic countries. In Mexico, for example, the number of Evangelical Protestants grew from nine hundred thousand to 4 million between 1970 and 1990, thanks largely to the efforts of local (Mexican) missionaries. The growth of evangelical Christianity may prove difficult to sustain. It makes considerable demands on its followers, so it remains to be seen whether the children of newly converted evangelicals will remain true to their faith once they become adults (Bowen, 1996).

The architectural differences between the Catholic Cathedral of St. John the Divine in New York City (left) and this Unitarian Church in Brewster, MA (right), are in many ways indicative of the doctrinal differences between these two sects of Christianity.

TABLE 17.1

Religions of the World by Percentage of Population, 1996

	NORTH AMERICA	LATIN AMERICA	EUROPE	ASIA/ PACIFIC	AFRICA	WORLDWIDE
Catholicism	25.5	83.4	37.0	2.9	16.8	16.9
Protestantism	41.0	7.1	10.9	1.5	15.3	7.0
Russian/Greek Orthodox	2.2	0.1	23.6	0.4	3.4	3.8
Other Christian	17.7	2.4	4.9	4.4	12.8	6.1
Judaism	2.0	0.2	0.3	0.1	0.0	0.2
Islam	1.9	0.3	4.4	22.0	41.3	19.4
Hinduism	0.5	0.2	0.2	22.2	0.3	13.7
Buddhism	0.3	0.1	0.2	9.1	0.0	5.6
Confucianism	0.0	0.0	0.0	0.1	0.0	0.1
Other religions	0.8	2.2	0.3	8.1	9.7	6.4
"New" religions	0.3	0.2	0.1	2.9	0.0	1.8
Nonreligious, atheism	7.8	3.9	18.0	26.3	0.5	19.1

SOURCE: U.S. Bureau of the Census, 1998a, Table 1333.

Islam

Islam is the second largest and fastest growing religion in the world today. There are as many as 1.3 billion Muslims (Muslim is the name for those who practice *al-islam,* an Arabic term meaning submission without reservation to God's will), and the number is increasing by 25 million each year. Islam began as and remains the official faith of Arabs and other peoples of the Middle East and has spread south into Africa, north into Europe and the former Soviet Union, and east into India, Pakistan, China, and Indonesia. Today there are more than sixty different ethnic groups of a million or more people who practice Islam. In fact, far more non-Arabs than Arabs identify themselves as Muslims. There are some 170 million Muslims in Indonesia alone, as well as 136 million in Pakistan, 106 million in Bangladesh, and 103 million in predominantly Hindu India. More than two out of five Africans, and one out of five Asians practice Islam, along with many immigrants from these regions to the United States. A large number of African Americans are Muslim as well.

Muslims believe in absolute, unquestioning, positive devotion to Allah (God). Although modern Islam dates to the Arab Prophet Muhammad (c. 570–632), Muslims trace their religion to the ancient Hebrew prophet Abraham, also regarded as the founder of Judaism. The precepts of Islam are believed to have been revealed to Muhammad and are contained in a sacred book dictated to his followers called the Koran (the common English form of the book's name, which means "recitation"; another is Qur'ān, which is closer to the Arabic pronunciation.) Muhammad's ideas were not initially accepted in his birthplace of Mecca, so in 622 he and his followers moved to Medina (both are located in what is today Saudi Arabia). This migration, called the *hijra,* marks the beginning of Islam, which soon spread throughout Arabia. Muhammad himself is not worshiped by Muslims. He is regarded not as a god or a messiah but as a great teacher and prophet, the last in a line that includes Abraham, Noah, Moses, and Jesus.

Islam is an all-encompassing religion. The sacred *sharia* ("way")—which governs all aspects of personal and social life—includes prescriptions for worship, daily life, ethics, and

Major Religions of the World

Missionaries and military force are two reasons that the majority of people in the world profess only a relative handful of religions today. Although Christianity (Catholicism and Protestantism) is the most widespread religion, it is rapidly being overtaken by Islam. Many of the predominantly Catholic countries of Central and South America have strong and, in some cases, growing Protestant minorities.

Legend:
- Japanese syncretism
- Chinese syncretism
- Catholic Christianity
- Oriental and Orthodox Christianity
- Protestant Christianity
- Buddhism
- Hinduism
- Islam (Sunni)
- Islam (Shiite)
- Animism and others

✝ Catholic concentrations in countries with other dominant religion

✡ Major Jewish concentrations

SOURCE: Chaliand and Rageau, 1992.

Every able-bodied Muslim who can afford to is obligated to make the pilgrimage to Mecca at least once in a lifetime. The pilgrims pictured here surround the *ka'aba*, a small cube-shaped building which houses the Hajar el Aswad (the Black Stone). Muslims believe that this stone fell from the sky during the time of Adam, and that it has the power to cleanse worshipers of their sins by absorbing them into itself. The stone is believed to have originally been white, but it is said to have turned black because of the sins it has absorbed over the years.

even government. Although by U.S. standards Muslim beliefs might be judged extremely restrictive, Muslims frequently view American life as spiritually undisciplined, corrupt, and immoral (Abdul-Rauf, 1975; MacEnoin and Al-Shahi, 1983; Martin, 1982; Esposito, 1984; Arjomand, 1988; Kedouri, 1992).

Just as Christianity is divided into different religious groups, so too is Islam. The principal division is between Sunnis (about 85 percent of all Muslims) and Shiites (15 percent). Sunni Muslims follow the "Beaten Path," a series of traditions deriving from the Qur'ān that tolerate a considerable diversity of opinion, in contrast to the more rigidly defined views of the Shiites. Shiism split from the main body of orthodox Islam early in its history and has remained influential ever since. Iran (once known as Persia) is the only major Islamic country that is overwhelmingly Shiite, although there are Shiite majorities in several other countries, including Iraq. There are large numbers of Shiites in other Middle Eastern countries, as well as in Turkey, Afghanistan, India, and Pakistan.

Shiism has been the official religion of Iran since the sixteenth century and was the source of the ideas behind the reli-giously conservative Iranian Revolution of 1978–1979. The Shiites trace their beginnings to Imam Ali, a seventh-century religious and political leader who is believed to have shown qualities of personal devotion to God and virtue outstanding among the worldly rulers of the time. Ali's descendants came to be seen as the rightful leaders of Islam, since they were held to belong to the prophet Muhammad's family, unlike the dynasties actually in power. The Shiites believed that the rule of Muhammad's rightful heir would eventually be instituted, doing away with the tyrannies and injustices associated with existing regimes. Muhammad's heir would be a leader directly guided by God, governing in accordance with the Qur'ān.

There is no separation of church and state in a few highly religious Islamic societies, such as Iran. In most Muslim countries, however, religious leaders live in a sometimes uneasy alliance with secular governments. Egypt, Algeria, Turkey, and Indonesia, for example, are all predominantly Muslim societies in which mosque and state are separate. In Algeria, religious groups that would have created an Islamic state won the popular vote, only to see the elections overturned by that country's military government. The result has been escalating violence and bloodshed (Juergensmeyer, 1995).

Judaism

With only 14 million followers worldwide, Judaism is by far the smallest of the world's major religions, yet it has exerted an influence greater than its limited numbers would suggest. First, as we have already mentioned, it is the source of the world's two largest religions, Islam and Christianity. Second, in European and U.S. culture, Jews have played a role disproportionate to their numbers in such diverse fields as music, literature, science, education, and business. Third, the existence of Israel as a Jewish state since 1948 has given the Jewish faith international prominence. Israel has existed in a near constant state of tension with many of its neighboring Arab countries since its founding and has seldom been out of the news.

Jews have often suffered persecution at the hands of the surrounding society. From the twelfth century on, European and Russian Jews were often forced to live in special districts termed "ghettos," where they lacked full rights as citizens and were sometimes the target of harassment, attacks, and murders. Partly in reaction to these conditions, and partly because the Torah identifies the city of Jerusalem as the center of the Jewish homeland, some Jews embraced *Zionism,* a movement calling for the return of Jews to Palestine and the creation of a Jewish state. (Zion is a biblical name for the ancient city of Jerusalem.) Although secular Zionists viewed Israel as a country where persecuted Jews could seek refuge, religious Zionists saw it as the one Jewish homeland, returning to which would fulfill biblical prophecies. Zionists established settlements in Palestine early in the twentieth century, living peacefully with their Arab and Palestinian neighbors. Following World War II and the Nazi extermination of 6 million Jews during the Holocaust, the state of Israel was created as a homeland for the survivors. This action, unfortunately, ended the once relatively peaceful relationship between Zionists and their neighbors.

Hinduism

Hinduism, which dates to about 2000 B.C.E., is one of the oldest religions in the world and is the source of Buddhism and Sikhism. It is not based on the teachings of any single individual, and its followers do not trace their national origins to a single god. Like other religions, Hinduism is an ethical religion that calls for an ideal way of life. Today nearly 900 million Hindus are found throughout the world, primarily in India, where Hindus make up the large majority of the population.

As we saw in Chapter 8, India's social structure is characterized by a caste system, in which people are believed to be born to a certain status that they must occupy for life. Although the caste system in India was officially abolished in 1949, it remains powerful to this day. The caste system has its origins in Hindu beliefs, which hold that an ideal life is partly achieved by performing the duties appropriate to one's caste.

Perhaps because Hinduism does not have a central organization or leader, its philosophy and practice are extremely diverse. Religious teachings direct all aspects of life but in a variety of ways, ranging from promoting the enjoyment of sensual pleasures to advising the stark renunciation of earthly pursuits. Mahatma Gandhi was a modern example of a man who led a virtuous life according to Hindu philosophy. Gandhi devoted his life to the Hindu virtues of "honesty, courage, service, faith, self-control, purity, and nonviolence" (Potter, 1992).

Despite the teaching that life is *maya,* or illusion, Hindu religious beliefs have an earthly quality. For example, Hindu religious services do not have to occur in a special place of worship. Although there are sacred sites on which temples and pilgrimage centers are located, any location may be a place of devotion. Hindus believe in the godlike unity of all things, yet their religion also has aspects of **polytheism,** the belief that different gods represent various categories of natural forces. For example, Hindus worship gods representing aspects of the whole, such as the divine dimension of a spiritual teacher (Schmidt, 1980; Kinsley, 1982; Basham, 1989; Potter, 1992).

Religion in the United States

In comparison with the citizens of other industrial nations, Americans are unusually religious. With few exceptions, "the United States has been the most God-believing and religion-adhering, fundamentalist, and religiously traditional country in Christendom [where] more new religions have been born . . . than any other country" (Lipset, 1991). Even though secularization may have weakened the power of religious institutions in the United States, it has not diminished the strength of religious beliefs.

More than half (55 percent) of all Americans surveyed in 1995–1996 claimed to be "strong believers" in God or the sacred (Roof, 1999). About two out of five report having attended religious services in the past week (U.S. Census Bureau, 2003, Table 80), and slightly more than half (54 percent) live in a household where at least one person is a member of a church, mosque, or synagogue (Kosmin, Mayer, and Keysar, 2001). According to public opinion polls, the overwhelming majority of Americans reportedly believe in God and claim they regularly pray, the majority one or more times a day (National Opinion Research Center, 1998). More than eight out of ten Americans report that they believe in an afterlife, and a substantial majority claim to believe in the devil as well (Roof, 1999: Table A-3).

Yet at the same time, one long-term measure of religiosity, based on indicators such as belief in God, religious membership, and attendance at religious services, found that the index reached its highest levels in the 1950s, and has declined ever since—in part because post–World War II "baby boomers" were less religious than their predecessors (Roof, 1999). As Table 17.2 shows, in one national survey overwhelming majorities of Catholics, liberal Protestants, and conservative Protestants reported attending church on a weekly basis while they were children, although their attendance had dropped sharply by the time they had reached their early twenties. Among the three groups, attendance had declined the most among liberal Protestants, and least among conservative Protestants (Roof, 1999).

One survey of more than fifty thousand adults in 2001 and nearly 114,000 adults in 1990 found that religious identification had declined sharply during the eleven-year period. In 1990, 90 percent of all adults identified with some religious group; in 2001, the figure was only 81 percent. The principal decline was among self-identified Christians (from 86 percent to 77 percent). This decline was not because a growing proportion of adults identified with other religions; rather, it was

TABLE 17.2

Weekly Attendance at Religious Services

	AGE	
	8–10	EARLY 20s
Roman Catholics	95	28
Liberal Protestants	82	18
Conservative Protestants	91	40

SOURCE: Roof, 1999, Table A–1, p. 319.

because the number of adults identifying with no religion whatever had grown from 8 percent to 14 percent of the population. Membership in religious institutions showed a parallel decline (Kosmin, Mayer, and Keysar, 2001).

"Civil Religion" in the United States

Although there is a constitutional separation of church and state in the United States, its presidents have all attended church, and some—such as the current president, George W. Bush—have been deeply and publicly religious. In fact, sociologists have argued that the United States has a **civil religion,** a set of religious beliefs through which a society interprets its own history in light of some conception of ultimate reality (Bellah, 1968, 1975). Civil religion usually consists of "god-language used in reference to the nation," including "historical myths about the society's divine origins, beliefs about its sacred historical purpose, and occasionally religious restrictions on societal membership" (Wuthnow, 1988).

The importance of civil religion in the United States is seen in the Pledge of Allegiance. By referring to "one nation, under God," the pledge seeks to infuse civic life with a religious belief derived from the Judeo-Christian heritage. The Pledge of Allegiance has been used for over a century, but the phrase "under God" was added by Congress only in 1954, during the height of cold war fears about "godless communism." Even though the Bill of Rights of the U.S. Constitution clearly calls for a separation of church and state, in the pledge a theistic religious belief was seen as central to U.S. citizenship.

Trends in Religious Affiliation

Roof's previously mentioned study (1993) of baby boomers found that even though two out of three had dropped out of church or synagogue in their teens, for the most part they still remain *A Generation of Seekers* (the title of his book). Although less than a quarter had formally reaffiliated with a religious organization, three out of four claimed to "definitely" believe in God, while one-third called themselves "born-again Christians." (For that matter, 70 percent also believed in "psychic powers.") Moreover, with many of the boomers raising families and approaching a midlife reexamination, Roof believed they were turning back to religion for themselves and their children. Increasingly, however, religious experience is being sought outside established religions, often in a highly personalized fashion.

It is difficult to estimate reliably the number of people belonging to churches, since the U.S. government does not officially collect such data. Nonetheless, based on occasional government surveys, public-opinion polls, and church records, sociologists of religion have concluded that church membership has grown steadily since the United States was founded. About one in six Americans belonged to a religious organization at the time of the Revolutionary War. That number had grown to about one in three at the time of the Civil War, one in two at the turn of the nineteenth century, and two in three in the 1990s (Finke and Stark, 1992).

One reason so many Americans are religiously affiliated is that religious organizations are an important source of social ties and friendship networks. Churches, synagogues, and mosques are communities of people who share the same beliefs and values, and who support one another during times of need. Religious communities thus often play a familylike role, offering help in times of emergency as well as more routine assistance such as child care.

Another reason so many people belong to religious organizations is simply that there are an enormous number of such organizations one can belong to. The United States is the most religiously diverse country in the world, with more than fifteen hundred distinct religions (Melton, 1989). Yet the vast majority of people belong to a relatively small number of religious denominations (see Figure 17.1). Fifty-three percent of Americans identify themselves as Protestants, 25 percent as Catholics, 2 percent as Jews, and 11 percent as "other," a category that

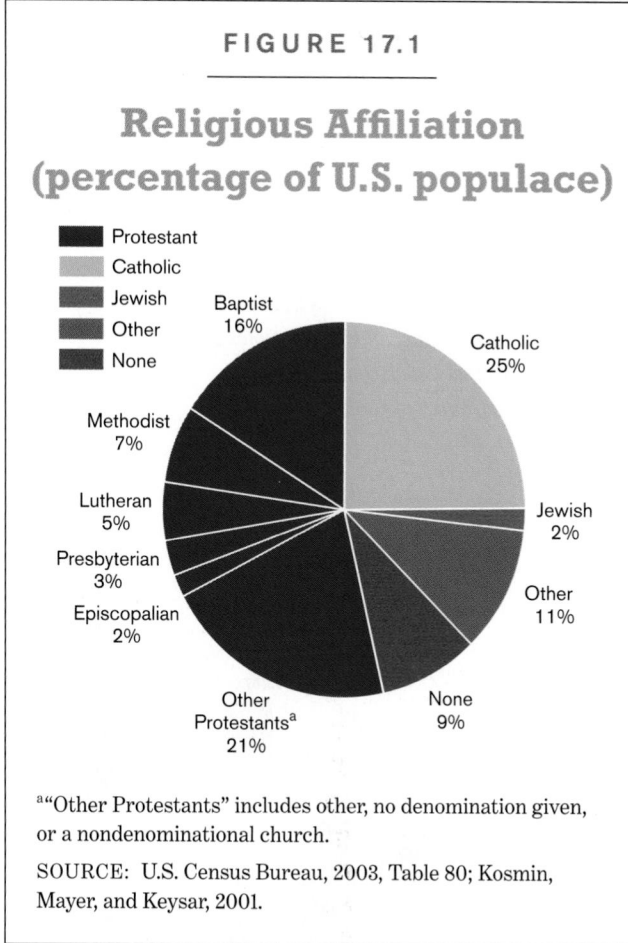

FIGURE 17.1

Religious Affiliation (percentage of U.S. populace)

- Protestant
- Catholic
- Jewish
- Other
- None

Baptist 16%

Catholic 25%

Methodist 7%

Lutheran 5%

Presbyterian 3%

Episcopalian 2%

Jewish 2%

Other 11%

Other Protestants[a] 21%

None 9%

[a]"Other Protestants" includes other, no denomination given, or a nondenominational church.

SOURCE: U.S. Census Bureau, 2003, Table 80; Kosmin, Mayer, and Keysar, 2001.

includes Eastern Orthodox, Mormons, and Muslims. The remainder (9 percent) say they have no religious affiliation at all (U.S. Census Bureau, 2003, Table 80).

PROTESTANTS: THE GROWING STRENGTH OF CONSERVATIVE DENOMINATIONS

A somewhat clearer picture of recent trends in American religion can be obtained if we break down the large Protestant category into major subgroups. According to the American Religious Identification Survey of more than fifty thousand households in 2001, the largest number of households were Baptist, accounting for 31 percent of all Protestants—nearly two and a half times the percentage of the second largest group, Methodists (13 percent). There were far fewer Lutherans (9 percent), Presbyterians (5 percent), and Episcopalians (3 percent) (Kosmin, Mayer, and Keysar, 2001). More than half of all Protestants today describe themselves as "born again" (*The Economist*, 2003).

These figures are important because they indicate the growing strength of conservative Protestants in the United States. Conservative Protestants emphasize a literal interpretation of the Bible, morality in daily life, and conversion through evangelizing. They can be contrasted with the more historically established liberal Protestants, who tend to adopt a more flexible, humanistic approach to religious practice. Somewhere in between are moderate Protestants.

Although all groups of Protestants showed a growth in membership from the 1920s through the 1960s, a major reversal has occurred since that time. Both liberal and moderate churches have experienced a decline in membership, whereas the number of conservative Protestants has exploded. The conservative denominations inspire deep loyalty and commitment, and they are highly effective in recruiting new members, particularly young people. Today twice as many people belong to conservative Protestant groups as liberal ones, and conservative Protestants may soon outnumber moderates as well (Roof and McKinney, 1990). Liberal Protestantism in particular has suffered. The aging members of the liberal Protestant denominations have not been replaced by new, young followers, commitment is low, and some current members are switching to other faiths. As Figure 17.2 indicates, from 1965 to 1989, declines were substantial for such liberal and moderate denominations as Evangelical Lutherans, United Methodists, the United Church of Christ, Episcopalians, Presbyterians, and Disciples of Christ. Together these six denominations lost nearly 23 million members—almost the same number that was gained by such conservative Protestant denominations as the Southern Baptists, the Church of the Nazarene, the Seventh-Day Adventists, the Assemblies of God, the Church of God, and the Mormon Church. Black Protestant churches also continue to thrive in the United States, as their members move into the middle class and a degree of economic and political prominence (Roof and McKinney, 1990; Finke and Stark, 1992).

Since the 1960s, the fastest-growing religious group has been self-identified evangelicals. Moreover, although all religious groups lose some converts to other denominations or beliefs, the more conservative religions experienced a net gain in converts during the 1990s, whereas the more liberal religions experienced a net loss (Kosmin, Mayer, and Keysar, 2001; see also Table 17.3).

CATHOLICISM

Although Catholics continue to grow in number, church attendance has shown a sharp decline over the past few decades, beginning in the 1960s and leveling off in the mid-1970s. One of the main reasons was the papal encyclical of 1968 that reaffirmed the ban on the use of contraceptives by Catholics. The encyclical offered no leeway for people whose conscience

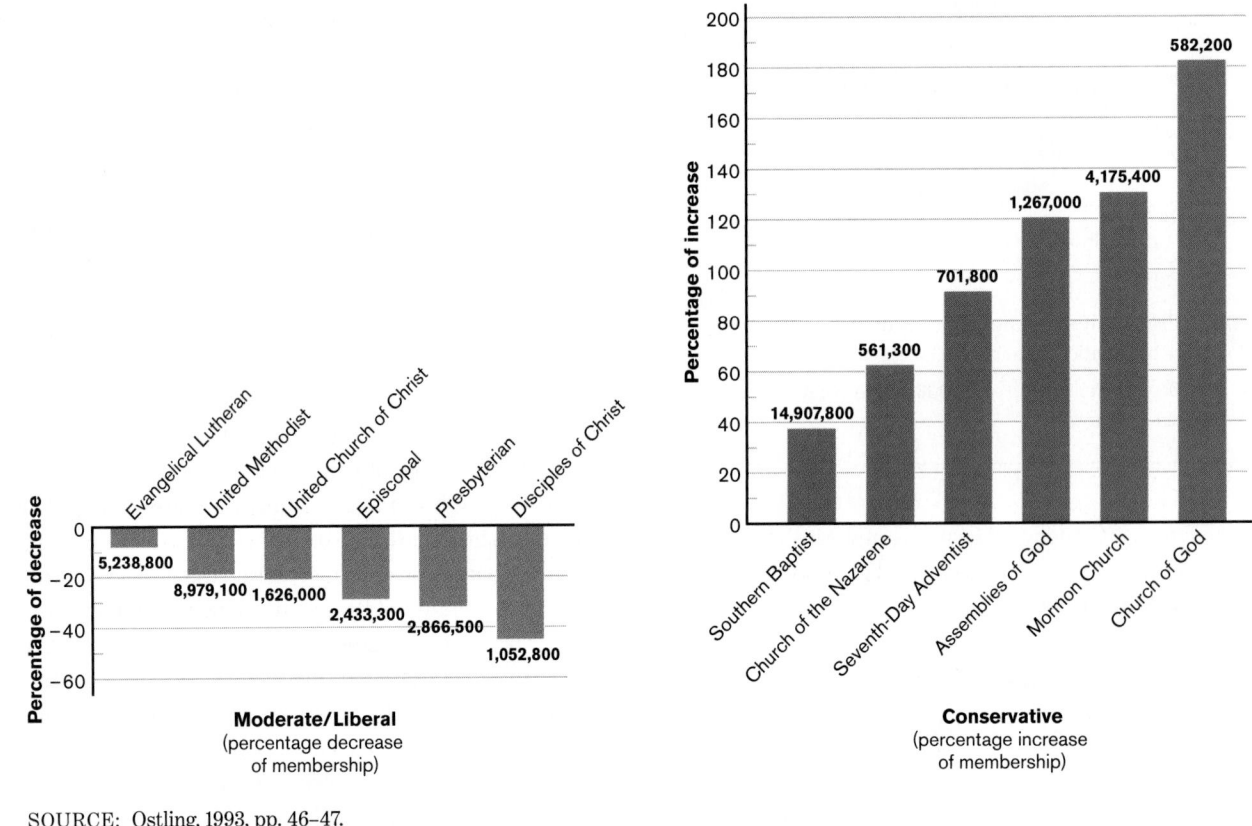

FIGURE 17.2

Loss and Gain in Church Membership, 1965–1989, for Selected Moderate Liberal and Conservative Protestant Churches

During the twenty-four-year period from 1965 to 1989, such mainstream denominations as the United Methodists, the United Church of Christ, the Episcopalians, the Presbyterians, and the Disciples of Christ lost between one-fifth and one-half of their membership. Conversely, such conservative Protestant churches as the Assemblies of God, the Mormons, and the Church of God more than doubled their membership.

SOURCE: Ostling, 1993, pp. 46–47.

allowed for the use of contraceptives. They were faced with disobeying the church, and many Catholics did just that. According to one study conducted by the Centers for Disease Control and Prevention, 96 percent of all Catholic women who have had sexual relations report having used contraceptives at one time or another; the General Social Survey found that three out of five Catholics say that contraceptives should be available to teens even without parental approval.

The Catholic Church has shown by far the largest increase in membership, partly because of the immigration of Catholics from Mexico and Central and South America. Yet the growth in Catholic Church membership has also slowed in recent years, as some followers have drifted away, either ceasing to identify themselves as Catholics or shifting to Protestantism.

OTHER RELIGIOUS GROUPS

The number of Jews has declined in recent years as a result of low birthrates, intermarriage, and assimilation. Yet even assimilated Jews often identify themselves as Jewish, and in

TABLE 17.3

Changes in Religious Self-Identification in the United States, 1999–2001

RELIGIOUS SELF-IDENTIFICATION	NET GAIN OR LOSS
Evangelical/Born Again	42%
Nondenominational	37%
No religion	23%
Pentecostal	16%
Buddhist	12%
Jehovah's Witness	11%
Seventh-Day Adventist	11%
Muslim/Islamic	8%
Assemblies of God	7%
Episcopalian/Anglican	5%
Church of God	5%
Mormon	0%
Baptist	−1%
Lutheran	−1%
Presbyterian	−2%
Churches of Christ	−2%
Jewish	−4%
Congregational/UCC	−6%
Methodist	−7%
Catholic	−9%

SOURCE: Kosmin, Mayer, and Keysar, 2001, exhibit 7.

or are African refugees from countries like Somalia and Ethiopia (Haddad, 1979; Roof and McKinney, 1990; Finke and Stark, 1992).

NEW CULTS

Since World War II, more religious movements have been founded in the United States than at any previous time in its history. Over this period, there has occurred an unprecedented series of mergers of and divisions between denominations. Most have proved short lived, but a few have achieved notable followings.

An example is the Unification Church, founded by the Korean Sun Myung Moon. This movement was introduced into the United States at the beginning of the 1960s, and it appealed to many who at the time were rejecting traditional religion and looking for insight in Eastern religious teachings. The Unification Church mixed Eastern ideas with elements of fundamentalist Christianity and showed a strong bent toward anticommunism.

The cult boasts a membership of fifty thousand in the United States today and 3 million worldwide (Melton, 1996). Its members are expected to fraternize only with each other, to donate their property to the cult, and to obey Moon's commands. Moon's doctrine of "heavenly deception" permits members to mislead the public when asking for money—for instance, by posing as a charity. Substantial funds were accumulated in this way.

Other examples of new religious movements include Scientology, Wiccan, Eckankar, Druid, Santería, and Rastafarianism. Their beliefs might seem unusual mixtures of traditional and modern religious ideas, but in fact all long-established religions mix elements taken from diverse cultural sources. The baby boomers studied by Wade Clark Roof, referred to earlier, are experimenting with a variety of mixed religious beliefs and practices.

Unification Church leader Reverend Sun Myung Moon and his wife marry 2,075 pairs of his followers at Madison Square Garden on New Year's Day, 1982.

recent years, there has been a resurgence of interest among some younger American Jews in rediscovering orthodox practices (Eisen, 1983; Goldberg and Rayner, 1987; Danzger, 1989; Blech, 1991; Davidman, 1991; Bamberger, 1992).

Among other denominations, growing immigration from Asia and Africa may somewhat change the U.S. religious profile. For example, estimates of the number of Muslims in the United States run as high as 3 million; many come from Asia

Religious Affiliation and Socioeconomic Status

Substantial socioeconomic and regional differences exist among the principal religious groupings in the United States (see Table 17.4 for differences among Protestants). *Liberal Protestants* tend to be well educated, somewhat upper income, and middle or upper class. They are concentrated in the northeastern states, and, to a small extent, in the West as well. Ethnically, they tend to be white Anglo-Saxon Protestants (WASPs) of British or German origins. *Moderate Protestants* fall at a somewhat lower level than liberal Protestants in terms of education, income, and social class. In fact, they are typical of the national average on these measures. They tend to live in the Midwest, and, to some extent, in the West. Moderate Protestants are from a variety of European ethnic backgrounds, including British, German, Scandinavian, Irish, and Dutch. *Black Protestants* are, on average, the least educated, poorest, and least middle class of any of the religious groups listed in Table 17.4. *Conservative Protestants* have a similar profile, although they fall at a marginally higher level on all these measures. Like moderate Protestants, they include a diverse profile of European ethnicities, although some are African American as well.

Catholics strongly resemble moderate Protestants (which is to say, average Americans) in terms of their socioeconomic profile. They are largely concentrated in the Northeast, although many live in the West and the Southwest as well. The largest ethnic group is European in origin (primarily German, Italian, Slavic, and Irish, and to a lesser extent English and French), followed by Latinos from Mexico and Central and South America.

Finally, Jews have the most successful socioeconomic profile. Jews tend to be college graduates in middle- or upper-income categories. One recent study found that Jewish educational and occupational attainment was significantly higher than that of other whites (Hartman and Hartman, 1996). Jews are largely European in origin, particularly Slavic and German, although some are from northern Africa (Roof

---

TABLE 17.4

Characteristics of Liberal, Moderate, Conservative, and Black Protestant Denominations

CHARACTERISTICS	LIBERAL	MODERATE	CONSERVATIVE	BLACK
Principal period of appearance	Historic "mainline" churches (pre–Revolutionary War)	Nineteenth century	Twentieth century	Nineteenth and twentieth centuries
Biblical interpretation	Humanistic, flexible	Fairly literal interpretation	Literal interpretation	Fairly literal interpretation, including emphasis on civil rights
Predominant income group	Middle and upper income	Middle income ("middle America")	Lower and middle income	Lower income
Higher education	Many college educated	Some college educated	Few college educated	Few college educated
Predominant region	Northeast, West	Midwest, West	South	South
Examples of denominations	Episcopalian, Presbyterian, United Church of Christ	Methodist, Lutheran, Disciples of Christ, Northern Baptist, Reformed churches	Southern Baptist Convention; Churches of Christ; Church of the Nazarene; Assemblies of God; Seventh-Day Adventist; Fundamentalist, Pentecostal and holiness groups	Black Methodist and Baptist churches

SOURCE: Adapted from Roof and McKinney, 1990.

and McKinney, 1990). Whereas the large majority of Jews once lived in the northeastern states, today only half do, since many have moved throughout the United States. One recent study suggests that this high degree of geographical mobility is associated with lowered involvement in Jewish institutions. Jews who move across the country are less likely to belong to synagogues or temples, have Jewish friends, or be married to Jewish spouses (Goldstein and Goldstein, 1996).

In sum, Jews and liberal Protestants are the most heavily middle and upper class; moderate Protestants and Catholics are somewhat in the middle (although the growing number of poor Catholic Latino immigrants may be changing this position); conservative and black Protestants are overwhelmingly lower class. These groupings correspond roughly to social and political liberalism and conservatism as well. In terms of civil liberties (such as the right of atheists to speak in public or homosexuals to teach), racial justice (such as support for interracial marriage), and women's rights (such as the right to have an abortion), Jews are by far the most tolerant. Liberal Protestants and Catholics are somewhat more tolerant than the average American, while moderate Protestants and black Protestants are somewhat less tolerant. Conservative Protestants are the least tolerant of all religious groupings (Roof and McKinney, 1990).

There are political differences across religious groups as well. Jews tend to be the most heavily Democratic of any major religious groups; fundamentalist and evangelical Christians the most Republican. The more moderate Protestant denominations are somewhere in between (Kosmin, Mayer, and Keysar, 2001, exhibit 14).

Secularization or Religious Revival in America?

According to Phillip Hammond (1992), there have been three principal historical periods in the United States during which religion has undergone **disestablishment,** that is, a period during which the political influence of established religions is successfully challenged. The first such disestablishment occurred with the 1791 ratification of the Bill of Rights—the first ten amendments to the U.S. Constitution—which calls for a firm separation of church and state. Some sociologists have seen this separation as part of a larger trend characteristic of the industrial societies of Europe and North America, in which different institutions come to specialize in different functions—from economics to medicine and from education to politics. Religion is no exception to this process (Parsons, 1951, 1960; Chaves, 1993, 1994). The second disestablishment occurred between the 1890s and 1920s, fed by an influx of

about 17 million immigrants (mainly European), many of whom were Catholic. For the first time, the notion of a predominantly Protestant United States was challenged, and the mainstream Protestant churches never regained their influence in politics or in defining national values. The third disestablishment occurred during the 1960s and 1970s, when core religious beliefs and values were further eroded by the anti–Vietnam war movement, the fight for racial equality, and experimentation with alternative lifestyles. Fundamental challenges came in such basic areas as sexuality, family authority, sexual and lifestyle preferences, women's rights, and birth control (Glock and Bellah, 1976; Wuthnow, 1976, 1978; Hunter, 1987; Roof and McKinney, 1990; Hammond, 1992).

The most recent disestablishment of religion resulted in a reduction in the political influence of religion. This does not mean, however, that religion is less important to individuals, or that secular influences are on the rise. On the contrary, the religious beliefs of many Americans appear to be stronger than ever (Roof, Carroll, and Roozen, 1995). In fact, some sociologists of religion have argued that the absence of an official state religion has forced religious groups to compete with each other for followers, the result being religious practices that are more likely to be tailored to public tastes (Moore, 1994). As we noted earlier, affiliations with conservative Protestant denominations have increased sharply in recent years. Furthermore, for many people, religious beliefs have become increasingly private as more and more people seek spiritual experiences outside established religious organizations. As noted above, in his study of baby boomers, Roof (1993) found that religion had become a highly personal (rather than public) experience for many people. From this he concluded that almost all Americans are religiously oriented, although often outside organized religion. Finally, counter to the overall trend toward religious disestablishment in the United States, some evidence indicates that in recent years conservative Protestant religious organizations have increasingly made their voices heard in U.S. politics.

In their 1992 book, *The Churching of America*, Roger Finke and Rodney Stark argue that disestablishment is a normal process through which mainstream groups become self-satisfied, losing followers to more aggressive sects and cults that promise to revitalize religious experience. In fact, Finke and Stark question whether the third disestablishment occurred at all, noting that cult formation in the 1960s was only slightly higher than in the 1950s. Some research (Melton, 1989; Kosmin, 1991) suggests that relatively minuscule numbers of people belong to groups such as the Unification Church (5,000 members), Krishna Consciousness (3,000), Scientology (55,000), or other New Age groups (20,000) (Melton, 1989; Kosmin, 1991; U.S. Census Bureau, 2003). What has happened, most scholars agree, is that the most liberal, intellectualized, and inclusive religious denominations have lost members, but the most conservative, traditional, and exclusive ones have thrived.

The Resurgence of Evangelicalism

Evangelicalism refers to a belief in spiritual rebirth (being "born again"). Evangelicalism can be seen in part as a response to growing secularism, religious diversity, and, in general, the decline of once-core Protestant values in American life (Wuthnow, 1988). In recent years, there has been an enormous growth in Evangelical denominations, paralleled by a decline in the more mainstream Protestant religious affiliations. Many Protestants are clearly seeking the more direct, personal, and emotional religious experience promised by Evangelical denominations.

Evangelical organizations are good at mobilizing resources to help achieve their religious and political objectives. In the businesslike language used by religious economists, they have proved to be extremely competitive "spiritual entrepreneurs" in the "religious marketplace" (Hatch, 1989). Radio and television have provided important new marketing technologies, used by some Evangelicals to reach a much wider audience than was previously possible. Called *televangelists* because they conduct their Evangelical ministries over television, these ministers depart from many earlier Evangelicals in preaching a "gospel of prosperity": the belief that God wants the faithful to be financially prosperous and satisfied, rather than to sacrifice and suffer. This approach differs considerably from the austere emphasis on hard work and self-denial ordinarily associated with traditional conservative Protestant beliefs (Bruce, 1970; Hadden and Shupe, 1987). Luxurious houses of worship, epitomized by Robert H. Schuller's Crystal

Interior of the Crystal Palace in Garden Grove, California.

Cathedral in Garden Grove, California, provide the televised settings for electronic churches, whose geographically dispersed congregants are united primarily by means of electronic technology. Theology and fund-raising are the staples of televangelism, which must support not only the television ministries themselves, but schools, universities, theme parks, and sometimes the lavish lifestyles of its preachers.

There is considerable debate over the number of people who watch such religious broadcasting. One of the most reliable studies (Bruce, 1990), conducted in 1985 at the height of televangelism's popularity, estimated that the average audience for the top ten programs was about 8 million people. During a typical month, at least 34 million *different* U.S. households—about 40 percent of all households—tuned in at least once. Yet, even at their peak, it is not clear that television ministries were actually bringing large numbers of new people "into the fold." Instead, they may have been merely providing an additional type of religious observation to those who were already well established in their local churches (Hadden and Swann, 1981; Hadden and Shupe, 1987; Hadden, 1990; Diekema, 1991).

During the late 1980s several prominent televangelists were involved in sexual and financial scandals. At the same time, the rising cost of television broadcasting made it more difficult to engage profitably in television ministries. Yet with the advent of cable and satellite television, it has been possible for televangelists to find a cost-effective market niche. The current large number of religious television networks include the American Christian Television System, the Christian Broadcasting Network, the Eternal Word Broadcasting Network, and Family Net. It is difficult to estimate how many people draw inspiration from television (and radio) ministries today, but some scholars argue that these ministries are stronger today than ever before (Hadden, 2004).

The electronic preaching of religion has become particularly prevalent in Latin America, where North American programs are shown. As a result, Protestant movements, most of them of the Pentecostal kind, have made a dramatic impact on such countries as Chile and Brazil, which are predominantly Catholic (Martin, 1990).

Although some Evangelicals combine a thoroughly modern lifestyle with traditional religious beliefs, others strongly reject many contemporary beliefs and practices. **Fundamentalists** are Evangelicals who are antimodern in many of their beliefs, calling for strict codes of morality and conduct. These frequently include taboos against drinking, smoking, and other "worldly evils"; a belief in biblical infallibility; and a strong emphasis on Christ's impending return to earth (Balmer, 1989). Their "old-time religion" clearly distinguishes good from evil and right from wrong (Roof and McKinney, 1990).

Beginning with the Reverend Jerry Falwell's Moral Majority in the 1970s, some groups of fundamentalists have become

On the campaign trail in 1999, presidential candidate George W. Bush addresses the Christian Coalition One Nation Under God Road to Victory Conference.

increasingly involved in what has been termed the New Christian Right in national politics, particularly in the conservative wing of the Republican Party (Simpson, 1985; Woodrum, 1988; Kiecolt and Nelson, 1991). Groups such as the Christian Voice and the Religious Roundtable have advanced a political agenda that is compatible with fundamentalist beliefs. Antiabortion groups such as the Christian Action Council, Focus on the Family, and Prayers for Life were effective in getting the federal government to greatly restrict abortions between 1989 and 1992, despite public opinion polls showing that a majority of Americans believed abortion to be an acceptable alternative in some cases.

Fundamentalist religious organizations helped to shape Republican party ideology and policies during the Reagan administration, as well as during both Bush administrations. White evangelical Protestants make up an estimated third of all registered voters, and they are overwhelmingly politically conservative. They have become a core constituency of the Republican party, contributing to its electoral success. The Republican party's program in turn reflects fundamentalist religious beliefs on such topics as opposition to gay marriage and abortion and a reduced role for government (*The Economist*, 2003).

Globalization and Religion

Religion is one of the most truly global of all social institutions, affecting many aspects of life in the United States. As previously mentioned, nearly half of the world's population follow one of two faiths: Christianity or Islam, religions that have long been unconstrained by national borders. The current globalization of religion is reflected in religious activism in poor countries, particularly on the part of Catholic priests and missionaries, and in the rise of religious nationalist movements in opposition to the modern secular state.

Activist Religion and Social Change Throughout the World

Religion has also played a particularly important role in global social changes of the past forty years. In Vietnam in the 1960s, Buddhist priests burned themselves alive to protest the policies of the South Vietnamese government. Their willingness to sacrifice their lives for their beliefs, seen on television sets around the world, contributed to growing U.S. opposition to the war. Buddhist monks in Thailand currently protest deforestation and care for victims of AIDS.

An activist form of Catholicism, termed **liberation theology,** combines Catholic beliefs with a passion for social justice for the poor, particularly in Central and South America and in Africa. Catholic priests and nuns organize farming cooperatives, build health clinics and schools, and challenge government policies that impoverish the peasantry. A similar role is played by Islamic socialists in Pakistan and Buddhist socialists in Sri Lanka (Berryman, 1987; Sigmund, 1990, Juergensmeyer, 1993). Many religious leaders have paid with their lives for their activism, which government and military leaders often regard as subversive.

In some Central and Eastern European countries once dominated by the former Soviet Union, long-suppressed religious organizations provided an important basis for the overturning of socialist regimes during the early 1990s. In Poland, for example, the Catholic Church was closely allied with the Solidarity movement, which toppled the socialist government in 1989. Yet, as the socialist regimes have crumbled, religion has also all too often played a central role in reviving ancient ethnic and tribal hatreds. In Bosnia and elsewhere in the former Yugoslavia, to cite one example, religious differences have helped to justify "ethnic cleansing," with Christian Serbs and to a lesser extent Croatians engaging in the mass murder, rape, and deportation of Muslims from communities and farmlands where they had lived for centuries.

The Global Rise of Religious Nationalism

Perhaps the most important trend in global religion today is the rise of **religious nationalism,** the linking of strongly held religious convictions with beliefs about a people's social and political destiny. In numerous countries around the world, religious nationalist movements reject the notion that religion, government, and politics should be separate and call instead for a revival of traditional religious beliefs that are directly embodied in the nation and its leadership (Beyer, 1994). These nationalist movements represent a strong reaction against the impact of technological and economic modernization on local religious beliefs. In particular, religious nationalists oppose what they see as the destructive aspects of "Western" influence on local culture and religion, ranging from U.S. television to the missionary efforts of foreign evangelicals. As one study notes, in the view of religious nationalists, "God's word is pure—not pluralist" (Marty and Appleby, 1995).

Religious nationalist movements accept many aspects of modern life, including modern technology, politics, and economics. For example, Islamic fundamentalists fighting the Russian army in Chechnya have developed Web sites to help promulgate their views. Osama bin Laden used video and television to reach millions of Muslims around the world. However, at the same time they emphasize a strict interpretation of religious values and completely reject the notion of secularization (Juergensmeyer, 1993, 2001). Nationalist movements do not simply revive ancient religious beliefs. Rather, nationalist movements partly "invent" the past, selectively drawing on different traditions and reinterpreting past events to serve their current beliefs and interests. Violent conflicts between religious groups sometimes result from their differing interpretations of the same historical event (Anderson, 1991; Juergensmeyer, 1993, 2001; Van der Veer, 1994).

Religious nationalism is on the rise throughout the world because in times of rapid social change, unshakable ideas have strong appeal. The collapse of the Soviet Union, the end of the cold war, and today's sweeping global economic and political changes have led many nations to reject the secular solutions offered by the United States and its former socialist enemies, and to look instead to their own past and cultures for answers (Juergensmeyer, 1995c). In the Middle East, many Palestinian Muslims as well as Israeli Orthodox Jews renounce the notion of a secular democratic state, arguing—often violently—for a religious nation purged of nonbelievers. In India, Hindus, Muslims, and Sikhs face off against each other. In India's nationwide elections held in early 1998, the religious nationalist Bharatiya Janata Party (BJP) got more votes than the Congress Party, which had dominated Indian politics since independence half a century earlier. (In 2004, the Congress party regained control of the government.)

Islamic nationalism has triumphed in Iran, Sudan, and until 2001, Afghanistan, where the United States overthrew the Islamist Taliban regime in response to its support for al Qaeda. Islamic nationalism has made significant inroads in Egypt, Algeria, Turkey, Pakistan, Palestine, Malaysia, and elsewhere (see Global Map 17.3). In the last thirty years, Islamic nationalism has shaped the contours of both national and international politics. In order to understand this phenomenon, we have to look both to aspects of Islam as a traditional religion and to secular changes that have affected countries where its influence is pervasive.

Islamic Nationalism

Islam, like Christianity, has continually stimulated activism. The Qur'ān is full of instructions to believers to "struggle in the way of God." This struggle is against both unbelievers and those within the Muslim community who introduce corruption. Over the centuries there have been successive generations of Muslim reformers, and Islam has become as internally divided as Christianity.

ISLAM AND THE WEST

During the Middle Ages, there was a more or less constant struggle between Christian Europe and the Muslim states. During the height of Islamic power, the *caliphs* (Islamic rulers, believed to be successors of Muhammad) ruled over an area that extended from what later became Spain, Greece, the former Yugoslavia, Bulgaria, and Romania to India, Pakistan, and Bangladesh (see Global Map 17.3). Most of the lands conquered by the Muslims were reclaimed by the Europeans, and many of their possessions in North Africa were in fact colonized as Western power grew in the eighteenth and nineteenth centuries. These reverses were catastrophic for Muslim religion and civilization, which Islamic believers held to be the highest and most advanced possible, transcending all others. In the late nineteenth century, the inability of the Muslim world effectively to resist the spread of Western culture led to reform movements seeking to restore Islam to its original purity and strength. A key idea was that Islam should respond to the Western challenge by affirming the identity of its own beliefs and practices.

This idea has been developed in various ways in the twentieth century and formed a backdrop to the Islamic revolution in Iran of 1978–1979. The revolution was fueled initially by internal opposition to the shah (the king), Mohammad Reza Pahlavi (1941–1979).

When the shah's premier, Mohammad Mossadeq, nationalized the oil industry in 1951, a conflict ensued between the pro-West shah and the supporters of the strongly nationalistic Mossadeq. The shah eventually fled the country but returned in 1953 when a U.S.- and British-led coup overthrew Mossadeq. The shah tried to promote forms of modernization

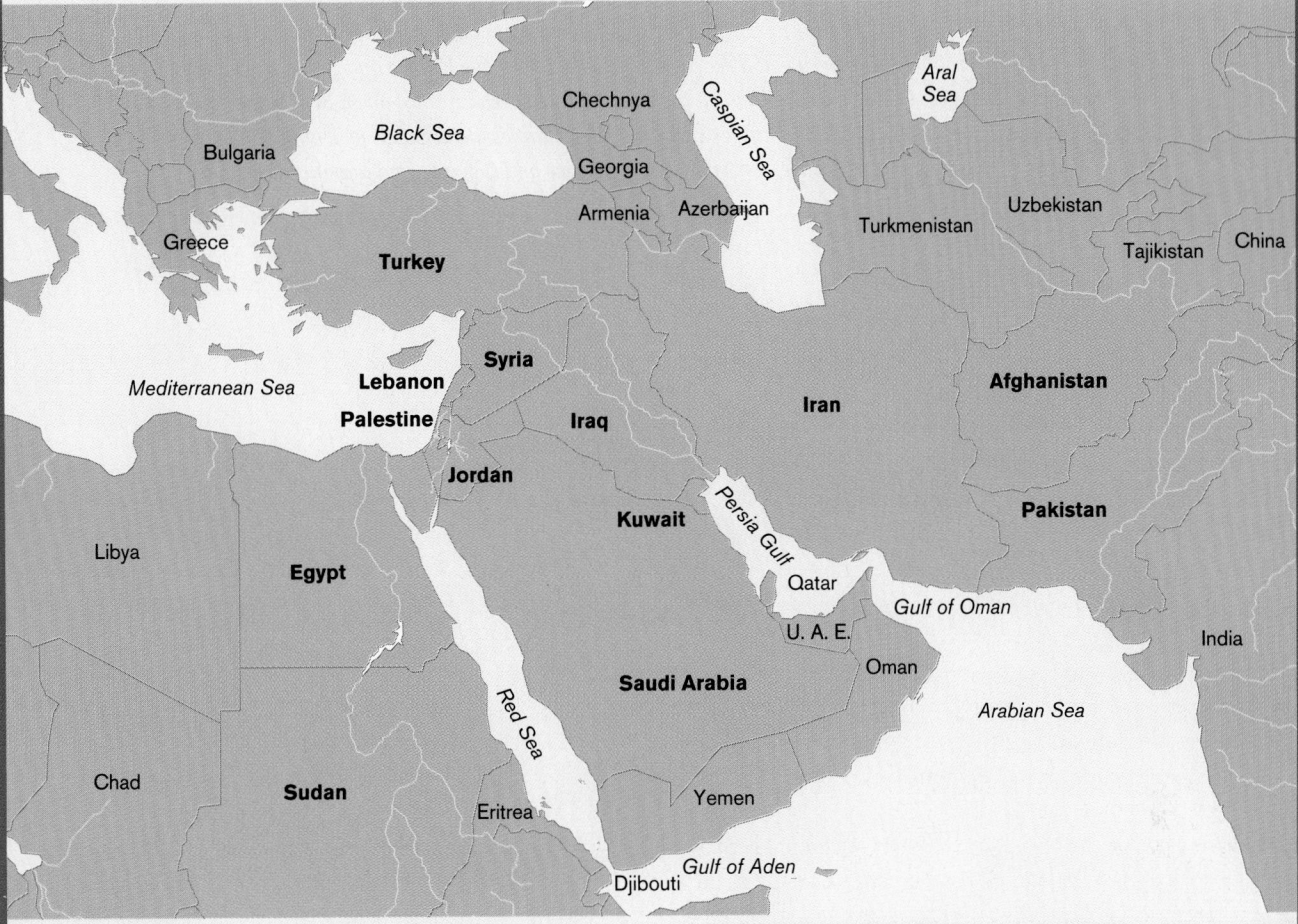

GLOBAL MAP 17.2

Islam in Power and in Opposition

Islamists in power

1 Iran: *Ayatollah Khomeini overthrew the shah in 1979*

2 Sudan: *Ruled since 1989 by a military regime now led by General Umar Hassan al-Bashir and backed by National Congress Party (formerly the National Islamic Front)*

Islamists deposed

Afghanistan: *The Taliban had consolidated their grip since 1996 and were deposed in 2001*

Islamists in opposition

1 Egypt: *The Muslim Brotherhood, with the Jamaat-e-Islam of Pakistan, was the fountainhead of "political Islam"*

2 Saudi Arabia: *An Islamic monarchy withstood an attempt by fanatics to overthrow it*

3 Turkey: *Western-style democracy has stripped its nonviolent Islamists of the power won by democratic means*

4 Iraq and Syria: *Totalitarian regimes have crushed Islamist uprisings savagely; Iraq regime overthrown by U.S.-led military invasion and occupation in 2003, constitutional democracy being introduced*

5 Palestine: *Hamas militants marry religious and patriotic zeal*

6 Pakistan: *"Moderate" Islamists have enjoyed more access to constitutional politics than those of any other Muslim country*

7 Chechnya: *A bitter struggle of independence from Moscow has provided a haven for Islamic extremists*

8 Nigeria and Malaysia: *Two of the "peripheral" countries of the Muslim world where Islam is a growing force*

SOURCES: *The Guardian*, February 15, 2000, p. 18, and authors' updates.

The Global Extent of Islamic Power at Its Height

Islam, which originated in the sixth century and is based on the teachings of the prophet Muhammad, rapidly spread throughout much of the world. Under the leadership of powerful caliphs believed to be direct descendants of the Prophet, Islamic rule had reached what was to become France and Spain by the eighth century; it was to remain in southern Spain until the end of the fifteenth century, when Ferdinand and Isabella succeeded in uniting all of Spain under Catholic rule. Islamic rule in Spain was noted for its high degree of culture and religious tolerance, contributions to science and the arts, and advanced economy.

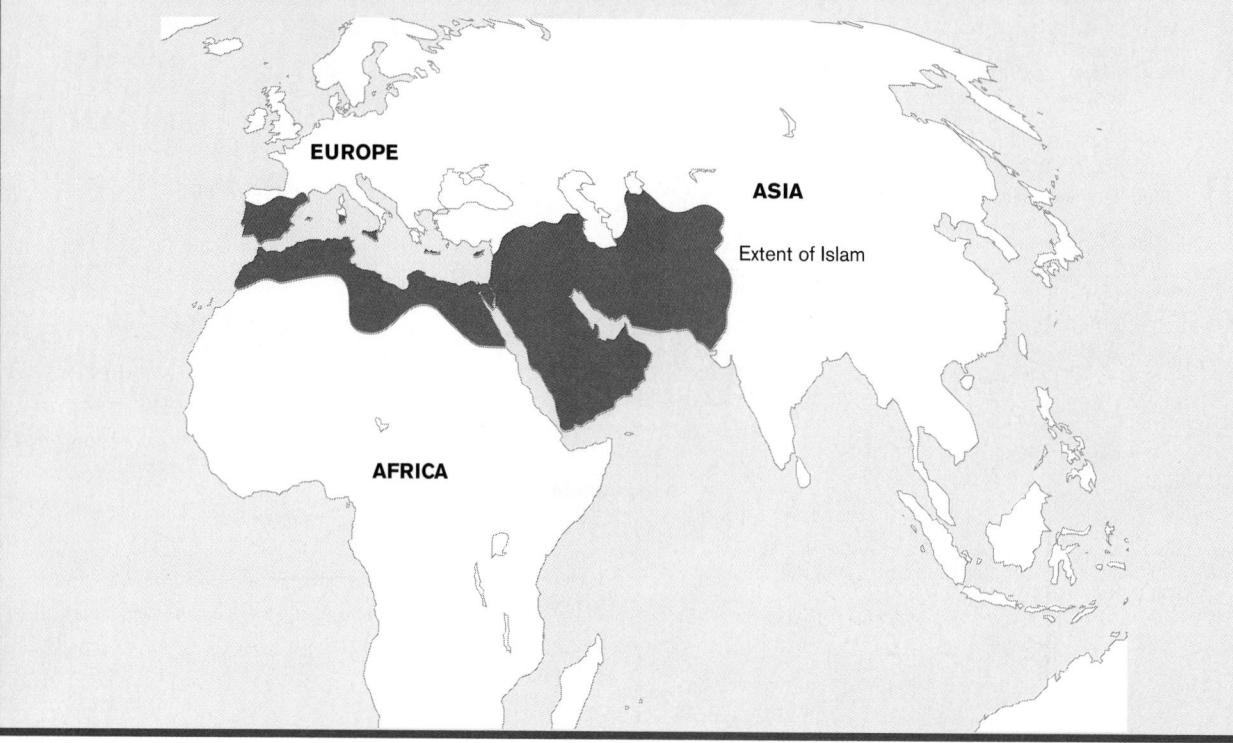

modeled on the West—for example, land reform, extending the vote to women, and developing secular education. He also used the army and secret police brutally to repress those who opposed his regime. The fact that he had been installed by Western powers helped fuel nationalist sentiments that eventually led to the revolution that overthrew him. That revolution brought together people of diverse interests, not all of whom were attached to Islamic fundamentalism. A dominant figure, however, was Ayatollah Ruhollah Khomeini, a religious leader exiled in France during the shah's reign, who provided a radical reinterpretation of Shiite ideas.

Khomeini established a government in strict accordance with traditional Islamic law, calling that government the "Representative of All." The Islamic revolution fused religion and the state. It made Islam, as specified in the Qur'ān, the direct basis of all political and economic life in Iran. Under re-

vived Islamic law, men and women were kept rigorously segregated, women were obliged to cover their heads in public, homosexuals faced the possibility of being shot by a firing squad, and women accused of adultery were stoned to death. The strict code was accompanied by a pronounced nationalistic outlook, strongly rejecting Western influences.

The aim of the Islamic Republic in Iran was to Islamize the state—to organize government and society so that Islamic teachings would become dominant in all spheres. A twelve-member Guardian Council of religious leaders has the last say in determining whether or not laws, policies, and even candidates for Parliament conform to Islamic beliefs, even though Iran has a U.S.-style constitution providing for elected officials and the separation of powers.

Recent years have seen a growing movement to liberalize the country. Mohammed Khatami, the reform-minded president, and his allies recaptured control of the Parliament in the February 2000 elections. But that victory may prove to be short-lived: the Guardian Council disqualified twenty-four hundred liberal candidates (nearly a third of all candidates) during the February 2004 elections. The result was a voters' boycott, resulting in low turnout by reform-minded voters. The reformist movement—which had effectively challenged the hard-liners four years earlier, taking control of Parliament—now controls less than a quarter of the seats.

THE SPREAD OF ISLAMIC REVIVALISM

Although the ideas underlying the Iranian revolution were supposed to unite the whole of the Islamic world against the West, governments of countries where the Shiites are in a minority have not aligned themselves closely with the Islamic Revolution in Iran. Yet Islamic fundamentalism (often referred to as "Islamism," the complete adherence to Islamic law along with rejection of most non-Islamic influences) has achieved significant popularity in most of these states, and various forms of Islamic revivalism elsewhere have been stimulated by it.

Although Islamic fundamentalist movements have gained influence in many countries in North Africa, the Middle East, and South Asia over the past ten to fifteen years, they have succeeded in coming to power in only two other states. Sudan has been ruled since 1989 by Hassan al-Turabi's National Salvation Front. The fundamentalist Taliban regime consolidated its hold on the fragmented state of Afghanistan in 1996 but was ousted from power at the end of 2001 by Afghan opposition forces and the U.S. military. In many other states, Islamic fundamentalist groups have gained influence but have been prevented from rising to power. In Egypt, Turkey, and Algeria, for example, Islamic fundamentalist uprisings have been suppressed by the state or the military.

Islamic opposition is building in states such as Malaysia and Indonesia. Several provinces in Nigeria have recently implemented *sharia* (strict Islamic law), and the war in Chechnya has attracted the participation of Islamic militants who support the establishment of an Islamic state in that region.

Al Qaeda is an example of a loosely knit transnational network of militant religious fundamentalists with a truly global vision. Founded by Osama bin Laden, al Qaeda seeks to overthrow what it regards as corrupt Muslim governments, drive Western influence from the Middle East, and eventually establish a religiously based government that would span half the globe, encompassing a billion Muslims in parts of Europe, Africa, and Asia. Its members envision a restoration of the original caliphates that controlled much of the world during the height of Islamic power. Islamic rule would be subject to strict religious discipline, much as it was during the rule of the Taliban in Afghanistan.

In 1998 Osama bin Laden issued a *fatwa*, saying that any American, whether Muslim or not, should be killed. A *fatwa* is a religious decree or judgment issued by a recognized Islamic legal authority. Upon bin Laden's issuing of the *fatwa*, Mullah Omar (the head of the Taliban in Afghanistan) issued a statement saying that bin Laden was not qualified to give a *fatwa* because he "had not undergone the requisite Islamic schooling."

Such Islamic revivalism plainly cannot be understood wholly in religious terms. It represents in large part a reaction against what the Iranian writer Jalal Al Ahmad forty years ago called "Weststruckedness" or "Westoxification"—the seductive (and, in his view, corrupting) power of Western cultural beliefs and practices (Al Ahmad, 1997). In countries where as much as half the population is under fifteen, where poverty is widespread and growing, and where many well-educated young men and women face a life of marginal employment and uncertainty, such beliefs are bound to find fertile ground.

The strong Western presence in the Middle East has provided additional fuel for anti-Western sentiments. In his *fatwas* (opinions that he claimed to be grounded in Islamic law), bin Laden repeatedly condemned U.S. troop presence in Saudia Arabia (which, as the land of Muhammad, is regarded by Islam as its most sacred place), U.S. support for Israel in its conflict with the Palestinians, the first Gulf War against Iraq, and what bin Laden claimed were a million deaths resulting from the postwar economic sanctions against Iraq. In a videotaped statement that was televised around the world following the September 11 attacks, bin Laden also stated that "what the United States tastes today is a very small thing compared to what we have tasted for tens of years. Our nation has been tasting this humiliation and contempt for more than 80 years" (BBC News, 2001). What he was referring to was the collapse of the Ottoman empire after World War I when more than a thousand years of Islamic rule—once spanning parts of Europe, the Middle East, Africa, and Asia—came to a humiliating end, with Islamic lands in the Middle East turned into European colonies (see Global Map 17.3).

To what extent are bin Laden's views shared in the Muslim world? In 2002 and 2003 the Pew Research Center conducted public opinion polls that reached a total of fifty thousand people around the world. Large majorities of people, including Muslims, reported that such things as television, the Internet, and cellular phones were actually making their lives better. (Pakistan, one of the world's largest Islamic countries, was a notable exception.) Most people (including most Muslims) felt that foreign TV, movies, and music were on balance a "good thing" (again, except for Pakistan). This generally positive view of Western influence was shared despite the fact that large majorities of Muslims and others also believed that their traditional ways of life were being lost and needed to be protected against foreign influence. Although the overwhelming majority of Muslim respondents polled did express concern that "there are serious threats to Islam today," the vast majority also rejected suicide bombings and other forms of violence against civilians as a legitimate means of "defending Islam against its enemies" (Pew, 2003).

Bin Laden's belief that "Westoxification" is a serious problem calling for a violent solution is clearly not widely shared among ordinary Muslims. Nonetheless, it is equally clear that he has a strong appeal among some Muslims—enough to make al Qaeda a serious threat. And his appeal appears to be strongest among Muslims whose religious convictions are sufficiently deep that they are willing to die for their beliefs.

How is it that Islamic religious views—or, for that matter, any religious views—could give rise to such a culture of violence? The sociologist Mark Juergensmeyer (2001), who has studied the relationship between violence and religion, has come to a startling conclusion: Even though virtually all major religious traditions call for compassion and understanding, violence and religion nonetheless go hand in hand. Juergensmeyer, who has studied religious violence among Muslims, Sikhs, Jews, Hindus, Christians, and Buddhists, argues that under the right conditions ordinary conflicts can become recast as religious "cosmic wars" between good and evil that must be won at all costs. Juergensmeyer argues that a violent conflict is most likely to seek religious justification as a "cosmic war" when:

- the conflict is regarded as decisive for defending one's basic identity and dignity—for example, when one's culture is seen as threatened; and
- losing the conflict is unthinkable, although
- winning the conflict is unlikely in any realistic sense. (2001)

If any of these three conditions is present, Juergensmeyer argues, it is more likely that:

a real-world struggle may be perceived in cosmic terms as a sacred war. The occurrence of all three simultaneously strongly suggests it. A struggle that begins on worldly terms may gradually take on the characteristics of a cosmic war as solutions become unlikely and awareness grows of how devastating it would be to lose. (2001)

In such instances, the proponents of cosmic warfare seek "terror in the mind of God" (the title of his book), justifying the loss of innocent lives as serving God's larger purpose. According to Juergensmeyer, bin Laden and al Qaeda exemplify such "cosmic warfare". They are seeking to defend Islam against an all-engulfing Westernization. He also argues that responding to al Qaeda's violence with still greater violence runs the risk of showing the Islamic world that the conflict is indeed cosmic, particularly if the most powerful nations on earth become embroiled. Based on his interviews with proponents of terrorism around the world, Juergensmeyer concludes that this is just what al Qaeda wants—to be elevated from the status of a minor criminal terrorist organization to a worthy opponent in a global war against the West. This, in the view of some of his interviewees, will increase the appeal of al Qaeda to a wider group of young Islamic men who blame the West for the decline of Islamic influence and the current hardships faced by many Muslims around the world.

Conclusion

In the shape of fundamentalism and in the diversity of new groups and sects found in the United States and elsewhere, religion remains a vital force in society. It might appear strange, therefore, to suggest that the influence of religion in the modern world is actually declining. However, sociologists generally agree that such a decline has taken place, considered at least as a long-term trend.

Until the modern period, churches rivaled and frequently surpassed monarchs and governments in the political power they wielded and the wealth they managed to accumulate. The priesthood maintained control over the skills of literacy, scholarship, and learning. As in other areas of social life, much of this changed as industrialization took hold. Churches and religious organizations in Western countries lost most of their secular power. Governments took over tasks that the churches had previously controlled, including education.

Toward the end of the nineteenth century, the German philosopher Friedrich Nietzsche announced, "God is dead." Religions, he argued, used to be a point of reference for our sense of purpose and meaning. Henceforth, we would have to live without this security, and indeed without any fixed moral reference points at all. Living in a world without God means creating our own values and getting used to what Nietzsche called "the loneliness of being"—understanding that our lives are without purpose and that no superior entities watch over our fate.

There can be little doubt that the hold of religious beliefs today is weaker than was generally the case in the past, particularly if we include under the term *religion* the whole range of supernatural phenomena in which people once believed. Most of us no longer see the world as permeated by spirits and demons.

Modern rationalist thought and religious outlook exist in an uneasy state of tension. A rationalist perspective permeates a good portion of our existence, and its hold in all probability will not become weakened in the foreseeable future. Yet there are bound to be reactions against rationalism, leading to periods of religious revivalism, as is happening today. Probably few individuals on the face of the earth have not been touched by religious sentiments at some time in their lives. Science and rationalist thinking remain silent on questions of the meaning and purpose of life, matters that have always been at the core of religion.

Study Outline

www.wwnorton.com/giddens5

The Sociological Study of Religion

- There are no known societies that do not have some form of religion, although religious beliefs and practices vary from culture to culture. All religions involve a set of shared beliefs and rituals practiced by a community of believers.
- The sociology of religion is not concerned with whether a particular religion is true or false, but with how it operates as an organization and its relationship to the larger society. Religions are viewed as arising from social relationships and providing a sense of social solidarity to followers.

How Sociologists Think About Religion

- Sociological approaches to religion have been most influenced by the ideas of the three "classical" thinkers: Marx, Durkheim, and Weber. All believed that religion is fundamentally an illusion. They held that the "other" world that religion creates is *our* world, distorted through the lens of religious symbolism.
- To Marx, religion contains a strong ideological element: Religion provides justification for the inequalities of wealth and power found in society. To Durkheim, religion is important because of the cohesive functions it serves, especially in ensuring that people meet regularly to affirm common beliefs and values. To Weber, religion is important because of the role it plays in social change, particularly the development of Western capitalism.
- According to the classical view, religion in modern society is threatened by a long-term process of *secularization* in which the challenge of scientific thinking, as well as the coexistence of numerous competing religions, inevitably leads to the complete demise of religion.

- The more recent *religious economy* approach draws the opposite conclusion: that competition among religious groups and the challenges of secularization force religions to work harder to win followers, thereby strengthening the various groups and countering any trend toward secularization.

Types of Religious Organizations

- Several different types of religious organization can be distinguished. A *church* is a large, established religious body, having a bureaucratic structure. *Sects* are small and aim at restoring the original purity of doctrines that have become "corrupted" in the hands of official churches. A *denomination* is a sect that has become institutionalized, having a permanent form. A *cult* is a loosely knit group of people who follow the same leader or pursue similar religious ideals.
- Although traditional churches have been experiencing a decline in membership in recent decades, many new religious movements have emerged alongside mainstream religions. New religious movements encompass a broad range of religious and spiritual groups, cults, and sects. They can be broadly divided into world-affirming movements, which are akin to self-help groups; world-rejecting movements, which withdraw from and criticize the outside world; and world-accommodating movements, which emphasize inner religious life over worldly concerns.
- The three most influential *monotheistic* religions (religions in which there is one God) in world history are Judaism, Christianity, and Islam. *Polytheism* (belief in several or many gods) is common in other religions, such as Hinduism.

Religion in the United States

- The United States is one of the most religious among the industrial nations. Although only about one quarter of all Americans report regularly attending church, the large majority claim to believe in God and to engage in regular prayer. Although church and state are legally separated by the U.S. Constitution, religious imagery and rituals pervade politics and civic life.

- Mainline liberal and moderate Protestant religious denominations in the United States have experienced declining membership recently, while more conservative or *evangelical* groups have seen an increase. These groups have sought to expand their direct influence in U.S. politics in recent years.

Religion as a Global Social Institution

- Religion has always been one of the most global of all social institutions. Fundamentalism has become common among some believers in different religious groups across the world. "Fundamentalists" are called this because they believe in returning to the fundamentals of their religious doctrines. Islamic fundamentalism has affected many countries in the Middle East following the 1979 Islamic revolution in Iran, which set up a religiously inspired government.

- Another important development is the role played by *liberation theologians* in fostering social justice and economic inequality, particularly in Latin America and Africa.

The Global Rise of Religious Nationalism

- Religious nationalism is an important force in the world today, existing in a precarious relationship with modern secular states. They often recast ordinary conflicts as religious "cosmic wars" between good and evil that must be won at all costs. This is especially likely to be the case when the conflict is seen as central to one's beliefs, losing it would be unthinkable, and winning it is unlikely.

Key Concepts

alienation (p. 508)
charisma (p. 516)
church (p. 513)
civil religion (p. 526)
cult (p. 513)
denomination (p. 513)
disestablishment (p. 531)
evangelicalism (p. 532)
fundamentalism (p. 532)
liberation theology (p. 533)
monotheism (p. 520)
New Age movement (p. 517)
new religious movement (p. 516)
polytheism (p. 525)

profane (p. 508)
religion (p. 506)
religious economy (p. 512)
religious movement (p. 516)
religious nationalism (p. 533)
sacred (p. 508)
sect (p. 513)
secular thinking (p. 510)
secularization (p. 510)
theism (p. 506)
total institution (p. 517)
world-accommodating movement (p. 518)
world-affirming movement (p. 517)
world-rejecting movement (p. 517)

Review Quiz

1. The linking of strongly held religious convictions with beliefs about a people's social and political destiny is
   a. religious economy.
   b. religious nationalism.
   c. civil religion.
   d. ethical religion.

2. When sociologists study religion, they are concerned with
   a. whether religious beliefs are true or false.
   b. whether religious beliefs are good or bad.
   c. the social organization of religion.
   d. all of the above.

3. What is a millenarian movement?
   a. A social movement, typically religious, that attaches some particular spiritual significance to the passage of thousand-year periods
   b. A group that anticipates immediate, collective salvation for believers, either because of some cataclysmic change in the present or through recovery of a golden age
   c. A movement of landless peasants who believe in a prophet's promises of salvation and eternal good harvests
   d. A type of ecstasy that is believed to overcome the body and soul at the movement of death and that represents the transition to a higher spiritual plane

4. The classical theories of religion argued that the key problem facing religions in the modern world is
   a. animism.
   b. the electronic church.
   c. fundamentalism.
   d. secularization.

5. Secularization can be evaluated according to a number of aspects or dimensions. Which of the following is *not* one of them?
   a. Level of industrialization
   b. Social influence of churches
   c. Level of membership
   d. Level of religiosity

6. Which of the following religions is polytheistic?
   a. Catholicism
   b. Protestantism
   c. Hinduism
   d. Islam
7. Which is the fastest-growing religion in the world today?
   a. Christianity
   b. Islam
   c. Judaism
   d. Hinduism
8. Which of the following statements is *true* about Sunni Muslims?
   a. There is a large Sunni Muslim population in Iraq.
   b. They tolerate a considerable diversity of opinion.
   c. They are Muhammad's direct heirs.
   d. They trace their beginnings to Imam Ali.
9. What is the most important trend in global religion today?
   a. Islamic revivalism
   b. The creation of the Israeli state
   c. Religious nationalism
   d. Secularization
10. Which of the following is *not* a characteristic of evangelicalism?
    a. A commitment to spreading "the Word" to others
    b. Admission of personal sin and salvation through acceptance of Christ
    c. A literal interpretation of the Bible
    d. An emphasis on collective (not personal) spiritual piety

Thinking Sociologically Exercises

1. Karl Marx, Émile Durkheim, and Max Weber each had different viewpoints on the nature of religion and its social significance.

Briefly explain the viewpoints of each. Which theorist's views have the most to offer in explaining the rise of national and international fundamentalism today? Why?

2. Drawing on this textbook's discussion, summarize the role of religion for most Americans today and assess whether religion is increasing or decreasing in importance for most people. Explain what it means for people to become more secular or fundamentalist in their religious practices. Are Americans becoming more secular or fundamentalist in their religious observances?

Data Exercises

www.wwnorton.com/giddens5
Keyword: Data17

- In this chapter you have read about the patterns of religious practices in the United States. The data exercise for this chapter will give you a further opportunity to explore not only the differences in religious affiliation and worship among groups within our society, but more importantly, how these patterns are changing.

PART FIVE

SOCIAL CHANGE IN THE MODERN WORLD

For virtually the whole of human history, the pace of social change was relatively slow; most people followed ways of life similar to those of their forebears. By contrast, we live today in a world subject to dramatic and continuous transformation. In the remaining chapters, we look at some of the major areas of change.

One of the most far-reaching influences of globalization is the focus of the growing field known as sociology of the body. Chapter 18 examines how global processes affect our bodies, including our diets, our health, and our sexual behavior.

The globalizing of social life both influences and is influenced by changing patterns of urbanization, the subject of Chapter 19. This chapter also analyzes two of the most far-reaching changes occurring in modern times, the tremendous growth in world population and the increasing threat of environmental problems. Population growth has been greatly affected by the spread of Western techniques of hygiene and medicine. At the same time, threats to the global environment brought on by social change require global solutions if human societies are to continue to thrive in the future.

The concluding chapter looks directly at processes of change. In this chapter, we study some of the major processes of social change from the eighteenth century to the present day. We also consider general interpretations of the nature of social change. What is social change actually, and why has it become so profound and constant? We also consider where present-day patterns of global change are likely to lead us in the twenty-first century. In doing so, we explore the factors contributing to globalization, the causes of increasing globalization, the impact of globalization on our lives, and the debate over its consequences.

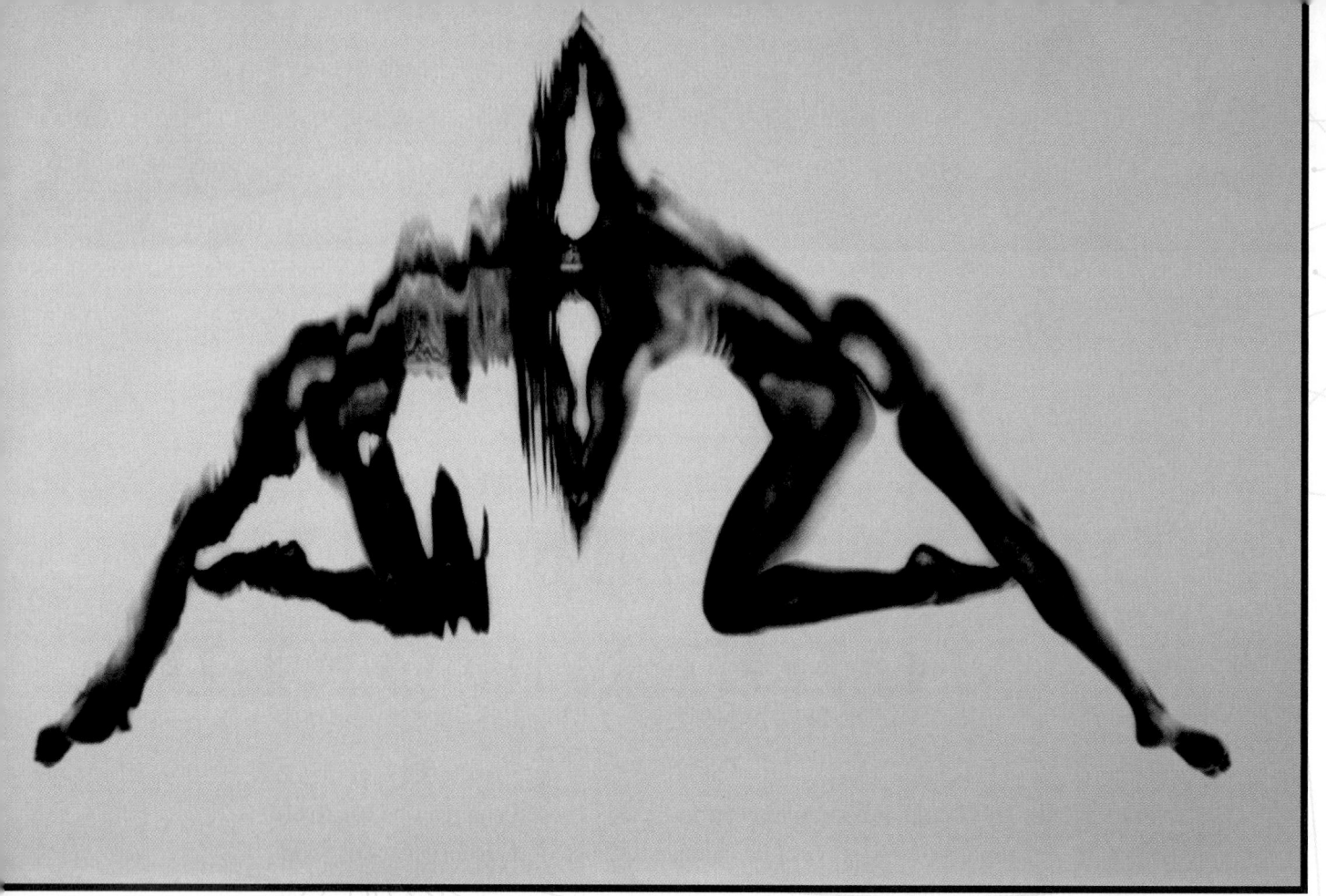

The Sociology of Health and Illness

Recognize that health and illness are culturally and socially determined. Learn the social and cultural differences in the distribution of disease. Learn more about HIV/AIDS as a sociological phenomenon.

Human Sexuality

Learn about the debate over the importance of biological versus social and cultural influences on human sexual behavior. Explore the cultural differences in sexual behavior and patterns of sexual behavior today.

CHAPTER EIGHTEEN

THE SOCIOLOGY OF THE BODY: HEALTH AND ILLNESS AND SEXUALITY

Look at the two photographs on the next page. The images of a sunken face and an emaciated body are almost identical. The young girl on the left is Somalian, dying from a simple lack of food. The young woman on the right is an American teenager, dying because, in a society with a superabundance of food, she chose not to eat or to eat so sparingly that her life was endangered.

The social dynamics involved in each case are utterly different. Starvation from lack of food is caused by factors outside people's control and affects only the very poor. The American teenager, living in the wealthiest country in the world, is suffering from anorexia, an illness with no known physical origin; obsessed with the ideal of achieving a slim body, she has eventually given up eating altogether. Anorexia and other eating disorders are illnesses of the affluent, not of those who have little or no food. It is completely unknown in the developing countries where food is scarce, such as Somalia.

Throughout much of human history, a few people such as saints or mystics have deliberately chosen to starve themselves for religious reasons. They were almost always men. Today, anorexia primarily affects women, and it has no specific connection to religious beliefs. It is an illness of the body, and thus we might think that we would have to look to biological or physical factors to explain it. But health and illness, like other topics we've studied, are also affected by social and cultural influences, such as the pressure to achieve a slim body.

Although it is an illness that expresses itself in physical symptoms, anorexia is closely related to the idea of being on a diet, which in turn is connected with changing views of physical

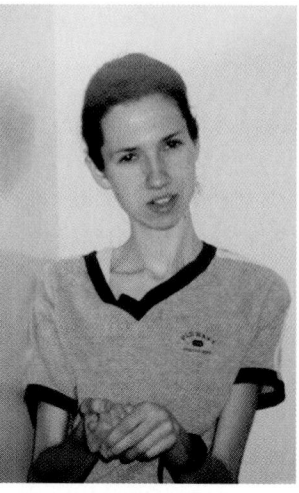

Take a look at the two women above: The first woman is painfully thin as a result of famine and malnutrition, sadly common problems in an area of the world plagued by frequent drought and crop failure. The second has become painfully thin by her own doing; people suffering from anorexia feel compelled by a variety of personal and social pressures to lose weight, and will often continue to view themselves as overweight even when they have reached a state of emaciation.

attractiveness, particularly of women, in modern society. In most premodern societies, the ideal female shape was a fleshy one. Thinness was not regarded as desirable at all—partly because it was associated with lack of food and therefore with poverty. Even in Europe in the 1600s and 1700s, the ideal female shape was well proportioned. Anyone who has seen paintings of the period, such as those by Rubens, will have noticed how curvaceous (even plump) the women depicted in them are. The notion of slimness as the desirable feminine shape originated among some middle-class groups in the late nineteenth century, but it has become generalized as an ideal for most women only recently.

Anorexia thus has its origins in the changing body image of women in the recent history of modern societies. It was first identified as a disorder in France in 1874, but it remained obscure until the past thirty or forty years (Brown and Jasper, 1993). Since then, it has become increasingly common among young women. So has bulimia—bingeing on food, followed by self-induced vomiting. Anorexia and bulimia are often found together in the same individual. Someone may become extremely thin through a starvation diet and then enter a phase of eating enormous amounts and purging in order to maintain a normal weight, followed by a period of again becoming very thin. Today, somewhere between 2 and 6 percent of the total U.S. population is afflicted with these conditions, over 85 percent of those affected are under the age of twenty (Rader Programs, 2003). Ninety percent of those who suffer

from these disorders are women. Anorexia has the highest mortality rate of any psychological disorder; 20 percent of those who suffer from anorexia will die from it (EDC, 2003).

Anorexia and other eating disorders are no longer obscure forms of illness in modern societies. The occurrence of eating disorders in the U.S. has doubled since 1960 (EDC, 2003). About 95 percent of U.S. college women say that they want to lose weight and up to 85 percent suffer serious problems with eating disorders at some point in their college careers. Around 25 percent experience bulimic episodes or anorexia. In American society, 60 percent of girls age thirteen have already begun to diet; this proportion rises to over 80 percent for young women of eighteen. College men also suffer similar experiences, though not in the same proportions. About 50 percent of American male college students claim that they want to lose weight, while about 30 percent are on diets (Hesse-Biber, 1997). Over 80 percent of ten-year-old children are afraid of being fat (EDC, 2003).

Nor is obsession with slenderness—and the resulting eating disorders—limited to women in the United States and Europe. As Western images of feminine beauty have spread to the rest of the world, so too have their associated illnesses. Eating disorders were first documented in Japan in the 1960s, a consequence of that county's rapid economic growth and incorporation into the global economy. Anorexia is now found among 2 percent of young Japanese women, and is occurring in younger and younger women (Curtin, 2003). During the past several years, eating problems have surfaced among young, primarily affluent women in Hong Kong and Singapore, as well as in urban areas in Taiwan, China, the Philippines, India, and Pakistan (Efron, 1997).

Once again, something that may seem to be a purely personal trouble—difficulties with food and despair over one's appearance—turns out to be a public issue. If we include not just life-threatening forms of anorexia but also obsessive concern with dieting and bodily appearance, eating disorders are now part of the lives of millions of people; they are found not only in the United States today but in all the industrial countries.

The astonishing spread of eating disorders brings home clearly the influence of social factors on our lives. The field known as **sociology of the body** investigates the ways in which our bodies are affected by these social influences. As human beings, we obviously all possess bodies. But the body isn't something we just have, and it isn't only something physical that exists outside of society. Our bodies are deeply affected by our social experiences, as well as by the norms and values of the groups to which we belong. It is only recently that sociologists have begun to recognize the profound nature of the interconnections between social life and the body. Therefore this field is quite a new area, but it is one of the most exciting.

Sociology of the body draws together a number of basic themes, which we will make use of throughout the chapter.

One major theme is the effects of social change on the body. A second theme is the increasing separation of the body from "nature"—from our surrounding environment and our biological rhythms. Our bodies are being invaded by the influence of science and technology, ranging from machines to diets, and this is creating new dilemmas. The invention of a range of reproductive technologies, for example, has introduced new options but has also generated intense social controversies. We will look at two such controversies, over genetic engineering and abortion, later in the chapter.

The term *technology* should not be understood in too narrow a way here. In its most basic sense, it refers to material technologies such as those involved in modern medicine—for example, the scanning machine that allows a doctor to chart a baby's development prior to birth. But we must also take account of what Michel Foucault (1988) has called "social technologies" affecting the body. By this phrase, he means that the body is increasingly something we have to "create" rather than simply accept. A **social technology** is any kind of regular intervention we make into the functioning of our bodies in order to alter them in specific ways. An example is dieting, so central to anorexia.

In this chapter, we will first analyze why eating disorders have become so common. From there, we will study the social dimensions of health and illness. Then we will turn to human sexuality, again by looking at the social and cultural influences on our sexual behavior.

The Sociology of Health and Illness

To understand why eating disorders have become so commonplace in current times, we should think back to the social changes analyzed earlier in the book. Anorexia actually reflects certain kinds of social change, including the impact of globalization.

The rise of eating disorders in Western societies coincides directly with the globalization of food production, which has increased greatly in the last three or four decades. The invention of new modes of refrigeration and container transportation have allowed food to be stored for long periods and to be delivered from one side of the world to the other. Since the 1950s, supermarket shelves have been abundant with foods from all parts of the world (for those who can afford it—now the majority of the population in Western societies). Most of them are available all the time, not just, as was true previously, when they are in season locally.

For the past decade or so, almost *everyone* in the United States and the other developed countries has been on a diet. This does not mean that everyone is desperately trying to get thin. Rather, when all foods are available more or less all the time, we must *decide* what to eat—in other words, construct a diet, where "diet" means the foods we habitually consume. First, we have to decide what to eat in relation to the many sorts of new medical information with which science now bombards us—for instance, that cholesterol levels are a factor in causing heart disease. Second, we can now worry about the calorie content of different foods. In a society in which food is abundant, we are able for the first time to design our bodies in relation to our lifestyle habits (such as jogging, bicycling, swimming, and yoga) and what we eat. Eating disorders have their origins in the opportunities, but also the profound strains and tensions, this situation produces.

Why do eating disorders affect women in particular and young women most acutely? To begin with, it should be pointed out that not all those suffering from eating disorders are women; about 10 percent are men. But men don't suffer from anorexia or bulimia as often as women, partly because widely held social norms stress the importance of physical attractiveness more for women than for men and partly because desirable body images of men differ from those of women.

Anorexia and other eating disorders reflect a situation in which women play a much larger part in the wider society than they used to but are still judged as much by their appearance as by their attainments. Eating disorders are rooted in feelings of shame about the body. The individual feels herself to be inadequate and imperfect, and her anxieties about how others perceive her become focused through her feelings about her body. Ideals of slimness at that point become obsessive—shedding weight becomes the means of making everything all right in her world. Once she starts to diet and exercise compulsively, she can become locked into a pattern of refusing food altogether or of vomiting up what she has eaten. If the pattern is not broken (some forms of psychotherapy and medical treatment have proved effective), the sufferer can actually starve herself to death.

The spread of eating disorders reflects the influence of science and technology on our ways of life today: Calorie counting has only been possible with the advance of technology. But the impact of technology is always conditioned by social factors. We have much more autonomy over the body than ever before, a situation that creates new possibilities of a positive kind as well as new anxieties and problems. What is happening is part of what sociologists call the **socialization of nature.** This phrase refers to the fact that phenomena that used to be "natural," or given in nature, have now become social—they depend on our own social decisions.

The Body Project

A century ago, American women were lacing themselves into corsets and teaching their adolescent daughters to do the same; today's teens shop for thong bikinis or midriff blouses on their own, and their middle-class mothers are likely to be uninvolved until the credit card bill arrives in the mail. These contrasting images might suggest a great deal of progress, but American girls at the end of the twentieth century actually suffer from body problems more pervasive and more dangerous than the constraints implied by the corset. Historical forces have made coming of age in a female body a different and more complex experience today than it was a century ago. Although sexual development—the onset of menstruation and the appearance of breasts—occurs in every generation, a girl's experience of these inevitable biological events is shaped by the world in which she lives, so much so, that each generation, at its own point in history, develops its own characteristic body problems and projects. Every girl suffers some kind of adolescent angst about her body; it is the historical moment that defines how she reacts to her changing flesh. From the perspective of history, adolescent self-consciousness is quite persistent, but its level is raised or lowered, like the water level in a pool, by the cultural and social setting. [***]

In a New Year's resolution written in 1982, a girl wrote: "I will try to make myself better in any way I possibly can with the help of my budget and baby-sitting money. I will lose weight, get new lenses, already got new haircut, good makeup, new clothes and accessories." This concise declaration clearly captures how girls feel about themselves in the contemporary

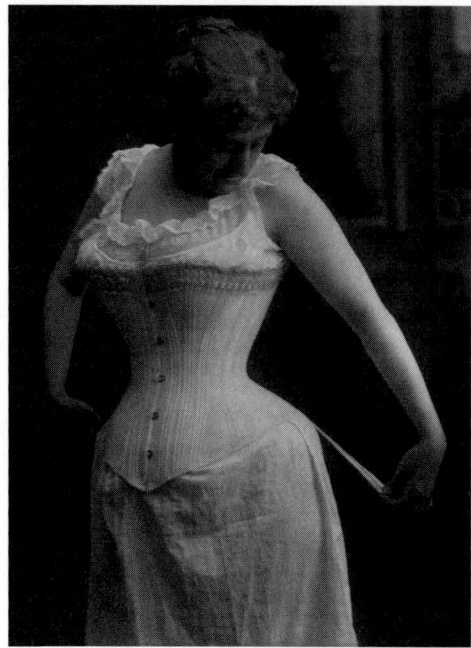

world. Like many adults in American society, girls today are concerned with the shape and appearance of their bodies as a primary expression of their individual identity. [***]

Today, unlike in the Victorian era, commercial interests play directly to the body angst of young girls, a marketing strategy that results in enormous revenues for manufacturers of skin and hair products as well as diet foods. Although elevated body angst is a great boost to corporate profits, it saps the creativity of girls and threatens their mental and physical health. Progress for women is obviously filled with ambiguities. [***]

Adolescent girls today face the issues girls have always faced—Who am I? Who do I want to be?—but their answers, more than ever before, revolve around the body. The increase in anorexia nervosa and bulimia in the past thirty years suggests that in some cases the body becomes an obsession, leading to recalcitrant eating behaviors that can result in death. But even among girls who never develop full-blown eating disorders, the body is so central to definitions of the self that psychologists sometimes use numerical scores of "body esteem" and "body dissatisfaction" to evaluate a girl's mental health. In the 1990s, tests that ask respondents to indicate levels of satisfaction or dissatisfaction with their own thighs or buttocks have become a useful key for unlocking the inner life of many American girls.

Why is the body still a girl's nemesis? Shouldn't today's sexually liberated girls feel better about themselves than their corseted sisters of a century ago? The historical evidence [***],

based on research that includes diaries written by American girls in the years between the 1830s and the 1990s, suggests that although young women today enjoy greater freedom and more options than their counterparts of a century ago, they are also under more pressure, and at greater risk, because of a unique combination of biological and cultural forces that have made the adolescent female body into a template for much of the social change of the twentieth century. I use the body as evidence to show how the mother-daughter connection has loosened, especially with regard to the experience of menstruation and sexuality; how doctors and marketers took over important educational functions that were once the special domain of female relatives and mentors; how scientific medicine, movies, and advertising created a new, more exacting ideal of physical perfection; and how changing standards of intimacy turned virginity into an outmoded ideal. The fact that American girls now make the body their central project is not an accident or a curiosity: it is a symptom of historical changes that are only now beginning to be understood.

SOURCE: Joan Jacobs Brumberg, *The Body Project* (New York: Vintage, 1997).

Questions

- What cultural and social factors may have driven girls to view their bodies as a primary source of their identities?
- How do the insecurities of adolescent girls affect the rest of the population, male and female?
- Can our culture avoid commodifying the body? Why are adolescent girls a primary target for marketers and manufacturers?

Sociological Perspectives on Health and Illness

One of the main concerns of sociologists is to examine the experience of illness—how being sick, chronically ill, or disabled is experienced and interpreted by sick persons and by those with whom they come in contact. If you have ever been ill, even for a short period of time, you know that patterns in everyday life are temporarily modified and your interactions with others become transformed. This is because the normal functioning of the body is a vital, but often unnoticed, part of our lives. We depend on our bodies to operate as they should; our very sense of self is predicated on the expectation that our bodies will facilitate, not impede, our social interactions and daily activities.

Illness has both personal and public dimensions. When we fall ill, not only do *we* experience pain, discomfort, confusion, and other challenges, but others are affected as well. People in close contact with us may extend sympathy, care, and support. They may struggle to make sense of the fact of our illness or to find ways to incorporate it into the patterns of their own lives. Others with whom we come into contact may also react to illness; these reactions in turn help to shape our own interpretations and can pose challenges to our sense of self.

Two ways of understanding the experience of illness have been particularly influential in sociological thought. The first, associated with the functionalist school, sets forth the norms of behavior that individuals are thought to adopt when sick. The second view, favored by symbolic interactionists, is a broader attempt to reveal the interpretations that are ascribed to illness and how these meanings influence people's actions and behavior.

THE SICK ROLE

The prominent functionalist thinker Talcott Parsons advanced the notion of the **sick role** in order to describe the patterns of behavior that the sick person adopts in order to minimize the disruptive impact of illness (Parsons, 1951). Functionalist thought holds that society usually operates in a smooth and consensual manner. Illness is therefore seen as a dysfunction that can disrupt the flow of this normal state of being. A sick individual, for example, might not be able to perform all of his or her standard responsibilities or might be less reliable and efficient than usual. Because sick people are not able to carry out their normal roles, the lives of people around them are disrupted: Assignments at work go unfinished and cause stress for coworkers, responsibilities at home are not fulfilled, and so forth.

According to Parsons, people learn the sick role through socialization and enact it—with the cooperation of others—when they fall ill. There are three pillars of the sick role:

1. **The sick person is not personally responsible for being sick.** Illness is seen as the result of physical causes beyond the individual's control. The onset of illness is unrelated to the individual's behavior or actions.

2. **The sick person is entitled to certain rights and privileges, including a withdrawal from normal responsibilities.** Since the sick person bears no responsibility for the illness, he or she is exempted from certain duties, roles, and behaviors that otherwise apply. For example, the sick person might be released from normal duties around the home. Behavior that is not as polite or thoughtful as usual might be excused. The sick person gains the right to stay in bed, for example, or to take time off from work.

3. **The sick person must work to regain health by consulting a medical expert and agreeing to become a patient.** The sick role is a temporary and conditional one that is contingent on the sick person's actively trying to get well. In order to occupy the sick role, the sick person must receive the sanction of a medical professional who legitimates the person's claim of illness. Confirmation of illness via an expert opinion allows those surrounding the sick person to accept the validity of his or her claims. The patient is expected to cooperate in his or her own recovery by following the doctor's orders. A sick person who refuses to consult a doctor or who does not heed the advice of a medical authority puts his or her sick-role status in jeopardy.

Parson's sick-role idea has been refined by other sociologists, who suggest that all illnesses are not the same as far as the sick role is concerned. They argue that the experience of the sick role varies with the type of illness, since people's reactions to a sick person are influenced by the severity of the illness and by their perception of it. Thus, everyone will not uniformly experience the added rights and privileges that are part of the sick role. Freidson (1970) has identified three versions of the sick role that correspond with different types and degrees of illness. The *conditional* sick role applies to individuals who are suffering from a temporary condition from which they can recover. The sick person is expected to get well and receives some rights and privileges according to the severity of the illness. For example, someone suffering from bronchitis would reap more benefits than the sufferer of a common cold. The *unconditionally legitimate* sick role refers to individuals who are suffering from incurable illnesses. Because the sick person cannot do anything to get well, he or she is automatically entitled to occupy the sick role. The unconditionally legitimate role might apply to individuals suffering from alopecia (total hair loss) or severe acne (in both cases there are no special privileges but rather an acknowledgment that the individual is not responsible for the illness), or from cancer or Parkinson's disease—which result in important privileges and the right to abandon many or most duties. The final sick role is the *illegitimate* role. The illegitimate role applies when an individual suffers from a disease or condition that is stigmatized by others. In such cases, there is a sense that the individual might somehow bear responsibility for the illness; additional rights and privileges are not necessarily granted. HIV/AIDS is perhaps the most vivid example of a stigmatized illness that affects a sufferer's right to assume the sick role.

A **stigma** is any characteristic that sets an individual or group apart from the majority of the population, with the result that the individual or group is treated with suspicion or hostility. As we have seen, most forms of illness arouse feelings of sympathy or compassion among nonsufferers, and the ill person receives special privileges. When an illness is seen as uncommonly infectious, however, or is perceived as somehow a mark of dishonor or shame, sufferers may be rejected by the healthy population. This was true in the Middle Ages of people afflicted with leprosy, who were popularly disowned and forced to live in separate leper colonies. HIV/AIDS often provokes such stigmatization today—in spite of the fact that, as with leprosy, the danger of contracting the disease in ordinary day-to-day situations is almost nil. For instance, the United Nations Joint Program with the World Health Organization on HIV/AIDS reports incidences in Kerala, India, where children infected with HIV have been barred from their schools and effectively denied any interaction with other children (UNAIDS, 2003). Stigmas, however, are rarely based on valid understandings. They spring from stereotypes or perceptions that may be false or only partially correct.

EVALUATION

The sick role model has been an influential theory that reveals clearly how the ill person is an integral part of a larger social context. But a number of criticisms can be levied against it. Some writers have argued that the sick-role formula is unable to capture the *experience* of illness. Others point out that it cannot be applied universally. For example, the sick role theory does not account for instances when doctors and patients disagree about a diagnosis or have opposing interests. It also fails to explain those illnesses that do not necessarily lead to a suspension of normal activity, such as alcoholism, certain disabilities, and some chronic diseases. Furthermore, assuming the sick role is not always a straightforward process. Some individuals suffer for years from chronic pain or from symptoms that are repeatedly misdiagnosed. They are denied the sick role until a clear diagnosis of their condition is made. In other cases, social factors such as race, class, and gender can affect whether and how readily the sick role is granted. The sick role cannot be divorced from the social, cultural, and economic influences that surround it.

The realities of life and illness are more complex than the sick role suggests. The increasing emphasis on lifestyle and health in our modern age means that individuals are seen as bearing ever greater responsibility for their own well-being. This contradicts the first premise of the sick role—that the individual is not to blame for his or her illness. Moreover, in modern societies the shift away from acute infectious disease toward chronic illness has made the sick role less applicable. Whereas the sick role might be useful in understanding acute illness, it is less useful in the case of chronic illness: There is no one formula for chronically ill or disabled people to follow. Living with illness is experienced and interpreted in a multiplicity of ways by sick people—and by those who surround them.

We will now turn to some of the ways that sociologists of the symbolic interactionist school have attempted to understand the experience of illness.

ILLNESS AS "LIVED EXPERIENCE"

Symbolic interactionists are interested in the ways people interpret the social world and the meanings they ascribe to it. Many sociologists have applied this approach to the realm of health and illness in order to understand how people experience being ill or perceive the illness of others. How do people react and adjust to news about a serious illness? How does illness shape individuals' daily lives? How does living with a chronic illness affect an individual's self-identity?

We have seen that patterns of disease have been changing in modern societies. Rather than dying of acute, infectious diseases as was once the case, people in industrialized societies are now living longer and suffering later in life from chronic illnesses. Medicine is able to relieve the pain and discomfort associated with some of these conditions, but a growing number of people are faced with the prospect of living with illness over a long period of time. Sociologists are concerned with how illness in such cases becomes incorporated into an individual's personal biography.

One theme that sociologists have explored is how chronically ill individuals learn to cope with the practical and emotional implications of their illness. Certain illnesses demand regular treatments or maintenance that can affect people's daily routines. Undergoing dialysis or insulin injections, or taking large numbers of pills demand that individuals adjust their schedules in response to illness. Other illnesses can have unpredictable effects on the body, such as the sudden loss of bowel or bladder control or violent nausea. Individuals suffering from such conditions often develop strategies for managing their illness in day-to-day life. These include both practical considerations—such as always noting the location of the toilet when in an unfamiliar place—as well as skills for managing interpersonal relations, both intimate and commonplace. Although the symptoms of the illness can be embarrassing and disruptive, people develop coping strategies to live life as normally as possible (Kelly, 1992).

At the same time, the experience of illness can pose challenges to and bring about transformations in people's sense of self. These develop both through the actual reactions of others to the illness and through imagined or perceived reactions. For the chronically ill or disabled, social interactions that are routine for many people become tinged with risk or uncertainty. The shared understandings that underpin standard everyday interactions are not always present when illness or disability is a factor, and interpretations of common situations may differ substantially. An ill person may be in need of assistance but not want to appear dependent, for example. An individual may feel sympathy for someone who has been diagnosed with an illness but be unsure whether to address the subject directly. The changed context of social interactions can precipitate transformations in self-identity.

Some sociologists have investigated how chronically ill individuals manage their illnesses within the overall context of their lives (Jobling, 1988; Williams, 1993). Illness can place enormous demands on people's time, energy, strength, and emotional reserves. Corbin and Strauss (1985) studied the *regimes of health* that the chronically ill develop in order to organize their daily lives. They identified three types of "work" contained in people's everyday strategies. *Illness work* refers to those activities involved in managing their condition, such as treating pain, doing diagnostic tests, or undergoing physical therapy. *Everyday work* pertains to the management of daily life—maintaining relationships with others, running household affairs, and pursuing professional or personal interests. *Biographical work* involves those activities that the ill person does as part of building or reconstructing their personal narrative. In other words, it is the process of incorporating the illness into one's life, making sense of it, and developing ways of explaining it to others. Such a process can help people restore meaning and order to their lives after coming to terms with the knowledge of chronic illness.

The work of symbolic interactionists on living with illness is one of the most relevant dimensions of the sociology of the body. We are living in a society in which individuals are living longer and leading more active lives in their later years than ever before, but in some cases this also means living longer with illness and anxiety.

Changing Conceptions of Health and Illness

Cultures differ in what they consider healthy and normal, as the discussion of eating disorders showed. All cultures have known concepts of physical health and illness, but most of what we now recognize as medicine is a consequence of developments in Western society over the past three centuries. In premodern cultures, the family was the main institution coping with sickness or affliction. There have always been individuals who specialized as healers, using a mixture of physical and magical remedies, and many of these traditional systems of treatment survive today in non-Western cultures throughout the world. For instance, Ayurvedic medicine (traditional healing) has been practiced in India for nearly two thousand years. It is founded on a theory of the equilibrium of psychological and physical facets of the personality, imbalances of which are treated by nutritional and herbal remedies. Chinese folk medicine is similarly based on a conception of the overall harmony of the personality, involving the use of herbs and acupuncture, a technique in which needles are strategically inserted into a patient's skin.

Modern medicine introduced a view of disease that sees its origins and treatment as physical and explicable in scientific terms. The application of science to medical diagnosis and cure was the major feature of the development of modern health care

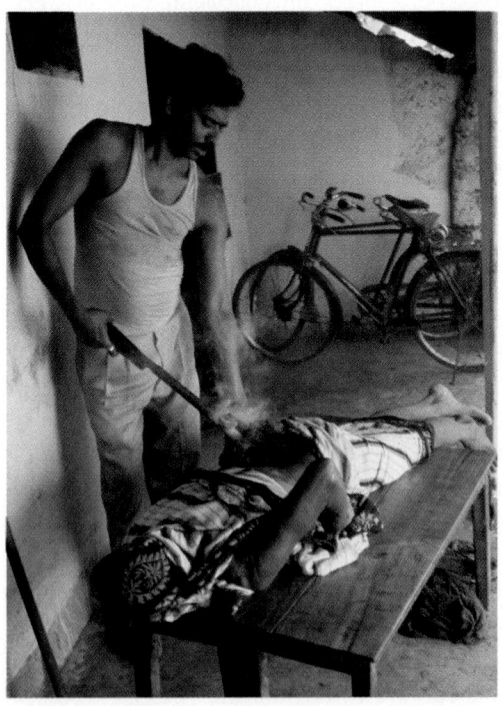

Ayurvedic treatment: Ayurvedic physician Kumar Das uses a hot iron rod and fabric soaked in herbs to heal an arthritic hip.

systems. Other, closely related features were the acceptance of the hospital as the setting within which serious illnesses were to be dealt with and the development of the medical profession as a body with recognized codes of ethics and significant social power. The scientific view of disease was linked to the requirement that medical training be systematic and long term; self-taught healers were excluded. Although professional medical practice is not limited to hospitals, the hospital provided an environment in which doctors for the first time were able to treat and study large numbers of patients, in circumstances permitting the concentration of medical technology.

In medieval times, the major illnesses were infectious diseases such as tuberculosis, cholera, malaria, and bubonic plague. The plague, or Black Death, epidemic of the fourteenth century (which was spread by fleas carried by rats) killed a quarter of the population of England and devastated large areas of Europe. Infectious diseases have now become a minor cause of death in industrialized countries, and several have been substantially eradicated. In industrialized countries, the most common causes of death are noninfectious diseases such as cancer and heart disease. Whereas in premodern societies the highest rates of death were among infants and young children, today death rates (the proportion of the population who die each year) rise with increasing age.

In spite of the prestige that modern medicine has acquired, improvements in medical care accounted for only a relatively minor part of the decline in death rates prior to the twentieth century. Effective sanitation, better nutrition, control of sewage, and improved hygiene were more consequential, particularly in reducing the infant mortality rate and the number of deaths of young children. Drugs, advances in surgery, and antibiotics did not significantly decrease death rates until well into the twentieth century. Antibiotics used to treat bacterial infections first became available in the 1930s and 1940s; most immunizations (against diseases such as polio) were developed later.

Alternative Medicine

Earlier in her life, Jan Mason enjoyed vibrant health. But when she began experiencing extreme fatigue and depression, she found that her regular doctor was unable to provide her much relief:

Before, I was a very fit person. I could swim, play squash, run, and suddenly I just keeled over. I went to the doctor but nobody could tell me what it was. My GP said it was glandular fever and gave me antibiotics which gave me terrible thrush. Then he kept saying that he did not know what is was either. . . I went through

all the tests. I was really very poorly. It went on for six months. I was still ill and they still did not know what it was. (Quoted in Sharma, 1992)

Jan's doctor suggested that she try antidepressants, concluding that she was suffering from the effects of stress. Jan knew that antidepressants were not the answer for her, even though she acknowledged that her undiagnosed condition had become a great stress in her life. After listening to a radio program, Jan suspected that her lethargy might be a result of postviral fatigue syndrome. On the advice of a friend, she sought out the assistance of a *homeopath*—an alternative medical practitioner who assesses the state of the whole body and then, using minuscule doses of substance, treats "like with like," on the assumption that the symptoms of a disease are part of a body's self-healing process. On finding a homeopath with whose approach she was comfortable, Jan was pleased with the treatment she received (Sharma, 1992).

Did it work? Did she get better? Jan is one of a growing number of people who incorporate nonorthodox medical practices into their health routines. In many industrialized societies over the last decade, there has been a surge of interest in the potential of *alternative medicine*. The number of alternative medical practitioners is expanding, as are the forms of healing that are available. From herbal remedies to acupuncture, from reflexology to chiropractic treatments, modern society is witnessing an explosion of health care alternatives that lie outside, or overlap with, the official medical system. It has been estimated that as many as one in ten Americans has consulted an alternative practitioner. The profile of the typical individual who seeks out alternative forms of healing is female, young to middle-aged, and middle class.

Industrialized countries have some of the best-developed, best-resourced medical facilities in the world. Why, then, are a growing number of people choosing to abandon the health care system for unscientific treatments such as aromatherapy and hypnotherapy? First, it is important to stress that not everyone who uses alternative medicine does so as a substitute for orthodox treatment (although some alternative approaches, such as homeopathy, reject the basis of orthodox medicine entirely). Many people combine elements of both approaches. For this reason, some scholars prefer to call nonorthodox techniques *complementary* medicine, rather than alternative medicine (Saks, 1992).

There are many reasons that individuals might seek the services of an alternative medicine practitioner. Some people perceive orthodox medicine to be deficient or incapable of relieving chronic, nagging pains or symptoms of stress and anxiety. Others are dissatisfied with the way modern health care systems function—long waits, referrals through chains of specialists, financial restrictions, and so forth. Connected to this are concerns about the harmful side effects of medication and the intrusiveness of surgery—both techniques favored by modern health care systems. The asymmetrical power relationship between doctors and patients is at the heart of some people's choice to avail themselves of alternative medicine. They feel that the role of the passive patient does not grant them enough input into their own treatment and healing. Finally, some individuals profess religious or philosophical objections to orthodox medicine, which tends to treat the mind and body separately. They believe that the spiritual and psychological dimensions of health and illness are often not taken into account in the practice of orthodox medicine. All these concerns are implicit or explicit critiques of the **biomedical model of health,** the foundation on which the Western medical establishment operates. The biomedical model of health defines disease in objective terms and believes that the healthy body can be restored through scientifically based medical treatment.

The growth of alternative medicine presents a number of interesting questions for sociologists to consider. First and foremost, it is a fascinating reflection of the transformations occurring within modern societies. We are living in an age where more and more information is available—from a variety of sources—to draw on in making choices about our lives. Health care is no exception in this regard. Individuals are increasingly becoming health consumers—adopting an active stance towards their own health and well-being. Not only are we able to make choices about the type of practitioners to consult, but we are also demanding more involvement in our own care and treatment. In this way the growth of alternative medicine is linked to the expansion of the self-help movement, which involves support groups, learning circles, and self-help books. People are now more likely than ever before to seize control of their lives and actively reshape them, rather than to rely on the instructions or opinions of others.

Another issue of interest to sociologists relates to the changing nature of health and illness in the late modern period. Many of the conditions and illnesses for which individuals seek alternative medical treatment seem to be products of the modern age itself. Insomnia, anxiety, stress, depression, fatigue, and chronic pain (caused by arthritis, cancer, and other diseases) are all on the rise in industrialized societies. Although these conditions have long existed, they appear to be causing greater distress and disruption to people's health than ever before. Recent surveys have revealed that stress has now surpassed the common cold as the biggest cause of absence from work. The World Health Organization predicts that within twenty years, depression will be the most debilitating disease in the world. Ironically, it seems that these consequences of modernity are ones that orthodox medicine has great difficulty in addressing. Alternative medicine is unlikely to overtake mainstream health care altogether, but indications are that its role will continue to grow.

The Social Basis of Health

The twentieth century witnessed a significant overall rise in life expectancy for people who live in industrialized countries. Diseases such as polio, scarlet fever, and tuberculosis have virtually been eradicated. Compared with those in other parts of the world, standards of health and well-being are relatively high. Many of these advances in public health have been attributed to the power of modern medicine. It is a commonly held assumption that medical research has been—and will continue to be—successful in uncovering the biological causes of disease and in developing effective treatments to control them. As medical knowledge and expertise grow, the argument runs, we can expect to see sustained and steady improvements in public health.

Although this approach to health and disease has been extremely influential, it is somewhat unsatisfactory for sociologists. This is because it ignores the important role of social and environmental influences on patterns of health and illness. The improvements in overall public health over the past century cannot conceal the fact that health and illness are not distributed evenly throughout the population. Research has shown that certain groups of people tend to enjoy much better health than others. These *health inequalities* appear to be tied to larger socioeconomic patterns.

Sociologists and scientists in social **epidemiology**—the science that studies the distribution and incidence of disease and illness within the population—have attempted to explain the link between health and variables such as social class, gender, race, age, and geography. While most scholars acknowledge the correlation between health and social inequalities, there is no agreement about the nature of the connection or about how health inequalities should be addressed. One of the main areas of debate concentrates on the relative importance of individual variables (e.g., lifestyle, behavior, diet, and cultural patterns) versus environmental or structural factors (e.g., income distribution and poverty; see Figure 18.1). In this section, we will look at variations in health patterns in the United States according to social class, gender, race, and geography, and review some of the competing explanations for their persistence.

SOCIAL CLASS-BASED INEQUALITIES IN HEALTH

Think about the way that we have previously defined "social class" in Chapter 8, as a concept that partakes of education,

FIGURE 18.1

Cultural and Material Influences on Health

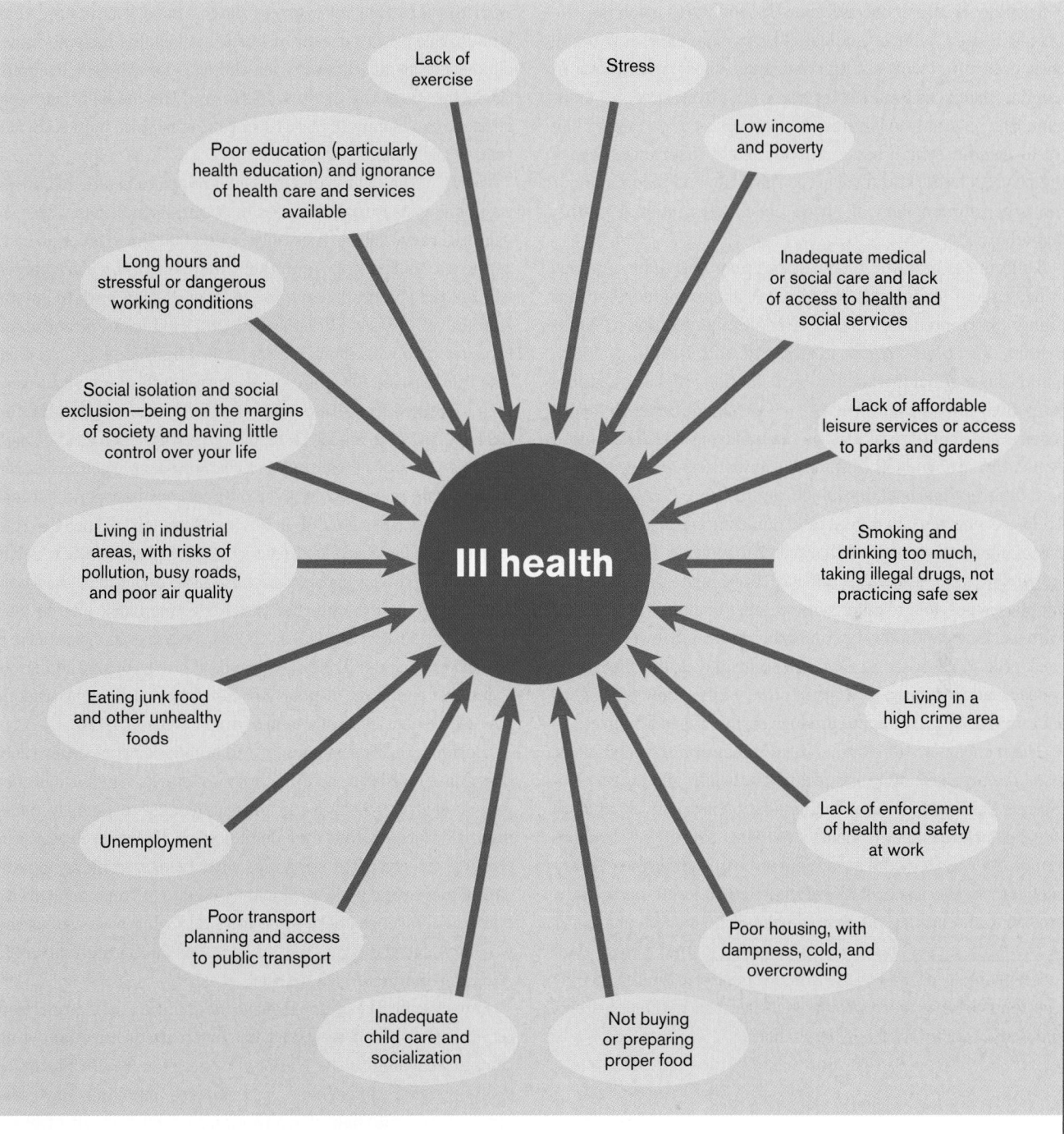

SOURCE: K. Browne, *An Introduction to Sociology,* 2nd ed. (Cambridge, UK: Polity, 1998). From *Sociology Review* 9.2 (November 1999), p. 5. Crown copyright.

income, and occupation. In American society, people with better educations, higher incomes, and more prestigious occupations have better health. What is fascinating is that each of these dimensions of social class may be related to health and mortality for different reasons.

Income is the most obvious. In countries such as the United States, where medical care is expensive and many persons are not covered by insurance, those with more financial resources have better access to physicians and medicine. But inequalities in health also persist in countries like Great Britain, which have national health insurance. One of the ways to understand this is to think beyond income about the other dimensions of social class, occupational status, and education.

Differences in occupational status may lead to inequalities in health and illness even when medical care is more or less evenly distributed. One study of health inequalities in Great Britain, *The Black Report* (Townsend and Davidson, 1982), found that manual workers had substantially higher mortality rates than professional workers, even though Britain's health service had made great strides in equalizing the distribution of health care. Indeed, different occupations are associated with different levels of on-the-job health risks.

Those who work in offices or in domestic settings are at less risk of injury or exposure to hazardous materials. The extent of industrial-based disease is difficult to calculate, because it is not always possible to determine whether an illness is acquired from working conditions or from other sources. However, some work-related diseases are well documented: Lung disease is widespread in mining, as a result of dust inhalation; work with asbestos has been shown to produce certain types of cancer.

Differences in education, a third dimension of social class, also are correlated with inequalities in health and illness. Numerous studies document that education is positively related to preventative health behaviors. One set of researchers found that better-educated people are significantly more likely to engage in aerobic exercise and to know their blood pressure, and are less likely to smoke or be overweight (Shea et al., 1991). Other researchers have found that poorly educated people tend to engage in more cigarette smoking; they also tend to have more problems associated with cholesterol and body weight (Winkleby et al., 1992).

RACE-BASED INEQUALITIES IN HEALTH

Life expectancy at birth in 2000 was about eighty years for white females but just seventy-five years for black females. Likewise, life expectancy at birth in 2000 was seventy-five years for white males yet just sixty-nine years for black males (U.S. Bureau of the Census, 2001d).

Health differences between blacks and whites are significant. When we note such differences, we are making use of a variable—race—that although different from social class, cannot be completely separated from it. One primary reason for inequalities of health between blacks and whites has to do with the fact that as a group blacks have less money than whites. Sixty-two percent of black households have no financial assets at all, almost twice the rate for white households (U.S. Bureau of the Census, 1998). And the median income of a black man is only 12 percent of that of a white man (U.S. Bureau of the Census, 2002).

Some of the differences in black and white health go beyond economic causes to differences in cultural conditions. Take, for example, racial gaps in mortality. Young black men are more susceptible to murder than any other group. In 2000, a black person was six times more likely to be murdered than a white person (Bureau of Justice Statistics, 2002a). Homicide victimization rates for both whites and blacks peaked between 1993 and 1994. The murder rate for white males between fourteen and seventeen increased from 9.4 per 100,000 in 1984 to a high of 22.4 in 1994. By 2000, the murder rate for young white men had declined to 7.9 per 100,000, lower than in 1984. For young black males, the murder rate increased by over 500 percent between 1984 and 1994 (from 47.6 per 100,000 in 1984 to 244 in 1993). Since then the murder rate for blacks has declined to 62.8 per 100,000, which is nearly 800 percent higher than for whites and still over 30 percent higher than the murder rate for young black men in 1984 (Bureau of Justice Statistics, 2002a). This rise in violent crime has accompanied the rise of widespread crack cocaine addiction, a cultural condition of poor African American neighborhoods plagued by high levels of unemployment (Wilson, 1996).

Besides the life expectancy and homicide rates, other race-based inequalities in health status are stark. There is a higher prevalence of hypertension among blacks—especially black men, a difference that may be biological. There are racial differences in cigarette smoking, with blacks smoking significantly more than whites. This may be due in some measure to cultural differences between blacks and whites, as well as the way in which the cigarette industry has deliberately targeted African Americans as a market.

But despite these depressing inequalities, it is important to note that some progress has been made in eradicating them. According to the National Center for Health Statistics (2003), racial differences in cigarette smoking have decreased. In 1965, half of white men and 60 percent of black men age eighteen and over smoked cigarettes. By 2001, only 25 percent of white men and 27 percent of black men smoked. In 1965, roughly equal proportions of black and white women age eighteen and older smoked (33–34 percent). In 2001, a smaller proportion of black women (20 percent) smoked than did white women (22 percent).

Prevalence of hypertension among blacks has been greatly reduced. In the early 1970s, half of black adults suffered from hypertension. By 1994, however, roughly 36 percent of black adults suffered from hypertension (National Center for Health Statistics, 2003).

Patterns of physician visitation, hospitalization, and preventive medicine have also changed. In 1987, only 30 percent of white women and 24 percent of black women aged forty and older reported having a mammogram within the past two years. By 2000, the rate for white women more than doubled to 71 percent, and that for black women increased over 2.5 times to 68 percent (National Center for Health Statistics, 2003c). Between 1983 and 2001, the proportion of blacks who had visited the dentist within the past year had increased from 39 percent to 57 percent, while the figure for whites increased from 57 percent to 67 percent (National Center for Health Statistics, 2003d).

How might the influence of poverty on health be countered? Extensive programs of health education and disease prevention are one possibility. But such programs tend to work better among more prosperous, well-educated groups and in any case usually produce only small changes in behavior. Increased accessibility to health services would help, but probably to a limited degree. The only really effective policy option is to attack poverty itself, so as to reduce the income gap between rich and poor (Najman, 1993).

GENDER-BASED INEQUALITIES IN HEALTH

Women in the United States are likely to live longer than men. This gender gap is, interestingly, a relatively recent phenomenon. In the United States, there was only a two-year difference in female and male life expectancies in 1900. By 1940, this gap increased to 4.4 years, and by 1970, the gap had widened to 7.7 years. The gender gap has since been stabilized at about 6 years (Cleary, 1987; National Center for Health Statistics, 2001).

How can we explain this changing gender gap? The main reason is that the leading cause of death has changed since the turn of the century. In 1900, the leading cause of death was infectious disease, which struck men, women, and children equally. Since mid-century, however, heart disease and cancer have been the leading causes of death for American adults. Heart disease and cancer are influenced by lifestyle, diet, and behavior—all of which are subject to gender differences.

Thus, social explanations for women's mortality advantage tend to focus on behavioral differences between men and women, including smoking, drinking, and preventive health behaviors. Men are more likely to smoke cigarettes than are women, and smoking is associated with heart disease and various types of cancer. Likewise, higher proportions of men than women drink alcoholic beverages, admit to "binge drinking," and smoke marijuana (National Center for Health Statistics, 1996).

Some researchers argue that male roles lead men to adopt the Coronary Prone Behavior Pattern, or Type A personality, and that Type A personalities (i.e., persons who are competitive, impatient, ambitious, and aggressive) are twice as likely as "laid back" (Type B) personalities to suffer heart attacks (Spielberger et al., 1991). Indirect evidence for this hypothesis comes from examining gender differences in hypertension (i.e., elevated blood pressure or taking antihypertensive medication). In the early 1990s, 25 percent of men and 20 percent of women aged twenty to seventy-four reported having hypertension (see National Center for Health Statistics, 1996). By 2000, however, the differences between genders in the occurrence of hypertension had been reduced to less than 1.5 percent (National Center for Health Statistics, 2003b). This may indicate that the "gender gap" in Type A personalities has declined, as more and more women enter the work force and pursue careers. Other factors (such as diet) may contribute to the convergence of hypertension between men and women. More research will have to be done before any firm conclusions can be drawn.

Sociologists tend to focus on societal factors in explaining these differences, but biological arguments should also be considered. One study tested the hypothesis that higher male mortality rates are due to the greater stresses of the male role in the 1950s (competitiveness of the work force, pressure for success and high earnings) compared with the "easy life" that wives and mothers were believed to have. The study was conducted on men and women who shared equal roles and equal stresses: nuns and monks. The nuns lived longer than the monks, and both had life expectancies essentially the same as the rest of the population. Because the environment was equalized for the two groups, lifestyle factors such as diet, drinking, and stress could be ruled out as explanatory factors (Madigan, 1957). However, critics of this study note that the monks smoked more than the nuns did, so that lifestyle differences were not entirely accounted for.

Biologists have also cited the existence of genetic factors. Humans have twenty-three pairs of chromosomes, one of which determines sex. Males have XY sex chromosomes, while females have two X chromosomes. The X chromosome carries more genetic information than the Y, including some defects that can lead to physical abnormalities. Instead of making females more vulnerable to X-linked disorders, this seems to give females a genetic advantage. A female typically needs two defective X chromosomes for most genetically linked disorders to manifest themselves; otherwise, one healthy X chromosome can override the abnormal one. A male who has a defective X chromosome will have a genetically linked disease no other X chromosome to cancel it out. This [ac]count for the higher number of miscarriages of [...] and for the greater ratio of male-to-female infant [...]d deaths at all ages due to congenital abnormalities [...]ck, 1994).

Despite the female advantage in mortality, most large surveys show women more often report poor health. Women have higher rates of illness from acute conditions and nonfatal chronic conditions, including arthritis, osteoporosis, and depressive and anxiety disorders. They are slightly more likely to report their health as fair to poor, they spend about 40 percent more days in bed each year, and their activities are restricted due to health problems about 25 percent more than men. In addition, they make more physician visits each year and have twice the number of surgical procedures performed on them as do men (National Center for Health Statistics, 1996, 2003e, 2003f).

There are two main explanations for women's poorer health, yet longer lives: (1) Greater life expectancy and age brings poorer health; (2) women make greater use of medical services including preventive care (Centers for Disease Control and Prevention, 2003a). In 2000, the average number of visits to physician offices, hospital emergency rooms, and hospital outpatient departments was 25 percent higher for women than for men. Men may experience as many or more health symptoms as women, but men may ignore symptoms, may underestimate the extent of their illness, or may utilize preventive services less often (Waldron, 1986).

Social Cohesion: The Key to Better Health?

In trying to unravel the causes of health inequalities, a growing number of sociologists are turning their attention to the role of social support and social cohesion in promoting good health. As you may recall from our discussion of Durkheim, social solidarity is one of the most important concepts in sociology. Durkheim saw the degree and type of solidarity within a culture as one of its most critical features. In his study of suicide, for example, he found that individuals and groups who were well integrated into society were less likely to take their own lives than were others.

In several articles and in his subsequent book, *Unhealthy Societies: The Afflictions of Inequality* (1996), Richard Wilkinson argues that the healthiest societies in the world are not the richest countries, but those in which income is distributed most evenly and levels of social integration are highest. High levels of national wealth, according to Wilkinson, do not necessarily translate into better health for the population. In surveying empirical data from countries around the world, Wilkinson notes a clear relationship between mortality rates and patterns of income distribution. Inhabitants of countries such as Japan and Sweden, which are regarded as some of the most egalitarian societies in the world, enjoy better levels of health on average than do citizens of countries where the gap between the rich and the poor is more pronounced, such as the United States.

In Wilkinson's view, the widening gap in income distribution undermines social cohesion and makes it more difficult for people to manage risks and challenges. Heightened social isolation and the failure to cope with stress is reflected in health indicators. Wilkinson argues that social factors—the strength of social contacts, ties within communities, availability of social support, a sense of security—are the main determinants of the relative health of a society.

Wilkinson's thesis has provoked energetic responses. Some claim that his work should become required reading for policy makers and politicians. They agree with Wilkinson that too much emphasis has been placed on market relations and the drive toward prosperity. This approach has failed many members of society, they argue; it is time to consider more humane and socially responsible policies to support those who are disadvantaged. Others criticize his study on methodological grounds and argue that he has failed to show a clear causal relationship between income inequality and poor health (Judge, 1995). Illness, critics contend, could be caused by any number of other mediating factors. They argue that the empirical evidence for his claims remains suggestive at best.

Whereas Wilkinson investigates the links between social cohesion and health at the level of society as a whole, other sociologists have focused on particular segments of the population. Heather Graham has studied the effects of stress on the health of white working-class women. She has highlighted the fact that women at the lower socioeconomic end of the spectrum have less access to support networks in times of life crisis than do middle-class women. Working-class women, she notes, tend to encounter life crises (such as job loss, divorce, eviction from housing, or the death of a child) more often than other groups but generally have weaker coping skills and fewer outlets for anxiety. Not only is the resulting stress harmful both physically and psychologically, but some of the coping strategies these women turn to—such as smoking—are also damaging. Graham argues that smoking is a way of reducing tension when personal and material resources are stretched to the breaking point. Thus, it occupies a paradoxical position in women's lives—increasing the health risk for women and their children while simultaneously allowing them to cope under difficult circumstances (Graham, 1987, 1994).

Ann Oakley and her colleagues have studied the role of social support in the health of socially disadvantaged women

and children in four English cities. They argue that the relationship between stress and health applies to both major life crises and smaller problems and that it is felt particularly acutely in the lives of working-class people. Oakley notes that social support—such as counseling services, hotlines, or home visits—can act as a buffer against the negative health consequences of stress commonly experienced by women (Oakley et al., 1994). Other studies have shown that social support is an important factor that can help people in adjusting to disease and illness (Ell, 1996).

The Developing World: Colonialism and the Spread of Disease

There is good evidence that the hunting and gathering communities of the Americas, prior to the arrival of the Europeans, were not as subject to infectious disease as the European societies of the period. Many infectious organisms only thrive when human populations are living above the density characteristic of hunting and gathering life. Permanently settled communities, particularly large cities, risk contamination of water supplies by waste products. Hunters and gatherers were less vulnerable in this respect because they moved continuously across the countryside.

The expansion of the West in the colonial era transmitted certain diseases into other parts of the world where they had not existed previously. Smallpox, measles, and typhus, among other major maladies, were unknown to the indigenous populations of Central and South America prior to the Spanish conquest in the early sixteenth century. The English and French colonists brought the same diseases to North America (Dubos, 1959). Some of these illnesses produced epidemics so severe that they ravaged or completely wiped out native populations, which had little or no resistance to them.

In Africa and subtropical parts of Asia, infectious diseases have almost certainly been rife for a long period of time. Tropical and subtropical conditions are especially conducive to diseases such as malaria, carried by mosquitoes, and sleeping sickness, carried by the tsetse fly. Yet it seems probable that prior to contact with the Europeans, levels of risk from infectious diseases were lower. There was always the threat of epidemics, drought, or natural disaster, but colonialism led to major changes in the relation between populations and their environments, producing harmful effects on health patterns. The Europeans introduced new farming methods, upsetting the ecology of whole regions. For example, wide tracts of East Africa today are completely devoid of cattle as a result of the uncontrolled spread of the tsetse fly, which multiplied as a result of the changes the intruders introduced. (The tsetse fly carries illnesses which are fatal to both humans and livestock.) Before the arrival of the Europeans, Africans successfully maintained large herds in these same areas (Kjekshus, 1977).

The most significant consequence of the colonial system was its effect on nutrition and therefore on levels of resistance to illness as a result of the changed economic conditions involved in producing for world markets. In many parts of Africa in particular, the nutritional quality of native diets became substantially depressed as cash-crop production supplanted the production of native foods.

This was not simply a one-way process, however, as the early development of colonialism also radically changed Western diets, having a paradoxical impact so far as health is concerned. On the one hand, Western diets were improved by the addition of a range of new foods either previously unknown or very rare, such as bananas, pineapples, and grapefruit. On the other hand, the importation of tobacco and coffee, together with raw sugar, which began increasingly to be used in all manner of foods, has had harmful consequences. Smoking tobacco, especially, has been linked to the prevalence of cancer and heart disease.

Infectious Diseases Today in the Developing World

Although major strides have been made in reducing, and in some cases virtually eliminating, infectious diseases in the developing world, they remain far more common there than in the West. The most important example of a disease that has almost completely disappeared from the world is smallpox, which, even as recently as the 1960s, was a scourge of Europe as well as many other parts of the world. Campaigns against malaria have been much less successful. When the insecticide DDT was first produced, it was hoped that the mosquito, the prime carrier of malaria, could be eradicated. At first, considerable progress was made, but this has slowed down because some strains of mosquito have become resistant to DDT.

Human Immunodeficiency Virus (HIV) and Acquired Immune Deficiency Syndrome (AIDS)

One devastating exception to the trend of eliminating infectious diseases in the developing world is HIV/AIDS, which has become a global epidemic. The true number of people infected

with HIV is unknown, but estimates put the figure at between 34 and 46 million worldwide, with 40 million being the most frequently cited. In 2003 alone, over 3 million people worldwide died from AIDS-related illnesses (UNAIDS, 2003). Using middle-range estimates, about 550,000 people are living with HIV/AIDS in Western Europe, 995,000 in North America, 2.1 million in Latin America and the Caribbean, and nearly 27 million in sub-Saharan Africa (see Global Map 18.1). The main impact of the epidemic is still to come, because of the time it takes for HIV infection to develop into full-blown AIDS. The majority of people affected in the world today are heterosexuals. As of 2002, more than half are women. In sub-Saharan Africa, young women are more than 2.5 times more likely than men to be infected with HIV/AIDS. Worldwide, at least four HIV infections are contracted heterosexually for every instance of homosexual spread. In high-income countries the rate of new infections has been on the decline, yet the demographics of who is infected with HIV/AIDS are striking. In the United States, there were 40,000 new infections in 2003. Of these, nearly half were in African Americans, who constitute only 12 percent of the total population. HIV/AIDS is now the leading cause of death among African American women aged twenty-five to thirty-four in the United States (UNAIDS, 2003).

Stigmatization of people with HIV/AIDS remains a major barrier to successful treatment programs. Stigma draws on preexisting prejudices to justify scapegoating and blaming in

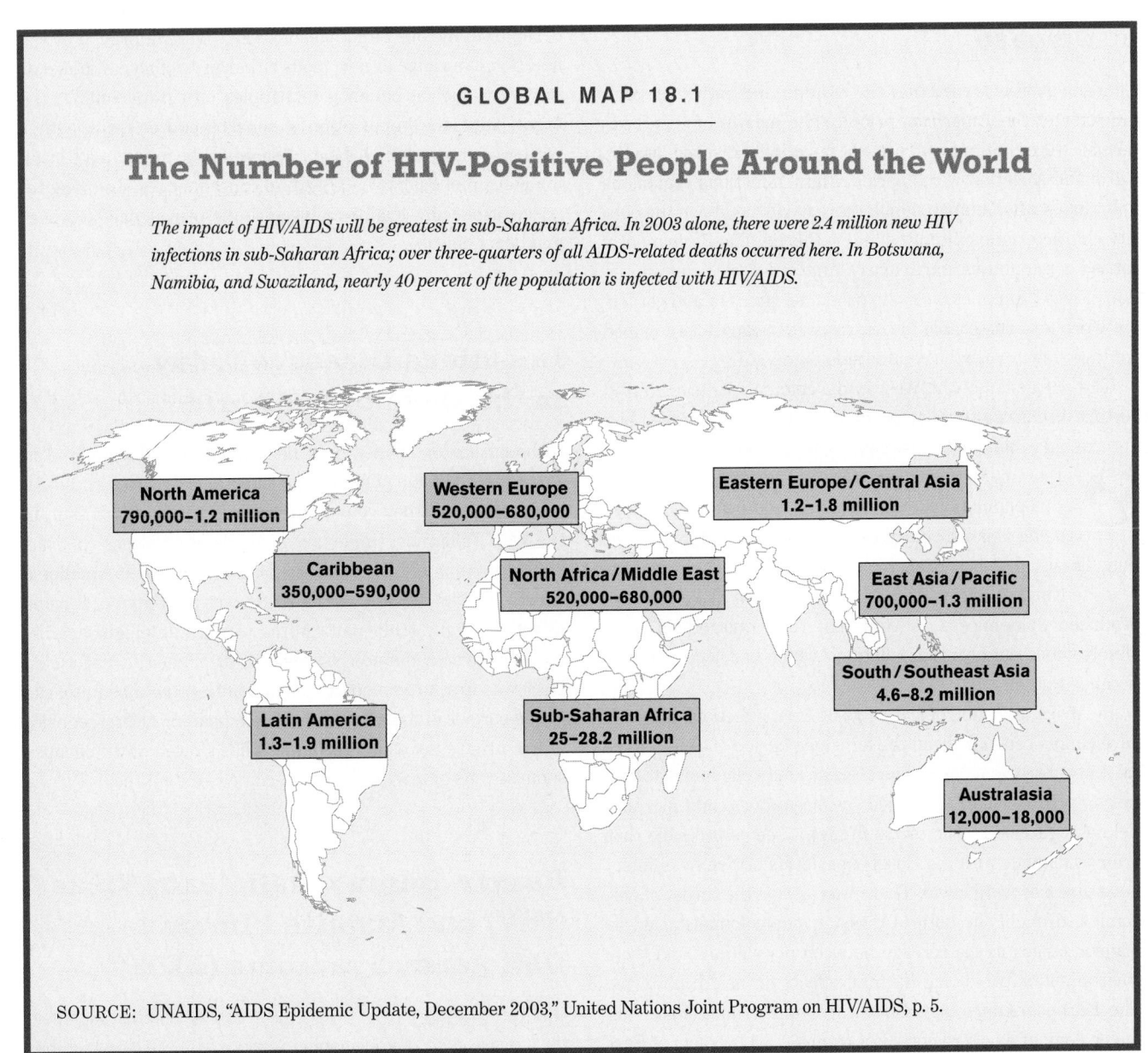

GLOBAL MAP 18.1

The Number of HIV-Positive People Around the World

The impact of HIV/AIDS will be greatest in sub-Saharan Africa. In 2003 alone, there were 2.4 million new HIV infections in sub-Saharan Africa; over three-quarters of all AIDS-related deaths occurred here. In Botswana, Namibia, and Swaziland, nearly 40 percent of the population is infected with HIV/AIDS.

North America
790,000–1.2 million

Western Europe
520,000–680,000

Eastern Europe/Central Asia
1.2–1.8 million

Caribbean
350,000–590,000

North Africa/Middle East
520,000–680,000

East Asia/Pacific
700,000–1.3 million

South/Southeast Asia
4.6–8.2 million

Latin America
1.3–1.9 million

Sub-Saharan Africa
25–28.2 million

Australasia
12,000–18,000

SOURCE: UNAIDS, "AIDS Epidemic Update, December 2003," United Nations Joint Program on HIV/AIDS, p. 5.

Looking AIDS in the Face: Anonymous (covering face) is a university student at Maputo University in Mozambique. Due to the extreme stigma he might face, he chose not to include any of his clothes in the photograph for fear of being identified. "I can't be identified because it may have a bad impact on my position as a university student. . . . Here in Mozambique there is discrimination promoted by the government. In one of his speeches the prime minister said Mozambique should not invest in educating people with AIDS as there is no hope for them. . . . If my faculty discovered my status there is real possibility that they would discriminate against me. Even if they don't expel me straight away, they would try all sorts of devious means to get rid of me."

victimized people. The stigma that associates HIV positive status with sexual promiscuity and immorality results in an avoidance of HIV/AIDS prevention and treatment programs. Clearly, the statistics cited above demonstrate that HIV/AIDS is not a "gay disease."

In the United States, an estimated 1 million people do not know that they are infected with HIV/AIDS (UNAIDS, 2003). Part of the reason why such a large group exists is the high level of fear and denial associated with being diagnosed as HIV positive. The stigma of having HIV/AIDS and the discrimination against people living with these infections are major barriers to the treatment of the epidemic worldwide. A 2002 survey found that 1 in 10 doctors and nurses in Nigeria have refused treatment to a person because of their HIV/AIDS status. In India, 70 percent of people living with HIV/AIDS have reported discrimination by health care workers (UNAIDS, 2003).

Discrimination is also seen at the level of government health care planning (UNAIDS, 2003). A case in point is South Africa, where President Thabo Mbeki, in a 2001 speech justifying his government's inaction on AIDS and unwillingness to spend government resources on AIDS prevention, declared that HIV did not cause AIDS and that, contrary to scientific opinion, antiretroviral medicines were ineffective

(Forrest and Streek 2001). Such attitudes have slowed progress in confronting the rapid expansion of the AIDS epidemic in South Africa, where at the end of 2002 5.3 million people were living with HIV/AIDS (UNAIDS, 2003).

Although the overall spread of AIDS in Western societies has slowed as the result of prevention programs, the opposite has been true in the developing world, where health education is limited and the medical establishment is poor.

In countries heavily affected by the HIV/AIDS epidemic, only 1 percent of pregnant women receives health care services aimed at preventing mother-to-child HIV transmission (UNAIDS, 2003). Besides the devastation caused by HIV/AIDS to individuals who suffer from it, the AIDS epidemic is creating a range of severe social consequences, including the explosion in the number of orphaned children stemming from the deaths of HIV-infected parents. In sub-Saharan Africa, the parents an estimated 13 million children have died as a result of HIV/AIDS (see Global Map 18.1). In Uganda alone, 77 percent of the population is under the age of eighteen; 30 percent of those are orphans (AIDS Orphans Educational Trust, 2003). The decimated population of working adults combined with the surging populations of orphans sets the stage for massive social instability, as economies break down and governments are unable to provide for the social needs of orphans who become targets for recruitment into gangs and armies who train them to fight as soldiers.

In fact, basic medical resources are still lacking in the vast majority of developing countries. The hospitals that do exist, together with trained doctors, tend to be heavily concen-

An eleven-year-old orphan girl sells her grandmother's brooms for $0.03 (U.S.) each in order to buy food in a shanty compound in Kitwe, Zambia. Seventy percent of the world's HIV-infected people live in sub-Saharan Africa and more than a million children in Zambia alone have been orphaned by parents who have succumbed to AIDS.

trated in urban areas, where their services are mostly monopolized by the affluent minority. Most developing countries have introduced some form of national health service, organized by the central government, but the medical services available are usually very limited. The small section of the wealthy utilizes private health care, sometimes traveling to the West when sophisticated medical treatment is needed. Conditions in many developing world cities, particularly in the shantytowns, make the control of infectious diseases very difficult: Many shantytowns almost completely lack basic services such as water, sewage, and garbage disposal.

Studies carried out by the World Health Organization suggest that more than two thirds of people living in urban areas in developing countries draw their water from sources that fail to meet minimal safety standards. It has been estimated that seventeen out of the twenty-five common water-related diseases in developing nations could either be cut by half or eradicated altogether simply by the provision of ready supplies of safe water (Doyal and Pennell, 1981). Only about a quarter of the city residents in developing countries have water-borne sewage facilities; some 30 percent have no sanitation at all. These conditions provide breeding grounds for diseases such as cholera (Dwyer, 1975).

Human Sexuality

The global AIDS epidemic and attempts to halt its spread are further examples of the socialization of nature. As with the study of health and illness, scholars have also differed over the importance of biological versus social and cultural influences on human sexual behavior, another important facet of the sociology of the body.

Social Influences on Sexual Behavior

Judith Lorber distinguishes as many as ten different sexual identities: straight (heterosexual) woman, straight man, lesbian woman, gay man, bisexual woman, bisexual man, transvestite woman (a woman who regularly dresses as a man), transvestite man (a man who regularly dresses as a woman), transsexual woman (a man who becomes a woman), and transsexual man (a woman who becomes a man). Sexual practices themselves are even more diverse. Freud argued that human beings are born "polymorphously perverse." By this he meant that human beings are born with a wide range of sexual tastes that are ordinarily curbed through socialization—although some adults may follow these even when, in a given society, they are regarded as immoral or illegal. Freud first began his research during the Victorian period, when many people were sexually prudish; yet his patients still revealed to him an amazing diversity of sexual pursuits.

Among possible sexual practices are the following: A man or woman can have sexual relations with women, men, or both. This can happen with one partner at a time or with two or more partners participating. One can have sex with oneself (masturbation) or with no one (celibacy). Someone can have sexual relations with transsexuals or people who erotically cross-dress; use pornography or sexual devices; practice sadomasochism (the erotic use of bondage and the inflicting of pain); have sex with animals; and so on (Lorber, 1994). In most societies, sexual norms encourage some practices and discourage or condemn others. Such norms, however, vary between different cultures. Homosexuality is a case in point. As will be discussed later, some cultures have either tolerated or actively encouraged homosexuality in certain contexts. Among the ancient Greeks, for instance, the love of men for boys was idealized as the highest form of sexual love.

Accepted types of sexual behavior also vary between different cultures, which is one way we know that most sexual responses are learned rather than innate. The most extensive study was carried out five decades ago by Clellan Ford and Frank Beach (1951), who surveyed anthropological evidence from more than two hundred societies. Striking variations were found in what is regarded as "natural" sexual behavior and in norms of sexual attractiveness. For example, in some cultures, extended foreplay, perhaps lasting hours, is thought desirable and even necessary prior to intercourse; in others, foreplay is virtually nonexistent. In some societies, it is believed that overly frequent intercourse leads to physical debilitation or illness. Among the Seniang of the South Pacific, advice on the desirability of spacing out lovemaking is given by the elders of the village—who also believe that a person with white hair may legitimately copulate every night!

In most cultures, norms of sexual attractiveness (held by both females and males) focus more on physical looks for women than for men, a situation that seems to be gradually changing in the West as women increasingly become active in spheres outside the home. The traits seen as most important in female beauty, however, differ greatly. In the modern West, a slim, small body build is admired, while in other cultures a much more generous shape is regarded as most attractive. Sometimes the breasts are not seen as a source of sexual stimulus, whereas in some societies great erotic significance is attached to them. Some societies place great store on the shape of the face, whereas others emphasize the shape and color of the eyes or the size and form of the nose and lips.

Sexuality in Western Culture

Western attitudes toward sexual behavior were for nearly two thousand years molded primarily by Christianity. Although different Christian sects and denominations have held divergent views about the proper place of sexuality in life, the dominant view of the Christian church was that all sexual behavior is suspect, except that needed for reproduction. During some periods, this view produced an extreme prudishness in society at large. But at other times, many people ignored or reacted against the church's teachings, commonly engaging in practices (such as adultery) forbidden by religious authorities. As was mentioned in Chapter 1, the idea that sexual fulfillment can and should be sought through marriage was rare.

In the nineteenth century, religious presumptions about sexuality became partly replaced by medical ones. Most of the early writings by doctors about sexual behavior, however, were as stern as the views of the church. Some argued that any type of sexual activity unconnected with reproduction causes serious physical harm. Masturbation was said to bring on blindness, insanity, heart disease, and other ailments, while oral sex was claimed to cause cancer. In Victorian times, sexual hypocrisy abounded. Virtuous women were believed to be indifferent to sexuality, accepting the attentions of their husbands only as a duty. Yet in the expanding towns and cities, prostitution was rife and often openly tolerated, "loose" women being seen as in an entirely different category from their respectable sisters.

Many Victorian men, who were on the face of things sober, well-behaved citizens, devoted to their wives, regularly visited prostitutes or kept mistresses. Such behavior was treated leniently, whereas "respectable" women who took lovers were regarded as scandalous and shunned in polite society if their behavior came to light. The differing attitudes toward the sexual activities of men and women formed a double standard, which has long existed and whose residues still linger on today.

In current times, traditional attitudes exist alongside much more liberal attitudes toward sexuality, which developed particularly strongly in the 1960s. Some people, particularly those influenced by Christian teachings, believe that premarital sex is wrong and generally frown on all forms of sexual behavior except heterosexual activity within the confines of marriage—although it is now much more commonly accepted that sexual pleasure is a desirable and important feature of marriage. Others, by contrast, condone or actively approve of premarital sex and hold tolerant attitudes toward different sexual practices. Sexual attitudes have undoubtedly become more permissive over the past thirty years in most Western countries. In movies and plays, scenes are shown that previously would have been completely unacceptable, while pornographic material is readily available to most adults who want it. (Pornography is reportedly the predominant use for the World Wide Web.)

Sexual Behavior: Kinsey's Study

We can speak much more confidently about public values concerning sexuality in the past than we can about private practices, for by their nature such practices mostly go undocumented. When Alfred Kinsey began his research in the United States in the 1940s and 1950s, it was the first time a major investigation of actual sexual behavior had been undertaken. Kinsey and his co-researchers faced condemnation from religious organizations, and his work was denounced as immoral in the newspapers and in Congress. But he persisted, and eventually obtained sexual life histories of 18,000 people, a reasonably representative sample of the white American population (Kinsey et al., 1948, 1953).

Kinsey's results were surprising to most and shocking to many, because they revealed a great difference between the public expectations of sexual behavior prevailing at that time and actual sexual conduct. He found that almost 70 percent of men had visited a prostitute, and 84 percent had had premarital sexual experience. Yet, following the double standard, 40 percent of men expected their wives to be virgins at the time of marriage. More than 90 percent of males had engaged in masturbation and nearly 60 percent in some form of oral sexual activity. Among women, about 50 percent had had premarital sexual experience, although mostly with their prospective husbands. Some 60 percent had masturbated, and the same percentage had engaged in oral-genital contacts.

The gap between publicly accepted attitudes and actual behavior that Kinsey's findings demonstrated was probably especially great at that particular period, just after World War II. A phase of sexual liberalization had begun rather earlier, in the 1920s, when many younger people felt freed from the strict moral codes that had governed earlier generations. Sexual behavior probably changed a good deal, but issues concerning sexuality were not openly discussed in the way that has become familiar now. People participating in sexual activities that were still strongly disapproved of on a public level concealed them, not realizing the full extent to which others were engaging in similar practices. The more permissive era of the 1960s brought openly declared attitudes more into line with the realities of behavior.

Sexual Behavior Since Kinsey

In the 1960s, the social movements that challenged the existing order of things, like those associated with countercultural, or "hippie," lifestyles, also broke with existing sexual norms. These movements preached sexual freedom, and the invention of the contraceptive pill for women allowed sexual pleasure to

The Spread of AIDS

There can be no question but that the threat of AIDS has significantly affected American sexual mores. Men and women, straight and gay, have come to realize the dangers posed by unprotected sex, and in many segments of the population, condom use has become the norm. As a result, the rate of transmission of HIV, the virus that causes AIDS, has dropped significantly in the United States. And although there remains no cure for the disease, the use of antiretroviral drugs has greatly increased the longevity of HIV-positive Americans.

The story is very different in the developing world. According to statistics released during the 1998 World AIDS Conference, 90 percent of those with HIV live in developing nations, with the vast majority living in Africa. Because condom availability in the developing world is low, because most governments in the developing world offer little in the way of sex

be clearly separated from reproduction. Women's groups also started pressing for greater independence from male sexual values, the rejection of the double standard, and the need for women to achieve greater sexual satisfaction in their relationships. Until recently it was difficult to know with accuracy how much sexual behavior had changed since the time of Kinsey's research.

In the late 1980s, Lillian Rubin interviewed a thousand Americans between the ages of thirteen and forty-eight to try to discover what changes have occurred in sexual behavior and attitudes over the past thirty years or so. According to her findings, there have indeed been significant changes. Sexual activity typically begins at a younger age than was true for the previous generation; moreover, the sexual practices of teenagers tend today to be as varied and comprehensive as those of adults. There is still a double standard, but it is not as powerful as it used to be. One of the most important changes is that women now expect, and actively pursue, sexual pleasure in relationships. They expect to receive, not only to provide, sexual satisfaction—a phenomenon that Rubin argues has major consequences for both sexes.

Women are more sexually available than once was the case; but along with this development, which most men applaud, has

come a new assertiveness many men find difficult to accept. The men Rubin talked to often said they "felt inadequate," were afraid they could "never do anything right," and found it "impossible to satisfy women these days" (Rubin, 1990).

Men feel inadequate? Doesn't this contradict much of what we have learned in this textbook so far? For in modern society, men continue to dominate in most spheres, and they are in general much more violent toward women than the other way around. Such violence is substantially aimed at the control and continuing subordination of women. Yet a number of authors have begun to argue that masculinity is a burden as much as a source of reward. Much male sexuality, they add, is compulsive rather than satisfying. If men were to stop using sexuality as a means of control, not only women but they themselves would gain.

In 1994, a team of researchers, led by Edward Laumann, published *The Social Organization of Sexuality: Sexual Practices in the United States,* the most comprehensive study of sexual behavior since Kinsey. To the surprise of many, their findings reflect an essential sexual conservatism among Americans. For instance, 83 percent of their subjects had had only one partner (or no partner at all) in the preceding year, and among married people the figure rises to 96 percent. Fidelity to one's spouse is

education, and because many mothers with HIV unknowingly pass the disease on to their children, in areas of Africa, one in four adults is infected with the AIDS virus. With rates of transmission showing no signs of decreasing, AIDS threatens to reduce the average life expectancy drastically in many developing nations. One sign of hope is that antiretroviral therapies—which can cost thousands of dollars per patient per year and thus could be out of reach for all but the wealthy few—are now being supplied by American pharmaceutical companies at little or no cost, thanks in part to protests and pressures placed on pharmaceutical companies by African governments and activists.

The specter of AIDS in the developing world also poses a direct threat to the West—because of globalization. Westerners are traveling to the developing world in record numbers, either as tourists or on business. Although HIV cannot be transmitted through casual contact, it is certainly the case that many Americans or Europeans who travel to developing countries will have sexual contacts while they are there, some by using the services of prostitutes. Thailand, for example, has a flourishing sex-tourism business, with some major hotels and tour companies catering to foreigners who wish to take advantage of the country's semilegal prostitution industry (Truong, 1990). Because many of these prostitutes are HIV positive, American tourists, businesspeople, or military personnel who employ

them and who fail to practice safe sex are at risk of contracting the virus and then spreading it on their return to the United States. Diseases, no less than people or goods, cross international borders more easily in a globalized world.

also quite common: Only 10 percent of women and less than 25 percent of men reported having an extramarital affair during their lifetime. According to the study, Americans average only three partners during their entire lifetime (see Table 18.1). Despite the apparent ordinariness of sexual behavior, some distinct changes emerge from this study, the most significant being a progressive increase in the level of premarital sexual experience, particularly among women. In fact, over 95 percent of Americans getting married today are sexually experienced.

In addition, sexual experience is increasing among high school students. Sexual permissiveness among young people is much greater today than it was thirty years ago. According to the Centers for Disease Control and Prevention, in 2001 nearly half (46 percent) of all high school students reported having had sexual intercourse; 14 percent reported having had four or more partners (CDC, 2003b). U.S. rates are far higher than those in Japan and China, where only a small percentage of all young people report having had sexual relationships (Toufexis, 1993; Tang and Zuo, 2000). Considering that the General Social Survey in 1998 reported that over 70 percent of respondents believed that teenage sex is "always wrong" and another 16 percent believed it is "almost always wrong" (GSS, 1998), parental beliefs and adolescent behavior are clearly in conflict.

One study of the sexual behavior of tens of thousands of American middle and high school students concluded that early sexual activity was higher among students who were from single-parent families, from a lower socioeconomic status, who demonstrated lower school performance and intelligence, and had lower religiosity—and among students with high levels of "body pride" (Halpern et al., 2000; Lammers et al., 2000).

Sexual Behavior in the United States: The Sociological Debate

Sociologists frequently rely on responses to survey questionnaires as their main source of information on human behavior. However, obtaining detailed information on sexual behavior and attitudes is often particularly difficult. The two most comprehensive studies of sexuality in the United States—the Kinsey studies (1948, 1953) and the Laumann study (Laumann et al., 1994)—offer very different portraits of sexual preferences and behaviors. Do these conflicting results reflect historical changes in sexual mores, or are the observed differences an outcome of methodological approaches?

TABLE 18.1

Sex in America: Social Influences on Sexual Behavior

TOTAL	SEX PARTNERS IN THE PAST 12 MONTHS				SEX PARTNERS SINCE AGE 18						MEDIAN NUMBER OF SEX PARTNERS SINCE AGE 18
	NONE	1	2–4	5+	NONE	1	2–4	5–10	11–20	21+	
	12%	71%	14%	3%	3%	26%	30%	22%	11%	9%	3
Men	10%	67%	18%	5%	3%	20%	21%	23%	16%	17%	6
Women	14	75	10	2	3	32	36	20	6	3	2
Ages 18–24	11%	57%	24%	9%	8%	32%	34%	15%	8%	3%	2
25–29	6	72	17	6	2	25	31	22	10	9	4
30–34	9	73	16	2	3	21	29	25	11	10	4
35–39	10	77	11	2	2	19	30	25	14	11	4
40–44	11	75	13	1	1	22	28	24	14	12	4
45–49	15	75	9	1	2	26	24	25	10	14	4
50–54	15	79	5	0	2	34	28	18	9	9	2
55–59	32	65	4	0	1	40	28	15	8	7	2
Never married, not living with someone	25%	38%	28%	9%	12%	15%	29%	21%	12%	12%	4
Never married, living with someone	1	75	20	5	0	25	37	16	10	13	3
Married	2	94	4	1	0	37	28	19	9	7	2
Divorced, separated, or widowed, not living with someone	31	41	26	3	0	11	33	29	15	12	5
Divorced, separated, or widowed, living with someone	1	80	16	3	0	0	32	44	12	12	6

As we just saw, in stark contrast to Kinsey's results, which found that a high proportion of men had premarital or extramarital sex, the Laumann study revealed that 83 percent of survey respondents had only one or no sexual partners in the year prior to the study. Moreover, only 10 percent of women and fewer than 25 percent of men reported ever having had an extramarital affair during their lifetime. Certainly, it's possible that Americans have become more sexually conservative over time. Perhaps the fear of AIDS and sexually transmitted diseases have frightened men and women away from extramarital affairs and multiple sex partners.

An alternative explanation for the wildly discrepant findings is that the researchers adopted different methodological approaches. Kinsey, an evolutionary biologist, first gave a ques-

TOTAL	SEX PARTNERS IN THE PAST 12 MONTHS				SEX PARTNERS SINCE AGE 18						MEDIAN NUMBER OF SEX PARTNERS SINCE AGE 18
	NONE	1	2–4	5+	NONE	1	2–4	5–10	11–20	21 +	
Less than high school degree	16%	67%	15%	3%	4%	27%	36%	19%	9%	6%	3
High school degree or equivalent	11	74	13	3	3	30	29	20	10	7	3
Some college or vocational school	11	71	14	4	2	24	29	23	12	9	4
College graduate	12	69	15	4	2	24	26	24	11	13	4
Advanced degree	13	74	10	3	4	25	26	23	10	13	4
No religion	11%	67%	17%	6%	3%	16%	29%	20%	16%	16%	5
Mainline Protestant	11	74	13	2	2	23	31	23	12	8	4
Conservative Protestant	13	70	14	3	3	30	30	20	10	7	3
Catholic	13	72	13	3	4	27	29	23	8	9	3
Jewish	4	78	15	4	0	24	13	30	17	17	6
Other religion	15	63	15	6	3	42	20	16	8	13	3
White	12%	73%	12%	3%	3%	26%	29%	22%	11%	9%	3
Black	13	60	21	6	2	18	34	24	11	11	4
Hispanic	11	70	17	3	3	36	27	17	8	9	2
Asian	15	77	8	0	6	46	25	14	6	3	1
Native American	12	76	10	2	5	28	35	23	5	5	3

SOURCE: Laumann et al., 1994.

tionnaire about sexual practices to students in his zoology classes at Indiana University. Finding this method unsatisfactory, he next conducted face-to-face interviews and then focused his study on specific social groups. He and his colleagues eventually interviewed nearly eighteen thousand people.

Kinsey recognized that the ideal survey would select people at random, and thus results would represent the general population. However, he did not believe it was possible to persuade a randomly selected group of Americans to answer deeply personal questions about their sexual behavior. Consequently, his survey respondents were primarily college students living in sorority and fraternity houses, prisoners, psychiatric patients, and friends. To make his data more credible, Kinsey made every effort to interview 100 percent of the members of each group, such as all students living in a given fraternity house. Because Kinsey's data are based on a convenience sample, they are not representative of the American public at large. Moreover, many of his survey respondents volunteered to participate in the study. Thus, these people may be unique from nonvolunteers in that they have wider sexual experiences or a greater interest in sexuality.

The Laumann study, in contrast, is based on data from the National Health and Social Life Survey (NHSLS). The NHSLS data were obtained from a nationally representative random sample of more than three thousand American men and women aged eighteen to fifty-nine who spoke English. In addition, the Laumann research team purposely oversampled among blacks and Hispanics so that they would have enough members of these minority groups to analyze their survey responses separately with confidence that findings were statistically reliable and valid.

Recognizing that people are often hesitant to discuss sexuality, the Laumann team paid particular attention to choosing nonjudgmental language in their questionnaire. The team also built several "checks" into their questionnaire to ensure the veracity of responses. Several questions were redundant, but were asked in different ways throughout the interview to gauge whether respondents were truthful in their answers. The research team also included eleven questions that had been asked previously on another national random sample survey of Americans. Comparisons of responses to the two sets of questions provided the Laumann researchers with assurance that their results were consistent with other researchers' findings.

Although the Kinsey and Laumann studies are influential works on human sexuality, the studies taken together also demonstrate that the process through which sociological knowledge is obtained often is as important as the actual research findings.

Sexual Orientation

Another important aspect of sexuality concerns *sexual orientation,* the direction of one's sexual or romantic attraction. The term *sexual preference,* which is sometimes incorrectly used instead of *sexual orientation,* is misleading and is to be avoided, since it implies that one's sexual or romantic attraction is entirely a matter of personal choice. As you will see below, sexual orientation results from a complex interplay of biological and social factors not yet fully understood.

The most commonly found sexual orientation in all cultures, including the United States, is *heterosexuality,* a sexual or romantic attraction for persons of the opposite sex (*hetero* comes from the Greek word meaning "other" or "different"). Heterosexuals in the United States are also sometimes referred to as "straight." It is important to bear in mind that although heterosexuality may be the prevailing norm in most cultures, it is not "normal" in the more fundamental sense that it is somehow dictated by some universal moral or religious standard. Like all forms of behavior, heterosexual behavior is socially learned within a particular culture.

Homosexuality involves a sexual or romantic attraction for persons of one's own sex. Today, the term *gay* is used to refer to male homosexuals, *lesbian* for female homosexuals, and *bi* as a shorthand for *bisexuals,* people who experience sexual or romantic attraction for persons of either sex. (*Lesbian* derives from the name of the Greek island Lesbos, the birthplace of

Sappho, the renowned ancient Greek poet who taught poetry to a devoted following of young women.) Although it is difficult to know for sure because of the stigma attached to homosexuality, which may result in the underreporting of sexuality in demographic surveys, current estimates find that from 2 to 5 percent of all women and 3 to 10 percent of all men in the United States are homosexual or bisexual (Burr, 1993; Laumann et al., 1994; GSS, 1997).

The term *homosexual* was first used by the medical community in 1869 to characterize what was then regarded as a personality disorder. The American Psychiatric Association did not remove homosexuality from its list of mental illnesses until 1973, nor from its highly influential *Diagnostic and Statistical Manual of Mental Disorders* (DSM) until 1980. These long-overdue steps were taken only after prolonged lobbying and pressure by homosexual rights organizations. The medical community was belatedly forced to acknowledge that no scientific research had ever found homosexuals as a group to be psychologically unhealthier than heterosexuals (Burr, 1993).

In some cultures, same-sex relationships are the norm in certain contexts and do not necessarily signify what today is termed "homosexuality." For example, the anthropologist Gilbert Herdt reported that among more than twenty tribes that he studied in Melanesia and New Guinea, ritually prescribed same-sex encounters among young men and boys were regarded as necessary for subsequent masculine virility (Herdt, 1981, 1984, 1986; Herdt and Davidson, 1988). Ritualized male-male sexual encounters also occurred among the Azande of Africa's Sudan and Congo (Evans-Pritchard, 1970), Japanese samurai warriors in the nineteenth century (Leupp, 1995), and highly educated Greek men and boys at the time of Plato (Rouselle, 1999).

IS SEXUAL ORIENTATION INBORN OR LEARNED?

Most sociologists currently believe that sexual orientation—whether homosexual, heterosexual, or something else—results from a complex interplay among biological factors and social learning. Since heterosexuality is the norm for most people in U.S. culture, a great deal of research has focused on why some people become homosexual. Some scholars argue that biological influences are the most important, predisposing certain people to become homosexual from birth (Bell, Weinberg, and Hammersmith, 1981; Green, 1987). Biological explanations for homosexuality have included differences in such things as brain characteristics of homosexuals (Maugh and Zamichow, 1991; LeVay, 1996) and the impact on fetal development of the mother's in utero hormone production during pregnancy (Blanchard and Bogaert, 1996; Manning, Koukourakis, and Brodie, 1997; McFadden and Champlin, 2000). Such studies, which are based on small numbers of cases, give highly inconclusive (and highly controversial) results (Healy, 2001). It is virtually impossible to separate biological from early social influences in determining a person's sexual orientation.

Studies of twins hold some promise for understanding if there is any genetic basis for homosexuality, since identical twins share identical genes. In two related studies, Bailey and Pillard (1991, 1993) examined 167 pairs of brothers and 143 pairs of sisters, with each pair of siblings raised in the same family, in which at least one sibling defined himself or herself as homosexual. Some of these pairs were identical twins (who share all genes), some were fraternal twins (who share some genes), and some were adoptive brothers or sisters (who share no genes). The researchers reasoned that if sexual orientation is determined entirely by biology, then all of the identical twins should be homosexual, since their genetic makeup is identical. Among the fraternal twins, some pairs would be homosexual, since some genes are shared. The lowest rates of homosexuality were predicted for the adoptive brothers and sisters.

The results of this study seem to show that homosexuality, like heterosexuality, results from a combination of biological and social factors. Among both the men and the women studied, roughly one out of every two identical twins was homosexual, compared with one out of every five fraternal twins, and one out of every ten adoptive brothers and sisters (Bailey and Pillard, 1991, 1993; see also Maugh, 1991, 1993; Burr, 1993). In other words, a woman or man is five times as likely to be lesbian or gay if her or his identical twin is lesbian or gay than if his or her sibling is lesbian or gay but related only through adoption. These results offer some support for the importance of biological factors, since the higher the percentage of shared genes, the greater the percentage of cases in which both siblings were homosexual. However, since approximately half of the identical twin brothers and sisters of homosexuals were not themselves homosexual, a great deal of social learning must also be involved; otherwise one would expect *all* identical twin siblings of homosexuals to be homosexual as well.

Its clear that even studies of identical twins cannot fully isolate biological from social factors. It is often the case that even in infancy, identical twins are treated more like one another by parents, peers, and teachers than are fraternal twins, who in turn are treated more like one another than are adoptive siblings. Thus, identical twins may have more than genes in common: They may share a higher proportion of similar socializing experiences as well.

HOMOPHOBIA

Homosexuality has long been stigmatized in the United States. **Homophobia,** a term coined in the late 1960s, refers to an aversion or hatred of homosexuals and their lifestyles, along with behavior based on such aversion. It is a form of prejudice that is reflected not only in overt acts of hostility and violence toward lesbians and gays, but also in various forms of verbal abuse that are widespread in American culture: for example, using terms like *fag* or *homo* to insult heterosexual males, or using female-related offensive terms such as *sissy* or *pansy* to put down gay men.

One recent study of homophobia in U.S. schools concluded that the estimated 2 million lesbian, gay, and bisexual middle and high school students are frequently the targets of humiliating harassment and sometimes physical abuse. *Hatred in the Hallways,* which was based on interviews with lesbian, gay, and bisexual students as well as youth service providers, teachers, administrators, counselors, and parents in seven states, found harassment to be a common and painful experience among lesbian, gay, and bisexual students (Bochenek and Brown, 2001). One gay student reported, "That's how you pick on someone, straight or gay. You call them a fag. I hear it a lot of times during the course of the day, a lot, at the very least ten to twenty times a day." A lesbian student reported getting threatening telephone calls at home, making her "hate every minute of school." The study cited a CBS poll reporting that a third of eleventh-grade students knew about incidents of sexual harassment of gays and lesbians, while more than a quarter admitted to engaging in harassment.

The study also found that verbal abuse often escalated into physical abuse. In one well-publicized incident, an openly gay Wisconsin student was verbally humiliated, spat and urinated upon, hit, subjected to a mock rape conducted by classmates in a science lab, and finally brutally beaten and seriously injured. When he complained to the school principal after the mock rape, she reportedly told him that "boys will be boys" and that his open gayness was causing the problem (Bochenek and Brown, 2001). This unhappy student twice attempted suicide—a tragically common occurrence, since lesbian, gay, and bisexual youths are at a four times greater risk for suicide than their straight peers (Gibson, 1989). Yet the vast majority of victims of antilesbian/gay violence never report the incident, for fear of being "outed" (New York City Gay and Lesbian Anti-Violence Project, 1996).

Such homophobia is widespread in U.S. culture: According to public opinion polls, three out of five Americans report believing that homosexuality is "morally wrong" (Gallup, 1998). In some states, homosexuality is still a legally punishable crime. Eighteen states, for example, have sodomy laws outlawing anal and oral sex. While in most cases these laws were originally written to apply to heterosexuals as well as homosexuals, in fact they are mainly used to justify taking children away from gay and lesbian parents or to arrest them for engaging in—or even discussing—homosexual sex. In four states—Kansas, Missouri, Oklahoma, and Texas—sodomy laws

Sexuality and the Mass Media

[***]

What does it take to capture the imagination of the country? Information that surprises us. Information that comes from solid research and credible sources, and that bears on the way we live, our common humanity (or, more often, inhumanity), and our desire to know about how well we are doing as individuals, parents, partners, and citizens. That is why an article such as the one sociologist Diane Lye wrote on parenting gets picked up by reporters: It went beyond the intuitive and taught us something. It was news.

Lye found that there was a lower divorce rate among men who had sons. If the research had stopped there, the presumptive meaning likely would have been that men still prefer sons over daughters, and attachment to sons will keep them home. It would have been a story, but not one that hit most major newspapers in the country. But Lye went further. She had data to indicate that American men did not prefer sons

over daughters, so she looked for other explanations. Her data allowed her to measure how much a father interacted with a child, and in what ways. She found that men interacted with sons more than with daughters—a fact she expected because men's traditional forms of leisure, spectator sports, and active participation in sports, might seem more appropriate for their sons than for their daughters. The next step: She decided to look at those fathers who broke the mold and did these activities with daughters and see what their rates of divorce were. She found that men who interacted with daughters in the same way as with sons also had lower divorce rates. She hypothesized that it is interaction that matters, and that men may feel they have fewer ways of interacting with a daughter, hence do less, and are thus less connected. If they do feel free to play with girl children in ways that are satisfying and comfortable, they will be equally attached to these children, creating an additional bond to support the marriage.

This finding was picked up by one reporter; again, wire services brought it to the attention of other newspapers and the story was repeated throughout the United States. It had a great deal of "play" in the various kinds of media (TV shows and magazine writers also crib from each other's stories) and showed an audience how children and sex role stereotypes about children might affect marital stability.

[***]

What does this tell us? That sociology not only needs to be the discoverer of truths and the corrector of politically expedient dogma or common myths, but it must be the framer of questions and the deliverer of memorable books and treatises of the journals and textbooks of academia. Right now, the common wisdom is skewing toward moral frames and explanations versus socioeconomic explanations, conflict theory, or cultural explanations. [***] Television programs and magazine articles have interpreted romantic and sexual patterns of today as genetic and evolutionary strategies. [***] Meanwhile, the public is buying millions of books by John Gray that tell us that men are from a different planet than women—and while sociologists feel that his assertions are easily torn apart, they do not choose a platform that reaches the same large audience that he does.

[***]

Why not? The answer to that involves, at least partly, the pretensions and customs of our discipline and, perhaps ironically, our ignorance about the way the world works. [***]

In general, writing about contemporary issues as they unfold is akin to being an ambulance chaser in our profession—the word "popularizer" is not an accolade. [***]

Yet, despite our attempts to ghettoize 95 percent of our work, journalists find us: Desperate for "fresh" information, they slog through our prose and latch on to our books and papers. They reduce research findings to two-minute segments and use us as talking heads in news clips or as part of their documentaries. [***]

[***]

I am asking us to package our work and to have a purpose to our work—to put it in appropriate places, in language that is compelling, and to connect it to the important events of our day. [***]

There is a huge emotional payoff in reaching the public with a sociological focus. I have had a couple of experiences where I felt that I was helping create a way of looking at things as well as supporting issues that meant a lot to me with evidence I believed in. I have worked as a journalist almost as much as I have worked as a sociologist. I have been on television in the Northwest for eighteen years in various capacities—as a "relationship expert," commentator, and as on-air support for news events. I write a column with sociologist Janet Lever for *Glamour* where each month 9 to 11 million women read what we feel is interesting and important about sex and health. In our two-page column, among other things, we comb books and the research literature looking for solid information for information-hungry readers. I have done this for several other media outlets as well—the most influential of which has been the *New York Times*—and I have found our journals crammed with good research upon which I could build a thesis and an article. I have also been an expert witness in a number of trials, the most satisfying of which have been trials involving custody cases, the right to serve in the army, and the right to marriage for gay men and lesbians. Much of the data that I used in my testimony was part of a study conducted in the late 1970s and early 1980s with my dear friend and colleague, Philip Blumstein, now deceased from AIDS. [***]

Was I the only one with this kind of information? No. But my work was still in the public eye because the book Phil and I wrote, *American Couples,* was published as a trade book, had been heavily promoted, and sold well. It had reached a number of publics, remained in the collective memory, not to mention Nexus and several rolodexes, and therefore was able to be put to good use. In the end, I felt that our ten years of work counted for something.

[***] If we continue to ignore the media, we can be sure that others will claim their attentions. But I believe that we need to vie for their affections. I would like us to be good citizens as well as good scholars and enter—and be powerful in—the debates and policies of our time.

[***]

SOURCE: Pepper Schwartz, "Stage Fright or Death Wish: Sociology in the Mass Media," *Contemporary Sociology*, 27, no. 5 (September 1998): pp. 439–445.

PEPPER SCHWARTZ is Professor of Sociology at the University of Washington in Seattle. She is the author of fourteen books, including The Great Sex Weekend, The Lifetime Love and Sex Quiz Book, *and* Everything You Know About Love and Sex is Wrong. *She currently writes columns for LifetimeTV.com, Classmates.com,* Lifetime Magazine *and* Classmates Magazine. *She lectures on relationship issues, women's issues, parent and child issues, communication between men and women, and maintaining personal and family well-being in the modern world.*

explicitly target same-sex sexual relations. In Oklahoma, sodomy is defined as a "crime against nature" and is punishable by up to ten years in prison. On the other hand, since the early 1960s, twenty-six states (and the District of Columbia) have repealed their sodomy laws. Laws in seven additional states have been invalidated by the courts, and those that remain are facing a variety of legal challenges (ACLU, 2003).

THE MOVEMENT FOR GAY AND LESBIAN CIVIL RIGHTS

Until recently, most gays and lesbians hid their sexual orientation, for fear that "coming out of the closet" would cost them their jobs, families, and friends and leave them open to verbal and physical abuse. Yet, since the late 1960s, many gays and lesbians have acknowledged their homosexuality openly, and in some cities the lives of lesbian and gay Americans has to a large extent been normalized (Seidman, Meeks, and Traschen, 1999). New York City, San Francisco, London, and other large metropolitan areas around the world have thriving gay and lesbian communities. "Coming out" may be important not only for the person who does so, but for others in the larger society: Previously "closeted" lesbians and gays come to realize they are not alone, while heterosexuals are forced to recognize that people whom they have admired and respected are homosexual.

The current global wave of gay and lesbian civil rights movements began partly as an outgrowth of the U.S. social movements of the 1960s, which emphasized pride in racial and ethnic identity. One pivotal event was the Stonewall riots in June 1969, when New York City's gay community—angered by continual police harassment—fought the New York Police Department for two days, a public action that for most people (gay or not) was practically unthinkable (Weeks, 1977; D'Emilio, 1983). The Stonewall riots became a symbol of gay pride, heralding the "coming out" of gays and lesbians, who insisted not only on equal treatment under the law, but also on a complete end to the stigmatization their lifestyle. In 1994, on the twenty-fifth anniversary of the Stonewall riots, one hundred thousand people attended the International March on the United Nations to Affirm the Human Rights of Lesbian and Gay People. It is clear that significant strides have been made, although discrimination and outright homophobia remain serious problems for many lesbian, gay, and bisexual Americans.

There are enormous differences among countries in the degree to which homosexuality is legally punishable. Sixty-eight countries still outlaw sex between males, and twenty-six outlaw sex between women. In Africa, for example, male homosexual acts have been legalized in only a handful of countries, while female homosexuality is seldom mentioned in the

The Stonewall Inn nightclub raid is regarded as the first shot fired in the battle for gay rights in the United States. The twenty-fifth anniversary of the event was commemorated in New York City with a variety of celebrations as well as discussions on the evolution and future of gay rights.

law at all. In South Africa, the official policy of the former white government was to regard homosexuality as a psychiatric problem that threatened national security. Once it took power, however, the black government legislated full equality. In Asia and the Middle East, the situation is similar: Male homosexuality is banned in the vast majority of countries, including all those that are predominantly Islamic. On the other hand, Europe has some of the most liberal laws in the world: Homosexuality has been legalized in nearly all countries, and Denmark legally recognizes same-sex marriages.

Today there is a growing movement around the world for the civil rights of gays and lesbians. The International Lesbian and Gay Association, which was founded in 1978, today has more than three hundred fifty member organizations in some eighty countries (ILGA, 2001). It holds international conferences, supports lesbian and gay social movement organizations around the world, and lobbies international organizations. For example, it convinced the Council of Europe to require all of its member nations to repeal laws banning homosexuality. In general, active lesbian and gay social movements tend to thrive in countries that emphasize individual rights and liberal state policies (Frank and McEneaney, 1999).

Sexuality and Procreative Technology

As with most of the topics in this chapter, the concept of "the socialization of nature" applies to a better sociological understanding of sexual behavior. An example is human reproduction. For hundreds of years, the lives of most women were dominated by childbirth and child rearing. In premodern times, contraception was ineffective or, in some societies, unknown. Even in Europe and the United States as late as the eighteenth century, it was common for women to experience as many as twenty pregnancies (often involving miscarriages and infant deaths). Improved methods of contraception have helped alter this situation in a fundamental way. Far from any longer being natural, it is almost unknown in the industrial countries for women to undergo so many pregnancies. Advances in contraceptive technology enable most women and men to control whether and when they choose to have children (see Global Map 18.2).

Contraception is only one example of a **procreative technology.** Some of the other areas in which natural processes have become social are described below.

CHILDBIRTH

Medical science has not always been involved with the major life transitions from birth to death. The medicalization of pregnancy and childbirth developed slowly, as local physicians and midwives were displaced by obstetric specialists. Today in industrialized societies, most births occur in a hospital with the help of a specialized medical team.

In the past, new parents had to wait until the day of birth to learn the sex of their baby and whether it would be healthy. Today, prenatal tests such as the sonogram (an image of the fetus produced by using ultrasonic waves) and amniocentesis (which draws off some of the amniotic fluid from around the fetus) can be used to discover structural or chromosomal abnormalities prior to birth. Such new technology presents couples and society with new ethical and legal decisions. When a disorder is detected, the couple are faced with the decision of whether or not to have the baby, knowing it may be seriously handicapped.

GENETIC ENGINEERING: DESIGNER BABIES

A great deal of scientific endeavor these days is being devoted to the expansion of genetic engineering; that is, intervening in the genetic makeup of the fetus so as to influence its subsequent development. The likely social impact of genetic engineering is starting to provoke debates almost as intense as those that surround the issue of abortion. According to its supporters, genetic engineering will bring us many benefits. It is possible, for example, to identify the genetic factors that make some people vulnerable to certain diseases. Genetic reprogramming will ensure that these illnesses are no longer passed on from generation to generation. It will be possible to "design" our bodies before birth in terms of skin color, color of hair and eyes, weight, and so forth.

There could be no better example of the mixture of opportunities and problems that the increasing socialization of nature creates for us. What choices will parents make if they can design their babies, and what limits should be placed on those choices? Genetic engineering is unlikely to be cheap. Will this mean that those who can afford to pay will be able to program out from their children any traits they see as socially undesirable? What will happen to the children of more deprived groups, who will continue to be born naturally?

Some sociologists have argued that differential access to genetic engineering might lead to the emergence of a "biological underclass." Those who don't have the physical advantages genetic engineering can bring might be subject to prejudice and discrimination by those who do enjoy these advantages. They might have difficulty finding employment and life or health insurance (Duster, 1990).

THE ABORTION DEBATE

The most controversial ethical dilemma created by modern reproductive technologies in modern societies is this: Under what conditions should abortion be available to women? The abortion debate has become so intense precisely because it centers on basic ethical issues to which there are no easy solutions. Those who are "prolife" believe that abortion is always wrong except in extreme circumstances, because it is equivalent to murder. For them, ethical issues are above all subject to the value that must be placed on human life. Those who are "prochoice" argue that the mother's control over her own body—her own right to live a rewarding life—must be the primary consideration.

The debate has led to numerous episodes of violence. Can it ever be resolved? At least one prominent social and legal theorist, Ronald Dworkin (1993), has suggested that it can. The intense divisions between those who are prolife and those who are prochoice, he argues, hide deeper sources of agreement between the two sides, and in this there is a source of hope. At previous periods of history, life was often relatively cheap. In current times, however, we have come to place a high value on the sanctity of human life. Each side agrees with this value, but they interpret it differently, the one emphasizing the interests of the child, the other the interests of the mother. If the two sides can be persuaded that they share a common ethical value, Dworkin suggests, a more constructive dialogue may be possible.

Percentage of Married Women Using Contraception

The socialization of nature is becoming more of a global phenomenon as contraception becomes more widely available around the world. Yet as this map indicates, strong cultural and social differences within societies determine whether women are likely to use contraception or not. What do you think some of the influences might be?

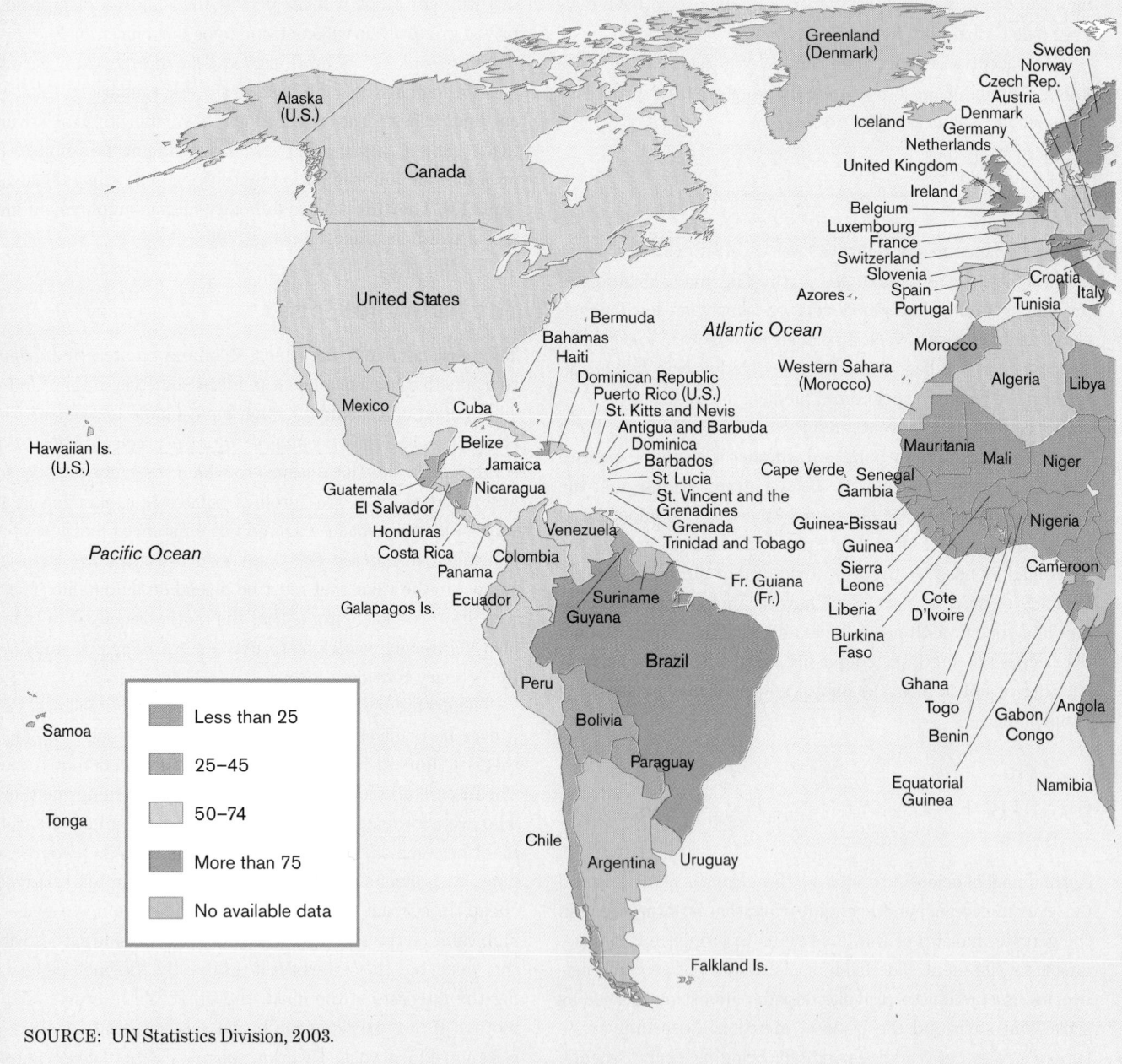

Legend:
- Less than 25
- 25–45
- 50–74
- More than 75
- No available data

SOURCE: UN Statistics Division, 2003.

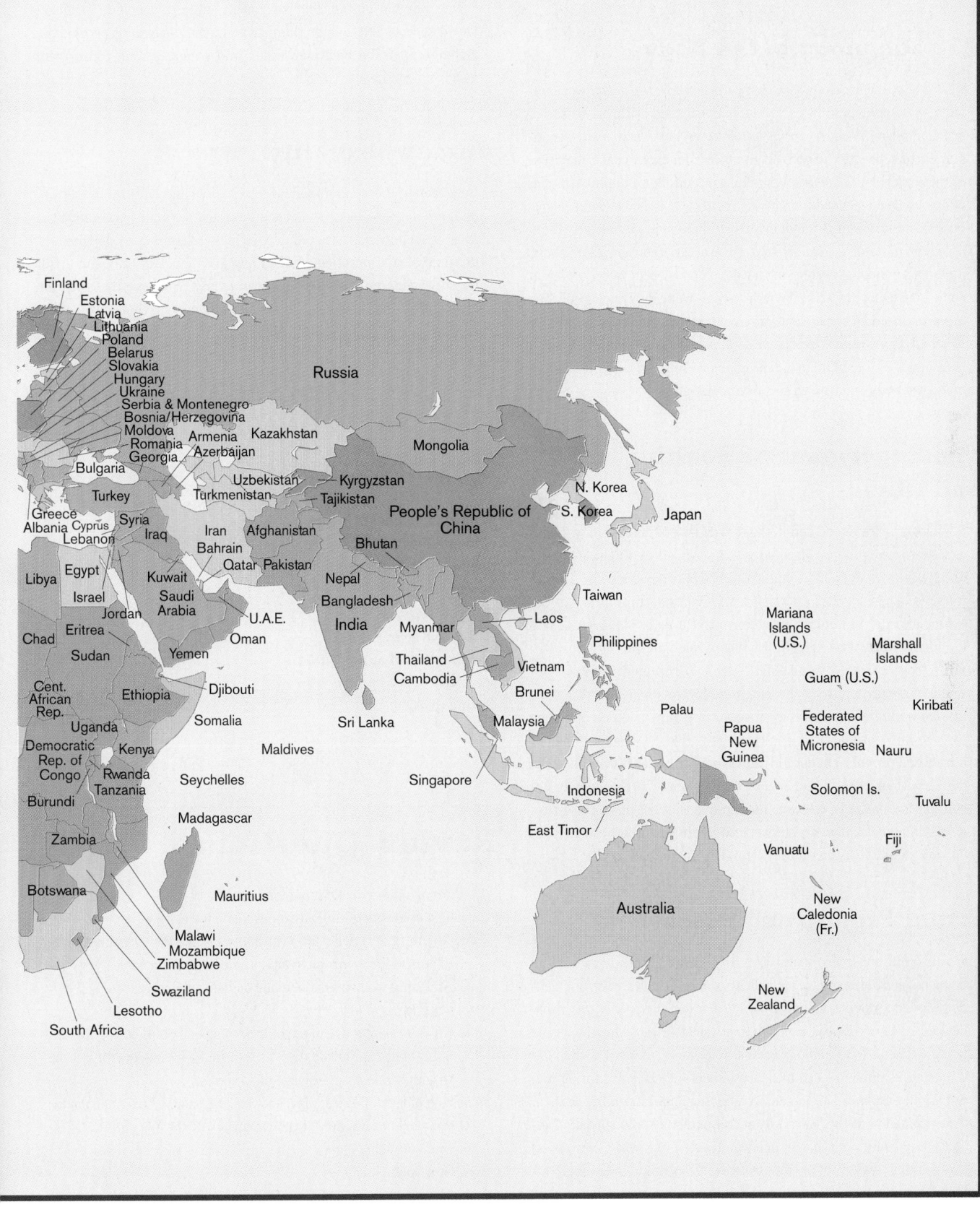

Study Outline

www.wwnorton.com/giddens5

The Sociology of the Body

- The field of the *sociology of the body* studies how the social world affects our bodies and is particularly concerned with processes of social change. Modern *social technologies* have managed, for instance, to separate the body from nature; an example is the notion of dieting, which involves planned interventions in the functioning of our bodies in order to modify or regulate them in various ways.
- Food production in the modern world has been globalized: Technologies of transportation and of storage (refrigeration) have meant that now everyone in the developed world is on a diet in some sense, having to *decide* what to eat every day. Such decisions are influenced by social relations. Women especially are judged by physical appearance, but feelings of shame about the body can lead anyone to compulsive dieting, exercising, or bodybuilding to make the body conform to social expectations.

The Experience of Health and Illness

- Sociologists are interested in the experience of illness—how being sick, chronically ill, or disabled is experienced by the sick person and by those nearby. The idea of the *sick role,* developed by Talcott Parsons, suggests that a sick person adopts certain forms of behavior in order to minimize the disruptive impact of illness. A sick individual is granted certain privileges, such as the right to withdraw from normal responsibilities, but in return must work actively to regain health by agreeing to follow medical advice.
- Symbolic interactionists have investigated how people cope with disease and chronic illness in their daily lives. The experience of illness can provoke changes in individuals' self-identity and in their daily routines. This dimension of the sociology of the body is becoming increasingly relevant for many societies; people are now living longer than ever before and tend to suffer more from chronic debilitating conditions than from acute illnesses.

Social Factors and Disease

- Health and illness are connected to population issues as well as being strongly affected by social factors such as class, race, and gender. Modern Western medicine, which arose in the past two or three centuries, views illness as having physical origins and hence as being explicable in scientific terms. In spite of modern medicine's importance, public health measures, such as better sanitation and nutrition, were more important in reducing infant mortality rates.
- The expansion of the West was accompanied by the spread of infectious diseases in what is now the developing world. Moreover, the colonial system, with its stress on cash crops, negatively affected the nutrition of developing-world people.

Status and Illness

- Susceptibility to the major illnesses is strongly influenced by socioeconomic status. For example, people in the industrialized world tend to live longer than those in the developing world; the richer tend to be healthier, taller, and stronger than those from less privileged backgrounds.

Human Sexuality

- Researchers have examined both biological and cultural influences on human sexual behavior, concluding that sexuality, like gender, is mostly socially constructed. There is an extremely wide range of possible sexual practices, but in any given society only some will be approved and reflected in social norms. Because these norms also vary widely, however, we can be quite certain that most sexual responses are learned rather than innate.

Key Concepts

biomedical model of health (p. 554)
epidemiology (p. 554)
homophobia (p. 569)
procreative technology (p. 573)
sick role (p. 550)
social technology (p. 547)
socialization of nature (p. 547)
sociology of the body (p. 546)
stigma (p. 551)

Review Questions

1. What are the "social technologies of the body"?
   a. The contents of the bathroom medicine cabinet
   b. Any kind of regular intervention we make into the functioning of our bodies in order to alter them in specific ways
   c. Anything we use to adorn our bodies, such as glasses, watches, and jewelry
   d. The increasing use of such devices as cell phones, pagers, and hand-held computing devices that make it possible for people to communicate over large distances
2. Which of the following diseases was transmitted to other parts of the world as a result of the expansion of the West in the colonial era?
   a. Smallpox
   b. Measles

c. Typhus

d. All of the above

3. Which of the following statements is true?

   a. About 95 percent of U.S. college women say that they want to lose weight.

   b. About 80 percent of U.S. college men say that they want to lose weight.

   c. About 50 percent of U.S. college women suffer serious problems with an eating disorder at some point in their college careers.

   d. About 50 percent of U.S. college men are on diets.

4. According to Talcott Parsons, which of the following is one of the three pillars of the sick role?

   a. The sick person is personally responsible for being sick.

   b. The sick person is not entitled to withdrawal from normal responsibilities.

   c. The patient should work to regain health by exercising and dieting.

   d. The sick person should consult a medical expert.

5. According to a recent study, how many lesbian, gay, and bisexual middle and high school students are frequently the targets of humiliating harassment, and sometimes physical abuse?

   a. A quarter million

   b. Half a million

   c. One million

   d. Two million

6. According to Frand and McEneancy, active lesbian and gay social movements tend to thrive in countries that emphasize

   a. polygamy.

   b. individual rights and liberal state policies.

   c. socialism.

   d. globalization.

7. According to Richard Wilkinson (1996), the healthiest societies in the world are located in

   a. the richest countries.

   b. countries in which income is distributed most evenly.

   c. countries in which levels of social integration are lowest.

   d. the United States.

8. Kinsey's findings from the 1940s and 1950s showed Americans to be much more liberal about sexuality than Laumann's findings from the 1990s. What best explains the differences in their results?

   a. Sexually transmitted disease has made Americans much more cautious about whom they have sex with.

   b. In the 1930s and 1940s people were much more prudish when asked about sex than they are today, but much more experimental in private. Today people are much more open when talking about sex, but much more conservative in what they are actually prepared to engage in.

   c. XXX-rated videos; nowadays everyone's seen it all, and figured out that much of it is not for them.

   d. Differences in methodology: Kinsey went looking for people he felt would talk about sexuality, whereas Laumann based his study on survey data from a national study.

9. According to statistics released during the 1998 World AIDS Conference, 90 percent of those with HIV live in developing nations, with the vast majority living in

   a. Africa.

   b. America.

   c. Asia.

   d. Europe.

10. Which of the following statements is true about the decline of death rates before the twentieth century?

   a. Medical innovation was the most important factor in bringing down death rates.

   b. Effective sanitation, better nutrition, control of sewage, and improved hygiene were the most important factors in bringing down death rates.

   c. Both a and b are true.

   d. Immunization and antibiotics were the most important factors in bringing down death rates.

Thinking Sociologically Exercises

1. Statistical studies of our national health persistently show a gap in life expectancies between the rich and the poor. Review all the major factors that would explain why rich people on average live about eight years longer than poor people.

2. This text discusses the biological and sociocultural factors associated with sexual orientation. Why are twin studies the most promising type of research on the genetic basis of sexual orientation? Briefly summarize the analysis of these studies and show whether it presently appears that sexual orientation results from genetic differences and/or sociocultural practices and experiences.

Data Exercises

www.wwnorton.com/giddens5
Keyword: Data18

• This chapter addressed many issues related to health and human sexuality. Without question, these two topics come together in discussing the contemporary HIV/AIDS pandemic. In this chapter you learned that those nations that are most disadvantaged economically are the very nations that have been hardest hit by HIV/AIDS. This exercise will give you a chance to learn more about those countries and how they are coping with the enormous consequences of the disease.

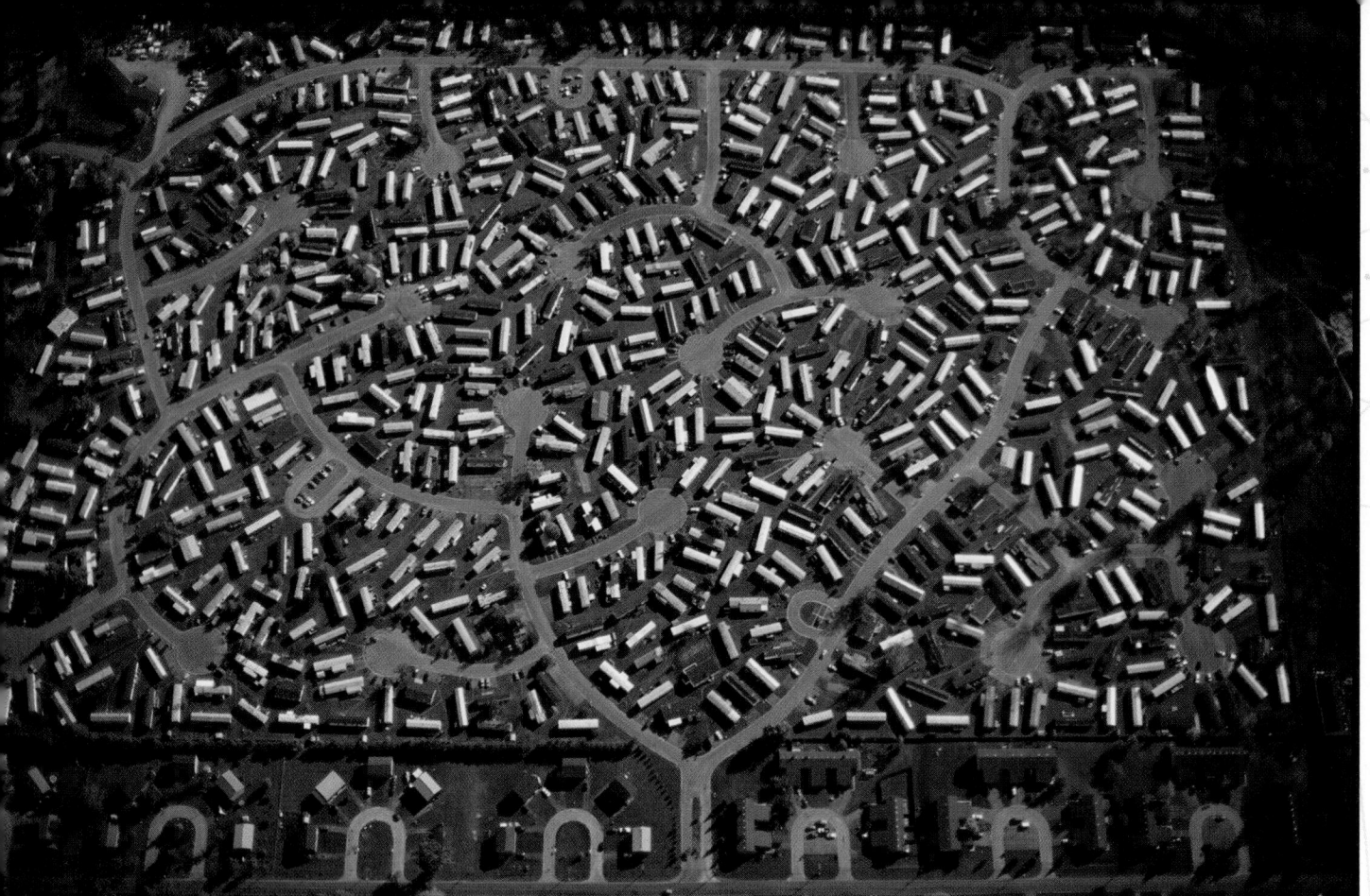

Living in Cities

Learn how cities have changed as a result of industrialization and urbanization.

Theories of Urbanism

Learn how theories of urbanism have placed increasing emphasis on the influence of socioeconomic factors on city life.

Urbanism in the United States

Learn about the recent key developments affecting American cities in the last several decades: suburbanization, urban decay, and gentrification.

Cities and Globalization

See that global economic competition has a profound impact on urbanization and urban life.

Urbanization in the Developing World

Recognize the challenges of urbanization in the developing world.

World Population Growth

Learn why the world population has increased dramatically and understand the main consequences of this growth.

Population Growth and the Environment

See that the environment is a sociological issue related to urbanization and population growth.

CHAPTER NINETEEN

URBANIZATION, POPULATION, AND THE ENVIRONMENT

nder the leadership of former Mayor Rudolph Giuliani, New York City became what urban sociologists call a "tourist city," attracting over 30 million visitors a year from all over the globe. As in many urban areas around the world, tourism has had a great effect on both the street life and the economic well-being of the city. For example, whereas the neighborhood around Times Square was once full of porn shops, X-rated theaters, strip joints, drug dealers, and cheap restaurants, it is now home to the Disney Store, theme restaurants, mainstream movie theaters, and other tourist attractions. In addition, the amount of money spent by tourists on theater tickets, hotel rooms, restaurant meals, and the like has pumped billions of dollars into the local economy. Once feared and shunned because of its so-called urban problems, New York is now one of the world's leading tourist destinations, where millions go for the "New York experience." The paradox of a "tourist city" like New York is that while the appeal of tourism is the opportunity to experience something different, cities that are remade to attract tourism seem more and more alike (Judd and Fainstein, 1999).

Nevertheless, cities like New York still offer people opportunities to escape the conformity and provincialism of life elsewhere. People who may have once flocked to Times Square now go to neighborhoods like the East Village, where they hang out on St. Marks Place or Eighth Street and have access to "hip" bars, music shops, and tattoo and piercing parlors. On a weekend night, a scene like Eighth Street is a destination for high school and college students—from both New York and its surrounding suburbs—from all different social and ethnic groups. Here, they move about

New York City's East Village has experienced a remarkable transformation. The neighborhood, which began as a prosperous residential area during colonial times and became a tenement district in the nineteenth century, later attracted artists and bohemians and thrived for many decades as an artists' colony within the city. Today rising rents make it increasingly unviable as an artists' district but it is still regarded as a haven for the city's counterculture.

among older white ethnics who are longtime neighborhood residents, college professors and other urban professionals of all races who have bought apartments in the neighborhood, gays of all classes and races, drug dealers who were forced out of nearby Washington Square Park, and homeless people who make a life for themselves on the sidewalks. Every fifteen minutes or so, double-decker buses drop off tourists who spend time strolling the Village's streets.

Eighth Street is an interesting location to a sociologist because it raises two central questions about urban life: Is social life in cities distinctive from social life outside cities? How much is urban life influenced by larger social forces? One defining characteristic of cities is the frequency of interactions between strangers. Even within the same neighborhood or apartment building, it's highly unlikely that people will know most of their neighbors. This fact alone makes life in cities today different from life elsewhere or during earlier times in history. Although city life is distinctive, cities are closely tied to social processes that cut across the globe. One of the processes that we will explore in this chapter is the movement of people. So while it is easy for one to assume that "urban" problems such as crime and homelessness are unique to cities, sociologists have shown they are neither distinctive to cities nor caused by city life.

The study of cities, and the understanding that a defining feature of urban life is the interaction between strangers, has been a central concern of American sociology since the early 1920s. This was when a group of sociologists at the University of Chicago did field studies of small social worlds within that city.

One such study, *The Taxi-Dance Hall* (Cressey, 1932), focused on the dance halls where immigrant men went for female companionship, buying tickets for dances with women. This early study looked at the dance hall as a place that could only exist in a city because such institutions depended on interaction between strangers. The early sociologists of the Chicago School argued that many people move from small towns to cities to get away from the suffocating atmosphere of "everyone knowing everyone else's business" and the social norms and moralistic codes that enforce conformity. But these same sociologists did not yet understand—as sociologists do today—that the conditions they observed in cities were socially constructed. They thought the patterns they observed were natural and would likely be the same in any city. In this chapter, we will see how urban sociologists ultimately came to a different understanding.

Living in Cities

An inescapable part of modern life, cities provide sociologists with a laboratory for studying the diversity of social life and conflict. Cities are the capitals of civilization: They are culturally lively, commercially dynamic, and alluring. They are efficient in providing for a large number of the population in a small amount of space. However, an entire literature has been devoted to the problems of city life, including poverty, racial and ethnic exclusion and antagonism, and crime.

In all modern societies, in contrast to the premodern era, most of the population live in urban areas, and even those who don't are affected by city life. We will first of all study the origins of cities and the vast growth in the numbers of city dwellers that has occurred over the past century. From there, we will review the most influential theories of urban life. We then move on to consider patterns of urban development in North America, compared with cities in the developing world. Cities in the developing world are growing at an enormous rate. We will consider why this is happening and at the same time look at changes now taking place in world population patterns. We will conclude by assessing the connections among urbanization, world population growth, and environmental problems.

Cities in Traditional Societies

The world's first cities appeared about 3500 B.C.E., in the river valleys of the Nile in Egypt, the Tigris and Euphrates in what is now Iraq, and the Indus in what is today Pakistan. Cities in traditional societies were very small by modern standards. Babylon, for example, one of the largest ancient Near Eastern cities, extended over an area of only 3.2 square miles and at its height, around 2000 B.C.E., probably numbered no more than fifteen to twenty thousand people. Rome under Emperor Augustus in the first century B.C.E. was easily the largest premodern city outside China, with some three hundred thousand inhabitants—the population of Birmingham, Alabama, or Tucson, Arizona, today.

Most cities of the ancient world shared certain features. They were usually surrounded by walls that served as a military defense and emphasized the separation of the urban community from the countryside. The central area of the city was almost always occupied by a religious temple, a royal palace, government and commercial buildings, and a public square. This ceremonial, commercial, and political center was sometimes enclosed within a second, inner wall and was usually too small to hold more than a minority of the citizens. Although it usually contained a market, the center was different from the business districts found at the core of modern cities, because the main buildings were nearly always religious and political (Sjoberg, 1960, 1963; Fox, 1964; Wheatley, 1971).

The dwellings of the ruling class or elite tended to be concentrated in or near the center. The less privileged groups lived toward the perimeter of the city or outside the walls, moving inside if the city came under attack. Different ethnic and religious communities were often allocated to separate neighborhoods, where their members both lived and worked. Sometimes these neighborhoods were also surrounded by walls. Communication among city dwellers was erratic. Lacking any form of printing press, public officials had to shout at the tops of their voices to deliver pronouncements. "Streets" were usually strips of land on which no one had yet built. A few traditional civilizations boasted sophisticated road systems linking various cities, but these existed mainly for military purposes, and transportation for the most part was slow and limited. Merchants and soldiers were the only people who regularly traveled over long distances.

Although cities were the main centers for science, the arts, and cosmopolitan culture, their influence over the rest of the country was always weak. No more than a tiny proportion of the population lived in the cities, and the division between cities and countryside was pronounced. By far the majority of people lived in small rural communities and rarely came into contact with more than the occasional state official or merchant from the towns.

Industrialization and Urbanization

The contrast in size between the largest modern cities and those of premodern civilizations is extraordinary. The most populous cities in the industrialized countries number over 26 million inhabitants. A **conurbation**—a cluster of cities and towns forming a continuous network—may include even larger numbers of people. The peak of urban life today is represented by what is called the **megalopolis,** the "city of cities." The term was originally coined in ancient Greece to refer to a city-state that was planned to be the envy of all civilizations. The current megalopolis, though, bears little relation to that utopia. The term was first applied in modern times to refer to the Northeast Corridor of the United States, an area covering some 450 miles from north of Boston to below Washington, D.C. In this region, about 40 million people live at a density of over 700 persons per square mile. An urban population almost as large and dense is concentrated in the lower Great Lakes region.

Britain was the first society to undergo industrialization, beginning in the mid-eighteenth century. The process of industrialization generated increasing **urbanization**—the movement of the population into towns and cities, away from the land. In 1800, fewer than 20 percent of the British population lived in towns or cities with more than ten thousand inhabitants. By 1900, this proportion had risen to 74 percent. London held about 1.1 million people in 1800; by the beginning of the twentieth century, it had increased in size to a population of over 7 million, at that date the largest city ever seen in the world. It was a vast manufacturing, commercial, and financial center at the heart of the still-expanding British empire.

The urbanization of most other European countries and the United States took place somewhat later. In 1800, the United States was more of a rural society than were the leading European countries. Fewer than 10 percent of Americans lived in communities with populations of more than 2,500 people. Today, well over three quarters of Americans are city dwellers. Between 1800 and 1900, as industrialization grew in the United States, the population of New York City leapt from 60,000 people to 4.8 million.

Urbanization in the twenty-first century is a global process, into which the developing world is being drawn more and more (Kasarda and Crenshaw, 1991). From 1900 to 1950, world urbanization increased by 239 percent, compared with a global population growth of 49 percent. The past fifty years have seen a greater acceleration in the proportion of people living in cities. From 1950 to 1986, urban growth worldwide was 320 percent, while the population grew by 54 percent. Most of this growth has occurred in cities in developing world societies. In 1975, 39 percent of the world's population lived in urban areas; the figure was around 50 percent in 2000 and is predicted to be 63 percent in 2025. Eastern and southern Asia will comprise about half of the world's people in 2025. By that date, the urban populations of the developing countries will exceed those of Europe or the United States.

Along with this worldwide urbanization come the effects of globalization. For example, the rise of urban-industrial areas in developing countries has brought intensified economic competition to industries in U.S. cities. South Korea's shoe industry has led to the impoverishment of urban areas in Massachusetts that formerly relied on that industry for their prosperity. Similarly, Baltimore has had to adjust to losing much of the market for its steel industry to Japan. We will examine later in the chapter how the global economy has influenced forms of city life in recent years.

Theories of Urbanism

The Chicago School

A number of writers associated with the University of Chicago from the 1920s to the 1940s—especially Robert Park, Ernest Burgess, and Louis Wirth—developed ideas that were for many years the chief basis of theory and research in urban sociology. Two concepts developed by the "Chicago School" are worthy of special attention. One is the so-called **ecological approach** to urban analysis; the other, the characterization of urbanism as a *way of life,* developed by Wirth (Park, 1952; Wirth, 1938). It is important to understand these ideas as they were initially conceived by the Chicago School and to see how they have been revised and even supplanted by later sociologists.

URBAN ECOLOGY

Ecology is a term taken from a physical science: the study of the adaptation of plant and animal organisms to their environment. In the natural world, organisms tend to be distributed in systematic ways over the terrain, such that a balance or equilibrium between different species is achieved. The Chicago School believed that the siting of major urban settlements and the distribution of different types of neighborhoods within them can be understood in terms of similar principles. Cities do not grow up at random, but grow in response to advantageous features of the environment. For example, large urban areas in modern societies tend to develop along the shores of rivers, in fertile plains, or at the intersection of trading routes or railways.

"Once set up," in Park's words, "a city is, it seems, a great sorting mechanism which . . . infallibly selects out of the population as a whole the individuals best suited to live in a particular region or a particular milieu" (Park, 1952). Cities become ordered into "natural areas," through processes of competition, invasion, and succession—all of which occur in biological ecology. If we look at the ecology of a lake in the natural environ-ment, we find that competition among various species of fish, insects, and other organisms operates to reach a fairly stable distribution among them. This balance is disturbed if new species invade—try to make the lake their home. Some of the organisms that used to proliferate in the central area of the lake are driven out to eke out a more precarious existence around its fringes. The invading species are their successors in the central sections.

Patterns of location, movement, and relocation in cities, according to the ecological view, have a similar form. Different neighborhoods develop through the adjustments made by inhabitants as they struggle to gain their livelihoods. A city can be pictured as a map of areas with distinct and contrasting social characteristics. Cities can be seen as formed in concentric rings, broken up into segments. In the center are the **inner-city** areas, a mixture of big business prosperity and decaying private houses. Beyond these are older established neighborhoods, housing workers employed in stable manual occupations. Further out still are the suburbs in which higher-income groups tend to live. Processes of invasion and succession occur within the segments of the concentric rings. Thus as property decays in a central or near-central area, ethnic minority groups might start to move into it. As they do so, more of the preexisting population start to leave, precipitating a wholesale flight to neighborhoods elsewhere in the city or out to the suburbs.

Another aspect of the **urban ecology** approach emphasized the *interdependence* of different city areas. *Differentiation*—the specialization of groups and occupational roles—is the main way in which human beings adapt to their environment. Groups on which many others depend will have a dominant role, often reflected in their central geographical position. Business groups, for example, such as large banks or insurance companies, provide key services for many in a community and hence are usually to be found in the central areas of settlements (Hawley, 1950, 1968).

As we noted in the chapter introduction, part of what it means to think like an urban sociologist today is to ask whether and how the conditions observed in cities are socially constructed or natural. We have seen that the early Chicago School leaned toward the idea that spatial patterns were natural outcomes. This all began to change when two black graduate students at the University of Chicago published the book *Black Metropolis* (1945), which posed a challenge to the human-ecology framework.

Drake and Cayton's massive study, based on extensive historical and ethnographic data, showed that the black residential neighborhoods of Chicago were by no means the result of natural forces, but were constructed by unnatural, social forces. These areas were called *ghettos,* a term that has come to mean many things to many people but that can be most usefully defined as a residential area where a racial or ethnic group initially comes to live as a consequence of systematic exclusion from more desirable places. Drake and Cayton showed that the ghetto was not in such a poor state because the people living there were black, but because blacks were given no choice but to live in the worst areas of the city. There was nothing natural about this placement and it would not have occurred if not for social forces such as exclusion, violence, and restrictive covenants where neighborhood "improvement" associations passed laws making it illegal to sell land in a community to blacks. After Drake and Cayton's *Black Metropolis,* it was harder for sociologists to think of the distributions of populations in urban areas as natural.

URBANISM AS A WAY OF LIFE

Wirth's thesis of **urbanism** as a *way of life* is concerned less with whether cities are natural or socially constructed than with what urbanism *is* as a form of social existence. Urbanism is related to the focus, identified earlier in this chapter, with how life in cities is distinctive or different from life elsewhere. Wirth also asserted that the effects of life in cities can be felt outside of cities as well. For example, have you ever noticed that many young people today dress in garments that were once thought to be distinctive to urban minority youth? It is not uncommon to find some teenagers in suburban high schools all over America dressing in baggy pants, untucked T-shirts, and hightop sneakers. If Wirth were writing today he might cite this as an example for his claim that the cultural life that begins in cities draws in the outerlying population, so that urbanism is "a way of life" in many places outside cities as well.

Wirth's theory is important for its recognition that urbanism is not just *part* of a society but expresses and influences the nature of the wider social system. Aspects of the urban way of life are characteristic of social life in modern societies as a whole, not just the activities of those who happen to live in big cities.

But another aspect to Wirth's argument focused more on an aspect of life that he did think was distinctive to cities. In cities, Wirth points out, large numbers of people live in close proximity to each other, without knowing most others personally—a fundamental contrast to small, traditional villages. Most contacts between city dwellers are fleeting and partial and are means to other ends rather than being satisfying relationships in themselves. Interactions with sales clerks in stores, cashiers in banks, passengers or ticket collectors on trains are passing encounters, entered into not for their own sake but as means to other aims.

Since those who live in urban areas tend to be highly mobile, there are relatively weak bonds between them. People are involved in many different activities and situations each day—the pace of life is faster than in rural areas. Competition prevails over cooperation. Wirth accepts that the density of social life in cities leads to the formation of neighborhoods having distinct characteristics, some of which may preserve the characteristics of small communities. In immigrant areas, for example, traditional types of connections between families are found, with most people knowing most others on a personal basis. The more such areas are absorbed into wider patterns of city life, however, the less these characteristics survive.

Wirth was among the first to address the "urban interaction problem" (Duneier and Molotch, 1999), the necessity for city dwellers to respect social boundaries when so many people are in close physical proximity all the time. Wirth elaborates that "the reserve, the indifference, and the blasé outlook that urbanites manifest in their relationships may thus be regarded as devices for immunizing themselves against the personal claims and expectations of others." Many people walk down the street in cities acting unconcerned about the others near them. Through such appearance of apathy they can avoid unwanted transgression of social boundaries.

Wirth's ideas have deservedly enjoyed wide currency. The impersonality of many day-to-day contacts in modern cities is undeniable—but to some degree this is true of social life in general in modern societies. Although one might assume that the "immunization" urban dwellers engage in to distance themselves from others is unique to city life, urban interaction may be only a subtype of the universal social condition. While the presence of strangers is more common in cities (Lofland, 1973, 1998), all people must manage social boundaries in their face-to-face interactions with others—as has been found as far afield as Western Samoa (Duranti, 1994) or among the African Poro people (Bellman, 1984). It is always necessary to ask whether the problems one associates with cities are aspects of social life more generally. In assessing Wirth's ideas, we must also ask whether his generalizations about urban life hold true for all cities during all times.

In assessing Wirth's idea, we should consider that neighborhoods involving close kinship and personal ties seem often to be actively *created* by city life; they are not just remnants of a preexisting way of life that survive for a period within the city. Claude Fischer has put forward an interpretation of why large-scale urbanism tends actually to promote diverse subcultures, rather than swamping everyone within an anonymous mass. Those who live in cities, he points out, are able to collaborate with others of like background or interests to develop local connections; and they can join distinctive religious, ethnic, political, and other subcultural groups. A small town or village does not allow the development of such subcultural diversity (Fischer, 1984). Those who form ethnic communities within cities, for instance, might have had little or no knowledge of one another in their land of origin. When they arrive in a new country, they gravitate to areas where others from a similar linguistic and cultural background are living, and new subcommunity structures are formed. An artist might find few others in a village or small town with whom to associate, but in a large city, on the other hand, he or she might become part of a significant artistic and intellectual subculture.

A large city is a world of strangers, yet it supports and creates personal relationships. This is not paradoxical. We have to separate urban experience into the public sphere of encounters with strangers and the more private world of family, friends, and work colleagues. It may be difficult to meet people when one first moves to a large city. But anyone moving to a small, established rural community may find the friendliness of the inhabitants largely a matter of public politeness—it may take years to become accepted. This is not the case in the city. Although one finds a diversity of strangers, each is a potential friend. And once within a group or network, the possibilities for expanding one's personal connections increase considerably.

Wirth's ideas retain some validity, but in the light of subsequent contributions it is clear that they are overgeneralized. Modern cities frequently involve impersonal, anonymous social relationships, but they are also sources of diversity—and, sometimes, intimacy.

JANE JACOBS: "EYES AND EARS UPON THE STREET"

Like most sociologists in the twentieth century, the Chicago School researchers were professors who saw their mission as contributing to a scholarly literature and advancing the field of social science.

At certain moments in the history of sociology, however, advances have also come from thinkers working outside universities without formal training in sociology. One such person was Jane Jacobs, who published *The Death and Life of Great American Cities* in 1961.

Jacobs was an architecture critic with a high school education, but through her own independent reading and research in the 1950s, she transformed herself into one of the most learned figures in the emerging field of urban studies. She is known as a public intellectual, because her main goal was to speak to the educated public, rather than to contribute to a scholarly literature. Nevertheless, her work has had an impact on scholarship in sociology as well.

Like sociologists such as Louis Wirth of the Chicago School before her, Jacobs argued that "cities are, by definition, full of strangers," some of whom are dangerous. She tried to explain what makes it possible for cities to meet the challenge of "assimilating strangers" in such a way that strangers can feel comfortable together. She argued that cities are most habitable when they feature a diversity of uses, thereby ensuring that many people will be coming and going on the streets at any time. When enough people are out and about, Jacobs argued, "respectable" eyes and ears dominate the street and are fixed on strangers, who will thus not get out of hand. Underneath the seeming disorder of a busy street is the very basis for order in "the intricacy of sidewalk use, bringing with it a constant succession of eyes." The more people are out, or looking from their windows at the people who are out, the more their gazes will safeguard the street.

Although Jacobs's ideas seem to cover a broad range of urban situations, there have also been notable exceptions: Only three years after her book was published, for example, a young woman named Kitty Genovese was stabbed to death in Queens, New York, while thirty-eight people watched from their windows (Rosenthal, 1999).

It is very common for people to make the mistake of believing that certain principles are natural to social life, only to discover later on that these principles only hold up under particular social conditions. The world has changed a great deal since Jacobs wrote *The Death and Life of Great American Cities*. Whereas when Jacobs was writing, most of the people on the sidewalks she discussed were similar in many respects, today homeless people, drug users, panhandlers, and others representing economic inequalities, cultural differences, and extremes of behavior can make sidewalk life unpredictable (Duneier, 1999). Under these conditions, strangers do not necessarily feel the kind of solidarity and mutual assurance she described. Sociologists today must ask, What happens to urban life when "the eyes and ears upon the street" represent vast inequalities and cultural differences? Do the assumptions Jacobs made still hold up? In many cases the answer is yes, but in other cases the answer is no. Four decades after her book was published, Jacobs's ideas remain extremely influential.

Urbanism and the Created Environment

Whereas the earlier Chicago School of sociology emphasized that the distribution of people in cities occurs naturally, we have seen that scholars such as Drake and Cayton showed this was not true with regard to the black population. They demonstrated that blacks often did not get to live where their incomes would naturally have led them to live, because of violence and restrictive covenants. More recent theories of the city have stressed that urbanism is not a natural process, but has to be analyzed in relation to major patterns of political and economic change.

According to this view, it is not the stranger on the sidewalk who is most threatening to many urban dwellers, especially the poor; instead, it is the stranger far away, working in a bank or real estate development company, who has the power to make decisions that transform whole blocks or neighborhoods (Logan and Molotch, 1987). This focus on the political economy of cities, and on different kinds of strangers, represented a new direction for urban sociology.

HARVEY: THE RESTRUCTURING OF SPACE

Urbanism, David Harvey emphasizes, is one aspect of the **created environment** brought about by the spread of industrial capitalism. In traditional societies, city and countryside were clearly differentiated. In the modern world, industry blurs the division between city and countryside. Agriculture becomes mechanized and is run according to considerations of price and profit, just like industrial work, and this process lessens the differences in modes of social life between urban and rural people.

In modern urbanism, Harvey points out, space is continually *restructured.* The process is determined by where large firms choose to place their factories, research and development centers, and so forth; the controls that governments operate over both land and industrial production; and the activities of private investors, buying and selling houses and land. Business firms, for example, are constantly weighing the relative advantages of new locations against existing ones. As production becomes cheaper in one area than another, or as the firm moves from one product to another, offices and factories will be closed down in one place and opened up elsewhere. Thus at one period, when there are considerable profits to be made, there may be a spate of office-block building in the center of large cities. Once the offices have been built and the central area redeveloped, investors look for the potential for further speculative building elsewhere. Often what is profitable in one period will not be so in another, when the financial climate changes.

The activities of private home buyers are strongly influenced by how far, and where, business interests buy up land, as well as by rates of loans and taxes fixed by local and central government. After World War II, for instance, there was vast expansion of suburban development outside major cities in the United States. This was partly due to ethnic discrimination and the tendency of whites to move away from inner-city areas. However, it was made possible, Harvey argues, only because of government decisions to provide tax concessions to home buyers and construction firms, and by the setting up of special credit arrangements by financial organizations. These provided the basis for the building and buying of new homes on the peripheries of cities and at the same time promoted de-

mand for industrial products such as the automobile (Harvey, 1973, 1982, 1985).

CASTELLS: URBANISM AND SOCIAL MOVEMENTS

Like Harvey, Manuel Castells stresses that the spatial form of a society is closely linked to the overall mechanisms of its development. But in contrast to the Chicago sociologists, Castells sees the city not only as a distinct *location*—the urban area—but as an integral part of processes of **collective consumption,** which in turn are an inherent aspect of industrial capitalism. Homes, schools, transport services, and leisure amenities are ways in which people consume the products of modern industry. The taxation system influences who is able to buy or rent where and who builds where. Large corporations, banks, and insurance companies, which provide capital for building projects, have a great deal of power over these processes. But government agencies also directly affect many aspects of city life, by building roads and public housing, planning parks, and so forth. The physical shape of cities is thus a product of both market forces and the power of government.

But the nature of the created environment is not just the result of the activities of wealthy and powerful people. Castells stresses the importance of the struggles of underprivileged groups to alter their living conditions. Urban problems stimulate a range of social movements, concerned with improving housing conditions, protesting against air pollution, defending parks, and combating building development that changes the nature of an area. For example, Castells has studied the gay movement in San Francisco, which succeeded in restructuring neighborhoods around its own cultural values—allowing many gay organizations, clubs, and bars to flourish—and gained a prominent position in local politics (Castells, 1977, 1983).

Cities, Harvey and Castells both emphasize, are almost wholly artificial environments, constructed by people. In some ways, the views set out by Harvey and Castells and those of the Chicago School usefully complement each other and can be combined to give a comprehensive picture of urban processes. The contrasts between city areas described in the urban ecology approach do exist, as does the overall impersonality of city life. But these are more variable than the members of the Chicago School believed, and are primarily governed by the social and economic influences analyzed by Harvey and Castells. John Logan and Harvey Molotch have suggested an approach that directly connects the perspectives of authors such as Harvey and Castells with some features of the ecological standpoint (Logan and Molotch, 1987). They agree with Harvey and Castells that broad features of economic development, stretching nationally and internationally, affect urban life in a quite

The Castro district in San Francisco is not only open but celebratory about its thriving gay and lesbian population.

direct way. But these wide-ranging economic factors, they argue, are focused through local organizations, including neighborhood businesses, banks, and government agencies, together with the activities of individual house buyers.

Places—land and buildings—are bought and sold, according to Logan and Molotch, just like other goods in modern societies, but the markets that structure city environments are influenced by how different groups of people want to *use* the property they buy and sell. Many tensions and conflicts arise as a result of this process—and these are the key factors structuring city neighborhoods. For instance, an apartment house is seen as a home by its residents but as a source of income by its landlord. Businesses are most interested in buying and selling property in an area to obtain the best production sites or to make profits in land speculation. Their interests and concerns are quite different from those of residents, for whom the neighborhood is a place to live.

Urbanism in the United States

What are the main trends that have affected city development in the United States over the past several decades? How can we explain the decay of central-city areas? These are questions we will take up in the following sections. One of the major changes in urban patterns in the period since World War II is the movement of large parts of city populations to newly constructed suburbs; this movement outward has been a particularly pronounced feature of American cities and is related directly to central-city decay. We therefore begin with a discussion of suburbia before moving on to look at the inner city.

Suburbanization

The word *suburb* has its origins in the Latin term *sub urbe,* or "under city control," an appropriate meaning throughout most of the history of urbanism. Suburbs were originally small pockets of dwellings dependent on urban centers for their amenities and livelihood. Today, they are any residential or commercial area adjoining a city, regardless of whether or not they are subject to central-city control. Many suburbs are effectively autonomous areas over which city administrations have little direct influence.

In the United States, **suburbanization,** the massive development and inhabiting of towns surrounding a city, rapidly increased during the 1950s and 1960s, a time of great economic growth. World War II had previously absorbed most industrial resources, and any development outside the war effort was restricted. But by the 1950s, war rationing had ended, automobiles instead of tanks were being mass produced, and people were encouraged to pursue at least one part of the "American dream"—owning a house and a piece of land. During that decade, the population in the cities increased by 10 percent, whereas in the suburban areas it grew by no less than 48 percent.

The prevailing economic scene also facilitated moving out of the city. The Federal Housing Administration (FHA) provided assistance in obtaining mortgage loans, making it possible in the early postwar period for families to buy housing in the suburbs for less than they would have paid for rent in the cities. The FHA did not offer financial assistance to improve older homes or to build new homes in the central areas of ethnically mixed cities; its large-scale aid went only to the builders and buyers of suburban housing. The FHA, together with the Veterans Administration, funded almost half of all suburban housing built during the 1950s and 1960s.

Early in the 1950s, lobbies promoting highway construction launched Project Adequate Roads, aimed at inducing the federal government to support the building of highways. President Eisenhower responded with a giant construction program for interstate roadways, and in 1956, the Highway Act was passed, authorizing $32 billion to be used for building such highways. This coincided with a period of expansion in the automobile in-

This aerial photograph taken in 1948 shows a portion of Levittown, New York, shortly after the mass-produced suburb was completed. Located on Long Island farmland just 25 miles east of Manhattan, William Levitt's concept to resolve the postwar housing crisis represented the future of suburbia— an entirely new kind of home and non-urban culture.

dustry such that families came to own more than one car; and the result was that previously out-of-the-way suburban areas, with lower property taxes, became accessible to places of work. At the same time, the highway program led to the establishment of industries and services in suburban areas themselves. Consequently, the movement of businesses from the cities to the suburbs took jobs from the manufacturing and service industries with them. Many suburban towns became essentially separate cities, connected by rapid highways to the other suburbs around them. From the 1960s on, the proportion of people commuting between suburbs increased more steadily than the proportion commuting to cities.

Although suburbia in the United States is white dominated, more and more members of racial and ethnic minorities are moving there. From 1980 to 1990, the suburban population of blacks grew by 34.4 percent, of Latinos by 69.3 percent, and of Asians by 125.9 percent. In contrast, the suburban white population grew by only 9.2 percent. In the following decade, from 1990 to 1999, the movement of racial and ethnic minority groups to the suburbs slowed, but remained diverse. The suburban population of blacks grew by 14.2 percent, Latinos by 40 percent, Asians by 45 percent, and whites by 7.6 percent (U.S. Bureau of the Census, 1999). Members of minority groups move to the suburbs for reasons similar to those who preceded them: better housing, schools, and amenities. Like the people who began the exodus to suburbia in the 1950s, they are mostly middle-class professionals. According to the chairman of the Chicago Housing Authority, "Suburbanization isn't about race now; it's about class. Nobody wants to be around poor people because of all the problems that go along with poor people: poor schools, unsafe streets, gangs" (DeWitt, 1994).

Nevertheless, the suburbs remain mostly white. Minority groups constituted only 18 percent of the total suburban population in 1999 (U.S. Bureau of the Census, 1999). Three out of every four African Americans continue to live in the center cities, compared with one in every four whites. Most black suburban residents live in black-majority neighborhoods in towns bordering the city.

While the last several decades saw a movement from the cities to the suburbs, they also witnessed a shift in the regional distribution of the U.S. population from north to south and east to west. As a percentage of the nation's total population, the Northeast dropped from 25 to 18.9 percent and the Midwest from 29 to 22.6 percent. Meanwhile the population of the South increased from 30.7 to 35.7 percent and that of the West from 15.6 to 22.8 percent (U.S. Bureau of the Census, 2002).

Urban Problems

Inner-city decay is partially a consequence of the social and economic forces involved in the movement of businesses, jobs, and middle-class residents from major cities to the outlying suburbs over the last fifty years. The manufacturing industries that provided employment for the urban blue-collar class largely vanished and were replaced by white-collar service industries. Millions of blue-collar jobs disappeared, and this affected in particular the poorly educated, drawn mostly from minority groups. Although the overall educational levels of minority groups improved over this period, the improvement was not sufficient to keep up with the demands of an information-based economy (Kasarda, 1993). William Julius Wilson has argued that the problems of the urban underclass grew out of this economic transformation (1991, 1996; see Chapter 8).

These economic changes also contributed to increased residential segregation of different racial and ethnic groups and social classes, as we saw in Chapter 11. Discriminatory practices by home sellers, real estate agents, and mortgage lending institutions further added to this pattern of segregation (Massey and Denton, 1993). In the early 1990s, more than 90 percent of African Americans in the United States lived in neighborhoods, both urban and suburban, that were 60 percent or more black (Farley and Frey, 1994). The social isolation of minority groups, particularly those in the underclass or "ghetto poor," can escalate urban problems such as crime, lack of economic opportunities, poor health, and family breakdown (Massey, 1996).

Adding to these difficulties is the fact that city governments today operate against a background of almost continual

Americans on the Move

How many times did your parents move from one residence to another while you were growing up? America has a high rate of residential mobility. In 1999–2000, 16.1 percent of Americans changed their place of residence at least once. Of these, over half (56 percent) moved to another home within the same county (U.S. Bureau of the Census, 2001). Although this number is no higher than the annual mobility rates of Canada, Australia, and New Zealand, Americans do tend to move more than residents of other industrially developed countries such as France, the United Kingdom, Japan, and Belgium. Yet except for a sharp increase in mobility in the mid-1980s, fueled by recovery from the recession of 1982–1983, mobility rates in the United States are in long-term decline. In the 1950s and 1960s, approximately 20 out of every 100 Americans moved at least once

every year. Mobility rates began to fall in the 1970s and, since the late 1980s, have consistently hovered around 17 percent.

Why do people move? According to a 1991 survey, the most commonly cited reason for moving was to improve one's housing situation: to buy a better home, to make the transition from renting to owning, and so on. Many respondents also cited employment factors as a reason for moving (Gober, 1993).

Because many Americans move for job-related reasons, migration patterns tend to reflect regional patterns of economic development. For example, the Northeast and Midwest, long home to much of the nation's industrial manufacturing, have suffered what demographers call an "out-migration" as a result of the deindustrialization of the American economy. Much of the growth in service-sector work and high-tech production has occurred in the South and West, and millions of Americans have left the Northeast and Midwest in search of jobs in these areas. The Midwest has slowly been able to recover from this situation, shifting its economic base to more viable forms of production and thus attracting enough new residents from other regions to counter the out-migration to the South and West. But the Northeast continues to lose residents at a rapid pace. In 1994, the Northeast lost a total of 61,000 residents, while the West gained 379,000 and the South gained 827,000 (Hansen, 1995). In 2000, the population of the Northeast continued to decline, with another 252,000 residents moving elsewhere. The South lost an additional 227,000, while the West also lost 57,000 residents. The Midwest received the only net gain of residents with 82,000 new people moving in (U.S. Bureau of the Census, 2001).

financial crisis. As businesses and middle-class residents moved to the suburbs, the cities lost major sources of tax revenue. High rates of crime and unemployment in the city require it to spend more on welfare services, schools, police, and overall upkeep. Yet because of budget constraints, cities are forced to cut back many of these services. A cycle of deterioration develops, in which the more suburbia expands, the greater the problems faced by city dwellers become.

Explaining Urban Poverty: The Sociological Debate

The plight of the American inner city has grown bleak in recent times. According to U.S. Census data, the proportion of our nation's poor who live in central cities increased from 34 percent in 1970 to 43 percent in 1990. By 2002, the proportion of the poor living in central cities had dropped slightly to 41

It is all too easy to view these demographic shifts as the result of natural and inevitable long-term processes: High-tech and service sector work comes to account for a greater share of the GNP, these industries naturally spring up in the South and West, making the regions attractive even for traditional manufacturing firms that wish to relocate, and the Northeast is depopulated.

A better explanation begins with—of all things—globalization. As globalization has proceeded, a number of important transformations have taken place in the economic sector. Changes in the financial infrastructure have made it easier for investors to put their money into enterprises anywhere on the globe, and corresponding improvements in communications technology, transportation, and managerial practices have made it more practical for businesses to move their production sites to wherever their costs will be minimized. Capital, economists and sociologists say, has become increasingly mobile under the influence of globalization.

Whereas the mobility of capital sometimes translates into American firms shifting the site of their production to the developing world, in other cases it means that firms will open in or relocate to regions of this country where their production costs will be low. All else being equal, if unions are strong in one region and weak in another, firms are more likely to do business in the region with the weak unions, because they will be able to get away with paying lower wages. Firms also prefer to operate in cities and states that are eager for new development and likely to grant substantial tax breaks. In general, state and local governments in the South and West have been more willing than governments in the Northeast to grant tax breaks to firms, and unions tend to be weaker in these regions than in the Northeast. These factors—in addition to cheaper land and energy—have helped pull some firms out of the Northeast and into the South and West, and have encouraged many startup firms to set up shop in the South and West. Although the dynamics involved are clearly complex, globaliza-

tion and the mobility of capital appear to lay behind recent trends in regional economic development and therefore underlie key patterns in regional migration.

Should attempts be made to halt these changes? What would migration patterns look like if unions were strong in all regions and if cities and states refused to grant generous tax breaks to corporate America? Is the depopulation of the Northeast a good or bad thing?

percent (U.S. Bureau of the Census, 2003). Not only are the poor increasingly concentrated in urban areas, but the poor living in the inner city are clustered in neighborhoods overwhelmingly inhabited by other poor families. The consequences are that the urban poor—particularly the black urban poor—are living in very poor, socially isolated, racially homogeneous neighborhoods, which are increasingly plagued with troubles such as joblessness, crime, and poor quality of life.

How is it possible that the living conditions of inner-city blacks have taken such a turn for the worse—especially in the three decades that followed the civil rights movements of the 1960s and progressive public policies such as the Fair Housing Act of 1968? Two books on inner-city poverty posit distinct—yet complementary—explanations for the state of urban poverty today. In *When Work Disappears: The World of the New Urban Poor* (1996), the sociologist William Julius Wilson argues, as we saw earlier in the chapter, that the loss of jobs is at the root of inner-city decline. Sociologists Douglas S. Massey and Nancy A. Denton, in their book *American Apartheid: Segregation and the Making of the Underclass* (1993), counter that the persistent poverty among urban blacks in the United States is due primarily to residential segregation.

Wilson's position can be described as the "economic restructuring" hypothesis. He argues that persistent urban poverty stems primarily from the structural transformation of the inner-city economy (1987, 1996). The decline of manufacturing industries, the "suburbanization" of employment, and the rise of a low-wage service sector have dramatically reduced the number of entry-level jobs that pay wages sufficient to support a family. The high rate of joblessness resulting from economic shifts has led to a shrinking pool of "marriageable" men (those financially able to support a family). Thus, marriage has become less attractive to poor women, unwed childbearing has increased, and female-headed families have proliferated. New generations of children are born into poverty, and the vicious cycle is perpetuated. Wilson argues that blacks suffer disproportionately due to past discrimination and because they are concentrated in locations and occupations particularly affected by economic restructuring.

Wilson elaborated that these economic changes were accompanied by an increase in the spatial concentration of poverty within black neighborhoods. This new geography of poverty, he felt, was due in part to the civil rights movement of the 1960s, which provided middle-class blacks with new opportunities outside the ghetto. The out-migration of middle-class families from ghetto areas left behind a destitute community lacking the institutions, resources, and values necessary for success in postindustrial society. He also acknowledges that such neighborhoods lack locally available training and education and have suffered from the dissolution of government and private support of local organizations that once supplied job information as well as employment opportunities. Thus, the urban underclass arose from a complex interplay of civil rights policy, economic restructuring, and a historical legacy of discrimination.

While Wilson emphasizes macro-level economic shifts as the cause underlying the concentration of urban poverty, Massey and Denton support the "racial residential segregation" hypothesis. This view holds that high levels of racial residential segregation may increase minority poverty by limiting access to employment opportunities. Segregation in ghettos exacerbates employment problems because it leads to weak informal employment networks and contributes to the social isolation of individuals and families, thereby reducing their chances of acquiring the skills, including adequate educational training, that facilitate mobility in a society. Since no other group in society experiences the degree of segregation, isolation, and poverty concentration that African Americans do, they are far more likely to be disadvantaged when they have to compete with other groups in society for resources and privileges.

Massey and Denton argue further that in the absence of residential segregation, the structural and economic changes observed by Wilson would not have produced the disastrous social and economic consequences observed in inner cities during the past thirty years. Although rates of black poverty were driven up by the economic dislocations Wilson identifies, it was segregation that confined the higher levels of deprivation to a small number of densely settled, tightly packed, and geographically isolated areas.

Massey and Denton also dispute Wilson's claim that concentrated poverty arose because the civil rights revolution allowed middle-class blacks to move out of the ghetto. Their principal objection to Wilson's focus on middle-class out-migration is that focusing on the flight of the black middle class deflects attention from the "real issue, which is the limitation of black residential options through segregation" (Massey and Denton, 1993).

Wilson, in turn, argues that "to focus mainly on segregation to account for the growth of concentrated poverty is to overlook some of the dynamic aspects of the social and demographic changes occurring in cities like Chicago." Instead, Wilson calls for an approach to studying inner-city poverty that "consider[s] the way in which other changes in society have interacted with segregation to produce the dramatic and social transformation of inner-city neighborhoods, especially since the 1970s" (Wilson, 1996).

Urban Renewal and Gentrification

Urban decay is not wholly a one-way process; it can stimulate countertrends, such as **urban renewal,** or **gentrification.** Dilapidated areas or buildings may become renovated as more affluent groups move back into cities. Such a renewal process is called gentrification because those areas or buildings become upgraded and return to the control of the urban "gentry"—high-income dwellers—rather than remaining in the hands of the poor.

In *Streetwise: Race, Class, and Change in an Urban Community* (1990), the sociologist Elijah Anderson analyzed the impact of gentrification on cities. Although the renovation of a neighborhood generally increases its value, it rarely improves the living standards of its current low-income residents, who are usually forced to move out. In the Philadelphia neighborhood that Anderson studied, close to the ghetto, many black residences were condemned, forcing over one thousand peo-

Does gentrification of a run-down inner-city area necessarily result in the dispossession of the existing population, or do renewed interest and an infusion of money in such areas promote a revitalization that works to their advantage? Not long ago, Clinton Street was a grim, graffiti-ridden streetscape (top) but it has evolved into a lively restaurant row on New York's Lower East Side (bottom).

ple to leave. Although they were told that their property would be used to build low-cost housing that they would be given the first opportunity to buy, large businesses and a high school now stand there.

The poor residents who continued to live in the neighborhood received some benefits in the form of improved schools and police protection, but the resulting increase in taxes and rents also forced them to leave for a more affordable neighborhood, most often deeper into the ghetto. African American residents Anderson interviewed expressed resentment at the influx of "yuppies," whom they held responsible for the changes that drove the poorer people away.

The white newcomers had come to the city in search of cheap "antique" housing, closer access to their city-based jobs, and a trendy urban lifestyle. They professed to be "open minded" about racial and ethnic differences; in reality, however, little fraternizing took place between the new and old residents unless they were of the same social class. Since the African American residents were mostly poor and the white residents were middle class, class differences were compounded by racial ones. Though some middle-class blacks lived in the area, most chose to live far from the ghetto, fearing that otherwise they would receive the same treatment that whites reserved for the black underclass. Over time, the neighborhood was gradually transformed into a white middle-class enclave.

It is important to note that the process of gentrification parallels another trend discussed earlier: the transformation of the urban economy from a manufacturing to a service-industries base. Addressing the concerns of the victims of these economic changes is critical for the survival of the cities.

Cities and Globalization

In premodern times, cities were self-contained entities that stood apart from the predominantly rural areas in which they were located. Road systems sometimes linked major urban areas, but travel was a specialized affair for merchants, soldiers, and others who needed to cross distances with any regularity. Communication between cities was limited. The picture at the start of the twenty-first century could hardly be more different. Globalization has had a profound effect on cities by making them more interdependent and encouraging the proliferation of horizontal links between cities across national borders. Physical and virtual ties between cities now abound and global networks of cities are emerging.

Some people have predicted that globalization and new communications technology might lead to the demise of cities as we know them. This is because many of the traditional functions of cities can now be carried out in cyberspace rather than in dense and congested urban areas. For example, financial markets have gone electronic, e-commerce reduces the need for both producers and consumers to rely on city centers, and telecommuting permits a growing number of employees to work from home rather than in an office building.

Yet, thus far, such predictions have not been borne out. Rather than undermining cities, globalization is transforming them into vital hubs within the global economy. Urban centers have become critical in coordinating information flows, managing business activities, and innovating new services and technologies. There has been a simultaneous *dispersion* and *concentration* of activity and power within a set of cities around the globe (Castells, 1996).

InnerCity Entrepreneurs

In the eight years since Roosevelt St. Louis launched Nouvelle Creation Catering, the Mattapan [Massachusetts] business has expanded from a two-person to a seven-person operation and become a leader in its field—catering of Caribbean and African American style food.

But Nouvelle Creation recently hit a wall. St. Louis, who has no formal business training and few well-connected friends,

was finding it difficult to fully capitalize on the market represented by the local minority community.

"My goal is to be the first professional, on-site catering facility in Boston that specializes in Caribbean and Southern cuisine," says St. Louis. "The biggest challenge I face is that when people hear about us, they assume that the quality of our food must be low, because top-quality catering for ethnic cuisine is uncommon. Expanding my business right now is going to require that I do a lot of social networking to get the word out."

It was to assist business owners like St. Louis that Daniel Monti, a [College of Arts and Science (CAS)] sociology professor, and Andrew Wolk, a [School of Management] research associate, recently launched InnerCity Entrepreneurs (ICE). A collaboration between the CAS sociology department, [Boston University's] Entrepreneurial Management Institute, and Roxbury Community College's Small Business Development Institute, ICE provides educational and networking resources to minority and inner-city business owners, with an eye toward helping them break into the city's larger business networks and at the same time strengthen their communities. It's supported by a $100,000 grant from Citizens Bank Foundation.

"There's a lot of technical assistance available out there for start-ups, but virtually nothing for established businesses that want to grow," says Monti. "We want to find owners of small businesses who have passed the three- to five-year survival

test, train them in how to grow their business, and put them in the same room so that by reaching a hand across the table, they can extend their markets."

So starting in January [2004], St. Louis and thirteen other business owners from around Boston have been attending a three-hour course at BU every two weeks that teaches skills in areas such as financial management, cost analysis, hiring and training, and goal-setting. Participants are required to create a three-year growth plan and during the yearlong course complete assignments that evaluate various aspects of their performance. They also agree to take part in a five-year panel study, headed by Monti, on the factors that enable small businesses in the inner city to grow, and the ways that the growth of businesses contributes to the vitality of inner-city communities, particularly by producing business leaders who become civic leaders.

"The course work gets the participants to step back and analyze their businesses in ways that most small business owners don't usually find the time to do," says Wolk, who directs ICE and teaches the course. "It's very interactive in that the participants use their own businesses as case studies, test out in their business what they learn in the course, and then come back and talk about it. The course has essentially become a part of their job now."

ICE also has developed a group of private industry experts from fields such as law, accounting, banking, equity financing, human resources, and real estate, who serve as guest speakers in the course and are available to answer the business owners' questions and help them network.

[***]

According to Monti, who says the idea for ICE stems from research he completed for his 1999 book *American City*, among the most revealing aspects of the project will be how its participants improve not just their businesses, but their neighborhoods.

"History has taught us that two important ways of building community in America are how businesspeople do it, and how members of ethnic groups do it," he says. "Those two strategies are very different, but I believe they can be complementary, and by combining them, ICE is trying to jump-start that entire community-building process. Business leaders tend to be very engaged in the community, in ways that most people don't observe. And in a city like Boston, which is perceived as being not particularly nurturing to new immigrant groups, the newer populations, such as the blacks, Latinos, and Asians, are going to be more successful economically, and culturally, if they learn to work together."

SOURCE: David J. Craig, "InnerCity Entrepeneurs Gives Small Businesses a Shot at the Big Leagues," *B.U.Bridge* VII, no. 26 (April 2, 2004), www.bu.edu/bridge.

Daniel Monti is Associate Professor of Sociology at Boston University. He is the author of The American City: A Social and Cultural History *and* Wannabe: Gangs in Suburbs and Schools. *He is currently involved in an ongoing study of American civic culture in cities across the United States. He is also working with minority and ethnic businesspeople in the Boston area to develop new businesses in minority communities and measure the impact of economic development programs.*

Global Cities

The role of cities in the new global order has been attracting a great deal of attention from sociologists. Globalization is often thought of in terms of a duality between the national level and the global, yet it is the largest *cities* of the world that comprise the main circuits through which globalization occurs (Sassen, 1998). The functioning of the new global economy is dependent on a set of central locations with developed informational infrastructures and a hyperconcentration of facilities. It is in such points that the "work" of globalization is performed and directed. As business, production, advertising, and marketing assume a global scale, there is an enormous amount of organizational activity that must be done in order to maintain and develop these global networks.

Saskia Sassen has been one of the leading contributors to the debate on cities and globalization. She uses the term **global city** to refer to urban centers that are home to the headquarters of large, transnational corporations and a superabundance of financial, technological, and consulting services. In *The Global City* (1991), Sassen bases her work on the study of three such cities: New York, London, and Tokyo. The contemporary development of the world economy, she argues, has created a novel strategic role for major cities. Most such cities have long been centers of international trade, but they now have four new traits:

1. They have developed into command posts—centers of direction and policy making—for the global economy.
2. Such cities are the key locations for financial and specialized service firms, which have become more important in influencing economic development than is manufacturing.
3. They are the sites of production and innovation in these newly expanded industries.
4. These cities are markets on which the "products" of financial and service industries are bought, sold, or otherwise disposed of.

New York, London, and Tokyo have very different histories, yet we can trace comparable changes in their nature over the past two or three decades. Within the highly dispersed world economy of today, cities like these provide for central control of crucial operations. Global cities are much more than simply places of coordination, however; they are also contexts of production. What is important here is not the production of material goods, but the production of the specialized services required by business organizations for administering offices and factories scattered across the world, and the production of financial innovations and markets. Services and financial goods are the "things" the global city makes.

The downtown areas of global cities provide concentrated sites within which whole clusters of "producers" can work in close interaction, often including personal contact, with one another. In the global city, local firms mingle with national and multinational organizations, including a multiplicity of foreign companies. Thus, 350 foreign banks have offices in New York City, plus 2,500 other foreign financial corporations; one out of every four bank employees in the city works for a foreign bank. Global cities compete with one another, but they also constitute an interdependent system, partly separate from the nations in which they are located.

Other authors have built on Sassen's work, noting that as globalization progresses, more and more cities are joining New York, London, and Tokyo in the ranks of the global cities. Castells has described the creation of a tiered hierarchy of world cities—with places such as Hong Kong, Singapore, Chicago, Frankfurt, Los Angeles, Milan, Zurich, and Osaka serving as major global centers for business and financial services. Beneath these, a new set of regional centers is developing as key nodes within the global economy. Cities such as Madrid, São Paulo, Moscow, Seoul, Jakarta, and Buenos Aires are becoming important hubs for activity within the so-called emerging markets.

Inequality and the Global City

The new global economy is highly problematic in many ways. Nowhere can this be seen more clearly than in the new dynamics of inequality visible within the global city. The central business district juxtaposed with impoverished inner-city areas in many global cities should be seen as interrelated phenomena, as Sassen and others remind us. The growth sectors of the new economy—financial services, marketing, high technology—are reaping profits far greater than any found within traditional economic sectors. As the salaries and bonuses of the very affluent continue to climb, the wages of those employed to clean and guard their offices are dropping. Sassen argues that we are witnessing the "valorization" of work located at the forefront of the new global economy and the "devalorization" of work that occurs behind the scenes (1998).

Disparities in profit-making capabilities are expected in market economies, but the magnitude of the disparities in the new global economy is having a negative effect on many aspects of the social world, from housing to the labor market. Those who work in finances and global services receive high salaries, and the areas where they live become gentrified. At the same time, orthodox manufacturing jobs are lost, and the very process of gentrification creates a vast supply of low-wage jobs—in restaurants, hotels, and boutiques. Affordable housing is scarce in gentrified areas, forcing an expansion of low-income neighborhoods. Whereas central business districts are the recipients of massive influxes of investment in real estate, development, and telecommunications, marginalized areas are left with few resources.

Within global cities, a geography of "centrality and marginality" is taking shape—as Mitch Duneier's study in New York's Greenwich Village revealed (Duneier, 1999). Alongside resplendent affluence there is acute poverty. Yet although these two worlds coexist side by side, the actual contact between them can be surprisingly minimal. As Mike Davis has noted in his study of Los Angeles, there has been a "conscious 'hardening' of the city surface against the poor" (1990). Accessible public spaces have been replaced by walled compounds, neighborhoods guarded by electronic surveillance, and "corporate citadels." In Davis's words:

> To reduce contact with untouchables, urban redevelopment has converted once vital pedestrian streets into traffic sewers and transformed public parks into temporary receptacles for the homeless and wretched. The American city . . . is being systematically turned inside out—or, rather, outside in. The valorized spaces of the new megastructures and super-malls are concentrated in the center, street frontage is denuded, public activity is sorted into strictly functional compartments, and circulation is internalized in corridors under the gaze of private police. (1990)

According to Davis, life is made as "unliveable" as possible for the poorest and most marginalized residents of Los Angeles. Benches at bus stops are short or barrel-shaped to prevent people from sleeping on them, the number of public toilets is

The city of Los Angeles has taken steps to dissuade the homeless from sleeping in public places. Notice that the bench pictured here is not long enough for a person to stretch out on and that the shape and placement of the slats would make it quite uncomfortable for any extended period of time.

fewer than in any other North American city, and sprinkler systems have been installed in many parks to deter the homeless from living in them. Police and city planners have attempted to contain the homeless population within certain regions of the city, but in periodically sweeping through and confiscating makeshift shelters, they have effectively created a population of "urban bedouins."

Urbanization in the Developing World

In 2000, 2.9 billion people, or 47 percent of the world's population, lived in cities. The world's urban population could reach 5 billion people, or over 60 percent of the world's population, by 2030. According to some estimates, 4 million of these urban dwellers will be residents of cities in the developing world. Currently, 40 percent of the populations of developing countries live in cities, but by 2030 urban dwellers are expected to account for 56 percent of the populations of developing countries. As Global Map 19.1 shows, most of the thirty-three cities projected to have more than 8 million residents in 2015 are located in the developing world. Most people in developed countries already live in cities. In 2000, 75 percent of the population of developed countries lived in cities, yet by 2030, 83 percent of people living in developed countries are anticipated to live in cities (UN Population Division, 2002).

Manuel Castells refers to **megacities** as one of the main features of third millennium urbanization (1996). They are defined not by their size alone—although they are vast agglomerations of people—but also by their role as connection points between enormous human populations and the global economy. Megacities are intensely concentrated pockets of activity through which politics, media, communications, finances, and production flow. According to Castells, megacities function as magnets for the countries or regions in which they are located. People are drawn toward large urban areas for various reasons; within megacities are those who succeed in tapping into the global system and those who do not. Besides serving as nodes in the global economy, megacities also become "depositories of all these segments of the population who fight to survive" (1996).

Why is the rate of urban growth in the world's lesser developed regions so much higher than elsewhere? Two factors in particular must be taken into account. First, rates of population growth are higher in developing countries than they are in industrialized nations. Urban growth is fueled by *high fertility rates* among people already living in cities.

Second, there is widespread *internal migration* from rural areas to urban ones—as in the case of the developing Hong

GLOBAL MAP 19.1

The Thirty-Three Cities Expected to Have More Than 8 Million Inhabitants in 2015

Los Angeles (United States) 14.4

Mexico City (Mexico) 20.4

New York (United States) 17.9

Bogotá (Colombia) 8.9

Lima (Peru) 9.3

Rio de Janeiro (Brazil) 11.5

São Paulo (Brazil) 21.2

Buenos Aires (Argentina) 13.1

Paris (France) 9.8

Moscow (Russia) 8.1

Istanbul (Turkey) 11.3

Cairo (Egypt) 11.5

Lagos (Nigeria) 15.9

Kinshasa (Democratic Republic of Congo) 9.8

Teheran (Iran) 8.1

Lahore (Pakistan) 8.7

Karachi (Pakistan) 16.1

Mumbai (Bombay) (India) 22.5

Bangalore (India) 8.3

Madras (India) 8.0

Delhi (India) 20.8

Dhaka (Bangladesh) 22.7

Calcutta (India) 16.7

Bangkok (Thailand) 9.8

Tianjin (China) 10.3

Beijing (China) 11.6

Seoul (Korea) 9.9

Tokyo (Japan) 27.1

Osaka (Japan) 11.0

Shanghai (China) 13.5

Hong Kong (China) 8.0

Metro Manila (Philippines) 12.5

Jakarta (Indonesia) 17.2

SOURCE: United Nations, World Urbanization Report, 2001 Revision, Ch. 6.

Kong–Guangdong megacity. People are drawn to cities in the developing world either because their traditional systems of rural production have disintegrated or because the urban areas offer superior job opportunities. Rural poverty prompts many people to try their hand at city life. They may intend to migrate to the city only for a relatively short time, aiming to return to their villages once they have earned enough money. Some actually do return, but most find themselves forced to stay, having for one reason or another lost their position in their previous communities.

Challenges of Urbanization in the Developing World

ECONOMIC IMPLICATIONS

As a growing number of unskilled and agricultural workers migrate to urban centers, the formal economy often struggles to absorb the influx into the work force. In most cities in the developing world, it is the *informal economy* that allows those who cannot find formal work to make ends meet. From casual work

The overcrowded streets of the Hong Kong–Guangdong megacity.

in manufacturing and construction to small-scale trading activities, the unregulated informal sector offers earning opportunities to poor or unskilled workers.

Informal economic opportunities are important in helping thousands of families to survive in urban conditions, but they have problematic aspects as well. The informal economy is untaxed and unregulated. It is also less productive than the formal economy. Countries where economic activity is concentrated in this sector fail to collect much-needed revenue through taxation. The low level of productivity also hurts the general economy—the proportion of the GDP generated by informal economic activity is much lower than the percentage of the population involved in the sector.

The OECD (Organization for Economic Cooperation and Development) estimates that a billion new jobs will be needed by 2025 to sustain the estimated population growth in cities in the developing world. It is unlikely that all of these jobs will be created within the formal economy. Some development analysts argue that attention should be paid to formalizing or regulating the large informal economy, where much of the excess work force is likely to cluster in the years to come.

ENVIRONMENTAL CHALLENGES

The rapidly expanding urban areas in developing countries differ dramatically from cities in the industrialized world. Al-

though cities everywhere are faced with environmental problems, those in developing countries are confronted by particularly severe risks. Pollution, housing shortages, inadequate sanitation, and unsafe water supplies are chronic problems for cities in less developed countries.

Housing is one of the most acute problems in many urban areas. Cities such as Calcutta and São Paulo are massively congested; the rate of internal migration is much too high for the provision of permanent housing. Migrants crowd into squatters' zones that mushroom around the edges of cities. In urban areas in the West, newcomers are most likely to settle close to the central parts of the city, but the reverse tends to happen in developing countries, where migrants populate what has been called the "septic fringe" of the urban areas. Shanty dwellings made of burlap or cardboard are set up around the edges of the city wherever there is a little space.

In São Paulo, it is estimated that there was a 5.4 million shortfall in habitable homes in 1996. Some scholars estimate that the shortage is as high as 20 million, if the definition of "habitable housing" is interpreted more strictly. Since the 1980s, the chronic deficit of housing in São Paulo has produced a wave of unofficial occupations of empty buildings. Groups of unhoused families initiate mass squats in abandoned hotels, offices, and government buildings. Many families believe that it is better to share limited kitchen and toilet facilities with hundreds of others than to live on the streets or in *favelas,* the makeshift shantytowns on the edges of the city. Still, 40 percent of the population live in *favelas* (Barcelona Field Studies Centre, 2003).

City and regional governments in less developed countries are hard pressed to keep up with the spiraling demand for housing. In cities such as São Paulo there are disagreements

Families sit on the sidewalk with their belongings after being evicted by police from a central São Paulo building. Hundreds of squatters had settled in São Paulo buildings until, facing forced eviction by riot police, they were compelled to leave.

Newspaper salesman Alvarado uses mask to protect himself from air pollution as he sells papers at a busy crossroad in Mexico City. Behind him a screen indicates the day's pollution levels.

among housing authorities and local governments about how to address the housing problem. Some argue that the most feasible route is to improve conditions within the *favelas*—to provide electricity and running water, pave the streets, and assign postal addresses. Others fear that makeshift shantytowns are fundamentally unhabitable and should be demolished to make way for proper housing for poor families.

Congestion and overdevelopment in city centers lead to serious environmental problems in many urban areas. Mexico City is a prime example. Ninety-four percent of Mexico City consists of built-up areas, with only 6 percent of land being open space. The level of green spaces—parks and open stretches of green land—is far below that found in even the most densely populated North American or European cities. Pollution is a major problem, coming mostly from the cars, buses, and trucks that pack the inadequate roads of the city, the rest deriving from industrial pollutants. It has been estimated that living in Mexico City is equivalent to smoking forty cigarettes a day. In March 1992, pollution reached its highest level ever. Whereas an ozone level of just under 100 points was deemed "satisfactory" for health, in that month the level climbed to 398 points. The government had to order factories to close down for a period, schools were shut, and 40 percent of cars were banned from the streets on any one day.

SOCIAL EFFECTS

Many urban areas in the developing world are overcrowded and underresourced. Poverty is widespread, and existing social services cannot meet the demands for health care, family planning advice, education, and training. The unbalanced age distribution in developing countries adds to their social and economic difficulties. Compared to industrialized countries, a much larger proportion of the population in the developing world is under the age of fifteen. A youthful population needs support and education, and during that time its members would not be economically productive. But many developing countries lack the resources to provide universal education. When their families are poor, many children must work full time, and others have to eke out a living as street children, begging for whatever they can. When the street children mature, most become unemployed, homeless, or both.

The Future of Urbanization in the Developing World

In considering the scope of the challenges facing urban areas in developing countries, it can be difficult to see prospects for change and development. Conditions of life in many of the world's largest cities seem likely to decline even further in the years to come. But the picture is not entirely negative.

First, although birthrates remain high in many countries, they are likely to drop in the years to come as urbanization proceeds. This in turn will feed into a gradual decrease in the rate of urbanization itself. In West Africa, for example, the rate of urbanization should drop to 3.4 percent per year by 2020, down from an annual rate of over 4.5 percent growth over the previous three decades (UN Population Division, 2002).

Second, globalization is presenting important opportunities for urban areas in developing countries. With economic integration, cities around the world are able to enter international markets, to promote themselves as locations for investment and development, and to create economic links across the borders of nation-states. Globalization presents one of the most dynamic openings for growing urban centers to become major forces in economic development and innovation. Indeed, many cities in the developing world are already joining the ranks of the world's global cities.

World Population Growth

There are currently over 6 billion people in the world. It was estimated that "baby number 6 billion" was born on October 12, 1999, although of course no one can know when and where this event happened. Paul Ehrlich calculated in the 1960s that if the rate of population growth at that time continued, nine hundred years from now (not a long period in world history as a whole) there would be 60,000,000,000,000,000 (60 quadrillion) people on the face of the earth. There would be one hundred people for every square yard of the earth's surface, including both land and water. The physicist J. H. Fremlin worked out that housing such a population would require a continuous two-thousand-story building covering the entire planet. Even such a stupendous structure would have only three or four yards of floor space per person (Fremlin, 1964).

Such a picture, of course, is nothing more than nightmarish fiction designed to drive home how cataclysmic the consequences of continued population growth would be. The real issue is what will happen over the next thirty or forty years, by which time, if current trends are not reversed, the world's population will already have grown to intolerable levels. Partly because governments and other agencies heeded the warnings of Ehrlich and others twenty years ago by introducing population-control programs, there are grounds for supposing that world population growth is beginning to trail off. Estimates calculated in the 1960s of the likely world population by the year 2000 turned out to be inaccurate. The World Bank estimated the world population was just over 6 billion in 2000, compared with some earlier estimates of over 8 billion. Nevertheless, considering that a century ago there were only 1.5 billion people in the world, this still represents growth of staggering proportions. Moreover, the factors underlying population growth are by no means completely predictable, and all estimates have to be interpreted with caution.

Population Analysis: Demography

The study of population is referred to as **demography.** The term was invented about a century and a half ago, at a time when nations were beginning to keep official statistics on the nature and distribution of their populations. Demography is concerned with measuring the size of populations and explaining their rise or decline. Population patterns are governed by three factors: births, deaths, and migrations. Demography is customarily treated as a branch of sociology, because the factors that influence the level of births and deaths in a given group or society, as well as migrations of population, are largely social and cultural.

Much demographic work tends to be statistical. All the industrialized countries today gather and analyze basic statistics on their populations by carrying out censuses (systematic surveys designed to find out about the whole population of a given country). Rigorous as the modes of data collection now are, even in these nations demographic statistics are not wholly accurate. In the United States there is a comprehensive population census every ten years, and sample studies are regularly conducted. Yet for various reasons, many people are not registered in the official population statistics, including illegal immigrants, homeless people, transients, and others who for one reason or another avoided registration.

In many developing countries, particularly those with recent high rates of population growth, demographic statistics are much more unreliable. For instance, some demographers have estimated that registered births and deaths in India may represent only about three quarters of the actual totals (Cox, 1976). The accuracy of official statistics is even lower in parts of central Africa.

Basic Demographic Concepts

Among the basic concepts used by demographers, the most important are crude birthrates, fertility, fecundity, and crude death rates. **Crude birthrates** are expressed as the number of live births per year per thousand of the population. They are called "crude" rates because of their very general character. Crude birthrates, for example, do not tell us what proportions of a population are male or female, or what the age distribution of a population is (the relative proportions of young and old people in the population). Where statistics are collected that relate birth or death rates to such categories, demographers speak of "specific" rather than "crude" rates. For instance, an age-specific birthrate might specify the number of births per thousand women in different age groups.

If we wish to understand population patterns in any detail, the information provided by specific birthrates is normally necessary. Crude birthrates, however, are useful for making overall comparisons between different groups, societies, and regions. Thus the crude birthrate in the United States is 15 per thousand. Other industrialized countries have lower rates, such as 9 per thousand in Germany, Russia, and Italy. In many other parts of the world, crude birthrates are much higher. In India, for instance, the crude birthrate is 25 per thousand; in Ethiopia it is 48 per thousand (World Bank, 1998).

Birthrates are an expression of the fertility of women. **Fertility** refers to how many live-born children the average woman has. A fertility rate is usually calculated as the average number of births per thousand women of childbearing age.

Fertility is distinguished from **fecundity,** which means the potential number of children women are biologically capable of bearing. It is physically possible for a normal woman to bear a child every year during the period when she is capable of conception. There are variations in fecundity according to the age at which women reach puberty and menopause, both of which differ among countries as well as among individuals. Although there may be families in which a woman bears twenty or more children, fertility rates in practice are always much lower than fecundity rates, because social and cultural factors limit breeding.

Urbanization and Migration

Population Movements

Notable shifts in population movement today involve rapid urbanization, the movement of refugees and displaced persons, and international migration. Movements of people, which will continue and increase in the future, affect patterns of development. Much of this movement is forced by conditions such as poverty or environmental degradation.

Virtually all population growth in the next decades will be concentrated in the urban areas of the world. Urban growth has outpaced employment and services and is often accompanied by poverty, yet cities offer opportunities for social change and economic development.

Although accounting for only 2 percent of the global population, a growing number—now 125 million people—are living outside the countries of their birth (including refugees and undocumented migrants). International migration is projected to remain high during the twenty-first century. The more developed regions are expected to remain net receivers of international migrants, with an average gain of about 2 million per year over the next 50 years.

Half the World in Cities

- As of 2000, 2.9 billion people were living in urban areas, comprising 47 percent of the world population.
- By 2030, 4.9 billion are expected to live in urban areas, or 60 percent of the world population.

Most of this population increase will be absorbed by the urban areas of less developed regions, while their rural populations will grow very slowly. By 2007, the number of urban dwellers is also expected to exceed the number of rural dwellers for the first time in history.

Rapid urban growth on today's scale strains the capacity of local and national governments to provide even the most

basic of services such as water, electricity and sewerage. The environment, natural resources, social cohesion and individual rights are at risk. Squatter settlements and overcrowded slums are home to tens of millions, like the *favelas* that cling to the hillsides of Rio de Janeiro and the tombs used as homes by tens of thousands in Cairo's "City of the Dead." In some developing countries, notably in Africa, this growth reflects rural crisis rather than urban-based development.

But cities also speed up social transformation, opening new avenues for human development, especially for women. Cities can give women greater access to schooling, to reproductive health services including family planning and sexual health, and to work with fair wages.

Causes That Motivate International Migration

- The search for a better life for oneself and family;
- Income disparities among and within regions;
- The labor and migration policies of sending and receiving countries;
- Political conflict (which drives migration across borders as well as within countries);
- Environmental degradation, including the loss of farmland, forests and pasture (most "environmental refugees" go to cities rather than abroad);

- "Brain drain," or the migration of more educated young people from developing countries to fill gaps in the work forces of industrialized countries.

SOURCE: United Nations Population Fund, "Urbanization and Migration," Population Issues Briefing Kit 2001, www.unfpa.org/modules/briefkit/07.htm.

Questions

- What political or social changes might reduce the pressure to migrate?
- What is the connection between environmental problems and the shift toward urbanization?
- The article mentions certain benefits from living in a city rather than in rural areas. What are they, and why do you think migrants seek them in spite of the many negative aspects of city life?

Crude death rates (also called "mortality rates") are calculated in the same way as birthrates—the number of deaths per thousand of population per year. Again, there are major variations among countries, but death rates in many societies in the developing world are falling to levels comparable to those of the West. The death rate in the United States in 1996 was 8 per thousand. In India it was 9 per thousand; in Ethiopia it was 17 per thousand. A few countries have much higher death rates. In Sierra Leone, for example, the death rate is 27 per thousand. Like crude birthrates, crude death rates only provide a very general index of **mortality** (the number of deaths in a population). Specific death rates give more precise information. A particularly important specific death rate is the **infant mortality rate:** the number of babies per thousand births in any year who die before reaching age one. One of the key factors underlying the population explosion has been reductions in infant mortality rates.

Declining rates of infant mortality are the most important influence on increasing **life expectancy**—that is, the number of years the average person can expect to live. In 1900, life expectancy at birth in the United States was about forty years. Today it has increased to nearly seventy-four years. This does not mean, however, that most people at the turn of the century died when they were about forty years of age. When there is a high infant mortality rate, as there is in many developing nations, the average life expectancy—which is a statistical average—is brought down (see Global Map 19.2). If we look at the life expectancy of only those people who survive the first year of life, we find that in 1900 the average person could expect to live to age fifty-eight. Illness, nutrition, and the influence of natural disasters are the other factors influencing life expectancy. Life expectancy has to be distinguished from **life span,** which is the maximum number of years that an individual could live. Although life expectancy has increased in most societies in the world, life span has remained unaltered. Only a small proportion of people live to be one hundred or more.

Dynamics of Population Change

Rates of population growth or decline are measured by subtracting the number of deaths per thousand over a given period from the number of births per thousand—this is usually calculated annually. Some European countries have negative growth rates—in other words, their populations are declining. Virtually all of the industrialized countries have growth rates of less than 0.5 percent. Rates of population growth were high in the eighteenth and nineteenth centuries in Europe and the United States but have since leveled off. Many developing countries today have rates of between 2 and 3 percent (see Global Map 19.3). These may not seem very different from the

rates of the industrialized countries, but in fact, the difference is enormous.

The reason is that growth in population is **exponential.** An ancient Persian myth helps to illustrate this concept. A courtier asked a ruler to reward him for his services by giving him twice as many grains of rice for each service than he had the time before, starting with a single grain on the first square of a chess board. Believing himself to be on to a good thing, the king commanded grain to be brought up from his storehouse. By the twenty-first square, the storehouse was empty; the fortieth square required ten billion grains of rice (Meadows et al., 1972). In other words, starting with one item and doubling it, doubling the result, and so on, rapidly leads to huge figures: 1:2:4:8:16:32:64:128, and so on. In seven operations the figure has risen by 128 percent. Exactly the same principle applies to population growth. We can measure this effect by means of the **doubling time,** the period of time it takes for the population to double. A population growth of 1 percent will produce a doubling of numbers in seventy years. At 2 percent growth, a population will double in thirty-five years, while at 3 percent it will double in twenty-three years.

Malthusianism

In premodern societies, birthrates were very high by the standards of the industrialized world today. Nonetheless, population growth remained low until the eighteenth century because there was a rough overall balance between births and deaths. The general trend of numbers was upward, and there were sometimes periods of more marked population increase, but these were followed by increases in death rates. In medieval Europe, for example, when harvests were bad, marriages tended to be postponed and the number of conceptions fell, while deaths increased. These complementary trends reduced the number of mouths to be fed. No preindustrial society was able to escape from this self-regulating rhythm (Wrigley, 1968).

During the period of the rise of industrialism, many looked forward to a new age in which scarcity would be a phenomenon of the past. The development of modern industry, it was widely supposed, would create a new era of abundance. In his celebrated work *Essay on the Principle of Population* (1976; orig. 1798), Thomas Malthus criticized these ideas and initiated a debate about the connection between population and food resources that continues to this day. At the time Malthus wrote, the population in Europe was growing rapidly. Malthus pointed out that whereas population increase is exponential, food supply depends on fixed resources that can be expanded only by developing new land for cultivation. Population growth therefore tends to outstrip the means of support available. The inevitable outcome is famine, which, combined with the influence of war and plagues, acts as a natural limit to population increase. Malthus predicted that human beings would always live in circumstances of misery and starvation, unless they practiced what he called "moral restraint." His cure for excessive population growth was for people to strictly limit their frequency of sexual intercourse. (The use of contraception he proclaimed to be a "vice.")

For a while, **Malthusianism** was ignored, since the population development of the Western countries followed a quite different pattern from that which he had anticipated—as we shall see below. Rates of population growth trailed off in the nineteenth and twentieth centuries. Indeed, in the 1930s there were major worries about population decline in many industrialized countries, including the United States. The upsurge in world population growth in the twentieth century has again lent some credence to Malthus's views, although few support them in their original version. Population expansion in developing countries seems to be outstripping the resources that those countries can generate to feed their citizenry.

The Demographic Transition

Demographers often refer to the changes in the ratio of births to deaths in the industrialized countries from the nineteenth century onward as the **demographic transition.** The notion was first worked out by Warren S. Thompson, who described a three-stage process in which one type of population stability would be eventually replaced by another as a society reached an advanced level of economic development (Thompson, 1929).

Stage one refers to the conditions characteristic of most traditional societies, in which both birth and death rates are high and the infant mortality rate is especially large. Population grows little if at all, as the high number of births is more or less balanced by the level of deaths. Stage two, which began in Europe and the United States in the early part of the nineteenth century—with wide regional variations—occurs when death rates fall while fertility remains high. This is therefore a phase of marked population growth. It is subsequently replaced by stage three, in which, with industrial development, birthrates drop to a level such that population is again fairly stable.

Demographers do not fully agree about how this sequence of change should be interpreted, or how long lasting stage three is likely to be. Fertility in the Western countries has not been completely stable over the past century or so; considerable differences in fertility remain among the industrialized nations, as well as between classes or regions within them. Nevertheless, it is generally accepted that this sequence accurately describes a major transformation in the demographic character of modern societies.

The theory of demographic transition directly opposes the ideas of Malthus. Whereas for Malthus, increasing prosperity would automatically bring about population increase, the thesis of demographic transition emphasizes that economic development, generated by industrialism, would actually lead to a new equilibrium of population stability.

Prospects for Change

Fertility remains high in developing-world societies because traditional attitudes to family size have been maintained. Having large numbers of children is often still regarded as desirable, providing a source of labor on family-run farms. Some religions are either opposed to birth control or affirm the desirability of having many children. Contraception is opposed by Islamic leaders in several countries and by the Catholic Church, whose influence is especially marked in South and Central America. The motivation to reduce fertility has not always been forthcoming even from political authorities. In 1974, contraceptives were banned in Argentina as part of a program to double the population of the country as fast as possible; this was seen as a means of developing its economic and military strength.

Yet a decline in fertility levels has at last occurred in some large developing countries. An example is China, which currently has a population of about 1.3 billion people—almost a quarter of the world's population as a whole. The Chinese government established one of the most extensive programs of population control that any country has undertaken, with the object of stabilizing the country's numbers at close to their current level. The government instituted incentives (such as better housing and free health care and education) to promote single-child families, whereas families who have more than one child face special hardships (wages are cut for those who have a third child). As a response to this government program, some families went to the extreme of killing their female infants. There is evidence that China's antinatal policies, however harsh they may appear, have had a substantial impact on its population (Mirsky, 1982). Yet there is also much resistance within the country. People are reluctant to regard parents with one child as a proper family.

China's program demands a degree of centralized government control that is either unacceptable or unavailable in most other developing countries. In India, for instance, many schemes for promoting family planning and the use of contraceptives have been tried but with only relatively small success. India in 1988 had a population of 789 million. In 2000, its population just topped 1 billion. And even if its population-growth rate does diminish, by 2050, India will be the most populous country in the world, with over 1.5 billion people.

Life Expectancies in Global Perspective, 2002

The United States presently ranks eighteenth in the world in life-expectancy rates—low among Western nations, but considerably higher than most Second World and developing nations. How much of a correlation do you find between life expectancy and income level?

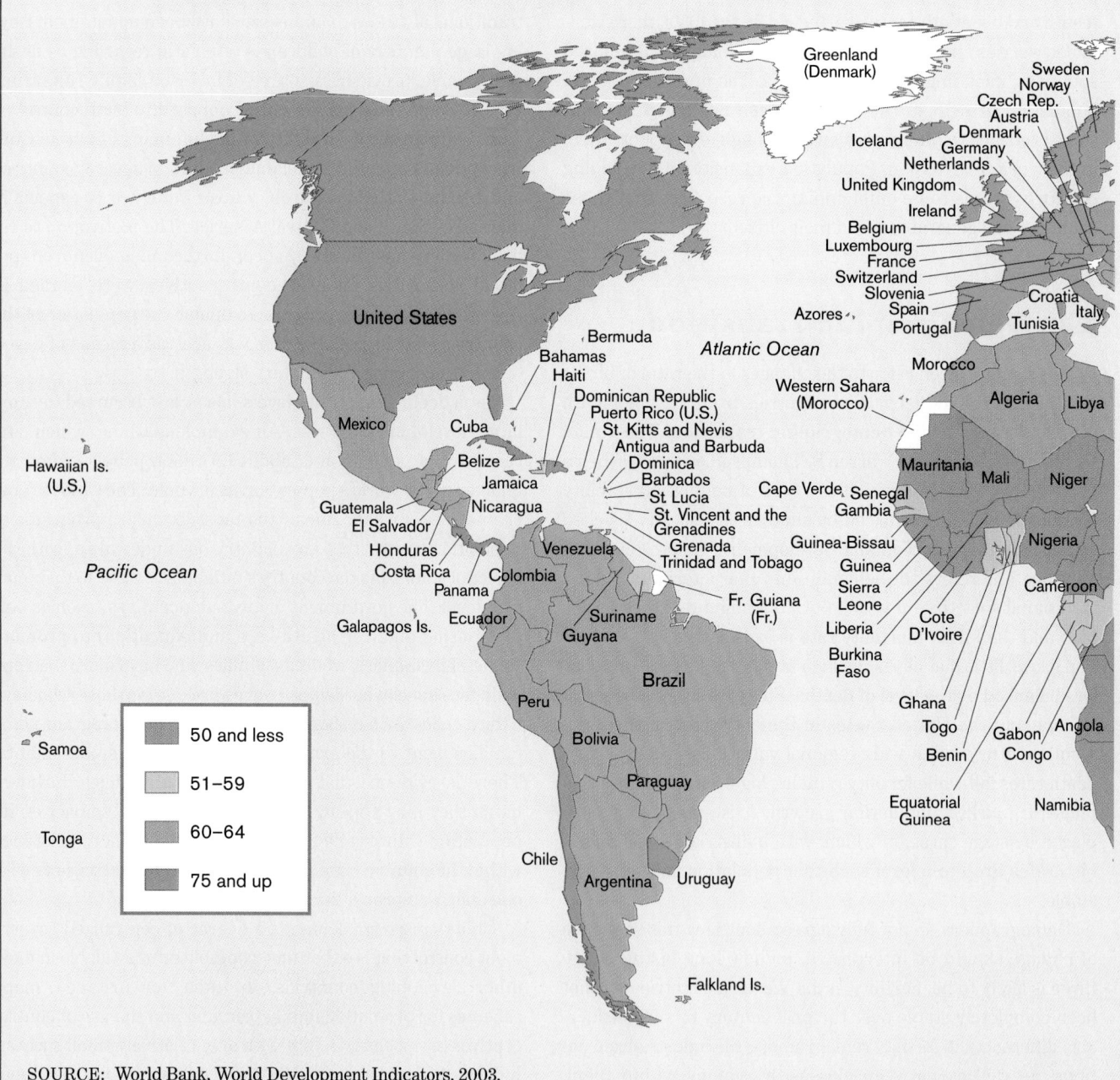

Legend:
- 50 and less
- 51–59
- 60–64
- 75 and up

SOURCE: World Bank, World Development Indicators, 2003.

Population Growth Rate, 1980–2002

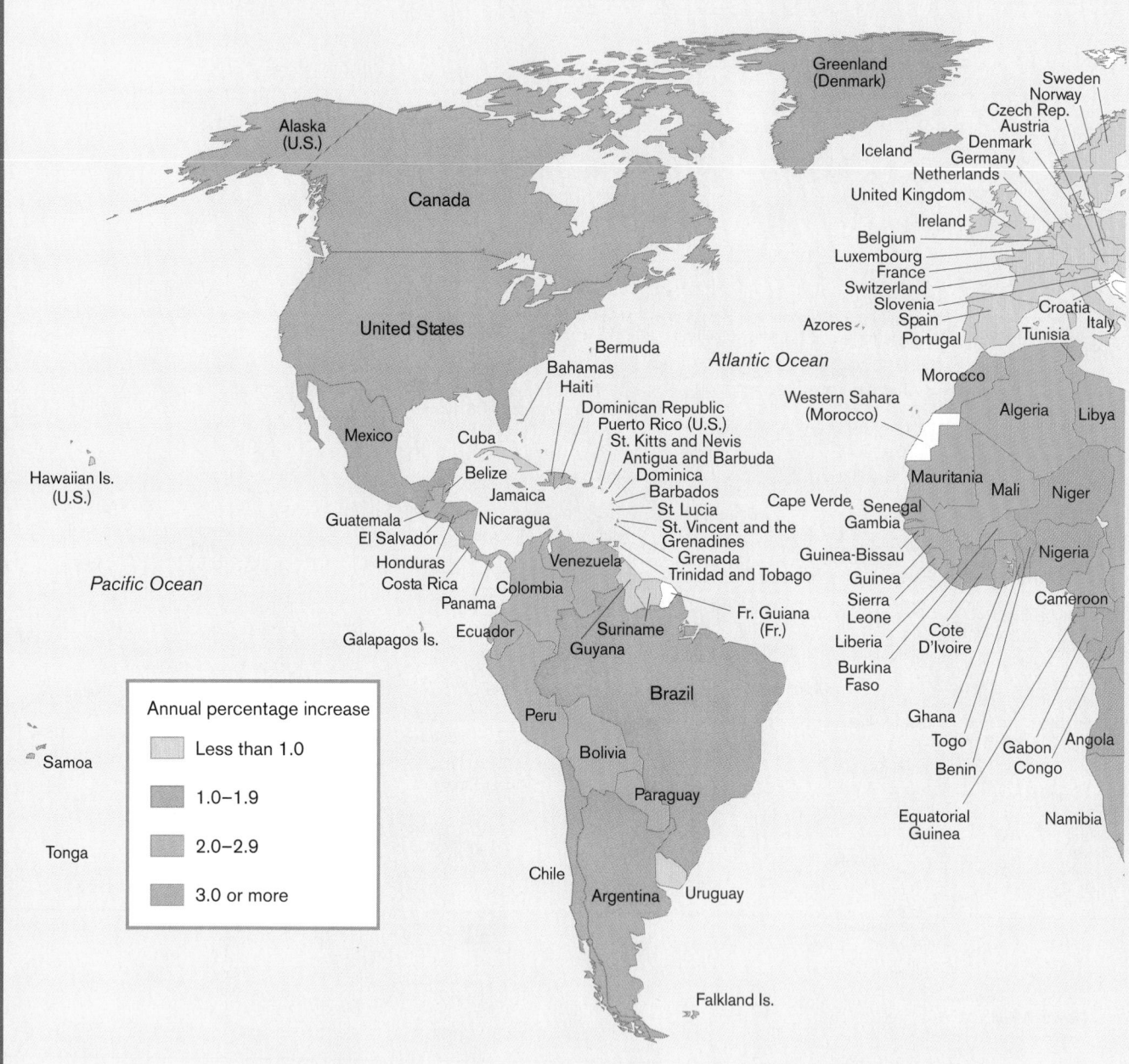

Annual percentage increase

- Less than 1.0
- 1.0–1.9
- 2.0–2.9
- 3.0 or more

SOURCE: World Bank, World Development Indicators, 2003.

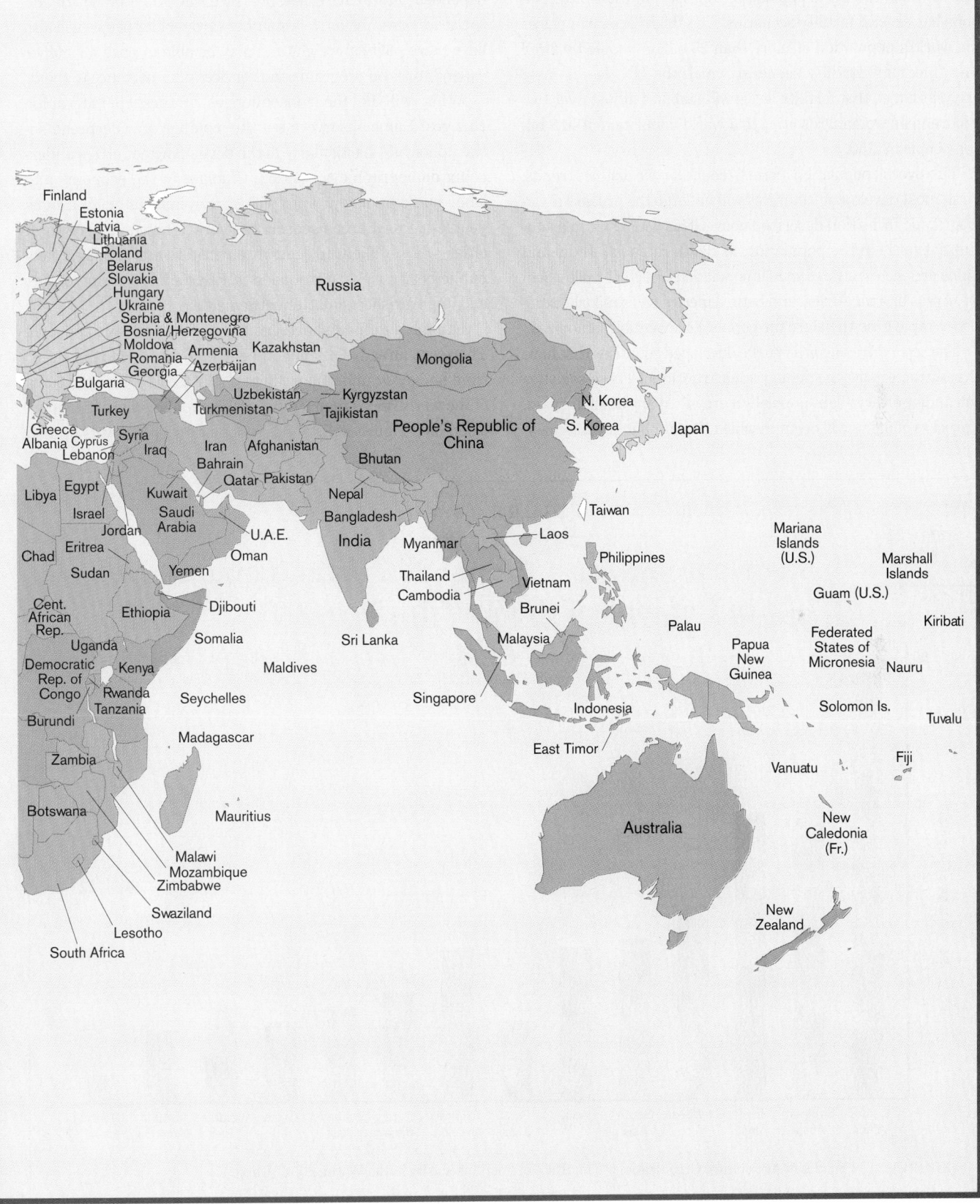

Some claim that the demographic changes that will occur over the next century will be greater than any before in all of human history. It is difficult to predict with any precision the rate at which the world population will rise, but the United Nations has several fertility scenarios. The "high" scenario places the world's population at more than 25 billion people by 2150! The "medium" fertility scenario, which the UN deems most likely, assumes that fertility levels will stabilize at just over two children per woman, resulting in a world population of 10.8 billion people in 2150.

This overall population increase conceals two distinct trends. First, most developing countries will undergo the process of demographic transition described above. This will result in a substantial surge in the population, as death rates fall. India and China are each likely to see their populations reach 1.5 billion people. Areas in Asia, Africa, and Latin America will similarly experience rapid growth before the population eventually stabilizes.

The second trend concerns the developed countries that have already undergone the demographic transition. These societies will undergo very slight population growth, if any at all. Instead, a process of aging will occur in which the number of young people will decline in absolute terms and the older segment of the population will increase markedly. This will have widespread economic and social implications for developed countries: As the dependency ratio increases, pressure will mount on health and social services. Yet, as their numbers grow, older people will also have more political weight and may be able to push for higher expenditures on programs and services of importance to them.

What will be the consequences of these demographic changes? Some observers see the makings of widespread social upheaval—particularly in the developing countries undergoing demographic transition. Changes in the economy and labor markets may prompt widespread internal migration as people in rural areas search for work. The rapid growth of cities will be likely to lead to environmental damage, new public-health risks, overloaded infrastructures, rising crime, and impoverished squatter settlements.

Famine and food shortages are another serious concern. There are already 842 million people in the world who suffer from hunger or undernourishment (FAO, 2003). In some parts of the world, more than a third of the population is undernourished (see Figure 19.1). As the population rises, levels of food

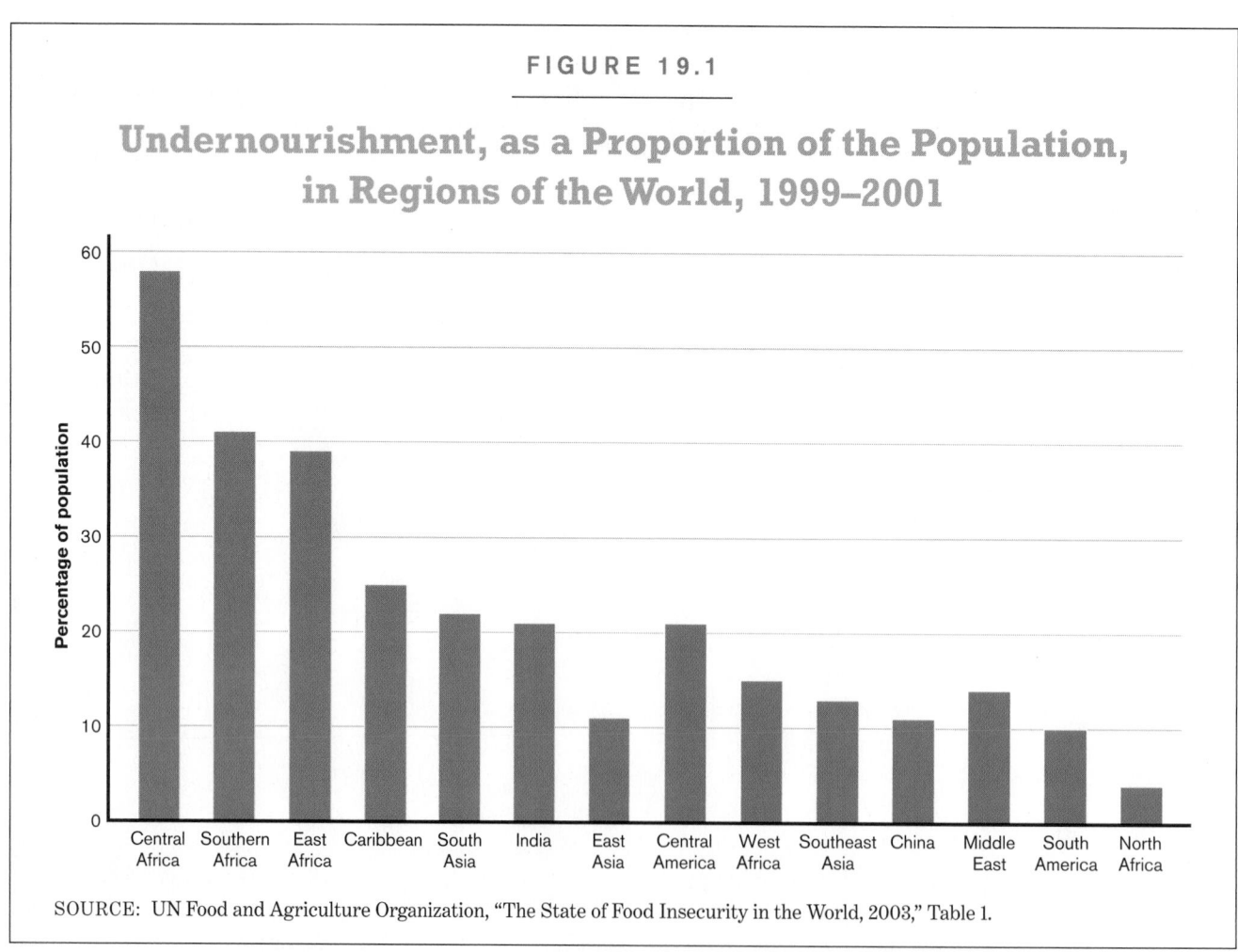

FIGURE 19.1

Undernourishment, as a Proportion of the Population, in Regions of the World, 1999–2001

SOURCE: UN Food and Agriculture Organization, "The State of Food Insecurity in the World, 2003," Table 1.

output will need to rise accordingly to avoid widespread scarcity. Yet this scenario is unlikely; many of the world's poorest areas are particularly affected by water shortages, shrinking farmland, and soil degradation—processes that reduce, rather than enhance, agricultural productivity. It is almost certain that food production will not occur at a level to ensure self-sufficiency. Large amounts of food and grain will need to be imported from areas where there are surpluses. According to the Food and Agricultural Organization (FAO), by 2010 industrialized countries will be producing 1,614 pounds of grain per person, compared to only 507 pounds per head in the developing world.

Technological advances in agriculture and industry are unpredictable, so no one can be sure how large a population the world might eventually be able to support. Yet even at current population levels, global resources may already be well below those required to create living standards in the less developed world comparable to those of the industrialized countries.

Population Growth and the Environment

Since the beginning of the practice of agriculture thousands of years ago, human beings have left an imprint on nature. Hunting and gathering societies mainly lived *from* nature; they existed on what the natural environment provided and made little attempt to change the world around them. With the coming of agriculture, this situation was altered. For crops to grow, land must be cleared, trees cut down, and encroaching weeds and wild foliage kept at bay. Even primitive farming methods can lead to soil erosion. Once natural forests are cut down and clearings made, the wind may blow away the topsoil. The farming community then clears some fresh plots of land, and so the process goes on. Some landscapes that we today think of as natural, such as the rocky areas and scrubland in southwestern Greece, are actually the result of soil erosion created by farmers five thousand years ago.

Yet before the development of modern industry, nature dominated human life far more than the other way round. Today the human onslaught on the environment is so intense that few natural processes are uninfluenced by human activity. Nearly all cultivable land is under agricultural production. What used to be almost inaccessible wildernesses are now often nature reserves, visited routinely by thousands of tourists. Modern industry, still expanding worldwide, has led to steeply climbing demands for sources of energy and raw materials. Yet the world's supply of such energy sources and

raw materials is limited, and some key resources are bound to run out if global consumption is not restricted. Even the world's climate, as we shall see, has probably been affected by the global development of industry.

Global Environmental Threats

One problem we all face concerns **environmental ecology.** The spread of industrial production may already have done irreparable damage to the environment. Ecological questions concern not only how we can best cope with and contain environmental damage, but also the very ways of life within industrialized societies. If the goal of continuous economic growth must be abandoned, new social institutions will probably be pioneered. Technological progress is unpredictable, and it may be that the earth will in fact yield sufficient resources for processes of industrialization. At the moment, however, this does not seem feasible, and if the developing countries are to achieve living standards comparable to those currently enjoyed in the West, global readjustments will be necessary.

"Green" movements and parties (such as Friends of the Earth or Greenpeace), which are themselves sometimes global organizations, have developed in response to the new environmental hazards. Although green philosophies are varied, a common thread concerns taking action to protect the world's environment, conserve rather than exhaust its resources, and protect the remaining animal species. Hundreds of animal

Greenpeace activists wearing targets protest outside the Brazilian Embassy in Hong Kong on October 18, 2001. The demonstrators urged the Brazilian government to guarantee the safety of environmentalists working to protect the Amazon following a telephoned death threat made against Greenpeace workers in Manaus, in the heart of the Amazon.

species have become extinct even over the past fifty years, and at the moment this is a continuing process.

Some environmental problems are particularly concentrated in specific areas. In the formerly communist societies of Eastern Europe and the Soviet Union, rivers, forests, and the air are highly polluted by industrial wastes. The consequences of such pollution, if it goes on unchecked, are potentially worldwide. As we have learned, the societies of the earth have become much more interdependent than ever before. As travelers on "spaceship earth," no matter where we live, we are all menaced by corrosion of the environment.

Global environmental threats are of several basic sorts: pollution, the creation of waste that cannot be disposed of in the short term or recycled, and the depletion of resources that cannot be replenished. The amount of domestic waste—what goes into our garbage cans—produced each day in the industrialized societies is staggering; these countries have sometimes been called the "throw-away societies" because the volume of items discarded as a matter of course is so large. For instance, food is mostly bought in packages that are thrown away at the end of the day. Some of these can be reprocessed and reused, but most cannot. Some kinds of widely employed plastics simply become unusable waste; there is no way of recycling them, and they have to be buried in garbage dumps.

When environmental analysts speak of waste materials, however, they mean not only goods that are thrown away, but also gaseous wastes pumped into the atmosphere. Examples are the carbon dioxide released into the atmosphere by the burning of fuels such as oil and coal in cars and power stations, and gases released into the air by the use of such things as aerosol cans, material for insulation, and air-conditioning units. Carbon dioxide is the main influence on the process of global warming that many scientists believe is occurring, while the other gases attack the ozone layer around the earth.

Global warming is thought to happen in the following way. The buildup of carbon dioxide in the earth's atmosphere functions like the glass of a greenhouse. It allows the sun's rays to pass through but acts as a barrier to prevent them from passing back. The effect is to heat up the earth; global warming is sometimes termed the "greenhouse effect" for this reason. If global warming is indeed taking place, the consequences are likely to be devastating. Among other things, sea levels will rise as the polar ice caps melt and the oceans will warm and expand. Cities that lie near the coasts or in low-lying areas will be flooded and become uninhabitable. Large tracts of fertile land will become desert.

The ozone layer, which is high in the earth's atmosphere, forms a shield that protects against ultraviolet radiation. The gases used in aerosols and refrigerants produce particles that react with the ozone layer in such a way as to weaken it. It is thought that these chemicals have produced detectable holes in the ozone layer at both poles and thinning elsewhere. The radiation that is let into the earth's atmosphere produces a variety of potentially harmful effects, including an increase in cataracts of the eyes (which can cause blindness) and in levels of skin cancer.

Modern industry, still expanding worldwide, has led to steeply climbing demands for sources of energy and raw materials. Yet the world's supply of such energy sources and raw materials is limited. Even at current rates of use, for example, the known oil resources of the world will be completely consumed by the year 2050. New reserves of oil may be discovered, or alternative sources of cheap energy invented, but there plainly is a point at which some key resources will run out if global consumption is not limited.

Sustainable Development

Rather than calling for a reining back of economic growth, more recent developments turn on the notion of **sustainable development.** Sustainable development means that growth should, at least ideally, be carried on in such a way as to recycle physical resources rather than deplete them and to keep levels of pollution to a minimum. The term *sustainable development* was first introduced in a 1987 report commissioned by the United Nations, *Our Common Future.* This is also known as the Brundtland Report, since the organizing committee which produced the report was chaired by G. H. Brundtland, at that time the prime minister of Norway. Sustainable development was defined as the use of renewable resources to promote economic growth, the protection of animal species and biodiversity, and the commitment to maintaining clean air, water, and land. The Brundtland Commission regarded sustainable development as "meeting the needs of the present, without compromising the ability of future generations to meet their own needs."

Following the publication of *Our Common Future,* the phrase *sustainable development* came to be widely used both by environmentalists and by governments. It was employed at the UN Earth Summit in Rio de Janeiro in 1992 and has subsequently appeared in other ecological summit meetings organized by the UN.

The Brundtland Report attracted much criticism. Critics see the notion of sustainable development as too vague and as neglecting the specific needs of poorer countries. According to the critics, the idea of sustainable development tends to focus attention only on the needs of richer countries; it does not consider the ways in which the high levels of consumption in the more affluent countries are satisfied at the expense of other people. For instance, demands on Indonesia to conserve its rainforests could be seen as unfair, because Indonesia has a greater need than the industrialized countries for the revenue it must forgo by accepting conservation.

Consumption, Poverty, and the Environment

Much of the debate surrounding the environment and economic development hinges on the issue of consumption patterns. *Consumption* refers to the goods, services, energy, and resources that are used up by people, institutions and societies. It is a phenomenon with both positive and negative dimensions. On the one hand, rising levels of consumption around the world mean that people are living under better conditions than in times past. Consumption is linked to economic development—as living standards rise, people are able to afford more food, clothing, personal items, leisure time, vacations, cars, and so forth. On the other hand, consumption can have negative impacts as well. Consumption patterns can damage the environmental resource base and exacerbate patterns of inequality.

The trends in world consumption over the course of the twentieth century are startling. According to the Human Development Report of the United Nations Development Program (UNDP, 1998), private and public consumption expenditures in 1998 reached 24 trillion dollars—twice the level of 1975 and six times that of 1950. In 1900, world consumption levels were just over 1.5 trillion dollars. Consumption rates have been growing extremely rapidly over the past twenty-five years. In industrialized countries, consumption per head has been growing at a rate of 2.3 percent annually; in East Asia growth has been even faster—6.1 percent annually. By contrast, the average African household consumes 20 percent *less* today than it did twenty-five years ago. There is widespread concern that the consumption explosion has passed by the poorest fifth of the world's population (UNDP, 1998).

The inequalities in consumption between rich and poor are significant. The richest 20 percent of the world's population accounts for 86 percent of private consumption expenditures, whereas the poorest 20 percent accounts for only 1.3 percent (see Figure 19.2). The richest 20 percent consumes 58 percent of total energy, 84 percent of all paper, 45 percent of all meat and fish, and owns 87 percent of all the vehicles.

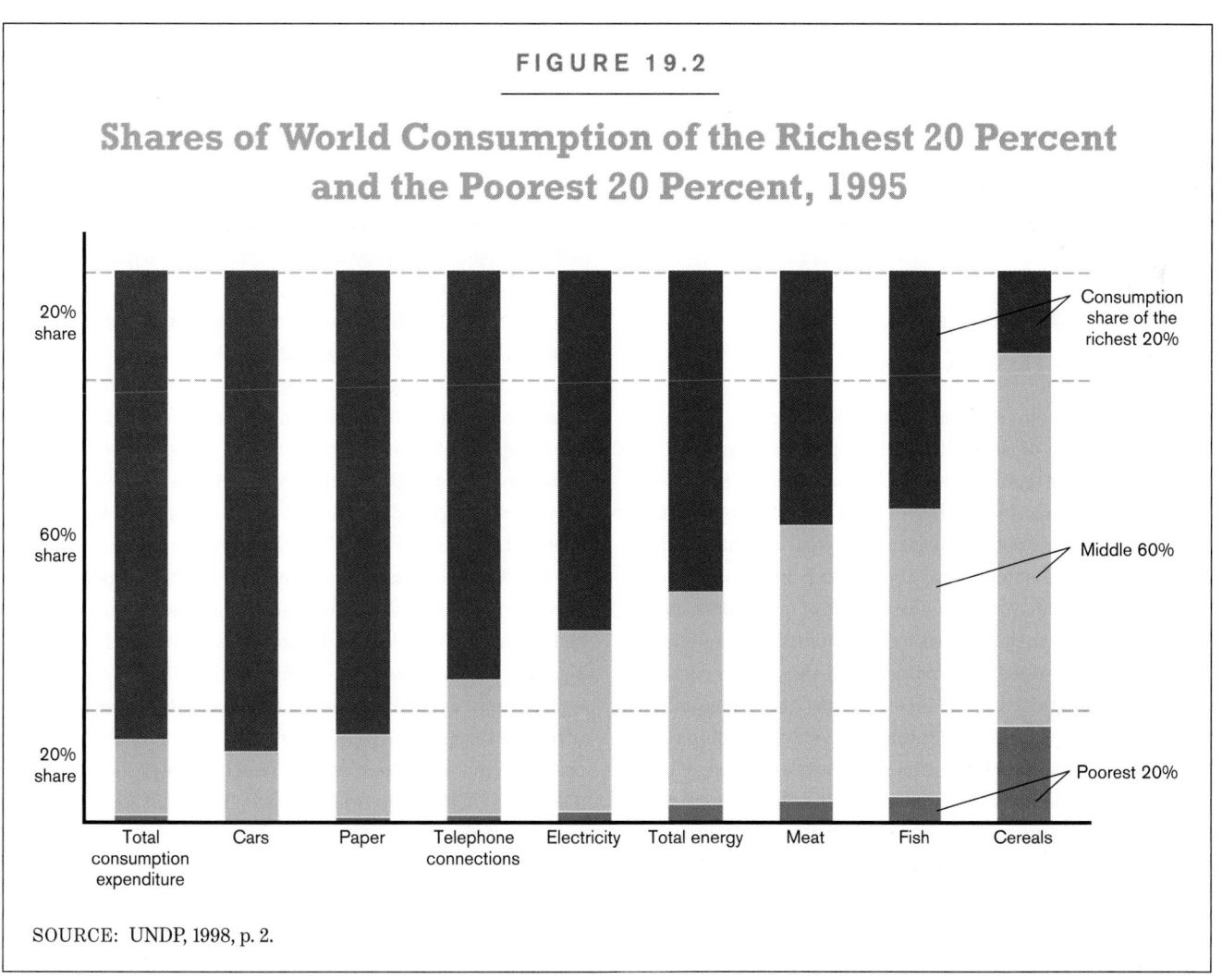

FIGURE 19.2

Shares of World Consumption of the Richest 20 Percent and the Poorest 20 Percent, 1995

SOURCE: UNDP, 1998, p. 2.

Current consumption patterns are not only highly unequal, but they also are having a severe impact on the environment. For example, the consumption of fresh water has doubled since 1960, the burning of fossil fuels has almost quintupled in the past fifty years, and the consumption of wood is up by 40 percent over twenty-five years ago. Fish stocks are declining, wild species are becoming extinct, water supplies are diminishing, and wooded areas are shrinking in size (UNDP, 1998). Patterns of consumption are not only depleting existing natural elements, but are also contributing to its degradation through waste products and harmful emissions.

Finally, although the rich are the world's main consumers, the environmental damage that is caused by growing consumption has the heaviest impact on the poor. The wealthy are in a better position to enjoy the many benefits of consumption without having to deal with its negative effects. On a local level, affluent groups can usually afford to move away from problem areas, leaving the poor to bear most of the costs. Chemical plants, power stations, major roads, railways, and airports are often sited close to low-income areas. On a global level, we can see a similar process at work: Soil degradation, deforestation, water shortages, lead emissions, and air pollution are all concentrated within the developing world. Poverty also intensifies these environmental threats. People with few resources have little choice but to maximize the resources that are available to them. As a result, more and more pressures are put on a shrinking resource base as the human population increases.

The Environment: A Sociological Issue?

Why should the environment be a concern for sociologists? Aren't we talking of issues that are the province purely of scientists or technologists? Isn't the impact of human beings on nature a physical one, created by modern technologies of industrial production? Yes, but modern industry and technology have come into being in relation to distinctive social institutions. The origins of our impact on the environment are social, and so are many of its consequences.

Rescuing the global environment will thus mean social as well as technological change. Given the vast global inequalities that exist, there is little chance that the poor developing countries will sacrifice their own economic growth because of environmental problems created largely by the rich ones. Yet the earth does not seem to possess sufficient resources for everyone on the planet to live at the standard of living most people in the industrialized societies take for granted. Hence, if the impoverished sectors of the world are to catch up with the richer ones, the latter are likely to have to revise their expectations about constant economic growth. Some "green" authors argue that people in the rich countries must react against consumerism and return to more simple ways of life if global ecological disaster is to be avoided.

Prospects for Change

There can be no question but that global warming is a global problem. Greenhouse gases released in the atmosphere do not simply affect the climate of the country in which they were produced, but alter climatic patterns for the entire world. For this reason, many policy makers and scientists believe that any viable solution to the problem must also be global in scale. Yet the political difficulties in negotiating an international treaty to reduce greenhouse gases are enormous and suggest that although globalization has ushered in a new era of international cooperation, the world is still far from being able to speak decisively with a unified political voice about many of the issues that it confronts.

In December 1997, delegates from 166 nations gathered in Kyoto, Japan, in an effort to hammer out an agreement to reduce global warming. The summit was the culmination of two years of informal discussion among the countries. World leaders, faced with mounting scientific evidence that global warming is indeed occurring, and under pressure from voters to adopt environmentally friendly policies, clearly recognized that international action of some kind was needed. But faced as well with intense lobbying by industry, which fears it will bear the brunt of the cost for reducing fossil fuel emissions, world leaders felt compelled to balance safeguarding the environment against the threat of economic disruption.

As a result, the pollution reductions agreed to by the countries are meager. Thirty-eight of the advanced industrial nations represented at the conference agreed to reduce total emission levels by 2010 to approximately 5 percent below what they were in 1990. But different countries agreed to different specific targets: The United States agreed (upon ratification by the U.S. Congress) to reduce emission levels by 7 percent, the fifteen countries of the European Union pledged an 8 percent reduction, and Japan promised a 6 percent cut. The nations also tentatively agreed to establish an emissions "trading" system whereby a country that has reduced emissions levels beyond its target will be able to sell emissions "credits" to countries that have been unable to meet their goals. The agreement also includes commitments on behalf of the industrialized countries to assist developing countries by providing technology and funding to help overcome their limited capacity to respond to climate change.

To become an active and enforceable treaty, the Kyoto Protocol must receive support from countries that emit 55 percent of global greenhouse emissions. This finally happened in November 2004 when Russia ratified the agreement. This brought the total number of ratifying countries to 127, including China, India, Japan, New Zealand, and the European Union. Notably, Australia and the United States have refused to ratify the treaty even though the United States is responsible for the largest single share of global greenhouse gases of any country.

While politicians hailed the accord as an important first step in dealing with global warming, there are three serious problems with the Kyoto agreement. First, while many newly industrialized countries, such as China, India, and Russia, have now ratified the treaty, the terms of the agreement largely exempt them from making emission reductions. Because the reduction of greenhouse gas emissions requires expensive technology upgrades for factories and other industrial infrastructure, opponents of the agreement have argued that the exemption for developing countries gives them an unfair competitive advantage in the global market. Yet this critique fails to take into account that developed countries produce over five times more emissions per person than developing countries (UN, 2004). This holds true even for China, which has the world's largest population and has been industrializing rapidly. The United States alone is responsible for over 25 percent of carbon dioxide emissions (BBC, 2001a). Second, many environmentalists warn that the reduction in greenhouse gases agreed to at Kyoto is not enough to reverse the trend toward global warming—only to slow its onset. Unless much greater emissions reductions are achieved, the world will still experience most of the disastrous consequences of global warming in the next century. Others, including President George W. Bush, have suggested that the science that supports the Kyoto Protocol is inconclusive and provides insufficient evidence that the measures adopted in the agreement would have their intended effect (White House Press Office, 2001). This is contrary to the United Nations Intergovernmental Panel on Climate Change (IPCC), which reviewed all of the available scientific research on climate change and determined that in fact, global warming is a result of human production of greenhouse gases and must be addressed immediately to avert a climatic disaster. Third, and most problematic, the Kyoto accord, which must be ratified by the legislative bodies of all the signatory countries, faces stiff political opposition. Industry leaders and conservative politicians in the United States, for example, claim that reaching even the 7 percent reduction agreed to by the U.S. delegation would be tremendously expensive and that the environmental regulations required to achieve even this modest goal would hamstring U.S. business and retard economic growth. The former House Speaker Newt Gingrich said the United States "surrendered" to pressure in Kyoto and called the proposed treaty an outrage that would cripple the American economy. In 2001, in an attempt to satisfy American business interests, President Bush proposed an alternative strategy to lower greenhouse gas emissions through a system of government incentives for voluntary emission reductions by private businesses. Countries that ratified the treaty denounced the Bush plan as ineffective and openly criticized the unwillingness of the United States to ratify the Kyoto Protocol or seriously address the global problems created in no small part by American industrialism.

It is clear that modern technology, science, and industry are not exclusively beneficial in their consequences. Sociologists perceive a responsibility to examine closely the social relations and institutions that brought about the current state of affairs, because rescuing the situation will require a profound consciousness of human authorship.

Study Outline

www.wwnorton.com/giddens5

Traditional Cities

- Traditional cities differed in many ways from modern urban areas. They were mostly very small by modern standards, were surrounded by walls, and their centers were dominated by religious buildings and palaces.

Living in Cities

- In traditional societies, only a small minority of the population lived in urban areas. In the industrialized countries today, between 60 percent and 90 percent do so. Urbanism is also increasing very rapidly in developing countries.

Theories of Urbanism

- Early approaches to urban sociology were dominated by the work of the Chicago School. The members of this school saw urban processes in terms of ecological models derived from biology. Louis Wirth developed the conception of urbanism as a "way of life." These approaches have more recently been challenged, though without being discarded altogether.
- Later approaches to urban theory have placed more emphasis on the influence of broader socioeconomic factors—particularly those deriving from industrial capitalism—on city life.

Suburbanization

- The expansion of suburbs—*suburbanization*—has contributed to *inner-city* decay. Wealthier groups and businesses tend to move out of the central city in order to take advantage of lower tax rates. This begins a cycle of deterioration, in which the more suburbia expands, the greater the problems faced by those living in the central cities. *Urban renewal* (also called *gentrification*)—the refurbishing of old buildings to put them to new uses—has become common in many large cities.

Urban Development

- Urban analysis today must be prepared to link global and local issues. Factors that influence urban development locally are sometimes part of much more international processes. The structure of local neighborhoods and their patterns of growth and decline often reflect changes in industrial production internationally.
- Massive urban development is occurring in developing countries. Cities in these societies differ in major respects from those characteristic of the West. The majority of the population live in illegal make-shift housing, in conditions of extreme poverty.
- Population growth is one of the most significant global problems currently faced by humanity. About a quarter of the world's population suffers from malnutrition, and over 10 million people die of starvation each year. This misery is concentrated in the developing countries.

Demography

- The study of population growth is called *demography*. Much demographic work is statistical, but demographers are also concerned with trying to explain why population patterns take the form they do. The most important concepts in population analysis are *birthrates, death rates, fertility,* and *mortality*.
- The changes in population patterns that have occurred in the industrialized societies are usually analyzed in terms of a process of *demographic transition*. Prior to industrialization, both birth and death rates were high. During the beginning of industrialization, there was population growth because death rates were reduced while birthrates took longer to decline. Finally a new equilibrium was reached with low birthrates balancing low death rates.
- World resources are finite, even if the limits of what can be produced are continually revised due to technological developments. Energy consumption and the consumption of raw materials and other goods are vastly higher in the Western countries than in other areas of the world. These consumption levels depend, moreover, on resources transferred from developing regions to the industrially developed nations. If resources were shared equally, there would be a significant drop in Western living standards.
- There are few aspects of the natural world that have not been affected by human activity. The industrialization of agriculture, the depletion of natural resources, the pollution of air and water, and the creation of vast mountains of unrecyclable waste are all sources of threat to the future survival of humanity. Addressing these issues will mean, among other things, that richer nations will have to revise their expectations of persistent economic growth.

Key Concepts

collective consumption (p. 585)
conurbation (p. 581)
created environment (p. 585)
crude birthrate (p. 599)
crude death rate (p. 602)
demographic transition (p. 603)
demography (p. 599)
doubling time (p. 602)
ecological approach (p. 582)
environmental ecology (p. 609)
exponential growth (p. 602)
fecundity (p. 599)
fertility (p. 599)
gentrification (p. 590)
global city (p. 594)
infant mortality rate (p. 602)
inner city (p. 582)
life expectancy (p. 602)
life span (p. 602)
Malthusianism (p. 603)
megacity (p. 595)
megalopolis (p. 581)
mortality (p. 602)
suburbanization (p. 586)
sustainable development (p. 610)
urban ecology (p. 582)
urban renewal (p. 590)
urbanism (p. 583)
urbanization (p. 581)

Review Questions

1. Most cities of the ancient world shared certain common features. Which one of the following is *not* one of those features?
   a. Cities were surrounded by walls.
   b. The central area of the city was occupied by a religious temple.
   c. The dwellings of the ruling class or elite tended to be concentrated in or near the center.
   d. Cities' influence over the rest of the countries was strong.
2. The inequalities in consumption between rich and poor are significant. The richest 20 percent of the world's population accounts for _____ percent of private consumption expenditures.
   a. 26
   b. 46
   c. 86
   d. 96

3. The Chicago School applied an ecological approach to the study of cities. What were the main concepts of this approach?

a. Cities became ordered into "natural areas"—concentric rings—through processes of competition, invasion, and succession.

b. The main concepts were differentiation and interdependence.

c. Urbanism is a specific "way of life."

d. Cities processed strangers by policing streets and pooling immigrants from the same backgrounds in their own neighborhoods.

4. What argument did Drake and Cayton make against the Chicago School with their book *Black Metropolis* (1945)?

a. They showed how blacks were treated as a lower species in the competition with whites for space and employment.

b. They demonstrated that the existence of black ghetto neighborhoods was the result not of natural competitive forces, but of segregation.

c. They found that blacks were evenly distributed in neighborhoods across the city when, according to the Chicago School's approach, they should have been specifically concentrated in ghettos.

d. They argued from their study of street interactions in mixed neighborhoods, and a comparison with interactions in the South, that there was no distinctive urban way of life.

5. According to Wirth, what function do "the reserve, the indifference, and the blasé outlook of urbanites" have in everyday living?

a. They are devices for immunizing urbanites against the personal claims and expectations of others.

b. They are devices for demonstrating the sophistication and critical acumen of the urbanite.

c. They are devices for reminding out-of-towners of their place as visitors.

d. They are devices for getting about town in a hurry.

6. What's the difference between *fertility* and *fecundity*?

a. *Fertility* refers to how many births the average woman has, whereas *fecundity* refers to how many of those births were of children who survived past one year of age.

b. *Fertility* refers to a woman's ability to ovulate, whereas *fecundity* refers to a man's ability to produce healthy sperm.

c. *Fertility* refers to how many live-born children the average woman has, whereas *fecundity* refers to the potential number of children women are biologically capable of having.

d. *Fertility* is the rate of live births of individuals, whereas *fecundity* is the rate of live birth of twins.

7. What is the Malthusian perspective on population?

a. Population growth will inevitably outstrip the food supply.

b. Food supply and population growth will always be in balance.

c. Agricultural technology will ensure enough food supply for the world's population.

d. All of the above.

8. What role can sociologists play in helping society come to terms with global warming?

a. Sociologists have a public duty to become actively engaged in the environmental movement and to put their unique perspective on social change to use for the public good.

b. Sociologists can help educate politicians and the public to understand the complex interdependencies of globalization and to show everyone that we are all in this together.

c. Sociologists can facilitate cross-cultural cooperation.

d. Sociologists can help make members of the public conscious of the wasteful choices they make in consumption—for example, by lobbying the local supermarket to reduce the bulk of packaging and by picketing car lots that sell notoriously fuel-inefficient sport utility vehicles.

9. According to Saskia Sassen, an urban center that is home to the headquarters of large, transnational corporations and a superabundance of financial, technological, and consulting service is called a

a. prime city.

b. modern city.

c. global city.

d. developed city.

10. Why is the rate of urban growth in the world's less-developed regions so much higher than elsewhere?

a. Rates of population growth are higher in developing countries than they are in industrialized nations.

b. Rates of population growth are lower in developing countries than they are in industrialized nations.

c. There is widespread internal migration from rural to urban areas.

d. a and c.

Thinking Sociologically Exercises

1. Explain what makes the urbanization now occurring in developing countries, such as Brazil and India, different from and more problematic than the urbanization that took place a century ago in New York, London, Tokyo, and Berlin.

2. Following analysis presented in this chapter, concisely explain how the expanded quest for cheap energy and raw materials and present-day dangers of environmental pollution and resource depletion threaten not only the survival of people in developed countries, but also that of people in less developed countries.

Data Exercises

www.wwnorton.com/giddens5
Keyword: Data19

• One of the basic concerns of a society is the quality of life of its citizens. The overall quality of life is reflected in a society's measure of life expectancy or how long its citizens can expect to live, given current mortality levels. The data exercise for this chapter explores the association between life expectancy and national income.

Influences on Social Change

Recognize that three main factors influence social change: the physical environment, the political organization, and cultural factors.

Change in the Modern Period

Analyze modern social change, particularly the impact of economic, political, and cultural factors.

Globalization

Recognize the dimensions, causes, and consequences of globalization.

CHAPTER TWENTY

GLOBALIZATION IN A CHANGING WORLD

human beings have inhabited the earth for about half a million years. Agriculture, the necessary basis of fixed settlements, is only around twelve thousand years old. Civilizations date back no more than six thousand years or so. If we were to think of the entire span of human existence thus far as a twenty-four-hour day, agriculture would have come into existence at 11:56 P.M. and civilizations at 11:57. The development of modern societies would not get under way until 11:59 and 30 seconds! Yet perhaps as much change has taken place in the last 30 seconds of this human day as in all the time leading up to it.

 The pace of change in the modern era is easily demonstrated if we look at rates of technological development. As the economic historian David Landes has observed:

> Modern technology produces not only more, faster; it turns out objects that could not have been produced under any circumstances by the craft methods of yesterday. The best Indian hand-spinner could not turn out yarn so fine and regular as that of the [spinning] mule; all the forges in eighteenth century Christendom could not have produced steel sheets so large, smooth and homogeneous as those of a modern strip mill. Most important, modern technology has created things that could scarcely have been conceived in the pre-industrial era: the camera, the motor car, the airplane, the whole array of electronic devices from the radio to the high-speed computer, the nuclear power plant, and so on almost ad infinitum. . . . The result has been an enormous increase in the output and

variety of goods and services and this alone has changed man's way of life more than anything since the discovery of fire: The Englishman of 1750 was closer in material things to Caesar's legionnaires than to his own great-grandchildren. (1969)

The modes of life and social institutions characteristic of the modern world are radically different from those of even the recent past. During a period of only two or three centuries—a minute sliver of time in the context of human history—human social life has been wrenched away from the types of social order in which people lived for thousands of years.

Far more than any generation before us, we face an uncertain future. To be sure, conditions of life for previous generations were always insecure: People were at the mercy of natural disasters, plagues, and famines. But though we are largely immune from plague and famine in the industrialized countries today, we must deal now with the social forces we ourselves have unleashed.

Defining Change

There is a sense in which everything changes, all of the time. Every day is a new day; every moment is a new instant in time. The Greek philosopher Heraclitus pointed out that a person cannot step into the same river twice. On the second occasion, the river is different, since the water has been flowing in the meantime, and the person has changed in subtle ways, too. Although this observation is in a sense correct, we do of course normally want to say that it is the same river and the same person stepping into it on two occasions. There is sufficient continuity in the shape of the river and in the physique and personality of the person with wet feet to say that each remains the same.

All accounts of change also involve showing what remains stable, as a baseline against which to measure changes. Even in the rapidly moving world of today, there are continuities with the distant past. Major religious systems, for example, such as Judaism, Christianity, or Islam retain their ties with ideas and practices initiated some two thousand years ago. Yet most institutions in modern societies clearly change much more rapidly than did institutions of the traditional world.

How should we define social change? **Social change** is the transformation over time of the institutions and culture of a society. In this chapter, we will look at attempts to interpret patterns of social change affecting human history as a whole; we will then consider why the modern period should be associated with such especially profound and rapid social change. This will be followed by a discussion of globalization, especially in terms of where the major lines of social change in modern societies and in the global order as a whole seem to be leading.

Influences on Social Change

Social theorists have tried for the past two centuries to develop a single grand theory that explains the nature of social change. But no single-factor theory has a chance of accounting for the diversity of human social development from hunting and gathering and pastoral societies to traditional civilizations and finally to the highly complex social systems of today. In analyzing social change, we can at most accomplish two tasks. We can identify the three main factors that have consistently influenced social change: the physical environment, political organization, and cultural factors. We can also develop theories that account for particular periods of change, such as modern times.

The Physical Environment

The physical environment often has an effect on the development of human social organization (Diamond, 1997). This is clearest in more extreme environmental conditions, where people must organize their ways of life in relation to weather conditions. People in polar regions necessarily develop different habits and practices from those living in subtropical areas. People who live in Alaska, where the winters are long and cold and the days very short, tend to follow different patterns of social life from people who live in the much warmer American South. Most Alaskans spend more of their lives indoors and, except for the summer months, plan outdoor activities carefully, given the frequently inhospitable environment in which they live.

Less extreme physical conditions can also affect society. The native population of Australia has never stopped being hunters and gatherers, since the continent contained hardly any indigenous plants suitable for regular cultivation or animals that could be domesticated to develop pastoral production. The world's early civilizations mostly originated in areas that contained rich agricultural land—for instance, in river deltas. The ease of communications across land and the availability of sea routes are also important: Societies cut off from others by mountain ranges, impassable jungles, or deserts often remain relatively unchanged over long periods of time.

Yet the direct influence of the environment on social change is not very great. People are often able to develop considerable productive wealth in relatively inhospitable areas. This is true, for example, of Alaskans, who have been able to develop oil and mineral resources in spite of the harsh nature of their surrounding environment. Conversely, hunting and gathering cultures have frequently lived in highly fertile regions without becoming involved in pastoral or agricultural production. For example, the Kwakiutl of Vancouver Island, whose way of life survived largely intact until about half a century ago, lived in an environment rich in fish, fruit, and edible plants. They were content with a hunting and gathering way of life in such favorable conditions and never sought to convert to settled agriculture.

There is little direct relation between the environment and the systems of production that develop. The evolutionists' emphasis on adaptation to the environment is thus less illuminating than Marx's ideas in explaining social development. For Marx stressed that human beings rarely just adapt to their surrounding circumstances, as animals do. Humans always seek to master the world around them rather than take it as given. Moreover, there is no doubt that types of production strongly influence the level and nature of social change, although they do not have the overriding impact Marx attributed to them.

Political Organization

A second factor strongly influencing social change is the type of political organization that operates in a society. In hunting and gathering societies, this influence is at a minimum, since there are no political authorities capable of mobilizing the community. In all other types of society, however, the existence of distinct political agencies—chiefs, lords, monarchs, and governments—strongly affects the course of development a society takes. Political systems are not, as Marx argued, direct expressions of underlying economic organization; quite different types of political order may exist in societies that have similar production systems. For instance, some societies based on industrial capitalism have had authoritarian political systems (Nazi Germany and South Africa under apartheid); others are much more democratic (the United States, Britain, and Sweden).

Military strength played a fundamental part in the establishment of most traditional states; it influenced their subsequent survival or expansion in an equally basic way. But the connections between the level of production and military strength are again indirect. A ruler may choose to channel resources into building up the military, for example, even when this impoverishes most of the rest of the population—as happened in Iraq in the 1980s under the rule of Saddam Hussein or in North Korea during the 1990s under Kim Jong-Il.

Cultural Factors

The third main influence on social change consists of cultural factors, which include the effects of religion, communication systems, and leadership. As we have seen, religion may be either a conservative or an innovative force in social life. Some forms of religious belief and practice have acted as a brake on change, emphasizing above all the need to adhere to traditional values and rituals. Yet, as Max Weber emphasized, religious convictions frequently play a mobilizing role in pressures for social change. For instance, American church leaders promote attempts to lessen poverty or diminish inequalities in society.

A particularly important cultural influence that affects the character and pace of change is the nature of communication systems. The invention of writing, for instance, allowed for the keeping of records, making possible increased control of material resources and the development of large-scale organizations. In addition, writing altered people's perception of the relation between past, present, and future. Societies that write keep a record of past events and know themselves to have a history. Understanding history can help in developing a sense of the overall movement or line of evolution a society is following, which people can then actively seek to promote further.

Under the general heading of cultural factors we should also place leadership. Individual leaders have had an enormous influence in world history. We have only to think of great religious figures (such as Jesus), political and military leaders (such as Julius Caesar), or innovators in science and philosophy (such as Isaac Newton) to see that this is the case. A leader capable of pursuing dynamic policies and generating a mass following or radically altering preexisting modes of thought can overturn a previously established order.

However, individuals can only reach positions of leadership and become effective if favorable social conditions exist. Adolf Hitler was able to seize power in Germany in the 1930s, for instance, partly as a result of the tensions and crises that beset the country at that time. If those circumstances had not existed, he would likely have remained an obscure figure within a minor political faction. The same was true at a later date of Mahatma Gandhi, the famous pacifist leader in India. Gandhi was able to be effective in securing his country's independence from Britain because World War II and other events had unsettled the existing colonial institutions in India.

Change in the Modern Period

What explains why the last two hundred years, the period of modernity, have seen such a tremendous acceleration in the speed of social change? This is a complex issue, but it is not difficult to pinpoint some of the factors involved. Not surprisingly, we can categorize them along lines similar to factors that have influenced social change throughout history, except that we will subsume the impact of the physical environment within the overall importance of economic factors.

Economic Influences

Of economic influences, the farthest reaching is the impact of industrial capitalism. Capitalism differs in a fundamental way from preexisting production systems, because it involves the constant expansion of production and the ever-increasing accumulation of wealth. In traditional production systems, levels of production were fairly static as they were geared to habitual, customary needs. Capitalism promotes the constant revision of the technology of production, a process into which science is increasingly drawn. The rate of technological innovation fostered in modern industry is vastly greater than in any previous type of economic order.

Consider the current development of information technology. Over the past fifteen years, the power of computers has increased by a factor of ten thousand. A large computer in the 1960s was constructed using thousands of handmade connectors; an equivalent device today is not only much smaller, but requires only a handful of elements in an integrated circuit.

The impact of science and technology on how we live may be largely driven by economic factors, but it also stretches beyond the economic sphere. Science and technology both influence and are influenced by political and cultural factors. Scientific and technological development, for example, helped create modern forms of communication such as radio and television. As we have seen, such electronic forms of communication have produced changes in politics in recent years. Radio, television, and the other electronic media have also come to shape how we think and feel about the world.

Political Influences

The most important political factor that has helped to speed up patterns of change in the modern era is the emergence of the modern state, which has proved a vastly more efficient mechanism of government than the types that existed in premodern societies. Government plays a much bigger role in our lives, for better or worse, than it did before modern industrial societies came on the scene.

Many changes in the political sphere have been spurred by economic transformations. For instance, the expanded role of government called for in the New Deal in the 1930s was a response to mass unemployment. But the political system affects economic life just as much as the other way around. Thus, the New Deal was a response to economic change, but the political programs it created in turn had a big impact on later economic development, serving to help reduce unemployment and introduce a period of increased prosperity before and after World War II.

Cultural Influences

Among the cultural factors affecting processes of social change in modern times, the development of science and the secularization of thought have each contributed to the *critical* and *innovative* character of the modern outlook. We no longer assume that customs or habits are acceptable merely because they have the age-old authority of tradition. On the contrary, our ways of life increasingly require a "rational" basis. For instance, a design for a hospital would not be based mainly on traditional tastes, but would consider its capability for serving the purpose of a hospital—effectively caring for the sick.

In addition to *how* we think, the *content* of ideas has also changed. Ideals of self-betterment, freedom, equality, and democratic participation are largely creations of the past two or three centuries. Such ideals have served to mobilize processes of social and political change, including revolutions. These ideas cannot be tied to tradition, but rather suggest the constant revision of ways of life in the pursuit of human betterment. Although they initially were developed in the West, such ideals have become genuinely universal in their application, promoting change in most regions of the world.

Current Change and Future Prospects

Where is social change leading us today? What are the main trends of development likely to affect our lives as the twenty-first century opens? Social theorists do not agree on the answers to these questions, which obviously involve a great deal of speculation. We will look at several different perspectives: the notion that we are a postindustrial society, the idea that we have reached a postmodern period, and finally and in the most detail, theories that have focused on the dimensions, causes, and consequences of globalization.

TOWARD A POSTINDUSTRIAL SOCIETY?

Some observers have suggested that what is occurring today is a transition to a new society no longer primarily based on industrialism. We are entering, they claim, a phase of development beyond the industrial era altogether. A variety of terms have been coined to describe this new social order, such as **information society, service society,** and **knowledge society.** The term that has come into most common usage, however—first employed by Daniel Bell in the United States and Alain Touraine in France—is **postindustrial society** (Touraine, 1974; Bell, 1976), the *post* (meaning "after") referring to the sense that we are moving beyond the old forms of industrial development.

The diversity of names is one indication of the myriad ideas put forward to interpret current social changes. But one theme that appears consistently is the significance of *information* or *knowledge* in the society of the future. Our way of life, based on the manufacture of material goods, centered on the power machine and the factory, is being displaced by one in which information is the basis of the productive system.

The clearest and most comprehensive classical portrayal of the postindustrial society is provided by Daniel Bell in *The Coming of the Post-Industrial Society* (1976). The postindustrial order, Bell argues, is distinguished by a growth of service occupations at the expense of jobs that produce material goods. The blue-collar worker, employed in a factory or workshop, is no longer the most essential type of employee. White-collar (clerical and professional) workers outnumber blue-collar, with professional and technical occupations growing fastest of all.

People working in higher-level white-collar occupations specialize in the production of information and knowledge. The production and control of what Bell calls "codified knowledge"—systematic, coordinated information—is society's main strategic resource. Those who create and distribute this knowledge—scientists, computer specialists, economists, engineers, and professionals of all kinds—increasingly become the leading social groups, replacing the industrialists and entrepreneurs of the old system. On the level of culture, there is a shift away from the "work ethic" characteristic of industrialism; people are freer to innovate and enjoy themselves in both their work and their domestic lives.

How valid is the view that the old industrial order is being replaced by a postindustrial society? Although the thesis has been widely accepted, the empirical assertions on which it depends are suspect in several ways.

1. The trend toward service occupations, accompanied by a decline in employment in other production sectors, dates back almost to the beginning of industrialism itself; it is not simply a recent phenomenon. From the early 1800s, manufacture and services both expanded at the expense of agriculture, with the service sector consistently showing a faster rate of increase than manufacture. The blue-collar worker never really was the most common type of employee; a higher proportion of paid employees has *always* worked in agriculture and services, with the service sector increasing proportionally as the numbers in agriculture dwindled. Easily the most important change has not been from industrial to service work but from farm employment to all other types of occupation.

2. The service sector is very heterogeneous. Service occupations cannot be simply treated as identical to white-collar jobs; many service jobs (such as that of gas-station attendant) are blue-collar, in the sense that they are manual. Most white-collar positions involve little specialized knowledge and have become substantially mechanized. This is true of most lower-level office work.

3. Many service jobs contribute to a process that in the end produces material goods and therefore should really be counted as part of manufacture. Thus, a computer programmer working for an industrial firm, designing and monitoring the operation of machine tools, is directly involved in a process of making material goods.

4. No one can be sure what the long-term impact of the spreading use of microprocessing and electronic communications systems will be. At the moment, these are integrated within manufacturing production, rather than displacing it. It seems certain that such technologies will continue to show high rates of innovation and will permeate more areas of social life. But how far we yet live in a society in which codified knowledge is the main resource is unclear (Gill, 1985; Lyon, 1989).

5. The postindustrial society thesis tends to exaggerate the importance of economic factors in producing social change. Such a society is described as the outcome of developments in the economy that lead to changes in other institutions. Most of those advancing the postindustrial hypothesis have been little influenced by, or are directly critical of, Marx; but their position is a quasi-Marxist one in the sense that economic factors are held to dominate social change.

Some of the developments cited by the postindustrial theorists are important features of the current era, but it is not obvious that the concept of the postindustrial society is the best way to come to terms with them. Moreover, the forces behind the changes going on today are political and cultural as well as economic.

POSTMODERNITY

Some authors have recently gone as far as saying that the developments now occurring are even more profound than signaling the end of the era of industrialism. They claim that what is happening is nothing short of a movement beyond modernity—the attitudes and ways of life associated with modern societies, such as our belief in progress, the benefits of science, and our capability to control the modern world. A **postmodern** era is arriving, or has already arrived.

The advocates of postmodernity claim that modern societies took their inspiration from the idea that history has a shape—it "goes somewhere" and leads to progress—and that now this notion has collapsed. There are no longer any "grand narratives"—overall conceptions of history—that make any sense (Lyotard, 1985). Not only is there no general notion of progress that can be defended, there is no such thing as history. The postmodern world is thus a highly pluralistic and diverse one. In countless films, videos, and TV programs, images circulate around the world. We come into contact with many ideas and values, but these have little connection with the history of the areas in which we live, or indeed with our own personal histories. Everything seems constantly in flux. As one group of authors expressed things:

> Our world is being remade. Mass production, the mass consumer, the big city, big-brother state, the sprawling housing estate, and the nation-state are in decline: flexibility, diversity, differentiation, and mobility, communication, decentralization and internationalization are in the ascendant. In the process our own identities, our sense of self, our own subjectivities are being transformed. We are in transition to a new era. (Hall et al., 1988)

History ends alongside modernity, it is said, because there is no longer any way of describing in general terms the pluralistic universe that has come into being.

Most contemporary social theorists accept that information technology and new communications systems, together with other technological changes, are producing major social transformations for all of us. However, the majority disagree with core ideas of the postmodernists, who argue that our attempts to understand general processes in the social world are doomed, as is the notion we can change the world for the better. Writers such as Ulrich Beck and one of the authors of this textbook, Anthony Giddens, claim that we need as much as ever to develop general theories of the social world and that such theories can help us intervene to shape it in a positive way. Such theories have focused on how contemporary societies are becoming globalized, while everyday life is breaking free from the hold of tradition and custom. But these changes should not spell the end of attempts at social and political reform. Marx's dreams of a socialist alternative to capitalism are dead. But some of the values that drove the socialist project—

Fredric Jameson describes the Westin Bonaventure Hotel, located in downtown Los Angeles, as an original postmodern space. The architecture distorts viewers' sense of place—the glass exterior mirrors the building's surroundings rather than permitting a view inside—and the symmetrical design of the interior challenges viewers' ability to comprehend the space through which they are walking.

those of social community, equality, and caring for the weak and vulnerable—are still very much alive.

Globalization

The concept of globalization has become widely used in debates in politics, business, and the media over the past few years. A decade ago, the term *globalization* was relatively unknown. Today it seems to be on the tip of everyone's tongue. Globalization refers to the fact that we all increasingly live in one world, so that individuals, groups, and nations become more *interdependent*.

Globalization is often portrayed solely as an economic phenomenon. Some make much of the role of transnational corporations whose massive operations stretch across national borders, influencing global production processes and the international distribution of labor. Others point to the electronic integration of global financial markets and the enormous volume of global capital flows. Still others focus on the unprecedented scope of world trade, involving a much broader range of goods and services than ever before.

Although economic forces are an integral part of globalization, it would be wrong to suggest that they alone produce it. Globalization is created by the coming together of political, social, cultural, and economic factors. It has been driven forward above all by the development of information and communication technologies that have intensified the speed and scope of interaction between people all over the world. As a simple example, think of the 2002 soccer World Cup. Because of global television links, some matches were watched by over 2 billion people across the world.

Factors Contributing to Globalization

The explosion in global communications has been facilitated by some important advances in technology and the world's telecommunications infrastructure. In the post–World War II era, there has been a profound transformation in the scope and intensity of telecommunications flows. Traditional telephonic communication, which depended on analog signals sent through wires and cables with the help of mechanical crossbar switching, has been replaced by integrated systems in which vast amounts of information are compressed and transferred digitally. Cable technology has become more efficient and less expensive; the development of fiber-optic cables has dramatically expanded the number of channels that can be carried. Whereas the earliest transatlantic cables laid in the 1950s were capable of carrying fewer than a hundred voice paths, by 1997 a single transoceanic cable could carry some 600,000 voice paths (Held et al., 1999). The spread of communications satellites, beginning in the 1960s, has also been significant in expanding international communications. Today a network of more than two hundred satellites is in place to facilitate the transfer of information around the globe.

The impact of these communications systems has been staggering. In countries with highly developed telecommunications infrastructures, homes and offices now have multiple links to the outside world, including telephones (both land lines and mobile phones), fax machines, digital and cable television, electronic mail, and the Internet. The Internet has emerged as the fastest-growing communication tool ever developed—some 140 million people worldwide were using the Internet in mid-1998. More than 604 million people were estimated to be online by 2003.

These forms of technology facilitate the compression of time and space: Two individuals located on opposite sides of the planet—in Tokyo and London, for example—not only can hold a conversation in real time, but can also send documents and images to one another with the help of satellite technology. Widespread use of the Internet and mobile phones is deepening and accelerating processes of globalization; more and more people are becoming interconnected through the use of these technologies and are doing so in places that have pre-

viously been isolated or poorly served by traditional communications (see Figure 20.1). Although the telecommunications infrastructure is not evenly developed around the world (see Table 20.1), a growing number of countries now have access to international communications networks in a way that was previously impossible.

Globalization is also being driven forward by the integration of the world economy. In contrast to previous eras, the global economy is no longer primarily agricultural or industrial in its basis. Rather, it is increasingly dominated by activity that is weightless and intangible (Quah, 1999). This *weightless economy* is one in which products have their base in information, as is the case with computer software, media and entertainment products, and Internet-based services. This new economic context has been described using a variety of terms that we have already discussed, including *postindustrial society, information society,* and *knowledge society.* The emergence of the knowledge society has been linked to the development of a broad base of consumers who are technologically literate and eagerly integrate new advances in computing, entertainment, and telecommunications into their everyday lives.

The very operation of the global economy reflects the changes that have occurred in the information age. Many aspects of the economy now work through networks that cross national boundaries, rather than stopping at them (Castells, 1996). In order to be competitive in globalizing conditions, businesses and corporations have restructured themselves to be more flexible and less hierarchical in nature. Production practices and organizational patterns have become more flexible, partnering arrangements with other firms have become commonplace, and participation in worldwide distribution networks has become essential for doing business in a rapidly changing global market.

The Causes of Increasing Globalization

POLITICAL CHANGES

A number of influences are driving forces behind contemporary globalization. One of the most significant of these is the collapse of Soviet-style communism, which occurred in a series of dramatic revolutions in Eastern Europe in 1989 and culminated in the dissolution of the Soviet Union itself in 1991. Since the fall of Communism, countries in the former Soviet bloc—including Russia, Ukraine, Poland, Hungary, the Czech Republic, the Baltic states, the states of the Caucasus and Central Asia, and many others—are moving toward Western-style political and economic systems. They are no longer isolated from the global community, but

FIGURE 20.1

The Multiplication of Television Sets and Telephones in Regions of the World, 1985–1995, and the Explosion in Online Communication

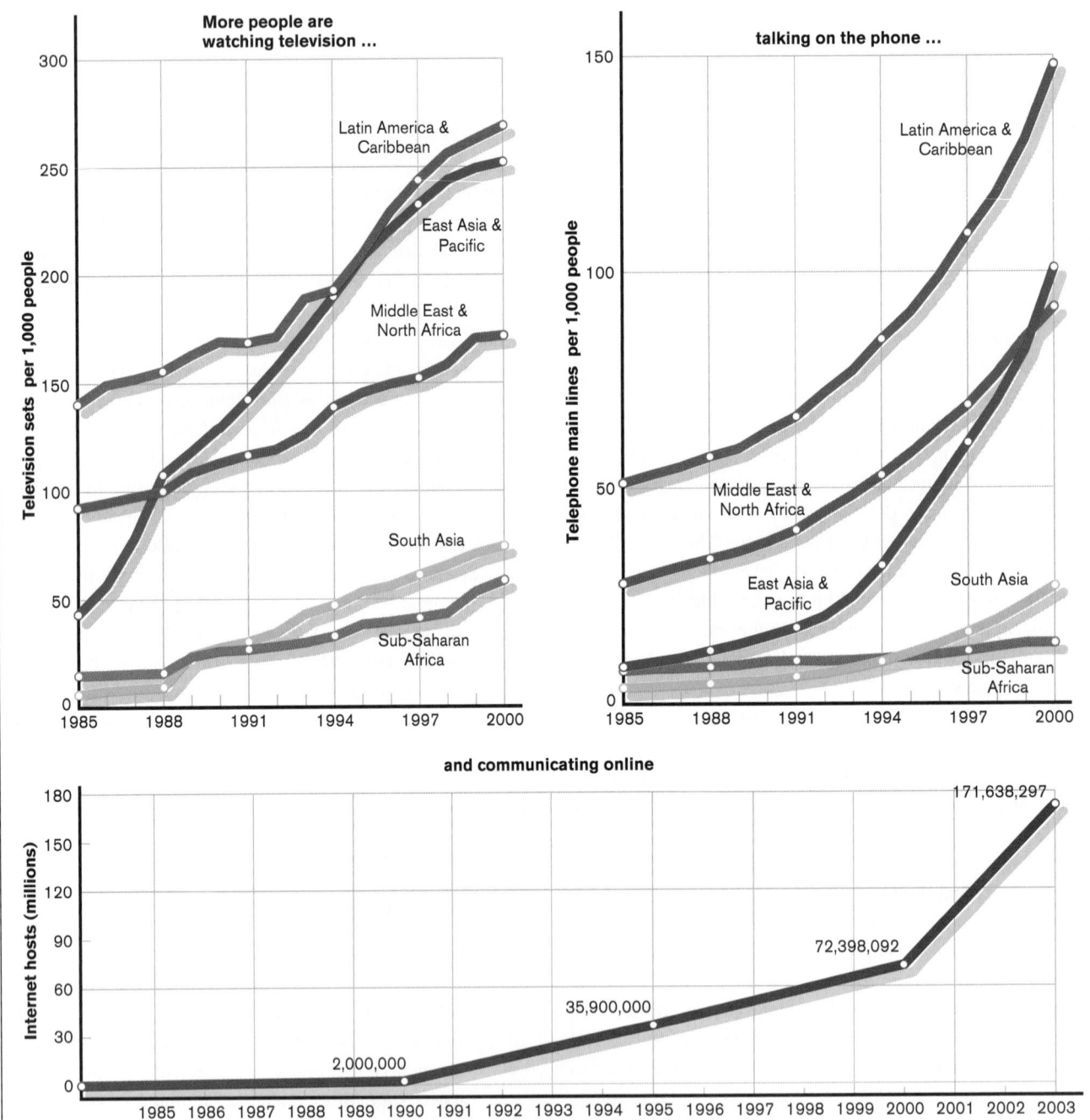

SOURCES: World Bank data from UNDP, 1999, p. 26; World Bank, World Development Indicators, 2002; United Nations, Human Development Report, 2003.

TABLE 20.1

Global Unevenness of Telecommunications Infrastructure and Use, 2002

	POPULATION (MILLIONS)	TELEPHONE MAINLINES (PER 1,000*)	CELLULAR SUBSCRIBERS (PER 1,000*)	PERSONAL COMPUTERS (PER 1,000)†
China	1,262.5	137	110	16
France	58.9	573	605	304
Germany	82.2	634	682	336
India	1,016.0	38	6	5
Japan	126.8	586	588	315
Sweden	8.9	739	790	507
United Kingdom	59.7	587	770	338
United States	281.6	667	451	585

*Data source: UN Human Development Report, 2003.

†2000 data; source: World Development Indicators, 2002.

are becoming integrated within it. This development has meant the end to the system that existed during the cold war, when countries of the First World stood apart from those of the Second World. The collapse of communism has hastened processes of globalization but should also be seen as a result of globalization itself. The centrally planned communist economies and the ideological and cultural control of communist political authority were ultimately unable to survive in an era of global media and an electronically integrated world economy.

A second important political factor leading to intensifying globalization is the growth of international and regional mechanisms of government. The United Nations and the European Union are the two most prominent examples of international organizations that bring together nation-states into a common political forum. Whereas the UN does this as an association of individual nation-states, the EU is a more pioneering form of transnational governance in which a certain degree of national sovereignty is relinquished by its member states. The governments of individual EU states are bound by directives, regulations, and court judgments from common EU bodies, but they also reap economic, social, and political benefits from their participation in the regional union.

Finally, globalization is being driven by international governmental organizations (IGOs) and international nongovernmental organizations (INGOs; see also Chapter 6). An *international governmental organization* is a body that is established by participating governments and given responsibility for regulating or overseeing a particular domain of activity that is transnational in scope. The first such body, the International Telegraph Union, was founded in 1865. Since that time, a great number of similar bodies have been created to regulate issues ranging from civil aviation to broadcasting to the disposal of hazardous waste. In 1909, there were 37 IGOs in existence to regulate transnational affairs; by 1996, there were 260 (Held et al., 1999).

As the name suggests, INGOs differ from international governmental organizations in that they are not affiliated with government institutions. Rather, they are independent organizations that work alongside governmental bodies in making policy decisions and addressing international issues. Some of the best-known INGOs—such as Greenpeace, Médecins San Frontières (Doctors Without Borders), the Red Cross, and Amnesty International—are involved in environmental protection and humanitarian relief efforts. But the activities of thousands of lesser-known groups also link together countries and communities (see Figure 20.2).

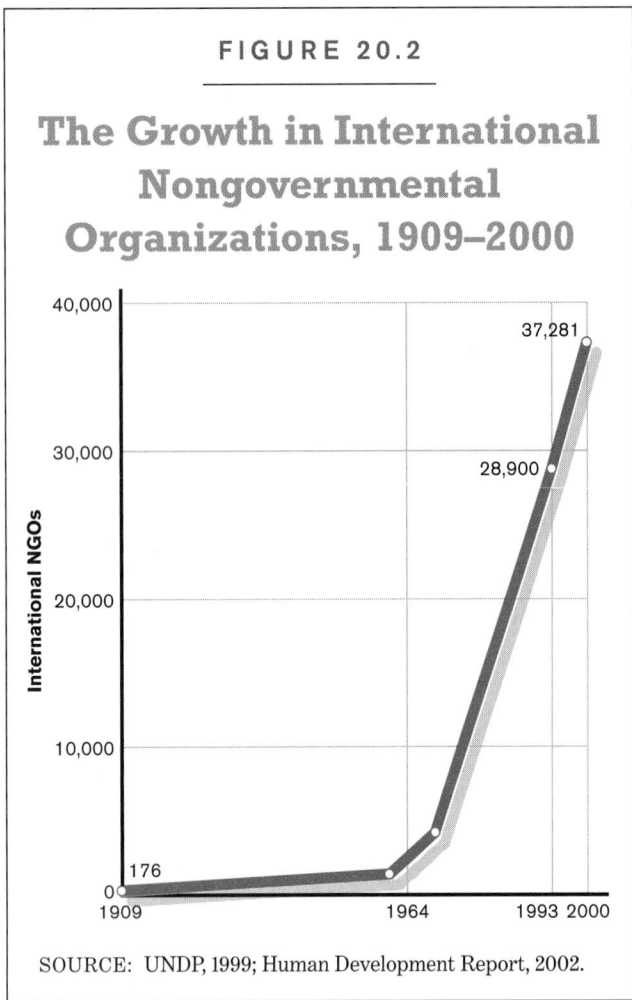

FIGURE 20.2

The Growth in International Nongovernmental Organizations, 1909–2000

SOURCE: UNDP, 1999; Human Development Report, 2002.

INFORMATION FLOWS

We have seen how the spread of information technology has expanded the possibilities for contact among people around the globe. It has also facilitated the flow of information about people and events in distant places. Every day, the global media bring news, images, and information into people's homes, linking them directly and continuously to the outside world. Some of the most gripping events of the past two decades—such as the fall of the Berlin Wall, the violent crackdown on democratic protesters in China's Tiananmen Square, and the terrorist attacks of September 11, 2001—have unfolded through the media before a truly global audience. Such events, along with thousands of less dramatic ones, have resulted in a reorientation in people's thinking from the level of the nation-state to the global stage. Individuals are now more aware of their interconnectedness with others and more likely to identify with global issues and processes than was the case in times past.

This shift to a global outlook has two significant dimensions. First, as members of a global community, people increasingly perceive that social responsibility does not stop at national borders but instead extends beyond them. Disasters and injustices facing people on the other side of the globe are not simply misfortunes that must be endured but are legitimate grounds for action and intervention. There is a growing assumption that the international community has an obligation to act in crisis situations to protect the physical well-being or human rights of people whose lives are under threat. In the case of natural disasters, such interventions take the form of humanitarian relief and technical assistance. In recent years, earthquakes in Armenia and Turkey, floods in Mozambique, famine in Africa, hurricanes in Central America, and the tsunami that hit Asia and Africa have been rallying points for global assistance.

There have also been stronger calls in recent years for interventions in the case of war, ethnic conflict, and the violation of human rights, although such mobilizations are more problematic than in the case of natural disasters. Yet in the case of the Gulf War in 1991 and the violent conflicts in the former Yugoslavia (Bosnia and Kosovo), military intervention was seen as justified by many people who believed that human rights and national sovereignty had to be defended.

Second, a global outlook means that people are increasingly looking to sources other than the nation-state in formulating their own sense of identity. This is a phenomenon that is both produced by and further accelerates processes of globalization. Local cultural identities in various parts of the world are experiencing powerful revivals at a time when the traditional hold of the nation-state is undergoing profound transformation. In Europe, for example, inhabitants of Scotland and the Basque region of Spain might be more likely to identify themselves as Scottish or Basque—or simply as Europeans—rather than as British or Spanish. The nation-state as a source of identity is waning in many areas as political shifts at the regional and global level loosen people's orientations toward the states in which they live.

TRANSNATIONAL CORPORATIONS

Among the many economic factors driving globalization, the role of **transnational corporations** is particularly important. Transnational corporations are companies that produce goods or market services in more than one country. These may be relatively small firms with one or two factories outside the country in which they are based or gigantic international ventures whose operations crisscross the globe. Some the biggest transnational corporations are companies known all around the world: Coca-Cola, General Motors, Colgate-Palmolive, Kodak, Mitsubishi, and many others. Even when transnational corporations have a clear national base, they are oriented toward global markets and global profits.

Transnational corporations are at the heart of economic globalization: They account for two thirds of all world trade, they are instrumental in the diffusion of new technology around the globe, and they are major actors in international financial markets. As one observer has noted, they are "the linchpins of the contemporary world economy" (Held et al., 1999). Some five hundred transnational corporations had annual sales of more than $10 billion in 2003, while only eighty-two *countries* could boast gross domestic products of at least that amount. In other words, the world's leading transnational corporations are larger economically than most of the world's countries (see Table 20.2). In fact, the combined sales of the world's largest five hundred transnational corporations totaled $13.7 trillion—nearly half (46 percent) of the value of goods and services produced by the entire world (calculated from World Bank, 2003 and *Fortune,* 2003).

Transnational corporations became a global phenomenon in the years following World War II. Expansion in the initial postwar years came from firms based in the United States, but by the 1970s, European and Japanese firms also began to invest abroad. In the late 1980s and 1990s, transnational corporations expanded dramatically with the establishment of three powerful regional markets: Europe (the Single European Market), Asia-Pacific (the Osaka Declaration guaranteed free and open trade by 2010), and North America (the North American Free Trade Agreement). Since the early 1990s, countries in other areas of the world have also liberalized restrictions on foreign investment. By the turn of the twenty-first century, few economies in the world were beyond the reach of transnational corporations. Over the past decade, transnational corporations based in industrialized economies have been particularly active in expanding their operations in developing countries and in the societies of the former Soviet Union and Eastern Europe.

The "electronic economy" is another factor that underpins economic globalization. Banks, corporations, fund managers, and individual investors are able to shift funds internationally with the click of a mouse. This new ability to move "electronic money" instantaneously carries with it great risks, however. Transfers of vast amounts of capital can destabilize economies, triggering international financial crises such as the ones that spread from the Asian "tiger economies" to Russia and beyond in 1998. As the global economy becomes increasingly integrated, a financial collapse in one part of the world can have an enormous effect on distant economies.

The political, economic, social, and technological factors described above are joining together to produce a phenomenon that lacks any earlier parallel in terms of its intensity and scope. The consequences of globalization are many and far reaching, as we will see later in this chapter. But first we will turn our attention to the main views about globalization that have been expressed in recent years.

The Globalization Debate

In recent years, globalization has become a hotly debated topic. Most people accept that important transformations are occurring around us, but the extent to which it is valid to explain these as "globalization" is contested. This is not entirely surprising. As an unpredictable and turbulent process, globalization is seen and understood very differently by observers. David Held and his colleagues (1999) have surveyed the controversy and divided its participants into three schools of thought: *skeptics, hyperglobalizers,* and *transformationalists.* These three tendencies within the globalization debate are summarized in Table 20.3.

THE SKEPTICS

Some thinkers argue that the idea of globalization is overrated—that the debate over globalization is a lot of talk about something that is not new. The skeptics in the globalization controversy believe that present levels of economic interdependence are not unprecedented. Pointing to nineteenth-century statistics on world trade and investment, they contend that modern globalization differs from the past only in the intensity of interaction between nations.

The skeptics agree that there may now be more contact among countries than in previous eras, but in their eyes the current world economy is not sufficiently integrated to constitute a truly globalized economy. This is because the bulk of trade occurs within three regional groups—Europe, Asia-Pacific, and North America. The countries of the European Union, for example, trade predominantly among themselves. The same is true of the other regional groups, thereby invalidating the notion of a single global economy (Hirst, 1997).

Many skeptics focus on processes of *regionalization* within the world economy—such as the emergence of major financial and trading blocs. To skeptics, the growth of regionalization is evidence that the world economy has become less integrated rather than more (Boyer and Drache, 1996; Hirst and Thompson, 1999). Compared with the patterns of trade that prevailed a century ago, they argue, the world economy is less global in its geographical scope and more concentrated on intense pockets of activity.

Skeptics reject the view held by some, such as the hyperglobalizers (see below), that globalization is fundamentally undermining the role of national governments and producing a

TABLE 20.2

Value of Sales of Top Corporations Compared with GDP of Selected Countries, 2001–2003

ECONOMY RANK	ECONOMY	GDP OR TOTAL SALES ($ BILLIONS)
20	**Wal-Mart Stores**	**246.5**
21	Belgium	230.0
22	Sweden	210.0
23	Austria	189.0
24	**General Motors**	**186.8**
25	Saudi Arabia	186.0
26	**ExxonMobil**	**182.5**
27	**Royal Dutch/Shell Group**	**179.4**
28	**BP**	**178.7**
29	Poland	176.0
30	Norway	166.0
31	**Ford Motor**	**163.9**
32	Denmark	162.0
33	Hong Kong	162.0
34	Turkey	148.0
35	Indonesia	145.0
36	**DaimlerChrysler**	**141.4**
37	**Toyota Motor**	**131.8**
38	**General Electric**	**131.7**
39	Venezuela	125.0
40	Finland	121.0
41	Greece	117.0
42	Thailand	115.0
43	Iran	114.0
44	South Africa	113.0
45	Portugal	110.0
46	**Mitsubishi**	**109.3**
47	**Mitsui**	**108.6**
48	Israel	108.0

SOURCE: World Bank, World Development Indicators, 2003 (2001 data); *Fortune,* July 21, 2003.

TABLE 20.3

Conceptualizing Globalization: Three Tendencies

	SKEPTICS	TRANSFORMATIONALISTS	HYPERGLOBALIZERS
WHAT'S NEW?	Trading blocs, weaker geogovernance than in earlier periods	Historically unprecedented levels of global interconnectedness	A global age
DOMINANT FEATURES	World less interdependent than in 1890s	"Thick" (intensive and extensive) globalization	Global capitalism, global governance, global civil society
POWER OF NATIONAL GOVERNMENTS	Reinforced or enhanced	Reconstituted, restructured	Declining or eroding
DRIVING FORCES OF GLOBALIZATION	Governments and markets	Combined forces of modernity	Capitalism and technology
PATTERN OF STRATIFICATION	Increased marginalization of global South	New architecture of world order	Erosion of old hierarchies
DOMINANT MOTIF	National interest	Transformation of political community	McDonald's, Britney Spears, etc.
CONCEPTUALIZATION OF GLOBALIZATION	As internationalization and regionalization	As the reordering of interregional relations and action at a distance	As a reordering of the framework of human action
HISTORICAL TRAJECTORY	Regional blocs/clash of civilizations	Indeterminate: global integration and fragmentation	Global civilization
SUMMARY ARGUMENT	Internationalization depends on government acquiescence and support	Globalization transforming government power and world politics	The end of the nation-state

SOURCE: Adapted from Held et al., 1999, p. 10.

world order in which they are less central. According to the skeptics, national governments continue to be key players because of their involvement in regulating and coordinating economic activity. Governments, for example, are the driving force behind many trade agreements and policies of economic liberalization.

THE HYPERGLOBALIZERS

The hyperglobalizers take an opposing position to that of the skeptics. They argue that globalization is a very real phenomenon whose consequences can be felt almost everywhere. They see globalization as a process that is indifferent to national borders. It is producing a new global order, swept along by powerful flows of cross-border trade and production. One of the best-known hyperglobalizers, the Japanese writer Kenichi Ohmae, sees globalization as leading to a "borderless world"— a world in which market forces are more powerful than national governments (Ohmae, 1990, 1995).

Much of the analysis of globalization offered by hyperglobalizers focuses on the changing role of the nation-state. It is argued that individual countries no longer control their economies because of the vast growth in world trade. National governments and the politicians within them, it is said, are increasingly unable to exercise control over the issues that cross their borders—such as volatile financial markets and environmental threats. Citizens recognize that politicians are limited in their ability to address these problems and, as a result, lose faith in existing systems of governance. Some hyperglobalizers believe that the power of national governments is also being challenged from above—by new regional and international institutions, such as the European Union, the World Trade Organization, and others.

Taken together, these shifts signal to the hyperglobalizers the dawning of a global age (Albrow, 1997) in which national governments decline in importance and influence.

THE TRANSFORMATIONALISTS

The transformationalists take more of a middle position. They see globalization as the central force behind a broad spectrum of changes that are currently shaping modern societies. According to them, the global order is being transformed, but many of the old patterns still remain. Governments, for instance, still retain a good deal of power in spite of the advance of global interdependence. These transformations are not restricted to economics alone, but are equally prominent within the realms of politics, culture, and personal life. Transformationalists contend that the current level of globalization is breaking down established boundaries between internal and external, international and domestic. In trying to adjust to this new order, societies, institutions, and individuals are being forced to navigate contexts where previous structures have been shaken up.

Unlike hyperglobalizers, transformationalists see globalization as a dynamic and open process that is subject to influence and change. It is developing in a contradictory fashion, encompassing tendencies that frequently operate in opposition to one another. Globalization is not a one-way process, as some claim, but a two-way flow of images, information, and influences. Global migration, media, and telecommunications are contributing to the diffusion of cultural influences. The world's vibrant "global cities" are thoroughly multicultural, with ethnic groups and cultures intersecting and living side by side. According to transformationalists, globalization is a decentered and reflexive process characterized by links and cultural flows that work in a multidirectional way. Because globalization is the product of numerous intertwined global networks, it cannot be seen as being driven from one particular part of the world.

Rather than losing sovereignty, as the hyperglobalizers argue, countries are seen by transformationalists as restructuring in response to new forms of economic and social organization that are nonterritorial in basis (e.g., corporations, social movements, and international bodies). They argue that we are no longer living in a state-centric world; governments are being forced to adopt a more active, outward-looking stance toward governance under the complex conditions of globalization (Rosenau, 1997).

Whose view is most nearly correct? Almost certainly that of the transformationalists. The skeptics are mistaken because they underestimate how far the world is changing; world finance markets, for example, are organized on a global level much more than they ever were before. The hyperglobalizers, on the other hand, see globalization too much in economic terms and as too much of a one-way process. In reality, globalization is much more complex.

The Impact of Globalization on Our Lives

Although globalization is often associated with changes within big systems—such as the world financial markets, production and trade, and telecommunications—the effects of globalization are felt equally strongly in the private realm. Globalization is not something that is simply out there, operating on a distant plane and not intersecting with individual affairs. Globalization is an "in here" phenomenon that is affecting our intimate and personal lives in many diverse ways. Inevitably, our personal lives have been altered as globalizing forces enter into our local contexts, our homes, and our communities through impersonal sources—such as the media, the Internet, and popular culture—as well as through personal contact with individuals from other countries and cultures.

Globalization is fundamentally changing the nature of our everyday experiences. As the societies in which we live undergo profound transformations, the established institutions that used to underpin them have become out of place. This is forcing a redefinition of intimate and personal aspects of our lives, such as the family, gender roles, sexuality, personal identity, our interactions with others, and our relationships to work. The way we think of ourselves and our connections with other people is being profoundly altered through globalization.

THE RISE OF INDIVIDUALISM

In our current age, individuals have much more opportunity to shape their own lives than once was the case. At one time, tradition and custom exercised a very strong influence on the path of people's lives. Factors such as social class, gender, ethnicity, and even religious affiliation could close off certain avenues for individuals or open up others. Being born the eldest son of a tailor, for example, would probably ensure that a young man would learn his father's craft and carry on practicing that craft throughout his lifetime. Tradition held that a woman's natural sphere was in the home; her life and identity were largely defined by those of her husband or father. In times past, individuals' personal identities were formed in the context of the community into which they were born. The values, lifestyles, and ethics prevailing in that community provided relatively fixed guidelines according to which people lived their lives.

Advancements such as laptop computers and the Internet have allowed those in remote areas, such as these Aboriginal children in rural Australia, unprecedented access to technology and the ability to communicate easily with people all around the world.

Under conditions of globalization, however, we are faced with a move toward a new *individualism* in which people have actively to construct their own identities. The weight of tradition and established values is retreating as local communities interact with a new global order. The social codes that formerly guided people's choices and activities have significantly loosened. Today, for example, the eldest son of a tailor could choose any number of paths in constructing his future, women are no longer restricted to the domestic realm, and many of the other signposts that shaped people's lives have disappeared. Traditional frameworks of identity are dissolving; new patterns of identity are emerging. Globalization is forcing people to live in a more open, reflexive way. This means that we are constantly responding and adjusting to the changing environment around us; as individuals, we evolve with and within the larger context in which we live. Even the small choices we make in our daily lives—what we wear, how we spend our leisure time, and how we take care of our health and our bodies—are part of an ongoing process of creating and recreating our self-identities.

WORK PATTERNS

Work is at the center of many people's lives—both on a day-to-day basis and in terms of larger life goals. Although we may regard work as a chore or a necessary evil, it is undeniable that work is a crucial element in our personal lives. We spend great amounts of time working or at work and find that many aspects of our existence—from our friends to our leisure pursuits—are shaped by our work patterns.

Globalization has unleashed profound transformations within the world of work. New patterns of international trade and the move to a knowledge economy have had a significant impact on long-standing employment patterns. Many traditional industries have been made obsolete by new technological advances or are losing their share of the market to competitors abroad whose labor costs are lower than in industrialized countries. Global trade and new forms of technology have had a strong effect on traditional manufacturing communities, where industrial workers have been left unemployed and without the types of skills needed to enter the new knowledge-based economy. These communities are facing a new set of social problems, including long-term unemployment and rising crime rates, as a result of economic globalization.

If at one time people's working lives were dominated by employment with one employer over the course of several decades—the so-called job-for-life framework—today many more individuals create their own career paths, pursuing individual goals and exercising choice in attaining them. Often this involves changing jobs several times over the course of a career, building up new skills and abilities, and transferring them to diverse work contexts. Standard patterns of full-time work are being dissolved into more flexible arrangements: working from home with the help of information technology, job sharing, short-term consulting projects, flextime, and so forth (Beck, 1992).

Women have entered the work force in large numbers, a fact that has strongly affected the personal lives of people of both sexes. Expanded professional and educational opportunities have led many women to put off marriage and children until after they have begun a career. These changes have also meant that many working women return to work shortly after having children, instead of remaining at home with young children as was once the case. These shifts have required important adjustments within families, in the nature of the domestic division of labor, in the role of men in child rearing, and with the emergence of more family-friendly working policies to accommodate the needs of dual-earner couples.

POPULAR CULTURE

The cultural impacts of globalization have received much attention. Images, ideas, goods, and styles are now disseminated around the world more rapidly than ever before. Trade, new information technologies, the international media, and global migration have all contributed to the free movement of culture across national borders. Many people believe that we now live in a single information order—a massive global network where information is shared quickly and in great volumes. A simple example should illustrate this point clearly.

Have you seen the film *Titanic*? It is quite likely that you have. It is estimated that hundreds of millions of people in countries around the world have seen *Titanic,* either in theaters, on cable, or on DVD. The 1997 film, which recounts the story of a

Internationalizing Public Sociologies

[***]

The SSF and Kibera Collaboration

Sociologists Without Borders/Sociólogos Sin Fronteras [SSF] is committed to building alliances in Third World countries, and while we encourage members to do this on their own, we are also building our own SSF partnerships to provide such opportunities. We will be seeking such a partnership in Quito,

Ecuador, with a relatively large NGO that is connected to many local communities, but like any new partnership, this will slowly evolve once it is off the ground. We are eager to start moving in that direction because our first partnership with CFK [Carolina for Kibera] in Kibera, Nairobi, has proven to be so successful for SSF.

So far the partnership has involved two steps: first, our becoming familiar with the programs of CFK, which include inter-tribal youth soccer teams, a girls' reproductive health center, health outreach programs, and the health clinic; and, second, setting up the Nairobi Fellowship, which, beginning in 2003, is awarded annually to a student. Our first recipient of the Fellowship was Olivier Crespel, who was selected by members from the Spanish chapter of SSF, and our next recipient will be an American student. When I visited Kibera in September, many people asked me when Olivier ("the nice young man with the guitar") would be coming back. We were truly fortunate with the choice of Olivier. He started an inter-tribal youth band with traditional African instruments, learned quite a bit of Swahili, and having traveled earlier in African countries, felt very comfortable in Kibera.

Kibera is the biggest slum in Africa, with an estimated population of over [750,000] people. It evolved from a Nubian refugee settlement into a multitribal community, without planning or city services. Kiberans are extremely poor and they have high rates of AIDS, malaria, and tuberculosis. There are no streets in Kibera. Instead, there are narrow dirt pathways on which people cook and carry out craft work, and vend things such as used articles of clothing, vegetables, and cassettes. When people can find work it is usually in textile factories located far away in an industrial park outside of Kibera, and the pay is abysmal.

SSF hopes to expand this partnership, anticipating grant proposals that will bring jobs to young people and promote innovative technologies, including recycling programs for plastics and Internet capabilities that use alternative energy sources. There are many opportunities for expanding this partnership to include youth programs, women's enterprises, and, especially, health programs. (Approximately 40 percent of the adult population is HIV positive.) In contrast with the charity model, SSF works hand-in-hand with the residents of Kibera so that they set the priorities in their own terms, and SSF tries to provide resources. It is a variation on service-learning, and it is our intent that the residents and the NGO are steering us. They are the experts.

It is important to stress the SSF-CKF partnership in Kibera is one that we hope will serve as a model for what Michael Burawoy refers to as "de-provincializing" American sociology. I stress three aspects of this. First, Kibera is the living expression of exploitation and oppression, not only in Africa, but on the entire planet. The casualties of colonial imperialism, capitalism, and globalization, Kiberans live lives deprived of all the basic human rights—the rights to food, security, health care, clean water, jobs, etc. They nevertheless live their lives with determination and great dignity. Second, African social science is very different from American social science, and if we are to pluralize our epistemology, we can learn from the residents of Kibera why this is the case. Third, if we are to participate in global political and social movements for justice and human rights, we need to share a language with Africans, Latin Americans, Asians, and Europeans.

Kibera was a good place for SSF to begin our international, collaborative projects. It will allow us to seek alliances with our African colleagues, provide students and ourselves with opportunities to advance human rights and social justice projects arm in arm with the poor residents of Kibera, and begin to work in

local, regional, and even global coalitions that are opposed to oppression and injustices. It is my hope that SSF can form alliances with other Nairobi NGOs that are working on issues related to socioeconomic, health, and environment rights, and that we make good use of our sociological expertise in these alliances. We learn a great deal about the dynamics of the pathologies of globalization and neoliberalism when we see first-hand how the multinationals, property owners, and pharmaceutical companies deny Kiberans of their basic human rights. It is one thing to theorize about the injustices of globalization, but it is quite another to jump in and engage in the politics and practices to battle these injustices. Kibera offers Sociologists Without Borders members opportunities to battle injustices where they are most acute and most chilling.

SOURCE: Judith Blau, "Internationalizing Public Sociologies," *Sociologists Without Borders*, www.sociologistswithoutborders.org.

JUDITH BLAU is Professor of Sociology at the University of North Carolina, Chapel Hill. She is the author of several books, including Race in the Schools: The End of White Dominance?, Social Contracts and Economic Markets, *and* The Shape of Culture: A Study of Contemporary Cultural Patterns in the United States, *as well as numerous articles. She is currently the editor of* Social Forces: An International Journal of Social Research.

young couple who fall in love aboard the ill-fated ocean liner, is one of the most popular films ever made. *Titanic* shattered all existing box-office records, grossing more than 1.8 billion dollars in revenues from screenings in fifty-five different countries. In many countries, when *Titanic* first opened in theaters, hundreds of people stood in line for tickets, and show after show was sold out. The film was popular with all age groups, but particularly with adolescent girls—many of whom paid to watch the film several times. The stars of *Titanic,* Leonardo DiCaprio and Kate Winslet, found their careers and futures utterly transformed; they had been elevated from little-known actors to global celebrities. *Titanic* is one of a handful of cultural products that has succeeded in cutting across national boundaries and creating a truly international phenomenon.

What can account for the enormous popularity of a film like *Titanic*? And what does its success tell us about globalization? At one level, *Titanic* was popular for very straightforward reasons: It combined a relatively simple plotline (a romance against the backdrop of tragedy) with a well-known historical event (the 1912 sinking of the *Titanic,* in which more than 1,600 people perished). The film was also lavishly produced, with great attention to detail, and included state-of-the-art special effects.

But another reason for *Titanic's* popularity is that it reflected a particular set of ideas and values that resonated with audiences worldwide. One of the film's central themes is the possibility of romantic love prevailing over class differences and family traditions. While such ideas are generally accepted in most Western countries, they are still taking hold in many other areas of the world. The success of a film like *Titanic* reflects the changing attitudes toward personal relationships and marriage, for example, in parts of the world where more traditional values have been favored. Yet *Titanic,* along with many other Western films, can also be said to *contribute* to this shift in values. Western-made films and television programs, which dominate the global media, tend to advance a set of political, social, and economic agendas that reflect specifically Western worldview. Some people worry that globalization is leading to the creation of a global culture in which the values of the most powerful and affluent—in this instance, Hollywood filmmakers—overwhelm the strength of local customs and tradition. According to this view, globalization is a form of cultural imperialism in which the values, styles, and outlooks of the Western world are being spread so aggressively that they smother individual national cultures.

Others, by contrast, have linked processes of globalization to a growing *differentiation* in cultural traditions and forms. Rather than cultural homogeneity, they claim that global society is now characterized by an enormous diversity of cultures existing side by side. Local traditions are joined by a host of additional cultural forms from abroad, presenting people with a bewildering array of lifestyle options from which to choose.

Rather than a unified global culture, what we are witnessing is the fragmentation of cultural forms (Baudrillard, 1988). Established identities and ways of life grounded in local communities and cultures are giving way to new forms of hybrid identity composed of elements from contrasting cultural sources (Hall, 1992). Thus, a black urban South African today might continue to be strongly influenced by the traditions and cultural outlooks of his tribal roots at the same time as he adopts cosmopolitan styles and tastes—in dress, leisure pursuits, hobbies, and so forth—that have been shaped by globalizing forces.

Globalization and Risk

The consequences of globalization are far reaching, affecting virtually all aspects of the social world. Yet because globalization is an open-ended and internally contradictory process, it produces outcomes that are difficult to predict and control. Another way of thinking of this dynamic is in terms of *risk*. Many of the changes wrought by globalization are presenting us with new forms of risk that differ greatly from those that existed in previous eras. Unlike risks from the past, which had established causes and known effects, today's risks are incalculable in origin and indeterminate in their consequences.

THE SPREAD OF "MANUFACTURED RISK"

Humans have always had to face risks of one kind or another, but today's risks are qualitatively different from those that came in earlier times. Until quite recently, human societies were threatened by **external risk**—dangers such as drought, earthquakes, famines, and storms that spring from the natural world and are unrelated to the actions of humans. Today, however, we are increasingly confronted with various types of **manufactured risk**—risks that are created by the impact of our own knowledge and technology on the natural world. As we shall see, many environmental and health risks facing contemporary societies are instances of manufactured risk—they are the outcomes of our own interventions into nature.

Environmental Risks One of the clearest illustrations of manufactured risk can be found in threats currently posed by the natural environment (see Chapter 19). One of the consequences of accelerating industrial and technological development has been the steady spread of human intervention into nature. There are few aspects of the natural world that remain untouched by humans—urbanization, industrial production and pollution, large-scale agricultural projects, the construction of dams and hydroelectric plants, and nuclear power are just some of the ways in which human beings have had an impact on their natural surroundings. The collective outcome of such processes has been the creation of widespread environmental destruction whose precise cause is indeterminate and whose consequences are similarly difficult to calculate.

In our globalizing world, ecological risk confronts us in many guises. Concern over global warming has been mounting in the scientific community for some years; it is now generally accepted that the earth's temperature has been increasing from the buildup of harmful gases within the atmosphere. The potential consequences of global warming are devastating: If polar ice caps continue to melt as they currently are, sea levels will rise and may threaten low-lying land masses and their human populations. Changes in climate patterns have been cited as possible causes of the severe floods that afflicted parts of China in 1998 and Mozambique in 2000.

Because environmental risks are diffuse in origin, it is unclear how they should be addressed or who bears responsibility for taking action to remedy them. A simple example demonstrates why this is so. Scientists have found that chemical pollution levels have had a harmful effect on certain Antarctic penguin colonies. But it is impossible to identify accurately either the exact origins of the pollution or its possible consequences for the penguins in the future. In such an instance—and in hundreds of similar cases—it is likely that effective action will not be taken to address the risk because the extent of both the cause and the outcome is unknown and unfixed (Beck, 1995).

Health Risks In the past decade, the dangers posed to human health by manufactured risks have attracted great attention. In the media and public health campaigns, for example, people have been urged to limit their exposure to the harmful ultraviolet rays of the sun and to apply sunscreen to prevent burning. In recent years, sun exposure has been linked to a heightened risk of skin cancer in many parts of the world. This is thought to be related to the depletion of the ozone layer—the layer of the earth's atmosphere that normally filters out ultraviolet light. Due to the high volume of chemical emissions that are produced by human activities and industry, the concentration of ozone in the atmosphere has been diminishing and, in some cases, ozone holes have opened up.

There are many examples of manufactured risk that are linked to food. Modern farming and food production techniques have been heavily influenced by advances in science and technology. For example, chemical pesticides and herbicides are widely used in commercial agriculture, and many animals (such as chickens and pigs) are pumped full of hormones and antibiotics. Some people have suggested that farming techniques such as these compromise food safety and could have an adverse effect on humans. In recent years, two particular

British Ministry of Agriculture officials watch as the carcasses of sheep and cattle are incinerated on a farm near Wigton in Cumbria, England, on March 16, 2001. Britain was compelled to kill tens of thousands of animals in order to prevent the spread of foot-and-mouth disease.

controversies have raised widespread public concern over food safety and manufactured risk: the debate over genetically modified foods and "mad cow disease."

The saga of genetically modified foods began only a few years ago when some of the world's leading chemical and agricultural firms decided that new knowledge about the workings of genes could transform the world's food supply. These companies had been making pesticides and herbicides, but wanted to move into what they saw as a major market for the future. The American firm Monsanto was the leader in developing much of the new technology. Monsanto bought up seed companies, sold off its chemical division and devoted much of its energy to bringing the new crops to the market. Led by its chief executive, Robert Shapiro, Monsanto launched a gigantic advertising campaign promoting the benefits of its genetically modified crops to farmers and to consumers. The early responses were just as the company had confidently anticipated. By early 1999, 55 percent of the soybeans and 35 percent of the maize produced in the United States contained genetic alterations. It is currently estimated that between 60 and 70 percent of all produce sold in grocery stores contains some genetically modified components (Safe-food.org, 2003). In addition to North America, genetically modified crops are being widely grown in China.

Since genetically modified crops are essentially quite new, no one can be certain about what their effects will be once they are introduced into the environment. Many ecological and consumer groups became concerned about the potential risks involved with the adoption of this largely untested technology.

The Manufactured Risks of Electronic Viruses and World Climate Change

Globalization comes with many unfamiliar, manufactured risks. Among them are two that may have had a direct impact on you. On May 4, 2000, chaos engulfed the electronic world when a virus nicknamed the "love bug" succeeded in overloading computer systems worldwide. Launched from a personal computer in Manila, the capital of the Philippines, the "love bug" spread rapidly across the globe and forced almost a tenth of the world's e-mail servers to shut down. The virus was carried worldwide through an e-mail message with the subject heading "I Love You." When recipients opened the file that was attached to the message, they unknowingly activated the virus in their own computer. The "love bug" would then replicate itself and automatically send itself on to all the e-mail addresses listed in the computerized address book, before attacking information and files stored on the computer's hard drive. The virus spread westward around the globe as employees, first in Asia, then in Europe and North America, arrived to work in the morning and checked their e-mail. By the end of day, the "love bug" was estimated to have caused more than $1.5 billion of damage worldwide.

The "love bug" was a particularly fast-spreading virus, but it was not the first of its kind. Electronic viruses have become

Bovine spongiform encephalopathy (BSE), known popularly as "mad cow disease," was first detected in British cattle in 1986. Scientists have linked BSE infection to the practice of raising cattle—normally herbivores—on feed containing traces of the parts of other animals. After the outbreak, the government took steps to control the disease among cattle, but it claimed that eating beef was safe and posed no danger to humans. Only in the mid-1990s was it admitted that several human deaths from Creutzfeldt-Jakob disease, a degenerative brain condition, had been linked to the consumption of beef from infected cattle. Thousands of British cattle were killed and strict legislation was passed to regulate cattle farming and the sale of beef products. Most recently cattle infected with BSE have been discovered in Canada and the United States sparking widespread fears about the safety of the food supply.

Although extensive scientific research has been launched to determine the risks to humans from BSE, the findings remain inconclusive. There is a risk that individuals who consumed British beef in the years preceding the discovery of BSE may have been exposed to infection. Yet as recently as December 1999 the European Union's Scientific Steering Committee declared that "the infectious dose to humans is currently not known." Calculating the risks humans run from BSE is an example of the complexity of risk assessment in the contemporary world. It is necessary to know if and when infected cattle were part of a certain food chain, the level and distribution of the infection that was present in the cattle, the way in which the beef was processed, and many other details. The sheer quantity of unknown factors has complicated the task and made any precise analysis of risk challenging.

THE GLOBAL "RISK SOCIETY"

Global warming, the BSE crisis, the debate over genetically modified foods, and other manufactured risks have presented individuals with new choices and challenges in their everyday lives. Because there is no roadmap to these new dangers, individuals, countries, and transnational organizations must nego-

more common—and more dangerous—as computers and electronic forms of communication have grown in importance and sophistication. Viruses such as the "love bug" demonstrate how interconnected the world has become with the advance of globalization. You might think that in this particular instance global interconnectedness proved to be quite a disadvantage, since a harmful virus was able to spread so rapidly around the globe. Yet many positive aspects of globalization are reflected in this case as well. As soon as the virus was detected, computer and security experts from around the world worked together to prevent its spread, protect national computer systems, and share intelligence about the virus's origins.

Another aspect of manufactured risk and one you likely have noticed—or been directly affected by—is the unusual weather in recent years. Scientists and disaster experts have pointed out that extreme weather events—such as unseasonably hot temperatures, droughts, floods, and cyclones—have been occurring with ever greater frequency. In 1998 alone, for example, eighty separate natural catastrophes were recorded at points around the globe, including devastating floods in China, hurricanes in Latin America, wildfires in Indonesia, and severe ice storms in North America. Since that time, drought has gripped regions as diverse as Ethiopia, southern Afghanistan, and the midwestern United States; floods have ravaged Venezuela and Mozambique; violent windstorms have battered parts of Europe; and a plague of locusts has swarmed through the Australian outback.

Although no one can be certain, many people believe that these natural disasters are caused in part by global warming (the heating up of the earth's atmosphere). If carbon dioxide emissions that contribute to global warming continue unchecked, it seems likely that the earth's climate will be irreversibly harmed. Who is to blame for global warming, and what can be done to slow its progress? As with so many aspects of our changing world, the risks associated with global warming are experienced worldwide, yet its precise causes are nearly impossible to pinpoint. In an age of globalization, we are constantly reminded of our interdependence with others: The actions of individuals or institutions in one part of the world can, and do, have significant consequences for people everywhere.

tiate risks as they make choices about how lives are to be lived. Because there are no definitive answers about the causes and outcomes of such risks, each individual is forced to make decisions about which risks he or she is prepared to take. This can be a bewildering endeavor! Should we use food and raw materials if their production or consumption might have a negative impact on our own health and on the natural environment? Even seemingly simple decisions about what to eat are now made in the context of conflicting information and opinions about the product's relative merits and drawbacks.

The German sociologist Ulrich Beck, who has written extensively about risk and globalization, sees these risks contributing to the formation of a global *risk society* (1992). As technological change progresses more and more rapidly and produces new forms of risk, we must constantly respond and adjust to these changes. The risk society, he argues, is not limited to environmental and health risks alone; it includes a whole series of interrelated changes within contemporary social life: shifting employment patterns, heightened job insecu-

rity, the declining influence of tradition and custom on self-identity, the erosion of traditional family patterns, and the democratization of personal relationships. Because personal futures are much less fixed than they were in traditional societies, decisions of all kinds present risks for individuals. Getting married, for example, is a riskier endeavor today than it was at a time when marriage was a lifelong institution. Decisions about educational qualifications and career paths can also feel risky: It is difficult to predict what skills will be valuable in an economy that is changing as rapidly as ours is.

According to Beck, an important aspect of the risk society is that its hazards are not restricted spatially, temporally, or socially (1995). Today's risks affect all countries and all social classes; they have global, not merely personal, consequences. Many forms of manufactured risk such as those concerning human health and the environment, cross national boundaries. The explosion at the Chernobyl nuclear power plant in Ukraine in 1986 provides a clear illustration of this point. Everyone living in the immediate vicinity of Chernobyl—regardless of age,

Global Health

An important aspect of the economic gap between developed and developing countries is the huge disparity in the health conditions experienced in the rich and poor parts of the world. The physical and economic burdens of diseases affect peoples in the developing world more significantly than they do those in developed countries. In its 1999 *World Health Report,* the World Health Organization (WHO) stated that "[d]espite the long list of success in health achieved globally during the 20th century, the balance sheet is indelibly stained by the avoidable burden of disease and malnutrition that the world's disadvantaged populations continue to bear." While WHO and other international organizations have tried to reduce the "health gap" between developed and developing countries, experts point to much evidence that the health gap still remains of daunting and, in some cases, worsening proportions. WHO argues that populations in developing countries now face not only continued threats from infectious diseases but also growing epidemics of non-communicable diseases, such as lung and heart disease. The continued presence of the global health gap becomes more worrisome when arguments that the processes of globalization are increasing, rather than narrowing, the gap are considered.

[***]

Not only has the "health gap" between developed and developing countries not disappeared, but it has also changed its nature. Previously, the gap was basically measured in terms of the burden of infectious diseases; countries were supposed to make the transition away from infectious diseases toward non-communicable diseases. Today and in the future, the gap is and will be measured in terms of the burdens of both infectious and non-communicable diseases. Any future "health transition" strategy now must aim to reduce the burdens of both infectious and non-communicable diseases—a public health undertaking of enormous proportions. The scale of the challenge can be glimpsed by briefly noting that it requires governments in developing countries (with international assistance) to improve basic sanitation and public health systems, making better use of

These photos illustrate responses to health issues in India. (Left) Protesters, many of them prostitutes and health care workers, march in New Delhi's red light district, calling for job opportunities and medical facilities on World AIDS Day 1997. The UN estimates that India has between 3 and 5 million HIV-positive citizens, making it the country with the most cases in the world. (Above right) Members of the Socialist Unity Center of India (SUCI) tangle with police in front of the West Bengal Legislative Assembly House in Calcutta, India to protest price hikes in electricity and health services in this eastern Indian state. (Right) According to UNICEF more than 53 million children under the age of five suffer from chronic and moderate malnutrition. (Far right) Postal staff handling foreign mail take precautions against anthrax at the Bombay airport in India.

antimicrobial treatments to prevent the development of resistant pathogens, and alter individual behavior patterns that produce morbidity and mortality, such as tobacco consumption, promiscuous sexual behavior, illicit drug use, and poor dietary habits. Where the economic resources to undertake such massive and expensive public health endeavors will originate remains a mystery. The mystery becomes even more forbidding when we begin to factor in the public health and health care implications of the globalization of markets and culture.

[***]

Public health and health care in developed and developing countries have not escaped the impact of the processes of globalization. In fact, experts have identified the phenomenon of the "globalization of public health," under which states are losing the ability to protect the health of their publics from disease threats. The loss of the ability to provide for public health because of global forces is, of course, a matter of concern for developed as well as developing countries. But as in other areas of globalization, the impact on developing countries is of a different magnitude in the health context because the health threats are greater and the financial, technological, and human resources to deal with them are smaller.

The relationship between globalization and health is complex; but it is necessary, even at the risk of oversimplification, to clarify how the processes of globalization adversely affect health in developing countries. From the broadest perspective, the adverse health effects from globalization in developing countries arise from structural imbalances in the international system that the processes of globalization exacerbate. The structural imbalances can be glimpsed through four features of globalization: (1) increases in international trade; (2) structural adjustment programs maintained by international financial organizations; (3) increases in international trade in services and in transnational investments in service industries; and (4) the international regime on intellectual property.

SOURCE: David P. Fidler, "Neither Science Nor Shamans: Globalization of Markets and Health in the Developing World," *Indiana Journal of Global Legal Studies* 7 (2001): 191.

Questions

- How might the economic and structural elements of international trade affect the society and health of a developing country?
- Name some ways that globalization can have a detrimental effect on health. How might we address and counteract these effects?
- Why might people participate in the globalizing trend, despite its negative aspects?

class, gender, or status—was exposed to dangerous levels of radiation. At the same time, the effects of the accident stretched far beyond Chernobyl itself—throughout Europe and beyond, abnormally high levels of radiation were detected long after the explosion.

Globalization and Inequality

Beck and other scholars have drawn attention to risk as one of the main outcomes of globalization and technological advance. New forms of risk present complex challenges for both individuals and whole societies that are forced to navigate through unknown terrain. Yet globalization is generating other important challenges as well.

Globalization is proceeding in an uneven way. The impact of globalization is experienced differentially, and some of its consequences are far from benign. Next to mounting ecological problems, the expansion of inequalities within and between societies is one of the most serious challenges facing the world at the start of the twenty-first century.

INEQUALITY AND GLOBAL DIVISIONS

As we learned in our discussion of types of society (Chapter 3), the vast majority of the world's wealth is concentrated in the industrialized or developed countries of the world, whereas the nations of the developing world suffer from widespread poverty, overpopulation, inadequate educational and health care systems, and crippling foreign debt. The disparity between the developed and the developing world widened steadily over the course of the twentieth century and is now the largest it has ever been.

The 1999 *Human Development Report,* published by the United Nations, revealed that the average income of the fifth of the world's population living in the richest countries was 74 times greater than the average income of the fifth living in the poorest. In the late 1990s, more than one fifth of the world's population accounted for 86 percent of the world's overall consumption, 82 percent of export markets, and 74 percent of telephone lines. The two hundred richest people in the world doubled their net worth between 1994 and 1998; the assets of the top three billionaires in the world in 1998 exceeded the combined gross domestic product (GDP) of all the least developed countries and the 600 million people who lived in them (UNDP, 1999).

In much of the developing world, levels of economic growth and output over the past century have not kept up with the rate of population growth, whereas the level of economic development in industrialized countries has far outpaced it. These opposing tendencies have led to a marked divergence between the richest and poorest countries of the world. The distance between the world's richest and poorest country was approximately 3 to 1 in 1820, 11 to 1 in 1913, 35 to 1 in 1950, 72 to 1 in 1992, and 173 to 1 in 2001 (see Figure 20.3). Over the past century, among the richest quarter of the world's population, income per head has increased almost sixfold, while among the poorest quarter, the increase has been less than threefold.

Globalization seems to be exacerbating these trends by further concentrating income, wealth, and resources within a small core of countries (see Figure 20.4). As we have seen in this chapter, the global economy is growing and integrating at an extremely rapid rate. The expansion of global trade has been central to this process—between 1990 and 1997, international trade grew by 6.5 percent. Even though this rate of growth has fallen to 3 percent in 2002 (WTO 2003), only a handful of developing countries had managed to benefit from that rapid growth, and the process of integration into the global economy has been uneven. Some countries—such as the East Asian economies, Chile, India, and Poland—have fared well, with growth in exports of over 5 percent. Other countries—such as Russia, Venezuela, and Algeria—have seen few benefits from expanding trade and globalization (UNDP, 1999). Findings from the World Bank support this picture: Among ninety-three nations in the developing world, only twenty-three can be said to be "rapid integrators." There is a danger that many of the countries most in need of economic growth will be left even further behind as globalization progresses (World Bank, 2000).

Free trade is seen by many as the key to economic development and poverty relief. Organizations such as the World Trade Organization (WTO) work to liberalize trade regulations and to reduce barriers to trade between the countries of the world. Free trade across borders is viewed as a win-win proposition for both developed and developing countries alike. While the industrialized economies are able to export their products to markets around the world, it is claimed that developing countries will also benefit by gaining access to world markets. This, in turn, is supposed to improve their prospects for integration into the global economy.

THE CAMPAIGN FOR GLOBAL JUSTICE

Not everyone agrees that free trade is the solution to poverty and global inequality. In fact, many critics argue that free trade is a rather one-sided affair that benefits those who are already well off and exacerbates existing patterns of poverty and dependency within the developing world. Recently, much of this criticism has focused around the activities and policies of the World Trade Organization (WTO), which is at the forefront of efforts to increase global trade.

In December 1999, more than fifty thousand people from around the world took to the streets of Seattle to protest during

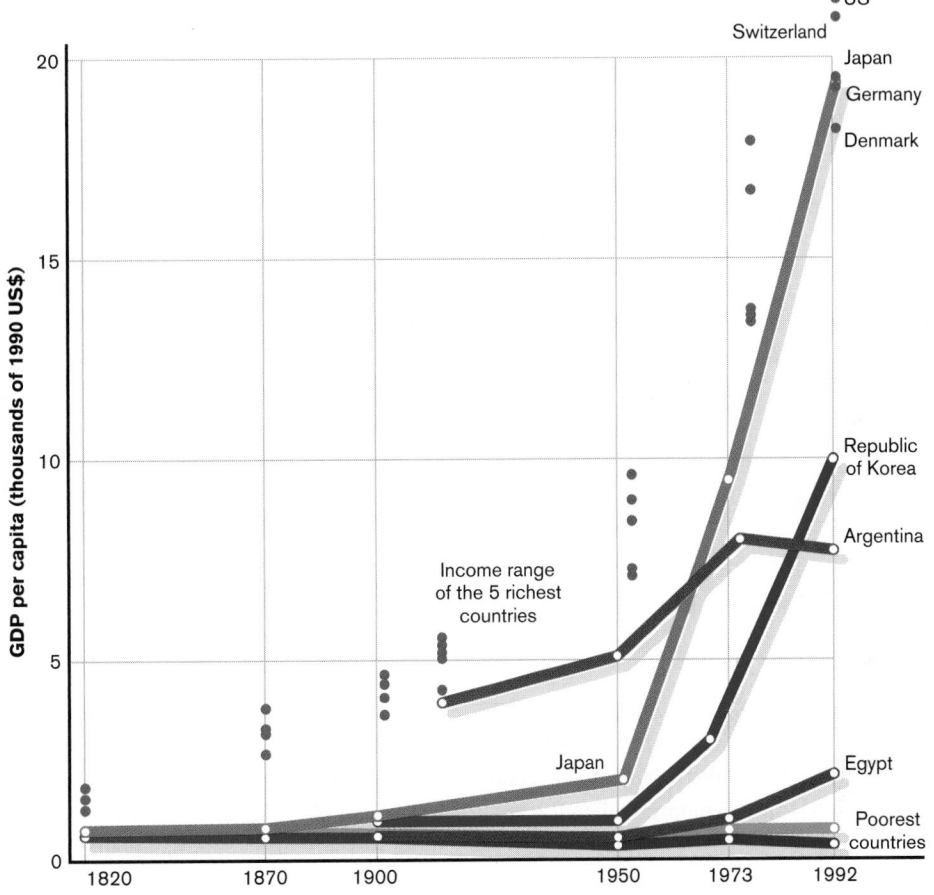

FIGURE 20.3

The Widening of the Gaps Between Richer and Poorer Countries Between 1820 and 1992

SOURCE: UNDP, 1999, p. 38; World Bank, World Development Indicators, 2003.

the WTO's so-called Millennium Round of trade talks. For four days, Seattle was awash with colorful demonstrations, street theater, acts of civil disobedience, marches, workshops, and teach-ins. Trade unionists, environmentalists, human rights campaigners, antinuclear activists, farmers, and representatives from hundreds of local and international nongovernmental organizations joined forces to voice their frustration with the WTO—an organization seen by many as favoring economic imperatives over all other concerns, including human rights, labor rights, the environment, and sustainable development. The protests were mostly peaceful, but violent clashes did break out between protesters and the local police force, which used tear gas and rubber bullets to control the crowds that brought downtown Seattle to a halt.

Negotiators from the WTO's 134 member states (the number of members has since risen to 146) had come together to discuss and agree on measures to liberalize conditions for global trade and investment in agriculture and forest products, among other issues. Yet the talks broke off early with no agreements reached. The organizers of the protests were triumphant—not only had the demonstrations succeeded in disrupting the talks, but internal disputes among delegates had also risen to the surface. The Seattle protests were heralded as the biggest victory to date for campaigners for "global justice." Since that time, every ministerial meeting of the WTO has been met by massive demonstrations by those excluded from the processes of setting the rules for global trade.

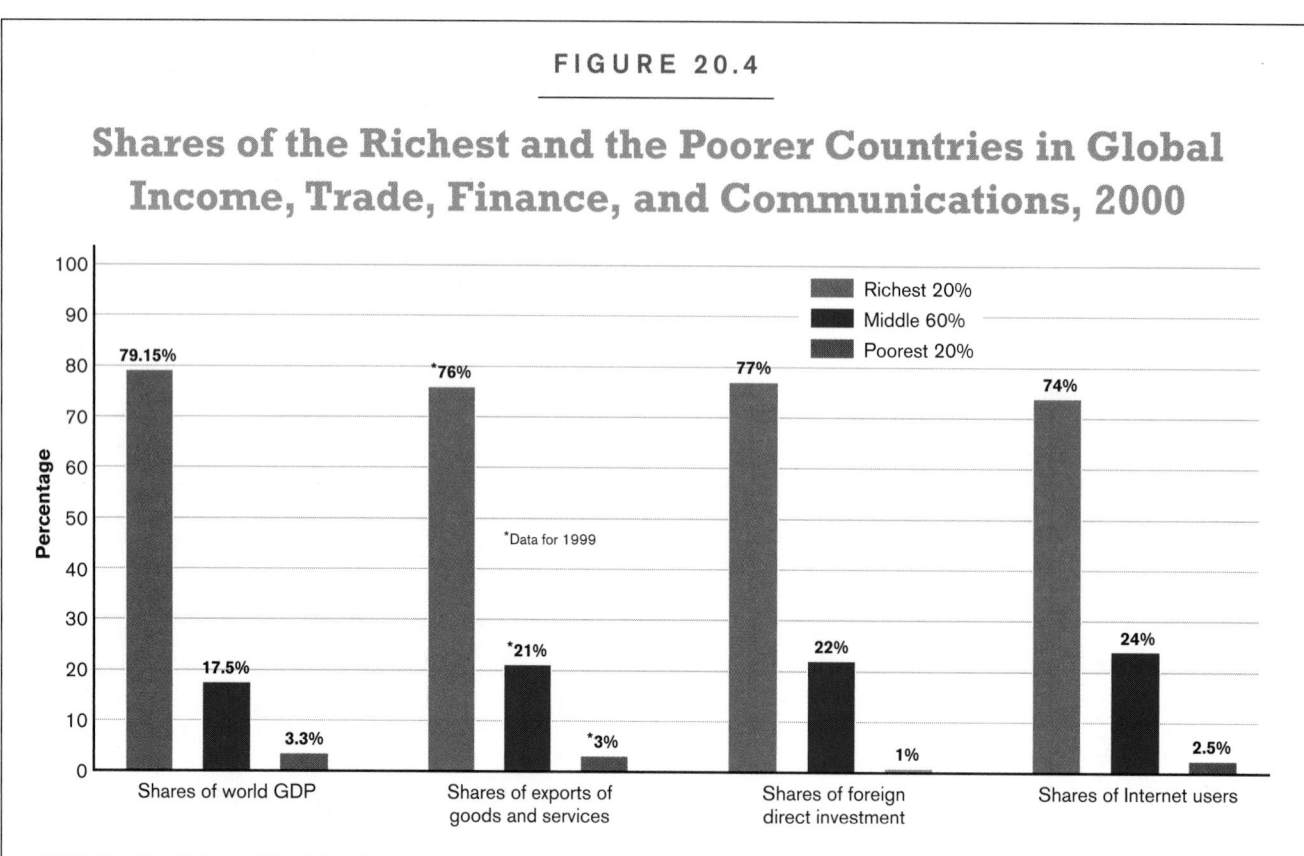

FIGURE 20.4

Shares of the Richest and the Poorer Countries in Global Income, Trade, Finance, and Communications, 2000

Legend:
- Richest 20%
- Middle 60%
- Poorest 20%

*Data for 1999

Shares of world GDP: 79.15%, 17.5%, 3.3%

Shares of exports of goods and services: *76%, *21%, *3%

Shares of foreign direct investment: 77%, 22%, 1%

Shares of Internet users: 74%, 24%, 2.5%

Y-axis: Percentage (0–100)

SOURCE: World Bank, World Development Indicators, 2002.

But what is this campaign about, and does it represent the emergence of a powerful antiglobalization movement, as some commentators have suggested? In the months following the Seattle protests, similar demonstrations were held in other cities around the world, such as London and Washington, D.C. These events were much smaller than those that took place in Seattle, but they were organized around similar themes. Protesters argued that free trade and economic globalization succeed in further concentrating wealth in the hands of a few, while increasing poverty for the majority of the world's population. Most of these activists agree that global trade is necessary and potentially beneficial for national economies, but they claim that it needs to be regulated by *different* rules from those favored by the WTO. They argue that trade rules should be oriented, first and foremost, to protecting human rights, the environment, labor rights, and local economies—not in ensuring larger profits for already rich corporations.

The protesters claim that the WTO is an undemocratic organization that is dominated by the interests of the world's richest nations—particularly the United States. Although the members of the WTO include many developing nations, many of them have virtually no practical influence over the organization's policies, because the agenda is set by the richest na-

tions. Poorer nations have many fewer resources, in terms of both money as well as trained personnel, to confront the many highly complex issues related to international trade. The president of the World Bank has pointed out that nineteen of the forty-two African states that are members of the WTO have little or no representation at its headquarters in Geneva (World Bank, 2000). Such imbalances have very real consequences. For example, although the WTO has insisted that developing nations open their markets to imports from industrialized countries, it has allowed developed countries to maintain high barriers to agricultural imports and provide vast subsidies for their domestic agriculture production in order to protect their own agricultural sectors. Between 1995 and 2001, the United States government spent $114 billion to boost the income of crop and livestock farmers (Environmental Working Group, 2003). This has meant that the world's poorest countries, many of which remain predominantly agricultural, do not have access to the large markets for agricultural goods in developed countries. This issue has been at the heart of a protracted breakdown in negotiating the expansion of WTO rules covering trade in services, foreign investment, government procurement, and other trade issues. Beginning with the 2003 WTO Ministerial Meeting, in Cancún, Mexico, the "Group of

21" developing nations led by Brazil and India have refused to consider the expansion of WTO rules until the United States and the European Union eliminate subsidies for agriculture production and allow greater access to other agriculture markets such as cotton. This led to the collapse of the Cancún Ministerial and contributed to slowed progress of other trade deals, such as the Free Trade Area of the Americas (FTAA), which is a plan to make both North and South America a free trading zone.

A similar divide exists over the protection of intellectual property rights—an issue monitored by a WTO multilateral agreement called TRIPS (Trade-Related Aspects of Intellectual Property Rights). Industrial countries own 97 percent of all patents worldwide, but the concept of intellectual property rights is alien to the developing world. There has been a significant increase in the number of patent claims over the past two decades as biotechnology companies and research institutes push to control and "own" more and more forms of knowledge, technology, and biodiversity. Many samples of plant material, for example, have been taken from biodiverse areas such as rain forests and developed by pharmaceutical companies into profitable—and patented—medicines. Local knowledge about the medicinal uses of the plants is often used in developing and marketing the medicines, yet the indigenous people of the area receive no compensation for their contribution. As industrialized countries within the WTO push to strengthen intellectual property laws, many people in developing countries argue that such a move works against the needs of their countries. Research agendas are dictated by profit interests, not human interests, and valuable forms of technology may end up out of the reach of poorer countries that could benefit greatly from their use.

Another criticism of the WTO is that it operates in secret and is not accountable to citizens who are directly affected by its decisions. In many ways, these criticisms are valid. Trade disputes between members of the WTO are decided behind closed doors by an unelected committee of "experts." When a decision is handed down, it is legally binding on all member states and enforceable through a mechanism that authorizes WTO member nations to enact punitive trade policies unless the losing nation complies with the decision. The WTO can also challenge or override laws in individual nations that are seen as barriers to trade. This includes national laws or bilateral agreements designed to protect the environment, conserve scarce resources, safeguard public health, or guarantee labor standards and human rights. For example, the WTO has ruled against the European Union, which refused to import U.S. hormone-treated beef because of its possible links to cancer, and has challenged a law passed in Massachusetts that prohibits companies from investing in Myanmar (Burma) because of its government's human rights violations. In another instance, the United States

and the European Union have attempted to use the Trade-Related Intellectual Property Rights (TRIPS) provision to block the importation of inexpensive generic HIV/AIDS medication into countries in sub-Saharan Africa, whose populations are being devastated by this epidemic. This was met with worldwide public outrage, which forced the WTO to reconsider its rules that regulate patent rights when public health is at stake.

A final concern shared by many activists is the undue influence wielded by the United States over the activities of the WTO and other international bodies such as the World Bank and the International Monetary Fund. In the years following the collapse of the Soviet Union, the United States has often been described as the world's only remaining superpower. In some respects, this is certainly true. With its overwhelming economic, political, and military might, the United States is able to influence debates and decision making in many international institutions. The unevenness of globalization must be seen in part as a reflection of the fact that political and economic power is concentrated in the hands of a few core states. Even with the significant influence of the United States on the formation and operation of the WTO, it is also subject to the rules and decisions of this organization. In fact, the United States almost always loses when it is forced to defend its trading practices before a World Trade Organization appellate panel (Conti, 2003). For example, in 2003 the WTO determined that high tariffs placed on imports of steel into the United States violated the rights of WTO member nations. Under heavy pressure from its trading partners, the United States eventually rescinded the tariffs and came into compliance with WTO law. This example highlights a fundamental tension about the nature of power and the processes of globalization: Can we expect the world's sole superpower to always play by the rules when the rules go against the interests of the superpower? What effect will this tension have on the creation of a just and equitable global legal and political system?

Protesters against the WTO and other international financial institutions such as the World Bank and the International Monetary Fund argue that exuberance over global economic integration and free trade is forcing people to live in an economy rather than a society. Many are convinced that such moves will further weaken the economic position of poor societies by allowing transnational corporations to operate with few or no safety and environmental regulations. Commercial interests, they claim, are increasingly taking precedence over concern for human well-being. Not only within developing nations, but in industrialized ones as well, there needs to be more investment in "human capital"—public health, education, and training—if global divisions are not to deepen even further. The key challenge for the twenty-first century is to ensure that globalization works for people everywhere, not only for those who are already well placed to benefit from it.

Conclusion: The Need for Global Governance

As globalization progresses, existing political structures and models appear unequipped to manage a world full of risks, inequalities, and challenges that transcend national borders. It is not within the capacity of individual governments to control the spread of HIV/AIDS, to counter the effects of global warming, or to regulate volatile financial markets. Many of the processes affecting societies around the world elude the grasp of current governing mechanisms. In light of this governing deficit, some have called for new forms of global governance that could address global issues in a global way. As a growing number of challenges operate above the level of individual countries, it is argued that responses to them must also be transnational in scope.

Although it may seem unrealistic to speak of governance above the level of the nation-state, some steps have already been taken toward the creation of a global democratic structure, such as the formation of the United Nations and the European Union. The EU in particular can be seen as an innovative response to globalization and could well become a model for similar organizations in other parts of the world where regional ties are strong. New forms of global governance could help to promote a cosmopolitan world order in which transparent rules and standards for international behavior, such as the defense of human rights, are established and observed.

The years that have passed since the end of the cold war have been marked by violence, internal conflict, and chaotic transformations in many areas of the world. Some have taken a pessimistic view, seeing globalization as accelerating crisis and chaos. Others see vital opportunities to harness globalizing forces in the pursuit of greater equality, democracy, and prosperity. The move toward global governance and more effective regulatory institutions is certainly not misplaced at a time when global interdependence and the rapid pace of change link all of us together more than ever before. It is not beyond our abilities to reassert our will on the social world. Indeed, such a task appears to be both the greatest necessity and the greatest challenge facing human societies at the start of the twenty-first century.

Study Outline

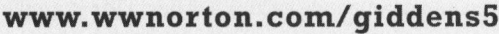

www.wwnorton.com/giddens5

Influences on Social Change

- *Social change* may be defined as the transformation, over time, of the institutions and culture of a society. The modern period, although occupying only a small fraction of human history, has shown rapid and major changes, and the pace of change is accelerating.

- The development of social organization and institutions, from hunting and gathering to agrarian to modern industrial societies, is far too diverse to be accounted for by any single-factor theory of social change. At least three broad categories of influences can be identified: The physical environment includes such factors as climate or the availability of communication routes (rivers, mountain passes); these are important to consider, especially as they affect early economic development, but should not be overemphasized. Political organization (especially military power) affects all societies, traditional and modern, with the possible exception of hunting and gathering societies. Cultural factors include religion (which can act as a brake on change), communication systems (such as the invention of writing), and individual leadership.

Change in the Modern Period

- The most important economic influence on modern social change is industrial capitalism, which depends on and promotes constant innovation and revision of productive technology. Science and technology also affect (and are affected by) political factors, the most important of which is the emergence of the modern state with its relatively efficient forms of government. Cultural influences include another effect of science and technology, the critical and innovative character of modern thinking, which constantly challenges tradition and cultural habits.

Current Changes and Future Prospects

- Social theorists have speculated on where social change will lead us. One influential line of thinking about where modern society is headed holds that the industrial era is being superseded by a *postindustrial society* based on the importance of information and service, rather than on manufacturing and industrialization. Some authors go further and speak not only of the end of industrialism, but of the end of modernity itself. Our beliefs in progress, in the benefits of science, and in our ability to control the modern world are diminishing, say the *postmodernists;* and there is such a diversity and plurality of individual concerns and points of view that it is no longer possible to have any overarching conception of history or of where we are headed.

Globalization

- Globalization is often portrayed as an economic phenomenon, but this view is too simplified. Globalization is produced by the coming together of political, economic, cultural, and social factors. It is driven forward above all by advances in information and communication technologies that have intensified the speed and scope of interaction among people around the world.
- Several factors are contributing to increasing globalization. First, the end of the cold war, the collapse of Soviet-style communism, and the growth of international and regional forms of governance have drawn the countries of the world closer together. Second, the spread of information technology has facilitated the flow of information around the globe and has encouraged people to adopt a global outlook. Third, transnational corporations have grown in size and influence, building networks of production and consumption that span the globe and link economic markets.
- Globalization has become a hotly debated topic. Skeptics believe that the idea of globalization is overrated and that current levels of interconnectedness are not unprecedented. Some skeptics focus instead on processes of regionalization that are intensifying activity within major financial and trade groups. Hyperglobalizers take an opposing position, arguing that globalization is a real and powerful phenomenon that threatens to erode the role of national governments altogether. A third group, the transformationalists, believes that globalization is transforming many aspects of the current global order—including economics, politics, and social relations—but that old patterns still remain. According to this view, globalization is a contradictory process, involving a multidirectional flow of influences that sometimes work in opposition.
- Globalization is not restricted to large, global systems. Its impact is felt in our personal lives, in the way we think of ourselves and our connections with others. Globalizing forces enter our local contexts and our intimate lives both through impersonal sources such as the media and the Internet and through personal contacts with people from other countries and cultures.

Globalization and Risk

- Globalization is an open-ended, contradictory process—it produces outcomes that are difficult to control and predict. Globalization is presenting us with new forms of risk that differ from those that existed previously. *External risk* refers to dangers that spring from the natural world, such as earthquakes. *Manufactured risks* are risks that are created by the impact of human knowledge and technology on the natural world. Some believe that we are living in a global-

risk society in which human societies everywhere are faced with risks (e.g., global warming) that have been produced by our own interventions into nature.
- Globalization is proceeding rapidly but unevenly. It has been marked by a growing divergence between the richest and poorest countries of the world. Wealth, income, resources, and consumption are concentrated among the developed societies, whereas much of the developing world struggles with poverty, malnutrition, disease, and foreign debt. Many of the countries most in need of the economic benefits of globalization are in danger of being marginalized.

World Trade Organization

- Barriers to international trade have been steadily reduced in recent decades, and many believe that free trade and open markets will allow developing countries to integrate more fully into the global economy. Opponents to this approach argue that international trade bodies, such as the World Trade Organization, are dominated by the interests of the richest countries and ignore the needs of the developing world. They claim that trade rules must, first and foremost, protect human rights, labor rights, the environment, and national economies, rather than simply ensuring larger profits for corporations.

Global Governance in the Future

- Globalization is producing risks, challenges, and inequalities that cross national borders and elude the reach of existing political structures. Because individual governments are unequipped to handle these transnational issues, there is a need for new forms of global governance that can address global problems in a global way. Reasserting our will on the rapidly changing social world may be the greatest challenge of the twenty-first century.

Key Concepts

external risk (p. 634)
information society (p. 621)
knowledge society (p. 621)
manufactured risk (p. 634)
postindustrial society (p. 621)
postmodernism (p. 622)
service society (p. 621)
social change (p. 618)
transnational corporation (p. 626)

Review Questions

1. What is the sociology of social change?
   a. The study of revolution
   b. The study of the transformation over time of the institutions and culture of society
   c. The study of social movements
   d. The study of collective behavior

2. According to hyperglobalizers, which one of the following statements is true?
   a. Internationalization depends on government acquiescence and support.
   b. Globalization is making national politics more powerful.
   c. Globalization means the end of the nation-state.
   d. Globalization has no impact on how nation-states or governments operate.

3. How do opponents of postindustrial theory refute the argument that the shift from manufacturing jobs to service jobs is a harbinger of postindustrialism?
   a. Such a shift has been going on since the beginning of the Industrial Revolution. Manufacturing and service employment have expanded at the expense of agriculture.
   b. Service jobs are not necessarily white-collar jobs. There are many blue-collar jobs in services.
   c. White-collar work isn't necessarily service work. A lot of white-collar work supports manufacturing.
   d. All of the above.

4. What is the argument of the "end of history" thesis?
   a. The "end of history" is the end of the Industrial Revolution and the coming of postindustrial society.
   b. The "end of history" is the end of the great ideological struggles that erupted in the wake of the Industrial Revolution: Capitalism has finally beaten socialism, and liberal democracy is unchallenged.
   c. The "end of history" is the end of the belief that humanity can make progress, through the application of science and the development of technology, toward controlling its own destiny.
   d. The "end of history" is the end of World War II.

5. Transnational corporations became a global phenomenon in the years following
   a. World War I.
   b. World War II.
   c. the collapse of the Soviet Union.
   d. the invention of the computer.

6. In 1992, the distance in terms of wealth between the world's richest and poorest countries was approximately
   a. 3 to 1.
   b. 11 to 1.
   c. 35 to 1.
   d. 72 to 1.

7. What is the relationship between science/technology and politics?
   a. Science and technology influence changes in politics.
   b. Politics influences how science and technology develop.
   c. Science and technology both influence and are influenced by political factors.
   d. Science and technology have no influence on politics.

8. According to Daniel Bell, what is postindustrial society's main strategic resource?
   a. The production and control of computers
   b. The production and control of nuclear weapons
   c. The production and control of food
   d. The production and control of codified knowledge

9. Which of the following can be controlled by individual governments?
   a. The spread of HIV/AIDS
   b. The effects of global warming
   c. Volatile financial markets
   d. None of the above

10. The "unevenness" of globalization is in part due to the fact that political and economic power is concentrated in the hands of
    a. the United States.
    b. the United Nations.
    c. a few core countries.
    d. oil-rich countries.

Thinking Sociologically Exercises

1. Discuss the many influences on social change: environmental, political, and cultural factors. Summarize how each element can contribute to social change.

2. According to this chapter, we now live in a society where we are increasingly confronted by various types of manufactured risks. Briefly explain what these risks consist of. Do you think the last decade has brought us any closer to or further away from confronting the challenges of manufactured risks? Explain.

Data Exercises

www.wwnorton.com/giddens5
Keyword: Data20

- What role have transnational corporations played in the development of a global economy? In what ways do they adapt their products and operations to local markets and in what ways do they ignore cultural differences? The data exercise for this chapter will give you an opportunity to investigate the global operations of a selected number of transnational corporations.

HOW TO USE LIBRARIES

ibraries, especially large ones, can seem like daunting places. People can feel somewhat lost when confronted with the apparently innumerable sources of information that libraries contain. They may therefore end up using only a small proportion of what a library has to offer, perhaps with damaging effects on their academic work. It is a good idea to get to know—at the beginning of your course—the range of resources libraries have. If you do this early on, the "lost" feeling will not last long!

All the information available in the library is stored and cataloged systematically, in order to make finding things easy. Most smaller libraries operate with *open stacks*—the books can be visibly inspected on the shelves, and the user can select whichever volume she wants directly. Most larger collections keep only a proportion of their books on open shelves and store others in vaults, where less space is required to keep them. In these libraries, anyone who wishes to use or borrow a book must ask for it or fill in a request slip.

If you are looking for a particular book, you will be able to look it up under author or title in the index or catalog. This may be a computerized list, drawers of index cards, or microfiche—or all three. Once you find the book's catalog number you can then either order it from library staff by quoting that number or find it on the open shelves, which are always arranged by catalog number. All—or most—sociology books will be in one area. Any librarian will be able to explain how the cataloging system works. To find books on a particular topic when you don't know any names or titles, you need to use a subject index (again, this may be computerized or on cards). A subject index lists books by topics—such as "class," "bureaucracy," etc.

Many of the larger libraries today have computer-trace systems, which are very easy to operate and are normally available to all library users. You simply key in the area about which you require bibliographical information, and the computer will display a list of relevant titles.

Most libraries provide similar services, but different libraries have their own ways of doing things, and there are variations in cataloging systems. Never be afraid to ask the librarian or assistants for their help if there is any procedure that puzzles you. You should not be worried about bothering them; librarians are trained professionals, committed to making sure that the library resources are available to everyone who wants to make use of them. They are usually highly knowledgeable about the range of material the library contains and only too willing to provide guidance.

Sources of General Information in Sociology

If you are beginning the study of a particular topic in sociology and want to find some general information about it, there are a number of useful sources. Several dictionaries of sociology are available. These provide brief discussions of major concepts and accounts of the ideas of some of the leading contributors to the discipline. The major encyclopedias—like the *World Book Encyclopedia*—contain many entries relevant to sociological topics, such as "city," "crime," "family," "middle class," "prejudice," "research," and "statistics." The entries in dictionaries and encyclopedias virtually always provide short lists of books or articles as a guide to further reading.

There are other ways in which books and articles relevant to a given issue can be traced. The *International Bibliography of the Social Sciences*, published annually by UNESCO, offers a comprehensive listing of works that have appeared in different social science subjects over the course of any year. Thus, for example, you can look up the heading "Sociology of education" and find a range of up-to-date materials in that field. An equally useful source is *Sociological Abstracts*, which not only lists books and articles in the different areas of sociology, but gives a short description of the contents of each.

Sociological Journals

It is worth familiarizing yourself with the main journals in sociology. Journals usually appear three or four times a year. The information and debates they contain are often more up to date than those in books, which take longer to write and publish. Journal articles are sometimes quite technical, and a person new to sociology may not find them readily understandable. But all the leading journals regularly publish articles of general interest, accessible to those with only limited knowledge of the subject.

The most important sociology journals include the *American Sociological Review* and the *American Journal of Sociology*.

Writing Research Papers

On some occasions, you may wish to use the library to pursue a particular research project, perhaps in the course of writing a thesis. Such a task might involve carrying out a more in-depth search for relevant sources than is required for normal study.

If you need statistical information concerning the United States, a good place to start is *Statistical Abstract of the United States*, which is available from the Government Printing Office in Washington, D.C. This volume contains selected statistical information on many areas of American social life.

Newspaper articles provide a mine of valuable information for the sociological researcher. A few newspapers are what are sometimes called "journals of record." That is to say, they not only carry news stories, but also record sections from congressional speeches, government reports, and other official sources. The *New York Times*, the *Washington Post*, and the *Los Angeles Times* are the most important examples, and each produces an index of topics and names that have appeared in its pages.

Once you start using a library regularly, you are likely to find that it is more common to feel overwhelmed by the number of works available in a particular area than to experience difficulty in tracing relevant literature. One way of dealing with this problem is to base your selection of books or articles on reading lists provided by professors. Where such lists are not available, the best procedure to follow is to define the information you require as precisely as possible. This will allow you to narrow the range of choice to feasible limits. If your library is an open-stack one, it is worth looking through a number of potentially useful books or articles before selecting those you decide to work with. In making the decision, keep in mind *when* the book was written. New developments are constantly taking place in sociology and in the other social sciences, and obviously older books will not cover these.

Words in bold type within entries refer to terms found elsewhere in the glossary.

AARP: American Association of Retired Persons.

absolute poverty: The minimal requirements necessary to sustain a healthy existence.

achieved status: Social status based on an individual's effort.

activity theory: A functionalist theory of aging which holds that busy, engaged people are more likely to lead fulfilling and productive lives.

affective individualism: The belief in romantic attachment as a basis for contracting **marriage** ties.

age-grades: The system found in small traditional cultures by which people belonging to a similar age-group are categorized together and hold similar rights and obligations.

ageism: Discrimination or **prejudice** against a person on the grounds of age.

agencies of socialization: Groups or social contexts within which processes of **socialization** take place.

aging: The combination of biological, psychological, and social processes that affect people as they grow older.

agrarian societies: Societies whose means of subsistence are based on agricultural production (crop growing).

alienation: The sense that our own abilities as human beings are taken over by other entities. The term was originally used by Marx to refer to the projection of human powers onto gods. Subsequently he used the term to refer to the loss of workers' control over the nature and products of their labor.

Alzheimer's disease: A degenerative disease of the brain resulting in progressive loss of mental capacity.

andragogy: Term coined by educators to refer to adult learning.

animism: A belief that events in the world are mobilized by the activities of spirits.

anomie: A concept first brought into wide usage in sociology by Durkheim, referring to a situation in which social **norms** lose their hold over individual behavior.

antiracism: Forms of thought and/or practice that seek to confront, eradicate and/or ameliorate racism.

apartheid: The system of racial **segregation** established in South Africa.

ascribed status: Social **status** based on biological factors such as **race, sex,** or age.

ascription: Placement in a particular social **status** based on characteristics such as family of origin, race, and gender.

assimilation The acceptance of a **minority group** by a majority population, in which the new group takes on the **values** and **norms** of the dominant **culture.**

authoritarian personality: A set of specific personality characteristics, including a rigid and intolerant outlook and an inability to accept ambiguity.

authority: A **government**'s legitimate use of **power.**

automation: Production processes monitored and controlled by machines with only minimal supervision from people.

back region: An area apart from **front region** performances, as specified by Erving Goffman, in which individuals are able to relax and behave informally.

biomedical model of health: The set of principles underpinning Western medical systems and practices. The biomedical model of health defines diseases objectively, in accordance with the presence of recognized symptoms, and believes that the healthy body can be restored through scientifically based medical treatment. The human body is likened to a machine that can be returned to working order with the proper repairs.

black feminism: A strand of **feminist theory** that highlights the multiple disadvantages of **gender, class,** and **race** that shape the experiences of nonwhite women. Black feminists reject the idea of a single, unified gender oppression that is experienced evenly by all women and argue that early feminist analysis reflected the specific concerns of white, middle-class women.

bureaucracy: A type of **organization** marked by a clear hierarchy of authority and the existence of written rules of procedure and staffed by full-time, salaried officials.

capitalism: An economic system based on the private ownership of **wealth,** which is invested and reinvested in order to produce profit.

capitalists: People who own companies, land, or stocks (shares) and use these to generate economic returns.

caste: A form of stratification in which a person's **social position** is fixed at birth and cannot be changed. There is virtually no intermarriage between the members of different castes.

caste society: A society in which different social levels are closed, so that all individuals must remain at the social level of their birth throughout life.

caste system: A social system in which one's social status is given for life.

causal relationship: A relationship in which one state of affairs (the effect) is brought about by another (the cause).

causation: The causal influence of one factor, or **variable,** upon another. A cause and effect relationship exists whenever a particular event or state of affairs (the effect) is produced by the existence of another (the cause). Causal factors in sociology include the reasons individuals give for what they do, as well as external influences on their behavior.

charisma: The inspirational quality capable of capturing the imagination and devotion of a mass of followers.

church: A large body of people belonging to an established religious organization. The term is also used to refer to the place in which religious ceremonies are carried out.

citizen: A member of a political community, having both rights and duties associated with that membership.

citizenship: A people's common rights and duties and consciousness of their relationship to the **state.**

civil inattention: The process whereby individuals in the same physical setting demonstrate to one another that they are aware of each other's presence.

civil religion: A set of religious beliefs through which a society interprets its own history in light of some conception of ultimate reality.

civil rights: Legal rights held by all **citizens** in a given national community.

civil society: The realm of activity that lies between the **state** and the market, including the **family,** schools, community associations, and noneconomic institutions. Civil society, or civic culture, is essential to vibrant democratic societies.

clan (business model): Work groups having close personal connections with one another, which some argue is more efficient and productive than other forms of business organization.

class: Although it is one of the most frequently used concepts in **sociology,** there is no clear agreement about how the notion should be defined. Most sociologists use the term to refer to socioeconomic variations between groups of individuals that create variations in their material prosperity and power.

clock time: Time as measured by the clock, in terms of hours, minutes, and seconds. Before the invention of clocks, time reckoning was based on events in the natural world, such as the rising and setting of the sun.

cognition: Human thought processes involving perception, reasoning, and remembering.

cohabitation: Two people living together in a sexual relationship of some permanence, without being married to one another.

collective action: Action undertaken in a relatively spontaneous way by a large number of people assembled together.

collective consumption: A concept used by Manuel Castells to refer to processes of urban consumption—such as the buying and selling of property.

colonialism: The process whereby Western nations established their rule in parts of the world away from their home territories.

communication: The transmission of information from one individual or group to another. Communication is the necessary basis of all social interaction. In face-to-face **encounters,** communication is carried on by the use of **language** and by bodily cues that individuals interpret. With the development of writing and electronic media such as radio, television, and computers, communication becomes in some part detached from immediate face-to-face social relationships.

communism: A set of political ideas associated with Marx, as developed particularly by Lenin and institutionalized in the Soviet Union, Eastern Europe, and some Third World countries.

community policing: A renewed emphasis on crime prevention rather than law enforcement to reintegrate policing within the community.

comparable worth: Policies that attempt to remedy the gender pay gap by adjusting pay so that those in female-dominated jobs are not paid less for equivalent work.

comparative questions: Questions concerned with drawing comparisons between different human societies for the purposes of sociological **theory** or research.

comparative research: Research that compares one set of findings on one society with the same type of findings on other societies.

compulsion of proximity: People's need to interact with others in their presence.

concrete operational stage: A stage of cognitive development, as formulated by Piaget, in which the child's thinking is based primarily on physical perception of the world. In this phase, the child is not yet capable of dealing with abstract concepts or hypothetical situations.

conflict theory: Argument that deviance is deliberately chosen and often political in nature.

conflict theory of aging: Argument that emphasizes the ways in which the larger social structure helps to shape the opportunities available to the elderly. Unequal opportunities are seen as creating the potential for conflict.

constitutional monarch: A king or queen who is largely a figurehead. Real power rests in the hands of other political **leaders.**

contradiction: A term used by Marx to refer to mutually antagonistic tendencies in a society.

contradictory class locations: Positions in the class structure, particularly routine white-collar and lower managerial jobs, that share characteristics of the class positions both above and below them.

control: A statistical or experimental means of holding some **variables** constant in order to examine the causal influence of others.

control theory: A **theory** that views **crime** as the outcome of an imbalance between impulses toward criminal activity and controls that deter it. Control theorists hold that criminals are rational beings who will act to maximize their own reward unless they are rendered unable to do so through either social or physical controls.

conurbation: An agglomeration of towns or cities into an unbroken urban environment.

conversational analysis: The empirical study of conversations, employing techniques drawn from **ethnomethodology.** Conversation analysis examines details of naturally occurring conversations to reveal the organizational principles of talk and its role in the production and reproduction of social order.

core countries: According to **world-systems theory,** the most advanced industrial countries, which take the lion's share of profits in the world economic system.

corporate crime: Offenses committed by large corporations in society. Examples of corporate crime include pollution, false advertising, and violations of health and safety regulations.

corporate culture: An organizational culture involving rituals, events, or traditions that are unique to a specific company.

corporations: Business firms or companies.

correlation: The regular relationship between two **variables,** often expressed in statistical terms. Correlations may be positive or negative. A positive correlation between two variables exists when a high rank on one variable is associated with a high rank on the other. A negative correlation exists when a high rank on one variable is associated with a low rank on the other.

correlation coefficient: A measure of the degree of **correlation** between **variables.**

created environment: Constructions established by human beings to serve their needs, derived from the use of man-made **technology**—including, for example, roads, railways, factories, offices, private homes, and other buildings.

crime: Any action that contravenes the **laws** established by a political authority. Although we may think of criminals as a distinct subsection of the population, there are few people who have not broken the law in one way or another during their lives. While laws are formulated by state authorities, it is not unknown for those authorities to engage in criminal behavior in certain situations.

crude birthrate: A statistical measure representing the number of births within a given population per year, normally calculated in terms of the number of births per thousand members. Although the crude birthrate is a useful index, it is only a general measure, because it does not specify numbers of births in relation to age distribution.

crude death rate: A statistical measure representing the number of deaths that occur annually in a given population per year, normally calculated as the ratio of deaths per thousand members. Crude death rates give a general indication of the **mortality** levels of a community or society, but are limited in their usefulness because they do not take into account the age distribution.

cult: A fragmentary religious grouping to which individuals are loosely affiliated, but which lacks any permanent structure.

cultural capital: The advantages that well-to-do parents usually provide their children.

cultural relativism: The practice of judging a **society** by its own standards.

cultural turn: **Sociology**'s recent emphasis on the importance of understanding the role of **culture** in daily life.

cultural universals: **Values** or modes of behavior shared by all human **cultures.**

culture: The **values, norms,** and **material goods** characteristic of a given group. Like the concept of **society,** the notion of culture is widely used in **sociology** and the other social sciences (particularly anthropology). Culture is one of the most distinctive properties of human social association.

culture of poverty: The thesis, popularized by Oscar Lewis, that poverty is not a result of individual inadequacies but is instead the outcome of a larger social and cultural atmosphere into which successive generations of children are socialized. The culture of poverty refers to the **values,** beliefs, lifestyles, habits, and traditions that are common among people living under conditions of material deprivation.

cybercrime: Criminal activities by means of electronic **networks** or involving the use of new information **technologies.** Electronic money laundering, personal identity theft, electronic vandalism, and monitoring electronic correspondence are all emergent forms of cybercrime.

cyberspace: Electronic networks of interaction between individuals at different computer terminals.

degree of dispersal: The range or distribution of a set of figures.

democracy: A political system that allows the **citizens** to participate in political decision making or to elect representatives to **government** bodies.

democratic elitism: A theory of the limits of **democracy,** which holds that in large-scale societies democratic participation is necessarily limited to the regular election of political **leaders.**

demographic transition: An interpretation of population change, which holds that a stable ratio of births to deaths is achieved once a certain level of economic prosperity has been reached. According to this notion, in preindustrial societies there is a rough balance between births and deaths, because population increase is kept in check by a lack of available food, by disease, or by war. In modern societies, by contrast, population equilibrium is achieved because **families** are moved by economic incentives to limit the number of children.

demography: The study of populations.

denomination: A religious **sect** that has lost its revivalist dynamism and become an institutionalized body, commanding the adherence of significant numbers of people.

dependency culture: A term popularized by Charles Murray to describe individuals who rely on state welfare provision rather than entering the labor market. The dependency culture is seen as the outcome of the "paternalistic" welfare state that undermines individual ambition and people's capacity for self-help.

dependency ratio: The ratio of people of dependent ages (children and the elderly) to people of economically active ages.

dependency theories: Marxist theories of economic development arguing that the poverty of low-income countries stems directly from their exploitation by wealthy countries and the **multinational corporations** that are based in wealthy countries.

dependent development theory: A Marxist-influenced theory holding that although low-income countries are poor because of their exploitation by high-income countries, under certain circumstances they can still develop economically, but only in ways shaped by their reliance on the wealthier countries.

dependent variable: A **variable,** or factor, causally influenced by another (the **independent variable**).

developing world: The less-developed societies, in which industrial production is either virtually nonexistent or only developed to a limited degree. The majority of the world's population live in less-developed countries.

developmental questions: Questions that sociologists pose when looking at the origins and path of development of **social institutions** from the past to the present.

deviance: Modes of action that do not conform to the **norms** or **values** held by most members of a group or **society.** What is regarded as deviant is as variable as the norms and values that distinguish different **cultures** and **subcultures** from one another. Forms of behavior that are highly esteemed by one group are regarded negatively by others.

deviant subculture: A **subculture** whose members hold values that differ substantially from those of the majority.

diaspora: The dispersal of an ethnic population from an original homeland into foreign areas, often in a forced manner or under traumatic circumstances.

differential association: An interpretation of the development of criminal behavior proposed by Edwin H. Sutherland, according to whom criminal behavior is learned through association with others who regularly engage in **crime.**

direct democracy: A form of **participatory democracy** that allows **citizens** to vote directly on **laws** and policies.

discourse: The framework of thinking in a particular area of social life. For instance, the discourse of criminality refers to the way people in a given **society** think and talk about **crime.**

discrimination: Behavior that denies to the members of a particular group resources or rewards that can be obtained by others. Discrimination must be distinguished from **prejudice:** Individuals who are prejudiced against others may not engage in discriminatory practices against them; conversely, people may act in a discriminatory fashion toward a group even though they are not prejudiced against that group.

disengagement theory: A functionalist theory of **aging** which holds that it is functional for society to remove people from their traditional roles when they become elderly, thereby freeing up those roles for others.

disestablishment: A period during which the political influence of established religions is successfully challenged.

displacement: The transferring of ideas or emotions from their true source to another object.

division of labor: The specialization of **work** tasks, by means of which different **occupations** are combined within a production system. All **societies** have at least some rudimentary form of division of labor, especially between the tasks allocated to men and those performed by women. With the development of industrialism, the division of labor became vastly more complex than in any prior type of production system. In the modern world, the division of labor is international in scope.

dominant group: The opposite of a **minority group;** the dominant group possesses more **wealth, power,** and **prestige** in a **society.**

doubling time: The time it takes for a particular level of population to double.

downward mobility: Social mobility in which individuals' **wealth, income,** or **status** is lower than what they or their parents once had.

dyad: A group consisting of two persons.

ecological approach: A perspective on urban analysis emphasizing the "natural" distribution of city neighborhoods into areas having contrasting characteristics.

economic interdependence: The fact that in the **division of labor,** individuals depend on others to produce many or most of the goods they need to sustain their lives.

economy: The system of production and exchange that provides for the material needs of individuals living in a given **society.** Economic institutions are of key importance in all social orders. What goes on in the economy usually influences other areas in social life. Modern economies differ substantially from traditional ones, because the majority of the population is no longer engaged in agricultural production.

egocentric: According to Piaget, the characteristic quality of a child during the early years of her life. Egocentric thinking involves understanding objects and events in the environment solely in terms of the child's own position.

emigration: The movement of people out of one country in order to settle in another.

empirical investigation: Factual inquiry carried out in any area of sociological study.

encounter: A meeting between two or more people in a situation of face-to-face interaction. Our daily lives can be seen as a series of different encounters strung out across the course of the day. In modern societies, many of these encounters are with strangers rather than people we know.

endogamy: The forbidding of marriage or sexual relations outside one's **social group.**

entrepreneur: The owner/founder of a business firm.

environmental ecology: A concern with preserving the integrity of the physical environment in the face of the impact of modern industry and **technology.**

epidemiology: The study of the distribution and incidence of disease and illness within a population.

ethnic cleansing: The creation of ethnically homogeneous territories through the mass expulsion of other ethnic populations.

ethnic-group closure: The maintenance of boundaries against others, the prohibition against intermarriage between groups, and restrictions on social contact with other groups.

ethnicity: Cultural **values** and **norms** that distinguish the members of a given group from others. An ethnic group is one whose members share a distinct awareness of a common cultural identity, separating them from other groups. In virtually all **societies,** ethnic differences are associated with variations in **power** and material **wealth.** Where ethnic differences are also racial, such divisions are sometimes especially pronounced.

ethnie: A term used to describe a group that shares ideas of common ancestry, a common cultural identity, and a link with a specific homeland.

ethnocentric transationals: Transnational corporations largely run directly from the headquarters of the parent company.

ethnocentrism: The tendency to look at other **cultures** through the eyes of one's own culture, and thereby misrepresent them.

ethnography: The firsthand study of people using **participant observation** or interviewing.

ethnomethodology: The study of how people make sense of what others say and do in the course of day-to-day social interaction. Ethnomethodology is concerned with the "ethnomethods" by which people sustain meaningful interchanges with one another.

evangelicalism: A form of Protestantism characterized by a belief in spiritual rebirth (being "born again").

exchange mobility: The exchange of positions on the socioeconomic scale such that talented people move up the economic hierarchy while the less talented move down.

experiment: A **research method** in which **variables** can be analyzed in a controlled and systematic way, either in an artificial situation constructed by the researcher or in naturally occurring settings.

exponential growth: A geometric, rather than linear, rate of progression, producing a fast rise in the numbers of a population experiencing such growth.

extended family: A **family** group consisting of more than two generations of relatives living either within the same household or very close to one another.

external risk: Dangers that spring from the natural world and are unrelated to the actions of humans. Examples of external risk include droughts, earthquakes, famines, and storms.

factual questions: Questions that raise issues concerning matters of fact (rather than theoretical or moral issues).

family: A group of individuals related to one another by blood ties, **marriage,** or adoption, who form an economic unit, the adult members of which are responsible for the upbringing of children. All known **societies** involve some form of family system, although the nature of family relationships varies widely. While in modern societies the main family form is the **nuclear family, extended family** relationships are also found.

family capitalism: Capitalistic enterprise owned and administered by entrepreneurial **families.**

family of orientation: The **family** into which an individual is born.

family of procreation: The **family** an individual initiates through **marriage** or by having children.

fecundity: A measure of the number of children that it is biologically possible for a woman to produce.

feminism: Advocacy of the rights of women to be equal with men in all spheres of life. Feminism dates from the late eighteenth century in Europe, and feminist movements exist in most countries today.

feminist theory: A sociological perspective that emphasizes the centrality of **gender** in analyzing the social world and particularly the uniqueness of the experience of women. There are many strands of feminist theory, but they all share the desire to explain **gender inequalities** in **society** and to work to overcome them.

feminization of poverty: An increase in the proportion of the poor who are female.

fertility: The average number of live-born children produced by women of childbearing age in a particular **society.**

field of action: The arena within which **social movements** interact with established **organizations,** the ideas and outlook of the members of both often becoming modified as a result.

First World: The group of **nation-states** that possesses mature industrialized economies based on capitalistic production.

flexible production: Process in which computers design customized products for a mass market.

focused interaction: Interaction between individuals engaged in a common activity or in direct conversation with one another.

Fordism: The system of production pioneered by Henry Ford, in which the assembly line was introduced.

formal operational stage: According to Piaget's theory, a stage of cognitive development at which the growing child becomes capable of handling abstract concepts and hypothetical situations.

formal organization: Means by which a group is rationally designed to achieve its objectives, often by means of explicit rules, regulations, and procedures.

formal relations: Relations that exist in groups and **organizations,** laid down by the **norms,** or rules, of the official system of authority.

front region: A setting of social activity in which people seek to put on a definite "performance" for others.

functionalism: A theoretical perspective based on the notion that social events can best be explained in terms of the functions they perform—that is, the contributions they make to the continuity of a **society.**

fundamentalism: A belief in returning to the literal meanings of scriptural texts.

fundamentalists: A group within **evangelicalism** that is highly antimodern in many of its beliefs, adhering to strict codes of morality and conduct.

gender: Social expectations about behavior regarded as appropriate for the members of each **sex.** Gender refers not to the physical attributes distinguishing men and women but to socially formed traits of masculinity and femininity. The study of gender relations has become one of the most important areas of **sociology** in recent years.

gender inequality: The inequality between men and women in terms of **wealth, income,** and **status.**

gender roles: Social roles assigned to each **sex** and labeled as masculine or feminine.

gender socialization: The learning of **gender roles** through social factors such as schooling, the media, and **family.**

gender typing: Women holding **occupations** of lower **status** and pay, such as secretarial and retail positions, and men holding **jobs** of higher status and pay, such as managerial and professional positions.

generalized other: A concept in the **theory** of George Herbert Mead, according to which the individual takes over the general **values** of a given group or **society** during the **socialization** process.

generational equity: The striking of a balance between the needs and interests of members of different generations.

genocide: The systematic, planned destruction of a racial, political, or cultural group.

gentrification: A process of **urban renewal** in which older, deteriorated housing is refurbished by affluent people moving into the area.

geocentric transnational: Transnational corporations whose administrative structure is global, rather than organized from any particular country.

geragogy: Term coined by educators to refer to older-adult learning.

glass ceiling: A promotion barrier that prevents a woman's upward mobility within an **organization.**

glass escalator: The process by which men in traditionally female professions benefit from an unfair rapid rise within an **organization.**

global city: A city—such as London, New York, or Tokyo—that has become an organizing center of the new global economy.

global commodity chain: A worldwide **network** of labor and production processes yielding a finished product.

global inequality: The systematic differences in **wealth** and **power** between countries.

globalization: The development of social and economic relationships stretching worldwide. In current times, we are all influenced by **organizations** and social **networks** located thousands of miles away. A key part of the study of globalization is the emergence of a **world system**—for some purposes, we need to regard the world as forming a single social order.

global village: A notion associated with Marshall McLuhan, who believed that the world has become like a small community as a result of the spread of electronic communication. For instance, people in many different parts of the world follow the same news events through television programming.

government: The enacting of policies and decisions on the part of officials within a political apparatus. We can speak of government as a process, or *the* government as the officialdom responsible for making binding political decisions. While in the past virtually all governments were headed by monarchs or emperors, in most modern **societies** governments are run by officials who do not inherit their positions of **power** but are elected or appointed on the basis of qualifications.

graying: A term used to indicate that an increasing proportion of a **society**'s population is becoming elderly.

group closure: The maintenance of boundaries against others, the prohibition of intermarriage between groups, and restrictions on social contact with other groups.

group production: Production organized by means of small groups rather than individuals.

groupthink: A process by which the members of a group ignore ways of thinking and plans of action that go against the group consensus.

heterosexism: The process by which nonheterosexual people are categorized and discriminated against on the basis of their sexual orientation.

hidden curriculum: Traits of behavior or attitudes that are learned at school but not included within the formal curriculum—for example, **gender** differences.

higher education: Education in colleges or universities.

high-trust systems: Organizations or **work** settings in which individuals are permitted a great deal of autonomy and control over the work task.

historicity: The use of an understanding of history as a basis for trying to change history—that is, producing informed processes of **social change.**

homeless: People who have no place to sleep and either stay in free shelters or sleep in public places not meant for habitation.

homophobia: An irrational fear or disdain of homosexuals.

housework (domestic labor): Unpaid work carried on, usually by women, in the home; domestic chores such as cooking, cleaning, and shopping.

human capital theory: Argument that individuals make investments in their own "human capital" in order to increase their productivity and earnings.

human resource management: A style of management that regards a company's work force as vital to its economic competitiveness.

hunting and gathering societies: Societies whose mode of subsistence is gained from hunting animals, fishing, and gathering edible plants.

hyperreality: An idea associated with Jean Baudrillard, who argued that as a result of the spread of electronic communication, there is no longer a separate "reality" to which TV programs and other cultural products

refer. Instead, what we take to be "reality" is structured by such communication itself. For instance, the items reported on the news are not just about a separate series of events, but actually define and construct what those events are.

hypothesis: An idea or a guess about a given state of affairs, put forward as a basis for empirical testing.

I: The pronoun used to refer used to refer to oneself as speaker or writer.

ideal type: A "pure type," constructed by emphasizing certain traits of a social item that do not necessarily exist in reality. An example is Max Weber's ideal type of bureaucratic organization.

identity: The distinctive characteristics of a person's or group's character that relate to who they are and what is meaningful to them. Some of the main sources of identity include **gender,** sexual orientation, nationality or **ethnicity,** and social **class.**

ideology: Shared ideas or beliefs that serve to justify the interests of **dominant groups.** Ideologies are found in all **societies** in which there are systematic and ingrained inequalities between groups. The concept of ideology connects closely with that of **power,** since ideological systems serve to legitimize the power that groups hold.

immigration: The movement of people into one country from another for the purpose of settlement.

impression management: Preparing for the presentation of one's **social role.**

income: Payment, usually derived from wages, salaries, or investments.

independent variable: A **variable,** or factor, that causally affects another (the **dependent variable**).

industrialism hypothesis: Theory that **societies** become more open to **social mobility** as they become more industrialized.

industrialization: The process of the machine production of goods. See also **industrialized societies.**

industrialized societies: Strongly developed **nation-states** in which the majority of the population work in factories or offices rather than in agriculture, and most people live in urban areas.

infant mortality rate: The number of infants who die during the first year of life, per thousand live births.

informal economy: Economic transactions carried on outside the sphere of orthodox paid employment.

informal relations: Relations that exist in groups and **organizations** developed on the basis of personal connections; ways of doing things that depart from formally recognized modes of procedure.

information poverty: The "information poor" are those people who have little or no access to information **technology,** such as computers.

information society: A **society** no longer based primarily on the production of **material goods** but on the production of knowledge. The notion of the information society is closely bound up with the rise of **information technology.**

information technology: Forms of **technology** based on information processing and requiring microelectronic circuitry.

in-group: A group toward which one feels particular loyalty and respect—the groups to which "we" belong.

inner city: The areas composing the central neighborhoods of a city, as distinct from the suburbs. In many modern urban settings in the **First World,** inner-city areas are subject to dilapidation and decay, the more affluent residents having moved to outlying areas.

instinct: A fixed pattern of behavior that has genetic origins and that appears in all normal animals within a given species.

institutional capitalism: Capitalistic enterprise organized on the basis of institutional shareholding.

institutional racism: Patterns of **discrimination** based on **ethnicity** that have become structured into existing social institutions.

intelligence: Level of intellectual ability, particularly as measured by **IQ (intelligence quotient)** tests.

interactional vandalism: The deliberate subversion of the tacit rules of conversation.

interest group: A group organized to pursue specific interests in the political arena, operating primarily by lobbying the members of legislative bodies.

intergenerational mobility: Movement up or down a social stratification hierarchy from one generation to another.

international division of labor: The interdependence of countries or regions that trade in global markets.

international governmental organization (IGO): An international organization established by treaties between **governments** for purposes of conducting business between the nations making up its membership.

international nongovernmental organization (INGO): An international organization established by agreements between the individuals or private **organizations** making up its membership.

intragenerational mobility: Movement up or down a **social stratification** hierarchy within the course of a personal career.

IQ (intelligence quotient): A score attained on tests of symbolic or reasoning abilities.

"iron law of oligarchy": A term coined by Weber's student Robert Michels meaning that large **organizations** tend toward centralization of **power**, making **democracy** difficult.

job: See **occupation.**

kinship: A relation that links individuals through blood ties, **marriage,** or adoption. Kinship relations are by definition part of marriage and the **family,** but extend much more broadly. While in most modern societies few social obligations are involved in kinship relations extending beyond the immediate family, in other cultures kinship is of vital importance to social life.

knowledge economy: A **society** no longer based primarily on the production of **material goods** but based instead on the production of knowledge. Its emergence has been linked to the development of a broad base of consumers who are technologically literate and have made new advances in computing, entertainment, and telecommunications part of their lives.

knowledge society: Another common term for **information society**—a **society** based on the production and consumption of knowledge and information.

Kuznets curve: A formula showing that inequality increases during the early stages of capitalist development, then declines, and eventually stabilizes at a relatively low level; advanced by the economist Simon Kuznets.

labeling theory: An approach to the study of **deviance** that suggests that people become "deviant" because certain labels are attached to their behavior by political authorities and others.

language: The primary vehicle of meaning and communication in a society, language is a system of **symbols** that represent objects and abstract thoughts.

latent functions: Functional consequences that are not intended or recognized by the members of a social system in which they occur.

law: A rule of behavior established by a political authority and backed by state **power.**

leader: A person who is able to influence the behavior of other members of a group.

legitimation crisis: The failure of a political order to generate a sufficient level of commitment and involvement on the part of its **citizens** to be able to govern properly.

liberal democracy: A system of **democracy** based on parliamentary institutions, coupled to the free-market system in the area of economic production.

liberalism feminism: Form of **feminist theory** that believes that **gender inequality** is produced by unequal access to **civil rights** and certain social resources, such as education and employment, based on **sex.** Liberal feminists tend to seek solutions through changes in legislation that ensure that the rights of individuals are protected.

liberation theology: An activist Catholic religious movement that combines Catholic beliefs with a passion for social justice for the poor.

life chances: A term introduced by Max Weber to signify a person's opportunities for achieving economic prosperity.

life course: The various transitions people experience during their lives.

life histories: Studies of the overall lives of individuals, often based on both self-reporting and documents such as letters.

life span: The maximum length of life that is biologically possible for a member of a given species.

linguistic relativity hypothesis: A **hypothesis,** based on the **theories** of Sapir and Whorf, that perceptions are relative to **language.**

local knowledge: Knowledge of a local community, possessed by individuals who spend long periods of their lives in it.

local nationalism: The belief that communities that share a cultural identity should have political autonomy, even within smaller units of a **nation-state.**

lower class: A social class comprised of those who work part time or not at all and whose household income is typically lower than $17,000 a year.

low-trust system: An organizational or **work** setting in which people are allowed little responsibility for, or control over, the work task.

macrosociology: The study of large-scale groups, **organizations,** or social systems.

Malthusianism: A doctrine about population dynamics developed by Thomas Malthus, according to which population increase comes up against "natural limits," represented by famine and war.

managerial capitalism: Capitalistic enterprises administered by managerial executives rather than by owners.

manifest functions: The functions of a type of social activity that are known to and intended by the individuals involved in the activity.

manufactured risk: Dangers that are created by the impact of human knowledge and **technology** on the natural world. Examples of manufactured risk include global warming and genetically modified foods.

market-oriented theories: Theories about economic development that assume that the best possible economic consequences will result if individuals are free to make their own economic decisions, uninhibited by governmental constraint.

marriage: A socially approved sexual relationship between two individuals. Marriage almost always involves two persons of opposite sexes, but in some cultures, types of homosexual marriage are tolerated. Marriage normally forms the basis of a **family of procreation**—that is, it is expected that the married couple will produce and bring up children. Some societies permit **polygamy,** in which an individual may have several spouses at the same time.

Marxism: A body of thought deriving its main elements from Marx's ideas.

mass media: Forms of communication, such as newspapers, magazines, radio, and television, designed to reach mass audiences.

master status: The **status**(es) that generally determine(s) a person's overall position in **society.**

material goods: The physical objects that a **society** creates, which influence the ways in which people live.

materialist conception of history: The view developed by Marx, according to which material, or economic, factors have a prime role in determining historical change.

matrilocal family: A **family** system in which the husband is expected to live near the wife's parents.

mean: A statistical measure of central tendency, or average, based on dividing a total by the number of individual cases.

means of production: The means whereby the production of **material goods** is carried on in a **society,** including not just **technology** but the social relations between producers.

measures of central tendency: The ways of calculating averages.

median: The number that falls halfway in a range of numbers—a way of calculating central tendency that is sometimes more useful than calculating a **mean.**

mediated interaction: Interaction between individuals who are not physically in one another's presence—for example, a telephone conversation.

mediated quasi-interaction: Interaction that is one-sided and partial—for example, a person watching a television program.

Medicare: A program under the U.S. Social Security Administration that reimburses hospitals and physicians for medical care provided to qualifying people over sixty-five years old.

megacities: A term favored by Manuel Castells to describe large, intensely concentrated urban spaces that serve as connection points for the global **economy.** It is projected that by 2015 there will be thirty-six megacities with populations of more than 8 million residents.

megalopolis: The "city of all cities" in ancient Greece—used in modern times to refer to very large **conurbations.**

melting pot: The idea that ethnic differences can be combined to create new patterns of behavior drawing on diverse cultural sources.

microsociology: The study of human behavior in contexts of face-to-face interaction.

middle class: A social **class** composed broadly of those working in white-collar and lower managerial occupations.

millenarian movement: Beliefs held by certain types of **religious movements,** according to which cataclysmic changes will occur in the near future, heralding the arrival of a new epoch.

minority group (or ethnic minority): A group of people in a minority in a given **society** who, because of their distinct physical or cultural characteristics, find themselves in situations of inequality within that society.

mode: The number that appears most often in a given set of data. This can sometimes be a helpful way of portraying central tendency.

modernization theory: A version of market-oriented development theory that argues that low-income societies develop economically only if they give up their traditional ways and adopt modern economic institutions, **technologies,** and cultural **values** that emphasize savings and productive investment.

monogamy: A form of **marriage** in which each married partner is allowed only one spouse at any given time.

monopoly: A situation in which a single firm dominates in a given industry.

monotheism: Belief in a single god.

mortality: The number of deaths in a population.

multiculturalism: Ethnic groups exist separately and share *equally* in economic and political life.

multimedia: The combination of what used to be different media requiring different **technologies** (e.g., visuals and sound) on a single medium, such as a CD-ROM or Web site.

multinational corporations: Business corporations located in two or more countries.

multiple sovereignty: A situation in which there is no single sovereign **power** in a **society.**

nationalism: A set of beliefs and **symbols** expressing identification with a national community.

nation-state: A particular type of **state,** characteristic of the modern world, in which a government has sovereign **power** within a defined territorial area, and the population are **citizens** who know themselves to be part of a single nation. Nation-states are closely associated with the rise of **nationalism,** although nationalist loyalties do not always conform to the boundaries of specific states. Nation-states developed as part of an emerging nation-state system, originating in Europe; in current times, they span the whole globe.

nations without states: Instances in which the members of a nation lack political **sovereignty** over the area they claim as their own.

neoliberalism: The economic belief that free market forces, achieved by minimizing government restrictions on business, provide the only route to economic growth.

network: A set of informal and formal social ties that links people to each other.

New Age movement: A general term to describe the diverse spectrum of beliefs and practices oriented on inner spirituality. Paganism, Eastern mysticism, shamanism, alternative forms of healing, and astrology are all examples of New Age activities.

new criminology: A branch of criminological thought, prominent in Britain in the 1970s, that regarded **deviance** as deliberately chosen and often political in nature. The new criminologists argued that **crime** and deviance could only be understood in the context of **power** and inequality within **society.**

new left realism: A strain of criminology, popularized in the 1980s by the work of Jock Young, that focused on the victims of **crime** and called for criminology to engage practically with issues of crime control and social policy.

newly industrializing economies (NIEs): Developing countries that over the past two or three decades have begun to develop a strong industrial base, such as Singapore and Hong Kong.

new racism: Racist outlooks, also referred to as "cultural racism," that are predicated on cultural or religious differences rather than biological ones.

new religious movements: The broad range of religious and spiritual groups, **cults,** and **sects** that have emerged alongside mainstream **religions.** New religious movements range from spiritual and self-help groups within the **New Age movement** to exclusive sects such as the Hare Krishnas.

new social movements: A set of **social movements** that have arisen in Western **societies** since the 1960s in response to the changing risks facing human societies. New social movements such as **feminism,** environmentalism, the antinuclear movement, protests against genetically modified food, and antiglobalization demonstrations differ from earlier social movements in that they are single-issue campaigns oriented to nonmaterial ends and draw support from across class lines.

nontheistic religions: Religions based on a belief in the existence of divine spiritual forces rather than a god or gods.

nonverbal communication: Communication between individuals based on facial expression or bodily gesture rather than on **language.**

norms: Rules of conduct that specify appropriate behavior in a given range of social situations. A norm either prescribes a given type of behavior or forbids it. All human groups follow definite norms, which are always backed by **sanctions** of one kind or another—varying from informal disapproval to physical punishment.

nuclear family: A **family** group consisting of a wife, a husband (or one of these), and dependent children.

occupation: Any form of paid employment in which an individual regularly works.

"old old": Sociological term for persons aged seventy-five to eighty-four.

"oldest old": Sociological term for persons aged eighty-five and older.

oligarchy: Rule by a small minority within an **organization** or **society.**

oligopoly: The domination of a small number of firms in a given industry.

oral history: Interviews with people about events they witnessed or experienced at some point earlier in their lives.

organic solidarity: According to Émile Durkheim, the social cohesion that results from the various parts of a **society** functioning as an integrated whole.

organization: A large group of individuals with a definite set of authority relations. Many types of organizations exist in **industrialized societies,** influencing most aspects of our lives. While not all organizations are bureaucratic, there are close links between the development of organizations and bureaucratic tendencies.

organized crime: Criminal activities carried out by **organizations** established as businesses.

out-group: A group toward which one feels antagonism and contempt—"those people."

pariah groups: Groups who suffer from negative **status discrimination**—they are looked down on by most other members of society. The Jews, for example, have been a pariah group throughout much of European history.

participant observation (fieldwork): A method of research widely used in **sociology** and anthropology, in which the researcher takes part in the activities of the group or community being studied.

participatory democracy: A system of **democracy** in which all members of a group or community participate collectively in making major decisions.

pastoral societies: Societies whose subsistence derives from the rearing of domesticated animals.

patriarchy: The dominance of men over women. All known **societies** are patriarchal, although there are variations in the degree and nature of the **power** men exercise, as compared with women. One of the prime objectives of women's movements in modern societies is to combat existing patriarchal institutions.

patrilocal family: A **family** system in which the wife is expected to live near the husband's parents.

peer group: A friendship group composed of individuals of similar age and social **status.**

peripheral countries: Countries that have a marginal role in the world **economy** and are thus dependent on the core producing societies for their trading relationships.

personality stabilization: According to the theory of **functionalism,** the **family** plays a crucial role in assisting its adult members emotionally. **Marriage** between adult men and women is the arrangement through which adult personalities are supported and kept healthy.

personal space: The physical space individuals maintain between themselves and others.

pilot study: A trial run in **survey** research.

pluralism: A model for ethnic relations in which all ethnic groups in the United States retain their independent and separate identities, yet share equally in the rights and **powers** of **citizenship.**

pluralist theories of modern democracy: **Theories** that emphasize the role of diverse and competing **interest groups** in preventing too much **power** from being accumulated in the hands of political **leaders.**

political rights: Rights of political participation, such as the right to vote in local and national elections, held by **citizens** of a national community.

politics: The means by which **power** is employed to influence the nature and content of governmental activities. The sphere of the political includes the activities of those in **government,** but also the actions of others. There are many ways in which people outside the governmental apparatus seek to influence it.

polyandry: A form of **marriage** in which a woman may simultaneously have two or more husbands.

polycentric transnationals: Transnational corporations whose administrative structure is global but whose corporate practices are adapted according to local circumstances.

polygamy: A form of **marriage** in which a person may have two or more spouses simultaneously.

polygyny: A form of **marriage** in which a man may simultaneously have two or more wives.

polytheism: Belief in two or more gods.

population: The people who are the focus of social research.

portfolio worker: A worker who possesses a diversity of skills or qualifications and is therefore able to move easily from **job** to job.

post-Fordism: A general term used to describe the transition from mass industrial production, characterized by **Fordist** methods, to more flexible forms of production favoring innovation and aimed at meeting market demands for customized products.

postindustrial society: A notion advocated by those who believe that processes of social change are taking us beyond the industrialized order. A postindustrial society is based on the production of information rather than **material goods.** According to postindustrialists, we are currently experiencing a series of social changes as profound as those that initiated the industrial era some two hundred years ago.

postmodernism: The belief that **society** is no longer governed by history or progress. Postmodern society is highly pluralistic and diverse, with no "grand narrative" guiding its development.

poverty line: An official **government** measure to define those living in poverty in the United States.

power: The ability of individuals or the members of a group to achieve aims or further the interests they hold. Power is a pervasive element in all human relationships. Many conflicts in **society** are struggles over power, because how much power an individual or group is able to achieve governs how far they are able to put their wishes into practice.

power elite: Small **networks** of individuals who, according to C. Wright Mills, hold concentrated **power** in modern **societies.**

prejudice: The holding of preconceived ideas about an individual or group, ideas that are resistant to change even in the face of new information. Prejudice may be either positive or negative.

preoperational stage: A stage of cognitive development, in Piaget's theory, in which the child has advanced sufficiently to master basic modes of logical thought.

prestige: The respect accorded to an individual or group by virtue of their **status.**

primary deviation: According to Edwin Lemert, the actions that cause others to label one as a deviant.

primary group: A group that is characterized by intense emotional ties, face-to-face interaction, intimacy, and a strong, enduring sense of commitment.

primary socialization: The process by which children learn the cultural **norms** of the **society** into which they are born. Primary socialization occurs largely in the **family.**

procreative technologies: Techniques of influencing the human reproductive process.

profane: That which belongs to the mundane, everyday world.

projection: Attributing to others feelings that a person actually has herself.

psychopath: A specific personality type; such individuals lack the moral sense and concern for others held by most normal people.

public sphere: The means by which people communicate in modern **societies,** the most prominent component of which is the **mass media**—movies, television, radio, videos, records, magazines, and newspapers.

quality circles (QCs): Types of industrialized **group production,** where workers use their expertise to participate actively in decision making.

race: Differences in human physical characteristics used to categorize large numbers of individuals.

racialization: The process by which understandings of **race** are used to classify individuals or groups of people. Racial distinctions are more than ways of describing human differences; they are also important factors in the reproduction of patterns of **power** and inequality.

"racial literacy": The skills taught to children of multiracial families to help them cope with racial hierarchies and to integrate multiple ethnic identities.

racism: The attribution of characteristics of superiority or inferiority to a population sharing certain physically inherited characteristics. Racism is one specific form of **prejudice,** focusing on physical variations between people. Racist attitudes became entrenched during the period of Western colonial expansion, but seem also to rest on mechanisms of **prejudice** and **discrimination** found in human **societies** today.

radical feminism: Form of **feminist theory** that believes that **gender inequality** is the result of male domination in all aspects of social and economic life.

random sampling: Sampling method in which a sample is chosen so that every member of the **population** has the same probability of being included.

rape: The forcing of nonconsensual vaginal, oral, or anal intercourse.

rational choice approach: More broadly, the **theory** that an individual's behavior is purposive. Within the field of criminology, rational choice analysis argues that deviant behavior is a rational response to a specific social situation.

rationality: See also **rationalization.** The belief that rules and efficiency should guide modern **societies.**

rationalization: A concept used by Max Weber to refer to the process by which modes of precise calculation and organization, involving abstract rules and procedures, increasingly come to dominate the social world.

reference group: A group that provides a standard for judging one's attitudes or behaviors.

reflexivity: This describes the connections between knowledge and social life. The knowledge we gain about **society** can affect the way in which we act in it. For instance, reading a **survey** about the high level of support for a political party might lead an individual to express support for that party too.

regionalization: The division of social life into different regional settings or zones.

relative deprivation: Feelings of deprivation a person feels by comparing himself with a group.

relative poverty: Poverty defined according to the living standards of the majority in any given society.

religion: A set of beliefs adhered to by the members of a community, incorporating **symbols** regarded with a sense of awe or wonder together with ritual practices. Religions do not universally involve a belief in supernatural entities.

religious economy: A theoretical framework within the sociology of **religion,** which argues that religions can be fruitfully understood as **organizations** in competition with one another for followers.

religious movement: An association of people who join together to seek to spread a new **religion** or to promote a new interpretation of an existing religion.

religious nationalism: The linking of strongly held religious convictions with beliefs about a people's social and political destiny.

representative sample: A sample from a larger **population** that is statistically typical of that population.

research methods: The diverse methods of investigation used to gather empirical (factual) material. Different research methods exist in **sociology,** but the most commonly used are fieldwork (or **participant observation**) and **survey** methods. For many purposes, it is useful to combine two or more methods within a single research project.

research process: The manner by which the study of a given subject proceeds from investigation to published findings.

resource allocation: Inequalities in the distribution of **wealth** and goods resulting from limited resources.

response cries: Seemingly involuntary exclamations individuals make when, for example, being taken by surprise, dropping something inadvertently, or expressing pleasure.

revolution: A process of political change, involving the mobilizing of a mass **social movement,** which by the use of violence successfully overthrows an existing regime and forms a new **government.**

role: The expected behavior of a person occupying a particular **social position.** The idea of **social role** originally comes from the theater, referring to the parts that actors play in a stage production. In every **society,** individuals play a number of social roles.

sacred: Describing something that inspires attitudes of awe or reverence among believers in a given set of religious ideas.

sample: A small proportion of a larger **population.**

sampling: Studying a proportion of individuals or cases from a larger **population** as representative of that population as a whole.

sanction: A mode of reward or punishment that reinforces socially expected forms of behavior.

scapegoat: An individual or group blamed for wrongs that were not of their doing.

science: In the sense of physical science, the systematic study of the physical world. Science involves the disciplined marshaling of empirical data, combined with **theoretical approaches** and **theories** that illuminate or explain those data. Scientific activity combines the creation of boldly new modes of thought with the careful testing of **hypotheses** and ideas. One major feature that helps distinguish science from other idea systems (such as **religion**) is the assumption that *all* scientific ideas are open to criticism and revision.

secondary deviation: According to Edwin Lemert, following the act of **primary deviation,** secondary deviation occurs when an individual accepts the label of deviant and acts accordingly.

secondary group: A group characterized by its large size and by impersonal, fleeting relationships.

Second World: Before the 1989 democracy movements, this included the industrialized Communist societies of Eastern Europe and the Soviet Union.

sect: A **religious movement** that breaks away from orthodoxy.

secularization: A process of decline in the influence of **religion.** Although modern **societies** have become increasingly secularized, tracing the extent of secularization is a complex matter. Secularization can refer to levels of involvement with religious organizations (such as rates of **church** attendance), the social and material influence wielded by religious organizations, and the degree to which people hold religious beliefs.

secular thinking: Worldly thinking, particularly as seen in the rise of **science, technology,** and rational thought in general.

segregation: The practices of keeping racial and ethnic groups physically separate, thereby maintaining the superior position of the **dominant group.**

self-consciousness: Awareness of one's distinct **social identity** as a person separate from others. Human beings are not born with self-consciousness but acquire an awareness of self as a result of early **socialization.** The learning of **language** is of vital importance to the processes by which the child learns to become a self-conscious being.

self-identity: The ongoing process of self-development and definition of our personal **identity** through which we formulate a unique sense of ourselves and our relationship to the world around us.

semiotics: The study of the ways in which nonlinguistic phenomena can generate meaning—as in the example of a traffic light.

semiperipheral countries: Countries that supply sources of labor and raw materials to the **core** industrial **countries** and the world economy but are not themselves fully **industrialized societies.**

sensorimotor stage: According to Piaget, a stage of human cognitive development in which the child's awareness of its environment is dominated by perception and touch.

service society: A concept related to the one of **postindustrial society,** it refers to a social order distinguished by the growth of service occupations at the expense of industrial jobs that produce **material goods.**

sex: The biological and anatomical differences distinguishing females from males.

sexual harassment: The making of unwanted sexual advances by one individual toward another, in which the first person persists even though it is clear that the other party is resistant.

shaming: A way of punishing criminal and deviant behavior based on rituals of public disapproval rather than incarceration. The goal of shaming is to maintain the ties of the offender to the community.

short-range downward mobility: Social **mobility** that occurs when an individual moves from one position in the **class** structure to another of nearly equal **status.**

sick role: A term associated with the functionalist Talcott Parsons to describe the patterns of behavior that a sick person adopts in order to minimize the disruptive impact of his or her illness on others.

signifier: Any vehicle of meaning and **communication.**

situational ethnicity: Ethnic identity that is chosen for the moment based on the social setting or situation.

slavery: A form of **social stratification** in which some people are literally owned by others as their property.

social age: The **norms, values,** and **roles** that are culturally associated with a particular chronological age.

social aggregate: A simple collection of people who happen to be together in a particular place but do not significantly interact or identify with one another.

social capital: The social knowledge and connections that enable people to accomplish their goals and extend their influence.

social category: People who share a common characteristic (such as **gender** or **occupation**) but do not necessarily interact or identify with one another.

social change: Alteration in basic structures of a **social group** or **society.** Social change is an ever-present phenomenon in social life, but has become especially intense in the modern era. The origins of modern **sociology** can be traced to attempts to understand the dramatic changes shattering the traditional world and promoting new forms of social order.

social closure: Practices by which groups separate themselves off from other groups.

social constraint: The conditioning influence on our behavior of the groups and **societies** of which we are members. Social constraint was regarded by Émile Durkheim as one of the distinctive properties of **social facts.**

social constructionism: Theory that social reality is a creation of the interaction of individuals and groups.

social construction of gender: The learning of **gender roles** through **socialization** and interaction with others.

social exclusion: The outcome of multiple deprivations that prevent individuals or groups from participating fully in the economic, social, and political life of the **society** in which they live.

social fact: According to Émile Durkheim, the aspects of social life that shape our actions as individuals. Durkheim believed that social facts could be studied scientifically.

social gerontology: The study of **aging** and the elderly.

social group: A collection of people who regularly interact with one another on the basis of shared expectations concerning behavior and who share a sense of common **identity.**

social identity: The characteristics that are attributed to an individual by others.

social institution: Basic modes of social activity followed by the majority of the members of a given **society.** Institutions involve **norms** and **values** to which large numbers of people conform, and all institutionalized modes of behavior are protected by strong **sanctions.** Institutions form the bedrock of a society, because they represent relatively fixed modes of behavior that endure over time.

social interaction: The process by which we act and react to those around us.

socialization: The social processes through which children develop an awareness of social **norms** and **values** and achieve a distinct sense of self. Although socialization processes are particularly significant in infancy and childhood, they continue to some degree throughout life. No individuals are immune from the reactions of others around them, which influence and modify their behavior at all phases of the **life course.**

socialization of nature: The process by which we control phenomena regarded as "natural," such as reproduction.

social mobility: Movement of individuals or groups between different **social positions.**

social movement: A large group of people who seek to accomplish, or to block, a process of **social change.** Social movements normally exist in conflict with **organizations,** whose objectives and outlook they oppose. However, movements that successfully challenge **power,** once they become institutionalized, can develop into organizations.

social position: The **social identity** an individual has in a given group or **society.** Social positions may be general in nature (those associated with **gender roles**) or may be more specific (occupational positions).

social rights: Rights of social and welfare provision held by all **citizens** in a national community, including, for example, the right to claim unemployment benefits and sickness payments provided by the **state.**

social roles: Socially defined expectations of an individual in a given **status,** or **social position.**

Social Security: A government program that provides economic assistance to persons faced with unemployment, disability, or agedness.

social self: The basis of **self-consciousness** in human individuals, according to the theory of G. H. Mead. The social self is the **identity** conferred upon an individual by the reactions of others. A person achieves self-consciousness by becoming aware of this **social identity.**

social stratification: The existence of **structured inequalities** between groups in **society,** in terms of their access to material or symbolic rewards. While all societies involve some forms of stratification, only with the development of state-based systems did wide differences in **wealth** and **power** arise. The most distinctive form of stratification in modern societies is **class** divisions.

social structure: The underlying regularities or patterns in how people behave and in their relationships with one another.

social technology: A means by which we try to alter our bodies in specific ways—for example, dieting.

society: A group of people who live in a particular territory, are subject to a common system of political **authority,** and are aware of having a distinct **identity** from other groups. Some societies, like **hunting and gathering societies,** are small, numbering no more than a few dozen people. Others are large, numbering millions—modern Chinese society, for instance, has a population of more than a billion people.

sociobiology: An approach that attempts to explain the behavior of both animals and human beings in terms of biological principles.

sociological imagination: The application of imaginative thought to the asking and answering of sociological questions. Someone using the sociological imagination "thinks himself away" from the familiar routines of daily life.

sociology: The study of human groups and **societies,** giving particular emphasis to analysis of the industrialized world. Sociology is one of a group of social sciences, which include anthropology, economics, political science, and human geography. The divisions between the various social sciences are not clear-cut, and all share a certain range of common interests, concepts, and methods.

sociology of the body: Field that focuses on how our bodies are affected by social influences. Health and illness, for instance, are determined by social and cultural influences.

sovereignty: The undisputed political rule of a **state** over a given territorial area.

standard deviation: A way of calculating the spread of a group of figures.

state: A political apparatus (**government** institutions plus civil service officials) ruling over a given territorial order, whose **authority** is backed by **law** and the ability to use force. Not all societies are characterized by the existence of a state. **Hunting and gathering societies** and smaller **agrarian societies** lack state institutions. The emergence of the state marked a distinctive transition in human history, because the centralization of political **power** involved in state formation introduced new dynamics into processes of **social change.**

state-centered theories: Development **theories** that argue that appropriate **government** policies do not interfere with economic development, but rather can play a key role in bringing it about.

state overload: A **theory** that holds that modern **states** face major difficulties as a result of being overburdened with complex administrative decisions.

status: The social honor or **prestige** that a particular group is accorded by other members of a **society.** Status groups normally display distinct styles of life—patterns of behavior that the members of a group follow. Status privilege may be positive or negative. **Pariah** status **groups** are regarded with disdain or treated as outcasts by the majority of the **population.**

status set: An individual's group of social **statuses.**

stepfamily: A **family** in which at least one partner has children from a previous **marriage,** living either in the home or nearby.

stereotype: A fixed and inflexible category.

stereotypical thinking: Thought processes involving rigid and inflexible categories.

stigma: Any physical or social characteristic that is labeled by **society** as undesirable.

strike: A temporary stoppage of **work** by a group of employees in order to express a grievance or enforce a demand.

structural mobility: Mobility resulting from changes in the number and kinds of **jobs** available in a **society.**

structural strain: Tensions that produce conflicting interests within **societies.**

structuration: The two-way process by which we shape our social world through our individual actions and by which we are reshaped by **society.**

structured inequality: Social inequalities that result from patterns in the **social structure.**

subculture: Values and **norms** distinct from those of the majority, held by a group within a wider **society.**

suburbanization: The development of suburbia, areas of housing outside **inner cities.**

suffragists: Members of early women's movements who pressed for equal voting rights for women and men.

surplus value: The value of a worker's labor power, in **Marxist** theory, left over when an employer has repaid the cost of hiring the worker.

surveillance: The supervising of the activities of some individuals or groups by others in order to ensure compliant behavior.

surveillance society: Term referring to how information about our lives and activities is maintained by **organizations.**

survey: A method of sociological research in which questionnaires are administered to the **population** being studied.

sustainable development: The notion that economic growth should proceed only insofar as natural resources are recycled rather than depleted; biodiversity is maintained; and clean air, water, and land are protected.

symbol: One item used to stand for or represent another—as in the case of a flag, which symbolizes a nation.

symbolic ethnicity: Ethnic **identity** that is retained only for symbolic importance.

symbolic interactionism: A **theoretical approach** in **sociology** developed by George Herbert Mead, which emphasizes the role of **symbols** and **language** as core elements of all human interaction.

Taylorism: A set of ideas, also referred to as "scientific management," developed by Frederick Winslow Taylor, involving simple, coordinated operations in industry.

technology: The application of knowledge of the material world to production; the creation of material instruments (such as machines) used in human interaction with nature.

theism: A belief in one or more supernatural deities.

theoretical approach: A perspective on social life derived from a particular theoretical tradition. Some of the major theoretical traditions in **sociology** include **functionalism, symbolic interactionism,** and **Marxism.** Theoretical approaches supply overall perspectives within which sociologists work and influence the areas of their research as well as the modes in which research problems are identified and tackled.

theoretical questions: Questions posed by sociologists when seeking to explain a particular range of observed events. The asking of theoretical questions is crucial to allowing us to generalize about the nature of social life.

theory: An attempt to identify general properties that explain regularly observed events. Theories form an essential element of all sociological works. While theories tend to be linked to broader **theoretical approaches,** they are also strongly influenced by the research results they help generate.

third generation theory of aging: Theory that views the elderly as playing an active role in determining their own physical and mental well-being rather than as merely adapting to the larger society or as victims of the stratification system.

Third World: A term used during the cold war to describe developing nations.

time-space: When and where events occur.

timetable: The means by which **organizations** regularize activities across time and space.

total institutions: Groups who exercise control over their members by making them subsume their individual **identities** in that of the group, compelling them to adhere to strict ethical codes or rules, and sometimes forcing them to withdraw from activity in the outside world.

tracking: Dividing students into groups according to ability.

transactional leader: A **leader** who is concerned accomplishing the group's tasks, getting group members to do their **jobs,** and making certain that the group achieves its goals.

transformational leader: A **leader** who is able to instill in the members of a group a sense of mission or higher purpose, thereby changing the nature of the group itself.

transnational corporations: Business **corporations** located in two or more countries.

triad: A group consisting of three persons.

triangulation: The use of multiple **research methods** as a way of producing more reliable empirical data than is available from any single method.

underclass: A **class** of individuals situated at the bottom of the class system, normally composed of people from **ethnic minority** backgrounds.

unfocused interaction: Interaction occurring among people present in a particular setting but not engaged in direct face-to-face **communication.**

union density: A statistic that represents the number of union members as a percentage of the number of people who could potentially be union members.

upper class: A social **class** broadly composed of the more affluent members of **society,** especially those who have inherited **wealth,** own businesses, or hold large numbers of stocks (shares).

urban ecology: An approach to the study of urban life based on an analogy with the adjustment of plants and organisms to the physical environment. According to ecological theorists, the various neighborhoods and zones within cities are formed as a result of natural processes of adjustment on the part of **populations** as they compete for resources.

urbanism: A term used by Louis Wirth to denote distinctive characteristics of urban social life, such as its impersonality.

urbanization: The development of towns and cities.

urban renewal: The process of renovating deteriorating neighborhoods by encouraging the renewal of old buildings and the construction of new ones.

values: Ideas held by individuals or groups about what is desirable, proper, good, and bad. What individuals value is strongly influenced by the specific **culture** in which they happen to live.

variable: A dimension along which an object, individual, or group may be categorized, such as income or height.

vertical mobility: Movement up or down a hierarchy of positions in a **social stratification** system.

wealth: Money and material possessions held by an individual or group.

welfare capitalism: Practice in which large **corporations** protect their employees from the vicissitudes of the market.

welfare state: A political system that provides a wide range of welfare benefits for its **citizens.**

white-collar crime: Criminal activities carried out by those in white-collar, or professional, **jobs.**

work: The activity by which people produce from the natural world and so ensure their survival. Work should not be thought of exclusively as paid employment. In traditional cultures, there was only a rudimentary monetary system, and few people worked for money. In modern **societies,** there remain types of work that do not involve direct payment (e.g., **housework**).

working class: A social **class** broadly composed of people working in blue-collar, or manual, **occupations.**

working poor: People who work, but whose earnings are not enough to lift them above the **poverty line.**

world-accommodating movements: Religious movements that emphasize the importance of inner religious life and spiritual purity over worldly concerns.

world-affirming movements: Religious movements that seek to enhance followers' ability to succeed in the outside world by helping them to unlock their human potential.

world information order: A global system of **communication** operating through satellite links, radio and TV transmission, and telephone and computer links.

world-rejecting movements: Religious movements that are exclusive in nature, highly critical of the outside world, and demanding of their members.

world-systems theory: Pioneered by Immanuel Wallerstein, this **theory** emphasizes the interconnections among countries based on the expansion of a capitalist world **economy.** This economy is made up of **core countries, semiperipheral countries,** and **peripheral countries.**

"young old": Sociological term for persons aged sixty-five to seventy-four.

BIBLIOGRAPHY

ABC. 1999. "Support for Gun Control Stable," ABC News Poll (May 18). http://more.abcnews.go.com/sections/us/DailyNews/guns_poll990518.html, accessed 5/18/99.

Abdul-Rauf, Muhammad. 1975. *Islam: Creed and Worship.* Washington, DC: Islamic Center.

Abeles, Ronald P.; and Riley, Matilda White. 1987. "Longevity, social structure, and cognitive aging," in Carmi Schooler and K. Warner Schaie, eds., *Cognitive Functioning and Social Structure over the Life Course.* Norwood, NJ: Ablex.

Aberle, David. 1966. *The Peyote Religion among the Navaho.* Chicago: Aldine Press.

Accad, Evelyne. 1991. "Contradictions for contemporary women in the Middle East," in Chandra Talpade Mohanty, Ann Russo, and Lourdes Torres, eds., *Third World Women and the Politics of Feminism.* Bloomington: Indiana University Press.

Adorno, Theodor W., et al. 1950. *The Authoritarian Personality.* New York: Harper and Row.

Ahmed, Akbar S.; and Donnan, Hastings. 1994. "Islam in the Age of Postmodernity," in Akbar S. Ahmed and Hastings Donnan, eds., *Islam, Globalization, and Postmodernity.* London: Routledge.

AIDS Orphans Educational Trust. 2003. "AIDS Orphans Educational Trust–Uganda." www.orphanseducation.org, accessed 12/28/04.

Akintoye, Stephen. 1976. *Emergent African States: Topics in Twentieth Century African History.* London: Longman.

Al Ahmad, Jalal. 1997; orig. 1962. *Gharbzadegi: Weststruckedness.* Costa Mesa, CA: Mazda Publications.

Albrow, Martin. 1997. *The Global Age: State and Society beyond Modernity.* Stanford, CA: Stanford University Press.

Aldrich, Howard E.; and Marsden, Peter V. 1988. "Environments and organizations," in Neil J. Smelser, ed., *Handbook of Sociology.* Newbury Park, CA: Sage.

Allen, Beverly. 1996. *Rape Warfare: The Hidden Genocide in Bosnia-Herzegovina and Croatia.* Minneapolis, MN: University of Minnesota Press.

Allen, Michael P. 1981. "Managerial power and tenure in the large corporation." *Social Forces,* vol. 60.

Alvarez, Rodolfo, et al. 1996. "Women in the professions: Assessing progress," in Paula J. Dubeck and Kathryn Borman, eds., *Women and Work: A Handbook.* New York: Garland.

Amenta, Edwin. 1998. *Bold Relief: Institutional Politics and the Origins of Modern American Social Policy.* Princeton, NJ: Princeton University Press.

American Association of Retired Persons (AARP) 2003. "Fact Sheet: What is AARP?" www.aarp.org/leadership/Articles/a2002-12-18-aarpfactsheet.html, accessed 1/10/05.

American Association for the Advancement of Retired People (AARP). 1997. "Report of Social Security Advisory Council." www.aarp.org/focus/ssecure/part2/advisory.htm, accessed 11/24/03.

American Association of University Women (AAUW). 1992. *How Schools Shortchange Girls.* Washington, DC: American Association of University Women Educational Foundation.

American Civil Liberties Union (ACLU). 2000. "Status of U.S. sodomy laws." www.aclu.org/issues/gay/sodomy.html, accessed 1/10/05.

American Council on Education, (ACE). 2001. *The American Freshman: National Norms for Fall 2000.* Los Angeles, California: UCLA Higher Education Research Institute and ACE. Results also published in "This year's freshmen at 4-year colleges: Their opinions, activities, and goals." *Chronicle of Higher Education,* January 26.

Amin, Samir. 1974. *Accumulation on a World Scale.* New York: Monthly Review Press.

Amsden, Alice H. 1989. *Asia's Next Giant: South Korea and Late Industrialization.* New York: Oxford University Press.

———; Kochanowicz, Jacek; and Taylor, Lance. 1994. *The Market Meets Its Match: Restructuring the Economies of Eastern Europe.* Cambridge, MA: Harvard University Press.

Anderson, Benedict. 1991. *Imagined Communities: Reflections on the Origin and Spread of Nationalism.* Revised ed. New York: Routledge.

Anderson, Elijah. 1990. *Streetwise: Race, Class, and Change in an Urban Community.* Chicago: University of Chicago Press.

Angier, Natalie. 1994. "Feminists and Darwin: Scientists try closing the gap." *New York Times,* June 21.

———. 1995. "If you're really ancient, you may be better off." *New York Times,* June 11.

Annie E. Casey Foundation. 2003. "Kids Count." www.aecf.org/cgi-bin/aeccensus.cgi?action=profileresults&area=39S, accessed 12/28/04.

Anzaldua, Gloria. 1990. *Making Face, Making Soul: Haciendo Caras: Creative and Cultural Perspectives by Feminists of Color.* San Francisco: Aunt Lute Foundation.

Appadurai, Arjun. 1986. "Introduction: commodities and the politics of value," in A. Appadurai, ed., *The Social Life of Things.* Cambridge: Cambridge University Press.

Appelbaum, Richard P. 1990. "Counting the homeless," in J. A. Momeni, ed., *Homeless in the United States,* vol. 2. New York: Praeger.

———; and Christerson, Brad. 1997. "Cheap labor strategies and export-oriented industrialization: Some lessons from the East Asia/Los Angeles apparel connection." *International Journal of Urban and Regional Research,* vol. 21, no. 2.

———; and Henderson, Jeffrey. eds., 1992. *States and Development in the Asian Pacific Rim.* Newbury Park, CA: Sage.

Apter, Terri. 1994. *Working Women Don't Have Wives: Professional Success in the 1990s.* New York: St. Martin's Press.

Ariès, Philippe. 1965. *Centuries of Childhood.* New York: Random House.

Arjomand, Said Amir. 1988. *The Turban for the Crown: The Islamic Revolution in Iran.* New York: Oxford University Press.

Arrighi, Giovanni. 1994. *The Long Twentieth Century: Money, Power, and the Origin of Our Times.* New York: Verso.

Asch, Solomon. 1952. *Social Psychology.* Englewood Cliffs, NJ: Prentice-Hall.

Aschenbrenner, Joyce. 1983. *Lifelines: Black Families in Chicago.* Prospect Heights, IL: Waveland Press.

Ashworth, Anthony E. 1980. *Trench Warfare: 1914–1918.* London: Macmillan.

Atchley, Robert C. 2000. *Social Forces and Aging: An Introduction to Social Gerontology.* 9th ed. Belmont, CA: Wadsworth.

Avins, Mimi. 2003. "MoveOn redefines party politics," *Los Angeles Times* December 9, p. A-1.

Ayres, Robert; and Miller, Steven. 1985. "Industrial robots on the line," in Tom Forester, ed., *The Information Technology Revolution.* Cambridge, MA: MIT Press.

Bahrami, Homa; and Evans, Stuart. 1995. "Flexible recycling and high-technology entrepreneurship." *California Management Review,* vol. 22.

Bailey, J. Michael. 1993. "Heritable factors influence sexual orientation in women." *Archives of General Psychiatry,* vol. 50.

———; and Pillard, Richard C. 1991. "A genetic study of male sexual orientation." *Archives of General Psychiatry,* vol. 48.

Bales, Kevin. 1999. *Disposable People: New Slavery in the Global Economy.* Berkeley, CA: University of California Press.

Bales, Robert F. 1953. "The egalitarian problem in small groups," in Talcott Parsons, ed., *Working Papers in the Theory of Action.* Glencoe, IL: Free Press.

———. 1970. *Personality and Interpersonal Behavior.* New York: Holt, Rinehart, and Winston.

Balmer, Randall. 1989. *Mine Eyes Have Seen the Glory: A Journey into the Evangelical Subculture in America.* New York: Oxford University Press.

Balswick, J. O. 1983. "Male inexpressiveness," in Kenneth Soloman and Norman B. Levy, eds., *Men in Transition: Theory and Therapy.* New York: Plenum Press.

Baltes, Paul B.; and Schaie, K. Warner. 1977. "The myth of the twilight years," in S. Zarit, ed., *Readings in Aging and Death: Contemporary Perspectives.* New York: Harper and Row.

Banfield, Edward. 1970. *The Unheavenly City.* Boston: Little, Brown.

Bankoff, Elizabeth A. 1983. "Aged parents and their widowed daughters: A support relationship." *Gerontologist,* vol. 38.

Barcelona Field Studies Centre. 2003. "Sao Paulo Growth and Management." www.geographyfieldwork.com/SaoPaulo Management.htm, accessed 12/28/04.

Barker, Martin. 1981. *The New Racism: Conservatives and the Ideology of the Tribe.* Frederick, MD: University Press of America.

Barlow, John, et al. 1995. "Harper's forum: what are we doing online?" *Harper's* (August).

Barnet, Richard J.; and Cavanagh, John. 1994. *Global Dreams: Imperial Corporations and the New World Order.* New York: Simon and Schuster.

Bart, Pauline B.; and O'Brien, Patricia H. 1985. *Stopping Rape: Successful Survival Strategies.* New York: Pergamon Press.

Barth, Frederick. 1969. *Ethnic Groups and Boundaries.* London: Allen and Unwin.

Basham, A. L. 1989. *The Origins and Development of Classical Hinduism.* Boston: Beacon Press.

Basu, Amrita, ed. 1995. *The Challenge of Local Feminisms: Women's Movements in Global Perspective.* Boulder, CO: Westview.

Baudrillard, Jean. 1988. *Jean Baudrillard: Selected Writings.* Stanford, CA: Stanford University Press.

Baxter, Jeanine; and Kane, Emily. 1995. "Dependence and independence: A cross national analysis." *Gender and Society,* vol. 9, no. 2.

BBC News. 2001. "Bin Laden's Warning: Full Text." http://news.bbc.co.uk/1/hi/world/ south_asia/1585636.stm, accessed 1/10/05.

———. 2001a. "Anger at US Climate Retreat." http://news.bbc.co.uk/1/hi/sci/tech/ 1248278.stm, accessed 1/10/05.

Beall, C.; and Goldstein, M. C. 1982. "Work, aging, and dependency in a Sherpa population in Nepal." *Social Science and Medicine,* vol. 16, no. 2.

Bean, Frank D., et al. 1994. *Illegal Mexican Migration and the U.S./Mexico Border.* Washington, DC: U.S. Commission on Immigration Reform.

Beck, Ulrich. 1992. *Risk Society.* London: Sage.

———. 1995. *Ecological Politics in an Age of Risk.* Cambridge, UK: Polity Press.

———; and Beck-Gernsheim, Elisabeth. 1995. *The Normal Chaos of Love.* Cambridge, UK: Polity Press.

Becker, Gary. 1964. *Human Capital.* New York: National Bureau of Economic Research.

———. 1991. *A Treatise on the Family.* Cambridge, MA: Harvard University Press.

Becker, Howard S. 1950. *Through Values to Social Interpretation.* Durham, NC: Duke University Press.

———. 1963. *Outsiders: Studies in the Sociology of Deviance.* New York: Macmillan.

Beechey, Veronica; and Perkins, Tessa. 1987. *A Matter of Hours: Women, Part-Time Work, and the Labour Market.* Cambridge, UK: Polity Press.

Beijing Women's Conference. 1995. "Declaration and Platform for Action." Critical Areas of Concern No. 43. Fourth World Conference on Women: Action for Equality, Development, and Peace, Beijing, September 15, 1995.

Belgrave, Linda Liska. 1988. "The effects of race difference in work history, work attitudes, economic resources, and health in women's retirement." *Research on Aging,* vol. 10.

Bell, A.; Weinberg, M.; and Hammersmith, S. 1981. *Sexual Preference: Its Development in Men and Women.* Bloomington: Indiana University Press.

Bell, Daniel. 1976. *The Coming of Post-Industrial Society: A Venture in Social Forecasting.* New York: Basic Books.

Bellah, Robert N. 1968. "Civil Religion in America," in William G. McLoughlin and Robert N. Bellah, eds., *Religion in America.* Boston: Houghton Mifflin.

———. 1975. *The Broken Covenant.* New York: Seabury Press.

———, et al. 1985. *Habits of the Heart: Individualism and Commitment in American Life.* New York: Harper and Row.

Bellman, Beryl. 1984. *The Language of Secrecy: Symbols and Metaphors in Poro Ritual.* New Brunswick, NJ: Rutgers University Press.

Bendick, Marc; Jackson, Charles; and Reinoso, Victor. 1993. "Measuring employment discrimination through controlled experiments," in *The Review of Black Political Economy.* Washington, DC: Fair Employment Council of Greater Washington.

Bengston, Vern L.; Rosenthal, Carolyn; and Burton, Linda. 1990. "Families and aging: Diversity and heterogeneity," in Robert H. Binstock and Linda K. George, eds., *Handbook of Aging and the Social Sciences.* 3rd ed. New York: Academic Press.

Bennet, James. 1992. "The old people sit and talk, about AIDS and secrecy." *New York Times,* September 21.

Bennett, John W. 1976. *The Ecological Transition: Cultural Anthropology and*

Human Adaptation. New York: Pergamon Press.

Berger, Peter L. 1963. *Invitation to Sociology.* Garden City, NY: Anchor Books.

———. 1967. *The Sacred Canopy: Elements of a Sociological Theory of Religion.* Garden City, NY: Anchor Books.

———. 1986. *The Capitalist Revolution: Fifty Propositions about Prosperity, Equality, and Liberty.* New York: Basic Books.

———; and Hsiao, Hsin-Huang Michael. 1988. *In Search of an East Asian Development Model.* New Brunswick, NJ: Transaction.

———; and Luckmann, Thomas. 1966. *The Social Construction of Reality: A Treatise in the Sociology of Knowledge.* Garden City, NY: Doubleday.

Berle, Adolf; and Means, Gardiner C. 1982. *The Modern Corporation and Private Property.* Originally published 1932. Buffalo, NY: Heim.

Bernhardt, Annett; Dresser, Laura; and Rogers, Joel. 2002. "Taking the high road in Milwaukee: The Wisconsin regional training partnership." *WorkingUSA* vol. 5, no. 3: 109.

Bernstein, Nina. 2001. "Homeless shelters in New York fill to highest levels since 80's." *New York Times,* February 7.

Berryman, Phillip. 1987. *Liberation Theology: Essential Facts About the Revolutionary Movement in Central America and Beyond.* Philadelphia: Temple University Press.

Bertelson, David. 1986. *Snowflakes and Snowdrifts: Individualism and Sexuality in America.* Lanham, MD: University Press of America.

Bertram, Eva, et al. 1996. *Drug War Politics.* Berkeley, CA: University of California Press.

Beyer, Peter. 1994. *Religion and Globalization.* Thousand Oaks, CA: Sage.

Birren, J. E.; and Bengston, V. L., eds. 1988. *Emerging Theories of Aging.* New York: Springer.

———; and Cunningham, W. 1985. "Research on the psychology of aging," in J. E. Birren and K. Warner Schaie, eds., *The Handbook of Aging.* 2nd ed. New York: Van Nostrand.

Blanchard, Ray; and Bogaert, A. F. 1996. "Homosexuality in men and number of older brothers." *American Journal of Psychiatry,* vol. 153.

Blankenhorn, David. 1995. *Fatherless America: Confronting Our Most Urgent Social Problem.* New York: Basic Books.

Blau, Joel. 1992. *The Visible Poor: Homelessness in the United States.* New York: Oxford University Press.

Blau, Judith. "Internationalizing public sociologies," *Sociologists Without Borders,* www.sociologistswithoutborders.org, accessed 12/27/04.

Blau, Peter. 1963. *The Dynamics of Bureaucracy.* Chicago: University of Chicago Press.

———. 1977. *Inequality and Heterogeneity: A Primitive Theory of Social Structure.* New York: Free Press.

———; and Duncan, Otis Dudley. 1967. *The American Occupational Structure.* New York: Wiley.

Blauner, Robert. 1964. *Alienation and Freedom.* Chicago: University of Chicago Press.

———. 1972. *Racial Oppression in America.* New York: Harper and Row.

Block, Fred. 1990. *Postindustrial Possibilities: A Critique of Economic Discourse.* Berkeley: University of California Press.

Blondet, Cecilia. 1995. "Out of the kitchen and onto the streets: Women's activism in Peru," in Amrita Basu, ed., *The Challenge of Local Feminisms.* Boulder, CO: Westview.

Bluestone, Barry. 1988. "Deindustrialization and unemployment in America." *Review of Black Political Economy,* vol. 17.

———; and Harrison, Bennett. 1982. *The Deindustrialization of America.* New York: Basic Books.

Blum, Linda M. 1991. *Between Feminism and Labor: The Significance of the Comparable Worth Movement.* Berkeley, CA: University of California Press.

Blumberg, Rae Lesser, ed. 1995. *Engendering Wealth and Well-Being: Empowerment for Global Change.* Boulder, CO: Westview.

Bobak, Laura. 1996. "India's Tiny Slaves," *Ottawa Sun,* October 23.

Bobo, Lawrence; and Kluegel, James R. 1991. "Modern American prejudice: Stereotypes, social distance, and perceptions of discrimination toward Blacks, Hispanics, and Asians." Paper presented at the 1991 meeting of the American Sociological Association.

Bochenek, Michael A.; and Brown, Widney. 2001. *Hatred in the Hallways: Violence and Discrimination against Lesbian, Gay, Bisexual, and Transgender Students in U.S. Schools.* New York: Human Rights Watch, www.hrw.org/reports/2001/uslgbt/toc.htm, May 30, accessed 12/28/04.

Boden, Deirdre; and Molotch, Harvey. 1994. "The compulsion of proximity," in Deirdre Boden and Roger Friedland, eds., *Nowhere: Space, Time, and Modernity.* Berkeley, CA: University of California Press.

Bohan, Suzanne. 1999. "Bohemian grove and global elite." *Sacramento Bee,* www.mt.net/~watcher/bohemiangrove.html, August 2, accessed 12/28/04.

Bonacich, Edna; and Appelbaum, Richard P. 2000. *Behind the Label: Inequality in the Los Angeles Garment Industry.* Berkeley, CA: University of California Press.

Bonnell, Victoria E.; and Hunt, Lynn, eds. 1999. *Beyond the Cultural Turn.* Berkeley, CA: University of California Press.

Bonney, Norman. 1992. "Theories of social class and gender." *Sociology Review,* vol. 1.

Booth, Alan. 1977. "Food riots in the northwest of England, 1770–1801." *Past and Present,* no. 77.

Borjas, George J. 1994. "The economics of immigration." *Journal of Economic Literature,* vol. 32.

Bosse, R., et al. 1987. "Mental health differences among retirees and workers: Findings from the normative aging study." *Psychology and Aging,* vol. 2.

Boswell, John. 1995. *The Marriage of Likeness: Same-Sex Unions in Pre-Modern Europe.* London: Fontana.

Bourdieu, Pierre. 1984. *Distinction: A Social Critique of Judgement of Taste.* Cambridge, MA: Harvard University Press.

———. 1988. *Language and Symbolic Power.* Cambridge, UK: Polity Press.

———. 1990. *The Logic of Practice.* Stanford, CA: Stanford University Press.

Bowen, Kurt. 1996. *Evangelism and Apostasy: The Evolution and Impact of Evangelicals in Modern Mexico.* Montreal: McGill-Queens University Press.

Bowlby, John. 1953. *Child Care and the Growth of Love.* Baltimore, MD: Penguin.

Bowles, Samuel; and Gintis, Herbert. 1976. *Schooling in Capitalist America.* New York: Basic Books.

Boyer, Robert; and Drache, Daniel. eds. 1996. *States against Markets: The Limits of Globalization.* New York: Routledge.

Braithwaite, John. 1996. "Crime, shame, and reintegration," in P. Cordella and L. Siegal, eds., *Readings in Contemporary Criminological Theory.* Boston: Northeastern University Press.

Bramlett, M.D.; and Mosher W.D. 2002. "Cohabitation, marriage, divorce, and remarriage in the United States." National Center for Health Statistics. *Vital Health Stat* vol. 23, no. 22.

Brass, Daniel J. 1985. "Men's and women's networks: A study of interaction patterns and influence in an organization." *Academy of Management Journal,* vol. 28.

Braverman, Harry. 1974. *Labor and Monopoly Capital.* New York: Monthly Review Press.

Brennan, Teresa. 1988. "Controversial discussions and feminist debate," in Naomi Segal and Edward Timms, eds., *The Origins and Evolution of Psychoanalysis.* New Haven, CT: Yale University Press.

Brewer, Rose M. 1993. "Theorizing race, class and gender: The new scholarship of black feminist intellectuals and black women's labor," in Stanlie M. James and Abena P. A. Busia, eds., *Theorizing Black Feminisms: The Visionary Pragmatism of Black Women.* New York: Routledge.

Brimelow, Peter. 1995. *Alien Nation: Common Sense About America's Immigration Disaster.* New York: Random House.

Britain, Samuel. 1975. "The economic contradictions of democracy." *British Journal of Political Science,* vol. 15.

Brookfield, Stephen. 1986. *Understanding and Facilitating Adult Learning.* San Francisco: Jossey-Bass.

Brown, Catrina; and Jasper, Karin, eds. 1993. *Consuming Passions: Feminist Approaches to Eating Disorders and Weight Preoccupations.* Toronto: Second Story Press.

Brown, Donald E. 1991. *Human Universals.* New York: McGraw-Hill.

Brown, Judith K. 1977. "A note on the division of labor by sex," in Nona Glazer and Helen Y. Waehrer, eds., *Woman in a Man-Made World.* 2nd ed. Chicago: Rand McNally.

Brownmiller, Susan. 1975. *Against Our Will: Men, Women, and Rape.* New York: Simon and Schuster.

———. 1986. *Against Our Will: Men, Women, and Rape.* Rev. ed. New York: Bantam.

Brownstein, Ronald. 2003. "Liberal group flexes online muscle in its very own primary," *Los Angeles Times,* June 23, p. A-9.

Brubaker, Rogers. 1992. *The Politics of Citizenship.* Cambridge, MA: Harvard University Press.

Bruce, Steve. 1990. *Pray TV: Televangelism in America.* New York: Routledge.

———; Kivisto, Peter; and Swatos, William H., eds. 1995. *The Rapture of Politics: The Christian Right as the U.S. Approaches the Year 2000.* New Brunswick, NJ: Transaction Publishers.

Bryan, Beverly; Dadzie, Stella; and Scafe, Suzanne. 1987. "Learning to resist: Black women and education," in Gaby Weiner and Madeleine Arnot, eds., *Gender under Scrutiny: New Inquiries in Education.* London: Hutchinson.

Buechler, Steven M. 2000. *Social Movements in Advanced Capitalism: The Political Economy and Cultural Construction of Social Activism.* New York: Oxford University Press.

Bull, Peter. 1983. *Body Movement and Interpersonal Communication.* New York: Wiley.

Bullock, Charles, III. 1984. "Equal education opportunity," in Charles S. Bullock III and Charles M. Lamb, eds., *Implementation of Civil Rights Policy.* Monterey, CA: Brooks and Cole.

Bumpass, Larry; and Lu, Hsien-Hen. 2000. "Trends in cohabitation and implications for children's family context in the United States." *Population Studies,* vol. 54.

———; and Sweet, James A. 1989. "National estimates of cohabitation: Cohort levels and union stability." *Demography,* vol. 26.

———; Sweet, James A.; and Cherlin, Andrew. 1991. "The role of cohabitation in declining rates of marriage." *Journal of Marriage and the Family,* vol. 53 (November).

Bureau of Justice Statistics. 2002a. "Racial differences exist with blacks disproportionately represented among homicide victims and offenders." www.ojp.usdoj.gov/bjs/homicide/race.htm, accessed 12/28/04.

———. 2002b. "Homicide trends in the U.S.: Age, gender, and race trends." www.ojp.usdoj.gov/bjs/homicide/tables/oarstab.htm, accessed 12/28/04.

Burghart, D. Brian. 2003. "About a Man," *Reno News and Review,* September 4.

Burns, James MacGregor. 1978. *Leadership.* New York: Harper and Row.

Burns, Thomas; and Stalker, G. M. 1994. *The Management of Innovation.* Rev. ed. Oxford, UK: Oxford University Press.

Burr, Chandler. 1993. "Homosexuality and biology." *Atlantic Monthly,* March.

Burris, Beverly H. 1993. *Technocracy at Work.* Albany: State University of New York Press.

———. 1998. "Computerization of the workplace," in *Annual Review of Sociology,* vol. 24. Palo Alto, CA: Annual Reviews.

Burt, Martha R. 1992. *Over the Edge: The Growth of Homelessness in the 1980s.* New York: Russell Sage.

Business Journal. 2000. "Judge tosses insurer's bid to keep redlining data secret." http://sanjose.bizjournals.com/sanjose/stories/2000/09/11/daily42.html, accessed 1/11/05.

BusinessWeek. 2001. "Executive pay." *BusinessWeek Online,* www.businessweek.com/magazine/content/01_16/b3728013.htm, April 16, accessed 12/28/04.

Butler, Judith. 1989. *Gender Trouble: Feminism and the Subversion of Identity.* New York: Routledge.

Butler, Tim; and Savage, Mike. 1995. *Social Change and the Middle Classes.* London: UCL Press.

Butterfield, Fox. 1998. "Decline of violent crimes is linked to crack market." *New York Times,* December 28, p. A18.

Byrd, Max. 1978. *London Transformed: Images of the City in the Eighteenth Century.* New Haven, CT: Yale University Press.

Byrne, David. 1995. "Deindustrialization and dispossession." *Sociology,* vol. 29.

Cairncross, Frances. 1997. *The Death of Distance: How the Communications Revolution Will Change Our Lives.* Boston: Harvard Business School Press.

Campbell, Beatrix. 1993. *Goliath: Britain's Dangerous Places.* London: Methuen.

Caplow, Theodore. 1956. "A theory of coalition in the triad." *American Sociological Review,* vol. 20.

———. 1959. "Further development of a theory of coalitions in triads." *American Journal of Sociology,* vol. 64.

———. 1969. *Two Against One: Coalitions in Triads.* Englewood Cliffs, NJ: Prentice Hall.

Capps, Walter H. 1990. *The New Religious Right: Piety, Patriotism, and Politics.* Columbia: University of South Carolina Press.

Cardoso, Fernando H.; and Faletto, Enzo. 1979. *Dependency and Development in Latin America.* Berkeley, CA: University of California Press.

Carnevale, Dan. 2000. "Brown U. and MCI WorldCom join to help colleges try to close the digital divide," *The Chronicle of Higher Education* (June 9).

Carr, Sarah. 1999. "U. of Nebraska's Class.com hooks up with a Kentucky school," *The Chronicle of Higher Education* (October 22).

———; and Young, Jeffrey R. 1999. "As distance-learning boom spreads, colleges help set up virtual high schools." *The Chronicle of Higher Education* (October 22).

Cashmore, E. Ellis. 1987. *The Logic of Racism.* New York: HarperCollins.

Castells, Manuel. 1977. *The Urban Question: A Marxist Approach.* Cambridge, MA: MIT Press.

———. 1983. *The City and the Grass Roots: A Cross-Cultural Theory of Urban Social Movements.* Berkeley, CA: University of California Press.

——. 1992. "Four Asian tigers with a dragon head: A comparative analysis of the state, economy, and society in the Asian Pacific Rim," in Richard P. Appelbaum and Jeffrey Henderson, eds., *States and Development in the Asian Pacific Rim.* Newbury Park, CA: Sage.

——. 1996. *The Rise of the Network Society.* Malden, MA: Blackwell.

——. 1997. *The Power of Identity.* Malden, MA: Blackwell.

——. 1998. *End of Millennium.* Malden, MA: Blackwell.

Castles, Stephen; and Miller, Mark J. 1993. *The Age of Migration: International Population Movements in the Modern World.* London: Macmillan.

CDI. 2003. "Highlights of the budget request," Washington, D.C.: Center for Defense Information (February 3). www.cdi.org/program/document.cfm?DocumentID=1041&StartRow=11&ListRows=10&appendURL=&Orderby=D.DateLastUpdated&ProgramID=15&from_page=index.cfm, accessed 1/11/05.

Center for American Women and Politics (CAWP). 2001. "Fact Sheets." Eagleton Institute of Politics, Rutgers University.

Center for Public Integrity. 2003. "How the feds stack up," Washington, D.C. : The Center for Public Integrity (May 15), www.publicintegrity.org/hiredguns/report.aspx?aid=167, accessed 1/10/05.

Centers for Disease Control and Prevention (CDC). 2003a. "National ambulatory care survey, 2001 summary." Advanced Data From Vital and Health Statistics, Number 337 (August 11), www.cdc.gov/nchs/data/ad/ad337.pdf, accessed 12/29/04.

——. 2003b. "Health topics: Sexual behavior." www.cdc.gov/nccdphp/dash/sexualbehaviors/index.htm, accessed 12/29/04.

——. 2000. *Youth Risk Behavior Trends from CDC's 1991, 1993, 1995, 1997, and 1999 Youth Risk Behavior Surveys.* www.cdc.gov/HealthYouth/yrbs/factsheet.htm, accessed 1/10/05.

Central Intelligence Agency (CIA). 2000. *CIA World Factbook.* www.cia.gov/cia/publications/factbook/geos/rs.html#Econ, accessed 12/29/04.

Chafe, William H. 1974. *The American Woman: Her Changing Social, Economic, and Political Roles, 1920–1970.* New York: Oxford University Press.

——. 1977. *Women and Equality: Changing Patterns in American Culture.* New York: Oxford University Press.

Chafetz, Janet Saltzman. 1990. *Gender Equity: An Integrated Theory of Stability and Change.* Newbury Park, CA: Sage.

——. 1997. "Feminist theory and sociology: Underutilized contributions for mainstream theory." *Annual Review of Sociology,* vol. 23.

Chambliss, William J. 1973. "The saints and the roughnecks." *Society,* November.

——. 1988. *On the Take: From Petty Crooks to Presidents.* Bloomington: Indiana University Press.

Chaney, David. 1994. *The Cultural Turn: Scene-Setting Essays in Contemporary Cultural History.* New York: Routledge.

Chang, Iris; and Kirby, William C. 1997. *The Rape of Nanking: The Forgotten Holocaust of World War II.* New York: Basic Books.

Charleston Business Journal. 2004. "Are 'all-American cars' still made in America?" www.charlestonbusiness.com/pub/6_18/news/2930-1.html, accessed 1/11/05.

Chase-Dunn, Christopher. 1989. *Global Formation: Structures of the World Economy.* Cambridge, MA: Basil Blackwell.

Chaves, Mark. 1993. "Intraorganizational power and internal secularization in Protestant denominations." *American Journal of Sociology,* vol. 99 (July): 1–48.

——. 1994. "Secularization as declining religious authority." *Social Forces,* vol. 72.

Cheng, Lucie; and Hsiung, Ping-Chun. 1992. "Women, export-oriented growth, and the state: The case of Taiwan," in Richard P. Appelbaum and Jeffery Henderson, eds., *States and Development in the Asian Pacific Rim.* Newbury Park, CA: Sage.

Chepesiuk, Ron. 1998. *Hard Target: The United States War against International Drug Trafficking, 1982–1997.* Jefferson, NC: McFarland and Company.

Cherlin, Andrew. 1990. "Recent changes in American fertility, marriage, and divorce." *Annals of the American Academy of Political and Social Science,* vol. 510 (July).

——. 1992. *Marriage, Divorce, Re-Marriage.* Rev. ed. Cambridge, MA: Harvard University Press.

——. 1999. *Public and Private Families: An Introduction.* 2nd ed. New York: McGraw Hill.

——, et al. 1998. "Effects of parental divorce on mental health throughout the life course." *American Sociological Review,* vol. 63.

Chicago Tribune. 2003. "Cost of a nursing home room jumps, study finds." www.chicagotribune.com/classified/realestate/over55/chi-0308300022aug31,0,364422.story?coll=chi-classifiedover55-hed (August 31, 2003), accessed 12/29/04.

Chodorow, Nancy. 1978. *The Reproduction of Mothering.* Berkeley, CA: University of California Press.

——. 1988. *Psychoanalytic Theory and Feminism.* Cambridge, UK: Polity Press.

Cicourel, Aaron V. 1968. *The Social Organization of Juvenile Justice.* New York: Wiley.

Clark, Philip G. 1993. "Public policy in the United States and Canada: Individualism, familial obligation, and collective responsibility in the care of the elderly," in Jon Hendricks and Carolyn J. Rosenthal, eds., *The Remainder of Their Days: Domestic Policy and Older Families in the United States and Canada.* New York: Garland Press.

Clawson, Dan, et al. 1999. *Dollars and Votes: How Business Campaign Contributions Subvert Democracy.* Philadelphia: Temple University Press.

Cleary, Paul D. 1987. "Gender differences in stress-related disorders," in Rosalind C. Barnett, ed., *Gender and Stress.* New York: Free Press.

Clegg, Stewart. 1990. *Modern Organizations: Organization Studies in the Postmodern World.* London: Sage.

Cleveland, Jeanette N. 1996. "Women in high-status nontraditional occupations," in Paula J. Dubeck and Kathryn Borman, eds., *Women and Work: A Handbook.* New York: Garland.

ClickZ Stats. 2003. "Population explosion!" www.clickz.com/stats/sectors/geographies/article.php/5911_151151, accessed 12/29/04.

Cloward, Richard A.; and Ohlin, L. 1960. *Delinquency and Opportunity.* New York: Free Press.

CNN. 2004. "Bush calls for ban on same-sex marriages." http://edition.cnn.com/2004/ALLPOLITICS/02/24/elec04.prez.bush.marriage/index.html (February 25), accessed 12/29/04.

Coate, J. 1994. "Cyberspace innkeeping: Building online community." Online paper, www.well.com:70/0/Community/innkeeping, accessed 12/29/04.

Cohen, Albert. 1955. *Delinquent Boys: The Culture of the Gang.* Glencoe, IL: Free Press.

Cohen, Lisa E.; Broschak, Joseph P.; and Haveman, Heather A. 1998. "And then there were more? The effect of organizational sex composition on the hiring and promotion of managers." *American Sociological Review,* vol. 63, no. 5.

Cohen, P.; and Bianchi, Suzanne. 1999. "Marriage, children and women's employment: What do we know?" *Monthly Labor Review,* vol. 122 no. 12: 22–30.

Cohen, Robin. 1997. *Global Diasporas: An Introduction.* London: UCL Press.

Cohen, Susan. 1997. "Old glory." *Washington Post Magazine,* June 1.

Cohn, Norman. 1970a. *The Pursuit of the Millennium.* London: Paladin.

———. 1970b. "Medieval millenarianism," in Sylvia L. Thrupp, ed., *Millennial Dreams in Action: Studies in Revolutionary Religious Movements.* New York: Schocken Books.

Coleman, James S. 1987. "Families and schools." *Educational Researcher,* vol. 16, no. 6.

———. 1988. "Social capital in the creation of human capital." *American Journal of Sociology,* supplement, vol. 94.

———. 1990. *The Foundations of Social Theory.* Cambridge, MA: Harvard University Press.

———, et al. 1966. *Equality of Educational Opportunity.* Washington, DC: U.S. Government Printing Office.

Collins, James; and Porras, Jerry. 1994. *Built to Last.* New York: Century.

Collins, Jane. 2000. "Quality by other means." Unpublished manuscript, Department of Sociology, University of Wisconsin–Madison.

Collins, Patricia Hill. 1990. *Black Feminist Thought: Knowledge, Consciousness, and the Politics of Empowerment.* Boston: Unwin Hyman.

Collins, Randall. 1971. "Functional and conflict theories of educational stratification." *American Sociological Review,* vol. 36.

———. 1979. *The Credential Society: An Historical Sociology of Education.* New York: Academic Press.

———, et al. 1993. "Toward an integrated theory of gender stratification." *Sociological Perspectives,* vol. 36.

Coltrane, Scott. 1992. "The micropolitics of gender in non-industrial societies." *Gender and Society,* vol. 6.

Combat 18. 1998. www.combat18.org, accessed 1/10/05.

Common Cause. 2002a. "The soft money laundromat: Top soft money donors 1/1/01 through 12/31/02." www.commoncause. org/laundromat/stat/topdonors01.htm, accessed 7/1/03.

———. 2002b. "Campaign finance reform: Election 2002—incumbent advantage," www.commoncause.org/news/default.cfm ?ArtID=38, accessed 11/6/02.

———. 2003. "Spending more than a half billion on political contributions, lobbying and ad campaigns, Phrma wins big on Medicare," www.commoncause.org/ action/070103_phrma_report.pdf, accessed 7/1/03.

Computer World. 2002. "The Best Places to Work in IT: United States," www.computerworld.com/departments/ surveys/bestplaces/bestplaces_us_region_ sort/0, 10984,,00.html, accessed 1/20/05.

Conley, Dalton. 1999. *Being Black, Living in the Red: Race, Wealth, and Social Policy in America.* Berkeley and Los Angeles: University of California Press.

———. 2003. "The cost of slavery," *New York Times,* February 15.

Connell, R. W. 1987. *Gender and Power: Society, the Person, and Sexual Politics.* Boston: Allen and Unwin.

Conner, K. A.; Dorfman, L. T.; and Tompkins, J. B. 1985. "Life satisfaction of retired professors: The contribution of work, health, income, and length of retirement." *Educational Gerontology,* vol. 11.

Conti, Joseph A. 2003. "Trade, power, and law: Dispute resolution in the World Trade Organization, 1995–2002." Masters Thesis. University of California, Santa Barbara.

Cooley, Charles Horton. 1964. *Human Nature and the Social Order.* Originally published 1902. New York: Schocken Books.

Coombs, Philip H. 1985. *The World Crisis in Education.* New York: Oxford University Press.

Coontz, Stephanie. 1992. *The Way We Never Were: American Families and the Nostalgia Trap.* New York: Basic Books.

Corbin, Juliet; and Strauss, Anselm. 1985. "Managing chronic illness at home: Three lines of work." *Qualitative Sociology,* vol. 8.

Corsaro, William. 1997. *The Sociology of Childhood.* Thousand Oaks, CA: Pine Forge Press.

Cosmides, Leda; and Tooby, John. 1997. "Evolutionary psychology: A primer." University of California at Santa Barbara: Institute for Social, Behavioral, and Economic Research Center for Evolutionary Psychology, available at www.psych.ucsb.edu/research/cep/ primer.htm, accessed 1/11/05.

Coward, Rosalind. 1984. *Female Desire: Women's Sexuality Today.* London: Paladin.

Cowgill, Donald O. 1968. "The social life of the aged in Thailand." *Gerontologist,* vol. 8.

———. 1986. *Aging around the World.* Belmont, CA: Wadsworth.

Cox, Oliver C. 1959. *Class, Caste, and Race: A Study in Social Dynamics.* New York: Monthly Review Press.

Cox, Peter R. 1976. *Demography.* 5th ed. New York: Cambridge University Press.

Cox, W. Michael; and Alm, Richard. 1999. *Myths of Rich and Poor: Why We're Better Off Than We Think.* New York: Basic Books.

Craig, David J. 2004. "InnerCity Entrepeneurs gives small businesses a shot at the big leagues." *B. U. Bridge,* vol. VII, no. 26 (April), www.bu.edu/bridge/archive/2004/04-02/innercity.html, accessed 12/29/04.

Craner, Lorne W. 2002. "Promoting corporate social responsibility abroad: The human rights and democracy perspective," Remarks at the 2002 Surrey Memorial Lecture, National Policy Association (June 18), www.state.gov/g/ drl/rls/rm/11405.htm, accessed 12/29/04.

Cressey, Paul. 1932. *The Taxi-Dance Hall.* Chicago: University of Chicago Press.

Crompton, Rosemary. 1998. *Class and Stratification: An Introduction to Current Debates.* 2nd ed. Cambridge, UK: Polity Press.

Crow, Graham; and Hardey, Michael. 1992. "Diversity and ambiguity among lone-parent households in modern Britain," in Catherine Marsh and Sara Arber, eds., *Families and Households: Divisions and Change.* London: Macmillan.

CRP. 2003a. "2000 Presidential Race: Total Raised and Spent," Center for Responsive Politics. www.opensecrets.org/2000elect/ index/AllCands.htm, accessed 12/29/04.

———. 2003b. "Election overview 2002 cycle: Business-labor-ideology split in PAC, soft & individual donations to candidates and parties" Center for Responsive Politics, based on data released by the FEC on Monday, June 9, 2003. www.opensecrets. org/overview/blio.asp?cycle=2002, accessed 12/29/04.

Cumings, Bruce. 1987. "The origins and development of the northeast Asian political economy: Industrial sectors, product cycles, and political consequences," in F. C. Deyo, ed., *The Political Economy of the New Asian Industrialism.* Ithaca, NY: Cornell University Press.

———. 1997. *Korea's Place in the Sun: A Modern History.* New York: Norton.

Cumming, Elaine. 1963. "Further thoughts on the theory of disengagement." *International Social Science Journal,* vol. 15.

———. 1975. "Engagement with an old theory." *International Journal of Aging and Human Development,* vol. 6.

————; and Henry, William E. 1961. *Growing Old: The Process of Disengagement.* New York: Basic.

Currie, Elliott. 1998. *Crime and Punishment in America.* New York: Henry Holt.

Curtin, J. Sean. 2003. "Youth trends in Japan: Part four—anorexia and other teenage eating disorders on the rise." Japanese Institute of Global Communications. www.glocom.org/special_topics/social_trends/20030701_trends_s46, accessed 12/29/04.

Curtiss, Susan. 1977. *Genie: A Linguistic Study of a Modern Day "Wild Child."* New York: Academic Press.

Cutler, Stephen J.; and Grams, Armin E. 1988. "Correlates of everyday self-reported memory problems." *Journal of Gerontology,* vol. 43.

Dahlburg, John-Thor. 1995. "Sweatshop case dismays few in Thailand." *Los Angeles Times,* August 27, p. A-4.

D'Andrade, Roy. 1995. *The Development of Cognitive Anthropology.* New York: Cambridge University Press.

Dannefer, Dale. 1989. "Human action and its place in theories of aging." *Journal of Aging Studies,* vol. 3.

Danziger, Sheldon H.; and Gottschalk, Peter. 1995. *America Unequal.* Cambridge, MA: Harvard University Press.

————, et al., eds. 1994. *Confronting Poverty: Prescriptions for Change.* Cambridge, MA: Harvard University Press.

Davenport, W. 1965. "Sexual patterns and their regulations in a society of the southwest Pacific," in F. Beech, ed., *Sex and Behavior.* New York: Wiley.

Davies, Bronwyn. 1991. *Frogs and Snails and Feminist Tales.* Sydney: Allen and Unwin.

Davies, James C. 1962. "Towards a theory of revolution." *American Sociological Review,* vol. 27.

Davis, Donald; and Polonko, Karen. 2001. "Telework America 2001 Summary," International Telework Association & Council, www.telecommute.org/telework/twa2001.htm, accessed 1/20/05.

Davis, Kingsley; and Moore, Wilbert E. 1945. "Some principles of stratification." *American Sociological Review,* vol. 10 (April).

Davis, Mike. 1990. *City of Quartz: Excavating the Future in Los Angeles.* New York: Verso.

Davis, Stanley M. 1987. *Future Perfect.* Reading, MA: Addison-Wesley.

————. 1988. *2001 Management: Managing the Future Now.* New York: Simon and Schuster.

Davis, Winston. 1987. "Religion and development: Weber and East Asia experience," in Myron Weiner and Samuel Huntington, eds., *Understanding Political Development.* Boston: Little, Brown.

Deacon, Terrance W. 1998. *The Symbolic Species: The Co-Evolution of Language and the Brain.* New York: Norton.

de Beauvoir, Simone. 1974. *The Second Sex.* Originally published 1949. New York: Random House.

Delany, Samuel R. 1999. *Times Square Red, Times Square Blue.* New York: New York University Press.

D'Emilio, John. 1983. *Sexual Politics, Sexual Communities: The Making of a Homosexual Minority in the United States, 1940–1970.* Chicago: University of Chicago Press.

Dertouzos, Michael L. 1989. *Made in America: Regaining the Productive Edge.* Cambridge, MA: MIT Press.

de Tocqueville, Alexis. 1969. *Democracy in America.* Originally published 1835. New York: Doubleday.

Devault, Marjorie L. 1991. *Feeding the Family: The Social Organization of Caring as Gendered Work.* Chicago: University of Chicago Press.

de Witt, Karen. 1994. "Wave of suburban growth is being fed by minorities." *New York Times,* August 15, pp. A1, B6.

Dey, Achintya N. 1997. "Characteristics of elderly nursing home residents: Data from the 1995 national nursing home survey." *Advance Data,* vol. 289 (July 2).

Deyo, Fred C. 1987. *The Political Economy of the New Asian Industrialism.* Ithaca, NY: Cornell University Press.

————. 1989. *Beneath the Miracle: Labor Subordination in the New Asian Industrialism.* Berkeley, CA: University of California Press.

Diamond, Jared. 1997. *Guns, Germs, and Steel: The Fates of Human Societies.* New York: Norton.

Dicken, Peter. 1992. *Global Shift: The Internationalization of Economic Activity.* 2nd ed. London: Chapman.

Dickman, Sharon. 1999. "Can life in nursing homes by meaningful?" University of Rochester press release, June 23.

Dicum, Gregory; and Luttinger, Nina. 1999. *The Coffee Book: Anatomy of an Industry from Crop to the Last Drop.* New York: New Press.

Diekema, David A. 1991. "Televangelism and the mediated charismatic relationship," *Social Science Journal,* vol. 28, no. 2: 143–62.

DiMaggio, Paul. 1997. "Culture and cognition." *Annual Review of Sociology,* vol. 23.

DiPrete, Thomas A.; and Grusky, David B. 1990. "Structure and trend in the process of stratification for American men and women." *American Journal of Sociology,* vol. 96.

————; and Nonnemaker, K. Lynn. 1997. "Structural change, labor market turbulence, and labor market outcomes." *American Sociological Review,* vol. 62.

————; and Soule, Whitman T. 1988. "Gender and promotion in segmented job ladder systems." *American Sociological Review,* vol. 53.

Dobash, R. Emerson; and Dobash, Russell P. 1992. *Women, Violence, and Social Change.* New York: Routledge.

Dolbeare, Cushing. 1995. *Out of Reach: Why Everyday People Can't Find Affordable Housing.* Washington, DC: Low Income Housing Information.

Domhoff, G. William. 1974. *The Bohemian Grove and Other Retreats.* New York: Harper and Row.

————. 1998 (earlier editions 1971, 1979, 1983). *Who Rules America?: Power and Politics in the Year 2000.* Belmont, CA: Mayfield.

Dore, Ronald. 1980. *British Factory, Japanese Factory: The Origins of National Diversity in Industrial Relations.* Berkeley, CA: University of California Press.

Doyal, Lesley; and Pennell, Imogen. 1981. *The Political Economy of Health.* Boston: South End Press.

Drake, St. Clair; and Cayton, Horace R. 1945. *Black Metropolis: A Study of Negro Life in a Northern City.* New York: Harcourt, Brace.

Draper, P. 1975. "!Kung women: Contrasts in sexual egalitarianism in foraging and sedentary contexts," in R. R. Reiter, ed., *Toward an Anthropology of Women.* New York: Monthly Review Press.

Dreier, Peter; and Appelbaum, Richard P. 1992. "The housing crisis enters the 1990s." *New England Journal of Public Policy,* spring–summer.

Drentea, Patricia. 1998. "Consequences of women's formal and informal job search methods for employment in female-dominated jobs." *Gender and Society,* vol. 12.

Du Bois, W. E. B. 1903. *The Souls of Black Folk.* New York: Dover.

Dubos, René. 1959. *Mirage of Health.* New York: Doubleday/Anchor.

Duignan, Peter; and Gann, L. H., eds. 1998. *The Debate in the United States over Immigration.* Stanford, CA: Hoover Institution Press.

Duncan, Greg J.; Brooks-Gunn, Jeanne; Yeung, W. Jean; Smith, Judith R. 1998. "How much does childhood poverty affect the life chances of children?" *American Sociological Review,* vol. 63, no. 3 (June): 406–23.

Duncan, Otis Dudley. 1971. "Observations on population." *New Physician,* April 20.

Duncombe, Jean; and Marsden, Dennis. 1993. "Love and intimacy: The gender division of emotion and emotion work: A neglected aspect of sociological discussion of heterosexual relationships." *Sociology,* vol. 27.

Duneier, Mitchell. 1999. *Sidewalk.* New York: Farrar, Straus, and Giroux.

———; and Molotch, Harvey. 1999. "Talking city trouble: Interactional vandalism, social inequality, and the urban interaction problem." *American Journal of Sociology,* vol. 104.

Dunn, Dana; Almquist, Elizabeth M.; and Saltzman Chafetz, Janet. 1993. "Macrostructural perspectives on gender inequality," in Paula England, ed., *Theory on Gender, Feminism on Theory.* New York: Aldine DeGrutyer.

Dunn, William. 1993. *The Baby Bust: A Generation Comes of Age.* Ithaca, NY: American Demographics Books.

Duranti, Alessandro. 1994. *From Grammar to Politics: Linguistic Anthropology in a Western Samoan Village.* Berkeley, CA: University of California Press.

Durkheim, Émile. 1964. *The Division of Labor in Society.* Originally published 1893. New York: Free Press.

———. 1965. *The Elementary Forms of the Religious Life.* Originally published 1912. New York: Free Press.

———. 1966. *Suicide.* Originally published 1897. New York: Free Press.

Duster, Troy. 1990. *Backdoor to Eugenics.* New York: Routledge.

Dutt, Mallika. 1996. "Some reflections on U.S. women of color and the United Nations fourth world conference on women and NGO forum in Beijing, China." *Feminist Studies,* vol. 22.

Dworkin, Andrea. 1981. *Pornography: Men Possessing Women.* New York: Pedigree.

———. 1987. *Intercourse.* New York: Free Press.

Dworkin, R. M. 1993. *Life's Dominion: An Argument About Abortion, Euthanasia, and Individual Freedom.* New York: Knopf.

Dwyer, D. J. 1975. *People and Housing in Third World Cities.* London: Longman.

Dychtwald, K. 1990. *Age Wave: How the Most Important Trend of Our Time Will Change Your Future.* New York: Bantam Books.

Dye, Thomas R. 1986. *Who's Running America?* 4th ed. Englewood Cliffs, NJ: Prentice Hall.

Eating Disorder Coalition (EDC). 2003. "Statistics." www.eatingdisorderscoalition. org/reports/statistics.html, accessed 12/29/04.

Ebomoyi, Ehigie. 1987. "The prevalence of female circumcision in two Nigerian communities." *Sex Roles,* vol. 17, nos. 3–4.

The Economist. 1990. *The Economist Book of Vital World Statistics.* New York: Times Books.

———. 2003. "A Nation Apart," May 6, www.economist.com/surveys/showsurvey. cfm?issue=20031108, accessed 12/29/04.

Edin, K.; and Lein, L. 1997. "Work, welfare, and single mothers' economic survival strategies." *American Sociological Review,* vol. 62, no. 2.

Efron, Sonni. 1997. "Eating disorders go global," *Los Angeles Times,* October 18, p. A-1.

Ehrenreich, Barbara; and Ehrenreich, John. 1979. "The professional-managerial class," in Pat Walker, ed., *Between Labor and Capital.* Boston: South End.

Eibl-Eibesfeldt, I. 1972. "Similarities and differences between cultures in expressive movements," in Robert A. Hinde, ed., *Nonverbal Communication.* New York: Cambridge University Press.

Eisenhower Library. 1961. "Farewell Address," Abilene, Kansas: The Dwight D. Eisenhower Presidential Library. www.eisenhower.utexas.edu/farewell.htm, accessed 12/29/04.

Ekman, Paul; and Friesen, W. V. 1978. *Facial Action Coding System.* New York: Consulting Psychologists Press.

el Dareer, Asma. 1982. *Woman, Why Do You Weep? Circumcision and Its Consequences.* Westport, CT: Zed.

Elias, Norbert. 1987. *Involvement and Detachment.* London: Oxford University Press.

———; and Dunning, E. 1987. *Quest for Excitement: Sport and Leisure in the Civilizing Process.* Oxford, UK: Blackwell.

Ell, Kathleen. 1996. "Social networks, social support, and coping with serious illness: The family connection." *Social Science and Medicine,* vol. 42.

Ellsworth American. 2001. "Laptop Computers for Students," editorial, *Ellsworth American,* www.ellsworthamerican. com/archive/edit2001/02_01/ea_edit2-02-08-01.html, accessed 1/10/05.

Elshtain, Jean Bethke. 1981. *Public Man: Private Woman.* Princeton, NJ: Princeton University Press.

Emmanuel, Arghiri. 1972. *Unequal Exchange: A Study of the Imperialism of Trade.* New York: Monthly Review Press.

England, Paula. 1992. *Comparable Worth: Theories and Evidence.* New York: Aldine de Gruyter.

Environmental Working Group. 2003. "EWG Farm Subsidy Database" www.ewg.org/farm/findings.php, accessed 12/29/04.

Epstein, Gene. 2003. "More women advance, but sexism persists," *Barron's* www. collegejournal.com/salaryhiring/industries/seniorexecs/20030605-epstein.html, accessed 1/11/05.

Equal Employment Opportunity Commission (EEOC). 1993. "National database fiscal year 1983 to fiscal year 1992." Washington, DC: Equal Employment Opportunity Commission.

———. 2003. "Sexual harassment charges, EEOC and FEPAs combined: FY1992–FY2002," www.eeoc.gov/stats/harass.html, accessed 7/5/03.

Erard, Michael. 2003. "Decoding the new cues in online society," *New York Times,* November 27.

Ericson, Richard; and Haggerty, Kevin. 1997. *Policing the Risk Society.* Toronto: University of Toronto Press.

Erikson, Kai. 1966. *Wayward Puritans: A Study in the Sociology of Deviance.* New York: Wiley.

Erikson, R.; and Goldthorpe, J. H. 1992. *The Constant Flux: A Study of Class Mobility in Industrial Societies.* Oxford, UK: Oxford University Press.

Esposito, John L. 1984. *Islam and Politics.* Syracuse, NY: Syracuse University Press.

Estes, Carol L. 1986. "The politics of aging in America." *Aging and Society,* vol. 6.

———. 1991. "The Reagan legacy: Privatization, the welfare state, and aging," in J. Myles and J. Quadagno, eds., *States, Labor Markets, and the Future of Old Age Policy.* Philadelphia: Temple University Press.

———; Binney, Elizabeth A.; and Culbertson, Richard A. 1992. "The gerontological imagination: Social influences on the development of gerontology, 1945–present." *Aging and Human Development,* vol. 35.

———; Swan, J.; and Gerard, L. 1982. "Dominant and competing paradigms in gerontology: Toward a political economy of aging." *Aging and Society,* vol. 2.

———, et al. 1984. *Political Economy, Health, and Aging.* Boston: Little, Brown.

Estrich, Susan. 1987. *Real Rape.* Cambridge, MA: Harvard University Press.

Etzioni-Halévy, Eva. 1985. *Bureaucracy and Democracy: A Political Dilemma.* New York: Routledge, Chapman and Hall.

Europa. 2000. "European enlargement: A historical opportunity." http://europa.eu.

int/comm/enlargement/docs/newsletter/ weekly_070700.htm, accessed 1/10/05.

Evans, David J. 1992. "Left realism and the spatial study of crime," in David J. Evans et al., eds., *Crime, Policing, and Place: Essays in Environmental Criminology.* New York: Routledge.

Evans, Peter. 1979. *Dependent Development.* Princeton, NJ: Princeton University Press.

———. 1987. "Class, state, and dependence in East Asia: Some lessons for Latin Americanists," in F. C. Deyo, ed., *The Political Economy of the New Asian Industrialism.* Ithaca, NY: Cornell University Press.

———. 1995. *Embedded Autonomy: States and Industrial Transformation.* Princeton, NJ: Princeton University Press.

Evans, Richard J. 1977. *The Feminists: Women's Emancipation Movements in Europe, America, and Australasia, 1840–1920.* New York: Barnes & Noble.

Evans-Pritchard, E. E. 1956. *Nuer Religion.* New York: Oxford University Press.

———. 1970. "Sexual inversion among the Azande." *American Anthropologist,* vol. 72.

Falk, G.; Falk, U.; and Tomashevich, V. 1981. *Aging in America and Other Cultures.* Saratoga, CA: Century Twenty-One.

Farley, Maggie. 1998. "Women in the new China." *Los Angeles Times,* November 22.

Farley, Reynolds; and Frey, William H. 1994. "Change in the segregation of whites from blacks during the 1980s: Small steps toward a more integrated society." *American Sociological Review,* vol. 59, no. 1.

Featherman, David L.; and Hauser, Robert M. 1978. *Opportunity and Change.* New York: Academic Press.

FEC. 2001. "PAC activity increases in 2000 election cycle," Federal Election Commission, News releases, Media Advisories (May 31), www.fec.gov/press/ press2001/053101pacfund/053101pacfund. html, accessed 1/11/05.

Ferguson, Kathy E. 1984. *The Feminist Case against Bureaucracy.* Philadelphia: Temple University Press.

Fernández, Kelly; and Patricia, María. 1987. "Technology and employment along the U.S.-Mexico border," in Cathryn L. Thorup, ed., *The United States and Mexico: Face to Face with the New Technology.* New Brunswick, NJ: Transaction Books.

Filkins, Dexter. 1998. "Afghans pay dearly for peace." *Los Angeles Times,* October 22, p. A-1.

FinanceAsia.com. 2003. "A week in tech," (July 5). www.financeasia.com/articles/

FF609444-A13D-11D7-81FC0090277 E174B.cfm, accessed 7/5/03.

Finke, Roger; and Stark, Rodney. 1988. "Religious economies and sacred canopies: Religious mobilization in American cities, 1906." *American Sociological Review,* vol. 53.

———. 1992. *The Churching of America, 1776–1990: Winners and Losers in Our Religious Economy.* New Brunswick, NJ: Rutgers University Press.

Firestone, Shulamith. 1971. *The Dialectic of Sex.* London: Paladin.

Fischer, Claude S. 1984. *The Urban Experience.* 2nd ed. New York: Harcourt Brace Jovanovich.

———, et al. 1996. *Inequality by Design: Cracking the Bell Curve Myth.* Princeton, NJ: Princeton University Press.

Fischer, David H. 1978. *Growing Old in America,* expanded ed. New York: Oxford University Press.

Fisher, Bonnie S.; Cullen, Francis T.; and Turner, Michael G. 2000. *The Sexual Victimization of College Women.* Washington, DC: U.S. Department of Justice, National Institute of Justice, Bureau of Justice Statistics (December), NJJ 182369, www.ncjrs.org/pdffiles1/ nij/182369.pdf, accessed 12/29/04.

Foner, Nancy. 1984. *Ages in Conflict: A Cross-Cultural Perspective on Inequality between Old and Young.* New York: Columbia University Press.

Forbes. 2000. "The world's richest people." (June 29).

———. 2001a. "The world's richest people." (June 21), www.forbes.com/2001/06/21/ billionairesindex.html, accessed 12/29/04.

———. 2001b. "Forbes top CEO's: Corporate America's most powerful people." http://www.forbes.com/lists/home.jhtml? passListID=12&passYear=2001&passList Type=Person, accessed 12/29/04.

———. 2002. (March 4).

———. 2003. "Survival of the richest" www. forbes.com/billionaires/freeforbes/2003/0 317/087.html, accessed 12/29/04.

Ford, Clellan S.; and Beach, Frank A. 1951. *Patterns of Sexual Behavior.* New York: Harper and Row.

Forrest, Drew; and Streek, Barry. 2001. "Mbeki in bizarre AIDS outburst" *Daily Mail and Guardian* (Johannesburg) October 26. www.aegis.com/news/dmg/ 2001/MG011021.html, accessed 12/29/04.

Fortune. 2003. "Global 500" (July 21), www.fortune.com/fortune/global500, accessed 12/14/03.

Foucault, Michel. 1971. *The Order of Things: An Archaeology of the Human Sciences.* New York: Pantheon.

———. 1978. *The History of Sexuality.* New York: Pantheon.

———. 1979. *Discipline and Punish: The Birth of the Prison.* New York: Random House.

———. 1987. *The Use of Pleasure.* Harmonds-worth, UK: Penguin.

———. 1988. "Technologies of the self," in Luther H. Martin, Huck Gutman, and Patrick H. Hutton, eds., *Technologies of the Self: A Seminar with Michel Foucault.* Amherst, MA: University of Massachusetts Press.

Fowles, Richard; and Merva, Mary. 1996. "Wage inequality and criminal activity: An extreme bounds analysis for the United States, 1975–1990." *Criminology,* vol. 34, no. 2.

Fox, Oliver C. 1964. "The pre-industrial city reconsidered." *Sociological Quarterly,* vol. 5.

Frank, Andre Gundar. 1966. "The development of underdevelopment." *Monthly Review,* vol. 18.

———. 1969a. *Latin America: Under-development or Revolution.* New York: Monthly Review Press.

———. 1969b. *Capitalism and Under-development in Latin America: Historical Studies of Chile and Brazil.* New York: Monthly Review Press.

———. 1979. *Dependent Accumulation and Underdevelopment.* London: Macmillan.

Frank, David John; and McEneaney, Elizabeth H. 1999. "The individualization of society and the liberalization of state policies on same-sex sexual relations, 1984–1995." *Social Forces,* vol. 7, no. 3.

Fredrickson, George M. 1998. *The Comparative Imagination: On the History of Racism, Nationalism, and Social Movements.* Berkeley and Los Angeles: University of California Press.

———. *Freedom in the World, 1997–1998.* New York: Freedom House.

Freeman, Richard B. 1999. *The New Inequality: Creating Solutions for Poor America.* Boston: Beacon Press.

———; and Rogers, Joel. 1999. *What Workers Want.* Ithaca, NY: ILR Press and Russell Sage Foundation.

Free the Children. 1998. www.freethechildren. org, accessed 12/29/04.

Freidson, Eliot. 1970. *Profession of Medicine: A Study of the Sociology of Applied Knowledge.* New York: Dodd, Mead.

Fremlin, J. H. 1964. "How many people can the world support?" *New Scientist,* (October 19).

French, Howard W. 2001a. "Diploma at hand, Japanese women find glass ceiling reinforced with iron." *New York Times,* January 1, p. A1.

———. 2001b. "Japan's new premier picks precedent-setting cabinet." *New York Times,* April 27, p. A1.

Freud, Sigmund. 1971. *The Psychopathology of Everyday Life.* New York: Norton.

Frey, William; and Liaw, Kao-Lee. 1998. "The impact of recent immigration on population redistribution in the United States," in James Smith and Barry Edmonston, eds., *The Immigration Debate.* Washington, DC: National Academy Press.

Friedan, Betty. 1963. *The Feminine Mystique.* New York: Norton.

Friedlander, Daniel; and Burtless, Gary. 1994. *Five Years After: The Long-Term Effects of Welfare-to-Work Programs.* New York: Russell Sage.

Fries, James F. 1980. "Aging, natural death, and the compression of morbidity." *New England Journal of Medicine,* vol. 303.

Frobel, Folker; Heinrichs, Jurgen; and Kreye, Otto. 1979. *The New International Division of Labor.* New York: Cambridge University Press.

Fry, C. L. 1980. *Aging in Culture and Society.* New York: Bergin.

Fryer, David; and McKenna, Stephen. 1987. "The laying off of hands—unemployment and the experience of time," in Stephen Fineman, ed., *Unemployment: Personal and Social Consequences.* London: Tavistock.

Fukuyama, Francis. 1989. "The end of history?" *National Interest,* vol. 16 (summer).

Furstenberg, Frank F., Jr.; and Cherlin, Andrew J. 1991. *Divided Families.* Cambridge, MA: Harvard University Press.

Gallup Organization. 1998. Gallup/CNN/*USA Today* Poll, July 21.

Gamoran, Adam, et al. 1995. "An organizational analysis of the effects of ability grouping." *American Educational Research Journal,* vol. 32, no. 4.

Gans, Herbert J. 1979. "Symbolic ethnicity: The future of ethnic groups and cultures in America." *Ethnic and Racial Studies,* vol. 2 (January).

Ganzeboom, H. B. G.; Luijkx, R.; and Treiman, D. 1989. "Intergenerational class mobility in comparative perspective." *Research in Social Stratification and Mobility,* vol. 8.

Gardner, Beatrice; and Gardner, Allen. 1969. "Teaching sign language to a chimpanzee." *Science,* no. 165.

———. 1975. "Evidence for sentence constituents in the early utterances of child and chimpanzee." *Journal of Experimental Psychology,* vol. 104.

Gardner, Carol Brooks. 1995. *Passing By: Gender and Public Harassment.* Berkeley and Los Angeles: University of California Press.

Garfinkel, Harold. 1963. "A conception of, and experiments with, 'trust' as a condition of stable concerted actions," in O. J. Harvey, ed., *Motivation and Social Interaction.* New York: Ronald Press.

Gavron, Hannah. 1966. *The Captive Wife: Conflicts of Housebound Mothers.* London: Routledge and Kegan Paul.

Geary, Dick. 1981. *European Labor Protest, 1848–1939.* New York: St. Martin's Press.

Geertz, Clifford. 1973. *The Interpretation of Cultures.* New York: Basic Books.

———. 1983. *Local Knowledge: Further Essays in Interpretative Anthropology.* New York: Basic Books.

Gelb, I. J. 1952. *A Study of Writing.* Chicago: University of Chicago Press.

Gelles, Richard; and Cornell, C. P. 1990. *Intimate Violence in Families.* 2nd ed. Newbury Park, CA: Sage.

Gellner, Ernest. 1983. *Nations and Nationalism.* Ithaca, NY: Cornell University Press.

General Social Survey (GSS). 1997. "General Social Surveys, 1972–1994: [Cumulative File]." Accessed and Analyzed online through the University of Michigan Inter-university Consortium for Political and Social Research (ICPSR), http:webapp.icpsr.umich.edu/cocoon/ICPSR-StUDY/03728.xml, accessed 1/10/05.

Gerbner, George, et al. 1985. "Television's mean world: violence profile no. 14–15." Philadelphia: Annenberg School of Communication, University of Pennsylvania.

Gereffi, Gary. 1995. "Contending paradigms for cross-regional comparison: Development strategies and commodity chains in East Asia and Latin America," in Peter H. Smith, ed., *Latin America in Comparative Perspective: New Approaches to Methods and Analysis.* Boulder, CO: Westview Press.

———. 1996. "Commodity chains and regional divisions of labor in East Asia." *Journal of Asian Business,* vol. 12, no. 1.

Gershuny, Jonathan, et al., 1994. "The domestic labor revolution: A process of lagged adaptation," in Michael Anderson, Frank Bechofer, and Jonathan Gershuny, eds., *The Social and Political Economy of the Household.* Oxford, UK: Oxford University Press.

———; and Miles, I. D. 1983. *The New Service Economy: The Transformation of Employment in Industrial Societies.* London: Francis Pinter.

Gibbons, John H. 1990. *Trading around the Clock: Global Securities Markets and Information Technology.* Washington, DC: Government Printing Office.

Gibson, P. 1989. "Gay male and lesbian youth suicide." Report of the Secretary's Task Force on Youth Suicide. Washington, D.C.: U.S. Department of Health and Human Services.

Giddens, Anthony. 1984. *The Constitution of Society.* Cambridge, UK: Polity Press.

———. 1995. *Beyond Left and Right: The Future of Radical Politics.* Stanford, CA: Stanford University Press.

———. 1998. *The Third Way: The Renewal of Social Democracy.* Cambridge, UK: Polity Press.

Gill, Colin. 1985. *Work, Unemployment, and the New Technology.* New York: Basic Blackwell.

Gilligan, Carol. 1982. *In a Different Voice: Psychological Theory and Women's Development.* Cambridge, MA: Harvard University Press.

Ginzburg, Carlo. 1980. *The Cheese and the Worms.* London: Routledge and Kegan Paul.

Gissing, George. 1983. *Demos: A Story of English Socialism.* Originally published 1892. New York: Routledge, Chapman and Hall.

Giuffre, Patti A.; and Williams, Christine L. 1994. "Boundary lines: Labeling sexual harassment in restaurants." *Gender and Society,* vol. 8.

Gladwell, Malcolm. 2000. "Designs for Working," *New Yorker,* December 11.

Glascock, A.; and Feinman, S. 1981. "Social asset or social burden: An analysis of the treatment for the aged in non-industrial societies," in C. L. Fry, ed., *Dimensions: Aging, Culture, and Health.* New York: Praeger.

———. 1986. "Toward a comparative framework: Propositions concerning the treatment of the aged in non-industrial societies," in C. L. Fry and J. Keith, eds., *New Methods for Old Age Research: Strategies for Studying Diversity.* South Hadley, MA: Bergin and Garvey.

Glassner, Barry. 1999. *The Culture of Fear: Why Americans Are Afraid of the Wrong Things.* New York: Basic Books.

Glenn, Evelyn Nakano. 1994. "Introduction," in Grace Change, Linda Rennie Forcey, and Evelyn Nakano Glenn, eds., *Mothering: Ideology, Experience, and Agency.* New York: Routledge.

Glock, Charles Y. 1976. "On the origin and evolution of religious groups," in Charles Y. Glock and Robert N. Bellah, eds., *The New Religious Consciousness.* Berkeley, CA: University of California Press.

Glueck, Sheldon W.; and Glueck, Eleanor. 1956. *Physique and Delinquency.* New York: Harper and Row.

Gober, Patricia. 1993. *Americans on the Move.* Washington, DC: Population Reference Bureau.

Goe, W. Richard. 1994. "The producer services sector and development within the deindustrializing urban community." *Social Forces,* vol. 72.

Goffman, Erving. 1967. *Interaction Ritual.* New York: Doubleday/Anchor.

———. 1971. *Relations in Public: Microstudies of the Public Order.* New York: Basic Books.

———. 1973. *The Presentation of Self in Everyday Life.* New York: Overlook Press.

———. 1981. *Forms of Talk.* Philadelphia: University of Pennsylvania Press.

Gold, T. 1986. *State and Society in the Taiwan Miracle.* Armonk, NY: M. E. Sharpe.

Goldberg, Carey. 1997. "Hispanic households struggle amid broad decline in income." *New York Times,* January 30, pp. A1, A16.

———. 2001. "School computer money approved," *New York Times,* July 27.

Goldin, Claudia Dale. 1990. *Understanding the Gender Gap: An Economic History of American Women.* New York: Oxford University Press.

Goldscheider, Frances K. 1990. "The aging of the gender revolution: What do we know and what do we need to know?" *Research on Aging,* vol. 12.

———; and Goldscheider, Calvin. 1999. *The Changing Transition to Adulthood: Leaving and Returning Home.* Thousand Oaks, CA: Sage.

———; and Waite, Linda J. 1991. *New Families, No Families? The Transformation of the American Home.* Berkeley, CA: University of California Press.

Goldstein, Sidney; and Goldstein, Alice. 1996. *Jews on the Move: Implications for Jewish Identity.* Albany, NY: SUNY Press.

Goldthorpe, John H. 1983. "Women and class analysis: In defense of the conventional view," *Sociology,* vol. 17.

Goode, William J. 1963. *World Revolution in Family Patterns.* New York: Free Press.

———. 1971. "Force and violence in the family," *Journal of Marriage and the Family,* vol. 33.

———. 1993. *World Changes in Divorce Patterns.* New Haven, CT: Yale University Press.

Goodhardt, G. J.; Ehrenberg, A. S. C.; and Collins, M. A. 1987. *The Television Audience: Patterns of Voting.* 2nd ed. London: Gower.

Gorz, Andre. 1982. *Farewell to the Working Class.* London: Pluto.

Gottfredson, Michael R.; and Hirschi, Travis. 1990. *A General Theory of Crime.* Stanford, CA: Stanford University Press.

Graham, Heather. 1987. "Women's smoking and family health." *Social Science and Medicine,* vol. 25.

———. 1994. "Gender and class as dimensions of smoking behavior: Insights from a survey of mothers." *Social Science and Medicine,* vol. 38.

Graham, Laurie. 1995. *On the Line at Subaru-Isuzu.* Ithaca, NY: Cornell University Press.

Granovetter, Mark. 1973. "The strength of weak ties." *American Journal of Sociology,* vol. 78.

Greeley, Andrew. 1977. *The American Catholic: A Social Portrait.* New York: Basic Books.

———. 1989. *Religious Change in America.* Cambridge, MA: Harvard University Press.

Green, F. 1987. *The "Sissy Boy" Syndrome and the Development of Homosexuality.* New Haven, CT: Yale University Press.

Greenberg, Jan S.; and Becker, Marion. 1988. "Aging parents as family resources." *Gerontologist,* vol. 28.

Greenfield, Patricia Marks. 1993. "Representational competence in shared symbol systems," in R. R. Cocking and K. A. Renninger, eds., *The Development and Meaning of Psychological Distance.* Hillsdale, NJ: Erlbaum.

Griffin, Susan. 1979. *Rape, the Power of Consciousness.* New York: Harper and Row.

Grint, Keith. 1991. *The Sociology of Work.* Cambridge, MA: Polity Press.

Gross, Jane. 1992. "Suffering in silence no more: Fighting sexual harassment." *New York Times,* July 13, p. A1.

Grusky, David B.; and Hauser, Robert M. 1984. "Comparative social mobility revisited: Models of convergence and divergence in 16 countries." *American Sociological Review,* vol. 49.

———; and Sorensen, J. B. 1998. "Can class analysis be salvaged?" *American Journal of Sociology,* vol. 103, no. 5.

The Guardian. 2002. "Top 1% earn as much as the poorest 57%" www.guardian.co.uk/business/story/0,,635292,00.html, accessed 1/10/05.

Gubrium, Jabber F. 1986. *Oldtimers and Alzheimer's: The Descriptive Organization of Senility.* Greenwich, CT: JAI Press.

———. 1991. *The Mosaic of Care: Frail Elderly and Their Families in the Real World.* New York: Springer.

———. 1993. *Speaking of Life: Horizons of Meaning for Nursing Home Residents.* Hawthorne, NY: Aldine de Gruyter.

———; and Sankar, Andrea, eds. 1994. *Qualitative Methods in Aging Research.* Newbury Park, CA: Sage.

Guibernau, Montserrat. 1999. *Nations without States: Political Communities in a Global Age.* Cambridge, MA: Blackwell.

Habermas, Jürgen. 1975. *Legitimation Crisis.* Trans. Thomas McCarthy. Boston: Beacon Press.

———. 1989. *The Structural Transformation of the Public Sphere: An Inquiry into a Category of Bourgeois Society.* Cambridge, UK: Polity Press.

Hacker, Andrew. 1992. *Two Nations: Black and White, Separate, Hostile, Unequal.* New York: Scribner.

Hadden, Jeffrey. 1990. "Precursors to the globalization of American televangelism," *Social Compass,* vol. 37 (March): 161–67.

———. 1997a. "The concepts 'cult' and 'sect' in scholarly research and public discourse." New Religious Movements Web site, http://religious movements.lib.virginia.edu/cultsect/concult.htm, accessed 1/10/05.

———. 1997b. "New religious movements mission statement." New Religious Movements Web site, http://religous movements.lib.virginia.edu/welcome/mission.htm, accessed 1/10/05.

———; and Shupe, Anson. 1987. "Televangelism in America," *Social Compass,* vol. 34, no. 1: 61–75.

———. 2004. Religious Broadcasting Web site, "Televangelism." http://religious broadcasting.lib.virginia.edu/televangelis m.html, accessed 1/3/05.

Hagan, John. 1992. "The poverty of a classless criminology." *Criminology,* vol. 30, no. 1.

———; and McCarthy, Bill. 1992. "Mean streets: The theoretical significance of situational delinquency among homeless youth." *American Sociological Review,* vol. 98.

Haggard, Stephan. 1990. *Pathways from the Periphery: The Politics of Growth in Newly Industrializing Countries.* Ithaca, NY: Cornell University Press.

Hall, Edward T. 1969. *The Hidden Dimension.* New York: Doubleday.

———. 1973. *The Silent Language.* New York: Doubleday.

Hall, Stuart. 1992. "The question of cultural identity," in Stuart Hall, David Held, and Tony McGrew, eds., *Modernity and Its Futures.* Cambridge, UK: Polity Press.

———, et al. 1978. *Policing the Crisis: Mugging, the State, and Law and Order.* London: Macmillan.

———, et al. 1982. *The Empire Strikes Back.* London: Hutchinson.

———, et al. 1988. "New times." *Marxism Today,* October.

Halpern, Carolyn Tucker, et al. 2000. "Smart teens don't have sex (or kiss much either)." *Journal of Adolescent Health,* vol. 26, no. 3.

Hamel, G. 1991. "Competition for competence and inter-partner learning within international strategic alliances." *Strategic Management Journal,* summer supplement, vol. 12.

Hamilton, Martha M. 2000. "Web retailer Kozmo accused of redlining; Exclusion of D.C. minority areas cited." *Washington Post,* April 14.

Hammond, Phillip E. 1992. *Religion and Personal Autonomy: The Third Disestablishment in America.* Columbia, SC: University of South Carolina Press.

Handy, Charles. 1994. *The Empty Raincoat: Making Sense of the Future.* London: Hutchinson.

Hansen, Kristin A. 1995. "Geographical mobility: March 1993 to March 1994," in U.S. Bureau of the Census, *Current Population Reports, P20–485.* Washington, DC: U.S. Government Printing Office.

Hare, A. Paul; Borgatta, Edgar F.; and Bales, Robert F. 1965. *Small Groups: Studies in Social Interaction.* New York: Knopf.

Harris, Judith Rich. 1998. *The Nurture Assumption: Why Children Turn Out the Way They Do.* New York: Free Press.

Harris, Marvin. 1975. *Cows, Pigs, Wars, and Riches: The Riddles of Culture.* New York: Random House.

———. 1978. *Cannibals and Kings: The Origins of Cultures.* New York: Random House.

———. 1980. *Cultural Materialism: The Struggle for a Science of Culture.* New York: Vintage Books.

Hartley, Eugene. 1946. *Problems in Prejudice.* New York: Kings Crown Press.

Hartman, Chris. 2000. "Facts and figures on wealth." Inequality.org, www.inequality. org/factsfr.html, accessed 1/3/05.

Hartman, Mary; and Banner, Lois, eds. 1974. *Clio's Consciousness Raised: New Perspectives on the History of Women.* New York: Norton.

Hartman, Moshe; and Hartman, Harriet. 1996. *Gender Equality and American Jews.* Albany: SUNY Press.

———; and Swann, Charles. 1981. *Prime Time Preachers: The Rising Tide of Televangelism.* Reading, MA: Addison-Wesley.

Hartmann, Heidi I., et al. 1985. "An agenda for basic research on comparable worth," in H. I. Hartmann et al., eds., *Comparable Worth: New Directions for Research.* Washington, DC: National Academy Press.

Harvard Magazine. 2000. "The world's poor: A Harvard Magazine roundtable." *Harvard Magazine,* vol. 103, no. 2. www.harvard-magazine.com/ on-line/1100134.html, accessed 1/11/03.

Harvey, David. 1973. *Social Justice and the City.* Oxford, UK: Blackwell.

———. 1982. *The Limits to Capital.* Oxford, UK: Blackwell.

———. 1985. *Consciousness and the Urban Experience: Studies in the History and Theory of Capitalist Urbanization.* Oxford, UK: Blackwell.

———. 1989. *The Condition of Postmodernity.* Cambridge, MA: Blackwell.

Hathaway. 1997. "Marijuana and tolerance: Revisiting Becker's sources of control." *Deviant Behavior,* vol. 18, no. 2.

Haugen, Einar. 1977. "Linguistic relativity: Myths and methods," in William C. McCormack and Stephen A. Wurm, eds., *Language and Thought: Anthropological Issues.* The Hague: Mouton.

Hauser, Robert M. 1999. "What if we ended social promotion?" *Education Week* (April 7).

Hawkes, Terence. 1977. *Structuralism and Semiotics.* Berkeley, CA: University of California Press.

Hawley, Amos H. 1950. *Human Ecology: A Theory of Community Structure.* New York: Ronald Press Company.

———. 1968. "Human ecology," in *International Encyclopedia of Social Science,* vol. 4. New York: Free Press.

Hayflick, Leonard. 1994. *How and Why We Age.* New York: Ballantine Books.

Hays, Sharon. 2000. "Constructing the centrality of culture—and deconstructing sociology?" *Contemporary Sociology,* vol. 29, no. 4.

Health Care Financing Administration (HCFA). 1997. Medicare. www.hcfa.gov/ stats/hstats96/stathili. htm.

Healy, Melissa. 2001. "Pieces of the puzzle." *Los Angeles Times,* http://pqasb. pqarchiver.com/latimes/results.html? RQT=511&sid=1&firstIndex= 460&PQACnt=1, accessed 1/10/05.

Heaven's Gate. 1997. Mirror of original Web site is available at TELAH Services, www.wave.net/upg/gate/, accessed 1/11/05.

Hebdige, Dick. 1987. *Cut 'n' Mix: Culture, Identity, and Caribbean Music.* London: Methuen.

Heelas, Paul. 1996. *The New Age Movement.* Oxford: Blackwell.

Heidensohn, Frances. 1985. *Women and Crime.* London: Macmillan.

Heise, David R. 1987. "Sociocultural determination of mental aging," in Carmi Schooler and K. Warner Schaie, eds., *Cognitive Functioning and Social Structure Over the Life Course.* Norwood, NJ: Ablex.

Held, David. 1987. *Models of Democracy.* Stanford, CA: Stanford University Press.

———, et al. 1999. *Global Transformations: Politics, Economics, and Culture.* Cambridge, UK: Polity Press.

Helm, Leslie. 1992. "Debt puts squeeze on Japanese." *Los Angeles Times,* November 21.

Hellman, Christopher. 2003. "Last of the big spenders: U.S. military budget still the world's largest, and growing," Washington, D.C.: Center for Defense Information (May 19). http://www.cdi.org/ program/document.cfm?DocumentID=10 40&StartRow=1&ListRows=10&append URL=&Orderby=D.DateLastUpdated& ProgramID=15&from_page=index.cfm, accessed 1/3/05.

Henderson, Jeffrey. 1989. *The Globalization of High Technology Production: Society, Space, and Semiconductors in the Restructuring of the Modern World.* London: Routledge.

———; and Appelbaum, Richard P. 1992. "Situating the state in the Asian development process," in Richard P. Appelbaum and Jeffrey Henderson, eds., *States and Development in the Asian Pacific Rim.* Newbury Park, CA: Sage.

Hendricks, Jon. 1992. "Generation and the generation of theory in social gerontology." *Aging and Human Development,* vol. 35.

———; and Hendricks, C. Davis. 1986. *Aging in Mass Society: Myths and Realities.* Boston: Little, Brown.

Henry, William E. 1965. *Growing Older: The Process of Disengagement.* New York: Basic Books.

Henslin, James M.; and Biggs, Mae A. 1971. "Dramaturgical desexualization: The sociology of the vaginal examination," in James M. Henslin, ed., *Studies in the Sociology of Sex.* New York: Appleton-Century-Crofts.

———. 1997. "Behavior in public places: The sociology of the vaginal examination," in James M. Henslin, ed., *Down to Earth Sociology: Introductory Readings.* 9th ed. New York: Free Press.

Hentoff, Nat. 2002. "The FBI's magic lantern: Ashcroft can be in your computer," *The Village Voice,* May 24.

Herdt, Gilbert. 1981. *Guardians of the Flutes: Idioms of Masculinity.* New York: McGraw-Hill.

———. 1984. *Ritualized Homosexuality in Melanesia.* Berkeley, CA: University of California Press.

———. 1986. *The Sambia: Ritual and Gender in New Guinea.* New York: Holt, Rinehart and Winston.

———; and Davidson, J. 1988. "The Sambia 'urnim-man': Sociocultural and clinical aspects of gender formation in Papua, New Guinea." *Archives of Sexual Behavior,* vol. 17.

Heritage, John. 1985. *Garfinkel and Ethnomethodology.* New York: Basil Blackwell.

Hernandez, D. J. 1993. *America's Children: Resources from Family, Government, and Economy.* New York: Russell Sage Foundation.

Herrnstein, Richard J.; and Murray, Charles. 1994. *The Bell Curve: Intelligence and Class Structure in American Life.* New York: Free Press.

Hess, John L. 1990. "The catastrophic health care fiasco." *The Nation,* vol. 250.

Hesse-Biber, Sharlene. 1997. *Am I Thin Enough Yet?: The Cult of Thinness and the Commercialization of Identity.* New York: Oxford University Press.

Hexham, Irvine; and Poewe, Karla. 1997. *New Religions as Global Cultures.* Boulder, CO: Westview Press.

Higginbotham, Elizabeth. 1992. "Making up with kin and community: Upward social mobility for black and white women." *Gender and Society,* vol. 6, no. 3.

Higher Education Research Institute (HERI). 1990. "The American freshman." Los Angeles: University of California.

Hirsch, Barry T.; and Macpherson, David A. 2004. "Union membership, coverage, density, and employment among all wage and salary workers, 1973–2003." www.trinity.edu/bhirsch/unionstats/All%20Wage%20and%20Salary%20Workers.xls, accessed 1/3/05.

Hirshci, Travis. 1969. *Causes of Delinquency.* Berkeley, CA: University of California Press.

Hirst, Paul. 1997. "The global economy: Myths and realities." *International Affairs,* vol. 73.

———; and Thompson, Grahame. 1992. "The problem of 'globalization': International economic relations, national economic management, and the formation of trading blocs." *Economy and Society,* vol. 24.

———. 1999. *Globalization in Question: The International Economy and the Possibilities of Governance.* Rev. ed. Cambridge, UK: Polity Press.

Ho, S. Y. 1990. *Taiwan: After a Long Silence.* Hong Kong: Asia Monitor Resource Center.

Hochschild, Arlie Russell. 1975. "Disengagement theory: A critique and proposal." *American Sociological Review,* vol. 40.

———. 1983. *The Managed Heart: Commercialization of Human Feeling.* Berkeley, CA: University of California Press.

———. 1997. *The Time Bind.* New York: Metropolitan Books.

———; with Machung, Anne. 1989. *The Second Shift: Working Parents and the Revolution at Home.* New York: Viking.

Hodge, Robert; and Tripp, David. 1986. *Children and Television: A Semiotic Approach.* Cambridge, MA: Polity Press.

Hofstede, Geert. 1997. *Culture's Consequences: International Differences in Work-Related Values.* Newbury Park: Sage.

Hogan, Beatrice. 2000. "U.N.: Women's conference presses for political parity." Radio Free Europe, June.

Holmes, L. D. 1983. *Other Cultures, Elder Years: An Introduction to Cultural Gerontology.* Minneapolis: Burgess.

Holmes, Steven A. 1996. "Quality of life is up for many blacks, data say." *New York Times,* November 18, p. A1.

———. 1997. "New reports say minorities benefit in fiscal recovery." *New York Times,* September 30, p. A1.

Holton, Robert J. 1978. "The crowds in history: Some problems of theory and method." *Social History,* vol. 3.

Homans, George. 1950. *The Human Group.* New York: Harcourt, Brace.

Homans, Hilary. 1987. "Man-made myth: The reality of being a woman scientist in the NHS," in Anne Spencer and David Podmore, eds., *In a Man's World: Essays on Women in Male-Dominated Professions.* London: Tavistock.

Honda Worldwide. 2002. "Honda Accord best-selling car in 2001 regains title after a decade." http://world.honda.com/news/2002/c020103_2.html, accessed 1/3/05.

Hooks, Bell. 1981. *Ain't I a Woman: Black Women and Feminism.* Boston: South End Press.

———. 1996. *Bone Black: Memories of Girlhood.* New York: Henry Holt.

Hopkins, Terence K.; and Wallerstein, Immanuel. 1996. *The Age of Transition: Trajectory of the World-System, 1945–2025.* London: Zed Books.

Horrigan, John, et al. 2003. *The Ever-Shifting Internet Population: A New Look at Internet Access and the Digital Divide.* Washington, D.C.: The PEW Internet and American Life Project (April 16). www.pewinternet.org/ppt/PIP_Ever_Shifting_Internet_Pop_NCI_NIH%206.25.03nn2.ppt, accessed 1/10/05.

Hotz, Robert Lee. 1998. "Boomers firing magic bullets at signs of aging." *Los Angeles Times,* May 4.

Hout, Michael. 1988. "More universalism, less structural mobility: The American occupational structure in the 1980s." *American Journal of Sociology,* vol. 93.

———. 1997. "Inequality at the margins: The effects of welfare, the minimum wage, and tax credits on low-wage labor markets." *Politics and Society* vol. 25 (December): 513–24.

———; and Lucas, Samuel R. 1996. "Education's role in reducing income disparities." *The Education Digest,* vol. 62, no. 3.

Howard, John H., et al. 1986. "Change in Type A behavior a year after retirement." *Gerontologist,* vol. 26.

Huber, Joan. 1990. "Macro-micro link in gender stratification," *American Sociological Review,* vol. 55.

———, ed. 1992. *Micro-Macro Linkages in Sociology.* Newbury Park, CA: Sage.

Hudson, Terese. 1995. "Medicaid's new crisis: Are we pitting the elderly against the poor?" *Hospitals and Health Networks,* May 20.

Hughes, Everett C. 1945. "Dilemmas and contradictions of status." *American Journal of Sociology,* vol. 50.

Hughes, Gordon. 1991. "Taking crime seriously?: A critical analysis of new left realism." *Sociology Review,* vol. 1.

Human Rights Watch. 1995. "The global report on women's human rights," www.hrw.org/about/projects/womrep/, accessed 1/3/05.

Humphreys, Laud. 1970. *Tearoom Trade: Impersonal Sex in Public Places.* Chicago: Aldine.

Hunter, James Davison. 1987. *Evangelism: The Coming Generation.* Chicago: University of Chicago Press.

Hunter, Lisa. 1990. *After Bereavement: A Study of Change in Attitudes about Life among Older Widows.* Ph.D. diss., The Fielding Institute, Santa Barbara, CA.

Huntington, Samuel P. 1991. *The Third Wave: Democratization in the Late Twentieth Century.* Norman, OK: University of Oklahoma Press.

——. 1996. *The Clash of Civilizations and the Remaking of World Order.* New York: Simon and Schuster.

Hurtado, A. 1995. "Variation, combinations, and evolutions: Latino families in the United States," in R. Zambrana, ed., *Understanding Latino Families.* Thousand Oaks, CA: Sage.

Hyman, Herbert H.; and Singer, Eleanor. 1968. *Readings in Reference Group Theory and Research.* New York: Free Press.

Hyman, Richard. 1984. *Strikes.* 2nd ed. London: Fontana.

Illich, Ivan D. 1983. *Deschooling Society.* New York: Harper and Row.

Infoplease.com. 2003. "Educational Attainment by Race and Hispanic Origin, 1940–2001" www.infoplease.com/ipa/A0774057.html, accessed 1/3/05.

Inglehart, Ronald. 1997. *Modernization and Postmodernization: Cultural, Economic and Political Change in 43 Societies.* Princeton, NJ: Princeton University Press.

Intelligence Report. 2001. "Reevaluating the Net." Summer, no. 102. Montgomery, AL: The Southern Poverty Law Center.

International Campaign to Ban Land Mines (ICBL). 2001. www.icbl.org, accessed 1/3/05.

——. 2003. "Ratifications update" www.icbl.org, accessed 1/3/05.

International Labor Organization (ILO). 1995. "Women work more, but are still paid less." Press release. www.ilo.org/public/english/bureau/pr/1995/22.htm, accessed 1/11/05.

——. 1997. "Women's progress in workforce improving worldwide, but occupational segregation still rife: 'Glass ceiling' separates women from top jobs." Geneva: ILO press release ILO/97/35. www.ilo.org/public/english/bureau/inf/pr/1997/35.htm, accessed 1/11/05.

——. 1999. C182 Worst Forms of Child Labour Convention, www.ilo.org/public/english/standards/ipec/ratification/convention/text.htm, accessed 1/11/05.

——. 2000. "Statistical information and monitoring programme on child labour (SIMPOC): Overview and strategic plan 2000–2002." Prepared by the International Program on the Elimination of Child Labour (IPEC) and Bureau of Statistics (STAT), January.

——. 2003a. "Facts on Women at Work" www.ilo.org/public/english/bureau/inf/download/women/pdf/factssheet.pdf, accessed 1/3/05.

——. 2003b. LABORSTA. http://laborsta.ilo.org/, accessed 1/3/05.

International Lesbian and Gay Association (ILGA). 2001. www.ilga.org, accessed 1/3/05.

International Telework Association & Council (ITAC). 2004. "Telework Facts and Figures," www.telecommute.org/resources/abouttelework.htm, accessed 1/20/05.

Internet Society (ISOC). 1997. "Web Languages Hit Parade," http://alis.isoc.org/palmares.en.html, accessed 1/11/05.

Iyer, Pico. 1989. *Video Nights in Katmandu.* New York: Vintage.

Jacobs, Jane. 1961. *The Death and Life of Great American Cities.* New York: Random House.

Jacoby, Sanford. 1997. *Modern Manors: Welfare Capitalism since the New Deal.* Princeton, NJ: Princeton University Press.

Jaher, Frederic Cople, ed. 1973. *The Rich, the Well Born, and the Powerful.* Urbana, IL: University of Illinois Press.

Jamieson, Amie; Shin, Hyon B.; and Day, Jennifer. 2002. "Voting and registration in the election of November 2000: Population characteristics." U.S. Department of Commerce, U.S. Census Bureau. February 2002. www.census.gov/prod/2002pubs/p20-542.pdf, accessed 1/3/05.

Janis, Irving L. 1972. *Victims of Groupthink.* Boston: Houghton Mifflin.

——. 1989. *Crucial Decisions: Leadership in Policy Making and Crisis Management.* New York: Free Press.

——; and Mann, Leon. 1977. *Decision Making: A Psychological Analysis of Conflict, Choice, and Commitment.* New York: Free Press.

Jencks, Christopher. 1994. *The Homeless.* Cambridge, MA: Harvard University Press.

——, et al. 1972. *Inequality: A Reassessment of the Effects of Family and School in America.* New York: Basic Books.

Jenkins, Henry. 1998. *From Barbie to Mortal Kombat: Gender and Computer Games.* Cambridge, MA: MIT Press.

Jensen, Arthur. 1967. "How much can we boost IQ and scholastic achievement?" *Harvard Educational Review,* vol. 29.

——. 1979. *Bias in Mental Testing.* New York: Free Press.

Jobling, Ray. 1988. "The experience of psoriasis under treatment," in Michael Bury and Robert Anderson, eds., *Living with Chronic Illness: The Experience of Patients and Their Families.* London: Unwin Hyman.

John, M. T. 1988. *Geragogy: A Theory for Teaching the Elderly.* New York: Haworth.

Johnson, Michael P. 1995. "Patriarchal terrorism and common couple violence: Two forms of violence against women in U.S. families." *Journal of Marriage and the Family,* vol. 57.

Johnson, M.; and Morton, J. 1991. *Biology and Cognitive Development: The Case of Face Recognition.* Oxford, UK: Blackwell.

Johnson-Odim, Cheryl. 1991. "Common themes, different contexts: Third World women and feminism," in Chandra Mohanty, et al., eds., *Third World Women and the Politics of Feminism.* Bloomington, IN: Indiana University Press.

——; and Strobel, Margaret, eds. 1992. *Expanding the Boundaries of Women's History: Essays on Women in the Third World.* Bloomington, IN: Indiana University Press.

Johnston, Hank; Larana, Enrique; and Gusfield, Joseph R. 1994. "Identities, grievances, and new social movements," in Enrique Larana, Hank Johnston, and Joseph R. Gusfield (eds.), *New Social Movements: From Ideology to Identity.* Philadelphia, PA: Temple University Press.

Joint Center for Housing Studies. 1994. *The State of the Nation's Housing.* Cambridge, MA: Harvard University Press.

Jones, Eric. 1998. "Globalism and the American tide." *National Interest,* vol. 53 (fall).

Jones, Jacqueline. 1986. *Labor of Love, Labor of Sorrow: Black Women, Work, and the Family from Slavery to the Present.* New York: Random House.

Jones, S. G. 1995. "Understanding community in the information age." in S. G. Jones, ed., *CyberSociety: Computer-Mediated Communication and Community.* Thousand Oaks, CA: Sage.

Jordan, Winthrop. 1968. *White over Black.* Chapel Hill: University of North Carolina Press.

Judd, Dennis R.; and Fainstein, Susan S., eds. 1999. *The Tourist City.* New Haven, CT: Yale University Press.

Judge, Ken. 1995. "Income distribution and life expectancy: A critical appraisal." *British Medical Journal,* vol. 311.

Juergensmeyer, Mark. 1993. *The New Cold War? Religious Nationalism Confronts the Secular State.* Berkeley, CA: University of California Press.

———. 2001. *Terror in the Mind of God: The Global Rise of Religious Violence.* Berkeley, CA: University of California Press.

Kamin, Leon J. 1974. *The Science and Politics of IQ.* Hillsdale, NJ: Erlbaum.

Kanter, Rosabeth Moss. 1977. *Men and Women of the Corporation.* New York: Basic Books.

———. 1983. *The Change Masters: Innovation for Productivity in the American Corporation.* New York: Simon and Schuster.

———. 1991. "The future of bureaucracy and hierarchy in organizational theory," in Pierre Bourdieu and James Coleman, eds., *Social Theory for a Changing Society.* Boulder, CO: Westview.

Kasarda, John. 1993. "Urban industrial transition and the underclass," in William Julius Wilson, ed., *The Ghetto Underclass.* Newbury Park, CA: Sage.

———; and Crenshaw, Edward M. 1991. "Third World urbanization: Dimensions, theories, and determinants," in *Annual Review of Sociology 1991.* Vol. 17. Palo Alto, CA: Annual Reviews.

———; and Janowitz, Morris. 1974. "Community attachment in mass society." *American Sociological Review,* vol. 39.

Katz, Jack. 1999. *How Emotions Work.* Chicago: University of Chicago Press.

Katz, Sidney, et al. 1983. "Active life expectancy." *New England Journal of Medicine,* vol. 309.

Kautsky, John J. 1982. *The Politics of Aristocratic Empires.* Chapel Hill, NC: University of North Carolina Press.

Kearny and *Foreign Policy.* 2001. "Measuring Globalization." A. T. Kearney, Inc. and *Foreign Policy* (January–February).

Kedouri, Elie. 1992. *Politics in the Middle East.* New York: Oxford University Press.

Keister, Lisa A. 2000. *Wealth in America: Trends in Wealth Inequality.* New York: Cambridge University Press.

Kelling, George L.; and Coles, Catherine M. 1997. *Fixing Broken Windows: Restoring Order and Reducing Crime in Our Communities.* New York: The Free Press.

Kelley, Jonathan; and Evans, M. D. R. 1995. "Class and class conflict in six western nations." *American Review of Sociology,* vol. 60, no. 2.

Kelly, Liz. 1987. "The continuum of sexual violence," in Jala Hanmer and Mary Maynard, eds., *Women, Violence, and Social Control.* Atlantic Highlands, NJ: Humanities Press.

Kelly, Michael P. 1992. *Colitis: The Experience of Illness.* London: Routledge.

Kelsey, Tim. 1996. "I want to live forever." *Sunday Times News Review,* January 7.

Kemp, Amanda, et al. 1995. "The dawn of a new day: Redefining South African feminism," in Amrita Basu, ed., *The Challenge of Local Feminisms.* Boulder, CO: Westview.

Kenway, Jane, et al. 1995. "Pulp fictions?: Education, markets, and the information superhighway." *Australian Educational Researcher,* vol. 22.

Kenworthy, Lane; and Malami, Melissa. 1999. "Gender inequality in political representation: A worldwide comparative analysis." *Social Forces,* vol. 78, no. 1.

Kern, Steven. 1983. *The Culture of Time and Space: 1880–1918.* Cambridge, MA: Harvard University Press.

Kerr, Clark, et al. 1960. *Industrialism and Industrial Man: The Problems of Labor and Management in Economic Growth.* Cambridge, MA: Harvard University Press.

Kiecolt, K. Jill; and Nelson, Hart M. 1991. "Evangelicals and party realignment, 1976–1988," *Social Science Quarterly,* vol. 72 (September).

King, Nancy R. 1984. "Exploitation and abuse of older family members: An overview of the problem," in J. J. Cosa, ed., *Abuse of the Elderly.* Lexington, MA: Lexington Books.

Kinsey, Alfred C., et al. 1948. *Sexual Behavior in the Human Male.* Philadelphia: Saunders.

———. 1953. *Sexual Behavior in the Human Female.* Philadelphia: Saunders.

Kinsley, David. 1982. *Hinduism: A Cultural Perspective.* Englewood Cliffs, NJ: Prentice Hall.

Kjekshus, H. 1977. *Ecology, Control, and Economic Development in East African History.* Berkeley, CA: University of California Press.

Kling, Robert. 1996. "Computerization at work," in R. Kling, ed., *Computers and Controversy.* 2nd ed. New York: Academic Press.

Kluckhohn, Clyde. 1949. *Mirror for Man.* Tucson: University of Arizona Press.

Knight, F. H. 1933. *Risk, Uncertainty, and Profit.* London: London School of Economics and Political Science.

Knoke, David. 1990. *Political Networks: The Structural Perspective.* New York: Cambridge University Press.

Knorr-Cetina, Karen; and Cicourel, Aaron V., eds. 1981. *Advances in Social Theory and Methodology: Towards an Integration of Micro- and Macro-Sociologies.* Boston: Routledge and Kegan Paul.

Kohn, Melvin. 1977. *Class and Conformity,* 2nd ed. Homewood, IL: Dorsey Press.

Kollock, P.; and Smith, M. A. 1996. "Managing the virtual commons: Cooperation and conflict in computer communities," in S. Herring, ed., *Computer-Mediated Communication.* Amsterdam: John Benjamins.

Kosmin, Barry A. 1991. *Research Report: The National Survey of Religious Identification.* New York: City University of New York Graduate Center.

———; Mayer, Egon; and Keysar, Ariela. 2001. *American Religious Identification Survey (ARIS).* New York: CUNY Graduate Center (December 19). www.gc.cuny.edu/studies/aris.pdf, accessed 1/3/05.

Kozol, Jonathan. 1991. *Savage Inequalities: Children in America's Schools.* New York: Crown.

Kroeger, Brooke. 2004. "When a dissertation makes a difference," *New York Times,* March 20.

Krueger, Colleen. 1995. "Retirees with company heath plans on decline." *Los Angeles Times,* September 22.

Kulkarni, V. G. 1993. "The productivity paradox: Rising output, stagnant living standards." *BusinessWeek,* February 8.

Kuznets, Simon. 1955. "Economic growth and income inequality." *Economic Review,* vol. XLV, no. 1.

Lacayo, Richard. 1994. "Lock 'em up!" *Time,* February 7.

Laing, R. D. 1971. *Self and Others.* London: Tavistock.

Lake, R. 1981. *The New Suburbanites: Race and Housing in the Suburbs.* New Brunswick, NJ: Center for Urban Policy Research, Rutgers University Press.

Lambert, Richard. 1995. "Foreign student flows and the internationalization of higher education," in Katharine Hanson and Joel Meyerson, eds., *International Challenges to American Colleges and Universities.* Phoenix: Orynx Press.

Lammers, Cristina, et al. 2000. "Influences on adolescents' decision to postpone onset of sexual intercourse: A survival analysis of virginity among youths aged 13 to 18 years." *Journal of Adolescent Health,* vol. 26, no. 1.

Land, Kenneth C.; Deane, Glenn; and Blau, Judith R. 1991. "Religious pluralism and church membership." *American Sociological Review,* vol. 56.

Landale, N., and Fennelly, K. 1992. "Informal unions among mainland Puerto Ricans: Cohabitation or an alternative to legal marriage?" *Journal of Marriage and the Family,* vol. 54.

Landes, David S. 1969. *The Unbound Prometheus.* New York: Cambridge University Press.

Landry, Bart. 1988. *The New Black Middle Class.* Berkeley, CA: University of California Press.

Lane, Harlan. 1976. *The Wild Boy of Aveyron.* Cambridge, MA: Harvard University Press.

Lane, James B. 1974. *Jacob A. Riis: The American City.* New York: Kennikat Press.

Lantenari, Vittorio. 1963. *The Religions of the Oppressed: A Study of Modern Messianic Cults.* New York: Knopf.

Lappe, France Moore, et al. 1998. *World Hunger: 12 Myths.* 2nd ed. New York: Grove Press.

Lash, Scott; and Urry, John. 1987. *The End of Organized Capitalism.* Madison, WI: University of Wisconsin Press.

Lashbrook, Jeff. 1996. "Promotional timetables: An exploratory investigation of age norms for promotional expectations and their association with job well-being." *Gerontologist,* vol. 36, no. 2.

Laslett, P. 1991. *A Fresh Map of Life.* Cambridge, MA: Harvard University Press.

Laumann, Edward O., et al. 1994. *The Social Organization of Sexuality: Sexual Practices in the United States.* Chicago: University of Chicago Press.

Lawrence, Bruce B. 1989. *Defenders of God: The Fundamentalist Revolt Against the Modern Age.* San Francisco: Harper & Row.

Lazarsfeld, Paul F.; Berelson, Bernard; and Gaudet, Hazel. 1948. *The People's Choice.* New York: Columbia University Press.

Lea, John; and Young, Jock. 1984. *What Is to Be Done about Law and Order?* London: Penguin.

Leach, Edmund. 1976. *Culture and Communication: The Logic by Which Symbols Are Connected.* New York: Cambridge University Press.

Leadbeater, Charles. 1999. *Living on Thin Air: The New Economy.* New York: Viking.

Lee, Gary. 1982. *Family Structure and Interaction: A Comparative Analysis.* 2nd ed. Minneapolis: University of Minnesota Press.

Lee, Richard B. 1968. "What hunters do for a living, or how to make out on scarce resources," in Richard B. Lee and Irven DeVore, eds., *Man the Hunter.* Chicago: Aldine.

———. 1969. "!Kung bushman subsistence: An input-output analysis," in A. P. Vayda, ed., *Environment and Cultural Behavior.* New York: Natural History Press.

Lees, Andrew. 1985. *Cities Perceived: Urban Society in European and American Thought, 1820–1940.* New York: Columbia University Press.

Lehrer, Warren; and Sloan, Judith. 2003. *Crossing the BLVD: Strangers, Neighbors, Aliens in a New America.* New York: Norton.

Lemert, Edwin. 1972. *Human Deviance, Social Problems, and Social Control.* Englewood Cliffs, NJ: Prentice-Hall.

Leonhardt, David. 2001. "Belt tightening seen as threat to the economy." *New York Times,* July 15, p. 1.

Lepkowsky, M. 1990. "Gender in an egalitarian society: A case study from the Coral Sea," in P. R. Sandy and R. G. Goodenough, eds., *Beyond the Second Sex.* Philadelphia: University of Pennsylvania Press.

Leupp, Gary P. 1995. *Male Colors, the Construction of Homosexuality in Tokugawa Japan.* Berkeley, CA: University of California Press.

Levay, Simon. 1996. *Queer Science: The Uses and Abuses of Research into Homosexuality.* Cambridge, MA: MIT Press.

Levin, William C. 1988. "Age stereotyping: College student evaluations." *Research on Aging,* vol. 10.

Lewis, Oscar. 1968. "The culture of poverty," in Daniel P. Moyhihan, ed., *On Understanding Poverty: Perspectives from the Social Sciences.* New York: Basic Books.

Liebow, Elliot. 1967. *Tally's Corner: A Study of Negro Streetcorner Men.* Boston: Little, Brown.

———. 1993. *Tell Them Who I Am: The Lives of Homeless Women.* New York: Free Press.

Lightfoot-Klein, Hanny. 1989. *Prisoners of Ritual: An Odyssey into Female Genital Circumcision in Africa.* New York: Haworth.

Lipset, Seymour Martin, ed. 1981. *Party Coalitions in the 1980s.* San Francisco: Institute for Contemporary Affairs.

———. 1991. "Comments on Luckmann," in Pierre Bourdieu and James S. Coleman, eds., *Social Theory in a Changing Society.* Boulder, CO: Westview.

———; and Bendix, Reinhard. 1959. *Social Mobility in Industrial Society.* Berkeley, CA: University of California Press.

Littlefield, Nick. 1992. "Education," in Mark Green, ed., *Changing America: Blueprint for the New Administration.* New York: New Market Press.

Locke, John. 2000. "Can a sense of community flourish in cyberspace?" *The Guardian,* March 11.

Lofland, Lyn H. 1973. *A World of Strangers.* New York: Basic Books.

———. 1998. *The Public Realm: Exploring the City's Quintessential Social Territory.* New York: Aldine de Gruyter.

Logan, John R.; and Molotch, Harvey L. 1987. *Urban Fortunes: The Political Economy of Place.* Berkeley, CA: University of California Press.

Long, Elizabeth, ed. 1997. *From Sociology to Cultural Studies: New Perspectives.* Malden, MA: Blackwell.

Longino, Charles F. 1995. *The Old Age Challenge to the Biomedical Model: Paradigm Strain and Health Policy.* Amityville, NY: Baywood Publications.

Loprest, Pamela. 1999. "Families who left welfare: Who are they and how are they doing?" Washington, DC: Urban Institute, www.urban.org/Template.cfm?NavMenu ID=24&template=/TaggedContent/View Publication.cfm&PublicationID=7297, accessed 1/3/05.

Lorber, Judith. 1994. *Paradoxes of Gender.* New Haven, CT: Yale University Press.

Loury, Glenn. 1987. "Why should we care about group inequality?" *Social Philosophy and Policy,* vol. 5.

Lowe, Graham S. 1987. *Women in the Administrative Revolution: The Feminization of Clerical Work.* Toronto: University of Toronto Press.

Lull, James. 1991. *China Turned On: Television, Reform, and Resistance.* New York: Routledge.

Lyman, Richard. 1995. "Overview," in Katharine Hanson and Joel Meyerson, eds., *International Challenges to American Colleges and Universities.* Phoenix: Orynx Press.

Lynd, Robert; and Lynd, Helen. 1929. *Middletown: A Study in Contemporary American Culture.* New York: Harcourt, Brace, and Co.

Lyon, David. 1989. *The Information Society: Issues and Illusions.* New York: Basil Blackwell.

———. 1994. *The Electronic Eye: The Rise of Surveillance Society.* Minneapolis: University of Minnesota Press.

Lyotard, Jean-François. 1985. *The Post-Modern Condition: A Report on Knowledge.* Minneapolis: University of Minnesota Press.

Macenoin, Deni; and al-Shahi, Ahmed, eds., 1983. *Islam in the Modern World.* New York: St. Martin's Press.

Maddox, G. L. 1965. "Fact and artifact: Evidence bearing on disengagement from the Duke Geriatrics Project." *Human Development,* vol. 8.

———. 1970. "Themes and issues in sociological theories of human aging." *Human Development,* vol. 13.

Madigan, F. C. 1957. "Are sex mortality differentials biologically caused?" *Millbank Memorial Fund Quarterly,* vol. 25.

Maharidge, Dale. 1996. *The Coming White Minority.* New York: Times Books.

Malinowski, Bronislaw. 1982. *"Magic: Science and Religion" and Other Essays.* London: Souvenir Press.

Malotki, Ekkehart. 1983. *Hopi Time: A Linguistic Analysis of the Temporal Concepts in the Hopi Language.* Berlin: Mouton.

Malthus, Thomas. 2003. *Essay on the Principle of Population: A Norton Critical Edition, Revised Edition.* Ed. Philip Appleman. Originally published 1798. New York: Norton.

Manning, John T.; Koukourakis, K.; and Brodie, D. A. 1997. "Fluctuating asymmetry, metabolic rate and sexual selection in human males." *Evolution and Human Behavior,* vol. 18, no. 1.

Manpower, Inc. 2003. "Facts & Figures." www.manpower.co.uk/about_manpower/main_facts_figures.asp, accessed 1/3/05.

Manton, Kenneth G.; Corder, Larry S.; and Stallard, Eric. 1993. "Estimates of change in chronic disability and institutional incidence and prevalence rates in the U.S. elderly population from the 1982, 1984, and 1989 national long term care survey." *Journal of Gerontology,* vol. 48, no. 466.

Mare, Robert D. 1991. "Five decades of educational assortative mating." *American Sociological Review,* vol. 56, no. 1.

Marsden, Peter. 1987. "Core discussion networks of Americans." *American Sociological Review,* vol. 52.

———; and Lin, Nan. 1982. *Social Structure and Network Analysis.* Beverly Hills, CA: Sage.

Marshall, T. H. 1973. *Class, Citizenship, and Social Development: Essays by T. H. Marshall.* Westport, CT: Greenwood Press.

Martin, David. 1990. *Tongues of Fire: The Explosion of Protestantism in Latin America.* Cambridge, UK: Blackwell.

Martin, Kay; and Voorhies, Barbara. 1975. *Female of the Species.* New York: Columbia University Press.

Martin, Richard C. 1982. *Islam: A Cultural Perspective.* Englewood Cliffs, NJ: Prentice Hall.

Martineau, Harriet. 1962. *Society in America.* Originally published 1837. Garden City, NY: Doubleday.

Marty, Martin E.; and Appleby, R. Scott, eds. 1995. *Fundamentalisms Comprehended.* Chicago, IL: University of Chicago Press.

Marx, Karl. 1977. *Capital: A Critique of Political Economy.* Vol. 1. Originally published 1864. New York: Random House.

Massey, Douglas S. 1996. "The age of extremes: Concentrated affluence and poverty in the twenty-first century." *Demography,* vol. 33, no. 4.

———; and Denton, Nancy A. 1993. *American Apartheid: Segregation and the Making of the Underclass.* Cambridge, MA: Harvard University Press.

Matsueda, Ross L. 1992. "Reflected appraisals, parental labeling, and delinquency: Specifying a symbolic interactionist theory." *American Journal of Sociology,* vol. 97.

Matthews, Roger; and Young, Jock, eds. 1986. *Confronting Crime.* London: Sage.

Maugh, Thomas H., II. 1991. "Survey of identical twins links biological factors with being gay." *Los Angeles Times,* December 15.

———. 1993. "Genetic compound found in lesbianism, study says." *Los Angeles Times,* March 12.

———; and Zamichow, Nora. 1991. "Medicine: San Diego's researcher's findings offer first evidence of a biological cause for homosexuality." *Los Angeles Times,* August 30.

Mayer, Susan; and Jencks, Christopher. 1994. "Trends in the economic well-being of children." Unpublished manuscript, cited in David Whitman, "The poor aren't poorer." *U.S. News and World Report* (July 25).

McCaffrey, Barry. 1998. "Prepared statement before the senate committee on the judiciary, 6/17/98." Federal News Service, n.p.

McFadden, Dennis; and Champlin, C. A. 2000. "Comparison of auditory evoked potentials in heterosexual, homosexual, and bisexual males and females." *Journal of the Association for Research in Otolaryngology,* vol. 1.

McKinlay, J. B. 1975. "A case for refocusing downstream: The political economy of illness," in P. Conrad and R. Kern, eds., *The Sociology of Health and Illness: Critical Perspectives.* New York: St. Martin's Press.

McLanahan, Sara; and Sandefur, Gary. 1994. *Growing Up with a Single Parent: What Hurts, What Helps.* Cambridge, MA: Harvard University Press.

McLuhan, Marshall. 1964. *Understanding Media.* London: Routledge and Kegan Paul.

McMichael, Philip. 1996. *Development and Social Change: A Global Perspective.* Thousand Oaks, CA: Pine Forge.

McNeely, Connie L. 1995. *Constructing the Nation-State: International Organization and Prescriptive Action.* Westport, CT: Greenwood.

Mead, Margaret. 1963. *Sex and Temperament in Three Primitive Societies.* Originally published 1935. New York: William Morrow.

———. 1972. *Blackberry Winter: My Earlier Years.* New York: William Morrow.

Meadows, Donnella H., et al. 1972. *The Limits to Growth.* New York: Universe Books.

Meatto, Keith. 2000. "Real reformers, real results: Our seventh annual roundup of student protest." *Mojo Wire Magazine,* September–October, www.mojones.com/mother_jones/SO00/activist_campuses.html, accessed 1/3/05.

Melton, J. Gordon. 1989. *The Encyclopedia of American Religions,* 3rd ed. Detroit, MI: Gale Research Co.

———. 1996. *The Encyclopedia of American Religions,* 5th ed. Detroit, MI: Gale Research Co.

Menn, Joseph. 2003. "The 'geeks' who once shunned activism amid the digital revolution are using their money and savvy to influence public policy," *Los Angeles Times,* August 11, p. A-1.

Merkyl, Peter H.; and Smart, Ninian, eds. 1983. *Religion and Politics in the Modern World.* New York: New York University Press.

Merton, Robert K. 1957. *Social Theory and Social Structure.* Rev. ed. New York: Free Press.

———. 1968. "Social structure and anomie." Originally published 1938. *American Sociological Review,* vol. 3.

———; and Rossi, Alice Kitt. 1968. "Contributions to the theory of reference group behavior," in Robert K. Merton, ed., *Social Theory and Social Structure.* Originally published 1949. Glencoe, IL: Free Press.

Meserve, Jason. 1999. "Bush takes to the Web." *Network World Fusion News* (December 9).

Meyer, John W.; and Rowan, Brian. 1977. "Institutionalized organizations: Formal structure as myth and ceremony." *American Journal of Sociology,* vol. 83.

Michels, Robert. 1967. *Political Parties.* Originally published 1911. New York: Free Press.

Milgram, Stanley. 1963. "Behavioral studies in obedience." *Journal of Abnormal Psychology,* vol. 67.

Milkman, Ruth. 1997. *Farewell to the Factory: Auto Workers in the Late Twentieth Century.* Berkeley, CA: University of California Press.

Mills, C. Wright. 1956. *The Power Elite.* New York: Oxford University Press.

———. 1959. *The Sociological Imagination.* New York: Oxford University Press.

Mills, Theodore J. 1967. *The Sociology of Small Groups.* Englewood, NJ: Prentice-Hall.

Miner, Horace. 1956. "Body ritual among the Nacirema." *American Anthropologist,* vol. 58.

Miniter, Richard. 1997. "This generation means business." *Reader's Digest,* vol. 151.

Mintzberg, Henry. 1979. *The Structuring of Organizations.* Englewood Cliffs, NJ: Prentice-Hall.

Mirsky, Jonathan. 1982. "China and the one child family." *New Society* (February 18), no. 59.

Mirza, H. 1986. *Multinationals and the Growth of the Singapore Economy.* New York: St. Martin's Press.

Mitchell, Juliet. 1975. *Psychoanalysis and Feminism.* New York: Random House.

Mitchell, W. 1995. *City of Bits: Space, Time and the Infobahn.* Cambridge, MA: MIT Press.

Mitnick, Kevin. 2000. "They call me a criminal." *The Guardian* (February 22).

Modood, Tariq, et al. 1997. *Ethnic Minorities in Britain: Diversity and Disadvantage.* London: Policy Studies Institute.

Moen, Phyllis. 1995. "A life course approach to postretirement roles and well-being," in Lynne A. Bond, Stephen J. Cutler, and Armin Grams, eds., *Promoting Successful and Productive Aging.* Newbury Park: Sage.

———. 1996. "Changing age trends: The pyramid upside down?" in U. Bronfenbrenner, P. McClelland, E. Wethington, P. Moen, and S. J. Ceci, eds., *The State of Americans.* New York: Free Press.

Moffitt, Terrie E. 1996. "The neuropsychology of conduct disorder," in P. Cordella and L. Siegel, eds., *Readings in Contemporary Criminological Theory.* Boston: Northeastern University Press.

Mohanty, Chandra Talpade. 1991. "Under Western eyes: Feminist scholarship and colonial discourse," in Chandra Talpade Mohanty, Ann Russo, and Lourdes Torres, eds., *Third World Women and the Politics of Feminism.* Bloomington, IN: Indiana University Press.

Molnar, Alex. 1996. *Giving Kids the Business: The Commercialization of America's Schools.* Boulder, CO: Westview.

Molowe, Jill. 1994. ". . . and throw away the key." *Time* (February 7).

Money, John; and Ehrhardt, Anke A. 1972. *Man and Woman, Boy and Girl.* Baltimore: Johns Hopkins University Press.

Moore, Barrington, Jr. 1966. *Social Origins of Dictatorship and Democracy: Lord and Peasant in the Making of the Modern World.* Boston: Beacon Press.

Moore, Gwen. 1990. "Structural determinants of men's and women's personal networks." *American Sociological Review,* vol. 55.

Moore, Laurence R. 1994. *Selling God: American Religion in the Marketplace of Culture.* New York: Oxford University Press.

Morawska, Eva. 1986. *For Bread with Butter: Life Worlds of East-Central Europeans in Johnstown, Pennsylvania, 1890–1940.* New York: Cambridge University Press.

Mor-Barak, Michal E., et al. 1992. "Employment, social networks, and health in the retirement years." *International Journal of Aging and Human Development,* vol. 35.

Morgan, S. Philip, et al. 1993. "Racial differences in household and family structure at the turn of the century." *American Journal of Sociology,* vol. 98.

Morris, Jan. 1974. *Conundrum.* New York: Harcourt Brace Jovanovich.

Moss, Miriam S.; Moss, Sidney Z.; and Moles, Elizabeth L. 1985. "The quality of relationships between elderly parents and their out-of-town children." *Gerontologist,* vol. 25.

Moynihan, Daniel Patrick. 1965. *The Negro Family: A Case for National Action.* Washington, DC: U.S. Government Printing Office.

———. 1993. "Defining deviancy down." *American Scholar,* vol. 62, no. 1.

Mumford, Lewis. 1973. *Interpretations and Forecasts.* New York: Harcourt Brace Jovanovich.

Muncie, John. 1999. *Youth and Crime: A Critical Introduction.* London: Sage.

Murdock, George Peter. 1949. *Social Structure.* New York: Macmillan.

Murray, Charles A. 1984. *Losing Ground: American Social Policy, 1950–1980.* New York: Basic Books.

Najman, Jake M. 1993. "Health and poverty: past, present, and prospects for the future." *Social Science and Medicine,* vol. 36, no. 2.

Narayan, Deepa. 1999. *Can Anyone Hear Us? Voices From 47 Countries.* Washington, DC: World Bank Poverty Group, PREM (December).

National Center for Health Statistics. 2001. *Health—United States 2001/2000* Washington, DC: U.S. Government Printing Office.

———. 2000. *Health, United States 2001/2000 with Adolescent Chartbook.* Hyattsville, MD: NCHS.

———. 2002a. "New report sheds light on trends and patterns in marriage, divorce, and cohabitation." www.cdc.gov/nchs/pressroom/02news/div_mar_cohab.htm, accessed 1/10/05.

———. 2002b. "Women are having more children, new report shows teen births continue to decline." www.cdc.gov/nchs/pressroom/02news/womenbirths.htm, accessed 1/10/05.

———. 2003a. "Table 61: Current cigarette smoking by adults according to sex, race, Hispanic origin, age and education: The United States, average annual 1990–92, 1995–98 and 1999–2001." www.cdc.gov/nchs/data/hus/tables/2003/03hus061.pdf, accessed 1/3/05.

———. 2003b. "Table 68: Hypertension among persons 20 years of age and over, according to sex, age, race, and Hispanic origin: United States, 1960–62, 1971–74, 1976–80, 1988–94 and 1999–2000." www.cdc.gov/nchs/data/hus/tables/2003/03husupdated.pdf, accessed 1/10/05.

———. 2003c. "Table 80: Use of mammography for women 40 years of age and over according to selected characteristics: United States, selected years 1987–2000." www.cdc.gov/nchs/data/hus/tables/2003/03hus080.pdf, accessed 1/3/05.

———. 2003d. "Table 78: Dental visits in the past year according to selected characteristics: United States, selected years 1997–2001." www.cdc.gov/nchs/data/hus/tables/2003/03hus078.pdf, accessed 1/3/05.

———. 2003e. "Women's health." www.cdc.gov/nchs/fastats/womens_health.htm, accessed 1/11/05.

———. 2003f. "Men's Health." www.cdc.gov/nchs/fastats/men.htm, accessed 1/3/05.

National Governors Association (NGA). 2003. "Trivia." www.nga.org/governors/1,1169,C_TRIVIA^D_2117,00.html, accessed 1/3/05.

National Interfaith Committee for Worker Justice (NICWJ). 1998. "Cross border blues: A call for justice for Maquiladora workers in Tehuacán." (July) Chicago, IL: NICWJ.

National Low Income Housing Coalition (NLIHC). 2000. *Out of Reach: The Growing Gap between Housing Costs and Income of Poor People in the United States.* (September) Washington, DC: The National Low Income Housing Coalition/Low Income Housing Information Service, www.nlihc.org/oor2000/index.htm, accessed 1/3/05.

National Opinion Research Center. 1994, 1998. *General Social Survey.* Chicago: National Opinion Research Center.

National Research Council. 1994. *Information Technology in the Service Society.* Washington, DC: National Academy Press.

NCES. 2000. *Teachers' Tools for the 21st Century: A Report on Teachers' Use of Technology.* National Center for Education Statistics, Office of Educational Research and Improvement, U.S. Department of Education. NCES 2000-102 (September) http://nces.ed.gov/pubs2000/2000102.pdf, accessed 1/3/05.

Negroponte, Nicholas. 1995. *Being Digital.* London: Hodder and Stoughton.

Nelson, E. Anne; and Dannefer, Dale. 1992. "Aged heterogeneity: Fact or fiction? The fate of diversity in gerontological research." *Gerontologist,* vol. 32.

NES. 2003. "The NES Guide to Public Opinion and Electoral Behavior, The National Election Studies, Graph 5A.1.2," Center for Political Studies, University of Michigan. Ann Arbor, MI: University of Michigan, Center for Political Studies. www.umich.edu/~nes/nesguide/graphs/g5a_1_2.htm, accessed 1/3/05.

———. 2003. *The National Election Studies,* "The NES Guide to Public Opinion and Electoral Behavior—Voter Turnout 1948–2002," Table 6A.2. www.umich.edu/~nes/nesguide/toptable/tab6a_2.htm, accessed 1/3/05.

Neuman, Johanna. 2003. "Liberals take a cue from Republicans and turn to big donors to set up think tanks and media outlets to counter the conservative message," *Los Angeles Times,* November 30, p. A-20.

Newman, Katherine S. 2000. *No Shame in My Game: The Working Poor in the Inner City.* New York: Vintage.

New York City Gay and Lesbian Anti-Violence Project. 1996. *Project Annual Report.* www.avp.org, accessed 1/3/05.

Niebuhr, H. Richard. 1929. *The Social Sources of Denominationalism.* New York: Holt.

Nielsen Media Research. 2001a. Nielsen/NetRatings, Weekly Top 10 Usage Data, May 3, www.nielsen-netratings.com, accessed 1/3/05.

———. 2001b. "Internet access for blue collar workers spikes 52 percent, according to Nielsen/Net-ratings," http://209.249.142.22/press_releases/PDF/pr_010412.pdf, accessed 5/3/01.

———. 2001c. "Lower income surfers are the fastest growing group on the web, according to Nielsen/Netratings." http://209.249.142.22/press_releases/PDF/pr_010313.pdf, accessed 5/3/01.

Nielson, Francois. 1994. "Income inequality and industrial development: Dualism revisited." *American Sociological Review,* vol. 59 (October).

Nordhaus, W. D. 1975. "The political business cycle." *Review of Economic Studies,* vol. 42.

Nua.com. 2000. www.nua.ie/surveys/how_many_online/index.html, accessed 1/3/05.

Nye, Joseph. 1997. "In government we don't trust." *Foreign Affairs* (fall).

Oakes, Jeannie. 1985. *Keeping Track: How Schools Structure Inequality.* New Haven, CT: Yale University Press.

———. 1990. *Multiplying Inequalities: The Effects of Race, Social Class, and Tracking on Opportunities to Learn Mathematics and Science.* Santa Monica, CA: Rand.

Oakley, Ann. 1974. *the Sociology of Housework.* New York: Pantheon.

———, et al. 1994. "Life stress, support, and class inequality: Explaining the health of women and children." *European Journal of Public Health,* vol. 4.

Offe, Claus. 1984. *Contradictions of the Welfare State.* Cambridge, MA: MIT Press.

———. 1985. *Disorganized Capitalism.* Cambridge, MA: MIT Press.

Ohmae, Kenichi. 1990. *The Borderless World: Power and Strategy in the Industrial Economy.* New York: HarperCollins.

———. 1995. *The End of the Nation State: The Rise of Regional Economies.* New York: Free Press.

Oliver, Melvin L.; and Shapiro, Thomas M. 1995. *Black Wealth/White Wealth: A New Perspective on Racial Inequality.* New York: Routledge.

Olson, M. H. 1989. "Work at home for computer professionals." *ACM Trans. Inf. Sys.,* vol. 7, no. 4.

———; and Primps, S. B. 1984. "Working at home with computers." *Journal of Social Issues,* vol. 40, no. 3.

Omi, Michael; and Winant, Howard. 1994. *Racial Formation in the United States: From the 1960s to the 1990s.* 2nd ed. New York: Routledge.

Oppenheimer, Valerie K. 1970. *The Female Labor Force in the United States.* Westport, CT: Greenwood Press.

———. 1988. "A theory of marriage timing." *American Journal of Sociology,* vol. 94.

Organization for Economic Cooperation and Development (OECD). 1996. *OECD Tourism Statistics.* Paris: OECD.

———. 2003. "OECD economic outlook, June, no. 73, annex table 26: General government total outlays."

Orloff, Ann Shola. 1993. *The Politics of Pensions: A Comparative Analysis of Britain, Canada, and the United States, 1880–1940.* Madison, WI: University of Wisconsin Press.

Ortiz, V. 1995. "The diversity of Latino families," in R. Zambrana, ed., *Understanding Latino Families.* Thousand Oaks, CA: Sage.

Ouchi, William G. 1979. "A conceptual framework for the design of organizational control mechanisms." *Management Science,* vol. 25.

———. 1982. *Theory Z: How American Business Can Meet the Japanese Challenge.* New York: Avon.

Packer, George. 2003. "Smart-mobbing the war," *New York Times,* May 9.

Pager, Devah. 2003. "The mark of a criminal record," *American Journal of Psychology* vol. 108, no. 5: 937–75.

Pahl, Jan. 1989. *Money and Marriage.* London: Macmillan.

Palley, Marian Lief. 1987. "The women's movement in recent American politics," in Sara E. Rix, *The American Woman, 1987–1988.* New York: Norton.

Palmore, Erdman B., et al. 1985. *Retirement: Causes and Consequences.* New York: Springer.

Paludi, Michele A., and Barickman, Richard B. 1991. *Academic and Workplace Sexual Harassment: A Resource Manual.* Albany, NY: SUNY Press.

Park, Robert E. 1952. *Human Communities: The City and Human Ecology.* New York: Free Press.

Parkin, Frank. 1971. *Class Inequality and Political Order: Social Stratification in*

Capitalist and Communist Societies. New York: Praeger.

———. 1979. *Marxism and Class Theory: A Bourgeois Critique.* London: Tavistock.

Parry, Noel; and Parry, Jose. 1976. *The Rise of the Medical Profession.* London: Croom Helm.

Parsons, Talcott. 1951. *The Social System.* Glencoe, IL: Free Press.

———. 1960. "Towards a healthy maturity." *Journal of Health and Social Behavior,* vol. 1.

———. 1964. *The Social System.* New York: Free Press.

———; and Bales, Robert F. 1955. *Family, Socialization, and Interaction Process.* Glencoe, IL: Free Press.

Pascoe, Eva. 2000. "Can a sense of community flourish in cyberspace?" *The Guardian* (March 11).

Patterson, Orlando. 1999. "When 'they' are 'us.'" *New York Times,* April 30, p. A31.

Paul, Diana Y. 1985. *Women in Buddhism: Images of the Feminine in the Mahayana Tradition.* Berkeley, CA: University of California Press.

Pearce, Frank. 1976. *Crimes of the Powerful: Marxism, Crime, and Deviance.* London: Pluto Press.

Perlmutter, Howard V. 1972. "Towards research on and development of nations, unions, and firms as worldwide institutions," in H. Gunter, ed., *Transnational Industrial Relations.* New York: St. Martin's Press.

Peterson, Candida C.; and Peterson, James L. 1988. "Older men's and women's relationships with adult kin: How equitable are they?" *International Journal of Aging and Human Development,* vol. 27.

Peterson, Richard. 1996. "A re-evaluation of the economic consequences of divorce." *American Sociological Review,* vol. 61.

Pew. 2003a. "The 2004 political landscape: evenly divided and increasingly polarized," The PEW Research Center for the People and the Press (November 5). http://people-press.org/reports/display. php3?ReportID=196, accessed 1/3/05.

———. 2003b. *Views of a Changing World 2003,* Washington, D.C.: The Pew Research Center for the People and the Press (June 3). http://people-press.org/reports/pdf/185.pdf, accessed 1/3/05 topline survey results http://people-press.org/reports/pdf/185topline.pdf, accessed 1/3/05.

Pilkington, Edward. 1992. "Hapless democratic experiment." *The Guardian* (January 28).

Pillemer, Karl. 1985. "The dangers of dependency: New findings in domestic violence against the elderly." *Social Problems,* vol. 33.

———; and Finkelhor, David. 1988. "The prevalence of elder abuse: A random sample survey." *Gerontologist,* vol. 28.

Pinkney, A. 1984. *The Myth of Black Progress.* New York: Cambridge University Press.

Pintor, Rafael López; and Gratschew, Maria. 2002. *Voter Turnout Since 1945: A Global Report.* Stockholm, Sweden: International Institute for Democracy and Electoral Assistance (International IDEA). www.idea.int/publications/turnout/VT_screenopt_2002.pdf, accessed 1/3/05.

Piore, Michael J.; and Sabel, Charles F. 1984. *The Second Industrial Divide: Possibilities for Prosperity.* New York: Basic Books.

Plett, P. C. 1990. *Training Report: Training of Older Workers in Industrialized Countries.* Geneva: International Labor Organization.

———; and Lester, B. T. 1991. *Training for Older People: A Handbook.* Geneva: International Labor Organization.

Plummer, Kenneth. 1975. *Sexual Stigma: An Interactive Account.* Boston: Routledge and Kegan Paul.

PoliticalMoneyLine. 2003. "Federal Lobby Directory" (December 14) www.tray.com, accessed 1/3/05.

Pollak, Otto. 1950. *The Criminality of Women.* Philadelphia: University of Pennsylvania Press.

Polletta, Francesca; and Jasper, James M. 2001. "Collective Identity and Social Movements," *Annual Review of Sociology* vol. 27: 283–305.

Popenoe, David. 1993. "American family decline, 1960–1990: A review and appraisal." *Journal of Marriage and Family,* vol. 55.

———. 1996. *Life without Father: Compelling New Evidence That Fatherhood and Marriage Are Indispensable for the Good of Children and Society.* New York: Martin Kessler Books.

Portes, Alejandro; and Stepik, Alex. 1993. *City on the Edge: The Transformation of Miami.* Berkeley, CA: University of California Press.

Potter, Karl H. 1992. "Hinduism," in the *American Academic Encyclopedia* (online edition). Danbury, CT: Grolier Electronic.

Powell, W. W.; and Brantley, P. 1992. "Competitive cooperation in biotechnology: Learning through networks?" in N. Nohria and R. Eccles, eds., *Networks and Organizations: Structure, Form and Action.* Boston: Harvard Business School Press.

———; Koput, K. W.; and Smith-Doerr, L. 1996. "Interorganizational collaboration and the locus of innovation: Networks of learning in biotechnology." *Administration Science Quarterly,* vol. 41.

Pratt, Joanne H. 2003. *Teleworking Comes of Age with Broadband.* International Telework Association & Council, www.telecommute.org/pdf/TWA2003_Executive_Summary.pdf, accessed 1/20/05.

Prebisch, Raul. 1967. *Hacia una dinamica del desarollo Latinoamericano.* Montevideo, Uruguay: Ediciones de la Banda Oriental.

———. 1971. *Change and Development—Latin America's Great Task: Report Submitted to the Inter-American Bank.* New York: Praeger.

President's Commission on Organized Crime. 1986. *Records of Hearings, June 24–26, 1985.* Washington, DC: U.S. Government Printing Office.

Provenzo, Eugene F., Jr. 1991. *Video Kids: Making Sense of Nintendo.* Cambridge, MA: Harvard University Press.

Public Broadcasting System (PBS). 2003. "AOL/Time-Warner merger." www.pbs.org/newshour/bb/business/aol_time_index.html, accessed 1/3/05.

Purser, Gretchen; Schalet, Amy; and Sharone, Ofer. 2004. *Berkeley's Betrayal: Wages and Working Conditions at Cal.* Berkeley, CA: University Labor Research Project.

Putnam, Robert. 1993. "The prosperous community: Social capital and public life." *American Prospect,* vol. 13.

———. 1995. "Bowling alone: America's declining social capital." *Journal of Democracy,* vol. 6.

———. 2000. *Bowling Alone: The Collapse and Revival of American Community.* New York: Simon and Schuster.

Quadagno, Jill. 1989. "Generational equity and the politics of the welfare state." *Politics and Society,* vol. 17.

Quah, Danny. 1999. *The Weightless Economy in Economic Development.* London: Centre for Economic Performance.

Quinn, Joseph F.; and Burkhauser, Richard V. 1994. "Retirement and labor force behavior of the elderly," in Linda G. Martin and Samuel H. Preston, eds., *Demography of Aging.* Washington, DC: National Academy Press.

Rader Programs. 2003. "Prevalence and Outcome." www.raderprograms.com/prevalen.htm, accessed 1/3/05.

Raines, Pat; and Leathers, Charles G. 2001. "Telecommuting: The New Wave of Workplace Technology Will Create a Flood of Change in Social Institutions," *Journal of Economic Issues,* vol. 35.

Rainie, Lee; Fox, Susannah; and Fallows, Deborah. 2003. *The Internet and the Iraq*

War: How Online Americans Have Used the Internet to Learn War News, Understand Events, and Promote Their Views . Washington, D.C.: The PEW Internet and American Life Project. http://www.pewinternet.org/PPF/r/87/report_display.asp, accessed 1/10/05.

Ramirez, Francisco O.; and Boli, John. 1987. "The political construction of mass schooling: European origins and worldwide institutionalism." *Sociology of Education,* vol. 60.

Ranis, Gustav. 1996. "Will Latin America now put a stop to 'stop-and-go?' " New Haven, CT: Yale University, Economic Growth Center.

———; and Mahmood, Syed Akhtar. 1992. *The Political Economy of Development Policy Change.* Cambridge, MA: Blackwell.

Redding, S. G. 1990. *The Spirit of Chinese Capitalism.* Berlin: De Gruyter.

Redman, Peter. 1996. "Empowering men to disempower themselves: Heterosexual masculinities, HIV, and the contradictions of anti-oppressive education," in Mairtin Mac an Ghaill, ed., *Understanding Masculinities.* Buckingham, UK: Open University Press.

Reich, Robert. 1991. *The Work of Nations: Preparing Ourselves for 21st-Century Capitalism.* New York: Knopf.

Renzetti, Claire M.; and Curran, Daniel J. 1995. *Women, Men, and Society.* 3rd ed. Needham Heights, MA: Allyn and Bacon.

———. 2000. *Living Sociology.* 2nd ed. Needham Heights, MA: Allyn and Bacon.

Reskin, Barbara; and Padavic, Irene. 1994. *Women and Men at Work.* Thousand Oaks, CA: Pine Forge Press.

———; and Roos, Patricia A. 1990. *Job Queues, Gender Queues: Explaining Women's Inroads into Male Occupations.* Philadelphia: Temple University Press.

Rhode, Deborah L. 1990. "Gender equality and employment policy," in Sara E. Rix, ed., *The American Woman, 1990–1991: A Status Report.* New York: Norton.

Richardson, Diane; and May, Hazel. 1999. "Deserving victims? Sexual status and the social construction of violence." *Sociological Review,* vol. 47.

Riddick, C. C. 1985. "Life satisfaction for older female homemakers, retirees, and workers." *Research on Aging,* vol. 7.

Rieff, David. 1991. *Los Angeles: Capital of the Third World.* New York: Simon and Schuster.

Riesman, David. 1961. *The Lonely Crowd: A Study of the Changing American Character.* New Haven, CT: Yale University Press.

Riis, Jacob A. 1957. *How the Other Half Lives: Studies among the Tenements of New York.* Originally published 1890. New York: Dover.

Riley, Matilda White; Foner, Anne; and Waring, Joan. 1988. "Sociology of age," in Neil J. Smelser, ed., *Handbook of Sociology.* Newbury Park, CA: Sage.

———; Johnson, Marilyn; and Foner, Anne. 1972. *Aging and Society.* New York: Russell Sage Foundation.

Ringer, Benjamin B. 1985. *"We the People" and Others: Duality and America's Treatment of Its Racial Minorities.* New York: Tavistock.

Ritzer, George. 1993. *The McDonaldization of Society.* Newbury Park, CA: Pine Forge Press.

Robinson, Paul. 1994. "The way we do the things we do." *New York Times Book Review,* October 30.

Roof, Wade Clark. 1993. *A Generation of Seekers: The Spiritual Journeys of the Baby Boom Generation.* San Francisco: Harper San Francisco.

———; Carroll, Jackson W.; and Roozen, David A., eds. 1995. *The Post-War Generation and Establishment Religion: Cross-Cultural Perspectives.* Boulder, CO: Westview Press.

———; and McKinney, William. 1990. *American Mainline Religion: Its Changing Shape and Future Prospects.* New Brunswick, NJ: Rutgers University Press.

Roscoe, W. 1991. *The Zuni Man-Woman.* Albuquerque, NM: University of New Mexico Press.

———. 2000. *Changing Ones.* New York, NY: Palgrave Macmillan.

Rosenau, James N. 1997. *Along the Domestic-Foreign Frontier: Exploring Governance in a Turbulent World.* Cambridge, UK: Cambridge University Press.

Rosenbaum, James E. 1979. "Organizational career mobility: Promotion chances in a corporation during periods of growth and contraction." *American Journal of Sociology,* vol. 85.

Rosener, Judy B. 1997. *America's Competitive Secret: Women Managers.* New York: Oxford University Press.

Rosenheck, Robert, et al. 1996. "Homeless veterans," in J. Baumohl, ed., *Homelessness in America.* Phoenix: Oryx Press.

Rosenthal, A. M. 1999. *Thirty-Eight Witnesses: The Kitty Genovese Case.* Berkeley, CA: University of California Press.

Rosenthal, Elisabeth. 1999. "Suicides reveal bitter roots of China's rural life." *New York Times,* January 24.

Ross, Patricia; and Reskin, Barbara. 1992. "Occupational desegregation in the

1970s—integration and economic equity." *Sociological Perspectives,* vol. 35.

Rossi, Alice. 1973. "The first woman sociologist: Harriett Martineau," in *The Feminist Papers: From Adams to de Beauvoir.* New York: Columbia University Press.

Rostow, W. W. 1961. *The Stages of Economic Growth.* Cambridge, UK: Cambridge University Press.

Rousselle, Robert. 1999. "Defining ancient Greek sexuality." *Digital Archives of Psychohistory,* vol. 26, no. 4, www.geocities.com/kidhistory/ja/defining.htm, accessed 1/11/05.

Rowe, R. H.; and Kahn, R. L. 1987. "Human aging: Usual and successful." *Science* (July 10).

Rowling, J. K. 1998. *Harry Potter and the Sorcerer's Stone.* New York: Scholastic.

Rubin, Lillian B. 1990. *Erotic Wars: What Happened to the Sexual Revolution?* New York: Farrar, Straus, and Giroux.

Rubinstein, W. D. 1986. *Wealth and Inequality in Britain.* Winchester, MA: Faber and Faber.

Rudé, George. 1964. *The Crowd in History: A Study of Popular Disturbances in France and England, 1730–1848.* New York: Wiley.

Ruggles, Patricia. 1990. *Drawing the Line: Alternative Poverty Measures and Their Implications for Public Policy.* Washington, DC: Urban Institute Press.

———. 1992. "Measuring poverty." *Focus,* vol. 14. University of Wisconsin-Madison, Institute for Research on Poverty.

Rusting, Ricki L. 1992. "Why do we age?" *Scientific American,* vol. 267.

Rutherford, Jonathan; and Chapman, Rowena. 1988. "Who's that man," in Rowena Chapman and Jonathan Rutherford, eds., *Male Order: Unwrapping Masculinity.* London: Lawrence and Wishart.

Rutter, M.; and Giller, H. 1984. *Juvenile Delinquency: Trends and Perspectives.* New York: Guilford Press.

RWB. 2003. *The Internet Under Surveillance: 2003 Report.* Paris, France: Reporters Without Borders. www.rsf.org/IMG/pdf/doc-2236.pdf, accessed 1/3/05.

Ryan, Tom. 1985. "The roots of masculinity," in Andy Metcalf and Martin Humphries, eds., *Sexuality of Men.* London: Pluto.

Sabel, Charles F. 1982. *Work and Politics: The Division of Labor in Industry.* New York: Cambridge University Press.

Sachs, Jeffrey. 2000. "A new map of the world." *The Economist* (June 22).

Sadker, Myra; and Sadker, David. 1994. *Failing at Fairness.* New York: Scribner.

Safe-food.org. 2003. "You are eating genetically engineered food. Is it good for you? Do you have a choice?" www.safe-food.org, accessed 1/3/05.

Sahliyeh, Emile, ed. 1990. *Religious Resurgence and Politics in the Contemporary World.* Albany, NY: SUNY Press.

Saks, Mike, ed. 1992. *Alternative Medicine in Britain.* Oxford, UK: Clarendon.

Salter, Howard. 1998. "Making a world of difference: Celebrating 30 years of development progress." U.S. AID press release, June 25.

Sampson, Robert J.; and Cohen, Jacqueline. 1988. "Deterrent effects of the police on crime: A replication and theoretical extension." *Law and Society Review,* vol. 22, no. 1.

Sandefur, Gary; and Libeler, Carolyn. 1997. "The demography of American Indian families." *Population Research and Policy Review,* vol. 16.

Sartre, Jean-Paul. 1965. *Anti-Semite and Jew.* Originally published 1948. New York: Schocken Books.

Sassen, Saskia. 1991. *The Global City: New York, London, Tokyo.* Princeton, NJ: Princeton University Press.

———. 1998. *Globalization and Its Discontents.* New York: New Press.

Savage, David G. 1998. "Same-sex harassment illegal, says high court." *Los Angeles Times,* March 5.

Savage, Mike, et al. 1992. *Property, Bureaucracy, and Culture: Middle Class Formation in Contemporary Britain.* London: Routledge.

Sawhill, Isabel V. 1989. "The underclass: An overview." *Public Interest,* vol. 96.

Sax, L. J., et al. 1999. "The American freshman: National norms for fall 1999." Los Angeles: Higher Education Research Institute, UCLA, www.gseis.ucla.edu/heri/heri.html, accessed 1/3/05.

Sax, L. J.; Lindholm, J. A.; Astin, A. W.; Korn, W. S.; and Mahoney, K. M. (2001) "The American freshman: National norms for fall 2001." Higher Education Research Institute, UCLA Graduate School of Education & Information Studies. www.gseis.ucla.edu/heri/norms_pr_01.html, accessed 1/3/05.

Sayers, Janet. 1986. *Sexual Contradiction: Psychology, Psychoanalysis, and Feminism.* New York: Methuen.

Schaie, K. Warner. 1979. "The primary mental abilities in adulthood: An exploration in the development of psychometric intelligence," in Paul B. Baltes and O. G. Brim, eds., *Lifespan Development and Behavior.* Vol. 2. New York: Academic Press.

———. 1983. *Longitudinal Studies of Adult Psychological Development.* New York: Guilford Press.

———. 1984. "Midlife influences upon intellectual functioning in old age." *International Journal of Behavioral Development,* vol. 7.

———; and Hendricks, Jon, eds. 2000. *The Evolution of the Aging Self: The Societal Impact on the Aging Process.* New York: Springer.

Scheff, Thomas. 1966. *Being Mentally Ill.* Chicago: Aldine.

Schiller, Herbert I. 1989. *Culture Inc.: The Corporate Takeover of Public Expression.* New York: Oxford University Press.

———. 1991. "Not yet the post-imperialist era." *Critical Studies in Mass Communication,* vol. 8.

Schmidt, Roger. 1980. *Exploring Religion.* Belmont, CA: Wadsworth.

Schooler, Carmi. 1987. "Cognitive effects of complex environments during the life span: A review and theory," in Carmi Schooler and K. Warner Schaie, eds., *Cognitive Functioning and Social Structure over the Life Course.* Norwood, NJ: Ablex.

Schor, Juliet. 1992. *The Overworked American.* New York: Basic Books.

Schuman, Howard; Steel, Charlotte; and Bobo, Lawrence. 1985. *Racial Attitudes in America: Trends and Interpretations.* Cambridge, MA: Harvard University Press.

Schumpeter, Joseph. 1934. *The Theory of Economic Development: An Inquiry into Profits, Capital, and Credit.* Cambridge, MA: Harvard University Press.

———. 1983. *Capitalism, Socialism, and Democracy.* Originally published 1942. Magnolia, MA: Peter Smith.

Schwartz, Gary. 1970. *Sect Ideologies and Social Status.* Chicago: University of Chicago Press.

Schwartz, Pepper. 1998. "Stage fright or death wish: Sociology in the mass media," *Contemporary Sociology,* vol. 27, no. 5 (September): 439–45.

Schwartzman, Kathleen. 1998. "Globalization and democracy." *Annual Review of Sociology,* vol. 24.

Schwarz, John E.; and Volgy, Thomas J. 1992. *The Forgotten Americans.* New York: Norton.

Scott, Catherine V. 1995. *Gender and Development: Rethinking Modernization and Dependency Theory.* London: Lynne Rienner Publishers.

Scott, Sue; and Morgan, David. 1993. "Bodies in a social landscape," in Sue Scott and David Morgan, eds., *Body Matters: Essays on the Sociology of the Body.* Washington, DC: Falmer Press.

Scott, W. Richard; and Meyer, John W. 1994. *Institutional Environments and Organizations: Structural Complexity and Individualism.* Thousand Oaks, CA: Sage.

Scully, Diana. 1990. *Understanding Sexual Violence: A Study of Convicted Rapists.* Boston: Unwin Hyman.

Sedlak, Andrea; and Broadhurst, Diane. 1996. *Third National Incidence Study of Child Abuse and Neglect.* Washington, DC: U.S. Department of Health and Human Services.

Seefeldt, C.; and Keawkungwal, S. 1985. "Children's attitudes toward the elderly in Thailand and the United States." *International Journal of Comparative Sociology,* vol. 26.

Segura, Denise A.; and Pierce, Jennifer L. 1993. "Chicana/o family structure and gender personality: Chodorow, familism, and psychoanalytic sociology revisited." *Signs,* vol. 19.

Seidman, Steven. 1997a. *Difference Troubles: Queering Social Theory and Sexual Politics.* Cambridge, UK: Cambridge University Press.

———. 1997b. "Relativizing sociology: The challenge of cultural studies," in Elizabeth Long, ed., *From Sociology to Cultural Studies: New Perspectives.* Malden, MA: Blackwell.

———; Meeks, Chet; and Traschen, Francie. 1999. "Beyond the closet? The changing social meaning of homosexuality in the United States." *Sexualities,* vol. 2, no. 1.

Seltzer, Judith. 2000. "Families formed outside of marriage." *Journal of Marriage and the Family* (November).

Sennett, Richard. 1998. *The Corrosion of Character: The Personal Consequences of Work in the New Capitalism.* New York: Norton.

"Seville Statement on Violence." 1990. *American Psychologist,* vol. 45, no. 10, www.lrainc.com/swtaboo/taboos/seville1.html, accessed 1/3/05.

Sewell, William H., Jr. 1992. "A theory of structure: Duality, agency, and transformation." *American Journal of Sociology,* vol. 98.

———. 1999. "The concept of culture," in Victoria E. Bonnell and Lynn Hunt, eds., *Beyond the Cultural Turn.* Berkeley, CA: University of California Press.

Sewell, William H.; and Hauser, Robert M. 1980. "The Wisconsin longitudinal study of social and psychological factors in aspirations and achievements." *Research in Sociology of Education and Socialization,* vol. 1.

Sharma, Ursula. 1992. *Complementary Medicine Today: Practitioners and Patients.* London: Routledge.

Sharp, H. 1981. "Old age among the Chipewyan," in Pamela T. Amoss and S. Harrells, eds., *Other Ways of Growing Old: Anthropological Perspectives.* Stanford, CA: Stanford University Press.

Shattuck, Roger. 1980. *The Forbidden Experiment: The Story of the Wild Boy of Aveyron.* New York: Farrar, Straus, and Giroux.

Shea, S.; Stein, A. D.; Basch, C. E.; Lantigua, R.; Maylahn, C.; Strogatz, D.; and Novick, L. 1991. "Independent associations of educational attainment and ethnicity with behavioral risk factors for cardiovascular disease." *American Journal of Epidemiology,* vol. 134, no. 6.

Sheldon, William A., et al. 1949. *Varieties of Delinquent Youth.* New York: Harper and Row.

Shelton, Beth Anne. 1992. *Women, Men, and Time: Gender Differences in Paid Work, Housework, and Leisure.* Westport, CT: Greenwood.

———; and John, Daphne. 1993. "Does marital status make a difference?: Housework among married and cohabiting men and women." *Journal of Family Issues,* vol. 14, no. 3.

Shepherd, Gill. 1987. "Rank, gender, and homo-sexuality: Mombasa as a key to understanding sexual options," in Pat Caplan, *The Social Construction of Sexuality.* New York: Tavistock.

Shinn, Marybeth; and Weitzman, Beth. 1996. "Homeless families are different," in J. Baumohl, ed., *Homelessness in America.* Phoenix: Oryx Press.

Siegel, Jacob. 1993. *A Generation of Change: A Profile of America's Older Population.* New York: Russell Sage Foundation.

Sigmund, Paul E. 1990. *Liberation Theology at the Crossroads: Democracy or Revolution?* New York: Oxford University Press.

Simmel, Georg. 1955. *Conflict and the Web of Group Affiliations.* Trans. Kurt Wolff. Glencoe, IL: Free Press.

Simon, Julian. 1981. *The Ultimate Resource.* Princeton, NJ: Princeton University Press.

———. 1989. *The Economic Consequences of Immigration.* Cambridge, MA: Basil Blackwell.

Simpson, George Eaton; and Yinger, J. Milton. 1986. *Racial and Cultural Minorities: An Analysis of Prejudice and Discrimination.* New York: Plenum Press.

Simpson, Ida H.; Stark, David; and Jackson, Robert A. 1988. "Class identification processes." *American Sociological Review,* vol. 53.

Simpson, John H. 1985. "Socio-moral issues and recent presidential elections," *Review of Religious Research,* vol. 27: 115–23.

Sjoberg, Gideon. 1960. *The Pre-Industrial City: Past and Present.* New York: Free Press.

———. 1963. "The rise and fall of cities: A theoretical perspective." *International Journal of Comparative Sociology,* vol. 4.

Sklar, Holly. 1999. "Brother, can you spare a billion?" *Z Magazine* (December), www.zmag.org/ZNET. htm, accessed 1/3/05.

Skocpol, Theda. 1979. *States and Social Revolutions: A Comparative Analysis of France, Russia, and China.* New York: Cambridge University Press.

———. 1992. *Protecting Soldiers and Mothers: The Political Origins of Social Policy in the United States.* Cambridge, MA: Harvard University Press.

Slapper, Gary; and Tombs, Steve. 1999. *Corporate Crime.* Essex, UK: Longman.

Smart, Ninian. 1989. *The World Religions.* Englewood Cliffs, NJ: Prentice Hall.

Smeeding, Timothy M. 2000. "Changing income inequality in OECD countries: Updated results from the Luxembourg income study (LIS)." Luxembourg Income Study Working Paper #252, March. Syracuse, New York: Maxwell School of Citizenship and Public Affairs, Syracuse University, www.lisproject.org/publications/liswps/252.pdf, accessed 1/11/05.

———; Rainwater, Lee; and Burtless, Gary. 2000. "United States poverty in a cross-national context." Luxembourg Income Study Working Paper #244, September. Syracuse, New York: Maxwell School of Citizenship and Public Affairs, Syracuse University, www.lisproject.org/publications/liswps/244.pdf, accessed 1/11/05.

Smelser, Neil J. 1963. *Theory of Collective Behavior.* New York: Free Press.

Smith, Philip; and West, Brad. 2000. "Cultural studies," in *Encyclopedia of Naturalism.* Vol. 1. San Diego, CA: Academic Press.

Smith, Vicki. 1997. "New forms of work organization." *Annual Review of Sociology,* vol. 23.

So, Alvin. 1990. *Social Change and Development: Modernization, Dependency, and World-Systems Theories.* Newbury Park, CA: Sage.

———; and Chiu, Stephen W. K. 1995. *East Asia and the World Economy.* Thousand Oaks, CA: Sage.

Sokolovsky, J., ed. 1990. *The Cultural Context of Aging: Worldwide Perspectives.* New York: Bergin and Garvey.

Sorokin, Pitirim A. 1927. *Social Mobility.* New York: Harper.

Soumerai, S. B.; and Avorn, J. 1983. "Perceived health, life satisfaction, and activity in urban elderly: A controlled study of the impact of part-time work." *Journal of Gerontology,* vol. 38.

Southwick, S. 1996. Liszt: *Searchable Directory of E-Mail Discussion Groups.* www.liszt.com, accessed 1/3/05.

Spain, Daphne; and Bianchi, Suzanne M. 1996. *Balancing Act: Motherhood, Marriage, and Employment among American Women.* New York: Russell Sage Foundation.

Spenner, Kenneth. 1983. "Deciphering Prometheus: Temporal change in the skill level of work." *American Sociological Review,* vol. 48.

Spielberger, C. D.; Crane, R. S.; Kearns, W. D.; Pellegrin, K. L.; Rickman, R. L.; and Johnson, E. H. 1991. "Anger and anxiety in essential hypertension." In C. D. Spielberger, I. G. Sarason, Z. Kulcs, and G. L. Van Heck, eds., *Stress and Emotion.* Vol. 14. New York: Hemisphere/Taylor & Francis.

Spilerman, Seymour. 1977. "Careers, labor market structure, and socioeconomic achievement." *American Journal of Sociology,* vol. 83.

Spinks, W. A.; and Wood J. 1996. "Office-Based Telecommuting: An International Comparison of Satellite Offices in Japan and North America," in *Proceedings of SIGCPR/SIGMIS '96.* Denver, CO: ACM.

Sreberny-Mohammadi, Annabelle. 1992. "Media integration in the third world," in B. Gronbeck et al., eds., *Media, Consciousness, and Culture.* London: Sage.

Stacey, Judith. 1990. *Brave New Families: Stories of Domestic Upheaval in Late Twentieth Century America.* New York: Basic Books.

———. 1993. "Good riddance to 'the family': A response to David Popenoe." *Journal of Marriage and Family,* vol. 55.

———. 1996. *In the Name of the Family: Rethinking Family Values in a Postmodern Age.* Boston: Beacon Press.

———. 2004. "Marital suitors court social science spin-sters: The unwittingly conservative effects of public sociology," *Social Problems,* vol. 51, no. 1: 131–45. © 2004, The Society for the Study of Social Problems, Inc.

Stampp, Kenneth. 1956. *The Peculiar Institution.* New York: Knopf.

Stark, Rodney; and Bainbridge, William Sims. 1980. "Towards a theory of religious commitment." *Journal for the Scientific Study of Religion,* vol. 19.

———. 1985. *The Future of Religion, Secularization, Revival, and Cult Formation.* Berkeley, CA: University of California Press.

———. 1987. *A Theory of Religion.* New Brunswick, NJ: Rutgers University Press.

Starrs, Paul F. 1997. "The sacred, the regional, and the digital." *Geographical Review,* vol. 87, no. 2.

Statham, June. 1986. *Daughters and Sons: Experiences of Non-Sexist Childraising.* New York: Basil Blackwell.

Steinberg, Ronnie J. 1990. "Social construction of skill: Gender, power, and comparable worth." *Work and Occupations,* vol. 17.

Steinmetz, Suzanne K. 1983. "Family violence toward elders," in Susan Saunders, Ann Anderson, and Cynthia Hart, eds., *Violent Individuals and Families: A Practitioner's Handbook.* Springfield, IL: Charles C. Thomas.

Sterling, Bruce. 1996. "Greetings from Burning Man," *Wired* 4.11, November.

Stetz, Margaret; and Oh, Bonnie, eds. 2001. *Legacies of the Comfort Women of World War II.* Armonk, NY: M. E. Sharpe.

Stillwagon, Ellen. 2001. "AIDS and poverty in Africa." *The Nation* (May 21).

Stone, Lawrence. 1980. *The Family, Sex, and Marriage in England, 1500–1800.* New York: Harper and Row.

Stone, Michael. 1993. *Shelter Poverty: New Ideas on Affordable Housing.* Philadelphia: Temple University Press.

Stouffer, Samuel A., et al. 1949. *The American Soldier: Adjustment during Army Life.* Princeton, NJ: Princeton University Press.

Straus, Murray; and Gelles, Richard. 1986. "Societal change and change in family violence from 1975 to 1985 as revealed by two national surveys." *Journal of Marriage and the Family,* vol. 48.

Strauss, William; and Howe, Neil. 1991. *Generations: The History of America's Future, 1584–2069.* New York: Quill.

Strinner, William F. 1979. "Modernization and the family extension in the Philippines: A social-demographic analysis." *Journal of Marriage and the Family,* vol. 41.

Stryker, Robin. 1996. "Comparable worth and the labor market," in Paula J. Dubeck and Kathryn Borman, eds., *Women and Work: A Handbook.* New York: Garland.

Sullivan, Andrew. 1995. *Virtually Normal: An Argument about Homosexuality.* New York: Knopf.

Sullivan, Oriel. 1997. "Time waits for no (wo)man: An investigation of the gendered experience of domestic time." *Sociology,* vol. 31.

Sutherland, Edwin H. 1949. *Principles of Criminology.* Chicago: Lippincott.

Swidler, Ann. 1986. "Culture in action: Symbols and strategies." *American Sociological Review,* vol. 51.

———. 2001. *Talk of Love: How Culture Matters.* Chicago: University of Chicago Press.

Tabor, James D.; and Gallagher, Eugene V. 1995. *Why Waco? Cults and the Battle for Religious Freedom in America.* Berkeley, CA: University of California Press.

Tang, Shengming; and Zuo, Jiping. 2000. "Dating attitudes and behaviors of American and Chinese college students." *Social Science Journal,* vol. 37, no. 1.

Tannenbaum, Frank. 1964. *The Fine Society: A Philosophy of Labour.* London: Cape.

Taylor, Ian; Walton, Paul; and Young, Jock. 1973. *The New Criminology: For a Social Theory of Deviance.* London: Routledge and Kegan Paul.

Tempest, Rone. 1996. "Barbie and the world economy." *Los Angeles Times,* September 22.

Tétreault, Mary Ann. ed. 1994. *Women and Revolution in Africa, Asia, and the New World.* Columbia, SC: University of South Carolina Press.

Thomas, G. M., et al. 1987. *Institutional Structure: Constituting State, Society and the Individual.* Newbury Park, CA: Sage.

Thomas, W. I.; and Znaniecki, Florian. 1966. *The Polish Peasant in Europe and America: Monograph of Our Immigrant Group.* 5 vols. Originally published 1918–20. New York: Dover.

Thompson, E. P. 1971. "The moral economy of the English crowd in the eighteenth century." *Past and Present,* vol. 50.

Thompson, John B. 1990. *Ideology and Modern Culture.* Cambridge, UK: Polity Press.

———. 1995. *The Media and Modernity: A Social Theory of the Media.* Cambridge, UK: Polity Press.

Thompson, Warren S. 1929. "Population." *American Journal of Sociology,* vol. 34.

Thorne, Barrie. 1993. *Gender Play: Girls and Boys in School.* New Brunswick, NJ: Rutgers University Press.

Tiano, Susan. 1994. *Patriarchy on the Line: Labor, Gender, and Ideology in the Mexican Maquila Industry.* Philadelphia: Temple University Press.

Tilly, Charles. 1978. *From Mobilization to Revolution.* Reading, MA: Addison-Wesley.

———. 1992. "How to detect, describe, and explain repertoires of contention." Working Paper No. 150. Center for the Study of Social Change. New York: New School for Social Research.

———. 1995. "Globalization threatens labor's rights." *International Labor and Working Class History,* vol. 47.

———. 1996. "The emergence of citizenship in France and elsewhere," in Charles Tilly, ed., *Citizenship, Identity, and Social History.* Cambridge, UK: Cambridge University Press.

Tinbergen, Niko. 1974. *The Study of Instinct.* Oxford, UK: Oxford University Press.

Tippet, Sarah. 2001. "Parents' Sexual Orientation Matters, Study Finds," Reuters News Agency, April 27.

Tittle, Charles R.; and Meier, Robert F. 1990. "Specifying the SES/delinquency relationship." *Criminology,* vol. 28, no. 2.

———, et al. 1978. "The myth of social class and criminality: An empirical assessment of the empirical evidence." *American Sociological Review,* vol. 43.

Totti, Xavier F. 1987. "The making of a Latino ethnic identity." *Dissent,* vol. 34 (fall).

Toufexis, Anastasia. 1993. "Sex has many accents." *Time* (May 24).

Touraine, Alain. 1974. *The Post-Industrial Society.* London: Wildwood.

———. 1977. *The Self-Production of Society.* Chicago: University of Chicago Press.

———. 1981. *The Voice and the Eye: An Analysis of Social Movements.* New York: Cambridge University Press.

Townsend, Peter; and Davidson, Nick, eds. 1982. *Inequalities in Health: The Black Report.* Harmondsworth, UK: Penguin.

Toyota.com. 2004. "Toyota by the numbers." www.toyota.com/about/operations/numbers/index.html#, accessed 1/3/05.

Treas, Judy. 1995. "Older Americans in the 1990s and beyond." *Population Bulletin,* vol. 5.

Treiman, Donald. 1977. *Occupational Prestige in Comparative Perspective.* New York: Academic Press.

Troeltsch, Ernst. 1931. *The Social Teaching of the Christian Churches.* 2 vols. New York: Macmillan.

Trow, Martin. 1961. "The second transformation of American secondary education." *Comparative Sociology,* vol. 2.

Truman, David B. 1981. *The Governmental Process.* Westport, CT: Greenwood Press.

Truong, Tranh-Dam. 1990. *Sex, Money, and Morality.* London: Zed Books.

Tumin, Melvin M. 1953. "Some principles of stratification: A critical analysis." *American Sociological Review,* vol. 18 (August).

Turnbull, Colin. 1983. *The Human Cycle.* New York: Simon and Schuster.

Turowski, Jan. 1977. "Inadequacy of the theory of the nuclear family: The Polish experience," in Luis Lenero Otero, ed., *Beyond the Nuclear Family Model: Cross-Cultural Perspectives.* Beverly Hills, CA: Sage.

Tuttle, Lisa. 1986. *Encyclopedia of Feminism.* New York: Facts on File.

UNAIDS. 2002. "Impact of AIDS on older populations." www.unaids.org/html/pub/publications/fact_shhets02/fs_older_en_pdf.htm, accessed 1/10/05.

———. 2003. "AIDS Epidemic Update, December 2003." Joint United Nations Program on HIV/AIDS. www.unaids.org/html/pub/publications/irc_pubOb/jc943-epiupdate2003_en_pdf.htm, accessed 1/10/05.

UN Chronicle. 1995. vol. 32, no. 4: 29.

UNICEF. 1997. *The State of the World's Children, 1997.* New York: Oxford University Press.

———. 2000. *State of the World's Children, 2000.* New York: United Nations Children's Fund.

Union of International Associations. 1996–97. "International organizations by year and by type, 1909–1996, in *Yearbook of International Organizations, 1996/97.* Statistics obtained from UIA Web site, www.uia.org/statistics/organizations-stybv296.php, accessed 1/3/05.

Union of International Organizations. 2003. "International organizations by type" www.uia.org/statistics/organizations/ytb199.php, accessed 1/3/05.

United Nations (UN). 1995. "Human Development Report, Gender and Human Development—Overview" http://hdr.undp.org/reports/global/1995/en/pdf/hdr_1995_overview.pdf, accessed 1/3/05.

———. 2000. *The World's Women, 2000: Trends and Statistics.* New York: United Nations.

———. 2003. Table 26. *United Nations Human Development Report,* 2003. www.undp.org/hdr2003/pdf/hdr03_HDI.pdf, accessed 1/3/05.

United Nations Conference on Trade and Development. 2002. *World Investment Report 2002: Transnational Corporations and Export Competitiveness.* New York: United Nations.

United Nations Department of Economic and Social Affairs. 2004. "Progress towards the millennium development goals, 1990–2004. Goal 7—Ensure environmental sustainability." http://unstats.un.org/unsd/mi/techgroup/goals_2004/goal_7-web_2004_fc3rev.doc, accessed 1/3/05.

United Nations Development Program (UNDP). 1998. *Human Development Report 1998.* New York: Oxford University Press.

———. 1999. *Human Development Report 1999.* New York: Oxford University Press.

———. 2000. *Human Development Report 2000.* New York: Oxford University Press.

———. 2002. *Human Development Report 2002.* http://hdr.undp.org/reports/global/2002/en/default.cfm, accessed 1/3/05.

United Nations Educational, Scientific, and Cultural Organization. 2003. "Institute for statistics." www.uis.unesco.org/ev.php?URL_ID=4926&URL_DO=DO_TOPIC&URL_SECTION=201, accessed 1/3/05.

United Nations Food and Agriculture Organization (UN FAO). 1996. "FAO/UNFPA expert group meeting on food production and population growth." United Nations: Food and Agriculture Organization, July 3–5.

———. 1999. "Food outlook, no. 5." United Nations: Food and Agriculture Organization, November.

———. 2001. "The impact of HIV/AIDS on food security." United Nations Food and Agriculture Organization, Conference on World Food Security, May 28–June 1.

———. 2003. "The state of food insecurity in the world, 2003." www.fao.org/docrep/006/j0083e/j0083e00.htm, accessed 1/3/05.

United Nations, Population Division. 2002. "World urbanization prospects, 2001 revision—Data tables and highlights." www.un.org/esa/population/publications/wup2001/wup2001dh.pdf, accessed 1/3/05.

United Nations Population Fund (UNFPA). 1998. *The State of World Population, 1998.* New York: United Nations.

———. 2003. "Ending widespread violence against women." www.unfpa.org/gender/violence.htm, accessed 1/3/05.

United Nations World Commission on Environment and Development (UNWCED). 1987. *Our Common Future.* New York: Oxford University Press.

United Nations World Food Program (UNWFP). 2001. "News release: WFP head releases world hunger map and warns of hunger 'hot spots' in 2001." (January 8) New York: UNWFP.

United Steel Workers of America. 2004. "Unprecedented manufacturing job losses cause worker mobility." www.uswa.org/uswa/program/content/915.php, accessed 3/3/2004.

Urban Institute. 2000. "America's homeless II: Populations and services." www.urban.org/template.cfm?Template=/TaggedContent/VicesPublication.cfm&PublicationID=6846&NavMenuID=95, accessed 1/10/05.

Urry, John. 1990. *The Tourist Gaze.* London: Sage.

U.S. Bureau of Justice. 2000. *Capital Punishment 1999, Statistics Bulletin.* Washington, DC: U.S. Government Printing Office.

U.S. Bureau of Justice Statistics. 2000. *Sourcebook of Criminal Justice Statistics.* Washington, DC: U.S. Government Printing Office.

U.S. Bureau of Labor Statistics. 1989. *Handbook of Labor Statistics.* Washington, DC: U.S. Government Printing Office.

———. 1991. *Employment and Earnings* (January). Washington, DC: U.S. Government Printing Office.

———. 1999. *Employment and Earnings* (January). Washington, DC: U.S. Government Printing Office.

———. 2001a. "Nonfarm payroll statistics from the current employment statistics (national): Total private average hourly earnings of production workers—seasonally adjusted (computed from series EES00500006)." http://146.142.4.24/cgi-bin/surveymost?ee, accessed 1/3/05.

———. 2001b. "Charts from the 'tomorrow's jobs' section of the 2000–2001 occupational outlook handbook." http://stats.bls.gov/oco/images/ocotjc04.gif, accessed 1/3/05.

———. 2003a. "Household data, annual averages" Tables 1 and 2. www.bls.gov/cps/cpsaat1.pdf and www.bls.gov/cps/cpsaat2.pdf, both accessed 1/3/05.

———. 2003b. "Household data annual averages" Table 11. www.bls.gov/cps/cpsaat11.pdf, accessed 1/3/05.

———. 2003c. "Household data annual averages" Table 37. www.bls.gov/cps/cpsaat37.pdf, accessed 1/3/05.

———. 2003d. "Women's earnings up relative to men's in 2002." www.bls.gov/opub/ted/2003/apr/wk3/art03.htm, accessed 1/3/05.

U.S. Bureau of the Census. 1991. "School enrollment: social and economic characteristics of students, October 1991," in *Current Population Reports,* series P-20, no. 469. Washington, DC: U.S. Government Printing Office.

———. 1992. *Statistical Abstract of the United States.* Washington, DC: U.S. Government Printing Office.

———. 1993. *Statistical Abstract of the United States.* Washington, DC: U.S. Government Printing Office.

———. 1994. *World Population Profile: 1994.* Report WP/94. Washington, DC: U.S. Government Printing Office.

———. 1996a. *P23-190 Current Population Reports: Special Studies—651 in the United States,* by Frank B. Hobbs with Bonnie L. Damon. Washington, DC: U.S. Government Printing Office.

———. 1996b. *Statistical Abstract of the United States.* Washington, DC: U.S. Government Printing Office.

———. 1997. "Historical poverty tables— Persons. Table 3. Poverty status of persons, by age, race, and hispanic origin: 1959 to 1996." www.census.gov/ftp/pub/hhes/poverty/histpov/ hstpov3. html, accessed 1/3/05.

———. 1998a. *Statistical Abstract of the United States.* Washington, DC: U.S. Government Printing Office.

———. 1998b. "Marital status and living arrangements," in *Current Population Reports.* Washington, DC: U.S. Government Printing Office.

———. 1998c. "Household and family characteristics (March)," in *Current Population Reports.* Washington, DC: U.S. Government Printing Office.

———. 1998d. "World population profile, 1998—Highlights." www.census.gov/ipc/www/wp98001.html, accessed 1/3/05.

———. 1998e. "Asset ownership of households, 1998." www.census.gov/hhes/www/wealth/1998_2000/wlth98-2.html, accessed 1/4/05.

———. 1999a. "FINC-03. Presence of related children under 18 years old—All families by total money income in 1999, type of family, work experience in 1999, race and Latino origin of reference person" (Current Population Survey, white families.) http://ferret.bls.census.gov/macro/032000/faminc/new03_000.htm, accessed 1/4/05.

———. 1999b. "Population profile of the United States, chapter 2" www.census.gov/population/pop-profile/1999/ chap02.pdf, accessed 1/4/05.

———. 2000a. "Money income in the United States: Current population surveys, table H-1. Income limits for each fifth and top 5 percent of households (all races): 1967 to 1999." www.census.gov/hhes/income/histinc/h01.html, accessed 1/4/05.

———. 2000b. "The changing shape of the nation's income distribution." www.census.gov/prod/2000pubs/p60-204.pdf, accessed 1/4/05.

———. 2000c. "Current population survey: Table A. People and families in poverty by selected characteristics: 1998 and 1999." www.census.gov/hhes/poverty/poverty99/pv99est1.html, accessed 1/4/05.

———. 2000d. "Current population survey: Poverty thresholds in 1999, by size of family and number of related children under 18 years." www.census.gov/hhes/poverty/threshld/thresh99.html, accessed 1/4/05.

———. 2000e. "Current population survey, table 18. Workers as a proportion of all poor people: 1978 to 1999." www.census.gov/hhes/poverty/histpov/hstpov18.html, accessed 1/4/05.

———. 2000f. "Current population survey, table 22. Number and percent of people below 50 percent of poverty level: 1975 to 1999." www.census.gov/hhes/poverty/histpov/hstpov/ 22.html, accessed 1/4/05.

———. 2000g. "Current population survey: 1959 to 1999, table 2. Poverty status of people by family relationship, race, and Latino origin: 1959 to 1999." www.census.gov/hhes/poverty/histpov/hstpov2.html, accessed 1/4/05.

———. 2000h. "Current population survey, poverty in the United States, figure 5. Poverty rate for people in families by family type and presence of work." www.census.gov/prod/2000pubs/p60-210.pdf, accessed 1/4/05.

———. 2000i. "Current population survey, historical poverty tables, table 3. Poverty status of people, by age, race, and Latino origin: 1959 to 1999." www.census.gov/hhes/poverty/histpov/hstpov3.html, accessed 1/4/05.

———. 2000j. "Money income in the United States: Current populations report, table H-2. Share of aggregate income received by each fifth and top 5 percent of households (all races): 1967 to 1999." www.census.gov/hhes/income/histinc/h02.html, accessed 1/4/05.

———. 2000k. "Money income in the United States: Current populations report, historical income tables: H-9, H-9B, H-9C, H-9D, and H-9E." www.census.gov/hhes/income/ histinc/inchhdet.html, accessed 1/4/05.

———. 2000l. "Current population survey, 1960– 2000." www.census.gov/hhes/poverty/poverty99/pov99.html, accessed 1/4/05.

———. 2000m. "Poverty in the United States: Current Population Reports." www.census.gov/prod/2000pubs/p60-210.pdf, accessed 1/4/05.

———. 2000n. "Poverty 1999: Table C. Percent of persons in poverty, by state: 1997, 1998, and 1999." www.census.gov/hhes/poverty/poverty99/pv99state.html, accessed 1/4/05.

———. 2000o. "Poverty in the United States 1999." www.census.gov/prod/2000pubs/p60-210.pdf, accessed 1/4/05.

———. 2000p. *Statistical Abstract of the United States.* Washington, DC: U.S. Government Printing Office.

———. 2000q. "P-12; Sex by age." Census 2000 Summary File 1 (SF-1). http://factfinder.census.gov/servlet/DTTable?geo_id=01000US&ds_name=DEC_2000_SF1_U&mt_name=DEC_2000_SF1_U_PCT012&_lang=en&_sse=on, accessed 1/4/05.

———. 2000r. "QT-P10. Households and Families: 2000." http://factfinder.census.gov/servlet/QTTable?geo_id=01000US&ds_name=DEC_2000_SF1_U&qr_name=DEC_2000_SF1_U_QTP10&_lang=en&_sse=on, accessed 1/4/05.

———. 2000s. "QT-P3. Race and Hispanic or Latino: 2000." http://factfinder.census. gov/servlet/QTTable?geo_id=01000US&ds_name=DEC_2000_SF1_U&qr_name=DEC_2000_SF1_U_QTP3&_lang=en&_sse=on, accessed 1/4/05.

———. 2001a. "Asset ownership of households: 1995." www.census.gov/hhes/www/wealth/ 1995/wlth95-1.html, accessed 1/4/05.

———. 2001b. "Household net worth and asset ownership: 1995." Current Population Reports: The Survey of Income and Program Participation, www.census.gov/prod/2001pubs/p70-71.pdf, accessed 1/4/05.

———. 2001c. "The older population in the United States: March 2000 detailed tables (PPL-147)." www.census.gov/population/www/socdemo/age/ppl-147.html, accessed 1/4/05.

———. 2001d. *Statistical Abstract of the United States.* Washington, DC: U.S. Government Printing Office.

———. 2002a. "Table IE-3. Household shares of aggregate income by fifths of the income distribution: 1967 to 2001" www.census.gov/hhes/income/histinc/ie3.html, accessed 1/4/05.

———. 2002b. "Table H-1. Income limits for each fifth and top 5 percent of households (all races): 1967 to 2001" www.census.gov/hhes/income/histinc/h01.html, accessed 1/4/05.

———. 2002c. "Historical income tables: Households; Tables H-9, H-9b, H-9c, H-9d, H-9e." www.census.gov/hhes/income/histinc/inchhdet.html, accessed 1/4/05.

———. 2002d. "Table 1a. Percent of high school and college graduates of the population 15 years and over, by age, sex, race, and Hispanic origin." www.census.gov/population/socdemo/education/ppl-169/tab01a.xls, accessed 1/4/05.

———. 2002e. "Table P-16. Educational attainment—people 25 years old and over by median income and sex: 1991 to 2001." www.census.gov/hhes/income/histinc/p16.html, accessed 1/4/05.

———. 2002f. "Historical income tables: Families, table F-2, share of aggregate income received by each fifth and the top five percent (all races) www.census.gov/hhes/income/histinc/f02.html, accessed 1/4/05.

———. 2002g. "No. 630. Labor union membership by state: 1983 and 2001." www.census.gov/prod/2003pubs/02statab/labor.pdf, accessed 1/4/05.

———. 2002h. "Children's living arrangements and characteristics, 2002." Table FG7. www.census.gov/population/www/socdemo/hh-fam/cps2002.html, accessed 1/4/05.

———. 2002i. "Statistical abstract of the United States, 2001." www.census.gov/prod/2002pubs/01statab/stat-ab01.html, accessed 1/4/05.

———. 2002j. *Statistical Abstract of the United States, 2002.* www.census.gov/prod/www/statistical-abstract-02.html, accessed 1/4/05.

———. 2002k. "Geographical mobility, population characteristics" Current Population Reports, PS20-538. www.census.gov/prod/2001pubs/p20-538.pdf, accessed 1/4/05.

———. 2002l. "Table 20a—Population by region, sex, race and Hispanic origin with percent distribution by race and Hispanic origin, March 2002." www.census.gov/population/socdemo/race/black/ppl-164/tab20.pdf, accessed 1/4/05.

———. 2003a. "Asset ownership of households: 2000." www.census.gov/hhes/www/wealth/1998_2000/wlth00-1.html, accessed 1/4/05.

———. 2003b. "Number in poverty and poverty rate by race and Hispanic origin: 2001 and 2002" www.census.gov/hhes/poverty/poverty02/table1.pdf, accessed 1/4/05.

———. 2003c. "Poverty 2002." www.census.gov/hhes/poverty/threshld/thresh02.html, accessed 1/4/05.

———. 2003d. "People and families by selected characteristics: 2001 and 2002." www.census.gov/hhes/poverty/poverty02/table2.pdf, accessed 1/4/05.

———. 2003e. "Table 4. Poverty status: Status of families, by type of family, presence of related children, race, and Hispanic origin: 1959 to 2002." www.census.gov/hhes/poverty/histpov/hstpov4.html, accessed 1/4/05.

———. 2003f. "Table 3. Poverty status of people, by age, race, and Hispanic origin: 1959 to 2002." www.census.gov/hhes/poverty/histpov/hstpov3.html, accessed 1/4/05.

———. 2003g. "Table 10. Related children in female householder families as a proportion of all related children, by poverty status: 1959 to 2002." www.census.gov/hhes/poverty/histpov/hstpov10.html, accessed 1/4/05.

———. 2003h. *Statistical Abstract of the United States 2000.* Washington, D.C.: U.S. Government Printing Office. www.census.gov/prod/2004pubs/03statab/pop.pdf, accessed 1/4/05.

———. 2003i. "Poverty in the United States, 2002" Current Population Reports, P60-222. Table 2. www.census.gov/prod/2003pubs/p60-222.pdf, accessed 1/4/05.

———. 2003j. "Table 1a. Percent of high school and college graduates of the population 15 years and over, by age, sex, race, and Hispanic origin: March 2002" www.census.gov/population/socdemo/education/ppl-169/tab01a.xls, accessed 1/4/05.

———. 2003k. "Table 7.2. Educational attainment of the population 25 years and over sex and Hispanic origin type: March 2002" www.census.gov/population/socdemo/hispanic/ppl-165/tab07-2.xls, accessed 1/4/05.

———. 2004. American Community Survey. Poverty Status in 1999 by Sex by Age, PCT49. www.census.gov/acs/www, accessed 1/4/05.

U.S. Bureau of Justice Statistics. 2004. "Capital Punishment Statistics," www.ojp.usdoj.gov/bjs/cp.htm, accessed 1/20/05.

U.S. Department of Education, National Center for Education Statistics. 1993. *Adult Literacy in America: A First Look at the Results of the National Adult Literacy Survey.* Washington, DC: U.S. Government Printing Office.

U.S. Department of Health and Human Services. 2000. *Child Maltreatment 1998: Reports from the States to the National Child Abuse and Neglect Data System.* Washington, DC: U.S. Government Printing Office.

———. 2003a. "Child maltreatment, 2001." www.acf.dhhs.gov/programs/cb/publications/cm01/chapterone.htm#highlight, accessed 1/4/05.

———. 2003b. "Child maltreatment, 1998." www.acf.dhhs.gov/programs/cb/publications/cm98/index.htm, accessed 1/4/05.

U.S. Department of Justice. 2000. "Criminal victimization 1999 changes 1998–99 with trends 1993–99." Washington, DC: U.S. Department of Justice, NCJ 182734 182734, www.ojp.usdoj.gov/bjs/pub/pdf/cv99.pdf, accessed 1/4/05.

———. 2003. "Criminal victimization, 2002." www.ojp.usdoj.gov/bjs/pub/pdf/cv02.pdf, accessed 1/4/05.

U.S. Federal Reserve Board. 2000. "Credit cards: Use and consumer attitudes, 1970 to 1998." *Federal Reserve Bulletin,* www.federalreserve.gov/pubs/bulletin/2000/0900lead.pdf, accessed 1/4/05.

U.S. House of Representatives. 2005. Office of the Clerk, Member FAQs, http://clerk.house.gov/members/memFAQ.html, accessed 1/20/05.

U.S. National Center for Health Statistics. 1993. "Childbearing patterns among selected racial/ethnic minority groups—United States, 1990." *Morbidity and Mortality Weekly Report,* May 28.

U.S. Social Security Administration. 1997a. "Highlights of Social Security data, October 1997," SSA Web site, www.ssa.gov/statistics/highlite.html, accessed 10/28/97.

———.1997b. "Social Security accountability report for fiscal year 1997." SSA Web site, www.ssa.gov/finance/97tblcon.pdf, accessed 1/4/05.

U.S. Surgeon General's Office. 2000. "Treating tobacco use and dependence, fact sheet." www.surgeongeneral.gov/tobacco/smokfact.htm, accessed 1/4/05.

Vallas, S.; and Beck, J. 1996. "The transformation of work revisited: The limits of flexibility in American manufacturing." *Social Problems,* vol. 43, no. 3.

van der Veer, Peter. 1994. *Religious Nationalism: Hindus and Muslims in India.* Berkeley, CA: University of California Press.

van Gennep, Arnold. 1977. *The Rites of Passage.* Originally published 1908. London: Routledge and Kegan Paul.

Vanneman, Reeve D.; and Cannon, Lynn W. 1987. *The American Perception of Class.* Philadelphia: Temple University Press.

Vaughan, Diane. 1986. *Uncoupling: Turning Points in Intimate Relationships.* New York: Oxford University Press.

———. 1996. *The Challenger Launch Decision: Risky Technology, Culture, and Deviance at NASA,* Chicago: University of Chicago Press.

———. 2003. "How theory travels: A most public public sociology," *Public Sociology in Action,* ASA Footnotes (Nov/Dec).

Viorst, Judith. 1986. "And the prince knelt down and tried to put the glass slipper on Cinderella's foot," in Jack Zipes, ed., *Don't Bet on the Prince: Contemporary Feminist Fairy Tales in North America and England.* New York: Methuen.

Vogel, Ezra F. 1979. *Japan as Number One: Lessons for America.* New York: Harper Colophon.

Wacquant, Loic J. D. 1993. "Redrawing the urban color line: The state of the ghetto in the 1980s," in Craig Calhoun and George Ritzer, eds., *Social Problems.* New York: McGraw-Hill.

———. 1996. "The rise of advanced marginality: Notes on its nature and implications." *Acta Sociologica,* vol. 39, no. 2.

———. 2002. "Scrutinizing the street: poverty, morality, and the pitfalls of urban ethnography," *American Journal of Sociology,* vol. 107 (May): 1468–1532.

———; and Wilson, William Julius. 1993. "The cost of racial and class exclusion in the inner city," in William Julius Wilson, ed., *The Ghetto Underclass: Social Science Perspectives.* Newbury Park, CA: Sage.

Wagar, Warren. 1992. *A Short History of the Future.* Chicago: University of Chicago Press.

Wajcman, Judy. 1998. *Managing Like a Man: Women and Men in Corporate Management.* Cambridge, UK: Polity Press.

Waldron, Ingrid. 1986. "Why do women live longer than men?" in Peter Conrad and

Rachelle Kern, eds., *The Sociology of Health and Illness.* New York: St. Martin's.

Wallerstein, Immanuel. 1974a. *Capitalist Agriculture and the Origins of the European World-Economy in the Sixteenth Century.* New York: Academic Press.

———. 1974b. *The Modern World-System.* New York: Academic Press.

———. 1979. *The Capitalist World Economy.* Cambridge, UK: Cambridge University Press.

———. 1990. *The Modern World-System II.* New York: Academic Press.

———. 1996a. *Historical Capitalism with Capitalist Civilization.* New York: Norton.

———, ed. 1996b. *World Inequality.* St. Paul, MN: Consortium Books.

Wallerstein, Judith S.; and Blakeslee, Sandra. 1989. *Second Chances: Men, Women, and Children a Decade After Divorce.* New York: Ticknor and Fields.

———; and Kelly, Joan Berlin. 1980. *Surviving the Break-Up: How Children and Parents Cope with Divorce.* New York: Basic Books.

Wallis, Roy. 1977. *The Road to Total Freedom.* New York: Columbia University Press.

———. 1984. *The Elementary Forms of New Religious Life.* London: Routledge and Kegan Paul.

Wallraff, Barbara. 2000. "What global language?" *Atlantic Monthly* (November).

Walum, Laurel Richardson. 1977. *The Dynamics of Sex and Gender: A Sociological Perspective.* Chicago: Rand McNally.

Warner, Stephen. 1993. "Work in progress toward a new paradigm for the sociological study of religion in the United States." *American Journal of Sociology,* vol. 98.

Warren, B. 1980. *Imperialism: Pioneer of Capitalism.* London: Verso.

Waters, Mary C. 1990. *Ethnic Options: Choosing Identities in America.* Berkeley, CA: University of California Press.

Wattenberg, Martin P. 1996. *The Decline of American Political Parties, 1952–1994.* Rev. ed. Cambridge, MA: Harvard University Press.

Waxman, Laura; and Hinderliter, Sharon. 1996. *A Status Report on Hunger and Homelessness in America's Cities.* Washington, DC: U.S. Conference of Mayors.

Weber, Max. 1947. *The Theory of Social and Economic Organization.* New York: Free Press.

———. 1963 (orig. 1921). *The Sociology of Religion.* Boston: Beacon Press.

———. 1977. *The Protestant Ethic and the Spirit of Capitalism.* New York: Macmillan.

———. 1979. *Economy and Society: An Outline of Interpretive Sociology.* 2 vols. Berkeley, CA: University of California Press.

Webster, Edward. 2004. "Sociology in South Africa: its past, present and future," *Society in Transition 2004,* vol. 35, no. 1: 27–41.

Weeks, Jeffrey. 1977. *Coming Out: Homosexual Politics in Britain, from the Nineteenth Century to the Present.* New York: Quartet.

———. 1986. *Sexuality.* New York: Routledge, Chapman and Hall.

Weinberg, Daniel H. 1996. "Press briefing on 1996 income, poverty, and health insurance estimates." U.S. Bureau of the Census: Housing and Household Economic Statistics Division, September 29.

Weismantle, Mai. 2001. *Reasons People Do Not Work: Household Economic Studies 1996.* U.S. Census Bureau, Current Population Reports, Series P70-76. Washington, DC: U.S. Government Printing Office.

Weiss, Rick. 1997. "Aging: New answers to old questions." *National Geographic,* vol. 192, no. 5.

Weitzman, Lenore. 1985. *Divorce Revolution: The Unexpected Social and Economic Consequences for Women and Children in America.* New York: Free Press.

———, et al. 1972. "Sexual socialization in picture books for preschool children." *American Journal of Sociology,* vol. 77.

Wellman, Barry S. 1994. "I was a teenage network analyst: The route from the Bronx to the information highway." *Connections,* vol. 17, no. 2.

———; Carrington, Peter J.; and Hall, Alan. 1988. "Networks as personal communities," in Barry Wellman and S. D. Berkowitz, eds., *Social Structures: A Network Approach.* New York: Cambridge University Press.

Wellman, Barry, et al. 1996. "Computer networks as social networks: Collaborative work, telework, and virtual community." *Annual Review of Sociology,* vol. 22.

Wellman, David T., ed. 1977. *Portraits of White Racism.* New York: Cambridge University Press.

———. 1987. *Portraits of White Racism.* New York: Cambridge University Press.

West, Candace; and Fenstermaker, Sarah. 1995. "Doing difference." *Gender and Society,* vol. 9, no. 1.

———; and Zimmerman, Don. 1987. "Doing gender." *Gender and Society,* vol. 1 (June).

Western, Bruce. 1997. *Between Class and Market: Postwar Unionization in the*

Capitalist Democracies. Princeton, NJ: Princeton University Press.

———; and Beckett, Katherine. 1999. "How unregulated is the U.S. labor market?: The penal system as a labor market institution." *American Journal of Sociology,* vol. 104, no. 4.

Wheatley, Paul. 1971. *The Pivot of the Four Quarters.* Edinburgh: Edinburgh University Press.

Wheeler, Deborah L. 1998. "Global culture or culture clash: New information technologies in the Islamic world—a view from Kuwait." *Communication Research,* vol. 25, no. 4.

White, Caroline. 2003. "China is top of the gaggers," *Dot Journalism* (June 27). www.journalism.co.uk/news/story673. html, accessed 1/4/05.

White House Press Office. 2001. "President Bush discusses global climate change," press release, June 11.

White, Lynn K. 1990. "Determinants of divorce: A review of research in the eighties." *Journal of Marriage and the Family,* vol. 52 (November).

White, Merry I. 1993. *The Material Child: Coming of Age in Japan and America.* New York: Free Press.

White, Michael; and Trevor, Malcolm. 1983. *Under Japanese Management: The Experience of British Workers.* New York: Gower.

Widom, Cathy Spatz; and Newman, Joseph P. 1985. "Characteristics of non-institutionalized psychopaths," in David P. Farrington and John Gunn, eds., *Aggression and Dangerousness.* Chichester, UK: Wiley.

Wiener, J. M.; Illston, J.; and Hanley, F. J. 1994. *Sharing the Burden: Strategies for Public and Private Long-Term Care Insurance.* Washington, DC: Brookings Institution.

Wilkinson, Richard. 1996. *Unhealthy Societies: The Afflictions of Inequality.* New York: Routledge.

Will, J.; Self, P.; and Datan, N. 1976. "Maternal behavior and perceived sex of infant." *American Journal of Orthopsychiatry,* vol. 46.

Williams, Christine L. 1992. "The glass escalator: Hidden advantages for men in the 'female' professions." *Social Problems,* vol. 39.

Williams, Simon J. 1993. *Chronic Respiratory Illness.* London: Routledge.

Willis, Paul. 1981. *Learning to Labor: How Working Class Kids Get Working Class Jobs.* New York: Columbia University Press.

Wilson, Bryan. 1982. *Religion in Sociological Perspective.* New York: Oxford University Press.

Wilson, Edward O. 1975. *Sociobiology: The New Synthesis.* Cambridge, MA: Harvard University Press.

———. 1978. *On Human Nature.* Cambridge, MA: Harvard University Press.

Wilson, James Q.; and Kelling, George. 1982. "Broken windows," *Atlantic* (March).

Wilson, William Julius. 1978. *The Declining Significance of Race: Blacks and Changing American Institutions.* Chicago: University of Chicago Press.

———. 1987. *The Truly Disadvantaged: The Inner City, the Underclass, and Public Policy.* Chicago: University of Chicago Press.

———. 1991. "Studying inner-city social dislocations: The challenge of public agenda research." *American Sociological Review,* vol. 56 (February).

———. 1996. *When Work Disappears: The World of the New Urban Poor.* New York: Knopf.

———, et al. 1987. "The changing structure of urban poverty." Paper presented at the annual meeting of the American Sociological Association.

Winkleby, Marilynn A., et al. 1992. "Socioeconomic status and health: How education, income, and occupation contribute to risk factors for cardiovascular disease." *American Journal of Public Health,* vol. 82.

Wirth, Louis. 1938. "Urbanism as a way of life." *American Sociological Review,* vol. 44 (July).

Witkowski, Stanley R.; and Brown, Cecil H. 1982. "Whorf and universals of number nomenclature." *Journal of Anthropological Research,* vol. 38.

Wolf, Naomi. 1992. *The Beauty Myth: How Images of Beauty Have Been Used against Women.* New York: Anchor Books.

Wolff, Edward N. 2000. "Recent trends in wealth ownership, 1983–1998." Tables 8 and 9. Jerome Levy Economic Institute, www.levy.org/default.asp?view= publications_view&pubID*f*73a204517, accessed 1/4/05.

Wong, Siu-Lun. 1986. "Modernization and Chinese culture in Hong Kong." *Chinese Quarterly,* vol. 106.

Woodrum, Eric. 1988. "Moral conservatism and the 1984 presidential election," *Journal for the Scientific Study of Religion,* vol. 27: 192–210.

Woolgar, Steve; and Pawluch, Dorothy. 1985. "Ontological gerrymandering: The

anatomy of social problems explanations." *Social Problems,* vol. 32, no. 3.

World Bank. 1994. *World Development Report, 1994.* New York: Oxford University Press.

———. 1995. "World development indicators," in *World Development Report 1995: Workers in an Integrating World.* New York: Oxford University Press.

———. 1996. "Poverty reduction: The most urgent task," Washington, DC: World Bank Brief, www.worldbank.org/html/ extdr/offrep/eca/pov.htm, accessed 8/14/96.

———. 1997. *World Development Report 1997: The State in a Changing World.* New York: Oxford University Press.

———. 1998. *World development indicators.* Washington, DC: World Bank.

———. 2000. *World Development Report.* New York: Oxford University Press.

———. 2000–2001. "World development indicators," in *World Development Report 2000–2001: Attacking Poverty.* http:// poverty.worldbank.org/library/topic/3389/ accessed 1/4/05.

———. 2001. "PovertyNet: Topics relevant to social capital."

———. 2003a. "Country classifications" www.worldbank.org/data/countryclass/ countryclass.html, accessed 1/4/05.

———. 2003b. "GNI per capita 2002, Atlas method" www.worldbank.org/data/ databytopic/GNIPC.pdf, accessed 1/4/05.

———. 2003c. "World development indicators 2003" www.worldbank.org/ data/onlinedatabases/onlinedatabases. html, accessed 1/4/05.

———. 2003d. *World Development Indicators.* www.worldbank.org/poverty/scapital/ topic/index.htm, accessed 1/4/05.

World Commission on Environment and Development (Brundtland Commission), 1987. *Our Common Future.* Oxford, UK: Oxford University Press.

World Trade Organization. 2003a. "International Trade Statistics, 2003— Table IV.20" www.wto.org/english/res_e/ statis_e/its2003_e/section4_e/iv20.xls, accessed 1/4/05.

———. 2003b. "International trade statistics, 2003." www.wto.org/english/res_e/statis_ e/its2003_e/its03_general_overview_e. htm, accessed 1/4/05.

Worrall, Anne. 1990. *Offending Women: Female Lawbreakers and the Criminal Justice System.* London: Routledge.

Worsley, Peter. 1968. *The Trumpet Shall Sound: A Study of Cargo Cults in Melanesia.* New York: Schocken.

Wright, Erik Olin. 1978. *Class, Crisis, and the State.* London: New Left Books.

———. 1985. *Classes.* New York: Shocken.

———. 1997. *Class Counts: Comparative Studies in Class Analysis.* New York: Cambridge University Press.

———. 2000. *Class Counts: Student Edition.* New York: Cambridge University Press.

Wright, Robin. 1995. "For women around the world, survival is problem no. 1." *Los Angeles Times,* September 3.

Wrigley, E. A. 1968. *Population and History.* New York: McGraw-Hill.

Wuthnow, Robert. 1976. *The Consciousness Reformation.* Berkeley, CA: University of California Press.

———. 1978. *Experimentation in American Religion.* Berkeley, CA: University of California Press.

———. 1988. "Sociology of religion," in Neil J. Smelser, ed., *Handbook of Sociology.* Newbury Park, CA: Sage.

Wyatt, Edward. 1999. "Investors are seeing profits in nation's demands for education." *New York Times,* November 4.

Yankelovich, Claney Shulman. 1991. "What's OK on a date." Survey for *Time* and CNN, May 8.

Young, Jock. 1998. "Breaking windows: Situating the new criminology," in Paul Walton and Jock Young, eds., *The New Criminology Revisited.* London: Macmillan.

———. 1999. *The Exclusive Society: Social Exclusion, Crime, and Difference in Late Modernity.* London: Sage.

Young, Michael; and Schuller, Tom. 1991. *Life after Work: The Arrival of the Ageless Society.* London: HarperCollins London.

———; and Willmott, Peter. 1973. *The Symmetrical Family: A Study of Work and Leisure in the London Region.* London: Routledge and Kegan Paul.

Zammuner, Vanda Lucia. 1986. "Children's sex-role stereotypes: A cross-cultural analysis," in Phillip Shaver and Clyde Hendrick, eds., *Sex and Gender.* Beverly Hills, CA: Sage.

Zeitlin, Irving. 1985. *Ancient Judaism: Biblical Criticism from Max Weber to the Present.* New York: Basil Blackwell.

———. 1988. *The Historical Jesus.* Cambridge, UK: Polity Press.

Zerubavel, Eviatar. 1979. *Patterns of Time in Hospital Life.* Chicago: University of Chicago Press.

———. 1982. "The standardization of time: A sociohistorical perspective." *American Journal of Sociology,* vol. 88.

Zhang, Naihu; and Xu, Wu. 1995. "Discovering the positive within the negative: The women's movement in a changing China," in Amrita Basu, ed., *The Challenge of Local Feminisms.* Boulder, CO: Westview.

Zimbardo, Philip G. 1969. "The human choice: Individuation, reason, and order versus deindividuation, impulse, and chaos," in W. J. Arnold and D. Levine, eds., *Nebraska Symposium on Motivation.* Vol. 17. Lincoln, NE: University of Nebraska Press.

———. 1972. "Pathology of imprisonment." *Society,* vol. 9.

———; Ebbesen, Ebbe B.; and Maslach, Christina. 1977. *Influencing Attitudes and Changing Behavior.* Reading, MA: Addison-Wesley.

Zubaida, Sami. 1996. "How successful is the Islamic Republic in Islamizing Iran?" in J. Beinen and J. Stork, eds., *Political Islam: Essays from the Middle East Report.* Berkeley, CA: University of California Press.

Zuboff, Shoshana. 1988. *In the Age of the Smart Machine: The Future of Work and Power.* New York: Basic Books.

PHOTO CREDITS

Chapter 1: p. 1: (left to right): Reuters/Corbis; Rodolfo Gonzalez/Rocky Mountain News/Corbis Sygma; Steve Prezant/Corbis; Bettmann/Corbis; Philip G. Zimbardo/Stanford Prison Experiment; Joseph Rodriguez/Blackstar; p. 2: Reuters/Corbis; p. 5: Reuters/Corbis; p. 6 (left): Bo Zaunders/Corbis; (right): Bettmann/Corbis; p. 7: © The New Yorker Collection 1969 Dana Fradon from cartoonbank.com. All Rights Reserved.; p. 8: Pablo Corral Vega/Corbis; p. 9: Thomas Hoepker/Magnum/PNI; p. 10: Rodolfo Gonzalez/Rocky Mountain News/Corbis Sygma; p. 11: (top left and right): George Kochaniec Jr./Rocky Mountain News/Corbis Sygma; (bottom right): Steve Liss/Corbis Sygma; p. 13: Corbis; p. 14 (all): Bettmann/Corbis; p. 15: The Granger Collection; p. 16: Bettman/Corbis; p. 17: The Warder Collection; p. 21: Steve Prezant/Corbis.

Chapter 2: p. 28: Bettmann/Corbis; p. 30: Aldine de Gruyter; p. 33: Staatliche Museen zu Berlin/Gemaldegalerie, Berlin; p. 39: Philip G. Zimbardo/Stanford Prison Experiment; p. 40 (left): Bettmann/Corbis; (right): A. Holbrooke/Corbis; p. 41 (left): Joseph Rodriguez/Black Star; (right): Benedict J. Fernandez.

Chapter 3: p. 49 (left to right): AP/Wide World Photos; AP/Wide World Photos; Photofest; AP/Wide World Photos; Picture Net/Corbis; Henry Diltz/Corbis; p. 50: AP/Wide World Photos; p. 53: Courtesy The BADvertising Institute; p. 54: Anna Clopet/Corbis; p. 55: (left): Peter Simon/IPN Stock; (right): Peter Turnley/Corbis; p. 56 (left): AP/Wide World Photos; (right): Clay Perry/Corbis; p. 57 (left): Kevin Fleming/Corbis; (right): Kelly-Mooney Photography/Corbis; p. 60: Courtesy of Danah Boyd; p. 61: Stephen Welstead/Corbis; p. 64: © Atsuko Tanaka www.atsukotanaka.com; p. 65: Rune Hellestad/Corbis; p. 66: Bettmann/Corbis; p. 67: Bettmann/Corbis; p. 69: Michael Yamashita/Corbis; p. 70: L. Clarke/Corbis; p. 79 (left): Jacques M. Chenet/Corbis; (right): AP/Wide World Photos; p. 80: Stephen Frink/Corbis; p. 82: Reuters/Corbis.

Chapter 4: p. 86: Photofest; p. 89: UCLA Library/Special Collections; p. 90: Courtesy Dan Bartell; p. 93: Reed Kaestner/Corbis; p. 95: Steve Rubin/The Image Works; p. 97: Jacques Langevin/Corbis; p. 98: Hulton-Deutsch/Corbis; p. 99: Lynn Goldsmith/Corbis; p. 101: Alinari Archives/Corbis; p. 102: © Dick Hemingway; p. 103: AP/Wide World Photos; p. 104 (left): Corbis; (right): Lucille Reyboz/Corbis; p. 105: Steve Prezant/Corbis.

Chapter 5: p. 108: AP/Wide World Photos; p. 110: Richard Perry/*New York Times*; p. 111: Paul Ekman; p. 114–115: Simon Bond; p. 118: © 1991 Mike Marland; p. 119: Dan Habib/Concord Monitor/Corbis; p. 122: David Samuel Robbins/Corbis; p. 123: AP/Wide World Photos; p. 126: © David Hoffman.

Chapter 6: p. 130: Picture Net/Corbis; p. 134: Dung Vo Trung/Coup D'Etat Productions/Corbis; p. 136 Philip Gould/Corbis; p. 138 (all): Courtesy Alexandra Milgram; p. 141: Owen Franken/Corbis; p. 144: AP/Wide World Photos; p. 145: Courtesy of Diane Vaughan; p. 147: Jim Sugar/Corbis; p. 148: University College Library, London; p. 151: Howard Grey/Getty Images; p. 154: Jon Feingersh/Masterfile; p. 155: Owen Franken/Corbis; p. 156: AP/Wide World Photos; p. 157: Masterfile; p. 161: Micheline Pelletier/Corbis.

Chapter 7: p. 166: Henry Diltz/Corbis; p. 170: J. Bounds/RNO/Corbis Sygma; p. 172 (left): Chris Stanford/*Washington Post*; (right): Craig Lovell/Corbis; p. 173 (left): © Gropp/Sipa; (right): AP/Wide World Photos; p. 176: Mark Peterson/Corbis; p. 190: Owen Franken/Corbis; p. 191: Ted Nebia/Corbis; p. 192: Courtesy of Devah Pager.

Chapter 8: p. 201 (left to right): Catherine Karnow/Corbis; AP/Wide World Photos; AP/Wide World Photos; Michael Smyth; Ruth Fremson/*New York Times*; Reuters/Corbis; p. 202: Catherine Karnow/Corbis; p. 206: © Johnston/Sipa; p. 212: AP/Wide World Photos; p. 213: Vince Streano/Corbis; p. 215: Vernier Jean Bernar/Corbis Sygma; p. 219: Robert Sorbo/Corbis; p. 222: Courtesy of Ofer Sharone; p. 223: AP/Wide World Photos; p. 226–227 (all): AP/Wide World Photos; p. 236: AP/Wide World Photos.

Chapter 9: p. 244: AP/Wide World Photos; p. 256: Reuters/Corbis; p. 257: Corbis; p. 260: Dean Conger/Corbis; p. 261: Danny Lehman/Corbis; p. 263: George Esiri/Reuters/Corbis; p. 265: Jacques Langevin/Corbis Sygma; p. 266 (left): AP/Wide World Photos; (right): Jack Kurtz/The Image Works; p. 267: AP/Wide World Photos; p. 270: Courtesy of Edward Webster; p. 271: Gideon Mendel/Corbis.

Chapter 10: p. 276: AP/Wide World Photos; p. 279: Corbis/Sygma; p. 281 (all): Bettmann/Corbis; p. 283: National Anthropological Archives/Smithsonian; p. 290: Gabe Palmer/Corbis; p. 292: Michael Keller/Corbis; p. 295: Courtesy of Jessie Klein; p. 299: Timothy McCarthy/Art Resource, NY; p. 304: Bettmann/Corbis; p. 306: *Chicago Tribune* photos by Ovie Carter; p. 307 (all): *Chicago Tribune* photos by Ovie Carter; p. 308: AP/Wide World Photos; p. 309: AP/Wide World Photos.

Chapter 11: p. 314: Michael Smyth; p. 317: Peter Marshall; p. 318: Alain Nogues/Corbis Sygma; p. 323: Mark Peterson/Corbis; p. 325: Penny Tweedle/Panos Pictures; p. 330: Corbis; p. 332: AP/Wide World Photos; p. 333: Bettmann/Corbis; p. 334: Hulton-Deutsch/Corbis; p. 336: © Warren Lehrer 2003 from the book *Crossing the BLVD: Strangers, Neighbors, Aliens in a new America* by Warren Lehrer and Judith Sloan; p. 337 (both): Erik Freeland/Corbis Saba; p. 344: bottom left: Photo Collection Alexander Alland/Corbis; bottom right: Jeff Greenberg/The Image Works; p. 345: Dalton Conley.

Chapter 12: p. 350: Ruth Fremson/*New York Times*; p. 355: Keren Su/Lonely Planet Images; p. 357: John Henley/Corbis; p. 364 (all): Courtesy of Thomas Roma; p. 365 (all): Courtesy of Thomas Roma.

Chapter 13: p. 370: Reuters/Corbis; p. 376: Danny Lehman/Corbis; p. 378: AP/Wide World Photos; p. 379: AP/Wide World Photos; p. 380: James Leynse/Corbis; p. 383: AP/Wide World Photos; p. 392: David Cunningham; p. 393: David Cunningham; p. 394: Giraudon/Art Resource, NY; p. 398: Hulton-Deutsch/Corbis; p. 402 (all): Tom Gralish/*Philadelphia Inquirer*; p. 403 (left): © Harvey Finkle; (right): Photo by Michael Mally/*Philadelphia Inquirer*.

Chapter 14: p. 411 (left to right): Jeff Zelevansky/Bloomberg News/Landov; Paul Barton/Corbis; Photo by Courteney Coolidge from *American Families: Beyond the White Picket Fence*, www.tenfamilies.com; Ed Kashi/Corbis; Scott Nelson/Getty Images; Raffi Alexander/Spiderbox; p. 412: Jeff Zelevansky/Bloomberg News/Landov; p. 417: Bettmann/Corbis; p. 420: Courtesy of Joel Rogers; p. 421: Courtesy of Laura Dresser; p. 422 AP/Wide World Photos; p. 426: AP/Wide World Photos; p. 432 (top): Joseph Sohm: ChromoSohm Inc./Corbis; (bottom): Courtesy of Dell, Inc.; p. 433: Charles E. Rotkin/Corbis; p. 438–439: Photographs by Bill Bamberger from *Closing: The Life and Death of an American Factory* (DoubleTake/ Norton, 1998).

Chapter 15: p. 444: Paul Barton/Corbis; p. 447: Paul Harrison/Panos Pictures; p. 450: Ariel Skelly/Corbis; p. 451: Philip Rostron/Masterfile; p. 460–461: Photos by Courteney Coolidge from *American Families: Beyond the White Picket Fence*, www.tenfamilies.com; p. 467: Najlah Feanny/Corbis; p. 468: Courtesy of Judith Stacey; p. 469: Koopman/Corbis; p. 470: Kimberly White/Reuters/Corbis

Chapter 16: p. 474: Ed Kashi/Corbis; p. 478: J.A. Giordano/Corbis; p. 480: Gary Connor/PhotoEdit/PNI; p. 481: Greg Meadors/Stock Boston/PNI; p. 484: Courtesy of Robert Hauser; p. 485: Will & Deni McIntyre/Corbis; p. 487: Ted Streshinsky/Corbis; p. 488 (left): Karen Stallwood/Dallas Morning News/KRT; (right): AP/Wide World Photos; p. 489 (top left and bottom): AP/Wide World Photos; (top right): Corbis; p. 495: Bill Nation/Corbis; p. 496: © 1997 Lloyd Dangle.

Chapter 17: p. 504: Scott Nelson/Getty Images; p. 510: Joseph Sohm, ChromoSohm Inc./Corbis; p. 511: © 1999 Joel Gordon; p. 514 (all): Rob Carr/*New York Times*; p. 515 (all): Rob Carr/*New York Times*; p. 519: Raffi Alexander/Spiderbox; p. 520 (left): Robert Holmes/Corbis; (right): CapeCodTravel.com; p. 524: World Religions Photo Library/Photos12.com; p. 529: Bettmann/Corbis; p. 532: Catherine Karnow/Corbis; p. 533: AP/Wide World Photos; p. 537: Reuters/Landov.

Chapter 18: p. 543 (left to right): © Howard Schatz/IPN Stock; Gideon Mendel/Corbis; Alex MacLean/Landslides Aerial Photography; Giry Daniel/Corbis Sygma; Guy Grenier/Masterfile; Reuters/Corbis; p. 544: © Howard Schatz/IPN Stock; p. 546 (left): C. Steele Perkins/Magnum Photos; (right): Ed Quinn/Corbis; p. 548: (left) Peter Morgan/Reuters/Time Pix/Getty Images; (right): Courtesy www.adbusters.org; p. 549 (left): Corbis; (right): Rachel Royse/Corbis; p. 552: Lindsay Hebberd/Corbis; p. 561 (left): Gideon Mendel/Corbis; (right): Louise Gubb/Corbis Saba; p. 564: Liba Taylor/Corbis; p. 565: Eye Ubiquitous/Corbis; p. 570: Courtesy of Pepper Schwartz; p. 572: *New York Daily News*.

Chapter 19: p. 578: Alex MacLean/Landslides Aerial Photography; p. 580: Jeff Greenberg/The Image Works; p. 586: Kat Wade/Corbis; p. 587: AP/Wide World Photos; p. 588: Philippa Lewis/Corbis; p. 589: AP/Wide World Photos; p. 591 (top): Arlene Gottfried/The Image Works; (bottom): Nicole Bengiveno/*New York Times*; p. 592: Courtesy of Boston University; p. 593: Corbis; p. 595: Dvir Bar-Gal/Zuma Press; p. 597 (top): Giry Daniel/Corbis Sygma; (bottom): AP/Wide World Photos; p. 598: AP/Wide World Photos; p. 600 (all): Sebastiao Salgado/Contact Press Images; p. 601 (all): Sebastiao Salgado/Contact Press Images; p. 609: Reuters/Corbis.

Chapter 20: p. 616: Guy Grenier/Masterfile; p. 622: Carl & Ann Purcell/Corbis; p. 631: Robert Essel NYC/Corbis; p. 632: Courtesy of Judith Blau; p. 633: Reuters/Corbis; p. 635: Reuters/Corbis; p. 636: AFP/Corbis; p. 637: AP/Wide World Photos; p. 638: AP/Wide World Photos; p. 639: AP/Wide World Photos.

INDEX

American Christian Television System, 532
American Psychiatric Association, 568
American Religious Identification Survey, 527
American Revolution, 373, 394
Americans for Generational Equity (AGE), 366
American Sociological Association, 343
America Online, 424
Amish and cell phones, 56–57
Amnesty International, 625
Anderson, Elijah, 126, 590–91
Anderson, Patty and Gary, 514
andragogy, 363
anomie, 14, 175
anorexia, 545–46, 547, 549
anthropology, 52
antidepressants, 186
antiracism, 319
    training for children, 316
antisweatshop movement, 402–3
AOL-Time Warner, 158–59
apartheid, 136, 205–6, 316, 319, 320, 322, 323
Appelbaum, Richard, 433
Apple, 152
Applewhite, Marshall Herff, 131, 132, 170
apprenticeships, 415
Apter, Terri, 292
Argentina, 378, 603
Ariès, Philippe, 102
Armed Forces Qualifying Test, 483
Armenian genocide, 323
arranged marriages, 4, 12, 103, 207
Asch, Solomon, 136–37
Aschbrenner, Joyce, 456
ascribed status, 118
ascription, 221
Ashworth, Anthony, 42
Asia
    colonialism in, 77
        spread of disease and, 559
        homosexuality in, 572
        population growth in, 581
        urbanization in, 581
Asian Americans, 329, 332, 335–38, 342–43
    families, 456
    poverty rates, 230
assembly line, 416, 417, 429
assimilation, 63, 321, 324

Association of Black Sociologists, 343–46
AT&T, 154, 423–24, 427, 438
Atta, Mohammed, 5
Aum Shinrikyo cult, 401, 518
Australia
    women in the work force in, 300
    women's movement in, 398
Austria
    working women in, 300
authority
    defined, 372
    obedience to, 137–38
    skepticism about traditional forms of, 389
Automat, 429
automation and skill debate, 429–30
automobiles and automobile industry, 53
    global production, 433–34
    highway construction and, 586–87
    international character of products of, 427, 428
    Japanese, 417
    mass production and mass marketing, 416
    robots used in manufacture of, 413, 429
    technology in the workplace, 413–14
Aviation Week and Space Technology, 144
ayurvedic medicine, 552
Azande of Africa, 568

Babylon, 580
back regions, 118–19
Bailey, J. Michael, 569
Balzac, Honoré de, 142
Bamberger, Bill, 439n
Bangladesh, 521
Baptists, 527
Barbie dolls, global commodity chain and, 264–68
Barnet, Richard, 426
Bart, Paulene, 296
Basque separatism, 404, 405, 626
Baudrillard, Jean, 20, 494–95
Bay of Pigs invasion, 138
Beach, Frank, 562
Beck, Ulrich, 622, 637
Becker, Gary, 288
Becker, Howard S., 177
Belgium, union density in, 418–19

Bell, Daniel, 390, 621
Bell, Genevieve, 61
Bell Curve: Intelligence and Class Structure in American Life, The (Herrnstein and Murray), 483
Bendix, Reinhard, 221
Benetton, 159
Benin, 378
Bentham, Jeremy, 147–48
berdaches, 283
Berger, Peter, 124, 510
Berle, Adolf, 423
Bernhardt, Annett, 421
Bhopal chemical plant, India, 187
Bianchi, Suzanne, 450
Biblarz, Timothy, 469
Biggs, Mae, 119–20
Bill of Rights, 526, 531
bin Laden, Osama, 4, 5, 534, 537
biological aging, 354
biological reductionism, 304
biological view of deviance, 174, 175
biomedical model of health, 554
birth control, *see* contraception
bisexuality, 568
black feminism, 304–5
Black Metropolis (Drake and Cayton), 582–83
Black Panthers, 64
black power, 319
Black Report, 556
blacks, *see* African Americans
Blades, Joan, 380
Blatch, Harriet Stanton, 398
Blau, Judith, 633n
Blau, Peter, 143, 151, 224
Blauner, Robert, 343, 429
blended families, 460
blue-collar jobs, 434, 440, 587, 621
blushing, 112
Boden, Deidre, 124
bodily posture, 112
body, sociology of the, 544–75
    basic themes of, 546–47
    health and illness, *see* health and illness
    as new field, 546
body image, 546, 547–49
body language, *see* nonverbal communication
Bohemian Grove, 139, 161
Bolivia, 378
Bonacich, Edna, 433
bonding social capital, 162
Bonnett, Alistair, 319
Borjas, George, 331

"born again" Christians, *see* Evangelical Protestantism
Bosnia, 299, 323, 371–72, 533, 626
Boston University, Entrepreneurial Management Institute, 592
Bourdieu, Pierre, 213–14, 224, 482
bovine spongiform encephalopathy (BSE), 636
Bowlby, John, 302
Bowles, Samuel, 482–83
Boyd, Danah, 60–61
Boyd, Wes, 380
Braithwaite, John, 196
Branch Davidians, 513–16, 518
Brandeis University, 392
Braverman, Harry, 155, 429
Brazil, 77, 78, 263, 643
bridging social capital, 162
Britain
    citizenship rights in, 373
    health inequalities in, 556
    industrialization in, 581
    introduction of sociology to, 17
    knowledge-based industries, 435
    "mad cow disease" in, 636
    religion in, 511, 512, 518
    social status in, 238
    women's suffrage in, 398
"broken windows" theory, 179
Brown, K., 555n
Brownmiller, Susan, 184–85, 298
Brown University, 227
Brown v. Board of Education, 206, 334
Brumberg, Joan Jacobs, 549n
Brundtland, G. H., 610
Buddhism, 525, 533
    gender and, 518–19
Buenos Aires, Argentina, 594
Buffett, Warren, 245–46
bulimia, 546, 549
Bumpass, Larry, 466
Bundy, Ted, 170
Burawoy, Michael, 633
bureaucracy, 18
    alternatives to, 151–59
    coining of term, 141
    Columbia Space Shuttle disaster and, 144–45
    defined, 142
    democracy and, 148–49

Evangelical Protestantism, 516, 520, 527, 532–33
Evelan, Joanna, 9
evidence, reviewing the, 32
exchange social mobility, 221
exclusion, social closure and, 239
experiments, 37, 38–39
explanatory comments or notes in a table, 44
exponential population growth, 602
extended family, 446, 452, 456
external risk, 634
extinction of species, 610, 612
Exxon, 423
eye contact, 117, 124
   civil inattention, 109–10
   cultural norms of, 52
   gender and, 112

face-to-face interactions, 495
Facial Action Coding System (FACS), 111–12
factual questions, 31
Fair Labor Association, 402
fairy tales, gender learning and, 98
family, 444–71
   alternatives to traditional forms of, 466–71
   dark side of, 464–65
   defined, 446
   extended, *see* extended family
   global patterns of change in the, 452–53
   historical perspective, 449–53
   myths of the traditional, 450–52
   nuclear, *see* nuclear family
   or orientation, 446–47
   power relationships, 448
   as primary social group, 133
   of procreation, 446, 447
   as reference group, 134
   as socializing agent, 91–92
   symmetrical, 448
   theoretical perspectives on, 447–49
   in the U.S., 453–64
      future of, 471
family capitalism, 424
family planning policies, state, 452
famine, 253–56
   population growth and global, 608–9

fatwas, 537
favelas, 597, 601
fecundity, 599
Federal Bureau of Investigation (FBI), Internet surveillance, 381
Federal Housing Administration (FHA), 586
Federalists, 382
Feeding the Family (Devault), 293
Feminine Mystique, The (Friedan), 451–52
femininity, *see* gender
feminism and feminist theory, 20, 30–31, 397–400
   central argument of, 20
   on crime and criminal justice system, 182–84
   family, perspectives on, 448–49
   Freud's theory of gender identity and, 100
   gender and organization, 149–51
   on gender inequality, 303–5
      black feminism, 304–5
      liberal feminism, 303
      radical feminism, 303–4
   human capital theory, criticism of, 289
   political power of feminists, 386
   on skill levels, 429–30
Feminist Case against Bureaucracy, The (Ferguson), 150
Feminist Studies, 309
feminization of poverty, 230–31
Fennelly, Kelly, 456
Ferguson, Kathy, 150
fertility rates, 595, 599, 603
feudalism, 396
Feuerbach, Ludwig, 508
Fidler, David P., 639*n*
fields of action, 396–97
fieldwork, 36
Filipino families, 456
financial markets, global integration of, 622, 628
Finke, Robert, 512, 531
Finland
   cohabitation in, 467
   union density in, 418–19
   women in politics in, 300
firearms, *see* guns
Firestone, Shulamith, 303

First World societies, 76, 77
Fischer, Claude, 583
527 organizations, 386
Flanders, 405
flexible production, 431
flexible working hours, 437
focused interaction, 117–18
Focus on the Family, 533
Food and Agricultural Organization (FAO), 609
foot-and-mouth disease, 635
Forbes, 219
Ford, Clellan, 562
Ford, Henry, 416, 417
Ford, William Clay, Jr., 424
Ford family, 424
Fordism, 416–17
Ford Motor Company, 416, 424, 427, 433
foreign aid, 262
foreign students in the U.S., 480–81
Forgotten Americans, The (Schwarz and Volgy), 225
formal operational stage of child development, 91
formal relations within organizations, 142–43
fossil fuels, 611, 612
fostering children, 460–61
Foucault, Michel, 146, 147, 148, 158, 498, 547
France, 404
   American "cultural imperialism" and, 51
   cohabitation in, 454, 467
   education in, 435
   ethnocentrism and, 67–68
   Internet and, 51
   Islam in, 536
   knowledge-based industries, 435
   labor conflicts in, 418
   length of workweek in, 451
   secularization of, 511
Frankfurt, Germany, 594
Frankfurt School of social thought, 494
Freedman, Rose, 351
freedom in global perspective, 374–75
Freeman, Richard, 422–23
"free-rider" problem, 400
free trade, *see* trade, globalization and world
Free Trade Area of the Americas (FTAA), 643

Fremlin, J. H., 599
French Revolution, 13, 42, 373, 394, 397
Freud, Sigmund, 562
   gender identity, theory of, 99–100
Friedan, Betty, 448, 451–52
Friedlander, Daniel, 233
Friedson, Eliot, 550
Friends of the Earth, 609
Friendster.com, 60–61
Friesen, W. V., 111–12
front regions, 118
functionalism, 18–19, 30, 404
   aging theories, 355–56
   crime and deviance theories, 175–77
   family, theories of, 447–48
   gender inequality theories, 302–3
   gender socialization theories, 280
   sick role, 550–51
   social stratification and, 238
fundamentalists
   Christian, 532–33
   Islamic, 4

Gamoran, Adam, 480–81
Gandhi, Mahatma, 525, 619
Gangi, Robert, 189
Gap, Inc., 219
Gardner, Carol Brooks, 125
Garfinkel, Harold, 113, 121
gated communities, 235
Gates, Bill, 215, 226, 245
Gates, Henry Louis, 334
gay rights movement, 31, 572
gays and lesbians, 568
   as crime victims, 185
   gay marriage, 466–67, 468–69, 533
   gay-parent families, 467–68
   Humphreys's study of "tearoom trade," 29–31, 42–43, 46
   see also homosexuality
Geerz, Clifford, 491
Gehman, Admiral Harold, 144, 145
Gelles, Richard, 465
Gellner, Ernest, 404
gender, 139
   crime and, 182–85
   defined, 278
   inequality, *see* gender inequality
   nature/nurture, 278–83
      biology's role, 278–79

Greenpeace, 160, 609, 625
Gross, Larry, 402
Group of 21, 642–43
group production, 431
groups, social, *see* social groups
groupthink, 138
Guangdong, China, 596, 597
guerrilla movements, 395
guest workers model of
        migration, 325
Guinea, hunger, malnutrition,
        and famine in, 253
guns
    gun control, 384
    violent crime and
        availability of, 182
gynecologist visits, study of,
        119–20

Habermas, Jürgen, 390, 491,
        494
Habibi, Shafiqa, 519, 520
hackers, 169–70
Hadden, Jeffrey K., 516
Haiti, 77
Hall, Edward T., 120
Hamilton, Alexander, 382
Hamilton, Andre, 488–89
Hamilton, Charles, 319
Hammond, Phillip, 531
Hanseatic League, 160
Hare Krishnas, 516, 531
Harris, Eric, 10
Harris, Marvin, 70–71
Harry Potter series, 87–88
Hartford Institute for Religious
        Research, 514
Hartig, Terry, 154
Harvey, David, 416, 585
Harvey, Larry, 173
hate crimes, 185, 319
hate groups, 140
Hatred in the Hallways, 569
Hauser, Robert M., 193, 224, 485*n*
Hawaii, same-sex marriage in,
        467
headings, table, 44
Head Start, 487
health and illness, 545–62
    aging and, 362–63
    alternative medicine, 553–54
    biomedical model of health,
        554
    changing conceptions of,
        552–53
    in the developing world,
        559–62
    global inequality, 252–53,
        638–39

manufactured risk, 635–36,
        638–39
    racial and ethnic inequality,
        340–41
    social basis of, 554–58
        gender-based
            inequalities, 557–58
        race-based inequalities,
            556–57
        social-class based
            inequalities, 554–56
    social cohesion and, 558–59
    sociological perspectives of,
        550–52
        illness as "lived
            experience," 551–52
        sick role, 550–51
health insurance, 358–59, 362,
        366
heart disease, 559
Heaven's Gate, 131–32, 136,
        137–38, 140, 170, 516
Heckman, James J., 193
Heelas, Paul, 510
Held, David, 376, 627
Henslin, James, 119–20
Heraclitus, 618
Herdt, Gilbert, 568
Herrnstein, Richard J., 483, 486
heterosexuality, 568
hidden curriculum, 481–82, 498
high-income countries, 248,
        250–52
"High Stakes: Testing for
        Tracking, Promotion
        and Graduation," 484
high-trust systems, 417
Highway Act of 1956, 586–87
highways, construction of
        interstate, 586–87
Hill, Anita, 290
Hinduism, 509, 525
hip-hop, 64
Hirschi, Travis, 179
Hispanics/Latinos, *see*
        Latinos/Hispanics
historical analysis, 42
    combining comparative
        research and, 42
historicity, 397
Hitachi, 152
Hitler, 619
HIV/AIDS, 362, 533, 559–62,
        564–65, 566
    in Africa, 252, 253, 560, 561,
        565, 633
    importation of generic
        medications, 643
    stigma of, 551, 560–61
Hochschild, Arlie, 292–93, 451

Hodge, Robert, 93
Holocaust, 323, 525
homeless, the, 240, 595
    deinstitutionalization
        movement and, 171
    as deviants and conformists,
        169, 170, 171–74
    reasons for becoming, 237
    social exclusion of, 236–37
    studies of the, 40–41
Homeless, The (Jencks), 40
homeopathy, 553
homeownership, *see* housing
homicide, 180–82
    mass, *see* mass murder
homicide rates, race and, 556
homophobia, 569–72
homosexuality, 568
    homophobia, 569–72
    international differences in
        legality of, 572
    sexual norms and, 562
    see also gays and lesbians
"homosexual panic" legal
        defense, 185
Hong Kong, 77, 78, 594, 596, 597
    eating disorders in, 546
    as high-income country, 248
    as newly industrializing
        economy, 257, 272
    steel production in, 437
Hooks, Bell, 304
hospitals, 141
housework, 292–93, 415
housing
    age-integrated, 364
    homeless, *see* homeless, the
    mortgages, discrimination
        in financing, 209,
        587
    residential mobility in the
        U.S., 588–89
    residential segregation, 341,
        587–88, 590
    social exclusion and, 234–35
    in urban areas of the
        developing world,
        597–98
    wealth and homeownership,
        208, 209
Hubbard, L. Ron, 517
human capital theory, 288–89
Human Development Report
        (UNDP), 499, 640
human resource management,
        153
Human Rights Watch, 193
human sexuality, *see* sexuality
Humphreys, Laud, 29–31,
        42–43, 46

Hungary, 76
    democracy in, 379
    women in the work force in,
        300
hunger, malnutrition, and
        famine, global,
        253–56
hunting and gathering
        societies, 71–72, 73,
        204, 609, 618–19
Hussein, Saddam, 506, 619
hyperreality, world of, 494–95
hypertension, 556–57
hypotheses, 32–33

IBM, 152, 158, 427, 438
ideal types, 142
identity, 96–97
ideology, 20
illegitimate sick role, 551
illiteracy, *see* education and
        literacy
illness, *see* health and illness
imagination, sociological, *see*
        sociological
        imagination
imitation, learning through, 90
immigration
    debate over social and
        economic costs of,
        330–31
    demographic structure of
        the U.S. and, 332–33
    port-of-entry settlement,
        333
    functional illiteracy in the
        U.S. and, 487
    illegal, 333, 376
        life on the work line,
            336–37
    quotas, 330
    U.S. policy, 331, 332, 338
    welfare state and, 374
    see also migration
Immigration and Nationality
        Act Amendments of
        1965, 331, 338
Immigration Reform and
        Control Act of 1986,
        331
impression management, 118,
        119–20
incarceration, *see* prisons
incest prohibition as cultural
        universal, 68
income
    of corporate executives
        versus their workers,
        217–18

income (*continued*)
    defined, 208
    educational attainment and,
        226
    inequality
        global, *see* global
            inequality
        health and, 556, 558
        in industrialized
            countries, 217, 218,
            390
        in the U.S., 208, 209,
            217–20, 338–40
    real, 208
independent variables, 35
India, 76, 619, 643
    affirmative action in, 319
    ayurvedic medicine in, 552
    caste system in, 205–6, 525
    eating disorders in, 546
    family planning in, 603
    health issues in, 638
    HIV/AIDS in, 561
    Islam in, 521
    as low-income country,
        246–47
    marriage in, 4, 207
    poverty in, 77
    projected population
        growth, 608
    religion in, 509, 534
    self-rule, 77
    violence against women in,
        296
individualism, 54, 631–32
    cultures valuing, 53, 55
Indonesia
    democracy in, 378
    hunger, malnutrition, and
        famine in, 253
    Islam in, 521, 524, 537
    as newly industrializing
        economy (NIE), 257
industrial conflicts, 418
industrialism hypothesis, 221
industrialization, 74
    deindustrialization, 432–33
    development of schooling
        and, 476–77
    education and, 432–33, 482
    mass media and, 495–96
    urbanization and, 581–82
    see also capitalism
industrialized societies, 74–75,
    76
    key features of, 74–75, 76
    social stratification in,
        204–5
Industrial Revolution, 13, 404,
    423

inequality
    in consumption, 611–12
    education and, *see* education
        and literacy,
        inequality and
    gender, *see* gender
    global, *see* global inequality
    globalization and, *see*
        globalization,
        inequality and
    in health and illness, 340–41,
        554–58, 638–39
    racial and ethnic, 338–46
    social stratification and, *see*
        social stratification
    in the U.S., gap between rich
        and poor, 208, 209,
        217–20, 240
*Inequality by Design: Cracking
    the Bell Curve Myth*
    (Fischer et al.),
    483–86
infanticide, 63, 296
infant mortality, 252–53, 340–41,
    449, 602
infectious disease, 553, 557, 559,
    638
    in the developing world
        today, 559–62
informal economy, 415, 596–97
informal relations within
        organizations, 142–43
information age, 434–35
information poverty, 499
information society, 621, 624
information technology, 158
    education and, 498–99
    electronic communications,
        see electronic
        communications
    global inequality and, 272
    globalization and, 622, 623,
        626
    hackers, 169–70
    organizational structures,
        influence on, 153–58
    social change and, 620
    social inequality and,
        226–227
    social movements and, 401
    the workplace and, 430
        computerization, 154–55,
        225, 434
in-groups, 133, 136
inner-city areas, 582
InnerCity Entrepreneurs (ICE),
    592–93
innovators, Merton's theory of
    deviance and, 176
instincts, 59, 62

institutional capitalism, 425
institutional discrimination,
    341, 346
institutional racism, 318–19, 346
Intel, 427
intellectual property rights, 643
intelligence, 483–86
    defining, 483
    IQ and genetic factors,
        debate over, 483–86
interactional vandalism, 113–17
interdependence, 5, 12, 141
    globalization and, 622
interest groups, 382, 383–86
    defined, 383
    pluralist theories of
        democracy and,
        387–88
intergenerational social
    mobility, 221
    downward, 225
International Campaign to Ban
    Landmines, 160–61
International Council of
    Women, 160
international division of labor,
    426
International Institute for
    Democracy and
    Electoral Assistance,
    383
International Labor
    Organization, 300
International Lesbian and Gay
    Association, 572
International March on the
    United Nations to
    Affirm the Human
    Rights of Lesbian and
    Gay People, 572
International Monetary Fund
    (IMF), 643
international organizations,
    159–61
    global culture and, 80
    governmental (IGO), 160,
        625
    nongovernmental (INGO),
        160–61, 625–26
International Planned
    Parenthood
    Federation, 160
International Sociological
    Association, 160
International Telegraph Union,
    625
International Telework
    Association and
    Council (ITAC),
    153–54

Internet, 51, 497–98
    access, 497
    censorship and surveillance
        on, 380–81
    cybercrime, 188
    as democratizing force,
        378–80
    English as unofficial
        language of, 51
    global map of number of
        Internet servers,
        1999, 81
    growth of the, 623, 624
    hate groups on the, 140
    mass customization and,
        431–33
    pornography on the, 563
    social interaction changed
        by, 60–61, 123–24
    as social network, 139–40
    subcultures, online, 60–61
    telecommuting and, 154
    traditional cultures,
        influence on, 80–82,
        631
internships, 476–77
intimacy, 445–46
intragenerational social
    mobility, 220–21
    downward, 225
Inuit of Greenland, 54–55
IQ (intelligence quotient), 483
    genetic factors and, 483–86
Iran, 405
    Guardian Council in, 537
    Revolution of 1978–79, 524,
        534–36
    Shiism in, 524, 534–37
Iraq, 405, 619
    first Gulf War, 537
    war on terror and, 506
Ireland, marriage in, 467
Irish Americans, 328, 329, 330,
    342
iron law of oligarchy, 149, 152
Islam, 521–24, 533
    global extent of Islamic
        power, 536
    sharia, 521–24
    Sunnis and Shiites,
        differences between,
        524
    in the U.S., 529
    women and, 519–20
Islamic fundamentalism, 4, 537
Islamic nationalism, 534–38
Island Juice, 203
Israel, 524–25, 534, 537
Isuzu, 427, 431
Italian Americans, 329, 342

mediated quasi-interaction, 495
Medicaid, 362
Medicare, 358, 359, 362, 366
    generational equity debate
        and, 366–67
Medicare Reform Act of 2003,
    385
medicine, *see* health and illness
megacities, 595–96
megalopolis, 581
Melanesia, 568
"melting pot," 321, 324
*Men and Women of the
    Corporation* (Kanter),
    149–50
mentally ill
    deinstitutionalization
        movement, 171
mentoring, 151
Merck, 272
mergers, corporate, 423–24
Merton, Robert K., 19, 21, 143
    on deviance, 175–76, 177
    on reference groups, 134
Methodists, 513, 527
Mexican Americans, 334, 335,
    343
    families, 456
    life on the work line, 336–37
Mexican Zapatista rebels, 401
Mexico, 78
    Evangelical Protestants in,
        520
    migration from, 331
Mexico City, Mexico, 598
Meyer, John, 143
Miami, Florida, 343, 456
Michels, Robert, 149
microsociology, 22, 41
    linking of macrosociology
        and, 125–26, 179–80
Microsoft, 427
middle class in the U.S., 215–16
Middle East
    homosexuality in, 572
    Islam in, 521
    personal space in the, 120
    women in politics in, 300
middle-income countries, 248,
    250–52
middle-range theories, 21–22
midlife crisis, 104
migration
    classic model of, 325
    colonial model of, 325
    from developing countries
        to the U.S., 77–78
    families in the developing
        world and rural-
        urban, 452

global, 325–28, 600, 601
    globalization and, 213,
        332–33
    guest workers model of, 325
    illegal models of, 325
    internal, in the developing
        world, 595–96
    macro-level factors, 326
    micro-level factors, 326
    pull factors, 325
    push factors, 325
    see also emigration;
        immigration
Milan, Italy, 594
Milgram, Stanley, 137–38
military, 619
    budgets, 389
    military-industrial complex,
        388
militia movement, 401
Miller, Mark, 326–27
Mills, C. Wright, 6, 7, 23
    The Power Elite, 388
Milosevic, Slobodan, 371–72
Milwaukee Jobs Initiative, 420,
    421
Miner, Horace, 65–66
minimum wage, 229–30, 232,
    236
minority groups, 320–21
    endogamy and, 320
    incarceration of, 167
    poverty rates and, 230
    wealth and income gaps,
        219–220
    see also individual groups
Mitnick, Kevin, 169–70
Mitsubishi Corporation, 425
Mobil Corporation, 423
mode, defined, 43
Model T Ford, 416
*Modern Corporation and Private
    Property, The* (Berle
    and Means), 423
modernization theory, 262
modern societies, 74–79
Mohave, gender roles of the,
    283
Molotch, Harvey, 124, 585–86
monarchies
    constitutional, 377
    liberal democracy and, 377
money laundering, 191
monogamy, 52, 447
monopoly, 423
monotheism, 520
Monsanto, 635
Monti, Daniel, 592–93
Moon, Reverend Sun Myung,
    516, 517, 529

Moore, Barrington, Jr., 379
Moore, Wilbert E., 238
morality, child development
    and, 90
Morawska, Eva, 330
Morris, Jan (James), 281–82
Morrison, Toni, 334
mortality, 602
mortality rates, 602
Moscow, Russia, 594
Moseley-Braun, Carol, 341
Moses, Bob, 393
Mossadeq, Mohammad, 534
MoveOn.org, 379–80, 386, 401
Moynihan, Daniel Patrick, 171,
    455
Mozambique, 378
Muhammad, Prophet, 521, 524
multiculturalism, 64, 321, 324
multinational corporations,
    425–27
multiparty systems, 381, 387
multiple sovereignty, 395
Murdock, George, 302, 447
Murray, Charles, 483, 486
Muslims, *see* Islam; Islamic
    fundamentalism
Myanmar (Burma), 77, 643
    Internet use and censorship
        in, 381

Najman, Jake, 340
Nanking, China, mass rape by
    Japanese soldiers in,
    299
National Aeronautics and
    Space
    Administration
    (NASA), 144–45
National Association for the
    Advancement of
    Colored People
    (NAACP), 17, 333–34
National Center for Health
    Statistics, 556
National Child Abuse and
    Neglect Reporting
    System, 465
National College Women Sexual
    Victimization Study,
    298
National Crime Victimization
    Survey, 180, 181
National Health and Social Life
    Survey (NHSLS),
    567–68
National Incidence Study of
    Child Abuse and
    Neglect, 465

National Institutes of Health,
    46
nationalism, 372, 404–406
    defined, 373
    in developing countries,
        405–6
    education and, 477
    local, 373, 626
    religious, 533–38
    resurgence of, 82
National Longitudinal Study of
    Youth, 483
National Organization for
    Women (NOW), 162,
    386, 398
National Research Council, 484
National Rifle Association
    (NRA), 384
National Science Foundation,
    46
National Urban League, 333,
    455
National Voting Rights
    Museum and
    Institute, 393
National Women's Political
    Caucus (NWPC), 398
nation-states, 74–75, 404
    citizenship in, 372–73
    defined, 373
    globalization and, 406, 626,
        629
    social change and, 620
    sovereignty of, 372
nations without states, 405
Native Americans, 328, 333,
    342, 343
    families, 456–57
nature
    interaction of nurture and,
        62–63
    /nurture debate, 59–63,
        278–83
    sexual orientation,
        568–69
    socialization of, 547
Navajos eye contact, cultural
    norm for, 52
Nazi Germany, 137, 619
neoliberalism, 262
Netherlands, 405
    women in the work force in,
        300
networks
    informal, within
        organizations, 142–43
    "old boys" network, 151
    organizations as, 158–59
    social, 138–40, 158
        Internet as, 139–40

Answer Key

Chapter 1	Chapter 5	Chapter 9	Chapter 13	Chapter 17
1. C	1. B	1. D	1. B	1. B
2. A	2. C	2. A	2. B	2. C
3. A	3. D	3. D	3. A	3. B
4. A	4. B	4. C	4. A	4. D
5. C	5. C	5. D	5. B	5. A
6. D	6. B	6. C	6. B	6. C
7. D	7. C	7. D	7. C	7. B
8. D	8. B	8. B	8. A	8. B
9. B	9. B	9. C	9. C	9. C
10. C	10. C	10. B	10. A	10. D

Chapter 2	Chapter 6	Chapter 10	Chapter 14	Chapter 18
1. B	1. C	1. A	1. C	1. B
2. B	2. D	2. B	2. C	2. D
3. C	3. B	3. D	3. B	3. A
4. A	4. B	4. D	4. A	4. D
5. A	5. D	5. D	5. C	5. D
6. C	6. A	6. D	6. C	6. B
7. D	7. C	7. C	7. B	7. B
8. C	8. C	8. B	8. D	8. D
9. D	9. C	9. A	9. B	9. A
10. A	10. B	10. C	10. C	10. B

Chapter 3	Chapter 7	Chapter 11	Chapter 15	Chapter 19
1. B	1. A	1. D	1. B	1. D
2. B	2. B	2. D	2. C	2. C
3. A	3. C	3. A	3. B	3. A
4. A	4. B	4. D	4. C	4. B
5. C	5. B	5. C	5. D	5. A
6. D	6. C	6. A	6. C	6. C
7. C	7. A	7. A	7. C	7. A
8. B	8. C	8. D	8. C	8. B
9. D	9. A	9. B	9. B	9. C
10. C	10. A	10. C	10. B	10. D

Chapter 4	Chapter 8	Chapter 12	Chapter 16	Chapter 20
1. B	1. A	1. C	1. B	1. B
2. D	2. B	2. D	2. B	2. C
3. A	3. C	3. A	3. B	3. D
4. B	4. C	4. C	4. A	4. B
5. B	5. C	5. B	5. A	5. B
6. B	6. A	6. C	6. C	6. D
7. B	7. B	7. D	7. B	7. C
8. D	8. C	8. B	8. D	8. D
9. A	9. B	9. B	9. A	9. D
10. C	10. A	10. A	10. C	10. C